Women's Information Directory

Highlights

The *Women's Information Directory (WID)* is a comprehensive guide to resources for and about women in the United States. *WID* provides current, detailed information on a wide range of print and "live" resources, including:

- Organizations
- Centers, Services, & Programs
- Library Collections
- Museums & Galleries
- Colleges, Universities, & Studies Programs
- Scholarships & Awards
- Research Centers
- Government Agencies & Programs
- Top Women-Owned Businesses
- Consultants & Consulting Organizations
- Publications, Publishers, & Booksellers
- Videos
- Electronic Resources

Detailed Information in a Convenient Arrangement

The first edition of *WID* offers:

▶ A convenient one-stop source of information.

▶ Nearly 10,800 descriptive listings organized into 26 separate chapters by type of resource.

▶ Listings that typically contain descriptive information and complete contact data, including addresses, telephone numbers, and personal names.

Easy Access to Information Resources

The combined Master Name and Subject Index provides quick and easy access to the descriptive listings through a single alphabetic arrangement of all resource names, as well as groupings of resources under subject categories, including topics such as:

- Abortion
- Battered Women
- Breast Cancer
- Displaced Homemakers
- Eating Disorders
- Equal Rights
- Feminism
- Lesbians
- Older Women
- Pay Equity
- Rape
- Sexual Harassment
- Women's Studies
- and more...

50887

ISSN 1063-0554

Women's Information Directory

First Edition

A Guide to Organizations, Agencies, Institutions, Programs, Publications, Services, and Other Resources Concerned with Women in the United States.

Shawn Brennan, Editor

 Gale Research Inc. · DETROIT · WASHINGTON DC · LONDON

Shawn Brennan, *Editor*
Kimberly Burton Faulkner, *Associate Editor*
Julie Anne Bilenchi and Sara Tal Waldorf, *Assistant Editors*
Amy Lucas, *Senior Editor*
Aided by: Susan Bartos, Sandra Doran, Kristin Kahrs, and Gwen E. Turecki

Victoria B. Cariappa, *Research Manager*
Gary Oudersluys, *Research Supervisor*
Lisa Lantz, *Editorial Associate*
Angela Artiaga, Melissa E. Brown, Antoinette Craig, Betty Davis, Sherita Grant,
Phyllis Shepherd, and Tracie A. Wade, *Editorial Assistants*

Mary Beth Trimper, *Production Manager*
Shanna Heilveil, *Production Assistant*

Benita Spight, *Data Entry Supervisor*
Gwendolyn Tucker, *Data Entry Group Leader*
Kenneth D. Benson, Virgil L. Burton III, Lysandra C. Davis,
Colin C. McDonald, and Nancy K. Sheridan, *Data Entry Associates*

Cynthia Baldwin, *Art Director*
Kelly Schwartz, *Graphic Designer*
C.J. Jonik, *Keyliner*

Theresa A. Rocklin, *Supervisor of Editorial Programming Services*
Timothy Richardson, *Programmer*

The paper used in this publication meets the minimum requirements of American National Standard for Information Sciences – Permanence Paper for Printed Library Materials, ANSI Z39.48-1984. ∞™

♻ This book is printed on recycled paper that meets Environmental Protection Agency Standards.

ISSN 1063-0554
ISBN 0-8103-8422-1

Printed in the United States of America

Published simultaneously in the United Kingdom
by Gale Research International Limited
(An affiliated company of Gale Research Inc.)

Contents

Acknowledgments

The editor would like to thank the following members of the *Women's Information Directory* Advisory Board for reviewing the scope, coverage, content, and arrangement of this volume:

- Joan Ariel, Women's Studies Librarian, University of California—Irvine.

- Sarah Pritchard, Director of Libraries, Smith College.

- Carol Seajay, Editor, *Feminist Bookstore News.*

- Susan E. Searing, Women's Studies Librarian, University of Wisconsin at Madison.

Preface

Women comprise over half of the U.S. adult population, yet, even in the '90s, American women still do not enjoy equal status with men and remain under-represented in many areas of society, including employment, education, politics, and even in the home. In her best-selling book, *Backlash: The Undeclared War Against American Women* (New York: Crown Publishers, Inc., 1991), Pulitzer Prize winning author Susan Faludi reported the following alarming statistics:

- American women represent two-thirds of all poor adults in the United States.
- The average American female college graduate earns less than a man with only a high school diploma; the average female high school graduate earns less than a male high school dropout.
- Three-fourths of all U.S. colleges violate federal law banning sex discrimination in education.
- Less than 8 percent of all U.S. federal and state judges are women; less than 6 percent are law partners; and less than one percent are top corporate managers.
- More than 99 percent of American private employers do not offer child care; the U.S. government mandates neither family-leave nor child care programs—unlike nearly every other industrialized nation in the world.
- In thirty states, it is still legal for husbands to rape their wives; only ten states have laws mandating arrest for domestic violence.
- Women are the fastest growing segment of the homeless—almost half of all homeless women are refugees of domestic violence.

In addition, national studies have found that:

- 4 million women are battered each year by a male partner.
- 1,500 women are killed each year by a male partner.
- The leading cause of death of female employees in the workplace is homicide by a male partner.

The reality of these statistics, fueled by controversy over recent events has thrust women's issues into the spotlight with renewed fervor. The U.S. Equal Employment Opportunity Commission reported a surge in formal sexual harassment complaints immediately following the well-publicized testimony of Prof. Anita Hill during the U.S. Supreme Court nomination hearings of Justice Clarence Thomas. According to two ABC News polls conducted before and after the Thomas hearings, the percentage of women saying they had been sexually harassed more than doubled. Formal complaints increased 70 percent over the same period during the previous year. In addition, reports of sexual harassment of women in the U.S. military have been making headlines ever since details of the 1991 "Tailhook" naval aviators convention were made public by 26 women who claimed they were sexually assaulted by male officers. The Senate Veterans Affairs Committee estimated that about 60,000 of the 1.2 million female U.S. veterans have been raped or assaulted while serving in the military. The celebrity rape trials of William Kennedy Smith and boxer Mike Tyson served to further demonstrate the controversy surrounding and the prevalence of this crime against women. And the U.S. Supreme Court's recent decision to increase the power of the states to restrict early-stage abortions, coupled with the recent controversies over the safety of silicone breast implants and the reliability and effectiveness of mammograms, has generated a renewed interest in women's health-related issues.

As these issues and controversies continue to gain attention, the need grows for information on all aspects of women in the United States. It was out of this need that *Women's Information Directory (WID)* was born.

Introduction

This first edition of the *Women's Information Directory (WID)* provides libraries, schools, businesses, organizations, and individuals with up-to-date information on a wide variety of organizations, agencies, institutions, programs, publications, services, and other resources for and about women, including:

- National and Regional, State, and Local Organizations
- Battered Women's Services
- Displaced Homemaker Programs
- Family Planning Services
- Women's Centers
- Library Collections, Museums, and Galleries
- Colleges, Universities, and Women's Studies Programs
- Scholarships, Fellowships, and Loans

- Awards, Honors, and Prizes
- Research Centers
- Federal and State Government Agencies
- Federal Domestic Assistance Programs
- Top U.S. Women-Owned Businesses
- Consultants and Consulting Organizations
- Directories and Newsletters
- Newspapers, Journals, and Magazines
- Publishers and Booksellers
- Videos and Electronic Resources

WID provides coverage of a wide variety of women's issues, including abortion, battered women, displaced homemakers, eating disorders, pay equity, sexual harassment, women's studies, and more.

Compiled with the Help of Experts

WID comprises more than 10,800 listings of resources carefully selected for inclusion based on their direct relevance to women or women's issues in such areas as education, employment, health, discrimination, equal rights, business and management, religion and theology, politics, minorities, and feminism. The process used to determine the scope, coverage, content, and arrangement of these listings was guided by an advisory board of prominent women's information specialists. *WID's* broad geographic scope, comprehensive coverage, and convenient single volume format eliminates the need to consult multiple, often hard-to-locate specialized sources.

Convenient Arrangement and Thorough Indexing Speed Access to Information Sources

WID consists of a main body of descriptive listings and a Master Name and Subject Index.

The descriptive listings are arranged into 26 separate chapters according to type of information resource, as outlined on the "Contents" page. Entries typically contain complete contact data, and many include descriptive information, enabling the user to easily determine relevant resources and then contact organizations by telephone or mail for further information.

The combined alphabetic Master Name and Subject Index provides quick and thorough access to all organizations, agencies, programs, institutions, publications, services, and other resources included in the descriptive listings section, either by subject terms or resource names. Citations to former/alternate names mentioned within the descriptive listings are also included.

For more information on the content, arrangement, and indexing of *WID*, consult the "User's Guide" following this Introduction.

Method of Compilation

WID was compiled from a variety of sources. Relevant entries were carefully selected from other Gale Research Inc. directories, government publications, and lists and directories supplied by numerous national and local organizations. Telephone inquiries were also employed to gather data and/or verify information.

WID Offered in Alternate Format

The information in *WID* is available in customized mailing list arrangements. Call 800-877-GALE for details.

Acknowledgments

The editor thanks Working Woman, Inc. and the National Displaced Homemakers Network for granting permission to use their publications in compiling this directory. In addition, the editor is also grateful to the National Council for Research on Women and the National Women's Studies Association for sharing their resources.

Thanks also to the following Gale editors for their valuable contributions to this directory: Karen Backus, Julia C. Furtaw, Linda S. Hubbard, Debra M. Kirby, John Krol, Amy Lucas, Kathleen Young Marcaccio, Charles B. Montney, Annette Piccirelli, and Julie Winklepleck.

Comments Welcome

We encourage users to bring new or unlisted organizations to our attention. Every effort will be made to provide information about them in subsequent editions of the directory. Comments and suggestions for improving the directory are also welcome. Please contact:

Women's Information Directory
Gale Research Inc.
835 Penobscot Bldg.
Detroit, MI 48226-4094
Telephone: (313)961-2242
Toll-Free: 800-347-GALE
FAX: (313)961-6815

Shawn Brennan

User's Guide

Women's Information Directory consists of a main body of descriptive listings arranged into separate chapters by type of information resource, and a Master Name and Subject Index, which provides a convenient alphabetical listing of, and subject access to, all organizations, agencies, institutions, programs, publications, and services included in *WID*. Each of these parts is described below.

Descriptive Listings

Listings are numbered sequentially within 26 separate chapters, as outlined on the "Contents" page. Details on the content, arrangement, sources, and indexing for each chapter follow:

1. National Organizations

- **Scope:** Primarily nonprofit membership organizations of national scope that are concerned with women or areas/issues of interest to women.
- **Entries include:** Organization name, address, telephone number, fax and toll-free numbers (when available), name of contact (when available), and a brief description of the organization's purpose and activities.
- **Arrangement:** Alphabetical by organization name.
- **Source:** *Encyclopedia of Associations, Volume 1, National Organizations of the U.S.*, 26th Edition, (published by Gale Research Inc.) and original research.
- **Indexed by:** Organization name.

2. Regional, State, and Local Organizations

- **Scope:** Nonprofit organizations that function at the regional, state, or local levels, including affiliates of selected national organizations.
- **Entries include:** Organization name, address, telephone number, name of contact (when available), fax, and toll-free numbers (when available), and, in some cases, a brief description of the organization's purpose and activities.
- **Arrangement:** Alphabetical by state and city, then alphabetical by organization name within city.
- **Source:** *Encyclopedia of Associations: Regional, State, and Local Organizations*, 3rd Edition (published by Gale Research Inc.) and original research.
- **Indexed by:** Organization name.

3. Battered Women's Services

- **Scope:** Local services and shelters for battered women and their children.
- **Entries include:** Sponsoring organization and/or program name, address, telephone number, and crisis phone line (when available).
- **Arrangement:** Alphabetical by state and city, then alphabetical by organization name within city.
- **Source:** *Medical and Health Information Directory*, 6th Edition, Volume 3 (published by Gale Research Inc.).
- **Indexed by:** Sponsoring organization name.

4. Displaced Homemaker Programs

- **Scope:** Local programs for displaced homemakers.
- **Entries include:** Sponsoring organization and/or program name, address, and telephone number.
- **Arrangement:** Alphabetical by state and city, then alphabetical by organization name within city.

- **Source:** *National Displaced Homemaker Directory* (published by National Displaced Home-makers Network, 1625 K St., N.W., Ste. 300, Washington, DC 20006).
- **Indexed by:** Sponsoring organization name.

5. Family Planning Services

- **Scope:** Offices, affiliates, and chapters of the Planned Parenthood Federation of America.
- **Entries include:** Organization name, address, and telephone number.
- **Arrangement:** Alphabetical by state and city, then alphabetical by organization name within city.
- **Source:** Planned Parenthood Federation of America (810 7th Ave., 14th Fl., New York, NY 10019).
- **Indexed by:** Sponsoring organization name.

6. Women's Centers

- **Scope:** University-affiliated women's centers which provide services to students on campus and to people in the nearby community, including career counseling, programs on sexuality and sexual identity, and activities that address campus violence against women.
- **Entries include:** Sponsoring organization name, center name, address, telephone number, and name of contact.
- **Arrangement:** Alphabetical by state and city, then alphabetical by organization name within city.
- **Source:** *NWSA Directory of Women's Studies Programs, Women's Centers, and Women's Research Centers* (published by the National Women's Studies Association, University of Maryland, College Park, MD 20742-1325).
- **Indexed by:** Sponsoring organization name.

7. Library Collections

- **Scope:** Libraries with special collections of interest to women, including historical, literary, and cultural archives.
- **Entries include:** Parent organization name, library name, address, telephone and fax numbers, name of contact, and a general description of special collections, holdings, and services.
- **Arrangement:** Alphabetical by library name.
- **Source:** *Directory of Special Libraries and Information Centers,* 16th Edition (published by Gale Research Inc.) and original research.
- **Indexed by:** Parent organization name and library name.

8. Museums and Galleries

- **Scope:** Museums and galleries featuring women's history, heritage, and art.
- **Entries include:** Organization name, address, telephone number, and a brief description of holdings.
- **Arrangement:** Alphabetical by organization name.
- **Source:** Original research.
- **Indexed by:** Organization name.

9. Colleges and Universities

- **Scope:** Currently operational U.S. colleges and universities founded for the education of women.
- **Entries include:** Institution name, address, telephone number, name of president, and brief descriptive information, including date founded and degrees offered.
- **Arrangement:** Alphabetical by institution name.
- **Source:** List provided by the Women's College Coalition (1090 Vermont Ave., N.W., 3rd Fl., Washington, DC 20005) and original research.
- **Indexed by:** Institution name.

10. Women's Studies Programs

- **Scope:** Colleges and universities that offer women's studies programs.
- **Entries include:** Institution name, address, telephone number, name of contact, and degrees and credits offered.
- **Arrangement:** Alphabetical by state and city, then alphabetical by institution name within city.
- **Source:** *NWSA Directory of Women's Studies Programs, Women's Centers, and Women's Research Centers* (published by the National Women's Studies Association, University of Maryland, College Park, MD 20742-1325) and original research.
- **Indexed by:** Institution name.

11. Scholarships, Fellowships, and Loans

- **Scope:** Sources of funding for women studying at postsecondary institutions.
- **Arrangement:** Alphabetical by program name.
- **Entries include:** Program name, administering organization name, address, telephone and fax numbers, and a description of the funding program, including selection criteria, application information and other details.
- **Source:** *Scholarships, Fellowships, and Loans*, 9th Edition (published by Gale Research Inc.).
- **Indexed by:** Program name.

12. Awards, Honors, and Prizes

- **Scope:** Awards and other distinctions bestowed by government, civic, professional, and business groups for service to women.
- **Arrangement:** Alphabetical by award name.
- **Entries include:** Award name, sponsoring organization name, address, telephone number, and a brief description of award.
- **Source:** *Awards, Honors, and Prizes*, 10th Edition (published by Gale Research Inc.).
- **Indexed by:** Award name.

13. Research Centers

- **Scope:** University-related and other nonprofit research centers studying topics of concern to women.
- **Entries include:** Sponsoring institution name, research center name, address, telephone number, name of contact, and a brief description of activities, facilities, and services.
- **Arrangement:** Alphabetical by institution and/or research center name.
- **Source:** *Research Centers Directory*, 17th Edition (published by Gale Research Inc.) and original research.
- **Indexed by:** Institution and/or research center name.

14. Federal Government Agencies

- **Scope:** Units of the federal government, including agencies, clearinghouses, committees, councils, and other advisory organizations concerned with women's rights, equal employment opportunity, and other areas of interest to women.
- **Entries include:** Agency name, address, telephone number, toll-free and fax numbers (when available), name of contact, and a brief description of agency programs and purposes.
- **Arrangement:** Alphabetical by agency name.
- **Source:** *Encyclopedia of Governmental Advisory Organizations*, 8th Edition, and *Clearinghouse Directory*, 1st Edition, (both published by Gale Research Inc.); *United States Government Manual* (published by the U.S. National Archives and Records Administration and available from the U.S. Government Printing Office); and original research.
- **Indexed by:** Parent agency name and specific unit name.

15. Federal Domestic Assistance Programs

- **Scope:** Federally-funded programs offering a wide variety of benefits and services to women in such areas as education, employment, and family assistance.

- **Entries include:** Sponsoring federal agency name, program name, address, telephone number, name of contact, and a brief program description. *Catalog of Federal Domestic Assistance* numbers are also included for easy cross-reference to complete *Catalog* listings.
- **Arrangement:** Alphabetical by agency name.
- **Source:** *Catalog of Federal Domestic Assistance* (published by the U.S. General Services Administration and available from the U.S. Government Printing Office).
- **Indexed by:** Sponsoring agency name and program name.

16. State Government Agencies

- **Scope:** State government agencies concerned with equal employment, civil rights, and other areas affecting women.
- **Entries include:** Agency name, address, telephone number, and name of contact.
- **Arrangement:** Alphabetical by state, then alphabetical by agency name within state.
- **Source:** Original research.
- **Indexed by:** Parent agency name and specific unit name.

17. Top U.S. Women-Owned Businesses

- **Scope:** The top 25 women-owned businesses in the United States, as listed in the May 1992 issue of *Working Woman Magazine* article (written by Ronit Addis Rose, Janet Bamford, and Alexandra Siegal). To be eligible for the list, which was compiled in cooperation with the National Foundation for Women Business Owners, each woman needs to own at least 20 percent of the stock for private companies and at least 10 percent for public companies, with no other institution or individual owning more. The woman stockholder also must be a top executive running the day-to-day operations.
- **Entries include:** Company name, address, telephone number, name of chief executive, year founded, number of staff, type of business, 1991 sales, and current ranking.
- **Arrangement:** By descending rank.
- **Source:** Reprinted with permission of *Working Woman Magazine,* copyright © 1992 by Working Woman, Inc.
- **Indexed by:** Company name.

18. Consultants and Consulting Organizations

- **Scope:** Individuals and organizations that offer consultation services on women's issues.
- **Entries include:** Organization name, address, telephone number, fax and toll- free numbers (when available), founding date, and a brief description of consulting activities.
- **Arrangement:** Alphabetical by organization name.
- **Source:** *Consultants and Consulting Organizations Directory,* 12th Edition (published by Gale Research Inc.).
- **Indexed by:** Company or personal name.

19. Directories

- **Scope:** Directories covering a wide variety of topics of interest to women, including business, lifestyle, family, health, and education.
- **Entries include:** Publication and publisher names, address, telephone number, and a brief description, including publication scope, frequency, and other details.
- **Arrangement:** Alphabetical by publication title.
- **Source:** *Directories in Print,* 10th Edition (published by Gale Research Inc.) and original research.
- **Indexed by:** Publication title.

20. Journals and Magazines

- **Scope:** Journals and magazines covering a wide variety of topics of interest to women, including business, lifestyle, family, health, and education.

- **Entries include:** Publication and publisher names, address, telephone number, fax number (when available), and a brief description, including publication scope, frequency, and other details.
- **Arrangement:** Alphabetical by publication title.
- **Source:** *Gale Directory of Publications and Broadcast Media,* 125th Edition (published by Gale Research Inc.) and original research.
- **Indexed by:** Publication title.

21. Newsletters

- **Scope:** Newsletters covering a wide variety of topics of interest to women, including business, lifestyle, family, health, and education.
- **Entries include:** Publication and publisher names, address, telephone number, fax number (when available), and a brief description, including publication scope, frequency, and other details.
- **Arrangement:** Alphabetical by publication title.
- **Sources:** *Newsletters in Print,* 6th Edition (published by Gale Research Inc.) and original research.
- **Indexed by:** Publication title.

22. Newspapers

- **Scope:** Newspapers covering a wide variety of topics of interest to women, including business, lifestyle, family, health, and education.
- **Entries include:** Publication and publisher names, address, telephone number, and a brief description, including publication scope, frequency, and other details.
- **Arrangement:** Alphabetical by publication title.
- **Source:** *Gale Directory of Publications and Broadcast Media,* 125th Edition (published by Gale Research Inc.) and original research.
- **Indexed by:** Publication title.

23. Publishers

- **Scope:** Large and small trade, academic, and independent publishers that publish books for, by, and about women or issues of interest to women.
- **Entries include:** Publisher name, address, telephone number, and a brief description of publishing activity.
- **Arrangement:** Alphabetical by publisher name.
- **Source:** *Publishers Directory,* 12th Edition (published by Gale Research Inc.) and original research.
- **Indexed by:** Publisher name.

24. Booksellers

- **Scope:** Booksellers and distributors that sell books for, by, and about women, including feminist and lesbian books.
- **Entries include:** Name, address, telephone number, and a brief description.
- **Arrangement:** Alphabetical by state and city, then alphabetical by organization name within city.
- **Source:** List of women's bookstores provided by *Feminist Bookstore News* (P.O. Box 882554, San Francisco, CA 94188) and original research.
- **Indexed by:** Store or distributor name.

25. Videos

- **Scope:** Educational and general interest videos for, by, and about women in the United States, including those covering the role of women in American society.

- **Entries include:** Video title, distributor name, address, telephone number, program description, and other details.
- **Arrangement:** Alphabetical by video title.
- **Source:** *Video Source Book,* 13th Edition (published by Gale Research Inc.).
- **Indexed by:** Video title.

26. Electronic Resources

- **Scope:** Databases, bulletin boards, and other electronic resources covering women's issues.
- **Entries include:** Database name and acronym, producer name, address, telephone number, resource description, and other details.
- **Arrangement:** Alphabetical by resource name.
- **Source:** *Computer-Readable Databases,* 8th Edition (published by Gale Research Inc.) and original research.
- **Indexed by:** Resource name.

Master Name and Subject Index

The alphabetical Master Name and Subject Index provides access to all entries included in *WID*, as well as to former or alternate names which appear within entry text. Each organization, agency, institution, program, publication, or service is indexed by the name listed. In addition, citations to resource names may appear under specific subject headings for quick access by topics. The terms "woman" and "women" have not been used as subject headings in the index, since, as a general category, they cover all the entries in the book.

Index references are to book entry numbers rather than page numbers. Entry numbers appear in the index in boldface type if the reference is to a main entry and in lightface type if the reference is to a program or former/alternate name included within the text of the cited entry.

If several entries have the same parent organization, as is the case with many of the groups listed in *WID*, related units are indexed individually by name and as a group under the name of the parent organization. The names of all federal government organizations are indexed under "U.S." Entries with identical names are differentiated in the index by city and state designations appended to the citations.

Sample entries that could appear in the index follow:

AAUW American Fellowships **145**
AAUW Career Development Grants **146**
Abortion (See also: Pro-choice; Reproductive Issues; Right-to-life)
    Abortion Alternative Organizations Directory **451**
    Coalition for Safety of Abortion Clinics **33**
    National Abortion Federation **249**
    Religious Coalition for Abortion Rights **267**
    Women Exploited by Abortion **123**
Battered women (See also: Domestic Violence; Rape; Violence Against Women; Chapter 3: Battered Women's Services)
    Bayou Area Family Violence Program **25**
    Center for Women and Families **321**
    Cove Domestic Violence and Sexual Assault Program **48**
    Women in Crisis Program **32**
    YWCA Shelter for Battered Women and their Children **19**

Women's Information Directory

(1) National Organizations

Entries in this chapter are arranged alphabetically by organization name. See the User's Guide at the front of this directory for additional information.

★1★ Abortion Rights Mobilization (ARM)
175 5th Ave., Ste. 814
New York, NY 10010
Phone: (212)673-2040
Lawrence Lader, Pres.

Description: Works to guarantee a woman's legal right to abortion as decreed by the U.S. Supreme Court.

★2★ Ad Hoc Committee in Defense of Life
1187 National Press Bldg.
Washington, DC 20045
Phone: (202)347-8686
Robert McFadden, Bureau Chief

Founded: 1974. **Description:** Seeks to have the Roe vs. Wade decision repealed. (The Roe vs. Wade decision, handed down by the Supreme Court in 1973, interpreted the concept of personal liberty guaranteed by the Constitution to include a woman's right to decide whether or not to terminate her pregnancy.) Disseminates information opposing abortion and euthanasia; lobbies for legislation against abortion and euthanasia. Maintains library of documents, clippings, and reports on pro-life issues. **Publications:** *Lifeletter*, 18/year. Newsletter; includes information on lobbying efforts. • Also publishes pamphlets.

★3★ The Advocacy Institute
Women vs. Smoking Network
1730 Rhode Island Ave., NW, Ste. 600
Washington, DC 20036
Phone: (202)659-8475
Michele Block M.D., Ph.D., Dir.

Description: Educates women about important issues and mobilizes them to fight against tobacco use. Provides information about advocacy and tobacco control.

★4★ Advocacy and Research Institute on Latino Women, Inc.
The Women's Bldg.
79 Central Ave.
Albany, NY 12206
Phone: (518)432-6498
Sonia Ivette Dueno, Executive Director

★5★ Affirmative Action Coordinating Center (AACC)
126 W. 119th St.
New York, NY 10026
Phone: (212)864-4000
Gerald Horne, Exec. Officer

Founded: 1978. **Description:** Network of organizations that believe affirmative action programs are legal and essential if the effects of hundreds of years of repression to minorities and women are to be overcome. Collects, indexes, and analyzes information on the status of pending litigation, and legislative and administrative rulings affecting affirmative action programs. Acts as clearinghouse and resource center in developing legal intervention strategies and sharing skills and reference materials among attorneys working to defend and expand affirmative action programs. **Members:** 150. **Publications:** *News*, quarterly. • Also publishes briefs.

★6★ AFL-CIO
Committee on Salaried and Professional Women
Department for Professional Employees
815 16th St., NW, No. 707
Washington, DC 20006
Phone: (202)638-0320
Gloria Johnson, Chair

Founded: 1974. **Description:** Explores the problems facing women in professional and technical occupations and encourages organizing and union participation among white collar women workers. **Publications:** *Interface*. • Also publishes statistics on white collar women.

★7★ AFL-CIO
Department of Civil Rights
815 16th St. NW
Washington, DC 20006
Phone: (202)637-5270
Richard Womack, Dir.

Founded: 1955. **Description:** Staff arm of AFL-CIO Civil Rights Committee. Serves as official liaison with women's and civil rights organizations and government agencies working in the field of equal opportunity; helps to implement state and federal laws and AFL-CIO civil rights policies; aids affiliates in the development of affirmative programs to expand opportunities for minorities and women; prepares and disseminates special materials on civil rights; speaks at union and civil rights institutes, conferences, and conventions; helps affiliates resolve com-

plaints involving unions under Title VII of the 1964 Civil Rights Act and Executive Order 11246. **Publications:** *AFL-CIO and Civil Rights*, biennial.

★8★ AFL-CIO
Women's Activities
815 16th St. NW
Washington, DC 20006
Phone: (202)637-5272
Cynthia McCaughan, Coordinator

Founded: 1955. Works with national and international unions to help carry out the c ivil rights and women's rights policies of the AFL-CIO. **Members:** 14,000,000.

★9★ Africa Studies Association
Women's Caucus
Credit Union Bldg.
Emory University
Atlanta, GA 30322
Phone: (404)329-6410
Edna Bay, Contact

Description: Promotes participation of women and attention to women's issues in African studies. The caucus works to bring women from Africa to attend the African Studies Association Conference; organize panels; exchange news about research and funding about women studies in Africa. **Publications:** *Women's Caucus Newsletter*.

★10★ African American Women's Association
PO Box 55122
Brightwood Station
Washington, DC 20011
Phone: (202)966-6645
Mary P. Doughterty, President

Description: A private, nonprofit organization dedicated to the establishment of closer relationships and understanding between the women of Africa and the Americas through cultural, educational, charitable, and social activities. Membership is open to all women who wish to support the objectives and goals of the association. Projects include giving clothes and necessities for Malawi (South Africa) earthquake victims, and Hurricane Hugo victims in South Carolina; supporting a language laboratory library at Africare House (Washington DC); providing annual scholarship to African and American undergraduate students attending a college or university in the Washington area; and sponsoring annual major fundraiser. Areas of focus include Africa Women, African American women, charities, community service, cultural exchange, ethnic groups, international issues, scholarships, volunteers, women in development, and women of color. **Publications:** *African American Women's Association Newsletter.*

★11★ African Methodist Episcopal Church (AME)
Women's Missionary Society
1134 11th St. NW
Washington, DC 20001
Phone: (202)371-8886
Fax: (202)371-8820
Delores L. Kennedy Wiliams, President

Description: The Women's Missionary Society of the African Methodist Episcopal Church provides leadership and ancillary services that enhance the outcome of training, education, and welfare of disadvantaged women, youth, and children throughout the United States, Bahamas, Burmuda, Canada, Central Africa, Dominican Republic, England, Guyana, Haiti, Jamaica, Namibia, Republic of South Africa, Suriname, Trinidad, and West Africa. The group works for the empowerment of women struggling to break the cycle of poverty and second class citizenship. They monitor and track legislation and trends to recommend public policy; conduct public workshops and seminars to educate women about the economic, social, and civil liberty issues affecting women and their families, publishes reports and specific information that assess the status and concerns of women; assists in the restoration and enrichment of family life. **Publications:** *Missionary Magazine.*

★12★ Alan Guttmacher Institute (AGI)
111 Fifth Ave.
New York, NY 10003
Phone: (212)254-5656
Fax: (212)254-9891
Jeannie I. Rosoff, Pres.

Founded: 1968. **Description:** Fosters sound public policies on voluntary fertility control and population issues and encourages responsive reproductive health programs through policy analysis, public education, and research. Compiles statistics on the provision of services relating to reproductive health care. Offers technical assistance. Until 1977, served as the Research and Development Division of Planned Parenthood Federation of America. **Publications:** *Annual Report.* • *Family Planning Perspectives*, bimonthly. Professional journal focusing on reproductive health issues. • *International Family Planning Perspectives* (in English, French, and Spanish), quarterly. Professional journal highlighting population and reproductive health research and program achievements in developing countries. • *Washington Memo*, 20/year. Newsletter covering legislative developments. Monitors federal appropriations for family planning and contraceptive research, congressional and Supreme Court actions on abortion, international population assistance, teenage pregnancy, maternal health, and pregnancy-related services. • Also publishes research reports. **Formerly:** (1975) Center for Family Planning Program Development.

★13★ Alcoholism Center for Women (ACW)
1147 S. Alvarado St.
Los Angeles, CA 90006
Phone: (213)381-8500
Brenda L. Underhill, Exec.Dir.

Founded: 1974. **Description:** Recovery center with services available to all women who have a primary problem with alcohol, with particular concern for the needs of women at high risk, including adult daughters of alcoholics, incest and battering survivors, and lesbians. Maintains 20-bed recovery facility and an outparticipant facility. Nonresidential services include various peer-oriented sobriety support groups. Provides: Prevention Services Program, which offers programs and services including workshops, referrals, alcohol-free social events, and community presentations designed to help women with histories of incest or child abuse, adult daughters of alcoholics, and women with compulsive behavior problems; Lapis Program, which offers workshops for women of color. Offers counseling and daily, evening, and weekend groups sessions. Recovery process emphasizes alcohol education, coping and survival skills, self-awareness, and esteem building. Maintains: Alcohol Free Living Center; New Journeys, a re-entry home for recovering alcoholic women and their children. Conducts prevention workshops, seminars, and professional and community education programs, including Psychotherapy and the Alcoholism Syndrome and Incest and Alcoholism: The Healing Process. Maintains speakers' bureau and 500 volume in-house library. **Local Groups:** 1. **Telecommunications Services:** Telecommunications Device for the Deaf. **Components:** AFLC; Out-Participant; Prevention Services; Residential. **Publications:** *Prevention and Community Services Newsletter*, bimonthly. Newsletter providing information on prevention-oriented workshops and topics in alcohol use and abuse; includes calendar of events. **Formerly:** (1975) Alcoholism Program for Women.

★14★ All About Issues American (AAIA)
PO Box 1350
Stafford, VA 22554
Phone: (703)659-4171
Judie Brown, Dir.

Description: Individuals interested in educating the public on alternatives to abortion. **Publications:** *All About Issues*, 6/year. Magazine. • Also publishes pamphlets, booklets, and educational materials.

★15★ All-Craft Foundation (ACF)
25 St. Marks Pl.
New York, NY 10003
Phone: (212)228-6421
Joyce Hartwell, Founder & Dir.

Founded: 1976. **Description:** Trains underprivileged poor women to enter the skilled construction trades. Provides physical and nutritional education counseling and job placement. Established All-Craft-MAWK Centers with the National Association of Women in Construction (see separate entry). Also offers evening and weekend classes open to the public.

★16★ All Nations Women's League (ANWL)
39-55 51st St., No. 2E
New York, NY 11377
Phone: (718)478-5566
Angela Miller, Founder

Founded: 1970. **Description:** Women over the age of 18 from all parts of the world. Purpose is to promote a mutual understanding of women's problems and the need for community integration. Seeks to improve the cultural, educational, and professional status of women throughout the world. Works to broaden public awareness of the goals, concerns, ideas, and problems of women. Sponsors cultural events, educational and health programs, and lectures. Educational activities for children include classes in music, painting, and crafts. Offers vocational rehabilitation programs for unemployed women; operates counseling office. Bestows awards; operates charitable program. **Members:** 1005. **State Groups:** 2. **Local Groups:** 2. **Publications:** *Bulletins*, periodic. • *Magazine*, periodic. • *Newsletter*, periodic.

★17★ Alliance of Minority Women for Business and Political Development
c/o Brenda Alford
Brassman Research
PO Box 13933
Silver Spring, MD 20911-3933
Phone: (301)565-0258
Brenda Alford, Pres.

Founded: 1982. **Description:** Minority women who own businesses in industries including manufacturing, construction, service, finance, insurance, real estate, retail trade, wholesale trade, transportation, and public utilities. Objectives are to unite minority women entrepreneurs and to encourage joint ventures and information exchange for political influence. **Members:** 650. **Formerly:** (1982) Task Force on Black Women Business Owners.

★18★ Alliance of Women Bikers (AWB)
PO Box 484
Eau Claire, WI 54702
Debby Berry, Contact

Founded: 1977. **Description:** International organization of women ages 18 to 65. Supports women motorcyclists; disdains a tough, macho, stay-out-of-my-way image; educates sexist motorcycle magazines; lobbies against laws that the alliance believes violate their rights as bikers and citizens. Has held motorcycle shows for inmates of women's prisons; seeks to provide social contact to incarcerated women. Motto is: "Sisters Helping Sisters." **Members:** 300.

★19★ Alpha Delta Kappa
1615 W. 92nd St.
Kansas City, MO 64114
Phone: (816)363-5525
Opal L. Lunsford, Executive Administrator

Description: The purposes of Alpha Delta Kappa are to recognize outstanding women educators actively engaged in teaching, administration, or some specialized fields of the teaching profession; to build a fraternal fellowship among educators; to promote high standards in education and assist in strengthening the status and advancement of the teaching profession; to promote education through the establishment of numerous scholarship and grant programs; and to contribute to world understanding, goodwill, and peace through an international fellowship of women educators united in the ideals of education; pursues scholarship and altruistic activities. **Publications:** *The Kappan.*

★20★ **Alpha Kappa Alpha, Inc. (AKA)**
5656 S. Stony Island Ave.
Chicago, IL 60637
Phone: (312)684-1282
Allison Harris, Executive Director

Description: The sorority is America's first Greek organization for black women. It is a service, action-oriented organization of 100,000 members, with 750 chapters in 47 states, West Africa, the Bahamas, West Germany, and the Virgin Islands. The organization is dedicated to improving the quality of life through service with a global perspective. It is an advocacy organization, providing public information and direct services through both its paid staff and its wide network of members who volunteer time to its programs. Issues currently being addressed include job discrimination, affirmative action, employment training, access to nontraditional jobs, pay equity, poverty, economic development, teenage pregnancy, education, child care, housing, domestic violence, families, health, and leadership development. The organization also targets higher education, with particular emphasis on the historically black colleges, voter education, and efforts to end apartheid. Sponsor grants, offers support, publication, and education.

★21★ **Alpha Phi International Fraternity**
1930 Sherman Ave.
Evanston, IL 60201
Phone: (312)475-0663
Mrs. Joyce Shumway, General Manager

Founded: 1872. **Description:** College women's fraternity. **Publications:** *Alpha Phi Quarterly.*

★22★ **Alpha Sigma Alpha Sorority**
1201 E. Walnut St.
Springfield, MO 65802
Phone: (417)869-0980
Rose Marie Fellin, Staff Dir.

Founded: 1901. **Description:** Social sorority. **Publications:** *Phoenix.*

★23★ **Alternatives to Abortion International/Women's Health and Education Foundation (AAI/WHEF)**
1213 1/2 S. James Rd.
Columbus, OH 43227-1801
Phone: (614)239-9433
Margaret H. Hartshorn, Ph.D., Chm.

Founded: 1971. **Description:** Affiliates are service groups offering alternatives to abortion. Assists persons with problem pregnancies and offers non-abortion personal and practical services. Rather than engage in legislative or judicial activities and/or lobbying, the groups develop programs to assist girls who may be contemplating abortion by offering emotional, medical, legal, and social support. Awards certificates to affiliates. Sponsors seminars. **Members:** 500. **Publications:** *Heartbeat,* quarterly. Newsletter including regional reports and news bulletin updates. • Also publishes directory. **Formerly:** (1975) Alternatives to Abortion. **Also known as:** World Federation of Prolife Emergency Pregnancy Service Centers.

★24★ **Always Causing Legal Unrest (ACLU)**
PO Box 2085
Rancho Cordova, CA 95741-2085
Phone: (408)427-2858
Steven Paskey, Contact

Founded: 1990. **Description:** Feminists; anti-pornography activists; individuals interested in an "alternative to First Amendment fundamentalism." Urges corporations to place public safety and welfare and women's rights over profit and the "fundamentalist" emphasis on trademark laws, private property rights, and individual privacy. Encourages women to learn self defense and weaponry. Sponsors Pushing Buttons Campaign, in which buttons bearing slogans against media violence and for women's self-defense are worn in an effort to gain widespread public and legislative awareness and support. Promotes the use of humor in generating public awareness of what the group sees as an overemphasis on conservative values. Disseminates information. **Members:** 200. **Local Groups:** 5. **Publications:** Leaflets and brochures.

★25★ **American Academy of Husband-Coached Childbirth (AAHCC)**
PO Box 5224
Sherman Oaks, CA 91413
Phone: (818)788-6662
Toll-free: 800-423-2397
Marjie Hathaway, Exec. Officer

Founded: 1970. **Description:** Trains instructors in the Bradley method of natural childbirth. **Members:** 1200. **Telecommunications Services:** Toll-free numbers, (800)423-2397 (outside California) and (800)42-BIRTH (inside California). **Publications:** *Directory of Instructors,* 2-3/year. • *Fetal Advocate,* periodic. • Also disseminates educational audiovisual materials.

★26★ **American Academy of Natural Family Planning (AANFP)**
615 S. New Ballas Rd.
St. Louis, MO 63141
Phone: (314)569-6495
Phyllis A. White, Pres.

Founded: 1982. **Description:** Individuals who participate in natural family planning instruction. (Natural family planning refers to methods that do not employ contraceptive devices of any kind, using instead the natural phases of fertility.) Seeks to improve the quality of natural family planning services by establishing specific certification and accreditation requirements for teachers and educational programs. Conducts training programs throughout the U.S. and England. Promotes public recognition and acceptance of natural family planning; disseminates information; bestows awards. **Members:** 300. **Computerized Services:** Mailing list. **Publications:** *Academy Activity,* quarterly. Newsletter. • *Client Connection,* quarterly. • *Membership Directory,* annual.

★27★ **American Academy of Religion Women's Caucus**
Washington University, Women's Studies
Box 1078
St. Louis, MO 63130-4899
Phone: (314)889-5000
Jacqueline Pastif, Co-Director

★28★ **American Agri-Women (AAW)**
c/o Sandy Greiner
Rte. 2, Box 193
Keota, IA 52248
Phone: (515)363-2293
Fax: (515)636-2293
Sandy Greiner, Pres.

Founded: 1974. **Description:** Farm and ranch women's organizations representing 35,000 interested persons. Promotes agriculture; seeks to present the real identity of American farmers to the rest of the population and to develop an appreciation of "the interdependence of the components of the agricultural system." Supports a marketing system which makes quality food and fiber available to all on a reasonable cost basis and at a fair profit to the farmer. Believes that the family farm system is the bulwark of the private enterprise system, and as such must be preserved. Works in areas of legislation, regulations, consumer relations, and education. Maintains resource center and speakers' bureau; bestows Leaven Award for outstanding achievement within AAW's guidelines. Is establishing an oral history project of America's farm and ranch women entitled From Mules to Microwaves; conducts research programs. **Members:** 42. **State Groups:** 20. **Publications:** *American Agri-Women–Directory,* annual. Contains listing of officers of affiliate organizations of farm and ranch women. • *Voice of the American Agri-Woman,* bimonthly. Newsletter concerned with farm and ranch women.

★29★ **American Agri-Women Resource Center (AAWRC)**
c/o Marjorie Wendzel
785 N. Bainbridge Center
Watervliet, MI 49098
Phone: (616)468-3649
Marjorie Wendzel, Treas.

Founded: 1974. **Description:** Farm women concerned with the advancement of agricultural production within the free enterprise system. Objectives are: to formulate and disseminate educational materials which accurately represent agripolitan America for use by teachers and the public; to initiate and promote an educational program to advance the interests and welfare of agriculture. Provides training for women in leadership, public relations, and self-esteem. Conducts the Agricultural Commodity Lessons which illustrates, explains, and informs in various subject areas from kindergarten to 8th grade levels. **Members:** 35,000. **Regional Groups:** 40. **Publications:** *American Agri-Women Resource Guide,* updated every 18 months.

★30★ **American Anorexia/Bulimia Association (AA/BA)**
418 E. 76 St.
New York, NY 10021
Phone: (212)734-1114
Randi Wirth, Ph.D., Exec.Dir.

Founded: 1978. **Description:** Anorectics, families of anorectics, psychiatric social workers, nurses, psychiatrists, physicians, and individuals interested in the problems of anorexia nervosa and bulimia. (Anorexia nervosa is a serious illness of deliberate self-starvation with profound psychiatric and physical components. Symptoms are excessive weight loss, cessation of menstruation in women, distorted body image, bingeing, continual constipation, and eventual muscle wasting. Bulimia is characterized by recurrent episodes of binge eating, followed by self-induced vomiting or purging by laxatives and diuretics. Symptoms are inconspicuous binge eating, menstrual irregularities, frequent significant weight fluctuations, and fear of inability to stop eating voluntarily.) Acts as information and referral service. Organizes selfhelp groups. Maintains speakers' bureau and small library; collects research information. **Members:** 2000. **State Groups:** 3. **Telecommunications Services:** Telephone referral service. **Publications:** *American Anorexia/Bulimia Association–Newsletter*, quarterly. Newsletter providing information on eating disorders; includes articles on selfhelp groups, current research, and recent conferences. Also includes book reviews and information on new publications. **Formerly:** (1980) Anorexia Nervosa Aid Society; (1983) American Anorexia Nervosa Association.

★31★ American Anthropological Association
Association for Feminist Anthropology
1703 New Hampshire Ave.
Washington, DC 20009
Phone: (202)232-8800
Jane Collins, Chair, AFA

Description: An interest group of anthropologists using or interested in feminist approaches within the discipline. Concerns of the association include research commissions on Women and Human Rights, Women's Body Control, Gender and the (Anthropology) Curriculum. **Publications:** *Anthropology Newsletter*.

★32★ American Association for Adult and Continuing Education
Women's Issues, Status and Education Unit
1112 16th St. NW, Ste. 420
Washington, DC 20036
Phone: (202)463-6333
Fax: (202)797-7225
Ellen Ironside, Director of Continuing Education

Description: Provides support for women in the field of adult and continuing education; calls attention to these women's issues as part of the national agenda; and provides support for those just entering the field to keep alive the grassroots work in the community. The Unit sponsors a yearly program presentation at the annual convention; provides a bibliography of recommended models; and evaluates all programs submitted for presentation at the conference.

★33★ American Association for the Advancement of Science (AAAS)
National Network of Women in Science (NWIS)
Office of Opportunities in Science
1333 H St., NW
Washington, DC 20005
Phone: (202)326-6670
Dr. Shirley Malcolm, Program Head

Founded: 1978. **Description:** A communication and support system to provide and promote full access to career information and education opportunities for minority and female students. Also promotes the professional advancement of American Indian, Asian, African American, Mexican American, and Puerto Rican women in science and engineering. **Publications:** Informational newsletter.

★34★ American Association for Counseling and Development (AACD)
Committee on Women
5999 Stevenson Ave.
Alexandria, VA 22304
Phone: (703)823-9800
Fax: (703)823-0252
Linda K. Kemp, Chairperson

Description: A special committee designed to enhance the identification, awareness, and response to women's issues within the profession, its divisions and members. The focus of this Committee is to develop and deliver training and orientation programs on gender-fair professional practices and issues which are currently endorsed by AACD; identify issues directly related to the welfare of women; disseminate information to AACD divisions, regions, branch leaders, and general membership. **Publications:** *GUIDEPOST*—a Newsletter published by the AACD and various other Division journals or newsletters.

★35★ American Association for Higher Education (AAHE)
Women's Caucus
1 Dupont Circle, Ste. 600
Washington, DC 20036
Phone: (202)293-6440
Fax: (202)293-0073
Judy Corcillo, Chair

Description: A network of AAHE members interested in women's issues in higher education; develops conference sessions and professional development workshops at the AAHE National Conference on Higher Education. **Publications:** Occasional newsletter sent free of charge to members.

★36★ American Association of Immunologists
Committee on the Status of Women
9650 Rockville Pike
Bethesda, MD 20814
Phone: (301)530-7178

★37★ American Association of Law Schools
Committee on Women
University of Southern California Law School
Los Angeles, CA 90089-0071
Phone: (213)743-7302
Judith Resnick, Chair

★38★ American Association for Maternal and Child Health (AAMCH)
c/o Harold J. Fishbein
233 Prospect, P-204
LaJolla, CA 92037
Phone: (619)459-9308
Harold J. Fishbein, Exec. Officer

Founded: 1919. **Description:** Interprofessional organization of obstetricians, generalists, pediatricians, anesthesiologists, public health MD's; maternity, public health, and pediatric nurses; nurse anesthetists; social service workers; nutritionists and dietitians; hospital administrators; and others concerned with maternal and newborn care. Sponsors reprints on prenatal and postnatal care. **Members:** 3000. **Regional Groups:** 3. **Local Groups:** 1000. **Formerly:** American Committee on Maternal Welfare; (1965) American Association for Maternal and Infant Health.

★39★ American Association of ProLife Obstetricians and Gynecologists (AAPLOG)
850 Elm Grove Rd.
Elm Grove, WI 53122
Phone: (414)789-7984
Fax: (414)782-8788
David V. Foley, M.D., Pres.

Founded: 1973. **Description:** Obstetricians and gynecologists who oppose abortions, perform no abortions, and take no part in arranging abortions. Seeks "to draw attention to the value of all human life from the moment of conception." Supports programs that assist unwed mothers who choose to have their babies. Conducts research on complications experienced by women who have had legal abortions and compiles statistics on illnesses and deaths; studies the long-range effects of abortion on fertility and reproductive capability. Presents awards to congresspersons and physicians who have demonstrated strong support for the protection of human life beginning with conception. Offers postgraduate course on the subject of care and concern for women experiencing mental and physical trauma after abortions. **Members:** 800. **Regional Groups:** 8. **Publications:** *Directory*, triennial. • *Newsletter*, quarterly.

★40★ American Association of Pro-Life Pediatricians (AAPLP)
2160 1st Ave.
Maywood, IL 60153
Phone: (708)216-4522
E. F. Diamond, M.D., Sec.

Founded: 1978. **Description:** Members of the American Academy of Pediatrics interested in issues such as abortion, infanticide, and definition of death. To coordinate member activities; to publicize political trends; and to educate members. **Members:** 510. **State Groups:** 50. **Publications:** *Newsletter*, quarterly. • Also publishes *This Curette for Hire* (book) and *Monograph on Fetal Pain*.

★41★ American Association of Retired Persons (AARP)
Women's Initiative Network (WIN)
1909 K St. NW
Washington, DC 20049
Phone: (202)434-2642
Margaret Arnold, Senior Program Specialist

Description: Advocates and supports policies, programs, and legislation that improve the status of mid-life and older women. Also works to remove barriers to productivity and achievement in all aspects of life; correct inequities in employment opportunities, practices, and policies; improve income support and pension programs; promote healthy lifestyles and provide access to universal quality health and long-term care; expand opportunities for personal growth and fullfillment; provide materials and resources for more informed consumer decisions; and promote greater recognition of the significant contributions of women to families, communities, the nation, and the world. Advocates legislation to remedy pension, social security, employment, and other inequities; sponsors conferences. **Publications:** *AARP WIN (Women's Initiative Network)*.

★42★ American Association of University Professors (AAUP)
Committee on the Status of Women in the Academic Profession
1012 14th St. NW, Ste. 500
Washington, DC 20005
Phone: (202)737-5900
Fax: (202)737-5526
Leslie Lee Francis, Associate Secretary

Description: With passage of the equal pay act and the 1972 amendments to Title VII of the 1964 Civil Rights Act prohibiting discrimination by sex in colleges and universities, female faculty members renewed their efforts to obtain equitable treatment in personnel decisions. The AAUP has used these laws in aggressive pursuit of its policy objectives of fair treatment for women. The Association has participated in major Title VII and pay equity suits around the country by furnishing expert witnesses and providing financial support from AAUP's Legal Defense Fund. AAUP has submitted amicus briefs in such landmark cases as Kunda vs. Muhlenberg College concerning tenure as a remedy. The Committee's operations at the state and local levels also provide support and assistance to individuals on campus and in the courts. **Publications:** *Academe.*

★43★ American Association of University Women (AAUW)
1111 16th St. NW
Washington, DC 20036
Phone: (202)785-7700
Anne L. Bryant, Exec.Dir.

Founded: 1881. **Description:** Graduates of regionally accredited colleges; colleges, universities, and two-year or community colleges. Works for advancement of women through advocacy and emphasis on lifelong learning; engages in research; lobbies Congress. Conducts a study-action program on topics such as women's work/women's worth and promoting individual liberties. Sponsors competitions; bestows awards. Maintains library and archive. **Members:** 140,000. **Regional Groups:** 10. **State Groups:** 51. **Local Groups:** 1900. **Publications:** *AAUW Outlook*, bimonthly. Magazine containing articles on issues such as equity in education and the workplace. Includes policy update on current legislative issues, newsnotes, and book reviews. • *American Association of University Women—Action Alert*, monthly. Newsletter covering legislative news and other issues, including pay equity, child care, and family law. • *Leader in Action*, quarterly. Magazine for leaders of AAUW branches and divisions. • *On Campus With Women*, 4/year. • Also publishes brochures, research studies, study guides, and booklets. **Formerly:** Association of Collegiate Alumnae.

★44★ American Association of University Women Educational Foundation (AAUWEF)
1111 16th St. NW
Washington, DC 20036
Phone: (202)785-7700

Founded: 1958. **Description:** An arm of the American Association of University Women (see separate entry). Established to: expand AAUW's primary emphasis on educational work; facilitate the building of endowments for fellowships, research, and public service projects; supplement and further specify areas of AAUWEF concern; assume administrative and managerial responsibilities in the AAUW Educational Center. Sponsors conferences; encourages development of the Educational Center in Washington, DC, as a center for women scholars throughout the world; seeks support from other foundations for research and educational projects; also receives contributions from AAUW members. Is especially concerned with women's participation in the community and in higher education. Administers Educational Foundation Library, American and International Fellowships Program, Research and Projects endowment funds, and the Eleanor Roosevelt Fund for Women and Girls Teacher Enrichment Sabbaticals. Enables 35 women from other countries to come to the U.S. for study each year. Presents 85 fellowship awards annually to American women for advanced study. Awards public service grants to member divisions and branches; presents individual women with project grants. Library contains 4000 volumes.

★45★ American Association of Women (AAW)
2210 Wilshire Blvd., Ste. 174
Santa Monica, CA 90403
Phone: (213)395-0244
Fax: (213)394-6470
Leslie C. Dutton, Pres. & Editor

Founded: 1984. **Advisory Boards:** Crime Prevention and Reporting; Family Health Issues; Health Care Costs and Quality; Illegal Immigration and Social Security; Insurance Rates for Women; Pension Fund Investment Practices; Public Health Crisis: The AIDS Epidemic; Safer Blood Products; Public Heal and Safety Issues. **Description:** Participants include retired career women, working mothers, and elected officials. Seeks to identify issues of particular interest to women and disseminate contrasting viewpoints on these matters. Encourages women to take part in the debate on public policy. Maintains collection of research papers, news clippings, and publications; bestows awards; operates speakers' bureau. Conducts issue workshops and conferences. **Publications:** *American Association of Women Newsletter*, 2-4/year. **Formerly:** (1986) American Association of Women Voters.

★46★ American Association of Women in Community and Junior Colleges (AAWCJC)
c/o Sharon Yaap
Grossmont Community College
8800 Grossmont College Dr.
El Cajon, CA 92020
Phone: (619)697-9090
Fax: (619)461-3396
Sharon Yaap, Pres.

Founded: 1973. **Description:** Women faculty members, administrators, staff members, students, and trustees of community colleges. Objectives are to: develop communication and disseminate information among women in community, junior, and technical colleges; encourage educational program development; obtain grants for educational projects for community college women. Disseminates information on women's issues and programs. Conducts regional and state professional development workshops and forums. Maintains placement services. Bestows Mildred Bulpitt Woman of the Year Award. A council of the American Association of Community and Junior Colleges. **Members:** 2300. **Regional Groups:** 10. **State Groups:** 51. **Publications:** *AAWCJC Journal*, annual. Covers research on women's issues. • *AAWCJC Quarterly*. Newsletter reporting on association and regional activities and programs involving women. Includes book reviews; calendar of events; educational opportunities; research updates. • *Directory*, annual. • Also publishes course outlines and program descriptions.

★47★ American Association of Women Dentists (AAWD)
401 N. Michigan Ave.
Chicago, IL 60611-4267
Phone: (312)644-6610
Fax: (312)245-1084
Christine Norris, Exec.Dir.

Founded: 1921. **Description:** Female dentists and dental students. Encourages young women to pursue an academic degree in dentistry and to advance the status of women already in the dental profession. Bestows Colgate-Palmolive Award. **Members:** 2000. **Regional Groups:** 17. **Publications:** *American Association of Women Dentists Chronicle*, bimonthly. Association newsletter; includes book reviews, listings of employment opportunities, obituaries, research updates, and statistics. • *Directory*, annual. **Formerly:** (1978) Association of American Women Dentists.

★48★ American Association for Women Podiatrists
1300 State Hwy.
Ocean Township, NJ 07712
Phone: (201)531-0490
Margaret Zakanycz, Contact

Description: Composed of women who are fully or partially engaged in the practice of podiatric medicine. Provides guidance, consultation and financial assistance to women students at the colleges of Podiatric Medicine and aids newly graduated women podiatrists in establishing their practices. **Publications:** *American Association for Women Podiatrists Newsletter.*

★49★ American Association of Women Radiologists (AAWR)
1891 Preston White Dr.
Reston, VA 22091
Phone: (703)648-8939
Ann Rosser Wieseneck, Exec.Dir.

Founded: 1980. **Description:** Physicians involved in diagnostic or therapeutic radiology, nuclear medicine, or radiologic physics. Facilitates exchange of knowledge and information as it relates to women in radiology; encourages publication of materials on radiology and medicine by members; supports women who are training in the field and encourages women at all levels to participate in radiological societies. Maintains ad hoc committees on affirmative action, radiation therapists, and policy on pregnancy. Conducts seminars and workshops; bestows awards. **Members:** 1200. **Publications:** *AAWR Focus*, quarterly. Newsletter. • *AAWR Membership Directory*, annual.

★50★ American Astronomical Society
Committee on the Status of Women in Astronomy
2000 Florida Ave. NW, Ste. 300
Washington, DC 20009
Phone: (202)328-2010
Roger Bell, Secretary

★51★ American Atheist Women (AAW)
PO Box 140195
Austin, TX 78714-0195
Phone: (512)458-1244
Dr. Madalyn Murray O'Hair, Sec.

Founded: 1960. **Description:** Female atheists united for the enrichment and beautification of life and to emphasize the need for quality living. Conducts leadership education/training program. Sponsors programs for children; maintains speakers' bureau and biographical archives; compiles statistics. **Members:** 35,000. **Publications:** Monographs.

★52★ American Bar Association (ABA)
Commission on Women in the Profession
750 N. Lakeshore Dr.
Chicago, IL 60611
Phone: (312)988-5676
Fax: (312)988-6281
Elaine Weiss, Director

Description: Assesses the status of women in the legal profession by identifying barriers to advancement and key issues of concern to women lawyers. The commission develops educational materials, programs, and research to address the discrimination women lawyers encounter and makes recommendations to the Association for action to address identified problems and barriers. The Commission has published a comprehensive manual, *Lawyers and Balanced Lives: A Guide to Drafting and Implementing Workplace Policies for Lawyers*; provides assistance to individuals and organizations interested in studying issues of concern to women lawyers; and conducts conferences on a variety of topics. **Publications:** National newsletter; Commission mailing list.

★53★ American Bar Association
Section on Individual Rights and
Responsibilities
Committee on the Rights of Women
1800 M St. NW
Washington, DC 20036
Phone: (202)822-6644
Leslie Harris, Co-Chair

Founded: 1970. **Description:** Committee educates the profession on issues affecting women and works to improve the status of women within the profession. **Publications:** *Human Rights Magazine*.

★54★ American Business Women's
Association (ABWA)
9100 Ward Pkwy.
PO Box 8728
Kansas City, MO 64114
Phone: (816)361-6621
Fax: (816)361-4991
Carolyn B. Elman, Exec.Dir.

Founded: 1949. **Description:** Women in business, including women owning or operating their own businesses, women in professions, and women employed in any level of government, education, or retailing, manufacturing, and service companies. Provides opportunities for businesswomen to help themselves and others grow personally and professionally through leadership, education, networking support, and national recognition. Presents national Top Ten Business Women of ABWA, and Local Woman of the Year awards to outstanding businesswomen. Offers leadership training and discounted CareerTrack programs, a resume service, credit card and member loan programs,

and various travel and insurance benefits. Annually Awards more than $2.5 million to women students through chapter scholarship programs; also awards scholarships nationally through the Stephen Bufton Memorial Educational Fund. Sponsors American Business Women's Day annually on Sept. 22. **Members:** 90,000. **Local Groups:** 2000. **Publications:** *CONNECT*, quarterly. Newsletter. • *Women in Business*, bimonthly. General interest magazine for businesswomen. • Also publishes training materials.

★55★ American Chemical Society (ACS)
Women Chemists Committee
1155 16th St. NW
Washington, DC 20036
Phone: (202)872-4456
Eileen Reilley, Staff Liason

Description: The Committee is concerned with the professional activities of the more than 23,000 women American Chemical Society members. Its goals are to develop programs to assure full participation of women chemists in their profession and in the Society at national, regional, and local levels and to stimulate the active interest of women chemists in the work of the Society. The committee prepares reports on the number of women in chemistry faculties of institutions granting Ph.D., M.S., and B.S. degrees in chemistry and studies of the economic status of women in the ACS; maintains resource file of women members willing to serve on the ACS Committee or review panels; monitors legislation affecting women chemists; publishes semi-annual newsletter; sponsors symposia. **Publications:** *Women Chemists*—semi-annual newsletter.

★56★ American Child Custody Alliance
(ACCA)
7400 E. 118th Pl.
Kansas City, MO 64134
Phone: (816)333-9911

★57★ American Citizens Concerned for
Life Education Fund (ACCL)
ACCL Communications Center
PO Box 179
Excelsior, MN 55331
Phone: (612)474-0885
Gloria Ford, Pres.

Founded: 1973. **Description:** Individuals engaged in educational, legislative, research, and service activities directed toward increasing respect, protection, and support for human life. Believes that society should encourage recognition of the humanity of the unborn. Purposes are: to encourage among the public an understanding of the dignity and worth of each human life whatever his or her circumstances; to foster respect for human life before and after birth, particularly for the defenseless, the incompetent, and the impaired and incapacitated; to promote, encourage, and sponsor legislative measures that will support these goals. Activities are focused in the area of education of the public on issues such as abortion, alternatives to abortion, euthanasia, ethics and morality, the disabled, and the elderly. Maintains resource center and speakers' bureau. **Publications:** *ACCL Communications Center Resource Catalog*, updated annually. • *Communications Center Update*, 3/year. Newsletter including book reviews and editorials. • Also publishes *Counseling the Individual Experiencing a Troubled Pregnancy* (manual for counselors), catalogs of books, pamphlets, and other pro-life materials;

makes available videotape and slide presentations on the abortion issue. **Formerly:** (1974) American Citizens for Life.

★58★ American Civil Liberties Union
(ACLU)
132 W. 43rd St.
New York, NY 10036
Phone: (212)944-9800
Fax: (212)354-5290
Ira Glasser, Exec.Dir.

Founded: 1920. **Description:** Champions the rights set forth in the Bill of Rights of the U.S. Constitution: freedom of speech, press, assembly, and religion; due process of law and fair trial; equality before the law regardless of race, color, sexual orientation, national origin, political opinion, or religious belief. Activities include litigation, advocacy, and public education. Maintains library of more than 3000 volumes. Sponsors litigation projects on topics such as women's rights, gay and lesbian rights, and children's rights. **Members:** 375,000. **State Groups:** 50. **Local Groups:** 200. **Publications:** *Civil Liberties*, quarterly. • *Civil Liberties Alert*, monthly. • Also publishes policy statements, handbooks, reprints, and pamphlets.

★59★ American Civil Liberties Union
Foundation (ACLUF)
132 W. 43rd St.
New York, NY 10036
Phone: (212)944-9800
Ira Glasser, Exec.Dir.

Founded: 1966. **Description:** Established as the tax-exempt arm of the American Civil Liberties Union (see separate entry). Purposes are legal defense, research, and public education on behalf of civil liberties including freedom of speech, press, and other First Amendment rights. Sponsors projects on topics such as children's rights, capital punishment, censorship, women's rights, immigration, prisoners' rights, national security, voting rights, and equal employment opportunity. Conducts research and public education projects to enable citizens to know and assert their rights. Seeks funds to protect liberty guaranteed by the Bill of Rights and the Constitution. **Regional Groups:** 2. **Publications:** *Annual Report*. • *Civil Liberties*, quarterly. Newsletter covering the legal defense, research, and public education projects of the foundation. Includes legislative news. • *First Principles*, monthly. **Formerly:** (1969) Roger Baldwin Foundation of ACLU.

★60★ American Coalition for Life (ACL)
PO Box 44415
Ft. Washington, MD 20749
Phone: (202)582-1343
Fax: (301)292-0609
Ray Allen, Exec. Officer

Founded: 1981. **Description:** Individuals and businesses dedicated to extending "compassion to the preborn." Concerned with human life issues, in particular abortion, infanticide, and euthanasia. Lobbies Congress. **Publications:** *Adopt A Congressman* (brochure) and *Congressional Life Index*.

★61★ American College of Nurse-Midwives (ACNM)
1522 K St. NW, Ste. 1000
Washington, DC 20005
Phone: (202)289-0171
Fax: (202)289-4395
Ronald E. Nitzsche, COO

Founded: 1955. **Description:** Registered nurses certified to extend their practice into providing gynecological services and care of mothers and babies throughout the maternity cycle; members have completed an ACNM accredited program of study and clinical experience in midwifery and passed a national certification exam. Cooperates with allied groups to enable nurse-midwives to concentrate their efforts in the improvement of services for mothers and newborn babies. Seeks to identify areas of nurse-midwifery practices as they relate to the total service and educational aspects of maternal and newborn care. Studies and evaluates activities of nurse-midwives in order to establish qualifications; cooperates in planning and developing educational programs. conducts research and continuing education workshops. sponsors research. Compiles statistics; bestows awards. Maintains speakers' bureau and archives; offers placement service. **Members:** 3000. **Regional Groups:** 6. **Local Groups:** 53. **Computerized Services:** Mailing list gravidata, software offering clinical data for nurses and midwives. **Publications:** *American College of Nurse-Midwives Membership Directory Supplement*, annual. • *Directory of Nurse-Midwifery Practices*, annual. Computer listing of certified nurse-midwives by state. • *Journal of Nurse-Midwifery*, bimonthly. Covers topics relevant to maternal and newborn health, obstetrics, well-woman gynecology, family planning, and midwifery education and clinical practice. Includes annual index and book and other media reviews. • *Quickening*, bimonthly. Newsletter; includes activities, calendar of events, employment listings, and legislative updates. • Also publishes pamphlets and brochures. **Formerly:** (1969) American College of Nurse-Midwifery.

★62★ American College of Obstetricians and Gynecologists (ACOG)
409 12th St. SW
Washington, DC 20024
Phone: (202)638-5577
Warren H. Pearse, M.D., Exec.Dir.

Founded: 1951. **Description:** Physicians specializing in childbirth and the diseases of women. Sponsors continuing professional development program. Maintains library of 8000 volumes. **Publications:** *Bulletin*, periodic. • *Directory of Fellows*, biennial. • *Newsletter*, monthly. • *Obstetrics and Gynecology*, monthly. • Also publishes manuals and patient booklets. **Formerly:** American Academy of Obstetrics and Gynecology.

★63★ American College of Obstetricians and Gynecologists (ACOG)
Nurses Association
409 12th St. SW
Washington, DC 20024-2188
Phone: (202)638-0026
Judith Serevino, Deputy Director

Description: Establishes and promotes the highest standards of prenatal women's health nursing practice, education, and research. Maintains a fetal heart rate monitoring national education program; intermediate nursing care

video and critical care obstetrics video; annual meetings; home-study modules; videos on teen pregnancy, childbirth, substance abuse, parenting. **Publications:** *NAACOG Newsletter*, *Journal of Obstetrics, Gynocologic and Neonatal Nursing*, *Clinical Issues in Perinatal and Women's Health Nursing*, *NAACOG's Women's Health Nursing Scan*.

★64★ American Collegians for Life (ACL)
PO Box 1112
Washington, DC 20013
Phone: (202)965-0699
Robert Salm, Chair

Founded: 1977. **Description:** Collegiate pro-life groups, individual collegiate pro-lifers, and persons interested in stimulating pro-life activity on college campuses. Provides communication link among collegiate pro-lifers and offers contacts, ideas, and suggestions to other groups planning similar programs. Maintains library of pro-life books and files for internal reference; operates speakers' bureau; bestows awards. **Members:** 1500. **Regional Groups:** 10. **State Groups:** 20. **Local Groups:** 150. **Computerized Services:** Mailing list. **Publications:** *VITA*, monthly. Newsletter. **Formerly:** (1987) Coalition of American Pro Life University Students.

★65★ American Council for Career Women (ACCW)
c/o Joan Savoy
PO Box 50825
New Orleans, LA 70150
Phone: (504)529-1116
Joan Savoy, Pres.

Founded: 1979. **Description:** Corporations, organizations representing 5000 individuals, and individuals concerned about the interests of career women. Purpose is to promote leadership and professional development among women. Seeks to enhance opportunities for career women in all educational and employment endeavors. Provides a forum for the discussion of issues, opportunities, and problems concerning women in business. Encourages higher business standards and improved business methods among men and women; works to maintain the integrity of and improve the business conditions for working women. Promotes heightened public awareness of and the demand for opportunities, products, and services for women; seeks to educate the public to the opportunities available to women. Bestows Achievers Award to outstanding business woman. Sponsors annual professional seminar. **Members:** 5175. **Computerized Services:** Accounting; mailing list. **Publications:** *American Council for Career Women Membership Roster*, annual. • *News/Views*, quarterly. • Also publishes *Women's Career Calendar*.

★66★ American Council on Education (ACE)
Office of Women in Higher Education (OWHE)
1 Dupont Circle
Washington, DC 20036-1193
Phone: (202)939-9390
Fax: (202)833-4760
Donna Shavlik, Director

Description: In 1971, the office established the National Identification Program (NIP) for the Avancement of Women in Higher Education Administration which seeks to advance Black, Hispanic, Asian Pacific, American Indian, and

white women in academic administration. A central objective of the program is to strengthen the state and national networks that have been established. The general plan of development of the program includes appointment of state coordinators who hold high-level administrative posts; formation of state panels of men and women who influence and shape educational policy; identification of women administrators within each state, and development of programs and strategies to promote their advancement; holding ACE national forums. ACENIP provides services regarding women, general information on programs, policies, ideas to advance women students, faculty, staff, and administrators in higher education. **Publications:** *Higher Education and National Affairs*, ACE newsletter. • *Educational Record*, quarterly magazine.

★67★ American Council of Railroad Women (ACRW)
Norfolk Southern Corp.
185 Spring St.
Atlanta, GA 30303
Phone: (404)529-2148
Deborah Harris, Pres.

Founded: 1944. **Description:** Women employed in the railroad industry as corporate officers or in management, professional, or high-level supervisory positions. **Members:** 175. **Publications:** *American Council of Railroad Women—Bulletin*, quarterly. **Formerly:** (1952) National Association of Railroad Women.

★68★ American Economics Association (AEA)
Committee on the Status of Women in the Economics Profession (CSWEP)
c/o Nancy M. Gordon
Congressional Budget Office
2nd & D Sts. SW, Rm. H2-418A
Washington, DC 20515
Phone: (202)226-2669
Nancy M. Gordon, Chair

Founded: 1973. **Description:** Maintains a presence at the annual meetings of the AEA and regional economics associations. Sponsors technical sessions and hosts social events. **Publications:** *Roster of Women Economists*. • *CSWEP Newsletter*. Contains topics such as job opportunities, research funds, scholarships, fellowships, conferences and women's progress within the profession.

★69★ American Educational Research Association (AERA)
Research on Women and Education Group (RWE)
San Jose State University
Department of Mathematics and Computer Science
San Jose, CA 95192-0103
Phone: (408)924-5112
Joanne Rossi Becker, Chair

Founded: 1973. **Description:** The Group operates in large part as one of approximately forty Special Interest Groups (SIGs) within the American Educational Research Association. This SIG was established with two major purposes: to provide a structure within AERA for the promotion of research concerning women and girls in education; and to provide a mechanism to facilitate communication among researchers and practitioners who are concerned about women in education. In addition to its own activities, the SIG works cooperatively with AERA officers as well as with other SIGs and divisions of the larger organization to promote research on women in education and equity within the profession. Activities have included co-sponsoring sessions and other events with other AERA groups. The SIG/RWE also works collaboratively with the Committee on the Role and Status of Women and Women Educators in co-sponsoring the Annual Willystine Goodshell Award. **Publications:** Periodic newsletter.

★70★ American Farm Bureau Federation Women's Committee
225 Touhy Ave.
Park Ridge, IL 60068
Phone: (312)399-5764
Marsha Purcell, Staff Director

Founded: 1919. **Description:** An indpendent, non-governmental, voluntary organization of farm and ranch families united for the purpose of analyzing problems and formulating action to achieve educational improvement, economic opportunity and social advancement.

★71★ American Federation of State, County and Municipal Employees (AFSCME)
Women's Rights Department
1625 L St. NW
Washington, DC 20036
Phone: (202)429-5090
Fax: (202)429-1293
Cathy Collette, Director

Description: Over 50 percent of AFSCME's membership is comprised of women. The union is one of few unions to have a department devoted to championing issues of concern to women and to helping women members achieve their leadership potential. The Women's Rights Department works with other AFSCME departments to ensure that the interests of women members are reflected throughout the union and provides direct services to members through workshops and technical assistance in dealing with issues such as pay equity, sexual harassment, and child abuse. **Publications:** *Public Employee*, six times per year. • *Leader*, weekly. • *Women's Letter*, four times per year.

★72★ American Federation of Teachers (AFT)
Women's Rights Committee
Human Rights Department
555 New Jersey Ave., NW
Washington, DC 20001
Phone: (202)879-4400
Barbara Van Blake, Director

Description: The Committee, comprised of AFT members that represent women across the United States, meets regularly to deal with topics affecting women, such as integrating women's history into the curriculum, sexual harassment, child care options, and pay equity. The Committee works to keep these issues before the membership, as well as lobbying for reform; conducts research and education programs; maintains a speakers bureau; and compiles statistics.

★73★ American Federation of Television and Radio Artists (AFTRA)
National Women's Division
260 Madison Ave.
New York, NY 10016
Phone: (212)532-0800
Virginia Williams, President

Founded: 1973. **Description:** Focuses on issues and concerns to women, including employment and upgrading the image of women in media.

★74★ American Film Institute
Directing Workshop for Women
2021 North Western Ave.
PO Box 27999
Los Angeles, CA 90027
Phone: (213)856-7722
Tess Martin, Director, Production/Training Division

Description: Provides an opportunity for women in the media arts to develop their talents as screen directors. The Workshop is structured as an intensive, hands-on learning experience that offers mid-career professional women their first opportunities to direct dramatic videotape projects.

★75★ American Folklore Society
Women's Section
George Mason University
Dept. of English
Fairfax, VA 22030
Phone: (703)323-2220
Peggy Yocum, Chair

★76★ American Foundation for Maternal and Child Health (AFMCH)
439 E. 51st St., 4th Fl.
New York, NY 10022
Phone: (212)759-5510
Doris Haire, Pres.

Founded: 1972. **Description:** Serves as a clearinghouse for interdisciplinary research on maternal and child health; focuses on the perinatal or birth period and its effect on infant development. Sponsors medical research designed to improve application of technology in maternal and child health; conducts educational programs; compiles statistics. Operates extensive reference library.

★77★ American Friends Service Committee
Nationwide Women's Program
1501 Cherry St.
Philadelphia, PA 19102
Phone: (215)241-7181
Joyce Miller, Co-chair

Founded: 1975. **Description:** Works to strengthen both ability and commitment of the Committee to address women's perspectives directly in all stages of program activities. The Committee provides encouragement and helps to locate and to create program resources for national and regional staff to engage constituencies of women throughout their work. **Publications:** *Listen Real Loud: News of Women's Liberation Worldwide.*

★78★ American GI Forum Women
c/o Marianne Martinez
9948 S. Plaza, Apt. 1-D
Omaha, NE 68127
Phone: (402)593-1248
Marianne Martinez, Chair

Founded: 1948. **Description:** Women ages 14 and over who are American citizens and are either married or related to members of the American GI Forum of United States. Seeks to "secure the blessing of American democracy at every level of life" for all citizens and support the interests of persons of Hispanic ancestry through upholding and defending the U.S. Constitution and fostering religious and political freedom. Sponsors competitions; provides scholarships. Presents awards for outstanding community service. **Members:** 6000. **Publications:** *The Forumeer*, monthly. Membership activities newsletter. **Formerly:** American GI Forum Auxiliary.

★79★ American Gold Star Mothers (AGSM)
2128 Leroy Pl. NW
Washington, DC 20008
Phone: (202)265-0991
Winona L. Tucker, Pres.

Founded: 1928. **Description:** Natural mothers whose sons or daughters died in the line of duty in the armed forces during World Wars I and II, the Korean Conflict, the Vietnam hostilities, or in other strategic areas. Seeks to: inspire patriotism and a sense of individual obligation to the community, state, and nation; assist veterans and their dependents with claims made to the Veterans Administration; perpetuate the memory of individuals who died in our wars; promote peace and good will for the U.S. and all other nations. Mothers work as volunteers in VA Medical Centers and at Vietnam Veterans Memorial Fund. **Members:** 4000. **State Groups:** 34. **Local Groups:** 385. **Publications:** *Gold Star Mother*, bimonthly.

★80★ American Gynecological and Obstetrical Society (AGOS)
c/o James R. Scott, M.D.
University of Utah
50 N. Medical Dr.
Salt Lake City, UT 84132
Phone: (801)581-5501
James R. Scott, M.D., Sec.

Founded: 1981. **Description:** To cultivate and promote knowledge concerning obstetrics and gynecology. Awards Association Foundation Prize for the gathering, promotion, and dissemination of theoretical and practical knowledge on subjects relating to obstetrics and gynecology. Holds learning workshops. **Members:** 300. **Publications:** *Transactions*, annual.

★81★ American History Association
400 A St. SE
Washington, DC 20003
Phone: (202)544-2422
Noralee Frankle, Asst. Dir. on Women and Minorities

Description: Promotes the status of women historians and the study and scholarship of the history of women and minorities. **Publications:** *Directory of Women Historians.* **Alternate phone number:** (703)569-2213.

★82★ American Home Economics
Association (AHEA)
1555 King St.
Alexandria, VA 25314
Phone: (703)706-4600
Karl Beddle, Interim Dir.

Founded: 1909. Description: Holds annual
meetings and provides discounts on products
and group insurance. Projects include Education for Pregnant Teenagers and "Home Safe"
for Latch-Key Children. Publications: AHEA
Action. • Journal of Home Economics. • Home
Economics Research Journal.

★83★ American Humanist Association
Feminist Caucus
Box 21506
San Jose, CA 95151
Phone: (408)924-5325
Meg Bowman, Chair

★84★ American Institute of Architects
Women in Architecture Committee
1735 New York Ave. NW
Washington, DC 20006
Phone: (202)626-7305
Fax: (202)626-7518
Jean Barber, Director, Special Programs

Description: The Committee reviews, monitors,
and develops for Board consideration policies
and programs that insure full opportunities for
women in the profession and at all levels of the
Institute. The Committee also aids in implementing Institute policy to pursue aggressively the
full integration of women in the profession with
equal opportunity. Activities of the Committee
include a women in architecture speakers'
bureau; promoting and publicizing women architects, developing a national liaison network; and
educational outreach.

★85★ American Institute of Certified
Planners
Women's Rights Committee
1776 Massachusetts Ave. NW
Washington, DC 20036
Phone: (202)872-0611

★86★ American Jewish Congress
Commission for Women's Equality
15 E 84th St.
New York, NY 10028
Phone: (212)360-1560
Fax: (212)249-3672
Harriet Kurlander, Director

Founded: 1985. Description: The Commission
was established to provide a forum for inquiry
and discussion of a wide range of issues
important to Jewish women. The American
Jewish Congress, which traditionally has had a
strong commitment to women's rights, established the Commission to place women's equality at the top of its agenda. The Commission
works to educate its constituencies on the
topics of reproductive freedom, economic equity, child care, equality in religious life, and the
equality of women in politics and in Jewish
Communal life.

★87★ American Legion Auxiliary
777 N. Merican St.
Indianapolis, IN 46204
Phone: (317)635-6291
Fax: (317)636-5590
Miriam Junge, National Secretary

Description: Women's auxiliary unit of the
national American Legion organization of veter-

ans. Offers scholarships and leadership development. Publications: National News Magazine.

★88★ American Library Association (ALA)
ACRL Women's Studies Section
50 E. Huron St.
Chicago, IL 60611
Phone: (312)944-6780
Margarete S. Klein, Contact

★89★ American Library Association (ALA)
Committee on Pay Equity
50 E. Huron St.
Chicago, IL 60611
Phone: (312)944-6780
Vivian W. Pinn, Dir.

★90★ American Library Association (ALA)
Committee on the Status of Women in
Librarianship (COSWL)
50 E Huron
Chicago, IL 60611
Phone: (312)944-6780
Fax: (312)440-9374
Margaret Myers, Staff Liaison

Description: COSWL is an umbrella organization that officially represents the diversity of
women's issues within the ALA. The Committee
coordinates collection and dissemination of
information on the status of women in librarianship; represents ALA concerns at interdisciplinary meetings on women's equality; establishes
and maintains contacts with other professional
groups; and produces programs and publications designed to enhance the opportunities and
image of women in the library profession.
Subcommittees of COSWL include Advancing
Women in Library Management, Bibliography
Clearinghouse, and Legislation. The Committee
is working on an oral history project of minority
women in librarianship. Publications: American
Libraries, for members. • Women in Libraries.

★91★ American Library Association
LAMA Women Administrators Discussion
Group
50 E. Huron St.
Chicago, IL 60611
Phone: (312)944-6780
Barbara Ferris, Contact

★92★ American Library Association (ALA)
RASD Discussion Group on Women's
Materials and Women Library Users
50 E. Huron St.
Chicago, IL 60611
Phone: (312)944-6780

★93★ American Library Association (ALA)
Social Responsibilities Round Table
(SRRT)
Feminist Task Force (FTF)
50 E. Huron St.
Chicago, IL 60611
Phone: (312)944-6780
Eunice Raigrodski, Technical Information

Founded: 1970. The Force addresses sexism in
libraries and librarianship and is concerned with
a broad set of feminist issues. Publications:
Women in Libraries, bimonthly newsletter.

★94★ American Library Association (ALA)
Social Responsibilities Round Table
(SRRT)
Gay and Lesbian Task Force
Office of Library Outreach Services
50 E. Huron
Chicago, IL 60611
Phone: (312)280-4294
Toll-free: 800-545-2433
Fax: (312)440-9374
Roland C. Hansen, Co-Chair

Founded: 1970. Description: Division of the
Social Responsibilities Round Table of the
American Library Association. Purposes are to
help get more and better materials concerning
gays into libraries and out to patrons and to deal
with discrimination against gay people in libraries. Bestows annual Gay/Lesbian Book Award
to recognize and honor books relating to the
gay experience. Maintains information clearinghouse. Publications: GLTF Newsletter, periodic. Formerly: (1979) Task Force on Gay Liberation; (1987) Gay Task Force of ALA.

★95★ American Life League (ALL)
c/o America's Family Center
PO Box 1350
Stafford, VA 22554
Phone: (703)659-4171
Fax: (703)659-2586
Judie Brown, Pres.

Founded: 1982. Description: Serves as a pro-
life service organization providing educational
materials, books, flyers, and programs for local,
state, and national pro-life, pro-family organizations. Sponsors international pro-life meetings,
training sessions, and seminars. Special fields
of interest: abortion; euthanasia; organ transplantation; population; world hunger. Sponsored Coalition for Unborn Children project.
Members: 250,000. Publications: All About
Issues, monthly. Magazine. • Also publishes
Choice in Matters of Life and Death and The
Living Will (books). Formerly: American Life
Education and Research Trust.

★96★ American Life Lobby (ALL)
PO Box 490
Stafford, VA 22554
Phone: (703)659-4171
Fax: (703)659-2586
Judie Brown, Pres.

Founded: 1979. Description: Pro-life individuals opposed to abortion. Primary goal is to
secure passage of a Human Life Amendment to
the U.S. Constitution that would effect legal
recognition of the "personhood" of the unborn,
and secure constitutional protection of human
beings from the moment of fertilization. Also
fights against euthanasia and infant homicide.
Strongly opposes tax-subsidized birth control
organizations. Works to end U.S. involvement in
population control of foreign countries. Seeks to
eliminate sex, violence, and profanity on television and radio; organizes and promotes boycotts of companies that advertise on shows
considered objectionable. Provides information
on the risks of abortion and the possible
adverse effects of some school and television
sex education programs. Promotes public participation in legislative decision making; monitors activities of Senate and House committees
dealing with pro-life issues; provides addresses
and reading lists for use by concerned citizens;
participates in pro-life symposia. Bestows annual Excellence in Journalism award; sponsors
semiannual high school essay contest. Con-

ducts education and research programs through American Life League (see separate entry). Maintains 17,000 volume library of flyers, leaflets, booklets, books, and audiovisual materials. **Members:** 75,000. **State Groups:** 50. **Publications:** *Communique*, Newsletter containing legislative alerts and updates. • Also publishes books, booklets, fact sheets, and information packets on current topics.

★97★ American Lutheran Church Women (ALCW)
422 S. Fifth St.
Minneapolis, MN 55415
Phone: (612)330-3100
Bonnie Jensen, Dir.

Founded: 1960. **Description:** Adult women of the American Lutheran church. "To serve as an auxiliary to the American Lutheran Church in the achievement of its objectives of making the Gospel of Jesus Christ known among all people." Conducts study program on the Bible and on the nature and mission of the church. **Members:** 700,000. **Regional Groups:** 19. **Local Groups:** 4800. **Publications:** *Scope*, monthly.

★98★ American Mathematical Society (AMS)
Joint Committee on Women in the Mathematics Sciences
Department of Mathematics
Texas A&M University
College Station, TX 77843
Phone: (409)845-7531
Susan Geller, Chair

Description: Acts to identify and recommend to the parent organization those activities that, in the Committee's opinion, should be taken to alleviate disadvantages that women in the mathematical sciences now experience and to document these recommendations and actions by presenting appropriate data; to identify, describe, and disseminate information on those activities and materials that enhance the status of women in the mathematical sciences; and to collect and disseminate data on the current status of women in the mathematical sciences. The Committee collects data on why students leave mathematics during graduate school; collects data on the rate of acceptance for males vs. females in various journals; and compiled a bibliography on career information, the history of women in mathematics, and programs to encourage women. Request reports and bibliography through Association for Women in Mathematics, Box 178, Wellesley, MA 02181.

★99★ American Medical Women's Association (AMWA)
801 N. Fairfax St., Ste. 400
Alexandria, VA 22314
Phone: (703)838-0500
Fax: (703)549-3864
Eileen McGrath, Exec.Dir.

Founded: 1915. **Description:** Women holding a M.D. or D.O. degree from approved medical colleges; women interns, residents, and medical students. Seeks to find solutions to problems common to women studying or practicing medicine, such as career advancement and the integration of professional and family responsibilities. Provides student members with educational loans and personal counseling. Gives Elizabeth Blackwell Medal for a major contribution to medicine by a woman physician; Janet

M. Glasgow Achievement Awards to women medical students graduating at the top of their class; Carroll L. Birch Manuscript Award to a medical student writing the best scientific research paper. Accredited to sponsor continuing medical education programs. Maintains Friends of American Medical Women's Association, an auxiliary organization for husbands, relatives, and supporters of AMWA. **Members:** 11,000. **Local Groups:** 160. **Publications:** *Journal*, bimonthly. • *Quarterly Newsletter*. • *What's Happening in AMWA*, semiannual. Membership activities newsletter.

★100★ American Medical Women's Association (AMWA)
American Women's Hospitals Service Committee (AWHSC)
801 N. Fairfax St., Ste. 400
Alexandria, VA 22314
Phone: (703)838-0500
Dr. Anne Barlow, Chwm.

Founded: 1917. **Description:** Committee of American Medical Women's Association (see separate entry). International philanthropic medical relief service that supports medical and hospital services conducted by women doctors and nurses for the care of the indigent sick and prevention of disease. Current activities, carried on in Bolivia, Haiti, and the U.S., include family planning and fostering health education through demonstrations, home visits, and giving financial aid to hospitals and clinics. **Formerly:** (1959) American Women's Hospitals; (1982) American Women's Hospitals Service.

★101★ American Meteorological Society (AMS)
Board on Women and Minorities
45 Beacon St.
Boston, MA 02108
Phone: (617)227-2425
Fax: (617)742-8718
Susan F. Zevin, Chair

Description: Activities of the Board include educational initiatives, scholarships, and restructuring toward the year 2000. Maintains a clearinghouse of resource information. **Publications:** AMS newsletter. • *Journal of Applied Meteorology (JAM)*. • *Weatherwise*. • *Weather and Forecasting*.

★102★ American Mothers, Inc. (AMI)
6843 Nashville Rd.
Lanham, MD 20706
Phone: (301)552-2712
Walterena R. Clack, Pres.

Founded: 1935. **Description:** Seeks to strengthen the moral and spiritual foundations of the American home and family and to give the observance of Mother's Day "a spiritual quality representative of ideal motherhood." Offers counselor service to young mothers; sponsors young mothers study groups. Sponsors Project Pledge, a program encouraging family commitment to integrity, honesty, a good work ethic, and prayer in the home. Selects American Mother of the Year; bestows Literary & Music and Arts & Crafts awards. Maintains Hall of Fame of Mothers and National Mothers Chapel (Colorado Springs, CO). **Members:** 5000. **State Groups:** 52. **Publications:** *The American Mother*, quarterly. Newsletter. Includes award news, book reviews, calendar of events, chapter news, legislative news, and obituaries. • *American Mothers, Inc.—Yearbook*. Includes conven-

tion news, short biographies, and reports on contest and award winners. • *Literary Awards Journal*, annual. Features recipients of the annual Gertrude Fogelson Cultural Arts Literary Contest. Contains articles, stories, and poetry written on the subject of motherhood. • Also publishes *Mothers of Achievement in American History, 1776-1976* (book). **Formerly:** (1981) American Mothers Committee.

★103★ American Musicological Society (AMS)
Committee on the Status of Women
Department of Music
Middlebury College
Middlebury, VT 05753
Phone: (802)388-3711
Susan Cook, Chair

Description: The Committee consists of five to six members of the Society appointed by the President and Board of AMS. The Committee holds open meetings at the annual conference which provides forums for the discussion of concerns related to women in musicology both professionally (as in women's studies/gender research in musicology) and the practical concerns of jobs, tenure, and career/family balance. Sponsors guest speakers and shares information about other organizations that will serve women in the field. **Publications:** *AMS Newsletter*, 3 per year. The Committee also produces a directory of women in the professional music societies.

★104★ American National Cattle Women (ANCW)
5420 S. Quebec
PO Box 3881
Englewood, CO 80155
Phone: (303)694-0313
Fax: (303)694-0313
Laurie Stotts, Exec.V.Pres.

Founded: 1952. **Description:** Women who are actively employed or interested in the cattle industry. Purposes are to assist the National Cattlemen's Association, the National Live Stock and Meat Board, and other beef-related organizations in carrying out all activities necessary for the betterment of the cattle industry in the U.S. and to serve as a public clearinghouse for information concerning that industry. Holds workshops; conducts National Beef Cook-Off each September. Sponsors Beef Cattle Drive for Hunger to raise funds for distribution of beef gift certificates to the needy. **Members:** 10,000. **Regional Groups:** 7. **State Groups:** 40. **Publications:** *ANCW Directory*, annual. • *ANCW Newsletter*, bimonthly. • Also publishes beef cookbook. **Formerly:** (1986) American National Cowbelles.

★105★ American News Women's Club (ANWC)
1607 22nd St., NW
Washington, DC 20008
Phone: (202)332-6770
Jane T. Lingo, Contact

Founded: 1932. **Description:** Women who write news for all media, government agencies, nonprofit organizations, or free-lance (300); women in the news as wives of ranking officials or as professional women in the arts, sciences, education, civic affairs, government, or social service are associates (100); women not currently working professionally (50) are nonactive members. Encourages friendly understanding between members and those whom they must contact in their profession. Sponsors social events; maintains club house. **Members:** 450. **Publications:** *American News Women's Club*, annual. Directory. • *Shop Talk*, monthly. **Formerly:** (1981) American Newspaper Women's Club.

★106★ **American Nurses Asociation (ANA)**
1101 14th St. NW, Ste. 200
Washington, DC 20005
Phone: (202)789-1800
Fax: (202)842-4375
Donna R. Richardson, Director, Government
& Agency Relations

Description: Advances the nursing profession by fostering high standards of nursing practice, promoting the economic and general welfare of nurses in the workplace, and by working with the U.S. Congress and regulatory agencies on issues affecting nurses and the public. **Publications:** *Capital Update*. • *The American Nurse*.

★107★ **American Pharmaceutical Association**
Committee on Women's Affairs
2215 Constitution Ave. NW
Washington, DC 20037
Phone: (202)429-7537
Maude Babington, Director of Professional
Affairs

★108★ **American Philological Association**
Committee on the Status of Women and Minorities
Department of Classics, Campus Box 248
University of Colorado, Boulder
Boulder, CO 80309
Phone: (303)492-6257
Joy K. King, Chair

★109★ **American Philological Association (APA)**
Women's Classical Caucus (WCC)
Department of Classics
College of New Rochelle
New Rochelle, NY 10801
Phone: (914)654-5399
Barbara McManus, Treasurer

Description: Provides annual forum for presentation of feminist work on classical antiquity and co-sponsors or instigates feminist panels at regional classical association meetings. The WCC also works to eliminate sexist, ageist, and homophobic practices and attitudes in the American Philological Association by co-sponsoring an annual election questionnaire through which candidates for office respond to issues about professional practices and ethics, and by raising comparable issues for APA discussion and consideration. WCC sponsors annual panels at national APA meetings; monitors employment practices and trends; and has established a fund to help members fight discriminatory behavior and communicate with colleges and universities involved in such issues. **Publications:** *WCC Newsletter*.

★110★ **American Philosophical Association (APA)**
Committee on the Status of Women
Department of Philosophy
University of Delaware
Newark, DE 19716
Phone: (302)451-1112
Alison Jaggar, Chair

Description: Assesses and reports on the status of women in the profession. Among its responsibilities are to identify unfair or discriminatory practices and to advise the Board and the members of the Association of ways in which they may be rectified; to advise women philosophers concerning means of overcoming discrimination that they may encounter; and to make reports and recommendations to the Board concerning ways in which full and meaningful equality of opportunity can be provided to all individuals who seek to study, teach, or conduct research in philosophy. The Committee is also concerned with teaching and research and seeks to facilitate an understanding of issues of gender and of the range of positions represented in feminist theories. Other Committee areas of focus include child care, the APA Congress, hiring women, curriculum revision, and mutually anonymous revising. **Publications:** *Feminism & Philosophy Newsletter*.

★111★ **American Physical Society (APS)**
Committee on the Status of Women in Physics (CSWP)
335 E. 45th St.
New York, NY 10017
Phone: (212)682-7341
Miriam A. Forman, Director

Description: The Committee addresses the production, retention, and career development of women physicists and gathers and maintains data on women in physics in support of these objectives. CSPW may recommend to the Council of APS various programs to carry out this charge and will supervise those programs and studies the Council approves. Maintains a roster of women in physics and provides a physics colloquium speakers' list. **Publications:** *GAZETTE*, newsletter. • Also publishes career literature.

★112★ **American Physiological Association (APA)**
Women in Physiology Society
Department of Comparative Biosciences
9650 Rockville Pike
Bethesda, MD 20814
Phone: (301)530-7164
Fax: (301)571-1814
Hannah Carey, Chair

Founded: 1982. **Description:** The Society is a committee composed of four or more members of the American Physiological Society, including a student member. The duties of the committee are to deal with issues pertaining to education, employment, and professional opportunities available to women physiologists; promote the discipline of physiology as a rewarding career to young women; coordinate activities with other such committees on women with the Federation of American Societies for Experimental Biology organization and those of other scientific societies that meet intermittently with the society; develop programs to provide incentives enabling graduate students to present research work at APS meetings; and administer the Caroline tum Suden Professional Opportunity Award. The Society maintains a current list of

women in the field available to employers. **Publications:** *The Physiologist*.

★113★ **American Planning Association**
Planning and Women Division
1776 Massachusetts Ave. NW
Washington, DC 20036
Phone: (202)872-0611
Carol Barrett, Director

★114★ **American Political Science Association (APSA)**
Committee on the Status of Women in Political Science
1527 New Hampshire Ave. NW
Washington, DC 20036
Phone: (202)483-2512
Sheila Mann, Asst.Dir.

Description: The Committee consists of academic political scientists working to advance the status of women in the field of political science. Publishes recommendations to academic departments to improve relations with women and to improve the representation of women authors in scholarly journals.

★115★ **American Postal Workers Union, AFL-CIO**
Post Office Women for Equal Rights
460 W. 34th St., 9th Fl.
New York, NY 10001
Phone: (212)563-7553
Josie McMillian, President

★116★ **American ProLife Council (APLC)**
1612 S. Prospect Ave.
Park Ridge, IL 60068
Phone: (708)692-2183
John de Paul Hansen, Pres.

Founded: 1980. **Description:** Provides right-to-life activists with insurance, credit union, and other programs containing pro-life provisions. Has established American Prolife Assurance Society and a general insurance agency, and uses profits to fund pro-life causes. **Members:** 50,000. **Publications:** *By Laws*.

★117★ **American Psychiatric Association (APA)**
Association of Women Psychiatrists
9802 Farnham Rd.
Louisville, KY 40223
Phone: (502)588-6185
Fax: (502)588-6849
Kathy Garvin, Executive Assistant

Description: The group's purpose is to form an international network of women psychiatrists; to improve communications and provide support to women psychiatrists; to promote women psychiatrists into leadership positions in all aspects of health care; to collect and disseminate information on women's mental health issues; to encourage and support activities and research into women's mental health issues; to advocate for just legislation for women; to encourage women psychiatrists to actively participate in the APA, both locally and nationally; and to influence the policy and procedures of the APA so it meets the needs of women. **Publications:** *Women in Psychiatry Newsletter*.

★118★ American Psychiatric Association (APA)
Committee on Women and Women's Caucus
1400 K St. NW
Washington, DC 20005
Phone: (202)682-2000
Fax: (202)682-6114
Jean Spurlock, Deputy Medical Director

Description: Defines and recommends action to meet the mental health needs of women; promotes the involvement of women psychiatrists in academic, research, administration, and professional organizations; reviews and stimulates research in the development of theories necessary to implement the aforementioned; and provides support systems for women colleges. The Women's Caucus nominates/elects representatives for the Assembly of District Branches. Concerns of the Committee include care of pregnant and newly-delivered women addicts; legislation to lift the ban on funding of total issue transplantation research; study of the psychiatric aspects of new reproductive technologies; promotion of reproductive choice. **Publications:** *American Journal of Psychiatry,* monthly. • *Psychiatric News,* twice monthly.

★119★ American Psychological Association (APA)
Committee on Women in Psychology
Department of Medical Psychology
4301 Jones Bridge Rd.
Bethesda, MD 20804
Phone: (301)295-3270
Sheryl Gallant, Chair

★120★ American Psychological Association (APA)
Division of the Psychology of Women
Women's Program Office
750 1st St. NE
Washington, DC 20002-4242
Phone: (202)336-6044
Fax: (202)336-6040
Gwendolyn Puryear Keita, Director, Women's Program Office

Description: The Association is devoted to the promotion of research and practice of feminist psychology. Division members work for the success of equitable treatment of women throughout society and within the discipline of psychology. These psychologists focus their work on issues related to and involving women at all stages of development and across all levels of society. Division maintains sections for members interested in issues relating to African American women, and for members in clinical training and practice. **Publications:** *Newsletter of Division of Psychology of Women Quarterly.*

★121★ American Psychological Association (APA)
Women's Caucus, Council of Representatives
1200 17th St. NW
Washington, DC 20036
Phone: (212)691-6587
Judith Alpert, Chair

Description: Objectives include improved research, education, training, and practice involving women and gender issues. The caucus also promotes the career status of women in psychology and in addition advocates the equality and well-being of women as members of society and the global community. Activities include the formulation and review of APA policy in

each of these areas and the endorsement of individuals who support these goals for election to APA boards and committees. All APA divisions and state coalitions, as well as individual Council members, are invited to join the women's Caucus.

★122★ American Public Health Association (APHA)
Women's Caucus
1015 15th St. NW
Washington, DC 20005
Phone: (202)789-5600
Shauna Heckert, Chair

Description: Formed to provide a forum for feminist input into the APHA through programs and resolutions. **Publications:** *Women's Caucus Newsletter,* two times per year.

★123★ American Rape Prevention Association (ARPA)
50 Muth Dr.
Orinda, CA 94563
Phone: (415)254-0963
Joseph Eugene Spott, Co-CEO

Founded: 1943. **Description:** Men, women, and children dedicated to preventing rape, incest, domestic violence and rape, sexual harassment, and kidnap/rape/murder (RIDS). Trains women and girls to respond to assault by using weapons against attackers, whom the association refers to as RIDS predators. ARPA believes that a female trained in RIDS prevention is "aggressive and offensive, forcing the RIDS predator to be defensive and try to escape from her." Asserts that rape crisis and battered women's programs encourage women to be dependent on law enforcement and social agencies for protection and discourage women from taking preventive measures in the event of an attack. Encourages local schools to offer doctoral degrees in RIDS prevention; accredits RIDS prevention programs and certifies individuals. Offers seminars and professional training programs. Lobbies; bestows awards; maintains biographical archives, museum, and hall of fame. Operates speakers' bureau and 200 volume library. Conducts children's services and charitable program; compiles statistics. Local groups are involved in programs, including: human and animal research to determine the causes, treatments, and cures of criminal sexual behavior; development of weapons for use against the assailant; private patrols that respond to emergencies and serve as protective escorts. **Members:** 60,000. **State Groups:** 17. **Publications:** *ARPA Newsletter,* monthly. • *Directory of Accredited RIDS Prevention Centers in the U.S.,* annual. • *Directory of Accredited Schools,* annual. • *Journal of the American Rape Prevention Association,* monthly. • *RPI Newsletter,* quarterly. • Also publishes news releases and books.

★124★ American Society of Allied Health Professions
Women's Issues Section
1101 Connecticut Ave., NW, Ste. 700
Washington, DC 20036
Phone: (202)857-1150
Carolyn M. Del Polito, Exec. Dir.

Founded: 1967. **Description:** Professional organization concerned with educational and professional interests of allied health. **Publications:** *Trends Newsletter.* • *Journal of Allied Health.*

★125★ American Society of Bio-Chemistry and Molecular Biology (ASBMB)
Committee on Equal Opportunities for Women
9650 Rockville Pike
Bethesda, MD 20814
Phone: (301)530-7145
Fax: (301)571-1824
Charles Hancock, Executive Officer

Description: Promotes career opportunities for women in bio-chemistry and molecular biology. Sponsors a panel at ASBMB national meeting.

★126★ American Society of Church History (ASCH)
Women in Theology and Church History (WITCH)
Lutheran Theological Seminary
7301 Germantown Ave.
Philadelphia, PA 19119
Phone: (215)248-4616
Fax: (215)248-4577
Faith Burgess, Chair

Description: The purpose of WITCH is to give a voice to women in the affairs of the Society for Church History as well as support to further the works of women's church history scholars and women's studies in church history.

★127★ American Society for Eighteenth Century Studies
Women's Caucus
Mail Location 368
University of Cincinnati
Cincinnati, OH 45221
Phone: (513)556-3820
Felicia Sturzer, Chair

Description: The Caucus selects seminar and paper topics for the society's annual meeting and discusses issues which affect women in the profession and makes suggestions to the executive board. Association and caucus activities include bibliographies, fellowships, and scholarly prizes. **Publications:** *Eighteenth Century Studies.*

★128★ American Society for Microbiology (ASM)
Committee on the Status of Women in Microbiology
1325 Massachusetts Ave., NW
Washington, DC 20005
Phone: (202)833-9680
Anne Morris Hooke, Contact

Founded: 1972. **Description:** Promotes status of women in microbiology and works to advance equal opportunity for women microbiologists at the national level. **Publications:** *Communicator,* quarterly.

★129★ American Society of Professional and Executive Women (ASPEW)
1429 Walnut St.
Philadelphia, PA 19102
Phone: (215)563-4415
Laurie Wagman, Exec.Dir.

Founded: 1979. **Description:** To promote, through practical information and benefits, a positive attitudinal environment for career women involved in all areas of American enterprise. Conducts seminars; provides discount library services and executive recruitment. **Members:** 25,200. **Computerized Services:** Data base. **Publications:** *Successful Woman in Business,* quarterly. Membership magazine for professional and executive women. Includes list of books and other resources on management, leadership, and business issues. • Also publishes guides.

★130★ **American Society for Psychoprophylaxis in Obstetrics (ASPO/LAMAZ)**
1101 Connecticut Ave. NW, Ste. 700
Washington, DC 20036
Phone: (202)857-1128
Toll-free: 800-368-4404
Fax: (703)524-8743
Linda Harmon, Exec.Dir.

Founded: 1960. **Description:** Physicians, nurses, nurse-midwives, certified teachers of psychoprophylatic (Lamaze) method of childbirth, other professionals, parents, and others interested in Lamaze childbirth preparation and family-centered maternity care. Disseminates information about the theory and practical application of psychoprophylaxis in obstetrics; administers teacher training courses and certifies qualified Lamaze teachers; sponsors prenatal classes in the Lamaze method for expectant parents; provides educational lectures, public forums, films, and written materials; maintains national and local teacher and physician referral service; bestows awards. Also presents materials to prospective parents concerning the demands of childrearing. Holds three to five continuing education workshops per year. Compiles statistics on the number of births and birth experiences of individuals using the Lamaze method. National office serves as information clearinghouse and houses small library. **Members:** 5000. **Local Groups:** 32. **Computerized Services:** Mailing lists for educational programs. **Publications:** *Genesis*, bimonthly. Newsletter. Contains book and film reviews and calendar of events. • *Lamaze Parents' Magazine*, semiannual. Supplements childbirth classes. • Also issues brochures, teaching aids, and films.

★131★ **American Society for Public Administration**
Section for Women in Public Administration
The Evergreen State College
3306 Windolp Loop, NW
Olympia, WA 98502
Phone: (206)866-6000
Camilla Stivers, Chair

★132★ **American Society for Training and Development (ASTD)**
Women's Network
1630 Duke St.
Box 1443
Alexandria, VA 22313
Phone: (703)683-8100
Fax: (703)683-8103
Mary Samsa, Director

Description: Serves as a catalyst and consulting resource regarding women in the human resource development profession by providing products and services; engaging in professional leadership development activities; providing liaison to other ASTD councils, network, and committees; providing a focal point and opportunity for linkages for those interested in issues of women in the human resource development field; and engaging in development, risk taking, outreach to other networks, and new forums for networking. The Women's Network provides programming for the ASTD National Conference; and presents national awards for leaders

in human resource development profession who support the resolution of gender issues in the workplace. **Publications:** *Women's Network*, sent to all national ASTD members who designate Women's Network affiliation.

★133★ **American Society of Women Accountants (ASWA)**
1755 Lynnfield Rd., Ste. 222
Memphis, TN 38119-7235
Phone: (901)680-0470
Fax: (901)680-0505
Allison Conte, Exec.Dir.

Founded: 1938. **Description:** Professional society of women accountants, educators, and others in the field of accounting. Assists women accountants in their careers and promotes development in the profession. Conducts educational and research programs; training seminars; bestows awards. **Members:** 8000. **Local Groups:** 140. **Publications:** *Coordinator*, monthly. Membership activities newsletter. Includes calendar of events, listings of new officers and directors, and recognizes distinguished members. • *Membership Directory*, annual.

★134★ **American Sociological Association (ASA)**
Committee on the Status of Women
1722 N St. NW
Washington, DC 20036
Phone: (202)833-3410
Fax: (202)785-0146
Carla B. Howery, Deputy Executive Officer

Description: The Committee monitors the participation of women in the Association, in the profession, and the impact of feminist work in sociology. The Committee is also concerned with representation of women at all ranks in sociology department faculties; gender as a variable in research; special issues of women of color; and curriculum materials for teaching about women. **Publications:** *Footnotes*, monthly newsletter.

★135★ **American Sociological Association**
Sex and Gender Section
Rutgers University, Sociology Department
PO Box 5072
New Brunswick, NJ 08904-5072
Phone: (908)932-2897
Judith M. Gerson, Chair

Description: The Sex and Gender Section brings together faculty researchers, practitioners, writers, students, and activists interested in the study of gender relations. Members of the section organize numerous panels and sessions at the annual meetings of the Association, presenting new research findings and analyses focused on gender. It has compiled and is currently updating a directory of its almost one thousand members and their areas of expertise and specialization. The Section also awards a prize annually for the best dissertation in the study of gender. **Publications:** *The Sex and Gender Newsletter*.

★136★ **American Speech-Language-Hearing Association**
Committee on the Equality of the Sexes
10801 Rockville Pike
Rockville, MD 20852
Phone: (301)897-5700
Peggy S. Williams, Deputy Executive Director

★137★ **American Statistical Association**
Caucus for Women in Statistics
Ohio State University
Statistics Department
1938 Neil Ave.
Columbus, OH 43210-1247
Phone: (614)292-2866
Sue Leurgans, President

Founded: 1970. **Description:** The Caucus is an independent association with membership open to men and women. It interacts with all statistical professional societies, and works closely with the Committee of Women in Statistics of the ASA. The Caucus fosters opportunities for the education, employment, and advancement of women in statistics, and the recruitment of women into the profession of statistics; promotes increased participation of women in professional meetings and publications and on governing boards and committees of statistical societies; stimulates professional and social contact among its members, and the interchange of concerns, ideas, and information related to its objectives; strives for the elimination of sex discrimination, and improvement of the status of professional women and female statisticians. Sponsors a fund drive for scholarships. **Publications:** *Newsletter of Caucus for Women in Statistics*.

★138★ **American Studies Association**
Women's Committee
University of Maryland
Taliafero Hall
College Park, MD 20742
Phone: (301)454-2533
Lee Chambers-Schiller, Chair

Description: The purpose of the Committee is to monitor and improve the status of women in the Association and in academe. This is accomplished through the gathering and analyzing of information collected from the membership and presented through panels at professional meetings. The Committee reports to the membership and makes recommendations for action by the governing body of the Association. The Committee is working on a study of integration of new research on women and gender into graduate training of American Studies programs. **Publications:** American Studies newsletter. • *American Quarterly*, academic journal of interdisciplinary American Culture Studies.

★139★ **American Victims of Abortion (AVA)**
419 7th St. NW, Ste. 500
Washington, DC 20004
Phone: (202)626-8800
Fax: (202)737-9189

Founded: 1985. **Description:** Individuals who have been affected by abortion including mothers, fathers, grandparents, and other relatives, doctors, nurses, and counselors. Works to expose "the truth of abortion's tragedy" and increase public awareness of "Post-Abortion Syndrome," which the association says is the physical, psychological, and emotional trauma suffered by the "secondary victims" of abortions. Conducts public awareness campaigns, legislative initiatives, and judicial activities. Maintains counseling referral service and speakers' bureau; encourages further research of "Post-Abortion Syndrome." **State Groups:** 50. **Publications:** *AVA Newsletter*, quarterly. • Also publishes brochures and pamphlets.

★140★ American War Mothers (AWM)
2615 Woodley Pl., NW
Washington, DC 20008
Phone: (202)462-2791
LaVita G. Orand, Contact

Founded: 1917. **Description:** Natural mothers of veterans, servicemen, and servicewomen. Holds Veterans' Day services at the U.S. Capitol and Mothers' Day services at Arlington Cemetery. Conducts volunteer services in VA hospitals. Presents biennial Award of Appreciation. **Members:** 3500. **State Groups:** 28. **Local Groups:** 195. **Publications:** *American War Mothers Newsletter*, quarterly.

★141★ American Woman's Economic Development Corporation (AWED)
641 Lexington Ave.
New York, NY 10022
Phone: (212)688-1900
Toll-free: 800-222-AWED
Fax: (212)688-2718
Roslyn Paaswell, CEO

Founded: 1975. **Description:** Women owning or planning to form small businesses. Sponsors 18-month training and technical assistance program. Provides management training, on-site analysis of businesses, volunteer advisers who work in specific problem areas, assistance in preparing a business plan, and continued support after the program is completed. Nine-week mini-programs are also available. Provides seminars. Staff is composed of experienced business people and specialists from university business schools and major corporations. Plans to expand to other cities and become a laboratory for research into the special problems and requirements of entrepreneurial women. **Members:** 6000. **Telecommunications Services:** Emergency business assistance hotline, (800)442-AWED in New York state; national telephone counseling service for women not enrolled in the training program. **Publications:** *Woman Entrepreneur*, monthly. Newsletter.

★142★ American Woman's Society of Certified Public Accountants (AWSCPA)
401 N. Michigan Ave.
Chicago, IL 60611
Phone: (312)644-6610
Fax: (312)321-6869
Bonnie Engle, Exec.Dir.

Founded: 1933. **Description:** Citizens of the U.S. who hold certified public accountant certificates; those who have passed the CPA examination but do not have certificates are associates; women holding degrees comparable to CPA certificates but who are not U.S. citizens are international associates. Works to improve the status of professional women and to make the business community aware of the professional capabilities of the woman CPA. Conducts semiannual statistical survey of members; offers scholarships and specialized education and research programs; bestows awards for public service and authorship; maintains biographical archives. **Members:** 4000. **Local Groups:** 45. **Publications:** *AWSCPA Newsletter*, quarterly. • *Issues Paper*, annual. • *Membership Roster*, annual.

★143★ American Women Buyers Club
225 W. 34th St.
New York, NY 10122
Phone: (212)564-7797
Marge Hafkin, Pres.

Founded: 1938. **Description:** Women who are buyers of apparel for stores and buying offices. **Members:** 70.

★144★ American Women Composers (AWC)
1690 36th St. NW, Ste. 409
Washington, DC 20007
Phone: (202)342-8179
Judith Shatin, Pres.

Founded: 1976. **Description:** Composers, performers, musicologists, and associate members. Seeks to help women attain recognition as composers by promoting and supporting the works of women composers and performers in the U.S. and by working to increase public awareness of women's contributions to American musical culture. Produces recordings of women's music. Maintains music library with over 3000 scores of women's music and biographical archives; sponsors live programs. Plans music festivals and seminars. **Members:** 350. **Regional Groups:** 3. **Publications:** *AWC News/Forum*, annual. Journal containing AWC news and activities, articles about women in music, and lists of competitions, contests, fellowships, and prizes. Also includes lists of professional opportunities and new works by contemporary women composers. • *AWC News—Update*, quarterly. **Formerly:** Female Composers of America.

★145★ American Women in Radio and Television (AWRT)
1101 Connecticut Ave. NW, Ste. 700
Washington, DC 20036
Phone: (202)429-5102
Fax: (202)223-4579
Donna Cantor, Exec.Dir.

Founded: 1951. **Description:** Professionals in administrative, creative, or executive positions in the broadcasting industry (radio, television stations, cable, and networks) as well as advertising, government, and charitable agencies, corporations, and service organizations, whose work is substantially devoted to radio and television. Maintains AWRT Educational Foundation, chartered 1960. Awards Silver Satellite for outstanding accomplishment in the field of broadcasting; also bestows awards of commendation for local and network programs. Maintains speakers' bureau and charitable program; sponsors competitions. **Members:** 3000. **Regional Groups:** 5. **Local Groups:** 52. **Computerized Services:** Mailing labels. **Publications:** *American Women in Radio & TV*, annual. Membership directory. • *News and Views*, bimonthly. • Also publishes *Women on the Job - Careers in the Electronic Media*, manuals, and treatises on the broadcasting industry.

★146★ American Women's Clergy Association (AWCA)
214 P St. NW
Washington, DC 20001
Phone: (202)797-7460
Rev. Imagene Stewart, Chairperson

Founded: 1969. **Description:** Lay and ordained women clergy. Seeks to promote and encourage the clergy as a profession for women. Operates shelter for homeless and battered

women in Washington, DC. Provides scholarships for women interested in the clergy; bestows Social Activist of the Year Award. **Members:** 167. **Local Groups:** 20.

★147★ Americans United for Life (AUL)
343 S. Dearborn, Ste. 1804
Chicago, IL 60604
Phone: (312)786-9494
Guy M. Condon, Pres.

Founded: 1971. **Description:** Pro-life educational organization concerned with protecting human life at all stages of development. Conducts legal and legislative activites including provision of testimony, model abortion statutes, and legal briefs in cases involving abortion and euthanasia. Offers summer internship to qualified law students. Maintains library of articles, books, and government publications. **Publications:** *AUL Briefing Memo*, periodic. Provides analysis of pro-life legal topics. • *AUL Forum*, quarterly. Newsletter for donors and friends. • *AUL Insights*, periodic. Includes a factual review of pro-life topics. • *Lex Vitae*, quarterly. • *Life Docket*, monthly. Contains summaries of legal news.

★148★ Americans United for Life (AULLDF)
Legal Defense Fund
343 S. Dearborn, Ste. 1804
Chicago, IL 60604
Phone: (312)786-9494
Guy M. Condon, Exec.Dir.

Founded: 1975. **Description:** Operated by Americans United for Life (see separate entry); public interest law firm and education organization. Works to reverse current U.S. laws governing abortion as defined in the 1973 U.S. Supreme Court Roe vs. Wade ruling which affirmed the legal rights of women to have an abortion during the entire nine months of pregnancy. Provides legal assistance to individuals wishing to challenge in court the Roe vs. Wade decision. Educates the public regarding euthanasia, infanticide, and abortion. Operates speakers' bureau. **Publications:** *AUL Forum*, quarterly. Newsletter. • *AUL Insights*, periodic. Includes an in-depth analyses of pertinent court cases and legislation. • *AUL Studies in Law, Medicine and Society*, periodic. Monograph series consisting of law review and other scholarly articles relating to abortion and euthanasia. • *Lex Vitae*, quarterly. Report on abortion and euthanasia litigation and legislation throughout the country. • *Life Docket*, quarterly. • Also publishes booklets.

★149★ Amit Women (AW)
817 Broadway
New York, NY 10003
Phone: (212)477-4720
Toll-free: 800-221-3117
Fax: (212)353-2312
Norma Holzer, Pres.

Founded: 1925. **Description:** Religious-Zionist organization of Jewish women. Provides child care, social welfare education, and vocational training programs for youth and newcomers to Israel in an atmosphere of Jewish tradition. Serves as Israel Ministry of Education's Official Reshet (network) for religious secondary technological and vocational education. Sponsors and maintains children's villages, vocational high schools, settlement houses, community centers, and other institutions in Israel. Distributes Passover supplies to the needy; conducts musicals and lectures for adults; provides aid to graduates. Participates in reforestation and land reclamation activities through Jewish National Fund. Conducts educational programs on life in Israel and the Jewish cultural and religious heritage; produces films and other materials. Maintains speakers' bureau. Presents annual America-Israel Friendship Award in the U.S. **Members:** 89,000. **Regional Groups:** 9. **Local Groups:** 425. **Community Councils:** 10. **Publications:** *Amit Woman*, 5/year. • *Not for Presidents Only*, 10/year. Newsletter. • *Program Guide*, bimonthly. • Also publishes biography of Bessie Gotsfeld, founder of AMW. **Formerly:** (1975) Mizrachi Women's Organization of America; (1983) American Mizrachi Women.

★150★ **ANAD—National Association of Anorexia Nervosa and Associated Disorders**
Box 7
Highland Park, IL 60035
Phone: (708)831-3438
Vivian Meehan, Exec.Dir.

Founded: 1976. **Description:** Anorectics and bulimics, their families, health professionals, and others interested in the problems of anorexia nervosa and bulimia. Maintains chapters in 45 states, Canada, Austria, South Africa, Italy, Saudi Arabia, Colombia, and Germany. Aims to: seek a better understanding of, prevent, and cure anorexia nervosa and associated eating disorders; educate the public and health professionals on illnesses relating to eating disorders and methods of treatment. Encourages and promotes research on the cause of eating disorders, methods of prevention, types of treatment and their effectiveness, and basic facts about victims. Acts as a resource center, compiling and providing information about eating disorders. Serves as an advocacy agency for those concerned with eating disorders. Works to end insurance discrimination against sufferers of eating disorders. Fights against the production, marketing, and distribution of dangerous diet aids and the use of misleading advertisements. Encourages and cosponsors local and regional meetings. Maintains speakers' bureau; provides children's services; compiles statistics. Conducts referral service, surveys, education, and early detection programs. Operates library of books, articles, and papers. Organizes selfhelp groups. **Publications:** *Working Together*, 4/year. Newsletter. **Formerly:** (1980) Anorexia Nervosa and Associated Disorders.

★151★ **Anorexia Nervosa and Related Eating Disorders (ANRED)**
PO Box 5102
Eugene, OR 97405
Phone: (503)344-1144
Dr. J. Bradley Rubel, Pres.

Founded: 1979. **Description:** Anorectics and bulimics; families and friends of anorectics and bulimics; medical and mental health professionals, school personnel, pastors, and community youth workers involved with anorectics and bulimics. Objectives are to: collect and disseminate information on anorexia nervosa, bulimia, and other eating disorders; provide support groups, medical referrals, and counseling for anorectics, bulimics, and their families. Conducts workshops, seminars, conferences, and training programs to help professionals identify, understand, and treat eating disorders. Conducts educational presentations for schools,

clubs, civic organizations, churches, and counseling agencies. **Members:** 20,000. **Publications:** *ANRED Alert*, monthly. Newsletter covering causes, symptoms, selfhelp, treatment, and diagnosis of eating disorders. • Also publishes pamphlets, brochures, and resource material.

★152★ **Arab-Jewish Women's Dialogue for Peace (AJWDFP)**
2116 Henderson Ave.
Wheaton, MD 20902
Phone: (301)946-9311
Susan Ryder, Founder

Founded: 1982. **Description:** Jewish and Arab women; non-Arab and non-Jewish women participate as facilitators, organizers, and advisory board members. Goals are to: open and enrich communication and understanding between the Arab and Jewish communities and cultures so that relations may improve in the U.S. and eventually in the Middle East; share experiences and emphasize unification of women worldwide. Focuses on the responsibility and capacity of women to create peaceful interaction worldwide. Aims to end the stereotypes and fears of Arab and Jewish women. Members plan to fast weekly until the fighting in the Middle East officially ends and a final settlement has been signed. Conducts bimonthly discussion groups; plans teenager programs and cultural events. **Formerly:** (1983) Women for Peace in the Middle East.

★153★ **Archconfraternity of Christian Mothers (ACM)**
220 37th St.
Pittsburgh, PA 15201
Phone: (412)683-2400
Rev. Bertin Roll, Dir.

Founded: 1881. **Description:** Parish confraternities interested in the home-education, character formation, and personality development of children guided primarily by mothers. **Members:** 3400. **Publications:** *The Christian Mother*, quarterly. Bulletin.

★154★ **Armenian Women's Welfare Association (AWWA)**
431 Pond St.
Jamaica Plain, MA 02130
Phone: (617)524-7024
Rosine Patterson, Pres.

Founded: 1921. **Description:** Women interested in helping with charitable work. Maintains nursing home to care for the aged. **Members:** 500.

★155★ **Art Libraries Society/North America (ARLIS/NA)**
Women and Art Round Table
3900 E. Timrod St.
Tucson, AZ 85711
Phone: (602)881-8479
Edith L. Crowe, Contact

Description: The group's members are concerned with documenting women's contributions to the visual arts and ensuring that materials related to women artists, curators, museums, and gallery directors, educators, and collections are accessible in libraries and visual resource collections. The Round Table's goal is to help scholars rediscover women in the history of the visual arts and encourage librarians and visual resource curators to collect materials on women artists for their institutions. The Round

Table participates in all ARLIS/NA activities by sponsoring sessions at the annual conference in cooperation with other ARLIS/NA groups (and with the Women's Caucus for Art or other related professional organizations).

★156★ **Asian-American Legal Defense and Education Fund**
99 Hudson St.
New York, NY 10013
Phone: (212)966-5932

Description: Provides legal assistance in employment discrimination and back wage claims through the Asian Community Labor Project and assistance on behalf of Asian working women through the Women's Rights Project.

★157★ **Asian-Indian Women in America (AIWA)**
RD 1, Box 98
Palisades, NY 10964
Phone: (914)365-1066
Fax: (914)425-5804
Ms. Uma Shah, Pres.

Founded: 1980. **Description:** Asian-Indian women, primarily professionals, who live in the U.S. Provides social, financial, and cultural services to Asian-Indian women in the U.S. Addresses issues affecting women in the U.S., including spouse abuse, single-parent families, and career development. Offers counseling for families and battered women; provides financial consultation services. Works with other groups on issues of concern to Asian-Indian women; sponsors social gatherings to aid the acculturation of members; conducts workshops. Monitors political developments in India. Maintains speakers' bureau. Plans to conduct support group. **Members:** 175. **Publications:** *AIWA Newsletter*, 3-4/year. • *Community News Bulletin*, monthly. Lists events of interest, job opportunities, and support information. • *Membership Directory*, annual. • Newsletter, 3-4/year. • Plans to publish *Asian-Indian Women's Directory*.

★158★ **Association of African-American Women Business Owners (BWE)**
c/o Brenda Alford
Brasman Research
PO Box 13933
Silver Spring, MD 20911-3933
Phone: (301)565-0258
Brenda Alford, Pres.

Founded: 1983. **Description:** Small business owners in all industries, particularly business services. Seeks to assist in developing a greater number of successful self-employed black women through business and personal development programs, networking, and legislative action. Is conducting a 2-year project identifying black women business owners as role models and historical figures; plans to establish an archive. **Members:** 1200. **Local Groups:** 10. **Publications:** *Black Business Women's News*, quarterly. • *Journal of Minority Business*, annual. **Formerly:** (1990) American Association of Black Women Entrepreneurs.

★159★ Association of American Colleges
Project on the Status and Education of
** Women**
1818 R Street, NW
Washington, DC 20009
Phone: (202)387-1300
Fax: (202)265-9532
Sherry Levy-Reiner, Director of Public
Information

Founded: 1971. **Description:** Project acts as a liaison between academic women, educational institutions, federal policy-makers and women's organizations. Develops materials that identify issues and provides recommendations for overcoming barriers to equity for women in higher education; monitors federal statutes, regulations, policies, enforcement, and litigation for possible impact on institutions and women in higher education; provides policy analyses of issues concerning women on campus; monitors journals, magazines, and newsletters to determine current campus policies, trends, and problems; serves as a clearinghouse on women in academe. Publishes original papers and provides information and other material upon request. Has produced summary chart of discrimination laws covering education. Also provides information on Hispanic women in education. **Publications:** *On Campus with Women.*

★160★ Association of American
** Geographers**
Committee on the Status of Women in
** Geography**
University of California, Los Angeles
Department of Urban Planning
Los Angeles, CA 90024
Phone: (213)825-1446
Margaret Fitzsimmons, Chair

★161★ Association of American
** Geographers (AAG)**
Specialty Group on Geographic
** Perspectives on Women**
Rutgers University
Lucy Stone Hall
Department of Geography
New Brunswick, NJ 08903
Phone: (201)932-4013
Joanna Regulska, Chair

Description: Promotes geographic research and education on topics relating to women and gender. Sponsors a best paper award and an assistance award and hosts special sessions on currently debated issues. **Publications:** The newsletter of the Geographic Perspectives on Women Specialty Group.

★162★ Association of American Law
** Schools**
Section on Women in Legal Education
1202 Connecticut Ave., NW
Washington, DC 20036-2065
Phone: (202)296-8851
Fax: (202)290-8869
Kathryn Venturatus Lorio, Chair

Description: The section provides networking and support services to women in legal education and law professors, presents an annual program focusing on legal issues relationg to women, and sponsors a resource bank on feminism and gender issues. **Publications:** The newsletter of the Section on Women in Legal Education, twice a year.

★163★ Association of American Medical
** Colleges (AAMC)**
Women in Medicine Program
1 Dupont Circle NW, Ste. 200
Washington, DC 20036
Phone: (202)828-0575
Fax: (202)785-5027
Janet Bickel, Director for Women's Programs

Description: The program initiates women's liaison programs for women in medicine. **Publications:** *Women in Medicine Update.* • *Building a Stronger Women's Program.* • *WLO Directory* (annual). • Also publishes women in medicine bibliography.

★164★ Association of Asian Studies
** (AAS)**
Committee of Women in Asian Studies
** (CWAS)**
State University of New York, Albany
Department of History
Albany, NY 12222
Phone: (518)442-4800
Fax: (518)442-4936
Sucheta Mazumdar, Chair

Description: The CWAS, which is open to the general membership of the Association, brings together those concerned with women's issues within the AAS and those involved in research on gender. **Publications:** *CWAS Newsletter*, 3/year.

★165★ Association for the Behavioral
** Treatment of Sexual Abusers (ABTSA)**
PO Box 66028
Portland, OR 97266
Phone: (503)494-6144
Fax: (503)494-6152
Sharon Siebert, Exec.Sec.

Founded: 1985. **Description:** Professionals working with sex offenders or victims of sexual assault. Provides training to professionals on the treatment of sex offenders; offers instruction in the operation of the penile plethysmograph, a device used to determine and record variations in the size of the penis due to the amount of blood present or passing through it. Maintains speakers' bureau. Offers consultation on program development and treatment of sex offenders; grants certification of behavioral therapists. **Members:** 250. **Formerly:** (1986) Association for the Behavioral Treatment of Sexual Aggression.

★166★ Association of Black Women in
** Higher Education (ABWHE)**
c/o Lenore R. Gall
Fashion Institute of Technology
Office of V.Pres. of Academic Affairs
227 W. 27th St. C-913
New York, NY 10001
Phone: (212)760-7911
Lenore R. Gall, Pres.

Founded: 1979. **Description:** Faculty members, education administrators, students, retirees, consultants, managers, and affirmative action officers. Objectives are to nurture the role of black women in higher education, and to provide support for the professional development goals of black women. Conducts workshops and seminars. **Members:** 350. **Computerized Services:** Mailing list. **Publications:** *ABWHE Newsletter*, quarterly.

★167★ Association of Black Women
** Historians**
PO Box 19753
Durham, NC 27707
Phone: (919)493-1024
Sylvia M. Jacobs, Director

Description: Works to establish a network among membership; promote black women in the profession; disseminate information by, for and about black women; share information about opportunities in the field; make suggestions concerning research topics and repositories.

★168★ Association for Childbirth at Home,
** International (ACHI)**
PO Box 430
Glendale, CA 91209
Phone: (213)663-4996
Tonya Brooks, Founder & Pres.

Founded: 1972. **Description:** Parents, midwives, doctors, childbirth educators, other professionals, and interested individuals, all of whom support childbirth at home. Purposes are to bring accurate information and competent support to parents seeking home birth and safe hospital birth; to identify and implement correct obstetrical and pediatric practice. Offers parent education classes, leader training programs, international resource and referral service, and professional education seminars and programs; instructs parents, childbirth educators, midwives, and physicians in safe home birth and noninterventive alternative techniques. Conducts research; compiles statistics. Presents Great Humanitarian and Outstanding Teacher and Trainee awards. Maintains speakers' bureau and reference library of 500 volumes. **Members:** 30,000. **Regional Groups:** 9. **State Groups:** 40. **Local Groups:** 120. **Publications:** *Birth Notes*, quarterly. Newsletter. • *Founders Letter*, 6/year. • Also publishes *Giving Birth at Home* (handbook) and brochures. **Formerly:** Association for Childbirth at Home.

★169★ Association for Children for
** Enforcement of Support (ACES)**
723 Phillips Ave., Ste. 216
Toledo, OH 43612
Phone: (416)476-2511
Toll-free: 800-537-7072
Fax: (419)478-1617
Geraldine Jensen, Pres.

Founded: 1984. **Description:** Custodial parents seeking legal enforcement of child support. Provides educational information about the legal rights involved in child support enforcement. Advocates improved child support enforcement services from the government. Seeks to increase public awareness of how a lack of child support affects children of divorced parents. Sponsors research and educational programs. Maintains speakers' bureau. **Members:** 18,000. **Local Groups:** 159. **Publications:** *Newsletter*, semiannual. • Also publishes *How to Collect Child Support* (handbook).

★170★ Association of College and Research Libraries (ACRL)
Women's Studies Section
American Library Association
50 E. Huron St.
Chicago, IL 60611
Toll-free: 800-545-2433
Jacqueline Marie, Chair

Description: The Section discusses, promotes, and sets standards for women's studies collections and services in academic and research libraries. Publications: College and Research Libraries News, monthly. • College and Research Libraries, 6/year.

★171★ Association of Contemplative Sisters (ACS)
Monastery Rd.
Carmelite Monastery
Elysburg, PA 17824
Phone: (717)672-2935
Sr. Joan Bourne, Pres.

Founded: 1969. Description: Women (most of whom are members of monastic communities and houses of prayer) dedicated to the service of the Roman Catholic church in the way of life known as contemplative. Goals are: to help contemporary men and women understand the meaning of life through affirmation of the contemplative dimension of humankind; to encourage contemplative women to unite in the vision of their role; to express the primacy of prayer in a diversity of life-styles; to foster the growth of each person in consciousness and freedom through authentic living-out of gospel values; to enable each sister to participate in the decision-making process affecting her life through sharing in the functioning of the association and of her own community. Conducts seminars and workshops. Members: 400. Regional Groups: 6. Publications: Newsletter, quarterly. • Also publishes brochure.

★172★ Association for Education in Journalism and Mass Communication
Committee on Status of Women
University of South Carolina
Columbia, SC 29208
Phone: (803)777-2005
Leslie Steeves, Chair

★173★ Association of Executive and Professional Women
The International Alliance
8600 LaSalle Rd., Ste. 308
Baltimore, MD 21204
Phone: (410)321-6699
Fax: (410)823-2410
Marian Goetze, Exec VP

Description: The Alliance serves worldwide as an umbrella organization that unites, supports, and promotes executive and professional women and their networks in the business, not-for-profit, and government sectors. It also maintains a speakers' bureau and a Directors Resource Database. Publications: The Alliance, bimonthly. • The group also publishes an annual member directory.

★174★ Association of Federal Woman's Award Recipients (AFWAR)
3529 Tilden St., NW
Washington, DC 20008

Founded: 1965. Description: Objectives are to: provide special recognition to women for their outstanding contributions to the efficiency and quality of career service in the federal government; encourage high standards of performance for all women in government; publicize career opportunities for women with the federal government. No new awards have been presented since 1976. Members: 75.

★175★ Association for Gay, Lesbian, and Bisexual Issues in Counseling (AGLBIC)
Box 216
Jenkintown, PA 19046
Robert Rohde, Sec.-Treas.

Founded: 1974. Description: Counselors and personnel and guidance workers concerned with lesbian and gay issues. Seeks to eliminate discrimination against and stereotyping of gay and lesbian individuals, particularly gay counselors. Works to educate heterosexual counselors on how to overcome homophobia and to best help homosexual clients. Provides a referral network and support for gay counselors and administrators; encourages objective research on gay issues. Maintains speakers' bureau. Members: 210. Publications: Caucus Comments, 4/year. Newsletter. Formerly: (1978) Caucus of Gay Counselors; (1986) National Caucus of Gay and Lesbian Counselors; (1988) Association for Gay and Lesbian Issues in Counseling.

★176★ Association of Girl Scout Executive Staff (AGSES)
10715 Hickman Rd.
Des Moines, IA 50322
Phone: (515)278-2881
Fax: (515)278-5988
Sandy Kautz, Pres.

Founded: 1939. Description: Executive/management staff employed by local Girl Scout Councils and the Girl Scouts of the U.S.A (see separate entry). Sections hold meetings semiannually on topics such as human relations, marketing, management, assertiveness training, supervision, fundraising, and pluralism. Members: 1200. Regional Groups: 8. Publications: Inter/Com, quarterly. • Has also published Survey of Girl Scout Executives. Formerly: (1955) National Association of Girl Scout Executives; (1975) Association of Girl Scout Professional Workers.

★177★ The Association of Junior Leagues International
1319 F St. NW, Ste. 604
Washington, DC 20004
Phone: (202)393-3364
Fax: (202)393-4517
Karen M. Hendricks, Dir., Department of Government Affairs

Description: The Association is an educational and charitable organization that comprises women committed to promoting volunteerism and improving the community. Association programs include Teen Outreach, an adolescent pregnancy prevention program, middle school improvement program, focusing on systemic changes in the middle grades, and Federal Legislative Advocacy, such as child care, family and medical leave, family violence, child abuse and neglect, and child welfare. Publications: Annual Report. • Homeless Women and Children's Report. • Report on Parental Leave. • Also publishes internal magazine for members only.

★178★ Association of Libertarian Feminists (ALF)
PO Box 20252, London Terrace
New York, NY 10011
Phone: (617)286-1719
Joan Kennedy Taylor, Coordinator

Founded: 1975. Description: Women and men who are both libertarians and feminists. Seeks to provide a libertarian alternative to those aspects of the women's movement that discourage independence and individuality; encourage women to become economically self-sufficient and psychologically independent; oppose the abridgement of individual rights by any government on the basis of sex; work toward changing sexist attitudes and behavior; publicize and promote realistic attitudes toward female competence, achievement, and potential. Distributes literature. Members: 200. Publications: Newsletter, quarterly. • Also publishes essays and brochures.

★179★ Association of Maternal and Child Health Programs (AMCHP)
2001 L St. NW, Ste. 308
Washington, DC 20036
Phone: (202)775-0436
Fax: (202)775-0061
Catherine Hess, Exec.Dir.

Founded: 1944. Description: Individuals responsible for or involved in the administration of state and territorial maternal and child health care programs and programs for children with special health care needs. Seeks to: inform public and private sector decision makers of the health care needs of mothers and children; develop and recommend maternal and child health policies and programs; develop coalitions with other interested organizations. Promotes exchange of ideas and experiences among members; studies and reports on the health of and services for mothers and children; develops models and standards for and provides technical assistance to maternal and child health care services. Members: 200. Publications: Caring for Mothers and Children: A Report of a Survey of 1987 State MCH Program Activities and Title V in Review: Two Decades of Analysis of Selected Aspects of the Title V Program. Formerly: Association of State and Territorial Maternal and Child Health and Crippled Children's Directors.

★180★ Association of Part-Time Professionals
Flow General Bldg.
7655 Old Springhouse Rd.
McLean, VA 22102
Phone: (703)734-7975
Diane Rothberg, President

★181★ Association for Population/Family Planning Libraries and Information Centers, International (APLIC-Intl)
c/o William Record
Association for Vol. Surgical Contraception
122 E. 42nd St., 18th Fl.
New York, NY 10168
Phone: (212)351-2504
Fax: (212)599-0959
William Record, Contact

Founded: 1968. Description: Population/family planning agencies and their librarians, information scientists, educators, and communicators. Works to professionally develop effective documentation, information systems, and services in the field of population/family planning. Objectives are to: strengthen professional contact among members; establish a cooperative network of population/family planning libraries and information centers; institute a program of continuing education in the field. Sponsors Duplicate Books Exchange Program. Coordinates training programs in librarianship and information science. **Members:** 115. **Publications:** *APLICommunicator*, quarterly. Newsletter. • *Proceedings of Annual Conference*. • Also publishes *National Population Census, 1945-1976: Some Holding Libraries, Tools for Population Information: Indexing and Abstracting Services*, and *Union List of Population/Family Planning Periodicals*.

★182★ Association for Professional Insurance Women
1 Liberty Plaza
New York, NY 10006
Phone: (212)225-7500
Marsha A. Cohen, President

★183★ Association on Programs for Female Offenders (APFO)
c/o South Dakota Department of Corrections
523 E. Capitol
Pierre, SD 57501
Phone: (605)773-3478
Lynne De Lano, Pres.

Description: Professionals in corrections or related fields and others interested in issues concerning female offenders. Develops and sponsors workshops on the topic of female offenders at the annual congress; facilitates sharing of information about programs and research on female offenders. Has sponsored conference workshops including Providing Services for Women in Jail: Whose Responsibility?; Mothers in Prison; and Education, Training, Employment: Resources for Women Inmates. **Members:** 80. **Publications:** *Newsletter*, periodic. **Formerly:** (1975) Women's Correctional Association.

★184★ Association of Romanian-American Orthodox Ladies Auxiliaries (ARAOLA)
c/o Pauline Trutza
1466 Waterbury Rd.
Lakewood, OH 44107
Phone: (216)221-2435
Pauline Trutza, Pres.

Founded: 1938. **Description:** Federation of women's organizations working for parishes of the Romanian Orthodox Episcopate of America. Conducts charitable program; maintains museum; offers scholarship to female graduate student of Romanian Orthodox Diocese annually. **Members:** 2600. **Auxiliaries:** 34. **Local Groups:** 39. **Publications:** *Newsletter*, quarterly. • Also publishes *ARFORA Cookbook*. **Also known as:** Asociatia Reuniunilor Femeilor Ortodoxe Romane-Americane.

★185★ Association for the Sexually Harassed (ASH)
PO Box 27235
Philadelphia, PA 19118
Phone: (215)952-8037
Cheryl Gomez-Tumpkins-Preston, Bd.Chm.

Founded: 1988. **Description:** Employers, organizations, victims of sexual harassment, and other interested individuals. Seeks to eliminate sexual harassment, which ASH defines as the "unwelcomed exposure to physical contact, pornography, sexual jokes, requests for dates, and demeaning comments, made by male or female, which causes an individual's environment or work place to become intimidating, hostile, or offensive." Works to educate the public about the effects of sexual harassment; offers policy recommendations. Provides assistance to businesses and victims in outlining problems of sexual harassment; conducts professional training on dealing with and preventing sexual harassment in the work environment. Conducts research on victims of sexual harassment and posttraumatic stress disorder. Operates support group for sexual harassment victims. Maintains newsclip collection on sexual harassment cases; conducts surveys and compiles statistics. Conducts statistical studies relating sexual harassment to homelessness, crime, unemployment, and workmen's compensation injuries. Operates speakers' bureau and children's services. **Members:** 100. **State Groups:** 2. **Local Groups:** 2.

★186★ Association of Teachers of Maternal and Child Health (ATMCH)
6505 Alvorado Rd., Ste. 205
San Diego, CA 92120-5011
Phone: (619)594-4493
Albert Chang, MD, Pres.

Founded: 1968. **Description:** Faculty and graduate students in maternal and child health. Promotes the teaching and research of maternal and child health programs in public health schools and professional schools in the U.S. and abroad. Participates in the development and support of policy initiatives related to the field. Bestows Academic Leadership in Maternal and Child Health Award. **Members:** 200. **Publications:** *ATMCH News*, semiannual. Newsletter.

★187★ Association for Theatre in Higher Education (ATHE)
Women and Theatre Program
English Department
Bowling Green State University
Bowling Green, OH 43403
Phone: (419)372-6831
Vicki Patraka, Contact

Description: Fosters the study of women in theatre, feminist theatre, and theatrical representation of women, and encourages standards of excellence in these pursuits; educates its members and others about the limitations resulting from sexism, homophobia, and class divisions as present in theatrical production, representation, and education. Makes available selected services, programs, meetings, and other activities designed to meet the needs of women working in theatre practice and criticism. Sponsors twenty or more panels at the main conference of the ATHE, a special graduate student caucus, and the Jane Chambers Memorial Playwriting Award. **Publications:** *Women and Theatre Program*.

★188★ Association for Union Democracy (AUD)
Women's Project for Union Democracy
YWCA Bldg.
30 3rd Ave.
Brooklyn, NY 11217
Phone: (718)855-6650
Fax: (718)855-6652
Susan Jennik, Executive Director

Description: The AUD Women's Project assists women fighting for equality on the job and in the union. As women increase their involvement and influence within their unions, and assists them in enforcing their legal rights on the job. Organizes conferences and workshops, publishes educational literature, and provides counseling and legal referrals. **Publications:** *Union Democracy Review*, bimonthly.

★189★ Association of Women in Architecture (AWA)
7440 University Dr.
St. Louis, MO 63130
Phone: (314)621-3484
Betty Lou Custer, Exec. Officer

Founded: 1922. **Description:** Women working in architecture or the allied arts. **Members:** 1150. **Undergraduate Chapters:** 11. **Professional Chapters:** 9.

★190★ Association for Women in Computing (AWC)
41 Sutter St., Ste. 1006
San Francisco, CA 94104
Pam Hinz, Pres.

Founded: 1978. **Description:** Individuals interested in promoting the education, professional development, and advancement of women in computing. Sponsors seminars at local and national levels. Maintains speakers' bureau; bestows awards; compiles statistics. **Members:** 650. **Local Groups:** 37. **Publications:** *Directory*, annual.

★191★ Association for Women in Development (AWID)
Virginia Tech
10 Sandy Hall
Blacksburg, VA 24061-0338
Phone: (703)231-3765
Fax: (703)231-6741
Norge Jerome, Pres.

Founded: 1982. **Description:** Individuals (600) and institutions (50) including government and United Nations agencies, private research and consulting firms, private voluntary agencies, and universities with a focus on international development, particularly as it affects women. Purpose is to ensure the participation of women as full and active partners in a more equitable process of development, and to guarantee them a share of its benefits. Seeks to: heighten public awareness of the interdependence among individuals, institutions, and nations in development; increase research and action by encouraging interaction among scholars, practitioners, and policymakers in women in development; improve communication and education on problems and solutions relating to women in development. **Members:** 650. **Publications:** *AWID Newsletter*, quarterly. • *Mailing List*, annual. • Also publishes *AWID Special Papers Series* and brochure.

★192★ Association of Women Gemologists (AWG)
PO Box 1844
Pearland, TX 77588
Phone: (713)485-1606
Anna Miller, Dir.

Founded: 1982. **Description:** Women gemologists. Provides a network for communication among women gemologists. Disseminates information concerning the industry, particularly information affecting women gemologists. **Members:** 135.

★193★ Association for Women Geoscientists (AWG)
10200 W. 44th Ave., Ste. 304
Wheat Ridge, CO 80033
Phone: (303)422-8527
Jane Willard, Pres.

Founded: 1977. **Description:** Men and women geologists, geophysicists, petroleum engineers, geological engineers, hydrogeologists, paleontologists, geochemists, and other geoscientists. Aims to: encourage the participation of women in the geosciences; exchange educational, technical, and professional information; enhance the professional growth and advancement of women in the geosciences. Provides information on opportunities and careers available to women in the geosciences. Conducts workshops and seminars on job hunting techniques, management skills, and career and professional development. Sponsors educational booths and programs at geological society conventions. Operates charitable program. Conducts Scholastic Awards Program for outstanding students in the geosciences; maintains hall of fame and Association for Women Geoscientists Foundation (educational arm). Compiles statistics. **Members:** 650. **Regional Groups:** 16. **Publications:** *Gaea*, bimonthly. Newsletter. • *Membership Directory*, annual. • Also publishes *Careers in the Geosciences*. **Formerly:** (1982) Association of Women Geoscientists.

★194★ Association for Women in Mathematics (AWM)
Wellesley College
Box 178
Wellesley, MA 02181
Phone: (617)237-7517
Tricia Cross, Exec.Dir.

Founded: 1971. **Description:** Mathematicians employed by universities, government, and private industry; students. Seeks to improve the status of women in the mathematical profession, and to make students aware of opportunities for women in the field. Membership is open to all interested individuals, regardless of sex. Maintains speakers' bureau and operates resource center at Wellesley College. **Members:** 4000. **Publications:** *Association for Women in Mathematics—Newsletter*, bimonthly. Contains articles by and about women in mathematics on topics such as employment, education, discrimination, law, mathematics, biography, and personal experience; also contains association news. Lists employment opportunities and honors and awards recipients. • *Association for Women in Mathematics—Speakers Bureau*, biennial. Directory listing women speakers, their topics, and suggested audience levels for talks related to mathematics. Arranged alphabetically by name. • *Directory of Women in the Mathematical Sciences*, periodic. • Also publishes *Careers for Women in Mathematics* (booklet). **Formerly:** (1973) Association of Women Mathematicians.

★195★ Association of Women in Natural Foods (AWIN)
10159 Brooke Ave.
Chatsworth, CA 91311
Phone: (818)718-6230
Roberta Fleischer, Exec. Officer

Founded: 1985. **Description:** Women wholesalers, retailers, salespersons, brokers, and suppliers to the natural foods industry. Acts as informational, philanthropic, and support network. Conducts seminars at trade shows. Be-

stows awards. **Members:** 140. **Publications:** *Association of Women in the Natural Foods Industry Newsletter*, quarterly. • *Directory*, annual. **Formerly:** (1989) Association of Women in the Natural Foods Industry.

★196★ Association for Women Psychiatrists
PO Box 191079-350
Dallas, TX 75219-0179
Phone: (214)855-5104
Ruth Barnhouse, Contact

★197★ Association for Women in Psychology (AWP)
c/o Angela R. Gillem, Ph.D.
Haverford College
370 Lancaster Ave.
Haverford, PA 19041-1392
Angela R. Gillem, Ph.D., Recorder

Founded: 1969. **Description:** Seeks to: end the role that the association feels psychology has had in perpetuating unscientific and unquestioned assumptions about the "natures" of women and men; encourage unbiased psychological research on sex and gender in order to establish facts and expose myths; encourage research and theory directed toward alternative sex-role socialization, child rearing practices, life-styles, and language use; educate and sensitize the science and psychology professions as well as the public to the psychological, social, political, and economic rights of women; combat the oppression of women of color; encourage research on issues of concern to women of color; achieve equality of opportunity for women and men within the profession and science of psychology. Conducts business and professional sessions at meetings of regional psychology associations. Holds local chapter and regional meetings. Maintains hall of fame, archives, and speakers' bureau; bestows Distinguished Publication, Women of Color Psychologies, Lesbian Psychologies Unpublished Manuscript Awards annually, and a student prize for research on women and gender. Monitors sexism in APA. **Caucuses** Jewish Women's; Women of Color. **Members:** 1500. **Publications:** *AWP Membership Directory*, annual. • Newsletter, quarterly. • Also publishes *A Feminist Mental Health Agenda for the Year 2,000*. **Formerly:** (1970) Association for Women Psychologists.

★198★ Association for Women in Science (AWIS)
1522 K St. NW, Ste. 820
Washington, DC 20005
Phone: (202)408-0742
Fax: (202)408-8321
Catherine Didion, Exec.Dir.

Founded: 1971. **Description:** Professional women and students in life, physical, and social sciences and engineering; men are also members. Promotes equal opportunities for women to enter the scientific workforce and to achieve their career goals; provides educational information to women planning careers in science; networks with other women's groups; monitors scientific legislation and the status of women in science. Provides advice and support to women involved in equal opportunity legislation; assists local chapters with programming and support services. Operates AWIS Educational Foundation, which awards thirteen $1,000 scholarships annually for predoctoral study; promotes appreciation of past accomplishments of women scientists. **Members:** 3500. **Local Groups:** 38.

Publications: *Association for Women in Science—Directory*, periodic. • *AWIS Magazine*, bimonthly. Features analytical articles on the status of women in science; includes book reviews and chapter news; lists employment, grant, and educational opportunities. • *Resources for Women in Science Series*, periodic. • Also publishes *Gender and Science, Bibliography of Science Education Resources, Grants-At-A-Glance, Careers in Science*, and list of local chapters.

★199★ Association for Women in Social Work (AWSW)
University of Pennsylvania
Women's Center
119 Houston Hall
3417 Spruce St.
Philadelphia, PA 19104-6306
Phone: (215)898-8611
Elena M. DiLapi, Director

Description: National organization of individuals concerned about women in social work. Facilitates regional chapters addressing issues of feminist/womanist social work practice and the concerns of women. Current activities include the Philadelphia Chapter organizing conference, Feminist/Womanist Visions of Social Work Practice in the 21st Century, and other chapters having support groups and local forums on social work for women. **Publications:** *Association for Women in Social Work*.

★200★ Association of Women Soil Scientists (AWSS)
c/o Margie Faber
PO Box 115
Ancram
New York, NY 12502
Phone: (914)677-3194
Margie Faber, Sec.-Treas.

Founded: 1981. **Description:** Women who are soil scientists, soil conservationists, soil agriculturists, research scientists, professors, and students. Identifies women in the field and provides them with communication opportunities, technical and career information, assistance, and encouragement. **Members:** 150. **Publications:** *Membership Directory*, periodic. • *Newsletter*, 3/year.

★201★ Association for Women in Sports Media (AWSM)
PO Box 4205
Mililami, HI 96789
Phone: (714)733-0558
Tracie Dodds, Pres.

Founded: 1986. **Description:** Women sportswriters, copy editors, and sports information directors; interested men and women. Supports and fosters advancement of women involved in sports media. Sponsors educational programs; awards college journalists summer internships. **Members:** 311. **Publications:** *AWSM Newsletter*, quarterly.

**★202★ Association for Women Students
(IAWS)**
c/o Laura Zimmerman
Student Services Bldg., Rm. 1118
Western Michigan University
Kalamazoo, MI 49008
Phone: (616)383-0075
Laura Zimmerman, Contact

Founded: 1923. **Description:** Campus organizations focusing on status and education of women, including intellectual, personal, and social development. To support and encourage women in higher education to use their individual potentials and fulfill their roles as educated and competent persons. Maintains extensive files on women's campus programming; conducts surveys; develops programs. Presents Athena Award to a person who has made an outstanding contribution to American womanhood in education, arts, sciences, and government. **Members:** 250,000. **Regional Groups:** 5. **Local Groups:** 50. **Publications:** *Feminine Focus*, bimonthly. • Also publishes programming book. **Formerly:** Midwestern Association of Women Students.

**★203★ Association for Women
Veterinarians (AWV)**
c/o Chris Stone Payne, D.V.M.
32205 Allison Dr.
Union City, CA 94587
Phone: (415)471-8379
Chris Stone Payne, D.V.M., Sec.

Founded: 1947. **Description:** Women veterinarians; students of veterinary medicine. Presents scholarships annually to second- or third-year veterinary students. Bestows AWV Service Award annually to individual contributing to the advancement of women in veterinary medicine; also awards Outstanding Woman Veterinarian annually for contributions to veterinary medicine. **Members:** 625. **Computerized Services:** Membership list. **Publications:** *AWV Bulletin*, quarterly. Association and professional newsletter. • *Roster of Women Veterinarians*, periodic. **Formerly:** (1981) Women's Veterinary Medical Association.

**★204★ Association of Women's Music
and Culture**
2124 Kittredge St., #104
Berkeley, CA 94704
Phone: (415)655-4334
Jim Cruise, Contact

Description: Feminist professional organization engaged in the enhancement of women's music and culture. Offers support, recognition, educational opportunities, networking, and resources for women as individuals, businesses, and organizations.

**★205★ Astraea National Lesbian Action
Foundation**
666 Broadway, Ste. 520
New York, NY 10012
Phone: (212)529-8021
Katherine T. Acey, Executive Director

Founded: 1977. **Description:** Astraea is the first nationwide lesbian foundation. It is a national, multi-cultural organization that seeks to empower women and girls through financial and organizational support. Funds projects that actively work to eliminate all forms of oppression that affect lesbians in the United States and sponsors a project that encourages and supports the work of lesbian writers.

**★206★ Auxiliaries of Our Lady of the
Cenacle (AOLC)**
900 S. Spoede Rd.
St. Louis, MO 63131
Phone: (314)432-2461
Sr. Agnes Sauer, Regional Dir.

Founded: 1878. **Description:** Catholic women of all ages and professions interested in a religious, but fully secular life. Vows are received through the Congregation of Our Lady of the Retreat in the Cenacle, and are renewed annually. Members serve God through their own professions, talents, lifestyles, or other apostolic works. Promotes apostolic and personal spiritual growth and development. Activities are usually church-related. **Members:** 140. **Regional Groups:** 2. **Publications:** *AC Highlights*, quarterly. Newsletter. • *Directory*, annual. • *Feuilles de Liaison des Auxiliares de Notre Dame Du Cenacle*, bimonthly. Newsletter. **Formerly:** (1960) Aggregation of Congresses of Our Lady of Cenacle.

★207★ Baltic Women's Council (BWC)
c/o Helga Ozolins
414 Abington Pl.
East Meadow, NY 11554
Phone: (718)672-5558
Helga Ozolins, Pres.

Founded: 1947. **Description:** Estonian, Latvian, and Lithuanian women's clubs in the U.S. and overseas. To unite the women of Estonian, Latvian, and Lithuanian origin; to preserve native culture; to assist with the development of their countries of birth; to promote the spirit of Baltic solidarity and friendship among the young generations. Sponsors literary, arts, and musical events. Works for reunification of Baltic refugee families. **Publications:** Pamphlets and book.

★208★ Baptists for Life (BFL)
2113 Alamo National Bldg.
105 S. St. Mary's
San Antonio, TX 78205
Phone: (512)227-2321
Rev. M. O. Turner, Sec.

Founded: 1976. **Description:** Baptists who support pro-life goals by using spiritual and scriptural approaches. Prepares and distributes literature and position statements on such issues as abortion and euthanasia.

**★209★ Barbara Deming Memorial Fund
Money for Women**
Box 40-1043
Brooklyn, NY 11240-1043
Pam McAllister, Administrator

Description: The fund provides small grants for individual feminists in the arts whose work "speaks for justice and peace" and addresses women's concerns.

**★210★ Berkshire Conference of Women
Historians**
Women's Studies Program
University of North Carolina, CB #3135
207 Caldwell Hall
Chapel Hill, NC 27599-3135
Phone: (919)962-3908
Barbara Harris, President

Description: The Conference supports the professional activities of women historians. Holds conferences and sponsors prizes.

**★211★ Biophysical Society
Committee on Professional Opportunities
for Women (CPOW)**
9650 Rockville Pike
Bethesda, MD 20814
Phone: (202)727-2280
Fax: (202)638-1736
Marial Prouty, Chair

Description: The Committee is a networking and mentoring body whose purpose is to assure full representation for women in the scientific and professional affairs of the Society as officers, Council members, speakers, symposium and workshop organizers, and committee chairs. Encourages students and post-doctoral and junior faculty. Sponsors a scientific symposium and program addressing the concerns of women scientists. **Publications:** *Spectrum*.

**★212★ Birthright, United States of
America**
686 N. Broad St.
Woodbury, NJ 08096
Phone: (609)848-1819
Toll-free: 800-848-LOVE
Fax: (609)848-2380
Denise F. Cocciolone, Exec.Dir.

Founded: 1968. **U.S. Chapters:** 540. **Description:** Groups operating independently in the U.S. to help pregnant women find alternatives to abortion. All chapters are private and interdenominational, supported by contributions, and operated by volunteers. Operates childbirth education classes and parenting programs. Maintains speakers' bureau. **Regional Groups:** 38. **Local Groups:** 617. **Publications:** *The Life-Guardian*, bimonthly. Newsletter. • Also publishes books.

★213★ Black Americans for Life
419 7th St. NW, Ste. 500
Washington, DC 20004
Phone: (202)626-8833

Description: Individuals working to educate the black community on pro-life and pro-family issues. Promotes alternatives to abortion for women with crisis pregnancies; strives to be a visible presence defending the rights of the unborn in the black community. Asserts that black women are twice as likely as white women to have abortions; believes that abortions are counterproductive to advances made through civil rights efforts. Provides information on resources and available speakers. **Publications:** Fact sheets.

**★214★ Black Professional Women's
Network**
123 W. 44th St., Ste. 2E
New York, NY 10036
Phone: (212)302-2924
Paulette M. Owens, President

Description: The Network provides information to black and hispanic women professionals, managers, and technical employers. Provides employment, health care, and financial information, distributes literature, and offers telephone referrals.

★215★ Black Women in Church and Society (BWCS)
c/o Interdenominational Theological Center
671 Beckwith St. SW
Atlanta, GA 30314
Phone: (404)527-7740
Jacquelyn Grant, Ph.D., Dir.
Founded: 1982. **Description:** Women in ministry, both ordained and laity. Seeks to provide: structured activities and support systems for black women whose goals include participating in leadership roles in church and society; a platform for communication between laywomen and clergywomen. Conducts research into questions and issues pivotal to black women in church and society. Sponsors charitable programs and semiannual seminar; compiles statistics. Maintains a research/resource center and a library with subject matter pertaining to liberation and black theology, feminism, and womanist movements. **Computerized Services:** Mailing list. **Publications:** *Black Women in Ministry*, quadrennial. Directory.

★216★ Black Women Organized for Educational Development (BWOED)
518 17th St., Ste. 202
Oakland, CA 94612
Phone: (510)763-9501
Fax: (510)763-4327
Dezie Woods-Jones, Exec.Dir.
Founded: 1984. **Description:** Fosters self-sufficiency in and encourages empowerment of low-income and socially disadvantaged women by establishing and maintaining programs that improve their social and economic well-being. Sponsors mentor program for junior high-age young women in low-income urban areas; offers support groups, workshops, and seminars. Maintains Black Women's Resource Center, an information and referral service for African American women and youth. **Publications:** *BWOED Newsletter*, quarterly.

★217★ Black Women in Publishing (BWIP)
PO Box 6275, F.D.R. Sta.
New York, NY 10150
Phone: (212)772-5951
Dolores Gordon, Pres.
Founded: 1979. **Description:** Designers, editors, financial analysts, freelancers, personnel directors, photographers, production managers, authors, entrepreneurs, and publicists within the print industry. A networking and support group whose purpose is to encourage minorities interested in all sectors of the print industry, including book, newspaper, and magazine publishing. Promotes the image of minorities working in all phases of the book, newspaper, and magazine industries; recognizes achievements of minorities in the media. Works for a free and responsible press. Facilitates the exchange of ideas and information among members, especially regarding career planning and job security. Keeps members informed about the publishing industry and their impact on it. Encourages and works to maintain high professional standards in publishing. Collaborates with other organizations in striving to improve the status of women and minorities. Sponsors lectures, panel discussions, seminars, workshops, radio talk shows, and other programs on topics such as computers in publishing, magazine publishing, trends in multicultural literature for children, career paths publishing, getting work published, starting a publishing firm, author readings, awards presentations, and women and stress. Organizes

social events. Maintains biographical archives, placement service, and a resume bank in collaboration with major corporations. **Publications:** *Interface*, bimonthly.

★218★ Black Women in Sisterhood for Action, Inc. (BISA)
PO Box 1592
Washington, DC 20013
Phone: (301)460-1565
Verna S. Cook, National President
Founded: 1980. **Description:** BISA is a nonprofit corporation whose purposes are to develop and promote alternative strategies for educational and career development for black women; provide scholarship assistance to qualifying applicants; provide support and social assistance to senior black women; share information and resources; and provide leadership, role models, and mentors for young people. Provides a forum for personal, professional, and collective growth in the areas of management, communication, and other areas. **Publications:** *The Black Woman.* • *Distinguished Black Women*, every five years. • Also publishes a calendar.

★219★ Black Women's Agenda, Inc.
208 Auburn Ave. NE
Atlanta, GA 30303
Phone: (404)524-8279
Dolly D. Adams, National President
Founded: 1977. **Description:** The Agenda is a nonprofit, volunteer organization whose purpose is to educate and advocate programs in the interest of black women's equity. It educates the public through workshops and others programs, about the economic, social, and civil liberties issues relevant to the needs and status of black women and recommends policy changes to secure rights for black women and their families. Publishes occasional papers, newsletters, and reports that assess the status and role of black women.

★220★ Black Women's Educational Alliance (BWEA)
6625 Greene St.
Philadelphia, PA 19119
Deidre Farmbey, Pres.
Founded: 1976. **Description:** Active and retired women in the field of education. Seeks a strong union among members in order to foster their intellectual and professional growth. Conducts public awareness programs to improve educational standards and delivery of educational services; works for equal opportunities for women. Bestows student scholarships and education and service awards; maintains speakers' bureau. Conducts instructional seminars and workshops. **Members:** 300. **Local Groups:** 2. **Publications:** *BWEA Bulletin*, periodic. • *BWEA Newsletter*, semiannual.

★221★ Black Women's Network (BWN)
PO Box 12072
Milwaukee, WI 53212
Phone: (414)562-4500
Joan Prince, Pres.
Founded: 1979. **Description:** Black professional women organized to improve the political, economic, and educational conditions of minority women. Offers support services and networking opportunities to address issues affecting African-American women. **Members:** 56.

Publications: *Cross Roads*, quarterly. Newsletter.

★222★ Black Women's Roundtable on Voter Participation (BWRVP)
1430 K St. NW, Ste. 401
Washington, DC 20011
Phone: (202)898-2220
Sonia R. Jarvis, Exec.Dir.
Founded: 1983. **Description:** A program of the National Coalition on Black Voter Participation. Black women's organizations committed to social justice and economic equity through increased participation in the political process. Organizes voter registration, education, and empowerment programs in the black community; emphasizes the importance of the women's vote. Seeks to: develop women's leadership skills through nonpartisan political participation; encourage black women's involvement in discussions concerning the influence of the women's vote in elections. Supports volunteer coalitions that work on voter registration, voter education, and get-out-the vote efforts. Conducts series of forums.

★223★ Blue Star Mothers of America (BSM)
c/o Margaret Wood
119 W. 2nd St., No. 706
Xenia, OH 45385
Phone: (513)372-9577
Margaret Wood, Pres.
Founded: 1942. **Description:** Mothers of current or past military service personnel. Members work in VA hospitals, assist veterans and their families, attempt to better the lives of servicemen abroad, participate in numerous community service and beautification projects, and promote patriotic sentiment. Studies and supports legislation concerning the welfare of veterans and national security. Collects money for the Chaplains Emergency Fund which provides for the needs of indigent, hospitalized veterans. Also sponsors child welfare programs and supports national civil defense projects. Maintains archives. **Members:** 2200. **State Groups:** 6. **Local Groups:** 166. **Publications:** *Blue Star Mother Yearbook*.

★224★ B'nai B'rith Women (BBW)
1828 L St. NW, Ste. 250
Washington, DC 20036
Phone: (202)857-1300
Fax: (202)857-1380
Elaine K. Binder, Exec.Dir.
Founded: 1897. **Description:** Jewish women's organizations. Engages in activities that support women and their families through public affairs advocacy and national and local education projects. Community activities include human relations, caregiving for older adults, philanthropy, and youth projects. Founded and maintains a home for emotionally disturbed boys in Jerusalem, Israel. Bestows the B'nai B'rith Women Perlman Award biennially to an individual or group for outstanding contributions to human advancement. **Members:** 120,000. **Regional Groups:** 12. **Local Groups:** 700. **Publications:** *Women's World*, 4/year. Newsletter; includes book reviews. **Formerly:** (1957) Women's Supreme Council.

★225★ Breast Cancer Advisory Center (BCAC)
PO Box 224
Kensington, MD 20895
Fax: (301)949-1132
Rose Kushner, Exec.Dir.

Founded: 1975. **Description:** Medical service group for people, mostly women, with breast cancer. Makes referrals; disseminates information; gives lectures. Maintains library on breast cancer. **Publications:** *Alternatives: New Developments in Breast Cancer* (book) and brochure.

★226★ Buddhist Churches of America (BCAFBWA)
Federation of Buddhist Women's Associations
c/o Buddhist Churches of America
1710 Octavia St.
San Francisco, CA 94109
Phone: (415)776-5600
Fax: (415)771-6293
Rev. Seikan Fukuma, Exec.Dir.

Founded: 1952. **Description:** Women members of Buddhist churches of Jodo Shinshu faith. Promotes American Buddhism through publications, community service, fundraising, and recreational and educational programs. Makes annual contributions to welfare organizations. **Members:** 15,000. **Formerly:** (1989) National Federation of Buddhist Women's Associations.

★227★ Business and Professional Women's Foundation (BPWF)
2012 Massachusetts Ave. NW
Washington, DC 20036
Phone: (202)293-1200
Linda Colvard Dorian, Exec.Dir.

Founded: 1956. **Description:** Dedicated to improving the economic status of working women through their integration into all occupations. Conducts and supports research on women and work, with special emphasis on economic issues. Provides Lena Lake Forrest Fellowship for research at the doctoral and postdoctoral level; Sally Butler Memorial Fund for Latina Research for women of Latin American descent/citizenship. Awards educational scholarships to mature women, including Clairol Loving Care Scholarship, Avon Products Foundation Scholarship, and New York Life Foundation Scholarship for women in health professions and health product sales careers. Sponsors BPW Foundation Loan Fund for Women in Engineering and BPW/Sears-Roebuck Loan Fund for Women in Graduate Business Studies. Maintains Marguerite Rawalt Resource Center of 20,000 items on economic issues involving women and work and provides public reference and referral service. Established by BPW/USA and the National Federation of Business and Professional Women's Clubs (see separate entry). **Publications:** *Annual Report.* • Also issues publications list.

★228★ Byelorussian-American Women Association (BAWA)
146 Sussex Dr.
Manhasset, NY 11030
Phone: (516)627-9195
Vera Bartul, Pres.

Founded: 1956. **Description:** Women of Byelorussian birth or descent and those related by marriage to Byelorussian-Americans. Aims to preserve national identity, cultural heritage, and traditions. Extends relief to needy Byelorussians at home and abroad in the form of packages and financial contributions. Organizes and supports school programs of Byelorussian supplementary schools. Also organizes shows and exhibitions of fine arts and ethnic crafts. Offers Byelorussian language classes. **Members:** 300. **State Groups:** 4. **Publications:** *Woman's Page in Belarus* (in Byelorussian), periodic Newspaper.

★229★ C/SEC
22 Forest Rd.
Framingham, MA 01701
Phone: (508)877-8266
Norma Shulman, Dir.

Founded: 1972. **Description:** Childbirth groups, doctors, laypersons, and nurses. Established out of concern for the lack of resources available to couples who anticipate or have had a cesarean delivery. Goals are to: improve the cesarean childbirth experience and make the cesarean delivery a good and meaningful childbirth experience for each couple; provide information and promote education on cesarean prevention and vaginal birth after cesarean; change attitudes and policies that affect the cesarean childbirth experience. Offers support for cesarean couples through informal discussion meetings, telephone contact, and personal reply to letters. Provides information on many aspects of cesarean childbirth in order to make couples aware of exactly what the procedure entails and what options are available. Works with doctors, hospitals, childbirth educators, and others in the medical community to effect policy changes and to promote family-centered maternity care for cesarean couples. Conducts in-service programs for hospital staffs and has spoken at conventions and workshops on childbirth. Acronym C/SEC stands for Cesareans/Support, Education and Concern. **Members:** 2000. **Publications:** *C/SEC Newsletter*, quarterly. Newsletter on cesarean childbirth, cesarean prevention, and vaginal birth after cesarean. Contains book reviews, calendar of events, research updates, and lists of resources available to women. • *Membership List*, periodic. • Also publishes guides, pamphlets, and manuals; has produced slide-cassette presentation. **Formerly:** (1976) C/SEC (Cesarean Sections: Education and Concern).

★230★ Campaign Fund for Republican Women (CFRW)
4203 S. 35th St.
Arlington, VA 22206
Phone: (703)931-8409
Wilma Goldstein, Founder

Founded: 1983. **Description:** Independent political action committee dedicated to raising funds for Republican women running for seats in the U.S. House and Senate. Does not require candidates to support particular issues.

★231★ Camping Women (CW)
7623 Southbreeze Dr.
Sacramento, CA 95828
Phone: (916)689-9326
Gail Sanabria, Pres.

Founded: 1976. **Description:** Individuals seeking to enhance women's camping skills; women interested in camping, backpacking, hiking, canoeing, white water rafting, biking, skiing, birdwatching, and other outdoor activities. Objectives are to: provide opportunities for women to experience an outdoor program in a supportive atmosphere; help women develop a sense of "at-homeness" in the outdoors; develop women's camping abilities and leadership skills. Provides skills training in campcraft, watercraft, snow camping, and leadership. Bestows awards and certificates. **Members:** 200. **Local Groups:** 6. **Publications:** *Camping Women Trails*, 10/year. Newsletter. • *Membership Directory*, annual.

★232★ Campus Ministry Women (CMW)
802 Monroe
Ann Arbor, MI 48104
Phone: (313)662-5189
Ann Marie Coleman, Treas.

Founded: 1970. **Description:** Protestant, Catholic, and Jewish women; interested men are associate members. To serve as a network to empower women to be effective ministers in college and university settings. Provides professional and educational resources to women as they locate and acquire campus ministry positions and develop their skills and careers. Promotes interfaith cooperation; enables women to participate in the development and teaching of a feminist theology reflecting interfaith awareness. Serves as a forum for sharing campus ministry programs and resources. Supports women who are victims of racism, religious bigotry, or discrimination because of their sexual preference; allots money for projects for such women. Advocates hiring and promoting women in religious and campus structures; provides grievance and crisis intervention. Assists in funding local projects by and for women. Bestows scholarships for meetings. **Members:** 250. **Publications:** *Directory*, periodic. • *Newsletter*, 5-6/year.

★233★ Catalyst
250 Park Ave., S.
New York, NY 10003
Phone: (212)777-8900
Felice N. Schwartz, Pres.

Founded: 1962. **Description:** A national research and advisory organization that helps corporations foster career and leadership development of women. Works to: identify and analyze human resource issues such as impediments to women's progress in the corporation, balancing work and family, and managing a diverse work force. Develops cost-effective and transferable models that help employers manage the two-gender work force. Services include: Corporate Board Resource to assist employers in locating qualified women for board directorships; speakers' bureau; Information Center, which holds current statistics, print media, and research materials on women in business. **Publications:** *Perspective on Current Corporate Issues*, monthly. • Also publishes research reports, career guidance books and pamphlets, policy planning tools for managing a diverse work force, and other publications on leadership development and career and family issues.

★234★ Catholic Daughters of the Americas (CDA)
10 W. 71st St.
New York, NY 10023
Phone: (212)877-3041
Lorraine McMahon, Exec.Sec.

Founded: 1903. **Description:** Society of Catholic women. Supports religious and charitable projects; awards scholarships to teachers of exceptional children; conducts study and discussion groups and poetry, essay, art, and poster contests. **Members:** 145,000. **State Groups:** 35. **Local Groups:** 1531. **Publications:** *Share Magazine*, 4/year. **Formerly:** (1979) Catholic Daughters of America.

★235★ **Catholics for a Free Choice (CFFC)**
1436 U St. NW, No. 301
Washington, DC 20009
Phone: (202)638-1706
Fax: (202)332-7995
Frances Kissling, Pres.

Founded: 1972. **Description:** Catholics within the Roman Catholic church who support the right to legal reproductive health care, especially to family planning and abortion. Goal is to preserve the right of women's choices in childbearing and child rearing. Advocates social and economic programs for women, families, and children. Engages in public education on being Catholic and pro-choice. **Publications:** *Conscience: A Newsjournal of Prochoice Catholic Opinion*, bimonthly. Serves as a forum for dialogue on ethical questions related to human reproduction; contains book reviews. • Also publishes monographs and pamphlets.

★236★ **Catholics United for Life (CUL)**
c/o Dennis Musk
3050 Gap Knob Rd.
New Hope, KY 40052
Phone: (502)325-3061
Fax: (502)325-3091
Dennis Musk, Treas.

Founded: 1975. **Description:** Subscribers: 100,000. **Board of Directors:** 9. Disseminates information on Catholic moral and social teachings regarding family life, marriage, and the value of human life. Provides speakers to family life, pro-life, or natural family planning conventions; suggests alternatives to abortion; teaches techniques of Sidewalk Counseling, through which individuals conduct legal vigils outside of abortion centers. Maintains chapel and holds daily services; sponsors regional and local conferences. Operates 10,000 volume library on theology, history, papal teachings, hagiology (literature dealing with venerated persons or writings), and related subjects. **Publications:** *Newsletter*, every 6 weeks. • Also publishes educational materials and books.

★237★ **Center for the American Woman and Politics (CAWP)**
Eagleton Inst. of Politics
Rutgers University
New Brunswick, NJ 08901
Phone: (908)828-2210
Fax: (908)932-6778
Ruth B. Mandel, Dir.

Founded: 1971. **Description:** Research, education, and public service center that aims to develop and disseminate information about U.S. women's political participation and to encourage women's involvement in public life. Sponsors workshops and courses. Maintains library of books, periodicals, papers, and reports concerning women's political participation. **Computerized Services:** National Information Bank of Women in Public Office, a listing of women elected officials. **Publications:** *CAWP News & Notes*, 3/year. Newsletter reporting on events, organizations, and news related to women in politics and public leadership. • *Subscriber*

Information Services, 3/year. Information packet containing fact sheets, reports, and timely information on the political status of women. • Also publishes books and monographs.

★238★ **Center for Humane Options in Childbirth Experiences (CHOICE)**
5426 Madison St.
Hilliard, OH 43026-2418
Phone: (614)771-0863
Abby Kinne, Dir.

Founded: 1977. **Description:** Medical professionals, paraprofessionals, and interested individuals. Purpose is to teach and encourage parents, parents-to-be, groups, and interested individuals working in family-oriented childbirth in hospital birth centers and out-of-hospital situations. Trains and certifies attendants to attend or coach births. Acts as consumer advocate for hospital births. Services include: medical referrals; childbirth education classes; supplementary prenatal care. Sponsors community educational programs; operates speakers' bureau; compiles statistics. Maintains small lending library. **Members:** 1200. **Local Groups:** 1.

★239★ **Center for International Studies Women in International Security (WIIS)**
University of Maryland
WIIS/CISSM, School of Public Affairs
College Park, MD 20742
Phone: (301)403-8109
Fax: (301)403-8107
Frances G. Burwell, Executive Director

Founded: 1987. **Description:** WIIS is a national, nonpartisan network and professional development program for women working on international issues. Acts to educate others about the roles and achievements of women in this field. Serves as a clearinghouse of information for and about women and maintains a computerized database of women working in international security. Hosts seminars on international relations issues and summer conferences for graduate students. **Publications:** *WIIS Words*, periodic. • *Internships in Foreign and Defense Policy: A Complete Guide for Women and Men*.

★240★ **Center for Law and Social Policy (CLASP)**
1616 P St. NW, Ste. 450
Washington, DC 20036
Phone: (202)328-5140
Fax: (202)328-5195
Paula Roberts, Acting Director

Founded: 1967. **Description:** CLASP is a national public interest law firm addressing the problems of low income families and the legal needs of the poor through policy advocacy, education, research, and legal representation. Seeks to develop new legislation that will address women's and consumer issues, education, the environment, mental health, rights of the disabled, mine health and safety, "feminization of poverty", international human rights, employment for poor people, marine and international environment, and health care for minorities and the poor. Monitors the implementation of the Family Support Act of 1988 and provides training and technical assistance on child support enforcement. **Publications:** *Family Matters*, quarterly. • *States Update*, monthly.

★241★ **Center for Loss in Multiple Birth (CLIMB)**
c/o Jean Kollantai
PO Box 1064
Palmer, AK 99645
Phone: (907)745-2706
Jean Kollantai, Exec. Officer

Founded: 1987. **Description:** Bereaved parents and other affected by multiple birth loss. Provides peer support for parents who have experienced the death of one or more twins or other multiple birth children during pregnancy, birth, infancy, or childhood. Promotes public awareness of the incidence of multiple birth loss and the needs of bereaved parents. Offers materials for professional twins clubs and other loss groups providing services to bereaved parents. Maintains collection of resources available on multiple birth loss; provides assistance to researchers and journalists. **Members:** 400. **Publications:** *Our Newsletter*, quarterly. Includes listings of articles available on multiple birth loss and names of parents who wish to share their experiences. **Formerly:** Multiple Birth Loss Support Network.

★242★ **Center for Population Options (CPO)**
1025 Vermont Ave. NW, Ste. 210
Washington, DC 20005
Phone: (202)347-5700
Fax: (202)347-2263
Judith Senderowitz, Exec.Dir. & Pres.

Founded: 1980. **Description:** Objectives are to: reduce the incidence of unintended teenage pregnancy and childbearing and promote adolescent health through education; to prevent the proliferation of the human immunodeficiency virus (HIV) among adolescents; motivate teens to think and act responsibly about birth control and parenting; conduct programs and advocacy campaigns to assure minors' access to family planning information and services. Provides technical assistance on program planning, implementation, and evaluation of sexuality education in the U.S. and, through International Clearinghouse on Adolescent Fertility, to health, education, and social service workers worldwide. Operates Support Center for School-Based Clinics and media project. Monitors legislative activities for various organizations concerned with youth issues. Conducts research to evaluate promising prevention strategies. Maintains 2500 volume library on sexuality education, family planning, and other adolescent fertility-related issues. Bestows awards. **Publications:** *Clinic News*, quarterly. • *Options*, quarterly. Newsletter. • *Passages* (in English, French, and Spanish), quarterly. • Also publishes fact sheets, reports, and resource guides.

★243★ **Center for Reproductive and Sexual Health (CRASH)**
Ten E. 21st St., 15th Fl.
New York, NY 10010
Phone: (212)758-7310
Roxanne Feldschuh, Adm.Dir.

Founded: 1970. **Description:** Outpatient facility providing health services, information, and counseling for women of all ages. Medical services include: pregnancy testing, birth control and family planning services, fertility counseling, testing and treatment for venereal disease, routine gynecological services, such as pap smears, pelvic and breast examinations, and abortions during the first trimester of pregnancy. All abortions are accompanied by a counseling session on the procedure, post-operative instructions, and information on alternative methods of birth control. According to CRASH, it was "the first outpatient ambulatory medical facility in the United States for the voluntary termination of unplanned pregnancies and became a model for similar facilities across the country." Sponsors educational seminars in cooperation with New York University School of Nursing.

★244★ Center for the Study, Education and Advancement of Women
University of California, Berkeley
Bldg. T-9, Rm. 112
Berkeley, CA 94720
Phone: (415)642-4786

Founded: 1972. **Description:** Aims to increase the educational and career opportunities of women. Sponsors lectures, workshops and discussion groups. Houses a library of resources for research on women, financial aid and job lists. **Publications:** *Connections.*

★245★ Center for the Study of Social Policy
1250 Eye St. NW, Ste. 503
Washington, DC 20005
Phone: (202)371-1565
Hilary Bender, Contact

Description: The Center conducts primary and secondary research on policy issues relating to women and children. Areas of interest include income security with respect to female-headed families and teenage pregnancy prevention programs. Provides technical assistance and evaluation to social service providers.

★246★ Center for Surrogate Parenting (CSP)
8383 Wilshire Blvd., Ste. 750
Beverly Hills, CA 90211
Phone: (213)655-1974
Toll-free: 800-696-4664
Fax: (213)852-1310
William Handle, Pres.

Founded: 1987. **Description:** Attorneys and psychologists who are experts in the field of surrogate parenting, an alternative method of childbearing employed when a woman is unable to conceive a child. Works to disseminate current and accurate information on the legal, moral, ethical, and psychological aspects of surrogate parenting. Advises legislators and establishes ethical and procedural guidelines regarding new laws protecting those involved. Provides information to law firms that handle surrogate parenting cases. Conducts research; maintains speaker's bureau; sponsors radio and television interviews. **Members:** 17. **Publications:** *Center for Surrogate Parenting,* semiannual. Newsletter. Provides information on new procedures and events; includes statistics. • Also distributes general information sheet and brochure. **Formerly:** (1986) Surrogate Parent Foundation.

★247★ Center for a Woman's Own Name
261 Kimberly
Barrington, IL 60010
Founded: 1973. **Description:** Clearinghouse of information, free counseling and educational materials.

★248★ Center for Women in Government
University at Albany
Draper 302
1400 Washington Ave.
Albany, NY 12222
Phone: (518)448-3900
Florence Bonner, Ph.D., Staff Dir.

Founded: 1978. **Description:** Offers research, training and public education, technical assistance, seminars and workshops. **Publications:** *News on Women in Government,* Newsletter.

★249★ Center for Women Policy Studies (CWPS)
2000 P St. NW, Ste. 508
Washington, DC 20036
Phone: (202)872-1770
Leslie R. Wolfe, Exec.Dir.

Founded: 1972. **Description:** Purpose is to educate the public and policymakers regarding issues of women's equity. Conducts studies of such issues as rape and domestic violence, occupational segregation and its roots in education, Social Security equity for women, and sexual harassment in the workplace. Conducts programs such as Educational Equity Policy Studies on math, science, and technology education for girls and women of color. Operates National Resource Center on Women and AIDS and the Law and Pregnancy Program. Has testified before congressional and governmental committees and commissions. Sponsors policy seminars; operates speakers' bureau; bestows awards. **Publications:** *Earnings Sharing in Social Security: A Model for Reform, The SAT Gender Gap, Violence Against Women as Bias-Motivated Hate Crime,* and *Guide to Resources on Women and AIDS* (books), and reports, articles, papers, and bibliographies.

★250★ Center for Women's Studies and Services (CWSS)
2467 E St.
San Diego, CA 92102
Phone: (619)233-8984
Carol Council, Dir.

Founded: 1969. **Description:** A feminist organization founded to meet the unmet needs of women via feminist services and programs and to advance the cause of women's rights. Offers: job referral; feminist-oriented counseling on a one-to-one basis or in groups; family and relationship counseling; legal counseling, and assistance for battered women and victims of sexual assault; crisis intervention; information on and referral to other women's programs and organizations and to human service agencies; information regarding educational programs; financial assistance. Conducts classes in the community and special workshops (Sexual Assault Prevention, Family Violence, and Assertiveness Training). Projects include: Dissolution Clinic - Uncontested Divorces, Rape Crisis Center, Shelter for Battered Women, and Temporary Restraining Order Legal Clinic. Maintains speakers' bureau. **Components:** Educational and Cultural; Storefront and Feminist Counseling. **Members:** 977. **Local Groups:** 2. **Telecommunications Services:** Hot line, (619)233-3088. **Publications:** *CWSS Newsletter,* quarterly. Analyzes current events with an emphasis on the women's and gay movements for equality. Covers such subjects as legislative and court actions, women artists, and the activities of women's, gay, and human rights organizations. • Has also published *Bylines by Women, The Year of the Fires, Double Jeopardy: Young and*

Female in America, and *Rainbow Snake* (book).
Formerly: (1971) Center for Women's Studies.

★251★ Cesarean Prevention Movement (CPM)
PO Box 152
Syracuse, NY 13210
Phone: (315)424-1942
Esther Booth Zorn, Pres.

Founded: 1982. **Description:** Men and women concerned with the increasing rate of cesarean births. Objectives are: to promote vaginal births; to offer encouragement, information, and support for women wanting vaginal births after cesarean (VBAC); to assist in organizing and informing new parents and cesarean parents on preventing future cesareans by opposing unnecessary medical intervention during the birth process and by working to make hospital routines more responsive to women in labor. Offers teacher training and course materials. Sponsors childbirth education certification program, Birth Works, a birth education program that emphasizes a holistic approach. Provides support network to link women anticipating a VBAC and VBAC mothers, supportive physicians, midwives, and childbirth educators. Maintains library of over 300 medical journals and articles. Compiles statistics. **Members:** 2000. **Regional Groups:** 80. **Computerized Services:** Mailing lists. **Publications:** *The Clarion,* quarterly. Includes research and informational articles, book reviews and chapter news. • Also publishes *Cesarean Facts.*

★252★ Chi Eta Phi Sorority, Inc.
3029 13th St., NW
Washington, DC 20005
Phone: (202)232-3858
Essis L. Rowser, Pres.

Founded: 1932. **Description:** Offers health screening, health education and scholarship aid for graduate and undergraduate nursing students. **Publications:** *The Glowing Lamp.*

★253★ Chicana Rights Project (CRP)
314 E. Commerce
San Antonio, TX 78205
Phone: (512)224-5476

Founded: 1974. **Description:** A project of the Mexican American Legal Defense and Educational Fund. Seeks to insure racial and sexual equality of opportunity for Chicana women in such areas as employment, education, and health. Petitions state and federal agencies and files suits to obtain enforcement and compliance with existing anti-discrimination laws; works to secure further gains for women regarding job training and placement, prison reform, maternity benefits, sexual harassment, and abortion funding for the economically disadvantaged. Conducts research in these areas to provide documentation on the problems faced by Chicana women. Participates in panels, legal workshops, and conferences dealing with women's rights on local, state, and national levels. Maintains library. Publishes monograph series, articles, fact sheets, and handbooks.

★254★ Child Care Action Campaign (CCAC)
330 7th Ave., 17th Fl.
New York, NY 10001
Phone: (212)239-0138
Barbara Reisman, Exec.Dir.

Founded: 1983. **Description:** Individuals and organizations interested and active in child care; corporations and financial institutions; labor organizations; editors of leading women's magazines; leaders in government and representatives of religious and civic organizations. Purposes are to: alert the country to the problems of and need for child care services; prepare and disseminate information responsive to inquiries resulting from publicity; analyze existing services and identify gaps; work directly with communities to stimulate the development of local task forces and long-range plans for improved and coordinated services. Brings pressing legislative action or inaction to public attention. Has worked to help make liability insurance available for child care provide rs. Compiles statistics. **Members:** 3000. **Publications:** *Childcare ActioNews*, bimonthly. Newsletter on innovations in the field of child care for working parents. Includes calendar of events, legislative update, and resource information. • Also publishes *Child Care: The Bottom Line*, distributes media kit, and produces audio training cassettes for family day care.

★255★ Childbirth Education Foundation (CEF)
PO Box 5
Richboro, PA 18954
Phone: (215)357-2792
James E. Peron, Founder & Exec.Dir.

Founded: 1972. **Description:** Physicians, nurses, childbirth educators, childbirth reform activists, concerned parents, and individuals dedicated to providing alternatives for a more meaningful childbirth experience, and to promoting reform in childbirth issues and in the treatment of the newborn. Promotes home births, birthing centers, certified nurse-midwife pregnancy management and delivery, family togetherness and infant bonding, "nonviolent birth" for mother and child, and breast-feeding. Distributes literature to libraries, parents, maternal care providers, and educators regarding childbirth, trends in childbirth, safe alternatives, the avoidance of "violence in birth," and the treatment of newborns and infants. Compiles statistics and conducts extensive research related to childbirth, newborn, and infant care; provides seminars and educational workshops for childbirth educators, Lamaze instructors, the La Leche League International (see separate entry), and right-to-life and birthright organizations. Provides referrals and film and videotape services to childbirth educators and maternal and child-care organizations. Maintains speakers' bureau and library. Sponsors charitable programs. **Members:** 18,000. **Computerized Services:** Mailing list of correspondents and maternal/child health groups in U.S. and Canada. **Publications:** *CEF Newsletter*, semiannual. • *Membership Directory*, periodic. • Also publishes a bibliography and educational bulletins.

★256★ Children's Foundation (TCF)
725 15th St. NW, Ste. 505
Washington, DC 20005
Phone: (202)347-3300
Kay Hollestelle, Exec.Dir.

Founded: 1969. **Description:** Concerned with social and economic issues, such as child support for low- and moderate-income women. Provides technical assistance to Child Care Food Program for family day care homes. **Publications:** *Directory of Family Day Care Associations and Support Groups*, annual. Lists over 500 groups involved in family day care issues nationwide. • *Directory of State and Local Child Support Advocacy Groups*, annual. Lists peer support groups for custodial parents having difficulties with child support issues; describes activities of each group. • *Family Day Care Bulletin*, quarterly. Newsletter providing current information on legislation, insurance, zoning, and other topics of interest to family day care providers. • Also publishes *Handbook of Family Day Care Associations*, *Fact Sheet on Family Day Care*, and *Child Support: An Overview of the Problem*.

★257★ Chimera Educational Foundation
59 E. Van Buren, No. 714
Chicago, IL 60605
Phone: (312)939-5341
Jolynn Doerr, Contact

Founded: 1976. **Description:** Women's self-defense organization. Seeks to prevent violence against women. Teaches self-defense techniques to women of all ages; provides certified instructors who are also competent in at least one martial art. Conducts seminars and workshops on the Chimera style of self-defense which involves kicking, blocking, and striking effectively without relying on pure physical strength. Provides educational programs. **Publications:** *Annual Report*. • *Chimera Newsletter*, periodic. Includes instructor profiles, book, television, and movie reviews, and consumer self-defense product test results.

★258★ CHOICE
1233 Locust St., Fl. 3
Philadelphia, PA 19107
Phone: (215)985-3355
Elizabeth Werthan, Exec.Dir.

Founded: 1971. **Description:** Concerned with reproductive health care and child care. Goal of CHOICE, which began as an outgrowth of the Clergy Consultation Service, is to make available, with dignity and concern, high-quality medical and social services to all people at every economic level. Operates resource information center; provides training and consulting services; sponsors teen improvisational theater group. Conducts training programs, seminars, and workshops. Maintains library. **Telecommunications Services:** Hot lines, (215)985-3300 (for health information), and (215)985-2437 for AIDS and HIV-related information; telephone counseling and referrals. **Publications:** *Where to Find*, periodic. Directory of family planning services. **Also known as:** Concern for Health Options - Information, Care and Education.

★259★ Christian Americans for Life (CAFL)
PO Box 977
Tulsa, OK 74102
Phone: (918)665-2345
Dr. Billy James Hargis, CEO

Founded: 1972. **Description:** Campaigns against abortion. Maintains program to support adoption instead of abortion. Compiles statistics, mails letters, and conducts research programs. **Members:** 10,000. **Publications:** *Hotline*, monthly. • Also publishes *Thou Shalt Not Kill.My Babies* and booklets. **Formerly:** (1985) Americans Against Abortion.

★260★ Christian Women's National Concerns (CWNC)
PO Box 100
Granbury, TX 76048
Phone: (817)573-2427
Kimberly Mathews, Dir.

Founded: 1981. **Description:** A division of Christian Voice. Educational service seeking to train women for involvement in grass roots politics, particularly in promotion of the rights of children and families. Attempts to foster public awareness for what the group sees as a need for spiritual repentance in America. Conducts seminars and letter writing campaigns in response to current events and issues.

★261★ Church Women United (CWU)
475 Riverside Dr., Rm. 812
New York, NY 10115
Phone: (212)870-2347
Doris Anne Younger, Gen.Dir.

Founded: 1941. **Description:** Ecumenical movement uniting Protestant, Roman Catholic, Orthodox, and other Christian church women into one Christian community. Supports peace, human rights, justice, and the empowerment of women. Works to strengthen the presence of ecumenical women in both the national and global arenas through offices in Washington, DC and the United Nations. Activities include Intercontinental Grants for Mission, Citizen Action, Assignment: Poverty of Women, and ecumenical and international relations. Sponsors World Day of Prayer (first Friday in March), May Fellowship Day (first Friday in May), and World Community Day (first Friday in November). **State Groups:** 52. **Local Groups:** 1750. **Publications:** *Church Woman*, quarterly. • *Lead Time*, bimonthly. Newsletter. **Formerly:** (1950) United Council of Church Women; (1966) Department of United Church Women of the National Council of Churches; (1969) Church Women United in the U.S.A.

★262★ Citizens' Commission on Civil Rights (CCCR)
2000 M St. NW, Ste. 400
Washington, DC 20036
Phone: (202)659-5565
Fax: (202)293-2672
Dr. Arthur Flemming, Chm.

Founded: 1982. **Description:** Bipartisan former federal cabinet officials concerned with achieving the goal of equality of opportunity. Objectives are to: monitor the federal government's enforcement of laws barring discrimination on the basis of race, sex, religion, ethnic background, age, or handicap; foster public understanding of civil rights issues; formulate constructive policy recommendations. **Members:** 16. **Publications:** *One Nation Indivisible: The*

Civil Rights Challenge For the 1990s, Barriers to Registration and Voting: An Agenda for Reform, and reports on fair housing, busing and the Brown Decision, and affirmative action; provides press releases.

★263★ Citizen's Committee to Amend Title 18
PO Box 936
Newhall, CA 91321
Phone: (805)259-4435
Beth Kurrus, Coordinator

Founded: 1972. **Description:** Custodial parents whose children have been kidnapped by the noncustodial parents. Goals are: to amend Title 18, Section 1201A of the U.S. Code, which exempts parents of minors of kidnapping charges; to obtain Federal Bureau of Investigation assistance when children are taken across state lines in violation of custody orders. Disseminates information about the problem to the public; assists those custodial parents whose children have been taken. **Members:** 300.

★264★ Clearinghouse on Family Violence Information
PO Box 1182
Washington, DC 20013
Phone: (703)385-7565
Fax: (703)385-3206
Candy Hughes, Dir.

Founded: 1987. **Description:** Provides information services to practitioners and researchers studying family violence prevention. Assists victims of family violence. Maintains library. **Computerized Services:** Data base accessible through DIALOG. **Publications:** *Family Violence: An Overview.*

★265★ Clearinghouse on Women's Issues (CWI)
PO Box 70603
Friendship Heights, MD 20813
Phone: (202)363-9795
Elaine L. Newman, Pres.

Founded: 1972. **Description:** Nonpartisan clearinghouse for national, regional, state, and local women's and civil rights organizations. Purpose is to exchange and disseminate educational information and materials on issues related to discrimination on the basis of sex and marital status, with particular emphasis on public policies affecting the economic and educational status of women. **Members:** 400. **Publications:** *Newsletter*, 9/year. **Formerly:** Clearinghouse on Women's Issues in Congress.

★266★ Coal Employment Project (CEP)
17 Emory Pl.
Knoxville, TN 37917
Phone: (615)637-7905
Fax: (615)637-3945
Carol J. Davis, Exec.Off.

Founded: 1977. **Description:** Female coal miners, their supporters, union members, and others who work in the coal industry. To help women obtain and retain coal mining jobs and to end discrimination against women in the coal industry. Works on issues vital to women coal miners such as legal rights, health and safety in the coal mines, sexual harassment, training for women miners, union support, child care, family leave, and pregnancy while employed as a miner. Pursues legal remedies for alleged injustices. Works closely with the Coal Mining

Women's Support Teams, founded by the CEP. Organizes local support groups and education in the fields of legal and occupational rights. Maintains collection of newspaper and magazine clippings and audiovisual materials about women miners. Conducts ongoing research and surveys on issues of importance to women miners and other nontraditional careers for women. **Local Groups:** 12. **Publications:** *Coal Mining Women's Support Team News*, 6/year.

★267★ Coalition of Labor Union Women (CLUW)
15 Union Sq. W
New York, NY 10003
Phone: (212)242-0700
Fax: (212)255-7230
Chrystl Lindo-Bridgeforth, Exec.Officer

Founded: 1974. **Description:** Aims to: unify all union women in order to determine common problems within unions and deal effectively with objectives; promote unionism and encourage unions to be more aggressive in their efforts to bring unorganized women under collective bargaining agreements; inform members about what can be done within the labor movement to achieve equal opportunity and correct discriminatory job situations; educate and inspire union brothers to help achieve affirmative action in the workplace. Seeks to encourage members, through action programs of the coalition, to become more active participants in the political and legislative processes of their unions, to seek election to public office or selection for governmental appointive office at local, county, state, and national levels, and to increase their participation in union policymaking. Bestows awards; operates speakers' bureau. Conducts training programs and project on empowerment of union women. Maintains Coalition of Labor Union Women Center for Education and Research **Members:** 18,000. **Local Groups:** 72. **Publications:** *Newsletter*, bimonthly.

★268★ Coalition of Leading Women's Organizations
825 8th Ave.
New York, NY 10019
Phone: (212)474-5000
Marcella Rosen, Chairperson

★269★ Coalition for Safety of Abortion Clinics (CSAC)
Planned Parenthood of Metropolitan Washington
1108 16th St., NW
Washington, DC 20036
Phone: (202)347-8500
Rosann Wisman, Exec.Dir.

Founded: 1984. **Description:** Organizations concerned with promoting the right of women to choose abortion. Protests the bombings of abortion-related facilities and attempts to secure resolutions from local governments condemning such bombings. Although the coalition operates in the Washington, DC area, it appeals to similar organizations nationally to organize. Maintains speakers bureau; compiles statistics on bombings in the Washington, DC area. **Members:** 22.

★270★ Coalition for Western Women's History (CWWH)
History Department
Washington State University
Pullman, WA 99614
Phone: (509)335-1560
Susan Armitage, Board Member

Description: The Coalition provides networking opportunities promotes the writing and publicizing of multi-cultural women's history in the American West. **Publications:** *CWWH Newsletter.*

★271★ Coalition on Women and the Budget (CWB)
National Women's Law
1616 P St., NW
Washington, DC 20036
Phone: (202)328-5160
Nancy Duff Campbell, Coordinator

Founded: 1981. **Description:** Civil rights, education, labor, religious, and women's organizations. Conducts annual assessments of the impact of budget cuts and the current U.S. administration's economic policies on women and children. Compiles statistics. **Members:** 80. **Publications:** *annual.* • Has also published report entitled Inequality of Sacrifice.

★272★ Coalition for Women in International Development (CWID)
c/o OEF International
1815 H St. NW, 11th Fl.
Washington, DC 20006
Phone: (202)466-3430
Fax: (202)775-0596
Nancy Rubin, Chwm.

Founded: 1976. **Description:** Organizations (50) and individuals (90). Promotes the participation of American women in U.S. foreign policy and of women throughout the world in the economic, social, and political development of their respective countries. Strives to inform and influence U.S. policymakers about issues affecting women and their families in developing countries. Conducts research programs. Lobbies and advises on issues concerning U.S. or foreign government policies. **Members:** 140. **Publications:** *Fact Sheet*, periodic. • *Minutes of the Quarterly Meetings.*

★273★ Coalition on Women and Religion (CWR)
4759 15th Ave. NE
Seattle, WA 98105
Phone: (206)525-1213
Carol Van Buren, Pres.

Founded: 1973. **Description:** Individuals and groups dedicated to claiming, exploring, and expanding the spirituality of women. Examines and reinterprets sacred texts from the feminist perspective. Maintains 200 volume library. **Members:** 400. **Regional Groups:** 1. **Publications:** *The Flame*, quarterly. Newsletter providing feminist and religious information, book reviews, and articles. • Also publishes *The Woman's Bible, The Word for Us, Study Guide for the Women's Bible, The FLAME Cartoons, and The Spirited Woman's Cartoon Book*, (books). **Formerly:** (1975) Coalition Task Force on Women and Religion.

★274★ Coalition for Women's Appointments (CWA)
c/o Natl. Women's Political Caucus
1275 K St. NW, Ste. 750
Washington, DC 20005-4051
Phone: (202)898-1100
Fax: (202)898-0458
Sharon Rodine, Pres.

Founded: 1976. **Description:** Organization coordinated by the National Women's Political Caucus (see separate entry). Seeks to promote the appointment and promotion of women to high level government positions and to assist women seeking appointment or election to the state or federal bench. The coalition evaluates and monitors appointments to determine their impact on issues affecting women. Compiles statistics and maintains biographical archives. **Members:** 84.

★275★ Coalition of Women's Art Organizations (CWAO)
123 E. Beutel Rd.
Port Washington, WI 53074
Phone: (414)284-4458
Dorothy Provis, Pres.

Founded: 1977. **Description:** Art organizations and professionals. Works to protect and improve the rights of all artists. In 1984, reorganized as an advocacy organization dedicated to alerting its national network to issues in the arts. Advocates for the passage of consignment legislation on the state level; supports the National Heritage Resource Act. **Publications:** *CWAO News*, monthly. Newsletter.

★276★ College Music Society Committee on the Status of Women
Butler University
Jordan College
Department of Music Theory and History
Indianapolis, IN 46208
Phone: (317)283-9231
S. Kay Hoke, Chair

★277★ Comision Femenil Mexicana Nacional (CFMN)
379 S. Loma Dr.
Los Angeles, CA 90017
Phone: (213)484-1515
Maggie Cervantes, Pres.

Founded: 1970. **Description:** Advocates Latin women's rights; works to advance Hispanic women politically, socially, economically, and educationally. Maintains: Chicana Service Action Center, which provides jobs skills training; Centro de Ninos, bilingual child development programs; Casa Victoria group home for teens. Bestows awards; maintains speakers' bureau; compiles statistics. Conducts research. **Members:** 5000. **Regional Groups:** 23. **State Groups:** 20. **Local Groups:** 10. **Computerized Services:** Data base of women's and Hispanic organizations and national Latina leaders. **Publications:** *Annual Report*. • *La Mujer*, semiannual. Includes statistics. • *Newsletter*, periodic.

★278★ Commission of the Status and Role of Women (CSRW)
1200 Davis St.
Evanston, IL 60201
Phone: (312)869-7330
Joetta Rinehart, Pres.

Founded: 1970. **Description:** A commission of the United Methodist Church. Laypersons and clergy interested in the status of women in the UMC. Works to protect the rights of women, both lay and clergy, in the UMC. Assists individuals with recognizing and bringing complaints of sexual harassment or discrimination to the appropriate church disciplinary body or civil authorities. Maintains speakers' bureau. **Members:** 48. **Regional Groups:** 72. **Publications:** *The Flyer*, 5/year. Newsletter.

★279★ Committee to Defend Reproductive Rights (CDRR)
25 Taylor St., Ste. 704
San Francisco, CA 94102
Phone: (415)441-4434
Lyn Farrugia, Coordinator

Founded: 1977. **Description:** Individuals interested in reproductive rights; health organizations. Conducts community education and activism concerning reproductive rights including abortion, sterilization, and prenatal care. Provides speakers for high schools, community colleges, and universities. Offers continuing education courses for nurses. **Members:** 1200. **Publications:** *CDRR News*, bimonthly.

★280★ Committee to Expose, Oppose, and Depose Patriarchy (CEODP)
8319 Fulham Ct.
Richmond, VA 23227
Phone: (804)266-7400
Donna Gorman, Exec. Officer

Founded: 1984. **Description:** Members who oppose institutions deemed to be "patriarchal" (administered exclusively for the benefit of males) and that "characteristically lie, practice double-think," "control and dominate" minorities, and are animated by a "love for death" (as in supporting militarism, war, and capital punishment). Monitors media sources. Disseminates information relative to partriarchal practices and events.

★281★ Committee for Mother and Child Rights (CMCR)
Rt. 1, Box 256A
Clear Brook, VA 22624
Phone: (703)722-3652
Elizabeth Owen, Natl.Coord.

Founded: 1980. **Description:** Concerned people, many of whom are mothers who have either lost custody, have been faced with contested custody of their children, or have other custody-related problems. Purposes are to help mothers and children who are going through the trauma of contested custody or who have been through it, or have custody but fear losing it, and to educate the public about some of the injustices that they believe occur to mothers and children. Aims to improve the status of mothers because "when mothers cease to be so powerless, children will thrive." **Members:** 6000.

★282★ Committee to Resist Abortion (CRA)
1626 2nd Ave.
New York, NY 10028
Hugo Carl Koch, Chm.

Founded: 1983. **Description:** Individuals who, after prolonged opposition to legalized abortion, created the committee as a means to intensify their protest. Seeks to: oppose abortion by mobilizing a nationwide anti-abortion income tax strike, during which participants would refuse to pay all or part of their federal income tax; prepare and present a petition to the U.N. General Assembly alleging that legalized abortion in the U.S. is an act of racial and class oppression constituting genocide under the terms of the U.N. charter. Maintains communication with antiabortion groups and interested individuals; collects supporting sociological and economic data. **Publications:** *Newsletter*, periodic.

★283★ Committee on the Role and Status of Women
c/o Emily Lowe Brizendine
California State University
Department of Educational Leadership
Hayward, CA 94542
Phone: (510)881-3106
Fax: (415)727-2283
Emily Lowe Brizendine, Chairperson

Founded: 1972. **Description:** A standing committee of the American Educational Research Association. Persons affiliated with elementary and secondary schools and universities. Established to assess and enhance the status of women in educational research at universities, research and development centers, and on an international level. Projects include preparation of a roster of women in educational research and development of career materials for educational research. Compiles statistics. **Members:** 5. **Publications:** *Directory*, periodic.

★284★ Committee on South Asian Women (COSAW)
Texas A&M University
Department of Psychology
College Station, TX 77843
Phone: (409)845-2576
Jyotsna Vaid, Contact

Founded: 1982. **Description:** Network of women of South Asian origin or interests. Supports efforts of South Asian women's groups and encourages cooperation with their Western counterparts. Disseminates information on the living and working conditions of women in South Asia, including Afghanistan, Bangladesh, Bhutan, India, Nepal, Pakistan, and Sri Lanka. Conducts research on issues of interest to South Asian women abroad. Sponsors lectures, films, conferences, seminars, and workshops. Maintains speakers' bureau and library. **Publications:** *COSAW Bulletin*, quarterly. Includes essays, creative writing, book and film reviews, news from South Asian women's groups, a research index, and a directory of organizations and individuals.

★285★ Committee on the Status of Women in the Economics Profession (CSWEP)
c/o Dr. Nancy M. Gordon
Congressional Budget Office
Second and D Sts., SW, Rm. H2-418A
Washington, DC 20515
Phone: (202)226-2669
Fax: (202)225-3149
Dr. Nancy M. Gordon, Chair

Founded: 1972. **Associates:** 4900. **Description:** A standing committee of American Economic Association. Women economists in the U.S. Purpose is to support and facilitate equality of opportunity for women economists. Disseminates information about job opportunities, research funding, and research related to the status of women in economics. Sponsors technical sessions. **Computerized Services:** Job roster; mailing list. **Publications:** *Newsletter*,

3/year. • *Women in Economics, The CSWEP Roster*, biennial.

★286★ Committee on the Status of Women in Linguistics (CSWL)
1325 18th St. NW, Ste. 211
Washington, DC 20036
Phone: (202)835-1714
Penelope Eckert, Chair

Founded: 1973. **Description:** A committee of the Linguistic Society of America. Purpose is to guarantee equality of opportunity in training and employment to all members. Studies and publicizes the official policies of institutions and organizations employing and representing linguists; investigates and makes reports on patterns of discrimination against women; makes available information about grievance and appeal agencies; communicates information about federal and state regulations regarding the status of women in academic institutions to colleges and universities employing linguists. Maintains up-to-date statistical data; presents recommendations for affirmative action at LSA meetings. **Members:** 6.

★287★ Committee on the Status of Women in Microbiology (CSWM)
c/o Dr. Anne Morris Hooke
Miami University
Dept. of Microbiology
Oxford, OH 45056
Phone: (513)529-2028
Fax: (513)529-3841
Dr. Anne Morris Hooke, Chairperson

Description: A committee of the American Society for Microbiology. Microbiologists investigating the status of women in microbiology in relation to their male counterparts in the work place and within their professional society. Reports findings and conducts seminars at the annual meeting of the ASM. Works toward full and equal opportunity for educational, career, and personal development for male and female microbiologists. **Members:** 6. Electronic mail accessible through Bitnet, AMHOOKEMIAMIU. **Publications:** *The Communicator*, 4/year. Newsletter. **Formerly:** (1985) Committee of Status of Women Microbiologists.

★288★ Committee on the Status of Women in Philosophy (CSWP)
c/o Alison Jaggar
University of Colorado
Dept. of Philosophy, No. 232
Boulder, CO 80309-0232
Phone: (303)492-6132
Alison Jaggar, Chairperson

Founded: 1970. **Description:** A committee of the American Philosophical Association. Individuals appointed by APA to report on and further the professional status of women in philosophy. Collects and disseminates information on the status of women in philosophy; works to facilitate an understanding of issues of gender and of the range of positions respresented in feminist theories. **Members:** 8. **Publications:** *Feminism and Philosophy Newsletter*, periodic. • Also publishes monographs, pamphlets, and other materials on sexist language, sexual discrimination in job interviews and hiring, and other topics.

★289★ Committee on the Status of Women in Sociology (CSWS)
c/o American Sociological Association
1722 N St. NW
Washington, DC 20036
Phone: (202)833-3410
Fax: (202)785-0146
Tahi L. Mottl, Ph.D., Asst.Exec. Officer

Founded: 1970. **Description:** A standing committee of the American Sociological Association. Primary task is to monitor and further the status of women in the sociological profession. **Members:** 6.

★290★ Committee of 200 (C200)
625 N. Michigan Ave., Ste. 500
Chicago, IL 60611-3108
Phone: (312)751-3477
Lydia Lewis, Exec.Dir.

Founded: 1982. **Description:** Women executives who are recognized as leaders in their industries. (Though originally intended to have a membership of 200 top-ranking businesswomen, the committee is no longer limited to 200). Encourages successful entrepreneurship by women and the active participation of women business owners and senior corporate executives in business, economic, social, and educational concerns. Seeks to strengthen the influence of women business leaders. Provides forum for exchange of ideas and enhancement of business opportunities for women. **Members:** 320. **Publications:** *Network*, monthly. Flier. • *Update*, semiannual. Newsletter.

★291★ Committee on Women in Asian Studies (CWAS)
c/o Sucheta Mazumdar
Dept. of History
State Univ. of New York Albany
Albany, NY 12203
Phone: (518)442-4795
Sucheta Mazumdar, Chair

Founded: 1972. **Description:** Scholars, students, writers, and professionals in any field that deals with male/female issues in Asia. Studies the social, economic, and political position of Asian women, including issues such as women and poverty in the Third World, sexual division of labor in south India, and women's education in the Third World. Seeks to further gender-disaggregated research, teaching, and publication concerning the lives of males and females in Asian populations; promotes the role of women in the Asian studies profession. Disseminates research results and information; sponsors workshops. **Publications:** *CWAS Newsletter*, 3/year. Includes book reviews, conference news and announcements, film and publications announcements, profiles of people in the field, and research reports. **Formerly:** (1982) Committee on the Status of Women in Asian Studies.

★292★ Committee for Women in Geophysics (CWG)
c/o Kathanne Lynch
Mobil Oil Corp.
1250 Poydras Bldg.
New Orleans, LA 70113
Phone: (504)566-5200
Kathanne Lynch, Chwm.

Founded: 1978. **Description:** A committee of the Society of Exploration Geophysicists. Objective is to increase the participation and recognition of women members of SEG in the field of geophysics. Activities include: encouraging and developing forms of communication among women members of SEG; developing programs which encourage women to enter the field of geophysics; assisting women members of SEG in their career goals. Offers scholarship awards. Maintains library of surveys and reports. Compiles statistics. Publishes Women Exploring the Earth (brochure). **Members:** 12.

★293★ Communication Workers of America, AFL-CIO (CWA)
Concerned Women's Advancement Committee
501 Third St. NW
Washington, DC 20001
Phone: (202)434-1100
Lela Foreman, Women's Director

Description: CWA has a national women's committee with one member from each of 12 districts. The Committee is concerned with job issues, job security, child care, and political issues. **Members:** 650,000. **Publications:** *CWA News*.

★294★ Communications Consortium
1333 H St. NW
Washington, DC 20005
Phone: (202)682-1270
Fax: (202)682-2154
Kathy Bonk, Co-Director

Description: The Consortium is a nonprofit media center whose purpose is to help public interest organizations maximize their use of media and telecommunications systems as tools for public education and policy change. Serves as a collaborative resource for public interest advocates who share policy change. Focuses on issues such as family policy, the environment, energy efficiency, women's rights, and reproductive health. **Publications:** The Consortium issues publications on the strategic use of media.

★295★ Concerned Women for America (CWA)
370 L'Enfant Promenade SW, Ste. 800
Washington, DC 20024
Phone: (202)488-7000
Fax: (202)488-0806
Beverly LaHaye, Pres.

Founded: 1979. **Description:** Educational and legal defense foundation that seeks to protect the rights of the family and preserve traditional American values. **Members:** 600,000. **Regional Groups:** 2500. **Publications:** *Newsletter*, 11/year.

★296★ Conference for Catholic Lesbians (CCL)
PO Box 436, Planetarium Sta.
New York, NY 10024
Phone: (718)921-0463
Karen Doherty, Outreach Coordinator

Founded: 1982. **Description:** Women of Catholic heritage and their non-Catholic women friends who recognize the importance of the Catholic tradition in shaping their lives, but who seek to develop and nurture a spiritual life which enhances and affirms their lesbian identity. Provides a forum for exploring spirituality through liturgies and rituals. Promotes Catholic lesbian visibility and community. Advocates women's and lesbian rights and social justice issues in the church and society. Serves as a support network worldwide. Sponsors lectures, retreats, and conferences. **Members:** 700. **Local Groups:** 20. **Publications:** *Images*, quarterly. Newsletter; provides a forum on current Catholic and lesbian issues.

★297★ Conference of Liberal Arts Colleges for Women (CLACW)
c/o Laura G. Stettner
869 Charles River St.
Needham, MA 02192
Phone: (617)239-3384
Laura G. Stettner, Coordinator

Founded: 1950. **Description:** Five colleges (Barnard, Bryn Mawr, Mt. Holyoke, Smith, and Wellesley) in Massachusetts, New York, and Pennsylvania. Conducts cooperative program for recruitment and admissions; informs students of opportunities at the five colleges. Coordinator is assisted by volunteer alumnae in each state. **Publications:** *Conference of Liberal Arts Colleges for Women—Recruitment Brochure*, periodic. • *Recruitment Brochure*, annual. **Formerly:** (1964) Seven College Conference Scholarship Program; (1969) Seven College Conference Program for Admission and Scholarships; (1973) Seven College Conference Program for Admission and Financial Aid; (1976) Six College Conference Admissions Programs; (1977) Five College Conference.

★298★ Congregation of Sisters of St. Agnes
475 Gillett St.
Fond du Lac, WI 54935
Phone: (414)923-2121
Sr. Jean Steffes, CSA, Gen. Superior

Founded: 1858. **Description:** Religious women serving rural and urban communities throughout the U.S. and Latin America. Promotes justice for the economically poor; works to further the role of women in the Catholic church and society; collaborates with the laity and clergy of other faiths in service programs. Provides staffing at 4 hospitals, a home for the aged, and a coeducational college. Places and supports missionaries in Nicaragua. **Members:** 487. **Local Groups:** 62. **Formerly:** (1991) Sisters of the Congregation of St. Agnes.

★299★ Congressional Caucus for Women's Issues (CCWI)
2471 Rayburn House Office Bldg.
Washington, DC 20515
Phone: (202)225-6740
Lesley Primmer, Exec. Officer

Founded: 1977. **Description:** Bipartisan legislative service organization of the U.S. House of Representatives with the goal of improving the status of American women and eliminating discrimination "built into many federal programs and policies." Supports legislation to improve women's status; has arranged regular meetings with cabinet officers and administration officials to establish a dialogue with the executive branch on issues concerning women. Focuses on equal treatment of women with regard to Social Security, federal and private pensions, insurance, and child support enforcement. Seeks recognition of the economic contributions and needs of all women. **Members:** 140. **Formerly:** (1982) Congresswomen's Caucus.

★300★ Congressional Club (CC)
2001 New Hampshire Ave. NW
Washington, DC 20009
Phone: (202)332-1155
Doris Matsui, Pres.

Founded: 1908. **Description:** Women's organization made up of wives of present and former U.S. Representatives, Senators, Cabinet members, and Supreme Court Justices. The wives of the President and Vice President of the U.S. and the wife of the Speaker of the House are honorary members. Holds weekly luncheon. **Members:** 650. **Publications:** *Directory*, biennial.

★301★ Congressional Wives for Soviet Jewry (CWSJ)
1522 K St. NW, Ste. 1100
Washington, DC 20005
Phone: (202)898-2500
Mrs. Henry Jackson, Founding Chwm.

Founded: 1978. **Description:** Spouses of members of the U.S. Congress. Purpose is to provide support for alleviating oppression of Jews in the former USSR. Sends telegrams and letters to U.S. officials and policy makers in the areas once governed by the Soviet Union; maintains contact with refuseniks in the former Soviet Union and members of their families who have emigrated. (Refuseniks are erstwhile Soviet citizens who have been refused exit visas.) Seeks to bring issues to international attention. Sponsors educational events for congressional spouses, such as briefings and seminars. Conducts informational mailings; maintains liaison with the National Conference on Soviet Jewry. Maintains library and speakers' bureau. **Members:** 150. **Publications:** Reports and pamphlets.

★302★ Congressional Wives Task Force
Box 1978, US House Representives
Washington, DC 20515

★303★ Consortium of Doctors (COD)
University System
PO Box 20402
Savannah, GA 31404
Phone: (912)354-4634
Dr. Abbie W. Jordan, Founder & Dir.

Founded: 1990. **Description:** Minority women who have earned a doctorate degree from an established, accredited institution. Assists members in finding jobs suitable to their training. Conducts charitable and educational programs; bestows awards. **Members:** 62. **Regional Groups:** 1. **State Groups:** 6. **Publications:** *COD*, annual. Membership activities newsletter.

★304★ Coordinating Committee on Women in the Historical Profession (CCWHP)
Conference Group on Women's History (CGWH)
c/o Lynn Weiner
527 Clinton
Oak Park, IL 60304
Phone: (708)386-1829
Lynn Weiner, Exec.Sec. & Treas.

Founded: 1969. **Description:** Women historians and others interested in women's history. Works to encourage and help develop research and instruction in the field of women's history, advance the status of women at all levels and increase their numbers, and to oppose discrimi-

nation against women in the profession. Assists members in establishing panels in different conferences; promotes networking. Bestows awards. **Members:** 800. **Regional Groups:** 14. **Publications:** *CCWHP/CGWH Newsletter*, 5/year. • Also publishes courses, bibliographies, conference reports, and job advertisements.

★305★ Cornell University Institute for Women and Work (IWW)
New York School of Industrial and Labor Relations
15 E. 26th St., 4th Fl.
New York, NY 10010
Phone: (212)340-2800
Francine Moccio, Director

Founded: 1972. **Description:** IWW promotes education and applied research and sponsors conferences and seminars on working women's issues. Programs may be conducted in association with unions, government, or other universities. Topics include training for union leadership positions and research on health care occupations, nontraditional work, women in trades, and work and family issues.

★306★ Cosmetic Executive Women (CEW)
217 E. 85th St., Ste. 214
New York, NY 10028
Phone: (212)759-3283
Lee MacCallum, Pres.

Founded: 1954. **Description:** Women who have served for more than three years in executive positions in the cosmetic and allied industries. Unites women executives in the cosmetic field for industry awareness and business advancement. Conducts seminars and luncheons. Presents the Cosmetic Executive Women Achiever Award annually. **Members:** 600. **Regional Groups:** 1. **Publications:** *CEW Wavelength*, periodic. Newsletter. • *Membership Roster*, periodic. **Formerly:** (1981) Cosmetic Career Women.

★307★ Cosmopolitan Associates (CA)
PO Box 1491
West Caldwell, NJ 07007
Phone: (201)992-2232
Gisela Lange, Pres.

Founded: 1947. **Description:** Foreign-born women living in the U.S. Purposes are to: retain affiliations with the homelands of members; provide for socialization and companionship; encourage formation of local chapters. Conducts charitable program. **Members:** 604. **Local Groups:** 13. **Publications:** *Newsletter*, monthly.

★308★ Council for Advancement and Support of Education (CASE) Commission for Opportunity and Equity (COE)
11 Dupont Circle NW, Ste. 400
Washington, DC 20036-1207
Phone: (202)328-5931
Susan VanGilder, Manager, Reference Center

Description: The Commission promotes equality in career access, promotion, pay, and recognition for minorities and women. To this end, it sponsors the annual Newcomers' Scholarship Program, forums on career advancement for women and minorities, such as the Forum for Institutional Advancement Officers, sessions at the Annual Assembly, and regional activities through district committees.

★309★ Council of Asian American Women
232 E. Capitol St., NE
Washington, DC 20003
Phone: (202)544-3181
Virginia Kee, Pres.

Founded: 1977. **Description:** Promotes the interests of Asian American women. Increases the awareness of Asian American women in the areas of politics, business and public policy.

★310★ Council of Communication Organizations (COCO)
A Woman's Network
Department of Communication, 248 Grehan Bldg.
University of Kentucky
Lexington, KY 40506
Phone: (606)257-7809
Ramona R. Rush, Professor of Communications

Founded: 1983. **Description:** Purpose is to network, using both high and low technology, about women's communication issues. Also encourages the electronic connection of art communities.

★311★ The Council of Presidents of United States Women's Organizations
American Nurses Association
1011 14th St. NW, Ste. 200
Washington, DC 20003
Phone: (202)789-1800
Chris deVries, Asst. Dir., Cong. and Agency Relations

Description: The Council coordinates public policy action for more than 50 groups representing diverse constituencies in the women's movement. Supports and reinforces the work of these organizations in order to increase impact on a progressive national policy agenda. Organizes meetings with leaders of Congress and the Administration and conducts media and public information campaigns.

★312★ Council of Women Chiropractors (CWC)
c/o Herbie McMennamy, D.C.
4002 Washington
Amarillo, TX 79110
Phone: (806)355-7217
Herbie McMennamy, D.C., Treas.

Description: A council of the American Chiropractic Association. Women chiropractors. Promotes the science, art, and practice of chiropractic and the professional welfare of its members; encourages women chiropractors to become members of the ACA; seeks to advance the prestige of women chiropractors; encourages women in this profession to give of their talents and accomplishments; tries to persuade young women to become chiropractors. **Members:** 150. **Formerly:** (1966) National Council of Women Chiropractors; American Council of Women Chiropractors.

★313★ Council for Women in Independent Schools (CWIS)
c/o National Association of Independent Schools
75 Federal St.
Boston, MA 02110
Phone: (617)451-2444
Dory Adams, Staff Liaison

Founded: 1974. **Description:** A special committee of the National Association of Independent Schools. Purpose is to examine and improve the situation of women in teaching and administration in independent schools. Studies curricula in independent schools; works to enhance the quality of education and to assist in faculty and administrative career advancement. **Publications:** *Newsletter,* annual.

★314★ Country Women's Council United States of America (CWC)
c/o Mrs. Henry Buff
3500 Henbet Dr.
West Columbia, SC 29169
Phone: (803)794-7548
Mrs. Henry Buff, Chm.

Founded: 1939. **Description:** Rural women's organizations. Aims are to: help in the economic, social, and cultural development of rural women; stimulate interest in the international aspects of rural and home life; further friendship and understanding among country women and homemakers of all nations. Awards the Ruth B. Sayre Scholarship to members who encourage leadership development. **Members:** 89. **Publications:** *News Sheet,* semiannual. • Has also published *United States of America - Our Way of Life* and *United States of America - People and Places.* **Formerly:** (1946) U.S. Liaison Committee of Associated Country Women of the World.

★315★ Couple to Couple League (CCL)
PO Box 111184
Cincinnati, OH 45211
Phone: (513)661-7612
John F. Kippley, Pres.

Founded: 1971. **Description:** Married and engaged couples interested in natural family planning (a method of spacing pregnancies through reliance on the woman's natural fertility cycle). Believes natural birth control strengthens family bonds and is healthier and more morally acceptable than artificial birth control devices. Sponsors local teaching groups where couples are taught basic natural family planning techniques. Provides special training program for those who wish to become CCL teaching couples. Promotes premarital chastity through speakers and materials. **Local Groups:** 450. **Publications:** *CCL Family Foundations,* bimonthly. Newsletter. • Also publishes *The Art of Natural Family Planning, Breastfeeding and Natural Child Spacing, Fertility, Cycles and Nutrition,* manual, and workbooks.

★316★ Custody Action for Lesbian Mothers (CALM)
PO Box 281
Narberth, PA 19072
Phone: (215)667-7508
Rosalie G. Davies, Coordinator

Founded: 1974. **Description:** Provides free legal and counseling services for lesbian mothers seeking child custody. Primary commitment is to aid the mother in keeping her children; broader goal is to bring cases to court so the

attitudes of judges and the courts may be challenged. Volunteers (usually lesbian mothers) advise mothers of their options, provide them with support and understanding, and accompany them through all phases of the legal process. Supports litigation addressing constitutional rights on the basis of sexual preference. Maintains nationwide contact with lesbian mother groups and attorneys who are either providing a similar counseling service or doing research in this area.

★317★ Dakota Women of All Red Nations (DWARN)
c/o Lorelei DeCora
PO Box 423
Rosebud, SD 57570
Lorelei DeCora, Chair

Founded: 1978. **Description:** Grass roots organization of American Indian women seeking to advance the Native American movement. Is establishing local chapters to work on issues of concern such as sterilization abuse and women's health, adoption and foster-care abuse, community education, political imprisonment, legal and juvenile justice problems, and problems caused by energy resource development by multinational corporations on Indian land. Supports leadership roles for American Indian women. **Publications:** Reports on health problems of American Indian women. **Formerly:** (1985) Women of All Red Nations.

★318★ Daughters of the American Colonists
2205 Massachusetts Ave., NW
Washington, DC 20008
Phone: (202)667-3076
Jame E. Crews, Pres.

Founded: 1920. **Description:** Concerned with researching colonial American. **Publications:** *The Colonial Courier.*

★319★ Daughters of the Cincinnati (DC)
122 E. 58th St.
New York, NY 10022
Phone: (212)319-6915
Caroline Slee, Contact

Founded: 1894. **Description:** Women descendants of the officers of George Washington's Continental Army or Navy. Works to preserve patriotic ideals and to award college scholarships to high school seniors who are daughters of commissioned officers of the armed services. **Members:** 550. **Publications:** *Year Book.*

★320★ Daughters of the Elderly Bridging the Unknown Together (DEBUT)
c/o Pat Meier
710 Concord St.
Ellettsville, IN 47429
Phone: (812)876-5319
Pat Meier, Pres.

Founded: 1981. **Description:** Women involved in caring for elderly parents; individuals preparing for future roles as caregivers. Provides: nonjudgmental support; education in all areas of caring, coping, and in the complex process of aging; an innovative model for interns, health service professionals, and caregivers. Stresses the importance of nursing center advocacy, community outreach, and intergenerational dialogue between adult children and their parents. Organizes seminars; delivers presentations at local and national gerontological functions. Educates the public through radio and television. **Members:** 100. **Local Groups:** 3. **Publications:** *Daughters of the Elderly: Building Partnerships in Caregiving*, (resource book).

★321★ **Daughters of Isabella, International Circle (DIIC)**
375 Whitney Ave.
New Haven, CT 06511
Phone: (203)865-2570
Janet Hagen, Office Mgr.

Founded: 1897. **Description:** Fraternal society of Catholic women who seek to emulate the accomplishments and virtues of Queen Isabella (1451-1504), ruler of Aragon and Castile. Promotes friendship and seeks to unite the energies and resources of members "for the advancement of all that is best and truest in life." Sponsors Queen Isabella Foundation, which provides scholarships in Social Service at Catholic University of America. Has established a family center at Catholic University of America. **Members:** 100,000. **Local Groups:** 800. **Formerly:** (1972) Daughters of Isabella, National Circle; (1977) Daughters of Isabella, Supreme Circle.

★322★ **Daughters of the Nile, Supreme Temple (DNST)**
c/o Geraldine Neely
9832 Watts Branch Dr.
Rockville, MD 20850
Phone: (301)279-2434
Geraldine Neely, Sec.

Founded: 1913. **Description:** Mothers, wives, sisters, daughters, and widows of Shriners. Assists with philanthropic work of the Shriners' hospitals for crippled children. **Members:** 81,000. **Local Groups:** 147.

★323★ **Daughters of Penelope (DP)**
1909 O St. NW, No. 500
Washington, DC 20009
Phone: (202)234-9741
Helen G. Pappas, Exec.Dir.

Founded: 1929. **Description:** Women's fraternal organization. Awards scholarships to girls of Greek descent and participates in other philanthropic activities. Sponsors Daughters of Penelope Foundation. **Members:** 14,000. **Local Groups:** 364.

★324★ **Daughters of the Republic of Texas (DRT)**
510 E. Anderson Ln.
Austin, TX 78753
Patti Cox, Custodian Gen.

Founded: 1891. **Description:** Women over age 16 who are lineal descendants of men or women who won independence for Texas from Mexico. Members are custodians of the Alamo, San Antonio, TX and the French Legation, Austin, TX. Maintains museum and library. **Members:** 6300. **Publications:** *Newsletter*, semiannual.

★325★ **Daughters of Scotia (DS)**
104 Buckingham Ave.
Syracuse, NY 13210
Phone: (315)472-4050
Marget Montgomery, Grand Rec.Sec.

Founded: 1895. **Description:** Women of Scottish descent or birth. **Members:** 7800. **Local Groups:** 96.

★326★ **Daughters of Union Veterans of the Civil War, 1861-1865 (DUV)**
503 S. Walnut St.
Springfield, IL 62704
Phone: (217)544-0616
Ms. Anna Kemison, Treas.

Founded: 1885. **Description:** Lineal descendants of Union veterans of the U.S. Civil War. Objectives are to perpetuate the memories of veterans of the U.S. Civil War, their loyalty to the Union, and their sacrifices for its preservation. Seeks to: keep alive the history of those who participated in the struggle for the maintenance of our free government; aid the descendants of Union veterans of the Civil War; assist those who are worthy and needy; cooperate in movements relating to veterans, civic, and welfare projects; inculcate a love of country and patriotism; promote equal rights and universal liberty; honor Union veterans of the Civil War by placing flowers on graves on Memorial Day. Conducts genealogical projects. Maintains heritage records and library. Supports and maintains public museum in Springfield, IL. Conducts charitable work in veterans' hospitals. Supports local historical societies. Takes part in patriotic ceremonial programs and holiday observances. Presents awards to one cadet at each of four military academies; grants scholarships to students. Conducts specialized education programs and sponsors competitions. **Members:** 6000. **Regional Groups:** 21. **Local Groups:** 194. **Publications:** *General Orders*, quarterly. • *Roster of National Members*, annual. • Is preparing local histories of the Civil War. **Formerly:** (1925) National Alliance Daughters of Veterans.

★327★ **Delegation for Friendship Among Women (DFW)**
2219 Caroline Ln.
South St. Paul, MN 55075
Phone: (612)455-5620
Fax: (612)445-5620
Mary Pomeroy, Sec.

Founded: 1962. **Description:** Women who have displayed leadership qualities in the fields of academia, architecture, business, journalism, law, and science. Promotes better understanding between women and women's organizations in developing nations and American women. Sponsors networks for the health, education, and welfare of women and children. Arranges programs for women visiting the U.S. from developing countries; provides speakers for women's activities. Maintains biographical archives and 600 volume library. **Members:** 144. **Publications:** *Bulletin*, periodic. • *Newsletter*, periodic.

★328★ **Delta Gamma Fraternity**
3250 Riverside Dr.
Columbus, OH 43221
Phone: (614)481-8169
Marilyn Monroe Fordham, Pres.

Founded: 1873. **Description:** Purpose is to foster high ideals of friendship among women, to promote education and cultural interests of members and to create a true sense of social responsibility. **Publications:** *ANCHORA*.

★329★ **Delta Kappa Gamma Society International**
PO Box 1589
Austin, TX 78767
Phone: (512)478-5748
Dr. Theresa Fachek, Staff Dir.

Founded: 1929. **Description:** Purposes are to advance and improve education, to endow scholarships and fellowships, and to honor women who have given distinctive service to education. **Publications:** *Bulletin News*.

★330★ **Delta Sigma Theta Sorority, Inc.**
1707 New Hampshire Ave. NW
Washington, DC 20009
Phone: (202)483-5460
Rosalind McKinney, Executive Director

Founded: 1913. **Description:** The Sorority's programs seek to promote educational and economic development, physical and mental health, political awareness and involvement, and international awareness and involvement. Awards scholarships and grants; supports the endowment of Distinguished Professor chairs at historically black colleges; sponsors tutoring and mentoring programs for youth; provides post-secondary career counseling for young adults. Maintains information pool on legislation and public policy issues.

★331★ **Delta Sigma Theta Sorority, Inc. Delta Research and Education Foundation (DREF)**
1707 New Hampshire Ave. NW
Washington, DC 20009
Phone: (202)483-5460
Lou Taylor, Director

Description: The Foundation offers programs in family welfare, educational development, and international awareness. Promotes cross cultural communication on college campuses and provides a leadership model for African American women's organizations. **Publications:** *Delta DREF Chapter Network News*, quarterly.

★332★ **Democratic National Committee Eleanor Roosevelt Fund**
1625 Massachusetts Ave. NW
Washington, DC 20036
Phone: (202)797-6543
Nancy Kirschner, Contact

★333★ **Depression After Delivery (DAD)**
PO Box 1282
Morrisville, PA 19067
Phone: (215)295-3994
Nancy Berchtold, Exec.Dir.

Founded: 1986. **Description:** Women who have experienced postpartum adjustment problems, depression, or psychosis; professionals in the health care industry. Provides support to members and their families. Acts as a clearinghouse for information on postpartum depression and psychosis. Maintains referral service. **Members:** 10,000. **State Groups:** 70. **Telecommunications Services:** Hot line. **Publications:** *Newsletter*, quarterly.

★334★ **DES Action, U.S.A.**
Long Island Jewish Med. Center
New Hyde Park, NY 11040
Phone: (516)775-3450
Andrea Goldstein, Pres.

Founded: 1977. **Description:** DES-exposed persons and others "working to try to ameliorate the problems caused by DES.'' DES (diethylstilbestrol) is a synthetic estrogen in use since 1940 and often prescribed for prevention of miscarriage, diabetes during pregnancy, difficulty in conceiving, staining during pregnancy, and cessation of premature labor. It has since been found that, in some cases, daughters born to women taking DES in the first five months of pregnancy have developed cervical and vaginal abnormalities, a very small percentage of which have resulted in cancer, and a greater number of DES daughters experience problems with first pregnancies, including seven times the rate of tubal pregnancy and twice the rate of miscarriage. DES mothers have a higher risk of breast cancer. There have been some reports of urinary problems and genital abnormalities among DES sons, although research has not been completed in this area. Goal is to reach DES-exposed persons and to stress to them the need for medical attention and monitoring; to educate professionals and the public; and to work for federal legislation. Worked for passage of the first DES legislation in the U.S., in New York State. Offers support, counseling, and doctor referral service. Maintains speakers' bureau and library. **State Groups:** 30. **Publications:** *DES Action Voice: A Focus on Diethylstilbestrol Exposure*, quarterly. Consumer health newsletter; includes medical question and answer column; book reviews; legislation and litigation news; conference reports. • Also publishes fact sheets, doctor referral sheet, bibliography, *Fertility and Pregnancy Guide for DES Daughters and Sons*, and *Reproductive Outcomes in DES Daughters*. **Formerly:** (1986) DES Action, National.

★335★ Dignity, Inc.
1500 Massachusetts Ave. NW, Ste. 11
Washington, DC 20005
Phone: (202)861-0017
Patrick E. Roche, Pres.

Founded: 1968. **Description:** Gays and lesbians who are members of the Roman Catholic church; individuals of other religious affiliations; theologians, priests, and nuns. Believes that: gay and lesbian Catholics are members of Christ's mystical body, numbered among the people of God; it is the right, duty, and privilege for a gay or lesbian person to live the sacramental life of the church; gays and lesbians can express their sexuality in a manner that is consonant with Christ's teaching; sexuality should be exercised in an ethically responsible and unselfish way. Seeks to: unite all gay and lesbian Catholics; develop leadership; be an instrument through which gay Catholics may be heard by the church and society. Works in the areas of spiritual development, education, and social events. Operates Dignity's Prison Ministry. **Members:** 5000. **Regional Groups:** 10. **Local Groups:** 110. **Publications:** *Dignity*, monthly. • Also publishes *Theological Pastoral Resources: A Collection of Articles on Homosexuality from a Catholic Perspective* and a chapter list.

★336★ Displaced Homemakers Network (DHN)
1411 K St. NW
Washington, DC 20005
Phone: (202)628-6767
Fax: (202)628-0123
Jill Miller, Executive Director

Description: DHN is dedicated to empowering displaced homemakers of all racial and ethic backgrounds and assisting them in achieving economic self-sufficiency. To this end, it works with lawmakers and business leaders to create and strengthen programs that support these efforts. DHN promotes public education on the needs of displaced homemakers. Collects and disseminates information on programs, agencies, and educational institutions that provide job training and other vital services to displaced homemakers in the United States. **Publications:** *Network News*, quarterly. • *Transition Times*, twice per year.

★337★ Domestic Violence Institute
50 S. Steele St., Ste. 850
Denver, CO 80209
Phone: (303)322-3444
Lenore Walker, Executive Director

Description: The Institute seeks to stop domestic violence through the actions of its Education and Training, Research, and Public Policy centers. Seeks to ''change the way people think about domestic violence''. Trains those who work with battered women and children; encourages the development of new forms of technology on behalf of battered women and children and their families; provides technical assistance to other domestic violence service organizations; encourages societal change at local, state, national, and international levels. Offers post graduate training, supervisory credentialing, and grants.

★338★ Donors' Offspring (DO)
PO Box 37
Sarcoxie, MO 64862
Phone: (417)548-3679
Candace Turner, Dir.

Founded: 1981. **Description:** Selfhelp support group for individuals involved in artificial fertilization, including donors, recipients, surrogate parents, offspring, parents of donor or recipient, and fertility experts and professionals. Assists in locating individual medical histories. Operates referral service and speakers' bureau; maintains biographical archives. Offers educational and research programs; provides children's services and peer counseling. **Publications:** *Donors' Offspring*, quarterly. Newsletter containing personal stories, search ads, and book reviews.

★339★ Eastern Women's Center (EWC)
38 E. 30th St.
New York, NY 10016
Phone: (212)686-6066
Adele Hughey, Acting Admin.

Founded: 1971. **Description:** Women's health facility. Serves women from all geographical areas. Activities include counseling and medical services (gynecology, family planning, pregnancy testing, and abortion up to 24 weeks). **Publications:** Pamphlets and information sheets on birth control methods, sexually transmitted diseases, common infections, and abortion rights and procedures.

★340★ Economic History Association (EHA)
Women of the Economic History Association
Department of Economics
University of Massachusetts
Amherst, MA 01003
Phone: (413)545-4883
Martha Olney, Assistant Professor of Economics

Description: The Association comprises the women in attendance at the Economic History Association annual meeting. Provides forum for the exchange of current research interests and efforts. **Publications:** Provides a directory containing all those who attended the meeting; available to members only.

★341★ Educational Equity Concepts (EEC)
114 E. 32nd St., Ste. 306
New York, NY 10016
Phone: (212)725-1803
Merle Froschl, Co-Dir.

Founded: 1982. **Description:** Organized to create educational programs and materials that are free of sex, race, and disability bias. Offers training programs for parents, teachers, and students; conducts seminars, symposia, and workshops. Provides conference planning, consulting, and materials development services. Conducts Women and Disability Awareness Project, which discusses and writes on matters concerning disabled women, feminism, and the links between the disability rights and women's movements. **Computerized Services:** National Clearinghouse on Women and Girls with Disabilities, a computerized means of identifying all programs that provide services for, or have an impact on, the lives of women and girls with disabilities. **Publications:** *Bridging the Gap: A National Directory of Services for Women and Girls with Disabilities*, periodic. • Also publishes guides including *Including All of Us: An Early Childhood Curriculum About Disability, What Will Happen If.Young Children and the Scientific Method, Non-Sexist Education for Young Children: A Practical Guide, Play Scenes Lotto, Playtime Is Science: Implementing a Parent/Child Activity Program*, and *Building Community: A Manual Exploring Issues of Women and Disability* and reprints on related educational topics; makes available activity kits for elementary school use; has produced *Equity Works: 5 to 50-plus, Equity Works: Vocational Education, Breaking Stereotypes: Teens Talk About Raising Children*, and *Mixed Messages: Teens Talk About Sex, Romance, Education, and Work* (videotapes) and posters.

★342★ Electrical Women's RoundTable (EWRT)
PO Box 292793
Nashville, TN 37229-2793
Phone: (615)890-1272
Ann Cox, Exec.Dir.

Founded: 1927. **Description:** Women holding positions connected with the electrical industry or allied fields in roles such as communicator, educator, information specialist, and researcher. Objectives are to: promote knowledge and expertise among members in the fields of electrical energy, energy resources, and energy conservation; increase recognition and encourage upward mobility of women in the electrical industry; advance consumer education. Acts as a forum, promotes research, conducts workshops, and reviews new audiovisual and printed materials. Bestows annual Julia Kiene and Lyle Mamer fellowship awards. **Members:** 425. **Local Groups:** 15. **Publications:** *Electrical Women's Round Table–Membership Directory*, annual. • *Electrical Women's Round Table–National Newsletter*, quarterly. Membership newsletter concerned with efficient use of electrical energy from an administrative standpoint. • Also publishes promotional brochures.

★343★ Elizabeth Cady Stanton Foundation
PO Box 603
Seneca Falls, NY 13148
Description: The guiding force behind the establishment of the Women's Rights National Historical Park; provides educational resources, sponsors conferences, workshops, and programs on women's history and women's issues. **Publications:** Newsletter.

★344★ EMILY's List
1112 16th St. NW, Ste. 750
Washington, DC 20036
Phone: (202)887-1957
Fax: (202)452-1997
Ellen Malcolm, Pres.
Founded: 1985. **Description:** Political network for Democratic women. Seeks to raise campaign funds for the election of pro-choice Democratic women to political office. (EMILY stands for Early Money is Like Yeast.) **Members:** 3400. **Publications:** *Notes from EMILY*, quarterly.

★345★ Emunah Women of America (EWA)
7 Penn Plaza
New York, NY 10001
Phone: (212)564-9045
Toll-free: 800-225-5528
Shirley Singer, Exec.Dir.
Founded: 1948. **Description:** A network of chapters throughout North America, with affiliated branches in 30 countries throughout the world. Supports and maintains 225 institutions in Israel where over 20,000 needy children are cared for in kindergartens, day care centers, nurseries, girls' homes, vocational training schools, and community colleges. Sponsors tours to Israel. **Members:** 38,000. **Local Groups:** 40. **Publications:** *Dinner Journal*, annual. • *The Emunah Connection*, quarterly. • *The Emunah Woman*, quarterly. • *Lest We Forget*, quarterly. **Formerly:** (1969) Women's Organization of Hapoel Hamizrachi; (1978) Hapoel Hamizrachi Women's Organization.

★346★ Endometriosis Association (EA)
8585 N. 76th Pl.
Milwaukee, WI 53223
Phone: (414)355-2200
Toll-free: 800-992-ENDO
Mary Lou Ballweg, Exec.Dir.
Founded: 1980. **Description:** Women who have endometriosis and others interested in the condition. (Endometriosis is a disorder in which endometrial tissue, which lines the uterus, is also found in other locations in the body, usually the abdomen. Symptoms can include extremely painful menstruation, infertility, painful sexual intercourse, and heavy or irregular bleeding.) Disseminates information on the treatment, research, and attitudes concerning endometriosis. Offers selfhelp support and informational meetings for women with endometriosis and others. Conducts public education programs;

maintains speakers' bureau; gathers data on individual experiences with endometriosis. Maintains library. **Computerized Services:** Research data bank. **Telecommunications Services:** Crisis counseling; toll-free numbers, (800)992-ENDO (in the United States) and (800)426-2END (in Canada). **Publications:** *Endometriosis Association Newsletter*, bimonthly. Includes news, tips, reviews, and research reports; also covers association and chapter news and activities. • Also publishes literature packets, reprints, and informational brochure; also distributes *Overcoming Endometriosis* (book), *You're Not Alone. Understanding Endometriosis* (videotape), and audio cassette set.

★347★ Episcopal Women's Caucus (EWC)
PO Box 5172
Laurel, MD 20726
Founded: 1971. **Description:** Lay and ordained men and women concerned with the full ministry of all women and minorities in the church. Provides network of people involved in similar issues. **Members:** 800. **Publications:** *RUACH*, quarterly. Newsletter. • Also publishes *A Collection of Statements, Papers and Resources on Inclusive Language*.

★348★ Equal Employment Advisory Council (EEAC)
1015 15th St. NW, Ste. 1220
Washington, DC 20005
Phone: (202)789-8650
Jeffrey A. Norris, Pres.
Founded: 1976. **Description:** Principal attorneys and personnel officers representing companies and trade associations. Promotes and presents the mutual interests of employers and the public regarding affirmative action and equal employment opportunity practices. Sponsors equal employment training courses and seminars.

★349★ Equal Rights Advocates (ERA)
1663 Mission St., Ste. 550
San Francisco, CA 94103
Phone: (415)621-0672
Fax: (415)621-6744
Nancy L. Davis, Exec.Dir.
Founded: 1974. **Description:** Public interest law center specializing in sex discrimination cases. To bring class action suits on behalf of plaintiffs focusing on discrimination issues in employment such as nontraditional work, sexual harassment, pregnancy-based discrimination, and pay equity. Lectures to professional groups; advises local, state, and national attorneys. Provides legal advice and counsel to victims of race- and sex-based discrimination; conducts public education programs on discrimination issues. Maintains law and research libraries. **Members:** 600. **Publications:** *Equal Rights Advocate*, quarterly. Newsletter reporting on women's legal issues; provides analyses of cases and legislation of concern to women. Also includes association news. • *Equal Rights Advocates—Annual Report*. Includes summaries of significant legal decisions affecting women. • Also publishes *Pay Equity Sourcebook*.

★350★ Equal Rights Congress (ERC)
4167 S. Normandy Ave.
Los Angeles, CA 90037
Phone: (213)291-1092
Nacho Gonzalez, Exec.Dir.
Founded: 1976. **Description:** National minority organizations united to struggle for equality of all people who have been discriminated against because of nationality, color, religion, sex, or economic status. Conducts educational program and seminars; provides training and technical assistance for organizing; maintains speakers' bureau and biographical archives; compiles statistics; sponsors competitions. **Regional Groups:** 2. **Local Groups:** 35. **Publications:** *Equal Rights Advocate*, bimonthly. • *Southern Advocate*, bimonthly. • Also publishes a series of pamphlets.

★351★ The Equity Institute, Inc.
4715 Cordell Ave.
PO Box 30245
Bethesda, MD 20814
Phone: (301)654-2904
Mary Ellen Verheyden-Hillard, Pres.
Founded: 1980. **Description:** Disseminates of information on equity for girls and women.

★352★ Equity Policy Center (EPOC)
2000 P St., NW, #508
Washington, DC 20036
Phone: (202)872-1770
Irene Tinker, Pres.
Founded: 1978. **Description:** Research, communications, and educational organizations concerned with global women's issues and developments. Identifies and studies critical areas in national and international development programs where women's interests have been neglected, and suggests policy and programmatic improvements. Provides assistance to planners and programmers in the review and analysis of ongoing projects and their impact on women. Offers internship program and represents women in development in U.S. and United Nations preparations for world conferences and meetings. Arranges seminars and provides speakers for universities and government agencies and foundations. Maintains library of unpublished materials on development issues. **Members:** 230. **Telecommunications Services:** Telex, 650 348 8207. **Publications:** Monographs and reports.

★353★ Eta Phi Beta Sorority, Inc.
1724 Mohawk Blvd.
Tulsa, OK 74110
Phone: (918)452-7717
Elizabeth Anderson, Grand Basileus

★354★ Evangelical and Ecumenical Women's Caucus (EEWC)
PO Box 209
Hadley, NY 12835
Phone: (518)696-2406
Florence Brown, Exec.Dir.
Founded: 1974. **Description:** Christian feminists, churches, seminaries, and colleges. Aims to: encourage evangelical women to work for change in their churches and in society; present God's teaching on female-male equality to the whole body of Christ's church; call men and women to "mutual submission and active discipleship." Believes that the Bible, when properly understood, supports the basic equality of the sexes. Holds special events and retreats. Main-

tains archives of EWCI activities. **Members:** 300. **Regional Groups:** 9. **Local Groups:** 12. **Publications:** *Update*, quarterly.

**★355★ Executive Women International
(EWI)**
Spring Run Executive Plaza
965 E. 4800 South, Ste. 1
Salt Lake City, UT 84117
Phone: (801)263-3296
Fax: (801)268-6127
Lois Trayner-Allinder, Pres.

Founded: 1938. **Description:** Individuals holding key positions in business professions. **Members:** 5000. **Local Groups:** 86. **Publications:** *Executive Women International Directory*, annual. • *Pulse*, quarterly. Newsletter. • Also publishes brochures. **Formerly:** (1977) Executives' Secretaries.

**★356★ Family of the Americas Foundation
(FAF)**
PO Box 219
Mandeville, LA 70470-0219
Phone: (504)626-7724
Fax: (504)626-4981
Mercedes Wilson, Exec.Dir.

Founded: 1977. **Description:** Promotes teaching of the Billings Ovulation Method of birth regulation in which a woman is taught to recognize the fertile phase of her menstrual cycle by analyzing the appearance of mucus secreted from the cervix. The method is named for its developers, Drs. John and Evelyn Billings of Melbourne, Australia. Maintains permanent teacher training centers; certifies instructors of the method. Conducts regional, national, and international workshops to present new scientific information concerning the method and to train new and existing teachers; assists in the planning and implementation of local workshops. Sponsors teacher training and preparation of instructional materials for developing countries. Holds conferences to educate the public about the use of natural family planning in developed and developing countries. Participates in conferences with medical, religious, government, and educational personnel. Assists parents in providing effective sex education for their children; teaches adolescents about fertility and the importance of accepting responsibility for their sexual behavior. Provides referral services and technical assistance; maintains library of natural family planning reference materials. Offers standard teacher certification programs for Master Teachers and Master Trainers. **Members:** 270. **Publications:** *Love and Fertility* (book, in English, French, and Spanish) and *BOM Teaching Posters and Client Charting Kit* (in Arabic, Chinese, English, French, Portuguese, and Spanish); makes available The Billings Method (introductory film). **Formerly:** (1982) World Organization of the Ovulation Method -Billings, U.S.A.

**★357★ Family Life and Population
Program/Church World Service
(FLPP/CWS)**
475 Riverside Dr., 6th Fl.
New York, NY 10115
Phone: (212)870-2061
Ms. Iluminada R. Rodriguez, M.P.H., Dir.

Founded: 1965. **Description:** A program of the National Council of Churches of Christ in the U.S.A. to provide funding for primary health care programs, family life educational programs,

family planning services, maternal-child health facilities, leadership training, development programs for women, educational programs, and some medical supplies. Supports seminars and workshops in family health leadership training. Provides technical resources in primary health care, maternal-child health care, and family planning. Distributes free printed material to the programs and hospitals it helps support. Concentrates efforts on developing countries. **Formerly:** (1976) Planned Parenthood Program.

★358★ Federally Employed Women (FEW)
1400 I St. NW, Ste. 425
Washington, DC 20005
Phone: (202)898-0994
Fax: (202)898-0998
Karen R. Scott, Exec.Dir.

Founded: 1968. **Description:** Men and women employed by the federal government; associate members are persons who support the goals and objectives of FEW. Seeks to end sex discrimination in government service; to increase job opportunities for women in government service and to further the potential of all women in the government; to improve the merit system in government employment; to assist present and potential government employees who are discriminated against because of sex; to work with other organizations and individuals concerned with equal employment opportunity in the government. Provides speakers and sponsors seminars to publicize the Federal Women's Program; furnishes members with information on pending legislation designed to end discrimination against working women; informs members of opportunities for training to improve their job potential; issues fact sheets interpreting civil service rules and regulations. Presents annual distinguished service award to a person who has done the most during the year to advance equality of opportunity for women; also sponsors several other awards. **Local Groups:** 200. **Publications:** *News and Views*, bimonthly.

**★359★ Federated Women in Timber
(FWIT)**
2543 Mt. Baker Hwy.
Bellingham, WA 98226
Phone: (206)592-5330
Judy Marr, Chm.

Founded: 1979. **Description:** Women from Alaska, California, Idaho, Montana, Colorado, Wyoming, Wisconsin, Oregon, Washington, Minnesota, and Michigan associated with the timber industry. Informs members of government, the communications media, and the public about the effect government-imposed restrictions on forest land have on timber communities. Lobbies against additional lands being designated as federal reserve or wilderness areas. Sponsors speakers' bureau; conducts research projects. **State Groups:** 11. **Publications:** *Newsletter*, periodic. • Also produces educational brochures and videotapes.

**★360★ Federation of Feminist Women's
Health Centers (FFWHC)**
1680 Vine St., Ste. 1105
Los Angeles, CA 90028-8837
Phone: (213)957-4062
Fax: (213)957-4064
Carol Downer, Exec.Dir.

Founded: 1975. **Description:** Women's health clinics (13); interested individuals (150). Works

to secure reproductive rights for women and men, educate women about the normal functions of their bodies, and improve the quality of women's health care. Coordinates activities of women's health centers. **Members:** 163. **Publications:** *A New View of a Woman's Body*, *Woman-Centered Pregnancy and Birth*, and *How to Stay Out of the Gynecologist's Office* (books).

**★361★ Federation of French American
Women (FFFA)**
240 Highland Ave.
Fall River, MA 02720
Phone: (508)678-1800
Marthe W. Whalon, Pres.

Founded: 1951. **Description:** Members of French fraternal organizations. Promotes French culture. Conducts oral history program, French speaking contests, youth festivals, ethnic vacations, and reunions. Maintains biographical archives and hall of fame. Bestows awards; compiles statistics. **Members:** 10,000. **Local Groups:** 49. **Publications:** *Le Bulletin*, semiannual. Journal reporting on membership activities. **Also known as:** Federation Feminine Franco-Americaine.

**★362★ Federation of Organizations for
Professional Women (FOPW)**
2001 S St. NW, Ste. 500
Washington, DC 20009
Phone: (202)328-1415
Fax: (202)462-5241
Dr. Viola Young-Horvath, Dir.

Founded: 1972. **Description:** Affiliate groups (30) and associates (200). Women's groups concerned with economic, educational, and social equality for women; interested individuals. Works to enhance the educational and emplcyment status of women. Acts as a forum for the exchange of ideas and to provide mutual support. Provides information on selected public policy issues to affiliate groups. Offers research and policy analyses. Accepts internships. Conducts seminars and training programs; compiles statistics. Maintains speakers' bureau and referral service. Sponsors networking events. Affiliated with 30 women's groups and organizations. **Members:** 230. **Computerized Services:** Mailing list (for members only). **Publications:** *A Woman's Yellow Book*, periodic. Directory. • *ALERT*, bimonthly. Newsletter. • *Washington Women Directory*, periodic. • Also publishes booklets.

**★363★ Federation of Woman's Exchanges
(FWE)**
231 Brattle Rd.
Syracuse, NY 13203
Phone: (315)472-2605
Kris Sammons, Pres.

Founded: 1934. **Description:** Groups known as Woman's Exchanges which operate voluntary nonprofit consignment shops. (Consignment shops provide a sales outlet for high-quality handcrafts and home-cooked foods; the profits from such shops are disbursed among other local voluntary nonprofit groups according to local needs.) Purposes are to: provide a market for handcrafted products; share information on effective shop management techniques; provide consultation to potential Woman's Exchanges; insure that the shops of prospective members are nonprofit and staffed by volunteers. **Mem-**

bers: 39. State Groups: 16. Publications: *Directory of Exchanges*, annual.

★364★ **Federation of Women Lawyers (FWL)**
Judicial Screening Panel
2000 P St., NW, Ste. 515
Washington, DC 20036
Phone: (202)822-6644
Estelle H. Rogers, Dir.

Founded: 1979. **Description:** Women attorneys who serve on a screening board to investigate and evaluate candidates under consideration for federal judgeships. Emphasis is placed on potential nominees' "demonstrated commitment to equal justice under law." Information and evaluations are transmitted to the Senate Committee on the Judiciary. **Members:** 30.

★365★ **Feminist Business and Professional Network (FBPN)**
PO Box 91214
Washington, DC 20090-1214
Chris Lundburg, Pres.

Founded: 1986. **Description:** Individuals and companies promoting cooperation, nurturing, and increased visibility of women in business and the professions. Provides technical assistance and networking support. Facilitates the sharing of information, problems, and successes among members. Offers community education and referral service. Believes that "feminism as a world-view of cooperation, equality, peace, and nurturing" can be part of a business philosophy, and that feminist businesses provide jobs and allow women the opportunity to realize individual goals and work in a nonoppressive atmosphere. Operates speakers' bureau. Although its activities are primarily local, the group plans to expand nationally. **Members:** 85. **Publications:** *FBPN Directory*, quarterly. • Also publishes brochure.

★366★ **Feminist Center for Human Growth and Development (FCHGD)**
300 E. 75th St., Ste. 26-D
New York, NY 10021
Phone: (212)686-0869
Charlotte Schwab, Ph.D., Exec.Dir.

Founded: 1976. **Description:** An educational organization that provides resources, information, and a referral support system for people who need personal or career counseling. Goal is to formulate a "new theory of personality development that will help to free women and men from the social, political and cultural limitations that now form the basis of existing psychological theories." Conducts nonsexist and feminist lectures, panels, and counseling. Sponsors participatory and experiential workshops and groups on such topics as relationships, self-identity, self-esteem, goal setting, risk taking, networking, assertiveness, and positive communication. Offers a nonsexist therapy training program for human resources personnel and others interested in counseling women and men. **Publications:** *A Model for Positive Self Identity and Self Defined Success, A Model for Effective Positive Communication*, brochures and articles on women and phobias and women and competence.

★367★ **The Feminist Institute, Inc.**
PO Box 30563
Bethesda, MD 20824
Phone: (301)951-9040
Carolyn H. Sparks, President

Description: The Institute is a nonprofit organization working for feminist social change through social action, education, and research projects that "illuminate and celebrate women's freedom and autonomy". Serves as a clearinghouse; maintains a speakers' bureau and a national database project; hosts a feminist tour of Capitol. **Publications:** *Friends of the Feminist Institute Program*. • *Feminist Institute Clearinghouse Catalog*.

★368★ **Feminist Karate Union (FKU)**
5429 Russell Ave. NW
Seattle, WA 98107
Phone: (206)789-4561
Jean Rogers, Contact

Founded: 1971. **Description:** To teach self-protection, self-defense, and karate to women and other victimized groups including children, senior citizens, physically and/or mentally disabled persons, and battered wives. Offers demonstrations, workshops, seminars, and in-service training to community and educational groups and social service agencies. **Members:** 150. **Local Groups:** 2. **Publications:** Publishes *Fear Into Anger: A Manual of Self-Defense for Women, Peace of Mind*, and *Acquaintance Rape*. **Formerly:** (1982) Feminist Karate Union; (1985) Feminist Karate Union/ Alternatives to Fear.

★369★ **Feminist Majority Foundation (FMF)**
186 South St.
Boston, MA 02111
Phone: (617)695-9688
Fax: (617)695-9747
Jennifer Jackson, Director

Description: FMF is a feminist think tank specializing in the development of creative new strategies to "empower women through direct action". It seeks to devise long term strategies and permanent solutions for social, political, and economic barriers to women. Conducts and disseminates information that exposes sources of opposition to women's equality. Campaigns for contraceptive research and has produced videos addressing abortion rights. **Publications:** *Feminist Majority Report*, five per year.

★370★ **The Feminist Press at the City University of New York (TFPNY)**
311 E. 94th St.
New York, NY 10128
Phone: (212)360-5790
Florence Howe, Pres.

Founded: 1970. **Description:** Nonprofit educational and publishing organization. Works to: eliminate sex-role and social stereotypes in education at all levels; further the rediscovery of the history of women; provide literature "with a broad vision of human potential." Researches the status of women's studies at colleges and universities throughout the country, and analyzes the teaching methods and curricula by which stereotypical attitudes can be changed. Provides texts for college courses and has created syllabi in which women's history and literature by women are introduced into traditional college courses. Reprints lost or neglected literature by women writers. Maintains Women's Studies International, a network of individu-

als and institutions that has published a report of its 1985 meeting in Nairobi, Kenya. **Publications:** *Women's Studies Quarterly*. Journal containing articles on research and teaching about women and on current projects to transform traditional curricula. Also includes annual reports, notices of grants and scholarships, and book reviews. • *The Feminist Press*, annual. Catalog. • Also publishes reprints of works by women authors, original anthologies, original autobiographies, biographies, nonsexist children's books, curricular materials, bibliographies, essays, and directories; makes available books for libraries, bookstores, classrooms, and the public.

★371★ **Feminist Teacher Editorial Collective (FTEC)**
Indiana University
Ballantine Hall 442
Bloomington, IN 47405
Phone: (812)855-5597
Elisabeth Daumer, Treas.

Founded: 1984. **Subscribers:** 900. **Description:** Teachers and students; schools, libraries, archives, and women's organizations. Opposes sexism, racism, and other forms of oppression in the classroom. Encourages innovative teaching practices that challenge traditional educational, disciplinary, and research methodologies. **Publications:** *Feminist Teacher*, 3/year. Provides a forum for new ideas in the classroom. Includes feminist teacher network news, information on teaching resources, book reviews, listings of conferences, and solicitations for papers.

★372★ **Feminist Writers' Guild (FWG)**
1742 W. Melrose
Chicago, IL 60657
Phone: (312)929-1326
Jorjet Harper, Admin.

Founded: 1977. **Description:** Women writers (published and unpublished) interested in sharing information and experiences. Areas of concern are the "politics of publishing," education, and political action. Maintains networking system for members' exchange of specific needs and services. Local chapters organize their own activities which include writers' retreats, publication of anthologies, workshops, and readings. Bestows annual Woman of Promise Award to a previously unpublished writer. **Members:** 1000. **Local Groups:** 10. **Publications:** *Newsletter*, 4/year. • Plans to publish *Words in Our Pocket: The Feminist Writers' Guild Handbook on How to Get Published and Get Paid*.

★373★ **Feministas Unidas (FU)**
2101 E. Coliseum Blvd.
Ft. Wayne, IN 46805
Phone: (219)481-6836
Stacey Schlau, Pres.

Founded: 1979. **Description:** Feminist scholars in Hispanic, Luso-Brazilian, Chicano, or Puerto Rican studies. Serves as a forum for discussion of Latin American studies. Conducts panel discussions in conjunction with the Modern Language Association of America. **Members:** 225. **Publications:** *Feministas Unidas Newsletter*, 2/year. Contains reports on current research and job postings.

★374★ Feminists Concerned for Better Feminist Leadership (FCBFL)
PO Box 1348, Madison Square Sta.
New York, NY 10159
Phone: (212)796-1467
Mia Albright, Dir.

Founded: 1986. **Description:** Participants include women's groups and individuals in the worldwide feminist community. Seeks to develop feminist citizenship and leadership roles. Acts as a liaison between women's groups, institutes, clinics, and leaders in the women's community. Conducts seminars and workshops. Maintains archives. **Publications:** *Gold Flag Bulletin*, periodic. • Also publishes and distributes books, pamphlets, and feminist educational cassettes.

★375★ Feminists Fighting Pornography (FFP)
PO Box 6731, Yorkville Sta.
New York, NY 10128
Page Mellish, Exec. Officer

Founded: 1984. **Description:** Combats pornography by lobbying the federal government. Maintains speakers' bureau; conducts slide shows. **Publications:** *Backlash Times*, annual. Magazine.

★376★ Feminists for Life of America (FFL)
811 E. 47th St.
Kansas City, MO 64110
Phone: (816)753-2130
Rosemary Bottcher, Exec.V.Pres.

Founded: 1972. **Description:** Individuals united to secure the right to life, from conception to natural death, of all human beings. Seeks legal and social equality of all persons regardless of sex. Supports a Human Life Amendment, Equal Rights Amendment, and other methods of achieving respect for life and equality of the sexes as necessarily compatible goals. Activities include workshops, speakers' bureau, debates, and research of current literature on abortion and feminism. **Members:** 3000. **State Groups:** 30. **Telecommunications Services:** Hot line news, (816)561-1365. **Publications:** *Sisterlife*, quarterly. • Also publishes *Profile Feminism: Different Voices* (book), position papers, and booklets on a variety of subjects.

★377★ Financial Women International (FWI)
7910 Woodmont Ave., Ste. 1430
Bethesda, MD 20814-3015
Phone: (301)657-8288
Susan Resh, Dir.

Founded: 1921. **Description:** Women officers and managers in the financial industry. Maintains FWI Educational Foundation. **Members:** 20,000. **State Groups:** 51. **Local Groups:** 350. **Publications:** *Financial Women Today*, monthly. **Formerly:** (1991) National Association of Bank Women.

★378★ First Catholic Slovak Ladies Association (FCSLA)
24950 Chagrin Blvd.
Beachwood, OH 44122
Phone: (216)464-8015
Anna S. Granchay, Pres.

Founded: 1892. **Description:** Fraternal benefit life insurance society. Owns home for the aged, Villa Sancta Anna, in Beachwood, OH. Presents scholarship awards and contributes to Slovak Catholic Churches, charities, and related organizations. **Members:** 87,000. **Regional Groups:** 9. **Local Groups:** 600. **Publications:** *Fraternally Yours*, monthly. **Formerly:** First Catholic Slovak Ladies Union.

★379★ For Our Children's Unpaid Support (FOCUS)
PO Box 2183
Vienna, VA 22180

★380★ ForLIFE
PO Drawer 1279
Tryon, NC 28782
Phone: (704)859-5392
Rev. Ralph D. Kuether, Exec.Dir.

Founded: 1973. **Description:** Purpose is to make available as wide a variety of pro-life materials as possible. Distributes material including films, videotapes, slide and filmstrip presentations, plays, puppet shows, stories, books, monographs, pamphlets, fundraising items, reprints, and transcripts; produces new material and assists others in printing and marketing material.

★381★ Forty Upward Network (FUN)
c/o YWCA
16915 Detroit Ave.
Lakewood, OH 44107
Phone: (216)521-8400
Florence Fubrer, Chm.

Founded: 1982. **Description:** Middle-aged women who are divorced, widowed, or have never been married. Purpose is to provide support, affirmation, and reinforcement of the personal validity of women as single people. Seeks to educate members in realistic financial/retirement planning. Advocates self-sufficiency in all areas; encourages members to take full responsibility for their futures. Sponsors discussions, monthly lectures, meetings, seminars, and travel and social activities. **Members:** 600. **Formerly:** (1986) Fifty Upward Network.

★382★ Forum for Women in Bridge (FWB)
c/o Joan Remey
21755 S. Tuller Ct.
Southfield, MI 48076
Phone: (313)356-2246
Joan Remey, Treas.

Description: Women bridge players. Seeks wider participation of women in bridge and the improvement of playing conditions. Encourages the further development of competitive bridge; seeks modifications in qualifying procedures for international events. Sponsors children's programs. Represents female members of the American Contract Bridge League. **Publications:** *Newsletter*, periodic.

★383★ Forum for Women Business Owners (FWBO)
703 Third St., SW
Washington, DC 20024

★384★ The Foundation for Women's Resources
700 N. Fairfax St., Ste. 302
Alexandria, VA 22314
Phone: (703)549-1102
Fax: (703)836-9205
Martha P. Farmer, National Executive Director

Founded: 1974. **Description:** The Foundation is a nonprofit educational organization which focuses on the achievements and advances of women. It is dedicated to improving the personal, economic, and professional status of women. Consults with other states interested in establishing programs similar to the Foundation's Leadership America and Leadership Texas programs. Sponsors exhibits and educational conferences. **Publications:** *Leadership America*, annual. *Alumnae Association Newsletter*. • Also publishes an annual program brochure.

★385★ Foundation for Women's Resources Leadership America
700 N. Fairfax St., Ste. 202
Alexandria, VA 22314
Phone: (703)549-1102
Kae B. Dakin, Exec.Dir.

Founded: 1988. **Description:** National, nonprofit leadership development program of the Foundation for Women's Resources (see separate entry) for women of achievement. Goal is to develop more women leaders and link them to the expanding network of their peers across the nation. Each year the program brings together a new group of 100 women of accomplishment from across the nation to participate in a year-long series of three professional development seminars. Through discussions with some of the country's most influential leaders, participants explore critical national and international issues while connecting with other women of achievement.

★386★ Freedom Information Service (FIS)
PO Box 3568
Jackson, MS 39207
Phone: (601)352-3398
Jan Hillegas, Treas.

Founded: 1965. **Description:** Researches activities of workers, blacks, and grass roots organizations through the FIS Deep South People's History Project. Maintains extensive Mississippi-centered library and archives. Distributes press releases on current southern news; reprints items on women's liberation and political education. **Publications:** *FIS Mississippi Newsletter*, periodic. • Has also issued political and economic publications relevant to the civil rights movement and black candidates. **Formerly:** (1965) Freedom Information Center.

★387★ Freedom Socialist Party (FSP)
5018 Rainier Ave., S.
Seattle, WA 98118
Phone: (206)722-2453
Guerry Hoddersen, Rep.

Founded: 1966. **Description:** Trotskyist socialist feminists who believe that women's leadership is essential for bringing about revolutionary social change. Participates in all social change movements; works to pull such movements together around a multi-issue, antiracist, antisexist, antihomophobic program designed to win fundamental social change. Holds public forums, classes, and study groups on Marxist theory, feminist history, world events, and revolutions. Sponsors educational programs; maintains library and speakers' bureau. **Publications:** *Freedom Socialist: Voice of Revolutionary Feminism*, periodic. Tabloid on "revolutionary socialist feminism" covering articles on topics such as gay resistance, women's revolutionary role in working class struggles, abortion rights, social and national freedom struggles, and imperialism. Includes book, music, and movie reviews and poetry. • Also publishes *AIDS Hysteria, A Marxist Analysis, Socialist Feminism, The First Decade 1966-1976, The War on the Disabled, Woman Sitting at the Machine, Thinking*, and position papers.

★388★ Friendly Hand Foundation (FHF)
347 S. Normandie
Los Angeles, CA 90020
Phone: (213)389-9964
Peggy Albrecht, Exec.Dir.

Founded: 1951. **Description:** Operates Friendly House, a home to aid in the rehabilitation of alcoholic women. Provides a home-like setting, love and understanding, and the companionship of individuals in similar situations to women recovering from alcohol dependence. Not officially affiliated with Alcoholics Anonymous World Services, but women in the home learn the principles of AA as part of group and individual therapy; the average stay at Friendly House is four weeks. Supported by contributions and through projects undertaken by affiliated groups of alcoholic and nonalcoholic women in California (known as Sweet Hearts and Grateful Hearts).

★389★ Friendly Peersuasion (FP)
33 E. 33rd St.
New York, NY 10016
Phone: (212)689-3700
Fax: (212)683-1253
Marilyn Russo, Project Dir.

Description: A project of Girls Incorporated (see separate entry). Seeks to prevent drug and alcohol abuse among girls 11 to 14 years old. Recognizes that girls are more socially apt to become users of substances such as tobacco and weight reduction stimulants containing amphetamines. Offers a peer leadership training course whereby older girls discourage younger ones from using addictive substances. Program consists of a flexible, 12-week course including instruction in managing stress, decision making, and techniques for alcohol and drug refusal.

★390★ Fund for the Feminist Majority (FFM)
1600 Wilson Blvd., Ste. 704
Arlington, VA 22209
Phone: (703)522-2214
Fax: (703)522-2219
Eleanor Smeal, Pres.

Founded: 1987. **Description:** Seeks to encourage women to fill leadership positions in business, education, media, law, medicine, and government. Sponsors Feminization of Power Campaign, which provides a vehicle for achieving FFM's goals and promotes a national feminist agenda; conducts national campus campaign; makes available internship programs. Promotes a national feminist agenda. Maintains speakers' bureau; compiles statistics. **Publications:** *Feminist Majority Report*, quarterly.

Newsletter. • Also makes available organizing kits, fact sheets, videos, and books.

★391★ G.O.P. Women's Political Action League (GOPAL)
2000 L St. NW, Ste. 200
Washington, DC 20036
Phone: (202)785-8242
Maureen E. Reagan, Chair

Founded: 1985. **Description:** Individual contributors to Republican female candidates' campaigns for public office. Promotes the election of Republican women to state and federal office primarily through contributions to their campaign committees. Sponsors fundraising activities and solicits direct contributions.

★392★ Gamma Phi Delta Sorority
2657 W. Grand Blvd.
Detroit, MI 48208
Phone: (313)872-8597
Willie B. Kennedy, Supreme Basileus

Founded: 1943. **Description:** The Sorority is a non-campus based service organization which supports the activities of business and professional black women. Its purpose is to enhance the social and economic welfare of the community by promoting high educational standards, encouraging business and job development, and strengthening support services to families. Awards scholarships and provides employment and training programs and child health, welfare and development services.

★393★ Gay AA (GAA)
84 Broadway
New Haven, CT 06511
Phone: (203)865-6354

Founded: 1976. **Description:** Provides a support system for gay and lesbian alcoholics. **Members:** 37.

★394★ Gay and Lesbian Media Coalition (GLMC)
8228 Sunset Blvd., Ste. 308
West Hollywood, CA 90046
Phone: (213)650-5133
Fax: (213)650-2226
Larry Horne, Exec.Dir.

Founded: 1981. **Description:** Individuals (10) and organizations (4). Purpose is to serve as a programming group focusing on independent fiction, documentary, and short films dealing with gay and lesbian situations. Promotes positive portrayal of gays and lesbians and avoidance of stereotypes. **Members:** 250. **Publications:** Plans to publish *Gay/Lesbian Media Anthology*.

★395★ General Commission on the Status and Role of Women (GCSRW - UM)
1200 Davis St.
Evanston, IL 60201
Phone: (708)869-7330
Kiyoko Kasai Fujiu, Gen. Secretariat

Founded: 1972. **Description:** Representatives of both sexes and each ethnic group within the United Methodist church. Purpose is to challenge the church to make a continuing commitment to the full and equal responsibility and participation of women in the total life and mission of the church, sharing fully in the power and policymaking at all levels of the church. Feels that the church cannot be an effective

witness to society until it has examined its own faithfulness to the full inclusiveness of all persons. Believes that many individuals feel excluded from a relationship with God when God is referred to only in masculine terms, but recognizes that some persons feel it necessary to use masculine gender in order to "be true to the sacred images of God." Works to foster an awareness of issues, problems, and concerns related to the status and role of women within the denomination; develops strategies to rectify adverse situations; recommends plans and curricula for new understanding of theological and biblical history. Acts as catalyst to achieve full utilization of women in total employment both in and out of the church. Holds leadership training sessions and annual Conference Constituency. **Members:** 48. **Publications:** *The Flyer*, 5/year. Newsletter providing a link between the national and the local commissions on the status and role of women in the United Methodist Church, in the church in general, and in society. Includes calendar of events; employment opportunities; new resources. • Also publishes brochures, including guidelines and procedures to be used in responding to the grievances of women who are members or employees of the church.

★396★ General Federation of Women's Clubs (GFWC)
1734 N St. NW
Washington, DC 20036-2990
Phone: (202)347-3168
Toll-free: 800-443-GFWC
Fax: (202)835-0246
Phyllis J. Dudenhotter, Pres.

Founded: 1890. **Description:** International women's volunteer service organization with members from 8500 U.S. clubs. Provides volunteer leadership training and development. Serves state and local clubs in community service programs in the following areas: the arts; conservation; education; home life; public affairs; international affairs. Has established Women's History and Resource Center to promote and document volunteer achievement. **Members:** 350,000. **Regional Groups:** 8. **State Groups:** 52. **Publications:** *GFWC Clubwoman Magazine*, quarterly.

★397★ Giarretto Institute (AMACU)
232 E Gish Rd.
San Jose, CA 95111
Phone: (408)453-7616
Fax: (408)453-9064
Brian Abbott, Ph.D., Exec.Dir.

Founded: 1971. **Description:** A program of Parents United. Purpose is to offer support and therapy to men and women unable to cope with the trauma of having been sexually abused as children. Offers group and individual therapy designed to help victims alleviate their guilt by giving responsibility for the abuse back to the abuser. Uses the Giarretto approach (named after group's executive director), a program for the humanistic treatment of sexual abuse victims that trains workers in techniques of coping with the revelation of abuse and the variety of stages of guilt and anger that follow. Experienced volunteers act as sponsors for one-on-one encouragement and advice; psychology students serve as volunteer interns in the second year of their master's degree programs. Currently treats women and men ages 18 and older. Maintains speakers' bureau; conducts training programs. **Publications:** *Chapter Contact List*, quarterly. Directory. • *Parents United*

Newsletter, bimonthly. • Also publishes fact sheets and brochures.

★398★ Girl Friends (GF)
c/o Rachel Norcom Smith
2228 Lansing Ave.
Portsmouth, VA 23704
Phone: (804)397-1339
Rachel Norcom Smith, Exec. Officer

Founded: 1927. **Description:** Black women "who have been friends over the years." Primary aim is to "keep the fires of friendship burning." Conducts charitable projects and contributes annually to a selected charity. Bestows awards. **Members:** 1200. **Local Groups:** 40. **Publications:** *The Chatterbox*, annual. • *Chatterletter*, biennial. • *Directory*, quinquennial. • *President's News and Friendship Letter*, annual.

★399★ Girl Scouts of the U.S.A. (GSUSA)
830 3rd Ave.
New York, NY 10022
Phone: (212)940-7500
Mary Rose Main, Exec.Dir.

Founded: 1912. **Description:** Daisy Girl Scouts (ages 5-6); Brownie Girl Scouts (ages 6-8); Junior Girl Scouts (ages 8-11); Cadette Girl Scouts (ages 11-14); Senior Girl Scouts (ages 14-17). Membership includes girls, adult volunteers, and professional workers. Purpose is to meet the special needs of girls and help girls develop as happy, resourceful individuals willing to share their abilities as citizens in their homes, their communities, their country and the world. Promotes ethical code through the Girl Scout Promise and Law. Has developed Program Emphases which encourage self-awareness, interaction with others, development of values, and service to society. Provides girls with opportunities to expand personal interests, learn new skills, and explore career possibilities. Offers leadership training, international exchange programs, and conferences and seminars on topics ranging from management to child development. Maintains library and archives. **Members:** 3,268,630. **Local Groups:** 333. **Publications:** *Environmental Scanning Report*. Contains U.S. and world statistics on demography, ecology and energy, economy, education, government and legislation, technology, and values and life-styles, and their implications for Girl Scouting in the U.S. • *Girl Scout Leader: For Adults in Girl Scouting*, quarterly. Magazine for all registerd adult Girl Scout members covering programs, troop activities, health and safety, and news about people and events in Girl Scouting/Girl Guiding. • *Girl Scouts of the U.S.A.—Annual Report*. Includes financial statements and membership statistics. • *GSUSA News*, monthly. Infomation addressed to Girl Scout councils covering Girl Scout-related items in the news, national and international highlights, programs and national meetings. Includes obituaries.

★400★ Girls Clubs of America, Inc.
30 E. 33rd St.
New York, NY 10016
Phone: (212)689-3700
Ellen Claire Wahl, Contact

Founded: 1945. **Description:** Provides assistance in helping girls overcome discrimination and develop self-sufficiency and responsibility. **Publications:** *Facts and Reflections on Careers for Today's Girls*. • *Sports Resource Kit*.

★401★ Girls Inc.
30 E. 33rd St.
New York, NY 10016
Phone: (212)689-3700
Margaret Gates, Dir.

Founded: 1945. **Description:** Girls ages six to 18. Conducts daily programs in careers and life planning, health and sexuality, leadership and communication, sports and adventure, and life skills and self-reliance. Represents girls on issues of equality. Works to create an environment in which girls can learn and grow to their fullest potential. More than 7000 adults participate in the program. Conducts series of local, regional, and national contests in photography, writing, citizenship, and scholarship. Majority of clubs supported by local United Way campaigns. Maintains Girls, Inc. National Resource Center in Indianapolis, IN that houses collection of materials and data base on girls. Rents films and videotapes. **Members:** 250,000. **Local Groups:** 200. **Publications:** *Girls Clubs of America—Annual Report*. Provides information of the club's financial status. • *Girls Ink*, 6/year. Newsletter providing information of interest to young girls and women including teen pregnancy and drug abuse. Includes calendar of events. **Formerly:** (1990) Girls Clubs of America.

★402★ Girls Nation (GN)
777 N. Meridian St.
Indianapolis, IN 46204
Phone: (317)635-6291
Fax: (317)636-5590
Miriam Junge, Sec.

Founded: 1947. **Description:** Youth citizenship training program conducted annually by the American Legion Auxiliary to give high school juniors practical experience in the processes of government and a clear understanding of their approaching citizenship responsibilities. Girls State sessions, sponsored by 49 state and territorial departments of the ALA, are held each June or July in state capitals or on centrally located campuses. From each Girls State, two senators are elected to represent their constituents at Girls Nation in July in Washington, DC. Girls States teach local, county, and state level government; at Girls Nation the emphasis is on national government. GN representatives organize political parties, hold conventions, run campaigns, elect officers, enact legislation, and visit government agencies.

★403★ The Global Fund for Women
2480 Sand Hill Rd., Ste. 100
Menlo Park, CA 94025-6941
Phone: (415)854-0420
Fax: (415)854-8050
Virgina Wright, Asst. to the President

Founded: 1987. **Description:** The Fund is a nonprofit, grantmaking institution that provides funds to seed, strengthen and link groups that are committed to women's well being internationally and "work for their full participation in society." Promotes greater donor understanding of the importance of funding women's activities internationally and encourages increased support for women's programs. Engages in philanthropic work and supports women's groups working on emerging controversial issues. Sponsors informational events and talks, international conferences, fundraising events, and organizational counseling for women's groups internationally.

★404★ Global Women of African Heritage (GWAH)
PO Box 1033, Cooper Station
New York, NY 10003
Phone: (212)547-5696
Thelma Dailey-Stout, Founder & Pres.

Founded: 1982. **Description:** Women of African heritage worldwide. Purpose is to bring together women of African heritage to share common experiences and knowledge. Also seeks to share this knowledge with women who are not of African heritage.

★405★ Gold Star Wives of America (GSW)
c/o Rose E. Lee
540 N. Lombardy St.
Arlington, VA 22203
Phone: (703)527-7706
Rose E. Lee, Pres.

Founded: 1945. **Description:** Widows of servicemen who died while on active duty or from service-connected disabilities. Promotes patriotism. Conducts volunteer work in veteran and civilian hospitals. Testifies before congressional committees on behalf of service widows. Notifies widows and their children of changes in VA benefits. **Members:** 13,000. **Regional Groups:** 8. **Local Groups:** 53. **Computerized Services:** Mailing list; membership records. **Publications:** *Gold Star Wives Newsletter*, quarterly. Covers the volunteer activities of the association. Includes legislation report. **Formerly:** American Widows of World War II; (1948) Gold Star Wives of World War II.

★406★ Grace of God Movement for the Women of the World (GGMWW)
c/o 3HO Found.
1620 Preuss Rd.
Los Angeles, CA 90035
Phone: (213)552-3416
Guru Amrit, Exec.Sec.

Founded: 1970. **Description:** Purpose is "to provide women with the techniques and knowledge to fulfill their divine potential to live healthy, happy and holy lives as the Grace of God." Provides specialized Kundalini Yoga exercises; recipes for diet; information on feminine health; training courses in vegetarian cooking; and literature for women regarding child training and male/female interpersonal relationships. Conducts annual training camp in New Mexico at which women learn music, cooking, martial arts, outdoor living, and psychological and sociological understanding of the self. **Local Groups:** 110. **Publications:** *Women in Training* (Khalsa women's training camp lectures). **Formerly:** Grace of God Movement for the Women of America.

★407★ Grandmothers for Peace International (GPI)
909 12th St., Ste. 118
Sacramento, CA 95814
Phone: (916)444-5080
Barbara Wiedner, Founder & Exec.Dir.

Founded: 1982. **Description:** Grandmothers and other individuals worldwide who seek an end to the nuclear arms race. Supports "peace-loving groups in communities across the nation and around the world." Promotes the elimination of all nuclear weapons. Encourages public involvement in campaigns against nuclear weapons, including vigils at military installations, armaments factories, and the Nevada nuclear weapons test site. Supports nonviolent resistance and efforts toward peaceful coexistence with the USSR. Corresponds with women sharing similar beliefs worldwide. Favors development of peace curricula for use in secondary schools; provides educational programs on peace and human rights issues. Maintains speakers' bureau. **Members:** 500. **Subscribers:** 3000. **Local Groups:** 11. **Publications:** *Grandmothers for Peace Newsletter*, quarterly. • Also makes available buttons and T-shirts. **Formerly:** (1991) Grandmothers for Peace.

★408★ Greek Orthodox Ladies Philoptochos Society (GOLPS)
345 E. 74th St.
New York, NY 10021
Phone: (212)744-4390
Fax: (212)861-1956
Dina Skouras-Oldknow, Pres.

Founded: 1931. **Description:** Women 18 years or older of the Greek Orthodox faith. Aim is to preserve the sacredness of the Orthodox family and perpetuate and promote the charitable and philanthropic purposes of the Greek Orthodox Archdiocese of North and South America. (The word "Philoptochos" is derived from "philo" meaning friend and "ptochos" meaning poor; hence, "friend of the poor.") Seeks to aid individuals in need of assistance. Supports educational institutions and offers scholarships and awards to needy and meritorious students of those institutions. Encourages wider religious activity and participation in the communal aspects of the church, especially among young people. Conducts seminars. **Members:** 40,000. **Regional Groups:** 11. **Local Groups:** 475.

★409★ Hadassah, The Women's Zionist Organization of America (HWZOA)
50 W. 58th St.
New York, NY 10019
Phone: (212)355-7900
Fax: (212)303-8282
Beth Wohlgelernter, Exec.Dir.

Founded: 1912. **Description:** Conducts many community services in the U.S. and Israel. Provides "basic Jewish education as a background for intelligent and creative Jewish living in America." Organizes programs in Jewish education, Zionist and American affairs, leadership development, career women, singles, and Young Judaea clubs and camps. Built and maintains Hadassah Medical Organization encompassing the Hadassah University Hospital on Mt. Scopus, Israel and the Hadassah Hebrew University Medical Center at Ein Karem, Israel. Maintains Hadassah College of Technology in Jerusalem, Israel, providing courses in computer science, medical and dental technology, electro-optics, printing, and graphics; operates Hadassah Career Counseling Institute for high school students, young adults, and new immigrants. Is the principal agency in the U.S. for support of Youth Aliyah villages and daycenters for immigrant and deprived youth. Participates in land purchase and reclamation programs of the Jewish National Fund. Maintains Hadassah International, which works worldwide to raise funds and support for medical activities and to encourage cooperation in public health and community medicine. Sponsors Young Judaea for American Jewish young people, ages 9 through 30. Conducts three month live-in program for adults wishing to live in Israel. Operates speakers' bureau; sponsors seminars and workshops; maintains 4000 volume library on Judaism and Zionism. **Members:** 385,000. **Re-**

gional Groups: 36. **State Groups:** 1500. **Computerized Services:** Fund-raising; membership. **Publications:** *The American Scene*, 3/year. • *Hadassah Associates Medbriefs*, quarterly. • *Hadassah Headlines*, quarterly. Newsletter. Contains medical news. • *Hadassah Magazine*, monthly, except combined June/July and August/September issues. Contains articles on art, medicine, parenting, and Hebrew education. • *Update*, 20/year. • *Textures: Hadassah National Jewish Studies Bulletin*, 3/year. Contains articles on Jewish art, culture, and thought. Examines daily life in Israel; discusses Hebrew texts, literature, and poetry; highlights important Jewish historic and contemporary topics. Includes book reviews and cultural reviews. • Also publishes study guides. **Formerly:** (1914) Daughters of Zion.

★410★ Happiness of Womanhood (HOW)
1335 Hancock Rd.
Riviera, AZ 86440
Phone: (602)758-7601
Jackie Davison, Natl.Dir.

Founded: 1971. **Description:** Men and women, both single and married, "dedicated to the preservation of the family, preservation of the masculine role as provider, and preservation of the feminine role as wife, mother and homemaker." Opposes the Equal Rights Amendment to the U.S. Constitution. Supports "God's divine plan, the family structure; removal of Communist and Socialist teachings from the schools; removal of radical elements of Women's Liberation Movement teachings from the schools; teaching of the joys of womanhood to young girls; preservation of femininity; restoration of morality; elimination of drug abuse; return to patriotism and the election to government of men and women dedicated to God, Family and Country." Encourages active participation in the political process. Sponsors lobbyists; maintains speakers bureau. **Members:** 15,000. **State Groups:** 6. **Publications:** *Legislative Review*, 9/year. • *Newsletter*, quarterly. • Also publishes I Am A Housewife (book) and brochure. **Also known as:** League of Housewives.

★411★ Health Policy Advisory Center
17 Murraly St.
5th Fl.
New York, NY 10007
Phone: (212)267-8890
Nancy McKenzie, Executive Director

Founded: 1968. **Description:** The Center is a nonprofit public interest organization that advocates appropriate, accessible health care for all. It seeks to bring about "a national health care system that serves public needs rather than professional prestige or private profit." Holds forums on public health issues, including homelessness, AIDS, and minority and women's health concerns. **Publications:** *Health/PAC Bulletin.*

★412★ Healthy Mothers, Healthy Babies (HMHB)
409 12th St. SW, Rm. 309
Washington, DC 20024
Phone: (202)863-2458
Toll-free: 800-673-8444
Fax: (202)863-2499
Lori Cooper, Exec.Dir.

Founded: 1980. **Description:** Coalition of national and state organizations concerned with

maternal and child health. Serves as a network through which members share ideas and information regarding issues such as prenatal care, nutrition for pregnant women, and infant mortality. **Members:** 104. **Publications:** • *Healthy Mothers, Healthy Babies Newsletter*, quarterly. • Also publishes *Compendium of Program Ideas for Serving Low-Income Women.*

★413★ Hispanic Women's Council (HWC)
5803 E. Beverly Blvd.
Los Angeles, CA 90022
Phone: (213)725-1657
Lourdes Saab, Executive Director

Description: Volunteer membership organization dedicated to the empowerment of hispanic women through education and career leadership development projects. Sponsors projects, including personal development leadership training, career development, youth outreach, and communication/advocacy. Seeks to provide young hispanic women with career role models and instill self esteem through Horizons, a one-day conference. Awards scholarships to qualifying applicants. **Publications:** *Hispa-News*, quarterly.

★414★ History of Science Society Women's Committee
35 Dean St.
Worcester, MA 01609
Phone: (508)831-5712
Fax: (508)831-5483
Michael Sokal, Exec. Sec.

Description: The Committee seeks to encourage women historians of science, technology, and medicine, and to promote work on the history of women in and affected by these fields. Conducts annual job survey. Maintains a directory of women in the profession.

★415★ History of Women Religious
c/o Karen Kennelly
12001 Chalon Rd.
Los Angeles, CA 90049

★416★ Hollywood Women's Political Committee (HWPC)
10536 Culver Blvd.
Culver City, CA 90232
Phone: (213)559-9334
Fax: (213)838-2367
Margery Tabankin, Exec.Dir.

Founded: 1984. **Description:** Women working in the entertainment industry and related fields. Raises funds for federal political candidates, grass roots organizations, and statewide initiatives that pledge to represent the group's beliefs on nuclear disarmament, increased environmental protection, improved public education, and expanded civil rights for women. Seeks to heighten community involvement in national politics. **Members:** 200.

★417★ Homemakers Equal Rights Association (HERA)
c/o Nancy Jean Seigle
48 Rollingwood Dr.
Voorhees, NJ 08043
Phone: (609)783-6102
Nancy Jean Seigle, Co-Chair

Founded: 1973. **Description:** Homemakers working both inside and outside of the home who support ratification of the Equal Rights Amendment. Endeavors to educate homemakers, legislators, and the public concerning the importance of the ERA. Seeks full partnership for homemakers in all laws. Affirms the value of the work women do in the home. Maintains speakers bureau. Conducts workshops, seminars, and specialized education. Compiles statistics; conducts research programs; maintains extensive collection of information on the ERA. **Members:** 2000. **State Groups:** 17. **Publications:** *Newsletter*, quarterly. • Also publishes brochures. **Formerly:** (1980) Housewives for ERA.

★418★ House of Ruth (HOR)
501 H St. NE
Washington, DC 20002
Phone: (202)547-6173
Ellen M. Rocks, Exec.Dir.

Founded: 1976. **Description:** Supported by individuals, churches, synagogues, service organizations, local businesses, private foundations, and local government service contracts. Provides shelter, on an emergency and temporary basis, for pregnant and battered women and homeless and destitute families; offers support services and individual and group counseling. Maintains second stage or transitional housing for former shelter residents. Sponsors speakers' bureau; holds volunteer training workshops. **Publications:** *Friends*, quarterly. Newsletter. Includes calendar of events and "needs" lists.

★419★ Human Lactation Center (HLC)
666 Sturges Hwy.
Westport, CT 06880
Phone: (203)259-5995
Dana Raphael, Ph.D., Dir.

Founded: 1975. **Description:** Dedicated to international education and research on lactation (breastfeeding). Current activities include: research into the effects of lactation as a factor that inhibits fertility; consultation for national and international government, industry, and medical institutions on food policy, indigenous weaning foods, and infant and maternal nutrition and feeding practices; design and management of conferences to encourage dialogue among professionals; cooperative meetings with health and family planning groups; development of methodology for use by researchers in anthropology, nutrition, and public health in field work on childbirth, breastfeeding, breast milk and AIDS virus. Maintains museum of items related to infant feeding including nursing chairs, amulet feeding bottles, animal skin milk carrying cases, and breastfeeding posters. Operates library of 6000 volumes and research. **Publications:** *The Lactation Review*, periodic. • Also published *Only Mothers Know: Infant Feeding Practices in Traditional Cultures*.

★420★ Human Life Center (HLC)
University of Steubenville
Steubenville, OH 43952
Phone: (614)282-9953
Fax: (614)282-0769
Mike & Rita Marker, Co-Dirs.

Founded: 1972. **Description:** Seeks to: promote the sanctity of human life from conception to natural death; help married couples, families, and individuals to lead value-oriented lives; offer an integrated approach to sexuality corresponding to Christian moral values; support teachings of the Catholic church on moral and social issues including contraception and sterilization;

support natural family planning; foster cooperation and serve as an educational and resource center for pro-life individuals and organizations. Holds seminars, educational programs, and workshops. Maintains 4000 volume library and speakers' bureau. HLC is the only university-based program of its kind in the U.S. **Publications:** *Human Life Issues*, quarterly. • *International Review*, quarterly. • Also publishes books and teen pamphlet series.

★421★ Human Life Foundation (HLF)
150 E. 35th St., Rm. 840
New York, NY 10016
Phone: (212)685-5210
J. P. McFadden, Pres.

Founded: 1977. **Description:** Serves as a charitable and educational foundation. Produces publications addressing issues such as abortion, euthanasia, infanticide, and family concerns. Offers financial support to organizations that provide women with alternatives to abortion. **Publications:** *Human Life Review*, quarterly. • Also publishes and distributes books and pamphlets on abortion, bioethics, and family issues.

★422★ Human Life International (HLI)
7845 Airparded, Ste. E
Gaithersburg, MD 20879
Phone: (301)670-7884
Fax: (301)869-7363
Paul Marx, Pres.

Founded: 1981. **Description:** Serves as a research, educational, and service program offering positive alternatives to what the group calls the antilife/antifamily movement. Explores and comments on various dimensions of human life issues. Provides research on topics such as: Christian sexuality, natural family planning, and all forms of mechanical and medical fertility control programs including abortion, infanticide, and euthanasia. Maintains 500 volume library; compiles statistics. Bestows awards; operates charitable program and speakers' bureau. **Members:** 500,000. **Regional Groups:** 32. **State Groups:** 8. **Publications:** *Escoge la Vida* (in Spanish), 4/year. • *HLI Reports*, monthly. Newsletter; includes information on population and developmental issues worldwide. • *Sorrow's Reward*, quarterly. Newsletter reporting on international developments in the study and treatment of what the group calls Post-Abortion Syndrome. Includes book reviews. • Also publishes *The Best of Natural Family Planning, Death Without Dignity, Deceiving Birth Controllers, Confessions of a Prolife Missionary*, and other reference materials.

★423★ Human Life and Natural Family Planning Foundation (HLNFPF)
PO Box 10419
Alexandria, VA 22310
Phone: (703)836-3377
Lawrence J. Kane, Exec.Dir.

Founded: 1978. **Description:** Established in response to the appeal of Pope Paul VI to world science for the initiation of research to improve methods of child spacing in keeping with the tenets of his encyclical, "Humanae Vitae." Purposes are: to sponsor scientific research, experimentation, investigation, and analysis pertaining to the following areas: the generation of human life and reproductive physiology (including ovulation, spermatogenesis, factors influencing the transmission of life at the ovulant

state and at the stage of fertilization; fertilization, nidation, what constitutes the beginning of human life); psychological and physiological ramifications of the human sexual act; medical implications of human fertility control; implications of human fertility control in relation to social and economic pressures upon family life and in relation to demographic problems; termination of the existence of the conceptus by abortion and otherwise, what constitutes abortion, abortifacients; what constitutes the end of human life; euthanasia; biological significance of the term "human"; medical and social implications of human transplantations. Also seeks to make available to the public scientific knowledge derived from such scientific research, experimentation, investigation, and analysis and to sponsor or carry out educational programs related to the foregoing areas; to cooperate with other organizations and persons performing research and education in the foregoing areas. Compiles statistics. Maintains library of 1000 volumes on natural family planning. **Publications:** *Private NFP Services*, annual. • *Report* (members only), monthly. • Also publishes Proceedings of Research Conference on Natural Family Planning, Natural Family Planning, Selected Bibliography and Natural Family Planning Curriculum, and training materials.

★424★ Human Rights Campaign Fund (HRCF)
1012 14th St., NW, Ste. 600
Washington, DC 20005
Phone: (202)628-4160
Tim McSeeley, Exec.Dir.

Founded: 1980. **Description:** To advance the cause of lesbian and gay civil rights by lobbying Congress and political candidates who support gay and lesbian civil rights and increased funding for AIDS research and treatment. Promotes responsible AIDS policy, including increased federal funding for AIDS research, education, and treatment programs, expedited release of promising AIDS drugs, and protection from discrimination for people with AIDS and HIV. Encourages: legislative protection for lesbian and gay men in employment, housing, public accomodations, military service, and immigration matters; recognition of the legitimacy of gay and lesbian families and the repeal of laws criminalizing the gay and lesbian lifestyle. Works for the elimination of anti-gay violence and the collection of data detailing crimes committed against gay men and lesbians. Provides financial contributions to supportive congressional candidates (over 100 candidates nationwide). Conducts fundraising events; bestows awards for contributions to the advancement of gay and lesbian civil rights. Maintains speakers' bureau. **Local Groups:** 13. **Computerized Services:** Records of the voting records of Congressmen. **Publications:** *Annual Report*. • *Momentum*, quarterly. Newsletter detailing legislative issues pertaining to lesbian and gay rights.

★425★ Hysterectomy Educational Resources and Services Foundation (HERS)
422 Bryn Mawr Ave.
Bala-Cynwyd, PA 19004
Phone: (215)667-7757
Nora W. Coffey, Pres.

Founded: 1982. **Description:** Seeks to help women make informed decisions regarding hysterectomy. Provides educational materials concerning hysterectomy and alternative procedures. Functions as a referral service matching women who have had or will have a hysterectomy for one-to-one sharing of experiences and concerns; offers referral list of doctors for second opinions; also provides legal referrals. Operates library of printed materials and videotapes; maintains speakers' bureau. Conducts seminars. **Publications:** *HERS Annual Hysterectomy Conference Proceedings.* • *HERS Newsletter*, quarterly. Contains book reviews, medical and scientific literature reviews, writer's chronicle of journal, and letters from readers. • Also makes available reading list and copies and reprints of articles; distributes audiocassettes and other related materials. **Also known as:** HERS Foundation.

★426★ Incest Survivors Anonymous
PO Box 5613
Long Beach, CA 90805-0613
Founded: 1980. **Description:** A self-help recovery program for victims of incest. Applies the twelve-step and twelve-tradition program of Alcoholics Anonymous World Service to assist with recovery.

**★427★ Incest Survivors Resource
Network, International (ISRNI)**
PO Box 7375
Las Cruces, NM 88006-7375
Phone: (505)521-4260
Anne-Marie Eriksson, Pres.
Founded: 1983. **Description:** Serves as a Quaker-affiliated resource service dedicated to the primary prevention of incest. Incest survivors from various professions offer awareness talks on the intergenerational transmission of verbal and physical violence associated with incest. Through programs such as Parents United, seeks resolution of incest trauma via education, professional therapeutic intervention, and selfhelp. Encourages the local development of Parents United chapters.

**★428★ Independent Federation of Flight
Attendants**
630 3rd Ave.
New York, NY 10017
Phone: (212)818-1130
Fax: (212)949-4058
Vicki Frankovich, President
Description: The Federation is a labor union representing 7500 flight attendants employed by Trans World Airlines. Negotiates contracts, processes grievances, and works on social issues, including family and medical leave, the protection of women's legal right to abortion, and others. **Publications:** *630 News*, quarterly.

**★429★ Indiana University, School of
Medicine**
Institute of Women's Health
Department of Obstetrics and Gynecology
926 W. Michigan St.
Indianapolis, IN 46202
Phone: (317)274-2014
Fax: (317)274-2014
Diane B. Brashear, Senior Officer
Description: The Institute studies women's health practices and advocates women's health self care through educational demonstration projects. Sponsors women's health and fitness project.

**★430★ Indigenous Women's Network
(IWN)**
PO Box 174
Lake Elmo, MN 55042
Phone: (612)770-3861
Winona LaDuke, Chair
Founded: 1989. **Description:** Individuals seeking to increase visibility of the indigenous women of the Western Hemisphere. Encourages the resolution of contemporary problems through traditional values. Opearates speakers' bureau; sponsors educational programs; conducts research. **Members:** 300. **Publications:** *Indigenous Woman*, semiannual. Magazine.

**★431★ Informed Homebirth/Informed Birth
and Parenting (IH/IBP)**
PO Box 3675
Ann Arbor, MI 48106
Phone: (313)662-6857
Rahima Baldwin, Pres.
Founded: 1977. **Description:** Expectant and new parents, childbirth educators, midwives, nurses, preschool and elementary school teachers, and others interested in safe childbirth alternatives. Seeks to provide information on alternatives in childbirth methods, parenting, and education. Sponsors Childbirth Educator Training Program leading to certification as Childbirth Educator; Childbirth Assistant Training emphasizing practical skills to help the birthing woman and the primary caregiver. Maintains mail order book service on alternative education. Offers cassette tape course for interested couples and childbirth educators who live in areas where classes are not available; conducts correspondence course to help students develop teaching outlines. **Members:** 1000. **Publications:** *Openings*, quarterly. Newsletter; includes association news, calendar of events, newly certified teacher listings, new resources, and schedule of upcoming workshops. • *Special Delivery*, quarterly. Newsletter; contains articles on midwifery and birth, book reviews, calendar of events, and schedule of upcoming workshops. **Formerly:** (1981) Informed Homebirth.

**★432★ Institute of Electrical and
Electronic Engineers**
Task Force on Women and Minorities
1111 19th St., Ste. 608
Washington, DC 20036
Phone: (202)785-0017
Vin O'Neill, Administrator, Professional Programs

★433★ Institute for Feminist Studies (IFS)
1005 Market St., Ste. 305
San Francisco, CA 94103
Phone: (415)621-4220
Ann Forfreedom, Exec.Dir.
Description: The Institute is a center for original research about historical and contemporary women's issues, including the suffrage movements in the United States and Britain, the ERA, violence against women, and other topics. Maintains an archive of feminist materials. Sponsors discussions, classes, and special events about feminist issues. **Publications:** *The Wise Woman*.

**★434★ Institute for Reproductive Health
(IRH)**
8721 Beverly Blvd.
Los Angeles, CA 90048
Phone: (213)854-7714
Fax: (213)854-4549
Vicki Hufnagel, M.D., Med.Dir.
Description: Persons supporting informed, responsible health care for women and working toward the passage of regulatory legislation. Conducts research and disseminates information on women's health issues including: technological advances, education, social and behavioral sciences, and belief systems; uterine endocrinology, female reconstructive surgery, sexually-transmitted diseases and their effect on female fertility; substance abuse and obstetrical problems; analysis of risks and losses due to hysterectomy. Holds seminars. **Members:** 500. **Computerized Services:** Maintains online database to the National Medical Library. **Publications:** *Women's Health* quarterly. • Also issues educational literature and audio- and videotapes.

**★435★ Institute for the Study of
Matrimonial Laws (ISML)**
c/o Sidney Siller
11 Park Pl., Ste. 1116
New York, NY 10007
Phone: (212)766-4030
Sidney Siller, Pres.
Founded: 1972. **Description:** To study the nation's divorce, alimony, custody, and visitation laws. Aims to: encourage rational and objective state and national laws that reflect contemporary life; aid local communities in establishing programs to help single parents and their children; encourage professional research. Proposes to undertake community service, such as conducting marriage seminars and providing training consultants; studies the emotional aspects of divorce; compiles demographic and statistical information. Sponsors educational programs. Maintains library of 10,000 volumes and other documents dealing with divorce, alimony, and custody. **Publications:** *Bulletin*, monthly (except summer).

**★436★ Institute for the Study of Sexual
Assault (ISSA)**
c/o San Francisco General Hospital
995 Potrero, Bldg. 80, Ward 83, Rm. 319
San Francisco, CA 94110
Judith L. Musick, Ph.D., Exec.Dir.
Founded: 1980. **Description:** Research group devoted to the study of civil-legal aspects of sexual assault. Provides consulting services to attorneys on matters including damage awards, pleadings, statutory analyses, expert witnesses, and other civil issues. Conducts grants review. Maintains national data base of pending and resolved civil sexual assault suits, a legal pleadings bank consisting of major pleadings in civil actions brought by sexual assault victims, and a specialized library containing articles and monographs on the social, political, psychological, and legal dimensions of rape. **Publications:** *Civil Sexual Assault Cases: Judgements and Settlements, Vols. I-III, Institutional Liability for Sexual Assault: An Annotated Bibliography of Selected Legal Cases*, and *Legal Handbook for Rape Crisis Centers*.

★437★ Institute of Women Today (IWT)
7315 S. Yale
Chicago, IL 60621
Phone: (312)651-8372
Sr. Margaret Ellen Traxler, Dir.

Founded: 1974. **Description:** Sponsored by church-related Protestant, Catholic, and Jewish women's organizations to examine religious and historical origins of women's liberation. Endeavors to bring church-related women into the women's movement so that the principles of faith will be reflected in the women's struggle for equality. Conducts workshops and research. Provides legal services to women in prisons. Maintains archives. **Members:** 889.

**★438★ Institute for Women and Work
NYSSILR**
Cornell University
15 E. 26th St.
New York, NY 10010
Phone: (212)340-2800
Anne H. Nelson, Contact

Description: Education programs for women members of labor unions and other working women on both a college credit and non-credit basis.

**★439★ Institute for Women's Studies in
the Arab World**
Beirut University College
475 Riverside Dr., Rm. 1846
New York, NY 10115
Phone: (212)870-2592
Fax: (212)870-2762
Dr. Julinda Abu Nasr, Dir.

Description: Conducts research, provides documentation, produces publications, and sponsors action programs to improve the condition of women and children in the Arab world.

★440★ Integrity
PO Box 19561
Washington, DC 20036
Phone: (404)892-3143
Bruce Garner, Pres.

Founded: 1974. **Description:** Gay and lesbian Episcopalians/Anglicans and supporters. Objectives are to: minister to the spiritual needs of gay men and lesbians; work for full participation of gay people in church and society; promote the study of human sexuality within a Christian context. Distributes educational materials for clergy and lay persons; sponsors conferences; offers counseling, AIDS ministries, and worship services. **Members:** 1700. **Regional Groups:** 4. **Local Groups:** 52. **Publications:** Integrity–Directory, annual. • Integrity Handbook, biennial. • Integrity–News and Notes, quarterly. Newsletter; includes book reviews, calendar of events, chapter news, and membership directory updates.

★441★ Intensive Caring Unlimited (ICU)
910 Bent Ln.
Philadelphia, PA 19118
Phone: (215)233-4723
Lenette S. Moses, Co-Founder

Founded: 1983. **Description:** Support organization for parents of children born prematurely or with special problems; parents experiencing a high-risk pregnancy or miscarriages health care professionals. Offers emotional and educational support and information on care of babies and young children with special medical or developmental problems. Conducts training courses on peer support, counseling, and in-house hospital informational programs. Provides referral services and speakers' bureau; maintains 2000 volume library. Activities are concentrated in Pennsylvania and southern New Jersey but ICU disseminates information nationwide. **Publications:** Intensive Caring Unlimited (in English and Spanish), bimonthly. Newsletter; includes medical reports. • Also publishes regional resource lists, training manuals, and information packets.

**★442★ Inter-American Commission of
Women (CIM)**
c/o Organization of American States
1889 F St. NW, Rm. 880
Washington, DC 20006
Phone: (202)458-6084
Linda J. Poole, Exec.Sec.

Founded: 1928. **Description:** Specialized agency of the Organization of American States dealing with issues concerning women. Commission is composed of one delegate for each member country of OAS. Mobilizes, trains, and organizes women "so that they may fully participate in all fields of human endeavor, on a par with men, as two beings of equal value, coresponsible for the destiny of humanity." Informs the OAS general assembly and member governments on: civil, political, social, economic, and cultural status of women in the Americas; progress achieved in the field as well as problems to be considered; development of a plan of action following the Decade of Women (1976-85) of strategies for full and equal participation by women by the year 2000. Serves as liaison for women's groups throughout the hemisphere and conducts research on laws affecting women. Maintains library; operates a regional information center in Santiago, Chile; finances development projects in Latin America and the Caribbean. **Members:** 32. **Publications:** Final Report-Assembly of Delegates, biennial. • Mujeres (in Spanish and English), 2-3/year. • Series: Studies, periodic.

**★443★ The International Alliance, An
Association of Executive and
Professional Women (TIA)**
8600 LaSalle Rd., Ste. 308
Baltimore, MD 21204
Phone: (301)321-6699
Fax: (301)823-2410
Marian E. Goetze, Exec.V.Pres.

Founded: 1980. **Description:** Local networks (20) comprising 5000 professional and executive women; individual businesswomen without a network affiliation (100) are alliance associates. Seeks to: promote recognition of the achievements of women in business; encourage placement of women in senior executive positions; maintain high standards of professional competence among members. Facilitates communication on an international scale among professional women's networks and their members. Represents members' interests before policymakers in business and government. Sponsors programs that support equal opportunity and enhance members' business and professional skills. Operates appointments and directors service. Conducts seminars, symposia, and workshops; maintains speakers' bureau. **Members:** 120. **Publications:** Membership Directory, annual. • The Alliance, bimonthly. Association professional newsletter. Includes calendar of events and research updates.

Formerly: (1986) National Alliance of Professional and Executive Women's Networks.

**★444★ International Association of Eating
Disorders Professionals (IAEDP)**
123 NW, 13th St., No. 206
Boca Raton, FL 33432
Phone: (407)338-6494
Fax: (714)248-8851
Shirley Klein, Exec.Dir.

Founded: 1985. **Description:** Eating disorders counselors and therapists. Establishes and develops curricula; operates and implements a system for certifying eating disorders counselors and therapists; provides public education and information on eating disorders counseling and therapy. Offers professional consulting and assistance to the medical community, hospitals, courts, law enforcement agencies, schools, churches, and social welfare agencies. Facilitates networking among members; makes available employment opportunity information. Sponsors workshops. **Publications:** The Counselor Quarterly. Includes association news and activities, treatment reports, and certification updates. • Also publishes certification manual and curriculum for higher education.

**★445★ International Association of
Ministers Wives and Ministers Widows
(IAMWMW)**
c/o Dr. Shirley Alexander Hart
305 Dexter St. E.
Chesapeake, VA 23324
Phone: (804)543-0427
Dr. Shirley Alexander Hart, Exec.Officer

Founded: 1941. **Description:** Wives and widows of ministers of 85 religious denominations. Seeks to erase barriers existing between religious communions. Offers annual Christian service scholarship and maintains student scholarship fund. Sponsors competitions; bestows awards; conducts research; compiles statistics. Maintains 10,000 volume library, museum, archives, hall of fame, and speakers' bureau. **Members:** 35,000. **Regional Groups:** 7. **Publications:** The Ministers' Wives Herald, quarterly. Journal. • Prayers for All Seasons, annual. • Also publishes books. **Formerly:** National Association of Ministers' Wives; (1978) National Association of Ministers' Wives and Ministers' Widows.

**★446★ International Association of
Parents and Professionals for Safe
Alternatives in Childbirth (NAPSAC)**
Rt. 1, Box 646
Marble Hill, MO 63764
Phone: (314)238-2010
Lee Stewart, Pres.

Founded: 1975. **Description:** Parents, midwives, physicians, nurses, health officials, social workers, and childbirth educators in 10 countries who are "dedicated to exploring, examining, implementing, and establishing family-centered childbirth programs which meet the needs of families as well as provide the safe aspects of medical science." Promotes education concerning the principles of natural childbirth; facilitates communication and cooperation among parents, medical professionals, and childbirth educators; assists in the establishment of maternity and childbearing centers. Provides educational opportunities to parents and parents-to-be, enabling them to assume more personal responsibility for pregnancy, childbirth, infant care, and child rearing. **Members:** 2000. **Computerized Services:** Data base; Mailing list. **Publications:** *NAPSAC Directory of Alternative Birth Services and Consumer Guide*, annual. Lists midwives, birth centers, noninterventive physicians, and educators for safe alternatives in childbirth. • *NAPSAC News*, quarterly. Newsletter; includes association news, book reviews, and calendar of events. • Also publishes books, monographs, and brochures. **Formerly:** (1979) National Association of Parents and Professionals for Safe Alternatives in Childbirth.

★447★ International Association for Personnel Women (IAPW)
PO Box 969
Andover, MA 01810-0017
Phone: (508)474-0750
Fax: (508)474-0750
Brenda Jackson, Pres.

Founded: 1950. **Description:** Professional association of personnel executives in business, industry, education, and government. Established to expand and improve the professionalism of women in personnel management. **Members:** 1500. **Local Groups:** 18. **Publications:** *Connections*, bimonthly. Newsletter. • *Membership Roster*, annual.

★448★ International Association of Physical Education and Sport for Girls and Women (IAPESGW)
c/o Ruth M. Schellberg
50 Skyline Dr.
Mankato, MN 56001
Phone: (507)345-3665
Ruth M. Schellberg, Exec.Officer

Founded: 1949. **Description:** Organizations in 54 countries with an interest in physical education for girls and women. Seeks to: bring together women working in physical education or sports; cooperate with organizations that encourage women's services; promote the exchange of persons and ideas between member organizations. Conducts research into problems affecting physical education and sport for women. **Members:** 400. **Publications:** *Report Following Congresses*, quadrennial.

★449★ International Association of Women Ministers (IAWM)
c/o Rev. Carol S. Brown
579 Main St.
Stroudsburg, PA 18360
Phone: (717)421-7751
Rev. Carol S. Brown, Treas.

Founded: 1919. **Description:** Women in 20 countries who are licensed, ordained, or otherwise authorized by any evangelical denomination to preach or who are preparing for the ministry. Promotes equal ecclesiastical rights for women and encourages young women to take up ministerial work. Conducts research on the ecclesiastical status of women. **Members:** 400. **Publications:** *Woman's Pulpit*, quarterly. Newsletter covering developments affecting the role of women in organized religion. **Formerly:** (1971) American Association of Women Ministers.

★450★ International Baby Food Action Network (IBFAN)
c/o ACTION
3255 Hennepin Ave., S., Ste. 220
Minneapolis, MN 55408
Phone: (612)823-1571
Janice Mantell, Exec. Officer

Founded: 1979. **Description:** To ban advertising and promotion of breast-milk substitutes, particularly in Third World countries. In May 1981, the World Health Organization voted on the adoption of a code restricting promotion of breast-milk substitutes. The vote was 118-1, the U.S. casting the only no vote. U.S. and Swiss corporations are the primary producers of the breast-milk substitutes. **Members:** 100. **Publications:** *Breastfeeding Briefs*, quarterly. • *IBFAN News*, bimonthly. Membership activities and issue newsletter.

★451★ International Black Women's Congress (IBWC)
1081 Bergen St.
Newark, NJ 07112
Phone: (201)926-0570
Fax: (201)761-1878
Dr. La Francis Rodgers-Rose, Pres.

Founded: 1983. **Description:** Women of African descent; interested individuals. Objective is to unite members for mutual support and socioeconomic development through: annual networking tours to Africa; establishing support groups; assisting women in starting their own businesses; assisting members in developing resumes and other educational needs; offering to answer or discuss individual questions and concerns. Conducts workshops and charitable program; compiles statistics. Bestows Oni Award annually to the person identified as "someone who protects, defends and enhances the general well being of African people." Operates speakers' bureau. Maintains 100 volume library. **Members:** 5800. **State Groups:** 5. **Undergraduate Chapters:** 3. **Publications:** *International Black Women's Directory*, periodic. • *Oni Newsletter*, quarterly.

★452★ International Center for Research on Women (ICRW)
1717 Massachusetts Ave. NW, Ste. 302
Washington, DC 20036
Phone: (202)797-0007
Fax: (202)797-0020
Mayra Buvinic, Dir.

Founded: 1977. **Description:** Purpose is to improve the productivity and incomes of women in developing countries worldwide. Provides technical services for the design, implementation, and evaluation of development projects that integrate women into mainstream economic roles. Disseminates research findings to policymakers and others throughout the world who are concerned with economic and socioeconomic issues of the Third World. Conducts policy roundtables. Compiles statistics on women in developing countries. Maintains 9500 volume library of published and unpublished studies on changing roles of women and on income generation for women in developing countries. **Publications:** *International Center for Research on Women–Papers*, periodic. Series of papers covering women's socioeconomic status, health, and nutrition in developing countries and women's participation in development projects. • Also has published *Women and Poverty in the Third World*.

★453★ International Childbirth Education Association (ICEA)
PO Box 20048
Minneapolis, MN 55420
Phone: (612)854-8660
Jean Rose, Pres.

Founded: 1960. **Description:** Purposes are: to further the educational, physical, and emotional preparation of expectant parents for childbearing and breastfeeding; to increase public awareness on current issues related to childbearing; to cooperate with physicians, nurses, physical therapists, hospitals, health, education, and welfare agencies, and other individuals and groups interested in furthering parental participation and minimal obstetric intervention in uncomplicated labors; to promote development of safe, low-cost alternatives in childbirth that recognize the rights and responsibilities of those involved. Develops, publishes, and distributes literature pertaining to family-centered maternity care. Offers a teacher certification program for childbirth educators. Conducts workshops. Bestows ICEA Virginia Larson Research Award. Operates mail order book store in Minneapolis, MN which makes available literature on all aspects of childbirth education and family-centered maternity care. **Members:** 12,000. **Local Groups:** 275. **Publications:** *ICEA Bookmarks*, 3/year. • *ICEA Sharing*, 3/year. Newsletter for childbirth educators covering parent education, perinatal nutrition, the mother/neonatal relationship, and labor and birth. Contains surveys, calendar of events, and research updates. • *International Journal of Childbirth Education*, 4/year. • *Membership Directory*, annual. • Also publishes pamphlets.

★454★ International Christian Women's Fellowship (ICWF)
PO Box 1986
Indianapolis, IN 46206
Phone: (317)353-1491
Janice R. Newborn, Exec.Sec.

Founded: 1949. **Description:** Women who are members of the Christian Church (Disciples of Christ) and others who accept the purpose of the CWF. Administered by Department of Church Women, Division of Homeland Ministries, and Christian Church. "To provide opportunities for spiritual growth, enrichment, education, and creative ministries to enable women to develop a sense of personal responsibility for the whole mission of the Church of Jesus Christ," through a program of study, worship, and service and through preparation of women for fuller participation in the total church life. Provides materials to local groups for programs on topics such as stewardship of life, Christian social relations, local church concerns, and the world mission of the church. **Members:** 136,870. **Publications:** *Guideposts for Christian Women's Fellowship*, annual. • *World CWF Newsletter*, annual. • *Yearbook*. • Also publishes program and Bible study materials and brochures.

★455★ International Committee for World Day of Prayer (ICWDP)
475 Riverside Dr., Rm. 812
New York, NY 10115
Phone: (212)870-3049
Fax: (212)870-2538
Eileen King, Exec.Dir.

Founded: 1967. **Description:** Christian women united to observe a common day of prayer established on the first Friday in March.

Through World Day of Prayer, which began in 1887, women "affirm their faith in Jesus Christ; share their hopes and fears, their joys and sorrows, their opportunities and needs." Encourages women to "become aware of the whole world and no longer live in isolation; to share the faith experience of Christians in other countries and cultures; to take up the burdens of other people and pray with and for them; to become aware of their talents and use them in the service of society." Affirms "that prayer and action are inseparable and that both have an imponderable influence in the world." **Regional Groups:** 100. **Publications:** *World Day of Prayer Journal*, annual. Reports on World Day of Prayer services.

★456★ **International Communication Association**
Feminist Scholarship Interest Group
University of Southern California
Department of Communication, Arts and Sciences
Los Angeles, CA 90089-1694
Phone: (213)787-9181
Karen Altman, Co-Chair

★457★ **International Congress on Women in Music (ICWM)**
PO Box 12164
La Crescenta, CA 91224-0864
Phone: (818)248-1249
Jeannie G. Pool, Coordinator
Founded: 1977. **Description:** Musicologists, scholars in women's studies, performers, composers, and feminist activists in 31 countries. Objectives are to: encourage performance, recording, and publication of classical concert music by women; establish courses on women in music on the college level; develop classroom materials at the primary and secondary school levels that include information on women's active and creative participation in music. Makes available information relating to the activities and accomplishments of women in music. Provides a forum for the discussion of issues and prospects for women in the music profession. Conducts performances, panels, and workshops. **Members:** 290. **Publications:** *Annual Membership Directory.* • *Newsletter*, quarterly. • *Working Papers on Women in Music*, quarterly. Journal. **Formerly:** (1983) National Congress of Women in Music.

★458★ **International Council of African Women (ICAW)**
PO Box 91812
Washington, DC 20090-1812
Phone: (202)546-8459
Nkenge Toure, Co-Coordinator
Founded: 1982. **Description:** The ICAW promotes worldwide networking and development of women of African descent. It focuses on bringing information to disadvantaged U.S. women of color about international women's conferences, developments, and events. The Council also works on domestic issues such as violence against women, reproductive rights, overcoming classism and racism, and voting, and foreign policy affecting women in South Africa and Central America. **Publications:** *African Women Rising.*

★459★ **International Council for Continuing Education and Training**
110 Connectictut Ave. NW, Ste. 700
Washington, DC 20036
Phone: (202)857-1122
Donna Cantor, Account Director
Description: Advises the President, Congress, and the Secretary of Education on matters concerning the education and educational equity of women and girls.

★460★ **International Council of Jewish Women (ICJW)**
53 W. 23 St.
New York, NY 10010
Phone: (212)645-4048
Stella Rozan, Pres.
Founded: 1912. **Description:** National organizations linking one million Jewish women. Objectives are to: promote friendly relations, understanding, and mutual support among Jewish women; uphold and strengthen the bonds of Judaism; show solidarity with Israel and support the efforts of Israel to secure a just and lasting peace; promote economic security and social, educational, and cultural development in Israel; further the highest interests of humanity; cooperate with national and international organizations working for goodwill among people and for equal rights for humanity. Supports the Universal Declaration of Human Rights of the United Nations, and encourages work for the improvement of the social, economic, and legal status of all women under Jewish and civil law. Conducts conferences, workshops, and seminars; sponsors field trips; maintains information and service center. **Members:** 37. **Telecommunications Services:** Telex, ICJW 612874F. **Publications:** *Directory of ICJW Affiliates*, triennial. • *Newsletter* (in English and Spanish), semiannual. • Also publishes bulletins and Kosher cookbook.

★461★ **International Council of Traditional Music**
Music and Gender Study Group
Hunter College
Department of Music
695 Park Ave.
New York, NY 10021
Phone: (212)772-5020
Barbara L. Hampton, Chair
Description: The Group's purpose is to conduct and report research into women and music globally. **Publications:** *Yearbook for Traditional Music.*

★462★ **International Curling Federation - Ladies Committee (ICFLC)**
c/o Mrs. Spencer VanEss
15085 Westover Rd.
Elm Grove, WI 53122
Phone: (414)786-2992
Mrs. Spencer VanEss, U.S. Rep.
Founded: 1977. **Description:** Women representatives of national curling associations united to govern and direct international curling for women. **Members:** 18.

★463★ **International Dalkon Shield Victims Education Association (IDEA)**
106 Pioneer Bldg.
Seattle, WA 98104
Phone: (206)329-1371
Fax: (206)623-4251
Constance Miller, Treas.
Founded: 1986. **Description:** Women who have contracted illnesses and/or been disabled through use of the Dalkon Shield intrauterine contraceptive device; their supporters. Promotes public education about the dangers of using the Dalkon Shield. Disseminates information regarding Dalkon Shield injuries, claim resolution, and related topics. Offers seminars. Maintains speakers' bureau. **Members:** 2000. **State Groups:** 2.

★464★ **International Federation for Family Life Promotion (IFFLP)**
1511 K St. NW, Ste. 326
Washington, DC 20005
Phone: (202)783-0137
Fax: (202)783-7351
Claude A. Lanctot, M.D., Exec.Dir.
Founded: 1974. **Description:** Organizations and individuals interested in natural family planning and family life education. Objectives are to: provide leadership, guidance, and education in fields of family life education; conduct research in natural family planning; stimulate and assist in the formation of natural family planning and family life education organizations. Maintains library. Offers educational programs in primary health care and breast-feeding promotion. Conducts training workshops for program coordinators. **Members:** 130. **Telecommunications Services:** telex, 4972704 FIDAF. **Publications:** *IFFLP Bulletin* (in English, French, and Spanish), semiannual. Newsletter featuring articles on family planning, zonal development programs, and primary health care. Includes information on meetings and conferences, book reviews, calendar of events, news of members, and research updates. • *Message to Members* (in English, French, and Spanish), annual. • *Presentation Summaries*, triennial. • Also publishes *Technical Series: NFP: Development of National Programs* (monograph), *NFP: Program Evaluation Instrument and Guide*, and *Family Life Education Selected Papers.*

★465★ **International Federation of Women Lawyers (IFWL)**
186 5th Ave.
New York, NY 10010
Phone: (212)206-1666
Dora Aberlin, Hon. Life Pres.
Founded: 1944. **Description:** Women lawyers in 70 countries. Seeks to: advance the science of jurisprudence and protect women and children; advance the diffusion of knowledge of the laws of various countries; create better international relations. Holds consultative status with the United Nations; maintains liaison representatives at the United Nations, the International Labour Organization, and the United Nations Educational, Scientific and Cultural Organization. **Publications:** *La Abogada Internacional*, biennial. • *La Abogada Newsletter*, quarterly.

★466★ International Federation of Women's Travel Organizations (IFWTO)
4545 N. 36th St., Ste. 126
Phoenix, AZ 85018
Phone: (602)956-7175
Fax: (602)957-0545
Paula Chavez, Exec.Dir.

Founded: 1969. **Description:** Travel clubs in 14 countries representing 5000 women engaged in the sale and promotion of travel. Seeks to: improve and make more effective the status of women within the travel industry; assist in the development of women's travel organizations in areas where none exist; be involved in the planning and development of industry affairs; further promote international goodwill and understanding. Presents Benger-Sullivan Award and SPIRIT award; maintains speakers' bureau. **Members:** 64. **Regional Groups:** 3. **Publications:** *Directory*, annual. 3/year. Membership activities newsletter; includes regional news. • *Federation Footnotes*, periodic.

★467★ International Institute for the Study of Women in Music
California State University
Music Department
Northridge, CA 91330
Phone: (818)885-3105
Beverly Grigsby, Director

Description: The Institiute maintains the Aaron I. Cohen Research Library. Areas of focus include arts, library collections, and women in music.

★468★ International Institute for Women's Political Leadership (IIWPL)
1511 K St. NW, Ste. 410
Washington, DC 20005
Phone: (202)842-1523
Fax: (202)347-1306
Audrey Sheppard, Exec.Dir.

Founded: 1988. **Description:** Promotes increased participation of women in politics and in political leadership roles in democratic governments worldwide. Believes if women become more active in public policy decision-making, they can improve world conditions and offer a unique perspective. Offers political education programs to women, especially those in democracies that are fragile, emergent, or under stress, to stabilize those democracies and enhance the position of women in those cultures. Conducts political skills workshops in African, South American, and Pacific countries. Sponsors survey project to collect data relevant to women in politics throughout the world. Provides training and networking opportunities.

★469★ International Lactation Consultant Association (ILCA)
201 Brown Ave.
Evanston, IL 60202-3601
Phone: (708)260-8874
Jan Barger, Pres.

Founded: 1985. **Description:** Lactation consultants, institutions, and health professionals from 20 countries interested in breastfeeding and lactation. Works to: establish and maintain quality educational and practice standards and ethical principles for lactation consultants; initiate and conduct continuing education and research in the field; promote work concerning lactation/breastfeeding issues; increase public and health care worker awareness of lactation and breastfeeding. Facilitates communication among members. Bestows ILCA Outstanding Achievement in Human Lactation Award. **Members:** 2500. **Regional Groups:** 33. **Computerized Services:** Mailing list. **Publications:** *Annual Syllabus of Conference*. • *ILCA Membership Directory*, annual. • *Journal of Human Lactation*, quarterly. Contains research and scientific articles, book reviews, association news, and film reviews. • Also publishes journal supplements, recommendations, papers, and brochure.

★470★ International Ladies' Garment Workers' Union (ILGWU)
1710 Broadway
New York, NY 10019
Phone: (212)265-7000
Jay Mazur, Pres.

Founded: 1900. **Description:** AFL-CIO. **Members:** 173,000. **Locals:** 348. **Publications:** *Justice*, 11/year. Tabloid newspaper informing members of union news, membership activities, and social and political issues.

★471★ International League of Women Composers (ILWC)
Southshore Rd., Box 670
Pt. Peninsula
Three Mile Bay, NY 13693
Phone: (315)649-5086
Elizabeth Hayden Pizer, Chairperson

Founded: 1975. **Description:** Established professional women composers representing 25 countries. Works to: obtain more commissions, recordings, and performances for women composers; develop areas which are insufficiently accessible to women composers. Holds concerts; sponsors radio series; conducts Search for New Music competition. **Members:** 400. **Publications:** *ILWC Journal*, 3/year. Covers the activities of women composers. Includes awards and competitions, book reviews, new recordings, and opportunities for members. • *ILWC Membership Directory*, annual. **Formerly:** (1978) League of Women Composers.

★472★ International Lutheran Women's Missionary League (ILWML)
3558 S. Jefferson Ave.
St. Louis, MO 63118-3810
Phone: (314)268-1531
Shirley Meckfessel, Office Mgr.

Founded: 1942. **Description:** Women's groups within the congregations of the Lutheran Church-Missouri Synod in the U.S. and Canada. Works to develop a program of mission education, inspiration, and service for the women of the Lutheran Church-Missouri Synod, and to gather voluntary funds for mission projects. **Members:** 200,000. **State Groups:** 44. **Local Groups:** 6000. **Publications:** *Convention Manual*, biennial. • *Lutheran Woman's Quarterly*. **Formerly:** (1976) Lutheran Women's Missionary League.

★473★ International Mothers' Peace Day Committee
PO Box 102
West Liberty, WV 26074
Phone: (304)336-7159
Jeanne V. Schramm, Chwm.

Founded: 1982. **Description:** Seeks to unite mothers and others worldwide to promote the establishment of the first Sunday in June as International Mothers' Peace Day, originated as Mothers' Peace Day, a day of observance established in 1872 by Julia Ward Howe (1819-1910), peace advocate and composer of The Battle Hymn of the Republic. Stages letter-writing campaigns and peace demonstrations. Observance based upon the motto, ''Those who nurture life on earth are of one mind in their opposition to those who would destroy it.''

★474★ International Nanny Association (INA)
PO Box 26522
Austin, TX 78755
Phone: (512)454-6462
Toll-free: 800-274-6462
Fax: (512)459-0070
Janet Shannon, Gen.Mgr.

Founded: 1987. **Description:** Nannies, nanny employers, educators, and nanny placement agencies. Promotes in-home professional child care; serves as a clearinghouse of information on nannies; conducts advocacy on behalf of members. Makes available educational programs; bestows awards; compiles statistics. **Members:** 1200. **Computerized Services:** Mailing list. **Publications:** *Directory of Nanny Placement Agencies, Training Programs and Special Services*, annual. • *INA Quarterly*. Association and industry newsletter. • Also publishes *A Nanny for Your Family* and *So You Want to Be a Nanny . . .* (brochures).

★475★ International Network for Women in Enterprise and Trade (INET)
PO Box 6178
McLean, VA 22106
Phone: (703)893-8541
Fax: (703)356-6655
Christina Lane, President

Description: The Network assists and supports women throughout the world to develop and implement effective business strategies and enterprise development initiatives. It has established the American German Library for Women in Enterprise and Trade at Humboldt University, Berlin. **Publications:** *Border Crossing*, bimonthly.

★476★ International Order of Job's Daughters, Supreme Guardian Council
233 W. 6th St.
Papillon, NE 68046-2210
Phone: (402)592-7987
Susan M. Goolsby, Exec.Mgr.

Founded: 1921. **Description:** Girls from 4 countries who are between the ages of 11 and 20 and are related to Master Masons. Promotes spiritual and character development. Conducts fraternal, patriotic, and educational activities; sponsors philanthropic project annually; bestows scholarship awards. **Members:** 50,000. **Regional Groups:** 46. **Publications:** *News Exchange*, 4/year. • *Proceedings*, annual.

★477★ International Organization of Women in Telecommunications
c/o Anne Bailey
2308 Oakwood Ln.
Arlington, TX 76012
Phone: (817)275-0683
Anne Bailey, Pres.

Founded: 1981. **Description:** Women and men involved in telecommunications; telecommunications students. To enhance the image of women in the telecommunications industry. Provides forums for exchange of information concerning education and job opportunities; acts as support group for persons in the field; provides credentials for members. Sponsors seminars on topics in telecommunications; maintains library in New York City. Plans to offer scholarships. **Members:** 350. **Regional Groups:** 20. **Publications:** (1) Report, monthly; (2) Newsletter, quarterly.

★478★ International Planned Parenthood Federation, Western Hemisphere Region (IPPF/WHR)
902 Broadway, 10th Fl.
New York, NY 10010
Phone: (212)995-8800
Fax: (212)995-8853
Hernan Sanhueza, Regional Dir.

Founded: 1952. **Description:** Division of International Planned Parenthood Federation. National family planning organizations in Canada, Latin America, Caribbean Islands, and the United States. Views family planning as "the expression of the human right of couples to have only the children they want and to have them when they want them." Works to extend the practice of voluntary family planning by providing information, education, and services to couples. Seeks to persuade governments to establish national family planning programs. Maintains 10,000 volume library. Conducts research programs; maintains speakers' bureau; sponsors specialized education programs. **Telecommunications Services:** Cable, WHIPPFE; telex, 620661. **Publications:** Annual Report. • Forum (in English and Spanish), quarterly. Magazine; includes calendar of events. Distributed primarily to affiliated family planning programs. • Also publishes occasional monographs, studies, and position papers.

★479★ International Prostitutes Collective U.S. PROStitutes Collective (US PROS)
PO Box 14512
San Francisco, CA 94114
Phone: (415)558-9628
Rachel West, Spokesperson

Founded: 1980. **Description:** US PROS is a multi-racial network of women campaigning for the abolition of prostitution laws; human, legal, and civil rights for prostitute women; and higher benefits, student grants, wages, housing for all women. The organizations opposes legislated police and government control of prostitutes. **Publications:** ECP Network, irregular. • Prostitutes—Our Life. • The Hooker and the Break—A Time to Break The Law? • Prostitute Women and AIDS—Resisting the Virus of Repression. • Anti-porn Is the Theory, Repression is the Practice. **Formerly:** New York Prostitutes Collective.

★480★ International Society of Women Airline Pilots (ISA)
PO Box 66268
Chicago, IL 60666-0268
Sue Nielsen, Sec.

Founded: 1978. **Description:** Women airline pilots employed as flight crew members or holding seniority numbers with a major air carrier that operates at least 1 aircraft with a gross weight of 90,000 pounds or more. Fosters international cooperation and exchange among women in the profession. Operates information bank for women interested in entering the field. Maintains speakers' bureau and biographical archives. Recognizes members attaining the rank of captain. Operates Husbands of Airline Pilots auxiliary. **Members:** 350. **Publications:** International Society of Women Airline Pilots Membership Roster, annual. • International Society of Women Airline Pilots Newsletter, quarterly. **Formerly:** (1984) International Social Affiliation of Women Airline Pilots.

★481★ International Women's Anthropology Conference (IWAC)
Anthropology Department
25 Waverly Pl.
New York University
New York, NY 10003
Phone: (212)998-8550
Dr. Linda Basch, Sec.-Treas.

Founded: 1978. **Mailing List:** 450. **Description:** Women anthropologists and sociologists who are researching and teaching topics such as women's role in development, feminism, and the international women's movement. Encourages the exchange of information on research, projects, and funding; addresses policies concerning women from an anthropological perspective. Conducts periodic educational meetings with panel discussions. **Publications:** Bulletin, periodic. • IWAC Newsletter, semiannual.

★482★ International Women's Fishing Association (IWFA)
PO Drawer 3125
Palm Beach, FL 33480

Founded: 1955. **Description:** Sportfisherwomen. Promotes angling competition among women anglers; encourages conservation; fosters fishing tournaments of all kinds. Bestows monthly and annual awards for outstanding fishing accomplishments. Has established a scholarship trust to help graduate students further their education in the marine sciences. **Members:** 260. **Publications:** Hooks and Lines, bimonthly. • Yearbook.

★483★ International Women's Forum (NWF)
1146 19th St. NW, Ste. 700
Washington, DC 20036
Phone: (202)775-8917
Cindy M. Ryan, Pres.

Founded: 1980. **Description:** Domestic (19) and international (10) women's networks that seek to bring together women of influence and achievement and allow them to share ideas, experiences, and resources, and to solidify relationships that can enhance their effectiveness. Each state or local network is autonomous and may have different goals. **Members:** 29. **Publications:** Connection, periodic. Newsletter. **Formerly:** (1987) National Women's Forum.

★484★ International Women's Media Project (IWPM)
c/o Madison Public Affairs Group
2033 M St., NW, Ste. 900
Washington, DC 20036
Phone: (202)233-0030
Ed Gabriel, Dir.

Founded: 1985. **Description:** A project of the Mid-American Foundation. Purpose is to establish international, cross-cultural exchange between women working in print, television, radio, and other communications media. **Publications:** International Women's Media Project Newsletter, quarterly.

★485★ International Women's Rights Action Watch (IWRAW)
University of Minnesota
Humphrey Institute of Public Affairs
301 19th Ave. S
Minneapolis, MN 55455
Phone: (612)625-2505
Fax: (612)625-6351
Arvonne Fraser, Dir.

Description: Loosely organized network of activists and academics. Monitors changes in law and public policy according to the principles of the Convention on the Elimination of All Forms of Discrimination Against Women. (The convention has been ratified by over 100 nations and sets standards for achieving equality between women and men. It also states the rights necessary for women to fully contribute to the development process.) Works to increase public awareness of and encourage conformity to the principles of the Convention. Encourages research and reporting on the Convention principles and violations. Supports and reviews the work of the Committee on the Elimination of Discrimination Against Women (CEDAW). Promotes the availability of legal services and literacy for women. Acts as a clearinghouse for information on the Convention, women's status worldwide, and women's organizations and activities. **Publications:** Women's Watch (in English and Spanish), periodic. • Also publishes Assessing the Status of Women: A Guide to Reporting Under the Convention (in Arabic, English, French, and Spanish), Women's Human Rights and Reproductive Rights: Capacity and Choice, Implementing the International Right to Sexual Nondiscrimination (bibliography), and reports. Distributes videotapes.

★486★ International Women's Tribune Centre (IWTC)
777 United Nations Plaza, 3rd Fl.
New York, NY 10017
Phone: (212)687-8633
Fax: (212)661-2704
Dr. Anne S. Walker, Ph.D., Dir.

Founded: 1976. **Description:** Women's development communications service responding to requests for information and technical assistance from individuals around the world who are involved in women's projects in the Third World. Seeks to develop communication methods and educational materials in collaboration with regional women's groups. Acts as a clearinghouse for and about women in development activities; conducts workshops; provides advisory services in low-cost media, women's resource centers, communications techniques, and organizational developments; compiles resource books; and maintains library of 5000 books, 550 periodicals, 52 file drawers of subject information and reports, a project data bank, and slide archives. **Telecommunications Services:** Cable, TRIBCEN NY. **Publications:** The Tribune (in English, French, and Spanish), quarterly. Newsletter covering women's projects throughout the developing world. Includes bibliographies and calendar of events. • The Women $hare Funding Newsnote (in English, French, and Spanish), periodic, Bulletin. Includes information on new grant programs and policy initiatives re: funding on books and funding initiatives. • Also publishes information on funding and proposal writing, appropriate technology for women, UN resolutions of interest to women, and networking activities linking women worldwide. **Formerly:** (1978) International Women's Year/Tribune Project.

★487★ International Women's Writing Guild (IWWG)
Box 810, Gracie Sta.
New York, NY 10028-0082
Phone: (212)737-7536
Hannelore Hahn, Exec.Dir.

Founded: 1976. **Description:** Women writers in 24 countries interested in expressing themselves through the written word professionally and for personal growth. Facilitates manuscript submissions to literary agents. Conducts writing workshops and educational conferences. Participates in international network. Maintains health insurance program at group rates; bestows Artist of Life Award. **Members:** 6000. **Publications:** *International Women's Writing Guild–Network*, bimonthly. Magazine helping women writers publish their work. Includes calendar of events; lists awards, employment opportunities, and current information on environmental issues.

★488★ Iota Sigma Pi
c/o Dr. Antoinette J. Hockman
634 Huson St.
Hoboken, NJ 07030
Dora C. Warren, President

Founded: 1902. **Description:** National honor society for women in chemistry. Major objectives are to promote interest in chemistry among women students and to foster mutual advancement in academic, business and social life. **Publications:** *The Iotan Newsletter*.

★489★ Iris Films/Iris Feminist Collective
Box 5353
Berkeley, CA 94705
Phone: (415)658-5763
Frances Reid, Pres.

Founded: 1975. **Description:** Produces realistic, entertaining films with strong positive images of women; seeks to share skills and to open the film field to more women. Produces films for women's groups, organizations, and companies. Conducts seminars, workshops, and classes in film and feminist film theory. **Members:** 3. **Formerly:** (1978) Iris Films.

★490★ Jewish Foundation for Education of Women (JFEW)
330 W. 58th St.
New York, NY 10019
Phone: (212)265-2565
Florence Wallach, Exec.Dir.

Founded: 1880. **Description:** Conducts charitable programs; bestows awards. **Members:** 32. **Formerly:** Educational Foundation for Jewish Girls; (1977) Jewish Foundation for Education of Girls.

★491★ Jewish War Veterans of the U.S.A.—National Ladies Auxiliary (JWVA)
1811 R St. NW
Washington, DC 20009
Phone: (202)667-9061
Charlotte Steinburg, Admin.

Founded: 1928. **Description:** Sisters, wives, mothers, daughters, widows, and lineal descendants of Jewish veterans of wars of the United States. Provides scholarships; sends gifts to servicemen overseas; conducts youth programs; provides service to hospitalized veterans. Has furnished a surgical wing at Chaim Sheba Medical Center in Israel and has contrib-

uted equipment to an amniotic laboratory there. Presents Humanity Awards annually to all military academies. Provides children's services; conducts charitable program. **Members:** 11,000. **Regional Groups:** 300. **Publications:** *Bulletin*, quarterly.

★492★ Johns and Call Girls United Against Repression (JACGUAR)
PO Box 021011
Brooklyn, NY 11202-0022
Hugh Montgomery, Pres.

Founded: 1978. **Description:** Seeks to: dispel "the notion that there is anything reprehensible or immoral in being a prostitute whose customers are adults, or in being the customer of an adult prostitute"; instill in adult prostitutes and their adult customers a sense of self-respect. Works to legally safeguard civil rights and liberties of prostitutes and their customers, and to repeal laws criminalizing prostitution. Speaks out on public issues affecting prostitutes and their customers; testifies at legislative hearings; maintains speakers' bureau. Sponsors litigation challenging antiprostitution laws. **Members:** 11.

★493★ Joint Custody Association (JCA)
10606 Wilkins Ave.
Los Angeles, CA 90024
Phone: (213)475-5352
James A. Cook, Pres.

Founded: 1980. **Description:** Psychologists, psychiatrists, physicians, social workers, marital and family counselors, attorneys, judges, concerned parents, authors of texts on joint custody, and others concerned with joint custody of children and related divorce issues. Disseminates information on joint custody for the children of divorce; surveys court decisions and their consequences. Assists children, parents, attorneys, counselors, and jurists with implementation of joint custody practices. Fosters introduction of legislation in several states regarding joint custody for children involved in divorce. Maintains bibliographical archives of joint custody and other materials. **Members:** 3000.

★494★ Judean Society (JS)
1075 Space Pkwy., No. 336
Mountain View, CA 94043
Phone: (415)964-8936
Mrs. Frances A. Miller, Foundress

Founded: 1952. **Description:** Divorced Catholic women who meet to offer personal comfort and inspiration to one another; other women of various religions concerned with divorce, separation, and their accompanying problems. Provides educational material regarding Catholic doctrine in terms of the Catholic divorced lifestyle. Encourages all divorced Catholics to remain in harmony with the church. Provides special counseling for marriage investigations and for the return to the sacraments for invalidly married Catholics. Sponsors retreats, workshops, Days of Recollection, and home masses to inspire and strengthen members' efforts to continue to do the will of God; also sponsors social activities. Maintains speakers' bureau. Conducts educational classes on Catholic doctrine regarding marriage and divorce, life after civil divorce, self-discovery, and personal growth. **Publications:** *Steps to Effective Living* and *Life After Civil Divorce*.

★495★ Junior Catholic Daughters of the Americas (JCDA)
Ten W. 71st St., Ste. 401
New York, NY 10023
Phone: (212)799-7870
Kathleen M. Gearey, Coordinator

Founded: 1926. **Description:** Sponsored by Catholic Daughters of the Americas (see separate entry) for girls ages six to 18. Conducts leadership training covering spiritual, charitable, cultural, and recreational activities. **Members:** 7000. **State Groups:** 16. **Local Groups:** 220. **Publications:** *Junior Catholic Daughters of the Americas—Spotlight*, three per year. Newsletter highlighting the leadership training provided by the organization for girls ages 6 to 18 covering the spiritual, charitable, cultural, and recreational facets of life. Provides news of the organization and its members. • *Spotlight* (newsletter), 3/year.

★496★ Justice for Women (JFW)
100 Witherspoon St., Rm. 4608A
Louisville, KY 40202
Phone: (502)569-5385
Fax: (502)569-5018
Rev. Mary J. Kuhns, Assoc.

Founded: 1988. **Description:** Division of United Presbyterian Church in the U.S.A. Women's Ministry Unit. Purpose is "to serve as the focal point for the identification of issues and church-wide policy relating to the status of women and their position within the church and society." Addresses issues of feminist theologies, inclusive language, and reproductive rights. Among its responsibilities are: evaluating programs of the church's agencies and governing units in terms of their compliance with denominational policies concerning the status of women; providing resources to task forces and committees on women in denomination's area structures. Conducts research on the status of women; sponsors training workshops. **Members:** 21. **Publications:** *Newsletter*, quarterly.

★497★ Ki-Wives International
c/o Myrna Bailey
17101 Quarter Horse Way
Olney, MD 20832
Phone: (301)570-0917
Myrna Bailey, Pres.

Founded: 1945. **Description:** Wives and widows of Kiwanis International club members and other women interested in community and civic improvement united to conduct civic service, social, and charitable projects. Encourages a closer fellowship among families of Kiwanis Clubs members; assists in the formation of new clubs. Conducts educational and charitable programs for battered wives, the homeless, the elderly, and needy children; bestows awards annually to the Ki-Wife of the Year, Ki-Wife Club of the Year, and the club with the greatest membership growth; makes available scholarships. Sponsors Keyette International for high school girls. **Members:** 400. **Local Groups:** 23. **Publications:** *Ki-Wives International Newsletter*, semiannual. **Formerly:** Ki-Wives National.

★498★ Know, Inc. (KI)
PO Box 86031
Pittsburgh, PA 15221
Phone: (412)241-4844
Phyllis Wetherby, Pres.

Founded: 1969. **Description:** "All members are dedicated to human equality." Objectives include: to publish articles about human rights; to discuss problems of discrimination where they exist; to investigate problems in human rights, particularly those unique to women's changing role in society; to educate with regard to changing roles of men and women. Maintains 1000 volume library of feminist books, periodicals, newsletters, and newspapers. **Members:** 1000. **Publications:** *Know News Service*, periodic. • Also issues books and pamphlets.

★499★ La Leche League International (LLLI)
9616 Minneapolis Ave.
PO Box 1209
Franklin Park, IL 60131
Phone: (708)455-7730
Toll-free: 800-LA-LECHE
Fax: (708)455-0125
Betty Wagner, Exec.Dir.

Founded: 1956. **Description:** Women in 49 countries interested in fostering good mothering through breastfeeding. Group maintains that breastfeeding infants will encourage closer family relationships. Has organized a professional advisory board and 485 breastfeeding resource centers in 40 countries. Supplies information through publications, telephone service, and correspondence. Conducts annual breastfeeding seminars for physicians and 7 lactation specialist workshops annually. Maintains library of 200 books and monographs on breast-feeding and parenting. **Members:** 40,000. **Local Groups:** 3009. **Computerized Services:** Membership list; online. **Publications:** *Alumnae News*, quarterly. • *Annual Report.* • *Breastfeeding Abstracts*, quarterly. Emphasizes clinical applications; includes book reviews. • *LaLeche League Directory*, annual. • *LaLeche League International Catalogue*, semiannual. • *Leaven*, bimonthly. • *LLLI Personnel Directory*, annual. • *New Beginnings*, bimonthly. Journal including articles about breastfeeding, parenting, family life, and nutrition, and book reviews. • Also publishes books, including *Breastfeeding Answer Book, The Womanly Art of Breastfeeding, Nighttime Parenting, Of Cradles and Careers: A Guide to Reshaping Your Job to Include a Baby in Your Life, Mothering Multiples, Safe and Healthy: A Parents Guide to Children's Illnesses and Accidents, Whole Foods for the Whole Family* (cookbook), and numerous pamphlets, booklets, and reprints. Publication catalog available.

★500★ Lact-Aid International (LAI)
PO Box 1066
Athens, TN 37303
Phone: (615)744-9090
Toll-free: 800-228-1933
Ms. Jimmie Lynne Avery, Exec.Dir.

Founded: 1983. **Description:** Company that produces nursing trainers and other products to assist in breastfeeding. Offers breastfeeding information to medical doctors and parents (for a fee). Distributes neonatal and pediatric home health care products. Conducts continuing education seminars and workshops. **Publications:** Makes available back issues of *Keeping Abreast Journal* and other publications dealing with breastfeeding.

★501★ Ladies Against Women (LAW)
48 Shattuck Sq., Ste. 70
Berkeley, CA 94704
Phone: (510)841-6500
Mrs. T. "Bill" Banks, Lady Chair-Man

Founded: 1980. **Description:** "Decent ladies with a moral imperative to return to the Good Old Days"; male authority figures; supporting groups such as Moral Sorority and Another Mother for World Domination. Conducts seminars for "uppity women" designed to promote stress reduction through apathy; sponsors consciousness-lowering sessions. Supports right-thinking with fundraiser, including an endangered accessories fashion show (Save the Stoles), bakesales for the Pentagon, guest disruptions of women's events, and picket-reception-lines for "real ladies." Advocates banning books, not bombs. Operates speakers' bureau on issues such as "repealing the women's vote, and the need for a national dress code." Bestows awards. Maintains library of tapes, interviews, newsclippings, and press releases. **Members:** 12,000. **Local Groups:** 26. **Publications:** *National Embroiderer*, periodic. • Also publishes *LAW Consciousness Lowering Kit* and *Ladyfesto*.

★502★ Ladies Apparel Contractors Association (LACA)
450 7th Ave.
New York, NY 10123
Phone: (212)564-6161
Sidney Reiff, Exec.Dir.

Founded: 1964. **Description:** Apparel contractors. Conducts labor negotiations, legislative activities, and other services for members. Sponsors seminars. **Members:** 175. **Formerly:** (1977) Popular Price Dress Contractors Association.

★503★ Ladies' Auxiliary of the American Beekeeping Federation (LAABF)
3927 North Rd. 3 W.
Monte Vista, CO 81144
Phone: (303)852-2301
Judy Haefeli, Pres.

Founded: 1953. **Description:** Mothers, wives, and daughters of beekeepers; other women interested in beekeeping. To promote the use and sale of honey, particularly honey's use in the home and community. Sponsors Honey Queen competition. **Members:** 200.

★504★ Ladies Auxiliary, Military Order of the Purple Heart, United States of America (LAMOPH)
419 Franklin St.
Reading, MA 01867
Phone: (617)944-1844
Nancy C. Klare, Sec.

Founded: 1932. **Description:** Female lineal descendants of veterans who have been wounded in combat and awarded the Purple Heart. Activities include: hospital work; child welfare; Americanism and community service; rehabilitation projects. Presents awards annually. **Members:** 3500. **Regional Groups:** 5. **State Groups:** 15. **Local Groups:** 130. **Computerized Services:** Magazine mailing list; membership notices. **Publications:** *Directory of Departments and Units*, annual. • *Newsletter*, 10/year. • *The Purple Heart Magazine*, bimonthly. • Plans to publish *Directory of Unit and Departments*.

★505★ Ladies Auxiliary to the Veterans of Foreign Wars of the United States (LAVFWUS)
406 W. 34th St.
Kansas City, MO 64111
Phone: (816)561-8655
Mrs. Glenn Grossman, Sec.-Treas.

Founded: 1914. **Description:** Wives, widows, mothers, stepmothers, grandmothers, daughters, foster daughters, stepdaughters, granddaughters, sisters, half sisters, stepsisters, and foster sisters of overseas campaign medal service veterans; women eligible for VFW. Conducts voluntary hospital and rehabilitation work and sponsors various patriotic, Americanism, and youth activities. Supports VFW National Home, Eaton Rapids, MI. Presents annual Better World, Unsung Heroine, and other humanitarian awards. Presents college scholarships to junior girls; also presents three cancer research fellowships. Sponsors patriotic art competition and bestows monetary awards. **Members:** 765,000. **State Groups:** 51. **Local Groups:** 7091. **Publications:** *Directory*, annual. • *National Auxiliary Magazine*, 8/year. • *Program Book*, annual.

★506★ Ladies of the Grand Army of the Republic (LGAR)
c/o Elizabeth B. Koch
204 E. Sellers Ave.
Ridley Park, PA 19078
Phone: (215)521-1328
Elizabeth B. Koch, Exec. Officer

Founded: 1885. **Description:** Female lineal descendants of soldiers, sailors, and marines honorably discharged as Union Civil War veterans. Programs include assistance to veterans and presentation of flags to youth and civic groups. Maintains museum; presents awards; compiles statistics. **Members:** 2000. **State Groups:** 26. **Local Groups:** 25. **Publications:** *Bugle Call*, quarterly. • *Journal*, annual. • *Roster*, annual. • *Roster of Officers - Past Officers*, annual. **Formerly:** (1886) Loyal Ladies League.

★507★ Ladies Kennel Association of America (LKA of A)
465 Edgewood Ave.
St. James, NY 11780
Mrs. Jack Provenzano, Sec.

Founded: 1901. **Description:** Holds an annual all-breed dog show and to encourage the intelligent breeding of purebred dogs. **Members:** 16.

★508★ LADIES - Life After Divorce Is Eventually Sane
PO Box 2974
Beverly Hills, CA 90213

Founded: 1983. **Description:** Ex-wives of famous men. Support group for divorced wives of celebrities that originated during a USA Cable show titled "Are You Anybody?" Seeks to form a network of support among other ex-wives in similar situations, and to assist in creating informal groups called LADIES Too whose members are ex-wives of non-famous men. Plans to offer discussion panels for other women's groups. **Members:** 15.

★509★ Ladies Oriental Shrine of North America (LOS of NA)
1111 E. 54th St., Ste. 111
Indianapolis, IN 46220
Phone: (317)259-1996
Fax: (317)253-4501
Betty J. Rathbun, Grand Recorder

Founded: 1914. **Description:** Wives, mothers, sisters, and daughters of members of the Imperial Council of the Ancient Arabic Order Nobles of the Mystic Shrine for North America. Conducts projects to raise funds for the Shriners' Hospitals for Crippled and Burned Children. **Members:** 32,000. **Publications:** *Proceedings*, annual.

★510★ Ladies Professional Bowlers Tour (LPBT)
7171 Cherryvale Blvd.
Rockford, IL 61112
Phone: (815)332-5756
Fax: (815)332-9636
John F. Falzone, Pres.

Founded: 1981. **Description:** Professional women bowlers. Conducts women's world-class championship professional bowling tournaments; presents special competition player awards for outstanding performances. Compiles annual and career competition statistics. Supplies photographic and other promotional services to the bowling industry. **Members:** 150. **Publications:** *Ladies Professional Bowlers Tour—Newsletter*, bimonthly. • *Ladies Professional Bowlers Tour—Official Rules and Regulations*, annual. Includes membership listing, policies, and procedures for all Ladies Pro Bowlers Tour tournaments, and tournaments conducted for others by the LPBT. • *LPBT Booster Club News*, quarterly. Contains news and highlights for bowling fans. • *LPBT Tour Guide*, annual. Program covering previous year's professional tournaments, records, statistics, and profiles of top women bowlers. Includes biographies of women professional bowling champions.

★511★ Ladies Professional Golf Association (LPGA)
2570 Vousia St., Ste. B
Daytona, FL 32114
Phone: (904)254-8800
Fax: (713)980-4352
Charles S. Mechem, Commissioner

Founded: 1950. **Description:** Professional women golfers and educators. Compiles statistics on tournaments, money winnings, and scoring. Assists members in finding golfing positions. Provides major retirement program for members; maintains hall of fame; bestows awards. **Members:** 678. **Publications:** *Fairway Magazine*, annual. Journal; includes player profiles, golf fashion section, statistics, tournament reports, and tournament schedule. • *Ladies Professional Golf Association-Schedule Directory*, annual. Lists tournament date, venue, purse, defending champion, and contact telephone number. • *Player Guide*, annual. Media guide including player biographies, tournament histories and information, LPGA records and statistics, information on LPGA awards, staff directory, and tournament schedule. **Formerly:** (1948) Women's Professional Golf Association.

★512★ Ladyslipper
PO Box 3124
Durham, NC 27715
Phone: (919)683-1570
Toll-free: 800-834-6044
Fax: (919)682-5601
Laurie Fuchs, Dir.

Founded: 1976. **Description:** Seeks to increase public awareness of the achievements of women artists and musicians and expand the scope and availability of musical and literary recordings by women. Makes available information on recordings by female musicians, writers, and composers. **Publications:** *Ladyslipper Catalog: Resource Guide to Records, Tapes, Compact Discs, and Videos by Women*, annual. Arranged by artist; includes music reviews. • Also distributes songbooks, pamphlets, audiocassettes, and audiodiscs.

★513★ Last Harvest (LH)
S. Tower, Ste. 810
2720 Stemmons Fwy.
Dallas, TX 75207
Phone: (214)630-6565
Ken Freeman, Pres.

Founded: 1984. **Description:** Offers information, counseling, and referrals to women who have had or are considering abortions. Operates speakers' bureau; produces radio programs. **Local Groups:** 80. **Computerized Services:** Data base listing locations of post-abortion recovery and support centers. **Publications:** *Ministry Memo*, monthly. Newsletter. • *Rachel's Circle*, monthly. Newsletter. • Also publishes *Healing Hurts of Abortion* (workbook) and *Behind Closed Doors*.

★514★ Latin American Professional Women's Association (LAPWA)
3516 N. Broadway
Los Angeles, CA 90031
Phone: (213)227-9060
Alicia Fuentes Unger, Treasurer

Founded: 1975. **Description:** The Association provides a mutual support group for Latin American women and promotes leadership, community awareness, professional development, and positive role models. LAPWA sponsors the Hermanita/Little Sister Program and the Adelante Mujer Hespana Conference, and offers a scholarship for women over 25 years of age. **Publications:** *Latin American Professional Women's Newsletter*. **Formerly:** Los Angeles Bilingual Secretaries Association (1978).

★515★ Latin American Studies Association
Task Force on Women in Latin American Studies
Darthmouth College
Faculty for the Social Sciences
Hanover, NH 03755
Marysa Navarro, Chair

★516★ Leadership Conference of Women Religious of the U.S.A. (LCWR)
8808 Cameron St.
Silver Spring, MD 20910
Phone: (301)588-4955
Fax: (301)587-4575
Sr. Janet Roesener, CSJ, Exec.Dir.

Founded: 1956. **Description:** Chief administrative officers of Roman Catholic communities of women religious in the U.S. Offers opportunity for discussion and exchange of ideas and information relative to women religious and to administration/leadership in religious orders. Organizes and promotes studies of matters of common interest. Provides information on matters affecting religious orders. Maintains national file of source references. **Members:** 820. **Regional Groups:** 15. **Publications:** *Directory*, annual. • *Newsletter*, monthly. **Formerly:** (1971) Conference of Major Religious Superiors of Women's Institutes of the United States of America.

★517★ League of Women Voters Education Fund (LWVEF)
1730 M St. NW
Washington, DC 20036
Phone: (202)429-1965

Founded: 1957. **Description:** Educational arm of the League of Women Voters of the United States (see separate entry). Conducts research on a variety of public policy issues including economic policy, nuclear and solid waste, social welfare, child care, and health care. Encourages more effective citizen participation in government. Organizes seminars. **Publications:** *Annual Report*. • Also publishes *Safety on Tap: A Citizen's Drinking Water Guide, Presidential Debates: 1988 and Beyond, The Nuclear Waste Primer, Understanding Economic Policy, America's Growing Dilemma: Pesticides in Food and Water*, guides, reports, and a catalog of educational pamphlets.

★518★ League of Women Voters of the United States (LWVUS)
1730 M St. NW
Washington, DC 20036
Phone: (202)429-1965
Fax: (202)429-0854
Gracia Hillman, Exec.Dir.

Founded: 1920. **Description:** Voluntary organization of citizens (men and women) 18 years old or over. Promotes political responsibility through informed and active participation of citizens in government and acts on selected governmental issues. Members select and study public policy issues at local, state, and national levels and take political action on these issues. Leagues at all levels distribute information on candidates and issues and campaign to encourage registration and voting. Does not support or oppose candidates or political parties. National concerns include government, international relations, natural resources, and social policy. Evolved from the National American Woman Suffrage Association, following the fight for woman suffrage. **Members:** 110,000. **Regional Groups:** 32. **State Groups:** 50. **Local Groups:** 1250. **Publications:** *Annual Report*. • *National Voter*, bimonthly. • *Report From the Hill*, bimonthly. • Also publishes leadership handbooks. **Formerly:** (1946) National League of Women Voters.

★519★ Legal Advocates for Women (LAW)
320 Clement
San Francisco, CA 94118
Ginny Foat, Exec.Dir.

Founded: 1984. **Description:** To educate women about their rights and responsibilities within the legal system; to improve the legal status and social condition of women. Works with and monitors legal cases such as those involving sexual harassment, discrimination, and physical abuse of wives by their husbands. Is currently developing a women's prison network to improve prison conditions and aid women following their release. Provides educational materials, expertise, and referrals; conducts research; maintains speakers' bureau. **Publications:** *Legal Case Studies*, periodic.

★520★ Legion of Young Polish Women (LYPW)
c/o Copernicus Center
5216 W. Lawrence
Chicago, IL 60630
Maria Ciesla, Pres.

Founded: 1939. **Description:** Women of Polish descent interested in promoting the cultural and social goals of the Polish American community and assisting Poles throughout the world. Provides financial assistance to Polish and American institutions and foundations. Sends medical supplies to Poland and participates in funding scholarships, exhibits, competitions, and publications. Since 1945, has sponsored the presentation of debutantes at the annual White and Red Ball. **Members:** 150.

★521★ Lesbian Feminist Liberation (LFL)
Gay Community Center
208 W. 13th St.
New York, NY 10011
Phone: (212)620-7310
Eleanor Cooper, Spokeswoman

Founded: 1973. **Description:** Women united to promote lesbian and women's rights. Works to change the attitudes and institutions that limit or deny women the control of their own lives and bodies. Activities include: coalitions with feminist and gay groups; lobbying; direct confrontation tactics (such as nonviolent demonstrations and sit-ins); educational programs. Conducts dances, concerts, sports events, and conferences. **Members:** 20.

★522★ Lesbian Herstory Educational Foundation, Inc. (LHEF)
PO Box 1258
New York, NY 10116
Phone: (212)874-7232
Joan Nestle, Sec.

Founded: 1974. **Description:** Works to gather, preserve, and share information on the lives and activities of lesbians worldwide. Maintains Lesbian Herstory Archives resource room including periodicals, diaries, tapes, photographs, poetry, prose, research papers, graphics, and other memorabilia on all aspects of the lesbian culture. Makes available guest speakers and offers slide shows for schools and community groups. **Publications:** *Lesbian Herstory Archives Newsletter*, periodic. Lists bibliographies and reviews lesbian cultural material; includes research updates. • Also publishes bibliographies.

★523★ Lesbian Mothers National Defense Fund (LMNDF)
PO Box 21567
Seattle, WA 98111
Phone: (206)325-2643
Jenny Sayward, Contact

Founded: 1974. **Description:** Provides legal, emotional, and financial support for lesbian mothers involved with custody problems. Monitors and reports on judicial and legislative activities and decisions affecting gay and lesbian parents. Conducts specialized education. Provides alternative conception and adoption

information, information bank, and lawyer referral service. Maintains speakers' bureau. **Members:** 450. **Telecommunications Services:** 24-hour answering service. **Publications:** *Mom's Apple Pie*, quarterly. Newsletter reporting on lesbian custody cases, current legislation, and other issues surrounding lesbian parenting. Includes book reviews.

★524★ Lesbian Resource Center (LRC)
1208 E. Pine St.
Seattle, WA 98122
Phone: (206)322-3953
Cherie Larson, Dir.

Founded: 1971. **Description:** Provides classes, support groups, workshops, social activities, and information on housing, employment, and lesbian community groups. Maintains lending library and collection of research materials; operates speakers' bureau. Represents the lesbian community in areas of political and social concern. **Telecommunications Services:** Telephone referral services. **Publications:** *Lesbian Resource Center Community News*, monthly. Newspaper covering community and center events; includes calendar, poetry, and news stories. • Also publishes informational brochure. **Formerly:** (1973) Gay Women's Alliance. **Also known as:** Pacific Women's Resources.

★525★ Lesbians United Non-Nuclear Action (LUNA)
46 Pleasant Street
Cambridge, MA 02138

★526★ Libertarians for Life (LFL)
13424 Hathaway Dr.
Department 25
Wheaton, MD 20906
Phone: (301)460-4141
Doris Gordon, Coordinator

Founded: 1976. **Description:** Purpose is to show that abortion, child abandonment, involuntary euthanasia, and involuntary medical experimentation constitute aggression under libertarian principles and that libertarianism is a pro-life philosophy. Supports libertarian view that aggression as a means of obtaining any goal, however worthy, is unjust. (Arguments are expressly philosophical rather than religious or pragmatic.) Explains the philosophical basis for parental obligation to provide care and protection for their children, born, and pre-born. Distributes literature; provides speakers; arranges or aids in arrangement of discussion and panel groups at libertarian and nonlibertarian functions. **Publications:** *LFL Reports*, periodic. Newsletter; includes book reviews and calendar of events. • Also publishes pamphlets.

★527★ Liberty Godparent Ministry (LGM)
1000 Villa Rd.
Lynchburg, VA 24503
Phone: (804)384-3043
Toll-free: 800-542-4453
Fax: (804)384-3730
Dr. Gregg Albers, Exec.V.Pres.

Founded: 1982. **Description:** Offers an alternative to abortion by meeting the immediate and long-term needs of teens in crisis pregnancy situations. Goal is "to change one life and save another through sharing the gospel of Jesus Christ" via the ministry's educational and outreach program. The program consists of three divisions: the Pregnancy Crisis Center offers a hot line, free pregnancy testing, educational

materials and counseling about alternatives to abortion; the Maternity Home, a residential care facility for women aged 12-21, offers life skills training, health services, counseling, and Christian education which centers on sharing the principles of the Bible and the claims of Jesus Christ and encouraging each woman to attend church regularly; the Adoption Agency places children in "dedicated, Bible-believing Christian families" which have been screened and spiritually prepared for the adoption by the ministry. Offers guidance in the establishment of local pregnancy crisis centers. Operates speakers' bureau. **Publications:** *What About Me.* **Formerly:** (1986) Save-A-Baby.

★528★ Linguistic Society of America (LSA)
Committee on the Status of Women in Linguistics
1325 18th St. NW, Ste. 211
Washington, DC 20036-6501
Phone: (202)835-1714
Penny Eckert, Chair

Description: The Committee is concerned with developing policy guidelines for the use of nonsexist language. It encourages research on women and language, as well as women in the linguistics profession.

★529★ The Links, Inc.
1200 Massachusetts Ave. NW
Washington, DC 20005
Phone: (202)842-8686
Mary P. Douglas, Chief Administrative Officer

Founded: 1946. **Description:** Links is an organization of African-American women committed to the community through educational, cultural, and civic activities. It provides enrichment experiences for those who are educationally disadvantaged and culturally deprived, and support for talented individuals. The organization also sponsors charitable activities and a National Grant-In-Aid program. **Publications:** *Link to Link*, quarterly newsletter. • *Links Directory*, quadrennial. • Also publishes journal.

★530★ Lithuanian Catholic Women (LCW)
3005 N. 124th St.
Brookfield, WI 53005
Phone: (508)756-0189
Dale Murray, Pres.

Founded: 1914. **Description:** Catholic-Lithuanian women or women married to Lithuanians who are interested in their heritage, and in the politics of Lithuania and America. Conducts regional seminars. Maintains archives at Kent State University in Ohio. Bestows membership and outstanding Lithuanian woman awards; presents scholarships. Operates speakers' bureau. **Members:** 2500. **Regional Groups:** 8. **State Groups:** 40. **Local Groups:** 40. **Publications:** *Newsletter*, semiannual. • *Women's Field*, bimonthly. • Also publishes Lithuanian cookbook. **Formerly:** (1990) American Lithuanian Roman Catholic Women's Alliance.

★531★ Looking Up (LU)
PO Box K
Augusta, ME 04332
Phone: (207)626-3402
Kathy Lamb, Exec.Dir.

Founded: 1983. **Description:** Survivors of incest and sexual and child abuse; individuals and groups meeting the needs of formerly and presently abused individuals. Fosters public awareness and concern over the plight of sexually abused victims and survivors of all ages. Encourages victims and survivors to apply the courage, creativity, and strength that enabled them to withstand the abuse to building full and satisfactory futures. Offers education, information, and advice to those abused and those concerned. Sponsors the Wilderness Program, workshops and retreats; maintains resource referral and trust fund. Does not serve sexual or child abuse offenders. **Publications:** *Looking Up Times*, semiannual. Journal. • *Survivor Resource Chronicle*, quarterly. Newsletter.

★532★ Love-N-Addiction (LNA)
PO Box 759
Willimantic, CT 06226
Phone: (203)423-2344
Carolyn C. Meister, Founder

Founded: 1986. **Description:** Selfhelp support groups; individual members are women who exhibit emotionally addictive and self-destructive behavior in relationships. Focuses on relationships that jeopardize the women's emotional and physical well-being. Members seek recovery through the sharing of knowledge and personal experiences. Offers consultations; maintains speakers' bureau. **Publications:** *Self-Help Group Starter Packet*.

★533★ Lubavitch Women's Organization (LWO)
398 Kingston Ave.
Brooklyn, NY 11225
Phone: (718)493-1773
Fax: (718)604-0594
Shterna Spritzer, Pres.

Founded: 1955. **Description:** Jewish women and girls. Sponsored by the Lubavitch Movement. Purposes are: to bring Jewish heritage and culture to Jewish women and girls; to enhance their knowledge and practice of Jewish traditions and customs, including religious candle lighting rituals, establishment and maintenance of Kosher homes, family and marriage laws, and holidays; to increase public awareness of Jewish culture, heritage, and tradition. Conducts adult education classes on Jewish laws and customs. Holds annual Week of the Jewish Woman seminars and workshops. Sponsors charitable programs; offers children's services; operates speakers' bureau. **Members:** 12,000. **Regional Groups:** 136. **Publications:** *Convention Journal*, annual. • *International N'shei Chabad Newsletter*, semiannual. • *N'shei Chabad Newsletter*, bimonthly. • *Yiddish Heim*, quarterly. • Also publishes *All the Days of Her Life* and *Shlichus - Meeting the Outreach Challenge* (books), *Aura, The Modern Jewish Woman: A Unique Perspective, The Spice and Spirit of Kosher Cooking, Key to Eternity, The Gift, A Candle of My Own*, brochure, and pamphlet. **Also known as:** Agudas Nshei Ubnos Chabad.

★534★ Lutherans for Life (LFL)
PO Box 819
Benton, AR 72015
Phone: (501)794-2212
Fax: (501)794-1437
Rev. Edward Fehskens, Exec.Dir.

Founded: 1978. **Description:** Pro-life, pan-Lutheran educational and outreach organization seeking to promote respect for life at all stages from conception to natural death. Assists Lu-

theran colleges, congregations, and seminaries in establishing programs that educate the public about euthanasia, abortion, infanticide, and related life issues; helps church bodies reexamine their stances on these issues; provides resources on life issues. Encourages participation in public policy-making processes. Offers referral services to individuals experiencing crises and need; supports creation of crisis pregnancy and post-abortion counseling services. Operates speakers' bureau; bestows awards. Maintains library of books, booklets, pamphlets, and files on abortion and related issues. Holds regional seminars. **Members:** 4000. **State Groups:** 12. **Local Groups:** 280. **Publications:** *Life Date*, quarterly. Newsletter reporting on the care of children, unwed mothers, disabled persons, the poor, and the repressed. Covers issues such as abortion, adoption, euthanasia, infanticide, church policies and policy-making, and counseling and research related to these issues. Includes book reviews and legislative updates. • *Living*, quarterly. Magazine covering pro-life issues. • Also publishes Bible studies and worship materials, brochures, and tracts; produces educational videotapes.

★535★ MADRE
121 W. 27th St., Rm. 301
New York, NY 10001
Phone: (212)627-0444
Fax: (212)675-3704
Vivian Stromberg, Exec.Dir.

Founded: 1983. **Description:** Project of the Women's Peace Network. Seeks to: draw public attention to common needs of women and children in Central America and the U.S.; end U.S. intervention in Central America and the Caribbean; build bonds of friendship. Operates "twinning" program wherein U.S. day care centers are paired with Nicaraguan counterparts, facilitating educational and cultural exchange. Conducts health campaign to raise funds for improved health care for women and children, including delivery of medical supplies and training workshops by midwives and health professionals. Maintains Visual and Performing Arts Peace Curriculum for elementary and secondary schools focusing on problems faced by youth in the U.S. ("Madre" is Spanish for "mother.") **Members:** 23,000. **Computerized Services:** PeaceNet. **Publications:** *MADRE* (in English and Spanish), quarterly. Newsletter. • Also publishes brochures and fact sheets.

★536★ March for Life (ML)
Box 90300
Washington, DC 20090
Phone: (202)543-3377
Nellie J. Gray, Pres.

Founded: 1974. **Description:** Seeks to protect the value and dignity of each human being, including the unborn, and advocates a mandatory Human Life Amendment to the U.S. Constitution. Sponsors annual March for Life whereby pro-lifers come from across the nation to march in Washington, D.C. in protest to the 1973 U.S. Supreme Court decision legalizing abortion. Each year on Jan. 22 (date of march), ML sends the President, each member of Congress, and the U.S. Supreme Court a typed message and red rose on behalf of the unborn. Conducts lobbying activities and presents testimony from the pro-life viewpoint. **Publications:** *Action Memo*, periodic. • *Journal*, annual.

★537★ Maryknoll Sisters of St. Dominic
Maryknoll Sisters Center
Maryknoll, NY 10545
Phone: (914)941-7575
Sr. Claudette LaVerdiere, Pres.

Founded: 1912. **Description:** Catholic women missionaries. Purpose is to "proclaim the Gospel of Jesus Christ" through life witness, pastoral ministry, communication, and community development, education, health, research, and social service programs. Members live and work in thirty countries of Africa, Asia, the Central Pacific Islands, and North, Central, and South America. Operates Mission Institute which provides continuing education for missioners and a forum for the discussion of mission trends and critical issues facing the Christian mission. Operates placement service. Compiles statistics; maintains museum, biographical archives, and 44,000 volume library. **Members:** 808. **Regional Groups:** 23. **Local Groups:** 3. **Computerized Services:** Direct mail fundraising program; donor/sponsor records; membership records. **Publications:** *Central Board Communique*, bimonthly. For congregational use. • *General Assembly Proceedings*, every 6 years. • *Membership Directory*, quarterly. • Also publishes *Women in Mission: Maryknoll Sisters Today* (book).

★538★ Mary's Pence
PO Box 29078
Chicago, IL 60629-9078
Phone: (312)783-3177
Maureen Gallagher, Contact

Description: A Catholic women's organization that collects and distributes funds for alternative ministries, such as women's shelters, legal services, housing advocacy, economic development, education and literacy programs, and centers for creative theology.

★539★ Maternity Center Association (MCA)
48 E. 92nd St.
New York, NY 10128
Phone: (212)369-7300
Ruth W. Lubic, Gen.Dir.

Founded: 1918. **Description:** Laypersons, physicians, nurses, nurse-midwives, and public health workers interested in improvement of maternity care, maternal and infant health, and family life. Maintains two Childbearing Centers for low-risk families. Conducts classes for expectant parents. Sponsors research; administers nurse-midwifery student assistance fund; maintains extensive reference library. Co-sponsors community-based Nurse-Midwifery Education Program. **Members:** 600. **Publications:** *Special Delivery*. Newsletter containing information on the activities of the organization. • Also publishes *The Birth Atlas, Preparation for Childbearing*, teaching aids for health professionals, and pamphlets for expectant parents.

★540★ Math/Science Network
Preservation Park
678 13th St., Ste. 100
Oakland, CA 946122
Phone: (510)893-6284
Rebecca Failor, Contact

Founded: 1974. **Description:** Works to promote the participation of women and girls in science and mathematics. Collects and disseminates information relating to the issues of the underrepresentation of women in math and science. **Publications:** *Broadcast Newsletter.*

★541★ Media Fund for Human Rights (MFHR)
PO Box 8185
Universal City, CA 91608
Phone: (818)902-1476
R. J. Curry, Exec.Dir.

Founded: 1983. **Description:** An educational foundation of the Gay and Lesbian Press Association. Seeks to: reeducate the media and the American public about gays; utilize the media to change attitudes that deny gays full benefits of citizenship; enable gays to report their news; promote the accessibility of gay history nationwide.

★542★ Media Watch (MW)
PO Box 618
Santa Cruz, CA 95061-0618
Phone: (408)423-6355
Fax: (408)423-9119
Ann Simonton, Dir.

Founded: 1984. **Description:** Individuals dedicated to improving the image of women in the media. Believes women and girls worldwide suffer from a lack of self-esteem which is instilled and maintained by the profusion of sexist, racist, and violent images of women in the media. Works to educate the public concerning the consequences of sexually objectifying women and children in the media with the goal of helping people become critical consumers of all forms of mass media. Stages public protests, boycotts, letter writing campaigns, and fundraising events. Maintains speakers' bureau, biographical archives, and small library; conducts children's programs and educational workshops and seminars. Compiles statistics. **Members:** 800. **Local Groups:** 3. **Publications:** *Media Watch News*, quarterly. Includes items illustrating the dehumanization of women by the media and announcements of current boycott campaigns.

★543★ Medical Mission Sisters (MMS)
8400 Pine Rd.
Philadelphia, PA 19111
Phone: (215)742-6100
Sarah Summers, Superior Gen.

Founded: 1925. **Description:** International women's religious community that combines religious life with practice of medicine, surgery, and obstetrics. Maintains 50 health centers and hospital in India, Pakistan, Ghana, Uganda, Venezuela, Indonesia, the Philippines, Kenya, Malawi, Ethiopia, Zaire, Brazil, Peru, Nicaragua, U.S., Canada, England, Netherlands, Belgium, Germany, Italy, and Mexico. Conducts local training programs for professional and managerial staffs. **Members:** 700. **Regional Groups:** 6. **Publications:** *Medical Mission Sisters News*, 4-6/year. Newsletter.

★544★ Melpomene Institute for Women's Health Research (MIWHR)
c/o Judy Mahle Lutter
1010 University Ave.
St. Paul, MN 55104
Phone: (612)642-1951
Judy Mahle Lutter, Pres.

Founded: 1981. **Description:** Individuals professionally trained in healthcare, physical activity, and sports for girls and women. Researches

and disseminates information on issues such as body image, osteoporosis, athletic amenorrhea, exercise and pregnancy, and aging. Offers undergraduate and graduate internships, and volunteer programs. Provides consulting services for program evaluations. Sponsors competitions and physical activities with children. Bestows awards; operates speakers' bureau; maintains library. **Members:** 1200. **Computerized Services:** Access to more than 3000 articles arranged by category and keyword. **Publications:** *Melpomene Journal*, 3/year. Examines the relationship between physical activity and lifestyles. Features research reports, scientific bibliographies, and personal profiles. • *Newsletter*, quarterly. • Also publishes *The Bodywise Woman*, information packets, and brochures; produces videotape on osteoporosis.

★545★ MEND - Mothers Embracing Nuclear Disarmament
PO Box 2309
La Jolla, CA 92038
Phone: (619)454-3343
Maureen King, Exec.Dir.

Founded: 1985. **Description:** Works to achieve global peace and understanding by teaching women and children to become peace educators and citizen diplomats. Utilizes the universal appeal of parenthood to inspire a mutual commitment among nations toward the reduction and eventual elimination of nuclear weapons. Acknowledges the need for a strong national defense, but believes that without a new approach toward national security, the human race is in danger. Supports a multilateral, verifiable disarmament agreement. Conducts Peace Educators Program, which provides international exchange opportunities and leadership skills training for women and children, and Kids Talk to Kids, a pen pal program between children of the United States and those in India and the Soviet Union. Sponsors workshops and information booths. Maintains speakers' bureau and travelling children's peace exhibit. Offers issue development and public awareness events. **Members:** 2300. **State Groups:** 12. **Publications:** *Newsletter*, quarterly. • Also publishes *A Concerned Citizens Introduction to National Security, Reflections on War and Peace - Children Speak Out* (books), and *Children Wish for Peace* (pamphlet).

★546★ Mexican American Women's National Association (MANA)
1030 15th St. NW, Ste. 468
Washington, DC 20005
Phone: (202)898-2036

Founded: 1974. **Description:** Promotes leadership and economic and educational development for Mexican-American and other Hispanic women. Areas of concern include pay equity, adolescent pregnancy, and children in poverty. Offers leadership development course, which includes training at the national and local levels; operates Hermanitas Project, an annual conference on self-image building and career counseling for high school Hispanic girls. Presents scholarship awards annually. **Members:** 2000. **Local Groups:** 12. **Publications:** *Quarterly Newsletter*. • Also distributes *Issue Updates*.

★547★ Middle East Studies Association (MESA)
Association of Middle East Women's Studies
University of Arizona
1232 N. Cherry Ave.
Tucson, AZ 85721
Phone: (602)621-5850
Nancy Dishaw, Secretary

★548★ Midwest Parentcraft Center (MPC)
3921 N. Lincoln
Chicago, IL 60613
Phone: (312)281-6638
Margaret Gamper, R.N., Exec.Dir.

Founded: 1950. **Description:** Prenatal instructors, parents, and professionals involved in parenting and pregnancy. To instruct and educate expectant mothers and others in the Gamper Method of childbirth. (The Gamper Method, based on the teachings of several 19th century physicians and developed by Margaret Gamper in 1946, is designed to prepare the prospective mother for childbirth by instilling self-determination and confidence in her ability to work with the physiological changes of her body during pregnancy, labor, and delivery.) Conducts prenatal and grandparenting classes and workshops; operates in-service programs for hospitals and clinics; sponsors programs on topics such as grieving and history of birth procedures. Disseminates teaching aids including slides, films, records, and tapes. Grants childbirth educator certificates to qualified applicants who have taught Gamper Method classes under the supervision of an instructor. Operates charitable program and speakers' bureau; maintains library of 6000 volumes on childbirth, midwifery, marriage, sex, and childcare. The center's activities are currently concentrated in Ohio, Illinois, Indiana, Wisconsin, and Michigan. **Publications:** *Heir Raising News*, quarterly. • Also publishes *Preparation for the Heir Minded* (book).

★549★ Midwives Alliance of North America (MANA)
PO Box 1121
Bristol, VA 24203
Phone: (615)764-5561
Karen Moran, Exec.Dir.

Founded: 1982. **Description:** Midwives, student/apprentice midwives, and persons supportive of midwifery. Seeks to expand communication and support among midwives. Works to promote basic competency in midwives; develops and encourages guidelines for their education. Offers legal, legislative, and political advice and resource referrals; conducts networking on local, state, and regional bases; provides advice regarding insurance issues. Operates speakers' bureau; bestows awards; compiles statistics. **Members:** 900. **Regional Groups:** 8. **Publications:** *MANA Directory*, annual. • *MANA News*, quarterly. • Also publishes brochures.

★550★ Minority Women's Network (MWN)
PO Box 02545
Detroit, MI 48202

★551★ Miss Mom/Mister Mom
PO Box 547
Moab, UT 84532
Phone: (801)259-5090
Tina L. Lopez, Exec.Dir.

Founded: 1986. **Description:** Selfhelp support group for single parents. Provides information and counseling on parenting, substance abuse prevention, building self-esteem, and other issues. Bestows awards; conducts research, charitable, and educational programs; offers children's services. **Members:** 5000. **State Groups:** 2. **Local Groups:** 1. **Publications:** *Miss Mom/Mister Mom*, bimonthly. Newsletter. **Formerly:** Miss Mom.

★552★ **Missionary Association of Catholic Women (MACW)**
3521 W. National Ave.
Milwaukee, WI 53215
Phone: (414)384-8047
Elizabeth Schneider, Exec. Officer
Founded: 1916. **Description:** Makes vestments and altar linens for missions and participates in other activities aiding missions including providing sacred vessels and rosaries. **Members:** 2973.

★553★ **Missionary Sisters of the Society of Mary - Marist Missionary Sisters (SMSM)**
349 Grove St.
Waltham, MA 02154
Phone: (617)893-0149
Sr. Virginia Fornasa, SMSM, Provincial Superior
Founded: 1845. **Description:** Women missionaries working primarily in Third World countries. Sponsors seminars; maintains libraries at congregation houses. **Members:** 700.

★554★ **Missionary Women International (MWI)**
60180 CR 113 S.
Elkhart, IN 46517
Phone: (219)875-3146
Opal Speicher, Pres.
Founded: 1944. **Description:** Promotes fellowship among church women. Raises funds for missions. Sponsors retreats and leadership training. Operates under the auspices of the Missionary Church. **Members:** 6000. **Publications:** *Corner to Corner Newsletter*, monthly. • *Prayer Projects*, annual. **Formerly:** Women's Missionary Society.

★555★ **Modern Language Association (MLA)**
Coalition of Women in German
Department of German and Russian
Carleton College
1 N. College St.
Northfield, MN 55057-4001
Phone: (507)663-4249
Fax: (507)663-4204
Julia Klassen, Newsletter Coord.
Description: The Coalition comprises students, teachers, and others interested in feminism and German studies. It sponsors conferences and workshops. **Publications:** *Women in German Yearbook*. • *Feminism in Film*.

★556★ **Modern Language Association (MLA)**
Commission on the Status of Women in the Profession
10 Astor Pl.
New York, NY 10003
Phone: (212)475-9500
Fax: (212)477-9863
Bettina Huber, Director of Research
Description: The Commission gathers, interprets, and reviews information on the status of women in modern languages and on related career strategies and ensures adequate representation of women in MLA activities. The Commission also maintains projects on intellectual harassment of feminist studies and teachers; the difficulties of combining an academic career with childbearing and family responsibilities; and age discrimination.

★557★ **Modern Language Association (MLA)**
Women's Caucus for the Modern Language (WCML)
Humanities Division
Drexel University
Philadelphia, PA 19104
Phone: (215)895-1820
Ellen Cronona Rose, President
Founded: 1970. **Description:** WCML promotes the interests of women within the Modern Language Association in the areas of professional advancement, scholarship, pedagogy, and related research. Sponsors panels and programs at MLA conventions; provides a scholarship fund for un/underemployed women in modern language, including graduate students; and sponsors the Florence Howe Award for essays in feminist literature scholarship. **Publications:** *Concerns*.

★558★ **Mothers of AIDS Patients (MAP)**
1811 Field Dr. NE
Albuquerque, NM 87112-2833
Phone: (619)544-0430
Barbara Peabody, Exec. Officer
Founded: 1985. **Description:** Family members of individuals with AIDS. Provides support for families of AIDS patients throughout the illness and following death. Acts as a resource network and assists in forming local groups. Conducts educational presentations on AIDS. **Local Groups:** 40.

★559★ **Mothers at Home**
8310-A Old Courthouse Rd.
Vienna, VA 22180
Phone: (703)827-5903
Cathy Myers, Pres.
Founded: 1983. **Description:** Dedicated to the support of mothers who choose to stay at home to raise their families. Serves as a forum for the exchange of information among members. Provides information at congressional hearings. Conducts research and seminars; compiles statistics; maintains speakers' bureau. **Publications:** *Welcome Home*, monthly. Magazine aimed at boosting the morale and image of mothers at home.

★560★ **Mothers' Home Business Network (MHBN)**
PO Box 423
East Meadow, NY 11554
Phone: (516)997-7394
Georganne Fiumara, Dir.
Founded: 1984. **Description:** Mothers choosing to work at home so they can earn income, maintain careers, and remain the primary caretakers of their children. Offers advice and support services on how to begin a successful business at home; helps members communicate with others who have chosen the same career option. Provides information on home business products and services, including home furnishings, raw materials and office supplies, and publications. **Members:** 5000. **Publications:** *Homeworking Mothers*, quarterly. • *Mothers' Home Businesspages: A Resource Guide*, annual. • Also publishes *Mothers' Money Making Manual*, *Mothering and Managing a Typing Service At Home*, and *Mothering and Managing a Mail Order Business At Home* (booklets).

★561★ **Mothers-in-Law Club International (MIL)**
420 Adelberg Ln.
Cedarhurst, NY 11516
Phone: (516)295-4744
Sylvia Parker, Pres.
Founded: 1970. **Description:** Mothers- and fathers-in-law, sons- and daughters-in-law. Serves as a common meeting ground for both present and future in-laws in an effort to solve problems that prevent a happy intrafamily relationship. Seeks to change the "false and unkind image of the mother-in-law" and to establish a holiday for mothers-in-law on the second Sunday in August, corresponding to Mother's Day. Promotes: a larger tax incentive for children who keep their aged parents at home with them; improvement of conditions in nursing and senior citizen homes; visitation rights for grandparents to visit grandchildren; foster homes for the aged who have no family; a change in Social Security laws so that people over 65 can collect benefits, still work, and receive normal salaries without being penalized. **Members:** 5000.

★562★ **Mothers Matter (MM)**
171 Wood St.
Rutherford, NJ 07070
Phone: (201)933-8191
Kay Willis, Founder & Dir.
Founded: 1975. **Description:** Seeks to increase enjoyment of parenting and improve childcare skills of parents. Offers educational programs. **Regional Groups:** 5. **State Groups:** 75.

★563★ **Mothers Without Custody (MWOC)**
PO Box 27418
Houston, TX 77256
Phone: (713)840-1622
Jennifer Isham, Pres.
Founded: 1981. **Description:** Women living apart from one or more of their minor children for any reason, including court decisions, exchange of custody with an ex-spouse, intervention by a state agency, or childnapping by an ex-spouse. Provides support to women currently exploring their child custody options during and after divorce. Helps establish local selfhelp groups that meet monthly and organize social events for mothers alone and mothers visiting their children. Has estimated that there are 1.5 million mothers living apart from minor children.

Provides member exchange. **Members:** 500. **Local Groups:** 100. **Publications:** *Mother-to-Mother*, bimonthly. Newsletter.

★564★ Ms. Foundation for Women (MFW)
141 5th Ave., Ste. 6-S
New York, NY 10010
Phone: (212)353-8580
Marie C. Wilson, Exec.Dir.
Founded: 1972. **Projects:** Ad Hoc Sexual Harassment Coalition, a broad-based coalition of women's and civil rights groups organized in response to the sexual harassment charges brought by Anita Hill against Justice Clarence Thomas during the U.S. Supreme Court nomination hearings. List of supporters. **Description:** Goals are to eliminate sex discrimination and to improve the status of women and girls in society. Provides funds and technical assistance to activist, community-based self-help feminist projects working on issues of economic development, nonsexist multicultural education, reproductive rights, health and AIDS, and prevention of violence to women and children. Evaluates community-based women's groups and helps them to strengthen their programs. **Publications:** *Newsletter*, quarterly. • *Report*, annual. • Also publishes periodic grant listings and summary brochures.

★565★ Mujeres Activas en Letras Y Cambio Social (MALCS)
c/o Ethnic Studies Program
Santa Clara Univ.
Santa Clara, CA 95053
Phone: (408)554-4511
Dr. Alma Garcia, Chairperson
Founded: 1982. **Description:** Hispanic women in higher education who conduct or foster research and writing on Chicanas and Latinas. Seeks to fight what MALCS views as race, class, and gender oppression in universities; strives to bridge the gap between intellectual work and active commitment to communities. Develops strategies for social change; works to organize, collect, and disseminate course materials useful to developing and teaching courses on Chicanas. Documents, analyzes, and interprets the Chicana experience in the U.S.; is concerned with women's conditions in the home and/or workplace, and their struggle for social and economic justice. Operates speakers' bureau; offers placement service; maintains biographical archives. **Members:** 90. **Regional Groups:** 7. **Computerized Services:** Mailing list. **Publications:** *Directory*, triennial. • *Noticiera de MALCS*, 3/year. Newsletter; includes information on educational placements and fellowships. • *Trabajos Monograficos: Studies in Chicana/Latina Research*, annual.

★566★ NAACOG: The Organization for Obstetric, Gynecologic, and Neonatal Nurses
409 12th St., SW
Washington, DC 20024
Phone: (202)638-0026
Sallye B. Shaw, Exec.Dir.
Founded: 1969. **Description:** Members are registered nurses; associate members are allied health workers with an interest in obstetric, gynecologic, and neonatal (OGN) nursing. Promotes and establishes the highest standards of OGN nursing practice, education, and research; cooperates with all members of the health team; stimulates interest in OGN nursing. Sponsors educational meetings, audiovisual programs, and continuing education courses. Maintains 1800 volume resource center on obstetrics, gynecology, neonatology, and general medicine. **Members:** 24,000. **Regional Groups:** 10. **State Groups:** 62. **Publications:** *Journal of Obstetric, Gynecologic, and Neonatal Nursing*, bimonthly. Includes advertisers' index and annual subject and author index. Contains book reviews, case studies, and employment opportunity listings. • *NAACOG Newsletter*, monthly. Includes annual index, calendar of events, employment opportunity listings, and legislative news. • Also publishes manual of standards and OGN nursing practice resources. **Formerly:** Nurses Association of the American College of Obstetricians and Gynecologists.

★567★ Na'amat U.S.A.
200 Madison Ave., 21st Fl.
New York, NY 10016
Phone: (212)725-8010
Founded: 1925. **Description:** Professional women and housewives. Cooperates with Na'amat Movement of Working Women and Volunteers for the rehabilitation, integration, and education of new immigrant women, children, and youth in Israel, as well as native born Israelis. Promotes Jewish education and culture in the United States and participates actively in American civic life. Is an authorized agency of Youth Aliyah. Maintains biographical archives and speakers' bureau; bestows awards. **Members:** 50,000. **Regional Groups:** 4. **State Groups:** 31. **Local Groups:** 500. **Publications:** *Na'amat Woman*, 5/year. Journal; includes book reviews. • Also publishes brochures. **Formerly:** (1982) Pioneer Women, The Women's Labor Zionist Organization of America; (1985) Pioneer Women/Na'amat, the Women's Labor Zionist Organization of America.

★568★ Najda: Women Concerned About the Middle East
PO Box 7152
Berkeley, CA 94707
Phone: (415)549-3512
Alice Kawash, Pres.
Founded: 1960. **Description:** Arab-Americans, Americans married to Arabs, and others interested in the Arab world. Promotes understanding between Americans and Arabs by offering educational programs and audiovisual presentations on Middle Eastern history, art, culture, and current events. Provides workshops on the Middle East. Provides scholarships to women in the Israeli-occupied territories of the Gaza Strip and the West Bank; raises funds for educational institutions in the Occupied Territories; provides humanitarian relief to Palestinian women and children. Sponsors poetry readings and other cultural performances. (Najda is an Arabic word meaning "assistance in time of need.") **Members:** 500. **Publications:** *Middle East Resources*, quarterly. Designed for teachers. • *Najda Newsletter*, bimonthly. • Also published *The Arabic Cookbook* and *The Arab World Notebook for the Secondary School Level*.

★569★ Nanny Pop-Ins Association (NPIA)
1110 Morgan's Landing Dr.
Atlanta, GA 30338
Phone: (404)395-7463
Barbara Adamek, Sec.
Founded: 1986. **Description:** Independent owner/operators of in-home child care services, and individuals who provide in-home child care. Seeks to aid would-be entrepreneurs in establishing new child care service outlets, and to standardize criteria for certification in the child care field. Promotes high standards of performance and ethics among child care professionals; conducts educational conferences and seminars. Provides group benefits for members including insurance, investigations, and employee benefit packages; offers certification and search and referral services. Operates placement service; maintains speakers' bureau; compiles statistics. **Members:** 15. **Computerized Services:** Membership list. **Publications:** *NPIA Newlsetter*, quarterly.

★570★ National Abortion Federation (NAF)
1436 U St. NW, Ste. 103
Washington, DC 20009
Phone: (202)667-5881
Toll-free: 800-772 9100
Fax: (202)667-5890
Barbara Radford, Exec.Dir.
Founded: 1977. **Description:** National professional forum for abortion service providers (physician offices, clinics, feminist health centers, planned parenthood affiliates) and others committed to making safe, legal abortions accessible to all women. Unites abortion service providers into a professional community dedicated to health care; upgrades abortion services by providing standards and guidelines; serves as clearinghouse of information on variety and quality of services offered; keeps abreast of educational, legislative, and public policy developments in reproductive health care. Provides consultations, training workshops, and seminars. Maintains 225 volume library on abortion, contraception, sexuality, sociology, and health and medical subjects. Bestows awards. **Members:** 300. **Computerized Services:** Data base regarding violence directed against abortion providers. **Telecommunications Services:** National toll-free consumer hot line to educate and inform women on how to choose an abortion facility, (800)772-9100. **Publications:** *Annual Meeting Workbook*. • *Membership Directory*, annual. Newsletter containing information pertinent to keeping abortion safe, legal, and accessible. Includes book reviews, calendar of events, and research updates. • *Risk Management Workbook*, semiannual. • Also publishes *Consumer's Guide to Abortion Services* (in English and Spanish), fact sheets, bulletins, books, and other materials.

★571★ National Abortion Rights Action League (NARAL)
1101 14th St. NW, 5th Fl.
Washington, DC 20005
Phone: (202)408-4600
Fax: (202)408-4698
Kate Michelman, Exec.Dir.
Founded: 1969. **Description:** To develop and sustain a pro-choice political constituency in order to maintain the right to legal abortion for all women. Initiates and coordinates political action of individuals and groups concerned with maintaining the 1973 Supreme Court abortion decision affirming the choice of abortion as a constitutional right. Maintains lobbyist; briefs members of Congress; testifies at hearings on abortion and related issues; organizes affiliates in states to build political awareness; trains field representatives. Supports pro-choice candidates for elected office. Maintains speakers' bureau; compiles statistics. **Members:** 400,000. **State Groups:** 41. **Publications:** *NARAL News-*

letter, quarterly. Provides updates on legislation regarding abortion. **Formerly:** (1973) National Association for Repeal of Abortion Laws.

★572★ National Academy of Sciences Committee on Women in Science and Engineering
2102 Constitution Ave. NW, Rm. GR412
Washington, DC 20418
Phone: (202)334-2709
Linda Dix, Study Dir.

★573★ National Action for Former Military Wives (NAFMW)
1700 Legion Dr.
Winter Park, FL 32789
Phone: (407)628-2801
Lois N. Jones, Pres.

Founded: 1979. **Description:** Seeks federal legislation that: provides for retroactive, pro-rata sharing of military retirement pay; requires mandatory assignment of the Survivors Benefit Plan to current and former spouses of service members; restores all medical, commissary, and exchange privileges to former spouses; prevents instances of double taxation on benefits shared by ex-spouses. Holds monthly support meeting to advise former military wives and those in the process of divorce. Offers children's services; compiles statistics. **Members:** 5000. **Publications:** *Newsletter*, 2-4/year. **Formerly:** (1983) Action for Former Military Wives.

★574★ National Action Forum for Midlife and Older Women (NAFOW)
Box 816
Stony Brook, NY 11790
Dr. Jane Porcino, Founder & Dir.

Founded: 1977. **Description:** People concerned with upgrading the quality of life for women over 40 years of age. Increases public awareness of the status and needs of women in midlife and late life. Provides national and international network and central resource exchange for those with interests in issues affecting older women. Supports the development of a broad spectrum of services and resources designed to enhance the quality of life for women in their later years. **Members:** 1600. **Publications:** *Hot Flash*, quarterly. Newsletter containing editorial and legislative alerts. **Formerly:** (1983) National Action Forum for Older Women.

★575★ National Alliance of Breast Cancer Organizations (NABCO)
1180 Ave. of the Americas, 2nd Fl.
New York, NY 10036
Phone: (212)719-0154
Fax: (212)719-0263
Amy Langer, Adm.Dir.

Founded: 1986. **Description:** Breast centers; hospitals; government health offices; and support and research organizations providing information about breast cancer and breast diseases from early detection through continuing care. Serves as a resource for: organizations requiring information about breast cancer programs and organizations and medical advances; individuals seeking information about research, developments, and treatment options for breast cancer. Seeks to influence public and private health policy on issues pertaining to breast cancer, such as insurance reimbursement, health care legislation, and research funding priorities. Offers advice on how to propose and

lobby for or against legislation regarding discrimination, informed consent, and third-party reimbursement. Disseminates educational materials and information on support groups, breast care centers, and hospital programs. **Members:** 700. **Publications:** *NABCO News*, quarterly. Newsletter monitoring developments relating to breast cancer. • *NABCO's Resource List*, annual. Contains information on materials and organizations that provide information about breast cancer.

★576★ National Alliance of Homebased Businesswomen (NAHB)
PO Box 306
Midland Park, NJ 07432
Phone: (201)423-9131
Marie MacBride, Staff Admin.

Founded: 1981. **Description:** Men and women who operate or plan to operate a homebased business; supporting members are interested individuals. Supports the right of every individual to operate a homebased business. Conducts national and local networking to combat the image of homebased businesses as "cottage industries" by emphasizing, encouraging, and stimulating personal, professional, and economic growth of members. Believes that homebased businesses deserve respect and should enjoy the same privileges and obligations as other businesses. Seeks the removal of federal, state, and local restrictions on homebased business. Keeps members abreast of legal, political, and business developments affecting homebased businesses. Serves as a forum for the discussion and exchange of information and experiences; provides a network of professional and educational contacts. Seeks to: influence planning boards to adopt zoning laws that are fair to homebased business; eliminate laws prohibiting homebased business; gain recognition of the legitimacy of homebased business; provide educational and business resources. Arranges and provides life insurance, car rentals, and hotel discounts for members; publicizes members' goods and services; conducts seminars. **Members:** 600. **Local Groups:** 15. **Computerized Services:** Mailing list. **Publications:** *Alliance*, bimonthly. Professional and association newsletter. Book reviews; classified ads. Directory of members, July. • *Alliance* (newsletter), bimonthly. • *Directory of Members*, annual, with semiannual updates. • *National Alliance of Homebased Businesswomen—Directory of Members*, annual in July with January update. Membership directory arranged by personal name, by company name, and geographically. • Also publishes Zoning for Homebased Business and Planning for Homebased Business (pamphlets).

★577★ National Anorexic Aid Society (NAAS)
1925 E. Dublin-Granville Rd.
Columbus, OH 43229
Phone: (614)436-1112
Arline Iannicello, Program Dir.

Founded: 1977. **Description:** Persons suffering from anorexia nervosa, bulimia, and related eating disorders; families of victims; educators, doctors, and mental health professionals. Provides community education programs and self-help groups for victims and their families; compiles state-by-state listing of doctors, hospitals, and clinics treating the disorders; offers information and referral services. Works with medical and mental health professionals to call attention to anorexia nervosa and bulimia so

that problems can be discussed and causes and treatments explored. Provides parents, educators, family physicians, and clergy with information that will aid in the early recognition, diagnosis, and treatment of eating disorders. **Members:** 500. **Publications:** *NAAS Newsletter*, quarterly. Includes book reviews. **Formerly:** (1979) Anorexic Aid Society.

★578★ National Assembly of Religious Women (NARW)
529 S. Wabash, Rm. 404
Chicago, IL 60605
Phone: (312)663-1980
Sr. Judy Vaughan, CSJ, Coordinator

Founded: 1970. **Description:** Women of faith; associate members are men. Organized to provide a forum for Catholic feminist women to network, speak out, and act on issues of social justice and ministry. Sponsors workshops; conducts leadership training programs for a Ministry for Justice. Offers resources and program materials on women's issues, concerns, and strategies for change. **Members:** 2400. **Publications:** *Probe*, bimonthly. Covers various justice issues having an impact on women in the church and society. **Formerly:** (1982) National Assembly of Women Religious.

★579★ National Association of Anorexia Nervosa and Associated Disorders
Box 7
Highland Park, IL 60035
Phone: (708)831-3438
Vivian Meehan, Exec.Dir.

Founded: 1976. **Description:** Anorectics and bulimics, their families, health professionals, and others interested in the problems of anorexia nervosa and bulimia. Maintains chapters in 45 states, Canada, Austria, South Africa, Italy, Saudi Arabia, Colombia, and Germany. Aims to: seek a better understanding of, prevent, and cure anorexia nervosa and associated eating disorders; educate the public and health professionals on illnesses relating to eating disorders and methods of treatment. Encourages and promotes research on the cause of eating disorders, methods of prevention, types of treatment and their effectiveness, and basic facts about victims. Serves as an advocacy agency for those concerned with eating disorders. Works to end insurance discrimination against sufferers of eating disorders. Fights against the production, marketing, and distribution of dangerous diet aids and the use of misleading advertisements. Acts as a resource center, compiling and providing information about eating disorders. Encourages and co-sponsors local and regional meetings. Maintains speakers' bureau; provides children's services; compiles statistics. Conducts referral service, surveys, education, and early detection programs. Operates library of books, articles, and papers. Organizes self-help groups. **Publications:** *Working Together*, 4/yr.

★580★ National Association of Bank Women
500 N. Michigan Ave., No. 1400
Chicago, IL 60611
Phone: (312)661-1700
Joan Carter, Admin. Dir.

★581★ National Association of Black Women Attorneys (NABWA)
3711 Macomb St., NW, 2nd Fl.
Washington, DC 20016
Phone: (202)966-9693
Fax: (202)244-6648
Mabel D. Haden, Pres.

Founded: 1972. **Description:** Black women who are members of the bar of any U.S. state or territory; associate members include law school graduates, paralegals, and law students. Seeks to: advance jurisprudence and the administration of justice by increasing the opportunities of black and non-black women at all levels; aid in protecting the civil and human rights of all citizens and residents of the U.S.; expand opportunities for women lawyers through education; promote fellowship among women lawyers. Provides pre-law and student counseling; serves as job placement resource for firms, companies, and others interested in the field. Holds regional seminars; sponsors scholarship awards competition and brief-writing contest. Maintains hall of fame; offers charitable program. **Members:** 500. **Regional Groups:** 8. **State Groups:** 10. **Local Groups:** 2. **Computerized Services:** Data base; mailing list. Telephone referral service. **Publications:** *Convention Bulletin*, annual. • *NABWA News*, quarterly. • Also publishes job announcements.

★582★ National Association of Black Women Entrepreneurs (NABWE)
PO Box 1375
Detroit, MI 48231
Phone: (313)341-7400
Fax: (313)342-3433
Marilyn French-Hubbard, Founder

Founded: 1979. **Description:** Black women who own and operate their own businesses; black women interested in starting businesses; organizations and companies desiring mailing lists. Acts as a national support system for black businesswomen in the U.S. and focuses on the unique problems they face. Objective is to enhance business, professional, and technical development of both present and future black businesswomen. Maintains speakers' bureau and national networking program. Offers symposia, workshops, and forums aimed at increasing the business awareness of black women. Shares resources, lobbies, and provides placement service. Bestows annual Black Woman Entrepreneur of the Year Award. **Members:** 3000. **Regional Groups:** 4. **State Groups:** 28. **Publications:** *Making Success Happen Newsletter*, bimonthly. • *Membership Directory*, annual.

★583★ National Association of Business and Industrial Saleswomen (NABIS)
90 Corona, Ste. 1407
Denver, CO 80218
Phone: (303)777-7257
A. K. Lovejoy, Acting Exec.Dir.

Founded: 1980. **Description:** Women who sell business and industrial products or services. Facilitates the exchange of ideas and experiences in an effort to further professional and personal development for women in business and industrial sales. Encourages women to enter the sales field; seeks recognition of saleswomen's needs through trade publications and other media. Provides resource services to corporations and individuals. Maintains career counseling and search services. **Publications:**

Interchange, periodic. Newsletter. • Also publishes brochure.

★584★ National Association of Chicano Studies
Mujeres Activas en Letras y Cambio Social (MALCS)
University of California, Davis
Chicano Studies Program
Davis, CA 95616
Phone: (916)758-8882
Ada Sosa Ridell, Chair

Description: MALCS is an association for Chicana and Latin American women in higher education. It promotes public policy research on Chicana and Latina issues and provides support to students and faculty. Supports Chicana public policy research center. **Publications:** Newsletter, quarterly. • Journal.

★585★ National Association of Childbearing Centers (NACC)
3123 Gottschall Rd.
Perkiomenville, PA 18074
Phone: (215)234-8068
Fax: (215)234-0994
Eunice K. M. Ernst, Admin.

Founded: 1983. **Description:** Birth centers; interested individuals and businesses that support the group's work. Acts as national information service on freestanding birth centers for state health departments, insurance companies, government agencies, consultants, hospitals, physicians, certified nurse-midwives, nurses, and families; promotes quality care in freestanding birth centers through state licensure and national standard-setting mechanisms, educational workshops, and support of professional education for midwives. Provides standards for certification of birth centers. Conducts regional workshops on financing, managing, operating, and marketing freestanding birth centers. Compiles statistics; maintains library. **Members:** 400. **Regional Groups:** 6. **State Groups:** 1. **Computerized Services:** Data bases. telephone referral. **Publications:** *Membership Directory*, periodic. • *NACC News*, annual.

★586★ National Association of Childbirth Assistants (NACA)
205 Copco Ln.
San Jose, CA 95126
Phone: (408)225-9167
Claudia Lowe, Pres.

Founded: 1985. **Description:** Professional organization of childbirth assistants. Provides information, resources, and referrals to childbearing families. Conducts training workshops. Awards childbirth assistant certification. Compiles statistics; maintains speakers' bureau. **Local Groups:** 12. **Publications:** *Childbirth Assistant Journal*, periodic. • *Professional Membership/Referral Directory*, periodic. • Also publishes *Becoming a Childbirth Assistant*, *Inside NACA*, and *Planning for a Positive Pregnancy*.

★587★ National Association of Childbirth Education (NACE)
3940 11th St.
Riverside, CA 92501
Phone: (714)686-0422
Rebecca Smith, Pres.

Founded: 1971. **Description:** Certified instructors who believe that through the proper knowledge, training, and work, childbirth can be an

enjoyable, participating experience for expectant parents. Provides an extensive and comprehensive program to train and certify childbirth educators. Teaches the Pavlov-Lamaze method and supports the growth in the field of childbirth education and community service. Works to promote better parent-child relationships and encourages breastfeeding and family-centered maternity care. Maintains lending library of information on pregnancy and childbirth, family planning, nutrition, breastfeeding, and child care. Sponsors workshops and conferences to update instructors on current trends. **Members:** 119. **Regional Groups:** 9. **Local Groups:** 4. **Publications:** *Focal Point*, bimonthly. Newsletter providing information on pregnancy and childbirth, family planning, nutrition, and child care. • *Focal Point* (newsletter), bimonthly. • *Membership Roster*, annual. • *National Association of Childbirth Education–Teacher Update*, bimonthly. Newsletter directed toward certified instructors who believe that through the proper knowledge, training, and work, childbirth can be an enjoyable, participatory experience for expectant parents. Articles on current trends; news of research; news of workshops and conferences. • *Teacher Update*, bimonthly. • Also publishes Expectant Parent Manual (in Spanish). **Formerly:** (1981) Childbirth Without Pain Education League.

★588★ National Association of Collegiate Women Athletic Administrators (NACWAA)
c/o Chriz Volez
University of Minnesota
Athletic Department
Minneapolis, MN 55455
Phone: (612)624-8000
Fax: (801)750-2615
Chriz Voelz, Pres.

Founded: 1979. **Description:** Women working in athletic administration at U.S. colleges and universities. Seeks to increase members' professional skills. Serves as a forum for the exchange of information among members and as an advocate for opportunities for women in sport. **Members:** 350. **Publications:** *CCWA Newsletter*, quarterly. **Formerly:** (1991) Council of Collegiate Women's Athletic Administrators.

★589★ National Association of Colored Women's Clubs (NACWC)
5808 16th St. NW
Washington, DC 20011
Phone: (202)726-2044
Carole A. Early, Hdqtrs.Sec.

Founded: 1896. **Description:** Federation of black women's clubs. Carries on program of civic service, education, social service, and philanthropy. Sponsors National Association of Girls Clubs (see separate entry). **Members:** 45,000. **State Groups:** 38. **Local Groups:** 1000. **Publications:** *National Notes*, quarterly.

★590★ National Association of Commissions for Women (NACW)
YWCA Bldg., 6th Fl.
624 9th St. NW
Washington, DC 20001
Phone: (202)628-5030
Claire Bigelow, Dir.

Founded: 1970. **Description:** State, city, and county commissions that focus on the status of women. To strengthen and coordinate the vital work of the state and local commissions, in seeking to further the legal, social, political, economic, and educational equality of American women, that they may make their fullest contribution in our nation. Works to: eliminate discrimination based on sex, race, age, religion, national origin, or marital status in all phases of American society; foster the dissemination of information and provide counsel on opportunities for the effective participation of women in the private and public sector; create greater public awareness of the role and function of commissions on the status of women and provide a national focus on issues affecting women; strenghten commissions, coordinate their efforts nationwide, and provide a unified voice; act as a central clearinghouse and networking resource for information and activities of commissions across the country; foster a closer relationship and fuller exchange of ideas among members. Offers guidance in the designing of new strategies and programs on critical contemporary issues of concern to women; assists efforts to broaden the base of involvement of women of color and those of different backgrounds; works with other national women's groups on issues requiring collective action. Presents testimony at public hearings; monitors legislation of special interest to women. Maintains speakers' bureau; compiles statistics. Conducts research, workshops, and leadership training programs. Operates resource library. **Members:** 128. **Regional Groups:** 33. **State Groups:** 40. **Local Groups:** 200. **Publications:** *Breakthrough*, quarterly. Newsletter reporting on news and activities of regional, state, and local commissions; includes legislative updates. • *Directory of National, Regional, State and Local Commissions*, periodic. • Also publishes informational pamphlets, organizational handbook, and federal legislative alerts. **Formerly:** (1975) Interstate Association of Commissions for Women.

★591★ **National Association of County Officials (NACO)**
**Women Officials of the National
Association of County Officials**
440 1st St. NW
Washington, DC 20001
Phone: (202)393-6226
Lena Palmer, Contact

Description: Women Officials of NACO is a women's caucus group that is concerned with the interests of women as they relate to county governments. **Publications:** *Women Officials of NACO Newsletter*, biennial.

★592★ **National Association of Cuban-American Women of the U.S.A. (NACAW-USA)**
2119 S. Webster
Ft. Wayne, IN 46802
Phone: (219)745-5421
Dr. G. F. del Cueto Beecher, Pres.

Founded: 1972. **Description:** To address current issues, concerns, and problems affecting Hispanic and minority women, and to achieve goals such as equal education and training, fair immigration policy, and meaningful work with adequate compensation. Coordinates activities with national Hispanic and other minority organizations; responds to female concerns from minority and majority populations; encourages participation in related task forces, legislative activities, and professional endeavors; acts as clearinghouse and referral center. Supports bilingual and bicultural education at the local, state, and national levels. Disseminates infor-

mation on postsecondary educational opportunities and sources of financial aid in particular cities. Produces biweekly bilingual radio program. Maintains library of 2000 volumes on subjects such as Cuban history, Cubans in the U.S., and human rights violations in Cuba. Conducts placement service; bestows awards; compiles statistics. **Members:** 5700. **State Groups:** 35. **Publications:** *Newsletter*, periodic. • Also publishes brochures. **Also known as:** Asociacion Nacional de Mujeres Cubanoamericanas, de los Estados Unidos de America.

★593★ **National Association of Extension Home Economists (NAEHE)**
100 E. Knox St.
Morrison, IL 61270
Phone: (804)357-3191
Mary Wells, Pres.

Founded: 1934. **Description:** Group of home economists employed by Land Grant·**Publications:** *The NAEHE Reporter*.

★594★ **National Association for Family Day Care (NAFDC)**
725 15th St. NW, Ste. 505
Washington, DC 20005
Phone: (202)347-3356
Toll-free: 800-359-3817
Barbara Taylor, Pres.

Founded: 1982. **Description:** Parents, advocates, and providers of family day care services. (Family day care offers provisions for child care within a household setting, allowing for flexible hours in supervision, personalized communication with parents, and greater individual attention to children.) Operates National Assessment and Credentialing Program, which provides accreditation for family day care providers and their homes. Serves as a national voice for family day care providers and promotes quality standards for all day care operations. **Members:** 2500. **Publications:** *National Association for Family Day Care–National Perspective*, bimonthly. Newsletter reporting on home child care. Includes book and material reviews, and calendar of events. • Also publishes *How to Start a Family Day Care Business*.

★595★ **National Association for Female Executives (NAFE)**
127 W. 24th St.
New York, NY 10011
Phone: (212)645-0770
Fax: (212)633-6489
Wendy Reid-Crisp, Dir.

Founded: 1972. **Description:** Career women in all phases of business. Purpose is to make women aware of the need to plan for career and financial success and to create tools to support these goals. Programs include: career-oriented conferences and seminars; management aptitude test; resume guide and writing service; discount prices for career books; group insurance plans; unsecured loans by mail; a credit handbook for women; venture capital funds. Sponsors NAFE Network, composed of 500 resource-sharing groups for career women nationwide. Conducts educational programs; sponsors competitions; maintains speakers' bureau. **Members:** 250,000. **Local Groups:** 400. **Publications:** *Executive Female*, bimonthly. Magazine; includes book reviews and calendar of events. • Also publishes *Networking, Stress Management, How to Get a Raise, Guide to a Winning Resume, Market Yourself for Success,*

Discover Your Opportunities, Achieve Your Goals, and *Master Your Future* (brochures).

★596★ **National Association of Full Figured Women (NAFFW)**
PO Box 27231
El Paso, TX 79926
C. B. Hart, Exec.Dir.

Founded: 1990. **Description:** Works to increase public awareness of the contributions of full-figured women to society and to prevent size discrimination. Sponsors charitable programs, children's services, and competitions; bestows awards. Maintains hall of fame, speakers' bureau, and biographical archives. Compiles statistics. **Members:** 445. **Chapters:** 23. **Publications:** *NAFFW News*, quarterly. • *NAFFW Register*, annual. Directory.

★597★ **National Association of Girls Clubs (NAGC)**
5808 16th St. NW
Washington, DC 20011
Phone: (202)726-2044
Carole A. Early, Hdqtrs.Sec.

Founded: 1930. **Description:** Sponsored by National Association of Colored Women's Clubs (see separate entry). Black girls, ages 6-18. Promotes the moral, mental, and material development of members; fosters positive attitudes toward health, beauty, love, home, and service among members. **Formerly:** (1976) National Association of Colored Girls Clubs.

★598★ **National Association for Girls and Women in Sport (NAGWS)**
1900 Association Dr.
Reston, VA 22091
Phone: (703)476-3450
Peggy Kellers, Exec.Dir.

Founded: 1899. **Description:** An association of the American Alliance for Health, Physical Education, Recreation and Dance. Teachers, coaches, athletic trainers, officials, athletic administrators, and students. NAGWS has 6 main structures: Advocacy and Liaison; Affiliated Boards of Officials; Coaching Enhancement; Minority Representation; Professional Development and Leadership; Publications and Communications. Supports and fosters the development of quality sports programs that will enrich the lives of all participants. Sponsors coaches clinics; holds seminars and training sessions. Maintains National Coaches Council which assists in organization and development of teams, offers grants, and emphasizes quality coaching. **Members:** 9,000. **Regional Groups:** 6. **State Groups:** 50. **Publications:** *Guides and Rulebooks*, annual. • *Newsletter*, quarterly. • Also publishes *Coaching the Female Athlete/Sport Leadership Conference Handbook*, and other related books. **Formerly:** (1971) Division of Girl's and Women's Sports of the American Association of Health, Physical Education, and Recreation.

★599★ National Association of Independent Schools (NAIS) Council for Women in Independent Schools (CWIS)
75 Federal St.
Boston, MA 02110
Phone: (617)451-2444
Dory Adams, Assoc. Director of Academic Services

Description: CWIS ensures that the needs of women and girls in independent schools are being met by the NAIS. The Council identifies and develops female leadership in member schools, the quality of life for women in independent schools, and the scope of the curriculum. Maintains list of women who are active candidates for leaderships in independent schools. **Publications:** *CWIS Newsletter*, annual. • *CWIS Newsnotes*, twice a year.

★600★ National Association of Insurance Women - International (NAIW)
1847 E. 15th
PO Box 4410
Tulsa, OK 74159
Phone: (918)744-5195
Toll-free: 800-766-6249
Fax: (918)743-1968
Jane R. Seago, Exec.V.Pres.

Founded: 1940. **Description:** Individuals in the insurance business. Sponsors insurance educational programs. Awards Certified Professional Insurance Woman (Man) certificate to qualified members who have passed one of several sets of national examinations. Sponsors competitions and bestows awards. **Members:** 20,000. **Regional Groups:** 9. **Local Groups:** 422. **Publications:** *Today's Insurance Woman*, bimonthly. Association and industry magazine providing members with information on decision-making, risk management, personal planning, and education. Includes membership profile and legislative updates. **Formerly:** National Association of Insurance Women.

★601★ National Association of MBA Women (NAMBAW)
7701 Georgia Ave. NW
Washington, DC 20012
Phone: (202)723-1267
Sharon Griffith, President

Description: The Association is dedicated to improving the career opportunities for women with M.B.A. degrees as well as providing networking and scholarship opportunities. Provides annual scholarship programs for women in MBA curricula and networking opportunities. **Publications:** *NAMBAW News*, bimonthly. • Also provides publications with job listings and other relevant news.

★602★ National Association of Media Women (NAMW)
1185 Niskey Lake Rd. SW
Atlanta, GA 30331
Phone: (404)344-5862
Mrs. Xernona Brady, Pres.

Founded: 1965. **Description:** Women professionally engaged in mass communications. Purposes are: to enrich the lives of members through an exchange of ideas and experiences; to sponsor studies, research, and seminars to find solutions to mutual problems; to create opportunities for women in communications. Grants annual scholarship to a woman who is pursuing a degree or specialized training in mass communications. Presents annual awards for national achievement to the Media Women of the Year and to the Outstanding Chapter of the Year. **Members:** 300. **Local Groups:** 14. **Publications:** *Media Woman*, annual. Journal.

★603★ National Association of Military Widows (NAMW)
4023 25th Rd. N.
Arlington, VA 22207
Phone: (703)527-4565
Jean Arthurs, Pres.

Founded: 1978. **Description:** Widows of careermen and reservists in all branches of the uniformed services whose husbands died either during active service or following disability or nondisability retirement. Seeks equitable legislation and survivor benefit programs, and monitors all legislation and programs affecting military widows in Congress, the Department of Defense, and Veterans Administration. **Members:** 2500. **Publications:** *National Association of Military Widows–Newsletter*, quarterly. Reports on issues affecting military widows.

★604★ National Association of Minority Political Women (NAMPW)
6120 Oregon Ave. NW
Washington, DC 20015
Phone: (202)686-1216
Mary E. Ivey, Pres.

Founded: 1983. **Description:** Professional women of all ages interested in the U.S. political process. Conducts research and educational programs. **Members:** 500.

★605★ National Association of Minority Women in Business (NAMWIB)
906 Grand Ave., Ste. 200
Kansas City, MO 64106
Phone: (816)421-3335
Fax: (816)421-3336
Inez Kaiser, Pres.

Founded: 1972. **Description:** Minority women in business ownership and management positions; college students. Serves as a network for the exchange of ideas and information on business opportunities for minority women in the public and private sectors. Conducts research and educational programs, as well as workshops, conferences, seminars, and luncheons. Maintains speakers' bureau, hall of fame, and placement service; compiles statistics; bestows awards to women who have made significant contributions to the field. **Members:** 5000. **Publications:** *Today*, bimonthly. Newsletter. • Also publishes brochures.

★606★ National Association of Mothers' Centers (NAMC)
336 Fulton Ave.
Hempstead, NY 11550
Phone: (516)486-6614
Toll-free: 800-645-3828
Lorri Slepian, Co-Dir.

Founded: 1981. **Description:** Encourages women and mothers to employ their knowledge and experiences for personal and societal changes benefiting mothers and families. Maintains local centers offering support groups. Conducts educational and research programs. **Formerly:** Mothers' Center Development Project.

★607★ National Association of Negro Business and Professional Women's Clubs (NANBPWC)
1806 New Hampshire Ave., NW
Washington, DC 20009
Phone: (202)483-4206
Fax: (202)462-7253
Ellen A. Graves, Exec. Officer

Founded: 1935. **Description:** Women actively engaged in a business or a profession who are committed to rendering service through club programs and activities. Seeks to direct the interest of business and professional women toward united action for improved social and civic conditions, and to provide enriching and ennobling experiences that will encourage freedom, dignity, self-respect, and self-reliance. Offers information and help regarding education, employment, health, housing, legislation, and problems of the aged and the disabled. Presents honors and awards for national and community service. Sponsors educational assistance program, which includes local and national scholarships. Conducts consumer education and prison reform programs. Maintains youth department clubs. Provides placement services; operates speakers' bureau; compiles statistics. **Members:** 10,000. **Regional Groups:** 6. **Local Groups:** 350. **Publications:** *Convention Proceedings*, annual. • *Directory*, annual. • *President's Newsletter*, monthly. • *Program Idea Exchange*, bimonthly. • *Responsibility*, quarterly. • Also publishes handbooks and manuals.

★608★ National Association of Professional Asian-American Women (NAPAAW)
PO Box 494
Washington Grove, MD 20880
Vivian Kim, Exec. Officer

Description: Represents the professional interests of Asian-American women. Promotes continued personal and professional development; works to enhance career opportunities. Encourages greater visibility of Asian-American women in public decision-making. Conducts educational programs. **Publications:** *NAPAAW Newsletter*, periodic.

★609★ National Association for Professional Saleswomen (NAPS)
5520 Cherokee Ave., Ste. 200
Aleandria, VA 22312
Phone: (703)256-9226
Fax: (703)658-8887
Gaye Garcia, Pres.

Founded: 1980. **Description:** Women actively involved or interested in professional sales and marketing careers. Conducts seminars, surveys, and research projects. Participates in television and radio programs. Maintains 450 volume library on business and sales. Operates speakers' bureau. Compiles statistics; sponsors competitions; bestows awards. **Members:** 2000. **Local Groups:** 30. **Publications:** *Successful Saleswoman*, monthly. Educational and informational newsletter; includes membership activities news and book reviews. • Has also published *On the Right Track: A Guide to a Successful Sales Career* (book).

★610★ **National Association of Railway Business Women (NARBW)**
c/o Carmen Taliaferro
2720 Mayfield Rd.
Cleveland Heights, OH 44106
Phone: (216)321-0971
Toll-free: 800-348-6272
Carmen Taliaferro, Pres.

Founded: 1921. **Description:** Women who work for railroads. Purposes are to: stimulate interest in the railroad industry; foster cooperation and understanding among members and people in related fields; promote good public relations for the railroad industry; further the educational, social, and professional interests of members. Conducts charitable, benevolent, and social welfare projects. Maintains a residence for retired members at Green Valley, AZ. Sponsors seminars and competitions. Bestows awards, including Railroad Woman of 10 Year. Offers ten scholarships annually. **Members:** 2500. **Regional Groups:** 6. **State Groups:** 46. **Publications:** *Capsule*, monthly. • Also publishes brochures. **Formerly:** (1954) Railway Business Women's Association.

★611★ **National Association of Surrogate Mothers (NASM)**
8383 Wilshire Blvd., Ste. 750D
Beverly Hills, CA 90211
Phone: (213)655-2015
Carol Sanchez, Exec. Officer

Founded: 1987. **Description:** Surrogate mothers. (Surrogate mothers carry and deliver children on behalf of infertile couples, usually for a fee). Seeks to educate the public concerning surrogate motherhood. Lobbies for legislation to regulate the surrogate motherhood industry and protect and define the legal rights of surrogate mothers. Acts as a forum through which members can share information and experiences. **Members:** 85. **Publications:** *NASM Newsletter*, quarterly.

★612★ **National Association of University Women (NAUW)**
1553 Pine Forest Dr.
Tallahassee, FL 32301
Phone: (904)878-4660
Ruth R. Corbin, Pres.

Founded: 1923. **Description:** Women college or university graduates. Works to promote constructive work in education, civic activities, and human relations; studies educational conditions with emphasis on problems affecting women; encourages high educational standards and stimulate intellectual attainment among women generally. Theme is Women of Action: Reaching, Risking, Responding. Offers tutoring and sponsors "After High School—What?" youth development program. Maintains placement service. Awards annual national fellowship; four sectional groups also award scholarships annually. **Members:** 4000. **Regional Groups:** 5. **Local Groups:** 92. **Publications:** *Bulletin*, biennial. • *Directory of Branch Presidents and Members*, annual. • *Journal of the National Association of University Women*, biennial. **Formerly:** (1974) National Association of College Women.

★613★ **National Association of Women Artists (NAWA)**
41 Union Sq. W.
New York, NY 10003
Phone: (212)675-1616
Ann Hermanson Chennault, Exec.Sec.

Founded: 1889. **Description:** Professional women artists (painters in oil, acrylic, and paper works; sculptors; printmakers). Sponsors foreign and national traveling shows. **Members:** 700. **Publications:** *National Association of Women Artists—Annual Exhibition Catalog*. Lists members, exhibiting members, and those receiving awards; includes black-and-white reproductions of prize-winning works. • *National Association of Women Artists—News*, semiannual. Newsletter; includes notices of exhibitions, shows, publications, awards, and corporate and museum purchases. **Formerly:** Association of Women Painters and Sculptors; Women's Art Club of the City of New York.

★614★ **National Association of Women Business Owners (NAWBO)**
600 S. Federal St., Ste. 400
Chicago, IL 60605
Phone: (312)922-6222
Natalie Holmes, Exec.Dir.

Founded: 1974. **Description:** Women who own and operate their own businesses. Purposes are: to identify and bring together women business owners in mutual support; to communicate and share experience and talents with others; to use collective influence to broaden opportunities for women in business. Services offered include: workshops and seminars; information clearinghouse, referral service, and reader service; representation before governmental bodies; liaison with groups of similar orientation. Bestows awards. **Members:** 3000. **Local Groups:** 44. **Computerized Services:** Data bank of women-owned businesses. **Publications:** *Annual Membership Roster*. • *Statement*, bimonthly. Association and membership activities newsletter. Includes calendar of events. **Formerly:** (1976) Association of Women Business Owners.

★615★ **National Association for Women in Careers (NAFWIC)**
PO Box 81525
Chicago, IL 60681-0525
Phone: (312)938-7662
Fax: (312)819-1220
Pat Surbella, CEO & Pres.

Founded: 1981. **Description:** Service organization for women representing various economic sectors including corporations, personally-owned businesses, nonprofit and sales organizations, retail outlets, financial institutions including government and health agencies, educational institutions, and associations. Provides support, networking, and skill-development services for all women to enhance their potential for greater success and enable them to meet future challenges for personal and career growth. Attempts to help women integrate who they are with what they do and to balance the demands of career growth and private life. Conducts seminars; provides job referral, career planning, and professional speakers. **Members:** 1500. **State Groups:** 8. **Publications:** *Directory*, periodic. **Formerly:** (1985) National Association of Future Women.

★616★ **National Association of Women in Chambers of Commerce (NAWCC)**
c/o Marie Davis Shope
PO Box 4552
Grand Junction, CO 81502-4552
Phone: (303)242-0075
Marie Davis Shope, Treas.

Founded: 1985. **Description:** Professional women affiliated with a chamber of commerce. Fosters members' growth and prosperity by providing education and management direction, information for business improvement, and opportunities for networking. Encourages women to work to realize their potential. Promotes and supports local chambers of commerce. **Members:** 100. **Computerized Services:** Membership list. **Publications:** *NAWCC Membership Directory*, annual. • *NAWCC Update*, quarterly. Newsletter. • Also publishes brochure.

★617★ **National Association of Women in Construction (NAWIC)**
327 S. Adams St.
Ft. Worth, TX 76104
Phone: (817)877-5551
Fax: (817)877-0324
Paula Clements-Zang, Exec.Dir.

Founded: 1954. **Description:** Professional women in the construction industry. Educates members in new construction techniques. Awards national and local scholarships to students of engineering construction or architecture; maintains scholarship trust fund, which currently assists five or more university students. Local chapters maintain employment services and sponsor career days, workshops, study courses, and educational programs. **Members:** 8800. **Regional Groups:** 14. **Local Groups:** 238. **Publications:** *NAWIC Image*, monthly. Magazine.

★618★ **National Association for Women Deans, Administrators and Counselors**
1325 18th St. NW, Ste. 210
Washington, DC 20036

★619★ **National Association for Women in Education (NAWE)**
1325 18th St. NW, Ste. 210
Washington, DC 20036-6511
Phone: (202)659-9330
Fax: (202)457-0946
Dr. Patricia A. Rueckel, Exec.Dir.

Founded: 1916. **Description:** Individuals holding positions in academic administration, student personnel, and counseling including student and academic deans, college presidents, professors of education, and directors of residence halls. Promotes study of trends in women's education. Bestows Ruth Strang Research Award. **Members:** 1900. **State Groups:** 21. **Publications:** *Directory*, annual. • *Journal*, quarterly. • *Newsletter*, quarterly. • Also publishes monographs. **Formerly:** (1956) National Association of Deans of Women; (1973) National Association of Women Deans and Counselors; (1991) National Association for Women Deans, Administrators, and Counselors.

★620★ National Association of Women Government Contractors
402 Maple Ave., W., Ste. C
Vienna, VA 22180
Phone: (703)281-1044
Nancy Stephens, Exec.Dir.

Founded: 1983. **Description:** Women entrepreneurs seeking business growth and profitability through effective competition with other groups for government contracts. Seeks "disadvantaged status" for women business owners by the Small Business Administration to increase women's access to government markets and to large government contracts. Goals are: protection of all women-owned businesses regardless of race, ethnicity, or cultural background; promotion of public policy that encourages professional women to lend expertise to the solution of problems affecting the nation's economy; establishment of programs utilizing women's training and talents; creation of a network for exchange of information, procedures, and ideas among current women business owners or those aspiring to start a business of their own. Aims to educate women entrepreneurs about the nation's political system and its legislative process as it works either to facilitate or to constrain fair access by the woman entrepreneur to federally-funded business opportunities. Compiles information on federal contract opportunities and awards and distributes such information to women entrepreneurs so they may better compete in the federal and/or private sector markets for goods and/or services. Offers marketing assistance including identification of government and industry buyers and explanation of sales protection techniques. Sponsors seminars on the procurement process, bidding, and other topics; conducts panels and lectures. Sponsors student interns who will provide technical support to a policy office in the federal government. Maintains small library of guides, membership and government directories, and small business publications. **Members:** 84. **Publications:** (1) Newsletter, bimonthly; (2) Directory, annual.

★621★ National Association of Women Highway Safety Leaders (NAWHSL)
721 Dragoon Dr.
Mt. Pleasant, SC 29464-3020
Phone: (803)884-7724
Mrs. Larry T. Riggs, Pres.

Founded: 1967. **Description:** Women and representatives of women's organizations with interests in traffic safety. Objectives are to reduce traffic crashes, injuries, and deaths by: supporting and implementing the National Highway Safety Standards in communities and states, and nationwide; encouraging each political subdivision to assume its responsibility for highway safety; aiming at more uniformity in traffic safety programs and regulations within the 50 states, the District of Columbia, and Puerto Rico. Conducts educational programs including seminars and workshops; maintains speakers' bureau. **Members:** 3,000,000. **Regional Groups:** 10. **State Groups:** 50. **Publications:** NAWHSL Directory, annual. • President's Newsletter, monthly. • Regional Director's Newsletter, monthly. • State Representatives Newsletter, periodic. • Also publishes Buckle Up, Look, Listen and Live, and High School Driver Education (brochures).

★622★ National Association of Women in Horticulture (NAWH)
c/o Lori Brown
PO Box 1483
Mt. Dora, FL 32757
Phone: (904)383-8811
Fax: (904)735-2688
Lori Brown, Exec.Sec.

Founded: 1985. **Description:** Men and women in the horticulture field; interested others. Serves as a networking vehicle for women holding professional positions in horticulture. Bestows Woman of the Year Award. Offers scholarship program. **Members:** 400. **State Groups:** 4. **Publications:** Directory of Women in Horticulture, annual. Directory of members and other women in horticulture. • The Forum, bimonthly. Newsletter. • Networking Directory, annual.

★623★ National Association of Women Judges (NAWJ)
c/o Natl. Center for State Courts
300 Newport Ave.
Williamsburg, VA 23187-8798
Phone: (804)253-2000
Fax: (804)220-1449
Karen S. Heroy, Staff Dir.

Founded: 1979. **Description:** Individuals holding judicial or quasi-judicial positions. Objectives are to: promote the administration of justice; discuss and formulate solutions to legal, educational, social, and ethical problems encountered by women judges; increase the number of women judges so that the judiciary more appropriately reflects the role of women in a democratic society; address other issues particularly affecting women judges. Conducts research and educational programs and referral services; compiles statistics. Presents Honoree of the Year Award. **Members:** 850. **Regional Groups:** 14. **Publications:** NAWJ Annual Directory. • NAWJ Newsletter, 3/year.

★624★ National Association of Women Lawyers (NAWL)
750 N. Lake Shore Dr.
Chicago, IL 60611
Phone: (312)988-6186
Fax: (312)988-6281
Patricia O'Mahoney, Exec.Dir.

Founded: 1911. **Description:** Lawyers who have been admitted to practice in any state or territory of the U.S. Presents Toch Membership Trophy annually to member who endorses most new members during the year. Maintains 17 committees. **Members:** 1200. **Publications:** Membership Directory, biennial. • Presidents Newsletter, quarterly. • Women Lawyers Journal, quarterly.

★625★ National Association of Women's Centers (NAWC)
c/o Sylvia Kramer
Women's Action Alliance
370 Lexington Ave., Ste. 603
New York, NY 10017
Phone: (212)532-8330
Fax: (212)779-2846
Sylvia Kramer, Contact

Founded: 1985. **Description:** Women's centers. Promotes a nonsexist society for women and men; provides a network for support; shares ideas and information; encourages legislative advocacy for battered women's shelters, rape crisis centers, marital and career counsel-

ing and training, and related concerns. Conducts research on the needs of women and women's issues. Maintains speakers' bureau. **Members:** 200. **Regional Groups:** 12. **Computerized Services:** Mailing list. **Publications:** Connections, 3/year. Newsletter; includes information on conferences. • Also plans to publish a directory.

★626★ National Bar Association (NBA) Association of Black Women Attorneys (ABWA)
134 W. 32nd St., Ste. 602
New York, NY 10001
Phone: (212)244-4270
Leslie R. Jones, President

Description: ABWA encourages minority women attorneys to develop their professional skills. ABWA programs and activities are designed with the following objectives: to establish and maintain an effective communication and information system for both members and the community; to conduct research and development in law-related areas; to assist in the development of legal assistance programs in the black community; to seek opportunities to provide input with respect to issues of concern to women; and to assist the legal education of minority students through the development of a scholarship fund. Provides seminars on professional skills and hosts fundraising activities for the Association's functions and programs. **Publications:** Association distributes monthly newsletter to membership.

★627★ National Bar Association Women Lawyers Division
c/o Brenda Girton
1211 Connecticut Ave. NW, Ste. 702
Washington, DC 20036
Phone: (202)291-1979
Fax: (202)347-7127
Brenda Girton, Pres.

Founded: 1972. **Description:** Women lawyers, law students, and other individuals. Purposes are to: provide a forum to discuss and address issues unique to women in the legal profession; promote professional growth and honor achievements of minority attorneys; promote admission to practice at all levels of the judicial system; foster interactions between minority and other bar associations; encourage participation in community service. Awards scholarships; holds seminars. **Members:** 300. **Publications:** Newsletter, periodic.

★628★ National Black Sisters' Conference (NBSC)
1001 Lawrence St. NE, Ste. 102
Washington, DC 20017
Phone: (202)529-9250
Sr. Gwynette Proctor, Exec.Dir.

Founded: 1968. **Description:** Black religious women. Seeks to develop the personal resources of black women; challenges society, especially the church, to address issues of racism in the U.S. Activities include: retreats; consulting, leadership, and cultural understanding; formation workshops for personnel. Maintains educational programs for facilitating change and community involvement in inner-city parochial schools and parishes. Operates Sojourner House to provide spiritual affirmation for black religious and laywomen. Bestows awards; maintains speakers' bureau. **Members:** 150. **Publications:** Signs of Soul, 4/year. Newsletter reporting on black members of the Catholic church. Includes employment opportunities and obituaries of members. • Also publishes *Joint Black Clergy and Black Sisters*, articles, and books.

★629★ National Black Women's Consciousness Raising Association (BWCR)
1906 N. Charles St.
Baltimore, MD 21218
Phone: (301)727-8900
Dr. Elaine Simon, Exec.Dir.

Founded: 1975. **Description:** Black women interested in women's rights and women's issues. Acts as a support group for women. Provides educational and informational workshops and seminars on subjects of concern to black women and women in general. Annually recognizes individuals, especially for academic achievement. **Members:** 750. **Publications:** *BWCR*, semiannual. Newsletter.

★630★ National Black Women's Health Project (NBWHP)
175 Trinity Ave. SW, 2nd Fl.
Atlanta, GA 30306
Phone: (404)681-4554
Toll-free: 800-ASK-BWHP
Fax: (404)752-6756
Cynthia Newbille-Marsh, Dir.

Founded: 1980. **Description:** Encourages mutual and selfhelp advocacy among women to bring about a reduction in health care problems prevalent among black women. Urges women to communicate with health care providers, seek out available health care resources, become aware of selfhelp approaches, and communicate with other black women to minimize feelings of powerlessness and isolation, and thus realize they have some control over their physical and mental health. Points out the higher incidence of high blood pressure, obesity, breast and cervical cancers, diabetes, kidney disease, arteriosclerosis, and teenage pregnancy among black women than among other racial or socioeconomic groups. Also notes that black infant mortality is twice that of whites and that black women are often victims of family violence. Offers seminars outlining demographic information, chronic conditions, the need for health information and access to services, and possible methods of improving the health status of black women. Maintains library,data base, and speakers' bureau. Conducts gender and race specific health research programs. Plans to: establish black women's wellness centers; develop Empowerment Though Wellness curriculum. **Members:** 2000. **Regional Groups:** 5. **State Groups:** 26. **Computerized Services:** Mailing list. **Publications:** *Annual Report*. • *Vital Signs*, quarterly. Newsletter. • Also publishes conference reports, brochure, and health fact sheet; plans to produce educational films and publish *Black Women's Health Issues* (manual). **Formerly:** (1984) Black Women's Health Project.

★631★ National Black Women's Political Leadership Caucus
3005 Bladensburg Rd., NE, No. 217
Washington, DC 20018
Phone: (202)529-2806
Juanita Kennedy Morgan, Dir.

Founded: 1971. **Description:** Women interested in understanding their political role and the need for females to work toward equality; auxiliary membership includes men, senior citizens, and youths. Works to educate and incorporate all black women and youth in the political and economic process through participation. Encourages women to familiarize themselves with the role of city, state, and federal governments. Presents awards for humanitarianism; trains speakers and conducts research on the black family and on topics concerning politics and economics; compiles statistics. Holds legislative, federal, state, and local workshops. Provides placement service; offers children's services; operates charitable program. **Regional Groups:** 3. **State Groups:** 33. **Publications:** *Newsletter*, semiannual. • Has published election tabloids.

★632★ National Catholic Women's Union (NCWU)
3835 Westminster Pl.
St. Louis, MO 63108-3492
Phone: (314)371-1653
Rev. John H. Miller, CSC, Dir.

Founded: 1916. **Description:** Individual Catholic women and affiliated societies interested in Catholic social action. Sponsors religious activities, works of charity, mission activities, and maternity guilds. Promotes vocations to the priesthood and the religious life. Headquarters, publications office, library, and various programs are maintained by Central Bureau, Catholic Central Union of America. **Members:** 10,900. **State Groups:** 7. **Local Groups:** 170.

★633★ National Center for Education in Maternal and Child Health (NCEMCH)
38th and R Sts. NW
Washington, DC 20057
Phone: (202)625-8400
Fax: (202)625-8404
Dr. Rochelle Mayer, Program Dir.

Founded: 1981. **Description:** Provides information services to professionals and the public on maternal and child health. Collects and disseminates information on available materials, programs, and research. Offers summer internships for graduate students in public health schools. Operates 8000 volume resource center containing books, journals, articles, teaching manuals, brochures, fact sheets, and audiovisual and educational materials. **Publications:** *Abstracts of Active Projects*, annual. Lists current grants of the Maternal and Child Health Bureau, U.S. Deptartment of Health and Human Services. • *MCH Program Interchange*, monthly. Lists new publications in maternal and child health. • *Reaching Out: A Directory of National Organizations Related to Maternal and Child Health*, annual. • *Starting Early: A Guide to Federal Resources in Maternal and Child Health*, annual. • Also publishes resource guides on selected topics, conference proceedings, and publications catalog. **Formerly:** (1982) National Clearinghouse for Human Genetic Diseases.

★634★ National Center for Lesbian Rights (NCLR)
1663 Mission St., 5th Fl.
San Francisco, CA 94103
Phone: (415)621-0674
Roberta Achtenberg, Exec.Dir.

Founded: 1977. **Description:** A public interest law firm specializing in sexual orientation discrimination cases, particularly those involving lesbians. Activities include: legal counseling and representation, community education, and technical assistance. Provides legal services to lesbians and gay men on issues of custody and foster parenting, employment, housing, the military, and insurance. **Publications:** *Lesbian Mother Litigation Manual, Lesbian Mothers and Their Children: An Annotated Bibliography of Cases and Law Review Articles, Recognizing Lesbian and Gay Families: Strategies for Extending Employment Benefits, Preserving and Protecting the Families of Lesbians and Gay Men, Lesbians Choosing Motherhood: Legal Issues in Donor Insemination*, and *AIDS and Child Custody*. **Formerly:** (1989) Lesbian Rights Project.

★635★ National Center for Policy Alternatives
Women's Economic Justice Center (WEJC)
1875 Connecticut Ave. NW, Ste. 710
Washington, DC 20009
Phone: (202)387-6030
Fax: (202)986-2539
Donna Talbert, Program Coordinator

Description: WEJC is dedicated to improving the lives of economically disadvantaged women and their families by creating sound state policies. The Center works with policymakers and advocates to identify policy alternatives on issues that include abortion, child care, economic development, economic equity, family and medical leave, low income women, teenage pregnancy, prochoice, and work and family. **Publications:** *WEJC UPDATE*.

★636★ National Center on Women and Family Law, Inc. (NCOWFL)
799 Broadway, Rm. 402
New York, NY 10003
Phone: (212)674-8200
Fax: (212)533-5104
Laurie Woods, Exec.Dir.

Founded: 1979. **Description:** Litigates and provides technical assistance to legal services staff and other advocates on women's issues in family law. Provides consultations and participates in impact litigation as co-counsel or amicus. Maintains files on custody, support, divorce, division of property, battery, and rape; other resources include a comprehensive state-by-state resource library on women's issues in family law. Compiles statistics. **Publications:** *Newsletter*, bimonthly. • Also publishes resource packets and manuals.

★637★ National Center for Women and Retirement Research (NCWRR)
Long Island University
Southampton Campus
Southampton, NY 11968
Toll-free: 800-426-7386
Fax: (516)283-4678
Christopher L. Hayes, Director

Description: The Center researches and prepares educational materials (handbooks, videos, cassettes, seminars) to assist women in addressing various issues related to aging; sponsors the PREP program (Pre-Retirement Educational Planning for women) to assist women in developing secure retirement plans; and conducts surveys relevant to women and aging. **Publications:** *National Center for Women and Retirement Research Newsletter* (quarterly).

★638★ National Chamber of Commerce for Women (NCCW)

10 Waterside Plaza, Ste. 6H
New York, NY 10010
Phone: (212)685-3454
Maggie Rinaldi, Exec.Dir.

Founded: 1977. **Description:** Coalition of corporations, state agencies, and concerned individuals. Works with local, regional, and state redevelopment agencies to expand business opportunities for women. Conducts pay comparison surveys. Compiles statistics. Maintains placement service and speakers' bureau. **Members:** 4700. **Computerized Services:** Business information bank. **Publications:** *Enrich!*, bimonthly. Newsletter analyzing opportunities, trends, and techniques for women who manage small businesses in commercial space or their homes. Includes information on how to bid, how to get consulting contracts, legal options, and pay comparisons. • Also publishes booklets.

★639★ National Child Support Enforcement Association (NCSEA)

Hall of States
444 N. Capitol NW, No. 613
Washington, DC 20001
Phone: (202)624-8180
Kathleen Duggan, Contact

Founded: 1952. **Description:** State and local officials and agencies responsible for enforcing reciprocal and family support enforcement laws for support of dependents. Bestows awards. **Members:** 1500. **State Groups:** 43. **Publications:** *National Roster and Interstate Referral Guide*, biennial. • *Newsletter*, bimonthly. **Formerly:** (1974) National Conference on Uniform Reciprocal Enforcement of Support; (1984) National Reciprocal and Family Support Enforcement Association.

★640★ National Clearinghouse for the Defense of Battered Women (NCDBW)

125 S. 9th St., Ste. 302
Philadelphia, PA 19107
Phone: (215)351-0010
Fax: (215)351-0779
Sue Osthoff, Director

Description: NCDBW aids battered women who have assaulted or killed their abusers in order to protect themselves and those who have been forced into crime and are unable to protect their children from their abuser. The Clearinghouse provides direct technical assistance and consultation to defense teams nationally, including attorneys, battered women advocates, and expert witnesses; it offers a comprehensive resource bank of information related to battered women's defense issues; provides support to abused women in prison; and provides a network of advocates working with battered women. **Publications:** *NCDBW Newsletter.* • Also publishes an annotated bibliography, a statistics packet, and working papers.

★641★ National Clearinghouse on Marital and Date Rape (NCOMDR)

2325 Oak St.
Berkeley, CA 94708
Phone: (415)524-1582
Laura X, Contact

Founded: 1980. **Description:** Students, attorneys, legislators, faculty members, rape crisis centers, shelters, and other social service groups. Operates as speaking/consulting firm. Is presently launching a nation-wide call for members to help marital, cohabitant, and date rape victims and to stop the rape of potential victims by vigorously educating the public and by providing resources to battered women's shelters, crisis centers, district attorneys and legislators through media appearances and lectures at college campuses and conferences. Ultimate goal is to "make intimate relationships truly egalitarian". Holds training sessions and workshops. Provides phone consultation (for a fee) for the media, prosecutors, expert witnesses, victim/witness advocates, legislators, police, rape crisis workers, and others. Offers sociological and legal research on court cases and legislation. Compiles statistics. **Members:** 500. **Formerly:** (1969) Women's History Research Center.

★642★ National Clearinghouse on Women and Girls with Disabilities

Educational Equity Concepts
114 E. 32nd St., Ste. 306
New York, NY 10016
Phone: (212)725-1803

Description: Provides information on programs and services concerned with women and girls with disabilities. **Publications:** *Bridging the Gap: A National Directory of Services for Women and Girls with Disabilities.* • *Building Community: A Manual Exploring Issues of Women and Disability.*

★643★ National Coalition Against Domestic Violence (NCADV)

PO Box 34103
Washington, DC 20043-4103
Phone: (202)638-6388
Deborah White, Coordinator

Founded: 1978. **Description:** Grass roots coalition of battered women's service organizations and shelters. Supplies technical assistance and makes referrals on issues of domestic violence. Provides training personnel; offers child advocacy training. Maintains speakers' bureau; operates a film loan library. Compiles statistics. **Members:** 1200. **State Groups:** 50. **Local Groups:** 1250. **Publications:** *National Coalition Against Domestic Violence—Voice*, quarterly. Newsletter. • Also publishes *A Step Toward Independence: Economic Self-Sufficiency*, *Naming the Violence: Speaking Out About Lesbian Battering*, and *Guidelines for Mental Health Practitioners in Domestic Violence Cases.*

★644★ National Coalition Against Sexual Assault (NCASA)

2428 Ontario Rd. NW
Washington, DC 20009
Phone: (202)483-7165
Marybeth Carter, Pres.

Founded: 1978. **Description:** Works to build a network through which individuals and organizations working against sexual assault can share expertise, experience, and information. Acts as an advocate for and on behalf of rape victims. Disseminates information on sexual assault. Sponsors Sexual Assault Awareness Month in April. Bestows awards; compiles statistics. **Members:** 500. **Regional Groups:** 6. **Publications:** *Newsletter*, quarterly.

★645★ National Coalition Against Surrogacy (NCAS)

1130 17th St. NW, Ste. 630
Washington, DC 20036
Phone: (202)466-2823
Jeremy Rifkin, Co-Chair

Founded: 1987. **Description:** Former contract surrogate mothers, lawyers, and legislators opposed to surrogate parenting. (Surrogate mothers are paid to bear children for infertile couples.) Provides legal and moral support to women who the coalition feel have been victimized by maternity contracts; advocates state and national legislation outlawing birth-for-pay arrangements; lobbies for rules and regulations to protect the rights and health of women who bear children for others. **Members:** 20.

★646★ National Coalition of American Nuns (NCAN)

7315 S. Yale
Chicago, IL 60621
Phone: (312)651-8372
Sr. Margaret Ellen Traxler, Dir.

Founded: 1969. **Description:** Dedicated to studying, working on, and speaking out on issues related to human rights and social justice. **Members:** 1800. **Publications:** *NCAN Newsletter*, quarterly.

★647★ National Coalition for Campus Child Care (NCCCC)

PO Box 258
Cascade, WI 53011
Phone: (414)528-7080
S. Lavernn Wilson, Chairperson

Founded: 1980. **Description:** Promotes child care centers on college campuses and provides information on organizing and operating these centers. Believes that campus child care programs should be an integral part of higher education systems and should provide safe and healthy environments for children, developmentally sound educational programs, and services to both parents and campus programs. **Members:** 300. **Publications:** *Newsletter*, semiannual. • Also publishes books, bibliographies, and brochure, and compiles list of campus child care centers.

★648★ National Coalition of 100 Black Women (NCBW)

300 Park Ave., 2nd Fl.
New York, NY 10022
Phone: (212)974-6140
Fax: (212)838-0542
Jewell Jackson-McCabe, Chm.

Founded: 1981. **Description:** African-American women actively involved with issues such as economic development, health, employment, education, voting, housing, criminal justice, the status of black families, and the arts. Seeks to provide networking and career opportunities for African-American women in the process of establishing links between the organization and the corporate and political arenas. Encourages leadership development; sponsors role-model and mentor programs to provide guidance to teenage mothers and young women in high school or who have graduated from college and are striving for career advancement. Bestows Candace Awards honoring outstanding African-American women and men. **Members:** 6000. **Chapters:** 59. **Publications:** *National Coalition of 100 Black Women–Statement*, semiannual.

Newsletter reporting on the activities and achievements of black women.

★649★ National Coalition for Women and Girls in Education (NCWGE)
c/o Displaced Homemakers Network
1411 K St. NW, Ste. 930
Washington, DC 20005
Phone: (202)628-6767
Jill Miller, Exec.Dir.

Founded: 1975. Description: National organizations opposing sex discrimination in education. Purpose is to promote national policies that assure educational equity for females. Monitors actions of agencies responsible for enforcing civil rights laws; advocates legislation guaranteeing women and girls equal opportunities in education. Bestows awards. Members: 60. Publications: Press packets and informational papers.

★650★ National Coalition for Women's Enterprise (HUB)
101 Alma St., Apt. 107-8
Palo Alto, CA 94301
Phone: (415)321-3503
Jing Lyman, Pres.

Founded: 1983. Description: Works with community-based women's organizations, women business owners, women actively interested in self-employment, and community leaders to develop local awareness, information, and support for minority and low-income women's self-employment. Offers technical assistance on: needs assessment; collecting data on women business owners; documenting existing community services; devising programs responsive to local needs. Helps to conduct surveys and compile statistics. Maintains speakers' bureau. (Group is named Hub "because women are at the hub of economic revitalization in their communities.") Regional Groups: 3. State Groups: 2. Local Groups: 6. Publications: Report of the National Strategy Session on Women's Self-Employment and Working Guide to Women's Self-Employment. Formerly: (1986) Hub Program for Women's Enterprise; (1988) Hub Co-Ventures for Women's Enterprise.

★651★ National Coalition for Women's Mental Health (NCWMH)
Women's Studies Program
Arizona State University
Tempe, AZ 85287
Phone: (602)965-2358
Nancy Felipe Russo, Director

Description: The NCWMH serves as a network to promote current women's issues from a psychological perspective. Coalition Report, twice yearly. • Also publishes pamphlets and works.

★652★ National Commission for Women's Equality (CWE)
c/o American Jewish Congress
15 E. 84th St.
New York, NY 10028
Phone: (212)879-4500
Fax: (212)249-3672
Harriet Kurlander, Dir.

Founded: 1984. Description: Feminists, elected officials, professionals, academics, and Jewish communal leaders working to define feminism within a context compatible with Judaism. Areas of concern include: reproductive freedom, economic equity, child care, equality in religious life, and the empowerment of women in politics and in Jewish communal life. A commission of the American Jewish Congress. Members: 200. Regional Groups: 15. Publications: none.

★653★ National Commission on Working Women (NCWW)
1325 G St., NW
Washington, DC 20005
Phone: (202)737-5764
Cindy Marano, Dir.

Founded: 1977. Description: A commission of Wider Opportunities for Women (see separate entry). Advocates for the needs and concerns of women in the work force, especially women in low-paying, low-status jobs in the service industry and in clerical occupations, retail stores, and factories and plants. Conducts public education on issues such as pay equity, child care, poor working women, age discrimination in employment, literacy, and the image of women on television. Works to mobilize corporate, congressional, labor, advocacy, media, and educational and training representatives to effectively respond to the needs of working women. Operates Women's Work Force Network. Conducts research. Bestows Women at Work Broadcast Awards. Maintains archives. Members: 30. Publications: Women at Work, quarterly. Newsletter. • Also publishes fact sheets and reports including No Way Out: Working Poor Women in the United States.

★654★ National Committee for Fair Divorce and Alimony Laws (NCFDAL)
11 Park Pl., Ste. 1116
New York, NY 10007
Phone: (212)766-4030
Sidney Siller, Gen. Counsel

Founded: 1965. Description: Individuals interested in having "antiquated divorce and alimony laws changed." Seeks to limit alimony, "alimony prison," and the concurrent jurisdiction of the Family Court and the Supreme Court (in New York). Advocates adequate child support with both parents contributing and equal visitation and responsibility for each parent. Supports a standard and uniform divorce code in every state, "thereby eliminating frauds, deceptions and injustices." Maintains extensive files of pertinent material, newspapers, and periodicals. Has formed the Institute for the Study of Matrimonial Laws (see separate entry). Provides personal assistance to those involved in marital difficulties. Conducts monthly symposium. Members: 2000. Publications: Newsletter, monthly. Formerly: (1965) Alimony Limited; Committee for Fair Divorce and Alimony Laws.

★655★ National Committee for a Human Life Amendment (NCHLA)
1511 K St. NW, Ste. 335
Washington, DC 20005
Phone: (202)393-0703
Fax: (202)347-1383
Michael A. Taylor, Exec.Dir.

Founded: 1974. Description: Seeks to overturn the U.S. Supreme Court decision on abortion by means of a Human Life Amendment. Is also involved in other pro-life legislation and education on the national level. Provides grass roots assistance on the effective organization of congressional districts.

★656★ National Committee on Pay Equity (NCPE)
1126 16th St. NW, Rm. 411
Washington, DC 20036
Phone: (202)331-7343
Fax: (202)331-7406
Claudia E. Wayne, Exec.Dir.

Founded: 1979. Description: Individuals (220) and organizations (140) such as women's groups, labor unions, professional associations, minority and civil rights groups, and governmental and educational groups. Educates the public about the historical, legal, and economic bases for pay inequities between men and women and white people and people of color. Sponsors speakers' bureau; acts as an information clearinghouse on pay equity activities. Members: 360. Publications: Newsnotes, 2-4/year. Newsletter; includes international news, federal legislation updates, and litigation reports. • Also publishes Pay Equity Activity in the Public Sector, 1979-1989, Pay Equity: An Issue of Race, Ethnicity, and Sex, Briefing Paper: The Wage Gap, Bargaining for Pay Equity: A Strategy Manual, Pay Equity Makes Good Business Sense, and Pay Equity Bibliography and Resource Listing. Formerly: (1980) National Pay Equity Committee.

★657★ National Conference of Puerto Rican Women (NACOPRW)
5 Thomas Circle
Washington, DC 20005
Phone: (202)387-4716
Nydia I. Santiago, Ph.D., Exec.Dir.

Founded: 1972. Description: Promotes full participation of Puerto Rican and other Hispanic women in the economic, social, and political life of the U.S. and Puerto Rico. Collaborates with other national organizations committed to equal rights for all. Encourages the formation of local chapters in all Puerto Rican communities and fosters closer ties among them. Sponsors competitions and bestows awards; maintains biographical archives and speakers' bureau. Members: 5000. State Groups: 16. Publications: Ecos Nacionales, 3/year. Newsletter covering issues affecting Puerto Rican and other Hispanic women; includes association news, book reviews, chapter news, employment opportunity listings. • Fact Sheets, periodic. • Membership Directory, annual. • Also publishes speeches, books, and articles.

★658★ National Conference of State Legislatures
The Women's Network
1560 Broadway, Ste. 700
Denver, CO 80202
Phone: (303)830-2200

Description: The Network strives to meet the needs of the women serving in state legislatures. The Network focuses on nation-wide, state-level adoption of policies benefiting women and their families. Publications: Women, Babies and Drugs: Family Centered Treatment Options. Remarks: Affiliated with National Conference of State Legislatures.

★659★ National Conference of Women's Bar Associations (NCWBA)
PO Box 77
Edenton, NC 27932-0077
Phone: (919)482-8202
Fax: (919)482-7642
Mary Ann Coffey, Exec.Dir.

Founded: 1981. **Description:** State and local women's bar associations. Promotes the interests of women lawyers. Serves as a forum for information exchange among women's bar associations. Maintains National Foundation for Women's Bar Associations. Conducts educational programs; maintains speakers' bureau; compiles statistics. Bestows community service awards. **Members:** 110. **Computerized Services:** National Clearinghouse of Women's Bar Associations. **Publications:** *NCWBA Newsletter*, quarterly.

★660★ National Congress of Neighborhood Women (NCNW)
249 Manhattan Ave.
Brooklyn, NY 11211
Phone: (718)388-6666
Deidra Ahran, Exec. Officer

Founded: 1975. **Description:** Low-and moderate-income women from diverse ethnic and racial backgrounds united to: bring about neighborhood stabilization and revitalization; raise awareness of women's roles in neighborhood activities and organizations as well as on issues affecting low-income women; provide a voice for a new women's movement that reflects family and neighborhood values while promoting women's empowerment. Current projects include: Neighborhood Women College Program, which offers associate arts degree programs; Project Prepare, which seeks to prepare individuals to get a job through adult education classes, work experience, resume writing, child care, and counseling support. Maintains local advisory board and support groups. Offers speakers' bureau and placement service. Bestows awards. Compiles statistics on women, poverty, and neighborhood development. Maintains library of articles, papers, reports, oral histories, newspapers, letters, and audiovisual materials. **Regional Groups:** 26. **Local Groups:** 26. **Computerized Services:** Mailing list. **Publications:** *Neighborhood Women Network News*, bimonthly. • Also publishes *Leadership Training Manual, Neighborhood Women: Putting It Together*, articles, and conference reports.

★661★ National Coordinating Committee for the Promotion of History (CCWHP)
NCC: 400 A St. SE
Washington, DC 20003
Phone: (301)544-2422
Page Putnam Miller, Director

Description: Central advocacy office for the historical profession in Washington dealing with federal legislation and policy that affects historians and the promotion of history. Promotes passage of legislation on Women's History Month and seeks representation of women in the National Park Service's National Historic Landmark Program. Projects include "Reclaiming our Past: Landmark Sites of Women's History." **Alternate phone number:** (301)622-2535.

★662★ National Council of Administrative Women in Education (NCAWE)
c/o Barbara Brooks, Ed.D.
5190 Roxbury Rd.
Pittsburgh, PA 15235
Phone: (619)223-3121
Barbara K. Brooks, Ed.D., Pres.

Founded: 1915. **Description:** Women educators in administrative or supervisory positions in a public or private school system, college or university, foundation, agency, government or nongovernment education programs; also offers auxiliary and associate memberships. Encourages women to prepare for careers in educational administration and to urge educational institutions, systems, and agencies to employ and advance women in this field. Monitors national and local legislation pertaining to women's education. Works to eliminate discrimination against women in educational administration. Circulates information on job openings. Maintains speakers' bureau; conducts research; presents awards. Sponsors competitions. **Members:** 1300. **Local Groups:** 7. **Publications:** *Administration Study on Status of Women Administration in Education*, periodic. • *Leadership in Education Journal*, semiannual. • *National Council of Administration in Education Directory*, annual. • *NCAWE News*, semiannual. Newsletter.

★663★ National Council of Career Women (NCCW)
3202 Gemstone Ct.
Oakton, VA 22124
Phone: (703)591-4359
Patricia Whittaker, Pres.

Founded: 1975. **Description:** Women interested in achieving maximum potential in the business world and individual careers (350); corporate sponsors (5). Seeks to enhance the image and role of women in the business and professional world, through professional skill development, education, mentoring, and networking. Bestows awards; operates placement services. **Members:** 355. **Publications:** *Membership Directory*, annual. • *NCCW News*, bimonthly. • Also publishes brochure.

★664★ National Council of Catholic Women (NCCW)
1275 K St. NW, Ste. 975
Washington, DC 20005
Phone: (202)682-0334
Fax: (202)682-0338
Annette Kane, Exec.Dir.

Founded: 1920. **Program Commissions:** Church Communities; Community Affairs; Family Affairs; International Affairs; Organizational Services. **Description:** Federation of 8000 national, state, diocesan, interparochial, and parochial organizations of Catholic women. Serves as a forum for Catholic women to share research, speak on current issues in the church and society, and develop leadership and management skills. Is engaged in initiating and developing programs in religious, educational, social, and economic areas. Members serve on private and public policymaking bodies monitoring a variety of social justice issues. Works to raise funds for foreign relief in conjunction with Catholic Relief Services, Works of Peace, Help-a-Child, and Madonna Plan. **Publications:** *Catholic Woman*, bimonthly. Newsletter. • Also publishes program kits.

★665★ National Council on Child Abuse and Family Violence (NCCAFV)
1155 Connecticut Ave. NW, Ste. 300
Washington, DC 20036
Phone: (202)429-6695
Toll-free: 800-222-2000
Fax: (818)914-3616
Alan Davis, Pres.

Founded: 1984. **Description:** To support community-based prevention and treatment programs that provide assistance to children, women, the elderly, and families who are victims of abuse and violence. Is concerned with the cyclical and intergenerational nature of family violence and abuse. Seeks to increase public awareness of family violence and promote private sector financial support for prevention and treatment programs. Collaborates with similar organizations to form an informal network; organized National Alliance on Family Violence. Provides technical assistance program to aid community-based organizations in obtaining nonfederal funding. Collects and disseminates information regarding child abuse, domestic violence, and elder abuse. **Telecommunications Services:** Toll-free number, (800)222-2000, providing referral service to persons seeking information or community services. **Publications:** *INFORUM*, periodic. Newsletter. • Also publishes information and brochure sheets.

★666★ National Council of Churches, USA Division of Church and Society: Justice for Women
475 Riverside Dr., Rm. 572
New York, NY 10115
Phone: (212)870-2421
Jane Kamp, Consultant

Description: The Division is an ecumenical effort of the Council which seeks to empower women in church and society. It is currently working on improving pay equity within the Council; sponsoring consultation for more funding to women's projects and programs; and developing resources on women in prostitution and women in prison.

★667★ National Council on Family Relations
Feminism and Family Studies (FFS)
3989 Central Ave. NE, Ste. 550
Minneapolis, MN 55421
Phone: (612)781-9331
Fax: (612)781-9348

Founded: 1985. **Description:** Family researchers and practitioners. Aims to integrate feminist perspectives into theory and family counseling. Is establishing a collection of teaching materials with a feminist perspective and a mentoring network. As a section of the National Council on Family Relations, organizes sessions on feminism and family studies and presents distinguished lecturers. **Publications:** *Newsletter*, periodic. **Formerly:** (1991) National Council on Family Relations Feminism and Family Studies Section.

★668★ National Council of Hispanic Women (NCHW)
20 F St., NW
PO Box 1655
Washington, DC 20013
Luisa A. Bras, Chairperson

Description: Hispanic women, universities, corporations, and government representatives interested in strengthening the role of Hispanic women in society. Seeks to: express the concerns and interests of Hispanic women by participating in the decision-making process; promote ideals that will keep the U.S. safe and strong; improve the social and economic conditions of the Hispanic community; assist Hispanics in establishing themselves in the mainstream of society; foster the exchange of ideas with other groups. Participates in public policy debates, conferences, and television interviews. **Members:** 175. **Publications:** *NCHW Newsletter*, quarterly.

★669★ **National Council of Jewish Women (NCJW)**
53 W. 23rd St.
New York, NY 10010
Phone: (212)645-4048
Fax: (212)645-7465
Iris Gross, CAE, Exec.Dir.

Founded: 1893. **Description:** Sponsors programs of education, social action, and community service for youth, the elderly, and women. Aims to improve the quality of life for individuals of all ages, races, religions, and socioeconomic levels. Advocates measures affecting social welfare, constitutional rights, civil liberties, and equality for women. Maintains the Research Institute for Innovation in Education at Hebrew University, Jerusalem, Israel. Established Center for the Child in New York to conduct research on issues and actions necessary to shape policies affecting children. Develops community service projects and training materials. **Members:** 100,000. **State Groups:** 39. **Local Groups:** 200. **Publications:** *NCJW Journal*, quarterly. Magazine covering constitutional rights, aging, family and child welfare, and Israeli and Jewish life. • *NCJW Washington Newsletter*, quarterly. Reports on legislative issues. • Also publishes program monographs, catalog, brochures, training manuals, and handbooks.

★670★ **National Council of La Roza**
810 First St., NE, Ste. 300
Washington, DC 20002-4205
Phone: (202)289-1380
Margarita Prieto, Contact

★671★ **National Council of Negro Women (NCNW)**
1211 Connecticut Ave., NW, Ste. 702
Washington, DC 20036
Phone: (202)659-0006
Dorothy I. Height, Pres.

Founded: 1935. **Description:** A coalition of 31 national organizations and concerned individuals. Assists in the development and utilization of the leadership of women in community, national, and international life. Provides a center of information for and about women in the black community; stimulates cooperation among women in diverse economic and social interests; acts as a catalyst for constructive advocacy on a number of women's issues. Maintains Women's Center for Education and Career Advancement in New York City, which offers programs designed to aid minority women pursuing nontraditional careers; also maintains the Bethune Museum and Archives for Black Women's History. Operates offices in west and southern Africa, which serve NCNW's international projects and which were designed to improve the social and economic status of rural women in Third World countries. Founded by Mary McLeod Bethune (1875-1955), black American educator and presidential advisor.

Members: 40,000. **Local Groups:** 240. **Publications:** *Black Woman's Voice*, periodic. • *Sisters Magazine*, quarterly.

★672★ **National Council for Research on Women (NCRW)**
Sara Delano Roosevelt Memorial House
47-49 E. 65th St.
New York, NY 10021
Phone: (212)570-5001
Mary Ellen Capek, Exec.Dir.

Founded: 1981. **Description:** National network of organizations representing the academic community, policymakers, and others interested in women's issues. Purpose is to bring institutional resources to bear on feminist research, policy analysis, and educational programs addressing legal, economic, and social inequities. Conducts and promotes collaborative research on women in development, and race, class, and gender issues; acts as clearinghouse. Houses the National Network of Women's Caucuses and Committees in the Disciplinary and Professional Associations. Operates the National Council Database Project that coordinates the development and application of current technology, software, and index standards to improve access to existing research, programs, and work in progress; is developing an online data base. Sponsors seminars. **Members:** 60. **Publications:** *Annual Report*. • *Directory of Members*, periodic. • *Women's Mailing List Directory*, periodic. • *Women's Research Network News*, 3-4/year. Newsletter reporting on member centers' activities, women's caucuses, and research; includes information on new books, fellowships, study and job opportunities, and conference announcements. • Also publishes *A Declining Federal Commitment to Research About Women, 1980-1984, International Centers for Research on Women, Mainstreaming Minority Women's Studies, Opportunities for Research and Study, 1989, Third World Women in Agriculture, an Annotated Bibliography, Transforming the Knowledge Base, Women in Academe: Progress and Prospects, A Task Force Report, Women in Development: Theory and Practice, Women's Thesaurus: An Index of Language Used to Describe and Locate Information By and About Women, Sexual Harassment: Research and Resources, A Report-in-Progress*.

★673★ **National Council for Research on Women (NCRW)**
National Network of Women's Caucuses (NNWC)
47-49 E. 65th St.
New York, NY 10021
Phone: (212)570-5001
Fax: (212)570-5380
Debra L. Schultz, Assist. Director

Founded: 1988. **Description:** NNWC is a coalition of more than 100 caucuses, commissions, committees, other groups in the academic disciplines, and professional associations. It is interested in curriculum transformation, feminist theory, gender issues, mentoring, networking, the professional status of women, sex discrimination, women in higher education, and women's studies. **Publications:** *Women's Research Network News*, quarterly.

★674★ **National Council of Teachers of English (NCTE)**
Women in Literature and Life Assembly (WILLA)
1111 Kenyon Rd.
Urbana, IL 61801
Phone: (217)328-3870
Sue Holbrook, Contact

Description: WILLA tries to ensure the equal treatment of women in the National Council of Teachers of English and the profession. The Assembly develops guidelines for using inclusive language and for forming a gender balanced curriculum in secondary schools. It also presents awards to outstanding women in the field. **Publications:** *WILLA*, annual. • *WILLA Newsletter*, twice yearly.

★675★ **National Council of Teachers of English**
Women's Committee
1111 Kenyon Rd.
Urbana, IL 61801
Phone: (217)328-3870

★676★ **National Council of Women of Free Czechoslovakia (NCWFC)**
77 Sprain Valley Rd.
Scarsdale, NY 10583
Phone: (914)723-9314
Betka Papanek, Pres.

Founded: 1951. **Description:** Women of Czechoslovak origin or background. "Carries on the democratic program of the National Council of Women of Czechoslovakia disbanded by the communists." Supports aged, ill, and disabled Czechoslovak refugees. Conducts cultural, educational, and welfare activities; sponsors exhibits of art and handcrafts. **Members:** 125. **Local Groups:** 4. **Publications:** *Bulletin*, 3/year.

★677★ **National Council on Women in Medicine, Inc.**
1300 York Ave., Rm. D-115
New York, NY 10021
Phone: (212)535-0031
Laura Scharf, Executive Director

Description: The Council tries to improve women's health through educating health professionals and the public. **Publications:** Newsletter.

★678★ **National Council of Women of the United States (NCW)**
777 United Nations Plaza
New York, NY 10017
Phone: (212)697-1278
Fax: (212)972-0164
Alicia Paolozzi, Pres.

Founded: 1888. **Description:** Works for the education, participation, and advancement of women in all areas of society. Serves as information center and clearinghouse for affiliated women's organizations. Conducts projects and sponsors conferences on national and international problems and matters of concern to women and shares the results with affiliated groups. Has observer status at the United Nations. Presents annual Woman of Conscience Award and various other awards to outstanding young women in careers or professions. **Members:** 500. **Publications:** *National Council of Women of the U.S.–Bulletin*, quarterly. Newsletter reporting on council programs and activities of member organizations. Includes awards announcements, book reviews, calendar of events, list of available resources, new member information, obituaries, and profiles of member organizations.

★679★ **National Deaf Women's Bowling Association (NDWBA)**
c/o Kathy M. Darby
33 August Rd.
Simsbury, CT 06070
Phone: (203)651-8234
Kathy M. Darby, Sec.-Treas.

Founded: 1974. **Description:** Hearing impaired bowlers. Promotes fellowship and fair play among participants. **Members:** 300. **Publications:** *NDWBA Constitution and By Laws.*

★680★ **National Defense Committee of the Daughters of the American Revolution (NDCDAR)**
1776 D St. NW
Washington, DC 20006-5392
Phone: (202)879-3261
Phyllis Schlafly, Chm.

Founded: 1926. **Description:** Objective is to assist members of the National Society, Daughters of the American Revolution (see separate entry) in carrying out their patriotic, educational, and historical purposes. Advocates a strong military defense as being essential for national sovereignty and independence. Provides information to alert its members of potential external and internal threats to national independence. Presents awards. **Local Groups:** 3000. **Publications:** *DAR National Defender,* 9/year.

★681★ **National Displaced Homemakers Network (NDHN)**
1625 K St. NW
Washington, DC 20006
Phone: (202)628-6767
Fax: (202)628-0123
Jill Miller, Exec.Dir.

Founded: 1978. **Description:** Displaced homemakers, displaced homemaker services, persons from related organizations, and supporters. Fosters development of programs and services for displaced homemakers. Acts as clearinghouse to provide communications, technical assistance, public information, data collection, legislative monitoring, funding information, and other services. Maintains program data library including annual reports, flyers, manuals, and descriptive material. Compiles statistics. Provides referrals, information on research in progress, and publication distribution; offers workshops. **Members:** 4000. **Regional Groups:** 10. **Local Groups:** 1100. **Publications:** *Displaced Homemaker Program Directory,* annual. • *Network News,* quarterly. Newsletter. • *Transition Times,* semiannual. Newsletter. • Also publishes *Guide to the Displaced Homemakers Self-Sufficiency Assistance Act, Transition to Triumph!, Overcoming Obstacles, Winning Jobs: Tools to Prepare Displaced Homemakers for Paid Employment,* program manual, press kit, and other materials.

★682★ **National Education Association (NEA)**
Women's Caucus
1202 16th St. NW
Washington, DC 20036
Phone: (202)373-1800
Trini Johannesen, Chairperson

Description: The Women's Caucus was established for the purpose of providing a channel through which NEA members can work to eliminate sexism and racism, especially in educational issues. Provides legislative alerts; promotes and encourages women into leadership positions; promotes and monitors affirmative action programs in the NEA, on the state and local level, and in school districts; develops programs for teaching awareness of sex role stereotyping; promotes implementation of Title IX and a woman's right to choose; and advocates ratification of the ERA. **Publications:** *NEA Womenspeak.*

★683★ **National Equal Rights Council (NERC)**
1170 Broadway
New York, NY 10001
Phone: (212)679-1259

★684★ **National Extension Homemakers Council (NEHC)**
5100 S. Atlanta
Tulsa, OK 74105-6600
Phone: (918)749-8383
Fax: (918)749-8703
Judy Weinkauf, Pres.

Founded: 1936. **Description:** Homemakers who are members of state extension homemakers councils in 43 states, the Virgin Islands, and Puerto Rico. Educational organization assisting individuals and family members in identifying and solving family and community problems, in cooperation with local resources, state land-grant universities, and the United States Department of Agriculture. Educational programs are concerned with children's issues, environmental problems, and literacy. Conducts leadership development programs. Presents awards for best educational programs and for outstanding projects in each of the work programs; sponsors Family Community Leadership Program. **Members:** 400,000. **State Groups:** 46. **Local Groups:** 28,000. **Publications:** *Handbook,* annual. • *The Homemaker Update,* bimonthly. Includes state group reports. • *NEHC Annual Report.* **Formerly:** National Home Demonstration Council.

★685★ **National Family Planning and Reproductive Health Association (NFPRHA)**
122 C St. NW, Ste. 380
Washington, DC 20001
Phone: (202)628-3535
Toll-free: 800-5NF-PRHA
Fax: (202)737-2690
Judith M. DeSarno, Exec.Dir.

Founded: 1971. **Description:** Hospitals, state and city departments of health, health care providers, private nonprofit clinics, and consumers concerned with the maintenance and improvement of family planning and reproductive health services. Serves as a national communications network and advocacy organization. Maintains contact with Congress and government agencies in order to monitor government policy and regulations. Bestows national and local public service awards. **Members:** 1000.

Publications: *NFPRHA Alert,* periodic. • *NFPRHA News,* bimonthly. • *NFPRHA Report,* bimonthly. • Also publishes professional papers and educational materials. **Formerly:** (1979) National Family Planning Forum.

★686★ **National Federation of Business and Professional Women's Clubs, Inc. of the U.S.A. (BPW/USA)**
2012 Massachusetts Ave. NW
Washington, DC 20036
Phone: (202)293-1100
Linda Colvard Dorian, Exec.Dir.

Founded: 1919. **Description:** Business and professional women and men representing 300 occupations. To promote full participation, equal opportunities, and economic self-sufficiency for working women. Has created Congressional Lobby Corps to influence elected officials on issues concerning women. Sponsors National Business Women Week, held the third week in October, and Business and Professional Women's Foundation (see separate entry) as research and education arm of the federation. Organizes the National Council on the Future of Women in the Workplace, which encourages corporate/private sector cooperation on issues such as dependent care and employer responsiveness to the needs of working women. Maintains 20,000 volume library. Provides nationwide career and personal training seminars. **Members:** 125,000. **Regional Groups:** 53. **Local Groups:** 3500. **Publications:** *National Business Woman,* bimonthly. Tabloid covering women's socioeconomic issues such as pay equity and child care; includes association news.

★687★ **National Federation of Business and Professional Women's Clubs**
Women's Clubs Political Action Committee (BPW/USA)
2012 Massachusetts Ave. NW
Washington, DC 20036
Phone: (202)293-1100
Mariwyn Heath, Chair

★688★ **National Federation of Cuban-American Republican Women (NFCARW)**
2904 Shawnee Dr.
Ft. Wayne, IN 46807
Phone: (219)456-8200
Graciela Beecher, Chair

Founded: 1983. **Description:** An auxiliary of the Republican National Committee. Promotes maintenance of the ideals of hard work, family life, religion, education, and strong defense, which are seen as an integral part of Cuban heritage and the Republican philosophy, as a means of continued improvement of life in the U.S. Encourages participation of women of Cuban origin in Republican Party activities; represents Cuban-American women on the RNC; works for advancement of Republican candidates, policies, and principles. Makes recommendations to the RNC on Cuban-American issues; organizes activities of state and local Republican Cuban-American groups; represents nations suffering under communist rule before the RNC.

★689★ National Federation of Democratic Women (NFDW)
828 Lemont Dr.
Nashville, TN 37216
Phone: (615)244-4270
Fax: (615)244-4281
Gwen McFarland, Exec. Officer
Founded: 1972. **Description:** Democratic women's organizations; state, local, and regional clubs; individuals. Organized to develop leadership among women locally and nationally, both as party workers and elected public officials. Goal is to unite the women of the party and to encourage full participation of women on every level of the party structure by promoting the exchange of ideas and communication. Maintains biographical archives and special study groups; conducts specialized education programs; offers an internship; bestows awards. **Members:** 300,000. **Regional Groups:** 4. **State Groups:** 42. **Publications:** *The Communicator*, quarterly. Newsletter. Includes president's message and regional reports. • *Directory*, semiannual.

★690★ National Federation of Grandmother Clubs of America (NFGCA)
203 N. Wabash Ave., Ste. 702
Chicago, IL 60601
Phone: (312)372-5437
Margaret Day, Office Mgr.
Founded: 1938. **Description:** Women who have grandchildren or have acquired them through marriage or adoption. Sponsors National Grandmother's Day (second Sunday in October). Raises funds to support research on children's diseases, especially leukemia. Bestows awards. **Members:** 8000. **Local Groups:** 300. **Publications:** *Autumn Leaves*, quarterly. Includes memorial list and club highlights.

★691★ National Federation of Officers for Life (NFOFL)
PO Box 892
Corpus Christi, TX 78403-0892
Phone: (512)992-1296
Fax: (512)992-1296
Sgt. Ruben Rodriguez, Pres.
Founded: 1990. **Description:** Active, reserve, and retired law enforcement officers from all levels of jurisdiction, public safety officers, and government officials who oppose abortion and the use of police to escort clients to abortion clinics. Seeks to extend existing conscience clauses which are aimed at protecting officers who for moral reasons refuse to escort women to medical abortion facilities. Maintains speakers' bureau; conducts research and educational programs. **Members:** 200. **State Groups:** 3. **Telecommunications Services:** Electronic bulletin board, (817)572-6397; electronic mail, via CompuServe, 72677,2605 and Prodigy, CJJS87A. **Publications:** *The APB*, bimonthly. Newsletter. • Also publishes *Law or Conscience* (pamphlet).

★692★ National Federation of Press Women (NFPW)
Box 99
Blue Springs, MO 64013
Phone: (816)229-1666
Marge Carpenter, Pres.
Founded: 1937. **Description:** Federation of state associations of professional women and men in all phases of communications on a full-time or free-lance basis. Purposes are to:

encourage the highest standards of professionalism in journalism; provide for exchange of ideas, knowledge, and experience. Conducts annual communications contest, presents minigrants and three scholarships in journalism, and bestows annual achievement award. Offers specialized education programs. **Members:** 5000. **State Groups:** 51. **Publications:** *Directory*, annual. • *Leader Letter*, monthly. • *Press Woman*, monthly.

★693★ National Federation of Republican Women (NFRW)
310 1st St. SE
Washington, DC 20003
Phone: (202)547-9341
Fax: (202)547-8485
Huda Jones, Pres.
Founded: 1938. **Description:** Purposes are: to provide an organization through which women who share the principles of the Republican Party can join in Republican activities; to distribute political educational materials; to recruit and support qualified and electable Republican candidates; to encourage more women to seek public office and to provide them with campaign expertise through NFRW-sponsored Campaign Management Schools across the country; to provide research material and legislative information to federation members. **Members:** 160,000. **State Groups:** 52. **Local Groups:** 2600. **Telecommunications Services:** Hot line network. **Publications:** *The Republican Woman*, bimonthly. Magazine containing articles on the Federation and the Republican Party, administrative policies, and legislative activities in Congress. • Also publishes *Consider Yourself for Public Office*, *Crime: You Don't Have to Live With It*, *Caring for America's Future*, *Lobby, Who Can? You Can!*, and other political education material and manuals. **Formerly:** National Federation of Women's Republican Clubs.

★694★ National Federation of Temple Sisterhoods (NFTS)
838 5th Ave.
New York, NY 10021
Phone: (212)249-0100
Fax: (212)861-0831
Eleanor R. Schwartz, Exec.Dir.
Founded: 1913. **Description:** Women of Reform or liberal Jewish congregations. Works "to intensify Jewish knowledge and to translate religious ideals into practical service to Jewish and humanitarian causes." Activities include: providing services to local affiliates; creating study material for Jewish parents and other adults; encouraging an appreciation of Jewish ceremonials and art; stimulating interest in modern Jewish and social problems; working for the blind; supporting Israel and Soviet Jewry. Also involved in youth activities, rabbinic and student scholarship aid, service to the elderly, education on U.N. affairs, and efforts to improve international understanding. Maintains speakers' bureau; bestows awards. Sponsors Jewish Braille Institute of America. **Members:** 125,000. **Regional Groups:** 13. **Local Groups:** 651. **Publications:** *Catalog for Sisterhood*, annual. • *Jewish Art Calendar*, annual. • *Leaders Line*, semiannual. • *Notes for Now*, quarterly.

★695★ National Fort Daughters of '98, Auxiliary United Spanish War Veterans
319 D. St.
Redwood City, CA 94063
Phone: (415)366-2801
Mary Rudd, Ft.Capt.
Founded: 1934. **Description:** Daughters, daughters-in-law, and other female descendants and legal relatives of veterans of the Spanish American War. Objective is to unite the descendants of Spanish American War veterans and perpetuate the memory of these veterans. Donates clothing and funds to homes for needy children. Bestows Clara Barton Nursing Scholarship Award. **Members:** 700. **State Groups:** 8. **Local Groups:** 40. **Publications:** *Bulletin*, periodic. Includes directory. • *Proceedings*, annual.

★696★ National Forum for Executive Women (NFEW)
1101 15th St., NW
Washington, DC 20005
Phone: (202)331-0270
Beth Neese, Dir.
Founded: 1974. **Description:** Women from middle and top level management within the savings industry. Recognizes the importance of women in executive level positions in business, particularly in the savings industry. Provides an environment for women to grow and improve professionally. Keeps members informed of events that affect the industry with an emphasis on legislative and regulatory changes in the economy and the competition. Offers members the opportunity to make contacts with others who can serve as resources for advice in solving problems, motivating employees', and increasing production. **Members:** 225. **Publications:** NFEW Newsletter, quarterly. **Formerly:** (1979) Executive Women's Division.

★697★ National Foundation for Women Business Owners (NFWBO)
1825 I St. NW, Ste. 800
Washington, DC 20006
Phone: (202)833-1854
Fax: (202)833-1938
Sharon Hardary, Exec.Dir.
Description: NFWBO is the nonprofit educational branch of the National Association of Business Owners. NFWBO is concerned with the leadership and career training of women entrepreneurs and women in management. Performs data collection and disseminates facts and statistics on women business owners; offers management and technical assistance programs; and provides workforce training and monitoring programs. **Publications:** *Newsletter of the National Foundation for Women Business Owners*, quarterly.

★698★ National Gold Star Mothers (NGSM)
c/o Myrtle Iseminger
606 1/2 E. Willow
Olivia, MN 56277
Phone: (612)523-2075
Myrtle Iseminger, Pres.
Founded: 1950. **Description:** Patriotic, civilian organization of mothers whose sons and daughters have died or may die as a result of wartime service in the Army, Navy, Marine Corps, Coast Guard, Merchant Marine, or Air Force of the U.S. and her allies. Conducts charitable work. **Members:** 200. **Publications:** *Bulletin*, quarterly.

★699★ **National Grange**
Department of Women's Activities
15 Meadowlark Rd.
West Simsbury, CT 06092
Phone: (203)658-2855
Betty Jane Gardiner, Director

Description: The National Grange Women's Activities Department functions include development in small rural communities. **Publications:** *National Grange Newsletter.* • *Jane's Jottings.* **Meetings:** Annual.

★700★ **National Hook-Up of Black Women**
(NHBW)
c/o Wynetta Frazier
5117 S. University Ave.
Chicago, IL 60615
Phone: (312)643-5866
Wynetta Frazier, Pres.

Founded: 1975. **Description:** Black women from business, professional, and community-oriented disciplines representing all economic, educational, and social levels. Purpose is to provide a communications network in support of black women who serve in organizational leadership positions, especially those elected or appointed to office and those wishing to elevate their status through educational and career ventures. Works to form and implement a Black Women's Agenda that would provide representation for women, families, and communities and that would help surmount economic, educational, and social barriers. Supports efforts of the Congressional Black Caucus in utilizing the legislative process to work toward total equality of opportunity in society. Seeks to highlight the achievements and contributions of black women. Sponsors workshops. Bestows Distinguished Community Service, Distinguished Family Service, Outstanding Leadership, and Hook-Up Member of the Year awards. Operates speakers' bureau. **Members:** 500. **Regional Groups:** 8. **Local Groups:** 9. **Publications:** *Hook-Up News and Views*, quarterly. Newsletter.

★701★ **National Housewives' League of**
America for Economic Security (NHLA)
3240 Gilbert
Cincinnati, OH 45207
Phone: (513)281-8822
Magnolia R. Silmond, Pres.

Founded: 1933. **Description:** Black women seeking to strengthen the economic base of their communities through a program of positive support for businesses and professions owned and operated by or employing blacks. Aids stores through increased purchasing; conducts tours of businesses; sponsors high school essay contest on business and economics. Maintains library of newspaper articles, bulletins, and minutes of meetings. Sponsors competitions; conducts research programs. **Members:** 250. **Local Groups:** 7. **Publications:** Souvenir conference program. **Formerly:** (1986) National Housewives' League of America.

★702★ **National Identification Program for**
the Advancement of Women in Higher
Education Administration (NIP)
American Council on Educ.
Office of Women in Higher Educ.
1 Dupont Circle NW
Washington, DC 20036
Phone: (202)939-9390
Fax: (202)833-4760
Donna Shavlik, Dir.

Founded: 1977. **Description:** Network of men and women administrators in higher education. Seeks to increase the recognition, acceptance, and promotion of women in policymaking positions in higher education. Program includes Black, Hispanic, American Indian, Asian Pacific, and white women. Conducts forums and invitational conferences that bring together women ready for college and university presidencies with established educational leaders. A program of the American Council on Education. **State Groups:** 50.

★703★ **National Infertility Network**
Exchange (NINE)
c/o Ilene Stargot
PO Box 204
East Meadow, NY 11554
Phone: (516)794-5772
Ilene Stargot, Pres.

Founded: 1988. **Description:** Peer support group for individuals and couples suffering from infertility. Offers education programs and referral service; advocates on behalf of participants. Maintains speakers' bureau. Although the group presently operates regionally, inquiries are answered on a national level. **Publications:** *News from NINE*, 6/year.

★704★ **National Institute for Women of**
Color (NIWC)
1301 20th St. NW Ste. 702
Washington, DC 20036
Phone: (202)296-2661
Sharon Parker, Bd.Chm.

Founded: 1981. **Description:** Aims to: enhance the strengths of diversity; promote educational and economic equity for black, Hispanic, Asian-American, Pacific-Islander, American Indian, and Alaskan Native women. Focuses on mutual concerns and needs, bringing together women who have traditionally been isolated. (NIWC uses the phrase "women of color" to convey unity, self-esteem, and political status and to avoid using the term "minority," which the institute feels has a negative psychological and social impact.) Serves as a networking vehicle to: link women of color on various issues or programs; promote women of color for positions on boards and commissions; ensure that women of color are visible as speakers or presenters at major women's conferences, as well as planners or program developers; support and initiate programs; educate women and the public about the status and culture of the various racial/ethnic groups they represent; promote cooperative efforts between general women's organizations and women of color, while raising awareness about issues and principles of feminism. Sponsors seminars and workshops. Provides technical assistance; conducts internship and leadership development programs. Bestows Outstanding Women of Color Awards; compiles statistics. **Publications:** Has published *Brown Papers*, *NIWC Network News*, bibliographies, bulletins, fact sheets, and other related resources.

★705★ **National Intercollegiate Women's**
Fencing Association (NIWFA)
3 Derby Lane
Dumont, NJ 07628
Phone: (201)384-1722
Sharon Everson, Pres.

Founded: 1929. **Description:** Degree-granting colleges and universities with varsity women's fencing teams. Promotes fencing for women in colleges and universities. Conducts fencing matches, workshops, and clinics. Sponsors and determines members of All-American Women's Fencing Team (chosen annually). Maintains archives. **Members:** 18. **Publications:** *Directory*, annual. • *National Intercollegiate Women's Fencing Association—Newsletter*, periodic. • Also publishes minutes and constitution. **Formerly:** (1970) Intercollegiate Women's Fencing Association.

★706★ **National Jewish Girl Scout**
Committee (NJGSC)
3556 Bedford Ave.
Brooklyn, NY 11210
Phone: (712)252-6072
Shirley W. Parker, Corr.Sec.

Founded: 1972. **Description:** Operates under the auspices of the Synagogue Council of America. Purposes are to: promote Girl Scouting within the Jewish community; encourage participation in Jewish award programs and religious services; promote exchanges with the Israeli Boy and Girl Scout Federation; advise Girl Scouts of the U.S.A. (see separate entry) on religious policy. Presents awards and provides religious education to Jewish Girl Scouts; offers scholarships to Girl Scouts participating in the Summer Scouting in Israel exchange program. **Members:** 100. **Publications:** *National Jewish Girl Scout Committee—Newsletter*, semiannual. Covers the annual meeting and activities of the committee. Includes annual membership list. • Also publishes *Craft Ideas for Jewish Holidays*, guidelines for award programs, and a leader's guide for the filmstrip *Wider-Op Israel - A Step Into History*.

★707★ **National Judicial Education**
Program to Promote Equality for Women
and Men in the Courts
99 Hudson St., 12th Fl.
New York, NY 10013
Phone: (212)925-6635
Fax: (212)226-1066
Lynn Hecht Schafran, Dir.

Founded: 1980. **Description:** A project of the NOW Legal Defense and Education Fund in cooperation with the National Association of Women Judges (see separate entries). Works to eliminate gender bias in the courts by making judges aware of stereotypes, myths, and biases pertaining to the roles of men and women, and how those biases can affect judicial decision-making and the courtroom environment. Serves as a clearinghouse for data on gender bias in the courts. Conducts courses, seminars, and other educational programs for judges, lawyers, and the public. Collaborates with state and national judicial colleges and state task forces; participates in legal conferences, law school programs, and continuing education projects.

★708★ National Ladies Auxiliary
Jewish War Veterans of the USA, Inc.
(JWVA)
1811 R St., NW
Washington, DC 20009
Phone: (202)667-9061
Ethyle K. Bornstein, Pres.
Founded: 1928. **Description:** Raises money for
the Medical Hospital in Israel and volunteers
hours to USVA Hospitals. **Publications:** *JWVA
Bulletin.*

★709★ National Ladies Auxiliary to
Veterans of World War I of the U.S.A.
PO Box 2907
Bay St. Louis, MS 39521-2907
Phone: (601)467-9799
Pauline Charping, Sec.-Treas.
Founded: 1953. **Description:** Female relatives
of Veterans of World War I of U.S.A. Conducts
patriotic, historical, and educational programs.
Members: 20,000. **Regional Groups:** 10. **State
Groups:** 48. **Local Groups:** 1000. **Publications:**
Torch, monthly.

★710★ National Latina Health Organization
(NLHO)
PO Box 7567
Oakland, CA 94601
Phone: (510)534-1362
Fax: (510)534-1364
Luz Alvarez Martinez, Dir.
Founded: 1986. **Description:** Puerto Rican,
Chicana, Mexican, Cuban, and South and Central American women. Works to increase awareness of health issues among Latin American
women. Promotes health education, self-help
methods, and bilingual access to health care.
Cooperates with other organizations to defend
reproductive choice, affordable birth control,
sex education, prenatal care, and freedom from
sterilization abuse. Offers technical training for
community health facilitators. Organizes conferences and forums. **Publications:** *Newsletter,*
periodic. Includes Latina health issues, legislation affecting Latinas, and calendar of events
and activities on health and reproductive rights.

★711★ National League of American Pen
Women (NLAPW)
1300 17th St., NW
Washington, DC 20036
Phone: (202)785-1997
Frances Hartman Mulliken, Pres.
Founded: 1897. **Description:** Writers, composers, artists, and professional women in the
creative arts. Promotes the professional development of members. Conducts and encourages
literary, educational, and charitable activites in
the fields of art, letters, and music. Fosters the
exchange of ideas and techniques through
workshops, discussion groups, and professional lecturers; sponsors art exhibit and contests.
Provides scholarships; bestows certificates of
proficiency and awards; received Literary Hall of
Fame Award. Maintains biographical archives,
hall of fame, research programs, and 3000
volume library. **Members:** 5000. **Regional
Groups:** 200. **State Groups:** 42. **Local Groups:**
5. **Computerized Services:** Data base; mailing
services. **Publications:** *National League of
American Pen Women—Roster,* biennial. Membership directory. • *The Pen Woman,* 5/year.
Membership activities magazine. Includes book
listings and obituaries. • Also publishes brochures.

★712★ National League of Cities (NLC)
Women in Municipal Government
1301 Pennsylvania Ave. NW
Washington, DC 20004
Phone: (202)626-3181
Fax: (202)626-3043
Kathryn Shane McCarty, Staff Liaison
Description: Encourages active participation of
women elected officials in NLC, identifies qualified women for service in NLC and in other
national positions; promotes issues of interest
to women and the status of women in U.S.
towns and cities. Issues of interest include
violence against women and their children, child
care, elected officials, public policy, women as
caregivers, and women in the government.
Publications: *NLC's Constituency Group
Newsletter,* quarterly.

★713★ National League for Nursing (NLN)
350 Hudson St.
New York, NY 10014
Phone: (212)989-9393
Toll-free: 800-669-1656
Fax: (212)989-3710
Peri Rosenfeld, Vice Pres.
Description: NLN is a nonprofit coalition of
nurses, other health care professionals, and
consumers working to maintain and improve
quality health care. Provides accreditation and
consultation services, continuing education programs, test services, research, publications,
videos, and lobbying efforts on behalf of nursing
and consumers. **Publications:** *Nursing and
HealthCare,* monthly journal. • *Executive Director's Wire.* • *Public Policy Bulletins.* • *Council
Updates,* all periodic newsletters.

★714★ National Master Farm
Homemakers' Guild (NMFHG)
c/o Eleanor Strait
RR 1 Box 72
Keosauqua, IA 52565
Phone: (319)293-3266
Eleanor Strait, Pres.
Founded: 1929. **Description:** Outstanding farm
women selected as leaders in local, state, or
national affairs by groups working with land
grant colleges. Works to: create a desire to give
service to home, community, state, and nation;
promote high standards of living in farm homes;
provide hospitality to international visitors.
Members: 525. **State Groups:** 6.

★715★ National Maternal and Child Health
Clearinghouse (NMCHC)
38th and R Sts. NW
Washington, DC 20057
Phone: (202)625-8410
Linda Cramer, Project Dir.
Founded: 1983. **Description:** Collects, and
disseminates information on maternal and child
health, human genetics, nutrition, and pregnan-
cy care, primarily from materials developed by
the U.S. Department of Health and Human
Services. **Computerized Services:** Mailing List.
Publications: *National Center for Education in
Maternal and Child Health and National Mater-
nal and Child Health Clearinghouse Publications
Catalog,* annual.

★716★ National Mother's Day Committee
1328 Broadway
New York, NY 10001
Phone: (212)594-6421
Fax: (212)594-9349
Theodore M. Kaufman, Exec.Dir.
Founded: 1941. **Description:** Individuals and
organizations "dedicated to building a permanently free democracy through wise parental
influence of the young." The U.S. president,
state governors, and former governors cooperate in observances of the committee. Sponsors
annual banquet in New York City to honor
Mother of the Year and mothers in special
categories. Mother's Day is a national holiday
by congressional act in 1914, observed on the
second Sunday of May. **Formerly:** (1978) National Committee for the Observance of Mother's Day.

★717★ National Network of Hispanic
Women
12021 Wilshire Blvd., Ste. 353
Los Angeles, CA 90025
Phone: (213)225-9895
Celia Torres, Chair
Founded: 1980. **Description:** The Network is
dedicated to the identification, preparation, and
advancement of outstanding Hispanic women in
business and the professions for leadership
positions in both the private and public sectors.
Publications: *Intercambios Femeniles,* quarterly
magazine.

★718★ National Network of Minority
Women in Science (MWIS)
c/o American Association for the
Advancement of Science
Directorate for Educ. and Human Resources
Programs
1333 H St. NW
Washington, DC 20005
Phone: (202)326-6670
Audrey B. Daniel, Coordinator
Founded: 1978. **Description:** Asian, Black,
Mexican American, Native American, and Puerto Rican women involved in science related
professions; other interested persons. Promotes the advancement of minority women in
science fields and the improvement of the
science and mathematics education and career
awareness of minorities. Supports public policies and programs in science and technology
that benefit minorities. Compiles statistics;
serves as clearinghouse for identifying minority
women scientists. Offers writing and conference presentations, seminars, and workshops
on minority women in science and local career
conferences for students. Local chapters maintain speakers' bureaus and placement services,
offer children's services, sponsor competitions,
and bestow awards. **Members:** 400. **Regional
Groups:** 1. **State Groups:** 2. **Local Groups:** 3.
Publications: *MWIS.* annual report. • Plans to
publish directory.

★719★ National Network for Women in
Prison
c/o CLAIM
205 W. Randolph St., Ste. 802
Chicago, IL 60606
Phone: (312)332-5537
Description: The Network is an outgrowth of
the Annual Roundtable for Women in Prison. It
publishes a newsletter and plans the Roundtable meetings.

★720★ National Network of Women in Sales (NNWS)
10613 Depot
Worth, IL 60482
Phone: 800-321-6697
Fax: (708)361-4726
Eloise Haverland, Founder

Founded: 1981. **Description:** Women who are in a sales or related career or seeking to enter the field. To further the careers of professional saleswomen by providing support and sharing expertise and experience. Conducts monthly programs and seminars in Chicago, IL, Cincinnati, OH, Houston, TX, Wilmington, NC, and northern Indiana; sponsors placement service and resume file; conducts job fairs; compiles data and statistics for researchers; offers counseling on resume writing, interview techniques, and career development; awards scholarships to women studying marketing/sales at colleges and universities. Operates speakers' bureau and library of 400 books and tapes on topics such as business and sales skills. Bestows annual leadership award and scholarships to women in a sales or marketing curriculum. **Members:** 750. **Regional Groups:** 8. **Computerized Services:** Member mailing lists. **Publications:** Contacts, quarterly. Membership activities newsletter. • Network News, monthly. • NNWS Membership Directory, annual.

★721★ National Network of Women's Funds (NNWF)
1821 University Ave. W., Ste. 409N
St. Paul, MN 55104
Phone: (612)641-0742
Carol Mollner, Exec. Officer

Founded: 1985. **Description:** Women's foundations and federations dedicated to generating increased resources for programs that benefit women and girls. Works to publicize what the network views as the low percentage of funds offered by foundations and corporations to programs serving women and girls. Works to increase funding for programs for women and girls, primarily by supporting the development and growth of women's foundations and federations. Maintains clearinghouse of information about women's funds.

★722★ National News Service for Women and Minorities
P. Box 27-572
San Francisco, CA 94127
Phone: (415)731-5913
Shirley Cohelan Burton, Director

★723★ National Order of Women Legislators
1300 Berkeley Rd.
Columbia, SC 29205
Phone: (803)734-0480
Joyce Hearn, President

Founded: 1938. **Description:** National organization for women legislators. Seeks to foster "a spirit of helpfulness" among past, present, and future members of various state legislators; promote and act as a clearinghouse of information; and encourage the election or appointment of women to public office.

★724★ National Organization of Adolescent Pregnancy and Parenting (NOAPP)
4421A East-West Hwy.
Bethesda, MD 20814
Phone: (301)913-0378
Fax: (301)913-0380
Kathleen Sheeran, Exec.Dir.

Founded: 1979. **Description:** Professionals, policymakers, community and state leaders, and other concerned individuals and organizations. Promotes comprehensive and coordinated services designed for the prevention and resolution of problems associated with adolescent pregnancy and parenthood. Supports families in expanding their capability of nurturing children and setting standards that encourage their healthy development through loving, stable relationships. Programs include: providing advocacy services at local, state, and national levels for pregnant adolescents and school-age parents (and their children); sharing information and promoting public awareness; conducting conferences and workshops to encourage the establishment of effective programs; coalition building assistance. **Members:** 2000. **Publications:** Directory of Adolescent Pregnancy and Parenting Program, periodic. • NOAPP Network Newsletter, quarterly. Contains resource reviews, state highlights, legislative focus, and successful program models.

★725★ National Organization of Episcopalians for Life (NOEL)
10523 Main St.
Fairfax, VA 22030
Phone: (703)591-6635
Mary Ann Dacey, Exec.Dir.

Founded: 1966. **Description:** Episcopalians organized to reaffirm their faith and reestablish moral responsibility in the Christian response to human life issues. Focuses on issues concerning the protection and enhancement of human existence in accordance with God's laws. Objectives are: to offer education within the Protestant Episcopal Church on the value, dignity, and sanctity of human life; to provide support for the church in teaching life issues; to offer viable alternatives to abortion; to disseminate information through educational programs of a religious, ethical, and scientific nature. Supports National Organization of Episcopalians for Life: Research and Education Foundation. Offers workshops, seminars, and a pro-life ministry. Maintains tape ministry and speakers' bureau. **Members:** 16,000. **Publications:** The Noel News, quarterly. Newsletter; includes calendar of events and member news. • Also publishes brochures and educational booklets. **Formerly:** (1983) Episcopalians for Life. **Also known as:** NOEL.

★726★ National Organization to Insure Survival Economics (NOISE)
c/o Diana D. DuBroff
12 W. 72nd St.
New York, NY 10023
Phone: (212)787-1070
Diana D. DuBroff, Dir.

Founded: 1972. **Description:** A "one woman crusade to help the victims of divorce"; to promote programs for and to find new ways and means to cope with support problems for a family after a divorce. Is forming research and education programs. Supports the idea of divorce insurance, to be given as a wedding gift by parents and grandparents or to be taken out at the time of marriage and to insure child support if the marriage should end in divorce. According to DuBroff, no enforcement laws would be necessary if support were insured and property settled before spouses file for divorce. DuBroff also advocates homemakers' services insurance. Seeks to persuade insurance companies to provide Single Parent Living in Poverty (SLIP) coverage by circulating a petition. Sponsors the Institute for Practical Justice, a nationwide educational service which helps people resolve disputes and avoid litigation. The institute produces Practical Justice by a Creative Lawyer (a cable television series) and sponsors seminars and lectures. The mailing list for NOISE and the institute contains over 10,000 names. **Formerly:** National Association to Improve Support Enforcement; (1981) National Organization to Insure Support Enforcement.

★727★ National Organization of Italian-American Women (NOIAW)
445 W. 59th St., Rm. 1248
New York, NY 10019
Phone: (212)237-8574
Fax: (212)489-6130
Barbara Gerard, Pres.

Founded: 1980. **Description:** Women who have at least one parent of Italian heritage. Objectives are to: foster interests and address problems and concerns of Italian-American women; provide network of resources and support for professional, political, and social advancement; increase cultural, educational, and financial opportunities of young people of Italian-American origin; promote awareness and perpetuation of Italian culture and ethnic identity; foster ethnic pride and develop role models for younger Italian-Americans; modify traditional images of women of Italian descent and expand their career choices; help serve the interests of Italian-American communities; provide liaison and promote greater unity with other Italian-American groups and women's ethnic groups. Encourages Italian-American women to monitor and participate in the political process and to serve health and welfare interests of the Italian-American community. Conducts film presentations; sponsors forums, workshops, seminars, cultural events, and networking meetings; conducts selfhelp programs. Sponsors Mentor Program for female college students whereby each student is "adopted" by a member who has a career in the student's chosen field. Provides scholarship program. **Members:** 800. **Regional Groups:** 4. **State Groups:** 21. **Publications:** NOIAW Newsletter, quarterly. Membership activities newsletter; contains regional updates and book reviews.

★728★ National Organization of Mothers of Twins Clubs (NOMOTC)
PO Box 23188
Albuquerque, NM 87192-1188
Phone: (505)275-0955
Lois Gallmeyer, Exec.Sec.

Founded: 1960. **Description:** Twin clubs seeking to broaden the understanding of those aspects of child development and rearing which relate especially to twins through the interchange of information among parents, educators, doctors, and others. Goals are: to make information about twins available to the public; to increase awareness of the individuality of each twin; to assist in medical research. Operates speakers' bureau; maintains bibliography of books on twin care. **Members:** 15,500. **Local**

Groups: 410. **Publications:** *MOTC's Notebook*, quarterly.

★729★ National Organization for Victim
  Assistance (NOVA)
1757 Park Rd. NW
Washington, DC 20010
Phone: (202)232-6682
Fax: (202)462-2255
Marlene A. Young, Ph.D., Exec.Dir.

Founded: 1975. **Description:** Victim counselors, district attorneys, police officials, mental health professionals, judges, crisis intervention specialists, domestic violence and rape crisis workers, former victims, and others whose purpose is "to express forcefully the victims' claims, too long ignored, for decency, compassion, and justice; to press those claims for the victims of crime and also for the victims of other stark misfortunes; and to ensure that victims' rights are honored by government officials and all others who can aid in the victims' relief and recovery." Offers technical counsel, referral services, and public support to victim assistance training programs; also provides services to victims directly. Serves as clearinghouse on state and federal legislation. Maintains library and speakers' bureau; conducts educational activities. Sponsors Regional Victim Assistance Training Program and National Victim Rights Week. Compiles staistics; annually presents awards. Establishes networks of service providers in 50 states to foster communications. **Members:** 4000. **Publications:** *Legislative Directory*, annual. • *National Organization for Victim Assistance–Newsletter*, monthly. Includes book reviews, calendar of events, and legislative and research updates. • *Program Directory*, annual. • *Victim Assistance Programs and Resources 1991*, annual. Lists 8,000 programs and resources, compensation programs, crisis centers and incest and abuse centers. • *Victim Rights Campaign*, annual. • *Victim Rights and Services: A Legislative Directory*, periodic. Provides state by state victim laws and legislation. • Also publishes *Victim Services System: A Guide to Action* and monthly newsletters and makes available Victim Rights Week kits.

★730★ National Organization for Women
  (NOW)
1000 16th St. NW, Ste. 700
Washington, DC 20036
Phone: (202)331-0066
Fax: (202)785-8576
Patricia Ireland, Pres.

Founded: 1966. **Description:** Men and women who support "full equality for women in truly equal partnership with men." Seeks to end prejudice and discrimination against women in government, industry, the professions, churches, political parties, the judiciary, labor unions, education, science, medicine, law, religion, "and every other field of importance in American society." Promotes passage of the Equal Rights Amendment and enforcement of federal legislation prohibiting discrimination on the basis of sex. Engages in lobbying and litigation. Works to increase the number of women elected to local, county, and state offices, the House of Representatives, and the Senate. Sponsors student essay contests. First president of NOW was Betty Friedan, author of the bestseller, *The Feminine Mystique*. **Members:** 250,000. **Regional Groups:** 9. **State Groups:** 50. **Local Groups:** 800. **Publications:** *NOW Times*, bimonthly. Newspaper. • Local groups publish monthly newspapers.

★731★ National Organization for Women
  (NOW)
Legal Defense and Education Fund (LDEF)
Project on Equal Education Rights (PEER)
99 Hudson St., 12th Fl.
New York, NY 10013
Phone: (212)925-6635
Walteen Grady Truely, Executive Director

Founded: 1974. **Description:** PEER promotes educational equity for women and girls. Seeks to achieve its goals through public policy analysis and advocacy at the federal and state levels; organization of committees for equity at the local level; and public information campaigns promoting equal education.

★732★ National Organization for Women
  Political Action Committee (NOW/PAC)
1000 16th St. NW, Ste. 700
Washington, DC 20036
Phone: (202)331-0066
Alice Cohan, Political Director

★733★ National Osteopathic Women
  Physician's Association (NOWPA)
c/o Marlene A. Wager, D.O.
Grosvenor Hall, Rm. 351
Athens, OH 45701
Phone: (614)593-2259
Marlene A. Wager, D.O., Exec. Officer

Founded: 1904. **Description:** Professional sorority - osteopathy. Gives Grant-in-Aid annually. Provides scholarship recognition awards to junior and senior osteopathic medical students. **Members:** 900. **Publications:** *The Alpha*, annual. **Formerly:** (1988) Delta Omega.

★734★ National Panhellenic Conference
  (NPC)
3901 W. 86th St., Ste. 380
Indianapolis, IN 46268
Phone: (317)872-3185
Fax: (317)872-3192
Rebecca Mitchell, Administrative Assistant

Description: The conference is a nonprofit umbrella organization of national Greek fraternities. Supports and promotes women's fraternities as a positive element of the higher education experience. Goals are to foster inter-fraternital relations; promote the welfare of the NPC member fraternities; work in concert with colleges and universities to maintain and advance high standards of conduct and scholarship; promote a positive image of women's fraternities to the public; provide a forum for the discussion of questions of interest to institutions of higher education and the fraternity world; and initiate appropriate programs and materials to carry out the mission of the conference. **Publications:** *The PH Factor*, 2/year. • *News Bulletin of the Alumnae Panhellenics Committee*, 2/year. • *Viewpoint*, 2/year.

★735★ National Political Congress of
  Black Women
PO Box 411
Rancocas, NJ 08073
Phone: (609)871-1500
Dempsey Portia, Exec.Dir.

★736★ National Pork Council Women
  (NPCW)
c/o National Pork Producers Council
PO Box 10383
Des Moines, IA 50306
Phone: (515)223-2600
Fax: (515)456-7675
Marjorie Ocheltree, Dir.

Founded: 1962. **Description:** Pork producers' wives and other interested women. Auxiliary of the National Pork Producers Council. Seeks to: support the pork industry; address issues as they affect the pork industry; protect and improve the image of pork; promote increased consumption of pork products. Maintains liaison with home economics teachers and school foodservice operators; carries out in-store pork promotion year-round. Encourages participation in state cookout contests. Assists the NPPC in sponsoring the National Pork Industry Queen Contest. Maintains speakers' bureau. **Members:** 14,000. **State Groups:** 27. **Publications:** *Newsletter*, semiannual. **Formerly:** (1985) National Porkettes.

★737★ National Pro-Life Democrats
  (NPLD)
PO Box 23467
Minneapolis, MN 55423
Phone: (612)825-4639
Mary Jo Cooley, Exec.Dir.

Description: Encourages pro-life Democrats to participate in the Democratic party. Provides education on becoming active in the Democratic party at the local level. Conducts workshops; develops educational materials. Compiles statistics.

★738★ National Puerto Rican Women's
  Caucus (NPRWC)
409 E. 84th St., Ste. 24
New York, NY 10028
Lydia M. Colon, Sec.-Treas.

Founded: 1983. **Description:** Puerto Rican professional women. Objectives are: to provide opportunities for the personal, professional, educational, and financial advancement of Puerto Rican women within an active and supportive network of other professional women; to serve as a forum for the exchange of information and resources; to promote a stronger sense of self-awareness, political sophistication, and cohesiveness among Puerto Rican professional women; and to increase the visibility of professional women as a group, ultimately creating change by influencing public policy decisions. Educational programs include seminars and lectures on personal financial management, career development, and personal growth. Promotes issues affecting the Puerto Rican community such as women's rights, employment opportunities, and community development. Maintains speakers bureau; compiles statistics. **Members:** 33. **Publications:** *Membership Directory*, periodic. • Also publishes brochure.

★739★ National Recreation and Parks
  Association (NRPA)
Women and Minority Programs
3101 Park Center Dr., Ste. 1200
Alexandria, VA 22302
Phone: (703)820-4940
Fax: (703)671-6772
Rikki Epstein, Program Manager

Description: The NRPA is a national, nonprofit organization engaged in a wide range of research, education, policy, and program initiatives. Seeks to meet the recreational needs of women and minorities through a variety of civic, professional, and technical projects. **Publications:** *Parks and Recreation.* • *Dateline.* • *Friends of the Parks and Recreation.*

★740★ **National Republican Coalition for Choice (NRCC)**
709 2nd St. NE, Ste. 100
Washington, DC 20002
Phone: (202)543-0676
Fax: (202)543-0676
Mary Dent Crisp, Natl. Chair

Founded: 1989. **Description:** Independent political committee founded to ensure a national voice for pro-choice Republicans. (Defines prochoice as an individual who opposes governmental, political, and legislative attempts to ban abortion.) Seeks to identify, organize, and elect pro-choice Republicans to office and to promote the pro-choice position as the official position of the Republican Party. **Members:** 4000. **Computerized Services:** Data base; mailing list.

★741★ **National Resource Center on Women and AIDS (NRCWA)**
Center for Women Policy Studies
2000 P St. NW, Ste. 508
Washington, DC 20036
Phone: (202)872-1770
Leslie R. Wolfe, Exec.Dir.

Founded: 1988. **Description:** A project of the Center for Women Policy Studies (see separate entry). Provides information to advocates, educators, and policymakers on issues involving women and AIDS. Focuses on AIDS among women of color and low-income women. Develops policy options through the National Collaboration for AIDS Policy for Women. Maintains speakers' bureau; provides assistance to other organizations working with women and/or AIDS. **Publications:** *Guide to Resources on Women and AIDS,* annual. Directory of AIDS education programs and local, state, and national AIDS related organizations; includes summaries of research, funding information for women and AIDS programs, and case studies of successful model programs. • *Policy Papers,* periodic. Defines a particular issue, summarizes the current state of research and policy development, and makes policy and advocacy recommendations. • Also publishes *Action Kit* and produces videotapes.

★742★ **National Right to Life Committee (NRLC)**
419 Seventh St., NW, Ste. 500
Washington, DC 20004
Phone: (202)626-8800
J. C. Willke, M.D., Pres.

Founded: 1973. **Description:** Pro-life organization that opposes abortion, euthanasia, and infanticide. Supports abortion alternative programs involving counseling and adoption. Provides ongoing public education programs on abortion, euthanasia, and infanticide. Lobbies before congressional committees; encourages passage and ratification of a constitutional amendment to protect all human life. Conducts research; compiles statistics; maintains speakers' bureau. Bestows awards. Has established library including 430 books, pamphlets, brochures, and audiovisual materials, and a vertical file of 1650 items. **State Groups:** 50. **Local Groups:** 3000. **Publications:** *National Right to*

Life News, biweekly. • Also publishes books and pamphlets.

★743★ **National Right to Life Educational Trust Fund (NRLETF)**
419 7th St. NW, Ste. 500
Washington, DC 20004
Phone: (202)626-8800
Fax: (202)737-9189
David O'Steen, Exec.Dir.

Description: Educational branch of the National Right to Life Committee (see separate entry). Fosters awareness of and responsibility for human life before and after birth, particularly those whom the group feels are "vulnerable" and "disadvantaged," such as the mentally retarded and the physically handicapped. Sponsors public awareness campaigns about bioethical issues, including abortion, human experimentation, infanticide, genetic engineering, and euthanasia. Encourages research and public education on parenthood and on the prevention of birth defects and mental retardation. Promotes "enlightened care and assistance" for pregnant women, children, handicapped, mentally retarded, and aged persons with special needs. Offers seminars and conferences. **Publications:** *The Challenge to be "Pro Life"* and *Abortion: Question and Answer Series* (booklets). Also publishes books and educational materials.

★744★ **National Rural Electric Cooperative Association (NRECA)**
National Rural Electric Women's Association (NREWA)
1800 Massachusetts Ave. NW
Washington, DC 20036
Phone: (202)257-9537
Linda R. Woodhouse, Manager, Women's Consumer Programs

Description: NREWA's goal is to further consumer and community understanding of rural electric cooperatives and to build unified, grassroots support for NRECA's legislative, political and communication objectives. Established in recognition of women's vital role in rural electrification programs. Unites women on the local and state level for networking and on national level for coordination of efforts in achieving goals. Sponsors projects on women's health, political fundraising, electricity safety, victim assistance, and youth scholarships. **Publications:** *Newsline,* quarterly.

★745★ **National Safety Council**
Women's Division
444 N. Michigan Ave.
Chicago, IL 60611
Phone: (312)527-4800

★746★ **National Senior Women's Tennis Association (NSWTA)**
1696 W. Calimjrna, No B
Fresno, CA 93711
Phone: (209)432-3095
Elaine Mason, Pres.

Founded: 1974. **Description:** Women over 30 years of age and others interested in senior women's competitive tennis. Promotes senior women's tennis events. Sponsors a national, intersectional, team competition event. **Members:** 800. **Publications:** *National Senior Women's Tennis Association Newsletter,* bimonthly.

★747★ **National Society, Daughters of the American Colonists (DAC)**
2205 Massachusetts Ave. NW
Washington, DC 20008
Phone: (202)667-3076
Mrs. James E. Crews, Pres.

Founded: 1921. **Description:** Women descended from men and women who gave civil or military service to the Colonies prior to the Revolutionary War. Awards scholarships; maintains library. **Members:** 10,700. **State Groups:** 51. **Local Groups:** 332. **Publications:** *Colonial Courier,* 3/year. • *Directory,* annual. • Also publishes handbook.

★748★ **National Society, Daughters of the American Revolution (DAR)**
1776 D St. NW
Washington, DC 20006-5392
Phone: (202)628-1776
Mrs. Eldred M. Yochim, Pres.Gen.

Founded: 1890. **Description:** Women descendants of Revolutionary War patriots. Conducts historical, educational, and patriotic activities. Maintains genealogical/historical research library, Americana museum, and documentary collections antedating 1830; organizes Junior American Citizens Clubs for schoolchildren; maintains two schools in the South and supports others; founded National Society of the Children of the American Revolution; initiated American History Month (February) and Constitution Week. Presents medals to school-age children for good citizenship, ROTC Medals to graduating cadets of outstanding ability and achievement, and occupational therapy and nursing scholarships. Bestows annual $8,000 American History Scholarship Award. **Members:** 204,000. **Local Groups:** 3152. **Publications:** *Daughters of the American Revolution Magazine,* 10/year. Covers association activities; includes information on genealogy, the American Revolutionary period, and current national defense issues. • *Directory of Committees,* annual. • *Proceedings,* annual. • Also publishes *Manual for Citizenship* and *Patriot Index,* plus supplements.

★749★ **National Society, Daughters of the British Empire in the United States of America (DBE)**
c/o Phyllis Blanco
Victoria Home
N. Malcolm Ave.
Ossining, NY 10562
Phone: (914)941-2450
Phyllis Blanco, Exec. Officer

Founded: 1909. **Description:** Women of British or British Commonwealth birth, or who are naturalized subjects of Britain or a Commonwealth country; women with proven British or British Commonwealth ancestry; wives of men born in Britain or the British Commonwealth. Maintains four retirement homes for both men and women. **Members:** 5000. **Regional Groups:** 4. **State Groups:** 32. **Local Groups:** 271. **Publications:** *National Society, Daughters of the British Empire in the United States of America—Yearbook.* • Also publishes pamphlets. **Formerly:** (1915) Imperial Order Daughters of the British Empire in the United States of America.

★750★ National Society Daughters of Founders and Patriots of America (DFPA)
Park Lane Bldg., No. 615
2025 I St. NW
Washington, DC 20006
Mrs. James Earl Haynes, Jr., Pres.

Founded: 1898. **Description:** Women who are lineal descendants, in the male line of either parent, from an ancestor who settled in any of the colonies between May 13, 1607 and May 13, 1687, and whose intermediate ancestors in the same line gave military service or assistance to the colonies during the American Revolution. Presents gifts annually to outstanding graduates of 5 U.S. service academies, gold medals to outstanding ROTC cadets in colleges and universities, and history awards. Also bestows annual Shadow-Box Award for outstanding contribution to education, restoration, or historical research. Restores records of the 13 original colonies. Maintains library for members only; places lineage books in libraries throughout the U.S. **Members:** 2250. **State Groups:** 53. **Publications:** *Yearbook-Directory of Chapter Officers.* • Also publishes *Gazette, Handbook,* and lineage books.

★751★ National Society Daughters of Utah Pioneers (NSDUP)
300 N. Main St.
Salt Lake City, UT 84103
Phone: (801)538-1050
Helen R. Grant, Pres.

Founded: 1901. **Description:** Descendants of Utah pioneers. Publishes the histories of Utah pioneers; places historical markers; preserves pioneer documents, relics, and craftsmanship. Maintains Pioneer Memorial Museum and Carriage House in Salt Lake City. Operates speakers' bureau and library. Conducts lectures. **Members:** 24,000. **Regional Groups:** 175. **Local Groups:** 1200. **Computerized Services:** Data base of membership, artifacts, and computers. **Publications:** *Historical Brochure,* monthly. • *Legacy,* quarterly. Newsletter. • Also publishes *An Enduring Legacy, Chronicles of Courage* (book series), and pamphlets.

★752★ National Society of New England Women (NSNEW)
PO Box 367
Union City, TN 38261
Phone: (901)885-3314
Shirley Ann Pease, Pres.Gen.

Founded: 1895. **Description:** Patriotic, educational, and charitable society of individuals descended from ancestors born in New England prior to 1789. Sponsors student loan funds. Provides endowment funds for children's homes and school for the deaf. Members work in veterans' hospitals, U.S.O., and Soldiers', Sailors', and Airmen's clubs in New York City. **Members:** 2500. **Regional Groups:** 63. **Publications:** *Clipper,* quarterly. Newsletter. • *National Society Year Book.*

★753★ National Society, United States Daughters of 1812
45 Indian Trail
Sanford, NC 27330
Phone: (919)499-2292
Mrs. George E. Lundeen, Pres.

Founded: 1892. **Description:** Women descendants of those who rendered civil, military, or naval service during the years 1784-1815.

Promotes patriotism and seeks to increase knowledge of American history by preserving documents and relics, marking historic spots, recording family histories and traditions, and celebrating patriotic anniversaries. Gives two annual awards to outstanding midshipmen graduates of the U.S. Naval Academy and one to West Point. Operates biographical archives and 400 volume library of 1812 historical period and genealogical books. Conducts speakers' bureau; operates children's services and charitable program; maintains museum; compiles statistics. **Members:** 4600. **State Groups:** 38. **Local Groups:** 144. **Publications:** *News-Letter,* 2/year. Includes membership list and obituaries. • Also publishes *1812 Ancestors Index* and *1812 Roster.*

★754★ National Society Women Descendants of the Ancient and Honorable Artillery Company (DAH)
c/o Mrs. Luther D. Swanstrom
9027 S. Damen Ave.
Chicago, IL 60620
Phone: (312)238-0423
Mrs. Luther D. Swanstrom, Pres.

Founded: 1927. **Description:** Women of lineal descent from members of the Ancient and Honorable Artillery Company (1637-1774) or from members of the General Court (Boston) of 1638. Compiles genealogical data; bestows scholarship to Hillside School for Boys to those who excel in history. **Members:** 1150. **Publications:** *Yearbook.* • Also issues biographical materials.

★755★ National Task Force on Prostitution (NTFP)
333 Valencia St., Ste. 101
San Francisco, CA 94103
Phone: (415)558-0450
Sharon Kiser, Exec.Dir.

Founded: 1973. **Description:** Prostitutes' rights organizations whose members include prostitutes, former prostitutes, lawyers, social service providers, and other individuals; women's groups and criminal justice and religious organizations. Long-range goal is the decriminalization of prostitution and "the removal of the stigmas associated with female sexuality." Seeks to protect working prostitutes from arrests for loitering and from entrapment by vice squad policemen. Activities include referrals to competent lawyers for arrested prostitutes, assistance in obtaining social aid, and coordinating a national campaign. Has created pressure groups to deal with the criminal justice system; lobbies in the state legislature. Conducts research; compiles statistics; prepares position papers ontopics related to prostitution. Maintains speakers' bureau, archives, and library on sex, women, and prostitution. **Local Groups:** 3. **Publications:** Reprints, research information, papers, and other information about prostitution and prostitutes; also publishes materials on pornography, violence against prostitutes, and AIDS and other health issues. Distributes materials produced by the International Committee for Prostitutes' Rights. **Formerly:** (1977) Coyote Howls. **Also known as:** COYOTE (Call Off Your Old Tired Ethics).

★756★ National Union of Eritrean Women—North America (NUEW)
PO Box 631
New York, NY 10025
Phone: (212)678-1977
Fax: (212)666-8022
Saba Issayas, Contact

Description: Women of Eritrean descent in North America united to support and publicize the activities of the Eritrean People's Liberation Front.

★757★ National United Women's Societies of the Adoration of the Most Blessed Sacrament (NUWSAMBS)
1127 Freida St.
Dickson City, PA 18519
Phone: (717)489-4364
Ceil D. Lallo, Pres.

Founded: 1933. **Description:** Women, 16 years and older, affiliated with the Polish National Catholic Church of America and Canada. Fosters and promotes Christian perfection through personal, family, and community development. Plans to establish library of historical data, Polish prose and poetry, and women's magazines. Sponsors charitable programs. **Members:** 5695. **Publications:** *Polka,* quarterly. Magazine. **Formerly:** (1988) United Women's Societies of the Adoration of the Most Blessed Sacraments.

★758★ National University Continuing Education Association
Division of Programs for Women
1 Dupont Circle, NW, Ste. 615
Washington, DC 20036
Phone: (202)659-3130
Kay Kohl, Executive Director

★759★ National Woman Abuse Prevention Project (NWAPP)
1112 16th St. NW, Ste. 920
Washington, DC 20036
Phone: (202)857-0216
Fax: (202)659-5597
Mary Pat Brygger, Dir.

Founded: 1986. **Description:** Works to prevent domestic violence and improve services offered to battered women. Seeks to increase public awareness of, and sensitivity to, domestic violence. Conducts educational programs; maintains library and operates speakers' bureau. **Publications:** *Exchange,* quarterly. Newsletter. Includes model program highlights and resource reviews. • Also publishes educational brochures, fact packets, and policy manuals.

★760★ National Woman's Christian Temperance Union (WCTU)
1730 Chicago Ave.
Evanston, IL 60201
Phone: (708)864-1396
Rachel B. Kelly, Pres.

Founded: 1874. **Description:** Nonpartisan, interdenominational Christian women dedicated to educate America's youth about what the group believes are the harmful effects of alcohol, narcotic drugs, and tobacco on the human body and American society. Seeks to build sentiment for total abstinence through teaching the relation of alcohol to the mental, moral, social, spiritual and physical well-being of the individual and the nation. Promotes essay, poster, and medal contests as well as intercollegiate oratorical contests on alcohol and related problems; produces films and filmstrips on temperance for use in schools and churches; sponsors total abstinence training camps for children and youth; makes available research materials to professionals and students; conducts philanthropic activities. Research and educational programs deal with such topics as alcohol and traffic accidents; consumer expenditures; teenage drinking; per capita consumption of alcohol; economic aspects; tobacco and health; gambling; and narcotics. Sponsors Youth's Temperance Council (ages 13-29) and Loyal Temperance Legion (ages 6-12). Maintains research library of 5000 volumes on alcohol, narcotics, tobacco, gambling, and prohibition; also maintains Frances E. Willard Home as a museum. **Members:** 50,000. **State Groups:** 48. **Local Groups:** 4000. **Publications:** *Annual Directory.* • *Monthly Promoter.* Contains excerpts of new literature. • *National Happenings,* periodic. Newsletter. • *The Union Signal,* monthly. Magazine; includes consumer and legislative updates and annual index. • *The Young Crusader,* monthly. Children's magazine. • Also publishes legislative updates.

★761★ National Woman's Party (NWP)
Sewall-Belmont House
144 Constitution Ave. NE
Washington, DC 20002
Phone: (202)546-1210
Sharon Griffith, Exec.Dir.

Founded: 1913. **Description:** Strives to raise the status of women. Directs attention toward equal rights matters; advocates ratification of the Equal Rights Amendment. Maintains NWP Equal Rights and Suffrage Art Gallery and Museum in the Sewall-Belmont House in Washington, DC, a designated national landmark filled with memorabilia of suffrage and ERA. **State Groups:** 8. **Publications:** *Equal Rights,* quarterly. Newsletter. • Also publishes *Answers to Questions about the ERA* (pamphlet).

★762★ National Woman's Relief Corps, Auxiliary to the Grand Army of the Republic
629 S. 7th
Springfield, IL 62703
Phone: (217)522-4373
Lurene I. Wentworth, Treas.-Sec.

Founded: 1883. **Description:** Patriotic women over age 13 who are citizens of the U.S., of good moral character, and are interested in perpetuating the principles of fraternity, charity, and loyalty for which the Grand Army of the Republic stood. Members are not required to be blood relatives of Civil War veterans. Original purpose was to urge the teaching of patriotism and the Pledge of Allegiance to the flag in private and public schools. Supports volunteer participation in treatment and rehabilitation programs for patients at Veterans Administration hospitals. Finances extensive scholarship program offering grants to members of veterans' families, loan funds at universities, annual gifts to honor students at military academies, and permanent scholarships. Promotes Americanism and patriotic education; cooperates with agencies serving the foreign-born; and sponsors national essay contest on patriotic topics. Maintains Grand Army of the Republic Memorial Museum. Has established patriotic and historical memorials and markers throughout the U.S. and has planted thousands of trees as "living memorials" to the Grand Army of the Republic. Promotes child welfare and sponsors a Junior Corps for girls ages 6 to 16. **Members:** 12,000.

State Groups: 33. **Local Groups:** 530. **Publications:** *General Orders,* bimonthly. • *Journal of the National Convention,* annual. • *Roster,* annual. • Also distributes flags and patriotic literature to schools.

★763★ National Women Bowling Writers Association (NWBW)
8061 Wallace Rd.
Baltimore, MD 21222
Phone: (410)284-6884
Theresa Ray, Sec.

Founded: 1948. **Description:** Professional (66) and nonprofessional (848) writers. Seeks to: promote the sport of bowling; foster communication and exchange of information among members; recognize outstanding publications by members; examine problems common to members. Sponsors writing and photography competitions; bestows awards. Operates charitable program. **Members:** 914. **Publications:** *Knows for News,* 5/year. • Also publishes *Writer's Digest* and *Publicity Guide.*

★764★ National Women of Color Association (NWCA)
Department of Women's Studies
336 North Hall
Universtiy of Wisconsin, LaCrosse
LaCrosse, WI 54601
Phone: (608)785-8357
Sondra O'Neil, Contact

Description: The Association is a fellowship of women of color, including, but not limited to four minority ethnic groups in the United States: Native American, African American, Latin American, and Asian American. Shares research on minority women and provides public education on various subjects, including women and health, politics, and community organizing. **Publications:** *Women of Color Newsletter,* 3/year.

★765★ National Women Student's Coalition (NWSC)
c/o USSA
815 15th St. NW, Ste. 838
Washington, DC 20005
Phone: (202)347-8772
Elizabeth Burpe, Co-Chair

Founded: 1978. **Description:** A subsidiary of the United States Student Association whose members are all women. Lobbies for women students' issues at the national level; acts as a network among members to accomplish such lobbying. Distributes *Affirmative Action* and *Entitled to IX* (manuals).

★766★ National Women's Anthropology Caucus
California State University
Department of Anthropology
Sacramento, CA 95819
Phone: (916)278-6452
Lorainne Heidecker, Contact

★767★ National Women's Automotive Association (NWAA)
11020 Ventura Blvd., Ste. 204
Studio City, CA 91604
Kaye Edelson, Pres.

Founded: 1981. **Description:** Women involved in management and sales in the automotive industry, primarily dealerships and leasing. Objective is to provide a network for women in the automotive industry to gain knowledge and

collect and disseminate information on management and sales. Conducts workshops. Activities are currently based in California, but the association plans to expand nationally. **Members:** 112. **Publications:** *Wheels,* periodic. Newsletter of interest to Association members. • *Wheels* (newsletter), quarterly.

★768★ National Women's Coalition (NWC)
The Heitman Group
1350 New York Ave., NW, Ste. 915
Washington, DC 20005
Phone: (202)347-3440
Betty Heitman, Chm.

Description: Professional and activist women drawn from business, the arts, academia, sports, and politics. Seeks to promote the rights, success, and independence of women. Believes "opportunity for all Americans can best be achieved through the policies of President Reagan, the current administration, and the Republican Party." Has initiated discussion on government policies that have benefited women. **Members:** 87.

★769★ National Women's Conference Center (NWCC)
16100 Golf Club Rd. No. 201
Ft. Lauderdale, FL 33326
Phone: (305)389-1879
Gene Boyer, President

Description: The Center is a nonprofit organization providing information to assist the National Women's Committee in monitoring and implementing its national plan of action, the Consensus Agenda of American Women, adopted in 1977 and updated regularly. Conducts and develops professional seminars and workshops. **Publications:** *The National Network Exchange.* • The Center also publishes informational materials on the National Plan of Action.

★770★ National Women's Conference Committee (NWCC)
PO Box 65605
Washington, DC 20035-5605
Phone: (202)842-2790
Dr. Elizabeth A. Abramowitz, Co-Chwm.

Description: Established by a mandate from the first National Women's Conference held in Houston, TX in 1977. Designed to represent and sustain grass roots involvement in women's equality. Purpose is to mobilize support for the National Plan of Action resulting from the conference addressing the need for legal, economic, and social changes to ensure equality. Maintains speakers' bureau; sponsors workshops and seminars. **Members:** 470. **State Groups:** 14. **Publications:** *NWCC Newsletter,* semiannual. • Also publishes *ERA Facts and Action Guide, Decade of Achievement: 1977-1987,* survey report, and monographs. **Formerly:** (1981) Continuing Committee of the National Women's Conference.

★771★ National Women's Economic Alliance Foundation (NWEAF)
1440 New York Ave. NW, Ste. 300
Washington, DC 20005
Phone: (202)393-5257
Fax: (202)639-8685
Patricia Harrison, Pres.

Founded: 1983. **Description:** Executive-level women and men. Promotes dialogue among men and women in industry, business, and government. Focuses on professional, economic, and career concerns and how to address these issues within the framework of the free enterprise system. Conducts research programs and leadership seminars; offers placement service; maintains biographical archives; bestows awards. **Members:** 750. **Computerized Services:** Data base of women on corporate boards. **Telecommunications Services:** telex, 756546. **Publications:** *NWEA Outlook*, semiannual. • *Policy Papers*, periodic. • *Women Directors of the Top 1000 Corporations*, annual. Directory of women who serve on corporate boards of Fortune 1000 companies. • Also publishes *America's New Women Entrepreneurs* (book).

★772★ **National Women's Education Fund**
(NWEF)
2000 P St., NW, Ste. 515
Washington, DC 20036
Phone: (202)822-6636
Rosalie Whelan, Exec.Dir.

Founded: 1972. **Description:** Nonpartisan training and information service for women and public leaders. Goals are to teach women to gain access to the public policy process, earn positions of influence within that process, and to develop and use the skills and resources necessary to lead effectively. Operates Resource and Technical Assistance Service for potential and current public leaders and organizations working with them. Disseminates information on women in public life to the media; operates Women's Election Central during election years offering coverage of the status of women candidates across the country. Conducts networking service; offers training programs. Publishes Catalogue of Training Programs and Materials, Campaign Workbook, and audiovisual training packages including How to Run for Office and Win and Making a Difference. **Formerly:** National Women's Educational Fund.

★773★ **National Women's Hall of Fame**
(NWHF)
76 Fall St.
Seneca Falls, NY 13148
Phone: (315)568-8060
Nancy Woodhull, Pres.

Founded: 1969. **Description:** Purpose is "to honor in perpetuity those women citizens of the United States whose contributions to the arts, athletics, business, education, government, the humanities, philanthropy, and science, have been of greatest value for the development of their country." Maintains hall of fame; plans special exhibits. Honorees are selected by National Honors Committee annually. Sponsors annual essay and poster contests. Conducts special activities with school age groups. Maintains museum, biographical archives, and 2000 volume library on American women's history and biography. Operates children's services. **Members:** 2000. **Publications:** *Newsletter*, quarterly. **Formerly:** (1979) Women's Hall of Fame.

★774★ **National Women's Health Network**
(NWHN)
1325 G St., NW
Washington, DC 20005
Phone: (202)347-1140
Fax: (202)347-1168
Beverly Baker, Exec.Dir.

Founded: 1976. **Description:** Individual consumers, organizations, and health centers. Represents the women's health movement. Monitors federal health policy as it affects women; testifies before Congress and federal agencies. Supports feminist health projects. Sponsors the Women's Health Clearinghouse, a national resource file on all aspects of women's health care. Operates speakers' bureau. **Members:** 15,000. **State Groups:** 5. **Local Groups:** 300. **Publications:** *National Women's Health Network–Network News*, bimonthly. Newsletter providing health information and medical alerts for women. Emphasizes matters affecting reproductive rights and occupational and environmental health. • *Newsalerts*, periodic. • Also publishes health information packets.

★775★ **National Women's Health Resource**
Center (NWHRC)
2440 M St. NW, Ste. 201
Washington, DC 20037
Phone: (202)293-6045
Fax: (202)293-7256
G. Patrick Kane, Pres. & CEO

Founded: 1988. **Description:** Healthcare professionals and consumers. Works to enable women to heighten their knowledge and increase their participation in their own healthcare and maintain healthy and productive lives. Promotes professional and public education and research that focuses on diseases or conditions that are unique, more prevalent, or more serious in women. Develops and provides models for clinical services, especially those that will meet the needs of under-served women. Provides advocacy on women's health issues; disseminates information. Maintains speakers' bureau. Bestows annual Breast Cancer Awareness Awards. **Publications:** *National Women's Health Report*, bimonthly. Newsletter containing features on current women's health issues.

★776★ **National Women's History Project**
(NWHP)
7738 Bell Rd.
Windsor, CA 95492
Phone: (707)838-6000
Fax: (707)838-0478
Molly MacGregor, Dir.

Founded: 1977. **Description:** Publishers of annual resource catalog promoting education on the history of women. Encourages multicultural study of women to reclaim contributions and impact of all groups of women and to persuade constructive and expansive social change. Focuses on the rich and inspiring heritage of women's contributions. Sponsors annual National Women's History Month. Maintains archive for National Women's History Month. Conducts workshops and educational training sessions introducing women into curricula and offers educational consulting for teachers, teacher trainers, administrators, and workplace organizers. Sponsors Women's History Network (see separate entry). Operates speakers' bureau. **Publications:** *Women's History Network Directory*, semiannual. Listing of network participants. Includes a brief biographical sketch and/or a description of women's history

activities in which each person has participated. • *Women's History Network News*, quarterly. Covers educational resources, commemorative holidays, traveling exhibits, and NWHP activities. Includes calendar of events, news of members, and lists of articles, books, and other resources. • *Women's History Resource Catalog*, annual. Includes books, films, records, posters, and program planning guides on women's history. Also includes subject index. • Also publishes *Community Organizing Guide, Lesson Plans*, posters, indexes, and curriculum units. **Formerly:** (1978) Education Taskforce on the Sonoma Commission; (1980) Women's History Week Project.

★777★ **National Women's Law Center**
(NWLC)
1616 P St. NW
Washington, DC 20036
Phone: (202)328-5160
Nancy Duff Campbell, Co-Pres.

Founded: 1972. **Description:** Works to guarantee equality for women under the law and to seek protection and advancement of their legal rights and issues at all levels. Areas of interest include employment, education, health, income security, tax reform, reproductive rights, child support enforcement, dependent care, and the family. Successful projects have included: obtaining a back-pay ruling on sex and race discrimination for employees of a major bank; securing court order that government must enforce laws prohibiting sex discrimination in schools; litigating to establish women's statutory and constitutional rights and ensure enforcement of those rights; securing enforcement of state child support laws without regard to family income. Conducts research on current and proposed policies and regulations to evaluate their impact on women's rights and determines the legality and constitutionality of practices and policies affecting women. **Publications:** *Sex Discrimination in Education, Dependent Care Tax Provisions in the States, Title IX: A Practical Guide to Achieving Sex Equity in Education*, and papers on dependent care tax credits. **Formerly:** (1981) Women's Rights Project of the Center for Law and Social Policy.

★778★ **National Women's Mailing List**
(NWML)
PO Box 68
Jenner, CA 95450
Phone: (707)632-5763
Fax: (707)632-5589
Jill Lippitt, Dir.

Founded: 1981. **Description:** A project of the Women's Information Exchange (see separate entry). Seeks to utilize information technology to facilitate outreach, communication networking, and resource-sharing among women. Individual women and women's organizations are able to sign up to receive mail in a variety of interest areas, such as politics, health, sports, women's culture, and spirituality. Names and addresses from this data bank are sorted according to geography, demography, organization type, and interest areas, and are made available to organizations conducting mailings of interest to women. Provides speakers on women and technology; offers two-day intensive computer literacy classes. **Members:** 70,000. **Computerized Services:** Data base of mailing labels on women's organizations.

★779★ National Women's Martial Arts Federation (NWMAF)
1377 Studer Ave.
Columbus, OH 43206
Phone: (614)443-1025
Melanie Fine, Treas.

Founded: 1972. **Description:** Female martial artists. Promotes excellence in martial arts. Encourages "the widest range of women" to train in the spirit of building individual and collective strength. Bestows awards; sponsors competitions, educational, and charitable programs. Maintains biographical archives. **Members:** 550. **Publications:** *NWMAF Newsletter*, quarterly. Includes articles and features on female maritial artists, and news about upcoming events. • Also publish *Disabilities Directory*.

★780★ National Women's Neckwear and Scarf Association (NWNSA)
c/o Jacob M. Weinstein
1350 Ave. of the Americas
New York, NY 10019
Phone: (212)708-0316
Jacob M. Weinstein, Counsel

Founded: 1933. **Description:** Manufacturers of women's neckwear and scarves. **Members:** 5.

★781★ National Women's Political Caucus (NWPC)
1275 K St. NW, Ste. 750
Washington, DC 20005
Phone: (202)898-1100
Linda Kaplan, Exec.Dir.

Founded: 1971. **Description:** Individuals supporting increased political influence of women. Multipartisan caucus seeking to gain an equal voice and place for women in the political process at local, state, and national levels. Supports women candidates for elective and appointive political offices. Raises women's issues in elections and seeks to ensure that women hold policymaking positions in political parties. Has lobbied in state legislatures to pass the Equal Rights Amendment, to protect women's rights of reproductive freedom, and to secure comparable worth on the job. Works for affirmative action within the major political parties. Compiles statistics. **Members:** 75,000. **Local Groups:** 300. **Publications:** *Women's Political Times*, quarterly. Newsletter covering political issues from a feminist viewpoint. Includes book reviews and legislative updates.

★782★ National Women's Studies Association (NWSA)
c/o Deborah Louis
University of Maryland
College Park, MD 20742-1325
Phone: (301)405-5573
Fax: (301)454-1572
Deborah Louis, Dir.

Founded: 1977. **Description:** Teachers, students, community activists, and interested individuals; academic and community-based programs, projects, and groups interested in feminist education. Works to further the social, political, and professional development of women's studies programs. Supports feminist causes; lobbies for women's studies at the elementary, secondary, and college level; encourages the development of a network for distributing information on women's studies; cooperates with women's projects in communities; administers graduate scholarships in women's studies. Offers prize money for best manuscript in women's studies. Compiles statistics. Conducts conferences to address topics such as: new developments and controversies in feminist research and theory in the humanities, social sciences, and sciences; curricular development; political and legal issues and strategies; intersection of race and gender; international women's studies. **Members:** 4000. **Regional Groups:** 12. **Computerized Services:** Mailing labels for women's studies programs and NWSA membership. **Caucuses:** African-American Women; Aging and Ageism; Community College; Disability; Jewish Women; Lesbian; Poor and Working Class Women; Prek-12 Educators; Student; Women of Color; Women's Centers/Services. **Publications:** *Annual Membership Directory*. • *Biannual Women's Studies Program Directory*. • *NWSA Journal*, quarterly. • *NWSAction*, quarterly. Newsletter containing calendar of events, conference reports, fellowship and employment opportunity listings, association news, and resources listings. Emphasizes multicultural and interdisciplinary perspectives.

★783★ National Youth Pro-Life Coalition (NYPLC)
5200 Shrewsbury
St. Louis, MO 63119
Phone: (314)781-7322
Mary Anne Hughes, Exec.Dir.

Founded: 1971. **Description:** Young adults who support pro-life issues. Conducts an eight-week legislative internship which includes training on pro-life issues, the legislative process, and lobbying. Arranges appointments with congressional offices to express pro-life concerns and support pro-life legislation. **Members:** 1500. **Local Groups:** 200.

★784★ Native Daughters of the Golden West (NDGW)
543 Baker St.
San Francisco, CA 94117
Phone: (415)563-9091
Julia Evans, Exec.Sec.

Founded: 1886. **Description:** Native born Californian women. Works to promote the history of the State of California, venerate California pioneers, promote child welfare programs, assist in marking and restoring historic landmarks, and participate in civic affairs. Presents annual scholarship. Maintains museum, historical collection, and reference library. **Members:** 13,500. **Publications:** *California Star*, bimonthly. Newsletter. • *Proceedings*, annual.

★785★ Navy Mothers' Clubs of America (NMCA)
c/o Peggy Rizzo
1718 Spruce St.
Philadelphia, PA 19103
Phone: (215)732-1566
Peggy Rizzo, Cmdr.

Founded: 1930. **Description:** Mothers of present or former servicemen and women in the active or reserve branches of the Navy, Marines, or Coast Guard. Conducts welfare activities; visits veterans' and naval hospitals; sponsors social programs for servicemen. Local groups maintain Servicemen's Center, Philadelphia, PA. **Members:** 3000. **State Groups:** 27. **Local Groups:** 185. **Publications:** *Navy Mothers' News*, bimonthly.

★786★ Navy Wifeline Association (NWA)
Washington Navy Yard, Bldg. 172
Washington, DC 20374
Phone: (202)433-2333
Fax: (202)433-2639
Peggy Mauz, Chwm.

Founded: 1965. **Description:** Spouses of both officers and enlisted men in the Navy, Marine Corps, and Coast Guard. Serves as a clearinghouse for information in an effort to better educate members on the importance of their spouses' careers. Fosters a sense of belonging among spouses of naval personnel by serving as a point of contact to help them combat the problems encountered due to separation from loved ones and constantly changing environments. Operates Family Ombudsman Program, which functions as a liaison between command family members and Navy, Marine Corps, and Coast Guard officials. Maintains Navy Family Service Center, which provides information and referral, counseling, family programs, and hospitality kits to active duty and retired Navy personnel and their families. Provides child care services; sponsors seminars. **Publications:** *Navy Family Lifeline*, quarterly. Magazine; includes articles from Navy wives worldwide. • Also publishes *Sea Legs, Social Customs and Traditions of the Naval Services, Guidelines for the Spouses of Commanding Officers and Executive Officers, Overseamanship, Financial and Personal Affairs*, and other guides, booklets, brochures, pamphlets, and leaflets.

★787★ Navy Wives Clubs of America (NWCA)
c/o Nancy Perry
149 Whitney St.
Auburn, ME 04210
Phone: (804)421-2180
Nancy Perry, Pres.

Founded: 1936. **Description:** Spouses of all enlisted persons in the Navy, Marine Corps, and Coast Guard, as well as their retired and active reserve components. Members participate in community projects and charitable programs. Scholarship Foundation provides funds to children of Navy, Marine Corps, and Coast Guard enlisted personnel; also awards member scholarship and enlisted dependent spouse scholarship. Presents annual President's Theme Award. **Members:** 1383. **Regional Groups:** 5. **Local Groups:** 83. **Publications:** *Mailing Directory*, periodic. • *Monthly Mimeo*. • Also publishes *Operating Manual*.

★788★ Network for Professional Women (NPW)
c/o JoAnne P. Smith
City Personnel
100 Committee Plaza, Ste. 220
Hartford, CT 06103
Phone: (203)727-1988
Fax: (203)727-9623
JoAnne P. Smith, Pres.

Founded: 1979. **Description:** To educate and motivate professional women in all facets of their lives. Sponsors seminars and workshops on topics including management of credit, employment networking, IRAs, and reentering the work force.

★789★ **Network of Women in Trade and Technical Jobs**
c/o Wentworth Inst
550 Huntington Ave.
Boston, MA 02115

★790★ **New Dawn (ND)**
PO Box 1849
Alexandria, VA 22313
Founded: 1980. **Description:** Lesbians interested in corresponding with other gay women. Functions as an exchange service through which members identify individuals with whom they wish to correspond. **Members:** 4000. **Publications:** *New Dawn*, quarterly. Magazine containing letters, art, and resources.

★791★ **New ERA Education/Child Care Parent Advocacy Program**
4516 Manordene Rd.
Baltimore, MD 21229
Phone: (301)233-5100

★792★ **New Trans-Century Foundation Secretariat for Women in Development**
1724 Kalorama Rd., NW
Washington, DC 20009
Phone: (202)328-4400
Warren W. Wiggins, Pres.
Founded: 1968. **Description:** Delivers technical assistance to the rural poor in international projects. *Job Opportunities Bulletin.*

★793★ **New Ways to Work (NWW)**
149 9th St.
San Francisco, CA 94103
Phone: (415)552-1000
Barney Olmsted, Co-Director
Founded: 1972. **Description:** A non-profit community based work resource center which focuses on promotion of alternative work schedules such as job sharing, permanent part-time and flextime.

★794★ **New York Academy of Science Women in Science Committee**
2 E. 63rd St.
New York, NY 10021
Phone: (212)838-0230
Anne Collins, Exec.Dir.
Founded: 1975. **Description:** Concerned with the human rights of women scientists. Offers workshops on various professional themes.

★795★ **9 to 5, National Association of Working Women**
614 Superior Ave. NW, Rm. 852
Cleveland, OH 44113
Phone: (216)566-9308
Toll-free: 800-522-0925
Fax: (216)566-0192
Karen Nussbaum, Exec.Dir.
Founded: 1973. **Description:** Women office workers. Seeks to build a national network of local office worker chapters that strives to gain better pay, proper use of office automation, opportunities for advancement, elimination of sex and race discrimination, and improved working conditions for women office workers. Works to introduce legislation or regulations at state level to protect video display terminal operators. Produces studies and research in areas such as reproductive hazards of Video Display Terminals (VDTs), automation's effect on clerical employment, family and medical leaves, and stress. Conducts annual summer school for working women. Maintains speakers' bureau. **Members:** 13,000. **Local Groups:** 25. **Publications:** *9 to 5 Newsletter*, 5/year. • Also publishes *9 to 5: Working Women's Guide to Office Survival, Hidden Victims: Clerical Workers, Automations, and the Changing Economy,* and other titles. **Formerly:** (1978) Working Women Organizing Project; (1982) Working Women, National Association of Officeworkers.

★796★ **9 to 5 Working Women Education Fund (WWEF)**
614 Superior Ave. NW
Cleveland, OH 44113
Phone: (216)566-1699
Tami O'Dell, Exec.Dir.
Founded: 1973. **Description:** Conducts research on the concerns of women office workers. Topics include: the future of office work; automation; health and safety issues; affirmative action; family and medical leave; pay equity; flex-time; job-sharing. Conducts public presentations and seminars upon request; provides speakers. Compiles statistics; has conducted a national survey on women and stress. Maintains biographical archives, and library on the history of working women. **Publications:** Reports. **Formerly:** (1989) Working Women Education Fund.

★797★ **Ninety-Nines, International Women Pilots**
Will Rogers Airport
PO Box 59965
Oklahoma City, OK 73159
Phone: (405)685-7969
Fax: (405)685-7985
Loretta Jean Gragg, Exec.Dir.
Founded: 1929. **Description:** Women pilots united to foster a better understanding of aviation. Encourages cross-country flying; provides consulting service and gives indoctrination flights; flies missions for charitable assistance programs; endorses air races. Develops programs and courses for schools and youth organizations and teaches ground school subjects. Participates in flying competitions. Maintains resource center, biographical archives, and a 700 volume library with a display area dedicated to the preservation of women's achievements in aviation. Bestows Amelia Earhart Memorial Scholarship Award, entitling winners to advanced flight training or courses in specialized branches of aviation; awards Amelia Earhart Research Scholar Grant to a specialized, professional scholar. Operates placement service. Conducts seminar on safety education, lecture on personal aviation experience, and charitable event. Compiles statistics. **Members:** 6900. **Computerized Services:** Information on women interested in aviation careers; membership listing. **Publications:** *Ninety-Nine News*, 10/year. • *Ninety-Nines, International Women Pilots—Membership Directory*, annual. • Also publishes brochures and *History of the Ninety-Nines—Sixty and Counting.* **Also known as:** International Group of Women Pilots.

★798★ **Non-Traditional Employment for Women (NEW)**
243 W. 20th St.
New York, NY 10011
Phone: (212)627-6252
Fax: (212)255-8021
Lola Snyder, Dir., Educational & Technical Assistance
Founded: 1978. **Description:** NEW is a training, placement, and advocacy organization dedicated to helping women find economic self-sufficiency through work in construction and other blue-collar trades. Provides information and technical assistance to other groups and those interested in increasing the number of women in trades. **Publications:** *NEWsletter*, quarterly. • *Training Women for Non-Traditional Jobs.* • *A Design for Success.*

★799★ **North American Indian Women's Association (NAIWA)**
9602 Maestor's Ln.
Gaithersburg, MD 20879
Phone: (301)330-0397
Ann French, Contact
Founded: 1970. **Description:** Women, 18 years and older, who are members of federally recognized tribes. Seeks to foster the general well-being of Indian people through unity of purpose. Promotes inter-tribal communication, awareness of the Native American culture, betterment of family life, health, and education, and strengthening of communication among Native Americans. **Regional Groups:** 6. **Local Groups:** 19. **Publications:** Brochure.

★800★ **North American Menopause Society (NAMS)**
University Hospitals of Cleveland
Departmentof OB/GYN
2074 Abington Rd.
Cleveland, OH 44106
Phone: (216)844-3334
Fax: (216)844-3348
Wulf H. Utian, M.D., Pres.
Founded: 1989. **Description:** Physicians, scientists, research and clinical personnel, and other health care professionals are active members; student or physicians serving residencies or fellowships are associate members. Promotes the study of the climacteric in men and women. Advances the exchange of research plans and experience between members. Offers educational programs. **Members:** 600. **Computerized Services:** Menopause Care Providers listing.

★801★ **North American Network of Women Runners (NANWR)**
PO Box 719
Bala-Cynwyd, PA 19004
Phone: (215)668-9886
Phoebe B. Jones, Dir.
Founded: 1979. **Description:** Women runners, fitness participants, racers, health professionals, women in sports, and women concerned about opportunities for health, fitness, and sport. Dedicated to winning the financial resources that will make athletic careers, physical fitness, and good health accessible to women internationally. Holds low-cost women's workouts with child care in various sports through community, school, and business facilities. **Members:** 500. **State Groups:** 10. **Publications:** *Newsletter*, quarterly.

★802★ NOW Legal Defense and Education Fund (NOW LDEF)
99 Hudson St., 12th Fl.
New York, NY 10013
Phone: (212)925-6635
Fax: (212)226-1066
Helen Neuborne, Exec.Dir.

Founded: 1970. **Description:** Functions as an educational and litigating sister group to the National Organization for Women (see separate entry) to provide legal assistance to women and to educate the public on gender discrimination and other equal rights issues. Purpose is to combat, by legal action and educational and community-based projects, discrimination based on race, sex, religion, or national origin. Conducts research; compiles and publishes facts and statistics concerning the legal, educational, and economic situation of women. Sponsors Women's Media Project, Project on Equal Education Rights, National Judicial Education Program to Promote Equality for Women and Men in the Courts, Women's Economic Rights Project (see separate entries), and Family Law Project. **Publications:** *State by State Guide to Women's Legal Rights*, reports, surveys, brochures, pamphlets, and legal resource kits.

★803★ Nuclear Energy Women (NEW)
c/o Patricia Bryant
1776 I St., Ste. 400
Washington, DC 20006-2495
Phone: (202)293-0770
Patricia Bryant, Program Coordinator

Founded: 1975. **Description:** Individuals in energy industries and citizen advocacy groups providing educational services. Disseminates information to women's groups and others concerned about energy. Seeks to provide a clearer understanding of energy choices, with emphasis on providing the facts about nuclear power. Goal is to establish a national network of women with energy expertise who will foster energy education and awareness among other women. Has developed and conducted national and regional energy workshops and seminars for representatives of major women's groups. Arranges energy tours, educational exhibits, and interviews for the news media with energy experts. Bestows Outstanding Woman in Energy Award annually. Maintains speakers' bureau. **Members:** 500. **Regional Groups:** 15. **State Groups:** 7. **Publications:** Issues publications and audiovisuals on energy subjects.

★804★ Nurturing Network (NN)
PO Box 2050
Boise, ID 83701
Phone: (208)344-7200
Toll-free: 800-TNN-4MOM
Fax: (208)344-4447
Mary Cunningham-Agee, Exec.Dir.

Founded: 1986. **Description:** Support group providing pregnant middle-class women with alternatives to abortion. Works to enable such women to have their children while continuing to pursue their educational and career goals. Contends that government financial aid is more readily available for pregnant low-income women and teenagers due to the assumption that middle-class families are more capable of providing financial and emotional support. Seeks the professional assistance of employers and doctors who can provide placement and medical services. Offers medical referral, counseling, and financial services.

★805★ OEF International (OEF)
1815 H St. NW, 11th Fl.
Washington, DC 20006
Phone: (202)466-3430
Fax: (202)775-0596
Cynthia A. Metzler, Exec. Officer

Founded: 1947. **Description:** Develops and provides training and technical assistance programs aimed at addressing the economic and social needs of Third World women. **Publications:** *Annual Report.* • Also publishes handbooks, reports, brochures, and studies. **Formerly:** (1961) Carrie Chapman Catt Memorial Fund; (1980) Overseas Education Fund of the League of Women Voters; (1984) Overseas Education Fund.

★806★ Of A Like Mind (OALM)
Box 6021
Madison, WI 53716
Phone: (608)838-8629

Founded: 1978. **Description:** Women who have signed an Affirmation of Women's Spirituality and define themselves as being on a positive path of spiritual growth. Acts as a network for the exchange of information and ideas; provides support and fellowship for women with similar interests. Operates round robin letter exchange. **Publications:** *Of A Like Mind*, quarterly. Newsletter covering wellness, astrology, tarot, psychic development, dreams, herbs, ethics, politics, the Craft, herstory, and related topics. Includes book reviews, announcements, and networking information.

★807★ Older Women's League (OWL)
730 11th St. NW, Ste. 300
Washington, DC 20001
Phone: (202)783-6686
Fax: (202)638-2356
Joan A. Kuriansky, Exec.Dir.

Founded: 1980. **Description:** Middle-aged and older women; persons of any age who support issues of concern to mid-life and older women. Primary issues include access to health care insurance, support for family caregivers, reform of social security, access to jobs and pensions for older women, effects of budget cuts on women, and maintaining self-sufficiency throughout life. Operates speakers' bureau; bestows awards; prepares educational materials; compiles statistics. **Members:** 21,000. **State Groups:** 2. **Local Groups:** 120. **Publications:** *OWL OBSERVER*, 6/year. Membership activities tabloid. • *Status Report*, annual. • Also publishes *Older Women and Job Discrimination*, *Gray Papers*, *Model State Bills*, and testimony statements on key issues and legislation; produces *A Matter of Life and Death* (videotape).

★808★ Older Women's League (OWLTFCG)
Task Force on Care Givers
730 11th St., NW, Ste. 300
Washington, DC 20001

★809★ Open Meadows Foundation
PO Box 197
Bronx, NY 10464
Phone: (212)885-1119
Nancy Dean, Project Coordinator

Description: The Foundation is a national funding organization for women's projects. It is a non-sexist, multi-racial, multi-ethnic group that offers small grants to projects that have limited financial access, are designed and implemented by women, reflect the cultural and ethnic diversity of society, and promote the well-being of women.

★810★ Operation Rescue (OR)
PO Box 1180
Binghamton, NY 13902
Phone: (607)723-4012
Fax: (607)723-4265

Founded: 1987. **Description:** Coalition of pro-life pastors and laypeople of all faiths. Organizes rescues/sit-ins at abortion clinics to block patient entry and: "save the lives of innocent children"; stop the exploitation of mothers from the "violence" of abortion; "call America to repent for allowing 25 million children to be slaughtered since 1973"; "rescue children and mothers in a way that produces political change." Activities have resulted in over 43,172 arrests of participants and over 634 abortions stopped.

★811★ Operation Sisters United (OSU)
1104 Allison St. NW
Washington, DC 20011
Phone: (202)726-7365
Eleanore Cox, Dir.

Founded: 1972. **Description:** A program of the National Council of Negro Women (see separate entry). Aids teenage girls who have had conflicts with the law; seeks to prevent incarceration and institutionalization of these girls, and help them avoid future legal problems. Works to keep teenage girls with their families. Operates cultural enrichment, counseling, sex education, and family planning programs. Conducts parenting classes for teenage parents. Compiles statistics; maintains placement service. Sponsors competitions and bestows awards.

★812★ Oral History Association Feminist Caucus
1093 Broxton Ave. #720
Los Angeles, CA 90024
Phone: (213)825-0597
Fax: (213)206-1864
Rebecca Sharpless, Contact

Description: The Caucus is a loosely-formed interest group designed to foster feminist inquiry within the subfield of oral history.

★813★ Order of the Daughters of the King (DOK)
4263 1st Ave.
Tucker, GA 30084
Phone: (404)934-5091
Elizabeth A. Hart, Pres.

Founded: 1885. **Description:** Lay order for women in the Episcopal church (and churches in communion with the Episcopal church or sharing the historic Episcopate) who have taken vows of prayer and service for the spread of Christ's Kingdom. Supports two missionaries; grants scholarships. **Members:** 12,000. **Regional Groups:** 51. **Provincial Assemblies:** 7. **Diocesan Assemblies:** 44. **Chapters:**. **Publications:** *The Royal Cross*, quarterly. **Also known as:** Daughters of the King.

★814★ Organization of American Historians (OAH)
Committee on the Status of Women in the Historical Profession (CSWHP)
300 Pompton Rd.
Wayne, NJ 07470
Phone: (201)595-2189
Dr. Carol S. Gruber, Chair

Description: Considers professional issues particular to women in the historical profession, discusses matters of concern to women and seeks to advance their status in the profession. **Alternate phone number:** (201) 595-2319.

★815★ Organization of Chinese American Women (OCAW)
1300 N St. NW, Ste. 100
Washington, DC 20005
Phone: (202)638-0330
Fax: (202)638-2196
Pauline W. Tsui, Exec.Dir.

Founded: 1977. **Description:** Advances the cause of Chinese American women in the U.S. and fosters public awareness of their special needs and concerns. Seeks to integrate Chinese American women into the mainstream of women's activities and programs. Addresses issues such as: equal employment opportunities at both the professional and nonprofessional levels; overcoming stereotypes; racial and sexual discrimination and restrictive traditional beliefs; assistance to poverty-stricken recent immigrants; access to leadership and policymaking positions. Develops training models for Chinese and Asian American women. Conducts training and job placement for class participants, widening teenage women's career choices, and networking for Chinese American women. Holds awards banquet. **Members:** 2000. **Publications:** *OCAW Speaks*, quarterly. Newsletter.

★816★ Organization for Equal Education of the Sexes (OEES)
PO Box 438
Blue Hill, ME 04614
Phone: (207)374-2489
Fax: (207)374-2489
Lucy Picco Simpson, Pres.

Founded: 1978. **Description:** Teachers, administrators, counselors, parents, students, and sex-equity professionals. Develops, publishes, and disseminates information and materials; promotes sharing of ideas for ensuring equal educational opportunities for all students. Maintains 1000 volume library on nonsexist curricula, women's history, and sexism in education. Provides a poster series on women's history, nontraditional careers, and dropout prevention. **Computerized Services:** Mailing list rental. **Publications:** *Teaching About Women in American History*, *Teaching About Women and Girls with Disabilities*, and other teaching packets.

★817★ Organization of PanAsian American Women (PANASIA)
PO Box 39128
Washington, DC 20016
Nguyen Minh Chau, Pres.

Founded: 1976. **Description:** To provide a voice for the concerns of Asian Pacific-American (APA) women and to encourage their full participation in all aspects of American society. Seeks to: promote an accurate and realistic image of APA women in America; develop the leadership skills and increase the occupational mobility of these women; maintain a national communications network. Produces legislative updates on national issues of concern to Asian Pacific Americans. Sponsors workshops and lectures; maintains speakers' bureau. **Members:** 100. **Publications:** *Membership Directory*, annual. • *Pan Asia News*, periodic. Newsletter. • Also publishes *Pan Asian Women: A Vital Force*.

★818★ Organization for the Study of Communication, Language and Gender (OSCLG)
Arizona State University, Communications Department
2607 S. Forest Ave.
Tempe, AZ 85282
Phone: (602)967-2817
Carol Valentine, Executive Secretary

Founded: 1981. **Description:** The organization provides a forum for professional discussion, presentation of research, and demonstration of creative projects in the areas of communication, language, and gender. Its focus is interdisciplinary and members include teachers, researchers, consultants, and practitioners from a variety of fields in the social sciences, humanities, and sciences. Provides Sexism in Language Guidelines and sponsors the Cheris Kramarae Award. **Publications:** *OSCLG News* (quarterly).

★819★ Original Cosmopolitans (OC)
217 Wilson Ave.
Westbury, NY 11590
Phone: (516)997-9871
Toll-free: 800-645-2996
Enid Kessler, Pres.

Founded: 1978. **Description:** Foreign-born women. Seeks closer ties between members and their families overseas. Conducts charitable program. **Members:** 1000. **Local Groups:** 15. **Publications:** *Cosmopolitan Courier*, monthly.

★820★ ORIGINS
PO Box 556
Whippanny, NJ 07981
Phone: (201)428-9683
Mary Anne Cohen, Co-Founder

Founded: 1980. **Description:** Women whose children have been adopted. Works to: recognize the emotional needs of these mothers and help them to deal with the continuing guilt, anguish, and concern for their lost children; unite women in similar situations; provide moral support and help in searching for their children, for the purpose of learning whether the children are alive, well, and in loving homes. Sponsors search clinics which include advice on methodology and contacts; provides search assistance to fathers, siblings, grandparents, and other relatives. Maintains collection of books and clippings on adoption, search, and contact; keeps mailing list and membership records. Operates speakers' bureau. Provides referrals. **Members:** 200. **Publications:** *Newsletter*, bimonthly. • Also publishes *Shedding Light On the Dark Side of Adoption*.

★821★ Ovulation Method Teachers Association (OMTA)
PO Box 101780
Anchorage, AK 99510-1780
Phone: (344)334-8606
Frances Butzke, Sec.

Description: Certifies teachers of the ovulation method of birth control. (The ovulation method is a means by which women can determine the fertile days of their menstrual cycle by analyzing the appearance of cervical mucus and charting the results.) Promotes the ovulation method as a safe and effective contraceptive. Upgrades the quality of ovulation method instruction through the evaluation and certification of teachers. Compiles and disseminates information for the continuing education of health professionals and the public. Provides a national teachers referral service to pair interested persons with teachers in their geographic area. **Publications:** *Ovulation Method Newsletter*, quarterly. Includes calendar of events, notices of the availability of educational materials, and news of the association's educational programs.

★822★ PanAmerican Liaison Committee of Women's Organizations (PALCO)
3203 Beech St., NW
Washington, DC 20015
Phone: (202)362-3274
Ruth Donaldson, Pres.

Founded: 1944. **Description:** Individuals and women's organizations in Western Hemisphere countries. Encourages closer friendship and understanding through cultural, educational, charitable, scientific, and literary projects and activities. Organizes training courses in leadership development; conducts workshops on the Laubach method of training literacy teachers and seminars on Pan-Americanism and parliamentary procedure. Awards scholarships; gives financial support to small, local self-help initiatives. **Members:** 200. **Publications:** *Newsletter*, monthly. • *Roster*, biennial.

★823★ PanAmerican Women's Association (PAWA)
c/o Frances R. Grant
310 West End Ave., Apt. 16C
New York, NY 10023
Phone: (212)362-0710
Frances R. Grant, Pres.

Founded: 1930. **Description:** Women united to foster greater inter-American understanding. Promotes common action for the well-being of the people of the Western Hemisphere through cultural and educational exchange. Organizes music, art, dance, and student programs; sponsors periodic panel discussions.

★824★ Panel of American Women (PAW)
c/o Nancy Boylan
205 19th St. NE, Apt. 108
Canton, OH 44714
Phone: (216)453-6160
Nancy Boylan, Exec. Officer

Founded: 1957. **Description:** Groups of women volunteers in cities all over the United States promoting understanding among people of all races and religions. Members present panel-type programs for church, school, and civic groups, discussing their personal experiences in confronting prejudice and discrimination. Each panel usually includes a moderator and four or five panelists representing Protestant, Catholic, Jewish, Black, Hispanic, Native American, and/or other ethnic groups, depending on the ethnic makeup of the community. The panels discuss issues affecting women and the prejudices they and their families have met in schools, housing, employment, and other situations; panels then answer questions from the audience. Also sponsors youth panels. Acts as a community resource, putting organizations in touch with agencies or providing them with resource materials. **Members:** 150. **Regional Groups:** 2. **Local Groups:** 14. **Publications:** *National Panel of American Women*, 3-4/year. • Also publishes handbook and brochure.

★825★ PanPacific and Southeast Asia Women's Association of the U.S.A. (PPSEAWA-US)
Box 1531, Madison Square Station
New York, NY 10159
Phone: (212)228-5307
Ann Allen, Pres.

Founded: 1928. **Description:** Seeks to strengthen peaceful ties by fostering international understanding and friendship among the women of Asia and the Pacific and women of the U.S.A. Promotes cooperation among women of these regions for the study and improvement of social, economic, and cultural conditions. Engages in studies on Asian and Pacific affairs; offers friendship, hospitality, and assistance to Asian and Pacific area women; presents programs of educational and social interest, dealing with the customs and cultures of Asian and Pacific countries; bestows scholastic awards. Conducts lectures, panels, and workshops. **Members:** 350. **Local Groups:** 5. **Publications:** *USA Newsletter*, semiannual. Informs members about association activities. • *International Bulletin*, semiannual. Provides information of significant activites in member countries and interest areas. **Formerly:** (1955) PanPacific Women's Association of United States of America.

★826★ Parents of Surrogate-Borne Infants and Toddlers in Verbal Exchange (POSITIVE)
PO Box 204
East Meadow, NY 11554
Phone: (516)794-5772
Ilene Stargot, Project Leader

Founded: 1988. **Description:** A special interest group of the National Infertility Network Exchange (see separate entry) providing peer support for parents raising children borne by a surrogate mother. Facilitates discussion of parenting issues. Although the group presently operates regionally, it answers inquiries on a national level and has addressed legislators from several states. Maintains speakers' bureau. **Publications:** *Positive Way Newsletter*, quarterly.

★827★ Peace Links
747 8th St. SE
Washington, DC 20003
Phone: (202)544-0805
Fax: (202)544-0809
Carol Williams, Director

Description: The organization is a network of over 30,000 Americans, mostly women, who work locally toward redirecting national policies away from nuclear weapons and war and into peaceful ways of resolving conflicts and also directing more of the country's resources to fund human needs. It conducts a letter-writing exchange between Americans and Soviets and an Action Network activating citizens. **Publications:** *Connection*. • *Action Network*.

★828★ Pension Rights Center
Women's Pension Project
918 16th St., NW, Ste. 704
Washington, DC 20006
Phone: (202)296-3776
Anne Moss, Dir.

Founded: 1981. **Description:** Works for pension reform for women and educates women about their pension rights.

★829★ PEO Sisterhood
3700 Grand Ave.
Des Moines, IA 50312
Phone: (515)255-3153
Fax: (515)255-3820
Deborah Cowan, CAO

Founded: 1869. **Description:** International women's organization seeking to further opportunities for higher education for women. Has established International Peace Scholarship Fund, Educational Loan Fund, Program for Continuing Education, and PEO Scholar Awards. Maintains Cottey Junior College for Women, Nevada, MO. **Members:** 247,000. **State Groups:** 50. **Local Groups:** 5596. **Publications:** *Directory of Presidents*, annual. • *PEO Record*, 10/year.

★830★ People Against Rape (PAR)
401 William St.
PO Box 5318
River Forest, IL 60305
Phone: (708)452-0737
Toll-free: 800-877-7252
Marie Howard, Pres.

Founded: 1976. **Description:** Seeks to help children avoid becoming the victims of sexual abuse. Sends instructors to schools across the United States to teach children and young adults the basic principles of self-defense. Offers drug/alcohol abuse assistance and teacher training programs. Conducts the Hands Off, I'm Special educational program. **Publications:** *Hands Off, I'm Special* (booklet), brochures, and pamphlets; also publishes books.

★831★ People for Life (PFL)
3375 N. Dousman
Milwaukee, WI 53212
Phone: (414)332-3423
Pam Cira, Chairperson

Founded: 1984. **Description:** A grass roots, pro-life organization. Provides counseling for anyone experiencing problems following an abortion, adoption placement, or miscarriage; matches counselor with similar experience to counselee. Facilitates postadoption support group for women who have placed their child up for adoption or are considering such a placement. Provides training for counselors. Sponsors seminars. Compiles statistics. **Publications:** *Annual Statistics*. • *Counselor Newsletter*, monthly. Organization activities newsletter. Includes calendar of events. • Also publishes postadoption, postmiscarriage, postabortion, and general information brochures.

★832★ Pharmacists for Life (PFL)
PO Box 130
Ingomar, PA 15127
Phone: (412)364-3422
Toll-free: 800-227-8359
Bogomir M. Kuhar, P.D., Pres.

Founded: 1984. **Description:** Pharmacists and interested groups and individuals. Seeks to educate pharmacists, other medical professionals, and the public about the "abortion holocaust." Defends the right to life from conception to natural death, regardless of biological stage, dependency, or residence. Provides medical supplies to individuals and crisis pregnancy centers. Provides children's services; sponsors charitable, educational, and research programs. Maintains library and speakers' bureau. Compiles statistics; bestows awards. **Telecommunications Services:** Financial, legal, and medical referrals. **Publications:** *Beginnings*, bimonthly. Newsletter; contains book and literature reviews, guest analyses and editorials, and news on current events. • Also publishes *Gambling with Life: the Birth Control Game*, *Can Cancer Pain be Relieved?*, *Pharmaceutical Companies: the New Abortionists*, and *IUD: Device of Death*.

★833★ Physicians for Choice (PFC)
c/o Planned Parenthood Federation of America
810 7th Ave.
New York, NY 10019
Phone: (212)541-7800
Fax: (212)261-4352
Laurie Novick, Coordinator

Founded: 1981. **Description:** Physicians who believe in preserving the right of American women to decide when or whether to bear a child. Conducts a variety of activities to educate legislators and the public on the health benefits of reproductive freedom. Testifies at congressional hearings; circulates petitions; lobbies legislators. Maintains speakers' bureau. **Members:** 3000.

★834★ Pi Lambda Theta
4101 E. 3rd St.
Bloomington, IN 47407
Phone: (812)339-3411
Fax: (812)339-3462
Leslie H. Kent, Executive Director

Description: The honor association is for outstanding education professionals and seeks to promote excellence at all academic levels, as well as provide leadership development for its members, an environment for professional growth, and leadership for the profession. It sponsors research awards and holds a biennial conference. **Publications:** *Educational Horizons* (quarterly). • *Newsletter* (5/year).

★835★ Pinochle Bugs Social and Civic Club
1624 Madison Ave.
Charlotte, NC 28216
Phone: (704)334-4802
Dr. Esther Page Hill, Pres.

Founded: 1955. **Description:** African American women. Promotes social and civic cooperation among various women's groups. Encourages social, economic, educational, and cultural advancement. Supports community projects. Holds pinochle tournaments; bestows civic awards; maintains speakers' bureau; awards scholarships. **Members:** 265. **Local Groups:** 20. **Publications:** *The Beetle*, biennial. Magazine; includes coverage of chapter activities and member profiles.

★836★ Planned Parenthood Federation of America (PPFA)
810 7th Ave.
New York, NY 10019
Phone: (212)541-7800
Toll-free: 800-829-PPFA
Fax: (212)245-1845
Faye Wattleton, Pres.

Founded: 1916. **Affiliates:** 171. **Description:** Organizations providing leadership in: making effective means of voluntary fertility regulation, including contraception, abortion, sterilization, and infertility services, available and fully accessible to all as a central element of reproductive health; stimulating and sponsoring relevant biomedical, socioeconomic, and demographic research; developing appropriate information, education, and training programs to increase knowledge about human reproduction and sexuality. Supports and assists efforts to achieve similar goals worldwide. Operates 900 centers that provide medically supervised family planning services and educational programs. Annually bestows: PPFA Margaret Sanger Award; PPFA Maggie Awards for media excellence; Arthur and Edith Wippman Scientific Research Award. Maintains 5000 volume library on contraception, abortion, sterilization, family planning, and population. **Publications:** *Annual Report.* • Also publishes books and pamphlets. **Formerly:** (1939) American Birth Control League. **Also known as:** Planned Parenthood; Planned Parenthood/World Population.

★837★ Polish Legion of American Veterans, U.S.A., Ladies Auxiliary (PLAVA)
2141 Vernon
Trenton, MI 48183
Phone: (313)675-1354
Wanda Swiecki, Treas.

Founded: 1921. **Description:** Women related to veterans of Polish descent who have served in the U.S. armed forces. Presents annual scholarships to graduating high school seniors. Conducts charitable and social service programs; assists hospitalized ex-servicemen; aids widows and orphans. **Members:** 10,000. **State Groups:** 16. **Local Groups:** 87. **Publications:** *Journal*, periodic. • *News*, quarterly.

★838★ Polish Women's Alliance of America (PWAA)
205 S. Northwest Hwy.
Park Ridge, IL 60068
Phone: (708)692-2247
Helen Wojcik, Pres.

Founded: 1898. **Description:** Fraternal benefit life insurance society administered by women. Supports and contributes to charitable and relief foundations in the U.S. and abroad. Maintains 7500 volume library of Polish, English, and American history and culture. **Members:** 65,000. **State Groups:** 17. **Local Groups:** 758. **Publications:** *Glos Polek* (in English and Polish), bimonthly.

★839★ Population Association of America (PAA)
Women's Caucus
1722 N St., NW
Washington, DC 20036
Phone: (703)875-4581
Fax: (202)785-0146
Ellen Starbird, Contact

Description: The Association is an international society of professionals working in the population field. The Women's Caucus provides an opportunity for women in the profession to discuss issues of concern to them and sponsors sessions at the annual meeting of the PAA.

★840★ The Population Council
1 Dag Hammarskjold Plaza
New York, NY 10023
Phone: (212)644-1300
Judith Bruce, Senior Associate/Program Division

Founded: 1952. **Description:** The Council is an international nonprofit organization that applies science and technology to the solution of population problems in developing countries by encompassing the social, health, and biomedical sciences. Collaborating with governments, nongovernmental organizations, and private foundations, it undertakes work on population policy, family planning and fertility, reproductive health survival, and women's roles and status. Projects include Family Formation, Female Headship and Poverty, and Quality Care, incorporating women's perspective in development of family planning services. **Publications:** *Annual Report.* • *SEEDS.* • *ZUALITE.*

★841★ Positive Pregnancy and Parenting Fitness (PPPF)
51 Saltrock Rd.
Baltic, CT 06330
Phone: (203)822-8573
Fax: 800-433-5523
Robert L. Olkin, Contact

Founded: 1982. **Description:** Nurses, childbirth educators, certified and lay midwives, yoga instructors, physical therapists, psychologists, healthcare providers, and others interested in pregnancy and parenting education. Promotes a holistic approach to pregancy to pregnancy and parenting; works to improve parent-child relationships in order to foster the development of strong family units. Supports increased availability of prenatal and neonatal health care. Conducts educational programs to certify childbirth and parenting instructors; develop midpregnancy and parenting classes. Conducts research programs; maintains speakers' bureau. **Members:** 350. **Regional Groups:** 10. **State Groups:** 10. **Local Groups:** 10. **Publications:** *Positive Pregnancy & Parenting Newsletter*, semiannual. Includes reviews of educational materials, recipes, workshop listing, and classified ads.

★842★ Postpartum Support, International (PSI)
927 N. Kellogg Ave.
Santa Barbara, CA 93111
Phone: (805)967-7636
Jane Honikman, Pres.

Founded: 1987. **Description:** Promotes public awareness about the mental health issues of childbearing. Encourages research and the formation of support groups; addresses legal and insurance coverage issues. Provides education-

al programs. **Publications:** *PSI News*, quarterly. Association and industry newsletter **Formerly:** (1987) International Post-Partum Mental Health Network; (1988) International Post-Partum Mental Health and Social Support.

★843★ Pregnancy and Infant Loss Center (PILC)
1421 E. Wayzata Blvd., No. 40
Wayzata, MN 55391
Phone: (612)473-9372
Susan Erling, Dir.

Founded: 1983. **Description:** Parents who have suffered a miscarriage, stillbirth, or infant death; concerned health care professionals and volunteers. Seeks to increase public awareness and establish a network of support for families affected by perinatal death. Provides referral services for parents who wish to contact support groups, counselors, or other couples who have also experienced a perinatal death. Offers assistance to speakers and workshop directors seeking to contact churches, schools, and service organizations interested in conducting perinatal bereavement assistance programs. Produces educational materials dealing with funeral arrangements, guidelines for the friends and families of bereaved parents, high-risk pregnancies, and the grief of surviving siblings. Offers perinatal bereavement seminars and consulting services. Maintains speakers' bureau and small library of material on perinatal bereavement. Conducts quarterly program on grief and loss. Sponsors annual Pregnancy and Infant Loss Awareness Month in October; distributes information packets. Compiles statistics; bestows awards. **Members:** 850. **Telecommunications Services:** Help line, at number listed above. **Publications:** *Loving Arms Newsletter*, quarterly. Features articles, poems, and resources on miscarriage, stillbirth, and infant death.

★844★ Premenstrual Syndrome Action
PO Box 16292
Irvine, CA 92713
Phone: (714)723-0232
Toll-free: 800-272-4PMS
Virginia Cassara, Contact

Founded: 1980. **Description:** Seeks to inform medical professionals and the public about the organic and biochemical causes of premenstrual syndrome. (Premenstrual syndrome, or PMS, is a hormonal disorder characterized by a variety of emotional and physical symptoms which recur during the same phase of each menstrual cycle. Symptoms include: tension, depression, irritability, crying for no apparent reason, forgetfulness or mental confusion, headaches, backaches, acne, cold sores, bloating, and breast tenderness. Some experts estimate that 40 percent of all women suffer from PMS, to varying degrees, at some time during their lives. Its exact cause is unknown.) Trains medicial professionals on the treatment of PMS. **Telecommunications Services:** Information line; toll-free numbers, (800)272-4PMS (outside California) and (800)3 32-4PMS (California). **Publications:** *PMS Connection*, periodic. **Also known as:** PMS Action.

★845★ Presbyterian Women (PW)
100 Witherspoon St.
Louisville, KY 40202
Phone: (502)569-5365
Toll-free: 800-872-3283
Fax: (502)569-5018
Gladys Strachan, Exec.Dir.

Founded: 1988. **Description:** Purposes are to promote the Presbyterian church and its teachings and to provide a forum for Presbyterian women. Administers to the needs of individuals through missions worldwide; defends the rights of those who are economically and politically powerless; makes political and social commitments to issues involving justice, peace, freedom, and world hunger; examines topics such as apartheid, child abandonment, rape, divorce, and displaced women. Participates in Presbyterian educational ministry and the training of church leaders. Offers economic justice consultations; organizes overseas study seminars and leadership and training events; conducts local, regional, and national workshops. Maintains speakers' bureau, biographical archives, and library; offers charitable program; compiles statistics. Bestows Women of Faith awards annually. **Members:** 400,000. **Regional Groups:** 187. **Local Groups:** 10,000. **Computerized Services:** Mailing lists of selected constituency. **Telecommunications Services:** Presbynet; Presbytel. **Publications:** *Crosswinds*, monthly. Newsletter providing updates and information on *Horizons*. • *Horizons*, bimonthly. Magazine; includes book reviews, Washington Watch, and information on regional groups and leaders. • *Women's Ministry Unit Newsletter*, 2/year. • Also publishes *Etchings of Diversity* (book). **Formerly:** (1988) United Presbyterian Women.

★846★ Pride
c/o Family and Children's Service
414 S. 8th St.
Minneapolis, MN 55404
Phone: (612)340-7634
Susan Battles, Coordinator

Founded: 1978. **Description:** Advocacy and support group for women attempting to get out of prostitution. Provides housing assistance, child protection services, and therapy programs. Maintains speakers' bureau. Conducts educational programs.

★847★ Priests for Equality (PFE)
PO Box 5243
West Hyattsville, MD 20782
Phone: (301)779-9298
Rev. Joseph A. Dearborn, Sec.

Founded: 1975. **Description:** Catholic priests seeking to achieve full equality for women both in the Catholic church and in society. Believes that women can and should be ordained as priests; that women and men are "equally precious to a loving Creator, equally bearing the image of that Creator, equally called to develop his or her human rights." Engages in sociological studies and surveys. Sponsors research studies, reports, and other activities designed to raise the consciousness of individuals and strengthen their commitment to equality. **Members:** 2300. **Supporters:** 1200. **Publications:** *Newsletter*, quarterly. • Also publishes pamphlets and papers.

★848★ Pro-Choice Defense League (PCDL)
131 Fulton Ave.
Hempstead, NY 11550
Phone: (516)538-2626
Bill Baird, Dir.

Founded: 1984. **Description:** Individuals seeking to protect reproductive freedom of choice. Serves as forum for information on reproductive rights. Sponsors public education programs and workshops; conducts training sessions for abortion clinic operators on methods of securing facilities against violence and harassment. **Members:** 300. **Publications:** *Newsletter*, periodic. • Also publishes pamphlets.

★849★ Pro-Family Press Association (PFPA)
PO Box 1584
Manassas, VA 22110
Phone: (703)368-5589
Pete Kelly, Exec.Dir.

Founded: 1981. **Description:** Pro-family publishers, writers, and artists; groups interested in pro-family publicity and publications. Seeks to: strengthen the pro-life movement and the American family by helping groups produce and improve pro-family publications; act as network among publishers of pro-life literature. Members share information and expertise. Conducts seminars. **Publications:** *Family Freedom Report*, monthly. Newsletter covering information of family-related disciplines and news relevant to American families. Monitors developments in the pro-life movement. • *Family News Digest*, monthly. Newsletter covering family-related developments in all sectors including legislation, health, education, and legal matters.

★850★ Pro-Life Action League (PLAL)
6160 N. Cicero, No. 600
Chicago, IL 60646
Phone: (312)777-2900
Fax: (312)777-3061
Joseph M. Scheidler, Exec.Dir.

Founded: 1980. **Description:** Individuals, including doctors, lawyers, business leaders, and students, who are pro-life. Purpose is "to stop abortions now, through effective, legal, nonviolent means" and to lay the groundwork for outlawing all abortions through a constitutional amendment. Conducts demonstrations and picketing against abortion clinics and pro-abortion agencies; appears on radio and television talk shows and demands equal media time to counter pro-abortion views; engages in lobbying. Sponsors seminars for community organizations; lectures student groups; holds workshops; trains volunteers to counsel women in front of clinics. Bestows annual National Protector Award; maintains library of 1000 volumes, tapes and videocassettes, and a filing system covering pro-life issues. Compiles statistics. **Members:** 12,000. **Telecommunications Services:** 24-hour Action Line, (312)777-2525. **Publications:** *Bulletin*, periodic. • *Pro-Life Action News*, quarterly. Newsletter. • Also publishes *Closed: 99 Ways to Stop Abortion*, video tapes on former abortion providers and sidewalk counseling, and brochures.

★851★ Pro-Life Alliance of Gays and Lesbians (GAA)
PO Box 33292
Washington, DC 20033-0292
Phone: (202)223-6697

Description: Gay men and women who oppose abortion. Works to enlighten gay men and women toward the understanding that "like homophobia, abortion tries to get rid of persons whose existence is considered undesirable." Encourages discussion and mutual respect; supports pro-life agencies and services. Works to assist pregnant women and their children. **Formerly:** (1991) Gays Against Abortion.

★852★ Pro-Life Direct Action League (PDAL)
PO Box 11881
St. Louis, MO 63105
Phone: (314)863-1022
Ann L. O'Brien, Pres.

Founded: 1984. **Description:** Opposes legalized abortion and promotes adherence to the "sanctity of life ethic." Group believes that this ethic is an integral part of Christian morality, and that abortion for any reason is in opposition to it; also believes that "law which deprives individuals of their basic human rights" is not valid, and that breaking such statutes is a Christian duty. Conducts sit-ins and other forms of nonviolent protest near abortion clinics. Maintains speakers' bureau. Holds seminars and training meetings; bestows awards. **Publications:** *Action News*, monthly. • Makes available brochures and films.

★853★ Pro-Life Nonviolent Action Project (PNAP)
PO Box 2193
Gaithersburg, MD 20886
Phone: (301)774-4043
Kathleen Kelly, Coordinator

Founded: 1975. **Description:** Goal is to protect human life by preventing abortions through nonviolent direct action. Conducts "sidewalk counseling" and sit-ins at abortion clinics; members submit to arrest when the situation arises in order to promote their beliefs. Holds annual Rachel's Rescue, led by parents of aborted children. **Members:** 1400. **Publications:** Pamphlets, brochures, handouts, and information packet.

★854★ Professional Older Women's Theatre Project (POWTP)
c/o Danse Mirage
153 Mercer St., Second Fl.
New York, NY 10012

★855★ Professional Secretaries International
301 E. Amour Blvd.
Kansas City, MO 64111-1299
Phone: (816)891-6600
Jerry Heitman, Exec.Dir.

Founded: 1942. **Description:** Promotes competence and recognition of persons in secretarial careers, conducts research studies and offers education and training for office workers. **Publications:** *The Secretary*.

★856★ Professional Women in Construction (PWC)
342 Madison Ave., Rm. 451
New York, NY 10173
Phone: (212)687-0610
Fax: (212)490-1213
Lenore Janis, Pres.

Founded: 1980. **Description:** Management-level women in construction and allied industries; owners, suppliers, architects, engineers, field personnel, office personnel, and bonding/surety personnel. Provides a forum for exchange of ideas and promotion of political and legislative action, education, and job opportunities for women in construction and related fields; forms liaisons with other trade and professional groups; develops research programs. Strives to reform abuses and to assure justice and equity within the construction industry. Sponsors mini-workshops; bestows awards. Maintains Action Line which provides members with current information on pertinent legislation and on the association's activities. **Members:** 500. **Regional Groups:** 2. **Publications:** *Calendar of Events*, monthly. • *Newsletter*, quarterly. **Formerly:** (1982) Association of Business and Professional Women in Construction.

★857★ Professional Women Photographers (PWP)
c/o Photographics Unlimited
17 W. 17th St., No. 14
New York, NY 10011
Phone: (212)255-9678
Mariette Allen, Chwm.

Founded: 1975. **Description:** Women professional photographers; other interested individuals. Conducts charitable, educational, and artistic activities to stimulate public interest in, support for, and appreciation of photographic art (particularly members' works). Encourages professional development of photographers. Has participated in New York City's first art parade and has sponsored The Me Generation, a traveling group exhibition. Maintains speakers' bureau. Conducts group shows and projects. **Members:** 500. **Computerized Services:** Mailing list. **Publications:** *PWP Newsletter*, 5/year. Includes meeting schedule and selected biographies.

★858★ Professional Women's Appraisal Association (PWAA)
8383 E. Evans Rd.
Scottsdale, AZ 85260
Phone: (602)998-4422
Fax: (602)998-8022
Deborah S. Johnson, Exec.Dir.

Founded: 1986. **Description:** Women appraisers in government agencies and national banks; independent professional appraisers. Goal is to provide a support system for women real estate appraisers. Offers continuing education classes in appraisal trends, technical methods, and legislation regarding the appraisal industry. Conducts research; maintains library. **Members:** 650. **Computerized Services:** Membership list.

★859★ Project on Equal Education Rights (PEER)
c/o NOW LDEF
99 Hudson St., 12th Fl.
New York, NY 10013
Phone: (212)925-6635
Fax: (212)226-1066
Walteen Grady Truely, Dir.

Founded: 1974. **Description:** Education division of the NOW (National Organization for Women) Legal Defense and Education Fund (see separate entry). Promotes stronger federal enforcement of laws (especially Title IX) against sex discrimination in public schools. Mobilizes coalitions of citizens' groups to work with their school districts for fair treatment of both sexes. Informs parents, community groups, and educators on developments in Congress, federal agencies, the courts, and throughout the country related to women and girls in education. **Publications:** *PEER Reports, Organizing for Change, Black Women in a High Tech World, Sex Bias at the Computer Terminal - How Schools Program Girls, Learning Her Place - Sex Bias in the Elementary School Classroom*, and other materials.

★860★ Project Priesthood (PP)
c/o Women's Ordination Conf.
PO Box 2693
Fairfax, VA 22031
Phone: (703)352-1006
Fax: (703)352-5181
Ruth Fitzpatrick, Coordinator

Founded: 1976. **Description:** Women who believe themselves called to the Roman Catholic priesthood. Aim is to create solidarity among participants and to promote the women's ordination movement. Conducts research programs; compiles statistics. **Members:** 500. **Computerized Services:** Data bases. **Publications:** *We Are Called*, periodic.

★861★ Project Return Foundation, Inc. Women in Crisis, Inc. (WIC)
133 W. 21st St., 11th Fl.
New York, NY 10011
Phone: (212)242-4880
Fax: (212)627-3483
Maria Da Silva, Director

Description: The nonprofit organization provides prevention programming, education, training, and resource materials, and targets its services primarily to Black and Latina women and their families. It promotes a holistic approach to women's health, emphasizes the relationship between alcohol and drug use and the risk of HIV infection, provides women with support and information on how to access a broad range of health and human services, conducts workshops, offers technical assistance to community agencies, and provides advocacy for women afflicated by alcohol, drugs, and AIDS-related problems. Funding is provided by the New York State Division of Alcoholism and Alcohol Abuse; the New York State Department of Health's AIDS Institute; Project Return Foundation; volunteer efforts; and corporate contributions.

★862★ Protect Life in All Nations (PLAN)
c/o America's Family Center
PO Box 1350
Stafford, VA 22554
Phone: (703)898-0729
Judie Brown, Exec.Sec.

Description: An international federation of individuals opposed to abortion. Disseminates information opposing abortion and euthanasia; organizes and promotes boycotts; offers information on what PLAN sees as complications and adverse effects of abortions. Works to eliminate use of sex, violence, and profanity in television and radio; publicizes what the group believes are detrimental effects of some school and television sex education programs. Demonstrates strong support against birth control organizations and for the protection of human life, beginning at conception. Participates in pro-life symposia. **Publications:** *Newsletter*, monthly.

★863★ Proutist Universal Women (PUW)
PO Box 114
Northampton, MA 01061
Phone: (413)586-3488
Jody Wright, Pres.

Founded: 1961. **Description:** Women and girls. Purpose is to enhance the dignity of women through economic independence, cultural renaissance, and lasting social change based on neo-humanism and a universal spiritual outlook. Encourages adherence to ideals outlined in PROUT, the Progressive Utilization Theory, which stresses decentralized economics, world government, and universalism. Sponsors classes, seminars, and a two-month training session in social and spiritual philosophy and organization. Organizes grass roots social service projects and fundraising events to benefit developing countries. **Members:** 10,000. **Regional Groups:** 4. **Local Groups:** 30. **Computerized Services:** Peoples' News Agency (network of PROUT newspapers in the U.S.). **Publications:** *Rising Sun Newsletter*, monthly. • *Tara: Journal of the Women's Prout Movement*, quarterly. • Also publishes leaflets, flyers, and local and regional publications. **Also known as:** Girls' Prout.

★864★ Radical Women (RW)
523-A Valencia St.
San Francisco, CA 94110
Phone: (415)864-1278
Constance Scott, Organizer

Founded: 1967. **Description:** Women with a socialist-feminist political orientation who believe that women's leadership is decisive for basic social change. Works toward reform in the areas of reproductive rights, child care, affirmative action, divorce, police brutality, rape, women of color, lesbians, and working women. Opposes efforts of conservative anti-feminist groups. **Local Groups:** 9. **Publications:** Papers.

★865★ Radio Free Women (RFW)
1213 N. Leithgow St.
Philadelphia, PA 19122
Phone: (215)763-4740
Eileen Kirby, Coordinator

Founded: 1972. **Description:** Women's feminist media collective. Produces feminist programs and tapes in order to raise the level of informational consciousness of women. Writes free-lance articles on women's issues. Maintains tape library. **Members:** 2.

★866★ Reach to Recovery
c/o American Cancer Society
1599 Cliffton Rd. NE
Atlanta, GA 30329
Phone: (404)320-3333
Claudia Bannon, Contact

Founded: 1952. **Description:** A short-term peer-visitor program sponsored by the American Cancer Society for women who have or have had breast cancer. Helps women meet the physical, emotional, and cosmetic needs related to their disease and its treatment. Visits are made at the request of patients or their physicians. Activities of selected and trained volunteer visitors include: providing support and information pre- and postoperatively; offering services to those who have undergone treatments such as chemotherapy, primary radiation, breast conservation, and breast reconstruction; providing information and support to patients' loved ones. **Publications:** brochure.

★867★ Read Natural Childbirth Foundation (RNCF)
PO Box 150956
San Rafael, CA 94915
Phone: (415)456-8462
Margaret B. Farley, Pres.

Founded: 1978. **Description:** Doctors, nurses, childbirth instructors, and parents. Promotes and teaches expectant parents the philosophies of natural childbirth pioneered by Grantly Dick-Read, a British doctor who began writing in 1932 about the then extremely controversial concept of natural childbirth and advocated relaxation as the key to comfortable labor. Techniques include abdominal and rib cage breathing and alleviation of fear, and thus pain, through knowledge. Acts as resource agency for the International Childbirth Education Association (see separate entry). Conducts charitable programs; awards scholarships. Offers speakers' bureau. Maintains 400 volume library on childbirth and parenting. **Members:** 30. **State Groups:** 2. **Publications:** *Newsletter*, periodic. • Also publishes *Preparation for Childbirth: Handbook for Use in Exercise Classes for Expectant Parents* and offers *A Time to Be Born* (film).

★868★ Redstockings of the Women's Liberation Movement
290 9th Ave., #2G
New York, NY 10001
Phone: (212)568-1834
Marisa Figueiredo, Secretary

Description: The movement is a grassroots research and education think tank founded by veteran activists of the 1960s committed to advancing and defending the women's liberation agenda. It develops and disseminates radical teach-ins, learn-ins, speak-outs, and conciousness raising groups. Redstockings' Archives for Action focuses on the 1960s, rebirth years of feminism, and offers catalog and research services.

★869★ Reformed Church Women (RCW)
475 Riverside Dr., Rm. 1825
New York, NY 10027
Phone: (212)870-2844
Diana Paulsen, Exec.Dir.

Founded: 1864. **Description:** Women of the Reformed Church in America dedicated to promoting fellowship for spiritual growth among members. Provides opportunities and avenues of service for community involvement in areas of concern such as the homeless and hungry. Encourages theological contemplation. Sponsors Footsteps Program which allows women to serve at missions. Conducts leadership seminars. **Members:** 25,000. **Publications:** *Reformed Church Women News*, quarterly. Newsletter. • *Resource Guide*, quarterly. **Formerly:** National Department of Women's Work.

★870★ Refugee Women in Development (RefWID)
810 1st St. NE, Ste. 300
Washington, DC 20002
Phone: (202)289-1104
Sima Wali, Dir.

Founded: 1981. **Description:** Refugee women who have resettled in the U.S. Seeks to enable Third World refugee women to attain social and economic independence and security through acculturation, economic security, ethnic preservation, and emotional support. Focuses on low-income working-age refugee women with limited skills and those suffering escape trauma. Sponsors education and research programs; advocates improvements in programs and services for refugee women. Develops program models, training curricula, and community involvement approaches. Represents refugees in national and international conferences. **Members:** 1200. **Computerized Services:** Data base on programs and materials for refuge women's programming. **Publications:** *Alert on Refugee Women in Crisis in Lebanon, Thailand, Pakistan*, *Understanding Family Violence Within U.S. Refugee Communities: A Training Manual*, and *The Production and Marketing of Ethnic Handcrafts in the U.S.*

★871★ Religious Coalition for Abortion Rights (RCAR)
100 Maryland Ave. NE, Ste. 307
Washington, DC 20002
Phone: (202)543-7032
Patricia Tyson, Exec.Dir.

Founded: 1973. **Description:** Religious organizations. Seeks to encourage and coordinate support for: safeguarding the legal option of abortion; ensuring the right of individuals to make decisions concerning abortion in accordance with their conscience and responsible medical practices; opposing efforts to deny these rights through constitutional amendment, or federal or state legislation. Educates on abortion issues within religious communities in order to prevent erosion or nullification of the 1973 Supreme Court decision on abortion. Monitors developments in Congress and state legislatures. Alerts members and individuals on both state and national levels. Organizes religious coalitions for abortion rights in key states. Bestows Religious Freedom Award. Maintains speakers' bureau and library. **Members:** 35. **State Groups:** 25. **Publications:** *Legislative Fact Sheet*, periodic. • *Religious Coalition for Abortion Rights–Dispatch*, periodic. Newsletter updating the public on proposed legislation affecting abortion and family planning. • *Religious Coalition for Abortion Rights–Options*, quarterly. Newsletter supporting a woman's right to an abortion. Monitors legislative, regulatory, and religious efforts to stop funding of state-financed abortions. • Also publishes pamphlets and booklets; distributes audiovisual resources.

★872★ Religious Network for Equality for Women (RNEW)
475 Riverside Dr., Rm. 812-A
New York, NY 10115
Phone: (212)870-2995
Fax: (212)870-2338
Dr. Zelle W. Andrews, Coordinator

Founded: 1976. **Description:** Interreligious coalition of faith groups committed to legal and economic justice for women. Engages in education and advocacy programs on behalf of women's rights, especially for the poor. Provides economic literacy program to educate women about the economic system. Lobbies for national legislation on civil rights and economic reform. Participates in the campaign to ratify the United Nations Convention on the Elimination of Discrimination Against Women. **Members:** 41. **Publications:** *RNEW Update*, 3/year. • Also publishes *Learning Economics*. **Formerly:** (1982) Religious Committee for the ERA.

★873★ Reproductive Rights National Network (RRNN)
17 Murray St., 5th Fl.
New York, NY 10007
Phone: (212)267-8891
Vienna Carroll, Dir.

Founded: 1979. **Description:** Organizations advocating reproductive freedom. Goals include abortion rights, adequate and safe birth control methods, child care, the right to live openly as a lesbian or gay man, freedom from sterilization abuse and reproductive hazards on the job, and an end to population control policies. Monitors legislation affecting reproductive rights, maintains liaison with similar organizations, and encourages the formation of new groups promoting reproductive freedom. Offers referral services on a national level; conducts public education/outreach at the local level; conducts slide shows and media campaign; produces organizer and public speaking packets. Conducts research. **Members:** 85. **Publications:** *Reproductive Rights* (newsletter), 4/year. • Also publishes brochure on anti-abortion legislation and plans to publish organizers' manual and brochures on sterilization abuse, child care, lesbian liberation, and Third World women.

★874★ Republican Women of Capitol Hill (RWCH)
160B Longworth House Office Bldg.
Washington, DC 20515
Phone: (202)224-3004
Ginny Sandahl, Pres.

Founded: 1963. **Description:** Social club for female employees of Republican representatives on Capitol Hill, Republican National Committee, or in the administration; associate members are women who have worked for one of the above. Provides members with the opportunity to establish contacts and meet influential leaders in Washington, DC. Holds monthly luncheons featuring speakers including ambassadors, White House staff members, and congressional representatives. Sponsors annual fashion show, Christmas bazaar, and embassy parties. **Members:** 250. **Publications:** *Trunk Line*, monthly. Newspaper.

★875★ Resolve Through Sharing (RTS)
La Crosse Lutheran Hospital
1910 South Ave.
La Crosse, WI 54601
Phone: (608)791-4747
Brenda Morgan, Admin.

Founded: 1981. **Description:** A perinatal bereavement program based in more than 500 hospitals. Addresses the individual needs of parents who have experienced miscarriages, stillbirths, or ectopic pregnancies. Offers counseling and support services to family members. **Publications:** *Counselor Connection*, quarterly. Newsletter.

★876★ Re'uth Women's Social Service (WSSI)
130 E. 59th St., Ste. 900
New York, NY 10022
Phone: (212)836-1570
Fax: (212)836-1114
Ursula Merrin, Pres.

Founded: 1951. **Description:** Raises funds for OHN hospital and homes for the aged in Israel by means of subscription social functions. **Members:** 1500. **Publications:** *Journal*, annual. **Formerly:** (1988) Women's Social Service for Israel.

★877★ Rosary Novena for Life Organization (RNL)
PO Box 40213
Memphis, TN 38174
Phone: (901)725-5937
Patrick V. Benedict, Chm.

Founded: 1988. **Description:** Promotes praying the Rosary as a means of "saving the lives of unborn babies." Assists in planning and conducting peaceful prayer demonstrations in front of abortion facilities for "pregnant mothers, abortionists and their supporters, and preborn babies who are routinely killed by surgical abortion as well as abortifacients such as the intrauterine device (IUD) and the so-called birth control pill." Supplies information and guidelines on how to coordinate a Rosary Novena for Life in local communities. **Publications:** *Rosary Novena for Life Newsletter*, periodic. • Has also published *Rosary Novena for Life Planning Manual*.

★878★ Roundtable for Women Food-Beverage-Hospitality (RWFBH)
145 W. 1st St., Ste. A
Tustin, CA 92680
Beverly Totman-Ham, Contact

Founded: 1983. **Description:** Individuals in the food and food service industries; persons providing services to these areas. Promotes advancement and success of women in the food industry. Acts as clearinghouse for food service, business, educational, and career information. Holds roundtables to clarify issues and promote entrepreneurial opportunities; provides practical counseling service for members entering, reentering, or advancing in the industry. Promotes recognition of products and services; maintains speakers' bureau; conducts seminars. Bestows annual Pacesetter Awards; operates job bank; compiles industry statistics. Plans include a hot line to provide information and counseling concerning food service entrepreneurship, and professional certification. **Members:** 1000. **Regional Groups:** 5. **Computerized Services:** Data base. **Publications:** *Pacesetter Journal*, periodic. • *Roundtable Journal*, periodic. • *RWF Membership Directory*, annual. Includes listing of services offered. • *RWF News*, quarterly. Newsletter. **Formerly:** Roundtable for Women in Foodservice.

★879★ Rural American Women (RAW)
50002 Old Jeanerette Rd.
New Iberia, LA 70560
Phone: (318)367-3277
Judy Voehringer, Pres.

Founded: 1977. **Description:** Federation of individuals (1000) and affiliated organizations (24) making up an ethnically, geographically, and economically diverse group of rural American women. Seeks to organize rural women of America to work together, develop their individual capabilities, contribute to the welfare of their families, improve their communities, tackle a broad range of issues in rural America, and give visibility to the contributions of rural women to our society. Believes rural women to be catalysts both for rekindling certain traditional values of which they feel the country has lost sight and for bringing about changes in the conditions of rural life. Offers rural community leadership training sessions and conducts food and energy workshops; provides home business aid. Maintains speakers' bureau. **Members:** 1024. **Publications:** *News Journal of Rural American Women*, bimonthly. • Also publishes *Annotated Bibliography on Rural Women*.

★880★ Rural Sociological Society (RSS) Women's Caucus
Louisiana State University
Baton Rouge, LA 70803
Dr. Virginia S. Purtle, Chair

Founded: 1937. **Description:** Professional organization of sociologists who specialize in rural areas. **Publications:** *Rural Sociology*. • *Rural Sociologist*.

★881★ Ruth Jackson Orthopaedic Society (RJS)
c/o Carole Murphy
222 S. Prospect Ave., Ste. 127
Park Ridge, IL 60068
Phone: (708)698-1632
Fax: (708)823-0536
Carole Murphy, Dir.

Founded: 1983. **Description:** Women orthopedic surgeons. Seeks to advance the science of orthopedic surgery and to provide support for women orthopedic surgeons. Named for practicing orthopedic surgeon Dr. Ruth Jackson (1902-), the first woman certified by the American Board of Orthopedic Surgery and the first female member of the American Academy of Orthopedic Surgeons. Compiles statistics; operates placement service, speakers' bureau, and biographical archives. **Members:** 189. **Publications:** *Membership List*, periodic. • *Ruth Jackson Society Newsletter*, semiannual. Includes articles on international members and careers and personal life; also contains calendar of events. **Formerly:** (1991) Ruth Jackson Society.

★882★ Sagaris, Inc.
10 2nd St. NE, No. 100
Minneapolis, MN 55413
Phone: (612)379-2640
Linda J. Harness, Admin.

Founded: 1974. **Description:** Feminist therapy collective. Offers psychotherapy to men, women, their partners, children, and families on issues including job problems, relationship problems, low self-esteem, and expression of anger or sadness. Offers consultation to organizations experiencing structural or interpersonal tensions. Sponsors workshops, short lecture series, and training in a feminist approach to therapy. **Members:** 7.

★883★ St. Joan's International Alliance (SJIA)
U.S. Section
2131 N. 37th St.
Milwaukee, WI 53208
Phone: (414)444-0976
C. Virginia Finn, Pres.

Founded: 1965. **Description:** Objectives are to secure legal and de facto equality between women and men in society, church, and state. Has worked for the passage of the Equal Rights Amendment since 1966. The International Alliance, founded in 1911, has worked with the United Nations (and earlier with the League of Nations) for: the abolition of child and forced marriages and slavery traffic and traffic in persons; the political rights of women; equal access to education and vocational training and economic opportunities; family law; elimination of discrimination against women. In the church, the alliance has petitioned for lay men and women observers and women auditors at the Second Vatican Council, for the revision of the nuptial liturgy, revision of those canons of the code that adversely affect women, and admission of women to the diaconate and priesthood on the same terms and under the same conditions as men. Seeks dialogue with bishops regarding the status of women in the church. **Publications:** *U.S. Bulletin*, quarterly. Reports on activities of Catholic feminists.

★884★ Save a Baby
PO Box 101
Orinda, CA 94563
Phone: (415)648-6436
Dr. James Fiatarone, Founder & Dir.

Founded: 1973. **Description:** Persons opposed to abortion. Purpose is to inform the public about the physical and emotional circumstances surrounding abortion and about what the group calls the sanctity of life and the threats posed by the anti-life and abortion-killing mentalities today. Encourages women to continue their pregnancies; offers counseling and coordinates assistance for women choosing to have their babies. Collects and distributes baby and maternity clothes and other supplies to women in need; broadcasts television and radio programs; sponsors anti-abortion programs and speeches for groups and organizations. Operates CARE-avan, an international humanitarian program in which volunteers provide medical and educational assistance and materials to needy people. Maintains speakers' bureau. **Publications:** *Save A Baby* and *Going Gentle* (books); also publishes pamphlets and distributes tapes of pro-life speeches and messages.

★885★ Screen Actors Guild (SAG)
National Women's Conference Committee
1515 Broadway, 44th Fl.
New York, NY 10036-8901
Phone: (212)827-1433
Fax: (212)944-6774
Elaine Brodey, Affirmative Action
Administrator
Description: The Committee promotes equal employment opportunities for female members of the Screen Actors Guild and positive imagery of women in television, film, and commercials.

★886★ Seamless Garment Network (SGN)
c/o Rose Evans
PO Box 210056
San Francisco, CA 94121-0056
Phone: (716)288-6146
Rose Evans, Sec.
Founded: 1987. **Description:** Organizations advocating a pro-life stand and peace. Promotes the protection of life which the group feels is threatened by war, abortion, the arms race, poverty, the death penalty, and euthanasia. Believes that these issues are linked under a "consistent ethic of life" and that individuals promoting these causes should "work together in a spirit of peace, justice, and reconciliation." The organization's name is derived from speeches by Cardinal Joseph Bernardin which alluded to pro-life work as being "like Christ's seamless garment". Operates speakers' bureau. Maintains small library. **Members:** 70. **Publications:** Consistent Ethic Resources, periodic. Directory of organizations, speakers, and publications.

★887★ Secretariat for Family, Laity,
Women, and Youth (SFLWY)
3211 4th St. NE
Washington, DC 20017
Phone: (202)541-3040
Fax: (202)541-3322
Dolores R. Leckey, Exec.Dir.
Description: Division of the National Conference of Catholic Bishops. Works to provide service in the areas of laity, marriage and family, women in church and society, and youth. Develops national policy in these area for the body of bishops. **Publications:** Newsletter, quarterly. **Formerly:** Secretariat on Laity and Family Life; Youth Ministry, United States Catholic Conference; Family Life Bureau; National Catholic Conference on Family Life; (1982) Family Life Division, United States Catholic Conference; (1987) Family Life Ministry United States Catholic Conference.

★888★ Section on Women in Legal
Education of the AALS
c/o Association of American Law Schools
1201 Connecticut Ave. NW, Ste. 800
Washington, DC 20036
Phone: (202)296-8851
Mary Becker, Chair
Description: Women law professors. Section of the Association of American Law Schools assisting women lawyers in teaching and scholarship. Provides information on the integration of women and women's concerns into the legal profession; makes recommendations on matters concerning the administration of law schools, the status of women in legal education, and improvement of law school curricula. Promotes communication of ideas and interests among members. **Publications:** Newsletter,

semiannual. • Also compiles bibliography on women in legal education.

★889★ Section for Women in Public
Administration (SWPA)
1120 G St. NW
Washington, DC 20005
Phone: (202)393-7878
Founded: 1971. **Description:** Established by the American Society for Public Administration to initiate action programs appropriate to the needs and concerns of women in public administration. Promotes equal educational and employment opportunities for women in public service, and full participation and recognition of women in all areas of government. Develops strategies for implementation of ASPA policies of interest to women in public administration; recommends qualified women to elective and appointive ASPA governmental leadership positions; acts as forum for communication among professional and laypeople interested in the professional development of women in public administration. Awards grants to local ASPA chapters initiating programs encouraging career growth and professional development for women in public administration; bestows the Joan Fiss Bishop Memorial Award. **Publications:** Bridging the Gap, semiannual. Newsletter. • Membership Directory, periodic. **Formerly:** (1973) Task Force for Women in Public Administration; (1982) National Committee for Women in Public Administration.

★890★ Service Employees International
Union (SEIU)
Women's Program
1313 L St., NW
Washington, DC 20005
Phone: (202)898-3365
Pat Thomas, Contact
Founded: 1921. **Description:** Focuses on issues like child care, parental leave, pay equity and career development. **Publications:** Service Employee's Union Magazine. • Politics is Union Business. • Legislative Newsletter.

★891★ The Seventh Generation Fund
Program for Native Women, Families and
Youth
Box 72
Nixon, NV 89424
Phone: (702)574-0157
Debra Harry, Field Representative

★892★ Sex Equity in Education Program
(SEEP)
c/o Women's Action Alliance
370 Lexington Ave., Rm. 603
New York, NY 10017
Phone: (212)532-8330
Fax: (212)779-2846
Jo Sanders, Dir.
Founded: 1971. **Description:** A program of the Women's Action Alliance (see separate entry) seeking to create a nonsexist environment for children. Provides information on nonsexist activities for children in elementary through secondary grades. Creates and distributes educational materials; conducts research and development projects; offers training and technical assistance. Manages the Computer Equity Program, aimed at encouraging school-age girls to make greater use of computers; develops strategies pursuant to that goal. **Publications:** Neuter Computer, a how-to guide to computer

equity, and other books. **Formerly:** (1983) Non-Sexist Child Development Project.

★893★ SHARE
St. Joseph's Health Center
300 1st Capitol Dr.
St. Charles, MO 63301
Phone: (314)947-5000
Liz Voegele, Contact
Founded: 1977. **Description:** Participants are parents who have suffered the loss of a child through miscarriage, stillbirth, or early infant death; supporters. Purposes are: to provide comfort and support to the bereaved parents; to continue reassurance and care beyond the hospital stay; to encourage the physical and emotional health of the parents and siblings. (SHARE stands for Source of Help in Airing and Resolving Experiences.) Makes presentations accompanied by films. Assists with formation of local groups. Local group activities include conducting bimonthly support meetings with speakers, providing lists of addresses and phone numbers to make resources readily available, developing keepsake kits, and facilitating parent-to-parent support. Sponsors presentations on grief. Maintains small library of topics relating to grief, newborn loss, and adoption. Plans to offer computerized services. **Regional Groups:** 280. **State Groups:** 55. **Local Groups:** 5. **Publications:** International Perinatal Support Groups Listing, periodic. • SHARE Newsletter, bimonthly. Concerned with bereavement especially following miscarriage, ectopic pregnancy, stillbirth, or newborn death for parents and professionals. Includes listing of books and resources, meetings schedule, and announcements of new groups. • Also publishes Bittersweet.hellogoodbye: a Resource for Planning Farewell Rituals when a Baby Dies, Starting Your Own Share Group (booklet), Thumpy's Story (in Spanish and English), a children's series of manuals and brochures on grief; makes available Thumpy's Story (video- and audiotapes in Spanish and English) and videotapes on perinatal grief.

★894★ Sigma Delta Epsilon, Graduate
Women in Science (SDE/GWIS)
111 E. Wacker Dr., No. 200
Chicago, IL 60601
Phone: (312)616-0800
Fax: (313)616-0226
Edna R. Bernstein, Sec.
Founded: 1921. **Description:** Professional organization - graduate women, science. Fosters research in science and seeks to increase the participation of women in science. Works to: improve science and mathematics education for women; encourage women with science degrees to enter the workforce; support study of the history of women in science; cooperate with organizations with similar goals; make use of the media to publicize the accomplishments of women in science. Presents Eloise Gerry Fellowship and fellowships for research projects. Sponsors competitions and bestows awards; conducts fundraising activities. **Members:** 1500. **Publications:** Bulletin, bimonthly. • Membership List, biennial. **Formerly:** (1977) Sigma Delta Epsilon.

★895★ **Sigma Gamma Rho Sorority, Inc.**
8800 S. Stony Island Ave.
Chicago, IL 60617
Phone: (312)873-9000
Bonita M. Herring, Executive Secretary

Founded: 1922. **Description:** The sorority dedicates itself to community service through programs designed to develop and support leadership in the black community and encourage educational opportunities for black youth. It works to promote human rights legislation; develop programs that enhance employment and training opportunities; provide greater access to nontraditional jobs at higher pay; attempt to emeliorate poverty; encourage economic development in the black community; and increase the supply of decent and affordable housing. Also emphasizes strengthening of the family through programs that address quality education, adequate child care, elimination of domestic violence, reduction in teenage pregnancies, and comprehensive health care.

★896★ **Single Mothers By Choice (SMC)**
PO Box 1642, Gracie Square Sta.
New York, NY 10028
Phone: (212)988-0993
Jane Mattes, Chairperson

Founded: 1981. **Description:** Primarily single professional women in their 30s and 40s who have either decided to have or are considering having children outside of marriage; also welcomes women who are considering adoption as single parents (does not include mothers who are widowed or divorced). Provides support for single mothers; disseminates information to women who choose to be single parents. Sponsors workshops and play groups for children. Offers the opportunity for single women to discuss the problems and benefits of being a single parent. Maintains resource files and speakers' bureau; conducts research programs, seminars, and workshops. **Members:** 1000. **State Groups:** 6. **Computerized Services:** Mailing list and information services. **Publications:** SMC Newsletter, 20/year. • Also disseminates literature packet of articles about single motherhood.

★897★ **Single Parent Resource Center**
141 W. 28th St., Ste. 302
New York, NY 10001
Phone: (212)947-0221
Suzanne Jones, Exec.Dir.

Founded: 1981. **Description:** Purpose is to establish a network of local single parent groups so that such groups will have a collective political voice. Is currently in the process of identifying existing single parent organizations. **Formerly:** (1985) National Single Parent Coalition.

★898★ **Sisterhood Is Global Institute (SIGI)**
370 Lexington Ave., Rm. 603
New York, NY 10017

★899★ **Slovenian Women's Union (SWU)**
431 N. Chicago St.
Joliet, IL 60432
Phone: (815)727-1926
Olga Ancel, Sec.

Founded: 1926. **Description:** Membership is composed primarily of Christian women and children of Slovenian ancestry. Conducts research programs; sponsors competitions. Main-

tains biographical archives and Slovenian Women's Union Heritage Museum in Joliet, IL. **Members:** 10,000. **State Groups:** 106. **Local Groups:** 1. **Publications:** ZARJA - The Dawn, monthly (except January, June, and August). Magazine; includes calendar of events, chapter news, and obituaries. • Also publishes Woman's Glory and Pots and Pans (cookbooks); Let's Sing (songbook); Flowers From My Garden (book of poems); From Here to Slovenia and Footsteps Thru Time (history and stories of immigrants).

★900★ **Society for the Advancement of Women's Health Research**
1601 Connecticut Ave. NW, Ste. 801
Washington, DC 20009
Phone: (202)328-2200
Fax: (202)667-0462
Joanne Howes, Director

Description: The coalition consists of women in health and medical sciences who seek to correct inequities in health research on women by working at public education institutions to guarantee the inclusion of women in clinical trials; developing a women's health agenda of the 1990s; and producing a report for the medical establishment about the inequities of women's health research.

★901★ **Society of American Archivists Women's Caucus**
4 Terrace Ave.
Ossining, NY 10562
Phone: (212)678-3072
Lucinda Manning, Editor, SAA Women's Caucus Newsletter

★902★ **Society of Daughters of Holland Dames (SDHD)**
c/o Mrs. Charles Irwin
139 E. 79th St.
New York, NY 10021
Phone: (212)288-4144
Mrs. Charles Irwin, Corr.Sec.

Founded: 1895. **Description:** Female descendants of settlers of New Netherlands (New York) prior to 1674. To promote the principles of Dutch ancestors; to collect documents, genealogical and historical, relating to the Dutch in America. **Members:** 150.

★903★ **Society of General Internal Medicine (SGIM) Women's Caucus**
Montefiore Medical Center, Department of Medicine
111 E. 210th St., Centennial 3
Bronx, NY 10467
Phone: (212)920-4784
Fax: (212)920-8375
Ellen Cohen, Contact

Description: The Caucus is an interest and advocacy group for women health care providers and patients, especially women of color and women of lower socioeconomic classes. Its scope includes birth control, gynecologic and breast cancers, menopause, hypertension, coronary artery disease, substance abuse, weight control/body image, depression, family and lifestyle issues, and problems of professional recognition and advancement. The Caucus encourages research on women's health and part-time work/academic promotion issues; serves as a resource network; and maintains a speakers' bureau. **Publications:** Column in the

monthly newsletter of the Society of General Internal Medicine.

★904★ **Society for Menstrual Cycle Research (SMCR)**
10559 N. 104th Pl.
Scottsdale, AZ 85258
Phone: (602)451-9731
Mary Anna Friederich, M.D., Sec.-Treas.

Founded: 1979. **Description:** Physicians, nurses, endocrinologists, geneticists, physiologists, psychologists, sociologists, researchers, educators, students, and others interested in the health needs of women as related to the menstrual cycle. Goals are: to identify research priorities, recommend research strategies, and promote interdisciplinary research on the menstrual cycle; to establish a communication network for facilitating interdisciplinary dialogue on menstrual cycle events; to disseminate information and promote discussion of issues among public groups. **Members:** 100. **Publications:** Membership Roster, annual. • Newsletter, quarterly. • Also publishes The Menstrual Cycle, Volume 1: A Synthesis of Interdisciplinary Research, The Menstrual Cycle, Volume 2: Research and Implications for Women's Health, Changing Perspectives on Menopause, Menarche: The Transition from Girl to Woman, and Menstrual Health in Women's Lives.

★905★ **Society of Military Widows (SMW)**
5535 Hempstead Way
Springfield, VA 22151
Phone: (703)750-1342
Maj.Gen. J. C. Pennington, USA, Contact

Founded: 1968. **Description:** Widows and adult children of deceased career or active duty military personnel; affiliate members are persons who support the society's goals. Seeks to obtain equity for military widows under the Survivor Benefit Plan and to educate the public concerning the problems and needs of military widows. Monitors federal legislation affecting military widows; provides members with fact sheets on changes in survivor benefits. Has introduced bills before Congress and testified before congressional committees. Conducts surveys; bestows awards. Local chapters maintain the ROTH (Reach Out To Help) Program, a support system for the newly widowed, and sponsor social and educational activities. **Members:** 6300. **Local Groups:** 21.

★906★ **Society of Our Lady of the Way (SOLW)**
147 Dorado Terrace
San Francisco, CA 94112
Phone: (415)585-3319
Blanche McNamara, Unit Dir.

Founded: 1936. **Description:** A secular society of laywomen who devote themselves by vow to the apostolate. Aims to Christianize the world and witness to Christ while living a secular life. Maintains archives and library. **Members:** 275. **Publications:** Witness, semiannual.

★907★ Society for the Study of Breast Disease (SSBD)
Sammons Tower
3409 Worth
Dallas, TX 75246
Phone: (214)821-2962
Fax: (214)827-7032
Gerorg N. Peters, M.D., Sec.

Founded: 1976. **Description:** Physicians and nurses, primarily those engaged in the fields of obstetrics and gynecology, surgery, radiology, family practice, and medical and radiation oncology. Seeks to further the study of diseases of the breast and to inform physicians and other health care professionals of developments in the diagnosis and treatment of breast cancer and benign diseases of the breast. Serves as a forum for discussion among members. Encourages research pertaining to breast disease. **Members:** 250. **Publications:** *Breast Disease - An International Journal*, quarterly. • *Newsletter*, periodic.

★908★ Society for the Study of Women in Legal History
619 Carroll St.
Brooklyn, NY 11215
Phone: (212)566-8334
Nancy S. Erickson, Esq., Coordinator

Description: Seeks to encourage research into the history of the status of women under the law, primarily in the U.S. **Alternate phone number:** (718) 783-8162.

★909★ Society of Women Engineers (SWE)
345 E. 47th St., Rm. 305
New York, NY 10017
Phone: (212)705-7855
Fax: (212)319-0947
B. J. Harrod, Acting Exec.Dir.

Founded: 1950. **Description: Student Sections:** 245. Educational service society of women engineers; membership is also open to men. Supplies information on the achievements of women engineers and the opportunities available to them; assists women engineers in preparing for return to active work following temporary retirement. Serves as an informational center on women in engineering. Administers several certificate and scholarship programs. Presents awards; offers tours, professional workshops, and career guidance; conducts surveys. Compiles statistics; maintains archives. **Members:** 15,000. **Local Groups:** 67. **Publications:** *U.S. Woman Engineer*, bimonthly. Journal. • Also publishes *Profile of the Woman Engineer* and career guidance pamphlets.

★910★ Society for Women in Philosophy, Eastern Division (SWIP)
c/o Peg Walsh
Bradford College
Dept. of Humanities
Bradford, MA 01835
Phone: (508)372-7161
Peg Walsh, Exec. Officer

Founded: 1971. **Description:** Students, faculty, and laypersons in the field or interested in the field of philosophy. Primary goal is to advance and support women in philosophy. Holds discussions on feminist and non-feminist topics. Offers placement services. Maintains archives. Bestows awards. The society has no national headquarters but operates through its divisions. **Members:** 850. **Regional Groups:** 3. **Publica-**

tions: *Directory of Women Available for Employment*, periodic. • *Hypatia*, quarterly. • *Newsletter*, semiannual.

★911★ Society for Women in Plastics (SWP)
PO Box 775
Sterling Heights, MI 48078-0775
Phone: (313)949-0440
Fax: (313)949-8400
Sharon A. Olejniczak, Pres.

Founded: 1979. **Description:** Women with education or employment experience in the field of plastics or related businesses. Promotes knowledge of the plastics industry. Conducts plant tours; operates speakers' bureau. **Members:** 138. **Publications:** *Dimensions*, monthly. Newsletter.

★912★ Sociologists for Women in Society (SWS)
c/o Ms. Carla Howery
American Sociological Association
1722 N St. NW
Washington, DC 20036
Phone: (202)833-3410
Dr. Catherine Berheide, Pres.

Founded: 1970. **Description:** Members are mainly female professional sociologists and female students of sociology, though membership is open to any woman or man interested in the purposes of the organization. Dedicated to: maximizing the effectiveness of and professional opportunities for women in sociology; exploring the contributions which sociology can, does, and should make to the investigation of and improvement in the status of women in society. Acts as watchdog of the American Sociological Association to ensure that it does not ignore the special needs of women in the profession. Has organized a job market service to bring potential jobs and applicants together; established a discrimination committee offering advice and organzational support for women who pursue cases charging sex discrimination; has aided women to establish social, professional, and intellectual contacts with each other. Conducts workshops and seminars at meetings of sociological societies. Bestows the annual Cheryl Miller Lecturer Award for outstanding feminist scholarship in sociology. **Members:** 1500. **Local Groups:** 20. **Computerized Services:** Mailing list. **Telecommunications Services:** Electronic mail, BITNET: CBH22VM. **Publications:** *Directory*, annual. • *Gender and Society*, quarterly. Journal; includes articles, research reports and book reviews. • *Network News*, quarterly. Newsletter; includes articles, letters to Editor, columns, minutes of meetings, job announcements. • Also publishes brochures on workfare and pay equity, directory of membership and *The Social Construction of Gender* (book). **Formerly:** (1970) Women's Caucus in Sociology.

★913★ Sons and Daughters of Oregon Pioneers (SDOP)
PO Box 6685
Portland, OR 97228
Phone: (503)222-1531
Jean Cusick, Pres.

Founded: 1901. **Description:** Lineal descendants of pioneers who arrived in the Oregon country prior to Feb. 14, 1859, the day Oregon became a state. Objectives are to pursue social and literary activities and to preserve historic

sites. Strives to perpetuate the memory of Oregon pioneers. Bestows annual Miss Pioneer Oregon scholarship. Holds six history study programs annually. **Members:** 800. **Computerized Services:** Mailing list. **Publications:** *Directory*, periodic. • *Newsletter*, quarterly.

★914★ Soroptimist International (SI)
1616 Walnut St., Ste. 700
Philadelphia, PA 19103
Phone: (215)732-0512
Leigh Wintz, Executive Director

Description: The world's largest classified service organization for executive and professional women. Achieves its community service goals through economic and social development; education; environment; health; human rights/status of women; and international goodwill and understanding. It conducts literacy projects; shelters for battered women; seminars on its service programs; and environmental clean-up projects. **Publications:** *The Soroptimists of the Americas*, bimonthly internal magazine.

★915★ Southern Baptist Convention Women's Missionary Union
PO Box 830010
Birmingham, AL 35283-0010
Phone: (205)991-8100
Fax: (205)991-4990
June Whitlow, Assoc. Exec. Dir.

Founded: 1888. The Union provides programs, publications, and promotions for mission education, action, and support to preschool children, girls, and women. Produces magazines and runs an image campaign. **Publications:** *Dimension.* • *Royal Service.* • *Contempo.* • *Accent.* • *Accent Leader.* • *Aware.* • *Discovery.* • *Start.* • *Share.* • *Nuestra Tarea.* • *Our Missions World.*

★916★ Southern Baptist Women in Ministry/Folio (SBWM/FOLIO)
2800 Frankfort Ave.
Louisville, KY 40206
Phone: (502)896-4425

Founded: 1983. **Description:** Ordained and unordained female Baptist ministers; students of the Baptist ministry; interested individuals. Promotes the image of women as ministers within the Southern Baptist Convention. Fosters support and communication among members. Conducts educational and research programs. Offers placement service; maintains speakers' bureau, library, and biographical archives. **Members:** 300. **State Groups:** 10. **Publications:** *Folio*, quarterly. Includes news and features pertaining to women ministers.

★917★ Southern Coalition for Educational Equity (SCEE)
PO Box 22904
Jackson, MS 39225-2904
Phone: (601)366-5351
Fax: (601)366-5351
Winifred Green, Pres.

Founded: 1978. **Description:** Coalition of parents, students, teachers, and administrators that operates in Alabama, Georgia, Louisiana, Mississippi, and North Carolina, with plans to include eight additional states. Works toward developing more efficient educational programs and eliminating racism and sexism within southern schools. Has organized projects including: Arkansas Career Resources Project, which provides minorities and single heads of households with marketable skills and jobs; New Orleans Effective Schools Project, which attempts to increase school effectiveness through high expectations, stressing academic achievement, and quality instruction; Project MiCRO, which seeks to provide computer access for, and sharpen analytical skills of, minority students; Summer Program, which focuses on students' reading comprehension skills. **Publications:** *Annual Report*.

★918★ **Southport Institute for Policy Analysis**
Project on Women and Population Aging
339 Hoyt St., Ground Fl.
Brooklyn, NY 11231
Phone: (718)643-6961
Jessie Allen, Project Director
Description: The Project examines and publicizes policy issues arising from the result of the rapid aging of the United States population combined with American women's changing social and economic status. It is involved in a working paper series covering work, health, and older women's socio-economic status and is producing a book.

★919★ **Speech Communications Association (SCA)**
Women's Caucus
5105 Backlick Rd., Ste. E
Annandale, VA 22003
Phone: (703)750-0533
Karen A. Foss, Chair
Description: The Caucus disseminates information about women in the communications discipline and supports scholarly research on women and gender. It also sponsors programs for the annual SCA convention and serves as a sounding board and resource for women in the SCA. **Publications:** *The Women's Caucus Newsletter* (biannual).

★920★ **The Spring Foundation for Research on Women in Contemporary Society**
316 El Verano Ave.
Palo Alto, CA 94306
Phone: (415)323-1778
Emily Lyon, Contact

★921★ **State University of New York at Albany**
Center for Women in Government
135 Western Ave.
Draper Hall, Rm. 302
Albany, NY 12222
Phone: (518)442-3900
Fax: (518)442-5232
Sharon Harlan, Director of Research
Founded: 1978. **Description:** The Center was established to improve employment opportunities for women and minorities in government. It conducts research and training, offers technical assistance and public education, and provides a forum for networking. Seeks to unite employees, union leaders, government officials, and representatives of advocacy, academic and professional organizations in cooperative efforts, including career development training, the elimination of sexual harassment, employment opportunities for inner city women in the public sector, and others. **Publications:** *News on Women in Government*, 1-2/year.

★922★ **Stop Equal Rights Amendment (SERA)**
c/o Eagle Forum
Box 618
Alton, IL 62002
Phone: (618)462-5415
Phyllis Schlafly, Chm.
Description: A project of Eagle Forum reactivated to defeat a proposed Equal Rights Amendment in the November, 1986 Vermont elections. Believes stopping ERA in Vermont will prevent its becoming a national political issue as it was prior to 1982. Raises funds for public education about "ERA's hidden agenda - gay rights and abortion." **Also known as:** Stop ERA.

★923★ **Stuntwomen's Association of Motion Pictures (SAMP)**
202 Vance
Pacific Palisades, CA 90272
Phone: (213)462-1605
Mary Peters, Pres.
Founded: 1968. **Description:** Stunt actresses and stunt coordinators who belong to the Screen Actors Guild and/or to the American Federation of Television and Radio Artists. **Members:** 21. **Formerly:** (1988) Stunt Women of America.

★924★ **Supportive Older Women's Network (SOWN)**
2805 N. 47th St., Ste. D
Philadelphia, PA 19131
Phone: (215)477-6000

★925★ **Supreme Assembly, International Order of Rainbow for Girls (SAIORG)**
Box 788
McAlester, OK 74501
Phone: (918)423-1328
Edna McLaurin, Supreme Advisor
Founded: 1922. **Description:** Girls' fraternal society composed of active members (unmarried girls from ages 11-20) and majority members (married women or members over 20 years old) in Australia, Canada, Germany, Japan, Panama, Philippines, and the United States. **Members:** 1,100,000.

★926★ **Supreme Caldron, Daughters of Mokanna (D of M)**
4240 Vernon NW
Canton, OH 44709
Phone: (216)782-7656
Ruby Kalkman, Supreme Rodeval Sec.
Founded: 1919. **Description:** Fraternal Masonic order for women relatives of Supreme Council, Mystic Order Veiled Prophets of Enchanted Realm members. Current project is the National Humanitarian Project for the Spastic Child and Dentistry for Handicap. Sponsors competitions for singing groups and drill teams; bestows awards. **Members:** 4822. **Local Groups:** 36. **Publications:** *Roster*, quinquennial. • *Supreme Caldron, Daughters of Mokanna—Proceedings*, annual.

★927★ **Supreme Ladies Auxiliary Knights of St. John (SLAKSJ)**
1606 Otis NE
Washington, DC 20018
Phone: (202)526-5322
Iris L. Nelson, Supreme Sec.
Founded: 1900. **Description:** Fraternal society of Catholic women. Sponsors competitions; provides children's services; conducts charitable and educational programs. **Members:** 14,521. **Publications:** *Convention Proceedings*, biennial. • *Grand*, annual. State proceedings.

★928★ **Supreme Lodge of the Danish Sisterhood of America (DSA)**
c/o Lorraine Zembinski
2916 N. 121 St.
Milwaukee, WI 53222
Lorraine Zembinski, Chwm.
Founded: 1883. **Description:** Women of, or related to those of, Danish birth or descent or those married to men of Danish descent; individuals interested in the Danish heritage. Bestows scholarships. **Members:** 4000. **Local Groups:** 77. **Publications:** *Danish Sisterhood News*, monthly. Includes national and lodge information.

★929★ **Supreme Temple Order Pythian Sisters (STOPS)**
c/o Wenonah Jones
PO Box 1257
Anaconda, MT 59711
Phone: (406)563-6433
Wenonah Jones, Supreme Sec.
Founded: 1888. **Description:** Women's auxiliary of the Supreme Lodge Knights of Pythias. Donates to many projects benefitting blood drives, retarded citizens, and patients suffering from cancer, cystic fibrosis, polio, cerebral palsy, and heart and kidney ailments. **Members:** 32,000. **State Groups:** 45. **Local Groups:** 647. **Publications:** *Pythian International*, 4/year.

★930★ **Surrogates by Choice (SBC)**
c/o Donna J. Regan
6212 Hickory
Oscoda, MI 48750
Donna J. Regan, Pres.
Founded: 1988. **Description:** Individuals interested in or concerned with the issue of surrogate parenting and who support surrogate parenting as an alternative to infertility. Acts as a support network for practical, emotional, moral, legal, and religious issues confronting surrogates. Promotes friendship and unity among surrogate mothers; maintains communication with organizations espousing similar beliefs and goals. Works to inform legislators and the public about the positive aspects of surrogate parenting. Seeks to protect the rights of members; assists with forming support groups. Conducts research. **Members:** 100. **Publications:** *SBC Newsletter*, annual.

★931★ **Survivors of Incest Anonymous (SIA)**
PO Box 21817
Baltimore, MD 21222
Phone: (301)433-2365
Linda L. Davis, Public Info. Officer
Founded: 1982. **Description:** Serves as a support group and selfhelp recovery program for any adult who was a victim of sexual abuse as a child. Follows a 12-step approach, modeled

after the program espoused by Alcoholics Anonymous World Services, to assist members in their recovery. Sponsors educational programs; maintains speakers' bureau; conducts workshops. **Members:** 10,000. **Local Groups:** 800. **Publications:** *Bulletin*, periodic. • *Meeting Directory*, bimonthly. • *S.I.A. World Service Bulletin*, bimonthly. • *S.I.A. World Service Directory*, bimonthly. • Also publishes *The Twelve Steps of S.I.A.*, *The Slogans of S.I.A.*, and other pamphlets and brochures.

★932★ Susan G. Komen Breast Cancer Foundation (SGKF)
5005 LBJ, Ste. 730
Dallas, TX 75244
Phone: (214)450-1777
Toll-free: 800-IM-AWARE
Fax: (214)450-7710
Patrick McDonough, Exec.Dir.

Founded: 1982. **Description:** Breast cancer patients, health care professionals, and other interested individuals. Works to: increase the recovery and survival rates of breast cancer patients; heighten public awareness of the risks of breast cancer and the need for early detection; promote legislative approval of breast cancer examination insurance coverage. Establishes breast screening and training in self-examination procedures; provides funding to research and treatment programs. Operates the Komen Alliance for Breast Disease Research, Education and Treatment, which conducts research into the genesis, progression, and treatment of the disease; sponsors educational programs. Bestows awards; sponsors competitions; maintains speakers' bureau. **Members:** 1000. **Publications:** Press kit. **Formerly:** (1989) Susan G. Komen Foundation. **Also known as:** Susan G. Komen Foundation for the Advancement of Cancer Research.

★933★ Swedish Women's Educational Association International (SWEA)
PO Box 2585
7414 Herschel Ave., No. 001
LaJolla, CA 92038-2585
Phone: (619)459-8435
Fax: (619)597-4111
Boel Alkdal, Admin.

Founded: 1979. **Description:** Women aged 18 and over who are fluent in the Swedish language and interested in preserving and promoting Swedish culture and tradition. Conducts public relations activities on behalf of Sweden. Awards scholarships for study in Sweden. **Members:** 2500. **Chapters:** 24. **Publications:** *Directory*, annual. • *SWEA Forum*, 3/year. Journal.

★934★ The Syvenna Foundation
Rte. 1, Box 193
Linden, TX 75563
Phone: (903)835-8252
Barbara Carroll, Associate Dir.

Description: Offers residencies for beginning and intermediate women writers, all genres. Accepts applications from all parts of the U.S.

★935★ Task Force on Equality of Women in Judaism (TFEWJ)
838 5th Ave.
New York, NY 10021
Phone: (212)249-0100
Eleanor Schwartz, Exec. Officer

Founded: 1972. **Description:** Task force of the New York Federation of Reform Synagogues. To promote religious equality for women within Reform Judaism; to eliminate sexism in the liturgy and educational curriculum; to encourage participation of women in leadership roles, as laypersons and as professionals in the synagogue. Conducts seminars on various subjects for Reform Judaism and interreligious groups. Plans training program for facilitation of the task force's consciousness-raising program. Compiles statistics on the position of women within the task force. **Members:** 200. **Publications:** Commentaries, rewrites, summaries, and other materials.

★936★ Task Force on Women and Judaism
838 Fifth Ave.
New York, NY 10021
Annette Daum, Contact

★937★ Theta Rho Girls' Club (TRGC)
422 Trade St., Ste. R
Winston-Salem, NC 27101
Phone: (919)725-6037
Janet Simmonds, Contact

Founded: 1931. **Description:** Girls between the ages of 8 and 18. Promotes citizenship and strength in character through "friendship, love, and truth." Teaches members "happiness through service." **Members:** 1915. **Local Groups:** 122. **Publications:** *Youth Reporter*, monthly. Newsletter containing activities schedule and report; information on youth exchange programs and United Nations trip.

★938★ Third World Women's Project (TWWP)
Institute for Policy Studies
1601 Connecticut Ave., NW
Washington, DC 20009
Phone: (202)234-9382
Fax: (202)387-7915
Isabel Letelier, Dir.

Founded: 1981. **Description:** A project of the Institute for Policy Studies. Universities, community and women's groups, and individuals. Strives to educate the public on Third World human rights and women's issues and to encourage dialogue between people in the Third World and people in the U.S. Establishes contacts for Third World women visiting the U.S., hoping that these contacts will benefit the work of such women in their respective countries. Maintains speakers' bureau and resource center on Third World women. Conducts local seminars, classes, and exhibits. Offers internships. **Publications:** *A Dialogue on Third World Women* (book); also makes available videotapes and filmstrip for rent or purchase.

★939★ Trade Union Women of African Heritage (TUWAH)
530 W. 23rd St., Ste. 4051
New York, NY 10011
Phone: (212)547-5696
Thelma Dailey, Pres.

Founded: 1969. **Description:** Black women union members. Supports various causes of

ethnic working women; participates in community activities; conducts alternative school programs. Maintains Global Women of African Heritage, Maverick Center for Self Development, and Leaders of the 21st Century. Operates speakers' bureau; compiles statistics; conducts research programs. **Publications:** *The Ethnic Woman*, periodic. Magazine. • *Newsletter*, periodic. • *Third World Women*, semiannual.

★940★ Tradeswomen, Inc.
PO Box 40664
San Francisco, CA 94140
Phone: (415)821-7334
Kai Douglas, Contact

Founded: 1979. **Description:** Women who work in nontraditional, blue-collar occupations including construction, transportation, and industrial work; women who seek to enter these fields or who support the right of others to do so. Serves as a network for women in the trades. Conducts social gatherings and local and regional forums and workshops on topics such as: health and safety on the job; racism and sexism in the trades; sexual harassment; working within unions. Makes available children's services; maintains library and speakers' bureau. Bestows awards annually to community activists and tradeswomen. Compiles statistics. Sponsored First National Conference of Women in the Trades. **Members:** 1000. **Publications:** *Trade Trax*, monthly. Newsletter. • *Tradeswomen Magazine*, quarterly. Features news on finding a job, contracting, networking, and tools; legislation and legal cases. Includes book and movie reviews. • Also publishes *What Are Journey Sisters?* (brochure) and *Little Tradeswomen Coloring Book*.

★941★ Turkish Women's League of America (TWLA)
821 UN Plaza, 2nd Fl.
New York, NY 10017
Phone: (212)682-8525
Ayten Sandikcioglu, Pres.

Founded: 1958. **Description:** Turkish women united to promote equality and justice for women. Organizes cultural and recreational activities to foster better understanding between the people of Turkey and the U.S.; brings together Turkic-speaking people in the U.S.; works to educate Turkish-Americans about their human and civil rights in the U.S. Operates Ataturk School, which offers courses in Turkish language, history, music, and folk dancing; sponsors workshops and seminars for high school teachers. **Members:** 300. **Publications:** *News Bulletin*, 10/year. • Also publishes brochures. **Also known as:** Amerika Turk Kadinlar Birligi.

★942★ Ukrainian National Women's League of America (UNWLA)
108 2nd Ave.
New York, NY 10003
Phone: (212)533-4646
Maria Savchak, Pres.

Founded: 1925. **Description:** Women of Ukrainian birth or descent living in the United States. Presents literary awards for works dealing with Ukrainian history and historical fiction. Sponsors prekindergarten for children ages three to five. Founded the Ukrainian Museum in New York City in 1976. Presents scholarships. Offers pen pal program for children and adults. **Members:** 5000. **Regional Groups:** 9. **Local Groups:** 119.

Publications: *Our Life Magazine* (in English and Ukrainian), monthly. • Also publishes children's books, embroidery books, crafts handbook, and cookbooks in Ukrainian and English.

★943★ **The Union Institute**
The Center for Women
1731 Connecticut Ave. NW
Washington, DC 20009-1146
Phone: (202)667-1313
Fax: (202)265-0492
Judith Arcana, Director

Description: The Union promotes cooperatively-developed projects that combine activism and scholarship in a multicultural and international perspective. It seeks to create a national network to facilitate community and academic collaboration. Areas of interest include cultural diversity, feminist theory, grassroots organizing, gender issues, and women's studies.

★944★ **Union of Palestinian Women's**
Association in North America (UPWA)
3148 W. 63rd St.
Chicago, IL 60629
Phone: (312)436-6060
Fax: (312)436-6460

Founded: 1986. **Description:** Promotes national and social self-determination and independence for Palestine. Encourages unity among Palestinian women; supports the women's movement worldwide. Works to raise social consciousness and develop women's self-reliance and leadership skills. Conducts educational programs in an effort to preserve Palestinian culture, heritage, and identity. Sponsors campaigns demanding release of Palestinian women political prisoners. Operates family sponsorship program and clothing collection and distribution program; assists Palestinian cooperatives. Offers counseling and support services. **Local Groups:** 26. **Publications:** *Voice of Palestinian Women*, periodic. • *UPWA Bulletin*, periodic.

★945★ **Unitarian Universalist Women's**
Federation (UUWF)
25 Beacon St.
Boston, MA 02108
Phone: (617)742-2100
Fax: (617)367-3237
Mairi Maeks, Exec.Dir.

Founded: 1963. **Description:** Federation of women's groups and individual members in local Unitarian Universalist Churches in the U.S. and Canada. Works for human rights for all, especially rights of women. Promotes: Supreme Court decision in favor of abortion; quality in childcare centers; concern for the family; work for and with the aging; work in area of women and religion. Sponsors volunteer representatives in Washington, DC. Presents annual Ministry to Women Award. Holds personal growth workshops; operates speakers' bureau. **Members:** 7000. **Local Groups:** 300. **Publications:** *Federation Communicator*, 5/year. • Also publishes books, pamphlets, studies, discussions, and other materials.

★946★ **Unite**
c/o Jeanes Hospital
7600 Central Ave.
Philadelphia, PA 19111
Phone: (215)728-3777
Janis Heil, Dir.

Founded: 1975. **Description:** Selfhelp support group for those experiencing grief after miscarriage or infant death. Services include counseling, educational programs for hospital staff, and training workshops for grief counselors and group facilitators. **Members:** 250. **Regional Groups:** 12. **Telecommunications Services:** Telephone support network. **Publications:** *Unite Note*, quarterly. Newsletter; includes articles and poetry on grieving and recovery.

★947★ **United Auto Workers (UAW)**
Women's Committee
505 8th Ave., 14th Fl.
New York, NY 10018
Phone: (212)736-6270
Fax: (212)629-3239
Beverley Gans, Sub-Regional Director

Description: The Committee seeks to activate and educate women within the Union. Currently working for abortion rights and campaigning against the "gag rule."

★948★ **United Auto Workers (UAW)**
Women's Department
8000 E. Jefferson
Detroit, MI 48214
Phone: (313)926-5237
Dorothy Jones, Assistant Director

Description: The Department's goal is to bring women into the mainstream of the Union through educational conferences, seminars, and workshops on women's issues in order to ensure that a "woman's place is in her union." **Publications:** *Women and United Auto Workers*, pamphlet updated every three weeks.

★949★ **United Church of Christ**
Coordinating Center for Women in
Church and Society (CCW)
700 Prospect Ave.
Cleveland, OH 44115
Phone: (216)736-2150
Fax: (216)736-2156
Mary Sue Gast, Contact

Founded: 1980. **Description:** Works to eliminate sexism in the church and society. Promotes advocacy for women's concerns through cooperative projects with United Church of Christ agencies; cooperates in projects by helping to establish a network to respond to legislation affecting women. Promotes consciousness-raising by contributing to other United Church of Christ publications. Maintains 200 volume library on women's issues, theology, economics, and employment. Bestows biennial Antoinette Brown Award to clergy women. Recognizes the contributions of lay women. Provides speakers; conducts workshops. **Publications:** *Common Lot*, quarterly. Journal. • Also publishes *Moms Morning Out* and *Women Pray* (books).

★950★ **United Daughters of the**
Confederacy (UDC)
328 N Blvd.
Richmond, VA 23220-4057
Phone: (804)355-1636
Mrs. Dan Bragg Cook, Pres.Gen.

Founded: 1894. **Description:** Women descendants of Confederate veterans of the Civil War. Maintains 2500 volume library primarily covering the Civil War years (1861-1865). **Members:** 28,000. **Local Groups:** 1000. **Publications:** *Magazine*, monthly.

★951★ **United Federation of Teachers**
(UFT)
Women's Rights Committee
260 Park Ave., S.
New York, NY 10010
Phone: (212)598-6879
Fax: (212)533-2704
Pearl Wolf, Chairperson

Description: The Committee provides curriculum information on teaching women's history to its members, develops a newsletter on women's issues, and organizes Women's History Month. **Publications:** Annual newsletter.

★952★ **United Food and Commercial**
Workers International Union
Civil Rights and Women's Affairs
1775 K St. NW
Washington, DC 20006
Phone: (202)223-3111

★953★ **The United Methodist Church**
General Board of Global Ministries
Women's Division
United Methodist Church
475 Riverside Dr., 15th Fl.
New York, NY 10115
Phone: (212)870-3752
Mary Kercherval Short, Exec.Sec., Women's Concerns

Description: The Division is a national membership organization that acts as an advocate for the oppressed and dispossessed, particularly women. It works to build a supportive community of women and foster the growth of Christianity through a campaign for children; charter for racial justice policies; ministries for older and incarcerated women and their children; pay equity; justice; Christian social responsibilities; and interpretation workshops. **Publications:** *Response*, bimonthly magazine.

★954★ **The United Methodist Church**
General Commission on the Status and
Role of Women (GCSRW)
1200 Davis St.
Evanston, IL 60201
Phone: (708)869-7330
Kioyoko Kasai Fujiu, General Secretariat

Founded: 1972. **Description:** The Commission creates methods and strategies to foster awareness of women's issues and problems throughout the church; seeks to redress inequities in personnel, program, policies, and publications; ensures inclusiveness of women in church power and policy-making at all levels; and encourages women to take leadership roles in the church mission and ministry through leadership training sessions and an annual Conference Constituency. Its programs include Education and Advocacy, Issue Development, and Monitoring and Research. **Publications:** *The Flyer*, 5/year.

**★955★ United Nations Development Fund
for Women (UNIFEM)**
304 E. 45th St., 6th Fl.
New York, NY 10017
Phone: (212)906-6400
Sharon Capeling-Alakija, Dir.

Founded: 1976. **Description:** Autonomous fund operating in association with the United Nations Development Programme and created by the U.N. General Assembly following the International Women's Year, 1975. Provides technical and financial support to educational programs in developing countries that benefit rural women or underprivileged women in urban areas. Funds numerous projects including: training in food preservation; training of child care workers; promotion and training of rural women in income-raising group activities; case studies. Organizes workshops to build skills in management of small-scale industries. Areas of interest include revolving loan funds, energy resource development, and community self-help activities for low-income women. **Regional Groups:** 5. **Telecommunications Services:** Cable, UN-DEVPRO NEW YORK. **Publications:** (in English, French, and Spanish) • *Development Review*, semiannual. • *Information Booklets*, periodic. • Also publishes *A Guide to Community Revolving Loan Funds* and occasional papers. **Formerly:** (1985) Voluntary Fund for the United Nations Decade for Women.

**★956★ United Nations Women's Guild
(UNWG)**
1 United Nations Plaza, Rm. DC-1-550
New York, NY 10017
Phone: (212)963-4149
Elsa Wurfl, Pres.

Founded: 1948. **Description:** Women employees of the United Nations; wives of those employed by the U.N. and its specialized agencies; individuals who contribute services to the guild. Goal is to send direct aid to underprivileged children worldwide. Members suggest projects involving institutions that provide assistance to young victims of poverty, disease, and war. Works with sister groups offering suggestions for projects or requesting aid in supporting their own local projects. Sponsors fundraising projects. **Publications:** *Directory*, annual. • *Newsletter*, annual. • Plans to publish *History of UNWG*.

★957★ United Order True Sisters (UOTS)
212 5th Ave, No. 1307
New York, NY 10010
Phone: (212)679-6790
Dorothy B. Giuriceo, Mgr.

Founded: 1846. **Description:** Women's charitable organization. Maintains cancer service, offers personal service to indigent patients and sends children with cancer to camp. **Members:** 12,000. **Publications:** *Echo*, quarterly. **Also known as:** UOTS, Inc.

**★958★ United Presbyterian Church
USA Women's Unit
Justice for Women**
100 Witherspoon St.
Louisville, KY 40202
Phone: (212)870-2019
Rev. Mary J. Kuhns, Associate

Description: The Unit promotes justice for women in the church by providing opportunities for women of all ages and races to participate in and hold leadership positions in the church. It conducts research on the status of women; sponsors training seminars; develops and implements strategies for addressing concerns of women throughout the church; develops and recommends policies and procedures to the General Assembly on issues of justice for women; and works for the fair representation of women in the church structure. **Publications:** *Newsletter of Justice for Women*, quarterly.

★959★ United Sisters (US)
PO Box 41
Garwood, NJ 07027
Founded: 1975. **Description:** "Lesbian/feminist group by lesbians for lesbians, although social services are available to all women 18 years or over." US is run by the collective whose members are "those women who give their time, energy and/or money to the organization and who have demonstrated that they support the aims and purposes of US." US will cooperate in research in the fields of anthropology and sociology if members feel the research is properly conducted. The group does not cooperate in psychiatric or psychological research, however, as it is their position that "lesbianism is in no way abnormal or unusual and therefore not a fit subject for these disciplines." Lesbianism is viewed by US as simply another valid lifestyle. US is neither a dating service nor an introduction service. Membership files and information are kept in strict confidence and anonymity is guaranteed to those who request it. Program includes social service, educational, and civil rights activities. Offers peer counseling and legal, medical, religious, and psychiatric referrals. Maintains information and speakers' bureaus. **Telecommunications Services:** Hot line.

**★960★ United States Army Mothers,
National (USAMN)**
c/o Barbara Mitchell
PO Box 124
Laclede, MO 64651
Phone: (816)963-2388
Barbara Mitchell, Exec. Officer

Founded: 1940. **Description:** Women relatives of persons who serve or have served in the armed forces since September, 1940. Sponsors charitable and educational programs in areas of rehabilitation of veterans, child welfare, and welfare of the American Indian; conducts legislative and civic activities. **Members:** 5000. **State Groups:** 4. **Local Groups:** 80. **Publications:** *National Organization Bulletin*, monthly.

★961★ U.S. Coalition for Life (USCL)
Box 315
Export, PA 15632
Phone: (412)327-7379
Randy V. Engel, Dir.

Founded: 1972. **Contacts:** 22,000. **Description:** Pro-life, anti-abortion organizations, hospitals, and government and health agencies. Research organization and clearinghouse on population control activities such as abortion, genetic engineering, and government family planning. Sponsors seminars; issues mailings on pro-life legislation. Maintains international reprint service. Aids in the development of research programs. **Publications:** *Pro-Life Reporter*, quarterly. • Also publishes monographs and reports.

**★962★ United States Delegation for
Friendship Among Women**
2219 Caroline Ln.
South St. Paul, MN 55075
Phone: (612)455-5620
Mary Pomeroy, Secretary Treasurer

Founded: 1970. **Description:** The Delegation is a nonprofit corporation which promotes cultural exchange and understanding among women leaders of the world. Objectives are to promote cultural and peaceful co-existence among peoples of the world. **Publications:** Newsletter for members.

**★963★ United States Student Association
Women's Coalition/Women of Color
Caucus**
815 15th St., NW
Washington, DC 20005
Phone: (202)347-8772
Glenda Francis, Co-Chair, Women's Coalition

Description: The Coalition works on federal legislation that empowers women on campuses by supporting the passage of the Violence Against Women Act, providing pressure for the passage of the Freedom of Choice Act, and supporting the national abortion rights marches in Washington, DC. The Caucus attempts to bring forth the women of color agenda of the women's movement and works for the advancement of women of color communities.

★964★ United States Women of Today
c/o Joy Hutchcraft
4601 Old Jacksonville Rd, No. 1
Springfield, IL 62704
Phone: (217)546-8819
Joy Hutchcraft, Pres.

Founded: 1985. **Description:** Individuals over the age of 18. Community service organization; conducts charitable activities. Promotes the personal development of members through programs such as Focus on Women, Success Through Enthusiastic Participation, Effective Writing, and Effective Speaking. **Members:** 5000. **Publications:** *Newsletter*, monthly.

**★965★ United States Women's Curling
Association (USWCA)**
c/o Luella M. Ansorge
4114 N. 53rd St.
Omaha, NE 68104
Phone: (402)453-6574
Luella M. Ansorge, Reference Chwm.

Founded: 1947. **Description:** Women amateur curlers. Maintains archive of association competition, awards, and administrative records. Bestows awards. **Members:** 3400. **Local Groups:** 73. **Publications:** *North American Curling News*, bimonthly. Newsletter containing results of national competition, sites and dates of upcoming Bonspiels (tournaments), and minutes of executive directors' meetings. • *Roster of USWCA*, annual. • Also publishes *Handbook of Rules and Regulations* and *Some Aspects of Curling* (booklet).

★966★ **United States Women's Lacrosse Association (USWLA)**
45 Maple Ave.
Hamilton, NY 13346
Phone: (315)824-2480
Fax: (315)824-4533
Susanna McVaugh, Exec.Sec.

Founded: 1931. **Description:** Promotes the sport of lacrosse for women. Establishes rules for competition; trains umpires; conducts seminars and clinics. Sponsors annual national tournament and competitive international events; bestows awards. **Members:** 2500. **Local Groups:** 50. **Publications:** *Directory*, annual. • *U.S. Women's Lacrosse Association—Newsletter*, 5/year. Includes calendar of events. • Also publishes coaching and umpiring manuals, and rule books; makes available instructional and game videos.

★967★ **United States Women's Track Coaches Association (USWTCA)**
c/o Karen Dennis
Michigan State University
Women's Athletic Dept.
East Lansing, MI 48824
Phone: (517)353-9299
Karen Dennis, Pres.

Founded: 1967. **Description:** A subcommittee of the Athletics Congress/USA. Track coaches interested in women's track and field. To provide information and serve as a forum for the discussion of issues involving women's track and field. Plans to compile statistics and develop awards program. **Members:** 100. **Publications:** *Membership Directory*, periodic. • *Newsletter*, quarterly.

★968★ **U.S.A. Petites (USAP)**
537 Newport Center Dr.
Newport Beach, CA 92660
Phone: (714)643-5008
Stephen Douglas, Co-Founder

Founded: 1989. **Description:** Promotes an attractive image of petites, women 5'5" and under. Sponsors Petite Model Pageants. Compiles statistics. Maintains Hall of Fame. **Members:** 15,000. **State Groups:** 50. **Computerized Services:** Data base. **Publications:** *Viva Petites!*, quarterly. Features petite fashions and modeling tips.

★969★ **University of California, Los Angeles (UCLA)**
Higher Education Research Institute (HERI)
320 Moore Hall
405 Hilgard Ave.
Los Angeles, CA 90024-1521
Phone: (213)825-2709
Fax: (213)206-6293
Helen S. Astin, Assoc. Dir.

Description: The Institute conducts empirical research on higher education utilizing national data on students, faculty, and administration. Studies focus on student development, equity in education, and gender differences in status attainment among faculty. Trains graduate students, sponsors visiting scholars, and holds seminars. **Publications:** *HERI Quarterly*.

★970★ **University of California, Santa Cruz (UCSC)**
Feminist Studies Focused Research Activity (FRA)
178 Kresge
Santa Cruz, CA 95064
Phone: (408)459-4052
Wendy Brown, Director

Description: FRA comprises feminist scholars, graduate students, and faculty from the humanities and social and natural sciences who share research, exchange ideas, and develop collaborative projects. It is committed to "inter-cultural, anti-racist, anti-homophobic theory and practice, and to a politics of pleasure and community in work." Sponsors research grants and lectures.

★971★ **Unwed Parents Anonymous (UPA)**
PO Box 44556
Phoenix, AZ 85064
Phone: (602)952-1463
Margot Sheahan, Exec. Officer

Founded: 1978. **Description:** Unwed parents; grandparents and others who are affected by an out-of-wedlock birth. Support group based on an adaptation of the Twelve Steps and Twelve Traditions of Alcoholics Anonymous World Services. Provides spiritual and emotional support for unwed parents during and after the pregnancy. While not endorsing any option, UPA offers guidance in making the decision to keep a baby or to place a child in an adoptive home. Provides information and advice about relationships, child care, dating problems, finances, housing, child rearing, and other issues affecting parent and child. Assists individuals in working through the feelings that may accompany a decision to relinquish a baby for adoption. Advocates abstinence from premarital sexual activity and a lifestyle of chastity. Maintains speakers' bureau. **Publications:** *Advice to Grandparents, Dating Guidelines from Unwed Mothers, It's OK to Say No, Should I Keep or Relinquish My Baby?*, and other pamphlets.

★972★ **Upper Midwest Women's History Center**
Central Community Center
6300 Walker St.
St. Louis Park, MN 55416
Phone: (612)925-3632
Susan Gross, Dir.

Founded: 1980. **Description:** Works on development of curriculum of the histories of women around the world for secondary through adult education. Also provides educatiuonal material to assist teachers interested in women's histories. **Publications:** *Glenhurst Collection* (bi-yearly newsletter). • *Women and Development Issues* (catalog).

★973★ **Urban Institute**
Program of Policy Research on Women and Families
2100 M St. NW
Washington, DC 20037
Phone: (202)857-8564
Elaine Sorensen, Senior Research Assoc.

Description: The Program is conducting research on a number of women's issues, including pay equity and child care.

★974★ **Valentine Foundation**
900 Old Gulph Rd.
Bryn Mawr, PA 19010
Phone: (215)525-6272
Alexander V.A. Walling, Admin.

Description: The Foundation makes grants to qualifying tax-exempt organizations that empower women and girls in order to recognize and develop to their full potential of achievement. Grants are given for endeavors which effect fundamental changes in attitudes, policies, or social patterns.

★975★ **Value of Life Committee (VOLCOM)**
637 Cambridge St.
Brighton, MA 02135
Phone: (617)787-4400
Marianne Rea-Luthin, Pres.

Founded: 1970. **Description:** Fosters respect for human life from fertilization to natural death and educates and informs the public on all issues concerning life. Maintains speakers' bureau and library of 300 medical and legal volumes concerning abortion, euthanasia, ethics, and genetics, including a complete newspaper file on life issues.

★976★ **Vietnam Women's Memorial Project (VWMP)**
2001 S St. NW, Ste. 302
Washington, DC 20009
Phone: (202)328-7253
Fax: (202)328-0063
Diane Carlson Evans, Chair & Founder

Founded: 1984. **Description:** Works to identify and document women who served during the Vietnam War, and promotes the placing of a memorial in Washington, DC to honor their service. Educates the public regarding the contributions of women during the Vietnam War; maintains speakers' bureau.

★977★ **Voices in Action**
PO Box 148309
Chicago, IL 60614
Phone: (312)327-1500
Vicki Polin, Contact

Description: Adult survivors of incest and sexual abuse, as children; relatives, concerned citizens, and human service, health care and legal professionals working to eradicate the incidence and alleviate the effects of incest and sexual abuse of children. Purpose is to provide a communication and peer support network for survivors of incest and those affected by it. Seeks to increase public understanding of the prevalence of incest, its consequences, and the possibility of prevention through the dissemination of information. Serves as liaison among survivors, medical and legal professionals, and social service agencies. Advocates the development of outreach, public education, and therapy programs; provides selfhelp and volunteer advocacy. Maintains speakers' bureau. Compiles statistics. Sponsors "rap" group leadership training and special interest groups. **Members:** 1000. **Telecommunications Services:** Resource and referral services. **Publications:** *The Chorus*, bimonthly. Newsletter. • Also publishes *How to Choose a Therapist, How to Confront Your Perpetrator: Dead or Alive, What Helps?* (pamphlets), *How to Organize Your Group, How to File a Civil Suite for Sexual Abuse, Surviving SOcial Situations,* and *Survival Kits I and II.* **Formerly:** (1982) Victims of Incest Concerned

Effort; (1984) VOICE -Victims of Incest Can Emerge (also known as VOICE, Inc.); (1985) VOICES -Victims of Incest Can Emerge Survivors.

★978★ Voters for Choice/Friends of Family Planning (VFC)
2000 P St. NW, Ste. 515
Washington, DC 20036
Phone: (202)822-6640
Fax: (202)822-6644
Julie Burton, Exec.Dir.

Founded: 1984. **Description:** Independent, bipartisan political committee. Seeks election and reelection of candidates to federal and state office who support the pro-choice position concerning abortion. Provides technical assistance and consulting services for favored candidates; offers direct financial contributions and services. **Publications:** *Winning With Choice* (campaign strategy handbook).

★979★ Wages for Housework Campaign (WFH)
PO Box 86681
Los Angeles, CA 90086-0681
Phone: (213)221-1698
Fax: (213)227-9353
Phoebe Jones Schellenberg, East Coast Coordinator

Founded: 1972. **Description:** The Campaign organizes for "the compensation of unwaged work women do, to be paid by dismantling the military- industrial complex." Compensation includes welfare, benefits, higher wages, Social Security, and child care. In 1985, the group succeeded in getting governments to agree to count women's unwaged work in agriculture, food production, reproduction, and household activities in the GNP and is now campaigning for the implementation of that decision. Active in circulating the international Women Count/Count Women's Work petition in 25 languages and Braille and coordinating the Women Count Network in the United States. **Publications:** *The Power of Women and the Subversion of the Community.* • *The Disinherited Family.* • *Sex, Race and Class.* • *The Global Kitchen.*

★980★ Wages for Housework Campaign
Black Women for Wages for Housework
PO Box 86681
Los Angeles, CA 90086-0681
Phone: (213)221-1698
Fax: (213)227-9353
Margaret Prescod, Co-founder

Description: International network of black women/women of color in Third World and metropolitan countries which aims to dismantle the "hierarchy of work and wealth by refusing forced labor and claiming reparations for slavery, imperialism, and unwaged work." It resists "divide and rule" among black people/people of color; and challenges racism and sexism. Campaign issues include racism, immigration controls, welfare, low wages, rape, prostitution, police accountability, civil and human rights, gays/lesbians, peace, and ecology. **Publications:** *Black Women: Bringing It All Back Home.* • *Black Women and the Peace Movement.* • *Roots: Black Ghetto Ecology.* • *Strangers and Sisters: Women, Race and Immigration.* • Periodic mailings on local, national, and international organizing work, literature, catalog, and speakers' bureau.

★981★ Wages for Housework Campaign
Wages Due Lesbians (WDL)
PO Box 14512
San Francisco, CA 94114
Phone: (415)558-9628
Lori Nairne, Contact

Founded: 1975. **Description:** Campaigns for wages for housework for all women and wants the physical and emotional housework of surviving as lesbian women in "a hostile and prejudiced society" to be recognized as work and paid for so that women have the economic power to afford sexual choices. It defends lesbian mothers' rights to custody of their children; initiated a Lesbian Teachers Fund and is fundraising to help cover legal costs of a lesbian teacher in Britain who fought and won her case against dismissal; helped to organize Time Off for Women; and advocates implementation of a 1985 United Nations agreement to count women's unwaged work in the GNP.

★982★ WAND Education Fund (WAND EF)
691 Massachusetts Ave.
Arlington, MA 02174
Phone: (617)643-4880
Marjorie Smith, Exec.Dir.

Founded: 1982. **Description:** Sponsored by Women's Action for Nuclear Disarmament (see separate entry). Seeks to improve public understanding of nuclear disarmament and other security issues. Sponsors lectures on nuclear disarmament and national security; holds annual media celebration on Mother's Day, seeking to restore the day to its original meaning as a call for women to speak out on issues of war and peace. Works to enhance the political influence of women in the U.S.; offers workshops on developing skills in speaking, lobbying, and grass roots organizing; promotes registration of female voters. Conducts training; maintains speakers' bureau; bestows awards. **Publications:** Brochures, fact sheets, and manuals.

★983★ WAVES National (WN)
c/o Berenice George
PO Box 6064
Clearwater, FL 34618
Phone: (813)447-0865
Berenice George, Pres.

Founded: 1979. **Description:** Women who have served on active duty in the U.S. Navy and can show proof of service and an honorable discharge; women who are currently on active duty or who have retired from duty in the U.S. Navy, Naval Reserve, Fleet Reserve, or Coast Guard. Encourages principles of patriotism and loyalty to God, country, and family among former WAVES Women Accepted for Volunteer Emergency Service who have served since World War II, and other women who have served in the Navy. Provides a network of support and assistance and an opportunity for locating, communicating, and associating with former WAVES; serves as a medium of exchange between its local units. Maintains collection of pictures, newspaper clippings, and military uniforms. Makes available World War II memorabilia to museums. Operates biographical archives. **Members:** 6700. **Local Groups:** 112. **Publications:** *White Caps,* bimonthly. Membership activities newsletter. **Formerly:** (1986) Waves National Corporation.

★984★ Whirly-Girls (International Women Helicopter Pilots)
PO Box 584840
Houston, TX 77058-8484
Phone: (713)474-3932
Colleen Nevius, Exec.Dir.

Founded: 1955. **Description:** Women helicopter pilots. Stimulates interest among women in rotary-wing aircraft. Members serve as standby pilots for search and rescue work. Awards 2 scholarships for helicopter flight training. **Members:** 790. **Publications:** *Membership List,* periodic. • *Newsletter,* quarterly.

★985★ Whisper
PO Box 8719, Lake St. Sta.
Minneapolis, MN 55408
Phone: (612)644-6301

Founded: 1985. **Description:** Seeks to: end commercial sexual exploitation of women; educate the public about prostitution as a form of violence against women; and assist women attempting to leave the sex industry. Conducts educational and research programs; maintains speakers' bureau and library. **Publications:** *Whisper Newsletter,* quarterly.

★986★ Wider Opportunities for Women (WOW)
1325 G St. NW, Lower Level
Washington, DC 20005
Phone: (202)638-3143
Fax: (202)638-4885
Cynthia Marano, Exec.Dir.

Founded: 1964. **Description:** To expand employment opportunities for women through information, employment training, and advocacy services. Works to overcome barriers to women's employment and economic equity, including occupational segregation, sex stereotypic education and training, discrimination in employment practices and wages. Sponsors Women's Work Force Network, a national network of 500 women's employment programs and advocates. The network monitors current policies to increase the priority given to employment needs of women; provides information to congressional staffs to clarify the impact of various legislative proposals on women; issues public policy alerts and informational materials when relevant federal policy is being proposed or undergoing revision; conducts investigative projects to assess how legislative programs are implemented and their impact on women. Offers technical assistance to education institutions and private industry on programs to increase women's participation in non-traditional employment and training. Maintains National Commission on Working Women (see separate entry) and Industry Advisory Council. **Publications:** *Women at Work,* quarterly. Newsletter. • Also publishes books and pamphlets.

★987★ Widows of World War I (WWWI)
c/o Helen Green
324 Gregory SW
Burleson, TX 76068
Phone: (817)295-1658
Helen Green, Pres.

Founded: 1946. **Description:** Widows of veterans of World War I. To obtain better legislation for widows of World War I. **Special Committees:** Americanism; Hospital and Rehabilitation; Legislation; Publicity. **Members:** 4000. **State Groups:** 4. **Local Groups:** 47. **Publications:**

Bulletin, quarterly. • *Newsletters to Chapters*, monthly.

★988★ **Wilshire Club (WC)**
607 S. Western Ave.
Los Angeles, CA 90005
Description: Private club for professional women that provides all the amenities of the traditional men's clubs - professional, social, and personal. Does not exclude men. Sponsors: contemporary and informative seminars and programs with speakers of national, regional, and local repute; classes in health, dance, the arts, fashion, and travel; telephone answering service; health spa; and conference facilities for members. Plans to open similar clubs in other major U.S. cities.

★989★ **Wishing Well (WW)**
PO Box 713090
Santee, CA 92072-3090
Laddie Hosler, Editor
Founded: 1974. **Description:** Network of lesbians interested in writing to other women. Serves as an exchange through which members identify other individuals with whom they wish to correspond. **Members:** 1000. **Publications:** *Wishing Well*, bimonthly. Includes descriptions of members, resources, and classified ads. • makes available *Well-Talk* series (audiotapes).

★990★ **Wives-SelfHelp Foundation (WSHF)**
Smylie Times Bldg., Ste. 205
8001 Roosevelt Blvd.
Philadelphia, PA 19152
Phone: (215)332-2311
Maxine Schnall, Pres.
Founded: 1974. **Description:** Persons with an interest in improving their marital, family, or personal lives through trained peer counseling via a Philadelphia, PA-based hot line. Offers immediate emotional support and guidance to clients; develops client potential for selfhelp. Operates professional in-house counseling which provides therapy for individuals, couples, and families in such areas as stress, depression, marital conflicts, physical abuse, anxiety, sexual problems, and drug and alcohol abuse. Offers services to children and adolescents experiencing difficulties in areas such as substance abuse and conflicts with parents and teachers. Provides information and referral services.

★991★ **The Woman Activist (TWA)**
2310 Barbour Rd.
Falls Church, VA 22043-2940
Phone: (703)573-8716
Flora Crater, Pres.
Founded: 1975. **Description:** Nonprofit consulting firm specializing in service on issues of political concern to women. Activities include research, program development, issue analysis, report writing, and statistics compilation. Rates members of Congress on women's issues and compares voting patterns of congressmen and congresswomen on civil and social rights issues. Compiles Woman Activist Mailing List of political feminists. Maintains library of feminist books and information. **Publications:** *The Woman Activist*, 10/year.

★992★ **The Woman Activist Fund (TWAF)**
2310 Barbour Rd.
Falls Church, VA 22043-2940
Phone: (703)573-8716
Flora Crater, Pres.
Founded: 1978. **Description:** Compiles information on representatives of individuals and groups in elected and appointed governmental bodies at local, state, and national levels, especially as such information affects women and minorities. Analyzes and publishes findings; conducts polls and surveys; educates the public, especially women and minorities, through programs and reports. **Members:** 11. **Publications:** *Almanac of Virginia Politics* (with supplements) and *Virginia General Assembly Voting Record*.

★993★ **WomanKraft**
PO Box 1005
Tucson, AZ 85702
Phone: (602)792-6306
Linn Lane, Program Dir.

★994★ **Woman's Education and Leadership Forum (WELF)**
918 16th St. NW, Ste. 403
Washington, DC 20006
Phone: (202)223-2908
Fax: (202)835-0968
Patricia Brockbank, Exec. Officer
Founded: 1986. **Description:** Encourages women to become self-sufficient by developing skills in areas including confident decision-making, health maintenance, and professionalism. Promotes the belief that each woman has the power to shape her own life in any way she chooses. Conducts seminars and workshops for government leaders and the public. **Publications:** none.

★995★ **Woman's Home and Foreign Mission Society (WHFMS)**
PO Box 23152
Charlotte, NC 28212
Phone: (704)545-6161
Fax: (704)753-0712
Caroline M. Michael, Dir.
Founded: 1897. **Description:** Administered by the Department of Women's Ministries of the Advent Christian Church. Christian women. Seeks to: unite members for action; encourage spiritual growth; involve women in evangelism and provide them with fellowship, mission education, and service opportunities. Works to provide leadership training and revitalize and increase the ministry potential of local member groups. Provides a means whereby members may share information and ideas. Raises funds to support worldwide Advent Christian ministries and field operations. Supports and encourages growth of children's groups in local ministries. Operates speakers' bureau. Holds training seminars and workshops. **Members:** 3000. **Regional Groups:** 5. **Local Groups:** 225. **Computerized Services:** Listings of organizational presidents, local spiritual life chairpersons, and local children's group leaders. **Publications:** *Advent Christian News*, monthly. • *Advent Christian Witness*, 10/year. • *Prayer and Praise*, monthly. Bulletin. • Also disseminates program kits, brochures, books, slides, and videotapes.

★996★ **Woman's Missionary Union (WMU)**
PO Box 830010
Birmingham, AL 35283-0010
Phone: (205)991-8100
Fax: (205)991-4990
Dellanna W. O'Brien, Exec.Dir.
Founded: 1888. **Description:** Female members of churches that are part of the Southern Baptist Convention. Purposes are to teach, support, and promote individual involvement in missions. Offers a limited number of scholarships for children of missionaries and for those preparing for missionary careers. Maintains library on missions, international studies, doctrine, and other religious materials. **Members:** 1,203,929. **State Groups:** 38. **Publications:** *Accent*, monthly. • *Aware*, quarterly. • *Contempo*, monthly. • *Dimension*, quarterly. • *Discovery*, monthly. • *Nuestra Tarea*, monthly. • *Royal Service*, monthly. • *Share*, quarterly. • *Start*, quarterly. • *Year Book*.

★997★ **Woman's National Auxiliary Convention of Free Will Baptists (WNACFWB)**
PO Box 1088
1134 Murfreesboro Rd.
Nashville, TN 37202
Phone: (615)361-1010
Mary R. Wisehart, Exec.Sec.-Treas.
Founded: 1935. **Description:** Provides opportunities for women to fulfill their role in the family, church, and community. Encourages involvement in prayer, study, and action through participation in local auxiliaries. Assists young people in making a commitment to Christianity. Contributes to the needs of missions; maintains a missionary provision closet with sheets, towels, and other household items for working missionaries; and participates in mission activities. Encourages the formation of local auxiliaries. Conducts district, state, and national workshops and seminars. Provides loans to qualified Christian students attending the Free Will Baptist College in Nashville, TN. Sponsors biennial retreat and creative writing contest. Historical materials are currently on loan to the Free Will Baptist College. **Members:** 10,223. **Regional Groups:** 3. **State Groups:** 23. **Local Groups:** 1500. **Publications:** *Co-Laborer*, bimonthly. Magazine. • Also publishes *Sparks into Flame: A History of WNAC, Leader's Guide*, and manuals.

★998★ **Woman's National Democratic Club (WNDC)**
1526 New Hampshire Ave., NW
Washington, DC 20036
Phone: (202)232-7363
Founded: 1922. **Description:** Democratic party members concerned with analyzing educational, social, and political issues to effect an informed democratic opinion. Purposes are to: study the processes of democracy and procedures of government; render educational and social services to the community; educate members in political science, economics, and the arts. Activities include twice weekly speaker luncheons, travel events, speaker dinners, panel discussions, and seminars. Bestows periodic award to an outstanding Democratic woman. Operates library on prominent Democrats and political leaders in the nation's history. Maintains Public Policy Committee composed of task force committees on subjects such as foreign policy, the economy, social security, education, energy, the environment, and human rights. **Members:**

2000. **Publications:** *WNDC Calendar Notes*, monthly. • *WNDC Membership Directory*, semi-annual. • *WNDC News*, monthly. Newsletter.

★999★ **Woman's National Farm and Garden Association (WNFGA)**
c/o Mrs. William R. Slattery
PO Box 608
Northville, MI 48167
Phone: (313)348-9175
Mrs. William R. Slattery, Pres.

Founded: 1914. **Description:** Seeks to stimulate interest in the conservation of natural resources and an appreciation and love for country life, herbs, and floral design. Awards 150 scholarships annually, through its local groups and national organization, to students interested in agriculture, horticulture, forestry, and related fields of study. Offers Tyson Graduate Scholarship to students interested in agriculture, horticulture, landscape, and architecture and McNaughton Scholarship. Bestows scholarships in the field of horticultural therapy to handicapped students. Provides funds for public school teachers to attend summer conservation conferences. Maintains program to train members as flower show judges, teach flower arrangement, and help branches organize and stage shows. Sponsors Gertrude Warren 4-H Leader Training Program and 4-H Club competitions for the best work in ecology and conservation. Planted Dogwood Gardens at the National Arboretum, Washington, DC. Maintains biographical archives. All publications and records are compiled at the Schlesinger Library at Radcliffe College. **Members:** 5000. **Regional Groups:** 10. **State Groups:** 8. **Local Groups:** 132. **Publications:** *Flower Show Guide*, periodic. • *WNFGA Directory*, periodic. • *WNFGA Magazine*, 3/year. • *Woman's National Farm and Garden Association—News Sheets*, periodic. • Also publishes *A Chronicle: The History of WNFGA*. **Formerly:** National Farm and Garden Association.

★1000★ **Woman's Organization of the National Association of Retail Druggists (WONARD)**
666 W. Willow Glen St.
Addison, IL 60101
Phone: (708)628-1729
Mildred A. Ragona, Contact

Founded: 1905. **Description:** Women and female relatives of men in the pharmaceutical business. Objective is to unite the families of persons interested in all aspects of the pharmaceutical profession. Promotes legislation for the betterment of the retail drug and pharmacy business. Maintains a scholarship fund; bestows awards; conducts charitable program. **Members:** 600. **Regional Groups:** 5. **Publications:** *WONARD Newsletter*, quarterly. Reports on legislation, education, and association activities.

★1001★ **Woman's Workshop (WWS)**
PO Box 843
Coronado, CA 92118
Phone: (619)437-1350
Christine Donovan, Co-Owner

Founded: 1987. **Description:** Women seeking information on combining motherhood and careers; membership includes at-home mothers and mothers who work part-time. Serves as an information exchange helping members explore alternatives to traditional full-time motherhood

and prepare for entry or return to work outside the home. Offers ideas for careers, hobbies, educational programs, and volunteer projects that do not conflict with the demands of full-time motherhood. **Publications:** *Woman's Workshop Quarterly*. Newsletter containing interviews and articles on personal enrichment and professional development.

★1002★ **Women Accepted for Volunteer Emergency Service National (WAVES)**
PO Box 6064
Clearwater, FL 34618
Phone: (813)447-0865
Berenice George, President

Description: The group consists of women who have served on active duty in the United States Navy and can show proof of service and an honorable discharge, women who are currently on duty, or women who have retired from duty. It encourages principles of patriotism and loyalty to God, country, and family; helps hospitalized women veterans; locates former Navy women; lends assistance to Navy women where needed; provides volunteer work and community services; maintains a collection of pictures, newspaper clippings, and military uniforms; and operates biographical archives. **Publications:** *White Caps*, 6/year.

★1003★ **Women Achieving Greater Economic Status (WAGE**
PO Box 585766
Orlando, FL 32858
Phone: (407)295-1941
Becky J. Cherney, Pres.

Founded: 1987. **Description:** Individuals interested in promoting and supporting pay equity for women. Researches businesses that depend primarily on women consumers to determine if women are represented throughout those businesses in relation to the economic contribution women make to the businesses. Provides emotional and economic support for women where proven discrimination exists. Operates speakers' bureau and placement service. Compiles statistics; conducts research. **Publications:** *WAGE$ Update*, quarterly. Newsletter. **Also known as:** WAGE$.

★1004★ **Women in Advertising and Marketing (WAM)**
4200 Wisconsin Ave. NW, Ste. 106-238
Washington, DC 20016
Phone: (301)369-7400
Hilary Lavine, Pres.

Founded: 1980. **Description:** Professional women in advertising and marketing. Serves as a network to keep members abreast of developments in advertising and marketing. Fosters professional contact among members. Conducts periodic seminar. Operates speakers' bureau and job bank. **Members:** 225. **Local Groups:** 1. **Publications:** *Membership Directory*, periodic. • *Newsletter*, quarterly.

★1005★ **Women in Aerospace (WIA)**
6352 Rolling Mill Pl., No. 102
Springfield, VA 22152
Phone: (703)644-7875
Fax: (703)866-3526
Linda Strine, Pres.

Founded: 1985. **Description:** Women and men working in aerospace and related fields; allied organizations and businesses. Seeks to in-

crease women's visibility as aerospace professionals and to expand their opportunities for career advancement. Goals are to: provide a forum for exchange of ideas and information among members and recognition of outstanding women in the field; assist members in meeting and maintaining contact with peers and key players in the profession; establish a positive public attitude toward the role of women as leaders in aerospace and related fields; influence the legislative process as it affects the industry; educate organization members about current issues in aerospace; encourage students to develop interests and abilities in the field. Bestows awards; maintains speaker s' bureau. **Members:** 250. **Publications:** *Newsletter*, quarterly. • *WIA Membership Directory*, annual.

★1006★ **Women Against Military Madness (WAMM)**
3255 Hennepin Ave. S.
Minneapolis, MN 55408
Phone: (612)827-5364
Lucia Wilkes, Co-Dir.

Founded: 1982. **Description:** Women and men seeking to bring an end to "systems perpetuating militarism and injustice." Supports higher priority of social concerns such as poverty and hunger. Conducts children's services and educational programs. Maintains small library of books and publications on military issues, disarmament, and related topics; operates speakers' bureau. **Members:** 3000. **Publications:** *WAMM Newsletter*, monthly. • Also publishes *Enpowerment of People for Peace* (booklet); produces videotape.

★1007★ **Women Against Pornography (WAP)**
321 W. 47th St.
New York, NY 10036
Phone: (212)307-5055
Mark Rose, Exec. Officer

Founded: 1979. **Description:** A feminist organization founded by author Susan Brownmiller and others that seeks to change public opinion about pornography so that Americans no longer view it as socially acceptable or sexually liberating. Offers tours of New York's Times Square district, which the group considers "the porn capital of the country," to women and men of all ages and backgrounds. The tour is intended to show firsthand that "the essence of pornography is about the degradation, objectification, and brutalization of women." Also offers adult and high school slide shows/lectures which show how pornographic imagery pervades popular culture. Offers referral service to victims of sexual abuse and sexual exploitation. Maintains speakers' bureau and biographical archives; compiles statistics; bestows awards; organizes protests. **Members:** 10,000. **Computerized Services:** Mailing list. **Publications:** *Women Against Pornography–Newsreport*, 2-4/year. Profiles feminist anti-pornography movements and events throughout the world. Discusses current and proposed pornography legislation, and reviews art, films, books, and advertisements in relation to sex role stereotyping and sexual violence. Includes calendar of events and research updates.

★1008★ Women Against Rape (WAR)
Box 02084
Columbus, OH 43202
Phone: (614)291-9751
Founded: 1972. **Description:** Works toward the prevention of rape. Sponsors crisis intervention services including a rape crisis hotline for support and referrals and rape survivor support groups. Also offers rape prevention training including self-defense classes for women. Maintains speakers' bureau. **Members:** 60. **Local Groups:** 1. **Publications:** *W.A.R. Newsletter*, quarterly. Includes current information on rape issues and calendar of events.

★1009★ Women in Agribusiness (WIA)
PO Box 10241
Kansas City, MO 64111
Dolores Emily, Pres.
Founded: 1985. **Description:** Women in agribusiness. Provides a forum for the discussion of ideas and information related to agribusiness. Offers placement, networking, and peer/mentor support services. Bestows annual awards to outstanding women in agribusiness. **Members:** 400. **Publications:** *Women in Agribusiness Bulletin*, quarterly.

★1010★ Women Airforce Service Pilots WWII (WASPWWII)
PO Box 9212
Ft. Wayne, IN 46899
Phone: (219)747-7933
Lt.Col. Marty Wyall, Pres.
Founded: 1945. **Description:** Women who graduated from or trained in the U.S. Army Air Corps between 1942 and 1944; military pilots of the Women Auxiliary Ferrying Squadron. Offers friendship and assistance to female pilots who flew together from training bases in Houston or Sweetwater, TX and army air bases throughout the U.S. Provides information to students conducting research on the history of the WASPWWII. Assists local WASP groups in organizing exhibits in schools and museums. Maintains biographical archives of old clippings, publications, and scrapbooks. **Members:** 981. **Publications:** *Newsletter*, semiannual. • *WASP Roster*, biennial. **Formerly:** (1980) Order of Fifinella.

★1011★ Women in the Arts (WITA)
University of Michigan School of Music
Ann Arbor, MI 48109
Phone: (313)764-0594
Doris Humphrey, Chair
Founded: 1982. **Description:** Individuals interested in women's contribution to the arts; initial emphasis is on the field of music; plans to extend membership to women in areas such as dance, art, and literature. To highlight accomplishments of women in performance, composition, research, and education; to establish a dialogue in support of such accomplishments. Promotes study in areas such as: ethnomusicology and anthropology; sociology; American, black, and women's studies; and popular culture. Presents recitals, lecture-recitals, and papers; conducts panel discussions and workshops on all women-related musical topics; offers tape-recordings of annual conferences. **Members:** 232. **Publications:** *Proceedings*, annual.

★1012★ Women in the Arts Foundation (WIA)
1175 York Ave., Apt. 2G
New York, NY 10021
Phone: (212)751-1915
Roberta Crown, Exec. Coordinator
Founded: 1971. **Description:** Women artists and women interested in the arts. Works to overcome discrimination against women artists, arrange exhibits of the work of women artists, and protest the underrepresentation of women artists in museums and galleries. Conducts specialized education programs, compiles statistics, and sponsors competitions. Maintains archives. **Members:** 300. **Publications:** *Women in the Arts Bulletin*, bimonthly. Newsletter. Includes book reviews, calendar of events, exhibit announcements, and lists of employment opportunities. • Also publishes *Artists Choice* and *Women Choose Women* (catalogs).

★1013★ Women Band Directors National Association (WBDNA)
345 Overlook Dr.
West Lafayette, IN 47906
Phone: (317)463-1738
Gladys Stone Wright, Sec. & Founder
Founded: 1969. **Description:** Women band directors. Objectives are: to develop a comprehensive program of musical and educational benefit to women band directors and their subjects; to work with administrators to provide the best music education program possible; to provide for equality of women in the profession; to establish a common meeting ground for an exchange of ideas, methods, and problems peculiar to women band directors. Encourages young women entering the instrumental musical field; recognizes the obligations of the school band to school and community, and encourages reciprocal support. Maintains hall of fame and biographical archives. Holds competitions; bestows awards, including the International Golden Rose Award to outstanding woman in the instrumental music profession and Silver Baton to outstanding educator; offers scholarship. Compiles statistics. **Members:** 380. **Regional Groups:** 6. **Publications:** *Newsletter*, quarterly. • *WBDNA Directory*, annual. • *The Woman Conductor*, quarterly. Journal reporting on career improvement, conducting techniques, and association news. Features employment opportunities. • *Women of the Podium*, periodic. Biographical directory.

★1014★ Women in Broadcast Technology (WBT)
c/o Susan Elisabeth
2435 Spaulding St.
Berkeley, CA 94703
Phone: (510)540-8640
Susan Elisabeth, Contact
Founded: 1983. **Description:** Women employed in broadcast-related technology fields; media students; interested individuals. Functions as a networking support group for women equipment operators and technicians in the television, radio, cable, video, and film industries. **Members:** 50. **Publications:** *Informational Flyer*, periodic. • *Newsletter*, periodic. • *Resources*, periodic. • *Women in Broadcast Technology Directory*, annual.

★1015★ Women in Cable (WIC)
c/o P.M. Haeger & Assocs.
500 N. Michigan Ave., Ste. 1400
Chicago, IL 60611
Phone: (312)661-1700
Fax: (312)661-0769
Pamela V. Williams, Exec.Dir.
Founded: 1979. **Description:** Individuals engaged in professional activity in cable television and related industries and disciplines. Encourages a high standard of professional business conduct; provides ongoing exchange of experience and opinions. Focuses attention on broadening the sphere in which women can contribute to the industry; highlights achievements of members. Provides speakers' bureau. **Members:** 2200. **Local Groups:** 20. **Publications:** *Membership Directory*, annual. • *Newsletter*, bimonthly.

★1016★ Women in Cell Biology (WICB)
c/o Dr. Mary Lou King
University of Miami R-124
Dept. of Anatomy and Cell Biology
1600 N.W. 10th Ave.
Miami, FL 33101
Phone: (301)496-7531
Fax: (301)480-2770
Dr. Mary Lou King, Chwm.
Description: Sponsored by the American Society of Cell Biology. Serves as a forum for the discussion of various women's issues. **Members:** 800. **Publications:** *How to Get a Job*, *How to Keep a Job*, *How to Get a Post-Doc*, *Alternate Careers in Cell Biology* (pamphlets), and list of female members of ASCB.

★1017★ Women Church Convergence (WCC)
c/o Loretto Staff Office
590 E. Lockwood Ave.
St. Louis, MO 63119
Phone: (314)962-8112
Sr. Virginia Williams, Contact
Founded: 1977. **Description:** National Catholic organizations concerned with the empowerment of women in society and the church. Seeks to create a political base that will bring a "gospel perspective" to issues of racism, classism, and sexism in the institutional church. Works to make women aware of the Catholic church's stance on these issues. **Members:** 2000. **Formerly:** (1988) Women in the Church Coalition.

★1018★ Women of the Church of God (WCG)
1303 E. 5th St.
Anderson, IN 46012
Phone: (317)642-0256
Doris Dale, Exec.Sec.-Treas.
Founded: 1932. **Description:** Female members of churches affiliated with the Church of God who are interested in individual stewardship and promotion of missions in the United States and abroad. Local groups meet at least monthly for Bible study, fellowship, and educational programs. Raises funds for mission work. **Members:** 46,000. **State Groups:** 57. **Local Groups:** 2000. **Publications:** *Church of God Missions*, 11/year. **Formerly:** (1975) National Woman's Missionary Society of the Church of God.

★1019★ Women of Color Partnership Program (WOCPP)
100 Maryland Ave. NE, Ste. 307
Washington, DC 20002
Phone: (202)543-7032
Fax: (202)543-7820
Elizabeth Castro, Dir.

Founded: 1985. **Description:** A division of the Religious Coalition for Abortion Rights (see separate entry). Educates women about reproductive health issues such as accessibility and cost of health care, role of the church, male responsibility, sterilization, and medical abuse of women. Conducts forums and workshops. Maintains speakers' bureau. **Publications:** *Common Ground - Different Planes*, semiannual. Newsletter.

★1020★ Women in Communications, Inc. (WICI)
2101 Wilson Blvd., Ste. 417
Arlington, VA 22201
Phone: (703)528-4200
Susan Lowell Butler, Exec.V.Pres.

Founded: 1909. **Description:** Professional society - journalism and communications. Offers placement service; compiles statistics. Sponsors National Clarion Awards Competition; presents Vanguard Award for to companies exhibiting positive action in the hiring and promotion of women to positions of equality. **Members:** 12,000. **Student Chapters:** 100. **Professional Chapters:** 85. **Publications:** *Leading Change*, periodic. Newsletter. • *Membership and Resource Directory*, biennial. • *The Professional Communicator*, 5/year. • Also publishes *Careers in Communications* (booklet). **Remarks:** Contact national headquarters for information on local chapters. **Formerly:** (1972) Theta Sigma Phi.

★1021★ Women in Community Service (WICS)
1900 N. Beauregard St., Ste. 103
Alexandria, VA 22311
Phone: (703)671-0500
Toll-free: 800-562-2677
Fax: (703)671-4489
Ruth C. Herman, Exec.Dir.

Founded: 1964. **Description:** Service coalition of five organizations: Church Women United; National Council of Catholic Women; National Council of Jewish Women; National Council of Negro Women; American GI Forum Women (see separate entries). Combines resources and efforts to coordinate programs of community welfare in the U.S. with special emphasis on services to young women. Creates and identifies employment opportunities; trains and supports individuals so they can take advantage of those opportunities. Recruits, screens, and provides support service before, during, and after Job Corps training to poor young women. Bestows annual Rosa Parks Award to commend the "extraordinary acts of ordinary people." **Publications:** *The Story of WICS*. • *This is WICS*, semiannual. Newsletter.

★1022★ Women in Crisis (WIC)
133 W. 21st St.
New York, NY 10011
Phone: (212)242-4880
Mari DaSilza, Program Coordinator

Founded: 1979. **Description:** National conference participants concerned with the plight of "women in crisis," including victims of sexual discrimination and poverty, battered wives, rape and incest victims, women offenders, and female drug abusers and alcoholics. Focuses efforts on women and work, mental health, women in leadership positions, drugs and alcohol, and justice. Seeks to create a network of professionals in these areas. Bestows awards.

★1023★ Women in Data Processing (WDP)
PO Box 880866
San Diego, CA 92108
Phone: (619)569-5615
Laurel Siegmund, Pres.

Founded: 1978. **Description:** Male and female technical personnel, managers, and students in data processing from corporations, government agencies, and colleges. Goals are to: provide a meeting place for data processing professionals in order to share common goals and experiences; promote the entry and advancement of women in the field of data processing; develop a network of professional associates; recognize individuals for professional achievement in data processing; and provide educational growth opportunities to women for personal and professional development. Offers occasional workshops on state-of-the-art technology, personal development, educational opportunities, and management practices. Maintains speakers' bureau of women who speak at schools and organization meetings about WDP and data processing. **Members:** 200. **State Groups:** 2. **Publications:** *Communique*, quarterly. • *Interface*, monthly. • *Link-Up*, monthly. • *Membership Directory*, annual.

★1024★ Women on Death Row Project National Coalition to Abolish the Death Penalty
1325 G St. NW (LL-B)
Washington, DC 20005
Phone: (202)347-2411
Leigh Dingerson, Dir.

Description: The Project has prepared an action oriented report, *Behind the Scenes—Women on Death Row* which has been prepared in cooperation with women's organizations.

★1025★ Women Educators (WE)
c/o Renee Martin
Coll. of Education's Allied Professions
The University of Toledo
Toledo, OH 43606-3390
Phone: (419)537-4337
Renee Martin, Chair

Founded: 1973. **Description:** Educational researchers and educators in institutions of higher education, school systems, government units, and private research organizations. Promotes equal opportunity for women in educational research. Bestows annual Research on Women in Education Award, Sex-Affirmative Curriculum Materials Award, and Scholar/Activist Award. Received grant from the Women's Educational Equity Act Program for a Project on Sex Stereotyping in Education. **Members:** 300. **Publications:** *Annual Awards Report*. • *Newsletter*, periodic (in conjunction with American Educational Research Association). • Also received grant to republish *Handbook for Achieving Sex Equity Through Education* and *Sex Equity Handbook for Scholars*. **Formerly:** (1975) American Educational Research Association Women's Caucus.

★1026★ Women Employed (WE)
22 W. Monroe, Ste. 1400
Chicago, IL 60603
Phone: (312)782-3902
Fax: (312)782-5249
Anne Ladky, Exec.Dir.

Founded: 1973. **Description:** Working women and women seeking employment. Helps women improve their jobs and employment opportunities. Conducts advocacy efforts on issues including pay equity, parental leave, and nontraditional jobs for women. Offers career development services that include seminars, counseling, and networking opportunities. Monitors government enforcement of equal opportunity laws. Conducts public education programs on issues concerning working women. Sponsors Women Employed Institute (see separate entry). **Members:** 1800. **Publications:** *Women Employed News*, quarterly. Newsletter. • Has published *Directory of Work/Family Benefits Offered by Chicago-Area Employers, Occupational Segregation: Economic Crisis for Women*, and *Workers and Families: Recommended Employer Policies* (monographs).

★1027★ Women Employed Institute (WEI)
22 W. Monroe, Ste. 1400
Chicago, IL 60603
Phone: (312)782-3902
Fax: (312)782-5249
Anne Ladky, Exec.Dir.

Founded: 1973. **Description:** Research and education division of Women Employed (see separate entry) devoted to promoting economic equity for women. Analyzes government programs and employer policies; develops recommendations for public and corporate policy to promote equal opportunity. Sponsors advocacy programs to increase women's accessibility to vocational education and training for higher paying, nontraditional jobs. Develops model employment awareness/readiness programs for disadvantaged women. Conducts research projects; compiles statistics on women's economic status. **Publications:** *Directory of Work/Family Benefits Offered by Chicago-Area Employers, Occupational Segregation: Understanding the Economic Crisis for Women*, and *Workers and Families: A Policy Guide for Employers*.

★1028★ Women and Employment (WE)
601 Delaware Ave.
Charleston, WV 25302
Phone: (304)345-1298
Fax: (304)342-0641
Pam Curry, Exec.Dir.

Founded: 1979. **Description:** Seeks to improve the economic position and quality of life for women, especially low-income and minority women. Works to provide access to job training and employment options to women. Supports self-employed women and small business owners by offering training and technical assistance and information. Advocates women's legal right to employment, training, education, and credit. Seeks to inform the public on economic issues related to women. While activities are conducted on local and state levels, group cooperates with national and international organizations on issues relating to employment and economic justice for women. Maintains speakers' bureau and library. Compiles statistics; conducts research. **Members:** 1450. **State Groups:** 2. **Computerized Services:** Data base of West Virginia non-profit and women's groups. **Tele-**

communications Services: Electronic mail; Rural Telecommunications via HandsNet. Publications: *Women & Employment News*, quarterly. Includes association activities and information on economic and employment issues relating to women.

★1029★ Women in Endocrinology
Dept. of Neurobiology and Physiology
Northwestern University
Hogan Hall, Rm. 2-120
2153 Sheridan Rd.
Evanston, IL 60208
Phone: (708)491-5767
Meena B. Schwartz, President

★1030★ Women in Energy (WE)
c/o Kim Flesher
555 N. Kensington
La Grange Park, IL 70525
Phone: (708)352-3746
Fax: (708)352-0499
Kim Flesher, Sec.
Founded: 1978. Description: Women and men working in energy-related fields such as science, engineering, and home economics; others interested in energy issues. Objectives are to educate the public about complex energy choices and issues and provide them with an understanding of the total energy/economy/environment picture to promote more informed and responsible decision-making on energy policy issues. Organizes energy briefings and seminars for local and regional organizations; operates speakers' bureau; sponsors exhibits; arranges tours of energy facilities. Judges high school science fairs and awards certificates of recognition. Members: 275. Regional Groups: 3. State Groups: 6. Local Groups: 10. Publications: *Membership Directory*, periodic. • *Women in Energy News*, quarterly. Newsletter. • Also issues educational publications and audiovisuals.

★1031★ Women Entrepreneurs (WE)
1275 Market St., Ste. 1300
San Francisco, CA 94103
Phone: (415)929-0129
Sharon Cannon, Pres.
Founded: 1974. Description: Women who actively own and operate a business (retail, service, manufacturing, consulting, publishing or other); associate members are persons with plans to start a business or who support the organization's goals. Offers the woman business owner support, recognition, and access to vital information and resources. Has participated in government studies and in the 1980 White House Conference on Small Business. Conducts monthly programs featuring speakers and technical assistance educational seminars and workshops; sponsors Advice Forum, providing business and problem-solving information; bestows Appreciation Awards. Members: 150. Computerized Services: Data base. Publications: *Membership Roster*, annual. • *Prospectus*, monthly.

★1032★ Women Executives International Tourism Association (WEXITA)
c/o SATH
347 5th Ave., Ste. 610
New York, NY 10016

★1033★ Women Executives in Public Relations (WEPR)
PO Box 20766
New York, NY 10025-1516
Phone: (212)721-9661
Alyce K. Noonan, Admin.
Founded: 1946. Description: Women and men senior-level executives in public relations (membership by invitation). Purposes are to: provide a support network for women in public relations; cooperate for mutual advancement and broaden professional knowledge; foster equality of opportunity, management development, training, promotion, and remuneration in public relations. Offers grants and scholarships for courses in public relations and internships to college students majoring in communications. Members: 110. Publications: *Network*, quarterly. Newsletter. Formerly: (1971) Committee on Women in Public Relations.

★1034★ Women Executives in State Government (WESG)
2000 M St. NW, Ste. 730
Washington, DC 20036
Phone: (202)293-7006
Fax: (202)223-3153
Susan Williams DeFife, Dir.
Founded: 1983. Description: Women executives employed in elected or appointed state government positions. Works to enhance members' skills in management, public policy development, government and business relations, and leadership. Encourages sharing of information and experiences among peers; provides mentors for members. Offers fellowships. Operates job search assistance and referral service; makes speakers available. Conducts roundtables, seminars, and government education programs such as federal cabinet-level briefings. Members: 200. Publications: *Annual Report*. • *WESG Membership and Sponsor Directory*, annual. • *WESG Newsletter*, bimonthly. Newsletter.

★1035★ Women Exploited (WE)
12105 Livingston St.
Wheaton, MD 20902
Phone: (301)942-1627
Dr. Olga Fairfax, Ph.D., Exec. Officer
Founded: 1975. Description: Women who have had abortions and regret having had them. To offer support and encouragement to these women; to encourage women considering abortion to keep their babies or give them up for adoption; to get women involved in antiabortion activities; to push for repeal of the Supreme Court decision on abortion. Promotes mutual support and sharing of experiences among women who have had abortions. Distributes antiabortion information to women entering abortion clinics. Counsels women contemplating abortion and women having difficulty coping with having had abortions. Believes that "abortion is a denial of a woman's right to be supported through a difficult pregnancy; of her right to give birth to the baby within her no matter what the circumstances may be ," and that women who have had abortions "were taken advantage of for someone else's monetary gain." Members speak at high schools and colleges, clubs, and right-to-life groups, and on television and radio. Maintains library of books, tapes on abortion by women who have had abortions, a slide-tape show, and files of material on abortion and pertinent legislation. Compiles statistics. Local Groups: 100.

★1036★ Women Exploited by Abortion (WEBA)
24823 Nogal St.
Moreno Valley, CA 92388
Phone: (714)924-4164
Kathy Walker, Pres.
Founded: 1982. Description: Christian-oriented organization of women who have had abortions and regret their action; associate members are concerned individuals who have not had abortions. Provides support and counseling for women suffering from emotional and physical problems as a result of their abortions. Offers counseling to pregnant women considering abortion; refers women who decide to have their babies to other groups that assist needy expectant mothers. Seeks to reeducate society about abortion and the effect it has on women. Provides speakers for pro-life groups, schools, churches, seminars, and television and radio programs. Sponsors seminars; conducts research; compiles statistics; maintains library. Members: 30,000. State Groups: 100. Local Groups: 300. Publications: *News for Life*, bimonthly. Newsletter covering pro-life issues. • Also publishes *Before You Make the Decision*, *Joy Comes in the Mourning* (pamphlets), and *Surviving Abortion* (booklet).

★1037★ Women in Film (WIF)
6464 Sunset Blvd., Ste. 900
Hollywood, CA 90028
Phone: (213)463-6040
Fax: (213)463-0963
Winona Holloway, President
Founded: 1973. Description: Purpose is to support women in the film and television industry and to serve as a network for information on qualified women in the entertainment field. Sponsors screenings and discussions of pertinent issues. Conducts workshops featuring lectures and discussions on such areas as directing, producing, contract negotiation, writing, production development, acting, and technical crafts. Presents Crystal Awards to outstanding women and men for their contributions toward improving the image and increasing participation of women in the industry. Provides speakers' bureau. Maintains Women in Film Foundation, which offers financial assistance to women for education, research, and/or completion of film projects and bestows grants for the employment of trainees as interns with major studios and independent film companies. Members: 1500. Publications: *WIF Directory*, annual. • *WIF Reel News*, monthly.

★1038★ Women in Fire Service (WFS)
PO Box 5446
Madison, WI 53705
Phone: (608)233-4768
Fax: (608)233-4768
Terese M. Floren, Exec.Dir.
Founded: 1983. Description: Women working in fire service, including career and volunteer firefighters, emergency medical technicians and paramedics, inspectors and arson investigators, fire safety educators, and administrators; women interested in careers in fire service; interested men. Provides support and advocacy for women in fire service; promotes professional development of members in an effort to make women more effective firefighters. Collects and disseminates information on issues affecting women in fire service; maintains resource bank on issues such as recruitment, physical agility

testing, promotional testing, fitness training, firefighting techniques, and maternity leave. Offers guidance in decisions concerning sexual harassment, sexual discrimination, and other issues. Supports and facilitates the development of local groups. Maintains speakers' bureau; compiles statistics; conducts charitable and educational programs. Awards scholarships. **Members:** 800. **Publications:** *Firework,* monthly. Newsletter. • *WFS Quarterly.* Journal for fire officers; focuses on gender integration of fire service. **Formerly:** (1990) Women in Fire Suppression.

**★1039★ Women and
Foundations/Corporate Philanthropy
(WAF/CP)**
141 5th Ave., Fl. 7-S
New York, NY 10010
Phone: (212)460-9253
Fax: (212)475-6206
Jane Ransom, Pres.

Founded: 1977. **Description:** Staff and trustees of grant-making organizations. Seeks to increase the amount of money for programs on behalf of women and girls and to enhance the status of women as decision-makers within private philanthropy. Builds regional networks of women and men in philanthropy; conducts research on grant-making patterns in the funding of programs; disseminates information to promote thoughtful decision-making with regard to the funding of programs that meet the needs of women. **Members:** 600. **Publications:** *Annual Report.* • *Newsletter,* 3/year. • *Papers,* 1-2/year. • Also publishes research studies, brochure, and special publications on needs of women and girls.

★1040★ Women in French (WIF)
Ball State University
Department of Foreign Languages
Muncie, IN 47306
Phone: (317)285-1374
Fax: (317)285-1027
Adele King, Secretary

Description: The organization is made up of scholars worldwide committed to the study of writing in French by women, both in metropolitan France and francophone countries. It produces publications, sponsors sessions at the conventions of the Modern Language Association, and seeks to promote the inclusion of more women in courses on literature and culture. **Publications:** *Women in French Newsletter.*

★1041★ Women in Government (WIG)
c/o Joy N. Stone
1101 30th St. NW, Ste. 500
Washington, DC 20006
Phone: (202)625-3479
Fax: (202)625-3445
Joy N. Stone, Exec.Dir.

Founded: 1988. **Description:** Coalition of elected women in state, national, and international governments. Promotes dialogue between the public and private sectors. Serves as an information clearinghouse. Conducts bimonthly seminars and discussions on issues affecting and affected by various legislative bodies. Conducts educational programs. **Members:** 1200. **Publications:** *Membership Directory,* annual. • *Newsletter,* quarterly. **Formerly:** (1991) National Order of Women Legislators.

**★1042★ Women in Government Relations
(WGR)**
1325 Massachusetts Ave. NW, Ste. 510
Washington, DC 20005-4171
Phone: (202)347-5432
Fax: (202)347-5434
Millicent Gorham, Pres.

Founded: 1975. **Description:** Professional women and men who have legislative or regulatory responsibilities involving federal, state, and local governmental bodies; members represent corporations, trade associations, the executive and legislative branches of government, and nonprofit organizations. Promotes the professional status of women; provides a forum for discussion of issues of national importance with political and business leaders; gives members the opportunity to develop contacts in the government relations field. Conducts workshops and educational seminars on improving communications skills, establishing professional credentials, achieving career objectives, and developing management techniques. Maintains speakers' bureau and job bank for government relations positions; compiles statistics. Presents annual Distinguished Member Award; sponsors Women in Government Relations LEADER Foundation (see separate entry). **Members:** 850. **Publications:** *Annual Report.* • *Membership Directory,* periodic. • *Women in Government Relations—Newsletter,* bimonthly.

**★1043★ Women in Government Relations
LEADER Foundation**
c/o Patricia Hill
American Paper Institute
1250 Connecticut Ave. NW, Ste. 210
Washington, DC 20038
Phone: (202)463-2581
Patricia Hill, Contact

Founded: 1979. **Description:** Seeks to provide women with management opportunities in business and government relations through leadership, education, advancement, development, endowment, and research (LEADER). Sponsors proposals and projects to enhance corporate management skills and increase knowledge. Provides resources, techniques, methods, information, and training opportunities not otherwise available to women. Maintains a central resource on career development programs related to business/government relations; sponsors internship programs and career seminars. Offers fellowships to professional women in the field of government relations. **Formerly:** (1986) Women in Government Relations Leader Fund.

**★1044★ Women Grocers of America
(WGA)**
1825 Samuel Morse Dr.
Reston, VA 22090
Phone: (703)437-5300
Thomas K. Zavcha, Pres.

Founded: 1983. **Description:** Serves as information and advisory arm to National Grocers Association. Supports and recognizes women in the food distribution industry and assists in the educational and professional needs of its members. Objectives include: organizing food donation programs for the needy; testifying before Congress on issues concerning the operations of independent retail groceries; coordinating programs with educational institutions that promote careers in the food distribution industry. **Members:** 200. **Publications:** *Exchange,* 3/year. Newsletter. • Also publishes brochure.

★1045★ Women for Guatemala (WG)
2119 S. Bennett St.
Seattle, WA 98108-1910
Phone: (301)977-1761
Patricia Ortiz, Coordinator

Founded: 1982. **Description:** Women working to improve life for Guatemalan women. Disseminates information to women in the U.S. on issues relating to the socioeconomic conditions, human rights, politics, and culture of Guatemalan women and children. Seeks to; broaden awareness and understanding among North American women of the complexity of Guatemalan women's situation; establish linkages between Guatemalan and North American women. Sponsors tours and exhibitions. Conducts charitable programs; maintains speakers' bureau; compiles statistics.

**★1046★ Women and Health Roundtable
(WHR)**
1000 Connecticut Ave. NW, Ste. 9
Washington, DC 20036
Phone: (301)953-4215
Lori Cooper, Co-Chwm.

Founded: 1976. **Description:** A monthly forum on women's health issues for representatives of health-related and women's organizations, consumer groups, and federal agencies. Monitors and attempts to improve federal and state health policies' responsiveness to women's health priorities. Exchanges information on policy developments, learns of new issues through informal briefings, and develops common strategies for accomplishing legislative or executive agency objectives. Disseminates information to universities, medical schools, health systems agencies, and women's health advocates. **Publications:** *Roundtable Report,* 11/year. Lists employment opportunities, conferences, and resources.

**★1047★ Women in Housing and Finance
(WHF)**
655 15th St. NW, Ste. 300
Washington, DC 20005
Phone: (202)639-4999

Founded: 1979. **Description:** Professionals employed in the fields of housing or finance. Purpose is to provide women finance professionals with the opportunity for continued professional development through interaction with others with similar interests. Promotes educational development of women in housing and finance; provides members with services and benefits to help them attain higher levels of expertise. Sponsors social events for members; holds receptions for congressional and regulatory leaders; conducts monthly luncheon and programs featuring speakers from federal agencies, Congress, and the private sector. Sponsors career development workshops. Activities are concentrated in the Washington, DC area. **Members:** 276. **Local Groups:** 1. **Publications:** *Newsletter,* 10/year. • *Women in Housing and Finance—Membership Directory,* annual.

★1048★ Women, Inc.
244 Townsend St.
Dorchester, MA 02121
Phone: (617)442-6166
Janet Walton, Interim Dir.

Founded: 1973. **Description:** Community service agency that provides for women with special needs. Programs include: Residential and Outpatient Drug and Alcohol Treatment Program, providing individual and group counseling and alcohol and drug education seminars; Parenting and Child Education Program, providing parenting seminars to mothers who maintain drug- and alcohol-free lifestyles. Also offers a comprehensive child care center for the children of parents with substance abuse histories, and provides a national research project on AIDS prevention among women.

★1049★ Women in Information Processing (WIP)
Lock Box 39173
Washington, DC 20016
Phone: (202)328-6161
Janice H. Miller, Pres.

Founded: 1979. Description: International organization of women who are professionals in computer fields, office automation, robotics, telecommunications, artificial intelligence, and related disciplines. Seeks to: advance the industry by helping women benefit from opportunities created by automation; attract additional qualified women; aid women in building professional contacts. Sponsors product demonstrations and exhibits. Offers speakers' bureau, career counseling, monthly seminar, resume guidance, discussions, and scholarship programs. Compiles statistics; bestows awards; offers group rate medical insurance. Presents annual award for meritorious achievements. Members: 4827. Regional Groups: 5. Computerized Services: Resume bank. Publications: Forumnet, quarterly. • Salary and Perception Survey, annual.

★1050★ Women in International Security (WIIS)
c/o Center for International Security Studies
University of Maryland - College Park
School of Public Affairs
College Park, MD 20742
Phone: (301)403-8109
Frances G. Burwell, Exec.Dir.

Founded: 1987. Description: A project of the Center for International Security Studies. Provides a forum for professional and social contact between women working on international issues in the military, academia, research and business organizations, and governmental and nonprofit groups. Acts as a nonpartisan network and professional development program. Serves as a clearinghouse for information for and about women, especially those working on international and foreign policy issues. Sponsors seminars and panel discussions. Maintains speakers' bureau. Computerized Services: Data base. Publications: WIIS Words, periodic. Newsletter; includes information on seminars and speakers. • Also publishes Internships in Foreign and Defense Policy (directory) and brochures; plans to publish directory of midcareer programs and fellowships and a resource directory.

★1051★ Women Involved in Farm Economics (WIFE)
Rt. 1, Box 224
Bradshaw, NE 68319
Phone: (402)736-4465
Elaine Stuhr, Pres.

Founded: 1976. Description: Committed to improving profitability in production agriculture through educational, legislative, and cooperative programs. Promotes public and governmental awareness of the importance of agriculture in the American economy; maintains that agriculture is the most vital renewable industry and that economic prosperity in the United States is dependent upon economic prosperity in agriculture. Upholds the "family farm" concept for the production of food and fiber in the U.S. Works with governmental agencies and Congress to promote stability in the agricultural industry. Encourages communication regarding agricultural issues. Cooperates with other agricultural organizations and commodity groups in an effort to provide a unified voice for the industry. Conducts educational activities including Ag in the Classroom program, seminars, and workshops. Sponsors National Ag Day promotions. Maintains archives. State Groups: 20. Local Groups: 140. Publications: Directory and Policy Summaries, annual. • Wifeline, monthly. Newspaper including editorials and reports on commodities. • Also publishes brochure.

★1052★ Women Judges' Fund for Justice (WJFJ)
733 15th St. NW, Ste. 700
Washington, DC 20005
Phone: (202)783-2073
Fax: (202)393-0079
Marilyn Negelski, Exec. Officer

Founded: 1980. Description: Participants are women judges committed to strengthening the role of women in the American judicial system. Primary goals are to: increase the number of women judges at all levels of the federal and state judiciary; minimize gender bias in the judicial system through support of special task forces, development of educational materials, and provision of training for male and female judges; increase the effectiveness of women judges through provision of education and other support programs. Has developed a curriculum on the judicial selection process and candidate skills, and has cosponsored and supported the National Judicial Education Program to Promote Equality for Women and Men in the Courts. Provides assistance in developing and funding education programs of the National Association of Women Judges (see separate entry). Sponsors institutes. Publications: Judicial Education: A Guide to State and National Programs and Operating a Task Force on Gender Bias in the Courts: A Manual for Action. Formerly: Foundation for Women Judges.

★1053★ Women in Legal Education
526 Pine St.
New Orleans, LA 70118
Phone: (504)861-5672
Kathy Lorio, Chair

★1054★ Women Library Workers (WLW)
c/o Women's Resource Center
Bldg. T-9, Rm. 112
University of California
Berkeley, CA 94720
Phone: (415)642-4786
Nancy Humphreys, Articles Editor

Founded: 1975. Description: Library and information workers united to combine the energies of credentialed and noncredentialed workers to change the existing distribution of power in libraries. Disseminates information to the public. Members: 500. Publications: Share, A Directory of Feminist Librarians, periodic. • WLW Journal, quarterly.

★1055★ Women Life Underwriters Confederation (WLUC)
1126 S. 70th St., No. S-100
Milwaukee, WI 53214
Phone: 800-776-3008
Fax: (414)475-2585
Liane L. Gonzalez, Exec. Officer

Founded: 1987. Description: Life and health underwriters. Objectives are to: advance the life insurance field; inform women members of opportunities in the profession; develop educational opportunities; provide peer support and sales motivational techniques; act as a forum for exchange of sales ideas and industry news. Conducts seminars; encourages development of local chapters. Maintains speakers' bureau. Members: 1500. Local Groups: 30. Publications: Roster, annual. • WLUC News, monthly. Newsletter. Available to members only. • Also publishes brochure.

★1056★ Women in the Mainstream (WM)
PO Box 66941
Baton Rouge, LA 70896
Phone: (504)928-7208
Neall Mitchell, Contact

Description: Organizations (100) and individuals (3000) united to create a women's exhibit for the 1984 World's Fair in honor of the exhibit shown at the 1884 Louisiana Exposition. The 1984 exhibit illustrated the many choices women have today as opposed to 100 years ago and honored women from the last century. Plans to organize other exhibits throughout the country. Operates hall of fame and museum. Offers a speakers bureau; sponsors competitions. Maintains biographical archives and an art collection. Members: 3100. Publications: Directory, annual. • Also publishes Women of Accomplishment 1884-1984.

★1057★ Women Make Movies (WMM)
225 Lafayette St., Ste. 207
New York, NY 10012
Phone: (212)925-0606
Fax: (212)925-2052
Debra S. Zimmerman, Dir.

Founded: 1972. Description: Individuals devoted to the development of a strong multicultural feminist media that accurately reflects the lives of women. Aim is the universal distribution of woman-made productions that encourage audiences to explore the changing and diverse roles women play in our society. Conducts sale or rental of films and videos made by women about issues important to women; filmmakers are available to attend screenings and to speak with audiences about the films and making process. Maintains library and distributes more than 200 films and videotapes on topics such as health, gender equity, cultural identity, and Latin America. Members: 300. Publications: News From Women Make Movies, periodic. Newsletter. • Also publishes film catalogs.

★1058★ Women in Management (WIM)
2 N. Riverside Plaza, Ste. 2400
Chicago, IL 60606
Phone: (312)263-3636
Fax: (312)263-0923
Patricia Kelps, Admin.

Founded: 1976. Description: Support network of women in professional and management positions that facilitates the exchange of experience and ideas. Promotes self-growth in management; provides speakers who are successful in management; sponsors workshops and special interest groups to discuss problems and share job experiences. Bestows awards. **Members:** 1700. **Publications:** *Memorandum*, quarterly. Newsletter. • *WIM National Newsletter*, quarterly. Includes chapter contacts. • *Women in Management—National Directory*, annual.

★1059★ **Women Marines Association (WMA)**
140 Merengo, No. 605
Forest Park, IL 60130
Phone: (708)366-6408
Helen H. Laukes, Pres.

Founded: 1960. **Description:** Women in the U.S. Marine Corps or the U.S. Marine Reserve, or those who have been discharged under honorable conditions; those separated or retired from the U.S. Marine Corps. Perpetuates comradeship among members and promotes the welfare of all women of the Marine Corps; encourages responsible civic leadership and citizenship; fosters patriotism in American youth through education; provides entertainment, care, and assistance to hospitalized veterans. Presents Molly Marine awards to women graduates of the Recruit Training program. Maintains charitable program. Sponsors competitions. Member of Navy-Marine Corps Council; Marine Corps Council. **Members:** 3000. **State Groups:** 78. **Publications:** *WMA 'Nouncements*, quarterly. Newsletter; includes information on membership, scholarships, chapters, and current leadership of the association and the Marine Corps. Includes listing of awards and scholarships. • *Women Marines Association—Membership Directory*, biennial. Includes application forms and scholarship information.

★1060★ **Women and Mathematics Education (WME)**
c/o Charlene Morrow
Mt. Holyoke College
302 Shattuck Hall
South Hadley, MA 01075
Phone: (413)538-2608
Charlene Morrow, Exec. Officer

Founded: 1978. **Description:** Individuals concerned with promoting the mathematical education of girls and women. Serves as a clearinghouse for ideas and resources in the area of women and mathematics. Establishes communications for networks focusing on doctoral students, elementary and secondary school teachers, and teacher educators. Encourages research in the area of women and mathematics, especially research that isolates factors contributing to the dropout rate of women in mathematics. Emphasizes the need for elementary and secondary school programs that help reverse the trend of avoidance of mathematics by females. Maintains speakers' bureau. **Members:** 500. **Computerized Services:** Mailing list. **Publications:** *Women and Mathematics*, annual. Resource list. • *Women and Mathematics Education—Newsletter*, 3/year. Supplies information on conferences, institutes, programs, and meetings significant to members, along with reports on the activities of the organization. Includes research reports, bibliography of resources, and lists of educational and professional opportunities for women. **Formerly:** (1979) Association for the Promotion of the Mathematics Education of Girls and Women.

★1061★ **Women for Meaningful Summits (WMS)**
c/o Beverly Stripling
YWCA
624 9th St. NW, 6th Fl.
Washington, DC 20001
Phone: (202)628-3636
Fax: (202)783-7123
Beverly Stripling, Pres.

Founded: 1985. **Description:** A network of women's peace organizations and individuals committed to reversing the arms race on earth and in space, and to creating a more just and peaceful world. Serves as a clearinghouse to inform the public on current activities and national and international programs. Offers grass roots educational programs. Maintains speakers' bureau. **Publications:** *Newsletter*, periodic. **Formerly:** (1989) Women for a Meaningful Summit.

★1062★ **Women Military Aviators (WMA)**
PO Box 396
Randolph AFB, TX 78148
Phone: (317)688-2167
Lt.Col. Kelly Hamilton-Barlow, USAF, Pres.

Founded: 1981. **Description:** Active duty pilots (375); navigators (72); former Women Air Force Service Pilots (245); those interested in or affiliated with military women pilots (40). Preserves, for educational purposes, the history of women who served their country as pilots and navigators. Conducts programs and offers slide presentations on women in the military. Sponsors Women Military Pilots Job Opportunity Network. Maintains biographical archives and speakers' bureau; offers seminars on career opportunities at conventions. **Members:** 732. **Telecommunications Services:** Membership mailing roster. **Publications:** *WMA Newsletter*, bimonthly. Contains information on changes of policy by uniformed services and historic articles on military women. Includes statistics and employment opportunities listings. • *WMA Roster*, annual. **Formerly:** (1989) Women's Military Pilots Association.

★1063★ **Women and the Military Project (WMP)**
c/o Women's Equity Action League
1250 I St., NW, Ste. 305
Washington, DC 20005
Phone: (202)898-1588
Vicki Almquist, Dir.

Founded: 1977. **Description:** To extend and protect the rights of women in the military (active and reserve), female veterans, families of military members, and civilian women employed by the military. Provides background papers, educational materials, and position statements. Conducts research and meets with federal officials in order to influence public policy to improve the status of women in the military. Maintains extensive files on the specific military branches, women in combat, military employment issues, military education, conscription, and current legislation; compiles statistics. **Publications:** Information packets, fact sheets, and news releases. **Formerly:** National Coalition for Women in Defense; (1983) National Clearinghouse on Women and the Military; (1987) National Information Center on Women and the Military.

★1064★ **Women in Mining National (WIM)**
1801 Broadway St., Ste. 400
Denver, CO 80202
Phone: (303)298-1535
Patricia A. Kemper, Pres.

Founded: 1972. **Description:** Individuals employed or interested in the mineral resource industry. Provides technical education and scientific programs fostering public awareness of economic and technical interrelationships between mineral production and the national economy. Monitors and participates in related legislative activities. Provides speakers at monthly meeting; conducts field trips and seminars; holds legislative receptions; participates in career days at local public schools. Encourages the growth of additional chapters. Sponsors competitions; bestows annual scholarship awards; maintains hall of fame. **Members:** 500. **Regional Groups:** 8. **Local Groups:** 7. **Publications:** *Women in Mining National—Membership Directory*, annual. • *Women in Mining—National Quarterly*. Newsletter covering legislative issues and national and chapter activities of the association. Includes calendar of events. • Also publishes brochures and chapter newsletters. **Formerly:** Women in Mining.

★1065★ **Women in Ministry Project**
475 Riverside Dr., Rm. 704
New York, NY 10115
Phone: (212)870-2144
Liz Vendesi, Dir.

Founded: 1974.

★1066★ **Women of the Motion Picture Industry, International (WOMPI)**
c/o Lili Beaudin
PO Box 900
Beverly Hills, CA 90213
Phone: (213)203-4083
Lili Beaudin, Pres.

Founded: 1953. **Description:** Federation of clubs of women employed in the production, distribution, and exhibition of motion pictures for theatres and television; those connected with supplier firms, concessionaires, and film transportation services. Seeks to: encourage active participation in service projects in the community; develop friendship as a means of broadening the field of opportunity for service; encourage fellowship and cultural relations. Presents awards; maintains charitable program; holds symposia. **Members:** 500. **Local Groups:** 10. **Publications:** *Newsletter from President and Bulletin Committee*, periodic. Membership newsletter including a bulletin reporting on the 10 local clubs. **Formerly:** International Association of Women of the Motion Picture Industry.

★1067★ **Women in Municipal Government (WIMG)**
National League of Cities
1301 Pennsylvania Ave. NW
Washington, DC 20004
Phone: (202)626-3000
Fax: (202)626-3043
Kathryn Shane McCarty, Coordinator

Founded: 1974. **Description:** Women who are elected and appointed city officials including mayors, council members, and commissioners. Seeks to: encourage active participation of women officials in the organizational and policy-making processes and programs of the National League of Cities and state municipal leagues; identify qualified women for service in the NLC and other national positions; promote issues of interest to women and the status of women in the nation's cities. **Members:** 400. **Publications:** *Constituency Report*, quarterly. Newsletter.

★1068★ **Women of the National Agricultural Aviation Association (WNAAA)**
Rt 1 Box 475
Greenwood, MS 38930
Phone: (601)455-3000
Fax: (601)455-1611
Dorothy Kimmel, Pres.

Founded: 1976. **Description:** Wives of members of the National Agricultural Aviation Association. Assists NAAA members with public relations and recreational activities. Provides scholarship program for children or grandchildren of agricultural aviators. **Members:** 1000.

★1069★ **Women Organizing Women (WOW)**
Political Action Committee
PO Box 1652
New Haven, CT 06507-1652
Phone: (203)281-3400
Barbara Pearce, Treasurer

★1070★ **Women Outdoors (WO)**
55 Talbot Ave.
Medford, MA 02155
D. J. Erb, Pres.

Founded: 1980. **Description:** Women whose vocation or interests include outdoor activity. Purpose is to maintain a network for women with a common interest in the outdoors. Encourages and holds professional training programs in development of leadership qualities and outdoor skills among women; promotes an ethic of care and respect for the environment. Conducts leadership development workshops. Maintains library of books on women's adventure travel. Offers scholarships. **Members:** 700. **State Groups:** 27. **Publications:** *Newsletter*, bimonthly. • *Women Outdoors Magazine*, quarterly. • Also publishes *Liability and Risk Management*, *Annotated Bibliography of Women's Travel and Adventure Literature*, *Getting a Job Out There*, *Women's Adventure and Skill Programs*, *Low Impact Use*, and *Female Hygiene in the Backwoods* (pamphlets).

★1071★ **Women in Psychology for Legislative Action (WPLA)**
Political Action Committee
436 N. Bedford Dr., No. 404
Beverly Hills, CA 90210
Phone: (213)458-1405
Fax: (213)394-4028
Gerry Simmons, Contact

★1072★ **Women for Racial and Economic Equality (WREE)**
198 Broadway, Rm. 606
New York, NY 10038
Phone: (212)385-1103
Sally Chaffee Maron, Co-Chair

Founded: 1975. **Description:** Multiracial and multinational group of working and working class women. Purposes include: to end race and sex discrimination in hiring, pay, and promotion practices; to support quality integrated public education and federally funded comprehensive child care; to promote peace and solidarity with women of all countries; to work for passage of the Women's Bill of Rights, a program of legislative demands that guarantees economic independence and social equality. Lobbies for equal employment, education, child care, and health issues. Conducts community education and action campaigns, conferences, seminars, forums, leadership training, and research projects. Bestows awards; maintains speakers' bureau. **Members:** 1600. **Local Groups:** 18. **Publications:** *WREE-View of Women*, bimonthly. Tabloid reporting on racism, affirmative action, child care, the environment, housing, and other issues. Includes book reviews. • Also publishes poetry books.

★1073★ **Women Refusing to Accept Tenant Harassment (WRATH)**
607 Elmira Rd., Ste. 299
Vacaville, CA 95687

★1074★ **Women in Sales Association (WIS)**
8 Madison Ave.
PO Box M
Valhalla, NY 10595
Phone: (914)946-3802
Fax: (914)946-3633
Marie T. Rossi, Chwm.

Founded: 1979. **Description:** Professional saleswomen; students aspiring to careers in sales. Promotes professional development of women in sales. Provides opportunity to establish business contacts, and to share information and ideas. Conducts work sessions on topics including personal communication skills and use of audiovisual aids in sales presentations; provides speakers on topics fundamental to sales skills; sponsors career guidance workshops and position referral service. Provides discounts to members on relevant publications; offers financial planning advice; presents Women in Sales Recognition Awards. **Members:** 1000. **Regional Groups:** 8. **Publications:** *Membership Directory*, periodic. • *Sales Leader*, quarterly. Newsletter promoting the professional development of women in sales. Includes position referral service. • Also publishes brochures.

★1075★ **Women in Scholarly Publishing (WISP)**
c/o Marilyn Campbell
Rutgers University Press
109 Church St.
New Brunswick, NJ 08901-1242
Phone: (908)932-7396
Fax: (704)693-1490
Marilyn Campbell, Contact

Founded: 1979. **Description:** Women involved in scholarly publishing and men who support the organization's goals. Promotes professional development and advancement, management skills, and opportunities for women in scholarly publishing. Concerns include career development, job sharing information, surveys of salaries and job opportunities for women, and practical workshops or other training opportunities. Provides a forum and network for communication among women in presses throughout the U.S. Sponsors educational workshops, programs, and seminars, in conjunction with the Association of American University Presses. Compiles statistics. **Members:** 300. **Computerized Services:** Mailing list. **Publications:** *WISP Newsletter*, quarterly. Includes association news, columns on benefit issues, calendar of events, and job openings; lists award recipients;

★1076★ **Women in Show Business (WiSB)**
PO Box 2535
North Hollywood, CA 91610
Phone: (213)271-3415
Fax: (818)994-6181
Scherr Lillico, Pres.

Founded: 1961. **Description:** Women employed in the entertainment industry and allied fields. Raises funds to pay for reconstructive and restorative surgery for poor children who are not eligible for state or federal aid and/or insurance coverage. Also provides for equipment, supplies, therapy, counseling, training services, prosthetics, and other materials. Bestows awards. **Members:** 100. **Publications:** *Newsletter*, monthly. **Formerly:** (1982) Girls Friday of Show Business.

★1077★ **Women for Sobriety (WFS)**
PO Box 618
Quakertown, PA 18951
Phone: (215)536-8026
Dr. Jean Kirkpatrick, Exec.Dir.

Founded: 1975. **Description:** Self-help groups of women alcoholics who use a program "based on abstinence, comprised of thirteen acceptance statements that, when accepted and used, will provide each woman with a new way of life through a new way of thinking.starts with coping first but then moves on to overcoming and a whole change in the approach to each day." Recognizes differences between male and female alcoholics in the method of successful recovery. Small groups organize and meet independently. Maintains speakers' bureau. Conducts seminars and workshops. **Members:** 5000. **Local Groups:** 450. **Publications:** *Newsletter*, monthly. • *Sobering Thoughts*, monthly. Newsletter; contains book reviews, calendar of events, and research updates. • Also publishes books, booklets, and pamphlets.

★1078★ **Women Strike for Peace (WSP)**
105 2nd St. NE
Washington, DC 20002
Phone: (202)543-2660
Ethel Taylor, Coordinator

Founded: 1961. **Description:** A movement and membership organization focusing on peace activism in the form of national campaigns, grass roots activities, and lobbying. Concentrates on disarmament, anti-interventionism, and mobilizing public opinion in the U.S. against current nuclear war-fighting plans. Local branches exercise autonomy in developing programs and adapting national action to local communities. **Members:** 5000. **Local Groups:** 10. **Publications:** *Women Strike for Peace-Legislative Alert*, monthly. Newsletter; informs readers of actions taken by the United States and other countries on disarmament and other foreign policy issues, and offers possible action that can be taken to alter objectionable policies. Includes news of research.

★1079★ **Women in Telecommunications**
1827 Haight St., #180
San Francisco, CA 94117
Phone: (415)751-4746
Jayne M. Snook, Dir.

Founded: 1981. **Description:** Users, manufacturers, and common carrier personnel in telecommunications. To establish national and international networks of professional men and women and to increase women's contributions to the field of telecommunications. Conducts seminars, monthly meetings, and educational programs. Offers telecommunications training. **Members:** 50. **Local Groups:** 2. **Publications:** Women in Telecommunications (newsletter), quarterly.

★1080★ **Women on Their Own (WOTO)**
PO Box 1026
Willingboro, NJ 08046
Phone: (609)871-1499
Maxine Karelitz, Exec.Dir.

Founded: 1982. **Description:** Participants are single, divorced, separated, or widowed women raising children on their own. Links participants together to help each other. Offers support and advocacy; provides referrals. Conducts workshops and seminars; maintains speakers' bureau. Makes available small, interest-free loans. Assists other organizations serving the same population. Bestows awards. **Publications:** *Directory*, periodic. • *Newsletter*, periodic. • Also publishes brochure. **Also known as:** WOTO.

★1081★ **Women in Transition (WIT)**
125 S. 9th St., Ste. 502
Philadelphia, PA 19107
Phone: (215)922-7177
Roberta L. Hacker, Exec.Dir.

Founded: 1971. **Description:** Offers services to women experiencing difficulties or distress in their lives. Facilitates selfhelp support groups for abused women and women recovering from substance abuse problems. Provides outreach, assessment, and referrals to women with drug and/or alcohol addiction; makes available individual, couple, and family counseling. Trains facilitators for selfhelp support groups. Offers consultation and training to mental health and social service agency personnel. Maintains speakers' bureau. **Telecommunications Services:** 24-hour telephone hot line for crisis counseling, information, and resource referrals, (215)922-7500. **Publications:** *Annual Report.* • *Volunteer Newsletter*, periodic. • Also publishes *Facilitator's Guide to Working with Separated and Divorced Women*, and *Stepping Out to Work: A Facilitator's Guide*, and *Child Support: How You Can Obtain and Enforce Support Orders.*

★1082★ **Women U.S.A. Fund**
845 3rd Ave., 15th Fl.
New York, NY 10022
Phone: (212)759-7982
Bella Abzug, Sec.

Founded: 1980. **Description:** Organizes activities around national and international policies, legislation and executive actions affecting women. Encourages women's participation in the political process; issues educational materials; holds drives; conducts conferences. Administers the Women's Foreign Policy Council, which works to increase the participation of women in the formulation and conduct of foreign policy, and the Women's Environment and Development Organization. **Publications:** *Directory of Women Foreign Policy Specialists*, periodic. • *News and Views*, periodic.

★1083★ **Women on Wheels (WOW)**
PO Box 5147
Topeka, KS 66605
Phone: (913)267-3779
Toll-free: 800-322-1969
Kathryn Greenwood, Exec.Dir.

Founded: 1982. **Description:** Women motorcyclists. Goals are to unite women motorcyclists and to gain recognition from the motorcycle industry concerning the needs of female consumers. Activities include compilation of statistics and participation in motorcycle events. Sponsors charity functions with the Motorcycle Safety Foundation. Plans to organize rallies, interchapter social affairs, fashion activities, and fundraising for public service projects. **Members:** 2000. **Computerized Services:** Online mailing list. **Publications:** *Membership Directory*, annual. • *Women on Wheels*, bimonthly. Magazine.

★1084★ **Women in the Wind (WW)**
PO Box 8392
Toledo, OH 43605
Becky Brown, Founder

Founded: 1979. **Description:** Women motorcyclists and enthusiasts united to promote a positive image of women motorcyclists. Educates members on motorcycle safety and maintenance. Conducts charitable programs; bestows awards. **Members:** 450. **Local Groups:** 34. **Publications:** *Shootin' the Breeze*, 9/year. Newsletter; contains membership activities news and calendar of events.

★1085★ **Women on Wine (WOW)**
6110 Sunset Ranch Dr.
Riverside, CA 92506-4621
Phone: (714)784-3096
Barbara Mader Ivey, Dir.

Founded: 1981. **Description:** Male and female consumers of wine and wine trade members. Seeks to educate the wine consumer and to recognize and encourage contributions of women to the wine trade. Provides scholarships for enology students; conducts monthly meetings; maintains speakers' bureau. Sponsors competitions and bestows awards. **Members:** 1000. **Publications:** *Women on Wine National News*, quarterly. Membership newsletter on activities in the wine industry. Includes regional news and calendar of events. • *WOW Chapter Flyer*, monthly.

★1086★ **Women World War Veterans (WWWV)**
Morgan Hotel
237 Madison Ave.
New York, NY 10016
Phone: (212)684-6728
Dorothy Frooks, Cmdr.

Founded: 1919. **Description:** Honorably discharged women who served in the Navy, Army, Coast Guard, Marine Corps, and Air Force during World Wars I and II. **Members:** 40,000. **Formerly:** (1932) Women of the U.S. Naval Reserve.

★1087★ **Women's Action Alliance (WAA)**
c/o Shazia Z. Rafi
370 Lexington Ave., Ste. 603
New York, NY 10017
Phone: (212)532-8330
Fax: (212)779-2846
Shazia Z. Rafi, Exec.Dir.

Founded: 1971. **Description:** Develops educational programs and services to assist women and women's organizations in achieving full equality for women. Maintains the Information Services Program, which provides information and referrals and disseminates publications on women's issues and programs to individuals and organizations. Administers the Women's Centers Program, which offers assistance in building networks among women's groups and has initiated projects including the Women's Centers and AIDS Project and the Women's Alcohol and Drug Education Project. Also conducts Sex Equity in Education Program (see separate entry) and the Computer Equity Training Project, which seeks to remediate girls' pattern of "computer avoidance" in the middle years by developing school strategies. Maintains 3000 volume research library of books, pamphlets, and periodicals on such subjects as children, education, and women's issues; also keeps profiles of national and professional women's groups and materials on program planning, organizational development, and fundraising. Maintains speakers' bureau. **Computerized Services:** Mailing list. **Telecommunications Services:** Telephone referral service. **Publications:** *Alliance Quarterly*. Newsletter; includes calendar of events. • *Equal Play*, semiannual. Journal for educators, parents, and others on nonsexist child raising and education of young children. Includes book reviews, research reports, and resource materials. • *Women's Action Alliance Catalog*, periodic. • *Women's Action Almanac*, periodic. • Also publishes magazines, resource material, and books including *Struggling Through Tight Times*, *The Neuter Computer*, *Does Your Daughter Say "No, Thanks" to the Computer*, *Do Your Female Students Say "No, Thanks" to the Computer*, and *Women Helping Women: A State by State Directory of Services.*

★1088★ **Women's Action Coalition (WAC)**
High School for the Humanities
351 W. 18th St.
New York, NY 10011
Phone: (212)967-7711

Description: WAC is "an open alliance of women committed to direct action on issues affecting the rights of all women." WAC "insists on economic parity and representation for all women, and an end to homophobia, racism, religious prejudice, and violence against women." WAC also "insists on every woman's right to health care, child care, and reproductive freedom" and seeks to "launch a visible and remarkable resistance." Organizes and participates in demonstrations and rallies for women's rights. **Membership:** 1500.

★1089★ **Women's Action for Nuclear Disarmament (WAND)**
691 Massachusetts Ave.
Arlington, MA 02174
Phone: (617)643-6740
Marjorie Smith, Contact

Founded: 1980. **Description:** Women's initiative uniting women and men in an effort to halt and reverse the nuclear arms race and redirect spending to meet domestic needs. Objectives are: to raise public awareness about nuclear issues; to support grass roots organizing for educational and political activities across the country; to monitor legislative activities that have an impact on nuclear weapons policy; to organize congressional district lobbying networks to be mobilized before key nuclear weapons votes. Offers workshops, fact sheets, and publications on the issues of nuclear arms and effective organizing and lobbying. Compiles statistics. Maintains library of printed and audiovisual materials on the effects of nuclear war, civil defense, and nuclear weapons. Has established WAND Education Fund (see separate entry). **Members:** 10,000. **Regional Groups:** 35. **Publications:** *WAND Bulletin*, quarterly. • Also publishes *Organizing for Nuclear Disarmament*, *Lobbying Manual*, *Voter Registration Manual*, *Speaker Training Manual*, *Turnabout - WAND Education Fund Report*, and *Grassroots Fundraising Manual*. **Formerly:** Women's Party for Survival.

★1090★ **Women's Africa Committee of the African-American Institute (WACAAI)**
c/o African-Amer. Institute
833 United Nations Plaza
New York, NY 10017
Phone: (212)949-5666
Warren Ruppel, Sec.-Treas.

Founded: 1959. **Description:** Volunteer organization of African and American women. Members seek to become better acquainted through social, educational, and cultural activities.

★1091★ **Women's Aglow Fellowship International (WAFI)**
PO Box 1548
Lynnwood, WA 98046
Phone: (206)775-7282
Fax: (206)778-9615
Jane Hansen, Pres.

Founded: 1967. **Description:** People in approximately 100 countries providing support, education, training, and ministry opportunities to help women "discover their true identity in Jesus Christ through the power of the Holy Spirit." **Members:** 36,000. **Local Groups:** 2600. **Publications:** *Connection*, quarterly. Newsletter. • Also publishes and distributes Bible studies, booklets, and books.

★1092★ **Women's All-Star Association (WASA)**
c/o Pearl Keller
29 Garey Dr.
Chappaqua, NY 10514
Phone: (914)241-0365
Pearl Keller, Exec.Dir.

Founded: 1971. **Description:** Amateur and professional women bowlers aged 17 and older with established minimum averages of 170 for one season in a sanctioned bowling league. Formed to provide tournaments for members and promote women bowlers and their accomplishments. Awards prize money and bestows Rookie and Sportswomen of the Year awards. Maintains hall of fame, biographical archives, and seniors group. Compiles statistics and updates and maintains historical records. **Members:** 440. **Publications:** *Newsletter*, 14/year. • Also publishes press releases and provides a program (with directory) at every tournament site.

★1093★ **Women's Alliance for Theology, Ethics and Ritual (WATER)**
8035 13th St., Stes. 1, 3, & 5
Silver Spring, MD 20910
Phone: (301)589-2509
Fax: (301)589-3150
Mary E. Hunt, Co-Dir.

Founded: 1983. **Description:** Participants include ministers, members of religious communities, and individuals seeking spiritual renewal from a feminist and liberation perspective. Promotes religious education inclusive of women's experiences and viewpoints of spirituality. Offers programs including Women Crossing Worlds, which unites women of the U.S. and Latin America for the purpose of sharing feminist theology and fostering international solidarity. Also offers special liturgies and rituals and counseling. Sponsors seminars and study groups. Provides consulting services; operates speakers' bureau. Maintains 1500 volume library. **Members:** 3000. **Computerized Services:** Mailing list. **Publications:** *Waterwheel*, quarterly. Newsletter. • *Women Crossing Worlds*, periodic. Directory. • Also publishes *Fierce Tenderness - A Feminist Theology of Friendship* and *From Woman-Pain to Woman-Vision - Writings in Feminist Theology* (books) and *Women and the Gospel Traditions - Feminist Celebrations* and *Women of Fire - A Pentecost Event* (liturgies); produces audio- and videotapes.

★1094★ **Women's American Basketball Association (WABA)**
2713 Mt. Moriah
Memphis, TN 38115
Phone: (512)523-7427
Larry Fuhrer, Chm.

Founded: 1984. **Description:** Owners of professional women's basketball teams. Goal is to promote organized women's basketball at the professional level. Seeks to expand women's basketball and to find sponsors for additional teams. Organizes WABA league schedule.

★1095★ **Women's American ORT**
315 Park Ave. S.
New York, NY 10010
Phone: (212)505-7700
Fax: (212)674-3057
Lorraine Blass, Exec.Dir.

Founded: 1927. **Description:** American Jewish women's organization supporting the Organization for Rehabilitation Through Training network of over 800 vocational and technical training installations in 32 countries. Seeks to end anti-Semitism and ensure democracy and pluralism in the U.S; Promotes women's rights and issues. Conducts education courses. Promotes quality public and upgraded vocational education in the U.S. and national literacy campaign. Operates technical institutes throughout the U.S. **Members:** 145,000. **State Groups:** 80. **Local Groups:** 1300. **Publications:** *Women's American ORT Reporter*, quarterly, magazine.

★1096★ **Women's Apparel Chains Associations (WACA)**
c/o Bernard Kyrovac
601 W. 25th St., 12th Fl.
New York, NY 10001
Phone: (212)675-6800
Bernard Kyrovac, Pres.

Founded: 1945. **Description:** Retail chain stores selling women's apparel and discount stores selling women's, men's, and children's apparel, as well as hard good lines, domestics, and other items. Members operate more than 1600 individual stores. **Members:** 35. **State Groups:** 44.

★1097★ **Women's Aquatic Network (WAN)**
PO Box 4993
Washington, DC 20008
Phone: (202)789-1201
Nancy Daves, Chwm.

Founded: 1983. **Description:** Individuals and institutions concerned with fresh water and marine affairs; persons involved in politics and private industries related to aquatic affairs. Focuses on policy issues related to marine and aquatic topics; promotes the importance of women taking an active part in the field. Serves as information clearinghouse. Maintains speakers' bureau. Conducts monthly forum. **Publications:** *Directory*, periodic. • *Women's Aquatic Network–Newsletter*, monthly. Membership activities newsletter covering issues of concern to the marine community. Includes calendar of events, employment opportunities, and legislative updates. • *Directory*, periodic. • Also publishes brochure. **Formerly:** (1984) Women's Network in Aquatic and Marine Affairs.

★1098★ **Women's Army Corps Veterans Association (WACVA)**
PO Box 5577
Ft. McClellan, AL 36205
Phone: (205)820-4019
Martha McBroom, Pres.

Founded: 1947. **Description:** Veterans of the United States Women's Army Corps and Women's Army Auxiliary Corps, women soldiers and officers of the line who are on a tour of active duty with, or have been honorably discharged from, the United States Army, and women who have served honorably or are serving in the United States Reserve or Army National Guard. Seeks "to be of service to all veterans and the communities in which we live and promote justice, tolerance, peace and goodwill." Conducts hospital and community service programs. Supports the Women's Army Corps Museum at Ft. McClellan, AL. Has assisted in the establishment of Women's Army Corps Veterans Redwood Memorial Grove in Big Basin Redwoods State Park, CA. Raises funds for Women's Memorial in Washington, DC. Presents annual Edith Nourse Rogers Scholarship at Boston University. Bestows four Pallas Athene Awards to outstanding ROTC cadets. Conducts charitable projects. **Members:** 4000. **Local Groups:** 56. **Publications:** *The Channel*, 10/year. Membership activities newsletter; includes directory listing national and chapter officers. • *The Yearbook*. Directory.

★1099★ **Women's Association for the Defense of Four Freedoms for Ukraine (WADFFU)**
136 2nd Ave.
New York, NY 10003
Phone: (716)882-2010
Dasha Procyk, Pres.

Founded: 1967. **Description:** American women of Ukrainian descent whose objectives are: to promote human and national rights in the Ukraine; to disseminate information and educate people on the plight of Ukrainians; to support efforts of Ukrainians to secure basic rights of freedom of speech, freedom of conscience, freedom from fear, and freedom from want. Encourages participation in legislative activities denouncing repression and supporting full implementation of the Helsinki Final Act, Human Rights Provision. Holds seminars; sponsors competitions and bestows awards; conducts charitable program. **Regional Groups:** 4. **State Groups:** 25. **Local Groups:** 4. **Publications:** *Between Death and Life*, *Ten Years of Work* (compilation of WASFFU activities), and *Poetry of Wasyl Stus*; also contributes articles to Ukrainian publications.

★1100★ **Women's Auxiliary to the Military Order of the Cootie (WAMOC)**
PO Box 809
Bryan, OH 43506
Phone: (419)636-3686
Patricia Fritch, Treas.

Founded: 1961. **Description:** Women who are members of the Ladies Auxiliary to the Veterans of Foreign Wars of the U.S.A. Activities include: volunteer work in VA hospitals and local hospitals, rest homes, and mental institutions; scholarship program for education of children from VFW National Home. **Members:** 17,022. **State Groups:** 40. **Local Groups:** 595. **Publications:** *Bulletin*, monthly. • *General Orders*, monthly. Published within *Cootie Courier*.

★1101★ **Women's Basketball Coaches Association (WBCA)**
1687 Tullie Circle, Ste. 127
Atlanta, GA 30329
Phone: (404)321-2922
Fax: (404)248-0451
Betty Jaynes, Exec.Dir.

Founded: 1981. **Description:** Head basketball coaches, assistants, athletic directors, officials, media personnel, organizations lending financial support to the association, and others interested in women's basketball. Purposes are to foster amateur sports competitions at both national and international levels, and to promote a reputable image of women's basketball by developing the game. Works to refine rules, regulations, and procedures that will enhance athletic leadership, sportsmanship, and women's participation in basketball. Encourages education and development of members and players; promotes health and welfare of participants in the sport. Sponsors eight national clinics in the fall and a Coaching Certification Program. Bestows All-America, Coach of the Year, Player of the Year, and Service awards. **Members:** 3000. **Computerized Services:** Mailing labels. **Publications:** *Backboard Bulletin*, bimonthly. • *Fast Break Alert*, monthly. • Also publishes *Coaching Women's Basketball* and *At the Buzzer*.

★1102★ **Women's Business Development Center**
205 Gurley Hall
Russell Sage College
Troy, NY 12180
Phone: (518)270-2302
Fax: (518)271-4545
Ruth Leverett, Chair, Board of Directors

Description: The Center acts as a catalyst for women to recognize and increase their business skills and ownership and to influence the business environment by providing access to a variety of resources.

★1103★ **Women's Campaign Fund (WCF)**
1601 Connecticut Ave. NW, Ste. 800
Washington, DC 20009
Phone: (202)234-3700
Jane Danowitz, Exec.Dir.

Founded: 1974. **Description:** Contributors to the fund. Purpose is to foster and support the election of qualified, progressive women to public offices. To achieve this aim, the WCF raises funds; makes direct cash contributions to the campaigns of endorsed candidates; provides campaign counsel and services (media, field organization, and polling) to candidates; recruits and develops progressive candidates; stimulates support for WCF-endorsed candidates by other groups and individuals; promotes public awareness of the need for more women in public office. **Members:** 23,000.

★1104★ **Women's Campaign Fund (WCF)**
Women's Campaign Research Fund (WCRF)
1601 Connecticut Ave. NW, Ste. 800
Washington, DC 20009
Phone: (202)462-3700
Fax: (202)462-3051
Pat Reuss, President

Description: The organization is dedicated to providing leadership and political skills to women running for political office by sponsoring Leadership 2000, leadership training seminars for women politicians at state and national levels.

★1105★ **Women's Caucus for Art (WCA)**
Moore Coll. of Art
20th The Parkway
Philadelphia, PA 19103
Phone: (215)854-0922
Essie Karp, Admin.

Founded: 1972. **Description:** Professional women in visual art fields: artists, critics, art historians, museum and gallery professionals, arts administrators, educators and students, and collectors of art. Objectives are to: increase recognition for contemporary and historical achievements of women in art; ensure equal opportunity for employment, art commissions, and research grants; encourage professionalism and shared information among women in art; stimulate and publicize research and publications on women in the visual arts. Conducts workshops, periodic affirmative action research, and statistical surveys. Presents annual honor awards to senior women in the visual arts. **Members:** 3500. **State Groups:** 35. **Publications:** *Chapter Newsletter*, periodic. • *WCA Honor Awards: Honor Awards for Outstanding Achievement in the Visual Arts*, annual. Catalog containing biographies of women artists and their works honored at the caucus' national conference. • *WCA National Directory*, biennial. Lists WCA membership. • *Women's Caucus for Art—National Update*, quarterly. Newsletter covering national and chapter news. Includes calendar of events and lists employment opportunities and exhibitions. • Also publishes resource books, exhibition catalogs, syllabi, and bibliographies. **Formerly:** (1974) Women's Caucus of the College Art Association.

★1106★ **Women's Caucus of the Endocrine Society (WE)**
University of Maryland School of Medicine
Department of Physiology
655 W. Baltimore St.
Baltimore, MD 21201
Phone: (301)328-3851
Phyllis Wise, Sec.-Treas.

Founded: 1975. **Description:** To promote professional advancement of women and younger members of the Endocrine Society. Maintains biographical archives; compiles statistics; conducts seminars and workshops. **Members:** 850. **Publications:** *Letter to Membership*, periodic.

★1107★ **Women's Caucus for the Modern Languages (WCML)**
c/o Emily Toth
Louisiana State University
Department of English - Women's Studies
Baton Rouge, LA 70803
Emily Toth, Contact

Founded: 1970. **Description:** Women working or studying in the modern languages, faculty, administrators, and graduate students. Seeks to improve the status of women in the profession. Disseminates information, organizes sessions, and workshops. **Members:** 700. **Regional Groups:** 7. **Publications:** *Women's Caucus for the Modern Languages—Concerns*, 3/year. Newsletter concerned with women's issues in the field of modern language scholarship. Includes listings of recent publications and films, regional reports, and research in progress.

★1108★ **Women's Caucus for Political Science (WCPS)**
c/o Karen O'Connor
Emory University
Department of Political Science
Atlanta, GA 30322
Phone: (404)727-6572
Fax: (404)874-6925
Karen O'Connor, Pres.

Founded: 1969. **Description:** Women professionally trained in political science. Purposes are to: upgrade the status of women in the profession of political science; promote equal opportunities for women political scientists for graduate admission, financial assistance in such schools, and in employment, promotion, and tenure. Advances candidates for consideration for APSA offices and committees; conducts specialized workshops and a program about women and politics at fall meeting. Bestows awards. **Members:** 500. **Regional Groups:** 5. **Publications:** *WCPS Quarterly*. Newsletter; includes information about the association and employment opportunities. • *Women's Caucus for Political Science Membership Directory*, biennial. Lists names, addresses, job title, and field of study.

★1109★ **Women's Caucus: Religious Studies**
c/o Boston Theological Institute
210 Herrick Rd.
Andover, MA 01810
Phone: (617)527-4880

Founded: 1971. **Description:** Women and institutions involved in academic religion. Aims to: facilitate the exchange of information among women in the field; promote research and teaching opportunities; encourage visibility and audibility of professional women. Offers speakers' bureau and provides placement information; maintains biographical archives. Conducts career development workshops. Is planning research program on status and professional development; hopes to procure grant for the study, placement, and training of women in religious studies. **Members:** 500. **Publications:** *Newsletter*, periodic. • *Placement News*, periodic. • *Registry of Women in Religious Studies*, biennial.

★1110★ **Women's Classical Caucus (WCC)**
c/o Prof. Barbara McManus
5 Chester Dr.
Rye, NY 10580
Phone: (914)698-5798
Prof. Barbara McManus, Treas.

Founded: 1972. **Description:** Ancient historians, archaeologists, art historians, and classicists. Works to support the professional status of women in the classics and related fields, and facilitates research on women in the areas of archaeology, ancient history, and ancient literature. Maintains speakers' bureau and editorial services. Makes available outlines for courses on Women in Antiquity and syllabi for other courses. **Members:** 200. **Computerized Services:** Mailing list. **Publications:** *Newsletter*, 2/year.

★1111★ **Women's College Coalition (WCC)**
1090 Vermont Ave. NW, 3rd Fl.
Washington, DC 20005
Phone: (202)842-3600
Jadwiga S. Sebrechts, Dir.

Founded: 1972. **Description:** Women's colleges concerned with their roles in supporting the intellectual, professional, and personal development of women. Raises public awareness of women's colleges and the educational needs of women. Disseminates information to the press, educational researchers, women's colleges, and the general public. Conducts research on women's colleges. **Members:** 71. **Publications:** *A Profile of Women's College Presidents, A Study of the Learning Environment at Women's Colleges, Alumnae Giving at Women's Colleges: A Ten year Study, '67/'77: A Profile of Recent Women's College Graduates, Enrollment Trends in Women's Colleges, The Case for Women's Colleges: A Review of the Literature*, and *Expanding Options: A Profile of Older Graduates of Women's Colleges*.

★1112★ **Women's Computer Literacy Center (WCLC)**
PO Box 68
Jenner, CA 95450
Phone: (707)632-5763
Deborah Brecher, Dir.

Founded: 1982. **Description:** Offers intensive two-day courses in computer literacy exclusively to women. Project is based upon a nonlinear teaching approach that emphasizes a holistic understanding of computer operations. Group believes that women's traditional computer phobia is best overcome when they fully understand all components of computer machinery and operation. Classes are held in New York, San Francisco, CA, Durham, NC, Portland, OR, and Denver, CO. Offers scholarships. **Publications:** *Women's Computer Literacy Handbook*. **Formerly:** (1988) Women's Computer Literacy Project.

★1113★ **Women's Council on Energy and the Environment (WCEE)**
PO Box 33211
Washington, DC 20033
Phone: (202)822-6755
Fax: (202)328-5002
Lori Wainright, Pres.

Founded: 1981. **Description:** Individuals, primarily women, who work for the federal government, consulting firms, private industry, and the environmental community and are involved in educating the public about national policy issues. Works to facilitate networking among members on public issues, particularly those concerning energy and the environment. Promotes the professional development of women interested in energy and environmental issues. Advocates informed decision-making on such issues by business and government officials. Maintains speakers' bureau. Sponsors monthly public programs that include roundtable and panel discussions and lectures. **Members:** 200. **Publications:** *Membership Directory*, annual. • *WCEE Newsletter*, monthly.

★1114★ **Women's Council of Realtors of the National Association of Realtors (WCR)**
430 N. Michigan Ave.
Chicago, IL 60611
Phone: (312)329-8483
Fax: (313)329-3290
Catherine M. Collins, Exec.V.Pres.

Founded: 1938. **Description:** Women real estate brokers and salespeople. Provides opportunity for women in real estate to participate at local, state, and national levels. Makes available programs and systems for personal and career growth. Encourages increased productivity, financial security, and the development of leadership skills among members. Offers courses in leadership training, and referral and relocation business. Maintains speakers' bureau and resource bank. **Members:** 18,000. **Regional Groups:** 12. **State Groups:** 38. **Local Groups:** 325. **Publications:** *Women's Council of Realtors of the National Association of Realtors—Communique*, 10/year. Newsletter. • *Women's Council on Realtors of the National Association of Realtors—Referral Roster*, annual. Membership directory.

★1115★ **Women's Distance Committee (WDC)**
306 River Isle Way
Sacramento, CA 95831
Phone: (916)392-5111
Karen Hunsaker, Chwm.

Founded: 1977. **Description:** Women and men who promote distance running for women. Encourages women's running nationally and internationally, for exercise and in preparation for the Olympics. Sponsors seminars and clinics at races or club meetings. Compiles statistics. **Members:** 10. **Publications:** *Running Women - The First Steps* (training brochure for beginning women runners). **Formerly:** Women's Olympic Distance Committee.

★1116★ **Women's Division of the Board of Global Ministries of the United Methodist Church**
475 Riverside Dr., Rm. 1504
New York, NY 10115
Phone: (212)870-3752
Fax: (212)870-3736
Joyce D. Sohl, Exec. Officer

Founded: 1940. **Description:** Women members of the United Methodist Church united to promote spiritual growth and leadership development among women worldwide. Makes available financial support to ministries and social programs benefitting women. **Members:** 1,200,000. **Publications:** *Response*, monthly. Magazine.

★1117★ **Women's Drug Research Project (WDR)**
c/o Beth G. Reed
Univ. of Michigan
School of Social Work
1065 Frieze Bldg.
Ann Arbor, MI 48109-1285
Phone: (313)763-5958
Beth G. Reed, Coordinator

Founded: 1973. **Description:** Has investigated differences in the needs and problems of men and women entering drug abuse treatment programs. Studied two outpatient methadone programs and two residential therapeutic communities, which were established to gather new information about women addicts, their needs, and possible methods for meeting those needs. Also collected data from 20 programs in five cities for studies on treatment organization and psychosocial characteristics of addicts.

★1118★ **Women's Economic Rights Project (WERP)**
c/o NOW Legal Defense and Educ. Fund
99 Hudson St., 12th Fl.
New York, NY 10013
Phone: (212)925-6635
Fax: (212)226-1066
Allison Weatherfield, Legal Dir.

Description: A project of the NOW Legal Defense and Education Fund (see separate entry) Legal Program. Participants include feminist attorneys involved in employment litigation or constitutional law. Seeks to aid women in attaining economic equality with men. Conducts public educational programs. **Publications:** Develops publications on sex discrimination and the legal rights of women.

★1119★ **Women's Economic RoundTable (WERT)**
866 United Nations Plaza, Ste. 4052
New York, NY 10017
Phone: (212)759-4360
Fax: (212)666-1625
Dr. Amelia Augustus, Pres.

Founded: 1978. **Description:** Business women and men who question economic policymakers in a public forum; economists, business executives, and unionists. To consolidate the voice of women in the formation of national economic policy and decisions. Conducts seminars; sponsors round tables to clarify national economic issues and make economic policy leaders accessible to members and the public; examines national and international economic issues; acts as resource center for the media and business and other institutions seeking experts and executives. Educates women on how to maintain control over the economic power they hold and stresses the importance of doing so. Bestows Maria and Sidney E. Rolfe Award to individual or group educating the public about business and economics or affecting economic and business policy. **Members:** 500.

★1120★ **Women's Equity Action League (WEAL)**
1250 I St., NW, Ste. 305
Washington, DC 20005
Phone: (202)898-1588
Mary L. McCain, Exec.Dir.
Founded: 1968. **Description:** To secure legal and economic rights for women through a program of research, public education, litigation, and legislative advocacy. Areas of interest include insurance, pensions, discrimination in employment and education, access to fellowship and training opportunities, women and the military, civil rights and affirmative action enforcement, and child care. Special projects include an intern program, which offers structured work experiences in the Washington, DC office for students, retired persons, job hunters, career changers, and others, and a national clearinghouse of information on women and the military. Bestows Elizabeth Boyer Award. **Publications:** *WEAL Informed*, periodic. Legislative alert. • *WEAL Washington Report/WEAL Report*, bimonthly. Newsletters focusing on issues of concern to women, including current legislation, Supreme Court decisions, and executive branch actions. Includes calendar of events and legislative reports. • Also publishes *Better Late Than Never: Financial Aid for Older Women*, fact sheets, reports, and action kits.

★1121★ **Women's Equity Program (WEP)**
Nelson House
University of Massachusetts
Amherst, MA 01003
Phone: (413)545-1558
Kathryn Lee Girard, Co-Dir.
Founded: 1976. **Description:** Nonmembership organization. To identify educational and economic equity issues of state, regional, and national importance and scope; to develop and disseminate model programs addressing those equities. Conducts research on women's centers, women's employment and small business development, and teacher preparation. Compiles statistics. Sponsored National Women's Centers Training Project that provided training to college and university women's centers in order to make them more effective in developing and gaining administrative and budgetary support. Coordinated Project S.E.E.D., a study of women's lives, particularly in the areas of underemployment and underutilization and Project TEAM, that provided non-sexist and non-racist teacher-training in Massachusetts. Operates Equity Information Network that provides information on legislation affecting educational and economic equity for women. Conducts Something Ventured, Something Gained, a training program in risk-taking for women business owners. Publishes Developing and Negotiating Budgets for Women's Programs, Developing Women's Programs, and To Make a Difference: A Guide to Working with Feminist Organizations (manuals); also publishes reports, research summaries, and working papers on women and employment. **Regional Groups:** 4.

★1122★ **Women's Fashion Fabrics Association**
PO Box 468, Midtown Station
New York, NY 10018
Phone: (212)947-4866
Amy S. Arrow, Pres.
Founded: 1959. **Description:** Women who are involved in the textile (fashion fabrics) or related areas united to serve as a communication center for the industry. Presents monthly educational programs. Sponsors charitable program; maintains speakers bureau and placement service. Bestows awards. **Members:** 150. **Publications:** (1) Sew What (newsletter), 6/year; (2) Directory, annual.

★1123★ **Women's Health Work Group (WHWG)**
Health Policy Advisory Center
17 Murray St.
New York, NY 10007

★1124★ **Women's History Alliance**
c/o Nancy Huppertz
4000 SW Griffith, No. 202
Beaverton, OR 97005

★1125★ **Women's History Network (WHN)**
7738 Bell Rd.
Windsor, CA 95492
Phone: (707)838-6000
Fax: (707)838-0478
Mary Ruthsdotter, Co-Dir.
Founded: 1983. **Description:** A project of the National Women's History Project (see separate entry). Coordinates the recognition and celebration of the contributions of women in U.S. history. Furnishes information, materials, referrals, technical assistance, and support services to aid those who seek to recognize and promote women's achievements and possibilities. Develops, discovers, and collects ideas and resources for women's history activities for educators, historians, community organizers, workplace activists, and unaffiliated individuals. Maintains a women's history performers bureau and biographical archives. **Members:** 500. **Computerized Services:** Networking services. **Publications:** Network News, quarterly. Newsletter. • Network Participant Directory, semiannual.

★1126★ **Women's Home and Overseas Missionary Society**
c/o Department of Overseas Missions AME, Zion Church
475 Riverside Dr., Rm. 1910
New York, NY
Phone: (212)870-2952
Mrs. Alcestis Coleman, Pres.
Founded: 1880. **Description:** Promotes growth in the knowledge of God and in Christian personhood. **Publications:** Missionary Seer.

★1127★ **Women's Independent Film Exchange (WIFE)**
c/o Cecile Starr
50 W. 96th St.
New York, NY 10025
Phone: (212)749-1250
Cecile Starr, Dir.
Founded: 1977. **Description:** Women who work on an independent or freelance basis in filmmaking and film-related activities including teaching, writing, and distribution. Promotes recognition of women's contributions to film directing and increased knowledge of women who have been denied creative credit for their films. Studies directors of commercial, independent, and educational films. Conducts research project on directors and director-producers of films made between 1910 and 1970; compiles materials from film studios, libraries, personal information files, locally initiated and funded research programs, and other sources; tapes and transcribes interviews with pioneer women directors and people who have personal knowledge of these women. Disseminates profiles of pioneer women filmmakers. Sponsors screenings in libraries, schools, and museums. Maintains biographical archives. Plans to establish a study center depository for the research data and issue book on results of research program. **Members:** 10.

★1128★ **Women's Independent Label Distribution Network (WILD)**
c/o Terry Grant
1712 E. Michigan Ave.
Lansing, MI 48912
Phone: (517)484-1712
Terry Grant, Exec. Officer
Founded: 1979. **Description:** Independent record distributors affiliated with the women's music industry. Disseminates information to improve distribution and women's business abilities. Holds annual roundtables and seminars on sales, bookkeeping, marketing, advertising, time management, cost analysis, and promotion. **Members:** 8. **Publications:** Newsletter, monthly. • Also publishes brochure.

★1129★ **Women's Information Bank (WIB)**
3918 W St. NW
Washington, DC 20007
Phone: (202)338-8163
Fax: (202)337-9091
Barbara Sylvester, Pres.
Founded: 1970. **Description:** Informal network of individuals who aid women seeking business partners and start-up capital, freelance work opportunities, and/or computer training and services. Operates Global Women Program, which helps women travelers locate individuals with similar interests in several American cities. Maintains library and placement services; conducts children's programs. **Computerized Services:** Data base. **Formerly:** (1988) Women's Travelers Center and Information Bank.

★1130★ **Women's Information Exchange (WIE)**
PO Box 68
Jenner, CA 95450
Phone: (707)632-5763
Fax: (707)632-5589
Jill Lippitt, Exec. Officer
Founded: 1980. **Description:** Feminist women computer specialists who believe that computer technology may be used to support the efforts of women and women's organizations nationwide. Promotes networking and communication between women and women's organizations. Provides speakers on such topics as gender-based learning differences, office automation, and women and technology. **Computerized Services:** Data base on women and women's service providers organized into categories such as health centers, women's centers, women's studies programs, and newspapers; data is available to organizations on peel-and-stick labels through the National Women's Mailing List (see separate entry).

★1131★ Women's Institute (WI)
5225 Pooks Hill Rd., Ste. 1718-N
Bethesda, MD 20814
Phone: (301)530-9192
Rita Z. Johnston, Pres.

Founded: 1975. **Description:** Serves as a vehicle for the development and presentation of programs on special problems and major issues of concern to women. Provides an educational and political forum for women's roles in economic, family, political and social life on a local, national, and international level. Conducts research. Presents the Myra E. Barrer Journalism Award for excellence and commitment to feminist journalism to a senior or graduate students at American University in Washington, DC. Maintains library. **Publications:** *Winds of Change: Korean Women in America, Convention on the Elimination of All Forms of Discrimination Against Women,* and *United Nations Decade for Women Plans of Action* (books).

★1132★ Women's Institute for Freedom of the Press
3306 Ross Pl. NW
Washington, DC 20008
Phone: (202)966-7783
Martha Leslie Allen, Director

Description: Conducts research and publishes documents directed toward "radical restructuring of the world's communication systems."

★1133★ Women's Interart Center (WIC)
c/o Margot Lewitin
549 W. 52nd St.
New York, NY 10019
Phone: (212)246-1050
Margot Lewitin, Artistic Dir.

Founded: 1969. **Description:** Professional women artists (painters, sculptors, actors, poets, photographers, filmmakers, video artists, writers, ceramists, and serigraphers). Offers opportunities for members to practice their crafts or explore new ones; exchange ideas; meet and work with other artists. Encourages members to explore new areas of expertise. Activities include film and video festival, panels, lectures, demonstrations, and workshops. Facilities include a theatre and a gallery which house events such as poetry readings, theatrical performances, painting, sculpture and photography exhibitions, and seminars and lectures. Maintains video documentary archives of women visual artists and a Fine Arts Museum. **Members:** 250. **Publications:** *Interart News,* quarterly.

★1134★ Women's International Bowling Congress (WIBC)
5301 S. 76th St.
Greendale, WI 53129-1191
Phone: (414)421-9000
Fax: (414)421-4420
Sandra Shirk, Chief Operat. Off.

Founded: 1916. **Description:** Women bowlers of American tenpins. Sanctions bowling for women and associations in 20 countries. Provides uniform qualifications, rules, and regulations to govern WIBC sanctioned teams, leagues, and tournaments. Conducts periodic leadership training seminars and lane inspectors' workshops; sponsors annual championship, Queens, and Queens Pro Am tournaments; bestows awards. Maintains hall of fame, museum, and biographical archives; compiles statistics. Supports BVL Fund to aid persons in Veterans Administration hospitals. Cosponsors Young American Bowling Alliance as well as collegiate and senior league programs and National Senior and National Mixed Tournaments. **Members:** 2,800,000. **State Groups:** 54. **Local Groups:** 2784. **Leagues:** 119,612. **Computerized Services:** Mailing lists. **Publications:** *Annual Report.* • *Media Guide,* annual. • *WIBC News,* monthly. Includes tournament results and calendar of events. • *WIBC Playing Rules and Bylaws Book,* annual. • *Woman Bowler Magazine,* 8/year. • Also publishes *Tournament Program, Bowlers Guide,* instruction and record brochure, handbooks, pamphlets, and printed forms. **Formerly:** (1925) Women's National Bowling Association.

★1135★ Women's International League for Peace and Freedom (WILPF)
U.S. Section
1213 Race St.
Philadelphia, PA 19107-1691
Phone: (215)563-7110
Fax: (215)864-2022
Mary Zepernick, Pres.

Founded: 1915. **Description:** Women working, through nonviolent means, to: eliminate U.S. economic and military intervention abroad, discrimination on any basis, and governmental surveillance and repression; establish total universal disarmament and unconditional amnesty for war resisters; improve and ensure civil rights; promote peace education in schools and communities; establish "an economy that puts people before profits." Bestows annual Jane Addams Children's Book Award for book that best promotes ideals of international friendship and understanding. Sponsors committee of educators and parents studying ways to teach peaceful attitudes in social relationships. Conducts research and seminar/training programs. U.S. section is one of 28 sections of the Women's International League for Peace and Freedom (see separate entry) in Geneva, Switzerland. **Members:** 15,000. **Regional Groups:** 4. **State Groups:** 33. **Local Groups:** 110. **Telecommunications Services:** Electronic mail, PEACENET: WILPFNATL and WILPFLEGIS. **Publications:** *Pax et Libertas,* quarterly. International newsletter. • *Peace and Freedom,* bimonthly. Journal containing news of the organization's activities. Includes book reviews and legislative news. • *Program and Legislative Action,* bimonthly. Newsletter. • Has also published *The Women's Budget* and *Women for All Seasons* (books). **Formerly:** (1919) Women's Peace Party.

★1136★ Women's International Motorcycle Association (WIMA)
360 E. Main St.
Waterloo, NY 13165
Phone: (315)539-8280
Louise Scherbyn, Pres.

Founded: 1950. **Description:** Women interested in international motorcycle competition. Promotes the sport of motorcycle racing among women. Conducts periodic competitions; bestows awards; compiles statistics. **Members:** 1200. **Regional Groups:** 6. **Publications:** *WIMA News,* quarterly. Newsletter.

★1137★ Women's International Network (WIN)
187 Grant St.
Lexington, MA 02173
Phone: (617)862-9431
Fax: (617)862-9431
Fran P. Hosken, Coordinator/Editor

Founded: 1975. **Description:** Goal is to encourage cooperation and communication between women of all backgrounds, beliefs, nationalities, and age groups through the compilation and dissemination of information on women's development. Participants voluntarily contribute news and information on women and health, environment, media, violence, female genital mutilation, and United Nations events of concern to women. The Network's Women and International Affairs Clearinghouse surveys career opportunities for women interested in working in international and development agencies. Conducts research on women's health and on women's development throughout the world. Maintains library of women's publications. **Publications:** *WIN News,* quarterly. Journal providing information on women and women's groups worldwide. • Has also published *Hosken Report: Genital and Sexual Mutilations of Females, Action Guide,* and *The Childbirth Picture Book* (series in Arabic, English, French, and Spanish), including flip charts and color slides.

★1138★ Women's International Professional Tennis Council (WIPTC)
100 Park Ave., 2nd Fl.
New York, NY 10017
Phone: (212)878-2250
Jane G. Brown, Mng.Dir.

Founded: 1975. **Description:** Goal is to sanction, administer, and promote women's professional tennis throughout the world. Sponsors tournaments worldwide. **Members:** 27. **Telecommunications Services:** Telex, 422609. **Publications:** *Virginia Slims World Championship Series Rules and Regulations.*

★1139★ Women's International Public Health Network (WIPHN)
7100 Oak Forest Ln.
Bethesda, MD 20817
Phone: (301)469-9210
Naomi Baumslag, National Pres.

Founded: 1986. **Description:** The Network is an umbrella organization of women's groups in health-related areas that seeks to improve the nutrition, health, and status of women worldwide. Offers women the opportunity to publish information in its newsletter, locate resources, and write articles which may be forbidden in their own countries; participates in women's health meetings; and supports grassroots women's health projects with funds and medical equipment. **Publications:** *WIPHN News,* 2/year.

★1140★ Women's International Resource Exchange (WIRE)
475 Riverside Dr., Rm. 570
New York, NY 10115
Phone: (212)870-2783
Sybil Wong, Admin.

Founded: 1981. **Description:** Collective whose objectives are to: confront sexism, racism, and classism; develop an understanding and global perspective of women's struggles and gains; provide low-cost information on the status of Third World women. **Publications:** Catalogue and information packets such as *Resistance,*

War and Liberation: Women of Southern Africa, Women and War in El Salvador, We Continue Forever: Sorrow and Strength of Guatemalan Women, Nicaragua Women: Unlearning the Alphabet of Submission, and *Voices of Women: Poetry by and about Third World Women.*

★1141★ **Women's International Surfing Association (WISA)**
30202 Silver Spur Rd.
PO Box 512
San Juan Capistrano, CA 92693
Phone: (714)493-2591
Mary Lou Drummy, Pres.
Founded: 1975. **Description:** Promotes the sport of surfing and the development of quality competition for amateur and professional women surfers of all ages. Sponsors surfing instructionals; presents slide and movie shows for school groups; conducts public relations work; supports beach preservation efforts; sponsors competitions. **Members:** 95. **Publications:** *Membership List*, semiannual. • *Women in Waves*, semiannual.

★1142★ **Women's Issues, Status, and Education (WISE)**
c/o Ellen Ironside
Meredith Coll.
Raleigh, NC 27607
Phone: (919)829-8353
Fax: (919)829-2828
Ellen Ironside, Dir.
Founded: 1983. **Description:** Women members of the American Association for Adult and Continuing Education. Purposes are: to plan and implement activities that will enhance opportunities for women in adult education; to increase channels of communication within the organization, with appropriate subdivisions of the parent organization and with other organizations; to identify needs and concerns of women in the field. Conducts research and reports activities on the status of women in adult education. **Members:** 100. **Publications:** *Minutes of Meeting*, annual. • *Newsletter*, 1-2/year.

★1143★ **Women's Jazz Festival (WJFI)**
PO Box 22321
Kansas City, MO 64113
Phone: (913)631-9511
Julie Hanson, Pres.
Founded: 1977. **Description:** Objectives are to create a market for the increasing number of female jazz artists and to stimulate a general interest in jazz. Serves as clearinghouse for individuals interested in jazzwomen and their aspirations, accomplishments, and availability. Conducts regular and continuous projects which include in-school clinics/workshops, sponsorship of Jazz Month, jam sessions for beginning and student jazz musicians, and lecture/film series. Bestows awards; sponsors charitable programs, competitions, and children's services. Maintains biographical archives. **Publications:** *Festival Program*, annual. • *Newsletter*, semiannual.

★1144★ **Women's Jewelry Association (WJA)**
11 2nd Ave.
New Hyde Park, NY 11040
Phone: (516)326-1369
Tina Segal, Pres.
Founded: 1983. **Description:** Women involved in jewelry design, manufacture, retail, and advertising; men may join as associate members. Aims to: enhance the status of women in the jewelry industry; make known the contribution of women to the industry; provide a network for women involved with fine jewelry. Bestows awards and scholarships; maintains hall of fame; offers placement services. **Members:** 700. **Computerized Services:** Membership information. **Publications:** *Jewelry Association Newsletter*, semiannual.

★1145★ **Women's Law Fund (WLF)**
c/o Nancy Krammer
57 E. Washington St.
Chagrin Falls, OH 44022
Phone: (216)247-6167
Nancy Krammer, Exec. Officer
Founded: 1972. **Description:** Purpose is to eradicate sex-based discrimination in education, employment, government benefits, and housing by providing legal assistance to individuals who have administrative charges pending before state and federal governmental agencies. Provides representation in court proceedings. Conducts lectures, speeches, and conferences; provides technical assistance to professionals and others; promotes full participation of women in American life by securing and protecting their Constitutional rights.

★1146★ **Women's Law Project (WLP)**
125 S. Ninth St., Ste. 401
Philadelphia, PA 19107
Phone: (215)928-9801
Fax: (215)928-9848
Linda Wharton, Acting Exec.Dir.
Founded: 1974. **Description:** Nonprofit feminist law firm working to challenge sex discrimination in the law and in legal and social institutions through litigation, public education, research and writing, representation of women's groups, and individual counseling. Conducts test case and class action litigation in the areas of family law, education, employment, prison reform, reproductive rights, and sex-based insurance rates. Maintains speakers' bureau. **Telecommunications Services:** Telephone counseling and referral services on women's legal rights concerns and community education. **Publications:** *Child Support Handbook: How You Can Obtain Child Support Orders in Philadelphia, Women's Rights and the Law,* and *Rights and Wrongs.*

★1147★ **Women's Law and Public Policy Fellowship Program (WLPPFP)**
600 New Jersey Ave., NW, Ste. 334
Washington, DC 20001
Phone: (202)662-9640
Susan Deller Ross, Director
Founded: 1983. **Description:** The Program offers law graduates an opportunity to work for a year in Washington, DC public interest organizations on women's legal and policy issues. Fellows have been placed in 33 organizations, including women's rights groups, civil rights groups, Congressional offices, governmental agencies, and the Georgetown University Law Center Sex Discrimination Clinic. Awards the Rita Charmatz Davidson Fellowship every other year to fund work specifically focused on poor women's legal issues.

★1148★ **Women's League for Conservative Judaism (WLCJ)**
48 E. 74th St.
New York, NY 10021
Phone: (212)628-1600
Fax: (212)772-3507
Bernice Balter, Exec.Dir.
Founded: 1918. **Description:** Composed of Sisterhoods affiliated with the Conservative movement, dedicated to the perpetuation of traditional Judaism and the translation of its ideals into practice. Purposes are: to guide its affiliates in local, national, and international activities, making them aware of their civic responsibilities; to foster Jewish education through study courses, Jewish Family Living Institutes and through the establishment of Synagogue and Sisterhood libraries. Supports Torah Fund - Residence Halls Project for the Jewish Theological Seminary. **Members:** 200,000. **Regional Groups:** 28. **Local Groups:** 750. **Publications:** *Ba' Olam*, bimonthly. Newsletter providing news and commentary on world affairs. • *Biennial Report.* • *Calendar Diary*, annual. Lists Hebrew and English dates and holidays. Includes prayers and readings. • *Outlook*, quarterly. Magazine for contemporary Jewish families covering programs of social action, health, education, history and culture, and Jewish lifestyles. • Also publishes *Welcome to the World: A Jewish Baby's Record Book, Hebrew Word Guide - Building Your Vocabulary, Count Your Blessings, A Doorway to Understanding, Quantity Kosher Cooking* and other books booklets, manuals, and catalogs; makes available teaching cassettes. **Formerly:** (1947) Women's League of the United Synagogue of America; (1973) National Women's League of the United Synagogue of America.

★1149★ **Women's League for Israel (WLI)**
160 E 56th St.
New York, NY 10022
Phone: (212)838-1997
Trudy Miner, Pres.
Founded: 1928. **Description:** Women interested in the redevelopment of Israel and in supporting educational, vocational, and social service programs for residents and newcomers. Maintains homes in Haifa, Jerusalem, Tel Aviv, and Nathanya, Israel and a vocational and rehabilitation center. Built women's dormitory, cafeteria, and student center at Hebrew University in Jerusalem, Israel, and two dormitories for women on Mount Scopus. Presents annual Freedom Cup Award. **Members:** 5000. **Local Groups:** 45. **Publications:** *Bulletin*, quarterly. • *Women's League for Israel—Newsletter*, 3/year. **Formerly:** Women's League for Palestine.

★1150★ **Women's Legal Defense Fund (WLDF)**
2000 P St. NW, No. 400
Washington, DC 20036
Phone: (202)887-0364
Fax: (202)861-0691
Judith Lichtman, Pres.
Founded: 1971. **Description:** Attorneys, paralegals, administrators, publicists, and secretaries. Purpose is to secure equal rights for women

through litigation, advocacy and monitoring, legal counseling and information, and public education. Works for women's rights in family law, employment, education, and other areas. Maintains speakers' bureau. **Members:** 1800. **Telecommunications Services:** Telephone referral services. **Publications:** *WLDF News*, semiannual. Newsletter reporting on women's legal rights in the areas of employment and family law, including Supreme Court decisions and legislative developments; also covers organization activities. • Also publishes handbooks, manuals, and brochures on discrimination in employment, domestic relations law, and others.

★1151★ Women's Media Project (WMP)
1333 H St., NW, 11th Fl.
Washington, DC 20005
Phone: (202)682-0940
Rosanna Landis, Contact

Founded: 1979. **Description:** A project of the NOW Legal Defense and Education Fund. Feminist activists united to eliminate sex role stereotyping of women and men in the media and to increase the participation of women and minorities in broadcasting. Purposes are to: conduct public education campaigns with up-to-date information on issues that affect women; guide individuals and groups in developing effective dialogues with local broadcasters and publishers through community action campaigns; monitor compliance with equal employment legislation in the communications industry; encourage development and distribution of quality television and radio programming that offers realistic and contemporary images of women. Identifies programming promoting equality between women and men. Conducts research in broadcast employment. **Publications:** *Women's Media Campaign Workbook*, annual. • Also publishes research reports. **Formerly:** (1987) Media Project.

★1152★ Women's Missionary Council of the Christian Methodist Episcopal Church (WMCCMEC)
623 San Fernando Ave.
Berkeley, CA 94707
Dr. Sylvia Faulk, Pres.

Founded: 1918. **Description:** Women members of the Christian Methodist Episcopal church. Seeks to: discover and share the mission of the church; promote cooperation, fellowship, and mutual counsel concerning the spiritual life and religious activities of the church; encourage Bible study and assist in spreading the Gospel; research and answer society's needs in order to develop programs and resources that will respond to that need. Awards Helena B. Cobb Scholarship Fund. **Members:** 100,000. **Publications:** *The Missionary Messenger*, monthly. • Also publishes handbooks.

★1153★ Women's Missionary and Service Commission of the Mennonite Church (WMSCMC)
421 S. 2nd St., Ste. 600
Elkhart, IN 46516-3243
Phone: (219)294-7131
Marian B. Hostetler, Exec.Sec.

Founded: 1915. **Description:** Encourages spiritual growth in women through prayer, Bible study, and community service. Operates speakers' bureau. Conducts educational programs on conflict resolution, poverty, and homelessness.

Bestows scholarships to Mennonite women for undergraduate work in Mennonite institutions and graduate work in seminary and non-Mennonite institutions. **Regional Groups:** 21. **Local Groups:** 500. **Publications:** *Resource Packet*, annual. In conjunction with Women in Mission of the General Conference Mennonite Church. Includes devotional lessons, how-to brochures, audio-visual materials, book list, and projects. • *Voice*, 11/year. Magazine featuring inspirational growth articles, service project opportunities, and chapter updates. • Makes available *Mennonite Women* (book).

★1154★ Women's Missionary Society, AME Church (WMS)
1134 11th St. NW
Washington, DC 20001
Phone: (202)371-8886
Delores L. Kennedy Williams, Pres.

Founded: 1944. **Description:** Women members of the African Methodist Episcopal Church. Seeks to: "help each woman and youth grow in the knowledge and experience of God through his son Jesus Christ; seek fellowship with women in other lands; make possible opportunities and resources to meet the changing needs and concerns of women and youth through intensive training, recruitment, and Christian witnessing; offer a fellowship so strong, a message so convincingly interpreted and imparted, and an enthusiasm so contagious, that the Gospel through us will be at work in the world so that we will be able to draw humankind into the fellowship of love." Sponsors administrative retreats, institutes, international exchanges, missionaries, leadership training programs, and educational programs for religious leaders. Operates information bureau; compiles statistics; maintains biographical archives. Organizes charitable activities; offers children's services. Sponsors competitions; bestows awards. Maintains 20 committees including: Christian Social Relations; Creative Arts; Family Life; Handy-Simmons Scholarship; Heath-Polk Rural Missions; Research on the Status of the Black Woman; Tanner-Turner Memorial. **Members:** 800,000. **Publications:** *Missionary Magazine*, 9/year. • *Young People's Division Newsletter*, quarterly. • Also publishes *Inspirational Preparatory Workbook*, *Women's Missionary Society Handbook* (books), resources guides, study books, and pamphlets.

★1155★ Women's Music Archives
208 Wildflower Ln.
Fairfield, CT 06430
Phone: (203)255-1348
Kim Kimber, Secretary/Curator

Description: Collects, preserves and shares materials relating to women's music (records, tapes, songbooks, periodicals, concert programs, and posters). Also maintains and collects all varieties of women's music memorabilia.

★1156★ Women's National Book Association (WNBA)
160 Fifth Ave., Rm. 604
New York, NY 10010
Phone: (212)675-7805
Fax: (212)989-7542
Sandra K. Paul, Exec. Officer

Founded: 1917. **Description:** Women and men professionally engaged in all phases of book publishing; booksellers, editors, authors, and

librarians. Encourages professional networking in order to facilitate exchange of information. Sponsors sessions on the book industry at meetings of related professional associations. Presents biennial award to a woman for outstanding contributions to the book industry; also presents annual Lucile Micheels Pannell Award in recognition of creative use of books with children. Maintains archives at Columbia University, New York City. **Members:** 1000. **Local Groups:** 8. **Publications:** *The Bookwoman*, 3/year. Covers association activities and women's issues in the publishing industry; includes book reviews and member profile.

★1157★ Women's National Republican Club (WNRC)
3 W. 51st St.
New York, NY 10019
Phone: (212)582-5454
Fax: (212)977-8972
Mrs. Lila Prounis, Exec. Officer

Founded: 1921. **Description:** Women interested in promoting the programs of the Republican Party and creating interest in political participation. Conducts educational, cultural, social, and political programs. Maintains the Henrietta Wells Livermore School of Politics, which provides political training and education on city, state, national, and international affairs. Bestows Republican Woman of the Year Award and Distinguished Political Service Award. Operates library and speakers' bureau. **Members:** 1300. **Publications:** *Guidon*, monthly. Newsletter.

★1158★ Women's Occupational Health Resource Center (WOHRC)
117 St. Johns Pl.
Brooklyn, NY 11217
Phone: (718)230-8822
Jeanne M. Stellman, Ph.D., Exec.Dir.

Founded: 1978. **Description:** Acts as clearinghouse for women's occupational health and safety issues. Aims to increase awareness of the health and safety hazards which women face in the workplace, and to raise management awareness of the need for improved workplace and equipment design. Advises manufacturers on design standards of safety equipment. Offers technical assistance in setting up programs designed to develop occupational health awareness; distributes questionnaires to assess occupational health and safety risks. Maintains library. **Members:** 2500. **Computerized Services:** Bibliographic information system. **Publications:** *WOHRC News*, quarterly. Newsletter; includes reviews of books and other resources and statistics. • Also publishes fact sheets, bibliographies, and fact packs; makes available mail-order books on topics such as reproductive hazards, health of health care workers, and industrial workers.

★1159★ Women's Ordination Conference (WOC)
PO Box 2693
Fairfax, VA 22031
Phone: (703)352-1006
Fax: (703)352-5181
Ruth Fitzpatrick, Coordinator

Founded: 1975. **Description:** Roman Catholic women and men, lay and ordained, who believe that women have the right to participate fully in church life, including the priestly ministry. Plans to continue prayer, support, networking, and lobbying until sexism is removed from the process of priestly ordination and from the structures and understandings of the Roman Catholic church. Conducts research; compiles documentation. Maintains national speakers' bureau and archives. Sponsors specialized education and research programs. **Members:** 3500. **Local Groups:** 100. **Publications:** *New Women/New Church*, bimonthly. Newspaper. • Also publishes *Liberating Liturgies* (book), *We Are Called*, monographs, promotional materials, and conference proceedings.

★1160★ **Women's Overseas Service League (WOSL)**
c/o Col. Doris M. Cobb
7400 Crest Way, No. 917
San Antonio, TX 78239
Phone: (512)654-8296
Col. Doris M. Cobb, Pres.

Founded: 1921. **Description:** Women who served overseas with the armed services, American Red Cross, Salvation Army, or other service organizations, or with any agency approved of by the U.S. government to work with the armed forces during World Wars I and II, Korean conflict, Vietnam, Persian Gulf, or aftermath; women of the U.S. Armed Forces or her allies. Carries on patriotic activities, services to disabled veterans, and aid to members in need. **Members:** 1250. **Local Groups:** 44. **Publications:** *Carry On*, quarterly.

★1161★ **Women's Press Collective**
PO Box 022337, Cadman Plaza Sta.
Brooklyn, NY 11202-0049
Phone: (718)852-0100
Fax: (718)852-0100
Diane Garrett, Contact

Description: Works toward the advancement of women in the media workforce and advancing minority low-income workers' organizations.

★1162★ **Women's Prison Association (WPA)**
110 2nd Ave.
New York, NY 10003
Phone: (212)674-1163
Fax: (212)677-1981
Ann L. Jacobs, Exec.Dir.

Founded: 1844. **Description:** Service agency that aids women who have been in conflict with the law. Sponsors Hopper Home, a halfway house in New York City. Offers individual and group counseling, work placement, and job development and referrals to other resources. Administers Hopper Academy, an academic and vocational training program for former women prisoners. Sponsors specialized parental education program and court diversion effort.

★1163★ **Women's Professional Racquetball Association (WPRA)**
153 S. 15th St.
Souderton, PA 18964
Phone: (215)723-7356
Molly O'Brien, Exec.Dir.

Founded: 1979. **Description:** Individuals interested in women's racquetball. Promotes the participation of women in sports. Organizes and implements a professional racquetball tour for women. Oversees all aspects of sanctioned tournaments; encourages communication among members regarding the rules of the game; provides a public relations service for women's racquetball. Conducts instructional seminars; compiles statistics; sponsors charitable program. **Members:** 500. **Publications:** *Women in Racquetball Newsletter*, bimonthly. Features profiles of players from across the country; includes tournament updates, professional rankings, and calendar of events. • *WPRA Handbook*, biennial. • *WPRA Official Tour Program*, annual.

★1164★ **Women's Professional Rodeo Association (WPRA)**
Rt. 5, Box 698
Blanchard, OK 73010
Phone: (405)485-2277
Lydia Moore, Sec.-Treas.

Founded: 1948. **Description:** To produce and compete in All Professional Girl Rodeos and Barrel Races in rodeo sanctioned by the Professional Rodeo Cowboys Association. Conducts seminars and clinics on fundamentals of horsemanship and rodeo events. Operates National Cowgirl Hall of Fame. Maintains library of films and photos. Annually awards $21,000 in prizes to the top 15 barrel racers and the champions in each of six rodeo events. **Members:** 2000. **Publications:** *News*, monthly. • *Reference Book*, annual. • *Rule Book*, annual. **Formerly:** (1980) Professional Women's Rodeo Association; (1981) Girls Rodeo Association.

★1165★ **The Women's Project**
6 W. 63rd St.
New York, NY 10023
Phone: (212)873-3040
Fax: (212)873-3788
Marjorie Oberlander, Marketing Associate

Description: The Project provides theatrial venues for plays written by women and sponsors readings and performances. **Publications:** A newsletter is sent to subscribers.

★1166★ **Women's Project & Productions (WP&P)**
220 W. 42nd St., 18th Fl.
New York, NY 10036
Phone: (212)382-3750
Julia Miles, Artistic Dir.

Founded: 1978. **Description:** Playwrights (132), directors (95), and composers (8). Promotes and produces new plays by women. Stages 3 major productions per year. Bestows awards. **Members:** 235. **Publications:** *Dialogues*, 3/year. Newsletter. • Has also published 3 anthologies of WP&P plays. **Formerly:** (1987) Women's Project at the American Place Theatre.

★1167★ **Women's Psychotherapy Institute**
1301 20th St., NW
Washington, DC 20036
Phone: (202)833-9026

Founded: 1984. **Description:** Mental health and psychotherapy.

★1168★ **Women's Research and Education Institute (WREI)**
1700 18th St. NW, Ste. 400
Washington, DC 20009
Phone: (202)328-7070
Fax: (202)328-3514
Jean Stapleton, Pres.

Founded: 1977. **Description:** Nonpartisan policy research organization. Provides a liaison between researchers and policymakers concerning issues of importance to women. Serves as information clearinghouse for legislators and women's research centers nationwide. Monitors administration and enforcement of existing laws; submits data to Congress on the impact upon women of pending legislation; suggests areas needful of congressional attention. Sponsors Graduate Fellowships on Women and Public Policy, an internship program placing women in congressional and committee offices to work on women's issues. Conducts workshops. **Publications:** *Annual Report on the Status of Women*. • *Directory of Women's Research and Policy Centers*, biennial. • Also publishes analyses of issues such as tax reform, women's employment, and social security reform. **Formerly:** (1980) Congresswomen's Caucus Corporation.

★1169★ **Women's Rights Committee (WRC)**
c/o Human Rights Department
555 New Jersey Ave. NW
Washington, DC 20001
Phone: (202)879-4400
Barbara Van Blake, Dir.

Founded: 1970. **Description:** Carries out policy resolutions of the American Federation of Teachers in the area of women's rights. Encourages programs on the local level that implement these policies; works with other feminist groups with the same views. Conducts research and education programs; maintains speakers' bureau; compiles statistics. **Publications:** *Action*, weekly. • *American Educator*, quarterly. • *American Teacher*, monthly.

★1170★ **Women's Rights Project (WRP)**
c/o American Civil Liberties Union
132 W. 43rd St.
New York, NY 10036
Phone: (212)944-9800
Isabelle Katz Pinzler, Dir.

Founded: 1972. **Description:** Strives to end sex discrimination in the U.S. through major class-action litigation in precedent-setting cases usually referred through affiliates. Emphasis is on nontraditional blue collar employment, exclusion of fertile women from the workplace, and equal pay for work of comparable value. **Publications:** Brochures and pamphlets.

★1171★ **Women's Roundtable (WR)**
2000 P St., NW, Ste. 515
Washington, DC 20036
Phone: (202)822-6636
Irene Natividad, Chair

Founded: 1982. **Description:** A loosely formed coalition of national women's organizations. Seeks to provide a national network to enhance and increase the power of women. Collects and disseminates information. Sponsors the Women's Vote Project (see separate entry), which works to register women voters. **Members:** 75.

★1172★ **Women's Spirituality Forum (WSF)**
PO Box 5143
Berkeley, CA 94705
Phone: (415)420-1454
Z. Budapest, Pres.

Founded: 1971. **Description:** Seeks to bring women's spirituality into the mainstream and feminist awareness. Promotes "the female side of one's concept of god, natural laws, and the empowerment of women." Conducts classes, workshops, and Sunday lecture series on topics such as women's spirituality, feminist history, craft skills, women's mysteries, European shamanism, women's holy days, and "the presence of the Goddess in everyday life." Performs rituals, rites of passage, blessings, memorials, and other community services. Conducts telephone inquiries and referrals; maintains speakers' bureau. **Computerized Services:** Mailing list. **Publications:** *Callisto*, 3-4/year. Newsletter; contains schedules of classes, workshops, retreats, rituals, festivals, and lecture series. **Formerly:** (1989) Susan B. Anthony Women's Spirituality Education Forum.

★1173★ **Women's Sports Foundation (WSF)**
342 Madison Ave., Ste. 728
New York, NY 10173
Phone: (212)972-9170
Toll-free: 800-227-3988
Fax: (212)949-8024
Deborah Anderson, Exec.Dir.

Founded: 1974. **Description:** Encourages and supports the participation of women in sports activities for their health, enjoyment, and mental development; educates the public about athletic opportunities and the value of sports for women. Activities include: conducting sports-related seminars and symposia; developing educational guides; providing travel and training grants and internship program; supporting the enforcement of the Title IX amendments of the 1972 Equal Education Act and the Amateur Sports Act. Sponsors an information and resource clearinghouse on women's sports and fitness. Presents awards for outstanding contributions and achievements in women's sports. Maintains International Women's Sports Hall of Fame. Maintains biographical archives; compiles statistics. **Members:** 300,000. **Publications:** *College Scholarship Guide*, annual. • *Headway*, quarterly. Newsletter. . • Also publishes *A Women's Guide To Coaching*. Parents Guide, *Aspire Higher - Careers in Sports for Women, The Winning Combination - Girls and Sports*, and *Tips For Teens*.

★1174★ **Women's Technical Assistance Project (WTAP)**
733 15th St. NW, Ste. 510
Washington, DC 20005
Phone: (202)638-0449
Fax: (202)783-1839
Eileen Paul, Dir.

Description: The Project facilitates the development of skills and resources among women who work for change by creating and leading community-based organizations. Its focus is the southeastern and southwestern United States and sponsors skills-sharing workshops for women-led community-based organizations on the topics of fundraising and organizational, program, and resource development. **Publications:** *Church Funding Resource Guide*, annual.

★1175★ **Women's Tennis Association (WTA)**
133 1st St. NE
St. Petersburg, FL 33701
Phone: (813)895-5000
Fax: (813)894-1982
Gerard Smith, CEO & Exec.Dir.

Founded: 1973. **Description:** Professional women tennis players. Purpose is to represent members with regard to professional tournaments. **Members:** 450. **Publications:** *Getting Started*, annual. • *Inside Women's Tennis*, monthly. • *Media Guide*, annual. • *Players Handbook*, annual. • *Tournament Guide*, annual. **Formerly:** (1986) Women's Tennis Association; (1991) Women's International Tennis Association.

★1176★ **Women's Theological Center**
PO Box 1200
Boston, MA 02117-1200
Phone: (617)536-8782

Description: Provides a forum for women from a variety of racial and ethnic backgrounds to engage in action-based community and educational programs. Aims to use feminist viewpoint to transform "oppressive" religious and social structures. Confronts racial, class, gender, and sexual orientation injustices. **Frequency:** Quarterly. **Publications:** *Women's Theological Center Newsletter*.

★1177★ **Women's Transportation Seminar—National (WTSN)**
808 17th St. NW, No. 200
Washington, DC 20006-3953
Phone: (202)223-9669
Fax: (202)223-9569
Helen Hall, Exec.Sec.

Founded: 1977. **Description:** Male and female transportation professionals. Assists women interested in transportation; advances the knowledge and training of transportation professionals; encourages communication among members of the transportation industry. Provides a neutral forum for business leaders and government executives to discuss transportation initiatives. Serves as vehicle for network development. Conducts seminars on career planning and management skills; sponsors legislative forums to provide members with the opportunity to hear congressional staff express views on upcoming transportation bills. Awards annual scholarships to outstanding female college and graduate students majoring in transportation; bestows awards annually to women and employers who have excelled in the field; sponsors roundtables to allow members to discuss developments with transportation specialists. Makes benefits discounts available to members. **Members:** 2500. **Local Groups:** 24. **Publications:** *Women's Transportation Seminar–National Membership Directory*, annual. • *WTS National Newsletter*, bimonthly. Newsletter covering current transportation issues, board meetings, and association activities. **Formerly:** (1988) Women's Transportation Seminar.

★1178★ **Women's Vote Project (WVP)**
1601 Connecticut Ave. NW, Ste. 801
Washington, DC 20009
Phone: (202)328-2312
Joanne Howes, Exec.Dir.

Founded: 1982. **Description:** A project of the Women's Roundtable and National Women's Education Fund. National women's organizations united to increase significantly the number of women voters to enhance their voice in public affairs. Focuses on office workers, displaced homemakers, senior citizens, lower income women, single heads of households, young working women, and black and ethnic women. Conducts a get-out-the-vote campaign by collecting and disseminating information, providing day-care services and transportation on election day, and maintaining phone banks to remind registered women to vote. **Members:** 75.

★1179★ **Woodswomen**
25 W. Diamond Lake Rd.
Minneapolis, MN 55419
Phone: (612)822-3809
Toll-free: 800-279-0559
Fax: (612)822-3814
Denise Mitten, Dir.

Founded: 1977. **Description:** Women who share an interest in outdoor activities including mountaineering, canoeing, and backpacking. Encourages members' sense of adventure and independence; sponsors educational programs in leadership training and the history of outdoorswomen; conducts wilderness trips. Provides children's services and educational programs. Maintains speakers' bureau and biographical archives; compiles statistics **Members:** 800. **Regional Groups:** 4. **Publications:** *International Women's Climbing Directory*, biennial. • *Woodswomen Membership Directory*, annual. • *Woodswomen News*, quarterly. Newsletter. Contains articles about outdoor trips, an adventure travel directory, and a trip calendar listing.

★1180★ **Working Women's Institute (WWI)**
c/o K.C. Wagner, Ph.D.
58 W. Eighth St., No. 3E
New York, NY 10011
K. C. Wagner, Ph.D., Exec.Dir.

Founded: 1975. **Description:** Provides research and education for working women on the problems of women in the workforce (especially the problem of sexual harassment on the job). Offers technical training and assistance and community education for employees, unions, universities, and organizations. **Formerly:** (1978) Working Women's United Institute.

★1181★ **World Federation of Doctors Who Respect Human Life (WFDRHL)**
U.S. Section
PO Box 508
Oak Park, IL 60303
Phone: (708)383-8766
Herbert Ratner, M.D., Sec.-Treas.

Founded: 1976. **Description:** Physicians united to restore the "traditional Hippocratic medical position" through firm opposition to abortion, suicide, and direct euthanasia. Sponsors educational programs and seminars. **Members:** 1400. **Publications:** *Primum Non Nocere*, quarterly. Newsletter.

★1182★ **World Federation of Estonian Women's Clubs in Exile (WFEWCE)**
c/o Mrs. Juta Kurman
68-50 Juno St.
Forest Hills, NY 11375
Phone: (718)261-9618
Mrs. Juta Kurman, Pres.

Founded: 1966. **Description:** Women's clubs and individuals in Australia, Canada, Germany, Sweden, and the United States. Seeks to preserve Estonian language and ethnic culture; supports the development of independent Estonia. Conducts charitable programs; maintains biographical archives and speakers' bureau; compiles statistics. Operates archive of local Estonian newspapers and bulletins. Maintains library of Estonian, Baltic, and American literature and reference books. **Members:** 1000. **Regional Groups:** 14. **State Groups:** 4. **Local Groups:** 3. **Publications:** *Shawl of Haapsalu* (booklet), circulars, and letters. **Formerly:** (1982) Federated Estonian Women's Clubs; (1985) World Federation of Estonian Women's Clubs.

★1183★ World Federation of Health Agencies for the Advancement of Voluntary Surgical Contraception (WFHAAVSC)
122 E. 42nd St.
New York, NY 10168
Phone: (212)351-2536
Fax: (212)599-0959
Ms. N. Lynn Bakamjian, Exec.Dir.

Founded: 1975. **Description:** Individual experts; national, regional, and local leadership groups. Fosters the inclusion of voluntary surgical contraception as a choice within basic health services and seeks to advance the understanding of issues involved. Promotes high quality health care and advocates the inclusion of procedures such as tubal ligation, vasectomy, and some nonpermanent, but long-lasting methods in family planning and basic medical programs worldwide. Serves as liaison among members and other international health and population organizations; maintains communications network. Encourages worldwide examination and comparison of educational, legal, professional, scientific, and social issues in the field; develops and disseminates policies and guidelines on pertinent issues; conducts seminars; establishes standards for data collection, education, equipment maintenance, medical surveillance, training, and other services. Maintains speakers' bureau. **Members:** 200. **Telecommunications Services:** Telex, 425604 AS-VUI. **Publications:** *Communique Newsletter*, (in Arabic, French, and Spanish), semiannual. • *Communique Newsletter*, (in English) annual. • Also publishes *Safe & Voluntary Surgical Contraception, Training Guidelines for Voluntary Surgical Contraception*, and abstracts of conference papers and background working papers.

★1184★ World Federation of Methodist Women, North America Area (WFMWNAA)
c/o Dr. Sylvia Faulk
623 San Fernanco Ave.
Berkeley, CA 94707
Phone: (415)526-5536
Dr. Sylvia Faulk, Pres.

Founded: 1939. **Description:** A division of World Federation of Methodist Women. Methodist women representing the United Methodist Church, United Church Women of Canada, Methodist Church in the Caribbean and the Americas, Christian Methodist Episcopal Church, African Methodist Episcopal Church, and African Methodist Episcopal Zion Church. Conducts evangelistic activities; sponsors healing ministries. Seeks an end to discrimination against women worldwide; supports the passage of legislation to prevent child abuse. Examines issues concerning women in the Third World. Promotes the development of literacy training and translation programs. Encourages the establishment of counseling and educational programs on family issues such as food production, malnutrition, hygiene, and family planning. Conducts quinquennial area seminar following the World Assembly; also holds regional and state seminars.

★1185★ World Woman's Party (WWP)
144 Constitution, NE
Washington, DC 20002

★1186★ World Women for Animal Rights/Empowerment Vegetarian Activist Collective
c/o Connie Salamone
616 6th St., No. 2
Brooklyn, NY 11215
Phone: (718)788-1362
Connie Salamone, Dir.

Founded: 1982. **Description:** Individuals interested in the preservation and conservation of animals and the environment. Promotes animal rights through the dissemination of information and promotional materials. Seeks to heighten women's "sensitivity to nature and ecology" through feminism. Conducts research; offers student intern program. Maintains archive of 4000 slides. **Formerly:** American Vegetarian Association.

★1187★ World Women in the Environment
1331 H St., NW, Ste. 903
Washington, DC 20005
Phone: (202)347-1514
Fax: (202)347-1524
Melissa Dann, Interim Executive Dir.

Description: The organization is a worldwide network of women concerned about environmental management and protection. It strives to educate the public and policy makers about "the vital linkages between women, natural resources and sustainable development"; promote the inclusion of women in the design and implementation of development policies; and mobilize and support women in enivronmental and natural resource programs. Also held a global assembly of women and the environment and provides an information service and worldwide forums. **Publications:** *Worldwide News*, bimonthly. • *Directory of Women and the Environment*.

★1188★ WORLD—Women Organized to Respond to Life-threatening Diseases
PO Box 11535
Oakland, CA 94611
Phone: (510)658-6939
Rebecca Denison, Founder

Founded: 1991. **Description:** Organization for women with HIV and AIDS. Members "share information about doctors, drugs, insurance, support groups, and life." Sponsors educational and social events and two annual retreats for HIV-positive women. **Publications:** *WORLD Newsletter*, monthly. • *Mujer Imagen de Vida*, quarterly Spanish-language newsletter written for and by HIV-positive Latina women.

★1189★ Y-ME National Organization for Breast Cancer Information and Support (Y-ME)
c/o Sharon Green
18220 Harwood Ave.
Homewood, IL 60430
Phone: (708)799-8338
Toll-free: 800-221-2141
Fax: (708)799-5937
Sharon Green, Exec.Dir.

Founded: 1978. **Description:** Purpose is to provide peer support and information to women who have or suspect they have breast cancer. Activities include presurgical counseling and referral service, inservice programs for health professionals, hot line volunteer training, and technical assistance. Offers seminars and workshops to organizations and businesses on all aspects of breast disease (in English and Spanish). Maintains small library. Administers the Deborah David Dewar Fund and the Billie Klein Memorial Fund. **Members:** 2000. **Telecommunications Services:** 24-hour hot line (708)799-8228. **Publications:** *Breast Cancer Bibliography*, annual. • *Y-ME Hotline*, bimonthly. Newsletter. • Also publishes *Guidelines for Breast Cancer Support Groups*. **Formerly:** (1989) Y-ME Breast Cancer Support.

★1190★ Young Ladies Institute (YLI)
PO Box 640687
San Francisco, CA 94164
Phone: (415)346-4367
Carol Marshall, Grand Sec.

Founded: 1887. **Description:** Catholic women on the West Coast and in Hawaii. Provides funds for charitable projects and religious activities. **Members:** 13,000. **Local Groups:** 140. **Publications:** *Voice of YLI*, bimonthly.

★1191★ Young Women of the Church of Jesus Christ of Latter-Day Saints (YW)
76 N. Main
Salt Lake City, UT 84150
Phone: (801)240-2141
Ardeth G. Kapp, Pres.

Founded: 1869. **Description:** Girls between the ages of 12 and 18. Seeks to strengthen the spiritual life of young women through Christian values and experiences. Reinforces the values of faith, divine nature, individual worth, knowledge, choice and accountability, good works, and integrity. Conducts service projects and leadership training. Bestows Young Womanhood Medallion for special achievement. **Members:** 400,000. **Formerly:** (1970) Young Women's Mutual Improvement Association.

★1192★ Young Women's Christian Association of the United States of America (YWCA-USA)
726 Broadway
New York, NY 10003
Phone: (212)614-2700
Fax: (212)677-9716
Gwendolyn Calvert Baker, Exec.Dir.

Founded: 1858. **Description:** Women and girls over 12 years of age and their families who participate in service programs of health education, recreation, clubs and classes, and counseling and assistance to girls and women in the areas of employment, education, human sexuality, self improvement, voluntarism, citizenship, emotional and physical health, and juvenile justice. Seeks to make contributions to peace, justice, freedom, and dignity for all people; works toward the empowerment of women and the elimination of racism. Conducts international advocacy program on human rights and on peace and development. Sponsors national advocacy programs on: international peace and justice; economic and social justice; improved environmental quality; individual rights and liberties. Local units include 366 community YWCA's, 39 student associations, 112 YWCA residences/shelters, and 24 resident camps. Men and boys participate in YWCA activities as associates or registrants. Maintains archives; compiles statistics. Bestows TWIN (Tribute to Women in Industry) Awards. Maintains library of 8000 books, pamphlets, and periodicals on contemporary American women and their concerns. **Members:** 2,000,000 (includes participants). **Volunteers:** 122,000. **Regional Groups:** 3. **Local Groups:** 446. **Computerized Services:** Data base on local YWCAs. **Board Committees:** Board Issues; Development; Public Policy; Racial Justice; World Relations. **Publications:** *Young Women's Christian Association of the U.S.A.—Annual Report.* • *Young Women's Christian Association of the U.S.A.—Directory*, triennial. • *YWCA Interchange*, quarterly. Newsletter covering national and local YWCA news. • Also publishes public policy bulletin, informational and instructional brochures, promotion packets, financial administration and development materials, and manuals and guides.

★1193★ **Zeta Phi Beta Sorority**
1734 New Hampshire, NW
Washington, DC 20009-2593
Phone: (202)387-3103
Fax: (202)232-4593
Linda Thompson, Exec. Dir.

Founded: 1920. **Description:** The Sorority, founded on the campus of Howard University in Washington, DC as a sister organization to the Phi Beta Sigma Fraternity, was the first to charter international chapters, which were located in West Africa and Germany, and to form adult and youth auxiliary groups. Its purpose is to foster the ideals of service, charity, scholarship, civic and cultural endeavors, sisterhood, and finer womanhood through national programs where its members provide voluntary service to staff community outreach programs, fund scholarships, support organized charities, and promote legislation for social and civic change. Sponsors a substance abuse prevention program; AIDS awareness; education and literacy tutoring; child care development centers owned and operated by chapters; scholarship awards to high school students; and leadership development projects. Members are predominantly black, educated women, collegiate and graduate, who are active in 500 chapters located on college campuses throughout 39 states and the District of Columbia, the Virgin Islands, the Bahamas, Germany, and West Africa. **Membership:** 65,000.

★1194★ **Zonta International**
557 W. Randolph St.
Chicago, IL 60606
Phone: (312)930-5848
Bonnie Koenig, Exec.Dir.

Founded: 1919. **Description:** Goals are to encourage high ethical standards in business and professions, to improve the legal, economic and professional status of women and to work for the advancement of understanding, good will and peace. **Publications:** *Zontian*.

(2) Regional, State, and Local Organizations

Entries in this chapter are arranged alphabetically by state and city, then by organization name within city. See the User's Guide at the front of this directory for additional information.

Alabama

Alabaster

★1195★ Sav-A-Life, Shelby
217 1st St. N.
PO Box 984
Alabaster, AL 35007
Phone: (205)664-1667
Fred McDuff, Pres.

Description: Individuals in Shelby County, AL interested in helping young women in a crisis pregnancy situation by providing free pregnancy counseling and testing, referrals for medical and financial assistance, and spiritual guidance. **Affiliated with:** Lifeline Children's Services; Sav-a-Life/Wales Goebal Ministries.

Auburn

★1196★ League of Women Voters of Alabama
Rte. 3, Box 99
Auburn, AL 36830
Phone: (205)821-1448
Carolyn Coker, President

Birmingham

★1197★ Alabama Abortion Rights Action League
PO Box 590033
Birmingham, AL 35259
Phone: (205)591-1319
Ed Higginbottom, Contact

★1198★ Alabama Federation of Women's Clubs
2728 Niazuma Ave., S.
Birmingham, AL 35205
Phone: (205)323-2392
Mrs. Robert W. Grames, Pres.

Description: Women's club members united to promote arts, education, philanthropy, public welfare, and high moral and spiritual values. Provides programs for the blind and handicapped and assistance in forming libraries. Sponsors scholarship program. **Affiliated with:** General Federation of Women's Clubs International.

★1199★ American Woman's Society of Certified Public Accountants of Alabama
1900 AmSouth/Harbert Plaza
Birmingham, AL 35203
Phone: (205)251-2000
Cathy Miller, Pres.

Description: Women certified public accountants united to advance their professional interests. Provides networking opportunities and speakers. **Affiliated with:** American Woman's Society of Certified Public Accountants.

★1200★ Birmingham Area Mothers of Twins Club
405 Shades Crest Rd.
Birmingham, AL 35226
Phone: (205)979-5529
Edna Rush, Pres.

Description: Serves as support group for mothers of multiple birth children.

★1201★ Foundation for Women's Health in Alabama
PO Box 7307-A
Birmingham, AL 35253
Phone: (205)933-9420
Fax: (205)933-9420
Laura Salmon, Exec.Dir.

Description: Works to improve access to medical care for women and children; encourages and supports scientific research and treatment of diseases and special conditions of women and infants; promotes education and research directed toward reducing infant mortality; and supports preventive medicine and the importance of nutrition in maintaining health. Provides education programs, health promotion activities, and legislative advocacy. Offers free cancer and health screenings. Produces *Women's Health: Answers for Today* television program. Sponsors annual Women's Health Issues Forum. Bestows Women's Health awards and annual Women's Health Volunteer Award. Holds luncheons and workshops. **Affiliated with:** Partners.

★1202★ National Association of Women in Construction, Greater Birmingham Chapter
401 S. 37th St.
Birmingham, AL 35222
Phone: (205)591-7189
Fax: (205)591-7304
Sandra S. Wallwork, Pres.

Description: Women involved in construction and related industries. To encourage women to pursue careers in construction; to contribute to the betterment of the construction industry; and to inform members of legislation as it relates to the industry. Provides educational programs and networking opportunities. Conducts charitable activities; participates in area festival. Holds trade shows. **Affiliated with:** National Association of Women in Construction.

★1203★ Older Women's League (OWL) Birmingham Chapter
PO Box 130264
Birmingham, AL 35213
Phone: (205)987-1452
Linda McCullough, Contact

★1204★ Women in Service and Politics
25 11th Ct. W.
Birmingham, AL 35204
Phone: (205)251-5566
Mrs. Armistrice Robinson, Pres.

Description: Professional women interested in serving the community of Jefferson County, AL and participating in the political process. Conducts charitable activities for homeless and other indigent persons. Conducts civic education.

★1205★ Women's Chamber of Commerce
5645 10th Ave. S.
Birmingham, AL 35222
Phone: (205)592-2171
Mrs. John L. Swindle, Consultant

Description: Women promoting community and cultural development in Birmingham, AL. Contributes funds to botanical gardens, library, and Arlington House historical preservation project.

★1206★ Women's Committee of the Alabama Symphony Association
PO Box 2125
Birmingham, AL 35201
Phone: (205)326-0100
Fax: (205)521-9070
Sahra Coxe, Pres.
Description: Individuals interested in supporting the Alabama Symphony Association.

Decatur

★1207★ Decatur Women's Chamber of Commerce
1039 Sherman St., SE
Decatur, AL 35601
Phone: (205)552-3067
Gloria R. Smith, Contact
Description: Women. Promotes business and community development in Decatur, AL. Conducts fundraising and service projects. Holds monthly board meeting. **Affiliated with:** Decatur Chamber of Commerce.

★1208★ United North Alabama Safe Alternatives in Childbirth
c/o Lynn Masters
Rte. 6, Box 18
Decatur, AL 35603
Phone: (205)350-4432
Lynn Masters, Leader
Description: Parents, nurses, and social workers seeking to educate the public about safe alternatives in childbirth. Provides information concerning breastfeeding, home or homelike births, natural childbirth, nutrition, and skillful midwifery.

Fairfield

★1209★ Alabama Association of Women's and Youth Clubs
7125 Westmoreland Dr.
Fairfield, AL 35064
Phone: (205)923-6093
Dr. Ethel H. Hall, Pres.
Description: Encourages women to reach their highest potential through intellectual, moral, and spiritual growth. Promotes youth training programs. **Affiliated with:** General Federation of Women's Clubs.

Huntsville

★1210★ Birthright of Huntsville
c/o Cynthia Franklin
13005 Camelot Dr.
Huntsville, AL 35803-1840
Description: Seeks to help pregnant women find alternatives to abortion. Conducts childbirth education and parenting programs.

Mobile

★1211★ National Association of Women Business Owners
Mobile Chapter
c/o Executive Suites of Mobile
PO Box 16944
Mobile, AL 36616-6944
Phone: (205)476-0457
Reba Steele, President

Montgomery

★1212★ Alabama Coalition Against Domestic Violence
PO Box 4762
Montgomery, AL 36101
Phone: (205)832-4842
Carol Gundlach, Contact

New Hope

★1213★ American Association of University Women, Alabama Division
PO Box 162
New Hope, AL 35760
Phone: (205)723-4761
Nancy L. Worley, Pres.
Description: Women graduates of regionally accredited four year colleges and universities. Works for the advancement of women through advocacy and emphasis on lifelong learning. Holds three board meetings per year. **Affiliated with:** American Association of University Women.

Alaska

Douglas

★1214★ League of Women Voters of Alaska
PO Box 423
Douglas, AK 99824
Rosemary Hagavig, President

Fairbanks

★1215★ Association for Women in Science, Alaska Chapter
c/o Phyllis Hunsucker
1618 Scenic Loop
Fairbanks, AK 99709-6734
Description: Works to improve education and employment opportunities for women in the sciences.

Juneau

★1216★ Alaska Network On Domestic Violence and Sexual Assault
419 6th St., No. 116
Juneau, AK 99801
Phone: (907)586-3650
Cindy Smith, Contact

Arizona

Bisbee

★1217★ Young Women's Christian Association of Bisbee
26 Howell Ave.
PO Box 968
Bisbee, AZ 85603
Phone: (602)432-3542
Description: Seeks to develop and improve the spiritual, social, mental, and physical well-being of young people and adults. **Affiliated with:** Young Women's Christian Association of the United States of America.

Chandler

★1218★ Cesarean Prevention Movement of Greater Phoenix
444 North Gila Spring Blvd., No. 2002
Chandler, AZ 85226
Phone: (602)961-1535
Rebecca Armstrong, Exec. Officer

Douglas

★1219★ Young Women's Christian Association of Douglas
341 Tenth St.
Douglas, AZ 85607
Phone: (602)364-5501
Pat Kehl, Contact
Description: Seeks to develop and improve the spiritual, social, mental, and physical well-being of young people and adults. **Affiliated with:** Young Women's Christian Association of the United States of America.

Flagstaff

★1220★ Arizona Association of Midwives
318 West Birch
Flagstaff, AZ 86001
Phone: (602)779-6064
Description: Promotes communication and support for midwives in AZ. Develops and encourages guidelines for midwifery education.

★1221★ Cesarean Prevention Movement of Northern Arizona
PO Box 22521
Flagstaff, AZ 86002
Phone: (602)774-2598
Kristie Pagel, Exec. Officer

★1222★ Flagstaff Association of Parents and Professionals for Safe Alternatives in Child Birth
318 West Birch, Ste. 5
Flagstaff, AZ 86001
Phone: (602)779-6064
Description: Parents and professionals supporting midwifery and other alternative childbirth options. **Affiliated with:** National Association of Parents and Professionals for Safe Alternatives in Child Birth.

Phoenix

★1223★ Arizona Coalition Against Domestic Violence
301 W. Hatcher Rd.
Phoenix, AZ 85201
Phone: (602)495-5429

★1224★ Arizona Family Planning Council
2920 North 24th Ave., Ste. 26
Phoenix, AZ 85015-5949
Phone: (602)258-5777
Description: Resource agency for information and services concerning family planning. Conducts lobbying activities; holds seminars and workshops.

★1225★ Hispanic Women's Conference
1112 East Buckeye Rd.
Phoenix, AZ 85034
Phone: (602)257-0700

★1226★ Older Women's League (OWL)
Arizona Chapter
1430 N. Maryland St.
Phoenix, AZ 85004
Phone: (602)838-0523
Jo Ann Pedrick, Contact

★1227★ Women's Overseas Service
League, Phoenix-Cholla Unit
c/o Patricia Pasbach
3232A W. Denton Ln.
Phoenix, AZ 85017
Phone: (602)973-6540
Patricia Pasbach, Pres.
Description: Women in the Phoenix, AZ area
who served overseas with the armed services,
American Red Cross, Salvation Army, or other
service organizations, or with any agency approved by the U.S. government to work with
the armed forces during World Wars I and II,
Korean War, the Vietnam War, or their aftermath. Conducts patriotic activities; foster friendship between nations. Issues publications. **Affi-
iated with:** Women's Overseas Service League.

★1228★ Young Women's Christian
Association of Maricopa County
755 East Willetta
Phoenix, AZ 85006
Phone: (602)258-0990
Judy M. Numbers, Contact
Description: Seeks to develop and improve the
spiritual, social, mental, and physical well-being
of young people and adults. **Affiliated with:**
Young Women's Christian Association of the
United States of America.

Prescott

★1229★ Arizona Women's Education and
Employment
107 North Cortez, No. 203
Prescott, AZ 86301
Phone: (602)778-3010
Ginger M. Johnson, Coordinator
Description: Displaced homemakers and single
parents in Maricopa and Yavapai counties, AZ.
Provides employment skills training, placement
assistance, and vocational education.

Scottsdale

★1230★ Arizona Business and
Professional Women's Foundation
c/o Nancy Guy
9832 N. Hayden Rd., Ste. 203
Scottsdale, AZ 85258-1235
Nancy Guy, Contact
Description: Business and professional wom-
en. To promote complete participation, equal
opportunities, and economic self-sufficiency for
working women.

★1231★ League of Women Voters of
Arizona
7239 E. Vista Dr.
Scottsdale, AZ 85250
Phone: (602)423-5440
Susan Ward, President

★1232★ National Association of Women
Business Owners
Phoenix Chapter
c/o Cactus Copier Supplies, Inc.
14435 N. Scottsdale Rd., No. 600
Scottsdale, AZ 85254
Phone: (602)994-8624
Linda Thrasher, President

★1233★ Women's Overseas Service
League, Scottsdale
7521 East Palm Ln.
Scottsdale, AZ 85257
Phone: (602)945-4723
Dorothy Jane Morris, Contact

Sun City West

★1234★ Sun City West Women's Golf
Association
14754 Yosemite Dr.
Sun City West, AZ 85375-5754
Description: Promotes women's golf in Sun
City West, AZ.

Tempe

★1235★ Arizona Woman Image Now
(WIN)
School of Art
Arizona State University
Tempe, AZ 85287
Phone: (602)965-3525
Founded: 1974. **Description:** A group of wom-
en affiliated with the university, composed of
students, faculty, alumnae, and local artists.
Provides information, resources, public relations, and affirmative action on behalf of its
members. It has successfully lobbied for additional women faculty and jurors. Has a program
of workshops, guest lecturers, and an art
exhibition.

Tucson

★1236★ Arizona Right to Choose
181 South Tucson Blvd., No. 103
Tucson, AZ 85716
Phone: (602)326-7111
Description: Promotes a woman's right to
terminate a pregnancy.

★1237★ La Leche League International,
Arizona Chapter
739 South Santa Ana
Tucson, AZ 85710
Phone: (602)885-1735
Chris Kraft, Coordinator
Description: Mothers and expectant mothers
interested in breastfeeding. Provides information and encouragement on breastfeeding
through informal meetings and telephone counseling. **Affiliated with:** La Leche League International.

★1238★ National Association of Women
Judges
Pima County Superior Court
110 W. Congress
Tucson, AZ 85701
Lina Rodriguez, Exec. Officer
Description: Individuals holding judicial or qua-
si-judicial positions. **Affiliated with:** National
Association of Women Judges.

★1239★ Sun City Vistoso Ladies 18 Hole
Golf Club
1495 East Rancho Visto Blvd.
Tucson, AZ 85737-9120
Description: Women golf players in Tucson,
AZ.

★1240★ Tucson Woman's Club
6245 East Bellevue St.
Tucson, AZ 85712
Phone: (602)296-3142
Ellie Davis, Pres.
Description: Women over the age of 40 inter-
ested in community service including philanthro-
py, and industrial, literary, and artistic culture.
Affiliated with: General Federation of Women's
Clubs.

★1241★ Tucson Women's Commission
240 North Court Ave.
Tucson, AZ 85701
Phone: (602)624-8318
Marcia Niemann, Exec.Dir.
Description: Appointed commissioners and volunteers. Assists women in achieving full equality
of opportunities in all aspects of life. Provides
information and referral services. Sponsors
seminars and workshops.

★1242★ Women's Transportation Seminar,
Tucson Chapter
Downtown Development Corp.
177 N. Church, Ste. 1010
Tucson, AZ 85701
Phone: (602)623-5427
Cathy McCoskey, Contact
Description: Women and men transportation
professionals united to assists and advance
women in the transportation industry. **Affiliated
with:** Women's Transportation Seminar-Nation-
al.

★1243★ Young Women's Christian
Association of Tucson
738 North 5th Ave.; Ste. 110
Tucson, AZ 85705
Phone: (602)884-7810
Janet C. Marcotte, Contact
Description: Seeks to develop and improve the
spiritual, social, mental, and physical well-being
of young people and adults. **Affiliated with:**
Young Women's Christian Association of the
United States of America.

Arkansas

Benton

★1244★ American Business Women's
Association, Pine Cone Chapter
Professional Bldg., Ste 2
Military Rd.
Benton, AR 72015
Phone: (501)776-0106
Dr. Darrellyn Williams, Pres.
Description: Business and working women in
Benton, AR. Provides scholarships for local
women. **Affiliated with:** American Business
Women's Association.

Crossett

★1245★ Ladies at Work
707 Cedar
Crossett, AR 71635
Phone: (501)364-2127
Betty DeLess, Pres.

Description: Professional women. Provides a social network for working women. Promotes continuing education; awards college scholarship. Bestows Woman of the Year Award.

El Dorado

★1246★ Young Women's Christian Association of El Dorado
410 E. Elm
El Dorado, AR 71730
Phone: (501)862-5442

Description: Seeks to develop and improve the spiritual, social, mental, and physical well-being of young people and adults. **Affiliated with:** Young Women's Christian Association of the United States of America.

Fayetteville

★1247★ Arkansas Coalition Against Violence to Women and Children
PO Box 2915
Fayetteville, AR 72702
Phone: (501)793-8111
Toll-free: 800-332-4443
Betty Eubanks, Contact

Ft. Smith

★1248★ Sebastian County Republican Women
1108 Adelaide St.
Ft. Smith, AR 72901
Phone: (501)785-3373
Susan Hutchinson, Pres.

Description: Women. Works to elect Republicans to local, state, and national office. Provides educational programs to women on political issues, responsibilities, and involvement. Works to inspire patriotism in young people through annual essay contest. Awards scholarships. **Affiliated with:** Arkansas Federation of Republican Women; National Federation of Republican Women.

★1249★ Young Women's Christian Association of Ft. Smith
401 Lexington Ave.
Ft. Smith, AR 72901
Phone: (501)782-4596
Anna Ruth Lovett, Contact

Description: Seeks to develop and improve the spiritual, social, mental, and physical well-being of young people and adults. Maintains crisis center houses for women and children. **Affiliated with:** Young Women's Christian Association of the United States of America.

Little Rock

★1250★ Association for Women in Science, Little Rock Chapter
500 Napa Valley Rd., 838
Little Rock, AR 72211-5061

Description: Works to improve education and employment opportunities for women in the sciences.

★1251★ Greater Little Rock Women's Chamber of Commerce
PO Box 2594
Little Rock, AR 72203-2594
Phone: (501)375-6310
Ruth A. Kirby, Pres.

Description: Business and professional women. To foster goodwill and fellowship. To secure cooperative action in advancing the cultural, business, and educational interests of women. **Affiliated with:** Arkansas State Chamber of Commerce.

★1252★ League of Women Voters of Arkansas
2020 W. 3rd St., Rm. 501
Little Rock, AR 72205-4466
Phone: (501)376-7760
Linda Polk, President

★1253★ National Association of Women Business Owners
Central Arkansas Chapter
c/o Copy Systems and Quik Print
1121 S. Spring St.
Little Rock, AR 72202
Phone: (501)376-2679
Mary Jane Rebick, President

★1254★ National Association of Women Judges
Pulaski County Courthouse, Rm. 307B
Little Rock, AR 72201
Phone: (501)663-6758
Ellen B. Brantley, Exec. Officer

★1255★ Young Women's Christian Association of Greater Little Rock
1200 Cleveland
Little Rock, AR 72204
Phone: (501)664-4268

Description: Seeks to develop and improve the spiritual, social, mental, and physical well-being of young people and adults. **Affiliated with:** Young Women's Christian Association of the United States of America.

Ozark

★1256★ North Franklin County Democratic Women
1007 W. School
Ozark, AR 72949
Phone: (501)667-2176
Ann Wiggins, Chwm.

Description: Women members of the Democratic Party. Works to elect Democrats to local, state, and national office.

California

Anaheim

★1257★ Older Women's League (OWL)
South Orange County Chapter
PO Box 52
Anaheim, CA 92815
Barbara Baldwin, Contact

Arbuckle

★1258★ Arbuckle Women's Club
600 Gale Ave.
Arbuckle, CA 95912-9702

Description: Women's volunteer service club.

Arcadia

★1259★ Woman's Club of Arcadia
324 South 1st Ave.
Arcadia, CA 91006
Phone: (818)445-9004
Pat Bowman, Exec. Officer

Description: Individuals in the Arcadia, CA area interested in philanthropy and social activities. Promotes intellectual and civic improvement. Provides assistance to local charities. **Affiliated with:** General Federation of Women's Clubs.

Arroyo Grande

★1260★ Central Coast Women's Soccer Association
PO Box 364
Arroyo Grande, CA 93420-0364

Description: Women soccer enthusiasts in Arroyo Grande, CA.

Auburn

★1261★ Placer Women's Center
PO Box 5462
Auburn, CA 95604
Phone: (916)885-0443
Barbara E. Webster, Exec.Dir.

Description: Provides services to women in Placer County, CA. Operates shelter, crisis intervention, and paralegal services for battered women and their children. Offers crisis intervention services, advocacy, and court and hospital accompaniment to survivors of sexual assault.

Bakersfield

★1262★ Young Women's Christian Association of Bakersfield
1130 17th St.
Bakersfield, CA 93301
Phone: (805)323-6072

Description: Seeks to develop and improve the spiritual, social, mental, and physical well-being of young people and adults. **Affiliated with:** Young Women's Christian Association of the United States of America.

Ben Lomond

★1263★ La Leche League International, North California/Hawaii Chapter
110 Taylor Rd.
Ben Lomond, CA 95005
Phone: (408)336-5873
Laura Maxson, Coordinator

Description: Mothers who are breastfeeding their babies. Provides information breast feeding, childbirth, parenting, and other subjects. **Affiliated with:** La Leche League International.

Berkeley

★1264★ Artistas Indigenas
48 Shattuck Sq.
Berkeley, CA 94704
Phone: (510)527-1492

Founded: 1982. **Description:** Nonprofit group formed to support and promote indigenous women artists and community activists of the American and Pacific Islands, with branches in

Oregon and Texas. Sponsors annual traveling exhibitions.

★1265★ **Center for Women and Religion**
2400 Ridge Rd.
Berkeley, CA 94709
Phone: (415)649-2490
Mary Cross, Contact
Founded: 1970. **Description:** Feminist curriculum, counseling program, resource library and special events. **Publications:** *Journal of Women and Religion* and *Membership Newsletter*.

★1266★ **Feminists for Animal Rights**
PO Box 10017, North Berkeley Sta.
Berkeley, CA 94709
Phone: (510)547-7251
Marti Kheel, Co-coordinator
Description: Promotes public education regarding animal abuse and the theoretical connection between abuse of women and that of animals. Conducts charitable activities.

★1267★ **Ohlone Older Women's League**
c/o Betty Soldz
6930 Norfolk Rd.
Berkeley, CA 94705
Phone: (510)845-9579
Betty Soldz, Co-Chair
Description: Middle-aged and older women in the East Bay area of California. Promotes equity for members in employment, health care, and housing. **Affiliated with:** Older Women's League.

★1268★ **Western Association of Women Historians (WAWH)**
1088 Cragmont Ave.
Berkeley, CA 94708
Alison Lingo, Newsletter Editor
Founded: 1969. **Description:** Promotes the professional achievement of women historians. WAWH is the largest of the regional women's historical associations. **Membership:** 500 active members. **Publications:** *The Networker* (Newsletter). **Meetings:** Annual spring conferences present scholarly work, new research, discussion of teaching methods, debate of issues important to women scholars.

★1269★ **Young Women's Christian Association of Berkeley**
2134 Allston Way
Berkeley, CA 94707
Phone: (510)848-1882
Chris McCray, Exec.Dir.
Description: Seeks to develop and improve the spiritual, social, mental, and physical well-being of young people and adults. Currently undergoing reorganization. **Affiliated with:** World Young Women's Christian Association; Young Women's Christian Association of the U.S.A.

Beverly Hills

★1270★ **Los Angeles Women's Campaign Fund**
150 El Camino Dr., Ste. 110
Beverly Hills, CA 90212
Phone: (213)275-4042
Nettie Becker, Co-Chair

★1271★ **Women For:**
8913 W. Olympic Blvd.
Beverly Hills, CA 90211
Phone: (213)657-7411
Marilyn Kizziah, Coordinator
Founded: 1964. **Description:** Bipartisan feminist political organization advocating social and economic rights for women and children. Advocate for ERA, abortion rights, public health, education, and environmental issues. Activities include fundraising, research, and action programs; supports local female pro-choice candidates for political office. **Members:** Over 2,000 active in the Los Angeles Area, including full-time homemakers, politicians, businesswomen, lawyers, architects, librarians, city planners, nuns, poets, and writers. **Publications:** Monthly newsletter.

Campbell

★1272★ **American Business Women's Association, Campbell Chapter**
621 East Campbell, Ste. 11E
Campbell, CA 95008
Phone: (408)370-6601
Diane D. Lowery, Sec.
Description: Business and executive women. Awards scholarships. **Affiliated with:** American Business Women's Association.

Castro Valley

★1273★ **Sullivan Political Action Committee for Women Democrats**
18600 Sheffield Rd.
Castro Valley, CA 94546
Phone: (510)886-3082
Stephanie Cartwright, Contact

Castroville

★1274★ **Girl Scouts, Monterey Bay Council**
10550 Merritt
Castroville, CA 95012
Phone: (408)633-4877
Brenda L. Whitsett, Exec.Dir.
Description: Daisy girl scouts (ages five to six); Brownie Girl Scouts (ages six to eight); Junior Girl Scouts (ages eight to 11); Cadette Girl Scouts (ages 11-14); Senior Girl Scouts (ages 14-17); and adult volunteer leaders in Monterey, San Benito, and Santa Cruz counties, CA. Works to develop girls to their highest potential. **Affiliated with:** Girl Scouts of the U.S.A.

Claremont

★1275★ **Association for Women in Science, Claremont Colleges Chapter**
c/o Dr. Regina Mooney
Dean of Students Office
Harvey Mudd College
301 E. 12th St.
Claremont, CA 91711
Phone: (714)621-8125
Description: Works to improve education and employment opportunities for women in the sciences.

Colton

★1276★ **Mothers for Race Unity and Equality**
c/o Lenise Gaertner
PO Box 851
Colton, CA 92324-0804
Description: Works to combat racism.

Concord

★1277★ **Business and Professional Women's Club of Todos Santos**
3112 Clayton Rd.
Concord, CA 94519
Phone: (510)672-3111
Wanda Harris, Pres.
Description: Business and professional women. To promote complete participation, equal opportunities, and economic self-sufficiency for working women. **Affiliated with:** National Federation of Business and Professional Women's Clubs of the U.S.A.

Covina

★1278★ **Covina Woman's Club**
128 South San Jose Ave.
Covina, CA 91723
Phone: (818)331-9180
Laura Brady, Pres.
Description: Women providing social, philanthropic, and educational services. **Affiliated with:** General Federation of Women's Clubs.

Culver City

★1279★ **Beta Pi Sigma Sorority, Alpha Chapter**
1216 Raintree Circle, Apt. 216
Culver City, CA 90230
Phone: (213)293-2860
Helene K. Bean, Contact
Description: Seeks to further the education and careers of female students studying in business and other professional fields. Offers scholarships.

★1280★ **Hollywood Women's Political Committee**
10536 Culver Blvd., No. 1
Culver City, CA 90232
Phone: (213)559-9334
Margery Tabankin, Exec.Dir.

★1281★ **Los Angeles Women's Community Chorus**
c/o Pat Dallam
11462 Patom Dr.
Culver City, CA 90230-5339
Description: Promotes appreciation and performance of women's choral music.

Dana Point

★1282★ **Dana Point Woman's Club**
24642 San Juan Ave.
Dana Point, CA 92629
Phone: (714)496-9061
Betty Matovich, Pres.
Description: Women. Promotes community affairs and organizations. Offers scholarship to high school senior. Sponsors charitable pro-

grams. **Affiliated with:** General Federation of Women's Clubs.

Danville

★1283★ Danville Women's Club
242 West Linda Mesa Ave.
Danville, CA 94526
Phone: (510)837-1165
Vivian Swarts, Pres.

Description: Women promoting education, philanthropy, public welfare, moral values, and culture and art. Raises funds for community services. **Affiliated with:** General Federation of Women's Clubs.

Davis

★1284★ Sacramento Women's Chorus
PO Box 92069
Davis, CA 95617-9010

El Cajon

★1285★ American Woman's Society of Certified Public Accountants of San Diego
2160 Valley Lake Dr.
El Cajon, CA 92020
Phone: (619)280-5102
Susan M. Ehrhardt, Contact

El Cerrito

★1286★ Older Women's League (OWL) Ohlone Chapter
2516 Mira Vista Dr.
El Cerrito, CA 94530
Phone: (510)236-0678
Joanna Selby, Contact

★1287★ Women's Club of El Cerrito
916 Kearney St.
El Cerrito, CA 94530
Phone: (510)525-2677
Pat Berndt, Pres.

Description: Women's volunteer service club. Works to develop intellectual and civic interests and promote community welfare. **Affiliated with:** Mount Diablo District Women's Clubs.

Fair Oaks

★1288★ General Federation of Women's Clubs, The Leisure Club
c/o Margaret Wolford
5417 Biltmore Way
Fair Oaks, CA 95628-2903

Description: Women in Fair Oakes, CA.

Fontana

★1289★ Young Women's Christian Association of Fontana
PO Box 483
Fontana, CA 92334
Phone: (714)822-6502
Christine A. Wiatt, Contact

Description: Seeks to develop and improve the spiritual, social, mental, and physical well-being of young people and adults. Bestows high school scholarships. Offers temporary shelter assistance. Conducts counseling, tutoring, and Vital English programs. **Affiliated with:** Young

Women's Christian Association of the United States of America.

Fremont

★1290★ Cesarean Prevention Movement of San Francisco Bay Area
33892 Abercrombie Pl.
Fremont, CA 94555
Phone: (510)796-8185
Joy Smith-Gomes, Exec. Officer

Fresno

★1291★ California Federation of Women's Clubs
2220 Tulare, Ste. 610
Fresno, CA 93721
Phone: (209)264-3690
Elizabeth Boragno, Sec.

Description: Women's volunteer service organization. Provides community, charitable, and educational services. Conducts board meetings. **Affiliated with:** General Federation of Women's Clubs.

★1292★ Older Women's League (OWL) Fresno County Chapter
4452 E. Terrace
PO Box 29
Fresno, CA 93703
Phone: (209)222-0981
Harriet Jowett, Contact

★1293★ Young Women's Christian Association of Fresno
1600 M St.
Fresno, CA 93721
Phone: (209)237-4706

Description: Seeks to develop and improve the spiritual, social, mental, and physical well-being of young people and adults. **Affiliated with:** Young Women's Christian Association of the United States of America.

Fullerton

★1294★ Association for Women in Science, Fullerton Chapter
c/o Dr. Diane Ross
Cal State Univ.
Dept. of Physical Education
Fullerton, CA 92634-0000

Description: Works to improve education and employment opportunities for women in the sciences.

★1295★ Young Women's Christian Association of North Orange County
321 North Pomona Ave.
Fullerton, CA 92632
Phone: (714)871-4488
Fax: (714)871-4709
Beverly R. Glen, Exec. Officer

Description: Seeks to develop and improve the spiritual, social, mental, and physical well-being of young people and adults. Promotes literacy, leadership development, and intercultural understanding. **Affiliated with:** Young Women's Christian Association of the United States of America.

Garden Grove

★1296★ Orange County Women's Bowling Association
13896 Harbor Blvd., Bldg. 5-A
Garden Grove, CA 92643
Phone: (714)554-0111

★1297★ Woman's Civic Club of Garden Grove
9501 Chapman Ave.
Garden Grove, CA 92643
Phone: (714)539-3134
Helen Cassity, Pres.

Description: Women's volunteer service club. Promotes education and spiritual values. Conducts benefit rummage sale and fashion shows. Sponsors Day at the Races. Operates thrift boutique. **Affiliated with:** General Federation of Women's Clubs.

Gardena

★1298★ Young Women's Christian Association of Gardena Valley
1341 West Gardena Blvd.
Gardena, CA 90247
Phone: (213)327-5356

Description: Seeks to develop and improve the spiritual, social, mental, and physical well-being of young people and adults. **Affiliated with:** Young Women's Christian Association of the United States of America.

Glendale

★1299★ National Association of Women Business Owners
Los Angeles Chapter
c/o Denny and Company
550 N. Brand Blvd., No. 1650
Glendale, CA 91203
Phone: (818)240-1800
Carolyn Denny, President

★1300★ Young Women's Christian Association of Glendale
735 East Lexington Ave.
Glendale, CA 91206
Phone: (818)242-4155

Description: Seeks to develop and improve the spiritual, social, mental, and physical well-being of young people and adults. **Affiliated with:** Young Women's Christian Association of the United States of America.

Glendora

★1301★ Glendora Woman's Club
PO Box 672
Glendora, CA 91740
Phone: (818)335-7010
Marilyn E. Edwards, Pres.

Description: Women in the Glendora, CA area. Seeks to develop cultural interests among members; addresses the civic, philanthropic, and educational needs of the community.

Hayward

★1302★ Young Women's Christian Association of Southern Alameda County
22366 Fuller Ave.
Hayward, CA 95441
Phone: (510)785-2736
Description: Seeks to develop and improve the spiritual, social, mental, and physical well-being of young people and adults. **Affiliated with:** Young Women's Christian Association of the United States of America.

Huntington Beach

★1303★ South Bay/Long Beach Woman's Society of Certified Public Accountants
Cline, Harduvel and Company
7755 Center Ave., Ste. 850
Huntington Beach, CA 92647
Phone: (213)597-4384
Jean L. Harduvel, Pres.

La Jolla

★1304★ Association for Women in Science, La Jolla Chapter
c/o Lynn Freedmann
PO Box 9143
La Jolla, CA 92038-9143
Description: Works to improve education and employment opportunities for women in the sciences.

★1305★ DES Action
c/o Dr. Wingard
Community Medicine M-007
Univ. of California-S.D.
La Jolla, CA 92093

★1306★ San Diego Coalition for School Age Mothers
c/o Kathryn Wachsberger
PO Box 948566
La Jolla, CA 92037-9406
Description: Supports and promotes the social programs for school-age mothers in San Diego, CA.

La Mesa

★1307★ La Mesa Community Welfare Association
8340 Lemon Ave.
La Mesa, CA 92041
Phone: (619)466-6678
Sandra Smith, Pres.
Description: Women volunteers. Provides emergency assistance to those in need. Offers assistance to senior citizens. Provides gifts during the Christmas season.

Laguna Beach

★1308★ National Association of Women Business Owners
Nashville Chapter
c/o Success Seminars
1289 S. Coast Hwy.
Laguna Beach, CA 92651
Phone: (714)433-6572
Rita Burgett, President

Lakewood

★1309★ Cesarean Prevention Movement of Long Beach
6309 Seaborn St.
Lakewood, CA 90713
Phone: (213)429-2015
Sandy Caves, Exec. Officer

Long Beach

★1310★ Greater Long Beach Girl Scout Council
4040 Bellflower Blvd.
Long Beach, CA 90808
Phone: (213)421-8456
Joan G. Blackmon, Exec.Dir.
Description: Girls aged five to 17 (7000) and adult volunteers (2000). Provides programs in which girls raise their self-esteem and learn to become happy and productive citizens. **Affiliated with:** Girl Scouts of the U.S.A.

★1311★ Young Women's Christian Association of Long Beach
PO Box 32107
Long Beach, CA 90832
Phone: (310)491-5362
Description: Seeks to develop and improve the spiritual, social, mental, and physical well-being of young people and adults. **Affiliated with:** Young Women's Christian Association of the United States of America.

Los Angeles

★1312★ Angeles Girl Scout Council
5057 West Adams Blvd.
Los Angeles, CA 90016
Phone: (213)933-4700
Florence Newsom, Exec.Dir.
Description: Girls ages five to 18 and adult volunteer leaders. Helps girls reach their full potential and become active, helpful citizens. **Affiliated with:** Girl Scouts of the U.S.A.

★1313★ Black Women Lawyers Association of Southern California
State Bar Court
818 W. 7th St.
Los Angeles, CA 90017
E. Jean Gary, Pres.

★1314★ Black Women's Forum
PO Box 01702
Los Angeles, CA 90001
Phone: (213)292-3009

★1315★ DES Action
Box 661653
Los Angeles, CA 90066

★1316★ Hispanic Women's Council
5803 East Beverly Blvd.
Los Angeles, CA 90022
Phone: (213)725-1657
Lourdes Z. Saab, Contact

★1317★ Los Angeles Jewish Feminist Center
American Jewish Congress
6505 Wilshire Blvd.
Los Angeles, CA 90048
Phone: (213)655-5619
Carol Plotkin, Contact
Description: Operated from the office of the American Jewish Congress, the library contains the West Coast's most comprehensive collection of publications about, by and for Jewish women. The center holds continuing education courses; community celebrations; consultations; speakers bureau. Sponsors a feminist research group.

★1318★ Los Angeles Women in Music
8489 West 3rd St.
Los Angeles, CA 90048-4194
Description: Women in the music industry; promotes professional advancement of members.

★1319★ Los Angeles Women's Foundation
6030 Wilshire Blvd., Ste. 303
Los Angeles, CA 90036
Phone: (213)938-9828
Jean Conger, Executive Director

★1320★ Southern Pacific Coast Region of Hadassah, The Women's Zionist Organization of America
6505 Wilshire Blvd., Ste. 404
Los Angeles, CA 90048
Phone: (213)653-9727
Molly Novak, Pres.
Description: Women providing social services and education in Israel and education and camps in the U.S. **Affiliated with:** Hadassah, The Women's Zionist Organization of America.

★1321★ Women's American ORT, Pacific Southwest District
6505 Wilshire Blvd., Ste. 512
Los Angeles, CA 90048
Phone: (213)655-2911
Evelyn Schecter, Exec.Dir.
Description: Provides technical and vocational support to the Organization for Rehabilitation through training. Issues publications. **Affiliated with:** Women's American ORT.

★1322★ Women's Political Committee
600 Hanley Way
Los Angeles, CA 90049
Phone: (213)655-2711
Marcia Herman, Treasurer

★1323★ Young Women's Christian Association of Los Angeles
1125 West Sixth St., Ste. 400
Los Angeles, CA 90017-1866
Phone: (213)482-3470
Fax: (213)482-1655
Laura S. Wiltz, PhD, Contact
Description: Seeks to develop and improve the spiritual, social, mental, and physical well-being of young people and adults. Sponsors local charities. **Affiliated with:** Young Women's Christian Association of the United States of America.

★1324★ Young Women's Christian Association Los Angeles, South Valley Center
1125 West 6th
Los Angeles, CA 90017
Phone: (818)766-1903
Description: Seeks to develop and improve the spiritual, social, mental, and physical well-being of young people and adults. **Affiliated with:**

Young Women's Christian Association of the U.S.A.

Mill Valley

★1325★ Cesarean Prevention Movement of Marin County
PO Box 2395
Mill Valley, CA 94942
Phone: (415)883-5049
Andrea Henkart, Pres.

Description: Mothers, pregnant women, nurses, and midwives in the Bay Area, CA. Seeks to decrease the rate of Cesarean births performed and to promote the natural approach to childbirth. Offers emotional support, information, and education. Conducts suppport groups; provides speakers. **Affiliated with:** Cesarean Prevention Movement.

Mission Viejo

★1326★ Saddleback Valley Business and Professional Women
28601 Marguerite Pkwy., #3
Mission Viejo, CA 92692
Phone: (714)364-2279

Description: Women in El Toro, Laguna Hills, Laguna Niguel, Mission Viejo, San Clemente, and San Juan Capistrano, CA. Promotes complete participation, equal opportunity, and economic self-sufficiency for working women. **Affiliated with:** National Federation of Business and Professional Women's Clubs of the U.S.A.

Modesto

★1327★ Central California Coalition On Domestic Violence
PO Box 3931
Modesto, CA 95352
Phone: (209)575-7037

Montclair

★1328★ Young Women's Christian Association of Greater Pomona Valley
5323 Holt Blvd.
Montclair, CA 91763
Phone: (714)624-4403

Description: Seeks to develop and improve the spiritual, social, mental, and physical well-being of young people and adults. **Affiliated with:** Young Women's Christian Association of the United States of America.

Monterey

★1329★ Young Women's Christian Association of the Monterey Peninsula
801 Lighthouse
Monterey, CA 93940
Phone: (408)649-0834

Description: Seeks to develop and improve the spiritual, social, mental, and physical well-being of young people and adults. **Affiliated with:** Young Women's Christian Association of the United States of America.

Monterey Park

★1330★ Southern California Nisei Women's Golf Association
c/o Masako Saisho
915 Ridgecrest St.
Monterey Park, CA 91754-4622

Description: Promotes women's golf in Southern California.

Mt. View

★1331★ Older Women's League (OWL) Palo Alto/Menlo Park Chapter
765 N. Rengstroff Ave. No. 24
Mt. View, CA 94043
Phone: (415)967-3074
Miriam Kusnierczyk, Contact

Napa

★1332★ Napa Emergency Women's Services
PO Box 427
Napa, CA 94559
Phone: (707)255-6397
Rosemary Dady, Program Dir.

Description: Provides emergency services to battered women and their children in Napa County, CA. Conducts charitable activities.

Oakdale

★1333★ Oakdale-Riverdale Branch of the American Association of University Women
1056 Maria Dr.
Oakdale, CA 95361-2663

Description: Oakdale-Riverdale, CA of the American Association of University Women.

Oakland

★1334★ Bay Area Black Women's Health Project
c/o Fleicia Ware
1051 Bella Vista, Ste. 3
Oakland, CA 94610-4036

Description: Individuals working on African-American women's health issues in the Bay area of Oakland-San Francisco, CA.

★1335★ Bay Area Evangelical and Ecumenical Women's Caucus
PO Box 9989
Oakland, CA 94613-0989
Phone: (510)635-5098
Margaret Arighi, Coordinator

Description: Christian feminists in northern California. Sponsors retreats, picnics, and quarterly support groups.

★1336★ Black Women Organized for Educational Development
518 17th St., Ste. 202
Oakland, CA 94612
Phone: (415)763-9501

★1337★ Black Women's Health Project
PO Box 10529
Oakland, CA 94601
Phone: (415)533-6923

★1338★ Black Women's Resource Center
518 17th St., Ste. 202
Oakland, CA 94612
Phone: (415)763-9501

★1339★ East Bay Women's Political Action Committee
5736 Chelton Dr.
Oakland, CA 94611
Phone: (510)482-4941
Helen Tirsell, Pres.

★1340★ Northern California Black Women Physicians Association
3022 East 14th St. 312
Oakland, CA 94601-2226

Description: African-American women physicians in northern California.

★1341★ Peninsula Women's Rugby
PO Box 10154
Oakland, CA 94610-0154

★1342★ Restored Women
c/o Sharon Montgomery
PO Box 5495
Oakland, CA 94605-0495

★1343★ Young Women's Christian Association of Oakland
1515 Webster St.
Oakland, CA 94612
Phone: (510)451-7900

Description: Seeks to develop and improve the spiritual, social, mental, and physical well-being of young people and adults. **Affiliated with:** Young Women's Christian Association of the United States of America.

Orange

★1344★ Orange County Crisis Pregnancy Centers
PO Box 2110
Orange, CA 92669-0110

Description: Provides support counseling, and other services for those affected by crisis pregnancy in Orange County, CA.

★1345★ Young Women's Christian Association of Central Orange County
146 North Grand St.
Orange, CA 92666
Phone: (714)633-4950

Description: Seeks to develop and improve the spiritual, social, mental, and physical well-being of young people and adults. **Affiliated with:** Young Women's Christian Association of the United States of America.

Pacific Palisades

★1346★ Pacific Palisades Woman's Club
PO Box 292
Pacific Palisades, CA 90272
Phone: (213)454-9012
June G. Blum, Pres.

Description: Women organized for philanthropic, political, and social activities. **Affiliated with:** California Federation of Women's Clubs; California Federation of Women's Clubs, Marina District; National Federation of Women's Clubs.

Palo Alto

★1347★ Association for Women in Science, Palo Alto Chapter
c/o Dr. Martha Murari
Varian Associates
3120 Hansen Way, M/S D-300
Palo Alto, CA 94304-1030
Phone: (415)424-5401
Description: Works to improve education and employment opportunities for women in the sciences.

★1348★ Mid-Peninsula Young Women's Christian Association
4161 Alma St.
Palo Alto, CA 94306
Phone: (415)494-0972
Description: Seeks to develop and improve the spiritual, social, mental, and physical well-being of young people and adults. **Affiliated with:** Young Women's Christian Association of the United States of America.

★1349★ Resource Center for Women
445 Sherman Ave.
Palo Alto, CA 94306
Phone: (415)324-1710
Gail Stypula, Contact
Founded: 1973. **Description:** Provides the information and guidance women need to make informed decisions about the direction of their lives. Offers career planning and employment services, a resource library, job listings, workshops and career counseling. **Publications:** *Career Connections.*

Pasadena

★1350★ Council of Women's Clubs
160 North Oakland Ave.
Pasadena, CA 91101
Phone: (818)796-5617
Inez T. Smith, Pres.
Description: Women's organizations in the Pasadena, CA area.

★1351★ Older Women's League (OWL) Foothill Area Chapter
PO Box
Pasadena, CA 94182
Phone: (818)792-9565
Addie Bossieux, Contact

★1352★ Pasadena Business and Professional Women's Club
319 Sierra Madre Blvd., Apt. J
Pasadena, CA 91107
Phone: (818)795-2904
Description: Business and professional women. To promote complete participation, equal opportunities, and economic self-sufficiency for working women. **Affiliated with:** National Federation of Business and Professional Women's Clubs of the U.S.A.

★1353★ Pasadena Commission on the Status of Women
234 East Colorado Blvd., Ste. 508
Pasadena, CA 91101
Phone: (818)796-6926
Fax: (818)405-4244
Cindy O. Kunisaki, Coordinator
Description: Women appointed by the city board of directors. Provides advice and recommendations on issues affecting women and families.

★1354★ Pasadena-Foothill Valley Young Women's Christian Association
78 North Marengo Ave.
Pasadena, CA 91101
Phone: (818)793-5171
Fax: (818)578-1359
Carol Bridges, CEO
Description: Seeks to develop and improve the spiritual, social, mental, and physical life of youth and adults in Arcadia, Durate, Monrovia, Pasadena, Sierra Madre, and South Pasadena, CA. Operates rape hotline crisis center. Offers child care services. Sponsors programs for senior citizens. Maintains child abuse prevention project, teen parenting project, thrift shop, and shelter for homeless women and children. **Affiliated with:** Young Women's Christian Association of the United States of America.

★1355★ Pasadena Interracial Women's Club
Pilgrim Tower, N., No. 710
560 E. Villa
Pasadena, CA 91101
Phone: (818)584-1611
Genevieve Valliere, Pres.
Description: Women working to achieve fellowship and positive results with women of all races. Provides scholarships to students in need and qualified students. Operates book review club. **Affiliated with:** Council of Women's Clubs.

★1356★ Woman's Civic League of Pasadena
160 North Oakland Ave.
Pasadena, CA 91101
Phone: (818)796-0560
Description: Women's volunteer service club.

Placentia

★1357★ Executive Women International, Orange County Chapter
620 South Placentia
Placentia, CA 92670
Phone: (714)961-0434
Description: Professional women organized to advance their firms and promote self-growth and community awareness. Makes available scholarship. **Affiliated with:** Executive Women International.

★1358★ National Association of Women Business Owners
Orange County Chapter
c/o Resumes, Etc.
2019 E. Orangethorpe, No. E
Placentia, CA 92670
Phone: (714)528-3765
Nita Busby, President

★1359★ Placentia Round Table Women's Club
PO Box 334
Placentia, CA 92670-0334

Pleasanton

★1360★ Older Women's League (OWL) Tri-Valley Chapter
4169 Churchill Dr.
Pleasanton, CA 945066
Marlene Osborne, Contact

Redlands

★1361★ Young Women's Christian Association of Redlands
16 East Olive Ave.
Redlands, CA 92373
Phone: (714)793-2957
Description: Seeks to develop and improve the spiritual, social, mental, and physical well-being of young people and adults. **Affiliated with:** Young Women's Christian Association of the United States of America.

Richmond

★1362★ Young Women's Christian Association of Contra Costa County
3230 MacDonald Ave.
Richmond, CA 94804
Phone: (510)234-1270
Fax: (415)234-2496
Bette Boatmun, Contact
Description: Seeks to develop and improve the spiritual, social, mental, and physical well-being of young people and adults. **Affiliated with:** Young Women's Christian Association of the United States of America.

Riverside

★1363★ Young Women's Christian Association of Riverside
8172 Magnolia Ave.
Riverside, CA 92504
Phone: (714)688-5531
Description: Seeks to develop and improve the spiritual, social, mental, and physical well-being of young people and adults. **Affiliated with:** Young Women's Christian Association of the United States of America.

Rockland

★1364★ Older Women's League (OWL) Placer County Chapter
4660 Arrowhead Dr.
Rockland, CA 95677
Phone: (916)624-2933
Jean Clawson, Contact

Rosemead

★1365★ Big Sisters of Los Angeles
6002 Willow Shore, Ste. 202
Rosemead, CA 90036
Phone: (213)933-5749
Fax: (213)933-6685
Janet Schulman, Exec.Dir.
Description: Provides volunteer adult role models to girls aged 6 to 18 from disadvantaged backgrounds. Works to maximize children's potential. **Affiliated with:** Big Brothers/Big Sisters of America.

Roseville

★1366★ Sunset Whitney Women's Golf Association
1106 Oakridge Dr.
Roseville, CA 95661-4618
Description: Promotes women's golf in Rose Ville, CA.

Sacramento

★1367★ American Association of University Women, California State Division
909 12th St., Ste. 114
Sacramento, CA 95814
Phone: (916)448-7795
Chris Winter, Pres.
Description: Women graduates of regionally accredited four year colleges and universities. Works for the advancement of women through advocacy and emphasis on lifelong learning. **Affiliated with:** American Association of University Women.

★1368★ California Women Lawyers
926 J St., Ste. 820
Sacramento, CA 95814
Phone: (916)441-3703
Description: Lawyers, law professors, judges, and law students. Conducts judicial evaluations and lobbying activities; offers referral services and networking opportunities.

★1369★ California Women Lawyers Education Foundation
926 J St.
Sacramento, CA 95814-2704

★1370★ Delta Chapter Gamma Phi Delta Sorority
PO Box 221221
Sacramento, CA 95822-8221

★1371★ League of Women Voters of California
926 J St., Ste. 1000
Sacramento, CA 95814
Phone: (916)442-7215
Robyn Prud'homme Bauer, President

★1372★ Matrix Workshop of Women Artists
1725 I St.
Sacramento, CA 95814
Phone: (916)441-4818
Description: Sponsors workshops and lectures on issues of interest to artists and community. Gallery and classroom space. **Membership:** 90.

★1373★ National Association of Women Business Owners
Sacramento Chapter
c/o Garcia Realty
2014 28th St., Ste. B
Sacramento, CA 95818
Phone: (916)452-7535
Eva Garcia, President

★1374★ Older Women's League (OWL)
California State Chapter
1127 11th St. No. 325
Sacramento, CA 95814
Phone: (916)444-2526
Theresa Johnson, Contact

★1375★ Older Women's League (OWL)
Sacramento Capitol Chapter
5717 8th Ave.
Sacramento, CA 95820
Phone: (916)455-6327
Elizabeth Perry, Contact

★1376★ Sacramento Black Women's Network
PO Box 162986
Sacramento, CA 95816
Phone: (916)427-7296

★1377★ Sacramento Women's Campaign Fund
PO Box 162212
Sacramento, CA 95816
Phone: (916)457-6721
Andrea Rosen, Contact

★1378★ Sacramento Women's Center
2306 J St., Ste. 200
Sacramento, CA 95816
Phone: (916)441-4207
Phyllis Hopkins, Exec.Dir.
Description: To improve the economic, social, and political status of women in the Sacramento County, CA area. Offers job training workshops and placement services for low income women. Provides employment information, referral program, and support groups. Conducts typing tests and community presentations. **Affiliated with:** National Association of Women Centers.

★1379★ Young Women's Christian Association of Sacramento
1122 17th St.
Sacramento, CA 95814
Description: Seeks to develop and improve the spiritual, social, mental, and physical well-being of young people and adults. **Affiliated with:** Young Women's Christian Association of the United States of America.

San Bernardino

★1380★ Young Women's Christian Association of San Bernardino
567 North Sierra Way
San Bernardino, CA 92404
Phone: (714)889-9536
Description: Seeks to develop and improve the spiritual, social, mental, and physical well-being of young people and adults. **Affiliated with:** Young Women's Christian Association of the United States of America.

San Bruno

★1381★ American Association of University Women, San Bruno Chapter
2500 Trenton Dr.
San Bruno, CA 94066
Kathleen Semenza, Pres.
Description: Women graduates of regionally accredited four year colleges and universities. Works for the advancement of women through advocacy and emphasis on lifelong learning. Co-chairs seminars and forums on women's issues. **Affiliated with:** American Association of University Women.

San Diego

★1382★ African-American Women's Conference
c/o Maria Denise Carothers
2415 56th St.
San Diego, CA 92105-5011

★1383★ Association for Women in Science, San Diego Chapter
c/o Barbara Armstrong
4484 Pocahontas Ave.
San Diego, CA 92117
Phone: (619)455-3366
Description: Works to improve education and employment opportunities for women in the sciences.

★1384★ Big Sister League of San Diego
115 Redwood
San Diego, CA 92103
Phone: (619)297-1172
Diane Williams Hymons, Exec.Dir.
Description: Provides guidance and companionship for young girls aged 6 to 15. Offers temporary shelter for women who are in crisis situations.

★1385★ Cesarean Prevention Movement of San Diego
c/o Kathy Shoecraft
13195 Capstone Dr.
San Diego, CA 92130
Phone: (619)259-6930
Kathy Shoecraft, Contact
Description: Provides education and support to childbearing women regarding cesarean birth and vaginal birth after cesarean. **Affiliated with:** Cesarean Prevention Movement.

★1386★ Childbirth Education Association
4175 Bonillo Dr., Ste. 2
San Diego, CA 92115
Phone: (619)583-9451
Cathy Hudson, Office Mgr.
Description: Childbirth educators in San Diego County, CA. Provides prenatal educational and excercise programs and early parenting classes to expectant parents. Conducts seminars. **Affiliated with:** International Childbirth Education Association.

★1387★ Girl Scouts of the U.S.A., San Diego-Imperial Council
1231 Upas
San Diego, CA 92103
Phone: (619)298-8391
Toll-free: 800-643-4798
Barbara J. Dickey, Exec.Dir.
Description: Girls aged five to 17 and adult volunteers in San Diego and Imperial counties, CA. Provides young girls with opportunities to develop their physical, intellectual, and spiritual potential, interpersonal skills, and values. **Affiliated with:** Girl Scouts of the U.S.A. **Telecommunications Services:** Toll-free number, (800)643-4798 (in San Diego County).

★1388★ **National Association of Women Business Owners**
San Diego Chapter
c/o Creative Capital Management
7428 Jackson Dr.
San Diego, CA 92119-2319
Phone: (619)464-2442
Peggy Eddy, President

★1389★ **National Association of Women in Construction, San Diego Chapter 21**
PO Box 880725
San Diego, CA 92168
Phone: (619)234-0080
Linda Ann Litle, Pres.

Description: Women in the construction industry. To educate and unite women in the field. Sponsors educational classes and scholarship awards. Conducts High School Drafting Contest. **Affiliated with:** National Association of Women in Construction.

★1390★ **National Association of Women Judges**
c/o Judge Janet Kintner
Dept 8M, 220 W. Broadway
San Diego, CA 92101
Janet Kintner, Exec. Officer

Description: Individuals holding judicial or quasi-judicial positions. **Affiliated with:** National Association of Women Judges.

★1391★ **National Women's Studies Association, Pacific Southwest Chapter**
San Diego State University
Women's Studies Department
San Diego, CA 92101
Phone: (619)594-5239
Dr. Bonnie Zimmerman, Coordinator

Description: Teachers, students, community activists, and interested individuals promoting feminist education. **Affiliated with:** National Women's Studies Association.

★1392★ **Older Women's League (OWL)**
San Diego Chapter
PO Box 12513
San Diego, CA 92112
Phone: (619)454-6230
Shirley Von Kalinowski, Contact

★1393★ **San Diego Career Women**
PO Box 880384
San Diego, CA 92108-0008

Description: Businesswomen in San Diego, CA.

★1394★ **San Diego Women's Association**
4550 Kearny Villa Rd.
San Diego, CA 92123-1574

★1395★ **Women's Institute for Continuing Jewish Education**
4079 54th St.
San Diego, CA 92105
Phone: (619)442-2666

★1396★ **Women's Overseas Service League, San Diego Unit**
2595 Murray Ridge Rd.
San Diego, CA 92123
Phone: (619)279-3797
Lezetta M. Davis, Pres.

Description: Women who served overseas with the armed services, American Red Cross, Salvation Army, or other service organizations.

Carries on patriotic activities, services to disabled veterans, and aid to members in need.

★1397★ **Young Women's Christian Association of San Diego County**
1012 C St.
San Diego, CA 92101
Phone: (619)239-0355
Janie Davis, Contact

Description: Seeks to develop and improve the spiritual, social, mental, and physical well-being of young people and adults. Conducts social service activities. **Affiliated with:** Young Women's Christian Association of the United States of America.

San Francisco

★1398★ **Advocates for Women (AFW)**
414 Mason St.
San Francisco, CA 94102
Phone: (415)391-4870
Barbara Woodward, Exec.Dir.

Founded: 1971. **Description:** Economic development center devoted exclusively to improving the economic status of women. Maintains additional offices in Oakland and Hayward, CA. Provides, through all three offices, Job Training Partnership Act funded services, such as job listings, resource library, community bulletin board, individual vocational counseling, and employment workshops. For women who are not economically disadvantaged, as defined by the Department of Labor, AFW offers a Worklife Options program providing vocational counseling and employment workshops on a sliding-scale fee basis. Oakland and Hayward offices serve primarily women who are seeking blue collar and nontraditional careers. Services include skills training, job development, placement counseling, and workshops on job search, resumes, interviewing techniques, and tutoring for blue collar employment testing. **Publications:** *Newsletter*, semiannual.

★1399★ **American Civil Liberties Union, Gay Rights Chapter**
1663 Mission St., No. 460
San Francisco, CA 94103
Phone: (415)621-2493

Description: Supporters of civil liberties and lesbian and gay rights in the San Francisco Bay area of California. Conducts activities to promote and protect civil liberties and gay rights. Lobbies on behalf of members. Sponsors ad hoc programs and activities. Conducts monthly board meetings. **Affiliated with:** American Civil Liberties Union; LIFE.

★1400★ **Asian-Pacific Sisters**
25 Clipper St.
San Francisco, CA 94114-3913

★1401★ **Association for Women in Science, San Francisco Chapter**
c/o Dr. Beth Hutchins
460 S. San Bruno Blvd.
San Francisco, CA 94110-1433

Description: Works to improve education and employment opportunities for women in the sciences.

★1402★ **Black Women Lawyers Association of Northern California**
State Bar of California
555 Franklin St.
San Francisco, CA 94102
Phyllis Culp, Pres.

★1403★ **California Abortion Rights Action League-North (CARAL)**
300 Brannan St., No. 501
San Francisco, CA 94107
Phone: (415)546-7211
Cynthia Carey-Grant, Contact

★1404★ **Korean American Women Artists and Writers Association**
c/o Min Paek
447 7th Ave., No. 4
San Francisco, CA 94118-3011

Description: Works to improve the status of Korean-American women in literacy and artistic field.

★1405★ **National Association of Women Business Owners**
San Francisco Chapter
c/o Jahn, Bayer and Assoc.
44 Montgomery St., No. 2865
San Francisco, CA 94104
Phone: (415)397-9393
Lela Jahn, President

★1406★ **National Organization for Women, San Francisco Chapter**
The Women's Bldg.
3543 18th St.
San Francisco, CA 94101
Phone: (415)861-8880
Helen L. Grieco, Exec.Dir.

Description: Men and women who support "full equality for women in truly equal partnership with men." **Affiliated with:** National Organization for Women.

★1407★ **Older Women's League (OWL)**
San Francisco Chapter
601 Dolores St.
San Francisco, CA 94110
Phone: (415)550-1660
Lillian Layman, Contact

★1408★ **Organization of Women Architects and Design Professionals (OWA)**
PO Box 26570
San Francisco, CA 94126
Phone: (415)550-6051

Founded: 1972. **Description:** A network for women designers in the San Francisco Bay Area that discusses current issues in the architectural profession. **Publications:** *OWA Newsletter*.

★1409★ **San Francisco Women Against Rape**
3543 18th St.
San Francisco, CA 94110-1699

Description: Women in San Francisco working to prevent rape.

★1410★   **Women in Community Service**
71 Stevenson, #1015
San Francisco, CA 94105
Phone: (415)744-7669
Ruth Herman, Dir.

Description: Regional office. Coalition of five national organizations serving low income youth. Recruits and screens youth for the Job Corps. Sponsors vocational training programs. **Affiliated with:** American GI Forum Women; Church Women United; National Council of Catholic Women; National Council of Jewish Women; National Council of Negro Women; Women in Community Service.

★1411★   **The Women's Building of the Bay Area/San Francisco Women's Centers**
3543 18th St.
San Francisco, CA 94110
Phone: (415)863-5255
Celeste Smeland, Arts Coordinator

Description: A nonprofit, women-owned and operated cultural resource and community center. Provides performance and exhibition space, meeting hall, and dining hall for dance, music, poetry, drama, and art. Houses seven women's organizations. **Publications:** Two newsletters and monthly report.

★1412★   **The Women's Foundation**
3543 18th St., No. 9
San Francisco, CA 94110
Phone: (415)431-1290
Kit Durgin, Executive Director

★1413★   **Women's International League for Peace and Freedom, San Francisco Branch**
50 Oak, Rm. 503
San Francisco, CA 94102
Phone: (415)863-7146
Stella M. Paton, Pres.

Description: Works to unite women in all countries who are opposed to war. Advocates on behalf of equality and freedom from racism and sexism. Seeks world disarmament and a change in government priorities. **Affiliated with:** Women's International League for Peace and Freedom, U.S. Section.

★1414★   **Women's Political Fund (WPF)**
PO Box 421811
San Francisco, CA 94142-1811
Phone: (415)474-6808
D.J. Seviero, Chair

Description: The organization is a bi-partisan political action committee which provides money to candidates.

★1415★   **Young Ladies Institute**
PO Box 640687
San Francisco, CA 94164-0687
Phone: (415)346-4367
Carol Marshall, Grand Sec.

Description: Catholic women on the West Coast and in Hawaii. Provides funds for charitable projects and religious activities.

San Jose

★1416★   **Campaign California/Women's Equity Fund**
40 N. 1st St., Ste. 204
San Jose, CA 95113
Phone: (408)286-6113
Barbara Perzigian, Contact

★1417★   **DES Action**
417 Avenida Abetos
San Jose, CA 95123

★1418★   **Society for Women in Philosophy, Pacific Division (SWIP)**
c/o Rita Manning
San Jose State University
Department of Philosophy
San Jose, CA 95192
Phone: (408)924-4501
Rita Manning, Exec.Sec.

Founded: 1975. **Description:** Women and men employed as philosophers or with degrees in philosophy. Facilitates the discussion of issues concerning philosophers, philosophy and academia, and related job issues; disseminates information involving women in philosophy. Offers career advice, support for women in the field, and a channel for socializing. **Members:** 140. **Publications:** Newsletter, semiannual.

★1419★   **Young Women's Christian Association of Santa Clara Valley**
440 North 1st St.
San Jose, CA 95112
Phone: (408)295-4011

Description: Seeks to develop and improve the spiritual, social, mental, and physical well-being of young people and adults. **Affiliated with:** Young Women's Christian Association of the United States of America.

San Juan Capistrano

★1420★   **Cesarean Prevention Movement of South Orange County**
26782 Via El Socorro
San Juan Capistrano, CA 92675
Phone: (714)492-7638
Krista Tiberio, Pres.

Description: Promotes natural childbirth. **Affiliated with:** Cesarean Prevention Movement.

San Leandro

★1421★   **Older Women's League (OWL) Peralta Chapter**
561 Warwick Ave.
San Leandro, CA 94577
Phone: (510)632-5360
Mimi Wilson, Contact

★1422★   **Women's Overseas Service League, Area 6**
2552 Williams St.
San Leandro, CA 94577
Phone: (415)357-3787
Georgia Boyd, Contact

Description: Women who served overseas during wartime or peace time. Promotes the welfare of the armed forces. Provides assistance to women veterans. Fosters better understanding between the U.S. and other nations. Provides funds for national projects, including Cathedral of Pines, Freedom Foundation Valley Forge, Hospitalized Veterans Weight Lifting Project,

and other charities. **Affiliated with:** Women's Overseas Service League.

San Luis Obispo

★1423★   **Older Women's League (OWL) Central Coast Chapter**
237 Del Mar Ct.
San Luis Obispo, CA 93405
Phone: (805)543-1024
Paula Ogren, Contact

San Marino

★1424★   **National Council of Jewish Women, San Gabriel Valley Chapter**
629 Santa Anita Ave.
San Marino, CA 91108
Phone: (818)792-8162

Description: Jewish women in the San Marino, CA providing community services. Advocates on behalf of the old and young, and Israel. **Affiliated with:** National Council of Jewish Women.

San Mateo

★1425★   **Friends of the San Mateo County Advisory Council on Women**
PO Box 6563
San Mateo, CA 94403-6563

Description: Supports and promotes the programs of the San Mateo County Advisory Council on Women.

★1426★   **Pro-Life of San Mateo County**
3615 East Laurel Creek Dr.
San Mateo, CA 94403
Phone: (415)341-8188
G. Gloria Gillogley, Chm.

Description: Individuals suppporting human life. Works to affirm the right-to-life of all human beings, including the unborn, the old and sick, and the disabled. Sponsors Birthright and other support groups and the San Mateo County Crisis Pregnancy Center. Conducts education programs and referral service. **Affiliated with:** California Pro-Life Council; National Right-to-Life.

San Pedro

★1427★   **Support for Harbor Area Women's Lives**
c/o Donald A. Smith
PO Box 948
San Pedro, CA 90733-0948
Donald A. Smith, Contact

★1428★   **Young Women's Christian Association of the Harbor Area**
437 West 9th St.
San Pedro, CA 90731
Phone: (213)547-0831

Description: Seeks to develop and improve the spiritual, social, mental, and physical well-being of young people and adults. Sponsors preschool and latchkey programs. **Affiliated with:** Young Women's Christian Association of the United States of America.

San Rafael

★1429★ Birthright of Marin
2144 4th St.
San Rafael, CA 94901
Phone: (415)456-4500
Toll-free: 800-848-LOVE
Margaret M. Farley, Dir.

Description: Volunteers in Marin County, CA providing pregnancy support services and alternatives to abortion to women, couples, and teenagers. Conducts childbirth classes for single women. **Affiliated with:** Birthright International.

★1430★ Northern California Coalition Against Domestic Violence
1717 5th Ave.
San Rafael, CA 94901
Phone: (415)457-2464
Donna Garske, Chair

Santa Ana

★1431★ Orange County Women For:
13681 Carlstad Dr.
Santa Ana, CA 92705
Phone: (714)544-1918
Francesjane Kapsch, Vice-chair

Founded: 1983. **Description:** Volunteer feminist organization supporting the women's movement on local, national, and world levels.

★1432★ Young Women's Christian Association of South Orange County
1411 North Broadway
Santa Ana, CA 92706
Phone: (714)542-3577

Description: Seeks to develop and improve the spiritual, social, mental, and physical well-being of young people and adults. **Affiliated with:** Young Women's Christian Association of the United States of America.

Santa Barbara

★1433★ Advocates for Girls
619 Olive St., Ste. No. 1
Santa Barbara, CA 93103-0000

Description: Represents members' interests; conducts lobbying activities. Holds seminars and workshops.

★1434★ Older Women's League (OWL)
Santa Barbara Chapter
1606 Grand No. 1
Santa Barbara, CA 93103
Phone: (805)966-9804
Estelle Schneider, Contact

★1435★ Santa Barbara Women's Political Committee
928 Las Palmas Dr.
Santa Barbara, CA 93110
Phone: (805)682-6767
Susan Rose, Vice President Elect

Santa Clara

★1436★ Cesarean Prevention Movement of Santa Clara Valley
2834 Ponderosa Way
Santa Clara, CA 95051
Phone: (408)984-0594
Diana Pierce, Exec. Officer

★1437★ Older Women's League (OWL)
Santa Clara County Chapter
PO Box 2683
Santa Clara, CA 95055
Phone: (415)968-5321
Faith Sandberg, Contact

Santa Cruz

★1438★ Young Women's Christian Association of Santa Cruz
303 Walnut Ave.
Santa Cruz, CA 95060
Phone: (408)426-3062

Description: Seeks to develop and improve the spiritual, social, mental, and physical well-being of young people and adults. **Affiliated with:** Young Women's Christian Association of the United States of America.

Santa Monica

★1439★ American Woman's Society of Certified Public Accountants of Los Angeles
Brenner, Levitt, and Gray
2951 28th St., No. 3040
Santa Monica, CA 90405
Phone: (213)399-8683
Corinne Pleger, Pres.

★1440★ California Abortion Rights Action League-South (CARAL)
225 Santa Monica Blvd. Ste. 406
Santa Monica, CA 90401
Phone: (310)393-0513
Kate Harris, Contact

★1441★ Southern California Coalition on Battered Women
PO Box 5036
Santa Monica, CA 90405
Phone: (213)578-1442

★1442★ Young Women's Christian Association of Santa Monica
2019 14th St.
Santa Monica, CA 90405
Phone: (213)452-3881

Description: Seeks to develop and improve the spiritual, social, mental, and physical well-being of young people and adults. **Affiliated with:** Young Women's Christian Association of the United States of America.

Santa Paula

★1443★ Ebell Club
13932 West Telegraph Rd.
Santa Paula, CA 93060
Phone: (805)525-6774
Hazel Keene Outland, Pres.

Description: Women's cultural enrichment society in Santa Paula, CA.

Santa Rosa

★1444★ Young Women's Christian Association of Sonoma County
PO Box 3506
Santa Rosa, CA 95402
Phone: (707)546-9922

Description: Seeks to develop and improve the spiritual, social, mental, and physical well-being of young people and adults. **Affiliated with:**

Young Women's Christian Association of the United States of America.

Sausalito

★1445★ Marin County Women's PAC
4 3rd St.
Sausalito, CA 94965
Phone: (415)331-7974
Johanna Willmann, Chair

★1446★ Sausalito Women's Club
c/o Gerry Beers
PO Box 3045
Sausalito, CA 94966-3045

Description: Women in Sausalito, CA.

★1447★ Sausalito Women's Club Preservation Society
PO Box 2488
Sausalito, CA 94966-2488

Description: Women in promoting preservation in Sausalito, CA.

Sebastopol

★1448★ Cesarean Prevention Movement of Sonoma
790 Daniel St.
Sebastopol, CA 95472
Phone: (707)823-1131
Meagan Pugh, Exec. Officer

Sierra Madre

★1449★ Sierra Madre Woman's Club
550 West Sierra Madre Blvd.
Sierra Madre, CA 91024
Phone: (818)355-9063
M. Guifford, Pres.

Description: Women over the age of 50. Promotes civic, cultural, and philanthropic activities. **Affiliated with:** California Federation of Women's Clubs.

South Pasadena

★1450★ Women's Overseas Service League, Pasadena Unit
401 El Centro
South Pasadena, CA 91030
Joan Moffet, Pres.

Description: Women U.S. veterans who served overseas during time of war. Makes services available to members and other veterans. Conducts charitable events. **Affiliated with:** Women's Overseas Service League.

South San Francisco

★1451★ National Association of Women Business Owners
Silicon Valley Chapter
c/o Events, Etc.
379 Oyster Pt. Blvd., Ste. 9
South San Francisco, CA 94080
Phone: (415)952-1110
Robbie Fakkema, President

Stockton

★1452★ Older Women's League (OWL)
Delta Chapter
PO Box 4836
Stockton, CA 95204
Phone: (209)946-2126
Georgie Whitney, Contact

Studio City

★1453★ Women's Division, Studio City
Chamber of Commerce
4243 Maryellen Ave.
Studio City, CA 91604
Phone: (818)990-0985
Joann Murphy, Contact
Description: Promotes business and community development in the San Fernando Valley area of California. **Affiliated with:** Studio City Chamber of Commerce.

Sun Valley

★1454★ La Leche League International,
South California/Nevada
c/o Joanne Snyder
9620 Clybourne Ave.
Sun Valley, CA 91352
Phone: (818)951-1961
Joanne Snyder, Coordinator
Description: Mothers who wish to breastfeed their babies. Provides breastfeeding and parenting education and support. **Affiliated with:** La Leche League International.

Sunnyvail

★1455★ Eleanor Roosevelt Fund of
California
1001-158 Evelyn Terr. E.
Sunnyvail, CA 94086
Phone: (408)773-9791
Andrea Leiderman, Contact

Tarzana

★1456★ Women's American ORT, Valley
Region
6002 Reseda Blvd.
Tarzana, CA 91356
Phone: (818)881-9370
Fax: (818)345-2941
Judy Weisman, Pres.
Description: Jewish women in the San Fernando Valley area of California united to raise funds for Organization for Rehabilitation Through Training (ORT) vocational and technical schools worldwide. **Affiliated with:** Women's American ORT.

Torrance

★1457★ Young Women's Christian
Association of Torrance
2320 West Carson St.
Torrance, CA 90501
Phone: (213)320-2255
Description: Seeks to develop and improve the spiritual, social, mental, and physical well-being of young people and adults. **Affiliated with:** Young Women's Christian Association of the United States of America.

Upland

★1458★ American Woman's Society of
Certified Public Accountants of Inland
Counties
Reardon and Associates
846 W. Foothill Blvd., Ste. C
Upland, CA 91786
Phone: (714)985-7286
Seren Schaich, Exec. Officer
Description: Works to improve the status of professional women and to make the business community aware of the professional capabilities of the woman CPA. Conducts networking activities. Offers educational programs and scholarships. **Affiliated with:** American Woman's Society of Certified Public Accountants.

★1459★ Cesarean Prevention Movement
of San Gabriel/San Bernardino
1130 East Arrow Hwy.
Upland, CA 91786
Phone: (714)982-5847
Melinda Jones, Exec. Officer

Valencia

★1460★ Santa Clarita Republican
Women's Club
PO Box 270
59 Rio Prodo
Valencia, CA 91355
Description: Women members of the Republican Party. Works to elect Republicans to local, state, and national office.

Visalia

★1461★ Coalition to Prevent Teenage
Pregnancy
c/o Cheryl Levitan
1900 E. Mineral King
Visalia, CA 93291-6907
Description: Works to alleviate the problem of teenage pregnancy through education and communication.

Watsonville

★1462★ Young Women's Christian
Association of Watsonville
40 Brennan St.
Watsonville, CA 95076
Phone: (408)724-6078
Lorraine Phillips, Contact
Description: Seeks to develop and improve the spiritual, social, mental, and physical well-being of young people and adults. **Affiliated with:** Young Women's Christian Association of the United States of America.

West Covina

★1463★ Young Women's Christian
Association of San Gabriel Valley
961 South Glendora Ave.
West Covina, CA 91790
Phone: (818)960-2995
Description: Seeks to develop and improve the spiritual, social, mental, and physical well-being of young people and adults. **Affiliated with:** Young Women's Christian Association of the United States of America.

Colorado

Aurora

★1464★ National Association of Women
Business Owners
Colorado Chapter
PO Box 460356
Aurora, CO 80046-0356
Phone: (303)394-2020
Linda Lodenkamper, President

Berthoud

★1465★ Older Women's League (OWL)
Greeley Regional Chapter
741 7th St.
PO Box 387
Berthoud, CO 80513
Phone: (303)532-2863
Mary Kathleen Spurling, Contact

Boulder

★1466★ Cesarean Prevention Movement
of Boulder
PO Box 3146
Boulder, CO 80307
Phone: (303)499-3050
Terra Palmarini Richardson, Exec. Officer

★1467★ Front Range/Women in the Visual
Arts
400 Brook Circle
Jamestown Star Route
Boulder, CO 80302
Phone: (303)443-6224
Sally Ellicot, Contact
Founded: 1974. **Description:** Non-profit group started by University of Colorado students to show the work of women artists in the Boulder area. Monthly meetings at members' homes. (Host member shows her work or slides.) There are special supper meetings in honor of visiting women artists and critics. **Membership:** 35.

★1468★ Women's International League for
Peace and Freedom, Boulder Chapter
1520 Euclid
Boulder, CO 80302
Phone: (303)444-6981
Description: Individuals working toward nuclear disarmament, world peace, and the elimination of racism in Boulder County, CO. **Affiliated with:** Women's International League for Peace and Freedom.

★1469★ Young Women's Christian
Association of Boulder County
2222 14th St.
Boulder, CO 80302
Phone: (303)443-0419
Description: Seeks to develop and improve the spiritual, social, mental, and physical well-being of young people and adults. **Affiliated with:** Young Women's Christian Association of the United States of America.

Cedaredge

★1470★ **Women's Surface Creek Saddle Club**
1871 2425 Dr.
Cedaredge, CO 81413
Phone: (303)856-6011
Melanie Son, Pres.

Description: Women in Delta County, CO working to further the care and enjoyment of horses and to promote horse events and activities.

Colorado Springs

★1471★ **DES Action**
PO Box 2645
Colorado Springs, CO 80901

★1472★ **Manitou Springs Women's Club**
c/o Naomi Yager
1006 S. Sierra Madre
Colorado Springs, CO 80903
Phone: (719)473-2905
Naomi Yager, Contact

Description: Women organized to conduct educational programs and fundraising events for charitable organizations.

★1473★ **Older Women's League (OWL) Colorado Springs Chapter**
4107 N Chestnut
Colorado Springs, CO 80907
Phone: (719)475-5170
Joanne Ruth, Contact

Denver

★1474★ **Colorado Abortion Rights Action League**
1210 E. Colfax, No. 203
Denver, CO 80218
Phone: (303)831-1973
Pat Blumenthal, Contact

★1475★ **Colorado Coalition Against Domestic Violence**
PO Box 18902
Denver, CO 80218
Phone: (303)573-9018
Jan Micksh, Contact

★1476★ **Denver Chapter of Hadassah, The Women's Zionist Organization of America**
c/o Marilyn S. Huttner
1786 S. Bellaire St., Ste. #516
Denver, CO 80222
Phone: (303)756-1440
Marilyn S. Huttner, Pres.

Description: Jewish women. Conducts fundraising for medical and educational projects in Israel. Sponsors Zionist youth program in the United States. **Affiliated with:** National Hadassah.

★1477★ **Denver Women's Press Club**
1325 Logan St.
Denver, CO 80211
Phone: (303)839-1519

★1478★ **Higher Education Resource Services, Mid-America (HERS)**
University of Denver
Colorado Women's College Campus
7150 Montview Blvd.
Denver, CO 80220
Phone: (303)871-6866
Fax: (303)871-6897
Cynthia Secor, Director

Founded: 1975. **Description:** HERS, Mid-America sponsors professional development activities designed to improve the status of women in higher education. Primarily focuses on the Summer Institute for Women in Higher Education Administration, co-sponsored with and held on the campus of Bryn Mawr College, a month-long program that offers women faculty and administrators intensive training in educational administration and a network of peers and mentors. **Publications:** Network.

★1479★ **League of Women Voters of Colorado**
1410 Grant St., Ste. B-204
Denver, CO 80203
Phone: (303)863-0437
Betsy McBride, President

★1480★ **National Abortion Rights Action League, Colorado Chapter**
1540 Vine St.
Denver, CO 80206
Phone: (303)388-4720
Pat Blumenthal, Exec. Officer

Description: To develop and sustain a pro-choice political constituency in order to maintain the right to legal abortion for all women. **Affiliated with:** National Abortion Rights Action League.

★1481★ **Older Women's League (OWL) Denver Chapter**
5585 E. Amherst Ave.
Denver, CO 80222
Phone: (303)758-9481
Eleanor Bent, Contact

★1482★ **Women's Foundation of Colorado**
1700 Broadway, Ste. 1820
Denver, CO 80290
Phone: (303)863-6012
Letty Bass, Executive Director

★1483★ **Young Women's Christian Association of Metropolitan Denver**
5356 West Mall
Denver, CO 80202
Phone: (303)825-7141

Description: Seeks to develop and improve the spiritual, social, mental, and physical well-being of young people and adults. **Affiliated with:** Young Women's Christian Association of the United States of America.

Estes Park

★1484★ **Journalism and Women Symposium**
PO Box 3100
Estes Park, CO 80517-3100

Description: Promotes greater and more effective participation by women in the journalism profession.

Ft. Collins

★1485★ **Association for Women in Science, Fort Collins Chapter**
c/o Karen Wedge
Colorado State University
Ft. Collins, CO 80523-0000
Karen Wedge, Contact

Description: Works to improve education and employment opportunities for women in the sciences.

Grand Junction

★1486★ **Mesa County Women's Network**
PO Box 1423
Grand Junction, CO 81502-1423

Greeley

★1487★ **Women's International League for Peace and Freedom, Greeley Chapter**
c/o Elaine Schmidt
1413 23rd Ave. Court
Greeley, CO 80631
Phone: (303)352-7765
Elaine Schmidt, Pres.

Description: Women working to end apartheid in South Africa. Seeks disarmament and a national policy of nonintervention. Conducts charitable activities. **Affiliated with:** Women's International League for Peace and Freedom.

Las Animas

★1488★ **Bent County Republican Women**
29007 Rd. 8-1/2
Las Animas, CO 31054
Phone: (719)456-2336
Louella Marlman, Exec. Officer

Description: Women members of the Republican Party. Works to elect Republicans to local, state, and national office.

Loveland

★1489★ **Women's Aglow Fellowship of Loveland**
c/o Vivian Tillotson
1554 Ranae Dr.
Loveland, CO 80537
Phone: (303)663-3908
Vivian Tillotson, Pres.

Description: Women from a variety of Christian denominations. Works to live and promote the Christian gospel, encourage church participation, and foster fellowship. Conducts 2 retreats per year and holds bible studies. **Affiliated with:** Women's Aglow Fellowship International.

McPherson

★1490★ **McPherson Women's International League for Peace and Freedom**
c/o Kaye Yoder
141 N. Charles
McPherson, CO 67460
Phone: (316)241-2935
Kaye Yoder, Pres.

Description: Individuals in McPherson County, Co interested in promoting world peace and justice. Maintains portable exhibit. **Affiliated with:** Women's International League for Peace and Freedom.

Monument

★1491★ Tri Lakes Women's Club
c/o E. June Dahlstrom
PO Box 669
Monument, CO 80132-0669
Description: Women's volunteer service club.

Pueblo

**★1492★ Young Women's Christian
Association of Pueblo**
801 North Santa Fe Ave.
Pueblo, CO 81003
Phone: (719)542-6904
Description: Seeks to develop and improve the spiritual, social, mental, and physical well-being of young people and adults. **Affiliated with:** Young Women's Christian Association of the United States of America.

Sterling

**★1493★ Church Women United Literacy
Council**
314 Bannock St.
Sterling, CO 80751
Phone: (303)522-3593
Mrs. Truth N. Colvard, Coordinator
Description: Volunteers organized to teach English, math, reading, and spelling to adults, teenagers, and students in northeastern Colorado. **Affiliated with:** Laubach Literacy Action; Logan County Literacy Coalition.

Connecticut

Bolton

★1494★ Connecticut Women Artists, Inc.
148 Hebron
Bolton, CT 06043
Phone: (203)646-1990
Diane Ursin, President
Founded: 1929. **Description:** Nonprofit organization of sculptors and painters. Has an annual, general-membership dinner meeting, and major juried exhibitions open to all women in the state. Membership is granted after being accepted by jury for three shows. One must submit work for jurying (no fee) for inclusion in the group's exhibition even after one becomes a member. **Membership:** 163.

Bridgeport

**★1495★ Young Women's Christian
Association of Greater Bridgeport**
753 Fairfield Ave.
Bridgeport, CT 06604
Phone: (203)334-6154
Laura Green, Exec.Dir.
Description: Seeks to develop and improve the spiritual, social, mental, and physical life of young people and adults. **Affiliated with:** Young Women's Christian Association of the United States of America.

Cornwall Bridge

**★1496★ Older Women's League (OWL)
Northwest Connecticut Chapter**
33 Dudleytown Rd., S.
Cornwall Bridge, CT 06754
Phone: (203)672-6089
Jeanne Russo, Contact

Coventry

★1497★ Homebirth Information Group
118 Old Tolland Tpke.
Coventry, CT 06238
Phone: (203)742-1417
Brenda Bearce, Treas.
Description: Interested persons. Disseminates information on home childbirth. Provides midwife referral.

Danbury

★1498★ Margaret Stroock Clinic
44 Main St.
Danbury, CT 06810
Phone: (203)743-2446
Margaret Blake, Exec.Dir.
Description: Provides gynocological care for needy individuals.

Darien

**★1499★ Young Women's Christian
Association of Darien-Norwalk**
49 Old Kingshighway N.
Darien, CT 06820
Phone: (203)655-2535
Rita Holmes Shaughnessy, Exec.Dir.
Description: Seeks to develop and improve the spiritual, social, mental, and physical life of youth and adults in the Darien-Norwalk, CT area. **Affiliated with:** Young Women's Christian Association of the United States of America.

East Hartford

**★1500★ East Hartford Junior Women's
Club**
1502 Forbes St.
East Hartford, CT 06118
Phone: (203)726-3192
Kathleen Jasak, Sec.
Description: Individuals 18 years of age and older. Works to stimulate and encourage members' civic, cultural, educational, and social growth as it related to the community. Sponsors annual spring Spelling Bee and annual fall Children's Fair. **Affiliated with:** Connecticut Junior Women.

Essex

**★1501★ American Association of
University Women, Lower Connecticut
Valley**
Benson Ln.
Essex, CT 06426
Phone: (203)767-2355
Barbara Dwyer, Contact
Description: Women graduates of regionally accredited four year colleges and universities. Works for the advancement of women through advocacy and emphasis on lifelong learning.

Fairfield

**★1502★ Cesarean Prevention Movement
of Fairfield County**
c/o Nancie O'Sullivan
1590 N. Benson Rd.
Fairfield, CT 06430
Phone: (203)255-4043
Nancie O'Sullivan, Pres.
Description: Physicians, midwives, childbirth instructors, labor support personnel, and women. Works to safely lower cesarean rate. Promotes education, conducts research, and provides support. Sponsors Birthworks holistic childbirth education program. Holds workshops. **Affiliated with:** Cesarean Prevention Movement.

Greenwich

**★1503★ Young Women's Christian
Association of Greenwich**
259 E. Putnam Ave.
Greenwich, CT 06830
Phone: (203)869-6501
Description: Seeks to develop and improve the spiritual, social, mental, and physical life of young people and adults. **Affiliated with:** Young Women's Christian Association of the United States of America.

Groton

**★1504★ Young Women's Christian
Association of New London**
476 Thames St.
Groton, CT 06340
Phone: (203)445-8151
Description: Seeks to develop and improve the spiritual, social, mental, and physical life of young people and adults. **Affiliated with:** Young Women's Christian Association of the United States of America.

Hamden

**★1505★ Junior Women's Club of Hamden-
North Haven**
PO Box 6283
Hamden, CT 06514-0000
Description: Young women united for community service.

**★1506★ League of Women Voters of
Connecticut**
1890 Dixwell Ave., Ste. 113
Hamden, CT 06514
Phone: (203)288-7996
Kay Maxwell, President

Hartford

**★1507★ Connecticut Abortion Rights
Action League**
135 Broad St.
Hartford, CT 06105
Phone: (203)246-0767
Anne Stanback, Contact

**★1508★ Connecticut Coalition Against
Domestic Violence**
22 Maple Ave.
Hartford, CT 06114
Phone: (203)524-5890
Anne Menard, Contact

★1509★ Connecticut Federation of Democratic Women's Clubs
634 Asylum Ave.
Hartford, CT 06105
Phone: (203)278-6080
Fax: (203)278-5879
Bernice E. Bowman, Pres.

Description: Registered women Democrats organized to educate and support women politically and to remain informed on legislative actions. **Affiliated with:** National Federation of Democratic Women's Clubs.

★1510★ Connecticut Women's Educational and Legal Fund
22 Maple Ave.
Hartford, CT 06114
Phone: (203)247-6090
Lucinda Finley, Pres.

Founded: 1973. **Description:** Non-profit organization that combines information and referral, community education and training, public policy research and legal strategies to work for women's legal rights.

Kensington

★1511★ Woman's Club of New Britain
c/o Margaret Klotz
181 Crater Ln.
PO Box 102
Kensington, CT 06037
Phone: (203)828-4667
Margaret Klotz, Pres.

Description: Interested persons organized for cultural and social activities.

Manchester

★1512★ Republican Women's Club of Manchester
90 Clover Ln.
Manchester, CT 06040
Phone: (203)643-4725
Donna Mercier, Pres.

Description: Seeks to elect Republican candidates to local, state, and national offices.

New Britain

★1513★ Young Women's Christian Association of New Britain
22 Glen St.
New Britain, CT 06051
Phone: (203)225-4681
Nancy Hruschke, Contact

Description: Seeks to develop and improve the spiritual, social, mental, and physical life of young people and adults. **Affiliated with:** Young Women's Christian Association of the United States of America.

New Haven

★1514★ DES Action
c/o Esposito
449 Townsend Ave.
New Haven, CT 06512

★1515★ Premenstrual Syndrome Group of New Haven
c/o Patricia Fling
Women's Health Services
911 State St.
New Haven, CT 06511
Phone: (203)789-1272
Patricia Fling, Exec.Dir.

Description: Interested women organized to provide support and PMS information.

★1516★ Young Women's Christian Association of New Haven
48 Howe St.
New Haven, CT 06511
Phone: (203)865-5171

Description: Seeks to develop and improve the spiritual, social, mental, and physical life of young people and adults. **Affiliated with:** Young Women's Christian Association of the United States of America.

New London

★1517★ Divorced and Separated Women's Group, New London Chapter
Women's Center
120 Broad St.
New London, CT 06320
Phone: (203)447-0366

Description: Provides crisis intervention counseling for victims of domestic violence and sexual assault. Maintains support groups.

★1518★ Mothers Support Group of New London
Women's Center
120 Broad St.
New London, CT 06320
Phone: (203)447-0366

Description: Provides short-term crisis intervention counseling for victims of domestic violence and sexual assault. Maintains support groups.

★1519★ Widows Support Group of New London
Women's Center
120 Broad St.
New London, CT 06320
Phone: (203)447-0366

Description: Provides support groups and crisis intervention counseling for victims of domestic violence and sexual assault.

Norwalk

★1520★ Norwalk Woman's Club
c/o Kathy Hagerty
136 Newtown Ave., No. 17
Norwalk, CT 06851
Phone: (203)847-4042
Kathy Hagerty, Pres.

Description: Interested women conducting community service. Awards scholarships. Conducts youth leadership programs. Gives assistance to shut-ins and the elderly in nursing homes. **Affiliated with:** General Federation of Women's Clubs.

Plainville

★1521★ Plainville Republican Women's Club
136 Whiting St.
Plainville, CT 06062
Phone: (203)747-3905
Helen Bergenty, Pres.

Description: Seeks to elect Republican candidates to local, state, and national offices.

South Windsor

★1522★ New England Lumber Women's Association
c/o Barbara Plamondon
PO Box 13
South Windsor, CT 06074
Barbara Plamondon, Acting Pres.

★1523★ South Windsor Junior Women's Club
c/o Anne Reilly
24 Carey Ln.
South Windsor, CT 06074-4256
Anne Reilly, Contact

Southport

★1524★ Women in Sales, Fairfield Chapter
c/o Thelma Hoyt
PO Box 1105
Southport, CT 06490-1105
Phone: (203)381-9327
Thelma Hoyt, Pres.

Description: Individuals in sales in Fairfield County, CT. Promotes continuing education and the general welfare of saleswomen. Develops sales skills, and provides support system. Seeks to maintain a high standard of ethics. Sponsors educational forum. **Affiliated with:** Women in Sales Association.

Stamford

★1525★ Women in Management
PO Box 691
Stamford, CT 06904
Phone: (203)329-0854
Dorota Bussey, Adm.Dir.

Description: Professional and corporate managers; entrepreneurs. Encourages identification and achievement of career and personal goals. Provides professional development opportunities and forum for exchange of information and ideas. Acknowledges members' achievements. Recognizes businesses and organizations that acknowledge achievements of their women managers. Commits expertise and resources to members' communities. Conducts skill-building workshops and high school outreach program; sponsors Junior Achievement competitions.

Waterbury

★1526★ Young Women's Christian Association of Waterbury
80 Prospect St.
Waterbury, CT 06702
Phone: (203)754-5136

Description: Seeks to develop and improve the spiritual, social, mental, and physical life of young people and adults. **Affiliated with:** Young Women's Christian Association of the United States of America.

West Haven

★1527★ West Haven Junior Women's Club
PO Box 126
West Haven, CT 06516
Phone: (203)934-4671
Betty Greenawalt, Treas.

Description: Women aged 18 and older interested in community service.

★1528★ West Haven Laurel Woman's Club
260 Howard Ave.
West Haven, CT 06516
Phone: (203)562-6067
Mrs. Robert Hauser, Pres.

Description: Women's volunteer service club.
Affiliated with: General Federation of Women's Clubs.

Westport

★1529★ Older Women's League (OWL) Fairfield County Chapter
8 Sturges Commons
Westport, CT 06880
Phone: (203)259-9416
Vidal S. Clay, Contact

Windsor

★1530★ Windsor Republican Women's Club
c/o Vi Nahabedian
103 Clover St.
Windsor, CT 06095
Phone: (203)688-3928
Vi Nahabedian, Pres.

Description: Supports Republican candidates and the Republican party.

Delaware

Claymont

★1531★ Delaware Association of American Mothers
8428 Society Dr.
Claymont, DE 19703
Phone: (302)798-8801
Mrs. B.W. LaDage, Contact

Description: Mothers united to strengthen moral, and spiritual values. **Affiliated with:** American Mothers.

Newark

★1532★ American Association of University Women, Delaware Chapter
100 St. Regis Dr.
Newark, DE 19711
Phone: (302)737-4686
Nancy Black, Pres.

Description: Women graduates of regionally accredited four year colleges and universities. Works for the advancement of women through advocacy and emphasis on lifelong learning. **Affiliated with:** American Association of University Women.

★1533★ New Castle County Crisis Pregnancy Center
Newark Med. Bldg., Ste. 303
325 E. Main St.
Newark, DE 19711
Phone: (302)366-0285
Sharon Bias, Exec.Dir.

Description: Assists young women in carrying their babies to term. **Affiliated with:** Christian Action Council.

★1534★ Sociologists for Women in Society, Delaware Chapter
c/o Margaret Anderson
University of Delaware
Department of Sociology
Newark, DE 19716
Phone: (302)451-2581
Margaret Anderson, Contact

Smyrna

★1535★ Older Women's League (OWL) First State Chapter
555 Kates Way
Smyrna, DE 19977
Phone: (302)653-2129
Kay O'Day Allen, Contact

Wilmington

★1536★ American Association of University Women, Wilmington Branch
1800 Fairfax Blvd.
Wilmington, DE 19803
Phone: (302)428-0939
Jeanne F. Rudy, Pres.

Description: Women graduates of regionally accredited four year colleges and universities. Works for the advancement of women through advocacy and emphasis on lifelong learning. **Affiliated with:** American Association of University Women.

★1537★ Association for Women in Science, Wilmington Chapter
c/o Maria Iarnos
7 Madelyn Ave.
Wilmington, DE 19803-3964

Description: Works to improve education and employment opportunities for women in the sciences.

★1538★ Birthright of Delaware
1311 N. Scott
Wilmington, DE 19806
Phone: (302)656-7080
Toll-free: 800-848-LOVE
Thomas Reynolds, Pres.

Description: Volunteer organization of professionals and nonprofessionals dedicated to providing services to women experiencing a crisis pregnancy who wish to carry the baby to term. Holds monthly board meeting.

★1539★ Delaware Commission for Women Department of Community Affairs
Carvel State Bldg.
820 N. French St., 4th Fl.
Wilmington, DE 19801
Phone: (302)571-2660

★1540★ League of Women Voters of Delaware
1800 N. Broom St., Rm. 201
Wilmington, DE 19802-3809
Phone: (302)571-8948
Joann Hasse, President

District of Columbia

Washington

★1541★ Advocates for Infants and Mothers
c/o Loretta Commodore
2500 Wisconsin Ave. NW 903
Washington, DC 20007-4526
Loretta Commodore, Contact

Description: Represents members' interests; conducts lobbying activities. Holds seminars and workshops.

★1542★ Alpha Chapter Chi Eta Phi Sorority
808 Nicholson St., NE
Washington, DC 20011-2733

★1543★ Association for Women in Science, Washington, DC Chapter
c/o Mary C. Barber
Science and Policy Associates, Inc.
W. Tower, Ste. 400
1333 H St., NW
Washington, DC 20005
Phone: (202)789-1201
Mary C. Barber, Contact

Description: Works to improve education and employment opportunities for women in the sciences.

★1544★ Capitol Hill Women's Political Caucus (CHWPC)
Longworth House Office Bldg.
PO Box 599
Washington, DC 20515
Phone: (202)986-0994
Liz Ryan, Co-Chwm.

Founded: 1971. **Description:** A chapter of the National Women's Political Caucus (see separate entry). Individuals dedicated to equal rights and equal opportunities for all people. Purpose is to promote and increase the election, appointment, and participation of women in local, state, and national political and governing processes. Works to increase the political power of women and to combat the inequities of employment and salaries for women on Capitol Hill. Believes equal political and governmental participation will enhance the quality of life for all Americans. Monitors and encourages the enactment of legislation beneficial to women, including the Equal Rights Amendment; acts as clearinghouse of legislative information. Sponsors job seminars and programs in personal and professional development. Promotes national organization's goals and works closely with NWPC in its efforts. Compiles statistics; operates speakers' bureau. **Members:** 250. **Publications:** *Directory*, annual. ● *Equal Times Newsletter*, bimonthly. ● Also publishes *The Last Plantation: How Women Fare on Capitol Hill*.

★1545★ D.C. Commission for Women
Reeves Center
2000 14th St., NW, Rm. 354
Washington, DC 20009
Phone: (202)939-8083
Carol Hill Lowe, Exec.Dir.

Description: Advocacy agency for women and their families. **Publications:** *Commission for Women Newsletters.*

★1546★ DC Feminists Against Pornography
2147 O St. NW, No. 305
Washington, DC 20037
Phone: (301)654-0176
Marty Langelan, Contact

Description: Activist/educational organization protesting sexism, racism, and violence against women, in the community, through pornography, and through the media. Sponsors speakers, slide shows, and public protest actions.

★1547★ District of Columbia Coalition Against Domestic Violence
c/o Emergency Domestic Relations Project
111 F St. NW
Washington, DC 20001
Phone: (202)662-9666
Meshall D. Thomas, Contact

★1548★ League of Women Voters of the District of Columbia
2025 Eye St. NW, Rm. 916
Washington, DC 20006
Phone: (202)331-4122
Anna Marsh, President

★1549★ National Association of Women Business Owners
Capital Area Chapter
c/o Professional Admin. Services
1900 L St., NW, Ste. 500
Washington, DC 20036
Phone: (202)659-8090
Brenda Billops, President

★1550★ National Child Day Care Association (NCDCA)
1501 Benning Rd. NE
Washington, DC 20002
Phone: (202)397-3800
Fax: (202)399-2666
Helen Taylor, Exec.Dir.

Description: A local, nonprofit group that seeks to provide quality day care services for the Washington, DC area.

★1551★ Older Women's League (OWL)
National Capitol Chapter
3973 Harrison St., NW
Washington, DC 20015
Phone: (202)966-8754
Sue Whitman, Contact

★1552★ Phyllis Wheatley Young Women's Christian Association
901 Rhode Island Ave. NW
Washington, DC 20001
Phone: (202)667-9100
Ruth Collins-Martin, Exec.Dir.

Description: Seeks to develop and improve the spiritual, social, mental, and physical well-being of young people and adults. Provides housing for single women. **Affiliated with:** Young Women's Christian Association of the United States of America.

★1553★ Sociologists for Women in Society, Capital Area
c/o Carla Howery
A.S.A.
1722 North St. NW
Washington, DC 20506
Phone: (202)833-3410
Carla Howery, Contact

Description: Sociologists committed to feminism. Promotes scholarly change and social action.

★1554★ Washington Area Women's Center
1350 Pennsylvania Ave., SE, Ste. 1
Washington, DC 20003
Phone: (202)546-0246
Angie Carrera, Contact
Founded: 1972. **Description:** Information and referral, support groups and affiliate groups. **Publications:** *In Our Own Write* and a newsletter.

★1555★ Washington Professional Women's Cooperative
1020 29th St., NW
Washington, DC 20007
Phone: (202)342-0101
Mary Lee Zetter, Pres.

Founded: 1977. **Description:** Promotes women in the arts, with the Worthy Gallery. Works with women's interest groups in feminist history, culture, myths, investments and financial management. **Publications:** *Worthy News.*

★1556★ Washington Women's Network (WWN)
c/o National Women's Education Fund
1410 Q St., NW
Washington, DC 20009
Phone: (202)462-8606
Rosalie Whelan, Coordinator

Founded: 1977. **Description:** Women leaders in government, nonprofit organizations, and the business community united to share ideas and information and to provide support and advice to potential women leaders. Members meet monthly for events, seminars, and discussions, often with speakers. Publishes Calendar of Washington Events that includes listing of job openings.

★1557★ Women's Bar Association of the District of Columbia
1819 H St., NW, Ste. 1250
Washington, DC 20006
Phone: (202)785-1540
Bettina Lawton, Contact

★1558★ Women's Growth and Therapy Center
3000 Connecticut Ave., NW
Washington, DC 20015
Phone: (202)483-9376
Rosalie Mandelbauae, Staff Dir.

Founded: 1978. **Description:** Mental health counseling for women and their partners.

★1559★ Women's Program Advisory Council (WPAC)
111 E. St., NW, Ste. 600
Washington, DC 20004
Phone: (202)727-2264
Vera M. Abbott, Contact
Founded: 1979.

★1560★ Young Women's Project
c/o Institute for Women Policy Research
1400 20th St. NW, Ste. 104
Washington, DC 20036
Phone: (202)785-5100
Nadia Moritz, Contact

Description: Network of young women from all ethnic backgrounds. Provides a forum in which to discuss issues, develop leadership skills, and strive for community improvements. Disseminates information.

Florida

Arcadia

★1561★ Arcadia Woman's Club
PO Box 204
Arcadia, FL 33821
Phone: (813)494-2966
Carolyn Pepper, Pres.

Description: Women in DeSoto County, FL interested in providing charitable and educational services to their community, state, and nation. Promotes good citizenship. Sponsors scholarship. **Affiliated with:** Florida Federation of Women's Clubs; General Federation of Women's Clubs.

Baker

★1562★ North Okaloosa Woman's Club
PO Box 621
Baker, FL 32531-0621

Description: Women in the North Okaloosa Island, FL area.

Boca Raton

★1563★ American Business Women's Association, Boca Raton Chapter
6461 NW 2nd Ave.
Boca Raton, FL 33487
Phone: (407)997-6727
Eileen Cioe, Contact

Description: Women's volunteer service club. Serves as a network linking women interested in learning about current business practices. Makes available scholarships.

★1564★ Junior Women's Club Boca Raton
Box 1005
Boca Raton, FL 33429
Phone: (407)368-8042
Gail McDonald, Contact

Description: Women's volunteer service group in the Boca Raton, FL area.

★1565★ Poinciana Republican Women's Club
Box 124
Boca Raton, FL 33429
Jessie Howard, Contact

Description: Women who belong to the Republican Party. Promotes knowledge of Republican office holders and their records, and Republican political activities. **Affiliated with:** Florida Federation of Republican Women; National Federation of Republican Women.

★1566★ Women's International Zionist Organization, Florida Chapter
Box 6288
Boca Raton, FL 33427

Description: Provides social welfare assistance to needy women in Florida.

Charlotte Harbor

★1567★ Women's Overseas Service League, Port Charlotte Unit
c/o Virginia D. McDaniel
23113 Bayshore Dr.
Charlotte Harbor, FL 33980
Phone: (813)625-7136
Virginia D. McDaniel, Pres.

Description: Women who have served overseas in the U.S. armed forces. Promotes community service and assists those incapacitated or wounded in the service. **Affiliated with:** Women Overseas Service League.

Clearwater

★1568★ American Association of University Women, Clearwater Branch
1866 Venetian Point Dr.
Clearwater, FL 34615
Althea Andersen, Exec. Officer

Description: Women graduates of regionally accredited four year colleges and universities. Works for the advancement of women through advocacy and emphasis on lifelong learning.

★1569★ Clearwater Women's Republican Club
2434 Australia Way, E., #46
Clearwater, FL 34623
Phone: (813)797-5620
Jana Krause, Exec.Dir.

Description: Works to elect Republicans to local, state, and national office.

★1570★ La Leche League of Clearwater
1450 Fairmont St.
Clearwater, FL 34615
Phone: (813)442-5946
Barbara Czipri, Leader

Description: Educational and support group for breastfeeding mothers in northern Pinellas County, FL. Provides speakers. **Affiliated with:** La Leche League International.

Coral Springs

★1571★ Cesarean Prevention Movement of Southeast Florida
c/o Lynn Jones
8393 NW 6 Ct.
Coral Springs, FL 33071
Phone: (305)752-3584
Lynn Jones, Contact

Description: Support group seeking to: lower rate of cesarean births through education; provide forum where women and men can express concerns about birth; and assist women healing from past births.

Deerfield Beach

★1572★ National Association of Women Business Owners
Ft. Lauderdale Chapter
c/o PMG Associates, Inc.
3880 NW 2nd Ct.
Deerfield Beach, FL 33442
Phone: (305)427-5010
Kathy Gonot, President

Del Ray Beach

★1573★ Older Women's League (OWL)
Tri City Chapter
c/o Saxony I No. 402
Del Ray Beach, FL 33446
Phone: (407)487-0483
Gladys Heller, Contact

Deltona

★1574★ Deltona Women's Club
1049 E. Normandy Blvd.
Deltona, FL 32725
Phone: (407)574-2311
Cappy Evans, Pres.

Description: Women's volunteer service club. Conducts charitable programs.

Ft. Lauderdale

★1575★ Ft. Lauderdale Woman's Club
15 SE 1st St.
Ft. Lauderdale, FL 33301
Phone: (305)462-3854
Mary Sheridan, Pres.

Description: Women's volunteer service club. Conducts community participation, educational, philanthropic, and self-improvement programs. Sponsors card parties, benefit luncheons, and other activities. **Affiliated with:** Florida Federation of Women's Clubs; General Federation of Women's Clubs.

★1576★ Healthy Mothers, Healthy Babies Coalition of Broward County
PO Box 030313
Ft. Lauderdale, FL 33303-0313

Description: Supports and promotes the proper care of infants.

★1577★ National Association of Women Business Owners
Boca/Delray Chapter
c/o W. Gozdz Enterprises, Inc.
PO Box 5711
Ft. Lauderdale, FL 33310
Phone: (305)741-3410
Wanda Gozdz, President

★1578★ Women's History Coalition
PO Box 4135
Ft. Lauderdale, FL 33338-4135
Annette Van Howe, Chair

Founded: 1986. **Description:** Coalition consists of Broward County organizations with a mission to "Celebrate Women: Their Accomplishments and Dreams." Public education through speakers, films, quizzes, videotapes, plays, posters, and exhibits with an eventual goal of a local Women's Hall of Fame.

Ft. Myers Beach

★1579★ Ft. Myers Beach Women's Club
175 Sterling St.
Ft. Myers Beach, FL 33931
Phone: (813)765-1417
Claire Doolittle, Contact

Description: Women's volunteer service club. Serves Lee County, FL.

Gainesville

★1580★ American Business Women's Association, Gainesville Chapter
4400 NW 23rd Ave., #C
Gainesville, FL 32606
Phone: (904)377-2225
Lois McCallum, Pres.

Description: Professional women.

★1581★ Gainesville Area Women's Network
PO Box 4066
Gainesville, FL 32613-4066
Phone: (904)378-2511
Fax: (904)378-9801
Jean Russell, Contact

Description: Women businesspersons and owners united to: promote spirit of cooperation and understanding among women; provide networking opportunities; achieve recognition of the contributions of women; and encourage personal and professional advancement. Provides employment listings; makes available scholarships.

★1582★ Gainesville Junior Woman's Club
PO Box 8337
Gainesville, FL 32605

Description: Women aged 18-45 in Alachua County, FL interested in community service. Conducts Festival of Trees fundraiser. **Affiliated with:** Florida Federation of Women's Clubs; General Federation of Women's Clubs.

★1583★ Gainesville Woman's Club
2809 W. University Ave.
Gainesville, FL 32607
Phone: (904)376-3901
Mrs. W. J. Gardner, Pres.

Description: Women's volunteer service club. Conducts charitable and educational programs; sponsors community events. **Affiliated with:** General Federation of Women's Clubs.

★1584★ **La Leche League International, Gainesville Florida Association**
2425 NW 36th Terr.
Gainesville, FL 32605
Phone: (904)372-6707
Carol Sarisky, Leader

Description: Seeks to provide information and support to new and expectant mothers in Alachua County, FL who want to breastfeed their babies. Maintains lending library. **Affiliated with:** La Leche League International. **Telecommunications Services:** Telephone counselling.

★1585★ **Older Women's League (OWL)**
Gainesville Chapter
3012 NW 28th Circle
Gainesville, FL 32605
Phone: (904)373-3427
Lynn Edgar, Contact

Hallandale

★1586★ **Women's American ORT, Southeast District**
2101 E. Hallandale Beach Blvd., Ste. 301
Hallandale, FL 33009
Phone: (305)458-1557
Dr. Terrie Temkin, Exec.Dir.

Description: Jewish women in Alabama, Florida, Georgia, Mississippi, North Carolina, and South Carolina. Supports network of technical and vocational schools. Works for quality public education and increased literacy. Fights against anti-Semitism and for human rights. Provides service and training. Holds semiannual board meeting. **Affiliated with:** Women's American ORT.

Hudson

★1587★ **Cotee River Women's Republican Club**
12217 Saddle Strap Row
Hudson, FL 34667
Phone: (813)868-3601
Clara Ann Smith, Pres.

Description: Works to elect Republicans to local, state, and national office.

Inverness

★1588★ **American Association of University Women, Crystal River Branch**
1208 Jones Ave.
Inverness, FL 32650
Phone: (904)637-0896
Mary Cotter, Contact

Description: Women graduates of regionally accredited four year colleges and universities. Works for the advancement of women through advocacy and emphasis on lifelong learning. Bestows scholarships. Conducts newsletter writing competitions. Assists spouse abuse center. **Affiliated with:** American Association of University Women; American Association of University Women, Florida Division.

Jacksonville

★1589★ **Florida Abortion Rights Action League (FARAL)**
1930 San Marco Blvd., No. 205
Jacksonville, FL 32207
Phone: (904)398-5588
Janis Compton, Contact

★1590★ **Girl Scouts Gateway Council**
1000 Shearer St.
Jacksonville, FL 32205
Phone: (904)388-4653
Wende S. Wilson, Exec.Dir.

Description: Girls aged five to 17 and adult volunteers in northeastern Florida. Provides leadership and citizen development training. Seeks to help young people develop values and reach their full potential. Provides volunteer training. **Affiliated with:** Girl Scouts of the U.S.A.

Lake Worth

★1591★ **Palm Glades Girl Scout Council**
2728 Lake Worth Rd.
Lake Worth, FL 33461
Phone: (407)582-5362
Sandra Patton, Exec.Dir.

Description: Girls aged five to 17 in 6.5 countries. Seeks to develop self-esteem through informal education and program activities chartered by Girl Scouts of the U.S.A.

Miami

★1592★ **Cubana Women's Club**
970 SW 1st St.
Miami, FL 33130
Phone: (305)324-5201

★1593★ **National Association of Women Business Owners**
Miami Chapter
c/o Amint, Inc.
8410 NW 53rd Terr., No. 101
Miami, FL 33166
Phone: (305)594-0870
Sandra Adams, President

★1594★ **National Bar Association, Women Lawyers Division - Dade Chapter**
c/o Cynthia Everett
155 S. Miami Ave., PH 1
Miami, FL 33158
Phone: (305)536-4797
Fax: (305)530-7139
Cynthia Everett, Pres.

Description: Professional association for black women lawyers. Promotes the improvement of legal practice for black women lawyers. Encourages black youths to enter law school. Represents the interests of members. Sponsors annual judicial page project for students to gain practical experience working in the legal profession. **Affiliated with:** National Bar Association.

North Miami

★1595★ **National Council of Jewish Women, Southern District**
12944 W. Dixie Hwy.
North Miami, FL 33161
Phone: (305)893-0001

Description: Jewish women in Alabama, Arkansas, Florida, Georgia, Louisiana, Mississippi, Oklahoma, South Carolina, Tennessee, and Texas interested in engaging in programs of advocacy, education, and service. **Affiliated with:** National Council of Jewish Women.

North Palm Beach

★1596★ **National Association of Women Business Owners**
Palm Beach Chapter
c/o Wojtusik, Smith and Assoc.
11760 U.S. Hwy. 1, Ste. 305
North Palm Beach, FL 33408
Phone: (407)624-0770
Mary Smith, President

Orlando

★1597★ **Florida Coalition Against Domestic Violence**
PO Box 532041
Orlando, FL 32853-2041
Phone: (407)425-8648
Sue Armstrong, Contact

★1598★ **Minority Women Business Enterprise**
201 S. Rosalind Ave.
Orlando, FL 32801
Phone: (407)836-7317

★1599★ **Pine Castle Woman's Club**
5901 S. Orange Ave.
Orlando, FL 32809
Phone: (407)855-8894
Ann Bennett, Pres.

Description: Women's volunteer service club. Supports Girl Scouts and contributes to other charitable causes. Sponsors Fine Arts and Crafts Show and essay contests for fifth graders and poster contests for middle school students. Rents building for community activities.

Palm Beach

★1600★ **Executive Women of the Palm Beaches**
8295 N. Military Trail, No. F
Palm Beach, FL 33410
Phone: (407)694-1882
Rita B. Craig, Pres.

Description: Executive and professional women dedicated to the advancement of women and the betterment of Palm Beach County, FL. Holds annual Red Tie Auction.

Pembroke Park

★1601★ **Park Lake Woman's Social Club**
108 E. Lake Shore Dr.
Pembroke Park, FL 33009-6021

Plantation

★1602★ **La Leche League International, Florida Chapter**
c/o Jeanne Beach
620 E. Acre Dr.
Plantation, FL 33317
Phone: (305)581-0327
Jeanne Beach, Coordinator

Description: Women breastfeeding or interested in breastfeeding their children. Encourages breastfeeding and provides educational programs. Provides assistance to mothers having difficulties in breastfeeding. **Affiliated with:** La Leche League International.

Pompano Beach

★1603★ Older Women's League (OWL)
Broward Chapter
1971 E. Discovery Circle
Pompano Beach, FL 33064
Phone: (305)428-5978
Dorcie Gallagher, Contact

Port Charlotte

★1604★ American Association of
University Women, Florida Division
4158 Tamiami Trail J-7
Port Charlotte, FL 33952
Phone: (813)625-6852
E. F. Penny Penner, Contact

Description: Women graduates of regionally accredited four year colleges and universities. Works for the advancement of women through advocacy and emphasis on lifelong learning. **Affiliated with:** American Association of University Women.

Port Richey

★1605★ Women Marines Association,
Orange Blossom Chapter Florida-5
6615 Clemens Blvd.
Port Richey, FL 34668
Phone: (813)868-4806
Diana L. Thornton, Pres.

Description: Former, retired, and active women Marines in the Springhill and West Pasco, FL areas. Works to counsel, assist, and promote the welfare of elderly, disabled, or needy active or veteran women Marines. Aids hospitalized veterans from all branches of the U.S. armed services. Promotes the civic and social welfare of the community. Sponsors elementary and secondary school essay contests. Makes monetary donations.

Santa Rosa Beach

★1606★ Birth Options in Pregnancy
PO Box 1654
Santa Rosa Beach, FL 32459
Phone: (904)267-2557

Description: Midwives, childbirth educators, and others interested in maternity care. Promotes public awareness and education of the risks and benefits of current medical trends in maternity care. Investigates physicians and hospitals and makes findings available to the public. Supports medical system reforms. Offers educational programs, including speakers.

Sarasota

★1607★ National Association of Women
Business Owners
Sarasota Chapter
c/o In Health, Inc.
3601 Azalea Ln.
Sarasota, FL 34240
Phone: (813)371-1213
Ruth Hochman, President

★1608★ Women's International League for
Peace and Freedom/Sarasota
c/o Pattie Lanier
2315 McClellan Pkwy.
Sarasota, FL 34239
Phone: (813)955-9623
Pattie Lanier, Exec. Officer

Description: Women in the Sarasota, FL area interested in achieving, through nonviolent means, elimination of war, want, and discrimination on any basis. **Affiliated with:** Women's International League for Peace and Freedom.

Surfside

★1609★ Florida Women's Political Caucus
c/o Dorie Lurie
9349 Abbott Ave.
Surfside, FL 33154
Phone: (305)866-1384
Dorie Lurie, Pres.

Description: Nonpartisan organization seeking to have qualified women appointed and elected to office. Conducts training workshops. **Affiliated with:** National Women's Political Caucus.

Tallahassee

★1610★ Association for Women in
Science, Tallahassee Chapter
c/o Dr. Nancy Marcus
Florida State Univ.
Dept. of Oceanography
Tallahassee, FL 32306-0000

Description: Works to improve education and employment opportunities for women in the sciences.

★1611★ League of Women Voters of
Florida
540 Beverly Ct.
Tallahassee, FL 32301
Phone: (904)224-2545
Kay Allen, President

★1612★ National Federation of Democratic
Women, Florida Chapter
4760 Gearhart Rd.
Tallahassee, FL 32303
Phone: (904)562-1999
Gwen Humphrey, Contact

Description: Works to elect Democrats to local, state, and national office.

Tampa

★1613★ American Business Women's
Association, Seminole Chapter
5616-C Granada Blvd.
Tampa, FL 33617
Phone: (813)988-8700
Edith Robinson Klein, Pres.

Description: Women in business in Temple Terrace, FL. Awards scholarships to women in business. **Affiliated with:** American Business Women's Association.

★1614★ Cesarean Prevention Movement
of Tampa
PO Box 82183
Tampa, FL 33612
Phone: (813)962-7238
Ruth Leaders, Sec.

Description: Seeks to provide education and support to families in order to decrease the number of cesarean births and promote positive and safe birthing experiences. **Affiliated with:** Cesarean Prevention Movement.

★1615★ Hillsborough Women's Republican
Club
PO Box 9151
Tampa, FL 33674
Phone: (813)989-8341
Helen K. Walker, Pres.

Description: Interested persons in Hillsborough County, FL. Promotes understanding of and participation in government and the ideals of the Republican party. Awards scholarships to women for use in leadership and campaign management study programs. **Affiliated with:** Florida Federation of Republican Women; National Federation of Republican Women.

★1616★ Insurance Women of Tampa
PO Box 23882
Tampa, FL 33623
Phone: (813)886-4444
Toll-free: 800-523-4040
Fax: (813)885-2823
Barbara Slawiak, Pres.

Description: Professional organization of women in the insurance industry. Promotes continuing education. Advocates on behalf of safety issues. Lobbies before state legislature. **Affiliated with:** National Association of Insurance Women - International.

Temple Terrace

★1617★ La Leche League International,
Temple Terrace Chapter
6624 Glencoe Dr.
Temple Terrace, FL 33617
Phone: (813)985-1227
Marcy Leber, Exec. Officer

Description: Peer support group for women who wish to breastfeed their children. Promotes parenting education and provides information. Holds four family oriented social events per year. **Affiliated with:** La Leche League International.

West Palm Beach

★1618★ Women's Club of the Arbours
2641 Gatley Dr. W. 708
West Palm Beach, FL 33415-7918
Description: Women's volunteer service club.

Winter Park

★1619★ Girl Scouts of the U.S.A., Citrus Council
1935 Woodcrest Dr.
Winter Park, FL 32792
Phone: (407)645-1020
Toll-free: 800-367-3906
Jan Richardson, Exec.Dir.

Description: Girls aged five to 17 and adult volunteers in Brevard, Flagler, Orange, Osceola, Seminole, and Volusia counties, FL. Seeks to develop potential of girls by providing leadership and learning opportunities. **Affiliated with:** Girl Scouts of the U.S.A.

Yulee

★1620★ Nassau County Pro-Life
300 Avant Rd.
Yulee, FL 32097
Phone: (904)225-8769
Vivian J. Aberson, Pres.

Description: Promotes education and information regarding abortion. Donates maternity and infant products to needy mothers. Distributes educational information upon request. **Affiliated with:** American Life Lobby.

Georgia

Albany

★1621★ National Association of Women in Construction, Albany Chapter
500 Whipporwill Rd.
Albany, GA 31707
Phone: (912)435-9659
Della Parrish, Contact

Description: Women in all areas of construction. To build better relations among construction workers.

Alpharetta

★1622★ Alpharetta Women's Club
PO Box 896
Alpharetta, GA 30239-0896

Description: Women's volunteer service club.

Atlanta

★1623★ Atlanta Lesbian Feminist Alliance
Box 5502
Atlanta, GA 30307
Phone: (404)378-9769

Description: Lesbian feminists. Provides social, political, educational, cultural, and recreational activities.

★1624★ Black Women's Coalition of Atlanta
PO Box 11367, Sta. A
Atlanta, GA 30310
Phone: (404)627-6000

★1625★ Georgia Abortion Rights Action League
1430 W. Peachtree, Ste. 505
Atlanta, GA 30309
Phone: (404)875-6338
Janelle Yamarick, Exec. Officer

★1626★ Georgia Advocates for Battered Women and Children
250 Georgia Ave. SE, Ste. 344
Atlanta, GA 30312
Phone: (404)524-3847
Dianne Winters, Contact

★1627★ Georgia Midwifery Association
PO Box 29633
Atlanta, GA 30359
Phone: (404)381-2339
Debbie Pulley, Pres.

Description: Midwives, doctors, nurses, and others supportive of homebirth options. Purpose is to make homebirth a legitimate and safe alternative.

★1628★ League of Women Voters of Georgia
100 Edgewood Ave. NE, Ste. 1010
Atlanta, GA 30303
Phone: (404)522-8683
Susan Whitney, President

★1629★ Older Women's League (OWL) Atlanta Chapter
957 N. Highland Ave.
Atlanta, GA 30306
Phone: (404)874-6430
Jeanne Scher, Contact

Augusta

★1630★ Central Savannah River Girl Scout Council
1325 Greene St.
Augusta, GA 30901-1031
Phone: (404)826-4516
Fax: (404)826-4504
Betty Dyches, Exec.Dir.

Description: Girls aged 5-17 in 15 Georgia and South Carolina counties. **Affiliated with:** Girl Scouts of the U.S.A.

★1631★ Older Women's League (OWL) Augusta CSRA Chapter
PO Box 5596
Augusta, GA 30906
Phone: (404)796-5025
Catherine Thompkins, Contact

Barnesville

★1632★ Lamar Coalition of Women
c/o June Danson
135 Atlanta St.
Barnesville, GA 30204-1201

Description: Social and civic service organization.

Brunswick

★1633★ American Association of University Women, Brunswick Chapter
c/o Dr. Arnetia Maasha
314 Ethridge Dr.
Brunswick, GA 31520
Phone: (912)262-0458
Dr. Arnetia Maasha, Pres.

Description: Graduates in Glynn County, GA of regionally accredited four year colleges and universities. Works for advancement of women through advocacy and emphasis on lifelong learning. Awards scholarships. **Affiliated with:** American Association of University Women.

Columbus

★1634★ American Business Women's Association, Georgian Chapter
6920 Fieldstone Ct.
Columbus, GA 31907
Phone: (404)568-3401
Meredith S. Tilly, Exec. Officer

Covington

★1635★ Newton County Task Force on Teenage Pregnancy Prevention
c/o Jane Atkinson
500 Mote Rd.
Covington, GA 30209-7188

Description: Individuals working to reduce the rate of teen pregnancies in Newton County, GA.

Dahlonega

★1636★ Dahlonega Woman's Club
106 Hilcrest Dr.
Dahlonega, GA 30533
Jessie Hudson, Exec. Officer

Description: Women's volunteer service club. Serves Lumpkin County, GA.

Decatur

★1637★ Association for Women in Science, Devry Atlanta Chapter
c/o Barbara R. Wilkins
250 N. Arcadia Ave.
Decatur, GA 30030
Phone: (404)292-7900

Description: Works to improve education and employment opportunities for women in the sciences.

Dunwoody

★1638★ DES Action
580 Spencer Tr.
Dunwoody, GA 30350

Fayetteville

★1639★ Fayette County Council on Battered Women
205 Brandywine Blvd., Ste. 100
Fayetteville, GA 30214-1561

Gadsden

★1640★ Goodyear Women's Club
509 Padenrich Ave.
Gadsden, GA 35903
Phone: (205)546-7989
Kathy Smith, Pres.

Description: Female employees and wives of male employees who work at the Goodyear Tire and Rubber Plant in Gasden, GA. Promotes and encourages social activities.

La Grange

★1641★ Bellevue/La Grange Woman's Club Charitable Trust
204 Ben Hill St.
La Grange, GA 30240
Phone: (404)884-1832
James A. Mann, Host
Description: Seeks to preserve the pre-Civil War home of Senator Benjamin H. Hill. Collects artifacts pertaining to the career of Senator Hill.

★1642★ La Grange Junior Woman's Club
PO Box 1135
La Grange, GA 30241-1135
Description: Social and civic service organization.

Macon

★1643★ Macon Woman's Club
725 Thurmond Dr.
Macon, GA 31204-1752
Description: Works to enhance the state of women in society.

Marietta

★1644★ American Woman's Society of Certified Public Accountants of Georgia
1290 Rockcrest Dr.
Marietta, GA 30062
Phone: (404)973-0651
Mary C. Porter, Exec. Officer
Description: Women certified public accountants. Promotes professionalism and high standards of practice. Sponsors shelter for battered women.

★1645★ Cesarean Prevention Movement of Marietta
2847 Pine Meadow Dr.
Marietta, GA 30066
Phone: (404)971-7713
Lori Vandegrift, Pres.
Description: Men and women interested in natural childbirth. Seeks to lower the rate of cesarean births through education. Offers a forum for the expression of thoughts on childbirth. Provides support to women who have had a cesarean. **Affiliated with:** Cesarean Prevention Movement.

★1646★ Young Women's Christian Association of Cobb County, Marietta Center
48 Henderson St. SW
Marietta, GA 30064
Phone: (404)427-2902
Fax: (404)429-8429
Barbara J. Bruegger, Exec.Dir.
Description: Seeks to develop and improve the spiritual, social, mental, and physical well-being of young people and adults. Provides emergency shelter and services for victims of domestic violence and crisis counseling for victims of sexual abuse; operates child care facilities. **Affiliated with:** Young Women's Christian Association of the United States of America.

Newnan

★1647★ Newnan Republican Women's Club
1 Pine Ridge
Newnan, GA 30263
Phone: (404)253-1629
Emma Hinesley, Chm.
Description: Works to elect Republicans to local, state, and national office.

Ringgold

★1648★ La Leche League International, Georgia Chapter
c/o Cindy Van Pelt
306 Calhoun St.
Ringgold, GA 30736
Phone: (404)935-5592
Cindy Van Pelt, Coordinator
Description: Gives information and support to health professionals and mothers interested in breastfeeding. Provides computer data. **Affiliated with:** La Leche League International.

St. Marys

★1649★ Birthright of St. Marys
100 Pine St.
St. Marys, GA 31558-2008
Description: Seeks to help pregnant women find alternatives to abortion. Conducts childbirth education and parenting programs.

Savannah

★1650★ American Association of University Women, Georgia Chapter
206 Varn Dr.
Savannah, GA 31405
Phone: (404)355-0615
Bettina B. Beecher, Pres.
Description: Women graduates of regionally accredited four year colleges and universities. Works for the advancement of women through advocacy and emphasis on lifelong learning. **Affiliated with:** American Association of University Women.

★1651★ Girl Scout Council of Savannah
428 Bull St.
Savannah, GA 31401
Phone: (912)236-1571
Gail Kiracofe, Exec.Dir.
Description: Girl scouts and adult volunteers organized to enable girls to achieve high levels of performance and efficiency. **Affiliated with:** Girl Scouts of the U.S.A.

★1652★ Older Women's League (OWL) Savannah Chapter
169 Vine St.
Savannah, GA 31401
Phone: (912)232-2349
Kathleen Scruggs, Contact

★1653★ Savannah Business and Professional Women's Club
c/o Kathryn Yocco
6906 Howard Foss Dr.
Savannah, GA 31406
Phone: (912)355-4336
Kathryn Yocco, Pres.
Description: Business and professional women. To promote complete participation, equal opportunities, and economic self-sufficiency for working women. Addresses the issues of women's multiple roles, lifetime economic security, and pay equity. **Affiliated with:** National Federation of Business and Professional Women's Clubs of the U.S.A.

★1654★ Savannah La Leche League
c/o Holly Lockard
731 Beechwood Ct.
Savannah, GA 31419
Phone: (912)920-0167
Holly Lockard, Accredited Leader
Description: Interested persons organized to promote breastfeeding and mothering through mother-to-mother support. Provides telephone counseling. **Affiliated with:** La Leche League International.

★1655★ Savannah Women's Network
PO Box 14326
Savannah, GA 31416
Phone: (912)355-1562
Nancy Walczyk, Contact
Description: Encourages women to reach their full potential. Seeks the enhancement and promotion of successful business and professional careers for women. Conducts networking activities.

Smyrna

★1656★ Older Women's League (OWL) Cobb County Chapter
32 Middleton Ct.
Smyrna, GA 30080
Phone: (404)319-8530
Benita Cohen, Contact

Statesboro

★1657★ Black Women of Profession - Statesboro Chapter
c/o Carolyn Postell
104 Harris Rd.
Statesboro, GA 30458
Phone: (912)764-4913
Carolyn Postell, Exec. Officer

★1658★ Statesboro Business and Professional Women
c/o Patricia McElwee
6 Adrian Ct.
Statesboro, GA 30458
Phone: (912)489-1068
Patricia McElwee, Pres.
Description: Business and professional women. To promote complete participation, equal opportunities, and economic self-sufficiency for working women. **Affiliated with:** National Federation of Business and Professional Women's Clubs of the U.S.A.

Valdosta

★1659★ Valdosta Women's Organization for Serving Youth
Rte. 2, Box 365
Valdosta, GA 31603
Phone: (912)559-5345
Barbara Colson, Pres.

Description: Provides encouragement and fundraising support to Georgia Christian School. Makes available scholarships; conducts annual charity auction.

West Point

★1660★ American Business Women's Association, West Point Chapter
PO Box 272
West Point, GA 31833

Description: Business and professional women. To promote complete participation, equal opportunities, and economic self-sufficiency for working women. Awards scholarships to women pursuing business degrees. **Affiliated with:** American Business Women's Association.

Weston

★1661★ Weston Woman's Club
PO Box 127
Weston, GA 31832
Phone: (912)828-2727
Mrs. Sonny Stapleton, Pres.

Description: Women's volunteer service club. Sponsors community activities.

Hawaii

Hilo

★1662★ Young Women's Christian Association of Hawaii Island
145 Ululani St.
Hilo, HI 96720
Phone: (808)935-7141

Description: Seeks to develop and improve the spiritual, social, mental, and physical well-being of young people and adults. **Affiliated with:** Young Women's Christian Association of the United States of America.

Honolulu

★1663★ Association for Women in Science, Hawaii Chapter
c/o Pat Convillan
1521 Olifander St. 1706
Honolulu, HI 96822-0000

Description: Works to improve education and employment opportunities for women in the sciences.

★1664★ Filipino Association of University Women
3968 Lurline Dr.
Honolulu, HI 96816-4006

Description: Women graduates of regionally accredited four year colleges and universities. Works for the advancement of women through advocacy and emphasis on lifelong learning.

★1665★ Hawaii Abortion Rights Action League
1290-D Maunakea St.
Honolulu, HI 96817
Phone: (808)599-5488
Tom Heinrich, Contact

★1666★ Hawaii State Committee on Family Violence
PO Box 31107
Honolulu, HI 96802-1107
Phone: (808)538-7216
Carol C. Lee, Contact

★1667★ League of Women Voters of Hawaii
49 S. Hotel St., No. 314
Honolulu, HI 96813
Phone: (808)531-7448
Evelyn Bender, President

★1668★ Young Women's Christian Association of Oahu
PO Box 337
Honolulu, HI 96809
Phone: (808)538-7061

Description: Seeks to develop and improve the spiritual, social, mental, and physical well-being of young people and adults. **Affiliated with:** Young Women's Christian Association of the United States of America.

Lihue

★1669★ Young Women's Christian Association of Kauai County
3094 Elua St.
Lihue, HI 96766
Phone: (808)245-5959
Fax: (808)245-5961

Description: Seeks to develop and improve the spiritual, social, mental, and physical well-being of young people and adults. **Affiliated with:** Young Women's Christian Association of the United States of America.

Idaho

Boise

★1670★ American Business Women's Association, Centennial Chapter
2067 South Springbrook Ln.
Boise, ID 83706
Phone: (208)338-8721
Kathy Stocker, Pres.

Description: Business and professional women. To promote complete participation, equal opportunities, and economic self-sufficiency for working women. Offers educational program.

★1671★ New Women Council of Boise
6205 Franklin Rd.
Boise, ID 83709
Phone: (208)375-1931

Description: Business and professional women. To promote complete participation, equal opportunities, and economic self-sufficiency for working women.

★1672★ Young Women's Christian Association of Boise
720 West Washington
Boise, ID 83702
Phone: (208)343-3688

Description: Seeks to develop and improve the spiritual, social, mental, and physical well-being of young people and adults. **Affiliated with:** Young Women's Christian Association of the United States of America.

Emmett

★1673★ Emmett Business and Professional Women's Club
302 East 2nd
Emmett, ID 83617
Phone: (208)365-2279
Marie Schneider, Contact

Description: Business and professional women. To promote complete participation, equal opportunities, and economic self-sufficiency for working women. **Affiliated with:** National Federation of Business and Professional Women's Clubs of the U.S.A.

★1674★ Girl Scouts of the U.S.A., Neighborhood Council
2783 Tom's Cabin Rd.
Emmett, ID 83617
Phone: (208)365-7338
Cynthia Landers, Exec. Officer

Description: Girls aged five to 17 years in Emmett, Garden Valley, and Horseshoe Bend, ID. **Affiliated with:** Girl Scouts of the U.S.A.

Grangeville

★1675★ League of Women Voters of Idaho
Rte. 2, Box 504
Grangeville, ID 83530
Jane Spencer, President

Idaho Falls

★1676★ American Association of University Women, Idaho Chapter
926 8th St.
Idaho Falls, ID 83401
Phone: (208)529-8945
Kay Snyder, Pres.

★1677★ Idaho Network to Stop Violence Against Women
PO Box 323
Idaho Falls, ID 83402
Phone: (208)529-4352
Lori McKenna, Contact

Lewiston

★1678★ Young Women's Christian Association of Lewiston-Clarkston
300 Main St.
Lewiston, ID 83501
Phone: (208)743-1535

Description: Seeks to develop and improve the spiritual, social, mental, and physical well-being of young people and adults. **Affiliated with:** Young Women's Christian Association of the United States of America.

Moscow

★1679★ American Association of University Women, Moscow Branch
723 North Lincoln
Moscow, ID 83843
Phone: (208)882-8209
Kathleen Hardcastle, Pres.

Description: Women graduates of regionally accredited four year colleges and universities. Works for the advancement of women through advocacy and emphasis on lifelong learning. Issues publications. **Affiliated with:** American Association of University Women.

★1680★ Moscow Business and Professional Women's Club
235 Home St.
Moscow, ID 83843
Phone: (208)883-1188
Andrea Beckett, Pres.

Description: Business and professional women. To promote complete participation, equal opportunities, and economic self-sufficiency for working women. **Affiliated with:** National Association of Business and Professional Women's Clubs of the U.S.A.

Pocatello

★1681★ Young Women's Christian Association of Pocatello
454 North Garfield Ave.
Pocatello, ID 83204
Phone: (208)232-0742

Description: Seeks to develop and improve the spiritual, social, mental, and physical well-being of young people and adults. **Affiliated with:** Young Women's Christian Association of the United States of America.

Illinois

Alton

★1682★ Young Women's Christian Association of Alton
304 E. 3rd St.
Alton, IL 62002
Phone: (618)465-7774
N. Joyce Lemoins, Exec.Dir.

Description: Seeks to develop and improve the spiritual, social, mental, and physical life of women and girls over the age of 12 in Madison County, IL. **Affiliated with:** Young Women's Christian Association of the United States of America.

Arlington Heights

★1683★ National Network of Women in Sales, Northwest Suburban Chicago Chapter
PO Box 1611
Arlington Heights, IL 60006
Phone: (708)253-2661
Janet Davie, Contact

Description: Salespersons, those interested in becoming salespersons, and entrepreneurs organized to provide support, information exchange, and educational opportunities. Sponsors the Shelter. **Affiliated with:** National Association for Executive Females; National Network of Women in Sales.

Ashmore

★1684★ American Business Women's Association, Charleston Branch
RR 1, Box 371
Ashmore, IL 61912
Phone: (217)349-8978
Margaret A. Paro, Pres.

Description: Seeks to improve the professional, educational, cultural, and social advancement of businesswomen. Bestows scholarships. **Affiliated with:** American Business Women's Association.

Aurora

★1685★ Older Women's League (OWL) Fox Valley Chapter
402 S. Fordham Ave.
Aurora, IL 60506
Phone: (708)892-9754
Maxine Fuller, Contact

★1686★ Young Women's Christian Association of Aurora
201 N. River St.
Aurora, IL 60506
Phone: (708)896-8588

Description: Seeks to develop and improve the spiritual, social, mental, and physical life of women and girls over the age of 12. **Affiliated with:** Young Women's Christian Association of the United States of America.

Barrington

★1687★ Birthrights
c/o Kimberly Van Fossan
112 Brinker Rd.
Barrington, IL 60010
Phone: (708)382-3529
Kimberly Van Fossen, Pres.

Description: Serves as a forum for individuals from the southern suburbs of Chicago, IL to discuss safe birth and related topics with qualified speakers. **Affiliated with:** International Association of Parents and Professionals for Safe Alternatives in Childbirth.

Beardstown

★1688★ Beardstown Business and Professional Women's Club
211 W. 9th St.
Beardstown, IL 62618
Phone: (217)323-1279
JoDeen Roley, Contact

Description: Business and professional women. To promote complete participation, equal opportunities, and economic self-sufficiency for working women. **Affiliated with:** National Federation of Business and Professional Women of the U.S.A.

★1689★ Beardstown Women's Club
c/o Eva Brown
1302 State St.
Beardstown, IL 62618
Phone: (217)323-2556
Eva Brown, Exec. Officer

Description: Women's volunteer service club.

Belleville

★1690★ Young Women's Christian Association of St. Clair County
9507 W. Main St.
Belleville, IL 62223
Phone: (618)397-0477

Description: Seeks to develop and improve the spiritual, social, mental, and physical life of women and girls over the age of 12. **Affiliated with:** Young Women's Christian Association of the United States of America.

Benton

★1691★ Benton Business and Professional Women's Club
c/o Verna Burminski
206 College
Benton, IL 62812
Phone: (618)439-0571
Verna Burminski, Treas.

Description: Business and professional women. To promote complete participation, equal opportunities, and economic self-sufficiency for working women. Sponsors Young Career Woman competition. Bestows scholarships. Conducts charitable activities; participates in Rend Lake Festival. **Affiliated with:** Illinois Federation of Business and Professional Women; International Federation of Business and Professional Women; National Federation of Business and Professional Women's Clubs of the U.S.A.

Bloomington

★1692★ Young Women's Christian Association of McLean County
1201 Hershey Rd.
Bloomington, IL 61704
Phone: (309)662-0461

Description: Seeks to develop and improve the spiritual, social, mental, and physical life of women and girls over the age of 12. **Affiliated with:** Young Women's Christian Association of the United States of America.

Canton

★1693★ Young Women's Christian Association of Canton
111 N. Avenue A
Canton, IL 61520
Phone: (309)647-0441

Description: Seeks to develop and improve the spiritual, social, mental, and physical life of women and girls over the age of 12. **Affiliated with:** Young Women's Christian Association of the United States of America.

Carbondale

★1694★ Southern Illinois Friends of Women's History
502 Orchard Dr.
Carbondale, IL 62901
Phone: (618)453-5141

Carthage

★1695★ American Association of University Women, Carthage Branch
c/o Nancy O'Hara
229 S. Madison
Carthage, IL 62321
Phone: (217)357-3246
Nancy O'Hara, Exec. Officer
Description: Women graduates of regionally accredited four year colleges and universities. Works for the advancement of women through advocacy and emphasis on lifelong learning. **Affiliated with:** American Association of University Women.

★1696★ Carthage Business and Professional Women's Club
c/o Danuta Huston
726 E. Main
Carthage, IL 62321
Phone: (217)357-3760
Danuta Huston, Exec. Officer
Description: Business and professional women. To promote complete participation, equal opportunities, and economic self-sufficiency for working women.

★1697★ Carthage Woman's Club
c/o Katharine Mensendick
736 Buchanan St.
Carthage, IL 62321
Phone: (217)357-2572
Katharine Mensendick, Pres.
Description: Women's literary club.

Centralia

★1698★ Centralia Woman's Club
c/o Bertha Pruett
PO Box 102
Centralia, IL 62801
Phone: (618)532-8597
Bertha Pruett, Exec. Officer
Description: Women's volunteer service club. Bestows scholarships. **Affiliated with:** General Federation of Woman's Clubs; Illinois Federation of Woman's Clubs.

Chambersburg

★1699★ Chambersburg Woman's Club
c/o Mary Cummings
Chambersburg, IL 62323
Phone: (217)327-4229
Mary Cummings, Pres.
Description: Women's volunteer service club. Sponsors local Community Chest.

Champaign

★1700★ Region 6 Breastfeeding Task Force and Resource Group
2125 S. 1st St.
Champaign, IL 61820-7401

★1701★ University of Illinois Young Women's Christian Association
1001 S. Wright St.
Champaign, IL 61820
Phone: (217)344-0721
Amy Schmidt Stowe, Exec.Dir.
Description: Seeks to develop and improve the spiritual, social, mental, and physical life of women, girls, and male associates over the age of 16. **Affiliated with:** Young Women's Christian Association of the United States of America.

Charleston

★1702★ American Association of University Women, Charleston-Mattoon Area Branch
c/o Fran Choate
2100 Meadow Lake Dr.
Charleston, IL 61920
Phone: (217)345-4435
Fran Choate, Contact
Description: Women graduates of regionally accredited four year colleges and universities. Works for the advancement of women through advocacy and emphasis on lifelong learning. **Affiliated with:** American Association of University Women.

★1703★ Charleston Business and Professional Women's Club
c/o Judy Winnett
1809 Garfield
Charleston, IL 61920
Phone: (217)345-6834
Judy Winnett, Pres.
Description: Business and professional women. To promote complete participation, equal opportunities, and economic self-sufficiency for working women. **Affiliated with:** National Federation of Business and Professional Women's Clubs of the U.S.A.

★1704★ Charleston Woman's Club
c/o Emily Nichols
531 Ashby Dr.
Charleston, IL 61920
Phone: (217)345-6493
Emily Nichols, Pres.
Description: Volunteer women involved in community service. Works to beautify the community, promote the fine arts, and support community projects. Bestows Woman of the Year award; presents summer scholarships. **Affiliated with:** General Federation of Women's Clubs; Illinois Federation of Women's Clubs.

Chicago

★1705★ Artemis Singers
Box 578296
Chicago, IL 60657
Phone: (312)764-4465
Description: Lesbians in the Chicago, IL area with an interest in choral music.

★1706★ Chicago Area Women's History Conference
c/o Jean S. Hunt
5485 S. Cornell
Chicago, IL 60615
Phone: (312)752-4369
Jean S. Hunt, Exec. Officer
Description: Individuals interested in research or study of women's history. Conducts programs on women's history which include lectures, slide presentations, movies, music, and tours. Bestows awards to educators who include women's history in their teaching program and to high school students for research projects. Holds special events during Women's History Month.

★1707★ Chicago Foundation for Women
230 W. Superior St., Ste. 400
Chicago, IL 60610
Phone: (312)266-1176
Marianne Philbin, Executive Director

★1708★ Chicago Society of Women Certified Public Accountants
Riverside Publishing Co.
8420 Bryn Mawr Ave.
Chicago, IL 60631
Phone: (312)693-0040
Robin Foltz, Exec. Officer

★1709★ Chicago Women in Government Relations
PO Box 641231
Chicago, IL 60664-1231

★1710★ Chicago Women in Publishing
2 N. Riverside Plaza, No. 2400
Chicago, IL 60606
Phone: (312)641-6311
Vanessa Poindexter, Contact
Description: Over 800 members from all aspects of publishing field, from publishers and editors to writers, proof-readers, sales representatives, and students. **Publications:** Newsletter, annual membership directory, annual free-lance directory. **Remarks:** Offers 24 programs in the publishing field for members and non-members. Also offers Jobline, a recorded listing of positions in the publishing field available in the Chicago area.

★1711★ Eleanor Association (EA)
1550 N. Dearborn Pkwy.
Chicago, IL 60610
Phone: (312)664-8245
Jill Goranson, Exec.Dir.
Founded: 1898. **Description:** To promote the advancement of women. Sponsors affordable residence for working women and full-time students in Chicago, IL. Offers scholarship program for senior undergraduates and graduate students who have demonstrated academic achievement and financial need. Bestows awards; maintains charitable program. Sponsors social and philanthropic club for mature women. **Members:** 500. **Publications:** Brochures and fliers.

★1712★ Feminists for Life of Chicago
1401 E. Hyde Blvd., Apt. 605
Chicago, IL 60615
Phone: (312)288-2596
Mary Krane Derr, Coordinator
Description: "People who believe that female and fetal liberation are complimentary, not diametrically opposed concerns." Promotes legislation and agencies that assist children and pregnant women; educates the public about pro-life feminism. Provides a forum for feminists who oppose the pro-choice issue. **Affiliated with:** Feminists for Life of America; Feminists for Life of Illinois.

★1713★ Hadassah, The Women's Zionist Organization of America, Chicago Chapter
111 N. Wabash
Chicago, IL 60602
Phone: (312)263-7473
Florence Chill, Pres.

Description: Jewish women and girls in the metropolitan Chicago, IL area working to support Hadassah hospitals in Israel, Youth Aliyah, and the Jewish National Fund. Sponsors summer camp, youth activities, and educational programs. **Affiliated with:** Hadassah, the Women's Zionist Organization of America.

★1714★ Illinois Women's Agenda
6 N. Michigan, Ste. 1313
Chicago, IL 60602
Phone: (312)704-1833
Ruth Sweetser, Pres.

Description: Individuals concerned with protecting the legal rights of women in Illinois. Provides women's rights advocacy; conducts public education programs. Holds monthly board meeting.

★1715★ Illinois Women's Funding Federation
22 W. Monroe, No. 1400
Chicago, IL 60603
Phone: (312)782-3902
Linda Moses, Executive Director

★1716★ Korean American Women in Need
PO Box 25139
Chicago, IL 60625-0139

Description: Provides assistance to Korean-American women in crisis.

★1717★ League of Black Women
18 S. Michigan Ave.
Chicago, IL 60603
Phone: (312)368-1329

★1718★ League of Women Voters of Illinois
332 S. Michigan Ave., No. 1142
Chicago, IL 60604-4301
Phone: (312)939-5935
Eleanor Revelle, President

★1719★ Lilac Tree Women in Transition
c/o Michael E. Pildes
2 N. Lasalle St., Ste. 1776
Chicago, IL 60602-3791
Michael E. Pildes, Contact

★1720★ Midwest Parentcraft Center
3921 N. Lincoln
Chicago, IL 60613
Phone: (312)281-6638
Margaret Gamper, R.N., Exec.Dir.

Description: Prenatal instructors, parents, and professionals involved in parenting and pregnancy. To instruct and educate expectant mothers and others in the Gamper Method of childbirth. (The Gamper Method, based on the teachings of several 19th century physicians and developed by Margaret Gamper in 1946, is designed to prepare the prospective mother for childbirth by instilling self-determination and confidence in her ability to work with the physiological changes of her body during pregnancy, labor, and delivery.) **Affiliated with:** International Childbirth Education Association.

★1721★ Midwest Women's Center
53 W. Jackson, Rm. 623
Chicago, IL 60604
Phone: (312)922-8530

Description: A non-profit organization that offers services to women, including employment counseling, job training, educational programs, public policy programs, professional women's services, and a referral service. **Publications:** *Illinois Women's Directory*.

★1722★ National Abortion Rights Action League of Illinois
100 E. Ohio, No. 426
Chicago, IL 60611
Phone: (312)644-0972
Sharon Powell, Contact

★1723★ Older Women's League (OWL) Chicago Loop Chapter
PO Box 641072
Chicago, IL 60664-1072
Phone: (312)786-1714

★1724★ Older Women's League (OWL) Chicago North Chapter
2626 W. Greenleaf
Chicago, IL 60645
Phone: (312)761-0930
Anita Cibelli, Contact

★1725★ Older Women's League (OWL) Chicago Southeast Chapter
7408 S. Chappel Ave.
Chicago, IL 60649
Phone: (312)324-0844
Anna Bettles, Contact

★1726★ Older Women's League (OWL) Hyde Park Chapter
5235 S. University Ave.
Chicago, IL 60615-4405
Phone: (312)332-1161
Judy Roothan, Contact

★1727★ Older Women's League (OWL) Illinois State Chapter
PO Box 25416
Chicago, IL 60625-0416
Phone: (312)296-2866
Pat Taylor, Contact

★1728★ Older Women's League (OWL) Marillac Chapter
2948 W. Jackson Blvd.
Chicago, IL 60612
Phone: (312)826-5842
Alice Seals, Contact

★1729★ Religious Coalition for Abortion Rights, Illinois Affiliate
PO Box 37-8654
Chicago, IL 60637
Phone: (312)924-1081
Patricia Camp, Exec.Dir.

Description: Seventeen religious organizations offering problem pregnancy counseling service. Sponsors women of color partnership program. Maintains speaker's bureau. **Affiliated with:** Religious Coalition for Abortion Rights.

★1730★ Right to Life of Illinois
343 S. Dearborn St., Ste. 1217
Chicago, IL 60604

Description: Promotes the rights of the unborn.

★1731★ Women's Transportation Seminar, Chicago Chapter
c/o Dorothy Martin
PO Box 804535
Chicago, IL 60680
Phone: (312)467-2669
Fax: (312)793-3481
Dorothy Martin, Pres.

Description: Transportation professionals organized to promote the professional development of women in transportation. Bestows Member of the Year and Woman of the Year awards; provides scholarships. Maintains job bank. **Affiliated with:** Women's Transporation Seminar.

★1732★ Young Women's Christian Association of Metropolitan Chicago
180 N. Wabash Ave., Ste. 301
Chicago, IL 60601
Phone: (312)372-6600

Description: Seeks to develop and improve the spiritual, social, mental, and physical life of women and girls over the age of 12. **Affiliated with:** Young Women's Christian Association of the United States of America.

Chrisman

★1733★ Edgar County Republican Woman's Organization
516 E. Madison
Chrisman, IL 61924
Phone: (217)269-2184
Virginia Johnson, Pres.

Description: Women supporting the goals of the Republican party.

Clinton

★1734★ DeWitt County Farm Bureau Women's Committee
c/o Dorothy Ferguson
Rte. 3
Clinton, IL 61727
Phone: (217)935-6993
Dorothy Ferguson, Chm.

Danville

★1735★ Older Women's League (OWL) Danville Chapter
215 S. Kansas St.
Danville, IL 61832
Phone: (217)443-2999
Christine Fitzsimmons, Contact

★1736★ Young Women's Christian Association of Danville
201 N. Hazel St.
Danville, IL 61832
Phone: (217)446-1217

Description: Seeks to develop and improve the spiritual, social, mental, and physical life of women and girls over the age of 12. **Affiliated with:** Young Women's Christian Association of the United States of America.

Decatur

★1737★ Young Women's Christian Association of Decatur
436 N. Main St.
Decatur, IL 62523
Phone: (217)423-3415
Description: Seeks to develop and improve the spiritual, social, mental, and physical life of women and girls over the age of 12. **Affiliated with:** Young Women's Christian Association of the United States of America.

Downers Grove

★1738★ Association for Women in Science, Illinois Chapter
c/o Patricia Finn
6925 Fairmont
Downers Grove, IL 60516-0000
Patricia Finn, Contact
Description: Works to improve education and employment opportunities for women in the sciences.

East Alton

★1739★ East Alton Woman's Club
209 McCasland Ave.
East Alton, IL 62024
Phone: (618)254-6291
Marie Brazier, Pres.
Description: Women's volunteer service club. Sponsors charitable activities.

Elgin

★1740★ Young Women's Christian Association of Elgin
220 E. Chicago St.
Elgin, IL 60120
Phone: (708)742-7930
Fax: (708)742-8217
Description: Seeks to develop and improve the spiritual, social, mental, and physical life of women and girls over the age of 12. **Affiliated with:** Young Women's Christian Association of the United States of America.

Evanston

★1741★ Pan Pacific and Southeast Asia Women's Association of the U.S.A., Chicago Chapter
3023 Pain St.
Evanston, IL 60201
Phone: (708)446-4998
Anita Yamada, Pres.
Description: Diplomatic corps wives, house-wives, professional women, university faculty wives, and interested individuals furthering the cause of peace by promoting friendship and the exchange of knowledge among women of the Pacific countries. **Affiliated with:** Pan Pacific and Southeast Asia Women's Association of the U.S.A.; Pan-Pacific and South-East Asia Women's Association.

★1742★ Young Women's Christian Association of Evanston/North Shore
1215 Church St.
Evanston, IL 60201
Phone: (708)864-8445
Description: Seeks to develop and improve the spiritual, social, mental, and physical life of women and girls over the age of 12. **Affiliated with:** Young Women's Christian Association of the United States of America.

Flossmoor

★1743★ Older Women's League (OWL) South Suburban Chapter
2129 Marston Ln.
Flossmoor, IL 60422
Phone: (708)798-0071
Virginia Jones, Contact

Geneseo

★1744★ National Association of Women Business Owners Quad Cities/Davenport Chapter
c/o Tamron Travel, Inc.
1021 S. Oakwood Ave.
Geneseo, IL 61254
Phone: (309)944-5158
Velma Wilkerson, President

Glen Ellyn

★1745★ Glen Ellyn Junior Woman's Club
PO Box 2234
Glen Ellyn, IL 60138
Phone: (708)469-8722
Bette Wagner, Pres.
Description: Women's volunteer service club. Conducts charitable activities. **Affiliated with:** General Federation of Women's Clubs; Illinois Federation of Women's Clubs.

★1746★ Glen Ellyn Woman's Club
PO Box 53
Glen Ellyn, IL 60137
Phone: (708)469-8791
LeAnn Steffee, Pres.
Description: Women's volunteer service club. Conducts scholarship drives. **Affiliated with:** General Federation of Women's Clubs.

Havana

★1747★ Havana Business and Professional Women's Club
c/o Betty Sinnock
RR 1, Box 485
Havana, IL 62644
Phone: (309)543-4950
Betty Sinnock, Exec. Officer
Description: Business and professional women. To promote complete participation, equal opportunities, and economic self-sufficiency for working women. **Affiliated with:** National Federation of Business and Professional Women's Clubs of the U.S.A.

Highland Park

★1748★ National Association of Women Business Owners Chicago Area Chapter
c/o My Kind of Town Tours, Inc.
266 Aspen Ln.
Highland Park, IL 60035
Phone: (708)432-4966
Marsha Goldstein, President

Homewood

★1749★ South Cook County Girls Scouts
1005 W. 175th St.
Homewood, IL 60430
Phone: (708)957-8100
Mary Drish, CEO
Description: Girls ages five to 17 and adult volunteers. Provides an information, educational program for girls. Sponsors training workshops for leaders. **Affiliated with:** Girl Scouts of the U.S.A.

Inverness

★1750★ Women's Club of Inverness
c/o Kathy Ross
1709 Appleby Rd.
Inverness, IL 60067
Phone: (708)358-3399
Kathy Ross, Exec. Officer
Description: Women's volunteer service club. Conducts charitable programs. **Affiliated with:** General Federation of Women's Clubs; Illinois Federation of Women's Clubs.

Jacksonville

★1751★ Alpha Iota Sorority, Jacksonville Alumnae Chapter
RR 2
Jacksonville, IL 62650
Phone: (217)243-2688
Elizabeth Hardy, V.Pres.
Description: Individuals who have attended business college or are currently working in business. Provides career guidance counseling; conducts charitable activities.

★1752★ Jacksonville Junior Women's Club
PO Box 4
Jacksonville, IL 62651
Phone: (217)673-5781
Bernie Hoagland, Pres.
Description: Women ages 21-45 united to perform community service. **Affiliated with:** General Federation of Women's Clubs.

Joliet

★1753★ Girl Scouts of the U.S.A., Trailways Council
RR 4
1533 Spencer Rd.
Joliet, IL 60433
Phone: (815)723-3449
Theresa Arneson, Exec. Officer

★1754★ La Leche League International, Illinois Chapter
105 Stadium Dr.
Joliet, IL 60435
Phone: (815)741-0354
Joan Woolwine, Coordinator

Description: Women interested in the breast-feeding of infants. **Affiliated with:** La Leche League International.

★1755★ Older Women's League (OWL) Will County Chapter
959 Cottage Pl.
Joliet, IL 60436
Phone: (815)729-4150
Esther Ferguson, Contact

Kankakee

★1756★ Kankakee Area Women on the Move
396 N. Industrial
Kankakee, IL 60901-2651

Description: Works to improve the position of women in society.

★1757★ National Association of Women in Construction, Kankakee Chapter
898 S. Washington
Kankakee, IL 60901
Phone: (815)939-1563
Mildred Woodall, Exec. Officer

★1758★ Older Women's League (OWL) Kankakee County Chapter
340 N. Dearborn, No. 223
Kankakee, IL 60901
Phone: (815)933-6109
Patricia Reynolds, Contact

★1759★ Young Women's Christian Association of Kankakee
1086 E. Court St.
Kankakee, IL 60901
Phone: (815)933-4516

Lemont

★1760★ Association for Women in Science, Chicago Area Chapter
PO Box 13
Lemont, IL 60439
Phone: (708)972-4341
Marie-Louise Saboungi, Pres.

Description: Professional women and men of the social and natural sciences united to promote equal opportunities for women to enter the professions and achieve their career goals. Bestows Science Fair Awards to public school students. Holds workshops. **Affiliated with:** Association for Women in Science.

Lincoln

★1761★ Chester Women's Club
Union St. Rd., Box 257
Lincoln, IL 62656
Phone: (217)732-7148
Virginia K. Johnson, Pres.

Description: Women's volunteer service club. Conducts card tournament.

Lisle

★1762★ Lisle Woman's Club
c/o Marianne Chittenden
569 Maywood Ln.
Lisle, IL 60532
Phone: (708)964-1489
Marianne Chittenden, Pres.

Description: Community service and philanthropic organization for women. Works to promote literacy. Sponsors charitable activities and essay and poster contests. Bestows art and music awards and scholarships. Holds annual fashion show fundraiser. Participates in Depot Days and Fourth of July activities. **Affiliated with:** General Federation of Women's Clubs; Illinois Federation of Women's Cluba; Illinois Federation of Women's Clubs, Fifth District; Literacy Volunteers of America.

Lombard

★1763★ Lombard Woman's Club
PO Box 14
Lombard, IL 60148
Phone: (708)620-7485
Bonnie Fiebrandt, Exec. Officer

Description: Women's volunteer service club. Conducts charitable activities. **Affiliated with:** General Federation of Women's Clubs; Illinois Federation of Women's Clubs.

★1764★ Older Women's League (OWL) DuPage Area Chapter
19 W 241-14th Place
Lombard, IL 60148
Phone: (708)620-0804
Joan Taylor, Contact

Mt. Prospect

★1765★ National Alliance of Homebased Businesswomen, Northern Illinois Chapter
c/o Janet V. Hansen
PO Box 283
Mt. Prospect, IL 60056
Phone: (708)253-9357
Janet V. Hansen, Pres.

Description: Male and female home-based business owners in the Chicago, IL metropolitan area organized as a support network for the exchange of information. Conducts monthly educational program. **Affiliated with:** National Alliance of Homebased Businesswomen.

Murphysboro

★1766★ Murphysboro Business and Professional Women's Club
c/o Phyllis Wallace
1630 Shomaker Dr.
Murphysboro, IL 62966
Phone: (618)687-3168
Fax: (618)687-3033
Phyllis Wallace, Pres.

Description: Business and professional women. To promote complete participation, equal opportunities, and economic self-sufficiency for working women. **Affiliated with:** National Federation of Business and Professional Women's Clubs of the U.S.A.

Oak Brook Terrace

★1767★ National Association for Women in Careers, West Suburban Chapter
c/o Ronald Danner
Superior Bank
1 Lincoln Center
Oak Brook Terrace, IL 60181
Phone: (708)916-4000
Ronald Danner, Exec. Officer

Oak Park

★1768★ Older Women's League (OWL) Near West Chapter
Box 3607
Oak Park, IL 60302
Phone: (708)383-3770
Marilyn Young, Contact

O'Fallon

★1769★ O'Fallon Woman's Club
c/o John Hendrickson
811 James Towne Rd.
O'Fallon, IL 62269
Phone: (618)632-6871
John Hendrickson, Pres.

Description: Women's volunteer service club. Maintains facilities for children and veteran's memorial; conducts fundraising activities for community parks. Bestows scholarship. **Affiliated with:** General Federation of Women's Clubs; Illinois Federation of Women's Clubs.

Oregon

★1770★ Rock River Women
c/o Janice L. Woodhouse
PO Box 313
Oregon, IL 61061
Phone: (815)732-7286
Janice L. Woodhouse, Exec. Officer

Description: Serves as a network to provide information and education beneficial to the improvement of life for rural women. Holds seminars and workshops.

Ottawa

★1771★ WISH List
1700 Champlin
Ottawa, IL 61350
Phone: (815)443-0534
Peg McDonnell Breslin, Representative

Founded: 1992. **Description:** Supports prochoice Republican female candidates for U.S. Congress and governorships. WISH stands for Women in the Senate and House.

Palatine

★1772★ Crawford County Federated Republican Women
317 S. Main
Palatine, IL 62451
Phone: (618)586-5115
Marsha Brock, Exec. Officer

Palos Heights

★1773★ **Chicago Women's Conference**
c/o Mary B. Bootsma
PO Box 311
Palos Heights, IL 60463-0311
Description: Works to advance the social and professional status of members.

Paris

★1774★ **Paris Business and Professional Woman's Club**
RR 2, Box 19
Paris, IL 61944
Phone: (217)463-2529
Gayla McDaniel, Exec. Officer
Description: Business and professional women. Promotes full participation in the workforce, equity, and economic self-sufficiency for working women. **Affiliated with:** Illinois Federation of Business and Professional Women; National Federation of Business and Professional Women's Clubs of the U.S.A.

★1775★ **Paris Woman's Club**
Rte. 2, Box 308
Paris, IL 61944
Phone: (217)463-3280
Gay Tegeler, Pres.
Description: Women interested in community service. Awards scholarships. Bestows Volunteer Woman of the Year award. **Affiliated with:** General Federation of Woman's Clubs; Illinois Federation of Woman's Clubs.

Pekin

★1776★ **Young Women's Christian Association of Pekin**
315 Buena Vista
Pekin, IL 61554
Phone: (309)347-2104
Jeanne Kimble, Contact
Description: Seeks to develop and improve the spiritual, social, mental, and physical life of women and girls over the age of 12. **Affiliated with:** Young Women's Christian Association of the United States of America.

Peoria

★1777★ **National Association of Women Business Owners**
Central Illinois Chapter
c/o JA-BO, Inc.
2235 W. Glen
Peoria, IL 61614
Phone: (309)691-3101
Bonnie Russell, President

★1778★ **Older Women's League (OWL)**
Central Illinois Chapter
139 E. Morningside Dr.
Peoria, IL 61614
Phone: (309)691-3781
Miriam Spitz-Domnitz, Contact

★1779★ **Young Women's Christian Association of Peoria**
301 NE Jefferson
Peoria, IL 61602
Phone: (309)674-1167
Marsha Creemeens, Exec.Dir.
Description: Seeks to develop and improve the spiritual, social, mental, and physical health of women and children over the age of 12. Operates emergency family shelter and women's residence. **Affiliated with:** Young Women's Christian Association of the United States of America.

Peoria Heights

★1780★ **Feminists for Life of Illinois**
PO Box 9098
Peoria Heights, IL 61614
Phone: (309)682-1876
Mary Ann Schaefer, Exec. Officer
Description: Feminists united to secure the right-to-life, from conception to natural death, of all human beings. **Affiliated with:** Feminists for Life of America.

Peru

★1781★ **Empty Arms**
c/o Debbie Boyd
Illinois Valley Community Hospital
925 West St.
Peru, IL 61354
Phone: (815)223-3300
Debbie Boyd, Facilitator
Description: Individuals who have suffered a miscarriage or the perinatal or neonatal loss of a child. Promotes healing of childbirth losses through one-to-one discussions; presents speakers. **Affiliated with:** SHARE.

Petersburg

★1782★ **Petersburg Town and Country Woman's Club**
c/o Carol Pope
521 N. 7th St.
Petersburg, IL 62675
Phone: (217)632-3709
Carol Pope, Contact
Description: Women's volunteer service club. Currently refurbishing city park. Conducts charitable activities. Participates in area festival.

★1783★ **Petersburg Woman's Club**
c/o Mrs. Robert Apken
Almond Ln.
Petersburg, IL 62675
Phone: (217)632-2313
Mrs. Robert Apken, Pres.
Description: Women's volunteer service club. **Affiliated with:** General Federation of Women's Clubs; Illinois Federation of Women's Clubs.

Pittsfield

★1784★ **Pittsfield Business and Professional Women's Club**
c/o Nancy Wessel
RR 3, Box 44
510 N. Jackson
Pittsfield, IL 62363
Phone: (217)285-6923
Nancy Wessel, Exec. Officer
Description: Business and professional women. To promote complete participation, equal opportunities, and economic self-sufficiency for working women. Sponsors Fall Festival and Young Careerist competition. Provides scholarships and loans. **Affiliated with:** National Federation of Business and Professional Women's Clubs of the U.S.A.

Polo

★1785★ **PEO Sisterhood, DW Chapter**
102 S. Jackson St.
Polo, IL 61064
Phone: (815)946-2814
Nancy Cline, Contact
Description: Promotes women's education; sponsors educational programs.

★1786★ **Polo Afternoon Women's Club**
107 N. Thomas St.
Polo, IL 61064
Phone: (815)946-3405
Mrs. Clark Huyett, Pres.
Description: Provides social, charitable, and educational events for women in Polo, IL.

★1787★ **Polo Evening Women's Club**
303 S. Union St.
Polo, IL 61064
Phone: (815)946-3807
Arlene Blum, Pres.
Description: Women interested in service to the community of Polo, IL.

Quincy

★1788★ **Older Women's League (OWL)**
Quincy Tri-State Chapter
1125 Hampshire St.
Quincy, IL 62301
Phone: (217)224-3633
Carla Gosney, Contact

★1789★ **Young Women's Christian Association of Quincy**
421 Jersey St.
Quincy, IL 62301
Phone: (217)222-4996
Description: Seeks to develop and improve the spiritual, social, mental, and physical life of women and girls over the age of 12. **Affiliated with:** Young Women's Christian Association of the United States of America.

Robinson

**★1790★ Crawford County Democratic
Women's Club**
204 E. 13th
Robinson, IL 62454
Phone: (618)544-7193
Marian Bonnell, Pres.

Description: Works to elect Democrats to local, state, and national office.

**★1791★ Crawford County Republican
Woman's Club**
c/o Mildred Storm
607 N. Jefferson
Robinson, IL 62454
Phone: (618)544-3219
Mildred Storm, Pres.

Description: Women who promote the Republican party. Conducts charitable activities; sponsors area festivals. **Affiliated with:** Illinois Federation of Republican Women; National Federation of Republican Women.

★1792★ Robinson Church Women United
508 E. Mefford Dr.
Robinson, IL 62454
Phone: (618)544-7528
Frances Cummins, Pres.

Description: Ecumenical movement uniting Protestant, Roman Catholic, Orthodox, and other churchwomen into one Christian community. Supports peace, human rights, justice, and the empowerment of women.

★1793★ Robinson Woman's Club
703 Beach
Robinson, IL 62454
Phone: (618)544-8791
Lois Goodwin, Pres.

Description: Women interested in community service.

Rock Island

**★1794★ American Association of
University Women, Illinois Division**
2936 36th St.
Rock Island, IL 61201
Phone: (309)786-7472
Jane Grahlmann, Pres.

Description: Women graduates from accredited colleges and universities in the U.S. Promotes equality for women and encourages continuing education and self development. **Affiliated with:** American Association of University Women.

**★1795★ Older Women's League (OWL)
Quad Cities Chapter**
1620 20th Ave.
Rock Island, IL 61201
George Anderson, Contact

**★1796★ Young Women's Christian
Association of Rock Island**
229 16th St.
Rock Island, IL 61201
Phone: (309)788-3479

Description: Seeks to develop and improve the spiritual, social, mental, and physical life of women and girls over the age of 12. **Affiliated with:** Young Women's Christian Association of the United States of America.

Rockford

★1797★ Rockford Woman's Club
323 Park Ave.
Rockford, IL 61101
Phone: (815)965-4233
Phyllis Smith, Pres.

Description: Philanthropic and community service organization for women.

**★1798★ Women in Illinois Needed Now
(WIINN)**
PO Box 1555
Rockford, IL 61105
Phone: (815)987-7555
Senator Joyce Holmberg, Chair

**★1799★ Young Women's Christian
Association of Rockford**
220 S. Madison St.
Rockford, IL 61104
Phone: (815)968-9681
Ann Garrity, Contact

Description: Seeks to develop and improve the spiritual, social, mental, and physical life of women and girls over the age of 12. **Affiliated with:** Young Women's Christian Association of the United States of America.

Rolling Meadows

★1800★ Northwest Action Against Rape
5005 Newport Dr.
Rolling Meadows, IL 60008
Phone: (708)253-0220
Laura Kaufman, Exec.Dir.

Description: Volunteers provide support, counseling, and crisis intervention to victims of sexual assault; seeks to end sexual assault and abuse. Provides training to social service organizations and law enforcement personnel. **Affiliated with:** Illinois Coalition Against Sexual Assault.

Springfield

**★1801★ Illinois Coalition Against Domestic
Violence**
937 S. 4th St.
Springfield, IL 62703
Phone: (217)789-2830
Joyce M. Pruitt, Contact

**★1802★ Illinois Federation of Business
and Professional Women**
528 S. 5th St., Ste. 209
Springfield, IL 62701
Phone: (217)528-8985
Christine LaFrance, Pres.

Description: Working women. Promotes women's advancement in the workplace. Lobbies; disseminates information; conducts training seminars.

**★1803★ National Association of Women
Business Owners**
Springfield Chapter
c/o The Minuteman
1820 W. Jefferson St.
Springfield, IL 62702
Phone: (217)793-8973
Deanna Langheim, President

**★1804★ Older Women's League (OWL)
Springfield Area Chapter**
PO Box 443
Springfield, IL 62705
Phone: (217)787-7778
Rita Whitney, Contact

**★1805★ Young Women's Christian
Association of Springfield**
421 E. Jackson St.
Springfield, IL 62701
Phone: (217)522-8828

Description: Seeks to develop and improve the spiritual, social, mental, and physical life of women and girls over the age of 12. **Affiliated with:** Young Women's Christian Association of the United States of America.

Sterling

**★1806★ Sterling-Rock Falls Young
Women's Christian Association**
412 1st Ave.
Sterling, IL 61081
Phone: (815)625-0333
Carol Fitzgerald, Exec.Dir.

Description: Social service organization for women and girls. Provides domestic violence and sexual assault victim programs and services; offers fitness, preschool, and special interest clubs and classes. **Affiliated with:** Young Women's Christian Association of the United States of America.

Sycamore

**★1807★ American Association of
University Women, De Kalb County
Branch**
c/o G.M. Crawford
515 Georjean Ct.
Sycamore, IL 60178
Phone: (815)895-9498
G. M. Crawford, Pres.

Description: Women graduates of regionally accredited four year colleges and universities. Works for the advancement of women through advocacy and emphasis on lifelong learning.

★1808★ Sycamore Woman's Club
1060 N. Main St.
Sycamore, IL 60178
Phone: (815)895-3832
Gladys L. Healy, Pres.

Description: Women's volunteer service club. **Affiliated with:** General Federation of Women's Clubs.

Urbana

**★1809★ Association for Women in
Science, Central Illinois Chapter**
c/o Dr. Karolyn Eisenstein
Stc. For Superconductivity
104 S. Goodwin Ave.
Urbana, IL 61801
Phone: (217)333-1744
Dr. Karolyn Eisenstein, Contact

Description: Works to improve education and employment opportunities for women in the sciences.

Waukegan

★1810★ **Young Women's Christian Association of Lake County**
2133 Belvedere Rd.
Waukegan, IL 60085
Phone: (708)662-4247

Description: Seeks to develop and improve the spiritual, social, mental, and physical life of women and girls over the age of 12. **Affiliated with:** Young Women's Christian Association of the United States of America.

Western Springs

★1811★ **American Association of University Women, Western Springs Branch**
c/o Margi Truckenbrodt
4062 Wolf Rd.
Western Springs, IL 60558
Phone: (708)246-0608
Margi Truckenbrodt, Exec. Officer

Description: Women graduates of regionally accredited four year colleges and universities. Works for the advancement of women through advocacy and emphasis on lifelong learning. **Affiliated with:** American Association of University Women.

Westmont

★1812★ **Club of Indian Women**
c/o Mrs. Jyotsna K. Kumar
17 W. 434 Sutton Pl.
Westmont, IL 60559-5114
Mrs. Jyotsna K. Kumar, Contact

Description: Social organization.

Willowbrook

★1813★ **Illinois Women for Agriculture**
4422 McArthur Dr.
Willowbrook, IL 60521
Phone: (708)887-1700
Amy Hartwick, Pres.

Description: Persons interested in promoting agriculture. **Affiliated with:** American Agriculture Women.

Indiana

Angola

★1814★ **Angola Business and Professional Women's Club**
Rte. 5
Angola, IN 46703
Phone: (219)665-9743
Judy Jones, Pres.

Description: Business and professional women. To promote complete participation, equal opportunities, and economic self-sufficiency for working women.

Arcadia

★1815★ **Hamilton County Republican Women's Club**
9331 E. 266th St.
Arcadia, IN 46030
Phone: (317)984-3716
Naomi Williamson, Contact

Description: Promotes Republican Party candidates for public office.

Auburn

★1816★ **Auburn Business and Professional Women's Club**
PO Box 6023
221 S. Main
Auburn, IN 46706
Phone: (219)925-0631

Description: Business and professional women. To promote complete participation, equal opportunities, and economic self-sufficiency for working women. Bestows scholarships. **Affiliated with:** BPW/Indiana; National Federation of Business and Professional Women's Clubs of the U.S.A.

Brownsburg

★1817★ **American Association of University Women, Brownsburg Chapter**
6370 North, 1000 East
Brownsburg, IN 46112
Phone: (317)852-8745
Joyce Compton, Exec. Officer

Description: Women graduates of regionally accredited four year colleges and universities. Works for the advancement of women through advocacy and emphasis on lifelong learning. American Association of University Women.

★1818★ **Older Women's League (OWL) Central Indiana Chapter**
419 William Dr.
Brownsburg, IN 46112
Phone: (317)852-4810
Dagmar L. Schilke, Contact

Carmel

★1819★ **DES Action**
Box 3158
Carmel, IN 46032

Elkhart

★1820★ **Young Women's Christian Association of Elkhart County**
200 E. Jackson Blvd.
Elkhart, IN 46516
Phone: (219)295-6915
Judith Beechy Dyck, Exec.Dir.

Description: Seeks to develop and improve the spiritual, social, mental, and physical life of women and girls. Operates Child Care Center and Goshen Program Center. **Affiliated with:** Young Women's Christian Association of the United States of America.

Elwood

★1821★ **General Federation of Women's Clubs, Elwood Department Club**
2127 S. K St.
Elwood, IN 46036
Phone: (317)552-2332
Ruth A. Murray, Pres.

Description: Promotes fine arts, education, and literature. Holds civics programs for elderly women.

Evansville

★1822★ **Evansville Career Women of Business and Professional Women's Club**
3308 Mt. Vernon Ave.
Evansville, IN 47712
Phone: (812)422-5434
Phyllis Roeder, Pres.

Description: Women administrators, bankers, nurses, teachers and others promoting the rights of working women and providing opportunities for networking. **Affiliated with:** National Federation of Business and Professional Women's Clubs of the U.S.A.

★1823★ **Evansville Young Women's Christian Association**
118 Vine St.
Evansville, IN 47708
Phone: (812)422-1191
Sylvia Neff Weinzapfel, Exec.Dir.

Description: Seeks to develop and improve the spiritual, social, mental, and physical life of women and children. **Affiliated with:** Young Women's Christian Association of the United States of America.

★1824★ **Girl Scouts of the U.S.A., Raintree Council**
2516 Washington
PO Box 14006
Evansville, IN 47728-6006
Phone: (812)473-8933
Janice K. Davies, Exec. Officer

★1825★ **La Leche League International of Evansville**
13400 Big Cynthiana Rd.
Evansville, IN 47720
Phone: (812)963-3865
Esther M. Kelley, Leader

Description: Mothers in southern Indiana who breastfeed their infants. Offers information and support. **Affiliated with:** La Leche League International.

Ft. Wayne

★1826★ **Project Comfort**
c/o Gerald C. Machgan
Parkview Hospital
2200 Randalia
Ft. Wayne, IN 46805
Phone: (219)484-6636
Gerald C. Machgan, Coordinator

Description: Support group in Allen County, IN for parents who have lost a child through stillbirth, miscarriage, or neonatal death. Provides information and counseling.

★1827★ **Young Women's Christian Association of Ft. Wayne**
2000 N. Wells St.
Ft. Wayne, IN 46808
Phone: (219)424-4908
Description: Seeks to develop and improve the spiritual, social, mental, and physical life of women and girls over the age of 12. **Affiliated with:** Young Women's Christian Association of the United States of America.

Franklin

★1828★ **American Business Women's Association, Franklin Chapter**
1060 W. Jefferson St.
Franklin, IN 46131
Phone: (317)736-8324
Alice Myers, Contact
Description: Educational association directed toward the professional, educational, cultural, and social advancement of businesswomen. **Affiliated with:** American Business Women's Association.

★1829★ **Big Sisters, Johnson County Chapter**
PO Box 813
Franklin, IN 46131
Phone: (317)738-3273
Ellen Annala, Exec. Officer
Description: Provides a girl from a single-parent home with an adult female volunteer who can offer regular guidance, understanding, and acceptance. **Affiliated with:** Big Brothers/Big Sisters of America.

★1830★ **Franklin Business and Professional Women's Club**
c/o Edna VanAntwerp
255 E. South St.
Franklin, IN 46131
Phone: (317)736-7288
Edna VanAntwerp, Exec. Officer
Description: Business and professional women. To promote complete participation, equal opportunities, and economic self-sufficiency for working women. **Affiliated with:** National Federation of Business and Professional Women's Club.

★1831★ **Franklin Women's Democrat Club**
320 King Arthur Dr.
Franklin, IN 46131
Phone: (317)736-9306
Phyllis Cantwell, Pres.
Description: To promote the Democratic party.

Fremont

★1832★ **Steuben County Business and Professional Women's Club**
RR 1, Box 79
Fremont, IN 46737
Phone: (219)495-7053
Ruth Edington, Exec. Officer
Description: Business and professional women. To promote complete participation, equal opportunities, and economic self-sufficiency for working women. **Affiliated with:** National Federation of Business and Professional Women's Clubs of the U.S.A.

Gary

★1833★ **Gary Business and Professional Women's Club**
PO Box 1286
Gary, IN 46407
Phone: (219)762-0743
Joan Morales, Pres.
Description: Business and professional women. To promote complete participation, equal opportunities, and economic self-sufficiency for working women. Makes charitable contributions to the Salvation Army and the local women's shelter. Awards scholarships to area students. Sponsors the Village Service Club Salute. **Affiliated with:** International Federation of Business and Professional Women; National Federation of Business and Professional Women's Club.

★1834★ **Young Women's Christian Association of Gary**
30 E. 6th Ave.
Gary, IN 46402
Phone: (219)886-9196
Description: Seeks to develop and improve the spiritual, social, mental, and physical life of women and girls over the age of 12. **Affiliated with:** Young Women's Christian Association of the United States of America.

Griffith

★1835★ **Griffith Woman's Club**
228 Woodlawn
Griffith, IN 46319
Phone: (219)924-2228
Description: Women's volunteer service club.

★1836★ **Ridgeland Federated Women's Club**
1306 N. Arbogiast
Griffith, IN 46319
Phone: (219)923-6069
Shirley Kapitan, Pres.
Description: Women's volunteer service club. Activities focus on areas of conservation, education, home life, international and public affairs, and the arts. **Affiliated with:** General Federation of Women's Clubs; GFWC Indiana Federation of Clubs.

Hagerstown

★1837★ **Association for Women in Science, Indiana Chapter**
c/o Dr. Joan Lafuze
100 W. Lane Dr.
Hagerstown, IN 47346
Phone: (317)274-2276
Dr. Joan Lafuze, Contact
Description: Works to improve education and employment opportunities for women in the sciences.

Hammond

★1838★ **Calumet Area Young Women's Christian Association**
250 Ogden St.
PO Box 1179
Hammond, IN 46325
Phone: (219)931-2922
Description: Seeks to develop and improve the spiritual, social, mental, and physical life of women and girls over the age of 12. **Affiliated with:** Young Women's Christian Association of the United States of America.

Indianapolis

★1839★ **Association for Women in Science, Indiana Chapter**
c/o Dr. Ellen Chernoff
Department of Biology, IUPUI
1125 E. 38th St.
Indianapolis, IN 46205
Phone: (317)274-0591
Dr. Ellen Chernoff, Pres.
Description: Professional women and men of the social and natural sciences united to promote equal opportunities for women to enter the professions and achieve their career goals. Maintain speakers' bureau. Judges science fairs. **Affiliated with:** Association for Women in Science.

★1840★ **Carmel Business and Professional Women's Club**
11010 Willowmere Dr.
Indianapolis, IN 46280
Phone: (317)576-9654
Donna Woodward, Pres.
Description: Business and professional women. To promote complete participation, equal opportunities, and economic self-sufficiency for working women. **Affiliated with:** National Federation of Business and Professional Women's Clubs of the U.S.A.

★1841★ **Christian Career Women**
c/o Mary Reynolds-Williams
PO Box 531152
Indianapolis, IN 46253-1152
Mary Reynolds-Williams, Contact
Description: Christians working women. Promotes ethics on the job.

★1842★ **Electrical Women's RoundTable, Indiana Chapter**
c/o Rebecca S. Horton
Indianapolis Power and Light
25 Monument Circle
Indianapolis, IN 46204
Phone: (317)261-8391
Rebecca S. Horton, Pres.
Description: Women who have careers in the electrical/energy fields. Promotes energy education and acts as a networking agency. Sponsors school grant and scholarship program. **Affiliated with:** Electrical Women's Round Table.

★1843★ **Indiana Abortion Rights Action League**
740 52nd St., Ste. 10
Indianapolis, IN 46205
Phone: (317)283-6033
Kevin Coughlin, Contact

★1844★ **Indiana Association for Child Care Resource and Referral**
c/o Wendy Schaffer
4460 Guion Rd.
Indianapolis, IN 46254-3113
Wendy Schaffer, Contact

★1845★ **Indiana Women's Political Caucus**
557 E. Washington
Indianapolis, IN 46041
Phone: (317)659-4535
Mary Ann Butters, Pres.

Description: Women and men committed to greater participation of women in politics and government. Promotes female candidates for public office and male candidates committed to women's rights; presents Good Guy awards to men who have advanced the status of, and regard for, women and children. **Affiliated with:** National Women's Political Caucus.

★1846★ **League of Women Voters of Indiana**
740 E. 52nd St.
Indianapolis, IN 46205
Phone: (317)925-8683
Melissa Durr, President

★1847★ **Right to Life of Indianapolis**
c/o Gordon R. Smith
8145 Ecole St.
Indianapolis, IN 46240-2726
Gordon R. Smith, Contact

Description: Promotes the rights of the unborn.

★1848★ **Young Women's Christian Association of Indianapolis**
4460 Guion Rd.
Indianapolis, IN 46254
Phone: (317)299-2750

Description: Seeks to develop and improve the spiritual, social, mental, and physical life of women and girls over the age of 12. **Affiliated with:** Young Women's Christian Association of the United States of America.

Kokomo

★1849★ **American Association of University Women, Kokomo Branch**
1310 Westbrook Dr.
Kokomo, IN 46902
Phone: (317)453-6443
Elaine C. Newman, Contact

Description: Women graduates of regionally accredited four year colleges and universities. Works for the advancement of women through advocacy and emphasis on lifelong learning.

★1850★ **Howard County Right to Life**
PO Box 2303
Kokomo, IN 46904-2303
Phone: (317)452-9300
Sheryl Dillman, Pres.

Description: Individuals and families united to protect human life from conception until natural death. Sponsors information booths and speakers' bureau. Issues publications.

★1851★ **Women of the Evangelical Lutheran Church in America**
1310 Westbrook Dr.
Kokomo, IN 46902
Phone: (317)453-6443
Elaine C. Newman, Contact

Description: Lutheran women promoting fellowship and spiritual growth.

★1852★ **Young Women's Christian Association of Kokomo**
406 E. Sycamore St.
Kokomo, IN 46901
Phone: (317)457-3293

Description: Seeks to develop and improve the spiritual, social, mental, and physical life of women and girls over the age of 12. **Affiliated with:** Young Women's Christian Association of the United States of America.

Lafayette

★1853★ **Indiana Coalition Against Domestic Violence**
605 N. 6th St.
Lafayette, IN 47901
Phone: (317)742-0075
Toll-free: 800-332-7385
Cheri Kilty, Contact

★1854★ **Young Women's Christian Association of Lafayette**
605 N. 6th St.
Lafayette, IN 47901
Phone: (317)742-0075

Description: Seeks to develop and improve the spiritual, social, mental, and physical life of women and girls over the age of 12. **Affiliated with:** Young Women's Christian Association of the United States of America.

Marion

★1855★ **Young Women's Christian Association of Marion**
615 S. Adams St.
Marion, IN 46953
Phone: (317)668-8995
Margaret Leza, Contact

Description: Seeks to develop and improve the spiritual, social, mental, and physical life of women and girls over the age of 12. **Affiliated with:** Young Women's Christian Association of the United States of America.

Martinsville

★1856★ **American Association of University Women, Mooresville Branch**
c/o Paula McKay
6950 Old SR 37 N.
Martinsville, IN 46151
Phone: (317)831-3018
Paula McKay, Exec. Officer

Description: Women graduates of regionally accredited four year colleges and universities. Works for the advancement of women through advocacy and emphasis on lifelong learning. **Affiliated with:** American Association of University Women.

Merrillville

★1857★ **Merrillville Business and Professional Women's Club**
6491 Hendricks St.
Merrillville, IN 46410
Phone: (219)769-2511
Gerry Chandler, Pres.

Description: Businesswomen, nurses, teachers, and interested individuals. To help working women gain equality. Offer scholarships. **Affiliated with:** National Federation of Business and Professional Women's Clubs of the U.S.A.

Muncie

★1858★ **Delaware County Democrat Women's Club**
c/o Democrat Headquarters
214 N. Walnut
Muncie, IN 47305
Phone: (317)282-9965

Description: Works to elect Democrats to local, state, and national office. Conducts fundraising activites.

★1859★ **Young Women's Christian Association of Muncie**
310 E. Charles St.
Muncie, IN 47305
Phone: (317)284-3345

Description: Seeks to develop and improve the spiritual, social, mental, and physical life of women and girls over the age of 12. **Affiliated with:** Young Women's Christian Association of the United States of America.

Plainfield

★1860★ **Hendricks County Democratic Women's Club**
706 E. Main St.
Plainfield, IN 46168
Phone: (317)839-0492
Esther Broyles, Co-Chm.

Rensselaer

★1861★ **Birthright of Rensselaer**
216 W. Washington, Ste. 6
Rensselaer, IN 47978-2822

Description: Seeks to help pregnant women find alternatives to abortion. Conducts childbirth education and parenting programs.

Richmond

★1862★ **Treaty Line Council of Girl Scouts**
713 Promenade
Richmond, IN 47374
Phone: (317)962-0225
Pamela Frazier, CEO

Description: Girls five to 18 years old and adult leaders in east central Indiana and west central Ohio organized for educational programs and activities. **Affiliated with:** Girl Scouts of the U.S.A.

★1863★ Young Women's Christian Association of Richmond
108 S. 9th St.
Richmond, IN 47374
Phone: (317)966-0538
Phyllis K. Morris, Exec.Dir.

Description: Seeks to develop and improve the spiritual, social, mental, and physical life of women and girls over the age of 12. Provides shelter for battered persons. **Affiliated with:** Young Womens Christian Association of the United States of America. **Telecommunications Services:** Phone Friendline.

Roachdale

★1864★ Indiana Women in Agriculture
Rte. 2, Box 25
Roachdale, IN 46172
Phone: (317)522-1441
Mrs. E. D. Brookshire, Pres.

Description: Seeks to educate nonfarmers on the problems faced by the farming family in America. **Affiliated with:** American Agri-Women.

Seymour

★1865★ Seymour Business and Professional Women's Club
108 E. Harrison Dr.
Seymour, IN 47274
Phone: (812)522-3434
Dolores Miller, Pres.

Description: Business and professional women. To promote complete participation, equal opportunities, and economic self-sufficiency for working women. **Affiliated with:** National Federation of Business and Professional Women's Clubs.

South Bend

★1866★ Young Women's Christian Association of St. Joseph County
802 N. Lafayette Blvd.
South Bend, IN 46601
Phone: (219)233-9491

Description: Seeks to develop and improve the spiritual, social, mental, and physical life of women and girls over the age of 12. **Affiliated with:** Young Women's Christian Association of the United States of America.

Sullivan

★1867★ Sullivan County Business and Professional Women's Club
804 N. Court St.
Sullivan, IN 47882
Phone: (812)268-5423
Michelle Faught, Exec. Officer

Description: Business and professional women. To promote complete participation, equal opportunities, and economic self-sufficiency for working women. **Affiliated with:** National Federation of Business and Professional Women's Clubs of the U.S.A.

Terre Haute

★1868★ Federation of Jewish Women, Terre Haute Chapter
United Hebrew Congregation
540 S. 6th St.
Terre Haute, IN 47807
Phone: (812)877-3043
Shirley Wormser, Pres.

Description: Members of the Jewish community in western Indiana and eastern Illinois. Seeks to foster and further the ideas of Judaism expressed through the synagogue; promote a closer fellowship among its members; and develop educational, religious, and social activities for the Jewish community. **Affiliated with:** National Federation of Temple Sisterhoods.

★1869★ Terre Haute Women's Club
c/o Patricia M. Cooke
PO Box 3217
Terre Haute, IN 47803-0217
Patricia M. Cooke, Pres.

Description: Women's volunteer service club.

★1870★ Young Women's Christian Association of Terre Haute
951 Dresser Dr.
Terre Haute, IN 47807
Phone: (812)232-3358

Description: Seeks to develop and improve the spiritual, social, mental, and physical life of women and girls over the age of 12. **Affiliated with:** Young Women's Christian Association of the United States of America.

Valparaiso

★1871★ Porter County Women's Democratic Club
256 Chicago St.
Valparaiso, IN 46384
Phone: (219)462-2886
Margaret Gold, Exec. Officer

Wabash

★1872★ Nurses Concerned for Life, Wabash Chapter
280 N. Wabash St.
Wabash, IN 46992
Phone: (219)563-7275
C. Jean Myers, Coordinator

Description: Nurses, volunteers, and interested individuals. Offers counseling for abortion alternatives, adoption information, free pregnancy testing, and referrals to community organizations. Donates infant and maternity clothes. Holds fundraisers. Sponsors annual Rally for Life. **Affiliated with:** Nurses Concerned for Life.

Walkerton

★1873★ Walkerton's Women's Community Club
c/o Ella Remus
RR 3
Walkerton, IN 46574
Phone: (219)586-3055
Ella Remus, Contact

Description: Women's volunteer service club. **Affiliated with:** General Federation of Women's Clubs.

Warsaw

★1874★ Heartline Pregnancy Care and Counseling
PO Box 1201
Warsaw, IN 46581-1201
Phone: (219)267-5110
Rene Hostetler, Exec.Dir.

Description: Doctors, lawyers, professional counselors, pastors, and business executives. Works to meet the needs of women in crisis pregnancies.

West Lafayette

★1875★ La Leche League International, Indiana Chapter
148 Thornbush
West Lafayette, IN 47906
Phone: (317)463-9946
Donna Larson, Coordinator

Description: Women interested in the breastfeeding of infants. **Affiliated with:** La Leche League International.

Iowa

Albia

★1876★ Albia Woman's Club
c/o Doris Mellick
RR 5
Albia, IA 52531
Phone: (515)932-2873
Doris Mellick, Pres.

Description: Women's volunteer service club. Works to preserve the Kendall Place. Sponsors annual school art show; bestows awards.

★1877★ American Association of University Women, Iowa Division
22 N. Main
Albia, IA 52531
Phone: (515)932-2540
Rowena Hardinger, Pres.

Description: Women graduates of regionally accredited four year colleges and universities. Works for the advancement of women through advocacy and emphasis on lifelong learning. **Affiliated with:** American Association of University Women.

Ames

★1878★ National Women Studies Association, Midwest Chapter
c/o Kathy Hickok
203 Ross Hall
Iowa State University
Ames, IA 50011
Kathy Hickok, Exec. Officer

★1879★ Older Women's League (OWL) Ames Chapter
1519 Top-O-Hollow
Ames, IA 50010
Phone: (515)232-1299
Pauline Williams, Contact

Bettendorf

**★1880★ Older Women's League (OWL)
Eastern Iowa Chapter**
204 Slavens Manor
Bettendorf, IA 52722
Phone: (319)355-0874
Dorothy Jensen, Contact

Bloomfield

★1881★ PEO Sisterhood, Chapter B
205 S. East St.
Bloomfield, IA 52537
Phone: (515)664-3603
Hildred L. Gordy, Sec.

Description: Women concerned with higher education. Offers educational programs. Makes charitable contributions. **Affiliated with:** PEO Sisterhood.

Burlington

**★1882★ Young Women's Christian
Association of Burlington**
2410 Mt. Pleasant St.
Burlington, IA 52601
Phone: (319)753-6734

Description: Seeks to develop and improve the spiritual, social, mental, and physical well-being of young people and adults. **Affiliated with:** Young Women's Christian Association of the United States of America.

Camanche

★1883★ Tri-S Women's Club
704 1st St.
Camanche, IA 52731
Phone: (319)259-1325
Dorothy Mayor, Pres.

Description: Service organization of women from Camanache and Clinton, IA.

Cedar Rapids

★1884★ New Encounters
5720 Johnson Ave., SW, No. 321
Cedar Rapids, IA 52404
Phone: (319)390-3026
Velma Seeley, Pres. & Founder

Description: Social organization for widows. Sponsors bus trips.

★1885★ Professional Women's Network
PO Box 2613
Cedar Rapids, IA 52406
Phone: (319)362-7475
Carol A. Burns, Exec.Dir.

Description: Provides networking opportunities for women.

**★1886★ Southern Association for Women
Historians**
c/o R. Carroll
COE College
Department of History
Cedar Rapids, IA 52402

Publications: Publishes newsletter three times a year. **Remarks:** Seeks to advance the status of women in the historical profession in the South; to provide communication among women historians regarding issues of professional concern; to stimulate interest in the study of Southern history and women's history; and to publicize and promote issues of concern to SAWH membership. Sponsored first Southern Conference on Women's History in 1988.

**★1887★ Women's Christian Temperance
Union**
141 17th St., SW
Cedar Rapids, IA 52404
Phone: (319)365-3732
Mary E. Rickey, Pres.

Description: Christian women. Promotes complete abstinence of alcohol, drugs, and tobacco. **Affiliated with:** Iowa Women's Christian Temperance Union.

**★1888★ Young Women's Christian
Association of Cedar Rapids and Linn
County**
318 5th St., SE
Cedar Rapids, IA 52403
Phone: (319)365-1458

Description: Seeks to develop and improve the spiritual, social, mental, and physical well-being of young people and adults. **Affiliated with:** Young Women's Christian Association of the United States of America.

Clarinda

**★1889★ American Association of
University Women, Clarinda Chapter**
311 N. 15th
Clarinda, IA 51632
Phone: (712)542-2217
Teresa Nook, Exec. Officer

Description: Women graduates of regionally accredited four year colleges and universities. Works for the advancement of women through advocacy and emphasis on lifelong learning. Conducts community service projects; makes available scholarships. Makes available scholarships for nontraditional students. Conducts symposia. **Affiliated with:** American Association of University Women.

Clear Lake

**★1890★ La Leche League International,
Mason City/Clear Lake Chapter**
c/o Anita Langholz
306 N. 10th St.
Clear Lake, IA 50428
Phone: (515)357-5097
Anita Langholz, Leader

Description: Mothers and infants of small children. Provides information and education regarding breastfeeding. Offers phone counseling. **Affiliated with:** La Leche League International.

Clinton

**★1891★ Clinton Business and
Professional Women's Club**
1822 1/2 Camanche Ave.
Clinton, IA 52732
Phone: (319)242-9181
Margaret Gideonsen, Exec. Officer

Description: Business and professional women. To promote complete participation, equal opportunities, and economic self-sufficiency for working women. Conducts charitable activities; sponsors young career woman contest; makes available scholarships. **Affiliated with:** National Federation of Business and Professional Women's Clubs of the U.S.A.

**★1892★ Young Women's Christian
Association of Gateway Branch**
317 7th Ave., S.
Clinton, IA 52732
Phone: (319)242-2110
Rita Dennis, Exec.Dir.

Description: Works to empower women, promote social change regarding equality, and eliminate racism. Conducts charitable activities. **Affiliated with:** Young Women's Christian Association of the United States of America.

Council Bluffs

**★1893★ National Association of Women
Business Owners
Omaha Chapter**
c/o Anthony Electric
3626 Birdsley Rd.
Council Bluffs, IA 51503
Phone: (712)328-1701
Cindy Anthony, President

Davenport

**★1894★ American Business Women's
Association, Three Bridges Chapter**
2128 E. 38th St.
Davenport, IA 52807
Phone: (319)359-4456
Barbara Humiston, Pres.

Description: Business and professional women. To promote complete participation, equal opportunities, and economic self-sufficiency for working women. Makes available scholarships. **Affiliated with:** American Business Women's Association.

Des Moines

**★1895★ American Association of
University Women, Des Moines Branch**
1815 69th St.
Des Moines, IA 50322
Phone: (515)276-6210
Silvey Barge, Pres.

Description: Women graduates of regionally accredited four year colleges and universities. Works for the advancement of women through advocacy and emphasis on lifelong learning. Networks with similar groups. Conducts classes for women inmates of correctional facilities. Sponsors benefits for homeless women's shelter. Conducts social events. **Affiliated with:** American Association of University Women. **Telecommunications Services:** Voice mail, (515)830-1199.

**★1896★ American Business Women's
Association, Challenge Chapter**
4031 E. 23rd St.
Des Moines, IA 50317
Phone: (515)262-0671
Carol A. Young, Pres.

Description: Women in business, including women owning or operating their own businesses, women in professions, and women employed in any level of government, education, or retailing, manufacturing, and service companies. **Affiliated with:** American Business Women's Association.

★1897★ Iowa Coalition Against Domestic Violence
Lucas Bldg., 1st Fl.
Des Moines, IA 50319
Phone: (515)281-7284
Dianne Fagner, Contact

★1898★ Iowa Federation of Womens Clubs
3839 Merle Hay Rd., Ste. 203
Des Moines, IA 50310
Phone: (515)276-0510
Sheryl J. Bobst, Sec.
Description: Service organization of women.

★1899★ Iowa Women in Natural Resources
PO Box 20083
Des Moines, IA 50320-9402
Description: Women employed in fields dealing with maintenance and use of natural resources.

★1900★ Iowa Women's Philatelic Society
c/o Audrey Harter
2200 36th St.
Des Moines, IA 50310
Phone: (515)255-3776
Audrey Harter, Rep.
Description: Women interested in philately. **Affiliated with:** American Philatelic Society; Federation of Iowa Stamp Clubs; Trans-Mississippi Philatelic Society.

★1901★ League of Women Voters of Iowa
4817 University Ave., Ste. 8
Des Moines, IA 50311
Phone: (515)277-0814
Jackie Manatt, President

★1902★ Moingona Girl Scout Council
10715 Hickman Rd.
Des Moines, IA 50322
Phone: (515)278-2881
Toll-free: 800-342-8389
Fax: (515)278-5988
Sharon L. Powell, Exec.Dir.
Description: Girls aged five through 17 and adults in central and southern Iowa. Conducts educational program which strives to teach girls the highest ideals of character and conduct. **Affiliated with:** Girl Scouts of the U.S.A.

★1903★ National Association of Women Business Owners
Central Iowa Chapter
c/o P.S. Pam Schoffner Writes
532 42nd St.
Des Moines, IA 50312
Phone: (515)279-6055
Pam Schoffner, President

★1904★ Older Women's League (OWL)
Mid-Iowa Chapter
3110 Cleveland
Des Moines, IA 50317
Phone: (515)265-8504

★1905★ Wedge Women's Economic Development Group Enterprises
2603 Ingersoll Ave.
Des Moines, IA 50312
Phone: (515)244-1502
Description: Assists women in central Iowa pursuing economic independence through business ownership. Provides individual and classroom instruction.

★1906★ Young Women's Christian Association of Greater Des Moines
717 Grand Ave.
Des Moines, IA 50309
Phone: (515)244-8961
Chris Hensley, Contact
Description: Seeks to develop and improve the spiritual, social, mental, and physical well-being of young people and adults. Conducts charitable activities. **Affiliated with:** Young Women's Christian Association of the United States of America.

Dubuque

★1907★ Birthright of Dubuque
701 Bluff St.
Dubuque, IA 52001
Phone: (319)556-1991
Toll-free: 800-848-LOVE
Description: Community volunteers from northeastern Iowa, southwestern Wisconsin, and northwestern Illinois helping pregnant women find alternatives to abortion. Operates emergency pregnancy service. **Affiliated with:** Birthright, U.S.A.

★1908★ Catholic Daughters of America, Chapter 1287
2 Julien Dubuque Dr., No. 18
Dubuque, IA 52001
Phone: (319)556-3497
Janaan Corken, Regent
Description: Catholic women in the Dubuque, IA area conducting religious, charitable, and educational activities. Affiliated with: Catholic Daughters of America.

★1909★ Dubuque Women's Club
375 Alpine
Dubuque, IA 52001
Phone: (319)582-4530
Sara Candy, Acting Pres.
Description: Women's volunteer service club. Areas of focus include education, music, art, literature, the environment, and travel safety. **Affiliated with:** General Federation of Women's Clubs; Iowa Federation of Women's Clubs.

★1910★ Girl Scouts of the U.S.A., Little Cloud Council
13284 Rte. 20
PO Box 26
Dubuque, IA 52004-0026
Phone: (319)583-9169
Susan O. Elder, Exec.Dir.
Description: Girls ages five to 17 and adult volunteers in Dubuque, IA. Promotes character development, good conduct, and patriotism among girls. Seeks to help girls become happy, resourceful citizens. **Affiliated with:** Girl Scouts of the U.S.A; United Way.

★1911★ National Association of Women in Construction, Dubuque Chapter
946 Southern Ave.
Dubuque, IA 52001
Phone: (319)583-5411
Dixie L. K. Lighthart, Past Dir.
Description: Women in construction and related fields. Provides educational opportunities for members. **Affiliated with:** National Association of Women in Construction.

★1912★ Women in Management, Dubuque Chapter
PO Box 1334
Dubuque, IA 52001
Phone: (319)588-2083
Fax: (319)588-0339
Mary Lou Baal, Pres.
Description: Women entrepreneurs, business administrators, attorneys, bank officers, and managers in eastern Iowa and northwestern Illinois. Promotes improvement of members' skills through exchange of ideas and information. Conducts seminars. **Affiliated with:** Women in Management.

★1913★ Young Women's Christian Association of Dubuque
35 N. Booth St.
Dubuque, IA 52001
Phone: (319)556-3371
Description: Seeks to develop and improve the spiritual, social, mental, and physical well-being of young people and adults. **Affiliated with:** Young Women's Christian Association of the United States of America.

Evansdale

★1914★ National Association of Women Business Owners
Waterloo/Cedar Falls Chapter
c/o Stoutner State Farm
PO Box 3145
Evansdale, IA 50707
Phone: (319)232-6630
Margaret Stoutner, President

Farragut

★1915★ Shenandoah Women's Service Club
R.R. 1, Box 104
Farragut, IA 51639
Phone: (712)385-8360
Betty Livingston, Pres.
Description: Business and professional women's service club. Bestows scholarships.

Glenwood

★1916★ Mills County Iowans for Life
601 S. Hazel
Glenwood, IA 51534
Phone: (712)527-3939
Paula A. Disterhaupt, Pres.
Description: Seeks to educate the public about the rights of the unborn. Sponsors Diaper Derby competition. Conducts charitable activities. **Affiliated with:** Iowans for Life.

Harlan

★1917★ Farm Bureau Women
R.R. 4
Harlan, IA 51537
Mrs. Horace Graves, Pres.
Description: Farm wives in the Harlan, IA area. Promotes knowledge of agricultural markets, safety, family farm corporate structure, and the farmer's role in providing a world food source.

Iowa City

★1918★ Lesbian Alliance
130 N. Madison
Iowa City, IA 48244
Phone: (319)335-1486
Description: Provides support, resources, and social opportunities to lesbians in Iowa.

★1919★ National Association of Women Business Owners
Cedar Rapids/Iowa City Chapter
c/o Weideman and Dilkes
PO Box 1576
Iowa City, IA 52244
Phone: (319)337-6444
Elanor Dilkes, President

Maquoketa

★1920★ Birthright of Maquoketa
108 1/2 W. Platt St.
Maquoketa, IA 52060-2239
Description: Seeks to help pregnant women find alternatives to abortion. Conducts childbirth education and parenting programs.

Marshalltown

★1921★ Young Women's Christian Association of Marshalltown
705 S. Center St.
Marshalltown, IA 50158
Phone: (515)752-4633
Description: Seeks to develop and improve the spiritual, social, mental, and physical well-being of young people and adults. **Affiliated with:** Young Women's Christian Association of the United States of America.

Mason City

★1922★ Bethlehem Lutheran Women's Missionary League
419 N. Delaware
Mason City, IA 50401
Phone: (515)423-0438
Mrs. Willis Handt, Pres.
Description: Seeks to develop a program of mission education, inspiration, and service for the women of the Bethlehem Lutheran Church. Fosters Christian fellowship. Conducts monthly meeting. **Affiliated with:** Lutheran Women's Missionary League.

★1923★ Daughters of Penelope, Mason City Chapter
836 E. State
Mason City, IA 50401
Phone: (515)423-0549
Genevieve Poulas, Exec. Officer
Description: Women's fraternal organization. Promotes social and ethical interests of members. Fosters citizenship and patriotism in the U.S. Affiliated with Ahepa.

★1924★ Girl Scouts of the U.S.A., North Iowa Council
307 N. Monroe
Mason City, IA 50401
Phone: (515)423-3044
Dawn Billings, Exec.Dir.
Description: Girls and adult volunteers involved in girl scouting programs. Addresses the developmental, emotional, and social needs and interests of young girls. **Affiliated with:** Girl Scouts of the U.S.A.

★1925★ Iowa Women's Traffic Safety Council
233 Seventh St., NW
Mason City, IA 50401
Phone: (515)423-2997
Maude Stackhouse, Chwm.
Description: Women's and men's organizations concerned with traffic safety. Sponsors safety and health education programs. **Affiliated with:** National Association of Women Highway Safety Leaders.

★1926★ Wampetuc Colony of New England Women
221 14th St., SE
Mason City, IA 50401
Phone: (515)423-5988
Betty Dillon, Pres.
Description: Patriotic, educational, and charitable society of women descended from ancestors born in New England prior to 1789. **Affiliated with:** National Society of New England Women.

★1927★ Women's Network of North Iowa
824 S. Tennessee Plaza
Mason City, IA 50401
Phone: (515)423-5568
Susan Evans, Exec. Officer
Description: Women in north central Iowa. Provides networking opportunities for members. Sponsors workshops and various social activities.

Milo

★1928★ Iowa Agri-Women
2045 Kirkwood St.
Milo, IA 50166
Phone: (515)942-6903
Marilea Chase, Pres.
Description: Farm and agri-business women. Promotes agriculture; seeks to educate consumers. **Affiliated with:** American Agri-Women.

Monticello

★1929★ Jones County Cattle Women
c/o Kathryn Peters
113 Shomont Dr.
Monticello, IA 52310
Phone: (319)465-4104
Kathryn Peters, Exec. Officer
Description: Women organized to promote the cattle industry.

★1930★ Monticello Business and Professional Women's Club
c/o Sharon Roller
RR 1
920 W. 1st St.
Monticello, IA 52310
Phone: (319)465-5281
Sharon Roller, Pres.
Description: Business and professional women. To promote complete participation, equal opportunities, and economic self-sufficiency for working women. **Affiliated with:** National Federation of Business and Professional Women's Clubs of the U.S.A.

Mt. Pleasant

★1931★ Birthright of Mt. Pleasant
205 N. Jefferson
Mt. Pleasant, IA 52641-2018
Description: Seeks to help pregnant women find alternatives to abortion. Conducts childbirth education and parenting programs.

Muscatine

★1932★ Young Women's Christian Association of Muscatine
1823 Logan
PO Box 998
Muscatine, IA 52761-0998
Phone: (319)263-7924
Description: Seeks to develop and improve the spiritual, social, mental, and physical well-being of young people and adults. **Affiliated with:** Young Women's Christian Association of the United States of America.

Oskaloosa

★1933★ Young Women's Christian Association of Oskaloosa
414 N. Third St.
Oskaloosa, IA 52577
Phone: (515)673-8411
Description: Seeks to develop and improve the spiritual, social, mental, and physical well-being of young people and adults. **Affiliated with:** Young Women's Christian Association of the United States of America.

Ottumwa

★1934★ Ottumwa Women Aglow Fellowship
522 Leighton
Ottumwa, IA 52501
Phone: (515)683-3513
Debbie Huffman, Pres.
Description: Christian women. Conducts Bible studies; assists nursing home. Issues publica-

tions. **Affiliated with:** Women's Aglow Fellowship International.

★1935★ Young Women's Christian Association of Ottumwa
133 W. Second St.
Ottumwa, IA 52501
Phone: (515)682-5473

Description: Seeks to develop and improve the spiritual, social, mental, and physical well-being of young people and adults. **Affiliated with:** Young Women's Christian Association of the United States of America.

Red Oak

★1936★ Red Oak Business and Professional Women's Club
Rte. 1, Box 231
Red Oak, IA 51566
Phone: (712)623-2933
Darlene Swanson, Pres.

Description: Business and professional women. To promote complete participation, equal opportunities, and economic self-sufficiency for working women. Stresses the need for equal rights/equal pay for women.

Rockwell

★1937★ Young at Heart Grandmother's Club
c/o Dorothy Austin
R.R. 1
Rockwell, IA 50469
Phone: (515)822-4514
Dorothy Austin, Organizer

Description: Women who have grandchildren. Promotes health and happiness for grandmothers. Assists disabled and underprivileged individuals; makes charitable contributions. **Affiliated with:** National Federation of Grandmother Clubs of America.

Shenandoah

★1938★ American Association of University Women, Shenandoah Branch
PO Box 310
Shenandoah, IA 51601
Deborah S. Rake, Pres.

Description: Women graduates of regionally accredited four year colleges and universities. Works for the advancement of women through advocacy and emphasis on lifelong learning. **Affiliated with:** American Association of University Women.

Washington

★1939★ Young Women's Christian Association of Washington
121 E. Main
Washington, IA 52353
Phone: (319)653-7281

Description: Seeks to develop and improve the spiritual, social, mental, and physical well-being of young people and adults. **Affiliated with:** Young Women's Christian Association of the United States of America.

Waterloo

★1940★ Young Women's Christian Association of Black Hawk County
425 Lafayette St.
Waterloo, IA 50703
Phone: (319)234-7589

Description: Seeks to develop and improve the spiritual, social, mental, and physical well-being of young people and adults. **Affiliated with:** Young Women's Christian Association of the United States of America.

Waukee

★1941★ Association of Women Contractors, Iowa Chapter
c/o Jean Wells
E.O. Dorsey and Associates
755 S. Fork Dr.
Waukee, IA 50263
Phone: (515)225-0976
Fax: (515)226-0220
Jean Wells, Pres.

Description: Women who own construction and construction related businesses. Works to strengthen the position of women in the industry.

Waverly

★1942★ Bremer Republican Women
c/o Helen B. Kelling
210 15th St., NW, #304
Waverly, IA 50677
Phone: (319)352-3459
Helen B. Kelling, Pres.

Description: Registered Republican women in Bremer County, IA. Works to elect Republicans to local, state, and national office. **Affiliated with:** Iowa Federation of Republican Women; National Federation of Republican Women.

West Des Moines

★1943★ National Abortion Rights Action League of Iowa
1001 Office Park Rd., No. 111
West Des Moines, IA 50265
Phone: (515)225-0731
Karin McElwain, Contact

Kansas

Brookville

★1944★ La Leche League International, Salina Chapter
12660 W. Armstrong Rd.
Brookville, KS 67425
Phone: (913)225-6787
Toll-free: 800-LA-LECHE
Betty Wagner, Pres.

Description: Provides information and support to women who wish to breastfeed their babies. Maintains speakers' bureau. **Affiliated with:** La Leche League International.

Ellsworth

★1945★ Kansas Business and Professional Women
414 N. Missouri
Ellsworth, KS 67439
Phone: (913)472-3271
Joann Briggs, Exec.Sec.

Description: Business and professional women. To promote complete participation, equal opportunities, and economic self-sufficiency for working women.

Junction City

★1946★ Church Women United of Geary County Chapter
231 W. 2nd
Junction City, KS 66441
Phone: (913)238-5670
Hermoine Milleson, Contact

Description: Church women in Geary County, KS. Promotes peace, human rights, justice, and the empowerment of women.

★1947★ Geary County Business and Professional Women's Clubs
Rte. 1, Box 93A
Junction City, KS 66441
Phone: (913)238-5725
Carla Dill, Contact

Description: Business and professional women. To promote complete participation, equal opportunities, and economic self-sufficiency for working women. **Affiliated with:** National Business and Professional Women.

Kansas City

★1948★ Young Women's Christian Association of Kansas City
1017 N. 6th St.
Kansas City, KS 66101
Phone: (913)371-1105

Description: Seeks to develop and improve the spiritual, social, mental, and physical well-being of young people and adults. **Affiliated with:** Young Women's Christian Association of the United States of America.

Kingman

★1949★ Kingman Business and Professional Women's Club
c/o Kathryn E. Vaughn
R.R. 1, Box 50
Kingman, KS 67068
Phone: (316)532-5657
Kathryn E. Vaughn, Pres.

Description: Business and professional women. To promote complete participation, equal opportunities, and economic self-sufficiency for working women. **Affiliated with:** National Federation of Business and Professional Women's Clubs of the U.S.A.

Larned

★1950★ **Women Involved in Farm Economics**
RR 2
Larned, KS 67550
Phone: (316)285-2574
Mrs. A. G. Crane, Contact

Description: Farm wives. Promotes education, and information on farming issues. Conducts lobbying activities.

Lawrence

★1951★ **Kansas Press Women**
1916 Countryside Ln.
Lawrence, KS 66044
Phone: (913)594-3846
Nora T. Cleland, Pres.

Description: Women in all communication occupations. Promotes the advancement of women in the communications industry. **Affiliated with:** National Federation of Press Women.

★1952★ **Older Women's League (OWL)**
Kaw Valley Chapter
1125 Cynthia St.
Lawrence, KS 66049
Phone: (913)842-1848
Margaret Gordon, Contact

Leavenworth

★1953★ **Young Women's Christian Association of Leavenworth**
520 S. Broadway
Leavenworth, KS 66048
Phone: (913)682-6404

Description: Seeks to develop and improve the spiritual, social, mental, and physical well-being of young people and adults. **Affiliated with:** Young Women's Christian Association of the United States of America.

Leawood

★1954★ **Older Women's League (OWL)**
Johnson County Chapter
8336 Sagamore
Leawood, KS 66206
Phone: (913)642-1614

Lenexa

★1955★ **Lenexa Republican Women's Club**
12517 W. 85th Terrace
Lenexa, KS 66215
Phone: (913)888-1708
Roberta Bridges, Pres.

Description: Works to elect Republicans to local, state, and national office. **Affiliated with:** Kansas Federation of Republican Women; National Federation of Republican Women.

Liberal

★1956★ **Petroleum Women's Club of Liberal**
c/o Cathy Wright
PO Box 1723
Liberal, KS 67905-1723
Cathy Wright, Contact

Manhattan

★1957★ **Association for Women in Science, Kansas Flint Hills Chapter**
c/o Dale Kennedy
Division of Biology
Kansas State University
Manhattan, KS 66506
Phone: (913)532-5929
Dale Kennedy, Contact

Description: Works to improve education and employment opportunities for women in the sciences.

Norton

★1958★ **Norton American Baptist Women**
605 N. Jones
Norton, KS 67654
Phone: (913)877-5340
Margaret Shelton, Pres.

Description: Women who belong to the Baptist Church. **Affiliated with:** American Baptist Women.

Overland Park

★1959★ **National Association of Women Business Owners**
Kansas City Chapter
c/o The Sterling Group
9300 W. 110th St., Ste. 440
Overland Park, KS 66210
Phone: (913)345-2228
Joan Wells, President

Salina

★1960★ **American Association of University Women, Salina Branch**
109 S. Hilldale Rd.
Salina, KS 67401
Phone: (913)827-1270
Gretchen Morgenstern, Pres.

Description: Women graduates of regionally accredited four year colleges and universities. Works for the advancement of women through advocacy and emphasis on lifelong learning. **Affiliated with:** American Association of University Women.

★1961★ **Salina County Democratic Women**
562 Berkshire
Salina, KS 67401
Phone: (913)823-3265
Martha Thomas, Exec. Officer

Description: Women members of the Democratic Party. Works to elect Democrats to local, state, and national office.

★1962★ **Young Women's Christian Association of Salina**
651 E. Prescott
Salina, KS 67401
Phone: (913)825-4626

Description: Seeks to develop and improve the spiritual, social, mental, and physical well-being of young people and adults. **Affiliated with:** Young Women's Christian Association of the United States of America.

Shawnee Mission

★1963★ **BusinessWomen United**
PO Box 14974
Shawnee Mission, KS 66215
Barbara Champion, Pres.

Description: Business and professional women. To promote complete participation, equal opportunities, and economic self-sufficiency for working women. Holds social events. **Affiliated with:** National Association of Female Executives.

Topeka

★1964★ **Girl Scouts of the United States of America, Kaw Valley Council**
PO Box 4314
Topeka, KS 66604
Phone: (913)776-1488
Rosemary Kutz, Exec.Dir.

Description: Girls ages 5 to 17 and adult volunteers in northeastern KS. Provides multifaceted informal educational programs to girls.

★1965★ **League of Women Voters of Kansas**
919 1/2 Kansas Ave.
Topeka, KS 66612
Phone: (913)234-5152
Patricia Pressman, President

★1966★ **Young Women's Christian Association of Topeka**
225 W. 12th St.
Topeka, KS 66612
Phone: (913)233-1750

Description: Seeks to develop and improve the spiritual, social, mental, and physical well-being of young people and adults. **Affiliated with:** Young Women's Christian Association of the United States of America.

Wichita

★1967★ **Alpha Phi Sorority**
3912 E. 21st, No. 40
Wichita, KS 67208
Phone: (316)683-5281
Cheryl K. McNutt, Contact

Description: Young women attending Wichita State University. Social sorority promoting unity, growth of character, and sisterly affection.

★1968★ **Kansas SER-Jobs for Progress Hispanic Women's Center**
709 E. 21st St.
Wichita, KS 67214
Phone: (316)264-5372
Maria Balderas, Exec.Dir.

★1969★ **National Association of Women Business Owners**
Wichita Chapter
c/o Higher Graphics, Inc.
310 W. Central, Ste. 209
Wichita, KS 67202
Phone: (316)267-6164
Joan Phillips, President

★1970★ **Wichita National Organization for Women**
PO Box 3940
Wichita, KS 67201
Phone: (316)269-0970
Fax: (316)263-8573
Colleen Kelly Johnston, Pres.

Description: Feminists in the southern half of Kansas. Seeks to secure equal rights for women. **Affiliated with:** National Organization for Women.

★1971★ **Young Women's Christian Association of Wichita**
350 N. Market St.
Wichita, KS 67202
Phone: (316)263-7501
V. Jane Gilchrist, Exec.Dir.

Description: Seeks to develop and improve the spiritual, social, mental, and physical well-being of young people and adults. **Affiliated with:** Young Women's Christian Association of the United States of America.

Winfield

★1972★ **Older Women's League (OWL) Walnut Valley Chapter**
700 Gary St., Ste. C
Winfield, KS 67156
Phone: (316)221-7020
Dorothy Neal, Contact

Kentucky

Ashland

★1973★ **Ashland Association of Insurance Women**
c/o Paula Webb
PO Box 1005
Ashland, KY 41105
Phone: (606)329-2200
Toll-free: 800-321-0923
Fax: (606)325-9677
Paula Webb, Contact

Description: Women employed in the insurance industry. Promotes continuing education, loyalty, and fellowship. **Affiliated with:** National Association of Insurance Women - International.

★1974★ **Ashland Democratic Woman's Club**
145 Blevins St.
Ashland, KY 41101
Phone: (606)324-5906
Mary Sweeney, Pres.

Description: Works to elect Democrats to local, state, and national office.

Bardstown

★1975★ **Electrical Women's RoundTable, Bluegrass Chapter**
c/o Melissa Brown
Salt River RECC
111 W. Brashear Ave.
Bardstown, KY 40004
Phone: (502)348-3931
Melissa Brown, Exec. Officer

Description: Offers professional growth and education for women in Kentucky employed in electrical and associated industries. Offers scholarships. **Affiliated with:** Electrical Women's Round Table.

Campbellsville

★1976★ **Campbellsville Woman's Club**
1502 Parkview Dr.
Campbellsville, KY 42718
Phone: (502)789-3287
Doris C. Taylor, Pres.

Description: Women's volunteer service club. Awards scholarships to high school students. Conducts charitable activities; sponsors community projects. Sponsors arts, crafts, and music competitions. **Affiliated with:** General Federation of Women's Clubs; Kentucky Federation of Women's Clubs.

Catlettsburg

★1977★ **Catlettsburg Woman's Club**
2400 Barbecue Rd.
Catlettsburg, KY 41129
Phone: (606)739-4214
Mrs. Ray Stewart, Pres.

Description: Women organized for fellowship and service. **Affiliated with:** General Federation of Women's Clubs.

Corbin

★1978★ **Tri-County Business and Professional Women's Luv Council**
PO Box 1291
Corbin, KY 40702
Phone: (606)528-4228
Cinda Proffitt, Coordinator

Description: Business and professional women, social workers, ministers, teachers, psychiatrists, and other individuals in Knox, Laurel, and Whitley counties, KY. Provides one-on-one instruction in English reading and writing skills to illiterate and partially illiterate adults. **Affiliated with:** Kentucky Literacy Commission.

Frankfort

★1979★ **Kentucky Commission on Women**
614-A Shelby St.
Frankfort, KY 40601
Phone: (502)564-6643
Phyllis J. Alexander, Exec.Dir.

Description: Individuals offering advice to the governor and other state officials on concerns and issues important to women. **Affiliated with:** National Association of Commissions on Women.

Highland Heights

★1980★ **United Campbell County Republican Women**
12 Dietrich Rd.
Highland Heights, KY 41076
Phone: (606)441-0672
Mary Spreher, Pres.

Description: Promotes the ideals of the Republican party and works for the election of Republican candidates to office. **Affiliated with:** National Federation of Republican Women.

Hopkinsville

★1981★ **League of Women Voters of Kentucky**
PO Box 87
Hopkinsville, KY 42241-0087
Phone: (502)885-3928
Elizabeth Spencer, Co-President

Independence

★1982★ **Women's Club - 620**
54 Roselawn Dr.
Independence, KY 41051
Phone: (606)356-3233
E. O. Jones, Pres.

Description: Women in Boone, Campbell, and Kenton counties, KY organized for social and cultural activities. Conducts field trips and charitable activities. Issues publications. **Affiliated with:** Baker-Hunt Foundation.

Lexington

★1983★ **Birthright of Lexington**
Medical Plaza Bldg.
2134 Nicholasville Rd., Ste. 6
Lexington, KY 40503
Phone: (606)277-2635
Toll-free: 800-848-LOVE
Elise Konwickza, Dir.

Description: Volunteers assisting pregnant women with maternity clothes, baby clothes, diapers, and prenatal care. Offers free pregnancy testing, referrals, and friendship. Maintains speakers' bureau.

★1984★ **National Association of Women Business Owners Lexington Chapter**
c/o Anglin and Co., C.P.A.'s
870 Corporate Dr., Ste. 403
Lexington, KY 40503
Phone: (606)224-4680
Carrie L. Anglin, President

★1985★ **Southeast Women's Employment Coalition (SWEC)**
382 Longview Dr.
Lexington, KY 40503
Phone: (606)276-1555
Wendy Johnson, Contact

Founded: 1979. **Description:** Focuses on the economic needs of low-income women in the Southeast. **Publications:** *Women of the the Rural South, Economic Status and Prospects, Job Development in Highway Construction: A Road Map for Women and Advocates* and *Generations*, quarterly newsletter.

Louisville

★1986★ **Fund for Women, Inc.**
239 S. 5th St. #1017
Louisville, KY 40202
Phone: (502)585-3434
Maxine Brown, Contact

Remarks: Serves Kentucky and Indiana.

★1987★ Kentucky Alliance for the Advancement of Midwifery
c/o Judy L. Ferry
PO Box 6414
Louisville, KY 40206-0414
Description: Promotes midwives as primary caregivers in normal pregnancies.

★1988★ Kentucky Federation of Women's Club
1228 Cherokee Rd.
Louisville, KY 40204
Phone: (502)451-8435
Description: Women's clubs.

★1989★ Kentucky Foundation for Women, Inc.
332 W. Broadway, No. 1215
Louisville, KY 40202
Phone: (502)562-0045
Ann Stewart Anderson, Executive Director

★1990★ National Association of Women Business Owners
Louisville Chapter
c/o Personnel Solutions, Inc.
Executive Park, Ste. 205
Louisville, KY 40207
Phone: (502)897-5160
Brenda Schissler, President

★1991★ Older Women's League (OWL)
Louisville Chapter
9614 Walnutwood Way
Louisville, KY 40299
Phone: (502)267-7203
Johnetta Marshall, Contact

★1992★ Pi Sigma-Sigma Gamma Rho Sorority
c/o Yvonne Young
2305 Date St.
Louisville, KY 40210-1135
Yvonne Young, Contact

★1993★ Right to Life of Louisville
134 Breckinridge Ln.
Louisville, KY 40207
Phone: (502)895-5959
Margie Montgomery, Exec.Dir.
Description: Volunteers educating the public regarding their belief in the sanctity of human life. Promotes alternatives to abortion, infanticide, and euthanasia. Initiates legislation to protect life. Maintains library and resource center.

Madisonville

★1994★ Madisonville Mothers of Twins
3014 Pond Rur Coll Rd.
Madisonville, KY 42431-9328
Phone: (502)825-1478
Donna Slaton, Contact
Description: Mothers of multiple births. Assists and educates expectant mothers with multiple births.

Newport

★1995★ Women's Crisis Center of Northern Kentucky
321 York St.
Newport, KY 41071
Phone: (502)491-3335
Edwina Walker, Exec.Dir.
Description: Provides crisis intervention, counseling, advocacy, information, and referral services to victims of rape and domestic violence. Operates emergency shelter for victims of spouse abuse. Conducts educational programs.

Somerset

★1996★ Friends of the Pulaski County Young Woman of the Year
c/o Yvonneda B. Gosser
PO Box 336
Somerset, KY 42502-0336
Description: Supports and promotes the Pulaski County Young Woman of the Year.

Varney

★1997★ American Association of University Women, Varney Branch
Box 8468
Brushy Road
Varney, KY 41571
Audrey Barkman, Contact
Description: Women graduates of regionally accredited four year colleges and universities. Works for the advancement of women through advocacy and emphasis on lifelong learning.

Louisiana

Abbeville

★1998★ Abbeville Women's Club
4016 Fairview
Abbeville, LA 70510
Phone: (318)893-2969
Mrs. Dixon, Contact
Description: Women's volunteer service club.

Alexandria

★1999★ Young Women's Christian Association of Alexandria-Pineville
5912 James St.
Alexandria, LA 71303
Phone: (318)442-3397
Description: Seeks to develop and improve the spiritual, social, mental, and physical well-being of young people and adults. **Affiliated with:** Young Women's Christian Association of the United States of America.

Baton Rouge

★2000★ American Association of University Women, Baton Rouge
3047 Yorktown Dr.
Baton Rouge, LA 70808-3472
Phone: (504)924-5618
Eleanor Earle, Pres.
Description: Women graduates of regionally accredited four year colleges and universities. Works for the advancement of women through advocacy and emphasis on lifelong learning. Sponsors fundraising activities. **Affiliated with:** American Association of University Women.

★2001★ American Society of Women Accountants, Baton Rouge Chapter
11011 Cal Rd., Ste. 134
Baton Rouge, LA 70809
Phone: (504)291-6968
Marianne Granier, CPA, Pres.
Description: Certified public accountants, accounting students, educational and governmental institutions, and women interested or working in accounting. Seeks to: promote women to enter or re-enter the profession; foster continuing professional education and certification; and inform the public of the role of women accountants. **Affiliated with:** American Society of Women Accountants; American Women's Society of Certified Public Accountants.

★2002★ Baton Rouge Association of Women Attorneys
PO Box 4394
Baton Rouge, LA 70821
Phone: (504)922-5000
Kathy Merkel, Pres.
Description: Women attorneys united to address issues affecting women and women attorneys. Provides networking opportunities; makes available scholarships.

★2003★ Federation of Woman's Exchanges, Baton Rouge Chapter
201 St. Charles St.
Baton Rouge, LA 70802
Phone: (504)383-7761
Kathleen D. Jeffcoat, Exec.Dir.
Description: Young women in the Baton Rouge, LA area. Promotes well rounded and religious socialization for girls and young women.

★2004★ League of Women Voters of Louisiana
850 N. 5th St.
Baton Rouge, LA 70802
Phone: (504)344-3326
Robin Rothrock, President

★2005★ Louisiana Choice
850 N. 5th St., No. 101
Baton Rouge, LA 70802
Phone: (504)383-2074
Ann Schiffman, Contact

★2006★ Young Women's Christian Association of Baton Rouge
2549 Druscilla Ln.
Baton Rouge, LA 70809
Phone: (504)926-3820
Description: Seeks to develop and improve the spiritual, social, mental, and physical well-being of young people and adults. **Affiliated with:** Young Women's Christian Association of the United States of America.

Breaux Bridge

★2007★ St. Martin Republican Women's Club
1111 Camp Bon Tent
Breaux Bridge, LA 70517
Phone: (318)332-3280
Carol Trosclair, Pres.

Description: Works to elect Republicans to local, state, and national office.

Chalmette

★2008★ DES Action
PO Box 804
Chalmette, LA 70044

De Ridder

★2009★ American Business Women's Association, De Ridder Chapter
c/o Bertha Owens
506 Magnolia
De Ridder, LA 70634
Phone: (318)462-0398
Bertha Owens, Treas.

Description: Business and professional women. To promote complete participation, equal opportunities, and economic self-sufficiency for working women. Provides scholarship to students from financially distressed families. **Affiliated with:** American Business Women's Association.

★2010★ De Ridder Business and Professional Women's Club
Rt. 1, Box 940
De Ridder, LA 70634
Phone: (318)463-3501
Anne M. Storms, Contact

Description: Business and professional women. To promote complete participation, equal opportunities, and economic self-sufficiency for working women. Sponsors Beauregard Princess Pageant and DeRidder Junior Miss contest. Assist with Beauregard Mental Health facility and Beauregard Parish Museum activities. Conducts workshops and semianrs. **Affiliated with:** Louisiana Federation of Business and Professional Women; National Federation of Business and Professional Women's Clubs of the U.S.A.

Houma

★2011★ Bayou Area Young Women's Christian Association
122 Prevost
Houma, LA 70364
Phone: (504)851-5950

Description: Seeks to develop and improve the spiritual, social, mental, and physical well-being of young people and adults. **Affiliated with:** Young Women's Christian Association of the United States of America.

Lafayette

★2012★ Older Women's League (OWL) Acadiana Chapter
105 Doug Dr.
Lafayette, LA 70508
Phone: (318)988-0360
Jane Temple, Contact

Lake Charles

★2013★ Business and Professional Women's Club of Lake Charles
PO Box 5717
Lake Charles, LA 70606-5717
Phone: (318)447-7989
Pat Moses, Pres.

Description: Business and professional women. To promote complete participation, equal opportunities, and economic self-sufficiency for working women. **Affiliated with:** National Federation of Business and Professional Women's Clubs of the U.S.A.

★2014★ Church Women United of Lake Charles
2121 Pin Oak Ln.
Lake Charles, LA 70605
Phone: (318)477-8745
Bertha Shea, President

Description: Churches and Christian women. Provides services and support to women and children. **Affiliated with:** Church Women United.

Metairie

★2015★ American Association of University Women, Louisiana Division
4217 Neyrey Dr.
Metairie, LA 70002
Phone: (504)454-3880
Freddie G. Landry, Pres.

Description: Women graduates of regionally accredited four year colleges and universities. Works for the advancement of women through advocacy and emphasis on lifelong learning. Sponsors Women's History Month in March, Teen Pregnancy Awareness Campaign in March, and annual Legislative Day. Operates AAUW educational funds. **Affiliated with:** American Association of University Women.

Monroe

★2016★ Girl Scouts of the U.S.A., Silver Waters Council
102 Arkansas Ave.
Monroe, LA 71201
Phone: (318)325-2691
Nan D. Salisbury, Exec.Dir.

Description: Girls between the ages of five-17 and adult volunteers in northeastern Louisiana. To inspire girls with the highest ideals of character, patriotism, and community service. **Affiliated with:** Girl Scouts of the U.S.A.

★2017★ Pregnancy Lifeline
1500 Royal Ave., Ste. A
Monroe, LA 71201-5688

★2018★ Young Women's Christian Association of Monroe
1515 Jackson St.
Monroe, LA 71202
Phone: (318)323-1505
Judy Bell, Contact

Description: Seeks to develop and improve the spiritual, social, mental, and physical well-being of young people and adults. Conducts therapy program; operates safe shelter. **Affiliated with:** Young Women's Christian Association of the United States of America.

Morgan City

★2019★ Morgan City-Berwick Business and Professional Women's Club
PO Box 1721
Morgan City, LA 70381
Phone: (504)384-0314
Peggy Odom, Chair

Description: Business and professional women. To promote complete participation, equal opportunities, and economic self-sufficiency for working women. Awards scholarships. Sponsors Pelican State mock government program.

New Orleans

★2020★ Young Women's Christian Association of New Orleans
601 S. Jefferson Davis Pkwy.
New Orleans, LA 70119
Phone: (504)482-9922

Description: Seeks to develop and improve the spiritual, social, mental, and physical well-being of young people and adults. **Affiliated with:** Young Women's Christian Association of the United States of America.

Shreveport

★2021★ American Woman's Society of Certified Public Accountants of Shreveport-Bossier City
Arkla Energy Resources
PO Box 21734
Shreveport, LA 71151
Phone: (318)429-2811
Liz Mulig, Pres.

Description: Professional society of women accountants. **Affiliated with:** American Woman's Society of Certified Public Accountants.

★2022★ Young Women's Christian Association of Northwest Louisiana
710 Travis St.
Shreveport, LA 71101
Phone: (318)222-2116

Description: Seeks to develop and improve the spiritual, social, mental, and physical well-being of young people and adults. **Affiliated with:** Young Women's Christian Association of the United States of America.

Maine

Augusta

★2023★ League of Women Voters of Maine
335 Water St.
Augusta, ME 04330
Phone: (207)622-0256
Marion S. Holshouser, President

★2024★ Maine Abortion Rights Action League
PO Box 5308
Augusta, ME 04330
Phone: (207)623-2729
Susanne Salkind, Contact

Bangor

★2025★ Young Women's Christian Association of Bangor-Brewer
17 2nd St.
Bangor, ME 04401
Phone: (207)941-2808
Description: Seeks to develop and improve the spiritual, social, mental, and physical well-being of young people and adults. **Affiliated with:** Young Women's Christian Association of the United States of America.

Bar Harbor

★2026★ Young Women's Christian Association of Mt. Desert Island
36 Mt. Desert St.
Bar Harbor, ME 04609
Phone: (207)288-5008
Description: Seeks to develop and improve the spiritual, social, mental, and physical well-being of young people and adults. **Affiliated with:** Young Women's Christian Association of the United States of America.

Brewer

★2027★ National Organization for Women, Greater Bangor Chapter
87 Sunset Strip
Brewer, ME 04412
Phone: (207)989-3306
JoAnne Dauphinee, Sec.
Description: Interested persons in northern and eastern Maine organized to promote equal rights and reproductive rights for women and to foster feminism. Conducts events, actions, and campaigns. Provides referrals.

Cape Elizabeth

★2028★ Girl Scouts of the United States of America, Kennebec Council
PO Box 207 CCB
Cape Elizabeth, ME 04107
Phone: (207)767-3317
Toll-free: 800-841-4600
Ingrid Ekdahl, Exec.Dir.
Description: Girls ages 5-17 and adult volunteers in southern and western Maine. Seeks to develop self-potential, values, and communication skills. Conducts community service. Maintains speakers' bureau, day and resident camps, and human relations program. **Affiliated with:** Girl Scouts of the United States of America.

Caribou

★2029★ Daughters of Isabella Caribou Chapter
79 E. River Rd.
Caribou, ME 04736
Phone: (207)498-8274
Dolores D. Martin, Regent
Description: Catholic women working to promote unity, friendship, and charity.

Dover-Foxcroft

★2030★ Womancare Aegis
86 Union Sq.
PO Box 192
Dover-Foxcroft, ME 04426
Phone: (207)564-8165
Juliana T. Plummer, Dir.
Description: Individuals in Piscataquis and southwestern Penobscot counties, ME. Assists women who are victims of domestic violence. Provides crisis intervention, short-term shelter, counseling, and support groups. Conducts educational programs.

East Winthrop

★2031★ Kennebec Valley Church Women United
c/o Evelyn Foster
Case Rd.
East Winthrop, ME 04343
Phone: (207)395-4656
Evelyn Foster, Exec. Officer

Ellsworth

★2032★ American Association of University Women, Maine Division
PO Box 1370
Ellsworth, ME 04605
Phone: (207)667-9416
Deborah Cravey, Pres.
Description: Works to achieve equality for women and raise the aspirations of youth. Offers postgraduate fellowships for women.

Lewiston

★2033★ Young Women's Christian Association of Lewiston-Auburn
130 East Ave.
Lewiston, ME 04240
Phone: (207)795-4050
Martha Breunig, Exec.Dir.
Description: Seeks to develop and improve the spiritual, social, mental, and physical life of youth and adults. Provides physical and counseling programs. **Affiliated with:** Young Women's Christian Association of the United States of America.

Norway

★2034★ Rape Education and Crisis Hotline
17 Winter St.
Norway, ME 04268-1142

Portland

★2035★ Greater Portland National Organization for Women
Box 4012, Sta. A
Portland, ME 04101
Phone: (207)871-0618
Jennifer Halm-Perazone, Co-Chair
Description: Interested women and men. Engages in activism that fosters equality, transforms patriarchy, insures women's reproductive rights, and supports rights for all people.

★2036★ Maine Women's Fund
PO Box 7445
Portland, ME 04112
Phone: (207)774-5513
JoAnne E. Peterson, Executive Director

★2037★ Pro-Life Education Association
22 Northwood Dr.
Portland, ME 04103
Phone: (207)878-3965
Deane S. Stevens, Pres.
Description: Interested persons promoting the belief that life begins at conception and that unborn children are entitled to the full protection of the law. Opposes abortion, infanticide, and euthanasia. Is concerned with the rising level of fetal alcohol syndrome. Gives lectures. Participates in forums and debates in the media. Lobbies and monitors legislation. Presents annual Pro-Life Award.

★2038★ Young Women's Christian Association of Portland
87 Spring St.
Portland, ME 04101
Phone: (207)874-1130
Description: Seeks to develop and improve the spiritual, social, mental, and physical well-being of young people and adults. **Affiliated with:** Young Women's Christian Association of the United States of America.

Presque Isle

★2039★ American Association of University Women, Presque Isle Branch
c/o Linda Graves
University of Maine at Presque Isle
Presque Isle, ME 04769
Phone: (207)764-0311
Linda Graves, Exec. Officer
Description: Women graduates of regionally accredited four year colleges and universities. Works for the advancement of women through advocacy and emphasis on lifelong learning. **Affiliated with:** American Association of University Women.

Sanford

★2040★ Sanford-Springvale Business and Professional Women's Club
c/o Ms. Lee Dupre
25 Riverside Ave.
Sanford, ME 04073
Phone: (207)324-5908
Ms. Lee Dupre, Parliamentarian
Description: Business and professional women. Works to promote complete participation, equal opportunities, and economic self-sufficiency for working women. Awards scholarships. Conducts charitable activities.

Waterville

★2041★ Lewiston-Auburn Business and Professional Women
11 Lawrence St.
Waterville, ME 04901
Phone: (207)784-2951
Clair G. Burgess, Pres.
Description: Business women and men organized to elevate standards for and promote the interests of working women. Seeks to bring about cooperative spirit among and extend

opportunities to working women. **Affiliated with:** International Federation of Business and Professional Women; Maine Federation of Business and Professional Women; National Federation of Business and Professional Women.

York

★2042★ Parent's Alternative to Latch Key
US Rte. 1
PO Box 148
York, ME 03909-0148

Maryland

Annapolis

★2043★ League of Women Voters of Maryland
200 Duke of Gloucester St.
Annapolis, MD 21401
Phone: (301)269-0232
Patricia Pollard, President

Baltimore

★2044★ Alliance of Black Women Attorneys
Legal Aid Bureau
714 E. Pratt St.
Baltimore, MD 21202
Phone: (301)539-5340
Harriette Taylor, Pres.

★2045★ American Association of University Women, Maryland Division
7400 Stanmore Ct.
Baltimore, MD 21212
Phone: (301)321-9830
Mary A. Peterson, Contact

Description: Women graduates of regionally accredited four year colleges and universities. Works for the advancement of women through advocacy and emphasis on lifelong learning. Sponsors math and science career day fair for girls. **Affiliated with:** American Association of University Women.

★2046★ Association for Women in Science, Baltimore Chapter
c/o Loretta Molitor
133 Regester Ave.
Baltimore, MD 21212
Phone: (301)830-2116
Loretta Molitor, Contact

Description: Works to improve education and employment opportunities for women in the sciences.

★2047★ Church Women United of Greater Baltimore
607 Park Ave.
Baltimore, MD 21201
Phone: (301)825-1520
Ruth Hall Smith, Exec. Officer

Description: Ecumenical organization of Christian women joined for worship and for the betterment of women and children.

★2048★ Coalition for Open Doors
2219 St. Paul St.
Baltimore, MD 21218
Phone: (301)889-8555
Fax: (301)576-0937
Susan Goering, Dir.

Description: Individuals and groups in Maryland working to open private club membership to women and minorities.

★2049★ Healthy Mothers, Healthy Babies, Maryland State Coalition
Mayor's Office for Children and Youth
10 South St., Ste. 100
Baltimore, MD 21202
Phone: (301)396-4848
Fax: (301)625-0743
Donna J. Petersen, Pres.

Description: Health, education, and social service organizations promoting the improvement of maternal and child health through education and advocacy. Sponsors professional education symposia for maternal and child health practitioners.

★2050★ Maryland Association for Anorexia Nervosa and Bulimia
6501 N. Charles St.
PO Box 6815
Baltimore, MD 21285-6815
Phone: (301)938-3000
Elizabeth Champney, Exec. Officer

Description: Promotes the healing of eating disorders through support group assistance, referral services, and community education. Operates speakers' bureau.

★2051★ National Association of Women Business Owners
Baltimore Chapter
c/o Marine Enterprises, Inc.
8800 A Kelao Dr.
Baltimore, MD 21221
Phone: (410)682-5303
Brenda Dandy, President

★2052★ Older Women's League (OWL)
Baltimore Chapter
6111 Fairdell Ave.
Baltimore, MD 21206
Phone: (301)426-2382
Mary Magri, Contact

Bethesda

★2053★ Older Women's League (OWL)
Glen Echo Chapter
6707 Rannoch Rd.
Bethesda, MD 20817
Phone: (301)229-0895
Grace DePalma, Contact

Easton

★2054★ Republican Women of Talbot County
Box 974
Easton, MD 21601
Phone: (301)820-7255
Kathryn Roepen, Rep.

Description: Works to elect Republicans to local, state, and national office.

★2055★ Talbot County Women's Club
PO Box 1632
Easton, MD 21601
Phone: (301)820-7078
Esther M. Henry, Pres.

Description: Women ages 42-94. Provides educational, cultural, and charitable programs to public schools and the community. Sponsors workshops. **Affiliated with:** General Federation of Women's Clubs.

Fallston

★2056★ American Woman's Society of Certified Public Accountants of Baltimore
2101 Givenswood Dr.
Fallston, MD 21047
Phone: (301)877-2941
Anna Vitale, Pres.

Description: Certified public accountants. Provides networking, support, and education. Holds seminars. **Affiliated with:** American Woman's Society of Certified Public Accountants.

Frederick

★2057★ Penn Laurel Girl Scout Council
3 Hillcrest Dr., Ste. A-103
Frederick, MD 21702
Phone: (301)662-5106
Judy Moore-Field, Dir.

Description: Girls aged 5 to 17 in western Maryland and southern Pennsylvania. Works to help girls develop into responsible adults. **Affiliated with:** Girl Scouts of the U.S.A.

Gaithersburg

★2058★ Woman Care of Washington
803 Russell Ave., Ste. 2A
Gaithersburg, MD 20879
Phone: (301)869-5550
Roger Vitrano, Director

Founded: 1986. **Description:** Dedicated to women's health currently specializing in breast diagnostics and breast ultra sounds.

Gambrills

★2059★ Four Seasons Women's Club
c/o Joan Frykman
PO Box 62
Gambrills, MD 21054-0062
Joan Frykman, Contact

Garrett Park

★2060★ Self Help for Equal Rights (SHER)
Box 105
Garrett Park Post Office
Garrett Park, MD 20896
Billie Mackey, Pres.

Founded: 1972. **Description:** Provides information and legislation concerning sex discrimination. Advises how to handle sexual discrimination and harassment and provides networking, support groups and weekly meetings.

Potomac

★2061★ Bethesda-Chevy Chase Business and Professional Women's Foundation
c/o Pat Cornish
10209 Lloyd Rd.
Potomac, MD 20854-1948

Description: Business and professional women. To promote complete participation, equal opportunities, and economic self-sufficiency for working women.

Rockville

★2062★ Maryland Mothers of Twins
PO Box 5846
Rockville, MD 20855-0846
Phone: (301)649-7868

Description: Mothers of twins. Provides support, information, and social activities. **Affiliated with:** National Organization of Mothers of Twins.

★2063★ A Woman's Place
Montgomery County Government Commission for Women
103 N. Adams St.
Rockville, MD 20850
Phone: (301)279-8346
Joan Ury, Manager

Description: A resource, activity and counseling center.

Silver Spring

★2064★ Maryland Abortion Rights Action League
817 Silver Spring Ave.
Silver Spring, MD 20910
Phone: (301)565-4154
Karyn Strickler, Contact

Upper Marlboro

★2065★ Maryland Association of Women Highway Safety Leaders
7206 Robin Hood Dr.
Upper Marlboro, MD 20772
Phone: (301)868-7583
Agnes D. Beaton, Exec.Dir.

Description: To create greater public awareness and support for safety belt use, reducing alcohol abuse, law enforcement, and education and engineering for safety. Conducts charitable programs. **Affiliated with:** National Association of Women Highway Safety Leaders.

★2066★ Older Women's League (OWL)
Prince George's County Chapter
48 Staton Dr.
Upper Marlboro, MD 20772
Phone: (301)249-1545
Angela Herron, Contact

Wheaton

★2067★ Birthright of Wheaton
11401 Grandview Ave.
Wheaton, MD 20902
Phone: (301)946-3339
Chris Cable, Dir.

Massachusetts

Allston

★2068★ National Council of Jewish Women, Greater Boston Section
75 Harvard Ave.
Allston, MA 02134
Phone: (617)783-9660
Myra Tattenbaum, Adm.Dir.

Description: Jewish women dedicated, in the spirit of Judaism, to advancing human welfare and the democratic way of life. Conducts social action, educational, and community service programs focusing on family issues, child welfare, and aging. Sponsors charitable programs. **Affiliated with:** International Council of Jewish Women; National Council of Jewish Women.

Andover

★2069★ Essex District Republican Women's Club
21 Enfield Dr.
Andover, MA 01810
Phone: (508)475-6765
Floranne Lovoi, Contact

Description: Seeks to elect Republican candidates to local, state, and national offices.

Arlington

★2070★ Massachusetts Citizens for Life, Arlington Chapter
346 Washington St.
Arlington, MA 02174
Phone: (617)646-2956
Bill Croke, Chm.

Description: Individuals dedicated to preserving the sanctity of human life from conception to natural death. Sponsors public education programs. **Affiliated with:** Massachusetts Citizens for Life.

Athol

★2071★ Athol Woman's Club
580 Spring St.
Athol, MA 01331
Phone: (508)249-3009
Barbara Robichard, Pres.

Description: Women who promote literary, educational, musical, and historical interest and contribute to the community's welfare. **Affiliated with:** General Federation of Women's Clubs; Massachusetts State Federation of Women's Clubs.

Boston

★2072★ Aid to Incarcerated Mothers (AIM)
32 Rutland St., 2nd fl.
Boston, MA 02118
Phone: (617)536-0058
Jean Fox, Exec.Dir.

Founded: 1980. **Description:** Helps incarcerated mothers in the Boston, MA area meet their parental responsibilities by providing them with the necessary information, resources, and support to do so. Furnishes transportation for family visits. Matches each mother with a volunteer in order to provide friendship and advocacy. Helps mothers learn self-help advocacy skills and their legal rights. Offers post-release support and services to mothers making the transition back to the community. Works to make the social services, the prison system, and the public more aware and responsive to incarcerated mothers' needs. Provides information, advice, and technical support to individuals and groups nationwide. Sends speakers to various groups, organizations, and schools in the community and, occasionally, to other states. **Publications:** *Staying Together*, 3/year. Newsletter.

★2073★ Association for Women in Science, Boston Chapter
c/o Virginia Wooter
179 Longwood Ave.
Boston, MA 02115-5896
Virginia Wooter, Contact

Description: Works to improve education and employment opportunities for women in the sciences.

★2074★ Big Sister Association of Greater Boston
161 Massachusetts Ave.
Boston, MA 02115
Phone: (617)236-8060
Jeraldine Martinson, Exec.Dir.

Description: Women volunteers who provide a stable, consistent role model relationship for girls aged seven to 15 from single parent homes. **Affiliated with:** Big Brothers/Big Sisters of America.

★2075★ Boston Women's Fund
Park Sq. Bldg.
31 St. James Ave., Ste. 902
Boston, MA 02116
Phone: (617)542-5955
Hayat Imam, Executive Director

★2076★ League of Women Voters of Massachusetts
133 Portland St., lower level
Boston, MA 02114
Phone: (617)523-2999
Risa Nyman, President

★2077★ Massachusetts Choice
Statler Bldg.
20 Park Plaza, No. 1129
Boston, MA 02116
Phone: (617)556-8800
Pam Nourse, Contact

★2078★ **Massachusetts Coalition of Battered Women's Service Groups**
20 East St.
Boston, MA 02111
Phone: (617)426-8492
Charlene Allen, Exec. Officer

★2079★ **Massachusetts Women's Political Caucus**
145 Tremont St., Ste. 607
Boston, MA 02111
Phone: (617)451-9294
Susan F. Brooks, Exec.Dir.

Description: Feminists who promote the election and appointment of qualified women to all levels of government. **Affiliated with:** National Women's Political Caucus.

★2080★ **Older Women's League (OWL) Greater Boston Chapter**
PO Box 1183
Boston, MA 02205-1183
Phone: (617)241-9566
Frances F. Wirta, Contact

★2081★ **Women's Exchange**
PO Box 581
Boston, MA 02117
Phone: (617)277-0200

★2082★ **Women's Transportation Seminar, Boston Chapter**
State Transportation Bldg. Library
10 Park Plaza
Boston, MA 02116
Phone: (617)973-8000
Mary Jane O'Meara, Pres.

Description: Professionals in public agencies and private firms. Seeks to: assist those interested in the transportation industry; advance the knowledge and training of transportation professionals; encourage communication among members of the transportation industry. **Affiliated with:** Women's Transportation Seminar.

★2083★ **Young Women's Christian Association of Boston**
140 Clarendon St.
Boston, MA 02116
Phone: (617)536-7940
Fax: (617)536-2708

Description: Seeks to develop and improve the spiritual, social, mental, and physical well-being of young people and adults. **Affiliated with:** Young Women's Christian Association of the United States of America.

Bradford

★2084★ **Society for Women in Philosophy, Eastern Division**
c/o Peg Walsh
Bradford College
Humanities Division
Bradford, MA 01835
Phone: (508)372-7161
Peg Walsh, Exec. Officer

Description: Students, faculty, and laypersons in the field or interested in the field of philosophy. Primary goal is to advance and support women in philosophy. Reads papers and holds discussions on feminist and non-feminist topics. Offers placement services. Maintains archives. Bestows awards.

Brockton

★2085★ **Massachusetts Association for Parents and Professionals for Safe Alternatives in Childbirth**
PO Box 2382
Brockton, MA 02403
Celine Colombo, Pres.

Description: Parents and professionals united to explore safe alternatives in childbirth.

★2086★ **Massachusetts Mothers of Twins Association**
50 South St.
Brockton, MA 02401
Phone: (508)587-2869
Alfreda M. Wright, Exec.Sec.

Description: Mothers, guardians, and grandmothers of multiple birth children. Encourages healthy individual development of multiple birth children through public education. Educates teachers to treat each child of a multiple birth as an individual. **Affiliated with:** National Organization of Mothers of Twins Clubs.

Brookline

★2087★ **Older Women's League (OWL) Northeast Regional Chapter**
312 Tappan St.
Brookline, MA 02146
Phone: (617)482-1390
Joan Lamphier, Contact

Cambridge

★2088★ **Women's Sales Network of Boston**
1753 Massachusetts Ave.
Cambridge, MA 02140
Phone: (617)576-8118
Janis Brubacher, Pres.

Description: Women in sales. Promotes communication and exchange of information. Sponsors educational programs and seminars.

★2089★ **Young Women's Christian Association of Cambridge**
7 Temple St.
Cambridge, MA 02139
Phone: (617)491-6050

Description: Seeks to develop and improve the spiritual, social, mental, and physical well-being of young people and adults. **Affiliated with:** Young Women's Christian Association of the United States of America.

Centerville

★2090★ **Cape Cod Women's Organization**
Box 771
Centerville, MA 02632-0771

Chestnut Hill

★2091★ **New England Women Business Owners**
99 Bellingham Rd.
Chestnut Hill, MA 02167
Phone: (617)566-3013
Janet Bentley, Pres.

Description: Women business owners. Supports women owned businesses and encourages women to establish new businesses. Promotes education and networking.

Concord

★2092★ **Birthright of Assabet Valley**
747 Main St.
Concord, MA 01742-3302

Description: Seeks to help pregnant women find alternatives to abortion. Conducts childbirth education and parenting programs.

Gardner

★2093★ **Gardner Woman's Club**
265 Sherman St.
Gardner, MA 01440
Phone: (508)632-5760
Marian Thatcher, Pres.

Description: Women in north central Massachusetts. Promotes civic and cultural interests. Awards scholarships for Gardner students. **Affiliated with:** General Federation of Women's Clubs.

Greenfield

★2094★ **Franklin County Women's Republican Club**
31 Lovers Ln.
Greenfield, MA 01301
Phone: (413)772-6984
Sylvia Hassett, Pres.

Description: Seeks to elect Republican candidates to local, state, and national offices.

★2095★ **Women's Fellowship of the First Congregational Church of Greenfield**
254 Green River Rd.
Greenfield, MA 01301
Phone: (413)773-8226
Luella B. McLaughlin, Contact

Description: Female members of First Congregational Church in Franklin County, MA. Promotes unity of women through worship, education, community service. Supports the Christian course. **Affiliated with:** United Church of Christ.

Haverhill

★2096★ **New England Women Historians**
c/o Mary Ault Harada
North Essex Community College
Haverhill, MA 01985

★2097★ **Young Women's Christian Association of Haverhill**
107 Winter St.
Haverhill, MA 01830
Phone: (508)374-6121

Description: Seeks to develop and improve the spiritual, social, mental, and physical well-being of young people and adults. **Affiliated with:** Young Women's Christian Association of the United States of America.

Holyoke

★2098★ **Holyoke Women's Club**
c/o Lorraine Gorham
19 Joanne Dr.
Holyoke, MA 01040
Lorraine Gorham, Exec. Officer

Description: Women united to form a center for moral, intellectual, and social betterment of area citizens. **Affiliated with:** General Federation of Women's Clubs.

Lawrence

★2099★ **Young Women's Christian Association of Greater Lawrence**
38 Lawrence St.
Lawrence, MA 01840
Phone: (508)687-0331

Description: Seeks to develop and improve the spiritual, social, mental, and physical life of youth and adults in the Greater Lawrence, MA area. **Affiliated with:** Young Women's Christian Association of the United States of America.

Leominster

★2100★ **Leominster Women's Republican Club**
215 West St.
Leominster, MA 01453
Phone: (617)537-2568
Nancy Piermarini, Contact

Description: Seeks to elect Republican candidates to local, state, and national offices.

Lexington

★2101★ **National League of American Pen Women, Wellesley Branch**
11 Tower Rd.
Lexington, MA 02173
Phone: (617)862-3834
Natalie Warshawer, Pres.

Description: Professional women writers, artists, and musicians in metropolitan Boston, MA. Encourages original production by members in the arts; exhibits completed/published projects. **Affiliated with:** National League of American Penwomen.

★2102★ **National Organization for Women, Lexington Area Chapter**
PO Box 511
Lexington, MA 02173
Phone: (508)371-7060
Linda H. Brown, Pres.

Description: Individuals promoting the feminist causes of equal rights, abortion rights, pay equity, and other pertinent issues that affect women. Conducts educational programs on feminist issues; sponsors voter information campaign; operates charitable projects. **Affiliated with:** National Organization for Women.

Longmeadow

★2103★ **Longmeadow Republican Women's Club**
73 Converse St.
Longmeadow, MA 01106
Anna L. Adam, Pres.

Description: Seeks to elect Republican candidates to local, state, and national offices.

Lowell

★2104★ **Young Women's Christian Association of Lowell**
206 Rogers St.
Lowell, MA 01852
Phone: (508)454-5405

Description: Seeks to develop and improve the spiritual, social, mental, and physical life of youth and adults in Lowell, MA. **Affiliated with:** Young Women's Christian Association of the United States of America.

Lynnfield

★2105★ **La Leche League of Massachusetts/Rhode Island/Vermont**
20 W. Tapley Rd.
Lynnfield, MA 01940
Phone: (617)334-3035
Mary G. Mahoney, Coordinator

Description: Nursing mothers, doctors, and other interested individuals. Encourages mothers to breastfeed their babies. Offers mother-to-mother help through meetings and telephone contacts. Provides speakers for high schools, hospitals, and clinics. **Affiliated with:** La Leche League International.

Malden

★2106★ **Young Women's Christian Association of Malden**
54 Washington St.
Malden, MA 02148
Phone: (617)322-3760

Description: Seeks to develop and improve the spiritual, social, mental, and physical life of youth and adults in Malden, MA. **Affiliated with:** Young Women's Christian Association of the United States of America.

Middleton

★2107★ **Spar and Spindle Girl Scout Council**
PO Box 1010
Middleton, MA 01949
Phone: (508)689-8015
Fax: (508)688-1846
Megan B. Shea, Exec.Dir.

Description: Girls aged 5-17 (10,000) and adult volunteers (3000) from 53 communities in northern Massachusetts and southern New Hampshire. Promotes individual development with high ideals of character, patriotism, and conduct. Encourages girls to become resourceful and happy citizens; participates in community service programs. **Affiliated with:** Girl Scouts of the U.S.A.

Needham

★2108★ **Massachusetts Citizens for Life, Needham Chapter**
c/o Laurie Goodrow
779 Highland Ave.
Needham, MA 02194
Phone: (617)444-8796
Laurie Goodrow, Chm.

Description: Opposes abortion. Works to educate the public on right-to-life issues. Provides speakers for local schools. Conducts fundrais-

ing and lobbying activities. Monitors legislation. Holds annual Walk for Life fundraiser.

New Bedford

★2109★ **Birthright of Greater New Bedford**
398 County St.
New Bedford, MA 02740
Phone: (508)996-6744
Gordon and Ann Baker, Dirs.

Description: Volunteers dedicated to pro-life ideals. Offers help and counseling to teenagers with unplanned pregnancies. Provides clothing and baby supplies free of charge. Provides free pregnancy testing. **Affiliated with:** Birthright, U.S.A.

★2110★ **New Bedford Young Women's Christian Association**
66 Spring St.
New Bedford, MA 02740
Phone: (508)999-3255
Nancy Carignan, Exec.Dir.

Description: Seeks to develop and improve the spiritual, social, mental, and physical life of youth and adults in New Bedford, MA. Offers programs for after school day care, displaced homemakers, exercise and swimming, empowerment of women, senior and community services. Holds support groups. Operates Next to New Shop and YWCA Standish House. **Affiliated with:** Young Women's Christian Association of the United States of America.

Newburyport

★2111★ **Older Women's League (OWL) Merrimac Valley Chapter**
3 Pond St.
Newburyport, MA 01950
Phone: (508)465-6304
Freda B. Muldoon, Contact

★2112★ **Young Women's Christian Association of Newburyport**
13 Market St.
Newburyport, MA 01950
Phone: (508)465-0981

Description: Seeks to develop and improve the spiritual, social, mental, and physical life of youth and adults in Newburyport, MA. **Affiliated with:** Young Women's Christian Association of the United States of America.

Newton

★2113★ **Boston Association for Childbirth Education**
PO Box 29
Newton, MA 02160
Phone: (617)244-5102

Description: Provides educational programs on family-centered childbirth, breastfeeding, and related issues. Offers counseling and support services.

★2114★ **Boston Network for Women in Politics and Government**
885 Centre St.
Newton, MA 02159-1156

Description: Women politicians, bureaucrats, lobbyists, and government workers in the Boston, MA area.

★2115★ **Nursing Mothers Council of the Boston Association for Childbirth Education**
PO Box 29
Newton, MA 02160
Phone: (617)244-5102
Carole Kavanagh, Coordinator
Description: Volunteers in eastern Massachusetts. Provides breastfeeding counseling and educational information. Sponsors counselor training programs. **Affiliated with:** Boston Association for Childbirth Education.

Newton Highlands

★2116★ **National Council of Jewish Women, Northeastern District**
950 Boylston St.
Newton Highlands, MA 02161
Phone: (617)244-8000
Ruth Rosenbaum, Chair
Description: Jewish women. Individuals providing advocacy and community service.

★2117★ **Northeast Association of Women Historians**
c/o Lilian Shiman
93 Carven Rd.
Newton Highlands, MA 02161

Northampton

★2118★ **Family Planning Council of Western Massachusetts**
16 Center St.
Northampton, MA 01060
Phone: (413)586-2016
Leslie T. Laurie, Exec.Dir.
Description: Promotes family planning. Makes available family planning, educational, and AIDS services; conducts teen parenting programs.

★2119★ **Flower Foundation**
PO Box 602
Northampton, MA 01061
Phone: (413)586-0622
Sue Krause, Contact

Northfield

★2120★ **Church Women United of Franklin County**
East St.
Northfield, MA 01360
Phone: (413)498-2081
Marian Holbrook, Pres.
Description: Women of all denominations. Encourages unity between denominations. Issues publications. **Affiliated with:** Church Women United.

Peabody

★2121★ **Female Benevolent Society at South Danvers**
63 Lynnfield St.
Peabody, MA 01960-5229

Raynham

★2122★ **Southeastern Massachusetts Business and Professional Women's Club**
1 Nottingham Dr.
Raynham, MA 02767
Phone: (508)823-7350
Patti Kelleher, Pres.
Description: Business and professional women. To promote complete participation, equal opportunities, and economic self-sufficiency for working women.

★2123★ **Taunton Business and Professional Women's Club**
280 Church St., No. 177
Raynham, MA 02767
Phone: (508)822-3217
Beverly A. Galvin, Exec. Officer
Description: Business and professional women. To promote complete participation, equal opportunities, and economic self-sufficiency for working women. Promotes women's issues such as better pay and quality day care. **Affiliated with:** National Federation of Business and Professional Women's Clubs of the U.S.A.

Salisbury

★2124★ **Newburyport Business and Professional Women's Organization**
c/o Diane Chatigny
320 Lafayette Rd.
Salisbury, MA 01912
Phone: (508)465-3856
Diane Chatigny, Exec. Officer
Description: Professional organization of working women in the Newburyport, MA area. Promotes interests of working women and continuing education as a means to improve opportunities in the business community. Encourages a spirit of cooperation among members. **Affiliated with:** Massachusetts Federation of Business and Professional Women's Clubs; National Federation of Business and Professional Women's Clubs of the U.S.A.

Shrewsbury

★2125★ **Women's Chief Executives of Massachusetts**
c/o Mary Coloril
Dimitria Delights
745 Main St.
Shrewsbury, MA 01545
Phone: (508)842-1113
Mary Coloril, Exec. Officer

Stoneham

★2126★ **Association for Women in Science, New England Chapter**
67 Pine St.
Stoneham, MA 02180
Phone: (617)438-6680
Virginia Wootten, Pres.
Description: Scientists, academics, and industrial and government employees joined to promote equal opportunities for women in the science field. Conducts charitable activities. **Affiliated with:** American Association for the Advancement of Science; Association for Women in Science.

Stoughton

★2127★ **DES Action**
PO Box 126
Stoughton, MA 02072

Sutton

★2128★ **Childbirth Education Services**
101 Leland Hill Rd.
Sutton, MA 01590
Phone: (508)865-4715
Kathyleen Kangas, Dir.
Description: Childbirth educators in Connecticut, Massachusetts, New Hampshire, and Rhode Island. Provides educational opportunities to parents and professionals relating to childbirth. **Affiliated with:** National Association of Parents and Professionals for Safe Alternatives in Childbirth.

Taunton

★2129★ **American Association of University Women, Taunton Area Branch**
22 Arbor Way
Taunton, MA 02780
Phone: (508)823-4316
Description: Women graduates of regionally accredited four year colleges and universities. Works for the advancement of women through advocacy and emphasis on lifelong learning. Sponsors community programs including used book sales, dinners, and first aid courses. **Affiliated with:** American Association of University Women.

★2130★ **Plymouth Bay Girl Scout Council**
140 Winthrop St.
PO Box 711
Taunton, MA 02780
Phone: (508)824-4034
Toll-free: 800-242-0925
Carolyn Mayo-Brown, Exec.Dir.
Description: Girls (19,000) and adult volunteers (4000) in southeastern Massachusetts. Encourages girls to develop their full potential as individuals through informal guidance, community service, and recreational activities. **Affiliated with:** Girl Scouts of the U.S.A.

Turners Falls

★2131★ **Women's Fellowship of the First Congregational Church of Turners Falls**
7th and L Sts.
Turners Falls, MA 01376
Phone: (413)863-9844
Helen Stotz, Exec. Officer
Description: Social organization of women of the First Congregational Church. Conducts annual church fair.

Wellesley

★2132★ **Higher Education Resource Services, New England (HERS)**
Wellesley College, Cheever House
828 Washington St.
Wellesley, MA 02181
Phone: (617)235-0320
Susan Knowles, Assistant Director
Description: HERS, New England seeks to improve the status of women in higher education administration. Sponsors the Management

Institute for Women in Higher Education which provides training for women college and university administrators. Provides network for members. **Publications:** *New England Network*, annual.

Wellesley Hills

★2133★ Hellenic Women's Club
166 Hampshire Rd.
Wellesley Hills, MA 02181-1240

West Roxbury

★2134★ Women's Overseas Service League, Boston Unit
11 Glenham St.
West Roxbury, MA 02132
Phone: (617)469-2643
Catherine A. M. Eachen, Pres.

Description: Women who served overseas with the armed services, American Red Cross, Salvation Army, or other service organizations during World Wars I and II, Korean and Vietnam war, or aftermath. Carries on patriotic activities, service to disabled veterans, and aid to members in need. **Affiliated with:** Women's Overseas Service League.

Winchendon

★2135★ Putnam Alliance Church of the Unity
PO Box 218
Winchendon, MA 01475
Phone: (508)297-0554
Fax: (508)297-0918
Mary W. White, Pres.

Description: Women of the Unitarian Universalist Church of Winchendon, MA. Serves as source for information on women's issues. Sponsors programs for the local church and holds fundraisers. Holds flea markets, programs, special events, and suppers. **Affiliated with:** Unitarian-Universalist Women's Federation.

Worcester

★2136★ Montachusett Girl Scout Council
81 Goldstar Blvd.
Worcester, MA 01606
Phone: (508)853-1070
Betty A. Stephenson, Exec.Dir.

Description: Girls aged five to 17 and adult volunteers in central Massachusetts. Encourages girls to develop their full potential as self-reliant and resourceful individuals. Operates 12 day camps and one residential camp. **Affiliated with:** Girl Scouts of the U.S.A.

★2137★ Young Women's Christian Association of Worcester
1 Salem Sq.
Worcester, MA 01608
Phone: (508)791-3181

Description: Seeks to develop and improve the spiritual, social, mental, and physical life of youth and adults in in Worcester, MA. **Affiliated with:** Young Women's Christian Association of the United States of America.

Michigan

Algonac

★2138★ American Business Women's Association, Vivon Chapter
6330 Marina Dr.
Algonac, MI 48001
Phone: (313)794-5154
Patricia Allen, Contact

Description: Works for the professional, educational, cultural, and social advancement of businesswomen. Sponsors local scholarships; conducts community service. **Affiliated with:** American Business Women's Association.

Allegan

★2139★ Allegan Business and Professional Women's Club
c/o Joann Zwerver
601 Ely St.
Allegan, MI 49010
Phone: (616)673-7036
Joann Zwerver, Pres.

Description: Business and professional women. To promote complete participation, equal opportunities, and economic self-sufficiency for working women. Awards scholarships. **Affiliated with:** National Federation of Business and Professional Women's Clubs of the U.S.A.

Ann Arbor

★2140★ DES Action
PO Box 2692
Ann Arbor, MI 48106

★2141★ Older Women's League (OWL) Washtenaw Chapter
PO Box 2162
Ann Arbor, MI 48106
Phone: (313)663-1842
Helen Metzner, Contact

★2142★ Washtenaw County Women's Action for Nuclear Disarmament
PO Box 1815
Ann Arbor, MI 48106
Phone: (313)761-1718
Sarah Cooleybeck, Contact

Description: Women united to lobby for nuclear disarmament and educate the public about nuclear war. Sponsors Mother's Day Festival of Peace and monthly educational programs. **Affiliated with:** Women's Action for Nuclear Disarmament.

Arcadia

★2143★ Arcadia Women's Club
c/o Eleanor Pilz
17023 3rd St.
PO Box 75
Arcadia, MI 49613
Phone: (616)889-4088
Eleanor Pilz, Exec. Officer

Description: Women's volunteer service club. Conducts charitable activities. Participates in area festival.

Bay City

★2144★ Bay County League of Democratic Women
2123 Center Ave.
Bay City, MI 48708
Phone: (517)893-2548
Karen Tighe, Pres.

Description: Professional, unionized, and other men and women working to advance women in politics. Dedicated to education and leadership within the Democratic Party.

★2145★ Young Women's Christian Association of Bay County
3405 E. Midland Rd.
Bay City, MI 48706
Phone: (517)686-4800
Cynthia A. Chadwick, Exec.Dir.

Description: Promotes personal and skill development, health, and fitness through various programs and services for the members and the community. Participates in Riverside Art Festival. **Affiliated with:** Young Women's Christian Association of the United States of America.

Benton Harbor

★2146★ American Association of University Women, Benton Harbor/St. Joseph Branch
1019 Fort
Benton Harbor, MI 49022
Phone: (616)925-3506
Virginia E. A. Maxwell, Pres.

Description: Women graduates of regionally accredited four year colleges and universities. Works for the advancement of women through advocacy and emphasis on lifelong learning. Awards annual scholarships. Supports local YWCA and Neighborhood Information Sharing Exchange. Sponsors book sale. **Affiliated with:** American Association of University Women.

Birmingham

★2147★ Birmingham Women Painters
32071 Rosevear Dr.
Birmingham, MI 48025-7199
Phone: (313)646-7199
Barbra Keidan, President

Founded: 1944. **Description:** Membership dues support a program of workshops and lectures. Group exhibition package available for travel. **Membership:** 50.

★2148★ Oakland Branch, American Association of University Women
18956 Devonshire
Birmingham, MI 48009
Phone: (313)646-7437
Nancy Kurchock, Pres.

Description: Women graduates of regionally accredited four year colleges and universities. Works for the advancement of women through advocacy and emphasis on lifelong learning. **Affiliated with:** American Association of University Women; International Association of University Women in Europe.

Cassopolis

★2149★ Cass County Coalition Against Domestic Violence
120 N. Broadway
Cassopolis, MI 49031-1302
Description: Works to prevent domestic violence in the Cassopolis, MI area.

Clawson

★2150★ General Federation of Women's Clubs, Michigan Chapter
659 S. Garantua
Clawson, MI 48017
Phone: (313)435-5767
Norma Johnson, Contact
Description: Works to improve the quality of life in the home, community, and the world. **Affiliated with:** General Federation of Women's Clubs.

Dearborn

★2151★ American Association of University Women, Dearborn Branch
2050 Russell
Dearborn, MI 48128
Phone: (313)278-8515
Beverly Bath, Pres.
Description: Women graduates of regionally accredited four year colleges and universities. Works for the advancement of women through advocacy and emphasis on lifelong learning. **Affiliated with:** American Association of University Women. Conducts charitable activities. Sponsors used book sale to provide scholarships.

Dearborn Heights

★2152★ General Federation of Women's Clubs, Dearborn
c/o Verna Holland
672 Norborne
Dearborn Heights, MI 48127
Phone: (313)562-7913
Verna Holland, Co-Pres.
Description: Women's volunteer service club. Conducts charitable activities for Girlstown of Belleville, Oakwood Hospital, and CARE. Assists with a crisis center. Awards scholarship. **Affiliated with:** General Federation of Women's Clubs - Michigan; General Federation of Women's Clubs.

★2153★ Women's International League for Peace and Freedom, Rouge Valley Branch
752 Charlesworth
Dearborn Heights, MI 48127
Phone: (313)565-2590
Julia Leedle, Chair
Description: Retirees, teachers, and individuals from southwestern Detroit, MI area. Strives to achieve world peace and justice. Promotes demonstrations with other groups. **Affiliated with:** Women's International League for Peace and Freedom.

Detroit

★2154★ Alternatives for Girls
1950 Trumbull
Detroit, MI 48216
Phone: (313)496-0938
Roberta Sharpe, Contact
Description: Provides support and opportunities to girls and young women who are considered at "high risk" for harmful activities and dangerous lifestyle choices.

★2155★ Childbirth Without Pain Education Association (CWPEA)
20134 Snowden
Detroit, MI 48235-1170
Phone: (313)341-3816
Flora Hommel, Exec.Dir.
Founded: 1958. **Description:** Former and current students of the Lamaze-Pavlov (psychoprophylactic) method of painless childbirth; physicians, nurses, and interested individuals. Membership centered in Detroit, MI. Sponsors lectures, classes, and films for women with or without partners, nurses, and medical and lay groups about the method, which is based on conditioning reflexes to help prevent pain, thus allowing for natural, usually drug-free childbirth. Works to provide a method-trained registered nurse (monitrice) in attendance at the birth where possible. Collects data for further development of the method; surveys maternity services; presents awards. Sponsors childbirth teacher and monitrice training and certification. Provides teen pregnancy programs. Offers referral service. Maintains library of more than 100 volumes on methods of childbirth preparation, particularly psychoprophylactic and family-centered maternity care. **Members:** 3000. **Publications:** *Childbirth Without Pain Education Association Memo*, bimonthly. Newsletter; includes association news and book reviews. **Also known as:** Lamaze Birth Without Pain Education Association.

★2156★ Detroit Women's Forum
163 Madison Ave.
Detroit, MI 48226
Phone: (313)965-3169
Ruth Driker Kroll, Dir.
Description: Academic, business, and professional women in the Ann Arbor and Detroit, MI areas focusing on today's economic, political, and social issues and their impact on women.

★2157★ EXCEL! The Initiative for Entrepreneurial Excellence
200 Renaissance Center, Ste. 1600
Detroit, MI 48243
Phone: (313)396-3576

★2158★ League of Catholic Women of Detroit
120 Parsons
Detroit, MI 48201
Phone: (313)831-1000
Marilyn F. Lundy, Exec. Officer
Description: Women dedicated to the faith and policies of the Roman Catholic Church.

★2159★ Michigan Federation of Democratic Women
19432 Burlington
Detroit, MI 48203
Virgie M. Rollins, Exec. Officer
Description: Women who support the Democratic party. Encourages political involvement by women; promotes women's issues. **Affiliated with:** National Federation of Democratic Women.

★2160★ Michigan Metro Girl Scout Council
28 W. Adams, Ste. 612
Detroit, MI 48226
Phone: (313)964-4475
Penny Bailer, Exec.Dir.
Description: Promotes the balanced development of girls in Wayne and southern Oakland counties, MI through informal educational, recreational, and community service activities supervised by adult volunteers. **Affiliated with:** Girl Scouts of the U.S.A.; United Foundation.

★2161★ National Association of Women Business Owners
Greater Detroit Chapter
200 Renaissance Center, Ste. 1600
Detroit, MI 48243
Phone: (313)396-3576
Chinyere Neal, Contact

★2162★ National Negro and Professional Women's Clubs, New Metropolitan Detroit Chapter
1411 Liebold
Detroit, MI 48217-1225
Description: African-American business women in Detroit, MI.

★2163★ Older Women's League (OWL)
Central Detroit Chapter
1550 Cherboneau Pl. 101
Detroit, MI 48207
Phone: (313)567-0429
Emmesia Frost, Contact

★2164★ Sojourner Foundation
20570 Evergreen Rd.
Detroit, MI 48219
Phone: (313)534-4263
Kate Davis, President

★2165★ Women's Justice Center (WJC)
23 E. Adams
Detroit, MI 48226
Phone: (313)961-4057
Carol Sullivan, Staff Dir.
Founded: 1975. **Description:** Works on family law, injunctions, divorce and custody for low income individuals in the area. It also provides domestic abuse shelters and career development help. **Publications:** Newsletter.

Dowagiac

★2166★ Tri-County Council of Women in Education Administration
Southwestern Michigan College
58900 Cherry Grove Rd.
Dowagiac, MI 49047
Toll-free: 800-456-8675
Fax: (616)782-8414
Gloria Cooper, Pres.

Description: Administrators of public and private schools from kindergarten through college levels. Promotes social and professional interaction among women in education.

East Lansing

★2167★ Association for Women in Science, Lansing Area Chapter
PO Box 6516
East Lansing, MI 48826
Phone: (517)353-5410
Karen Strickler, Pres.

Description: Women working in scientific industries or teaching science at the postsecondary level. Promotes advancement of women in scientific fields.

★2168★ Michigan Democratic Women's Caucus
501 Rampart Way, No. 304
East Lansing, MI 48823
Liza Estlund Olson, Chair

Description: Women members of the Democratic Party. Promotes the involvement of women in the Democratic party and its decision making process. Works to increase the number of women holding public office.

★2169★ Take Back the Night Task Force
Michigan State University
319 Student Union
East Lansing, MI 48824
Phone: (517)353-5255
Theresa Nash, Dir.

Description: Organization interested in issues of concern to women (feminist theory, violence against women and children, and pornography) in Michigan. Sponsors a statewide "Take Back The Night" protest march. **Affiliated with:** Women's Council.

★2170★ Women's Overseas Service League, Lansing Unit
6091 Brook Haven Ln., No. 33
East Lansing, MI 48823
Phone: (517)351-2518
Betty L. Leiby, Pres.

Description: Women who have served overseas with the Armed Forces, including nurses, WACs, and Red Cross workers during World Wars I and II, Korean War, and Vietnam War. Seeks to maintain ties of friendship and to perform charitable work. Assists with veterans' hospitals in Michigan. **Affiliated with:** Women's Overseas Service League.

Farmington

★2171★ National Organization for Women, Great Lakes Region
32321 Shiawassee
Farmington, MI 48336
Phone: (313)474-2526
Marian McCracken, Contact

Description: Men and women who support "full equality for women in true, equal partnership with men." **Affiliated with:** National Organization for Women.

★2172★ Older Women's League (OWL) Michigan State/Farmington Hills Chapter
35281 Drakeshire, Apt. 204
Farmington, MI 48335
Phone: (313)474-3094
Virginia Nicoll, Contact

Farmington Hills

★2173★ Association for Women in Science, Detroit Area Chapter
PO Box 3445
Farmington Hills, MI 48333-3445
Phone: (313)851-3702
Ruth Reck, Ph.D., Pres.

Description: Professional women and men of the social and natural sciences united to promote equal opportunities for women to enter the professions and achieve their career goals. Sponsors educational activities, workshops, seminars, and speakers. **Affiliated with:** National Association for Women in Science.

Fenton

★2174★ Older Women's League (OWL) Flint/Fenton Chapter
2035 Front St.
Fenton, MI 48430
Phone: (313)629-2474
Marilyn Hoover, Contact

Flint

★2175★ Flint Associated Chapter of Endometriosis
Flint Osteopathic Hospital
Dept. of Education
Flint, MI 48502
Phone: (313)762-4608
Charaine Manwell, Contact

Description: Women in Genessee County, MI who have endometriosis. Provides education concerning endometriosis and other women's health issues. Offers person to person group support.

★2176★ Foundation for the Young Women's Christian Association of Greater Flint
c/o Kathryn K. Mcclanahan
310 E. 3rd St.
Flint, MI 48502-1786
Kathryn K. Mcclanahan, Contact

★2177★ Young Women's Christian Association of Flint
310 E. 3rd St.
Flint, MI 48502
Phone: (313)238-7621
Carol W. Anselm, Ph.D., Exec. Officer

Description: Seeks to develop and improve the spiritual, social, mental, and physical life of women and girls over the age of 12 in Genesee and Lapeer counties, MI. Operates pre-school. Bestows awards. **Affiliated with:** Young Women's Christian Association of the United States of America.

Grand Rapids

★2178★ Alliance of Women Entrepreneurs
PO Box 6731
Grand Rapids, MI 49506
Phone: (616)455-2424
Allison Kaufman, Contact

Description: Women business owners from western Michigan dedicated to support, educate, and provide networking opportunities for each other.

★2179★ American Association of University Women, Grand Rapids Chapter
1645 Millbank SE
Grand Rapids, MI 49508
Phone: (616)243-6400
Phyllis Pomeroy, Past Pres.

Description: Women graduates of regionally accredited four year colleges and universities. Works for the advancement of women through advocacy and emphasis on lifelong learning. Sponsors fundraisers for scholarships, fellowships, and grants. **Affiliated with:** American Association of University Women.

★2180★ American Business Women's Association, Hopewell Chapter
7305 Driftwood SE
Grand Rapids, MI 49546
Phone: (616)676-1062

Description: Professional organization for business women. Awards college scholarships.

★2181★ DES Action
2205 Rosewood SE
Grand Rapids, MI 49506

★2182★ Grand Rapids Right-to-Life
2340 Porter SW
Grand Rapids, MI 49509
Phone: (616)532-2300
Fax: (616)451-9842
Barbara Schwartz, Exec.Sec.

Description: Individuals working to educate people, assist members, and coordinate local projects concerning anti-abortion. Advocates for protective legislation on behalf of the unborn. Conducts charitable activities; sponsors annual Bike 'n Hike for Life.

★2183★ National Association of Women in Construction, Grand Rapids Chapter
2824 3 Mile Rd. NW
Grand Rapids, MI 49504
Phone: (616)453-8610
Marcia VanDyke, Contact

★2184★ Right to Life of Michigan
PO Box 901
Grand Rapids, MI 49509-0901

Description: Promotes the rights of the unborn.

★2185★ Young Women's Christian Association of Grand Rapids
25 Sheldon Rd. SE
Grand Rapids, MI 49503
Phone: (616)459-4681

Description: Seeks to develop and improve the spiritual, social, mental, and physical life of women and girls over the age of 12. **Affiliated with:** Young Women's Christian Association of the United States of America.

Harbor Springs

★2186★ La Leche League International, Michigan
819 Ottawa
Harbor Springs, MI 49740
Phone: (517)484-5005
Sue Grimm, Coordinator

Description: Breastfeeding mothers, health professionals, and volunteer leaders. Offers monthly support groups and telephone help. Provides information and support to breastfeeding mothers. Maintains lending library. **Affiliated with:** La Leche League International.

Hesperia

★2187★ Michigan Midwives Association
c/o Patrice Bobier
4220 Loop Rd.
Hesperia, MI 49421
Phone: (616)861-2234.
Patrice Bobier, Treas.

Description: Midwives, midwives-in-training, birth educators, and interested individuals. Seeks to better inform the public regarding midwifery and childbirth. Responds to legal needs and encourages further relations between the profession and other health care professions. Facilitates communication among members; encourages the education of midwives. Sponsors Healthy Mothers/Healthy Babies Coalition. Holds public information sessions. **Affiliated with:** Midwives Alliance of North America.

Holland

★2188★ Birthright of Holland
21 W. 16th St.
Holland, MI 49423
Phone: (616)396-5840
Anne H. Stitt, Financial Sec.

Description: Volunteers provide guidance for pregnant women. Offers free pregnancy testing, counseling, maternity clothing, layettes and referrals. Operates hotline. Provides a speaker for local groups. **Affiliated with:** Alternatives of Abortion, Inc.; International Birthright; Pro-Life Emergency Pregnancy Services.

Holly

★2189★ American Association of University Women, Fenton Branch
7355 Fish Lake Rd.
Holly, MI 48442
Phone: (313)634-8102
Darlyne Stanczyk, Pres.

Description: Women graduates of regionally accredited four year colleges and universities. Works for the advancement of women through advocacy and emphasis on lifelong learning.

Conducts educational and community services. Awards grants. Holds annual book sale. **Affiliated with:** American Association of University Women.

Inkster

★2190★ Michigan State Association of Colored Women's Clubs
26842 Hopkins
Inkster, MI 48141
Phone: (313)561-4694
Gertrude Warren, Pres.

Description: Professionals and others interested in promoting youth education and international understanding, and improving home standards. Fosters unity among cultural and social women's clubs. Supports events in all human service areas. Awards scholarships. **Affiliated with:** Central Region Association of Colored Women's Clubs; National Association of Colored Women's Clubs.

★2191★ Young Women's Christian Association of Western Wayne County
26279 Michigan Ave.
Inkster, MI 48141
Phone: (313)561-4110

Description: Seeks to develop and improve the spiritual, social, mental, and physical life of women and girls over the age of 12. **Affiliated with:** Young Women's Christian Association of the United States of America.

Ionia

★2192★ Ionia Area Council Church Women United
c/o Margaret F. Seidelman
1877 N. State Rd.
Ionia, MI 48846-9502
Margaret F. Seidelman, Contact

Description: Promotes community improvement.

Kalamazoo

★2193★ American Association of University Women, Kalamazoo Branch
5140 Greenhill
Kalamazoo, MI 49808
Phone: (616)382-2345
Virginia Norton, Exec. Officer

Description: Men and women graduates of regionally accredited four year colleges and universities. Works for the advancement of women through advocacy and emphasis on lifelong learning. Awards scholarships. **Affiliated with:** American Association of University Women; American Association of University Women, Michigan Division.

★2194★ Older Women's League (OWL) Kalamazoo Chapter
8620 Tozer Ln.
Kalamazoo, MI 49002
Phone: (616)327-1392
Betty Lee Ongley, Contact

★2195★ Young Women's Christian Association of Kalamazoo
353 E. Michigan
Kalamazoo, MI 49007
Phone: (616)345-5595
Karen L. V'Soske, Exec.Dir.

Description: Provides shelter and services to victims of domestic violence; services for sexual assault victims; child care; physical fitness and educational programs to women. **Affiliated with:** Young Women's Christian Associations of the U.S.A.

Kentwood

★2196★ American Society of Women Accountants, Grand Rapids Chapter
5960 Cristmoor, SE
Kentwood, MI 49508
Phone: (616)455-3592
Barb Hazlett, Pres.

Description: Accoutants, bookkeepers, and certified public accountants organized to promote the interest of women in accounting. **Affiliated with:** American Society of Women Accountants; American Society of Woman's Certified Public Accoutants.

Lansing

★2197★ American Association of University Women, Michigan Division
200 Museum Dr.
Lansing, MI 48933
Phone: (517)372-8302
Toll-free: 800-821-4364
Susan Stepnitz, Pres.

Description: Women graduates of regionally accredited four year colleges and universities. Works for the advancement of women through advocacy and emphasis on lifelong learning. **Affiliated with:** American Association of University Women.

★2198★ League of Women Voters of Michigan
200 Museum Dr., Ste. 202
Lansing, MI 48933-1997
Phone: (517)484-5383
Frances Parker, President

★2199★ Michigan Council for Maternal and Child Health
318 W. Ottawa
Lansing, MI 48933
Phone: (517)482-5807
Paul N. Shaheen, Exec.Dir.

Description: Acts as an advocate for maternal and child health issues.

★2200★ Michigan Federation of Business and Professional Women's Clubs
204 S. Museum Dr.
Lansing, MI 48933
Phone: (517)372-2688
Barbara N. Deleeuw, Admin.Asst.

Description: Promotes the interests of business women.

★2201★ Michigan Women's Foundation
119 Pare Marquette, Ste. 2A
Lansing, MI 48912
Phone: (517)374-7270
Susan Church, Executive Director

★2202★ **Michigan Women's Historical Center and Hall of Fame**
213 W. Main St.
Lansing, MI 48933
Phone: (517)484-1880
Description: Serves as a community resource, drawing people to exhibits, lectures, concerts, poetry readings and similar events. **Publications:** Has published books and educational resource packet, established a theme trail.

★2203★ **Michigan Women's Studies Association**
213 W. Main St.
Lansing, MI 48933
Phone: (517)484-1880
Gladys Beckwith, Pres.
Description: Educators, education institutions, and others interested in promoting women's studies in schools and universities. Works to: promote information on American women; eliminate bias against and stereotyping of women. Promotes nonracist and nonsexist education in schools; encourages research by, for, and about women. Maintains Women's Hall of Fame and Women's Historical Center. **Affiliated with:** Friends of Michigan Women's Historical Center and Hall of Fame; National Women's Studies Association.

★2204★ **National Organization for Women, Michigan Chapter**
217 Townsend
PO Box 18063
Lansing, MI 48901
Phone: (517)485-9687
Description: Individuals concerned about women's issues and rights. Works to achieve equality of the sexes worldwide.

★2205★ **Older Women's League (OWL) Greater Lansing Chapter**
2344 Tecumseh River Rd.
Lansing, MI 48906
Phone: (517)321-4877
Fran Ryan, Contact

★2206★ **St. Jude Women's Club of Lansing**
c/o Barbara L. Grissom
439 Spector 913
Lansing, MI 48917-1030
Barbara L. Grissom, Contact

★2207★ **Women in State Government**
Box 14133
Lansing, MI 48901
Sandra I. Slee, Pres.
Description: Provides advancement opportunities for women in all branches of government. Conducts educational programs.

★2208★ **Young Women's Christian Association of Greater Lansing**
217 Townsend St.
PO Box 14163
Lansing, MI 48901
Phone: (517)485-7201
Mary E. Aikey, Exec.Dir.
Description: Seeks to develop and improve the spiritual, social, mental, and physical life of women and girls over the age of 12 in Clinton, Eaton, and Ingham counties, MI. Conducts charitable activities. **Affiliated with:** Young

Women's Christian Association of the United States of America.

Livonia

★2209★ **Garden City Business and Professional Women's Club**
17207 Country Club Dr.
Livonia, MI 48152
Phone: (313)462-2654
Maureen McDonald, Pres.
Description: Business and professional women. To promote complete participation, equal opportunities, and economic self-sufficiency for working women. Sponsors young career women competitions. Awards scholarships. Participates in Garden City Community Festival. **Affiliated with:** National Federation of Business and Professional Women's Clubs.

★2210★ **Winning Women**
18770 Farmington Rd.
Livonia, MI 48152
Phone: (313)474-7271
Peggy Burdick, Pres.
Description: Inter-denominational church women. "Provide speakers who can share effectively the reality of Jesus Christ, His power, and His love."

Manistee

★2211★ **American Association of University Women, Manistee Branch**
1921 Cherny Rd.
Manistee, MI 49660
Phone: (616)723-2420
Dorothy Lundbom, Exec. Officer
Description: Women graduates of regionally accredited four year colleges and universities. Works for the advancement of women through advocacy and emphasis on lifelong learning. Honors local high school women graduating with a grade point average of 3.5 or better. **Affiliated with:** American Association of University Women; American Association of University Women, Michigan Division.

Marshall

★2212★ **American Association of University Women, Marshall Branch**
c/o Patrice Elms
140 River Park Dr.
Marshall, MI 49068
Phone: (616)781-8344
Patrice Elms, Exec. Officer
Description: Women graduates of regionally accredited four year colleges and universities. Works for the advancement of women through advocacy and emphasis on lifelong learning. Offers scholarships. **Affiliated with:** American Association of University Women.

Marysville

★2213★ **Marysville Women's Club**
125 Cuttle Rd., B-10
Marysville, MI 48040
Phone: (313)364-5675
Betty Ann Trumble, Pres.
Description: Women's volunteer service club. Sponsors civic, intellectual, and social activities.

Works towards city beautification. Awards music and tuition scholarships.

Midland

★2214★ **Michigan Women's Bowling Association**
PO Box 1705
Midland, MI 48641-1705
Phone: (517)631-7260
Shirley Thomas, Exec.Sec.
Description: Women bowlers and women's bowling organizations. Conducts state bowling tournament. Holds three board meetings per year.

Milan

★2215★ **Milan Woman's Club**
390 Everett
Milan, MI 48160
Phone: (313)439-1619
Nina Pemberton, Pres.
Description: Women's volunteer service club. **Affiliated with:** General Federation of Women's Clubs.

Mt. Clemens

★2216★ **American Association of University Women, Utica Branch**
c/o Catherine Barlow
19383 Briarwood Dr.
Mt. Clemens, MI 48043
Phone: (313)463-7838
Catherine Barlow, Exec. Officer
Description: Women graduates of regionally accredited four year colleges and universities. Works for the advancement of women through advocacy and emphasis on lifelong learning. **Affiliated with:** American Association of University Women.

★2217★ **Michigan Coalition Against Domestic Violence**
PO Box 463100
Mt. Clemens, MI 48046
Phone: (313)954-1180
Carol Sullivan, Contact

★2218★ **Otsikita Council of Girl Scouts**
42804 Garfield
Mt. Clemens, MI 48044
Phone: (313)263-0220
Peggy Beach, Exec.Dir.
Description: To promote positive character development, good conduct, and patriotism in girls who live in Macomb County, MI. **Affiliated with:** Girl Scouts of the U.S.A.

Northville

★2219★ **Michigan ERAmerica**
PO Box 434
Northville, MI 48167
Phone: (313)420-3270
Harriet B. Sawyer, Chair
Description: Interested individuals and organizations. Works to obtain the passage and ratification of the Equal Rights Amendment.

Owosso

★2220★ Young Women's Christian Association of Shiawassee County
621 W. Oliver St.
Owosso, MI 48867
Phone: (517)725-2136
Sherry Kewish, Exec.Dir.

Description: Seeks to develop and improve the spiritual, social, mental, and physical life of women and girls over the age of 12. Sponsors classes, childcare, and seminars. **Affiliated with:** Young Women's Christian Association of United States of America.

Pigeon

★2221★ General Federation of Women's Clubs, Huron County
c/o Marie Leipprandt
7107 Dunn Rd.
Pigeon, MI 48755-9735
Marie Leipprandt, Contact

Description: Women's clubs in Huron County, MI.

Plymouth

★2222★ Woman's Club of Plymouth
PO Box 670
Plymouth, MI 48170
Phone: (313)453-5925
Joyce Roebuck, Pres.

Description: Individuals who work to contribute to the community. Provides civic funds through benefit programs. Awards academic scholarships.

Pontiac

★2223★ Young Women's Christian Association of Pontiac-North Oakland
269 W. Huron
Pontiac, MI 48053
Phone: (313)334-0973

Description: Seeks to develop and improve the spiritual, social, mental, and physical life of women and girls over the age of 12. **Affiliated with:** Young Women's Christian Association of the United States of America.

Rochester

★2224★ Chi Upsilon Sorority
c/o Stephan Edens
49 Oakland Center
Rochester, MI 48309-0000
Stephan Edens, Contact

Description: Promotes scholarship and fellowship among members.

★2225★ Michigan Religious Coalition for Abortion Rights
PO Box 081794
Rochester, MI 48308
Phone: (313)375-5150
Sarah Smith Redmond, Exec.Dir.

Description: Clergy and laypersons of 35 denominations and faith groups in Michigan. Works to ensure that legal abortions will remain available to women who choose that option. Sponsors public educational events. Issues publications. Conducts meetings.

Royal Oak

★2226★ Older Women's League (OWL) Royal Oak Chapter
1422 Hickory
Royal Oak, MI 48073
Phone: (313)288-3391
Viola Wagner, Contact

St. Clair Shores

★2227★ Shores Women's Club
21600 Broadway
St. Clair Shores, MI 48080
Phone: (313)777-2594
Margaret J. Sullivan, Treas.

Description: Women's volunteer service club.

St. Joseph

★2228★ Church Women United of St. Joseph
1731 Anthony Dr.
St. Joseph, MI 49085
Phone: (616)429-3580
Mrs. James D. Stark, Contact

Description: Represents women involved in the church.

★2229★ Southwestern Michigan Women's Political Coalition
2727 S. Lakeshore, No. C-12
St. Joseph, MI 49085
Phone: (616)429-9634
Dorothy Golze, Pres.

Description: Grassroots organization of elected women and men officials. Invites speakers on a monthly basis to talk to the community on controversial topics.

★2230★ Young Women's Christian Association of St. Joseph-Benton Harbor
508 Pleasant St.
St. Joseph, MI 49085
Phone: (616)983-1561

Description: Seeks to develop and improve the spiritual, social, mental, and physical life of women and girls over the age of 12. **Affiliated with:** Young Women's Christian Association of the United States of America.

Sanford

★2231★ Clare Business and Professional Women's Club
4762 Verity Ct.
Sanford, MI 48657
Phone: (517)687-5878
Marilyn Hunter, Pres.

Description: Business and professional women. To promote complete participation, equal opportunities, and economic self-sufficiency for working women. Conducts charitable activites. Promotes educational programs. **Affiliated with:** Michigan Federation of Business and Professional Women; National Federation of Business and Professional Women of the U.S.A.

Saugatuck

★2232★ Saugatuck Women's Club
PO Box 909
303 Butler
Saugatuck, MI 49453
Phone: (616)857-2484
Lillian Dalman, Pres.

Description: Women's volunteer service club.

South Haven

★2233★ American Association of University Women, South Haven
15595 76th St.
South Haven, MI 49090
Phone: (616)637-4166
Kathleen Haines, Pres.

Description: Women college graduates. Sponsors educational and cultural activities. **Affiliated with:** American Association of University Women.

Southfield

★2234★ Michigan Abortion Rights Action League
19400 W. 10 Mile Rd., Ste. 107
Southfield, MI 48075
Phone: (313)827-4550
Carol King, Exec. Officer

★2235★ Michigan Women's Political Caucus
25015 Oakbrooke Dr.
Southfield, MI 48034
Phone: (313)357-5805

★2236★ National Association of Childbearing Centers
c/o Marylou Longeway, R.N.
Providence Hospital
16001 W. 9 Mile Rd.
PO Box 2043
Southfield, MI 48075
Phone: (313)424-3919
Marylou Longeway, R.N., Dir.

Description: Provides safe alternative birth experience.

★2237★ Society of Women Engineers, Detroit Area
Lawrence Technical University
Mechanical Engineering Department
21000 W. 10 Mile Rd.
Southfield, MI 48075
Phone: (313)356-0200
Patricia Shamamy, Contact

Description: Women engineers in southern Michigan. Seeks to inform young women and others about the engineering profession; encourage women engineers to obtainhigh levels of achievement; serve as a center of information on women in engineering. **Affiliated with:** Society of Women Engineers.

★2238★ Women's Action for Nuclear Disarmament, Metropolitan Detroit
PO Box 2577
Southfield, MI 48037
Phone: (313)851-0984
Jean Prokopow, Exec. Officer

Description: Women's initiative to halt and reverse the nuclear arms race by raising public awareness and supporting nuclear disarmament activities. **Affiliated with:** Women's Action for Nuclear Disarmament.

★2239★ **Women's National Book Association, Detroit Chapter**
25343 Maplebrooke
Southfield, MI 48034
Phone: (313)577-1825
Edith Phillips, Pres.

Description: Librarians, editors, publishers, book retailers, and others in a book-related profession. Promotes the status of women in the world of books and the importance of reading. Holds three to four dinner meetings per month. **Affiliated with:** Women's National Book Association.

Swartz Creek

★2240★ **American Association of University Women, Flint Branch**
7464 Diane Ct.
Swartz Creek, MI 48473
Phone: (313)635-2186
Janet Orr, Exec. Officer

Description: Women graduates of regionally accredited four year colleges and universities. Works for the advancement of women through advocacy and emphasis on lifelong learning. **Affiliated with:** American Association of University Women.

Troy

★2241★ **Michigan Association of American Mothers**
1766 Chatham
Troy, MI 48084
Phone: (313)643-8258
Judy Ehrer, Pres.

Description: Seeks to strengthen the moral and spiritual foundations of the American family.

Twin Lake

★2242★ **Older Women's League (OWL) Muskegon Chapter**
3175 1st St.
Twin Lake, MI 49457
Phone: (616)828-6675
Mary C. Payne, Contact

Union Lake

★2243★ **Michigan Press Women**
917 Sherbrooke
Union Lake, MI 48917
Phone: (517)363-5583
Patricia Riccobono, Pres.

Description: Professional communicators organized to discuss common problems, exchange ideas, and improve professional skills. Sponsors high school journalism contest and professional journalism contest. Awards scholarships. **Affiliated with:** National Federation of Press Women.

Utica

★2244★ **General Federation of Women's Clubs, Macomb**
PO Box 604
Utica, MI 48087
Phone: (313)781-9691
Susan Roberts, Pres.

Description: Women's volunteer service club. Works with children and senior citizens. Conducts charitable activities. Participates in area festival. **Affiliated with:** General Federation of Women's Clubs; General Federation of Women's Clubs - Michigan.

Wyoming

★2245★ **Women's Overseas Service League, Grand Rapids Unit**
2207 Porter SW, No. 208
Wyoming, MI 49509
Phone: (616)532-4107
Cornelia L. Ooms, Pres.

Description: Women who served overseas with the armed services or attached services. Promotes patriotism, comradeship, and a sense of obligation. Conducts services for disabled veterans. **Affiliated with:** Women's Overseas Service League.

Minnesota

Alden

★2246★ **Minnesota Pork Council Women**
RR 1, Box 71
Alden, MN 56009
Phone: (507)265-3317

Austin

★2247★ **American Association of University Women, Austin Branch**
405 NW 5th St.
Austin, MN 55912
Phone: (507)433-9423
Leslie Albers, Pres.

Description: Women graduates of regionally accredited four year colleges and universities. Works for the advancement of women through advocacy and emphasis on lifelong learning. conducts educational programs. Awards scholarships.

★2248★ **Austin Business and Professional Women's Club**
PO Box 355
Austin, MN 55912
Phone: (507)433-6577
Jan Larson, Pres.

Description: Business and professional women. To promote complete participation, equal opportunities, and economic self-sufficiency for working women.

Brooklyn Center

★2249★ **Greater Minneapolis Girl Scout Council**
5601 Brooklyn Blvd.
Brooklyn Center, MN 55429
Phone: (612)535-4602
Fax: (612)535-7524
Kathleen C. Pickering, CEO

Description: Girls between the ages of 5-17. Seeks to inspire girls with the highest ideals of character, conduct, patriotism, and service so that they may become resourceful citizens. **Affiliated with:** Girl Scout Council of St. Croix Valley; Girl Scouts of the U.S.A.

Buffalo

★2250★ **General Federation of Women's Clubs, Buffalo**
802 S. 2nd Ave.
Buffalo, MN 55313
Phone: (612)682-2520
Flora Mohring, V.Pres.

Description: Women's volunteer service club.

Burnsville

★2251★ **American Association of University Women, Minnesota Division**
13121 Highpoint
Burnsville, MN 55337
Phone: (612)432-9769
Fax: (612)627-4280
Barbara Halweg, Pres.

Description: Women graduates of regionally accredited four year colleges and universities. Works for the advancement of women through advocacy and emphasis on lifelong learning. **Affiliated with:** American Association of University Women.

Chokio

★2252★ **Stevens County Pork Council Women**
c/o Betty Zierke
Chokio, MN 56221
Phone: (612)324-7473
Betty Zierke, Contact

Cloquet

★2253★ **Rural Women's Advocates of Carlton County**
1412 Summit Ave.
Cloquet, MN 55720-1346

Description: Supports and promotes the interests of women living in rural areas of Carlton County, MN.

Crookston

★2254★ **Minnesota Women for Agriculture**
Rte. 3, Box 54
Crookston, MN 56716
Phone: (218)926-5651
Donna Ulseth, Exec. Officer

Crystal

★2255★ Northside Mothers of Multiples
5655 Rhode Island N.
Crystal, MN 55428-3308
Description: Mothers of twins, triplets and other multiple births.

Detroit Lakes

★2256★ Detroit Lakes Women of Today
PO Box 861
Detroit Lakes, MN 56502
Phone: (218)847-8693
Ann Jenning, Dir.
Description: Women aged 21-40. Provides leadership training and promotes community service. Conducts fundraisers. **Affiliated with:** Minnesota Women of Today; United States Women of Today.

Duluth

★2257★ Association for Women in Science, Lake Superior Chapter
c/o Sabra Anderson
Coll. of Science and Engineering
University of Minnesota, Duluth
Duluth, MN 55812
Phone: (218)726-7201
Fax: (218)726-6360
Sabra Anderson, Pres.
Description: Women in the fields of science and engineering. Promotes and supports the participation of women in these fields.

Eagan

★2258★ La Leche League International, Minnesota/Dakotas
c/o Lynda G. Mader
1362 Wilderness Run Dr.
Eagan, MN 55123-1854
Phone: (612)922-4996
Lynda G. Mader, Treas.
Description: Provides support and encouragement to women who breastfeed their babies. Services include: phone counseling, up-to-date medical and practical information, and educational classes. **Affiliated with:** Le Leche League International.

Eden Prairie

★2259★ National Association of Women Business Owners
Minnesota Chapter
c/o Lariat Companies, Inc.
11800 Singletree Ln., No. 210
Eden Prairie, MN 55344
Phone: (612)943-1404
Julie Skarda, President

Edina

★2260★ Edina Women of Today
PO Box 24241
Edina, MN 55424
Phone: (612)822-6778
Heather Southam, Pres.
Description: Women's community service organization.

Eveleth

★2261★ Eveleth United Methodist Women
204 Adams Ave.
Eveleth, MN 55734
Phone: (218)744-2802
Alice Nettell, Pres.
Description: Women from the United Methodist Church and other interested individuals working together to create a supportive fellowship. Works to expand the concept of mission by participation in global church ministries. Encourages involvement in the church and community.

Faribault

★2262★ Daughters of Isabella Faribault Council
111 SW 2nd St.
Faribault, MN 55021
Phone: (507)332-7674
Helen Hanegraaf, Regent
Description: Fraternal society of Catholic women who emulate the accomplishments and virtues of Queen Isabella (1451-1504, ruler of Aragon and Castile). Conducts charitable activities. **Affiliated with:** Daughters of Isabella; Our Lady of Victory Circle 559.

Forest Lake

★2263★ St. Croix Valley Mothers of Multiples
10860 191st St., N.
Marine on St. Croix
Forest Lake, MN 55047
Phone: (612)433-3050
Betty Houdek, V.Pres.
Description: Mothers of multiple birth children from Centerville, Chisago, Forest Lake, Hugo, Lino Lakes, Marine On St. Croix, North Branch, Scandia, and Wyoming, MN. Dedicated to help others with raising the children. Serves as a forum to exchange ideas. Holds semiannual clothing exchanges; conducts charitable programs.

Golden Valley

★2264★ Minnesota Korean Women's Association
c/o Yun C. Huffman
5126 Minnaqua Dr.
Golden Valley, MN 55422-4014
Description: Korean-American women united for mutual support.

Hastings

★2265★ Daughters of Isabella Hastings Chapter
1517 Tyler St.
Hastings, MN 55033
Phone: (612)437-3784
Alice O'Connor, Red.Sec.
Description: Fraternal society of Catholic women who seek to emulate the accomplishments and virtues of Queen Isabella (1451-1504, ruler of Aragon and Castile). Affiliated with Daughters of Isabella, International Circle.

Lake Elmo

★2266★ Indigenous Women's Network
PO Box 174
Lake Elmo, MN 55042-0174
Description: Works to improve the position of women in society.

Mankato

★2267★ Sociologists for Women in Society, Mankato Chapter
c/o Barb Keating
Mankato State University
Department of Sociology
Box 49
Mankato, MN 56001
Phone: (507)388-6360
Barb Keating, Contact

Minneapolis

★2268★ Abortion Rights Council of Minnesota
3255 Hennepin Ave., #227
Minneapolis, MN 55408
Phone: (612)827-5827
Lee Roper-Batker, Exec. Officer

★2269★ American Woman's Society of Certified Public Accountants of Minnesota
PO Box 2642
Minneapolis, MN 55402
Phone: (612)475-3383
Betsy O'Berry, Pres.
Description: Women CPAs. Promotes leadership development and networking. **Affiliated with:** American Woman's Society of Certified Public Accountants.

★2270★ Birth Community
PO Box 6207
Minneapolis, MN 55406
Phone: (612)426-8880

★2271★ Calliope Women's Chorus
3211 35th Ave. S.
Minneapolis, MN 55406-2115
Description: Women in Minneapolis who promote and perform choral music.

★2272★ DES Action
Box 3102, Butler Quarter Sta.
Minneapolis, MN 55403

★2273★ Electrical Women's RoundTable, North Central Chapter
c/o Janice R. Wallraff
Northern States Power Co.
414 Nicollet Mall
Minneapolis, MN 55401
Phone: (612)330-5529
Janice R. Wallraff, Chwm.

★2274★ Harmony Women's Fund
PO Box 300105
Minneapolis, MN 55403
Phone: (612)377-8431
Marilyn Crawford, Contact

★2275★ Minnesota NARAL
3255 Hennepin Ave., No. 227
Minneapolis, MN 55408
Phone: (612)827-5827
Lisa Goodman, Contact

★2276★ Minnesota Women's Center
University Counseling Services
192 Pillsbury Dr., SE
5 Eddy Hall
Minneapolis, MN 55455
Phone: (612)625-2874
Kevin Nutter, Contact
Founded: 1960. **Description:** Offers counseling based on a full understanding of issues affecting women.

★2277★ Minnesota Women's Fund
Foshay Tower, Ste. A 200
821 Marquette Ave.
Minneapolis, MN 55402
Phone: (612)339-7343
Sharon Chapman, Manager

★2278★ Woodswomen
25 W. Diamond Lake Rd.
Minneapolis, MN 55419
Phone: (612)822-3809
Denise Mitten, Exec.Dir.
Description: Women of all ages interested in outdoor activities.

Minnetonka

★2279★ Feminists for Life of Minnesota
16309 Pine St.
Minnetonka, MN 55345
Phone: (612)935-2887
Kay Castonguay, Pres.
Description: Men and women united to secure the right-to-life, from conception to natural death. Seeks to eliminate sexism, injustice, and violence within our society. Conducts fundraising activities on behalf of crisis pregnancy centers. **Affiliated with:** Feminists for Life of America.

Rochester

★2280★ Rochester Women of Today
c/o Becky Nelson
PO Box 6792
Rochester, MN 55903-6792

St. Louis Park

★2281★ Upper Midwest Women's History Center for Teachers
c/o Susan Hill Gross
6300 Walker St.
St. Louis Park, MN 55416

St. Paul

★2282★ American Business Women's Association, Key Wakota Chapter
1202 Niles Ave.
St. Paul, MN 55116
Phone: (612)699-9140
Dolores Sullivan, Pres.
Description: Working women and men from Dakota, Ramsey, and Washington counties, MN. Works to advance women in the work force. Sponsors scholarships. Holds social events. **Affiliated with:** American Business Women's Association; American Business Women's Association, Twin City Council.

★2283★ Human Life Alliance of Minnesota
3570 N. Lexington Ave., Ste. 301
St. Paul, MN 55126
Phone: (612)484-1040
Marlene Reid, Pres.
Description: Individuals seeking to "restore legal protection to the unborn and protect the disabled, elderly, and vulnerable". Lobbies congress. Promotes "action through education, political action, and alternatives to violence in order to create a society in which all human life is held sacred". Conducts seminars.

★2284★ League of Women Voters of Minnesota
550 Rice St., Ste.201
St. Paul, MN 55103
Phone: (612)224-5445
Kay Erickson, President

★2285★ Minnesota Coalition for Battered Women
Physicians Plaza, Ste. 201
570 Asbury St.
St. Paul, MN 55104
Phone: (612)646-6177
Marcia Frey, Dir.

★2286★ Minnesota Women's Campaign Fund
550 Rice St., Ste. 206
St. Paul, MN 55103
Phone: (612)222-1603
Tracy Whitehead, Chair

★2287★ Minnesota Women's Consortium
550 Rice St.
St. Paul, MN 55103
Phone: (612)228-0338
Gloria Griffin, Coordinator
Founded: 1981. **Description:** Consortium represents 155 member organizations dealing with women's issues and rights; serves as a resource center for members and general public. **Publications:** *Capitol Bulletin*, a weekly newsletter and *Legislative Reporter*, a weekly newsletter covering women's issues in local, state, and federal government.

★2288★ Older Women's League (OWL) Minnesota Chapter
550 Rice St.
St. Paul, MN 55103
Phone: (612)228-9990
Toni Tschann, Contact

★2289★ WARM: A Women's Collective Art Space
2402 University Ave. W., 2nd Fl.
St. Paul, MN 54114
Phone: (612)649-0059
Robin Madrid, Coordinator
Description: A nonprofit collective dedicated to improving the visibility of women artists, facilitating women's artistic careers, and educating the public on the historical and contemporary contributions of women artists. Provides exhibition space for members of the collective and visiting artists, houses a slide registry open to all Minnesota women's artists, and sponsors an annual Minnesota women juried exhibition. WARM also has slide/tape educational packages about women artists, past and present, for rental. **Membership:** 40; 200 supporting and associate members. **Publications:** Journal of art reviews, poetry, and feminist essays.

★2290★ Women Historians of the Midwest
PO Box 8138, Como Station
St. Paul, MN 55108
Phone: (612)649-0059
Description: Historians and scholars interested in promoting women's history in Iowa, Minnesota, and Wisconsin. Holds history programs.

★2291★ Women's Transportation Seminar, Twin Cities Chapter
PO Box 65794
St. Paul, MN 55165-0794
Phone: (612)298-2907
Fax: (612)223-8003
Terrie Williams, Pres.
Description: Professional planners, engineers, managers in the transportation industry, and others in the Minneapolis-St. Paul, MN area. Promotes professional and educational development of transportation professionals. Offers programs on transportation issues, projects, key legislation, and tours. Sponsors fundraising activities; makes available job bank services. Awards scholarship. **Affiliated with:** Women's Transportation Seminar.

Sauk Rapids

★2292★ Sauk Rapids Women of Today
PO Box 123
Sauk Rapids, MN 56379
Phone: (612)253-8627
Connie Ness, Pres.
Description: Women between the ages of 18-40. Provides leadership training and community service. **Affiliated with:** United States Women of Today.

White Bear Lake

★2293★ White Bear Lake Business & Professional Women's Club
2551 Sumac Circle
White Bear Lake, MN 55110
Phone: (612)773-0937
Evelyn Staus, Pres.
Description: Business and professional women. To promote complete participation, equal opportunities, and economic self-sufficiency for working women. **Affiliated with:** Minnesota Federation of Business and Professional Women's Clubs.

Mississippi

Cleveland

★2294★ Women Band Directors National Association, Mississippi Chapter
Rte. 1, Box 521
Cleveland, MS 38732
Phone: (601)843-2019
Hanna Cook, Pres.
Description: Female band directors. Provides support to women entering the field and service to entire music education field. Maintains scholarship fund for prospective instrumental music students. Sells t-shirts to raise funds. **Affiliated with:** Women Band Directors National Association.

Greenville

★2295★ American Association of University Women, Mississippi Division
1821 S. Main Ext.
Greenville, MS 38701
Phone: (601)335-5972
Juanita Gray, Pres.
Description: Women graduates of regionally accredited four year colleges and universities. Works for the advancement of women through advocacy and emphasis on lifelong learning. **Affiliated with:** American Association of University Women.

Jackson

★2296★ League of Women Voters of Mississippi
PO Box 55505
Jackson, MS 39296-5505
Phone: (601)352-4616
Barbara Powell, President

★2297★ Mississippi Federation of Women's Club
2407 N. State St.
Jackson, MS 39216
Phone: (601)875-4139
Mary G. Arndt, Pres.
Description: Women's clubs. Promote civic and community improvement and involvement.

★2298★ Southern Coalition for Educational Equity
PO Box 22904
Jackson, MS 39225
Phone: (601)355-7398
Winifred Green, Pres.
Description: Coalition of parents, students, teachers, and administrators that operates in Alabama, Georgia, Louisiana, Mississippi, and North Carolina, with plans to include eight additional states. Works toward developing more efficient educational programs and eliminating racism and sexism within southern schools. Has organized projects including: New Orleans Effective Schools Project, which attempts to increase school effectiveness through high expectations, stressing academic achievement, and quality instruction; Project MiCRO, which seeks to provide computer access for, and sharpen analytical skills of, minority students; Summer Program, which focuses on students' reading comprehension skills.

Pascagoula

★2299★ Business and Professional Women's Club of Pascagoula
PO Box 521
Pascagoula, MS 39568-7255
Phone: (601)762-7255
Linda Towns Eiland, Pres.
Description: Business and professional women. To promote complete participation, equal opportunities, and economic self-sufficiency for working women. National Federation of Business and Professional Women's Clubs of the U.S.A.

Sallis

★2300★ Attala County Lady Landowner League
c/o Virginia Robertson
Rt. 4
Sallis, MS 39160
Phone: (601)289-2791
Virginia Robertson, Pres.
Description: Women landowners interested in land management and litter control.

★2301★ National Council of Negro Women, Kosciusko-Attala Section
Rt. 1, Box 131
Sallis, MS 39160
Phone: (601)289-6016
Virginia Clark, Pres.
Description: Black women in central Mississippi. Seeks to improve quality of life for black women, their families, and their communities. Sponsors annual Fall Tea. **Affiliated with:** National Council of Negro Women.

Missouri

Blue Springs

★2302★ Lake Tapawingo Women's Club
c/o Joyce Maggard
Box 104, 64A
Lake Tapawingo
Blue Springs, MO 64015
Phone: (816)229-1300
Joyce Maggard, Pres.
Description: Community service organization. Offers scholarship loans; conducts charitable activities.

Clarksdale

★2303★ Missouri Pork Council Women
PO Box 115
Clarksdale, MO 64430
Phone: (314)456-2168
Dixie Crider, Pres.
Description: Pork producers and associate persons organized to promote the industry.

Clayton

★2304★ DES Action
7647 Carswold
Clayton, MO 63105

Gravois Mills

★2305★ American Business Women's Association, Ozark Paradise Chapter
Rt. 1, Box 992
Gravois Mills, MO 65037
Bernice Kleindienst, Exec. Officer
Description: Women in business, including women owning or operating their own businesses, women in professions, and women employed in any level of government, education, or retailing, manufacturing, and service companies. Bestows scholarships. **Affiliated with:** American Business Women's Association.

Hannibal

★2306★ Oakwood Women's Club
c/o Marie Allen
4924 Paies Gravel Rd.
Hannibal, MO 63401
Phone: (314)221-2594
Marie Allen, Pres.
Description: Women's volunteer service club. **Affiliated with:** General Federation of Women's Clubs.

Harrisonville

★2307★ Harrisonville Business and Professional Women's Club
PO Box 382
Harrisonville, MO 64701
Phone: (816)884-4850
Mary Parker, Pres.
Description: Business and professional women. To promote complete participation, equal opportunities, and economic self-sufficiency for working women.

Houston

★2308★ Girl Scouts of the U.S.A., Houston Council
444 S. Hwy. 63
PO Box 276
Houston, MO 65483
Phone: (417)967-3915
Gayla Bratton, Organizer
Description: Girls aged five to 17 years in Houston, Licking, Raymondville, and Success, MO. Service organization. **Affiliated with:** Dogwood Trails Girl Scouts Council; Girl Scouts of the U.S.A.

Jefferson City

★2309★ Missouri Coalition Against Domestic Violence
311 E. McCarty, No. 34
Jefferson City, MO 65101
Phone: (314)634-4161
Colleen Coble, Contact

Kansas City

★2310★ Association of Women Lawyers of Greater Kansas City
4420 Madison Ave.
Kansas City, MO 64111
Phone: (816)931-2700
Description: Women lawyers. Promotes the role of women in the legal profession.

★2311★ Mexican American Women's National Association - Kansas City Office
706 W. 42nd St.
Kansas City, MO 64111
Phone: (816)931-6283

★2312★ Missouri Branch of National Abortion Rights Action League
West Port Allen Center
706 W. 42nd St.
Kansas City, MO 64111
Phone: (816)531-7304

★2313★ Older Women's League (OWL)
Metro Kansas City Chapter
PO Box 10463
Kansas City, MO 64111
Phone: (816)587-0248
Janice Williams, Contact

★2314★ Young Women's Christian
Association of Kansas City
1000 Charlotte St.
Kansas City, MO 64106
Phone: (816)842-7538
Eva Martin Blythe, Exec.Dir.
Description: Seeks to develop and improve the spiritual, social, mental, and physical well-being of young people and adults. **Affiliated with:** Young Women's Christian Association of the United States of America.

Kirksville

★2315★ Birthright of Kirksville
111 N. Main, Ste. 102
Kirksville, MO 63501
Phone: (816)665-5688
Nancy Darrow, Co-Dir.
Description: To assist women with problem pregnancies. Provides free pregnancy testing and maternity and baby clothing. Offers emotional support and resource referrals. **Affiliated with:** Birthright International.

Mountain Grove

★2316★ Mountain Grove Business and
Professional Women's Club
c/o Karen Rogers
R.R. No. 2, Box 185G
Mountain Grove, MO 65711
Phone: (417)926-3207
Karen Rogers, Sec. & Dir.
Description: Business and professional women. To promote complete participation, equal opportunities, and economic self-sufficiency for working women.

St. Joseph

★2317★ Young Women's Christian
Association of St. Joseph
304 N. 8th St.
St. Joseph, MO 64501
Phone: (816)232-4481
Description: Seeks to develop and improve the spiritual, social, mental, and physical well-being of young people and adults. Operates: shelter for abused women; rape crisis center; child day care facility. **Affiliated with:** Young Men's Christian Association of the United States of America.

St. Louis

★2318★ Home Birth Support Group
PO Box 23924
St. Louis, MO 63119
Phone: (314)962-3051
Barb Roussin, Dir.
Description: Parents in eastern Missouri preparing for home birth or who have had home births. Provides members with information necessary to having a successful home birth. Offers referrals; maintains library. **Affiliated with:** International Association of Parents and Professionals for Safe Alternatives in Childbirth.

★2319★ League of Women Voters of
Missouri
6665 Delmar, Rm. 304
St. Louis, MO 63130
Phone: (314)727-8674
Elaine Blodgett, President

★2320★ Missouri Abortion Rights Action
League
393 N. Euclid, No. 310
St. Louis, MO 63108
Phone: (314)367-9680
Laura Cohen, Contact

★2321★ Missouri Women's Action Fund
1108 Hillside Dr.
St. Louis, MO 63117
Phone: (314)781-1081
Vivian Eveloff, First Vice-Chair

★2322★ Missouri Women's Network
138 Kings
St. Louis, MO 63034
Phone: (314)966-7518
Shirley Breeze, Chairperson
Description: Women's organizations united to promote and improve the status of women in employment, education, health, child care and reproductive rights, and public office. Other areas of interest include child support, teenage pregnancy, domestic violence, and the Equal Rights Amendment.

★2323★ National Association of Women
Business Owners
St. Louis Chapter
c/o EBS Properties
1247 Hampton Park Dr.
St. Louis, MO 63117
Phone: (314)647-9464
Brenda Stedronsky, President

★2324★ National Association of Women
Judges
U.S. Coast Guard
1430 Olive St.
St. Louis, MO 63103
Phone: (314)773-1724
Rosemary Denson, Exec. Officer

★2325★ Older Women's League (OWL)
Gateway St. Louis Chapter
4533 Moonglow
St. Louis, MO 63128
Phone: (314)892-1255
Bea Renna, Contact

★2326★ Religious Coalition for Abortion
Rights, Missouri Chapter
8129 Dolmar, Ste. 208
St. Louis, MO 63130
Phone: (314)721-2446
Anne Cox, Exec. Officer

★2327★ Young Women's Christian
Association of Metropolitan St. Louis
4232 Forest Park, No. 204
St. Louis, MO 63108
Phone: (314)531-1115
Fax: (314)531-5008
Marilyn Robinson, CEO
Description: Seeks to develop and improve the spiritual, social, mental, and physical well-being of young people and adults. **Affiliated with:** Young Women's Christian Association of the United States of America.

Washington

★2328★ Washington Federated Republican
Women's Club
820 Camp St.
Washington, MO 63090
Phone: (314)239-4208
Joy Gerstein, Exec. Officer

Montana

Billings

★2329★ Young Women's Christian
Association of Billings
909 Wyoming Ave.
Billings, MT 59101
Phone: (406)252-6303
Description: Seeks to develop and improve the spiritual, social, mental, and physical well-being of young people and adults. **Affiliated with:** Young Women's Christian Association of the United States of America.

Bozeman

★2330★ League of Women Voters of
Montana
5555 Black Bear Rd.
Bozeman, MT 59715
Jenny Younger, President

★2331★ Montana Coalition Against
Domestic Violence
PO Box 5096
Bozeman, MT 59715
Phone: (406)586-7689
Kate McInnerny, Contact

Corvallis

★2332★ Ravalli County Democratic
Women
877 McWilliams Dr.
Corvallis, MT 59828
Phone: (406)961-4683
Mildred Sullivan, Pres.
Description: Works to elect Democrats to local, state, and national office.

★2333★ Ravalli County Republican
Women
1050 Coal Pit Rd.
Corvallis, MT 59828
Phone: (406)961-4283
Marion B. Deeths, Pres.
Description: Supports Republican projects and campaigns for public office. **Affiliated with:** Montana State Republican Women. Provides public education.

Dillon

★2334★ La Leche League International,
Dillon Chapter
510 Monroe
Dillon, MT 59725
Phone: (406)683-4034
Mary Karlsgodt, Exec. Officer
Description: Women with babies, women expecting babies, and health professionals. Promotes breastfeeding through education and distribution of educational materials. **Affiliated with:** La Leche League International; La Leche League of Montana.

Great Falls

★2335★ Young Women's Christian Association of Great Falls
220 Second St., North
Great Falls, MT 59401
Phone: (406)452-1315

Description: Seeks to develop and improve the spiritual, social, mental, and physical well-being of young people and adults. **Affiliated with:** Young Women's Christian Association of the United States of America.

Hamilton

★2336★ Hamilton Women's Club
395 Zimmerman Ln.
Hamilton, MT 59840
Phone: (406)363-4167
Dorothy Boaska, Pres.

Description: Community service organization. Sponsors charitable activities. **Affiliated with:** National Federation of Women's Clubs; State of Montana Women's Clubs.

Helena

★2337★ American Association of University Women, Montana Chapter
Box 5731
Helena, MT 59604
Phone: (406)444-6576
Claudette Morton, Pres.

★2338★ Lewis and Clark Republican Women's Club
PO Box 9192
Helena, MT 59604
Phone: (406)442-6483
Dorothea Neath, Pres.

Description: Women members of the Republican party. Works to elect Republicans to local, state, and national office. Promotes increased female representation in government. Voices the principles of liberty, freedom, and equality. **Affiliated with:** National Federation of Republican Women.

★2339★ Montanas for Choice/National Abortion Rights Action League
PO Box 279
Helena, MT 59624
Phone: (406)443-0276
Jan Lombardi, Contact

Livingston

★2340★ American Baptist Women, Livingston Chapter
202 East Lewis
Livingston, MT 59047
Phone: (406)222-1603
Edna I. Lanning, Pres.

Description: Women affiliated with the local Baptist church of Livingston, MT. Supports the mission of the Baptist faith and works to unite the women of the church community. **Affiliated with:** American Baptist Women.

Missoula

★2341★ Montana Women's History Project
University of Montana
Mansfield Library
Missoula, MT 59812
Phone: (406)243-4153

Description: Offers oral histories, tapes, video programs, speakers.

★2342★ Young Women's Christian Association of Missoula
1130 West Broadway
Missoula, MT 59802
Phone: (406)543-6691

Description: Seeks to develop and improve the spiritual, social, mental, and physical well-being of young people and adults. **Affiliated with:** Young Women's Christian Association of the United States of America.

Nebraska

Alliance

★2343★ American Association of University Women, Alliance Branch
1011 Mississippi Ave.
Alliance, NE 69301
Phone: (308)762-4284
Carol Phipps, Pres.

Description: Women graduates of regionally accredited four year colleges and universities. Works for the advancement of women through advocacy and emphasis on lifelong learning. **Affiliated with:** American Association of University Women.

Battle Creek

★2344★ Norfolk Woman's Club
204 Highland Dr.
Battle Creek, NE 68715
Phone: (402)675-7265
Norma Cole, Exec. Officer

Description: To improve educational, civic, and social standing for women. **Affiliated with:** General Federation of Women's Clubs.

Beatrice

★2345★ Young Women's Christian Association of Beatrice
PO Box 126
405 N. 5th
Beatrice, NE 68310
Phone: (402)223-5314

Description: Seeks to develop and improve the spiritual, social, mental, and physical well-being of young people and adults. **Affiliated with:** Young Women's Christian Association of the United States of America.

Columbus

★2346★ Twice Blessed Mothers of Twins Club
675 Louis Pl.
Columbus, NE 68601
Cindy Hoadley, Exec.Sec.

Description: Support group for mothers of twins in the Midwest.

Falls City

★2347★ Falls City General Women's Club
1717 Valley
Falls City, NE 68355
Mrs. Ralph Seward, Contact

Description: Women's volunteer service club. **Affiliated with:** National Federated Women's Club.

Gering

★2348★ American Association of University Women, Scottsbluff Branch
1700 Beverly Blvd.
Gering, NE 69341
Phone: (308)436-5291
Wanda Mowry, Pres.

Description: Women graduates of regionally accredited colleges living in Scotts Bluff County, NE; colleges, universities, and two-year or community colleges. Works for advancement of women through advocacy and emphasis on lifelong learning. **Affiliated with:** American Association of University Women.

Grand Island

★2349★ Young Women's Christian Association of Grand Island
234 E. 3rd St.
Grand Island, NE 68801
Phone: (308)384-8170
Linda Stanislav, Contact

Description: Seeks to develop and improve the spiritual, social, mental, and physical well-being of young people and adults. **Affiliated with:** Young Women's Christian Association of the United States of America.

Hastings

★2350★ Young Women's Christian Association of Adams County
604 N. St. Joseph
Hastings, NE 68901
Phone: (402)462-8821

Description: Seeks to develop and improve the spiritual, social, mental, and physical well-being of young people and adults. **Affiliated with:** Young Women's Christian Association of the United States of America.

Lincoln

★2351★ League of Women Voters of Nebraska
808 P St., Ste. 207
Lincoln, NE 68508
Phone: (402)475-1411
Karren Kerr, President

★2352★ Nebraska Domestic Violence and Sexual Assault Coalition
1630 K St., Ste. H
Lincoln, NE 68508
Phone: (402)476-6256
Sarah O'Shea, Contact

★2353★ **Nebraska Religious Coalition for Abortion Rights**
PO Box 6043
Lincoln, NE 68506
Phone: (402)488-5625
Shirley Marsh, Chairperson

Description: Supports legal abortion information and services. Conducts lobbying activities; operates speakers' bureau. Provides Clergy Counsel Referral Service for pregnant women. **Affiliated with:** Pro-Choice Coalition; Religious Coalition for Abortion Rights.

★2354★ **Older Women's League (OWL)**
Lincoln Chapter
7120 Eastborough Ln.
Lincoln, NE 68505
Phone: (402)483-5585
Beth Higer, Contact

★2355★ **Young Women's Christian Association of Lincoln**
1432 N St.
Lincoln, NE 68508
Phone: (402)476-2802
Cathy Kushner, Contact

Description: Seeks to develop and improve the spiritual, social, mental, and physical well-being of young people and adults. **Affiliated with:** Young Women's Christian Association of the United States of America.

Minden

★2356★ **Minden Federated Woman's Club**
c/o Carol King
Rte. 1
Minden, NE 68959
Phone: (308)833-2361
Carol King, Contact

Description: Women's volunteer service club. **Affiliated with:** Nebraska Federation of Women's Clubs.

Norfolk

★2357★ **Norfolk Business and Professional Women's Club**
412 Ridgeway
Norfolk, NE 68701
Phone: (402)379-4390
Mary Meyer, Pres.

Description: Business and professional women. To promote complete participation, equal opportunities, and economic self-sufficiency for working women. Sponsors Women's Issues Resource Center; makes available scholarship.

Omaha

★2358★ **American Business Women's Association, Triple Crown Chapter**
4730 S. 52nd
Omaha, NE 68117
Phone: (402)733-3856
Helen Ryan, Pres.

Description: Women in business, including women owning or operating their own businesses, women in professions, and women employed in any level of government, education, or retailing, manufacturing, and service companies. **Affiliated with:** American Business Women's Association.

★2359★ **Executive Women International, Omaha Chapter**
Maenner Company
444 Regency Circle Park Dr.
Omaha, NE 68114
Phone: (402)393-3200
Shari Fredrickson, Pres.

★2360★ **Omaha Business and Professional Women**
5929 S. 151st St.
Omaha, NE 68137
Phone: (402)896-1597
Gail M. Formanack, Pres.

Description: Business and professional women. To promote complete participation, equal opportunities, and economic self-sufficiency for working women. Conducts seminars. **Affiliated with:** National Federation of Business and Professional Women's Clubs of the U.S.A.

★2361★ **Young Women's Christian Association of Omaha**
222 S. 29th St.
Omaha, NE 68131
Phone: (402)345-6555

Description: Seeks to develop and improve the spiritual, social, mental, and physical well-being of young people and adults. **Affiliated with:** Young Women's Christian Association of the United States of America.

Osceola

★2362★ **American Association of University Women, Nebraska Division**
PO Box 257
Osceola, NE 68651
Phone: (402)747-2672
Barbara Griffith, Pres.

Description: Graduates of regionally accredited colleges; colleges, universities, and two year or community colleges. Works for advancement of women through advocacy and emphasis on lifelong learning. **Affiliated with:** American Association of University Women.

Plattsmouth

★2363★ **American Business Women's Association, Heritage Hills Chapter**
412 S. 8th St.
PO Box 88
Plattsmouth, NE 68048
Phone: (402)296-2871
Mildred Buethe, Exec. Officer

Description: Women in business, including women owning or operating their own businesses, women in professions, and women employed in any level of government, education, or retailing, manufacturing, and service companies. **Affiliated with:** American Business Women's Association.

Scottsbluff

★2364★ **Compassionate Friends, Nebraska Panhandle Chapter**
PO Box 1101
Scottsbluff, NE 69361
Phone: (308)632-4039
Richard and Linda Landrigan, Exec. Officers

Description: Self-help organization for parents who have experienced the death of a child. **Affiliated with:** Compassionate Friends.

Sidney

★2365★ **La Leche League International, Western Nebraska Chapter**
Rte. 1, Box 16
Sidney, NE 69162
Phone: (308)254-3313
Barbara Mock, Contact

Description: Support group in the Nebraska Panhandle area for breastfeeding mothers.

Nevada

Hawthorne

★2366★ **Mineral County Advocates to End Domestic Violence**
c/o Clydell G. Wert
PO Box 331
Hawthorne, NV 89415-0331
Clydell G. Wert, Contact

Description: Works to prevent domestic violence; assists domestic violence victims.

Las Vegas

★2367★ **Association for Women in Science, Southern Nevada Chapter**
c/o Dr. Delyle E.wood
Lockheed, Ste. 301
1050 E. Flamingo
Las Vegas, NV 89119
Phone: (702)734-3287

Description: Works to improve education and employment opportunities for women in the sciences.

★2368★ **League of Women Voters of Nevada**
1874 Camino Verde Ln.
Las Vegas, NV 89119
Susan J. Petz, President

★2369★ **National Association of Women Business Owners**
Northern Nevada Chapter
c/o Beckley, Singleton, Delanoy
3070 S. Tioga
Las Vegas, NV 89117
Phone: (702)598-3133
Patricia Brown, President

McGill

★2370★ **American Association of University Women, Nevada Chapter**
PO Box 1075
McGill, NV 89318
Phone: (702)289-1460
Sharron R. Oleson, Pres.

Reno

★2371★ **Executive Women International, Reno Chapter**
c/o Harrah's Reno
PO Box 10
Reno, NV 89520
Phone: (702)788-2619
Fax: (702)788-3705
Carol Barton, Pres.

Description: Business women united to promote networking. Awards scholarships. **Affiliated with:** Executive Women International.

★2372★ **Nevada Women's Fund**
PO Box 50428
Reno, NV 89513
Phone: (702)786-2335
Fritsi H. Ericson, Exec. Vice Pres.

★2373★ **Young Women's Christian Association of Reno-Sparks**
1301 Valley Rd.
Reno, NV 89512
Phone: (702)322-4531

Description: Seeks to develop and improve the spiritual, social, mental, and physical well-being of young people and adults. **Affiliated with:** Young Women's Christian Association of the United States of America.

Sparks

★2374★ **Nevada Network Against Domestic Violence**
2100 Capurro Way, Ste. 21-1
Sparks, NV 89431
Phone: (702)746-2700
Toll-free: 800-992-5757

New Hampshire

Claremont

★2375★ **Claremont Women's Republican Club**
39 Myrtle St.
Claremont, NH 03743
Phone: (603)542-8050
Mrs. G. L. Walsemann, Exec. Officer

Description: Seeks to elect Republican candidates to local, state, and national offices.

Concord

★2376★ **League of Women Voters of New Hampshire**
207 N. Main St.
Concord, NH 03301
Phone: (603)225-5344
Ginger Culpepper, President

★2377★ **National Abortion Rights Action League of New Hampshire**
30 S. Main St.
Concord, NH 03301
Phone: (603)228-1224
Peg Dobbie, Contact

★2378★ **New Hampshire Coalition Against Domestic and Sexual Violence**
PO Box 353
Concord, NH 03302
Phone: (603)224-8893
Toll-free: 800-852-3311
Grace Mattern, Contact

★2379★ **Women's Club of Concord**
44 Pleasant St.
Concord, NH 03301
Phone: (603)224-0598
Roioli Schweiker, Pres.

Description: Retired teachers, office workers, and homemakers. Seeks to become center for social service and civic activities and to create broader fellowship among women in the community. **Affiliated with:** General Federation of Women's Clubs; New Hampshire Federation of Women's Clubs.

Durham

★2380★ **Association for Women in Science, University of New Hampshire Chapter**
c/o Judith Spiller
University of New Hampshire
Orientation Program
Huddleston Hall
Durham, NH 03824
Phone: (603)862-3979
Judith Spiller, Co-Coordinator

Description: Works to improve education and employment opportunities for women in the sciences. Acts as referral service for students on campus interested in science careers. Sponsors annual science reception. **Affiliated with:** Association for Women in Science.

East Rochester

★2381★ **Rochester Women's Club**
15 Walnut Ave.
East Rochester, NH 03868
Phone: (603)332-0519
Estelle Winkley, Pres.

Description: Women. Performs community and volunteer services. **Affiliated with:** General Federation of Women's Clubs; New Hampshire Federation of Women's Clubs.

Gilford

★2382★ **Women's Club of Lakeport**
c/o Donalda Richards
87 Sleeper Hill Rd.
Gilford, NH 03246
Phone: (603)524-1087
Donalda Richards, Pres.

Description: Women's volunteer service club.

Hanover

★2383★ **Association for Women in Science, Dartmouth Chapter**
c/o Dr. Judy Stern
Maternal Child Health & Pathology
Clinic 500
Dartmouth-Hitchcock Medical Ctr.
Hanover, NH 03755
Phone: (603)646-8218
Dr. Judy Stern, Contact

Description: Works to improve education and employment opportunities for women in the sciences.

Keene

★2384★ **Country Acres Women's Association**
c/o Fannie Guion
PO Box 193
Keene, NH 03431-0193
Fannie Guion, Contact
Description: Social organization.

★2385★ **National Women's Studies Association, New England Region**
c/o Eleanor M. Vander Haegen
Keene State College
Department of Sociology
Keene, NH 03431
Phone: (603)358-2519
Eleanor M. Vander Haegan, Coordinator

Description: Community and academic women interested in furthering women's studies. **Affiliated with:** National Women's Studies Association.

Laconia

★2386★ **Laconia Woman's Club**
176 Pleasant St.
Laconia, NH 03246
Phone: (603)524-6222
Mario Hawkins, Pres.

Description: Women's volunteer service club. Their motto is: In principal, like our granite, In Aspiration, like our mountains, In Sympathy, swift and far-reaching like our rivers. **Affiliated with:** General Federation of Women's Clubs.

Manchester

★2387★ **Birthright Counseling**
227 S. Main St.
Manchester, NH 03102-4838

Description: Seeks to help pregnant women find alternatives to abortion. Conducts childbirth education and parenting programs.

★2388★ **Girl Scouts of the U.S.A., Swiftwater Council**
88 Harvey Rd., No. 4
Manchester, NH 03103
Phone: (603)627-4158
Toll-free: 800-654-1270
Jane Behlke, Exec.Dir.

Description: Girls aged 5 to 17 and adults in New Hampshire and Vermont. Provides girls with character building activities and services. Sponsors camp. **Affiliated with:** Girl Scouts of the U.S.A.

★2389★ **Young Women's Christian Association of Manchester**
72 Concord St.
Manchester, NH 03101
Phone: (603)625-5785

Description: Seeks to develop and improve the spiritual, social, mental, and physical life of young people and adults. **Affiliated with:** Young Women's Christian Association of the United States of America.

Nashua

★2390★ **Women in Touch**
Box 3541
Nashua, NH 03061
Phone: (603)883-9228
Mona Jewell, Exec. Officer

Description: Lesbians. Promotes networking and social support in chemical free environment. Presents annual Gay and Lesbian Community Awards.

★2391★ Young Women's Christian
Association of Nashua
17 Prospect St.
Nashua, NH 03060
Phone: (603)883-3081
Description: Seeks to develop and improve the
spiritual, social, mental, and physical life of
young people and adults. Affiliated with: Young
Women's Christian Association of the United
States of America.

New London

★2392★ Women in Business of the New
London Area
PO Box 481
New London, NH 03257
Phone: (603)526-9450
Barbara M. Herbert, Contact
Description: Provides a network of resources
for businesswomen in Sullivan and Merrimack
counties, NH. Sponsors seminars, speakers,
and community projects.

Portsmouth

★2393★ Piscataqua Business and
Professional Women's Club
PO Box 5461
Portsmouth, NH 03801
Joan E. Hudson, Pres.
Description: Business and professional wom-
en. To promote complete participation, equal
opportunities, and economic self-sufficiency for
working women. Affiliated with: Federation of
Business and Professional Women's Clubs of
New Hampshire; National Federation of Busi-
ness and Professional Women's Clubs of the
U.S.A.

★2394★ Portsmouth College Women's
Club
RFD 1
276 Aldrich Rd.
Portsmouth, NH 03801
Phone: (603)436-6788
Mrs. Richard Hay, Pres.
Description: Women with college degrees in
Hampton, New Castle, Portsmouth, and Rye,
NH and Kittery and York, ME. Promotes fellow-
ship. Raises funds for high school scholarships.

★2395★ Portsmouth Women's Chorus
PO Box 234
Portsmouth, NH 03802-0234
Priscilla Stevens French, Music Dir.
Description: Women interested in vocal music.
Presents concerts in southern Maine and coast-
al areas of New Hampshire.

★2396★ Portsmouth Women's City Club
375 Middle St.
Portsmouth, NH 03801
Phone: (603)436-1228
Joan E. Hudson, Pres.
Description: Women. To establish network of
women to promote the city and state and
provide a forum for discussion. Affiliated with:
General Federation of Women's Clubs; General
Federation of Women's Clubs, New Hampshire.

New Jersey

Atlantic City

★2397★ Atlantic City Women's Chamber
of Commerce
PO Box 1397
Atlantic City, NJ 08404
Phone: (609)484-0151
Barbara Holz, Pres.
Description: Promotes business and commu-
nity development in Atlantic City, NJ. Conducts
charitable activities. Co-sponsors civic events.

Bayonne

★2398★ Young Women's Christian
Association of Bayonne
44 W. 32nd St.
Bayonne, NJ 07002
Phone: (201)339-7676
Description: Seeks to develop and improve the
spiritual, social, mental, and physical life of
young people and adults. Affiliated with: Young
Women's Christian Association of the United
States of America.

Belleville

★2399★ Essex County Women's Bowling
Association
679 Washington Ave.
Belleville, NJ 07109
Phone: (201)751-7425
Mary N. Ross, Sec.
Description: Promotes bowling in a friendly,
competitive environment. Affiliated with: Wom-
en's International Bowling Congress.

Bloomfield

★2400★ Birthright, Essex County Chapter
623 Bloomfield Ave.
Bloomfield, NJ 07003
Phone: (201)743-2061
Toll-free: 800-848-LOVE
Dorothy Zins, Dir.
Description: Housewives and nurses. To help
pregnant women carry their unborn child to a
full term. Offers assistance for crisis pregnan-
cies.

Bradley Beach

★2401★ National Association of Women
Business Owners
New Jersey Chapter
c/o Independent Insurance Planner
205 McCabe Ave.
Bradley Beach, NJ 07720
Phone: (908)988-7256
Eileen Shrem, President

Cherry Hill

★2402★ Hispanic Women's Task Force of
New Jersey
401 The Woods
Cherry Hill, NJ 08034
Phone: (609)757-6348

★2403★ National Organization for Women,
Alice Paul Chapter
PO Box 2801
Cherry Hill, NJ 08034
Phone: (609)778-8320
Judy Buckman, Contact
Description: Women and men in Burlington,
Camden, and Gloucester counties, NJ. Pro-
motes the legal, economic, and political equality
of women. Sponsors support groups for sepa-
rated and divorced women. Maintains library
and operates legal referral service.

Cinnaminson

★2404★ Coalition for Burlington County
Women
319 Parry Rd.
Cinnaminson, NJ 08077
Eleanor Peterman, Contact
Description: Women and women's organizations. Seeks to identify issues of particular
interest to women; assists women in making
use of county services.

★2405★ New Jersey Women's Political
Caucus
702 Wood Ln.
Cinnaminson, NJ 08077
Phone: (609)829-5885
Jeanne Fox, Pres.
Description: Individuals working to increase the
number of women holding political office. Con-
ducts training workshops; maintains New Jer-
sey Women's Political Caucus Political Action
Committee.

Dunellen

★2406★ Association for Women in
Science, NJS Chapter
c/o Dr. Marian Glenn
343 New Market Rd.
Dunellen, NJ 08812-1536
Description: Works to improve education and
employment opportunities for women in the
sciences.

Edison

★2407★ Women's Political Action
Committee of New Jersey (WPACNJ)
PO Box 170
Edison, NJ 08818
Phone: (908)638-6784
Patricia Connolly, President
Description: Bipartisan group of business and
professional women. Primary activity is to raise
and distribute funds to support female candidates who share the Group's goals for local,
county, and state government, including pay
parity and child care options, training, and
protection from domestic violence.

Englewood

★2408★ Girl Scouts of the U.S.A., Englewood
77 Oakland St.
Englewood, NJ 07631
Phone: (201)871-4418
Lorraine Washington, Contact

Description: Girls aged five to 18 and women volunteers. To help develop self-respect, and respect for others and the environment. Promotes good citizenship and community awareness. **Affiliated with:** Girl Scout Council of Bergen County.

Ft. Lee

★2409★ DES Action
Box 762
Ft. Lee, NJ 07024

Freehold

★2410★ Birthright-Freehold
8 Spring St.
Freehold, NJ 07728
Phone: (201)462-2888
Claire McCarthy, Dir.

Description: Volunteers. Supports pregnant women. **Affiliated with:** Birthright International.

Hackensack

★2411★ Coalition of 100 Black Women of Bergen-Passaic New Jersey
185 Prospect Ave., No. 3R
Hackensack, NJ 07601-2210

Description: African-American professional women; promotes community improvement through social action.

★2412★ Young Women's Christian Association of Hackensack
285 Passaic St.
Hackensack, NJ 07601
Phone: (201)487-2224

Description: Seeks to develop and improve the spiritual, social, mental, and physical life of young people and adults. **Affiliated with:** Young Women's Christian Association of the United States of America.

Hackettstown

★2413★ Girl Scouts of the United States of America, Hackettstown Council
Willow Grove St.
Hackettstown, NJ 07840
Ms. Phillips, Pres.

Description: Girls ages 5 through 18 and adult volunteers. Seeks to inspire girls with the highest ideals of character, conduct, and patriotism. **Affiliated with:** Girl Scouts of the United States of America.

Haddonfield

★2414★ La Leche League International, New Jersey Chapter
766 Mt. Vernon Ave.
Haddonfield, NJ 08033
Phone: (609)795-2092
Peggy Stedman, Pres.

Description: Women who breastfeed or have breastfed their babies. Provides information, support, and encouragement to mothers who want to breastfeed their babies. **Affiliated with:** La Leche League International.

Hammonton

★2415★ Women's Civic Club of Hammonton
Broadway & Liberty Sts.
Hammonton, NJ 08037
Phone: (609)561-1780
Geraldine Caputo, Pres.

Description: Women promoting civic and charitable activities. Awards scholarships. **Affiliated with:** General Federation of Women's Clubs.

Jersey City

★2416★ Young Women's Christian Association of Jersey City
270 Fairmount Ave.
Jersey City, NJ 07306
Phone: (201)333-5700

Description: Seeks to develop and improve the spiritual, social, mental, and physical lives of young people and adults. **Affiliated with:** Young Women's Christian Association of the United States of America.

Lakewood

★2417★ Young Women's Christian Association of Lakewood and Ocean County
299 Monmouth Ave.
Lakewood, NJ 08701
Phone: (908)363-1158

Description: Seeks to develop and improve the spiritual, social, mental, and physical life of young people and adults. **Affiliated with:** Young Women's Christian Association of the United States of America.

Lindenwold

★2418★ Birthright of Lindenwold
24 N. White Horse Pike
Lindenwold, NJ 08021
Phone: (609)627-6344
Mildred Wilson, Dir.

Description: Volunteers who help pregnant women. Issues publications.

Livingston

★2419★ National Council of Jewish Women, Essex County Section
513 W. Mt. Pleasant Ave.
Livingston, NJ 07039
Phone: (201)740-0588
Marsha Atkind, Pres.

Description: Participates in policy making, resolutions, and programming decisions. Sponsors community service projects and programs for the elderly, developmentally disabled children, and others. **Affiliated with:** National Council of Jewish Women.

Lodi

★2420★ Italian American Woman's Forum of Lodi
PO Box 872
Lodi, NJ 07644-0872

Description: Promotes appreciation of Italian history and culture.

Maplewood

★2421★ Essex County National Organization for Women
Box 201
Maplewood, NJ 07040
Phone: (201)761-4479

Description: Individuals advocating for equal rights of women and ending sex discrimination. **Affiliated with:** National Organization for Women; National Organization for Women, New Jersey.

Merchantville

★2422★ Merchantville Woman's Club
Community Center of Merchantsville
Somerset Ave. and Greenwich Ct.
Merchantville, NJ 08109
Phone: (609)727-4902
Elvie Chvilz, Pres.

Description: Women's volunteer service club.

Middletown

★2423★ Women's Club of Middletown
34 Michael Dr.
Middletown, NJ 07701
Phone: (201)671-1285
Mary G. Powell, Pres.

Description: Community service organization of women over the age of 35. Awards scholarships for women going back to school and to the Rainbow Foundation.

Montclair

★2424★ American Association of University Women, Montclair Chapter
26 Warren Pl.
Montclair, NJ 07042
Phone: (201)509-0461
Sheryl King Lazzarotti, Pres.

Description: Women graduates of regionally accredited four year colleges and universities. Works for the advancement of women through advocacy and emphasis on lifelong learning. **Affiliated with:** American Association of University Women.

★2425★ NARAL New Jersey
29 Valley Rd.
Montclair, NJ 07042
Phone: (201)783-0100
Timothy L. Wright, Contact

★2426★ Young Women's Christian Association of Montclair-North Essex
159 Glenridge Ave.
Montclair, NJ 07042
Phone: (201)746-5400
Description: Seeks to develop and improve the spiritual, social, mental, and physical life of young people and adults. **Affiliated with:** Young Women's Christian Association of the United States of America.

Montvale

★2427★ Adventures for Women
PO Box 515
Montvale, NJ 07645
Phone: (201)930-0557
Betsy Thomason, Dir.
Description: Women in New York and New Jersey. Promotes personal growth through wilderness challenges. Provides a foundation in outdoor and interpersonal skills to foster participation in decision-making with confidence.

Moorestown

★2428★ Evergreen Woman's Club
c/o Pauline E. Mietz
Community House
E. Main St.
Moorestown, NJ 08057
Pauline E. Mietz, Pres.
Description: Women's volunteer service club. Promotes civic and social activities in Burlington County, NJ.

Mountainside

★2429★ Feminists for Life of New Jersey
244 Pembrook Rd.
Mountainside, NJ 07092
Phone: (908)232-7537
Grace O. Dermody, Exec. Officer
Description: Seeks to achieve equal opportunity for all women and the rights of unborn children.

★2430★ Religious Coalition for Abortion Rights, New Jersey Chapter
370 Central Ave.
Mountainside, NJ 07092
Phone: (908)232-6054
Fax: (908)467-7867
Myra Terry, Coordinator
Description: Religious organizations and faith groups. Seeks to encourage and coordinate support for self-guarding the legal option of abortion. **Affiliated with:** Religious Coalition for Abortion Rights.

New Brunswick

★2431★ New Jersey State Federation of Women's Clubs
55 Clifton Ave.
New Brunswick, NJ 08901
Phone: (201)249-5474
Olga Mackaronis, Exec.Sec.
Description: Women organized to improve their social, cultural, and physical environment. Provides fellowship and networking opportunities. Sponsors projects. Holds monthly board of directors meeting. **Affiliated with:** General Federation of Women's Clubs.

★2432★ Rutgers, The State University of New Jersey
Consortium for Educational Equity
The Women's Project
Livingston Campus 4090
New Brunswick, NJ 08903
Phone: (908)548-8600
Founded: 1984. **Description:** A non-profit organization dedicated to the retrieval and documentation of New Jersey women's history. **Publications:** *Past and Promise: Lives of New Jersey Women.*

★2433★ Young Women's Christian Association of Central Jersey
51 Livingston Ave.
New Brunswick, NJ 08901
Phone: (908)545-6622
Description: Seeks to develop and improve the spiritual, social, mental, and physical life of young people and adults. **Affiliated with:** Young Women's Christian Association of the United States of America.

Orange

★2434★ Young Women's Christian Association of Essex and West Hudson
395 Main St.
Orange, NJ 07050
Phone: (201)672-9500
Description: Seeks to develop and improve the spiritual, social, mental, and physical life of young people and adults. **Affiliated with:** Young Women's Christian Association of the United States of America.

Passaic

★2435★ Young Women's Christian Association of Passaic-Clifton
114 Prospect St.
Passaic, NJ 07055
Phone: (201)779-1770
Description: Seeks to develop and improve the spiritual, social, mental, and physical life of young people and adults. **Affiliated with:** Young Women's Christian Association of the United States of America.

Paterson

★2436★ Young Women's Christian Association of Paterson
185 Carroll St.
Paterson, NJ 07501
Phone: (201)684-6408
Margo McRae, Exec.Dir.
Description: Seeks to develop and improve the spiritual, social, mental, and physical life of young people and adults. **Affiliated with:** Young Women's Christian Association of the United States of America.

Peapack

★2437★ Municipal Bond Women's Club of New York
c/o Bethzaida Cruz
Asch-Dwyer Municipal Securities
87 Main St., PO Box 315
Peapack, NJ 07977
Phone: (908)781-6900
Bethzaida Cruz, Pres.
Founded: 1942. **Description:** Women in New York City who are associated with investment firms dealing in municipal bonds. Sponsors social gatherings. **Members:** 281.

Penns Grove

★2438★ Woman's Club of Penns Grove and Carneys Point
Franklin and Harmony St.
Penns Grove, NJ 08069-1317
Description: Women's volunteer service club.

Plainfield

★2439★ Young Women's Christian Association of Plainfield/North Plainfield
232 E. Front St.
Plainfield, NJ 07060-1387
Phone: (908)756-3836
Joan L. Retzlaff, Exec.Dir.
Description: Seeks to develop and improve the spiritual, social, mental, and physical life of young people and adults. **Affiliated with:** Young Women's Christian Association of the United States of America.

Port Murray

★2440★ American Association of University Women, Port Murray Branch
RD, Penwell
Port Murray, NJ 07865
Phone: (201)852-0436
Patricia A. Nichols, Pres.
Description: Women graduates of regionally accredited four year colleges and universities. Works for the advancement of women through advocacy and emphasis on lifelong learning. **Affiliated with:** American Association of University Women.

Ridgewood

★2441★ Ridgewood Unit of Republican Women
PO Box 334
Ridgewood, NJ 07450
Phone: (201)445-5710
Description: Seeks to elect Republican candidates to local, state, and national offices.

★2442★ Woman's Club of Ridgewood
215 W. Ridgewood Ave.
Ridgewood, NJ 07450
Phone: (201)444-5722
Gloria Andriuolo, Pres.
Description: Women working together to promote improvement in the community and to provide a social network of mutual support. **Affiliated with:** General Federation of Women's Clubs; New Jersey State Federation of Women's Clubs.

★2443★ Young Women's Christian Association of Ridgewood
112 Oak St.
Ridgewood, NJ 07450
Phone: (201)444-5600
J. Robert Sheppard, Gen.Exec.

Description: Seeks to develop and improve the spiritual, social, mental, and physical life of young people and adults. **Affiliated with:** Young Women's Christian Association of the United States of America.

Roselle

★2444★ Older Women's League (OWL) Central New Jersey Chapter
453 Broookside Dr.
Roselle, NJ 07203
Phone: (908)245-4884
Sara Ann Currie, Contact

Shrewsbury

★2445★ Older Women's League (OWL) Monmouth County Chapter
126 Trafford St.
Shrewsbury, NJ 07702
Phone: (908)741-9446
Alvina M. Johnston, Contact

Somerville

★2446★ American Association of University Women, New Jersey Division
30 Putnam St.
Somerville, NJ 08876
Phone: (908)685-7550
Jacqueline D'Alessio, Pres.

Description: Women graduates of regionally accredited four year colleges and universities. Works for the advancement of women through advocacy and emphasis on lifelong learning. Sponsors annual Legislative Day. **Affiliated with:** American Association of University Women.

Sparta

★2447★ Young Women's Christian Association of Sussex County
200 Woodport Rd.
Sparta, NJ 07871
Phone: (201)729-6474

Description: Seeks to develop and improve the spiritual, social, mental, and physical life of young people and adults. **Affiliated with:** Young Women's Christian Association of the United States of America.

Summit

★2448★ Young Women's Christian Association of Summit
79 Maple St.
Summit, NJ 07901
Phone: (201)273-4242

Description: Seeks to develop and improve the spiritual, social, mental, and physical life of young people and adults. **Affiliated with:** Young Women's Christian Association of the United States of America.

Teaneck

★2449★ Media Women
PO Box 3327
Teaneck, NJ 07666-9106

Description: Women working in the communication industry.

★2450★ National Council of Jewish Women, Greater Teaneck Section
405 Cedar Ln.
Teaneck, NJ 07666
Phone: (201)836-4973

Description: Furthers human welfare in Jewish and other communities through volunteer activities. Sponsors monthly study group. **Affiliated with:** National Council of Jewish Women.

Totowa

★2451★ Women's American ORT, Northwest Jersey Region
205 U.S. Hwy. 46
Totowa, NJ 07512
Phone: (201)785-0440
Naomi Lilien, Pres.

Description: Jewish women in Essex, Moris, and Passaic counties, NJ. Sponsors fundraisers for vocational and technical schools. **Affiliated with:** Women's American ORT.

Trenton

★2452★ Family Planning Association of New Jersey
132 W. State
Trenton, NJ 08608
Phone: (609)393-8423
Katharine Pinneo, Exec.Dir.

Description: Promotes family planning.

★2453★ League of Women Voters of New Jersey
204 W. State St.
Trenton, NJ 08608
Phone: (609)394-3303
Ann Auerbach, President

★2454★ New Jersey Coalition for Battered Women
2620 Whitehorse Hamilton Sq. Rd.
Trenton, NJ 08690-2718
Phone: (609)584-8107
Toll-free: 800-572-7233
Barbara M. Price, Contact

★2455★ New Jersey Healthy Mothers, Healthy Babies
New Jersey State Department of Health
MIH Program
CN 364
Trenton, NJ 08625
Phone: (609)292-5616
Sandra Huneke, Coordinator

Description: Clergy, consumers, nurses, nutritionists, outreach workers, physicians, and social workers. Seeks to reduce the infanity mortality rate. **Affiliated with:** Healthy Mothers, Healthy Babies Coalition.

★2456★ Young Women's Christian Association of Trenton
140 E. Hanover St.
Trenton, NJ 08608
Phone: (609)396-8291
Fax: (609)989-8696

Description: Seeks to develop and improve the spiritual, social, mental, and physical life of young people and adults. **Affiliated with:** Young Women's Christian Association of the United States of America.

Union City

★2457★ New Jersey Federation of Democratic Women
301 Manhattan Ave.
Union City, NJ 07087
Phone: (201)867-4801
Clara Allen, Pres.

Description: Seeks to elect Democratic candidates to local, state, and national offices.

Upper Montclair

★2458★ Woman's Club of Upper Montclair
200 Cooper Ave.
Upper Montclair, NJ 07043
Phone: (201)744-9138

Description: Women in Essex County, NJ. Promotes education and charitable activities. **Affiliated with:** General Federation of Women's Clubs; New Jersey State Federation of Women's Clubs.

Wayne

★2459★ New Jersey Child Support Council
5 Fay Ct.
Wayne, NJ 07470-6556

Description: Individuals involved in child support in New Jersey.

Westwood

★2460★ Westwood Woman's Club
205 Kinderkamack Rd.
Westwood, NJ 07675
Phone: (201)666-9755
Helen Kremen, Pres.

Description: Women in Bergen County, NJ. Works to form a recognized center for active engagement in movements for civic and philanthropic betterment of the community. **Affiliated with:** General Federation of Women's Clubs; General Federation of Women's Clubs, District 9.

Willingboro

★2461★ General Federation of Women's Clubs, Willingboro
c/o Anna Burkhardt
24 Fireside Ct.
Willingboro, NJ 08046
Phone: (609)871-9703
Anna Burkhardt, Contact

Description: Women over the age of 35. Promotes women's rights; conducts charitable programs.

New Mexico

Albuquerque

★2462★ American Association of University Women, New Mexico Division
1611 Bayita Ln., NW
Albuquerque, NM 87107
Phone: (505)344-2590
Margaret H. Dike, Pres.
Description: Women graduates of regionally accredited four year colleges and universities. Works for the advancement of women through advocacy and emphasis on lifelong learning. **Affiliated with:** American Association of University Women.

★2463★ Cesarean Prevention Movement of New Mexico
1534 Larkin Rd., SW
Albuquerque, NM 87105
Phone: (505)247-8928
Elaine Miller, Pres.
Description: Men and women concerned with the increasing rate of casarean births. Works to: prevent unnecessary cesareans; offer encouragement, support, and information to women wanting vaginal births after cesarean. Conducts political action activities; maintains library. **Affiliated with:** Cesarean Prevention Movement.

★2464★ Eleanor Roosevelt Fund of New Mexico
1820 Gabaldon NW
Albuquerque, NM 87104
Phone: (505)242-6516
Kathleen Casey, Treasurer

★2465★ New Mexico Right to Choose
PO Box 14126
Albuquerque, NM 87191
Phone: (505)294-0171
Nancy Ellefson, Contact

★2466★ New Mexico Women in the Arts
c/o Janice Raithel
New Mexico in the Arts
University of New Mexico
Department of Art and Art History
Albuquerque, NM 87131-1401
Phone: (505)277-0111
Janice Raithel, Contact
Membership: 50.

★2467★ New Mexico Women's Foundation
5200 Copper NE
Albuquerque, NM 87108
Phone: (505)268-3996
Diane Wood, Executive Director

★2468★ Religious Coalition for Abortion Rights, New Mexico Chapter
PO Box 14144
Albuquerque, NM 87191
Phone: (505)275-3001

★2469★ Women's Support Group
c/o Full Circle Books
2205 Silver Ave., SE
Albuquerque, NM 87106
Phone: (505)266-0022
Description: Support group for women.

★2470★ Young Women's Christian Association of Albuquerque
7201 Taseo Del Norte, NE
Albuquerque, NM 87113
Phone: (505)822-9922
Description: Seeks to develop and improve the spiritual, social, mental, and physical well-being of young people and adults. **Affiliated with:** Young Women's Christian Association of the United States of America.

Santa Fe

★2471★ Girl Scouts of the U.S.A., Sangre de Christo Girl Scout Council
450 St. Michael Dr.
Santa Fe, NM 87501
Phone: (505)983-6339
Jaclyn Libowitz, Exec.Dir.
Description: Girls and adult volunteers in New Mexico and southern Colorado. Seeks to inspire girls to the highest ideals of character, conduct, patriotism, and service. **Affiliated with:** Girl Scouts of the U.S.A.

★2472★ League of Women Voters of New Mexico
440 Cerrillos Rd., Ste. G
Santa Fe, NM 87501
Phone: (505)982-9766
Hanna Lattman, President

★2473★ New Mexico State Coalition Against Domestic Violence
La Casa, Inc.
PO Box 5698
Santa Fe, NM 87502-5698
Phone: (505)624-0666

Tucumcari

★2474★ American Association of University Women, Tucumcari Chapter
c/o Maxine Elliot
1815 S. Fourth
Tucumcari, NM 88401
Phone: (505)461-1478
Maxine Elliot, Pres.
Description: Women graduates of regionally accredited four year colleges and universities. Works for the advancement of women through advocacy and emphasis on lifelong learning. Awards annual scholarship. **Affiliated with:** American Association of University Women.

★2475★ Tucumcari Business and Professional Women's Club
PO Box 1107
Tucumcari, NM 88401
Phone: (505)461-3602
Patsy Gresham, Pres.
Description: Business and professional women. To promote complete participation, equal opportunities, and economic self-sufficiency for working women. **Affiliated with:** National Federation of Business and Professional Women's Clubs of the U.S.A.

New York

Albany

★2476★ Holding Our Own: A Fund For Women
79-81 Central Ave.
Albany, NY 12206
Phone: (518)462-2871
Naomi Jaffe, Contact
Remarks: Funds capitol district of New York state.

★2477★ League of Women Voters of New York
35 Maiden Ln.
Albany, NY 12207-2712
Phone: (518)465-4162
Shirley Eberly, President

★2478★ New York State Branch of National Abortion Rights Action League
The Women's Bldg.
79 Central Ave.
Albany, NY 12206
Phone: (518)465-3076
Laurie Nichols, Contact

★2479★ New York State Coalition Against Domestic Violence
Women's Bldg.
79 Central Ave.
Albany, NY 12206
Phone: (518)432-4864
Toll-free: 800-942-6906
Gwen Wright, Contact

★2480★ Young Women's Christian Association of Albany
28 Colvin Ave.
Albany, NY 12206
Phone: (518)438-6608
Description: Seeks to develop and improve the spiritual, social, mental, and physical life of young people and adults. **Affiliated with:** Young Women's Christian Association of the United States of America.

★2481★ Young Women's Christian Association of Lea County
28 Bolbin Ave.
Albany, NY 12206
Phone: (518)438-6608
Description: Seeks to develop and improve the spiritual, social, mental, and physical well-being of young people and adults. **Affiliated with:** Young Women's Christian Association of the United States of America.

Amherst

★2482★ National Council of Jewish Women, Queens Chapter
4242 Judge St.
Amherst, NY 11373
Phone: (718)457-9207
Sylvia Schwartzburg, Pres.
Description: Women advocating the tenets of Judaism. Promotes education. Conducts fundraisers and community service, and public affairs. **Affiliated with:** National Council of Jewish Women.

Barker

★2483★ La Leche League International, Newfane Chapter
1091 Quaker Rd.
Barker, NY 14012
Phone: (716)795-3709
Margo Sue Bittner, Leader

Description: To support, encourage, and help mothers who choose to breastfeed their babies. **Affiliated with:** La Leche League International.

Batavia

★2484★ Young Women's Christian Association of Genesee County
301 North St.
Batavia, NY 14020
Phone: (716)343-5808

Description: Seeks to develop and improve the spiritual, social, mental, and physical life of young people and adults. **Affiliated with:** Young Women's Christian Association of the United States of America.

Binghamton

★2485★ Broome County Coalition for Free Choice
PO Box 705
Binghamton, NY 13902
Phone: (607)772-1476
Rev. Marcel Duhamel, Pres.

Description: Works to maintain the legal right of women to have an abortion.

★2486★ Broome County Republican Women's Club
c/o Broome County Republican Committee
O'Neil Bldg., Rm. 307
State St.
Binghamton, NY 13901
Phone: (607)797-1350

Description: Seeks to elect Republican candidates to local, state, and national offices.

★2487★ Day Nursery Association
32 Stuyvesant St.
Binghamton, NY 13901
Phone: (607)722-4529
Timothy T. Stephenson, Exec.Dir.

Description: To provide affordable, high-quality child care to working families and single parents in Broome County, NY.

★2488★ Young Women's Christian Association of Binghamton and Broome County
80 Hawley St.
Binghamton, NY 13901
Phone: (607)772-0340

Description: Seeks to develop and improve the spiritual, social, mental, and physical life of young people and adults. **Affiliated with:** Young Women's Christian Association of the United States of America.

Brewster

★2489★ Cesarean Prevention Movement of Westchester/Putnam
R.D. 2, Joe's Hill Rd.
Brewster, NY 10509
Phone: (914)279-9028
Mia Thelen, Co-Coordinator

Description: Mothers, childbirth educators, midwives, and families planning their child's birth in upper Westchester, Putnam, and Dutchess counties, NY. Seeks to lower the number of cesarean sections through education. Provides support to women who have had cesareans and a forum where parents-to-be can express their thoughts and concerns about childbirth. Operates a lending library with information on childbirth and vaginal birth after a cesarean. **Affiliated with:** Cesarean Prevention Movement.

Bronx

★2490★ Bronx Puerto Rican Ladies Action
1274 Castle Hill Ave.
Bronx, NY 10462
Phone: (212)829-8300
Margarita Valazquez, Pres.

Brooklyn

★2491★ Alpha Kappa Alpha Sorority, Delta Rho Omega Chapter
PO Box 070-155
Brooklyn, NY 11207
Phone: (718)778-7801
Emma St. Bernard, Pres.

Description: Social service sorority. Seeks to improve the social and economic conditions of the disadvantaged. Promotes high scholastic achievement and ethical standards among college women. **Affiliated with:** Alpha Kappa Alpha Sorority.

★2492★ Association for Women in Science, Brooklyn Chapter
c/o Alice Miller
227 Ingersoll Hall
Brooklyn, NY 11237-1512
Alice Miller, Contact

Description: Works to improve education and employment opportunities for women in the sciences.

★2493★ DES Action
PO Box 331
Brooklyn, NY 11229

Description: Educational organization dedicated to reaching women who took the synthetic estrogen compound DES. Provides networking and an outreach program. **Affiliated with:** DES Action, U.S.A.

★2494★ Neighborhood Women of Williamsburg-Greenpoint
249 Manhattan Ave.
Brooklyn, NY 11211-4905

Description: Neighborhood cooperation group in Brooklyn, NY.

★2495★ Older Women's League (OWL) Brooklyn Chapter
867 E. 24th St.
Brooklyn, NY 11210
Phone: (718)253-3326
Annabelle Staber, Contact

★2496★ Young Women's Christian Association of Brooklyn
30 3rd Ave.
Brooklyn, NY 11217
Phone: (718)875-1190
Donna Ceravolo, Exec.Dir.

Description: Seeks to develop and improve the spiritual, social, mental, and physical life of young people and adults. Provides skills training and job placement. Operates residence for single women, Montessori school, and day care. Conducts Shawdow Box Theatre and community activities. Advocates for women's issues. **Affiliated with:** Young Women's Christian Association of the United States of America.

Buffalo

★2497★ Association for Women in Science, Buffalo Chapter
c/o Mary Bisson
SUNY Buffalo
Biological Sciences
623 Cooke Hall
Buffalo, NY 14226
Phone: (716)636-2550
Fax: (716)636-2975
Mary Bisson, Sec.

Description: Professional women in the field of science. Seeks to enhance the role of women in science. Offers networking. Works to make women visible as speakers. Holds and judges science fairs. Introduces science to girls and encourages young women to enter the field. **Affiliated with:** Association for Women in Science.

★2498★ Buffalo Women's Bowling Association
251 Comstock Ave.
Buffalo, NY 14215
Phone: (716)832-5470
Stell Kolis, Sec.

Description: Women bowlers. Promotes the game of ten-pin bowling. Sponsors tournaments. Contributes to local charities. **Affiliated with:** Women's International Bowling Congress.

★2499★ DES Action
56 Maple View
Buffalo, NY 14225

★2500★ Every Woman Opportunity Center, Inc.
237 Main St., Ste. 330
Buffalo, NY 14203
Phone: (716)847-1120
Myrna F. Young, Exec.Dir.

Founded: 1977. **Description:** Concerned with career counseling, remediation/skills development and alcohol/substance abuse. **Publications:** Newsletter.

Canandaigua

★2501★ American Association of University Women, Ontario County Branch
c/o Carol Zanghi
54 Cove Rd.
Canandaigua, NY 14424
Phone: (716)394-7216
Carol Zanghi, Exec. Officer

Description: Women graduates of regionally accredited four year colleges and universities. Works for the advancement of women through advocacy and emphasis on lifelong learning. Sponsors local scholarship for women graduates of two year colleges going on to four year colleges. **Affiliated with:** American Association of University Women.

Carle Place

★2502★ Association for Women in Science, Long Island Chapter
AWIS - Long Island
c/o Lorraine Bondi-Goldsmith
3 Madison Ln., Apt. 1-G
Carle Place, NY 11514
Phone: (516)876-2758
Lorraine Bondi-Goldsmith, Contact

Description: Works to improve education and employment opportunities for women in the sciences.

Central Valley

★2503★ Maternal-Infant Services Network of Orange, Sullivan and Ulster Counties
340 Rte. 32
Central Valley, NY 10917-9802
Description: Works to improve maternal and child health.

Corning

★2504★ La Leche League International, Corning Chapter
34 Pershing St.
Corning, NY 14830
Phone: (607)962-1303
Marcella Masteller, Leader

Description: Nursing mothers. Provides information and education on breastfeeding. **Affiliated with:** La Leche League International.

Cortland

★2505★ Young Women's Christian Association of Cortland
14 Clayton Ave.
Cortland, NY 13045
Phone: (607)753-9651

Description: Seeks to develop and improve the spiritual, social, mental, and physical life of young people and adults. Provides aid to battered women; conducts foot rally and antique show. **Affiliated with:** Young Women's Christian Association of the United States of America.

Deer Park

★2506★ Cesarean Prevention Movement of Suffolk
92 Oak St.
Deer Park, NY 11729
Phone: (516)242-3897
Sandi Koltzau, Sec.-Treas.

Description: Prospective parents, pregnant women, new parents, childbirth educators, and health care professionals. Provides support and encouragement for the childbearing experience with an emphasis on encouraging vaginal birth for women who have had a cesarean during a previous birth. Seeks to diminish the number of cesarean births. **Affiliated with:** Cesarean Prevention Movement.

East Hampton

★2507★ Ladies Village Improvement Society
95 Main St.
PO Box 1196
East Hampton, NY 11937
Phone: (516)324-1220
James Briggs, Pres.

Description: Women interested in maintaining historic landmarks, parks, greens and trees in the village East Hampton, NY area.

East Setauket

★2508★ Association for Women in Science, New York State Chapter
c/o Victoria McLane
PO Box 204
East Setauket, NY 11733-0204

Description: Works to improve education and employment opportunities for women in the sciences.

Elmira

★2509★ Young Women's Christian Association of Chemung County
211 Lake St.
Elmira, NY 14901-3193
Phone: (607)733-5575
Judith H. Clovsky, Contact

Description: Seeks to develop and improve the spiritual, social, mental, and physical well-being of young people and adults. **Affiliated with:** Young Women's Christian Association of the United States of America.

Elmont

★2510★ B'nai B'rith Women, Queens/Long Island Region
1975 Linden Blvd., No. 208
Elmont, NY 11003
Phone: (516)285-9494
Rita Shliselberg, Dir.

Description: To unite Jewish women. To promote the principles of social advancement through education, service, and advocacy. **Affiliated with:** B'nai B'rith Women.

Fishkill

★2511★ DES Action
Box 597
Fishkill, NY 12524

Flushing

★2512★ Women United
65-30 Kissena Blvd. Student Union 210A
Caller Box 6703, SU Box 26
Queens College
Flushing, NY 11367
Phone: (718)263-5668
Katy German, Pres.

Description: Students and faculty. To educate the Queens College community on the social, legal, and academic role of women and to raise awareness of sanctioned stereotypes. Operates library with feminist materials.

Fredonia

★2513★ American Association of University Women, Dunkirk-Fredonia Branch
10185 Patterson Ln.
Greencrest
Fredonia, NY 14063
Phone: (716)672-4077
Cindy Coon, Treas.

Description: Women graduates of regionally accredited four year colleges and universities. Works for the advancement of women through advocacy and emphasis on lifelong learning. **Affiliated with:** American Association of University Women.

Garden City

★2514★ Women's Direct Response Group - New York Chapter (WDRG)
224 7th St.
Garden City, NY 11530
Phone: (516)746-6700
Deb Glasserow, Pres.

Founded: 1970. **Description:** Direct marketing professionals. Seeks to: advance the interests and influence of women in the direct response industry; provide for communication and career education; assist in advancement of personal career objectives; serve as professional network to develop business contacts and foster mutual goals. Maintains career talent bank; bestows awards. Sponsors monthly seminar, workshops, and summer internship program. Distributes information nationally; maintains offices in Washington, DC and Chicago, IL. **Members:** 600. **Publications:** *Women's Direct Response Group—Membership Roster*, annual. • *Women's Direct Response Group—Newsletter*, quarterly. Membership activities newsletter with information on career developments. Includes calendar of events and profiles of new members.

Glen Head

★2515★ National Association of Women Business Owners
Long Island Chapter
c/o Market Makers Public Relations
1 Robert Ln., No. 10
Glen Head, NY 11545
Phone: (516)674-0068
Susan Parker, President

★2516★ Ninety-Nines, International Organization of Women Pilots, New York-New Jersey Section
2 Exeter Pl.
Glen Head, NY 11545-1115
Phone: (516)676-7852
Fax: (516)676-7971
Lu Hollander, Sec.

Description: Works for the advancement of aviation. Sponsors educational, charitable, and scientific programs. Issues publications.

Glens Falls

★2517★ Birthright of Greater Glens Falls
22 Center St.
Glens Falls, NY 12801-3607

Description: Seeks to help pregnant women find alternatives to abortion. Conducts childbirth education and parenting programs.

Gloversville

★2518★ Young Women's Christian Association of Gloversville
33 Bleecker Sq.
Gloversville, NY 12078
Phone: (518)725-5316
Ruth H. Carey, Exec.Dir.

Description: Seeks to develop and improve the spiritual, mental, and physical life of young people and adults. **Affiliated with:** Young Women's Christian Association of the United States of America.

Great Valley

★2519★ Beta Sigma Phi Sorority, Xi Beta Tau Chapter
175 Whalen Dr.
Great Valley, NY 14741
Phone: (716)945-4368
Evelyn Sum, Pres.

Description: Women's organization comprised of homemakers and working women. Offers women cultural and social enrichment through the liberal arts. Participates in annual Founder's Day celebration.

Groton

★2520★ American Association of University Women, Cortland Chapter
299 Locke Rd.
Box 44
Groton, NY 13073
Phone: (607)898-5198
Dr. Lucille S. Baker, Pres.

Description: Women graduates of regionally accredited four year colleges and universities. Works for the advancement of women through advocacy and emphasis on lifelong learning. **Affiliated with:** American Association of University Women.

Hamburg

★2521★ Hamburg Business and Professional Women's Club
3921 Monroe Ave.
Hamburg, NY 14075
Dorothy A. Romanczuk, Pres.

Description: Women in business, industry, and professional positions. Studies issues concerning women, the family, employment, and the place of women in American society.

Hampton Bays

★2522★ National Organization for Women, East End Chapter
PO Box 766
Hampton Bays, NY 11946
Phone: (516)728-4256
Lynn Buck, Pres.

Description: Feminists. Promotes equality of rights and freedom of choice for women. **Affiliated with:** National Organization for Women.

Henrietta

★2523★ Older Women's League (OWL) Greater Rochester Chapter
44 Horseshoe Ln. N.
Henrietta, NY 14467
Phone: (716)461-1959
Lois Zakia, Contact

Ithaca

★2524★ Cesarean Prevention Movement of Ithaca
1191 Ellis Hollow Rd.
Ithaca, NY 14850
Phone: (607)272-3204
Yvonne LaMontagne, Exec. Officer

★2525★ Upstate New York Women's History Organization
1202 E. State St.
Ithaca, NY 14850
Patricia Foster Haines, Contact

Description: Network of historians interested in women's history. **Publications:** Bimonthly newsletter to disseminate information on topics of interest to membership. **Meetings:** Holds a conference each year in different parts of upstate New York.

Jamestown

★2526★ Westside Women's Club
c/o Evalyn Paulson
243 Hallock St.
Jamestown, NY 14701
Phone: (716)484-7271
Evalyn Paulson, Pres.

Description: Women's volunteer service club.

★2527★ Young Women's Christian Association of Jamestown
401 N. Main St.
Jamestown, NY 14701
Phone: (716)488-2237

Description: Seeks to develop and improve the spiritual, social, mental, and physical life of young people and adults. **Affiliated with:** Young Women's Christian Association of the United States of America.

Kingston

★2528★ Girl Scouts of the U.S.A., Ulster County Council
65 St. James St.
PO Box 3039
Kingston, NY 12401
Phone: (914)338-5367
Gail A. Widholm, Exec. Officer

Description: Girls ages seven-18 and adult volunteers. To inspire girls with the highest ideals and personal conduct. **Affiliated with:** Girl Scouts of the U.S.A.

★2529★ Young Women's Christian Association of Ulster County
209 Clinton Ave.
Kingston, NY 12401
Phone: (914)338-6844
Dianne T. Craig, Exec.Dir.

Description: Seeks to develop and improve the spiritual, social, mental, and physical life of young people and adults. Operates child care center, nursery school program, teen parents services, and senior reassurance services. **Affiliated with:** Young Women's Christian Association of the United States of America.

Lindenhurst

★2530★ La Leche League International, East New York Chapter
334 S. 3rd St.
Lindenhurst, NY 11757
Phone: (516)957-1986
Ronnie McEntee, Coordinator

Description: Offers assistance, support, and information to mothers interested in breastfeeding. **Affiliated with:** La Leche League International.

Lockport

★2531★ Girl Scouts of the U.S.A., Niagara County Council
5000 Cambria Rd.
Lockport, NY 14094-9755
Phone: (716)434-6212
Nancy J. Marshanke, Exec.Dir.

Description: Girls aged five-17 and adult volunteers providing the Girl Scout Program. **Affiliated with:** Girl Scouts of the U.S.A.

★2532★ Young Women's Christian Association of Lockport
32 Cottage St.
Lockport, NY 14094
Phone: (716)433-6714
Mary Carol Marotta, Exec.Dir.

Description: Seeks to develop and improve the spiritual, social, mental, and physical life of young people and adults. **Affiliated with:** Young Women's Christian Association of the United States of America.

Locust Valley

★2533★ Ladies' Kennel Association of New York
10 Millford Dr.
Locust Valley, NY 11560
Patricia G. Spear, Delegate

Description: Dog kennel club. Promotes pure-bred dogs. **Affiliated with:** American Kennel Club.

Medford

★2534★ Lady Reelers
2320 Rte. 112
Medford, NY 11763-3196

Description: Women with an interest in fishing.

Mineola

★2535★ Sunken Meadow Ladies Golf Club Thursday
c/o K. Libassi
190 Mineola Blvd.
Mineola, NY 11501-2532
K. Libassi, Contact

Description: Women golf players in Mineola, NY.

Montour Falls

★2536★ Watkins Glen Business and Professional Women's Club
c/o Judith A. Coyle
200 E. South St.
Montour Falls, NY 14865
Phone: (607)535-6585
Judith A. Coyle, Pres.

Description: Business and professional women. To promote complete participation, equal opportunities, and economic self-sufficiency for working women. **Affiliated with:** Business and Professional Women's Clubs of New York State; National Federation of Business and Professional Women's Clubs of the U.S.A.

New Rochelle

★2537★ Westchester Association of Women Business-Owners
121 Clove Rd.
New Rochelle, NY 10801
Phone: (914)235-3744

New Windsor

★2538★ Young Women's Christian Association of Newburgh
565 Union Ave.
New Windsor, NY 12550
Phone: (914)561-8050

Description: Seeks to develop and improve the spiritual, social, physical, and mental well-being of young people and adults. **Affiliated with:** Young Women's Christian Association of the United States of America.

New York

★2539★ Advertising Women of New York (AWNY)
153 E. 57th St.
New York, NY 10022
Phone: (212)593-1950
Fax: (212)759-2865
Peggy R. Urso, Exec.Dir.

Founded: 1912. **Description:** Women engaged in an executive or administrative capacity in advertising, publicity, marketing, research, or promotion. Conducts professional development seminars and a career clinic to provide personal job counseling. The affiliated Advertising Women of New York Foundation funds scholarship programs and conducts an annual career conference for college seniors and graduate students and other educational and charitable programs. Membership concentrated in the New York City area. Maintains speakers' bureau. **Members:** 850. **Publications:** *Advertising Women of New York—Annual Roster.* Membership directory. • *AWNY Matters: A Monthly Report from the Advertising Women of New York.* Newsletter informing members of social events and trends impacting the advertising industry. • *AWNY News,* 3/year. Membership activities newsletter.

★2540★ Association of Black Women Attorneys
134 W. 32nd St., Ste. 602
New York, NY 10001
Phone: (212)815-0478
Leslie R. Jones, Pres.

★2541★ Association for Women in Science, Metropolitan New York Chapter
c/o Barbara Gerolimatos, Ph.D
Harlem Hospital
New York, NY 10037-0000
Barbara Gerolimatos, Ph.D, Contact

Description: Works to improve education and employment opportunities for women in the sciences.

★2542★ Berkshire Conference of Women Historians
Rutgers University
History Department
3133 W. 17th St.
New York, NY 10011
Phone: (212)243-6418
Judith Walkowitz, President

★2543★ Chinese Women's Benevolent Association (CWBA)
22 Pell St., No. 3
New York, NY 10013
Phone: (212)267-4764
Mrs. Louis F. S. Hong, Pres.

Founded: 1942. **Description:** Chinese women who volunteer in fundraising drives, aid students, and conduct other philanthropic activities. Provides interpreting and translating services when needed. Activities centered in New York City area. **Members:** 100.

★2544★ Club of Printing Women of New York (CPW)
c/o Expertype
44 W. 28th St.
New York, NY 10001
Phone: (212)532-6222
Annette Wolf Bensen, Pres.

Founded: 1930. **Description:** Women of executive or semi-executive level in printing plants or allied fields such as publishing, advertising, and printing supplies; includes plant owners, production managers, bindery workers, salespersons, and buyers of printing and paper, estimators, cost accountants, mill representatives, and designers. Enables women in printing to keep informed of developments in the graphic arts, through monthly dinner meetings and lectures by industry leaders and field trips to plants in New York metropolitan area. Presents annual education award to a student in the graphic arts. Maintains resource library. Organization is currently in the process of reorganization. **Members:** 100.

★2545★ Coordinating Committee on Women in the Historical Profession, New York Metropolitan Region
501 W. 123rd St., No. 10-H
New York, NY 10027
Beatrice Gottlieb, Sec.-Treas.

Description: Women historians and women interested in history. Promotes the interests of women historians and provides opportunities for members to meet and discuss their work and common interests. **Affiliated with:** Coordinating Committee on Women in the Historical Profession.

★2546★ Electrical Women's RoundTable, New York Chapter
c/o Loretta DiCamillo
Consolidated Edison
4 Irving Pl., Rm. 1625-S
New York, NY 10003
Phone: (212)460-3106
Loretta DiCamillo, Chwm.

Description: Women employed in the electrical industry or related fields. To establish professional associations among women in the electrical field. To promote: the growth potential of women within the field; research and education in the electrical field; greater emphasis concerning the work women are doing. To advance consumer education on the wise and efficient use of electricity. Operates speakers' bureau. **Affiliated with:** Electrical Women's Round Table.

★2547★ Federation of Jewish Women's Organizations (FJWO)
1265 Broadway, Rm. 608
New York, NY 10001
Phone: (212)684-2888
Sylvia N. Rachlin, Pres.

Founded: 1896. **Description:** Jewish women's organizations representing 120,000 individuals in the New York City area. Serves as clearinghouse of information; maintains liaison between member groups and municipal and recognized private agencies; encourages interest in education, health, religion, social service, civic improvements, and city, state, and national welfare legislation; promotes efficiency by providing guidance and preventing duplication of efforts. Holds forums and lectures; equips synagogues in municipal institutions; conducts activities for armed forces and veterans. **Members:** 300. **Publications:** *Horizons*, monthly. **Formerly:** (1920) Federation of Sisterhoods.

★2548★ The Feminist Press at the City University of New York
311 E. 94th St., 2nd Fl.
New York, NY 10128
Phone: (212)360-5790
Fax: (212)348-1241
Florence Howe, Pres.

Description: Nonprofit educational and publishing organization. Seeks to eliminate sex-role and social stereotypes in education at all levels; to further the rediscovery of the history of women; to provide literature "with a broad vision of human potential." Researches the status of women's studies at colleges and universities, and analyzes the teaching methods and curricula by which stereotypical attitudes can be changed. Provides texts for college courses and has created syllabi in which women's history and literature by women are introduced into traditional college courses. Reprints lost or neglected literature by women writers.

★2549★ Financial Women's Association of New York (FWA)
215 Park Ave. S, Ste. 2010
New York, NY 10003
Phone: (212)533-2141
Nancy Sellar, Exec.Dir.

Founded: 1956. **Description:** Persons of professional status in the field of finance in the New York metropolitan area. Works to: promote and maintain high professional standards in the financial and business communities; provide an opportunity for members to enhance one another's professional contacts; achieve recognition of the contribution of women to the financial and business communities; encourage other women to seek professional positions within the financial and business communities. Activities include: educational trips to foreign countries; seminars; college internship program including foreign student exchange; high school mentorship program; Washington and international briefings; placement service for members. Bestows annual FWA Woman of the Year Award and community service awards. Maintains speakers' bureau. **Members:** 800. **Publications:** *Financial Women's Association of New York–Directory*, annual. Membership directory including listings by firm and occupation. Includes photographs. • *Financial Women's Association of New York—Newsletter*, 11/year. Includes listing of new members. **Formerly:** (1968) Young Women's Investment Association of New York; (1971) Young Women's Financial Association of New York.

★2550★ Girl Scout Council of Greater New York
43 W. 23rd St.
New York, NY 10010
Phone: (212)645-4000
Judith F. Kehoe, Exec. Officer

Description: Promotes scouting in the metropolitan New York City area.

★2551★ HACER - National Hispanic Women's Center
611 W. 177 St.
New York, NY 10033
Phone: (212)927-2800

★2552★ Hispanic Women's Center
545 8th Ave., 11th Fl.
New York, NY 10018
Phone: (212)594-7640

★2553★ Lesbian Switchboard of New York City
The Center
208 W. 13th St.
New York, NY 10011
Phone: (212)741-2610
Naomi E. Goodhart, Pres.

Description: To provide confidential information and crisis counseling to women who are lesbians.

★2554★ Metropolitan New York Right to Life Foundation
19 W. 34th St., Rm. 1207
New York, NY 10001-3006

Description: Seeks to help pregnant women find alternatives to abortion. Conducts childbirth education and parenting programs.

★2555★ Municipal Bond Women's Club of New York
c/o Terry Aromondo
Smith Barney Harris & Upham
1345 Ave. of the Americas
New York, NY 10019
Phone: (212)698-6676
Terry Aromondo, Pres.

Description: Women who are associated with investment firms dealing in municipal bonds. Sponsors social gatherings.

★2556★ National Association of Women Business Owners
New York Chapter
c/o Arthur D. Levy and Company
276 5th Ave.
New York, NY 10001
Phone: (212)684-7999
Rosann Levy, President

★2557★ National Council of Jewish Women, New York Section (JWRC)
Jewish Women's Resource Center
9 E. 69th St.
New York, NY 10021
Phone: (212)535-5900
Amy Gershenson, Coordinator

Founded: 1978. **Description:** The Center serves as an information collective on Jewish women. Maintains 5000 item library, including special collections on birth ceremonies, egalitarian marriage contracts, and Passover Haggadot; also maintains a directory (in file form) of Jewish women in the arts and Rosh Chodesh groups. Sponsors Jewish Women's Poetry Project, women's selfhelp groups, film festival and lectures. **Publications:** *JWRC Newsletter*, 3/year. • Also publishes books, bibliographies, and study guides.

★2558★ National Council of Negro Women, Greater New York
777 United Nations Plaza, 10th Fl.
New York, NY 10017
Phone: (212)687-5870

★2559★ National Organization for Women, New York Chapter
15 W. 18th St.
New York, NY 10011
Phone: (212)989-7230
Melodie Bahan, Pres.

Description: Individuals who support women's rights. Promotes and advocates for the full participation of women in American society. Operates Service Fund. **Affiliated with:** National Organization for Women.

★2560★ Networking Project for Disabled Women and Girls (NPDWG)
c/o YWCA of City of New York
610 Lexington Ave.
New York, NY 10022
Phone: (212)735-9767
Angela Perez, Dir.

Founded: 1984. **Description:** A project of the Young Women's Christian Association (see separate entry) of New York City. Purpose is to increase the educational, social, and career aspirations of adolescent girls with disabilities by linking them to successful, disabled role models. Provides support groups; offers advocacy training, pre-employment skills development, and one-to-one mentoring. Organizes visits to the role model's workplace. Currently operates in the New York City area and is providing technical assistance to facilitate replication at several sites throughout the country. **Publications:** *Replication Manual*, books, and videotapes.

★2561★ New York Exchange for Woman's Work (NYEWW)
1095 3rd Ave. & 64th St.
New York, NY 10021
Phone: (212)753-2330
Mrs. Manie Van Doren, Pres.

Founded: 1878. **Description:** Philanthropic organization providing a sales outlet for handwork and foods made by people in need of income. Helps about 1100 women earn a livelihood. **Members:** 34. **Publications:** *Exchange Revue*, monthly.

★2562★ New York Feminist Art Institute
91 Franklin
New York, NY 10013
Phone: (212)219-9590
Regina Tierney, Assoc.Dir.

Description: School and resource center for women in the arts in the tri-state area of New York City. Offers classes and workshops, special events and symposia, exhibitions and performances. Rents studio space at affordable rates to emerging artists. Sponsors annual benefit.

★2563★ New York Metro Roundtable for Women in Foodservice
205 E. 78th St., No. 1A
New York, NY 10021
Phone: (212)439-0580
Suellen Schussel, Pres.

Description: Women working in the foodservice industry. Serves as a clearinghouse for information. Provides support and recognition. Offers developmental programs and seminars. Maintains mentoring program and scholarship fund. Bestows annual Pacesetter Award. **Affiliated with:** Roundtable for Women in Foodservice.

★2564★ New York Metropolitan Region CCWHP
c/o Betty Boyd Caroli
30 5th Ave.
New York, NY 10011
Phone: (212)260-1321

Description: Serves as a network for women historians in the New York City area. **Members:** About 100. **Meetings:** Six times per year. Members use these meetings to discuss their own research projects and exchange information about issues relevant to women historians.

★2565★ New York Society of Women Artists
450 West End Ave.
New York, NY 10024
Phone: (212)877-1902

Founded: 1924. **Description:** Holds annual group exhibition in public space. **Membership:** 60.

★2566★ New York State Abortion Rights Action League
2 W. 64th St.
New York, NY 10023
Phone: (212)724-5770
Kelli Conlin, Contact

★2567★ New York Women's Bar Association
245 5th Ave., Ste. 2103
New York, NY 10016
Phone: (212)889-7873

Description: Professional association of women attorneys. Promotes networking and education. Holds social activities and committee meetings. Rates candidates for judicial office. **Affiliated with:** Women's Bar Association of the State of New York.

★2568★ New York Women's Foundation
120 Wooster St.
New York, NY 10012
Phone: (212)226-2220
Sheila Holderness, Executive Director

★2569★ Newswomen's Club of New York (NCNY)
15 Gramercy Pk. S
New York, NY 10003
Phone: (212)777-1610
Sylvia Carter, Pres.

Founded: 1922. **Description:** Women journalists working full-time or freelancing for New York City and metropolitan daily newspapers, wire services, syndicates, national news and news/feature magazines published in New York City, and radio and television stations or networks whose broadcasts originate in New York City; associate members are former actives who have left the newspaper business. Sponsors professional, educational, social, and charitable activities; arranges for speeches by news headliners; invites journalism students to various events to learn about the field from professionals. Gives graduate scholarships to women students at Columbia University School of Journalism. Funded by the Eleanor Roosevelt and Anne O'Hare McCormick Travel-Work Scholarship Funds. Sponsors annual Front Page Awards for best stories of the year by women journalists. **Members:** 206. **Publications:** *Bulletin*, periodic. **Formerly:** New York Newspaper Women's Club; Newspaper Women's Club of New York.

★2570★ Older Women's League (OWL) Greater New York Chapter
Box 1242, Ansonia Sta.
New York, NY 10023
Phone: (212)496-1409
Sandy Warshaw, Contact

★2571★ The Pen and Brush
16 E. 10 St.
New York, NY 10003
Phone: (212)475-3669

Founded: 1893. **Description:** Organization with close to 300 sculptors, craftswomen and writers. Members receive a bulletin with news and information on exhibits and events.

★2572★ Soho Twenty
469 Broome St.
New York, NY 10013
Phone: (212)226-4167
Eugenia Foxworth, Professional Director

Founded: 1973. **Description:** Provides gallery space to members, sponsors dance performances, poetry readings, slide shows, and invitational exhibitions. **Membership:** 20.

★2573★ Women and AIDS Resource Network (WARN)
c/o Washington Square Church
135 W. 4th St.
New York, NY 10012
Phone: (212)475-6713

Founded: 1987. **Description:** Focuses on AIDS specific to women and children. The initial purpose of the agency is to assemble and enhance resources for women and children affected by AIDS and to facilitate their access to these resources.

★2574★ Women in Need
323 W. 39th St.
New York, NY 10018
Phone: (212)695-4758
Rita Zimmer, Exec. Dir.

Founded: 1982. **Description:** Provides services, access to resources and opportunities to foster and enhance the quality of life for women and children in the city. Assists women and children with transitional and permanent housing, employment, training and placement, alcohol and substance abuse and child care services.

★2575★ Women in Production (WIP)
347 5th Ave., No. 1008
New York, NY 10016-5010
Phone: (212)481-7793
Margaret Glos, CAE, Exec.Dir.

Founded: 1977. **Description:** Persons involved in all phases of print and graphics, including those working in magazine and book publishing, agency production and print manufacturing, print-related vending and buying, and advertising production. To improve job performance by sharing information with each other and with suppliers of printing services. Acts as a network of contacts for those in the printing professions; offers assistance to persons with production problems. Membership is concentrated in the New York City area. Sponsors competitions, charitable program, and placement service; maintains speakers' bureau. Bestows awards and scholarships; compiles statistics. Conducts seminars and educational tours of printing and printing-related facilities. **Members:** 702. **Computerized Services:** Mailing list. **Publications:** *Women in Production*, quarterly. Newsletter. • *WIP Roster*, annual.

★2576★ Women's City Club
35 E. 21st St., No. 7W
New York, NY 10010
Phone: (212)353-8070

Founded: 1916. **Description:** Feminist civic and educational organization involved with many issues, including the status of women, women's health, arts, the environment, and transportation. **Publications:** Include newsletters, brochures, and pamphlets.

★2577★ Women's Employment and Training Association
213 E. 31st St., Ste. 2D
New York, NY 10016
Phone: (212)685-0865
Simone Charlop, Chairperson

Remarks: Serves New York City.

★2578★ Women's Interart Center
549 W 52nd St.
New York, NY 10019
Phone: (212)246-1050
Margot Lewitin, Artistic Director

Description: The center supports workshops, performances, and exhibitions in the visual arts, film, video, music, dance, ceramics, writing, and theater.

★2579★ Women's National Book Association New York City Chapter
PO Box 237, FDR Sta.
New York, NY 10022
Phone: (212)675-7805

★2580★ Women's Overseas Service League, New York Unit
283 Lexington Ave.
New York, NY 10016
Edda Cushman, Pres.

Description: Women living in Connecticut, New Jersey, and New York who have served overseas during war. Works to keep alive the spirit of overseas voluntarism. Maintains ties of friendship. Promotes patriotism. **Affiliated with:** Women's Overseas Service League.

★2581★ Women's Student Association (WSA)
c/o Hebrew Union Coll.
Jewish Inst. of Religion
1 W. 4th St.
New York, NY 10012
Phone: (212)674-5300
Amy Schwartzman, Chairperson

Description: Female rabbinic, cantorial, and education students and rabbis in the New York City area. Acts as an educational, political action, and support group for women in the rabbinate and cantorate. Holds seminars and topical discussions with speakers. **Members:** 35. **Regional Groups:** 2. **Formerly:** (1984) Women's Rabbinic Alliance.

★2582★ Young Women's Christian Association of the City of New York
610 Lexington Ave.
New York, NY 10022
Phone: (212)755-4500
Lenore Parker, Contact

Description: Seeks to develop and improve the spiritual, social, mental, and physical well-being of young people and adults. **Affiliated with:** Young Women's Christian Association of the United States of America.

North Syracuse

★2583★ Coordinating Council on Women in the Historical Profession, Upstate New York Chapter
c/o Suzanne Etherington
595 Thompson Rd.
North Syracuse, NY 13212
Phone: (315)458-3203
Suzanne Etherington, Exec. Officer

North Tonawanda

★2584★ Young Women's Christian Association of the Tonawandas
49 Tremont St.
North Tonawanda, NY 14120
Phone: (716)692-5580
Merrie Manganello, Exec.Dir.

Description: Seeks to develop and improve the spiritual, social, mental, and physical life of young people and adults. **Affiliated with:** Young Women's Christian Association of the United States of America.

Old Westbury

★2585★ Women in Theology and Church History
c/o Prof. Anne Barstow
SUNY College at Old Westbury
Old Westbury, NY 11568
Phone: (516)876-3110

Description: Support for women in the historical profession: shares news of job openings and research; secures nomination of women to posts in American Society of Church History; secures panels on women's history at meetings of ASCH; appoints feminist commentators to panels. **Meetings:** Meets twice a year. **Alternate phone number:** (212)662-8209.

Orchard Park

★2586★ Kins (Mothers) of Twins Southtowns
24 Old Orchard Ln.
Orchard Park, NY 14127
Phone: (716)648-6756
Diane Aberte, Pres.

Description: Mothers of multiple birth children. Serves as a forum of discussion of the joys and problems associated with raising multiples; conducts educational programs. Maintains library; operates clothing and equipment exchange services.

★2587★ New York State Women's Bowling Association
3552 Southwestern Blvd.
Orchard Park, NY 14127
Phone: (716)662-0018

Pittsford

★2588★ National Association of Women Business Owners Rochester Chapter
c/o College Preparatory Service
26 Wood Hill Rd.
Pittsford, NY 14534
Phone: (716)586-7399
Iris Metz, President

Plainview

★2589★ Nassau County Women's Services
1425 Old Country Rd.
Plainview, NY 11803
Phone: (516)564-6880

Description: Organization provides career counseling services to women.

Pleasantville

★2590★ Girl Scouts of Westchester Putnam
2 Great Oak Ln.
Pleasantville, NY 10570
Phone: (914)747-3080
Ellie Waechter, Exec.Dir.

Description: Girls ages five-17 and adult volunteers. To provide girls the opportunity to develop their full potential through girl scout activities. Operates day and resident camps, outreach program for low income, inner-city, and homeless girls, and training and skill enrichment program for adults. **Affiliated with:** Girl Scouts of the U.S.A.

Poughkeepsie

★2591★ Older Women's League (OWL) Hudson Valley Chapter
7 Monroe Dr.
Poughkeepsie, NY 12601
Phone: (914)297-7836
Sally Klein, Contact

★2592★ Young Women's Christian Association of Dutchess County
18 Bancroft Rd.
Poughkeepsie, NY 12601
Phone: (914)454-6770

Description: Seeks to develop and improve the spiritual, social, mental, and physical life of young people and adults. **Affiliated with:** Young Women's Christian Association of the United States of America.

Riverhead

★2593★ East End Women's Network
PO Box 1227
Riverhead, NY 11901
Phone: (516)727-3274
Carolyn London, Pres.

Description: Professional women; women in the work force. Provides networking opportunities. Offers seminars and special events. Fosters individual growth and encourages self-improvement.

Rochester

★2594★ Black Women's Support Group
280 Valiant Dr.
Rochester, NY 14623
Phone: (716)359-2302
Merlina Moore, Exec. Officer

★2595★ DES Cancer Network
PO Box 10185
Rochester, NY 14610

★2596★ Greater Rochester Women's Fund
c/o Rochester Area Foundation
335 Main St. E. No. 402
Rochester, NY 14604
Phone: (716)325-4353
Phyllis Collier, Chair

★2597★ Young Women's Christian Association of Rochester and Monroe County
175 Clinton Ave., N.
Rochester, NY 14604
Phone: (716)546-5820

Description: Seeks to develop and improve the spiritual, social, mental, and physical life of young people and adults. **Affiliated with:** Young Women's Chrisitan Association of the United States of America.

Rosedale

★2598★ The Women's Studio Workshop
PO Box 489
Rosedale, NY 12472
Phone: (914)658-9133
Ann Kalmbach, Director

Description: A nonprofit organization supported by state and federal arts funds, fees, and membership dues. Provide teaching programs of studio arts instruction and work experience in the visual arts. Has workshops, dialogs, and film and video showings.

Scarsdale

★2599★ Older Women's League (OWL) Westchester Chapter
162 Wyndcliff Rd.
Scarsdale, NY 10583
Phone: (914)472-3340
Elaine Wilk Cohen, Contact

Schenectady

★2600★ Girl Scouts, Mohawk Pathways Council
945 Palmer Ave.
Schenectady, NY 12309
Phone: (518)374-3345
Pamela Hyland, Exec.Dir.

Description: Girls ages five-18 and adult volunteers. To inspire girls with the highest ideals of character, conduct, and patriotism. **Affiliated with:** Girl Scouts of the U.S.A.

★2601★ Schenectady County Right to Life
PO Box 9231
Schenectady, NY 12309
Phone: (518)374-4588
Robert E. Griesemer, Exec.Dir.

Description: Individuals opposed to abortion. Works to restore legal protection to all "human life", from conception to natural death. Maintains education office; provides referral services.

★2602★ Young Women's Christian Association of Schenectady
44 Washington Ave.
Schenectady, NY 12305
Phone: (518)374-3394
Description: Seeks to develop and improve the spiritual, social, mental, and physical life of young people and adults. **Affiliated with:** Young Women's Christian Association of the United States of America.

Selden

★2603★ Older Women's League (OWL) Suffolk County Chapter
36 Kings Ave.
Selden, NY 11784
Phone: (516)261-0460
Kay Murphy, Contact

Seneca Falls

★2604★ Stanton Foundation (KCSF)
PO Box 603
Seneca Falls, NY 13148
Phone: (315)568-8486
Mary Ellen Snyder, Exec. Officer
Founded: 1978. **Description:** Participants include educators and activists from Seneca Falls and central New York who work to interpret the works of Elizabeth Cady Stanton (1815-1902), the suffragist responsible for the first women's rights convention held in 1848. Supports the Women's Rights National Historical Park in Seneca Falls, NY. Has purchased the home of Stanton and donated it to the National Park Service in 1982. Has administered national design competition for architectural restoration of the Wesleyan Chapel, site of the first convention; has produced video documentary about the chapel. Sponsors lectures, forums, and artistic presentations that relate the history of women's rights activities to contemporary concerns. **Regional Groups:** 1. **Local Groups:** 1. **Publications:** *Newsletter*, 2/year. Includes information on foundation activities, book reviews, and reprints of lectures. • Also publishes *Upstate New York Women's History Trail* and *Seneca Falls, 1848: All Men and Women Are Created Equal*; produces *The Wesleyan Chapel: Birthplace of Women's Rights* (video documentary).

Snyder

★2605★ Amherst Business and Professional Women's Club
99 Hallwill Dr.
Snyder, NY 14226
Phone: (716)839-9630
Constance Bridges, Pres.
Description: Business and professional women. To promote complete participation, equal opportunities, and economic self-sufficiency for working women. Offers scholarships. **Affiliated with:** National Federation of Business and Professional Women's Clubs of the U.S.A.

Staten Island

★2606★ Teen Pregnancy Network of Staten Island
392 Forest Ave.
Staten Island, NY 10301
Phone: (718)447-5660
Fax: (718)720-8092
Jo Kelly, Exec.Dir.
Description: Youth service providers. Coordinates services to pregnant, parenting, and at risk teenagers. Facilitates information exchange between agencies. Provides educational forums for service providers and community members. Seeks to improve youth services.

Syracuse

★2607★ Association for Women in Science, Syracuse Chapter
c/o Susan Anagnost
SUNY Health Science Center
Syracuse, NY 13210-0000
Susan Anagnost, Contact
Description: Works to improve education and employment opportunities for women in the sciences.

★2608★ Religious Coalition for Abortion Rights, New York State
3049 E. Genessee St.
Syracuse, NY 13224
Phone: (315)446-6151
Fax: (315)446-5789
Audrey R. Kutil, Admin.
Description: Interfaith representatives organized to support the right to choose whether and when to bear children based on individual conscience and personal faith. Opposes legislation intended to make abortion inaccessible. **Affiliated with:** Religious Coalition for Abortion Rights.

★2609★ Young Women's Christian Association of Syracuse and Onondaga County
960 Salt Springs Rd.
Syracuse, NY 13224
Phone: (315)445-1418
Shirley M. Ward, Exec.Dir.
Description: Seeks to develop and improve the spiritual, social, mental, and physical life of young people and adults. **Affiliated with:** Young Women's Christian Association of the United States of America.

Troy

★2610★ Young Women's Christian Association of Troy-Cohoes
21 1st St.
Troy, NY 12180
Phone: (518)274-7100
Lynn Holley-Mayer, Exec. Officer
Description: Seeks to develop and improve the spiritual, social, mental, and physical life of adults and young people over the age of 12 in Troy, NY. Sponsors day care, preschool, and after school program. Operates shelter for women in transition. **Affiliated with:** Young Women's Christian Association of the United States of America.

Utica

★2611★ Young Women's Christian Association of Utica
1000 Cornelia St.
Utica, NY 13502
Phone: (315)732-2159
Description: Seeks to develop and improve the spiritual, social, mental, and physical life of young people and adults. **Affiliated with:** Young Women's Christian Association of the United States of America.

Wappingers Falls

★2612★ National Organization for Women, Mid-Hudson Chapter
PO Box 1173
Wappingers Falls, NY 12590
Phone: (914)227-7750
Laurette Giardino, Co-Pres.
Description: Feminists in Dutchess County, NY and parts of Putnam and Ulster counties, NY. To ensure equality of women. Sponsors demonstrations.

Watertown

★2613★ Cesarean Prevention Movement of Northern New York
129 Haney St.
Watertown, NY 13601
Phone: (315)788-2182
Sally A. Dear, Pres.
Description: Individuals seeking consumer oriented childbirth information, support, and planning. Provides support to women who do not want a cesarean delivery. **Affiliated with:** Cesarean Prevention Movement.

★2614★ Jefferson County Women's Democratic Club
c/o Rose M. Ward
522 Mohawk St.
Watertown, NY 13601
Phone: (315)788-7583
Rose M. Ward, Pres.
Description: Women democrats. Promotes the election of democrats to local, state, and national office. **Affiliated with:** Jefferson County Democratic Committee.

★2615★ Young Women's Christian Association of Watertown
50 Public Sq.
Watertown, NY 13601
Phone: (315)788-6610
L. T. Lynes, Contact
Description: Seeks to develop and improve the spiritual, social, mental, and physical life of young people and adults. **Affiliated with:** Young Women's Christian Association of the United States of America.

Webster

★2616★ Women's Club of Webster
631 Lake Rd.
Webster, NY 14580
Phone: (716)671-4799
Margaret S. Brown, Pres.
Description: Women aged 35-70 providing community service.

West Berne

★2617★ Association for Women in Science, Albany Area Chapter
c/o Kathy Moore
Bradt Hollow Rd.
Box 116
West Berne, NY 12023-0116
Kathy Moore, Contact

Description: Works to improve education and employment opportunities for women in the sciences.

Westfield

★2618★ Young Women's Christian Association of Westfield
58 S. Portage St.
Westfield, NY 14787
Phone: (716)326-2011
Carol Best, Contact

Description: Seeks to develop and improve the spiritual, social, mental, and physical life of young people and adults. **Affiliated with:** Young Women's Christian Association of the United States of America.

White Plains

★2619★ Women in SelfHelp
468 Rosedale Ave.
White Plains, NY 10605
Phone: (914)946-5757
Mildred Kaplan, Dir.

Description: Support group for women. Sponsors Japanese connection and mothers connection. Holds annual fundraiser and monthly staff meeting. Offers referral service.

★2620★ Young Women's Christian Association of White Plains and Central Westchester
515 North St.
White Plains, NY 10605
Phone: (914)949-6227
Betty J. Grosse, Contact

Description: Seeks to develop and improve the spiritual, social, mental, and physical life of young people adults. **Affiliated with:** Young Women's Christian Association of the United States of America.

Whitesboro

★2621★ Older Women's League (OWL) Mohawk Valley Chapter
1 Symphony Dr.
Whitesboro, NY 13490
Phone: (315)736-0728
Charlene Heath, Contact

Yonkers

★2622★ Young Women's Christian Association of Yonkers
87 S. Broadway
Yonkers, NY 10701
Phone: (914)963-0640
Fax: (914)963-7103

Description: Seeks to develop and improve the spiritual, social, mental, and physical life of young people and adults. **Affiliated with:** Young Women's Christian Association of the United States of America.

North Carolina

Ahoskie

★2623★ Center for Women's Economic Alternatives
PO Box 1033
Ahoskie, NC 27910
Phone: (919)332-4179
Sarah Fields-Davis, Exec.Dir.

Description: Provides workplace and benefits education. Maintains referral service.

Albemarle

★2624★ La Leche League North Carolina
2222 Monza Dr.
Albemarle, NC 28001
Phone: (704)983-1559
Karen McAlister, Contact

Description: Organized to assist women in breastfeeding. **Affiliated with:** La Leche League International.

Asheboro

★2625★ Randolph County Council on Adolescent Pregnancy Prevention
c/o Patricia A Chamberlin
1438 E. Dixie Dr, Ste. 180
Asheboro, NC 27203-6008

Beaufort

★2626★ Carteret County Domestic Violence Program
c/o Joan Cloutier
402 W. Turner St.
Beaufort, NC 28516-1838

Description: Works to eliminate domestic violence.

Durham

★2627★ National Abortion Rights Action League of North Carolina
PO Box 908
Durham, NC 27702
Phone: (919)687-4959
Faulkner Fox, Contact

★2628★ North Carolina Coalition Against Domestic Violence
PO Box 51875
Durham, NC 27717-1875
Phone: (919)490-1467
Diane Hall, Contact

★2629★ Women-In-Action Clearinghouse
112 N. Queen St.
Box F
Durham, NC 27701
Kathereen Johnson, Exec. Dir.

Founded: 1968. **Description:** Coordinates community resources to aid people in times of crisis. **Publications:** Brochures and a newsletter.

Eden

★2630★ American Business Women's Association, Eden Charter Chapter
Rte. 2, Box 903
Eden, NC 27288
Phone: (919)623-9724
Fax: (919)623-2023
Lucille S. Johnson, Pres.

Description: Interested persons working to unite women of diverse backgrounds and raise funds for scholarships. **Affiliated with:** American Business Women's Association.

★2631★ Women's League of Eden
606 Briarwood Dr.
Eden, NC 27288-5241

Description: Women's volunteer service club.

Fayetteville

★2632★ Cumberland Council on Adolescent Pregnancy
308 Green St.
Fayetteville, NC 28301-5057

Description: Individuals working to reduce the rate of adolescent pregnancy.

Gastonia

★2633★ Pioneer Girl Scout Council
324 N. Highland St.
Gastonia, NC 28052-2194
Phone: (704)864-3245
Toll-free: 800-629-6031
Fax: (704)864-9020
Sylvia L. Holmes, Exec.Dir.

Description: Girls aged five to 17 in Cleveland, Gaston, Lincoln, and Rutherford counties, NC. Offers informal educational and recreational programs. Seeks to promote good citizenship. **Affiliated with:** Girl Scouts of the U.S.A.

Goldsboro

★2634★ Girl Scout Council of Coastal Carolina
108 E. Lockhaven Dr.
Goldsboro, NC 27530
Phone: (919)734-6231
Ursula M. Pombier, Exec.Dir.

Description: Girls aged five to 17. Provides informal program of education, recreation, and leadership training. **Affiliated with:** Girl Scouts of the U.S.A.

Greensboro

★2635★ North Carolina Branch of National Abortion Rights Action League
819 N. Elm St., No. 4
Greensboro, NC 27401
Phone: (919)273-7566

Henderson

★2636★ Vance County Coalition on Adolescent Pregnancy
PO Box 2504
Henderson, NC 27536-6504

Hendersonville

★2637★ **American Association of University Women, North Carolina Chapter**
c/o Elizabeth S. Black
150 7-K Greenville Hwy.
Hendersonville, NC 28792
Phone: (704)692-0618
Elizabeth S. Black, Pres.
Description: Women graduates of regionally accredited four year colleges and universities. Works for the advancement of women through advocacy and emphasis on lifelong learning. **Affiliated with:** American Association of University Women.

Jacksonville

★2638★ **Onslow County Young Woman of the Year Scholarship Foundation**
c/o Wanda Snowdon
309 Luan Dr.
Jacksonville, NC 28546-6628

Moravian Falls

★2639★ **National Federation of Democratic Women, North Carolina Chapter**
Rt. 1, Box 100
Moravian Falls, NC 28654
Phone: (919)667-2744
Betty S. Winslow, Pres.
Description: Democratic women registered to vote. Teaches philosophy of Democratic Party, explores issues, and assists Democratic candidates in general elections. **Affiliated with:** National Federation of Democratic Women.

Raleigh

★2640★ **League of Women Voters of North Carolina**
801 Oberlin Rd., Ste. 325
Raleigh, NC 27605
Phone: (919)839-5532
Claudia Kadis, President

★2641★ **National Association of Women Business Owners North Carolina Chapter**
c/o Absolute Typography
6512 Falls of Neuse Rd., No. 100
Raleigh, NC 27615
Phone: (919)878-6631
Vickie Cribb, President

★2642★ **North Carolina Child Support Council**
PO Box 2084
Raleigh, NC 27602-2084
Description: Supports and promotes the child support issues in North Carolina.

★2643★ **Young Women's Christian Association of Wake County**
1012 Oberlin Rd.
Raleigh, NC 27605
Phone: (919)828-3205
Pamela J. Dowdy, Exec.Dir.
Description: Seeks to develop and improve the spiritual, social, mental, and physical well-being of young people and adults. Active in the fight against racism.

Reidsville

★2644★ **American Business Women's Association, Carolina Morning Chapter**
Rt. 3, Box 643
Reidsville, NC 27320
Doris Meacher, Contact
Description: Business and professional women. To promote complete participation, equal opportunities, and economic self-sufficiency for working women. Bestows scholarships to young women in Rockingham County, NC.

Research Triangle Park

★2645★ **Association for Women in Science, Triangle Area Chapter**
c/o Jane Ellen Simmons
Enviromental Protection Agency, Md74
Research Triangle Park, NC 27711-0000
Description: Works to improve education and employment opportunities for women in the sciences.

Roaring Gap

★2646★ **Sparta Women's Club**
c/o Genia J. George
PO Box 42
Roaring Gap, NC 28668
Phone: (919)363-2312
Genia J. George, Sec.-Treas.
Description: Women organized for civic activities. Conducts beautification projects and charitable activities. Awards scholarship to high school senior. Sponsors child at agricultural extension camp. Makes monetary contributions.

Rockingham

★2647★ **Richmond County Council on the Status of Women**
908 Morningside Dr.
Rockingham, NC 28379
Phone: (919)997-5866
Svea E. Strong, Chairperson
Description: Interested persons working to address women's issues, initiate programs, and promote observances of women's achievements. **Affiliated with:** North Carolina Council on the Status of Women.

Statesville

★2648★ **American Business Women's Association, Metrolina Chapter**
c/o Jean Harpe
Rte. 2, Box 51
Statesville, NC 28677
Phone: (704)876-2878
Jean Harpe, Pres.
Description: Business and professional women. To promote complete participation, equal opportunities, and economic self-sufficiency for working women. Raises money for scholarships for young women. Issues publications. **Affiliated with:** American Business Women's Association.

Stoneville

★2649★ **Eden Business and Professional Women's Club**
PO Box 214
Stoneville, NC 27048
Phone: (919)573-9133
Jane A. Yount, Pres.
Description: Business and professional women. To promote complete participation, equal opportunities, and economic self-sufficiency for working women. Fosters cooperation and seeks to increase industrial, scientific, and other vocational opportunities for women. **Affiliated with:** National Federation of Business and Professional Women's Clubs of the U.S.A.

Whiteville

★2650★ **A Woman's Choices of Columbus County**
107 Powell Building
Whiteville, NC 28472-3123

Williamston

★2651★ **Martin County Women's Council**
c/o Pauline Savage
PO Box 1405
Williamston, NC 27892
Phone: (919)792-3587
Pauline Savage, Chairperson
Description: Women organized to address needs and concerns of women and disseminate information.

Wilson

★2652★ **American Association of University Women, Wilson County Branch**
PO Box 545
Wilson, NC 27894
Phone: (919)237-1498
Brenda Thorne, Pres.
Description: Women graduates of regionally accredited four year colleges and universities. Works for the advancement of women through advocacy and emphasis on lifelong learning. **Affiliated with:** American Association of University Women; American Association of University Women, North Carolina Chapter.

Winston-Salem

★2653★ **Older Women's League (OWL) Winston-Salem Chapter**
1220 Forsyth St.
Winston-Salem, NC 27101
Phone: (919)777-3000
Peggy Matthews, Contact

North Dakota

Bismarck

★2654★ **North Dakota Council on Abused Women's Services**
State Networking Office
418 E. Rosser Ave., Ste. 320
Bismarck, ND 58501
Phone: (701)255-6240
Toll-free: 800-472-2911
Bonnie Palacek, Contact

Drayton

★2655★ North Dakota Agri-Women
Rte. 1, Box 25
Drayton, ND 58285
Phone: (701)454-3413
Vivian Emanuelson, Exec. Officer

Fargo

★2656★ Fargo Women of Today
PO Box 503
Fargo, ND 58107
Phone: (701)235-8581
Margaret Kloster, Pres.

Description: Women over 17 years old. Encourages community service and leadership development. Participates in local charitable programs. Conducts competitions. Sponsors Casino Night.

**★2657★ League of Women Voters of
North Dakota**
15 Broadway, No. 600
Fargo, ND 58102-4907
Phone: (701)232-6696
Genevieve Durben, President

**★2658★ National Association of Women in
Construction, Fargo/Moorhead Chapter
246**
2208 2nd. Ave S.
Fargo, ND 58103
Phone: (701)235-4441
Fax: (701)235-3435
Amy Bertsch, Pres.

Description: Women affiliated with the construction industry. Encourages professional cooperation and communication among members. Promotes education and service to the construction industry.

**★2659★ North Dakota Abortion Rights
Action League**
PO Box 284
Fargo, ND 58102
Phone: (701)239-8237

**★2660★ Young Women's Christian
Association of Fargo-Moorhead**
1616 12th Ave., N.
Fargo, ND 58102
Phone: (701)232-2547

Description: Seeks to develop and improve the spiritual, social, mental, and physical well-being of young people and adults. **Affiliated with:** Young Women's Christian Association of the United States of America.

Grand Forks

**★2661★ American Business Women's
Association, Grand Forks Chapter**
c/o Marlene Maxon
3107 E. Elmwood Dr.
Grand Forks, ND 58201
Phone: (701)772-8106
Marlene Maxon, Contact

Description: Business and professional women. Awards scholarships to women.

★2662★ Law Women's Caucus
University of North Dakota School of Law
Grand Forks, ND 58202
Phone: (701)777-2104
Fax: (701)777-2104
Carol Brekke, Pres.

Description: Law students and members of the North Dakota Bar Association. Promotes the position of women in the legal profession and in society through furthering civil and human rights.

**★2663★ North Dakota Coalition for
Healthy Mothers, Healthy Babies**
RD 1, Box 139
Grand Forks, ND 58201-9775

Description: Supports and promotes the Prenatal care in North Dakota.

Jamestown

**★2664★ American Association of
University Women, North Dakota**
911 9th Ave. SW
Jamestown, ND 58401
Phone: (701)252-7852
Kathleen Enzminger, Pres.

Description: Women graduates of regionally accredited four year colleges and universities. Works for the advancement of women through advocacy and emphasis on lifelong learning. **Affiliated with:** American Association of University Women.

Litchville

**★2665★ Valley City Christian Women's
Club**
c/o Evelyn Kluvers
Litchville, ND 58461
Phone: (701)762-3650
Evelyn Kluvers, Chm.

Description: Interdenominational Christian women's organization. Offers luncheon programs, with speakers. Provides Bible study materials. **Affiliated with:** Stone Croft Ministries.

Minot

**★2666★ Girl Scouts of the U.S.A., Minot
Council**
1515 24th Ave. SW
Minot, ND 58701
Phone: (701)852-5611
Nancy Heskin Rakness, Contact

Description: Girls and adult volunteers in 14 North Dakota counties. Inspires girls to the highest ideals of character, conduct, patriotism, and service so that they may become happy and resourceful citizens. **Affiliated with:** Girl Scouts of the U.S.A.

**★2667★ Young Women's Christian
Association of Minot**
205 3rd Ave., SE
Minot, ND 58701
Phone: (701)838-1812
Shirley A. Olson, Exec.Dir.

Description: Seeks to develop and improve the spiritual, social, mental, and physical well-being of young people and adults. **Affiliated with:**

Young Women's Christian Association of the United States of America.

Portland

**★2668★ North Dakota Federation of
Republican Women**
RR 1, Box 29
Portland, ND 58274
Phone: (701)543-3303
Eileen D. Larson, Pres.

Description: Works to elect Republicans to local, state, and national office.

Williston

★2669★ Williston Chapter Right to Life
303 W. Boradway
Williston, ND 58801
Kathy Eretn, Contact

Description: Individuals in Williston, ND with strong moral and religious objections to abortion and euthenasia. Conducts education programs and lobbying activities.

Ohio

Akron

**★2670★ Akron Business and Professional
Women**
1325 Weathervane Ln., Apt. 1B
Akron, OH 44313
Phone: (216)867-2821
Fax: (216)666-7559
Mary Ann Leonino, Pres.

Description: Business and professional women. To promote complete participation, equal opportunities, and economic self-sufficiency for working women. Bestows two scholarships, Young Careerist Award, and Individual Development Program Award. Sponsors Women's History Week and takes part in Keep Akron Beautiful campaign. **Affiliated with:** International Federation of Business and Professional Women's Clubs; National Federation of Business and Professional Women's Clubs of the U.S.A.

**★2671★ Western Reserve Girl Scout
Council**
108 Fir Hill
Akron, OH 44304
Phone: (216)376-6876
Toll-free: 800-852-4474
Fax: (216)434-0662
Jody Johnston, Exec.Dir.

Description: Girls ages 5 to 18 and adult volunteers in Medina, Portage, northern Wayne, and Summit counties, OH. Seeks to help girls develop their potential through group activities. **Affiliated with:** Girl Scouts of the U.S.A.

Alliance

**★2672★ Young Women's Christian
Association of Alliance**
239 E. Market St.
Alliance, OH 44601
Phone: (216)823-1840

Description: Seeks to develop and improve the quality of life for women, children, and families in the Alliance Community. **Affiliated with:**

Young Women's Christian Association of the United States of America.

Bexley

★2673★ **Religious Coalition for Abortion Rights, Ohio Affiliate**
201 S. Cassady Ave.
Bexley, OH 43209
Phone: (614)236-8453
Jo Anne Grossman, Coordinator

Bowling Green

★2674★ **American Association of University Women, Bowling Green Branch**
133 Wolfly
Bowling Green, OH 43402
Phone: (419)353-5001
Evelyn Bachman, Pres.

Description: Women graduates of regionally accredited four year colleges and universities. Works for the advancement of women through advocacy and emphasis on lifelong learning. **Affiliated with:** American Association of University Women.

Bucyrus

★2675★ **Bucyrus Business and Professional Women's Club**
500 S. Spring St.
Bucyrus, OH 44820
Phone: (419)562-7285
Marilyn Gottfried, Pres.

Description: Employed women united to elevate their standards and promote their interests. Seeks to bring about cooperation among and extend opportunities to working women. **Affiliated with:** National Federation of Business and Professional Women's Clubs of the U.S.A.

Cambridge

★2676★ **Guernsey County Right to Life Society**
PO Box 174
Cambridge, OH 43725
Phone: (614)439-4047
Jane Grimm, Pres.

Description: Pro-life organization opposed to abortion, euthanasia, and infanticide. Conducts educational programs. Provides maternity clothes to pregnant mothers, and baby clothes and other items to persons who request assistance.

Canton

★2677★ **Lake Cable Women's Club**
5725 Fulton Dr. NW
Canton, OH 44718-1732
Description: Social and civil service organization.

★2678★ **National Association of Women Highway Safety Leaders, Ohio Chapter**
c/o Barbara J. Bailey
3042 16th St., NW
Canton, OH 44708
Phone: (216)456-6737
Barbara J. Bailey, Exec. Officer

Description: Women interested in traffic safety seeking to reduce the number of traffic accidents, injuries, and deaths. **Affiliated with:** National Association of Women Highway Safety Leaders.

★2679★ **Young Women's Christian Association of Canton**
231 6th St., NE
Canton, OH 44702
Phone: (216)453-7644

Description: Seeks to develop and improve the spiritual, social, mental, and physical life of women and girls over the age of 12. **Affiliated with:** Young Women's Christian Association of the United States of America.

Chagrin Falls

★2680★ **The Chagrin Valley Woman's Exchange**
88 N. Main St.
Chagrin Falls, OH 44022
Phone: (216)247-5033
Judy Tremain, Pres.

Description: Homemakers and retired businesswomen. Maintains shop for the promotion and sale of arts and crafts. **Affiliated with:** Federation of Women's Exchanges.

Cincinnati

★2681★ **Cincinnati Coalition of Domestic Violence**
c/o Jan Day
7374 Reading Rd., Ste. A-1
Cincinnati, OH 45237-3401
Jan Day, Contact

Description: Works to prevent domestic violence; provides support services to the abused.

★2682★ **Prenatal Care Alliance**
c/o Joy Lawrence-Slater
11340 Kenn Rd.
Cincinnati, OH 45240-2526
Joy Lawrence-Slater, Contact

Description: Professionals and interested individuals united in the Cincinnati, OH area to ensure qulaity prenatal care for needy mothers.

★2683★ **Women's American ORT, Greater Cincinnati Region**
7536 Reading Rd., No. 2
Cincinnati, OH 45237
Phone: (513)821-7744
Laura Foster, Pres.

Description: Membership is primarily composed of Jewish women. Seeks to raise money for the Organization for Rehabilitation Through Training (ORT) network of vocational and technical schools. Provides volunteer services for community projects. **Affiliated with:** Allegheny/Great Lakes Field Service; Women's American ORT; Women's American ORT, District VII.

★2684★ **Young Women's Christian Association of Cincinnati**
898 Walnut St.
Cincinnati, OH 45202
Phone: (513)241-7090
Charlene Ventura, Exec.Dir.

Description: Works to empower women and eliminate racism. Conducts job readiness and literacy programs; makes available shelters for battered women, counseling programs for spouse abusers, and teen pregnancy prevention programs; operates emergency food distribution center and fitness facilities. **Affiliated with:** Young Women's Christian Association of the United States of America.

Cleveland

★2685★ **DES Action**
Box 21625
Cleveland, OH 44121

★2686★ **Ohio Branch of National Abortion Rights Action League**
604 Rockefeller Bldg.
614 Superior Ave. NW
Cleveland, OH 44113
Phone: (216)522-0169
Ellen Ackerman, Contact

★2687★ **Women Space**
1021 Euclid Ave., 7th Fl.
Cleveland, OH 44115
Phone: (216)696-6967
Susan Haas, Contact

Founded: 1977. **Description:** Dedicated to serving the needs of women in the greater Cleveland community.

★2688★ **Women's City Club**
3813 Euclid Ave.
Cleveland, OH 44115
Phone: (216)881-1101
Judith Makaryk Rosen, Exec.Dir.

Description: Women in Cuyahoga County and six surrounding counties in Ohio. Conducts civic and social programs, lectures, panel discussions, and presentations. Sponsors charitable activities benefitting blind people and the homeless.

★2689★ **Women's Community Foundation**
12200 Fairhill Rd., Rm. E-008
Cleveland, OH 44120
Phone: (216)229-5001
Emily Ford, Executive Director
Remarks: Serves Cuyahoga county.

★2690★ **Young Women's Christian Association of Cleveland**
3201 Euclid Ave.
Cleveland, OH 44115
Phone: (216)881-6878
Carol Rowngardt, Exec.Dir.

Description: Seeks to develop and improve the spiritual, social, mental, and physical life of women and girls over the age of 12 in Cuyahoga County, OH. **Affiliated with:** Ohio Council of Young Women's Christian Associations; Young Women's Christian Association of the United States of America.

Cleveland Heights

★2691★ Childbirth Education Association of Cleveland
c/o Chris Moore
3566 Fenley Rd.
Cleveland Heights, OH 44121-1346
Chris Moore, Contact
Description: Promotes knowledge of childbirth among women.

★2692★ Greater Cleveland Community Shares
3130 Mayfield Rd., Ste. W207
Cleveland Heights, OH 44118
Phone: (216)371-0209
Joan Farragher, Sec.
Description: Advocacy groups for employees, minorities, and senior citizens. Works to improve neighborhoods; assists victims of domestic violence, mental illness, divorce, learning disabilities, and unemployment; promotes world peace, environmental protection, healthy race relations, and fair housing policies. **Affiliated with:** Community Shares U.S.A.

Columbus

★2693★ Action Ohio Coalition for Battered Women
PO Box 15673
Columbus, OH 43215
Phone: (614)221-1255

★2694★ American Society of Women Accountants, Columbus Chapter
1810-B Northwest Ct.
Columbus, OH 43212
Phone: (614)268-1504
Helen Haigner, Exec. Officer

★2695★ Association for Women in Science, Central Ohio Chapter
PO Box 21772
Columbus, OH 43221-0772
Description: Works to improve education and employment opportunities for women in the sciences.

★2696★ Columbus Woman's Club
1039 Stoney Creek Rd.
Columbus, OH 43235
Phone: (614)436-3535
Eleanor Botkin, Exec. Officer
Description: Women's volunteer service club. Contributes to Creative Living, a quadroplegic complex. **Affiliated with:** General Federation of Women's Clubs.

★2697★ Columbus Women's District Golf Association
c/o Vivian M. Shively
4551 Lanercost Way
Columbus, OH 43220-2916
Vivian M. Shively, Treas.
Description: Promotes women's golf.

★2698★ Epsilon Kappa Tau Alumnae Sorority
c/o Rebecca C. Princehorn
100 S. 3rd St.
Columbus, OH 43215-4214
Rebecca C. Princehorn, Contact
Description: Members of the Epilson Kappa Tau Sorority who have graduated.

★2699★ League of Women Voters of Ohio
65 S. 4th St.
Columbus, OH 43215
Phone: (614)469-1505
Marilyn Shearer, President

★2700★ National Abortion Rights Action League of Ohio
760 E. Broad St.
Columbus, OH 43205
Phone: (614)221-2594
Jane Larson, Contact

★2701★ National Anorexic Aid Program, Ohio Chapter
1925 E. Dublin-Granville Rd.
Columbus, OH 43229
Phone: (614)436-1112
Arline Iannicello, Dir.

★2702★ Ohio Federation of Republican Women
172 E. State St., Ste. 400
Columbus, OH 43215
Phone: (614)228-2481
Karen Whitcraft, Exec.Sec.

★2703★ Ohio Women
65 S. 4th St.
Columbus, OH 43215
Phone: (614)463-9558
Joyce Garver Keller, Pres.
Description: Seeks to provide education and conduct research on issues of interest to women. Serves as a network for progressive women's organizations in Ohio.

★2704★ Ohio Women's Division Council
c/o Marcia Miller
Ohio Bureau of Employment Services
Columbus, OH 43215
Phone: (614)466-4496
Marcia Miller, Dir.

★2705★ Women's Information Center
c/o Ohio General Assembly
State House
Columbus, OH 43215
Phone: (614)466-5580
Toll-free: 800-282-3040
Description: Serves as a clearinghouse for information on laws affecting women. Provides referral service to resources to help young women and to appropriate state and federal agencies handling discrimination complaints and disseminates a variety of topical brochures published by various agencies free of charge. **Publications:** *WIC Status Report* (newsletter) and *Legislative Update*.

★2706★ Women's Outreach for Women
1950-H N. 4th St.
Columbus, OH 43201
Phone: (614)291-3639
Cheryl Carter, Exec.Dir.
Description: Women from Franklin County, OH recovering from alcohol abuse, narcotic abuse,

or incest. Provides educational workshops and films and peer support services. Sponsors social activities. **Telecommunications Services:** Crisis telephone line.

★2707★ Women's Overseas Service League, Columbus Unit
438 N. Westmoor Ave.
Columbus, OH 43204
Description: Women who served overseas with the armed services or attached services. Promotes patriotism, comradeship, and a sense of obligation. Conducts services for disabled veterans. **Affiliated with:** Women's Overseas Service League.

★2708★ Young Women's Christian Association of Columbus
65 S. 4th St.
Columbus, OH 43215
Phone: (614)224-9121
Karen Schwarzwalder, Contact
Description: Seeks to develop and improve the spiritual, social, mental, and physical life of women and girls over the age of 12. **Affiliated with:** Young Women's Christian Association of the United States of America.

Coshocton

★2709★ Young Women's Christian Association of Coshocton
623 Main St.
Coshocton, OH 43812
Phone: (614)622-3542
Description: Seeks to develop and improve the spiritual, social, mental, and physical life of women and girls over the age of 12. **Affiliated with:** Young Women's Christian Association of the United States of America.

Dayton

★2710★ Dayton Childbirth Education Association
3809 Wilmington Pike
Dayton, OH 45429
Phone: (513)294-5772

★2711★ Girl Scouts of the U.S.A., Buckeye Trails Council
450 Shoup Mill Rd.
Dayton, OH 45415
Phone: (513)275-7601
Toll-free: 800-233-4845
Fax: (513)275-1147
S. Annelle Lewis, Exec. Officer
Description: Young women and girls, ages 5-18. Seeks to develop moral values through community service, citizenship training, and mental and physical fitness. **Affiliated with:** Girl Scouts of the U.S.A.

★2712★ Miami Valley Aborted Women
Wright Bros.
PO Box 9284
Dayton, OH 45409-0000
Description: Women who have had abortions united for mutual support.

★2713★ Older Women's League (OWL)
Montgomery County Chapter
628 Cambridge Ave.
Dayton, OH 45407
Phone: (513)277-7901
Lulu Jackson, Contact

★2714★ Older Women's League (OWL)
Southwestern Ohio Chapter
8100 Clyo Rd.
Dayton, OH 45458
Connie Goss, Contact

★2715★ Women's Overseas Service
League, Dayton Unit
524 Daytona Pkwy., No. 9
Dayton, OH 45406
Phone: (513)278-9560
Ruth M. Wysor, Pres.

Description: Women who served overseas with the armed services or attached services. Promotes patriotism, comradeship, and a sense of obligation. Conducts services for disabled veterans. **Affiliated with:** Women's Overseas Service League; Veterans Administration Voluntary Service of Dayton.

★2716★ Young Women's Christian
Association of Dayton
141 W. 3rd St.
Dayton, OH 45402
Phone: (513)461-5550

Description: Seeks to develop and improve the spiritual, social, mental, and physical life of women and girls over the age of 12. **Affiliated with:** Young Women's Christian Association of the United States of America.

Delaware

★2717★ American Association of
University Women, Delaware Branch
130 Pinecrest Dr.
Delaware, OH 43015
Phone: (614)363-0478
Judy Allen, Pres.

Description: Women graduates of regionally accredited four year colleges and universities. Works for the advancement of women through advocacy and emphasis on lifelong learning. Conducts home tours. **Affiliated with:** American Association of University Women.

Elyria

★2718★ Young Women's Christian
Association of Elyria
318 West Ave.
Elyria, OH 44035
Phone: (216)322-6308

Description: Seeks to develop and improve the spiritual, social, mental, and physical life of women and girls over the age of 12. **Affiliated with:** Young Women's Christian Association of the United States of America.

Fairborn

★2719★ American Association of
University Women, Fairborn Branch
c/o Georgia Hale
51 S. Wright
Fairborn, OH 45324
Phone: (513)878-0575
Georgia Hale, Exec. Officer

Description: Women graduates of regionally accredited four year colleges and universities. Works for the advancement of women through advocacy and emphasis on lifelong learning. Promotes the Greene County Domestic Violence Center. **Affiliated with:** American Association of University Women.

Hillsboro

★2720★ American Association of
University Women, Hillsboro Branch
c/o Sandra Nartker
6295 SR 138
Hillsboro, OH 45133
Phone: (513)393-2294
Sandra Nartker, Educ. Chair

Description: Women graduates of regionally accredited four year colleges and universities. Works for the advancement of women through advocacy and emphasis on lifelong learning. Sponsors local scholarship, woman's recognition banquet, tasting luncheon, and annual Festival of Bells fundraiser. **Affiliated with:** American Association of University Women; International Federation of University Women.

★2721★ Hillsboro Woman's Club
c/o Virginia Morrow
8739 Dragoo Rd.
Hillsboro, OH 45133
Phone: (513)393-2643
Virginia Morrow, Exec. Officer

Description: Women interested in community service. Participates in cultural and charitable events.

Lakewood

★2722★ Older Women's League (OWL)
Greater Cleveland Chapter
Lakewood Office on Aging
16024 Madison Ave.
Lakewood, OH 44107
Phone: (216)521-1515
Joyce Vega, Contact

Lima

★2723★ Young Women's Christian
Association of Lima
649 W. Market St.
Lima, OH 45801
Phone: (419)228-8664

Description: Seeks to develop and improve the spiritual, social, mental, and physical life of women and girls over the age of 12. **Affiliated with:** Young Women's Christian Association of the United States of America.

Lorain

★2724★ Young Women's Christian
Association of Lorain
200 9th St.
Lorain, OH 44052
Phone: (216)244-1919
Camille Havris, Contact

Description: Seeks to develop and improve the spiritual, social, mental, and physical life of women and girls over the age of 12. **Affiliated with:** Young Women's Christian Association of the United States of America.

Mansfield

★2725★ Young Women's Christian
Association of Mansfield
455 Park Ave., W.
Mansfield, OH 44906
Phone: (419)522-1300

Description: Seeks to develop and improve the spiritual, social, mental, and physical life of women and girls over the age of 12. **Affiliated with:** Young Women's Christian Association of the United States of America.

Marion

★2726★ Ohio Domestic Violence Network
PO Box 1433
Marion, OH 43301-1433

Description: Works to reduce the incidence of domestic violence in Ohio.

Massillon

★2727★ Young Women's Christian
Association of Massillon
131 Tremont St., SE
Massillon, OH 44646
Phone: (216)837-5116

Description: Seeks to develop and improve the spiritual, social, mental, and physical life of women and girls over the age of 12. **Affiliated with:** Young Women's Christian Association of the United States of America.

Medina

★2728★ Young Women's Christian
Association of Medina County
4046 Medina Rd.
Medina, OH 44256
Phone: (216)722-2020

Description: Seeks to develop and improve the spiritual, social, mental, and physical life of women and girls over the age of 12. **Affiliated with:** Young Women's Christian Association of the United States of America.

Middletown

★2729★ Middletown Area Federation of
Women's Clubs
2009 Tullis Dr.
Middletown, OH 45042-2962

Description: Women's volunteer service club.

Napoleon

★2730★ Cesarean Prevention Movement of Northwest Ohio
Rte. 1, S-236 Rd. 11
Napoleon, OH 43545
Phone: (419)599-4780
Sherry Oberhaus, Contact
Description: Educators, parents, and couples from the Toledo, Dayton, and Findlay, OH areas dedicated to educating the public about natural childbirth. Purposes are to help couples avoid unnecessary cesareans; attempt to inform others that natural childbirth is possible after one or more cesareans; and to provide a forum where couples can discuss their concerns about the birthing process. Also functions as a support network for women healing from their last cesarean. Members are available for telephone support. Operates a small lending library which includes books and other resources. **Affiliated with:** Cesarean Prevention Movement.

Newark

★2731★ Young Women's Christian Association of Licking County
140 W. Church & 6th Sts.
Newark, OH 43055
Phone: (614)345-4084
Description: Seeks to develop and improve the spiritual, social, mental, and physical life of women and girls over the age of 12. **Affiliated with:** Young Women's Christian Association of the United States of America.

Novelty

★2732★ Russell Women's Civic Club Scholarship Fund
PO Box 124
Novelty, OH 44072-0124

Piqua

★2733★ Young Women's Christian Association of Piqua
418 N. Wayne St.
Piqua, OH 45356
Phone: (513)773-6626
Description: Seeks to develop and improve the spiritual, social, mental, and physical life of women and girls over the age of 12. **Affiliated with:** Young Women's Christian Association of the United States of America.

Rocky River

★2734★ Women's Welsh Clubs of America (WWCA)
c/o The Welsh Home
22199 Center Ridge Rd.
Rocky River, OH 44116
Phone: (216)331-0420
Kathy Lloyd, Sec.
Founded: 1914. **Description:** Organized to maintain a home for aged people of Welsh descent in Rocky River, OH. **Members:** 805. **Local Groups:** 23. **Publications:** *Annual Report.*

Salem

★2735★ Young Women's Christian Association of Salem
364 N. Lincoln Ave.
Salem, OH 44460
Phone: (216)332-9944
Barbara Cope, Exec.Dir.
Description: Seeks to develop and improve the spiritual, social, mental, and physical life of women and girls over the age of 12. **Affiliated with:** Young Women's Christian Association of the United States of America.

Springfield

★2736★ American Association of University Women, Springfield Branch
c/o Mrs. Quinn
1812 Crescent Dr.
Springfield, OH 45504
Phone: (513)399-7250
Mrs. Quinn, Sec.
Description: Women graduates of regionally accredited four year colleges and universities. Works for the advancement of women through advocacy and emphasis on lifelong learning. Makes available scholarships. **Affiliated with:** American Association of University Women.

Steubenville

★2737★ Young Women's Christian Association of Steubenville
320 N. 4th St.
Steubenville, OH 43952
Phone: (614)282-1261
Description: Seeks to develop and improve the spiritual, social, mental, and physical life of women and girls over the age of 12. **Affiliated with:** Young Women's Christian Association of the United States of America.

Toledo

★2738★ Toledo Area Association of Parents and Professionals for Safe Alternatives in Childbirth
3873 Monroe
Toledo, OH 43623
Phone: (419)472-0107
Tracy L. Meiring, Sec.-Treas.
Description: Parents, parents-to-be, and professionals in northwestern Ohio and southwestern Michigan seeking safe alternatives in childbirth. Keeps public informed on all aspects of childbirth. **Affiliated with:** International Association of Parents and Professionals for Safe Alternatives in Childbirth.

★2739★ Women in Cable, Michigan Chapter
c/o Ellen Jackson
The Cable System
5566 Southwyck Blvd.
Toledo, OH 43614
Phone: (419)866-5802
Ellen Jackson, Dir.
Description: Individuals engaged in professional activity in cable television and related industries interested in developing a high standard of professional business conduct. **Affiliated with:** Women in Cable.

★2740★ Young Women's Christian Association of Toledo
1018 Jefferson Ave.
Toledo, OH 43624
Phone: (419)241-3235
Description: Seeks to develop and improve the spiritual, social, mental, and physical life of women and girls over the age of 12. **Affiliated with:** Young Women's Christian Association of the United States of America.

Trenton

★2741★ Middletown Business and Professional Women's Club
105 E. Roger Dr.
Trenton, OH 45067
Phone: (513)988-0229
Mary Wysong, Exec. Officer
Description: Business and professional women. To promote complete participation, equal opportunities, and economic self-sufficiency for working women. Sponsors charitable events and competitions. **Affiliated with:** Middletown Area Federation Clubs; National Federation of Business and Professional Women of the U.S.A.

Van Wert

★2742★ Young Women's Christian Association of Van Wert County
408 E. Main St.
Van Wert, OH 45891
Phone: (419)238-6639
Description: Seeks to develop and improve the spiritual, social, mental, and physical life of women and girls over the age of 12. **Affiliated with:** Young Women's Christian Association of the United States of America.

Vandalia

★2743★ American Business Women - Crossroads of America Chapter
455 Glenrose
Vandalia, OH 45377
Phone: (513)890-0906
Arlene Sailer, Pres.
Description: Business and professional women. To promote complete participation, equal opportunities, and economic self-sufficiency for working women.

Wapakoneta

★2744★ Ohio Federation of Women's Clubs
709 Douglas St.
Wapakoneta, OH 45895
Phone: (614)264-0288
Shirley A. Mitchell, Pres.
Description: Women's organization promoting their common interest for the welfare of the state. Acts as a forum for the exchange of ideas. **Affiliated with:** General Federation of Women's Clubs; Great Lakes Conference.

Warren

★2745★ **Warren Young Women's Christian Association**
375 N. Park Ave.
Warren, OH 44481
Phone: (216)373-1010
Rebecca Altdoerffer, Exec.Dir.

Description: Seeks to develop and improve the spiritual, social, mental, and physical life of women and girls over the age of 12. **Affiliated with:** Young Women's Christian Association of the United States of America.

Youngstown

★2746★ **Young Women's Christian Association of Downtown Youngstown**
25 W. Rayen Ave.
Youngstown, OH 44503
Phone: (216)746-6361
Janet E. Schweitzer, Exec.Dir.

Description: Seeks to develop and improve the spiritual, social, mental, and physical life of women and girls over the age of 12. Operates shelter for battered women and residence. Provides resource referral. **Affiliated with:** Young Women's Christian Association of the United States of America.

Zanesville

★2747★ **Young Women's Christian Association of Zanesville**
49 N. 6th St.
Zanesville, OH 43701
Phone: (614)452-2717
Nancy Graham, Contact

Description: Seeks to develop and improve the spiritual, social, mental, and physical life of women and girls over the age of 12. **Affiliated with:** Young Women's Christian Association of the United States of America.

Oklahoma

Ardmore

★2748★ **Young Women's Christian Association of Ardmore**
27 W. Broadway
Ardmore, OK 73401
Phone: (405)223-2027

Description: Seeks to develop and improve the spiritual, social, mental, and physical well-being of young people and adults. **Affiliated with:** Young Women's Christian Association of the United States of America.

Bartlesville

★2749★ **American Association of University Women, Bartlesville Branch**
1432 S. Osage
Bartlesville, OK 74003-5936

Description: Women graduates of regionally accredited four year colleges and universities. Works for the advancement of women through advocacy and emphasis on lifelong learning.

★2750★ **Bartlesville Women and Children in Crisis**
PO Box 5016
Bartlesville, OK 74005
Phone: (918)336-1188
Faye Marlowe-Holden, Exec.Dir.

Description: Individuals in Washington, Nowata, and Osage counties, OK. Provides support and services to victims of domestic violence and their families.

★2751★ **Young Women's Christian Association of Bartlesville**
411 S. Johnstone Ave.
Bartlesville, OK 74003
Phone: (918)336-0503
Junie C. Janzen, Exec.Dir.

Description: Seeks to develop and improve the spiritual, social, mental, and physical life of youth and adults in the Bartlesville, OK area. Conducts charitable activities. **Affiliated with:** Young Women's Christian Association of the United States of America.

Edmond

★2752★ **DES Action**
2404 Pawnee Crossing
Edmond, OK 73034

Enid

★2753★ **Young Women's Christian Association of Enid**
525 S. Quincy
Enid, OK 73701
Phone: (405)234-7581

Description: Seeks to develop and improve the spiritual, social, mental, and physical well-being of young people and adults. **Affiliated with:** Young Women's Christian Association of the United States of America.

Muskogee

★2754★ **American Business Women's Association, Indian Capital Chapter**
3111 Tull Pl.
Muskogee, OK 74402
Phone: (918)683-6128
Jan Stevenson, Pres.

Description: Women in business, including women owning or operating their own businesses, women in professions, and women employed in any level of government, education, or retailing, manufacturing, and service companies. **Affiliated with:** American Business Women's Association.

★2755★ **American Business Women's Association, Tuit Chapter**
PO Box 605
Muskogee, OK 74402
Phone: (918)687-0230
Sharron Barns, Pres.

Description: Women in business, including women owning or operating their own businesses, women in professions, and women employed in any level of government, education, or retailing, manufacturing, and service companies. **Affiliated with:** American Business Women's Association.

★2756★ **Muskogee Women of Prayer**
c/o Mickey L. Madewell
Rte. 1, Box 391D
Muskogee, OK 74401-9801

Description: Religious women in Muskogee, OK.

Norman

★2757★ **Oklahoma Coalition on Domestic Violence and Sexual Assault**
PO Box 5089
Norman, OK 73070
Phone: (405)360-7125
Toll-free: 800-522-SAFE
Sherry Ford, Contact

Oklahoma City

★2758★ **League of Women Voters of Oklahoma**
525 NW 13th St.
Oklahoma City, OK 73103
Phone: (405)236-5338
Kathryn B. Hinkle, President

★2759★ **National Association of Women Business Owners**
Oklahoma City Chapter
c/o Freedom Personnel, Inc.
5100 N. Brookline, Ste. 175
Oklahoma City, OK 73112
Phone: (405)943-7677
Ginny Kidwell, President

★2760★ **Red Lands Council of Girl Scouts**
121 NE 50
Oklahoma City, OK 73105
Phone: (405)528-3535
Fax: (405)528-3535
Barbara Naranche, Exec.Dir.

Description: Adult volunteers and girls between 5 and 17 in northern central OK. Helps develop young girl's potential. Promotes partnership and friendship between all youth. **Affiliated with:** Girl Scouts of America.

★2761★ **Young Women's Christian Association of Oklahoma City**
2460 NW 39th St.
Oklahoma City, OK 73112
Phone: (405)948-1770

Description: Seeks to develop and improve the spiritual, social, mental, and physical well-being of young people and adults. **Affiliated with:** Young Women's Christian Association of the United States of America.

Tulsa

★2762★ **American Business Women's Association, Tulsey Town High Noon Chapter**
PO Box 871
Tulsa, OK 74102
Phone: (918)588-7161
Margaret Metcalf, Pres.

Description: Businesswomen in Tulsa, OK. Promotes the professional, educational, cultural, and social advancement of women. Conducts special events and community service activities. **Affiliated with:** American Business Women's Association.

★2763★   American Society of Women Accountants, Tulsa Chapter
c/o Nancy B. Arch
PO Box 3708
Tulsa, OK 74102-3708
Phone: (918)588-7789
Pat Philpot, Pres.

Description: Women accountants in the public, industrial, governmental, and educational sectors. Promotes and assists women entering, returning to, or employed in accounting. **Affiliated with:** American Society of Women Accountants.

★2764★   DES Action
3155 E. 68th St.
Tulsa, OK 74136

★2765★   Executive Women International, Tulsa Chapter
PO 645
Tulsa, OK 74101-0645
Phone: (918)599-3711
Fax: (918)581-1534
Marilyn Cinocca, Pres.

Description: Professional and business firms in Tulsa County, OK. Promotes member firm's interests through professional representatives. **Affiliated with:** Executive Women International.

★2766★   Federation of Colored Women's Clubs - Tulsa Chapter
c/o Fannie Bryant
1612 N. Boston
Tulsa, OK 74106
Phone: (918)584-1546
Fannie Bryant, Sec.

★2767★   Girl Scouts of the U.S.A., Magic Empire Council
2432 E. 51st St.
Tulsa, OK 74105
Phone: (918)749-2551
Bonnie R. Brewster, Exec.Dir.

Description: Girls ages five to 17 in seven counties in northeastern Oklahoma. Promotes the growth and development of members by providing leadership and lifelong skills. **Affiliated with:** Girl Scouts of the U.S.A.

★2768★   National Association of Women Business Owners
Tulsa Chapter
c/o Askins and Assoc.
1232 S. Columbia Pl.
Tulsa, OK 74104
Phone: (918)592-1466
Diana Askins, President

★2769★   Oklahoma Abortion Rights Action League
PO Box 14284
Tulsa, OK 74159
Phone: (918)254-4023
Stephanie Grogan, Contact

★2770★   Older Women's League (OWL) Tulsa Chapter
3274 S. Lakewood
Tulsa, OK 74135
Phone: (918)472-3598
Janice Meredith, Contact

★2771★   Religious Coalition for Abortion Rights, Oklahoma Chapter
PO Box 35194
Tulsa, OK 74153-0194
Phone: (918)743-8444
Virginia Van Pelt, Contact

Description: Supports legal abortion information and services. Sponsors educational events and public forums. Conducts lobbying activities; holds workshops.

★2772★   Women's Overseas Service League, Tulsa Chapter
c/o Margaret West
4643 E. 24 Pl.
Tulsa, OK 74114
Phone: (918)744-8521
Margaret West, Pres.

Description: Women who served overseas with the armed services, American Red Cross, Salvation Army, or other service organizations. Seeks to carry on the spirit of service that originally prompted members to serve overseas. **Affiliated with:** Women's Overseas Service League.

★2773★   Young Women's Christian Association of Tulsa
4900 S. Lewis
Tulsa, OK 74105
Phone: (918)749-1074

Description: Seeks to develop and improve the spiritual, social, mental, and physical well-being of young people and adults. **Affiliated with:** Young Women's Christian Association of the United States of America.

Oregon

Ashland

★2774★   Southern Oregon Women Writer's Group
200 Ashland Rd.
Ashland, OR 97520
Phone: (503)482-8864
Tangren Alexander, Contact

Founded: 1981. **Description:** Group meets to share writing, music and art.

Corvallis

★2775★   Association for Women in Science, Corvallis Chapter
3145 Seneca
Corvallis, OR 97330
Phone: (503)757-1728
Dr. Ann E. Brodie, Pres.

Description: Women scientists. Promotes equal opportunities for women entering the science profession. Works to help women achieve their career goals. Sponsors career workshop for girls in the seventh and eighth grade.

★2776★   Center Against Rape and Domestic Violence
PO Box 914
Corvallis, OR 97339
Phone: (503)758-0219
Sue Parrott, Adm.Dir.

Description: Individuals in Benton and Linn counties, OR working to change society's attitude on rape and domestic violence. Operates

safe shelter. Advocates for victims of rape and domestic violence. Sponsors support groups, counseling, and children's program. **Telecommunications Services:** Crisis hotline.

Eugene

★2777★   Older Women's League (OWL) Emerald Chapter
1515 Polk No. 6
Eugene, OR 97402
Phone: (503)344-4934
Carmen Yokum, Contact

★2778★   Oregon Branch of National Abortion Rights Action League
PO Box 11542
Eugene, OR 97440
Phone: (503)342-1922
Judith Schoap, Contact

Gresham

★2779★   American Association of University Women, Oregon Chapter
914 Washburn Ln.
Gresham, OR 97080
Phone: (503)773-8846
Gayle Clawson, Pres.

Description: Women graduates of regionally accredited four year colleges and universities. Works for the advancement of women through advocacy and emphasis on lifelong learning. **Affiliated with:** American Association of University Women.

Junction City

★2780★   Junction City Business and Professional Women's Club
PO Box 261
Junction City, OR 97448
Phone: (503)688-9541
Amanda Marker, Pres.

Description: Business and professional women. To promote complete participation, equal opportunities, and economic self-sufficiency for working women. Awards scholarships to young women. Supports community youth and holiday activities. **Affiliated with:** National Federation of Business and Professional Women of the U.S.A.; Oregon State Business and Professional Women Federation.

★2781★   Lane County Women for Agriculture
94705 Oakely Dr.
Junction City, OR 97448
Phone: (503)998-8784
Gerry Ottosen, Exec. Officer

Description: Educational organization for women in agriculture. **Affiliated with:** Oregon Women in Agriculture.

★2782★   Oregon Women for Agriculture
94705 Oaklea Dr.
Junction City, OR 97448
Phone: (503)998-8784
Gerry Ottosen, Exec. Officer

Description: Individuals with agricultural interests. Promotes public education regarding agriculture. Holds monthly board meeting. **Affiliated with:** American Agri-Women.

Marylhurst

★2783★ **International Registry for Religious Women Artists, Marylhurst Chapter**
Liturgical Arts Resource Center
Marylhurst, OR 97036
Phone: (503)697-3097
Sr. Patricia Baxter, Dir.

Description: Musical, dance, visual arts, and dramatic artists and their supporters. Offers exhibits, workshops, classes, events, and festivals. **Affiliated with:** International Registry for Religious-Wo/Men-Artists.

Merlin

★2784★ **Cesarean Prevention Movement of Southern Oregon**
464 Connie Ln.
Merlin, OR 97532
Phone: (503)474-9728
Christi Siedlecki, Pres.

Description: Women who have experienced a cesarean birth. Seeks to lower the occurence of cesarean sections through education. Acts as a forum and support network. **Affiliated with:** Cesarean Prevention Movement.

Milwaukie

★2785★ **National Association of Childbearing Centers**
Milwaukie Birth Center
10423 SE 23rd Ave.
Milwaukie, OR 97222
Phone: (503)652-2311
Karen J. Hubbard, Dir.

Portland

★2786★ **American Woman's Society of Certified Public Accountants of Portland**
Schnitzer Steel Products Company
3200 NW Yeon Ave.
Portland, OR 97210
Phone: (503)224-9900
Ursula Luckert, Pres.

★2787★ **Imani Women's Support Project**
PO Box 11688
Portland, OR 97211-0688

Description: Provides assistance to Imani women in need.

★2788★ **Institute for Managerial and Professional Women**
PO Box 40324
Portland, OR 97240
Phone: (503)292-0175

★2789★ **Older Women's League (OWL) Portland Chapter**
4749 SE 104th Ave.
Portland, OR 97266
Phone: (503)761-7447
Lois Bjorklund, Contact

★2790★ **Oregon Abortion Rights Action League**
921 SW Morrison, No. 427
Portland, OR 97205
Phone: (503)223-4510
Diane Linn, Contact

★2791★ **Oregon Coalition Against Domestic and Sexual Violence**
2336 SE Belmont St.
Portland, OR 97214
Phone: (503)239-4486
Holly Pruett, Contact

★2792★ **Oregon Committee of the National Museum of Women in the Arts**
c/o Paula M. Madden
PO Box 855
Portland, OR 97207-0855

Description: Promotes public awareness and appreciation of the arts in Oregon.

★2793★ **Oregon Healthy Mothers Healthy Babies Coalition**
1220 SW Morrison 620
Portland, OR 97205-2225

Description: Provides educational programs for parents in Oregon. Promotes good health.

★2794★ **Oregon Symphony Women's Association**
711 SW Alder, No. 210
Portland, OR 97205
Phone: (503)223-8455
Harriet Laird, Exec. Officer

★2795★ **Oregon Women's Caucus for Arts**
c/o Jeri Sofka
605 SE 18th
Portland, OR 97214-2743

Description: Promotes public awareness and appreciation of the arts in Oregon.

★2796★ **Oregon Women's Political Caucus**
534 SW 3rd, No. 716
Portland, OR 97204
Phone: (503)224-2588

Description: Promotes the election and appointment of women to all levels of government. **Affiliated with:** National Women's Political Caucus.

★2797★ **Religious Coalition for Abortion Rights, Oregon Chapter**
PO Box 86472
Portland, OR 97286
Phone: (503)774-1586
Donna McFall, Coordinator

Description: Religious individuals engaged in education and advocacy for abortion rights and reproduction, for religious freedom. **Affiliated with:** Religious Coalition for Abortion Rights.

★2798★ **SisterSpirit**
Box 9246
Portland, OR 97207
Phone: (503)294-0645
Rev. Frodo Okulum, Coordinator

Description: Women from different spiritual and/or religious backgrounds in the pacific northwestern area of the U.S. Seeks to develop a common bond in spirituality among members. Holds monthly celebrations and small group discussions; maintains emergency fund and library; conducts spiritual counseling and information and referral programs. Sponsors Lammas Women's Festival. **Affiliated with:** Universal Fellowship of Metropolitan Community Churches.

★2799★ **Women's Investment Network Political Action Committee (WIN PAC)**
PO Box 8432
Portland, OR 97207
Phone: (503)253-6639
Jewel A. Lansing, CPA, Co-director

Founded: 1988. **Description:** Bipartisan group helps non-incumbent, pro-choice women get elected to the Oregon State Legislature.

★2800★ **Young Women's Christian Association of Portland**
1111 SW 10th Ave.
Portland, OR 97205
Phone: (503)223-6281

Roseburg

★2801★ **American Association of University Women, Roseburg Branch**
1276 SE Jackson
Roseburg, OR 97470
Phone: (503)672-8883
Sonia Wright-Holt, Pres.

Description: Women graduates of regionally accredited four year colleges and universities. Works for the advancement of women through advocacy and emphasis on lifelong learning. **Affiliated with:** American Association of University Women.

★2802★ **American Business Women's Association, Roseburg Chapter**
PO Box 725
Roseburg, OR 97470
Phone: (503)679-6451
Shirley J. McSperitt, V.Pres.

Description: Businesswomen. Promotes the educational advancement of members. Provides scholarships, personal loans, and insurance programs. **Affiliated with:** American Business Women's Association.

★2803★ **Roseburg Women's Bowling Association**
520 SW Wilson-Collins Rd.
Roseburg, OR 97470
Phone: (503)672-5045
Deborah Wallace, Sec.

Description: Bowlers united to promote the sport.

Salem

★2804★ **League of Women Voters of Oregon**
2659 Commercial St. SE, No. 220
Salem, OR 97302
Phone: (503)581-5722
Katherine Eaton, President

★2805★ **Young Women's Christian Association of Salem**
768 State St.
Salem, OR 97301
Phone: (503)581-9922
Jo Rita Gann, Exec.Dir.

Description: Seeks to develop and improve the spiritual, social, mental, and physical life of youth and adults in Marion and Polk Counties, OR. Programs offered include adult education, day care, and resource assistance for the homeless and needy. Bestows awards to outstanding women and their employers. **Affiliated**

with: Young Women's Christian Association of the United States of America.

Winchester

★2806★ Roseburg Woman's Club
PO Box 1142
Winchester, OR 97495
Phone: (503)672-4567
Becky Chitwood, Pres.

Description: Ladies in the Roseburg, OR area organized to promote educational and civic improvement opportunities. Sponsors studies and involvement in the arts; encourages young talent. Promotes good citizenship, spiritual values, and health. Advocates world peace and international understanding. **Affiliated with:** General Federation of Women's Clubs; Oregon Federation of Women's Clubs.

Pennsylvania

Allentown

★2807★ Girl Scouts of the U.S.A., Great Valley Council
2633 Moravian Ave.
Allentown, PA 18103
Phone: (215)791-2411
Elizabeth Browne, Exec.Dir.

Description: Girls aged five to 17 and adult volunteers. Seeks to "inspire girls with the highest ideals of character, conduct, patriotism, and service that they may become happy and resourceful citizens." **Affiliated with:** Girl Scouts of the U.S.A.

Altoona

★2808★ Young Women's Christian Association of Altoona
224 Union Ave.
Altoona, PA 16602
Phone: (814)944-8119
Cynthia Baney, Contact

Description: Seeks to develop and improve the spiritual, social, mental, and physical life of young people and adults. **Affiliated with:** Young Women's Christian Association of the United States of America.

Beaver

★2809★ Girl Scouts of the U.S.A., Beaver-Castle Council
443 Third St.
Beaver, PA 15009
Phone: (412)774-3553
Gail M. Sudore, Exec.Dir. and CEO

Description: Girls aged five to 17 and adult volunteers in Beaver and Lawrence counties, PA. Seeks to inspire girls with the highest ideals of character, conduct, patriotism, and service. Offers day and resident camping. Holds events and program activities. **Affiliated with:** Girl Scouts of the U.S.A.

Bedford

★2810★ Bosom Buddies
RD 4, Box 58
Bedford, PA 15522
Phone: (814)847-2446
Vera M. Beegle, Pres.

Description: Women in Bedford, PA who have had breast cancer and a mastectomy. **Affiliated with:** American Cancer Society.

Bethlehem

★2811★ Young Women's Christian Association of Bethlehem
Seven E. Market St.
Bethlehem, PA 18018
Phone: (215)867-4669
Kathleen A. Widner, Exec.Dir.

Description: Seeks to develop and improve the spiritual, social, mental, and physical life of young people and adults in Lehigh and Northampton counties, PA. Promotes the empowerment of women and the elimination of racism. Provides adult and child daycare, wellness service, and health promotion and recreational activities. **Affiliated with:** Young Women's Christian Association of the United States of America.

Bradford

★2812★ Young Women's Christian Association of Bradford
24 W. Corydon St.
Bradford, PA 16701
Phone: (814)368-4235
Donna Dennis, Contact

Description: Seeks to develop and improve the spiritual, social, mental, and physical life of young people and adults. Operates Women's Resource Center which provides social services to children and women. **Affiliated with:** Young Women's Christian Association of the United States of America.

Bushkill

★2813★ Saw Creek Women's Club
PO Box 574
Bushkill, PA 18324-0574

Butler

★2814★ Young Women's Christian Association of Butler
120 W. Cunningham St.
Butler, PA 16001
Phone: (412)287-5709

Description: Seeks to develop and improve the spiritual, social, mental, and physical life of young people and adults. **Affiliated with:** Young Women's Christian Association of the United States of America.

Camp Hill

★2815★ Pennsylvania Federation of Women's Clubs
3310 Market St.
Camp Hill, PA 17011
Phone: (717)761-5063
Edith Rathbun, Exec.Sec.

Description: Women's civic groups. Holds annual Festival of Arts.

Carlisle

★2816★ Young Women's Christian Association of Carlisle
301 W. G St.
Carlisle, PA 17013
Phone: (717)243-3818
Barbara Kohutiak, Exec.Dir.

Description: Seeks to develop and improve the spiritual, social, mental, and physical life of young people and adults. Promotes the empowerment of women and the elimination of racism. **Affiliated with:** Young Women's Christian Association of the United States of America.

Carnegie

★2817★ Association of Women in the Metal Industries, Pittsburgh Chapter
PO Box 309
Carnegie, PA 15106
Phone: (412)279-3534
Sally Conley, Pres.

Description: Women employed in management, purchasing, or sales in metal industries in the Pittsburgh, PA area. Seeks to develop and promote educational and professional backgrounds of women in metal industries and provide support. **Affiliated with:** Association of Women in the Metal Industries.

★2818★ Young Women's Christian Association of Greater Pittsburgh, Carnagie Center
510 Washington Ave.
Carnegie, PA 15106
Phone: (412)923-2669
Jeanne Berrington, Program Exec.

Description: Seeks to develop and improve the spiritual, social, mental, and physical life of young people and adults. Promotes the empowerment of women and the betterment of the community. **Affiliated with:** Young Women's Christian Association of the United States of America.

Chambersburg

★2819★ Women's Network
c/o Paula Matthews
Office of College Advancement
Wilson College
Chambersburg, PA 17201
Phone: (717)264-4141

Description: Organization of women professionals in the Chambersburg area. **Publications:** Newsletter.

Chester

★2820★ Young Women's Christian Association of Chester
7th and Sproul Sts.
Chester, PA 19013
Phone: (215)876-8226

Description: Seeks to develop and improve the spiritual, social, mental, and physical life of young people and adults. **Affiliated with:** Young Women's Christian Association of the United States of America.

Coatesville

★2821★ Young Women's Christian
Association of Coatesville
423 E. Lincoln Hwy.
Coatesville, PA 19320
Phone: (215)384-9591
Description: Seeks to develop and improve the
spiritual, social, mental, and physical life of
young people and adults. Affiliated with: Young
Women's Christian Association of the United
States of America.

Conyngham

★2822★ Greater Hazleton Business &
Professional Women
3 Frederick Dr.
Conyngham, PA 18219
Phone: (717)788-1727
Helen Braskie, Pres.
Description: Working women in the Hazleton,
PA area. Seeks to elevate employment stan-
dards, interest, and cooperation of businesses
regarding professional women.

East Stroudsburg

★2823★ Junior Women's Club of the
Stroudsburgs
PO Box 122
East Stroudsburg, PA 18301
Phone: (717)421-7323
Georgelyn Blake, Pres.
Description: Works to advance the welfare of
the community and promote civic, educational,
and social progress. Affiliated with: General
Federation of Women's Clubs; Pennsylvania
Federation of Women's Clubs.

Easton

★2824★ Young Women's Christian
Association of Easton
41 N. 3rd St.
Easton, PA 18042
Phone: (215)258-6271
Description: Seeks to develop and improve the
spiritual, social, mental, and physical life of
young people and adults. Affiliated with: Young
Women's Christian Association of the United
States of America.

Ellwood City

★2825★ Lawrence County Deanery
Council of Catholic Women
629 Hazel Ave.
Ellwood City, PA 16117
Joan DiCarlo, Pres.
Description: Carries out the work of the Bishop
of the Diocese of Pittsburgh, PA. Affiliated
with: National Council of Catholic Women;
Pittsburgh Diocesan Council of Catholic Wom-
en.

★2826★ Lawrence County Federation of
Women's Clubs
416 Argonne Blvd.
Ellwood City, PA 16117
Phone: (412)758-3192
Mrs. Pat Robert Hines, Contact
Description: Women's volunteer service club.

Erie

★2827★ Young Women's Christian
Association of Erie
4247 W. Ridge Rd.
Erie, PA 16506
Phone: (814)838-9671
Description: Seeks to develop and improve the
spiritual, social, mental, and physical life of
young people and adults. Affiliated with: Young
Women's Christian Association of the United
States of America.

Flourtown

★2828★ B'nai B'rith Women, Tri-State
Office
1107 Bethlehem Pike
Flourtown, PA 19031
Phone: (215)233-4442
Honey Forman, Dir.
Description: Jewish women united to promote
social advancement through action, education,
and service. Issues publications. Affiliated with:
B'nai B'rith International.

Gettysburg

★2829★ Young Women's Christian
Association of Gettysburg
909 Fairfield Rd.
Gettysburg, PA 17325
Phone: (717)334-9171
Fax: (717)334-1491
Description: Seeks to develop and improve the
spiritual, social, mental, and physical life of
women and their families. Affiliated with:
Young Women's Christian Association of the
United States of America.

Greensburg

★2830★ Birthright of Central
Westmoreland
121 N. Main St.
Greensburg, PA 15601
Phone: (412)832-2577
Toll-free: 800-848-LOVE
Sheila A. Shogan, Dir.
Description: Individuals interested in promoting
alternatives to abortion for pregnant women in
central Westmoreland County, PA. Affiliated
with: Birthright, United States of America.

★2831★ Young Women's Christian
Association of Greensburg
424 N. Main St.
Greensburg, PA 15601
Phone: (412)834-9390
Bonnie Lewis, Exec.Dir.
Description: Seeks to develop and improve the
spiritual, social, mental, and physical life of
young people and adults. Committed to empowering women and eliminating racism. Affiliated
with: Young Women's Christian Association of
the United States of America.

Grove City

★2832★ American Business Women's
Association, Wolf Creek Carter Chapter
PO Box 706
Grove City, PA 16127
Phone: (412)458-5573
Merle Reeseman, Pres.
Description: Professional in western Pennsyl-
vania united to assist women with their personal
and professional growth. Conducts educational
programs. Issues publications.

★2833★ Penn's Agri-Women
136 Old Mill Site Rd.
Grove City, PA 16127
Phone: (412)458-8181
Carol Ann Gregg, Pres.
Description: Farm and ranch women in Penn-
sylvania. Promotes agriculture through commu-
nication with consumers and schoolchildren.
Conducts social activities. Affiliated with:
American Agri-Women.

Hanover

★2834★ Young Women's Christian
Association of Hanover
23 W. Chestnut St.
Hanover, PA 17331
Phone: (717)637-2125
Description: Seeks to develop and improve the
spiritual, social, mental, and physical life of
young people and adults. Affiliated with: Young
Women's Christian Association of the United
States of America.

Harrisburg

★2835★ League of Women Voters of
Pennsylvania
226 Forster St.
Harrisburg, PA 17102-3220
Phone: (717)234-1576
Diane Edmundson, President

★2836★ Pennsylvania Coalition Against
Domestic Violence
2505 N. Front St.
Harrisburg, PA 17110-1111
Phone: (717)234-7353
Nancy Durborow, Contact

★2837★ Program for Female Offenders of
South Central Pennsylvania
2337 N. 3rd St.
Harrisburg, PA 17110-1891

★2838★ Young Women's Christian
Association of the Greater Harrisburg
Area
215 Market St.
Harrisburg, PA 17101
Phone: (717)234-7931
Description: Seeks to develop and improve the
spiritual, social, mental, and physical life of
young people and adults. Affiliated with: Young
Women's Christian Association of the United
States of America.

Hazleton

★2839★ Agudas Israel Sisterhood
Pine & Oak Sts.
Hazleton, PA 18201
Phone: (717)455-2851
Rhoda Starker, Pres.

Description: Women in the Hazleton, PA area. Promotes and supports conservative Judaism. **Affiliated with:** Women's League for Conservative Judaism.

★2840★ Hazleton Woman's Club
705 Grant St.
Hazleton, PA 18201
Phone: (717)454-2238
Dorothy Bresnock, Contact

Description: Women's volunteer service club. Develops the educational, civic, and social interests of members. **Affiliated with:** General Federation of Women's Clubs; Pennsylvania State Federation of Women's Clubs.

★2841★ Young Women's Christian Association of Hazleton
75 S. Church St.
Hazleton, PA 18201
Phone: (717)455-2046

Description: Seeks to develop and improve the spiritual, social, mental, and physical life of young people and adults. **Affiliated with:** Young Women's Christian Association of the United States of America.

Hermitage

★2842★ General Federation of Women's Clubs, Hermitage Woman's Club
c/o Debbie Wilcox
223 Boyd Dr.
Hermitage, PA 16148-1661

Johnstown

★2843★ Young Women's Christian Association of Johnstown
526 Somerset St.
Johnstown, PA 15901
Phone: (814)536-3519
Doris Lichtenfels, Exec.Dir.

Description: Seeks to develop and improve the spiritual, social, mental, and physical life of young people and adults. **Affiliated with:** Young Women's Christian Association of the United States of America.

Lafayette Hill

★2844★ Childbirth Education Association of Greater Philadelphia
706 Ridge Pike
Lafayette Hill, PA 19444
Phone: (215)828-0131
Carol Sigel, Pres.

Description: Childbirth educators, counselors, health care professionals, nursing mothers, and individuals interested in promoting freedom of choice in childbirth through awareness of alternatives. Provides breastfeeding counseling, childbirth educator training, support for parents of infants with a cleft lip/palate, labor and delivery classes, and refresher and VBAC courses. Operates referral service. **Affiliated with:** International Childbirth Education Association.

Lancaster

★2845★ Young Women's Christian Association of Lancaster
110 N. Lime St.
Lancaster, PA 17602
Phone: (717)393-1735
Maureen Powers, Contact

Description: Seeks to enable young women to reach their full potential and to create a society free from sexism and racism. Provides counseling. Conducts charitable activities; sponsors town fair. **Affiliated with:** Young Women's Christian Association of the United States of America.

Lebanon

★2846★ Domestic Violence Intervention of Lebanon County
RR 4, Box 180
Lebanon, PA 17042-9408

Description: Attempts to prevent domestic violence.

Levittown

★2847★ Bucks County Emergency Pregnancy Service
PO Box 713
Levittown, PA 19058
Phone: (215)943-2131
Sandra Peoples, Pres.

Description: Provides assistance services such as medical care referrals, housing, food, clothing, adoption, and 24-hour hotline to pregnant women in Bucks County, PA and the surrounding area.

★2848★ Older Women's League (OWL) Bucks County Chapter
5 Park Ln.
Levittown, PA 19054
Phone: (215)946-9697
Shirley Milgram, Contact

Loyalhanna

★2849★ Latrobe Business and Professional Women's Club
215 Richmond St.
Loyalhanna, PA 15661-9720
Phone: (412)834-5000
Theresa Revicky, Pres.

Description: Business and professional women. To promote complete participation, equal opportunities, and economic self-sufficiency for working women. **Affiliated with:** National Federation of Business and Professional Women's Clubs of the U.S.A.

McKeesport

★2850★ Young Women's Christian Association of McKeesport
410 9th Ave.
McKeesport, PA 15132
Phone: (412)664-7146

Description: Seeks to develop and improve the spiritual, social, mental, and physical life of young people and adults. **Affiliated with:** Young Women's Christian Association of the United States of America.

Meadville

★2851★ Young Women's Christian Association of Meadville
378 Chestnut St.
Meadville, PA 16335
Phone: (814)337-4279

Description: Seeks to develop and improve the spiritual, social, mental, and physical life of young people and adults. **Affiliated with:** Young Women's Christian Association of the United States of America.

Mechanicsburg

★2852★ Concerned Women for America, Pennsylvania Chapter
PO Box 381
Mechanicsburg, PA 17055
Phone: (717)697-5496
Karen Keckler, Rep.

Description: Seeks to preserve, promote, and protect traditional Judeo-Christian values through education, legal defense procedures, and legislative advocacy. Conducts educational programs; assists crisis pregnancy centers. **Affiliated with:** Concerned Women for America.

Nescopech

★2853★ DES Action
Box 286
Nescopech, PA 18635

New Castle

★2854★ New Castle Area Church Women United
1603 Wilson Ave.
New Castle, PA 16101
Phone: (412)654-0908
Mary McClain, Pres.

Description: Churches. Conducts charitable activities. Holds celebrations and luncheon programs.

★2855★ New Castle Jewish Ladies Relief Society
409 E. Sheridan Ave.
New Castle, PA 16105
Phone: (412)658-8044
Mary Kohler, Pres.

Description: Women in Lawrence County, PA united to provide financial assistance to those in need in the local Jewish community. Conducts nursing home visits.

New Town

★2856★ Young Women's Christian Association of Bucks County
Stockingsworth Complex
301 S. State St.
New Town, PA 18940
Phone: (215)860-9922

Description: Seeks to develop and improve the spiritual, social, mental, and physical life of young people and adults. **Affiliated with:** Young Women's Christian Association of the United States of America.

Oil City

★2857★ **Young Women's Christian Association of Oil City**
109 Central Ave.
Oil City, PA 16301
Phone: (814)676-6528

Description: Seeks to develop and improve the spiritual, social, mental, and physical life of young people and adults. **Affiliated with:** Young Women's Christian Association of the United States of America.

Philadelphia

★2858★ **Association for Women in Science, Philadelphia Chapter**
c/o Elizabeth Bingham
ERRC, USDA
600 E. Mermaid Ln.
Philadelphia, PA 19118
Phone: (215)832-3472

Description: Works to improve education and employment opportunities for women in the sciences.

★2859★ **Cesarean Prevention Movement of Greater Philadelphia**
11171 Hendrix
Philadelphia, PA 19116
Phone: (215)698-9206
Kathy Malamut, Pres.

Description: Parents, childbirth educators, nurses, and midwives in Philadelphia and Bucks and Montgomery counties, PA. Seeks to lower the number of cesarean sections performed. Provides education, support for women recovering from cesareans, and a forum for exchange of ideas. Offers information on area hospital maternity services. Maintains library of books and medical journal reprints. **Telecommunications Services:** Telephone counseling.

★2860★ **Community Women's Education Project (CWEP)**
Frankford Ave. at Somerset St.
Philadelphia, PA 19134
Phone: (215)426-2200

Description: The Project trains and educates poor and low-income women who seek preparation for employment that will enable them to be self-supporting. Entry-level college programs, computer training, basic skills and career education are offered.

★2861★ **Maternity Care Coalition of Greater Philadelphia (MCC)**
511 N. Broad St., 9th Fl.
Philadelphia, PA 19123
Phone: (215)922-6300

Description: Advocates for medical, social and nutritional services for low-income pregnant women to reduce the incidence of preventable infant illness and death. Model programs include MOMobile and Community Maternity Project.

★2862★ **National Abortion Rights Action League of Pennsylvania**
1218 Chestnut St., Ste. 1007
Philadelphia, PA 19107
Phone: (215)923-3172
Fax: (215)923-0749
Jenny Daughtry, Exec. Dir.

Description: Supports the constitutional right to choose a safe, legal abortion. Endorses candidates and lobbies for favorable legislation. Affiliated with: National Abortion Rights Action League.

★2863★ **Northeast Women's Center**
2751 Comly Rd.
Philadelphia, PA 19154
Phone: (215)464-2225

★2864★ **Options**
215 S. Broad St.
Philadelphia, PA 19107
Phone: (215)735-2202

Description: Provides career and human resources counseling.

★2865★ **Philadelphia Black Women's Health Project**
1415 N. Broad, Rm. 227-D
Philadelphia, PA 19122
Phone: (215)232-1115

★2866★ **The Plastic Club**
247 S. Camac St.
Philadelphia, PA 19107
Phone: (215)545-9324

Founded: 1897. **Description:** A nonprofit group with an elected board of officials, giving artists an opportunity to show their works, and furthering art in the greater Philadelphia area.

★2867★ **Tradeswomen of Philadelphia/Women in Non-Traditional Work (TOP/WIN)**
3001 Dickinson St.
Philadelphia, PA 19146
Phone: (215)551-1808

Description: Provides support services, job training, networking, job placement and advocacy for women in blue-collar, non-traditional work.

★2868★ **Women in Community Service, Region III**
3535 Market St., Rm. 2250
Philadelphia, PA 19104
Phone: (215)596-4540
Toll-free: 800-JOB-CORPS
Lyanne L. Wassermann, Dir.

Description: Service coalition of five organizations: Church Women United; National Council of Catholic Women; National Council of Jewish Women; National Council of Negro Women; American GI Forum. Provides disadvantaged youth aged 16-22 in Delaware, Maryland, Pennsylvania, Virginia, Washington, DC, and West Virginia with opportunities in education and vocational training through Job Corps. Offers job placement and support services. Maintains speakers' bureau. **Affiliated with:** Women in Community Service.

★2869★ **Women Organized Against Rape (WOAR)**
1233 Locust St., Ste. 202
Philadelphia, PA 19107
Phone: (215)985-3315

Description: Offers critical services to adult and child survivors of sexual assault, including a 24-hour hotline, hospital and court accompaniment, individual counseling and support groups for survivors and their families, and community education.

★2870★ **Women's Alliance for Job Equity (WAJE)**
1422 Chestnut St., Ste. 1100
Philadelphia, PA 19102
Phone: (215)561-1873

Description: The Alliance provides direct services, public education, peer support and advocacy on behalf of non-management working women. WAJE counsels women experiencing unlawful employment practices and provides sexual harassment prevention training.

★2871★ **Women's Way**
1233 Locust St., Ste. 300
Philadelphia, PA 19107
Phone: (215)985-3322
Lynn H. Yeakel, President

Founded: 1976. **Description:** Coalition of Philadelphia organizations supporting equal opportunity, women's rights, and other issues that pertain to its goal of creating a "more just and humane society." Allocates funds annually to member organizations and to non-members through a grant-making process. **Members:** Eleven member and four associate member organizations include Community Women's Education Project, Domestic Abuse Project of Delaware County, Elizabeth Blackwell Health Center for Women, Tenant's Action Group, Philadelphia Lesbian and Gay Task Force, and Women's Law Project. **Remarks:** Over 200 corporate contributors and 6,500 individual donors support the coalition.

★2872★ **Young Women's Christian Association of Philadelphia**
1831 Chestnut St., 2nd Fl.
Philadelphia, PA 19103
Phone: (215)564-3430
Fax: (215)636-0167
Prudence K. Vipiani, Exec.Dir. & CEO

Description: Seeks to develop and improve the spiritual, social, mental, and physical life of young people and adults. **Affiliated with:** Young Women's Christian Association of the United States of America.

Pittsburgh

★2873★ **Business and Professional Women's Club of Pittsburgh**
5867 Burchfield
Pittsburgh, PA 15217
Phone: (412)421-1867
Patricia Waddington, Pres.

Description: Business and professional women. To promote complete participation, equal opportunities, and economic self-sufficiency for working women. Provides job networking. Awards scholarship. **Affiliated with:** National Federation of Business and Professional Women's Clubs of the U.S.A.

★2874★ Girl Scouts of Southwestern Pennsylvania
100 5th Ave.
Pittsburgh, PA 15222
Phone: (412)566-2570
Marlene Szary, Exec.Dir.

Description: Girls aged five to 17 and adult volunteers in northeastern Maryland and West Virginia and western Pennsylvania. Assist girls in developing interpersonal skills, self-esteem, sense of community, and values. **Affiliated with:** Girl Scouts of the U.S.A.

★2875★ La Leche League International, West Pennsylvania Chapter
537 Bellaire Ave.
Pittsburgh, PA 15226
Phone: (412)344-7891
Mary McNulty, Coordinator

Description: Breastfeeding women in western Pennsylvania. Provides encouragement, information, and support for women who want to breastfeed their babies. Conducts educational programs for medical professionals and the public. **Affiliated with:** La Leche League International.

★2876★ National Association of Women Business Owners
Pittsburgh Chapter
c/o Tresbri Development Company
745 Gaywood Dr.
Pittsburgh, PA 15235
Phone: (412)244-1021
Bridget Canedy, President

★2877★ National Organization for Women, Pennsylvania State Organization
PO Box 17326
Pittsburgh, PA 15235
Phone: (412)795-3972
Fax: (412)795-3369
Chris Niebrzydowki, Pres.

Description: Women and men who support equality for women. **Affiliated with:** National Organization for Women.

★2878★ Pennsylvania Branch of National Abortion Rights Action League
c/o YWCA
305 Wood St.
Pittsburgh, PA 15222
Phone: (412)471-1507
Carol Sylvestry, Contact

★2879★ Pennsylvania Organization for Women in Early Recovery
7445 Church St.
Pittsburgh, PA 15218-2484

★2880★ Pittsburgh Action Against Rape
3712 Forbes Ave.
Pittsburgh, PA 15213
Phone: (412)682-0219
Molly Knox, Exec.Dir.

Description: Seeks to eliminate all forms of sexual assault. Provides child, individual, and volunteer counseling. Conducts professional training and community education and prevention programs. **Telecommunications Services:** 24-hour hot line, (412)765-2731.

★2881★ Pittsburgh Conference of Jewish Women's Organizations
180 Penhurst Dr.
Pittsburgh, PA 15235
Phone: (412)829-1525
Shirley Farbman, Pres.

Description: Presidents and delegates of local Jewish women's organizations. Serves as a clearinghouse of information on religious and community events. **Affiliated with:** National Bureau of Federated Jewish Women's Organizations.

★2882★ Pittsburgh Credit and Financial Women's Association
c/o Jack Picio
NACM Western Pennsylvania
3737 Library Rd.
Pittsburgh, PA 15234
Phone: (412)344-1400
Jack Picio, Exec.V.Pres.

★2883★ Young Women's Christian Association of Greater Pittsburgh
305 Wood St.
Pittsburgh, PA 15222
Phone: (412)391-5100
Margaret Tyndall, Exec.Dir.

Description: Seeks to develop and improve the spiritual, social, mental, and physical life of young people and adults. Works to eliminate racism. **Affiliated with:** Young Women's Christian Association of the United States of America.

Pottstown

★2884★ Young Women's Christian Association of Pottstown
315 King St.
Pottstown, PA 19464
Phone: (215)323-1888

Description: Seeks to develop and improve the spiritual, social, mental, and physical life of young people and adults. **Affiliated with:** Young Women's Christian Association of the United States of America.

Pottsville

★2885★ Young Women's Christian Association of Pottsville
325 S. Center St.
Pottsville, PA 17901
Phone: (717)622-0551

Description: Seeks to develop and improve the spiritual, social, mental, and physical life of young people and adults. **Affiliated with:** Young Women's Christian Association of the United States of America.

Reading

★2886★ Birthright of Berks County
124 S. 5th Ave.
Reading, PA 19611
Phone: (215)374-8545
Margaret Vath, Pres.

Description: Seeks to provide positive alternatives to abortion for pregnant women and their families. Provides education, fetal development counseling, infant and maternity clothes and supplies, pregnancy testing, and speakers. **Affiliated with:** Birthright International.

★2887★ Woman's Club of Reading
140 N. 5th St.
Reading, PA 19601
Phone: (215)372-3714
Elizabeth Evans, Pres.

Description: Women engaged in charitable, cultural, and educational activities.

Scranton

★2888★ Pennsylvanians for Human Life
506 Broadway
PO Box 895
Scranton, PA 18501
Phone: (717)343-5099
Helen Gohsler, Exec.Dir. & Pres.

Description: Seeks to protect the right-to-life of all persons from conception to natural death. Provides public information courses on abortion, euthanasia, and infanticide. Distributes and lends educational and resource materials. Sponsors educational exhibits and speakers' bureau for churches, civic organizations, and schools. **Affiliated with:** National Right-to-Life Committee; Pennsylvania Pro-Life Federation.

Springdale

★2889★ Springdale-Cheswick Woman's Club
848 Pittsburgh St.
Springdale, PA 15144
Phone: (412)274-4718
Edna M. Acken, Pres.

Description: Women's volunteer service club.

Springhouse

★2890★ National Association of Women Business Owners
Philadelphia Chapter
c/o Ridgaway Philips Company
321 Norristown Rd.
Springhouse, PA 19477
Phone: (215)540-0200
Jacqueline S. Moore, President

State College

★2891★ State College Woman's Club
PO Box 984
State College, PA 16804
Phone: (814)238-2322
Nancy Spannuth, Pres.

Description: Women's volunteer service club. **Affiliated with:** General Federation of Women's Clubs; Pennsylvania Federation of Women's Clubs.

Stroudsburg

★2892★ Women in Business, Pocono Mountains Chamber of Commerce
556 Main St.
Stroudsburg, PA 18360
Phone: (717)421-4433
Joan Hunter, Chair

Description: Women members of the Pocono Mountains Chamber of Commerce interested in exchanging information and networking.

Titusville

★2893★ Young Women's Christian Association of Titusville
201 N. Franklin St.
Titusville, PA 16354
Phone: (814)827-2746
Mary Ann Forbes, Contact
Description: Seeks to develop and improve the spiritual, social, mental, and physical life of young people and adults. **Affiliated with:** Young Women's Christian Association of the United States of America.

Warren

★2894★ Warren County Women's History
116 Jefferson St.
Warren, PA 16365

★2895★ Woman's Club of Warren
310 Market St.
Warren, PA 16365
Phone: (814)723-5910
Elizabeth A. Jones, Pres.
Description: Women over the age of 21 organized to provide social, cultural, business, and educational focus.

★2896★ Young Women's Christian Association of Warren
207 2nd Ave.
Warren, PA 16365
Phone: (814)723-6350
Description: Seeks to develop and improve the spiritual, social, mental, and physical life of young people and adults. **Affiliated with:** Young Women's Christian Association of the United States of America.

Washington

★2897★ Girl Scouts of the United States of America, Southwestern Pennsylvania Council
Cherry Ave.
Washington, PA 15301
Phone: (412)225-5800
Description: Girls ages 5 to 18 and adult volunteers. Seeks to help girls develop their potential through group activities.

★2898★ Young Women's Christian Association of Washington
42 W. Maiden St.
Washington, PA 15301
Phone: (412)222-3200
Description: Seeks to develop and improve the spiritual, social, mental, and physical life of young people and adults. **Affiliated with:** Young Women's Christian Association of the United States of America.

West Chester

★2899★ Business and Professional Women's Club of West Chester
709 Timber Ln.
West Chester, PA 19380
Phone: (215)363-1664
Linda Reilly, Pres.
Description: Professional business owners. Business and professional women. To promote complete participation, equal opportunities, and economic self-sufficiency for working women. Conducts public speaking contest; bestows awards; holds social functions. **Affiliated with:** Business and Professional Women's Club of Pennsylvania; National Federation of Business and Professional Women's Club of the U.S.A.

★2900★ Chester County Citizens Concerned About Life
PO Box 2102
West Chester, PA 19380
Phone: (215)692-4463
Alberta Horrocks, Pres.
Description: Individuals. Educates, lobbies, and promotes concern for human life. Counsels pregnant women and offers support to health-care agencies. Organizes and participates in marches. Works closely with the Pro-Life Coalition of Southeastern Pennsylvania.

★2901★ Crime Victim's Center of Chester County
PO Box 738
West Chester, PA 19382
Phone: (215)692-7273
Margaret Gusz, Exec.Dir.
Description: Provides supportive services and assistance to crime victims and witnesses and their families on an immediate and ongoing basis. Offers supportive counseling and emergency services. If necessary, members accompany crime victims and witnesses to court, to the police station, and to medical facilities. Offers prevention education programs for schools in the community and training workshops for area professionals (school, medical, police, court, and social service professionals).

★2902★ Young Women's Christian Association of Greater West Chester
123 N. Church St.
West Chester, PA 19380
Phone: (215)692-3737
Nancy Bernhardt, Exec. Officer
Description: Seeks to develop and improve the spiritual, social, mental, and physical life of women and girls. Sponsors charitable programs. **Affiliated with:** Young Women's Christian Association of the United States of America.

West Hazleton

★2903★ Pennsylvania Women's Campaign Fund
115 E. Broad St.
West Hazleton, PA 18201
Phone: (717)445-3100
Susan Nenstiel, Treasurer

Wilkes-Barre

★2904★ Girl Scouts of the United States of America, Penn Woods Council
10 S. Sherman St.
Wilkes-Barre, PA 18702
Phone: (717)829-2631
Sally A. Jervis, Exec.Dir.
Description: Girl scouts and adult leaders in Carbon, Columbia, Luzerne, Northumberland, Schuykill, and Wyoming counties, PA. Promotes character development and improvement of leadership skills among girl scouts.

★2905★ Ladies Pennsylvania Slovak Catholic Union
69 Public Sq., Ste. 922
Wilkes-Barre, PA 18701
Phone: (717)823-3513
Rita Simalchik, Sec.-Treas.
Description: Social organization of men and women. Contributes to seminaries, churches, institutions, and national and local community drives. Provides aid to indigent and bereaved individuals. Awards college scholarships.

Wilkinsburg

★2906★ Young Women's Christian Association of Greater Pittsburgh, Wilkinsburg Center
742 Ross Ave.
Wilkinsburg, PA 15221
Phone: (412)371-2712
Ada Ezekoye, Dir.
Description: Seeks to develop and improve the spiritual, social, mental, and physical life of young people and adults. **Affiliated with:** Young Women's Christian Association of the United States of America.

Williamsport

★2907★ Preventing Teen Pregnancy
815 W. 4th St.
Williamsport, PA 17701-5891

★2908★ Young Women's Christian Association of Williamsport
815 W. 4th St.
Williamsport, PA 17701
Phone: (717)322-4637
Leslie Mowen Miller, Exec.Dir.
Description: Seeks to develop and improve the spiritual, social, mental, and physical life of young people and adults. Works to eliminate racism and sexism. Conducts charitable and educational programs; sponsors Ways Garden Art Festival. **Affiliated with:** Young Women's Christian Association of the United States of America.

York

★2909★ Mother and Unborn Baby Care of York
c/o Lorraine Mitrick
PO Box 2232
York, PA 17405-2232
Description: Promotes maternal and child health.

★2910★ Young Women's Christian Association of York
320 E. Market St.
York, PA 17403
Phone: (717)845-2631
Description: Seeks to develop and improve the spiritual, social, mental, and physical life of young people and adults. **Affiliated with:** Young Women's Christian Association of the United States of America.

Puerto Rico

Bayamon

**★2911★ Puerto Rico Coalition Against
Domestic Violence**
N-11 Calle 11
San Souci
Bayamon, PR 00619

Old San Juan

**★2912★ Comision Para los Asuntos de la
Mujer**
San Francisco St. 151153
Old San Juan, PR 00905
Phone: (809)722-2977
Toll-free: 800-462-7155
Yolanda Zamas, Exec.Dir.

Description: Seeks to increase public awareness of women's issues. Provides crisis intervention; offers legal counseling. Maintains library. Organizes discussion groups and workshops.

Rio Piedras

**★2913★ Coordinadora de Organizaciones
Feministas**
Apartado 21939, Estacion UPR
Rio Piedras, PR 00931
Phone: (809)728-5480

Description: Coordinates efforts of feminist activist organizations, especially for the International Day of the Working Woman (Mar. 8) and the International Day of No More Violence Against Women (Nov. 25).

★2914★ Feministas en Marcha
Apartado 21939, Estacion UPR
Rio Piedras, PR 00931
Phone: (809)751-7833
Ana Riuera-Lassen, Contact

Description: Is concerned with legal processes and political work affecting women. Conducts periodic discussion groups.

Santurce

**★2915★ League of Women Voters of
Puerto Rico**
PO Box 13485
Santurce, PR 00908
Phone: (809)722-3948
Marianne Maldonado, President

**★2916★ Puerto Rico Association of
Women Executives**
Box 11374, Fdez. Juncos Sta.
Santurce, PR 00910
Anna Martin Alfaro, Pres.

Rhode Island

Bristol

**★2917★ Bristol County Business and
Professional Women's Club**
14 Charles St.
Bristol, RI 02809
Phone: (401)253-8981
Ingrid Kleckner, Pres.

Description: Working women and men. To promote women's role in the work force and society by helping them to recognize and achieve their potential. **Affiliated with:** National Federation of Business and Professional Women.

Central Falls

**★2918★ Rhode Island Council on
Domestic Violence**
324 Broad St.
Central Falls, RI 02863
Phone: (401)723-3051
Donna Nesselbush, Contact

**★2919★ Young Women's Christian
Association of Greater Rhode Island**
324 Broad St.
Central Falls, RI 02863
Phone: (401)723-9922

Description: Seeks to develop and improve the spiritual, social, mental, and physical life of young people and adults. **Affiliated with:** Young Women's Christian Association of the United States of America.

Coventry

**★2920★ La Leche League International,
Rhode Island Chapter**
4 Laurie Ave.
Coventry, RI 02816
Phone: (401)821-7465
Christine Malouin, Coordinator

Description: Parents and professionals interested in furthering the goal of "good mothering through breastfeeding." Offers information and support for mothers who breastfeed through phone counseling and group meetings. **Affiliated with:** La Leche League International.

North Scituate

**★2921★ National Association of Women
Business Owners**
Rhode Island Chapter
c/o Going Places, Inc.
Box 9, Village Plaza Way
North Scituate, RI 02857
Phone: (401)934-2300
Connie Paquin, President

Portsmouth

**★2922★ American Association of
University Women, Rhode Island Division**
293 W. Main Rd.
Portsmouth, RI 02871
Phone: (401)683-0896
Cathleen Speer, Pres.

Description: Women graduates of regionally accredited four year colleges and universities. Works for the advancement of women through advocacy and emphasis on lifelong learning. **Affiliated with:** American Association of University Women.

Providence

**★2923★ League of Women Voters of
Rhode Island**
PO Box 28678
Providence, RI 02908-0678
Phone: (401)453-1111
Suzette Gebhard, President

Warren

**★2924★ Democratic Women's Club of
Warren**
781 Main St.
Warren, RI 02885
Phone: (401)245-7480
Irene McVey, Exec. Officer

Description: Seeks to elect Democratic candidates to local, state, and national offices.

Woonsocket

**★2925★ Young Women's Christian
Association of Northern Rhode Island**
514 Blackstone St.
Woonsocket, RI 02895
Phone: (401)769-7450

Description: Seeks to develop and improve the spiritual, social, mental, and physical life of young people and adults. **Affiliated with:** Young Women's Christian Association of the United States of America.

South Carolina

Abbeville

**★2926★ Abbeville County Republican
Women**
c/o Ethel Hughes
Woodland Way
Abbeville, SC 29260
Phone: (803)459-4739
Ethel Hughes, Contact

Description: Works to elect Republicans to local, state, and national office.

Anderson

**★2927★ Anderson County Republican
Women**
1105 Trammell Rd.
Anderson, SC 29621
Phone: (803)226-3617
Mrs. William Trammell, Contact

Description: Works to elect Republicans to local, state, and national office.

★2928★ Anderson County Woman's Club
809 W. Market St.
Anderson, SC 29624
Phone: (803)226-7576
Mrs. L. B. Hopkins, Jr., Pres.

Description: Interested women organized to foster and encourage the educational, literary, cultural, and civic growth of Anderson County, SC. Bestows scholarships to fine arts students.

★2929★ Anderson-Oconee Council on Teen Pregnancy Prevention
PO Box 2623
Anderson, SC 29622-2623
Description: Works to educate the public about and reduce the incidence of teen pregnacy in the Anderson, SC area.

Columbia

★2930★ General Federation of Women's Clubs, South Carolina
1511 Laurel St.
Columbia, SC 29201
Phone: (803)252-6756
Elise Cain, Pres.

Description: Women organized for community improvement. **Affiliated with:** General Federation of Women's Clubs.

★2931★ Girl Scouts of the United States of America - Congaree Council
2712 Middleburg Dr.
Columbia, SC 29204
Sue Eleazor, Contact

★2932★ League of Women Voters of South Carolina
1314 Lincoln St., Ste. 212
Columbia, SC 29201
Phone: (803)771-0063
Margaret West, President

★2933★ Midlands Ad-Hoc Committee for Women's History
c/o YWCA of the Midlands
1505 Blanding St.
Columbia, SC 29201
Phone: (803)252-2151
Diane Solmonson, Director

Description: Goals: to introduce students and teachers to women's history through activities, programs, exhibits, curricula and events, including a year-round speakers bureau.

★2934★ National Women's Studies Association, Southeast Chapter
1710 College St.
University of South Carolina
Columbia, SC 29208
Phone: (803)777-4007
Fax: (803)777-5415
Sue V. Rosser, Dir.

Description: Academicians in women's studies programs promoting women's studies. **Affiliated with:** National Women's Studies Association.

★2935★ Older Women's League (OWL) Central South Carolina Chapter
1410 Beaver Dam Rd.
Columbia, SC 29212
Phone: (803)781-6878
Terri Whirrett, Contact

★2936★ South Carolina Coalition Against Domestic Violence and Sexual Assault
PO Box 7776
Columbia, SC 29202-7776
Phone: (803)669-4694
Ellen Hamilton, Contact

Easley

★2937★ National League of American Pen Women, Carolina-Piedmont Branch
c/o Madeline Canup
100 Kilarney Way
Easley, SC 29642
Phone: (803)855-5276
Madeline Canup, Pres.

Description: Artists, writers, and musicians in Greenville, SC and surrounding area organized to promote the arts. **Affiliated with:** National League of American Pen Women.

Greenville

★2938★ American Association of University Women, South Carolina Chapter
18-C Knoxbury Terrace
Greenville, SC 29601
Phone: (803)235-3285
Betsy Moseley, Pres.

Description: Women graduates of regionally accredited four year colleges and universities. Works for the advancement of women through advocacy and emphasis on lifelong learning. **Affiliated with:** American Association of University Women.

★2939★ Greenville Professional Women's Forum
PO Box 10463
Greenville, SC 29603
Phone: (803)242-8325
Joanne East Batson, Pres.

Description: Professional women in significant management positions. Conducts networking and community contribution activities with an emphasis on the development of women in leadership positions.

★2940★ Rape Crisis Council of Greenville
104 Chapman St.
Greenville, SC 29605
Phone: (803)232-8633

Description: Provides assistance to victims of sexual assault through peer counseling, information, and victim advocacy programs.

Greer

★2941★ American Business Women's Association, Greer Charter Chapter
c/o Jimmie Lou West
801 Ansel School Rd.
Greer, SC 29651-9434
Phone: (803)877-8200
Jimmie Lou West, Pres.

Description: Promotes the general welfare of its members. Issues publications. **Affiliated with:** American Business Women's Association.

Heath Springs

★2942★ Zeta Phi Beta Sorority, Lambda Epsilon Zeta Chapter
PO Box 396
Heath Springs, SC 29058
Towanna Ealey, Contact

Description: Professional women. Provides community service to the Heath Springs, SC area.

Inman

★2943★ Carolina Home Birth Alliance
105 Hunter Ridge Ct.
Inman, SC 29349
Phone: (803)578-2428
Susan Smart, Sec.

Description: Midwives and other interested persons organized to educate the public on the benefits of home birthing. Provides educational opportunities for midwives. Conducts film showings. Operates convention booths.

Mauldin

★2944★ Society of Women Engineers, Mauldin Chapter
302 Murray Dr.
Mauldin, SC 29662
Phone: (803)297-6341
Pam Wilkinson, Sec.

Description: Engineers and scientists organized to encourage women to achieve full professional potential and to present the engineering profession as a positive force in improving the quality of life and demonstrating the value of diversity. Issues publications.

Roebuck

★2945★ Spartanburg Christian Women's Club II
189 Winchester Dr.
Roebuck, SC 29376
Phone: (803)574-0907
Sandra West, Contact

Description: Interdenominational women's group working to spread the message of Christianity. **Affiliated with:** Stonecroft Ministries.

Simpsonville

★2946★ La Leche League of the Golden Strip
c/o June Augustine
104 Saddletree Pl.
Simpsonville, SC 29681
Phone: (803)234-7141
June Augustine, Exec. Officer

Description: Interested persons organized to promote and disseminate information on breastfeeding. Provides telephone counseling. **Affiliated with:** La Leche League International.

★2947★ La Leche League of Greenville County
104 Saddletree Ct.
Simpsonville, SC 29681
Phone: (803)234-7141
June Augustine, Contact

Description: Mothers, nurses, and physicians working to promote breastfeeding. **Affiliated with:** La Leche League.

Spartanburg

★2948★ Democratic Women of Spartanburg County
147 Harmony Dr.
Spartanburg, SC 29301
Phone: (803)576-9105
Detria E. Long, Pres.

Description: Works to elect Democrats to local, state, and national office.

★2949★ Ninety-Nines, International Organization of Women Pilots, Blue Ridge Chapter
PO Box 1023
Spartanburg, SC 29304
Phone: (803)576-9642
A. Lee Orr, Chm.

Description: Women pilots organized to promote women in aviation. **Affiliated with:** Ninety Nines, International Organization of Women Pilots.

York

★2950★ Western York Business and Professional Women's Club
601 N. Congress St.
York, SC 29745
Sue Jonas, Contact

Description: Business and professional women. To promote complete participation, equal opportunities, and economic self-sufficiency for working women.

South Dakota

Agency Village

★2951★ South Dakota Coalition Against Domestic Violence and Sexual Assault
PO Box 689
Agency Village, SD 57262
Phone: (605)789-4169
Brenda Hill, Contact

Beresford

★2952★ Beresford Study Club
410 S. 1st
Beresford, SD 57004
Opal E. Fitzgerald, Pres.

Description: Women in the Beresford, SD area. Promotes community improvement, music, and the arts. Participates in volunteer programs. **Affiliated with:** General Federation of Women's Clubs.

Brandon

★2953★ Republican Women of Minnehaha County
316 6th St.
Brandon, SD 57005
Louella Jellema, Contact

Description: Republican women in Minnehaha County, SD. Works to elect Republicans to local, state, and national office. **Affiliated with:** National Federation of Republican Women; South Dakota Federation of Republican Women.

Brookings

★2954★ General Federation of Women's Clubs, South Dakota
819 6th Ave.
Brookings, SD 57006
Phone: (605)697-5170
Fax: (605)697-6472
Doris Roden, Pres.

Description: Women and men involved in community improvement projects. Promotes the advancement of art, conservation, education, home life, and public and international affairs. **Affiliated with:** General Federation of Women's Clubs.

Huron

★2955★ Young Women's Christian Association of Huron
17 5th St., SW
Huron, SD 57350
Phone: (605)352-2793
Donna Houghton, Exec.Dir.

Description: Seeks to develop and improve the spiritual, social, mental, and physical well-being of young people and adults. **Affiliated with:** Young Women's Christian Association of the United States of America.

Midland

★2956★ South Dakota Cattlewomen
PO Box 228
Midland, SD 57552
Phone: (605)843-2242
Maxine Jones, Pres.

Description: Women interested in promoting beef and the cattle industry. **Affiliated with:** American National Cattle Women.

Mitchell

★2957★ Young Women's Christian Association of Mitchell
201 W. Third Ave.
Mitchell, SD 57301
Phone: (605)996-4311
Carol A. Metzger, Contact

Description: Seeks to develop and improve the spiritual, social, mental, and physical well-being of young people and adults. Conducts Race at Your Pace competition. Sponsors Pampered Pink Health Fair. **Affiliated with:** Young Women's Christian Association of the United States of America.

Mobridge

★2958★ American Association of University Women, Mobridge Chapter
1214 W. Tenth Ave.
Mobridge, SD 57601
Phone: (605)845-2679
Shirley N. Berry, Chairperson

Description: Graduates of regionally accredited colleges living in the Mobridge, SD area; colleges, universities, and two-year or community colleges. Works for advancement of women through advocacy and emphasis on lifelong learning. Conducts annual community project. **Affiliated with:** American Association of University Women, Gettysburg Branch.

Rapid City

★2959★ Black Hills Branch, National League of American Pen Women
926 College Ave.
Rapid City, SD 57701
Phone: (605)343-8509
Irene Kverne, Pres.

Description: Professional artists, composers, and writers in the Black Hills area of South Dakota. Promotes literary and educational work for professional recognition. Conducts charitable activities in the arts. Sponsors art and writing competitions; holds art shows. Hosts autograph parties for authors. Issues publications. **Affiliated with:** National League of American Pen Women.

★2960★ General Federation of Women's Clubs, Fortnightly Club
802 6th St.
Rapid City, SD 57701
Phone: (605)342-3016
Marjorie Hann, Sec.

Description: Community service organization of women. Promotes the arts. Volunteer activities include involvement in local girl's club, children's centers, veterans' services, and center working to end violence against women. Awards music scholarship. **Affiliated with:** General Federation of Women's Clubs.

★2961★ Girl Scouts of the U.S.A., Rapid City Council
PO Box 1846
Rapid City, SD 57709
Phone: (605)343-6355
J. David Miller, Exec.Dir.

Description: Girls aged five to 17 years and adult volunteers in western South Dakota. Promotes the highest ideals of character, conduct, patriotism, and service. Encourages girls to become happy and resourceful citizens through social and recreational activities. **Affiliated with:** Girl Scouts of the U.S.A.

★2962★ South Dakota Women's Bowling Association
1306 N. 7th St.
Rapid City, SD 57701
Phone: (605)343-4442
Jerrie Peterson, Sec.

Description: Serves the member associations and leagues through guidance and services. Sponsors annual state tournament. **Affiliated with:** Women's International Bowling Congress.

★2963★ Women's Christian Temperance Union, Rapid City Chapter
c/o Alberta Pashby
2130 Wisconsin Ave.
Rapid City, SD 57701
Phone: (605)343-0432
Alberta Pashby, Exec. Officer

Description: Christian women. Supports the abolition of drug and alcohol use. Promotes protection of the home through Christian values. Sponsors poster, essay, and speech contests. Provides films and printed educational materials. Conducts lobbying activities.

Sioux Falls

★2964★ League of Women Voters of South Dakota
2500 Harriet Lea St.
Sioux Falls, SD 57103
Deanna Knudson, President

★2965★ South Dakota Abortion Rights Action League
4320 S. Louise Ave.
Sioux Falls, SD 57106
Phone: (605)361-5014
Thelma Underberg, Contact

★2966★ Young Women's Christian Association of Sioux Falls
300 W. 11th St.
Sioux Falls, SD 57102
Phone: (605)336-3660

Description: Seeks to develop and improve the spiritual, social, mental, and physical well-being of young people and adults. Affiliated with: Young Women's Christian Association of the United States of America.

Spearfish

★2967★ La Leche League International, Spearfish Chapter
1414 5th
Spearfish, SD 57783
Phone: (605)642-4529

Description: Mothers, mothers-to-be, health care professionals, and other interested individuals. Promotes breastfeeding through education.

★2968★ Women in Crisis Coalition
PO Box 486
Spearfish, SD 57783
Phone: (605)642-7825
Cindy Lloyd, Exec.Dir.

Description: Provides shelter and aid to victims of domestic and sexual abuse. Offers weekly support group.

Yankton

★2969★ Yankton Christian Women's Council
1306 Maple
Yankton, SD 57078
Phone: (605)665-8750
Deborah Stevens, Rep.

Description: Women in Yankton County, SD interested in promoting Christian values. Affiliated with: Yankton Christian Couples Club.

Tennessee

Chattanooga

★2970★ National Association of Women Business Owners Chattanooga Chapter
c/o Bottom Line Building
PO Box 11494
Chattanooga, TN 37401-2492
Phone: (615)622-3563
Vivienne Harris, President

Hendersonville

★2971★ National Association of Women Business Owners Tidewater Chapter
c/o Miclar, Inc.
104 Edgewood Dr.
Hendersonville, TN 37075
Phone: (615)822-7508
Michele Schulman, President

Kingsport

★2972★ American Association of University Women, Kingsport Branch
1224 Watauga St.
Kingsport, TN 37660
Phone: (615)245-4958
Lydia C. Haseltine, Contact

Description: Women graduates of regionally accredited four year colleges and universities. Works for the advancement of women through advocacy and emphasis on lifelong learning. Provides scholarships to women. Sponsors bookfair and taster's tour. Affiliated with: American Association of University Women.

★2973★ La Leche League International, Kingsport Chapter
2245 Bruce St.
Kingsport, TN 37664
Phone: (615)245-5979
Carolyn C. Barry, Pres.

Description: Nursing mothers. Provides support and information on breastfeeding. Affiliated with: La Leche League International.

Knoxville

★2974★ Southern Association for Physical Education for College Women
c/o Dr. Joy Di Sensi
University of Tennessee
Human Performance and Sports Studies
1914 Andy Holt Ave.
Knoxville, TN 37996
Phone: (615)974-5111
Dr. Joy Di Sensi, Pres.

★2975★ Tanasi Girl Scout Council
1600 Breda Dr.
Knoxville, TN 37918
Phone: (615)688-9440
Fax: (615)688-9442
Diana Steinfield-Hicks, Exec.Dir.

Description: Adult volunteers and girls aged 5-17 in eastern Tennessee. Promotes scouting. Affiliated with: Girl Scouts of the U.S.A.

★2976★ Tennessee American Association of University Women
3705 Terrace View Dr.
Knoxville, TN 37918
Phone: (615)574-5276
Peggy Emmett, Pres.

Description: Women graduates of regionally accredited four year colleges and universities. Works for the advancement of women through advocacy and emphasis on lifelong learning. Affiliated with: American Association of University Women.

Madison

★2977★ Nash Club of National Association of Negro Business and Professional Women's Clubs
c/o Mrs. Lady Etherly Drake
400 Farris Ave.
Madison, TN 37115-4125
Mrs. Lady Etherly Drake, Contact

Description: African-American business women in Madison, TN.

Madisonville

★2978★ National Association of Childbearing Centers, Monroe Maternity Center
Hwy. 68-Lost Sea Pike
PO Box 115
Madisonville, TN 37354
Phone: (615)442-4453
Becky Bell, Admin.

Description: County commissioners, physicians, and concerned individuals. To provide maternity care in rural areas. Affiliated with: National Association of Childbearing Centers.

Memphis

★2979★ Older Women's League (OWL) Greater Memphis Chapter
1261 Wedgewood
Memphis, TN 38111
Phone: (901)744-7274
Martha Lewelling, Contact

★2980★ Woman's Exchange of Memphis
88 Racine St.
Memphis, TN 38811
Phone: (901)327-5681
Mrs. Marti Edwards, Mgr.

Description: Volunteer organization providing support to local artisans.

Morristown

★2981★ American Association of University Women, Morristown Branch
1560 Daniel Boone Dr.
Morristown, TN 37814
Phone: (615)586-2081
Jo Ann Kell, Pres.

Description: Women graduates of regionally accredited four year colleges and universities. Works for the advancement of women through advocacy and emphasis on lifelong learning.

Nashville

★2982★ League of Women Voters of Tennessee
1701 21st Ave., S., No. 425
Nashville, TN 37212
Phone: (615)297-7134
Theresa Mauer, President

★2983★ Tennessee Task Force on Family Violence
PO Box 120972
Nashville, TN 37212-0972
Phone: (615)242-8288
Kathy England, Contact

★2984★ TKALS
PO Box 120871
Nashville, TN 37212
Phone: (615)327-0821
Cathy Fenner, Contact

★2985★ Women's National Book Association
Nashville Chapter
Nashville Public Library, Nashville Room
Nashville, TN 37203
Phone: (615)862-5800
Mary Hearne, Contact

★2986★ Women's National Book Association, Nashville Chapter
Davis Kidd Booksellers
4007 Hillsboro Rd.
Nashville, TN 37215
Phone: (615)385-2645
Donna Paz, Pres.
Description: Individuals in the publishing industry and librarians. To promote books and the role of women in the publishing fields. **Affiliated with:** Women's National Book Association.

Oak Ridge

★2987★ Association for Women in Science, East Tennessee Chapter
PO Box 278
Oak Ridge, TN 37831-0278
Description: Works to improve education and employment opportunities for women in the sciences.

Texas

Abilene

★2988★ Young Women's Christian Association of Abilene
1350 N. 10th St.
Abilene, TX 79601
Phone: (915)677-5321
Jerita Sayre, Contact
Description: Seeks to develop and improve the spiritual, social, mental, and physical well-being of young people and adults. **Affiliated with:** Young Women's Christian Association of the United States of America.

Amarillo

★2989★ Top of Texas Safe Alternatives in Childbirth
2411 W. 3rd
Amarillo, TX 79106
Phone: (806)376-4800
Sally Moss, Chm.
Description: Parents in the Texas panhandle region promoting the study of alternative methods of childbirth. **Affiliated with:** International Association of Parents and Professionals for Safe Alternatives in Childbirth.

Arlington

★2990★ American Association of University Women, Arlington Branch
c/o Marsha Abeson
511 Franklin Dr.
Arlington, TX 76011
Phone: (817)461-2096
Marsha Abeson, Pres.
Description: Women graduates of regionally accredited four year colleges and universities. Works for the advancement of women through advocacy and emphasis on lifelong learning. Sponsors Career Guidance Fair and charity book fair. **Affiliated with:** American Association of University Women.

★2991★ Texas Federation of Business and Professional Women's Clubs
3019 Medlin Dr., Ste. 200
Arlington, TX 76015
Phone: (817)467-0712
Myra J. Schmitt, Exec.Dir.
Description: Federation of business and professional women's clubs. **Affiliated with:** National Federation of Business and Professional Business Clubs of the U.S.A.

★2992★ Texas Rangers Woman's Club
c/o Forresteen Musser
2216 Lincoln Green, No. 1707
Arlington, TX 76011
Phone: (817)860-9907
Forresteen Musser, Pres.
Description: Individuals united to support and promote the Texas Rangers baseball club. Conducts charitable activities. Sponsors annual picnic.

Austin

★2993★ Austin AAU Women's Basketball Club
6542 Needham Ln.
Austin, TX 78739-1514
Description: Women in the Austin, TX area who play in basketball leaues affiliated with the (Amateur Athletic Union of the United States).

★2994★ Daughters of the Republic of Texas
5758 Balcones Dr., Ste. 201
Austin, TX 78731
Phone: (512)452-8977
Virginia T. Mecredy, Custodian Gen.
Description: Women over age 16 who are lineal descendants of men or women who won independence for Texas from Mexico. Members are custodians of the Alamo, San Antonio, TX, and

the French Legation, Austin, TX. Maintains museum and library.

★2995★ Electrical Women's RoundTable, South Texas Chapter
PO Box 220
Austin, TX 78769
Phone: (512)473-4088
Fax: (512)475-4097
Janelle H. Jones, Contact
Description: Women holding positions in the electrical industry. **Affiliated with:** Electrical Women's Round Table.

★2996★ League of Women Voters of Texas
1212 Guadalupe, No. 107
Austin, TX 78701-1801
Phone: (512)472-1100
Evelyn Bonavita, President

★2997★ National Association of Women Business Owners
Austin Chapter
c/o Color Marks
2525 Wallingwood Dr., No. 503A
Austin, TX 78746
Phone: (512)328-3216
Susan Pauley, President

★2998★ Texas Abortion Rights Action League (TARAL)
905 W. Oltorf, Ste. D
Austin, TX 78704
Phone: (512)462-1661
Phyllis Dunham, Contact

★2999★ Texas Council on Family Violence
3415 Greystone, Ste. 220
Austin, TX 78731
Phone: (512)794-1133
Judy Reeves, Contact

★3000★ Texas Family Planning Association
PO Box 3868
Austin, TX 78764
Phone: (512)448-4857
Peggy Romberg, Exec.Dir.
Description: Promotes and provides strategies for family planning.

★3001★ Texas Federation of Women's Clubs
2312 San Gabriel
Austin, TX 78705
Phone: (512)472-1456
Margie L. Brown, Exec.Sec.
Description: Union of women's clubs in Texas. Promotes activities in the areas of conservation, education, home life, public affairs, the arts, and Texas heritage. Holds annual board meeting.

★3002★ Texas Feminists for Life of America
3109 Lafayette
Austin, TX 78722
Phone: (512)478-2494
Maurine McClean, Contact
Description: Feminists united to promote alternatives to abortion. Supports positive social attitudes toward women and children. Seeks to educate the public about what the group feels are the ways that abortion erodes women's

rights. **Affiliated with:** Feminists for Life of America.

★3003★ **Women and Their Work**
1137 W. 6th St.
Austin, TX 78703
Phone: (512)477-1064
Chris Cowden, Coordinator

Description: A multidisciplinary arts and cultural organization including the literary, visual, and performing arts. Has annual festival for the arts, traveling exhibitions, statewide slide files, workshops, and public performance activities.

★3004★ **Young Women's Christian Association of Austin**
405 W. 18th St.
Austin, TX 78701
Phone: (512)478-9873

Description: Seeks to develop and improve the spiritual, social, mental, and physical well-being of young people and adults. **Affiliated with:** Young Women's Christian Association of the United States of America.

Baytown

★3005★ **Texas Foundation for Intercollegiate Athletics for Women**
4419 Country Club View
Baytown, TX 77521-3037

Description: Supports and promotes women's intercollegiate athletic programs in Texas.

Beaumont

★3006★ **Young Women's Christian Association of Beaumont**
660 Calder St.
Beaumont, TX 77701
Phone: (409)832-7765

Description: Seeks to develop and improve the spiritual, social, mental, and physical well-being of young people and adults. **Affiliated with:** Young Women's Christian Association of the United States of America.

Big Spring

★3007★ **American Business Women's Association, Scenic Cactus Chapter**
c/o Connie Gatliff
2508 Allendale
Big Spring, TX 79720
Phone: (915)263-5544
Connie Gatliff, Pres.

Description: Business women organized to further the personal and economic well-being of women. Funds scholarship. **Affiliated with:** American Business Women's Association.

Bonham

★3008★ **Fannin County Church Women United**
1300 E. 9th
Bonham, TX 75418
Phone: (214)583-4335
Betty Wood, Pres.

Description: Churchgoing women in Fannin County, TX. Works to teach the Christian gospel, help the needy, and further the cause of

ecumenism. **Affiliated with:** Church Women United.

Corpus Christi

★3009★ **Young Women's Christian Association of Corpus Christi**
4601 Corona
Corpus Christi, TX 78411
Phone: (512)857-5661

Description: Seeks to develop and improve the spiritual, social, mental, and physical well-being of young people and adults. **Affiliated with:** Young Women's Christian Association of the United States of America.

Dallas

★3010★ **Dallas Women's Coalition**
1445 Ross At Field, Ste. 1700
Dallas, TX 75202-0000

Description: Works to enhance the social and professional status of women.

★3011★ **Dallas Women's Foundation**
9400 N. Central Expy., No. 1215
Dallas, TX 75231
Phone: (214)750-6363
Pat Nicklaus Sabin, Executive Director

★3012★ **National Association of Women Business Owners**
Dallas/Ft. Worth Chapter
c/o LDSI
2001 Bryan Tower, No. 3857
Dallas, TX 75201
Phone: (214)747-0209
Wanda Tomas, President

★3013★ **National Women's Studies Association, South Central Chapter**
PO Box 670-665
Dallas, TX 75367-0665
Phone: (214)352-8356
Mariam K. Harris, Contact

★3014★ **Reel Women**
c/o Janetta Walls
5900 Junius St.
Dallas, TX 75214-4428
Janetta Walls, Contact

★3015★ **T-Bar M Women's Tennis Association**
6060 Dilbeck
Dallas, TX 75240-5399

Description: Supports and promotes the women's tennis in Dallas, TX.

★3016★ **Young Women's Christian Association of Metropolitan Dallas**
4621 Ross Ave.
Dallas, TX 75204
Phone: (214)827-6850
Fax: (214)826-4548

Description: Seeks to develop and improve the spiritual, social, mental, and physical well-being of young people and adults. **Affiliated with:** Young Women's Christian Association.

El Paso

★3017★ **American Business Women's Association, El Paso New Horizons Chapter**
c/o Patricia Statton
324 Caporal Ct.
El Paso, TX 79932
Phone: (915)533-1727
Patricia Statton, Sec.

Description: Women owners or managers of businesses in Arizona, California, Colorado, Nevada, New Mexico, and Texas. Business and professional women. To promote complete participation, equal opportunities, and economic self-sufficiency for working women. Bestows scholarships. **Affiliated with:** American Business Women's Association.

★3018★ **Congregation B'nai Zion Sisterhood, El Paso Chapter**
805 Cherry Hill Ln.
El Paso, TX 79912
Phone: (915)833-2222
Sandra Dula, Exec. Officer

Description: Jewish women organized to promote conservative Judaism, comradeship, and good community relations. Conducts fundraising and charitable activities for children and the elderly. Co-manages synagogue.

★3019★ **Lebanese American Women's Club of El Paso**
901 Galena
El Paso, TX 79930
Phone: (915)755-7358
Susan Nabhan, Pres.

Description: Persons of Lebanese descent or spouses of Lebanese Americans. Seeks to preserve Lebanese heritage. Raises funds for Lebanese war victims. Conducts charitable activities for the larger community. **Affiliated with:** Southern Federation of Lebanese Syrian American Clubs.

★3020★ **Young Women's Christian Association, Central Branch**
1918 Texas Ave.
El Paso, TX 79901
Phone: (915)533-2311
Myrna J. Deckert, Exec.Dir.

Description: Seeks to develop and improve the spiritual, social, mental, and physical well-being of young people and adults. Provides health, child care, and cooperative services, services to teen parents, and counseling. Conducts seminars and workshops. **Affiliated with:** Young Women's Christian Association of the U.S.A.

Flower Mound

★3021★ **Lewisville Area Republican Women's Club**
c/o Ramona Kennedy
4718 Lloyd Ct.
Flower Mound, TX 75028
Phone: (214)539-9654
Ramona Kennedy, Exec. Officer

Description: Works to elect Republicans to local, state, and national office. Conducts training courses and workshops on political skills. Encourages women to seek leadership roles. Educates on issues and political processes. Conducts canvassing, fundraising, and other activities for Republican candidates. Encourages participation in the political process. Conducts literacy tutoring; sponsors festival. Affiliated with: National Federation of Republican Women.

Ft. Worth

★3022★ American Society of Women Accountants, Ft. Worth Chapter
500 Throckmorton, Ste. 2408
Ft. Worth, TX 76102
Phone: (817)332-1923
Gina Grikis, Pres.

Description: Seeks to advance the interests of women in accounting. **Affiliated with:** American Women's Society of Certified Public Accountants.

★3023★ Electrical Women's RoundTable, North Texas Chapter
Texas Utilities Electric Company
PO Box 970
Ft. Worth, TX 76101-0970
Mariolyn Jackson, Exec. Officer

Description: Women holding positions in the electrical industry. **Affiliated with:** Electrical Women's Round Table.

★3024★ Ft. Worth Alumnae Chapter, Delta Sigma Theta Sorority
c/o Margie H. Major
5908 Goodman Ave.
Ft. Worth, TX 76107-6913
Phone: (817)732-1583
Margie H. Major, Pres.

Description: College graduates united for community service and social action projects. Operates Teen Lift program. Awards scholarships. **Affiliated with:** Delta Sigma Theta Sorority.

★3025★ Ft. Worth Business and Professional Women's Club
c/o Bonnie Swafford
611 Throckmorton
Ft. Worth, TX 76102
Phone: (817)332-1171
Bonnie Swafford, Pres.

Description: Business and professional women. To promote complete participation, equal opportunities, and economic self-sufficiency for working women.

★3026★ Hispanic Women's League of Fort Worth
1820 Harrington
Ft. Worth, TX 76106
Phone: (817)625-0986
Maggie Cagigal, Sec.

★3027★ Young Women's Christian Association of Ft. Worth and Tarrant County
512 W. 4th St.
Ft. Worth, TX 76102
Phone: (817)332-6191
Judi Voirin Bishop, Exec. Officer

Description: Seeks to develop and improve the spiritual, social, mental, and physical well-being of young people and adults. **Affiliated with:** Young Women's Christian Association of the United States of America.

Galveston

★3028★ American Business Women's Association, Sand Dollar Chapter
4820 Ave. S
Galveston, TX 77551
Phone: (409)744-8188
Edith Cridland, Contact

Description: Women in business, including women owning or operating their own businesses, women in professions, and women employed in any level of government, education, or retailing, manufacturing, and service companies. **Affiliated with:** American Business Women's Association.

★3029★ Galveston Republican Women's Club
1515 Harbor View Circle
Galveston, TX 77550
Phone: (409)763-2261
Rose Farmer, Pres.

Description: Women Republicn party members. Works to elect Republicans to local, state, and national office. Provides public education on issues and candidates. **Affiliated with:** National Federation of Republican Women; Texas Federation of Republican Women.

★3030★ Propeller Club Women, Galveston Chapter
c/o Mrs. A. D. Suderman, Jr.
5530 Gull Dr.
Galveston, TX 77551
Phone: (409)744-8285
Mrs. A. D. Suderman, Jr., Pres.

Description: Works to promote and support the American Merchant Marine and other maritime interests. Sponsors Marine Science Fair. **Affiliated with:** Women's Propeller Club of the U.S.

Houston

★3031★ Association for Women in Science, Gulf Court/Houston Chapter
c/o Karen Wendler
3402 Tangley St.
Houston, TX 77005-2248

Description: Works to improve education and employment opportunities for women in the sciences.

★3032★ Cesarean Prevention Movement of Houston
PO Box 79103
Houston, TX 77279-9103
Phone: (713)580-0048
Betsy Eades, Pres.

Description: Pediatricians, nurses, midwives, obstetricians, parents, childbirth educators, and professional labor assistants. Promotes vaginal births and education on pregnancy and birthing procedures. **Affiliated with:** Cesarean Prevention Movement.

★3033★ Concerned Women for America, Southeast Texas
3604 Meadow Lake
Houston, TX 77027
Betty Lou Martin, Exec. Officer

★3034★ Greater Houston Women's Foundation
3040 Post Oak Blvd., Ste. 350
Houston, TX 77056
Phone: (713)623-4493
Linda May, Executive Director

**★3035★ National Association of Women Business Owners
Houston Chapter**
c/o Kainer and Company, P.C.
1 Greenway Plaza, Ste. 650
Houston, TX 77043
Phone: (713)552-9475
Deborah Kainer, President

★3036★ Young Women's Christian Association of Houston
3621 Willia
Houston, TX 77007
Phone: (713)868-9922

Description: Seeks to develop and improve the spiritual, social, mental, and physical well-being of young people and adults. **Affiliated with:** Young Women's Christian Association of the United States of America.

Junction

★3037★ Leti Study Club
c/o Edith Allen
PO Box 394
Junction, TX 76849
Edith Allen, Pres.

Description: Women in Kimble and surrounding counties, TX working to advance women's interests and activities in civics, education, fine arts, philanthropy, and values. Awards scholarships to graduating high school seniors. Conducts annual Tasting Luncheon.

Kerrville

★3038★ American Business Women's Association, Kerrville Chapter
1st National Bank
301 Junction Hwy.
Kerrville, TX 78028
Phone: (512)896-2424
Nita Ernst, Contact

Description: Business and professional women. To promote complete participation, equal opportunities, and economic self-sufficiency for working women. Awards scholarships. **Affiliated with:** American Business Women's Association.

★3039★ Women's Division, Kerrville Area Chamber of Commerce
1200 Sidney Baker St.
Kerrville, TX 78028
Phone: (512)896-1155
Barbara Steward, Pres.

Description: Women in the business community working to foster a spirit of cultural and commercial progress and encourage goodwill and fellowship. Seeks to advance industrial, educational, and civic interests. Bestows Outstanding Woman of the Year award. Conducts beautification and Christmas in the Hills projects. **Affiliated with:** Kerrville Area Chamber of Commerce.

Lake Jackson

★3040★ South Texas Girl Scout Council
231 W. Hwy 332
Lake Jackson, TX 77566
Phone: (409)297-5556
Betty Bednare, Exec.Dir.
Description: Girls, adult volunteers, and professional workers. Seeks to develop girls into happy, resourceful individuals willing to share their abilities as citizens in their homes and their communities. **Affiliated with:** Girl Scouts of the U.S.A.

Lubbock

★3041★ Young Women's Christian Association of Lubbock
3101 35th St.
Lubbock, TX 79413
Phone: (806)792-2723
Betty E. Wheeler, Contact
Description: Seeks to develop and improve the spiritual, social, mental, and physical well-being of young people and adults. Conducts charitable and educational events for women and their families. **Affiliated with:** Young Women's Christian Association of the United States of America.

McQueeney

★3042★ Guadalupe County Democratic Women's Forum
51 Spyglass
McQueeney, TX 78155
Phone: (512)557-5524
Mrs. John Taylor, Exec. Officer
Description: Women members of the Democratic Party. Works to elect Democrats to local, state, and national office.

Midland

★3043★ American Association of University Women, Odessa Branch
10600 W. County Rd. 145
Midland, TX 79703
Phone: (915)335-5129
Dorothy Hudman, Pres.
Description: Women graduates of regionally accredited four year colleges and universities. Works for the advancement of women through advocacy and emphasis on lifelong learning. Issues publications. **Affiliated with:** American Association of University Women.

Mission

★3044★ Texas Agri-Women
2101 Scout Ln.
Mission, TX 78572
Phone: (512)581-5869
Fax: (512)487-2844
Karen Peterson, Pres.
Description: Women's agricultural businesses, farms, and ranches. Seeks to educate the public on the importance of agriculture. **Affiliated with:** American Agri-Women.

Montgomery

★3045★ Ladies Association of Walden
PO Box 262
Montgomery, TX 77356-0262
Description: Social and civic service organziation.

Muleshoe

★3046★ American Association of University Women, Muleshoe Branch
c/o Virginia Bowers
407B W. 17th
Muleshoe, TX 79347
Phone: (806)272-3233
Virginia Bowers, Exec. Officer
Description: Women graduates of regionally accredited four year colleges and universities. Works for the advancement of women through advocacy and emphasis on lifelong learning. **Affiliated with:** American Association of University Women; Texas Association of University Women.

Odessa

★3047★ American Business Women's Association, Howdy Pardner Chapter
4200 Maple
Odessa, TX 79762
Phone: (915)362-2567
Ms. Billie Reagan, Contact
Description: Women in business, including women owning or operating their own businesses, women in professions, and women employed in any level of government, education, or retailing, manufacturing, and service companies. **Affiliated with:** American Business Women's Association.

★3048★ Permian Basin Girl Scout Council
5217 N. Dixie
Odessa, TX 79762
Phone: (915)563-0634
Toll-free: 800-594-5618
Susan G. Rutherford, Exec.Dir.
Description: Girls and adult volunteers. Works to enable girls to develop their potential and become contributors to their communities. **Affiliated with:** Girl Scouts of the U.S.A.

Orange

★3049★ American Association of University Women, Orange Branch
4440 Memorial
Orange, TX 77630
Phone: (409)886-7224
Sandra Wickersham, Pres.
Description: Women graduates of regionally accredited four year colleges and universities. Works for the advancement of women through advocacy and emphasis on lifelong learning. Conducts periodic special interest meetings. **Affiliated with:** American Association of University Women.

Paris

★3050★ Young Women's Christian Association of Paris and Lamar County
308 S. Main
Paris, TX 75460
Phone: (903)785-5221
Description: Seeks to develop and improve the spiritual, social, mental, and physical well-being of young people and adults. **Affiliated with:** Young Women's Christian Association of the United States of America.

Richardson

★3051★ Society for Women in Philosophy, Southwestern Division (SW-SWIP)
c/o Nancy Tuana
University of Texas, Dallas
Department of Philosophy
PO Box 830688
Richardson, TX 75083-0688
Phone: (214)690-2980
Nancy Tuana, Exec. Officer
Founded: 1975. **Description:** Professional women with a background or interest in philosophy and women's issues. Promotes interaction among women in philosophy in the Southwest and the involvement of women in the philosophical community. Supports the development of philosophical issues with an emphasis on feminist theory. Conducts seminars. **Members:** 40. **Publications:** *Hypatia: A Journal of Feminist Philosophy*, quarterly.

San Angelo

★3052★ Assault Victim Services
3034 W. Beauregard
San Angelo, TX 76901
Phone: (915)944-8728
Fax: (915)658-6504
Linda Shelton, Dir.
Description: Persons in the Tom Green County, TX area. Provides sexual assault prevention and intervention services. Offers counseling and professional training and community education programs; provides court and hospital accompaniment. Operates Child Assault Prevention Project; maintains speakers' bureau. **Affiliated with:** MHMR Services for Concho Valley.

★3053★ San Angelo Business and Professional Women's Club
PO Box 2476
San Angelo, TX 76902
Phone: (915)949-9511
Melda Calvert, Contact
Description: Business and professional women. To promote complete participation, equal opportunities, and economic self-sufficiency for working women. **Affiliated with:** National Federation of Business and Professional Women's Clubs of the U.S.A.

San Antonio

★3054★ Concerned Women for America, South Texas Chapter
PO Box 160422
San Antonio, TX 78280
Paulette Brack, Exec. Officer
Description: Women in southern Texas. Promotes the preservation of traditional Judeo-Christian values.

★3055★ Young Women's Christian Association of San Antonio
8601 Cinnamon Creek
San Antonio, TX 78240
Phone: (512)692-9973
Fax: (512)692-3704
Ida Givens, Contact
Description: Seeks to develop and improve the spiritual, social, mental, and physical well-being of young people and adults. **Affiliated with:** Young Women's Christian Association of United States of America.

Seguin

★3056★ Guadalupe County Republican Women's Club
Rte. 3, Box 490
Seguin, TX 78155
Phone: (512)379-7722
Kay Hoerman, Exec. Officer
Description: Women members of the Republican Party. Works to elect Republicans to local, state, and national office.

Stamford

★3057★ Girl Scouts of the United States of America, Stamford Council
1402 Wells
Stamford, TX 79553
Phone: (915)773-5070
Nelda Hopkins, Dir.
Description: Provides program of physical, emotional, and spiritual growth for girls and young women. **Affiliated with:** Girl Scouts of the U.S.A.

Texarkana

★3058★ Young Women's Christian Association of Texarkana
3410 Magnolia
Texarkana, TX 75503
Phone: (903)793-6769
Description: Seeks to develop and improve the spiritual, social, mental, and physical well-being of young people and adults. **Affiliated with:** Young Women's Christian Association of the United States of America.

Tyler

★3059★ Briarwood Women's Golf Association
4511 Briarwood Dr.
Tyler, TX 75709-2009
Description: Women in Tyler, TX interested in golf.

Waco

★3060★ Bluebonnet Girl Scout Council
3700 W. Waco Dr.
Waco, TX 76710-5347
Phone: (817)756-4497
Mary Everett, Exec. Officer
Description: Girl scouts in 13 counties in central Texas. Seeks to inspire girls to the highest ideals of character, conduct, and patriotism.

★3061★ DES Action
8230 Shadowwood Dr.
Waco, TX 76712

★3062★ Young Women's Christian Association of Waco
2601 Franklin Ave.
Waco, TX 76710
Phone: (817)753-3881
Description: Seeks to develop and improve the spiritual, social, mental, and physical well-being of young people and adults. **Affiliated with:** Young Women's Christian Association of the United States of America.

Wichita Falls

★3063★ Young Women's Christian Association of Wichita Falls
801-03 Burnett St.
Wichita Falls, TX 76301
Phone: (817)723-2124
Coralee Hester, Exec.Dir.
Description: Seeks to develop and improve the spiritual, social, mental, and physical well-being of young people and adults. **Affiliated with:** Young Women's Christian Association of the United States of America.

The Woodlands

★3064★ Older Women's League (OWL) East Texas Chapter
PO Box 9456
The Woodlands, TX 77387
Phone: (713)292-6503
Yvette Crudgington, Contact

Utah

Brigham City

★3065★ Utah Federation of Women's Clubs
c/o LaRaine Petersen
634 East 200 South
Brigham City, UT 84302
Phone: (801)723-6904
LaRaine Petersen, Pres.
Description: Represents members' interests. Conducts seminars and workshops.

★3066★ Women in Business
94 South 400 West
Brigham City, UT 84302
Phone: (801)723-8521
Description: Business and professional women. To promote complete participation, equal opportunities, and economic self-sufficiency for working women. **Affiliated with:** Brigham City Chamber of Commerce.

Logan

★3067★ Association for Women in Science, Northern Utah Chapter
c/o Terrie Wierenga
1150 E. 1400 N.
Logan, UT 84321
Phone: (801)752-2941
Description: Works to improve education and employment opportunities for women in the sciences.

Mt. Pleasant

★3068★ Utah Midwives' Association
438 South State
Mt. Pleasant, UT 84647
Phone: (801)462-2532
Katherine Tarr, Pres.
Description: To preserve the art of midwifery as a nonmedical profession.

Ogden

★3069★ Cesarean Prevention Movement of Ogden/Northern Utah
635 East 2300 North
Ogden, UT 84404
Phone: (801)782-5967
Betty Pankiewicz, Exec. Officer

★3070★ Young Women's Christian Association of Ogden/Northern Utah
2261 Adams Ave.
Ogden, UT 84401
Phone: (801)394-9456
Description: Seeks to develop and improve the spiritual, social, mental, and physical well-being of young people and adults. **Affiliated with:** Young Women's Christian Association of the United States of America.

Salt Lake City

★3071★ Girl Scouts of America, Utah Council
PO Box 57280
Salt Lake City, UT 84109
Phone: (801)265-8472
Sharon Stetz, Exec.Dir.
Description: Girls aged five to 17 years in Arizona, Nevada, and Utah. To inspire high ideals of character, conduct, patriotism, and service. Provides youth services. **Affiliated with:** Girl Scouts of the U.S.A.

★3072★ Higher Education Resources Services, West (HERS)
Women's Center
University of Utah
Salt Lake City, UT
Phone: (801)581-8030
Kathy Brooks, Contact
Description: HERS, West sponsors a research group which examines issues of women and power.

★3073★ League of Women Voters of Utah
3804 Highland Dr., Ste. 9
Salt Lake City, UT 84106-4209
Phone: (801)272-8683
Karil Frohboese, Co-President

★3074★ Utah Abortion Rights Action League
287 D St.
Salt Lake City, UT 84103
Phone: (801)328-9355
Susanne Millsaps, Contact

★3075★ **Utah Association of Women**
PO Box 195
Salt Lake City, UT 84110
Phone: (801)363-3420
Susan Roylance, Pres.

Description: To strengthen society by protecting, elevating, and supporting the traditional family.

★3076★ **Utah Women's History**
Association
300 Rio Grande
Salt Lake City, UT 84101

★3077★ **Young Women's Christian**
Association of Salt Lake City
322 East 3rd, South
Salt Lake City, UT 84111
Phone: (801)862-7520

Description: Seeks to develop and improve the spiritual, social, mental, and physical well-being of young people and adults. **Affiliated with:** Young Women's Christian Association of the United States of America.

Vermont

Bennington

★3078★ **American Association of**
University Women, Bennington Chapter
117 Imperial Ave.
Bennington, VT 05201
Celine Hoffman, Exec. Officer

Description: Works for advancement of women through advocacy and emphasis on lifelong learning.

Brattleboro

★3079★ **Green Mountain Women's Action**
for Nuclear Disarmament
3 Tyler Ave.
Brattleboro, VT 05301
Phone: (802)257-5179
Deedee Jones, Pres.

Description: Individuals in southeastern Vermont and southwestern New Hampshire dedicated to educating others on the arms race and the importance of disarmament. **Affiliated with:** Women's Action for Nuclear Disarmament.

★3080★ **Women's Crisis Center**
PO Box 933
Brattleboro, VT 05302
Phone: (802)257-7364
Dorothy Green, Exec.Dir.

Description: Provides services to battered and sexually abused women in Windham County, VT. Maintains shelter for abused women and their children.

Burlington

★3081★ **American Association of**
University Women, Burlington Branch
272 Church St.
Burlington, VT 05401
Phone: (802)864-4932
Pat Allen Morgan, Pres.

Description: Group sponsors educational programs, lobbying activities, and social gatherings.

★3082★ **Champlin Valley Birthright**
c/o James H. Marihugh, Jr.
229 Curtis Ave.
Burlington, VT 05401-2407

Description: Individuals maintaining a right-to-life position.

★3083★ **Vermont Young Women's**
Christian Association
278 Main St.
Burlington, VT 05401
Phone: (802)862-7520

Description: Seeks to develop and improve the spiritual, social, mental, and physical well-being of young people and adults. **Affiliated with:** Young Women's Christian Association of the United States of America.

East Middlebury

★3084★ **League of Women Voters of**
Vermont
PW Box 529
East Middlebury, VT 05740
Phone: (802)388-0870
Nelda Holder, President

Montpelier

★3085★ **Pro-Choice Vermont**
43 State St.
Montpelier, VT 05602
Phone: (802)229-9207
Elaine Alfano, Contact

★3086★ **Vermont Network Against**
Domestic Violence and Sexual Assault
PO Box 405
Montpelier, VT 05601
Phone: (802)223-1302
Garnett Harrison, Contact

★3087★ **Vermont Right to Life Committee**
PO Box 1079
Montpelier, VT 05601
Phone: (802)229-4885
Margaret Barnes, Pres.

Description: Interested persons working to educate the community regarding abortion, infanticide, and euthanasia. Promotes legislation to protect human life. Maintains pregnancy support and adoption committees. Provides pro-life resources and information. **Affiliated with:** National Right to Life Committee.

Saxtons River

★3088★ **American Association of**
University Women, Vermont Branch
Box 444
Saxtons River, VT 05154
Phone: (802)869-2566
Louise Luring, Contact

Description: Group sponsors educational programs, lobbying activities, and social gatherings.

Waterbury

★3089★ **Older Women's League (OWL)**
Green Mountain Chapter
201 Acorn Dr. Oakwood
Waterbury, VT 05676
Phone: (802)244-8838
Mary Fries, Contact

Virgin Islands

St. Thomas

★3090★ **League of Women Voters of**
Virgin Islands
PO Box 638, Charlotte Amalie
St. Thomas, VI 00801
Phone: (809)774-8620
Helen Gjessing, President

Virginia

Alexandria

★3091★ **American Association of**
University Women, Falls Church Branch
6337 Hillcrest Place
Alexandria, VA 22312-1246
Anne Baxter, Pres.

Description: Women graduates of regionally accredited four year colleges and universities. Works for the advancement of women through advocacy and emphasis on lifelong learning.

★3092★ **Friends of Guest House, Inc.**
1 E. Luray Ave.
Alexandria, VA 22301
Phone: (703)549-8072
Ronald Hagar, Staff Director

Founded: 1974. **Description:** Re-entry and alternative to incarceration services to women ex-offenders.

Arlington

★3093★ **Chesapeake Area Group of**
Women Historians
c/o Judy Howard
4542 N. 40th St.
Arlington, VA 22207

★3094★ **Healthy Mothers, Healthy Babies**
Virginia State Coalition
March of Dimes Birth Defects Foundation
2700 S. Quincy St., Ste. 220
Arlington, VA 22206
Phone: (703)824-0111
Fax: (703)578-4928

Description: Volunteers in the District of Columbia, Maryland, and Virginia. Works to prevent birth defects through medical services and educational programs. Encourages research into the causes, treatments, and prevention of birth defects.

★3095★ Organized Women Voters of Arlington
1600 N. Oak St., No. 415
Arlington, VA 22209
Phone: (703)538-6750
Mrs. Renfro, Contact
Description: Encourages citizens to become involved in government through voting and lobbying efforts.

Bedford

★3096★ American Association of University Women, Bedford Chapter
PO Box 423
Bedford, VA 24523
Janet Adams, Pres.
Description: Women graduates of regionally accredited four year colleges and universities. Works for the advancement of women through advocacy and emphasis on lifelong learning. Sponsors annual art show. Awards scholarship. **Affiliated with:** American Association of University Women.

★3097★ Bedford Business and Professional Women's Club
1214 W. Hills Dr.
Bedford, VA 24523
Phone: (703)586-4476
Janet Cofer, Contact
Description: Business and professional women. To promote complete participation, equal opportunities, and economic self-sufficiency for working women. Awards scholarships to female high school seniors. Presents educational programs on legal issues, politics, self improvement, and other topics of interest. **Affiliated with:** National Business and Professional Women's Clubs.

Burke

★3098★ Older Women's League (OWL) Northern Virginia Chapter
9152 Bloom Ct.
Burke, VA 22015-1643
Phone: (703)764-2887
Dorothy Pond Morris, Contact

Danville

★3099★ Danville Business Women's Club
215 Roberts St.
Danville, VA 24541
Phone: (804)793-9184
Bertha H. Bruce, Sec.
Description: Business and professional women. To promote complete participation, equal opportunities, and economic self-sufficiency for working women.

Dunn Loring

★3100★ Fairfax County YWCA Women's Network
PO Box 86
Dunn Loring, VA 22027
Phone: (703)560-1111
Valerie Ducker, Program Specialist
Founded: 1982. **Description:** Provides a forum for learning ways for career and economic advancement. Holds monthly meetings with speakers, workshops and seminars.

★3101★ Family Life and Maternity Education of Dunn Loring
PO Box 379
Dunn Loring, VA 22027
Phone: (703)276-9248
Toll-free: 800-776-9248
Lori Flowers, Pres.
Description: Childbirth educators and volunteers. Promotes the Lamaze method of natural childbirth. Offers educational seminars; makes available scholarships. **Affiliated with:** International Childbirth Education Association.

Fairfax

★3102★ DES Action
12494 Alexander Cornell Dr.
Fairfax, VA 22033

Falls Church

★3103★ Virginia Abortion Rights Action League
PO Box 489
Falls Church, VA 22046
Phone: (703)532-3448
Erika Goodman, Contact

★3104★ Woman's Club of Falls Church
PO Box 165
Falls Church, VA 22046
Phone: (703)525-4274
Libby Holland, Pres.
Description: Women in Falls Church, VA promoting the improvement of the community through fundraising activities and volunteer work.

Hampton

★3105★ American Association of University Women, Virginia Division
4205 Chesapeake Ave.
Hampton, VA 23669
Phone: (804)722-0069
Susan H. Hoover, Pres.
Description: Women graduates of regionally accredited four year colleges and universities. Works for the advancement of women through advocacy and emphasis on lifelong learning. **Affiliated with:** American Association of University Women.

Herndon

★3106★ American Association of University Women, Reston Chapter
1139 Bandy Run Rd.
Herndon, VA 22070
Phone: (703)450-5360
Jackie Brown, Pres.
Description: Women graduates of regionally accredited four year colleges and universities. Works for the advancement of women through advocacy and emphasis on lifelong learning. Offers special interest groups such as book discussion, gourmet cooking, and bridge playing. **Affiliated with:** American Association of University Women.

Manassas

★3107★ AAA Women for Choice
9380A Forestwood Ln.
Manassas, VA 22110-4702
Description: Women united to maintain the right to legal abortion.

Marion

★3108★ Marion Junior Woman's Club
590 Look Ave.
Marion, VA 24354
Patty P. Blevins, Treas.
Description: Volunteer civic organization promotes community development through service. Promotes education, safety, health, the arts, and home life. **Affiliated with:** General Federation of Women's Clubs; Virginia Federation of Women's Clubs.

Midlothian

★3109★ National Association of Women Business Owners Richmond Chapter
c/o Jennings and Jennings
10138 Hull St. Rd.
Midlothian, VA 23112
Phone: (804)276-8011
Debbie Jennings, President

Newport News

★3110★ Woman's Club of Hilton Village
PO Box 1005
Newport News, VA 23601
Phone: (804)596-3722
Mrs. Clyde H. Base, Pres.
Description: Registered voters in Newport News, VA. Non-partisan non-profit organization encourages and promotes fine arts, education, and public welfare.

Oakton

★3111★ Virginia Organization to Keep Abortion Legal
PO Box 152
Oakton, VA 22124
Phone: (703)532-3448
Maria Briancon, Coordinator
Description: Individuals working to maintain and expand abortion rights. Conducts grassroots organizing. Monitors legislation. **Affiliated with:** National Abortion Rights Action League.

Reston

★3112★ Network of Entrepreneurial Women
1810 Michael Faraday Dr., Ste. 101
Reston, VA 22090
Phone: (703)435-4449
Mary Keel, Pres.
Description: Women business owners. Promotes networking, education, and visibility of women in business.

★3113★ **Virginia Association for Female Executives**
PO Box 3308
Reston, VA 22090
Phone: (703)476-0089
Martha B. Walters, President
Founded: 1986. **Description:** Provides a forum for professional women to meet each other. **Publications:** Newsletter.

Richmond

★3114★ **League of Women Voters of Virginia**
2805 McRae Rd., A-5
Richmond, VA 23235
Phone: (804)320-7528
Patricia Szabo, President

★3115★ **National Federation of Democratic Women, Virginia Chapter**
313 N. Granby St.
Richmond, VA 23220
Phone: (804)355-7628
Sophie Salley, Exec. Officer
Description: Works to elect Democrats to local, state, and national office. **Affiliated with:** National Federation of Democratic Women.

★3116★ **Older Women's League (OWL) Greater Richmond Chapter**
1215 E. Marshall
Richmond, VA 23298
Phone: (804)786-1525
Debbie Snyder, Contact

★3117★ **Virginia Council on the Status of Women**
8007 Discovery Dr.
Richmond, VA 23229-8699
Phone: (804)662-9200
Connie C. Gendron, Chair Woman
Founded: 1970. **Description:** Promotes equal opportunity for women in the Commonwealth of Virginia. **Publications:** *Virginia Women.*

★3118★ **Virginia Federation of Women's Clubs**
300 W. Franklin St., Ste. 402, W.
Richmond, VA 23220
Phone: (804)644-2558
Vicki Marks, Exec.Sec.
Description: Women's clubs. Promotes education and community service.

★3119★ **Virginians Against Domestic Violence**
PO Box 5692
Richmond, VA 23220
Phone: (804)780-3505
Ruth Micklem, Contact

Springfield

★3120★ **Black Women United**
6551 Loisdale Ct., Ste. 714
Springfield, VA 22150
Phone: (703)922-5757
Virginia Williams, President
Founded: 1985.

★3121★ **Fairfax County Mothers of Multiples**
8522 Bauer Dr.
Springfield, VA 22152
Karen Setia, Pres.
Description: Mothers of twins, triplets, and quadruplets in northern Virginia. Provides education and support for families with multiple birth children.

★3122★ **Re-Entry Women's Employment Center**
County of Fairfax
5501 Backlick Rd., Ste. 110
Springfield, VA 22151
Phone: (703)750-0633
Leia Franciso, Dir.
Founded: 1979. **Description:** A career development agency providing workshops and other services. **Publications:** *Connections.*

Strasburg

★3123★ **La Leche League International, Front Royal Chapter**
Ft. Valley Rt., Box 68
Strasburg, VA 22657
Phone: (703)635-1678
Abbe Mulvena, Leader
Description: Pregnant women, nursing mothers, and family oriented individuals. Promotes breastfeeding. Maintains library. Issues publications. **Affiliated with:** La Leche League International.

Stuart

★3124★ **Moorefield Store Women's Auxiliary**
Pine St.
Stuart, VA 24171
Mrs. Ruby Handy, Pres.
Description: Women's volunteer service club.

Virginia Beach

★3125★ **Tidewater Mothers of Twins**
c/o Vickie Dyer
2004 Convoy Ct.
Virginia Beach, VA 23454
Phone: (804)481-3541
Vickie Dyer, Contact
Description: Support group for parents of multiple birth children. Provides help, understanding, and encouragement to parents. **Affiliated with:** Tri-State Mothers of Twins Clubs Association.

★3126★ **Virginia Beach Jr. Women's Club**
c/o Katherine P. King
PO Box 9744
Virginia Beach, VA 23450-9744
Description: Women's volunteer service club. Conducts youth programs.

Wytheville

★3127★ **Wytheville Ladies Puritan Club**
295 Chapman Rd.
Wytheville, VA 24382
Phone: (703)228-3823
Peggy P. Duncan, Sec.
Description: Community service organization. **Affiliated with:** Ruritan National.

★3128★ **Wytheville Lady Golfers**
1405 N. 11th St.
Wytheville, VA 24382
Phone: (703)228-4813
Janet Lester, Pres.
Description: Lady golfers in Wytheville, VA. Promotes golf as a leisure activity.

Washington

Battle Ground

★3129★ **Women's Study Club of Battle Ground**
302 West E St.
Battle Ground, WA 98604
Phone: (206)687-3026
Lynette Sargent, Pres.
Description: Women working to make public aware of civic problems and possible solutions to those problems. Provides aid to scholastically eligible students. Works in cooperation with local American Association of Retired Persons chapter and Retired Senior Volunteer Program. Sponsors annual tea for girls graduating class. Welcomes newcomers.

Bellingham

★3130★ **Older Women's League (OWL) Mt. Baker Chapter**
206 Bayside Pl.
Bellingham, WA 98225
Phone: (206)733-2539
Maggie Hanson, Contact

★3131★ **Young Women's Christian Association of Bellingham**
1026 North Forest St.
Bellingham, WA 98225
Phone: (206)734-4820
Description: Seeks to develop and improve the spiritual, social, mental, and physical well-being of young people and adults. **Affiliated with:** Young Women's Christian Association of the United States of America.

Bremerton

★3132★ **Young Women's Christian Association of Kitsap County**
PO Box 559
Bremerton, WA 98310
Phone: (206)479-5116
Barbara P. Malich, Contact
Description: Seeks to develop and improve the spiritual, social, mental, and physical well-being of young people and adults. Sponsors A.L.I.V.E. House for battered women, legal referral service, and various women's programs. **Affiliated with:** Young Women's Christian Association of the United States of America.

Des Moines

★3133★ American Association of University Women, Washington Division
816 South 216th St., No. 604-06
Des Moines, WA 98198-6395
Phone: (206)870-8604
Thelma G. Soltman, Pres.

Description: Women graduates of regionally accredited four year colleges and universities. Works for the advancement of women through advocacy and emphasis on lifelong learning. Sponsors Expanding Your Horizons program. Lobbies for favorable legislation. **Affiliated with:** American Association of University Women.

Federal Way

★3134★ American Association of University Women, Federal Way Branch
500 South 321st, No. 2A
Federal Way, WA 98003
Phone: (206)838-5963
Elaine Cook, Contact

Description: University graduates in southern King County, WA. Seeks to provide women with assistance and equity, in education and the workplace. Conducts workshops. **Affiliated with:** American Association of University Women; Washington Division of University Women.

Issaquah

★3135★ Christian Counseling for Women
c/o Aurelio P. Simon
5116 W. Lake, Sammamish Pkwy. SE
Issaquah, WA 98027-9329

Description: Provides Christian counseling to women.

Kelso

★3136★ Older Women's League (OWL) Cowlitz County Chapter
208 NW 8th, No. 3
Kelso, WA 98626
Phone: (206)425-4031

Kent

★3137★ Riverbend Ladies Golf Association
c/o Susan Boros
PO Box 1091
Kent, WA 98035-1091

Description: Promotes the sport of golf.

Kirkland

★3138★ Kirkland Business and Professional Women's Club
6714 Lake Washington Blvd., NE
Kirkland, WA 98033
Phone: (206)822-7720
Evelyn Burnett, Liaison

Description: Business and professional women. To promote complete participation, equal opportunities, and economic self-sufficiency for working women. **Affiliated with:** National Federation of Business and Professional Women's Clubs of the U.S.A.

Lynnwood

★3139★ Older Women's League (OWL) Snohomish County Chapter
PO Box 5627
Lynnwood, WA 98046
Phone: (206)568-8306
Kathy McElhaney, Contact

★3140★ Women's Transportation Seminar, Seattle Chapter
6909 185th Pl., SW
Lynnwood, WA 98037
Phone: (206)771-3271
Louise Stanton-Mason, Consultant

Description: Women and men transportation professionals united to assist and advance women in the transportation industry. Makes available scholarships. **Affiliated with:** Women's Transportation Seminar-National.

Naselle

★3141★ Washington State Domestic Violence Hotline
c/o Pacific County Crisis Support Network
HCR 78 Box 336
Naselle, WA 98638
Phone: (206)484-7191
Toll-free: 800-562-6025
Jeri Varila, Contact

Olympia

★3142★ Thurston County Women Can Do Committee
6431 Rich Rd. SE
Olympia, WA 98501-5319

Description: Women's volunteer service club.

★3143★ Young Women's Christian Association of Olympia
220 Union SE
Olympia, WA 98501
Phone: (206)352-0593

Description: Seeks to develop and improve the spiritual, social, mental, and physical well-being of young people and adults. **Affiliated with:** Young Women's Christian Association of the United States of America.

Pasco

★3144★ Mid-Columbia Women's Bowling Association
4208 West Ruby
Pasco, WA 99301
Phone: (509)547-6321
Shirley Hansen, Exec. Officer

Description: Women interested in the sport of bowling.

Port Townsend

★3145★ National Organization for Women, Jefferson County Chapter
PO Box 500
Port Townsend, WA 98368
Phone: (206)385-2285
Julia Cochrane, Exec. Officer

Description: Feminists in eastern Jefferson County, WA. To improve the political, legal, and economic position of women. **Affiliated with:** National Organization for Women.

Proseer

★3146★ Washington Women for the Survival of Agriculture
1043 Elm
Proseer, WA 99350
Phone: (509)786-2489
Nancy Boettcher, Sec.

Description: Women in agriculture or related businesses and industries united to promote agriculture and provide education on agricultural issues. **Affiliated with:** American Agri-Women.

Renton

★3147★ Coalition of Labor Union Women
19822 104th SE
Renton, WA 98055
Phone: (206)852-7774
Susan Moyer, V.Pres.

Description: Women who are members of labor unions. Promotes increased participation of women in union activities. **Affiliated with:** National Coalition of Labor Union Women.

★3148★ King County Sexual Assault Resource Center
PO Box 300
Renton, WA 98057
Phone: (206)226-5062
Mary Ellen Stone, Exec.Dir.

Description: Seeks to eliminate sexual assault. Offers educational and direct victim services. Maintains speakers' bureau. Sponsors program on public television.

Richland

★3149★ Girl Scouts of the U.S.A., Mid-Columbia Council
710A George Washington Way
Richland, WA 99352-4211
Phone: (509)943-1187
Fax: (509)946-8746
Avis J. DeRuyter, Exec.Dir.

Description: Girls aged five through 17 and adults in central Washington and northeastern Oregon. Sponsors leadership and character building programs. **Affiliated with:** Girl Scouts of the United States of America.

★3150★ National Organization for Women, Tri-Cities Chapter
PO Box 11
Richland, WA 99352
Phone: (509)943-9730
Judith M. Johannesen, Contact

Description: Feminist activists. Seeks to end prejudice and discrimination against women in government, industry, the professions, and labor unions.

Seattle

★3151★ Associated Lesbians of Puget Sound
PO Box 20424
Seattle, WA 98102
Phone: (206)233-8145

Description: Serves as a social and educational network for lesbians.

★3152★ **Association for Women in Science, Seattle Chapter**
c/o Reitha Weeks
2410 Dexter Ave. N., 102
Seattle, WA 98109-2260
Description: Works to improve education and employment opportunities for women in the sciences.

★3153★ **Birthright of Seattle**
c/o Roberta Gleason
4000 Aurora Ave. N., Ste. 219
Seattle, WA 98103-7853
Description: Seeks to help pregnant women find alternatives to abortion. Conducts childbirth education and parenting programs.

★3154★ **League of Women Voters of Washington**
1411 4th Ave. Bldg., No. 803
Seattle, WA 98101-2216
Phone: (206)622-8961
Margaret Colony, President

★3155★ **Northwest Women's Law Center**
119 S. Main St., Ste. 330
Seattle, WA 98104
Phone: (206)682-9552
Lindy Cater, Staff Dir.
Founded: 1978. **Description:** Works to advance and strengthen the legal rights of women. **Publications:** Equal Times and Family Law in Washington State.

★3156★ **Older Women's League (OWL) Seattle/King County Chapter**
c/o Wallingford Sr. Ctr.
4649 Sunnyside Ave. N
Seattle, WA 98103
Pat Melgard, Contact

★3157★ **Religious Coalition for Abortion Rights, Washington Chapter**
PO Box 2075, Broadway Sta.
Seattle, WA 98112
Phone: (206)324-8219
Madelene Crook, Exec. Officer

★3158★ **Seattle Women Act for Peace**
2524 16th, South
Seattle, WA 98144
Phone: (206)329-3666
Ethel Boyar, Co-Chair
Description: Works for disarmament and military budget cuts. Conducts lobbying activities. Sponsors educational programs. **Affiliated with:** Women Strike for Peace.

★3159★ **Washington State Abortion Rights Action League**
105 S. Main St., No. 326
Seattle, WA 98104
Phone: (206)624-1990
Esther Herst, Contact

★3160★ **Women Certified Public Accountants of Seattle**
c/o Patricia L. Scanlon
Group Health Cooperative
521 Wall St.
Seattle, WA 98121
Phone: (206)448-5109
Patricia L. Scanlon, Pres.
Description: Professional organization for women accountants.

★3161★ **Women's Caucus for Art**
4057A Roosevelt-Wayne
Seattle, WA 98105
Phone: (206)632-4747
Description: Provides well known women artists as speakers, exhibition space for women's artwork; sponsors classes on feminist art theory and History of American women in art.

★3162★ **Women's Funding Alliance**
219 1st Ave. S., Ste. 120
Seattle, WA 98104
Phone: (206)467-6733
Karen Campbell, Executive Director

★3163★ **Women's Spirituality Center**
4135 Bagley Ave., North
Seattle, WA 98103
Phone: (206)547-3374
Rev. Lita Artis, Exec.Dir.
Description: Resource center comprised of religious and Christian feminists working to create a dialogue between spirituality and feminism through programs, reading groups, liturgies, and workshops. Conducts charitable activities.

★3164★ **Young Women's Christian Association of Seattle-King County**
1118 5th Ave.
Seattle, WA 98101
Phone: (206)461-4888
Description: Seeks to develop and improve the spiritual, social, mental, and physical well-being of young people and adults. **Affiliated with:** Young Women's Christian Association of the United States of America.

Spokane

★3165★ **American Woman's Society of Certified Public Accountants of Spokane**
Elliott, Clevenger, and Nelson
S. 612 Bernard
Spokane, WA 99204
Phone: (509)838-2949
Barbara Clevenger, Pres.

★3166★ **Older Women's League (OWL) Greater Spokane Chapter**
4224 N. Calispel
Spokane, WA 99205
Phone: (509)328-0287
Madeline Kardong, Contact

★3167★ **Washington Branch of National Abortion Rights Action League**
S. 9 Washington, No. 519
Spokane, WA 99204
Phone: (509)455-6310
Leslie Farris, Contact

★3168★ **Young Women's Christian Association of Spokane**
829 West Broadway
Spokane, WA 99201
Phone: (509)326-1190
Kelly Honeychurch, Contact
Description: Seeks to develop and improve the spiritual, social, mental, and physical well-being of young people and adults. **Affiliated with:** Young Women's Christian Association of the United States of America.

Tacoma

★3169★ **Tacoma Lesbian Concern**
Box 947
Tacoma, WA 98401
Phone: (206)472-0422
Mary DeSanto, Treas.
Description: Social, educational and support group for lesbians in Kitsap, Pierce, Thurston, and south King counties, WA.

★3170★ **Women's Overseas Service League, Tacoma Chapter**
c/o Winifred A. Walker
10023 107 Ave., SW
Tacoma, WA 98498
Phone: (206)582-3006
Winifred A. Walker, Pres.
Description: Women in Oregon and Washington who served overseas with the armed forces. To maintain the spirit and camaraderie born of overseas service; to further patriotic work; to assist the men and women wounded in service of their country.

★3171★ **Young Women's Christian Association of Tacoma and Pierce County**
405 Broadway Ave.
Tacoma, WA 98402
Phone: (206)272-4181
Description: Seeks to develop and improve the spiritual, social, mental, and physical well-being of young people and adults. **Affiliated with:** Young Women's Christian Association of the United States of America.

Vancouver

★3172★ **Older Women's League (OWL) Columbia River Chapter**
1115 Esther
Vancouver, WA 98660
Phone: (206)573-9493
Lora Allred, Contact

★3173★ **Young Women's Christian Association of Vancouver-Clark County**
1115 Esther St.
Vancouver, WA 98660
Phone: (206)696-0167
Description: Seeks to develop and improve the spiritual, social, mental, and physical well-being of young people and adults. **Affiliated with:** Young Women's Christian Association of the United States of America.

Walla Walla

★3174★ **Birthright of Washington**
118 South 2nd
Walla Walla, WA 99362-3001
Description: Seeks to help pregnant women find alternatives to abortion. Conducts childbirth education and parenting programs.

★3175★ **Young Women's Christian Association of Walla Walla**
213 South 1st St.
Walla Walla, WA 99362
Phone: (509)525-2570
Description: Seeks to develop and improve the spiritual, social, mental, and physical well-being of young people and adults. **Affiliated with:**

Young Women's Christian Association of the United States of America.

Wenatchee

★3176★ Teen Awareness in Prevention-Pregnancy-Parenting
316 Washington St.
Wenatchee, WA 98801
Phone: (509)664-5306
Suzanne Gaukroger, Dir.
Description: To improve the health outcome of pregnant and parenting teens in Chelan and Douglas counties, WA. Seeks to reduce the rate of second pregnancies and encourage self-reliance through education and training.

★3177★ Young Women's Christian Association of Wenatchee Valley
212 1st St.
Wenatchee, WA 98801
Phone: (509)662-3531
Description: Seeks to develop and improve the spiritual, social, mental, and physical well-being of young people and adults. **Affiliated with:** Young Women's Christian Association of the United States of America.

Yakima

★3178★ American Association of University Women, Yakima Branch
105 East Shamrock Dr. North
Yakima, WA 98908
Phone: (509)966-3409
Description: Women graduates of regionally accredited four year colleges and universities. Works for the advancement of women through advocacy and emphasis on lifelong learning. **Affiliated with:** American Association of University Women.

★3179★ Yakima Business and Professional Women's Club
621 South 71st Ave.
Yakima, WA 98908
Phone: (509)965-0713
Pauline King, Pres.
Description: Business and professional women. To promote complete participation, equal opportunities, and economic self-sufficiency for working women. Issues publications.

★3180★ Yakima Woman's Century Club
304 North 2nd St.
Yakima, WA 98901
Phone: (509)453-3921
Description: Conducts cultural, educational, and social activities.

★3181★ Young Women's Christian Association of Yakima
15 North Naches Ave.
Yakima, WA 98901
Phone: (509)248-7796
Description: Seeks to develop and improve the spiritual, social, mental, and physical well-being of young people and adults. **Affiliated with:** Young Women's Christian Association of the United States of America.

West Virginia

Bluefield

★3182★ American Association of University Women, Bluefield Branch
PO Box 367
Bluefield, WV 24701
Phone: (304)327-7337
Margaret Murphy, Pres.
Description: Women graduates of regionally accredited four year colleges and universities. Works for the advancement of women through advocacy and emphasis on lifelong learning. Provides scholarships to Bluefield State College. Sponsors Women in Art exhibition. **Affiliated with:** American Association of University Women.

★3183★ Bluefield Junior Women's Club
403 Hillcrest
Bluefield, WV 24605
Phone: (304)327-0127
Ora Damagio, Pres.
Description: Business, family, career, and single women age 18-40. Works to improve family and community life.

Charleston

★3184★ American Association of University Women, West Virginia Division
722 Chappell Rd.
Charleston, WV 25304
Phone: (304)925-5792
Shirley Randolph, Pres.
Description: Women graduates of regionally accredited four year colleges and universities. Works for the advancement of women through advocacy and emphasis on lifelong learning. Advocates on behalf of women. Alerts women on issues affecting their welfare. Makes available scholarships. **Affiliated with:** American Association of University Women.

★3185★ West Virginia Abortion Rights Action League
PO Box 11076
Charleston, WV 25339
Phone: (304)343-5002
Karen Hannah, Contact

Fairmont

★3186★ Marion County Democratic Woman's Club
1099 Charles Ave.
Fairmont, WV 26554
Phone: (304)366-6168
Joyce Morris, Contact
Description: Woman Democrats. Works to elect Democrats to local, state, and national office.

Fayetteville

★3187★ Fayetteville Junior Woman's Club
c/o Kay Wendell
506 W. Maple Ave.
Fayetteville, WV 25840-1420
Description: Women's volunteer service club.

Glen Dale

★3188★ Moundsville Business and Professional Women's Club
608 Washington Ave.
Glen Dale, WV 26038
Phone: (304)845-4367
Joyce Hummel, Pres.
Description: Business and professional women. To promote complete participation, equal opportunities, and economic self-sufficiency for working women.

Granville

★3189★ Older Women's League (OWL) Morgantown Chapter
502 Michigan Ave.
PO Box 394
Granville, WV 26534
Cathy Zara, Contact

Huntington

★3190★ Association for Women in Science, West Virginia Chapter
c/o Dr. Susan Demesquita
Marshall University
Dept. of Physiology, School of Medicine
1542 Spring Valley Dr.
Huntington, WV 25755-9340
Phone: (304)696-7365
Description: Works to improve education and employment opportunities for women in the sciences.

Martinsburg

★3191★ Shawnee Girl Scout Council
PO Box 3239
Martinsburg, WV 25401
Phone: (304)263-8833
Anna Claire Chacknes, Exec.Dir.
Description: Young girls and adult volunteers in Maryland, Pennsylvania, Virginia, and West Virginia. Promotes individual development with high ideals of character, patriotism, and conduct. Encourages girls to become happy and resourceful citizens. **Affiliated with:** Girl Scouts of the U.S.A.

Pipestem

★3192★ Princeton Junior Women's Club
PO Box 120
Pipestem, WV 25979
Phone: (304)466-5961
Debbie Griffith, Contact
Description: Women 18-40 years old. Women's volunteer service club.

Princeton

★3193★ National Association of Insurance Women of Virginia/West Virginia
c/o Murphy Insurance Agency
PO Box 5069
Princeton, WV 24740
Phone: (304)425-8793
Fax: (304)425-4083
Rita G. Kidd, AAI, C, Pres.
Description: Women employed in the insurance industry in southwestern Virginia and southern West Virginia. Promotes insurance education.

Affiliated with: National Association of Insurance Women - International.

Shepardstown

★3194★ **West Virginia Branch of National Abortion Rights Action League**
PO Box 1601
Shepardstown, WV 25443
Kate Lowman, Contact

South Charleston

★3195★ **League of Women Voters of West Virginia**
1127 Montrose Dr.
South Charleston, WV 25303
Karen Lukens, President

Sutton

★3196★ **West Virginia Coalition Against Domestic Violence**
PO Box 85
Sutton, WV 26601
Phone: (304)765-2250
Sue Julian, Contact

Wisconsin

Antigo

★3197★ **Birthright of Antigo**
Langlade Memorial Hospital
Antigo, WI 54409
Phone: (715)623-4119
Kathleen Payant, Dir.

Description: Women who promote the belief that "every woman has the right to have her baby and every baby has the right to be born". Assists pregnant women in need of support.

Appleton

★3198★ **Religious Coalition for Abortion Rights, Wisconsin Affiliate**
838 W. Prospect Ave.
Appleton, WI 54911
Phone: (414)731-4010
Cathy Boardman, Coordinator

★3199★ **Women Exploited by Abortion, Wisconsin Chapter**
PO Box 712
Appleton, WI 54912
Phone: (414)734-2966
Shelly Banda, Pres.

Description: Women who regret having had an abortion; associate members are concerned individuals. Seeks to inform people about abortion. Sponsors support groups. **Affiliated with:** Women Exploited by Abortion International.

Beaver Dam

★3200★ **Wisconsin Business Women's Coalition**
PO Box 455
Beaver Dam, WI 53916
Phone: (414)887-1078
Gene Boyer, Contact

Description: Business and professional women. To promote complete participation, equal opportunities, and economic self-sufficiency for working women.

Beloit

★3201★ **Young Women's Christian Association of Stateline Area**
246 W. Grand Ave.
Beloit, WI 53511
Phone: (608)364-4438
Virginia Young-Meyer, Contact

Description: Seeks to develop and improve the spiritual, social, mental, and physical life of women and girls over the age of 12. Sponsors abused family shelter, Tribute to Women festival, and other programs. **Affiliated with:** Young Women's Christian Association of the United States of America.

Brookfield

★3202★ **Brookfield Junior Woman's Club**
PO Box 261
Brookfield, WI 53008-0261

Description: Women 21-45 years old. Women's volunteer service club. Issues children's cookbook. **Affiliated with:** General Federation of Woman's Club.

Chippewa Falls

★3203★ **American Business Women's Association, Chippewa Falls Chapter**
c/o Jeanne Hintz
948 1st Ave., No. 3
Chippewa Falls, WI 54729
Phone: (715)723-6961
Jeanne Hintz, Exec. Officer

Description: Works for the professional, educational, cultural, and social advancement of business women. **Affiliated with:** American Business Women's Association.

★3204★ **Chippewa Falls Women's Club**
c/o Marlys Holmes
728 Mansfield St.
Chippewa Falls, WI 54729
Phone: (715)723-2851
Marlys Holmes, Exec. Officer

Description: Women's volunteer service club. Conducts charitable activities. Provides scholarships for high school students. **Affiliated with:** Chippewa County Federation of Women's Clubs.

Green Bay

★3205★ **Young Women's Christian Association of Green Bay-De Pere**
230 S. Madison St.
Green Bay, WI 54301
Phone: (414)432-5581

Description: Seeks to develop and improve the spiritual, social, mental, and physical life of women and girls over the age of 12. **Affiliated with:** Young Women's Christian Association of the United States of America.

Greenfield

★3206★ **Women in Cable, Wisconsin Chapter**
c/o Faye DeLaurier
VIACOM Cablevision
5475 W. Abbott Ave.
Greenfield, WI 53220
Phone: (414)282-6300
Faye DeLaurier, Pres.

Description: Individuals engaged in professional activity in cable television and related industries interested in developing a high standard of professional business conduct. **Affiliated with:** Women in Cable.

Hilbert

★3207★ **Wisconsin Association of Women Highway Safety Leaders**
N. 5874 Van Rd.
Hilbert, WI 54129
Phone: (414)439-1645
Cecilia Van Daalwyk, Pres.

Description: Concerned individuals united to promote highway safety through mature driver programs and alcohol and drug prevention programs in the public schools. **Affiliated with:** National Association of Women Highway Safety Leaders.

Janesville

★3208★ **Wisconsin Women's Political Caucus**
2020 S. Crosby
Janesville, WI 53546
Phone: (608)754-7004
Carolyn Brandeen, Exec. Officer

★3209★ **Young Women's Christian Association of Janesville**
220 St. Lawrence Ave.
Janesville, WI 53545
Phone: (608)752-5445
Kathi Madsen, Contact

Description: Seeks to develop and improve the spiritual, social, mental, and physical life of women and girls over the age of 12. **Affiliated with:** Young Women's Christian Association of the United States of America.

Kenosha

★3210★ **Pleasant Prairie Woman's Club**
c/o Carol Thiele
7908 104th St.
Kenosha, WI 53142
Phone: (414)694-6320
Carol Thiele, Exec. Officer

Description: Women's volunteer service club. **Affiliated with:** General Federation of Women's Clubs; Wisconsin Federation of Women's Clubs.

★3211★ **Woman's Club of Kenosha**
6028 8th Ave.
Kenosha, WI 53143
Phone: (414)652-1731
Marianne Gavel, Pres.

Description: Women's volunteer service club. Conducts charitable activities. Holds workshops. **Affiliated with:** General Federation of Women's Clubs; Wisconsin Federation of Women's Clubs.

La Crosse

★3212★ Young Women's Christian Association of La Crosse
1140 Main St.
La Crosse, WI 54601
Phone: (608)784-5479
Brenda K. Haug, Contact

Description: Seeks to develop and improve the spiritual, social, mental, and physical life of women and girls over the age of 12. **Affiliated with:** Young Women's Christian Association of the United States of America.

Lake Geneva

★3213★ Lake Geneva Woman's Club
c/o Elaine Schiess
Rte. 4, Box 750
Lake Geneva, WI 53147
Phone: (414)248-4472
Elaine Schiess, Exec. Officer

Description: Women's volunteer service club. Awards scholarships; makes donations to YMCA, public library, community improvement projects, and social services. **Affiliated with:** General Federation of Women's Clubs; Wisconsin Federation of Women's Clubs.

Lake Tomahawk

★3214★ American Association of University Women, Rhinelander Branch
c/o Patricia A. Harrington
7059 Loon Rd.
Lake Tomahawk, WI 54539
Phone: (715)277-3476
Patricia A. Harrington, Pres.

Description: Women graduates of regionally accredited four year colleges and universities. Works for the advancement of women through advocacy and emphasis on lifelong learning. Awards scholarships. **Affiliated with:** American Association of University Women.

Madison

★3215★ Central Wisconsin Women's Caucus for Art
PO Box 7441
Madison, WI 53707-7441

Description: Women promoting appreciation of the arts.

★3216★ League of Women Voters of Wisconsin
122 State St., Ste. 405
Madison, WI 53703-2500
Phone: (608)256-0827
Mona Steele, President

★3217★ Wisconsin Coalition Against Domestic Violence
1051 Williamson St.
Madison, WI 53703
Phone: (608)255-0539
Bonnie Brandl, Contact

★3218★ Young Women's Christian Association of Madison
101 E. Mifflin St.
Madison, WI 53703
Phone: (608)257-1436
Fax: (608)257-1439
Melanie G. Ramey, Contact

Description: Seeks to empower women, regardless of faith, race, or ethnic origin. Provides affordable housing to women, and shelter to homeless families. **Affiliated with:** Young Women's Christian Association of the United States of America.

Manitowoc

★3219★ Manitowoc-Two Rivers Business and Professional Women's Club
844 Wilson St.
Manitowoc, WI 54220
Phone: (414)682-6676
Ruth Anne Longmeyer, Past Pres.

Description: Business and professional women. To promote complete participation, equal opportunities, and economic self-sufficiency for working women. **Affiliated with:** National Federation of Business and Professional Women's Clubs of the U.S.A.

Milwaukee

★3220★ DES Action
PO Box 17102
Milwaukee, WI 53217
Phone: (414)352-1949

Description: DES-exposed persons and others working to relieve the problems caused by DES (diethylstilbestrol). Offers support, counseling, and doctor referral service. **Affiliated with:** DES Action, U.S.A.

★3221★ Milwaukee Business and Professional Women's Club
PO Box 92175
Milwaukee, WI 53202
Diane Jones Meier, V.Pres.

Description: Business and professional women. To promote complete participation, equal opportunities, and economic self-sufficiency for working women. Conducts charitable activities. Awards scholarships and special gifts for civic purposes. Holds workshops and board meetings. **Affiliated with:** National Federation of Business and Professional Women's Clubs of the U.S.A.

★3222★ The Milwaukee Foundation Women's Fund
1020 N. Broadway
Milwaukee, WI 53202
Phone: (414)272-5805
Joan Underberg, Executive Director

★3223★ Older Women's League (OWL) Milwaukee Chapter
1831 W. Cambridge
Milwaukee, WI 53202
Jean Browning, Contact

★3224★ Wisconsin Abortion Rights Action League
301 N. Water St., 4th Fl., SE
Milwaukee, WI 53202
Phone: (414)271-4811
Chris Korsmo, Contact

★3225★ Wisconsin Right to Life
4840 Fond du Lac
Milwaukee, WI 53216
Phone: (414)447-8333
Barbara L. Lyons, Exec.Dir.

Description: Fosters respect for human life from conception to natural death. **Affiliated with:** National Right to Life Committee.

Muskego

★3226★ Muskego Woman's Club
PO Box 143
Muskego, WI 53150-0143

Description: Women's volunteer service club.

Nashotah

★3227★ Older Women's League (OWL) Waukesha County Chapter
4935 Woodfield Ct., Apt. 1
Nashotah, WI 53058
Phone: (414)367-5004
Lou Lyon, Contact

New Berlin

★3228★ New Berlin Junior Women's Club
c/o Faye A. Germain
14565 Fairfield Dr.
New Berlin, WI 53151
Phone: (414)785-1023
Faye A. Germain, Pres.

Description: Women ages 18-45. Provides community service through volunteering time to the police department, library, and hospital. Holds fundraisers, craft fair, lunch with Santa, sales, and monthly board meeting.

★3229★ Women's Club of West Allis
c/o Dorothy Yanke
12845 W. Brentwood Dr.
New Berlin, WI 53151
Phone: (414)782-1698
Dorothy Yanke, Pres.

Description: Women's volunteer service club. Awards college scholarships. Holds arts and crafts show. **Affiliated with:** General Federation of Women's Clubs; Wisconsin Federation of Women's Clubs.

Oconto

★3230★ Oconto Woman's Club
c/o Jean Davidson
1424 Main St.
Oconto, WI 54153
Phone: (414)834-2375
Jean Davidson, Exec. Officer

Description: Women's volunteer service club. **Affiliated with:** General Federation of Women's Clubs; Wisconsin Federation of Women's Clubs.

Poynette

★3231★ Columbia County Right to Life
312 N. Franklin St.
Poynette, WI 53955
Phone: (608)635-4936
Fred & Betty Cook, Co-Chairs

Description: Individuals in Columbia county, WI. Promotes the right to life for all people from conception to natural death. **Affiliated with:** Wisconsin Right to Life.

Racine

★3232★ **Girl Scouts of the United States of America, Racine County Council**
816 6th St.
Racine, WI 53403
Phone: (414)633-2409
Mary I. Charles, Exec. Dir.

Description: Provides leadership and growth programs to girls ages five through 17. Affiliated with: Girls Scouts of the U.S.A.

★3233★ **Young Women's Christian Association of Racine**
740 College Ave.
Racine, WI 53403
Phone: (414)633-3503
Sandra Tait, Exec.Dir.

Description: Seeks to develop and improve the spiritual, social, mental, and physical life of women and girls over the age of 12. **Affiliated with:** Young Women's Christian Association of the United States of America.

Rhinelander

★3234★ **Northland Childbirth Education Association**
c/o Deb Blackstone
316 E. Kemp
Rhinelander, WI 54501
Phone: (715)369-4910
Deb Blackstone, Exec. Officer

Description: Childbirth educators, nurses, doctors, and parents in the Rhinelander, WI area. Provides informational programs for the public; holds prepared childbirth and sibling classes. **Affiliated with:** International Childbirth Education Association.

★3235★ **Rhinelander Business and Professional Women's Club**
43 S. Brown St.
Rhinelander, WI 54501
Phone: (715)362-3900
Jacci Csee, Contact

Description: Business and professional women. To promote complete participation, equal opportunities, and economic self-sufficiency for working women. **Affiliated with:** National Federation of Business and Professional Women's Clubs of the U.S.A.

Richland Center

★3236★ **Organization for the Enforcement of Child Support, Wisconsin Chapter**
c/o Sharon Clark
Rte. 3, Box 180
Richland Center, WI 53581
Phone: (608)647-4673
Sharon Clark, Acting Pres.

Description: Individuals organized to promote the enforcement of child support laws. Disseminates information about problems with child support collection and parental rights under existing child support laws; provides referrals and legislative advocacy. **Affiliated with:** Organization for the Enforcement of Child Support.

Ripon

★3237★ **American Association of University Women, Ripon Branch**
c/o Esther Bent
722 Park St.
Ripon, WI 54971
Phone: (414)748-2929
Esther Bent, Sec.

Description: Women graduates of regionally accredited four year colleges and universities. Works for the advancement of women through advocacy and emphasis on lifelong learning. **Affiliated with:** American Association of University Women.

Shawano

★3238★ **Shawano Business and Professional Women's Club**
PO Box 435
Shawano, WI 54166
Phone: (715)526-3913
Darlene Ross, Pres.

Description: Businesswomen united to promote their interests. **Affiliated with:** National Federation of Business and Professional Women's Clubs of the U.S.A.

★3239★ **Shawano Woman's Club**
c/o Jeannene Teskey
Rte. 4, Box 61
Shawano, WI 54166
Phone: (715)526-6083
Jeannene Teskey, Pres.

Description: Women involved in social, cultural, and civic activities. Sponsors Helen Mears Art Contest and Hugh O'Brien Student competition. Conducts annual Oktoberfest. **Affiliated with:** General Federation of Women's Clubs; Wisconsin Federation of Women's Clubs.

Sheboygan

★3240★ **National Association of Women Highway Safety Leaders, Wisconsin Chapter**
c/o LaVerne Hoerig
1321 Clara Ave.
Sheboygan, WI 53081
Phone: (414)452-0905
LaVerne Hoerig, Exec. Officer

Description: Women interested in traffic safety seeking to reduce the number of traffic accidents, injuries, and deaths. Sponsors safety programs and projects. **Affiliated with:** National Association of Women Highway Safety Leaders.

Waukesha

★3241★ **Wisconsin Sportwomen's Club**
W. 237 N. 1480 Busse Rd.
Waukesha, WI 53188
Phone: (414)547-8013
Genevieve M. Ebert, Pres.

Description: Women who enjoy hunting and fishing. Offers instruction.

Waupaca

★3242★ **Gorgonas Women's Club**
c/o Mrs. Glenn Robbins
E. 1505 Rural Rd.
Waupaca, WI 54981
Phone: (715)258-3423
Mrs. Glenn Robbins, Pres.

Description: Women's volunteer service club.

Wausau

★3243★ **Older Women's League (OWL) North Central Wisconsin Chapter**
PO Box 37
Wausau, WI 54402
Phone: (715)842-2467
Christine Clarke-Epstein, Contact

★3244★ **Young Women's Christian Association of Wausau**
613 5th St.
Wausau, WI 54401
Phone: (715)842-3381

Description: Seeks to develop and improve the spiritual, social, mental, and physical life of women and girls over the age of 12. **Affiliated with:** Young Women's Christian Association of the United States of America.

Wyoming

Casper

★3245★ **Wyoming Coalition Against Domestic Violence and Sexual Assault**
341 E. E St., Ste. 135A
Casper, WY 82601

Cheyenne

★3246★ **American Association of University Women, Wyoming Chapter**
2531 Crazy Horse
Cheyenne, WY 82009
Phone: (307)635-3788
Betty Jo Mainwaring, Pres.

Description: Women graduates of regionally accredited four year colleges and universities. Works for the advancement of women through advocacy and emphasis on lifelong learning. Conducts seminars; makes available scholarships. **Affiliated with:** American Association of University Women.

★3247★ **League of Women Voters of Wyoming**
PO Box 2862
Cheyenne, WY 82003
Linda L. Kirkbride, President

★3248★ **Woman's Club of Cheyenne**
3821 Cribbon Ave.
Cheyenne, WY 82001-1052
Phone: (307)634-1991
Helen R. Clark, Pres.

Description: To stimulate intellectual development and promote fellowship and involvement in the community. Maintains art, bridge, gardening, and reading groups. **Affiliated with:** General Federation of Women's Clubs; General Federation of Women's Clubs of Wyoming.

Lander

★3249★ Lander Women's Bowling Association
365 North 10th St.
Lander, WY 82520
Phone: (307)332-5830
Estelle Halbert, Sec.
Description: Women bowlers. To promote team competition.

Larmie

★3250★ Wyoming Abortion Rights Action League
819 Harney
Larmie, WY 82070
Phone: (307)742-9189
Sharon Breitweiser, Contact

Riverton

★3251★ GFWC-W Progressive Women's Club
PO Box 1373
Riverton, WY 82501
Phone: (307)856-1128
Faye Cox, Pres.
Description: To improve the political, social, and professional status of women. Conducts charitable activities; sponsors quarterly blood drive. Assists with Community Entry Services of Riverton. **Affiliated with:** General Federation of Women's Clubs of Wyoming.

★3252★ National Organization for Women, Fremont County Chapter
HC 36, Box 2108
Riverton, WY 82501
Phone: (307)856-5047
Gwenda Urbigkit, Exec. Officer
Description: To promote full equality for women. **Affiliated with:** National Organization for Women.

Rock Springs

★3253★ Young Women's Christian Association of Sweetwater County
PO Box 1667
Rock Springs, WY 82902
Phone: (307)362-7923
Christie DeGrendele, Contact
Description: Seeks to develop and improve the spiritual, social, mental, and physical well-being of young people and adults. **Affiliated with:** Young Women's Christian Association of the United States of America.

Worland

★3254★ Birthright of Worland
204 South 7th
Worland, WY 82401-3308
Description: Attorneys in good standing. Seeks to improve the administration of civil and criminal justice, and the availability of legal services to the public.

★3255★ La Leche League International, Worland Chapter
1501 Crestway
Worland, WY 82401
Phone: (307)347-4478
Pam Arps, Leader
Description: Provides information and support to mothers who breastfeed their babies. Conducts seminars for medical professionals. Issues publications. **Affiliated with:** La Leche League International.

(3) Battered Women's Services

Entries in this chapter are arranged alphabetically by state and city, then by organization name within city. See the User's Guide at the front of this directory for additional information.

Alabama

Anniston

★3256★ The Salvation Army Women's Shelter
PO Box 218
Anniston, AL 36201
Phone: (205)236-5644

Crisis Phone(s): (205)236-5644.

★3257★ Second Chance
PO Box 2714
Anniston, AL 36202
Phone: (205)236-7381

Crisis Phone(s): (205)236-7233.

Auburn

★3258★ East Alabama Task Force for Battered Women
PO Box 1104
Auburn, AL 36831-1104
Phone: (205)821-9417

Crisis Phone(s): (205)887-9330.

Birmingham

★3259★ Family Violence Center
PO Box 11865
Birmingham, AL 35202
Phone: (205)521-9646

Crisis Phone(s): (205)322-4878.

Columbiana

★3260★ Safehouse of Shelby County
PO Box 762
Columbiana, AL 35051
Phone: (205)669-1320

Crisis Phone(s): (205)669-1320.

Dothan

★3261★ House of Ruth
PO Box 968
Dothan, AL 36302
Phone: (205)793-5214

Crisis Phone(s): (205)793-2232 (collect calls accepted).

Florence

★3262★ Safeplace
PO Box 1456
Florence, AL 35631
Phone: (205)767-3076

Crisis Phone(s): (205)767-6210.

Gadsden

★3263★ The Shelter
PO Box 1548
Gadsden, AL 35900
Phone: (205)543-2408

Crisis Phone(s): (205)543-3059.

Huntsville

★3264★ HOPE Place
PO Box 687
Huntsville, AL 35804
Phone: (205)534-4052

Crisis Phone(s): (205)539-1000.

Jasper

★3265★ Daybreak Family Resource Center of Northwest Alabama
PO Box 3429
Jasper, AL 35502-3429
Phone: (205)387-1186

Crisis Phone(s): (205)387-1157.

Mobile

★3266★ Penelope House
PO Box 9127
Mobile, AL 36691-0127
Phone: (205)342-2809

Crisis Phone(s): (205)342-8994.

Montgomery

★3267★ Montgomery Area Family Violence Program
Kiwanis Domestic Abuse Shelter
802 Forest Ave.
Montgomery, AL 36106
Phone: (205)263-0677

Crisis Phone(s): (205)263-0218.

Pelham

★3268★ Safehouse of Shelby County
PO Box 574
Pelham, AL 35124
Phone: (202)664-4357

Phenix City

★3269★ Russell County Shelter for Battered Women
PO Box 2835
Phenix City, AL 36868-3835
Phone: (205)297-4401

Crisis Phone(s): (205)297-4401.

Selma

★3270★ Black Belt Regional Domestic Violence Program
2104 Franklin St.
Selma, AL 36701
Phone: (205)874-8711

Tuscaloosa

★3271★ San, Inc.
PO Box 1165
Tuscaloosa, AL 35403
Phone: (205)758-0808

Crisis Phone(s): (205)758-0808.

Alaska

Anchorage

★3272★ Abused Women's Aid in Crisis
100 W. 13th Ave.
Anchorage, AK 99501
Phone: (907)279-9581

Crisis Phone(s): (907)272-0100.

★3273★ Alaska Women's Resource Center
111 W. 9th Ave.
Anchorage, AK 99501
Phone: (907)276-0528

★3274★ Standing Together Against Rape
1057 W. Firewood Ln., Ste. 230
Anchorage, AK 99503
Phone: (907)276-7279

Crisis Phone(s): (907)276-RAPE.

Barrow

★3275★ Arctic Women in Crisis
PO Box 69
Barrow, AK 99723
Phone: (907)852-2942

Crisis Phone(s): (907)852-4357.

Bethel

★3276★ Tundra Women's Coalition
PO Box 1537
Bethel, AK 99559
Phone: (907)543-3444
Toll-free: 800-478-7799

Crisis Phone(s): (907)543-3456.

Dillingham

★3277★ Safe and Fear-Free Environment
PO Box 94
Dillingham, AK 99576
Phone: (907)842-2320
Toll-free: 800-478-2316

Crisis Phone(s): (907)842-2316.

Emmonak

★3278★ Emmonak Women's Shelter
General Delivery
Emmonak, AK 99581
Phone: (907)949-1434

Fairbanks

**★3279★ Tanana Chiefs Conference
Domestic Violence Program**
201 1st Ave.
Fairbanks, AK 99701
Phone: (907)452-8251

**★3280★ Women in Crisis Counseling and
Assistance**
702 10th Ave.
Fairbanks, AK 99701
Phone: (907)452-2293

Crisis Phone(s): (907)452-2293.

Homer

**★3281★ South Peninsula Women's
Services**
PO Box 2328
Homer, AK 99603
Phone: (907)235-7712

Crisis Phone(s): (907)235-8101.

Hooper Bay

★3282★ Bering Sea Coastal Shelter
Box 137
Hooper Bay, AK 99604
Phone: (907)758-4135

Crisis Phone(s): (907)758-4135.

Juneau

**★3283★ Aiding Women in Abuse and
Rape Emergencies**
1547 Old Glacier Hwy.
PO Box 020809
Juneau, AK 99802-0809
Phone: (907)586-6623

Crisis Phone(s): (907)283-7257.

★3284★ Parent Aid Family Support Center
427 W. 12th St.
Juneau, AK 99801
Phone: (907)586-3785

Kenai

**★3285★ Women's Resource and Crisis
Center**
325 S. Spruce St.
Kenai, AK 99611
Phone: (907)283-9479

Crisis Phone(s): (907)283-7257.

Ketchikan

★3286★ Women in Safe Homes
PO Box 6552
Ketchikan, AK 99901
Phone: (907)225-0202

Crisis Phone(s): (907)225-9474.

Kodiak

**★3287★ Women's Resource and Crisis
Center**
PO Box 2122
Kodiak, AK 99615
Phone: (907)486-6171

Crisis Phone(s): (907)486-3625.

Kotzebue

**★3288★ Maniilaq Regional Women's Crisis
Program**
PO Box 38
Kotzebue, AK 99572
Phone: (907)442-3311

Crisis Phone(s): (907)442-3969; (800)478-
3312 (Monday through Friday, 8am - 5pm).

Nome

★3289★ Bering Sea Women's Group
PO Box 1596
Nome, AK 99762
Phone: (907)443-5491

Crisis Phone(s): (907)443-5444.

Palmer

★3290★ Valley Women's Resource Center
403 S. Alaska St.
Palmer, AK 99645-6339
Phone: (907)746-4080
Toll-free: 800-478-1090

Crisis Phone(s): (907)746-4080.

Seward

★3291★ Seward Life Action Council
PO Box 1045
Seward, AK 99664
Phone: (907)224-5257

Sitka

★3292★ Sitkans Against Family Violence
PO Box 6136
Sitka, AK 99835
Phone: (907)747-3370

Unalaska

**★3293★ Unalaskans Against Sexual
Assault and Family Violence**
PO Box 36
Unalaska, AK 99685
Phone: (907)581-1500
Toll-free: 800-47U-SAVV

Crisis Phone(s): (800)47U-SAVV.

Valdez

**★3294★ Advocates for Victims of
Violence**
PO Box 524
Valdez, AK 99696
Phone: (907)835-2980

Crisis Phone(s): (907)835-2999.

Arizona

Bullhead City

**★3295★ Safe House/Shelter of Bullhead
City**
1155 E. Hancock Rd., No. 5
Bullhead City, AZ 86442
Phone: (602)763-7233

Crisis Phone(s): (602)763-SAFE; (602)763-
7233.

Casa Grande

★3296★ Against Abuse, Inc.
PO Box 733
Casa Grande, AZ 85222
Phone: (602)836-1239

Crisis Phone(s): (602)836-0858.

Chandler

★3297★ My Sister's Place
961 W. Ray Rd., No. 4
Chandler, AZ 85224
Phone: (602)821-1024

Cottonwood

**★3298★ Catholic Social Services
Battered Women's Services**
507 E. Main St.
Cottonwood, AZ 86326
Phone: (602)634-4254

Crisis Phone(s): (602)634-3632.

★3299★ Verde Valley Community
Guidance Clinic
19 E. Beech
PO Box 925
Cottonwood, AZ 86326
Phone: (602)634-2236

Flagstaff

★3300★ Center Against Domestic
Violence, Inc.
2501 N. 4th St., Ste. 18
Flagstaff, AZ 86001
Phone: (602)744-4503
Crisis Phone(s): (602)774-7353.

Glendale

★3301★ Faith House
4506 W. Citrus Way
Glendale, AZ 85301
Crisis Phone(s): (602)939-6798.

★3302★ Organization for Non-Violence
Education
PO Box 863
Glendale, AZ 85311
Phone: (602)934-0696
Crisis Phone(s): (602)263-8856.

Globe

★3303★ The Caring Place
2601 W. Dunlap, Ste. 10
Globe, AZ 85821
Phone: (602)473-2406
Crisis Phone(s): (602)473-2406.

Kayenta

★3304★ Kayenta Health Center
PO Box 368
Kayenta, AZ 86033
Phone: (602)697-3211

★3305★ Tohdenasshai Shelter Home
PO Drawer 8
Kayenta, AZ 86033
Phone: (602)697-3211

Kingman

★3306★ Kingman Association for Abused
People
PO Box 1046
Kingman, AZ 86402
Phone: (602)753-6222
Crisis Phone(s): (602)753-4242.

★3307★ Mohave Mental Health Clinics
PO Box 4179
Kingman, AZ 86412
Phone: (602)757-8111

Lake Havasu City

★3308★ Mohave Mental Health Clinics
2178 McCulloch Blvd., Ste. 10
Lake Havasu City, AZ 86403
Phone: (602)855-3432

Mesa

★3309★ Pre-Hab of Arizona
Autumn House
PO Drawer 5860
Mesa, AZ 85211-5860
Crisis Phone(s): (602)835-5555.

Miami

★3310★ The Caring Place
Advocate House
PO Box 786
Miami, AZ 85539
Phone: (602)473-3752
Crisis Phone(s): (602)473-3752.

Nogals

★3311★ Santa Cruz Family Guidance
Center
Domestic Violence Program
489 N/ Arrovo Blvd.
Nogals, AZ 85621
Phone: (602)287-4713
Crisis Phone(s): (602)287-4713.

Page

★3312★ Page Guidance Center
PO Box 3049
Page, AZ 86040
Phone: (602)645-8843
Crisis Phone(s): (602)645-2554.

Phoenix

★3313★ Chicanos por la Causa
De Colores
PO Box 6553
Phoenix, AZ 85005-6553
Phone: (602)269-1515

★3314★ Chrysalis
PO Box 9956
Phoenix, AZ 85068
Phone: (602)944-4999

★3315★ DOVE
c/o de Novo
Phoenix, AZ 85012
Phone: (602)258-0564

★3316★ The Salvation Army
Family Services
2707 E. Van Buren
Phoenix, AZ 85072
Phone: (602)267-4130
Crisis Phone(s): (602)267-4130.

★3317★ Sojourner Center
PO Box 2649
Phoenix, AZ 85002
Phone: (602)258-5344
Crisis Phone(s): (602)258-5344.

★3318★ YWCA
Women in Transition
755 E Willetta
Phoenix, AZ 85006
Phone: (602)258-0990

Prescott

★3319★ Faith House
1535 Private Rd.
Prescott, AZ 86301
Phone: (602)445-4705
Crisis Phone(s): (602)445-4673.

Riviera

★3320★ Mohave Mental Health Clinics
2135 Hwy. 95, Ste. 241
Riviera, AZ 86442
Phone: (602)758-5905

Safford

★3321★ Graham/Greenlee Counseling
Center
Domestic Violence Program
PO Box 956
Safford, AZ 85546
Phone: (602)428-4550
Crisis Phone(s): (602)428-5711.

Scottsdale

★3322★ Chrysalis
PO Box 1551
Scottsdale, AZ 85251
Phone: (602)481-0402

Show Low

★3323★ White Mountain SAFE House
201 W. Brady
Show Low, AZ 85901
Phone: (602)537-7707

Sierra Vista

★3324★ Forgach House
PO Box 1961
Sierra Vista, AZ 85636
Crisis Phone(s): (602)458-9096.

Tempe

★3325★ Maricopa County Task Force
Against Domestic Violence
Box 27571
Tempe, AZ 85282
Phone: (602)835-5817
Crisis Phone(s): (602)835-5555.

Tuba City

★3326★ Tuba City Against Domestic
Violence
PO Box 67
Tuba City, AZ 86045
Phone: (602)283-6211

Tucson

★3327★ AVA Crisis Shelter
PO Box 40878
Tucson, AZ 85717
Phone: (602)795-4266
Crisis Phone(s): (602)795-4880.

★3328★ Brewster Center for Victims of Family Violence
PO Box 3425
Tucson, AZ 85722
Phone: (602)623-0951
Crisis Phone(s): (602)622-6347.

★3329★ Tucson Center for Women and Children
PO Box 40878
Tucson, AZ 85717
Phone: (602)795-8001
Crisis Phone(s): (602)795-4266; (602)795-4880.

Whiteriver

★3330★ White Mountain Indian Hospital White Mountain Apache Committee for Family Peace
PO Box 860
Whiteriver, AZ 85941
Phone: (602)338-4911

Yuma

★3331★ Safe House
1700 S. 1st Ave., No. 100
Yuma, AZ 85364
Phone: (602)782-0077
Crisis Phone(s): (602)782-0044.

Arkansas

Arkadelphia

★3332★ Abused Women and Children, Inc.
PO Box 924
Arkadelphia, AR 77923
Crisis Phone(s): (501)246-2587.

Batesville

★3333★ Family Violence Protection, Inc.
PO Box 2943
Batesville, AR 72503
Phone: (501)793-4011
Crisis Phone(s): (501)793-8111.

Camden

★3334★ Women's Crisis Center
PO Box 1149
Camden, AR 71701
Phone: (501)836-0325
Crisis Phone(s): (501)836-8272.

Fayetteville

★3335★ Project for Victims of Family Violence
PO Box 2915
Fayetteville, AR 72702
Crisis Phone(s): (501)442-9811.

Ft. Smith

★3336★ Women's Crisis Center for Battered Women
401 Lexington
Ft. Smith, AR 72901
Crisis Phone(s): (501)782-4956.

Harrison

★3337★ Sanctuary, Inc.
PO Box 762
Harrison, AR 72601
Phone: (501)741-2121
Crisis Phone(s): (501)741-2121.

Jonesboro

★3338★ Northeast Arkansas Council on Family Violence
PO Box 721
Jonesboro, AR 72403
Phone: (501)933-9449
Crisis Phone(s): (501)935-2090.

★3339★ Northeast Arkansas Task Force on Family Violence
PO Box 234
Jonesboro, AR 72403
Phone: (501)935-3658
Crisis Phone(s): (501)932-5555.

Little Rock

★3340★ Advocates for Battered Women
PO Box 1954
Little Rock, AR 72203
Toll-free: 800-332-4443
Crisis Phone(s): (501)376-3219.

Pine Bluff

★3341★ Women's Shelter
PO Box 6705
Pine Bluff, AR 71611
Phone: (501)535-2955
Crisis Phone(s): (501)535-0287.

Russelville

★3342★ River Valley Shelter for Battered Women and Children
PO Box 2066
Russelville, AR 72801
Crisis Phone(s): (501)968-3110.

Texarkana

★3343★ Domestic Violence Prevention
PO Box 712
Texarkana, AR 75504
Phone: (214)794-4000
Crisis Phone(s): (214)793-4357.

Yellville

★3344★ SAFE
PO Box 605
Yellville, AR 72687
Phone: (501)449-4019
Crisis Phone(s): (501)449-6278.

California

Artesia

★3345★ Su Casa Family Crisis and Support
PO Box 998
Artesia, CA 90702
Phone: (213)402-7081
Crisis Phone(s): (213)402-4888; (310)402-4888.

Auburn

★3346★ Placer Women's Center
PO Box 5462
Auburn, CA 95604
Phone: (916)885-0443
Crisis Phone(s): (916)652-6558.

Bakersfield

★3347★ Alliance Against Family Violence
PO Box 2054
Bakersfield, CA 93303
Phone: (805)322-0931
Crisis Phone(s): (805)327-1091; (800)273-7713 (Kern County).

Barstow

★3348★ Desert Sanctuary, Inc.
Haley House
PO Box 1781
Barstow, CA 92312-1781
Phone: (619)252-3441
Crisis Phone(s): (619)252-3441.

Belmont

★3349★ Battered Women's Services of San Mateo County
604 Mountain View Ave.
Belmont, CA 94002
Phone: (415)593-8622
Crisis Phone(s): (415)342-0850.

Berkeley

★3350★ Family Violence Law Center
PO Box 209
Berkeley, CA 94701
Phone: (510)540-5354

★3351★ Women's Refuge
PO Box 3298
Berkeley, CA 94703
Phone: (415)658-7231
Crisis Phone(s): (415)547-4663.

Big Bear Lake

★3352★ DOVES, Inc.
PO Box 3646
Big Bear Lake, CA 92315
Phone: (714)866-1546

Crisis Phone(s): (714)866-5723.

Bishop

★3353★ Wild Iris Women's Services
PO Box 57
Bishop, CA 93515
Phone: (619)873-6601

Crisis Phone(s): (619)873-7384.

Canoga Park

★3354★ Haven Hills
PO Box 260
Canoga Park, CA 91305
Phone: (818)887-7481

Crisis Phone(s): (818)887-6589.

Carson

★3355★ Carson Shelter/Employment
  Readiness Support Center
23013 S. Avalon Blvd.
Carson, CA 90745-5018
Phone: (213)549-0137

Crisis Phone(s): (213)549-1375.

Chico

★3356★ Catalyst Women's Advocates
PO Box 4184
Chico, CA 95927
Phone: (916)343-7711

Crisis Phone(s): (916)895-8476.

★3357★ Rape Crisis Intervention
PO Box 423
Chico, CA 95927
Phone: (916)891-1331

Crisis Phone(s): (916)342-7273.

Claremont

★3358★ House of Ruth
PO Box 457
Claremont, CA 91711
Phone: (714)623-4364

Crisis Phone(s): (714)988-5559.

Concord

★3359★ Battered Women's Alternatives
PO Box 6406
Concord, CA 94524
Phone: (415)676-2845

Crisis Phone(s): (415)930-8300.

Costa Mesa

★3360★ Safety Net
1695 W. MacArthur Blvd.
Costa Mesa, CA 92626
Phone: (714)540-9293

Crisis Phone(s): (714)540-9293.

Davis

★3361★ Sexual Assault/Domestic Violence
  Center
Harper House
222 D St.
Davis, CA 95616
Phone: (916)758-0540

Crisis Phone(s): (916)371-1907.

Dinuba

★3362★ Open Gate Ministries
511 N. K St.
Dinuba, CA 93618
Phone: (209)591-3890

Crisis Phone(s): (209)591-1241.

El Centro

★3363★ Womanhaven
PO Box 2219
El Centro, CA 92244
Phone: (619)353-6922

Crisis Phone(s): (619)353-8530.

Escondido

★3364★ California Youth Encounter
165 E. Lincoln Ave.
Escondido, CA 92026
Phone: (619)744-3117

Crisis Phone(s): (619)744-3117.

Eureka

★3365★ Humboldt Women for Shelter
PO Box 969
Eureka, CA 95501
Phone: (707)444-9255

Crisis Phone(s): (707)443-6042.

Fairfield

★3366★ SCEOC, Inc.
Domestic Violence Program
PO Box 2589
Fairfield, CA 94533
Phone: (707)422-7763

Crisis Phone(s): (707)429-HELP; (707)645-7854.

Ft. Bragg

★3367★ Community Assistance in Assault
  and Rape Emergency
PO Box 764
Ft. Bragg, CA 95434
Phone: (707)964-4055

Crisis Phone(s): (707)964-4357.

Fremont

★3368★ Shelter Against Violent
  Environments
PO Box 8283
Fremont, CA 94537
Phone: (415)794-6056

Crisis Phone(s): (415)794-6055.

French Camp

★3369★ Haven of Peace
Women's Shelter
7070 S. Hailan Rd.
French Camp, CA 95231
Phone: (209)982-0396

Crisis Phone(s): (209)982-0396.

Fresno

★3370★ YWCA
Marjaree Mason Center
PO Box 1895
Fresno, CA 93718-1895
Phone: (209)237-4706

Crisis Phone(s): (209)237-4701.

Gilroy

★3371★ South County Alternatives
La Isla Pacifica
7700 Monterey Rd.
Gilroy, CA 95021
Phone: (408)842-3118

Crisis Phone(s): (408)683-4118.

Glendale

★3372★ YWCA
Phoenix House
735 E. Lexington St.
Glendale, CA 91206
Phone: (818)242-4155

Crisis Phone(s): (818)242-1106.

Grass Valley

★3373★ Domestic Violence Coalition
PO Box 484
Grass Valley, CA 95945
Phone: (916)272-2045

Crisis Phone(s): (916)272-3467.

Hanford

★3374★ Kings County Community Action
  Organization
Domestic Violence Prevention Program
1222 W. Lacey Blvd.
Hanford, CA 93230
Phone: (209)582-4386

Crisis Phone(s): (209)582-4386.

Hayward

★3375★ Emergency Shelter Program
22634 2nd St., No. 205
Hayward, CA 94541
Phone: (510)581-5626

Crisis Phone(s): (510)786-1246.

Hermosa Beach

★3376★ **Women's Refuge**
PO Box 3298
Hermosa Beach, CA 90254
Phone: (213)372-5843
Crisis Phone(s): (213)547-4663.

Hollister

★3377★ **San Benito County Victim Witness Program**
483 5th St.
Hollister, CA 95023
Phone: (408)637-8244
Crisis Phone(s): (408)637-8244.

Jackson

★3378★ **Operation Care**
Amador County Crisis Line
PO Box 592
Jackson, CA 95642
Crisis Phone(s): (209)223-2600.

Joshua Tree

★3379★ **Unity Home**
PO Box 1662
Joshua Tree, CA 92252
Phone: (619)366-8233
Crisis Phone(s): (619)366-9663.

La Habra

★3380★ **The Klein Center for the Prevention of Domestic Violence**
PO Box 1174
La Habra, CA 90633-1174
Phone: (213)905-9782
Crisis Phone(s): (213)697-1000.

Lakeport

★3381★ **Aware**
460 S. Main St., No. 7
Lakeport, CA 95453-5355
Crisis Phone(s): (707)263-1133.

Lancaster

★3382★ **Valley Oasis Shelter**
PO Box 4226
Lancaster, CA 93539
Phone: (805)945-5509
Crisis Phone(s): (805)945-6736.

Livermore

★3383★ **Tri-Valley Haven for Women**
PO Box 2190
Livermore, CA 94551
Phone: (510)449-5845
Crisis Phone(s): (510)449-5842.

Lompoc

★3384★ **Shelter Services for Women**
PO Box 1366
Lompoc, CA 93436
Crisis Phone(s): (805)736-0965.

Long Beach

★3385★ **YWCA**
Women's Shelter
853 Atlantic Ave.
Long Beach, CA 90832-2107
Phone: (213)491-5362
Crisis Phone(s): (213)437-4663.

Los Angeles

★3386★ **Battered Service Action Center**
108 N. Bonnie Beach
Los Angeles, CA 90063
Phone: (213)268-7568
Crisis Phone(s): (213)268-7564.

★3387★ **Center for the Pacific Asian Family**
543 N. Fairfax Ave.
Los Angeles, CA 90036
Crisis Phone(s): (213)653-4042; (800)339-3940.

★3388★ **Chicana Service Action Center**
East Los Angeles/Free Spirit Shelter
134 E. 1st St.
Los Angeles, CA 90012
Phone: (213)253-5959
Crisis Phone(s): (213)268-7564; (213)937-1312.

★3389★ **Good Shepherd Shelter**
2561 Venice Blvd.
Los Angeles, CA 90019
Phone: (213)373-6111

★3390★ **Jenesse Center**
PO Box 73837
Los Angeles, CA 90003-0837
Phone: (213)751-1145
Crisis Phone(s): (213)755-8636.

Mammoth Lakes

★3391★ **Wild Iris Women's Services**
PO Box 7732
Mammoth Lakes, CA 93546
Phone: (619)934-2491

Merced

★3392★ **A Woman's Place**
PO Box 822
Merced, CA 95341
Phone: (209)725-7900
Crisis Phone(s): (209)722-HELP.

Modesto

★3393★ **Haven Women's Center of Stanislaus**
219 McHenry Ave.
Modesto, CA 95354-0543
Phone: (209)522-0331
Toll-free: 800-834-1990
Crisis Phone(s): (209)577-5980.

Monterey

★3394★ **YWCA**
Domestic Violence Program
801 Lighthouse Ave., Ste. 109
Monterey, CA 93940-1011
Phone: (408)649-0834
Crisis Phone(s): (408)372-6300.

Mountain View

★3395★ **Mid-Peninsula Support Network for Battered Women**
200 Blossom Ln., 3rd Fl.
Mountain View, CA 94041-1358
Phone: (415)940-7850
Crisis Phone(s): (415)940-7855.

Napa

★3396★ **Napa Emergency Women's Service**
1157 Division St.
Napa, CA 94559
Phone: (707)252-3687
Crisis Phone(s): (702)255-NEWS.

Newhall

★3397★ **Santa Clarita Valley Battered Women's Association**
PO Box 186
Newhall, CA 91322
Phone: (805)259-2332
Crisis Phone(s): (805)259-4357.

Oakhurst

★3398★ **Safe House**
PO Box 1658
Oakhurst, CA 93669
Phone: (209)683-3533
Crisis Phone(s): (209)683-3533.

Oakland

★3399★ **A Safe Place**
PO Box 275
Oakland, CA 94604
Phone: (415)444-7255
Crisis Phone(s): (415)536-7233.

Oceanside

★3400★ **Women's Resource Center**
3355 Mission Ave., Ste. 111
Oceanside, CA 92054
Phone: (619)757-3500
Crisis Phone(s): (619)757-3500.

Orange

★3401★ Women's Transitional Living
  Center
PO Box 6103
Orange, CA 92667
Phone: (714)992-1939

Crisis Phone(s): (714)992-1931.

Pasadena

★3402★ Haven House
PO Box 50007
Pasadena, CA 91115-0007
Phone: (818)564-8880

Crisis Phone(s): (213)681-2626.

Placerville

★3403★ El Dorado Women's Center
3133 Gilmore St.
Placerville, CA 95667
Phone: (916)626-1450

Crisis Phone(s): (916)626-1131.

Porterville

★3404★ Porterville Mission Project
Mary Baker Mission Shelter/Porterville
  Women's Shelter
PO Box 2033
Porterville, CA 93258

Crisis Phone(s): (209)784-0192.

Red Bluff

★3405★ DOVE
PO Box 286
Red Bluff, CA 96080
Phone: (916)529-1102

Crisis Phone(s): (916)529-1102.

Redding

★3406★ Shasta County Women's Refuge
1800 Shasta
Redding, CA 96001
Phone: (916)244-0117

Crisis Phone(s): (916)244-0117.

Redondo Beach

★3407★ 1736 Family Crisis Center
103 W. Torrance Blvd., No. 101
Redondo Beach, CA 90277-3633
Phone: (310)372-4674

Crisis Phone(s): (310)379-3620.

★3408★ South Bay Coalition
ALIVE
320 Knob Hill
Redondo Beach, CA 90277
Phone: (213)372-9855

Crisis Phone(s): (213)372-9855.

Ridgecrest

★3409★ Women's Shelter Network
815 E. Inyokern Rd.
Ridgecrest, CA 93555
Phone: (619)446-7491

Crisis Phone(s): (619)375-7525.

Riverside

★3410★ Alternatives to Domestic Violence
Horizon House
PO Box 910
Riverside, CA 92502
Phone: (714)684-1720
Toll-free: 800-752-7233

Crisis Phone(s): (714)683-0829.

Rosemead

★3411★ International Institute of Los
  Angeles
Refuge Relocation and Domestic Violence
  Program
3257 Delmar Ave.
Rosemead, CA 91770
Phone: (818)307-1084

Sacramento

★3412★ Women Escaping a Violent
  Environment
PO Box 161356
Sacramento, CA 95816
Phone: (916)448-2321

Crisis Phone(s): (916)920-2952.

Salinas

★3413★ Shelter Plus
PO Box 3584
Salinas, CA 93912
Phone: (408)422-2201
Toll-free: 800-339-8228

Crisis Phone(s): (408)422-2201.

★3414★ Women's Crisis Center
PO Box 1805
Salinas, CA 93902
Phone: (408)757-1002

Crisis Phone(s): (408)757-1001.

San Andreas

★3415★ Calaveras Women's Crisis-Line
PO Box 623
San Andreas, CA 95249
Phone: (209)754-3114

Crisis Phone(s): (209)736-4011.

San Bernardino

★3416★ Domestic Violence Outreach
  Center
1616 N. D St.
San Bernardino, CA 92405
Phone: (714)881-1290

★3417★ Option House
PO Box 970
San Bernardino, CA 92402
Phone: (714)381-3471

Crisis Phone(s): (714)381-3471.

San Diego

★3418★ Center for Women's Studies and
  Services
2467 E St.
San Diego, CA 92102
Phone: (619)233-8984

Crisis Phone(s): (619)267-8023.

★3419★ YWCA
Battered Women's Services
PO Box 126398
San Diego, CA 92112-6398
Phone: (619)234-3164

Crisis Phone(s): (619)234-3164.

San Francisco

★3420★ Asian Women's Shelter
Box 19
San Francisco, CA 94110
Phone: (415)731-7100

★3421★ Cameron House
920 Sacramento St.
San Francisco, CA 94108
Phone: (415)781-0401

★3422★ Family Violence Prevention Fund
Bldg. 1, Ste. 200
San Francisco, CA 94110
Phone: (415)821-4553

★3423★ La Casa de las Madres
965 Mission St., No. 218
San Francisco, CA 94103
Phone: (415)777-1808

Crisis Phone(s): (415)333-1515.

★3424★ St. Vincent De Paul Society
Rosalie House
1745 Folsom St.
San Francisco, CA 94103
Phone: (415)255-0166

Crisis Phone(s): (415)255-0165.

★3425★ Women Organized to Make
  Abuse Non-Existent
333 Valencie St., Ste. 251
San Francisco, CA 94103
Phone: (415)864-4777

Crisis Phone(s): (415)864-4722.

San Jose

★3426★ Next Door
1181 N. 4th St., Ste. A
San Jose, CA 95112-4945
Phone: (408)298-3505

Crisis Phone(s): (408)279-2962.

San Leandro

**★3427★ San Leandro Community
Counseling**
296 Broadmoor Blvd.
San Leandro, CA 94577
Phone: (415)638-6603

San Luis Obispo

★3428★ Women's Shelter Program
PO Box 125
San Luis Obispo, CA 93406
Phone: (805)544-2321

Crisis Phone(s): (805)544-6163.

San Pedro

★3429★ Rainbow Shelter
PO Box 1925
San Pedro, CA 90733
Phone: (213)548-5450

Crisis Phone(s): (213)547-9343.

San Rafael

★3430★ Marin Abused Women's Services
1717 5th Ave.
San Rafael, CA 94901
Phone: (415)457-2464

Crisis Phone(s): (415)924-3456 (Spanish);
(415)924-6616.

Santa Barbara

★3431★ Shelter Services for Women
PO Box 1536
Santa Barbara, CA 93102
Phone: (805)963-4458

Crisis Phone(s): (805)964-5245; (805)736-
0965; (805)925-2160; (805)686-4390.

Santa Cruz

★3432★ Women's Crisis Support
1025 Center St.
Santa Cruz, CA 95060
Phone: (408)425-5525

Crisis Phone(s): (408)429-1478; (408)728-
2295.

Santa Maria

★3433★ Family Violence Counseling
815 S. Park View Ave.
Santa Maria, CA 93454
Phone: (805)346-7226

★3434★ Shelter Services for Women
PO Box 314
Santa Maria, CA 93456
Phone: (805)925-2160

Santa Monica

★3435★ Sojourn
237 Hill St.
Santa Monica, CA 90405
Phone: (213)399-9239

Crisis Phone(s): (213)392-9896.

Santa Rosa

**★3436★ YWCA
Women's Emergency Shelter**
PO Box 7164
Santa Rosa, CA 95407
Phone: (707)546-7115

Crisis Phone(s): (707)546-1234.

Seal Beach

★3437★ Interval House
PO Box 3356
Seal Beach, CA 90740
Crisis Phone(s): (310)594-4555; (714)891-
8121.

Selma

★3438★ Good Samaritan House
1927 Young St.
Selma, CA 93662
Crisis Phone(s): (209)896-9927.

Sonora

★3439★ Mother Lode Women's Center
PO Box 663
Sonora, CA 95370
Phone: (209)532-4746

Crisis Phone(s): (209)532-4707.

South Laguna

★3440★ Human Options
PO Box 9445
South Laguna, CA 92677-9455
Phone: (714)497-7017

Crisis Phone(s): (714)494-5367.

South Lake Tahoe

★3441★ Womenspace Unlimited
3140 Lake Tahoe Blvd.
South Lake Tahoe, CA 96150
Phone: (916)544-2118

Crisis Phone(s): (916)544-4444.

Stockton

**★3442★ Directions for Abused Women in
Need**
620 N. San Joaquin St.
Stockton, CA 95202
Phone: (209)941-2611

Crisis Phone(s): (209)465-4878.

Susanville

★3443★ Lassen Family Services, Inc.
PO Box 701
Susanville, CA 96130
Phone: (916)257-4599

Crisis Phone(s): (916)257-5004.

Truckee

★3444★ Domestic Violence Coalition
PO Box 1105
Truckee, CA 96160-1105
Phone: (916)582-9117

Crisis Phone(s): (916)587-3101.

Ukiah

★3445★ Project Sanctuary
PO Box 995
Ukiah, CA 95482
Phone: (707)462-9196

Crisis Phone(s): (707)463-HELP.

Vallejo

**★3446★ Sanctuary in Abused Family
Emergencies**
502 Virginia St.
Vallejo, CA 94590
Phone: (707)648-7233

Van Nuys

★3447★ Family Violence Project
6851 Lennox Ave.
Van Nuys, CA 91401
Phone: (818)908-5007

Ventura

**★3448★ Ventura County Coalition Against
Household Violence**
4882 McGrath, Ste. 240
Ventura, CA 93003
Phone: (805)656-3443

Crisis Phone(s): (805)656-1111; (805)656-
4861; and (805)656-4810.

Victorville

**★3449★ High Desert Domestic Violence
Program**
15579 8th St.
Victorville, CA 92392
Phone: (619)241-0035

Crisis Phone(s): (619)245-4211.

Visalia

**★3450★ The Battered Women's Shelter of
Visalia**
PO Box 510
Visalia, CA 93279
Crisis Phone(s): (209)732-5941.

Weaverville

**★3451★ Human Response Network
Family Crisis Services**
PO Box 2370
Weaverville, CA 96093
Phone: (916)623-2024

Crisis Phone(s): (916)623-4357.

West Covina

★3452★ Women in Need Growing Strong
PO Box 1464
West Covina, CA 91793
Phone: (818)915-5191
Crisis Phone(s): (818)967-0658.

West Sacramento

★3453★ Harper House
PO Box 725
West Sacramento, CA 95605
Phone: (916)661-6336
Crisis Phone(s): (916)758-8400; (916)371-1907; (916)662-1133.

Whittier

★3454★ Women's and Children's Crisis Shelter
PO Box 404
Whittier, CA 90608
Phone: (310)945-3937
Crisis Phone(s): (310)945-3939.

Yreka

★3455★ Siskiyou County Domestic Violence Program
PO Box 1679
Yreka, CA 96097
Phone: (916)842-6629
Crisis Phone(s): (916)842-4068.

Yuba City

★3456★ Casa de Esperanza
PO Box 56
Yuba City, CA 95992
Phone: (916)674-5400
Crisis Phone(s): (916)674-2040; (916)674-5400.

Colorado

Alamosa

★3457★ Tu Casa
PO Box 473
Alamosa, CO 81101
Phone: (719)589-4729
Crisis Phone(s): (719)589-2465.

Arvada

★3458★ Women in Crisis
PO Box 1586
Arvada, CO 80001
Phone: (303)420-6752
Crisis Phone(s): (303)420-6752.

Aspen

★3459★ Response
PO Box 1340
Aspen, CO 81612
Phone: (303)925-5347
Crisis Phone(s): (303)925-SAFE.

Aurora

★3460★ Gateway Battered Women's Shelter
PO Box 914
Aurora, CO 80040
Phone: (303)343-1856
Crisis Phone(s): (303)343-1851.

Boulder

★3461★ Boulder County Safehouse
PO Box 4157
Boulder, CO 80306
Phone: (303)449-8623
Crisis Phone(s): (303)449-8623.

Canon City

★3462★ Family Crisis Service
PO Box 308
Canon City, CO 81212
Phone: (719)275-2429
Crisis Phone(s): (719)275-2429.

Castle Rock

★3463★ Women's Crisis Center of Douglas County
PO Box 367
Castle Rock, CO 80104
Phone: (303)688-1094
Crisis Phone(s): (303)688-8484.

Colorado Springs

★3464★ Center for Prevention of Domestic Violence
PO Box 2662
Colorado Springs, CO 80901
Phone: (719)633-1462
Crisis Phone(s): (719)633-3819.

Commerce City

★3465★ Alternatives to Family Violence
PO Box 385
Commerce City, CO 80037
Phone: (303)289-4441
Crisis Phone(s): (303)289-4441; (303)280-0111.

Cortez

★3466★ Renew, Inc.
PO Box 169
Cortez, CO 81321
Phone: (303)565-2100
Crisis Phone(s): (303)565-4631.

Craig

★3467★ Abused and Battered Humans
PO Box 1050
Craig, CO 81626
Phone: (303)824-9709
Crisis Phone(s): (303)824-2400.

Denver

★3468★ Amend
777 Grant St., No. 600
Denver, CO 80203
Phone: (303)832-6363
Crisis Phone(s): (303)832-6363.

★3469★ Brandon Center
1865 Larimer St.
Denver, CO 80204
Phone: (303)620-9190
Crisis Phone(s): (303)620-9190.

★3470★ Domestic Violence Initiative for Women with Disabilities
PO Box 300535
Denver, CO 80203
Crisis Phone(s): (303)839-5510.

★3471★ Elder Abuse Prevention Project
770 Grant St., No. 234
Denver, CO 80203
Phone: (303)832-2900

★3472★ Empowerment Program
1245 E. Colfax Ave., No. 404
Denver, CO 80218
Phone: (303)863-7817
Crisis Phone(s): (303)863-7817.

★3473★ Safe House for Battered Women
PO Box 18014
Denver, CO 80218
Phone: (303)830-8181
Crisis Phone(s): (303)830-6800; (303)832-2929 (TDD).

★3474★ Servicios de la Raza
4055 N. Tejon St.
Denver, CO 80211
Phone: (303)458-5851
Crisis Phone(s): (303)458-7088.

Durango

★3475★ Alternative Horizons
PO Box 503
Durango, CO 81302
Phone: (303)247-4374
Crisis Phone(s): (303)247-9619.

★3476★ Volunteers of America Southwest Safehouse
PO Box 2107
Durango, CO 81302
Phone: (303)259-5443
Crisis Phone(s): (303)259-5443.

Ft. Collins

★3477★ Crossroads
PO Box 993
Ft. Collins, CO 80522
Phone: (303)482-3502
Crisis Phone(s): (303)482-3502.

Ft. Morgan

★3478★ SHARE, Inc.
PO Box 414
Ft. Morgan, CO 80701
Phone: (303)867-4444
Crisis Phone(s): (303)867-3411.

Frisco

★3479★ Advocates for Victims of Assault
PO Box 1859
Frisco, CO 80443
Phone: (303)668-3906
Crisis Phone(s): (303)668-3906.

George Town

★3480★ Clear Creek County Advocates
PO Box 21
George Town, CO 80444
Phone: (303)569-3126
Crisis Phone(s): (303)567-4844.

Glenwood Springs

★3481★ Advocates/Safehouse Project
PO Box 2036
Glenwood Springs, CO 81602
Phone: (303)945-2632
Crisis Phone(s): (303)945-3939.

Golden

★3482★ Family Violence Intervention Program
1726 Cole Blvd., Ste. 115
Golden, CO 80401
Phone: (303)278-6950

Grand Junction

★3483★ Individual and Family Counseling
1425 N. 5th St.
Grand Junction, CO 81501
Phone: (303)242-4414
Crisis Phone(s): (303)243-4414.

**★3484★ The Resource Center
Domestic Violence Program**
1129 Colorado Ave.
Grand Junction, CO 81502
Phone: (303)243-0190
Crisis Phone(s): (303)241-6704.

Greeley

★3485★ A Woman's Place
PO Box 71
Greeley, CO 80632
Phone: (303)351-0476
Crisis Phone(s): (303)356-4226.

Hot Sulphur Springs

★3486★ Advocates/Victim Assistance Team
PO Box 155
Hot Sulphur Springs, CO 80451-0155
Phone: (303)725-3442
Crisis Phone(s): (303)725-3393.

La Junta

★3487★ Arkansas Valley Women's Resource Center
PO Box 716
La Junta, CO 81050
Crisis Phone(s): (719)384-7764.

Lamar

★3488★ Sunrise Shelter
PO Box 953
Lamar, CO 81052
Phone: (719)336-4357
Crisis Phone(s): (719)336-4357.

Leadville

★3489★ Advocates of Lake County
PO Box 325
Leadville, CO 80461
Phone: (719)486-1178
Crisis Phone(s): (719)486-3530.

Longmont

★3490★ Longmont Coalition for Women in Crisis
PO Box 231
Longmont, CO 80502-0231
Phone: (303)772-0432
Crisis Phone(s): (303)772-4422.

Loveland

★3491★ Alternatives to Violence
320 N. Cleveland, No. 5
Loveland, CO 80537
Phone: (303)669-5150
Crisis Phone(s): (303)669-5150.

Meeker

★3492★ Safe House, Inc.
PO Box 1152
Meeker, CO 81641
Phone: (303)878-5670
Crisis Phone(s): (303)878-3131.

Montrose

★3493★ Women's Resource Center
307 Main, Ste. 1
Montrose, CO 81401
Phone: (303)249-2486
Crisis Phone(s): (303)249-2486.

Pueblo

**★3494★ YWCA
Family Crisis Shelter**
801 N. Santa Fe
Pueblo, CO 81003
Crisis Phone(s): (719)545-8195.

Rangely

★3495★ Aid to Victims of Domestic Violence
PO Box 194
Rangely, CO 81648
Phone: (303)675-5220
Crisis Phone(s): (303)675-8466; (303)675-8467.

Salida

★3496★ Alliance Against Domestic Violence
PO Box 173
Salida, CO 81201
Phone: (719)539-7347
Crisis Phone(s): (719)539-2596 (Salida); (719)395-2451 (Buena Vista).

Steamboat Springs

★3497★ Advocates Against Battering and Abuse
PO Box 1424
Steamboat Springs, CO 80477
Phone: (303)879-2034
Crisis Phone(s): (303)879-8888.

Sterling

★3498★ Help for Abused Partners
PO Box 1286
Sterling, CO 80751
Phone: (303)522-2307
Crisis Phone(s): (303)522-2844.

Trinidad

★3499★ Advocates Against Domestic Assault
PO Box 696
Trinidad, CO 81082
Phone: (303)846-6665
Crisis Phone(s): (303)846-4357.

Vail

★3500★ The Resource Center
PO Box 3414
Vail, CO 81658
Phone: (303)476-7384
Crisis Phone(s): (303)476-7384.

Walsenburg

★3501★ Domestic Violence Elimination Program
206 W. 6th
Walsenburg, CO 81089
Phone: (719)738-2852
Crisis Phone(s): (719)738-1044.

Yuma

★3502★ Yuma Community Resource
Center
New Directions
708 S. Cedar, Ste. B
Yuma, CO 80759
Phone: (303)848-3867

Crisis Phone(s): (303)848-5441.

Connecticut

Ansonia

★3503★ Umbrella Project
435 E. Main St.
Ansonia, CT 06401
Phone: (203)736-9944

Crisis Phone(s): (203)736-9944.

Bridgeport

★3504★ YWCA
Shelter Services for Abused Families
753 Fairfield Ave.
Bridgeport, CT 06604
Phone: (203)334-6154

Crisis Phone(s): (203)334-6154; (203)222-0151 (Westport). After 5 p.m. and on weekends: (2 03)333-7555 (Bridgeport); (203)853-2525 (Norwalk); (203)324-1010 (Stamford).

Danbury

★3505★ Women's Center
Battered Women Services
256 Main St.
Danbury, CT 06810
Phone: (203)731-5200

Crisis Phone(s): (203)731-5206; (203)731-5204 (Rape Crisis).

Dayville

★3506★ United Services, Inc.
Domestic Violence Program
PO Box 251
Dayville, CT 06241
Phone: (203)774-2020

Crisis Phone(s): (203)774-8648.

Enfield

★3507★ Network Against Domestic Abuse
of North Central Connecticut
PO Box 531
Enfield, CT 06083-0531
Phone: (203)745-3363

Crisis Phone(s): (203)763-4542.

Greenwich

★3508★ YWCA
Domestic Abuse Service
259 E. Putman Ave.
Greenwich, CT 06830
Phone: (203)869-6501

Crisis Phone(s): (203)622-0003.

Hartford

★3509★ Hartford Interval House
PO Box 6207
Hartford, CT 06106
Phone: (203)246-9149

Crisis Phone(s): (203)527-0550.

Meriden

★3510★ Meriden/Wallingford Chrysalis
PO Box 663
Meriden, CT 06450
Phone: (203)238-1501

Crisis Phone(s): (203)238-1501.

Middletown

★3511★ New Horizons
PO Box 1076
Middletown, CT 06457
Phone: (203)347-6971

Crisis Phone(s): (203)347-6971.

New Britain

★3512★ Prudence Crandall Center for
Women
PO Box 895
New Britain, CT 06050
Phone: (203)225-5187

Crisis Phone(s): (203)225-6357; (203)583-6272; (203)747-2030.

New Haven

★3513★ Domestic Violence Services
PO Box 1329
New Haven, CT 06505
Phone: (203)865-1957

Crisis Phone(s): (203)789-8104.

New London

★3514★ Women's Center of Southeast
Connecticut
Genesis House
PO Box 572
New London, CT 06320
Phone: (203)447-0366

Crisis Phone(s): (203)447-0366.

Norwalk

★3515★ Women's Crisis Center
5 Eversley Ave.
Norwalk, CT 06851
Phone: (203)853-0418

Crisis Phone(s): (203)852-1980.

Sharon

★3516★ Women's Emergency Services
PO Box 1029
Sharon, CT 06069
Phone: (203)364-0223

Crisis Phone(s): (203)364-0844.

Stamford

★3517★ Stamford Domestic Violence
Services
65 High Ridge Rd., Ste. 378
Stamford, CT 06905
Phone: (203)965-0049

Crisis Phone(s): (203)357-8162.

Torrington

★3518★ Susan B. Anthony Project
PO Box 846
Torrington, CT 06790
Phone: (203)489-3798

Crisis Phone(s): (203)482-7133.

Waterbury

★3519★ Women's Emergency Shelter
PO Box 1503
Waterbury, CT 06721
Phone: (203)575-0036

Willimantic

★3520★ United Services, Inc.
Domestic Violence Program
132 Mansfield Ave.
Willimantic, CT 06226
Phone: (203)456-2261

Crisis Phone(s): (203)456-9476.

Delaware

Milford

★3521★ People's Place, II
Families in Transition Center
219 S. Walnut St.
Milford, DE 19963
Phone: (302)856-4919

Crisis Phone(s): (302)422-8058 (Kent County and Sussex County).

Wilmington

★3522★ CHILD, Inc.
Family Violence Program
507 Philadelphia Pike
Wilmington, DE 19809-2177
Phone: (302)762-8989

Crisis Phone(s): (302)762-6110.

★3523★ Parents Anonymous of Delaware
124-D Senatorial Dr.
Wilmington, DE 19807
Phone: (302)654-1102

Crisis Phone(s): (302)654-1102.

District of Columbia

Washington

★3524★ Family Stress Services of the
District of Columbia
Fact Hotline
PO Box 57194
Washington, DC 20037
Phone: (202)223-2255

Crisis Phone(s): (202)223-0020.

★3525★ House of Imagene
214 P St. NW
Washington, DC 20001
Crisis Phone(s): (202)797-7460.

★3526★ House of Ruth
Herspace
651 10th St. NE
Washington, DC 20002
Phone: (202)347-0737
Crisis Phone(s): (202)347-2777.

★3527★ My Sister's Place
PO Box 29596
Washington, DC 20017
Crisis Phone(s): (202)529-5991.

★3528★ Women's Legal Defense Fund
1875 Connecticut Ave. NW, Ste. 710
Washington, DC 20009
Phone: (202)986-2600

Florida

Bartow

★3529★ Peace River Center for Personal Development
Domestic Violence Services
1745 Hwy. 17S
Bartow, FL 33830
Phone: (813)682-7270
Crisis Phone(s): (813)682-7270.

Bradenton

★3530★ HOPE Family Services
PO Box 1624
Bradenton, FL 34206
Phone: (813)747-7790
Crisis Phone(s): (813)755-6805.

Bunnell

★3531★ Family Life Center
PO Box 2058
Bunnell, FL 32110
Phone: (904)437-3505
Crisis Phone(s): (904)437-3505.

Clearwater

★3532★ Spouse Abuse Shelter
PO Box 37
Clearwater, FL 34617
Phone: (813)442-4128
Crisis Phone(s): (813)531-4664 (after hours).

Cocoa

★3533★ The Salvation Army
Domestic Violence Program
PO Box 1540
Cocoa, FL 32923
Phone: (407)631-2764

Dade City

★3534★ Sunrise Spouse Abuse Shelter
PO Box 928
Dade City, FL 33526
Phone: (904)521-3120
Crisis Phone(s): (904)521-3120.

Daytona Beach

★3535★ Domestic Abuse Council
PO Box 142
Daytona Beach, FL 32015
Phone: (904)255-2102

Delray Beach

★3536★ Aid to Victims of Domestic Assault
PO Box 667
Delray Beach, FL 33447-0667
Phone: (407)265-2900

Ft. Lauderdale

★3537★ Women in Distress of Broward County
PO Box 676
Ft. Lauderdale, FL 33302
Phone: (305)760-9800
Crisis Phone(s): (305)761-1133.

Ft. Myers

★3538★ ACT
PO Box 06401
Ft. Myers, FL 33906
Phone: (813)939-3112
Crisis Phone(s): (813)939-3112.

Gainesville

★3539★ Sexual and Physical Abuse Resource Center
PO Box 12367
Gainesville, FL 32604
Phone: (904)378-1762
Crisis Phone(s): (904)377-8255.

Homestead

★3540★ South Dade Victims' Center
49 W. Mowry St.
Homestead, FL 33030
Crisis Phone(s): (305)247-4249.

Inverness

★3541★ Citrus County Abuse Shelter Association
PO Box 205
Inverness, FL 32651
Phone: (904)344-8112
Crisis Phone(s): (904)344-8111.

Jacksonville

★3542★ Hubbard House
PO Box 4909
Jacksonville, FL 32201
Phone: (904)354-3122
Toll-free: 800-76-ABUSE
Crisis Phone(s): (904)354-3114.

Kissimmee

★3543★ Help NOW
806 W. Verona St., Ste. 5
Kissimmee, FL 32741
Phone: (407)847-8562
Crisis Phone(s): (407)847-8811.

Lakeland

★3544★ Peace River Center for Personal Development
1835 N. Gilmore Ave.
Lakeland, FL 33805
Phone: (813)683-5701
Crisis Phone(s): (813)682-7270.

Leesburg

★3545★ Haven of Lake and Sumter Counties, Inc.
PO Box 492335
Leesburg, FL 32749-2335
Phone: (904)753-5800

Marathon

★3546★ Domestic Abuse Shelter
PO Box 1145
Marathon, FL 33050
Phone: (305)743-9465
Crisis Phone(s): (305)294-5463; (305)743-4440 (Middle Keys); (305)852-6195; (305)294-082 4 (Lower Keys); (305)852-6222 (Upper Keys).

Miami

★3547★ Advocates for Victims
Safespace
7831 NE Miami Ct.
Miami, FL 33138
Crisis Phone(s): (305)758-2546.

★3548★ Domestic Intervention Program
Family and Victim Services
1515 NW 7th St., Ste. 220
Miami, FL 33125
Phone: (305)547-5482

★3549★ Metro/Dade Advocates for Victims
7831 NE Miami Ct.
Miami, FL 33138
Phone: (305)728-2546
Crisis Phone(s): (305)728-2546.

Naples

★3550★ Shelter for Abused Women of Collier County
PO Box 10102
Naples, FL 33941
Phone: (813)775-2011

Ocala

★3551★ Creative Services
Rape Crisis/Spouse Abuse Center
PO Box 21193
Ocala, FL 32670
Phone: (904)622-8495
Crisis Phone(s): (904)622-8495.

Orlando

★3552★ Spouse Abuse, Inc.
PO Box 536276
Orlando, FL 32853-6276
Phone: (407)886-2244
Crisis Phone(s): (407)886-2856; (407)740-0017.

Panama City

★3553★ The Salvation Army
Domestic Violence Program
651-H W. 14th St.
Panama City, FL 32402-0540
Phone: (904)769-7989
Crisis Phone(s): (904)763-0706.

Pensacola

★3554★ Favorhouse of Northwest Florida, Inc.
1207 W. Moreno St.
Pensacola, FL 32501
Phone: (904)434-1177
Crisis Phone(s): (904)434-6600.

Port Richey

★3555★ The Salvation Army
Domestic Violence Shelter
PO Box 1050
Port Richey, FL 34673-1050
Phone: (813)856-5797

Punta Gorda

★3556★ Center for Abuse and Rape
Emergency of Charlotte County
PO Box 234
Punta Gorda, FL 33951-0234
Phone: (813)639-5499
Crisis Phone(s): (813)627-6000.

Ruskin

★3557★ Mary and Martha House
PO Box 1251
Ruskin, FL 33570
Phone: (813)645-7874

St. Petersburg

★3558★ Center Against Spouse Abuse
PO Box 414
St. Petersburg, FL 33731
Phone: (813)895-4912
Crisis Phone(s): (813)898-3671.

Sarasota

★3559★ Safe Place and Rape Crisis
Center of Sarasota
PO Box 1675
Sarasota, FL 33578
Crisis Phone(s): (813)365-1976.

Tallahassee

★3560★ Refuge House
PO Box 4356
Tallahassee, FL 32315
Phone: (904)681-2111

Tampa

★3561★ The Spring
PO Box 4772
Tampa, FL 33677
Phone: (813)621-7233
Crisis Phone(s): (813)247-7233.

Vero Beach

★3562★ Safespace
PO Box 2822
Vero Beach, FL 32961
Crisis Phone(s): (407)569-7233.

West Palm Beach

★3563★ Domestic Assault Program
307 N. Dixie Hwy., 4th Fl. Annex
West Palm Beach, FL 33401-6593
Phone: (407)820-2383
Crisis Phone(s): (407)820-2383.

★3564★ YWCA
Harmony House
901 S. Olive Ave.
West Palm Beach, FL 33401-6593
Crisis Phone(s): (407)655-6106.

Georgia

Albany

★3565★ Liberty House
PO Box 273
Albany, GA 31702
Phone: (912)439-7094
Crisis Phone(s): (912)439-7065.

Athens

★3566★ Project SAFE
1394 S. Milledge Ave.
Athens, GA 30604
Phone: (404)549-0922
Crisis Phone(s): (404)543-3331.

★3567★ The Salvation Army
Shelter
399 Meigs St.
Athens, GA 30601
Phone: (404)543-5350

Atlanta

★3568★ Council on Battered Women
PO Box 54383
Atlanta, GA 30308
Phone: (404)873-1766

★3569★ Families First, Inc.
Domestic Crisis Intervention Unit
250 Georgia Ave., Rm. 212
Atlanta, GA 30312
Phone: (404)658-6074

★3570★ Women's Crisis Center
PO Box 160109
Atlanta, GA 30316
Phone: (404)659-6977

Augusta

★3571★ Safe Homes of Augusta
PO Box 3187
Augusta, GA 30914-3187
Phone: (404)736-2499

Blairesville

★3572★ SAFE
PO Box 11
Blairesville, GA 31501
Phone: (912)285-5850

Blue Ridge

★3573★ North Georgia Mountain Crisis
Network
PO Box 1249
Blue Ridge, GA 30513
Phone: (404)632-8401
Crisis Phone(s): (404)632-8400.

Brunswick

★3574★ Amity House
PO Box 278
Brunswick, GA 31521
Crisis Phone(s): (912)264-4357.

Calhoun

★3575★ Calhoun/Gordon Council on
Battered Women
PO Box 2315
Calhoun, GA 30703
Phone: (404)629-1111

Carrollton

★3576★ Carroll County Emergency
Services
815 Dixie St.
Carrollton, GA 30117
Phone: (404)834-1141

Catersville

★3577★ Christian League for Battered
Women
Tranquility House
PO Box 1383
Catersville, GA 30120
Phone: (404)386-8779
Crisis Phone(s): (404)386-8779.

Clarksville

★3578★ Circle of Hope
PO Box 371
Clarksville, GA 30523
Phone: (404)776-3406
Crisis Phone(s): (404)776-3406.

Columbus

★3579★ Columbus Alliance for Battered Women
PO Box 5804
Columbus, GA 31906
Phone: (404)324-3850
Crisis Phone(s): (404)324-3850.

Cumming

★3580★ Family Haven
PO Box 1160
Cumming, GA 30130
Phone: (404)889-6384

Dalton

★3581★ Northwest Georgia Family Crisis Center
PO Box 554
Dalton, GA 30722
Phone: (404)278-6595
Crisis Phone(s): (404)278-5586.

Decatur

★3582★ Women's Resource Center of De Kalb County
PO Box 171
Decatur, GA 30031
Phone: (404)688-9436
Crisis Phone(s): (404)688-9436.

Douglasville

★3583★ Share House
PO Box 723
Douglasville, GA 30133
Phone: (404)942-2720

Fayetteville

★3584★ Fayette County Council on Battered Women
PO Box 854
Fayetteville, GA 30214
Phone: (404)460-1604
Crisis Phone(s): (404)487-8717.

Ft. Benning

**★3585★ U.S. Army
Family Advocacy Program**
Slinter Village, Bldg. 2640
Ft. Benning, GA 31905
Phone: (404)545-7517
Crisis Phone(s): (404)545-5222.

Gainesville

★3586★ Gateway House
PO Box 2962
Gainesville, GA 30503
Phone: (404)536-5850
Crisis Phone(s): (404)536-5850 (collect calls accepted).

Griffin

**★3587★ Christian Women's Center of Griffin
Crisis Care Shelter**
PO Box 803
Griffin, GA 30224
Phone: (404)227-3700
Crisis Phone(s): (404)227-3700.

Hinesville

★3588★ Coastal Area Community Mental Health/Mental Retardation/Substance Abuse Center
PO Box 1489
Hinesville, GA 31313
Phone: (912)368-3344
Crisis Phone(s): (912)368-HELP.

★3589★ Tri-County Protective Agency Domestic Violence Emergency Shelter
PO Box 1937
Hinesville, GA 31313
Crisis Phone(s): (912)368-9200.

La Grange

★3590★ Project LOVE
PO Box 2107
La Grange, GA 30240
Phone: (404)882-1000
Crisis Phone(s): (404)882-1000.

Lebanon

★3591★ Cherokee Family Violence Center
PO Box 424
Lebanon, GA 30146
Phone: (404)479-1703

Macon

★3592★ Macon Rescue Mission Battered Women Division
PO Box 749
Macon, GA 31202
Phone: (912)935-8626

Marietta

**★3593★ YWCA
Battered Women's Program**
48 Henderson St.
Marietta, GA 30064
Crisis Phone(s): (404)427-3390; (404)428-2666.

McDonough

★3594★ The Association for the Prevention of Domestic Violence
PO Box 1241
McDonough, GA 30253
Phone: (404)954-9229
Crisis Phone(s): (404)954-9229.

Rome

★3595★ Hospitality House
216 S. Broad St.
Rome, GA 30161
Phone: (912)235-4673
Crisis Phone(s): (404)235-4673.

St. Mary's

★3596★ Camben Community Crisis Center
PO Box 1223
St. Mary's, GA 31558
Phone: (912)882-7858
Crisis Phone(s): (912)882-7858.

Savannah

★3597★ Safe Shelter
PO Box 22487
Savannah, GA 31403
Phone: (912)232-2342
Crisis Phone(s): (912)234-9999

Tifton

★3598★ Brother Charlie Rescue Center
PO Box 783
Tifton, GA 31794
Phone: (912)382-0577
Crisis Phone(s): (912)386-0645.

Warner Robbins

★3599★ The Salvation Army Safe House
PO Box 2408
Warner Robbins, GA 31099
Phone: (912)923-6294

Waycross

★3600★ Shelter for Abused Women and Children
PO Box 1824
Waycross, GA 31501
Phone: (912)285-5850

Hawaii

Hilo

★3601★ Family Crisis Shelter
PO Box 612
Hilo, HI 96720
Phone: (808)959-5825
Crisis Phone(s): (808)959-8400 (east Hawaii); (808)322-SAFE (west Hawaii).

Honolulu

★3602★ Developing Options to Violence
200 N. Vineyard Blvd., Ste. 20
Honolulu, HI 96817
Phone: (808)521-2377
Crisis Phone(s): (808)841-0822.

★3603★ Family Peace Center
1370 Kapiolani Blvd.
Honolulu, HI 96814
Phone: (808)944-0900
Crisis Phone(s): (808)944-0900.

★3604★ Hawaii Women Lawyers
Domestic Violence Legal Hotline
1154 Fort St. Mall, No. 402
Honolulu, HI 96813
Phone: (808)531-3771
Crisis Phone(s): (808)531-3771.

★3605★ Honolulu Department of the
Prosecuting Attorney
Victim/Witness Assistance Division
1164 Bishop St., Ste. 1009
Honolulu, HI 96813
Phone: (808)523-4158

★3606★ Military Family Abuse Shelter
PO Box 2218
Honolulu, HI 96804
Crisis Phone(s): (808)533-7125.

★3607★ Shelter for Abused Spouses and
Children
200 N. Vinyard Blvd., Ste. 20
Honolulu, HI 96817
Phone: (808)847-4602
Crisis Phone(s): (808)841-0822.

★3608★ Waikiki Community Center
Family Violence Program
310 Paoakalani Ave.
Honolulu, HI 96815
Phone: (808)823-1802

Hoolehua

★3609★ Hale Laiku
PO Box 157
Hoolehua, HI 96729
Phone: (808)567-6420
Crisis Phone(s): (808)567-6420.

Kaunakaki

★3610★ Alternatives to Violence
PO Box 589
Kaunakaki, HI 96748
Phone: (808)553-3202
Crisis Phone(s): (808)553-3202.

Lihue

★3611★ YWCA
Family Violence Shelter
3094 Elva St.
Lihue, HI 96746
Phone: (808)245-8404
Crisis Phone(s): (808)245-6362.

Paia

★3612★ Women Helping Women
PO Box 760
Paia, HI 96779
Phone: (808)579-8474
Crisis Phone(s): (808)579-9581.

Wailuku

★3613★ Alternatives to Violence
PO Box 909
Wailuku, HI 96893
Phone: (808)244-1564

★3614★ Wailuku Department of the
Prosecuting Attorney
Victim/Witness Assistance Program
200 S. High St.
Wailuku, HI 96793
Phone: (808)243-7777

Idaho

American Falls

★3615★ Power County Domestic Violence
Support Group
659 Gifford Ave.
American Falls, ID 83211
Phone: (208)226-2409
Crisis Phone(s): (208)226-2311.

Blackfoot

★3616★ Bingham Crisis Center for
Women
PO Box 714
Blackfoot, ID 83221
Phone: (208)785-1047
Crisis Phone(s): (208)785-3811.

Boise

★3617★ Emergency Housing Services
815 N. 7th St.
Boise, ID 83701
Phone: (208)384-0162

★3618★ Family Advocate Program, Inc.
Parent Aids and CASA Programs
1134 North Orchard, Ste. 1
Boise, ID 83706
Phone: (208)345-3344

★3619★ SANE
1010 N. Orchard, Ste. 7
Boise, ID 83706
Phone: (208)345-1170

★3620★ Southwest Center for New
Directions
1910 University Dr.
Boise, ID 83725
Phone: (208)385-3126

★3621★ YWCA
Boise Women's Crisis Center
720 W. Washington St.
Boise, ID 83702
Phone: (208)343-3688
Crisis Phone(s): (208)343-7025.

Bonners Ferry

★3622★ Boundary County Bonners Ferry
Alternatives to Domestic Violence
1524 Sherman Ave.
Bonners Ferry, ID 83805
Crisis Phone(s): (208)267-3141.

Challis

★3623★ Mainstay Council
PO Box 341
Challis, ID 83226
Phone: (208)774-3321
Crisis Phone(s): (208)528-1932.

Coeur d'Alene

★3624★ Women's Center
Alternatives to Domestic Violence
2201 Government Way, Ste. L
Coeur d'Alene, ID 83814
Phone: (208)664-1443
Crisis Phone(s): (208)664-1443.

Idaho Falls

★3625★ Sexual Assault and Rape Relief
of Bonneville County
Help, Inc.
545 Shoup Ave., Ste. 339
Idaho Falls, ID 83402
Phone: (208)522-7016
Crisis Phone(s): (208)525-1831.

★3626★ Women Against Domestic
Violence
PO Box 50323
Idaho Falls, ID 83402
Phone: (208)529-4352
Crisis Phone(s): (208)525-1820.

Ketchum

★3627★ Crisis Hotline
PO Box 939
Ketchum, ID 83340
Phone: (208)726-3597
Crisis Phone(s): (208)788-3596; (208)726-3596.

Lewiston

★3628★ Nez Perce County Victim
Advocacy Project
PO Box 1267
Lewiston, ID 83501
Phone: (208)799-3073

★3629★ YWCA
Crisis Services
300 Main St.
Lewiston, ID 83501
Phone: (208)743-1535
Crisis Phone(s): (208)746-9655.

McCall

★3630★ Support for Women in Crisis
PO Box 1369
McCall, ID 83638
Crisis Phone(s): (208)382-4201.

Moscow

★3631★ Alternatives to Violence
PO Box 8517
Moscow, ID 83843
Phone: (509)332-0552
Crisis Phone(s): (208)883-HELP; (509)332-HELP.

★3632★ University of Idaho
Women's Center
Moscow, ID 83843
Phone: (208)885-6616

Mountain Home

★3633★ Elmore County Family Crisis
Intervention
955 North, 8th East
Mountain Home, ID 83647
Phone: (208)587-5507
Crisis Phone(s): (208)587-5507.

Nampa

★3634★ Mercy House
PO Box 558
Nampa, ID 83653
Phone: (208)467-4130
Crisis Phone(s): (208)465-5011.

★3635★ SANE
1503 3rd St. N
Nampa, ID 83687
Phone: (208)467-7654

Pocatello

★3636★ YWCA
Women's Advocates
454 N. Garfield
Pocatello, ID 83204
Phone: (208)232-0742
Crisis Phone(s): (208)232-9169.

St. Maries

★3637★ Crisis Intervention Center
137 N. 8th St.
St. Maries, ID 83861-1845

Sandpoint

★3638★ Bonner County Crisis-Line
PO Box 1213
Sandpoint, ID 83864
Phone: (208)263-1241
Crisis Phone(s): (208)263-1241.

Soda Springs

★3639★ Caribou County Domestic
Violence Committee
481 S. 3rd E.
Soda Springs, ID 83276
Phone: (208)547-3238
Crisis Phone(s): (208)547-2561.

Twin Falls

★3640★ Volunteers Against Violence
PO Box 2444
Twin Falls, ID 83303-2444
Phone: (208)733-5054
Crisis Phone(s): (208)733-0100.

Wallace

★3641★ Women's Resource Center
524 Bank St., Ste. 205
Wallace, ID 83873
Phone: (208)556-6101
Crisis Phone(s): (208)556-6101.

Weiser

★3642★ Project ROSE
PO Box 527
Weiser, ID 83672
Phone: (208)549-1330
Crisis Phone(s): (208)549-0740.

Illinois

Aledo

★3643★ Coalition Against Domestic
Violence
PO Box 122
Aledo, IL 61231
Phone: (309)582-7233
Crisis Phone(s): (309)582-7233.

Alton

★3644★ Oasis Women's Center
111 Market St.
Alton, IL 62002
Phone: (618)465-1978
Crisis Phone(s): (618)465-1978.

Aurora

★3645★ Mutual Ground
PO Box 843
Aurora, IL 60507
Phone: (708)897-0084
Crisis Phone(s): (708)897-0080 (domestic violence); (708)897-8383 (sexual assault).

Belleville

★3646★ Women's Crisis Center of Metro
East
PO Box 284
Belleville, IL 62222
Phone: (618)236-2531
Toll-free: 800-924-0096
Crisis Phone(s): (618)235-0892.

Bloomington

★3647★ Mid-Central Community Action,
Inc.
Countering Domestic Violence
923 E. Grove
Bloomington, IL 61701
Phone: (309)829-0691
Crisis Phone(s): (309)827-4005; (309)827-8913; (309)827-7070.

Cairo

★3648★ Women's Shelter
529 Cross
Cairo, IL 62914
Phone: (618)734-4200
Crisis Phone(s): (618)734-4357.

Canton

★3649★ Women's Crisis Service
700 E. Oak St., Rm. 203-A
Canton, IL 61520
Phone: (309)647-7487
Crisis Phone(s): (309)647-8311.

Carbondale

★3650★ Women's Center
408 W. Freeman St.
Carbondale, IL 62901-2725
Phone: (618)529-2324
Crisis Phone(s): (618)529-2324; (618)997-2277.

Centralia

★3651★ People Against Violent
Environments
PO Box 342
Centralia, IL 62801
Phone: (618)533-7233
Crisis Phone(s): (618)533-7233 (collect calls accepted).

Charleston

★3652★ Coalition Against Domestic
Violence
PO Box 732
Charleston, IL 61920
Phone: (217)348-5931
Crisis Phone(s): (217)345-4300.

Chicago

★3653★ Chicago Abused Women Coalition
PO Box 477166
Chicago, IL 60647-7916
Phone: (312)278-4110
Crisis Phone(s): (312)278-4566; (312)278-4114 (TDD).

★3654★ **Chicago Department of Human Services**
Domestic Violence Services
510 N. Peshtigo Ct.
Chicago, IL 60611
Toll-free: 800-654-8595
Crisis Phone(s): (312)744-5829; (312)744-8418.

★3655★ **Family Rescue**
3234 E. 91st St.
Chicago, IL 60617
Phone: (312)375-1918
Crisis Phone(s): (312)375-8400; (312)375-6863.

★3656★ **Harriet Tubman Shelter**
4844 S. State
Chicago, IL 60609
Phone: (312)924-3151
Crisis Phone(s): (312)924-3152.

★3657★ **Mujeres Latinas en Accion**
1823 W 17th St.
Chicago, IL 60608
Phone: (312)226-1544
Crisis Phone(s): (312)226-1544.

★3658★ **Neopolitan Lighthouse**
PO Box 24709
Chicago, IL 60624
Phone: (312)638-0228
Crisis Phone(s): (312)638-0227.

★3659★ **Rainbow House/Arco Iris**
PO Box 29019
Chicago, IL 60629
Phone: (312)521-5501
Crisis Phone(s): (312)762-6611; (312)762-6802 (TDD).

★3660★ **St. Francis Shelter**
78th St.
Chicago, IL 60619
Phone: (312)487-8615

★3661★ **The Salvation Army**
Emergency Lodge
800 W. Lawrence Ave.
Chicago, IL 60640
Phone: (312)275-9383

★3662★ **Sarah's Inn**
4909 W. Division St.
Chicago, IL 60651
Phone: (708)287-2400
Crisis Phone(s): (708)386-4225.

★3663★ **Southwest Women Working Together**
3201 W. 63rd St.
Chicago, IL 60629
Phone: (312)436-0550

★3664★ **Travelers and Immigrants Aid**
327 S. LaSalle
Chicago, IL 60604
Phone: (312)435-4500
Crisis Phone(s): (312)686-7562.

★3665★ **United Charities of Chicago**
Family Options Program
14 E. Jackson Blvd.
Chicago, IL 60604
Phone: (312)436-4273
Crisis Phone(s): (312)829-1402.

★3666★ **Uptown Center Hull House**
Woman Abuse Action Project
4520 N. Beacon
Chicago, IL 60640
Phone: (312)561-3500
Crisis Phone(s): (312)561-3500 (voice and TDD); (312)521-4865.

★3667★ **YWCA**
Women's Services
180 N. Wabash
Chicago, IL 60601
Phone: (312)372-6600

Clay City

★3668★ **Stopping Women Abuse NOW**
PO Box 504
Clay City, IL 62824
Phone: (618)676-1912
Crisis Phone(s): (618)676-1911.

Danville

★3669★ **YWCA**
Women's Shelter
201 N. Hazel
Danville, IL 61832
Phone: (217)446-1217
Crisis Phone(s): (217)443-5566.

De Kalb

★3670★ **Safe Passage**
PO Box 621
De Kalb, IL 60115
Phone: (815)756-7930
Crisis Phone(s): (815)756-5228.

Decatur

★3671★ **DOVE**
788 E. Clay
Decatur, IL 62521
Phone: (217)428-6616
Crisis Phone(s): (217)423-2238 and (217)935-6072.

Des Plaines

★3672★ **Life Span**
PO Box 445
Des Plaines, IL 60016
Phone: (708)824-0382
Crisis Phone(s): (312)824-4454.

East St. Louis

★3673★ **Women's Crisis Center of Metro East**
East St. Louis Outreach Office
327 Missouri Ave., Ste. 625
East St. Louis, IL 62201
Toll-free: 800-924-0096
Crisis Phone(s): (618)875-7970.

Elgin

★3674★ **Community Crisis Center**
PO Box 1390
Elgin, IL 60121
Phone: (708)697-2380
Crisis Phone(s): (708)697-2380.

Evanston

★3675★ **YWCA**
Shelter for Battered Women and Their Children
PO Box 5164
Evanston, IL 60204
Phone: (708)864-8445
Crisis Phone(s): (708)864-8780.

Freeport

★3676★ **YWCA**
Domestic Violence Services
641 W. Stephenson St.
Freeport, IL 61032
Phone: (815)235-1681
Crisis Phone(s): (815)235-1641; (815)777-3680.

Glen Ellyn

★3677★ **Family Shelter Service**
PO Box 646
Glen Ellyn, IL 60138
Phone: (708)469-5652
Crisis Phone(s): (708)469-5650; (708)469-4878 (TDD).

Harrisburg

★3678★ **Anna Bixby Women's Center**
213 S. Shaw St.
Harrisburg, IL 62946
Phone: (618)252-8380
Crisis Phone(s): (618)252-8389.

Homewood

★3679★ **South Suburban Family Shelter**
PO Box 937
Homewood, IL 60430
Phone: (708)335-4125
Crisis Phone(s): (708)335-3028.

Jacksonville

★3680★ **Women's Crisis Center**
446 E. State
Jacksonville, IL 62650
Phone: (217)245-4357
Crisis Phone(s): (217)243-4357.

Joliet

**★3681★ Guardian Angel Home of Joliet
Groundwork**
1550 Plainfield Rd.
Joliet, IL 60435
Phone: (815)729-0930
Crisis Phone(s): (815)722-3344; (815)729-1228.

Kankakee

**★3682★ Coalition Against Domestic
Violence**
Harbor House
PO Box 1824
Kankakee, IL 60901
Phone: (815)932-5814
Crisis Phone(s): (815)932-5800 (Kankakee); (815)432-3500 (Watseka).

Lincoln

**★3683★ Logan County Committee Against
Domestic Violence and Sexual Assault**
1609 Broadway
Lincoln, IL 62656
Crisis Phone(s): (217)732-7011.

Macomb

**★3684★ Coalition Against Domestic
Violence**
PO Box 157
Macomb, IL 61455
Phone: (309)837-2997
Crisis Phone(s): (309)837-5555.

Moline

**★3685★ Domestic Violence Advocacy
Program**
111 19th Ave.
Moline, IL 61265
Phone: (309)797-1777

Oak Park

★3686★ Sarah's Inn
212 S. Marian, Ste. 11
Oak Park, IL 62450
Phone: (708)386-3305
Crisis Phone(s): (708)386-4225.

Olney

★3687★ Stopping Woman Abuse NOW
1114 S. West St.
Olney, IL 62450
Phone: (618)392-3556
Crisis Phone(s): (618)392-3556.

Peoria

★3688★ Tri-County WomenStrength
PO Box 3172
Peoria, IL 61612-3172
Phone: (309)691-0551
Crisis Phone(s): (309)691-4111.

Princeton

★3689★ Freedom House
PO Box 544
Princeton, IL 61356
Phone: (815)872-0087
Crisis Phone(s): (815)875-8233; (309)853-4961.

Quincy

★3690★ Quanada
c/o The Woodland Center
Quincy, IL 62301
Phone: (217)222-0069
Toll-free: 800-396-2287
Crisis Phone(s): (217)222-2873.

Rochelle

★3691★ HOPE
PO Box 131
Rochelle, IL 61068
Phone: (815)562-4323
Crisis Phone(s): (815)562-8890.

Rock Island

★3692★ Christian Family Care Center
PO Box 4176
Rock Island, IL 61204
Phone: (309)788-2276
Crisis Phone(s): (309)788-2273.

Rockford

★3693★ PHASE
Working Against Violent Environments
319 S. Church
Rockford, IL 61101
Phone: (815)962-0871
Crisis Phone(s): (815)962-6102.

Springfield

★3694★ Sojourn Women's Center
PO Box 4626
Springfield, IL 62708-4626
Phone: (217)544-0203
Crisis Phone(s): (217)544-2484.

Sterling

★3695★ YWCA
**Cove Domestic Violence and Sexual
Assault Program**
412 1st Ave.
Sterling, IL 61081
Phone: (815)625-0343
Crisis Phone(s): (815)626-7277; (815)288-1011; (815)772-7959.

Streator

★3696★ Alternatives to Domestic Violence
PO Box 593
Streator, IL 61364
Phone: (815)673-1555
Toll-free: 800-892-3375

Summit

**★3697★ Des Plaines Valley Community
Center**
Constance Morris House
6125 S. Archer Rd.
Summit, IL 60501
Phone: (708)485-0069
Crisis Phone(s): (708)485-5254; (708)485-5257 (TDD).

Tinley Park

★3698★ Crisis Center for South Suburbia
7700 Timber Dr.
Tinley Park, IL 60477
Phone: (708)429-7255
Crisis Phone(s): (708)429-7233.

Urbana

★3699★ A Woman's Fund
A Woman's Place
505 W. Green
Urbana, IL 61801
Phone: (217)384-4462
Crisis Phone(s): (217)384-4390.

Waukegan

★3700★ A Safe Place
PO Box 1067
Waukegan, IL 60079
Phone: (708)249-5147
Crisis Phone(s): (708)249-4450.

Woodstock

★3701★ Turning Point
PO Box 723
Woodstock, IL 60098
Phone: (815)338-8081
Toll-free: 800-892-8900
Crisis Phone(s): (800)897-8900 (in McHenry County).

Worth

★3702★ Crisis Center for South Suburbia
PO Box 304
Worth, IL 60482
Phone: (312)974-1091
Crisis Phone(s): (312)974-1791.

Wyanet

★3703★ Freedom House
PO Box 414
Wyanet, IL 61379
Phone: (815)699-7714
Crisis Phone(s): (815)875-8233.

Indiana

Anderson

★3704★ WAI: Center for Victim Services
PO Box 1302
Anderson, IN 46015-1302
Crisis Phone(s): (317)643-0200.

Bloomington

★3705★ Middle Way House
PO Box 95
Bloomington, IN 47402
Phone: (812)333-7404
Crisis Phone(s): (812)336-0846.

Columbus

★3706★ Turning Point
PO Box 103
Columbus, IN 47202
Toll-free: 800-221-6311
Crisis Phone(s): (812)379-9844.

Crawfordsville

★3707★ Family Crisis Shelter
PO Box 254
Crawfordsville, IN 47933
Crisis Phone(s): (317)362-2030.

Elkhart

★3708★ Elkhart County Women's Shelter
PO Box 2684
Elkhart, IN 46515
Phone: (219)294-1811
Crisis Phone(s): (219)293-8671.

★3709★ YWCA
Assist Women's Resource Center
200 E. Jackson Blvd.
Elkhart, IN 46516
Phone: (219)295-6915
Crisis Phone(s): (219)293-8671.

Evansville

★3710★ Albion Fellows Bacon Center
PO Box 3164
Evansville, IN 47731
Phone: (812)422-9372
Crisis Phone(s): (812)424-7273.

★3711★ YWCA
Shelter
118 Vine St.
Evansville, IN 47708
Crisis Phone(s): (812)422-1191.

Ft. Wayne

★3712★ YWCA
Shelter for Women Victims of Violence
PO Box 11242
Ft. Wayne, IN 46856-1242
Toll-free: 800-441-4073
Crisis Phone(s): (219)447-7233.

Gary

★3713★ Gary Commission for Women
The Ark Shelter
475 Broadway, Ste. 508
Gary, IN 46402
Phone: (219)882-0021
Crisis Phone(s): (219)882-0021.

★3714★ Gary Commission for Women
The Rainbow
475 Broadway, Ste. 508
Gary, IN 46402
Phone: (219)883-4155
Crisis Phone(s): (219)886-1600.

Hammond

★3715★ Haven House
834 Chicago Ave.
Hammond, IN 46327
Crisis Phone(s): (219)931-2090.

Hobart

★3716★ Caring Place
Brickyard Plaza
Hobart, IN 46342
Phone: (219)465-0164
Crisis Phone(s): (219)464-2128.

Indianapolis

★3717★ The Salvation Army
Social Service Center
540 N. Alabama St.
Indianapolis, IN 46204
Phone: (317)637-5551

★3718★ Sojourner
PO Box 88062
Indianapolis, IN 46208
Crisis Phone(s): (317)251-7575.

Kokomo

★3719★ YWCA
Family Intervention Center
PO Box 1303
Kokomo, IN 46903
Crisis Phone(s): (317)459-0314.

Lafayette

★3720★ YWCA
Women in Crisis Program
605 N. 6th St.
Lafayette, IN 47901
Phone: (317)423-1118
Crisis Phone(s): (317)423-1118.

Marion

★3721★ Women's Services
428 S. Washington
Marion, IN 46953
Crisis Phone(s): (317)664-0701.

Michigan City

★3722★ Stepping Stone
PO Box 1045
Michigan City, IN 46360
Crisis Phone(s): (219)879-4615 (Michigan City); (219)362-7777 (La Porte).

Muncie

★3723★ A Better Way
PO Box 734
Muncie, IN 47308
Phone: (317)747-9107
Crisis Phone(s): (317)747-9107.

New Albany

★3724★ The Center for Women and Families
Spouse Abuse Center
2818 Grant Line Rd.
New Albany, IN 47150-3492
Phone: (812)944-6743
Crisis Phone(s): (812)944-6743.

New Castle

★3725★ Lifeline for the Battered
PO Box 814
New Castle, IN 47362
Phone: (317)529-4866
Crisis Phone(s): (317)529-5313.

Richmond

★3726★ YWCA
Genesis/Friends of the Battered Shelter
1900 S. L St.
PO Box 2430
Richmond, IN 47375-2430
Phone: (317)935-3920
Crisis Phone(s): (317)935-3920; (800)243-4508.

South Bend

★3727★ YWCA
Women's Shelter
802 N. LaFayette Blvd.
South Bend, IN 46601
Phone: (219)233-9491
Crisis Phone(s): (219)232-9558.

Terre Haute

★3728★ Catholic Charities
Bethany House
Tribune Bldg.
Terre Haute, IN 47807
Phone: (812)232-1447
Crisis Phone(s): (812)232-4978.

★3729★ Council on Domestic Abuse
PO Box 392
Terre Haute, IN 47808
Phone: (812)232-0870
Crisis Phone(s): (812)232-1736.

Vincennes

★3730★ Harbor House
PO Box 601
Vincennes, IN 47591
Phone: (812)882-7900
Crisis Phone(s): (812)882-7900.

Warsaw

★3731★ The Beaman House
PO Box 12
Warsaw, IN 46580
Phone: (219)267-7701
Crisis Phone(s): (219)267-7701.

Iowa

Ames

★3732★ Assault Care Center Extending Shelter and Support
PO Box 1965
Ames, IA 50010
Phone: (515)232-5418
Crisis Phone(s): (515)232-2303.

Atlantic

★3733★ Family Violence Support Network
PO Box 11
Atlantic, IA 50022
Phone: (712)243-6615
Crisis Phone(s): (712)243-5123.

Burlington

★3734★ YWCA
Shelter and Sexual Assault Center
2410 Mount Pleasant
Burlington, IA 52601
Phone: (319)752-0606
Crisis Phone(s): (319)752-4475.

Carroll

★3735★ Domestic Abuse Prevention Center
PO Box 451
Carroll, IA 51401
Crisis Phone(s): (712)792-6722.

Cedar Rapids

★3736★ Intervention in Violence Against Women Project
PO Box 5201
Cedar Rapids, IA 52406
Phone: (319)362-9148

★3737★ YWCA
Domestic Violence Program and Shelter
318 5th St., SE
Cedar Rapids, IA 52401
Phone: (319)365-1458
Crisis Phone(s): (319)363-2093.

Cherokee

★3738★ Council Against Domestic Abuse
PO Box 962
Cherokee, IA 51012
Phone: (712)225-5003
Toll-free: 800-225-5003

Clarinda

★3739★ Waubonsie Mental Health Center
PO Box 457
Clarinda, IA 51632
Phone: (712)542-2388
Crisis Phone(s): (712)542-2388.

Clinton

★3740★ YWCA
Women's Resource Center
317 7th Ave., S.
Clinton, IA 52732
Phone: (319)242-2118
Crisis Phone(s): (319)243-STOP.

Council Bluffs

★3741★ Domestic Violence Program
315 W. Pierce
Council Bluffs, IA 51501
Phone: (712)328-3087
Crisis Phone(s): (712)328-0266.

Davenport

★3742★ Family Resources Domestic Violence Advocacy Program
PO Box 190
Davenport, IA 52805
Phone: (319)323-1852
Crisis Phone(s): (319)326-9191; (319)797-1777.

Decorah

★3743★ Helping Services for Northeast Iowa
Services for Abused Women
PO Box 372
Decorah, IA 52101
Phone: (319)382-2989
Toll-free: 800-383-2988

Des Moines

★3744★ Family Violence Center
1111 University Ave.
Des Moines, IA 50314-2329
Phone: (515)243-6147
Crisis Phone(s): (515)243-6147; (800)942-0333 (Iowa).

★3745★ Polk County Victim Services
1915 Hickman Rd.
Des Moines, IA 50314
Phone: (515)288-1050
Crisis Phone(s): (515)288-1750.

Dubuque

★3746★ YWCA
Battered Women Program
35 N. Booth
Dubuque, IA 52001
Phone: (319)556-3371
Crisis Phone(s): (319)588-4016.

Eldora

★3747★ Mid-Iowa Stepping Stones
Box 122
Eldora, IA 50627
Crisis Phone(s): (515)858-2618.

Estherville

★3748★ Council for the Prevention of Domestic Violence
16 N. 7th
PO Box 151
Estherville, IA 51334
Crisis Phone(s): (712)362-4612.

Ft. Dodge

★3749★ Family Violence Center
PO Box 173
Ft. Dodge, IA 50501
Phone: (515)955-2273
Crisis Phone(s): (515)955-5456.

Iowa City

★3750★ Domestic Violence Intervention Program
PO Box 733
Iowa City, IA 52244
Phone: (319)351-1042
Crisis Phone(s): (319)351-1043.

Keokuk

★3751★ Tri-State Coalition Against Family Violence
PO Box 494
Keokuk, IA 52632
Crisis Phone(s): (319)524-4445.

Malvern

★3752★ Stepping Stones
Domestic Abuse Program
PO Box 76
Malvern, IA 51551
Toll-free: 800-468-7333

Marshalltown

★3753★ Domestic Violence Alternatives
PO Box 1507
Marshalltown, IA 50158
Phone: (515)753-9332
Crisis Phone(s): (515)753-3513 (Marshall County); (800)779-3512 (Tama, Poweshiek, and Jasper Counties).

Mason City

★3754★ Crisis Intervention Service
22 N. Georgia, Ste. 216
Mason City, IA 50401
Phone: (515)424-9071
Crisis Phone(s): (515)424-9133.

Muscatine

★3755★ **Muscatine County Rape/Assault Care Services**
Medical Arts Bldg.
Muscatine, IA 52761
Phone: (319)263-0067
Crisis Phone(s): (319)263-8080.

Ottumwa

★3756★ **Adult Life/Family Crisis Association**
PO Box 446
Ottumwa, IA 52501
Phone: (515)683-3123
Crisis Phone(s): (515)683-3122.

Pella

★3757★ **Turning Point**
PO Box 302
Pella, IA 50219
Phone: (515)628-4901
Toll-free: 800-433-SAFE

Sioux City

★3758★ **Council Against Domestic Abuse**
237 Commerce Blvd.
Sioux City, IA 51101
Phone: (712)225-5003
Crisis Phone(s): (712)434-2343.

★3759★ **Council on Sexual Assault and Domestic Violence**
PO Box 1565
Sioux City, IA 51102
Phone: (712)258-7233
Toll-free: 800-982-7233
Crisis Phone(s): (712)258-7233.

★3760★ **Domestic Violence Aid Center**
128 3rd St. NW
Sioux City, IA 51250
Phone: (712)722-4404
Crisis Phone(s): (712)737-3307.

Waterloo

★3761★ **Crisis Services**
2530 University Ave.
Waterloo, IA 50701
Phone: (319)233-8484
Crisis Phone(s): (319)233-8484.

Kansas

Colby

★3762★ **Northwest Kansas Family Shelter**
PO Box 502
Colby, KS 67701
Crisis Phone(s): (913)462-8161.

Concordia

★3763★ **Domestic Violence Task Force**
c/o Concordia Police Department
103 W. 9th St.
PO Box 402
Concordia, KS 66901
Crisis Phone(s): (913)243-3131.

Dodge City

★3764★ **Crisis Center**
PO Box 1173
Dodge City, KS 67801
Phone: (316)225-6987
Crisis Phone(s): (316)225-6510.

Emporia

★3765★ **SOS, Inc.**
PO Box 1191
Emporia, KS 66801
Phone: 800-825-1295
Crisis Phone(s): (316)342-1870.

Garden City

★3766★ **Family Crisis Service Domestic Violence Program**
PO Box 1092
Garden City, KS 67846
Phone: (316)275-2018
Crisis Phone(s): (316)275-5911.

Great Bend

★3767★ **Family Crisis Center**
PO Box 1543
Great Bend, KS 67530
Phone: (316)792-3672
Crisis Phone(s): (316)792-1885.

Hays

★3768★ **Northwest Kansas Family Shelter**
PO Box 284
Hays, KS 67601
Toll-free: 800-794-4624
Crisis Phone(s): (913)625-3055.

Hiawatha

★3769★ **Northeast Kansas Family Violence Intervention Program**
PO Box 264
Hiawatha, KS 66434
Phone: (913)486-2825
Crisis Phone(s): (913)486-2131.

Hutchinson

★3770★ **Reno County Victims of Abuse Network**
PO Box 2856
Hutchinson, KS 67504
Phone: (316)663-2522
Crisis Phone(s): (316)663-2522.

★3771★ **Sexual Assault/Domestic Violence Center**
1 E. 9th St.
Hutchinson, KS 67501
Phone: (316)663-3630
Crisis Phone(s): (316)663-2522.

Iola

★3772★ **Hope Unlimited**
PO Box 12
Iola, KS 66749
Phone: (316)365-7566

Kansas City

★3773★ **Friends of Yates Rebecca Vincson Battered Women's Center**
PO Box 1514
Kansas City, KS 66117
Phone: (913)321-1566
Crisis Phone(s): (913)321-0951.

Lawrence

★3774★ **Women's Transitional Care Services**
PO Box 633
Lawrence, KS 66044
Crisis Phone(s): (913)841-6887.

Leavenworth

★3775★ **Alliance Against Family Violence**
PO Box 465
Leavenworth, KS 66408
Phone: (913)682-1752
Crisis Phone(s): (913)682-9131.

Manhattan

★3776★ **Crisis Center**
PO Box 1526
Manhattan, KS 66502
Crisis Phone(s): (913)539-2785.

McPherson

★3777★ **McPherson County Council on Violence Against Persons**
PO Box 406
McPherson, KS 67460
Phone: (316)241-1650
Crisis Phone(s): (316)241-6615.

Pittsburg

★3778★ **Safehouse**
101 E. 4th, Ste. 214
Pittsburg, KS 66762
Phone: (316)231-8692
Toll-free: 800-794-9148
Crisis Phone(s): (316)231-8251.

Salina

★3779★ Domestic Violence Association of Central Kansas
1700 E. Iron
Salina, KS 67401
Phone: (913)827-5862
Crisis Phone(s): (913)827-4747.

Scott City

★3780★ Help Everyone Live Peaceably
301 Court St.
Scott City, KS 67871
Crisis Phone(s): (316)872-2133.

Topeka

★3781★ YWCA
Battered Women Task Force
PO Box 1883
Topeka, KS 66601
Phone: (913)354-7927
Crisis Phone(s): (913)233-1730.

Wichita

★3782★ YWCA
Women's Crisis Center/Safehouse
PO Box 1740
Wichita, KS 67201
Phone: (316)263-9806
Crisis Phone(s): (316)263-2313.

Winfield

★3783★ Cowley County Safe Homes
PO Box 181
Winfield, KS 67156
Phone: (316)221-7300
Crisis Phone(s): (316)221-4357.

Kentucky

Ashland

★3784★ Safe Harbor of Northeast Kentucky
PO Box 2163
Ashland, KY 41101
Phone: (606)329-9304
Crisis Phone(s): (606)329-9304; (800)926-2150 (Kentucky).

Beattyville

★3785★ Resurrection Home
68 Resurrection Rd.
Beattyville, KY 41311
Phone: (606)464-8481
Crisis Phone(s): (606)464-8481.

Bowling Green

★3786★ Brass, Inc.
PO Box 1945
Bowling Green, KY 42102-1945
Phone: (502)843-1183
Crisis Phone(s): (502)843-1183.

Danville

★3787★ Collins, Kubale, and Miles
219 S. 4th St.
Danville, KY 40422
Phone: (606)236-0853
Crisis Phone(s): (606)236-0853.

Elizabethtown

★3788★ Lincoln Trail Domestic Violence Program
PO Box 2047
Elizabethtown, KY 42701
Phone: (502)765-4057
Crisis Phone(s): (502)769-1234; and (800)767-5838.

Hopkinsville

★3789★ Sanctuary, Inc.
PO Box 1265
Hopkinsville, KY 42240
Phone: (502)885-4572
Crisis Phone(s): (502)886-8174.

Lexington

★3790★ YWCA
Spouse Abuse Center
PO Box 8028
Lexington, KY 40533-8028
Phone: (606)255-9808
Crisis Phone(s): (800)544-2022 (Kentucky).

Louisville

★3791★ YWCA
Center for Women and Families
226 W. Breckenridge St.
Louisville, KY 40203-2232
Phone: (502)581-7225
Crisis Phone(s): (502)581-7222.

Martin

★3792★ Big Sandy Family Abuse Center
Box 1166
Martin, KY 41649
Phone: (606)285-5004
Crisis Phone(s): (606)285-9193.

Maysville

★3793★ Women's Crisis Center
PO Box 484
Maysville, KY 41056
Phone: (606)564-6708
Crisis Phone(s): (800)928-6708.

Mt. Vernon

★3794★ Family Life Abuse Center
PO Box 674
Mt. Vernon, KY 40456
Phone: (606)256-9511
Crisis Phone(s): (606)256-2724.

Murray

★3795★ Spouse Abuse Hotline and Safehouse
PO Box 910
Murray, KY 42071
Phone: (502)753-4050
Crisis Phone(s): (502)759-4050.

Newport

★3796★ Women's Crisis Center
321 York St.
Newport, KY 41071
Crisis Phone(s): (606)491-3335.

Owensboro

★3797★ Owensboro Area Spouse Abuse and Information Center
1316 W. 4th St.
Owensboro, KY 42301
Crisis Phone(s): (502)685-0260.

Paducah

★3798★ Purchase Area Spouse Abuse Center
PO Box 98
Paducah, KY 42002-0098
Phone: (502)443-6001
Crisis Phone(s): (502)443-6001.

Red Fox

★3799★ LKLP Women and Children's Safe House
HC 32, Box 2150
Red Fox, KY 41847
Phone: (606)439-1552
Crisis Phone(s): (606)439-5129.

Somerset

★3800★ Bethany House
PO Box 864
Somerset, KY 42501
Phone: (606)679-1553
Toll-free: 800-755-2071
Crisis Phone(s): (606)679-8852.

Williamstown

★3801★ Women's Crisis Center
PO Box 294
Williamstown, KY 41097
Toll-free: 800-928-3335
Crisis Phone(s): (606)824-7697.

Louisiana

Alexandria

★3802★ Family Counseling Agency
Battered Women's Program
PO Box 1908
Alexandria, LA 71309-1908
Phone: (318)442-7196
Toll-free: 800-960-9436

Baton Rouge

★3803★ Capital Area Family Violence
Intervention Center
Battered Women's Program
PO Box 2133
Baton Rouge, LA 70821
Toll-free: 800-541-9706

Crisis Phone(s): (504)389-3001.

Franklin

★3804★ Chez Hope, Inc.
PO Box 98
Franklin, LA 70538
Phone: (318)923-4537
Toll-free: 800-331-5303

Hammond

★3805★ Southeast Spouse Abuse
Program
PO Box 1946
Hammond, LA 70404
Phone: (504)542-8384
Toll-free: 800-256-1143

Crisis Phone(s): (504)542-8384.

Houma

★3806★ YWCA
Bayou Area Family Violence Program
PO Box 9014
Houma, LA 70361-9014
Phone: (504)851-5950

Crisis Phone(s): (504)851-5950; (504)872-1111.

Jefferson

★3807★ Metropolitan Battered Women's
Program
PO Box 10775
Jefferson, LA 70181
Phone: (504)837-5400

Crisis Phone(s): (800)738-8900 (Louisiana
only).

Lafayette

★3808★ Faith House
PO Box 93145
Lafayette, LA 70509
Phone: (318)232-2770

Crisis Phone(s): (318)232-8954.

Lake Charles

★3809★ Calcasieu Women's Shelter
PO Box 276
Lake Charles, LA 70602
Toll-free: 800-223-8066

Crisis Phone(s): (318)436-4552.

Monroe

★3810★ YWCA
Family Violence Program
1515 Jackson St.
Monroe, LA 71202
Phone: (318)323-1505

Crisis Phone(s): (318)323-1543; (318)387-4357.

New Iberia

★3811★ Safety Net for Abused Persons
PO Box 10207
New Iberia, LA 70562
Phone: (318)367-7627

New Orleans

★3812★ Crescent House
1231 Prytania St.
New Orleans, LA 70130
Phone: (504)523-3755

★3813★ YWCA
Battered Women's Program
601 S. Jefferson Davis Pkwy.
New Orleans, LA 70119
Phone: (504)486-7666

Crisis Phone(s): (504)486-0377.

Shreveport

★3814★ YWCA
Family Violence Program
710 Travis St.
Shreveport, LA 71101
Phone: (318)222-2117
Toll-free: 800-338-6536

Crisis Phone(s): (318)222-2117.

Slidell

★3815★ YWCA
St. Tammany Battered Women's Program
PO Box 634
Slidell, LA 70459

Crisis Phone(s): (504)643-9407.

Maine

Auburn

★3816★ Abused Women's Advocacy
Project
PO Box 713
Auburn, ME 04210

Crisis Phone(s): (207)795-4020.

Augusta

★3817★ Family Violence Project
PO Box 304
Augusta, ME 04332
Phone: (207)623-3569
Toll-free: 800-452-1930

Crisis Phone(s): (207)623-3569.

Bangor

★3818★ Spruce Run
PO Box 653
Bangor, ME 04402
Phone: (207)945-5102

Crisis Phone(s): (207)947-0496.

Caribou

★3819★ Family Support Center
Battered Women's Project
PO Box 1358
Caribou, ME 04736-1358
Phone: (207)498-6570
Toll-free: 800-439-2323

Crisis Phone(s): (207)769-8251.

Dover-Foxcroft

★3820★ Womancare/Aegis Association
PO Box 192
Dover-Foxcroft, ME 04426
Phone: (207)564-8165

Crisis Phone(s): (207)564-8165 (business hrs.);
(207)564-8401 (evenings & weekends).

Ellsworth

★3821★ Spruce Run
PO Box 524
Ellsworth, ME 04605
Phone: (207)667-2426

Crisis Phone(s): (207)667-9489; and (207)723-5664.

Houlton

★3822★ Battered Women's Project
PO Box 986
Houlton, ME 04730
Phone: (207)532-4004

Crisis Phone(s): (207)769-8251.

Machias

★3823★ Womankind
PO Box 493
Machias, ME 04654
Phone: (207)255-4785
Toll-free: 800-432-7303

Portland

★3824★ Family Crisis Shelter
PO Box 704
Portland, ME 04104
Phone: (207)874-1197
Toll-free: 800-537-6066

Crisis Phone(s): (207)774-HELP.

Presque Isle

★3825★ Family Support Center
PO Box 22
Presque Isle, ME 04769
Phone: (207)498-6146

Crisis Phone(s): (207)769-8251.

Rockland

★3826★ New Hope for Women
PO Box 642
Rockland, ME 04841
Phone: (207)594-2128

Crisis Phone(s): (207)594-2128.

Sanford

★3827★ Caring Unlimited
York County Domestic Violence Center
PO Box 590
Sanford, ME 04073
Phone: (207)490-3900

Crisis Phone(s): (207)282-2182; (207)324-1802.

Skowhegan

★3828★ Family Violence Project
PO Box 3104
Skowhegan, ME 04976
Phone: (207)474-8860
Toll-free: 800-452-1930

Maryland

Annapolis

★3829★ YWCA
Women's Center
167 Duke of Gloucester St.
Annapolis, MD 21401

Crisis Phone(s): (301)268-4393; (301)269-0378.

Baltimore

★3830★ Family and Children's Services of Central Maryland
Battered Spouse Program
7131 Liberty Rd., Ste. 202
Baltimore, MD 21207
Phone: (410)281-1334

★3831★ Family Crisis Center
PO Box 3909
Baltimore, MD 21222
Phone: (410)285-4357

Crisis Phone(s): (410)828-6398.

★3832★ House of Ruth
2201 Argonne Dr.
Baltimore, MD 21218
Phone: (410)889-0840

Crisis Phone(s): (410)889-7884.

Bel Air

★3833★ Sexual Assault/Spouse Abuse Resource Center
101 Thomas St.
Bel Air, MD 21014
Phone: (301)836-8430

Crisis Phone(s): (301)836-8430; (301)879-3486 (Baltimore).

Bethesda

★3834★ Community Crisis Center
Abused Persons Program
4905 Del Ray Ave., No. 200
Bethesda, MD 20814
Phone: (301)986-5885

Crisis Phone(s): (301)654-1881, and (301)657-4110 (TDD).

Brentwood

★3835★ Family Crisis Center
3611 43rd Ave.
Brentwood, MD 20722-1926
Phone: (301)864-9101

Crisis Phone(s): (301)864-9101.

California

★3836★ Walden-Sierra Inc.
PO Box 1238
California, MD 20619-1238
Phone: (301)863-6661

Columbia

★3837★ Citizens Against Spouse Abuse
8950 Gorman Plaza, Ste. 116
Columbia, MD 21045
Phone: (301)997-0304

Crisis Phone(s): (301)997-2272.

Cumberland

★3838★ Family Crisis Resource Center
153 Baltimore St., 3rd Fl.
Cumberland, MD 21502-2398
Phone: (301)759-9246

Crisis Phone(s): (301)759-9244.

Denton

★3839★ Mid-Shore Council on Family Violence
PO Box 5
Denton, MD 21629
Phone: (301)759-9246
Toll-free: 800-479-HOPE

Crisis Phone(s): (301)759-9244.

Elderburg

★3840★ The Unity Group
PO Box 753
Elderburg, MD 21784
Phone: (301)795-4849

Crisis Phone(s): (301)795-4849.

Elkton

★3841★ Cecil County Department of Social Services
Domestic Violence Program
PO Box 2137
Elkton, MD 21922
Phone: (410)392-5030

Crisis Phone(s): (301)392-5030.

Frederick

★3842★ Heartly House, Inc.
PO Box 831
Frederick, MD 21701

Crisis Phone(s): (301)662-8800.

Hagerstown

★3843★ Citizens Against Spouse Abuse
116 W. Baltimore St.
Hagerstown, MD 21740
Phone: (301)739-4990

Crisis Phone(s): (301)739-8975.

Prince Frederick

★3844★ Calvert County Health Department
Abused Persons Program
Rte. 4 at Stoakley Rd.
Prince Frederick, MD 20678
Phone: (301)535-5400

Crisis Phone(s): (410)535-1121; (301)855-1075.

Salisbury

★3845★ Life Crisis Center
PO Box 387
Salisbury, MD 21803
Phone: (301)749-4357

Crisis Phone(s): (301)749-4357; (301)749-0632 (TDD).

Towson

★3846★ Sexual Assault/Domestic Violence Center
6229 N. Charles St.
Towson, MD 21212
Phone: (410)337-8111

Crisis Phone(s): (410)828-6391.

Waldorf

★3847★ Community Crisis and Referral Center
PO Box 1291
Waldorf, MD 20604
Phone: (301)843-1110

Crisis Phone(s): (301)645-3336.

Westminster

★3848★ Family and Children's Services of Central Maryland
Battered Spouse Program
22 N. Court St.
Westminster, MD 21157
Phone: (410)876-1233

Crisis Phone(s): (301)857-0077.

White Plains

★3849★ Community Crisis and Referral Center
6311 Theodore Green Blvd., No. B
White Plains, MD 20695-9552
Phone: (301)843-1110

Crisis Phone(s): (301)645-3336.

Massachusetts

Attleboro

★3850★   New Hope Center
PO Box 1036
Attleboro, MA 02703
Phone: (617)226-4015
Crisis Phone(s): (617)695-2113.

Boston

★3851★   Casa Myrna Vazquez
PO Box 18019
Boston, MA 02118
Phone: (617)262-9581
Crisis Phone(s): (800)992-2600.

Brockton

★3852★   Womansplace
PO Box 4206
Brockton, MA 02403
Phone: (508)588-2042
Crisis Phone(s): (508)588-2041.

Cambridge

★3853★   Transition House
PO Box 530, Harvard Square Sta.
Cambridge, MA 02238
Phone: (617)354-2676
Crisis Phone(s): (617)661-7203.

Chelsea

★3854★   Harbor Me
PO Box 191
Chelsea, MA 02150
Phone: (617)884-8974
Crisis Phone(s): (617)889-2111.

Dorchester

★3855★   Mary Lawson Foreman House of CMV
PO Box 49
Dorchester, MA 02125
Crisis Phone(s): (617)262-9764.

Fall River

★3856★   GFRFP/Rape Crisis
337 Hanover St.
Fall River, MA 02706
Phone: (617)673-2400
Crisis Phone(s): (617)673-2400.

★3857★   Stanley Street Treatment and Resources Women's Center
386 Stanley St.
Fall River, MA 02720
Phone: (508)675-0087
Crisis Phone(s): (508)675-0087.

Fitchburg

★3858★   Women's Resources
PO Box 2503
Fitchburg, MA 01420
Phone: (508)342-2919
Crisis Phone(s): (508)342-9355; (508)630-1031; and (508)368-1311.

Greenfield

★3859★   New England Learning Center for Women in Transition
25 Forest Ave.
Greenfield, MA 01301-1916
Phone: (413)772-0871
Crisis Phone(s): (413)772-0806.

Haverhill

★3860★   Women's Resource Center
26 White St.
Haverhill, MA 01860
Phone: (617)373-4041
Crisis Phone(s): (617)373-4041.

Holyoke

★3861★   Womanshelter/Companeras
PO Box 6099
Holyoke, MA 01041
Crisis Phone(s): (413)536-1628.

Hyannis

★3862★   Independence House
105 Pleasant St.
Hyannis, MA 02601-3126
Phone: (617)771-6507
Crisis Phone(s): (617)428-4720.

Jamaica Plain

★3863★   Boston Indian Council Native Women Against Violence
105 S. Huntington Ave.
Jamaica Plain, MA 02130
Phone: (617)232-0343

★3864★   Elizabeth Stone House
PO Box 59
Jamaica Plain, MA 02130
Crisis Phone(s): (617)522-3417.

Lawrence

★3865★   Women's Resource Center Latinos Against Sexual Assault
454 N. Canal St.
Lawrence, MA 01840
Phone: (508)685-2480
Crisis Phone(s): (508)685-2480.

Lowell

★3866★   Alternative House
PO Box 2096, Highland Sta.
Lowell, MA 01851
Phone: (508)458-0274
Crisis Phone(s): (508)454-1436.

Malden

★3867★   Adult/Adolescent Counseling in Development Services Against Family Violence
110 Pleasant St.
Malden, MA 02148
Crisis Phone(s): (617)324-2221.

Natick

★3868★   Women's Protective Services
251 W. Central St.
Natick, MA 01760
Phone: (617)653-4464
Crisis Phone(s): (617)651-3300.

New Bedford

★3869★   New Bedford Women's Center Battered Women's Project
252 County St.
New Bedford, MA 02740
Crisis Phone(s): (508)992-4222.

Newburyport

★3870★   Women's Crisis Center
8 Prince Pl.
Newburyport, MA 01950
Phone: (617)465-2155
Crisis Phone(s): (617)465-2155.

Northampton

★3871★   Necessities/Necesidades
55 Fairview Ave.
Northampton, MA 01060-3857
Phone: (413)586-1125
Crisis Phone(s): (413)586-5066.

Plymouth

★3872★   South Shore Women's Center
85 Samoset St.
Plymouth, MA 02360-4557
Phone: (617)746-2664
Crisis Phone(s): (508)746-2664.

Roxbury Crossing

★3873★   Renewal House
PO Box 919
Roxbury Crossing, MA 02120
Phone: (617)277-4194
Crisis Phone(s): (617)566-6881.

Salem

★3874★   Help for Abused Women and Their Children
9 Crombie St.
Salem, MA 01970
Phone: (508)744-8552
Crisis Phone(s): (508)744-6841.

Somerville

★3875★ RESPOND
PO Box 555
Somerville, MA 02143
Crisis Phone(s): (617)623-5900.

Springfield

★3876★ Hotline to End Rape and Abuse
PO Box 80632
Springfield, MA 01138
Crisis Phone(s): (413)733-7100.

Waltham

**★3877★ Waltham Battered Women
Support Committee**
PO Box 24
Waltham, MA 02251
Crisis Phone(s): (617)891-0724.

Westfield

★3878★ New Beginnings
PO Box 1835
Westfield, MA 01086
Phone: (413)562-5739
Crisis Phone(s): (413)562-1920.

Worcester

★3879★ Abby's House
21-23 Crown St.
Worcester, MA 01609
Crisis Phone(s): (508)756-5486.

★3880★ Daybreak, Inc.
72 Cambridge St., No. 222
Worcester, MA 01603-2369
Phone: (508)755-5371
Crisis Phone(s): (508)755-9030.

Michigan

Adrian

**★3881★ Call Someone Concerned
Domestic Violence Program**
227 N. Winter St.,Ste. 215
Adrian, MI 49221-2043
Phone: (517)263-6739
Crisis Phone(s): (517)263-6737; (800)322-0044 (517 area only).

**★3882★ Family Counseling and Children's
Services**
213 Toledo St.
Adrian, MI 49221
Phone: (517)265-5352
Crisis Phone(s): (313)265-6776.

Alpena

★3883★ Shelter, Inc.
PO Box 797
Alpena, MI 49707
Phone: (517)356-6265
Crisis Phone(s): (517)356-9650.

Ann Arbor

**★3884★ Domestic Violence Project, Inc.
Safe House**
PO Box 7052
Ann Arbor, MI 48107
Phone: (313)973-0242
Crisis Phone(s): (313)995-5444.

Battle Creek

**★3885★ Battle Creek Area Organization
Against Domestic Violence
Safe Place**
PO Box 199
Battle Creek, MI 49016
Phone: (616)965-6093
Crisis Phone(s): (616)965-7233.

Bay City

★3886★ Bay County Women's Center
PO Box 1458
Bay City, MI 48706
Phone: (517)686-4551
Crisis Phone(s): (517)893-4555.

Benton Harbor

★3887★ Safe Shelter
275 Pipestone
Benton Harbor, MI 49022
Phone: (616)925-2280
Crisis Phone(s): (616)983-4275.

Big Rapids

★3888★ Women's Information Service
PO Box 1074
Big Rapids, MI 49307
Phone: (616)796-6692
Crisis Phone(s): (616)796-6600.

Cadillac

★3889★ OASIS
PO Box 955
Cadillac, MI 49601
Phone: (616)775-7299
Crisis Phone(s): (616)775-7233.

Calumet

★3890★ Barbara Kettle Gundlach Shelter
PO Box 8
Calumet, MI 49913
Phone: (906)337-5632
Crisis Phone(s): (906)337-5623.

Caro

**★3891★ Thumb Area Assault Crisis
Center**
c/o Human Development Commission
Caro, MI 48723
Phone: (517)673-4121
Toll-free: 800-292-3666

Coldwater

**★3892★ Branch County Coalition Against
Domestic Violence**
PO Box 72
Coldwater, MI 49036
Phone: (517)278-7432
Crisis Phone(s): (517)278-7432.

Detroit

★3893★ My Sister's Place
PO Box 13500
Detroit, MI 48213
Phone: (313)921-3902

★3894★ RESPOND
2727 2nd Ave.
Detroit, MI 48201-2627
Phone: (313)342-0300

**★3895★ YWCA
Interim House**
PO Box 21904
Detroit, MI 48221
Phone: (313)861-5300

East Lansing

★3896★ Gateway Community Services
910 Abbott Rd., Ste. 100
East Lansing, MI 48823
Phone: (517)337-4000
Toll-free: 800-292-4517

Escanaba

**★3897★ Delta County Alliance Against
Violence and Abuse, Inc.**
1019 Ludington
Escanaba, MI 49829
Phone: (906)789-9207

Flint

★3898★ Domestic Violence Connection
PO Box 74
Flint, MI 48501-0074
Phone: (313)767-9236
Crisis Phone(s): (313)767-9236.

★3899★ Violence Injures All
PO Box 3297
Flint, MI 48502
Phone: (313)767-5958
Crisis Phone(s): (313)767-5958.

**★3900★ YWCA
Safe House**
310 E. 3rd St.
Flint, MI 48502
Phone: (313)238-7621
Crisis Phone(s): (313)238-7233.

Grand Rapids

**★3901★ YWCA
Domestic Crisis Center**
25 Sheldon Blvd. SE
Grand Rapids, MI 49503
Phone: (616)451-2744
Crisis Phone(s): (616)451-2744 (9 am - 5 pm); (616)774-3535 (after 5 pm).

Grayling

★3902★ River House
PO Box 661
Grayling, MI 49738
Phone: (517)348-3169
Crisis Phone(s): (517)348-8972.

Hillsdale

★3903★ Domestic Harmony
PO Box 231
Hillsdale, MI 49242
Phone: (517)439-1454
Crisis Phone(s): (517)439-1454.

Holland

★3904★ Center for Women in Transition
304 Garden Ave.
Holland, MI 49424
Phone: (616)842-4357
Toll-free: 800-851-4054
Crisis Phone(s): (616)842-4357.

Howell

★3905★ Livingston Area Council Against Spouse Abuse
PO Box 72
Howell, MI 48843
Phone: (517)548-1350
Crisis Phone(s): (313)227-7100.

Ionia

★3906★ Eight Cap, Inc.
Ionia/Montcalm Domestic Violence Program
PO Box 93
Ionia, MI 48846
Phone: (616)527-3351
Crisis Phone(s): (616)527-3351 (before 5pm); (616)527-5252 (after 5pm & weekends).

Iron Mountain

★3907★ Caring House
PO Box 184
Iron Mountain, MI 49801
Phone: (906)774-1337
Crisis Phone(s): (906)774-1112; (800)232-3226 (in area codes 906, 715, and 414).

Ironwood

★3908★ Domestic Violence Escape
PO Box 366
Ironwood, MI 49938
Phone: (906)932-4990
Crisis Phone(s): (906)932-0310.

Jackson

★3909★ AWARE
PO Box 1526
Jackson, MI 49204
Phone: (517)783-2861
Crisis Phone(s): (517)783-2861.

Kalamazoo

★3910★ YWCA
Domestic Assault Program
353 E. Michigan Ave.
Kalamazoo, MI 49007
Phone: (616)385-2869
Crisis Phone(s): (616)385-3587.

L'Anse

★3911★ Baraga County Shelter Home
11 S. 4th St.
L'Anse, MI 49946
Phone: (906)524-5017

Lansing

★3912★ Council Against Domestic Assault
PO Box 14149
Lansing, MI 48901
Phone: (517)372-5976
Crisis Phone(s): (517)372-5572; (517)372-5576 (TDD).

Lawrence

★3913★ Van Cas Cap
Youth and Domestic Violence Program
488 S. Paw Paw St.
Lawrence, MI 49064
Phone: (616)674-3905

Ludington

★3914★ Region Four Community Services
210 N. Harrison St.
Ludington, MI 49431
Phone: (616)843-2539
Crisis Phone(s): (616)845-5808.

Manistee

★3915★ CHOICES
PO Box 604
Manistee, MI 49660
Phone: (616)723-6597
Crisis Phone(s): (616)723-6004.

Marquette

★3916★ Harbor House/Women's Center
PO Box 517
Marquette, MI 49855
Phone: (906)225-1346
Crisis Phone(s): (906)226-6611.

Midland

★3917★ Council on Domestic Violence and Sexual Assault
PO Box 2289
Midland, MI 48641
Phone: (517)835-6771

Monroe

★3918★ Family Counseling and Shelter Services
502 W. Elm Ave., Ste. G
Monroe, MI 48161-2833
Phone: (313)241-2380
Crisis Phone(s): (313)242-7233.

Mt. Clemens

★3919★ Turning Point
PO Box 1123
Mt. Clemens, MI 48043
Phone: (313)463-4430
Crisis Phone(s): (313)463-6990.

Mt. Pleasant

★3920★ Women's Aid Service
Domestic Violence Project
PO Box 743
Mt. Pleasant, MI 48804
Phone: (517)773-0078
Crisis Phone(s): (517)772-9168.

Muskegon

★3921★ Catholic Social Services
Battered Women's Services
1095 3rd St.
Muskegon, MI 49441
Phone: (616)726-4735
Crisis Phone(s): (616)726-4735.

★3922★ Child and Family Services
1352 Terrace St.
Muskegon, MI 49442
Phone: (616)726-3582

★3923★ Circuit Court Family Counseling Services
440 S. Quarterline
Muskegon, MI 49441
Phone: (616)726-4493
Crisis Phone(s): (616)726-4493.

★3924★ Every Woman's Place
Crisis Center
1706 Peck St.
Muskegon, MI 49441
Phone: (616)726-4493
Crisis Phone(s): (616)722-3333 (after 5pm).

★3925★ Muskegon County Community Mental Health Services
125 E. Southern St.
Muskegon, MI 49442
Phone: (616)726-5266

★3926★ Women's Aid Service
1706 Peck St.
Muskegon, MI 49441
Phone: (616)726-4493
Crisis Phone(s): (616)722-3333 after 5:00 p.m. and weekends.

Petoskey

★3927★ Women's Resource Center of Northern Michigan
Domestic Violence Shelter Project
1515 Howard St.
Petoskey, MI 49770
Phone: (616)347-0067
Crisis Phone(s): (616)347-0082.

Pontiac

★3928★ HAVEN
PO Box 787
Pontiac, MI 48343
Phone: (313)334-1284
Crisis Phone(s): (313)334-1274.

Port Huron

★3929★ Domestic Assault and Rape Elimination Services
1625 Pine Grove Ave.
Port Huron, MI 48060
Phone: (313)985-4950
Crisis Phone(s): (313)985-5538.

Saginaw

★3930★ Underground Railroad
PO Box 565
Saginaw, MI 48606
Crisis Phone(s): (517)755-0411.

St. Johns

★3931★ Relief After Violent Encounters
PO Box 472
St. Johns, MI 48879
Phone: (517)224-4662
Crisis Phone(s): (517)224-7283.

Sault Ste. Marie

★3932★ Eastern Upper Peninsula Domestic Violence Program
PO Box 636
Sault Ste. Marie, MI 49783
Phone: (906)635-0566

Three Rivers

★3933★ St. Joseph County Domestic Assault Shelter Coalition
PO Box 402
Three Rivers, MI 49093
Phone: (616)279-5122
Toll-free: 800-828-2023
Crisis Phone(s): (616)279-5122; (800)828-2023.

Traverse City

★3934★ Women's Resource Center of Grand Traverse
1017 Hannah
Traverse City, MI 49684
Phone: (616)941-1210
Crisis Phone(s): (616)941-1210; and (616)946-1211 (TDD).

Westland

**★3935★ First Step
Project on Domestic Violence and Sexual Assault**
8381 Farmington Rd.
Westland, MI 48185
Phone: (313)525-2230
Crisis Phone(s): (313)459-5900.

Ypsilanti

**★3936★ Washtenaw County Community Mental Health Center
Assault Crisis Center**
1866 Packard
Ypsilanti, MI 48197
Phone: (313)483-7942
Crisis Phone(s): (313)483-7273.

Minnesota

Aitkin

★3937★ Aitkin County Women's Advocates
PO Box 153
Aitkin, MN 56431-0153
Phone: (218)927-2327
Crisis Phone(s): (218)828-1216.

Albert Lea

★3938★ Freeborn County Victims's Crisis Center
PO Box 649
Albert Lea, MN 56007
Phone: (507)373-2223
Crisis Phone(s): (507)373-2223.

Austin

**★3939★ Victim's Crisis Center
St. Olaf Mental Health and Treatment Center**
101 14th St. NW
Austin, MN 55912
Crisis Phone(s): (507)437-6680.

Belle Plaine

★3940★ Southern Valley Alliance for Battered Women
PO Box 102
Belle Plaine, MN 56011
Phone: (612)873-4214

Bemidji

★3941★ Northwoods Coalition for Battered Women
PO Box 563
Bemidji, MN 56601
Crisis Phone(s): (218)751-0211.

Bloomington

★3942★ Cornerstone Advocacy Service
2131 W. Old Shakopee Rd.
Bloomington, MN 55431
Phone: (612)884-0376
Crisis Phone(s): (612)884-0330.

★3943★ United Battered Families Network
PO Box 31147
Bloomington, MN 55431
Phone: (612)881-1872

Brainerd

★3944★ Mid-Minnesota Women's Center
PO Box 602
Brainerd, MN 56401
Crisis Phone(s): (218)828-1216.

Brooklyn Center

**★3945★ Brooklyn Center
Domestic Abuse Intervention Project**
6301 Shingle Creek Pkwy.
Brooklyn Center, MN 55430
Phone: (612)569-3434
Crisis Phone(s): (612)569-3339.

Burnsville

**★3946★ Womankind
Support Systems for Battered Women**
Fairview Ridges Hospital
201 E. Nicollet Blvd.
Burnsville, MN 55337
Phone: (612)892-2500
Crisis Phone(s): (612)892-2500.

Caledonia

★3947★ Houston County Women's Resources
PO Box 422
Caledonia, MN 55921
Phone: (507)724-2676
Toll-free: 800-356-9588

Cambridge

★3948★ The Refuge for Battered Adults
PO Box 323
Cambridge, MN 55008
Phone: (612)689-3532
Crisis Phone(s): (612)689-3532.

Chisholm

★3949★ Range Women's Advocates
PO Box 2
Chisholm, MN 55719
Phone: (218)254-3377
Crisis Phone(s): (800)232-1300 (Information and Referral).

Circle Pines

★3950★ Alexandra House
PO Box 424
Circle Pines, MN 55014-0424
Phone: (612)780-2332
Crisis Phone(s): (612)780-2330.

Cloquet

★3951★ Rural Women's Advocates
1412 Summit Ave.
Cloquet, MN 55720
Phone: (218)389-6065
Crisis Phone(s): (800)232-1300.

Crookston

★3952★ Project Safe
223 E. 7th St., No. 39
Crookston, MN 56716
Phone: (218)281-2864
Crisis Phone(s): (218)281-2864.

Detroit Lakes

★3953★ Lakes Area Service for Rape and Domestic Violence
PO Box 394
Detroit Lakes, MN 56501
Phone: (218)847-0521
Crisis Phone(s): (218)847-7446.

Duluth

★3954★ Domestic Abuse Intervention Project
206 W. 4th St.
Duluth, MN 55806
Phone: (218)722-2781
Crisis Phone(s): (218)722-4134.

★3955★ Women's Coalition
PO Box 3558
Duluth, MN 55803
Phone: (218)728-6481

Eagan

★3956★ B. Robert Lewis House
4345 Nichols Rd.
Eagan, MN 55122
Crisis Phone(s): (612)452-7288.

Elk River

★3957★ Rivers of Hope
PO Box 142
Elk River, MN 55330
Phone: (612)441-0792

Fairmont

★3958★ Southern Minnesota Crisis Support Center
115 S. Main St.
Fairmont, MN 56031
Phone: (507)238-2814
Crisis Phone(s): (507)235-3456.

Fergus Falls

★3959★ Women's Crisis Center
PO Box 815
Fergus Falls, MN 56537
Crisis Phone(s): (218)739-3359.

Forest Lake

★3960★ Forest Lake Area New Beginnings
PO Box 211
Forest Lake, MN 55025
Phone: (612)462-4844

Grand Marais

★3961★ Center for Family Crisis
PO Box 134
Grand Marais, MN 55604
Phone: (218)386-2831

★3962★ Cook County Collective
120 11th Ave., W.
Grand Marais, MN 55604
Phone: (218)387-1262
Crisis Phone(s): (218)387-1237.

Grand Rapids

★3963★ Advocates Against Domestic Abuse
Courthouse
Grand Rapids, MN 55744
Phone: (218)326-0388
Crisis Phone(s): (218)326-8565.

Hopkins

★3964★ Sojourner Shelter
PO Box 272
Hopkins, MN 55343
Phone: (612)933-7433
Crisis Phone(s): (612)933-7422.

International Falls

★3965★ Friends Against Abuse
PO Box 1271
International Falls, MN 56649
Phone: (218)285-7220
Crisis Phone(s): (218)285-7220.

Inver Grove Heights

★3966★ Lewis House
7150 Clayton Ave., E.
Inver Grove Heights, MN 55077
Phone: (612)457-0707
Crisis Phone(s): (612)457-0707.

Kellogg

★3967★ Domestic Abuse Advocates of Wabasha County
PO Box 143
Kellogg, MN 55945
Phone: (507)767-4525
Crisis Phone(s): (507)767-4525.

Lake Elmo

★3968★ Family Violence Network
PO Box 854
Lake Elmo, MN 55042
Phone: (612)770-8544
Crisis Phone(s): (612)770-0777.

Mankato

★3969★ Commission Against Domestic Abuse
CADA House
PO Box 466
Mankato, MN 56001
Crisis Phone(s): (507)625-7233.

Marshall

★3970★ Community Intervention Program
PO Box 122
Marshall, MN 56258
Phone: (507)532-7288
Crisis Phone(s): (507)532-2350.

★3971★ Southwest Rural Rainbow
210 S. 1st St.
PO Box 838
Marshall, MN 56258
Phone: (507)532-4604
Crisis Phone(s): (507)532-2350.

McGregor

★3972★ Aiken County Women's Advocates
PO Box 162
McGregor, MN 55760
Phone: (218)768-3701
Crisis Phone(s): (218)828-1216.

Minneapolis

★3973★ BIHA
Women in Action
122 W. Franklin Ave., No. 306
Minneapolis, MN 55404
Phone: (612)870-1193
Crisis Phone(s): (612)870-1193.

★3974★ Community University Health Care Center
2016 16th Ave., S.
Minneapolis, MN 55404
Phone: (612)627-4774
Crisis Phone(s): (612)627-4774.

★3975★ Domestic Abuse Project
204 W. Franklin Ave.
Minneapolis, MN 55404
Phone: (612)874-7063

★3976★ Eastside Neighborhood Service Family Violence Program
1929 2nd. St., NE
Minneapolis, MN 55418
Phone: (612)781-6011

★3977★ Education for Cooperative Living
1700 Penn Ave., N.
Minneapolis, MN 55411
Phone: (612)521-3646

★3978★ Family and Children's Services
414 S. 8th St.
Minneapolis, MN 55404
Phone: (612)340-7444

★3979★ Family Violence Program
Division of Indian Work
3045 Park Ave. S.
Minneapolis, MN 55407
Phone: (612)827-1795

★3980★ Harriet Tubman Shelter
PO Box 7026
Minneapolis, MN 55407
Phone: (612)827-6105
Crisis Phone(s): (612)827-2841.

★3981★ ICBA Battered Women's Program
2614 Nicollet Ave., S.
Minneapolis, MN 55408
Phone: (612)871-7878

★3982★ Incarnation House
3754 Pleasant Ave., S.
Minneapolis, MN 55409
Phone: (612)827-5776

**★3983★ Indian Health Board of
Minneapolis
Counseling and Support Clinics**
1315 E. 24th St.
Minneapolis, MN 55407
Crisis Phone(s): (612)721-9800.

**★3984★ Minnesota Citizens Council on
Crime and Justice
Crime Victim Center**
822 S. 3rd St., Ste. 100
Minneapolis, MN 55415
Phone: (612)340-5432
Crisis Phone(s): (612)340-5400.

**★3985★ Twin Cities Women for Take
Back the Night**
PO Box 8974
Minneapolis, MN 55408
Phone: (612)872-6221

★3986★ Walk-In Counseling Center
2421 Chicago Ave.
Minneapolis, MN 55404-3393
Phone: (612)870-0565

**★3987★ Womankind
Support Services for Battered Women**
Fairview Southdale Hospital
Minneapolis, MN 55435
Phone: (612)924-5774
Crisis Phone(s): (612)924-5775.

Moorhead

**★3988★ Hispanic Battered Women's
Project**
Townsite Centre
810 4th Ave., S.
Moorhead, MN 56560
Phone: (218)236-6502
Crisis Phone(s): (800)842-8693.

Morris

**★3989★ Stevens County Committee for
Battered Women**
PO Box 352
Morris, MN 56267
Phone: (612)589-1481

Naytahwaush

**★3990★ Northwoods Coalition for Battered
Women**
White Earth Reservation/Women Alive
Crisis Center
PO Box 28
Naytahwaush, MN 56566
Phone: (218)938-2276
Crisis Phone(s): (218)935-2276.

Onamia

**★3991★ American Indian Women's Circle
Against Domestic Abuse**
HCR 67
Onamia, MN 56359
Phone: (612)532-3183

Park Rapids

**★3992★ Battered Women's Services of
Hubbard County, Inc.**
PO Box 564
Park Rapids, MN 56470
Phone: (218)732-7413
Crisis Phone(s): (218)732-5035.

Plainview

**★3993★ Domestic Abuse Advocates of
Wabasha County**
PO Box 272
Plainview, MN 55964
Phone: (507)767-4525
Crisis Phone(s): (507)534-2234.

Plymouth

★3994★ Home Free Shelter
3405 E. Medicine Lake Blvd.
Plymouth, MN 55441
Phone: (612)559-9008
Crisis Phone(s): (612)559-4945.

Preston

★3995★ Fillmore Family Resources
PO Box 303
Preston, MN 55965
Phone: (507)765- 2316
Crisis Phone(s): (507)768-3874.

Rochester

★3996★ Women's Shelter
PO Box 457
Rochester, MN 55901
Phone: (507)285-1010

St. Cloud

**★3997★ Minnesota Migrant Council
Hispanic Battered Women Program**
PO Box 1231
St. Cloud, MN 56302
Phone: (218)281-7893
Crisis Phone(s): (612)253-7010.

★3998★ St. Cloud Intervention Project
523 Mall Germain, Ste. 210
St. Cloud, MN 56301
Phone: (612)251-7203

★3999★ Woman House
PO Box 195
St. Cloud, MN 56301
Crisis Phone(s): (612)252-1603.

St. Paul

★4000★ Casa de Esperanza
PO Box 75177
St. Paul, MN 55175
Phone: (612)772-1723
Crisis Phone(s): (612)772-1611.

**★4001★ Children's Home Society
Crisis Nursery**
2230 Como Ave.
St. Paul, MN 55108
Phone: (612)646-6393
Crisis Phone(s): (612)641-1300.

★4002★ Family and Children's Services
166 4th St. E., No. 330
St. Paul, MN 55101
Phone: (612)222-0311

**★4003★ Lesbian Battering Intervention
Project**
Hamline Park Plaza, Ste. 201
St. Paul, MN 55104
Phone: (612)646-6177
Crisis Phone(s): (612)646-0994.

**★4004★ Midway Family Service and
Abuse Center**
4235 Aldine St.
St. Paul, MN 55104
Phone: (612)641-5584
Crisis Phone(s): (612)641-5584.

★4005★ St. Paul Intervention Project
435 Aldine St.
St. Paul, MN 55104
Phone: (612)645-2824

★4006★ Survivor's Network
PO Box 4721
St. Paul, MN 55104
Phone: (612)645-5679

★4007★ W.H.I.S.P.E.R.
1821 University, No. 214S
St. Paul, MN 55104
Phone: (612)644-6301

**★4008★ Wider Community Assistance
Program**
650 Marshall Ave.
St. Paul, MN 55104
Phone: (612)221-0048

★4009★ Women of Nations
PO Box 40309
St. Paul, MN 55104
Phone: (612)222-5830
Crisis Phone(s): (612)222-5836.

★4010★ Women's Advocates
584-588 Grand Ave.
St. Paul, MN 55102
Phone: (612)227-9966
Crisis Phone(s): (612)227-8284.

**★4011★ Women's Association of Hmong
and Lao**
1544 Timberlake Rd.
St. Paul, MN 55102
Phone: (612)487-3871

★4012★ YWCA
Progressive Housing Program
198 Western Ave. N.
St. Paul, MN 55102
Phone: (612)222-7290

Sanstone

★4013★ W.I.N.D.O.W.
PO Box 545
Sanstone, MN 55072
Phone: (612)245-5224

Shakopee

★4014★ Minnesota Correctional Facility
PO Box 7
Shakopee, MN 55379
Phone: (612)496-4471

Silver Bay

★4015★ North Shore Horizons
99 Edison Blvd.
Silver Bay, MN 55614
Phone: (218)226-4443

Thief River Falls

★4016★ Violence Intervention Project
PO Box 96
Thief River Falls, MN 56701
Toll-free: 800-660-6667
Crisis Phone(s): (218)681-5557.

Two Harbors

★4017★ North Shore Horizons
607 2nd Ave.
Two Harbors, MN 55616
Phone: (218)834-5924
Toll-free: 800-232-1300

Virginia

★4018★ Range Mental Health Center
Domestic Abuse Program
624 13th St., S.
Virginia, MN 55792
Phone: (218)749-2881
Toll-free: 800-450-2273
Crisis Phone(s): (800)450-2273; Alternate toll-free: (800)972-4567.

Wilmar

★4019★ Shelter House
PO Box 787
Wilmar, MN 56201
Phone: (612)235-4613
Toll-free: (808)992-1716

Windon

★4020★ Cottonwood County Crisis Center
225 9th St.
Windon, MN 56101
Phone: (507)831-2244

Winona

★4021★ Women's Resource Center
Battered Women's Task Force
77 E. 5th St.
Winona, MN 55987
Phone: (507)452-4440

Worthington

★4022★ Southwest Crisis Center
Domestic Violence Program
927 6th Ave.
Worthington, MN 56187
Phone: (507)376-4311

Mississippi

Biloxi

★4023★ Gulf Coast Women's Center
PO Box 333
Biloxi, MS 39533
Phone: (601)436-3809
Crisis Phone(s): (601)435-1968 (Hancock County); (601)435-1968 (Harrison County); (601)875-5433 (Jackson County).

Columbus

★4024★ SAFE HAVEN
PO Box 5354
Columbus, MS 39701
Phone: (601)327-6118
Crisis Phone(s): (601)328-0200.

Greenville

★4025★ The Salvation Army
Domestic Violence Shelter
PO Box 1144
Greenville, MS 38701
Phone: 800-898-0834
Crisis Phone(s): (601)334-3249.

Jackson

★4026★ Catholic Charities
Shelter for Battered Families
PO Box 2248
Jackson, MS 39225-2248
Phone: (601)366-0222
Crisis Phone(s): (800)273-9012; and (601)366-0222.

Laurel

★4027★ Domestic Abuse Family Shelter
PO Box 273
Laurel, MS 39441
Crisis Phone(s): (601)428-8821.

Meridian

★4028★ Care Lodge
PO Box 5331
Meridian, MS 39302
Phone: (601)693-4673
Crisis Phone(s): (601)693-4673.

Oxford

★4029★ Domestic Violence Project
PO Box 286
Oxford, MS 38655
Toll-free: 800-227-5764
Crisis Phone(s): (601)234-7521.

Tupelo

★4030★ SAFE, Inc.
PO Box 985
Tupelo, MS 38802-0985
Phone: (601)841-9138
Crisis Phone(s): (601)841-CARE.

Vicksburg

★4031★ The Family Shelter
PO Box 57
Vicksburg, MS 39181-0057
Phone: (601)638-0555
Crisis Phone(s): (601)638-0555.

Missouri

Bowling Green

★4032★ Northeast Community Action
Corporation
Family Violence Prevention
PO Box 470
Bowling Green, MO 63334
Phone: (314)324-2231

Camdenton

★4033★ Citizens Against Domestic
Violence
PO Box 673
Camdenton, MO 65020
Phone: (314)346-2633
Crisis Phone(s): (314)346-2633.

Cape Girardeau

★4034★ WISER, Inc.
1111 Linden
Cape Girardeau, MO 63701
Phone: (314)334-7794
Crisis Phone(s): (314)334-7794.

Columbia

★4035★ The Shelter
PO Box 1367
Columbia, MO 65205
Phone: (314)875-1369
Toll-free: 800-548-2480
Crisis Phone(s): (314)875-1370.

Festus

★4036★ A Safe Place
PO Box 519
Festus, MO 63028
Phone: (314)942-3730
Crisis Phone(s): (314)937-3000; and (314)942-3730.

Fulton

★4037★ SERVE, Inc.
Treatment Services
302 Market St.
Fulton, MO 65251-1639
Phone: (314)642-8363

Hannibal

★4038★ Avenues, Inc.
PO Box 284
Hannibal, MO 63401
Phone: (314)221-4280
Toll-free: (808)678-7713
Crisis Phone(s): (800)678-7713; and (314)221-4280.

Independence

★4039★ Hope House
PO Box 1170
Independence, MO 64051
Phone: (816)461-4188
Crisis Phone(s): (816)461-4673.

Jefferson City

★4040★ Rape and Abuse Crisis Service
PO Box 416
Jefferson City, MO 65102
Phone: (314)634-8346
Crisis Phone(s): (314)634-4911.

Joplin

★4041★ Lafayette House
1809 Connor Ave.
Joplin, MO 64802-1765
Phone: (417)782-1772
Crisis Phone(s): (417)782-1772.

Kansas City

★4042★ NEWS House
PO Box 240019
Kansas City, MO 64124
Phone: (816)231-7378
Crisis Phone(s): (816)241-0311.

★4043★ Northland Battered Persons Program
PO Box 11055
Kansas City, MO 64119
Phone: (816)753-6268
Crisis Phone(s): (816)452-8535.

★4044★ Parents Anonymous of Kansas City
PO Box 27067
Kansas City, MO 64110
Phone: (816)861-3460
Crisis Phone(s): (816)861-6100.

★4045★ Rose Brooks Center
PO Box 27067
Kansas City, MO 64110
Phone: (816)861-3460
Crisis Phone(s): (816)861-6100.

★4046★ SafeHaven
PO Box 11055
Kansas City, MO 64119
Phone: (816)452-8910
Crisis Phone(s): (816)452-8535.

Kirksville

★4047★ Violence Intervention Services
PO Box 439
Kirksville, MO 63501-0439
Phone: (816)665-0021
Crisis Phone(s): (816)665-1617.

Malden

★4048★ Liberty Shelter
PO Box 207
Malden, MO 63863
Phone: (314)276-5500

Montgomery City

★4049★ Tri-County Council Against Domestic Violence
120 N. Sturgeon
Montgomery City, MO 63361
Phone: (314)456-7867

Nevada

★4050★ Council on Families in Crisis
PO Box 851
Nevada, MO 64772
Phone: (417)667-3733

Poplar Bluff

★4051★ Haven House
921 Harper St.
Poplar Bluff, MO 63901
Phone: (314)686-4873
Crisis Phone(s): (314)686-4873.

St. Charles

★4052★ Women's Center Domestic Violence Services
PO Box 51
St. Charles, MO 63301
Phone: (314)946-6854
Crisis Phone(s): (314)946-3257.

St. Joseph

★4053★ YWCA Shelter for Abused Women and Victims of Domestic Violence
304 N. 8th St.
St. Joseph, MO 64501
Phone: (816)232-4481
Crisis Phone(s): (816)232-1225.

St. Louis

★4054★ Abused Women's Support Project
PO Box 63010
St. Louis, MO 63163
Phone: (314)772-4535

★4055★ Advocate Services for Abused Women
PO Box 499A, Field Sta.
St. Louis, MO 63018
Phone: (314)454-6940
Toll-free: 800-444-0514

★4056★ ALIVE
PO Box 11201
St. Louis, MO 63105
Phone: (314)993-2777

★4057★ Educational Center of Family Violence
1040 S. Taylor
St. Louis, MO 63310
Phone: (314)534-1010

★4058★ Raven: Ending Men's Violence
PO Box 24159
St. Louis, MO 63130
Phone: (314)725-6137

★4059★ St. Martha's Hall
PO Box 4950
St. Louis, MO 63108
Phone: (314)533-1313

★4060★ Victim Service Council
7900 Carondelet, 4th Fl.
St. Louis, MO 63105
Phone: (314)889-3075

★4061★ Women's Self-Help Center
2838 Olive
St. Louis, MO 63103
Phone: (314)531-9100
Crisis Phone(s): (314)531-2003.

Sedalia

★4062★ Citizens Against Spouse Abuse
PO Box 1371
Sedalia, MO 65302-1371
Phone: (816)827-5559
Crisis Phone(s): (816)827-5555.

Springfield

★4063★ Family Violence Center
PO Box 5972
Springfield, MO 65801
Phone: (417)865-0373
Crisis Phone(s): (417)865-1728.

Trenton

★4064★ North Central Missouri Mental Health Center
1601 E. 28th
Trenton, MO 64683
Phone: (816)359-4487
Crisis Phone(s): (816)359-3297.

University City

★4065★ University City Police Department Victim Services Unit
6801 Delmar Blvd.
University City, MO 63130
Phone: (314)863-0924

Warrensburg

★4066★ Survival
PO Box 344
Warrensburg, MO 64093
Phone: (816)429-2847
Crisis Phone(s): (816)429-2847.

Warsaw

★4067★ SAFE Council
PO Box 1374
Warsaw, MO 65355
Phone: (816)438-5393
Crisis Phone(s): (816)438-5393.

West Plains

★4068★ Christos House
PO Box 822
West Plains, MO 65775
Phone: (417)256-9255

Montana

Billings

★4069★ YWCA
Gateway House
909 Wyoming Ave.
Billings, MT 59101
Crisis Phone(s): (406)259-8100.

Bozeman

★4070★ Battered Women's Network
PO Box 752
Bozeman, MT 59715
Phone: (406)586-0263
Toll-free: 800-225-9789
Crisis Phone(s): (416)586-4111.

★4071★ Bozeman Help Center
323 S. Wallace
Bozeman, MT 59715
Crisis Phone(s): (406)586-3333.

Butte

★4072★ Butte Christian Community Center
Safespace
1131 W. Copper
Butte, MT 59703
Phone: (406)782-2111
Crisis Phone(s): (406)782-8511.

Colstrip

★4073★ Alert
Battered Women's Task Force
PO Box 826
Colstrip, MT 59323
Phone: (406)748-4357
Crisis Phone(s): (406)748-2211.

Dillon

★4074★ Women's Resource Center
PO Box 888
Dillon, MT 59725
Phone: (406)683-6106
Crisis Phone(s): (406)683-6106; (800)772-2333.

Ft. Benton

★4075★ Hi-Lines Help for Abused Spouses
Box 1029
Ft. Benton, MT 59442
Phone: (406)734-5266
Crisis Phone(s): (406)759-5170.

Glendive

★4076★ Dawson County Spouse Abuse Program
Box 505
Glendive, MT 59330
Phone: (406)365-6477
Crisis Phone(s): (406)365-6477.

Great Falls

★4077★ Golden Triangle CMHC
PO Box 3048
Great Falls, MT 59403
Phone: (406)761-2100
Crisis Phone(s): (406)761-2100.

★4078★ Mercy Home
PO Box 886
Great Falls, MT 59403
Phone: (406)453-1018
Crisis Phone(s): (406)453-1018.

Harlem

★4079★ Ft. Belknap
PO Box 459
Harlem, MT 59526
Phone: (406)353-2205
Crisis Phone(s): (406)353-2933.

Havre

★4080★ The Haven
PO Box 1509
Havre, MT 59501
Phone: (406)265-6744
Crisis Phone(s): (406)265-2222.

Helena

★4081★ Friendship Center
1503 Gallatin
Helena, MT 59601
Phone: (406)442-6800
Crisis Phone(s): (406)442-6800.

Kalispell

★4082★ Violence Free Crisis-Line
PO Box 1385
Kalispell, MT 59903-1385
Phone: (406)752-4735
Crisis Phone(s): (406)752-7273.

Lewiston

★4083★ Saves
PO Box 404
Lewiston, MT 59457
Crisis Phone(s): (406)538-2281.

Libby

★4084★ Women's Help-Line
PO Box 2
Libby, MT 59923
Phone: (406)293-9141
Crisis Phone(s): (406)293-3223.

Missoula

★4085★ Women's Place
521 N. Orange St.
Missoula, MT 59802
Crisis Phone(s): (406)543-7606.

★4086★ YWCA
Domestic Violence Assistance Center
1130 W. Broadway
Missoula, MT 59802
Phone: (406)542-0028
Crisis Phone(s): (406)542-1944.

Polson

★4087★ Family Crisis Center
PO Box 1158
Polson, MT 59860
Phone: (406)883-3350
Toll-free: 800-228-1038
Crisis Phone(s): (406)676-2518.

Sidney

★4088★ Richland County Coalition Against Domestic Violence
PO Box 822
Sidney, MT 59270
Phone: (406)482-7421
Crisis Phone(s): (406)482-2120.

Twin Bridges

★4089★ Madison County Unit Against Spouse Abuse
PO Box 72
Twin Bridges, MT 59754
Phone: (406)684-5400

Nebraska

Bayard

★4090★ Alliance Task Force on Domestic Violence
PO Box 466
Bayard, NE 69301
Phone: (308)762-7939
Crisis Phone(s): (308)762-5788.

Bellevue

**★4091★ Family Service Domestic Abuse
Program**
Multi-Service Center at Bellevue
116 E. Mission Ave.
Bellevue, NE 68005
Phone: (402)291-6065
Toll-free: 800-523-3666

Crisis Phone(s): (402)444-4433.

Benkelman

**★4092★ Task Force on Domestic Violence
and Sexual Assault**
Box 302
Benkelman, NE 69021
Phone: (308)423-2498

Crisis Phone(s): (308)423-2676.

Broken Bow

**★4093★ Central Nebraska Task Force on
Domestic Abuse and Sexual Assault**
PO Box 183
Broken Bow, NE 68822
Phone: (308)538-2510

Crisis Phone(s): (308)872-5988.

Columbus

**★4094★ Center for Sexual Assault and
Domestic Violence Survivors**
PO Box 42
Columbus, NE 68601
Phone: (402)564-2155
Toll-free: 800-658-4482

Crisis Phone(s): (402)564-2155.

**★4095★ Columbia Area Domestic Violence
and Sexual Assault Program**
1472 28th Ave.
Columbus, NE 68601
Phone: (402)564-1616

Crisis Phone(s): (402)564-1616.

Crete

**★4096★ Coordinated Intervention System
for Domestic Abuse**
PO Box 73
Crete, NE 68333
Phone: (402)826-2332

Fremont

**★4097★ Domestic Abuse/Sexual Assault
Crisis Center**
PO Box 622
Fremont, NE 68025
Phone: (402)721-4340

Crisis Phone(s): (402)727-7777.

Gordon

★4098★ DAWN
Family Rescue Shelter
309 N. Main
Gordon, NE 69343
Phone: (308)282-2492

Crisis Phone(s): (308)282-2492.

★4099★ Family Rescue Services
107 E. 2nd.
Gordon, NE 69343
Phone: (308)282-0125

Crisis Phone(s): (308)282-0125; (308)282-
0126; (308)432-4433 (Chadron).

Grand Island

★4100★ The CRISIS Center
PO Box 1008
Grand Island, NE 68802
Phone: (308)381-0555

Crisis Phone(s): (308)381-0555.

Hastings

**★4101★ Spouse Abuse/Sexual Assault
Crisis Center**
422 N. Hastings, Ste. B-2
Hastings, NE 68901
Phone: (402)463-5810

Crisis Phone(s): (402)463-4677.

Kearney

**★4102★ The Spouse/Sexual Abuse Family
Education Center**
3720 Ave. A, Ste. C
Kearney, NE 68847
Phone: (308)237-2599

Crisis Phone(s): (308)237-2599.

Lexington

**★4103★ Dawson County Parent/Child
Center**
PO Box 722
Lexington, NE 68850
Phone: (308)324-2336

Crisis Phone(s): (308)324-3040.

Lincoln

★4104★ Friendship Home
PO Box 30268
Lincoln, NE 68503-0268

Crisis Phone(s): (402)475-7273.

★4105★ Rape/Spouse Abuse Crisis Center
2545 N St.
Lincoln, NE 68510-1250
Phone: (402)476-2110

Crisis Phone(s): (402)475-7273.

McCook

**★4106★ Domestic Abuse/Sexual Assault
Services**
322 Norris, Rm. 5
McCook, NE 69001

Crisis Phone(s): (308)345-5534.

Norfolk

**★4107★ Norfolk Task Force on Domestic
Violence and Sexual Assault**
PO Box 1711
Norfolk, NE 68701
Phone: (402)379-3975

Crisis Phone(s): (402)379-3798.

North Platte

★4108★ Rape/Domestic Abuse Program
PO Box 393
North Platte, NE 69101
Phone: (308)532-0624

Crisis Phone(s): (308)534-3495.

Ogallala

**★4109★ Sandhills Crisis Intervention
Program**
PO Box 22
Ogallala, NE 69153
Phone: (308)284-8311

Crisis Phone(s): (308)284-6055.

Omaha

★4110★ The Salvation Army
Emergency Shelter
3612 Cuming St.
Omaha, NE 68131-1900
Phone: (402)544-5943

★4111★ The Shelter
PO Box 4346
Omaha, NE 68104
Phone: (402)558-5700

★4112★ YWCA
Women Against Violence
222 S. 29th St.
Omaha, NE 68131
Phone: (402)345-6555

Crisis Phone(s): (402)345-7273.

Scottsbluff

**★4113★ Domestic Violence Emergency
Services**
PO Box 434
Scottsbluff, NE 69361
Phone: (308)632-3683

Crisis Phone(s): (308)436-4357.

Taylor

**★4114★ Loup Valley Task Force on
Domestic Violence**
HC 65, Box 8
Taylor, NE 68879
Phone: (308)942-3191

Crisis Phone(s): (308)728-7040.

Wayne

★4115★ Haven House
Family Services Center
PO Box 44
Wayne, NE 68787
Phone: (402)375-4633

Crisis Phone(s): (402)375-4633.

Nevada

Battle Mountain

★4116★ Lander County Committee
Against Domestic Violence
PO Box 624
Battle Mountain, NV 89820
Phone: (702)635-2500

Carson City

★4117★ Advocates to End Domestic
Violence
PO Box 2529
Carson City, NV 89701
Phone: (702)883-7654

Crisis Phone(s): (702)883-7654.

Elko

★4118★ Committee Against Domestic
Violence
PO Box 2531
Elko, NV 89801
Phone: (702)738-6524

Crisis Phone(s): (702)738-9454.

Ely

★4119★ Support, Inc.
PO Box 583
Ely, NV 89301
Phone: (702)289-2270

Fallon

★4120★ Domestic Violence Intervention
PO Box 2231
Fallon, NV 89406
Phone: (702)423-1313

Hawthorne

★4121★ Mineral County Advocates to End
Domestic Violence
PO Box 331
Hawthorne, NV 89415
Phone: (702)945-2472

Las Vegas

★4122★ Temporary Assistance for
Domestic Crisis
Domestic Crisis Shelter
PO Box 43264
Las Vegas, NV 89116
Phone: (702)646-4981

Crisis Phone(s): (702)646-4981.

Lovelock

★4123★ Pershing County Domestic
Violence Intervention
PO Box 1203
Lovelock, NV 89419
Phone: (702)273-7373

Crisis Phone(s): (703)273-7373.

Minden

★4124★ Family Support Council of
Douglas County
PO Box 810
Minden, NV 89423
Phone: (702)782-7565

Crisis Phone(s): (702)782-8692; (702)588-7171.

Sparks

★4125★ Committee to Aid Abused
Women
101 15th St.
Sparks, NV 89431
Phone: (702)358-4150

Crisis Phone(s): (702)358-4150.

Tonopah

★4126★ Tonopah Goldfield Intervention
for Families
PO Box 891
Tonopah, NV 89849
Phone: (702)482-3891

Winnemucca

★4127★ Committee Against Family
Violence
PO Box 583
Winnemucca, NV 89445
Phone: (702)623-3974

Crisis Phone(s): (702)623-6429.

Yerington

★4128★ ALIVE
PO Box 130
Yerington, NV 89447
Phone: (702)463-5843

Crisis Phone(s): (702)463-4009.

New Hampshire

Berlin

★4129★ Coos County Family Health
Services
RESPONSE to Sexual and Domestic
Violence
54 Willow St.
Berlin, NH 03570
Phone: (603)752-2040
Toll-free: 800-984-7888

Claremont

★4130★ Women's Supportive Services
11 School St.
Claremont, NH 03743
Phone: (603)543-0155

Crisis Phone(s): (603)543-0155.

Concord

★4131★ Rape and Domestic Violence
Crisis Center
PO Box 1344
Concord, NH 03302-1344
Phone: (603)225-7376
Toll-free: 800-852-3388

Conway

★4132★ Carroll County Against Domestic
Violence and Rape
PO Box 1972
Conway, NH 03818
Phone: (603)356-7993

Crisis Phone(s): (603)356-6849.

Keene

★4133★ Women's Crisis Service of the
Monadnock Region
69Z Island St.
Keene, NH 03431-3529
Phone: (603)352-3844

Crisis Phone(s): (603)352-3782.

Laconia

★4134★ Lakes Region Stop Family
Violence Program
95 Water St.
Laconia, NH 03246-3313
Phone: (603)524-5835

Crisis Phone(s): (603)524-5835.

Lebanon

★4135★ Women's Information Service
79 Hanover St., Ste. 1
Lebanon, NH 03766-1000
Phone: (603)448-5922

Crisis Phone(s): (603)448-5525.

Littleton

★4136★ Support Center Against Domestic
Violence and Sexual Assault
PO Box 965
Littleton, NH 03561
Phone: (603)444-0624

Crisis Phone(s): (603)444-0544.

Manchester

★4137★ YWCA
Women's Crisis Service
72 Concord St.
Manchester, NH 03101
Phone: (603)625-5785

Crisis Phone(s): (603)688-2299.

Nashua

★4138★ Rape and Assault Support
Services
PO Box 217
Nashua, NH 03061
Phone: (603)883-5521

Crisis Phone(s): (603)883-3044.

Plymouth

★4139★ Task Force Against Domestic
and Sexual Violence
PO Box 53
Plymouth, NH 03264
Phone: (603)536-3423

Crisis Phone(s): (603)536-1659.

Portsmouth

★4140★ Seacoast Task Force on Family
  Violence
A Safe Place
PO Box 674
Portsmouth, NH 03802
Phone: (603)436-7924
Toll-free: 800-852-3388

★4141★ Sexual Assault Support Services
1 Junkins Ave.
Portsmouth, NH 03801
Phone: (603)436-4107
Crisis Phone(s): (603)436-4107.

New Jersey

Belvidere

★4142★ Domestic Abuse and Rape Crisis
  Center
PO Box 423
Belvidere, NJ 07823
Phone: (908)453-4121
Crisis Phone(s): (908)475-8408; and (908)453-
4181.

Blackwood

★4143★ YWCA
SOLACE
PO Box 1309
Blackwood, NJ 08012
Phone: (609)227-1800
Crisis Phone(s): (609)227-1234.

Bloomfield

★4144★ Safe House
PO Box 1887
Bloomfield, NJ 07003
Phone: (201)759-2378
Crisis Phone(s): (201)759-2154.

Burlington

★4145★ Providence House
Willingboro Shelter
PO Box 424
Burlington, NJ 08016
Phone: (609)871-2003
Crisis Phone(s): (609)871-7551.

Caldwell

★4146★ PEACE Suburban Center
Family Violence Project
c/o Caldwell College
Caldwell, NJ 07006
Phone: (201)226-6166

Cape May Court House

★4147★ Coalition Against Rape and
  Abuse
Crest Haven Complex
Cape May Court House, NJ 08210
Phone: (609)463-0947
Crisis Phone(s): (609)522-6489.

Elizabeth

★4148★ YWCA
Project Protect
1131 E. Jersey St.
Elizabeth, NJ 07201
Phone: (201)355-1500
Crisis Phone(s): (201)355-4399.

Flemington

★4149★ Women's Crisis Services
47 E. Main St.
Flemington, NJ 08822
Phone: (201)788-7666
Crisis Phone(s): (201)788-4044.

Glassboro

★4150★ People Against Spouse Abuse
PO Box 755
Glassboro, NJ 08028
Crisis Phone(s): (609)848-5557; (609)881-
3335.

Hackensack

★4151★ Alternatives to Domestic Violence
21 Main St., Rm. 111
Hackensack, NJ 07601
Phone: (201)487-8484
Crisis Phone(s): (201)487-8484.

★4152★ Shelter Our Sisters
PO Box 202
Hackensack, NJ 07602
Phone: (201)836-1075
Crisis Phone(s): (201)944-9600.

Hazlet

★4153★ Women's Center of Monmouth
  County
Bethany Commons Bldg. 3, Ste. 42
Hazlet, NJ 07703
Crisis Phone(s): (908)264-4111.

Jersey City

★4154★ YWCA
Hudson County Battered Women's Project
270 Fairmount Ave.
Jersey City, NJ 07306
Phone: (201)333-5700
Crisis Phone(s): (201)333-5700.

Lawrenceville

★4155★ Womanspace, Inc.
Outreach Office
1860 Brunswick Ave.
Lawrenceville, NJ 08648
Phone: (609)394-0136
Crisis Phone(s): (609)394-9000.

Morris Plains

★4156★ Jersey Battered Women's
  Services
PO Box 363
Morris Plains, NJ 07950-0363
Phone: (201)455-1256
Crisis Phone(s): (201)267-4763.

New Brunswick

★4157★ Women Aware
PO Box 312
New Brunswick, NJ 08903
Phone: (908)249-4504
Crisis Phone(s): (908)937-9525.

★4158★ Women Aware
Outreach Office
96 Paterson St.
New Brunswick, NJ 08901
Phone: (908)937-9525

Newark

★4159★ Essex County Family Violence
  Program
755 S. Orange Ave.
Newark, NJ 07106
Phone: (201)484-1704
Crisis Phone(s): (201)484-4446.

Newton

★4160★ Domestic Abuse Services, Inc.
PO Box 805
Newton, NJ 07860
Phone: (201)875-1211
Crisis Phone(s): (201)579-2386.

Northfield

★4161★ Atlantic County Women's Center
PO Box 311
Northfield, NJ 08225
Crisis Phone(s): (609)646-6767.

Paterson

★4162★ Passaic County Women's Center
PO Box 244
Paterson, NJ 07513
Crisis Phone(s): (201)881-1450.

Rio Grande

★4163★ Coalition Against Rape and
  Abuse
1128 Rt. 47, S.
Rio Grande, NJ 08242
Phone: (609)522-6489
Crisis Phone(s): (609)391-9146.

Salem

★4164★ Salem County Women's Services
PO Box 125
Salem, NJ 08079
Crisis Phone(s): (609)935-6655.

Somerville

★4165★ **Resource Center for Women and Their Families**
205 W. Main St.
Somerville, NJ 08876
Phone: (908)685-1126

Crisis Phone(s): (908)685-1122.

Toms River

★4166★ **Domestic Violence Crisis Intervention Unit**
CN 2191
Toms River, NJ 08753
Phone: (908)244-5353

★4167★ **Providence House**
PO Box 104
Toms River, NJ 08754
Crisis Phone(s): (908)244-8259; and (609)698-0005.

Trenton

★4168★ **Womanspace, Inc.**
PO Box 7070
Trenton, NJ 08628
Toll-free: 800-572-7233
Crisis Phone(s): (609)394-9000.

Vineland

★4169★ **Cumberland County Women's Center**
PO Box 921
Vineland, NJ 08360
Crisis Phone(s): (609)691-3713.

Woodbury

★4170★ **People Against Spouse Abuse**
Carpenter St./Allen Ln.
Woodbury, NJ 08096
Phone: (609)848-5557
Crisis Phone(s): (609)848-5557.

New Mexico

Alamogordo

★4171★ **COPE**
PO Box 1180
Alamogordo, NM 88310
Phone: (505)434-3622
Crisis Phone(s): (505)437-2673.

Albuquerque

★4172★ **Shelter for Victims of Domestic Violence**
PO Box 1336
Albuquerque, NM 87103
Phone: (505)247-4219
Crisis Phone(s): (505)247-4219.

Carlsbad

★4173★ **Carlsbad Battered Families Shelter**
PO Box 2396
Carlsbad, NM 88220
Phone: (505)885-4615
Crisis Phone(s): (505)885-4615.

Clovis

★4174★ **Shelter for Victims of Domestic Violence**
PO Box 1732
Clovis, NM 88101
Phone: (505)762-0050
Crisis Phone(s): (505)769-0305.

Farmington

★4175★ **Family Crisis Center**
115 Corcorran
Farmington, NM 87401
Phone: (505)325-3549
Crisis Phone(s): (505)325-1906.

Gallup

★4176★ **Battered Families Services**
650 Vanden Bosch Pkwy.
Gallup, NM 87301
Phone: (505)722-6389
Crisis Phone(s): (505)722-7483.

Hobbs

★4177★ **OPTIONS**
PO Box 2213
Hobbs, NM 88240
Phone: (505)393-2495
Crisis Phone(s): (505)397-1576.

Laguna

★4178★ **Laguna Family Shelter Program**
PO Box 194
Laguna, NM 87026
Phone: (505)552-9701
Crisis Phone(s): (505)552-9701.

Las Cruces

★4179★ **La Casa**
PO Box 2463
Las Cruces, NM 88004
Phone: (505)526-2819
Crisis Phone(s): (505)526-9513.

Roswell

★4180★ **The Refuge for Battered Adults**
PO Box 184
Roswell, NM 88202
Phone: (505)624-0666

Ruidoso

★4181★ **Family Crisis Center**
PO Box 3004 HS
Ruidoso, NM 88345
Phone: (505)624-0666
Crisis Phone(s): (505)257-7365.

Santa Fe

★4182★ **Esperanza**
PO Box 5701
Santa Fe, NM 87502-5701
Crisis Phone(s): (505)473-5200; (505)425-9383 (Las Vegas); (505)753-5142 (Espanola).

Silver City

★4183★ **El Refugio**
PO Box 679
Silver City, NM 88062
Phone: (505)538-2135

Socorro

★4184★ **El Puente del Socorro**
PO Box 663
Socorro, NM 87801
Phone: (505)835-0928
Crisis Phone(s): (505)835-1150.

Taos

★4185★ **Battered Women's Project**
PO Box 169
Taos, NM 87571
Phone: (505)758-8082
Crisis Phone(s): (505)758-9888.

New York

Albany

★4186★ **Albany Arbor House**
302 Western Ave.
Albany, NY 12203
Phone: (518)489-6030

★4187★ **Albany Catholic Family and Community Services**
Domestic Violence Services
214 Lark St.
Albany, NY 12210
Phone: (518)432-7865

★4188★ **Equinox**
Domestic Violence Services
214 Lark St.
Albany, NY 12210
Phone: (518)432-7865

★4189★ **Mercy House**
12 St. Joseph Terr.
Albany, NY 12210
Phone: (518)434-3531

Albion

★4190★ **Orleans County Probation Department**
Domestic Violence Program
34 E. Park St.
Albion, NY 14411
Phone: (716)589-5538
Crisis Phone(s): (716)589-5528.

Amsterdam

★4191★ Women's Resource and Crisis Center
PO Box 636
Amsterdam, NY 12010
Phone: (518)842-6145
Crisis Phone(s): (518)842-3384.

Auburn

★4192★ Cayuga County Action Program Battered Women's Project
87 North St.
Auburn, NY 13021
Phone: (315)255-1703
Crisis Phone(s): (315)253-3356.

Batavia

★4193★ Catholic Charities Domestic Violence Services
113 Main St., 2nd Fl.
Batavia, NY 14020
Phone: (716)343-0614

★4194★ YWCA Domestic Violence Program
301 North St.
Batavia, NY 14020
Phone: (716)343-7513
Crisis Phone(s): (716)343-7513.

Bath

★4195★ Victim Crisis Center of the Neighborhood Justice Program
122 Liberty St.
Bath, NY 14810
Phone: (607)776-4077
Crisis Phone(s): (800)346-2211.

Binghamton

★4196★ The Alternative Counseling Center Domestic Violence Services
37 Mill St.
Binghamton, NY 13903
Phone: (607)722-1836

★4197★ Crime Victims Assistance Center
PO Box 836
Binghamton, NY 13902
Crisis Phone(s): (607)722-4256.

★4198★ Family and Children's Services
257 Main St.
Binghamton, NY 13905
Phone: (607)729-6206

★4199★ First Call for Help
PO Box 550
Binghamton, NY 13902
Phone: (607)729-9100
Crisis Phone(s): (607)729-9100.

★4200★ Women's Center
PO Box 354
Binghamton, NY 13902
Phone: (607)770-9014

★4201★ YWCA Emergency Housing/Interfaith Rooms
80 Hawley St.
Binghamton, NY 13901
Crisis Phone(s): (607)772-0340.

Breman

★4202★ Help Hotline
Rte. 812, Box 111
Breman, NY 13367
Phone: (315)376-8202
Crisis Phone(s): (315)376-4357.

Bronx

★4203★ Fordham/Tremont Community Mental Health Center Domestic Violence Services
2021 Grand Concourse, 8th Fl.
Bronx, NY 10453
Phone: (212)960-0408

★4204★ Jewish Board of Family and Children's Services Domestic Violence Services
990 Pelham Pkwy. S.
Bronx, NY 10461
Phone: (212)931-2600

★4205★ Project Return Aegis
PO Box 905, Morris Heights Sta.
Bronx, NY 10453
Crisis Phone(s): (212)733-4443.

★4206★ Tremont Improvement Program
819 E. 178th St.
Bronx, NY 10460
Phone: (212)583-1090

★4207★ Victims Services Agency Project Oasis
2530 Grand Concourse
Bronx, NY 10458
Phone: (212)365-9500
Crisis Phone(s): (212)577-7777.

Brooklyn

★4208★ Brooklyn College Womens Center
227 New Ingersoll
Brooklyn, NY 11210
Phone: (718)780-5777

★4209★ Center for the Elimination of Violence in the Family
PO Box 279
Brooklyn, NY 11220
Phone: (718)439-4612
Crisis Phone(s): (718)439-1000.

★4210★ House of Mercy
1230 63rd St.
Brooklyn, NY 11219
Phone: (718)256-1469

★4211★ Neighborhood Women of Williamsburg-Greenpoint
249 Manhattan Ave.
Brooklyn, NY 11211
Phone: (718)388-6666

★4212★ Park Slope Safe Homes Project
PO Box 429, Van Brunt Sta.
Brooklyn, NY 11215
Crisis Phone(s): (718)499-2151 (M-F, 9 am - 9 pm, Sat., 12 pm - 4 pm).

★4213★ Victims Services Agency
50 Court, 8th Fl.
Brooklyn, NY 11201
Phone: (718)858-9078
Crisis Phone(s): (718)783-3700.

★4214★ Women's Survival Space
PO Box 200279
Brooklyn, NY 11220-0006
Phone: (718)439-4612
Crisis Phone(s): (718)439-7281.

Buffalo

★4215★ Child and Family Services Domestic Violence Treatment Program
330 Delaware Ave.
Buffalo, NY 14202
Phone: (716)842-2750
Crisis Phone(s): (716)884-6000.

★4216★ Haven House
PO Box 45, Ellicott Sta.
Buffalo, NY 14205
Phone: (716)884-6002
Crisis Phone(s): (716)884-6000.

★4217★ The Salvation Army Family Services
960 Main St.
Buffalo, NY 14202
Phone: (716)883-9800
Crisis Phone(s): (716)883-9800.

★4218★ YWCA Residence
245 North St.
Buffalo, NY 14201
Phone: (716)884-4761
Crisis Phone(s): (716)884-4761.

Canandaigua

★4219★ New York Department of Social Services Domestic Violence Services
3871 County Road 46
Canandaigua, NY 14424
Phone: (716)396-4111

Canton

★4220★ Renewal House
PO Box 468
Canton, NY 13617
Phone: (315)379-9845
Crisis Phone(s): (315)379-9845 (days); (315)265-2422 or (315)764-1900 (evenings and weekends).

Catskill

★4221★ Columbia/Greene Domestic
Violence Program
2 Franklin St.
Catskill, NY 12414
Phone: (518)943-3385
Crisis Phone(s): (518)943-9211.

Corning

★4222★ Victim Crisis Center of the
Neighborhood Justice Program
147 E. 2nd St.
Corning, NY 14830
Phone: (607)936-8807
Toll-free: 800-540-8177
Crisis Phone(s): (607)962-6774.

Cortland

★4223★ YWCA
Aid to Women Victims of Violence
14 Clayton Ave.
Cortland, NY 13045
Phone: (607)753-3639
Crisis Phone(s): (607)756-6363.

Delhi

★4224★ Delaware Opportunity
Safe Against Violence
47 Main St.
Delhi, NY 13753
Phone: (607)746-2992
Crisis Phone(s): (607)746-6278.

East Meadow

★4225★ Nassau County Coalition Against
Domestic Violence
c/o Nassau County Medical Center, Bldg. G
East Meadow, NY 11554
Phone: (516)542-2596
Crisis Phone(s): (516)542-0404.

Elizabethtown

★4226★ End Domestic Violence Program
PO Box 115
Elizabethtown, NY 12932-0715
Phone: (518)873-9240
Crisis Phone(s): (518)873-9240.

Elmira

★4227★ Info-Line
425 Pennsylvania Ave., Rm. 201
Elmira, NY 14904
Crisis Phone(s): (607)737-2077.

★4228★ The Salvation Army
Victims of Domestic Violence Program
PO Box 293
Elmira, NY 14902
Phone: (607)732-0314
Crisis Phone(s): (607)737-2077.

Endicott

★4229★ SOS Shelter
PO Box 393
Endicott, NY 13760
Phone: (607)748-7453
Crisis Phone(s): (607)754-4340.

Far Rockaway

★4230★ YWCA
Transition Center
1800 Seagirt Blvd.
Far Rockaway, NY 11691
Phone: (718)327-7660
Crisis Phone(s): (718)520-8045 (8 am - 5 pm, M-F).

Flushing

★4231★ Korean Family Counseling and
Research Center
142-01 38th Ave.
Flushing, NY 11354
Phone: (718)961-7226

Fredonia

★4232★ Amicae
Hotline for Rape and Battering
PO Box 0023
Fredonia, NY 14063
Phone: (716)672-8423
Crisis Phone(s): (716)672-8484; (800)836-5940.

Geneseo

★4233★ Chances and Changes
PO Box 326
Geneseo, NY 14454
Phone: (716)658-3940
Crisis Phone(s): (716)658-2660.

Geneva

★4234★ Family Counseling Service of the
Finger Lakes
Domestic Violence Services
671 S. Exchange St.
Geneva, NY 14456
Phone: (315)789-2613
Crisis Phone(s): (315)789-2613; and (315)539-9241.

Glen Falls

★4235★ Catholic Family and Community
Services
Domestic Violence Project
12 E. Washington St.
Glen Falls, NY 12801-3009
Phone: (518)793-9496
Toll-free: 800-287-3836

Gloversville

★4236★ Family Counseling Center
Family Violence Project
PO Box 94
Gloversville, NY 12078
Phone: (518)725-4310
Crisis Phone(s): (518)725-5300.

Harlem

★4237★ Urban Women's Retreat
PO Box 804
Harlem, NY 10037
Phone: (212)690-6494
Crisis Phone(s): (212)696-6490.

Hauppauge

★4238★ Victims Information Bureau of
Suffolk
515 Route 111, Ste. 201
Hauppauge, NY 11788-4333
Phone: (516)360-3730
Crisis Phone(s): (516)360-3606.

Hempstead

★4239★ Center for Psychological and
Physically Abused Persons
Hofstra University
Hempstead, NY 11550
Phone: (516)829-8838

Hogansburg

★4240★ St. Regis Mohawk Community
Health Services
Domestic Violence Program
Community Bldg.
Hogansburg, NY 13655
Phone: (518)358-2272
Crisis Phone(s): (315)769-9242.

Hornell

★4241★ Victim Crisis Center of the
Neighborhood Justice Program
238 Main St., 2nd Fl.
Hornell, NY 14843
Phone: (607)324-4433
Toll-free: 800-346-2211

Ilion

★4242★ Catholic Family and Community
Services
Domestic Violence Program
61 West St.
Ilion, NY 13357
Crisis Phone(s): (315)866-0458; (800)942-6906; and (315)866-0458 (Herkimer County).

Islip Terrace

★4243★ Long Island Women's Coalition
PO Box 183
Islip Terrace, NY 11752
Phone: (516)666-7181
Crisis Phone(s): (516)666-8833.

Ithaca

★4244★ Suicide Prevention and Crisis
Service
PO Box 312
Ithaca, NY 14851
Phone: (607)272-1505
Crisis Phone(s): (607)272-1616.

★4245★ Tompkins County Task Force for Battered Women
PO Box 164
Ithaca, NY 14851
Phone: (607)277-3203
Crisis Phone(s): (607)277-5000.

Jackson Heights

**★4246★ Victims Services Agency
Travelers Aid Services**
74-09 37th Ave., Rm. 412
Jackson Heights, NY 11372
Phone: (718)899-1233
Crisis Phone(s): (212)577-7777.

Jamaica

★4247★ Allen Women's Resource Center
PO Box 316
Jamaica, NY 11434
Crisis Phone(s): (718)739-6202.

★4248★ Lutheran Community Services of Queens
89-13 161st St.
Jamaica, NY 11432
Phone: (718)657-5851

★4249★ Women Helping Women
PO Box 3002
Jamaica, NY 11431
Phone: (718)539-9111
Crisis Phone(s): (718)539-9111 (M-F, 8 am - 11 pm).

Jamestown

**★4250★ YWCA
Family Violence/Sexual Assault Network**
401 N. Main St.
Jamestown, NY 14701
Phone: (716)488-2237
Crisis Phone(s): (716)484-0052.

Kingston

**★4251★ Family of Woodstock
Family Shelter**
UPO Box 3817
Kingston, NY 12401
Phone: (914)331-7080
Crisis Phone(s): (914)338-2370.

**★4252★ U.C. Crime Victims
Assistance Program**
1 Pearl St.
Kingston, NY 12401
Phone: (914)331-9300
Crisis Phone(s): (914)437-0020.

Lockport

**★4253★ YWCA
Domestic Violence Program**
32 Cottage St.
Lockport, NY 14094
Phone: (716)433-6714
Crisis Phone(s): (716)433-6716.

Long Beach

**★4254★ Circulo de la Hispanidad
Salva**
54 W. Park Ave.
Long Beach, NY 11561
Phone: (516)889-3831
Crisis Phone(s): (516)889-3831.

Mahopac

**★4255★ Putnam/North Westchester
Women's Resource Center**
2 Mahopac Plaza
Mahopac, NY 10541
Phone: (914)628-9284
Crisis Phone(s): (914)628-2166.

Manhattan

**★4256★ East Harlem Council for Human Service
Victims Intervention Project**
2253 3rd. Ave.
Manhattan, NY 10035
Phone: (212)410-9080
Crisis Phone(s): (212)360-5090.

Middletown

★4257★ Middletown Family Counseling
9 Academy Ave.
Middletown, NY 10940-5101
Phone: (914)342-6767

Monticello

★4258★ Sullivan County Alternatives to Family Violence
PO Box 248
Monticello, NY 12701
Phone: (914)794-4600
Crisis Phone(s): (914)794-4600.

Mt. Kisco

**★4259★ Northern Westchester Guidance Clinic
Domestic Violence Services**
344 Main St.
Mt. Kisco, NY 10549
Phone: (914)666-4646

New Hyde Park

**★4260★ Long Island Jewish Medical Center
Abused Spouse Counseling Center**
New Hyde Park, NY 11042
Phone: (718)470-7540

New York

**★4261★ Chinese-American Planning Council
Project Help**
480 Broadway, 2nd Fl.
New York, NY 10013
Phone: (212)941-0978

★4262★ Henry Street Settlement Shelter
PO Box 2
New York, NY 10002
Phone: (212)475-6400
Crisis Phone(s): (212)475-6400.

★4263★ Hotline Cares
2037 3rd Ave.
New York, NY 10029
Crisis Phone(s): (212)831-7050.

**★4264★ Institute for Modern Psychoanalysis
Domestic Violence Services**
112 W. 87th St.
New York, NY 10024
Phone: (212)496-9043

★4265★ Jewish Board of Family and Children's Services
120 W. 57th St.
New York, NY 10019
Phone: (212)582-9100

★4266★ New York Asian Women's Center
39 Bowery
New York, NY 10002
Phone: (212)732-5230
Crisis Phone(s): (212)732-5230.

★4267★ Sanctuary for Families
PO Box 413, Times Square Sta.
New York, NY 10108
Phone: (212)582-2091
Crisis Phone(s): (212)582-2091.

**★4268★ Urban Resource Institute
Urban Women's Retreat**
PO Box 804
New York, NY 10037
Phone: (212)690-6490
Crisis Phone(s): (212)690-6490.

★4269★ Victim Services Agency
2 Lafayette St.
New York, NY 10007
Phone: (212)577-7700
Crisis Phone(s): (212)577-7777; (212)619-6884 (New York City Runaway Hotline).

**★4270★ Victim Services Agency
Project Oasis**
60 Lafayette St.
New York, NY 10007
Phone: (212)964-0116
Crisis Phone(s): (212)577-7777.

★4271★ Victims Intervention Project
PO Box 136, Triboro Sta.
New York, NY 10035
Phone: (212)410-9080
Crisis Phone(s): (212)360-5090.

**★4272★ Volunteer Counseling Service of Rockland County
Batterers Intervention Project**
151 S. Main St.
New York, NY 10956
Phone: (914)634-5729

Newark

★4273★ **Family Counseling Service of the Finger Lakers**
Domestic Violence Services
703 E. Maple Ave.
PO Box 550
Newark, NY 14513
Phone: (315)331-1700
Crisis Phone(s): (315)331-4879.

Newburgh

★4274★ **Family Counseling Service of Orange County**
21 Grand St.
Newburgh, NY 12550
Phone: (914)561-0301

★4275★ **Orange County Safe Homes**
PO Box 649
Newburgh, NY 12550
Phone: (914)562-5340

★4276★ **Our Lady of Comfort**
91 Ann St.
Newburgh, NY 12550
Phone: (914)561-6267

Niagara Falls

★4277★ **Community Missions**
1570 Buffalo Ave.
Niagara Falls, NY 14303
Phone: (716)285-3403
Crisis Phone(s): (716)285-3403.

★4278★ **Family and Children's Services**
Passage Program
826 Chilton Ave.
Niagara Falls, NY 14301
Crisis Phone(s): (716)285-6984.

North Tonawanda

★4279★ **YWCA**
Domestic Violence Program
49 Tremont St.
North Tonawanda, NY 14120
Phone: (716)692-5580
Crisis Phone(s): (716)692-5643.

Norwich

★4280★ **Chenango County Mental Health Clinic**
Domestic Violence Services
5 Court St.
Norwich, NY 13815
Phone: (607)337-1600
Crisis Phone(s): (607)335-4362.

★4281★ **Crime Victims Program**
19 Prospect St.
Norwich, NY 13815
Phone: (607)336-1528
Crisis Phone(s): (607)336-1101.

Olean

★4282★ **Cattaraugus Community Action, Inc.**
Domestic Violence Program
210 E. Elm St.
Olean, NY 14760
Phone: (716)373-4027
Crisis Phone(s): (716)945-3970.

Oneida

★4283★ **Victims of Violence**
134 Vanderbilt Ave.
Oneida, NY 13421
Phone: (315)366-5000

Oneonta

★4284★ **Aid to Battered Women**
32 Main St.
Oneonta, NY 13820-2519
Phone: (607)433-8320
Crisis Phone(s): (607)432-4855.

Oswego

★4285★ **Services to Aid Families**
101 W. Utica St.
Oswego, NY 13126
Phone: (315)342-1609
Crisis Phone(s): (315)342-1600.

Owego

★4286★ **Victim/Witness Assistance Center of Tioga County**
55 North Ave.
Owego, NY 13827
Phone: (607)687-6866
Crisis Phone(s): (607)687-6866.

Plattsburgh

★4287★ **Stop Center on Domestic Violence**
159 Margaret St.
Plattsburgh, NY 12901
Phone: (518)563-6904

Pleasantville

★4288★ **Northern Westchester Shelter**
Non-residential Services
70 Memorial Plaza
Pleasantville, NY 10570
Phone: (914)747-4029
Crisis Phone(s): (914)747-0707.

Potsdam

★4289★ **Reachout of St. Lawrence County**
PO Box 5051
Potsdam, NY 13676
Phone: (315)265-2422

Poughkeepsie

★4290★ **Grace Smith House**
PO Box 5205
Poughkeepsie, NY 12602
Crisis Phone(s): (914)471-3033.

★4291★ **YWCA**
Battered Women Services
18 Bancroft Ave.
Poughkeepsie, NY 12601
Crisis Phone(s): (914)485-5550.

Queensbury

★4292★ **Giant Step Hotline for Rape and Domestic Violence**
PO Box 4085
Queensbury, NY 12804-0085
Crisis Phone(s): (518)793-5888.

Rochester

★4293★ **Alternatives for Battered Women**
PO Box 39601
Rochester, NY 14604
Crisis Phone(s): (716)232-7353.

★4294★ **YWCA**
Battered Women's Services
175 N. Clinton Ave.
Rochester, NY 14604
Crisis Phone(s): (716)546-5820.

Salamanca

★4295★ **Cattaraugus Community Action, Inc.**
Domestic Violence Program
25 Jefferson St.
Salamanca, NY 14779
Phone: (716)945-1041
Crisis Phone(s): (716)945-3970.

Saranac Lake

★4296★ **Tri-Lakes Community Center**
PO Box 589
Saranac Lake, NY 12983
Phone: (518)891-3173
Crisis Phone(s): (518)891-3173.

Saratoga Springs

★4297★ **Domestic Violence Services**
480 Broadway, LL20
Saratoga Springs, NY 12866
Phone: (518)583-0280
Crisis Phone(s): (518)584-8188.

Schenectady

★4298★ **YWCA**
Services to Families in Violence
44 Washington Ave.
Schenectady, NY 12305
Crisis Phone(s): (518)374-3394.

Shirley

★4299★ **Brighter Tomorrow**
PO Box 382
Shirley, NY 11967
Phone: (516)395-1801
Crisis Phone(s): (516)395-1800.

Spring Valley

★4300★ **Rockland Family Shelter**
39 S. Main St.
Spring Valley, NY 10977
Crisis Phone(s): (914)425-0112.

Staten Island

★4301★ **Victims Services Agency**
Bailey Seton Hospital
Staten Island, NY 10304
Phone: (718)447-5454
Crisis Phone(s): (212)577-7777.

Syracuse

★4302★ **Abused Person's Unit**
407 S. State St., 2nd Fl.
Syracuse, NY 13202
Phone: (315)425-3092
Crisis Phone(s): (315)425-2111.

★4303★ **Dorothy Day House**
145 W. Beard Ave.
Syracuse, NY 13205
Phone: (315)476-0617
Crisis Phone(s): (315)474-7011.

★4304★ **The Salvation Army
Counseling and Residential Services**
749 S. Warren St.
Syracuse, NY 13202
Crisis Phone(s): (315)475-1688.

★4305★ **Vera House**
PO Box 365
Syracuse, NY 13209
Phone: (315)425-0818
Crisis Phone(s): (315)468-3260.

★4306★ **YWCA**
Residence
960 Salt Springs Rd.
Syracuse, NY 13224
Phone: (315)445-1418
Crisis Phone(s): (315)445-1418.

Thornwood

★4307★ **Northern Westchester Shelter**
PO Box 105
Thornwood, NY 10594
Crisis Phone(s): (914)747-0707.

Tonawanda

★4308★ **YWCA**
Domestic Violence Program
49 Tremont St.
Tonawanda, NY 14120
Phone: (716)692-5580
Crisis Phone(s): (716)692-5643.

Troy

★4309★ **Unity House**
Families in Crisis
3215 6th Ave.
Troy, NY 12180-1205
Phone: (518)272-5917
Crisis Phone(s): (518)272-2370.

Tuckahoe

★4310★ **My Sisters' Place**
PO Box 337
Tuckahoe, NY 10702
Phone: (914)779-3900
Crisis Phone(s): (914)969-5800.

Utica

★4311★ **YWCA**
Hall House
1000 Cornelia St.
Utica, NY 13502
Phone: (315)793-0057
Crisis Phone(s): (315)797-7740.

Warsaw

★4312★ **Wyoming County Battered
Women's Services**
64 Main St.
Warsaw, NY 14569
Phone: (716)786-2010
Crisis Phone(s): (716)786-3300.

Watertown

★4313★ **Family Counseling Services of
Jefferson County**
643 Woolworth Bldg.
Watertown, NY 13601
Phone: (315)782-4483

★4314★ **Jefferson County Women's
Center**
131 Franklin St.
Watertown, NY 13601
Phone: (315)782-1823
Crisis Phone(s): (315)782-1855.

Wellsville

★4315★ **Family Violence Task Force of
Allegany County**
PO Box 521
Wellsville, NY 14895
Phone: (716)268-7605
Crisis Phone(s): (716)593-5322.

White Plains

★4316★ **Abused Spouse Assistance
Services**
29 Sterling Ave.
White Plains, NY 10606
Phone: (914)949-6741
Crisis Phone(s): (914)997-1010.

★4317★ **Samaritan House**
33 Church St.
White Plains, NY 10601
Phone: (914)948-3075
Crisis Phone(s): (914)949-4008.

North Carolina

Albemarle

★4318★ **Stanly County Department of
Social Services**
201 S. 2nd St.
Albemarle, NC 28001
Phone: (704)983-7300

Asheboro

★4319★ **Randolph County Family Crisis
Center**
PO Box 2161
Asheboro, NC 27203
Phone: (919)629-4159

Asheville

★4320★ **Helpmate, Inc.**
31 College Pl., No. D105
Asheville, NC 28801-2458
Phone: (704)254-2698
Crisis Phone(s): (704)254-0516.

Bakersville

★4321★ **Mitchell County Social Services
Domestic Violence Program**
PO Box 365
Bakersville, NC 28705
Phone: (704)688-2175

Boone

★4322★ **Oasis**
PO Box 1591
Boone, NC 28607
Phone: (704)264-1532
Crisis Phone(s): (704)262-5035.

Brevard

★4323★ **Safe Program**
PO Box 2013
Brevard, NC 28712
Phone: (704)885-7233

Bryson City

★4324★ **Safe Program**
PO Box 1416
Bryson City, NC 28713
Phone: (704)488-6809
Crisis Phone(s): (704)497-3930.

Burlington

★4325★ **Family Abuse Services of
Alamance County**
PO Box 2192
Burlington, NC 27216
Phone: (919)226-5982
Crisis Phone(s): (919)227-6220.

Charlotte

★4326★ The Shelter
PO Box 220312
Charlotte, NC 28222
Phone: (704)332-2513
Crisis Phone(s): (704)332-2513.

★4327★ Victim Assistance/Rape Crisis
Program
825 E. 4th St.
Charlotte, NC 28202
Phone: (704)336-2190
Crisis Phone(s): (704)375-9900.

Columbus

★4328★ Steps to Hope, Inc.
PO Box 518
Columbus, NC 28722
Phone: (704)894-2340
Crisis Phone(s): (704)894-2340.

Concord

★4329★ CVAN Battered Women's Shelter
PO Box 1749
Concord, NC 28026
Phone: (704)788-1108
Crisis Phone(s): (704)788-2826.

Durham

★4330★ Orange/Durham Coalition for
Battered Women
PO Box 51848
Durham, NC 27717
Phone: (919)489-1955
Crisis Phone(s): (919)929-0479; (919)732-2796; (919)683-8628.

Elizabeth City

★4331★ Crimes Against Women Task
Force
Albemarle Hopeline
PO Box 2064
Elizabeth City, NC 27906-2064
Phone: (919)338-5338
Crisis Phone(s): (919)338-3011.

Fayetteville

★4332★ Cumberland County Department
of Social Services
Domestic Violence Services
1101 Hay St.
Fayetteville, NC 28305
Phone: (919)323-4187
Crisis Phone(s): (919)323-4187.

Forest City

★4333★ Prevention of Abuse in the Home
PO Box 1075
Forest City, NC 28043
Phone: (704)245-8595
Crisis Phone(s): (704)245-8595.

Gastonia

★4334★ Gaston County Department of
Social Services
Battered Spouse Program
PO Box 10
Gastonia, NC 28053
Phone: (704)866-3679
Crisis Phone(s): (704)866-3300; and (704)865-2323.

Goldsboro

★4335★ Shelter of Wayne County
PO Box 11008
Goldsboro, NC 27532
Phone: (919)736-1313
Crisis Phone(s): (919)736-1313; (919)735-4357.

Greensboro

★4336★ Family and Children's Services
Turning Point
301 E. Washington St.
Greensboro, NC 27401-2911
Phone: (919)333-6910
Crisis Phone(s): (919)274-7316; and (919)273-7273.

Greenville

★4337★ Pitt County Family Violence
Program
PO Box 13
Greenville, NC 27835
Phone: (919)752-3811

★4338★ Real Crisis Intervention, Inc.
312 E. 10th St.
Greenville, NC 27858
Crisis Phone(s): (919)758-4357; (919)758-1976 (teen hotline).

Henderson

★4339★ Family Violence Intervention
Program
PO Box 1988
Henderson, NC 27536
Phone: (919)492-9693
Crisis Phone(s): (919)492-9693.

Hickory

★4340★ Family Guidance Center
First Step Spouse Abuse Program
17 Hwy. 70 SE
Hickory, NC 28602
Phone: (704)322-1400

High Point

★4341★ High Point Women's Shelter
323 Boulevard Ave.
High Point, NC 27260
Phone: (919)883-7474
Crisis Phone(s): (919)889-7273.

Jacksonville

★4342★ Onslow County Women's Center
PO Box 1622
Jacksonville, NC 28541
Phone: (919)347-4000
Crisis Phone(s): (919)347-4000.

Kingston

★4343★ SAFE
PO Box 3092
Kingston, NC 28502-3092
Phone: (919)523-5573
Crisis Phone(s): (919)523-5573.

Lenoir

★4344★ Shelter Home of Caldwell County
PO Box 426
Lenoir, NC 28645
Phone: (704)758-0888

Lexington

★4345★ Davidson County Domestic
Violence Services
PO Box 1231
Lexington, NC 27293
Phone: (704)243-1628
Crisis Phone(s): (704)249-8974.

Lumberton

★4346★ Southeastern Family Violence
Center
PO Box 642
Lumberton, NC 28359
Phone: (919)739-8622
Crisis Phone(s): (919)739-8622; (919)277-7660.

Manteo

★4347★ Outer Banks Hotline
PO Box 1417
Manteo, NC 27954
Phone: (919)473-5121
Crisis Phone(s): (919)473-3366; (919)995-4555.

Marion

★4348★ Family Services
PO Box 1572
Marion, NC 28752
Phone: (704)652-8538
Crisis Phone(s): (704)652-6150.

Morehead City

★4349★ Carteret County Domestic
Violence Program
408 Arendell St., Ste. 3
Morehead City, NC 28557
Phone: (919)726-3788
Crisis Phone(s): (919)247-3023.

Morganton

★4350★ OPTIONS
PO Box 2512
Morganton, NC 28655
Phone: (704)438-9444

Crisis Phone(s): (704)438-9444.

Mt. Airy

**★4351★ Surry Task Force on Domestic
Violence**
PO Box 1643
Mt. Airy, NC 27030
Phone: (919)789-6808

Crisis Phone(s): (919)386-4046.

Murphy

★4352★ Reach, Inc.
PO Box 977
Murphy, NC 28906
Phone: (704)837-8064

Crisis Phone(s): (704)837-7477.

New Bern

★4353★ Coastal Women's Shelter Board
PO Box 13081
New Bern, NC 28561
Phone: (919)638-4509

Crisis Phone(s): (919)638-5995.

**★4354★ Craven County Council on
Women**
Rape/Sexual Assault Program
PO Box 1285
New Bern, NC 28560
Phone: (919)636-3381

Crisis Phone(s): (919)638-5995.

Pittsboro

**★4355★ Family Violence and Rape Crisis
Services in Chatham County**
PO Box 1105
Pittsboro, NC 27312
Phone: (919)542-5445

Crisis Phone(s): (919)542-4422; (919)742-
5612; (919)929-0479.

Raleigh

★4356★ Interact, Inc.
1100 Wake Forest Rd.
Raleigh, NC 27604
Phone: (919)828-7501

Crisis Phone(s): (919)828-7740 (domestic violence); (919)828-3005 (rape crisis).

Reidsville

★4357★ HELP, Inc.
119 N. Scales
Reidsville, NC 27320
Phone: (919)342-3331

Crisis Phone(s): (919)342-3331.

Roanoke Rapids

**★4358★ Halifax County Mental Health
Center**
Services for Battered Women
PO Drawer 1199
Roanoke Rapids, NC 27870
Phone: (919)537-6174

Crisis Phone(s): (919)537-2909.

★4359★ Hannah's Place
PO Box 1392
Roanoke Rapids, NC 27870
Phone: (919)537-6312

Crisis Phone(s): (919)537-2556.

Salisbury

**★4360★ Rape, Child and Family Abuse
Crisis Council**
131 W. Council St.
Salisbury, NC 28144
Phone: (704)636-4718

Crisis Phone(s): (704)636-9222.

Sanford

**★4361★ Lee County Family Violence and
Rape Crisis Center**
PO Box 3191
Sanford, NC 27331-3191
Phone: (919)774-8923

Crisis Phone(s): (919)774-4520.

Shelby

★4362★ Abuse Prevention Council
PO Box 2895
Shelby, NC 28150
Phone: (704)487-7129

Smithfield

★4363★ Harbor, Inc.
PO Box 1903
Smithfield, NC 27577
Phone: (919)934-0233

Crisis Phone(s): (919)934-6161.

Sylva

★4364★ REACH of Jackson County
PO Box 1828
Sylva, NC 28779
Phone: (704)586-8969

Crisis Phone(s): (704)586-2459.

Taylorsville

★4365★ Crisis Council, Inc.
103 S. Center St.
Taylorsville, NC 28681
Phone: (704)632-7364

Crisis Phone(s): (704)685-2900.

Wadesboro

★4366★ Anson County Crisis Council
209 E. Wade St.
Wadesboro, NC 28170

Crisis Phone(s): (704)694-2273.

★4367★ Sandhills Center, Anson Unit
303 Eastview St.
Wadesboro, NC 28170
Phone: (704)694-6588

Washington

★4368★ OPTIONS
PO Box 1387
Washington, NC 27889
Phone: (919)946-3219
Toll-free: 800-682-0767

Waynesville

★4369★ REACH of Haywood County
PO Box 206
Waynesville, NC 28786
Phone: (704)456-7898

Crisis Phone(s): (704)456-7898.

Whiteville

**★4370★ Citizens Against Spouse Abuse
(CASA)**
PO Box 623
Whiteville, NC 28472
Phone: (919)642-2762

Crisis Phone(s): (919)642-3388.

Wilkesboro

★4371★ SAFE, Inc.
PO Box 445
Wilkesboro, NC 28697
Phone: (919)667-7656

Crisis Phone(s): (919)838-SAFE; (919)838-
7233.

Wilmington

**★4372★ Domestic Violence Shelter and
Services**
PO Box 1555
Wilmington, NC 28402
Phone: (919)343-0703

Crisis Phone(s): (919)343-0703.

Wilson

★4373★ Wesley Shelter
209 Douglas St.
Wilson, NC 27893
Phone: (919)291-2344

Crisis Phone(s): (919)237-5156.

Winston-Salem

★4374★ Family Services
PO Box 604
Winston-Salem, NC 27102
Phone: (919)724-3979

Crisis Phone(s): (919)723-8125.

★4375★ Family Services
610 Coliseum Dr.
Winston-Salem, NC 27106
Phone: (919)722-8173

Yanceyville

★4376★ Caswell Family Violence
Prevention Program
PO Box 639
Yanceyville, NC 27379
Phone: (919)694-5655

Crisis Phone(s): (919)694-5198.

North Dakota

Beulah

★4377★ Women's Action and Resource
Center
207 Hwy. 49 NW
Beulah, ND 58523
Phone: (701)873-2274

Crisis Phone(s): (701)748-2274 (nights and weekends); (701)873-2274.

Bismarck

★4378★ Abused Adult Resource Center
PO Box 167
Bismarck, ND 58502
Phone: (701)222-8370

Crisis Phone(s): (800)472-2911.

★4379★ North Dakota Council on Abused
Women's Services
418 E. Rosser, No. 320
Bismarck, ND 58501
Phone: (701)255-6240
Toll-free: 800-472-2911

Bottineau

★4380★ Bottineau County Coalition
Against Domestic Violence
PO Box 371
Bottineau, ND 58318
Phone: (701)228-2028

Crisis Phone(s): (701)228-3171.

Devils Lake

★4381★ Safe Alternatives for Abused
Families
Mercy Hospital, 4th Fl.
Devils Lake, ND 58301
Phone: (701)662-7378

Crisis Phone(s): (701)662-5323.

Dickinson

★4382★ Domestic Violence and Rape
Crisis Center
PO Box 1081
Dickinson, ND 58601
Phone: (701)225-4506

Crisis Phone(s): (701)225-4506.

Ellendale

★4383★ Kedish House
PO Box 322
Ellendale, ND 58436
Phone: (701)349-4729
Toll-free: 800-472-2911

Crisis Phone(s): (701)349-3611.

Fargo

★4384★ Rape and Abuse Crisis Center of
Fargo/Moorhead
PO Box 2984
Fargo, ND 58108
Phone: (701)293-7273

Crisis Phone(s): (701)293-7273.

★4385★ YWCA
Fargo/Moorhead Services for Battered
Women
1616 12th Ave. N.
Fargo, ND 58102
Phone: (701)232-2547

Ft. Yates

★4386★ Tender Hearts Against Family
Violence
PO Box 478
Ft. Yates, ND 58538
Phone: (701)854-3402

Grafton

★4387★ Domestic Violence Program of
Walsh County
422 Hill Ave.
Grafton, ND 58237
Phone: (701)352-0647

Crisis Phone(s): (701)352-3059.

Grand Forks

★4388★ Abuse and Rape Crisis Center
111 S. 4th St.
Grand Forks, ND 58201
Phone: (701)746-0405

Crisis Phone(s): (701)746-8900.

Jamestown

★4389★ Safe Shelter
PO Box 1934
Jamestown, ND 58402
Phone: (701)251-2300

Crisis Phone(s): (701)251-2300.

Lisbon

★4390★ Women's Advocacy Network
PO Box 919
Lisbon, ND 58054
Phone: (701)683-5061

Crisis Phone(s): (701)683-5061.

Minot

★4391★ Domestic Violence Crisis Center
PO Box 881
Minot, ND 58702
Phone: (701)852-2258

Crisis Phone(s): (701)857-2200.

New Town

★4392★ Ft. Berthold Coalition Against
Domestic Violence
PO Box 935
New Town, ND 58763
Phone: (701)627-4171

Crisis Phone(s): (701)627-3617.

Stanley

★4393★ Action Resource Center
PO Box 538
Stanley, ND 58784
Phone: (701)628-3233

Crisis Phone(s): (701)628-3233.

Valley City

★4394★ Abused Persons Outreach Center
PO Box 508
Valley City, ND 58072
Phone: (701)845-0078

Crisis Phone(s): (701)845-0072.

Washburn

★4395★ McLean Family Resource Center
PO Box 506
Washburn, ND 58577
Phone: (701)462-8643

Crisis Phone(s): (701)462-8643.

Williston

★4396★ Family Crisis Shelter
PO Box 1893
Williston, ND 58801
Phone: (701)572-0757

Crisis Phone(s): (701)572-9111; (701)664-3305 (Tioga); (701)842-3000 (Watford City).

Ohio

Akron

★4397★ Battered Women's Shelter of
Akron
PO Box 9074
Akron, OH 44305
Phone: (216)374-0740

Crisis Phone(s): (216)374-1111.

Alliance

★4398★ Alliance Area Domestic Violence
Shelter
PO Box 3622
Alliance, OH 44601
Phone: (216)823-7223

Ashtabula

★4399★ Homesafe, Inc.
PO Box 702
Ashtabula, OH 44004
Phone: (216)992-2727

Crisis Phone(s): (216)992-2727.

Athens

★4400★ My Sister's Place
PO Box 1158
Athens, OH 45701
Phone: (614)594-8337
Toll-free: 800-443-3402
Crisis Phone(s): (614)593-3402.

Batavia

★4401★ YWCA
House of Peace
55 S. 4th St.
Batavia, OH 45103
Phone: (513)753-7281

Beachwood

★4402★ The Center for Prevention of
Domestic Violence
23875 Commerce Park Rd.
Beachwood, OH 44122
Phone: (216)831-5440
Crisis Phone(s): (216)391-4357.

Cambridge

★4403★ Haven of Hope
PO Box 948
Cambridge, OH 43725
Phone: (614)432-3542
Crisis Phone(s): (614)432-3542.

Canton

★4404★ Domestic Violence Project
PO Box 9432
Canton, OH 44711-9432
Phone: (216)453-7233
Crisis Phone(s): (216)452-6000.

Celina

★4405★ Family Crisis Network
PO Box 632
Celina, OH 45822
Phone: (419)586-1133
Crisis Phone(s): (419)586-1133.

Chardon

★4406★ Women Safe
PO Box 656
Chardon, OH 44024
Toll-free: 800-752-1995
Crisis Phone(s): (216)564-9555.

Chillicothe

★4407★ Ross County Coalition Against
Domestic Violence
PO Box 1727
Chillicothe, OH 45601
Phone: (614)773-4357

Cincinnati

★4408★ YWCA
Alice Paul House
898 Walnut St.
Cincinnati, OH 45202
Crisis Phone(s): (513)241-2757.

Cleveland

★4409★ Templum House
PO Box 5466
Cleveland, OH 44101
Phone: (216)631-2275

★4410★ Witness/Victim Service Center
Family Violence Program of Cuyahoga
County
Justice Center
Cleveland, OH 44113
Phone: (216)443-7345

Columbus

★4411★ Action Ohio Coalition for Battered
Women
PO Box 15673
Columbus, OH 43215
Phone: (614)221-1255
Nancy Evans, Exec.Dir.
Description: Advocates and service providers
for domestic violence victims and their families.
Promotes changes in public policy.

★4412★ CHOICES
PO Box 06157
Columbus, OH 43206
Phone: (614)224-6080
Crisis Phone(s): (614)224-4663.

Dayton

★4413★ Artemis House
Violence Resource Center
224 N. Wilkinson St., Ste. 303
Dayton, OH 45402
Phone: (513)461-4357
Crisis Phone(s): (513)461-4357.

★4414★ YWCA
Battered Women Project
141 W. 3rd St.
Dayton, OH 45402
Phone: (513)222-0874

Defiance

★4415★ Northwestern Ohio Crisis-Line
PO Box 13
Defiance, OH 43512-0013
Phone: (419)782-1314
Crisis Phone(s): (419)782-1100.

Elyria

★4416★ Genesis House
42707 N. Ridge Rd.
Elyria, OH 44035
Phone: (216)244-1853

Findlay

★4417★ Open Arms Domestic Violence
Shelter and Rape Crisis Services
PO Box 496
Findlay, OH 45839
Phone: (419)422-4766
Crisis Phone(s): (419)422-4766.

Fostoria

★4418★ First Step
PO Box 1103
Fostoria, OH 44830
Phone: (419)435-7300
Crisis Phone(s): (419)435-7300.

Gallipolis

★4419★ Serenity House
PO Box 454
Gallipolis, OH 45631
Crisis Phone(s): (800)252-5554 (Meigs and
Jackson Counties); 446-5554 (Gallia County).

Greenville

★4420★ Shelter From Violence
PO Box 988
Greenville, OH 45331
Phone: (513)548-2020
Crisis Phone(s): (513)548-2020.

Hamilton

★4421★ YWCA
Shelter for Battered Persons and Their
Children
244 Dayton St.
Hamilton, OH 45011
Phone: (513)863-7099

Hillsboro

★4422★ Highland County Domestic
Violence Task Force
1111 Northview Dr.
Hillsboro, OH 45133
Phone: (513)393-8118
Crisis Phone(s): (513)393-9904; (513)981-
7020.

Lancaster

★4423★ Lighthouse
PO Box 215
Lancaster, OH 43130
Phone: (614)687-4423
Crisis Phone(s): (614)687-4423.

Lebanon

★4424★ Family Abuse Shelter
570 N. State Rte. 741
Lebanon, OH 45036
Phone: (513)932-6301
Toll-free: 800-932-3366

Lima

★4425★ Crossroads
PO Box 643
Lima, OH 45802
Crisis Phone(s): (419)228-4357.

Mansfield

★4426★ The Shelter
PO Box 1524
Mansfield, OH 44901
Crisis Phone(s): (419)526-4450.

Marietta

★4427★ Ex-Victims Empowered, Inc.
PO Box 122
Marietta, OH 45750
Phone: (614)374-5819

Marion

★4428★ Turning Point
PO Box 822
Marion, OH 43301-0822
Phone: (614)382-8988
Crisis Phone(s): (614)382-8988; (800)232-6505 (Crawford, Delaware, Marion, Morrow, Union, and Wyandot Counties only).

Mt. Vernon

★4429★ New Directions
PO Box 453
Mt. Vernon, OH 43050
Phone: (614)397-4357
Crisis Phone(s): (614)397-4357.

New Philadelphia

★4430★ Harbor House
PO Box 435
New Philadelphia, OH 44663
Phone: (216)364-1374
Crisis Phone(s): (216)364-1374.

Newark

★4431★ Family Counseling Services of Newark
New Beginnings Shelter
68 W. Church St., 3rd Fl.
Newark, OH 43055
Phone: (614)349-7066
Crisis Phone(s): (614)345-4498.

Ottawa

★4432★ Crime Victims Services and Crisis Assistance in Putnam County
PO Box 453
Ottawa, OH 45875
Phone: (419)523-1111
Crisis Phone(s): (419)523-1111.

Painesville

★4433★ Forbes House
PO Box 702
Painesville, OH 44077
Phone: (216)357-7321
Crisis Phone(s): (216)357-1018; (216)953-9779.

Portsmouth

★4434★ Southern Ohio Task Force on Domestic Violence
PO Box 754
Portsmouth, OH 45662
Phone: (614)456-8217
Crisis Phone(s): (614)354-1010.

Ravenna

★4435★ Woman Shelter
206 N. Main St.
Ravenna, OH 44266
Phone: (216)297-7868
Crisis Phone(s): (216)297-9999.

St. Clairsville

★4436★ Women's Tri-County Help Center
PO Box 494
St. Clairsville, OH 43942
Phone: (614)695-5441
Crisis Phone(s): (304)234-8161; (800)695-1639.

Sandusky

★4437★ Citizens Council on Domestic Violence
Lilith Place Shelter
PO Box 823
Sandusky, OH 44870
Phone: (419)625-4878
Crisis Phone(s): (419)625-4878.

Sidney

★4438★ New Choices
129 E. Court St.
PO Box 452
Sidney, OH 45365
Phone: (513)498-7261

Springfield

★4439★ Project Woman Crisis Services
1316 E. High St.
Springfield, OH 45505
Phone: (513)325-3707
Toll-free: 800-634-9893

Steubenville

★4440★ ALIVE
PO Box 866
Steubenville, OH 43952
Phone: (614)283-3444
Crisis Phone(s): (614)283-3444.

Toledo

★4441★ Bethany House—Long Term Shelter
PO Box 4221
Toledo, OH 43609
Phone: (419)241-5331

★4442★ Family Service of Northwest Ohio
1 Stranahan Sq., Ste. 414
Toledo, OH 43604
Phone: (419)244-5511

★4443★ YWCA
Battered Women Shelter
1018 Jefferson Ave.
Toledo, OH 43624
Phone: (419)241-3235
Crisis Phone(s): (419)241-7386.

Troy

★4444★ Family Abuse Shelter
16 E. Franklin St.
Troy, OH 45373
Phone: (513)339-6761
Crisis Phone(s): (800)351-7347 (county-wide).

Van Wert

★4445★ Crisis Care Line
PO Box 266
Van Wert, OH 45891
Phone: (419)238-0784
Crisis Phone(s): (419)238-4357.

Warren

★4446★ Someplace Safe
PO Box 282
Warren, OH 44482
Phone: (216)393-3003
Crisis Phone(s): (216)393-1565; (216)545-4371.

Waverly

★4447★ Service and Assistance for Victims of Spouse Abuse
408 Walnut St.
Waverly, OH 45690
Phone: (614)947-5555

Wooster

★4448★ Every Woman's House
237 N. Walnut St.
Wooster, OH 44691
Phone: (216)263-6021
Crisis Phone(s): 263-1020.

Xenia

★4449★ Domestic Violence Project
PO Box 271
Xenia, OH 45385
Phone: (513)372-4552

Youngstown

★4450★ YWCA
Barbara M. Wick Transitional House
25 W. Raven
Youngstown, OH 44503
Phone: (216)746-6361
Crisis Phone(s): (216)746-6361.

Zanesville

★4451★ Transitions
PO Box 226
Zanesville, OH 43702
Phone: (614)454-3214
Crisis Phone(s): (614)454-3213.

Oklahoma

Ada

★4452★ Services for Battered Women
PO Box 2274
Ada, OK 74820
Phone: (405)436-3504
Crisis Phone(s): (405)436-3504.

Altus

★4453★ ACMI House
PO Box 397
Altus, OK 73521
Phone: (405)482-7449
Crisis Phone(s): (405)482-3800.

Bartlesville

★4454★ Women and Children in Crisis
PO Box 5016
Bartlesville, OK 74005
Phone: (918)336-1188
Crisis Phone(s): (918)336-1188.

Broken Arrow

**★4455★ Domestic Violence Intervention
Services**
116 W Dallas
Broken Arrow, OK 74012
Phone: (418)251-2933
Crisis Phone(s): (918)585-3143.

Chickasha

**★4456★ Women's Service and Family
Resource Center**
PO Box 1539
Chickasha, OK 73023
Phone: (405)222-1819
Toll-free: 800-734-4117
Crisis Phone(s): (405)222-1818.

Clinton

★4457★ ACTION Associates
PO Box 1534
Clinton, OK 73601
Phone: (405)323-0838
Crisis Phone(s): (405)323-2604; (405)225-1313 (Elk City); (405)928-2122 (Sayre).

Durant

★4458★ Crisis Control Center
PO Box 113
Durant, OK 74702
Phone: (405)924-3030
Crisis Phone(s): (405)924-3030.

Enid

★4459★ YWCA
Option House
525 S. Quincy
Enid, OK 73701
Phone: (405)234-7581
Crisis Phone(s): (405)234-7644.

Idabel

**★4460★ Southeastern Oklahoma Services
for Battered Women**
PO Box 394
Idabel, OK 74745
Phone: (405)286-3369
Toll-free: (808)522-7233

Lawton

★4461★ New Directions
PO Box 1684
Lawton, OK 73502
Phone: (405)357-6141
Crisis Phone(s): (405)357-2500.

McAlester

★4462★ Area Women's Center
PO Box 1356
McAlester, OK 74502
Phone: (918)423-3444
Crisis Phone(s): (918)423-3444.

★4463★ Women in Safe Homes
PO Box 3182
McAlester, OK 74502
Phone: (918)423-3700
Crisis Phone(s): (918)423-3700.

Miami

★4464★ Community Crisis Center
PO Box 905
Miami, OK 74355
Phone: (918)540-2432
Crisis Phone(s): (918)542-1001.

Muskogee

★4465★ Women in Safe Homes
PO Box 487
Muskogee, OK 74402
Phone: (918)682-7879
Crisis Phone(s): (918)682-7878.

Norman

★4466★ Women's Resource Center
Norman Shelter for Battered Women
PO Box 5089
Norman, OK 73070
Phone: (405)360-0306
Crisis Phone(s): (405)360-0590.

Oklahoma City

★4467★ YWCA
Crisis Intervention Services
2460 NW 39th Expy.
Oklahoma City, OK 73112
Phone: (405)948-1770
Crisis Phone(s): (405)949-1866 (crisis); (405)949-0907 (shelter); (405)943-7273 (rape).

Ponca City

★4468★ Domestic Violence Program
PO Box 85
Ponca City, OK 74602
Phone: (405)762-3603
Crisis Phone(s): (405)762-2873.

Poteau

**★4469★ Women's Crisis Center of La
Flore County**
PO Box 774
Poteau, OK 74953
Phone: (918)647-2810
Crisis Phone(s): (918)647-9800.

Sapulpa

**★4470★ Domestic Violence Intervention
Services**
16 E Lee
Sapulpa, OK 74066
Phone: (918)224-9290
Crisis Phone(s): (918)585-3143.

Shawnee

★4471★ Project SAFE
322 N. Broadway
Shawnee, OK 74801
Phone: (405)273-9953
Crisis Phone(s): (405)273-2420.

Stillwater

**★4472★ Stillwater Domestic Violence
Services**
PO Box 1059
Stillwater, OK 74076
Phone: (405)624-3028
Crisis Phone(s): (405)642-3020.

Tahlequah

★4473★ Help-in-Crisis
PO Box 1975
Tahlequah, OK 74464
Phone: (918)456-0673
Crisis Phone(s): (918)456-HELP.

Tulsa

★4474★ Domestic Violence Intervention
  Services
1419 E. 15th St.
Tulsa, OK 74120-5840
Phone: (918)585-3163
Crisis Phone(s): (918)585-3143.

Woodward

★4475★ Northwest Domestic Crisis
  Services
1323 Kansas
Woodward, OK 73801
Phone: (405)256-1215
Toll-free: 800-545-0518
Crisis Phone(s): (405)256-8712.

Oregon

Ashland

★4476★ Dunn House
PO Box 369
Ashland, OR 97520
Phone: (503)779-4357
Crisis Phone(s): (503)779-4357; (503)779-2112.

Astoria

★4477★ Women's Crisis Service
883 Astor St., No. 3
Astoria, OR 97103
Phone: (503)325-3426
Crisis Phone(s): (503)325-5735.

Baker

★4478★ May Day, Inc.
2101 Main St., No. 12
Baker, OR 97814
Phone: (503)523-4134
Crisis Phone(s): (503)523-5903.

Bend

★4479★ Central Oregon Battering and
  Rape Alliance
PO Box 1086
Bend, OR 97709
Phone: (503)382-9227
Crisis Phone(s): (800)356-2369.

Burns

★4480★ Harney Helping Organization for
  Personal Emergencies
PO Box 24
Burns, OR 97720
Phone: (503)573-7176
Crisis Phone(s): (503)573-7176.

Coos Bay

★4481★ Coos County Women's Crisis
  Service
PO Box 3521
Coos Bay, OR 97420
Phone: (503)888-6911
Crisis Phone(s): (503)267-2020.

Corvallis

★4482★ Center Against Rape and
  Domestic Violence
PO Box 914
Corvallis, OR 97339
Phone: (503)758-0219
Crisis Phone(s): (503)754-0110.

The Dalles

★4483★ Haven from Domestic Violence
PO Box 576
The Dalles, OR 97058
Phone: (503)296-1662
Crisis Phone(s): (503)298-4789.

Eugene

★4484★ Family Shelter House
969 Hwy. 99 N.
Eugene, OR 97402
Phone: (503)689-7156

★4485★ Womenspace
PO Box 5485
Eugene, OR 97405
Phone: (503)485-8232
Toll-free: (808)281-2800
Crisis Phone(s): (503)485-6513 and (503)485-7262 (TDD).

Grants Pass

★4486★ Illinois Valley Counseling Center
714 NW A St.
Grants Pass, OR 97526-1865
Phone: (503)592-3172
Crisis Phone(s): (503)592-3172.

★4487★ Women's Crisis Support Team
748 NW 5th St.
Grants Pass, OR 97526
Phone: (503)479-9349
Crisis Phone(s): (503)479-9349.

Hillsboro

★4488★ Shelter/Domestic Violence
  Resource Center
PO Box 494
Hillsboro, OR 97123
Phone: (503)640-5352
Crisis Phone(s): (503)640-1171.

Hood River

★4489★ Project Helping Hands Against
  Violence
PO Box 441
Hood River, OR 97031
Phone: (503)386-6603
Crisis Phone(s): (503)386-6603.

John Day

★4490★ Society Against Battering, Rape,
  and Abuse
166 SW Brent
John Day, OR 97845
Phone: (503)575-2500
Crisis Phone(s): (503)575-2255.

Klamath Falls

★4491★ Klamath Crisis Center
1014 Main
Klamath Falls, OR 97601
Phone: (503)884-0636
Crisis Phone(s): (800)452-3669 (Oregon only).

La Grande

★4492★ Shelter from the Storm
PO Box 173
La Grande, OR 97850
Phone: (503)963-7226
Crisis Phone(s): (503)963-9261.

Lakeview

★4493★ Crisis Intervention Center
513 Center St.
Lakeview, OR 97630
Phone: (503)947-2449
Toll-free: 800-338-7590
Crisis Phone(s): (503)947-2449.

Lincoln City

★4494★ Lincoln Shelter and Services
PO Box 426
Lincoln City, OR 97367
Phone: (503)994-3365
Crisis Phone(s): (503)994-5959; (503)265-7726.

McMinnville

★4495★ Henderson House
PO Box 26
McMinnville, OR 97128
Phone: (503)472-0244
Crisis Phone(s): (503)472-1503.

Mill City

★4496★ Canyon Crisis Service
PO Box 500
Mill City, OR 97360
Phone: (503)897-2327
Crisis Phone(s): (503)897-2327.

Milwaukie

★4497★ Clackamas Women's Services
PO Box 22547
Milwaukie, OR 97222
Phone: (503)654-2807
Crisis Phone(s): (503)654-2288.

North Bend

★4498★ Women's Crisis Service/Shelter
PO Box 791
North Bend, OR 97459
Phone: (503)756-7864
Crisis Phone(s): (503)756-7000.

Ontario

★4499★ Project DOVE
PO Box 745
Ontario, OR 97914
Phone: (503)889-6316
Crisis Phone(s): (503)889-2000.

Pendleton

**★4500★ Domestic Violence Services
Awakening House Shelter**
PO Box 152
Pendleton, OR 97801
Phone: (503)276-3322
Toll-free: 800-833-1161
Crisis Phone(s): (503)278-0241.

Portland

★4501★ Bradley/Angle House
PO Box 14694
Portland, OR 97214
Phone: (503)281-3540
Crisis Phone(s): (503)281-2442.

★4502★ Portland Women's Crisis-Line
PO Box 42610
Portland, OR 97242
Phone: (503)232-9751
Crisis Phone(s): (503)235-5333.

★4503★ Raphael House
PO Box 10797
Portland, OR 97210
Phone: (503)222-6507
Crisis Phone(s): (503)222-6222.

**★4504★ The Salvation Army
West Women's and Children's Shelter**
PO Box 2398
Portland, OR 97208
Phone: (503)224-7718

**★4505★ YWCA
Women's Resource Center**
1111 SW 10th
Portland, OR 97205
Phone: (503)223-6281

Roseburg

**★4506★ Battered Person's Advocacy
Project**
PO Box 1942
Roseburg, OR 97470
Phone: (503)673-7867
Toll-free: 800-464-6543
Crisis Phone(s): (503)673-6641.

St. Helens

**★4507★ Columbia County Women's
Resource Center**
PO Box 22
St. Helens, OR 97051
Phone: (503)397-7110
Crisis Phone(s): (503)397-6161.

Salem

**★4508★ Mid-Valley Women's Crisis
Service**
PO Box 851
Salem, OR 97308
Phone: (503)378-1572
Crisis Phone(s): (503)399-7722.

Tillamook

★4509★ Women's Crisis Center
PO Box 187
Tillamook, OR 97141
Phone: (503)842-9486

Pennsylvania

Allison Park

★4510★ Crisis Center North
PO Box 75
Allison Park, PA 15101
Phone: (412)487-4700
Crisis Phone(s): (412)487-4700.

Altoona

★4511★ Domestic Abuse Project
Altoona, PA 16601
Phone: (814)944-3583

Beaver

★4512★ Women's Center
PO Box 397
Beaver, PA 15009
Phone: (412)775-2032
Crisis Phone(s): (412)775-0131.

Bedford

★4513★ Bedford County Abuse Center
PO Box 496
Bedford, PA 15522
Phone: (814)623-7767
Crisis Phone(s): (814)623-5682.

Bethlehem

★4514★ Turning Point
PO Box 5355
Bethlehem, PA 18015
Phone: (215)437-0222
Crisis Phone(s): (215)437-3369.

Bloomsburg

★4515★ Women's Center
Bloomsburg, PA 17815
Toll-free: (808)544-8293
Crisis Phone(s): (717)784-6631.

Bradford

**★4516★ YWCA
Victim's Resource Center**
24 W. Corydon St.
Bradford, PA 16701
Phone: (814)368-4235
Crisis Phone(s): (814)368-6325.

Carmichaels

**★4517★ Fayette County Family Abuse
Council**
226 S. Market St.
Carmichaels, PA 15320
Phone: (412)966-2200

Chambersburg

★4518★ Women in Need
PO Box 25
Chambersburg, PA 17201
Phone: (717)264-3056
Crisis Phone(s): (717)264-4444.

Clarion

★4519★ SAFE
PO Box 108
Clarion, PA 16214
Phone: (814)226-8481
Toll-free: 800-992-3039
Crisis Phone(s): (814)226-7233.

Clearfield

★4520★ Marian House
Clearfield, PA 16830
Phone: (814)765-5646

Doylestown

★4521★ A Woman's Place
PO Box 299
Doylestown, PA 18901
Phone: (215)343-9241
Crisis Phone(s): (215)348-9780; (215)752-8035; (215)538-7760.

Du Bois

★4522★ Hope for Victims of Violence
PO Box 896
Du Bois, PA 15801
Phone: (814)371-0207
Toll-free: 800-773-1223
Crisis Phone(s): (814)371-1223.

Erie

★4523★ Hospitality House
PO Box 1436
Erie, PA 16512-1436
Phone: (814)454-8161
Crisis Phone(s): (814)454-8161.

Evans City

★4524★ Volunteers Against Abuse Center
PO Box 293
Evans City, PA 16033
Phone: (412)776-5910
Crisis Phone(s): (412)776-6790; (412)282-3672.

Franklin

★4525★ YWCA
Women's Center Satellite Office
1235 Liberty St., No. 5
Franklin, PA 16323
Phone: (814)432-7491
Crisis Phone(s): (814)432-7491.

Gettysburg

★4526★ Survivors
PO Box 3572
Gettysburg, PA 17325
Phone: (717)334-0589
Crisis Phone(s): (717)334-9777; (717)633-6005.

Hanover

★4527★ YWCA
Battered Women's Services
23 W. Chestnut St.
Hanover, PA 17331
Phone: (717)637-2125
Crisis Phone(s): (717)632-0007.

Harrisburg

★4528★ Women's Services of
Westmoreland County
7629 Timber Ln.
Harrisburg, PA 17112-9005
Phone: (412)837-9540
Crisis Phone(s): (412)836-1122.

★4529★ YWCA
Rape and Domestic Violence Services
215 Market St.
Harrisburg, PA 17101
Phone: (717)234-7931
Toll-free: 800-654-1211

Honesdale

★4530★ Victims Intervention Program
PO Box 986
Honesdale, PA 18431
Phone: (717)253-4431
Crisis Phone(s): (717)253-4401.

Huntingdon

★4531★ Huntingdon House
PO Box 217
Huntingdon, PA 16652
Phone: (814)643-2801
Crisis Phone(s): (814)643-1190.

Indiana

★4532★ Alice Paul House
PO Box 417
Indiana, PA 15701
Phone: (412)349-4444
Toll-free: 800-435-7249
Crisis Phone(s): (412)349-4444.

Jenkintown

★4533★ Women's Center of Montgomery
County
Benson East, Ste. B-7
Jenkintown, PA 19046
Phone: (215)885-5020
Crisis Phone(s): (215)885-5020.

Johnstown

★4534★ Women's Help Center
809 Napoleon St.
Johnstown, PA 15901
Phone: (814)536-5361
Toll-free: 800-999-7406
Crisis Phone(s): (814)536-5361 (Cambria County); (814)443-2824 (Somerset County).

Kittanning

★4535★ HAVIN
PO Box 983
Kittanning, PA 16201
Phone: (412)543-1180
Crisis Phone(s): (412)548-8888.

Lancaster

★4536★ Lancaster Shelter for Abused
Women
PO Box 359
Lancaster, PA 17604
Phone: (717)299-9677
Crisis Phone(s): (717)299-1249; (717)299-1240.

Laporte

★4537★ Wise Options for Women
Laporte, PA 18626
Phone: (717)946-4215

Lehighton

★4538★ Carbon County Women in Crisis
PO Box 155
Lehighton, PA 18235
Crisis Phone(s): (215)377-0760; (215)377-0880; (800)424-5600.

Lewisburg

★4539★ Susquehanna Valley Women in
Transition
PO Box 170
Lewisburg, PA 17837
Phone: (717)523-1134
Crisis Phone(s): (717)523-6482; (717)374-7773.

Lewistown

★4540★ Mifflin County Abuse Network
PO Box 268
Lewistown, PA 17044
Phone: (717)242-0715
Crisis Phone(s): (717)242-2444 (Mifflin County); (717)436-2402 (Juniata County).

Lock Haven

★4541★ Clinton County Women's Center
151 Susquehanna Ave.
Lock Haven, PA 17745
Phone: (717)748-9539
Crisis Phone(s): (717)748-9509.

McKeesport

★4542★ Womansplace
PO Box 144
McKeesport, PA 15134
Phone: (412)678-7831
Crisis Phone(s): (412)678-4616.

Meadville

★4543★ Women's Services
The Greenhouse
PO Box 637
Meadville, PA 16335
Phone: (814)724-4637
Crisis Phone(s): (814)333-9766.

Media

★4544★ Domestic Abuse Project
PO Box 174
Media, PA 19063
Phone: (215)565-6272
Crisis Phone(s): (215)565-4590.

Milford

★4545★ Women's Resources
413 Broad St.
Milford, PA 18337
Crisis Phone(s): (717)296-HELP.

Montrose

★4546★ Women's Resource Center
Box 202
Montrose, PA 18801
Crisis Phone(s): (717)278-1800.

New Castle

★4547★ Women's Shelter of Lawrence County
PO Box 1422
New Castle, PA 16103
Phone: (412)652-9206
Crisis Phone(s): (412)652-9036.

Norristown

★4548★ Laurel House
PO Box 764
Norristown, PA 19401
Phone: (215)643-3150
Toll-free: 800-642-3150
Crisis Phone(s): (215)643-3150.

★4549★ Women's Center of Montgomery County
1 Montgomery Plaza, Ste. 1002
Norristown, PA 19404
Crisis Phone(s): (215)279-1548.

North Warren

★4550★ YWCA
Women's Center
207 2nd Ave.
North Warren, PA 16365
Phone: (814)723-6350
Toll-free: 800-338-3460
Crisis Phone(s): (814)726-1030.

Philadelphia

★4551★ Lutheran Social Mission's Society Women's Program
Philadelphia, PA 19125
Phone: (215)426-8610
Crisis Phone(s): (215)739-9999; (215)235-9992 (Spanish).

★4552★ Women Against Abuse
PO Box 13758
Philadelphia, PA 19101
Phone: (215)386-1280
Crisis Phone(s): (215)386-7777.

★4553★ Women in Transition
172 S. 9th St., Ste. 502
Philadelphia, PA 19107
Phone: (215)922-7177
Crisis Phone(s): (215)922-7500.

Pittsburgh

★4554★ Crisis Center North
PO Box 101093
Pittsburgh, PA 15237-8093
Phone: (412)364-8340
Crisis Phone(s): (412)364-5556.

★4555★ Women's Center and Shelter of Greater Pittsburgh
PO Box 9024
Pittsburgh, PA 15224
Phone: (412)687-8017
Crisis Phone(s): (412)687-8005.

Pottstown

★4556★ Women's Center of Montgomery County
546 High St.
Pottstown, PA 19464
Crisis Phone(s): (215)970-7363.

Pottsville

★4557★ Schuylkill Women in Crisis
PO Box 96
Pottsville, PA 17901
Phone: (717)622-3991
Toll-free: 800-282-0634
Crisis Phone(s): (717)622-6220.

Punxsutawney

★4558★ Crossroads
JCCEDA, Inc.
Punxsutawney, PA 15767
Phone: (814)849-1617
Toll-free: 800-648-3381
Crisis Phone(s): (814)938-3302; (814)849-1617; (814)438-3580 (Shelter).

Reading

★4559★ Berks Women in Crisis
PO Box 803
Reading, PA 19603
Phone: (215)373-2053
Crisis Phone(s): (215)372-9540.

Ridgway

★4560★ CAPSEA
PO Box 464
Ridgway, PA 15853
Phone: (814)772-3838
Crisis Phone(s): (814)772-1227; (814)486-1227.

Scranton

★4561★ Women's Resource Center
Domestic Violence Program
PO Box 975
Scranton, PA 18501-0975
Phone: (717)346-4672
Crisis Phone(s): (717)346-4671; (717)278-1800.

Sharon

★4562★ AWARE
PO Box 662
Sharon, PA 16146
Phone: (412)981-3753
Crisis Phone(s): (412)981-1457.

State College

★4563★ Centre County Women's Resource Center
State College, PA 16801
Phone: (814)238-7066
Crisis Phone(s): (814)234-5050.

Stroudsburg

★4564★ Women's Resources
112 Park Ave.
Stroudsburg, PA 18360-1549
Phone: (717)421-4200
Crisis Phone(s): (717)421-4000.

Tarentum

★4565★ Alle-Kiski Area Hope Center
PO Box 67
Tarentum, PA 15084-0067
Phone: (412)224-1100
Crisis Phone(s): (412)224-4673; (412)339-4673.

Titusville

★4566★ Titusville Women's Center
201 N. Franklin St.
Titusville, PA 16354
Phone: (814)827-2746
Toll-free: 800-828-7474
Crisis Phone(s): (814)827-9777; (814)432-7491.

Towanda

★4567★ Abuse and Rape Crisis Center
PO Box 186
Towanda, PA 18848
Phone: (717)265-5333
Crisis Phone(s): (717)265-1901.

Tunkhannock

★4568★ Victims Resource Center
86 E. Tioga St.
Tunkhannock, PA 18657
Phone: (717)836-5544
Toll-free: 800-331-3261
Crisis Phone(s): (717)836-5544.

Union City

★4569★ Horizon House
Union City, PA 16438
Phone: (814)438-2675
Crisis Phone(s): (814)438-2675.

Uniontown

★4570★ Fayette County Family Abuse Council
215 Searight Ave.
Uniontown, PA 15401
Phone: (412)427-2530
Crisis Phone(s): (412)439-9500.

Washington

★4571★ Washington Women's Shelter
PO Box 503
Washington, PA 15301
Crisis Phone(s): (412)223-9190.

Wawa

★4572★ Women's Alternative Center
Station Rd.
Wawa, PA 19063
Crisis Phone(s): (215)459-9177.

Waynesburg

★4573★ Greene County Domestic Violence Program
County Office Bldg., Rm. 202
Waynesburg, PA 15370
Phone: (412)852-2893
Crisis Phone(s): (412)627-9099.

Wellsboro

★4574★ Tioga County Women's Coalition
PO Box 933
Wellsboro, PA 16901-0933
Phone: (717)724-3549
Crisis Phone(s): (717)724-3554; (717)724-7911.

West Chester

★4575★ Domestic Violence Center of Chester County
PO Box 832
West Chester, PA 19381
Phone: (215)431-3546
Crisis Phone(s): (215)431-1430.

West Hazleton

★4576★ Victims Resource Center
107 Madison Ave.
West Hazleton, PA 18201
Toll-free: 800-331-3261
Crisis Phone(s): (717)454-7200.

Wilkes-Barre

★4577★ Domestic Violence Service Center
PO Box 1662
Wilkes-Barre, PA 18703
Phone: (717)823-5834
Crisis Phone(s): (717)455-9971; (717)823-7312.

★4578★ Victims Resource Center
68 S. Franklin
Wilkes-Barre, PA 18701
Phone: (717)823-0765
Toll-free: 800-331-3261
Crisis Phone(s): (717)823-0765; (717)836-5544; (717)454-7200.

Williamsport

★4579★ Wise Options for Women
Williamsport, PA 17701
Phone: (717)323-8167

York

★4580★ ACCESS, York, Inc.
PO Box 743
York, PA 17405
Phone: (717)845-8816
Toll-free: 800-262-8444
Crisis Phone(s): (717)846-5400.

Zelienople

★4581★ Volunteers Against Abuse Center of Butler County
PO Box 27
Zelienople, PA 16063
Phone: (412)452-5710
Crisis Phone(s): (412)776-6790.

Rhode Island

Central Falls

★4582★ Blackstone Shelter
324 Broad St.
Central Falls, RI 02863
Phone: (401)723-3057

Newport

★4583★ Newport County Women's Resource Center
114 Touro St.
Newport, RI 02840-2912
Phone: (401)846-5263
Crisis Phone(s): (401)847-2533.

Providence

★4584★ Sojourner House
PO Box 3413, Wayland Square Sta.
Providence, RI 02906
Phone: (401)431-1870
Crisis Phone(s): (401)765-3232.

★4585★ Women's Center
45 E. Transit St.
Providence, RI 02906
Crisis Phone(s): (401)861-2760.

Tiverton

★4586★ Tiverton Outreach Office of Women's Resource Center
346 Judson
Tiverton, RI 02878
Phone: (401)625-1144
Crisis Phone(s): (401)625-1144.

Wakefield

★4587★ Women's Resource Center of South County
61 Main St.
Wakefield, RI 02879
Phone: (401)782-3990

Warwick

★4588★ Elizabeth Buffum Chace House
PO Box 9476
Warwick, RI 02889
Phone: (401)738-1700
Crisis Phone(s): (401)738-1700.

South Carolina

Aiken

★4589★ Coalition to Assist Abused Persons
PO Box 1293
Aiken, SC 29802-1293
Phone: (803)649-0480
Crisis Phone(s): (803)648-9900.

Beaufort

★4590★ Citizens Opposed to Domestic Abuse
PO Box 1775
Beaufort, SC 29202
Phone: (803)525-1009

Columbia

★4591★ SISTERCARE, Inc.
PO Box 1029
Columbia, SC 29202
Phone: (803)765-5477
Crisis Phone(s): (803)765-9428.

Florence

★4592★ Pee Dee Coalition Against Domestic and Sexual Assault
PO Box 2152
Florence, SC 29503
Phone: (803)669-4694
Crisis Phone(s): (803)669-4600.

Greenville

★4593★ Family Service of Greenville Women in Crisis
301 University Ridge, Ste. 5500
Greenville, SC 29601-3674
Phone: (803)232-2434
Crisis Phone(s): (803)235-2224.

Myrtle Beach

★4594★ Citizens Against Spouse Abuse
PO Box 912
Myrtle Beach, SC 29578
Phone: (803)626-7595
Crisis Phone(s): (803)448-6206 (Myrtle Beach).

North Charleston

★4595★ My Sister's House
PO Box 5341
North Charleston, SC 29406
Phone: (803)747-4069
Toll-free: 800-273-4673
Crisis Phone(s): (803)744-3242.

Orangeburg

★4596★ **Sister United**
PO Box 2554
Orangeburg, SC 29116-2554
Phone: (803)533-1289

Rock Hill

★4597★ **SISTER-HELP**
PO Box 10876
Rock Hill, SC 29731
Phone: (803)324-5141
Crisis Phone(s): (803)329-2800.

Spartanburg

★4598★ **Spartanburg County Safe Homes Network**
163 Union St.
Spartanburg, SC 29302
Phone: (803)583-9803
Crisis Phone(s): (803)583-9803.

Sumter

★4599★ **YWCA**
Family Violence Programs
246 Church St.
Sumter, SC 29150
Phone: (803)773-7158

South Dakota

Aberdeen

★4600★ **Resource Center for Women**
317 S. Kline
Aberdeen, SD 57401
Phone: (605)226-1212
Crisis Phone(s): (605)226-1212.

Agency Village

★4601★ **The Women's Circle**
Old Agency Box 689
Agency Village, SD 57262
Phone: (605)698-4129
Crisis Phone(s): (605)698-4129.

Brookings

★4602★ **Brookings Women's Center**
802 11th Ave.
Brookings, SD 57006
Phone: (605)688-4518

Eagle Butte

★4603★ **Sacred Heart Center Women's Shelter**
Landmark St., Box 2000
Eagle Butte, SD 57625-2000
Phone: (605)964-6062
Crisis Phone(s): (605)964-SAFE.

Flandreau

★4604★ **Wholeness Center**
115 2nd Ave. E.
Flandreau, SD 57028
Phone: (605)997-3661
Crisis Phone(s): (605)997-3535.

Ft. Thompson

★4605★ **Project SAFE**
PO Box 49
Ft. Thompson, SD 57339
Phone: (605)245-2471
Crisis Phone(s): (605)245-2471.

Gregory

★4606★ **Gregory Shelter**
PO Box 408
Gregory, SD 57533
Phone: (605)835-8394
Crisis Phone(s): (605)835-8893.

Hot Springs

★4607★ **Fall River Crisis Intervention Team**
906 N. River St.
Hot Springs, SD 55747-0995
Phone: (605)745-5859
Crisis Phone(s): (605)745-6070.

Huron

★4608★ **YWCA**
Family Violence Program
17 5th Ave., SW
Huron, SD 57350
Crisis Phone(s): (605)352-9433 (days); (605)353-6200 (evenings & weekends).

Lake Andes

★4609★ **Native American Women's Health Education Resource Center**
PO Box 572
Lake Andes, SD 57356
Phone: (605)487-7072
Crisis Phone(s): (605)487-7072.

Lower Brule

★4610★ **Services to Victims of Crime**
PO Box 299
Lower Brule, SD 57548-0299
Phone: (605)473-5662

Madison

★4611★ **Madison Area Help-Line**
115 N. Chicago
Madison, SD 57042
Crisis Phone(s): (605)256-3336.

Martin

★4612★ **People Against Violence**
PO Box 903
Martin, SD 57551
Phone: (605)685-6829
Crisis Phone(s): (605)685-6829.

Mission

★4613★ **White Buffalo Calf Woman Society Shelter**
PO Box 227
Mission, SD 57555
Phone: (605)856-2317

Mitchell

★4614★ **Mitchell Area Safe House**
219 W. 3rd
Mitchell, SD 57301
Phone: (605)996-2765
Crisis Phone(s): (605)996-4440.

Pierre

★4615★ **Missouri Shores Women's Resource Center**
Hughes County Courthouse
Pierre, SD 57501
Phone: (605)224-0256
Crisis Phone(s): (605)224-7187; (605)224-3932.

Pine Ridge

★4616★ **Sacred Shawl Women's Society**
PO Box 273
Pine Ridge, SD 57770
Phone: (605)867-5138
Crisis Phone(s): (605)867-5008.

Rapid City

★4617★ **Women Against Violence**
PO Box 3042
Rapid City, SD 57709
Crisis Phone(s): (605)341-4808.

Redfield

★4618★ **Family Crisis Center**
723 E. 7th Ave.
Redfield, SD 57469
Crisis Phone(s): (605)472-3097.

Sioux Falls

★4619★ **Children's Inn**
409 North Western Ave.
Sioux Falls, SD 57104
Phone: (605)338-0116
Crisis Phone(s): (605)338-4880.

★4620★ **Citizens Against Rape and Domestic Violence**
PO Box 876
Sioux Falls, SD 57101
Phone: (605)339-0116
Crisis Phone(s): (605)339-4357.

★4621★ YWCA
Crisis and Transition Shelter
300 W. 11th St.
Sioux Falls, SD 57102
Phone: (605)336-3660
Crisis Phone(s): (605)336-3660.

Spearfish

★4622★ Victims of Violence Intervention
Program
PO Box 486
Spearfish, SD 57783
Phone: (605)642-7825

Vermillion

★4623★ Coalition Against Domestic
Violence
PO Box 144
Vermillion, SD 57069
Crisis Phone(s): (605)624-5311.

Watertown

★4624★ Women's Resource Center
PO Box 781
Watertown, SD 57201
Phone: (605)886-4300
Crisis Phone(s): (605)886-4300.

Winner

★4625★ Winner Area Crisis-Line
PO Box 322
Winner, SD 57580
Crisis Phone(s): (605)842-0888.

Yankton

★4626★ Women's Center/Shelter
510 Broadway
Yankton, SD 57078-0675
Phone: (605)665-4811
Crisis Phone(s): (605)665-1448.

Tennessee

Alcoa

★4627★ Haven House
PO Box 134
Alcoa, TN 37701
Phone: (615)982-1087
Crisis Phone(s): (615)982-1087.

Bristol

★4628★ Abuse Alternatives
PO Box 3388
Bristol, TN 37625
Phone: (615)968-7957
Crisis Phone(s): (615)764-2287.

Chattanooga

★4629★ Family and Children's Services
Domestic Violence Program
PO Box 6234-37401
Chattanooga, TN 37401
Phone: (615)755-2840
Crisis Phone(s): (615)755-2700.

Cookville

★4630★ Upper Cumberland Alliance
Against Domestic Violence
PO Box 1183
Cookville, TN 38503
Phone: (615)526-5197
Crisis Phone(s): (615)526-4730.

Crossville

★4631★ Battered Women, Inc.
PO Box 3063
Crossville, TN 38557
Phone: (615)456-0747
Crisis Phone(s): (615)484-4642.

Gallatin

★4632★ Home Safe
650 N. Water
Gallatin, TN 37202
Phone: (615)452-5439
Crisis Phone(s): (615)452-4315 (Summer
County); (615)382-0829 (Robeertson County);
(615)444-8955 (Wilson County).

Jackson

★4633★ WRAP
416 E. Lafayette
Jackson, TN 38301
Phone: (901)423-0700
Toll-free: 800-273-8712

Johnson City

★4634★ The Salvation Army
Services for Battered Women
c/o Vicki Gibson
Johnson City, TN 37604
Phone: (615)926-8901

Kingsport

★4635★ Safe House, Inc.
PO Box 3426
Kingsport, TN 37664
Phone: (615)246-2273
Crisis Phone(s): (615)246-2273.

Knoxville

★4636★ Child and Family Services
Family Crisis Center
2535 Magnolia Ave.
Knoxville, TN 37914
Phone: (615)673-3066
Crisis Phone(s): (615)637-8000.

★4637★ Serenity Shelter
PO Box 3352
Knoxville, TN 37927
Phone: (615)523-4800
Crisis Phone(s): (615)971-4673.

Lawrenceburg

★4638★ The Shelter
PO Box 894
Lawrenceburg, TN 38464
Phone: (615)523-4800
Crisis Phone(s): (615)762-1115.

Marion

★4639★ Women's Services of Family
Services
428 S. Washington, Box 9
Marion, TN 46953
Phone: (317)662-9971
Crisis Phone(s): (317)664-0701.

Memphis

★4640★ The Salvation Army
Emergency Family Shelter
200 Monroe
Memphis, TN 38103
Phone: (901)526-1066

★4641★ YWCA
Abused Women's Services
766 S. Highland
Memphis, TN 38111
Phone: (901)725-5861
Crisis Phone(s): (901)458-1661.

Morristown

★4642★ CEASE
PO Box 3359
Morristown, TN 37815-3359
Phone: (615)581-7029
Crisis Phone(s): (615)581-2220.

Murfreesboro

★4643★ Domestic Violence Program
PO Box 2652
Murfreesboro, TN 37130
Phone: (615)896-2012
Crisis Phone(s): (615)896-2012.

Nashville

★4644★ The Salvation Army
Services for Battered Women
600 Demonbreun
Nashville, TN 37203
Phone: (615)242-0411

★4645★ Tennessee Task Force Against
Domestic Violence
PO Box 120972
Nashville, TN 37212-0972
Phone: (615)242-8288
Kathy England, Exec.Dir.
Description: Battered women's programs and
shelters for women. To end all forms of violence
against women and their children. Seeks

changes in societies acceptance of wife and child abuse. Sponsors training program.

★4646★ YWCA
Shelter and Domestic Violence Program
1608 Woodmont Blvd.
Nashville, TN 37215
Crisis Phone(s): (615)297-8833.

Newport

★4647★ Cosby Coalition Against Domestic Violence
Safe Space
PO Box 831
Newport, TN 37821
Phone: (615)623-3125
Toll-free: 800-244-5968

Oak Ridge

★4648★ YWCA
Battered Women's Services
1660 Oak Ridge Tpke.
Oak Ridge, TN 37830
Phone: (615)482-9922
Crisis Phone(s): (615)482-0005.

Tullahoma

★4649★ Haven of Hope
PO Box 1671
Tullahoma, TN 37388
Phone: (615)857-3909

Texas

Abilene

★4650★ Noah Project
PO Box 875
Abilene, TX 79604
Phone: (915)676-7107
Toll-free: 800-444-3551
Crisis Phone(s): (915)676-7107.

Alpine

★4651★ Rio-Pecos Family Crisis Center
109 N. 6th
Alpine, TX 79831
Phone: (915)837-2242
Crisis Phone(s): (915)837-2242 (collect calls accepted).

Alvin

★4652★ Women's Center of Brazoria County
Outreach
1111 Adoue
Alvin, TX 77511
Phone: (713)331-0703
Toll-free: 800-243-5788
Crisis Phone(s): (409)849-5166.

Amarillo

★4653★ Rape Crisis/Domestic Violence Center
804 S. Bryan, No. 214
Amarillo, TX 79106
Phone: (806)373-8533
Toll-free: 800-749-9026
Crisis Phone(s): (806)373-8022.

Angleton

★4654★ Women's Center of Brazoria County
PO Box 476
Angleton, TX 77516-0476
Phone: (409)849-9553
Toll-free: 800-243-5788
Crisis Phone(s): (409)849-5166.

Austin

★4655★ Center for Battered Women
PO Box 19454
Austin, TX 78760
Phone: (512)385-5181
Crisis Phone(s): (512)928-9070.

★4656★ Family Violence Diversion Network
2001 Chicon
Austin, TX 78722
Phone: (512)478-1648

★4657★ Texas Council on Family Violence
3415 Graystone, Ste. 220
Austin, TX 78731
Phone: (512)794-1133
Toll-free: 800-444-1978

Bastrop

★4658★ Family Crisis Center
PO Box 736
Bastrop, TX 78602
Phone: (512)321-7760
Crisis Phone(s): (512)321-7755.

Bay City

★4659★ Matagorda County Women's Crisis Center
PO Box 1820
Bay City, TX 77414
Phone: (409)245-9299
Crisis Phone(s): (409)245-9109.

Baytown

★4660★ Bay Area Women's Center
PO Box 3735
Baytown, TX 77522
Phone: (713)424-3300
Crisis Phone(s): (713)422-2292.

Beaumont

★4661★ Women's and Children's Shelter of Southeast Texas
PO Box 6606
Beaumont, TX 77705-0606
Phone: (409)883-2545
Toll-free: 800-621-8882
Crisis Phone(s): (409)832-7575.

Boerne

★4662★ Hill Country Crisis Council
PO Box 1817
Boerne, TX 78028
Phone: (512)249-8379
Crisis Phone(s): (512)249-8379.

Bonham

★4663★ Crisis Center
PO Box 787
Bonham, TX 75418-0787
Phone: (903)583-7740

Brenham

★4664★ Faith Mission and Help Center
305 College
Brenham, TX 77833
Phone: (409)830-1488

Brownsville

★4665★ Friendship of Women
PO Box 3112
Brownsville, TX 78523
Phone: (512)544-7412

Brownwood

★4666★ Noah Project
PO Box 250
Brownwood, TX 76804
Phone: (915)646-9574
Crisis Phone(s): (915)646-9574.

Bryan

★4667★ Phoebe's Home
PO Box 3490
Bryan, TX 77805
Phone: (409)775-2471
Crisis Phone(s): (409)775-5355.

Burleson

★4668★ Johnson County Women's Shelter
PO Box 453
Burleson, TX 76028
Phone: (817)295-3855
Crisis Phone(s): (817)295-9396.

Cleburne

★4669★ Family Crisis Center
PO Box 43
Cleburne, TX 76031
Phone: (817)641-2343
Toll-free: 800-848-3206
Crisis Phone(s): (817)641-2332.

Corpus Christi

★4670★ Women's Shelter
PO Box 3368
Corpus Christi, TX 78463-3368
Phone: (512)881-8888
Crisis Phone(s): (512)881-8888.

Dallas

★4671★ The Family Place
4211 Cedar Springs, No. 100
Dallas, TX 75219
Phone: (214)559-2170
Crisis Phone(s): (214)941-1991.

★4672★ Genesis Women's Shelter
Drawer G
Dallas, TX 75208
Phone: (214)942-2998
Crisis Phone(s): (214)942-2998.

★4673★ The Salvation Army
Family Violence Program
PO Box 35928
Dallas, TX 75235
Phone: (214)688-4494
Crisis Phone(s): (214)688-4494.

Denton

★4674★ Denton County Friends of the Family
PO Box 623
Denton, TX 76202
Phone: (817)387-5131
Crisis Phone(s): (817)382-7273.

Dumas

★4675★ Safe Place
PO Box 317
Dumas, TX 79029
Phone: (806)935-7585
Crisis Phone(s): (806)935-2828.

El Paso

★4676★ Center for Battered Women
PO Box 26219
El Paso, TX 79926
Phone: (915)593-1000
Crisis Phone(s): (915)593-7300.

Ft. Stockton

★4677★ Rio-Pecos Family Crisis Center
502 N Spring
Ft. Stockton, TX 79735
Phone: (915)336-5584
Crisis Phone(s): (915)837-2242 (collect calls accepted).

Ft. Worth

★4678★ Women's Haven of Tarrant County
PO Box 1456
Ft. Worth, TX 76101
Phone: (817)535-6462
Crisis Phone(s): (817)535-6464; (817)535-6465.

Fredericksburg

★4679★ Hill Country Crisis Council
PO Box 835
Fredericksburg, TX 78624
Phone: (512)997-9756
Crisis Phone(s): (512)997-9855.

Gainesville

★4680★ Crisis Center
Cooke County Friends of the Family
PO Box 1221
Gainesville, TX 76240
Phone: (817)665-2873

Galveston

★4681★ Women's Resource and Crisis Center
PO Box 1545
Galveston, TX 77553
Phone: (409)763-1441
Crisis Phone(s): (409)765-SAFE; (409)948-HELP; (409)925-HELP; (713)332-HELP.

Garland

★4682★ New Beginning Center
218 N. 10th St.
Garland, TX 75040-6172
Phone: (214)276-0057
Crisis Phone(s): (214)276-0057.

Grand Prairie

★4683★ Brighter Tomorrow
PO Box 532151
Grand Prairie, TX 75053
Phone: (214)262-8383

Greenville

★4684★ Women in Need
PO Box 349
Greenville, TX 75401
Phone: (214)455-4612
Toll-free: 800-7-HELPME
Crisis Phone(s): (214)454-HELP.

Harlingen

★4685★ Family Crisis Center
2220 Haine Dr., Ste. 32
Harlingen, TX 78550
Phone: (512)423-9304
Crisis Phone(s): (512)423-9304.

Haskell

★4686★ Noah Project
PO Box 52
Haskell, TX 79521
Phone: (817)864-2551
Toll-free: 800-444-3551
Crisis Phone(s): (817)864-2551.

Hereford

★4687★ Rape Crisis/Domestic Violence Center
Deaf Smith County Courthouse, No. 301
Hereford, TX 79045
Phone: (806)364-7822
Crisis Phone(s): (806)373-8022.

Hondo

★4688★ Medina County Women's Crisis Center
PO Box 393
Hondo, TX 78861
Phone: (512)426-5972
Crisis Phone(s): (512)426-5131.

Houston

★4689★ Aid to Victims of Domestic Abuse
2626 South Loop W., Ste. 420
Houston, TX 77054
Phone: (713)664-2832

★4690★ The Bridge Over Troubled Waters
18301-A Egret Bay Blvd.
Houston, TX 77058
Phone: (713)333-9815

★4691★ Family Service Center
4625 Lillian
Houston, TX 77007
Phone: (713)861-4849

★4692★ Family Violence Center
4610 SM 1960 W.
Houston, TX 77069
Phone: (713)583-0652
Crisis Phone(s): (713)583-2539.

★4693★ Houston Area Women's Center Shelter for Abused Women and Their Children
Houston, TX 77098
Phone: (713)528-6798
Crisis Phone(s): (713)528-2121.

★4694★ Houston Area Women's Shelter Non-residential Family Violence Program
3101 Richmond Ave., No. 150
Houston, TX 77098-3013
Phone: (713)528-6798
Crisis Phone(s): (713)528-5785.

★4695★ The Roseate, Inc.
Dept. 382
Houston, TX 77290
Phone: (713)444-1367
Crisis Phone(s): (713)351-4357.

Huntsville

★4696★ **Walker County Family Violence Council**
SAAFE House
PO Box 1893
Huntsville, TX 77342-1893
Phone: (409)291-3529
Crisis Phone(s): (409)291-3369.

Hurst

★4697★ **The Women's Shelter**
1241 Southridge Ct., Ste. 103
Hurst, TX 76503
Phone: (817)282-2211
Crisis Phone(s): (817)460-5624.

Irving

★4698★ **New Tomorrows**
PO Box 157214
Irving, TX 75017-7214
Phone: (214)594-1772

Jacksonville

★4699★ **Cherokee County Crisis Center**
PO Box 8371
Jacksonville, TX 75766
Toll-free: 800-442-1691

Kilgore

★4700★ **Kilgore Community Crisis Center**
905 Broadway
Kilgore, TX 75662
Phone: (903)984-3019
Toll-free: 800-333-9148
Crisis Phone(s): (903)984-2377.

Killeen

★4701★ **Families in Crisis**
PO Box 25
Killeen, TX 76541
Phone: (817)634-1184
Toll-free: 800-373-2774
Crisis Phone(s): (817)634-8309.

Laredo

★4702★ **Laredo Family Violence Center**
PO Box 3305
Laredo, TX 78041
Phone: (512)724-5051
Crisis Phone(s): (512)727-7888.

Longview

★4703★ **Women's Center of East Texas**
PO Box 347
Longview, TX 75606
Phone: (903)757-9308
Toll-free: 800-441-5555
Crisis Phone(s): (903)757-9308.

Lubbock

★4704★ **Women's Protective Services**
1706 23rd St., No. 104
Lubbock, TX 79411
Phone: (806)747-6491
Toll-free: 800-736-6491
Crisis Phone(s): (806)747-6491.

Lufkin

★4705★ **New Angelinas County Outreach Office**
304 N. Rauet
Lufkin, TX 75901
Phone: (409)639-1681

Marble Falls

★4706★ **Crisis Center**
PO Box 805
Marble Falls, TX 78654
Phone: (512)693-3656
Crisis Phone(s): (512)693-5600.

Marfa

★4707★ **Rio-Pecos Family Crisis Center**
MAC Bldg.
Marfa, TX 79843
Phone: (915)729-3388
Crisis Phone(s): (915)837-2242 (collect calls accepted).

McAllen

★4708★ **Mujeres Unidas/Women Together**
420 N. 21st St.
McAllen, TX 78501
Phone: (512)630-4878
Crisis Phone(s): (512)630-HURT.

Midland

★4709★ **Permian Basin Center for Battered Women**
PO Box 2942
Midland, TX 79702
Phone: (915)683-1300
Crisis Phone(s): (915)683-1300.

Minerals Wells

★4710★ **Hope Inc.**
PO Box 1622
Minerals Wells, TX 76067
Phone: (817)325-1308
Crisis Phone(s): (817)325-1306.

Nacogdoches

★4711★ **Women's Shelter of East Texas**
PO Box 569
Nacogdoches, TX 75963-0569
Phone: (409)569-1018
Toll-free: 800-828-SAFE
Crisis Phone(s): (409)569-8850.

New Braunfels

★4712★ **Comal County Women's Center**
PO Box 310344
New Braunfels, TX 78131-0344
Phone: (512)620-7520
Crisis Phone(s): (512)620-HELP.

★4713★ **Family Violence Shelter**
150 N. Seguin, Ste. 306
New Braunfels, TX 78130
Phone: (512)620-5533

Pampa

★4714★ **Tralee Crisis Center for Women**
PO Box 2880
Pampa, TX 79066
Phone: (806)669-1131
Crisis Phone(s): (800)658-2796.

Paris

★4715★ **Family Haven**
1220 Main St.
Paris, TX 75460
Phone: (214)784-6842
Toll-free: 800-444-2836
Crisis Phone(s): (214)784-6842.

Pasadena

★4716★ **The Bridge Over Troubled Waters**
1414 E. Southmore
Pasadena, TX 77501
Phone: (713)472-0753
Crisis Phone(s): (713)473-2801.

Pearland

★4717★ **Women's Center of Brazoria County**
Outreach
2335 N. Texas
Pearland, TX 77581
Phone: (713)485-0934
Toll-free: 800-243-5788
Crisis Phone(s): (409)849-5166.

Perryton

★4718★ **Panhandle Crisis Center**
PO Box 502
Perryton, TX 79070
Phone: (806)435-5013
Toll-free: 800-753-5308
Crisis Phone(s): (806)435-5008.

Plainview

★4719★ **Hale County Crisis Center**
PO Box 326
Plainview, TX 79073-0326
Phone: (806)293-9772
Crisis Phone(s): (806)293-7273.

Plano

★4720★ Collin County Women's Shelter
2701 W. 15th, Ste. 12
Plano, TX 75075
Phone: (214)422-2911
Crisis Phone(s): (214)422-7233.

Richmond

★4721★ Ft. Bend County Women's Center
PO Box 183
Richmond, TX 77469
Phone: (713)342-0251
Crisis Phone(s): (713)342-4357.

Round Rock

★4722★ Williamson County Crisis Center
211 Commena, No. 103
Round Rock, TX 78664
Phone: (512)255-1278
Crisis Phone(s): (512)255-1212.

San Angelo

★4723★ Family Shelter
PO Box 5018
San Angelo, TX 76902
Phone: (915)655-5775
Crisis Phone(s): (915)655-5774; (800)749-8631.

San Antonio

★4724★ Battered Women's Shelter of Bexar County
PO Box 10393
San Antonio, TX 78210
Phone: (512)733-8810
Crisis Phone(s): (512)733-8810.

★4725★ Battered Women's Shelter of Bexar County
Outreach: Women's and Children's Resource Center
800 NW Loop 410, Ste. 378
San Antonio, TX 78216
Phone: (512)525-9834

San Marcos

★4726★ Hays County Women's Center
PO Box 234
San Marcos, TX 78667-0234
Phone: (512)396-3404
Crisis Phone(s): (512)396-4357.

Seguin

★4727★ Guadalupe County Women's Shelter
PO Box 1302
Seguin, TX 78155
Phone: (512)372-2780
Crisis Phone(s): (512)372-2780.

Sherman

★4728★ Grayson County Women's Crisis-Line
PO Box 2112
Sherman, TX 75091-2112
Phone: (903)893-3909
Crisis Phone(s): (903)893-5615.

Snyder

★4729★ Noah Project
PO Box 425
Snyder, TX 79549
Phone: (915)573-1822
Toll-free: 800-444-3551

Texarkana

★4730★ Domestic Violence Prevention
PO Box 712
Texarkana, TX 75504
Phone: (903)794-4000
Crisis Phone(s): (903)793-4357.

Tyler

★4731★ East Texas Crisis Center
3027 SSE Loop 323
Tyler, TX 75701
Phone: (903)595-3199
Toll-free: 800-333-0358
Crisis Phone(s): (903)595-5591.

Uvalde

★4732★ Medina County Women's Crisis Center
PO Box 514
Uvalde, TX 78802
Phone: (512)278-1067
Crisis Phone(s): (512)278-6310.

Vernon

★4733★ First Step, Inc.
Outreach Office
1600 Pease St., Ste. 214
Vernon, TX 76384
Phone: (817)553-4384

Victoria

★4734★ Women's Crisis Center
PO Box 395
Victoria, TX 77901
Phone: (512)573-4357

Waco

★4735★ Family Abuse Center
PO Box 20395
Waco, TX 76702-0395
Phone: (817)753-8401
Crisis Phone(s): (817)753-8401.

★4736★ Sanctuary Home
PO Box 952
Waco, TX 76701
Phone: (817)754-0730

Wichita Falls

★4737★ First Step, Inc.
PO Box 773
Wichita Falls, TX 76307
Phone: (817)767-3330
Toll-free: 800-658-2683
Crisis Phone(s): (817)767-4933.

The Woodlands

★4738★ Montgomery County Women's Center
1600 Lake Front Circle, No. 200
The Woodlands, TX 77387-8666
Phone: (713)367-8003
Crisis Phone(s): (713)292-4338; (409)539-5757.

Utah

Blanding

★4739★ San Juan Social Services
Domestic Violence Program
522 North 100 East
Blanding, UT 84511
Phone: (801)678-3211

Logan

★4740★ Citizens Against Physical and Sexual Abuse
PO Box 3617
Logan, UT 84321
Phone: (801)752-4493
Crisis Phone(s): (801)753-2500.

Ogden

★4741★ Your Community Connection of Ogden/Northern Utah
Women's Crisis Center
2261 Adams Ave.
Ogden, UT 84401
Phone: (801)394-9456
Crisis Phone(s): (801)392-7273.

Park City

★4742★ The Counseling Institute
Domestic Violence Program
1725 Bonanza Dr., Ste. D
Park City, UT 84060
Phone: (801)649-2426

Price

★4743★ Utah Department of Social Services
Domestic Violence Shelter
90 N. 1st E.
Price, UT 84501
Crisis Phone(s): (801)637-6850.

Provo

★4744★ Legal Center for Victims of Domestic Violence
PO Box 353
Provo, UT 84603
Phone: (801)375-1031

★4745★ **Women and Children in Crisis**
PO Box 1075
Provo, UT 84603-1075
Phone: (801)374-9351
Crisis Phone(s): (801)377-5500.

Richfield

★4746★ **Utah Office of Human Services
Domestic Violence Program**
PO Box 610
Richfield, UT 84701
Phone: (801)896-5411

St. George

★4747★ **Utah Office of Human Services
Domestic Violence Program**
168 North 100 East
St. George, UT 84770
Phone: (801)673-9691

Salt Lake City

★4748★ **Community Counseling Center
Domestic Violence Treatment Program**
660 South 200 East, Ste. 308
Salt Lake City, UT 84111
Phone: (801)355-2846

★4749★ **Legal Aid Society
Domestic Violence Victim Assistance**
225 South 200 East, Ste. 230
Salt Lake City, UT 84111
Phone: (801)355-4357

★4750★ **YWCA
Women in Jeopardy Program**
322 East 300 South
Salt Lake City, UT 84111
Phone: (801)355-2804
Crisis Phone(s): (801)355-2804.

Vernal

★4751★ **Utah Basin Counseling
Women's Crisis Center**
559 N. 1700, W.
Vernal, UT 84078
Toll-free: 800-325-4709
Crisis Phone(s): (801)781-0743.

Vermont

Bennington

★4752★ **Project Against Violent
Encounters**
PO Box 227
Bennington, VT 05201
Phone: (802)442-2370
Crisis Phone(s): (802)442-2111.

Brattleboro

★4753★ **Women's Crisis Center**
PO Box 933
Brattleboro, VT 05302
Phone: (802)257-7364
Crisis Phone(s): (802)254-6954.

Bristol

★4754★ **Addison County Women in Crisis**
6 Main St.
Bristol, VT 05443
Phone: (802)453-4754

Burlington

★4755★ **Women Helping Battered Women**
PO Box 1535
Burlington, VT 05402
Phone: (802)658-3131
Crisis Phone(s): (802)658-1996.

★4756★ **YWCA
Battered Women's Services**
278 Main St.
Burlington, VT 05401
Phone: (802)862-7520

Chelsea

★4757★ **Chelsea Help for Battered
Women**
Box 36
Chelsea, VT 05038
Crisis Phone(s): (802)685-3000.

★4758★ **Safeline**
PO Box 254
Chelsea, VT 05038
Phone: (802)685-4514
Toll-free: 800-639-7233

Hardwick

★4759★ **AWARE**
PO Box 307
Hardwick, VT 05843
Phone: (802)472-6463

Montpelier

★4760★ **Battered Women's Services of
Montpelier**
PO Box 828
Montpelier, VT 05601
Phone: (802)223-0855

★4761★ **Central Vermont Shelter Project**
137 Berry St.
Montpelier, VT 05602-3539
Crisis Phone(s): (802)476-5022.

Morrisville

★4762★ **Clarina Howard Nichols Center**
PO Box 517
Morrisville, VT 05661
Phone: (802)888-5256
Crisis Phone(s): (802)888-5256.

Newport

★4763★ **Step ONE**
63 Main St.
Newport, VT 05855
Phone: (802)334-0148
Crisis Phone(s): (802)334-6744.

Rutland

★4764★ **Rutland County Women's
Network**
PO Box 313
Rutland, VT 05701
Phone: (802)775-6788
Crisis Phone(s): (802)775-3232.

St. Albans

★4765★ **Abuse and Rape Crisis Services**
86 N. Main St.
St. Albans, VT 05478
Phone: (802)524-4911
Crisis Phone(s): (802)524-6575.

★4766★ **The Family Center
Domestic Violence/Sexual Assault
Prevention Program**
86 N. Main St.
St. Albans, VT 05478
Phone: (802)524-6574
Crisis Phone(s): (802)524-6575.

St. Johnsbury

★4767★ **The Umbrella**
1 Prospect Ave.
St. Johnsbury, VT 05819
Phone: (802)748-8645
Crisis Phone(s): (802)748-8141 (evenings and weekends).

Springfield

★4768★ **New Beginnings**
100 River St., Rm. 308
Springfield, VT 05156
Phone: (802)885-2368
Crisis Phone(s): (802)885-2050.

Virginia

Alexandria

★4769★ **Domestic Violence Program**
Alexandria Office on Women
Alexandria, VA 22314-3234
Crisis Phone(s): (703)838-4911.

★4770★ **Fairfax County Victim Assistance
Network**
8119 Holland Rd.
Alexandria, VA 22306
Phone: (703)360-6910
Crisis Phone(s): (703)360-7273.

★4771★ **Northern Virginia Family Service**
3321 Duke St.
Alexandria, VA 22314
Phone: (703)370-3223

★4772★ **Route One Corridor Housing**
PO Box 6465
Alexandria, VA 22306
Phone: (703)768-3400

Arlington

★4773★ Arlington Community Temporary Shelter
PO Box 1285
Arlington, VA 22210
Crisis Phone(s): (703)237-0881.

★4774★ Arlington County Victims of Violence Program
1725 N. George Mason Dr.
Arlington, VA 22205
Phone: (703)358-5150
Crisis Phone(s): (703)358-4848.

Carrolton

★4775★ The Genieve Shelter
PO Box 231
Carrolton, VA 23314
Phone: (804)238-2852
Crisis Phone(s): (804)238-3581.

Charlottesville

★4776★ Shelter for Help in Emergency
PO Box 3013
University Sta.
Charlottesville, VA 22903
Phone: (804)293-6155
Crisis Phone(s): (804)293-8509.

Chesterfield

★4777★ Chesterfield County Victim/Witness Assistance Office
101000 Iron Bridge Rd.
Chesterfield, VA 23832
Phone: (804)796-7087

Clifton Forge

★4778★ Alleghany Highlands Community Services Board
601 Main St.
Clifton Forge, VA 24422
Phone: (703)862-2806
Crisis Phone(s): (703)962-2181; (703)962-5713.

Culpeper

★4779★ Services to Abused Families, Inc.
PO Box 402
Culpeper, VA 22701
Crisis Phone(s): (703)825-8876; (703)349-0309.

Danville

★4780★ Domestic Violence Emergency Services
PO Box 2381
Danville, VA 24541
Phone: (804)799-3683
Crisis Phone(s): (804)791-1400.

Dumfries

★4781★ Turning Points
Domestic Violence Program/ACTS
PO Box 74
Dumfries, VA 22026
Phone: (703)221-4951
Crisis Phone(s): (703)221-3186.

Farmville

★4782★ Domestic Assistance for You
PO Box 238
Farmville, VA 23901
Phone: (804)392-8228
Crisis Phone(s): (804)392-9696.

Fredericksburg

★4783★ Rappahannock Council on Domestic Violence
PO Box 5923
Fredericksburg, VA 22403
Phone: (703)373-9373
Crisis Phone(s): (703)373-9373.

Front Royal

★4784★ Warren County Council on Domestic Violence
PO Box 1831
Front Royal, VA 22630
Phone: (703)635-9062
Crisis Phone(s): (703)635-9062.

Glen Allen

★4785★ Henrico County Area Mental Health Center
Domestic Violence Treatment Program
10299 Woodman Rd.
Glen Allen, VA 23060
Phone: (804)266-4991
Crisis Phone(s): (804)737-9427.

Gloucester

★4786★ Cope
PO Box 427
Gloucester, VA 23061
Crisis Phone(s): (804)693-2673; (800)542-2673.

Hampton

★4787★ Virginia Peninsula Council on Domestic Violence
PO Box 561
Hampton, VA 23669
Phone: (804)722-2261
Crisis Phone(s): (804)723-7774.

Harrisonburg

★4788★ First Step, Inc.
PO Box 621
Harrisonburg, VA 22801
Phone: (703)434-0295
Crisis Phone(s): (703)434-0295.

Hopewell

★4789★ Ex-Victims Empowered, Inc.
1107 W. Broadway
Hopewell, VA 22801
Phone: (804)458-9226
Crisis Phone(s): (804)796-8843.

Leesburg

★4790★ Victims/Witness Office of Loudoun County
20 E. Market St.
Leesburg, VA 22075
Phone: (703)777-0417
Crisis Phone(s): (703)777-3399.

Lexington

★4791★ Project Horizon
PO Box 529
Lexington, VA 24450
Phone: (703)463-7861
Crisis Phone(s): (703)463-2594.

Lynchburg

★4792★ YWCA
Family Violence Prevention Program
600 Monroe St.
Lynchburg, VA 24504
Phone: (804)528-1041
Crisis Phone(s): (804)528-1041.

Martinsville

★4793★ Citizens Against Family Violence
13 Cleveland Ave.
Martinsville, VA 24114
Phone: (703)632-8701
Crisis Phone(s): (703)632-8701.

Middlesex

★4794★ Domestic Violence Hotline in Middlesex
PO Box 427
Middlesex, VA 23061
Phone: (804)293-2673
Crisis Phone(s): (800)542-2673.

Norfolk

★4795★ YWCA
Women in Crisis Program
253 W. Freemason St.
Norfolk, VA 23510
Phone: (804)625-4248
Crisis Phone(s): (804)625-5570.

Norton

★4796★ Family Crisis Support Services
Hope House
PO Box 447
Norton, VA 24273
Phone: (703)679-6188
Toll-free: 800-572-2278

Onancock

★4797★ Eastern Shore Coalition Against Domestic Violence
PO Box 3
Onancock, VA 23417
Phone: (804)787-1329
Crisis Phone(s): (804)787-1329.

Petersburg

★4798★ Crisis Assistance Response Emergency Shelter
102 N. Union St.
Petersburg, VA 23804
Phone: (804)861-0849
Crisis Phone(s): (804)733-6247.

Portsmouth

★4799★ Child and Family Services
Domestic Violence Program
1805 Airline Blvd.
Portsmouth, VA 23707
Phone: (804)397-2121
Crisis Phone(s): (804)399-6393.

★4800★ Help and Emergency Response
PO Box 1515
Portsmouth, VA 23705
Phone: (804)393-7833
Crisis Phone(s): (804)393-9449.

Purceville

★4801★ Loudoun Abused Women's Shelter
PO Box 875
Purceville, VA 22132
Crisis Phone(s): (703)777-6552.

Radford

★4802★ Women's Resource Center of the New River Valley
PO Box 306
Radford, VA 24141
Phone: (703)639-9592
Crisis Phone(s): (703)639-1123.

Richmond

★4803★ Family Counseling Center
1100 W. Franklin St.
Richmond, VA 23220
Phone: (804)358-1974

★4804★ Richmond Mental Health Center
Domestic Violence Intervention Project
501 N. 9th St.
Richmond, VA 23219
Phone: (804)780-6900
Crisis Phone(s): (804)780-5924.

★4805★ Virginia Department of Social Services
Spouse Abuse Program
8007 Discovery Dr.
Richmond, VA 23229-8699
Phone: (804)662-9029

★4806★ Virginians Against Domestic Violence
PO Box 5592
Richmond, VA 23220
Phone: (804)780-3505

★4807★ YWCA
Women's Advocacy Program
6 N. 5th St.
Richmond, VA 23219
Phone: (804)643-6761
Crisis Phone(s): (804)643-0888 (Richmond area); (804)796-3066 (Chesterfield).

Roanoke

★4808★ Family Services
Domestic Violence Program
3208 Hershberger Rd. NW
Roanoke, VA 24017
Phone: (703)563-5316

★4809★ The Salvation Army
The Turning Point
PO Box 1631
Roanoke, VA 24008
Phone: (703)344-5765
Crisis Phone(s): (703)345-0400.

★4810★ Women's Resource Center
PO Box 2868
Roanoke, VA 24001
Phone: (703)345-6781

Rocky Mount

★4811★ Family Resource Center
PO Box 4
Rocky Mount, VA 24151
Phone: (703)483-5088
Crisis Phone(s): (703)483-1234.

South Boston

★4812★ Halifax County Community Action
Domestic Violence Program
Riverdale Hwy. 501 S.
South Boston, VA 24592
Phone: (804)575-7916
Crisis Phone(s): (804)476-1374.

Stanley

★4813★ Council on Domestic Violence for Page County
Choices, Inc.
PO Box 317
Stanley, VA 22851
Phone: (703)743-5739
Crisis Phone(s): (703)743-3733.

Staunton

★4814★ Alternatives for Abused Adults
PO Box 1414
Staunton, VA 24401
Phone: (703)886-4001
Crisis Phone(s): (703)886-6800; (703)942-HELP.

Suffolk

★4815★ Western Tidewater Mental Health Center
Domestic Violence Services
538 E. Constance Rd.
Suffolk, VA 23434
Crisis Phone(s): (804)925-2484.

Tazewell

★4816★ Family Violence Prevention Program
PO Box 487
Tazewell, VA 24651
Phone: (703)988-5583
Crisis Phone(s): (703)988-6790.

Vienna

★4817★ Fairfax County Women's Shelter
Northwest Center for Community Mental Health
Vienna, VA 22183
Crisis Phone(s): (703)435-4940.

Virginia Beach

★4818★ Family Advocacy Network
Virginia Beach rt. Service Unit
Virginia Beach, VA 23456-9002
Phone: (804)427-4426
Crisis Phone(s): (804)427-4426.

★4819★ Virginia Beach Department of Social Services
3432 Virginia Beach Blvd.
Virginia Beach, VA 23452
Phone: (804)431-3373
Crisis Phone(s): (804)463-2000.

Warsaw

★4820★ Family Focus of Richmond County
Haven
PO Box 713
Warsaw, VA 22572
Phone: (804)333-5370

Williamsburg

★4821★ Avalon: A Center for Women and Children
PO Box 1079
Williamsburg, VA 23187
Phone: (804)258-5022
Crisis Phone(s): (804)258-5051.

Winchester

★4822★ The Shelter for Abused Women
PO Box 14
Winchester, VA 22601
Phone: (703)667-6466
Crisis Phone(s): (703)667-6466.

Woodstock

★4823★ Response
PO Box 287
Woodstock, VA 22664
Phone: (703)459-5161
Crisis Phone(s): (703)459-5161.

Wytheville

★4824★ Family Resource Center
PO Box 612
Wytheville, VA 24382
Phone: (703)228-8431
Crisis Phone(s): (703)228-7141.

Washington

Bellevue

★4825★ Eastside Domestic Violence
Program
PO Box 6398
Bellevue, WA 98009
Phone: (206)562-8840
Crisis Phone(s): (206)746-1940.

Bellingham

★4826★ Whatcom County Crisis Services
Domestic Violence Program
1407 Commercial St.
Bellingham, WA 98225-4309
Phone: (206)676-5714
Crisis Phone(s): (206)384-1485.

★4827★ Womencare Shelter
2505 Cedarwood, No. 5
Bellingham, WA 98225
Phone: (206)671-8539
Crisis Phone(s): (206)734-3438.

Bremerton

★4828★ YWCA
Alternatives to Living in Violence
611 Highland Ave.
Bremerton, WA 98310
Phone: (206)479-5118
Crisis Phone(s): (206)479-1980.

Chehalis

★4829★ CARE Services
PO Box 337
Chehalis, WA 98532
Phone: (206)748-0547
Toll-free: 800-244-7414
Crisis Phone(s): (206)748-6601.

Colville

★4830★ Alternatives to Violence
605 S. Infirmary Rd.
Colville, WA 99114
Phone: (509)684-3796
Crisis Phone(s): (509)684-6139.

Davenport

★4831★ Family Resource Center
PO Box 907
Davenport, WA 99122
Phone: (509)725-4357

Ellensburg

★4832★ CWCMH
Kittitas Services
220 W. 4th St.
Ellensburg, WA 98926
Phone: (509)925-9861
Crisis Phone(s): (509)925-4168.

Everett

★4833★ Snohomish County Center for
Battered Women
PO Box 2086
Everett, WA 98203
Phone: (206)258-3543
Crisis Phone(s): (206)252-2873 (TDD 8am -
12am).

Forks

★4834★ Forks Abuse Program
PO Box 1775
Forks, WA 98331
Crisis Phone(s): (206)374-2273.

Ft. Lewis

★4835★ Ft. Lewis Family Advocacy
Army Community Services
Ft. Lewis, WA 98433
Phone: (206)967-7166
Toll-free: 800-562-6025

Hoquian

★4836★ Domestic Violence Center of
Grays Harbor
2306 Sumner Ave.
Hoquian, WA 98550-3927
Phone: (206)538-0733
Toll-free: 800-562-6025

Kelso

★4837★ Emergency Support Shelter
PO Box 877
Kelso, WA 98626
Phone: (206)425-1176
Crisis Phone(s): (206)636-8471.

Kennewick

★4838★ Columbia Basin Domestic
Violence Services
5917 W. Clearwater Ave.
Kennewick, WA 99336-1847
Phone: (509)943-2649
Toll-free: 800-648-1277

Kent

★4839★ DAWN
PO Box 1521
Kent, WA 98035
Phone: (206)656-4305
Crisis Phone(s): (206)656-7867.

Langler

★4840★ Citizens Against Domestic Abuse
PO Box 796
Langler, WA 98260
Phone: (206)321-4181
Crisis Phone(s): (206)675-2232 (Langler);
(206)321-4181 (S. Whidbey).

Lopez Island

★4841★ Volunteers Against Violence
Rte. 1, Box 1813
Lopez Island, WA 98261
Toll-free: 800-562-6025

Lynwood

★4842★ Pathways for Women
PO Box 5627
Lynwood, WA 98046
Phone: (206)774-9843
Crisis Phone(s): (206)259-4357.

Moses Lake

★4843★ Our Place
1008 E. Broadway Ext.
PO Box 1394
Moses Lake, WA 98837
Phone: (509)765-1214
Crisis Phone(s): (509)765-1791.

Mt. Vernon

★4844★ Skagit Rape Relief and Battered
Women's Services
PO Box 301
Mt. Vernon, WA 98273
Phone: (206)336-9591
Crisis Phone(s): (206)336-2162; (206)293-
3232 (Anacortes).

Naselle

★4845★ Pacific County Crisis Support
Network
HCR 78, Box 336
Naselle, WA 98638
Phone: (206)484-7191
Toll-free: 800-435-7276

Newport

★4846★ Family Crisis Network
PO Box 944
Newport, WA 99156
Phone: (509)447-2274
Crisis Phone(s): (509)447-LIVE; (800)548-
3133.

Oak Harbor

★4847★ Citizens Against Domestic Abuse
PO Box 190
Oak Harbor, WA 98277
Phone: (206)675-7781
Crisis Phone(s): (206)675-2232.

Olympia

★4848★ The Equal Defense Alliance
1023 S. Adams, FF286
Olympia, WA 98501
Phone: (206)459-5989
Toll-free: 800-562-6025

★4849★ Refugee Center
309 4th Ave. E.
Olympia, WA 98501-1106
Phone: (206)754-7197

★4850★ Safeplace
PO Box 1605
Olympia, WA 98507
Phone: (206)786-8754
Crisis Phone(s): (206)754-6300.

Omak

★4851★ The Support Center
PO Box 2058
Omak, WA 98841
Phone: (509)826-3221
Crisis Phone(s): (509)826-3221.

Port Angeles

★4852★ Safehome/Substance Abuse and Domestic Violence
PO Box 1858
Port Angeles, WA 98362
Phone: (206)452-3811
Crisis Phone(s): (206)452-HELP.

Port Townsend

★4853★ Domestic Violence/Sexual Assault Program
PO Box 743
Port Townsend, WA 98368
Crisis Phone(s): (206)385-5291.

Republic

★4854★ Ferry County Domestic Violence Program
PO Box 406
Republic, WA 99166
Phone: (509)775-3341
Crisis Phone(s): (509)775-3132.

Seattle

★4855★ Broadview
PO Box 31151
Seattle, WA 98103
Phone: (206)622-3108
Crisis Phone(s): (206)622-4933.

★4856★ Center for Prevention of Sexual Abuse and Domestic Violence
1914 N. 34th St., No. 105
Seattle, WA 98103
Phone: (206)634-1903

★4857★ Family Services
615 2nd Ave., Ste. 150
Seattle, WA 98104
Phone: (206)461-3883

★4858★ New Beginnings Shelter
PO Box 75125
Seattle, WA 98125
Phone: (206)783-4520
Crisis Phone(s): (206)522-9472.

★4859★ The Salvation Army Catherine Booth House
PO Box 20128
Seattle, WA 98102
Phone: (206)324-7271
Crisis Phone(s): (206)324-4943; (206)324-7271.

★4860★ The Salvation Army Hickman House
PO Box 20128
Seattle, WA 98102
Phone: (206)932-5341
Crisis Phone(s): (206)932-5341.

★4861★ Stop Abuse, Capo
CAPO Bldg., Ste. 2086
12351 Lake City Way, NE
Seattle, WA 98125
Phone: (206)258-3543
Crisis Phone(s): (206)252-2873

★4862★ YWCA Emergency Shelter for Women and Children in Crisis
1118 5th Ave.
Seattle, WA 98101
Crisis Phone(s): (206)461-4882.

Shelton

★4863★ RECOVERY
PO Box 1132
Shelton, WA 98584
Phone: (206)426-5878
Toll-free: 800-562-5062

Spokane

★4864★ YWCA Alternatives to Domestic Violence
829 W. Broadway
Spokane, WA 99201
Phone: (509)327-9534
Crisis Phone(s): (509)838-4428 (evenings and weekends).

Stevenson

★4865★ Skamania County Council on Domestic Violence and Sexual Assault
PO Box 477
Stevenson, WA 98648
Phone: (509)427-4210
Toll-free: 800-526-6025

Sunnyside

★4866★ CWCMH Kittitas Services
1319 Saul Rd. S.
Sunnyside, WA 98944
Phone: (509)837-2089
Toll-free: 800-572-8122

★4867★ Lower Valley Crisis and Support Services
PO Box 93
Sunnyside, WA 98944-0093
Crisis Phone(s): (509)837-6689.

Tacoma

★4868★ Evergreen Human Services
PO Box 8004
Tacoma, WA 98408
Phone: (206)474-2294
Toll-free: 800-562-6025

★4869★ Family Renewal Shelter
PO Box 98318
Tacoma, WA 98498
Phone: (206)564-8998

★4870★ YWCA Women's Support Shelter
405 Broadway
Tacoma, WA 98402
Phone: (206)383-3263
Crisis Phone(s): (206)383-2593.

Vancouver

★4871★ YWCA Safechoice
1115 Esther St.
Vancouver, WA 98660
Phone: (206)696-0167
Crisis Phone(s): (206)695-0501.

Wenatchee

★4872★ Wenatchee Rape Crisis and Domestic Violence Center
PO Box 2704
Wenatchee, WA 98807
Phone: (509)663-1952
Toll-free: 800-356-4533
Crisis Phone(s): (509)663-7446.

White Salmon

★4873★ Klickitat County DV/SA Council
PO Box 1850
White Salmon, WA 98672
Phone: (509)493-2662
Toll-free: 800-562-6025

Yakima

★4874★ CWCMH Kittitas Services
321 E. Yakima Ave.
Yakima, WA 98901
Phone: (509)575-4084
Toll-free: 800-572-8122

★4875★ YWCA Family Crisis Program
15 N. Naches Ave.
Yakima, WA 98901
Crisis Phone(s): (509)248-7796.

West Virginia

Beckley

★4876★ Women's Resource Center
PO Box 1476
Beckley, WV 25802-1476
Crisis Phone(s): (304)255-2559.

Charleston

★4877★ YWCA
Resolve Family Abuse Program
1114 Quarrier St.
Charleston, WV 25301
Phone: (304)340-3550
Toll-free: 800-352-6513

Elkins

★4878★ Women's Aid in Crisis
PO Box 2062
Elkins, WV 26241
Phone: (304)636-8433
Toll-free: 800-339-1185

Fairmont

★4879★ HOPE
PO Box 626
Fairmont, WV 26555
Crisis Phone(s): (304)367-1100.

Huntington

★4880★ Branches
PO Box 403
Huntington, WV 25708
Crisis Phone(s): (304)529-2382.

Keyser

★4881★ Family Crisis Center
PO Box 207
Keyser, WV 26726
Phone: (304)788-6061
Toll-free: 800-698-1240
Crisis Phone(s): (304)788-6061.

Lewisburg

★4882★ Family Refuge Center
PO Box 249
Lewisburg, WV 24901
Phone: (304)645-6334
Crisis Phone(s): (304)645-6334.

Martinsburg

★4883★ Shenandoah Women's Center
PO Box 1083
Martinsburg, WV 25401
Phone: (304)263-8292
Crisis Phone(s): (304)263-8292.

Morgantown

**★4884★ Rape and Domestic Violence
Information Center**
PO Box 4228
Morgantown, WV 26505
Toll-free: 800-554-9743
Crisis Phone(s): (304)292-5100.

Parkersburg

**★4885★ Family Crisis Intervention Center
of Region V**
PO Box 695
Parkersburg, WV 26102
Phone: (304)428-3707
Crisis Phone(s): (304)428-2333.

Welch

**★4886★ Stop Abusive Family
Environments**
70 McDowell St., Ste. 414
Welch, WV 24801
Crisis Phone(s): (304)436-8117.

Weston

★4887★ HOPE
Task Force on Domestic Violence
PO Box 52
Weston, WV 26452
Phone: (304)269-5130
Crisis Phone(s): (304)367-1100.

Wheeling

★4888★ YWCA
Domestic Violence Services
1100 Chapline St.
Wheeling, WV 26003
Crisis Phone(s): (304)232-0511.

Williamson

**★4889★ Tug Valley Recovery Shelter
Association**
PO Box 863
Williamson, WV 25661
Crisis Phone(s): (304)235-6121.

Wisconsin

Antigo

★4890★ AVAIL
PO Box 355
Antigo, WI 54409
Phone: (715)623-5177
Crisis Phone(s): (715)623-5767.

Appleton

**★4891★ Outagamie County Domestic
Abuse Program**
401 S. Elm St.
Appleton, WI 54911
Phone: (414)832-1667
Crisis Phone(s): (414)832-1666.

Ashland

★4892★ Northwoods Women
New Day Shelter
PO Box 88
Ashland, WI 54806
Phone: (715)682-9566
Toll-free: 800-924-4132
Crisis Phone(s): (715)682-9565.

Balsam Lake

★4893★ Community Referral Agency
Box 182
Balsam Lake, WI 54810
Phone: (715)485-3171
Crisis Phone(s): (715)485-3171.

Baraboo

★4894★ Hope House
PO Box 432
Baraboo, WI 53913
Phone: (608)356-9123
Crisis Phone(s): (608)356-7500; (800)584-6790.

Beaver Dam

**★4895★ People Against a Violent
Environment**
PO Box 561
Beaver Dam, WI 53916
Phone: (414)887-3785
Crisis Phone(s): (414)386-3500; (414)887-3785; (414)262-0990.

Beloit

★4896★ YWCA
Family Shelter
246 W. Grand Ave.
Beloit, WI 53511
Phone: (608)364-1914
Crisis Phone(s): (608)364-1025.

Chippewa Falls

★4897★ Family Support Center
PO Box 143
Chippewa Falls, WI 54729
Phone: (715)723-1138
Toll-free: 800-400-7020
Crisis Phone(s): (715)723-1138.

Eau Claire

★4898★ Bolton Refuge House
PO Box 482
Eau Claire, WI 54702
Phone: (715)834-0628
Crisis Phone(s): (715)834-9578.

Elkhorn

**★4899★ Association for the Prevention of
Family Violence**
PO Box 1007
Elkhorn, WI 53121
Phone: (414)723-4653
Crisis Phone(s): (414)723-4653.

Fond du Lac

★4900★ Friends Aware of Violent
Relationships
PO Box 1752
Fond du Lac, WI 54936
Phone: (414)922-7760

Crisis Phone(s): (414)923-1700.

Green Bay

★4901★ Family Violence Center
PO Box 13536
Green Bay, WI 54307
Phone: (414)498-8282

Crisis Phone(s): (414)432-4244.

★4902★ Positive Indian Development
Center
PO Box 11064
Green Bay, WI 54303
Phone: (414)494-2961

Janesville

★4903★ YWCA
Alternatives Program
220 St. Lawrence Ave.
Janesville, WI 53545
Phone: (608)752-5445

Crisis Phone(s): (608)752-2583.

Jefferson

★4904★ Jefferson County Human Services
N-3995 Annex Rd.
Jefferson, WI 53549
Phone: (414)674-3105

Crisis Phone(s): (414)674-4945.

Kenosha

★4905★ Women's Horizons
PO Box 792
Kenosha, WI 53141
Phone: (414)652-1846

Crisis Phone(s): (414)652-1846.

Keshena

★4906★ Menominee County Domestic
Violence Program
PO Box 280
Keshena, WI 54135
Phone: (715)799-3861

Crisis Phone(s): (715)799-3861.

★4907★ Ne-Naiah-Kaha-Kok
PO Box 82
Keshena, WI 54135

Lac du Flambeau

★4908★ Lac du Flambeau Domestic
Abuse Program
PO Box 67
Lac du Flambeau, WI 54538
Phone: (715)588-7660
Toll-free: 800-236-7660

Ladysmith

★4909★ Time-Out Family Abuse Shelter
PO Box 406
Ladysmith, WI 54848
Phone: (715)532-6976

Crisis Phone(s): (715)532-7089 (voice/TDD).

Madison

★4910★ Dane County Advocates for
Battered Women
PO Box 1145
Madison, WI 53701
Phone: (608)251-1237
Toll-free: 800-747-4045

Crisis Phone(s): (608)251-4445.

Manitowoc

★4911★ Manitowoc County Domestic
Violence Center
PO Box 1142
Manitowoc, WI 54221-1142
Phone: (414)684-5770

Crisis Phone(s): (414)684-5770.

Marinette

★4912★ Newcap Rainbow House
1530 Main St.
Marinette, WI 54143
Phone: (715)735-6656

Crisis Phone(s): (715)735-6656.

Marshfield

★4913★ North Wood County Domestic
Violence Project
Personal Development Center
604 E. 4th St.
Marshfield, WI 54449
Phone: (715)384-2971

Crisis Phone(s): (715)384-5555.

Medford

★4914★ Taylor County Citizens Against
Domestic Abuse
PO Box 224
Medford, WI 54451
Phone: (715)748-5140

Crisis Phone(s): (715)748-5140.

Menomonie

★4915★ West Central Domestic Abuse
Project
PO Box 700
Menomonie, WI 54751
Phone: (715)235-9074
Toll-free: 800-924-9188

Crisis Phone(s): (715)235-9074.

Merrill

★4916★ HAVEN
PO Box 32
Merrill, WI 54452
Phone: (715)536-9563

Crisis Phone(s): (715)536-1300.

Milltown

★4917★ Community Referral Agency
PO Box 365
Milltown, WI 54858
Phone: (715)825-4414
Toll-free: 800-261-SAFE

Crisis Phone(s): (715)825-4404.

Milwaukee

★4918★ Milwaukee Women's Center
611 N. Broadway, No. 230
Milwaukee, WI 53202
Phone: (414)272-6199

Crisis Phone(s): (414)671-6140.

★4919★ Sojourner Truth House
PO Box 08110
Milwaukee, WI 53208
Phone: (414)643-1777

Crisis Phone(s): (414)933-2722.

★4920★ Task Force on Battered Women
1228 W. Mitchell
Milwaukee, WI 53204
Phone: (414)643-1911

Crisis Phone(s): (414)643-5455.

Monroe

★4921★ Green Haven Family Advocates
PO Box 181
Monroe, WI 53566
Phone: (608)325-6489

Crisis Phone(s): (608)325-7711.

Neenah

★4922★ Regional Domestic Abuse
Services
PO Box 99
Neenah, WI 54957
Phone: (414)729-5727

Crisis Phone(s): (414)729-6395; (414)235-5998 (Oshkosh).

Oneida

★4923★ Oneida Tribe Domestic Abuse
Program
PO Box 365
Oneida, WI 54155
Phone: (414)869-4410

Crisis Phone(s): (414)432-4244.

Platteville

★4924★ Family Advocates
PO Box 705
Platteville, WI 53818
Phone: (608)348-5995
Toll-free: 800-924-2624

Crisis Phone(s): (608)348-3838.

Portage

★4925★ Columbia County Advocates for Battered Women
PO Box 758
Portage, WI 53901
Phone: (608)742-7677

Crisis Phone(s): (608)742-7677.

★4926★ STRIVE
PO Box 758
Portage, WI 53901
Phone: (608)742-7677

Crisis Phone(s): (608)742-7677.

Racine

★4927★ Women's Resource Center
PO Box 1764
Racine, WI 53401
Phone: (414)633-3274

Crisis Phone(s): (414)633-3233.

Rhinelander

★4928★ Tri-County Council on Domestic Violence and Sexual Assault
PO Box 233
Rhinelander, WI 54501
Phone: (715)362-6841
Toll-free: 800-236-1222

Crisis Phone(s): (715)362-6800.

Richland Center

★4929★ Passages
PO Box 546
Richland Center, WI 53581-0546
Phone: (608)647-6317
Toll-free: 800-236-HEAL

Crisis Phone(s): (608)647-3616.

River Falls

★4930★ Turningpoint
PO Box 304
River Falls, WI 54022
Phone: (715)425-6751
Toll-free: 800-338-2882

Crisis Phone(s): (715)425-6751.

Saukville

★4931★ Advocates Helping Battered Women and Families
PO Box 166
Saukville, WI 53080
Phone: (414)284-6902

Crisis Phone(s): (414)284-6902.

Sheboygan

★4932★ Safe Harbor
PO Box 582
Sheboygan, WI 53082
Phone: (414)452-8611

Crisis Phone(s): (414)452-7640.

★4933★ St. Nicholas Hospital Domestic Violence Center
1601 N. Taylor Dr.
Sheboygan, WI 53081
Phone: (414)459-4621

Crisis Phone(s): (414)459-8300.

★4934★ Sheboygan County Advocates for Battered Women
1048 Janewood Lane
Sheboygan, WI 53081
Phone: (414)452-7009

Crisis Phone(s): (414)452-7009.

Stevens Point

★4935★ Family Crisis Center
1503 Water St.
Stevens Point, WI 54481
Phone: (715)344-8508
Toll-free: 800-472-3377

Crisis Phone(s): (715)344-8508.

Sturgeon Bay

★4936★ HELP of Door County
PO Box 319
Sturgeon Bay, WI 54235
Phone: (414)743-8818

Crisis Phone(s): (414)743-8818.

Superior

★4937★ Center Against Sexual and Domestic Abuse
2231 Catlin Ave.
Superior, WI 54880
Phone: (715)392-3136
Toll-free: 800-649-2921

Crisis Phone(s): (715)392-3136.

★4938★ Human Resource Center
39 N. 25th St. E.
Superior, WI 54880
Phone: (715)392-8216
Toll-free: 800-924-0772

Crisis Phone(s): (715)392-8216.

Viroqua

★4939★ Vernon County Domestic Abuse Project
PO Box 149
Viroqua, WI 54665
Phone: (608)637-7052

Crisis Phone(s): (608)637-7007.

Waukesha

★4940★ Women's Center Sister House
726 N. East Ave.
Waukesha, WI 53186
Phone: (414)542-6777

Crisis Phone(s): (414)542-3828.

Waupaca

★4941★ Safe-T
PO Box 124
Waupaca, WI 54981
Phone: (715)467-2273
Toll-free: 800-472-3377

Wausau

★4942★ The Women's Community Domestic Abuse Program and Sexual Assault Victim Services
PO Box 6215
Wausau, WI 54402
Phone: (715)842-5663

Crisis Phone(s): (715)842-7323.

Wauwatosa

★4943★ Task Force on Battered Women
4067 N. 92nd St.
Wauwatosa, WI 53222
Phone: (414)466-1660

Crisis Phone(s): (414)643-5455.

West Bend

★4944★ Friends of Abused Families
PO Box 117
West Bend, WI 53095
Phone: (414)334-5598

Crisis Phone(s): (414)334-7298.

Wisconsin Rapids

★4945★ The Family Center
531 10th Ave. N.
Wisconsin Rapids, WI 54494
Phone: (715)421-1511

Crisis Phone(s): (715)421-1511.

Wyoming

Basin

★4946★ Crisis and Referral Emergency Services
220 S. 4th St.
Basin, WY 82410
Phone: (307)568-2020

Crisis Phone(s): (307)568-3334 (Basin); (307)548-2333 (Lovell).

Casper

★4947★ Self Help Center
341 E. E St., Ste. 135-A
Casper, WY 82601
Phone: (307)235-2814

Crisis Phone(s): (307)235-2814.

Cheyenne

★4948★ Safehouse/Sexual Assault Services, Inc.
PO Box 1885
Cheyenne, WY 82003
Phone: (307)634-8655

Crisis Phone(s): (307)632-2072; (307)637-7233.

Cody

★4949★ Crisis Intervention Services
PO Box 1324
Cody, WY 82414
Phone: (307)587-3545

Crisis Phone(s): (307)527-7801 (Cody); (307)754-3737 (Powell).

Douglas

★4950★ Converse County Coalition
PO Box 692
Douglas, WY 82633
Crisis Phone(s): (307)358-4800.

Ethete

★4951★ Circle of Respect
PO Box 741
Ethete, WY 82520
Phone: (307)332-7046
Crisis Phone(s): (307)332-7046.

Evanston

**★4952★ Sexual Assault/Family Violence
Task Force**
35 City View Dr., Ste. 208
Evanston, WY 82930
Crisis Phone(s): (307)789-3628.

Gillette

★4953★ Gillette Abuse Refuge
PO Box 3110
Gillette, WY 82717
Phone: (307)686-8071
Toll-free: 800-233-2965
Crisis Phone(s): (307)686-8070.

Jackson

★4954★ Teton County Task Force
PO Box 1328
Jackson, WY 83001
Phone: (307)733-3711
Crisis Phone(s): (307)733-7466.

Kemmerer

★4955★ The Turning Point
Lincoln County's Self-Help Center
PO Box 64
Kemmerer, WY 83101
Phone: (307)877-6834

Crisis Phone(s): (307)877-9209 (Kemmerer); (307)886-9491 (Afton).

Laramie

★4956★ Project SAFE
312 Steele
Laramie, WY 82070
Phone: (307)742-7273
Crisis Phone(s): (307)745-3556.

Lovell

**★4957★ Crisis and Referral Emergency
Services**
441 Montana Ave.
Lovell, WY 82431
Phone: (307)548-6543
Crisis Phone(s): (307)548-2333.

Lusk

★4958★ Helpmate Crisis Center
PO Box 89
Lusk, WY 82225
Phone: (307)334-3416
Crisis Phone(s): (307)334-2608.

Newcastle

★4959★ Focus
PO Box 818
Newcastle, WY 82701
Phone: (307)746-2748
Crisis Phone(s): (307)746-3630.

Pinedale

**★4960★ Sexual Assault/Family Violence
Task Force**
PO Box 1236
Pinedale, WY 82941
Phone: (307)367-6305
Toll-free: 800-445-7233

Rawlins

★4961★ Carbon County COVE
PO Box 713
Rawlins, WY 82301
Phone: (307)324-7071
Crisis Phone(s): (307)324-7144.

Riverton

★4962★ Fremont Alliance
PO Box 1127
Riverton, WY 82501
Phone: (307)856-0942
Crisis Phone(s): (307)856-4734.

Rock Springs

★4963★ YWCA
Support and Safe House Program
PO Box 1667
Rock Springs, WY 82902
Phone: (307)362-7674

Crisis Phone(s): (307)382-6925 (Rock Springs); (307)875-7666 (Green River).

Sheridan

★4964★ Women's Center
PO Box 581
Sheridan, WY 82801
Phone: (307)672-7471
Crisis Phone(s): (307)672-3222.

Sundance

**★4965★ Family Violence and Sexual
Assault Services**
PO Box 128
Sundance, WY 82729
Phone: (307)283-2415
Crisis Phone(s): (307)283-2620.

Thermopolis

**★4966★ Office Against Family Violence
and Sexual Assault**
Hot Springs Crisis-Line
PO Box 824
Thermopolis, WY 82443
Phone: (307)864-2131
Crisis Phone(s): (307)864-2131.

Torrington

**★4967★ Goshen County Task Force on
Domestic Violence and Sexual Assault**
PO Box 561
Torrington, WY 82240
Phone: (307)532-2118
Crisis Phone(s): (307)532-2118.

Wheatland

★4968★ Project SAFE
PO Box 8
Wheatland, WY 82201
Phone: (307)322-4794
Crisis Phone(s): (307)322-4794.

Worland

★4969★ Community Crisis Services
PO Box 872
Worland, WY 82401
Phone: (307)347-4992
Crisis Phone(s): (307)347-4991.

(4) Displaced Homemaker Programs

Entries in this chapter are arranged alphabetically by state and city, then by organization name within city. See the User's Guide at the front of this directory for additional information.

Alabama

Andalusia

★4970★ **Wallace State Junior College**
Displaced Homemakers Program
PO Drawer 1418
Andalusia, AL 36420
Phone: (205)222-6591
Lynn Krudop, Contact

Atmore

★4971★ **Jeff Davis Community College**
Displaced Homemaker/Single Parent
  Program
PO Box 1119
Atmore, AL 36504
Phone: (205)368-8118
Sandra Majors, Contact

Bessemer

★4972★ **Bessemer State Technical**
  College
Displaced Homemakers Program
PO Box 308
Bessemer, AL 35021
Phone: (205)428-6391
Betty Batson, Contact

Birmingham

★4973★ **Lawson State Community College**
Displaced Homemakers Program
3060 Wilson Rd.
Birmingham, AL 35221
Phone: (205)925-1666
Deborah Walker, Contact

Childersburg

★4974★ **Central Alabama Community**
  College, Childersburg Campus
Displaced Homemakers Program
PO Box 389
Childersburg, AL 35044
Phone: (205)378-5576
Joyce Gideons, Contact

Deatsville

★4975★ **Ingram State Technical Institute**
Displaced Homemakers Program
PO Box 209
Deatsville, AL 36022
Phone: (205)285-5177
Becky Mullins, Contact

Decatur

★4976★ **Calhoun State Community College**
Displaced Homemakers Program
PO Box 2216
Decatur, AL 35609-2216
Phone: (205)353-3102
Patty Smith, Contact

Dothan

★4977★ **Wallace State Community**
  College, Dothan Campus
Programs for Women
Displaced Homemaker Programs
Napier Field Rd.
Dothan, AL 36303
Phone: (205)983-3521
Kay Roney, Contact

Enterprise

★4978★ **Enterprise State Junior College**
Displaced Homemakers Program
PO Box 1300
Enterprise, AL 36331
Phone: (205)347-2623
Mary Bauer, Contact

Eufaula

★4979★ **Sparks State Technical College**
WISH (Women In Self-Help)
Displaced Homemaker Program
PO Box 580
Eufaula, AL 36027
Phone: (205)687-3543
Becky Day, Contact

Fayette

★4980★ **Brewer State Junior College**
Displaced Homemakers Program
Highway 43 N.
2631 Temple Ave., N.
Fayette, AL 35555
Phone: (205)932-3221
Delisa Brown, Contact

Gadsden

★4981★ **Gadsen State Community College**
Women's Educational Training and
  Orientation Center
1001 George Wallace Dr.
Gadsden, AL 35999
Phone: (205)547-5451
Helen P. Jaggears, Contact

Hanceville

★4982★ **Wallace State Community College**
Displaced Homemakers Program
PO Box 250
Hanceville, AL 35077
Phone: (205)352-6403
M. Lea Kelly, Contact

Huntsville

★4983★ **Drake State Technical College**
Displaced Homemaker Program
3421 Meridian St., N.
Huntsville, AL 35811
Phone: (205)539-8161
Bernehl Tibbs, Contact

Mobile

★4984★ **Bishop State Junior College**
Displaced Homemaker/Single Parent
  Project
351 N. Broad St.
Mobile, AL 36690
Phone: (205)690-6805
Mary Taylor, Contact

★4985★ **Carver State Technical College**
Displaced Homemaker Programs
414 Stanton St.
Mobile, AL 36617
Phone: (205)473-8692
Sadie Armstead, Contact

Monroeville

★4986★ **Patrick Henry State Junior**
  College
Displaced Homemakers Program
PO Box 2000
Monroeville, AL 36460
Phone: (205)575-3158
Carole Prouty, Contact

Montgomery

★4987★ **Patterson Technical College**
Displaced Homemaker Programs
3920 Troy Hwy.
Montgomery, AL 36116
Phone: (205)288-1080
Sharon Bretherick, Contact

★4988★ Trenholm State Technical
Program
Displaced Homemakers Program
1225 Air Base Blvd.
Montgomery, AL 36108
Phone: (205)832-9000
Sara Boyd, Contact

Muscle Shoals

★4989★ Shoals Community College
Choices for Success
George Wallace Blvd.
PO Box 2545
Muscle Shoals, AL 35662
Phone: (205)381-2813
Ann O. Anderson, Contact

Opelika

★4990★ MacArthur Technical College
Displaced Homemaker Program
PO Box 649
Opelika, AL 36467
Phone: (205)493-6631
Peggy Linton, Contact

★4991★ Southern Union State Junior
College
Displaced Homemaker Program
2900 Waverly Parkway
Opelika, AL 36801
Phone: (205)821-8838
Olga Williams, Contact

Ozark

★4992★ Alabama Aviation and Technical
College
Displaced Homemaker/Single Parent
Program
PO Box 1209
Ozark, AL 36361
Phone: (205)774-5113
Eva Sasser, Contact

Phenix City

★4993★ Chattahoochee Valley State
Community College
Displaced Homemakers Program
2602 College Dr.
Phenix City, AL 36867
Phone: (205)291-4991
Nicole Ceccato, Contact

Phil Campbell

★4994★ Northwest Alabama State
Community College
Displaced Homemakers Program
Rte. 3, Box 77
Phil Campbell, AL 35581
Phone: (205)993-5331
Karen Newton, Contact

Selma

★4995★ Wallace State Community College
Displaced Homemaker/Single Parent
Program
PO Box 1049
Selma, AL 36701
Phone: (205)875-2634
Angelia Stephens, Contact

Sumiton

★4996★ Walker State Technical College
Displaced Homemakers Program
Drawer K
Sumiton, AL 35148
Phone: (205)648-3271
Susan Bush, Contact

Tuscaloosa

★4997★ Fredd State Technical College
Career Alternatives
3401 Martin L. King, Jr. Blvd.
Tuscaloosa, AL 35401
Phone: (205)758-3361
Shirley C. Johnson, Contact

★4998★ Shelton State Community College
New Options Program
202 Skyland Blvd.
Tuscaloosa, AL 35401
Phone: (205)759-1541
Paula Sue Hayes, Contact

Wadley

★4999★ Southern Union State Junior
College
Women's ADEPT
Roberts St.
Wadley, AL 36276
Phone: (205)395-2211
Joanne Jordan, Contact

Alaska

Anchorage

★5000★ Nine Star Enterprises, Inc.
Single Parent Career Enhancement
650 W. International Airport Rd.
Anchorage, AK 99518
Phone: (907)563-3174
David Alexander, Contact

★5001★ University of Alaska, Anchorage
Center for Women and Men
3211 Providence Drive K-106
Anchorage, AK 99508
Phone: (907)786-1441
Shari Olander, Contact

Fairbanks

★5002★ Fairbanks Native Association
Careers in Nontraditional Occupations for
Single Parent Homemakers
201 1st Ave.
Fairbanks, AK 99701
Phone: (907)452-1648
Dorothy Haskins, Contact

Homer

★5003★ Southern Peninsula Women's
Services
PO Box 2328
Homer, AK 99603
Phone: (907)235-7712
Jane Andreen, Contact

Juneau

★5004★ Gastineau Human Services
Single Parent/Displaced Homemaker
Corrections Program
5597 Aisek St.
Juneau, AK 99801
Phone: (907)780-4338
Greg Pease, Contact

★5005★ Southeast Regional Resource
Center
Single Parent/Displaced Homemaker
Programs
210 Ferry Way, #200
Juneau, AK 99801
Phone: (907)586-6806
Mark Hanson, Contact

Kenai

★5006★ Women's Resource/Crisis Center
Single Parent/Homemakers Program
325 South Spruce St.
Kenai, AK 99611
Phone: (907)283-9479
Joni Weymer, Contact

Arizona

Coolidge

★5007★ Central Arizona College
Displaced Homemaker Program
8470 N. Overfield Rd.
Coolidge, AZ 85004
Phone: (602)426-4432
Sharon Stinard, Contact

Douglas

★5008★ Cochise College
Single Parent Homemaker Program
Douglas, AZ 85607
Phone: (602)364-0340
Maggie McGrail, Contact

Glendale

★5009★ Center for New Directions
6010 W. Northern #109
Glendale, AZ 85301
Phone: (602)435-8530
Pat Scheib, Contact

Kingman

★5010★ Mohave Community College
Women's Center
REACH Program
1971 Jagerson Ave.
Kingman, AZ 86401
Phone: (602)757-4331
Jane Barkhurst, Contact

Mesa

★5011★ Center for New Directions
616 East Southern #101
Mesa, AZ 85204
Phone: (602)844-0187
Janet Lilly, Contact

★5012★ Mesa Community College
Displaced Homemaker Program
1833 West Southern
Mesa, AZ 85202
Phone: (602)461-7429
Carolyn O'Conner, Contact

Phoenix

★5013★ Arizona Women's Education &
Employment (AWEE)
1111 N. First St.
Phoenix, AZ 85004
Phone: (602)258-0864
Jean Rosenberg, Contact

★5014★ Center for New Directions
1430 N. Second St.
Phoenix, AZ 85004
Phone: (602)252-0918
Johanna Phalen, Contact

★5015★ Job Training Service
Displaced Homemaker Program
6201 N. 35th Ave.
Phoenix, AZ 85017
Phone: (602)841-9049
John Shamrock, Contact

Prescott

★5016★ Arizona Women's Employment
and Education (AWEE)
Northern Arizona Council of Governments
107 N. Cortez
Prescott, AZ 86301
Phone: (602)778-3010
Ginger Johnson, Contact

Riviera

★5017★ Mohave Community College
Women's Center
REACH Program
3259 Highway 95
Riviera, AZ 86442
Phone: (602)758-3926
Barbara Wetherill, Contact

Scottsdale

★5018★ Scottsdale Community College
Women's Services
9000 East Chaparral
Scottsdale, AZ 85253
Phone: (602)968-9933
Sue Cheuvret, Contact

Somerton

★5019★ Chicano Por LaCausa
Displaced Homemaker/Single Parent
Program
PO Box 517
Somerton, AZ 85350
Phone: (602)627-2042
Yoland Rios, Contact

Thatcher

★5020★ Eastern Arizona College
Displaced Homemaker Program
688 Church St.
Thatcher, AZ 85552
Phone: (602)428-8317
Hopi Fritz-William, Contact

Tucson

★5021★ Adult Vocational Training
Program
Single Parent/Homemaker Program
531 W. Plata
Tucson, AZ 85705
Phone: (602)884-8686
Edith Manning, Contact

★5022★ Pima Community College
Displaced Homemaker Program
2202 West Anklam Rd.
Tucson, AZ 85705
Phone: (602)884-6645
Mini Montez, Contact

★5023★ University of Arizona
College of Agriculture
Project for Homemakers Seeking
Employment
1230 N. Park Ave., Rm. 209
Tucson, AZ 85721
Phone: (602)621-3902
Diane L. Wilson, Contact

Yuma

★5024★ SER (Service Employment
Redevelopment) Jobs for Progress
Displaced Homemaker Program
285 Main St.
Yuma, AZ 85364
Phone: (602)783-4414
Amanda Males, Contact

Arkansas

Bald Knob

★5025★ Bald Knob School District
CHOICES: Career Development Center
Rte. 3, Box 33
Bald Knob, AR 72010
Phone: (501)724-6306
Glen Cooley, Contact

Batesville

★5026★ Gateway Vocational Technical
School
CHOICES: Career Development Center
PO Box 3350
Batesville, AR 72501
Phone: (501)793-3677
Ann W. Spragins, Contact

Camden

★5027★ Southern Arkansas University
CHOICES: Career Development Center
133 Jackson St.
Camden, AR 71701
Phone: (501)836-0117
Roselyn Dorton, Contact

Dewitt

★5028★ Rice Belt Vocational Technical
School
CHOICES: Career Development Center
PO Box 427
Dewitt, AR 72042
Phone: (501)946-3506
Julia K. Eldridge, Contact

Fayetteville

★5029★ Economic Opportunity Agency
Nontraditional Occupations
2325 N. Gregg
Fayetteville, AR 72703
Phone: (501)521-1394
Marjorie Marugg, Contact

Forrest City

★5030★ Crowley's Ridge Vocational-
Technical School
Single Program/Homemaker Program
PO Box 925
Forrest City, AR 72205
Phone: (501)633-5411
Brenda McBride, Contact

Ft. Smith

★5031★ Westark Community College
CHOICES: Career Development Center
PO Box 3649
Ft. Smith, AR 72913
Phone: (501)452-8994
Kathy Phillips, Contact

Harrison

★5032★ Twin Lakes Vocational-Technical
School
CHOICES: Career Development Center
PO Box 1496
Harrison, AR 72601
Phone: (501)741-6175
Judy Nickens, Contact

Hot Springs

★5033★ Garland County Community
College
CHOICES: Career Development Center
No. 1 College Drive
Mid-America Park
Hot Springs, AR 71913
Phone: (501)767-9371
Linda Holmes, Contact

Little Rock

★5034★ Pulaski Vocational-Technical
School
CHOICES: Career Development Center
Executive Building-Suite 516
2020 W. 3rd St.
Little Rock, AR 72205
Phone: (501)372-7161
Sylvia Crockett, Contact

Springdale

★5035★ Northwest Technical Institute
Single Parent/Homemaker Program
PO Drawer A
Springdale, AR 72764
Phone: (501)751-8824
Shirley M. Sutton, Contact

California

Alameda

★5036★ College of Alameda
Resources and Supportive Programs
555 Atlantic Ave.
Alameda, CA 94501
Phone: (510)748-2208
Ruth Phillip, Contact

Anaheim

★5037★ North Orange County Regional Occupational Program
SOLO Single Parent/Displaced Homemaker Project
2360 W. La Palma
Anaheim, CA 92801
Phone: (714)776-2170
Laurie Manseau, Contact

Aptos

★5038★ Cabrillo College
Single Parent/Displaced Homemaker Programs
6500 Soquel Drive
Aptos, CA 95003
Phone: (408)479-6249
Shirley Flores-Munoz, Coptact

Auburn

★5039★ Placer Womens Center
Displaced Homemaker Programs
PO Box 5462
Auburn, CA 95604
Phone: (916)885-0443
Barbara Webster, Contact

Bakersfield

★5040★ YWCA
Displaced Homemaker Program
1130 17th St.
Bakersfield, CA 93301
Phone: (805)823-6072
Trish Sanderson, Contact

Berkeley

★5041★ YWCA
Turning Point Career Center
2600 Bancroft Way
Berkeley, CA 94704
Phone: (415)848-6370
Winnie Froehlich, Contact

Capitola

★5042★ Santa Cruz County Regional Occupational Programs
SOLO Single Parent/Displaced Homemaker Project
809 Bay Ave., Ste. H
Capitola, CA 95010
Phone: (408)476-7140
Patricia Johns, Contact

Colton

★5043★ Somos Hermanas Unidas
Project Redirect
254 East E St.
Colton, CA 92324
Phone: (714)824-5350
Emma Lechuga, Contact

Columbia

★5044★ Columbia College
Single Parent/Displaced Homemaker Project
PO Box 1849
Columbia, CA 95310
Phone: (209)533-5106
Judy Strattan, Contact

Compton

★5045★ YWCA Los Angeles
Displaced Homemaker Program
509 East Compton Blvd.
Compton, CA 90220
Phone: (213)636-1429
Elaine Harris, Contact

Concord

★5046★ Mount Diablo Adult Education
Women in Transition
1936 Carlotta Dr.
Concord, CA 94519-1397
Phone: (415)685-7340
Joanne Durkee, Contact

Costa Mesa

★5047★ Orange Coast College
Single Parent/Displaced Homemaker Project
2701 Fairview Rd.
Costa Mesa, CA 92628-0120
Phone: (714)432-5162
Nicolette Jackson, Contact

Culver City

★5048★ West Los Angeles College
Single Parent/Displaced Homemaker Project
4800 Freshman Dr.
Culver City, CA 90230-3500
Phone: (213)287-4363
Victoria van Tamelen-Hall, Contact

El Cajon

★5049★ Grossmont College
Single Parent/Displaced Homemaker Project
8800 Grossmont College Dr.
El Cajon, CA 92020-1799
Phone: (619)465-1700
Dawn Wellspeak, Contact

El Centro

★5050★ Imperial Valley Regional Occupation Program
Single Parent/Displaced Homemaker Project
1398 Sperber Rd.
El Centro, CA 92243
Phone: (619)339-6434
Ellie Kussman, Contact

Eureka

★5051★ College of the Redwoods
Single Parent/Displaced Homemaker Project
7351 Tompkins Hills Rd.
Eureka, CA 95501
Phone: (707)445-6737
Rodney Kaloostain, Contact

Fairfield

★5052★ Solano County Regional Occupational Program
SOLO Single Parent/Displaced Homemaker Project
655 Washington St.
Fairfield, CA 94533
Phone: (707)429-6445
Seretha Jefferson, Contact

Fontana

★5053★ Fontana Indian Center
Displaced Homemaker Program
9680 Citrus Ave.
Fontana, CA 92335
Phone: (714)850-7500
Mary Fuller, Contact

Fremont

★5054★ Fremont-Newark Regional Occupational Program
Single Parent/Homemaker Project
40230 Laiolo Rd.
Fremont, CA 94538
Phone: (415)656-0533
Randi Fewel, Contact

Fresno

★5055★ Fresno City College
Single Parent/Displaced Homemaker Program
1101 E. University Ave.
Fresno, CA 93741
Phone: (209)442-4600
Deborah Ikeda, Contact

★5056★ YWCA
Displaced Homemakers Program
1600 M St.
Fresno, CA 93721
Phone: (209)237-4701
Cheryl Deboise, Contact

Glendora

★5057★ Citrus College
Single Parent/Displaced Homemaker Project
1000 W. Foothill Blvd.
Glendora, CA 91740-1899
Phone: (818)914-8501
Diane Hinds, Contact

Hanford

★5058★ Kings Regional Occupational Program
Single Parent/Displaced Homemaker Project
1144 W. Lacey Blvd.
Hanford, CA 93230
Phone: (209)582-2823
Darlene Stankovich, Contact

Hayward

★5059★ Chabot College
Women in Transition
Displaced Homemakers Program
25555 Hesperian Blvd.
Hayward, CA 94545
Phone: (415)786-6716
Lois Button, Contact

Kentfield

★5060★ College of Marin
Single Parent/Displaced Homemaker Project
College Ave.
Kentfield, CA 94904
Phone: (415)485-9409
Patricia Hurley, Contact

Livermore

★5061★ Las Positas College
Single Parent/Displaced Homemaker
  Project
3033 Collier Canyon Rd.
Livermore, CA 94550-9797
Phone: (415)373-5810
John Rath, Contact

Long Beach

★5062★ Long Beach City College
Displaced Homemaker Program
4901 E. Carson St.
Long Beach, CA 90808
Phone: (213)420-4180
Lynne Miller, Contact

Los Angeles

★5063★ Gender Equity Program
1320 W. 3rd St., Rm. 101
Los Angeles, CA 90017
Phone: (213)625-4555
Juanita McDonald, Contact

★5064★ National Council of Jewish
  Women
Women Helping Women
543 N. Fairfax Ave.
Los Angeles, CA 90036
Phone: (213)651-2930
Lori Karny, Contact

★5065★ Pasadena Unified School District
SOLO Single Parent/Displaced Homemaker
  Project
351 S. Hudson
Los Angeles, CA 91109
Phone: (818)793-2092
Kathy Moore, Contact

Menlo Park

★5066★ OICW (Opportunity Industralized
  Center West)
Displaced Homemaker Program
1100 O'Brien Dr.
Menlo Park, CA 94025
Phone: (415)322-8431
Sharon Williams, Contact

Merced

★5067★ Merced College
Single Parent/Displaced Homemaker
  Project
3600 M St.
Merced, CA 95348-2898
Phone: (209)384-6230
Anne Newins, Contact

★5068★ Merced County Regional
  Occupational Program
SOLO Single Parent/Displaced Homemaker
  Project
632 W. 13th St.
Merced, CA 95340
Phone: (209)385-8346
Ida May Johnson, Contact

Mission Viejo

★5069★ Saddleback College
Single Parent/Displaced Homemaker
  Project
28000 Marguerite Parkway
Mission Viejo, CA 92692
Phone: (714)582-4611
Alma Vanasse, Contact

Monterey

★5070★ Monterey Peninsula College
Single Parent/Displaced Homemaker
  Project
980 Fremont St.
Monterey, CA 93940-4799
Phone: (408)646-4276
Phyllis Peet, Contact

Monterey Park

★5071★ East Los Angeles College
Single Parent/Displaced Homemaker
  Project
1301 Brooklyn Ave.
Monterey Park, CA 91754
Phone: (213)265-8747
Olga Dominguez-Gary, Contact

Napa

★5072★ Napa Valley College
Single Parent/Displaced Homemaker
  Project
Napa, CA 94558
Phone: (707)253-3021
Jill Schrutz, Contact

Norwalk

★5073★ Norwalk-La Mirada Adult Center
SOLO Single Parent/Displaced Homemaker
  Project
14800 South Jersey Ave.
Norwalk, CA 90650
Phone: (213)868-9858
Ramona Lopez, Contact

Novato

★5074★ Novato Human Needs Center
Displaced Homemaker Program
1907 Novato Blvd.
Novato, CA 94947
Phone: (415)897-4147
Jean Conrad, Contact

Oakland

★5075★ Merritt College
Women's Center/Career Center
12500 Campus Dr.
Oakland, CA 94619
Phone: (510)436-2444
Debra Jacks, Contact

Orange

★5076★ Friendly Center
Displaced Homemaker Programs
147 W. Rose St.
Orange, CA 93033
Phone: (714)771-5300
Mary Garcia, Contact

Oroville

★5077★ Butte College
Single Parent/Displaced Homemaker
  Project
3536 Butte Campus Dr.
Oroville, CA 95965
Phone: (916)895-2396
Verla Winslow, Contact

Pasadena

★5078★ Career and Job Resource Center
Women at Work
78 N. Marengo Ave.
Pasadena, CA 91101
Phone: (818)796-6870
Betty Ann Jansen, Contact

Pittsburg

★5079★ Pittsburg Adult Education Center
Single Parent, Displaced Homemaker
  Program
20 E. 10th St.
Pittsburg, CA 94565
Phone: (415)439-2031
Bridgette Warren-Moffett, Contact

Pleasant Hill

★5080★ Diablo Valley College
Single Parent/Displaced Homemaker
  Project
321 Golf Club Rd.
Pleasant Hill, CA 94523
Phone: (415)685-1230
Sandra Holman, Contact

Pomona

★5081★ Pomona Unified School District
SOLO Single Parent/Displaced Homemaker
  Program
605 N. Park Ave.
Pomona, CA 91768
Phone: (714)629-2551
Barbara Price, Contact

Porterville

★5082★ Porterville College
Single Parent/Displaced Homemaker
  Project
900 S. Main St.
Porterville, CA 93257
Phone: (209)781-3130
Charles Guerrero, Contact

Rancho Cucamonga

★5083★ Chaffey College
Single Parent/Displaced Homemaker
  Project
5885 Haven Ave.
Rancho Cucamonga, CA 91701
Phone: (714)460-1522
Donna Warren, Contact

Redwood City

★5084★ San Mateo County Office of
  Education
SOLO Single Parent/Displaced Homemaker
  Project
333 Main St.
Redwood City, CA 94002
Phone: (415)363-5439
Pat Kurtz, Contact

★5085★ The Women's Center of San
  Mateo
300 Bradford St.
Redwood City, CA 94063
Phone: (415)363-4471
Janet Frakes, Contact

Richmond

★5086★ YWCA of Contra Costa
Displaced Homemaker Program
3230 MacDonald Ave.
Richmond, CA 94804
Phone: (415)234-1270
Nancy Vandenberg, Contact

Riverside

★5087★ Riverside County Schools
Regional Occupational Program
SOLO Single Parent/Displaced Homemaker
 Project
3939 13th St.
PO Box 868
Riverside, CA 92502
Phone: (714)788-6516
Diane E. Rose, Contact

Rocklin

★5088★ Sierra College
Single Parent/Displaced Homemaker
 Project
5000 Rocklin Rd.
Rocklin, CA 95677
Phone: (916)624-3333
Paulette Perfumo-Kreiss, Contact

Sacramento

★5089★ American River College
Single Parent/Displaced Homemaker
 Project
4700 Coll. Oak Dr.
Sacramento, CA 95841
Phone: (916)484-8547
Esther Nelson, Contact

★5090★ Asian Resources Center
Displaced Homemaker Program
2251 Florin Rd., Ste. E
Sacramento, CA 95822
Phone: (916)452-3601
May Lee, Contact

★5091★ YWCA of Sacramento
Displaced Homemaker Program
1122 17th St.
Sacramento, CA 95814
Phone: (916)442-4741
Barbara Thalacker, Contact

Salinas

★5092★ Hartnell College
Re-Entry Center
156 Homestead
Salinas, CA 93901
Phone: (408)755-6865
Gail Marmor, Contact

San Diego

★5093★ San Diego Community College
 District
Displaced Homemaker Program
3375 Camino del Rio South
San Diego, CA 92108-3883
Phone: (619)230-2152
Lori Erreca, Contact

★5094★ San Diego Mesa College
Single Parent/Displaced Homemaker
 Project
7250 Mesa College Dr.
San Diego, CA 92111-4998
Phone: (619)566-2697
Ricki Block, Contact

San Fernando

★5095★ Los Angeles Mission College
Single Parent/Displaced Homemaker
 Project
1212 San Fernando Rd.
San Fernando, CA 91340
Phone: (818)364-7600
Penny Jarecke, Contact

San Jose

★5096★ Center for Training and Careers
Displaced Homemakers Program
1600 Las Plumas Dr.
San Jose, CA 95133
Phone: (408)251-3165
Rose Amador, Contact

★5097★ YWCA Career Development
 Center of Santa Clara Valley
440 N. First St.
San Jose, CA 95112
Phone: (408)295-4011
Jean Perera, Contact

San Lorenzo

★5098★ Southern Alameda County YWCA
Displaced Homemaker Program
22366 Fuller Ave.
San Lorenzo, CA 94541
Phone: (415)537-2736
Jeanie Pina, Contact

San Pablo

★5099★ Contra Costa College
Single Parent/Displaced Homemaker
 Project
2600 Mission Bell Dr.
San Pablo, CA 94806
Phone: (415)235-7800
Wanda Gallerson, Contact

San Rafael

★5100★ Marin County Office of Education
SOLO Single Parent/Displaced Homemaker
 Project
1111 Las Gallinas Ave.
PO Box 4925
San Rafael, CA 94913
Phone: (415)472-4110
Dedo Priest, Contact

Santa Barbara

★5101★ Santa Barbara City College
Single Parent/Displaced Homemaker
 Project
721 Cliff Dr.
Santa Barbara, CA 93109-2394
Phone: (805)965-0581
Carole Purdie, Contact

Santa Clara

★5102★ Mission College
Single Parent/Displaced Homemaker
 Project
3000 Mission Blvd.
Santa Clara, CA 95054
Phone: (408)748-2725
Nancy Wright, Contact

Santa Maria

★5103★ Allan Hancock College
Single Parent/Displaced Homemaker
 Project
800 S. College Dr.
Santa Maria, CA 93454
Phone: (805)922-6966
Rosemary Arnold, Contact

Santa Monica

★5104★ Santa Monica College
Single Parent/Displaced Homemaker
 Project
1900 Pico Blvd.
Santa Monica, CA 90405
Phone: (213)450-5150
Tina Feiger, Contact

Santa Rosa

★5105★ Santa Rosa Junior College
Displaced Homemaker Program
1501 Mendocino Ave.
Santa Rosa, CA 95401
Phone: (707)527-4375
Evelyn Pollard, Contact

Saratoga

★5106★ West Valley College
Single Parent/Displaced Homemaker
 Project
14000 Fruitvale Ave.
Saratoga, CA 95070
Phone: (408)741-2022
Arlene Herman, Contact

Stockton

★5107★ Women's Center of San Joaquin
 County
620 N. San Joaquin St.
Stockton, CA 95202
Phone: (209)941-2611
Linda K. Fawcet, Contact

Taft

★5108★ Taft College
Single Parent/Displaced Homemaker
 Project
29 Emmons Park Dr.
Taft, CA 93268
Phone: (805)763-4282
Patricia Bench, Contact

Torrance

★5109★ Southern California Regional
 Occupational Center
SOLO Single Parent/Displaced Homemaker
 Project
2300 Crenshaw Rd.
Torrance, CA 90501
Phone: (213)320-6700
Linda Pope, Contact

Tulare

★5110★ Tulare Adult School
SOLO Single Parent/Displaced Homemaker
 Program
700 E. Kern St.
Tulare, CA 93274
Phone: (209)686-0225
Mary H. Heist, Contact

Ukiah

★5111★ Bright Center
North Coast Opportunities
413 A. N. State St.
Ukiah, CA 95482
Phone: (707)462-1954
Mary T. Brown, Contact

★5112★ Mendocino County Office of Education
Regional Occupational Programs
SOLO Single Parent/Displaced Homemaker Project
2240 E. Side Rd.
Ukiah, CA 95482
Phone: (707)463-4900
Pat Gein, Contact

Walnut

★5113★ Mount San Antonia College
Single Parent/Displaced Homemaker Project
1100 N. Grand Ave.
Walnut, CA 91789
Phone: (714)594-5611
Kay Ragan, Contact

Weed

★5114★ College of the Siskiyous
Displaced Homemaker Program
800 College Ave.
Weed, CA 96094
Phone: (916)938-5297
Karen Zeigler, Contact

Whittier

★5115★ Tri-Cities ROP (Regional Occupational Program)
SOLO Single Parent/Displaced Homemaker Project
9401 S. Painter Ave.
Whittier, CA 90605
Phone: (310)698-9571
Arlene Olivis, Contact

Wilmington

★5116★ Los Angeles Harbor College
Single Parent/Displaced Homemaker Project
1111 Figueroa Place
Wilmington, CA 90744
Phone: (213)518-1000
Pauline Zaich, Contact

Woodland Hills

★5117★ Los Angeles Pierce College
Adults in Transition
6201 Winnetka Ave.
Woodland Hills, CA 91371
Phone: (818)347-0551
Bonnie West-Caruson, Contact

Yreka

★5118★ Yreka Union High School District
SOLO Single Parent/Displaced Homemaker Project
431 Knapp St.
Yreka, CA 96097
Phone: (916)467-3756
Pat McIntyre, Contact

Yuba City

★5119★ Sutter County Career Placement Center
256 Wilbur Ave.
PO Box F
Yuba City, CA 95991
Phone: (916)741-5120
Linda Protine, Contact

Colorado

Aurora

★5120★ Community College of Aurora
Displaced Homemaker Program
16000 E. CentreTech Parkway
Room A102
Aurora, CO 80011
Phone: (303)360-4790
Karla Gabriel, Contact

Boulder

★5121★ Boulder County YWCA
Displaced Homemaker Program
2222 14th St.
Boulder, CO 80304
Phone: (303)443-0419
Mary Garvey, Contact

★5122★ Project Self-Sufficiency
Displaced Homemaker Program
PO Box 471
Boulder, CO 80306
Phone: (719)441-3929
Nancy Consolloy, Contact

Colorado Springs

★5123★ Pikes Peak Community College
Displaced Homemaker Program
5675 S. Academy Blvd.
Colorado Springs, CO 80906
Phone: (719)540-7112
Marilyn Kastel, Contact

★5124★ Women's Resource Agency, Inc. of Colorado Springs
1011 N. Weber, Ste. C
Colorado Springs, CO 80903
Phone: (719)471-3170
Dolores Quinlisk, Contact

Craig

★5125★ Colorado Northwestern Community College
Options and Opportunities Program
50 Spruce Dr.
Craig, CO 81625
Phone: (303)824-4078
Kathleen Martynowicz, Contact

Delta

★5126★ Delta-Montrose Area Vocational-Technical School
Displaced Homemaker Program
1765 Highway 50
Delta, CO 81416
Phone: (303)874-7671
Frank Kline, Contact

★5127★ Western Colorado Employment and Training
Single Parent/Displaced Homemaker Program
540 Main St., Ste. 7
Delta, CO 81416
Phone: (303)874-8634
Diana Clayton, Contact

Denver

★5128★ Community College of Denver
Women's Resource Center
Box 203
1111 W. Colfax Ave.
Denver, CO 80204
Phone: (303)556-3610
Juanita Guitierrez, Contact

★5129★ Emily Griffith Oppurtunity School
Single Parent Program
1250 Welton St.
Denver, CO 80204
Phone: (303)572-8218
Peggy Campbell, Contact

★5130★ Empowerment Program
1245 E. Colfax Ave., Ste. 404
Denver, CO 80218
Phone: (303)863-7817
Carol Lease, Contact

★5131★ Mi Casa Resource Center For Women
571 Galapago St.
Denver, CO 80204
Phone: (303)573-1302
Judy Patrick, Contact

★5132★ Northeast Women's Center
2247 Oneida
Denver, CO 80207
Phone: (303)355-3486
Hazel Whitsett, Contact

★5133★ YWCA Metropolitan Denver
Displaced Homemaker Program
535 16th St., Ste. 700
Denver, CO 80202
Phone: (303)825-7141
Dagnija Langberg, Contact

Durango

★5134★ Western Colorado Employment and Training Service
Displaced Homemaker Program
PO Box 2024
Durango, CO 81302
Phone: (303)259-0376
Delores Barela, Contact

★5135★ Women's Resource Center
PO Box 2132
Durango, CO 81302
Phone: (303)247-1242
Chris Bauch, Contact

Englewood

★5136★ Hope Unlimited
Displaced Homemaker Program
7000 E. Belleview, #201
Englewood, CO 80111
Phone: (303)220-0100
Pat Mercure, Contact

Ft. Collins

**★5137★ Front Range Community College
Larimer County Center
Single Parent/Homemaker Program**
PO Box 2397
Ft. Collins, CO 80522
Phone: (303)226-2500
Kay Hood, Contact

**★5138★ The Women's Center of Larimer
County**
424 Pine St. No. 102
Ft. Collins, CO 80524
Phone: (303)484-1902
Carol Plock, Contact

Ft. Lupton

**★5139★ Aims Community College—South
Campus
Displaced Homemakers Program**
PO Box 949
Ft. Lupton, CO 80621
Phone: (303)857-4022
Karen Kimble, Contact

Ft. Morgan

**★5140★ Morgan Community College
Single Parent/Homemaker Center**
17800 County Rd. No. 20
Ft. Morgan, CO 80701
Phone: (303)867-3081
Carolyn Helget, Contact

Grand Junction

★5141★ The Resource Center, Inc.
1129 Colorado Ave.
Grand Junction, CO 81501
Phone: (303)243-0190
Jackie Jacobs, Contact

Hot Sulphur Springs

**★5142★ Grand County Resource Center
Single Parent/Homemaker Program**
PO Box 276
612 Hemlock
Hot Sulphur Springs, CO 80451
Phone: (303)725-3257
Eric Renz, Contact

Lakewood

**★5143★ Red Rocks Community Center
Displaced Homemakers Program
Women's Resource Center**
12600 W. Sixth Ave.
Lakewood, CO 80401-5398
Phone: (303)988-6160
Caryll Cramm, Contact

Lamar

**★5144★ Lamar Community College
Displaced Homemaker Program**
2401 S. Main St.
Lamar, CO 81052
Phone: (719)336-2248
Cindy Baer, Contact

Littleton

★5145★ Transitions Program
2500 W. College Dr.
PO Box 9002
Littleton, CO 80160-9002
Phone: (303)797-5805
Mickie D. Axtell, Contact

Loveland

★5146★ The Women's Center
320 E. Third St.
Loveland, CO 80537
Phone: (303)663-2288
Carol Plock, Contact

Pagosa Springs

**★5147★ Archuleta County Educational
Center, Inc.
Displaced Homemaker Program**
PO Box 1066
Pagosa Springs, CO 81147
Phone: (303)264-2835
Tom Steen, Contact

Rangely

**★5148★ Colorado Northwestern
Community College
Displaced Homemaker Program**
500 Kennedy Dr.
Rangely, CO 81648
Phone: (303)675-2261
Judy Allred, Contact

Sterling

**★5149★ Northeastern Junior College
Displaced Homemaker Program**
100 College Lane
Sterling, CO 80751
Phone: (303)522-6600
Polly Gregory, Contact

Trinidad

**★5150★ Rocky Mountain SER (Service
Employment Redevelopment) Region VIII
Displaced Homemaker Program**
304 N. Commercial
Trinidad, CO 81082
Phone: (719)846-4438
Judy Gallegos, Contact

Walsenburg

**★5151★ Rocky Mountain SER (Service
Employment Redevelopment) Region VIII
Displaced Homemakers Program**
600 Main St.
Walsenburg, CO 81089
Phone: (719)738-3004
Mary Anderson, Contact

Westminster

**★5152★ Front Range Community College
Displaced Homemakers Program**
3645 W. 112th Ave.
Westminster, CO 80030
Phone: (303)466-8811
Judy Fernandez, Contact

Yuma

**★5153★ Yuma Community Resource
Center**
708 S. Cedar, Ste. B
Yuma, CO 80759
Phone: (303)246-3610
Patricia Brewster-Willeke, Contact

Connecticut

Bridgeport

**★5154★ YWCA of Greater Bridgeport
Job Re-entry Program
Displaced Homemakers Program**
753 Fairfield Ave.
Bridgeport, CT 06604
Phone: (203)334-6154
Esther Nagy, Contact

Danbury

**★5155★ Women's Center of Greater
Danbury
RESCUE**
256 Main St.
Danbury, CT 06810
Phone: (203)743-3010
Mary McInerney, Contact

Danielson

**★5156★ NEAC—Northeast Action
Committee
Displaced Homemaker Program**
16-H Maple St.
Danielson, CT 06239
Phone: (203)774-0418
Gina Smith, Contact

Darien

**★5157★ YWCA of Darien/Norwalk
Displaced Homemakers Program**
49 Old Kings Highway N.
Darien, CT 06820
Phone: (203)655-2535
Wendy Woods, Contact

Greenwich

**★5158★ YWCA of Greenwich
Displaced Homemakers Program**
259 E. Putnam Ave.
Greenwich, CT 06830
Phone: (203)869-6501
Elaine Murray, Contact

Hartford

**★5159★ Hartford College for Women
The Counseling Center
Look Forward**
50 Elizabeth St.
Hartford, CT 06105
Phone: (203)236-5838
Carol Berman, Contact

Litchfield

★5160★ R.E.S.C.U.E.
Goshen Rd.
Litchfield, CT 06759
Phone: (203)567-0863
Pat Doolan, Contact

Manchester

★5161★ Manchester Community College
Look Forward/Beginning Again
Bidwell Ave.
Manchester, CT 06040
Phone: (203)647-6175
Pat Reading, Contact

Meriden

★5162★ YWCA of Meriden
Open DOHR Program
169 Colony St.
Meriden, CT 06450
Phone: (203)235-9297
Jennifer Meligonis-DeJohn, Contact

New Britain

★5163★ YWCA of New Britain
Look Forward
22 Glen St.
New Britain, CT 06051
Phone: (203)225-4681
June Rosen, Contact

New Haven

★5164★ YWCA of Greater New Haven
Women in Transition
48 Howe St.
New Haven, CT 06511
Phone: (203)865-5171
Magalene Bowling, Contact

New London

★5165★ Consortium for Women's Career
Development and Training
106 Truman St.
New London, CT 06320
Phone: (203)442-4630
Renee Main, Contact

Stamford

★5166★ YWCA of Stamford
Displaced Homemakers Program
141 Franklin St.
Stamford, CT 06901
Phone: (203)348-7727
Diane Monti, Contact

Torrington

★5167★ Susan B. Anthony Project
S.T.R.I.V.E.
367 Goshen Rd.
Torrington, CT 06790
Phone: (203)489-3798
Claudette Baril, Contact

Waterbury

★5168★ Waterbury Job Training Agency
Displaced Homemakers Program
29 Leavenworth St.
Waterbury, CT 06702
Phone: (203)574-6971
Valerie Leal, Contact

★5169★ YWCA
Women On Their Way
80 Prospect St.
Waterbury, CT 06702
Phone: (203)754-5136
Jane Allen, Contact

Willimantic

★5170★ NEAC—North East Action
Committee
Displaced Homemaker Program
872 Main St.
Willimantic, CT 06226
Phone: (203)423-2539
Dawn Niles, Contact

Delaware

Dover

★5171★ Delaware Technical and
Community College, Terry Campus
Displaced Homemaker Program
1832 N. Dupont Parkway
Dover, DE 19901
Phone: (302)739-5401
Jean Close, Contact

★5172★ Women's Vocational Services
211 Carroll's Plaza
Dover, DE 19901
Phone: (302)739-4540
Diane Donnelly, Contact

Georgetown

★5173★ Delaware Technical College
Women in Transition
PO Box 610
Georgetown, DE 19947
Phone: (302)856-5384
Pat Fleetwood, Contact

★5174★ Women's Vocational Services
Rte. 113, Box 548
Georgetown, DE 19947
Phone: (302)856-5325
Betsy Archer, Contact

Newark

★5175★ Institute for the Development of
Human Resources
Displaced Homemakers Program
325 E. Main St.
Newark, DE 19711
Phone: (302)737-7488
Connie Stanton, Contact

Wilmington

★5176★ Delaware Skills Center
Displaced Homemaker Program
13th and Poplar Streets
Wilmington, DE 19801
Phone: (302)654-5325
Robert Marshall, Contact

★5177★ Delaware Technical and
Community College, Stanton/Wilmington
Campus
Displaced Homemaker Program
333 Shipley St.
Wilmington, DE 19801
Phone: (302)571-5313
Stephanie Brondt, Contact

★5178★ Women's Vocational Services
Displaced Homemakers Program
3301 Lancaster Ave.
Wilmington, DE 19805
Phone: (302)577-6192
Mary Dunn, Contact

★5179★ YWCA of New Castle County
Woman Power
233 King St.
Wilmington, DE 19801
Phone: (302)658-7161
Maxine Jackson, Contact

District of Columbia

Washington

★5180★ D.C. Public Schools
Office of Sex Equity
A Step Towards Employment Program
415 12th St., NW, Room 1010
Washington, DC 20004
Phone: (202)727-1037
Joy Jones, Contact

★5181★ Harrison Center for Career
Education
624 9th St. N.W., 6th Floor
Washington, DC 20005
Phone: (202)628-5672
Karen Bright, Contact

★5182★ Wider Opportunities for Women
1325 G St., N.W., Lower Level
Washington, DC 20005
Phone: (202)638-3143
Cindy Marano, Contact

Florida

Apopka

★5183★ Justice and Peace Office, Inc.
SMILE (Single Mothers in a Learning
Environment)
52 E. Main St.
Apopka, FL 32703
Phone: (407)889-0100
Deborah Sims, Contact

Avon Park

★5184★ South Florida Community College
Visions-Single Parent/Displaced
Homemakers Program
600 W. College Dr.
Avon Park, FL 33825
Phone: (813)382-6900
Shannon Beck, Contact

Bradenton

★5185★ Manatee Community College
Single Parents or Homemakers
Rm. 639, Technology Bldg.
PO Box 1849
Bradenton, FL 34207
Phone: (813)755-1511
June Barber, Contact

★5186★ Manatee County
Displaced Homemakers Program
New Options Center
5603 34th St. W.
Bradenton, FL 34210
Phone: (813)751-7922
Margot Jones, Contact

Brooksville

★5187★ Pasco-Hernando Community College
Single Parent/Homemaker Training
11415 Ponce de Leon Blvd.
Brooksville, FL 34601
Phone: (904)796-2235
Joy Johnson, Contact

Chipley

★5188★ Vocational Technical Center
Washington-Holmes Area
Single Parent/Homemakers Program
209 Hoyt St.
Chipley, FL 32428
Phone: (904)638-1180
Rose Adams, Contact

Clearwater

★5189★ PTEC—Pinellas Technical Education Center Clearwater
Single Parent/Homemaker Program
6100 154th Ave. N.
Clearwater, FL 34620
Phone: (813)531-3531
Neysa Steveson, Contact

Cocoa

★5190★ Brevard Community College
Displaced Homemaker Program
Bldg. U-112
Cocoa, FL 32922
Phone: (407)632-1111
Sandra G. Keene, Contact

★5191★ Brevard Community College
Women in Transition
1519 Clearlake Rd.
Cocoa, FL 32922
Phone: (407)632-1111
Kieta O. Culp, Contact

Coconut Creek

★5192★ Broward Community College
WINGS (Women Investigating New Goals and Services)
1000 Coconut Creek Blvd.
Coconut Creek, FL 33066
Phone: (305)973-2256
Carol Faber, Contact

Cross City

★5193★ Dixie District Schools
Single Parents or Homemakers
PO Box 1268
Cross City, FL 32628
Phone: (904)498-3358
Skipper Jones, Contact

Daytona Beach

★5194★ Daytona Beach Community College
Fresh Start for Displaced Homemakers—Women's Center
PO Box 2811
Daytona Beach, FL 32120-2811
Phone: (904)254-3068
Lucy B. Bell, Contact

★5195★ Daytona Beach Community College
Women's Center
Single Parent/Homemaker Program
PO Box 2811
Daytona Beach, FL 32115-2811
Phone: (904)254-3068
Lisa Edwards, Contact

Eustis

★5196★ Lake County Area Vocational-Technical Center
DAWN (Dealing Affirmatively With Needs Program)
2001 Kurt St.
Eustis, FL 32726
Phone: (904)357-8222
Sarah Burkert, Contact

Ft. Lauderdale

★5197★ Broward Community College
Project You
1000 Coconut Creek Blvd.
Ft. Lauderdale, FL 33066
Phone: (305)973-2232
Marcia Camerano, Contact

★5198★ School Board of Broward County
Single Parent/Displaced Homemakers Program
600 SE 3rd Ave., 4th Floor
Ft. Lauderdale, FL 33316
Phone: (305)760-7400
Dee Raulens, Contact

Ft. Myers

★5199★ Lee County Area Vocational Technical Center
Rediscovery Program
3800 Michigan Ave.
Ft. Myers, FL 33916
Phone: (813)334-4544
Paula Peterson, Contact

Ft. Pierce

★5200★ Indian River Community College
Single Parent/Displaced Homemakers Program
3209 Virginia Ave.
Ft. Pierce, FL 34981
Phone: (407)468-4739
Susan Jespersen, Contact

Gainesville

★5201★ Santa Fe Community College
Focus on the Future: Displaced Homemaker Program
3000 NW 83rd St.
Gainesville, FL 32606
Phone: (904)395-5047
Nancy Griffin, Contact

★5202★ Santa Fe Community College
Single Parents/Homemakers
Focus on Careers
PO Box 1530, #R222
Gainesville, FL 32606
Phone: (904)395-5581
Andrea S. Ashley, Contact

Immokalee

★5203★ Collier County Vocational-Technical Center
Immokalee High School
Center for Career Development
701 Immokalee Dr., Trailer #4
Immokalee, FL 33934
Phone: (813)657-3671
Gloria Dominguez, Contact

Kissimmee

★5204★ Osceola County School District
Family Resource Center
PO Box 1948
Kissimmee, FL 32742-1948
Phone: (407)847-3147
Sally David, Contact

Lake Butler

★5205★ Union County High School
Single Parent/Homemakers Program
1000 South Lake Ave.
Lake Butler, FL 32054
Phone: (904)496-2648
Joyce Gill, Contact

Lake City

★5206★ Lake City Community College
Continuing Education Department
Displaced Homemakers Program
Rte. 3, Box 7
Lake City, FL 32055
Phone: (904)752-1822
Jo Halley, Contact

Lake Worth

★5207★ Palm Beach Community College
Division of Continuing Education
Crossroads Program
4200 Congress Ave.
Lake Worth, FL 33461
Phone: (407)433-5995
Pat Jablonski, Contact

★5208★ Palm Beach Community College
Single Parent/Homemaker Program
4200 Congress Ave.
Lake Worth, FL 33461
Phone: (407)439-8181
Bobbi Marsh, Contact

Lakeland

★5209★ Polk County
Single Parent Displaced Homemaker Program
New Beginnings
1108 E. Memorial Blvd.
Lakeland, FL 33801
Phone: (813)665-3002
Trudy Horigan, Contact

Largo

★5210★ Resource Center for Women
12945 Seminole Blvd.
Twin Towers II, Ste. 8
Largo, FL 34648
Phone: (813)586-1110
Dolores K. Benjamin, Contact

Leesburg

★5211★ Lake Sumter Community College
Women's Program
9501 S. Highway 441
Leesburg, FL 32788
Phone: (904)365-3570
Janice Adkinson, Contact

Marianna

★5212★ Chipola Junior College
Single Parents/Displaced Homemakers
Program
College St.
Marianna, FL 32446
Phone: (904)526-2761
Addie Summers, Contact

★5213★ Jackson County Adult Education
Single parent/Homemakers Program
444 Guyton St.
Marianna, FL 32446
Phone: (904)482-9100
Carolyn Saunders, Contact

Melbourne

★5214★ South Brevard Women's Center
901 E. New Haven Ave. #2
Melbourne, FL 32901
Phone: (407)727-2200
Marca Fronk, Contact

Miami

★5215★ Institute for Human Research and
Development
Displaced Homemaker Center
42 NW 27th Ave., Ste. 302
Miami, FL 33125
Phone: (305)541-7887
Sara Krets, Contact

★5216★ Miami-Dade Community College
Vocational Educational Opportunity Grant
Single Parent/Homemaker Program
11011 Southwest 104th St.
Miami, FL 33176
Phone: (305)347-2497
Teresita Gaudy, Contact

★5217★ Miami-Dade Community College
Vocational Training for Single Parents and
Homemakers
11380 Northwest 27th Ave.
Miami, FL 33167-3495
Phone: (305)237-1149
Sue Lerner, Contact

Milton

★5218★ Locklin Vocational Technical
Center
Single Parents and Displaced Homemakers
2216 Berryhill Rd.
Milton, FL 32570
Phone: (904)623-3663
Suzanne Locklin, Contact

Monticello

★5219★ Jefferson County High School
Single Parent/Homemaker Program
425 W. Washington St.
Monticello, FL 32344
Phone: (904)997-3555
Anita Fierro, Contact

Niceville

★5220★ Okaloosa-Walton Community
College
Displaced Homemaker/Single Parent
Program
100 College Blvd.
Niceville, FL 32578
Phone: (904)729-5291
Johanna Adkins, Contact

Ocala

★5221★ Central Florida Community
College
Single Parent/Homemakers Program
PO Box 1388
State Road 200 W.
Ocala, FL 32678
Phone: (904)237-2111
Karen Williams, Contact

Orlando

★5222★ Valencia Community College
Displaced Homemaker Program
PO Box 3028 5-1
Orlando, FL 32802
Phone: (407)628-3511
Virginia Stuart, Contact

Panama City

★5223★ Gulf Coast Community College
Returning Woman Program
5230 W. Highway 98
Panama City, FL 32401
Phone: (904)769-1551
Dawyn Hudson, Contact

★5224★ Haney Vocational Technical
Center
Single Parent/Displaced Homemaker
Program
3016 Highway 77
Panama City, FL 32405
Phone: (904)769-2191
Janice Spencer, Contact

Pensacola

★5225★ George Stone Vocational-
Technical Center
Single Parent/Displaced Homemaker
Program
2400 Long Leaf Dr.
Pensacola, FL 32506
Phone: (904)944-1424
Betty McDermott, Contact

★5226★ Pensacola Junior College
Single Parent/Displaced Homemaker
Program
1000 College Blvd.
Pensacola, FL 32504
Phone: (904)484-1764
Debi Bick, Contact

★5227★ YWCA
Center for Displaced Homemakers
875 Royce St.
Pensacola, FL 32503
Phone: (904)474-3993
Lois Silberstein, Contact

Perry

★5228★ Taylor Technical Institute
Displaced Homemakers Program
3233 Highway 19 S.
Perry, FL 32347
Phone: (904)584-7603
Diana Chaffin, Contact

Pompano Beach

★5229★ Pompano Multi-Purpose Center
Single Parent/Homemaker Program
1400 Northeast 6th St.
Pompano Beach, FL 33060
Phone: (305)786-7620
Dee Raulins, Contact

Port Charlotte

★5230★ Charlotte Vocational Technical
School Center
ENCORE!
18300 Toledo Blade Blvd.
Port Charlotte, FL 33948-3399
Phone: (813)629-6819
Carol Watters, Contact

Quincy

★5231★ Gadsen Vocational Technical
School
Single Parent/Homemakers Association
201 Experiment Station Rd.
Quincy, FL 32351
Phone: (904)627-7591
Charlene Gre, Contact

St. Augustine

★5232★ St. Augustine Technical Center
Single Parents/Homemaker Program
Collins Ave. at Del Monte Dr.
St. Augustine, FL 32084
Phone: (904)824-4401
M. A. Allman, Contact

St. Petersburg

★5233★ Pinellas Vocational-Technical
Center
Single Parent Program
901 34th St. S.
St. Petersburg, FL 33711
Phone: (813)791-2474
Barbara H. Giffin, Contact

★5234★ St. Petersburg Junior College
Women on the Way Challenge Center
PO Box 13489
St. Petersburg, FL 33733
Phone: (813)791-2546
Lorna Minewiser, Contact

Sanford

★5235★ Seminole Community College
New Directions
100 Weldon Blvd.
Sanford, FL 32773
Phone: (407)323-1450
Midge Mycoff, Contact

Sarasota

★5236★ Women's Resource Center
Challenge Program
340 S. Tuttle Ave.
Sarasota, FL 34237
Phone: (813)366-1700
Susan Prefton, Contact

Stuart

★5237★ Vocational Assessment Center
CASH (Career Awareness for Single
Homemakers)
2300 E. Ocean Blvd., Bldg. 20
Stuart, FL 34994
Phone: (407)288-2760
Megan Horrigan, Contact

Tallahassee

★5238★ Tallahassee Community College
Begin Exploring New Directions (BEND)—
Displaced Homemakers Program
444 Appleyard Dr.
Tallahassee, FL 32304
Phone: (904)488-9200
Cheryl D. Roberts, Contact

Tampa

★5239★ Center for Women
305 S. Hyde Park Ave.
Tampa, FL 33606
Phone: (813)251-8437
Lee Ann Cox, Contact

★5240★ Hillsborough Community College
Single Parent/Homemakers Program
PO Box 5096
Tampa, FL 33675
Phone: (813)253-7659
Jean Stewart, Contact

★5241★ Single Parent/Displaced
Homemakers Program
2010 E. Hillsborough Ave.
Tampa, FL 33610
Phone: (813)272-4221
Bea Seymour, Contact

West Palm Beach

★5242★ Palm Beach County School
District
Single Parents/Displaced Homemaker
Program
1235 15th St.
West Palm Beach, FL 33401
Phone: (407)655-8407
Carolyn Helm, Contact

★5243★ Women's Horizons
901 S. Olive
West Palm Beach, FL 33401
Phone: (407)833-0817
Bobbye Duke, Contact

Winter Park

★5244★ Valencia Community College
Single Parent/Homemaker Program
1010 N. Orlando Ave.
Winter Park, FL 32789
Phone: (407)628-1976
Terri Rofter, Contact

Georgia

Albany

★5245★ Albany Technical Institute
New Connections
1021 Lowe Rd.
Albany, GA 31708
Phone: (912)430-3548
Francine Shuman, Contact

Athens

★5246★ Athens Area Technical Institute
New Connections
U.S. Highway 29, N.
Athens, GA 30601
Phone: (404)549-2360
Judy Taylor, Contact

Atlanta

★5247★ Atlanta Area Vocational Technical
School
New Connections
1560 Stewart Ave. Southwest
Atlanta, GA 30310
Phone: (404)758-9451
Sandra Bush, Contact

Augusta

★5248★ Augusta Technical Institute
New Connections
3116 Deans Bridge Rd.
Augusta, GA 30906
Phone: (404)796-6900
Shirley Norman, Contact

Bainbridge

★5249★ Bainbridge College
Vocational-Technical Education
STEP/New Connections
US Highway 84 E.
Bainbridge, GA 31717
Phone: (912)248-2530
Joan Beers, Contact

Carrollton

★5250★ Carroll Technical Institute
New Connections
997 S. Highway 16
Carrollton, GA 30117
Phone: (404)834-2611
Sue Jones, Contact

Clarkston

★5251★ Dekalb Technical Institute
New Connections
495 N. Indian Creek Dr.
Clarkston, GA 30021
Phone: (404)297-9522
Elizabeth Todd, Contact

Clarksville

★5252★ North Georgia Technical College
New Connections
Highway 197 N.
PO Box 65
Clarksville, GA 30523
Phone: (404)754-7766
Sandra Shore, Contact

Columbus

★5253★ Columbus Technical Institute
New Connections
928 45th St.
Columbus, GA 31995
Phone: (404)649-1818
Lee Fuller, Contact

Dalton

★5254★ Dalton College
New Connections
213 N. College Dr.
Dalton, GA 30720
Phone: (404)272-4464
Reba Olsen, Contact

★5255★ Dalton Vocational School of
Health Occupations
CHIPS/New Connections
1221 Elkwood Dr.
Dalton, GA 30720
Phone: (404)278-8922
Becky Fowler, Contact

Dublin

★5256★ Heart of Georgia Technical
Institute
Create Success/New Connections
Rte. 5, Box 136A-1
Dublin, GA 31021
Phone: (912)275-6589
Sara A. Swida, Contact

Griffin

★5257★ Griffin Technical Institute
New Connections
501 Varsity Rd.
Griffin, GA 30223
Phone: (404)228-7386
Nancy Duncan, Contact

Jasper

★5258★ Pickens Technical Institute
New Connections
240 Burnt Mountain Rd.
Jasper, GA 31043
Phone: (404)692-3411
Glenda Young, Contact

LaGrange

★5259★ West Georgia Technical Institute
New Connections
303 Fort Dr.
LaGrange, GA 30240
Phone: (404)883-8324
Frances Stroud, Contact

Lawrenceville

★5260★ Gwinnett Technical Institute
New Connections
PO Box 1505
Lawrenceville, GA 30245
Phone: (404)962-7580
Lora Novak, Contact

Macon

★5261★ Macon Technical Institute
New Connections
3300 Macon Technical Dr.
Macon, GA 31206
Phone: (912)781-0551
Carol G. Lystlund, Contact

Marietta

★5262★ Chattahoochee Technical College
New Connections
980 S. Cobb Dr.
Marietta, GA 30060
Phone: (404)528-4484
Stella Sessum, Contact

★5263★ Cobb YWCA
Women in Transition
48 Henderson St.
Marietta, GA 30064
Phone: (404)427-4795
Sharol Lee, Contact

Moultrie

★5264★ Moultrie Technical Institute
New Connections
PO Box 520
Moultrie, GA 31776
Phone: (912)985-2297
Janie Nash, Contact

Oakwood

★5265★ Lanier Technical Institute
New Connections
PO Box 58
Oakwood, GA 30566
Phone: (404)531-6346
Lisa Wilson, Contact

Rock Springs

★5266★ Walker County Area Vocational-
Technical School
CHIPS/New Connections
Rte. 2, Box 185, Merry Meadow Ln.
Rock Springs, GA 30739
Phone: (404)764-1016
Beverly Harris, Contact

Rome

★5267★ Coosa Valley Technical Institute
CHIPS/New Connections
112 Hemlock St.
Rome, GA 30161
Phone: (404)235-1142
Emily Eidson, Contact

Savannah

★5268★ Savannah Area Vocational-
Technical School
New Connections
5717 White Bluff Rd.
Savannah, GA 31499
Phone: (912)351-6362
Lynn Player, Contact

Statesboro

★5269★ Georgia Southern University
The Job Network Center
LB 8084
Statesboro, GA 30460
Phone: (912)681-6785
Sue Stephens-Fleuren, Contact

Swainsboro

★5270★ Swainsboro Technical Institute
New Connections
201 Kite Rd.
Swainsboro, GA 30401
Phone: (912)237-6465
Jan Brantley, Contact

Thomaston

★5271★ Upson Technical Institute
New Connections
PO Box 1089
Thomaston, GA 30286
Phone: (404)646-9616
Lisa Ingram, Contact

Thomasville

★5272★ Thomas Technical School
New Connections
PO Box 1578
Thomasville, GA 31799
Phone: (912)225-5093
Susanne Boykins, Contact

Valdosta

★5273★ Valdosta Technical Institute
New Connections
Rte. 1, Box 202
Valdosta, GA 31602
Phone: (404)333-2100
Michael Rayburn, Contact

Warner Robbins

★5274★ Middle Georgia Technical
Institute
New Connections
1311 Corder Rd.
Warner Robbins, GA 31056-3199
Phone: (912)929-6800
Jack Payne, Contact

Waycross

★5275★ Okefenokee Technical Institute
New Connections
1701 Carswell Ave.
Waycross, GA 31501
Phone: (912)283-2002
Barbara Howard, Contact

Hawaii

Hilo

★5276★ University of Hawaii at Hilo
Single Parent/Homemaker Program
UHH-HCC Bldg. 379, Room 3
Hilo, HI 96749
Phone: (808)933-3495
Annette Maeda, Contact

Honolulu

★5277★ Honolulu Community College
Single Parent/Homemaker Program
874 Dillingham Blvd.
Honolulu, HI 96817
Phone: (808)845-9120
Cheryl Chekpell-Long, Contact

★5278★ Kapiolani Community College
Single Parent/Homemaker Program
4302 Diamond Head Rd.
Honolulu, HI 96816
Phone: (808)734-9500
Cathy Chow, Contact

★5279★ YWCA
Network/SPAN
Single Parent Family Advocacy
1040 Richard St.
Honolulu, HI 96813
Phone: (808)538-7061
Pat Lau, Contact

Kahului

★5280★ Maui Community College
Single Parent/Homemaker Program
310 Kaahumanu Ave.
Kahului, HI 96732
Phone: (808)242-1278
Priscilla Mikell, Contact

Kaneohe

★5281★ Windward Community College
Single Parent/Homemaker Program
45-720 Keaahala Rd.
Kaneohe, HI 96744
Phone: (808)235-7471
Norma Higa, Contact

Lihue

★5282★ Kauai Community College
Single Parent/Homemaker Program
3-1901 Kaumualii Highway
Lihue, HI 96766
Phone: (808)245-8259
Jeni Ahn, Contact

Pearl City

★5283★ Leeward Community College
Adults in Transition
96-045 Ala Ike
Pearl City, HI 96782
Phone: (808)455-0233
Diane Sebring, Contact

Idaho

Boise

★5284★ YWCA
Career Center
720 W. Washington St.
Boise, ID 83702
Phone: (208)336-7306
Joyce Martin, Contact

Coeur d'Alene

★5285★ North Idaho College
Center for New Directions
1000 W. Garden Ave.
Coeur d'Alene, ID 83814
Phone: (208)769-3445
Carol Joseph-Haught, Contact

Idaho Falls

★5286★ Eastern Idaho Technical College
Southeastern Center for New Directions
1600 Hitt Rd.
Idaho Falls, ID 83401
Phone: (208)524-3000
Yvonne Booty, Contact

Lewiston

★5287★ Lewis-Clark State College
Center for New Directions
6th St. & 8th Ave.
Lewiston, ID 83501
Phone: (208)799-2331
Nina Woods, Contact

Nampa

★5288★ Boise State University
Canyon County Division
Center for New Directions
2407 Caldwell Blvd.
Nampa, ID 83651
Phone: (208)467-5707
Ranelle Nabring, Contact

Pocatello

★5289★ Idaho State University
Center for New Directions
PO Box 8380
Pocatello, ID 83209-0009
Phone: (208)236-2454
Mary Nelle Whitenack, Contact

Twin Falls

★5290★ College of Southern Idaho
Center for New Directions
1060 Washington St. N.
PO Box 1238
Twin Falls, ID 83303-1238
Phone: (208)736-0070
Rita Larom, Contact

Illinois

Aurora

★5291★ Waubonsee Community College
Building Opportunity Project
5 E. Galena Blvd.
Aurora, IL 60506
Phone: (312)892-3334
Sharon Gilmour, Contact

Belleville

★5292★ Belleville Area College
Every Women's Center
2500 Carlyle Rd.
Belleville, IL 62223
Phone: (618)235-2700
Patricia Brian, Contact

★5293★ College Vocational System
St. Clair County Belleville Area
Building Opportunity Project
500 Wilshire Dr.
Belleville, IL 62223
Phone: (618)398-5280
Shirley Gasparich, Contact

Canton

★5294★ Spoon River College
Single Parent/Displaced Homemakers
Program
Rural Rte. #1
Canton, IL 61520
Phone: (309)647-4645
Jody McCamey, Contact

Carbondale

★5295★ GENESIS
Displaced Homemaker Program
500-C Lewis
Carbondale, IL 62901
Phone: (618)453-2331
Ruth Ann Ramey, Contact

Carmi

★5296★ Regional Vocational Delivery
Service
Displaced Homemakers Program
PO Box 520
Carmi, IL 62821
Phone: (618)382-2830
Judy Brewster, Contact

Carterville

★5297★ John A. Logan College
Building Opportunity Project
Rte. 2
Carterville, IL 62918
Phone: (618)985-3741
Marjorie Jack, Contact

Centralia

★5298★ Kaskaskia College
Regional Delivery System for Vocational
Education
Building Opportunity Project
Shattuc Rd.
Centralia, IL 62801
Phone: (618)532-1981
Jane Kimberly, Contact

Chicago

★5299★ Assignment House of Chicago
Single Parent/Displaced Homemaker
Building Opportunity Project
1116 N. Kedzie Ave.
Chicago, IL 60647
Phone: (312)486-4489
Ana Romero, Contact

★5300★ Chicago City-Wide College
Displaced Homemaker Program
226 W. Jackson Blvd., 4th Fl.
Chicago, IL 60606-6997
Phone: (312)368-8836
Yvonne Johnson, Contact

★5301★ Chicago City-Wide College
Single Parent/Displaced Homemaker
Building Opportunity Project
226 W. Jackson Blvd., 4th Fl.
Chicago, IL 60606-6997
Phone: (312)368-8841

★5302★ Harry S. Truman College
Single Parent/Displaced Homemaker
Building Opportunity Program
1145 W. Wilson Ave.
Chicago, IL 60640
Phone: (312)989-6797
Tina Page, Contact

★5303★ Jewish Vocational Services
Single Parent/Displaced Homemaker
Building Opportunity Project
One S. Franklin St.
Chicago, IL 60606
Phone: (312)346-6700
Gerald Silverstein, Contact

★5304★ Kennedy-King College
Single Parent/Displaced Homemaker
Building Opportunity Project
6800 S. Wentworth Ave.
Chicago, IL 60621
Phone: (312)962-3200
Rebecca Browder, Contact

★5305★ Southwest Women Working
Together
3201 W. 63rd St.
Chicago, IL 60629
Phone: (312)436-0550
Joy Aruguete, Contact

★5306★ Women Employed Institute
22 W. Monroe, Ste. 1400
Chicago, IL 60603
Phone: (312)782-3902
Linda S. Hannah, Contact

Crystal Lake

★5307★ McHenry County Community
College
Building Opportunity Project
Rte. 14 & Lucas Rd.
Crystal Lake, IL 60012
Phone: (815)455-8769
Shelly Kaplan, Contact

Danville

★5308★ Vermillion Vocational Education
Building Opportunity Project
Delivery Sys., Co. Service Bldg.
Rte. 1, Box 12E
Danville, IL 61832
Phone: (217)442-0461
Cynthia Moore, Contact

Decatur

★5309★ Richland Community College
Options for Displaced Homemakers
One College Park
Decatur, IL 62521
Phone: (217)875-7200
Fax: (217)875-6961
Kathy Sorensen, Contact

East Moline

★5310★ Black Hawk College
Women's Resource Program
301 42nd Ave.
East Moline, IL 61244
Phone: (309)755-2200
Kathy Kessler, Contact

Elgin

★5311★ Elgin Community College
Alternatives
1700 Spartan Dr.
Elgin, IL 60120
Phone: (708)697-1000
Cindy Moehrlin, Contact

Freeport

★5312★ Martin Luther King Center
Building Opportunity Project
511 S. Liberty Ave.
Freeport, IL 61032
Phone: (815)233-9915
Anne Pulley, Contact

Glen Ellyn

★5313★ YWCA-West Suburban
Target Program
739 Roosevelt Rd., Bldg. 8
Glen Ellyn, IL 60137
Phone: (312)790-6600
Lois Ulreich, Contact

Grays Lake

★5314★ Lake County Area Vocational System
Building Opportunity Project
19525 W. Washington St.
Grays Lake, IL 60030
Phone: (708)223-6681
Barbara Oilsellager, Contact

Greenville

★5315★ Bond, Fayette, and Effingham, Vocational Education System
Bond County Community Unit 2
Building Opportunity Project
800 N. Dewey
Greenville, IL 62246
Phone: (618)664-5009
Cindy Adkins, Contact

Harrisburg

★5316★ Southeastern Illinois College
Building Opportunity Project
3575 College Rd.
Harrisburg, IL 62946
Phone: (618)252-6376
Barbara Luce-Turner, Contact

Hillsboro

★5317★ Christian-Montgomery Education for Employment System
Building Opportunity Project
200 S. Main St.
Hillsboro, IL 62049
Phone: (217)532-9344
Helene Huber, Contact

Ina

★5318★ Rend Lake College
Building Opportunity Project
Rte. 1
Ina, IL 62846
Phone: (618)437-5321
Elaine Johnson, Contact

Jerseyville

★5319★ Lewis & Clark Community College
Building Opportunity Project
Community Education Center
519 S. State St.
Jerseyville, IL 62052
Phone: (618)498-6279
Stephanie Von Almen, Contact

Kankakee

★5320★ Kankakee Community College
Building Opportunity Project
Box 888, River Rd.
Kankakee, IL 60901
Phone: (815)933-0250
Julie Kyrouac, Contact

Macomb

★5321★ LaMoine Valley Vocational System
Building Opportunity Project
130 1/2 S. Lafayette
PO Box 562
Macomb, IL 61455
Phone: (309)837-4821
Ann Johnson, Contact

Malta

★5322★ Kishwaukee College
Building Opportunity Project
Rte. 38 & Malta Rd.
Malta, IL 60150
Phone: (815)825-2086
Joy Gulotta, Contact

Mattoon

★5323★ Lake Land College
Building Opportunity Project
South Rte. 45
Mattoon, IL 61938
Phone: (217)235-3131
Beverly Luft, Contact

Olney

★5324★ Olney Central College
Displaced Homemakers Program
305 NW St.
Olney, IL 62450
Phone: (618)395-4351
Pam Schwartz, Contact

Palatine

★5325★ Harper College
Project Turning Point
Algonquin and Roselle Rds.
Palatine, IL 60067
Phone: (708)397-3000
Danares Reid, Contact

Palos Hills

★5326★ Moraine Valley Community College
Building Opportunity Project
10900 S. 88th Ave.
Palos Hills, IL 60465
Phone: (708)974-4300
Cheryl Washington, Contact

Peoria

★5327★ Project Redirection
317 S. MacArthur
Peoria, IL 61605
Phone: (309)672-4363
Annie Gordon, Contact

Perkin

★5328★ Building Opportunity Project
Taxewell County
Box 489
Perkin, IL 61554
Phone: (309)353-5011
Carol Leach, Contact

Quincy

★5329★ John Wood Community College
Building Opportunity Project
150 S. 48th St.
Quincy, IL 62301
Phone: (217)224-6500
Rita Buddemeyer, Contact

Rantoul

★5330★ Champaign/Ford Vocational System
Building Opportunity Project
200 S. Frederick St., Box 919
Rantoul, IL 61866
Phone: (217)893-3219
Ruth Stevens, Contact

Rockford

★5331★ Rock Valley College
Fresh Beginnings
3350 North Bell School Rd.
Rockford, IL 61111
Phone: (815)654-4273
Nancy Conner, Contact

Romeoville

★5332★ Displaced Homemaker Program
201 Normantown Rd.
Romeoville, IL 60441
Phone: (815)886-3324
Gloria Hollister, Contact

Skokie

★5333★ Oakton Community College
Displaced Homemaker Program
7701 Lincoln
Skokie, IL 60076
Phone: (708)982-9888
Gail Grossman, Contact

Springfield

★5334★ Lincoln Land Community College
Project Fresh Start Displaced Homemakers Program
Shepherd Rd.
Springfield, IL 62794-9256
Phone: (217)786-2231
Lanette Nies, Contact

Urbana

★5335★ Building Opportunity Project
Single Parent/Displaced Homemakers Program
Univ. of IL-549 Bevier Hall
905 S. Goodwin Ave.
Urbana, IL 61801
Phone: (217)244-2849
Jane Scherer, Contact

Indiana

Bloomington

★5336★ South Central Indiana PIC— Private Industry Council
Single Parent/Displaced Homemaker Program
405 W. 7th St.
Bloomington, IN 47402
Phone: (812)332-3777
Anne Bright, Contact

Columbus

★5337★ McDowell Education Center
Single Parent/Homemaker Program
2700 McKinley Ave.
Columbus, IN 47201
Phone: (812)376-4451
Anya Cutter, Contact

Connersville

★5338★ Single Parent/Homemakers Program of Southeastern Indiana
200 W 5th St.
Connersville, IN 47331
Phone: (317)825-8581
Carolyn Bunzendahl, Contact

Evansville

★5339★ Evansville-Vanderburgh School
  Corporation
Single Parent/Homemaker Program
1900 Stringtown Rd.
Evansville, IN 47711
Phone: (812)424-0904
Joanne Reid, Contact

Ft. Wayne

★5340★ Ft. Wayne Women's Bureau, Inc.
Single Parent/Homemaker Program
303 E. Washington Blvd.
Ft. Wayne, IN 46802
Phone: (219)424-7977
Rikki Goldstein, Contact

★5341★ Northeast Indiana PIC—Private
  Industry Council
Single Parent Displaced Homemaker
  Program
201 W. Wayne St.
Ft. Wayne, IN 46802
Phone: (219)426-5006
Margo Altevogt, Contact

Hammond

★5342★ Hammond Client Service Center
Single Parent/Displaced Homemaker
  Program
5217 Hohman Ave.
Hammond, IN 46320
Phone: (219)937-0381
Ida Rancifer, Contact

Indianapolis

★5343★ J. Everett Light Career Center
Career Advancement Training Center for
  Single Parents/Homemakers
1901 E. 86th St.
Indianapolis, IN 46240
Phone: (317)251-0041
Carol Strum, Contact

Lafayette

★5344★ Tecumseh Area Partnership, Inc.
Single Parent/Homemaker Program
PO Box 4729
Lafayette, IN 47903
Phone: (317)448-2772
Bob Brelsford, Contact

New Albany

★5345★ Extended Services Center
Single Parent/Homemakers Program
506 W. Spring St.
New Albany, IN 47150
Phone: (812)949-4262
Jack Womack, Contact

New Castle

★5346★ New Castle Area Vocational
  School
Single Parent/Homemaker Program
1305 G Ave.
New Castle, IN 47362
Phone: (317)529-7227
Laura K. Mogg, Contact

Peru

★5347★ North Central PIC—Private
  Industry Council
Single Parent Displaced Homemaker
  Program
36 W. 5th St., Ste. 102A
Peru, IN 46970
Phone: (317)473-6688
Evelyn Lindsey, Contact

South Bend

★5348★ Workforce Development Services
115 N. William St.
PO Box 1048
South Bend, IN 46624
Phone: (219)239-2380
Susan Gadacz, Contact

Terre Haute

★5349★ Wabash Valley Single
  Parent/Homemakers Project
7377 S. Dixie Bee Rd.
Terre Haute, IN 47802
Phone: (812)299-1121
Casey Chaney, Contact

Valparaiso

★5350★ Kankakee Valley Job Training
Displaced Homemakers Program
150 Lincoln Square, Ste. 20001
PO Box 450
Valparaiso, IN 46384
Phone: (219)464-4861
Ethel Walker, Contact

Vincennes

★5351★ New Directions
525 N. 4th St.
PO Box 450
Vincennes, IN 47591
Phone: (812)885-5306
Jill Littell, Contact

Iowa

Boone

★5352★ Des Moines Area Community
  College
Project Self-Support/Displaced Homemaker
  Center
1125 Hancock Dr.
Boone, IA 50036
Phone: (515)432-7203
Maggie Stone, Contact

Calmar

★5353★ Northeast Iowa Community
  College
Adult Re-Entry Program
Box 400
Calmar, IA 52132
Phone: (319)562-3263
Mary Rausch, Contact

Carroll

★5354★ Des Moines Area Community
  College
Project Self-Support
906 N. Grant Rd.
Carroll, IA 51401
Phone: (712)792-1755
Renee Schon, Contact

Cedar Rapids

★5355★ Kirkwood Community College
Displaced Homemaker Program
6301 Kirkwood Blvd. S. W.
PO Box 2068
Cedar Rapids, IA 52406
Phone: (319)398-5471
Regina Dudley, Contact

Council Bluffs

★5356★ Iowa Western Community College
New Horizons
2700 College Rd., Box 4C
Council Bluffs, IA 51502
Phone: (712)325-3441
Marie Elkin, Contact

Creston

★5357★ Displaced Homemaker and Single
  Parent Program
1501 W. Townline
Creston, IA 50801
Phone: (515)782-7081
Sharon Bennett, Contact

Davenport

★5358★ Eastern Iowa Community College
Displaced Homemaker Program
306 W. River Dr.
Davenport, IA 52801
Phone: (319)326-5319
Sara Wissing, Contact

Des Moines

★5359★ Des Moines Area Community
  College
Project Self-Sufficiency
1100 7th St.
Des Moines, IA 50314
Phone: (515)244-4226
Denise Hotopp, Contact

★5360★ Homes of Oakridge
Displaced Homemaker Program
926 Oakridge Dr.
Bldg. 45 - #123
Des Moines, IA 50314
Phone: (515)244-7702
Margaret Toomey, Contact

Dubuque

★5361★ Displaced Homemakers Program
330 Nesler Center
PO Box 1140
Dubuque, IA 52004
Phone: (319)556-4166
Ron Axtel, Contact

★5362★ Operation: New View
1449 Central Ave.
Dubuque, IA 52001
Phone: (319)556-5130
Karen McCarthy, Contact

Estherville

★5363★ **Iowa Lakes Community College**
Displaced Homemaker/Single Parent
  Program
300 South 18th St.
Estherville, IA 51334
Phone: (712)362-2604
Linda J. Wiegman, Contact

Ft. Dodge

★5364★ **Iowa Central Community College**
Displaced Homemaker Program
330 Ave., M.
Ft. Dodge, IA 50501
Phone: (515)576-7459
Elaine Weidlein, Contact

Maquoketa

★5365★ **Maquoketa Community Center**
Project Stepping Stone
506 S. Eliza
Maquoketa, IA 52060
Phone: (319)652-4958
Joanne Evans, Contact

Marshalltown

★5366★ **Iowa Valley Community College**
Displaced Homemakers Network
3700 S. Center St., Box 536
Marshalltown, IA 50158
Phone: (515)752-7106
Gladys Ebert, Contact

★5367★ **Iowa Valley Community College**
Mequaki Indian Project
Displaced Homemaker Program
Box 536
Marshalltown, IA 50158
Phone: (515)752-4693
Mark Steinberg, Contact

Kansas

Arkansas City

★5368★ **Cowley County Community**
  College
Single Parent/Homemaker Program
125 S. 2nd
Arkansas City, KS 67005
Phone: (316)442-0430
Judy Queen, Contact

Chanute

★5369★ **Neosho County Community**
  College
Single Parent/Homemaker Program
1000 S. Allen
Chanute, KS 66720
Phone: (316)431-2820
Martha McCoy, Contact

Coffeyville

★5370★ **Coffeyville Community College**
Single Parent/Homemaker Program
11th & Willow Streets
Coffeyville, KS 67337
Phone: (316)251-4090
Allene Knedlik, Contact

Concordia

★5371★ **Cloud County Community College**
Single Parent/Displaced Homemaker
  Program
2221 Campus Drive
PO Box 1002
Concordia, KS 66901
Phone: (913)243-1435
Sherri Orr, Contact

Dodge City

★5372★ **Dodge City Community College**
Single Parent/Displaced Homemaker
  Program
2501 N. 14th Ave.
Dodge City, KS 67801
Phone: (316)225-1321
Sam Seybold, Contact

El Dorado

★5373★ **Butler County Community College**
Resource Center
Second Chance/Displaced Homemakers
  Program
613 N. Main
El Dorado, KS 67042
Phone: (316)321-4030
Karen Hasting, Contact

Ft. Scott

★5374★ **Fort Scott Community College**
Single Parent/Homemaker Program
2108 S. Horton
Ft. Scott, KS 66701
Phone: (316)223-2700
Connie Corbett-Whittier, Contact

Garden City

★5375★ **Garden City Community College**
Single Parent Homemaker Program
801 Campus Dr.
Garden City, KS 67846
Phone: (316)276-7611
JoAnn Garrier, Contact

Independence

★5376★ **Independence Community College**
Single Parent/Homemaker Program
PO Box 708
Independence, KS 67301
Phone: (316)331-4100
Joy Barta, Contact

Iola

★5377★ **Allen County Community College**
Single Parent/Homemaker Program
1801 N. Cottonwood
Iola, KS 66749
Phone: (316)365-5116
Donna Culver, Contact

Kansas City

★5378★ **Kansas City Kansas Community**
  College
Women's Resource Center
7250 State Ave.
Kansas City, KS 66112
Phone: (913)334-1100
Andrea Chastain, Contact

Manhattan

★5379★ **Kansas State University**
New Directions
407 Bluemont Hall
Manhattan, KS 66506
Phone: (913)532-6561
Shirley Marshall, Contact

★5380★ **Manhattan Area Vocational**
  Technical School
Single Parent/Homemaker Program
3136 Dickens Ave.
Manhattan, KS 66502
Phone: (913)539-7431
Jule Kuhn, Contact

Ottawa

★5381★ **Adult Education Center**
Single Parent Program
1418 S. Main, Ste. 4
Ottawa, KS 66067
Phone: (913)242-6719
Susan Padfield, Contact

Parsons

★5382★ **Labette Community College**
Single Parent/Displaced Homemaker
  Program
200 S. 14th
PO Box 957
Parsons, KS 67357
Phone: (316)421-6700
Kathy Stotts, Contact

Shawnee Mission

★5383★ **Broadmoor Center**
Johnson County Area Vocational-Technical
  School
Single Parent/Homemaker Program
6701 W. 83rd
Shawnee Mission, KS 66204
Phone: (913)642-3130
Barbara Johnson, Contact

Topeka

★5384★ **YWCA**
Career Assistance Network
225 W. 12th
Topeka, KS 66607
Phone: (913)233-1750
Jan Brunton, Contact

Wichita

★5385★ **Wichita YWCA**
Employment and Resource Network
350 N. Market
Wichita, KS 67202
Phone: (316)263-7501
Claudia Moeder, Contact

Kentucky

Ashland

★5386★ **Ashland Community College**
Re-Entry Program
1400 College Dr.
Ashland, KY 41101
Phone: (606)329-2999
Louise Shytle, Contact

Elizabethtown

★5387★ Elizabethtown Community College
REWARD
College Street Rd.
Elizabethtown, KY 42701
Phone: (502)769-2371
Beth Moore, Contact

Hazard

★5388★ Hazard Community College
Career Awareness for the Single Parents
and Homemakers
Hwy. 15 South
Hazard, KY 41701
Phone: (606)436-5721
Judy Johnson, Contact

Henderson

★5389★ Henderson Community College
Career Development Center
Displaced Homemaker Program
2660 S. Green St.
Henderson, KY 42420
Phone: (502)827-1867
Sandra Smith, Contact

Highland Heights

★5390★ Northern Kentucky University
Vocational Preparation for Single
Parent/Homemakers in Northern
Kentucky
225 Albright Health Center
Highland Heights, KY 41076
Phone: (606)572-5595
Candace Sellers, Contact

Hopkinsville

★5391★ Hopkinsville Community College
Single Parent/Homemaker Department
PO Box 2100
Hopkinsville, KY 42240
Phone: (502)886-3921
Joyce Boren, Contact

London

★5392★ I Can Do Career Awareness
235 S. Laurel Rd.
London, KY 40741
Phone: (606)864-5141
Francine Mosley, Contact

Louisville

★5393★ Center for Women and Families
Creative Employment Project
PO Box 2048
Louisville, KY 40201-2048
Phone: (502)581-7237
Diane Guenther, Contact

Madisonville

★5394★ Madisonville Community College
Single Parent/Displaced Homemaker
Program
College Dr.
Madisonville, KY 42431
Phone: (502)821-2250
Beth Moore, Contact

Maysville

★5395★ Maysville Community College
Displaced Homemakers Program
U.S. Highway 68
Maysville, KY 41056
Phone: (606)759-7141
Beverly Levay, Contact

Owensboro

★5396★ Career Development Program
2641 S. Griffith Ave.
Owensboro, KY 42301
Phone: (502)686-1036
Paddy Miller, Contact

Paducah

★5397★ Paducah Community College
Single Parent/Homemakers Program
Alben Barkley Dr.
PO Box 7380
Paducah, KY 42002-7380
Phone: (502)554-9200
Janice Foust, Contact

Prestonsburg

★5398★ Prestonsburg Community College
Single Parent/Homemaker Career
Development Program
H.C. 69, Box 230
Prestonsburg, KY 41653
Phone: (606)886-3863
Jean Rosenberg, Contact

Somerset

★5399★ Somerset Community College
Transitional Support Services
Displaced Homemakers Program
808 Monticello Rd.
Somerset, KY 42501
Phone: (606)679-8501
Peg Taylor, Contact

Louisiana

Baton Rouge

★5400★ Center for Displaced
Homemakers
7393 Florida Blvd.
Bon Marche Mall
Baton Rouge, LA 70806
Phone: (504)925-6922
Joan Didier, Contact

Lafayette

★5401★ Center for Displaced
Homemakers
1304 Bertrand Dr., Ste. C-1
Lafayette, LA 70506
Phone: (318)265-5191
Janet Melancon, Contact

Lake Charles

★5402★ Center for Displaced
Homemakers
1202 Common St.
Lake Charles, LA 70601
Phone: (318)491-2656
Mary June Malus, Contact

New Orleans

★5403★ New Orleans Regional Vocational
Technical Institute
Center for Displaced Homemakers
980 Navarre Ave.
New Orleans, LA 70124
Phone: (504)483-4664
Barbara Connors, Contact

Shreveport

★5404★ Center For Displaced
Homemakers
752 Dalzell St.
Shreveport, LA 71104
Phone: (318)226-7137
Daphne Rushe, Contact

Maine

Augusta

★5405★ University of Maine—Augusta,
Stoddard House
Displaced Homemaker Program
Augusta, ME 04330
Phone: (207)621-3438
Judy Gallant, Contact

Bangor

★5406★ Bangor Hall, University College
Transitions: A Displaced Homemaker
Program
355 Maine Ave.
Bangor, ME 04401
Phone: (217)581-6132
Ilze Petersons, Contact

East Millinocket

★5407★ Katahdin Area Training and
Education Center
Displaced Homemaker Program
1 Industrial Dr.
East Millinocket, ME 04430
Phone: (207)746-5741
Sue D'Alessandro, Contact

Farmington

★5408★ University of Maine—Farmington
Look House Basement
Displaced Homemakers Program
Farmington, ME 04938
Phone: (207)778-9050
Carol Millay, Contact

Houlton

★5409★ Displaced Homemakers Program
106 Main St.
PO Box 382
Houlton, ME 04730
Phone: (207)532-9313
Audrey Zimmerman, Contact

Lewiston

★5410★ Lewiston/Auburn College
University of Southern Maine/University
of Maine—Augusta
Displaced Homemakers Program
15-55 Westminster Street
Lewiston, ME 04240
Phone: (207)783-4860
Karen Ronquist, Contact

Portland

★5411★ Displaced Homemakers Resource Center
865 Forest Ave.
Portland, ME 04103
Phone: (207)773-3537
Jane Pease, Contact

Presque Isle

★5412★ Northern Maine Technical College Transitions
33 Edgemont Dr.
Presque Isle, ME 04769
Phone: (207)764-0050
Linda Senechal, Contact

Skowhegan

★5413★ Displaced Homemakers Program
20 High St.
PO Box 930
Skowhegan, ME 04976
Phone: (207)872-9482
Thia Hamilton, Contact

Thomaston

★5414★ University of Maine Thomaston Center Displaced Homemakers Program
42 Main St.
Thomaston, ME 04861
Phone: (207)354-6906
Nancy Anderson, Contact

Maryland

Annapolis

★5415★ YWCA Woman's Center Displaced Homemakers Program
167 Duke of Gloucester St.
Annapolis, MD 21401
Phone: (410)269-0378
Lora D. Junkin, Contact

Baltimore

★5416★ Community College of Baltimore Re-Entry Program
Harbor Campus, Rm. B-112
Lombard St. & Market Place
Baltimore, MD 21202
Phone: (410)333-5555
Shirley Robinson, Contact

★5417★ Essex Community College Turning Point
7201 Rossville Blvd.
Baltimore, MD 21237
Phone: (410)522-1746
Maureen O'Brien, Contact

★5418★ Maryland New Directions, Inc.
2220 N. Charles St.
Baltimore, MD 21218
Phone: (410)235-0350
Joan Patterson, Contact

Bel Air

★5419★ Open Doors Career Center, Inc.
432 S. Main St.
Bel Air, MD 21014
Phone: (410)879-9627
Judith Kole, Contact

Bowie

★5420★ New Ventures, Inc.
3501 Moylan Dr., Rm. 18
Bowie, MD 20716
Phone: (301)464-2622
Eileen Waters, Contact

Capitol Heights

★5421★ United Communities Against Poverty Crossroads, Displaced Homemaker Program
1400 Doewood Ln.
Capitol Heights, MD 20743
Phone: (301)322-5700
Mona Harding, Contact

Catonsville

★5422★ Catonsville Community College Project Second Start
800 S. Rolling Rd.
Catonsville, MD 21228
Phone: (410)455-4719
Joan Swiston, Contact

Columbia

★5423★ Howard Community College Single Parent/Homemakers Program
Little Patuxent Pkwy.
Columbia, MD 21044
Phone: (410)992-4841
Dale Flint, Contact

Cumberland

★5424★ Allegany Community College Displaced Homemaker Program
Willowbrook Rd.
PO Box 1695
Cumberland, MD 21502
Phone: (301)724-7700
Ellen Durr, Contact

Dundalk

★5425★ Dundalk Community College Single Parent/Homemakers Project
7200 Sellers Point Rd.
Dundalk, MD 21222
Phone: (410)285-9774
Alice Moore, Contact

Elkton

★5426★ The Career Connection
107 Railroad Ave.
Elkton, MD 21921
Phone: (410)392-3366
Adina Ruvel, Contact

Frederick

★5427★ Frederick Community College Project Forward Step
7932 Oppossumtown Pike
Frederick, MD 21702
Phone: (301)846-2483
Sandra Cavalier, Contact

Hagerstown

★5428★ CASA, Inc.
116 W. Baltimore St.
Hagerstown, MD 21740
Phone: (301)739-4990
Vicki A. Sadehvandi, Contact

★5429★ Hagerstown Junior College Chapter II Homemakers in Transition
751 Robinwood Dr.
Hagerstown, MD 21740
Phone: (301)790-2800
Robin L. Spaid, Contact

La Plata

★5430★ Charles County Community College Project Transition
269 Smallwood Village Center
PO Box 910
La Plata, MD 20604
Phone: (301)870-3008
Patricia Schroeder, Contact

Largo

★5431★ Prince George's Community College Crossroads
Bladen Hall
Largo, MD 20772
Phone: (301)322-0485
Judy Dubose, Contact

McHenry

★5432★ Garrett Community College New Horizons
PO Box 151
McHenry, MD 21541
Phone: (301)387-6666
Barbara Frey, Contact

Rockville

★5433★ Jewish Social Service Agency Displaced Homemakers Program
6123 Montrose Rd.
Rockville, MD 20852
Phone: (301)881-3700
Debra Ekman, Contact

★5434★ Montgomery College Project Next Step
51 Mannakee St.
Rockville, MD 20850
Phone: (301)279-5064
Maureen Busher, Contact

★5435★ New Phase Career Center Montgomery County Government
255 N. Washington St., 4th Fl.
Rockville, MD 20850
Phone: (301)279-1800

Founded: 1977. **Description:** Services include individual career counseling appointments and special career seminars.

★5436★ Women Counseling and Career Center
255 N. Washington St.
Rockville, MD 20850
Phone: (301)279-1800
Thyra Packett, Contact

Salisbury

★5437★ Shore Up, Inc. Project Renaissance
520 Snow Hill Rd.
PO Box 430
Salisbury, MD 21801
Phone: (410)749-1142
Margaret Antal, Contact

★5438★ **Wor-Wic Community College**
Step Two
30 Wesley Dr.
Salisbury, MD 21801
Phone: (410)749-8181
Carol Childs, Contact

Westminster

★5439★ **Carroll Community College**
Displaced Homemaker Program
1601 Washington Rd.
Westminster, MD 21157
Phone: (410)876-9617
Sherry Glass, Contact

Wye Mills

★5440★ **Chesapeake College**
New Horizons
PO Box 8
Wye Mills, MD 21679
Phone: (410)822-4850
Elizabeth Jones, Contact

Massachusetts

Beverly

★5441★ **North Shore Community College**
Single Parent/Displaced Homemakers
Program
3 Essex St.
Beverly, MA 01915
Phone: (508)927-4850
Marquerile McLellan, Contact

Billerica

★5442★ **Shawsheen Valley Technical High**
School
Single Parent/Displaced Homemakers
Progam
100 Cook St.
Billerica, MA 01852-5499
Phone: (508)667-2111
Dan Trainor, Contact

Boston

★5443★ **Franklin Institute**
Displaced Homemakers Program
41 Berkeley St.
Boston, MA 02116
Phone: (617)262-3240
Richard Fields, Contact

★5444★ **Higher Education Information**
Center
Bay State Centers for Displaced
Homemakers
666 Boyston St.
Boston, MA 02116
Phone: (617)536-0200
Pat Dacey, Contact

Brockton

★5445★ **Massasoit Community College**
Single Parent/Displaced Homemakers
Program
1 Massasoit Blvd.
Brockton, MA 02402
Phone: (508)588-9100
Donna Malley, Contact

Cambridge

★5446★ **Women's Job Counseling Center**
34 Follen St.
Cambridge, MA 02138
Phone: (617)547-1123
Sheila G. Cook, Contact

Charlestown

★5447★ **Bunker Hill Community College**
Single Parent/Homemakers Program
Rutherford Ave.
Charlestown, MA 02129
Phone: (617)241-8600
Kathleen Teehan, Contact

Fitchburg

★5448★ **Montachusett Opportunity Council**
Learning Center
Displaced Homemakers Program
100 Main St.
Fitchburg, MA 01420
Phone: (508)345-7317
Jenny Morris, Contact

Holyoke

★5449★ **Holyoke Community College**
Single Parent/Homemakers Program
303 Homestead Ave.
Holyoke, MA 01040
Phone: (413)538-7000
Helen Kapinos, Contact

Hyannis

★5450★ **Bay State Centers for Displaced**
Homemakers
270 Communications Way
Hyannis, MA 02601
Phone: (508)771-0141
Mary Morreale, Contact

Lowell

★5451★ **Greater Lowell, YWCA**
Bay State Centers for Displaced
Homemakers
206 Rogers St.
Lowell, MA 01852
Phone: (508)454-5405
Rosemary Hawkins, Contact

★5452★ **Middlesex Community College**
Displaced Homemakers Program
650 Suffolk St.
Lowell, MA 01854
Phone: (508)937-5454
Barbara Rubin, Contact

Lynn

★5453★ **North Shore Community College**
Single Parent/Displaced Homemaker
Program
3 Essex St.
Lynn, MA 01915
Phone: (617)593-6722
Patricia Neilson, Contact

New Bedford

★5454★ **New Bedford YWCA**
Bay State Centers for Displaced
Homemakers
66 Spring St.
New Bedford, MA 02740
Phone: (508)999-3255
Nancy Haley, Contact

Northampton

★5455★ **Bay State Centers for Displaced**
Homemakers
16 Center St., No. 312
Northampton, MA 01060
Phone: (413)584-9111
Lyndell Rowe, Contact

Pittsfield

★5456★ **Berkshire Community College**
Single Parent/Homemakers Progam
West St.
Pittsfield, MA 01201
Phone: (413)499-4660
Barbara Hockberg, Contact

★5457★ **Women's Services Center,**
Bay State Centers for Displaced
Homemakers
146 1st St.
Pittsfield, MA 01201
Phone: (413)499-2425
Bernyce Goettinger, Contact

Quincy

★5458★ **Quincy Junior College**
Bay State Centers for Displaced
Homemakers
34 Coddington St.
Quincy, MA 02169
Phone: (617)984-1675
Diane Canino, Contact

Springfield

★5459★ **Bay State Centers for Displaced**
Homemakers
1113 Main St., 2nd Fl.
Springfield, MA 01103
Phone: (413)737-6841
Susan Manott, Contact

★5460★ **Springfield Technical Community**
College
Single Parent/Homemakers Program
1 Armory Sq.
Springfield, MA 01105
Phone: (413)781-7822
Shirley Willer, Contact

Tyngsborough

★5461★ **Greater Lovell Regional**
Vocational and Technical School
Single Parent/Displaced Homemaker
Program
Pawtucket Blvd.
Tyngsborough, MA 01879
Phone: (508)454-5411
Nelson Burns, Contact

Wellesley

★5462★ **Massachusetts Bay Community**
College
Single Parent/Homemakers Program
50 Oakland St.
Wellesley, MA 02181
Phone: (617)237-1100
Armand Potenza, Contact

West Barnstable

★5463★ **Cape Cod Community College**
Single Parent/Homemakers Program
West Barnstable, MA 02068
Phone: (508)362-2131
Dot Burrill, Contact

Worcester

★5464★ Worcester Community Action
County
**Bay State Centers for Displaced
Homemakers**
340 Main St.
Worcester, MA 01608
Phone: (508)754-1176
Priscilla Holmes, Contact

Michigan

Alpena

★5465★ Alpena Community College
Displaced Homemakers Program
666 Johnson St.
Alpena, MI 49707
Phone: (517)356-9021
Bonnie Erlaub, Contact

★5466★ Shelter, Inc.
Displaced Homemaker Program
PO Box 797
Alpena, MI 49707
Phone: (517)356-6569
Sharon J. Beaufore, Contact

Ann Arbor

★5467★ Soundings
PO Box 7372
Ann Arbor, MI 48104
Phone: (313)663-6689
Jill MacDonald, Contact

★5468★ Washtenaw Community College
Adult Resource Center
Single Parent/Homemaker Program
4800 E. Huron River Dr., Box D-1
Ann Arbor, MI 48106
Phone: (313)973-3397
David Beaumont, Contact

Battle Creek

★5469★ Community Action Agency of
South Central Michigan
Single Parent/Homemaker Program
PO Box 1026
Battle Creek, MI 49016
Phone: (616)965-0711
Ginger Hentz, Contact

★5470★ Kellogg Community College
Single Parent/Homemaker Program
450 North Ave.
Battle Creek, MI 49017-3397
Phone: (616)965-3931
Sherry Rial, Contact

Benton Harbor

★5471★ Lake Michigan College
Single Parent/Homemaker Program
2755 E. Napier Ave.
Benton Harbor, MI 49022-1899
Phone: (616)927-3571
Carol Head, Contact

Big Rapids

★5472★ Ferris State University
School of Technology
Single Parent/Homemaker Program
Big Rapids, MI 49307
Phone: (616)592-2890
Joyce Hawkins, Contact

Centreville

★5473★ Glen Oaks Community College
Single Parent/Homemaker Program
62249 Shimmel Rd.
Centreville, MI 49032-9719
Phone: (616)467-9945
Jill Peck, Contact

Dearborn

★5474★ Henry Ford Community College
Focus on Women Program
5101 Evergreen Rd.
Dearborn, MI 48128
Phone: (313)845-9629
Grace Stewart, Contact

Detroit

★5475★ Wayne County Community
College
Displaced Homemaker Program
801 W. Fort
Detroit, MI 48226
Phone: (313)496-2866
Patricia Crumpler, Contact

Dowagiac

★5476★ Southwestern Michigan College
Single Parent Projects
Cherry Grove Rd.
Dowagiac, MI 49047
Phone: (616)782-5113
Roger Campbell, Contact

Escanaba

★5477★ Bay De Noc Community College
Single Parent/Homemaker Program
2001 N. Lincoln Rd.
Escanaba, MI 49829-2511
Phone: (906)786-5802
Robert Yirka, Contact

Flint

★5478★ C.S. Mott Community College
Single Parent/Homemaker Program
1401 E. Court St.
Flint, MI 48502-2394
Phone: (313)762-0315
Angela Reeves, Contact

Grand Rapids

★5479★ Grand Rapids Junior College
Single Parent/Homemaker Project
143 Bostwick Ave., NE
Grand Rapids, MI 49503
Phone: (616)456-4407
Audrey Mayfield, Contact

★5480★ Women's Resource Center
Displaced Homemaker Program
252 State St. SE
Grand Rapids, M! 49503
Phone: (616)458-5443
Patricia Pope, Contact

Harrison

★5481★ Mid Michigan Community College
Single Parent/Homemaker Program
1375 S. Clare Ave.
Harrison, MI 48625
Phone: (517)386-7792
Barbara Richards, Contact

Highland Park

★5482★ Highland Park Community College
Center for Instructional Support
Glendale at Third
Highland Park, MI 48203
Phone: (313)252-0475
Jeanette Floyd, Contact

Holland

★5483★ Center for Women in Transition
Displaced Homemakers Program
304 Garden Ave.
Holland, MI 49423
Phone: (616)392-2829
Suzanne Nummerdor, Contact

Ironwood

★5484★ Gogebic Community College
Displaced Homemakers Program
Jackson and Greenbush Sts.
Ironwood, MI 49938
Phone: (906)932-4231
Cheryl Barth, Contact

Jackson

★5485★ Jackson Community College
**Single Parent/Displaced Homemaker
Program**
2111 Emmons Rd.
Jackson, MI 49201
Phone: (517)787-0800
Susan DeChant, Contact

Kalamazoo

★5486★ Kalamazoo Valley Community
College
Displaced Homemakers Program
6767 West "O" St.
Kalamazoo, MI 49009
Phone: (616)372-5340
Roger K. Miller, Contact

Lansing

★5487★ Lansing Community College
Women's Resource Center
419 N. Capitol Ave.
PO Box 40010
Lansing, MI 48901-7201
Phone: (517)483-1199
Andrea Belkin, Contact

★5488★ YWCA
Displaced Homemakers Program
PO Box 14163
Lansing, MI 48901
Phone: (517)485-7201
Meredee Vaughn, Contact

Livonia

★5489★ Schoolcraft College
Women's Resource Center
Displaced Homemakers Program
18600 Haggerty Rd.
Livonia, MI 48152-2696
Phone: (313)462-4400
Nancy Swanborg, Contact

Marquette

★5490★ Women's Center Marquette
Displaced Homemakers Program
1310 S. Front St.
Marquette, MI 49855
Phone: (906)225-1346
Sharon Denk, Contact

Monroe

★5491★ Monroe County Community College
Single Parent/Homemaker Program
1555 S. Raisinville Rd.
Monroe, MI 48161
Phone: (313)242-7300
Saundra Etue, Contact

Mt. Clemens

★5492★ Turning Point
PO Box 1123
Mt. Clemens, MI 48046
Phone: (313)463-4430
Karen Phillips, Contact

Muskegon

★5493★ Every Woman's Place, Inc.
1706 Peck St.
Muskegon, MI 49442
Phone: (616)726-4493
Addie Randall, Contact

★5494★ Muskegon Community College
Single Parent/Homemaker Program
221 S. Quarterline Rd.
Muskegon, MI 49442
Phone: (616)777-0309
Eunice Merwin, Contact

Petoskey

★5495★ Women's Resource Center
1515 Howard St., Rm. 52, NCMC
Petoskey, MI 49770
Phone: (616)347-0067
Mary Hyslop, Contact

Port Huron

★5496★ St. Clair County Community College
Student Learning Center
Single Parent/Homemaker Program
323 Erie St.
Port Huron, MI 48061-5015
Phone: (313)984-3881
Gerri Barber, Contact

Roscommon

★5497★ Kirtland Community College
Single Parent/Displaced Homemakers Project
10775 North St., Helen Rd.
Roscommon, MI 48653
Phone: (517)275-5121
Jenny Walker, Contact

Saginaw

★5498★ Averill Career Center
2101 Weiss
Saginaw, MI 48602
Phone: (517)797-4836
Julie A. Walker, Contact

Sault Ste. Marie

★5499★ Inter-Tribal Council of Michigan
Single Parent/Homemaker Program
405 E. Easterday Ave.
Sault Ste. Marie, MI 49783
Phone: (906)632-6896
Cindy Paymant, Contact

Scottville

★5500★ West Shore Community College
Single Parent/Homemaker Program
3000 N. Stiles Rd., Box 277
Scottville, MI 49454-0277
Phone: (616)845-6211
Victoria Oddo, Contact

Sidney

★5501★ Montcalm Community College
Single Parent/Homemaker Program
2800 College Dr.
Sidney, MI 48885
Phone: (517)328-2111
Carol Krumbach, Contact

Southfield

★5502★ Jewish Vocational Service
Displaced Homemaker Program
29699 Southfield Rd.
Southfield, MI 48076
Phone: (313)559-5000
Mary Ellen Stack, Contact

Traverse City

★5503★ Northwestern Michigan College
Single Parent Projects
1701 E. Front St.
Traverse City, MI 49684
Phone: (616)922-1052
Blaike Vance, Contact

University Center

★5504★ Delta College
Single Parent/Sex Equity Project
University Center, MI 48710
Phone: (517)686-9390
Diane Cooley, Contact

Warren

★5505★ Macomb Community College
Displaced Homemaker Program
14500 12 Mile Rd., Rm. G312
Warren, MI 48093
Phone: (313)445-7868
Kathleen McInerney, Contact

Minnesota

Austin

★5506★ Austin Area Vocational Technical Institute
Expanded Career Choices
1900-8th Ave. NW
Austin, MN 55912
Phone: (507)433-0600
Pat Capek, Contact

Brainerd

★5507★ Brainerd Community College
Meta Five
College Drive and SW 4th St.
Brainerd, MN 56401
Phone: (218)828-2538
Arlyne Forsberg, Contact

Duluth

★5508★ Project SOAR of Northeast Minnesota
205 W. 2nd St., Ste. 101
Duluth, MN 55802
Phone: (218)722-3126
Fran Hubert, Contact

Elbow Lake

★5509★ West Central Community Action
Pathfinders
10 E. Sixth St. Box 127
Theater Arcade Bldg.
Elbow Lake, MN 56267
Phone: (612)589-2556
Holly Witt, Contact

Mankato

★5510★ Life-Work Planning Center
Nichols Office Center
410 Jackson St.
Mankato, MN 56001
Phone: (507)345-1577
Sue Bruss, Contact

Marshall

★5511★ MAINSTAY, Inc.
1105 E. College Dr.
PO Box 816
Marshall, MN 56258
Phone: (507)537-1546
Kathleen Nightskye, Contact

Morris

★5512★ Pathfinders
215 Atlantic Ave.
Morris, MN 56267
Phone: (612)589-2556
Kate Ouverson, Contact

New York Mills

★5513★ Otter Tail-Wadena Community Action Inc.
New Directions
PO Box L
New York Mills, MN 56567
Phone: (218)385-2900
Pat Fredley, Contact

Rochester

★5514★ Rochester Community College
CHOICES of Southeast Minnesota
851 30th Ave., SE
Rochester, MN 55904-4999
Phone: (507)285-7210
Fax: (507)285-7496
Maureen Hart, Contact

St. Cloud

★5515★ Wings
Tri-County Action Program Inc.
700 Mall Germain
St. Cloud, MN 56301
Phone: (612)251-1612
Judy Stene, Contact

St. Louis Park

★5516★ Lenox Community Center
Women in Transition
6715 Minnetonka Blvd.
St. Louis Park, MN 55426
Phone: (612)925-9193
Sharon Hill, Contact

St. Paul

★5517★ Working Opportunities for Women
New Careers
2700 University Ave., Ste. 120
St. Paul, MN 55114
Phone: (612)647-9961
Helene Lockhart, Contact

Thief River Falls

★5518★ Displaced Homemakers Program,
Inc.
Crossroads
403 N. Labree
Thief River Falls, MN 56701
Phone: (218)681-8158
Sally Erickson, Contact

Virginia

★5519★ Arrowhead Economic Opportunity
Agency
Lives in Transition
702 3rd Ave. S
Virginia, MN 55792-2797
Phone: (218)749-2912
Kim Milne, Contact

Willmar

★5520★ Heartland Community Action
Agency
Stepping Stones
310 1st St., Box 1359
Willmar, MN 56201
Phone: (612)235-0850
Terry Van Derk, Contact

Mississippi

Batesville

★5521★ South Panola School District
Displaced Homemaker Program
PO Box 749
Batesville, MS 38606
Phone: (601)563-9361
Martha L. Johnson, Contact

Belzoni

★5522★ Humphreys Vocational Complex
Educational Intervention for the Single
Parent in a Rural Setting
PO Box 672
Belzoni, MS 39038
Phone: (601)247-2764
Bessie Smith, Contact

Canton

★5523★ Canton Vocational-Technical
Center
Displaced Homemakers Program
487 N. Union Extension
Canton, MS 39046
Phone: (601)859-3984
Bobbie Love, Contact

★5524★ Madison County Schools
Single Parent Displaced Homemaker
Program
Rte. 1, Box 47-A
Canton, MS 39046-4706
Phone: (601)355-9893
Marie Smith, Contact

Clarksdale

★5525★ Coahoma Community College
Displaced Homemakers Program
Rte. 1, Box 616
Clarksdale, MS 38614
Phone: (601)627-2571
Delores Robinson, Contact

Corinth

★5526★ Alcorn County Vocational Center
Single Parent Displaced Homemaker
Program
Rte. 5, Box 66
Corinth, MS 38834
Phone: (601)286-7727
Rodger Conn, Contact

Ellisville

★5527★ Jones County Junior College
Single Parent/Displaced Homemaker
Program
900 Court St.
Ellisville, MS 39437
Phone: (601)477-4115
Jackie Stennett, Contact

Fayette

★5528★ Jefferson County Vocational
Technical Center
Single Parent/Displaced Homemaker
Program
Rte. 2, Box 35-E
Fayette, MS 39069
Phone: (601)786-6125
Inez Coleman, Contact

Gautier

★5529★ Mississippi Gulf Coast Community
College, Jackson County Campus
Displaced Homemaker/Single Parent
PO Box 100
Gautier, MS 39553
Phone: (601)497-9602
Jean McCool, Contact

Goodman

★5530★ Holmes Community College
Single Parent/Displaced Homemakers
Program
PO Box 409
Goodman, MS 39079
Phone: (601)472-2312
Alva Cobb, Contact

Gulfport

★5531★ Mississippi Gulf Coast Community
College, Jefferson Davis Campus
Displaced Homemaker/Single Parent
Program
Courthouse Rd. Sta.
Gulfport, MS 39507
Phone: (601)896-3355
Edna Boone, Contact

Hollandale

★5532★ Simmons High School
Single Parent Displaced Homemaker
Program
PO Box 128
Hollandale, MS 38748
Phone: (601)827-2276
Doris Thompson, Contact

Holly Springs

★5533★ Holly Springs Vocational
Technical School
Displaced Homemaker Program
531 N. Walthall
Holly Springs, MS 38635
Phone: (601)252-4271
Rose Stone, Contact

★5534★ Marshall County Vocational
Center
Displaced Homemaker/Single Parent
Program
PO Box 38
Holly Springs, MS 38635
Phone: (601)838-2591
Barbara Longest, Contact

Jackson

★5535★ Hinds Community College,
Jackson Campus
Single Parent/Displaced Homemaker
Program
3925 Sunset Dr.
Jackson, MS 39213
Phone: (601)366-1405
Pat Sumrail, Contact

★5536★ Hinds Community College
Nursing Allied Health Center
Displaced Homemaker/Single Parent
1750 Chadwick Dr.
Jackson, MS 39204-3490
Phone: (601)372-6507
Janice Cornelius, Contact

Laurel

★5537★ R.H. Watkins Vocational Center
Single Parent/Displaced Homemaker
Program
110 W. 11th St.
Laurel, MS 39440
Phone: (601)649-4141
Mary Jo Blackledge, Contact

Mayhew

★5538★ East Mississippi Community
College, Golden Triangle Campus
Single Parent/Displaced Homemaker
Program
PO Box 100
Mayhew, MS 39753
Phone: (601)327-1112
Brenda Wilson, Contact

Meridian

★5539★ Meridian Community College
Single Parent/Displaced Homemaker
Program
910 Hwy. 19 N
Meridian, MS 39307
Phone: (601)484-8840
Betty T. Henry, Contact

Moorhead

★5540★ Mississippi Delta Community
College
Displaced Homemakers Program
PO Box 668
Moorhead, MS 38761
Phone: (601)246-5631
Linda L. Gray, Contact

Natchez

★5541★ Copiah-Lincoln Community
College—Natchez Campus
Single Parent/Homemaker Program
61 North, Rte. 4, Box 115
Natchez, MS 39120
Phone: (601)445-8299
Myra Washington, Contact

Oxford

★5542★ Northwest Mississippi Junior
College
Lafayette-Yalobusha Technical Center
Displaced Homemaker/Single Parent
Program
1310 Belk St.
Oxford, MS 38655
Phone: (601)236-2023
Jeanette Stone, Contact

Perkinston

★5543★ Mississippi Gulf Coast Community
College, Parkinston Campus
Single Parent Displaced Homemaker
Program
PO Box 67
Perkinston, MS 39753
Phone: (601)928-5211
Suzan Bounds, Contact

Poplarville

★5544★ Pearl River Community College
Single Parent/Displaced Homemaker
Program
Poplarville Campus
PO Box 5026
Poplarville, MS 39470
Phone: (601)795-6801
Beverly Tynes, Contact

Rolling Fork

★5545★ Sharkey-Issaquena School District
Single Parent/Displaced Homemaker
Program
600 S. Pkwy.
Rolling Fork, MS 39159
Phone: (601)873-2029
Lela Ware, Contact

Scooba

★5546★ East Mississippi Junior College
Single Parent/Displaced Homemakers
Program
Box 158
Scooba, MS 39358
Phone: (601)476-8442
Joyce Clair, Contact

Senatobia

★5547★ Northwest Mississippi Community
College
Displaced Homemakers Program
Drawer E
Senatobia, MS 38668
Phone: (601)562-5262
Gloria Lyons, Contact

Tupelo

★5548★ Itawamba Community College
Single Parent/Displaced Homemakers
Program
653 Eason Blvd.
Tupelo, MS 38801
Phone: (601)842-5621
Gloria H. McKinney, Contact

Utica

★5549★ Hinds Community College, Utica
Campus
Displaced Homemaker/Single Parent
Program
Utica, MS 39175
Phone: (601)354-2327
Christine Tanner-Watkins, Contact

Wesson

★5550★ Copiah-Lincoln Community
College
Single Parent/Homemaker Program
PO Box 649
Wesson, MS 39191
Phone: (601)643-5101
Brenda Westbrook, Contact

Woodville

★5551★ Wilkinson County Vocational
Center
Single Parent/Displaced Homemaker
Program
PO Box 1
Woodville, MS 39669
Phone: (601)888-4394
Sherryl Plummer, Contact

Missouri

Ballwin

★5552★ St. Louis Community College
Displaced Homemaker Program
15444 Clayton Rd., Ste. 222
Ballwin, MO 63011
Phone: (314)394-8600
Marlene Hanks, Contact

Columbia

★5553★ Columbia Area Career Center
New Directions/New Perspectives
4203 S. Providence Rd.
Columbia, MO 65203
Phone: (314)886-2629
Roseann Cochran, Contact

Flat River

★5554★ Mineral Area College
Career Connections
PO Box 1000
Flat River, MO 63601
Phone: (314)431-1951
Nancy Wegge, Contact

Hillsboro

★5555★ Jefferson College
Career Connection
1000 Viking Dr.
Hillsboro, MO 63050
Phone: (314)789-3951
Debbie Shores, Contact

Jefferson City

★5556★ Nichols Career Center
Displaced Homemaker Program
609 Union
Jefferson City, MO 65101
Phone: (314)659-3049
Sharon Bullard, Contact

Joplin

★5557★ Franklin Technical School
Region VI Western Consortium
New Perspectives
2020 Iowa Ave.
Joplin, MO 64804
Phone: (417)625-5265
Linda Koehler, Contact

Kansas City

★5558★ Maple Woods Community College
Displaced Homemakers Program
2601 N.E. Barry Rd.
Kansas City, MO 64156
Phone: (816)436-6500
Janet Weaver, Contact

★5559★ Penn Valley Community College
Displaced Homemakers Program
3201 SW Trafficway
Kansas City, MO 64111
Phone: (816)932-7602
Thada Sorenson, Contact

Kirksville

★5560★ Kirksville Area Vocational Center
New Perspectives
1103 S. Cottage Grove
Kirksville, MO 63501
Phone: (816)665-2865
Cheryl Lock, Contact

Lee's Summit

★5561★ Longview Community College
Displaced Homemakers Program
500 Longview Rd. SW
Lee's Summit, MO 64081
Phone: (816)763-7777
Connie Flick-Hraska, Contact

Linn

★5562★ Linn Technical College
Careers Unlimited
1212 E. Main
Linn, MO 65051
Phone: (314)897-3603
Roberta Buschjost, Contact

Maryville

★5563★ Northwest Technical School
New Perspectives
1515 S. Munn
Maryville, MO 64468
Phone: (816)562-2777
Shirley Twombly, Contact

Moberly

★5564★ Moberly Area Junior Community
  College
New Perspectives
College and Rollins Ave.
Moberly, MO 65270
Phone: (816)263-4110
Sharon Nelson, Contact

Neosho

★5565★ Crowder College
New Horizons
Displaced Homemakers Program
Neosho, MO 64850
Phone: (417)451-3584
Barbara O'Shea, Contact

O'Fallon

★5566★ St. Charles Community College
Displaced Homemakers Program
507 S. College Spring Rd.
O'Fallon, MO 63366
Phone: (314)281-2020
Liz Clemensen, Contact

Platte City

★5567★ Northland Career Center at Platte
  County Area Vocational-Technical School
New Perspective
Box 1700, Hwy. 92 and I-29
Platte City, MO 64079
Phone: (816)464-2484
Cheryl Parks, Contact

Poplar Bluff

★5568★ Three Rivers Community College
New Perspectives
Three Rivers Blvd.
Poplar Bluff, MO 63901
Phone: (314)686-4101
Doris Pearson, Contact

Rolla

★5569★ Rolla Area Vocational Technical
  School
New Perspectives
1304 E. 10th St.
Rolla, MO 65401
Phone: (314)364-0767
Laura Hendley, Contact

St. Louis

★5570★ Florissant Valley Community
  College
Careers for Homemakers
3400 Pershall Rd.
St. Louis, MO 63135
Phone: (314)595-4565
Karen Lyon, Contact

★5571★ Forest Park Community College
Careers for Homemakers
5600 Oakland Ave.
St. Louis, MO 63110
Phone: (314)644-9262
Sandra Knight, Contact

★5572★ Meramec Community College
Careers for Homemakers
11333 Big Bend Blvd.
St. Louis, MO 63122
Phone: (314)984-7568
Bernadette Dignan, Contact

Springfield

★5573★ Heart of the Ozarks Community
  Technical College
New Perspectives
PO Box 5958
Springfield, MO 65801
Phone: (417)863-0333
Shawn Arnold, Contact

Trenton

★5574★ North Central Missouri College
Displaced Homemakers Program
1301 Main St.
Trenton, MO 64683
Phone: (816)359-3948
Ginny Wikoff, Contact

Union

★5575★ East Central College
Career Connection
Box 529
Union, MO 63084
Phone: (314)583-5193
Dot Schowe, Contact

Montana

Billings

★5576★ YWCA Women's Center
Displaced Homemakers Program
909 Wyoming Ave.
Billings, MT 59101
Phone: (406)245-6879
Lynn Davis-Rightmuir, Contact

Bozeman

★5577★ Career Transitions
321 E. Main, Ste. 215
Bozeman, MT 59715
Phone: (406)587-1721
Beverly Barnhart, Contact

Butte

★5578★ Career Futures, Inc.
44 E. Park Plaza
Butte, MT 59701
Phone: (406)723-9101
Gayle Howell, Contact

Glendive

★5579★ Action for Eastern Montana
111 West Bell
Glendive, MT 59330
Phone: (406)365-3364
April Sutor, Contact

★5580★ Dawson Community College
New Directions
PO Box 421
Glendive, MT 59330
Phone: (406)365-3396
Irene Fabian, Contact

Great Falls

★5581★ YWCA
Work Place
104 2nd St. S, Ste. 200
Great Falls, MT 59405
Phone: (406)727-0966
Danna Duffy, Contact

Havre

★5582★ Displaced Homemaker Program
PO Box 1509
District 4 HRDC
Havre, MT 59501
Phone: (406)265-6743
Mark Tollefson, Contact

Helena

★5583★ Career Training Institute
Displaced Homemakers Program
17 1/2 S. Last Chance Gulch
Helena, MT 59601
Phone: (406)443-0800
Donna Porter, Contact

Kalispell

★5584★ Northwest Montana Human
  Resources
Serving Displaced Homemakers
1st & Main
PO Box 1058
Kalispell, MT 59903-1058
Phone: (406)752-6565
Mary Danford, Contact

Lewistown

★5585★ District VI HRDC—Human
  Resources Development Council
Displaced Homemakers Center
300 1st Ave. N
Centennial Plaza, Ste. 203
Lewistown, MT 59457
Phone: (406)538-7488
Pam Higgins, Contact

Miles City

★5586★ Miles Community College
Career Development Program
2715 Dickinson
Miles City, MT 59301
Phone: (406)232-3031
Sharon Kearnes, Contact

Missoula

★5587★ Word, Inc.
127 N. Higgins
Missoula, MT 59802
Phone: (406)543-3550
Laura Rose, Contact

★5588★ YWCA
New Horizons Program
1130 W. Broadway
Missoula, MT 59802
Phone: (406)543-6768
Paula Hoffman, Contact

Nebraska

Chadron

★5589★ Northwest Community Action
Single Parent Program
300 W. 2nd St.
Chadron, NE 69337
Phone: (308)432-3393
Becky Casellie, Contact

Grand Island

★5590★ YWCA—Transitions
Displaced Homemakers Program
234 E. 3rd
Grand Island, NE 68801
Phone: (308)384-8170
Ann Herbig, Contact

Hastings

★5591★ Central Community College
Explore Your World
Displaced Homemaker Program
PO Box 1024
Hastings, NE 68901
Phone: (402)461-2478
Cammie Farrell, Contact

Kearney

★5592★ Kearney State College
Vocational Education Center
Workers in Transition
West Campus
Kearney, NE 68849
Phone: (308)234-8465
Carolyn Daughtery, Contact

Lincoln

★5593★ Southeast Community College
Single Parent/Displaced Homemaker
 Program
8800 "O" St.
Lincoln, NE 68520
Phone: (402)471-3333
Karen Sachtleben, Contact

McCook

★5594★ McCook Community College
Bright Beginnings Program
1205 E. 3rd
McCook, NE 69001
Phone: (308)345-6303
Tyler Esch, Contact

Milford

★5595★ Southeast Community College
Single Parent Program
Milford Campus
RR 2, Box D
Milford, NE 68405
Phone: (402)761-2131
Joan Sterns, Contact

Norfolk

★5596★ Northeast Technical Community
College (NTCC)
New Beginning/Displaced Homemakers and
 Single Parent Programs
801 E. Benjamin Ave.
PO Box 469
Norfolk, NE 68702-0469
Phone: (402)644-0471
Susan Tucker, Contact

North Platte

★5597★ Mid-Plains Community College
Displaced Homemakers and Single Parents
 Program
Rte. 4, Box 1
North Platte, NE 69101
Phone: (308)532-8740
Wanda Vybralek, Contact

Omaha

★5598★ Metropolitan Community College
Expanded Services for Homemakers and
 Single Parents
PO Box 3777
Omaha, NE 68103
Phone: (402)449-8386
Angela M. McPherson, Contact

★5599★ YWCA
Displaced Homemakers Center
222 S. 29th St.
Omaha, NE 68131
Phone: (402)345-6555
Doralee Rogier, Contact

Scottsbluff

★5600★ Western Nebraska Community
College
Displaced Homemakers and Single Parent
 Program
1601 E. 27th St.
Scottsbluff, NE 69361
Phone: (308)635-6121
Joyce Jeary, Contact

Sidney

★5601★ Western Nebraska Community
College
Vocational Education for Homemakers
Sidney, NE 69162
Phone: (308)254-5450
Liz Johnson, Contact

Nevada

Carson City

★5602★ Western Nevada Community
College
Single Parent/Displaced Homemaker
 Program
2201 W. Nylane
Carson City, NV 89701
Phone: (702)887-3000
Josephine Gonzales, Contact

Elko

★5603★ North Nevada Community College
Single Parent/Displaced Homemaker
 Program
901 Elm St.
Elko, NV 89801
Phone: (702)738-8493
Patrick Collins, Contact

Las Vegas

★5604★ Women's Development Center
216 S. 7th St., Ste. 2
Las Vegas, NV 89101
Phone: (702)382-7311
Candace Ruisi-Murphy, Contact

North Las Vegas

★5605★ Community College of Southern
Nevada
Re-Entry Center
3200 E. Cheyenne Ave.
North Las Vegas, NV 89030
Phone: (702)643-6060
N.J. Pettit, Contact

Reno

★5606★ Truckee Meadows Community
College
Single Parent/Displaced Homemaker
 Program
7000 Dandini Blvd.
Reno, NV 89512
Phone: (702)673-7056
Michelle Glazier, Contact

New Hampshire

Berlin

★5607★ New Hampshire Technical
College—Berlin
Assisting People in Transition
Berlin, NH 03570
Phone: (603)752-1113
Christine Mulcahey, Contact

★5608★ New Hampshire Vocational
Technical College at Berlin
Making Informed Career Choices
2020 Riverside Dr.
Berlin, NH 03584
Phone: (603)752-1113
Christine Mulcahey, Contact

Claremont

★5609★ New Hampshire Technical
College—Claremont
Project Rise
One College Dr.
Claremont, NH 03743
Phone: (603)542-7744
Sandra Cole, Contact

Concord

★5610★ New Hampshire Technical
Institute
A.I.D.E. (Assistance, Information, Direction
 and Education)
Institute Dr.
PO Box 2039
Concord, NH 03302
Phone: (603)275-1864
Lorraine Good, Contact

★5611★ Project Second Start
17 Knight St.
Concord, NH 03301
Phone: (603)228-1341
Patricia Nelson, Contact

Dover

★5612★ Dover School District
Displaced Homemakers Program
SAU No. 11, Municipal Bldg.
Dover, NH 03820
Phone: (603)742-1030
Deborah Tasker, Contact

Keene

★5613★ Keene State College
Project EDGE (Educational Development
for Gainful Employment)
229 Main St.
Keene, NH 03431
Phone: (603)352-1909
Judith Perry, Contact

Laconia

★5614★ New Hampshire Technical
College—Laconia
Project Renew
Prescott Hill
Laconia, NH 03246
Phone: (603)524-3207
Maureen Houghton, Contact

Manchester

★5615★ New Hampshire Vocational-
Technical College
Project STRIDE
1066 Front St.
Manchester, NH 03102
Phone: (603)668-6706
Martha Long, Contact

Nashua

★5616★ Nashua Adult Learning Center
**Project PLACE (People Learning About
Careers and Entry)**
4 Lake St.
Nashua, NH 03060
Phone: (603)882-9080
Marianne O'Malley, Contact

★5617★ New Hampshire Vocational
Technical College
Project REDIRECTION
505 Amherst St.
Nashua, NH 03061
Phone: (603)882-6923
Mary Gillette, Contact

New Jersey

Asbury Park

★5618★ Brookdale Community College
Education Resource Center
500 Grand Ave.
Asbury Park, NJ 07712
Phone: (908)774-3363
Mickie McSwieney, Contact

Bayonne

★5619★ Bayonne Public Schools
**Project RITE (Reaching Independence
Through Employment)**
Avenue A & 29th St.
Bayonne, NJ 07002
Phone: (201)858-5925
Agnes Gillespie, Contact

Brant Beach

★5620★ St. Francis Community Center
Single Parent/Homemaker Program
4700 Long Beach Blvd
Brant Beach, NJ 08008
Phone: (609)494-1554
Karen Hauer, Contact

Bridgewater

★5621★ Somerset County Vocational-
Technical School
Twilights Single Parents Program
N. Bridge St. & Vogt Dr.
PO Box 6350
Bridgewater, NJ 08807
Phone: (201)526-8900
Karen Glass, Contact

Camden

★5622★ Hispanic Health and Mental
Health Association of Southern New
Jersey, Inc.
Hispanic Women's Resource Center
425 Broadway
Camden, NJ 08103
Phone: (609)541-6985
Laura Hernandez-Paine, Contact

★5623★ Hispanic Women's Resource
Center
2700 Westfield St.
Camden, NJ 08105
Phone: (609)365-7393
Yolanda Neely, Contact

★5624★ Urban Women's Center
501-B Cooper St., 2nd Fl.
Camden, NJ 08102
Phone: (609)963-8180
Rosemary Jackson, Contact

Cape May Court House

★5625★ Cape May Community Vocational
Schools
Single Parents/Homemakers Program
Crest Haven Rd.
Cape May Court House, NJ 08210
Phone: (609)465-3064
Daniel L. Money, Contact

Carney's Point

★5626★ Salem Community College
Women's Center
W.I.S.H. Program
460 Hollywood Ave.
Carney's Point, NJ 08069
Phone: (609)299-2100
Katherine Smalley, Contact

East Brunswick

★5627★ Middlesex Community Vocational
Technical High School
Urban Women's Job Center
112 Rues Ln.
PO Box 1070
East Brunswick, NJ 08816
Phone: (908)247-3832
Karen McCloud, Contact

Englewood

★5628★ Women's Rights Information
Center
Displaced Homemaker Program
Women's Center Bldg.
108 W. Palisades Ave.
Englewood, NJ 07631
Phone: (201)568-1166
Phoebe Seham, Contact

Flemington

★5629★ Hunterdon County Career and
Life Planning Center
Hunterdon County Adult Education Bldg.
Rte. 12
Flemington, NJ 08822
Phone: (201)788-1405
Shannon Brennan, Contact

Freehold

★5630★ Brookdale Community College
Displaced Homemakers Program
36 W. Main St., 3rd Fl.
Freehold, NJ 07728
Phone: (201)780-0020
Rita Toro, Contact

Glassboro

★5631★ Glassboro State College
Continuing Education
**South Jersey Outreach, Training and
Counseling Center**
Glassboro, NJ 08028
Phone: (609)863-5000
Dolores Harris, Contact

Hackensack

★5632★ Bergen County Technical School
Career Development Center for Women
280 Hackensack Ave.
Hackensack, NJ 07601
Phone: (201)343-6000
Rena Grasso, Contact

Jersey City

★5633★ Jersey City Public Schools
SUCCESS
346 Claremont Ave.
Jersey City, NJ 07305
Phone: (201)915-6344
Elizabeth Shurina, Contact

★5634★ Jersey City State College
**Women's Opportunity to Retain for
Careers (WORC)/Women's Center**
2039 Kennedy Blvd.
Jersey City, NJ 07305
Phone: (201)547-3198
Karen DeAngelis, Contact

Lincroft

★5635★ Brookdale Community College
Community Service Division
AVENUES
Newman Springs Rd.
Lincroft, NJ 07738
Phone: (201)842-1900
Norma Kline, Contact

Livingston

★5636★ National Council of Jewish
Women
Center for Women
2 E. Mount Pleasant Ave.
Livingston, NJ 07039
Phone: (201)994-4994
Phyllis Korsten, Contact

Long Branch

★5637★ Brookdale Community College
Long Branch Learning Center
Displaced Homemaker Program
213 Broadway
Long Branch, NJ 07740
Phone: (201)229-8440
Frances Williams, Contact

Marlboro

★5638★ Monmouth County Vocational
School District
Single Parent Homemaker Project
2 Bucks Lane
PO Box 191
Marlboro, NJ 07746
Phone: (201)431-7942
Sandra Carine, Contact

Montville

★5639★ Montville Township Board of
Education
Adult Resource Center
Displaced Homemaker Program
100 Horseneck Rd.
Montville, NJ 07045
Phone: (201)335-6516
Elaine Muller, Contact

Mt. Laurel

★5640★ YWCA
Women's Opportunity Center
5001 Centerdon Rd.
Mt. Laurel, NJ 08054
Phone: (609)234-6200
Mary Yakabosky, Contact

New Brunswick

★5641★ Middlesex County Vocational
School
Urban Women's Job Center
256 Easton Ave.
New Brunswick, NJ 08901
Phone: (201)247-9304
Bridget Hill, Contact

Newark

★5642★ Essex County College
WISE Women's Center
303 University Ave.
Newark, NJ 07102
Phone: (201)877-3399
Patricia Palmeri, Contact

★5643★ La Cosa de Don Pedro
Vocational Outreach for Single Parents
and Homemakers
23 Broadway
Newark, NJ 07104
Phone: (201)483-2703
Talia E. Bernal, Contact

Plainfield

★5644★ YWCA of Plainfield
Urban Women
232 E. Front St.
Plainfield, NJ 07060
Phone: (201)756-3500
April Miller-Hardge, Contact

Sewell

★5645★ Gloucester County College
Center for People in Transition
Tanyard Rd.
Sewell, NJ 08080
Phone: (609)468-1445
Meredith Flynn, Contact

Sparta

★5646★ Project Self Sufficiency
Displaced Homemaker Program
PO Box 322
Sparta, NJ 07871
Phone: (201)383-5129
Deborah Berrytoon, Contact

Trenton

★5647★ Mercer County Vocational-
Technical School
Single Parent Homemaker Program
1085 Old Trenton Rd.
Trenton, NJ 08690
Phone: (609)586-2121
Michelle Bovasso, Contact

★5648★ New Jersey State Federation of
Colored Women's Clubs, Inc.
Urban Women's Center
40 Fowler St.
Trenton, NJ 08618
Phone: (609)392-5959
Carol Clark, Contact

★5649★ Trenton Board of Education
New Century Program
108 N. Clinton Ave.
Trenton, NJ 08650
Phone: (609)989-2608
Lourdes Ochoa, Contact

★5650★ YWCA of Trenton
Displaced Homemakers Program
140 E. Hanover St.
Trenton, NJ 08608
Phone: (609)396-8291
Pamela Smith-Chambers, Contact

Union City

★5651★ Catholic Community Services
Hispanic Women's Resource Center
533 35th St.
Union City, NJ 07087
Phone: (201)866-3208
Marta San Martin, Contact

Upper Montclair

★5652★ Montclair State College
Life Skills Center—Economics Department
Normal Ave. and Valley Rd.
Upper Montclair, NJ 07043
Phone: (201)893-4172
Joanne Cote-Bonnano, Contact

★5653★ Montclair State College
Occupational Resource Center
Life Skills Center
Single Parents and Homemakers
Upper Montclair, NJ 07043
Phone: (201)893-5235
Marie Caruso, Contact

Washington

★5654★ Warren County Adult Education
Transitions Displaced Homemakers
Program
R.D. 1, Box 168A
Washington, NJ 07882
Phone: (201)689-0604
Elaine Molnar, Contact

West Keansburg

★5655★ Brookdale Community College
Bayshore Learning Center
Displaced Homemaker Program
311 Laurel Ave.
West Keansburg, NJ 07734
Phone: (201)787-0019
Robin Vogel, Contact

Woodstown

★5656★ Salem County Vocational-
Technical School
Vocational Opportunities for Single Parents
and Homemakers
RD 2, Box 350
Woodstown, NJ 08098
Phone: (609)769-0101
Hannah McDonough, Contact

New Mexico

Albuquerque

★5657★ New Mexico Association for
Community Education Development
Homemakers Information Project
PO Box 4368
Albuquerque, NM 87196
Phone: (505)247-2329
Tamra Ivy, Contact

★5658★ New Mexico Commission on the
Status of Women
Displaced Homemakers Programs
4001 Indian School Rd. NE Ste. 220
Albuquerque, NM 87110
Phone: (505)841-4662
Renie Garcia y Griego, Contact

★5659★ YWCA
Career Services Center
7201 Paseo del Norte NE
Albuquerque, NM 87113
Phone: (505)266-9922
Jennifer White, Contact

Carlsbad

★5660★ New Mexico State University
Single Parent/Displaced Homemaker
  Program
1500 University Dr.
Carlsbad, NM 88220
Phone: (505)885-8831
Bethe Orrell, Contact

Clovis

★5661★ Clovis Community College
Adult Re-Entry Program
417 Schepps Blvd.
Clovis, NM 88101
Phone: (505)769-4087
Barbara Martinez, Contact

Espanola

★5662★ Northern New Mexico Community
  College
Pathways Program
1002 N. Onate St.
Espanola, NM 87532
Phone: (505)753-7141
Jessica Brooks, Contact

Farmington

★5663★ San Juan College
Single Parent/Displaced Homemaker
  Program
4601 College Blvd.
Farmington, NM 87401
Phone: (505)599-0211
Linda Coy, Contact

Gallup

★5664★ University of New Mexico—Gallup
Sex Equity Program
200 College Rd.
Gallup, NM 87301
Phone: (505)863-7500
Kennard Van Brott, Contact

Los Alamos

★5665★ University of New Mexico—Los
  Alamos
Single Parent/Low Income Homemakers
  Internship Program
4000 University Dr.
Los Alamos, NM 87544-1999
Phone: (505)662-5919
Lucia Ortiz y Garcia, Contact

Roswell

★5666★ Eastern New Mexico University,
  Roswell Campus
Single Parent/Displaced Homemaker
  Project
PO Box 6000
Roswell, NM 88202
Phone: (505)624-7440
Kay Liakos, Contact

Santa Fe

★5667★ Santa Fe Community College
Women in Transition
PO Box 4187
Santa Fe, NM 87502
Phone: (505)471-8200
Francis Kean, Contact

Silver City

★5668★ Western New Mexico University
Pathways to Success
PO Box 680
Silver City, NM 88061
Phone: (505)538-6286
Patti Donaldson, Contact

Tucumcari

★5669★ Tucumcari Area Vocational
  School
New Transitions
PO Box 1143
Tucumcari, NM 88401
Phone: (505)461-4413
Bob Bowers, Contact

New York

Albany

★5670★ Albany Displaced Homemakers
  Center
315 Hamilton St.
Albany, NY 12210
Phone: (518)434-3103
Pat McLean, Contact

★5671★ Albany-Schoharie-Schenectady
  Board of Cooperative Education Service
Jobs for Success
1015 Watervliet-Shaker Rd.
Albany, NY 12205
Phone: (518)456-9255
Michele Wierzgac, Contact

Alfred

★5672★ State University of New York—
  Alfred
Board of Cooperative Educational Services
Displaced Homemaker Program
Victorian House
Alfred, NY 14802
Phone: (607)587-4541
Marie Babcock, Contact

Angola

★5673★ Erie No. 2 BOCES—Board of
  Cooperative Educational Services
Project New Ventures
8685 Erie Rd.
Angola, NY 14006
Phone: (716)549-4454
Nancy Sabatini, Contact

Bath

★5674★ Steuben-Allegheny Board of
  Cooperative Educational Service
Project Sphere
Rd. #1
Bath, NY 14810
Phone: (607)776-7631
Susan Edington, Contact

Bellport

★5675★ Board of Cooperative Educational
  Services
Displaced Homemaker Program
2 Suffolk
360 Martha Ave.
Bellport, NY 11713
Phone: (516)563-6079
Linda Murksamer, Contact

Binghamton

★5676★ Broome Community College
Displaced Homemaker Program
PO Box 1017
Binghamton, NY 13902
Phone: (607)771-5350
Barbara Kane-Lewis, Contact

★5677★ Broome-Tioga Board of
  Cooperative Educational Services
Displaced Homemaker Program
421 Upper Glenwood Rd.
Binghamton, NY 13905
Phone: (607)729-9301
Paula Calavito, Contact

Bronx

★5678★ Bronx Community College
Displaced Homemakers Program
Gould Hall, Rm 509
University Ave. and West 181 St.
Bronx, NY 10453
Phone: (212)220-6395
Olga Martinez, Contact

★5679★ Hostos Community College
Career Development Program
475 Grand Concourse
Bronx, NY 10451
Phone: (212)960-1136
Acte Maldonado, Contact

Brooklyn

★5680★ Aqudath Israel of America
Fresh Start
1756 Ocean Ave.
Brooklyn, NY 11230
Phone: (718)338-9200
Risa Silverman, Contact

★5681★ Bensonhurst Tenants Council
Displaced Homemakers Program
82 Quentin Rd.
Brooklyn, NY 11223
Phone: (718)372-2413
Barbara Ann DiGeronimo, Contact

★5682★ New York City Technical College
Access for Women
300 Jay St., Rm M407
Brooklyn, NY 11201
Phone: (718)260-5730
Linda Silverman, Contact

★5683★ WISH (Women in Self Help)
421 5th Ave.
Brooklyn, NY 11215
Phone: (718)768-9700
Carol Marsh, Contact

Buffalo

★5684★ Everywoman Opportunity Center
237 Main St., Ste. 330
Buffalo, NY 14203
Phone: (716)847-1120
Dorothy Carey-Mattar, Contact

Cazenovia

★5685★ Cazenovia College
Continuing Education Department
Vocational Education Program
Cazenovia, NY 13035
Phone: (315)655-9446
Virginia Felleman, Contact

Cobleskill

**★5686★ State University of New York—
Cobleskill**
Adult Center for Education
Cobleskill, NY 12043
Phone: (518)234-5528
Marsha Foster, Contact

Dix Hills

**★5687★ Board of Cooperative Educational
Services, 3 Suffolk**
L.A. Wilson Technical Center
Adult Career Center
17 Westminister Ave.
Dix Hills, NY 11746
Phone: (516)595-1402
Sandra Hoffman, Contact

Dunkirk

★5688★ Everywoman Opportunity Center
314 Central Ave.
Dunkirk, NY 14048
Phone: (716)366-7020
Margaret McDonnell, Contact

Elmira

★5689★ Cope House
161 DeWitt Ave.
Elmira, NY 14901
Phone: (607)737-7431
Lorraine Welliver, Contact

★5690★ YWCA
Suddenly Single
211 Lake St.
Elmira, NY 14901
Phone: (607)733-5575
Debbie Farnbaugh, Contact

Fairport

**★5691★ Monroe Board of Cooperative
Educational Services No. 1**
Bridge to Employment
41 O'Connor Rd.
Fairport, NY 14450
Phone: (716)377-4660
Joyce Ebmeyer, Contact

Garden City

★5692★ Nassau Community College
AIMS Program
Bldg. H. Rm 105
Garden City, NY 11530
Phone: (516)222-7436
Helen Kaftain, Contact

Goshen

**★5693★ Orange-Ulster BOCES—Board of
Cooperative Educational Services**
The Adult Center
Gibson Rd.
Goshen, NY 10924
Phone: (914)294-5431
Doris Buck, Contact

Hauppauge

**★5694★ Federation Employment and
Guidance Service**
Displaced Homemakers Programs
1455 Veterans Way
Hauppauge, NY 11788
Phone: (516)234-0300
Renee Lazer, Contact

Hempstead

**★5695★ Multi-Service Center/Nassau City
E.O.C. Displaced Homemakers**
106 Main Street
Hempstead, NY 11550
Phone: (516)481-2103
Terri Banks, Contact

**★5696★ Nassau County Office of
Women's Services**
250 Fulton Ave.
Hempstead, NY 11550
Phone: (516)564-8250
Geraldine Linton, Contact

Ithaca

★5697★ Displaced Homemakers Center
301 S. Geneva St.
Ithaca, NY 14850
Phone: (607)272-1520
Sandra Lyons, Contact

Jamaica

**★5698★ Queen's Women's Network
Displaced Homemaker Program**
161-10 Jamaica Ave., Ste. 416
Jamaica, NY 11432
Phone: (718)657-6200
Irene Hammel, Contact

Johnstown

**★5699★ Fulton-Montgomery Community
College**
First Place/Lift
Rte. 67
Johnstown, NY 12095
Phone: (518)762-4651
Cheryl Arcolano, Contact

Loch Sheldrake

**★5700★ Sullivan County Community
College**
Single Parent/Homemakers Program
Loch Sheldrake, NY 12759
Phone: (914)434-5750
Onalie Pettit, Contact

Long Island

★5701★ LaGuardia Community College
Project Enable
29-10 Thomson Ave.
Long Island, NY 11101
Phone: (718)482-5322
Laurel Scott, Contact

Mahopac

**★5702★ Putman/Northern Westchester
Women's Resource Center**
2 Mahopac Plaza
Mahopac, NY 10541
Phone: (914)628-9284
Joanne DePaola, Contact

Middletown

**★5703★ Orange County Community
College**
Women in Technology
115 South St.
Middletown, NY 10940
Phone: (914)344-6222
Lynn Sheven, Contact

New York

**★5704★ New York Women's Center for
Education and Career Advancement**
198 Broadway, Ste. 200
New York, NY 10038
Phone: (212)964-8934
Carmen Applewhaite, Contact

**★5705★ YWCA of New York City
Reentry Employment Program**
610 Lexington Ave.
New York, NY 10022
Phone: (212)735-9727
Claire Harnan, Contact

Niagara Falls

**★5706★ Niagara County Community
College**
Project New Ventures
1001 11th St.
Niagara Falls, NY 14301
Phone: (716)731-3271
Carla Volpe, Contact

**★5707★ Niagara Falls Center
Everywoman Opportunity Center**
473 3rd St., Ste. 207
Niagara Falls, NY 14301
Phone: (716)282-8472
Ann Basile, Contact

Nyack

**★5708★ Rockland County Guidance
Center**
Displaced Homemaker Program
83 Main St.
Nyack, NY 10960
Phone: (914)358-9390
Margaret Anderson, Contact

Olean

**★5709★ BOCES—Board of Cooperative
Educational Services**
Career Services
Winfall Rd.
Olean, NY 14760
Phone: (212)372-8293
Patricia Finocchio, Contact

★5710★ Everywoman Opportunity Center
Executive South Bldg. Ste. 210
407 N. Union St.
Olean, NY 14760
Phone: (716)373-4013
Mary Snodgrass, Contact

Orchard Park

**★5711★ Adult Education Department
Erie—Cattaraugus**
Single Parent/Homemakers Program
Board of Coop., Ed Services
3340 Baker Rd.
Orchard Park, NY 14127
Phone: (716)549-4454
Joanne Hess, Contact

Port Ewen

**★5712★ Ulster BOCES—Board of
Cooperative Educational Services**
Rt. 9W
PO Box 601
Port Ewen, NY 12466
Phone: (914)331-0902
Fereshte Nikfetrat, Contact

Poughkeepsie

★5713★ Dutchess Community College
Day II
Pendell jRd.
Poughkeepsie, NY 12601
Phone: (914)471-4500
Wendy Walker, Contact

★5714★ Program Transitions
100 Cannon St.
Poughkeepsie, NY 12601
Phone: (914)471-6665
Marianna E. Martin, Contact

Rochester

★5715★ GROW
Displaced Homemakers Center
79 N. Clinton Ave.
Rochester, NY 14604
Phone: (716)454-3224
Peg Steffan, Contact

★5716★ Monroe Community College
Automotive Technology for Women
1000 E. Henrietta Rd.
Rochester, NY 14623
Phone: (716)292-2000
Jessica Levy, Contact

Sanborn

★5717★ Niagara County Community
College
Women in Technology Program
3111 Saunders Settlement Rd.
Sanborn, NY 14132
Phone: (716)731-3271
Virginia Taylor, Contact

★5718★ Orleans-Niagara, BOCES—Board
of Cooperative Educational Services
Continuing Education Division
Bridge to Employment
3181 Saunders Settlement Rd.
Sanborn, NY 14132
Phone: (716)731-4176
Gretchen Skurski, Contact

Scarsdale

★5719★ Legal Awareness for Women
Box 35H
Scarsdale, NY 10583
Phone: (914)472-2371
Diane White, Contract

Schenectady

★5720★ Schenectady Community Action
Program
First Place Displaced Homemakers
Program
148 Clinton St.
Schenectady, NY 12305
Phone: (518)374-9181
Barbara Rivenburgh, Contact

Smithtown

★5721★ Suffolk County Department of
Labor
Resource Center for Displaced
Homemakers
PO Box 1319
Smithtown, NY 11787
Phone: (516)661-8600
Joan Fischer, Contact

Syracuse

★5722★ Onondaga Community College
Displaced Homemakers Program
Onondaga Hill
Syracuse, NY 13215
Phone: (315)469-7741
Elaine Taggert, Contact

★5723★ Regional Learning Service
Displaced Homemaker Program
Program #4
405 Oak Street
Syracuse, NY 13202
Phone: (315)425-5290
Peggy Hanousek, Contact

Tonawanda

★5724★ Everywoman Opportunity Center
Green Acres Bldg.
205 Yorkshire Rd.- Rm. 108
Tonawanda, NY 14150
Phone: (716)837-2260
Betty Belschner, Contact

Uniondale

★5725★ Nassau Community College
Adult Students Multi-Service Center (AIMS)
1137 Braxton St.
Uniondale, NY 11553
Phone: (516)483-4683
Pamela McLean-Wainwright, Contact

Utica

★5726★ Access Center
Project New Ventures
508 2nd Center
Utica, NY 13501
Phone: (315)732-8807
Elizabeth Gillis, Contact

★5727★ Utica Displaced Homemaker
Program, AFL/CIO
State Office Bldg. Rm 209
207 Genesee St.
Utica, NY 13501
Phone: (315)736-8271
Laura Bradigan, Contact

Valhalla

★5728★ Westchester Community College
Project Transition-AAB 302
75 Grasslands Rd.
Valhalla, NY 10595
Phone: (914)285-6825
Marilyn Wald, Contact

White Plains

★5729★ Westchester Office for Women
Displaced Homemaker Program
112 E. Post Rd., Rm 216
White Plains, NY 10601
Phone: (914)285-5972
Leslie Marioka, Contact

Yorktown Heights

★5730★ Putnam North Westchester Board
of Cooperative Education Services
Project Success
Pine Ridge Rd.
Yorktown Heights, NY 10598
Phone: (914)245-2700
Andria Cassidy, Contact

North Carolina

Asheboro

★5731★ Randolph Community College
Displaced Homemakers Program
Asheboro, NC 27204-1009
Phone: (919)629-1471
Mary Morgan, Contact

Chapel Hill

★5732★ Orange County Woman's Center,
Inc.
210 Henderson St.
PO Box 1057
Chapel Hill, NC 27514
Phone: (919)968-4610
Catherine Dickman, Contact

Charlotte

★5733★ Central Piedmont Community
College
Wider Opportunities for Women
PO Box 35009
Charlotte, NC 28235
Phone: (704)342-6633
Sara Graham, Contact

★5734★ WomanReach, Inc.
The Gallery, Ste. 605
Midtown Square
Charlotte, NC 28204
Phone: (704)334-3614
Lynn Crenshaw, Contact

Durham

★5735★ Durham Technical Community
College
Single Parent/Homemaker Program
1637 Lawson St.
Durham, NC 27703
Phone: (919)598-9206
Maggie McLaughlin, Contact

Fayetteville

★5736★ Fayetteville Technical Institute
Single Parent/Homemaker Program
PO Box 35236
Fayetteville, NC 28303
Phone: (919)678-8413
Helen Winstead, Contact

★5737★ Women's Center of Fayetteville
PO Box 2384
Fayetteville, NC 28302
Phone: (919)323-3377
Slyvia G. Ray, Contact

Greensboro

★5738★ Displaced Homemaker Program
1400 Battleground Ave., Ste. 202
Greensboro, NC 27408
Phone: (919)334-5094
Katherine Harrelson, Contact

★5739★ YWCA
Displaced Homemaker Program
1 YWCA Place
Greensboro, NC 27402
Phone: (919)273-3461
Jackie Sharp, Contact

Hickory

★5740★ Women's Resource Center
328 N. Center St.
Hickory, NC 28601
Phone: (704)322-6333
Marian C. Belk, Contact

Jacksonville

★5741★ Coastal Carolina Community
College
Displaced Homemaker Program
444 Western Blvd.
Jacksonville, NC 28546
Phone: (919)445-1221
Laura Payne, Contact

Jamestown

★5742★ Guilford Technology Community
College
Displaced Homemaker Program
PO Box 309
Jamestown, NC 27282
Phone: (919)334-4822
Katie Strickland, Contact

Pittsboro

★5743★ Joint Orange-Chatham Community
Action Agency, Inc.
Displaced Homemaker Program
PO Box 27
Pittsboro, NC 27312
Phone: (919)542-4781
Faye S. Hall, Contact

Raleigh

★5744★ Women's Center
128 E. Hargett St., #10
Raleigh, NC 27601
Phone: (919)829-3711
Anne Britt, Contact

Wentworth

★5745★ Rockingham Community College
Displaced Homemaker Program
Human Resources Development
PO Box 38
Wentworth, NC 27375
Phone: (919)342-4261
Carolyn Loftins, Contact

Winston-Salem

★5746★ Displaced Homemaker Program
2100 Silas Creek Parkway
Winston-Salem, NC 27103-1009
Phone: (919)723-0371
Gloria Sexton, Contact

★5747★ Planned Parenthood of the Triad
Displaced Homemaker Program
939 Burke St.
Winston-Salem, NC 27101
Phone: (919)761-1058
Ellen B. Olson, Contact

North Dakota

Belcourt

★5748★ Turtle Mount Community College
Single Parent/Displaced Homemaker
PO Box 340
Belcourt, ND 58316-0340
Phone: (701)477-5605
June Parisien, Contact

Bismarck

★5749★ Single Parent/Homemakers
Program
South Central High School
222 W. Bowen
Bismarck, ND 58504
Phone: (701)221-3790
Marilyn Brucker, Contact

★5750★ United Tribes Technical College
Displaced Homemakers Program
3315 University Dr.
Bismarck, ND 58504-7596
Phone: (701)255-3285
Vernes Johnson, Contact

Bottineau

★5751★ Bottineau Public School
Single Parent/Homemakers Program
301 Branden St.
Bottineau, ND 58318
Phone: (701)228-2266
Del Rothman, Contact

Devils Lake

★5752★ Lake Area Vocational Technical
School
Single Parent/Homemakers Program
Devils Lake, ND 58301
Phone: (701)662-7596
Pat Kurtz, Contact

★5753★ University of North Dakota
Devils Lake Regional Area Learning
Center
Displaced Homemakers Program
North College Dr.
Devils Lake, ND 58301
Phone: (701)662-8683
Marlene Krack, Contact

Dickinson

★5754★ Dickinson Adult Learning Center
Single Parent/Homemaker Program
Box 1057
Dickinson, ND 58602
Phone: (701)225-1550
Lee Aljets-Lemen, Contact

Fargo

★5755★ Displaced Homemakers Program
1104 2 Ave., S
Fargo, ND 58103
Phone: (701)241-4907
Dianne Hill, Contract

Grafton

★5756★ North Valley Vocational Center
Single Parent/Homemakers Program
Rte., 1 Box 4
Grafton, ND 58237
Phone: (701)352-3705
Elizabeth Daby, Contact

Grand Forks

★5757★ Adult Learning Center
Displaced Homemakers Program
911 Cottonwood
Grand Forks, ND 58201
Phone: (701)746-2425
Crystal Roy, Contact

Jamestown

★5758★ Jamestown Valley Vocational
Center
Jamestown Region Area Learning Center
Displaced Homemakers Program
910 12th Ave., NE
Jamestown, ND 58401
Phone: (701)252-8841
Elizabeth Hanson, Contact

Minot

★5759★ Minot Regional Area Learning
Center
Displaced Homemakers Program
1609 4th Ave., NW
Minot, ND 58701
Phone: (701)857-4498
Vicky Campbell, Contact

New Town

★5760★ Fort Berthold Community College
Single Parent/Homemaker Program
PO Box 490
New Town, ND 58763
Phone: (701)627-4738
Marcia Azure, Contact

Ohio

Akron

★5761★ Akron City Schools
Displaced Homemakers Program
147 Park St.
Akron, OH 44307
Phone: (216)253-5142
Jane Nichols, Contact

Alliance

★5762★ Alliance City Schools
Displaced Homemaker Program
200 Glamorgan St.
Alliance, OH 44601
Phone: (216)821-2100
Kathy Smith, Contact

Canton

★5763★ Pyramid Career Services
Displaced Homemaker Program
2400 Cleveland Ave. N
Canton, OH 44709
Phone: (216)453-3767
Sherry Cini-Putnam, Contact

Carroll

★5764★ **Fairfield Career Center**
Discover
4000 Columbus-Lancaster Rd.
Carroll, OH 43112
Phone: (614)837-9443
Marcy J. Happeney, Contact

Celina

★5765★ **Tri Star Career Compact**
Single Parent/Homemaker Program
1011 N. Brandon Ave.
Celina, OH 45822
Phone: (419)586-8833
Suzanne Taylor, Contact

Chesapeake

★5766★ **Lawrence County Joint Vocational**
   School
New Horizons
Rte. 2, Box 262
Chesapeake, OH 45619
Phone: (614)867-6641
Kim Day, Contact

Chillicothe

★5767★ **Pickaway-Ross Joint Vocational**
   School
Starting A New Life
895 Crouse Chapel Rd.
Chillicothe, OH 45601
Phone: (614)642-2550
Sherrie Tener, Contact

Cincinnati

★5768★ **Cincinnati Public Schools**
Women Taking Action
425 Ezzard Charles Dr.
Cincinnati, OH 45203
Phone: (513)381-6521
Alexa Noel, Contact

★5769★ **Great Oak Joint Vocational**
   School District
YWCA —Women's Opportunities Center
Lifestrides
898 Walnut St.
Cincinnati, OH 45202
Phone: (513)241-7090
Diane Marowitz, Contact

★5770★ **Great Oaks Junior Vocational**
   School
A.W.A.K.E. Second Careers
3254 E. Kemper Rd.
Cincinnati, OH 45241
Phone: (513)771-8925
Donna Willard, Contact

Circleville

★5771★ **Pickaway County Community**
   Action
Displaced Homemakers Program
Recycling Bldg.
1080 Rte. 22 W
PO Box 67
Circleville, OH 43113
Phone: (614)477-1655
Esta Wells, Contact

Clayton

★5772★ **Montgomery County Joint**
   Vocational School
Changes and Choices in Transition
6800 Hoke Rd.
Clayton, OH 45315
Phone: (513)837-7781
Sandra Raines, Contact

Cleveland

★5773★ **Cuyahoga Community College,**
   Metropolitan Campus
Displaced Homemaker Program
2900 Community College Ave.
Cleveland, OH 44115
Phone: (216)987-5091
Steve Chylinski, Contact

Columbus

★5774★ **Center for New Directions**
51 Jefferson Ave.
Columbus, OH 43215-3859
Phone: (614)461-6117
Sharon Sachs, Contact

Greensburg

★5775★ **Portage Lakes Career Center**
Displaced Homemaker Program, New
Visions
4401 Shriver Rd.
PO Box 248
Greensburg, OH 44232
Phone: (216)896-3757
Linda Glover, Contact

Groveport

★5776★ **Eastland Career Center**
Discover
4464 S. Hamilton Rd.
Groveport, OH 43125
Phone: (614)836-3903
Mary Whitehead, Contact

Highland Hills Village

★5777★ **Cuyahoga Community College**
Displaced Homemaker Program
4250 Richmond Rd.
Highland Hills Village, OH 44122
Phone: (216)987-2270
Nita Leff, Contact

Lima

★5778★ **Apollo Career Center**
Displaced Homemaker Program
3325 Shawnee Rd.
Lima, OH 45806
Phone: (419)999-3015
Connie Plikerd, Contact

Lisbon

★5779★ **Columbian County Vocational**
   School District
Career Development for Displaced
Homemakers
9364 State Rte. 45
Lisbon, OH 44432
Phone: (216)424-9561
Karen J. Arbogast, Contact

Lorain

★5780★ **Charleston Career Center**
Displaced Homemakers Program
2350 Pole Ave.
Lorain, OH 44052
Phone: (216)233-2234
Christine Bucholz, Contact

Mansfield

★5781★ **Madison Local Schools**
New Directions
600 Esley Ln.
Mansfield, OH 44905
Phone: (419)589-6363
Elizabeth Huggins, Contact

Marion

★5782★ **Tri Rivers Career Center**
Adult Education/Changing Roles
Career and Job Readiness Program
2222 Marion-Mt. Gilead Rd.
Marion, OH 43302
Phone: (614)389-6347
Judy Williams, Contact

Medina

★5783★ **Medina County Vocational Center**
Women's Connection
1101 W. Liberty St.
Medina, OH 44256
Phone: (216)725-1191
Barbara Holley, Contact

Mentor

★5784★ **Lakeland Community College**
Displaced Homemaker Program
Mentor, OH 44060
Phone: (216)953-7322
Meredith Ring, Contact

Milan

★5785★ **Ehove Career Center**
New Life Options
316 W. Mason Rd.
Milan, OH 44846
Phone: (419)499-4663
Sandra Jankowski, Contact

Nelsonville

★5786★ **Tri-County Joint Vocational**
   School
On My Own
Rt. 1, State Rte. 691
Nelsonville, OH 45764
Phone: (614)753-3511
Sharon Frame, Contact

New Philadelphia

★5787★ **Buckeye Joint Vocational School**
Displaced Homemaker Program
545 University Dr. NE
New Philadelphia, OH 44663
Phone: (216)339-2288
Helen Hoover, Contact

Newark

★5788★ **Licking County Employment Training Office**
Displaced Homemaker Program
743 E. Main St.
Newark, OH 43055
Phone: (614)366-3351
Chris Franklin-Panek, Contact

Piqua

★5789★ **Upper Valley Joint Vocational School**
Discovering Hope
8811 Career Dr.
Piqua, OH 45356
Phone: (513)778-0674
Rose Hemm, Contact

Rio Grande

★5790★ **Gallia-Jackson-Vinton Joint Vocational School District**
S.U.C.C.E.S.S.
Buckeye Hills Rd.
PO Box 157
Rio Grande, OH 45674
Phone: (614)245-5334
Betty Adkins, Contact

St. Clairsville

★5791★ **Belmont Career Center Vocational School District**
Learning to Earn
110 Fox/Shannon Pl.
St. Clairsville, OH 43950
Phone: (614)695-5330
Ginny E. Moore, Contact

Sandusky

★5792★ **Sandusky City Schools**
New Horizons
407 Decatur St.
Sandusky, OH 44870
Phone: (419)621-2717
Lee Anna Caswell, Contact

Sardinia

★5793★ **Southern State Community College**
Hillsboro City Schools
Your Place
12681 U.S. Rte. 62
Sardinia, OH 45171
Phone: (513)695-0700
Karen Sheeley, Contact

Springfield

★5794★ **Springfield/Clark Joint Vocational School**
Displaced Homemakers Program
1901 Selma Rd.
Springfield, OH 45505
Phone: (513)325-5461
Peggy Kelly, Contact

Toledo

★5795★ **Jefferson Center for Change No. 235**
A New Beginning
1300 Jefferson Ave., Rm. 213
Toledo, OH 43624
Phone: (419)255-7196
Kay Porter, Contact

★5796★ **University of Toledo**
Catharine S. Eberly Center for Women
Project Succeed
2801 W. Bancroft St.
Toledo, OH 43606
Phone: (419)537-2058
Jan Floate-Kott, Contact

★5797★ **YWCA**
55+ Pre-Employment Program
1018 Jefferson Ave.
Toledo, OH 43624
Phone: (419)241-3235
Pamela Broyles, Contact

Van Wert

★5798★ **Vantage Vocational School**
New Beginnings
818 N. Franklin St.
Van Wert, OH 45891
Phone: (419)238-5411
Marilyn Mead, Contact

Warren

★5799★ **Trumbull County Joint Vocational School**
Focus On the Future
528 Educational Hwy.
Warren, OH 44483
Phone: (216)847-0503
Terry Shifflet, Contact

Wilmington

★5800★ **Southern State Community College**
Your Place
2698 Old State Rte. 73
Wilmington, OH 45177
Phone: (513)382-6645
Nancy Wolford, Contact

Xenia

★5801★ **Greene County Vocational School District**
Greene County Career Center
Focus
2960 W. Enon Rd.
Xenia, OH 45385-9545
Phone: (513)372-6941
Carol Shaw, Contact

Youngstown

★5802★ **Youngstown City Schools**
Choffin Career Center
STEP-UP
200 E. Wood St.
Youngstown, OH 44503
Phone: (216)744-8782
Vicki Book, Contact

Oklahoma

Altus

★5803★ **Southwest Oklahoma Skills Center**
Displaced Homemakers Program
1121 N. Spurgeon
Altus, OK 73521
Phone: (405)477-2439
Susan Brown, Contact

Ardmore

★5804★ **Southern Oklahoma Area Vocational Technical School**
Displaced Homemakers Program
Rte 1, Box 14M
Ardmore, OK 73401
Phone: (405)223-2070
Dona Farr, Contact

Bartlesville

★5805★ **Tri-County Area Vocational Technical School**
Displaced Homemakers Program
6107 Nowata Rd.
Bartlesville, OK 74006
Phone: (918)333-2422
Mary Miller, Contact

Burns Flat

★5806★ **Western Vocational Technical School**
Displaced Homemaker Program
621 Kliewer Dr.
PO Box 1469
Burns Flat, OK 73624
Phone: (405)562-3181
May Estraca, Contact

Chickasha

★5807★ **Canadian Valley Area Vocational-Technical School**
Single Parent/Homemaker Program
1401 Michigan Ave.
Chickasha, OK 73018
Phone: (405)224-7220
Margie Albin, Contact

Choctaw

★5808★ **Eastern Oklahoma County Area Vocational Technical Center**
New Directions
4601 N. Chowtaw Rd.
Choctaw, OK 73020
Phone: (405)390-9591
Linda Christian, Contact

Duncan

★5809★ **Red River Area Vocational-Technical School**
Single Parent Homemaker Program
3300 W. Boise D'Arc
PO Box 1807
Duncan, OK 73534
Phone: (405)255-2903
Monica McCarley, Contact

Enid

★5810★ **O.T. Autry Area Vocational Technical School**
Displaced Homemaker Program
1201 W. Willow
Enid, OK 73703
Phone: (405)242-2750
Bea Paul, Contact

★5811★ **YWCA**
Women in Transition
525 S. Quincy
Enid, OK 73701
Phone: (405)234-7581
Judith Kirk, Contact

Ft. Cobb

★5812★ Caddo-Kiowa Area Vocational-Technical Center
Displaced Homemaker Programs
PO Box 190
Ft. Cobb, OK 73038
Phone: (405)643-2387
Pam McEachern, Contact

Idabel

★5813★ Kiamichi Area Vocational Technical School
Displaced Homemakers Program
Rte. 3, Box 177
Idabel, OK 74745
Phone: (405)286-7555
Pat Baggs, Contact

Lawton

★5814★ Great Plains Area Vocational Technical School
Single Parent/Displaced Homemaker Program
4500 West Lee Blvd.
Lawton, OK 73501
Phone: (405)355-6371
Beverly Horse, Contact

McAlester

★5815★ Kiamichi Area Vocational-Technical School
Displaced Homemaker Program
PO Box 308
McAlester, OK 73501
Phone: (918)426-0940
Peggy Lawrence, Contact

Muskogee

★5816★ Indian Capital Area Vocational Technical School
Displaced Homemaker Program
Rte. 6, Box 206
Muskogee, OK 74401
Phone: (918)687-6383
Jan Stevenson, Contact

Norman

★5817★ Moore-Norman Area Vocational-Technical School
Options
4701 12th Ave. NW
Norman, OK 73069
Phone: (405)364-5763
Ann Baccus, Contact

Oklahoma City

★5818★ Francis Tuttle Vocational Technical Center
Single Parent/Displaced Homemaker Program
12777 N. Rockwell
Oklahoma City, OK 73142
Phone: (405)722-7799
Jennifer Haile-Egbert, Contact

★5819★ Metro Tech
Displaced Homemaker Program
1900 Springlake Dr.
Oklahoma City, OK 73111
Phone: (405)424-8324
Carmaleta Walker, Contact

Ponca City

★5820★ Pioneer Area Vocational Technical School
Displaced Homemakers Programs
2101 N. Ash
Ponca City, OK 74601
Phone: (405)762-8336
Dee Brown, Contact

Poteau

★5821★ Kiamichi Area Vocational Technical School
Single Parent/Homemaker Center
PO Box 825
Poteau, OK 74953
Phone: (918)647-4525
Pat Kidd, Contact

Pryor

★5822★ Northeast Oklahoma Area Vocational Technical School
Single Parent/Displaced Homemaker Program
PO Box 825
Pryor, OK 74362
Phone: (918)825-5555
Sandra McElroy, Contact

Sapulpa

★5823★ Central Oklahoma Vocational Technical School
Displaced Homemaker/Single Parent Program
1720 S. Main
Sapulpa, OK 74066
Phone: (918)352-2551
Linda Brewster, Contact

Shawnee

★5824★ Gordon Cooper Vocational Technical School
Displaced Homemaker/Single Parent Program
PO Drawer 848
Shawnee, OK 74801
Phone: (405)273-7493
Robin Hall, Contact

Stillwater

★5825★ Indian Meridian Area Vocational Technical School
Displaced Homemaker Program
1312 S. Sangre Rd.
Stillwater, OK 74074
Phone: (405)377-3333
Nancy Hughlett, Contact

Tahlequah

★5826★ Bill Willis Skills Center
Displaced Homemaker Program
1400 S. Hensley Dr.
Tahlequah, OK 74464
Phone: (918)456-2594
Evelyn Epperson, Contact

Tulsa

★5827★ Tulsa County Area Vocational Technical School
Displaced Homemaker Program
3420 S. Memorial
Tulsa, OK 74145-1390
Phone: (918)627-7200
Karen Griffith, Contact

★5828★ YWCA
Women's Resource Center
823 S. Gary Place
Tulsa, OK 74104
Phone: (918)582-7555
Penny Painter, Contact

Wayne

★5829★ Mid America Vocational Technical School
Rediscovery for Displaced Homemakers
Box H
Wayne, OK 73095
Phone: (405)449-3391
Rita Morris, Contact

Woodward

★5830★ High Plains Area Vocational Technical School
Displaced Homemaker Program
3921 34th St.
Woodward, OK 73801-0009
Phone: (405)256-6618
Patty McGuire, Contact

Oregon

Albany

★5831★ Linn-Benton Community College
Turning Point Transition Program
6500 Pacific Blvd. SW
Albany, OR 97321
Phone: (503)967-0581
Mary Lou Bennett, Contact

Astoria

★5832★ Clatsop Community College
Lives In Transition
1653 Jerome St.
Astoria, OR 97103
Phone: (503)325-0910
Alice Morten, Contact

Bend

★5833★ Central Oregon Community College
Changing Directions
2600 NW College Way
Bend, OR 97701
Phone: (503)382-6112
Midge Cross, Contact

Coos Bay

★5834★ Southwestern Oregon Community College
Vocational Education Opportunities for Single Parents/Displaced Homemakers
1988 Newmark
Coos Bay, OR 97420
Phone: (503)888-7297
Brenda Brecke, Contact

The Dalles

★5835★ The Visit Center
VISIT (Vocational Improvement Services for Individuals in Transition)
606 Court St.
The Dalles, OR 97058
Phone: (503)296-4677
Sandra Gittman, Contact

Eugene

★5836★ Lane Community College
Transition to Success
Displaced Homemaker/Single Parent
  Project
4000 E. 30th Ave.
Eugene, OR 97405
Phone: (503)747-4501
Charleen Maclean, Contact

Grants Pass

★5837★ Rouge Community College
Moving On Program
3345 Redwood Hwy.
Grants Pass, OR 97526
Phone: (503)479-5541
Serena Sinclair, Contact

Newport

★5838★ Pathways
163 N.E. 11th St.
Newport, OR 97365
Phone: (503)265-3087
Muril Demory, Contact

Oregon City

★5839★ Clackamas Community College
Life and Career Options Program
19600 S. Molalla Ave.
Oregon City, OR 97045
Phone: (503)657-6958
Lynne Maloney, Contact

Phoenix

★5840★ Training and Resources for
  Women
S. Pacific & Fern Valley Rd.
PO Box 667
Phoenix, OR 97535
Phone: (503)535-7050
Mollie Owens-Stevenson, Contact

Portland

★5841★ Centennial Center
Women In Transition
14750 S.E. Clinton St.
Portland, OR 97236
Phone: (503)760-4007
Toni Partington, Contact

★5842★ Portland Community College
New Directions
Rock Creek Campus
Bldg. 2, Rm. 102
PO Box 19000
Portland, OR 97219-0990
Phone: (503)244-6111
Joanne Truesdell, Contact

★5843★ Portland Community College
Project Independence
Cascade Campus
Bldg. C/H. Rm. B49
PO Box 19000
Portland, OR 97219-0990
Phone: (503)244-6111
Terry Greenfield, Contact

Roseburg

★5844★ Confidence Clinic
308 Jackson
Roseburg, OR 97470
Phone: (503)672-5392
Barbara Nordin, Contact

Salem

★5845★ Chemeketa Community College
Services for the New Workforce
Skills for Independence
4000 Lancster Dr. NE
Salem, OR 97309
Phone: (503)399-5236
Sandra Nelson, Contact

Pennsylvania

Aliquippa

★5846★ Pennsylvania State University
New Choices
Franklin Center Annex
524 Franklin Ave.
Aliquippa, PA 15001
Phone: (412)378-4227
Claudia Brown, Contact

Allison Park

★5847★ YWCA
Women's Resource Center
8500 Thompson Run Rd.
Allison Park, PA 15101
Phone: (412)364-3844
Alayne Rosenfeld, Contact

Altoona

★5848★ Altoona Area Vocational
  Technical School
New Choices
1500 4th Ave.
Altoona, PA 16602
Phone: (814)946-8454
Frances Stevenson, Contact

Bedford

★5849★ New Choices
122 E. Penn St.
Bedford, PA 15522
Phone: (814)623-6222
Jenny Gardene, Contact

Bellefonte

★5850★ Centre County Area Vocational-
  Technical School
New Choices
Central Intermediate Unit No. 10
Development Center for Adults
Bellefonte, PA 16823
Phone: (814)359-3069
Susan Antram, Contact

Bethel Park

★5851★ Bethel Park School District
New Choices
301 Church Rd.
Bethel Park, PA 15102
Phone: (412)854-8415
Mary Ann Eisenreich, Contact

Bethlehem

★5852★ Northampton County Area
  Community College
New Choices
3835 Green Pond Rd.
Bethlehem, PA 18017
Phone: (215)861-5350
Sandra Wiens, Contact

Bloomsburg

★5853★ Women's Center
Voice/Train Counselor
Bloomsburg, PA 17815
Phone: (717)784-6631
Terry Jacques, Contact

Blue Bell

★5854★ Montgomery County Community
  College
New Choices
340 Dekalb Pike
Blue Bell, PA 19422-0758
Phone: (215)641-2310
Brighid Blake, Contact

Braddock

★5855★ Community College of Allegheny
  County, Braddock Campus
New Choices
424 George St.
Braddock, PA 15146
Phone: (412)271-0239
Mary Pat Brennan, Contact

Bradford

★5856★ Second Ward School
New Choices
72 Congress St.
Bradford, PA 16701
Phone: (814)362-3854
Janice Himes, Contact

Bristol

★5857★ New Choices
1200 New Rogers Rd.
Bristol, PA 19007
Phone: (215)781-3937
Marilyn Ebert, Contact

Bryn Mawr

★5858★ Harcum Junior College
New Choices
Montgomery Ave.
Bryn Mawr, PA 19010
Phone: (215)526-6037
Louise Burroughs, Contact

Butler

★5859★ Butler County Community College
New Choices
College Dr., Oak Hills
PO Box 1203
Butler, PA 16001
Phone: (412)287-8711
Laurie Allen, Contact

Chambersburg

★5860★ Wilson College
Directions Unlimited
1015 Philadelphia Ave.
Chambersburg, PA 17201
Phone: (717)264-4141
Sandra Slifko, Contact

Clairton

★5861★ Steel Center Area Vocational-
Technical School
New Choices
565 Lewis Run Rd.
Clairton, PA 15025
Phone: (412)469-2249
Martha Meister, Contact

Clarion

★5862★ Clarion Office Complex
New Choices
214 S. 7th Ave.
Clarion, PA 16214
Phone: (814)226-4631
Michele Takei, Contact

Clearfield

★5863★ Clearfield County Area
Vocational-Technical School
New Choices
RR No. 1, Box 5
Central Intermediate Unit 10
Development Center for Adults
Clearfield, PA 16830
Phone: (814)765-1131
Francey Gelfand, Contact

Cresson

★5864★ Mount Aloysius Junior College
New Choices, Displaced Homemaker
Program
Cresson, PA 16630
Phone: (814)886-4131
Debbie Mutz, Contact

Dimock

★5865★ Susquehanna County Area
Vocational-Technical School
New Choices
Box 133
Dimock, PA 18816
Phone: (717)278-9229
Alice Davis, Contact

East Stroudsburg

★5866★ East Stroudsburg University
New Choices
Women's Center
East Stroudsburg, PA 18301
Phone: (717)424-3375
Kathryn LeSoire, Contact

Erie

★5867★ Erie County Technical School
New Choices
8500 Oliver Rd.
Erie, PA 16509
Phone: (814)868-0837
Mary Ellen Camp, Contact

Exton

★5868★ New Choices
150 James Hance Ct.
Exton, PA 19341
Phone: (215)524-5108
Goldie Levin, Contact

Harrisburg

★5869★ PROBE
589 S. Front St.
Harrisburg, PA 17104
Phone: (717)233-6262
Kathryn Towns, Contact

★5870★ PROBE/New Choices
2101 N. Front St.
Bldg. 1, Ste. 301
Harrisburg, PA 17101
Phone: (717)236-2414
Pat Geissel, Contact

Indiana

★5871★ Indiana University of
Pennsylvania
Center for Vocational Personnel
Preparation
New Choices
Reschini House
Indiana, PA 15705
Phone: (412)357-4738
Linda Schaeffer, Contact

Jim Thorpe

★5872★ Carbon County Area Vocational-
Technical School
New Choices
150 W. 13th St.
Jim Thorpe, PA 18229
Phone: (717)325-3682
Grace Dunn, Contact

Lancaster

★5873★ Lancaster County, Area
Vocational-Technical School at the
YWCA
New Directions-Employment and
Counseling Center.
110 N. Lime St.
Lancaster, PA 17602
Phone: (717)393-1735
Nora Rosa-Cleary, Contact

Lebanon

★5874★ PROBE/New Choices
815 Cumberland St.
Lebanon, PA 17042
Phone: (717)273-2090
Lee Brennan, Contact

Lewisburg

★5875★ New Choices
CSIU No. 16
Box 213
Lewisburg, PA 17837
Phone: (717)523-1155
Diane Johnson, Contact

Lewistown

★5876★ Juniata-Mifflin County Area
Vocational-Technical School
Adult Education & Job Training Center
New Choices
1020 Belle Vernon Ave.
Lewistown, PA 17044
Phone: (717)248-4942
Suzanne Fischer, Contact

Lock Haven

★5877★ Development Center for Adults
Clinton County Development
New Choices
110 East Bald Eagle St., 2nd Fl.
Lock Haven, PA 17745
Phone: (717)893-4038
Linda Hinman, Contact

Meadville

★5878★ Crawford County Area Vocational
Technical School
New Choices
860 Thurston Rd.
Meadville, PA 16335
Phone: (814)724-6024
Alice Dalmaso, Contact

Media

★5879★ Delaware County Community
College
New Choices
Rte. 252 & Media Line Rd.
Media, PA 19063
Phone: (215)359-5296
Suzanne Whitaker, Contact

Mercer

★5880★ Mercer County Area Vocational-
Technical School
New Choices
PO Box 152
Mercer, PA 16137
Phone: (412)662-3000
Ann Burdette, Contact

Mill Creek

★5881★ Huntingdon Area Vocational-
Technical School
New Choices Program
Box E
Mill Creek, PA 17060
Phone: (814)643-0951
Linda Hoenstine, Contact

Monroeville

★5882★ Forbes Road East Area
Vocational Technical School
New Choices
Beatty & Cooper Road
Monroeville, PA 15146
Phone: (412)373-8100
Renee King, Contact

Nanticoke

★5883★ Luzerne County Community
College
New Choices
Prospect St. & Middle Rd.
Nanticoke, PA 18634
Phone: (717)829-7485
Susan Spry, Contact

Oil City

★5884★ Venango County Area Vocational-
Technical School
New Choices
1 Vocational Technical Dr.
Oil City, PA 16301
Phone: (814)677-3097
Anne Wachob, Contact

Philadelphia

★5885★ Community College of Philadelphia
New Choices
1700 Spring Garden St.
Philadelphia, PA 19130
Phone: (215)751-8922
Cynthia Walls, Contact

★5886★ Community Women's Education Project
New Horizons
Somerset at Frankford Ave.
Philadelphia, PA 19134
Phone: (215)426-2200
Pat Haff, Contact

★5887★ Educational Services for Adults
1616 Walnut St., 1st Fl.
Philadelphia, PA 19103
Phone: (215)787-1536
Wendy Slegal, Contact

★5888★ Lutheran Settlement House Women's Program
1340 Frankford Ave.
Philadelphia, PA 19125
Phone: (215)426-8610
Carol Goertzel, Contact

★5889★ Temple University
Home to Work
New Choices
1500 N. Broad St.
Ed Whitehall, Rm. 103
Philadelphia, PA 19121
Phone: (215)787-7491
Priscilla Woods, Contact

Pittsburgh

★5890★ Community College of Allegheny County, College Center—North
New Choices
808 Ridge Ave.
Pittsburgh, PA 15208
Phone: (412)237-2595
Shelia Johnson, Contact

Quakertown

★5891★ New Choices
515 S. West End Blvd.
Quakertown, PA 18951
Phone: (215)538-1944
Sharon Shaw, Contact

Reading

★5892★ Reading Area Community College
New Choices
PO Box 1706
Reading, PA 19603
Phone: (215)372-4721
Beverly Thompson, Contact

Schnecksville

★5893★ Lehigh Count Vocational Technical School
New Choices
2300 Main St.
Schnecksville, PA 18078
Phone: (215)799-1452
Maryann Haytmanek, Contact

Scranton

★5894★ Employment Opportunity Training Center
116 N. Washington Ave., Suite 3D-Kane Building
Scranton, PA 18503
Phone: (717)348-6484
Sharon McCrone, Contact

Washington

★5895★ YWCA
New Choices
42 W. Maiden St., Ste. 23
Washington, PA 15301
Phone: (412)223-4305
Joyce Blackburn, Contact

Waynesburg

★5896★ New Choices Program
22 W. High St., Rm. 20
Waynesburg, PA 15370
Phone: (412)627-7985
Kate Thompson, Contact

Wellsboro

★5897★ Pennsylvania College of Technology
New Choices
RD 3, Box 436
Wellsboro, PA 16901
Phone: (717)724-7703
Linda S. Williams, Contact

West Mifflin

★5898★ Community College of Allegheny County, South Campus
New Choices
1750 Clairton Rd.
West Mifflin, PA 15122
Phone: (412)673-7221
Susan Kantrowitz, Contact

Williamsport

★5899★ Pennsylvania College of Technology
New Choices
1 College Ave.
Williamsport, PA 17701-5799
Phone: (717)326-3761
Cheri Reagle, Contact

York

★5900★ New Choices
320 E. Market St.
York, PA 17402
Phone: (717)848-2729
Marla Butcher, Contact

Rhode Island

Cranston

★5901★ Cranston Adult Education
Single Parent Program
70 Metropolitan Ave.
Cranston, RI 02920
Phone: (401)785-8177
Doris Kushner, Contact

Lincoln

★5902★ Community College of Rhode Island
Project Sphere
1762 Louisquisset Pike
Lincoln, RI 02865
Phone: (401)333-7092
Corinne Conde, Contact

Providence

★5903★ Community College of Rhode Island, Providence Campus
Project Sphere
Providence Campus
Providence, RI 02905
Phone: (401)333-7206
Marsha Healy-Cohen, Contact

★5904★ Rhode Island Displaced Homemaker Program
275 Westminster Mall
Providence, RI 02903
Phone: (401)277-2862
Suzanne Merkin, Contact

Warwick

★5905★ Community College of Rhode Island
Project Sphere
400 East Ave.
Warwick, RI 02886
Phone: (401)825-2000
Linda Benvenuti, Contact

South Carolina

Aiken

★5906★ Aiken Technical College
Single Parents/Displaced Homemakers Program
PO Box 696
Aiken, SC 29801
Phone: (803)593-9231
Francis Syblewski, Contact

Charleston

★5907★ College of Charleston
Displaced Workers Counseling and Undergraduate Studies
66 George St.
Charleston, SC 29424
Phone: (803)792-5674
Olivia G. White, Contact

★5908★ Florence Crittenton Home, Inc.
Single Parent/Displaced Homemaker Program
19 St. Margaret St.
Charleston, SC 29403
Phone: (803)722-7526
Dorothy Meacham, Contact

★5909★ Trident Technical College
Single Parents/Homemakers Program
PO Box 10367
Charleston, SC 29411
Phone: (803)572-6009
Claire O'Neill, Contact

Cheraw

★5910★ **Chesterfield-Marlboro Technical College**
Single Parent/Displaced Homemaker Program
PO Box 1007
Cheraw, SC 29520
Phone: (803)537-5286
Jean Page Watson, Contact

Columbia

★5911★ **The Columbia Urban League**
Single Parent/Displaced Homemaker Programs
PO Drawer J
Columbia, SC 29526
Phone: (803)347-3186
Centuri Watson, Contact

★5912★ **Midlands Technical College**
Center for Adult Learners
WO/MEN in Transition
PO Box 2408
Center for Adult Learners
Columbia, SC 29202
Phone: (803)738-7630
Mary Kendrick, Contact

Conway

★5913★ **Horry County School District**
Single Parent/Displaced Homemaker Program
Rte. 6, Box 201
Adult Education Center
Conway, SC 29526
Phone: (803)347-4688
Gaye Ducker, Contact

★5914★ **Horry-Georgetown Technical College**
Single Parents/Displaced Homemakers Program
PO Box 1966
Conway, SC 29526
Phone: (803)347-3186
Olis Jayroe, Contact

Denmark

★5915★ **Denmark Technical College**
Single Parent/Displaced Homemakers Program
PO Box 327
Denmark, SC 29042
Phone: (803)793-3301
Peggy S. Faust, Contact

Elloree

★5916★ **Orangeburg School District No.7**
Single Parent/Displaced Homemakers Program
Drawer L
Elloree, SC 29047
Phone: (803)897-2211
Frances Bowers, Contact

Florence

★5917★ **Florence-Darlington Technical College**
Single Parent/Displaced Homemaker Program
PO Drawer F-8000
Florence, SC 29501
Phone: (803)661-8174
Bonnie Fanning, Contact

★5918★ **Pee Dee Community Action Agency**
Single Parents/Displaced Homemakers Program
364 N.B. Baroody St.
PO Box 935
Florence, SC 29501
Phone: (803)678-3424
Mildred Thomas, Contact

Greenville

★5919★ **Greenville Technical College**
Single Parents/Displaced Homemaker Program
Career Advancement Center
PO Box 5616, Sta. B
Greenville, SC 29606
Phone: (803)239-2971
Flora M. Rogers, Contact

★5920★ **Sunbelt Human Advancement Resources, Inc.**
Single Parent/Displaced Homemaker Program
PO Box 10204, FS
Greenville, SC 29603
Phone: (803)242-3712
Karen McIntyre, Contact

Greenwood

★5921★ **Piedmont Technical College**
Single Parent/Displaced Homemaker Program
PO Box 1467
Greenwood, SC 29646
Phone: (803)223-8357
Ann Howell, Contact

Kingstree

★5922★ **Williamsburg Technical College**
Single Parents/Displaced Homemakers Program
601 Lane Rd.
Kingstree, SC 29556
Phone: (803)354-7423
Donald Melton, Contact

Lexington

★5923★ **Lexington Vocational Center**
Single Parent/Displaced Homemaker Program
2421 Augusta Hwy.
Lexington, SC 29072
Phone: (803)359-4151
Linda Jacobus, Contact

Orangeburg

★5924★ **Orangeburg-Calhoun Technical College**
Single Parent/Homemaker Program
3250 St. Matthews Rd.
Orangeburg, SC 29115
Phone: (803)536-0311
Martha Ann Weeks, Contact

Pendleton

★5925★ **Tri-County Technical College**
Single Parents/Displaced Homemakers Program
PO Box 587
Pendleton, SC 29670
Phone: (803)646-8361
Ollie Chappell-Smith, Contact

Rock Hill

★5926★ **York Technical College**
Single Parents/Displaced Homemaker Program
Women's Center
452 S. Anderson Rd.
Rock Hill, SC 29730
Phone: (803)327-8004
Sally Herlong, Contact

Spartanburg

★5927★ **Spartanburg Technical College**
Single Parents/Displaced Homemaker Program
Women's Program
PO Box 4386
Spartanburg, SC 29305
Phone: (803)591-3600
Molly Wilkes, Contact

Sumter

★5928★ **Sumter Area Technical College**
Single Parent/Displaced Homemaker Program
506 N. Guignard
Sumter, SC 29150
Phone: (803)778-6634
Jill L. Webster, Contact

Union

★5929★ **Union County Schools**
Get Set for Job Success
Single Parent/Displaced Homemaker Program
PO Box 907
Union, SC 29379
Phone: (803)429-0581
Elaine Delk, Contact

Williamston

★5930★ **The Career Center**
702 Belton Hwy.
Williamston, SC 29697
Phone: (803)847-4121
Cathey White, Contact

South Dakota

Beresford

★5931★ **Displaced Homemaker Program**
301 W. Oak
Beresford, SD 57004
Phone: (605)763-2145
Sheridan Swee, Contact

Brookings

★5932★ **Career Learning Center**
Single Parent/Homemaker Project
2308 E. 6th St.
Brookings, SD 57006
Phone: (605)688-4374
DiAnn Kothe, Contact

Lemmon

★5933★ **Northwest Area Schools Multi-District**
Single Parent/Homemaker Project
310 11th St. W
Lemmon, SD 57638
Phone: (605)374-3811
Connie Hermann, Contact

Mitchell

★5934★ Mitchell Vocational Technical
Single Parent/Homemaker Project
821 N. Capital
Mitchell, SD 57301
Phone: (605)995-3024
Tina Bennett, Contact

Pierre

★5935★ Missouri Shores Women
 Resource Center
Single Parent/Homemaker Project
104 E. Capital
Pierre, SD 57501
Phone: (605)224-0256
Kayle Rice Tibbs, Contact

Rapid City

★5936★ Career Learning Center
Single Parent/Homemaker Program
514 Mt. Rushmore Rd.
Rapid City, SD 57701
Phone: (605)394-5120
Kathy Cornelison, Contact

★5937★ Western Dakota Vocational
 Technical Institute
Displaced Homemakers Programs
1600 Sedivy Ln.
Rapid City, SD 57701
Toll-free: 800-544-8765
Donna Belitz, Contact

Sioux Falls

★5938★ Southeast Vocational Technical
 Project
Displaced Homemaker Program
2301 Career Place
Sioux Falls, SD 57104
Phone: (605)339-7175
Nancy Gacke, Contact

Springfield

★5939★ Correctional Facility
Displaced Homemaker Program
Box 322
Springfield, SD 57062
Phone: (605)369-2201
Tari Tielke, Contact

Sturgis

★5940★ Black Hills Special Services
Single Parent/Homemaker Program
PO Box 218
Sturgis, SD 57785
Phone: (605)347-4467
Char Madsen-Clark, Contact

Watertown

★5941★ Lake Area Vocational Technical
 Institute
Single Parent/Homemaker Project
230 11th St. NE
PO Box 730
Watertown, SD 57201
Phone: (605)886-5872
Linda Schurmann, Contact

Tennessee

Alcoa

★5942★ East Tennessee Human Resource
 Agency
Displaced Homemaker/Single Parent
 Program
266 Joule St.
Alcoa, TN 37701
Phone: (615)983-8411
Patricia S. Ford, Contact

★5943★ Second Start
Alcoa Education Bldg.
Farraday St.
Alcoa, TN 37701
Phone: (615)983-1121
Janet Sayler, Contact

Algood

★5944★ Displaced Homemakers Program
150 W. Church St.
Algood, TN 38501
Phone: (615)537-6542
Phyllis R. Bennett, Contact

Blountville

★5945★ Northeast Street Technical
 Community College
Displaced Homemaker/Single Parent
 Programs
PO Box 246
Blountville, TN 37617
Phone: (615)323-3191
Judy Reed, Contact

Chattanooga

★5946★ Chattanooga Urban League
Single Parent/Displaced Homemaker
 Program
730 Martin Luther King Blvd.
PO Box 11106
Chattanooga, TN 37401
Phone: (615)756-1762
Edyth Kelly, Contact

★5947★ Hamilton County Schools
Displaced Homemaker Program
201 Broad St.
Chattanooga, TN 37402
Phone: (615)757-1700
Jane Teeter, Contact

★5948★ University of Tennessee at
 Chattanooga
Life Planning Services for Displaced
 Homemakers
Center for Community Career Education
615 McCallie Ave.
Chattanooga, TN 37403-2598
Phone: (615)755-4475
Beverly Gibson, Contact

Cokeville

★5949★ Cumberland Career Equity Center
Box 5161 TTU
Cokeville, TN 38505
Phone: (615)243-3310
Beverly Heath, Contact

Columbia

★5950★ Columbia State Community
 College
Single Parent/Displaced Homemaker
 Program
Working Opportunities for Women
PO Box 1315
Columbia, TN 38401
Phone: (615)388-0120
Ann Tidwell, Contact

Covington

★5951★ Tri-County Family and Children
 Services
420 Long Ave.
PO Box 45
Covington, TN 38019
Phone: (901)476-2364
Minnie Bommer, Contact

Dresden

★5952★ Weakley County Board of
 Education
Single Parents Success Program
309 Courthouse
Dresden, TN 38225
Phone: (901)364-2247
Julia Rich, Contact

Dyersburg

★5953★ Dyersburg State Community
 College
Single Parent/Displaced Homemaker
 Program
PO Box 648
Dyersburg, TN 38025-0648
Phone: (901)286-3358
Varetta Haskin, Contact

Etowah

★5954★ Etowah City School District
Displaced Homemaker/Single Parent
 Programs
858 Eighth St.
Etowah, TN 37331
Phone: (615)263-5483
Nancy Boardman, Contact

Gallatin

★5955★ Sumner County Board of
 Education
Displaced Homemaker Program
117 E. Winchester
Gallatin, TN 37066
Phone: (615)451-5200
Ron Hosse, Contact

★5956★ Volunteer State Community
 College
Displaced Homemaker/Single Parent
 Programs
Nashville Pike
Gallatin, TN 37066
Phone: (615)741-3215
Patti Powell, Contact

Greeneville

★5957★ Greeneville City Schools
Displaced Homemaker/Single Parent
  Programs
PO Box 1420
Greeneville, TN 37744
Phone: (615)639-0171
Gayle Greene, Contact

Harriman

★5958★ Roane State Community College
Special Projects
Displaced Homemaker/Single Parent
  Programs
Harriman, TN 37748
Phone: (615)354-3000
Maureen Magnan, Contact

Jackson

★5959★ Jackson Area Vocational Training
  School
Single Parent/Displaced Homemaker
  Program
McKellar Field
Jackson, TN 38301
Phone: (901)424-0691
Mary Boyd, Contact

Knoxville

★5960★ East Tennessee Human Resource
  Agency
Single Parent/Displaced Homemaker
  Program
408 N. Cedar Bluff Rd., Ste. 150
Knoxville, TN 37923
Phone: (615)691-2551
Patricia Ford, Contact

★5961★ Knoxville Women's Center
Single Parent/Displaced Homemaker
  Program
220 Carrick St.
Knoxville, TN 37921
Phone: (615)546-1873
Faith Willis, Contact

★5962★ Pellissippi State Technical
  Community College
Second Start
Division Street Campus
PO Box 22990
Knoxville, TN 37933
Phone: (615)971-5222
Mary Ann Piper, Contact

Manchester

★5963★ Central High School
Single Parent/Displaced Homemaker
  Program
COPE
2001 McAuthur St.
Manchester, TN 37355
Phone: (615)728-1994
Marianne Brandon, Contact

★5964★ Coffee County Schools
Displaced Homemaker/Single Parents
  Program
300 Hillsboro Hwy.
Manchester, TN 37355
Phone: (615)728-3309
Charlotte Philpot, Contact

Memphis

★5965★ Memphis City Schools
Single Parent/Displaced Homemakers
  Program
320 Carpenter St.
Lester Annex
Memphis, TN 38112
Phone: (901)425-5295
Susan Companiotte, Contact

★5966★ Memphis YWCA
PEP
1044 Mississippi Blvd.
Memphis, TN 38126
Phone: (901)942-4653
Patricia Thompson, Contact

★5967★ Shelby State Community College
Displaced Homemaker/Single Parent
  Program
PO Box 40568
Memphis, TN 38174-0568
Phone: (901)528-8912
Sue Field, Contact

★5968★ State Technical Institute at
  Memphis
Displaced Homemaker/Single Parent
  Program
PREP
5983 Macon Cove
Memphis, TN 38134
Phone: (901)377-4145
James Franklin, Contact

Morristown

★5969★ Douglas-Cherokee Economic
  Authority
Single Parent/Displaced Homemakers
  Program
PO Box 1218
Morristown, TN 37816-1218
Phone: (615)587-4500
Joyce Carpenter, Contact

★5970★ Hamblen County Board of
  Education
Single Parent/Displaced Homemaker
  Program
210 E. Morris Blvd.
Morristown, TN 37919
Phone: (615)586-7700
Bob Howard, Contact

Murfreesboro

★5971★ Rutherford County Board of
  Education
Displaced Homemaker Program
502 Memorial Blvd.
Murfreesboro, TN 37310
Phone: (615)893-5812
Bruce Frizzell, Contact

Nashville

★5972★ Metro Nashville Public Schools
Career Directions Program
2601 Bradsford Ave.
Nashville, TN 37204
Phone: (615)259-8545
Victor Baggett, Contact

★5973★ Nashville State Technical Institute
Displaced Homemaker/Single Parent
  Program
120 White Bridge Rd.
Nashville, TN 37209
Phone: (615)353-3229
Kathy Emery, Contact

★5974★ OIC (Opportunity Industralized
  Center)
Displaced Homemakers Program
1507 Meharry Blvd.
PO Box 5506
Nashville, TN 37208
Phone: (615)321-0021
Betty Cunningham, Contact

★5975★ YWCA of Nashville
Displaced Homemaker Program
1608 Woodmont Blvd.
Nashville, TN 37215
Phone: (615)269-9922
Duann Kier, Contact

Oak Ridge

★5976★ Oak Ridge YWCA
Displaced Homemaker Program
1660 Oak Ridge
Oak Ridge, TN 37830
Phone: (615)482-9922
Phyllis Scalf, Contact

Sneedville

★5977★ Hancock County Schools
Displaced Homemaker Program
PO Box 629
Sneedville, TN 37869
Phone: (615)733-2591
Kay Greene, Contact

Tazewell

★5978★ Claiborne County Board of
  Education
Displaced Homemaker/Single Parent
  Programs
PO Box 179
Tazewell, TN 37879
Phone: (615)626-0264
Pat Tartar, Contact

★5979★ Clinch-Powell Education
  Cooperative
Employability Development and Placement
  Program
Single Parent/Displaced Homemaker
  Program
PO Box 79
Tazewell, TN 37879
Phone: (615)626-4677
Dwight Snodgrass, Contact

Tullahoma

★5980★ Motlow State Community College
Displaced Homemakers/Single Parent
  Program
Tullahoma, TN 37388
Phone: (615)455-8511
Lee Austin, Contact

Whiteville

**★5981★ Whiteville State Area Vocational-
Technical School**
**Displaced Homemaker/Single Parent
Program**
PO Box 489
Whiteville, TN 38075
Phone: (901)254-8521
Assie Walker, Contact

Texas

Alvin

★5982★ Alvin Community College
**Displaced Homemaker/Single Parent
Program**
3110 Mustang Rd.
Alvin, TX 77511-4898
Phone: (713)331-6111
Sandra Houne, Contact

Amarillo

★5983★ Amarillo College
Displaced Homemakers Program
Adult Students and Women's Service
PO Box 447
Amarillo, TX 79178
Phone: (806)371-5450
Donna Moore, Contact

**★5984★ Texas State Technical Institute—
Amarillo Campus**
TOT Program
PO Box 11197
Amarillo, TX 79111
Phone: (806)335-2316
Debbie Bailey, Contact

Austin

★5985★ Austin Community College
**Displaced Homemaker/Single Parent
Program**
PO Box 2285
Austin, TX 78768
Phone: (512)832-4726
Diane Cramer, Contact

Baytown

★5986★ Lee College
**Single Parent/Displaced Homemaker
Program**
511 S. Whiting St.
Baytown, TX 77520-4703
Phone: (713)425-6400
Ed Moak, Contact

Beeville

★5987★ Bee County College
**Displaced Homemaker/Single Parent
Program**
3800 Charco Rd.
Beeville, TX 78102
Phone: (512)358-3130
Patricia Myers, Contact

Brownsville

★5988★ Texas Southmost College
Single Parent/Homemaker Program
80 Fort Brown
Brownsville, TX 78520-4993
Phone: (512)544-8930
Alexa Pfister, Contact

Carthage

★5989★ Panola College
**Single Parent/Displaced Homemaker
Program**
W. Panola St.
Carthage, TX 75663
Phone: (214)693-2032
Ronald Johnston, Contact

Cisco

★5990★ Cisco Junior College
**Displaced Homemaker/Single Parent
Program**
Rte. 3, Box 3
Cisco, TX 76437
Phone: (817)698-2212
David Allen, Contact

Clarendon

★5991★ Clarendon College
**Displaced Homemaker/Single Parent
Program**
PO Box 968
Bugbee St. at Hwy. 287
Clarendon, TX 79226
Phone: (806)874-3574
Don Smith, Contact

College Station

**★5992★ Texas Engineering Extension
Service**
**Single Parent/Displaced Homemaker
Program**
College Station, TX 77843-8000
Phone: (409)845-7225
Margaret Halsema, Contact

Corpus Christi

★5993★ Del Mar College
**Single Parent/Displaced Homemaker
Program**
Edwin & Ayers
Corpus Christi, TX 78404
Phone: (512)886-1298
Jo Ann Luckie, Contact

Corsicana

★5994★ Navarro College
Carl Perkins Career Center
Single Parent/Homemkaker Program
3200 W. 2nd Ave.
Corsicana, TX 75110
Phone: (903)874-6501
Mary Dickerson, Contact

Dallas

★5995★ Bill J. Priest Institute
Kahn Job Training Center
1402 Corinth
Dallas, TX 75215
Phone: (214)565-5736
Alecia B. Cobb, Contact

★5996★ Mountain View College
Displaced Homemaker Program
4849 W. Illinois Ave.
Dallas, TX 75211-6599
Phone: (214)333-8672
Marietta Kane, Contact

★5997★ Richland College
Adult Resource Center
12800 Abrams Rd.
Dallas, TX 75243-2199
Phone: (214)238-6034
Patsy A. Shockley, Contact

El Paso

★5998★ El Paso Community College
Women's Center
100 W. Rio Grande
PO Box 20500
El Paso, TX 79998
Phone: (915)534-4121
Olga Chavez, Contact

★5999★ YWCA
Women's Resource Center
1600 N. Brown
El Paso, TX 79902
Phone: (915)533-7492
Lupe Castaneda, Contact

Farmers Branch

★6000★ Brookhaven College
Displaced Homemaker Program
3939 Valley View Lane
Farmers Branch, TX 75244
Phone: (214)620-4849
Janice Groeneman, Contact

Ft. Worth

**★6001★ Women's Center of Tarrant
County**
1723 Hamphill St.
PO Box 11860
Ft. Worth, TX 76110
Phone: (817)927-4006
Karen Perkins, Contact

Gainesville

★6002★ Cooke County College
Returning Students
Highway 51 South
PO Box 815
Gainesville, TX 76240
Phone: (817)668-7731
Bill Caver, Contact

Galveston

★6003★ Galveston College
**Single Parent/Displaced Homemaker
Program**
4015 Avenue Q
Galveston, TX 77550
Phone: (409)763-6551
Thelma White, Contact

Harlingen

★6004★ Texas State Technical Institute
**Single Parent/Displaced Homemaker
Program**
PO Box 2628
Harlingen, TX 78550
Phone: (512)425-0677
Irma Penn, Contact

Houston

★6005★ Houston Area Women's Center
WIRES—New Resources
3101 Richmond Ave., Ste. 150
Houston, TX 77098
Phone: (713)528-2121

★6006★ **Houston Community College**
  System
Support Services
PO Box 7849
Houston, TX 77270-7849
Phone: (713)868-0773
Eileen Hatcher, Contact

★6007★ **North Harris County College**
Single Parent/Displaced Homemaker
  Program
2700 W.W. Thorne Dr.
Houston, TX 77073
Phone: (713)443-5480
Karen Blankner, Contact

★6008★ **North Harris County College**
  District
Single Parent/Displaced Homemaker
250 N. Belt East
Houston, TX 77060
Phone: (713)591-3524
Sondra Whitlow, Contact

★6009★ **San Jacinto College—North**
  Campus
Single Parent/Displaced Homemaker
  Program
5800 Uvalde Rd.
Houston, TX 77049
Phone: (713)458-4050
Mary Froh, Contact

★6010★ **San Jacinto College—South**
  Campus
Single Parent/Displaced Homemaker
  Program
13735 Beamer Rd.
Houston, TX 77089
Phone: (713)484-1900
Marvin Wittrock, Contact

Irving

★6011★ **North Lake College**
Center for Returning Adults
5001 N. MacArthur Blvd.
Irving, TX 75038
Phone: (214)659-5375
Yvonne Abatso, Contact

Keller

★6012★ **Keller Independent School District**
Support Services for Single Parents
101 Indian Trail Dr.
Keller, TX 76248
Phone: (817)431-2585
Debbie Kelly, Contact

Kilgore

★6013★ **Kilgore College**
Displaced Homemaker Program
1100 Broadway
Kilgore, TX 75662
Phone: (214)983-8178
Susan Atchley, Contact

Killeen

★6014★ **Central Texas College**
American Education Complex System
Single Parent Homemaker Program
PO Box 1800
Killeen, TX 76540-9990
Phone: (817)526-1355
Louella Tate, Contact

Lake Jackson

★6015★ **Brazosport College**
Displaced Homemaker/Single Parent
  Program
500 College Dr.
Lake Jackson, TX 77566
Phone: (409)265-6131
Connie Zettel, Contact

Lancaster

★6016★ **Cedar Valley College**
Special Services Department
Displaced Homemaker Program
3030 N. Dallas Ave.
Lancaster, TX 75134
Phone: (214)372-8262
Vicki Lawson, Contact

Laredo

★6017★ **Laredo Junior College**
Single Parent/Homemaker Program
Women's Center
West End Washington St.
Laredo, TX 78040-4395
Phone: (512)721-5137
Ramiro Ramirez, Contact

Lufkin

★6018★ **Angelina College**
Women's Support Services
Hwy. 59 S
PO Box 1768
Lufkin, TX 75901
Phone: (409)639-1301
Mary Jo Gordon, Contact

Mesquite

★6019★ **Eastfield College**
Single Parent/Homemaker Program
3737 Motley Dr.
Mesquite, TX 75150
Phone: (214)324-7020
Gloria Dean, Contact

Mt. Pleasant

★6020★ **Northeast Texas Community**
  College
Single Parent/Homemaker Program
PO Box 1307
Mt. Pleasant, TX 75455
Phone: (903)572-1911
Carolyn Duke, Contact

Odessa

★6021★ **Odessa College**
Single Parent/Displaced Homemaker
201 W. University
Odessa, TX 79764
Phone: (915)335-6583
Jennifer Cochran, Contact

Paris

★6022★ **Paris Junior College**
Center for Women
2400 Clarksville St.
Paris, TX 75460
Phone: (903)784-9423
Cindy Miles, Contact

Pasedena

★6023★ **San Jacinto College—Central**
  Campus
Single Parent/Displaced Homemaker
  Program
8060 Spencer Hwy.
Pasedena, TX 77505
Phone: (713)476-1501
Mary Stevens, Contact

Plano

★6024★ **Collin County Community College**
Single Parent/Displaced Homemaker
  Program
2800 E. Springcreek
Plano, TX 75074
Phone: (214)881-5852
Karen Rose, Contact

Ranger

★6025★ **Ranger Junior College**
Displaced Homemakers Program
College Circle
Ranger, TX 76460
Phone: (817)647-3234
Lyndell Cockburn, Contact

San Antonio

★6026★ **Alamo Community College District**
Displaced Homemaker/Single Parent
  Program
811 W. Houston St.
San Antonio, TX 78284
Phone: (512)220-1500
Linda Silva, Contact

★6027★ **Bexas County Women's Center**
Displaced Homemakers Program
1401 N. Main
San Antonio, TX 78212
Phone: (512)225-4387
Randi Hargrove, Contact

★6028★ **Palo Alto College**
Single Parent/Homemaker Program
1400 W. Villaret
PO Box 3800
San Antonio, TX 78224
Phone: (512)921-5260
Cessie Sanchez, Contact

★6029★ **St. Phillips College**
Equity Center
Single Parent/Homemaker Program
1801 Martin Luther King Dr.
San Antonio, TX 78203
Phone: (512)531-3474
Sandra Moore-Pope, Contact

★6030★ **San Antonio College**
Women's Center
1300 San Pedro
San Antonio, TX 78284
Phone: (512)733-2299
Helen Vera, Contact

Santa Fe

★6031★ **Santa Fe Independent School**
  District
Single Parent Program
13304 Hwy. 6
PO Box 370
Santa Fe, TX 77510
Phone: (409)925-3526
Edwina Campbell, Contact

Sweetwater

**★6032★ Texas State Technical College
Support Services/Displaced Homemaker
Program**
Rte. 3, Box 18
Sweetwater, TX 79556
Phone: (915)235-7300
Susie Alford, Contact

Temple

**★6033★ Temple Junior College
Gender Equity Program**
2600 S. 1st St.
Temple, TX 76504
Phone: (817)773-9961
Mercedes Wolff, Contact

**★6034★ Temple Junior College
Single Parent/Displaced Homemaker
Program**
2600 S. 1st St.
Temple, TX 76504-6599
Phone: (817)336-7851
Norman Steward, Contact

Texas City

**★6035★ College of the Mainland
Displaced Homemaker Program**
Women's Center
1200 Auburn Rd.
Texas City, TX 77591
Phone: (409)938-1211
Barbara Crews, Contact

Tomball

**★6036★ North Narris County College—
Tomball
Single Parent/Displaced Homemaker
Program**
30555 Tomball Pkwy.
PO Box 1969
Tomball, TX 77377-1979
Phone: (713)351-3380
Mary Shafer, Contact

Tyler

**★6037★ Tyler Junior College
Displaced Homemakers Program**
PO Box 9020
Tyler, TX 75711
Phone: (903)510-2615
Vickie Geisel, Contact

Vernon

**★6038★ Vernon Regional Junior College
Single Parent/Displaced Homemaker
Program**
4400 College Dr.
Vernon, TX 76384
Phone: (817)552-6291
Deana Lehman, Contact

Waco

**★6039★ McLennan Community College
Displaced Homemaker and Handicapped
Services**
1400 College Dr.
Waco, TX 76708
Phone: (817)750-3591
Marylea Henderson, Contact

**★6040★ Texas State Technical Institute
Single Parent/Homemaker Program**
3801 Campus Dr.
Waco, TX 76705
Phone: (817)799-3611
Leotia Howard, Contact

Weatherford

**★6041★ Weatherford College
Single Parent/Displaced Homemaker
Program**
308 E. Park Ave.
Weatherford, TX 76086
Phone: (817)594-5471
Barbara Schrank, Contact

Wharton

**★6042★ Wharton County Junior College
Single Parent/Displaced Homemaker
Program**
911 Boling Hwy.
Wharton, TX 77488
Phone: (409)532-4560
John Judd, Contact

Wichita Falls

**★6043★ YWCA
New Directions**
801 Burnett St.
Wichita Falls, TX 76301
Phone: (817)723-2124
Trudie Tirey, Contact

Utah

Cedar City

**★6044★ Southern Utah State College
University Student Support Services
Turning Point**
South Hall
Cedar City, UT 84720
Phone: (801)586-7855
Daphne Dalley, Contact

Ephraim

**★6045★ Snow College
Turning Point**
325 W. 100 North
Ephraim, UT 84627
Phone: (801)283-4021
Barbara Wood, Contact

Kaysville

**★6046★ Davis Area Vocational-Technical
School
Turning Point**
550 E. 300 South
Kaysville, UT 84037
Phone: (801)546-4134
Linda Stevens, Contact

Logan

**★6047★ Bridgerland Applied Technology
Center
Turning Point**
1301 N. 600 West
Logan, UT 84321
Phone: (801)753-6780
Susan K. Price, Contact

Ogden

**★6048★ Ogden-Weber Area Vocational-
Technical School
Applied Technology Center
Turning Point**
559 A.V.C. Lane
Ogden, UT 84404
Phone: (801)621-2373
Ra Nea Johnson, Contact

Price

**★6049★ College of Eastern Utah
Turning Point**
451 E. 400 North
Price, UT 84501
Phone: (801)637-2120
Sherril Burge, Contact

Roosevelt

**★6050★ Utah Basin Applied Technology
Center
Turning Point**
1100 East Lagoon St.
Box 124-5
Roosevelt, UT 84066
Phone: (801)722-4526
Vickie Jenkins, Contact

St. George

**★6051★ Dixie College
Turning Point**
225 S. 700 East
Home Ec. 138
St. George, UT 84770
Phone: (801)673-4811
Fran Kannard, Contact

Salt Lake City

**★6052★ Salt Lake Community College
Turning Point**
4600 S. Redwood Rd.
PO Box 30808
Salt Lake City, UT 84130
Phone: (801)967-4184
Bernadette Martinez-Astorga, Contact

Vermont

Bennington

**★6053★ Southwest Vermont Career
Development Center
Single Parent/Displaced Homemaker
Program
Expand Your Horizons**
Park St.
Bennington, VT 05201
Phone: (802)447-0220
Tina Callabro, Contact

Bradford

**★6054★ Oxbow Area Vocational Center
Displaced Homemaker Program**
PO Box 618
Bradford, VT 05033
Phone: (802)222-9645
Al Stevens, Contact

Brattleboro

★6055★ Community Action Brattleboro
Displaced Homemaker Program
53 Frost St.
PO Box 1769
Brattleboro, VT 05302
Phone: (802)257-7051
Kathleen Maisto, Contact

★6056★ Southeast Vermont Career
Education Center
Adult Services
Fairground Rd.
Brattleboro, VT 05301
Phone: (802)257-7335
Mary Rowell O'Brien, Contact

Bristol

★6057★ Addison County Adult Basic
Education
Displaced Homemakers Program
14 School St.
Bristol, VT 05443
Phone: (802)453-3459
Ann Crocker, Contact

Burlington

★6058★ Burlington Area Vocational
Technical Center
Displaced Homemaker Program/National
Skill Building: Working in Vermont
52 Institute Rd.
Burlington, VT 05401
Phone: (802)864-8463
Pat DiLego, Contact

★6059★ Champlain College
Displaced Homemaker Program
PO Box 670
Burlington, VT 05402
Phone: (802)658-0800
Nancy Boldt, Contact

Burre

★6060★ Barre Regional Vocational
Technical Center
Single Parent Displaced Homemaker
Program
155 Ayers St.
Burre, VT 05461
Phone: (802)476-6237
Donna Stratton, Contact

Enosburg Falls

★6061★ Enosburg Falls Area Vocational
Center
Adult Vocational Education for Single
Parents/Homemakers
Missisquoi St.
PO Box 278
Enosburg Falls, VT 05450
Phone: (802)933-4943
Barbara Irish-Paradee, Contact

Essex Junction

★6062★ Essex Junction Area Vocational
Center
Single Parent/Homemakers Program
Essex Junction, VT 05452
Phone: (802)879-5564
John Shingler, Contact

Hyde Park

★6063★ Lamoille Area Vocational Center
Displaced Homemaker Program
PO Box 304
Hyde Park, VT 05655
Phone: (802)888-4447
Yvonne Martin, Contact

Johnson

★6064★ Johnson State College
Displaced Homemaker Program
Johnson, VT 05656
Phone: (802)635-2356
Bari Gladstone, Contact

Middlebury

★6065★ Addison County Vocational
Technical Center
Success
Charles Ave.
Middlebury, VT 05753
Phone: (802)388-3115
Herb Shipman, Contact

Montpelier

★6066★ Futures Program
214 Main St.
Montpelier, VT 05602
Phone: (802)223-7902
Susan Griffin, Contact

★6067★ Woman Centered
17 Northfield St.
Montpelier, VT 05602
Phone: (802)229-6202
Clotilde Pitkin, Contact

Morrisville

★6068★ Clarina Howard Nichols Center
Displaced Homemakers Program
PO Box 517
Morrisville, VT 05661
Phone: (802)888-5256
Shelia D'Amico, Contact

Newport

★6069★ North County Career Center
Adult Services
Veterans Ave.
Newport, VT 05855
Phone: (802)334-9469
Lynn Anner-Bolieu, Contact

Rutland

★6070★ Rutland Area Vocational-Technical
Center
Career Counseling and Training
Stratton Ave.
Rutland, VT 05701
Phone: (802)773-1990
Sharon Crowley, Contact

★6071★ Rutland County Parent/Child
Center
Project Future
261 N. Church St.
Rutland, VT 05701
Phone: (802)775-9711
Sharon Comstock, Contact

★6072★ Southwest Vermont Adult Basic
Education
Displaced Homemaker Program
128 Merchants Row, Rm. 205
Rutland, VT 05701
Phone: (802)775-0617
Judith Lashof, Contact

St. Albans

★6073★ Bellows Free Academy Area
Vocational Center
Single Parent/Homemakers Project
South Main St.
St. Albans, VT 05478
Phone: (802)527-7576
Bernard O'Keefe, Contact

St. Johnsbury

★6074★ Northeast Kingdom Community
Action
Project Future
13 Cherry St.
St. Johnsbury, VT 05819
Phone: (802)748-8997
Madelyne Wight, Contact

★6075★ St. Johnsbury Academy
Vocational Center
Skill Development for Self-Sufficiency
24 Western Ave.
St. Johnsbury, VT 05819
Phone: (802)748-4744
Sandra Taylor, Contact

★6076★ Umbrella, Inc.
1 Prospect Ave.
St. Johnsbury, VT 05819
Phone: (802)748-8645
Rachel Desilets, Contact

Springfield

★6077★ Springfield Area Vocational
Center
Skills for Independence
Single Parent/Homemakers Project
303 South St.
Springfield, VT 05156
Phone: (802)885-8485
Michele Delhaye, Contact

White River Jct.

★6078★ Hartford Area Vocational Center
Single Parents/Homemaker Project
Saunders Ave.
White River Jct., VT 05001
Phone: (802)295-8630
Charles Reibel, Contact

Virginia

Alberta

★6079★ Southside Virginia Community
College
Vocational Preparation for Single Parents
and Homemakers
Christinna Campus
Rte. 1, Box 60
Alberta, VA 23821
Phone: (804)949-7111
Sheila Wilson, Contact

Alexandria

★6080★ The Campagna Center
418 S. Washington St.
Alexandria, VA 22314
Phone: (703)549-0111
Liz Ward, Contact

Big Stone Gap

★6081★ Mountain Empire Community
College
WINS (Women/Men In Need of Skills)
Drawer 700
Big Stone Gap, VA 24219
Phone: (703)523-2400
Carol Moore, Contact

Charlottesville

★6082★ Piedmont Virginia Community
College
Jobsight Focus
1705 Gordon Ave.
Charlottesville, VA 22903
Phone: (804)295-8336
Joan Velliquette, Contact

Clifton Forge

★6083★ Dabney S. Lancaster Community
College
Single Parent/Displaced Homemaker
Program
PO Box 1000
Clifton Forge, VA 24422-1000
Phone: (703)862-4246
Donna Forbes, Contact

Danville

★6084★ Danville Area Community College
Project Hope
1008 S. Main St.
Danville, VA 24541
Phone: (804)797-3553
Janet Tate, Contact

Dublin

★6085★ New River Community College
Displaced Homemaker Program
Rte. 100, PO Drawer 1127
Dublin, VA 24084
Phone: (703)674-3600
Linda Capone-Claussen, Contact

Emporia

★6086★ Southside Virginia Community
College Campus without Walls
Vocational Preparation Center for Single
Parents and Homemakers
184 Pleasant Shade Dr.
Emporia, VA 23847
Phone: (804)634-5147
Melody L. Moore, Contact

Falls Church

★6087★ Project Update
7510 Lisle Ave.
Falls Church, VA 22043
Phone: (703)506-2225
Jan Clement, Contact

Franklin

★6088★ Paul D. Camp Community College
The Opportunity Center—Vocational
Education for Single Parents and
Homemakers
PO Box 737
Franklin, VA 23851
Phone: (804)562-2171
Fran Flythe, Contact

Glenns

★6089★ Rappahannock Community
College
The Equal Opportunities for Employability
Project
Box 787
Glenns, VA 23149
Phone: (804)758-5324
Reba B. Bolden, Contact

Hampton

★6090★ Thomas Nelson Community
College
Regional Center for Project 2000
PO Box 9407
Hampton, VA 23670
Phone: (804)825-2890
Kay Olinger, Contact

Harrisonburg

★6091★ Career Development Consultants,
Inc.
TAP for Single Heads of
Households/Displaced Homemakers
245 Newman Ave.
Harrisonburg, VA 22801
Phone: (703)434-8579
Suzanne Garrett, Contact

Keysville

★6092★ Southside Virginia Community
College—John H. Daniel Campus
Southside Center for Vocational
Preparation for Single
Parents/Homemakers
Rte. 1, Box 15
Keysville, VA 23947
Phone: (804)736-8484
Kathy Ebbitt, Contact

Locust Grove

★6093★ Germanna Community College
Germanna Regional Center for Single
Parents and Displaced Homemakers
2130 Germanna Hwy.
PO Box 339
Locust Grove, VA 22508
Phone: (703)423-1333
Lisa L. Pauli, Contact

Martinsville

★6094★ Patrick Henry Community College
Center for Single Parent/Displaced
Homemakers
PO Drawer 5311
Martinsville, VA 24115-5311
Phone: (703)638-8777
Karen Lackey, Contact

Middletown

★6095★ Lord Fairfax Community College
Project CARE
PO Box 47
Middletown, VA 22645
Phone: (703)869-1120
Pat Groff, Contact

Norfolk

★6096★ Step Up, Inc.
983 Ingleside Rd., Ste. 2
Norfolk, VA 23502
Phone: (804)461-8525
Sandra Brandt, Contact

★6097★ YWCA of the Tidewater Areas
Women in Transition
253 W. Freemason St.
Norfolk, VA 23510
Phone: (804)625-4248
Kathy Froede, Contact

Richlands

★6098★ Southwest Virginia Community
College
Southwest Virginia Regional Center for
Single Parents/Displaced Homemakers
PO Box SVCC
Richlands, VA 24641
Phone: (703)964-7545
Linnea L. Olson, Contact

Richmond

★6099★ J. Sargeant Reynolds Community
College
Single Parent/Homemaker Center
Downtown Campus
PO Box C-32040
Richmond, VA 23261-2040
Phone: (804)786-1105
Erlene Carter-Dabney, Contact

Springfield

★6100★ Fairfax County Career
Development Center for Women
5501 Backlick Rd., Ste. 110
Springfield, VA 22151
Phone: (703)750-0633
Mary Fairchild, Contact

Suffolk

★6101★ Paul D. Camp Community College
Project ADVANCE
530 E. Pinner St.
Suffolk, VA 23434
Phone: (804)925-2283
Mary Phillips, Contact

Vienna

★6102★ Women's Center of Northern
Virginia
Public Relations Department
133 Park St. NE
Vienna, VA 22180
Phone: (703)281-2657
Virginia Marshall, Contact

Warsaw

★6103★ Rappahannock Community College
The Equal Opportunities for Employability Program
PO Box 318
Warsaw, VA 22572
Phone: (804)333-4024
Robert B. Worthy, Jr., Contact

Wytheville

★6104★ Wytheville Community College
Project NOVA (Non-Traditional Opportunities for Vocational Advancement)
1000 E. Main St.
Wytheville, VA 24382
Phone: (703)288-5541
Linda Mitchem, Contact

Washington

Aberdeen

★6105★ Coastal Action
117 E. 3rd
PO Box 1827
Aberdeen, WA 98520
Phone: (206)633-3316
Paul D. Youmans, Contact

★6106★ Grays Harbor College
Women's Programs
Aberdeen, WA 98520
Phone: (206)532-9020
Diane Murry, Contact

Auburn

★6107★ Green River Community College
Women's Programs
12401 Southeast 320th St.
Auburn, WA 98002
Phone: (206)833-9111
Majd J. Adams, Contact

Bellevue

★6108★ Bellevue Community College
Women's Programs
3000 Landerholm Circle, SE
Rm. A-102
Bellevue, WA 98007
Phone: (206)641-2279
Sutapa Basu, Contact

Bellingham

★6109★ Bellingham Technical College
Displaced Homemaker Program
3028 Lindbergh Ave.
Bellingham, WA 98225
Phone: (206)676-6490
Carole Shanahan, Contact

★6110★ Whatcom Community College
Women's Programs
237 W. Kellogg Rd.
Bellingham, WA 98226
Phone: (206)676-2170
Laurel Kunesh, Contact

Bremerton

★6111★ Kitsap County Job Training Center
Project Transition Adult Training Program
3721 Kitsap Way, Ste. 8
Bremerton, WA 98312
Phone: (206)478-4620
Barbara Davis, Contact

★6112★ Olympic College
Women's Programs
1600 Chester
Bremerton, WA 98310
Phone: (206)478-4798
Dorothy Bristow, Contact

Clarkston

★6113★ Walla-Walla—Clarkston Center
Displaced Homemakers Center
Box 700
Clarkston, WA 99403
Phone: (509)758-3339
Petrova Ashby, Contact

Des Moines

★6114★ Highline Community College
Women's Programs
PO Box 98000
Des Moines, WA 98198
Phone: (206)878-3710
Julie Burr, Contact

Everett

★6115★ Everett Community College
Women's Programs
801 Wetmore Ave.
Everett, WA 98201-1327
Phone: (206)259-7151
Laura Hedges, Contact

Kirkland

★6116★ Lake Washington Vocational Technical Institute
Displaced Homemakers Program
11605 132nd Northeast
Kirkland, WA 98034
Phone: (206)828-5647
Judith Goodman, Contact

Longview

★6117★ Lower Columbia College
Women's Programs
1600 Maple
Longview, WA 98632
Phone: (206)577-2300
Julia Armstrong, Contact

Lynnwood

★6118★ Edmonds Community College
Women's Programs
20000 - 68th Ave. W
Lynnwood, WA 98036
Phone: (206)771-1500
Cheryl Cole, Contact

Moses Lake

★6119★ Big Bend Community College
Women's Programs
28th and Chanute Streets
Moses Lake, WA 98837
Phone: (509)762-5351
Kathy Tracy, Contact

Mt. Vernon

★6120★ Stagit Valley College
Displaced Homemaker Program
2405 E. College Way
Mt. Vernon, WA 98273
Phone: (206)428-1253
Audrey Brainard, Contact

Mountlake Terrace

★6121★ Pathways for Women
6205 222nd St. SW
Mountlake Terrace, WA 98043
Phone: (206)774-9843
Anne Gordon, Contact

Newport

★6122★ Pathways
Displaced Homemaker Program
163 N.E. 11th St.
Newport, WA 97365
Phone: (503)265-3087
Muril Demory, Contact

Olympia

★6123★ YWCA Discovery Program
Displaced Homemaker Program
220 Union Ave. S.E.
Olympia, WA 98501
Phone: (206)352-0593
Pamela Norris, Contact

Pasco

★6124★ Columbia Basin College
Displaced Homemakers Program
2600 N. 20th Ave.
Pasco, WA 99301
Phone: (509)547-0511
Susan Gilbert, Contact

★6125★ Columbia Basin College
Women's Programs
2600 N. 20th
Pasco, WA 99301
Phone: (509)547-0511
Sylvia Schneidmiller, Contact

Port Angeles

★6126★ Peninsula College
Women's Programs
1502 Lauridsen Blvd.
Port Angeles, WA 98362
Phone: (206)452-9277
Diane Johnson, Contact

Seattle

★6127★ North Seattle Community College
Women's Programs
9600 College Way N
Seattle, WA 98103
Phone: (206)527-1249
Nancy Verheyden, Contact

★6128★ Seattle Central Community College
Women's Programs
1701 Broadway
Box 2BE 1140
Seattle, WA 98122
Phone: (206)587-3854
Lexie Evans, Contact

★6129★ Shoreline Community College
Women's Programs
16101 Greenwood Ave. N
Seattle, WA 98133
Phone: (206)546-4606
Dianne Dailey, Contact

★6130★ South Seattle Community College
Women's Programs
6000-16th Ave. S.W.
Seattle, WA 98106
Phone: (206)764-5339
Ginna Seese, Contact

★6131★ Urban League
Displaced Homemaker Program
104-14th St.
Seattle, WA 98122
Phone: (206)461-3792
Casaundra Bradford-Yitref, Contact

★6132★ Widowed Information and
Consultation Services
15407-1st Ave. S., #D
Seattle, WA 98148
Phone: (206)246-6142
Diane Bingham, Contact

Spokane

★6133★ Community Colleges of Spokane
Displaced Homemaker Program
W. 3305 Ft. George Wright Dr.
Mail Stop-3090
Spokane, WA 99204
Phone: (509)533-3756
Brenda Von Branch, Contact

Tacoma

★6134★ Clover Park Technical College
Displaced Homemaker Program
4500 Steilacoom Blvd. SW
Tacoma, WA 98499
Phone: (206)584-7611
John Wilson, Contact

★6135★ Metropolitan Development Council
Displaced Homemaker Program
622 Tacoma Ave. S, Ste. 6
Tacoma, WA 98402
Phone: (206)383-3921
Rose Stidham, Contact

★6136★ Pierce College
Displaced Homemaker Program
9401 Farwest Dr., SW
Tacoma, WA 98498
Phone: (206)964-6500
Mikel Ann Robinson, Contact

★6137★ Tacoma Community College
Women's Programs
5900 S. 12th St.
Tacoma, WA 98465
Phone: (206)566-5018
Tanya Brunke, Contact

★6138★ YWCA Women's Resource Center
Women in Transition Program
405 Broadway
Tacoma, WA 98402
Phone: (206)272-4181
Irene Fruzzetti, Contact

Vancouver

★6139★ Clark College
Women's Programs
1800 E. McLoughlin Blvd.
Vancouver, WA 98663
Phone: (206)694-6521
Terry Woodward, Contact

★6140★ Network
1950 Ft. Vancouver Way
Vancouver, WA 98668
Phone: (206)696-8409
Joyce Smith, Contact

Walla Walla

★6141★ Walla Walla Community College
Women's Programs
500 Tausick Way
Walla Walla, WA 99362
Phone: (509)522-2500
Barbara Colburn, Contact

Wenatchee

★6142★ Wenatchee Valley College
Community Services
1300 - 5th St.
Wenatchee, WA 98801
Phone: (509)664-2558
David Lindelad, Contact

★6143★ Women in Transition
20 Adams St.
PO Box 2051
Wenatchee, WA 98801
Phone: (509)662-0121
Patricia A. Smiths, Contact

Yakima

★6144★ People for People
Reach for Success
PO Box 1665
Yakima, WA 98902
Phone: (509)248-6726
Helen Bradley, Contact

★6145★ Yakima Valley Community
College
Women's Programs
PO Box 1647
Yakima, WA 98907
Phone: (509)575-2915
Mary Kowalsky, Contact

West Virginia

Bluefield

★6146★ Bluefield State College
Displaced Homemaker Program
219 Rock St.
Bluefield, WV 25038
Phone: (304)327-4500
Roger Neil, Contact

Charleston

★6147★ Career Works Associates, Ltd.
1033 Quarrier St.
Charleston, WV 25301
Phone: (304)344-2273
Jacquelin Artz, Contact

★6148★ Women and Employment
601 Delaware Ave.
Charleston, WV 25302
Phone: (304)345-1298
Pam Curray, Contact

Danville

★6149★ Boone County Career Center
Single Parent/Displaced Homemaker
Program
Box 50B
Danville, WV 25053
Phone: (304)369-4585
Rodney Smith, Contact

Eleanor

★6150★ Putnam County Technical Center
Displaced Homemaker Program
PO Box 640
Eleanor, WV 25070-0640
Phone: (304)586-3494
Malinda Legg, Contact

Huntington

★6151★ Cabell County Vocational-
Technical Center
OH NOW
1035 Norway Ave.
Huntington, WV 25705-2897
Phone: (304)528-5108
David Groves, Contact

Keyser

★6152★ Mineral County Vocational-
Technical Center
Displaced Homemakers Program
600 W. Water St.
Keyser, WV 26726-2897
Phone: (304)788-4240
Terry L. Cannon, Contact

Leroy

★6153★ Roane-Jackson Technical Center
Displaced Homemaker Program
4800 Spencer Rd.
Leroy, WV 25252
Phone: (302)372-7335
Dean Fisher, Contact

Martinsburg

★6154★ James Rumsey Technical
Institute
Project Success
Rte. 6, Box 268
Martinsburg, WV 25401
Phone: (304)754-7925
Pauline Custer, Contact

Montgomery

★6155★ West Virginia Institute of
Technology Community and Technical
College
Options for Adult Women
Montgomery, WV 25136
Phone: (304)442-3277
Jan Young, Contact

St. Marys

★6156★ PRT—Pleasants, Ritchie and
Tyler Vocational-Technical Center
Displaced Homemakers Program
PO Box 329
St. Marys, WV 26170-0029
Phone: (304)684-2464
Elizabeth Loughner, Contact

Wheeling

★6157★ West Virginia Northern
Community College
Wider Opportunities for Women
College Square
Wheeling, WV 26003
Phone: (304)233-5900
Bettie Steele, Contact

Wisconsin

Cleveland

★6158★ Lakeshore Technical College
Life Work Planning
1290 North Ave.
Cleveland, WI 53015
Phone: (414)458-4183
Kathy McNellis, Contact

Eau Claire

★6159★ Chippewa Valley Technical
College
**Turnaround: Helping Displaced
Homemakers**
620 W. Clairemont Ave.
Eau Claire, WI 54701
Phone: (715)833-6257
Judy Ristow, Contact

Fennimore

★6160★ Southwest Technical College
Project PIVOT
Bronson Blvd
Fennimore, WI 53809
Phone: (608)822-3262
Jean Holzer, Contact

Fond du Lac

★6161★ Moraine Park Technical College
Women's Reentry Program
235 N. National Ave.
PO Box 1940
Fond du Lac, WI 54935
Phone: (414)922-8611
Joan Visintainer, Contact

Green Bay

★6162★ Northeast Wisconsin Technical
College
Turnaround
2740 W. Mason St.
PO Box 19042
Green Bay, WI 54307
Phone: (414)498-5693
Jean O'Keefe, Contact

Janesville

★6163★ Blackhawk Technical College
**Reentry and Job Development Center for
Displaced Homemakers**
6004 Prire Rd., Co. Trk. G
PO Box 5009
Janesville, WI 53547
Phone: (608)757-7655
Cynthia Bagley, Contact

LaCrosse

★6164★ Western Wisconsin Technical
College
Displaced Homemaker Program
304 N. 6th St.
LaCrosse, WI 54602-0908
Phone: (608)785-9144
Judith Erickson, Contact

Madison

★6165★ Employment Options, Inc.
Forward View
2095 Winnebago St.
Madison, WI 53704
Phone: (608)244-5181
Kathy Schmidt, Contact

★6166★ Madison Area Technical College
Forward View
3550 Anderson St.
Madison, WI 53704
Phone: (608)246-6261
Deb Reichert, Contact

Milwaukee

★6167★ Interfaith Employment Services
Displaced Homemaker Network
1200 E. Capital Dr.
Milwaukee, WI 53211
Phone: (414)963-1200
Elene Speeris, Contact

★6168★ Milwaukee Area Technical
College
Displaced Homemaker Program
700 W. State St.
Milwaukee, WI 53233
Phone: (414)278-6214
Gloria Gonzales, Contact

Pewaukee

★6169★ Waukesha County Technical
College
**Cooperative Employment Services for
Displaced Homemakers**
800 Main St.
Pewaukee, WI 53072
Phone: (414)691-5445
Libby Sellars, Contact

Racine

★6170★ Gateway Technical College
**Wisconsin Displaced Homemakers
Networth**
1001 S. Main St.
Racine, WI 53403
Phone: (414)631-7300
Esta Lewin, Contact

★6171★ Women's Resource Center
PO Box 1764
Racine, WI 53401
Phone: (414)633-3233
Kathy Rippon, Contact

Rhinelander

★6172★ Nicolet Area Technical College
Project Access
PO Box 518
Rhinelander, WI 54501
Phone: (715)369-4478
Teresa Mayfield Nitzel, Contact

Shell Lake

★6173★ Wisconsin Indianhead Technical
College
New Perspectives
505 Pine Ridge Dr.
PO Box 452, HC 69 Box 10B
Shell Lake, WI 54871
Phone: (715)468-2815
Claudeen Hepburn-Oebser, Contact

Waukesha

★6174★ The Women's Center, Inc.
726 N. East Ave.
Waukesha, WI 53186
Phone: (414)547-4600
Jane DeGeorge, Contact

Wausau

★6175★ Northcentral Technical College
**Northcentral Wisconsin Displaced
Homemaker Program**
1000 Campus Dr.
Wausau, WI 54401
Phone: (715)675-3331
Judy Foster, Contact

★6176★ The Women's Community, Inc.
329 4th St.
PO Box 6215
Wausau, WI 54402-6215
Phone: (715)842-5663
Gail Wirsbenski, Contact

Wisconsin Rapids

★6177★ Mid-State Technical College
Turn Around/New Challenges
500 32nd St. N
Wisconsin Rapids, WI 54494
Phone: (715)422-5450
Deb McDonald, Contact

Wyoming

Casper

★6178★ Casper College
**Project for Single Parents and
Homemakers in Transition**
125 College Dr.
Casper, WY 82601
Phone: (307)268-2696
Barbara Ochiltree, Contact

Cheyenne

★6179★ Laramie County Community
College
**Displaced Homemakers/Single Parent
Program**
1400 E. College Dr.
Cheyenne, WY 82007
Phone: (307)778-5222
Terri Fiorilli, Contact

Powell

★6180★ **Northwest Community College**
Single Parent/Displaced Homemaker
 Program
231 W. 6th St.
Powell, WY 82435
Phone: (307)754-6111
Carolyn McIntyre, Contact

Rawlins

★6181★ **Carbon County Agricultural**
 Extension Service
Displaced Homemaker Program
PO Box 280
Rawlins, WY 82301
Phone: (307)328-2642
Ceil Miner, Contact

Riverton

★6182★ **Central Wyoming College**
Single Parent/Homemaker Project
2660 Peck Ave.
Riverton, WY 82501
Phone: (307)856-9291
Mohamed Waheed, Contact

Rock Springs

★6183★ **Western Wyoming College**
Women's Center
PO Box 428
Rock Springs, WY 82901
Phone: (307)382-2121
Gayle Yamasaki, Contact

★6184★ **YWCA of Sweetwater County**
Transitional Services
PO Box 1667
Rock Springs, WY 82902
Phone: (307)362-7923
Joanna Johnson, Contact

Sheridan

★6185★ **Sheridan College**
Transitional Support Services for Single
 Parent/Displaced Homemakers
PO Box 1500
Sheridan, WY 82801
Phone: (307)674-6446
Tena Hanes, Contact

Torrington

★6186★ **Eastern Wyoming College**
Re-Entry Program
PO Box 428
Torrington, WY 82240
Phone: (307)532-7111
Ann Gardetto, Contact

Wheatland

★6187★ **Project Safe**
Single Parent/Homemaker Project
PO Box 1078
Wheatland, WY 82201
Phone: (307)322-4794
Vonnie Elliott, Contact

★6188★ **Wheatland Career Center**
Displaced Homemakers Program
1950 South St.
Wheatland, WY 82201
Phone: (307)322-2063
Phyllis Hale, Contact

(5) Family Planning Services

Entries in this chapter are arranged alphabetically by state and city, then alphabetically by organization name within city. See the User's Guide at the front of this directory for additional information.

Alabama

Birmingham

★6189★ **Planned Parenthood of Alabama**
1211 27th Pl., S.
Birmingham, AL 35205
Phone: (205)322-0111

Alaska

Anchorage

★6190★ **Planned Parenthood of Alaska**
1008 W. Northern Lights Blvd.
Anchorage, AK 99503
Phone: (907)563-2229

Arizona

Phoenix

★6191★ **Planned Parenthood of Central and Northern Arizona**
5651 N. 7th St.
Phoenix, AZ 85014
Phone: (602)277-7526

Tucson

★6192★ **Planned Parenthood of Southern Arizona**
127 S. 5th Ave.
Tucson, AZ 85701
Phone: (602)628-7201

Arkansas

Little Rock

★6193★ **Planned Parenthood of Greater Arkansas**
5512 W. Markham
Little Rock, AR 72205
Phone: (501)666-7526

California

Eureka

★6194★ **Six Rivers Planned Parenthood**
2316 Harrison Ave.
Eureka, CA 95501
Phone: (707)442-2961

Fresno

★6195★ **Planned Parenthood of Central California**
255 N. Fulton, Ste. 106
Fresno, CA 93701
Phone: (209)486-2647

Los Angeles

★6196★ **Planned Parenthood/World Population Los Angeles**
1920 Marengo St.
Los Angeles, CA 90033
Phone: (213)223-4462

Monterey

★6197★ **Planned Parenthood of Monterey County**
5 Via Joaquin
Monterey, CA 93940
Phone: (408)373-1709

Pasadena

★6198★ **Pasadena Planned Parenthood Committee**
1045 N. Lake Ave.
Pasadena, CA 91104
Phone: (818)794-5679

Sacramento

★6199★ **Planned Parenthood of Sacramento Valley**
501 S St., Ste. 3
Sacramento, CA 95814
Phone: (916)446-5037

San Diego

★6200★ **Planned Parenthood of San Diego and Riverside Counties**
2100 5th Ave.
San Diego, CA 92101
Phone: (619)231-6760

San Francisco

★6201★ **Planned Parenthood of Alameda/San Francisco**
815 Eddy St., Ste. 300
San Francisco, CA 94109
Phone: (415)441-7858

★6202★ **Planned Parenthood Federation of America**
Western Region Office
333 Broadway, 3rd Fl.
San Francisco, CA 94133
Phone: (415)956-8856
Territory Includes: AK, AZ, CA, CO, HI, ID, MT, NV, NM, ND, OR, SD, UT, WA, and WY.

San Jose

★6203★ **Planned Parenthood Association of Santa Clara County**
1691 The Alameda
San Jose, CA 95126
Phone: (408)287-7532

San Mateo

★6204★ **Planned Parenthood of San Mateo County**
2211-2215 Palm Ave.
San Mateo, CA 94403-1857
Phone: (415)574-5823

San Rafael

★6205★ **Planned Parenthood of Marin, Sonoma, and Mendocino**
20 H St.
San Rafael, CA 94901
Phone: (415)454-0476

Santa Ana

★6206★ **Planned Parenthood of Orange and San Bernardino Counties**
1801 N. Broadway
Santa Ana, CA 92706
Phone: (714)973-1733

Santa Barbara

★6207★ **Planned Parenthood of Santa Barbara, Ventura, and San Luis Obispo Counties**
518 Garden St.
Santa Barbara, CA 93101
Phone: (805)963-2445

Santa Cruz

★6208★ **Planned Parenthood of Santa Cruz County**
212 Laurel St.
Santa Cruz, CA 95060
Phone: (408)425-1551

Stockton

★6209★ **Planned Parenthood of San Joaquin Valley**
19 N. Pilgrim St.
Stockton, CA 95205
Phone: (209)466-9220

Walnut Creek

★6210★ **Planned Parenthood of Shasta/Diablo**
1291 Oakland Blvd.
Walnut Creek, CA 94596
Phone: (415)935-4066

Colorado

Aurora

★6211★ **Planned Parenthood of the Rocky Mountains**
1537 Alton St.
Aurora, CO 80010
Phone: (303)360-0006

Connecticut

New Haven

★6212★ **Planned Parenthood of Connecticut**
129 Whitney Ave.
New Haven, CT 06510
Phone: (203)865-5158

Delaware

Wilmington

★6213★ **Planned Parenthood of Delaware**
625 Shipley St.
Wilmington, DE 19801
Phone: (302)655-7293

District of Columbia

Washington

★6214★ **Planned Parenthood of Metropolitan Washington, DC**
1108 16th St., NW
Washington, DC 20036
Phone: (202)347-8500

Florida

Boca Raton

★6215★ **Planned Parenthood of South Palm Beach and Broward Counties**
455 NW 35th St.
Boca Raton, FL 33431
Phone: (407)394-3540

Gainesville

★6216★ **Planned Parenthood of North Central Florida**
914 NW 13th St.
Gainesville, FL 32601
Phone: (904)377-0856

Jacksonville

★6217★ **Planned Parenthood of Northeast Florida**
603 N. Market St.
Jacksonville, FL 32202
Phone: (904)358-2244

Lakeland

★6218★ **Planned Parenthood of Central Florida**
PO Box 1482
Lakeland, FL 33802
Phone: (813)665-4422

Miami

★6219★ **Planned Parenthood Association of Greater Miami**
11632 N. Kendall Dr.
Miami, FL 33176
Phone: (305)595-1213

Sarasota

★6220★ **Planned Parenthood of Southwest Florida**
1958 Prospect St.
Sarasota, FL 34239
Phone: (813)365-3913

Tallahassee

★6221★ **Planned Parenthood of Tallahassee**
1315-B E. Lafayette St.
Tallahassee, FL 32301
Phone: (904)656-7799

West Palm Beach

★6222★ **Planned Parenthood of the Palm Beach Area**
5312 Broadway
West Palm Beach, FL 33407
Phone: (407)848-6402

Georgia

Atlanta

★6223★ **Planned Parenthood Association of the Atlanta Area**
100 Edgewood Ave., NE, Ste. 1604
Atlanta, GA 30303
Phone: (404)688-9300

★6224★ **Planned Parenthood Federation of America**
Southern Region Office
3340 Peachtree Rd., NE, Rm. 1620
Atlanta, GA 30326
Phone: (404)262-1128
Territory Includes: AL, AR, FL, GA, KY, LA, MS, NC, OK, SC, TN, TX, and VA.

Augusta

★6225★ **Planned Parenthood of East Central Georgia**
1289 Broad St.
Augusta, GA 30901
Phone: (404)724-5557

Hawaii

Honolulu

★6226★ **Hawaii Planned Parenthood**
1441 Kapiolani Blvd., Ste. 1400
Honolulu, HI 96813
Phone: (808)944-1591

Idaho

Boise

★6227★ **Planned Parenthood Association of Idaho**
4301 Franklin Rd.
Boise, ID 83705
Phone: (208)345-0839

Illinois

Bloomington

★6228★ **Planned Parenthood of Mid-Central Illinois**
318 W. Washington St., 3rd Fl.
Bloomington, IL 61701
Phone: (309)827-4368

Champaign

★6229★ **Planned Parenthood Association of Champaign County**
314 S. Neil St.
Champaign, IL 61820
Phone: (217)359-8022

Chicago

★6230★ **Planned Parenthood Association of the Chicago Area**
17 N. State St., 15th Fl.
Chicago, IL 60602
Phone: (312)781-9550

Decatur

★6231★ **Planned Parenthood of Decatur**
3201 N. Oakland Ave.
Decatur, IL 62526
Phone: (217)877-6474

Oak Brook

★6232★ **Planned Parenthood Federation of America**
Northern Region Office
635 Butterfield Rd., Ste. 120
Oak Brook, IL 60181
Phone: (708)627-9270
Territory Includes: CT, DE, DC, IL, IN, IA, KS, ME, MD, MA, MI, MN, MO, NE, NH, NJ, NY, OH, PA, RI, VT, WV, and WI.

Peoria

★6233★ Planned Parenthood Association of the Greater Peoria Area
705 NE Jefferson St.
Peoria, IL 61603
Phone: (309)673-0907

Springfield

★6234★ Planned Parenthood of the Springfield Area
1000 E. Washington St.
Springfield, IL 62703
Phone: (217)544-7050

Indiana

Bloomington

★6235★ Planned Parenthood of Southern Indiana
421 S. College Ave.
Bloomington, IN 47401
Phone: (812)336-7050

Evansville

★6236★ Planned Parenthood of Southwestern Indiana
971 Kenmore Dr.
Evansville, IN 47715
Phone: (812)473-8800

Indianapolis

★6237★ Planned Parenthood of Central Indiana
3209 N. Meridian St.
Indianapolis, IN 46208
Phone: (317)926-4662

Lafayette

★6238★ Tecumseh Area Planned Parenthood Association
1016 E. Main
Lafayette, IN 47902
Phone: (317)742-7281

Merrillville

★6239★ Planned Parenthood of Northwest/Northeast Indiana
8645 Connecticut
Merrillville, IN 46410
Phone: (219)769-3500

Muncie

★6240★ Planned Parenthood of East Central Indiana
110 N. Cherry St. at W. Main
Muncie, IN 47305
Phone: (317)282-3546

South Bend

★6241★ Planned Parenthood of North Central Indiana
201 S. Chapin St.
South Bend, IN 46625
Phone: (219)289-7062

Iowa

Burlington

★6242★ Planned Parenthood of Southeast Iowa
403 Tama Bldg.
Burlington, IA 52601
Phone: (319)753-6209

Cedar Rapids

★6243★ Planned Parenthood of Linn County
1500 2nd Ave., SE, Ste. 100
Cedar Rapids, IA 52403
Phone: (319)363-8572

Des Moines

★6244★ Planned Parenthood of Mid-Iowa
PO Box 4557
Des Moines, IA 50306
Phone: (515)280-7000

Sioux City

★6245★ Planned Parenthood Committee of Sioux City
4700 Gordon Dr.
Sioux City, IA 51106
Phone: (712)276-6292

Kansas

Wichita

★6246★ Planned Parenthood of Kansas
2226 E. Central
Wichita, KS 67214
Phone: (316)263-7575

Kentucky

Berea

★6247★ Mountain Maternal Health League Planned Parenthood
122 Main St.
Berea, KY 40403
Phone: (606)986-2326

Lexington

★6248★ Lexington Planned Parenthood Center
508 W. 2nd St.
Lexington, KY 40508
Phone: (606)252-8494

Louisville

★6249★ Planned Parenthood of Louisville
1023 S. 2nd St.
Louisville, KY 40203
Phone: (502)584-2471

Louisiana

New Orleans

★6250★ Planned Parenthood of Louisiana
4018 Magazine St.
New Orleans, LA 70115
Phone: (504)891-8013

Maryland

Baltimore

★6251★ Planned Parenthood Association of Maryland
610 N. Howard St.
Baltimore, MD 21201
Phone: (301)576-1400

Massachusetts

Cambridge

★6252★ Planned Parenthood League of Massachusetts
99 Bishop Richard Allen Dr.
Cambridge, MA 02139
Phone: (617)492-0519

Michigan

Ann Arbor

★6253★ Planned Parenthood of Mid-Michigan
3100 Professional Dr.
Ann Arbor, MI 48106
Phone: (313)973-0710

Benton Harbor

★6254★ Planned Parenthood Association of Southwestern Michigan
785 Pipestone Rd.
Benton Harbor, MI 49022
Phone: (616)925-1306

Detroit

★6255★ Planned Parenthood League of Detroit
1249 Washington Blvd., Ste. 1900
Detroit, MI 48226
Phone: (313)963-2870

Flint

★6256★ Flint Community Planned Parenthood Association
310 E. 3rd St.
Flint, MI 48503
Phone: (313)234-1659

Grand Rapids

★6257★ Planned Parenthood Centers of West Michigan
425 Cherry, SE
Grand Rapids, MI 49503
Phone: (616)774-7005

Kalamazoo

★6258★ Reproductive Health Care Center of South Central Michigan
4201 W. Michigan Ave.
Kalamazoo, MI 49007
Phone: (616)372-1205

Marquette

★6259★ Marquette/Alger Planned Parenthood
228 W. Washington
Marquette, MI 49855
Phone: (906)225-5070

Petoskey

★6260★ Northern Michigan Planned Parenthood Association
820 Arlington
Petoskey, MI 49770
Phone: (616)347-9692

Minnesota

St. Paul

★6261★ Planned Parenthood of Minnesota
1965 Ford Pkwy.
St. Paul, MN 55116
Phone: (612)698-2401

Mississippi

Hattiesburg

★6262★ Planned Parenthood of Mississippi
PO Box 893
Hattiesburg, MS 39403
Phone: (601)545-9264

Missouri

Columbia

★6263★ Planned Parenthood of Central Missouri
711 N. Providence Rd.
Columbia, MO 65203
Phone: (314)449-2475

Kansas City

★6264★ Planned Parenthood of Greater Kansas City
1001 E. 47th St.
Kansas City, MO 64110
Phone: (816)756-2277

Kirksville

★6265★ Planned Parenthood of Northeast Missouri
PO Box 763
Kirksville, MO 63501
Phone: (816)665-5672

Rolla

★6266★ Planned Parenthood of the Central Ozarks
1032-B Kings Hwy.
Rolla, MO 65401
Phone: (314)364-1509

St. Louis

★6267★ Planned Parenthood of the St. Louis Region
7415 Manchester
St. Louis, MO 63143
Phone: (314)781-3800

Montana

Billings

★6268★ Intermountain Planned Parenthood
721 N. 29th St.
Billings, MT 59101
Phone: (406)248-3636

Missoula

★6269★ Planned Parenthood of Missoula
219 E. Main
Missoula, MT 59802
Phone: (406)728-5490

Nebraska

Lincoln

★6270★ Planned Parenthood of Lincoln
2246 O St.
Lincoln, NE 68510
Phone: (402)476-7521

Omaha

★6271★ Planned Parenthood of Omaha/Council Bluffs
4610 Dodge St.
Omaha, NE 68132
Phone: (402)554-1045

Nevada

Las Vegas

★6272★ Planned Parenthood of Southern Nevada
3220 W. Charleston Blvd.
Las Vegas, NV 89102
Phone: (702)878-3622

Reno

★6273★ Planned Parenthood of Northern Nevada
455 W. 5th St.
Reno, NV 89503
Phone: (702)329-1781

New Jersey

Camden

★6274★ Planned Parenthood of the Greater Camden Area
590 Benson St.
Camden, NJ 08103
Phone: (609)365-3519

Morristown

★6275★ Planned Parenthood of Greater Northern New Jersey
196 Speedwell Ave.
Morristown, NJ 07960
Phone: (201)539-9580

New Brunswick

★6276★ Planned Parenthood League of Middlesex County
211 Livingston Ave., 2nd Fl.
New Brunswick, NJ 08901
Phone: (201)246-2411

Newark

★6277★ Planned Parenthood of Essex County
151 Washington St.
Newark, NJ 07102
Phone: (201)622-3900

Paterson

★6278★ Passaic County Committee for Planned Parenthood
171-175 Market St.
Paterson, NJ 07505
Phone: (201)345-3883

Shrewsbury

★6279★ Planned Parenthood of Monmouth County
69 E. Newman Springs Rd.
PO Box 95
Shrewsbury, NJ 07701
Phone: (201)842-9300

Trenton

★6280★ Planned Parenthood Association of the Mercer Area
437 E. State St.
Trenton, NJ 08608
Phone: (609)599-3736

New Mexico

Albuquerque

★6281★ Rio Grande Planned Parenthood
203 Hermosa, NE
Albuquerque, NM 87108
Phone: (505)265-5976

Las Cruces

★6282★ Planned Parenthood of Southern New Mexico
1882 S. Espina
Las Cruces, NM 88001
Phone: (505)524-4471

New York

Albany

★6283★ Upper Hudson Planned Parenthood
259 Lark St.
Albany, NY 12210
Phone: (518)434-4979

Binghamton

★6284★ Planned Parenthood of Broome and Chenango Counties
168 Water St.
Binghamton, NY 13901
Phone: (607)723-9692

Buffalo

★6285★ Planned Parenthood of Buffalo and Erie County
210 Franklin St.
Buffalo, NY 14202
Phone: (716)853-1779

Commack

★6286★ Planned Parenthood of Suffolk County
6500 Jericho Tpke.
Commack, NY 11725
Phone: (516)462-6214

Elmira

★6287★ Planned Parenthood of the Southern Tier
200 E. Market St.
Elmira, NY 14901
Phone: (607)734-3921

Geneva

★6288★ Planned Parenthood of the Finger Lakes
601 W. Washington St.
Geneva, NY 14456
Phone: (315)781-1749

Ithaca

★6289★ Planned Parenthood of Tompkins County
314 W. State St.
Ithaca, NY 14850
Phone: (607)273-1526

Mineola

★6290★ Planned Parenthood of Nassau County
107 Mineola Blvd.
Mineola, NY 11501
Phone: (516)248-6357

New York

★6291★ Planned Parenthood of New York City
380 2nd Ave., 3rd Fl.
New York, NY 10010
Phone: (212)777-2002

Newburgh

★6292★ Planned Parenthood of Orange/Sullivan
91 DuBois St.
Newburgh, NY 12550
Phone: (914)562-5748

Niagara Falls

★6293★ Planned Parenthood of Niagara County
The Haeberle Plaza
Niagara Falls, NY 14301
Phone: (716)282-2501

Oneonta

★6294★ Planned Parenthood Association of Delaware and Otsego Counties
48 Market St.
Oneonta, NY 13820
Phone: (607)432-2252

Plattsburgh

★6295★ Northern Adirondack Planned Parenthood
66 Brinkerhoff St.
Plattsburgh, NY 12901
Phone: (518)561-4430

Poughkeepsie

★6296★ Planned Parenthood of Dutchess/Ulster
178 Church St.
Poughkeepsie, NY 12601
Phone: (914)471-1530

Rochester

★6297★ Planned Parenthood of Rochester and Genesee Valley
114 University Ave.
Rochester, NY 14605
Phone: (716)546-2595

Schenectady

★6298★ Planned Parenthood Health Services of Northeastern New York
414 Union St.
Schenectady, NY 12305
Phone: (518)374-5353

Syracuse

★6299★ Planned Parenthood Center of Syracuse
1120 E. Genesee St.
Syracuse, NY 13210
Phone: (315)475-5532

Utica

★6300★ Planned Parenthood Association of the Mohawk Valley
1424 Genesee St.
Utica, NY 13502
Phone: (315)724-6146

Watertown

★6301★ Planned Parenthood of Northern New York
220 Sherman St., 2nd Fl.
Watertown, NY 13601
Phone: (315)782-1818

White Plains

★6302★ Planned Parenthood of Westchester and Rockland Counties
175 Tarrytown Rd.
White Plains, NY 10607
Phone: (914)428-7876

North Carolina

Chapel Hill

★6303★ Planned Parenthood of Orange County
93 Elliott Rd.
Chapel Hill, NC 27515-3258
Phone: (919)929-5402

Charlotte

★6304★ Planned Parenthood of Greater Charlotte
700 E. Stonewall St., Ste. 430
Charlotte, NC 28202
Phone: (704)377-0841

Raleigh

★6305★ Planned Parenthood of Greater Raleigh
Bryan Bldg., Ste. 233
Raleigh, NC 27605
Phone: (919)833-7534

Winston-Salem

★6306★ Planned Parenthood of the Triad
939 Burke St.
Winston-Salem, NC 27101
Phone: (919)761-1058

Ohio

Akron

★6307★ Planned Parenthood of Summit, Portage and Medina Counties
34 S. High St.
Akron, OH 44308-1805
Phone: (216)535-2674

Athens

★6308★ Planned Parenthood of Southeast Ohio
396 Richland Ave.
Athens, OH 45701
Phone: (614)593-3375

Canton

★6309★ Planned Parenthood of Stark County
626 Walnut Ave., NE
Canton, OH 44702
Phone: (216)456-7191

Cincinnati

★6310★ Planned Parenthood Association of Cincinnati
2314 Auburn Ave.
Cincinnati, OH 45219
Phone: (513)721-7635

Cleveland

★6311★ Planned Parenthood of Greater Cleveland
3135 Euclid, Ste. 102
Cleveland, OH 44115
Phone: (216)881-7742

Columbus

**★6312★ Planned Parenthood of Central
Ohio**
206 E. State St.
Columbus, OH 43215
Phone: (614)224-2235

Dayton

**★6313★ Planned Parenthood Association
of Miami Valley**
224 N. Wilkinson St.
Dayton, OH 45402
Phone: (513)226-0780

Hamilton

**★6314★ Planned Parenthood Association
of Butler County**
11 Ludlow St.
Hamilton, OH 45011
Phone: (513)856-8335

Mansfield

**★6315★ Planned Parenthood of North
Central Ohio**
35 N. Park St.
Mansfield, OH 44902
Phone: (419)525-3075

Newark

**★6316★ Planned Parenthood Association
of East Central Ohio**
843 N. 21st St.
Newark, OH 43055
Phone: (614)366-3377

Springfield

**★6317★ Planned Parenthood of West
Central Ohio**
Arcue Bldg.
Springfield, OH 45502
Phone: (513)325-6416

Toledo

**★6318★ Planned Parenthood of Northwest
Ohio**
1301 Jefferson
Toledo, OH 43624
Phone: (419)255-1123

Youngstown

**★6319★ Planned Parenthood of Mahoning
Valley**
77 E. Midlothian Blvd.
Youngstown, OH 44507
Phone: (216)788-6506

Oklahoma

Oklahoma City

**★6320★ Planned Parenthood of Central
Oklahoma**
619 NW 23rd St.
Oklahoma City, OK 73103
Phone: (405)528-0221

Tulsa

**★6321★ Planned Parenthood of Eastern
Oklahoma and Western Arkansas**
1007 S. Peoria
Tulsa, OK 74120
Phone: (918)587-7674

Oregon

Eugene

**★6322★ Planned Parenthood Association
of Lane County**
134 E. 13th Ave.
Eugene, OR 97401
Phone: (503)344-2632

Medford

**★6323★ Planned Parenthood of Southern
Oregon**
650 Royal Ave., Ste. 18
Medford, OR 97504
Phone: (503)773-8285

Portland

**★6324★ Planned Parenthood of
Columbia/Willamette**
3231 SE 50th
Portland, OR 97206
Phone: (503)775-4931

Pennsylvania

Bristol

**★6325★ Planned Parenthood Association
of Bucks County**
721 New Rodgers Rd.
Bristol, PA 19007
Phone: (215)785-4591

Harrisburg

**★6326★ Planned Parenthood of the
Capitol Region**
1514 N. 2nd St.
Harrisburg, PA 17102
Phone: (717)234-2479

Lancaster

**★6327★ Planned Parenthood of Lancaster
County**
31 S. Lime St.
Lancaster, PA 17602
Phone: (717)299-2891

Philadelphia

**★6328★ Planned Parenthood Association
of Southeastern Pennsylvania**
1144 Locust St.
Philadelphia, PA 19107
Phone: (215)351-5500

Pittsburgh

**★6329★ Planned Parenthood of Western
Pennsylvania**
209 9th St., Ste. 400
Pittsburgh, PA 15222
Phone: (412)434-8958

Trexlertown

**★6330★ Planned Parenthood of North
East Pennsylvania**
Trexler Mall
Trexlertown, PA 18087
Phone: (215)481-0481

West Chester

**★6331★ Planned Parenthood of Chester
County**
8 S. Wayne St.
West Chester, PA 19382
Phone: (215)436-8645

York

**★6332★ Planned Parenthood of Central
Pennsylvania**
728 S. Beaver St.
York, PA 17403
Phone: (717)845-9681

Rhode Island

Providence

**★6333★ Planned Parenthood of Rhode
Island**
111 Point St.
Providence, RI 02903
Phone: (401)421-7820

South Carolina

Columbia

**★6334★ Planned Parenthood of Central
South Carolina**
2712 Middleburg Dr., Ste. 106
Columbia, SC 29204
Phone: (803)256-4908

Hilton Head

**★6335★ Planned Parenthood of the Low
Country**
PO Box 22329
Hilton Head, SC 29925
Phone: (803)681-7774

Tennessee

Memphis

★6336★ Memphis Planned Parenthood
1407 Union Ave.
Memphis, TN 38104
Phone: (901)725-1717

Nashville

**★6337★ Planned Parenthood Association
of Nashville**
University Plaza
112 21st Ave., S., 3rd Fl.
Nashville, TN 37203
Phone: (615)327-1095

Oak Ridge

★6338★ Planned Parenthood of East Tennessee
162 Ridgeway Center
Oak Ridge, TN 37830
Phone: (615)482-3406

Texas

Amarillo

★6339★ Panhandle Planned Parenthood Association
604 W. 8th St.
Amarillo, TX 79101
Phone: (806)372-8731

Austin

★6340★ Planned Parenthood Center of Austin
1209 Rosewood Ave.
Austin, TX 78702
Phone: (512)472-0868

Brownsville

★6341★ Planned Parenthood of Cameron and Willacy Counties
370 Old Port Isabel Rd.
Brownsville, TX 78521
Phone: (512)546-4572

Corpus Christi

★6342★ Planned Parenthood of South Texas
3536 Holly Rd.
Corpus Christi, TX 78415
Phone: (512)855-9107

Dallas

★6343★ Planned Parenthood of Dallas and Northeast Texas
7515 Greenville Ave., Ste. 707
Dallas, TX 75231
Phone: (214)363-2004

El Paso

★6344★ Planned Parenthood Center of El Paso
2817 E. Yandell
El Paso, TX 79903
Phone: (915)566-1613

Ft. Worth

★6345★ Planned Parenthood of North Texas
155 Merrimac Circle, Ste. 200
Ft. Worth, TX 76107
Phone: (817)332-7966

Houston

★6346★ Planned Parenthood of Houston and Southeast Texas
3601 Fannin
Houston, TX 77004
Phone: (713)522-6240

Lubbock

★6347★ Planned Parenthood Association of Lubbock
3821 22nd St.
Lubbock, TX 79413
Phone: (806)795-7123

McAllen

★6348★ Planned Parenthood Association of Hidalgo County
1017 Pecan
McAllen, TX 78501
Phone: (512)686-0585

Odessa

★6349★ Planned Parenthood of West Texas
910-B S. Grant St.
Odessa, TX 79761
Phone: (915)333-4133

San Antonio

★6350★ Planned Parenthood Center of San Antonio
104 Babcock Rd., Ste. A
San Antonio, TX 78201
Phone: (512)736-2244

Waco

★6351★ Planned Parenthood of Central Texas
1121 Ross Ave.
Waco, TX 76703
Phone: (817)754-2391

Utah

Salt Lake City

★6352★ Planned Parenthood Association of Utah
654 South 900 East
Salt Lake City, UT 84102
Phone: (801)532-1586

Vermont

Burlington

★6353★ Planned Parenthood of Northern New England
23 Mansfield Ave.
Burlington, VT 05401
Phone: (802)862-9637

Virginia

Hampton

★6354★ Planned Parenthood of Southeastern Virginia
1520 Aberdeen Rd., Rm. 101
Hampton, VA 23666
Phone: (804)826-2198

Richmond

★6355★ Virginia League for Planned Parenthood
517 W. Grace St.
Richmond, VA 23220
Phone: (804)788-6742

Roanoke

★6356★ Planned Parenthood of Southwest Virginia
2708 Liberty Rd., NW
Roanoke, VA 24012
Phone: (703)362-3968

Washington

Bellingham

★6357★ Mt. Baker Planned Parenthood
1800 C St., Ste. C-6
Bellingham, WA 98225
Phone: (206)734-9007

Everett

★6358★ Planned Parenthood of Snohomish County
32nd and Hoyt
PO Box 1051
Everett, WA 98206-1051
Phone: (206)339-3392

Seattle

★6359★ Planned Parenthood of Seattle/King County
2211 E. Madison
Seattle, WA 98112
Phone: (206)328-7734

Spokane

★6360★ Planned Parenthood of Spokane and Whitman Counties
PO Box 9460
Spokane, WA 99209-9460
Phone: (509)326-2142

Tacoma

★6361★ Planned Parenthood of Pierce County
813 S. K St., Ste. 200
Tacoma, WA 98405
Phone: (206)572-4321

Walla Walla

★6362★ Planned Parenthood Center of Walla Walla
136 E. Birch St.
Walla Walla, WA 99362
Phone: (509)529-3570

Yakima

★6363★ Planned Parenthood of Central Washington
208 N. 3rd Ave.
Yakima, WA 98902
Phone: (509)248-3628

West Virginia

Vienna

★6364★ **Planned Parenthood of the Rocky Mountains**
1100 9th St., Bldg. I
Vienna, WV 26105
Phone: (304)295-3331

Wisconsin

Milwaukee

★6365★ **Planned Parenthood of Wisconsin**
744 N. 4th St., Ste. 444
Milwaukee, WI 53203
Phone: (414)271-8045

(6) Women's Centers

Entries in this chapter are arranged alphabetically be state and city, then by organization name within city. See the User's Guide at the front of this directory for additional information.

Alabama

Enterprise

★6366★ Enterprise State Junior College
Women's Center
Continuing Education
PO Box 1300
600 Plaza Dr.
Enterprise, AL 36331
Phone: (205)347-2623
Fax: (205)347-2623
Mary D. Bauer, Contact

Alaska

Anchorage

★6367★ Alaska Pacific University
Women's Resource Center
4101 University Dr.
Anchorage, AK 99508
Phone: (907)564-8241
Fax: (907)562-4276
Diana Caldwell, Contact

★6368★ University of Alaska
Center for Women and Men
3211 Providence Dr., K-106
Anchorage, AK 99508
Phone: (907)786-1060
Holly Sample, Contact

Arizona

Mesa

★6369★ Mesa Community College
Mesa Community College Re-Entry Center
1833 W. Southern Ave.
Mesa, AZ 85702
Phone: (602)461-7430
Carolyn O'Connor, Contact

Tucson

★6370★ University of Arizona
Associated Studies of the University of
Arizona
Student Union
Tucson, AZ 85721
Phone: (602)621-3919
Carrie Adams, Contact

California

Alameda

★6371★ College of Alameda
Women's Resource Center
555 Atlantic Blvd.
Alameda, CA 94501
Phone: (415)748-2208
Fax: (415)769-6019
Ruth Phillips, Contact

Aptos

★6372★ Cabrillo College
Women's Center
6500 Soquel Dr.
Aptos, CA 95003
Phone: (408)479-6249
Maxine R. White, Contact

Arcta

★6373★ Humboldt State University
Women's Center
House 55
Arcta, CA 95521
Phone: (707)826-4216
Karen Foss, Contact

Berkeley

★6374★ Graduate Theological Union
Center for Women and Religion
2400 Ridge Rd.
Berkeley, CA 94709
Phone: (415)649-2400
Mary Cross, Contact

★6375★ University of California, Berkeley
Women's Resource Center
Bldg. T-9
Berkeley, CA 94720
Phone: (415)642-4786
Alice Jordan, Contact

★6376★ Vista Community College
Gender Equity Program
2020 Milvia St.
Berkeley, CA 94704
Phone: (415)841-8431
Lin Davis, Contact

Carson

★6377★ California State University,
Dominguez Hills
Women's Center
100 E. Victoria St.
Carson, CA 90747
Phone: (213)516-3759
Elizabeth Cook, Contact

Chico

★6378★ California State University, Chico
Educational Support Programs for Women
ESPW-755
Chico, CA 95929
Phone: (916)895-5724
Cindy Peterson, Contact

Claremont

★6379★ Pitzer College
Women's Center
1050 N. Mills Ave.
Claremont, CA 91711
Phone: (714)621-8000
Mychal Rosenbaum, Contact

★6380★ Pomona College
Women's Union
Walker Hall
Claremont, CA 91711
Phone: (714)621-8000
Toni Clark, Contact

★6381★ Scripps College
Women's Resource Center
Dean of Students Office
Claremont, CA 91711
Phone: (714)621-8000
Sally Law, Contact

Culver City

★6382★ West Los Angeles College
Center for New Options
4800 Freshman Dr.
Culver City, CA 90004
Phone: (213)836-7110
Victoria Van Tameley-Hall, Contact

Fullerton

**★6383★ California State University,
Fullerton
Women's Center**
MH-33
Fullerton, CA 92634
Phone: (714)773-2594
Fax: (714)449-7090
Barbara McDowell, Contact

Irvine

**★6384★ University of California, Irvine
Women's Center**
Irvine, CA 92717
Phone: (714)856-6000
Fax: (714)856-6685
Paula Goldsmid, Contact

La Jolla

**★6385★ University of California, San
Diego
Women's Resource Center**
Price Center
La Jolla, CA 92075
Phone: (619)534-2023

Long Beach

**★6386★ California State University, Long
Beach
Women's Resource Center**
RM LA3-105
1250 Bellflower Blvd.
Long Beach, CA 90840
Phone: (213)985-5466
Jean Caveness, Contact

Los Angeles

**★6387★ California State University, Los
Angeles
The Women's Resource Center**
5151 State University Dr.
Los Angeles, CA 90032
Phone: (213)343-3370
Fax: (213)343-2670
Virginia Cooper, Contact

**★6388★ Mount St. Mary's College
Women's Leadership Center**
12001 Chalon Rd.
Los Angeles, CA 90049
Phone: (213)476-2237
Fax: (213)476-9296
Cheryl Mabey, Contact

**★6389★ University of California, Los
Angeles
Women's Resource Center**
2 Dodd Hall
405 Hilgard Ave.
Los Angeles, CA 90024-1452
Phone: (213)825-3945
Kathy Rose-Mockry, Contact

**★6390★ University of Southern California
Women's Issues Advocate Office**
Student Union 202
Los Angeles, CA 90089-0890
Phone: (213)740-2311
Kathleen Bartle-Schulweis, Contact

Mission Vejo

**★6391★ Saddleback College
Adult Opportunity/Women's Center**
28000 Marguerite Parkway
Mission Vejo, CA 92692
Phone: (714)582-4611
Alma Van Asse, Contact

Moorpark

**★6392★ Moorpark College
Women's Center**
7075 Campus Road
Moorpark, CA 93021
Phone: (805)378-1497
Mary Baird, Contact

Napa

**★6393★ Napa Valley College
Women's Re-Entry Center**
Napa, CA 94558
Phone: (707)253-3051
Lauralyn Bauer, Contact

Northridge

**★6394★ California State University,
Northridge
Women's Studies Program**
Life House
18111 Nordhoff St.
Northridge, CA 91330
Phone: (818)885-1200
Julie Pearl, Contact

Oakland

**★6395★ Mills College
Career, Counseling and Health Centers**
5000 MacArthur Blvd.
Oakland, CA 94613
Phone: (415)430-2255
Marilyn Bowles, Contact

Pittsburg

**★6396★ Los Medanos College
Women's Center**
2700 E. Leland St.
Pittsburg, CA 94565
Phone: (415)439-2181
Carlton Williams, Contact

Pleasant Hill

**★6397★ Diablo Valley College
Women's Center**
321 Golf Club Rd.
Pleasant Hill, CA 94523
Phone: (415)685-1230
Sandra Trujillo-Holman, Contact

Pomona

**★6398★ California State Polytechnic
University, Pomona
Re-Entry Center**
3801 Temple Avenue
Pomona, CA 91758
Phone: (714)869-3205
Pat Martinez, Contact

Porterville

**★6399★ Porterville Community College
CARE-Entry Center**
900 Main
Porterville, CA 93257
Phone: (209)781-3130
Norma Jean Rogers, Contact

Redlands

**★6400★ University of Redlands
Women's Center**
1200 E. Colton Ave.
Redlands, CA 92373
Phone: (714)793-2121

Riverside

**★6401★ University of California, Riverside
Women's Resource Center**
990 University Ave.
Riverside, CA 92521
Phone: (714)787-3337
Barbara Gardner, Contact

Rohnert Park

**★6402★ Sonoma State University
Women's Resource Center**
Rohnert Park, CA 94928
Phone: (707)664-2845
Karen Markowitz, Contact

Sacramento

**★6403★ California State University,
Sacramento
Women's Resource Center**
6000 J St.
Sacramento, CA 95819
Phone: (916)278-7388
Ashley Sinclaire, Contact

**★6404★ Sacramento City College
Re-Entry Center**
3835 Freeport Blvd.
Sacramento, CA 95822
Phone: (916)449-7534
Maureen White, Contact

San Bruno

**★6405★ Skyline College
Women in Transition Program**
3300 College Dr.
San Bruno, CA 94066
Phone: (415)355-7000
Joyce Unger, Contact

San Diego

**★6406★ Center for Women's Studies and
Services**
2467 E. St.
San Diego, CA 92102
Phone: (619)233-8984

Description: Provides services for domestic
violence and sexual assault victims. Serves San
Diego area.

**★6407★ San Diego State University
Women's Resource Center**
Aztec Center
San Diego, CA 92182
Phone: (619)594-5230

San Francisco

★6408★ San Francisco State University
Women's Center
1600 Holloway Ave.
San Francisco, CA 94132
Phone: (415)338-2235
Julie Mau, Contact

San Jose

★6409★ San Jose State University
Women's Resource Center
1 Washington Sq.
San Jose, CA 95192
Phone: (408)924-6500

Santa Barbara

★6410★ University of California, Santa
Barbara
Women's Center
Santa Barbara, CA 93106
Phone: (805)961-3778
Janet Vandervender, Contact

Santa Clara

★6411★ Santa Clara University
Women Student Resource Center
Benson 207
Santa Clara, CA 95053
Phone: (408)554-4109
Denise Priestley, Contact

Santa Cruz

★6412★ University of California, Santa
Cruz
Women's Center
Cardiff House
Santa Cruz, CA 95064
Phone: (408)459-2072
Beatriz Lopez Florez, Contact

Santa Monica

★6413★ Santa Monica College
Women's Center
1900 Pico Blvd.
Santa Monica, CA 90405
Phone: (213)452-9338
Tina Felger, Contact

Thousand Oaks

★6414★ California Lutheran University
Women's Resource Center
60 W. Olsen Rd.
Thousand Oaks, CA 91360
Phone: (805)493-3345
Kathryn Swanson, Contact

Whittier

★6415★ Rio Hondo College
Career and Equity Services
3600 Workman Mill Rd.
Whittier, CA 90608
Phone: (213)908-3407
Barbara Booth, Contact

Colorado

Boulder

★6416★ University of Colorado, Boulder
Multicultural Center for Counseling and
Community Development
Campus Box 103
Boulder, CO 80309
Phone: (303)492-6766
Doris Olsen, Contact

Denver

★6417★ Metropolitan State College of
Denver
Women's Services
1006 Eleventh St., Box 36
Denver, CO 80204
Phone: (303)556-8441
Fax: (303)556-4941
Mackie Faye Hill, Contact

Englewood

★6418★ Denver Seminary
Office of Women's Concerns
3401 S. University Blvd.
Englewood, CO 80110
Alice Mathews, Contact

Ft. Collins

★6419★ Colorado State University
Women's Programs and Studies
112 Student Services
Ft. Collins, CO 80523
Phone: (303)491-6384
Karen J. Wedge, Contact

Pueblo

★6420★ University of Southern Colorado
Women's Center
Pueblo, CO 81001
Phone: (719)549-2100

Sterling

★6421★ Northeastern Junior College
Women's Resource Center
100 College Dr.
Sterling, CO 80751
Phone: (303)522-6600
Fax: (303)522-4945
Polly Gregory, Contact

Connecticut

Bridgeport

★6422★ Housatonic Community College
Women's Center
510 Barnum Ave.
Bridgeport, CT 06608
Phone: (203)255-4396
Lillie Margaret Lazaruk, Contact

Enfield

★6423★ Asnuntuck Community College
Student Services
170 Elm St.
Enfield, CT 06082
Phone: (203)745-1603

Fairfield

★6424★ Fairfield University
Women's Resource Center
Nyselius Library
Fairfield, CT 06430
Phone: (203)254-4000
Sharlene McEvoy, Contact

★6425★ Sacred Heart University
University Center for Women
5151 Park Ave.
Fairfield, CT 06432
Phone: (203)371-7845

Hamden

★6426★ Quinnipiac College
Women's Center
Boc 392
Hamden, CT 06518
Phone: (203)288-5251

Manchester

★6427★ Manchester Community College
Women's Center
60 Bidwell St.
Manchester, CT 06423
Phone: (203)647-6056
Gail A. Dunnrowicz, Contact

Middletown

★6428★ Wesleyan University
Women's Resource Center
287 High St.
Middletown, CT 06423
Phone: (203)347-9411

New Britain

★6429★ Central Connecticut State
University
Women's Center
1615 Stanley St.
New Britain, CT 06050
Phone: (203)827-7000
Doris Hornig Gunther, Contact

New Haven

★6430★ Albertus Magnus College
Continuing Education
700 Prospect St.
New Haven, CT 06511
Phone: (203)773-8550
Sister Jane McDermott, Contact

★6431★ Yale University
Women's Center
PO Box 5051
Yale Station
80 Wall St.
New Haven, CT 06570
Phone: (203)432-0388

New London

★6432★ Connecticut College
Women's Center
Box 4286, 270 Mohegan Ave.
New London, CT 06320-4196
Phone: (203)447-7909

Storrs

★6433★ University of Connecticut
Women's Center
U Box 181, 417 Whitney Rd.
Storrs, CT 06268
Phone: (203)486-4738
Myra Hindus, Contact

Trinity

★6434★ Trinity College
Women's Center
Trinity, CT 06457
Phone: (203)297-2408
Diane Martell, Contact

Willimantic

★6435★ Eastern Connecticut State
University
Women's Center
Winthrop Hall
Willimantic, CT 06226
Phone: (203)456-5552
Ann Marie Orza, Contact

Winsted

★6436★ Northwestern Connecticut
Community College
Women's Resource Center
Park Pl.
Winsted, CT 06098
Phone: (203)379-8543
Joanne Keiller, Contact

District of Columbia

Washington

★6437★ George Washington University
Women's Center
2201 G St. NW, 217 Funger Hall
Washington, DC 20052
Phone: (202)994-6942
Natalie Krochenhauer, Contact

★6438★ Union Institute
The Women's Project
1731 Connecticut Ave. NW, #300
Washington, DC 20077-5927
Phone: (202)667-1313
Judith Arcana, Contact

Florida

Gainesville

★6439★ Santa Fe Community College
Resource Center: Focus on Women
3000 NW 83rd St.
Gainesville, FL 32606
Phone: (904)395-5507
Fax: (904)395-5581
Ann Bromley, Contact

Jacksonville

★6440★ Florida Community College at
Jacksonville
Women's Center
101 W. State St.
Jacksonville, FL 32202-3056
Phone: (904)633-8390
Fax: (904)633-8435
Margaret Heanue Bard, Contact

★6441★ Florida Junior College
Center for Continuing Education
3939 Roosevelt Blvd.
Jacksonville, FL 32205
Phone: (904)387-8205

★6442★ University of North Florida
Women's Center
4567 St. Johns Bluff Rd.
Jacksonville, FL 32216
Phone: (904)646-2528
Shirley Webb, Contact

Leesburg

★6443★ Lake-Sumter Community College
Women's Program
9501 U.S. Hwy. 441
Leesburg, FL 34788
Phone: (904)365-3501
Janice Adkinson, Contact

Ocala

★6444★ Central Florida Community
College
Women and Family Center
Box 1388
Ocala, FL 32678
Phone: (904)237-2111
Marty Nugent, Contact

St. Petersburg

★6445★ Eckerd College
Women Resources Committee
4200 54th Ave., S.
St. Petersburg, FL 33771
Phone: (813)867-1166
Judith Greene, Contact

Tallahassee

★6446★ Florida State University
Women's Education and Cultural Center
112 N. Woodward
Tallahassee, FL 32373
Phone: (904)644-4007

Tampa

★6447★ University of South Florida
Everywoman's Center
Student Union
Tampa, FL 33620
Phone: (813)974-3332

Hawaii

Hilo

★6448★ University of Hawaii at Hilo
Women's Center
Hilo, HI 96720-4091
Phone: (808)933-3422
Fax: (808)933-3622
Noelie Rodriguez, Contact

Honolulu

★6449★ University of Hawaii at Manoa
Women's Center
2424 Maile Way, Porteus 722
Honolulu, HI 96822
Phone: (808)956-7464
Fax: (808)942-5710

Illinois

Carbondale

★6450★ Southern Illinois University at
Carbondale
Women's Services
Woody Hall, B-244
Carbondale, IL 62901
Phone: (618)453-3655
Beth Firestein, Contact

Charleston

★6451★ Eastern Illinois University
Women's Resource Center
Rm. 209, MLK Union
Charleston, IL 61920
Phone: (217)581-5947
Genie Lenihan, Contact

Chicago

★6452★ Northeastern Illinois University
New Directions
5500 N. St. Louis Ave.
Chicago, IL 60625
Phone: (312)583-4050
Fax: (312)794-6243
Jacquie Harper, Contact

Decatur

★6453★ Richland Community College
Options for Displaced Homemakers and
Single Parents
One College Park
Decatur, IL 62521
Phone: (217)875-7200
Fax: (217)875-6961
Kathy Sorenson, Contact

DeKalb

★6454★ Northern Illinois University
University Resources for Women
DeKalb, IL 60115
Phone: (815)753-0320
Sharon Howard, Contact

Evanston

★6455★ Northwestern University
Women's Center
2000 Sheridan Rd.
Evanston, IL 60208
Phone: (708)491-5871
June Terpstra, Contact

Macomb

★6456★ Western Illinois University
Women's Center
Sallee Hall
Macomb, IL 61455
Phone: (309)298-2242
Linnea High, Contact

Romeoville

★6457★ Lewis University
Women's Studies Center
Rte. 53
Romeoville, IL 60441
Phone: (815)838-0500
Karen K. Lockyer, Contact

Indiana

Elkhart

★6458★ Associated Mennonite Seminary
Women's Advisory Council
3003 Benham
Elkhart, IN 46517
Phone: (219)295-3726
Mary Schertz, Contact

Ft. Wayne

★6459★ Indiana University—Purdue
University at Fort Wayne
Center for Women and Returning Adults
2101 Coliseum Blvd.
Ft. Wayne, IN 46805
Phone: (219)481-6029
Linda Johnson, Contact

Hammond

★6460★ Purdue University Calumet
Woman to Woman
2233 171st St.
Hammond, IN 46323
Phone: (219)989-2993
Jackie Larson, Contact

Indianapolis

★6461★ Indiana University—Purdue
University at Indianapolis
Office of Women's Research
425 University Blvd. (CA 001E)
Indianapolis, IN 46202
Phone: (317)274-7611
Pat Boer, Contact

New Albany

★6462★ Indiana University Southeast
Adult Student Center
Student Affairs
4201 Grant Line Rd.
New Albany, IN 47150
Phone: (812)941-2420
Tom Mitchell, Contact

Richmond

★6463★ Earlham College
Womyn's Center
Box 62
Richmond, IN 47374
Phone: (317)983-1505

South Bend

★6464★ Indiana University at South Bend
Women's Resource Center
PO Box 7111
South Bend, IN 46634
Phone: (219)237-4494
Gloria Kaufman, Contact

Terre Haute

★6465★ Indiana State University
Women's Resource Center
Student Services Bldg.
Terre Haute, IN 47809
Phone: (812)237-3939
Chavonda Marshall, Contact

Vincennes

★6466★ Vincennes University
Women in Transition
1002 N. Forest St.
Vincennes, IN 47591
Phone: (812)885-4313
Kaye Gegenheimer, Contact

Iowa

Ames

★6467★ Iowa State University
Women's Center
Ames, IA 50011
Phone: (515)294-4154
Judy Jones, Contact

Ankeny

★6468★ Des Moines Area Community
College
Student and Education Development
2006 S. Ankeny Blvd.
Ankeny, IA 50021
Phone: (515)964-6474
Carolyn Waddell, Contact

Iowa City

★6469★ University of Iowa
Women's Research and Action Center
Iowa City, IA 52242
Phone: (319)335-1486
Papusa Molina, Contact

Ottumwa

★6470★ Indian Hills Community College
Women's Center
525 Grandview Ave.
Ottumwa, IA 52501
Phone: (515)683-5172
Ann Griffin, Contact

Sioux City

★6471★ Morningside College
Center for Women
1501 Morningside Ave.
Sioux City, IA 51106
Phone: (712)274-5100
Rev. Penny Bunger, Contact

Kansas

Emporia

★6472★ Emporia State University
Women's Resource Center
1200 Commercial, Box 6
Emporia, KS 66801
Phone: (316)343-5388
Fax: (316)343-5979
Sally S. Torrey, Contact

Lawrence

★6473★ Haskell Indian Junior College
Academic Support Center
155 Indian Ave.
Lawrence, KS 66049-4800
Phone: (913)864-8470
Dawn Yonally, Contact

★6474★ University of Kansas
Women's Resource Center
118 Strong Hall
Lawrence, KS 66045
Phone: (913)864-3552
Fax: (913)864-4120
Barbara Ballard, Contact

Manhattan

★6475★ Kansas State University
Women's Resource Center
Holton Hall
Manhattan, KS 66506
Phone: (913)532-6444
Judy Davis, Contact

Wichita

★6476★ Wichita State University
Center for Women's Studies Program
Campus Box 82
Wichita, KS 67208
Phone: (316)689-3358
Sally L. Kitch, Contact

Kentucky

Highland Heights

★6477★ Northern Kentucky University
Women's Center
BFP 301
Highland Heights, KY 41076
Phone: (606)572-5498
Fax: (606)572-5566
Katherine Meyer, Contact

Midway

★6478★ Midway College
Women's Studies
512 E. Stephens St.
Midway, KY 40347-1120
Phone: (606)846-5364
Fax: (606)846-5349
Kristina Minister, Contact

Owensboro

★6479★ Brescia College
Contemporary Woman Program
717 Frederica St.
Owensboro, KY 42301
Phone: (502)686-4275
Fax: (502)686-4213
Marita Greenwell, Contact

Louisiana

New Orleans

★6480★ Tulane University
Newcomb College Center for Research on
Women
1229 Broadway
New Orleans, LA 70118
Phone: (504)865-5238
Beth Willinger, Contact

★6481★ **University of New Orleans**
Women's Center
UNO Library
New Orleans, LA 70148
Phone: (504)286-7285
Pam Jenkins, Contact

Maine

Auburn

★6482★ **Central Maine Technical College**
Women Unlimited
Auburn, ME 04210
Phone: (207)784-2385
Dale McCormick, Contact
Specialization: Research on personal and career development.

Bar Harbor

★6483★ **College of the Atlantic**
Women's Advisory Group
Eden St.
Bar Harbor, ME 04609
Phone: (207)288-5015
Susan Lerner, Contact

Portland

★6484★ **University of Southern Maine**
Women's Forum
96 Falmouth St.
Portland, ME 04103
Phone: (207)874-6593

Maryland

Baltimore

★6485★ **Johns Hopkins University**
Women's Center
Levering Hall
Baltimore, MD 21218
Phone: (301)338-7681

College Park

★6486★ **University of Maryland at College Park**
Women's Center
Student Union
College Park, MD 20742
Phone: (301)405-1000

Frostburg

★6487★ **Frostburg State University**
Women's Resource Center
Old Main
Frostburg, MD 21532
Phone: (301)689-4234
Fax: (301)689-4737
Lisa Morshead, Contact

Hagerstown

★6488★ **Hagerstown Business College**
Women's Center
1050 Crestwood Dr.
Hagerstown, MD 21740
Phone: (301)739-2670
Fax: (301)791-7661
Lynne Diehl, Contact

Towson

★6489★ **Goucher College**
Women's Center
Towson, MD 21204
Phone: (301)337-6570
Charlotte Crosson, Contact

★6490★ **Towson State University**
Women's Center
Towson, MD 21204
Phone: (301)830-2666
Leah Schofield, Contact

Massachusetts

Amherst

★6491★ **Amherst College**
Women's Center
Campus Center
Amherst, MA 01002
Phone: (413)542-2000

★6492★ **Hampshire College**
Women's Center
Amherst, MA 01002
Phone: (413)549-4600
Nanette Sawyer, Contact

★6493★ **University of Massachusetts at Amherst**
Everywomen's Center
Wilder Hall
Amherst, MA 01002
Phone: (413)545-0883
Carol Wallace, Contact

Beverly

★6494★ **North Shore Community College**
Student Life
3 Essek St.
Beverly, MA 01915
Phone: (617)922-6722
Lisa Milso, Contact

Boston

★6495★ **Boston University**
Women's Studies Program
Women's Center
226 Bay State Rd.
Boston, MA 02215
Phone: (617)353-2000

★6496★ **Northeastern University**
Women's Center
23 Dodge Hall
Boston, MA 02115
Phone: (617)437-3442
Carol Lyons, Contact

★6497★ **Simmons College**
Women's Center
300 The Fenway
Boston, MA 02115
Phone: (617)738-2000
Terry Delahunty, Contact

★6498★ **Suffolk University**
Women's Center
8 Ashburton Pl.
Boston, MA 02108
Phone: (617)573-8327
Doris Clausen, Contact

★6499★ **University of Massachusetts at Boston Harbor Campus**
Women's Center
Boston, MA 02125
Phone: (617)287-5000

★6500★ **Wentworth Institute of Technology**
Women's Task Force
8-004 Beatty Hall
550 Huntington Ave.
Boston, MA 02115
Phone: (617)442-9010
Joyce Indelicato, Contact

Bridgewater

★6501★ **Bridgewater State College**
Women's Center
Bridgewater, MA 02325
Phone: (508)697-1200
Nancy Meymand, Contact

Brockton

★6502★ **Massasoit Community College**
Center for Women
1 Massasoit St.
Brockton, MA 02402
Phone: (508)588-9100
Judy Flynn, Contact

Cambridge

★6503★ **Joint Committee on the Status of Women**
Harvard Medical Area
221 Longwood Ave., Ste. 219
Cambridge, MA 02115
Phone: (617)432-0719
Laura Spernzi, Contact
Founded: 1973. **Description:** Documents and evaluates the status of women at Harvard School of Public Health, Harvard Medical School and Harvard School of Dental Medicine.

★6504★ **Radcliffe College**
Radcliffe Union of Students
Fay House
10 Garden St.
Cambridge, MA 02138
Phone: (617)495-8102

Chestnut Hill

★6505★ **Boston College**
Women's Resource Center
Boston College
Chestnut Hill, MA 02167
Phone: (617)552-3480
Sister Ann Morgan, Contact

Great Barrington

★6506★ **Simon's Rock of Bard College**
Women's Center
Alford Rd.
Great Barrington, MA 01230
Phone: (413)528-0771
Fran Mascia-Less, Contact

Lowell

★6507★ **University of Lowell**
Women's Center
1 University Ave.
Lowell, MA 01854
Phone: (508)934-4000

Medford

★6508★ **Tufts University**
Women's Center
55 Talbot Ave.
Medford, MA 02155
Phone: (617)381-3184
Peggy Barrett, Contact

North Dartmouth

★6509★ **Southeastern Massachusetts**
University
Women's Center
Old Westport Rd.
North Dartmouth, MA 02747
Phone: (508)999-3653
Susan Mitchell, Contact

Northampton

★6510★ **Smith College**
Women's Resource Center
Hatfield Hall
Northampton, MA 01063
Phone: (413)585-3336

Salem

★6511★ **Salem State College**
Women's Center
Salem, MA 01970
Phone: (508)741-6555
Florence Luscom, Contact

South Hadley

★6512★ **Mount Holyoke College**
Women's Center
PO Box 3206
South Hadley, MA 01075
Phone: (413)538-2000
A. Elizabeth Anema, Contact

South Hamilton

★6513★ **Gordon Conwell Theological**
Seminary
Women's Concerns
130 Essex St.
South Hamilton, MA 01982
Phone: (508)468-7111

Springfield

★6514★ **Springfield Technical Community**
College
Women's Center
One Armory Sq.
Springfield, MA 01105
Phone: (413)781-7822
Shirley A. Willer, Contact

Williamstown

★6515★ **Williams College**
Feminist Alliance
Williamstown, MA 01267
Phone: (413)597-3131

Worcester

★6516★ **Clark University**
Women's Center
950 Main St.
Worcester, MA 01520
Phone: (508)756-8582
Melanie Orhant, Contact

★6517★ **Quinsigamond Community College**
Women's Center
670 W. Boylston St.
Worcester, MA 01606
Phone: (508)853-2300
Elaine Fallon, Contact

Michigan

Albion

★6518★ **Albion College**
Women's Center
Albion, MI 49224
Phone: (517)629-0340
Virginia Tunnicliff, Contact

Ann Arbor

★6519★ **University of Michigan**
Center for Education of Women
330 E. Liberty
Ann Arbor, MI 48109-2289
Phone: (313)998-7080
Carol Hollenshead, Contact

★6520★ **Washtenaw Community College**
Adult Resource Center
4800 E. Huron River Dr.
Ann Arbor, MI 48106-0978
Phone: (313)973-3300

Dearborn

★6521★ **Henry Ford Community College**
Focus on Women
5101 Evergreen Rd.
Dearborn, MI 48128
Phone: (313)845-9629
Grace Stewart, Contact

Detroit

★6522★ **Wayne State University**
Women's Resource Center
Student Services Bldg.
Detroit, MI 48202
Phone: (313)577-4103
Kay A. Hartley, Contact

East Lansing

★6523★ **Michigan State University**
Division of Women's Programs
380 Administration Bldg.
East Lansing, MI 48824
Phone: (517)355-3922
Judy McQueen, Contact

Flint

★6524★ **University of Michigan, Flint**
Re-Entry Program
280 UCEN
Flint, MI 48502-2186
Phone: (313)762-3085
Jan Worth, Contact

Grand Rapids

★6525★ **Aquinas College**
Women's Center
1607 Robinson Rd.
Grand Rapids, MI 49506
Phone: (616)459-8981
Mary Alice Williams, Contact

Kalamazoo

★6526★ **Kalamazoo College**
Women's Equity Coalition
Hicks Center
Kalamazoo, MI 49007
Phone: (616)383-8400

Minnesota

Bemidji

★6527★ **Bemidji State University**
Women's Resource Center
Bemidji, MN 56601
Phone: (218)755-3770
Fax: (218)755-4048
Kristine Cannon, Contact

Duluth

★6528★ **University of Minnesota, Duluth**
Women's Resource and Action Center
10 University Dr.
Duluth, MN 55812
Phone: (218)726-6232
Fax: (218)726-6331
Holly Nordquist, Contact

Mankato

★6529★ **Mankato State University**
Women's Centre
Box 107
Mankato, MN 56002
Phone: (507)389-6146
Neala Schlenning, Contact

Minneapolis

★6530★ **Augsburg College**
Women's Awareness House
731 21st Ave., S.
Minneapolis, MN 55454
Phone: (612)330-1000

★6531★ **University of Minnesota, Twin**
Cities
Women's Center
192 Pillsbury Dr. SE
Minneapolis, MN 55455
Phone: (612)625-2874
Anne Thorsen Truax, Contact

Moorhead

★6532★ **Moorhead State University**
Women's Center
Dhall Hall, Rm. 115
Moorhead, MN 56560
Phone: (218)236-3792
Lora Bertelsen, Contact

Northfield

★6533★ **St. Olaf College**
Women's Resource Center
Northfield, MN 55057
Trish Lewis, Contact

Rochester

★6534★ **Rochester Community Program**
Choices—Displaced Homemakers Program
851 30th Ave. SE
Rochester, MN 55904
Phone: (507)285-5510
Fax: (507)285-7496
Maureen Hart, Contact

St. Cloud

★6535★ St. Cloud University
Women's Center
Colbert House North
St. Cloud, MN 56301-4498
Phone: (612)255-4958
Jane Olsen, Contact

St. Paul

★6536★ College of St. Catherine
Abigail Quigley McCarthy Center for
Women
2004 Randolph Ave.
St. Paul, MN 55105
Phone: (612)690-6783
Fax: (612)690-6024
Catherine Lupori, Contact

★6537★ Macalester College
Women's Resource Center
St. Paul, MN 55105
Phone: (612)696-6000

★6538★ Metropolitan State University
Women's Program
121 7th Pl. E.
St. Paul, MN 55409
Phone: (612)296-1002
Fax: (612)296-1187
Linda Fancher-White, Contact

St. Peter

★6539★ Gustavus Adolphus College
Womyn's Center
St. Peter, MN 56082
Phone: (507)931-7061
Kirsten Gilderhus, Contact

Willmar

★6540★ Willmar Community College
Non-Traditional Student Center
PO Box 797
Willmar, MN 56201
Phone: (612)231-5176
Fax: (612)235-5114
Bernice Grabber-Tintes, Contact

Winona

★6541★ St. Mary's College
Women's Issues Office
Campus Box 1458
Winona, MN 55987
Phone: (507)454-3426
Susan Edel, Contact

Missouri

Columbia

★6542★ University of Missouri, Columbia
Women's Center
229 Brady
Columbia, MO 65211
Phone: (314)882-6601
Laura Hacquard, Contact

Kansas City

★6543★ University of Missouri, Kansas
City
Women's Center
1638 Scoffield Hall, Rm. 1638
Kansas City, MO 64110-2499
Phone: (816)235-1409
Linda Rodriguez, Contact

St. Joseph

★6544★ Missouri Western State College
Women's Educational Resource Center
4525 Downs Dr.
St. Joseph, MO 64507-2294
Phone: (816)271-4280
Ellen Harpst, Contact

St. Louis

★6545★ University of Missouri, St. Louis
Women's Center
8001 Natural Bridge Rd.
St. Louis, MO 63121-4499
Phone: (314)553-5380

★6546★ Washington University
Women's Resource Center
One Brookings Dr.
Campus Box 1068
St. Louis, MO 63130
Phone: (314)889-5943
Fax: (314)889-5799
Tammy Gocial, Contact

★6547★ Webster University
Women's Resource Center
470 E. Lockwood
St. Louis, MO 63119
Phone: (314)968-6920
Peg McCurthy, Contact

Montana

Billings

★6548★ Eastern Montana College
Women's Studies Center
1500 N. 30th St.
Billings, MT 59101-0298
Phone: (406)657-2202
Sue Hart, Contact

Bozeman

★6549★ Montana State University
Women's Resource Center
Hamilton Hall
Bozeman, MT 59717
Phone: (406)994-3836
Fax: (406)994-2893
Michelle Dennis, Contact

Missoula

★6550★ University of Montana
Women's Center
Missoula, MT 59812
Phone: (406)243-0211

Nebraska

Bellevue

★6551★ Bellevue College
Women's Center
Galvin Rd. at Harvell Dr.
Bellevue, NE 68005
Phone: (402)293-3772
Roxanne L. Sullivan, Contact

Lincoln

★6552★ University of Nebraska, Lincoln
Women's Resource Center
Nebraska Union 117
Lincoln, NE 68588
Phone: (402)472-2597
Gina Matkin, Contact

Nevada

Reno

★6553★ University of Nevada, Reno
Women's Center
Reno, NV 89557
Phone: (702)784-4661
Helen Jones, Contact

New Hampshire

Hanover

★6554★ Dartmouth College
Women's Resource Center
6 Choate Rd.
Hanover, NH 03755
Phone: (603)646-3456
Judith White, Contact

Keene

★6555★ Keene State College
Women's Resource Center
229 Main St.
Keene, NH 03431
Phone: (603)352-1909

New Jersey

Hackettstown

★6556★ Centenary College
Women's Center
400 Jefferson St.
Hackettstown, NJ 07840
Phone: (201)852-9365
Fax: (201)850-9508
Jill D. Zahniser, Contact

Jersey City

★6557★ **Jersey City State College**
Women's Center
2309 Kennedy Memorial Blvd.
Jersey City, NJ 07305
Phone: (201)547-3189
Karen DeAngelis, Contact

Lawrenceville

★6558★ **Rider College**
Women's Center
2083 Lawrenceville Rd.
Lawrenceville, NJ 08648
Phone: (609)896-5255
Arlene Wilner, Contact

Mahwah

★6559★ **Ramapo College of New Jersey**
Women's Center
505 Ramapo Valley Rd.
Mahwah, NJ 07430
Phone: (201)529-7468
Barbara Harrison, Contact

New Brunswick

★6560★ **Rutgers, The State University of**
New Jersey, Douglass College
Douglass College Advisory Services for
Women
132 George St.
New Brunswick, NJ 08903
Phone: (201)932-9603
Viola Van Jones, Contact

Princeton

★6561★ **Princeton Theological Seminary**
Women's Center
CN 821
Princeton, NJ 08542
Phone: (609)924-3879
Fax: (609)924-2973

★6562★ **Princeton University**
Women's Center
201 Aaron Burr Hall
Princeton, NJ 08544
Phone: (609)258-5565
Jan Strout, Contact

Trenton

★6563★ **Trenton State College**
Women's Center
Hillwood Lakes/CN 4700
Trenton, NJ 08650
Phone: (609)771-2120

Upper Montclair

★6564★ **Montclair State College**
Women's Center
Student Center
Upper Montclair, NJ 07043
Phone: (201)893-7031
Fax: (201)893-5455
Sharon Olson, Contact

New Mexico

Albuquerque

★6565★ **University of New Mexico**
Women's Center
Mesa Vista Hall
Albuquerque, NM 87131
Phone: (505)277-3716
Johanna Clayton, Contact

Las Cruces

★6566★ **New Mexico State University**
Women's Center
Box 3WSP
Las Cruces, NM 88003
Phone: (505)646-4633
Rebecca Spillman, Contact

New York

Annandale-on-Hudson

★6567★ **Bard College**
Women's Center
Bard College
Annandale-on-Hudson, NY 12504
Phone: (914)758-6822
Hester Baer, Contact

Aurora

★6568★ **Wells College**
Women's Resource Center
Route 90
Aurora, NY 13206
Phone: (315)364-3278

Binghampton

★6569★ **State University of New York**
College at Binghamton
Women's Center
Vestal Parkway W.
Binghampton, NY 13790
Phone: (607)777-2458

Bronx

★6570★ **Hostos Community College of the**
City University of New York
Center for Women and Immigrants Rights
475 Grand Concourse
Bronx, NY 10463
Phone: (212)960-1204
Marta Rivera, Contact

Brooklyn

★6571★ **Brooklyn College of the City**
University of New York
Women's Center
Bedford Ave. & H Ave.
Brooklyn, NY 11210
Phone: (718)780-5777

★6572★ **Medgar Evers College of the City**
University of New York
Women's Studies Program
Center for Women's Development
1650 Bedford Ave.
Brooklyn, NY 11225
Phone: (718)270-5020
Safiya Bandele, Contact

★6573★ **New York City Technical College**
of the City University of New York
Access for Women
250 Jay St.
Brooklyn, NY 11201
Phone: (718)643-4626

Buffalo

★6574★ **Buffalo State College**
Women's Resource Center
Cassita Hall
Buffalo, NY 14222
Phone: (716)878-4000
Molly Kerwin, Contact

★6575★ **State University of New York**
College at Buffalo
Women's Center
101 Wende Hall
Buffalo, NY 14260
Phone: (716)831-3405

Clinton

★6576★ **Hamilton College**
Women's Center
College Hill Rd.
Clinton, NY 13323
Phone: (315)859-4279

Cortland

★6577★ **State University of New York**
College at Cortland
Minority and Women's Studies Center
College at Cortland
Cortland, NY 13045
Phone: (607)753-5784
Fax: (607)753-5999
Patty Francis, Contact

Flushing

★6578★ **Queens College of the City**
University of New York
Women's Center
Student Union
Flushing, NY 11367
Katie German, Contact

Hamilton

★6579★ **Colgate University**
Women's Resource Center
Hamilton, NY 13346
Phone: (315)824-1000

Ithaca

★6580★ **Cornell University**
Women's Center
Box 71
Ithaca, NY 14853
Phone: (607)255-9611

Jamaica

**★6581★ York College of the City
University of New York**
Women's Center
Jamaica, NY 11451
Phone: (718)262-2008
Elaine Baruch, Contact

New Rochelle

★6582★ Iona College
Women's Resource Center
New Rochelle, NY 10801
Phone: (914)633-2328
Fax: (914)633-2020
Gloria Moldow, Contact

New York

**★6583★ The City College of the City
University of New York**
Women's Resource Center
NAC 4-150B, Convent Ave. at 138th St.
New York, NY 10031
Phone: (212)650-8269
Mary Jackson, Contact

★6584★ Columbia University
Women's Center
Broadway & W. 116th St.
New York, NY 10027
Phone: (212)854-4907

**★6585★ Hunter College of the City
University of New York**
Women's Center
695 Park Ave.
New York, NY 10021
Phone: (212)772-4931
Myrna Fader, Contact

★6586★ New York Theological Seminary
**Resource Center for African-American
Women in Ministry**
Southwest 29th St.
New York, NY 10001
Phone: (212)532-40127
Rev. Joan Speaks, Contact

★6587★ New York University
Womyn's Center
21 Washington Pl.
New York, NY 10003
Phone: (212)998-4712
Nancy Brooks, Contact

★6588★ Union Theological Seminary
Women's Center
3041 Broadway
New York, NY 10027
Phone: (212)662-7100

Old Westbury

**★6589★ State University of New York
College at Old Westbury**
Women's Center
Box 210
Old Westbury, NY 11568
Phone: (516)876-3294
Barbara Tutungian, Contact

Orchard Park

**★6590★ Erie Community College, South
Campus**
Women's Center
4140 Southwestern Blvd.
Orchard Park, NY 14127
Phone: (716)648-5400
Marion Perry, Contact

Oswego

**★6591★ State University of New York
College at Oswego**
Women's Center
Hewitt Union
Oswego, NY 13126

Poughkeepsie

★6592★ Vassar College
Women's Center
Poughkeepsie, NY 12601

Schenectady

★6593★ Union College
Women's Center
Schenectady, NY 12308
Phone: (518)370-6143
Sharon Gmelch, Contact

Selden

**★6594★ Suffolk County Community
College**
Adult Center
Adult Student Center
Selden, NY 11784
Phone: (516)451-4222
Glenda Rosenblum, Contact

Stony Brook

**★6595★ State University of New York
College at Stony Brook**
Center for Womyn's Concerns
Langmuir College
Stony Brook, NY 11794
Phone: (516)632-4219
Esther Lastique, Contact

Syracuse

★6596★ Syracuse University
Women's Center
Schine Student Center
Syracuse, NY 13244
Phone: (315)443-1870
Ann Sheedy, Contact

Williamville

**★6597★ Erie Community College, North
Campus**
Women's Center/Caucus
Main St. & Youngs Rd.
Williamville, NY 14221
Phone: (716)634-0800
Roberta Bothwell, Contact

North Carolina

Charlotte

**★6598★ Central Piedmont Community
College**
Womenshare
PO Box 35009
Charlotte, NC 28235
Phone: (704)342-6532

Durham

★6599★ Duke University
Women's Center
101-5 Bryan Center
Durham, NC 27706
Phone: (919)684-3897
Martha Abshire Simmons, Contact

Goldsboro

★6600★ Wayne Community College
Second Wind
Caller Box 8002
Goldsboro, NC 27530
Phone: (919)735-5151
Fax: (919)736-3204
M. Annette Lewis, Contact

Grantsboro

★6601★ Pamlico Community College
A Place for Women
PO Box 185, Highway 306
Grantsboro, NC 28529
Phone: (919)249-1851
Almuria M. Credle, Contact

Polkton

★6602★ Anson Community College
Women's Center
PO Box 126
Polkton, NC 28135
Phone: (704)272-7635
Pat Taylor, Contact

Swannanoa

★6603★ Warren Wilson College
Women's Center
701 Warren Wilson Rd.
Swannanoa, NC 28778
Phone: (704)298-5721
Louise Solomon, Contact

North Dakota

Grand Forks

★6604★ University of North Dakota
Women's Center
105 Hamline
Grand Forks, ND 58202
Phone: (701)777-4300
Nancy Nienhaus, Contact

Ohio

Celina

**★6605★ Wright State University, Lake
Campus**
Women's Center
7600 State, Rte. 703
Celina, OH 45822
Phone: (419)586-2365
Fax: (419)586-9048
Barbara Wourms, Contact

Cincinnati

★6606★ University of Cincinnati
Women's Programs and Services
Cincinnati, OH 45221-0179
Phone: (513)556-4401
Nancy Spence, Contact

Columbus

★6607★ The Ohio State University
Women's Students Services
2040 Drake Hall
1849 Cannon Dr.
Columbus, OH 43210
Phone: (614)292-8473
Cynthia M.Z. Harris, Contact

Delaware

★6608★ Ohio Wesleyan University
Women's Resource Center
Memorial Union Building
Delaware, OH 43015
Phone: (614)368-3182
Alice Crawford, Contact

Gambier

★6609★ Kenyon College
Crozier Center
Gambier, OH 43022
Phone: (614)427-5140
Cheryl Steele, Contact

Granville

★6610★ Denison University
Women's Resource Center
Fellows Hall
Granville, OH 43023
Phone: (614)587-6366
Fax: (614)587-6417
Lisa Ransdell, Contact

Mount St. Joseph

★6611★ College of Mount St. Joseph
Women's Center
Mount St. Joseph, OH 45051
Phone: (513)244-4312
Fax: (513)244-4222

Newark

★6612★ The Ohio State University,
Newark Campus
ALL Women
Newark, OH 43062
Phone: (614)366-3321

Oberlin

★6613★ Oberlin College
Women's Information and Resource Center
Wilder Hall
Oberlin, OH 44074
Phone: (216)775-8121

Salem

★6614★ Kent State University, Salem
Regional Campus
Women's Center
2491 State Route 45 S.
Salem, OH 44460
Phone: (216)332-0361
Stephanie Elise Booth, Contact

Springfield

★6615★ Wittenberg University
Womyn's Center
Box 720
Springfield, OH 45501
Phone: (513)327-7323
Christine L. Matusik, Contact

Toledo

★6616★ University of Toledo
Center for Women
Scott House
Toledo, OH 43606
Phone: (419)537-2058
Fax: (419)537-4940
Dianne K. Mills, Contact

Wooster

★6617★ College of Wooster
Women's Center
Wooster, OH 44691
Phone: (216)263-2000

Yellow Springs

★6618★ Antioch College
Women's Center
Livermore St.
Yellow Springs, OH 45387
Phone: (513)767-7331

Youngstown

★6619★ Youngstown State University
Women's Resource Center
Youngstown, OH 44555
Phone: (216)742-7309
Danna Bozick, Contact

Oregon

Albany

★6620★ Linn-Benton Community College
Women's Center
6500 Southwest Pacific Blvd.
Albany, OR 97321
Phone: (503)967-6112
Marian Roberts, Contact

Ashland

★6621★ Southern Oregon State College
Women's Center
1077 Ashland St.
Ashland, OR 97520
Phone: (503)482-6216
Glenda Galaba, Contact

Corvallis

★6622★ Oregon State University
Women's Center
Corvallis, OR 97331-2503
Phone: (503)737-3186
Sue Adams, Contact

Eugene

★6623★ Lane Community College
Women's Awareness Center
4000 E. 30th Ave.
Eugene, OR 97405
Phone: (503)747-4501
Kate Barry, Contact

★6624★ University of Oregon
Women's Center
Suite 2 EMU
Eugene, OR 97403
Phone: (503)346-4095
Fax: (503)346-3127
Hasani Kudura, Contact

La Grande

★6625★ Eastern Oregon State College
Student Development Center
La Grande, OR 97850
Phone: (503)963-1392
Fax: (503)962-1849
Theresa Jordan, Contact

McMinnville

★6626★ Linfield College
Abigail Scott Duniway Women's Center
McMinnville, OR 97128
Phone: (503)472-4121
Anne Hardin, Contact

Oregon City

★6627★ Clackamas Community College
Focus on Women
19600 S. Mollala Ave.
Oregon City, OR 97045
Phone: (503)657-6958
Gaye O'Toole, Contact
Specialization: Life careers option program.

Portland

★6628★ Mt. Hood Community College
Centennial Center
14750 SE Clinton
Portland, OR 97236
Phone: (503)760-4007
Nan Poppe, Contact

★6629★ Portland Community College
Women's Resource Center
PO Box 19000
Portland, OR 97219-0990
Phone: (503)244-6111
Terry Greenfield, Contact

★6630★ Portland State University
Women's Union and Resource Center
PO Box 751
Portland, OR 97207
Phone: (503)725-4452
Fax: (503)725-4882
A.J. Arriola, Contact

Salem

★6631★ Willamette University
Women's Center
Salem, OR 97301
Phone: (503)370-6471
Gwen Ellyn Anderson, Contact

Pennsylvania

Annville

★6632★ Lebanon Valley College
Women's Counseling Center
PO Box R
Annville, PA 17003
Phone: (717)867-6181
Barbara Denison, Contact

Bethlehem

★6633★ Lehigh University
Women's Center
Johnson Hall #35
Bethlehem, PA 18015
Kathy Calabrese, Contact

Bryn Mawr

★6634★ Bryn Mawr College
Women's Center
Bryn Mawr, PA 19010
Phone: (215)526-5000
Donna Vettwiller, Contact

California

★6635★ California University of
Pennsylvania
Women's Center
114 Clyde Hall
California, PA 15419
Phone: (412)938-5857
Albertha Graham, Contact

Carlisle

★6636★ Dickinson College
Women's Center
Box 743
Carlisle, PA 17013-2896
Phone: (717)245-1451
Leah Goldfarb, Contact

East Stroudsburg

★6637★ East Stroudsburg University of
Pennsylvania
Women's Center
309 Stroud Hall
East Stroudsburg, PA 18301
Phone: (717)424-3211

Gettysburg

★6638★ Gettysburg College
"A Room of Our Own" Women's Center
53 W. Stevens St.
Gettysburg, PA 17325
Phone: (717)337-6991
Jessica Mong, Contact

Haverford

★6639★ Haverford College
Women's Center
Haverford, PA 19004
Phone: (215)896-1292
Fax: (215)896-1224
Marilou Allen, Contact

Lewisburg

★6640★ Bucknell University
Women's Resource Center
200 Roberts Hall
Lewisburg, PA 17837
Phone: (717)524-1375
Janice Butler, Contact

Philadelphia

★6641★ Lincoln University
Women's Technical Program
4601 Market St.
Philadelphia, PA 19139
Phone: (215)476-6666
Roslie Grant, Contact

★6642★ University of Pennsylvania
Women's Center
119 Houston Hall
Philadelphia, PA 19104-6306
Phone: (215)898-8611
Elena Dilapi, Contact

Pittsburgh

★6643★ Community College of Allegheny
County, North Campus
Women's Center
808 Ridge Ave.
Pittsburgh, PA 15212
Phone: (412)237-2595
Janice Kelly, Contact

Reading

★6644★ Albright College
Women's Center
PO Box 15234
Reading, PA 19612
Phone: (215)921-2381
Karen M. Hicks, Contact

Shippenburg

★6645★ Shippenburg University of
Pennsylvania
Women's Center
Shippenburg, PA 17257
Phone: (717)532-1790
Jean L. McBride, Contact

University Park

★6646★ Pennsylvania State University,
University Park
Center for Women Students
University Park, PA 16802
Phone: (814)863-2027
Sabrina Chapman, Contact

West Chester

★6647★ West Chester University of
Pennsylvania
Women's Center
100 Lawrence Hall
West Chester, PA 19383
Phone: (215)436-2122
Robin Garrett, Contact

Williamsport

★6648★ Pennsylvania College of
Technology
Women's Forum
1005 W. 3rd ·
Williamsport, PA 17701
Phone: (717)326-3761
Veronica Muzic, Contact

Rhode Island

Kingston

★6649★ University of Rhode Island
Women's Center
Plains and Alumni Rds.
Kingston, RI 02881
Phone: (401)792-1000
Leni Silverstein, Contact

Providence

★6650★ Brown University
Sarah Doyle Center
185 Meeting St.
Providence, RI 02912
Phone: (401)863-2189
Gigi DiBello, Contact

★6651★ Johnson & Wales University
Women's Concerns Center
8 Abbott Park Pl.
Providence, RI 02903
Phone: (401)456-1000
Nancy Jackson, Contact

★6652★ Rhode Island College
Women's Center
Donovan - Mall Level
Providence, RI 02908
Phone: (401)456-8474
Anna Grady, Contact

South Carolina

Columbia

★6653★ University of South Carolina
Women's Student Services
Russell House
Columbia, SC 29208
Phone: (803)777-7000
Leigh Stanton, Contact

Tennessee

Knoxville

★6654★ University of Tennessee,
Knoxville
Women's Center
301 University Center
Knoxville, TN 37996-4102
Phone: (615)974-1029
Maureen Nikolas, Contact

Murfreesboro

★6655★ Middle Tennessee State
University
Women's Center
Box 295
Murfreesboro, TN 37132
Phone: (615)898-2193
Rebecca Rice, Contact

Nashville

★6656★ Vanderbilt University
Women's Center
Box 1315, Station B
Nashville, TN 37235
Phone: (615)322-4843
Nancy Ransom, Contact

Texas

Arlington

★6657★ University of Texas at Arlington
Women and Minorities Research and
Resource Center
Box 1529
Arlington, TX 76019-0529
Phone: (817)273-2861
Fax: (817)273-3392

Austin

★6658★ Austin Community College
Women's Center—Northridge Campus
PO Box 140707
Austin, TX 78714
Phone: (512)832-4726
Diane Kramer, Contact

Beeville

★6659★ Bee County College
Adult Outreach Program
3800 Charco Rd.
Beeville, TX 78102
Phone: (512)358-3130
Dolores Perez, Contact

Dallas

★6660★ Southern Methodist University
Women's Center
3116 Fondren Dr.
Dallas, TX 75275
Phone: (214)987-4997
Lindley Doran, Contact

El Paso

★6661★ El Paso Community College
Women's Center
110 W. Rio Grande
El Paso, TX 79902
Phone: (915)534-4121
Olga Chavez, Contact

★6662★ University of Texas at El Paso
Women's Center
Student Union
El Paso, TX 79968
Phone: (915)747-5291
Tricia Tague Miller, Contact

Laredo

★6663★ Laredo Junior College
Special Population
West End Washington St.
Laredo, TX 78040
Phone: (512)722-0521
Ramiro Ramirez, Contact

Mesquite

★6664★ Eastfield College
Adult Resource Center
3737 Motley
Mesquite, TX 75150
Phone: (214)324-7619
Carolyn Stock, Contact

Midland

★6665★ Midland College
Reassessment Program
3600 N. Garfield
Midland, TX 79701
Phone: (915)685-4568
Fax: (915)685-4714
Wanda Phillips, Contact

San Antonio

★6666★ Our Lady of the Lake University
of San Antonio
Center for Women in Church and Society
411 Southwest 24th St.
San Antonio, TX 78207
Phone: (512)434-6711
Fax: (512)436-0824
Jane Shafer, Contact

★6667★ St. Philip's College
Equity Center—Educational Support
Service
2111 Nevada
San Antonio, TX 78212
Phone: (512)531-3474
Sandra Moore-Pope, Contact

Texas City

★6668★ College of the Mainland
Women's Center
1200 Auburn
Texas City, TX 77591
Phone: (409)938-1211
Fax: (409)938-1306
Barbara K. Crews, Contact

Utah

Logan

★6669★ Utah State University
Women's Center for Lifelong Learning
Logan, UT 84322-0185
Phone: (801)750-1728
Janet Osborne, Contact

Orem

★6670★ Utah Valley Community College
Center for Personal and Career
Development
800 W. 1200 South
Orem, UT 84058
Phone: (801)222-8000
Linda Barlow, Contact

Salt Lake City

★6671★ University of Utah
Women's Resource Center
295 Union
Salt Lake City, UT 84112
Phone: (801)581-8030
Kathy Brooks, Contact

Vermont

Brattleboro

★6672★ School for International Training
Center for Women and Gender Issues
Kipling Rd.
Brattleboro, VT 05301
Phone: (802)257-7751
Cathy Armstrong, Contact

Middlebury

★6673★ Community College of Vermont
Gender Equity Task Force
Middlebury, VT 05753
Phone: (802)388-3032
Bette Makowski, Contact

Plain Field

★6674★ Goddard College
Wimmin's Center
Plain Field, VT 05667
Phone: (802)454-8311
Shelley Smith, Contact

Virginia

Bristol

★6675★ Virginia Intermont College
Women's Resource Center
Moore St.
Bristol, VA 24201
Phone: (703)669-8754
Betsie A. Cole, Contact

Buena Vista

★6676★ Southern Seminary College
Student Development and Academic
Assistance
Buena Vista, VA 24416
Phone: (703)261-8400
Mollie Messimer, Contact

Charlottesville

★6677★ University of Virginia
Women's Center
Box 323
Charlottesville, VA 22908
Phone: (804)982-2250
Sharon Davie, Contact

Danville

★6678★ Averett College
Women's Resource Center
425 W. Main St.
Danville, VA 24541
Phone: (804)791-5726
Joan R. Sprinkle, Contact

Fairfax

★6679★ George Mason University
Women's Studies Research and Resource
Center
4400 University Dr.
Fairfax, VA 22030
Phone: (703)323-2921
Karen Rosenblum, Contact

Harrisonburg

★6680★ Eastern Mennonite College
Student Women's Association
1200 Park Rd.
Harrisonburg, VA 22801
Phone: (703)432-4208

Keysville

★6681★ Southside Virginia Community
College
Vocational Preparation Center
Rte. 1, Box 15
Keysville, VA 23947
Phone: (804)736-8484
Fax: (804)736-8578
Melody Moore, Contact

Lynchburg

**★6682★ Lynchburg College
Women's Network**
Lynchburg, VA 24503
Phone: (804)522-8433
Janice Rice, Contact
Specialization: Older women and aging.

**★6683★ Randolph-Macon Woman's
College
Woman's Resource Center**
Lynchburg, VA 24503
Phone: (804)847-0258
Sarah Snead, Contact

Norfolk

**★6684★ Old Dominion University
Women's Center**
1521 W. 49th St.
Norfolk, VA 23529
Phone: (804)683-4109
Julie Dodd, Contact

Richmond

**★6685★ University of Richmond
Women's Resource Center**
Richmond, VA 23173
Phone: (804)289-8025

Roanoke

**★6686★ Hollins College
Women's Center**
PO Box 9603
Roanoke, VA 24020
Phone: (703)362-6270
Fax: (703)362-6642
Lucy Lee, Contact

Washington

Auburn

**★6687★ Green River Community College
Women's Center**
12401 SE 320th
Auburn, WA 98002
Phone: (206)833-9111
Maid Adams, Contact

Bellingham

**★6688★ Western Washington University
Women's Center**
VU 211
Bellingham, WA 98225
Phone: (206)676-3460

Cheney

**★6689★ Eastern Washington University
Women's Studies Center**
MS 166
Cheney, WA 99004
Phone: (509)359-2409
Fax: (509)359-6927
Lee Swedberg, Contact

Ellensburg

**★6690★ Central Washington University
Women's Resource Center**
Ellensburg, WA 98926
Phone: (509)963-2127
Linda Buffer, Contact

Everett

**★6691★ Everett Community College
Women's Programs**
801 Wetmore Ave.
Everett, WA 98201
Phone: (206)259-7151
Laura Hedges, Contact

Olympia

**★6692★ The Evergreen State College
Women's Center**
Olympia, WA 98505
Phone: (206)866-6000

Pasco

**★6693★ Columbia Basin College
Women's Resource Center**
2600 N. 20th
Pasco, WA 99301
Phone: (509)547-0511
Susan Gilbert, Contact

Pullman

**★6694★ Washington State University
Women's Resource and Research Center**
Pullman, WA 99164-7204
Phone: (509)335-6830
Beth Prinz, Contact

Seattle

**★6695★ North Seattle Community College
Women's Center**
9600 College Way N.
Seattle, WA 98103
Phone: (206)527-3696
Irma Levin, Contact

**★6696★ Shoreline Community College
Women's Center**
16101 Greenwood Ave., N.
Seattle, WA 98133
Phone: (206)546-4676
Fax: (206)546-4599
Dianne Dailey, Contact

**★6697★ University of Washington
Women's Information Center**
AJ-50, Cunningham Hall
Seattle, WA 98195
Phone: (206)543-1090
Angela Ginorio, Contact

Tacoma

**★6698★ Pacific Lutheran University
Women's Center**
East Campus G-10
Tacoma, WA 98447
Phone: (206)535-8759
Fax: (206)535-8320
Linda Curtis-Downey, Contact

Toppenish

**★6699★ Heritage College
Women as Resources**
Rte. 3, Box 3540
Toppenish, WA 98948
Phone: (509)865-2244

Vancouver

**★6700★ Clark College
Women's Center**
1800 E. McLoughlin Blvd.
Vancouver, WA 98663
Phone: (206)699-0366
Patricia Watne, Contact

Walla Walla

**★6701★ Whitman College
Women's Resource Center**
Walla Walla, WA 99362
Phone: (509)527-5906
Meg Robinson, Contact

Yakima

**★6702★ Yakima Valley Community
College
Women's Center**
PO Box 1647
Yakima, WA 98907
Phone: (509)575-2915
Mary Doherty Kowalsky, Contact

Wisconsin

Appleton

**★6703★ Lawrence University
Downer Feminist Council**
Coleman Hall
Appleton, WI 54912
Phone: (414)832-6530

Beloit

**★6704★ Beloit College
Women's Center**
700 College St.
Beloit, WI 53511
Phone: (608)363-2500
John Winkleman, Contact

Cleveland

**★6705★ Lakeshore Technical College
Life Work Planning**
1290 North Ave.
Cleveland, WI 53015
Phone: (414)457-4183
Fax: (414)457-6211
Maureen Simon, Contact

Eau Claire

**★6706★ University of Wisconsin—Eau
Claire
Women's Center**
Eau Claire, WI 54701
Phone: (715)836-5717
Fax: (715)836-2380
Sarah Harder, Contact

Green Bay

**★6707★ University of Wisconsin—Green
Bay
Women's Center**
2420 Nicolet Dr.
Green Bay, WI 54311-2355
Phone: (414)465-2582
Patricia Maguire, Contact

Kenosha

★6708★ University of Wisconsin—Parkside
Women's Center
Kenosha, WI 53141
Phone: (414)553-2170
Susan Burns, Contact

La Crosse

★6709★ University of Wisconsin—La
Crosse
Women's Center
306 North Hall
La Crosse, WI 54601
Phone: (608)785-8753
Sondra O'Neale, Contact

★6710★ Western Wisconsin Technical
College
The Opportunity Center
304 N. Sixth St.
La Crosse, WI 54602-0908
Phone: (608)785-9585
Jeanne Potter, Contact

Madison

★6711★ University of Wisconsin—Madison
Women's Center
710 University Ave., No. 202
Madison, WI 53706
Phone: (608)263-8093
Kristen Wilson, Contact

Milwaukee

★6712★ Alverno College
Research Center on Women
3401 S. 39th St.
Milwaukee, WI 53215
Phone: (414)382-6061
Lola Stuller, Contact

★6713★ Marquette University
Women's Center
Carpenter Hall
Milwaukee, WI 53233
Phone: (414)288-1413
Stephanie Quade, Contact

★6714★ Milwaukee Area Technical
College
Family and Women's Resource Center
700 W. State St.
Milwaukee, WI 53233
Phone: (414)278-6219
Gloria Gonzales, Contact

Oskosh

★6715★ University of Wisconsin—Oshkosh
**M.F. Berry Women's Resource Center
Board**
Oskosh, WI 54901
Phone: (414)424-1491
Kelly Heppner, Contact

Pewaukee

★6716★ Waukesha County Technical
College
Women's Development Center
800 Main St.
Pewaukee, WI 53072
Phone: (414)691-5445
Fax: (414)691-5593
Libby Sellars, Contact

Platteville

★6717★ University of Wisconsin—
Platteville
Women's Center
126 Doudna Hall
Platteville, WI 53818
Phone: (608)342-1453
Amy Zolot, Contact

River Falls

★6718★ University of Wisconsin—River
Falls
Women's Center
Hathorne Hall
River Falls, WI 54022
Phone: (715)425-3808
Carol Ryan, Contact

Stevens Point

★6719★ University of Wisconsin—Stevens
Point
Women's Resource Center
Nelson Hall
Stevens Point, WI 54481
Phone: (715)346-4851
Deb Gustafson, Contact

Superior

★6720★ University of Wisconsin—Superior
Women's Resource Center
Superior, WI 54880
Phone: (715)394-8290
Michelle Stronach, Contact

Wyoming

Laramie

★6721★ University of Wyoming
Women's Center
PO Box 3808
Laramie, WY 82071
Phone: (307)766-6258
Cindy Omsburg, Contact

Rock Springs

★6722★ Western Wyoming Community
College
Women's Center
PO Box 428
Rock Springs, WY 82901
Phone: (307)382-1646

(7) Library Collections

Entries in this chapter are arranged alphabetically by library name. See the User's Guide at the front of this directory for additional information.

★6723★ **ALA Gay & Lesbian Task Force Clearinghouse**
c/o American Library Association
Office of Library Outreach Services
50 E. Huron
Chicago, IL 60611
Phone: (312)944-6780
JoAnn Segal, Assoc.Dir. for Prog.

Subjects: Homosexuality, lesbianism/feminism, gay rights. **Holdings:** 2000 books, pamphlets, periodical titles. **Publications:** *Gay Bibliography*—for sale; list of additional publications—available on request. **Remarks:** Affiliated with the American Library Association, Social Responsibilities Round Table. For further information, write to GLTF c/o Roland Hansen, Sec./Treas., 3824 N. Fremont, Chicago, IL 60613. **Formerly:** Gay Task Force of ALA-Information Center, located in Philadelphia, PA.

★6724★ **Alliant Health System Library/Media Services**
Box 35070
Louisville, KY 40232
Phone: (502)629-8125
Fax: (502)629-8138
Wenda Webster Fischer, Dir.

Subjects: Medicine, nursing, hospital administration, psychiatry, pediatrics, women's health, orthopedics. **Special Collections:** Flexner Historical Collection. **Holdings:** 5000 books; pamphlets; audio and video cassettes. **Subscriptions:** 300 journals and other serials.

★6725★ **Alverno College Research Center on Women**
3401 S. 39th St.
Milwaukee, WI 53215
Phone: (414)382-6061
Lola Stuller, Libn.

Subjects: Women - careers/professions, education, religion, life styles, employment; women's movement. **Holdings:** 3000 books; 110 bound periodical volumes; 100 AV program/microform titles. **Subscriptions:** 250 journals and other serials.

★6726★ **Alza Corporation Research Library**
950 Page Mill Rd.
Palo Alto, CA 94304
Phone: (415)494-5548
Fax: (415)494-8811
Helen T. Rolen, Mgr., Lib.Serv.

Subjects: Pharmacology, biochemistry, medicine, dermatology, veterinary medicine, pharmaceuticals, obstetrics, gynecology, physiology, polymer science, analytical chemistry, chemical engineering. **Holdings:** 20,000 books; 20,000 bound periodical volumes; 5000 reels of microfilm; 500 microfiche; 20 VF drawers. **Subscriptions:** 550 journals and other serials; 6 newspapers.

★6727★ **American Association of University Women Educational Foundation Library and Archives**
111 16th St., N.W.
Washington, DC 20036
Phone: (202)785-7763

Subjects: Education and higher education; women's activities and achievements; status of women. **Special Collections:** *Graduate Woman* (formerly *AAUW Journal*), complete bound collection since its beginning in 1898 as *ACA Journal* (also on microfilm). **Holdings:** 400 archival and records boxes relating to history and formation of the association; work done on research education projects; study topics and issues; bound volumes of board meetings for both association and foundation; biennial reports for association, 1933 to present, and foundation, 1958 to present; 158 reels of microfilm of archival materials, 1881-1976. **Subscriptions:** 150 journals and other serials; 5 newspapers.

★6728★ **American Bar Association Center on Children and the Law**
1800 M. St., N.W.
Washington, DC 20036
Phone: (202)331-2250
Sally Inada, Dir. of Pubns.

Subjects: Child abuse and neglect, foster care, adoption, parental kidnapping of children, child support, grandparents' rights, developmentally disabled children's rights, child exploitation. **Holdings:** 5000 books, periodicals, reports, and training and conference materials. **Subscriptions:** 12 journals and other serials.

★6729★ **American College of Obstetricians and Gynecologists Resource Center**
409 12th St., S.W.
Washington, DC 20024
Phone: (202)638-5577
Pamela Van Hine, Assoc.Dir.

Subjects: Obstetrics, gynecology, medical socioeconomics, medical education, women's health care, abortion, contraception, venereal disease, sex education, patient education. **Special Collections:** Archives; history of obstetrics-gynecology. **Holdings:** 8000 books; reprints. **Subscriptions:** 300 journals and other serials.

★6730★ **American Federation of Teachers Library**
555 New Jersey Ave. NW
Washington, DC 20001
Phone: (202)879-4481
Fax: (202)879-4545
Paula O'Connor, Dir., Info.Serv.

Subjects: Labor, childcare, education, women's rights. **Holdings:** 20,000 books. **Subscriptions:** 450 journals and other serials; 7 newspapers. **Publications:** Convention Report.

★6731★ **American Foundation for the Blind Helen Keller Archives**
15 W. 16th St.
New York, NY 10011
Phone: (212)620-2157
Alberta J. Lonergan, Archv.

Subjects: Helen Keller; Anne Sullivan Macy; John Albert Macy; Polly Thomson; work on behalf of the blind, deaf-blind, and deaf; children and women in factories; planned parenthood; labor movements; peace; suffrage. **Holdings:** 65,000 manuscripts, sound recordings, photographs, films, slides, letters, speeches, literary manuscripts, legal and genealogical material.

★6732★ **American Humane Association American Association for Protecting Children National Resource Center on Child Abuse and Neglect**
63 Inverness Dr., E.
Englewood, CO 80112-5117
Phone: (303)792-9900
Toll-free: 800-227-5242
Fax: (303)792-5333
Robyn Alsop, Coord.Info.Serv.

Subjects: Children - abuse, neglect, sexual abuse; risk assessment; case decision making;

staffing; caseload management; community resource integration; reasonable efforts. **Special Collections:** Child protective services policies and procedures manuals for all states. **Holdings:** 1000 books; 5 VF drawers of subject files; 5 VF drawers of organizations; 50 state child protective service newsletters. **Subscriptions:** 100 journals and other serials. **Publications:** *Protecting Children*, quarterly - available by subscription or membership; *Child Sexual Abuse Curriculum*; *Framework for Advocacy*; *Research Issues in Risk Assessment*; *Understanding Medical Diagnosis of Child Maltreatment*; list of publications - available on request. **Remarks:** Member of National Child Welfare Resource and Research Centers and National Child Abuse Coalition. Affiliated with the Clearinghouse on Child Abuse and Neglect (Federal).

★6733★ American Life Lobby
Library
PO Box 490
Stafford, VA 22554
Phone: (703)659-4171
Fax: (703)659-2586
Robert Marshall, Contact

Subjects: Abortion; euthanasia; infanticide; opposition to tax-subsidized birth control organizations, population control in foreign countries; opposition to sex, violence, and profanity on television and radio; opposition to school and television sex education programs. **Holdings:** 17,000 flyers, leaflets, booklets, books, audiovisual materials, and other items.

★6734★ Americans United for Life
Library
343 S. Dearborn St., Ste. 1804
Chicago, IL 60604
Phone: (312)786-9494
Jeanette M. O'Connor, Pubns. Mgr.

Subjects: Abortion, euthanasia, infanticide. Holdings: Books, articles, government publications.

★6735★ Association for Voluntary Surgical
Contraception
Library
79 Madison Ave.
New York, NY 10016
Phone: (212)561-8040
Fax: (212)779-9439
William J. Record, Libn.

Subjects: Sexual sterilization. **Holdings:** 3010 books; 80 feet of vertical files. **Subscriptions:** 118 journals and other serials.

★6736★ Atlanta Lesbian Feminist Alliance
Southeastern Lesbian Archives
Box 5502
Atlanta, GA 30307
Phone: (404)378-9769

Subjects: Lesbian feminism, women's theory, lesbianism, feminism. **Holdings:** 800 books; 435 periodical titles; 10 linear feet of archives. **Subscriptions:** 192 journals and other serials. **Publications:** *Atalanta*, monthly—by subscription or membership.

★6737★ Augusta Technical Institute
Library
3116 Deans Bridge Rd.
Augusta, GA 30906
Phone: (404)796-6900
Fax: (404)796-8810
Dr. Robert W. Duttweiler, Lib.Dir.

Subjects: Telecommunications, electronics, engineering, business. **Special Collections:** Women's Studies Collection. **Holdings:** 50,000 books; 5000 bound periodical volumes; government documents depository; industry standards. **Subscriptions:** 300 journals and other serials; 25 newspapers.

★6738★ Barnard College
Barnard Center for Research on Women
Birdie Goldsmith Ast Resource Collection
101 Barnard Hall
3009 Broadway
New York, NY 10027
Phone: (212)854-2067
Fax: (212)854-7491
Leslie Coleman, Dir., Women's Ctr.

Subjects: Feminist theory; sex roles and sex differences; women's movement; education; employment; legal status; health; violence and sexual exploitation; women in other countries, history, and the arts; women and development. **Special Collections:** Bobbye Ortiz Collection on Women in Developing Nations; Helen Marieskind health files; Working Women's Institute files on sexual harassment; Professor Ruth Milkman's Materials on Comparable Worth & Pay Equity; Norma Wikler files on reproductive technology. **Holdings:** 1800 volumes; 5700 journal articles, reports, clippings, fact sheets, pamphlets, conference proceedings, unpublished papers, government documents; bibliographies; handbooks; directories; special issues of journals. **Subscriptions:** 160 periodicals, newspapers, and newsletters. **Publications:** List of publications - available on request. Maintains current information on internships and job opportunities in fields related to women's issues, as well as information on graduate and undergraduate programs in women's studies.

★6739★ Bayfront Medical Center, Inc.
Health Sciences Library
701 6th St., S.
St. Petersburg, FL 33701
Phone: (813)893-6136
Fax: (813)893-6797
Sylvia Cesanek, Hea.Sci.Libn.

Subjects: Medicine, family practice, geriatrics, nursing, obstetrics, gynecology, oncology, physical rehabilitation. **Holdings:** 1500 books; 3000 bound periodical volumes; 25,000 microfiche cards; 200 Audio-Digest tapes; 310 video cassettes. **Subscriptions:** 200 journals.

★6740★ Bennett College
Thomas F. Holgate Library
Special Collections
900 E. Washington
Campus Box M
Greensboro, NC 27401
Phone: (919)273-4431

Special Collections: Afro-American Women's Collection (480 books; 2 VF drawers); Norris Wright Cuney Papers (personal and business correspondence, diaries, and newspaper clippings); College Archives (51 boxes; 3 file cabinets; 28 shelves; 1 bookcase).

★6741★ Bethune Museum and Archives
for Black Women's History
1318 Vermont Ave., NW
Washington, DC 20005
Phone: (202)332-1233

Founded: 1979. **Description:** Promotes greater public awareness of Black women's history and serves as a resource for scholarly research. **Holdings:** Contains the largest manuscript collection of materials pertaining to organizational and individual contributions of Black women in America, and over 3000 photographs. **Publications:** A pamphlet details available books, kits, posters, films and exhibits.

★6742★ Birmingham Public and Jefferson
County Free Library
Linn-Henley Library for Southern Historical
Research
Department of Archives and Manuscripts
2100 Park Place
Birmingham, AL 35203
Phone: (205)226-3645
Fax: (205)226-3743
Marvin Y. Whiting, Archv./Cur., Mss.

Subjects: Birmingham, Alabama - history, civil rights, real estate development, politics and government, private utilities, industry, civic organizations, photographic history, women's history. **Special Collections:** Birmingham Municipal Records (510 linear feet); Jefferson County Public Records (1550 linear feet); Civil Rights in Alabama (90 linear feet and microforms); Robert Jemison, Jr. papers (250 linear feet); Birmingham Water Works Company records (180 linear feet); Southern Women's Archives (500 linear feet). **Holdings:** 1055 books; 405 bound periodical volumes; 9000 linear feet of archives and manuscripts; 923 reels of microfilm of archives and manuscripts; 2106 microfiche; 600 oral history cassette tapes; 215,000 photographic prints and negatives. **Subscriptions:** 9 journals and other serials; 21 newspapers. **Publications:** *A Guide to the Collections of the Department of Archives and Manuscripts*, Linn-Henley Research Library - for sale.

★6743★ Birmingham Southern College
Charles Andrew Rush Learning
Center/Library
Special Collections
800 8th Ave., W.
Box A-20
Birmingham, AL 35254-9990
Phone: (205)226-4744
Billy Pennington, Dir.

Holdings: Methodism (880 volumes); Americana (1920 items); Alabama History and Authors (1314 volumes); Branscomb Collection For, By, About Women (335 volumes).

★6744★ Black Women in Church and
Society
Research/Resource Center
Inter Denominational Theological Center
671 Beckwith St. SW
Atlanta, GA 30314
Phone: (404)527-7740

Subjects: Liberation theology, feminism, women's movements, women in ministry. **Holdings:** 250 volumes.

★6745★ **Boston Public Library**
Rare Books and Manuscripts
Copley Sq.
PO Box 286
Boston, MA 02117
Phone: (617)536-5400
Fax: (617)267-8273
Dr. Laura V. Monti, Kpr.

Special Collections: Includes Galatea Collection of History of Women (5200 volumes).

★6746★ **Boston University**
Women's Center
Library
GSU Student Center
775 Commonwealth Ave., Ste. 9
Boston, MA 02215
Phone: (617)353-9800
Maureen Hurley, Adv.

Subjects: Women's studies, lesbianism, sociology, psychology, fiction, health, poetry. **Holdings:** 300 books; 40 reports; 100 back issues of *MS*, magazine; 3 drawers of clippings and acrhival materials.

★6747★ **Bowling Green State University**
Center for Archival Collections
Library, 5th Fl.
Bowling Green, OH 43403-0175
Phone: (419)372-2411
Fax: (419)372-7966
Paul D. Yon, Dir.

Subjects: State and local history, rare books, university archives, historic preservation. **Special Collections:** State and local government records; manuscripts (4000 cubic feet); newspapers (1000 cubic feet); published materials; archives (1000 cubic feet); Ohio Labor History (400 cubic feet); Sam Pollock Collection (150 cubic feet); Women's History (300 cubic feet); National Student Affairs Archives (400 cubic feet); Ray Bradbury Collection (1500 volumes); Franklin D. Roosevelt Collection (1000 volumes; 1000 pieces of ephemera). **Holdings:** 10,000 volumes; 1500 volumes of newspapers from 19 counties of northwest Ohio; 3000 volumes of local government records; 20,000 microforms; 200,000 photographs; 3800 other cataloged items. **Subscriptions:** 77 journals and other serials; 55 newspapers. **Publications:** *Archival Chronicle*, 3/year—free upon request.

★6748★ **Brooklyn Public Library**
Social Science/Philosophy Division
Grand Army Plaza
Brooklyn, NY 11238
Phone: (718)780-7746
Madeline Kiner, Div.Chf.

Subjects: Economics, education, demography, philosophy, psychology, sociology, womens' history, politics and government, labor, law. **Special Collections:** College histories; comparative folklore (in English); railroads. **Holdings:** 200,000 books; 7000 periodicals, bound and on microfilm; ERIC on microfiche, 1980 to present; U.S. government documents; New York State documents (partial depository); 4 VF drawers of pamphlets. **Subscriptions:** 850 journals and other serials.

★6749★ **Brown University**
Christine Dunlap Farnham Archives
John Hay Library
Box A
Providence, RI 02912
Phone: (401)863-2148

Subjects: History of women at Brown University and Pembroke College; history of Brown alumnae; women in Rhode Island; women's higher education, literature, and social history. **Holdings:** Manuscripts; organizational records; photographs; ephemera; Pembroke College records; student papers, correspondence, diaries, lecture notes, photographs, memorabilia, films, and scrapbooks. **Publications:** *Research Guide to the Christine Dunlap Farnham Archives.*

★6750★ **Brown University**
Pembroke Center for Teaching and
Research on Women
Library
Rockefeller Library
Box A
Providence, RI 02912
Phone: (401)863-3581
Jodi Caldwell, Libn.

Subjects: Women, cultural concepts of gender, and the ways those concepts are related to other cultural, social, political, and economic factors. **Holdings:** Figures not available. **Remarks:** Alternate telephone number(s): (401)863-2643.

★6751★ **Business and Professional**
Women's Foundation
Marguerite Rawalt Resource Center
2012 Massachusetts Ave. NW
Washington, DC 20036
Phone: (202)293-1200
Ms. J. Lyle Martin, Cons.Libn.

Subjects: Women, with special emphasis on economic issues of importance to working women: jobs, careers, occupational segregation, comparable worth, sexual harassment, displaced homemakers, women's legal status. **Holdings:** 5000 books; 650 dissertations on microfilm; 12,000 VF materials; archival materials. **Subscriptions:** 113 journals and other serials. **Publications:** *Selected Acquisitions*, bimonthly.

★6752★ **C. Henry Kempe National Center**
for the Prevention and Treatment of
Child Abuse and Neglect
Library
University of Colorado Health Sciences
Center
Department of Pediatrics
1205 Oneida
Denver, CO 80220-2944
Phone: (303)321-3963

Subjects: Child abuse - diagnosis, prevention, treatment, intervention; sexual abuse; parenting. **Holdings:** Books; bound periodical volumes; reports; files. **Subscriptions:** 6 journals and other serials.

★6753★ **California Family Study Center**
Library
5433 Laurel Canyon Blvd.
North Hollywood, CA 91607-2114
Phone: (818)509-5959
Fax: (818)762-6547
Mark Stover, Dir.

Subjects: Marriage and family counseling, psychotherapy, psychology, research methods. **Holdings:** 5000 books; 1000 professional papers; 110 journals; 40 journal titles on microfiche; 500 audio cassettes; 175 video cassettes; 21 films; 6 VF drawers. **Subscriptions:** 150 journals and other serials. TSS Electronic mail address: enq4mes@mvs.oac.ucla.edu (InterNet).

★6754★ **California School of Professional**
Psychology
Los Angeles Campus Library
1000 S. Fremont Ave.
Alhambra, CA 91803-1360
Phone: (818)284-2777
Fax: (818)284-1682
Tobeylynn Birch, Dir. of Lib.

Subjects: Psychology-clinical, industrial/organizational, health, community; public policy; women's issues; homosexuality and lesbianism; minority mental health. **Holdings:** 20,000 books; 2000 bound periodical volumes; 4000 microfiche; 1800 dissertations; 80 reels of microfilm; 450 audiotapes; 125 video cassettes; 7 films. **Subscriptions:** 330 journals and other serials.

★6755★ **California State University,**
Northridge
Urban Archives Center
Oviatt Library, Rm. 4
Northridge, CA 91330
Phone: (818)885-2487

Subjects: Los Angeles County and San Fernando Valley history, Chambers of Commerce, education, labor and guild history, political history, minority and ethnic groups, women's studies, social service organizations, environment, journalism. **Special Collections:** California Association for the Education of Young Children (10 linear feet); California Federation of Teachers, AFT, AFL-CIO (60 linear feet); Senator Thomas C. Carrell Collection (12 linear feet); Congressman James C. Corman papers (300 linear feet); League of Women Voters, Los Angeles Chapter (30 linear feet); The Los Angeles Newspaper Guild (25 linear feet); The United Way of Los Angeles (50 linear feet); The YWCA of Los Angeles Collection (22 linear feet); Bustop Campaign Collection (86 linear feet); The Jewish Family Service Collection (13.5 linear feet); Agness M. Underwood Collection (12 linear feet); Dorothy Boberg Collection (15 linear feet); John and LaRee Caughey's ACLU Papers on School Integration (1 linear foot). **Holdings:** 2100 linear feet of documents, minutes, labor newspapers; photographs; oral histories. **Publications:** *The UAC Newsletter*, 3/year; finding guides to collections.

★6756★ Carolina Population Center
Library
University of North Carolina at Chapel Hill
CB No. 8120
Chapel Hill, NC 27516-3997
Phone: (919)962-3081
Fax: (919)966-6638
Patricia E. Shipman, Hd.Libn.

Subjects: Population dynamics, policy, education; abortion; family planning; fertility. **Special Collections:** Collected papers of the Population Associations of America, 1968 to present; Bibliography File (350). **Holdings:** 9000 books; 1500 bound periodical volumes; 40,000 analytics; 15,000 documents, technical reports, manuscripts; 90 documents on microfiche. **Subscriptions:** 375 journals and other serials. **Telecommunications Services:** Electronic mail address: CLWARD@UNCVM1 (BITNET).

★6757★ Catalyst
Information Center
250 Park Ave., S., 5th Fl.
New York, NY 10003-1459
Phone: (212)777-8900
Fax: (212)477-4252
Mary C. Mattis, V.Pres. Res.

Subjects: Corporate women. **Special Collections:** Work and family (two career families); leadership development and management. **Holdings:** 5000 books; 8000 vertical files of periodical articles, government documents, studies. **Subscriptions:** 200 journals and other serials.

★6758★ Catholics United for Life
c/o Dennis Musk
3050 Gap Knob Rd.
New Hope, KY 40052
Phone: (502)325-3061
Fax: (502)325-3091

Subjects: Catholic moral and social teachings - family life, marriage, the value of human life, natural family planning; alternatives to abortion; theology; papal teachings; hagiology; and related subjects. **Holdings:** 10,000 volumes.

★6759★ Caylor-Nickel Medical Center
Library
1 Caylor-Nickel Square
Bluffton, IN 46714
Phone: (219)824-3500
Patricia Niblick, Med.Libn.

Subjects: Surgery, internal medicine, pathology, radiology, pediatrics, obstetrics, gynecology, urology, nursing, pharmacology, endocrinology. **Special Collections:** Complete set of the Collected Papers in Medicine and Surgery from the Mayo Clinic and the Mayo Foundation. **Holdings:** 9782 books; 5126 bound periodical volumes; 1 VF drawer of staff reprints; 902 tapes; 10 films. **Subscriptions:** 417 journals and other serials. **Publications:** New Acquisitions list.

★6760★ Cedar Crest College
Women's Center
Library
100 College Dr.
Allentown, PA 18104
Phone: (215)437-4471
Patricia Sacks, Dir.

Subjects: Psychology and sociology of women, job opportunities, education, the women's movement, elderly women. **Holdings:** 300

books; college guides; occupational reference materials.

★6761★ Center for the American Woman & Politics
Library
Eagleton Institute, Rutgers University
Wood Lawn, Neilson Campus
New Brunswick, NJ 08901
Phone: (908)932-9384
Fax: (908)932-6778
Kathy Kleeman, Sr.Prog.Assoc.

Subjects: Women and American politics and government. **Holdings:** 700 books; 2000 papers, pamphlets, clippings. **Subscriptions:** 75 journals and other serials. **Publications:** List of publications - available on request. **Remarks:** CAWP is a research and education center committed to increasing knowledge about American women's participation in government and politics.

★6762★ Center for Humane Options in Childbirth Experiences (CHOICE)
Library
5426 Madison St.
Hilliard, OH 43026
Abby Kinne, Founder

Subjects: Home birth, Lamaze method, natural childbirth, breast feeding, birth alternatives, nutrition, midwifery, Monitrice program for hospital coaches. **Holdings:** 400 books; films; pamphlets; statistical reports.

★6763★ Center for Population Options
Resource Center
1012 14th St. NW, Suite 1200
Washington, DC 20005
Phone: (202)347-5700
Fax: (202)347-2263

Subjects: Adolescent fertility issues - sexuality education, birth control, teenage pregnancy and child bearing, health, human immunodeficiency virus (HIV) among adolescents, condom availability; school-based clinics. **Holdings:** 2500 volumes.

★6764★ Chicago Historical Society
Library and Archives
Clark St. at North Ave.
Chicago, IL 60614
Phone: (312)642-4600
Cheryl Bezio-Gorham, Executive Director

Subjects: History of women in Chicago, Illinois and the U.S.; women in various professions and occupations; women's societies and clubs; women's rights; social service; suffrage and the temperance movements; biographies of leading Chicago women. **Special Collections:** Papers of the Board of Lady Managers of the World's Columbian Exposition (1893); archives of the Chicago Women's Liberation Union (formed 1968). **Publications:** Exhibition catalogs; illustrated quarterly journal; research monographs. **Remarks:** The Prints and Photographs Department maintains collection of 500,000 prints, photographs, broadsides, and posters relating to Chicago history.

★6765★ Chicago Public Library
Central Library
400 N. Franklin St.
Chicago, IL 60602
Phone: (312)269-2900

Description: Maintains holdings on women and women's organizations in general. Collections include Business/Science/Technology, Social Sciences and History, Literature and Language, Government Publications, Visual and Performing Arts, and General Information Services. Administers Film/Video Center at the Cultural Center, which circulates films and videotapes on various topics, including rape prevention and changing roles of women. **Special Collections:** Mrs. Harlan Ward Cooley Papers—a collection of correspondence relating to the planning of a lecture series presented by The Chicago Women's Club in conjuction with The National Council of Women, at the Century of Progress Exposition in Chicago, 1934. **Telecommunications Services:** DIAL-LAW—telephone information service that supplies taped information on such topics as child custody, spouse abuse, and marriage/divorce. **Publications:** Monthly Calendar of Events for the Branches and The Cultural Center—available at Chicago Public Library agency.

★6766★ Chicana Research & Learning Center, Inc.
Library
44 East Ave., Suite 201
Austin, TX 78701
Phone: (512)477-1604
Fax: (512)477-1767
Martha P. Cotera, Dir.

Subjects: Hispanic women. **Holdings:** 400 books; 500 reports.

★6767★ Child Custody Services of Philadelphia, Inc.
Resource Center
PO Box 202
Glenside, PA 19038-0202
Phone: (215)576-0177
Dr. Ken Lewis, Dir.

Subjects: Child custody, single-parent families, divorce, child-snatching, mental health and law. **Special Collections:** Father's rights movement; women's liberation. **Holdings:** 828 books; 50 bound periodical volumes; 16 dissertation abstracts; 25 special reports; 12 grant narratives; 28 television and radio news documentaries; 50 monographs. **Subscriptions:** 75 journals and other serials; 58 newspapers. **Telecommunications Services:** Electronic mail address: 354-0356 (MCI Mail). **Publications:** CCES Workshop Series; CCES Monograph Series.

★6768★ Child Trends, Inc.
Library
2100 M St. NW, Rm. 610
Washington, DC 20037-1207
Phone: (202)223-6288
Fax: (202)728-4142
Dr. Nicholas Zill, Exec.Dir.

Subjects: Physical, social, emotional, and psychological development of children; influence of family, school, peers, neighborhood, religion, media on children; teen pregnancy; family strengths; statistics. **Holdings:** Statistics and reports from U.S. Bureau of the Census, National Center for Health Statistics, National Center for Education Statistics.

★6769★ The Claremont Colleges
Ella Strong Denison Library
Scripps College
Claremont, CA 91711
Phone: (714)621-8000
Fax: (714)621-4733
Judy Harvey Sahak, Libn.

Subjects: Humanities and fine arts. **Special Collections:** Perkins and Kirby Collection (history of the book and book arts); Macpherson Collection (women); Metcalf Collection (Gertrude Stein); Pacific Coast Browning Foundation (Browning); Hanna Collection (Southwest); Miller-Howard Collection (Latin America); Ament Collection (Melville); Louise Seymour Jones Collection (4600 bookplates); original and revised versions of Richard W. Armour (62 titles, including 44 manuscripts); Scripps College Archives (including Alexander and Hartley Burr, Scripps, Ellen Browning). **Holdings:** 100,129 books. **Subscriptions:** 106 journals and other serials.

★6770★ Clearinghouse on Child Abuse
and Neglect Information
PO Box 1182
Washington, DC 20013
Phone: (703)821-2086
Fax: (703)506-0384

Subjects: Child abuse and neglect, child protective services. **Special Collections:** State statutes; directory of program directories. **Holdings:** 12,000 books, articles, and reports. **Subscriptions:** 30 journals and other serials. **Publications:** Listing of the National Center on Child Abuse and Neglect publications - available upon request. **Remarks:** Maintained by the U.S. Department of Health & Human Services—National Center on Child Abuse and Neglect (NCCAN) and the Office of Policy, Planning and Legislation (OPPL).

★6771★ Clearinghouse on Family Violence
Information
PO Box 1182
Washington, DC 20013
Phone: (703)385-7565
Fax: (703)385-3206

Subjects: Spouse abuse, elder abuse, sibling abuse, parent abuse. **Holdings:** 700 books, articles, and reports. **Subscriptions:** 10 journals and other serials. **Publications:** List of publications - available upon request. **Remarks:** Maintained by the U.S. Department of Health & Human Services - National Center on Child Abuse and Neglect (NCCAN) and the Office of Policy, Planning and Legislation (OPPL).

★6772★ College of St. Catherine
Library
Ade Bethune Collection
2004 Randolph Ave.
St. Paul, MN 55105
Phone: (612)690-6650
Fax: (612)690-6024
Janet Kinney, Lib.Dir.

Subjects: Ade Bethune, sacred art, liturgy and art, women artists, liturgical movement, Catholic church history, Catholic radicalism, Catholic Worker Movement. **Special Collections:** Ade Bethune Collection. **Holdings:** 23 VF drawers; 10 map drawers.

★6773★ College of St. Catherine
Library
Women's Collection
Saint Catherine Library
2004 Randolph Ave.
St. Paul, MN 55105
Phone: (612)690-6648
Fax: (612)690-6024
Janet Kinney, Lib.Dir.

Subjects: Sociological and economic studies on women published in the early 20th century; psychological liberation of women; history, education, status of women in all phases of public and private life. **Special Collections:** Herstory (collection of 300 women's journals, newspapers, newsletters, 1956-1971; 23 reels of microfilm); U.S. Dept. of Labor, *Women's Bureau Bulletin*, 1918-1954 (microfiche). **Holdings:** 5400 books; 20 bound periodical volumes; 8 VF drawers of pamphlets and clippings. **Subscriptions:** 40 journals and other serials.

★6774★ College of Saint Mary
Library
Special Collections
1901 S. 72nd St.
Omaha, NE 68124
Phone: (402)399-2471
Fax: (402)399-2686
Sr. Susan Severin, Dir.

Subjects: Spirituality, literature, education. **Special Collections:** Women's Studies (5000 volumes). **Holdings:** Figures not available.

★6775★ Columbia Hospital for Women
Medical Library
2425 L St. NW
Washington, DC 20037
Phone: (202)293-6560
Elizabeth M. Haggart, Libn.

Subjects: Gynecology, obstetrics. **Holdings:** 1800 books. **Subscriptions:** 280 journals and other serials.

★6776★ Columbia University
Center for Population & Family Health
Library/Information Program
60 Haven Ave.
New York, NY 10032
Phone: (212)305-6960
Fax: (212)305-7024
Susan K. Pasquariella, Ph.D, Hd.Libn.

Subjects: Family planning, evaluative methodology, operations research, demography. **Special Collections:** Developing countries family planning program evaluations. **Holdings:** 7000 books; 30,000 published and unpublished reports, manuscripts, reprints, documents. **Subscriptions:** 200 journals and other serials. **Telecommunications Services:** Telex: 971913 POPFAMHLTH. **Publications:** *POPLINE Thesaurus; CPFH Working Papers.* **Remarks:** Center for Population & Family Health is a part of International Institute for the Study of Human Reproduction, Columbia University.

★6777★ Columbia University
Whitney M. Young, Jr. Memorial Library of
Social Work
309 International Affairs Bldg.
New York, NY 10027
Phone: (212)854-5159
Laura Delaney, Contact

Subjects: Social work; community organization; social policy development and administration;

health, mental health, mental retardation; social services - family and children, homemaker, day care, legal; aging; corrections and court services - probation, parole, diversionary treatment; alcoholism and drug addiction; industrial social welfare and manpower programs; urban education; intergroup relations; social and physical rehabilitation. **Special Collections:** The Mary Richmond Archives; The Homer Folks Archives; The Whitney M. Young, Jr. Papers; The Dorothy Hutchinson Collection on the Child; The Brookdale Collection on Gerontology. **Holdings:** 130,000 volumes; student projects; dissertations; agency reports. **Subscriptions:** 646 journals and other serials. **Telecommunications Services:** Electronic mail address: LD16@CUNIXF.CC.COLUMBIA.EDU (InterNet).

★6778★ Commission on Civil Rights
National Clearinghouse Library
1121 Vermont Ave. NW
Washington, DC 20425
Phone: (202)376-8110
Fax: (202)376-8315
Barbara J. Fontana, Libn.

Subjects: Civil rights, economics, education, sex discrimination, sociology, law. **Special Collections:** The aged and the handicapped; commission publications. **Holdings:** 65,000 books; 1100 bound periodical volumes; 1200 state and federal codes and statutes; 110 legal periodical titles; 500 reels of microfilm of minority periodicals; 300 journals on microfiche. **Subscriptions:** 300 journals and newspapers. **Publications:** Monthly acquisitions list; bibliographies.

★6779★ Cornell University
New York State School of Industrial and
Labor Relations
Sanford V. Lenz Library
15 E. 26th St.
New York, NY 10010-1565
Phone: (212)340-2845
Fax: (212)340-2822
Donna L. Schulman, Dir.

Subjects: Industrial relations, labor relations, collective bargaining, arbitration, women and work. **Special Collections:** Trade Union Women (1000 books; 200 subject files). **Holdings:** 6000 books. **Subscriptions:** 125 journals and other serials; 65 newspapers. **Publications:** Acquisitions list, irregular.

★6780★ Dayton and Montgomery County
Public Library
Adult Services Department
215 E. Third St.
Dayton, OH 45402-2103
Phone: (513)227-9500
Glenna Reynolds, Dept.Hd.

Subjects: General collection. **Special Collections:** Dayton and Montgomery County history, genealogy; Women's Suffrage Collection; Shaker Collection; Dayton and Montgomery County photographs (2000 items); large print (4200 items); foreign languages (French, German, Italian, Spanish, Vietnamese, Slavic; 4000 items); sheet music (12 VF drawers); adult literacy and English as a second language (1200 titles). **Holdings:** 500,000 books. **Telecommunications Services:** TTY: (513)224-9433. **Publications:** *BITS* (Business Industry Technology Service), 10/year; Dayton/Miami Valley Clearinghouse, annual.

★6781★ Deaconess Community Lutheran Church of America
Lutheran Deaconess Community Library
801 Merion Square Rd.
Gladwyne, PA 19035
Phone: (215)642-8838
Sr. Catharine Stirewalt, Libn.

Subjects: Religion, theology, Christian education, church history, Bible, psychology, education, social work, women's work in the church. **Special Collections:** Historical and archival collection of Deaconess Community, LCA (26 VF drawers; 95 documentary storage boxes; 2 memorabilia cabinets; 150 volumes). **Holdings:** 9000 volumes; 30 pamphlet cases of audiovisual and curriculum material for Christian education; 6 VF drawers of miscellanea. **Subscriptions:** 38 journals and other serials.

★6782★ Defense for Children International—United States of America
Library
210 Forsyth St.
New York, NY 10002
Phone: (212)353-0951

Subjects: Child maltreatment and abuse, children's rights legislation, children and war, refugees, juvenile justice. **Holdings:** 1000 volumes; statistical materials.

★6783★ Delegation for Friendship Among Women
Library
2219 Caroline Ln.
South St. Paul, MN 55075
Phone: (612)455-5620
Mary Pomeroy, Delegation Sec.

Subjects: Activities of women in the Third World. **Special Collections:** Womens' organizations in third world or developing countries. **Holdings:** 1000 books; 30 other cataloged items. **Subscriptions:** 20 journals and other serials; 6 newspapers.

★6784★ Diocese of Allentown
Pro-Life Library
1135 Stefko Blvd.
Bethlehem, PA 18017
Phone: (215)691-0380
Suzanne Mello, Contact

Subjects: Bioethics, abortion, sexuality, death and dying. **Special Collections:** United States Catholic Conference Documentary Service; Origins Documentary Service. **Holdings:** 700 volumes; 600 audiotapes; 40 videotapes; 100 pamphlets and booklets; 50 government statistics and reports; newspaper clippings. **Subscriptions:** 11 journals and other serials. **Publications:** pamphlets and tracts, irregular; curriculum publications.

★6785★ Duke University
Special Collections Department
344 Perkins Library
Durham, NC 27706
Phone: (919)684-3372
Fax: (919)684-2855
Robert L. Byrd, Dir., Spec.Coll.

Subjects: Southern history and literature; U.S. history; history of advertising; history of economic theory; British history and literature, women's studies; English and American literature; Utopian literature; Wesleyana and Methodistica; German Baroque literature; parapsychology; juvenile literature; Nazi and Fascist propaganda and literature; American popular sheet music. **Holdings:** 137,000 books; 11,000 maps, broadsides, and pieces of sheet music; 9.5 million manuscripts. **Publications:** *Guide to the Cataloged Collections in the Manuscript Department of the William R. Perkins Library* (1980; 1005 pages).

★6786★ Eastern Washington State Historical Society
Research Library and Special Collections
Cheney Cowles Museum
W. 2316 1st Ave.
Spokane, WA 99204
Phone: (509)456-3931
Glenn Mason, Dir.

Subjects: History of Eastern Washington, Spokane, the Inland Empire; Inland Empire mining; Eastern Washington social, agricultural, women's history; Spokane business history; Native American plateau cultures. **Holdings:** 7000 books; 100,000 historical photographs; 140 bound periodical volumes; 2100 linear feet of manuscripts; 45 VF drawers of newspaper clippings; 750 oral history tapes; 35 videotapes; 3 music tapes; 9 reels of microfilm; 12 drawers of maps. **Subscriptions:** 18 journals and other serials.

★6787★ Educational Center for Life
Professional Bldg., Suite 19
909 Woodward Ave.
Pontiac, MI 48341-2977
Phone: (313)338-1910
Phyllis Sullivan, R.N., B.S.N., Dir.

Subjects: Abortion, infanticide, euthanasia, chastity, medical ethics, alternatives to abortion. **Holdings:** 220 books; 12 bound periodical volumes; 9 VF drawers; films; videotapes; audiotapes. **Subscriptions:** 20 journals and other serials. **Publications:** *Pregnancy Services of Southeastern Michigan Directory; Teen Alert Card;* coloring books.

★6788★ Emory University
Special Collections Department
Woodruff Library
Atlanta, GA 30322
Phone: (404)727-6887
Fax: (404)727-0053
Linda M. Matthews, Hd., Spec.Coll.

Subjects: Methodism, Confederate history, Southern history, Southern journalists, Southern literature, Southern women, British and Irish literature, American and Asian Communism, Emory archives. **Holdings:** 30,000 books; 300 bound periodical volumes; 800 maps; 7500 linear feet of manuscripts; 7000 volumes of Emory University dissertations and theses; 325 reels of microfilm. **Telecommunications Services:** Electronic mail address: LIBBDB@EMUVM1 (BITNET). **Publications:** *Manuscript Sources for Women's History: A Descriptive List of Holdings in the Special Collections Department* (revised 1987).

★6789★ ERIC Clearinghouse on Elementary and Early Childhood Education
University of Illinois
805 W. Pennsylvania Ave.
Urbana, IL 61801
Phone: (217)333-1386
Fax: (217)333-3767
Lilian G. Katz, Ph.D., Dir.

Subjects: Early childhood education, elementary education, day care, parent education, infants, child development and education through early adolescence. **Holdings:** ERIC microfiche collection; VF drawers; small resource library of early childhood materials. **Subscriptions:** 150 journals and other serials. **Telecommunications Services:** Electronic mail address: ericeece@ux1 (BITNET). **Publications:** ERIC/EECE Newsletter; resource lists and digests—free upon request; list of additional publications—for sale, available upon request.

★6790★ Family Health International
Library
P.O. Box 13950
Research Triangle Park, NC 27709
Phone: (919)544-7040
Fax: (919)544-7261
William Barrows, Info. Serv. Mgr.

Subjects: Reproductive medicine, family planning, contraception, population, developing countries. **Special Collections:** AIDS; breast cancer. **Holdings:** 5500 books; 800 unbound periodical volumes; 9000 reprints and unpublished documents; 330 patents. **Subscriptions:** 425 journals and other serials; 280 newsletters. **Publications:** *Network* (newsletter), quarterly; *Magdelene Messenger*, 2/year; Annual List of FHI Publications and Reprints.

★6791★ The Family Institute
Crowley Library
680 N. Lake Shore Dr., Suite 1306
Chicago, IL 60611
Phone: (312)908-7854
Phyllis Anne Miller, Libn.

Subjects: Therapy - family, marital, divorce, step-family, adolescent; adoption issues; death and mourning; anorexia; schizophrenia; dysfunctional families; ethnic issues. **Special Collections:** Family therapy. **Holdings:** 2500 books; 5000 reprints; 60 videotapes; 200 audio cassettes. **Subscriptions:** 25 journals and other serials.

★6792★ Family Life Information Exchange
P.O. Box 37299
Washington, DC 20013-7299
Phone: (301)585-6636
Florence Lehr, Proj.Mgr.

Subjects: Family planning, sexually transmitted diseases, adolescent pregnancy, adoption, contraception, reproductive health. **Holdings:** 5000 monographs. **Subscriptions:** 60 journals and other serials. **Remarks:** The exchange was created to serve federally supported service agencies. It provides information to family-planning workers, educators, and trainers.

★6793★ Florida State University
Center for the Study of Population
659 Bellamy
Tallahassee, FL 32306-4063
Phone: (904)644-1762
Fax: (904)644-8818
Robert McCann, Libn.

Subjects: Migration, urbanization, fertility, mortality, population education, family planning. **Special Collections:** World Fertility Survey Comparative Studies, Scientific Reports and Occasional Papers (200); Acquired Immune Deficiency Syndrome; U.S. Population & Housing Census, 1950-1990 (2100 volumes); Gahna Selegen Collection of Soviet Population Materials (50 volumes). **Holdings:** 9700 books; 3500 bound periodical volumes; 3200 vertical files. **Subscriptions:** 100 journals and other serials. **Publications:** Working Papers series, irregular—by subscription.

★6794★ Forbes Health System
Forbes Regional Health Center
Medical Library
2570 Haymaker Rd.
Monroeville, PA 15146
Phone: (412)858-2422
Elena Hartmann, Med.Libn.

Subjects: Medicine, nursing, family practice, obstetrics, gynecology, pediatrics, oncology. **Holdings:** 1614 books; 462 bound periodical volumes; Audio-Digest tapes. **Subscriptions:** 111 journals and other serials. **Publications:** Forbes Libraries Booktales, irregular.

★6795★ Foundation for Citizen Education
Anna Lord Strauss Library
35 Maiden Ln.
Albany, NY 12207
Phone: (518)465-4162
Fax: (518)465-0812
Rita Lashway, Exec.Dir.

Subjects: Woman's suffrage, government, politics, international relations. **Holdings:** 500 books; other cataloged items. **Remarks:** Affiliated with the League of Women Voters of New York State.

★6796★ Freedom Information Service
(FIS)
PO Box 3568
Jackson, MS 39207
Phone: (601)352-3398
Jan Hillegas, Treas.

Founded: 1965. **Description:** Researches activities of workers, blacks, and grass roots organizations through the FIS Deep South People's History Project. Maintains extensive Mississippi-centered library and archives. Distributes press releases on current southern news; reprints items on women's liberation and political education. **Publications:** FIS Mississippi Newsletter, periodic. • Has also issued political and economic publications relevant to the civil rights movement and black candidates. **Formerly:** (1965) Freedom Information Center.

★6797★ Gay Alliance of the Genesee
Valley Inc.
Library
179 Atlantic Ave.
Rochester, NY 14607
Phone: (716)244-8640
Tom Krolak, Libn.

Subjects: Gay and lesbian literature, history, male and female fiction, feminism, sex, religion and philosophy. **Holdings:** 1400 books; periodicals; newspapers. **Subscriptions:** 5 journals and other serials; 6 newspapers. **Publications:** Empty Closet, monthly.

★6798★ General Federation of Women's
Clubs
Women's History and Resource Center
1734 N St. NW
Washington, DC 20036
Phone: (202)347-3168
Fax: (202)835-0246
Cynthia N. Swanson, Dir.

Subjects: Women's history, women's issues, women's clubs, public affairs, the arts, home life. **Special Collections:** Archives of the General Federation of Women's Clubs (1890 to present; 850 linear feet); Good Housekeeping "Women in Passage" Collection on the UN Decade for Women (1975-1985; 25 linear feet). **Holdings:** 1000 volumes; 68 bound periodical volumes; 100 AV programs; 1 reel of microfilm; VF drawers; manuscripts. **Publications:** Brochure. **Remarks:** Center is dedicated to women's history, with emphasis on women in volunteerism.

★6799★ Girls Incorporated
National Resource Center
441 W. Michigan St.
Indianapolis, IN 46202
Phone: (317)634-7546
Mary Maschino, Libn.

Subjects: Girls' issues, including development, single sex environments, girls in math and science, health and sexuality, preventing adolescent pregnancy, sports, career education, nontraditional jobs, gender roles and relationships. **Holdings:** 3000 books; 25 filmstrips and slide sets; 240 vertical files; 650 dissertations on microfiche; 55 posters; 30 video cassettes; 120 program models. **Subscriptions:** 150 journals and other serials. **Publications:** Choices: Teen Woman's Journal for Self-awareness and Personal Planning; What Do We Know About Girls; Facts and Reflections on Female Adolescent Sexuality; Facts and Reflections on Careers for Today's Girls; monographs; specialized bibliographies; Facts and Reflections on Girls and Substance Use. **Formerly:** Girls Clubs of America.

★6800★ The Hastings Center
Library
255 Elm Rd.
Briarcliff Manor, NY 10510
Phone: (914)762-8500
Fax: (914)762-2124
Marna Howarth, Libn.

Subjects: Medical ethics, ethics, ethics in life and social sciences, reproductive technologies, congressional ethics, teaching of ethics, abortion, death/dying, AIDS, genetics, public policy, health ethics. **Holdings:** 6000 books; 40 VF drawers. **Subscriptions:** 120 journals and other serials. **Publications:** IRB: A Review of Human

Subjects Research, bimonthly; Hastings Center Report, bimonthly.

★6801★ Hebrew College
Jacob and Rose Grossman Library
43 Hawes St.
Brookline, MA 02146
Phone: (617)232-8710
Maurice S. Tuchman, Dir., Lib.Serv.

Subjects: Education, Jewish history, Hebrew literature, Bible, Israel, children's literature, Rabbinic literature. **Special Collections:** Response literature; Kabbalah and Hassidic literature; Jewish education; large-print Judaica; Dr. Harry A. and Beatrice Savitz Jewish Medical History Collection; Russian Judaica; Japanese Judaica; women's studies collection. **Holdings:** 100,000 books; 2000 bound periodical volumes; 2 incunabula; 320 16th and 17th century rare books; 75 manuscripts; 1020 phonograph records; 60 maps and charts; 649 reels of microfilm; 100 slides; 134 audio cassettes. **Subscriptions:** 252 journals and other serials; 12 newspapers.

★6802★ Highland Hospital
John R. Williams, Sr. Health Sciences
Library
1000 South Ave.
Rochester, NY 14620
Phone: (716)461-6761
Fax: (716)473-1613
Diane Dayton Robbins, Lib.Dir.

Subjects: Medicine, surgery, family medicine, nursing, hematology/oncology, radiation therapy, obstetrics, gynecology. **Holdings:** 6000 books and bound periodical volumes; 7 VF drawers of archives; AV programs. **Subscriptions:** 200 journals and other serials.

★6803★ Homosexual Information Center
Library
115 Monroe St.
Bossier City, LA 71111
Phone: (318)742-4709
Leslie Colfax, Libn.

Subjects: Homosexuality, civil liberties, censorship, sexual freedom, lesbiana, prostitution, abortion. **Special Collections:** Homosexual Movement Collection (papers from 1948 to present). **Holdings:** 9800 books and bound periodical volumes; 32 VF drawers of manuscripts, clippings, pamphlets, documents; 86 legal briefs and court opinions; 30 boxes. **Subscriptions:** 32 journals and other serials; 21 newspapers. **Publications:** Directory of Homosexual Organizations; Seeds of the American Sexual Revolution; Prostitution is Legal; HIC Newsletter; Selected Bibliography of Homosexuality; selected bibliographies; reading lists; subject heading guides; list of other publications—available upon request. **Remarks:** Provides information and referral services at Homosexual Information Center, Box 8252, Universal City, CA 91608. **Also known as:** The Tangent Group.

★6804★ Howard University
Social Work Library
6th St. & Howard Pl. NW
Washington, DC 20059
Phone: (202)806-7316
Julia C. Player, Libn.

Subjects: Social work theory and practice; social policy, planning, administration; social welfare problems of black community; urban-oriented problems; human development; women's issues; gerontology. **Holdings:** 37,881 books; 8880 bound periodical volumes. **Subscriptions:** 804 journals and other serials.

★6805★ **Human Lactation Center, Ltd.**
Library
666 Sturges Hwy.
Westport, CT 06880
Phone: (203)259-5995
Fax: (203)259-7667
Dana Raphael, Ph.D., Dir.

Subjects: Breastfeeding, maternal and infant nutrition, social science, demography, childbirth, women in development, supportive behavior, mammalian reproduction, incest and child sexual abuse. **Holdings:** 4000 volumes; 7 VF drawers of reports, manuscripts, dissertations; 40 tapes; 4 films. **Subscriptions:** 70 journals and other serials; 5 newspapers. **Publications:** *Only Mothers Know: Patterns of Infant Feeding in Traditional Cultures; Being Female: Reproduction, Power and Change; Breastfeeding and Food Policy in a Hungry World; The Tender Gift: Breastfeeding.*

★6806★ **Human Life Center**
Library
University of Steubenville
Steubenville, OH 43952
Phone: (614)282-9953
Fax: (614)282-0769

Subjects: Abortion, euthanasia, and allied "sanctity of human life" issues; sexuality corresponding to Christian moral values; Catholic moral and social teachings; natural family planning; pro-life organizations. **Holdings:** 4000 volumes.

★6807★ **Human Life International**
Library
7845 E. Airpark Rd.
Gaithersburg, MD 20879
Phone: (301)670-7884
Fax: (301)869-7363
Vernon L. Kirby, Dir., Pubns.

Subjects: Abortion, contraception, post-abortion stress, euthanasia, population control, chastity. **Holdings:** 1000 books; 3 bound periodical volumes; 30 reports. **Subscriptions:** 50 journals and other serials; 20 newspapers.

★6808★ **Hutzel Hospital**
Medical Library
4707 St. Antoine Blvd.
Detroit, MI 48201
Phone: (313)745-7178
Fax: (313)993-0152
Jean M. Brennan, Dir., Lib.Serv.

Subjects: Obstetrics and gynecology, orthopedics, ophthalmology, substance abuse, arthritis/rheumatology. **Holdings:** 2500 books; 10,000 bound periodical volumes; 6 VF drawers; Audio-Digest tapes in surgery, internal medicine, obstetrics, gynecology; state medical association journals. **Subscriptions:** 450 journals and other serials.

★6809★ **Intensive Caring Unlimited**
Library
910 Bent Lane
Philadelphia, PA 19118
Phone: (215)233-4723

Subjects: Premature and high-risk infants, children with medical or developmental problems, high-risk pregnancy, infant and neonatal death. **Holdings:** 1200 volumes. **Remarks:** The activities of this parent support organization are concentrated in Pennsylvania and southern New Jersey, but it disseminates information nationwide.

★6810★ **Interfaith Medical Center**
St. John's Episcopal Hospital
Nursing and Medical Library
1545 Atlantic Ave.
Brooklyn, NY 11216
Phone: (718)604-6030
Dallas C. Hopson, Dir.

Subjects: Pediatrics, obstetrics/gynecology. **Holdings:** 2500 books; 200 bound periodical volumes. **Subscriptions:** 105 journals and other serials.

★6811★ **International Center for Research on Women**
Resource Center
1717 Massachusetts Ave. NW, Ste. 302
Washington, DC 20036
Phone: (202)797-0007
Fax: (202)797-0020
Patricia Martin, Prog.Asst.

Subjects: Women's issues - credit, income generation, development projects, access to agricultural extension services, survival strategies, heads of households, structural adjustment, recession, maternal health, child welfare, women's health. **Holdings:** 2000 books; 8500 other cataloged items. **Subscriptions:** 75 journals and other serials.

★6812★ **International Child Resource**
Institute
Information Clearinghouse
1810 Hopkins
Berkeley, CA 94707
Phone: (510)644-1000
Fax: (510)525-4106
Susan Gordon, Off.Mgr.

Subjects: Children - health, abuse, care, advocacy. **Holdings:** 10,000 pieces of information. **Telecommunications Services:** Electronic mail address: icri@igc.org (PeaceNet).

★6813★ **International Federation of Family Life Promotion**
Library
1511 K St., N.W., Suite 326
Washington, DC 20005
Phone: (202)783-0137
Fax: (202)783-7351
Richard Sevigny, Contact

Subjects: Natural family planning, sexuality. **Holdings:** 1000 books; 5 bound periodical volumes; 250 reports. **Subscriptions:** 20 journals and other serials; 4 newspapers. **Publications:** *Listings of Natural Family Planning Centers* (worldwide); *NFP reports; Congress Proceedings.* Telex: 497-2704 FIDAF.

★6814★ **International Planned Parenthood**
Federation
Western Hemisphere Region
Library
902 Broadway, 10th Fl.
New York, NY 10010
Phone: (212)995-8800
Fax: (212)995-8853
Abigail Hourwich, Libn.

Subjects: Family planning, population, demography, maternal-child health. **Special Collections:** Population and family planning in Latin America and the Caribbean. **Holdings:** 5000 books; AV programs. **Subscriptions:** 200 journals and other serials. Telex: 620661. **Publications:** *FORUM* - to family planners in Latin America and the Caribbean; occasional essays and other publications.

★6815★ **International Reference**
Organization in Forensic Medicine &
Sciences
Library and Reference Center
PO Box 8282
Wichita, KS 67208
Phone: (316)685-7612
Dr. William G. Eckert, Dir.

Subjects: Abortion, accidents, alcohol, alcoholism, drugs and drug abuse, forensic sciences, medicolegal history, homicide, iatrogenic problems, legal medicine, pediatric medicine, poisoning, suicidology, sex problems, thanatology, toxicology, trauma, war crimes, war wounds. **Special Collections:** Texts in forensic medicine from 20 countries; journals in forensic and legal medicine from 20 countries; reference materials on forensic medical problems in 80 countries. **Holdings:** 1700 books; 1500 bound periodical volumes; 2000 papers; 2000 miscellaneous reports; 100 bibliographies; 500 hours of videotapes; 1000 hours of magnetic tapes; AV programs; microfilm. **Subscriptions:** 30 journals and other serials. **Publications:** *INFORM Newsletter*, quarterly; list of other publications - available on request. **Remarks:** Center acts as the Secretariat for the Pan-American Association of Forensic Sciences. It is affiliated with the William G. Eckert Medico-Legal Institute, Sao Paulo, Brazil. **Also known as:** INFORM.

★6816★ **International Women's Tribune**
Centre
Library
777 United Nations Plaza, 3rd Fl.
New York, NY 10017
Phone: (212)687-8633
Fax: (212)661-2704
Alice Mastrangelo, Contact

Subjects: Women in development, appropriate technology, community economic development, communication, media, training, funding, financial management, gender, small business. **Special Collections:** Violence Against Women; Women and Environment.

★6817★ **Irene Josselyn Clinic**
Mental Health Library
405 Central
Northfield, IL 60093
Phone: (708)441-5600
Fax: (708)441-7968
Jean M. Peterson, Libn.

Subjects: Child development, adolescence, parenting, divorce, psychoanalysis, psychotheraphy. **Special Collections:** Films and videotapes on suicide. **Holdings:** Figures not available.

★6818★ **Jersey Shore Medical Center**
Ann May School of Nursing Library &
   Media Center
1945 Rte. 33
Neptune, NJ 07754
Phone: (201)776-4195
Darlene Robertelli, Lib.Serv.Coord.

Subjects: Nursing, women's health, consumer education and health, allied health sciences. **Holdings:** 4000 books; 650 bound periodical volumes; 20 VF drawers; computer programs; 500 AV programs; National League for Nurses' and American Nursing Association publications. **Subscriptions:** 175 journals and other serials. **Publications:** Bimonthly acquisitions lists; *Library Handbook*; vertical file subject headings list; periodical holdings list; subject bibliographies.

★6819★ **Johns Hopkins University**
Population Information Program
527 St. Paul Pl.
Baltimore, MD 21202
Phone: (301)659-6300
Fax: (301)659-6266
Dr. Phyllis T. Piotrow, Dir.

Subjects: Population, family planning, human fertility, contraception, allied health, law, and policy issues. **Holdings:** 1000 books; 110,000 documents. **Subscriptions:** 500 journals and other serials. **Publications:** *Population Reports*, bimonthly—to worldwide mailing list; *POPLINE Thesaurus*. **Remarks:** The purpose of the program is to provide accurate, continuing, systematic, and up-to-date information on new developments in population, family planning, and allied issues. The program is supported primarily by the United States Agency for International Development.

★6820★ **Johns Hopkins University**
School of Hygiene and Public Health
Population Center Collection
615 N. Wolfe St., Rm. 2300
Baltimore, MD 21205
Phone: (301)955-3573
Fax: (301)955-1215
L. Terri Singer, Libn.

Subjects: Population dynamics, demography, family planning, physiology of reproduction, statistics. **Special Collections:** U.S. Census publications, 1790 to present; U.S. vital and health statistics, 1935 to present. **Holdings:** 16,000 books; 700 bound periodical volumes; 175 theses; 675 National Center for Health Statistics pamphlets; 600 Population Association of America documents. **Subscriptions:** 170 journals and other serials. **Publications:** Current contents of journals received, bimonthly - to faculty and students; acquisitions list, monthly - to students, faculty, and university libraries; serials holdings list.

★6821★ **June Mazer Lesbian Collection**
Connexus Women's Center
626 N. Robertson Blvd.
West Hollywood, CA 90069
Phone: (213)659-2478
Degania Golove, Coord.

Subjects: Lesbianism-history, culture, thought, organizations, writers, writing, the arts. **Special Collections:** Margaret Cruikshank Collection; Lillian Faderman Collection; Reid/Hyde papers; Sue Prosin papers; Joanne Parrent papers; Diana Press Archive; Telewoman archive;

SCWU archive. **Holdings:** 2000 books; 300 periodical titles; 3 VF drawers of manuscripts; 1 VF drawer of archives; 1 VF drawer of dissertations; magnetic tapes; videotapes. **Formerly:** Connexxus Womens Center

★6822★ **Katharine Gibbs School, Boston**
Library
126 Newbury St.
Boston, MA 02116
Phone: (617)578-7177
Fax: (617)262-2010
Cynthia W. Alcorn, Libn.

Subjects: Business careers including travel, hotel/restaurant, secretarial; women in the workplace; American woman. **Holdings:** 4000 books; 800 cassette tapes. **Subscriptions:** 72 journals and other serials; 5 newspapers.

★6823★ **Kinsey Institute for Research in**
   Sex, Gender & Reproduction, Inc.
Library and Information Service
313 Morrison Hall
Indiana University
Bloomington, IN 47405
Phone: (812)855-7686
Fax: (812)855-8277

Subjects: Sexual behavior and attitudes, erotic literature and art, gender, reproduction. **Special Collections:** Multimedia/nonbook sex-related materials; unpublished behavioral data. **Holdings:** 75,000 books, reprints, bound periodical volumes; 39 VF drawers; 209 reels of microfilm; 105 tapes; 108 phonograph records; 3500 objects; 55,000 photographs; 5000 slides; 6500 films. **Subscriptions:** 100 journals and other serials. **Telecommunications Services:** Electronic mail address: harlerm@iubacs (BITNET).

★6824★ **La Leche League International**
Library
9616 Minneapolis Ave.
PO Box 1209
Franklin Park, IL 60131
Phone: (708)455-7730
Fax: (708)455-0125

Subjects: Breast-feeding, parenting. **Holdings:** 200 books and monographs.

★6825★ **Lambda, Inc.**
Barnes Library
Box 55913
Birmingham, AL 35255
Phone: (205)326-8600
Ron Joullian, Coord.

Subjects: Gay and lesbian literature. **Special Collections:** Alabama Gay Archives; Lady B.J. Memorial Collection (gay and lesbian books and records from the entertainment world). **Holdings:** 805 books; 150 folders of gay and lesbian information; 25 subject binders. **Subscriptions:** 30 newsletters; 15 newspapers. **Telex:** (205)326-8600. **Remarks:** Library located at 516 S. 27th St., Birmingham, AL 35233.

★6826★ **Lesbian Herstory Educational**
   Foundation, Inc.
Archives
Box 1258
New York, NY 10116
Phone: (212)874-7232

Subjects: Lesbian history and culture, women's history. **Special Collections:** Manuscript collection; oral history collection; international lesbian

collection; lesbian organizations (files on 400 groups); biographical collection (files on 1000 individuals); art and music collection; button, T-shirt, and photography collections. **Holdings:** 8500 books; 30 bound periodical volumes; 350 unbound periodical volumes; 700 tapes; 500 subject files; dissertations. **Subscriptions:** 200 journals and other serials; 50 newspapers. **Publications:** *L.H.A. Newsletter*, irregular—to mailing list; occasional bibliographies.

★6827★ **Library of Congress**
Public Service and Collections
   Management I
Manuscript Division
10 First St., SE
Washington, DC 20540
Phone: (202)707-5325
James H. Hutson, Chief

★6828★ **Library of Congress**
Public Service and Collections
   Management I
Music Division
10 First St., SE
Washington, DC 20540
Phone: (202)707-5325
James W. Pruett, Chief

Remarks: Includes collections on women composers.

★6829★ **Library of Congress**
Public Service and Collections
   Management I
Prints and Photographs Division
10 First St., SE
Washington, DC 20540
Phone: (202)707-5000
Stephen E. Ostrow, Chief

★6830★ **Library of Congress**
Public Service and Collections
   Management II
Microform Reading Room
10 First St., SE
Washington, DC 20540
Phone: (202)707-5471

Remarks: Includes holdings in women's history and literature.

★6831★ **Library of Congress**
Rare Book & Special Collections Division
Thomas Jefferson Bldg., Rm. 204
Washington, DC 20540
Phone: (202)707-5434
Larry E. Sullivan, Chf.

Contains collections on woman's suffrage, including the Susan B. Anthony and National American Woman Suffrage Association collections.

★6832★ **Los Angeles Public Library**
Social Sciences, Philosophy and Religion
   Department
630 W. 5th St.
Los Angeles, CA 90071
Phone: (213)612-3250
Fax: (213)612-0536
Marilyn C. Wherley, Dept.Mgr.

Subjects: Philosophy, religion, psychology, social problems, government, foreign affairs, international relations, law, criminology, education, women's movements, family relations, ethnic groups, psychology, interpersonal relations. **Special Collections:** California, U.S., and U.N. documents depository; Black history; Mexican-

American Affairs; women; education; the occult; cults and sects; Eastern religions. **Holdings:** 389,000 volumes. **Subscriptions:** 2850 journals and other serials. **Remarks:** Library located at 433 S. Spring St., Los Angeles, CA 90013.

★6833★ Los Angeles Regional Family Planning Council, Inc.
Library
3600 Wilshire Blvd., Ste. 600
Los Angeles, CA 90010-0605
Phone: (213)386-5614
Fax: (213)383-0973
Selda Roth, Libn.

Subjects: Family planning, family life education, birth control, reproductive health, sexually transmitted diseases, AIDS, breast feeding, international family planning, natural family planning. **Holdings:** 1500 books; 400 AV programs; pamphlets, VF drawers of newspaper and journal articles, reports, studies. **Subscriptions:** 70 journals and other serials. **Publications:** Bilingual Bibliography of Spanish Resources; annotated bibliographies; technical assistance lists.

★6834★ Loyola University of Chicago
E.M. Cudahy Memorial Library
Lake Shore Campus
6525 N. Sheridan Rd.
Chicago, IL 60626
Phone: (312)508-2658
S. Rita Stalzer, Women's Studies Bibliog.

Subjects: Women in religion, literature, antiquity, U.S. history, and cinema. **Remarks:** Maintains also Julia Deal Lewis Memorial Library at Water Tower Campus.

★6835★ Lutheran Deaconess Association
Center for Diaconal Ministry
Library
1304 LaPorte Ave.
Valparaiso, IN 46383
Phone: (219)464-0909
Deaconess Louise Williams, Exec.Dir.

Subjects: Theology, Christian education, pastoral care and counseling, women in the church, history of diaconate. **Holdings:** 850 volumes. **Subscriptions:** 30 journals and other serials; 10 newspapers.

★6836★ Lutheran Medical Center
Medical Library
150 55th St.
Brooklyn, NY 11220
Phone: (718)630-7200
Fax: (718)630-8918
Estela Longo, Med.Libn.

Subjects: Nursing, medicine, surgery, gynecology, obstetrics, pediatrics, dentistry, family practice. **Holdings:** 8072 books; 2977 AV programs; 468 videotapes; 40 VF drawers; 312 other cataloged items. **Subscriptions:** 236 journals and other serials.

★6837★ Lutherans For Life
Library
PO Box 819
Benton, AR 72015
Phone: (501)794-2212
Fax: (501)794-1437
Jewell Rapier, Contact

Subjects: Abortion, infanticide, euthanasia, theology. **Holdings:** 50 books; 10 filing drawers;

newsletters; clippings. **Subscriptions:** 30 journals and other serials; 10 newspapers. **Publications:** *Living* (magazine), quarterly; *Lifedate* (newsletter), quarterly.

★6838★ Madison Pharmacy Associates
PMS Access
Library
P.O. Box 9326
Madison, WI 53715
Phone: (608)833-4767
Marla Ahlgrimm, Contact

Subjects: Premenstrual syndrome. **Holdings:** Current literature; audio cassettes; slide programs, videotapes. **Publications:** Newsletter.

★6839★ Magee-Womens Hospital
Howard Anderson Power Memorial Library
Forbes Ave. & Halket St.
Pittsburgh, PA 15213
Phone: (412)647-4288
Bernadette Kaelin, Dir., Lib.Serv.

Subjects: Obstetrics, gynecology, gynecological oncology, neonatology, perinatology, genetics. **Holdings:** 1000 books; 1000 bound periodical volumes; 200 pamphlets and documents. **Subscriptions:** 201 journals and other serials. **Publications:** *Powerline* (newsletter).

★6840★ Maimonides Medical Center
George A. Degenshein, M.D. Memorial Library
4802 10th Ave.
Brooklyn, NY 11219
Phone: (718)283-7406
Lydia Friedman, Chf.Med.Libn.

Subjects: Medicine, dentistry, gynecology, surgery, pediatrics, obstetrics, nursing, pharmacology, psychiatry, anatomy, physiology. **Holdings:** 4969 books; 10,859 bound periodical volumes; 8 Audio-Digest series; 961 video programs; 188 slide programs. **Subscriptions:** 279 journals and other serials.

★6841★ March of Dimes Birth Defects Foundation
Reference Room
1275 Mamaroneck Ave.
White Plains, NY 10605
Phone: (914)428-7100

Subjects: Birth defects, pediatrics, obstetrics, maternal and child health. **Special Collections:** Reprints of March of Dimes Grantees; birth defects original article series. **Holdings:** 2500 books; 1722 bound periodical volumes; 5 VF drawers. **Subscriptions:** 108 journals and other serials. **Publications:** Journal holdings list, semiannual.

★6842★ Margaret Sanger Center-Planned Parenthood New York City
Abraham Stone Library
380 Second Ave.
New York, NY 10010
Phone: (212)677-6474

Subjects: Abortion, adolescent sexuality, infertility, sex, family living, demography, population, sexuality of the handicapped, women's health. **Holdings:** 6000 books; 3000 bound periodical volumes; 60 VF drawers of reprints and newspaper clippings. **Subscriptions:** 85 journals and other serials.

★6843★ Marquette University
Department of Special Collections and University Archives
Manuscript Collections Memorial Library
Memorial Library
1415 W. Wisconsin Ave.
Milwaukee, WI 53233
Phone: (414)288-7256
Fax: (414)288-5324
Charles B. Elston, Hd.

Subjects: Catholic social thought and action, Catholic Indian ministry, Marquette University history, Jesuits and Jesuit institutions, recent U.S. political history, Catholic religious formation and vocation ministries. **Special Collections:** National Catholic Conference for Interracial Justice Collection, 1956 to present (200 feet); Project Equality, Inc. Collection, 1971 to present (45 feet); Sr. Margaret Ellen Traxler papers, 1909-1919, 1950 to present (17 feet); National Coalition of American Nuns Collection, 1969 to present (10 feet); Sister Formation Conference/Religious Formation Conference Archives, 1954 to present (28 feet); The Madonna Center (Chicago) Records, 1865-1964 (10 feet); Women's Ordination Conference Records, 1975 to present (16 feet); The Dorothy Day-Catholic Worker Collection, 1933 to present (100 feet); Catholic Association for International Peace Archives, 1926-1970 (30 feet); National Sisters Vocation Conference Archives, 1967 to present (6 feet); Holdings: 12,000 volumes; 3000 bound periodical volumes; 8100 cubic feet of archives and manuscripts; 450 reels of microfilm; 3700 feet of manuscript collections relating primarily to Catholic social action and the history of Jesuits and Jesuit institutions, 1880 to present; 3750 cubic feet of Marquette University Archives, 1881 to present; 350 cubic feet of Catholic Indian mission records, 1848 to present. Subscriptions: 45 journals and other serials; 20 newpapers.

★6844★ Maryland Committee for Children, Inc.
MCC Resource Center
608 Water St.
Baltimore, MD 21202
Phone: (301)752-7588
Fax: (301)752-6286
Sandra Skolnik, Exec.Dir.

Subjects: Day care, early childhood growth and development, child advocacy. **Special Collections:** Work/Family Initiatives Collection. **Holdings:** 1450 books; 115 file boxes. **Subscriptions:** 38 journals and other serials. **Publications:** List of publications available on request.

★6845★ Massachusetts Institute of Technology
Humanities Library
Rm. 14S-200
Cambridge, MA 02139
Phone: (617)253-5683
Fax: (617)253-3109
Theresa Tobin, Contact

Subjects: Anthropology, archeology, education, foreign languages, history, history of science and technology, library and information science, linguistics, literature, philosophy, psychology, religion, women's and men's studies. **Holdings:** 139,658 books; 22,900 bound periodical volumes; 67,170 bound serial volumes; 467 M.I.T. theses; 2389 technical reports; 2057 pamphlets; 4195 reels of microfilm; 24,515 microfiche; 545 maps and plans. **Subscriptions:** 3908 journals and other serials. **Telecommuni-**

cations Services: Electronic mail address: ALA1764 (ALANET).

★6846★ Maternity Center Association Reference Library
48 E. 92nd St.
New York, NY 10028
Phone: (212)369-7300
Esther Hanchett, Act.Libn.

Subjects: Obstetrics, maternal and infant care, family life, nurse-midwifery, preparation for child-bearing. Holdings: 2300 books. Subscriptions: 31 journals and other serials.

★6847★ Medical College of Pennsylvania Archives and Special Collections on Women in Medicine
3300 Henry Ave.
Philadelphia, PA 19129
Phone: (215)842-7124
Fax: (215)843-6862
Janet Miller, Dir./Archv.

Subjects: Women physicians, health care for women, Medical College of Pennsylvania, education, medicine. Special Collections: College archives; women in medicine; Black Women Physicians Collection; Asian American Women Physicians Project; Oral History Project (43 interviews); American Women's Hospitals Records (25 linear feet); Medical Women's International Association Records (10 linear feet). Holdings: 1000 books; 6000 reprints; 15,000 photographs; 1500 linear feet of archival materials and manuscripts; memorabilia. Publications: Newsletter, biannual, available on request; *Guide to Collections in the Archives & Special Collections on Women in Medicine.*

★6848★ Meiklejohn Civil Liberties Institute Library
Box 673
Berkeley, CA 94701
Phone: (510)848-0599
Ann Fagan Ginger, Exec.Dir.

Subjects: Peace law, civil rights and liberties, due process, sex discrimination, juries, police misconduct. Special Collections: Peace Law Brief and Issues Bank; Angela Davis case (20,000 pages); Pentagon Papers Case (35,000 pages); official repository for National Lawyers Guild Archives; Draft and Military Law Collection (188 microfiche). Holdings: 200 books; legal documents from over 9000 cases. Subscriptions: 130 journals and other serials; 20 newspapers. Publications: *Human Rights Organizations and Periodicals Directory*, biennial, for sale; list of other publications available upon request. Remarks: Library located at 1715 Francisco St., Berkeley, CA 94703.

★6849★ Mexican-American Opportunity Foundation Resource and Referral Service Lending Library
6252 E. Telegraph Rd.
Commerce, CA 90040
Phone: (213)722-7842
Yolanda Franco, Prog.Coord.

Subjects: Infant development, parenting, domestic and child abuse, self-esteem, emotional and physical handicaps; displaced homemakers. Special Collections: Mayan & Aztec History; Mexican History; Child Psychology and Development. Holdings: 2500 volumes; filmstrips; cassettes; records; audiophonic media cards; arts and crafts materials. Publications: Newsletter, quarterly - to mailing list and by public contact. Remarks: The Resource and Referral Service is funded by the California State Department of Education - Office of Child Development. Program is geared to the needs of the Hispanic community of East Los Angeles and surrounding communities.

★6850★ Michigan Department of Civil Rights Civil Rights Library
1200 6th St., 7th Fl.
Detroit, MI 48226
Phone: (313)256-2622
Fax: (313)256-2680
Ellen B. McCarthy, Contact

Subjects: Civil rights; discrimination - employment, housing; minority groups. Holdings: 10,000 books; 13,000 microfiche; unbound periodicals. Subscriptions: 200 journals and other serials; 10 newspapers.

★6851★ Midwest Lesbian and Gay Resource Center Gerbar-Hart Library
3238 N. Sheffield Ave.
Chicago, IL 60657
Phone: (312)883-3003
Ruth Ketchem, Co-dir. & Libn.

Description: Serves as a depository for resources and information on lesbianism and homosexuality. Subjects: AIDS, health and legal rights of lesbians and gay men. Special Collections: Arno Press reprint series, including *The Ladder* and *The Mattachine Review*—two of the oldest publications of the U.S. Gay and Lesbian Movement. Publications: Newsletter (irregular).

★6852★ Midwest Women's Center
53 W. Jackson, Ste. 1015
Chicago, IL 60604
Phone: (312)922-8530
Yolanda Marino, Libn.

Founded: 1979. Subjects: Occupational health, trade skills, sex equity. Special Collections: Teen Mother Employment Collection—includes materials for service providers working with pregnancy and parenting teen women. Holdings: 1000 files; 200 ephemera files; 2000 monographs.

★6853★ Mills College F.W. Olin Library Special Collections
5000 MacArthur Blvd.
Oakland, CA 94613
Phone: (510)430-2047
Fax: (510)430-3314
Renee Jadushlever, Spec.Coll.Libn.

Subjects: English and American literature, printing, dance, Shakespeare, women's history, bookbinding. Special Collections: Albert M. Bender Collection; Jane Bourne Parton Collection; Elias Olan James Collection; Mills College Archives. Holdings: 12,000 books.

★6854★ Missing Children Minnesota Resource Center
1025 W. Broadway
Minneapolis, MN 55411
Phone: (612)521-1188
Fax: (612)521-1743
Carol Watson, Exec.Dir.

Subjects: Missing children, preventing abduction, parental kidnapping. Special Collections: Missing children clippings file from Minnesota daily and weekly papers, 1989 to present. Holdings: 40 books; 3 AV programs; pictures of missing children. Subscriptions: 5 journals and other serials. Publications: Posters of missing children; information packets on parental abduction and runaways; bibliographies. Remarks: Missing Children Minnesota is an all volunteer organization that acts as a local resource and information center, helps parents locate and recover missing children, and works to effect legislative change for better child protection.

★6855★ Mohawk Valley Community College Library Special Collections
1101 Sherman Dr.
Utica, NY 13501
Phone: (315)792-5408
Raul Huerta, Lib.Dir.

Special Collections: Women's Resource Collection (1100 titles); Minorities Studies Collection (800 titles).

★6856★ Montclair State College Women's Center Library
Student Center, 4th Fl.
Upper Montclair, NJ 07043
Phone: (201)893-5114
Sharon Olson, Ph.D., Dir.

Subjects: Women - literature, family, health, sexuality, career, psychology, education, feminism, aging, society. Holdings: 575 books; 5 VF drawers of clippings.

★6857★ Moore College of Art and Design Library
20th & Benjamin Franklin Parkway
Philadelphia, PA 19103
Phone: (215)568-4515
Fax: (215)568-8017
Paula A. Feid, Dir.

Subjects: Fine arts, professional arts, art education, art history, women's studies, humanities. Special Collections: John Sartain Collection (engravings and prints); Sartain family correspondence (one drawer); Bookworks Collection (artist's books). Holdings: 38,500 books; 2500 bound periodical volumes; 400 folios; 98 VF drawers of pictures, prints, clippings, plates; 110,000 slides; 1000 phonograph records. Subscriptions: 227 journals and other serials; 8 newspapers.

★6858★ Mount Zion Hebrew Congregation Temple Library
1300 Summit Ave.
St. Paul, MN 55105
Phone: (612)698-3881
Fax: (612)698-4780
Robert A. Epstein, Libn.

Subjects: Jews - history, religion, literature, biography, philosophy; Israel. Special Collections: Clara Margolis Collection (Jewish feminism; 140 titles); children's collection (950 titles); Rabbi Harry Sterling Margolis Collection (memorial collection on 20th century American Judaism; 1000 titles). **Holdings:** 7250 books; 125 phonograph records; 50 cassette tapes; 75 videotapes. **Subscriptions:** 20 journals and other serials.

★6859★ Multnomah School of the Bible
John and Mary Mitchell Library
8435 NE Glisan St.
Portland, OR 97220
Phone: (503)255-0332
James F. Scott, Dir.

Subjects: Bible, doctrine, missions, Christian education, New Testament Greek, journalism, music, women's ministries, pastoral ministries. **Holdings:** 49,687 books; 2734 bound periodical volumes; 7135 AV programs; 6937 microforms. **Subscriptions:** 629 journals and other serials.

★6860★ Naiad Press, Inc.
Lesbian and Gay Archives
Box 10543
Tallahassee, FL 32302
Phone: (904)539-5965
Fax: (904)539-9731
Donna J. McBride, Hd.Libn.

Subjects: Lesbian, gay, and feminist literature. **Holdings:** 18,000 books; 1000 bound periodical volumes; 4000 unbound periodicals; 450 manuscripts; 8 boxes of clippings; 300 videotapes. **Subscriptions:** 62 journals and other serials; 111 newspapers. **Publications:** *The Lesbian in Literature*, 1982; *Black Lesbians: An Annotated Bibliography*, 1981.

★6861★ National Abortion Federation
Resource Center
1436 U St., N.W., Suite 103
Washington, DC 20009
Phone: (202)667-5881
Fax: (202)667-5890

Subjects: Abortion, contraception, sexuality, sociology, health, medicine, sexually transmitted diseases. **Holdings:** 225 volumes; symposia publications; clippings; audio cassattes. **Subscriptions:** 5 journals and other serials; 3 newspapers.

★6862★ National Association for the
Advancement of Colored People
NAACP Legal Defense and Educational
Fund
Law Library
99 Hudson St., 16th Fl.
New York, NY 10013
Phone: (212)219-1900
Donna Gloeckner, Contact

Subjects: Civil rights law - discrimination against blacks, other racial minorities, and women in employment, education, housing, and other areas. **Holdings:** 15,000 volumes.

★6863★ National Center on Women and
Family Law, Inc.
Information Center
799 Broadway, Rm. 402
New York, NY 10003
Phone: (212)674-8200
Fax: (212)533-5104
Laurie Woods, Dir.

Subjects: Battered women and law, marital rape, rape, single mothers, divorce, custody, child snatching, child and wife support. **Hold-**

ings: 500 books; 50 VF drawers; 200 resource packets. **Subscriptions:** 1500 newspapers. **Publications:** Newsletter, bimonthly.

★6864★ National Chamber of Commerce
for Women, Inc.
Elizabeth Lewin Business Library &
Information Center
10 Waterside Plaza, Suite 6H
New York, NY 10010-2610
Phone: (212)685-3454
Maggie Rinaldi, Dir.

Subjects: Law and women, labor-management relations, small business, consumerism, women in education. **Holdings:** 1800 books; 650 bound periodical volumes; 100 cassette tapes; 800 market research reports and proposals; 500 annual reports and quarterly brochures; 2 VF drawers of press clippings. **Subscriptions:** 10 journals and other serials. **Publications:** *National Chamber of Commerce for Women Research Digest*, monthly for members.

★6865★ National Clearinghouse on Marital
and Date Rape
2325 Oak St.
Berkeley, CA 94708
Phone: (510)524-1582
Laura X, Exec.Dir.

Subjects: Rape - marital, date, cohabitation, legislation; marital rape legislation and prosecution. **Holdings:** 20 books; 1000 files of briefs, testimony, clippings, reports, newsletters, studies, research, dissertations. **Subscriptions:** 10 journals and other serials. **Publications:** *Bibliographic Guide to the Files on Marital Rape*; Newsletter; *Summary of Greta Rideout's Story*; pamphlet; sociolegal case chart; prosecution statistics chart; state law chart. **Remarks:** Affiliated with the Women's History Research Center, Inc. Holdings housed at University of Illinois Women's Studies Library. Publications available from them as well.

★6866★ National Committee for Adoption
Library
1930 17th St., N.W.
Washington, DC 20009-6207
Phone: (202)328-1200
Fax: (202)332-0935

Subjects: Adoption - voluntary agencies, adoptive parents, adoptees, birthparents, maternity services; legislation for the adoption process; infertility. **Holdings:** 2000 volumes and files; statistics. **Remarks:** Alternate telephone number(s): National Adoption Hotline, (202)628-8072.

★6867★ National Ecumenical Coalition,
Inc.
Library
4300 Old Dominion Dr., Suite 502
Arlington, VA 22207-3246
Phone: (703)522-9759
Bro. Scott R. Desmond, S.J.

Subjects: Civil and constitutional rights, ecumenical programs, juvenile delinquency, drug abuse, law, gay rights, AIDS advocacy, human rights, Equal Rights Amendment (ERA), refugee programs. **Holdings:** 6000 books; 7500 bound periodical volumes; 340 boxes of civil rights archives; 51 boxes of gay rights archives; 200 boxes of ecumenical archives; U.N. publications. **Subscriptions:** 350 journals and other serials; 72 newspapers. **Publications:** *N.E.C.*

Today, monthly—by subscription; bibliography on civil rights, gay rights, AIDS education, ecumenical organizations, and drug abuse (computer printout).

★6868★ National Museum of Women in
the Arts (NMWA)
NMWA Library and Research Center
1250 New York Ave. NW
Washington, DC 20005
Phone: (202)783-5000
Fax: (202)393-3235
Krystyna Wasserman, Dir., Lib. & Res.Ctr.

Subjects: Art by women - painting, sculpture, printmaking, photography, book art. **Special Collections:** Women artists (14,000 vertical files); artists' books (120); collection of bookplates by women; personal library of Irene Rice Pereira; Archives of the International Conference of Women Artists in Copenhagen, 1985. **Holdings:** 6000 volumes; manuscripts; artists' correspondence; slides; 1100 institution files; 400 subject files. **Subscriptions:** 70 journals and other serials. **Publications:** *The NMWA News* (newsletter), quarterly for members.

★6869★ National Religious Vocation
Conference
Library
1603 S. Michigan Ave., Suite 400
Chicago, IL 60616
Phone: (312)663-5454
Fax: (312)663-5030
Mary Ann Hamer, Adm.Asst.

Subjects: Church-related careers. **Special Collections:** Brochures that are specific to the various religious communities of women and men in the United States. **Holdings:** 125 audio cassettes; 5 statistical studies and research documents. **Publications:** *Guide to Religious Communities for Women* (1983); *Woman Song I* (1986); *Woman Song II* (1987); *Who's Entering Religious Life* (1987); *Turning Parables and Paradigms* (1986); *Ministries For The Lord* (1985); *Horizon*, quarterly; *Directory of Resources*; *Woman Song III* (1989).

★6870★ National Right to Life Committee
Library
419 7th St., N.W., Suite 500
Washington, DC 20004
Phone: (202)626-8800

Subjects: Abortion, euthanasia, and infanticide. **Holdings:** 1000 books, pamphlets, brochures, and audiovisual materials; vertical file containing 20,000 items. **Subscriptions:** 20 journals and other serials; 6 newspapers.

★6871★ National Society, Daughters of
the American Revolution
Library
1776 D St. NW
Washington, DC 20006-5392
Phone: (202)879-3229
Fax: (202)879-3252
Eric G. Grundset, Lib.Dir.

Subjects: Genealogy, U.S. local history, U.S. history, American Indian history, American women's history. **Special Collections:** Genealogies; United States, state, county, local histories; published rosters of Revolutionary War soldiers; published vital records; cemetery inscriptions; Bible records; transcripts of various county records (such as wills), compiled by the Genealogical Records Committees of DAR;

published archives of some of the thirteen original states; abstracts of some Revolutionary War pension files; American Indian history, genealogy, culture; U.S. City Directory Collection, 20th century. **Holdings:** 110,000 books; 10,000 bound periodical volumes; 250,000 files of manuscript material, genealogical records, pamphlets. **Subscriptions:** 550 journals and other serials.

★6872★ National Sudden Infant Death Syndrome Clearinghouse
8201 Greensboro Dr., Ste. 600
McLean, VA 22102
Phone: (703)821-8955
Fax: (703)506-0384
Liz Eckel, Info.Spec.

Publications: Subject-specific publications (Sudden Infant Death Syndrome, monitoring, family grief and loss).

★6873★ National Woman's Christian Temperance Union
Frances E. Willard Memorial Library
1730 Chicago Ave.
Evanston, IL 60201
Phone: (708)864-1396
Alfred H. Epstein, Contact

Subjects: History of temperance; biographies of temperance leaders; influence of alcohol, tobacco, and narcotics on the human body; history of prohibition; alcohol education; history of women's movement; social reform history. **Special Collections:** Works by and about Frances Willard (correspondence; journals; scrapbooks). **Holdings:** 5000 books; 500 bound periodical volumes; photographs; archives; song books; reports; documents. **Subscriptions:** 15 journals and other serials.

★6874★ National Women and Media Collection
Western Historical Manuscript Collection
University of Missouri, Columbia
23 Ellis Library
Columbia, MO 65201
Phone: (314)882-6028
Nancy Lankford, Assoc.Dir.

Subjects: History - Missouri, political, economic, agricultural, urban, labor, black, women's, frontier, religious, literary, social, science, steamboating, social reform and welfare, business. **Holdings:** 12,500 linear feet of manuscripts; 7300 reels of microfilm; 3400 audiotapes and audio cassettes; 675 phonograph records; 190 video materials. **Publications:** *Guide to the Western Historical Manuscripts Collection*, 1952; supplement, 1956; finding aids (index, shelf list, and chronological file). **Remarks:** Collection contains the manuscript holdings of both the University of Missouri and the State Historical Society of Missouri. Offices are located at the four branches of the University of Missouri. Materials may be loaned among the four branches.

★6875★ National Women's Health Network
Women's Health Information Service Library
1325 G St., N.W.
Washington, DC 20005
Phone: (202)347-1140

Subjects: Women's health issues - general, abortion, breast cancer, cervical cancer, childbirth, contraceptives, menopause, occupational and environmental health, osteoporosis, pregnancy, premenstrual syndrome, sexually transmitted diseases, teen pregnancy, toxic shock syndrome, women and alcohol.

★6876★ National Women's History Project (NWHP)
7738 Bell Rd.
Windsor, CA 95492
Phone: (707)838-6000
Fax: (707)838-0478
Molly MacGregor, Dir.

Founded: 1977. **Description:** Publishers of annual resource catalog promoting education on the history of women. Encourages multicultural study of women to reclaim contributions and impact of all groups of women and to persuade constructive and expansive social change. Focuses on the rich and inspiring heritage of women's contributions. Sponsors annual National Women's History Month. Maintains archive for National Women's History Month. Conducts workshops and educational training sessions introducing women into curricula and offers educational consulting for teachers, teacher trainers, administrators, and workplace organizers. Sponsors Women's History Network (see separate entry). Operates speakers' bureau. **Publications:** *Women's History Network Directory*, semiannual. Listing of network participants. Includes a brief biographical sketch and/or a description of women's history activities in which each person has participated. • *Women's History Network News*, quarterly. Covers educational resources, commemorative holidays, traveling exhibits, and NWHP activities. Includes calendar of events, news of members, and lists of articles, books, and other resources. • *Women's History Resource Catalog*, annual. Includes books, films, records, posters, and program planning guides on women's history. Also includes subject index. • Also publishes *Community Organizing Guide, Lesson Plans*, posters, indexes, and curriculum units. **Formerly:** (1978) Education Taskforce on the Sonoma Commission; (1980) Women's History Week Project.

★6877★ New College of California
New College Library
50 Fell St.
San Francisco, CA 94102-5298
Phone: (415)626-1694
Janet Talleman, Dir.

Subjects: Law, alternative humanities, psychology, poetics, women's studies, homosexuality/lesbianism, minorities, Third World. **Special Collections:** Modern American poetry. **Holdings:** 30,000 books; unbound periodicals. **Subscriptions:** 100 journals and other serials.

★6878★ New York Hospital-Cornell Medical Center
Medical Archives
1300 York Ave.
New York, NY 10021
Phone: (212)746-6072
Fax: (212)746-6494
Adele A. Lerner, Archv.

Subjects: Medical education; health care; history - medicine, nursing, psychiatry; women's history. **Special Collections:** New York Hospital-Cornell Medical Center records, 1927 to present; Society of the New York Hospital records, 1771 to present; Cornell University Medical College records, 1898 to present; Cor-

nell University Graduate School of Medical Sciences records, 1952 to present; Cornell University-New York Hospital School of Nursing records, 1877-1979; Society of the Lying-In Hospital of the City of New York records, 1799 to present; Manhattan Maternity and Dispensary records, 1905-1939; Nursery for the Children of Poor Women and Nursery and Child's Hospital records, 1854-1910; New York Infant Asylum records, 1865-1910; New York Nursery and Child's Hospital records, 1910-1947; New York Asylum for Lying-In Women records, 1823-1899; Women's Medical Association of New York City records, 1902 to present; American Medical Women's Association Archives, 1915 to present (76 linear feet). **Holdings:** 4600 linear feet of archival materials and manuscripts; 217 films; 22 videotapes; 844 audiotapes and cassettes. **Subscriptions:** 8 journals and other serials (for archival reference). **Telecommunications Services:** Electronic mail address: CLASS.CORNELLMED (OnTyme Electronic Message Network Service). **Publications:** *An Introduction to the Medical Archives of the New York Hospital-Cornell Medical Center*, 1976. **Remarks:** Maintained by Cornell University Medical College. Affiliated with the C.V. Starr Biomedical Information Center.

★6879★ New York Public Library
Carl H. Pforzheimer Shelley and His Circle Collection
Fifth Ave. & 42nd St., Rm. 319
New York, NY 10018
Phone: (212)930-0717
Fax: (212)302-4815
Mihai Handrea, Cur.

Subjects: Outstanding English literature material on Shelley and his circle, including Byron, Leigh Hunt, Peacock, Godwin, Thomas Moore, women writers of 1790-1840 (Mary Wollstonecraft, Mary Hays, Lady Blessington). **Holdings:** 13,000 books; 8000 manuscripts; 6 VF drawers. **Subscriptions:** 45 journals and other serials.

★6880★ New York Public Library
Early Childhood Resource and Information Center
66 Leroy St., 2nd Fl.
New York, NY 10014
Phone: (212)929-0815
Hannah Nuba, Supv.Libn.

Subjects: Early childhood and parent education, prenatal care, parent-child activities, language and intellectual development, multicultural and multilingual education, adoption and foster care. **Special Collections:** Adult collection on child development, parenting, education, and special needs; circulating collection of books and puzzles for young children. **Holdings:** 14,198 books; 72 noncirculating filmstrip kits; 52 noncirculating films; 345 sound recordings; 114 video cassettes; toys; pamphlets. **Subscriptions:** 125 journals and other serials.

★6881★ New York Public Library
Microforms Division
Fifth Ave. & 42nd St.
New York, NY 10018
Phone: (212)930-0838
Thomas Bourke, Chf.

Subjects: Literature, psychology, social science, science. **Special Collections:** FBI files on the Assassination of President Kennedy; American Civil Liberties Union papers; History of

Women Collection; History of Photography Collection; papers pertaining to the Amistad Schooner case. **Holdings:** 170,000 reels of microfilm; 400,000 microfiche; 103,309 microcards; city directories; newspapers. **Subscriptions:** 4000 journals and other serials; 200 newspapers.

★6882★ New York Theological Seminary
Library
5 W. 29th St.
New York, NY 10001
Phone: (212)532-4012
Eleanor Soler, Libn.

Subjects: Bible, theology, pastoral counseling, parish ministry, African-American church studies, women in the church. **Holdings:** 20,000 volumes; 700 audio cassettes; 20 video cassettes; 300 Spanish books; 200 Korean books; 2 drawers of periodicals on microfiche. **Subscriptions:** 40 journals and other serials.

★6883★ Ninety-Nines, Inc.
Library
Will Rogers Airport
Box 59965
Oklahoma City, OK 73159
Phone: (405)685-7969
Fax: (405)685-7985
Dorothy Niekamp, Libn.

Subjects: Aviation, women in aviation. **Special Collections:** Archives of the Ninety-Nines; records from the Powder Puff Derby. **Holdings:** 900 books. **Publications:** 99 News. **Also known as:** International Women Pilots Association.

★6884★ Northwestern University
Special Collections
Women's Collection
University Library
1935 Sheridan Rd.
Evanston, IL 60208-2300
Phone: (708)491-3635
Fax: (708)491-8306
Russell Maylone, Cur. of Spec.Coll.

Subjects: Domestic and international Women's Liberation Movement, Equal Rights Amendment (ERA), women in society. **Special Collections:** Domestic and foreign feminist periodicals, 1960 to present; feminist position papers; ephemeral materials covering over 100 major subject areas. **Holdings:** 1000 books; 4000 periodicals titles; 6000 VF folders of conference papers, notices, syllabi, bibliographies, clippings; 300 posters. **Subscriptions:** 350 journals and other serials. **Publications:** Women's Collection Newsletter, semiannual, free upon request.

★6885★ Oberlin College—Library
Archives
420 Mudd Center
Oberlin, OH 44074-1532
Phone: (216)775-8014
Fax: (216)775-8739
Roland M. Baumann, Coll.Archv.

Subjects: Higher education, 19th century reform, temperance, women's history, black education, architecture, Ohio history. **Special Collections:** Missions, the antislavery movement, and temperance in Oberlin; papers of Oberlin College faculty and graduates; Congressman Charles Mosher papers; Congressman Don J. Pease papers; Oberlin municipal government records; photographs of Oberlin College and

Oberlin. **Holdings:** 4400 linear feet of manuscripts and archival materials. **Subscriptions:** 6 journals and other serials. **Telecommunications Services:** Electronic mail address: PBAUMANN@OBERLIN (BITNET). **Publications:** Library of Congress Rule Interpretation for AACR2; Guide to the Women's History Sources in the Oberlin College Archives (1990); Current Scholarship in Women's Studies (1987).

★6886★ Ohio State University
Women's Studies Collection
220 Main Library
1858 Neil Ave. Mall
Columbus, OH 43210
Phone: (614)292-3035
Fax: (614)292-7859
Linda Krikos, Hd., Women's Stud.Lib.

Subjects: Women's studies. **Holdings:** 15,000 volumes; 2500 pamphlets and newsletters; 50 microform collections. **Subscriptions:** 100 journals and other serials. **Publications:** Feminisms, (in conjunction with the Center for Women's Studies).

★6887★ ONE, Inc.
Blanche M. Baker Memorial Library
3340 Country Club Dr.
Los Angeles, CA 90019
Phone: (213)735-5252
Luis Balmaseda, Libn.

Subjects: Homosexuality, homophile movement, gay liberation movement, gay and lesbian literature, women's and lesbian studies. **Holdings:** 20,000 titles; 60 VF drawers of other cataloged items; archival collections of many organizations; personal papers; foreign language periodicals. **Subscriptions:** 200 journals; 46 newspapers.

★6888★ Organization for Equal Education
of the Sexes
Library
PO Box 438
Blue Hill, ME 04614
Phone: (207)374-2489
Lucy Simpson, Pres.

Subjects: Nonsexist curricula, women's history, sexism in education. **Holdings:** 1000 volumes.

★6889★ Pacifica Foundation
Pacifica Program Service
Pacifica Radio Archive
3729 Cahuenga Blvd. W.
North Hollywood, CA 91604
Phone: (818)506-1077
Bill Thomas, Dir.

Subjects: Politics and government, social sciences, Third World, minorities, women's studies, philosophy. **Special Collections:** Noncommercial radio programs, 1950 to present. **Holdings:** 28,000 magnetic audiotapes.

★6890★ Pennsylvania State University
Gerontology Center
Human Development Collection
S109 Henderson Human Development Bldg.
University Park, PA 16802
Phone: (814)863-0776
Faye Wohlwill, Coll.Dir.

Subjects: Gerontology, adolescent and child psychology, marriage and family. **Holdings:** 3500 volumes. **Subscriptions:** 25 journals and other serials.

★6891★ Pinellas County Juvenile Welfare
Board
Mailande W. Holland Library
4140 49th St., N.
St. Petersburg, FL 33709
Phone: (813)521-1853
Fax: (813)528-0803
Alison R. Birmingham, Libn.

Subjects: Child welfare, marriage and family therapy, juvenile delinquency, substance abuse, child abuse and neglect, day care and early childhood education, primary prevention, adolescent health, mental health, advocacy for economically disadvantaged, legislation, administration, funding and grant writing, community planning and development, community education. **Special Collections:** Intergenerational relations; funding collection (20 volumes). **Holdings:** 2000 books; 300 government documents; 300 AV programs. **Subscriptions:** 120 journals and other serials. **Publications:** Bulletin, quarterly.

★6892★ Planned Parenthood Association
Leslie Resource Center
17 N. State St., 15th Fl.
Chicago, IL 60602
Phone: (312)781-9550
Kerry Reid, Volunteer/Lib.Assoc.

Description: Maintains audio-visual lending library of films and other educational aids on health, family life, and sexuality education. The center also provides research and curriculum development assistance. **Subjects:** Family planning, contraception, sexuality and family life education, reproductive rights. **Publications:** Comprehensive series of brochures in English and Spanish; annual reports; fact sheets.

★6893★ Planned Parenthood of Central
Indiana
Resource Center
3209 N. Meridian St.
Indianapolis, IN 46208
Phone: (317)925-6686
Fax: (317)927-3663
Betsy Lambie, Libn.

Subjects: Birth control, human sexuality, teen pregnancy, human reproduction, abortion, sex education, women's health, STDs, AIDS. **Holdings:** 1200 books; 130 films and videotapes; vertical files; poster collection. **Subscriptions:** 55 journals and other serials.

★6894★ Planned Parenthood of Cleveland,
Inc.
Library
3135 Euclid Ave., No. 101
Cleveland, OH 44115
Phone: (216)881-7742
Fax: (216)881-1834
Betsey C. Kaufman, Exec.Dir.

Subjects: Birth control and contraceptives, family planning, population, sexuality, family life education. **Special Collections:** Historical information on the birth control movement. **Holdings:** 900 books; 10 films; 103 videotapes. **Subscriptions:** 10 journals and other serials. **Publications:** The Source, a directory of services and holdings.

★6895★ **Planned Parenthood Federation of America, Inc.**
Katharine Dexter McCormick Library
810 7th Ave.
New York, NY 10019
Phone: (212)541-7800
Fax: (212)245-1845
Gloria A. Roberts, Hd.Libn.

Subjects: Family planning in the U.S., contraceptives, abortion and sterilization, history of birth control, population, sexuality, sexuality education, reproductive rights, teen sexuality. **Holdings:** 4000 books; 35 VF drawers of journal articles, reprints, unpublished mimeographs. **Subscriptions:** 125 journals and other serials. **Publications:** *A Family Planning Library Manual; A Small Library in Family Planning; Current Literature in Family Planning* (review of books and journal articles in the field, annotated and classified), monthly; *Directory of Population Research and Family Planning Training Centers in the U.S.A., 1980-1981; LINK Line* (newsletter) for sexuality educators and other professionals. **Alternate phone number:** (212)603-4637.

★6896★ **Planned Parenthood of Houston & Southeast Texas, Inc.**
Mary Elizabeth Hudson Library
3601 Fannin St.
Houston, TX 77004
Phone: (713)522-6363
Natalie H. Thrall, Volunteer Libn.

Subjects: Sexuality education, family planning, parenting, reproductive health, reproductive rights, population, women's issues. **Holdings:** 2500 books; 100 bound periodical volumes; 400 file folders of reprints and newspaper clippings. **Subscriptions:** 23 journals and other serials.

★6897★ **Planned Parenthood of Minnesota**
Phyllis Cooksey Resource Center
1965 Ford Pkwy.
St. Paul, MN 55116
Phone: (612)698-2401
Fax: (612)698-2401
Debra Bauer, Rsrc.Ctr.Coord.

Subjects: Family planning, population growth, human sexuality, abortion, sex education. **Special Collections:** Works of Margaret Sanger (8 volumes). **Holdings:** 1500 books; 12 VF drawers of pamphlets and ephemera; 100 films, video- and audio cassettes. **Subscriptions:** 100 journals and other serials. **Telex:** 612 698-1183. **Publications:** Acquisitions lists, newsnotes, semiannual - free upon request; educational brochure catalog; AV catalog, both available upon request; list of other publications available upon request.

★6898★ **Planned Parenthood of Northern New England**
PPNNE Resource Center
23 Mansfield Ave.
Burlington, VT 05401
Phone: (802)862-9637
Fax: (802)863-5284
Tracy Fisk, Res.Coord.

Subjects: Family life education, sexual development, parenting and child care, women's health, infertility. **Special Collections:** Agency history; sex education. **Holdings:** 2300 books; 4 VF drawers of articles. **Subscriptions:** 30 journals and other serials; 30 newsletters. **Publications:** *Edsource,* 3/year for area educators; *K-12 Family Life Curriculum* for sale.

★6899★ **Planned Parenthood of the St. Louis Region**
Education Department
Library
7415 Manchester Rd.
St. Louis, MO 63143
Phone: (314)781-3800
Denise Page, Dir. of Pub.Educ.

Subjects: Family planning, human reproduction, sexually transmitted diseases, pregnancy, homosexuality, human sexuality, abortion, parenting. **Special Collections:** Birth Control Review, 1922-1927 (complete); Social Welfare Forum, 1948-1965. **Holdings:** 500 books; 20 bound periodical volumes; clippings and articles. **Subscriptions:** 11 journals and other serials. **Formerly:** Planned Parenthood Association of St. Louis - Family Planning Library.

★6900★ **Planned Parenthood of San Antonio and South Central Texas**
Library
104 Babcock Rd.
San Antonio, TX 78201
Phone: (512)736-2244
Patricia Sidebottom, Exec.Dir.

Subjects: Birth control, population, human sexuality, sex education, family planning, AIDS, ecology, environment, women's health, teenage pregnancy. **Holdings:** 1500 books; 500 periodicals; pamphlets; vertical files; 100 films, filmstrips, slide sets. **Subscriptions:** 35 journals and other serials. **Publications:** Pamphlets on venereal disease and birth control.

★6901★ **Planned Parenthood Southeastern Pennsylvania**
Resource Center
1144 Locust St.
Philadelphia, PA 19107-5740
Phone: (215)351-5590
Fax: (215)351-5595
Wanda Mial, Rsrc.Ctr.Coord.

Subjects: Family planning, reproductive health, venereal diseases, childbearing and pregnancy options, sex education. **Holdings:** 2500 books; 40 bound periodical volumes; 12 VF drawers; 100 slides, videotapes, films, filmstrips. **Subscriptions:** 65 journals and other serials. **Publications:** List of publications available on request.

★6902★ **Planned Parenthood of Southwestern Indiana, Inc.**
Resource Center
Hebron Plaza
971 Kenmore Dr.
Evansville, IN 47715-7503
Phone: (812)473-8800
Toni Godeke, Dir. of Educ.

Subjects: Contraceptives, sexuality, family life education curriculum, women's health, infertility, population. **Holdings:** 300 books; 5 VF drawers. **Subscriptions:** 6 journals and other serials. **Alternate phone number:** (812)473-8807.

★6903★ **Planned Parenthood of Wisconsin Maurice Ritz Resource Library and Bookstore**
302 N. Jackson St.
Milwaukee, WI 53202
Phone: (414)271-7930
Fax: (414)271-1935
Ann H. McIntyre, Libn.

Subjects: Family planning, reproductive health, sexuality education, contraception, obstetrics/gynecology nursing education, population. **Holdings:** 1500 books; 12 VF drawers of clippings and reports; 100 pamphlets, booklets, reprints; 80 films, slides, tapes, videotapes. **Subscriptions:** 55 journals and other serials. **Publications:** Audiovisual list; pamphlets list; material available for rent or purchase; subject bibliographies.

★6904★ **Plymouth Congregational Church**
Library
1900 Nicollet Ave., S.
Minneapolis, MN 55403
Phone: (612)871-7400
Joanne Lee, Libn.

Subjects: Religion and theology, global concerns, social and women's issues, art, children's literature. **Special Collections:** Free to Be collection (women's issues; 40 books); Global Concerns collection (60 books and pamphlets); art lending library (35 framed pictures). **Holdings:** 2000 books; 100 tapes. **Subscriptions:** 12 journals and other serials.

★6905★ **Population Council**
Library
1 Dag Hammarskjold Plaza
New York, NY 10017
Phone: (212)644-1620
Fax: (212)755-6052
Hue Neil Zimmerman, Libn.

Subjects: Population; demography; family planning; contraception; statistics; public health; development - economic, social, agricultural. **Holdings:** 20,000 books; 6,000 pamphlets, mimeographs, reprints, other cataloged items. **Subscriptions:** 350 journals and other serials. **Publications:** Acquisitions List, irregular.

★6906★ **Population Crisis Committee/Draper Fund**
Library
1120 19th St., N.W., Suite 550
Washington, DC 20036
Phone: (202)659-1833
Anne Marie B. Amantia, Sr.Libn./Info.Mgr.

Subjects: Family planning, demography, contraceptive technology, status of women, food, environment. **Special Collections:** Female circumcision; history of population legislation. **Holdings:** 5000 books; 65 VF drawers. **Subscriptions:** 500 journals and other serials. **Telecommunications Services:** Telex: 440450. **Publications:** Serials holdings list, - free upon request.

**★6907★ Pregnancy and Infant Loss
    Center**
Lending Library
1415 E. Wayzata Blvd., No. 105
Wayzata, MN 55391
Phone: (612)473-9372
Sherokee Ilse, Pres.

Subjects: Perinatal bereavement, coping with grief, children and death. **Holdings:** 100 books. **Subscriptions:** 30 newspapers.

★6908★ Presbyterian Church (U.S.A.)
Department of History (Montreat)
Library and Archives
Box 849
Montreat, NC 28757
Phone: (704)669-7061
Fax: (704)669-5369
Robert Benedetto, Dp.Dir.

Subjects: Presbyterianism in the South, Reformed Churches of the world. **Special Collections:** History of churches and women's work in the Presbyterian Church, U.S.A. (6000 volumes); records and minutes of Presbyterian and Reformed Churches of the world (7500 volumes). **Holdings:** 40,000 books; 25,000 bound periodical volumes; 75,000 other cataloged items; 6500 linear feet of archival materials and manuscripts; 3000 reels of microfilm. **Subscriptions:** 150 journals and other serials. **Publications:** *Presbyterian Heritage,* 3/yr.; *Survey of Records and Minutes in the Historical Foundation; The Historical Foundation and its Treasures; Guide to the Manuscript Collection of the Presbyterian Church, U.S.; Eighteenth-Century American Publications; Conservation of Church Records.*

★6909★ Princeton University
Rare Books and Special Collections
Firestone Library
Princeton, NJ 08544
Phone: (609)258-3184
William L. Joyce, Assoc.Libn.

Special Collections: Includes Miriam Y. Holden Collection on the History of Women (Rare Books Section).

★6910★ Pro-Life Action League
Library
6160 N. Cicero, No. 210
Chicago, IL 60646
Phone: (312)777-2900

Subjects: Abortion - pro-life perspective, legal aspects, proposed constitutional amendment, public protests and demonstrations, sidewalk counseling, statistics. **Special Collections:** Biographical archives. **Holdings:** 1000 volumes, tapes, videocassettes, and vertical files. **Remarks:** Alternate telephone number(s): (312)777-2525 (24-hour Action Line).

★6911★ Radcliffe College
Arthur and Elizabeth Schlesinger Library
on the History of Women in America
10 Garden St.
Cambridge, MA 02138
Phone: (617)495-8647
Dr. Patricia M. King, Dir.

Subjects: Women - suffrage, medicine, education, law, social service, labor, family, organizations; history of American women in all phases of public and private life. **Special Collections:** Beecher-Stowe; Woman's Rights; Blackwell Family; Charlotte Perkins Gilman; Emma Gold-

man; Somerville-Howorth; Dr. Martha May Eliot; Jeannette Rankin; National Organization for Women; National Women's Political Caucus; Black Women Oral History Project; Culinary Collection (9000 volumes); etiquette books; picture collection (50,000). **Holdings:** 35,000 volumes; 3000 bound periodical volumes; 850 major collections of papers on individual American women, families, women's organizations; 9500 reels of microfilm; 2250 magnetic tapes; 70 VF drawers; 2500 reels of audio- and videotapes; 6500 linear feet of manuscripts; 50,000 photographs. **Subscriptions:** 495 journals and other serials. **Publications:** Occasional Reports, sent on request. **Remarks:** Library located at 3 James St., Cambridge, MA, 02138.

★6912★ Radcliffe College
Henry A. Murray Research Center
10 Garden St.
Cambridge, MA 02138
Phone: (617)495-8140
Fax: (617)495-8422
Anne Colby, Dir.

Subjects: Human development and social change; women - work, careers, education, mental health, political participation, family life, widowhood, aging. **Special Collections:** Archival materials dealing with data sets of raw and computer-accessible social science research studies. **Holdings:** 190 data sets; 150 books; 500 boxes of raw data; 50 dissertations; 300 unpublished reports; 150 computer magnetic tapes. **Publications:** *Murray Center News,* semiannual - free upon request.

★6913★ Right to Life League of Southern
    California
Library
50 N. Hill Ave., Suite 306
Pasadena, CA 91106
Phone: (818)449-8408
Fax: (818)449-4822
Lori Hougens, Dir., Educ.

Subjects: Abortion, pre-natal development, euthanasia, genetic engineering, infanticide, human experimentation. **Special Collections:** The Human Life Review, 1975-1986. **Holdings:** Books; periodicals; clippings; pamphlets; cassettes; videotapes. **Publications:** *Life Issues Report* (newsletter) - free upon request.

★6914★ Right to Life of Michigan
Macomb County Education/Resource
Center
27417 Harper
St. Clair Shores, MI 48081
Phone: (313)774-6050
Andrea Treall, Contact

Subjects: Abortion, euthanasia, infanticide, legislation. **Holdings:** 37 books; 30 videotapes; 12 16mm films; 125 audio cassettes; slides; booklets; pamphlets.

★6915★ Right to Life of Michigan
Resource Center
43000 9 Mile Rd., Suite 213
Novi, MI 48375
Phone: (313)347-1601
Barbara Lowman, Contact

Subjects: Abortion, euthanasia, infanticide, legislation. **Holdings:** Books; videotapes; 16mm films; audio cassettes; slides; VF files; booklets; newspaper clippings; pamphlets.

★6916★ Right to Life of Michigan
Resource Center
Knapp's Centre, Suite 588
300 S. Washington Sq.
Lansing, MI 48933
Phone: (517)487-3376
Malika Abdur-Rashid, Contact

Subjects: Abortion, euthanasia, infanticide, legislation. **Holdings:** Books; videotapes; 16mm films; audio cassettes; slides; VF files; booklets; newspaper clippings; pamphlets.

★6917★ Right to Life of Michigan
Resource Center
1574 Fort St.
Lincoln Park, MI 48146
Phone: (313)381-2180
Betty Pevovar, Region 4 Dir. & Off.Mgr.

Subjects: Abortion, euthanasia, infanticide, legislation. **Holdings:** Books; videotapes; 16mm films; audio cassettes; slides; VF files; booklets; newspaper clippings; pamphlets.

★6918★ Right to Life of Michigan
State Central Resource Center
920 Cherry, S.E.
Grand Rapids, MI 49506
Phone: (616)451-0225
Sheri Hicks, Dir.

Subjects: Abortion, euthanasia, infanticide, legislation. **Holdings:** Books; videotapes; 16mm films; audio cassettes; slides; VF files; booklets; newspaper clippings; pamphlets.

★6919★ Riverside Regional Medical
    Center
Health Sciences Library
J. Clyde Morris Blvd.
Newport News, VA 23601
Phone: (804)599-2175
Fax: (804)599-2986

Subjects: Family practice, medicine, pediatrics, obstetrics-gynecology, nursing, allied health sciences. **Holdings:** 4038 books; 6742 bound periodical volumes. **Subscriptions:** 203 journals and other serials. **Remarks:** Alternate telephone number(s): 599-2682.

★6920★ Rockefeller University
Rockefeller Archive Center
15 Dayton Ave.
Pocantico Hills
North Tarrytown, NY 10591
Phone: (914)631-4505
Fax: (914)631-6017
Dr. Darwin H. Stapleton, Dir.

Subjects: American philanthropy; Rockefeller family; education; medicine; physical, natural, and social sciences; public health; arts; humanities; agriculture; Black history; international relations and economic development; labor; politics; population; religion; social welfare; women's history. **Holdings:** 23,000 cubic feet of archival and manuscript collections; 250,000 photographs; 4000 microfiche; 1600 films. **Publications:** Newsletter, annual; occasional papers; *Research Reports from the Rockefellar Archive Center.*

★6921★ Rutgers University
Special Collections and Archives
Alexander Library
College Ave. & Huntington St.
New Brunswick, NJ 08903
Phone: (908)932-7006
Fax: (908)932-7637
Ronald L. Becker, Dir.

Subjects: History of education, social policy and social welfare, labor, exploration and travel, Puritanism, genealogy, Latin America, history of science and technology. **Special Collections:** Women's Archives (including the records of SIGNS and the Womens Caucus for Art). **Holdings:** 152,000 volumes; 1000 newspaper titles; 2000 manuscript collections (6500 cubic feet); 200,000 pictures; 5500 almanacs; 4400 maps; 12,500 broadsides; 500 reels of microfilm; genealogical materials; ephemera; museum objects. **Subscriptions:** 842 journals and other serials. **Telecommunications Services:** Electronic mail address: BECKER@ZODIAC.RUTGERS.EDU (BITNET). **Publications:** Acquisitions reports; user guides.

★6922★ Salem State College
Library of Social Alternatives
Salem, MA 01970
Phone: (508)741-6000
Margaret Andrews, Coord.

Subjects: Alternative lifestyles, Third World, social change, ecology, gays/lesbians, health care, women, hobbies, radical left. **Special Collections:** Community Resource Referral File. **Holdings:** 3000 books; magazine archives. **Subscriptions:** 20 journals and other serials. **Publications:** Community Resource File: A Directory.

★6923★ Schoolcraft College
Women's Resource Center
18600 Haggerty Rd.
Livonia, MI 48152
Phone: (313)462-4443
Nancy K. Swanborg, Dir.

Subjects: Women and single parents - career information, education, employment, counseling, health. **Holdings:** 500 books; 1000 newsletters, pamphlets, government publications, research reports, reprints; 6 VF drawers. **Subscriptions:** 18 journals and other serials. **Publications:** Reprints, irregular; Newsletter, quarterly - free upon request.

★6924★ Searle Research Library
4901 Searle Pkwy.
Skokie, IL 60077
Phone: (708)982-8285
Fax: (708)982-4701
Anthony Petrone, Mgr.

Subjects: Chemistry, biology, gastroenterology, gynecology and contraception, hypertension, pharmacology. **Holdings:** 6500 books. **Subscriptions:** 700 journals and other serials; 35 newsletters. **Publications:** Acquisitions List, monthly - for internal distribution only. **Formerly:** G.D. Searle & Company - Research Library.

★6925★ Seneca Falls Historical Society
Jessie Beach Watkins Memorial Library
55 Cayuga St.
Seneca Falls, NY 13148
Phone: (315)568-8412
Sylvia Farrer-Bornarth, Exec.Dir.

Subjects: Local and area history, Victoriana, Civil War. **Special Collections:** Women's Rights Collection (documents, 1848 to present). **Holdings:** 1500 books; 4 VF drawers; local newspaper, 1839 to present, on microfilm. **Subscriptions:** 10 journals and other serials.

★6926★ Sharon Long - Private Collection
104-06 85th Ave.
Richmond Hill, NY 11418
Phone: (718)441-8917
Sharon Long, Contact

Subjects: Abortion. **Special Collections:** Pro-Life Anti-Abortion Feminism. **Holdings:** 25 books; 50 bound periodical volumes; 5 VF drawers of articles and pamphlets. **Remarks:** Collection of articles, focusing on empirical studies of abortion, is organized by subject and by pro-life and pro-choice points of view.

★6927★ Simmons College
Archives
300 The Fenway
Boston, MA 02115
Phone: (617)738-3141
Fax: (617)738-2099
Megan Sniffin-Marinoff, Arch.Hd.

Subjects: Social welfare, nursing, home economics, children's literature, library science, women's history. **Special Collections:** Donald Moreland Collection (history of social welfare; 1500 volumes); Knapp Collection (19th and early 20th Century children's literature); public health nursing collection (200 volumes). **Holdings:** 3200 books; 100 linear feet of archival materials. **Publications:** Guides to archives; guides to manuscript collections.

★6928★ Sisters of St. Joseph of Carondelet
St. Paul Province
Archives
1884 Randolph Ave.
St. Paul, MN 55105
Phone: (612)690-7000
Mary E. Kraft, C.S.J., Archv.

Subjects: Religious life, education, health care, social justice, women. **Holdings:** Archival collections.

★6929★ Smith College
Sophia Smith Collection
Women's History Archive
Northampton, MA 01063
Phone: (413)585-2970
Susan Grigg, Dir.

Subjects: U.S. women's history, 1820 to present, especially birth control, social work, women's suffrage and rights, journalism, medicine, international service; 19th century families. **Special Collections:** 200 major collections of personal papers and organizational records, including: Margaret Sanger; Planned Parenthood of America and Massachusetts; Hale, Ames, and Garrison families; Ellen Gates Starr; Mary van Kleeck; Pauline Frederick. **Holdings:** 3600 linear feet of manuscripts, archives, periodicals, printed ephemera, photographs, books. **Subscriptions:** 65 serials.

★6930★ Southern Illinois University at Carbondale
Undergraduate Library
Morris Library
Carbondale, IL 62901
Phone: (618)453-2818
Fax: (618)453-8109
Dr. Judith Ann Harwood, Libn.

Subjects: Automotive technology, thanatology, cinema and photography, women's studies, radio and television, general studies. **Holdings:** 120,000 books; 9533 bound periodical volumes; 2437 reels of microfilm. **Subscriptions:** 433 journals and other serials.

★6931★ Southern Regional Council, Inc.
Reference Library
60 Walton St., N.W., 2nd Fl.
Atlanta, GA 30303-2199
Phone: (404)522-8764
Fax: (404)522-8791
Stephen T. Suitts, Exec.Dir.

Subjects: Civil rights, civil liberties, poverty, politics, suffrage. **Holdings:** 1200 books; civil rights movement newspaper collection on microfilm; newsclip collection, 1946-1975; special studies. **Publications:** Southern Changes, bimonthly - by subscription; SRC House Record, Voting Rights Review, Legislative Bulletin - all quarterly; Special Reports and Studies.

★6932★ State Historical Society of Wisconsin
Library
816 State St.
Madison, WI 53706-1482
Phone: (608)264-6534
Fax: (608)264-6520
R. David Myers, Dir.

Subjects: History—American, Canadian, state, local, labor, U.S. church; radical/reform movements and groups in the U.S. and Canada; ethnic and minority groups in North America; genealogy; women's history; military history; religious history. **Holdings:** 2.8 million items. **Subscriptions:** 8500 periodicals; 320 newspapers. **Publications:** Wisconsin Public Documents (checklist of state government documents) free upon request; bibliographies; guides. **Remarks:** This library is a U.S. Federal Government regional depository, a Wisconsin State official depository, and a Canadian Federal Government selective depository for government publications.

★6933★ State University of New York at Buffalo
University Archives
420 Capen Hall
Buffalo, NY 14260
Phone: (716)636-2916
Fax: (716)636-3844
Shonnie Finnegan, Univ.Archv.

Subjects: Archives of the State University of New York at Buffalo and its predecessor, University of Buffalo, 1846 to present. **Special Collections:** Documents pertaining to the Darwin D. Martin House and other Buffalo buildings designed by Frank Lloyd Wright; records of social action and women's organizations; history of Buffalo area in the 20th century; Fran Striker Collection (early radio scripts, including The Lone Ranger, 1932-1937). **Holdings:** 7000 linear feet of manuscripts, papers, and other archival materials.

★6934★ Staten Island Institute of Arts and Sciences
Archives and Library
75 Stuyvesant Place
Staten Island, NY 10301
Phone: (718)727-1135
John-Paul Richiuso, Archv./Hist.

Subjects: Natural history, Staten Island history, archeology, black history, women's history, urban planning. **Special Collections:** Architecture; N.L. Britton; G.W. Curtis; J.P. Chapin; W.T. Davis (total of 1000 cubic feet); photographs and prints of old Staten Island; local black history; repository for U.S. Geological Survey publications; complete list of special collections available on request. **Holdings:** 12,000 books; 22,000 bound periodical volumes; 3000 maps; 1200 prints; 50,000 photographs; 1500 art museum and gallery catalogs; 1500 cubic feet of manuscripts, letters, and documents; 80 reels of microfilm of Staten Island newspapers. **Subscriptions:** 200 journals and other serials. **Publications:** Proceedings, 2/year by subscription and exchange; *Guide to Special Collections*, 16 volumes. **Remarks:** Basic library has been divided into two sections, a Science Library and a History Library.

★6935★ Stowe-Day Foundation
Library
77 Forest St.
Hartford, CT 06105
Phone: (203)728-5507
Joseph S. Van Why, Dir.

Subjects: Art, architecture, decorative arts, history, literature, slavery, women's suffrage. **Special Collections:** William H. Gillette papers, plays, and photographs, 1853-1937; suffrage papers of Isabella Beecher Hooker; Katharine S. Day Collection; Saturday Morning Club Collection; literary manuscripts of Mark Twain and Harriet Beecher Stowe; 19th century wallpaper samples. **Holdings:** 15,000 books; 1500 bound periodical volumes; 150,000 manuscripts, especially Beecher family; 1500 pamphlets, 1850-1900; 3500 miscellaneous 19th century pamphlets; photographs. **Subscriptions:** 10 journals and other serials. **Remarks:** The books, manuscripts, and photographs of the Mark Twain Memorial, Hartford, Connecticut, are also cataloged and housed in the Stowe-Day Library. The Stowe-Day Foundation maintains an active publishing program, consisting of original and reprint works, which reflects the interests of the library.

★6936★ Swarthmore College
Friends Historical Library
500 College Ave.
Swarthmore, PA 19081-1399
Phone: (215)328-8496
Fax: (215)328-8673
J. William Frost, Dir.

Subjects: Quaker faith, history, and genealogy; Quaker social concerns - abolition of slavery, race relations, women's rights, peace, education, prison reform, mental health, Indian rights, temperance. **Special Collections:** Friends Meeting records (4000 volumes of manuscripts); Whittier (1700 books, 900 manuscripts); Quaker manuscripts (277 collections); Lucretia Mott manuscripts (7 boxes); Samuel Janney manuscripts (7 boxes); Elias Hicks manuscripts (12 boxes); journals of Quaker ministers (18 boxes); Charles F. Jenkins Autograph Collection (6 boxes). **Holdings:** 39,192

books; 1897 bound periodical volumes; 240 boxes of pictures; 81 chart case drawers of pictures, maps, broadsides, deeds, genealogical charts, marriage certificates; 2536 reels of microfilm; 750 microfiche. **Subscriptions:** 185 journals and other serials. **Telecommunications Services:** Electronic mail address(es): MCHIJIOL@CC.SWARTHMORE.EDU (InterNet); TRIPOD.BRYNMAWR.EDU (public access catalog, InterNet). **Publications:** Descriptive leaflet; Guide to the Manuscript Collections of Friends Historical Library of Swarthmore College, 1982; Guide to the Records of Philadelphia Yearly Meeting, 1989.

★6937★ Temple University
Central Library System
Contemporary Culture Collection
13th & Berks Sts.
Philadelphia, PA 19122
Phone: (215)787-8667
Elaine Cox Clever, Cur.

Subjects: Social change, peace and disarmament, small press poetry, fringe politics, alternative life styles, animal rights, feminism, gays. **Special Collections:** Counter culture and peace movement newspapers from the Vietnam era; early second wave feminist publications and literary chapbooks; Liberation News Service Archive (160 linear feet); Youth Liberation Archive (40 linear feet); Committee of Small Press Editors and Publishers Archive (32 linear feet); small presses archives (83 linear feet); personal papers of poet Lyn Lifshin (36 linear feet). **Holdings:** 8000 books and pamphlets; 4000 periodical, newspaper, and newsletter titles; 730 reels of microfilm; 70 linear feet of ephemera. **Subscriptions:** 290 journals and other serials; 90 newspapers. **Publications:** Periodical holdings lists, 1972, 1976; *Alternative Press Periodicals: A Listing of Periodicals Microfilmed at The Collection, 1976*; Exhibits with related bibliographies.

★6938★ Texas Woman's University
Blagg-Huey Library
Special Collections
TWU Sta., Box 23715
Denton, TX 76204-1715
Phone: (817)898-3751
Fax: (817)898-3726
Dawn Weston, Hd., Spec.Coll.

Subjects: Women's biography, history, and literature; suffrage; cookery. **Special Collections:** Woman's Collection (45,467 books and bound periodical volumes, including the Madeleine Henrey Collection and the LaVerne Harrell Clark Collection); Sarah Weddington Collection; Claire Myers Owens Collection; Texas Women: A Celebration of History collection; Texas Federation of Women's Clubs papers; Delta Kappa Gamma—Texas papers; Cookbook and Menu Collection (8817 books and bound periodical volumes; 2000 menus, 1844 cookbooklets, including the Julie Bennell Cookbook Collection and the Margaret Scruggs Cookbook Collection); The Ribbon Archives; Genevieve Dixon Collection (1126 books); university archives and manuscript collection (2200 cubic feet). **Holdings:** 65,729 books and bound periodical volumes; 27,125 items in microforms; 575 AV programs. **Subscriptions:** 98 journals and other serials. **Alternate phone number:** 898-2665.

★6939★ Tulane University
Newcomb College Center for Research on Women
Vorhoff Library
New Orleans, LA 70118
Phone: (504)865-5238
Susan Tucker, Contact

Subjects: Women's education, women's labor, Southern women, motherhood. **Special Collections:** Archives of Newcomb College (300 cubic feet of archival materials); Scrapbooks of Southern Women Collection; Cookbook Collection. **Holdings:** 3055 books; 450 cubic feet of archival materials. **Subscriptions:** 76 journals and other serials. **Publications:** *Contents Service*; *Bibliography and Reference Series*; subject guide, biennial; *Working Papers Series in Women's Studies*.

★6940★ United Nations Population Fund
Library
220 E. 42nd St., Rm. DN-1763
New York, NY 10017
Phone: (212)297-5069
Fax: (212)297-4914
Audun Gythfeldt, Chf.

Subjects: Population, demography, family planning, economic development, population assistance, contraception. **Holdings:** 5500 books; 2500 reprints. **Subscriptions:** 400 journals and other serials; 5 newspapers.

★6941★ U.S. Department of Justice
National Institute of Justice
Library
633 Indiana Ave. NW, Rm. 900
Washington, DC 20531
Phone: (202)307-5883
Fax: (202)307-6394
Barbara L. Owen, Libn.

Subjects: Law enforcement, police science, criminology, juvenile delinquency, courts, corrections, white collar crime, spouse and child abuse, victims. **Holdings:** 5500 books; 1000 U.S. Government documents. **Subscriptions:** 100 journals and other serials. **Remarks:** Affiliated with National Criminal Justice Reference Service in Rockville, MD.

★6942★ U.S. Department of Labor
Women's Bureau
Reference Library on Women and Women's Employment
230 S. Dearborn St., 10th Fl.
Chicago, IL 60604
Phone: (312)353-6985
Sandra K. Frank, Reg.Adm.

Description: Works to improve women's employment status through policy and program development within U.S. Department of Labor and by working cooperatively with other government, public, private, and community organizations. **Subjects:** Women's employment—training, affirmative action, safety and health, work and family, nontraditional employment, equal opportunity, career information.

★6943★ U.S. Equal Employment Opportunity Commission (EEOC) Library
1801 L St. NW, Rm. 6502
Washington, DC 20507
Phone: (202)663-4630
Fax: (202)663-4629
Susan D. Taylor, Lib.Dir.

Subjects: Employment discrimination, minorities, women, aged, handicapped, testing, labor law, civil rights. **Special Collections:** Equal Employment Opportunity Commission Publications. **Holdings:** 25,000 books. **Subscriptions:** 300 journals and other serials; 8 newspapers. **Publications:** Library service and selected bibliographies, brochure. **Also known as:** EEOC.

★6944★ U.S. National Institutes of Health National Institute of Allergy & Infectious Diseases
Rocky Mountain Laboratory Library
Hamilton, MT 59840
Phone: (406)363-3211
Leza Serha Hamby, Med.Libn.

Subjects: Medicine, virology, bacteriology, immunology, entomology, chemistry, parasitology, pathology, microbiology, biochemistry, biology, sexually transmitted disease. **Holdings:** 6000 books, 22,000 bound periodical volumes. **Subscriptions:** 287 journals and other serials. **Alternate phone number:** (406)363-6406.

★6945★ U.S. National Park Service Frederick Douglass National Historic Site Library
1411 W St. SE
Washington, DC 20020
Phone: (202)426-5962
Fax: (202)472-9227
Douglas E. Stover, Musm.Cur.

Subjects: History, biography, science, geography, philosophy. **Special Collections:** History of Women's Suffrage (4 volumes); Executive Documents, 1820-1895. **Holdings:** 2000 books. **Subscriptions:** 14 journals and other serials. **Also known as:** National Capital Park-East—Douglass Private Collection.

★6946★ U.S. Navy Naval Air Station Library
Bldg. 2, Wing 3
Alameda, CA 94501-5051
Phone: (510)263-3028
Mrs. Ranjan Bhashyam-Tambe, Sta. Libn.

Subjects: Navy and other military branches, careers and education, women and minorities. Special Collections: Materials on and about California; Janes' books. Holdings: 29,766 volumes; 200 bound periodical volumes; 10 VF drawers of pamphlets and clippings; 10 shelves of periodicals; 1345 phonograph records/tapes (mainly popular music). Subscriptions: 60 journals and other serials; 7 newspapers. Publications: *Library News* - basewide distribution.

★6947★ University of California, Davis Women's Resources & Research Center Library
10 Lower Freeborn Hall
Davis, CA 95616
Phone: (916)752-3373
Joy Fergoda, Libn.

Subjects: Women's issues, concerns, and research. **Special Collections:** Native and Pioneer Women in Yolo and Solano Counties, California (oral history collection; 28 tapes; 2 photograph albums). **Holdings:** 4500 books; 7500 vertical file materials; 650 audiotapes. **Subscriptions:** 130 journals and other serials; 14 newspapers.

★6948★ University of California, Riverside Special Collections
Box 5900
Riverside, CA 92517-5900
Phone: (714)787-3233
Fax: (714)787-3285
Sidney E. Berger, Hd., Spec.Coll.

Special Collections: 20th century English literature; Ezra Pound (700 volumes); Juan Silvano Godoi Collection (45 volumes; 57 boxes); Eaton Collection of Fantasy and Science Fiction (65,000 volumes; 6500 periodicals; 25,000 items of fanzines); historical collection of children's literature (2000 volumes); Thomas Hardy Theater Collection; Skinner-Ropes Collection (7000 manuscripts, 1843-1917, including 5 Civil War diaries and extensive Californiana); Sadakichi Hartmann Collection (47 boxes); Oswald Jonas/Heinrich Schenker Collection (71 boxes); Jack Hirschman poetry (2700 sheets of manuscripts); William Blake Collection (900 volumes); Niels Gade Collection (600 scores); German National Socialism (5000 volumes); photography (3000 volumes); Osuna Photographic Archive on the Mexican Revolution (427 glass plates); Tomas Rivera Archive, (192 boxes); utopias (500 volumes); women (5000 volumes); history of citriculture; date growing; Paraguay (1000 volumes); B. Traven (240 volumes; 1 box of manuscripts); William Walker (75 volumes); manuscripts and papers of Robert L. Forward, Gregory Benford, and others; university archives (1300 items; 52 tapes); Riverside City Archives (on deposit). **Holdings:** 110,000 volumes; 150,000 manuscripts; 13,000 photographs. **Telecommunications Services:** ELectronic mail address: SPCOLSEB@UCRVMS (BITNET). **Publications:** *Dictionary Catalog of J. Lloyd Eaton Collection of Science Fiction and Fantasy Literature; Oswald Jonas Memorial Collection; The Sadakichi Hartmann Papers: A Descriptive Inventory*

★6949★ University of California, Santa Cruz
Dean E. McHenry Library
Santa Cruz, CA 95064
Phone: (408)459-2711
Fax: (408)459-8206
Allan J. Dyson, Univ.Libn.

Subjects: Astronomy, women's studies, literature, local history. **Special Collections:** Thomas Carlyle; Kenneth Patchen; Gregory Bateson; Robert Heinlein; South Pacific; Santa Cruz local history including pre-statehood and Mexican local government archives; Trianon Press Archive; fine printing; Californiana. **Holdings:** 1,004,772 volumes; 2149 manuscript units; 161,677 maps; 19,685 reels of microfilm; 453,199 microfiche; 75,331 microprints; 72,112 government documents; 24,833 audio items; 2041 videotapes; 33 multi-media kits; 610 motion pictures; 24 filmstrips; 14,447 pictures; 229,647 slides. **Subscriptions:** 10,004 journals and other serials. **Telecommunications Services:** Electronic mail address: LIBOFF@UCSCM (BITNET).

★6950★ University of Colorado—Boulder Western Historical Collections/University Archives
Campus Box 184
Boulder, CO 80309-0184
Phone: (303)492-7242
Fax: (303)492-2185

Subjects: Colorado history, 19th and 20th century American West, political leadership, organized labor, professional organizations, women's history, environmental history, business and industry. **Special Collections:** Women's International League for Peace and Freedom Papers; National Farmers Union Archives; Edward P. Costigan Papers; Western Federation of Miners and International Union of Mine, Mill and Smelter Workers Archives; James G. Patton Papers; Herrick Roth Papers; Elwood Brooks Papers; Western History Association Papers; Colorado Library Association Archives; Oil, Chemical and Atomic Workers Union; Wayne Aspinall Papers; Ray Kogovsek Papers; Frank Delaney Papers; Gary Hart Papers; Friends of the Earth Papers. **Holdings:** 15,000 linear feet of historical manuscripts; 4000 linear feet of university archives; 2000 linear feet of newspapers; 13,000 volumes; 250,000 photographs; pamphlets; maps; microfilm. **Publications:** *A Guide to Manuscript Collections* (1982); guides to individual manuscript collections for sale.

★6951★ University of Illinois at Chicago University Library
Midwest Women's Historical Collection (MWHC)
Box 8198
801 N. Morgan
Chicago, IL 60680
Phone: (312)996-2742
Mary Ann Bamberger, Asst.Spec.Coll.Libn.

Description: Focuses on 19th and 20th century Chicago and Midwestern women active in various areas, including literature, education, social welfare and social work, design, the arts, health sciences, politics and social reform; papers of anarchist Emma Goldman; records of the YWCA of Metropolitan Chicago, the League of Women Voters of Chicago, the Chicago Urban League, and the Women's Advertising Club of Chicago; Jane Addams Memorial Collection—contains information on the activities and programs of Hull-House, women's role in immigration, social and child welfare, trade unions, and peace movements; the Gutter Collection of Chicagoana; Swallow Press Archives; Society of Midland Authors Collection—comprises records pertaining to women in higher education, nursing, and hospital care. **Publications:** Guides and bibliographies—available upon request.

★6952★ University of Illinois at Urbana-Champaign
Women in International Development Library
Women's Studies/WID Reading Rm.
415 Library
1408 W. Gregory
Urbana, IL 61801
Phone: (217)333-7998
Beth Stafford-Vaughn, Contact

★6953★ University of Massachusetts at Lowell
Center for Lowell History
40 French St.
Lowell, MA 01852
Phone: (508)934-4998
Martha Mayo, Dir.

Subjects: Middlesex Canal; Lowell, Massachusetts; hydraulics; women in industry; textile manufacturing; immigrants; Warren H. Manning. **Special Collections:** Lowell Historical Society Collection; Middlesex Canal Collection; Proprietors of Locks & Canals Collection; Manning Collection; University Archives; Olney Collection (textile books); Boston & Maine Railroad Historical Society Collection; Lowell Museum Collection; Greater Lowell Chapter of the American Association of University Women Records; John I. Coggeshall Collection; Katherine Davis Collection; Paul E. Tsongas Collection; Jack Kerouac Collection; Flather Collection; Lambert Collection; Oral History Collection; Commodore Collection; Nursing Collection; Riddick Collection. **Holdings:** 28,000 volumes; records and manscripts; 6000 maps and plans; 1000 hours of oral histories; 30,000 photographs; 25 paintings; 2000 reels of microfilm. **Alternate phone number:** 934-4998. **Formerly:** University of Lowell.

★6954★ University of Michigan
Center for the Education of Women Library
330 E. Liberty
Ann Arbor, MI 48104-2289
Phone: (313)998-7080
Fax: (313)936-7787
Mary Lee Jensen, Libn.

Subjects: Women - employment, education, status, counseling, career development. **Special Collections:** Women's organizations collection (3 cubic feet); women in science series (20 audio- and videotapes). **Holdings:** 700 books; 2000 organizational reports, government publications, dissertations, manuscripts, unpublished papers; 1 cubic foot of clippings; Michigan Occupational Information System computer software and microfiche. **Subscriptions:** 50 journals and other serials. **Publications:** *Acquisition List*, quarterly; selected topical bibliographies free upon request; *Directory of Special Collections/Libraries Independent of the University of Michigan Library System*, irregular.

★6955★ University of Michigan—School of Public Health
Department of Population Planning and International Health
Reference Collection
Ann Arbor, MI 48109
Phone: (313)763-5732

Subjects: National and international population policy and family planning; educational and medical aspects of family planning; family planning systems; demography. **Holdings:** 500 books; 6000 unbound reports and documents; 1000 country files representing 70 countries; family planning program data; reprints; documents; conference proceedings. **Subscriptions:** 100 journals and other serials.

★6956★ University of Minnesota
Department of Obstetrics and Gynecology
Litzenberg-Lund Library
PO Box 395 UMHC
420 Delaware St. SE
Minneapolis, MN 55455
Phone: (612)626-2645
Sarah Sturey, Lib.Mgr.

Subjects: Obstetrics, gynecology, reproductive endocrinology, gynecologic oncology, gynecologic surgery, maternal-fetal medicine. **Special Collections:** Historical medical and obstetrics-gynecology books. **Holdings:** 330 books; 300 bound periodical volumes. **Subscriptions:** 14 journals and other serials. **Remarks:** The Litzenberg-Lund Library is sponsored by the University of Minnesota Obstetrics & Gynecology, University Women's Health Physicians, and donations.

★6957★ University of Minnesota
Social Welfare History Archives
101 Walter Library
117 Pleasant St. SE
Minneapolis, MN 55455
Phone: (612)624-6394
David Klaassen, Cur./Archv.

Subjects: Social welfare, settlement movement, professional social work, voluntary associations, recreation, health. **Special Collections:** records and files of Survey Associates, National Federation of Settlements, Young Men's Christian Association (YMCA) of the U.S.A., National Association of Social Workers, United Neighborhood Houses of New York, and others; social service organization materials (600 linear feet); contemporary feminist periodicals and pamphlets (100 linear feet). **Holdings:** 10,134 books; 7213 feet of manuscripts; 1563 microforms; 20,044 AV programs. **Subscriptions:** 65 journals and other serials. **Publications:** *Guide to Holdings*, 1979; *Descriptive Inventories of Collections in the Social Welfare History Archives*.

★6958★ University of Missouri—St. Louis
Women's Center
211 Clark Hall
8001 Natural Bridge Rd.
St. Louis, MO 63121
Phone: (314)553-5380
Joanne Grubb, Dir.

Subjects: Women—politics, psychology, medicine; male sex roles. **Holdings:** 450 books; 500 unbound periodicals; 8 VF drawers of clippings and reports. **Subscriptions:** 6 newspapers.

★6959★ University of Nevada—Reno
Special Collections Department/University Archives
University Library
Reno, NV 89557-0044
Phone: (702)784-6538
Fax: (702)784-4529
Robert E. Blesse, Hd.

Subjects: Nevada history, 20th century poetry and fiction, anthropology, ethnography, architecture, women in the trans-Mississippi West, magic, witchcraft, history of printing, university archives, mining, water and land use. **Special Collections:** Nevada Collection; Great Basin Anthropological Collection; Nevada fiction; Women in the West; Modern Authors Collection (170 English and American writers prominent after 1910); University of Nevada, Reno archives; History of Printing and the Book Arts Collection; Nevada Architectural Archives; Senator Alan Bible papers; Virginia & Truckee Railroad Collection; Samuel Johnson; Robert Burns; George Stewart. **Holdings:** 52,000 books; 600 bound periodical volumes; 4100 linear feet of manuscripts; 110,000 photographs; 4800 maps; 17,000 architectural drawings. **Subscriptions:** 31 journals and other serials. **Telecommunications Services:** Electronic mail address: SPECARCH@EQUINOX.UNR.EDU (InterNet).

★6960★ University of North Carolina at Greensboro
Woman's Collection
Jackson Library, Special Collections
Greensboro, NC 27412
Phone: (919)334-5246

Subjects: Women - education, history, suffrage; history of costume; women authors; manners and morals; child raising and family life. **Special Collections:** Women in the 17th-19th centuries. **Holdings:** 5000 books; 254 bound periodical volumes. **Publications:** The Woman's Collection, A Check-list of Holdings, 1975.

★6961★ University of North Carolina at Greensboro
Woman's Detective Fiction Collection
Jackson Library, Special Collections
Greensboro, NC 27412
Phone: (919)334-5246

Subjects: Women detectives in American fiction, 1867-1967. **Holdings:** 1800 books.

★6962★ University of North Dakota
Elwyn B. Robinson Department of Special Collections
Chester Fritz Library
Grand Forks, ND 58202
Phone: (701)777-4625
Fax: (701)777-3319
Sandra Beidler, Hd., Archv. & Spec.Coll.

Subjects: History - North and South Dakota, Northern Great Plains, Plains Indian, women, environmental; agrarian radicalism; Nonpartisan League (North Dakota); genealogy; oral history. **Special Collections:** North Dakota Book Collection (13,250 volumes); Fred G. Aandahl Book Collection (1350 volumes); Family History/Genealogy Collection (2300 volumes); North Dakota State Documents (40,000); university archives (1200 linear feet); Orin G. Libby Manuscript Collection (6000 linear feet). **Holdings:** 16,900 books; 7200 linear feet of manuscript material; 3725 reels of microfilm; 44,000 photographs; 2000 AV items. **Publications:** *University of North Dakota Theses and Dissertations on North Dakota, 1895-1971, 1972*; *Reference Guide to North Dakota History and Literature, 1979*; *Reference Guide to the Orin G. Libby Manuscript Collection* (Volume 1, 1975; Volume 2, 1983; Volume 3, 1985).

★6963★ University of Oregon
Knight Library
Special Collections Department
Eugene, OR 97403-1299
Phone: (503)346-3053

★6964★ **University of Rochester**
Government Documents and Microtext
Center
Rush Rhees Library
Rochester, NY 14627
Phone: (716)275-4484
Fax: (716)473-1906
Kathleen E. Wilkinson, Govt.Docs.Libn.

Subjects: Documents - U.S. Congress, U.S. Bureau of the Census, New York State, women's studies, black studies, North American Indians, American and British literature. **Special Collections:** Goldsmiths'-Kress Collection (economic literature); slavery; papers of William Henry Seward and of the National Association for the Advancement of Colored People (NAACP); Early English Books; American Fiction; History of Women; Early British Periodicals. **Holdings:** 380 books; 391,000 uncataloged government documents in paper; 914,200 uncataloged government documents in microform; 2.4 million other microforms.

★6965★ **University of Toledo**
Ward M. Canaday Center
William S. Carlson Library
Toledo, OH 43606
Phone: (419)537-4480
Fax: (419)537-2726
Richard W. Oram, Dir.

Subjects: 20th century American poetry, Southern authors, and black American literature; university history; history of books and printing; women's social history; Toledo glass industry. **Special Collections:** Ezra Pound Collection (400 volumes); William Faulkner Collection (500 volumes); Black American Poetry, 1920 to present (1000 volumes); William Dean Howells Collection (150 volumes); Herbert W. Martin Collection (15 feet); Etheridge Knight Collection (10 feet); Libbey-Owens-Ford Corporation archives (150 feet); Richard T. Gosser Collection (20 feet); Jean Gould Collection (11 feet); university archives (2000 feet); J.H. Leigh Hunt (100 volumes); Scott Nearing Collection (50 volumes); T.S. Eliot (200 volumes); William Carlos Williams (75 volumes); Marianne Moore (75 volumes); Broadside Press (200 items); Women's Social History, 1840-1920 (1200 volumes). **Holdings:** 25,000 books; 3000 linear feet of archives and manuscripts. **Telecommunications Services:** Electronic mail address: FAC1734@UOFT1 (BITNET). **Publications:** *Friends of the University of Toledo Libraries*; exhibition catalogs.

★6966★ **University of Wisconsin Green**
Bay
Women's Center
Library
IS 1144
Green Bay, WI 54302
Phone: (414)465-2582
Michelle Krajnik, Women's Ctr.Coord.

Subjects: Women's history, women's movement, biography, resources available to women. **Holdings:** 400 books; periodicals, information files.

★6967★ **University of Wisconsin—Madison**
Memorial Library
Department of Special Collections
728 State St.
Madison, WI 53706
Phone: (608)262-3243
John Tedeschi, Cur.

Subjects: History of science, 19th and 20th century American literature, English literature, Socialistica, Russian history, 16th-18th century European history and literature. **Special Collections:** Thordarson Collection (history of science; 5000 volumes); Duveen Collection (history of chemistry; 2900 titles); Cole Collection (history of chemistry; 700 titles); Bassett-Brownell Mark Twain Collection (500 volumes; periodicals; manuscripts); Sukov Collection of Little Magazines (5500 titles); Russian Underground Collection (1800 items); French pamphlet collection (2500 titles); Cairns Collection (American women writers; 4100 titles); Tank Collection (Dutch culture, 16th-18th centuries; 4800 volumes); medieval manuscripts. **Holdings:** 108,000 books; 38,800 periodical volumes. **Subscriptions:** 1200 journals and other serials. **Formerly:** Department of Rare Books & Special Collections.

★6968★ **Value of Life Committee**
Library
637 Cambridge St.
Brighton, MA 02135
Phone: (617)787-4400

Subjects: Medical and legal aspects of abortion, euthanasia, ethics, and genetics. **Holdings:** 600 books, newspaper clippings, and other items. **Subscriptions:** 10 journals and other serials; 7 newspapers.

★6969★ **Vassar College—Library**
Department of Special Collections
Box 20
Poughkeepsie, NY 12601
Phone: (914)437-5799
Nancy S. MacKechnie, Cur., Rare Bks./Mss.

Subjects: College history, women's history, American and British literature, etiquette and household, fine printing, early atlases and maps. **Special Collections:** Papers of Elizabeth Bishop, Ruth Benedict, Mary McCarthy, John Burroughs, Mark Twain, Maria Mitchell, Lucy Maynard Salmon, Alma Lutz, Elizabeth Cady Stanton, Susan B. Anthony, Hallie Flanagan Davis, Robert Owens; women's suffrage collection; household manuals; cookbooks; Courtesy Books; children's literature; gardening and herbal books; Village Press Collection; Jean Webster McKinney Collection of Mark Twain Manuscripts and Family Papers. **Holdings:** 16,000 books; 1152 linear feet of documents.

★6970★ **Vermont State Office of the**
Secretary of State
State Archives
26 Terrace St.
Montpelier, VT 05602
Phone: (802)828-2308
Fax: (802)828-2496
D. Gregory Sanford, State Archv.

Subjects: Governors' official papers, legislative records, surveyors' general papers, original acts and resolves, Vermont state papers, 1744 to present, municipal charters. **Special Collections:** Stevens Collection of Vermontiana (60 feet); Vermont/New Hampshire Boundary Case (30 feet); Vermont Bicentennial Commission (30 feet); Order of Women Legislators (2 feet); Records of the Governor's Commission on the Status of Women (20 feet); Houston Studio/Country Camera Photograph Collection; Agency of Transportation and Department of Agriculture Photograph and Film Collections (35 feet); various state officers' papers (20 feet). **Holdings:** 500 books; 250 volumes of bound manuscripts; 60 volumes of maps, surveys, and charters; 500 cartons of manuscript material; 60 boxes of original acts and resolutions; 57 boxes of legislative committee records. **Publications:** *State Papers of Vermont*.

★6971★ **Vigo County Public Library**
Special Collections
1 Library Square
Terre Haute, IN 47807
Phone: (812)232-1113
Clarence Brink, Coord., Ref.Serv.

Subjects: State and local history, genealogy. **Special Collections:** Baertich Collection (2 VF drawers); Shriner Collection (4 VF drawers); family files (36 VF drawers); community affairs (116 VF drawers); local club and association records (62 boxes); Dr. Charles N. Combs Memorabilia (1 box); Eugene V. Debs Collection (2 boxes); Jane Dabney Shackelford Collection (10 boxes); Joseph Jenckes Collection (1 box); Theodore Dreiser/Paul Dresser Collection (1 box); J.A. Wickersham Scrapbook (1 box); League of Women Voters of Terre Haute Collection; Rotary Club of Terre Haute Collection; Ida Husted Harper Collection (5 boxes); Terre Haute Chamber of Commerce Collection (30 boxes). **Holdings:** 7200 books; 1440 bound periodical volumes; 425 maps and charts; 244 archival collections; 3744 reels of microfilm. **Subscriptions:** 84 journals and other serials.

★6972★ **Virginia Polytechnic Institute and**
State University
International Archive of Women in
Architecture
Special Collections Dept.
University Libraries
PO Box 90001
Blacksburg, VA 24062-9001
Phone: (703)231-9215
Laura H. Katz, Archv.

Subjects: Architecture, women. **Special Collections:** Papers of Han Schroeder (10 cubic feet), Hilde Westrom (2 cubic feet), Association for Women in Architecture (9 cubic feet), Sena Sekulic (1.5 cubic feet), Elsa Leviseur (6 cubic feet), Susana Torre (3 cubic feet), Diana Lee-Smith (.4 cubic feet). **Holdings:** 107 collections of architectural drawings, photographs, specifications, brochures, and articles.

★6973★ **Washington University**
George Warren Brown School of Social
Work
Library & Learning Resources Center
Campus Box 1196
St. Louis, MO 63130
Phone: (314)935-6633
Fax: (314)935-8511
Michael E. Powell, Dir.

Subjects: Alcoholism, women, women's issues, social work, gerontology, mental health, health, aging, gerontology, minorities, children and youth services, social and economic development, family therapy, management, special populations. **Holdings:** 40,266 volumes; 5000 government documents; 250 theses; 4122 pamphlets; 113 reels of microfilm; 9 films, filmstrips, slides; 496 videotapes; 132 audiotapes. **Subscriptions:** 665 journals and other serials; 14 newspapers. **Telecommunications Services:** Electronic mail address: MIKEOP@WULIBS (BITNET); MIKEOP@WULIBS.WUST.EDU (InterNet). **Publications:** Acquisitions list, monthly; bibliographies. **Remarks:** Maintains computing facility for campus use.

★6974★ Wellesley College
Archives
Wellesley, MA 02181
Phone: (617)235-0320
Fax: (617)239-1139
Wilma R. Slaight, Archv.

Subjects: Wellesley College, women's education. **Holdings:** 4290 linear feet of archival material.

★6975★ West Virginia Library Commission
Film Services Department
Science and Cultural Center
Charleston, WV 25305
Phone: (304)348-3976
Steve Fesenmaier, Hd. Film Serv.

Special Collections: Appalachia (250 films); astronomy (10 films); women (100 films); feature films (2000); Les Blank Collection (30 films); foreign feature films (300); black history and culture (200 films); independent animation (500 titles). **Holdings:** 5000 16mm sound films. **Subscriptions:** 12 journals and other serials. **Publications:** *WVLC Film Services Newsletter*, quarterly - to WV public libraries; *Pickflick Papers* (online); *Library Trustees Manual*, 1989. **Remarks:** Conducts state and local film workshops and annual film festival.

★6976★ Western Historical Manuscript
Collection
Thomas Jefferson Library
University of Missouri, St. Louis
8001 Natural Bridge Rd.
St. Louis, MO 63121
Phone: (314)553-5143
Ann Morris, Assoc.Dir.

Subjects: History - state and local, women's, Afro-American, ethnic, education, immigration; socialism; 19th century science; environment; peace; religion; Missouri politics; social reform and welfare; photography; journalism; business; labor. **Special Collections:** Socialist Party of Missouri records; Oral History Program (1000 tapes); Photograph Collection (200,000 images); League of Women Voters of Missouri; papers of Irving Dilliard, Dr. Thomas A. Dooley, Margaret Hickey, Leo Drey, Judge Noah Weinstein, Charles Guenther, Marlin Perkins, Ernest and Deverne Calloway, Theodore Lentz, Alberta Slavin, Rep. William Hungate, Rep. Robert Young, Rep. James Symington, Lt. Governor Harriet Woods, Paul Preisler, Joseph Pulitzer (copy), Virginia Irwin, and Kay Drey; Coalition for the Environment; Committee for Environmental Information; KETC-TV; Metropolitan Church Federation; Sierra Club - Ozark Chapter; Nuclear Weapons Freeze Campaign; Health and Welfare Council; Bureau for Men; Dismas House; St. Louis Labor Council; Family and Children's Service of Greater St. Louis; Regional Commerce and Growth Association; Missouri Public Interest Research Group; Ethical Society of St. Louis; YMCA and YWCA of St. Louis; Amalgamated Clothing and Textile Workers Union - Southwest Region. **Holdings:** 5500

linear feet of manuscripts, photographs, oral history tapes, and university archives. **Remarks:** Collection contains the manuscript holdings of both the University of Missouri and the State Historical Society of Missouri. Offices are located at the four branches of the University of Missouri. Materials may be loaned among the four branches.

★6977★ Western Michigan University
Women's Center
Library
A-331 Ellsworth Hall
Kalamazoo, MI 49008
Phone: (616)387-2990
Gwen Raaberg, Dir. of Women's Ctr.

Subjects: Women - health, financial status, careers, discrimination; displaced homemakers; nontraditional students and jobs; reentry women; equal pay for equal work. **Special Collections:** Local history of women's groups and causes; sex bias in textbooks in local public schools; local history of women in education. **Holdings:** 1000 books; 9 VF drawers of clippings. **Subscriptions:** 20 journals and other serials.

★6978★ Women Artists News/Midmarch
Arts
Archives
Grand Central Sta., Box 3304
New York, NY 10163
Phone: (212)666-6990
L. Greenberg, Contact

Subjects: Art, women artists, women in art, women's organizations, art exhibitions. **Holdings:** 24 VF drawers of archival material on women in the arts; ephemera. **Subscriptions:** 25 journals and other serials. **Publications:** *Women Artists News*, quarterly; *Guide to Women's Art Organizations*, biennial; *Whole Arts Directory*, biennial with quarterly update; *Voices of Women* (criticism, poetry, graphics); *Women Artists of the World* (essays, photographs, and reproductions of art works of women artists worldwide); *Pilgrims & Pioneers: New England Women in the Arts* (historical and contemporary; essays and photographs); *American Women in Art: Works on Paper, No Bluebonnets, No Yellow Roses: Essays on Texas Women in the Arts* (historical and contemporary essays and photographs); *California Women in the Arts, 1869-1988* (historical and contemporary; essays and photographs); *Camera Fiends & Kodak Girls: Women in Photography, 1840-1930*; *The Lady Architects: Howe, Manning & Aling, 1843-1937*. **Remarks:** Published by Midmarch Associates.

★6979★ Women Exploited by Abortion
Library
International Headquarters
Rte. 1, Box 821
Venus, TX 76084
Phone: (214)366-3600
Kathy Walker, Pres.

Subjects: Abortion, post abortion syndrome (PAS) counseling, physical and psychological aftereffects of abortion. **Special Collections:** Research and data information on post abortion syndrome; personal stories. **Holdings:** 100 books; 1000 pamphlets and other items. **Publications:** *Post-Abortion Newsletter*.

★6980★ Women's Action Alliance. Inc.
Library
370 Lexington Ave., Suite 603
New York, NY 10017
Phone: (212)532-8330
Fax: (212)779-2846
Paulette Brill, Info.Serv.

Subjects: Women's issues - child care, sex discrimination, marriage, divorce, family, health, employment, affirmative action, reproductive rights, legislation, organizations and centers, chemical dependency, AIDS, teenage pregancy. **Special Collections:** Files of national women's organizations and women's centers organized by state. **Holdings:** 2000 books; 2000 bound periodical volumes; 40 VF drawers. **Subscriptions:** 200 journals and other serials. **Publications:** List of publications - available upon request.

★6981★ The Women's Collection
Northwest University Library
Special Collections Dept.
Evanston, IL 60208
Phone: (708)491-2895

Description: Collection of women's periodicals, ephemera, and monographs.

★6982★ Women's Health Resources
1003 W. Wellington and 7331 N. Sheridan
Chicago, IL 60657
Phone: (312)525-1177
Nancy Curran, Educ.Coord.

Subjects: Women's health—battered women, breast cancer, disabled women, mental health, nutrition, occupational health, stress. **Holdings:** 140 subject files—contains media clippings, brochures, medical journal reprints, articles; books; resource guides; research reports; magazines; journals; newsletters; pamphlets. **Publications:** Tailor-made information packets; Women's Health Resources brochures.

★6983★ Women's History Research
Center
Women's History Library
2325 Oak St.
Berkeley, CA 94708
Phone: (510)524-1582
Laura X, Exec.Dir.

Founded: 1969. **Subjects:** Women's health and mental health, women and law, black and Third World women, female artists, children, films by and/or about women, Soviet women. **Special Collections:** International Women's History Archive (850 periodical titles on microfilm). **Holdings:** 2000 books; 300 tapes; 54 reels of microfilm on health and law; 90 reels of microfilm of women's periodicals in Herstory Collection. **Publications:** *Directory of Films by and/or about Women*; *Female Artists Directory*; *Women & Health/Mental Health, Women & Law, and Herstory serials* (microfilm) - all for sale.

★6984★ Women's International Network
187 Grant St.
Lexington, MA 02173
Phone: (617)862-9431
Fran P. Hosken, Ed.

Subjects: Women's development and health, women's economic development, property rights of women worldwide. **Special Collections:** Female circumcision, genital mutilation. **Holdings:** Books; Network publications; foreign journals; uncataloged items. **Subscriptions:** 40

journals and other serials; 10 newspapers. **Publications:** *Childbirth Picture Book/Program*; *WIN News*, quarterly; list of additional publications - available on request.

★6985★ **Women's Movement Archives**
Women's Educational Center, Inc.
46 Pleasant St.
Cambridge, MA 02139
Phone: (617)354-8807
Libby Bouvier, Contact

Subjects: Houses a collection of Boston area women's organizations, including Bread & Roses (1969-1971), Female Liberation (1970-1974), Cell 16 (1968-1975), and Th e Women's Center (1971-present).

★6986★ **Women's Resource and Action Center**
Sojourner Truth Women's Resource Library
130 N. Madison
Iowa City, IA 52242
Phone: (319)335-1486
Laura K. Stokes, Libn.

Subjects: Feminism. **Special Collections:** Complete holdings of Ain't I A Woman, 1970-1973 (feminist periodical). **Holdings:** 1700 books. **Subscriptions:** 100 journals and other serials. **Publications:** *Women's Resource & Action Center News*, monthly - by subscription and free local distribution.

★6987★ **Women's Resource Center**
Library
250 Golden Bear Ctr.
University of California
Berkeley, CA 94720
Phone: (510)643-8367
Dorothy Lazard, Lib.Coord.

Subjects: Women's studies, women and work, financial aid, comparable worth, women of color, international issues. **Special Collections:** Catherine Scholten Collection on Women in American History (100 books); Bea Bain Collection on the Women's Movement (100 books); Margaret Monroe Drews Collection of Working Papers (the status of women in the U.S., 1950-1970; 12 VF drawers); Constance Barker Collection on Lesbian History (700 books); women's movement magazines of the 1970s. **Holdings:** 3000 books; 20,000 other uncataloged items. **Subscriptions:** 60 journals and other serials. **Publications:** Acquisitions list, quarterly; bibliographies, irregular. **Remarks:** Alternate telephone number(s): (510)643-5727.

★6988★ **Working Opportunities for Women**
W.O.W. Resource Center
2700 University Ave. W., Suite 120
St. Paul, MN 55114
Phone: (612)647-9961

Subjects: Women - employment, careers, job seeking skills, networking, occupational resources, divorce, minorities. **Special Collections:** Vocational Biographies (100 booklets). **Holdings:** 700 books; 2 shelves of educational bulletins. **Subscriptions:** 13 journals and other serials.

★6989★ **World Federation of Doctors Who Respect Human Life**
Library
PO Box 508
Oak Park, IL 60303
Phone: (708)383-8766

Subjects: Medical opposition to abortion, suicide, and direct euthanasia. **Holdings:** 700 volumes.

★6990★ **Wyoming Department of Health**
Division of Public Health
Film Library
Hathaway Bldg.
Cheyenne, WY 82002-0710
Phone: (307)777-7363
Ramona L. Nelson, Film Libn.

Subjects: Nursing, mental health, childbirth education, venereal diseases, dental health, school health, AIDS. **Special Collections:** Rape Prevention; Family Violence. **Holdings:** 431 16mm films; 500 videotape and filmstrip programs.

★6991★ **Y-ME National Organization for Breast Cancer Information and Support**
Library
18220 Harwood Ave.
Homewood, IL 60430
Phone: (708)799-8338
Fax: (708)799-5937
Kay Mueller, Contact

Subjects: Breast cancer - medicine, personal narratives, psychology. **Holdings:** 140 books; clippings. **Subscriptions:** 15 journals and other serials; 15 newsletters.

★6992★ **Young Women's Christian Association**
National Board
Library
726 Broadway
New York, NY 10003
Phone: (212)614-2716
Fax: (212)677-9716
Elizabeth D. Norris, Libn./Hist.

Subjects: Women, racism, sexism, civil rights, women's health, youth, voluntarism. **Special Collections:** Woman's Press Publications, 1918-1952 (2500 volumes). **Holdings:** 10,000 books; 25 VF drawers of subject files, clippings, pamphlets, reports, catalogs. **Subscriptions:** 175 journals and other serials. **Publications:** New Library Books, monthly - for internal distribution only. **Also known as:** YWCA.

(8) Museums and Galleries

Entries in this chapter are arranged alphabetically by organization name. See the User's Guide at the front of this directory for additional information.

★6993★ A.I.R. Gallery
63 Crosby St.
New York, NY 10012
Phone: (212)966-0799
Description: A nonprofit cooperative gallery for women artists. Publishes exhibition catalogs. Reaches market through direct mail and reviews. **Selected Titles:** *American Women: The Depression Era; A.I.R. Gallery Invitational: Japan; Patsy Norvell: Ten Years 1969-79; Detail: The Special Task; Women Artists of the '80's: New Talent.* **Principal Officials and Managers:** Sarah Savidge, Director.

★6994★ Coalition for Western Women's History
Washington State University
Women's Studies Program
Pullman, WA 99163
Sue Armitage, Newsletter Editor
Description: Networking and information about research in Western women's history.

★6995★ The Collective Gallery
1626 SW Central Park
Topeka, KS 66604
Phone: (913)234-4254
Kathleen Seery, President
Description: Artist's co-op gallery.

★6996★ Gallery 25
1936 Echo St.
Fresno, CA 93704
Phone: (209)266-6244
Founded: 1974. **Description:** Storefront co-op gallery sponsoring group and solo shows for a limit of up to 25 women artists.

★6997★ Hera Gallery
327 S. Main St.
PO Box 336
Wakefield, RI 02880
Phone: (401)789-1488
Alexandra Broches, Coordinator
Description: Features the art work of past and present Hera members.

★6998★ In Her Image
3208 SE Hawthorne
Portland, OR 97214
Phone: (503)231-3726
Description: Features feminist art.

★6999★ Kentucky Women's Heritage Museum
108 Paddock Dr.
Nicholasville, KY 40356
Liz Saum, President
Description: Museum's goal is to establish a permanent, visible display honoring/recognizing the achievements of Kentucky women.

★7000★ Minnesota Historical Society Minnesota Women's History Project
c/o Minnesota Historical Society
690 Cedar
St. Paul, MN 55101
Phone: (612)297-4467
Holdings: Collection of oral histories, books, papers, photographs, artworks, artifacts of Minnesota women.

★7001★ National Women's Hall of Fame
76 Fall St.
PO Box 335
Seneca Falls, NY 13148
Phone: (315)568-2936
Description: A non-profit membership organization to educate, motivate, and provide inspiration to women by presenting outstanding American women as role models. Offers a variety of education programs, services, and materials. Gallery houses an exhibition of women of achievement. Travelling exhibitions are also available.

★7002★ National Women's Military Museum
c/o Isobel Van Lom
PO Box 68687
Portland, OR 97268
Phone: (503)292-4046
Description: Museum honors women who served in all branches of the military.

★7003★ The New Art Center
6925 Willow St. NW
Washington, DC 20016
Phone: (202)291-2999
Description: Women's art center and gallery.

★7004★ Pioneer Woman Museum
701 Monument
Ponca City, OK 74604
Phone: (405)765-6108
Description: Exhibits collections from pioneer homes and a statue dedicated to the pioneer woman.

★7005★ Prudence Crandall Museum
PO Box 47
Routes 14 & 169
Canterbury, CT 06331
Phone: (203)546-9916
Description: Site of New England's first Black female academy. Permanent and changing exhibits includes themes on African-Americans in pre-Civil War Connecticut. Research library open to public for in-house study.

★7006★ Sewall-Belmont House
144 Constitution Ave. NE
Washington, DC 20002
Phone: (202)546-3989
Description: Headquarters for the National Woman's Party. Artifacts from the suffrage movement are also housed and exhibited.

★7007★ Smithsonian Institution Museum of American History Division of Political History National Women's History Collection
Washington, DC 20560
Phone: (202)357-2008
Founded: 1920. **Description:** Established with the deposit of materials from the National American Woman Suffrage Association, the collection reflects the changing role and status of women in politics and society, from the Women's Rights Convention of 1848 to the present. It includes the nation's most outstanding collection of material objects, political images of women reflected in prints, cartoons, posters. Serves as a clearinghouse of information concerning women's history repositories and materials, current scholarship on the history of women, and on women's political organizations.

★7008★ Susan B. Anthony House
17 Madison St.
Rochester, NY 14608
Description: Museum displays much of Susan B. Anthony's furniture and artifacts, as well as mementos of other suffragettes.

★7009★ Webb House Museum
303 Granville St.
Newark, OH 43055
Phone: (614)345-8540
Founded: 1976. **Description:** Includes collection of artwork from arts and crafts movement by 12 early Ohio women artists. Sponsors two art exhibits yearly focusing on women artists.

★7010★ Western University
Fairhaven College
Chrysalis Art Gallery
Bellingham, WA 98225
Phone: (206)676-3692
Carin Graupe, Director
Description: Exhibits work by women artists.

★7011★ Womencrafts
376 Commercial
Box 190
Provinceton, MA 02657
Description: Gallery/shop handling art and crafts by women.

★7012★ Women's Army Corps Museum
WAC Foundation
PO Box 5339
Ft. McClellan, AL 36205
Phone: (205)238-3512
Description: Honors members of the Women's Army Auxiliary Corps, the Women's Army Corps, and women serving in today's Army through displays, exhibits, films and archives.

★7013★ Women's Heritage Museum
1509 Portola Ave.
Palo Alto, CA 94306
Phone: (415)321-5260
Founded: 1985. **Description:** Maintains "Museum-Without-Walls," lending exhibits, and displays. **Remarks:** Collecting information and laying plans for permanent exhibit space.

★7014★ Women's Heritage Museum
University of Kentucky
c/o Mackelene G. Smith
404 King Library S.
Lexington, KY 40506-0391
Remarks: Developing a traveling exhibit, Hall of Fame, and women's history museum.

★7015★ Women's History Museum
Box 209
West Liberty, WV 26074
Phone: (304)335-7159
Jeanne V. Schramm, Contact
Description: Mobile museum featuring seven women from U.S. history with costumed performances about the life of each woman.

★7016★ Women's Project of New Jersey, Inc.
34 Maynard Crt.
Ridgewood, NJ
Phone: (201)652-4440
Delight Dodyk, President
Description: Bio-History and traveling exhibit of New Jersey women. Project documents available at Women's Archives, Rutgers University; exhibit flyers available from Drew University, Madison, New Jersey.

★7017★ Women's Rights National Historical Park
PO Box 70
Seneca Falls, NY 13148
Phone: (315)568-2991
Founded: 1980. **Description:** Established by Congress to commemorate the first Women's Rights Convention, held in Seneca Falls in 1848, and to preserve the Wesleyan Chapel (site of the convention), the home of Elizabeth Cady Stanton, and the McClintock House where the "Declaration of Sentiments" was written. **Remarks:** A visitors' center is now under construction.

(9) Colleges and Universities

Entries in this chapter are arranged alphabetically by institution name. See the User's Guide at the front of the directory for additional information.

★7018★ **Agnes Scott College**
Decatur, GA 30030
Phone: (404)371-6280
Founded: 1889. **Description:** Presbyterian four-year college. **Degree(s) Offered:** BA.

★7019★ **Alverno College**
3401 S. 39th St.
Milwaukee, WI 53215-4020
Phone: (414)382-6000
Sr. Joel Read, President
Founded: 1887. **Description:** Independent women's institution. **Degree(s) Offered:** AA, BA, BS.

★7020★ **Aquinas Junior College—Milton**
303 Adams St.
Milton, MA 02186
Phone: (617)696-3100
Dorothy Mulcahy-Oppenheim, President
Founded: 1956. **Description:** Roman Catholic junior college. **Degree(s) Offered:** AS.

★7021★ **Aquinas Junior College—Newton**
15 Walnut Pk.
Newton, MA 02158
Phone: (617)969-4400
Sr. Marian Batho, President
Founded: 1961. **Description:** Roman Catholic junior college. **Degree(s) Offered:** AS.

★7022★ **Barnard College**
606 W. 120th St.
New York, NY 10027
Phone: (212)854-2021
Ms. Ellen V. Futter, President
Founded: 1889. **Description:** Independent four-year women's college. **Degree(s) Offered:** BA.

★7023★ **Bay Path College**
588 Longmeadow St.
Longmeadow, MA 01106
Phone: (413)567-0621
Dr. Jeanette T. Wright, President
Founded: 1897. **Description:** Independent junior college. **Degree(s) Offered:** AS.

★7024★ **Bennett College**
900 E. Washington St.
Greensboro, NC 27401-3239
Phone: (919)370-8607
Dr. Gloria R. Scott, President
Founded: 1873. **Description:** United Methodist women's college. **Degree(s) Offered:** BA, BS.

★7025★ **Blue Mountain College**
Box 338
Blue Mountain, MS 38610
Phone: (601)685-4771
Dr. E. Harold Fisher, President
Founded: 1873. **Description:** Southern Baptist primarily women's institution. **Degree(s) Offered:** BA, BS, BM, BSEd.

★7026★ **Brenau College**
204 Boulevard
Gainesville, GA 30501
Phone: (404)534-6299
Dr. John S. Burd, President
Founded: 1878. **Description:** Independent college. **Degree(s) Offered:** Academic & Professional.

★7027★ **Bryn Mawr College**
Bryn Mawr, PA 19010
Phone: (215)526-5000
Dr. Mary Patterson McPherson, President
Founded: 1885. **Description:** Independent primarily women's institution. **Degree(s) Offered:** Academic & Professional.

★7028★ **Carlow College**
3333 Fifth Ave.
Pittsburgh, PA 15213-3109
Phone: (412)578-6000
Grace Ann Geibel, R.S.M., President
Founded: 1929. **Description:** Roman Catholic primarily women's college. **Degree(s) Offered:** BA, BS, BSN, MA.

★7029★ **Cedar Crest College**
100 College Dr.
Allentown, PA 18104-6196
Phone: (215)437-4471
Dr. Dorothy Gulbenkian Blaney, President
Founded: 1867. **Description:** United Church of Christ primarily women's college. **Degree(s) Offered:** BA, BS.

★7030★ **Chatham College**
Woodland Rd.
Pittsburgh, PA 15232
Phone: (412)365-1100
Dr. Esther L. Barazzone, President
Founded: 1869. **Description:** Independent four year women's college. **Degree(s) Offered:** BA, BS.

★7031★ **Chestnut Hill College**
9601 Germantown Ave.
Philadelphia, PA 19118
Phone: (215)248-7000
Sr. Matthew Anita MacDonald, President
Founded: 1924. **Description:** Roman Catholic comprehensive primarily women's institution. **Degree(s) Offered:** AA, AS, BA, BS, MA, MS.

★7032★ **College of New Rochelle**
New Rochelle, NY 10801
Phone: (914)632-5300
Sr. Dorothy Ann Kelly, O.S.U., President
Founded: 1904. **Description:** Independent primarily women's college. **Degree(s) Offered:** BA, BS, BSN, BFA, MA, MS.

★7033★ **College of Notre Dame of Maryland**
4701 N. Charles St.
Baltimore, MD 21210
Phone: (301)435-0100
Sr. Kathleen Feeley, President
Founded: 1873. **Description:** Independent Roman Catholic women's institution. **Degree(s) Offered:** BA, BS, MA.

★7034★ **College of Saint Benedict**
St. Joseph, MN 56374
Phone: (612)363-5505
Sr. Colman O'Connell, President
Founded: 1887. **Description:** Independent Roman Catholic women's college. **Degree(s) Offered:** BA, BS.

★7035★ **College of Saint Catherine**
2004 Randolph Ave.
St. Paul, MN 55105
Phone: (612)690-6000
Dr. Anita M. Pampusch, President
Founded: 1905. **Description:** Roman Catholic women's college. **Degree(s) Offered:** BA, MA.

★7036★ College of Saint Elizabeth
Convent Station, NJ 07961
Phone: (201)539-1600
Sr. Jacqueline Burns, President
Founded: 1899. **Description:** Roman Catholic primarily women's college. **Degree(s) Offered:** BA, BS, BSN.

★7037★ College of Saint Mary
1901 S. 72nd St.
Omaha, NE 68124
Phone: (402)399-2438
Dr. Kenneth Nielsen, President
Founded: 1923. **Description:** Roman Catholic women's college. **Degree(s) Offered:** BA, BS, AA, AS.

★7038★ Columbia College
Columbia College Dr.
Columbia, SC 29203
Phone: (803)786-3012
Dr. Peter T. Mitchell, President
Founded: 1854. **Description:** United Methodist comprehensive women's institution. **Degree(s) Offered:** BA, BFA, BMus, MM, MEd.

★7039★ Converse College
580 E. Main St.
Spartansburg, SC 29301
Phone: (803)596-9000
Dr. Ellen Wood Hall, President
Founded: 1889. **Description:** Independent women's institution. **Degree(s) Offered:** Academic & Professional.

★7040★ Cottey College
1000 West Austin
Nevada, MO 64772-1000
Phone: (417)667-8181
Dr. Helen R. Washburn, President
Founded: 1884. **Description:** Independent junior college. **Degree(s) Offered:** AA.

★7041★ Douglass College
Rutgers University
New Brunswick, NJ 08903
Phone: (908)932-9721
Dr. Mary S. Hartman, Dean
Founded: 1918. **Description:** State-supported four-year women's institution. **Degree(s) Offered:** BA, BS.

★7042★ Elms College
291 Springfield St.
Chicopee, MA 01013-2839
Phone: (413)594-2761
Sr. Mary A. Dooley, S.S.J., President
Founded: 1928. **Description:** Roman Catholic women's college. **Degree(s) Offered:** BA, BS, BSN, MA.

★7043★ Emmanuel College
400 The Fenway
Boston, MA 02115
Phone: (617)735-9825
Sr. Janet Eisner, S.N.D., President
Founded: 1919. **Description:** Roman Catholic women's college. **Degree(s) Offered:** AA, BA, BS, BFA, MA.

★7044★ Endicott College
376 Hale St.
Beverly, MA 01915
Phone: (508)927-0585
Mr. Richard E. Wylie, President
Founded: 1939. **Description:** Independent junior college. **Degree(s) Offered:** AA, AS.

★7045★ Fisher Junior College
118 Beacon St.
Boston, MA 02116
Phone: (617)262-3240
Dr. Scott Fisher, President
Founded: 1903. **Description:** Independent junior college. **Degree(s) Offered:** AA, AS.

★7046★ Georgian Court College
900 Lakewood Ave.
Lakewood, NJ 08701-2697
Phone: (201)364-2200
Sr. Barbara Williams, R.S.M., President
Founded: 1908. **Description:** Roman Catholic primarily women's institution. **Degree(s) Offered:** BA, BS, MA.

★7047★ Harcum Junior College
Morris & Montgomery Aves.
Bryn Mawr, PA 19010-3476
Phone: (215)526-6050
Dr. Norma F. Furst, President
Founded: 1915. **Description:** Independent junior college. **Degree(s) Offered:** AA, AS.

★7048★ Hartford College for Women
1265 Asylum Ave.
Hartford, CT 06105
Phone: (203)236-1215
Dr. Jane Barstow, Dean
Founded: 1939. **Description:** Independent women's college. **Degree(s) Offered:** AA.

★7049★ Hollins College
Hollins College, VA 24020
Phone: (703)362-6321
Dr. Jane Margaret O'Brien, President
Founded: 1842. **Description:** Independent women's institution. **Degree(s) Offered:** BA, MA, MALS.

★7050★ Hood College
Rosemont Ave.
Frederick, MD 21701
Phone: (301)663-3131
Dr. Martha E. Church, President
Founded: 1893. **Description:** Independent primarily women's institution. **Degree(s) Offered:** Academic & Professional.

★7051★ Immaculata College
Immaculata, PA 19345-0901
Phone: (215)647-4400
Sr. Marian William, President
Founded: 1920. **Description:** Roman Catholic primarily women's institution. **Degree(s) Offered:** AA, BA, BS, BMus, MA.

★7052★ Judson College
PO Box 120
Marion, AL 36756
Phone: (205)683-6161
Dr. David E. Potts, President
Founded: 1838. **Description:** Independent Southern Baptist four-year women's college. **Degree(s) Offered:** BA, BS.

★7053★ Lasell College
Newton, MA 02166
Phone: (617)243-2221
Dr. Thomas E.J. de Witt, President
Founded: 1851. **Description:** Independent junior college. **Degree(s) Offered:** AA, AS.

★7054★ Lesley College
29 Everett St.
Cambridge, MA 02138-2790
Phone: (617)349-8500
Ms. Margaret A. McKenna, Esq., President
Founded: 1909. **Description:** Independent comprehensive women's college. **Degree(s) Offered:** Academic & Professional.

★7055★ Marian Court Junior College
35 Littles Point Rd.
Swampscott, MA 01907-2896
Phone: (617)595-6768
Sr. Joanne Bibeau, President
Founded: 1964. **Description:** Roman Catholic junior college.

★7056★ Mary Baldwin College
Staunton, VA 24401
Phone: (703)887-7000
Dr. Cynthia H. Tyson, President
Founded: 1842. **Description:** Independent Presbyterian four-year women's college. **Degree(s) Offered:** BA, BS, BFA.

★7057★ Marymount College
Tarrytown, NY 10591
Phone: (914)631-3200
Sr. Brigid Driscoll, RSHM, President
Founded: 1907. **Description:** Independent women's college. **Degree(s) Offered:** BA, BS.

★7058★ Marymount Manhattan College
221 E. 71st St.
New York, NY 10021
Phone: (212)517-0400
Dr. Regina Peruggi, President
Founded: 1936. **Description:** Independent primarily women's college. **Degree(s) Offered:** BA, BLS, BFA.

★7059★ Meredith College
Raleigh, NC 27607-5298
Phone: (919)829-8600
Dr. John E. Weems, President
Founded: 1891. **Description:** Southern Baptist-affiliated women's institution. **Degree(s) Offered:** BA, BS, BMus, MA, MS.

★7060★ Midway College
Midway, KY 40347-9731
Phone: (606)846-5310
Dr. Robert R. Botkin, President

Founded: 1847. **Description:** Disciples of Christ four-year womens institution. **Degree(s) Offered:** AA, BA, BSN.

★7061★ Mills College
5000 MacArthur Blvd.
Oakland, CA 94613
Phone: (415)430-2255
Dr. Janet Holmgren McKay, President

Founded: 1852. **Description:** Independent comprehensive women's institution. **Degree(s) Offered:** Academic & Professional.

★7062★ Mississippi University for Women
PO Box W-1602
Columbus, MS 39701
Phone: (601)329-7100
Dr. Clyda S. Rent, President

Founded: 1884. **Description:** State-supported primarily women's institution. **Degree(s) Offered:** ASN, BA, BS, MSN.

★7063★ Moore College of Art and Design
20th & The Parkway
Philadelphia, PA 19103
Phone: (215)568-4515
Dr. Mary-Linda Merriam, President

Founded: 1844. **Description:** Independent four-year women's college. **Degree(s) Offered:** BFA.

★7064★ Mount Holyoke College
South Hadley, MA 01075-1496
Phone: (413)538-2000
Dr. Elizabeth T. Kennan, President

Founded: 1837. **Description:** Independent four-year women's institution. **Degree(s) Offered:** BA, BS.

★7065★ Mount Mary College
2900 N. Menomonee River Pkwy.
Milwaukee, WI 53222
Phone: (414)258-4810
Sr. Ruth Hollenbach, SSND, President

Founded: 1913. **Description:** Roman Catholic women's college. **Degree(s) Offered:** BA, BS, MA.

★7066★ Mount St. Mary's College
12001 Chalon Rd.
Los Angeles, CA 90049
Phone: (213)476-2237
Sr. Karen M. Kennelly, President

Founded: 1925. **Description:** Independent Roman Catholic comprehensive primarily women's institution. **Degree(s) Offered:** Academic & Professional.

★7067★ Mount Vernon College
2100 Foxhall Rd. NW
Washington, DC 20007
Phone: (202)625-4600
Dr. Lucy Ann Geiselman, President

Founded: 1875. **Description:** Independent four-year college. **Degree(s) Offered:** AA, BA.

★7068★ Newcomb College
Tulane University
New Orleans, LA 70118
Phone: (504)865-5421
Dr. Ann H. Die, Dean

Founded: 1886. **Description:** Independent college. **Degree(s) Offered:** BS, BA, BFA.

★7069★ Notre Dame College of Ohio
4545 College Rd.
Cleveland, OH 44121
Sr. Marla Loehr, S.N.D., President

Founded: 1922. **Description:** Roman Catholic women's college. **Degree(s) Offered:** BA, BS, AA, AS.

★7070★ Peace College
15 E. Peace St.
Raleigh, NC 27604
Phone: (919)832-2881
Dr. Garrett Briggs, President

Founded: 1857. **Description:** Presbyterian junior college. **Degree(s) Offered:** AA, AAMus, ASBus.

★7071★ Pine Manor College
400 Heath St.
Chestnut Hill, MA 02167
Phone: (617)731-7000
Mrs. Rosemary G. Ashby, President

Founded: 1911. **Description:** Independent four-year women's institution. **Degree(s) Offered:** AA, BA.

★7072★ Radcliffe College
10 Garden St.
Cambridge, MA 02138
Phone: (617)495-8601
Dr. Linda S. Wilson, President

Founded: 1879. **Description:** Independent co-educational institution. **Degree(s) Offered:** AB, BS.

★7073★ Randolph-Macon Woman's College
2500 Rivermont Ave.
Lynchburg, VA 24503
Phone: (804)846-7392
Mrs. Linda Koch Lorimer, President

Founded: 1891. **Description:** United Methodist four-year women's college. **Degree(s) Offered:** BA, BS.

★7074★ Regis College
235 Wellesley St.
Weston, MA 02193
Phone: (617)893-1820
Sr. Therese Higgins, C.S.J., President

Founded: 1927. **Description:** Independent Roman Catholic women's college. **Degree(s) Offered:** BA, BS.

★7075★ Rosemont College
Rosemont, PA 19010
Phone: (215)527-0200
Ms. Ofelia Garcia, President

Founded: 1921. **Description:** Roman Catholic four-year women's college. **Degree(s) Offered:** BA, BS, BFA, MEd.

★7076★ Russell Sage College
45 Ferry St.
Troy, NY 12180
Phone: (518)270-2000
Dr. Sara S. Chapman, President

Founded: 1916. **Description:** Independent women's college. **Degree(s) Offered:** Academic & professional.

★7077★ Saint Joseph College
1678 Asylum Ave.
West Hartford, CT 06117
Phone: (203)232-4571
Ms. Winifred E. Coleman, President

Founded: 1932. **Description:** Independent Roman Catholic comprehensive women's institution. **Degree(s) Offered:** Academic & Professional.

★7078★ Saint Mary-of-the-Woods College
St. Mary-of-the-Woods, IN 47876
Phone: (812)535-5151
Sr. Barbara Doherty, S.P., President

Founded: 1840. **Description:** Independent Roman Catholic women's college. **Degree(s) Offered:** AA, BA, BS, BSW, MA.

★7079★ Saint Mary's College
Notre Dame, IN 46556
Phone: (219)284-4000
Dr. William A. Hickey, President

Founded: 1844. **Description:** Independent Roman Catholic four-year women's college. **Degree(s) Offered:** BA, BS, BBA, BFA, BMus.

★7080★ Saint Mary's College
900 Hillsborough
Raleigh, NC 27603-1689
Phone: (919)828-2521
Dr. Clauston Jenkins, President

Founded: 1842. **Description:** Episcopal junior college. **Degree(s) Offered:** AA.

★7081★ Salem College
Winston-Salem, NC 27108
Phone: (919)721-2600
Dr. Julianne Still Thrift, President

Founded: 1772. **Description:** Independent Moravian women's institution. **Degree(s) Offered:** BA, BS, BM, MA.

★7082★ Scripps College
1030 Columbia Ave.
Claremont, CA 91711-3948
Phone: (714)621-8000
Mrs. Nancy Y. Bekavac, President

Founded: 1926. **Description:** Independent four-year women's college. **Degree(s) Offered:** BA.

★7083★ Seton Hill College
Greensburg, PA 15601
Phone: (412)834-2200
Dr. JoAnne W. Boyle, President

Founded: 1883. **Description:** Roman Catholic four-year women's institution. **Degree(s) Offered:** BA, BFA, BMus, BS.

★7084★ Simmons College
300 The Fenway
Boston, MA 02115
Phone: (617)738-2000
Dr. William J. Holmes, President
Founded: 1899. **Description:** Independent women's institution. **Degree(s) Offered:** Academic & Professional.

★7085★ Smith College
College Hall
Northampton, MA 01063
Phone: (413)584-2700
Mary Maples Dunn, President
Founded: 1871. **Description:** Independent women's college. **Degree(s) Offered:** Academic & Professional.

★7086★ Southern Seminary Junior College
Buena Vista, VA 24416
Phone: (703)261-6181
Dr. Joyce O. Davis, President
Founded: 1867. **Description:** Independent junior college.

★7087★ Spelman College
350 Spelman Ln. SW
Atlanta, GA 30314
Phone: (404)681-3643
Dr. Robert K. Ackerman, President
Founded: 1836. **Description:** Independent college. **Degree(s) Offered:** BA, BS.

★7088★ Stephens College
1200 E. Broadway
Columbia, MO 65215-0001
Phone: (314)442-2211
Dr. Patsy H. Sampson, President
Founded: 1833. **Description:** Independent, primarily women's college. **Degree(s) Offered:** BA, BS, BFA.

★7089★ Sweet Briar College
Sweet Briar, VA 24595
Phone: (804)381-6100
Dr. Barbara Ann Hill, President
Founded: 1901. **Description:** Independent four-year women's institution. **Degree(s) Offered:** BA.

★7090★ Texas Woman's University
Box 23925 TWU Station
Denton, TX 76204
Phone: (817)898-3201
Dr. Shirley S. Chater, President
Founded: 1901. **Description:** State-supported primarily women's university. **Degree(s) Offered:** Academic & Professional.

★7091★ Trinity College
125 Michigan Ave., NE
Washington, DC 20017-1094
Phone: (202)939-5000
Ms. Patricia A. McGuire, President
Founded: 1897. **Description:** Roman Catholic four-year college. **Degree(s) Offered:** Academic & Professional.

★7092★ Trinity College of Vermont
208 Colchester Ave.
Burlington, VT 05401
Phone: (802)658-0337
Sr. Janice E. Ryan, President
Founded: 1925. **Description:** Roman Catholic primarily women's institution. **Degree(s) Offered:** AA, AS, BA, BS.

★7093★ Ursuline College
2550 Lander Rd.
Pepper Pike, OH 44124
Phone: (216)449-4200
Dr. Anne Marie Diederich, O.S.U., President
Founded: 1871. **Description:** Roman Catholic primarily women's institution. **Degree(s) Offered:** AA, AS, BA, BSN, MA.

★7094★ Wellesley College
Wellesley, MA 02181-8201
Phone: (617)235-0320
Dr. Nannerl O. Keohane, President
Founded: 1870. **Description:** Independent women's institution.

★7095★ Wells College
Aurora, NY 13026-0500
Phone: (315)364-3370
Dr. Robert A. Plane, President
Founded: 1868. **Description:** Independent women's institution. **Degree(s) Offered:** BA.

★7096★ Wesleyan College
4760 Forsyth Rd.
Macon, GA 31297-4299
Phone: (912)477-1110
Dr. Robert K. Ackerman, President
Founded: 1836. **Description:** Independent United Methodist four-year women's college. **Degree(s) Offered:** BA, BS, BFA, BMus, MedTech.

★7097★ Westhampton College
University of Richmond
Richmond, VA 23173-1903
Phone: (804)289-8468
Dr. Patricia C. Harwood, Dean
Founded: 1830. **Description:** Southern Baptist four-year college.

★7098★ William Smith College
Smith Hall
Geneva, NY 14456
Phone: (315)789-5500
Ms. Rebecca MacMillan Fox, Dean
Founded: 1908. **Description:** Independent women's college. **Degree(s) Offered:** BA, BS.

★7099★ William Woods College
200 W. 12th St.
Fulton, MO 65251
Phone: (314)642-2251
Dr. Jahnae H. Barnett, President
Founded: 1870. **Description:** Disciples of Christ four-year women's institution. **Degree(s) Offered:** BA, BFA.

★7100★ Wilson College
1015 Philadelphia Ave.
Chambersburg, PA 17201-1285
Phone: (717)264-4141
Dr. Gwendolyn E. Jensen, President
Founded: 1869. **Description:** Presbyterian four-year primarily women's college. **Degree(s) Offered:** AA, BA, BS.

★7101★ Wood School
8 E. 40th St.
New York, NY 10016
Phone: (212)686-9040
Mrs. Rosemary H. Duggan, President
Founded: 1879. **Description:** Junior college.

(10) Women's Studies Programs

Entries in this chapter are arranged alphabetically by state and city, then by institution name within city. See the User's Guide at the front of this directory for additional information.

Alabama

Auburn

★7102★ Auburn University
Women's Studies Program
Department of Foreign Language
8030 Haley Center
Auburn, AL 36849
Phone: (205)844-6373
Louise Katainen, Contact

Undergraduate: Minor in Women's Studies.

Birmingham

★7103★ University of Alabama at Birmingham
Women's Studies Program
Humanities Bldg., Rm. 204
Birmingham, AL 35294
Phone: (205)934-8599
Fax: (205)934-9896
Dr. Sherry Sullivan, Contact

Undergraduate: Minor.

Tuscaloosa

★7104★ University of Alabama
Women's Studies Program
109 Manly Hall
Box 870272
Tuscaloosa, AL 35487-0272
Phone: (205)348-5782
Fax: (205)348-9642
Dr. Alice Parker, Contact

Undergraduate: Minor, Area of Concentration.
Graduate: Major, Minor, Area of Concentration.
Degree(s) Offered: BA, MA.

Alaska

Anchorage

★7105★ University of Alaska
Center for Women and Men
3211 Providence Dr., K-106
Anchorage, AK 99508
Phone: (907)786-1066
Fax: (907)786-1563
Sherry Lander, Contact

Undergraduate: Minor

Arizona

Douglas

★7106★ Cochise College
Women's Studies Program
Douglas, AZ 85607
Phone: (602)364-0336

Degree(s) Offered: AA in Women's Studies.

Flagstaff

★7107★ Northern Arizona University
Women's Studies Program
Box 5695
Flagstaff, AZ 86011-5695
Phone: (602)523-3300
Joseph Boles, Contact

Undergraduate: Minor, Area of Concentration.

Tempe

★7108★ Arizona State University
Women's Studies Program
Tempe, AZ 85287-1801
Phone: (602)965-2358
Fax: (602)965-1093
Nancy Felipe Russo, Contact

Undergraduate: Major, Certificate. **Graduate:** MA and PHD Concentration. **Degree(s) Offered:** BA, BS.

Tucson

★7109★ University of Arizona
Women's Studies Program
Douglass 102
Tucson, AZ 85721
Phone: (602)621-7338
Fax: (602)621-9424
Karen Anderson, Contact

Undergraduate: Major. **Graduate:** Minor in English/History, specialization in Sociology. **Degree(s) Offered:** BA.

Arkansas

Little Rock

★7110★ University of Arkansas at Little Rock
Women's Studies Program
2801 S. University
Little Rock, AR 72204
Phone: (501)569-3234
Fax: (501)569-8775
John S. Miller, Contact

Undergraduate: Minor.

California

Aptos

★7111★ Cabrillo College
Women's Center/Studies
6500 Soquel Dr.
Aptos, CA 95003
Phone: (408)479-6249
Rosemary Brogan, Contact

Undergraduate: Major. **Degree(s) Offered:** AA in Women's Studies.

Arcata

★7112★ Humboldt State University
Women's Studies Program
House 55
Arcata, CA 95521
Phone: (707)826-4925
Karen Foss, Contact

Undergraduate: Minor, Certificate. **Specialization:** Student can write a special Major in which Women's Studies is one of three areas.

Bakersfield

★7113★ Bakersfield Community College
Women's Studies Program
1801 Panorama Dr.
Bakersfield, CA 93305
Phone: (805)395-4011
Phyllis Hullett, Contact

★7114★ California State University, Bakersfield
Women's Studies Program
9001 Stockdale Highway
Bakersfield, CA 93311
Phone: (805)664-2011
Fax: (805)664-3194
Anita DuPratt, Contact

Berkeley

★7115★ Graduate Theological Union Center for Women and Religion
Women's Studies Program
2400 Ridge Rd.
Berkeley, CA 94769
Phone: (416)649-2490
Mary Cross, Contact

Degree(s) Offered: MA, PhD in Theology.

★7116★ University of California, Berkeley
Women's Studies Department
301 Campbell Hall
Berkeley, CA 94720
Phone: (510)642-2767
Fax: (510)642-4607

Undergraduate: Major, Minor. **Graduate:** Area of concentration. **Degree(s) Offered:** BA.

★7117★ Vista Community College
Women's Studies Program
2020 Milvia St.
Berkeley, CA 94704
Phone: (510)841-8431
Fax: (415)841-7333
Jenny Lowood, Contact

Carson

★7118★ California State University, Dominguez Hills
Women's Studies Program
1000 E. Victoria St.
Carson, CA 90747
Phone: (213)516-3759
Linda Pomerantz, Contact

Undergraduate: Minor.

Chico

★7119★ California State University, Chico
Center for Ethnic Women's Studies
Chico, CA 95929
Phone: (916)345-8118
Gayle Kimball, Contact

Undergraduate: Minor. **Graduate:** Minor.

Claremont

★7120★ Claremont Colleges Consortium
Office of Women's Studies of the Claremont Colleges
c/o Claremont Graduate School
Benezet 229
Claremont, CA 91711
Phone: (714)621-8274
J'nan Morse Sellery, Coordinator

Remarks: All six campuses offer Women's Studies Courses. Program is administratively headquartered at Claremont Graduate School. Coordinating Committee has a member from each college: Harvey Mudd, Pomona, Pitzer, Scripps, Claremont McKenna, and Claremont Graduate School.

★7121★ Harvey Mudd College
Women's Studies Program
Kingston Hall
301 E. 12th St.
Claremont, CA 91711
Phone: (714)621-8000
Fax: (714)621-8360
J'nan Morse Sellery, Contact

★7122★ Pitzer College
Women's Studies Program
1050 N. Mills Ave.
Claremont, CA 91711
Phone: (714)621-8000
Ann Stromberg, Contact

Undergraduate: Major. **Degree(s) Offered:** BA.

★7123★ Pomona College
Women's Studies Program
550 Harvard Ave.
Claremont, CA 91711
Phone: (714)621-8000
Deborah Burke, Contact

Undergraduate: Major. **Degree(s) Offered:** BA.

★7124★ Scripps College
Women's Studies Program
1030 Columbia Ave.
Claremont, CA 91711-3948
Phone: (714)621-8000
Sue Mansfield, Contact

Undergraduate: Major, Minor, Area of Concentration. **Graduate:** Major, Minor, Area of Concentration,.

Cupertino

★7125★ DeAnza College
Women's Studies Program
21250 Stevens Creek Blvd.
Cupertino, CA 95014
Phone: (408)864-8554
Julie Nash, Contact

Specialization: Courses taken here may lead to a degree at San Jose University.

Davis

★7126★ University of California, Davis
Women's Studies Program
307 Young Hall
Davis, CA 95616
Phone: (916)752-4686
Linda Morris, Director

Degree(s) Offered: BA in Women's Studies; undergraduate major, minor in Women's Studies; graduate designated emphasis in PhD program through Anthropology, Comparative Literature, Italian, Spanish, French, English, History, and Sociology Departments.

El Cajon

★7127★ Christian Heritage College
El Cajon, CA 92019
Phone: (619)588-7747
Description: Women's studies major.

Fremont

★7128★ Ohlone College
Women's Studies Program
43600 Mission Blvd.
PO Box 3909
Fremont, CA 94539-0390
Phone: (510)659-6011
E.J. Foster-Hillard, Contact

Fresno

★7129★ California State University, Fresno
Women's Studies Program
Fresno, CA 93740-0078
Phone: (209)278-2858
Dr. Lillian Faderman, Contact

Undergraduate: Minor.

★7130★ Fresno City College
Women's Studies Program
1101 E. University Ave.
Fresno, CA 93741
Phone: (209)442-8210
James Walsh, Contact

Degree(s) Offered: AA in Women's Studies.

Fullerton

★7131★ California State University, Fullerton
Women's Studies Program
MH-103
Fullerton, CA 92634
Phone: (714)773-2594
Fax: (714)773-3314
Diane Ross, Contact

Undergraduate: Minor.

★7132★ Fullerton College
Women's Studies Committee
321 E. Chapman Ave.
Fullerton, CA 92634-9480
Phone: (714)773-2011

Hayward

★7133★ California State University, Hayward
Women's Studies Program
Hayward, CA 94542
Phone: (510)881-3221
Fax: (510)727-2276
Emily Stoper, Contact; Elsa Garcia

Undergraduate: Minor.

Irvine

★7134★ University of California, Irvine
Women's Studies Program
403 Social Science Tower
Irvine, CA 92717
Phone: (714)856-4234
Fax: (714)856-8441
Leslie Rabine, Contact

Undergraduate: Major, Minor. **Degree(s) Offered:** BA.

Kentfield

★7135★ College of Marin
Women's Program
Student Services Bldg., Rm. 201
Kentfield, CA 94904
Phone: (415)485-9641

La Jolla

★7136★ University of California, San Diego
Women's Studies Program
c/o John Muir College-0006
La Jolla, CA 92093
Phone: (619)534-7127
Stephanie Jed, Contact

Undergraduate: Minor, Area of Concentration; interdisciplinary major. **Degree(s) Offered:** BA in Women's Studies.

Long Beach

★7137★ California State University, Long Beach
Women's Studies Program
FO2-226
Long Beach, CA 90840
Phone: (213)985-4839
Sharon L. Sievers, Contact

Undergraduate: Major, Minor. **Graduate:** Minor, Concentration in American Studies. **Degree(s) Offered:** BA as special Major, BA in American Studies with Concentration in Women's Studies; MA as special Major.

Los Altos

★7138★ Foothill College
Women's Studies Program
12345 Elmonte St.
Los Altos, CA 94022
Phone: (415)949-7322

Los Angeles

★7139★ California State University, Los Angeles
Women's Studies Program
5151 State University Dr.
Los Angeles, CA 90032
Phone: (213)343-3000
Sharon Bassett, Contact

Undergraduate: Minor.

★7140★ Loyola Marymount University
Women's Studies Program
Loyola Boulevard at W. 80th St.
Los Angeles, CA 90045
Phone: (213)338-2757
Fax: (213)338-2706
Joanne Fisher, Contact

Undergraduate: Minor.

★7141★ Mount St. Mary's College
Women's Leadership Program
12001 Chalon Rd.
Los Angeles, CA 90049
Phone: (213)476-2237
Fax: (213)476-9296
Cheryl Mabey, Contact

Undergraduate: Minor.

★7142★ Occidental College
Women's Studies Program
1600 Campus Rd.
Los Angeles, CA 90041
Phone: (213)259-2787
Karen L. King, Contact

Undergraduate: Minor, Area of Concentration.
Specialization: Independent Pattern of Study.

★7143★ University of California, Los Angeles
Women's Studies Program
240 Kinsey Hall
405 Hilgard Ave.
Los Angeles, CA 90024-1453
Phone: (213)206-8101
Karen Brodkin Sacks, Contact

Undergraduate: Major, Specialization (Area of concentration), Certificate. **Degree(s) Offered:** BA.

★7144★ University of Southern California
Study of Women/Men in Society
Social Science B-15
Los Angeles, CA 90089-0036
Phone: (213)743-8286
Lois Banner, Contact

Undergraduate: Minor. **Graduate:** Certificate.
Degree(s) Offered: BA. **Specialization:** Individualized Major.

Marysville

★7145★ Yuba Community College
Women's Studies Program
Fine Arts and Social Science Division
2088 N. Beale Rd.
Marysville, CA 95901
Phone: (916)741-6829
Cal Gower, Contact

Undergraduate: Area of concentration in Women's Studies. **Degree(s) Offered:** AA in Women's Studies.

Mission Viejo

★7146★ Saddleback College
Women's Studies Program
28000 Marguerite Pkwy.
Mission Viejo, CA 92692
Phone: (714)582-4388
Anne Clasby, Contact

Degree(s) Offered: AA.

Monterey

★7147★ Monterey Peninsula College
Women's Studies Program
980 Fremont St.
Monterey, CA 93940
Phone: (408)646-4160
Phyllis Peet, Contact

Undergraduate: Major.

Moorpark

★7148★ Moorpark College
Women's Studies Program
7075 Campus Rd.
Moorpark, CA 93021
Phone: (805)378-1452
Carole Ginet, Contact

Northridge

★7149★ California State University, Northridge
Women's Studies Program
18111 Nordhoff St.
Northridge, CA 91330
Phone: (818)885-3110
Dr. Sondra Hale, Contact

Undergraduate: Major, Minor, Area of Concentration, Certificate. **Degree(s) Offered:** BA.

Oakland

★7150★ Laney College
Women's Studies Program
Oakland, CA 94606-4170
Phone: (510)834-5740

★7151★ Mills College
Women's Studies Program
Oakland, CA 94613
Phone: (510)430-2233
Carol George, Contact

Undergraduate: Major, Minor, Area of Concentration. **Degree(s) Offered:** BA.

Pleasant Hill

★7152★ Diablo Valley College
Women's Studies Program
321 Golf Club Rd.
Pleasant Hill, CA 94523
Phone: (510)685-1230
Diane Scott-Summers, Contact

Undergraduate: Area of Concentration, Certificate. **Degree(s) Offered:** AA in Women's Studies.

Pomona

★7153★ California State Polytechnic University, Pomona
Ethnic and Women's Studies Program
3801 W. Temple Ave.
Pomona, CA 91768
Phone: (714)869-3593
Patricia Lin, Contact

Undergraduate: Minor.

Redlands

★7154★ University of Redlands
Women's Studies Program
PO Box 3080
Redlands, CA 92373-0999
Phone: (714)793-2121
Fax: (714)793-2029
Dr. Emily Culpepper, Contact

Undergraduate: Individualized Major, Minor.
Degree(s) Offered: BA.

Redwood City

★7155★ Canada College
Women's Programs
4200 Farm Hill Blvd.
Redwood City, CA 94061
Phone: (415)364-1212

Riverside

**★7156★ University of California, Riverside
Women's Studies Program**
990 University Ave.
Riverside, CA 92521
Phone: (714)787-6427
Carole Shammus, Chair

Undergraduate: Major, minor. **Graduate:** Emphasis in gender studies through Sociology and English Departments; departmental emphasis in History. **Degree(s) Offered:** BA in Women's Studies.

Rocklin

**★7157★ Sierra College
Women's Studies Program**
5000 Rocklin Road
Rocklin, CA 95677
Phone: (916)624-3333
Mary Moon, Contact

Degree(s) Offered: AA through Liberal Studies.

Rohnert Park

**★7158★ Sonoma State University
Women's Studies Program**
1801 E. Cotati Ave.
Rohnert Park, CA 94928
Phone: (707)664-2840
Ellen Kay Trimberger, Contact

Undergraduate: Minor. **Specialization:** Interdisciplinary Independent Major with an emphasis on women.

Sacramento

**★7159★ California State University, Sacramento
Women's Studies Program**
6000 J Street
Sacramento, CA 95819
Phone: (916)278-6817
Filomina Steady, Contact

Undergraduate: Major, Minor. **Graduate:** Minor. **Degree(s) Offered:** BA, Specialized MA.

**★7160★ Cosumnes River College
Women's Studies Program**
8401 Center Pkwy.
Sacramento, CA 95823
Phone: (916)688-7354
A. Christine Harris, Contact

Undergraduate: Major, Minor, Area of Concentration, Certificate. **Degree(s) Offered:** AA in Women's Studies. **Specialization:** Interdisciplinary Studies; Women's Studies Option.

**★7161★ Sacramento City College
Women's Studies**
Social Science Division
3835 Freeport Blvd.
Sacramento, CA 95822
Phone: (916)558-2431
Suzanne Nissen, Contact

Undergraduate: Major. **Degree(s) Offered:** AA in Women's Studies.

Salinas

**★7162★ Hartnell College
Women's Programs**
156 Homestead Ave.
Salinas, CA 93901
Phone: (408)755-6700
Allison Paul, Contact

San Bernardino

**★7163★ California State University, San Bernardino
Women's Studies Program**
c/o Department of Anthropology
5500 University Parkway
San Bernardino, CA 92407
Phone: (714)880-5503
Ellen Gruenbaum, Contact

Undergraduate: Minor, Area of Concentration, Certificate. **Graduate:** Minor, Certificate.

San Diego

**★7164★ Beacon College
Women's Studies Program**
814 Morena Blvd., Ste. 103
San Diego, CA 92102
Phone: (619)233-8984

**★7165★ San Diego State University
Women's Studies Department**
San Diego, CA 92182-0437
Phone: (619)594-6524
Bonnie Zimmerman, Contact

Undergraduate: Major, Minor. **Graduate:** MA. **Degree(s) Offered:** BA; MA in Liberal Arts; MA in Special Major.

**★7166★ University of San Diego
Women's Studies Program**
Alcala Park
San Diego, CA 92110
Phone: (619)260-4506
Fax: (619)260-6836
Dr. Linda Perry, Contact

San Francisco

**★7167★ City College of San Francisco
Women's Studies Program**
50 Phelan Ave.
Box L206
San Francisco, CA 94112
Phone: (415)239-3442
Fax: (415)239-3919
Susan Evans, Contact

Degree(s) Offered: AA in General Education; AA in Women's Studies.

**★7168★ New College
Feminist Psychology Program**
777 Valencia St.
San Francisco, CA 94110
Phone: (415)861-4168
Fax: (415)864-2560
Betsy Kassoff, Contact

Graduate: Area of Concentration. **Degree(s) Offered:** MA in Psychology, MA in Feminist Psychology.

**★7169★ San Francisco State University
Women's Studies Program**
1600 Holloway Ave.
San Francisco, CA 94132
Phone: (415)338-1388
Dr. Chinosole, Contact

Undergraduate: Minor in Women's Studies. **Graduate:** Individualized major in Women's Studies. **Degree(s) Offered:** BA in Women's Studies; MA.

San Jose

**★7170★ San Jose State University
Women's Studies Program**
1 Washington Sq.
San Jose, CA 95192-0121
Phone: (408)924-5590
Lois Rita Helmbold, Contact

Undergraduate: Major, Minor, Area of Concentration. **Graduate:** Minor, Area of Concentration. **Degree(s) Offered:** BA; MA; official degree is in Social Sciences with a focus on Women's Studies.

San Luis Obispo

**★7171★ California Polytechnic State University, San Luis Obispo
Women's Studies Program**
San Luis Obispo, CA 93407
Phone: (805)756-2706
John Ericson, Contact

Undergraduate: Minor.

**★7172★ Cuesta Community College
Women's Studies Program**
Box 8106
San Luis Obispo, CA 93403-8106
Phone: (805)546-3100

San Pablo

**★7173★ Contra Costa College
Women's Studies Programs**
2600 Mission Bell Dr.
San Pablo, CA 94806
Phone: (510)235-7800

Santa Ana

**★7174★ Rancho Santiago Community College
Women's Studies Program**
17th at Bristol St.
Santa Ana, CA 92706
Phone: (714)564-6500
Sharon Wayland, Contact

Degree(s) Offered: AA in Women's Studies.

Santa Barbara

**★7175★ Santa Barbara City College
Women's Studies Program**
721 Cliff Dr.
Santa Barbara, CA 93109
Phone: (805)963-4091
Alison Venliner, Contact

★7176★ **University of California, Santa Barbara**
Women's Studies Program
Sonth Hall, Rm. 3709
Santa Barbara, CA 93106
Phone: (805)893-4330
Patricia Cohen, Contact
Undergraduate: Major. **Degree(s) Offered:** BA.

Santa Clara

★7177★ **Santa Clara University**
Women's Studies Program
11 O'Connor Hall, Rm. 329
Santa Clara, CA 95053
Phone: (408)554-4461
Alma N. Garcia, Contact
Degree(s) Offered: Minor in Women's Studies.

Santa Cruz

★7178★ **University of California, Santa Cruz**
Women's Studies Program
186 Kresge College
Santa Cruz, CA 95064
Phone: (408)459-4324
Gloria Hull, Contact
Undergraduate: Major. **Degree(s) Offered:** BA; PhD through History of Consciousness.

Saratoga

★7179★ **West Valley College**
Women's Studies Program
14000 Fruitvale Ave.
Saratoga, CA 95070
Phone: (408)867-2200
Julia Maia, Contact
Degree(s) Offered: AA in Women's Studies.

Stanford

★7180★ **Stanford University**
Program in Feminist Studies
Stanford, CA 94305-8640
Phone: (415)723-2412
Jeane Collier, Contact
Undergraduate: Major, Minor. **Specialization:** Honors Certification in Feminist Studies.

Stockton

★7181★ **San Joaquin Delta College**
Women's Program
5151 Pacific Ave.
Stockton, CA 95207
Phone: (209)474-5151
Naomi Fitch, Contact

Thousand Oaks

★7182★ **California Lutheran University**
Women's Studies Task Force
60 W. Olsen Rd.
Thousand Oaks, CA 91360-2787
Phone: (805)493-3345
Kathryn Swanson, Contact
Undergraduate: Minor. **Degree(s) Offered:** BA. **Specialization:** Interdisciplinary Major.

Turlock

★7183★ **California State University, Stanislaus**
Ethnic and Women's Studies Department
801 Monte Vista Ave.
Turlock, CA 95380
Phone: (209)667-3347
J.J. Hendricks, Contact
Undergraduate: Minor, Area of Concentration.

Ventura

★7184★ **Ventura College**
Women's Studies Program
History Department
4667 Telegraph Rd.
Ventura, CA 93003
Phone: (805)654-6400
Margaret O'Neil, Contact

Weed

★7185★ **College of the Siskiyous**
Women's Studies Program
800 College Ave.
Weed, CA 96094
Phone: (916)938-4461

Woodland Hill

★7186★ **International College**
Women's Studies Program
4409 Willens Ave.
Woodland Hill, CA 91364
Phone: (818)786-9637

Colorado

Boulder

★7187★ **University of Colorado, Boulder**
Women's Studies Program
Campus Box 246
Boulder, CO 80309
Phone: (303)492-8923
Marcia Westkott, Contact
Undergraduate: Major, Certificate. **Degree(s) Offered:** BA.

Colorado Springs

★7188★ **Colorado College**
Women's Studies Program
Economics Department
14E Cache La Poudre, Rm. 132
Colorado Springs, CO 80903
Phone: (719)389-6412
Ester Redmount, Contact
Undergraduate: Minor.

★7189★ **University of Colorado, Colorado Springs**
Women's Studies Program
Austin Bluffs Pkwy.
PO Box 7150
Colorado Springs, CO 80933
Phone: (719)593-3538
Michelle Baldwin, Contact
Undergraduate: Major-Distributed Studies.

Denver

★7190★ **Metropolitan State College of Denver**
Women's Studies Program
PO Box 173362
Denver, CO 80217-3362
Phone: (303)556-8441
Fax: (303)556-4941
Jodi Wetzel, Contact
Undergraduate: Major by contract. **Degree(s) Offered:** BA, BS.

★7191★ **University of Denver**
Women's Studies Program
2130 S. Race, Rm. 119
Denver, CO 80208
Phone: (303)871-2406
M.E. Warlick, Contact
Undergraduate: Major, Minor. **Degree(s) Offered:** BA.

Englewood

★7192★ **Denver Seminary**
Women's Studies Program
3401 S. University Blvd.
Englewood, CO 80110
Phone: (303)761-2482
Fax: (303)761-8060
Alice Matthews, Contact
Graduate: Area of Concentration.

Ft. Collins

★7193★ **Colorado State University**
Women's Programs & Studies
112 Student Services Bldg.
Ft. Collins, CO 80523
Phone: (303)491-6384
Karen J. Wedge, Contact
Undergraduate: Certificate. **Graduate:** Certificate.

Greeley

★7194★ **University of Northern Colorado**
Women's Studies Program
Greeley, CO 80639-2983
Phone: (303)351-2607
Fax: (303)351-1837
Marcia Willcoxon, Contact
Undergraduate: Major, Minor. **Graduate:** Minor. **Degree(s) Offered:** BA. **Specialization:** MA, EdD-Interdisciplinary Studies Program, Women's Studies emphasis; Graduate Interdisciplinary Degree Program, Women's Studies emphasis.

Pueblo

★7195★ **University of Southern Colorado**
Women's Studies Program
Pueblo, CO 81001
Phone: (719)549-2729
B.A. Bassien, Contact
Undergraduate: Area of Concentration.

Connecticut

Danbury

**★7196★ Western Connecticut State
University**
Women's Studies Program
181 White St.
Danbury, CT 06810
Phone: (203)797-4094
Jerry Bannister, Contact

Undergraduate: Minor. **Specialization:** Interdisciplinary Minor.

Hamden

★7197★ Quinnipiac College
Women's Studies Program
Box 119
Hamden, CT 06518
Phone: (203)281-8703
Michele Hoffnung, Contact

Undergraduate: Minor, Independent Major. **Degree(s) Offered:** BA.

Hartford

★7198★ Trinity College
Women's Studies Program
Hartford, CT 06106
Phone: (203)297-2131
Joan D. Hedrick, Contact

Undergraduate: Major (Individually designed), Minor. **Degree(s) Offered:** BA.

Middletown

★7199★ Wesleyan University
Women's Studies Program
287 High St.
Middletown, CT 06459
Phone: (203)347-9411
Gertrude Hughes, Contact

Undergraduate: Major, Minor, Area of Concentration. **Graduate:** Area of Concentration. **Degree(s) Offered:** BA, MA.

New Britain

**★7200★ Central Connecticut State
University**
Women's Studies Program
1615 Stanley St.
New Britain, CT 06050
Phone: (203)827-7000
June Higgins, Contact

Undergraduate: Area of Concentration.

New Haven

**★7201★ Southern Connecticut State
University**
Women's Studies Committee
501 Crescent St.
New Haven, CT 06515
Phone: (203)397-4204
Katherine McCarthy, Contact

★7202★ Yale University
Women's Studies Program
Yale Station
80 Wall St.
PO Box 5046
New Haven, CT 06520
Phone: (203)432-0845
Emily Honig, Contact

Undergraduate: Major, Area of Concentration.
Degree(s) Offered: BA.

New London

★7203★ Connecticut College
Women's Studies Program
PO Box 5542
New London, CT 06320-4196
Phone: (203)447-1911
Jane W. Torrey, Contact

Undergraduate: Major, Minor. **Specialization:** Student Designed Interdisciplinary Major.

Storrs

★7204★ University of Connecticut
Women's Studies Program
417 Whitney Rd.
Storrs, CT 06269-1181
Phone: (203)486-3970
Fax: (203)486-4789
Lucy Creevey, Contact

Undergraduate: Major, Minor. **Degree(s) Offered:** BA.

West Hartford

★7205★ St. Joseph College
Interdisciplinary Studies
Women's Studies Program
1678 Asylum Ave.
West Hartford, CT 06117
Phone: (203)232-4571
Barbara E. Lacey, Contact

Undergraduate: Minor.

★7206★ University of Hartford
Women's Studies Program
200 Bloomfield Ave.
West Hartford, CT 06117
Phone: (203)243-4528
Fax: (203)286-5043
Marsha Moen, Contact

Undergraduate: Minor.

Willimantic

**★7207★ Eastern Connecticut State
University**
Women's Studies Program
Knight House
Willimantic, CT 06226
Phone: (203)456-5535
Fax: (203)456-5571
Marcia Phillips McGowan, Contact

Undergraduate: Minor.

Delaware

Dover

★7208★ Delaware State College
Women's Studies Program
Dover, DE 19901
Phone: (302)739-4000
Ann Jenkins, Contact

Newark

★7209★ University of Delaware
Women's Studies Program
333 Smith Hall
Newark, DE 19716
Phone: (302)831-8474
Sandra Harding, Contact

Undergraduate: Major, Minor. **Degree(s) Offered:** BA.

District of Columbia

Washington

★7210★ The American University
Women's Studies Program
4400 Massachusetts Ave. NW
Washington, DC 20016
Phone: (202)885-2485
Fax: (202)885-2013
Muriel Cantor, Contact

Undergraduate: Minor, Area of Concentration. **Graduate:** Area of Concentration. **Specialization:** Minor within discipline; Area of Concentration within discipline.

★7211★ George Washington University
Women's Studies Program
2201 G St. NW, 217 Funger Hall
Washington, DC 20052
Phone: (202)994-6942
Sonya Quitslund, Contact

Undergraduate: Minor. **Graduate:** MA, Concentration. **Degree(s) Offered:** MA in women's studies.

★7212★ Georgetown University
Women's Studies Program
Department of English
Washington, DC 20057
Phone: (202)687-7558
Leona M. Fisher, Contact

Undergraduate: Minor. **Degree(s) Offered:** Interdisciplinary BA.

★7213★ Howard University
Women's Studies Program
2400 Sixth St. NW
Washington, DC 20059
Phone: (202)686-6634

★7214★ Trinity College
Women's Studies Program
125 Michigan Ave. NE
Washington, DC 20017-5074
Phone: (292)939-5000
Fax: (202)885-2494
Roxanne Moayedi, Contact

Undergraduate: Minor, Area of Concentration.

Florida

Boca Raton

★7215★ Florida Atlantic University
Women's Studies Center
Humanities Bldg. 243E
Boca Raton, FL 33431
Phone: (407)367-3865
Helen Bannan, Contact
Undergraduate: Certificate.

Ft. Lauderdale

★7216★ Nova University
Women's Studies Program
3301 College Ave.
Ft. Lauderdale, FL 33314
Phone: (305)475-7343
Kathleen Waites Lamm, Contact
Undergraduate: Area of Concentration, Certificate.

Ft. Pierce

★7217★ Indian River Community College
Women's Program
3209 Virginia Ave.
Ft. Pierce, FL 34981-5599
Phone: (407)468-4700
Fax: (407)468-4720
Patti Williams, Contact

Gainesville

★7218★ University of Florida
Women's Studies Program
8 Anderson Hall
Gainesville, FL 32611
Phone: (904)392-3365
Helga Kraft, Contact
Undergraduate: Certificate.

Jacksonville

★7219★ University of North Florida
Women's Studies Program
College of Arts and Sciences
4567 St. John's Bluff Rd.
Jacksonville, FL 32216
Phone: (904)646-2666
Shirley Webb, Contact
Undergraduate: Minor.

Miami

★7220★ Florida International University
Women's Studies Center
University Park
Miami, FL 33199
Phone: (305)348-2408
Marilyn Hoder-Salmon, Contact
Undergraduate: Area of Concentration, Certificate.

Miami Shores

★7221★ Barry University
Women's Studies Program
Psychology Dept.
11300 NE 2nd Ave.
Miami Shores, FL 33161
Phone: (305)899-3419
Lillian Schanfield, Contact
Undergraduate: Minor, Certificate.

Pensacola

★7222★ University of West Florida
Women's Studies Program
Department of Sociology
11000 University Pkwy.
Pensacola, FL 32514
Phone: (904)474-2797
Mary F. Rogers, Contact
Undergraduate: Minor.

St. Petersburg

★7223★ Eckerd College
Women's Studies Program
4200 54th Ave. S.
St. Petersburg, FL 33771
Phone: (813)867-1166
Carolyn Johnston, Contact
Undergraduate: Major. **Degree(s) Offered:** BA.

Tallahassee

★7224★ Florida State University
Women's Studies Program
R-126A
Tallahassee, FL 32306
Phone: (904)644-9514
Jean G. Bryant, Contact
Undergraduate: Minor. **Graduate:** Concentration, Minor.

★7225★ Tallahassee Community College
Women's Studies Program
444 Appleyard Dr.
Tallahassee, FL 32304
Phone: (904)488-9200

Tampa

★7226★ University of South Florida
Women's Studies Program
4202 E. Fowler Ave., HMS 413
Tampa, FL 33620
Phone: (813)974-3496
Fax: (813)974-2668
Janice B. Snook, Contact
Undergraduate: Major, Minor. **Graduate:** Courses. **Degree(s) Offered:** BA.

★7227★ University of Tampa
Women's Studies Program
Social Science Department
401 W. Kennedy Department
Tampa, FL 33606
Phone: (813)253-3333
Richard Piper, Contact
Undergraduate: Minor.

Winter Park

★7228★ Rollins College
Women's Studies Program
Box 2604
Winter Park, FL 32789
Phone: (407)646-2666
Rosemary Curb, Contact
Undergraduate: Minor, Area of Concentration.

Georgia

Athens

★7229★ University of Georgia, Athens
Women's Studies Program
230-F Main Library
Athens, GA 30602
Phone: (404)542-2846
Patricia Del Rey, Contact
Undergraduate: Certificate. **Specialization:** Graduate Specialization, College of Home Economics, Child and Family Development; Department graduate minor in Women's Studies.

Atlanta

★7230★ Clark Atlanta University
African Women's Studies Program
223 Chestnut St. SW
Atlanta, GA 30314
Phone: (404)880-8733
Alma Vinyard, Contact
Undergraduate: Major, Minor.

★7231★ Emory University
Women's Studies Program
210 Physics Bldg.
Atlanta, GA 30322
Phone: (404)727-0096
Fax: (404)727-0251
Martine Brownley, Contact
Undergraduate: Major, Minor, Area of Concentration. **Degree(s) Offered:** BA, BS, MA, PhD through the Institute for Liberal Arts, PhD certificate.

★7232★ Georgia State University
Women's Studies Program
Department of Political Science
University Plaza
Atlanta, GA 30303
Phone: (404)651-3152
Diane L. Fowlkes, Contact
Undergraduate: Minor (as interdisciplinary minor), Area of Concentration (in Bachelor of Interdisciplinary Studies). **Graduate:** Minor (Cognate for PhD in Education, as field in political science by petition). **Degree(s) Offered:** BS in Women's Studies.

★7233★ Spelman College
Women's Research and Resource Center
350 Spelman Ln. SW
Box 115
Atlanta, GA 30311
Phone: (404)681-3643
Fax: (404)753-8383
Beverly Guy-Sheftall, Contact
Undergraduate: Minor.

Decatur

★7234★ Agnes Scott College
Women's Studies Program
College Ave.
Decatur, GA 30030
Phone: (404)371-6221
Christine Cozzens, Contact
Undergraduate: Minor.

Gainsville

★7235★ Brenau Women's College
Women's Studies Program
Humanities Dept.
Gainsville, GA 30501
Phone: (404)534-6192
Leslie Jones, Contact
Specialization: Women's Leadership Development Program.

Macon

★7236★ Mercer University
Women's Studies Program
College of Liberal Arts
1400 Coleman Ave.
Macon, GA 31207
Phone: (912)752-2700
Kenneth Hammond, Contact

Marietta

★7237★ Kennesaw State College
Women's Studies Program
History Department
Box 444
Marietta, GA 30061
Phone: (404)423-6245
Ann W. Ellis, Contact
Undergraduate: Minor.

Milledgeville

★7238★ Georgia College
Women's Studies Program
Box 486
Milledgeville, GA 31060
Phone: (912)543-4504
Rosemary Begemann, Contact
Undergraduate: Minor.

Oxford

**★7239★ Oxford College of Emory
University**
Southern Institute of Gender Studies
Oxford, GA 30267
Phone: (404)784-4444
Theodore Davis, Contact
Undergraduate: Women's studies major.

Hawaii

Hilo

★7240★ University of Hawaii at Hilo
Women's Studies Program
Chancellor's Office
Hilo, HI 96720-4091
Phone: (808)933-3422
Trina Nahm-Mijo, Contact
Undergraduate: Minor.

Honolulu

★7241★ Chaminade University of Honolulu
Women's Studies
3140 Waialae Ave.
Honolulu, HI 96816
Phone: (808)735-4711

★7242★ Kapiolani Community College
Women's Studies
4303 Diamond Head Rd., No. 203
Honolulu, HI 96816
Phone: (808)734-9123

★7243★ University of Hawaii at Manoa
Women's Studies Program
2424 Maile Way, Porteus 722
Honolulu, HI 96822
Phone: (808)956-7464
Fax: (808)942-5710
Meda Chesney-Lind, Contact
Undergraduate: Area of concentration in Women's Studies; individualized major in Women's Studies; Certificate. **Degree(s) Offered:** BA in Women's Studies. **Specialization:** Asian, Pacific and Hawaiian Women.

Kaneohe

★7244★ Windward Community College
Women's Studies Program
45-720 Keaahala Rd.
Kaneohe, HI 96744
Phone: (808)235-0077
Janice Nuckols, Contact

Illinois

Aurora

★7245★ Aurora University
Women's Studies Program
347 S. Gladstone Ave.
Aurora, IL 60506
Phone: (708)844-4890
Dr. Tony Olejnik, Contact

Carbondale

★7246★ Southern Illinois University at Carbondale
Women's Studies Program
806 Chautauqua
Carbondale, IL 62901
Phone: (618)453-5141
Kathryn Ward, Contact
Undergraduate: Minor in Women's Studies. **Graduate:** Minor, Departmental emphasis, Concentration for MA and PhD. **Degree(s) Offered:** BA, BS.

Champaign

★7247★ Parkland College
Women's Studies Program
2400 W. Bradley
Champaign, IL 61821-1899
Phone: (217)351-2217
Pauline Kayes, Contact

★7248★ University of Illinois at Urbana-Champaign
Women in International Development
801 S. Wright
Champaign, IL 61820
Phone: (217)333-1977
Kathleen Cloud, Contact
Undergraduate: Major (Independent Basis), Area of Concentration.

Charleston

★7249★ Eastern Illinois University
Women's Studies Council
Rm. 209, MLK Union
Charleston, IL 61920
Phone: (217)581-5947
Ruth Hoberman, Coordinator
Undergraduate: Minor.

Chicago

★7250★ DePaul University
Women's Studies Program
802 W. Beldon Ave.
McGaw Bldg. Rm. 245
Chicago, IL 60614-3214
Phone: (312)341-8000
Carol Zyganowski, Contact
Undergraduate: Minor.

★7251★ Harold Washington University
Women's Studies Program
30 E. Lake St.
Chicago, IL 60601
Phone: (312)781-9430
Robin Herndobler, Contact

★7252★ Loyola University of Chicago
Women's Studies Program
6525 N. Sheridan Rd.
Chicago, IL 60626
Phone: (312)508-2934
Judith Wittner, Contact
Undergraduate: Minor, Certificate.

★7253★ Mundelein College
Women's Studies Program
6363 N. Sheridan Rd.
Chicago, IL 60660
Phone: (312)262-8100
Prudence A. Moylan, Coordinator
Undergraduate: Individualized major in Women's Studies; minor in Women's Studies. **Degree(s) Offered:** BA in Women's Studies.

★7254★ Northeastern Illinois University
Women's Studies Program
5500 N. St. Louis Ave.
Chicago, IL 60625
Phone: (312)583-4050
Fax: (312)794-6243
Irene Campos Carr, Contact
Undergraduate: Major, Minor.

★7255★ Roosevelt University
Women's Studies Program
430 S. Michigan Ave.
Chicago, IL 60605
Phone: (312)341-3860
Carol Traynor Williams, Contact

Degree(s) Offered: BA General Studies, MA General Studies.

★7256★ University of Illinois at Chicago
Women's Studies Program
Box 4348, Mail Code 360
Chicago, IL 60680
Phone: (312)996-2441
Peg Strobel, Contact

Undergraduate: Minor. **Graduate:** Concentration. **Degree(s) Offered:** BA (interdisciplinary designed degree).

DeKalb

★7257★ Northern Illinois University
Women's Studies Program
107 Reavis Hall
DeKalb, IL 60115
Phone: (815)753-1038
Lois S. Self, Contact

Undergraduate: Minor.

Des Plaines

★7258★ Oakton Community College
Women's Studies Program
1600 E. Golf Rd., Rm. 1186
Des Plaines, IL 60016
Phone: (708)635-1600
Kathy Calabrese, Contact

Edwardsville

★7259★ Southern Illinois University at
Edwardsville
Women's Studies Program
Box 1350
Edwardsville, IL 62026
Phone: (618)692-2003
T. Bagchi, Contact

Undergraduate: Minor. **Degree(s) Offered:** MA Specialization through Department of Philosophical Studies.

Elgin

★7260★ Elgin Community College
Women's Programs
1700 Spartan Dr.
Elgin, IL 60123
Phone: (708)697-1000
Gretchen Roche, Contact

Evanston

★7261★ Northwestern University
Women's Studies Program
2000 Sheridan Rd.
Evanston, IL 60208
Phone: (708)491-5871
Rae A. Moses, Contact

Undergraduate: Individualized major; minor in Women's Studies; certificate in Women's Studies. **Degree(s) Offered:** BA in Women's Studies.

Galesburg

★7262★ Knox College
Women's Studies Program
Galesburg, IL 61401
Phone: (309)343-0112
Penny S. Gold, Contact

Undergraduate: Area of Concentration.

Glen Ellyn

★7263★ College of Dupage
Focus on Women Program
22nd St. Lamberg Rd.
Glen Ellyn, IL 60137
Phone: (708)858-2800

Lake Forest

★7264★ Barat College
Committee on Women
700 E. Westleigh Rd.
Lake Forest, IL 60045
Phone: (708)234-3000
Laura Spernzi, Staff Dir.

Founded: 1973. **Description:** Documents and evaluates the status of women at Harvard School of Public Health, Harvard Medical School and Harvard School of Dental Medicine.

★7265★ Lake Forest College
Women's Studies
555 N. Sheridan Rd.
Lake Forest, IL 60045
Phone: (708)234-3100
A. Eskilson, Contact

Undergraduate: Minor, Area of Concentration.

Macomb

★7266★ Western Illinois University
Women's Studies Program
Department of English and Journalism
Simpkins Hall
Macomb, IL 61455
Phone: (309)298-1422
Janice Welsch, Contact

Undergraduate: Minor.

Monmouth

★7267★ Monmouth College
Women's Studies Program
700 E. Broadway
Monmouth, IL 61462
Phone: (309)457-2165
Carolyn Tyirin Kirk, Contact

Undergraduate: Minor.

Normal

★7268★ Illinois State University
Women's Studies Program
604 S. Main
Normal, IL 61761
Phone: (309)438-2947
Cynthia Huff, Contact

Undergraduate: Minor.

Palatine

★7269★ William Rainey Harper College
Women's Programs
1200 W. Algonquin
Palatine, IL 60067
Phone: (708)397-3000
Rena Tevor, Contact

Park Forest South

★7270★ Governors State University
Family & Women's Studies Program
Sociology Dept.
Park Forest South, IL 60466
Phone: (708)534-4581
Harriet Gross, Contact

Degree(s) Offered: BA, MA in Sociology with emphasis in Women's Studies.

Peoria

★7271★ Bradley University
Women's Studies Program
Bradley Ave.
Peoria, IL 61625
Phone: (309)677-3538
Toll-free: 800-447-6460
Bonnie Gordon, Contact

Undergraduate: Minor.

Rock Island

★7272★ Augustana College
Women's Studies Program
Rock Island, IL 61201
Phone: (309)794-7384
Nancy Huse, Contact

Undergraduate: Major, Minor, Area of Concentration.

Romeoville

★7273★ Lewis University
Women's Programs
Rt. 23
Romeoville, IL 60441
Phone: (815)838-0500
Barbara E. Maddex, Contact

Springfield

★7274★ Sangamon State University
Women's Studies Program
Shepherd Rd.
Springfield, IL 62794-9243
Phone: (217)786-6706
Pat Langley, Contact

Undergraduate: Major, Minor. **Graduate:** Individualized MA. **Degree(s) Offered:** BA, MA.

Urbana

★7275★ University of Illinois at Urbana-
Champaign
Women's Studies Program
708 S. Mathews
Urbana, IL 61801
Phone: (217)333-2990
Marianne Ferber, Contact

Undergraduate: Minor.

Indiana

Bloomington

★7276★ Indiana University Bloomington
Women's Studies Program
Memorial Hall E. 131
Bloomington, IN 47405
Phone: (812)855-0101
Jean Robinson, Contact
Undergraduate: Minor, Area of Concentration,
Certificate. **Graduate:** PhD Minor, Law Minor.

Ft. Wayne

★7277★ Indiana University—Purdue
University at Ft. Wayne
Women's Studies Program
2101 Coliseum Blvd., Rm. CM272
Ft. Wayne, IN 46805-1499
Phone: (219)481-6100
Judi Dilorio, Director
Undergraduate: Minor, Area of Concentration.

Franklin

★7278★ Franklin College of Indiana
Women's Studies Program
501 E. Monroe St.
Franklin, IN 46131
Phone: (317)738-8000
Emily Stauffer, Contact

Gary

★7279★ Indiana University Northwest
Women's Studies Program
3400 Broadway
Gary, IN 46408
Phone: (219)980-6500
Stephanie Shanks-Meiley, Contact

Goshen

★7280★ Goshen College
Women's Studies Program
Goshen, IN 46526
Phone: (219)535-7000
Anna Bowman, Contact
Undergraduate: Minor.

Greencastle

★7281★ DePauw University
Women's Studies Program
109 Asbury Hall
Greencastle, IN 46135
Phone: (317)658-4177
Fax: (317)658-2177
Meryl Altman, Coordinator
Undergraduate: Minor.

Hammond

★7282★ Purdue University Calumet
Women's Studies Program
2233 171st St.
Hammond, IN 46323
Phone: (219)989-2489
Jane R. Shoup, Contact
Undergraduate: Minor, Certificate.

Indianapolis

★7283★ Indiana University—Purdue
University at Indianapolis
Women's Studies Program
425 University Blvd. (CA 001E)
Indianapolis, IN 46202
Phone: (317)274-7611
Ann Donchin, Director
Undergraduate: Minor.

Muncie

★7284★ Ball State University
Women's Studies and Gender Studies
Muncie, IN 47306
Phone: (317)285-5451
Michael Stevenson, Contact
Undergraduate: Minor.

New Albany

★7285★ Indiana University Southeast
Women's Studies Certificate
4201 Grant Line Rd.
New Albany, IN 47150
Phone: (812)941-2412
Susan Moffett Matthias, Contact
Undergraduate: Minor, Certificate.

Notre Dame

★7286★ St. Mary's College
Women's Studies Program
71 Madelva
Notre Dame, IN 46556
Phone: (219)284-4000
Fax: (219)284-4716
Linnea Vacca, Contact
Undergraduate: Minor.

★7287★ University of Notre Dame
Gender Studies
104 O'Shaughnessy
Notre Dame, IN 46556
Phone: (219)239-8635
Ava Collins, Director
Undergraduate: Area of Concentration.

Richmond

★7288★ Earlham College
Women's Studies Program
Box 62
Richmond, IN 47374
Phone: (317)983-1505
Barbara Caruso, Contact
Undergraduate: Major, area of Concentration.
Degree(s) Offered: BA. **Specialization:** Areas
of Concentration: Peace and Global Studies;
Human Development and Social Relations.

South Bend

★7289★ Indiana University at South Bend
Women's Studies Program
1700 Mishawaka Ave.
South Bend, IN 46634
Phone: (219)237-4308
Gloria Kaufman, Director
Undergraduate: Minor.

Terre Haute

★7290★ Indiana State University
Women's Studies Program
Dreiser Hall
Terre Haute, IN 47809
Phone: (812)237-3658
Darlene Hantzis, Contact
Undergraduate: Minor.

Valparaiso

★7291★ Valparaiso University
Women's Studies Program
Valparaiso, IN 46383
Phone: (219)464-5011
D. Nuechterlein, Contact

West Lafayette

★7292★ Purdue University
Women's Studies Program
Pierce Hall, Rm. 170
West Lafayette, IN 47907
Phone: (316)494-4600
Berenice A. Carroll, Contact
Undergraduate: Minor.

Westville

★7293★ Purdue University North Central
Women's Studies Program
History Department
1401 S. US 421
Westville, IN 46391
Phone: (219)785-5200
Howard Jablon, Contact

Iowa

Ames

★7294★ Iowa State University
Women's Studies Program
203 Ross Hall
Ames, IA 50011
Phone: (515)294-3286
Kathleen K. Hickok, Contact
Undergraduate: Major, Minor, Area of Concentration. **Graduate:** Area of Concentration. **Degree(s) Offered:** BA, BS.

Cedar Falls

★7295★ University of Northern Iowa
Women's Studies Program
Cedar Falls, IA 50614
Phone: (319)273-2731
Fax: (319)273-3509
Martha Reineke, Director
Undergraduate: Minor.

Davenport

★7296★ St. Ambrose University
Women's Studies Program
518 W. Locust St.
Davenport, IA 52803
Phone: (319)383-8758
Fred Holman, Director

Decorah

★7297★ Luther College
Gender Studies
Decorah, IA 52101
Phone: (319)387-1369
Jackie Wilkie, Contact

Undergraduate: Area of Concentration.

Des Moines

★7298★ Drake University
Women's Studies Program
2700 University Ave.
Des Moines, IA 50311
Phone: (515)271-3563
Susan Wright, Contact

Grinnell

★7299★ Grinnell College
Committee on Gender and Women's
  Studies
Women Studies Program
Harry Hopkins House
Grinnell, IA 50112
Phone: (515)269-4000
Mary Lynn Broe, Director

Undergraduate: Area of Concentration. Specialization: Independent Major.

Indianola

★7300★ Simpson College
Women's Studies Program
701 N. C St.
Indianola, IA 50125
Phone: (515)961-1567
Nancy Sinclair, Director

Iowa City

★7301★ University of Iowa
Women's Studies Program
202 Jefferson Bldg.
Iowa City, IA 52242
Phone: (319)335-0322
Susan Birrell, Contact

Undergraduate: Minor in Women's Studies; area of concentration in Women's Studies; Graduate: Individualized major in Women's Studies; Area of Concentration in Women's Studies. Degree(s) Offered: MA in Feminist Anthropology; PhD in Women's Studies; Ad Hoc Interdisciplinary PhD.

Mt. Vernon

★7302★ Cornell College
Women's Studies Program
600 1st St. W.
Mt. Vernon, IA 52314
Phone: (319)895-4260
Tom Shaw, Contact

Undergraduate: Major, Minor. Degree(s) Offered: BA.

Pella

★7303★ Central College
Committee on the Role of Women
812 University St.
Pella, IA 50219
Phone: (515)628-9000

Waverly

★7304★ Wartburg College
Women's Studies Program
PO Box 1003
222 9th St. NW
Waverly, IA 50677
Phone: (319)352-8201
Cheryl Jacobsen, Director

Undergraduate: Minor.

Kansas

Emporia

★7305★ Emporia State University
Women's Studies Program
1200 Commercal
Emporia, KS 66801
Phone: (316)343-1200

Lawrence

★7306★ University of Kansas
Women's Studies Program
2120 Wescoe Hall
Lawrence, KS 66045-2117
Phone: (913)864-4011
Sandra Albrecht, Director

Degree(s) Offered: BA, BGS in Women's Studies; double major with a field in Humanities, Sociology, or Natural Science.

Manhattan

★7307★ Kansas State University
Women's Studies Program
22 Eisenhower Hall
Manhattan, KS 66506-1001
Phone: (913)532-5738
Fax: (913)532-7004
Sandra Coyner, Director

Undergraduate: Major, Area of Concentration.

Midway

★7308★ Midway College
Women's Studies
512 E. Stephens St.
Midway, KS 40347-1120
Phone: (606)846-5364
Fax: (606)846-5349
Kristina Minister, Contact

Pittsburg

★7309★ Pittsburg State University
Women's Studies Program
1701 S. Broadway
Pittsburg, KS 66762
Phone: (316)231-7000
Kathleen L. Nichols, Contact

Undergraduate: Certificate in Women's Studies.

Wichita

★7310★ Wichita State University
Center for Women's Studies Program
Campus Box 82
Wichita, KS 67208
Phone: (316)689-3358
Sally L. Kitch, Contact

Undergraduate: Minor in Women's Studies; individualized major in Women's Studies; Graduate: Minor in Women's Studies; individualized major in Women's Studies. Degree(s) Offered: BA in Women's Studies, MA in Liberal Studies with concentration in Women's Studies; BGS with an emphasis in Women's Studies.

Kentucky

Frankfort

★7311★ Kentucky State University
Women's Studies Program
Frankfort, KY 40601-0020
Phone: (502)227-6022

Highland Heights

★7312★ Northern Kentucky University
Women's Studies Program
537 Laudrum
Highland Heights, KY 41099
Phone: (606)572-5100
Fax: (606)572-5566
Judith Bechtel, Director

Undergraduate: Minor.

Lexington

★7313★ University of Kentucky
Women's Studies Program
241 Patterson Office Tower
Lexington, KY 40506-0027
Phone: (606)257-1388
Bonnie Cox, Contact

Undergraduate: Minor. Degree(s) Offered: PhD in Sociology and Psychology with emphasis on Women's Studies.

Louisville

★7314★ University of Louisville
Women's Studies Program
College of History
Louisville, KY 40292
Phone: (502)588-6831
Dr. Ann T. Allen, Director

Undergraduate: Minor.

Owensboro

★7315★ Brescia College
Contemporary Woman Program
717 Frederica St.
Owensboro, KY 42301
Phone: (502)686-4275
Fax: (502)686-4213
Marita Greenwell, Contact

Undergraduate: Minor.

Louisiana

Baton Rouge

★7316★ Louisiana State University
Women's Studies
Allen Hall
Baton Rouge, LA 70803
Phone: (504)388-2236
Michelle Masse, Director
Graduate: Departmental Emphasis in English.

New Orleans

★7317★ Loyola University at New Orleans
Women's Studies Minor
Box 65
6363 St. Charles Ave.
New Orleans, LA 70118
Phone: (504)865-2567
Nancy Fix Anderson, Contact
Degree(s) Offered: Undergraduate minor in Women's Studies.

★7318★ Tulane University
Women's Studies Program
1229 Broadway
New Orleans, LA 70118
Phone: (504)865-5238
Beth Willinger, Director
Undergraduate: Major (self-designed), Minor.
Degree(s) Offered: BA.

★7319★ University of New Orleans
Women's Studies Program
Department of Sociology
New Orleans, LA 70148
Phone: (504)286-6301
Susan Archer Mann, Director
Undergraduate: Minor.

Maine

Bar Harbor

★7320★ College of the Atlantic
Women's Studies Program
105 Eden St.
Bar Harbor, ME 04609
Phone: (207)288-5015
Susan Lerner, Director
Degree(s) Offered: BA in Human Ecology.

Biddeford

★7321★ University of New England
Women's Studies Program
11 Hills Beach Rd.
Biddeford, ME 04005
Phone: (207)283-0171
Roxie B. Hamlin, Director

Brunswick

★7322★ Bowdoin College
Women's Studies Program
Brunswick, ME 04011
Phone: (207)725-3724
Sarah McMahon, Director
Undergraduate: Minor.

Lewiston

★7323★ Bates College
Women's Studies Program
Lewiston, ME 04240
Phone: (207)786-6071
Elizabeth H. Tobin, Director
Undergraduate: Major. **Degree(s) Offered:** BA.

Orono

★7324★ University of Maine
Women's Studies Program
101 Fernald Hall
Orono, ME 04469
Phone: (207)581-1228
Ann Schonberger, Director
Undergraduate: Major, Area of Concentration, Certificate. **Degree(s) Offered:** BA.

Portland

★7325★ University of Southern Maine
Women's Studies Program
96 Falmouth St.
Portland, ME 04103
Phone: (207)780-4289
Fax: (207)780-4933
Diana Long, Contact
Undergraduate: Major, Minor. **Degree(s) Offered:** BA.

Waterville

★7326★ Colby College
Women's Studies Program
Mayflower Hill Dr.
Waterville, ME 04901
Phone: (207)872-3566
Debra Cambeu, Contact
Undergraduate: Major. **Specialization:** Individualized Major.

Maryland

Baltimore

★7327★ Johns Hopkins University
Women's Studies Program
300 Jenkins Hall
Baltimore, MD 21218
Phone: (301)516-6166
Judith Walkowitz, Contact

★7328★ Notre Dame College of Maryland
Continuing Education
4701 N. Charles St.
Baltimore, MD 21210
Phone: 800-435-0300
Judy Sabalauskas, Contact

★7329★ University of Baltimore
Women's Studies Program
1420 N. Charles at Mt. Royal
Baltimore, MD 21201
Phone: (301)625-3246
Nijole Benokraitis, Contact
Undergraduate: Major.

★7330★ University of Maryland, Baltimore County
Women's Studies Program
Fine Arts, Rm. 452
5401 Wilkens Ave.
Baltimore, MD 21228-5398
Phone: (301)455-2001
Joan Korenman, Director
Undergraduate: Major, Minor. **Degree(s) Offered:** BA (Interdisciplinary Studies).

College Park

★7331★ University of Maryland at College Park
Women's Studies Program
1121 Mill Bldg.
College Park, MD 20742
Phone: (301)405-6877
Evelyn T. Beck, Contact
Undergraduate: Individualized major in Women's Studies; certificate in Women's Studies.
Degree(s) Offered: BA in Women's Studies; American Studies, Economics, Government, and Politics, History, and Sociology Departments offer graduate degrees with an emphasis on women or gender roles.

Frostburg

★7332★ Frostburg State University
Women's Studies Program
Frostburg, MD 21532
Phone: (301)689-4445
Fax: (301)689-4737
Joy Kroeger Mappes, Contact
Undergraduate: Minor.

Rockville

★7333★ Montgomery College
Women's Studies Program
51 Mannakee St.
Rockville, MD 20850
Phone: (301)279-5000
Myrna Goldenberg, Director

Towson

★7334★ Goucher College
Women's Studies Program
1021 Dulaney Valley Rd.
Towson, MD 21204
Phone: (301)337-6274
Marianne Githens, Contact
Undergraduate: Major. **Degree(s) Offered:** BA.

★7335★ Towson State University
Women's Studies Program
English Dept.
Towson, MD 21204
Phone: (301)830-2660
Fax: (301)296-8782
Elaine Hedges, Director
Undergraduate: Minor in Women's Studies.
Degree(s) Offered: BGS with concentration in Women's Studies.

Westminster

★7336★ Western Maryland College
Women's Studies Program
2 College Hill
Westminster, MD 21157-4390
Phone: (410)857-2593
Tim Weinfeld, Contact
Undergraduate: Minor.

Massachusetts

Amherst

★7337★ Amherst College
Department of Women and Gender
Studies
14 Grosvenor House
Amherst, MA 01002
Phone: (413)542-5781
Amrita Basu, Contact
Undergraduate: Major, Minor. **Degree(s) Offered:** BA.

★7338★ Five Colleges Consortium
Women's Studies Committee
Box 740
Amherst, MA 01004
Phone: (413)256-8316
Fax: (413)256-0249
Lorna Peterson, Contact

★7339★ Hampshire College
Feminist Studies
Amherst, MA 01002
Phone: (413)549-4600
Rhonda Blair, Contact
Undergraduate: Minor. **Degree(s) Offered:** BA in Women's Studies.

★7340★ University of Massachusetts at
Amherst
Women's Studies Program
208 Bartlett Hall
Amherst, MA 01003
Phone: (413)545-1922
Jan Raymond, Contact
Undergraduate: Major, Minor, Certificate. **Degree(s) Offered:** Bachelor's Degree with Individual Concentration (BDIC); PhD in English with emphasis on Women's Studies.

Boston

★7341★ Boston University
Women's Studies Program
718 Commonwealth Ave., Rm. 405
Boston, MA 02215
Phone: (617)353-2948
Dorothy Kelly, Contact
Undergraduate: Minor in Women's Studies. **Degree(s) Offered:** PhD in American Studies with a concentration/dissertation in Women's Studies.

★7342★ Emerson College
Women's Studies Program
100 Beacon St.
Boston, MA 02116
Phone: (617)578-8600
Fax: (617)578-8509
Undergraduate: Minor.

★7343★ Emmanuel College
Women's Studies Program
400 The Fenway
Boston, MA 02115
Phone: (617)735-9975
Mary Mason, Contact
Undergraduate: Minor.

★7344★ Northeastern University
Women's Studies Program
524 HO/360 Huntington Ave.
Boston, MA 02115
Phone: (617)437-4442
Fax: (617)437-2942
Laura L. Frader, Contact
Undergraduate: Minor.

★7345★ Simmons College
Women's Studies Program
300 The Fenway
Boston, MA 02115
Phone: (617)738-2160
Pam Bromberg, Contact
Undergraduate: Minor in Women's Studies; area of concentration. **Graduate:** Area of concentration. **Degree(s) Offered:** BA and MA in Women's Studies.

★7346★ Suffolk University
Women's Studies Minor Program
8 Ashburton Pl.
Boston, MA 02108
Phone: (617)573-8327
C. Rubb, Contact
Undergraduate: Minor in Women's Studies.

★7347★ University of Massachusetts at
Boston Harbor Campus
Women's Studies Program
Boston, MA 02125
Phone: (617)287-6780
Catherine Manton, Contact
Undergraduate: Major, Minor, Certificate. **Degree(s) Offered:** BA.

★7348★ Women's Theological Center
Women's Studies Program
PO Box 1200
Boston, MA 02117
Phone: (617)536-8782
Undergraduate: Certificate. **Specialization:** Independent Program.

Bridgewater

★7349★ Bridgewater State College
Women's Advisory Committee
Bridgewater, MA 02325
Phone: (508)697-1200
Evelyn Pezzulich, Contact
Undergraduate: Minor.

Cambridge

★7350★ Episcopal Divinity School
Feminist Liberation Theology Program
99 Brattle St.
Cambridge, MA 02138
Phone: (617)868-3450
Alison Cheek, Contact
Degree(s) Offered: MA in Feminist Liberation Theology, Doctor of Ministry in Fem. Lib. Theo.

★7351★ Harvard Divinity School
Women's Studies in Religion
45 Francis Ave.
Cambridge, MA 02138
Phone: (617)495-5705
Constance Buchanan, Contact
Degree(s) Offered: ThD in Religion, Gender and Culture.

★7352★ Harvard Extension School
Women's Studies Program
20 Garden St.
Cambridge, MA 02138
Phone: (617)495-9413
Suzanne Spreadbury, Contact
Undergraduate: Area of Concentration. **Degree(s) Offered:** MA in Liberal Arts.

★7353★ Harvard University
Women's Studies Program
34 Kirkland St.
Cambridge, MA 02138
Phone: (617)495-9199
Fax: (617)495-9855
Barbara Johnson, Contact
Undergraduate: Major, Minor, Area of Concentration. **Degree(s) Offered:** BA, PhD.

★7354★ Massachusetts Institute of
Technology
Women's Studies Program
14E-316
Cambridge, MA 02139
Phone: (617)253-8844
Undergraduate: Major (by special request), Minor (by request), Area of Concentration. **Graduate:** Major (by request), Minor (by request), Area of Concentration. **Degree(s) Offered:** BA, MA.

★7355★ Radcliffe College
Women's Studies Program
Cambridge, MA 02138
Phone: (617)495-8608

Chestnut Hill

★7356★ Boston College
Women's Studies Program
Department of Sociology
McGuinn Hall
Chestnut Hill, MA 02167
Phone: (617)552-4139
Sharlene Hesse-Biber, Contact
Undergraduate: Minor.

★7357★ Pine Manor College
Women's Studies Program
400 Heath St.
Chestnut Hill, MA 02167
Phone: (617)731-7000
Melinda Ponder, Contact
Undergraduate: Minor.

Chicopee

★7358★ Elms College
Women's Studies Program
Continuing Education
291 Springfield St.
Chicopee, MA 01013
Phone: (413)594-2761
Fax: (413)592-4871
Kathleen Kirlen, Contact

Fitchburg

★7359★ Fitchburg State College
Women's Studies Program
Fitchburg, MA 01420
Phone: (508)345-3398
Harriet Alonso, Contact

Great Barrington

★7360★ Simon's Rock of Bard College
Women's Studies Program
Alford Rd.
Great Barrington, MA 01230
Phone: (413)528-0771
Fran Mascia-Less, Contact
Undergraduate: Major, Area of Concentration.
Degree(s) Offered: BA.

Haverhill

★7361★ Northern Essex Community
College
Women's Studies Program
100 Elliot St.
Haverhill, MA 01830
Phone: (508)374-3900
Priscilla B. Bellairs, Contact
Undergraduate: Area of Concentration. **Degree(s) Offered:** AA in Liberal Arts with Women's Studies Specialization.

Longmeadow

★7362★ Bay Path College
Women's Studies Program
588 Longmeadow St.
Longmeadow, MA 01106
Phone: (413)567-0621

Lowell

★7363★ University of Lowell
Women's Studies Program
1 University Ave.
Lowell, MA 01854
Phone: (508)934-4600
Undergraduate: Minor.

Medford

★7364★ Tufts University
Women's Studies Program
55 Talbot Ave.
Medford, MA 02155
Phone: (617)381-3184
Peggy Barrett, Contact
Undergraduate: Minor. **Degree(s) Offered:**
PhD with emphasis on Women's Issues.

Milton

★7365★ Curry College
Women's Studies Program
1071 Blue Hill Ave.
Milton, MA 02186
Phone: (617)333-0500
Fax: (617)333-6860
Marlene Samuelson, Contact
Undergraduate: Major (individually initiated),
Minor, Certificate. **Degree(s) Offered:** BA (individually initiated).

North Adams

★7366★ North Adams State College
Women's Studies Program
Interdisciplinary Studies Department
Church St.
North Adams, MA 01247
Phone: (413)664-4511
Fax: (413)664-4511
Undergraduate: Minor.

North Andover

★7367★ Merrimack College
Women's Studies Program
Turnpike Rd.
North Andover, MA 01845
Phone: (508)683-7111
Fax: (508)837-5222
Marguerite P. Kane, Contact

North Dartmouth

★7368★ University of Massachusetts at
Dartmouth
Women's Studies Program
Old Westport Rd.
North Dartmouth, MA 02747
Phone: (508)999-8000
Fax: (508)999-8901
Betty Mitchell, Contact
Undergraduate: Major, Minor. **Degree(s) Offered:** BA. **Specialization:** Major through Multidisciplinary Studies.

Northampton

★7369★ Smith College
Women's Studies Program
Hatfield Hall
Northampton, MA 01063
Phone: (413)585-3336
Fax: (413)585-2075
Susan Van Dyne, Contact
Undergraduate: Major, Minor. **Degree(s) Offered:** BA.

Norton

★7370★ Wheaton College
Women's Studies Program
E. Main St.
Norton, MA 02766
Phone: (508)285-7722
Fax: (508)285-2908
Frances A. Maher, Contact
Undergraduate: Minor in Women's Studies;
individualized major in Women's Studies. **Degree(s) Offered:** BA in Women's Studies.

Salem

★7371★ Salem College
Women's Studies Program
352 Lafayette St.
Salem, MA 01970
Phone: (508)741-2324
Alice Stadthaus, Contact
Undergraduate: Minor in Women's Studies;
Interdisciplinary Perspectives offers an emphasis in Women's Studies.

South Hadley

★7372★ Mount Holyoke College
Women's Studies Program
104 Dickinson House
South Hadley, MA 01075
Phone: (413)538-2339
Fax: (413)538-2391
Jean Grossholt, Contact
Undergraduate: Major, Minor. **Degree(s) Offered:** BA.

South Hamilton

★7373★ Gordon Conwell Theological
Seminary
Women's Studies Program
130 Essex St.
South Hamilton, MA 01982
Phone: (508)468-7111
Dr. Spencer, Contact

Waltham

★7374★ Bentley College
Gender Issues
G-076/English Deprtment
175 Forest St.
Waltham, MA 02154-6720
Phone: (617)891-2962
Jane Buchanan, Contact

★7375★ Brandeis University
Women's Studies Program
Waltham, MA 02254-9110
Phone: (617)736-3033
Joyce Antler, Contact
Undergraduate: Individualized major in Women's Studies; certificate in Women's Studies.
Degree(s) Offered: BA in Women's Studies.

Wellesley

★7376★ Wellesley College
Women's Studies Program
106 Central St.
Wellesley, MA 02181-8201
Phone: (617)235-0320
Susan Reverby, Contact
Undergraduate: Major. Degree(s) Offered: BA.

Westfield

★7377★ Westfield State College
Women's Studies Program
Western Avenue
Westfield, MA 01086
Phone: (413)568-3311
John Loughney, Contact
Undergraduate: Minor, Area of Concentration.

Weston

★7378★ Regis College
Women's Studies Program
235 Wellesley St.
Weston, MA 02193
Phone: (617)893-1820
Louise Levesque Lopman, Contact
Undergraduate: Individualized Major in Women's Studies.

Williamstown

★7379★ Williams College
Women's Studies Program
Department of English
Stetson Hall
Williamstown, MA 01267
Phone: (413)597-2564
Dona Bell, Contact
Undergraduate: Minor, Area of Concentration.
Specialization: Contract Major.

Worcester

★7380★ Clark University
Women's Studies Program
950 Main St.
Worcester, MA 01610
Phone: (508)793-7358
Rachel Joffe Falmagne, Contact
Undergraduate: Area of Concentration.

★7381★ Holy Cross College
Women's Studies Program
1 College St.
Worcester, MA 01610
Phone: (508)793-2011
Fax: (508)793-3030
Prof. Diane Bell, Contact

★7382★ Quinsigamond Community College
Women's Studies Program
670 W. Boylston St.
Worcester, MA 01606
Phone: (508)853-2300
Fax: (508)852-6943
Elaine Fallon, Contact
Undergraduate: Minor.

★7383★ Worcester State College
Women's Studies Program
486 Chandler St.
Worcester, MA 01602
Phone: (508)793-8000
Michael Burke, Contact

Michigan

Albion

★7384★ Albion College
Women's Studies Program
Albion, MI 49224
Phone: (517)629-1000
Fax: (517)629-0509
Judith Lockyear, Contact
Undergraduate: Major, Area of Concentration.

Allendale

★7385★ Grand Valley State University
Women's Studies Program
Campus Drive
Allendale, MI 49401
Phone: (616)895-3416
Doris Rucks, Contact
Undergraduate: Minor.

Alma

★7386★ Alma College
Women's Studies Program
614 W. Superior St.
Alma, MI 48801-1599
Phone: (517)463-7111

Ann Arbor

★7387★ Great Lakes Colleges Association
Women's Studies Program
2929 Plymouth Rd. No. 207
Ann Arbor, MI 48105
Phone: (313)761-4833
Fax: (313)761-3939
Jeanine L. Elliott, Vice President

★7388★ University of Michigan
Women's Studies Program
234 W. Engineering Bldg.
Ann Arbor, MI 48109-1092
Phone: (313)763-2047
Abigail Stewart, Contact
Undergraduate: Major. Graduate: Certificate.
Degree(s) Offered: BA.

★7389★ Washtenaw Community College
Women's Studies Program
Continuing Education/Community Service
4800 E. Huron River Dr.
PO Box D-1
Ann Arbor, MI 48106-0978
Phone: (313)677-5030
Judith Swan, Contact

Benton Harbor

★7390★ Lake Michigan College
Women's Studies Program
2755 E. Napier Ave.
Upper Level
Benton Harbor, MI 49022
Phone: (616)927-3571
Sherry Hoadley-Pries, Contact

Dearborn

★7391★ Henry Ford Community College
Focus on Women Program
5101 Evergreen Rd.
Dearborn, MI 48128
Phone: (313)271-2750
Undergraduate: Concentration in Women's Studies. Degree(s) Offered: AA with Concentration in Women's Studies.

★7392★ University of Michigan, Dearborn
Women's Studies Program
4901 Evergreen Rd.
Dearborn, MI 48128
Phone: (313)927-1245
Fax: (313)593-5552
Christopher Dahl, Contact
Undergraduate: Minor in Women's Studies.

Detroit

★7393★ University of Detroit
Women's Studies Program
4001 W. McNichols
Detroit, MI 48221
Phone: (313)993-1000
Lyn Lewis, Contact

★7394★ Wayne County Community College
Women's Studies Program
801 W. Fort St.
Detroit, MI 48226
Phone: (313)496-2758
Fax: (313)961-2791

★7395★ Wayne State University
Women's Studies Program
51 Warren Ave.
Detroit, MI 48202
Phone: (313)577-7556
Effie Ambler, Contact
Undergraduate: Individualized Major, Minor.
Degree(s) Offered: BA.

East Lansing

★7396★ Michigan State University
Women's Studies Program
301 Linton Hall
East Lansing, MI 48824
Phone: (517)355-4495
Fax: (517)353-5368
Joyce Ladenson, Contact
Undergraduate: Area of Concentration, Certificate. Graduate: Departmental Emphasis.

Flint

★7397★ University of Michigan, Flint
Women's Studies Program
285 University Pavillion
Flint, MI 48502-2186
Phone: (313)762-3085
Jan Worth, Contact
Undergraduate: Minor.

Grand Rapids

★7398★ Aquinas College
Women's Center
1607 Robinson Rd., SE
Grand Rapids, MI 49506
Phone: (616)459-8281
Mary Alice Williams, Contact
Degree(s) Offered: Undergraduate area of concentration in Women's Studies; Sociology, Religious Studies, Philosophy, and English Departments offer an emphasis in Women's Studies.

Holland

★7399★ Hope College
Women's Studies and Program Committee
Holland, MI 49423
Phone: (616)392-5111
Anne Larsen, Contact
Degree(s) Offered: Undegraduate minor in Women's Studies; undergraduate individualized major in Women's Studies.

Kalamazoo

★7400★ Kalamazoo College
Women's Studies Program
1200 Academy St.
Kalamazoo, MI 49007
Phone: (616)383-8494
Gail B. Griffin, Contact
Degree(s) Offered: Undergraduate area of concentration in Women's Studies; undergraduate individualized major in Women's Studies.

★7401★ Western Michigan University
Women's Studies Program
Kalamazoo, MI 49008-3899
Phone: (616)387-4900
Owen Laaberg, Contact
Undergraduate: Individualized Major, Minor.
Degree(s) Offered: BA.

Mt. Pleasant

★7402★ Central Michigan University
Women's Studies Program
118 Pearce Hall
Mt. Pleasant, MI 48859
Phone: (517)774-3601
Donna Grave, Contact
Undergraduate: Minor.

Port Huron

★7403★ St. Clair County Community College
Women's Studies Program
323 Erie St.
Port Huron, MI 48060
Phone: (313)984-3881
Fax: (313)984-4730
Linda E. Flickinger, Contact

Rochester

★7404★ Oakland University
Women's Studies Concentration
521 Wilson Hall
Rochester, MI 48309
Phone: (313)370-3389
Susan Hawkins, Contact
Undergraduate: Area of Concentration.

Saginaw

★7405★ Saginaw Valley State University
Women's Studies Program
2250 Pierce Rd.
PO Box 5825
Saginaw, MI 48710
Phone: (517)790-4200
Fax: (517)790-0186

Ypsilanti

★7406★ Eastern Michigan University
Women's Studies Program
720 Pray-Harrold
Ypsilanti, MI 48197
Phone: (313)487-1177
Margaret Crouch, Contact
Undergraduate: Minor. **Graduate:** Area of Concentration. **Degree(s) Offered:** MA (MLS).

Minnesota

Bemidji

★7407★ Bemidji State University
Women's Studies Program
1500 Birchmont Dr. NE
Bemidji, MN 56601-2699
Phone: (218)755-2766
Fax: (218)755-4048
Patricia A. Rosenbrock, Contact
Undergraduate: Minor.

Brooklyn Park

★7408★ North Hennepin Community College
Women's Studies Program
7411 85th Ave. N.
Brooklyn Park, MN 55445
Phone: (612)424-0811
Gayla Shoemake, Contact

Collegeville

★7409★ St. John's University
Women's Studies Program
Collegeville, MN 56321
Phone: (612)363-2138
Annette Atkins, Contact

Coon Rapids

★7410★ Anoka-Ramsey Community College
Women's Studies Program
Coon Rapids, MN 55433
Phone: (612)422-3328
Dorothy Sauber, Contact

Duluth

★7411★ College of St. Scholastica
Women's Studies Program
1200 Kenwood Ave.
Duluth, MN 55811
Phone: (218)723-6000
E. Stich, Contact
Undergraduate: Minor in women's studies.

★7412★ University of Minnesota, Duluth
Women's Studies Program
209 Bohannon Hall
10 University Dr.
Duluth, MN 55812-2496
Phone: (218)726-7953
Fax: (218)726-6331
Susan Coultrap, Contact
Undergraduate: Major, Minor. **Graduate:** Departmental Emphasis. **Degree(s) Offered:** BA.

Mankato

★7413★ Mankato State University
Women's Studies Program
PO Box 8400
MSU Box 64
Mankato, MN 56002-8400
Phone: (507)389-2077
Mary VanVoorhis, Contact
Undergraduate: Major, Minor, Area of Concentration. **Degree(s) Offered:** BA, BS, MS in Continuing Studies.

Minneapolis

★7414★ Augsburg College
Women's Studies Program
731 21st Ave. S.
Minneapolis, MN 55454
Phone: (612)330-1063
Beverly J. Stratton, Contact
Undergraduate: Major, Minor. **Degree(s) Offered:** BA in process (Individually Designed).

★7415★ Minneapolis Community College
Women's Studies
1501 Hennepin Ave. S.
Minneapolis, MN 55403
Phone: (612)341-7020
Fax: (612)341-7075
Mary C. Pruitt, Contact

★7416★ University of Minnesota, Twin Cities
Women's Studies Program
489 Ford Hall
Minneapolis, MN 55455
Phone: (612)624-6006
Susan Geiger, Contact
Undergraduate: Major, Minor, Area of Concentration. **Graduate:** Minor. **Degree(s) Offered:** BA.

Moorhead

★7417★ **Moorhead State University**
Women's Studies Program
S. Eleventh St.
Moorhead, MN 56560
Phone: (218)236-4685
Sheila Coghill, Contact

Undergraduate: Minor in Women's Studies; individualized major in Women's Studies. **Degree(s) Offered:** BA in Women's Studies.

Morris

★7418★ **University of Minnesota, Morris**
Women's Studies Program
600 E. 4th St.
Morris, MN 56267-2211
Phone: (612)589-2116
Mariam Darce Frenier, Contact

Undergraduate: Minor.

Northfield

★7419★ **Carleton College**
Women's Studies Program
1 N. College St.
Northfield, MN 55057
Phone: (507)663-4000
Barbara Allen, Contact

Undergraduate: Area of Concentration.

★7420★ **St. Olaf College**
Women's Studies Program
Northfield, MN 55057
Phone: (507)646-3231
Olivia Frey, Contact

Undergraduate: Major, Minor, Area of Concentration. **Degree(s) Offered:** BA.

Rochester

★7421★ **Rochester Community College**
Women's Studies Program
851 30th Ave. SE
Rochester, MN 55904
Phone: (507)285-7218
Fax: (507)285-7496
Arlouene Olson, Contact

Undergraduate: Area of Concentration.

St. Cloud

★7422★ **St. Cloud State University**
Women's Studies Program
8th St., Education Bldg. B120
St. Cloud, MN 56301-4498
Phone: (612)255-0121
Pat A. Samuel, Director

Undergraduate: Minor. **Degree(s) Offered:** BA Elective Studies, MA or MS: Special Studies.

St. Paul

★7423★ **College of St. Catherine**
Abigail Quigley McCarthy Center for Women
2004 Randolph Ave.
St. Paul, MN 55105
Phone: (612)690-6783
Fax: (612)690-6024
Catherine Lupori, Director

Undergraduate: Minor. **Degree(s) Offered:** BA with Special Major.

★7424★ **Hamline University**
Women's Studies Program
1536 Hewitt St.
St. Paul, MN 55104
Phone: (612)641-2207
Margaret Jensen, Contact

Undergraduate: Minor, Women's Studies. **Specialization:** Individualized major in Women's Studies.

★7425★ **Macalester College**
Women's and Gender Studies
St. Paul, MN 55105
Phone: (612)696-6318
Jan Seary, Director

Undergraduate: Minor, Area of Concentration. **Specialization:** Individually Designed, Interdepartmental Major (IDIM).

★7426★ **Metropolitan State University**
Women's Program
700 E. 7th St.
St. Paul, MN 55106-5000
Phone: (612)772-7650
Fax: (612)772-7652
Linda Fancher-White, Contact

St. Peter

★7427★ **Gustavus Adolphus College**
Women's Studies Program
St. Peter, MN 56082
Phone: (507)933-7397
Deoborah Downs-Miers, Contact

Undergraduate: Minor.

Willmar

★7428★ **Willmar Community College**
Women's Studies Program
PO Box 797
Willmar, MN 56201
Phone: (612)231-5102
Bernice Grabber-Tintes, Contact

Undergraduate: Area of Concentration. **Degree(s) Offered:** AA in Women's Studies.

Mississippi

Columbus

★7429★ **Mississippi University for Women**
Women's Studies Program
Box W-1603
Columbus, MS 39701
Phone: (601)329-7142

Jackson

★7430★ **Millsaps College**
Women's Studies Program
1701 N. State St.
Jackson, MS 39210
Phone: (601)974-1000
Judith W. Page, Contact

Undergraduate: Area of Concentration.

Oxford

★7431★ **University of Mississippi**
Women's Studies Program
Sarah Isom Center
Oxford, MS 38677
Phone: (601)232-5916
Joanne V. Hawks, Contact

Undergraduate: Area of Concentration. **Degree(s) Offered:** History Department offers MA with minor in Women's Studies.

Starkville

★7432★ **Mississippi State University**
Women's Studies Concentration
PO Drawer E.
Starkville, MS 39762
Phone: (601)325-2224
Susan Shelly, Contact

Undergraduate: Area of Concentration, Certificate.

Missouri

Cape Girardeau

★7433★ **Southeast Missouri State University**
Women's Studies Program
Cape Girardeau, MO 63701
Phone: (314)651-2625
Pamela Hearn, Contact

Columbia

★7434★ **Stephens College**
Women's Studies Program
Box 2013
Columbia, MO 65215
Phone: (314)876-7103
Fax: (314)876-7248
Carol Perkins, Contact

Undergraduate: Minor, Area of Concentration.

★7435★ **University of Missouri, Columbia**
Women's Studies Program
309 Switzler Hall
Columbia, MO 65211
Phone: (314)882-2703
Mary Jo Neitz, Contact

Undergraduate: Major, Minor, Area of Concentration. **Degree(s) Offered:** BA.

Hillsboro

★7436★ **Jefferson College**
Women's Studies Program
1000 Viking Dr.
Hillsboro, MO 63050
Phone: (314)789-3951
Trish Loomis, Contact

Kansas City

★7437★ Avila College
Women's Studies Program
11901 Wornall Rd.
Kansas City, MO 64145
Phone: (816)942-8400
Dona Neuman, Contact
Undergraduate: Minor. **Degree(s) Offered:**
BA.

★7438★ University of Missouri, Kansas City
Women's Studies Program
5204 Rockhill Rd.
Kansas City, MO 64110-2499
Phone: (816)235-1000
Kristen Esterberg, Contact
Undergraduate: Minor.

St. Louis

★7439★ Clayton University
Women's Studies Program
PO Box 16941
St. Louis, MO 63105
Phone: (314)727-6100

★7440★ St. Louis University
Women's Studies Program
221 N. Grand Blvd.
St. Louis, MO 63103
Phone: (314)658-2295
J. Gibbons, Contact
Undergraduate: Certificate.

★7441★ University of Missouri, St. Louis
Women's Studies Program
8001 Natural Bridge Rd.
St. Louis, MO 63121
Phone: (314)553-5581
Suzanna Rose, Contact
Undergraduate: Certificate. **Graduate:** Concentration; Certificate.

★7442★ Washington University
Women's Studies Program
One Brookings Dr.
Campus Box 1078
St. Louis, MO 63130
Phone: (314)935-5102
Fax: (314)889-5799
Joyce Trebilcot, Contact
Undergraduate: Major, Minor. **Degree(s) Offered:** BA.

★7443★ Webster University
Women's Studies Advisory Committee
470 E. Lockwood St.
St. Louis, MO 63119
Phone: (314)968-7074
Britt Marie Shiller, Contact
Undergraduate: Minor, Certificate; individualized Major in Women's Studies. **Graduate:** Certificate.

Warrensburg

★7444★ Central Missouri State University
Women's Studies Program
Wood Bldg., No. 136
Warrensburg, MO 64093
Phone: (816)543-4404
Patricia Ashman, Contact
Undergraduate: Minor; individualized Major in Women's Studies.

Montana

Billings

★7445★ Eastern Montana College
Women's Studies Program
1500 N. 30th St.
Billings, MT 59101-0298
Phone: (406)657-2202
Sue Hart, Contact

Bozeman

★7446★ Montana State University
Women's Studies Program
College of Letters and Science
Bozeman, MT 59717
Phone: (406)994-4248
Undergraduate: Minor in Women's Studies.

Missoula

★7447★ University of Montana
Women's Studies Program
Philosophy Department
Missoula, MT 59812
Phone: (406)243-2845
Maxine Van de Wetering, Contact
Undergraduate: Area of Concentration.

Nebraska

Bellevue

★7448★ Bellevue College
Women's Studies
Galvin Rd. at Harvell Dr.
Bellevue, NE 68005
Phone: (402)293-3736
Roxanne Sullivan, Contact
Undergraduate: Minor.

Kearney

★7449★ Kearney State College
Women's Studies Program
Department of English
Kearney, NE 68849
Phone: (308)234-8294
Kathryn N. Benzel, Contact
Undergraduate: Minor.

Lincoln

★7450★ University of Nebraska, Lincoln
Women's Studies Program
202 Andrews Hall
Lincoln, NE 68588-0333
Phone: (402)472-6357
Maureen Honey, Contact
Undergraduate: Major, Minor. **Graduate:** Area of Concentration. **Degree(s) Offered:** BA.

Nevada

Las Vegas

★7451★ University of Nevada, Las Vegas
Women's Studies Program
4505 Maryland Pkwy.
Las Vegas, NV 89154
Phone: (702)739-3322
Catherine Bellver, Contact
Undergraduate: Major, Minor. **Degree(s) Offered:** BA.

Reno

★7452★ University of Nevada, Reno
Women's Studies Program
090 UNR
Reno, NV 89557
Phone: (702)784-1560
Elaine Enarson, Contact
Undergraduate: Minor.

New Hampshire

Durham

★7453★ University of New Hampshire
Women's Studies Program
304A Dimond Library
Durham, NH 03824
Phone: (603)862-2194
Cathryn Adamsky, Contact
Undergraduate: Minor. **Degree(s) Offered:** BA (student-designed); AA in Women's Studies.

Hanover

★7454★ Dartmouth College
Women's Studies Program
2 Carpenter Hall
Hanover, NH 03755
Phone: (603)646-2722
Anne Brooks, Contact
Undergraduate: Modified Major, Minor, Certificate. **Degree(s) Offered:** BA in Women's Studies.

Henniker

★7455★ New England College
Women's Studies Program
Henniker, NH 03242
Phone: (603)428-2223
Elizabeth Alexander, Contact

Keene

★7456★ Keene State College
Women's Studies Program
229 Main St.
Keene, NH 03431
Phone: (603)352-2357
Eleanor VanderHaegen, Contact
Undergraduate: Minor.

Nashua

★7457★ Rivier College
Women's Studies Program
S. Main St.
Nashua, NH 03060
Phone: (603)888-1314
Marjorie Marcourx Faiia, Contact
Undergraduate: Minor.

Plymouth

★7458★ Plymouth State College
Center for Women's Services
Bagley House
Plymouth, NH 03264
Phone: (603)535-5000
Bev Hart, Contact
Undergraduate: Minor.

Rindge

★7459★ Franklin Pierce College
Women's Studies Program
PO Box 60
Rindge, NH 03461
Phone: (603)899-4200
Margaret Madden, Contact

New Jersey

Caldwell

★7460★ Caldwell College
Women's Studies Program
Department of Psychology
Ryerson Ave.
Caldwell, NJ 07006-1695
Phone: (201)228-4424
Marie Hudson, Contact
Undergraduate: Certificate.

Camden

★7461★ Rutgers, The State University of
New Jersey
Camden College of Arts and Sciences
Women's Studies
Sociology Department
Camden, NJ 08102
Phone: (609)757-6013
Sheila Cosminsky, Contact
Undergraduate: Minor.

Glassboro

★7462★ Glassboro State College
Women's Studies Program
Triad Bldg.
Glassboro, NJ 08028
Phone: (609)863-5249
Fax: (609)863-6553
Corann Okorodudu, Contact
Undergraduate: Area of Concentration.

Hackettstown

★7463★ Centenary College
Women's Studies Program
400 Jefferson
Hackettstown, NJ 07840
Phone: (908)582-1400
Norman Muir, Contact
Undergraduate: Minor.

Jersey City

★7464★ Jersey City State College
Women's Studies Program
2039 Kennedy Memorial Blvd.
Jersey City, NJ 07305
Phone: (201)200-2000
Barbara Rubin, Director
Undergraduate: Minor, Area of Concentration.

Lakewood

★7465★ Georgian Court College
Women's Studies Program
Lakewood, NJ 08701
Phone: (908)364-2200
Fax: (908)905-8571
Judith Beck, Contact
Undergraduate: Minor.

Lawrenceville

★7466★ Ride College
Women's Studies Program
2083 Lawrenceville Rd.
Lawrenceville, NJ 08648
Phone: (609)895-5570
Dr. Virginia Cyrus, Contact
Undergraduate: Minor, Certificate.

Madison

★7467★ Drew University
Women's Studies Program
36 Madison Ave.
Bowne Bldg.
Madison, NJ 07940
Phone: (201)408-3632
Fax: (201)408-3939
Wendy Kolmar, Contact
Undergraduate: Minor.

Mahwah

★7468★ Ramapo College of New Jersey
Women's Studies Program
505 Ramapo Valley Rd.
Mahwah, NJ 07430
Phone: (201)529-7576
Donna Crawley, Contact
Undergraduate: Minor.

Morris Township

★7469★ College of St. Elizabeth
Women's Studies Program
Convent Sta.
Morris Township, NJ 07960
Phone: (201)292-6351
Barbara Bari, Contact

New Brunswick

★7470★ Rutgers, The State University of
New Jersey
Douglass College
Women's Studies Program
Voorhess Chapel, Lower Level, Rm. 9
New Brunswick, NJ 08903
Phone: (908)932-9331
Alice Kessler-Harris, Contact
Undergraduate: Major, Minor, Certificate.
Graduate: Certificate. Degree(s) Offered: BA,
MA/PhD in Women's History (History), MA/PhD
in Women in Politics.

★7471★ Rutgers, The State University of
New Jersey
Livingston College
Women's Studies Program
Lucy Stone Hall
New Brunswick, NJ 08903
Phone: (201)932-2065
Judith M. Gerson, Contact
Undergraduate: Women's studies major

Newark

★7472★ Rutgers, The State University of
New Jersey, Newark
Women's Studies Program
360 M.L. King Blvd., Rm. 310
Newark, NJ 07102
Phone: (201)648-5817
Fran Bartkowski, Contact
Undergraduate: Minor, Area of Concentration.

Paramus

★7473★ Bergen Community College
Women's Studies Program
400 Paramus Rd.
Paramus, NJ 07652
Phone: (201)447-7100
Judith Friedman, Contact
Degree(s) Offered: AA in Women's Studies.

Pomona

★7474★ Stockton State College
Women's Studies Program
Jim Leeds Rd.
Pomona, NJ 08240
Phone: (609)652-1776
Nancy Ashton, Contact
Undergraduate: Certificate.

Princeton

★7475★ Princeton Theological Seminary
Women's Studies Program
CN 821
Princeton, NJ 08542
Phone: (609)497-7911
Freda A. Gardner, Contact
Undergraduate: Major, Area of Concentration.
Degree(s) Offered: ThM of Theology.

★7476★ Princeton University
Women's Studies Program
113 Dickinson
Princeton, NJ 08544
Phone: (609)258-5430
Laura Engelstein, Contact
Undergraduate: Certificate.

Randolph

★7477★ County College of Morris
Women's Studies Program
214 Center Grove Rd.
Randolph, NJ 07867
Phone: (201)328-5000

Teaneck

★7478★ Fairleigh Dickinson University
Women's Studies Program
1000 River Rd.
Teaneck, NJ 07666
Phone: (201)692-2465
Theresa Marciano, Contact
Degree(s) Offered: Sociology Department offers undergraduate area of concentration in Women's Studies.

Toms River

★7479★ Ocean County College
Women's Program
College Dr.
Toms River, NJ 08754
Phone: (408)255-4000

Trenton

★7480★ Mercer County Community College
Women's Studies Concentration
PO Box B
Trenton, NJ 08690
Phone: (609)586-4800
Angela McClym, Contact
Undergraduate: Area of Concentration.

★7481★ Trenton State College
Women's Studies Program
Hillwood Lakes, CN 4700
Trenton, NJ 08650
Phone: (609)771-2539
Ellen G. Friedman, Contact
Undergraduate: Minor.

Union

★7482★ Kean College of New Jersey
Women's Studies Program
History Department
Union, NJ 07083
Phone: (908)527-2039
Sylvia Straus, Contact
Undergraduate: Minor.

Upper Montclair

★7483★ Montclair State College
Women's Studies Program
433 Partridge Hall
Upper Montclair, NJ 07043
Phone: (206)893-7416
Fax: (201)893-5455
Adele McCollum, Contact
Undergraduate: Minor. **Degree(s) Offered:** MA Liberal Studies, Concentration on Gender Studies.

Wayne

★7484★ William Paterson College of New Jersey
Women's Studies Program
Political Science Department
Wayne, NJ 07470
Phone: (201)595-2000
Carole Sheffield, Director
Undergraduate: Minor; general education requirement in Women's Studies.

West Long Branch

★7485★ Monmouth College
Women's Studies Program
West Long Branch, NJ 07764
Phone: (908)571-3421
Donna Dolphin, Contact
Undergraduate: Minor.

New Mexico

Albuquerque

★7486★ University of New Mexico
Women's Studies Program
2142 Mesa Vista Hall
Albuquerque, NM 87131
Phone: (505)277-3854
Elizabeth Jameson, Contact
Graduate: Minor. **Degree(s) Offered:** MA and PhD with a Minor in Gender Studies in Educational Foundations.

Las Cruces

★7487★ New Mexico State University
Women's Studies Program
Box 30001, Dept. 3WSP
Las Cruces, NM 88003-0001
Phone: (505)646-3448
Cookie Stephan, Contact
Undergraduate: Minor, Area of Concentration.

Portales

★7488★ Eastern New Mexico University
Women's Studies Committee
Station 19
Portales, NM 88130
Phone: (505)562-2421
Janet Owens Frost, Contact
Undergraduate: Minor, Certificate.

New York

Albany

★7489★ Albany Law School
Women's Studies Program
80 New Scotland Ave.
Albany, NY 12208
Phone: (518)445-2311
Bernard Evans Harvith, Contact

★7490★ State University of New York College at Albany
Women's Studies Program
1400 Washington Ave.
HUM 117
Albany, NY 12222
Phone: (518)442-4221
Fax: (518)442-4188
Bonnie Spencer, Contact
Undergraduate: Major, Minor, Certificate. **Graduate:** Concentration, Certificate. **Degree(s) Offered:** BA, MA in Liberal Studies.

Alfred

★7491★ Alfred University
Women's Studies Program
PO Box 806
Alfred, NY 14802
Phone: (607)871-2256
Susan Mayberry, Contact
Undergraduate: Minor.

Annandale-on-Hudson

★7492★ Bard College
Women's Studies Program
Annandale-on-Hudson, NY 12504
Phone: (914)758-6822
Fax: (914)758-7544
Michele D. Domini, Contact
Undergraduate: Area of Concentration. **Degree(s) Offered:** BA with a Concentration in Women's Studies.

Aurora

★7493★ Wells College
Women's Studies Program
Rte. 90
Aurora, NY 13206
Phone: (315)364-3240
Prof. Ann Rush, Director
Undergraduate: Minor in Women's Studies; individualized major in Women's Studies through Special Academic Programs. **Degree(s) Offered:** BA in Women's Studies.

Batavia

★7494★ **Genessee Community College**
Women's Studies Program
College Rd.
Batavia, NY 14020
Phone: (716)492-5265

Binghamton

★7495★ **State University of New York**
College at Binghamton
Women's Studies Program
PO Box 6000
Library N. 1105
Binghamton, NY 13902
Phone: (607)777-2815
Bat-Ami Bar On, Director

Undergraduate: Minor in Women's Studies; area of concentration in Women's Studies; individualized major in Women's Studies through Independent Project Board; certificate in Women's Studies. **Degree(s) Offered:** History Department offers MA and PhD in Women's History.

Brockport

★7496★ **State University of New York**
College at Brockport
Women's Studies Program
Brockport, NY 14420
Phone: (716)395-2628
Evelyn Newlyn, Director

Undergraduate: Major, Minor. **Graduate:** Area of Concentration.

Bronx

★7497★ **Fordham University**
Women's Studies Program
Rose Hill Campus
414 E. Fordham Rd.
Bronx, NY 10458
Phone: (212)579-2245
Diane S. Isaacs, Contact

Undergraduate: Major. **Degree(s) Offered:** BA.

★7498★ **Herbert Lehman College**
Women's Studies Program
250 Bedford Park Blvd. W.
Bronx, NY 10468
Phone: (212)960-8847
Fax: (212)960-8935
Joan P. Mencher, Contact

Undergraduate: Minor, Area of Concentration.

Bronxville

★7499★ **Concordia College**
Women's Studies Program
171 White Plains Rd.
Bronxville, NY 10468
Phone: (914)337-9300
Doris Anthony, Contact

★7500★ **Sarah Lawrence College**
Women's Studies Program
Bronxville, NY 10708
Phone: (914)395-2405
Amy Swerdlow, Director

Undergraduate: Area of Concentration. **Degree(s) Offered:** MA in Women's History.

Brooklyn

★7501★ **Brooklyn College of the City**
University of New York
Women's Studies Program
Bedford Ave. and H Ave.
227 Ingersoll Extension
Brooklyn, NY 11210
Phone: (718)780-5485
Nancy Romer, Contact

Undergraduate: Co-Major in Women's Studies.

★7502★ **Kingsborough Community College**
of the City University of New York
Women's Studies Program
2001 Oriental Blvd.
Brooklyn, NY 11235
Phone: (718)368-5000
Isabel Krey, Director

★7503★ **Medgar Evers College of the City**
University of New York
Women's Studies Program
1650 Bedford Ave.
Brooklyn, NY 11225
Phone: (718)270-5051
Andrea Nicola-McLaughlin, Contact

Cross-Cultural Black Women's Studies Summer Institute (Overseas Program).

Brookville

★7504★ **Long Island University**
Women's Studies Program
C.W. Post Campus
Brookville, NY 11548
Phone: (516)299-2404
Alice Scourby, Contact

Undergraduate: Minor.

Buffalo

★7505★ **Buffalo State College**
Women's Studies Program
Philosophy Dept.
Buffalo, NY 14222
Phone: (716)878-6403
Dr. Marianne Ferguson, Contact

Undergraduate: Minor.

★7506★ **Canisius College**
Women's Studies
2001 Main St.
Buffalo, NY 14208
Phone: (716)888-2150
Fax: (716)888-2525

★7507★ **State University of New York**
College at Buffalo
Women's Studies Program
1010 Clemens Hall
Buffalo, NY 14260
Phone: (716)636-2810
Elizabeth Kennedy, Contact

Undergraduate: Major, Minor. **Degree(s) Offered:** BA, MA/ PhD in American Studies.

Canton

★7508★ **St. Lawrence University**
Gender Studies
15 Hepburn Hall
Canton, NY 13617
Phone: (315)379-5524
Valerie Lehr, Contact

Undergraduate: Minor.

Clinton

★7509★ **Hamilton College**
Women's Studies Program
College Hill Rd.
Clinton, NY 13323
Phone: (315)859-4285
Fax: (315)859-4648
Margaret Gentry, Director

Undergraduate: Major, Minor. **Degree(s) Offered:** BA.

Cortland

★7510★ **State University of New York**
College at Cortland
Women's Studies Program
Department of Communication
Cortland, NY 13045
Phone: (607)753-4099
Fax: (607)753-5999
Jina Daddario, Contact

Undergraduate: Minor.

Dobbs Ferry

★7511★ **Mercy College**
Women's Studies Program
555 Broadway
Dobbs Ferry, NY 10522
Phone: (914)693-4500
Fay Greenwald, Director

Undergraduate: Major, Minor.

Dryden

★7512★ **Tompkins Cortland Community**
College
Women's Studies Program
170 North St.
Dryden, NY 13053
Phone: (607)844-8211
Sandra Pollack, Contact

Undergraduate: Minor, Major. **Degree(s) Offered:** AA in Women's Studies.

Flushing

★7513★ **Queens College of the City**
University of New York
Women's Studies Program
Department of English
Flushing, NY 11367
Phone: (718)520-7651
Susan K. Harris, Contact

Undergraduate: Major, Minor. **Degree(s) Offered:** BA.

Fredonia

★7514★ State University of New York College at Fredonia
Women's Studies Concentration
Thompson Hall
Fredonia, NY 14063
Phone: (716)673-3111
James Hurtgen, Contact

Undergraduate: Major, Minor. **Degree(s) Offered:** BA. **Specialization:** Individualized Major.

Garden City

★7515★ Adelphi University
Women's Studies Program
1 South Ave.
Garden City, NY 11530
Phone: (516)877-3000
Ann Alter, Director

Geneseo

★7516★ State University of New York College at Geneseo
Women's Studies Program
1 College Circle
Geneseo, NY 14454
Phone: (716)245-5209
Margaret Matlin, Contact

Undergraduate: Minor. **Graduate:** Minor.

Geneva

★7517★ Hobart and William Smith Colleges
Women's Studies Program
Geneva, NY 14456
Phone: (315)789-5500
Toni Flores, Contact

★7518★ William Smith College
Women's Studies Program
Geneva, NY 14456
Phone: (315)781-3472
Toll-free: 800-245-0100

Undergraduate: Women's studies major.

Hamilton

★7519★ Colgate University
Women's Studies Program
Hamilton, NY 13346-1398
Phone: (315)824-1000
Fax: (315)824-1000
Kay Johnston, Contact

Undergraduate: Major, Minor. **Degree(s) Offered:** BA.

Hempstead

★7520★ Hofstra University
Women's Studies
1000 Fulton Ave.
Hempstead, NY 11550
Phone: (516)463-5828
Linda Longmierl, Contact

Undergraduate: Minor in Women's Studies; area of concentration in Women's Studies; individualized major in Women's Studies; certificate in Women's Studies; **Graduate:** Area of concentration in Women's Studies; individualized major in Women's Studies. **Degree(s) Offered:** BA and MA in Women's Studies.

Hudson

★7521★ Columbia Green Community College
Women's Studies Program
Rt. 23
Box 1000
Hudson, NY 12534
Phone: (518)828-4181
Mary Davidson, Director

Undergraduate: Minor in Women's Studies; area of concentration in Women's Studies.

Ithaca

★7522★ Cornell University
Women's Studies Program
384 Uris Hall
Ithaca, NY 14853
Phone: (607)255-6480
Nelly Furman, Director

Undergraduate: Major, Area of Concentration. **Graduate:** Minor.

Jamaica

★7523★ York College of the City University of New York
Women's Studies Program
Foreign/Humanities Department
94-20 Guy Brewer Blvd.
Jamaica, NY 11451
Phone: (718)262-2430
Fax: (718)262-2027
Gloria Waldman, Contact

Undergraduate: Area of Concentration.

Long Island

★7524★ Friends World College
Women's Studies Program
Long Island, NY 11101
Phone: (516)549-5000
Rivka Polatnick, Contact

Long Island City

★7525★ LaGuardia Community College
Women's Studies Program
31-10 Thomson Ave.
C-711
Long Island City, NY 11101-5351
Phone: (718)482-5293
Sandra M. Watson, Contact

Loudonville

★7526★ Siena College
Women and Minority Studies
Rte. 9
Loudonville, NY 12211
Phone: (518)783-4129
Jennifer McErlean, Contact

New Paltz

★7527★ State University of New York College at New Paltz
Women's Studies Program
Hohmann House
New Paltz, NY 12561
Phone: (914)257-2975
Fax: (914)257-3009
Amy Kesselman, Contact

Undergraduate: Major, Minor, Area of Concentration. **Degree(s) Offered:** BA, MA with emphasis in Women's Studies.

New Rochelle

★7528★ College of New Rochelle
Women's Studies Program
New Rochelle, NY 10801
Phone: (914)654-5000
Kristen Wenzel, Contact

Undergraduate: Minor. **Degree(s) Offered:** BA through Interdisciplinary Studies.

★7529★ Iona College
Women's Studies Program
715 North Ave.
New Rochelle, NY 10801
Phone: (914)633-2328
Fax: (914)633-2020
Susan Toliver, Director

Undergraduate: Minor.

New York

★7530★ Barnard College
Women's Studies Program
203 Barnard Hall
New York, NY 10027
Phone: (212)854-2108
Natalie Kampen, Contact

Undergraduate: Major. **Degree(s) Offered:** BA.

★7531★ Boricua College
Women's Studies Program
3755 Broadway
New York, NY 10032
Phone: (212)694-1000

★7532★ The City College of the City University of New York
Women's Studies Program
Convent Ave. at 138th St.
New York, NY 10031
Phone: (212)650-8269
Mary Jackson, Contact

Degree(s) Offered: BS; BA through Interdisciplinary Studies with Concentration in Women's Stu dies.

★7533★ City University of New York Graduate School
Women's Studies Program
33 W. 42nd St., Rm. 4004 GB
New York, NY 10036-8099
Phone: (212)642-2416
Fax: (212)642-2642
Judith Lorber, Contact

Degree(s) Offered: PhD, Certificate, MA in Liberal Studies.

★7534★ Columbia University
Women's Studies Program
763 Schermerhorn Extension
116th St. & Broadway
New York, NY 10027
Phone: (212)854-1754
Martha Howell, Director
Undergraduate: Major. **Degree(s) Offered:**
BA.

★7535★ Empire State College of the
State University of New York College
Working Women's Studies Program
330 W. 42nd St.
New York, NY 10036-6901
Phone: (212)598-0640
Susan Hallgarth, Director
Undergraduate: Area of Concentration. **Specialization:** Labor Studies.

★7536★ Eugene Lang College
New School for Social Research
Women's Studies Program
65 W. 11th St.
New York, NY 10011
Phone: (212)741-5665
Undergraduate: Women's studies major.

★7537★ Hunter College of the City
University of New York
Women's Studies Program
695 Park Ave.
New York, NY 10021
Phone: (212)772-5680
Fax: (212)772-4941
Michelle Paludi, Director
Undergraduate: Co-Major, Minor. **Degree(s)**
Offered: BA.

★7538★ New York University
Women's Studies Program
10 Washington Place
New York, NY 10003
Phone: (212)998-7999
Carol Sternhill, Contact
Undergraduate: Major, Minor, Area of Concentration. **Graduate:** Area of Concentration. **Degree(s) Offered:** BA; MA in Women's History offered through History Department. **Specialization:** Gallatin Division Curriculum Model (Individually designed).

★7539★ Parsons School of Design
New School for Social Research
Vera List Center
66 W. 12th St., Rm. 507
New York, NY 10011
Phone: (212)229-5620
Sandra Farginis, Director
Undergraduate: Certificate. **Degree(s) Offered:** BA with an individualized major or through interdisciplinary Studies.

Old Westbury

★7540★ State University of New York
College at Old Westbury
Women's Studies Program
Box 210
Old Westbury, NY 11568
Phone: (516)876-3103
Laura Anchor, Director
Undergraduate: Area of Concentration. **Degree(s) Offered:** BA through American Studies.

Oneonta

★7541★ Hartwick College
Women's Studies Program
Oneonta, NY 13820
Phone: (607)431-4200
Winifred D. Wandersee, Contact

★7542★ State University of New York
College at Oneonta
Women's Studies Program
Milne Library, Rm. 315A
Oneonta, NY 13820
Phone: (607)431-3500
Fax: (607)431-2107
Kathleen O'Mara, Director
Undergraduate: Minor.

Oswego

★7543★ State University of New York
College at Oswego
Women's Studies Program
Mahar Hall
Oswego, NY 13126
Phone: (315)341-3443
Dr. Karen Halbersleben, Director
Undergraduate: Minor.

Plattsburgh

★7544★ State University of New York
College at Plattsburgh
Women's Studies Program
Hawkins Hall
Plattsburgh, NY 12901
Phone: (518)564-3301
Eleanor P. Stoller, Director
Undergraduate: Minor.

Potsdam

★7545★ State University of New York
College at Potsdam
Women's Studies Program
Potsdam, NY 13676
Phone: (315)267-2180

Poughkeepsie

★7546★ Marist College
Women's Studies Program
North Rd.
Poughkeepsie, NY 12601-1387
Phone: (914)575-3000
JoAnne Myers, Contact

★7547★ Vassar College
Women's Studies Program
Raymond Ave.
Box 205
Poughkeepsie, NY 12601
Phone: (914)437-7144
Eileen Leonard, Contact
Undergraduate: Major, Minor. **Degree(s) Offered:** BA.

Purchase

★7548★ Manhattanville College
Women's Studies Program
125 Purchase St.
Purchase, NY 10577
Phone: (914)694-2200
Nancy S. Harris, Director
Undergraduate: Minor. **Graduate:** Minor.

★7549★ State University of New York
College at Purchase
Women's Studies Program
Social Sciences Bldg.
Purchase, NY 10577
Phone: (914)251-6600
Esther Newton, Contact

Rochester

★7550★ Nazareth College of Rochester
Women's Studies Concentration
4245 E. Ave.
Rochester, NY 14610
Phone: (716)586-2525
Fax: (716)586-2452
Catherine G. Valentine, Contact
Undergraduate: Minor, Area of Concentration.

★7551★ University of Rochester
Susan B. Anthony Center for Women's
Studies Program
538 Lattimore Hall
Rochester, NY 14627
Phone: (716)275-8318
Sharon Willis, Director
Undergraduate: Major, Minor. **Degree(s) Offered:** BA.

Saranac Lake

★7552★ North Country Community College
Women's Studies Program
20 Winona Ave.
Saranac Lake, NY 12983
Phone: (518)891-2915

Saratoga Springs

★7553★ Skidmore College
Women's Studies Program
North Broadway
Saratoga Springs, NY 12866
Phone: (518)584-5000
Mary Stange, Director
Undergraduate: Minor/Major.

★7554★ State University of New York at
Empire State College
Women's Studies Program
2 Union Ave.
Saratoga Springs, NY 12866
Phone: (518)587-2100
Carolyn Forrey, Contact

Schnectady

★7555★ Union College
Women's Studies
27 N. College, Rm. 106
Schnectady, NY 12308
Phone: (518)370-6423
Sharon Gmelch, Contact

Undergraduate: Major, Area of Concentration.
Degree(s) Offered: BA.

Selden

**★7556★ Suffolk County Community
College**
Women's Studies Program
Humanities Department
533 College Rd.
Selden, NY 11784
Phone: (516)451-4365
Alice Goode-Elman, Contact

Undergraduate: Major, Area of Concentration,
Certificate. **Degree(s) Offered:** AA (Humanities
degree with an emphasis in Women's Studies).

Staten Island

**★7557★ College of Staten Island of the
City University of New York**
Women's Studies Program
130 Stuyvesant Pl.
Rm. I-621
Staten Island, NY 10301
Phone: (718)390-7818
Florence C. Parkinson, Contact

Undergraduate: Major, Minor. **Degree(s) Offered:** BA. **Specialization:** Independent study.

Stony Brook

**★7558★ State University of New York
College at Stony Brook**
Women's Studies Program
Old Chemical Bldg., Rm. 105
Stony Brook, NY 11794-3456
Phone: (516)632-9176
Adriene Munich, Contact

Undergraduate: Minor in Women's Studies.
Graduate: Certificate in Women's Studies. **De-
gree(s) Offered:** BA/BS/EdD in Women's Studies; History and English Departments offer MA
and PhD with emphasis in Women's Studies.

Syracuse

★7559★ Onondaga Community College
Women's Studies Program
Graphic Arts Department
Syracuse, NY 13215
Phone: (315)469-7741
Patricia Brooke, Contact

★7560★ Syracuse University
Women's Studies Program
Hall of Languages, Rm. 307
Syracuse, NY 13244-1170
Phone: (315)443-3707
Diane Murphy, Contact

Undergraduate: Major/Minor, Area of Concentration. **Graduate:** Certificate.

Tarrytown

★7561★ Marymount College
Women's Studies Program
Tarrytown, NY 10591
Phone: (914)631-3200
Bernice W. Liddie, Contact

Undergraduate: Minor. Individualized major in
Women's Studies.

Troy

★7562★ Russell Sage College
Women's Studies Program
Troy, NY 12180
Phone: (518)270-2306
Kris Anderson, Contact

Undergraduate: Minor.

North Carolina

Asheville

★7563★ University of North Carolina
Southeastern Women's Studies
1 University Heights
Asheville, NC 28804-3299
Phone: (704)251-6550
Pam Nickless, Contact

Undergraduate: Women's studies major

Boone

★7564★ Appalachian State University
Women's Studies Program
East Hall
Boone, NC 28608
Phone: (704)262-2144
Melissa Barth, Contact

Undergraduate: Major (Interdisciplinary Studies), Minor (only self-designed), Area of Concentration. **Graduate:** Minor.

Chapel Hill

**★7565★ University of North Carolina at
Chapel Hill**
Women's Studies Program
207 Caldwell Hall/CB 3135
Chapel Hill, NC 27599-3135
Phone: (919)962-3908
Barbara J. Harris, Contact

Undergraduate: Area of Concentration, Certificate. **Graduate:** Courses. **Degree(s) Offered:**
BA in Women's Studies through Interdisciplinary Studies.

Charlotte

**★7566★ Central Piedmont Community
College**
Women's Studies Program
Charlotte, NC 28235
Phone: (704)342-6888
Beth Willinger, Dir.

Degree(s) Offered: AA in Women's Studies.

**★7567★ University of North Carolina at
Charlotte**
Women's Studies Program
301 Kennedy
Charlotte, NC 28223
Phone: (704)547-4312
Dr. Lorrine M. Getz, Contact

Undergraduate: Minor.

Durham

★7568★ Duke University
Women's Studies Program
207 E. Duke Bldg.
Durham, NC 27706
Phone: (919)684-5683
Jean O'Barr, Contact

Undergraduate: Area of Concentration, Certificate. **Graduate:** Certificate. **Specialization:**
Honors at Undergraduate Level.

Elon College

★7569★ Elon College
Women's Studies Program
Campus Box 2219
Elon College, NC 27244
Phone: (919)584-2260
Martha Smith, Contact

Undergraduate: Minor.

Greensboro

★7570★ Bennett College
Women's Studies Program
900 E. Washington St.
Greensboro, NC 27401
Phone: (919)370-8690

Undergraduate: Area of Concentration in Wom-
en's Studies.

★7571★ Guilford College
Women's Studies Program
5800 W. Friendly Ave.
Greensboro, NC 27410
Phone: (919)292-5511
Carol Stoneburner, Contact

Undergraduate: Minor.

**★7572★ University of North Carolina at
Greensboro**
Women's Studies Program
108 Foust
Greensboro, NC 27412
Phone: (919)334-5673
Jodi Bilinkoff, Contact

Undergraduate: Major, Minor. **Degree(s) Offered:** BA.

Greenville

★7573★ East Carolina University
Women's Studies Program
Tenth St., Brewster A204
Greenville, NC 27858
Phone: (919)757-6268
Fax: (919)757-4263
Marie T. Farr, Contact

Undergraduate: Minor.

Wilmington

★7574★ University of North Carolina at Wilmington
Women's Studies Program
601 S. College Rd.
Wilmington, NC 28403
Phone: (919)395-3000
K. Berkeley, Contact

Winston-Salem

★7575★ Salem College
Women's Studies Program
Main Hall/Old Salem
Winston-Salem, NC 27018
Phone: (919)725-5411
Gary Ljungquist, Contact
Undergraduate: Certificate.

★7576★ Wake Forest University
Women's Studies Program
PO Box 7365, Reynolds Sta.
Winston-Salem, NC 27109
Phone: (919)759-5139
Mary DeShazer, Contact
Undergraduate: Minor. Graduate: Area of Concentration.

North Dakota

Fargo

★7577★ North Dakota State University
Women's Studies Program
English Department
Minard Hall, Rm. 320
Fargo, ND 58105
Phone: (701)237-7156
Jean Strandness, Contact
Undergraduate: Minor.

Grand Forks

★7578★ University of North Dakota
Women's Studies Program
Box 42, University Sta.
Grand Forks, ND 58202
Phone: (701)777-4115
Sandra J. Parsons, Contact
Undergraduate: Minor.

Ohio

Akron

★7579★ The University of Akron
Women's Studies Program
Spicer 120
Akron, OH 44325-6216
Phone: (216)972-7396
Carole Gozansky Garrison, Contact
Undergraduate: Certificate. Graduate: Certificate.

Athens

★7580★ Ohio University
Women's Studies Program
Scott 320
University Terrace
Athens, OH 45701
Phone: (614)593-4686
Linda Hunt, Contact
Undergraduate: Individualized major in Women's Studies. Degree(s) Offered: English Department offers MA with concentration in Women's Studies.

Bowling Green

★7581★ Bowling Green State University
Women's Studies Program
Union Bldg.
Bowling Green, OH 43402
Phone: (419)372-7133
Karen Gould, Contact
Undergraduate: Major, Minor. Degree(s) Offered: BA.

Cincinnati

★7582★ Union Institute
Women's Studies Program
440 E. McMillan St.
Cincinnati, OH 45206
Phone: (513)861-6400
Dr. Judith Arcana, Contact
Graduate: Concentration. Degree(s) Offered: BA, Individualized PhD.

★7583★ University of Cincinnati
Center for Women's Studies Program
ML-164
Cincinnati, OH 45221
Phone: (513)556-6776
Fax: (513)556-0128
Hilda Smith, Contact
Undergraduate: Certificate. Graduate: Minor. Degree(s) Offered: MA.

★7584★ Xavier University
Women's Studies Program
3800 Victory Pkwy.
Cincinnati, OH 45207
Phone: (513)745-2042
Fax: (513)745-1954
Carol Winkleman, Contact
Undergraduate: Minor.

Cleveland

★7585★ Case Western Reserve University
Women's Studies Program
American Studies
Cleveland, OH 44106
Phone: (216)368-2000
Roberta Wollons, Contact

★7586★ Cleveland State University
Women's Comprehensive Program
UC #363
1983 E. 24th St.
Cleveland, OH 44115
Phone: (216)687-3755
Mareyjoyce Green, Contact

★7587★ Cuyahoga Community College
Institute on Human Relations
2900 Community College Ave.
Cleveland, OH 44115
Phone: (216)987-4515
Dorothy Salem, Contact
Undergraduate: Concentration in Women's Studies.

Columbus

★7588★ The Ohio State University
Center for Women's Studies
286 University Hall
230 W. 17th Ave.
Columbus, OH 43210
Phone: (614)292-1021
Susan Hartmann, Contact
Undergraduate: Major, Minor. Graduate: Concentration; interdisciplinary programs with emphasis in Women's Studies. Degree(s) Offered: BA, BS, MA, PhD.

Dayton

★7589★ University of Dayton
Women's Studies Program
300 College Park
Dayton, OH 45469
Phone: (513)229-4285
Judith Martin, Contact
Undergraduate: Minor.

Delaware

★7590★ Ohio Wesleyan University
Women's Studies Program
215 Sturgis Hall
Delaware, OH 43015
Phone: (614)368-3577
Laurie Churchill, Contact
Undergraduate: Major, Minor. Degree(s) Offered: BA.

Gambier

★7591★ Kenyon College
Gender Studies
Gambier, OH 43022
Phone: (614)427-5374
Linda Smolak, Coordinator
Undergraduate: Individualized major in Women's Studies.

Granville

★7592★ Denison University
Women's Studies Program
Granville, OH 43023
Phone: (614)587-6536
Annette Van Dyke, Contact
Undergraduate: Major, Minor. Degree(s) Offered: BA/BS.

Hiram

★7593★ **Hiram College**
Gender Studies Program
PO Box 306
Hiram, OH 44234
Phone: (216)569-5328
Sandra Parker, Contact

Undergraduate: Minor in Gender Studies; certificate in Gender Studies.

Kent

★7594★ **Kent State University**
Women's Studies Program
308 Bowman Hall
Kent, OH 44242
Phone: (216)672-2060
Trudy Steuernagel, Contact

Undergraduate: Minor, Certificate.

Marietta

★7595★ **Marietta College**
Women's Studies Program
Marietta, OH 45750
Phone: (614)373-4643
Sara Shute, Contact

Undergraduate: Minor.

Mentor

★7596★ **Lakeland Community College**
Women's Studies Program
Department of Psychology
7700 Clock Tower Dr.
Mentor, OH 44060-7594
Phone: (216)953-7000
Mary Ring, Contact

Mount St. Joseph

★7597★ **College of Mount St. Joseph**
Women's Studies Program
5701 Delphi Pike
Mount St. Joseph, OH 45023-1670
Phone: (513)244-4939
K. Clifton, Contact

Undergraduate: Major, Minor. **Degree(s) Offered:** BA.

Newark

★7598★ **The Ohio State University,**
Newark Campus
Women's Studies Program
University Dr.
Newark, OH 43055
Phone: (614)366-9293
Judith Johnson, Contact

Oberlin

★7599★ **Oberlin College**
Women's Studies Program
Rice Hall 16
Oberlin, OH 44074
Phone: (216)775-8409
Fax: (216)775-8124
Sandra Zagarell, Contact

Undergraduate: Major, Minor. **Degree(s) Offered:** BA.

Oxford

★7600★ **Miami University**
Women's Studies Program
152 Upham Hall
Oxford, OH 45056
Phone: (513)529-4616
Karen Maitland, Contact

Undergraduate: Minor. **Degree(s) Offered:** English Department offers BA with emphasis on Women's Studies.

Painesville

★7601★ **Lake Erie College**
Women's Studies Program
391 Washington St.
Painesville, OH 44077
Phone: (216)352-3361
Caroline Zillboorg, Contact

Salem

★7602★ **Kent State University, Salem**
Regional Campus
Women's Studies Program
2491 State, Rte. 45 S.
Salem, OH 44460
Phone: (216)332-0361
Stephane Elise Booth, Contact

Undergraduate: Certificate.

Springfield

★7603★ **Wittenberg University**
Women's Studies Progam
Box 720
Springfield, OH 45501
Phone: (513)327-7323
Christine L. Matusik, Contact

Sylvania

★7604★ **Loudes College**
Women's Studies Program
6835 Convent Blvd.
Sylvania, OH 43560
Phone: (419)885-3211
Ruth Zellers, Contact

Toledo

★7605★ **University of Toledo**
Women's Studies Program
2801 W. Bancroft
Toledo, OH 43606-3390
Phone: (419)537-2164
Fax: (419)537-2157
Scott G. McNall, Contact

Degree(s) Offered: BA Program in Women's Studies.

University Heights

★7606★ **John Carroll University**
Men and Women: Perspectives on Sex
and Gender
University Heights, OH 44118
Phone: (216)397-4294
Marian J. Morton, Contact

Wooster

★7607★ **College of Wooster**
Women's Studies Program
Wooster, OH 44691
Phone: (216)263-2575
Susan Figge, Contact

Undergraduate: Major, Minor. **Degree(s) Offered:** BA.

Yellow Springs

★7608★ **Antioch College**
Women's Studies Program
Yellow Springs, OH 45387
Phone: (513)767-6364
Marianne Welchel, Contact

Undergraduate: Area of Concentration. **Degree(s) Offered:** BA (Self Designed Major). **Specialization:** European term abroad in Women's Studies.

Youngstown

★7609★ **Youngstown State University**
College of Arts and Sciences
Women's Studies Advisory Committee
DeBartolo Hall 435
410 Wick Ave.
Youngstown, OH 44555
Phone: (216)742-1687
Dr. Pat Gilmartin-Zena, Contact

Undergraduate: Minor. **Degree(s) Offered:** History Department offers Master's theses with emphasis in Women's Studies.

Oklahoma

Norman

★7610★ **University of Oklahoma**
Women's Studies Program
530 Physical Science Center
Norman, OK 73019
Phone: (405)325-3481
Judith S. Lewis, Contact

Undergraduate: Minor. **Graduate:** Interdisciplinary.

Stillwater

★7611★ **Oklahoma State University**
Women's Studies Program
College of Arts and Sciences
Stillwater, OK 74078
Phone: (405)624-5663
Nuala Archer, Contact

Degree(s) Offered: Undergraduate certificate in Women's Studies.

Tulsa

★7612★ **University of Tulsa**
Center for Study of Women's Literature
600 S. College Ave.
Tulsa, OK 74104
Phone: (918)631-2000
Shari Benstock, Contact

Graduate: Departmental Emphasis in English.

Oregon

Ashland

★7613★ **Southern Oregon State College**
Women's Studies
Psychology Department
250 Siskoy
Ashland, OR 97520
Phone: (503)482-6206
Shelley Eriksen, Contact

Undergraduate: Minor, Area of Concentration.
Degree(s) Offered: MA Concentration in Inter-
disciplinary Studies; MA-Interdisciplinary, MS-
Interdisciplinary.

Corvallis

★7614★ **Oregon State University**
Women's Studies Program
Social Science 200
Corvallis, OR 97331-6208
Phone: (503)737-2826
Janet Lee, Contact

Undergraduate: Minor, Area of Concentration,
certificate. **Graduate:** Major, Minor, Area of
Concentration. **Degree(s) Offered:** MA (Interdisciplinary Studies). **Specialization:** All Doctoral Programs offer a Minor in Women's Studies.

Eugene

★7615★ **Lane Community College**
Women's Studies Program
4000 E. 30th Ave.
Eugene, OR 97405
Phone: (503)747-4501
Kate Barry, Contact

★7616★ **University of Oregon**
Women's Studies Program
636 Prince L. Campbell Hall
Eugene, OR 97403
Phone: (503)346-5529
Fax: (503)346-3127
Marsha Ritzdorf, Contact

Undergraduate: Minor, Certificate. **Graduate:**
Certificate. **Specialization:** Interdisciplinary
Master's Degree.

Forest Grove

★7617★ **Pacific University**
Women's Programs
2043 College Way
Forest Grove, OR 97116
Phone: (503)357-6151

Gresham

★7618★ **Mount Hood Community College**
Women's Program
26000 SE Stark
Gresham, OR 97030
Phone: (503)667-6422

Marylhurst

★7619★ **Marylhurst College**
Women's Studies Programs
Marylhurst, OR 97036
Phone: (503)636-8141

McMinnville

★7620★ **Linnfield College**
Women's Programs
McMinnville, OR 97128
Phone: (503)472-4121

Oregon City

★7621★ **Clackamas Community College**
Women's Program
19600 S. Malloa
Oregon City, OR 97045
Phone: (503)657-6958

Pendleton

★7622★ **Blue Mountain Community**
College
Women's Programs
Pendleton, OR 97801
Phone: (503)276-1260

Portland

★7623★ **Lewis and Clark College**
Gender Studies
Portland, OR 97219
Phone: (503)768-7000
Jean M. Ward, Contact

Undergraduate: Major, Minor. **Degree(s) Offered:** BA (student-designed), BS (student-designed).

★7624★ **Portland Community College**
BFIT Program
12000 SW 49th Ave.
Portland, OR 97219-0990
Phone: (503)244-6111
Fax: (503)293-4947
Gail Smith, Contact

★7625★ **Portland State University**
Women's Studies Program
PO Box 751
Portland, OR 97207
Phone: (503)725-3516
Fax: (503)725-4882
Johanna Brenner, Contact

Undergraduate: Minor, Certificate.

★7626★ **University of Portland**
Women's Studies Program
5000 N. Willamette Blvd.
Portland, OR 97203
Phone: (503)283-7147
Loretta Zimmerman, Contact

★7627★ **Warner Pacific College**
Women's Programs
2219 SE 69th Ave.
Portland, OR 97215
Phone: (503)775-4366

★7628★ **Western Evangelical Seminary**
Women's Studies Program
4200 SE Jennings Ave.
Portland, OR 97267
Phone: (503)654-5466
Susie Stanley, Contact

Salem

★7629★ **Chemeketa Community College**
Women's Studies Program
PO Box 14007
Salem, OR 97309
Phone: (503)399-3921

Pennsylvania

Allentown

★7630★ **Cedar Crest College**
Women's Studies Program
100 College Dr.
Allentown, PA 18104
Phone: (215)395-5580
Ann Hill-Beuf, Contact

Undergraduate: Minor in Women's Studies;
area of concentration in Women's Studies;
individualized major in Women's Studies; certificate. **Degree(s) Offered:** BA.

Aston

★7631★ **Neumann College**
Gender Studies
Aston, PA 19014-1297
Phone: (215)558-5579
Martha Boston, Contact; Stephanie Marek

Undergraduate: Minor.

Bethlehem

★7632★ **Lehigh University**
Women's Studies Program
Art and Architecture
Bethlehem, PA 18103
Phone: (215)758-5619
Lucy Ganns, Contact

Undergraduate: Minor.

Bryn Mawr

★7633★ **Bryn Mawr College**
Feminist and Gender Studies
Department of History
Thomas Hall
Bryn Mawr, PA 19010
Phone: (215)526-5066
Fax: (215)525-4739
Jane Caplan, Contact

Undergraduate: Minor, Area of Concentration,
Independent Major in Women's Studies.

California

★7634★ **California University of**
Pennsylvania
Women's Studies Program
California, PA 15419
Phone: (412)938-5788
Margaret Spratt, Contact

Carlisle

★7635★ Dickinson College
Women's Studies Program
PO Box 1773
Carlisle, PA 17013-2896
Phone: (717)245-1231
Margaret Carroll, Contact
Undergraduate: Individualized major in Women's Studies.

Chambersburg

★7636★ Wilson College
Women's Studies Program
1015 Philadelphia Ave.
Chambersburg, PA 17201
Phone: (717)264-4141
Fax: (717)264-1578
Beverly Ayers-Nachamkin, Contact
Undergraduate: Certificate.

Collegeville

★7637★ Ursinus College
Women's Studies Program
Department of Modern Language
Rm. 1000
Collegeville, PA 19426
Phone: (215)489-4111
Colette Hall, Contact
Specialization: Interdisciplinary Course.

East Stroudsburg

★7638★ East Stroudsburg University of Pennsylvania
Women's Studies Program
309 Stroud Hall
East Stroudsburg, PA 18301
Phone: (717)424-3542
Anne Berkman, Contact
Undergraduate: Area of Concentration.

Easton

★7639★ Lafayette College
Women's Studies Program
Psychology Department
Easton, PA 18042
Phone: (215)250-5294
Susan A. Basow, Contact
Undergraduate: Minor, Individualized Major.

Gettysburg

★7640★ Gettysburg College
Women's Studies Program
PO Box 2450
Gettysburg, PA 17325
Phone: (717)337-6788
Fax: (717)337-6251
Jean Potuchek, Contact
Undergraduate: Minor.

Greensburg

★7641★ Seton Hill College
Women's Studies Program
Greensburg, PA 15601
Phone: (412)834-2200
Vivien Linkhauer, Contact
Undergraduate: Area of Concentration in Women's Studies; individualized major in Women's Studies.

Grove City

★7642★ Grove City College
Women's Studies Program
100 Campus Dr.
Grove City, PA 16127-2104
Phone: (412)458-2100
Dr. M. Barbara Akin, Contact

Haverford

★7643★ Haverford College
Feminism and Gender Studies
Haverford, PA 19041
Phone: (215)896-1156
Fax: (215)896-1224
Elaine Tuttle Hansen, Contact
Undergraduate: Area of Concentration.

Indiana

★7644★ Indiana University of Pennsylvania
Women's Studies Program
352 Sutton Hall
Indiana, PA 15705
Phone: (412)357-4753
Maureen C. McHugh, Contact
Undergraduate: Minor, Certificate. **Graduate:** Area of Concentration.

Lancaster

★7645★ Franklin and Marshall College
Women's Studies Program
Department of Anthropology
Lancaster, PA 17604
Phone: (717)291-4193
Nancy McDowell, Contact
Undergraduate: Minor. **Specialization:** Special Studies Major.

Lewisburg

★7646★ Bucknell University
Women's Studies Program
Lewisburg, PA 17837
Phone: (717)524-1545
Catherine Blair, Contact; Karen Dugger
Undergraduate: Minor.

McKeesport

★7647★ Pennsylvania State University, McKeesport
Women's Studies Program
University Dr.
McKeesport, PA 15132
Phone: (412)675-9461
Dr. Margaret L. Signorella, Contact
Undergraduate: Minor.

Meadville

★7648★ Allegheny College
Women's Studies Program
Meadville, PA 16335
Phone: (814)332-2395
Ellen Gray, Contact
Undergraduate: Minor, Area of Concentration.

Middletown

★7649★ Pennsylvania State University Harrisburg Capitol College
Women's Studies Program
777 W. Harrisburg Pike
Middletown, PA 17057-4898
Phone: (717)948-6250

Philadelphia

★7650★ Chestnut Hill College
Women's Studies Program
9601 Germantown Ave.
Philadelphia, PA 19118
Phone: (215)248-7001

★7651★ Drexel University
Women's Studies Program
McAlister Hall
33rd and Chestnut Sts.
Philadelphia, PA 19104
Phone: (215)895-2400
Ellen Rose, Contact

★7652★ LaSalle University
Women's Studies Program
20th and Olney Sts.
Philadelphia, PA 19141
Phone: (215)951-1161
Linda E. Merians, Contact
Undergraduate: Minor.

★7653★ St. Joseph's University
Women's Studies Program
5600 City Ave.
Philadelphia, PA 19131
Phone: (215)660-1000

★7654★ Temple University
Women's Studies Program
Gladfelter Hall
Broad St. 12 and Berks
Philadelphia, PA 19122-6954
Phone: (215)787-6753
Sherri Grasmuck, Contact
Undergraduate: Minor in Women's Studies. **Graduate:** Individualized major in Women's Studies. **Degree(s) Offered:** BA in Women's Studies.

★7655★ University of Pennsylvania
Women's Studies Program
3440 Market, Rm. 590
Philadelphia, PA 19104-3325
Phone: (215)898-8740
Demi Kurz, Contact
Undergraduate: Major, Minor. **Degree(s) Offered:** BA.

Pittsburgh

★7656★ Carlow College
Women's Studies Program
3333 Fifth Ave.
Pittsburgh, PA 15213
Phone: (412)578-6208
Ellie Wymard, Contact

Undergraduate: Minor. **Degree(s) Offered:** BA
Individualized Major.

★7657★ Community College of Allegheny
County, North Campus
Women's Studies
808 Ridge Ave.
Pittsburgh, PA 15212
Phone: (412)237-2627
Edna McKenzie, Contact

Undergraduate: Certificate.

★7658★ LaRoche College
Women's Studies Program
9000 Babcock Blvd.
Pittsburgh, PA 15237
Phone: (412)367-9241

★7659★ University of Pittsburgh
Women's Studies Program
2632 Cathedral of Learning
Pittsburgh, PA 15260
Phone: (412)624-6485
Susan Hansen, Contact

Undergraduate: Certificate. **Graduate:** Area of
Concentration.

Radnor

★7660★ Cabrini College
Women's Studies Program
610 King of Prussia
Radnor, PA 19087-3699
Phone: (215)971-8356
Kathleen Daley, Contact

Undergraduate: Area of Concentration. **Spe-**
cialization: Concentration under Sociology.

Scranton

★7661★ University of Scranton
Women's Studies Program
Scranton, PA 18510
Phone: (717)941-7400
Jean Harris, Contact

Shippensburg

★7662★ Shippensburg University of
Pennsylvania
Women's Studies Program
Shippensburg, PA 17257
Phone: (717)532-9121

Undergraduate: Minor.

Slippery Rock

★7663★ Slippery Rock University of
Pennsylvania
Women's Studies Program
B106 Bailey Library
Slippery Rock, PA 16057
Phone: (412)794-7451
Jace Condravy, Contact

Undergraduate: Minor, Certificate.

Swarthmore

★7664★ Swarthmore College
Women's Studies Program
500 College Ave.
Swarthmore, PA 19081-1397
Phone: (215)328-8135
Marjorie Murphy, Contact

Undergraduate: Area of Concentration. **Gradu-**
ate: Area of Concentration.

University Park

★7665★ Pennsylvania State University,
University Park
Women's Studies Program
13 Sparks Bldg.
University Park, PA 16802
Phone: (814)863-4025
Lynne Goodstein, Contact

Undergraduate: Major, Minor. **Graduate:** Department Minor. **Degree(s) Offered:** BA.

Villanova

★7666★ Villanova University
Women's Studies Program
Villanova, PA 19085
Phone: (215)645-4483
Dr. Barbara Wall, Contact

Graduate: MSA Concentration. **Degree(s) Of-**
fered: BA through interdisciplinary studies.

West Chester

★7667★ West Chester University of
Pennsylvania
Women's Studies Program
211 Main Hall
West Chester, PA 19383
Phone: (215)436-2464
Stacey Schlau, Contact

Undergraduate: Minor, Area of Concentration.
Graduate: Area of Concentration. **Degree(s)**
Offered: AA in Women 's Studies.

Wilkes-Barre

★7668★ Wilkes University
Women's Studies Program
Liberal Arts and Human Sciences
South River St.
PO Box 111
Wilkes-Barre, PA 18766
Phone: (717)824-4651
Patricia B. Heaman, Contact

Undergraduate: Minor.

Williamsport

★7669★ Lycoming College
Women's Studies Program
Williamsport, PA 17701
Phone: (717)321-4000
Emily R. Jensen, Contact

Undergraduate: Major, Minor.

Rhode Island

Kingston

★7670★ University of Rhode Island
Women's Studies Program
315 Roosevelt Hall
Kingston, RI 02881-0806
Phone: (401)792-5150
Fax: (401)792-2892
Mary Ellen Reilly, Contact

Undergraduate: Major, Minor, Area of Concentration. **Graduate:** Departmental Emphasis.

Providence

★7671★ Brown University
Women's Studies Program
Pembroke Center, Box 1958
Providence, RI 02912
Phone: (401)863-2643
Elizabeth Weed, Contact

Degree(s) Offered: BA.

★7672★ Johnson & Wales University
Women's Studies Program
8 Abbott Park Place
Providence, RI 02903
Phone: (401)456-1000
Nancy Jackson, Contact

★7673★ Providence College
Women's Studies Program
Sociology Department
Providence, RI 02918
Phone: (401)865-1000
Charlotte O'Kelly, Contact

★7674★ Rhode Island College
Women's Studies Program
600 Mt. Pleasant Ave.
Providence, RI 02908
Phone: (401)456-8377
Maureen T. Reddy, Contact

Undergraduate: Major, Minor, Area of Concentration. **Degree(s) Offered:** BA.

South Carolina

Charleston

★7675★ College of Charleston
Women's Studies Program
Philosophy Department
Charleston, SC 29424
Phone: (803)792-5687
June McDaniel, Contact

Undergraduate: Minor.

Clemson

★7676★ Clemson University
Women's Studies Program
Department of Language
Strode Tower
Clemson, SC 29634
Phone: (803)656-2287
Judith M. Melton, Contact

Undergraduate: Minor in Women's Studies.

Columbia

★7677★ Columbia College
Women's Studies Program
1301 Columbia College Dr.
Columbia, SC 29203
Phone: (803)786-3871
Lesley Diehl, Contact

★7678★ University of South Carolina
Women's Studies Program
1710 College St.
Columbia, SC 29208
Phone: (803)777-4007
Sue V. Rosser, Contact
Undergraduate: Major, Minor, Area of Concentration. **Graduate:** Certificate, Area of Concentration. **Degree(s) Offered:** BA.

Rock Hill

★7679★ Winthrop College
Women's Studies Program
Sociology Department
Rock Hill, SC 29733
Phone: (803)323-2181
Dr. April Gordon, Contact
Undergraduate: Minor.

South Dakota

Brookings

★7680★ South Dakota State University
Women's Studies Program
Political Science Department
Brookings, SD 57007
Phone: (605)688-4914
Eleanor A. Schwab, Contact
Undergraduate: Minor.

Vermillion

★7681★ University of South Dakota
Women's Studies Program
414 E. Clark St.
Vermillion, SD 57069
Phone: (605)677-5229
Fax: (605)677-5073
Susan Wolfe, Contact
Undergraduate: Minor, Area of Concentration. **Degree(s) Offered:** BA, BS, MS; MA Selected Studies.

Tennessee

Clarksville

★7682★ Austin Peay State University
Women's Studies Program
Clarksville, TN 37040
Phone: (615)648-7011
Betty Jo Wallace, Contact

Knoxville

★7683★ University of Tennessee, Knoxville
Women's Studies Program
2012 Lake Ave.
Knoxville, TN 37996-4102
Phone: (615)974-2409
Martha Lee Osborne, Contact
Undergraduate: Area of Concentration. **Degree(s) Offered:** BA in Women's Studies.

Memphis

★7684★ Memphis State University
Women's Studies Program
Department of History
Memphis, TN 38152
Phone: (901)678-2515
Margaret Caffrey, Contact
Undergraduate: Minor, individualized major in Women's Studies.

★7685★ Shelby State Community College
Women's Studies Program
PO Box 40568
Memphis, TN 38174-0568
Phone: (901)528-6700

★7686★ University of Tennessee, Memphis
Women's Studies Program
Memphis, TN 38163
Phone: (901)528-5560

Murfreesboro

★7687★ Middle Tennessee State University
Women's Studies Program
Box 498
Murfreesboro, TN 37132
Phone: (615)898-2645
Nancy Rupprecht, Contact
Undergraduate: Minor.

Nashville

★7688★ Fisk University
Women's Studies Program
1000 17th Ave. N.
Nashville, TN 37203
Phone: (615)329-8502

★7689★ Vanderbilt University
Women's Studies Program
Box 86, Sta. B
Nashville, TN 37235
Phone: (615)343-7808
Nancy Walker, Contact
Undergraduate: Minor.

Texas

Amarillo

★7690★ Amarillo College
Women's Programs
PO Box 447
Amarillo, TX 79178
Phone: (806)371-5450
Donna Moore, Contact

Arlington

★7691★ University of Texas at Arlington
Center for Women's Studies Program
Department of Psychology
Box 19529
Arlington, TX 76019-0529
Phone: (817)273-2861
Fax: (817)273-3392
Kathleen Underwood, Contact
Undergraduate: Area of Concentration. **Graduate:** Area of Concentration. **Specialization:** Interdisciplinary Studies.

Austin

★7692★ Austin Community College
Women's Studies Program
Social and Behavioral Sciences
PO Box 140707
Austin, TX 78714
Phone: (512)832-4729
E. Allen Poe, Contact

★7693★ University of Texas at Austin
Women's Studies Program
WMB 206B
Austin, TX 78712
Phone: (512)471-1122
Susan Marshall, Contact
Undergraduate: Minor, Area of Concentration.

College Station

★7694★ Texas A & M University
Women's Studies Program
217 CD Blocker Bldg.
College Station, TX 77843-4227
Phone: (409)845-9670
Harriette Andreadis, Contact
Undergraduate: Minor. **Graduate:** Departmental Emphasis.

Dallas

★7695★ Southern Methodist University
Women's Studies Program
Dallas Hall 227
Dallas, TX 75275
Phone: (214)692-2000
Caroline Brettell, Contact
Undergraduate: Minor.

Denton

★7696★ Texas Woman's University
Women's Studies Program
PO Box 23029
Denton, TX 76204
Phone: (817)898-2241
Jean Saul, Contact
Undergraduate: Area of Concentration, Minor.

El Paso

★7697★ **El Paso Community College**
Women's Studies Program
PO Box 20500
El Paso, TX 79998
Phone: (915)594-2595
Rebecca Moore, Contact

Undergraduate: Area of Concentration. **Degree(s) Offered:** AA through Psychology and English departments.

★7698★ **University of Texas at El Paso**
Women's Studies Program
401 Liberal Arts
University Ave.
El Paso, TX 79968
Phone: (915)747-5200
Sandra Beyer, Contact

Undergraduate: Area of Concentration.

Georgetown

★7699★ **Southwestern University**
Women's Studies Program
PO Box 770
Georgetown, TX 78626-0770
Phone: (512)863-6511
Fax: (512)863-5788
Mary Visser, Contact

Undergraduate: Major, Minor. **Degree(s) Offered:** BA.

Houston

★7700★ **Rice University**
Women's Studies Program
PO Box 1892
Houston, TX 77251
Phone: (713)527-8101
Helen Longino, Contact

Undergraduate: Minor.

★7701★ **University of Houston, Clear Lake**
Women's Studies Program
2700 Bay Area Blvd.
Houston, TX 77058
Phone: (713)283-3319
Fax: (713)488-2408
Cynthia Miller, Contact

Undergraduate: Area of Concentration. **Degree(s) Offered:** MA Concentration.

Lubbock

★7702★ **Texas Tech University**
Women's Studies Program
PO Box 4170
Lubbock, TX 79409-1162
Phone: (806)742-3001
Gwendolyn T. Sorell, Contact

Undergraduate: Minor. **Degree(s) Offered:** MA Concentration in Interdisciplinary Studies.

Nacogdoches

★7703★ **Stephen F. Austin State University**
Women's Studies Program
Nacogdoches, TX 75962
Phone: (409)568-4405
Joy B. Reeves, Contact

Undergraduate: Minor.

Richardson

★7704★ **University of Texas at Dallas**
Women's Studies Program
Box 688
Richardson, TX 75080
Phone: (214)690-2365
Nancy Tawana, Contact

Undergraduate: Area of Concentration. **Graduate:** Area of Concentration.

San Marcos

★7705★ **Southwest Texas State University**
Multicultural and Gender Studies
Flowers Hall
San Marcos, TX 78666
Phone: (512)245-2361
Fax: (512)245-3040
Lydia Blanchard, Contact

Undergraduate: Minor. **Graduate:** Minor.

Utah

Cedar City

★7706★ **Southern Utah State College**
Women's Resource Committee
Cedar City, UT 84720
Phone: (801)586-7740

Logan

★7707★ **Utah State University**
Women's Studies Committee
Logan, UT 84322-3510
Phone: (801)750-1256
Fax: (801)750-1240
Caryn Beck-Dudley, Contact

Undergraduate: Minor, Certificate.

Ogden

★7708★ **Weber State College**
Women in Higher Education
Ogden, UT 84408
Phone: (801)626-6000
Neila Seshachari, Contact

Povo

★7709★ **Brigham Young University**
Women's Studies Program
970 SWKT
Povo, UT 84602
Phone: (801)378-4636

Salt Lake City

★7710★ **University of Utah**
Women's Studies Program
217 Bldg. 44
Salt Lake City, UT 84112
Phone: (801)581-8094
Fax: (801)581-5580
Patty Reagan, Contact

Undergraduate: Major, Minor. **Graduate:** Concentration. **Degree(s) Offered:** BA/BS, AB. **Specialization:** Graduate Literary Criticism (English).

Vermont

Bennington

★7711★ **Bennington College**
Women's Resource Group
Bennington, VT 05201
Phone: (802)442-5401
Joan Goodrich, Contact

Undergraduate: Individualized Major.

Burlington

★7712★ **Burlington College**
Feminist Studies
95 N. Ave.
Burlington, VT 05401
Phone: (802)862-9616
Anna Blackner, Contact

Undergraduate: Major, Minor. **Degree(s) Offered:** BA.

★7713★ **Trinity College of Vermont**
Women's Studies Program
Colchester Ave.
Burlington, VT 05401
Phone: (802)658-0337
Barbara Davis Cheng, Contact

Degree(s) Offered: BA through Special Studies.

★7714★ **University of Vermont**
Women's Studies Program
Living and Learning Center
225 Commons
PO Box 14
Burlington, VT 05405-0348
Phone: (802)656-4282
Joan Smith, Contact

Undergraduate: Minor, Area of Concentration.

Marlboro

★7715★ **Marlboro College**
Women's Studies Program
Marlboro, VT 05344
Phone: (802)257-4333
Willene Clark, Contact

Degree(s) Offered: BA, BS, and MA in Women's Studies; undergraduate and graduate minors in Women's Studies; undergraduate and graduate areas of concentration in Women's Studies; undergraduate and graduate individualized majors in Women's Studies; Literature, History, American Studies, Theater, Art History, Sociology, Anthropology and Interdisciplinary Liberal Arts Departments offer BA and MA with emphasis in Women's Studies.

Middlebury

**★7716★ Middlebury College
Women's Studies Program**
Munroe Hall
Middlebury, VT 05753
Phone: (802)388-3711
Margaret K. Nelson, Contact
Undergraduate: Major, Area of Concentration.
Degree(s) Offered: BA.

Montpelier

**★7717★ Vermont College of Norwich
  University
Women's Studies Program**
College Street
Montpelier, VT
Phone: (802)485-2000
Rhoda Carroll, Contact

Plainfield

**★7718★ Goddard College
Feminist Studies**
Plainfield, VT 05667
Phone: (802)454-8311
Shelley Smith, Contact
Degree(s) Offered: BFA, MFA.

Virginia

Ashland

**★7719★ Randolph Macon College
Women's Studies Focus**
Henry St.
Ashland, VA 23005
Phone: (804)798-8372
Charlotte Fitzgerald, Contact
Undergraduate: Minor.

Blacksburg

**★7720★ Virginia Polytechnic Institute and
  State University
Women's Studies Program**
10 Sandy Hall
Blacksburg, VA 24061
Phone: (703)231-7615
Dr. Anne Killkelly, Contact
Undergraduate: Area of Concentration.

Charlottesville

**★7721★ University of Virginia
Women's Studies Program**
11 Miner Hall
Charlottesville, VA 22901
Phone: (804)982-2961
Ann J. Lane, Contact
Undergraduate: Area of Concentration. Individualized major in Women's Studies. **Degree(s)
Offered:** BA.

Fairfax

**★7722★ George Mason University
Women's Studies Program**
4400 University Dr.
Fairfax, VA 22030
Phone: (703)993-1000
Karen Rosenblum, Contact
Undergraduate: Minor.

Fredricksburg

**★7723★ Mary Washington College
Race and Gender Project**
Fredricksburg, VA 22401
Phone: (703)899-4117
Fax: (703)899-4373
Carole Corcoran, Contact
Undergraduate: Special Major.

Lynchburg

**★7724★ Randolph-Macon Woman's
  College
Women's Studies Program**
2500 Rivermont Ave.
Box 952
Lynchburg, VA 24503
Phone: (804)845-9583
Pamela Quaggiotto, Contact
Undergraduate: Minor.

Norfolk

**★7725★ Old Dominion University
Women's Studies Program**
Hampton Blvd.
Norfolk, VA 23529
Phone: (804)683-3823
Fax: (804)683-3241
Anita Clair Fellman, Contact
Undergraduate: Major, Minor, Certificate.
Graduate: MA Departmental Emphasis Certificate. **Degree(s) Offered:** BA, BS, MA, MS.

Richmond

**★7726★ University of Richmond
Women's Studies Program**
Richmond, VA 23173
Phone: (804)289-8307
Suzanne W. Jones, Contact
Undergraduate: Major, Minor. **Degree(s) Offered:** BA, BS.

**★7727★ Virginia Commonwealth University
Women's Studies Program**
Box 2040
Richmond, VA 23284
Phone: (804)367-6641
Diana Scully, Contact
Undergraduate: Minor.

Stuanton

**★7728★ Mary Baldwin College
Women's Studies Program**
Stuanton, VA 24401
Phone: (703)887-7000
Fax: (703)886-5561
Martha Noel Evans, Contact
Undergraduate: Minor; Independent Major.

Washington

Bellingham

**★7729★ Western Washington University
Women's Studies**
Bellingham, WA 98225
Phone: (206)676-3680
Kathryn Anderson, Contact
Undergraduate: Minor in Women's Studies.

Cheney

**★7730★ Eastern Washington University
Women's Studies Program**
MS 166
Cheney, WA 99004
Phone: (509)359-2409
Fax: (509)359-6927
Lee Swedberg, Contact
Undergraduate: Minor. **Graduate:** Courses.

Ellensburg

**★7731★ Central Washington University
Women's Studies Program**
Ellensburg, WA 98926
Phone: (509)963-1858
Christine Sutphin, Contact
Undergraduate: Minor.

Everett

**★7732★ Everett Community College
Women's Programs**
801 Wetmore Ave.
Everett, WA 98201
Phone: (206)388-9292

Lynwood

**★7733★ Edmonds Community College
Women's Programs**
Lynwood, WA 98036
Phone: (206)672-6309
Ruth McCormick, Contact

Mt. Vernon

**★7734★ Skagit Valley College
Women's Program**
2405 College Way
Mt. Vernon, WA 98221
Phone: (206)428-1135
Linda Woiwod, Contact

Olympia

**★7735★ The Evergreen State College
Women's Studies Program**
Library 2211
Olympia, WA 98505
Phone: (206)866-6000
Pris Bowerman, Contact
Undergraduate: Area of Concentration. **Degree(s) Offered:** BA.

Pullman

★7736★ **Washington State University**
Women's Studies Program
Pullman, WA 99164-4171
Phone: (509)335-1794
Fax: (509)335-4032
Jo Hockenhull, Contact

Undergraduate: Minor. **Graduate:** Minor.

Seattle

★7737★ **Shoreline Community College**
Women's Program
16101 Greenwood Ave. N.
Seattle, WA 98133
Phone: (206)546-4676
Fax: (206)546-4599
Dianne Dailey, Contact

★7738★ **University of Washington**
Women's Studies Program
GN-45
Seattle, WA 98195
Phone: (206)543-6900
Sydney J. Kaplan, Contact

Undergraduate: Major. **Degree(s) Offered:** BA (General Studies with a Women's Studies Major).

Spokane

★7739★ **Gonzaga University**
Women's Studies Program
Spokane, WA 99258
Phone: (509)484-6484

Undergraduate: Minor.

Tacoma

★7740★ **Pacific Lutheran University**
Women's Studies Program
Tacoma, WA 98447
Phone: (206)535-8744
Fax: (206)535-8320
Elizabeth Brusco, Contact

Undergraduate: Minor, Area of Concentration. **Degree(s) Offered:** BA-Individualized Major for Special Honors, MA in Social Sciences-Individualized Study.

★7741★ **Tacoma Community College**
Women's Studies Program
5900 S. Twelfth St.
Tacoma, WA 98456
Phone: (206)566-5000
Lee Morrison, Contact

★7742★ **University of Puget Sound**
Women's Studies Program
Tacoma, WA 98416
Phone: (206)756-3431
Fax: (206)756-3500
Nancy Bristow, Contact

Undergraduate: Minor.

Vancouver

★7743★ **Clark College**
Women's Studies Program
1800 E. McLoughlin Blvd.
Vancouver, WA 98663
Phone: (206)694-6521
Pat Watne, Contact

Walla Walla

★7744★ **Whitman College**
Women's Studies Program
Walla Walla, WA 99362
Phone: (509)527-5111

Yakima

★7745★ **Yakima Valley Community College**
Women's Studies Program
PO Box 1647
Yakima, WA 98907
Phone: (509)575-2915
Mary Doherty Kowalsky, Contact

Undergraduate: Area of Concentration.

West Virginia

Bethany

★7746★ **Bethany College**
Women's Studies Program
Bethany, WV 26032
Phone: (304)829-7611
Lenora Balla Cayard, Contact

Huntington

★7747★ **Marshall University**
Women's Studies Program
Huntington, WV 25701
Phone: (304)696-3170
Dee Cockrille, Contact

Morgantown

★7748★ **West Virginia University**
Women's Studies Program
218 Eiesland Hall
Morgantown, WV 26506
Phone: (304)293-2339
Dr. Lillian Waugh, Contact

Undergraduate: Certificate. **Degree(s) Offered:** MA in Liberal Studies with a Concentration in Women's Studies.

Wisconsin

Appleton

★7749★ **Lawrence University**
Gender Studies
Appleton, WI 54912
Phone: (414)832-7000
Anne Schutte, Contact

Undergraduate: Area of Concentration. **Specialization:** Interdisciplinary Area in Gender Studies that functions like a minor.

Beloit

★7750★ **Beloit College**
Women's Studies Program
700 College St.
Beloit, WI 53511
Phone: (608)363-2000
Fax: (608)365-0806
Diane Lichtenstein, Contact

Undergraduate: Minor. **Specialization:** Individually constructed Major.

Cleveland

★7751★ **Lakeshore Technical College**
Women's Studies Program
Cleveland, WI 53015
Phone: (414)458-4180
Dr. Elaine Hedges, Chairperson

Degree(s) Offered: AA in Women's Studies.

Eau Claire

★7752★ **University of Wisconsin—Eau Claire**
Women's Studies Program
Eau Claire, WI 54701
Phone: (715)836-5717
Fax: (715)836-2380
Sarah Harder, Contact

Undergraduate: Minor.

Green Bay

★7753★ **University of Wisconsin—Green Bay**
Women's Studies Program
2420 Nicolet Dr.
Green Bay, WI 54311-7001
Phone: (414)465-2355
Julie Brickley, Contact

Undergraduate: Minor, Area of Concentration. **Degree(s) Offered:** AA in Women's Studies.

Kenosha

★7754★ **University of Wisconsin—Parkside**
Women's Studies Program
Kenosha, WI 53141
Phone: (414)595-2162
Frank Kavenik, Contact

Undergraduate: Minor.

La Crosse

★7755★ **University of Wisconsin—La Crosse**
Women's Studies Program
336 North Hall
La Crosse, WI 54601
Phone: (608)785-8357
Sondra O'Neal, Contact

Undergraduate: Minor.

★7756★ **Viterbo College**
Women's Studies Program
815 S. 9th St.
La Crosse, WI 54601
Phone: (608)791-0040
Sandra Krajewski, Contact

Undergraduate: Minor.

Madison

★7757★ **Edgewood College**
Women's Studies Program
855 Woodrow St.
Madison, WI 53711
Phone: (608)257-4861
Fax: (608)257-1455
Esther Heffernan, Contact

Undergraduate: Minor; individualized Major.

★7758★ Madison Area Technical College
Women's Studies Program
3550 Anderson St.
Madison, WI 53704
Phone: (608)246-6250
Fax: (608)246-6644
Sara Sherkow, Contact
Undergraduate: Area of Concentration.

★7759★ University of Wisconsin—Madison
Women's Studies Program
209 North Brooks St.
Madison, WI 53715
Phone: (608)263-4703
Fax: (608)263-6448
Betsy Draine, Contact
Undergraduate: Individualized major in Women's Studies; Major, Certificate. **Graduate:** Minor, Departmental Emphasis; individualized Major in Women's Studies; Minor (PhD) in Women's Studies. **Degree(s) Offered:** BA in Women's Studies; History department offers MA in Women's History.

Menomonie

★7760★ University of Wisconsin—Stout
Women's Studies Program
School of Liberal Studies
Menomonie, WI 54751
Phone: (715)232-1122
Sharon Nero, Contact
Undergraduate: Minor.

Milwaukee

★7761★ Marquette University
Women's Studies Program
Marquette University
Milwaukee, WI 53233
Phone: (414)288-1430
Rebecca Bardwell, Contact
Undergraduate: Minor/Major.

★7762★ University of Wisconsin—Milwaukee
Center for Women's Studies
PO Box 413
Milwaukee, WI 53201
Phone: (414)229-5918
Merry Wiesner-Hanks, Contact
Specialization: Certificate.

Oshkosh

★7763★ University of Wisconsin—Oshkosh
Women's Studies Program
Oshkosh, WI 54901
Phone: (414)424-0384
Eleanor Amico, Contact
Undergraduate: Minor.

Platteville

★7764★ University of Wisconsin—Platteville
Women's Studies Program
446 Gardner Hall
Platteville, WI 53818
Phone: (608)342-1750
Helen Tierney, Contact
Undergraduate: Major-Individually constructed, Minor Certificate. **Degree(s) Offered:** BA/BS.

Ripon

★7765★ Ripon College
Women's Studies Program
300 Seward St.
Ripon, WI 54971
Phone: (414)748-8131
Vance Cope-Kasten, Contact
Undergraduate: Minor.

River Falls

★7766★ University of Wisconsin—River Falls
Women's Studies Program
Cascade Ave.
River Falls, WI
Phone: (715)425-3115
Meg Swenson, Contact
Undergraduate: Minor.

Sheboygan

★7767★ Lakeland College
Women's Studies Program
Sheboygan, WI
Phone: (414)565-2111
Patricia Bonnet, Contact

Stevens Point

★7768★ University of Wisconsin—Stevens Point
Women's Studies Program
English Department - WWSP
Stevens Point, WI 54481
Phone: (715)346-4347
Katherine Ackley, Contact
Undergraduate: Minor.

Superior

★7769★ University of Wisconsin—Superior
Women's Studies Program
Superior, WI 54880
Phone: (715)394-8101
Delores Harms, Contact
Undergraduate: Minor.

Waukesha

★7770★ Carroll College
Women's Studies Program
Waukesha, WI 53186
Phone: (414)547-1211
Lori Kelly, Contact
Undergraduate: Minor.

Whitewater

★7771★ University of Wisconsin—Whitewater
Women's Studies Program
423 Heide Hall
Whitewater, WI 53190
Phone: (414)472-1042
Aubrey Roberts, Contact
Undergraduate: Major, Minor, Certificate. **Degree(s) Offered:** BA, BS.

Wyoming

Casper

★7772★ Casper College
Women's Studies Program
125 College Dr.
Casper, WY 82601
Phone: (307)268-2491
Carolyn Logan, Contact
Specialization: 2-year Major with Liberal Arts Option.

Laramie

★7773★ University of Wyoming
Women's Studies Program
PO Box 4297
Laramie, WY 82071
Phone: (307)766-6870
Patricia Taylor, Contact
Undergraduate: Minor.

(11) Scholarships, Fellowships, and Loans

Entries in this chapter are arranged alphabetically by program name. See the User's Guide at the front of this directory for additional information.

★7774★ AAUW American Fellowships
American Association of University Women—
Educational Foundation (AAUW)
1111 16th St. NW
Washington, DC 20006
Phone: (202)728-7603
Fax: (202)872-1425

Study Level: Doctorate, Postdoctorate. **Award Type:** Fellowship. **Applicant Eligibility:** Applicants must be women who are citizens or permanent residents of the United States. There are no restrictions on the place of study or age of the applicant. A postdoctoral fellowship candidate must hold a doctoral degree at the time of application. Scholars in any field of study may apply. One fellowship is designated for a woman from an underrepresented minority group. Dissertation fellowships are for women who are in the final year of writing their dissertation. Applicants must have successfully completed all required course work, passed all preliminary examinations, and have their dissertation research proposal (or plan) approved by November 15 of the year of application. Applicants are expected to receive a doctoral degree at the end of the fellowship year. The fellowship is not intended to fund extended field research. Students holding a fellowship for the purpose of writing a dissertation the year before the AAUW fellowship year are ineligible. This category is open to applicants in all fields of study except engineering. **Selection Criteria:** Selection is based primarily on scholarly excellence of applicants' proposals, and their commitment to helping women through service in their community, profession, and/or field of research. **Funds Available:** Nine postdoctoral fellowships ranging from $20,000 to $25,000. Dissertation fellowships of $12,500 each. **Application Details:** American Fellowships (postdoctoral and dissertation) applications are available from August 1 through November 1. Applicants may apply up to 2 times for a dissertation fellowship on the same topic. **Application Deadline:** November 15. Fellowship year starts July 1.

★7775★ AAUW Career Development Grants
American Association of University Women—
Wilmington, Delaware Branch (AAUW)
1800 Fairfax Blvd.
Wilmington, DE 19803

Study Level: Doctorate, Graduate, Professional Development. **Award Type:** Grant. **Applicant Eligibility:** Grants are awarded to women who, through higher education, are reentering the work force, making a career change, or advanc-

ing their current career. Applicants must be U.S. citizens or permanent residents who hold a baccalaureate degree; have received their most recent degree on or before June 30, 1986; plan to pursue course work at a fully accredited two- or four-year college or university or at a technical school that is licensed, accredited, or approved by the federal Veteran's Administration; and enroll in courses that are prerequisites for professional employment plans. Candidates who fulfill eligibility requirements for other fellowship programs offered by the AAUW Educational Foundation will not be considered for Career Development Grants. Minority women are encouraged to apply. **Selection Criteria:** Special consideration is given to qualified AAUW members, and preference is given to applicants pursuing course work that will prepare them for careers that are nontraditional for women. **Funds Available:** Non-renewable $1,000 to $5,000 grants provide for tuition, books, transportation (to/from/at school), and dependent care. Funds are not available for the final year of terminal professional degree programs (i.e., M.B.A., J.D., M.D). Doctoral students may apply for funding only for course work, not for dissertation research or writing. **Application Deadline:** Postmarked by January 1. **Contact(s):** AAUW Educational Foundation, 1111 16th St., NW, Washington, D.C.; (202)872-1430.

★7776★ AAUW Career Development Grants
American Association of University Women—
Educational Foundation (AAUW)
1111 16th St. NW
Washington, DC 20006
Phone: (202)728-7603
Fax: (202)872-1425

Study Level: Professional Development. **Award Type:** Grant. **Purpose:** To prepare women for re-entry into the work force, career changes, or career advancement. **Applicant Eligibility:** Candidates must hold a baccalaureate degree and have completed their most recent degree no more than five years prior to the award year. Applicants must be U.S. citizens or permanent residents. Candidates must plan to pursue course work at a fully-accredited 2- or 4-year college or university or at a technical school that is licensed, accredited, or approved by the Veteran's Administration. Applicants must enroll in courses that are prerequisites for professional employment plans. **Selection Criteria:** Candidates for grants who seek to enter nontraditional career fields receive preference. Special consideration is given to AAUW members.

Minority students are encouraged to apply. **Funds Available:** These are seed money grants (not full funding grants) ranging from $1,000 to $5,000. **Application Details:** Application forms must be requested from the AAUW between August 1 and December 15. **Application Deadline:** Completed applications must be filed by January 1. Applicants are notified by April 15.

★7777★ AAUW Community Action Grants
American Association of University Women—
Educational Foundation (AAUW)
1111 16th St. NW
Washington, DC 20006
Phone: (202)728-7603
Fax: (202)872-1425

Study Level: Other. **Award Type:** Grant. **Purpose:** To provide seed money to AAUW branches or divisions or to individual women for nondegree research or other projects that address the contemporary needs of women and girls or provide information to educate and benefit the public on those issues. **Applicant Eligibility:** Applicants must be U.S. citizens or permanent residents; project directors must hold a baccalaureate degree; proposed activity must have direct community or public impact and support the advancement of education and equity for women and girls; proposals from AAUW branches and divisions must be approved and signed by the branch or division president. Applicants conducting nondegree research or preparing literary work for publication that is in the public interest are also eligible. **Funds Available:** Grants between $500 to $5,000 are awarded for office and mailing expenses, promotional materials, honoraria, and transportation costs. Unsuccessful proposals may be resubmitted; however a branch, division, or individual may reapply only once for funding for the same project. **Application Deadline:** Postmark deadlines are February 1 and September 1 for winter and fall terms respectively. Notifications are made by April 15 and November 15 for respective terms.

★7778★ AAUW Dissertation Fellowships in Engineering
American Association of University of
Women—Educational Foundation (AAUW)
1111 16th St. NW
Washington, DC 20006
Phone: (202)728-7603
Fax: (202)872-1425

Study Level: Doctorate. **Award Type:** Fellowship. **Applicant Eligibility:** Awarded to women who are citizens or permanent residents of the

United States and who will complete all required course work and have passed all preliminary exams by November 15. Dissertation research proposals should be approved by the November 15 deadline or, at the latest, by December 15. Doctoral degree is expected at the end of the fellowship year. Students holding any fellowship for the purpose of writing a dissertation in the year prior to the AAUW fellowship year are ineligible. **Selection Criteria:** Special consideration will be given to applicants who demonstrate professional promise in innovative or neglected areas of research and/or practice, public interest concerns, or those specialties in which women remain underrepresented. **Funds Available:** Fellowships stipends are $12,500 each for full-time work on the dissertation. **Application Details:** Applications available August 1 - November 1. Application form requests must be received by the Fellowship at least two weeks before the deadline. Candidates may request only one application and apply for only one fellowship. **Application Deadline:** November 15. Fellowship year starts on July 1.

★7779★ **AAUW Focus Professions Fellowships**
American Association of University Women— Educational Foundation (AAUW)
111 16th St. NW
Washington, DC 20006
Phone: (202)728-7603
Fax: (202)872-1425

Study Level: Graduate. **Award Type:** Fellowship. **Applicant Eligibility:** Awarded to minority women who are citizens or permanent residents of the United States and who are graduate professional degree candidates completing their final year of study in the fellowship year in the fields of business administration, law, or medicine. **Selection Criteria:** Special consideration will be given to applicants who demonstrate professional promise in innovative or neglected areas of research and/or practice, areas of public interest, or those specialties in which women remain underrepresented. **Funds Available:** Fellowships stipends range from $5,000 to $9,500 for full-time study. **Application Details:** Applications available August 1 - December 1 (except M.B.A.); August 1 - December 15 (M.B.A. only). **Application Deadline:** December 15; February 1 (M.B.A. only).

★7780★ **AAUW Science/Technology Fellowships**
American Association of University of Women—Educational Foundation (AAUW)
1111 16th St. NW
Washington, DC 20006
Phone: (202)728-7603
Fax: (202)872-1425

Study Level: Graduate. **Award Type:** Fellowship. **Applicant Eligibility:** Awarded to women who are citizens or permanent residents of the United States for the final year of a master's degree program (including one-year programs) in architecture, computer information science, engineering, mathematics/statistics. **Selection Criteria:** Special consideration will be given to applicants who demonstrate professional promise in innovative or neglected areas of research and/or practice, areas of public interest, or those specialties in which women remain underrepresented. **Funds Available:** Fellowships stipends range from $5,000 to $9,500 for full-time study. **Application Details:** Applications available August 1 - December 1. **Application Deadline:** December 15.

★7781★ **AAUW Travelships**
American Association of University Women— Educational Foundation (AAUW)
1111 16th St. NW
Washington, DC 20006
Phone: (202)728-7603
Fax: (202)872-1425

Applicant Eligibility: Applicants must be AAUW members who can demonstrate an appropriate interest or expertise. Candidates must plan to attend the IFUW Triennial Conference for the benefit of her branch and community. **Funds Available:** Awards are based on applicant's one-way mileage. **Application Details:** One Application per triennium year may be submitted by an AAUW member.

★7782★ **ACLS Fellowships**
American Council of Learned Societies (ACLS)
228 E. 45th St.
New York, NY 10017-3398
Phone: (212)697-1505
Fax: (212)949-8058

Study Level: Postdoctorate. **Award Type:** Fellowship. **Purpose:** To help scholars devote 6 to 12 continuous months to full-time research. **Applicant Eligibility:** Candidates must hold the Ph.D. or its equivalent as of the application deadline date. They must be United States citizens or permanent legal residents of the United States. Three years must have elapsed between the conclusion of the last supported research leave and July 1 of fellowship year. **Selection Criteria:** Applications are particularly invited from women and members of minority groups. Younger scholars and independent scholars who do not hold academic appointments are also encouraged to apply. **Funds Available:** Fellowships do not exceed $20,000 and are intended primarily as salary replacement for the provision of time free for research. The ACLS Fellowship stipend, plus any sabbatical salary and other grants, may not exceed the candidate's normal academic year salary. **Application Details:** Individuals must request application forms in writing and provide the following information: highest academic degree held and date received; country of citizenship or permanent legal residence; academic or other position; field of specialization; proposed subject of research or study; proposed date for beginning tenure of the award and duration requested; specific award program for which application is requested. **Application Deadline:** Completed application forms must be postmarked no later than October 1. Decisions are announced in late February. Fellowships are tenable during 6-12 months between July 1 of the award year and December 31 of the following year. **Contact(s):** Office of Fellowships and Grants.

★7783★ **ACLS Grants for East European Studies—Dissertation Fellowships**
American Council of Learned Societies (ACLS)
228 E 45th St.
New York, NY 10017-3398
Phone: (212)697-1505
Fax: (212)949-8058

Study Level: Doctorate. **Award Type:** Fellowship. **Applicant Eligibility:** Applications must be doctoral candidates. Dissertation research and writing may be undertaken at any university or institution outside of East Europe. Applicants must be United States citizens or permanent

legal residents of the United States. Three years must have elapsed between the conclusion of the last supported research leave and July 1 of Fellowship year. These programs are not intended to support research within East Europe. **Selection Criteria:** Applications are particularly invited from women and members of minority groups. Younger scholars and independent scholars who do not hold academic appointments are also encouraged to apply. Fellows will be selected on the basis of the scholarly merit of the proposal, its importance to the development of East European studies, and the scholarly potential, accomplishments, and financial need of the applicants. **Funds Available:** Stipends are up to $12,000 plus expenses per year. Candidates may apply initially for support for one year, with reapplication for a second year. **Application Details:** Individuals must request application forms in writing and provide the following information: highest academic degree held and date received; country of citizenship or permanent legal residence; academic or other position; field of specialization; proposed subject of research or study; proposed date for beginning tenure of the award and duration requested; specific award program for which application is requested. **Application Deadline:** Completed application forms must be postmarked no later than November 15. Decisions are announced in early May. **Contact(s):** Office of Fellowships and Grants.

★7784★ **ACLS Grants for East European Studies—East European Language Training Grants**
American Council of Learned Societies (ACLS)
228 E 45th St.
New York, NY 10017-3398
Phone: (212)697-1505
Fax: (212)949-8058

Study Level: Undergraduate, Graduate, Postdoctorate. **Award Type:** Grant. **Purpose:** To support summer language training for students and scholars who cannot receive such training in their home institution. **Applicant Eligibility:** Advanced undergraduates, graduate students, and postdoctoral scholars are eligible to apply. They must be United States citizens or permanent legal residents of the United States. Three years must have elapsed between the conclusion of the last supported research leave and July 1 of the fellowship year. **Selection Criteria:** Applications are particularly invited from women and members of minority groups. Younger scholars and independent scholars who do not hold academic appointments are also encouraged to apply. **Funds Available:** Grants of $2,000 each will be offered for the first-or second-year of study of any East European language (except the Russian language). Grants of $2,500 each will be offered for intermediate or advanced training in these languages in Eastern Europe. Grants of $7,500 will be offered to support instruction in certain of the least commonly taught East European languages at summer programs in the U.S. One award each will be for instruction in Czech and in Hungarian. One award will be for instruction in either Albanian, Bulgarian, Macedonian, Romanian, Slovak. or Slovenian. Both schools willing to offer these languages and teachers of them will be eligible to apply. **Application Details:** Individuals must request application forms in writing and provide the following information: highest academic degree held and date received; country of citizenship or permanent legal residence; academic or other position; field of specialization; proposed subject of research or study; proposed date for beginning tenure of the award and duration requested; specific award program for which application is requested. **Application Deadline: d Completed application forms must be postmarked no later than March 1. Contact(s):** Office of Fellowships and Grants.

★7785★ ACLS Grants for East European Studies—Fellowships for Advanced Graduate Training
American Council for Learned Studies (ACLS)
228 E 45th St.
New York, NY 10017-3398
Phone: (212)697-1505
Fax: (212)949-8058

Study Level: Doctorate. **Award Type:** Fellowship. **Applicant Eligibility:** Candidates must be graduate students currently enrolled in a degree program who will have completed at least two years of work toward the doctorate by June 30 of the fellowship year. They are intended for students who need extra training before beginning their dissertation because of the difficulties of combining area studies with work in a discipline. They must be United States citizens or permanent legal residents of the United States. Three years must have elapsed between the conclusion of the last supported research leave and July 1 of Fellowship year. All proposals should be for scholarly work, the product of which is to be disseminated in English. These programs are not intended to support research within East Europe. **Selection Criteria:** Applications are particularly invited from women and members of minority groups. Younger scholars and independent scholars who do not hold academic appointments are also encouraged to apply. Fellows will be selected on the basis of the scholarly merit of the proposal, its importance to the development of East European studies, and the scholarly potential, accomplishments, and financial need of the applicants. **Funds Available:** Stipends of up to $10,000 plus expenses. **Application Details:** Individuals must request application forms in writing and provide the following information: highest academic degree held and date received; country of citizenship or permanent legal residence; academic or other position; field of specialization; proposed subject of research or study; proposed date for beginning tenure of the award and duration requested; specific award program for which application is requested. **Application Deadline:** Completed application forms must be postmarked no later than November 15. Decisions are announced in early May. **Contact(s):** Office of Fellowships and Grants. en

★7786★ ACLS Grants for East European Studies—Fellowships for Postdoctoral Research
American Council of Learned Societies (ACLS)
228 E 45th St.
New York, NY 10017-3398
Phone: (212)697-1505
Fax: (212)949-8058

Study Level: Postdoctorate. **Award Type:** Fellowship. **Purpose:** To enable scholars to undertake a period of at least six consecutive months of full-time research. **Applicant Eligibility:** Candidates must hold a Ph.D. or its equivalent as of the application deadline date. They must be United States citizens or permanent legal resi-

dents of the United States. Three years must have elapsed between the conclusion of the last supported research leave and July 1 of Fellowship year. All proposals should be for scholarly work, the product of which is to be disseminated in English. These programs are not intended to support research with East Europe. In special circumstances untenured scholars or younger independent scholars without an academic appointment may apply for support to be used over any period of one to three years. **Selection Criteria:** Applications are particularly invited from women and members of minority groups. Younger scholars and independent scholars who do not hold academic appointments are also encouraged to apply. Fellows will be selected on the basis of the scholarly merit of the proposal, its importance to the development of East Europe studies, and the scholarly potential, accomplishments, and financial need of the applicants. **Funds Available:** Stipends of up to $25,000 are intended primarily as salary replacement to provide time for free research; the funds may be used to supplement sabbatical salaries or awards from other sources, provided they would intensify or extend the contemplated research. **Application Details:** Individuals must request application forms in writing and provide the following information: highest academic degree held and date received; country of citizenship or permanent legal residence; academic or other position; field of specialization; proposed subject of research or study; proposed date for beginning tenure of the award and duration requested; specific award program for which application is requested. **Application Deadline:** Completed application forms must be postmarked no later than November 15. Decisions are announced in early May. Fellowships are tenable during 6-12 months between July 1 and September 1. **Contact(s):** Office of Fellowships and Grants.

★7787★ ACLS Grants-in-Aid
American Council of Learned Societies (ACLS)
228 E. 45th St.
New York, NY 10017-3398
Phone: (212)697-1505
Fax: (212)949-8058

Study Level: Postdoctorate. **Award Type:** Grant. **Purpose:** To assist scholars with the expenses of specific programs of research. **Applicant Eligibility:** Candidates must hold the Ph.D. or its equivalent as of the application deadline date. They must be United States citizens or permanent legal residents of the United States. For ACLS Fellowship, three years must have elapsed between the conclusion of the last supported research leave and July 1 of Fellowship year. **Selection Criteria:** Applications are particularly invited from women and members of minority groups. Younger scholars and independent scholars who do not hold academic appointments are also encouraged to apply. **Funds Available:** Grants will not exceed $3,000 and may be used for personal travel and maintenance away from home necessary to gain access to materials. Awards for living expenses at home to relieve the applicant of the necessity of teaching beyond the conventional academic year will be made only in exceptional cases. Grants are not ordinarily made for the purchase of personal computers, books, or other non-expendable materials. **Application Details:** Individuals must request application forms in writing and provide the following information: highest academic degree held and date received; country of citizenship or

permanent legal residence; academic or other position; field of specialization; proposed subject of research or study; proposed date for which application is requested. **Application Deadline:** Completed application form must be postmarked by November 1. Decisions are announced in late April. Fellowships are tenable during a 12-month period starting May 1. **Contact(s):** Office of Fellowships and Grants.

★7788★ ACLS Grants for Latin American Studies—Doctoral Research Fellowships
American Council of Learned Societies (ACLS)
228 E 45th St.
New York, NY 10017-3398
Phone: (212)697-1505
Fax: (212)949-8058

Study Level: Doctorate. **Award Type:** Fellowship. **Applicant Eligibility:** Candidates must be enrolled in full-time graduate study at a university in the United States, and have all Ph.D. requirements, except the dissertation, before going to the field. There are no citizenship requirements. Fellowships are offered for doctoral dissertation research in the social sciences and the humanities. Proposals on any topic are eligible for support, including projects comparing Latin American or Caribbean Countries to others located outside this region. Recipients of fellowships are expected to devote a minimum of 9 and a maximum of 18 months to field research in the country or countries relevant to their proposals. While abroad, fellows are required to affiliate with a university, research institute, or another appropriate institution in the country where they will be conductiong research. Support for dissertation write-up is available for up to 6 months after return from the field. **Selection Criteria:** Applications are particularly invited from women and members of minority groups. Younger scholars and independent scholars who do not hold academic appointments are also encouraged to apply. **Application Details:** Individuals must request application forms in writing and provide the following information: university and department affiliation; date of completion of all requirements except the dissertation; brief statement of the dissertation topic; and proposed site of research. **Application Deadline:** The deadline for receipt of application is November 1 and decisions are announced on April 1. Research supported by the program must begin by January 1. **Contact(s):** Latin American and Caribbean Program, Social Science Research Council, 605 3rd Ave., New York, NY 10158.

★7789★ ACLS Grants for Latin American Studies—Advanced Grants Competition
American Council of Learned Societies (ACLS)
228 E 45th St.
New York, NY 10017-3398
Phone: (212)697-1505
Fax: (212)949-8058

Study Level: Postdoctorate. **Award Type:** Grant. **Purpose:** To support research in the social sciences and humanities for all aspects of the societies and cultures of Latin America or the Caribbean. **Applicant Eligibility:** Candidates must hold Ph.D. degree or another degree suitable for a university career, or completed work equivalent to a doctoral dissertation. No repeat postdoctoral awards are granted. There are no citizenship requirements. Research proposals on any topic are eligible for support including projects involving more than one area or country in Latin American or the Caribbean. Comparative projects dealing with Latin American and non-Latin American country are also accepted. Collaborative advanced grants are also awarded to 2 scholars of approximately equal scholarly attainment who wish to collaborate on a research project. For collaborative awards, each researcher must meet the eligibility requirements. One of the collaborators must be a citizen of a Latin American or the Caribbean country, the other may hold any citizenship. If both are citizens of the same Latin American or Caribbean country, they must propose to do research in another country. Advanced grants support individual scholars for a minimum of 2 and maximum of 12 months of research. Regardless of the length of the grant period, grantees are expected to devote all or a major part of the time to research. **Selection Criteria:** Applications are particularly invited from women and members of minority groups. Younger scholars and independent scholars who do not hold academic appointments are also encouraged to apply. **Funds Available:** Individual grants of up to $15,000. Grants may not be used for the following; course work; revision of doctoral dissertations; preparation of texbooks, anthologies, dictionaries, translations, or abstracts; editing or publication of manuscripts; completion of course requirements for a degree; nor for travel to meetings or conferences. **Application Details:** Individuals must request application forms in writing and provide the following information: university, discipline, and date of Ph.D. or equivalent degree; current affiliation and position; brief statement of the proposed research project; and proposed site of research, if travel is involved. For collaborative awards, two individual application forms must be completed, even if the proposal is the same. **Application Deadline:** The deadline for receipt of applications is December 1. **Contact(s):** Latin American and Caribbean Program, Social Science Research Council, 605 3rd Ave., New York, NY 10158.

★7790★ **Air Products and Chemicals, Inc. Scholarship**
Society of Women Engineers (SWE)
United Engineering Center, Rm. 305
345 E. 47th St.
New York, NY 10017
Phone: (212)705-7855

Study Level: Undergraduate. **Award Type:** Scholarship. **Applicant Eligibility:** Applicants must be women junior or sophomore students majoring in chemical engineering. Applicants must be United States citizens, preferably members of ethnic minorities. **Funds Available:** One $1,000 award. **Application Details:** Scholarship information and applications are sent to the deans of accredited engineering schools in October and March of each year. Applications and information can be obtained from the dean of engineering or from the SWE Headquarters in New York. Requests to SWE Headquarters must be accompanied by a self-addressed, stamped envelope. Applications are available from October through January only. **Application Deadline:** Completed applications, including all supportive materials, must be postmarked no later than February 1. Recipient only will be notified by May 1.

★7791★ **Alexandra Apostolides Sonenfeld Award**
Daughters of Penelope
AHEPA Senior Women's Auxiliary
1909 Q St., NW, Ste. 500
Washington, DC 20009

Study Level: Undergraduate. **Award Type:** Scholarship. **Applicant Eligibility:** Candidate must be a female high school graduate or an undergraduate at the college level and must be of Greek descent, or related to an AHEPAN or a Daughter of Penelope, or be a member of the Maids of Athena. She must be sponsored by her local or nearest Daughters of Penelope chapter; if there is no Daughters of Penelope chapter, the local or nearest Order of AHEPA chapter may sponsor the candidate and endorse the application. Applicants must be residents of the United States, Canada, Greece or wherever there is an established Daughters of Penelope chapter in good standing. **Selection Criteria:** Scholarships are awarded according to merit, without regard to other scholarships an applicant may receive. Financial need is also considered. **Funds Available:** $1,000 per scholarship. Scholarships are renewable for up to three years at rate of $300-$500. **Application Details:** Applications must be accompanied by the recommendation of the principal or counselor of the high school the candidate attended or the dean of the college she is attending, SAT or ACT results, and high school transcript. In addition, all applicants must submit a Parents' Confidential Statement or Financial Aid Form. **Application Deadline:** Applications must be submitted by the beginning of June. Recepients are announced by July 15. **Contact(s):** Chairman, National Scholarship Committee; Chapter of Daughters of Penelope that is sponsoring the applicant; or Mrs. Mary Plumides, National Chairman, Scholarship Committee, 4642 Sharon View Rd., Charlotte, NC 28201.

★7792★ **Alice E. Smith Fellowship**
The State Historical Society of Wisconsin
816 State St.
Madison, WI 53706
Phone: (608)262-3266
David Myers, Library Director

Study Level: Graduate. **Award Type:** Fellowship. **Applicant Eligibility:** Women conducting research in American history are eligible to apply. **Selection Criteria:** Preference is given to applicants involved in graduate research in the history of Wisconsin or of the Middle West. Fellows are chosen by a committee of the State Historical Society of Wisconsin. **Funds Available:** An outright grant of $2,000 is awarded. Recipients are generally not eligible for more than one award. **Application Details:** Applicants need only submit a letter briefly describing their background or interest in historical research and, in some detail, descriptions of current research work, which should include a proposal, sources to be used, possible conclusions, and applicant's conception of the work's significance. The society does not require nor seek references, transcripts, or examples of previous work. **Application Deadline:** July 15. Notification is sent to all applicants in August.

★7793★ **Alpha Epsilon Iota Scholarship Fund**
Alpha Epsilon Iota Scholarship
c/o Betty Kelsea
Trustcorp Society Bank
100 S. Main St.
Ann Arbor, MI 48104
Phone: (313)994-5555

Study Level: Doctorate. **Award Type:** Scholarship. **Purpose:** To financially support women medical students enrolled in any accredited institution in the United States. **Applicant Eligibility:** Must be a female degree candidate in an accredited, United States college of medicine. **Selection Criteria:** Applicants will be judged on scholastic achievement, financial data, work and research experience, and publications. **Funds Available:** Maximum award is $3,000 per year. **Application Deadline:** May 1.

★7794★ **Amaranth Fund Awards**
California Masonic Foundation
1111 California St.
San Francisco, CA 94108

Study Level: Undergraduate. **Award Type:** Scholarship. **Applicant Eligibility:** Applicants must be United States citizens, show evidence of financial need and be legal residents of California. Candidates must be young women under 21 who ar living in California and attending a California college. **Funds Available:** The maximum award is generally $1,000. Awards may be renewed on evidence of satisfactory academic progress and continuing financial need. **Application Details:** The first step in making application is for the student to personally write a letter describing family, community, fraternal, athletic and scholastic activities, academic standing and personal goals. A stamped-self addressed envelope must be provided. If eligible, an application and letter of instructions will be forwarded. **Contact(s):** Scholarship Committee.

★7795★ **Amelia Earhart Fellowship Awards**
Zonta International Foundation
557 W. Randolph St.
Chicago, IL 60606-2284
Phone: (312)930-5848
Fax: (312)930-0951
Lily A. Klinger, Contact

Study Level: Graduate. **Award Type:** Fellowship. **Applicant Eligibility:** Candidates are women who hold the bachelor's degree in a science acceptable as preparatory for graduate work in aerospace-related fields. They must have a superior academic record, career goals, and evidence of potential. Applicant must be accepted by an institution that offers fully accredited graduate courses and degrees in aerospace-related science or engineering. Past recipients may apply for renewed grants. **Selection Criteria:** Special attention is given to the candidate's applications, transcripts, recommendations, publications, and related activities. **Funds Available:** 40 fellowships of $6,000 each are awarded annually. **Application Details:** Applications are available in September for the next academic year. **Application Deadline:** Applications must be filed by December 31. Recipients are announced by May 1.

★7796★ **Amelia Greenbaum Scholarship Fund**
National Council of Jewish Women (NCJW)
Greater Boston Section
75 Harvard Ave.
Allston, MA 02134

Study Level: Undergraduate. **Award Type:** Scholarship. **Applicant Eligibility:** Applicants must be female students of the Jewish faith who reside in the Greater Boston area. Applicants must be attending or planning to attend a degree granting institution within the Commonwealth of Massachusetts on an undergraduate level. **Selection Criteria:** Financial need and academic record. Priority will be given to women who are returning to school after at least a five year absence; are new Americans with competency in English; and intend to pursue studies in areas related to the objectives of NCJW, such as social work, public policy and administration, law, and early childhood education. **Funds Available:** The amount of a scholarship is individually determined. **Application Details:** Applications may be requested in writing after January 1. A transcript and letter of recommendation from the applicant's principal, guidance counselor, or professor must accompany the application. **Application Deadline:** All application materials must be received by April 30. Interviews are held shortly thereafter. Recipients are notified the end of June. **Contact(s):** Administrative Director.

★7797★ **American Society for Microbiology Fellowships**
American Society for Microbiology (ASM)
1325 Massachusetts Ave. NW
Washington, DC 20005
Phone: (202)737-3600

Description: The following fellowships are awarded: (1) Raymond W. Sarber Fellowship - to enable five students, one for each divisional group, to attend the Annual Meeting and present their work. The awards consist of predetermined funds up to $400 toward transportation plus the cost of hotel expenses and a certificate to be presented at the Annual Meeting during the luncheon of the branch officers; (2) Congressional Science Fellowship - To make practical contributions to more effective use of scientific knowledge in government, to educate the scientific communities regarding the public policy process, and to broaden the perspective of both the scientific and governmental communities regarding the value of such science-government interaction. Fellows must be citizens of the United States and be members of ASM for at least one year. The ASM Fellow functions as a special legislative assistant within the congressional staff system. The program is defrayed to the maximum extent funded by the estate of Martin Frobisher; (3) Loretta Leive Memorial Fellowship - To inspire and encourage women in science. The recipient must be pre- or postdoctoral, must be a Ph.D. or a candidate for Ph.D., must be involved in 100 percent research activity, and must have graduated from or be matriculated at an accredited university. Candidates need not be American citizens, but the fellowship must be awarded to an American citizen in alternate years. Consideration is given to candidates in the disciplines of microbiology, immunology, and biochemistry and to postdoctorals within three to five years of their degree and no older than 40 years of age. The amount of the fellowship will be determined by the total funds raised and the investment program; (4) Predoctoral Minority Fellowship - To support graduate students in microbiology who are members of recognized racial and ethnic minorities in the population of the United States. A Fellow must be a citizen of the United States, a member of a minority as defined by the National Institutes of Health Minority Access to Research Careers (MARC) program, and formally admitted for a graduate academic degree in microbiology in an accredited institution of higher learning in the United States. A stipend up to $5,000 and an additional amount up to $5,000 to cover tuition and fees at the institution chosen by the awardee are awarded annually. Grants are renewable; and (5) President's Fellowship - To support predoctoral graduate students and junior research workers in microbiology. Members of the Society residing in the United States are eligible. Transportation and subsistence expenses for short visits to other laboratories in the United States for the purpose of acquiring new research skills and techniques are awarded.

★7798★ **America's National Teenager Scholarship**
National Teen-Ager Foundation
1001 W. Euless Blvd., Ste. 208
Euless, TX 76040
Phone: (817)540-0313

Study Level: Undergraduate. **Award Type:** Scholarship. **Purpose:** To encourage scholastic and leadership achievements of America's teenagers by providing cash, tuition scholarships, and other awards. **Applicant Eligibility:** Candidates must be females between 13 and 18 years of age. **Selection Criteria:** Applicants are judged on: leadership ability, scholastic achievement, poise, appearance, and personality. **Funds Available:** The Foundation awards more than $20,000 in cash scholarships. Additionally, academic institutions often provide state or national winners with further scholarships. **Application Deadline:** Dates vary. **Contact(s):** For information on local and state pageant sponsors write to National Teen-Ager Foundation, 215 Piedmont Ave., NE, Atlanta, GA 30308.

★7799★ **AMWA Medical Education Loans**
American Medical Women's Association, Inc. (AMWA)
National Office
801 N. Fairfax, Ste. 400
Alexandria, VA 22314
Phone: (703)838-0500
Fax: (703)549-3864

Study Level: Doctorate. **Award Type:** Loan. **Applicant Eligibility:** Applicants must be women who are enrolled in accredited U.S. medical or osteopathic medicine schools; U.S. citizens or permanent residents; and Student Life members of national AMWA. **Funds Available:** Loans of $1,000 or $2,000 per student per year. Student can receive a maximum of $4,000 during medical school. Payment on the principal commences nine months after graduation and must be completed within three years. **Application Details:** Formal application must be filed. **Application Deadline:** April 15.

★7800★ **Anne O'Hare McCormick Scholarship**
Newswomen's Club of New York
15 Gramercy Park S.
New York, NY 10003
Phone: (212)777-1610
Joan O'Sullivan, Contact

Study Level: Graduate. **Award Type:** Scholarship. **Applicant Eligibility:** Open only to women students who have been accepted for enrollment at Columbia University's Graduate School of Journalism. **Selection Criteria:** Financial need and the candidate's potential for success in the media. **Funds Available:** Awards range from $2,500 to $3,100. **Application Deadline:** June 1.

★7801★ **ASOR National Endowment for the Humanities Post-Doctoral Research Fellowships, Jerusalem**
American Schools of Oriental Research (ASOR)
711 W. 40th St., Ste. 354
Baltimore, MD 21211
Phone: (301)889-1383
Fax: (301)889-1157

Study Level: Postdoctorate. **Award Type:** Fellowship. **Applicant Eligibility:** Candidates must be United States citizens or aliens residing in the United States continuously for the three years preceding application deadline date. Applicants must hold the Ph.D. degree by January 1 of the academic year application is filed. Research must be carried out at the Albright Institute of Archaeological Research in Jerusalem. The research may be in any humanities discipline and should contribute to the understanding of the cultures and peoples of the Middle East. Qualified minorities and women are encouraged to apply. **Funds Available:** Stipends are up to $27,500 for a research period of one year. Six-month period stipends are up to $13,750. Two fellowships are awarded for study in Jerusalem. **Application Details:** Formal application required. **Application Deadline:** October 15.

★7802★ **ASOR National Endowment for the Humanities Post-Doctoral Research Fellowships, Nicosia**
American Schools of Oriental Research (ASOR)
711 W 40th St., Ste. 354
Baltimore, MD 21211
Phone: (301)889-1383
Fax: (301)889-1157

Study Level: Postdoctorate. **Award Type:** Fellowship. **Applicant Eligibility:** Applicants must be humanities scholars holding a Ph.D. degree by January 1 of the academic year application is filed. Research must be carried out at the Cyprus American Archaeological Research Institute (CARRI). Qualified minorities and women are encouraged to apply. **Funds Available:** Stipend of up to $30,000 for a research period on one year. **Application Details:** Formal application required. **Application Deadline:** October 15.

★7803★ AT&T Bell Laboratories Dual Degree Scholarships
AT&T Bell Laboratories—Special Progams
Crawfords Corner Rd., Rm. 1E-209
Holmdale, NJ 07733-1988
Phone: (908)949-4301
Fax: (908)949-6800

Study Level: Undergraduate. **Award Type:** Scholarship. **Applicant Eligibility:** Candidates must be outstanding members of underrepresented minority groups, i.e., Blacks, Hispanics, Native American Indians, and women who are interested in engineering or computer science and in a five year engineering program. **Funds Available:** The Five-Year Program offers full tuition including books, fees, room and board, and summer employment at AT&T. **Application Details:** The applicant must supply information on educational and work background, a statement of career goals and three letters of recommendation preferably from math or science teachers. Remarks: Anticipated number of candidates selected each year is three, with a maximum total of 15 in the program. Through a coordinated effort with the Atlanta University Center, students earn a BA in Mathematics or Physics from Spelman, Morehouse, Clark or Morris Brown Colleges in three years and then go on to earn a BS degree in Engineering or Computer Science in two years at Georgia Institute of Technology, Auburn University, Rochester Institute of Technology or Boston University. **Application Deadline:** Application deadline is December 31. **Contact(s):** Dual Program Administrator.

★7804★ AT&T Bell Laboratories Engineering Scholarships
AT&T Bell Laboratories—Special Programs
Crawfords Corner Rd., Rm. 1E-209
Holmdale, NJ 07733-1988
Phone: (908)949-4301
Fax: (908)949-6800

Study Level: Undergraduate. **Award Type:** Scholarship. **Purpose:** To encourage and assist Blacks, Hispanics, Native Americans, and women to enter engineering and computer science professions. **Applicant Eligibility:** Candidates are academically qualified Black, Hispanic, Native American minority groups and women who will enter the engineering and computer science professions. They must be United States citizens or permanent residents. **Funds Available:** Scholars begin with the first year of college or engineering school and include tuition, mandatory fees, room and board or living allowance, and a stipend for books and supplies. These scholarships are renewable each year until completion of the B.S. degree subject to the student's continued interest in engineering or computer science, the maintenance of a B average in college and satisfactory preformance during summer employment. Summer employment is provided at an appropriate Bell Laboratory where the participant works with a company engineer who also serves as the student's year-round advisor. Qualified participants are given full consideration for regular employment at the conclusion of their undergraduate studies. **Application Details:** The application requires information about cumulative grade point average, class rank, scholastic honors, employment and/or other activities, statement of interests, and how candidate expects to use technical training. Transcripts, three letters of recommendation, and SAT scores must be submitted. **Application Deadline:** January 15. **Contact(s):** ESP Administrator.

★7805★ AT&T Bell Laboratories Graduate Research Fellowships for Women
AT&T Bell Laboratories—Special Programs
Crawfords Corner Rd., Rm. 1E-209
Holmdel, NJ 07733-1988
Phone: (908)949-4301
Fax: (908)949-6800

Study Level: Doctorate. **Award Type:** Fellowship. **Purpose:** To identify and develop research ability in women and to increase their representation in science and engineering. **Applicant Eligibility:** Applicants must be women students who are pursuing full-time doctoral studies in the following disciplines: chemistry, chemical engineering, communications, science, computer science/engineering, electrical engineering, information science, materials science, mathematics, mechanical engineering, operations research, physics, and statistics. Awards are made only to women who are U.S. citizens or permanent residents, and who are admitted to full-time study in a doctoral program agreed to by AT&T Bell Laboratories. The program is primarily directed to graduating seniors, but applications from first year graduate students will be considered. **Selection Criteria:** Participants are selected on the basis of scholastic attainment in their field of specialization, and other evidence of their ability and potential as research scientists. **Funds Available:** Four fellowships are awarded annually. The fellowship provides full tuition, an annual stipend of $13,200 (paid bi-monthly September through May), books, fees, and related travel expenses. Fellowship recipients may not accept any other fellowship support. Fellowships may be renewed on a yearly basis for the normal duration of the graduate program, subject to the participant's satisfactory progress toward the doctoral degree. **Application Details:** Applications should include a statement of interest, information on scholastic background, academic standing, and related job experience. Candidates should arrange for official transcripts of grades to be sent from their institutions, and three letters of recommendation from college professors who can evaluate the applicant's scientific aptitude and potential for research. In addition, Graduate Record Examination scores on the Aptitude Test and the appropriate Advanced Test are required. **Application Deadline:** Applications and all supporting documentation must be received by January 15.

★7806★ AT&T Bell Laboratories Graduate Research Grants for Women
AT&T Bell Laboratories—Special Programs
Crawfords Corner Rd., Rm. 1E-209
Holmdel, NJ 07733-1988
Phone: (908)949-4301
Fax: (908)949-6800

Study Level: Doctorate. **Award Type:** Grant. **Purpose:** To identify and develop research ability in women and to increase their representation in science and engineering. **Applicant Eligibility:** Applicants must be women students who are pursuing full-time doctoral studies in the following disciplines: chemistry, chemical engineering, communications, science, computer science/engineering, information science, materials science, mathematics, mechanical engineering, operations research, physics, and statistics. Awards are made only to women who are U.S. citizens or permanent residents, and who are admitted to full-time study in a doctoral program approved by AT&T Bell Laboratories. The program is primarily directed to graduating Seniors, but applications from first year gradu-

ate students will be considered. **Selection Criteria:** Participants are selected on the basis of scholastic attainment in their field of specialization and other evidence of their ability and potential as research scientists.

★7807★ AT&T Bell Laboratories Summer Research Program for Minorities & Women
AT&T Bell Laboratories—Special Programs
Crawfords Corner Rd., Rm. 1E-209
Holmdel, NJ 07733-1988
Phone: (908)949-4301
Fax: (908)949-6800

Study Level: Undergraduate. **Award Type:** Fellowship. **Purpose:** To attract students into scientific careers, including patent law, by placing participants in working contact with experienced research scientists, engineers, and patent lawyers. **Applicant Eligibility:** Applicants must be women and/or members of underrepresented minority groups (Blacks, Native American Indians, and Hispanics). The program is primarily directed toward undergraduate students who have completed their third year of college. Emphasis is placed on the following disciplines: ceramic engineering, electrical engineering, information science, materials science, mathematics, mechanical engineering, operations research, physics, and statistics. Applicants should be U.S. citizens or permanent residents of the U.S. **Selection Criteria:** Candidates are selected based on academic achievement, personal motivation, and compatibility of student interests with current AT&T Bell Laboratories activities. **Funds Available:** From 60 to 100 awards are given annually. Salaries are commensurate with those of regular AT&T Bell Laboratories employees of comparable education. **Application Deadline:** Application and all supporting documentation, preferably in one package, must be received by December 1.

★7808★ AWIS Predoctoral Awards
Association for Women in Science—Educational Foundation (AWIS)
1522 K St., NW, Ste. 820
Washington, DC 20005
Phone: (202)408-0742

Study Level: Doctorate. **Award Type:** Award. **Applicant Eligibility:** Applicants must be female students enrolled in any life, physical, or social science or engineering program leading to a Ph.D. degree. Winners have traditionally been at the dissertation level of their graduate work. U.S. citizens may use the money for study in the U.S. or abroad. Non-U.S. citizens must be enrolled in a U.S. institution of higher education to be eligible for these awards. **Funds Available:** Four awards of $500. Honorable mentions of $100 are sometimes awarded. Awards can be used for any aspect of education, including tuition, books, housing, research, expenses, and equipment. **Application Details:** Application forms for the awards are available from AWIS Headquarters between September 1 and December 15 of each year. The application includes a basic form, a two-to three-page summary of the candidate's dissertation research, and two recommendation report forms. Applicants must submit official transcripts of all course work conducted at postsecondary institutions. **Application Deadline:** All materials must be received by January 15. Winners are notified by mail and announced publicly in the July/August issue of the *AWIS Newsletter*. Applicants may call the AWIS around June 15 for results.

★7809★ **BPW Career Advancement Scholarships**
Business and Professional Women's Foundation—Educational Programs (BPW)
2012 Massachusetts Ave. NW
Washington, DC 20036

Study Level: Undergraduate. **Award Type:** Scholarship. **Purpose:** To assist women seeking the education necessary for entry or re-entry into the workforce or advancement within a career field. The program was conceived as a concrete, practical means to achieve the Foundation's mission of improving the economic status of all working women. **Applicant Eligibility:** Scholarships are awarded for full-time or part-time programs of study in the fields of computer science, education, paralegal, or science (health care fields are not covered). Applicants must: be women 30 years of age or older; be citizens of the United States; be officially accepted into an accredited program or course of study at a United States institution; be graduating within 24 months from August 31 of the application year; demonstrate critical need for financial assistance to upgrade skills or complete education for career advancement; and have a definite plan to use the desired training to improve chances for advancement, to train for a new career field, or to re-enter the job market. This scholarship program does not cover study at the doctoral level, correspondence courses, or non-degree programs. **Funds Available:** Scholarships range from $500 to $1,000. 100 scholarships are awarded per year. **Application Details:** To receive application packet, application request form must be submitted to the BPW Foundation. **Application Deadline:** Application materials are available between October 1 and April 1. Completed application materials must be returned by April 15.

★7810★ **BPW Loans for Women in Engineering Studies**
Business and Professional Women's Foundation—Educational Programs (BPW)
2012 Massachusetts Ave. NW
Washington, DC 20036

Study Level: Graduate, Undergraduate. **Award Type:** Loan. **Purpose:** To assist women in their final two years of any accredited engineering program, including undergraduate, refresher, and conversion programs, as well as graduate studies. **Applicant Eligibility:** Studies may be full or part-time, but applicants must carry at least six semester hours or the equivalent during each semester for which a loan is required. Applicants must: be citizens of the United States; have written notice of acceptance for a course of study in engineering accredited by the Accreditation Board of Engineering and Technology; have academic and/or work experience records showing career motivation and ability to complete course of study; and demonstrate financial need. **Funds Available:** Loans of up to $5,000 are made for an academic year. Interest of seven percent per annum begins immediately after graduation. Loans are repaid in five equal installments commencing 12 months after graduation. **Application Details:** To receive application packet, applicants must submit an application request form to the BPW Foundation. **Application Deadline:** Application materials are available between October 1 and April 1. Application request forms must be received between October 1 and April 1. Completed application materials must be returned by April 15.

★7811★ **BPW/Sears Roebuck Loans for Women in Graduate Business Studies**
Business and Professional Women's Foundation—Educational Programs (BPW)
2012 Massachusetts Ave. NW
Washington, DC 20036

Study Level: Graduate. **Award Type:** Loan. **Purpose:** The loan fund was established in 1974 jointly by the BPW Foundation and the Sears-Roebuck Foundation for women seeking their Master's in Business Administration. **Applicant Eligibility:** Studies may be full or part-time, but applicants must carry at least six semesters hours or equivalent during each semester for which a loan is requested. Applicants must: be citizens of the United States; have written notice of acceptance or enrollment at a school accredited by the American Assembly of Collegiate Schools of Business; have academic and/or work experience records showing career motivation and ability to complete course of study; and demonstrate financial need. BPW Foundation and Sears-Roebuck Foundation employees are not eligible. **Funds Available:** Loans of up to $2,500 are made for tuition and fees for an academic year and are paid directly to the school. Interest of seven percent per annum begins immediately after graduation. Loans are repaid in five equal installments commencing 12 months after graduation. **Application Details:** To receive application packet, applicants must submit an application request form to the BPW Foundation. **Application Deadline:** Application materials are available between October 1 and April 1. Application request forms must be received between October 1 and April 1. Completed application materials must be returned by April 15.

★7812★ **Bunting Fellowship**
Mary Ingraham Bunting Institute of Radcliffe College
34 Concord Ave.
Cambridge, MA 02138
Phone: (617)495-8212
Fax: (617)495-8136
Chiho Tokita, Contact

Study Level: Postdoctorate, Professional development. **Award Type:** Fellowship. **Applicant Eligibility:** Women scholars, creative writers, and visual artists are eligible. Scholars must have held the Ph.D. or appropriate terminal degree at least two years prior to appointment. Non-academic applicants, such as artists, writers, social workers, lawyers, and journalists, need to have a significant record of accomplishment, professional experience equivalent to a doctorate, and some-doctoral work. **Selection Criteria:** Applications are judged on the significance and quality of the project proposal, the applicant's record of accomplishment, and on the difference the fellowship may make in the applicant's career. **Funds Available:** $21,500 stipend for a one-year appointment, July through June. Ten fellowships are awarded annually. **Application Details:** Applicants should provide the names of three intended recommenders on the Summary Application Information sheet. In December or January the Institute will solicit three letters of recommendation from finalists. Recommendation forms will be sent to applicants with notification of selection as finalists. **Application Deadline:** Applications must be postmarked by October 15. Fellows and alternates are notified in the beginning of April.

★7813★ **Bunting Institute Affiliation Program**
Mary Ingraham Bunting Institute of Radcliffe College
34 Concord Ave.
Cambridge, MA 02138
Phone: (617)495-8212
Fax: (617)495-8136

Study Level: Postdoctorate, Professional development. **Applicant Eligibility:** Women scholars, creative writers, and visual artists are eligible. Scholars must have held the Ph.D. or appropriate terminal degree at least two years prior to appointment. Non-academic applicants, such as artists, writers, social workers, lawyers, and journalists need to have a significant record of accomplishment, and professional experience equivalent to a doctorate, and some postdoctoral work. **Selection Criteria:** Applications are judged on the significance and quality of the project proposal, the applicant's record of accomplishment, and on the difference the fellowship may make in the applicant's career. **Funds Available:** Appointment is without stipend, but includes office or studio space and other resources available to all fellows. Appointments are made for Fall (July 1 through September 30), Spring (January 1 through June 30), or full year (July 1 through June 30). **Application Details:** Three letters of recommendation must be submitted with application. **Application Deadline:** Applications must be postmarked by January 15. Notification is made by April.

★7814★ **Bunting Institute Peace Fellowships**
Mary Ingraham Bunting Institute of Radcliffe College
34 Concord Ave.
Cambridge, MA 02138
Phone: (617)495-8212
Fax: (617)495-8136

Study Level: Postgraduate. **Award Type:** Fellowship. **Applicant Eligibility:** Women actively involved in finding peaceful solutions to conflict or potential conflict among groups or nations; involvement with peace issues may be of an activist or scholarly nature. **Selection Criteria:** Applications are reviewed by a committee of scholars and activists. **Funds Available:** $21,500 stipend for a one-year appointment, July 1 through June 30. One fellowship is awarded annually. **Application Details:** Applicants should include three letters of recommendation with application. **Application Deadline:** January 15.

★7815★ **Bunting Institute Science Scholars Fellowships**
Mary Ingraham Bunting Institute of Radcliffe College
34 Concord Ave.
Cambridge, MA 02138
Phone: (617)495-8212
Fax: (617)495-8136

Study Level: Postdoctorate. **Award Type:** Fellowship. **Applicant Eligibility:** Women scientists who are U.S. citizens are eligible to apply. Applicants must have held a Ph.D. for two years prior to the date of appointment. Applications are accepted in the following fields: molecular and cellular biology; biochemistry; chemistry; cognitive and neural sciences; mathematics; physics; astronomy; computer science; electrical engineering; aerospace/mechanical engineering; materials science; naval architecture and ocean engineering; and oceanography.

Selection Criteria: Applications are judged on the significance and quality of the project proposal and the difference the fellowship may make in the applicant's career. **Funds Available:** $27,600 stipend for a one-year appointment, July 1 through June 30. Eight fellowships are awarded annually. **Application Details:** Applicants should include three letters of recommendation with application. **Application Deadline:** October 15.

★7816★ Circle Key Grants of Rose McGill
Kappa Kappa Gamma Fraternity
PO Box 2079
Columbus, OH 43216-2079
Study Level: Professional Development, Undergraduate. **Award Type:** Grant. **Applicant Eligibility:** These grants are available only to Kappa Kappa Gamma Fraternity alumnae who need educational assistance. The grants are awarded on the basis of need, merit, and individual goals for study for the purpose of aiding career qualifications. Recipients may study at colleges, universities, career, vocational, or technical schools. **Funds Available:** Grants are available in varying amounts up to $750. **Application Details:** Alumnae may apply for Circle Key Grants any time during the year. Grants are awarded throughout the year as long as funds are available. **Contact(s):** Chairman of the Circle Key Alumnae Grants.

★7817★ Congressional Fellowships on Women and Public Policy
Women's Research and Education Institute
1700 18th St. NW, Ste. 400
Washington, DC 20009
Phone: (202)328-7070
Study Level: Graduate. **Award Type:** Fellowship. **Applicant Eligibility:** Candidates must be graduate students anywhere in the United States interested in participation in the formation of public policy. They must have approval of their academic advisor to register for six hours fellowship credit at the home institution. **Funds Available:** A stipend of $9,000 for the academic year, $500 for the purchase of health insurance, and a maximum of $1,500 for the cost of six hours tuition at the home institution are awarded to each fellow. **Application Details:** Applications must be requested in writing after November 1. Three copies of applications and supporting materials must be filed. **Contact(s):** Fellowship Director.

★7818★ Daughters of Penelope Past Grand Presidents Award
Daughters of Penelope
AHEPA Senior Women's Auxiliary
1909 Q St., Ste. 500
Washington, DC 20009
Study Level: Undergraduate. **Award Type:** Scholarship. **Applicant Eligibility:** Candidate must be a female high school graduate or an undergraduate at the college level and must be of Greek descent, or related to an AHEPAN or a Daughter of Penelope, or be a member of the Maids of Athena. She must be sponsored by her local or nearest Daughters of Penelope chapter; if there is no Daughters of Penelope chapter, the local or nearest Order of AHEPA chapter may sponsor the candidate and endorse the application. Applicants must be residents of the United States, Canada, Greece or wherever there is an established Daughters of Penelope chapter in good standing. **Selection**

Criteria: Scholarships are awarded according to merit, without regard to other scholarships an applicant may receive. Financial need is also a criteria. **Funds Available:** Each scholarship is $500. Scholarships are renewable for up to three years at rate of $300-$500. **Application Details:** Applications must be accompanied by the recommendation of the principal or counselor of the high school the candidate attended or the dean of the college she is attending. Parents' Confidential Statement or Financial Aid Form. **Application Deadline:** Applications must be submitted by the beginning of June. Recepients are announced by July 15. **Contact(s):** Chairman, National Scholarship Committee; Chapter of Daughters of Penelope that is sponsoring the applicant; or Mrs. Mary Plumides, National Chairman, Scholarship Committee, 4642 Sharon View Rd., Charlotte, NC 28201.

★7819★ David Sarnoff Research Center Scholarship
Society of Women Engineers (SWE)
United Engineering Center, Rm. 305
345 E. 47th St.
New York, NY 10017
Phone: (212)705-7855
Study Level: Undergraduate. **Award Type:** Scholarship. **Applicant Eligibility:** Applicants must be women engineering students entering their junior year. Applicants must be United States citizens. **Funds Available:** One $1,500 award. **Application Details:** Scholarship information and applications are sent to the deans of accredited engineering schools in October and March of each year. Applications and information can be obtained from the dean of engineering or from the SWE Headquarters in New York. Requests to SWE Headquarters must be accompanied by a self-addressed, stamped envelope. Applications are available from October through January only. **Application Deadline:** Completed applications, including all supportive materials, must be postmarked no later than February 1. Recipient only will be notified by May 1.

★7820★ Digital Equipment Corporation Scholarship
Society of Women Engineers (SWE)
United Engineering Center, Rm. 305
345 E. 47th St.
New York, NY 10017
Phone: (212)705-7855
Study Level: Undergraduate. **Award Type:** Scholarship. **Applicant Eligibility:** Scholarship is awarded at the end of the freshman year to a woman student member of the SWE majoring in electrical, mechanical, or computer engineering who is attending a university in New York or New England. Applicants must be United States citizens or permanent residents. **Funds Available:** One $1,000 award. The scholarship is renewable for two consecutive years, contingent upon maintaining an appropriate grade point average. **Application Details:** Scholarship information and applications are sent to the deans of accredited engineering schools in October and March of each year. Applications and information can be obtained from the dean of engineering or from the SWE Headquarters in New York. Requests to SWE Headquarters must be accompanied by a self-addressed, stamped envelope. Applications are available from October through January only. **Application Deadline:** Completed applications, including all supportive materials, must be post-

marked no later than February 1. Recipient only will be notified by May 1.

★7821★ Dr. B. Olive Cole Graduate Educational Grant
Lambda Kappa Sigma—International Office
6250 Mountain Vista, Ste. 1
Henderson, WV 89014
Phone: (702)456-3186
Fax: (702)456-4309
Study Level: Graduate, Doctorate. **Award Type:** Grant. **Applicant Eligibility:** Candidates must be members of Lambda Kappa Sigma Fraternity who are enrolled in programs of graduate study and research at accredited colleges or universities in order to advance their careers in the pharmaceutical sciences. Applicants must have successfully completed one academic year of graduate study toward Master of Science, Doctor of Philosophy, or Master of Science/Doctor of Philosophy degrees and must have the endorsements of their respective department directors. Candidates must also be members in good standing with collegiate or alumni chapters, or be Stray Lambs of Lambda Kappa Sigma and must be current in their dues. Applicants' graduate records must be filed with the Fraternity's Educational Grant Committee. **Funds Available:** One grant of $1,000 is awarded annually and may be used for tuition, books, living or travel expenses, or thesis expenses. **Application Deadline:** Applications must be filed by November 1. Awards are made by January 15. **Contact(s):** Chairman, Educational Grant Committee, above address.

★7822★ Doris Mullen Memorial Flight Scholarship
International Women Helicopter Pilots
c/o Jean Roth-Howard
1619 Duke St.
Alexandria, VA 22314
Phone: (703)683-4646
Study Level: Professional Development. **Award Type:** Scholarship. **Purpose:** To assist a deserving Whirly-Girl in obtaining advanced add-on or transition helicopter ratings and to further her degree of professionalism as an experienced pilot in the helicopter industry. **Applicant Eligibility:** Applicants must have proof of financial need and have demonstrated a strong desire and effort to pursue a career as a helicopter pilot. **Funds Available:** $5,000. **Application Deadline:** Applications must be postmarked on or before October 31. **Contact(s):** Captain Diane C. Dowd, International President, The Whirly-Girls Scholarship Fund, Inc., Green Pond Rd., RR No. 2, PO Box 67B, Sherman, CT 06784.

★7823★ E.K. Wise Loan
American Occupational Therapy Foundation, Inc.
1383 Piccard Dr.
PO Box 1725
Rockville, MD 20750-4375
Phone: (301)948-9626
Study Level: Graduate. **Award Type:** Loan. **Purpose:** To assist eligible students with the expenses of their occupational therapy education. **Applicant Eligibility:** Must be female citizen of the United States or a permanent resident, member of the American Occupational Therapy Association, have a bachelor's degree, be enrolled in an occupational therapy curriculum leading to a certificate or graduate degree in

occupational therapy, and plan to seek future employment in the field of occupational therapy. **Funds Available:** Loans up to $2,000 which must be repaid within three years after graduation or earlier should the recipient withdraw from the approved course of study before graduation. **Application Details:** Formal application required. **Application Deadline:** Application for a loan may be made at any time.

★7824★ **Edith H. Henderson Scholarship**
Landscape Architecture Foundation
4401 Connecticut Ave. NW, Ste. 500
Washington, DC 20008
Phone: (202)686-2752

Study Level: Graduate, Undergraduate. **Award Type:** Scholarship. **Purpose:** The prize is awarded to a student committed to the goal of developing practical communication skills in her role as a landscape architect. **Applicant Eligibility:** Must be a female landscape architecture student enrolled at the University of Georgia. Applicants must be entering their final year of undergraduate work, or in any year of their graduate career. **Funds Available:** $1,000. **Application Details:** Applicants should submit the completed application form with a typed, double-spaced essay describing the candidates viewpoint on the value of a two-hour client consultation in residential design. Included in the essay should be how such a consultation would be developed and the way in which this session would be conducted. Participation in a class in public speaking or creative writing is also requested. **Application Deadline:** May 15.

★7825★ **Edith Nourse Rogers Scholarship Fund**
Women's Army Corps Veterans Association
PO Box 5577
McClellan, AL 36205
Phone: (205)820-4019
Mary Callahan, Contact

Study Level: Graduate. **Award Type:** Scholarship. **Purpose:** To assist selected students at a Massachusetts university in the completion of their studies. **Applicant Eligibility:** Female dependants of United States veterans majoring in government or political science who are enrolled full-time. **Selection Criteria:** The award is based on merit with need as a secondary factor. **Funds Available:** $1,500. **Application Deadline:** April 1.

★7826★ **Edwin G. and Lauretta M. Michael Scholarship**
Christian Church (Disciples of Christ)
Division of Homeland Ministries
222 S. Downey Ave.
PO Box 1986
Indianapolis, IN 46206
Phone: (317)353-1499

Study Level: Undergraduate. **Award Type:** Scholarship. **Applicant Eligibility:** Candidates must be wives of ministers; members of the Christian Church (Disciples of Christ); better than average students with at least a C plus average; able to provide evidence of financial need; enrolled as full-time students in an accredited school or seminary. **Application Details:** Applicants must provide a transcript of academic work and references. Recipients must make a renewal application each year if eligible. Write for an application. **Application Deadline:** March 15.

★7827★ **Eleanor Roosevelt Teacher Fellowship**
American Association of University Women— Educational Foundation (AAUW)
1111 16th Ave. NW
Washington, DC 20006
Phone: (202)728-7603
Fax: (202)872-1425

Study Level: Professional Development. **Award Type:** Fellowship. **Purpose:** Eleanor Roosevelt Teacher Fellowships are designed for elementary and secondary school teachers who are seeking to advance gender equity in the classroom, increase their effectiveness at teaching math and science to girls, and/or tailor their teaching to the needs of minority students and girls at risk of dropping out. **Applicant Eligibility:** Women teachers who are U.S. citizens or permanent residents, teach full-time at U.S. public schools in grades K-12, have at least five consecutive years full-time teaching experience, plan to continue teaching for the next five years, and can demonstrate commitment to educational opportunities for women and girls through work in the classroom are eligible. **Funds Available:** Fellowships range from $1,000 to $10,000. The amount of each fellowship depends on the period of study undertaken. Applicants are not required to take leave from their school districts. Course work and/or research can be conducted during the summer or part time. **Application Deadline:** December 1.

★7828★ **Eleanor Scholar Grant**
Eleanor Association
1550 N. Dearborn Pkwy.
Chicago, IL 60610
Phone: (312)664-8245
Theresa Isquierdo, Contact

Study Level: Undergraduate. **Award Type:** Grant. **Purpose:** To assist women in completing their education by lessening the financial burden. **Applicant Eligibility:** Applicant must be a woman currently attending a participating college or university and have been nominated by their school officials. They must be at the senior level and planning to graduate in the year that the grant will be awarded. **Selection Criteria:** Selection is based on scholastic achievement, community/school activities, and financial need. Finalists are interviewed by the Association's board of directors. **Funds Available:** Ten awards of $5,000 each. **Application Details:** Contact the financial aid officer of any participating school: Elmhurst College; Lake Forest College; North Central College; Loyola University of Chicago; Wheaton College; Mundelein College; Rosary College; Northwestern University; University of Chicago; or University of Illinois, Chicago. **Application Deadline:** March 1.

★7829★ **Eloise Gerry Fellowships**
Sigma Delta Epsilon Graduate Women in Science, Inc. (SDE)
PO Box 4748
Ithaca, NY 14852

Study Level: Postgraduate. **Award Type:** Fellowship. **Purpose:** To increase knowledge in the chemical and biological sciences and to encourage research by women. **Applicant Eligibility:** Candidates must be women holding a science degree from an accredited college or university. Gerry Fellowships are for research in the biological and chemical sciences. Applicants must have demonstrated outstanding ability and potential in research. **Funds Available:** The

amount of the fellowship may vary from $1,500 to $4,000. Grants may not be used for tuition, administrative overhead, or equipment of general use. The fellowship period depends upon the option exercised at the time the fellowship is granted. If it extends beyond a year, submission of an annual progress report is required. **Application Details:** Candidates must submit a formal application, a 4-page description of the project, evidence of research ability and experience (these may include a list of publications, short papers or reports, a detailed budget, statement of other financial support, two letters of recommendation and two self-addressed stamped envelopes). Applications are reviewed based on scientific question, presentation, methodology, experience, and budget. **Application Deadline:** Applications are due December 1; awards are announced on June 1. **Contact(s):** Chairman, Eloise Gerry Fellowships Committee.

★7830★ **ETS Postdoctoral Fellowship**
Educational Testing Service (ETS)
Mail Stop 30-B
Princeton, NJ 08541-0001
Phone: (609)734-1124

Study Level: Postdoctorate. **Award Type:** Fellowship. **Purpose:** To allow recent doctorates the opportunity to conduct research. ETS also hopes to increase the number of female and minority professionals with careers in the following areas: cognitive psychology, educational psychology, psychometrics, statistics, higher education, technology, occupational/vocational testing, policy studies, testing issues, and minority issues. **Applicant Eligibility:** Applicant must have a doctorate in a related discipline and provide evidence of prior research. **Selection Criteria:** Preference is given to women and minority students. **Funds Available:** Four stipends of $27,000 with limited relocation and family expenses allowed. **Application Deadline:** December or January.

★7831★ **Foreign Policy Studies Advanced Research Fellowships**
Social Science Research Council
605 Third Ave.
New York, NY 10158
Phone: (212)661-0280

Study Level: Postdoctorate. **Award Type:** Fellowship. **Purpose:** To recruit research scholars from fields or disciplines which have not traditionally viewed the making of foreign policy as part of their substantive domain. The fellowships are also intended to support innovative research on the making of foreign policy within the field of international relations. **Applicant Eligibility:** The fellowship is open to individual researchers who hold the doctoral degree (Ph.D. or its equivalent) or to others with professional backgrounds in law, journalism, or government. The program supports empirical research that applies theories and insights from diverse social science disciplines, including anthropology, economics, history, political science, psychology, sociology, and foreign area studies. Applicants should have demonstrated their ability to contribute to the research literature through the publication of books or articles. Some preference is given to researchers in the early stages of their careers. Applicants are welcome without regard to the prospective fellow's citizenship or country of residence. The program particularly encourages applications from members of minority groups, from women, and from researchers who are citizens of Third

World countries. **Application Deadline:** Applications (including letters of reference and language competency forms) must be received at the Council by December 1. Awards are announced April 1.

★7832★ **General Electric Foundation Scholarships**
Society of Women Engineers (SWE)
United Engineering Center, Rm. 305
345 E. 47th St.
New York, NY 10017
Phone: (212)705-7855

Study Level: Undergraduate. **Award Type:** Scholarship. **Applicant Eligibility:** Applicants must be women students who will be incoming freshmen in a school, college or university accredited by the Accreditation Board for Engineering and Technology. Applicants must be United States citizens. **Funds Available:** Three $1,000 awards. The scholarships are renewable for three years with continued academic achievements. In addition, the General Electric Foundation provides $500 for each entering freshman recipient so that she can attend the annual National Convention/Student Conference and/or provide support to the local Section. **Application Details:** Scholarship information and applications are sent to the deans of accredited engineering schools in October and March of each year. Applications and information can be obtained from the dean of engineering or from the SWE Headquarters in New York. Requests to SWE Headquarters must be accompanied by a self-addressed, stamped envelope. Applications are available from March through June only. **Application Deadline:** Completed applications, including all supportive materials, must be postmarked no later than May 15. Recipients only will be notified by September 15.

★7833★ **Georgia Harkness Scholarship**
The United Methodist Church
Office of Loans and Scholarships
General Board of Higher Education and Ministry
PO Box 871
Nashville, TN 37202
Phone: (615)340-7344

Study Level: Graduate. **Award Type:** Scholarship. **Applicant Eligibility:** Scholarships are awarded to women over 35 preparing for the ordained ministry in the United Methodist Church as a second career. Scholarships may be used for study toward the basic seminary degree only in an accredited school of theology. **Funds Available:** Awards of up to $1,000 are available. **Application Details:** Applicants must submit a formal application. **Application Deadline:** March 1. **Contact(s):** A United Methodist seminary or Division of the Ordained Ministry, Georgia Harkness Scholarship Award.

★7834★ **Gini Richardson Memorial Flight Scholarship**
International Women Helicopter Pilots
c/o Jean Roth-Howard
1619 Duke St.
Alexandria, VA 22314
Phone: (703)683-4646

Study Level: Professional Development. **Award Type:** Scholarship. **Purpose:** To enable a deserving woman airplane, balloon, or glider pilot to obtain her initial helicopter rating. **Applicant Eligibility:** Applicants must have proof of finan-

cial need and have demonstrated a strong desire and effort to pursue a career as a helicopter pilot. **Funds Available:** $5,000. **Application Deadline:** Applications must be postmarked on or before October 31. **Contact(s):** Captain Diane C. Dowd, International President, The Whirly-Girls Scholarship Fund, Inc., Green Pond Rd., RR No. 2, PO Box 67B, Sherman, CT 06784.

★7835★ **Gladys Anderson Emerson Scholarship**
Iota Sigma Pi
c/o Dr. Barbara A. Sawrey
Department of Chemistry B-003
University of California
La Jolle, CA 92093
Phone: (619)534-6479
Fax: (619)534-7687

Study Level: Undergraduate. **Award Type:** Scholarship. **Applicant Eligibility:** Nominees must be women undergraduate students with junior or senior standing in their curriculum at an accredited college or university, and must have at least one semester of work to complete as of August 1 following the announcement. Nominees must be members of Iota Sigma Pi. **Selection Criteria:** Excellence in chemistry or biochemistry. **Funds Available:** $1,000. **Application Details:** Nomination forms are available from the Senior National Director. **Application Deadline:** January 1. **Contact(s):** Dr. Martha Thompson, Dept. of Physiology and Pharmacology, Oregon Health Sciences University, School of Dentistry, 611 S.W. Campus Dr., Portland, OR 97201-3097.

★7836★ **Gladys C. Anderson Scholarship**
American Foundation for the Blind, Inc.
15 West 16th St.
New York, NY 10011
Phone: (212)620-2000
Mrs. Leslye S. Piqueras, Contact

Study Level: Undergraduate. **Award Type:** Scholarship. **Applicant Eligibility:** Candidates must be women who are United States citizens, legally blind, and studying religious or classical music at the college level. **Funds Available:** Two $1,000 scholarships are awarded annually. **Application Details:** Applicants must submit evidence of legal blindness; official transcripts of grades; proof of acceptance at a college or university; three letters of recommendation; a sample performance tape of voice or instrumental selection (not to exceed 30 minutes); and a typewritten statement of no more than two double-spaced pages describing educational and personal goals, work experience, extracurricular activities, and how scholarship monies will be used.

★7837★ **Harriett Barnhardt Wimmer Scholarship**
Landscape Architecture Foundation
4401 Connecticut Ave. NW, Ste. 500
Washington, DC 20008
Phone: (202)686-2752

Study Level: Undergraduate. **Award Type:** Scholarship. **Applicant Eligibility:** Must be a woman going into her final year of undergraduate landscape studies who has demonstrated excellence in her design ability and sensivity to the environment. **Funds Available:** $500. **Application Details:** An application consists of the following: a 500-word autobiography and statement of personal and professional goals; one

letter of recommendation from a design instructor; a sample of design work; and a completed application form. **Application Deadline:** May 15.

★7838★ **Helen Miller Malloch Scholarship**
National Federation of Press Women, Inc. (NFPW)
PO Box 99
Blue Springs, MD 64013
Phone: (816)229-1666

Study Level: Graduate, Undergraduate. **Award Type:** Scholarship. **Applicant Eligibility:** Applicants must be female college students who are majoring in communication and seeking a degree in journalism. Candidates must be junior, senior, or graduate level students. **Selection Criteria:** Recipient is selected on the basis of career potential, scholarship, and financial need. **Funds Available:** One $1,000 scholarship is awarded annually. **Application Details:** Applications must include a transcript of college credit, work samples and letters of recommendation in sealed envelopes from at least two persons acquainted with the applicant's work and/or school achievements. A photograph, a description of the study plan, a timetable for completion, a budget for use of the scholarship, and how the scholarship will be augmented to achieve study goals are also required. **Application Deadline:** May 1. **Contact(s):** Professional Education Scholarships.

★7839★ **Helene Overly Scholarship**
Women's Transportation Seminar (WTS)
808 17th St. NW, Ste. 200
Washington, DC 20006-3953
Phone: (202)223-9669

Study Level: Graduate. **Award Type:** Scholarship. **Purpose:** To support female students in studies related to transportation. **Applicant Eligibility:** Applicant must be a woman enrolled in a graduate degree program at an accredited United States institution. Candidate must have a GPA of 3.0 or higher and must intend to pursue a transportation-related career. **Funds Available:** $3,000. **Application Details:** Application materials are available from, and should be submitted to, the chapter of Women's Transportation Seminar in the candidate's home state. After reviewing applications, each chapter may nominate one candidate for consideration by the national scholarship committee. If a candidate lives in a state that does not have a chapter, then she may write to the national headquarters for an application form and guidelines. **Application Deadline:** February.

★7840★ **Holly A. Cornell Scholarship**
American Water Works Association
6666 W. Quincy Ave.
Denver, CO 80235
Phone: (303)794-7711
Fax: (303)794-7310
Kimberley M. Knox, Contact

Study Level: Graduate. **Award Type:** Scholarship. **Purpose:** To encourage minority or female students to pursue a Masters in Engineering. **Applicant Eligibility:** Applicants must anticipate the completion of a Masters in Engineering no sooner that December 1 of the following year. **Selection Criteria:** Selection is determined by grades, recommendations, and career plan. **Funds Available:** The Scholarship provides $5,000 for the recipient. **Application Deadline:** March 1.

★7841★ IBM Fellowships for Women
International Business Machines (IBM)
T.J. Watson Research Center
PO Box 218
Yorktown Hgts., NY 10598
Study Level: Graduate. **Award Type:** Fellowship. **Purpose:** To assist universities in training graduate students in areas of central interest to the electronics industry. **Applicant Eligibility:** Applicants must be women graduate students in the following fields: computer science, electrical engineering, mechanical engineering, mathematics, physics, manufacturing engineering, industrial engineering, materials science, chemistry, chemical engineering. **Selection Criteria:** Academic excellence and relevance to ongoing research in the electronics industry. **Funds Available:** 15 fellowships are awarded. Duration of award is one year. **Application Deadline:** February 1.

★7842★ Iota Sigma Pi Undergraduate Award for Excellence in Chemistry
Iota Sigma Pi
c/o Dr. Barbara A. Sawrey
Department of Chemistry B-003
University of California
La Jolla, CA 92093
Phone: (619)534-6479
Fax: (619)534-7687
Study Level: Undergraduate. **Award Type:** Award. **Applicant Eligibility:** Nominees must be senior women chemistry students in an accredited college or university that grants a four-year degree. Nominees must have attained senior standing. Nominees may be, but need not be, members of Iota Sigma Pi. **Selection Criteria:** Excellence in the field of chemistry. **Funds Available:** $300. **Application Details:** Nomination for the award must be made by members of the institution's undergraduate faculty. Only one nomination may be submitted by each department. The nomination dossier must contain: the nominee's permanent and school addresses; an official transcript of the student's college record, including grade point average; department head certification of most recent grades if they are not included in the official transcript; a list of the student's activities while in college and a statement of plans after graduation; two or more recommendations by faculty members. Six copies of the dossier should be sent to the Junior National Director. **Application Deadline:** February 1.

★7843★ Irene Stambler Vocational Opportunities Grant
Jewish Social Service Agency
6123 Montrose Rd.
Rockville, MD 20852
Phone: (301)816-2676
Study Level: Undergraduate. **Award Type:** Grant. **Purpose:** To assist women who need to become self-supporting after a recent separation, divorce, widowhood, or the catastrophic illness of a spouse. **Applicant Eligibility:** Candidates must be Jewish women in the Washington, DC area who have been divorced, widowed, or seperated within the last five years. They must demonstrate financial need, and have a specific, feasible vocational plan that can be implemented within two years. Women whose husbands have become disabled and who are financially in need may also apply. **Funds Available:** One time grants of up to $2,500 are awarded. **Application Details:** Can-

didates should request written criteria, application, and financial statement forms. Staff from the Jewish Social Service Agency are available to help complete the forms. **Contact(s):** Scholarship and Loan Coordinator, (301)816-2676.

★7844★ Ivy Parker Memorial Scholarship
Society of Women Engineers (SWE)
United Engineering Center, Rm. 345
345 E. 47th St.
New York, NY 10017
Phone: (212)705-7855
Study Level: Undergraduate. **Award Type:** Scholarship. **Applicant Eligibility:** Applicants must be women engineering students entering their junior or senior year. Applicants must demonstrate financial need. **Funds Available:** One $1,000 award. If awarded to a junior student, the recipient may reapply for continued support the following year. **Application Details:** Scholarship information and applications are sent to the deans of accredited engineering schools in October and March of each year. Applications and information can be obtained from the dean of engineering or from the SWE Headquarters in New York. Requests to SWE Headquarters must be accompanied by a self-addressed, stamped envelope. Applications are available from October through January only. **Application Deadline:** Completed applications, including all supportive materials, must be postmarked no later than February 1. Recipient only will be notified by May 1.

★7845★ Jeanne Humphrey Block Dissertation Award
The Henry A. Murray Research Center—Radcliffe College
10 Garden St.
Cambridge, MA 02138
Phone: (617)495-8140
Study Level: Doctorate. **Award Type:** Award. **Applicant Eligibility:** Applicants must be women enrolled in a doctoral program in a field relevant to girls' or womens' psychological development. They must complete course work by the time the award is made. Dissertation proposals should focus on the development of sex differences or some other developmental issues of particular concern to girls or women. **Selection Criteria:** Preference is given to projects that draw on or contribute to the resources of the Henry A. Murray Research Center of Radcliffe College. Recipient selection is based on the importance of the research question and its potential contribution to the field of study; the adequacy of the research design; the extent to which the project creatively uses or contributes to the Murray Center's resources; and general academic excellence. **Funds Available:** One grant of $2,500 is awarded annually. **Application Details:** Applicant should submit a cover page with name, affiliation, and title of the proposed research. A description of the research to be undertaken, including statements of background significance and rationale of the project should be detailed in the body of the proposal. Descriptions may consist of up to 6 double-spaced pages. A proposed time table and budget should also be included. **Application Deadline:** April 1.

★7846★ Judith Resnik Memorial Scholarship
Society of Women Engineers (SWE)
United Engineering Center, Rm. 305
345 E. 47th St.
New York, NY 10017
Phone: (212)705-7855
Study Level: Undergraduate. **Award Type:** Scholarship. **Applicant Eligibility:** Applicants must be rising women seniors studying an engineering field with a space-related major, who will pursue a career in the space industry. Applicants must be SWE members. **Funds Available:** One $1,000 award. **Application Details:** Scholarship information and applications are sent to the deans of accredited engineering schools in October and March of each year. Applications and information can be obtained from the dean of engineering or from the SWE Headquarters in New York. Requests to SWE Headquarters must be accompanied by a self-addressed, stamped envelope. Applications are available from October through January only. **Application Deadline:** Completed applications, including all supportive materials, must be postmarked no later than February 1. Recipient only will be notified by May 1.

★7847★ Julia Kiene Fellowship
Electrical Women's Round Table (EWRT)
PO Box 292793
Nashville, TN 37229-2793
Study Level: Graduate. **Award Type:** Fellowship. **Purpose:** To honor accomplishments of women in the electrical field and to encourage high caliber women to study toward advanced degrees in preparation for leadership in fields such as electrical utilities, electrical engineering, electric home appliance and home equipment manufacturing, journalism, radio-television, research, education, cooperative extension service, and communication. **Applicant Eligibility:** Candidates must be women who are graduating from an accredited college or university. Candidates should be planning to pursue graduate studies in any phase of electrical energy at a college or university that is approved by EWRT Fellowship Committee. **Selection Criteria:** Applications are judged on the basis of scholarship, character, financial need, and professional interest in electrical energy. **Funds Available:** Up to $2,000 for graduate work in electrical energy. **Application Details:** Applications, which must include statements about the candidates' interest in graduate work and how they propose to contribute to the field of electrical energy upon completion of graduate study, should be submitted with references and official transcripts. **Application Deadline:** March 1.

★7848★ Junior Native Daughter Scholarship
Native Daughters of the Golden West
543 Baker St.
San Francisco, CA 94117-1405
Phone: (415)563-9091
Study Level: Undergraduate. **Award Type:** Scholarship. **Applicant Eligibility:** Applicant must have been an active participating member of the Junior Daughters as of October 12, 1985, have a letter of acceptance from a school of choice (university, college, vocational school, junior college) and a grade point average of at least 2.5 in the seventh semester of high school or the fall of senior year. **Funds Available:** Scholarships of $100 are awarded. **Application Details:** Application forms may be obtained

from the Chairman of the Committee on Education and Scholarships or from the Grand Parlor Office of the Native Daughters of the Golden West.

★7849★ Kansas City Speech Pathology Award
Kappa Kappa Gamma Fraternity
PO Box 2079
Columbus, OH 43216-2079

Study Level: Graduate. **Award Type:** Scholarship. **Purpose:** To finance eight weeks of clinical training in the Speech Pathology Service of the Institute of Rehabilitation Medicine, New York University Medical Center. This Advanced Clinic Practicum is a comprehensive and intensive clinical experience in the language rehabilitation of brain-damaged adults especially geared toward speech pathology students who intend to specialize in this area. **Applicant Eligibility:** Candidates need not be members of Kappa Kappa Gamma, but must have completed at least two years of study on campuses with chapters or be enrolled in graduate work on campuses with chapters of Kappa Kappa Gamma Fraternity. Candidates must be women, United States or Canadian citizens, and in need of financial assistance. **Funds Available:** $2,000. **Contact(s):** Additional information about the course of study may be obtained by writing to Dr. Martha Taylor Sarno, Institute of Rehabilitation Medicine, New York University Medical Center, New York.

★7850★ Kappa Kappa Gamma Chapter Consultant Scholarships
Kappa Kappa Gamma Fraternity
PO Box 2079
Columbus, OH 43216-2079

Study Level: Graduate. **Award Type:** Scholarship. **Applicant Eligibility:** These scholarships are available to graduating Kappa Kappa Gamma Fraternity members who have held major office in their own chapters and who are interested in assisting other chapters while doing additional study. Candidates must be women and United States or Canadian citizens who have completed at least two years of study on campuses with Kappa Kappa Gamma chapters or who will be graduate students on campuses with chapters of Kappa Kappa Gamma Fraternity. **Funds Available:** The amounts of the awards are determined on an individual basis. **Application Deadline:** December 1. **Contact(s):** Director of Field Representatives.

★7851★ Kappa Kappa Gamma Emergency Assistance Grants
Kappa Kappa Gamma Fraternity
PO Box 2079
Columbus, OH 43216-2079

Study Level: Undergraduate. **Award Type:** Grant. **Applicant Eligibility:** These grants are intended for Kappa Kappa Gamma Fraternity upperclassmen who face sudden financial emergencies. Applicants must be members of Kappa Kappa Gamma Fraternity, women, United States or Canadian citizens and have completed two years of study on campuses with chapters of Kappa Kappa Gamma Fraternity. **Funds Available:** Grants of up to $500 are determined on an individual basis. **Application Details:** Applicants must be recommended by the Kappa Kappa Gamma Advisory Board. Applications are accepted and grants awarded throughout

the year. **Contact(s):** Chapter Council adviser or Chairman of Emergency Assistance Grants.

★7852★ Kappa Kappa Gamma Graduate Fellowships
Kappa Kappa Gamma Fraternity
PO Box 2079
Columbus, OH 43216-2079

Study Level: Graduate. **Award Type:** Fellowship. **Applicant Eligibility:** Applicants must be women college students who are citizens of the United States or Canada. They must have received their bachelor's degree, or will have obtained it prior to July 1st. They must have attended an institution for two years that has a chapter of Kappa Kappa Gamma, or will attend as a graduate student an institution where there is a chapter. Both members and nonmembers are eligible. Applicants with high academic standing who need assistance in training and careers, are eligible. **Funds Available:** Graduate Fellowships of $1,000 each are awarded annually. **Application Details:** Candidates must request application forms before February 1. Applications must be filed by February 15.

★7853★ Kappa Kappa Gamma Rehabilitation Scholarships
Kappa Kappa Gamma Fraternity
PO Box 2079
Columbus, OH 43216-2079

Study Level: Undergraduate, Graduate. **Award Type:** Scholarship. **Purpose:** To assist students in preparation for work with the mentally retarded, physically handicapped, socially deprived, emotionally disturbed, and aged. **Applicant Eligibility:** These scholarships are awarded to both undergraduate and graduate female students. Undergraduate students must have completed two years of study on campuses with chapters of Kappa Kappa Gamma. Graduate recipients must be enrolled for study on campuses with chapters of Kappa Kappa Gamma. Applicants for the undergraduate scholarships must be majoring in any phase of rehabilitation. Graduate student applicants must be pursuing advanced study in some field of rehabilitation. Applicants must be United States or Canadian citizens, but may or may not be members of Kappa Kappa Gamma Fraternity. **Funds Available:** Undergraduate scholarships are $750; graduate scholarships are $1,000. **Application Deadline:** Completed applications must be filed by February 15.

★7854★ Kappa Kappa Gamma Student Loan Fund
Kappa Kappa Gamma Fraternity
PO Box 2079
Columbus, OH 43216-2079

Study Level: Graduates, Undergraduates. **Award Type:** Loan. **Applicant Eligibility:** The fund is for junior, senior, and graduate women college students who are in need of additional assistance to finance their academic studies. Applicants must be members of Kappa Kappa Gamma and United States or Canadian Citizens. **Funds Available:** Loans of up to $1,000 per year are available. A maximum of $2,000 may be borrowed over a two-year period at low interest rates. **Application Details:** Applications may be filed at any time.

★7855★ Kappa Kappa Gamma Undergraduate Scholarships
Kappa Kappa Gamma Fraternity
PO Box 2079
Columbus, OH 43216-2079

Study Level: Undergraduate. **Award Type:** Scholarship. **Applicant Eligibility:** Candidates are required to be Kappa Kappa Gamma members, women, and United States or Canadian citizens. Applicants should have completed at least two years of study on campuses with chapters of Kappa Kappa Gamma Fraternity. Candidates must have at least a B average, no F's, and must have made important contributions to their chapters and campuses. Applicants must demonstrate need for financial assistance. **Funds Available:** $750 per scholarship. **Application Deadline:** February 15. **Contact(s):** Chairman of Undergraduate Scholarships.

★7856★ Katherine J. Schutze Memorial Scholarship
Christian Church (Disciples of Christ)
Division of Homeand Ministries
222 S. Downey Ave.
PO Box 1986
Indianapolis, IN 46206
Phone: (317)353-1499

Study Level: graduate. **Award Type:** Scholarship. **Applicant Eligibility:** Applicant must be a woman seminary student; a member of the Christian Church (Disciples of Christ); planning to prepare for the ordained ministry Christian Church (Disciples of Christ); at least a C plus student; able to provide evidence of financial need; enrolled full-time in an accredited school or seminary. **Application Details:** Applicants must provide a transcript of academic work; make a renewal application each year if eligible; provide references from a regional minister, pastor, lay leaders, and/or professors; be under care of a regional Commission on the Ministry or in the process of coming under care. Write for application. **Application Deadline:** March 15.

★7857★ Kathryn G. Siphers Scholarship
Women Band Directors National Association (WBDNA)
344 Overlook Dr.
West Lafayette, IN 47906
Phone: (317)463-1738

Study Level: Undergraduate. **Award Type:** Scholarship. **Purpose:** To support young college women currently preparing to be band directors. **Applicant Eligibility:** Must be women instrumental music majors enrolled in a university and working toward a degree in music education with the intention of becoming band directors. **Application Details:** Write for application. **Application Deadline:** December 1.

★7858★ Ladies Auxiliary to the VFW Junior Girls Scholarship
Ladies Auxiliary to the VFW
406 W. 34th St.
Kansas City, MO 64111
Phone: (816)561-8655
Fax: (815)931-4753
Brenda H. Hampton, Contact

Study Level: Undergraduate. **Award Type:** Scholarship. **Applicant Eligibility:** Applicant must have been an active member for one year, holding an office in her Junior Girls Unit. Applicants must be in school grades 9 through

12. Previous prize winners are not eligible, but former unsuccessful applicants may re-apply. **Selection Criteria:** Judging is based on a point system; junior unit activities 30 points, school activities and community activities 25 points each, and scholastic grades 20 points. **Funds Available:** Two scholarships, one of $3,000 and one of $2,000 are awarded annually. Scholarships are paid to the recipients' college of choice upon their acceptance. In addition, $100 is awarded to each Junior Girl who is selected as Department winner and entered in the National Championship. **Application Details:** Application must be accompanied by school grades transcript, letters of recommendation from a school teacher, Junior Girls leader, and one other person of applicant's choice. These papers must be submitted to the auxiliary Junior Girls Unit Chairman for initial judging. **Application Deadline:** One application from each unit is sent to the Department Junior Girls chairman by April 15. The winning department application is forwarded to the National Headquarters for national competition by May 15.

★7859★ **Lillian Moller Gilbreth Scholarship**
Society of Women Engineers (SWE)
United Engineering Center, Rm. 305
35 E. 47th St.
New York, NY 10017
Phone: (212)705-7855

Study Level: Undergraduate. **Award Type:** Scholarship. **Applicant Eligibility:** Applicants must be junior or senior women engineering students of outstanding potential and achievement. **Funds Available:** One $4,000 award. **Application Details:** Scholarship information and applications are sent to the deans of accredited engineering schools in October and March of each year. Applications and information can be obtained from the dean of engineering or from the SWE Headquarters in New York. Requests to SWE Headquarters must be accompanied by a self-addressed, stamped envelope. Applications are available from October through January only. **Application Deadline:** Completed applications, including all supportive materials, must be postmarked no later than February 1. Recipient only will be notified by May 1.

★7860★ **Lucy Corbett Scholarship**
Women in Communications, Inc.—Detroit Chapter (WICI)
35918 Rewa
Mt. Clemens, MI 48043
Phone: (313)226-9282

Study Level: Graduate, Undergraduate. **Award Type:** Scholarship. **Applicant Eligibility:** Applicant must be a female Michigan resident, a junior, senior or graduate student majoring in journalism or communications at a Michigan college or university. Applicant must be recommended by a faculty member and a department chairman. **Selection Criteria:** The scholarship is not awarded solely on financial need, although the applicant's financial status will be considered. At least a 3.0 grade point average on 4.0 scale is required. **Funds Available:** $1,000. **Application Details:** Application forms can be obtained from Lynn C. Anderson, WICI Scholarship Center, 1212 Griswold, Detroit, MI 48226-1899. **Application Deadline:** Beginning of April.

★7861★ **Luise Meyer-Schutzmeister Award**
Award for Women in Science—Educational Foundation (AWIS)
1522 K St., NW, Ste. 820
Washington, DC 20005
Phone: (202)408-0742

Study Level: Graduate. **Award Type:** Award. **Applicant Eligibility:** Applicants must be female graduate students in physics. Winners have traditionally been at the dissertation level of their graduate work. U.S. citizens may use the money for study in the U.S. or abroad. Non-U.S. citizens must be enrolled in a U.S. institution of higher education to be eligible for these awards. **Funds Available:** One award of $500. Award can be used for any aspect of education, including tuition, books, housing, research, expenses, and equipment. Honorable mentions of $100 are sometimes awarded. **Application Details:** Application forms for the awards are available from AWIS Headquarters between September 1 and December 15 of each year. The application includes a basic form, a two-to three-page summary of the candidate's dissertation research, and two recommendation report forms. Applicants must submit official transcripts of all course work conducted as postsecondary institutions. **Application Deadline:** All materials must be received by January 15. Winner is notified by mail and announced publicly in the July/August issue of the *AWIS Newletter*. Applicants may call the AWIS around June 15 for results.

★7862★ **Lyle Mamer Fellowship**
Electrical Women's Round Table (EWRT)
PO Box 292793
Nashville, TN 37229-2793

Study Level: Graduate. **Award Type:** Fellowship. **Purpose:** To honor the accomplishments of women in the electrical field and to encourage high caliber women to study towards advanced degrees in preparation for leadership in fields such as electric utilities, electrical engineering, electric home appliances and home equipment manufacturing, journalism, radio-television, research, communications, cooperative extension service and education. **Applicant Eligibility:** Candidates must be women who are graduating seniors from an accredited college or university. Candidates should be planning to pursue graduate studies in any phase of electrical energy at a college or university that is approved by EWRT Fellowship Committee. **Selection Criteria:** Applications are judged on the basis of scholarship, character, financial need, and professional interests in electrical energy. **Funds Available:** Up to $1,000 for graduate work in electrical energy. **Application Details:** Applications, which should include statements about the candidates' interest in graduate work and how they propose to contribute to the field of electrical energy upon completion of graduate study, should be submitted with references and official transcripts. **Application Deadline:** March 1.

★7863★ **Mary Butler Scholarship**
Women in Communications, Inc.—Detroit Chapter (WICI)
35918 Rewa
Mt. Clemens, MI 48043
Phone: (313)226-9282

Study Level: Graduate, Undergraduate. **Award Type:** Scholarship. **Applicant Eligibility:** Applicant must be a female Michigan resident at a Michigan college or university and a junior,

senior, or graduate student majoring in journalism or communications. The applicant must be recommended by a faculty member and department chairman. Applicant must be a first-rate student who has already demonstrated communications skill. **Selection Criteria:** The scholarship is not awarded solely on financial need, although the applicant's financial status will be considered. At least a 3.0 average on a 4.0 scale is required. Special consideration will be given to students who have faced personal challenge. **Funds Available:** $500. **Application Details:** Application forms can be obtained from Lynn C. Anderson, WICI Scholarship Center, 1212 Griswold, Detroit, MI 48226-1899. **Application Deadline:** Beginning of April.

★7864★ **Mary Connolly Livingston Grant**
Lambda Kappa Sigma—International Office
6250 Mountain Vista, Ste. 1
Henderson, WV 89014
Phone: (702)456-3186
Fax: (702)456-4309

Study Level: Doctorate. **Award Type:** Grant. **Purpose:** To advance the careers of students in the pharmaceutical sciences. **Applicant Eligibility:** Candidates must be members of Lambda Kappa Sigma who are enrolled in programs leading to the Pharm.D. degree at an accredited college or university. They must be in the upper half of their class. Preference is given to applicants enrolled in the last two years of the professional curriculum. Applicants must provide evidence of financial need. **Funds Available:** Currently, one award of $500 is presented. **Contact(s):** Chairman, Educational Grant Committee.

★7865★ **Mary Isabel Sibley Fellowship**
Phi Beta Kappa Society
1811 Q St., NW
Washington, DC 20009
Phone: (202)265-3808

Study Level: Doctorate, Postdoctorate. **Award Type:** Fellowship. **Applicant Eligibility:** Applicants must be unmarried women between 25 and 35 years of age. They must have demonstrated ability to carry out original research. They must hold the doctorate or have fulfilled all the requirements for the doctorate except the dissertation. Applicants must plan to devote full-time work to research during the fellowship year. Eligibility is not limited to members of Phi Beta Kappa. In odd years, the fellowship is offered for the study of Greek language, literature, history or archaeology; in the even years, the fellowship is offered for the study of French language or literature. **Funds Available:** One fellowship in the amount of $7,000 is awarded annually. **Application Deadline:** Applications must be filed before January 15 of the year in which the award is granted; recipients are notified by April 1. **Contact(s):** Mary Isabel Sibley Fellowship Committee.

★7866★ **MASWE Memorial Scholarship**
Society of Women Engineers (SWE)
United Engineering Center, Rm. 305
345 E. 47th St.
New York, NY 10017
Phone: (212)705-7855

Study Level: Undergraduate. **Award Type:** Scholarship. **Applicant Eligibility:** Applicants must be sophomore women pursuing an engineering degree. Applicants must be SWE student members. United States citizens are preferred. **Funds Available:** One $1,000 award. **Application Details:** Scholarship information and applications are sent to the deans of accredited engineering schools in October and March of each year. Applications and information can be obtained from the dean of engineering or from the SWE Headquarters in New York. Requests to SWE Headquarters must be accompanied by a self-addressed, stamped envelope. Applications are available from October through January only. **Application Deadline:** Completed applications, including all supportive materials, must be postmarked no later than February 1. Recipient only will be notified by May 1.

★7867★ **McKnight Junior Faculty**
Development Fellowships
Florida Endowment Fund for Higher
Education
201 E. Kennedy Blvd., Ste. 1525
Tampa, FL 33602
Phone: (813)221-2772
Fax: (813)224-0192

Study Level: Graduate, Professional Development. **Award Type:** Fellowship. **Purpose:** The program is intended to encourage excellence in teaching and research for minority junior faculty members with special emphasis on African-Americans and women in fields where they are severely under represented by affording a full academic year to enable participants to pursue special interests or research directly related to their teaching area. **Applicant Eligibility:** The awards are open to teachers in public and private colleges, universities, and community colleges in Florida. Applicants are required to have a minimum of two years and no more than six years in a non-tenured position. Proof of legal residency in Florida is required. Candidates must be United States citizens. **Funds Available:** Twenty fellowships of $15,000 are awarded annually. The recipient receives normal salary and benefits. The awardee's institution receives $15,000 to cover teaching replacement cost. **Application Deadline:** February 1.

★7868★ **Miss America Pageant**
Scholarships
Miss America Pageant Scholarship
Foundation
PO Box 119
Atlantic City, NJ 08404

Study Level: Graduate, Undergraduate. **Award Type:** Scholarship. **Purpose:** "To encourage and foster young American women in becoming the leaders of tomorrow." **Applicant Eligibility:** Entrant must be a female between the ages of 17 and 26, a high school graduate, single and never been married, of good moral character, and a citizen of the United States. A complete list of eligibility requirements is available from the local or state pageants. **Selection Criteria:** Based on a series of pageants at the local, state, and national levels. Contestants are judged on talent, interview, evening gown, and swimsuit competitions. **Funds Available:** More than $5,000,000 is awarded annually in scholarships presented at the local, state, and national Miss America pageants. The scholarships are intended for tuition, room, board, supplies, and other educational expenses. **Contact(s):** Local pageant organization.

★7869★ **Monticello College Foundation**
Fellowship for Women
The Newberry Library
60 W. Walton St.
Chicago, IL 60610-3380

Study Level: Postdoctorate. **Award Type:** Fellowship. **Applicant Eligibility:** Applicants must have the Ph.D. at the time of application, and must be a United States citizen or permanent resident. The award is primarily for women at an early stage in their professional careers whose work gives clear promise of scholarly productivity and whose career would be significantly enhanced by six months of research and writing. Applicants may propose a study in any field appropriate to the Newberry's collections. Preference, other matters being equal, will be given to an applicant whose scholarship is particularly concerned with the study of women. **Funds Available:** The six month fellowship carries a stipend of $12,500. **Application Deadline:** January 10.

★7870★ **NABWA Scholarship Award**
National Association of Black Women
Attorneys (NABWA)
3711 Macomb St. NW, 2nd Fl.
Washington, DC 20016
Phone: (202)966-9693
Fax: (202)244-6648
Robin Alexander, Contact

Study Level: Graduate. **Award Type:** Scholarship. **Purpose:** To provide financial assistance to black female law students. **Applicant Eligibility:** Applicant must be a black female in her first, second, or third year of a four year program at an accredited law school. **Selection Criteria:** Applicants are judged through a writing competition. **Application Deadline:** October 1.

★7871★ **National Association for Women**
in Education Women's Research Awards
National Association for Women in Education
1325 18th St. NW, Ste. 210
Washington, DC 20036

Study Level: Graduate. **Award Type:** Award. **Purpose:** To encourage and support excellence in research by, for, and about women. **Applicant Eligibility:** The graduate student competition is open to any student enrolled in a graduate study program. Any person may enter the open competition. **Funds Available:** Awards are in the amount of $500. **Application Details:** Contact the Association for application. **Application Deadline:** November 1.

★7872★ **National League of American Pen**
Women Scholarships for Mature Women
The National League of American Pen
Women, Inc.
1300 17th St., N.W.
Washington, DC 20036

Study Level: Professional Development. **Award Type:** Scholarship. **Purpose:** To further the creative goals of women at a time in their lives when encouragement can lead to realization of long-term goals. **Applicant Eligibility:** Applicants must be women 35 years of age or older as of the beginning of January of even-numbered years. Candidate cannot be a Pen Woman or related to a Pen Woman. **Funds Available:** Three $1,000 scholarships are awarded in even-numbered years in Art, Letters, and Music. **Application Details:** Candidates must submit a letter stating that they will be 35 or over by the application deadline date, a $5.00 fee, and a

self-addressed stamped envelope. They must also submit slides, manuscripts, or musical compositions depending upon their field of interest. **Application Deadline:** January 15 in even-numbered years. Awards are usually made by April.

★7873★ **National Miss Indian U.S.**
Scholarship
American Indian Heritage Foundation
6501 Arlington Blvd.
Falls Church, VA 22044
Barbara Butler, Pageant Director

Study Level: Undergraduate, Graduate. **Award Type:** Scholarship, Award. **Applicant Eligibility:** Women must be 18-26 years old, never married, pregnant, or cohabitated, and must be high school graduates. Applicant must have an Indian sponsor such as: tribe, business, or organization with a valid governing board. The women must also have a belief in and practice tribal culture and heritage. They must exhibit such positive characteristics as: listening to their elders, joining in pow-wows, and promoting Indian language if possible. **Funds Available:** First place winner receives a $10,000 cash award, $7,000 to the school of choice, $5,000 for wardrobe ($2,500 for traditional clothing and $2,500 for cultural/heritage clothing). Four runners-up receive the same kinds of prizes in descending amounts. **Application Details:** Send a request for an application. **Application Deadline:** September 15.

★7874★ **NCAA Ethnic Minority and**
Women's Enchancement Programs
National Collegiate Athletic Association
(NCAA)
6201 College Blvd.
Overland, KS 66211-2422
Phone: (913)339-1906

Study Level: Graduate. **Award Type:** Scholarship. **Purpose:** To increase the pool of and opportunities for qualified minority and women candidates in intercollegiate athletics. **Applicant Eligibility:** The applicant must be accepted into a sports-administration program or a related program that will assist the applicant in obtaining a career in athletics. **Funds Available:** 10 scholarships to ethnic minorities and 10 scholarships to women are available annually to college graduates who will be entering into the first semester of their postgraduate studies. Each award is valued at $6,000. **Application Details:** All application folders for the postgraduate scholarships and internships, with supporting transcripts, must be to the NCAA national office. **Application Deadline:** Applications are available in December. Application folders must be mailed to the NCAA national office no later than March 15.

★7875★ **NCAR Graduate Research**
Assistantships
National Center for Atmospheric Research—
Advanced Study Program (NCAR)
PO Box 3000
Boulder, CO 80307
Phone: (303)497-1601

Study Level: Graduate, Doctorate. **Award Type:** Award. **Applicant Eligibility:** Candidates must declare their intention of working on a Ph.D. thesis in cooperation with a National Center for Atmospheric Research (NCAR) program. Applicants must be enrolled in a university graduate program having common interests with NCAR facility project or research group concerned. Fields of study are atmospheric dynamics, climatology and paleoclimatology, oceanography, atmospheric physics, radiation, cloud physics, atmospheric chemistry, solar and space physics, astrophysics, environmental and societal impact assessment, and atmospheric technology. Recipient is expected to be in residence at NCAR for thesis work except when research requires residence elsewhere. For students having a limited amount of course work to complete, support may be available if they can assist in NCAR research for at least nine months out of each 12 month period of support. There are no restrictions for foreign applicants, and applications from women and minorities are encouraged. **Selection Criteria:** Research proposal, applicant's scientific potential and ability to take advantage of research opportunities at NCAR. **Funds Available:** For the student who passes the doctoral level comprehensive examination or its equivalent, the salary is $13,150. For those who have not passed the comprehensive exam and for those still working on an M.S. degree, the salary is $12,400. Funding for field trips relating to thesis research is negotiable; funds are available for two trips per year to the applicant's home institution or to appropriate scientific meeting (usually to the amount of under $1,200 per year) **Application Details:** The awards are made on the basis of a proposal submitted jointly by a university scientist and an NCAR scientist. The proposal should include a brief description and time table for the project, supervisory arrangements, and NCAR facilities required. Biographical data and background, a transcript of all undergraduate and graduate work, and the names of four persons excluding the university scientist and the NCAR scientist who will serve as the student's adviser to whom ASP can write for references are also required. **Application Deadline:** Proposals are competitively evaluated quarterly beginning January 1. All materials should be submitted to NCAR in Boulder.

★7876★ **New Mexico Graduate Fellowships**
New Mexico Educational Assistance Foundation
3900 Osuna, NE
PO Box 27020
Albuquerque, NM 87125-7020
Phone: (505)345-3371

Study Level: Graduate. **Award Type:** Fellowship. **Purpose:** To increase graduate enrollment, particularly minorities and women in academic fields of high regional and national priority in the state's public universities. **Applicant Eligibility:** Applicants must be U.S. citizens and New Mexico residents. They must be willing to serve ten hours per week in an unpaid internship or assistantship. Preference will be given to students enrolled in business, engineering, computer science, mathematics, and agriculture. **Funds Available:** The Fellowship will pay a maximum of $7,200 per year ($600 per month); it is renewed annually based on good academic standing as determined by the institution. **Application Details:** Formal application form required. **Contact(s):** Financial aid officer of the New Mexico post-secondary school of their choice.

★7877★ **New Mexico Minority Doctoral Assistance**
New Mexico Eudcational Assistance Foundation
3900 Osuna, NE
PO Box 27020
Albuquerque, NM 87125-7020
Phone: (505)345-3371

Study Level: Doctorate. **Award Type:** Loan. **Purpose:** To increase the number of ethnic minorities and women teaching engineering, physical or life sciences, mathematics, and other academic disciplines in which ethnic minorities and women are demonstrably underrepresented. **Applicant Eligibility:** This is a loan-for-service program. Applicants must be citizens of the United States and residents of New Mexico. They must have successfully completed all requirements for a baccalaureate degree and/or master's degree at a New Mexico four-year public post-secondary institution. They must meet admission requirements and be accepted for enrollment as full-time doctoral students at an eligible out-of state institution. Applicants must be sponsored by a New Mexico four-year institution. Recipients must agree to return to teach at the sponsoring institution. **Contact(s):** Those interested should contact the graduate dean of the sponsoring institution of their choice.

★7878★ **New York Life Foundation Scholarships for Women in the Health Professions**
Business and Professional Women's Foundation—Educational Programs (BPW)
2012 Massachusetts Ave. NW
Washington, DC 20036

Study Level: Undergraduate. **Award Type:** Scholarship. **Purpose:** To assist women seeking the education necessary for entry or re-entry into the workforce or advancement within a career in the health-care field. **Applicant Eligibility:** Scholarships are awarded for full-time or part-time programs of study in one of the health care fields. Applicants must: be women 30 years of age or older; citizens of the United States; officially accepted into an accredited program or course of study at a United States institution; graduating within 24 months from August 31 of the application year; demonstrate critical need for financial assistance to upgrade skills or complete education for career advancement; and have a definite plan to use the desired training to improve chances for advancement, to train for a new career field, or to re-enter the job market. This scholarship program does not cover study at the doctoral level, correspondence courses, or non-degree programs. Relatives or officials of the New York Life Insurance Company are not eligible to participate in this program. **Funds Available:** Scholarships range from $500 to $1,000. 100 scholarships are awarded per year. **Application Details:** To receive application packet, application request form must be submitted to the BPW Foundation. **Application Deadline:** Application Materials are available between October 1 and April 1. Application request forms must be received between October 1 and April 1. Completed application materials must be returned by April 15.

★7879★ **NFPW Junior/Senior Scholarships**
National Federation of Press Women, Inc. (NFPW)
PO Box 99
Blue Springs, MD 64013
Phone: (816)229-1666

Study Level: Undergraduate. **Award Type:** Scholarship. **Applicant Eligibility:** Applicants must be female college students who are majoring in communication and seeking a degree in journalism. Candidates must be junior or senior level students. **Selection Criteria:** Recipients are selected on the basis of career potential, scholarship, and financial need. **Funds Available:** One $1,000 scholarship is awarded annually. **Application Details:** Applications must include a transcript of college credit, work samples, and letters of recommendation in sealed envelopes from at least two persons acquainted with the applicant's work and/or school achievements. A photograph, a description of the study plan, a timetable for completion, a budget for use of the scholarship, and how the scholarship will be augmented to achieve study goals are also required. **Application Deadline:** May 1. **Contact(s):** Professional Education Scholarships.

★7880★ **NIAAA Individual National Research Service Awards**
National Institute on Alcohol Abuse and Alcoholism (NIAAA)
5600 Fishers Ln.
Rockville, MD 20857
Phone: (301)443-4223

Study Level: Doctorate, Postdoctorate. **Award Type:** Fellowship. **Purpose:** To provide fellowships for pre- and postdoctral scholars for research training in both basic and applied alcohol research projects for a wide range of disciplines as related to alcohol abuse and alcoholism. **Applicant Eligibility:** Applicants must be U.S. citizens, noncitizen nationals, or lawfully admitted to the U.S. for permanent residence at the time of application. They must be willing to engage in biomedical or behavioral health-related research and/or health-related teaching within two years after termination of the Award. Such service shall be on a continuous basis and average more than 20 hours per week for a period equal to the total NRSA support in excess of 12 months. Women and minority candidates are particularly encouraged to apply. **Selection Criteria:** Applicant qualifications and potential for both a scuessful career as an independent researcher and successful fellowship experience. **Funds Available:** Awards include stipends for awardees and a small allowance to the sponsoring institution to defray some of the awardee's training expenses. Individuals sponsored by foreign institutions also receive travel funds. **Application Details:** Formal applications comprised of two parts (part 1 to be completed by the applicant; part 2 by the sponsor and sponsoring institution officials). **Application Deadline:** January 10, May 10, and September 10 for projects to begin no earlier than June, October, and February respectively. **Contact(s):** Office of Grants Inquiries, Division of Research Grants, National Institutes of Health, Bethesda, MD 20892.

★7881★ NRC/ACRS Science and Engineering Fellowships
U.S. Nuclear Regulatory Commission
Advisory Committee on Reactor
Safeguards (NRC/ACRS)
Washington, DC 20555

Study Level: Doctorate, Postdoctorate. **Award Type:** Fellowship. **Purpose:** To assist the Committee in carrying out its functions in the nuclear power safety field, and to provide an opportunity for young engineers and scientists to develop an understanding of nuclear power production and expertise in the nuclear reactor safety area. **Applicant Eligibility:** Applications are accepted from persons with the following educational backgrounds: a doctorate in a scientific or engineering field; students in science or engineering who are in the final steps of their Ph.D. work; engineers or scientists with experience in the nuclear field who are at a stage in their careers where they can undertake a one-to-two year fellowship program on a full-time basis. Applicants must be United States citizens. Applications from minorities and women are especially encouraged. **Funds Available:** Stipend ranges from $32,000 to $65,000. Duration of award is two years.

★7882★ NSF Graduate Research Fellowships for Women in Engineering
National Science Foundation (NSF)
2101 Constitution Ave.
Washington, DC 20418
Phone: (202)357-9598

Study Level: Doctorate, Graduate. **Award Type:** Fellowship. **Purpose:** To encourage women to undertake graduate study in engineering. NSF annually awards 65 Fellowships for study and research in engineering leading to master's or doctoral degrees. Fellowships are intended for students at or near the beginning of their graduate study in engineering. **Applicant Eligibility:** Applicants must be female citizens or nationals of the United States. They must have, by the beginning of the Fall term of the application year, completed no more than 30 semester hours, 45 quarter hours, or the equivalent of graduate study in the science and engineering fields since completion of their last baccalaureate degree in science or engineering. Applicants are not disqualified by reason of holding a master's degree unless they have exceeded the semester and quarter hour limitations stipulated above. **Selection Criteria:** Ability and special aptitude training in science and engineering as judged by considering academic records, recommendations regarding applicant's qualifications, and GRE scores. **Funds Available:** Fellowships for a three-year tenure (usable over a five-year period). Stipends for 12 months are $13,500 (prorated monthly at $1,125 for lesser periods). Additionally, cost-of-education allowances of $6,000 per fellow are awarded to sponsoring institutions, as well as a special international research travel allowance for fellows who qualify. **Application Details:** In addition to completed applications (comprised of two parts), candidates are required to provide a proposed plan of study/research, description of previous research experience, course reports and academic transcripts, reference reports, and GRE scores. **Application Deadline:** Part 1 of the application is due in early November; part 2 in early December. **Contact(s):** The Fellowship Office, National Research Council, 2101 Constitution Ave., Washington, DC 20418; (202) 334-2872.

★7883★ NSF Minority Graduate Fellowships for Women
National Science Foundation (NSF)
2101 Constitution Ave.
Washington, DC 20418
Phone: (202)357-9498

Study Level: Doctorate, Graduate. **Award Type:** Fellowship. **Purpose:** To increase the number of practicing female scientists and engineers who are members of ethnic minority groups that traditionally have been underrepresented in the advanced levels of the nation's engineering talent pool. NSF annually awards 15 fellowships to support graduate studies in engineering leading to master's or doctoral degrees. Fellowships are intended for students at or near the beginning of their graduate study in engineering. **Applicant Eligibility:** Applicants must be female citizens or nationals of the United States and members of minority groups underrepresented in the advanced levels of the United States engineering pool. Such groups currently include American Indian, Black, Hispanic, Native Alaskan (Eskimo and Aleut), and Native Pacific Islander (Polynesian or Micronesian). They must have, by the beginning of the Fall term of the application year, completed no more than 30 semester hours, 45 quarter hours, or the equivalent of graduate study in the science and engineering fields since completion of their last baccalaureate degree in science or engineering. Applicants who have earned any medical degree are not eligible. **Selection Criteria:** Ability and special aptitude for advanced training in science and engineering as judged by considering academic records, recommendations regarding applicant's qualifications, and GRE scores. **Funds Available:** Fellowships for a three-year tenure (usable over a five-year period). Stipends for 12 months periods are $13,500 (prorated monthly at $1,125 for lesser periods). Additionally, cost-of-education allowances of $6,000 per fellow are awarded to sponsoring institutions, as well as a special international research travel allowance for fellows who qualify. **Application Details:** In addition to completed applications (comprised of two parts), candidates are required to provide a proposed plan of study/research, description of previous research experience, course reports and academic transcripts, reference reports, and GRE scores. **Application Deadline:** Part 1 of the application is due in early November; part 2 in early December. **Contact(s):** The Fellowship Office, National Research Council, 2101 Constitution Ave., Washington, DC 20418; (202)334-2872.

★7884★ Olive Lynn Salembier Scholarship
Society of Women Engineers (SWE)
United Engineering Center, Rm. 305
345 E. 47th St.
New York, NY 10117
Phone: (212)705-7855

Study Level: Graduate, Undergraduate. **Award Type:** Scholarship. **Applicant Eligibility:** Applicants must be women who have been out of the engineering job market a minimum of two years and seek to obtain the credentials necessary to re-enter the job market as an engineer. **Funds Available:** One $1,500 award. **Application Details:** Scholarship information and applications are sent to the deans of accredited engineering schools in October and March of each year. Applications and information can be obtained from the dean of engineering or from the SWE Headquarters in New York. Requests to SWE Headquarters must be accompanied by a self-

addressed, stamped envelope. Applications are available from March through June only. **Application Deadline:** Completed applications, including all supportive materials, must be postmarked no later than May 15. Recipients will be notified by September 15.

★7885★ Patricia Robert Harris Public Service Fellowship
U.S. Department of Education
Office of Student Financial Assistance
Washington, DC 20202
Phone: (202)732-3154

Study Level: Postdoctorate, doctorate. **Award Type:** Fellowship. **Purpose:** To provide the historically underrepresented (women, minorities, and others) with fellowships for study leading to an advanced degree in a graduate or professional program in specific academic areas. **Applicant Eligibility:** Recipients are women, minorities, or other members of an underrepresented group who plan to study full-time in postbaccalaureate professional degree at an institution that has received a fellowship allocation. Applicants must also be nationals of the U.S. or intend to become permanent residents. **Selection Criteria:** Applicants are selected by the institution. **Funds Available:** The $10,000 12-month stipend is prorated on a monthly basis at the rate of $500. **Contact(s):** Division of Higher Education, 400 Maryland Ave., SW, Washington, DC 20202; (202) 732-4389.

★7886★ Post Doctoral Support in the Atmospheric Sciences
National Center for Atmospheric Research—
Advanced Study Program
PO Box 3000
Boulder, CO 80307
Phone: (303)497-1601
Fax: (303)497-1137

Study Level: Postdoctorate. **Award Type:** Fellowship. **Purpose:** The program seeks to provide an opportunity for atmospheric scientists to continue their research interests and develop skills in new areas. **Applicant Eligibility:** Applicants must be just receiving the Ph.D. or equivalent or have more than four years applicable experience beyond the doctoral degree. Applications are encouraged from women and minorities, and there are no restrictions for foreign applicants. Highly qualified Ph.D. physicists, chemists, applied mathematicians, engineers, and specialists from other natural scientific disciplines as well as those interested in the environmental and societal impact of atmosphere-related issues are encouraged to apply. **Funds Available:** Fellowships for those with more than one year's experience receive $31,200. Appointees with regular positions (such as faculty members) receive stipends matching their salaries. Travel expenses and other benefits are also included. **Application Details:** Undergraduate and graduate transcripts; a list of honors, awards, scholarships and fellowships; an abstract of the doctoral dissertation; list of publications; summary of scientific work experience; four persons who can provide references directly to ASP; and a statement of interest in the atmospheric sciences are required. **Application Deadline:** Applications must be filed by mid-January; recipients are announced in March.

★7887★ R.L. Gillette Scholarship
American Foundation for the Blind, Inc.
15 West 16th St.
New York, NY 10011
Phone: (212)620-2000
Mrs. Leslye S. Piqueras, Contact

Study Level: Undergraduate. **Award Type:** Scholarship. **Applicant Eligibility:** Candidates must be women who are legally blind and enrolled in a four-year undergraduate degree program in literature or music. Applicants must be United States citizens. **Funds Available:** Two $1,000 scholarships are awarded annually. **Application Details:** Applicants must submit evidence of legal blindness; official transcripts of grades; proof of acceptance at a college or university; three letters of recommendation; a sample performance tape (not over 30 minutes) or a creative writing sample; and a typewritten statement of no more than two double-spaced pages describing educational and personal goals, work experience, extra-curricular activities, and how scholarship monies will be used.

★7888★ Renate W. Chasman Scholarship
Brookhaven Women in Science
PO Box 183
Upton, NY 11973
Phone: (516)282-7226

Study Level: Graduate, Undergraduate. **Award Type:** Scholarship. **Purpose:** To support women who are pursuing degrees in the sciences, engineering, or mathematics and who have had their studies interrupted through family, financial, or other pressures. **Applicant Eligibility:** Candidates must be re-entry women, must be citizens of the United States or permanent resident aliens, and must be residents of Nassau or Suffolk counties of Long Island, New York. Applicants must be accepted for credit in a degree-oriented program in the sciences, engineering or mathematics at an accredited institution. The program of study must be at the junior or senior undergraduate level, or first-year graduate level. **Selection Criteria:** Selection is based on academic and life/career record, letters of reference, and a short essay on career goals. Finalists will be chosen on merit. Financial need may be a consideration in the selection of winners. **Funds Available:** One-time awards of $1,000 are made directly to recipients, to be applied towards expenses associated with an academic program pursued on a half-time or greater basis. **Application Deadline:** June 1.

★7889★ Root Foreign Languages Scholarship
Kappa Kappa Gamma Fraternity
PO Box 2079
Columbus, OH 43216-2079

Study Level: Graduate. **Award Type:** Scholarship. **Applicant Eligibility:** This scholarship is open only to Kappa Kappa Gamma graduate students who wish to study a foreign language in the country of that language for one year. Candidates must be women, United States or Canadian citizens, and in need of financial assistance. **Funds Available:** $1,000 per scholarship. **Application Deadline:** Completed applications must be filed by February 15. **Contact(s):** Chairman of Graduate Fellowships.

★7890★ Ruth Buxton Sayre Scholarship
Country Women's Council, USA
c/o Betty Buff
3500 Henbet Dr.
West Columbia, SC 29169
Phone: (803)794-7548

Award Type: Scholarship. **Applicant Eligibility:** Applicant must be a female resident of the Americas. She should show potential leadership ability. **Funds Available:** Scholarship money will be sent to recipient's chosen educational institution or to the ACWW affiliated organization. **Application Details:** Application should be submitted through an ACWW affiliated organization. A list of sponsoring organizations can be obtained by contacting the Council.

★7891★ Sarah Bradley Tyson Memorial Fellowship
Woman's National Farm and Garden Association
c/o Mrs. Elmer Braun
13 Davis Dr.
Saginaw, MI 48602
Phone: (517)793-1714

Study Level: Doctorate. **Award Type:** Fellowship. **Purpose:** To recognize leadership in cooperative extension work and initiative in scientific research. **Applicant Eligibility:** Young women who have proved their ability by several years experience in agriculture, horticulture, or related subjects. **Funds Available:** $500 award to be used for advanced study at an educational institution of recognized standing within the United States. **Application Details:** A letter of application should include an account of the applicant's educational training; a statement in full of the object in view and the plan of study; a certificate of degrees received by the applicant from the registrar of the school awarding the degree; testimonials as to character, ability, personality, and scholarship; thesis, papers, or reports of investigations, published or unpublished if available; a health certificate; and a small recent photograph. **Application Deadline:** April 15.

★7892★ SDE Fellowships
Sigma Delta Epsilon Graduate Women in Science, Inc. (SDE)
PO Box 4748
Ithaca, NY 14852

Study Level: Postgraduate. **Award Type:** Fellowship. **Purpose:** To increase knowledge in the fundamental sciences and to encourage research by women. **Applicant Eligibility:** Candidates must be women holding a science degree from an accredited college or university. SDE Fellowships are for research in the natural sciences, i.e., physical, environmental, mathematical, computer, and life sciences. Applicants must have demonstrated outstanding ability and potential in research. **Selection Criteria:** Applications are reviewed based on scientific question, presentation, methodology, experience and budget. **Funds Available:** The amount of the fellowship may vary from $1,500 to $4,000. Grants may not be used for tuition, administrative overhead, or equipment of general use. The fellowship period depends upon the option exercised at the time the fellowship is granted. If it extends beyond a year, submission of an annual progress report is required. **Application Details:** Candidates must submit a formal application, a 4-page description of the project, evidence of research ability and experience (these may include a list of publications, short papers or reports), a detailed budget, statement of other financial support, two letters of recommendation and two self-addressed, stamped envelopes. **Application Deadline:** Applications are due December 1; awards are announced on June 1.

★7893★ Seattle Municipal Internships
Seattle Personnel Department
710 2nd Ave.
Seattle, WA 98104
Phone: (206)684-7999
Jerene Kelly, Contact

Study Level: Undergraduate, Graduate. **Award Type:** Internship. **Purpose:** To provide work experience in municipal government. **Applicant Eligibility:** Must be a graduate or undergraduate student majoring in engineering, business, or another professional field. **Selection Criteria:** Preference is given to women and minorities. **Funds Available:** Salary varies with position.

★7894★ Sigma Alpha Iota Inter-American Music Awards
Sigma Alpha Iota Philanthropies, Inc.
c/o Eugenia L. Dengel
165 W. 82nd St.
New York, NY 10024
Phone: (212)724-2809

Study Level: Professional Development. **Award Type:** Award. **Applicant Eligibility:** Candidates must be women composers from North, Central, or South America. Their composition must be a work for instrumental solo or instrumental solo with piano that has a performance time of seven to ten minutes and has not been published or performed publicly prior to its submission for this award. **Funds Available:** The composer of the winning composition receives: a $500 award; publication by C.F. Peters Corporation and a sharing of the royalties with Sigma Alpha Iota; first performance at the National Convention; and transportation and two nights lodging to attend the first performance. **Application Details:** A candidate may submit more than one composition and must pay an entry fee of $10 for each manuscript submitted. Contestants must sign each composition and entry blank with the same pseudonym. Manuscript must be written in black ink or heavy black pencil on vellum or opaque manuscript paper.

★7895★ Society of Daughters of the United States Army Scholarship
Society of Daughters of the United States Army
c/o Mary Louise Bishop
4242 East-West Hwy., Apt. 910
Chevy Chase, MD 20815

Study Level: Undergraduate. **Award Type:** Scholarship. **Applicant Eligibility:** Applicants must be a daughter or granddaughter (including adopted or stepdaughter) of a career commissioned officer of the United States Army (Warrant Officer through General) who is currently on active duty; retired after at least 20 years of active service or for medical reasons; or died while on active duty or after retiring with 20 or more years of active service. Applicants must be enrolled in, or planning to enroll in undergraduate study at any accredited college, university, or vocational school. **Selection Criteria:** A board of judges selects recipients based on a combination of financial need and personal record (scholastic standing, test scores, school community activities, etc.). First consideration each year is given to those recipients of the previous year who have not finished their course of study. **Funds Available:** One-year, renewable awards of $750 per year. **Application Details:** Three references, a current transcript showing above average standing in academic work to date, and an essay are required. Name, rank, social security number, and inclusive dates of active duty of the qualifying parent/grandparent are required with each candidate's request for an application. **Application Deadline:** March 31.

★7896★ Sportsgirl of the Year Scholarship
Teen Magazine
8490 Sunset Blvd.
Los Angeles, CA 90069
Phone: (213)854-2950

Study Level: Undergraduate. **Award Type:** Scholarship. **Purpose:** To encourage teenage females who are interested in pursuing postsecondary education and are outstanding athletes. **Applicant Eligibility:** Applicants must be athletes between 12 and 19 who excel in sports, have strong leadership skills, and have satisfactory academic progress. **Funds Available:** The winner receives a $10,000 scholarship that may be used at the school of her choice. **Application Details:** Applications are available in the March through June issues of Teen Magazine. Winner is announced the following February. **Application Deadline:** June.

★7897★ SSRC-MacArthur Foundation Fellowships on Peace and Security in a Changing World Dissertation Fellowships
Social Science Research Council (SSRC)
605 Third Ave.
New York, NY 10158
Phone: (212)661-0280

Study Level: Doctorate. **Award Type:** Fellowship. **Purpose:** To support research on the implications for security issues of worldwide cultural, social, economic, and political changes. **Applicant Eligibility:** The competition is open to researchers who are finishing course work, examinations, or similar requirements for the Ph.D. or its equivalent. Applicants should expect to complete all requirements for the doctoral degree except the dissertation by the spring of the award year. The competition is open to researchers in the social and behavioral sciences (including history and area studies), the humanities, or the physical and biological sciences. Persons doing their research in non-academic settings are welcome to apply. There are no citizenship, residency, or nationality requirements. The Council especially encourages women and members of minority groups to apply. **Funds Available:** Approximately eight fellowships are awarded. Fellowships pay a stipend of from $12,500 to $17,500 depending upon the cost of living in the area where the recipient will be working. **Application Deadline:** December 1.

★7898★ Susan B. Anthony Post-doctoral Fellowship
Susan B. Anthony Center for Women's Studies
c/o University of Rochester
583 Lattimore Hall
Rochester, NY 14627
Phone: (716)275-8318

Study Level: Postdoctorate. **Award Type:** Fellowship. **Purpose:** A Susan B. Anthony Fellow will work on a project, will be appointed in an existing academic department, and will teach two courses during the year. Content is open subject to the interests of the Fellow and the needs of the Center. The courses will bridge a standard academic discipline and women's studies. **Applicant Eligibility:** Must have Ph.D. in any discipline. Applicant's work should be closely related to women's studies. **Selection Criteria:** Based on merit of application received. **Funds Available:** $24,000 for one academic year beginning in September. **Application Details:** Submit vita, a course proposal, three letters of recommendation, a 1-2 page project proposal, and samples of published or unpublished work. **Application Deadline:** February 1. **Contact(s):** Director.

★7899★ TRW Scholarships
Society of Women Engineering (SWE)
United Engineering Center, Rm. 305
345 E. 47th St.
New York, NY 10017
Phone: (212)705-7855

Study Level: Undergraduate. **Award Type:** Scholarship. **Purpose:** To encourage freshmen women to major in engineering. **Applicant Eligibility:** Applicants must be women students who will be incoming freshmen in an accredited school, college or university. **Funds Available:** Awards total $2,500. **Application Details:** Scholarship information and applications are sent to the deans of accredited engineering schools in October and March of each year. Applications and information can be obtained from the dean of engineering or from the SWE Headquarters in New York. Requests to SWE Headquarters must be accompanied by a self-addressed, stamped envelope. Applications are available from March through June only. **Application Deadline:** Completed applications, including all supportive materials, must be postmarked no later than May 15. Recipients only will be notified by September 15.

★7900★ United Telephone Corporation Scholarships
Society of Women Engineers (SWE)
United Engineering Center, Rm. 305
345 E. 47th St.
New York, NY 10017
Phone: (212)705-7855

Study Level: Undergraduate. **Award Type:** Scholarship. **Applicant Eligibility:** Applicants must be women sophomore students majoring in engineering. Applicants must be United States citizens. **Funds Available:** Two $1,000 awards. The scholarships are renewable for two years with continued academic achievement. **Application Details:** Scholarship information and applications are sent to the deans of accredited engineering schools in October and March of each year. Applications and information can be obtained from the dean of engineering or from the SWE Headquarters in New York. Requests to SWE Headquarters must be accompanied by a self-addressed, stamped enve-

lope. Applications are available from October through January only. **Application Deadline:** Completed applications, including all supportive materials, must be postmarked no later than February 1. Recipients only will be notified by May 1.

★7901★ Virginia Volkwein Memorial Scholarship
Women Band Directors National Association (WBDNA)
344 Overlook Dr.
West Lafayette, IN 47906
Phone: (317)463-1738

Study Level: Undergraduate. **Award Type:** Scholarship. **Purpose:** To support young college women currently preparing to be band directors. **Applicant Eligibility:** Applicants must be women instrumental music majors enrolled in a university and working toward a degree in music education with the intention of becoming band directors. **Application Details:** Write for application. **Application Deadline:** December 1.

★7902★ Westinghouse Bertha Lamme Scholarship
Society of Women Engineers (SWE)
United Engineering Center, Rm. 305
345 E. 47th St.
New York, NY 10017
Phone: (212)705-7855

Study Level: Undergraduate. **Award Type:** Scholarship. **Purpose:** To attract entering freshmen women to the field of engineering. **Applicant Eligibility:** Applicants must be women majoring in engineering in a school, college or university with an accredited engineering program, who will be in their freshmen year of study during the academic year following presentation of the grant. Applicants must be United States citizens. **Funds Available:** Three $1,000 awards. **Application Details:** Scholarship information and applications are sent to the deans of accredited engineering schools in October and March of each year. Applications and information can be obtained from the dean of engineering or from the SWE Headquarters in New York. Requests to SWE Headquarters must be accompanied by a self-addressed, stamped envelope. Applications are available from March through June only. **Application Deadline:** Completed applications, including all supportive materials, must be postmarked no later than May 15. Recipients only will be notified by September 15.

★7903★ Women of the ELC Scholarship
Women of the Evangelical Lutheran Church (ELC) in America
8765 W. Higgins Rd.
Chicago, IL 60631-4189
Phone: (312)380-2700

Study Level: Undergraduate. **Award Type:** Scholarship. **Purpose:** To provide financial assistance to ELC women who wish to pursue postsecondary school education. **Applicant Eligibility:** Must be ELC laywoman, 21 years or older, cannot be a current high school student, must have 2-year interruption in schooling. Cannot be studying for ordination, deaconess, or church-certified position. Must provide some academic record beyond high school, have clear educational goals, demonstrate Christian commitment, scholastic ability, and financial need. **Funds Available:** $500 to $3,000. **Application Deadline:** February.

★7904★ **Women Marines Association**
    Scholarships
Women Marines Association (WMA)
WMA Scholarship Committee
282 San Dimas Ave.
Oceanside, CA 92056
Phone: (619)439-1447
Eleanor L. Judge, Chair

Study Level: Undergraduate. **Award Type:**
Scholarship. **Applicant Eligibility:** Must have at
least a B grade point average during the last
three years of high school and must be sponsored by a member of the Women Marines
Association who has at least two years membership completed. College applicants must
maintain at least a B grade point average at any
junior college, college, university or college-level
trade school. No more than two scholarships
will be awarded to any individual. **Funds Available:** $500 scholarships. **Application Details:**
Formal application required. **Application Deadline:** Postmarked by March 31.

★7905★ **Women in United Methodist**
    History Research Grant
General Commission on Archives and History
of the United Methodist Church
36 Madison Ave.
PO Box 127
Madison, NJ 07940
Phone: (201)822-2787
Fax: (201)408-3909

Award Type: Grant. **Purpose:** To provide seed
money for research projects relating specifically
to the history of women in the United Methodist
Church or its antecedents. **Selection Criteria:**
Criteria include the project's potential contribution to the body of knowledge in the field,
availability of the results to interested persons,
and the quality of the applicant's scholarship.
Proposals on women of color and history at the
grass roots level are especially encouraged.
Funds Available: $1,000 for one person or
$500 each for two persons is awarded each
year at the discretion of the selection committee. Funds are to be used for travel, secretarial
services, etc., but not for equipment, publications costs, or the researcher's salary. **Application Details:** Candidates must submit a curriculum vita, a description of the project, a timetable, a budget, an indication of how the
research results will be disseminated, and three
letters of recommendation from persons providing evidence of the scholarly capabilities of
candidates. Applicants are encouraged to consider a variety of formats (written, audiovisual,
oral history, bibliographies, archival guides). The
final product does not necessarily have to be
formally published, but the information must be
made available to the public in some way. All
materials should be submitted to Susan M.
Eltscher, Director, Women's and Ethnic History,
General Commission on Archives and History.
Application Deadline: December 31.

★7906★ **Women's Week Scholarship**
Rochester Area Foundation
335 E. Main St.
Rochester, NY 14604
Phone: (716)325-4353

Study Level: Undergraduate. **Award Type:**
Scholarship. **Purpose:** To provide mature wom-
en in New York with financial aid for pursuing
postsecondary education. **Applicant Eligibility:**
Adult women living in Monroe County, New
York, who are interested in reentering to start or

resume postsecondary education. Recipients
must attend a postsecondary institution in
Monroe County, New York.

★7907★ **Women's Western Golf**
    Foundation Scholarship
Women's Western Golf Foundation
c/o Mrs. Peter C. Marshall
348 Graiville Rd.
Cedarburg, WI 53012

Study Level: Undergraduate. **Award Type:**
Scholarship. **Purpose:** To provide financial support to female high school seniors who are
involved in golf. **Applicant Eligibility:** Graduating, female high school seniors who are accepted at an accredited university are eligible.
Selection Criteria: Applicants will be judged on
academic records, financial status, involvement
with (not excellence in) the sport, and character.
Funds Available: Stipend of $2,000 per year
may be renewed given satisfactory academic
progress. **Application Deadline:** April 1.

★7908★ **Woodrow Wilson Women's**
    Studies Research Grant
Woodrow Wilson National Fellowship
Foundation
PO Box 642
Princeton, NJ 08542
Phone: (609)924-4713
Fax: (609)497-9064

Study Level: Doctorate. **Award Type:** Grant.
Purpose: To encourage original and significant
research about women on such topics as the
evolution of women's role in science (particularly contemporary America), women in history,
the psychology of women, and women as seen
in literature. **Applicant Eligibility:** Must be
students in doctoral programs who have completed all predissertation requirements in any
field of study at a graduate school in the United
States. **Funds Available:** Winners will receive
grants averaging $1,000 to be used for re-
search expenses connected with the dissertation. These may include, but are not limited to
travel, books, microfilming, taping, and computer related services. The number of awards is
based on available funds. **Application Details:**
Forms are available in late summer by writing.
Applications must be endorsed by the candidate's dissertation director and graduate dean.
Supporting documents consist of graduate
school transcripts, letters of reference, a dissertation prospectus, a statement of career plans,
and a timetable for completion of the dissertation. **Application Deadline:** November.

★7909★ **WTS Chapters' Undergraduate**
    Scholarship
Women's Transportation Seminar (WTS)
808 17th St., NW, Ste. 200
Washington, DC 20006-3953
Phone: (202)223-9669

Study Level: Undergraduate. **Award Type:**
Scholarship. **Purpose:** To support undergraduate female students in studies related to transportation. **Applicant Eligibility:** Applicant must
be a woman enrolled in an undergraduate
degree program at an accredited United States
institution. Candidate must have a GPA 0f 3.0
or higher and must intend to pursue a transportation-related career. **Funds Available:** $2,000.
Application Details: Application materials are
available from, and should be submitted to, the
chapter of Women's Transportation Seminar in
candidate's home state. After reviewing applica-

tions, each chapter may nominate one candidate for consideration by the national scholarship committee. If a candidate lives in a state
that does not have a chapter, then she may
write the national headquarters for an application and guidelines. **Application Deadline:** February.

★7910★ **Zelds Walling Vicha Memorial**
    Scholarship
American Society of Podiatric Medical
Assistants
36 E. Church St.
Lock Haven, PA 17745
Phone: (717)748-5527
Joan Gordon, Chair

Study Level: Graduate. **Award Type:** Scholarship. **Purpose:** To assist with educational costs.
Applicant Eligibility: Applicant must be a fourth
year female podiatry student. **Selection Criteria:** Outstanding scholastic achievement and
financial need. **Funds Available:** Two $500
scholarships are awarded annually. **Application
Details:** Applications are sent to each of the
seven podiatry colleges in February of each
year. They must be obtained at the financial aid
offices of those colleges or by contacting the
chairman of the scholarship fund. **Application
Deadline:** May 1.

(12) Awards, Honors, and Prizes

Entries in this chapter are arranged alphabetically by award name. See the User's Guide at the front of this directory for additional information.

★7911★ **Advertising Women of New York President's Award**
Advertising Women of New York (AWNY)
153 E. 57th St.
New York, NY 10022
Phone: (212)593-1950

Description: To recognize a member who has made an important contribution to the growth and success of the Association. Awarded annually when merited. Established in 1968.

★7912★ **Agnes Faye Morgan Research Award**
Iota Sigma Pi
634 Hudson St.
Hoboken, NJ 07030
Phone: (201)963-7968

Description: For recognition of outstanding research achievements in chemistry or biochemistry by young women chemists. Women under 40 years of age who are members or are qualified to be members are eligible. The deadline for nominations is February 1. A monetary prize of $300 and a certificate are awarded every three years. The awardee presents a summary of her research at the National Convention in June. Established in 1951. Additional information is available from Sister Mary Rose Stockton, Chair, Agnes Fay Morgan Research Award Committee, Marian College, 3200 Cold Spring Road, Indianapolis, IN 46222.

★7913★ **AHSA Horsewoman of the Year**
American Horse Shows Association (AHSA)
220 E. 42nd St., Ste. 409
New York, NY 10017
Phone: (212)972-2472

Description: To recognize the most outstanding horsewoman competing in recognized shows throughout the United States. Female members of the Association who have ridden or driven in at least two recognized shows during the year are eligible. A sterling trophy is awarded annually. Established in 1959.

★7914★ **ALA Equality Award**
American Library Association (ALA)
50 E. Huron St.
Chicago, IL 60611
Phone: (312)944-6780

Description: To recognize an outstanding contribution by an individual or group towards promoting equality between women and men in the library profession. The contribution may be either a sustained one or a single outstanding accomplishment. The award may be given for an activist or scholarly contribution in such areas as pay equity, affirmative action, legislative work, and nonsexist education. The deadline for nominations is December 15. A monetary award of $500 and a certificate are awarded. Established in 1984. Sponsored by the OScarecrow Press, Inc.

★7915★ **Alberta E. Crowe Star of Tomorrow**
Young American Bowling Alliance
5301 S. 76th St.
Greendale, WI 53129
Phone: (414)421-4700

Description: To honor a young woman who displays outstanding bowling ability and potential, sportsmanship, a pleasant personality and scholastic accomplishment. Candidates must be amateur as defined by the Young American Bowling Alliance. The nominees must be 17 to 21 years of age and show high bowling potential and an outstanding record of bowling achievements. Applications may be submitted by January 15. A scholarship of $1,000 and a symbolic award are presented annually at the Women's International Bowling Congress convention. Established in 1961 in honor of Alberta E. Crowe, former president of the Women's International Bowling Congress.

★7916★ **Alice Paul Award**
National Woman's Party
144 Constitution Ave. NE
Washington, DC 20002
Phone: (202)546-1210

Description: To recognize a woman's outstanding efforts to secure passage of the Equal Rights Amendment. Women are considered for continuous past efforts and support in working for the ERA. A plaque is awarded infrequently. Established in 1985.

★7917★ **Alpha Kappa Alpha National Achievement Awards**
Alpha Kappa Alpha Sorority
5656 S. Stony Island Ave.
Chicago, IL 60637
Phone: (312)684-1282

Description: To honor women who have distinguished themselves in their fields, rendered unselfish and outstanding service to humanity, and demonstrated Alpha Kappa Alpha's belief in "Service To All Mankind." Members may submit nominations by February 15. The following awards are presented: (1) Anna Eleanor Roosevelt Medallion of Honor; (2) Founders' Graduate Service Award; (3) Founders' Undergraduate Service Award; (4) International Service Award to a Foreign Woman; and (5) Septima Poinsette Clark Award. A plaque is awarded biennially at the National Convention in even-numbered years. Established in 1964.

★7918★ **America/Israel Friendship Award**
AMIT Women
817 Broadway
New York, NY 10003
Phone: (212)477-4720

Description: To recognize distinguished contributions toward the development and furtherance of America-Israel friendship. Distinguished Americans who are not of the Jewish faith are eligible. An inscribed plaque is awarded. Established in 1948.

★7919★ **American Agri-Women Awards**
American Agri-Women
PO Box 127
New Park, PA 17352
Phone: (717)382-4878

Description: For recognition of outstanding achievements in promoting agriculture for the benefit of the American people and the world. The following awards are given: (1) Agri-Women of the Year - established in 1976; (2) Communications Award - established in 1977; (3) President's Award - established in 1978; and (4) Special Recognition - established in 1978. Plaques are awarded.

★7920★ **American Woman of the Year**
St. Joan's International Alliance U.S. Section
2131 N. 37th St.
Milwaukee, WI 53208
Phone: (414)444-0976

Description: To recognize an American woman for extraordinary accomplishment that benefits the cause of security de jure and de facto equality between women and men in State, Society and Church. A letter of appreciation is awarded as merited. Established in 1979.

★7921★ American Women in Radio and Television Achievement Award
American Women in Radio and Television
1101 Connecticut Ave. NW, Ste. 700
Washington, DC 20036
Phone: (202)429-5102

Description: For recognition of a member who has earned the respect of peers, strengthened the role of women in the industry, and contributed to the betterment of the community. Awarded annually.

★7922★ American Women in Radio and Television Commendation Awards
American Women in Radio and Television
1101 Connecticut Ave. NW, Ste. 700
Washington, DC 20036
Phone: (202)429-5102

Description: To honor excellence in programming and commericals that presents a positive portrayal of women. Entries in both the local and network radio and television categories are accepted. The deadline for applications is January 5. A black lucite plaque is awarded at a ceremony in New York City. Established in 1976.

★7923★ AMIT Women Silver Medallion Award
AMIT Women
817 Broadway
New York, NY 10003
Phone: (212)477-4720

Description: Silver Medallion Award of American Mizrachi Women. To recognize Jewish women who have made distinguished contributions to the building of Israel and the development of Jewish life and culture through individual talent or organizations contributing towards those goals. An inscribed plaque is awarded. Established in 1963. Occasionally men are honored. **Formerly:** Silver Medallion Award of American Mizrachi Women.

★7924★ Angel of the Year
Women in Show Business (WISB)
PO Box 2535
Toluca Lake, CA 91610
Phone: (213)271-3415
Fax: (818)994-4661

Description: To recognize a member of the entertainment community who has given time, energy and support to WISB. Members of the organization make the selection through ballot. A crystal angel is awarded annually at the Celebrity Benefit Ball in the fall. Established in 1970.

★7925★ Anna Louise Hoffman Award for Outstanding Achievement in Graduate Research
Iota Sigma Pi
634 Hudson St.
Hoboken, NJ 07030
Phone: (201)963-7968

Description: To recognize original research which can be described by one of the main chemical divisions (e.g., analytical, biochemical, inorganic, organic, physical, and/or ancillary divisions of chemistry). Nominations may be made by members of the institution's graduate faculty. The deadline is February 1. A monetary award of $300 and a certificate are awarded annually. Established in 1979. Additional information is available from Linda Munchausen,

Chair, Professional Excellence Award Committee, Department of Chemistry and Physics, Box 372, Southeastern Louisiana University, Hammond, La 70402.

★7926★ Annie Jump Cannon Award in Astronomy
American Association of University Women
  Educational Foundation
2401 Virginia Ave. NW
Washington, DC 20037
Phone: (202)785-7700

Description: To recognize a young woman for achievement and potential for research in the field of astronomy. Applicants must be in the early stages of their careers and have as career goals the pursuit of research in astronomy. Preference is given to applicants who have held a Ph.D. in astronomy or a related field for at least one year. There are no restrictions on nationality or the location of the research. The deadline is February. A monetary award of $5,000 is presented annually in the spring. Established in 1934 by the American Astronomical Society in honor of Annie Jump Cannon, a prominent early 20th century woman astronomer. Ms. Cannon established the classification of stars now used by astronomers. Additional information is available from Anna Fiets, Education Department.

★7927★ Antoinette Brown Award
United Church of Christ Coordinating Center
  for Women
105 Madison Ave.
New York, NY 10016
Phone: (212)683-5656

Description: To lift up the gifts and the ministries of ordained women. A medal is presented biennially at the General Synod. Established in 1975 by the Task Force on Women to honor Antoinette Brown, the first woman in the United States to be ordained.

★7928★ Arthur and Edith Wippman Scientific Research Award
Planned Parenthood Federation of America
  (PPFA)
c/o Barbara Snow
810 7th Ave.
New York, NY 10019
Phone: (212)541-7800

Description: To recognize significant contributions in scientific research, which have enhanced reproductive freedom for the people of the world. Established in 1987.

★7929★ ASA - deBeer Richard H. Pollack Memorial Award
Amateur Softball Association of America
  (ASA)
2801 NE 50th St.
Oklahoma City, OK 73111
Phone: (405)424-5266
Fax: (405)424-5288

Description: To honor the women's softball Sportswoman of the Year. ASA State/Metro Associations are eligible to nominate. Awarded annually. Established in 1985 to honor Richard H. Pollack, a former deBeer employee who died of cancer. Sponsored by the J. deBeer Company, Albany, NY.

★7930★ Association for Women Veterinarians Distinguished Service Award
Association for Women Veterinarians
Box 1051
Littleton, CO 80160-1051
Phone: (303)795-0130

Description: To recognize an individual for contributing toward advancing the status of women veterinarians. Awarded annually when merited. Established in 1976.

★7931★ Augusta Ada Lovelace Award
Association for Women in Computing
1133 15th St. NW
Washington, DC 20005
Phone: (213)540-7027

Description: To recognize individuals who have excelled in either, or both, of two areas: (1) outstanding scientific and technical achievement; and (2) extraordinary service to the computing community through their accomplishments and contributions on behalf of women in computing. Any person who has rendered extraordinary service to the computing industry through contributions on behalf of women in computing, or whose technical and scientific accomplishments are outstanding, is eligible for nomination. A certificate is awarded annually when merited. Established in 1981 in memory of Augusta Ada, Countess of Lovelace, considered to be the first woman in computing for her work with Charles Babbage, inventor of the "analytical engine," the first computer. She programmed the machine and understood its implications for the future.

★7932★ AWNY Advertising Woman of the Year
Advertising Women of New York (AWNY)
153 E. 57th St.
New York, NY 10022
Phone: (212)593-1950

Description: To recognize a woman who has made outstanding contributions to advertising throughout her professional career. Awarded annually when merited. Established in 1965.

★7933★ Barbara V. Ferraro Award
Gamma Sigma Sigma National Service
  Sorority
4 Kirkland Court
Yalesville, CT 06492
Phone: (203)265-1410

Description: To recognize the undergraduate chapter with the most outstanding service program.

★7934★ Barnard New Women Poets Prize
Women Poets of Barnard
English Dept.
Barnard College
3009 Broadway
New York, NY 10007
Phone: (212)280-2110

Description: To recognize a woman poet. Manuscripts may be submitted by any woman poet who has not previously published work. A monetary award of $1,000 and a publishing contract in the *Barnard New Women Poet Series* by Beacon Press are awarded annually. Established in 1986 by Chris Baswell and Celeste Schenck.

★7935★ Bertha Tickey Award
Amateur Softball Association of America
(ASA)
2801 NE 50th St.
Oklahoma City, OK 73111
Phone: (405)424-5266
Fax: (405)424-5288

Description: To honor the outstanding pitcher in the Women's Major Fast Pitch National Championship. The award is named in honor of former Raybestos Brakette, Bertha Tickey. Established in 1967.

★7936★ Bertha Van Hoosen Award
American Medical Women's Association
(AMWA)
801 N. Fairfax St., Ste. 400
Alexandria, VA 22314
Phone: (703)838-0500

Description: To recognize a woman physician who has been an active member of the Association for at least five years and who has demonstrated exceptional leadership and service to AMWA. Established in 1983 in honor of Bertha Van Hoosen, co-founder and first president of AMWA, by Dolores J. Shelfoon, M.D. The first Award was presented in 1990.

★7937★ Billie Jean King Contribution Award
Women's Sports Foundation (WSF)
342 Madison Ave., Ste. 728
New York, NY 10173
Phone: (212)972-9170

Description: To recognize an individual, organization or corporation for significant contributions to the development of women's sports. Demonstration of a continuing, lasting commitment and dedication to the growth of sports for women is necessary. Recipients are selected by the Trustees and Advisory Board members of the Women's Sports Foundation.

★7938★ BUDDY Award (Bring Up Daughters Differently)
NOW Legal Defense and Education Fund
(NOWLDEF)
99 Hudson St.
New York, NY 10013
Phone: (212)925-6635
Fax: (212)226-1066

Description: To recognize corporate families who, through their commitment to equal opportunity, have inspired their own daughters to believe they can accomplish whatever they set their minds to. A nominating committee makes the selection. A cast bronze sculpture and plaque are awarded annually at a luncheon. Established in 1986.

★7939★ C.C. Jackson Awards
The Athletics Congress of the USA
PO Box 120
Indianapolis, IN 46206-0120
Phone: (317)638-9155
Fax: (317)261-0481

Description: To recognize outstanding women in track and field. A plaque is awarded annually at the National Convention. Established in 1978 in memory of C.C. Jackson, one of the foremost promoters of women's track and field.

★7940★ Camille Mermod Award
American Medical Women's Association
(AMWA)
801 N. Fairfax St., Ste. 400
Alexandria, VA 22314
Phone: (703)838-0500

Description: To honor a non-physician for outstanding contributions to the American Medical Women's Association. A medal is awarded as merited. Established in 1969.

★7941★ Candace Award
National Coalition of 100 Black Women
50 Rockefeller Plaza
New York, NY 10020
Phone: (212)974-6140

Description: To recognize the achievements of black women in various fields of endeavor.

★7942★ Carroll L. Birch Award
American Medical Women's Association
(AMWA)
801 N. Fairfax St., Ste. 400
Alexandria, VA 22314
Phone: (703)838-0500

Description: For recognition of the best scientific research paper written by a woman medical student. A monetary award of $500 and possible publication in the *Journal of the American Medical Women's Association* are awarded. Established in 1965. Sponsored by AMWA's Branch 2, Chicago.

★7943★ Catalyst Corporate Leadership Award
Catalyst
250 Park Ave. S.
New York, NY 10003-1459
Phone: (212)777-8900
Fax: (212)477-4252

Description: To celebrate corporate initiatives to promote women's leadership. Awarded annually in March. Established in 1976.

★7944★ Catherine "Cathy" Hensel Award
Driving School Association of the Americas
111 W. Pomona Blvd.
Monterey Park, CA 91754
Phone: (213)728-2100

Description: For recognition of contributions to the field of traffic safety during the past year over and above what is normally asked for. Female members of the industry are eligible. A monetary prize of $500 and a plaque are awarded annually in November. Established in 1987 by Catherine P. Hensel Trust in memory of "Cathy" Hensel, co-founder of the California Driving School, Inc., one of the largest in the nation, and the first woman mayor of the city of Montebello, CA.

★7945★ Catherine Lorillard Wolfe Art Club Annual Open Exhibition
Catherine Lorillard Wolfe Art Club
33 E. 35th St.
Patterson, NJ 07514

Description: To recognize outstanding women artists whose works exemplify the finest representations of contemporary traditional art. Awards are given in some of the following categories: oil; watercolor; pastel or graphics; and sculpture. Some of the awards presented are: the Catharine Lorillard Wolfe Medal of Honor - a $250 award in each of the four

categories; the Anna Hyatt Huntington Bronze Medals - awarded in each of the four categories; the M. Grumbacher - Silver Medallion - $200 for an oil or watercolor painting; and the Harriet W. Frishmuth Memorial Award - $200 for an oil or watercolor painting. Awarded annually. Established in 1896 by a group of women at Grace Church in New York to help the struggling young women art students.

★7946★ Champion Player of the Year Award
Naismith Memorial Basketball Hall of Fame
PO Box 179
1150 W. Columbus Ave.
Springfield, MA 01101-0179
Phone: (413)781-6500

Description: To recognize the outstanding women basketball players in NCAA Divisions I, II, III, the NAIA, and the NJCAA. The award honors individual excellence, leadership, sportsmanship, and contribution to the team's overall standing.

★7947★ Charlotte Danstrom Award
Women in Management
2 N. Riverside Plaza, Ste. 2400
Chicago, IL 60606
Phone: (312)263-3636

Description: To recognize women of outstanding achievement in each of the following categories: Corporate, Academia, Entrepreneur, and Government/Not For Profit/Social Services. Members may be nominated by their individual chapter. They must have professional leader experiences, community contributions/activities and have helped others develop professionally. A plaque is awarded annually. Established in 1982 in honor of Charlotte Danstrom, for her dedication to leadership skills and unflagging support.

★7948★ Churchman, Churchwoman of the Year
Religious Heritage of America
7900 Jerome Ave.
St. Louis, MO 63143
Phone: (314)781-7888

Description: To recognize a layman and laywoman active within their churches. Their service should have been of national importance. Success in their chosen field of endeavor is considered as part of the criteria. Nominees should be in good standing within the local assembly (church or synagogue) of their denomination. The deadline for nominations is April 1. A plaque is awarded annually. Established in 1951.

★7949★ Clairol Mentor Program
National Women's Economic Alliance Foundation (NWEA)
1440 New York Ave. NW, Ste. 300
Washington, DC 20005
Phone: (202)393-5257
Fax: (202)639-8685

Description: To encourage the growth of mentoring relationships among women by matching aspiring women in a variety of professions with established, successful women in the same fields. Women, at least 22 years old who feel they would benefit from a mentor relationship in one of the eleven career categories offering mentors each year, may apply for an award. Eleven winning aspirants receive awards of

$1,000 each and are flown to New York City to personally meet their mentors and to be honored at a special awards luncheon. There, each receives a framed certificate and has the opportunity for a one-to-one session with her new mentor. Ideally, it will be the first of many such career-strategy discussions between each pair.

★7950★ Clairol Scholarship Program
Business and Professional Women's
   Foundation
c/o Clairol Scholarship Program
2012 Massachusetts Ave. NW
Washington, DC 20036
Phone: (202)293-1200

Description: To provide financial aid to women over 30 who are returning to school in order to achieve career goals. Study may be part-time or full-time, and for either academic degree work (with the exception of Ph.D. or Ed.D.) or vocational training. The deadlines are April 15 for the fall term and September 15 for the spring term. Approximately a hundred women receive a total of $50,000 in scholarships annually. Individual awards average $750-$1,000. The money may be used for education-related expenses, such as child care, transportation or books, as well as for tuition and fees. Established in 1974.

**★7951★ Clairol Take Charge Awards
   Program**
National Women's Economic Alliance
   Foundation (NWEA)
1440 New York Ave. NW, Ste. 300
Washington, DC 20005
Phone: (202)393-5257
Fax: (202)639-8685

Description: To recognize the achievements of seemingly ordinary women who, after the age of 30, have overcome obstacles and taken charge of their own lives. These are women who have successfully changed the courses of their lives and have gone on to make significant contributions to the field in which they work or to their communities. An important goal of the program is to spotlight the recipients as role models who will inspire women everywhere. Nominations are due by July 15. Every year, 25 women receive Take Charge Awards and grants of $1,000 each. The individual grants may be used in any way the award recipients choose.

★7952★ Clarion Awards
Women in Communications (WIC)
National Headquarters
PO Box 17460
Arlington, VA 22216
Phone: (703)528-4200

Description: National Awards Contest. To recognize excellence in all areas of communications, to provide incentive for further achievement, and to demonstrate the role of communications in dealing with current issues. The deadline for entries is March 1. Awards are presented in the categories of: broadcast; print; public relations; newspapers; magazines; special publications; photography; and advertising. Materials published, broadcast or implemented between January 1 and December 31 of the preceding year are eligible. Plaques are awarded annually at the National Professional Conference. Established in 1973. **Formerly:** National Awards Contest.

★7953★ Coach of the Year
Ladies Professional Golf Association (LPGA)
2570 Volusia Ave., Ste. B
Daytona Beach, FL 32114

Description: To honor a woman golf professional who is actively engaged in the teaching and coaching of golf at the college or high school level. Members in good standing of the Teaching Division, presently serving in the position of head coach at an accredited educational institution, who have demonstrated responsibility in the areas of coaching, recruiting, program development, instruction, tournament organization, and professional involvement in Associations governing athletics are eligible. Awarded annually. Established in 1981.

★7954★ Crystal Award
Women in Film
6464 Sunset Blvd., Ste. 900
Los Angeles, CA 90028
Phone: (213)463-6040
Fax: (213)463-0963

Description: To honor outstanding individuals who, through their endurance and the excellence of their work, have helped to expand the role of women within the entertainment industry. The recipients are chosen for both the diversity of their accomplishments and their contributions to the support and advancement of women within the entertainment industry. A crystal block is awarded annually. Established in 1977.

**★7955★ Delta Kappa Gamma Educator's
   Award**
Delta Kappa Gamma Society International
PO Box 1589
Austin, TX 78767
Phone: (512)478-5748

Description: To recognize outstanding contributions of women authors whose works may influence the direction of thought and action necessary to meet the needs of today's complex society. Contributions should be of more than local interest with relationship - direct or implied - to education everywhere. The book must be written by one woman or by two women who are citizens of any country where the Society is organized - Canada, Costa Rica, El Salvador, Finland, Great Britain, Guatemala, Iceland, Mexico, The Netherlands, Norway, Puerto Rico, Sweden, or the United States. Methods and skills-books, textbooks, unpublished manuscripts, and books written specifically for children are not considered. A monetary award of $2,000 is presented annually when merited. Established in 1946.

**★7956★ Diana Fell Gilmore - Behind the
   Scenes Award**
United States Auto Club
4910 W. 16th St.
Speedway, IN 46224
Phone: (317)247-5151
Fax: (317)247-0123

Description: To recognize the woman behind the scenes in the sport of auto racing who best exemplifies the dedication, support and undying spirit of Diana Fell Gilmore. Established in 1980.

★7957★ Directors' Choice Awards
National Women's Economic Alliance
   Foundation (NWEA)
1440 New York Ave. NW, Ste. 300
Washington, DC 20005
Phone: (202)393-5257
Fax: (202)639-8685

Description: To honor ten women who serve on corporate boards for their outstanding achievements. Through their work and accomplishments, these women are representative of the talent and commitment available to business, industry and government. Selection is based on the results of a poll the Alliance conducts of its members, Board of Directors, Executive Committee and Directors Resource Council, and chief executive officers of the top 500 service and industrial corporations. Representing business, industry, the arts, academia, government, and science, the honorees collectively oversee more than $522 billion as directors on boards of Fortune 1000 corporations. Awarded annually. Established in 1987.

**★7958★ Disabled Professional Woman of
   the Year**
Pilot International
PO Box 4844
244 College St.
Macon, GA 31213
Phone: (912)743-7403
Fax: (912)743-2173

Description: Handicapped Professional Woman of the Year. To select outstanding executive or professional women in the United States and Canada in order to dramatize the abilities of handicapped people and recognize their achievements. Any disabled woman who, having surmounted her handicap, is serving successfully in an executive or professional position, and who actively participates in community betterment programs is eligible. Selection is based on community service contributions, occupational and employment achievements, nature and severity of disability, persistence and initiative in surmounting the handicap, and level of education, training and/or experience. The nominations deadline is January 15. Awards are given in the following categories: (1) Community Recognition - Each year communities in which Pilot Clubs exist select one or more winners who each receive an engraved trophy from OSears, Roebuck and Company; (2) District Recognition - District winners (21) are chosen from among community winners and honored at Pilot district conventions. They become nominees for the international award. (Pilot Clubs outside established districts enter nominees directly on the international level.) Sears, Roebuck and Company provides U.S. $100 to the sponsoring club of each district winner; and (3) International Recognition - The international winner and first runner-up receive expense-paid trips to the Pilot International convention where they are recognized and honored. They are also guests of Sears, Roebuck and Company at the annual meeting of the President's Committee. The international winner receives U.S. $1,000 from Sears, Roebuck and Co., an engraved silver bowl from the President's Committee, a U.S. $100 savings bond and engraved plaque from Pilot International, and has her name engraved on a plaque displayed at Pilot International Headquarters in Macon, GA. From these same sponsors the first runner-up receives 500, a silver bowl and an engraved plaque. Cash awards are used to benefit people with disabilities. Awarded annually. Established in 1970 to recognize and applaud disabled women. Co-sponsored by the OPresident's Committee on Employment of People with Disabilities and Sears, Roebuck and Company. **Formerly:** Handicapped Professional Woman of the Year.

★7959★ **Distinguished American Woman Award**
College of Mount Saint Joseph
Office of the Pres.
5701 Delhi Pike
Mount St. Joseph, OH 45051
Phone: (513)244-4232

Description: To recognize an American woman who has made a national and/or international impact through excellence in her profession, achievement in her career, and influence as an inspiration to fellow men/women. The President of the College, with the recommendation of the Board of Trustees, makes the selection. An engraved free-standing carved glass plate is awarded biennially. Established in 1985.

★7960★ **Distinguished Engineering Educator Award**
Society of Women Engineers (SWE)
United Engineering Center
345 E. 47th St., Rm. 305
New York, NY 10017
Phone: (212)705-7855

Description: To recognize a woman who, as a full time or emerita engineering educator, has demonstrated excellence in teaching and the ability to inspire students to high levels of accomplishments, has shown evidence of scholarship through contributions to research and technical literature, and who, through active involvement in professional engineering societies, has made significant contributions to the engineering profession. Candidates must have at least one earned engineering or engineering related degree, be a full time or emerita faculty member in a school of engineering or engineering technology, have at least ten years teaching experience, hold the rank of at least associate professor, and be a member of SWE. An inscribed memento and plaque are awarded at the annual student award luncheon or banquet. Established in 1986.

★7961★ **Distinguished Women of Northwood Institute**
Northwood Institute
3225 Cook Rd.
Midland, MI 48640-2398
Phone: (517)832-4364

Description: To honor ten women who serve as examples by their achievement and high ideals in business, government, media, the arts, academic life or in the voluntary private sector. Nominations may be made by someone familiar with the nominee's qualifications. Selection is by a special committee of Northwood officers and trustees. The winners receive a medal, designed by sculptor Giulio Tamassy, and a book, entitled *Distinguished Women*, at the annual recognition luncheon which is held in various cities of the United States. Established in 1970 by the co-founder of the Northwood Institute, Dr. Arthur E. Turner, and the College Board of Trustees.

★7962★ **Dr. J. Frances Allen Scholarship**
American Fisheries Society
5410 Grosvenor Ln., Ste. 110
Bethesda, MD 20814-2199
Phone: (301)897-8616

Description: To provide funds for a female fisheries science student with a Ph.D. Established in 1986 at the annual meeting during a caucus of Women in Fisheries. The award honors Dr. Allen, who pioneered women's involvement in AFS.

★7963★ **Doctoral Dissertation Grants in Women's Studies**
Woodrow Wilson National Fellowship Foundation
PO Box 642
Princeton, NJ 08542
Phone: (609)924-4666

Description: To encourage original and significant research on women's roles. Graduate students in their dissertation year enrolled in U.S. graduate schools may apply by November 10. Grants of $1,000 are awarded annually. Established in 1974 by the Ford Foundation.

★7964★ **E.C. Bouey Memorial Award**
International Ministers' Wives and Widows
128 Pennsylvania Ave.
Roosevelt, NY 11575
Phone: (516)379-2541

Description: To recognize the person who best emulates the characteristics and services of the founder, E.C. Bouey. A plaque is awarded annually. Established in 1958.

★7965★ **Elizabeth Blackwell Medal**
American Medical Women's Association (AMWA)
801 N. Fairfax St., Ste. 400
Alexandria, VA 22314
Phone: (703)838-0500

Description: To recognize the physician who has made the most outstanding contribution to the cause of women in the field of medicine. A medal is awarded annually. Established in 1949.

★7966★ **Elizabeth Boyer Award**
Women's Equity Action League (WEAL)
1250 I St. NW, Ste. 305
Washington, DC 20005
Phone: (202)898-1588

Description: To recognize the outstanding contributions of the unsung heroines of the women's movement. A plaque is presented at the awards luncheon. Awarded annually the day before the annual meeting in Washington, D.C. Established in 1974 in honor of Elizabeth Boyer, founder of WEAL, and a women's rights attorney and activist.

★7967★ **Elizabeth Cutter Morrow Award**
Young Women's Christian Association of the City of New York
922 9th Ave.
New York, NY 10019
Phone: (212)564-1300

Description: For recognition of women who make a difference in the quality of life in New York and who, by their leadership and ability, elevate the status of women everywhere. The award, which varies, is an item designed by a craft student league instructor. Presented annu-

ally. Established in 1977 by Polly Gordon to honor Elizabeth Cutter Morrow.

★7968★ **Elizabeth Lewin Award**
National Chamber of Commerce for Women (NCCW)
10 Waterside Plaza, Ste. 6H
New York, NY 10010
Phone: (212)685-3454

Description: To recognize women entrepreneurs whose business success is due to management and marketing skill, not to money infusions. Active members of the Chamber who use the NCCW Infobank are eligible. Free advertising in the bimonthly publication *ENRICH* is awarded annually. Established in 1987 in memory of Elizabeth Lewin, a woman entrepreneur who succeeded in a man's world.

★7969★ **Entrepreneur Awards**
Women Business Owners of New York
La Concierge Services Inc.
322 E. 86th St.
New York, NY 10028
Phone: (212)737-5289

Description: For recognition of achievement by women in business. Consideration for awards is based on yearly gross sales of the candidate's business, length of time in business, and the fact that the business is solely owned by a woman. Crystal engraved paperweights from Tiffany's are awarded annually at the Entrepreneurial Woman Awards Luncheon. Established in 1977.

★7970★ **Equal Employment Opportunity Award**
United States Department of State
Rm. 2429
Washington, DC 20520
Phone: (202)647-7236

Description: For recognition of outstanding contributions toward improving employment opportunities for minorities and women. It is given to an employee of the Department of State who has made the most significant achievements in the futherance of affirmative action and equal employment opportunity. The award consists of a certificate signed by the Secretary and $5,000 in cash. Awarded annually.

★7971★ **Erv Lind Award**
Amateur Softball Association of America (ASA)
2801 NE 50th St.
Oklahoma City, OK 73111
Phone: (405)424-5266
Fax: (405)424-5288

Description: To honor the top defensive player in the women's major fast pitch national tournament. The winner is determined by a vote of a selection committee at the tournament. A plaque is awarded annually. Established in 1966 by the Amateur Softball Association in honor of Erv Lind, former sponsor of women's fast pitch teams.

★7972★ **Esther Haar Award**
American Academy of Psychoanalysis
30 E. 40th St., Ste. 206
New York, NY 10016
Phone: (212)679-4105

Description: To recognize the author of the best unpublished paper on either adolescents' or women's issues. The deadline for submission is November 15. A monetary prize of $400 is awarded. Additionally, the award-winning paper is presented at the annual meeting of the Academy and then submitted to the *Journal of the American Academy of Psychoanalysis.* Awarded annually. Established in 1984.

★7973★ Evelyn Bauer Prize
International Psychohistorical Association (IPA)
627 Dakota Trail
Franklin Lakes, NJ 07417

Description: To recognize the woman whose work on psychohistory is most outstanding. If the award is given for a book, research paper, or presentation that is delivered elsewhere, the recipient will then give a presentation based upon her work at the annual IPA convention, although the winner need not be a member of the IPA. A monetary award of $100 to $500 is presented annually. Established in 1988 in memory of Evelyn Bauer, a pioneer in the field of psychohistory and a former member of the Executive Committee. Additional information is available from Henry Lawton, M.A., M.L.S., 266 Monroe Avenue, Wyckoff, NJ 07481.

★7974★ Exceptional Merit Media Award (EMMA)
National Women's Political Caucus (NWPC)
Leadership, Development, & Education Fund
1275 K St. NW, Ste. 750
Washington, DC 20005
Phone: (202)898-1100
Fax: (202)898-0458
Jean Shackelford, Contact

Description: To recognize individuals for outstanding media contributions to women's quest for equality. EMMA Awards are presented in several categories, including cartoons and newspaper articles. Established in 1990.

★7975★ FEW Distinguished Service Award
Federally Employed Women (FEW)
1400 Eye St. NW, Ste. 425
Washington, DC 20005
Phone: (202)898-0994

Description: To recognize an individual who most notably has shown courage and leadership in furthering the cause of federally employed women. Nominations may be submitted by a FEW chapter or a member-at-large by April 15. A framed hand-lettered certificate is awarded annually at the National Training Program in July. Established in 1971.

★7976★ Frances Pomeroy Naismith Hall of Fame Award
Naismith Memorial Basketball Hall of Fame
PO Box 179
1150 W. Columbus Ave.
Springfield, MA 01101-0179
Phone: (413)781-6500

Description: To honor an outstanding senior female college basketball player under five foot six inches, who has exhibited outstanding skill, character and leadership. The award is selected by the Women's Basketball Coaches Association. Wood plaques are awarded annually. Established in 1984 by James S. Naismith, son of the founder of basketball, in memory of his wife, Frances Pomeroy Naismith. Sponsored by Shawmut First Bank. (An award for men is also given)

★7977★ Front Page Awards
Newswomen's Club of New York
15 Gramercy Park
New York, NY 10003
Phone: (212)777-1610
Harriet Coleman, Contact

Description: For recognition of journalistic excellence in the following categories: (1) best story on deadline; (2) best newspaper feature; (3) best newspaper series; (4) best feature on family living; (5) best magazine news story; (6) best magazine feature; (7) best magazine column; (8) best radio reporting; (9) best television news feature; (10) best television documentary; and (11) best news or news feature photograph. Newswomen whose material is published or broadcast in or from the Greater New York area within the preceding year are eligible. A scroll is awarded annually. Established in 1936 with variation in categories at times.

★7978★ Frontrunner Award
Sara Lee Corporation
3 First National Plaza
Chicago, IL 60602-4260
Phone: (312)726-2600

Description: To recognize women whose outstanding achievements forge new pathways, contribute to the betterment of society and motivate others to do the same. The Frontrunner is a woman who: (1) holds a pre-eminent position in her field; (2) benefits others through her achievements; (3) receives recognition often from her peers; and (4) demonstrates a continuous commitment to her work. Awards are presented in four categories: business; government; the arts (communications, media, and the fine and performing arts); and the humanities (social or charitable work, medicine, science or research). A corporate donation of $10,000 is made in each Frontrunner's name to a nonprofit women's organization of her choice. Established in 1987.

★7979★ Fulltime Homemaker Award
Eagle Forum
PO Box 618
Alton, IL 62002

Description: To recognize fulltime career homemakers. Each nominee must be a Fulltime Homemaker who: (1) lives in the traditional family life-style - husband-breadwinner with wife-homemaker; (2) has at least one child under age 18 currently living at home; (3) uses her husband's name; and (4) did not have earned income in excess of $500 during the preceding year. Award recipients need not be Eagle Forum members or nominated by Eagle Forum members. Nominations may be submitted by the nominee, a friend, or a family member. One award is presented to a Fulltime Homemaker in each of the 50 states, and one National award is presented in Washington, DC. Established to honor traditional families who have made the commitment to give their children something very special - a resident mother in the home to provide constancy, stability, and emotional security to her children.

★7980★ Gamma Sigma Sigma Distinguished Service Award
Gamma Sigma Sigma National Service Sorority
4 Kirkland Court
Yalesville, CT 06492
Phone: (203)265-1410

Description: To honor both alumnae and undergraduate members of the sorority for outstanding service, over and above sorority commitments, to either one organization or to a variety of organizations. Nominations by sorority chapters or members may be submitted by April 1 of odd-numbered years. A plaque and a donation of $100 made on behalf of the recipient to a service organization of their choice are awarded biennially at the national convention. Established in 1985.

★7981★ Gamma Sigma Sigma Woman of the Year Award
Gamma Sigma Sigma National Service Sorority
4 Kirkland Court
Yalesville, CT 06492
Phone: (203)265-1410

Description: To recognize women of national prominence for outstanding contributions in volunteer service. Nominations may be submitted prior to the National Board of Directors' meeting between conventions. A commemorative gift or donation, and a certificate or plaque are awarded biennially at the national convention. Established in 1971.

★7982★ Garvan Medal
American Chemical Society
1155 16th St. NW
Washington, DC 20036
Phone: (202)872-4408
Fax: (202)872-6206

Description: To recognize distinguished service to chemistry by women chemists who are citizens of the United States. The deadline for nominations is February 1. A monetary prize of $4,000, an inscribed gold medal, a bronze replica of the medal, and an allowance of $1,000 for travel expenses to attend the meeting at which the award is presented are awarded annually. Established in 1936 through a donation from Francis P. Garvan. Sponsored by Olin Corporation.

★7983★ Gatorade Rookie of the Year
Ladies Professional Golf Association (LPGA)
2570 Volusia Ave., Ste. B
Daytona Beach, FL 32114

Description: To recognize a player who, in her first season, leads all other first-year players on the LPGA money list. A trophy, which is a Georgian silver cup, is awarded annually. Established in 1962.

★7984★ Georgina Smith Award
American Association of University Professors
1012 14th St. NW, Ste. 500
Washington, DC 20005
Phone: (202)737-5900

Description: To recognize a person who has provided exceptional leadership in a given year in improving the status of academic women or in the advancement of academic collective bargaining and, through that work, in improving the profession in general.

★7985★ Gertrude Fogelson Cultural and Creative Arts Program
American Mothers
Waldorf Astoria
301 Park Ave.
New York, NY 10022
Phone: (212)755-2539

Description: To encourage and honor all mothers in their artistically creative pursuits. The program's purpose is to strengthen the moral and spiritual values in the family and in the home. The exhibit offers an expression of the beauty and meaning of art in the life of the mother and family today. Entries may be submitted in the following categories: (1) Fine Arts; (2) Literature; and (3) Vocal Music. Entries are limited to one in each category per state. The following monetary awards are presented annually: (1) Fine Arts: (a) sculpture - $1,000; (b) painting - $1,000; (c) graphics - $1,000; and (d) crafts - $500; (2) Literature: (a) poetry - $100 for first place and $25 for second place; (b) short story - $100 for first place and $25 for second place; and (c) essay or article - $100 for first place and $25 for second place; and (3) Vocal Music - $1,000. Established in 1971 by the Joe and Emily Lowe Foundation.

★7986★ Gladys G. Shute Award
Oakton Community College
1600 E. Golf Rd.
Des Plaines, IL 60016
Phone: (312)635-1600

Description: For recognition of a significant contribution to the advancement of women. A man or a woman who has worked to provide advancement opportunities for women in education, journalism, the media or other areas is eligible for consideration. A plaque is presented annually in early May. Established in 1976 by the Women's Program Advisory Committee at Oakton Community College. The award commemorates Gladys G. Shute, a former Oakton Community College administrator, who helped initiate the Women's Program at the college.

★7987★ Golden Gazelle Awards
NOW Legal Defense and Education Fund (NOWLDEF)
Project on Equal Education Rights
1333 H St. NW
Washington, DC 20005
Phone: (202)682-0940

Description: To recognize individuals and organizations who have been amazingly quick-footed in promoting equity in education. Schools, government agencies, policymakers and other individuals and organizations are eligible for performance in preventing discrimination. Nominations are judged by a panel of committed individuals active in the civil and education rights community. Awards may be presented in the following categories: (1) Flo Hyman Memorial Golden Gazelle; (2) State and National Golden Gazelles; and (3) Sports Gazelles. Soft sculpture models of gazelles are awarded annually. Established in 1979.

★7988★ Good Guys Awards
National Women's Political Caucus (NWPC)
Leadership, Development, & Education Fund
1275 K St. NW, Ste. 750
Washington, DC 20005
Phone: (202)898-1100
Fax: (202)898-0458

Description: To honor men who have contributed significantly to women's quest for equality - an equality for all. Selection is by nomination by the NWPC. An appropriate award is chosen each year. In 1985, the award was an original print of the caricatures of the awardees. Awarded annually, usually in the fall. Established in 1985.

★7989★ Hasty Pudding Theatricals Woman of the Year
Hasty Pudding Theatricals
12 Holyoke St.
Cambridge, MA 02138
Phone: (617)495-5205

Description: To recognize an individual who has made a lasting and impressive contribution to the world of entertainment. Actors, dancers, directors and writers may be considered. The traditional Hasty Pudding Pot, a symbol of the Theatricals, is awarded annually. Established in 1951.

★7990★ Headliner Award
Women in Communications (WIC)
National Headquarters
PO Box 17460
Arlington, VA 22216
Phone: (703)528-4200

Description: This, the highest honor WIC can bestow on a member, is given to recognize distinguished recent achievements as well as continued excellence of women in the field of communications. Active members of the organization are eligible. Selection is made by WIC Board of Directors. A plaque is awarded annually at the National Professional Conference. Established in 1939.

★7991★ Heart of America
American Legion Auxiliary
777 N. Meridian St., 3rd Fl.
Indianapolis, IN 46204
Phone: (317)635-6291

Description: Golden Press Awards. To recognize the creative excellence of those who are students or working members of the firm or print media who have given positive attention to the concerns of women and the family unit. Awards are given in the following categories: (1) radio; (2) television; (3) movie; (4) magazine; and (5) newspaper. Nominations of students or working members of the film or print media must be submitted by May 15. Submissions published or broadcast between April 1 of the previous year and April 1 of the current year are eligible. Trophies are awarded annually at the National Convention. The Golden Mike Awards were established in 1957 and the Golden Press Awards in 1968. The two awards were combined in 1989 as the Heart of America. **Formerly:** Golden Press Awards.

★7992★ Helen Caldicott Leadership Award
Women's Action for Nuclear Disarmament Education Fund (WAND)
691 Massachusetts Ave.
Arlington, MA 02174
Phone: (617)617-4880

Description: For recognition of a contribution to the Women's Action for Nuclear Disarmament and the cause of nuclear disarmament, and for recognition of leadership on behalf of women in society. An engraved piece of sculptured jewelry is awarded annually. Established in 1982 in honor of Helen Caldicott, founder of WAND, disarmament spokesperson, and woman leader.

★7993★ Helen Copeland Scholarship
United States Association for Blind Athletes (USABA)
33 North Institute
Brown Hall, Ste. 015
Colorado Springs, CO 80903
Phone: (719)630-0422

Description: To provide financial assistance to a female USABA member based on athletic participation and academic achievement. Legally blind scholar/athletes, active with the Association for at least 2 years, and entering or already in an academic, vocational, technical, professional or certification program at the postsecondary level may submit applications by May 10. A monetary award of $500 is presented annually. Established in 1988 to honor Arthur and Helen Copeland, who founded USABA in 1976 and are instrumental in blind sports.

★7994★ History of Women in Science Prize
History of Science Society
35 Dean St.
Worcester, MA 01609
Phone: (508)831-5712
Fax: (508)831-5483

Description: To encourage the development of the growing specialty of women in science within the history of science and to recognize those scholars who are pioneering and developing this field. A monetary prize of $500 is awarded annually, granted in alternate years for: (1) an outstanding book published in the previous four years; and (2) an outstanding article published in the previous four years. Established in 1987.

★7995★ Honoree of the Year (Women's Long Distance Running)
The Athletics Congress of the USA
PO Box 120
Indianapolis, IN 46206-0120
Phone: (317)638-9155
Fax: (317)261-0481

Description: Woman of the Year. To recognize an outstanding contribution by both men and women to the development of the sport of long distance running. A plaque is awarded annually at the National Convention. Established in 1977. **Formerly:** Woman of the Year.

★7996★ Humanist Heroine Award
American Humanist Association (AHA)
7 Harwood Dr.
PO Box 146
Amherst, NY 14226-0146
Phone: (716)839-5080

Description: To recognize a woman who has made a significant contribution to humanism and feminism. Nominations are accepted from members of the AHA Feminist Caucus and Association members. Selection is made by the AHA Feminist Caucus. A bronze plaque on hardwood is awarded annually. Established in 1983.

★7997★ International Federation of Women's Travel Organizations Berger - Sullivan Award
International Federation of Women's Travel Organizations (IFWTO)
c/o IFWTO Exec. Office
4545 N. 36th St., Ste. 126
Phoenix, AZ 85018
Phone: (602)956-7175

Description: To recognize an individual or entity for an outstanding and ongoing contribution to worldwide travel and tourism. An individual or a business entity, such as cruise line, airline, tour operator, travel magazine or paper, etc., demonstrating long involvement in a prominent way in the travel industry is considered. A plaque or trophy is awarded when merited. Established in 1986.

★7998★ International Federation of Women's Travel Organizations Spirit Award
International Federation of Women's Travel Organizations (IFWTO)
c/o IFWTO Exec. Office
4545 N. 36th St., Ste. 126
Phoenix, AZ 85018
Phone: (602)956-7175

Description: Woman of the Year. For recognition of outstanding service to the Federation. Candidate must be a member in good standing. A trophy is awarded when merited at the Annual Conference. Established in 1974. **Formerly:** Woman of the Year.

★7999★ International Golden Rose Award
Women Band Directors National Association (WBDNA)
344 Overlook Dr.
West Lafayette, IN 47906
Phone: (317)463-1738

Description: To honor women of outstanding achievement and/or international reputation in the field of instrumental music. A trophy with a baton and a certificate are awarded biennially. Established in 1971.

★8000★ International Ministers' Wives and Widows Community Service
International Ministers' Wives and Widows
128 Pennsylvania Ave.
Roosevelt, NY 11575
Phone: (516)379-2541

Description: To recognize achievement by a non-member to the community, either locally, nationally or world-wide. Any member of Society may make a nomination. A trophy and/or a plaque are awarded annually at the Conference in June. Established in 1982.

★8001★ International Minister's Wives and Widows President's Award
International Ministers' Wives and Widows
128 Pennsylvania Ave.
Roosevelt, NY 11575
Phone: (516)379-2541

Description: To recognize person(s) who give the best all around service to the organization. Plaques are awarded annually. Established in 1960.

★8002★ International Women's Sports Hall of Fame
Women's Sports Foundation (WSF)
342 Madison Ave., Ste. 728
New York, NY 10173
Phone: (212)972-9170

Description: For recognition of great female athletes of the world. Becoming a member of the Women's Sports Hall of Fame requires international recognition of an athlete's sports performance and of her continuing commitment to the development of women's sports. Athletes whose major accomplishments were achieved prior to 1960 are inducted as Pioneers, while the Contemporary category recognizes athletes whose greatest success has been since 1960. Nominations for both categories are received from sport historians, international and national sport organizations, and the public. A Selection Committee, comprised of current Hall of Fame members, selects the new inductees. Only one person from a specific sport may be nominated in each category each year. Awarded annually at the Award Dinner. Established in 1980.

★8003★ Iota Sigma Pi Award for Professional Excellence
Iota Sigma Pi
634 Hudson St.
Hoboken, NJ 07030
Phone: (201)963-7968

Description: To recognize outstanding contributions to chemistry and allied fields. Nominees are judged on the significance of their accomplishments in academic, governmental, or industrial chemistry; in education; in administration; or in a combination of these areas. Achievements may include innovative design, development, application, or promotion of a principle or practice which has widespread significance to the scientific community or society on a national level. The nominee may be a member of Iota Sigma Pi. The deadline is February 1. A monetary prize of $300 and a certificate are presented at the National Convention in June. Established in 1984. Additional information is available from Linda Munchausen, Chair, Professional Excellence Award Committee, Department of Chemistry and Physics, Box 372, Southeastern Louisiana University, Hammond, LA 70402.

★8004★ Iota Sigma Pi National Honorary Member
Iota Sigma Pi
634 Hudson St.
Hoboken, NJ 07030
Phone: (201)963-7968

Description: This, the highest honor of Iota Sigma Pi, is given for recognition of exceptional and significant achievement in chemistry or an allied field of such nature as to merit international recognition. The nominee may be a member of Iota Sigma Pi. The deadline is February 1. The honor and a certificate are presented at the

Triennial Convention in convention years, or at a suitable time arranged by the Chairman of the National Honorary Membership Committee in non-convention years. Established in 1921. Additional information is available from Doris C. Warren, Chair, National Honorary Member Committee, Department of Chemistry, Houston Baptist University, 7502 Fondren Road, Houston, TX 77074-3298.

★8005★ Jacqueline Z. Radin Memorial Award
Newswomen's Club of New York
15 Gramercy Park
New York, NY 10003
Phone: (212)777-1610

Description: For recognition of the talents and promise of a newcomer to the journalism profession. Newswomen with no more than three years of newspaper experience are eligible. A scroll is awarded annually. Established in 1973 in memory of Mrs. Radin of *Newsday* who had a deep concern for and involvement with young people.

★8006★ Jane Addams Medal
Rockford College
5050 E. State St.
Rockford, IL 61108-2393
Phone: (815)226-4000

Description: To recognize women who are pioneers in their professions, who are outstanding in character and vision, and who are widely recognized for their contributions to society. A large bronze medallion of Jane Addams, by Chicago artist Andrene Kauffman, is awarded as merited. Established in 1944 by Mr. George E. Frazer in honor of Jane Addams, a noted alumna, social reformer, winner of the 1931 Nobel Peace Prize, and founder of Hull House in Chicago.

★8007★ Jane Dempsey Douglass Prize
American Society of Church History
328 Deland Ave.
Indialantic, FL 32903

Description: To recognize the author of the best unpublished essay on some aspect of the role of women in the history of Christianity. Entries may be submitted by August 1. A monetary award of $250 and publication of the essay in *Church History* are awarded annually when merited at the annual meeting of the Society in December. Established in 1990. Additional information is available from Richard L. Greaves, Chair, Committee on Research, American Society of Church History, c/o Department of History, Florida State University, Tallahassee, FL 32306-2029.

★8008★ Janet Heidinger Kafka Prize
University of Rochester
Susan B. Anthony Center
538 Lattimore Hall
Rochester, NY 14627
Phone: (716)275-8318

Description: To recognize an American woman who has written the best recently published book-length work of prose fiction, whether novel, short stories, or experimental writing. Works written primarily for children and publications from private and vanity presses cannot be considered. Only under the most unusual circumstances will a writer be considered for a subsequent award within a ten-year span. All entries are submitted by publishers who wish to have the work of their authors considered. Entries must be submitted before December 31 of any given year, and the works must have been assembled for the first time, or at least one-third of the material must be previously unpublished. A monetary award of $1,000 and a certificate are awarded annually in the fall. Established in 1975 by the family and friends of Janet Heidinger Kafka, a young editor who was killed in an auto accident. **Formerly:** Janet Kafka Prize.

★8009★ **Janet M. Glasgow Certificate Award**
American Medical Women's Association (AMWA)
801 N. Fairfax St., Ste. 400
Alexandria, VA 22314
Phone: (703)838-0500
Description: To recognize women medical students graduating first or in the top ten per cent of their classes. Established in 1941. In addition, a Janet M. Glasgow Essay award of $1,500 is awarded to a medical student who has written the best essay identifying a woman physician who has been a significant role model. Established in 1958.

★8010★ **Jessie Bernard Award**
American Sociological Association
1722 N St. NW
Washington, DC 20036
Phone: (202)833-3410
Description: For recognition of a work that has enlarged the horizons of the discipline of sociology to encompass fully the role of women in society. The award may be given for an exceptional single work, for several pieces of work, or for significant cumulative work done throughout a professional lifetime. A certificate is awarded biennially in odd-numbered years. Established in 1976.

★8011★ **Joan Fiss Bishop Award**
Section for Women in Public Administration
1120 G St. NW, Ste. 500
Washington, DC 20005
Phone: (202)393-7878
Description: To recognize members of the American Society of Public Administration who have contributed to increased involvement by women in the public sector, and who have distinguished careers in public administration. Practitioners or educators in public administration with leadership qualities, career accomplishment, and commitment to public administration are eligible. A plaque is awarded annually at the National ASPA convention. Established in 1985 in honor of Joan Fiss Bishop. Additional information is available from Debra Martin, phone: (313) 257-3707.

★8012★ **Joan Kelly Memorial Prize in Women's History**
American Historical Association
400 A St. SE
Washington, DC 20003
Phone: (202)544-2422
Description: To recognize an outstanding work in any chronological period, geographical location, or in any area of feminist theory that incorporates a historical perspective. Books published during the preceding year are eligible to be submitted by June 15. A monetary award

of $1,000 is presented annually. Established in 1984 by the Coordinating Committee on Women in the Historical Profession and the Conference Group on Women's History.

★8013★ **Joan Orr Award**
Air Force Association
1501 Lee Hwy.
Arlington, VA 22209-1198
Phone: (703)247-5810
Fax: (703)247-5855
Description: To recognize the outstanding Air Force wife each year. Awarded annually. Established in 1987.

★8014★ **Ladies Professional Golf Association Hall of Fame**
Ladies Professional Golf Association (LPGA)
2570 Volusia Ave., Ste. B
Daytona Beach, FL 32114
Description: To honor the best professional women golfers. Association members in good standing for 10 consecutive years who have won 30 official Tour events including at least two different major championships, or 35 official Tour events including at least one major championship, or 40 official Tour events are eligible. Established in 1967, after being a part of the Women's Golf Hall of Fame since 1950.

★8015★ **Ladies Professional Golf Association Leading Money Winners**
Ladies Professional Golf Association (LPGA)
2570 Volusia Ave., Ste. B
Daytona Beach, FL 32114
Description: To recognize the professional women golfers with the highest earnings from tournament play during the award year. Established in 1954.

★8016★ **Ladies Professional Golf Association Professional of the Year**
Ladies Professional Golf Association (LPGA)
2570 Volusia Ave., Ste. B
Daytona Beach, FL 32114
Description: To recognize a woman professional who manages a total golf program. An individual who manages a shop, has shown exceptional leadership and dedication to the game, and who has been active in LPGA sectional and national events, tournament supervision and promotion of junior and women's golf, is eligible. Awarded annually. Established in 1980.

★8017★ **Leaven Award**
American Agri-Women
PO Box 127
New Park, PA 17352
Phone: (717)382-4878
Description: To recognize individuals who, to an outstanding degree, have acted as "leaven," a truly feminine concept since "lady" means "giver of bread." A plaque is awarded. Established in 1977.

★8018★ **Lillian Gish Award**
Women in Film
6464 Sunset Blvd., Ste. 900
Los Angeles, CA 90028
Phone: (213)463-6040
Fax: (213)463-0963
Description: To recognize the overall achievement of women's work in film, television, music video, shorts, animation, and documentaries. Women who direct, write, or produce works that have not had a theatrical release prior to the festival are considered. A trophy is awarded annually. Established in 1987 in memory of Lillian Gish.

★8019★ **Loretta Richards Alumni Award**
College of Mount Saint Joseph
Office of the Pres.
5701 Delhi Pike
Mount St. Joseph, OH 45051
Phone: (513)244-4232
Description: To recognize an alumna distinguished for achievement in vocation, dedication to community service, and loyalty to the College of Mount Saint Joseph. Members are eligible for nomination and final confirmation by the College president. A plaque is awarded annually at Homecoming. Established in 1979 in honor of Loretta Richards, first alumnae president.

★8020★ **Loyola Camellia**
Loyola University of Chicago
829 N. Michigan Ave.
Chicago, IL 60611
Phone: (312)670-3000
Description: To recognize distinguished women for dedicated and responsible participation in the community's social, cultural or educational programs. Awarded annually. Established in 1965.

★8021★ **Luminas Awards**
Women in Film
6464 Sunset Blvd., Ste. 900
Los Angeles, CA 90028
Phone: (213)463-6040
Fax: (213)463-0963
Description: To recognize outstanding creative achievement in the depiction of multi-dimensional women characters in feature film and television programming. Established in 1986.

★8022★ **Lyle Mamer Fellowship**
Electrical Women's Round Table (EWRT)
PO Box 292793
Nashville, TN 37229-2793
Description: To promote the efficient use of electricity and to encourage high calibre women college graduates to further study toward an advanced degree in the field of electrical energy. Applications may be submitted by March 1. A monetary award up to $1,000 is presented annually. Established in 1982 in memory of Lyle Mamer, retired Associate Professor at the University of Tennessee College of Home Economics.

★8023★ **M. Carey Thomas Award**
Alumnae Association of Bryn Mawr College
Wyndham
Bryn Mawr, PA 10910
Phone: (215)645-5227
Description: To recognize American women who have made both eminent and outstanding

achievements. A monetary award is presented approximately every five years. Established in 1922 in honor of M. Carey Thomas, a former President of Bryn Mawr College.

★8024★ **Margaret H. Zimmerman Award**
Gamma Sigma Sigma National Service
    Sorority
4 Kirkland Court
Yalesville, CT 06492
Phone: (203)265-1410

Description: To recognize an alumnae chapter for activities and accomplishments in the community, and towards undergraduate chapters and the national organization.

★8025★ **Margaret M. Linton Award**
Gamma Sigma Sigma National Service
    Sorority
4 Kirkland Court
Yalesville, CT 06492
Phone: (203)265-1410

Description: To recognize an undergraduate chapter for activities and accomplishments on campus, in the community, and to the national organization.

★8026★ **Marguerite Ferdinand Award**
California Agricultural Aircraft Association
    (CAAA)
1100 N St., Ste. 5A
Sacramento, CA 95814
Phone: (916)447-1171

Description: To recognize women for outstanding contributions to the aerial application industry. Women affiliated with the aerial application industry including, but not limited to, members of the CAAA are eligible. A plaque is awarded annually at the convention. Established in 1984 in honor of Marguerite Ferdinand, a prime mover in ladies' activities in California.

★8027★ **Maria Goeppert-Mayer Award**
American Physical Society
335 E. 45th St.
New York, NY 10017-3483
Phone: (212)682-7341
Fax: (212)687-2532

Description: To recognize and enhance outstanding achievements by a woman physicist in the early years of her career, and to provide opportunities for her to present these achievements to others through public lectures. Women who are not later than ten years after the granting of the Ph.D. degree or the equivalent career stage are eligible for scientific achievements that demonstrate her potential as an outstanding physicist. The award is open to women of any nationality, and the lectures may be given at institutions in any country within two years after the award is made. The award consists of $2,000 plus a $3,000 travel allowance to provide opportunities for the recipient to give lectures in her field of physics at four institutions of her choice and at the meeting of the Society at which the award is bestowed, and a certificate citing the contributions made by the recipient. Established in 1985 by the General Electric Foundation, to be first awarded in 1986.

★8028★ **Martin Abzug Memorial Award**
National Women's Political Caucus (NWPC)
Leadership, Development, & Education Fund
1275 K St. NW, Ste. 750
Washington, DC 20005
Phone: (202)898-1100
Fax: (202)898-0458
Cathy Quick, Contact

Description: To recognize the spouse of a feminist leader whose constant support reflects his personal commitment to the goals and ideals of the Caucus. Established to honor Martin Abzug, husband, friend and staunch supporter of the Honorable Bella Abzug, whose advice and aid helped Bella through many political struggles and triumphs.

★8029★ **Mary Egging Memorial Award**
American Mothers
Waldorf Astoria
301 Park Ave.
New York, NY 10022
Phone: (212)755-2539

Description: To recognize a young mother who has shown outstanding service to American Mothers, Inc. in the program for mothers of young children. The following factors are considered: (1) leadership among mothers; (2) organizing new chapters; (3) increasing membership; and (4) serving as an example of quality mothering to other young women. A medallion is awarded. Established about 1978.

★8030★ **Matrix Award**
Women in Communications, New York
    Chapter (WIC)
245 5th Ave., Ste. 2103
New York, NY 10016-8728
Phone: (212)370-1866

Description: This, one of the industry's most prestigious awards, is given to honor the outstanding achievements of women who work in the New York area in the field of communications based on a high degree of professional competence in the fields of books, advertising, newspapers, magazines, broadcasting and public relations. Nominations are accepted. The deadline is usually the end of January. A symbolic Matrix (a metal mold used to cast type for printed material which represents the beginning of mass communication) in a paperweight or a shadow box is awarded yearly at the New York Women in Communications' annual Matrix Awards luncheon. Established in 1970.

★8031★ **Mature Women Scholarship Grant**
National League of American Pen Women
1300 17th St. NW
Washington, DC 20036
Phone: (202)785-1997

Description: To encourage the development of women in the fields of art, letters and music. Women over the age of 35 who are neither members of the League nor the immediate family of members are eligible. Three monetary awards of $1,000 each are presented biennially in even-numbered years in art, letters and music. Established in 1974. Additional information is available from Shirley Holden Helberg, National Scholarship Chairperson, phone: (717) 225-3023 or (301) 522-2557. Diskette and magnetic tape.

★8032★ **Maureen Connolly Brinker Award**
United States Tennis Association (USTA)
1212 Avenue of the Americas
New York, NY 10036-9998
Phone: (212)302-3322

Description: Maureen Connolly Brinker Outstanding Junior Girl Award. To recognize the girl player considered by the selection committee to have had the most outstanding full season performance. Selection is based on exceptional ability, sportsmanship, and competitive spirit. The winner's name is inscribed on a large silver bowl kept at the Philadelphia Cricket Club; each recipient receives a silver tray and lifetime enrollment in the USTA. Awarded annually at the Philadelphia Cricket Club. Established in 1969 by the Maureen Connolly Brinker Foundation. **Formerly:** Maureen Connolly Brinker Outstanding Junior Girl Award.

★8033★ **McElligott Medallion**
Association of Marquette University Women
Marquette Univ.
1212 West Wisconsin Ave.
Milwaukee, WI 53233
Phone: (414)288-1590

Description: To recognize a woman of national prominence who has emulated the ideals of the Association's founders in advancing the educational and cultural interests of women. A silver medal is awarded when merited. Established in 1963 in honor of Mabel Mannix McElligott, a longtime Dean of Women at the University and founder of the alumnae association.

★8034★ **McKinney Award**
National Newspaper Association
1627 K St. NW, Ste. 400
Washington, DC 20006
Phone: (202)466-7200

Description: To recognize a woman for distinguished contributions to journalism. Active, working women associated with a non-metropolitan weekly or daily newspaper, may be nominated by June 1 of the awarding year. A plaque is awarded annually at the Convention. Established in 1966 in memory of Emma McKinney, an Oregon pioneering newswoman.

★8035★ **Mickey Wright Award**
Golf Digest
Public Relations
5520 Park Ave.
PO Box 395
Trumbull, CT 06611
Phone: (203)373-7000
Fax: (203)373-7170

Description: To recognize the female golfer who has won the most events during the previous year. Players on the professional golf circuit are eligible. A Tiffany crystal trophy is awarded annually. Established in 1955.

★8036★ **Minister's Wife of the Year**
International Ministers' Wives and Widows
128 Pennsylvania Ave.
Roosevelt, NY 11575
Phone: (516)379-2541

Description: To recognize a minister's wife for distinguished services to church, community, state and national objectives. A plaque is awarded annually. Established in 1950.

★8037★ Ministry to Women Award
Unitarian Universalist Women's Federation (UUWF)
25 Beacon St.
Boston, MA 02108
Phone: (617)742-2100

Description: To recognize an individual or organization that has served the cause of women in an outstanding manner. Prior to 1985, the award was given only to non-Unitarian Universalists. The administrative board of UUWF is currently rethinking the criteria. An honorarium of $500, travel expenses to the meeting where the award is given, and a citation are awarded annually. Established in 1974.

★8038★ Miss America Women's Achievement Award
Miss America Organization
PO Box 119
Atlantic City, NJ 08404
Phone: (609)345-7571

Description: To recognize American women who demonstrate exemplary commitment to a cause or issue of benefit to American society and who serve as role models for others. A $15,000 grant and a commemorative crystal sculpture entitled "Soaring Eagle," a limited edition piece created by Steuben, are awarded annually. Established in 1989. Sponsored by the Miss America Foundation.

★8039★ Mobil Cup
The Athletics Congress of the USA
PO Box 120
Indianapolis, IN 46206-0120
Phone: (317)638-9155
Fax: (317)261-0481

Description: To recognize the outstanding female athlete at both the National Women's Indoor and Outdoor Championships. A trophy is awarded annually at the National Convention. Established in 1973.

★8040★ Mortar Board National Citation
Mortar Board
Natl. Hon. Soc. for Col. Srs. for Ldrship., Scholar. & Serv.
1250 Chambers Rd., Ste. 170
Columbus, OH 43212
Phone: (614)292-3319

Description: To recognize distinguished contributions to the nation within the ideals of scholarship, service, and leadership; and to promote equal opportunities among all peoples while emphasizing the advancement of the status of women. Presented to no more than two persons at one time at the biennial national conference. Established in 1973.

★8041★ Mother of the Year
American Mothers
Waldorf Astoria
301 Park Ave.
New York, NY 10022
Phone: (212)755-2539

Description: To encourage the strengthening of the moral and spiritual foundations of the home, and to give to the observance of Mother's Day a spiritual quality which highlights the standards of ideal motherhood in the home, community, nation and the world. A citation and diamond pin are awarded annually. Established in 1935. Additional information is available from Waltere-

na R. Cark, President, 6843 Nashville Road, Lanham, MD, 20706, phone: (301) 552-2712.

★8042★ Mrs. Lyndon B. Johnson Award
Keep America Beautiful
Mill River Plaza
9 W. Broad St.
Stamford, CT 06902
Phone: (203)323-8987

Description: To recognize an outstanding woman-volunteer leader of the movement to improve the quality of American life at the grassroots level. This highly selective award is given only if judges decide a nominee has contributed substantially in the movement for a cleaner, more beautiful America. Awarded annually at the National Awards Luncheon.

★8043★ *MS.* Magazine Making a Difference Advertising Award
Ms. Magazine
c/o Matilda Publications, Inc.
1 Times Sq., 9th Fl.
New York, NY 10036
Phone: (212)719-9800

Description: To recognize positive portrayals of women in advertising. Established in 1989.

★8044★ *Ms.* Magazine Woman of the Year
Ms. Magazine
c/o Matilda Publications, Inc.
1 Times Sq., 9th Fl.
New York, NY 10036
Phone: (212)719-9800

Description: To recognize women for excellence. Awarded annually. Established in 1983.

★8045★ Myra E. Barrer Journalism Award
American University
School of Communication
4400 Massachusetts Ave. NW
Washington, DC 20016
Phone: (202)885-2060

Description: To recognize journalistic efforts that best demonstrate knowledge and interest in the women's movement and the historical and contemporary efforts for the provision of equal rights and equal opportunities for women. Entries may be submitted in the form of a journalism news story, feature story, or editorial; television or radio production; and monograph, or research paper. Graduating seniors at The American University are eligible. The entry deadline is March 6. A monetary prize of $400 and a certificate are awarded annually. Established in 1979 in memory of Myra Barrer, a member of the Women's Institute Advisory Council during its initial years.

★8046★ Naismith All-American Teams
Atlanta Tipoff Club
3820 Satellite Blvd., Ste. 100
Duluth, GA 30136
Phone: (404)476-9700
Fax: (404)476-4651

Description: To recognize the top five male and female collegiate basketball players and their coaches. The final ballot is taken prior to the NCAA tournament.

★8047★ Naismith College Coach of the Year
Atlanta Tipoff Club
3820 Satellite Blvd., Ste. 100
Duluth, GA 30136
Phone: (404)476-9700
Fax: (404)476-4651

Description: To recognize the outstanding male and female college basketball coach of the year. Established in 1987.

★8048★ Naismith High School Awards
Atlanta Tipoff Club
3820 Satellite Blvd., Ste. 100
Duluth, GA 30136
Phone: (404)476-9700
Fax: (404)476-4651

Description: To recognize the nation's male and female prep player of the year based on a nationwide poll of sportswriters, broadcasters, coaches and administrators and a special Tipoff Club selection committee. A bronze trophy is awarded. The program also honors the boy and girl player of the year in each state. Established in 1987. Sponsored by Days Inn of America.

★8049★ Naomi Berber Memorial Award
Graphic Arts Technical Foundation
4615 Forbes Ave.
Pittsburgh, PA 15213-3796
Phone: (412)621-6941

Description: To recognize a woman who has made a major contribution to the development of the graphic communications industries. Women who have worked in the graphic arts industry for at least ten years, are actively working in the industry, and have an outstanding record of accomplishments and leadership are eligible. The deadline for nominations is July 15. A hand engraved, ivory pendant watch is awarded annually. Established in 1975 in memory of Naomi Berber, former administrative director, and the first woman to be elected to the Fellows.

★8050★ National Agriculture Aviation Association Most Active Woman Award
National Agricultural Aviation Association
1005 E St. SE
Washington, DC 20003
Phone: (202)546-5722
Fax: (202)546-5726

Description: To recognize an outstanding contribution of a woman who is active in the affairs of the industry or the Association. Established in 1971 by Mrs. Shirley Carroll in memory of her son, William Carroll.

★8051★ National Association of Black Women Attorneys Scholarship Award
National Association of Black Women Attorneys
3711 Macomb St. NW
Washington, DC 20016
Phone: (202)966-9693
Fax: (202)244-6648

Description: To provide a scholarship for black women law students. Several scholarships are presented annually at the Red Dress Ball at the Convention. Established in 1978 by Attorney Mabel D. Haden, Washington, DC, with contributions from various businesses, lawyers and concerned citizens.

★8052★ National Association of Negro Business and Professional Women's Club National Achievement Award
National Association of Negro Business and
Professional Women's Club
1806 New Hampshire Ave. NW
Washington, DC 20009
Phone: (202)483-4206
Fax: (202)462-7253

Description: For recognition of achievement by a woman. A plaque is awarded annually at the convention.

★8053★ National Association of Negro Business and Professional Women's Club National Appreciation Award
National Association of Negro Business and
Professional Women's Club
1806 New Hampshire Ave. NW
Washington, DC 20009
Phone: (202)483-4206
Fax: (202)462-7253

Description: For recognition for service to the Association. Members are eligible. Awarded annually at the Convention.

★8054★ National Association of Negro Business and Professional Women's Club National Community Service Award
National Association of Negro Business and
Professional Women's Club
1806 New Hampshire Ave. NW
Washington, DC 20009
Phone: (202)483-4206
Fax: (202)462-7253

Description: To recognize an oustanding woman, non-member, who resides in the city where the convention is held for a contribution to the community. A plaque is awarded annually at the convention.

★8055★ National Association of Negro Business and Professional Women's Club National Scholarship Award
National Association of Negro Business and
Professional Women's Club
1806 New Hampshire Ave. NW
Washington, DC 20009
Phone: (202)483-4206
Fax: (202)462-7253

Description: To encourage professional development. Members are eligible. A plaque is awarded annually at the convention.

★8056★ National Association of Negro Business and Professional Women's Club National Youth Award
National Association of Negro Business and
Professional Women's Club
1806 New Hampshire Ave. NW
Washington, DC 20009
Phone: (202)483-4206
Fax: (202)462-7253

Description: For recognition of achievement. Outstanding young women under 30 years of age are eligible. A plaque is awarded annually at the Convention.

★8057★ National Association for Professional Saleswomen Achievers' Circle
National Association for Professional
Saleswomen (NAPS)
PO Box 2606
Novato, CA 94948
Phone: (415)898-2606
Fax: (415)897-5347

Description: Cross Pen Awards for Professional Sales Achievement. To recognize women for service to NAPS, service to their industries, personal career achievement, and professionalism. Honorees must have been NAPS members for a minimum of two years and served in a NAPS leadership position for at least one year. The honoree should have at least five years experience in sales and have a minimum annual income of $50,000. A plaque and recognition at the annual conference and in the national newsletter, *Successful Saleswoman*, are awarded annually. Established in 1983 and sponsored by A.T. Cross Company. Renamed in 1988. Formerly: Cross Pen Awards for Professional Sales Achievement.

★8058★ National Association of Women Judges Honoree of the Year Award
National Association of Women Judges
300 Newport Ave.
Williamsburg, VA 23187-8798
Phone: (804)253-2000
Fax: (804)220-0449

Description: Judge of the Year Award. To recognize individuals who have assisted women judges to become more proficient in their professions to solve the legal, social and ethical problems associated with the profession; assisted in increasing the number of women judges; and addressed important issues affecting women judges. Individuals, male or female, judges or non-judges, may be nominated. A plaque and other appropriate gifts are awarded at the annual conference in the fall. Established in 1982. Formerly: Judge of the Year Award.

★8059★ National Collegiate Athletic Association National Championships
National Collegiate Athletic Association
(NCAA)
PO Box 1906
Nall Ave. at 63rd St.
Mission, KS 66201
Phone: (913)384-3220
Fax: (913)831-8425

Description: The NCAA sponsors 76 national championships annually of which nine are National Collegiate Championships for which all divisions are eligible, 23 are National Collegiate Division I Championships, 20 are National Collegiate Division II Championships and 24 are National Collegiate Division III Championships. It oversees tournaments to determine team and individual National Collegiate Champions in the following sports: baseball, basketball, cross country, football, rifle, softball, fencing, golf, gymnastics, ice hockey, lacrosse, skiing, soccer, swimming and diving, tennis, track and field, volleyball, water polo, field hockey and wrestling. To be eligible to enter a team or individual in NCAA championship competition, an institution must be an active member in good standing in the appropriate division or have its sport so classified and be eligible under the rules of the intercollegiate athletics conference of which it is a member, provided the confer-

ence is a conference member of the Association. The championships are held annually.

★8060★ National Conference of Puerto Rican Women Award
National Conference of Puerto Rican Women
5 Thomas Circle
Washington, DC 20005
Phone: (202)387-4716

Description: For recognition of service to the advancement of Puerto Rican and Hispanic women. A plaque or the organization's emblem in gold is awarded when merited at the annual conference. Established in 1978.

★8061★ National Council of Administrative Women in Education Leadership Award
National Council of Administrative Women in
Education
331 Churchill Rd.
Pittsburgh, PA 15235
Phone: (412)824-7950

Description: For recognition of outstanding research pertaining to women in educational administration or to the development of leadership skills. Application must be submitted by December 30. A monetary award plus transportation to the National Conference are awarded biennially. Established in 1984.

★8062★ National Federation of Press Women Honorary Member
National Federation of Press Women
Box 99
Blue Springs, MO 64015
Phone: (816)229-1666

Description: To recognize a woman for an outstanding contribution in the field of communications. Awarded occasionally when merited. Established in 1971.

★8063★ National Federation of Press Women Sweepstakes Winner
National Federation of Press Women
Box 99
Blue Springs, MO 64015
Phone: (816)229-1666

Description: For recognition of contributions to the field of communications. Awarded annually. Established in 1969.

★8064★ National Planning Awards - Diana Donald Award
American Planning Association
1776 Massachusetts Ave. NW
Washington, DC 20036
Phone: (202)872-0611

Description: To recognize outstanding male or female planners who have made a substantial contribution to furthering the advancement of women in the planning field. The recipient should have demonstrated significant contributions to the profession, held a responsible management position in planning, and devoted substantial effort to community service - particularly service involving the attainment of women's rights both in the planning profession and in the community at-large. Nominations of members and non-members may be made by any person or organization. Awarded annually. This award honors the late APA Board of Directors member for her contributions to the Association.

★8065★ National Women's Hall of Fame
National Women's Hall of Fame
PO Box 335
76 Fall St.
Seneca Falls, NY 13148
Phone: (315)568-2936
Linda Lopez McAlister, Contact

Description: To honor American women of achievement and struggles in the fields of arts, athletics, business, education, government, humanitarianism, philanthropy, and science which have been of great value to the development of their country. Nominations of women whose achievements are of national significance and enduring value and whose efforts promote the progress and freedom of women are accepted. Living honorees receive a Steuben Star Crystal. The honor given to all honorees is perpetual. Presented annually at a mid-July ceremony. Established in 1973.

★8066★ NAWA Annual Exhibition Awards
National Association of Women Artists
(NAWA)
41 Union Sq., W., Ste. 906
New York, NY 10003-3278
Phone: (212)675-1616

Description: To encourage women in the arts and provide a means of showing their works. Members of the Association may submit works of art in oils and acylics, works on paper, sculpture, and printmaking. An invited Jury of Awards makes the final selections. Medals of Honor and monetary prizes are awarded annually in the spring.

★8067★ Ninety-Nines NIFA Achievement Award
Ninety-Nines
International Women Pilots Association
PO Box 59965
Will Rogers World Airport
Oklahoma City, OK 73159
Phone: (405)685-7969

Description: To encourage active participation by women in aviation. Female university students in good standing who have Private Pilot Certificates are eligible. The following prizes are awarded: first place - a monetary prize of $200 and the Gold Amelia Earhart Medal; second place - $150 and the Silver Amelia Earhart Medal; and third place - $100 and the Bronze Amelia Earhart Medal. In addition, the Top Female Pilot award is presented. Awarded annually. Established in the late 1940s.

★8068★ Nissan FOCUS Awards Competition
Nissan FOCUS Awards
Films of College & Univ. Students (FOCUS)
10 E. 34th St., 6th Fl.
New York, NY 10016
Phone: (212)779-0404
Fax: (212)779-1985

Description: The FOCUS (Films of College and University Students) film competition is designed to recognize excellence in college-level film training and to forge a major link between university film students and the professional film world. It provides more than $100,000 in prizes and scholarship funds to students for outstanding achievement in the following categories: (1) narrative film; (2) documentary film; (3) animated/experimental film; (4) screenwriting; (5) film editing; (6) sound achievement; (7) cinematography; (8) Women in Film Foundation Award; and

(9) Renee Valente Producers Award. Film entries must be 16mm, must be made on a non-commercial basis, and must have been recently completed in conjunction with courses at American colleges and universities, art institutes, or professional film schools. The deadline varies annually, and is usually in April. Either a Nissan automobile or a monetary prize is awarded. In addition, all winners receive trophies and a five day all-expenses paid trip to Los Angeles to attend various industry seminars and a Premiere and Awards Ceremony. The corresponding college or university of the First Place winners in the three Filmmaking Categories will receive the FOCUS Institutional Award, $1,000 in Eastman motion picture film and video tape from Eastman Kodak Company for their film department's use. The competition is held annually. Established in 1977 by TRG Communications, Inc. for Nissan Motor Corporation in U.S.A., the competition's principal sponsor. Co-sponsored in 1989 by Steven Spielberg's Amblin Entertainment, John Badham's Films, Dolby Laboratories, Eastman Kodak Company, and Benihana of Tokyo, Inc.

★8069★ NNWS Beverly Kievman Leadership Award
National Network of Women in Sales
(NNWS)
PO Box 59269
Schaumburg, IL 60195-0269
Phone: (312)577-2537

Description: For recognition of outstanding leadership abilities within the organization. Members who are active in the organization may be nominated by June. A monetary award, a plaque, and motivational tapes are awarded annually. Established in 1984 by Beverly Kievman.

★8070★ NOW Foundation Essay Contest
NOW Foundation
1000 16th St. NW, Ste. 700
Washington, DC 20036-5705
Phone: (202)331-0066

Description: To recognize the outstanding essays on the topic of women's rights. In 1989, the specific topic was: "The Continuing Struggle for Women's Equality in the United States." Within this broad subject essays dealt with, but were not limited to: Earliest Voices for Women's Equality; The Beginning of the Women's Rights Movement; Last Days Winning the Vote for Women; The Introduction of the Equal Rights Amendment; and Why We Need the ERA The contest is open to all students enrolled in one of the following: (1) Senior High School (grades 9 through 12); (2) College; and (3) Continuing Education. Essays of not more than 1,500 words may be submitted by October 15. The competition is judged by a national panel composed of leaders of the women's rights movement. The national winners in each category are awarded scholarships of $1,000. In addition, the NOW Foundation has the right to publish winning entries either in the *National NOW Times*, or another appropriate publication. Established in 1987.

★8071★ NOW LDEF Equal Opportunity Award
NOW Legal Defense and Education Fund
(NOWLDEF)
99 Hudson St.
New York, NY 10013
Phone: (212)925-6635
Fax: (212)226-1066
Anita Borg, Contact

Description: To salute individuals and corporate leaders dedicated to full equality for women; and to focus attention on NOW LDEF's work to end sex discrimination and achieve full equality through institutional change by legal reform and educational campaigns. A nominating committee makes the selection. An engraved silver photo frame is awarded annually at a dinner. Established in 1979.

★8072★ Outstanding Elected Democratic Woman Holding Public Office
National Federation of Democratic Women
3311 NW Roosevelt
Corwallis, OR 97330
Phone: (503)752-5708

Description: To recognize a current statewide, regional or national woman office holder who has demonstrated support of the Federation, the Democratic Party and its principles and commitment to the success of other Democratic women. Established in 1987. In addition, special awards are presented at the Convention.

★8073★ Outstanding Mother Award
National Mother's Day Committee
1328 Broadway, Ste. 1023
New York, NY 10001
Phone: (212)594-6421
Fax: (212)594-9349

Description: To recognize a mother who serves as a role model to influence the American public with a perception of contemporary motherhood as a vital and growing factor in our social fabric. Motherhood - biological, adoptive or foster; a good record of interest in children's related activities, not just in the family, but in the community; involvement in some aspect of public service; and a good tradition of solid family ties are considered. A sculpture, designed by Henry Dunay, is presented annually in April. Established in 1979.

★8074★ Outstanding NFDW Member of the Year
National Federation of Democratic Women
(NFDW)
3311 NW Roosevelt
Corwallis, OR 97330
Phone: (503)752-5708

Description: For recognition of an active member who has made a significant contribution to the growth, development, and promotion of the Federation. Members of national scope and stature are eligible. A certificate is awarded annually at the Convention. Established in 1985.

★8075★ Outstanding Woman Veterinarian Award
Association for Women Veterinarians
Box 1051
Littleton, CO 80160-1051
Phone: (303)795-0130

Description: For recognition of a woman veterinarian who has made a significant contribution to the field of veterinary medicine. Nominations are accepted. A plaque is presented annually. Established in 1951 and awarded annually between 1951 and 1958. The award was reinstituted in 1972.

★8076★ Outstanding Women of Color
National Institute for Women of Color
1301 20th St. NW, Ste. 702
Washington, DC 20036-6042
Phone: (202)296-2661

Description: To recognize individuals for achievement in an area of service and contributions to a community or a field of activity, and to encourage professional development. Women of color may be nominated by the board of directors of the Institute, may apply, or may be referred. A plaque is awarded every two years at the National Conference. Established in 1982.

★8077★ Outstanding Women in Music Award
Tau Beta Sigma
122 Seretean Center
Oklahoma State Univ.
Stillwater, OK 74078
Phone: (405)372-2333

Description: To honor a woman who has made a distinct or unique contribution to the field of band music in some way. The candidate must be out of college, and have at least five years experience in her particular area. A trophy is awarded biennially. Established in 1969.

★8078★ Patty Berg Award
Ladies Professional Golf Association (LPGA)
2570 Volusia Ave., Ste. B
Daytona Beach, FL 32114

Description: To recognize outstanding contributions to women's golf. Any person, a member or non-member, may be nominated for the Award. The selection committee is composed, by appointment from the Commissioner's office, of a Hall of Fame member, past President, member of Sponsor association, Board of Directors member, and media representative. The Berg Trophy is a spiral structure of clear crystal mounted on a black leather base. The crystal is a Steuben called "Tetrahedra." Awarded when merited. Established in 1979 to honor Patty Berg and recognize her diplomacy, sportsmanship, goodwill and contributions to the game.

★8079★ Pearl S. Buck Woman's Award
Pearl S. Buck Foundation
Green Hills Farm
Perkasie, PA 18944
Phone: (215)249-0100
Fax: (215)249-9657

Description: To recognize a woman who emulates Pearl Buck, whether in professional success, humanitarian effort or familial devotion. Pearl Buck was a humanitarian, a teacher, a translator, a civil-rights pioneer, an art lover, a gardener, a homemaker, and the mother of eight children. A bronze statuette created by sculptor Madeline Smith is awarded annually. The statuette portrays an Amerasian child holding a rice bowl, symbolizing the plight of the thousands of half-American children living throughout Southeast Asia, whom Pearl Buck helped through the establishment of the Pearl S. Buck Foundation in 1964. Established in 1979.

★8080★ PEN/Jerard Fund Award
PEN American Center
568 Broadway
New York, NY 10012
Phone: (212)334-1660
Fax: (212)334-2181

Description: To recognize a woman writer at an early point in her career for a work-in-progress of general nonfiction. Applicants must have published at least one magazine article in a national publication or in a major literary magazine. However, she must not have published more than one book in any field. Each applicant should submit no more than 75 pages of her English-language booklength nonfiction work-in-progress accompanied by a personal bibliography. There are no restrictions upon the content of the work, nor on the age of the applicant. Applicants must be residents of the United States. The deadline for submissions is February 15. A monetary prize of $3,000 is awarded. Established in 1987 in cooperation with the New York Community Trust.

★8081★ Phyllis B. Marriott President's Award
American Mothers
Waldorf Astoria
301 Park Ave.
New York, NY 10022
Phone: (212)755-2539

Description: To recognize a state chapter for outstanding achievement in the field of record keeping of events within their state organization that year. Awarded annually.

★8082★ Pioneer Achiever Award
National Woman's Party
144 Constitution Ave. NE
Washington, DC 20002
Phone: (202)546-1210

Description: To recognize "women pioneers" and their professional accomplishments as "firsts" in their field as women. Distinguished professional achievements by women are considered. A plaque is awarded annually at the celebration of Alice Paul's birthday on January 11. Established in 1986.

★8083★ Pioneer Award
Women Business Owners of New York
La Concierge Services Inc.
322 E. 86th St.
New York, NY 10028
Phone: (212)737-5289

Description: For recognition of achievement by women in business. Nomination for award is based on the candidate's significant contribution to business for women in an area that had not yet been pioneered. A crystal engraved paperweight from Tiffany's is awarded annually at the Entrepreneurial Woman Awards Luncheon. Established in 1977.

★8084★ Planned Parenthood Federation of America (PPFA) Margaret Sanger Award
Planned Parenthhood Federation of America (PPFA)
c/o Barbara Snow
810 7th Ave.
New York, NY 10019
Phone: (212)541-7800

Description: This, the highest honor in the family planning movement, is given in recogni-

tion of excellence and leadership in the field. The deadline for nominations is usualy April 1. A bronze statuette titled *Children of the World*, by the American artist Stanley Bleifeld, is awarded each year. Established in 1966.

★8085★ Psychological Research on Women Award
Association for Women in Psychology
48 Wallingford
Brighton, MA 02130
Phone: (617)381-3244

Description: For recognition of outstanding psychological research on women by graduate or undergraduate students. The subjects of research eligible for this award are construed very broadly, and may represent work in social, developmental, personality, clinical, experimental, or any other area of psychology. The research should be relevant in some significant way to women's lives, or more generally, to the emerging psychological understanding of gender role influences on human behavior. The research may be basic or applied. Jointly authored papers are eligible, but the first author must have been a student at the time the research was done. Entries should be of approximately journal length and written in APA style. Papers which have been submitted for publication or presented at a professional meeting are eligible along with papers which have been previously published or accepted for publication. A monetary prize of $150 is awarded annually. Established in 1985. Additional information is available from Maureen McHugh, Women's Studies Program, Indiana University of Pennsylvania, Indiana, PA 15705.

★8086★ Resnik Challenger Medal
Society of Women Engineers (SWE)
United Engineering Center
345 E. 47th St., Rm. 305
New York, NY 10017
Phone: (212)705-7855

Description: To recognize exceptional engineering contributions in broadening the frontiers of space exploration. Any woman engineer who has been practicing for ten or more years; who is an analytical visionary; and who has expanded the horizons of space exploration through an engineering breakthrough in aeronautics, astronautics, materials, electronics, structures, health or other space-related engineering accomplishment may be nominated by January 1. A medal bearing the likeness of Dr. Resnik and a space shuttle, and a certificate are awarded as merited. Established in 1986 to honor Judith A. Resnik, mission specialist on the ill fated Challenger space shuttle flight on January 28, 1986.

★8087★ Rodney D. Chipp Memorial Award
Society of Women Engineers (SWE)
United Engineering Center
345 E. 47th St., Rm. 305
New York, NY 10017
Phone: (212)705-7855

Description: To recognize an individual or corporation for significant contributions to the acceptance and advancement of women in the engineering profession. An engraved plaque and a citation are awarded as merited. Established in 1967 in memory of Dr. Chipp, a prominent engineer, and the late husband of Dr. Beatrice A Hicks, first President of the Society.

★8088★ **Rolex Player of the Year**
Ladies Professional Golf Association (LPGA)
2570 Volusia Ave., Ste. B
Daytona Beach, FL 32114

Description: To recognize the player who, during a current Tour year, has had the most consistent and outstanding record. Members of LPGA are eligible. The honoree's name is inscribed on a permanent trophy - an Irish silver cup made in the 1900s in Dublin. Awarded annually. Established in 1966. Sponsored by Rolex Watch U.S.A., Inc.

★8089★ **Rosetta LeNoire Award**
Actors' Equity Association
165 W. 46th St.
New York, NY 10036
Phone: (212)869-8530

Description: To recognize those theatres and producing organizations under an equity contract which are exemplary in the hiring of ethnic minority and female actors through affirmative action, multi-racial and non- traditional casting. Nominations of a theatre producing organization are accepted by October 31.

★8090★ **Runner of the Year**
The Athletics Congress of the USA
PO Box 120
Indianapolis, IN 46206-0120
Phone: (317)638-9155
Fax: (317)261-0481

Description: To honor the woman runner of the year. Consideration is based upon the runner's performances and/or achievements in competitions. A plaque is awarded annually at the National Convention. Established in 1981.

★8091★ **Sales Leader of the Year Award**
Women in Sales Association
8 Madison Ave.
Valhalla, NY 10595
Phone: (914)946-3802

Description: To provide recognition for women's achievements in sales. Nomination or validation of a sales manager are accepted. A plaque is awarded at a seminar. Established in 1981.

★8092★ **Sally Deaver Award**
United States Ski Association
PO Box 100
1500 Kearns Blvd.
Park City, UT 84060
Phone: (801)649-9090
Fax: (801)649-3613

Description: To recognize the winner of the National Women's Slalom competition. Awarded annually. Established in 1965 by the Deaver family in memory of Sally Deaver, an outstanding slalom champion.

★8093★ **Sarah Palfrey Danzig Award**
United States Tennis Association (USTA)
1212 Avenue of the Americas
New York, NY 10036-9998
Phone: (212)302-3322

Description: To recognize a female player who by character, sportsmanship, manners, spirit of cooperation and contribution to the growth of the game ranks first in the opinion of the Selection Committee. The name of the winner is engraved on the trophy and a silver tray suitably inscribed is given to the recipient as a memento of the award. Established in 1986 in honor of Sarah Palfrey Danzig as an award comparable to the William M. Johnston Award for men.

★8094★ **Scholarships and Research Grants for Women Doing Behavioral Studies**
National Chamber of Commerce for Women (NCCW)
10 Waterside Plaza, Ste. 6H
New York, NY 10010
Phone: (212)685-3454

Description: Woman of the Year. For recognition of outstanding achievement in labor-management relations and to provide funds for further education. Applicants may submit research programs or curricula that examine organizational behavior or business ethics. Scholarships based on need are awarded. Established in 1981. **Formerly:** Woman of the Year.

★8095★ **Search for New Music**
International League of Women Composers
Southshore Rd., Box 670
Point Peninsula
Three Mile Bay, NY 13693
Phone: (315)649-5086

Description: To encourage women composers of music in any style or medium. Full-time student women composers of any age are eligible. The award consists of a first prize of $250, and a second prize of $150, and honorable mentions. Awarded annually. Established in 1978. In addition, the Ellen Zwilich Award is given to recognize younger women composers (21 years of age or younger). A monetary award of $150 is presented annually. Established in 1989 to honor Ellen Zwilich, who received the Pulitzer Prize for Music in 1983 - the first woman to achieve this distinction. Additional information is available from Jane Weiner Le Page, 30 Thistle Path, Williamstown, MA 02167.

★8096★ **Service Bowl Award**
United States Tennis Association (USTA)
1212 Avenue of the Americas
New York, NY 10036-9998
Phone: (212)302-3322

Description: To recognize the female player who most notably contributes to the sportsmanship, fellowship and service of tennis. Nominations may be submitted by June 15. A Service Bowl Trophy is awarded annually. Established in 1940 by Mrs. Lyman H.B. Olmstead in honor of Mrs. Hazel H. Wightman.

★8097★ **Seventh Day Baptist Historical Society Robe of Achievement**
Seventh Day Baptist Historical Society
PO Box 1678
Janesville, WI 53547
Phone: (608)752-5055

Description: To recognize Seventh Day Baptist women who have made an outstanding contribution beyond the local church life and community. Custodianship of the traditional robe for one year and a plaque are awarded annually at the General Conference sessions by the Seventh Day Baptist Women's Society. Established in 1964.

★8098★ **Sheila Scott Memorial Scholarship**
Whirly-Girls
7551 Callaghan Rd., Ste. 330
San Antonio, TX 78229
Phone: (512)344-4825

Description: Tony Page Memorial Scholarship. To assist a deserving woman to acquire her initial helicopter rating. A woman who currently has an airplane, balloon or glider pilot license, and shows financial need and commitment to aviation is eligible. A scholarship of $4,000 is awarded annually. Established in 1978 by the Whirly-Girls Men's Auxiliary in memory of different individuals each year who have contributed to the Whirly-Girls and the Helicopter Industry. **Formerly:** Tony Page Memorial Scholarship.

★8099★ **Sigma Delta Epsilon Fellowships**
Sigma Delta Epsilon
Graduate Women in Science
PO Box 4748
Ithaca, NY 14852

Description: To increase knowledge in all the natural sciences, and to encourage research by women. Individuals who hold a degree from a recognized institution of higher learning; give evidence of outstanding ability and promise in one of the mathematical, physical, environmental, computer or life sciences; and are currently involved in research may submit applications by December 1. Monetary fellowships of $1,500 to $4,000 are awarded annually at the summer meeting.

★8100★ **Sigma Delta Epsilon Honorary Member**
Sigma Delta Epsilon
Graduate Women in Science
PO Box 4748
Ithaca, NY 14852

Description: To recognize women for outstanding achievement in all fields of scientific research. Membership is not a requirement. Women who have demonstrated outstanding achievement may be nominated. A certificate and exemption from membership dues are awarded. Established in 1926.

★8101★ **Silver Baton Award**
Women Band Directors National Association (WBDNA)
344 Overlook Dr.
West Lafayette, IN 47906
Phone: (317)463-1738

Description: To honor outstanding women in the field of instrumental music. The criteria for selection are that the woman: (1) consistently produces bands of high performance level; (2) consistently performs programs of high musical quality; (3) has made an outstanding contribution to the community and the country through music; (4) has made an outstanding contribution to the improvement of bands in America through participation and leadership in professional organizations; and (5) must be an active member of WBDNA, and have made an outstanding contribution to the Association through participation. A certificate and plaque are awarded annually. Established in 1972.

★8102★ Silver Satellite Award
American Women in Radio and Television
1101 Connecticut Ave. NW, Ste. 700
Washington, DC 20036
Phone: (202)429-5102

Description: To recognize an individual who has made outstanding contributions to the field of broadcast communication. A silver sculpture is awarded at the Annual Convention. Established in 1967.

★8103★ Silver Snail Award
NOW Legal Defense and Education Fund (NOWLDEF)
Project on Equal Education Rights
1333 H St. NW
Washington, DC 20005
Phone: (202)682-0940

Description: To recognize individuals and organizations who have been exceptionally sluggish in promoting equity in education. Schools, government agencies, policymakers and other individuals and organizations are eligible for nonperformance in preventing discrimination. Nominations are judged by a panel of committed individuals active in the civil and education rights community. Awards may be presented in the following categories: (1) Supreme Snail; (2) Lifetime Underachievement Award; (3) Garden Snail; and (4) Sports Snail - Grand Slime Sluggers. A Royal Order of the Snail Certificate is awarded annually. In addition, repeat winners are inducted into the Snail Hall of Fame. Established in 1979.

★8104★ Small Business Advocates of the Year
U.S. Small Business Administration
c/o Office of Public Communicators
1441 L St. NW
Washington, DC 20416
Phone: (202)653-6365

Description: To recognize individuals in various professions who have significantly increased awareness of small business concerns or created opportunities for small business to succeed. Advocates of the Year are recognized in each of the 50 states, the District of Columbia, and Puerto Rico for their efforts in the following areas of importance to small businesses: (1) accountant advocate; (2) banker advocate; (3) media advocate; (4) minority advocate; (5) veteran advocate; and (6) women in business advocate. State winners are then eligible for national recognition. The criteria for selection are: engaging in civic and community activities that promote small business; volunteering services to assist small firms experiencing management, financial, or legal problems; sponsoring or participating in legislative or regulatory initiatives; communicating publicly through speech or the written word; actively participating in small business organizations; or pursuing initiatives that will help a large number of small businesses. Nominations are accepted. Awards are presented during Small Business Week in May. Established in 1978.

★8105★ Society of Woman Geographers Gold Medal Award
Society of Woman Geographers
1619 New Hampshire Ave. NW
Washington, DC 20009
Phone: (202)265-2669

Description: To recognize a member of the Society whose original, innovative, or pioneering contributions are of major significance to the world's knowledge and understanding of the universe in which we live. Only members of the Society are eligible. A gold medal is awarded when merited. It has been presented only eight times since it was established in 1933.

★8106★ Society of Woman Geographers Outstanding Achievement Award
Society of Woman Geographers
1619 New Hampshire Ave. NW
Washington, DC 20009
Phone: (202)265-2669

Description: To recognize a member of the Society for an outstanding contribution or service of lasting benefit to science, the arts, or humanity. Only members of the Society are eligible. A certificate is awarded annually when merited. Established in 1978.

★8107★ Society of Women Engineers Achievement Award
Society of Women Engineers (SWE)
United Engineering Center
345 E. 47th St., Rm. 305
New York, NY 10017
Phone: (212)705-7855

Description: To recognize a woman for significant contributions to engineering in the field of engineering practice, research, education or administration. An engraved plaque, a gold pin, an engraved Steuben crystal bowl, and life membership in the Society are awarded annually. Established in 1952.

★8108★ Sons of the American Revolution Martha Washington Award Medal
National Society
Sons of the American Revolution (SAR)
1000 S. 4th St.
Louisville, KY 40203
Phone: (502)589-1776

Description: To recognize women who have rendered outstanding service to the Society. A gold filled medal is awarded irregularly. Established in 1971.

★8109★ Sons of the American Revolution Medal of Appreciation
National Society
Sons of the American Revolution (SAR)
1000 S. 4th St.
Louisville, KY 40203
Phone: (502)589-1776
David Hill, Contact

Description: To recognize members of the Daughters of the American Revolution who have rendered outstanding service to the SAR. A gold filled medal is awarded irregularly. Established in 1955.

★8110★ Soroptimist Training Awards Program
Soroptimist International of the Americas
1616 Walnut St., Ste. 700
Philadelphia, PA 19103
Phone: (215)732-0512
Fax: (215)732-7508

Description: McCall Life Pattern Fund (Training Award). To aid the mature woman who, as head of a household, must enter or return to the job market or further her skills and training in order to upgrade her employment status. Recipients are chosen on the basis of financial need as well as their statement of clear career goals, with primary consideration given to women entering vocational or technical training, or completing an undergraduate degree. Individuals must apply through a local Soroptimist club. Clubs choose their own recipients, giving awards at their own discretion. Club recipients then become eligible for the annual regional award. Established in 1972 by the Soroptimist International Foundation. Sponsored by the Soroptimist Foundation, Inc. and the Soroptimist Foundation of Canada. **Formerly:** McCall Life Pattern Fund (Training Award).

★8111★ Sportswomen of the Year Awards
Women's Sports Foundation (WSF)
342 Madison Ave., Ste. 728
New York, NY 10173
Phone: (212)972-9170

Description: To recognize the outstanding amateur and professional female athletes whose performances over a twelve-month span have been exceptional. Criteria for these awards are new records, new precedents, breakthroughs, and/or new styles in a particular sport. There are two Sportswoman Awards. One honors the outstanding amateur athlete; the other recognizes the outstanding professional athlete. Athletes from different sports are nominated in each of the categories by the Nominating Committee. Nominations are received from sport organizations and the public, and the winners are selected by Voting Members of the WSF. Established in 1980.

★8112★ Susan R. Hellings Award
National Christian College Athletic Association (NCCAA)
PO Box 1312
Marion, IN 46952-7712
Phone: (317)674-8401
Fax: (317)674-8487

Description: To honor the outstanding female volleyball player selected from the NCCAA member colleges. Athletes in their junior or senior year who excel on an outstanding team, are excellent students, demonstrate leadership ability and have a clear Christian testimony both on and off the court are eligible. An award to commemorate the occasion is presented annually to the recipient and to the institution she represents. Established in 1986. The award honors Susan R. Hellings, who played volleyball in the mid 1970's at Houghton College.

★8113★ Susan Smith Blackburn Prize
Susan Smith Blackburn Prize, Inc.
3239 Avalon Pl.
Houston, TX 77019
Phone: (713)522-8529

Description: To recognize a woman for having written a full-length play of outstanding quality for the English-speaking theatre. Prominent professionals in the English-speaking theatre may make nominations by September. A monetary award of $5,000, and a signed and numbered lithograph by William de Kooning, created especially for the occasion, are presented annually in February. Established in 1978 by the family and friends of Susan Smith Blackburn, the noted American actress and writer who lived in London the last 15 years of her life.

★8114★ Susi Pryor Award
Arkansas Women's History Institute
Dept. of History
Univ. of Arkansas at Little Rock
Little Rock, AR 72204
Phone: (501)569-3235

Description: To recognize the best unpublished essay or article in Arkansas women's history. Manuscripts not longer than 35 pages may be submitted by February 15. Manuscripts are judged on the basis of: (1) contribution to the knowledge of women in Arkansas history; (2) judicious use of primary and secondary materials; (3) creative interpretation and originality; and (4) stylistic excellence. A monetary award of $1,000 is presented annually. Established in 1986 to honor Susie Pryor, an inspiring and energetic woman whose activities touched on all aspects of women's experience in Arkansas.

★8115★ TAC Heptathlon Award
The Athletics Congress of the USA
PO Box 120
Indianapolis, IN 46206-0120
Phone: (317)638-9155
Fax: (317)261-0481

Description: Multi-Event Outstanding Women Award. To recognize the most outstanding woman in the seven track and field events of the Heptathlon. A special trophy is presented as merited. Established in 1982. Formerly: Multi-Event Outstanding Women Award.

★8116★ Tau Beta Sigma Scroll of Honor
Tau Beta Sigma
122 Seretean Center
Oklahoma State Univ.
Stillwater, OK 74078
Phone: (405)372-2333

Description: To honor the top band member in each summer session band camp. The award is designed and offered by bandswomen to a young musician, in recognition of outstanding performance, attendance, diligence and proficiency. A certificate is awarded to one female camper per session. Established in 1974.

★8117★ Teacher of the Year
Ladies Professional Golf Association (LPGA)
2570 Volusia Ave., Ste. B
Daytona Beach, FL 32114

Description: To recognize the woman teaching professional who has best exemplified her profession during the year. The awardee must be a member in good standing of the Class A Division who is presently engaged in the teaching of golf at a country club, golf club or approved driving range. Awarded annually. Established in 1958.

★8118★ Team Championship Award
The Athletics Congress of the USA
PO Box 120
Indianapolis, IN 46206-0120
Phone: (317)638-9155
Fax: (317)261-0481

Description: To recognize the team scoring the most points in women's competition in the USA Indoor Track and Field Championships. A plaque is awarded annually at the National Convention. Established in 1974.

★8119★ Undergraduate Award for Excellence in Chemistry
Iota Sigma Pi
634 Hudson St.
Hoboken, NJ 07030
Phone: (201)963-7968

Description: For recognition of excellence in chemistry. The nominee shall be a senior woman chemistry student in an accredited college or university and may be a member of Iota Sigma Pi. The deadline for nominations is February 1. A monetary award of $200 and a certificate are presented. Established in 1975.

★8120★ U.S. Catholic Award
U.S. Catholic
Claretian Publications
205 W. Monroe St.
Chicago, IL 60606
Phone: (312)236-7782
Toll-free: 800-328-6515

Description: To recognize individuals for furthering the cause of women in the church. Nominations may be submitted to the editors of the national magazine, U.S. Catholic by December 31. An engraved Steuben glass is awarded annually, at a special luncheon. Established in 1978.

★8121★ Unsung Heroine Award
Veterans of Foreign Wars Ladies Auxiliary
34th & Broadway
VFW Bldg.
Kansas City, MO 64111
Phone: (816)561-8655

Description: This award, which was originally presented to women in service for valiant acts, is now given to recognize any American woman who performs an heroic act. A monetary award of $3,000 and a plaque are awarded annually at the National Convention. Established in 1965.

★8122★ Upward Mobility Award
Society of Women Engineers (SWE)
United Engineering Center
345 E. 47th St., Rm. 305
New York, NY 10017
Phone: (212)705-7855

Description: To recognize a woman who has made an outstanding contribution in the field of engineering and/or technical management such that she has, as a minimum, achieved the level of general manager or equivalent upper management position within her organization (industry, academia or government service). Her academic training may be in either science or engineering, and she need not be a member of SWE. The qualifications are: (1) an engineering degree from a recognized college or university, and not less than six years of increasingly important engineering/technical management experience; or a degree in science related to engineering from a recognized college or university, and not less than eight years of increasingly important engineering/technical management experience; and (2) not less than eleven years of increasingly important engineering/technical management experience indicating outstanding competency and achievement. A Citation and a Longines ATMOS clock are awarded annually. Established in 1989.

★8123★ USO Woman of the Year
USO of Metropolitan New York
1457 Broadway, Mezzanine Level
New York, NY 10036
Phone: (212)719-5433

Description: To recognize a woman who has contributed significantly to help support active duty military personnel and their families. Financial, entertainment, or volunteer contributions by residents of the New York metropolitan area are considered. Awarded annually at the Spring Fund Raiser Dinner. Established in 1961.

★8124★ USRowing Athlete of the Year (Female)
United States Rowing Association (USRowing)
201 S. Capital Ave., Ste. 400
Indianapolis, IN 46225
Phone: (317)237-5656
Fax: (317)237-5646

Description: To recognize the outstanding female athlete in U.S. rowing. Individuals who participate on the U.S. National Rowing Team are eligible. An etched glass bowl is awarded annually. Established in 1985.

★8125★ USRowing Woman of the Year
United States Rowing Association (USRowing)
201 S. Capital Ave., Ste. 400
Indianapolis, IN 46225
Phone: (317)237-5656
Fax: (317)237-5646

Description: NWRA Woman of the Year. To honor the woman who has made the greatest contribution to the advancement of women's rowing in the past year. Women active in the sport of rowing are eligible. A Revere bowl is awarded annually at the Convention. Established in 1982 by the National Women's Rowing Association which merged with USRowing in 1986. Formerly: NWRA Woman of the Year.

★8126★ USTA/ITHOF Tennis Educational Merit Award for Women
International Tennis Hall of Fame (ITHOF)
194 Bellevue Ave.
Newport, RI 02840
Phone: (401)849-3990
Fax: (401)849-8780

Description: Special Educational Merit Award for Women. To recognize the female teaching professional and/or instructor who has rendered outstanding service to the tennis educational program through leadership, inspiration and devotion. The permanent trophy is a large silver bowl, on which the winner's name is engraved. A small sterling memento, suitably inscribed, is awarded to the recipient. Awarded annually at the USTA annual meeting. Established in 1972 by the National Tennis Foundation. Formerly: Special Educational Merit Award for Women.

★8127★ USWCA Senior Ladies Trophy
United States Women's Curling Association (USWCA)
4114 N. 53rd St.
Omaha, NE 68104
Phone: (402)453-6574

Description: To recognize the winner of the Senior Ladies Bonspiel. Members of local clubs affiliated with USWCA are eligible. A traveling trophy (a silver teapot) is awarded. Team members receive a pin. Established in 1983.

★8128★ Vanguard Award
Women in Communications (WIC)
National Headquarters
PO Box 17460
Arlington, VA 22216
Phone: (703)528-4200

Description: To recognize a firm or institution for positive non-stereotypical portrayals of women, and to heighten the general awareness of factors that enhance the image and status of women. Any individual or organization may submit nominations by January 25. A plaque is presented annually. Established in 1979.

★8129★ Vare Trophy
Ladies Professional Golf Association (LPGA)
2570 Volusia Ave., Ste. B
Daytona Beach, FL 32114

Description: To recognize the player with the lowest scoring average at the end of each year. Vare Trophy scoring averages are computed on the basis of a players' total yearly score in official LPGA tournaments divided by the number of offical rounds she played during the year. A player must compete in 70 official rounds of tournament competition during the LPGA tour year. The trophy is awarded annually. The Vare Trophy was presented to the Ladies' Professional Golf Association by Betty Jameson in 1952 in honor of the great American player, Glenna Collett Vare.

★8130★ Volunteer of Distinction Award
Gamma Sigma Sigma National Service
  Sorority
4 Kirkland Court
Yalesville, CT 06492
Phone: (203)265-1410

Description: To recognize women of local prominence for outstanding volunteer service in their community/state. Nominations by sorority chapters or members may be submitted four to six weeks prior to each conference. The recipient must attend the conference and address the assembly. A commemorative plaque and expenses for conference attendance are awarded biennially. Established in 1985.

★8131★ Wade Trophy
National Association for Girls and Women in
  Sports (NAGWS)
1900 Association Dr.
Reston, VA 22091
Phone: (703)476-3450

Description: To recognize the top player in women's collegiate basketball. The recipient is chosen based on the following criteria: (1) senior college basketball player; (2) Kodak All-American; (3) positive role model for women in sport; (4) commitment to academics; (5) demonstrated leadership; and (6) sportsmanlike conduct. The winner is announced and presented the Wade Trophy at a NAGWS awards luncheon at the national convention of the American Alliance for Health, Physical Education, Recreation and Dance. The trophy is permanently displayed in the Basketball Hall of Fame in Springfield, MA. Established in 1978 to honor Lilly Margaret Wade, a member of the National Basketball Hall of Fame, who dedicated her life to women's athletics, education and basketball.

★8132★ Wauwatosa Event
United States Women's Curling Association
  (USWCA)
4114 N. 53rd St.
Omaha, NE 68104
Phone: (402)453-6574

Description: To recognize the first place winners in a 32-game competition. Members of local clubs affiliated with the USWCA are eligible. A traveling trophy (the Wauwatosa Trophy - a large silver punch bowl) is awarded annually. Each of four team members receives a pin. Established in 1947 by the Wauwatosa Club of Wisconsin. The trophy was donated by the Wauwatosa Club, one of the charter members of the National Association.

★8133★ Wava Turner Award
Tau Beta Sigma
122 Seretean Center
Oklahoma State Univ.
Stillwater, OK 74078
Phone: (405)372-2333

Description: To honor individuals who have made outstanding contributions to the sorority through continued support of chapter activities and national programs. An organizational crest on walnut is awarded annually. Established in 1977.

★8134★ WCA Honors
Women's Caucus for Art (WCA)
National Office
Moore College of Art
20th & The Parkway
Philadelphia, PA 19103
Phone: (215)854-0922

Description: For recognition of contributions to the visual arts by senior women artists. Nominations are made by the Honors Committee. A plaque and lifetime membership in the Women's Caucus for Art are presented annually at the Conference along with a retrospective exhibition with catalogue that includes monograph, chronology, and reproductions. Established in 1979.

**★8135★ Western Political Science
  Association Awards**
Western Political Science Association (WPSA)
c/o Dept. of Political Science
Univ. of Utah
Salt Lake City, UT 84112
Phone: (916)278-7737
Fax: (916)278-6959

Description: To recognize outstanding unpublished papers in the field of political science. The following awards are presented: (1) Dissertation Award - $250 for the best doctoral dissertation completed at a university within the regional groupings of the WPSA between July 1 and June 30 of the previous academic year; (2) Pi Sigma Alpha Award - $200 for the best paper presented at the last WPSA annual meeting; (3) WPSA Women and Politics Awards - $100 for an outstanding paper on women and politics; (4) WPSA Best Paper Award on Chicano Politics - $100 for an outstanding paper by a Chicano scholar on Chicano politics and its relative aspects; and (5) Award by Committee on the Status of Blacks - $100 for an outstanding paper discussing issues and problems which concern most Black Americans. Entries must be submitted by January 15. Established in 1976.

★8136★ William and Mousie Powell Award
Ladies Professional Golf Association (LPGA)
2570 Volusia Ave., Ste. B
Daytona Beach, FL 32114

Description: To recognize an LPGA member who, in the opinion of her playing peers, by her behavior and deeds, best exemplifies the spirit, ideals and values of the LPGA. A bracelet designed by Tiffany's is awarded annually. Established in 1986.

**★8137★ WISE Award for Engineering
  Achievement**
National Science Foundation (NSF)
Interagency Committee for Women in
  Science and Engineering (WISE)
1800 G St. NW, Rm. 546
Washington, DC 20550
Phone: (202)357-9819

Description: To recognize a specific or special engineering/technical contribution by a woman engineer in the federal service; and to recognize a specific contribution made by a woman engineer in the federal service in promoting the entry of girls and/or the advancement of women in engineering. Factors included in evaluating the nominations include: (1) a significant engineering achievement which has led to an advancement in the state of the art in a particular field; (2) an invention, patent, or design of equipment which has significantly enhanced a field of work or opened up new fields; (3) an exceptionally innovative and/or creative research paper or project which has either significantly improved or led to a new field of research, or the results of which are considered by that discipline as having made a major breakthrough in relation to that particular field of engineering; and (4) an unusual act which facilitated the entry of girls and/or the advancement of women in science or engineering. Nominations may be submitted by January 16. A plaque and an honorary citation are awarded annually at the annual awards luncheon at the WISE National Training Conference. Established in 1988.

**★8138★ WISE Award for Scientific
  Achievement**
National Science Foundation (NSF)
Interagency Committee for Women in
  Science and Engineering (WISE)
1800 G St. NW, Rm. 546
Washington, DC 20550
Phone: (202)357-9819

Description: To recognize a specific or special scientific or technical contribution by a woman scientist in the federal service; and to recognize a specific contribution made by a woman scientist in the federal service in promoting the entry of girls and/or the advancement of women in science. All women scientists employed by the Federal Government in either a civilian or non-civilian status are eligible. Factors included in evaluating the nominations include: (1) a significant scientific achievement which has led to an advancement in the state of the art in a particular field; (2) an invention, patent, or design of equipment which has significantly enhanced a field of work or opened up new fields; (3) an exceptionally innovative and/or creative research paper or project which has either significantly improved or led to a new field of research, or the results of which are considered by that discipline as having made a major breakthrough in relation to that particular field of science; and (4) an unusual act which facilitated the entry of girls and/or advancement of women in science or engineering. Nominations may be submitted by January 16. A plaque and an honorary citation are awarded annually at the annual awards luncheon at the WISE National Training Conference. Established in 1985.

★8139★ WISE Lifetime Achievement Award
National Science Foundation (NSF)
Interagency Committee for Women in
 Science and Engineering (WISE)
1800 G St. NW, Rm. 546
Washington, DC 20550
Phone: (202)357-9819
Janet Boles, Contact

Description: To recognize the sustained scientific and technical contributions by a woman scientist or engineer in the federal service; and to recognize the contributions made by a woman scientist or engineer in the federal service in promoting the entry of girls and/or in facilitating the advancement of women in science or engineering. All women scientists or engineers with 20 years service in the Federal Government in either a civilian or non-civilian status are eligible. Factors included in evaluating the nominations include: (1) exceptional scientific or engineering achievements as evidenced by publications, inventions, patents or awards; (2) recognition as a scientist or engineer at national and international levels; (3) unusual degree of imagination, innovation, and initiative in the pursuit of science/engineering; and (4) unusual dedication to facilitating the entry of girls and/or the advancement of women in science and engineering. Nominations may be submitted by January 16. A plaque and an honorary citation are awarded annually at the annual awards luncheon at the WISE National Training Conference. Established in 1985.

★8140★ WMA National Service Award
Women Marines Association (WMA)
140 Marengo, Ste. 605
Forest Park, IL 60130
Phone: (312)366-6408

Description: For recognition of outstanding service over a period of several years in keeping with the purposes and objectives of the Association. Members may nominate other members who must be approved by the Board. Established in 1974.

★8141★ Woman of Achievement Award
National Federation of Press Women
Box 99
Blue Springs, MO 64015
Phone: (816)229-1666

Description: To recognize a woman who has excelled in the field of communications. A gold medallion and framed scroll are awarded annually. Established in 1957.

★8142★ Woman Lawyer of the Year
Women's Bar Association of the District of
 Columbia
1819 H St. NW, Ste. 1250
Washington, DC 20006
Phone: (202)785-1540

Description: For recognition of achievement in, significant contributions to the legal profession, and dedication to the advancement of justice in the District of Columbia. Nominations are accepted. A plaque is presented at the Annual

Membership Meeting in May. Established in 1964.

★8143★ Woman Officer of the Year
International Association of Women Police
 (IAWP)
20-25 45th St.
Astoria, NY 11105
Phone: (718)721-6494

Description: To recognize outstanding women of the law enforcement profession by a professional network of peer officers. In addition, the award has the following objectives: (1) to provide the members with the benefit of learning about achievements of sister officers; (2) to increase understanding and awareness of women in law enforcement and the International Association of Women Police; (3) to encourage police administrators to support the organization with their own membership as well as that of officers in their agencies; (4) to promote the annual training conference; and (5) to promote membership by all women law enforcement officers in IAWP. Women who are sworn law enforcement officers with the power of arrest, and who are currently employed may be nominated with the approval of the highest ranking official of the agency where the woman is employed. Nominations may be made when a woman officer has demonstrated meritorious police service, i.e., has at imminent risk of life performed deeds of valor or has rendered invaluable police service and is dedicated to her daily tasks. Travel and expenses to attend the annual conference are awarded annually in September or October. Established in 1977.

★8144★ Women in the Arts Crown Award
Women in the Arts Foundation
325 Spring St., Rm. 200
New York, NY 10013
Phone: (212)691-0988

Description: Women in the Arts Award. For recognition of achievement in promoting and protecting visual artists and fighting discrimination against women visual artists. Nomination is by the Society's Membership Executive Board by February of the award year. A plaque is awarded every ten years. Established in 1976.
Formerly: Women in the Arts Award.

★8145★ Women Band Directors National Association Achievement Award
Women Band Directors National Association
 (WBDNA)
344 Overlook Dr.
West Lafayette, IN 47906
Phone: (317)463-1738

Description: To recognize outstanding women graduating from high school for their work in instrumental music. A certificate is awarded. Established in 1971.

★8146★ Women Band Directors National Association Citation of Merit Award
Women Band Directors National Association
 (WBDNA)
344 Overlook Dr.
West Lafayette, IN 47906
Phone: (317)463-1738

Description: To honor outstanding members of WBDNA. Criteria for selection are that the woman: (1) consistently produces bands of high performance level; (2) consistently performs programs of high musical quality; (3) has made

an outstanding contribution to the community through music; and (4) must be an active member of WBDNA. At least one and no more than three certificates are given annually. Established in 1976.

★8147★ Women Band Directors National Association Performing Artists Award
Women Band Directors National Association
 (WBDNA)
344 Overlook Dr.
West Lafayette, IN 47906
Phone: (317)463-1738

Description: To identify talented young female soloists in their junior year which will enhance their profile in the community, state, and universities of their choice. Any outstanding young woman soloist who is enrolled in a high school band program is eligible for recommendation. A certificate with a gold seal and a lapel pin are awarded. Established in 1986 in honor of Dorothy Stewart Jones for her outstanding work with young soloists.

★8148★ Women Band Directors National Association Scroll of Excellence
Women Band Directors National Association
 (WBDNA)
344 Overlook Dr.
West Lafayette, IN 47906
Phone: (317)463-1738

Description: To honor outstanding women band directors, preferably not members of WBDNA. The criteria for selection are that the woman: (1) consistently produces bands of high performance level with programs of high musical quality, and/or has contributed significantly in other ways to instrumental music education; and (2) must actively participate in regional and/or state events; and (3) must be sponsored by one WBDNA member with the endorsement of two other WBDNA members. Only one award per state may be given annually and no more than ten nationally each year. A scroll signed by the President is presented at a public concert or other public event whenever possible. Established in 1985.

★8149★ Women Business Owners of New York Corporate Awards
Women Business Owners of New York
La Concierge Services Inc.
322 E. 86th St.
New York, NY 10028
Phone: (212)737-5289

Description: For recognition of achievement by women in business. Consideration for award is based on the candidate's position of responsibility, length of time in business, and the entrepreneurial nature of her position. Crystal engraved paperweights from Tiffany's are awarded annually at the Entrepreneurial Woman Awards Luncheon. Established in 1977.

★8150★ Women Business Owners of New York Up and Coming Award
Women Business Owners of New York
La Concierge Services Inc.
322 E. 86th St.
New York, NY 10028
Phone: (212)737-5289

Description: For recognition of achievement by women in business. Consideration for award is based on the candidate's age, the length of time in business, yearly gross sales, and the fact that the business is solely owned or started by a woman. A crystal engraved paperweight from Tiffany's is awarded annually at the Entrepreneurial Woman Awards Luncheon. Established in 1977.

★8151★   **Women of Conscience Award**
National Council of Women of the United
   States
777 United Nations Plaza, 7th Fl.
New York, NY 10017
Phone: (212)697-1278

Description: To recognize an American woman who best exemplifies the merits of innovation, leadership and dedication toward improving the world in which we live. Professionals or full-time volunteers are eligible. A monetary award of $1,500 and a scroll are awarded annually. Established in 1963 and funded by Clairol, Inc.

★8152★   **Women in Development Award**
OEF International
1815 H St. NW
Washington, DC 20006
Phone: (202)466-3430

Description: To recognize an individual who has made a significant contribution to the economic development of women in the Third World. The decision is made by the Board of Directors. A trophy, a crystal pyramid on an ebony base, is awarded annually at the spring luncheon. Established in 1985.

★8153★   **Women of Enterprise Awards**
Avon Products
Women of Enterprise Awards
9 West 57th St.
New York, NY 10019
Phone: (212)546-6015

Description: To recognize women business owners who have been profitably self- employed for a minimum of five years and have overcome significant hardship to achieve success. Candidates for the award may be nominated by women's and civic organizations or may apply directly. The deadline for applications is February 1. Five winners each receive a monetary prize of $1,000, a Tiffany-designed crystal award and an all-expense paid trip to New York City. They will also have the opportunity to speak at self-employment seminars and conferences for women. A matching $1,000 grant is also awarded to organizations which nominate winning candidates. Avon's Women of Enterprise Awards is the first corporate-sponsored awards program exclusively for women entrepreneurs. Established in 1987 by Avon Products in conjunction with the U.S. Small Business Administration.

★8154★   **Women in Film International
   Award**
Women in Film
6464 Sunset Blvd., Ste. 900
Los Angeles, CA 90028
Phone: (213)463-6040
Fax: (213)463-0963

Description: To recognize a woman working internationally who represents the highest ideals of the film industry. Established in 1987.

★8155★   **Women in Government Relations
   Distinguished Member Award**
Women in Government Relations
1325 Massachusetts Ave. NW, Ste. 510
Washington, DC 20005-4171
Phone: (202)347-5432
Fax: (202)347-5434

Description: For recognition of special leadership, service and contributions to the ideals and goals of Women in Government Relations. Members may be nominated by January of each year. A plaque is presented at the annual meeting in March. Established in 1977.

★8156★   **Women at Work Broadcast
   Awards**
National Commission on Working Women of
   Wider Opportunities for Women
1325 G St. NW, Lower Level
Washington, DC 20005
Phone: (202)737-5764

Description: To reward outstanding radio and television programs about working women's issues. Awards are presented in the following categories: spot feature; news feature; public affairs or documentary; editorial; news series; and entertainment. Programs which focus generally on the participation of women in the workforce as well as on specific aspects of women and work, such as child care, occupational health and safety, job training and education, sexual harassment, pay equity, and other related issues are eligible. The award is open to all television and radio stations in the United States. The deadline for nominations, which may be made by producers, reporters, or station officials, is August 15. First place winners receive an ''Alice,'' a Tiffany crystal award named after the waitress portrayed by Linda Lavin in the CBS television series. Second and third places and Honorable Mentions receive a certificate. In addition, the Commissioners' Award may be presented. Awarded annually at a gala awards ceremony in Washington, D.C., in the fall. Established in 1979.

★8157★   **Women's National Book
   Association Award**
Women's National Book Association (WNBA)
160 5th Ave.
New York, NY 10010
Phone: (212)675-7805

Description: Constance Lindsay Skinner Award. To recognize a distinguished bookwoman for outstanding contributions to the world of books and, through books, to society. The nominee must be a living American, and derive her income from books and the allied arts. A citation is awarded biennially in even-numbered years. Established in 1940 in memory of Constance Lindsay Skinner, author/editor and founder of the WNBA publication, *The Bookwoman*. **Formerly:** Constance Lindsay Skinner Award.

★8158★   **Women's National Collegiate
   Awards**
United States Tennis Association (USTA)
1212 Avenue of the Americas
New York, NY 10036-9998
Phone: (212)302-3322

Description: To recognize winners of the annual tennis tournaments for women players. The following prizes are awarded: Treesh bowl - singles winner; Pat Yeomans Bowl - doubles

winners; and Catharine Sample Bowl - team winner. Established in 1974.

★8159★   **Women's Network National Award
   for Outstanding Achievement**
American Society for Training and
   Development (ASTD)
1630 Duke St.
Box 1443
Alexandria, VA 22313
Phone: (703)683-8100
Fax: (703)683-8103

Description: To recognize a human resource development professional who has made significant contributions to the growth and development of women. Selection is based in part on an individual who: demonstrates ongoing commitment to the growth and development of women in the human resource development field through networking, career development counseling, and mentoring; and creates and maintains a climate of mutual support and respect between men and women both in the work environment and in other professional activities. The award is open to any human resource professional. The entry deadline is December 1. Awarded annually by the Women's Network at the ASTD National Conference.

★8160★   **Women's Network Professional
   Development Leadership Award**
American Society for Training and
   Development (ASTD)
1630 Duke St.
Box 1443
Alexandria, VA 22313
Phone: (703)683-8100
Fax: (703)683-8103

Description: To recognize a woman who has participated and contributed to the Women's Network at the local, regional or national level. Selection is based on contribution to the professional development of women; leadership in the Women's Network; and representing standards of professionalism to which the network aspires. Individuals must be members of national ASTD and the Women's Network. The entry deadline is December 1. Awarded annually by the Women's Network at the ASTD National Conference.

★8161★   **Women's Open Cup—United
   States Soccer Federation**
United States Soccer Federation
1750 E. Boulder St.
Colorado Springs, CO 80909
Phone: (719)578-4678

Description: To recognize outstanding women's soccer teams. Awarded annually.

★8162★   **Women's Research Award**
National Association for Women Deans,
   Administrators, and Counselors
1325 18th St. NW, Ste. 210
Washington, DC 20036
Phone: (202)659-9330

Description: To encourage and support excellence in research by, for, and about women. Research considered for the awards may be on any topic relevant to the education and personal and professional development of women and girls. The research may be historical, philosophical, experimental, evaluative, or descriptive. Two awards are presented annually: (1) Graduate Student Competition - for research by a graduate student; and (2) Open Competition - for persons at any career/professional level. Manuscripts may be submitted by November 1. A $500 honorarium and an engraved plaque are awarded in each category at the annual conference. Winners who are not members are also given a one year membership in the Association. Additional information is available from: Women's Research Awards Committee, c/o Mary Dawn Bailey, Associate Director, Urban Institute, University of North Carolina at Charlotte, Charlotte, NC 28223, phone: (704) 547-2307.

★8163★ **Women's Sports Foundation Flo Hyman Award**
Women's Sports Foundation (WSF)
342 Madison Ave., Ste. 728
New York, NY 10173
Phone: (212)972-9170

Description: To recognize a woman athlete who captures the dignity, spirit and commitment to excellence of the late Flo Hyman. It honors an athlete who recognizes the far-reaching benefits of sport and who is determined to share these values with others. Awarded on National Girls and Women in Sports Day, celebrated the second Thursday in February. Established in 1987.

★8164★ **Women's Sports Foundation Up and Coming Award**
Women's Sports Foundation (WSF)
342 Madison Ave., Ste. 728
New York, NY 10173
Phone: (212)972-9170

Description: To recognize up and coming women athletes. Talented young women coming up through the ranks, who have distinguished themselves by making regional or national teams, are eligible. Awards are given in the following categories: (1) artistic; (2) individual versus individual; (3) women versus nature; (4) team sports; (5) speed/power sports; (6) speed/endurance; (7) standard of perfection;(8) combination sports; (9) explosive strength; and (10) physically/mentally challenged. Established in 1984.

★8165★ **WTS National Member of the Year**
Women's Transportation Seminar - National (WTS)
PO Box 7408, Ben Franklin Sta.
Washington, DC 20044

Description: To recognize achievement and contribution by a WTS member, who has demonstrated outstanding support of the organization. Selection is based on the following criteria: (1) a woman who is a member of WTS; (2) a woman who supports the ideas and has demonstrated an interest in WTS; (3) a woman who has demonstrated a willingness to work with the Chapter structure and promote intra-Chapter communication and development; and (4) a woman who has enhanced the reputation of WTS within the transportation industry. Nominations may be submitted through local WTS Chapters. A crystal obelisk is awarded annually at the annual conference in May. In addition, the winner's name is added to a plaque honoring all recipients. Established in 1981.

★8166★ **WTS National Woman of the Year**
Women's Transportation Seminar - National (WTS)
PO Box 7408, Ben Franklin Sta.
Washington, DC 20044

Description: To recognize achievement and contribution to the transportation industry. Selection is based on the following criteria: (1) a woman who has made an outstanding contribution to the transportation industry; (2) a woman who has made a significant contribution toward the advancement of women in developing a career in transportation and/or enhancing their career paths; (3) a woman who has overcome substantial obstacles in order to achieve career successes in the transportation field; and (4) a woman who supports the ideas and has demonstrated an interest in WTS. A crystal obelisk is awarded annually at the annual conference in May. Established in 1980.

★8167★ **Young Achievers Award**
National Council of Women of the United States
777 United Nations Plaza, 7th Fl.
New York, NY 10017
Phone: (212)697-1278

Description: To honor women under the age of 35 who have achieved recognition in their chosen fields, have demonstrated leadership ability, have made contributions in other areas as well as in their chosen profession, and are involved currently in their careers. Awarded annually.

★8168★ **YWCA of Houston Outstanding Women's Award**
YWCA of Houston
3621 William
Houston, TX 77007
Phone: (713)868-9922

Description: To recognize the outstanding achievements and superlative contributions of Houston area women in the areas of business, arts, public service, media, education, science and technology, volunteerism and medicine. Any woman, 21 years of age and over, who lives in the Houston area and has made important contributions to her field of expertise, is eligible. A crystal trophy is presented annually at the Outstanding Women's Luncheon. Established in 1976.

(13) Research Centers

Entries in this chapter are arranged alphabetically by institution name. See the User's Guide at the front of this directory for additional information.

★8169★ Alan Guttmacher Institute
111 5th Ave.
New York, NY 10003
Phone: (212)254-5656
Jeannie Rosoff, President

Founded: 1968. **Research Activities and Fields:** Issues related to human reproduction, especially concerning the economically and socially disadvantaged, including family planning, sex education, abortion, teenage pregnancy, maternal and prenatal health care, contraceptive development and use, and reproductive health services. The Institute submits its research program to a scientific advisory panel whose members are drawn from academic research centers throughout the U.S. **Publications:** *Family Planning Perspectives* (bimonthly); *International Family Planning Perspectives* (quarterly); *Washington Memo* (20 per year); *State Reproductive Health Monitor: Legislative Proposals and Action* (quarterly); Annual Report. **Formerly:** Center for Family Planning Program Development, at the time a division of the Planned Parenthood Federation of America (1977).

★8170★ Alverno College
Research Center on Women
3401 S. 39th St.
Milwaukee, WI 53215
Phone: (414)382-6084
Austin Doherty, Vice President for Academic Affairs

Founded: 1970. **Research Activities and Fields:** Status and role of women in American society and economic, political, psychological, social, physiological, and religious factors that have influenced the past history of women and contribute to contemporary lifestyles. Mainstreams women's studies in the college curriculum and monitors women's contributions in academic disciplines. **Publications:** *RCD Reporter* (irregularly). **Meetings/Educational Activities:** Cosponsors Woman to Woman Conference (annually). **Library:** Maintains books, research reports, pamphlets, periodicals, and audiovisual resources. Lola Stuller, librarian.

★8171★ Barnard College
Barnard Center for Research on Women
3009 Broadway
New York, NY 10027-6598
Phone: (212)854-2067
Dr. Leslie J. Calman, Director

Founded: 1971. **Research Activities and Fields:** Culture, art, the humanities, and social policy as issues of gender affect them. Offers guidance to researchers, writers, and artists. Studies include women and science, women as immigrants and refugees, and social movements of women in quality of life issues. **Publications:** *The Barnard Occasional Papers on Women's Issues* (three times a year). **Meetings/Educational Activities:** Sponsors the Scholar and the Feminist Conference (annually in spring, open to the public) and a colloquia series, including Conversations About Women, Women's Issues Luncheons, and the Women's History Seminars. Also sponsors the Reid Lecture Series. **Library:** 12,000 items; 1,500 books, 110 periodicals, 7,500 factsheets and periodicals.

★8172★ Boston College
Women's Research Center for the Study of Women's Lives
Chestnut Hill, MA 02167
Phone: (617)552-8529
Sharlene Hesse-Biber, Contact

★8173★ Brigham Young University
Women's Research Institute
945 SWKT
Provo, UT 84602
Phone: (801)378-4609
Dr. Marie Cornwall, Director

Founded: 1978. **Research Activities and Fields:** Multidisciplinary women's studies, including lives and experiences, women's issues, and gender. **Publications:** Newsletter (semiannual). **Meetings/Educational Activities:** Sponsors conferences in conjunction with other departments of the University.

★8174★ Brown University
Pembroke Center for Teaching and Research on Women
Alumnae Hall
194 Meeting St.
Providence, RI 02912
Phone: (401)863-2643
Karen Newman, Director

Founded: 1981. **Research Activities and Fields:** Gender, race, ethnicity, and class emphasizing the ways in which cultural differences define and organize knowledge. The theme for 1991-92 is Scientific Knowledge and "Difference," which will focus on the production of scientific knowledge and the discontinuities of humanistic and scientific discourses on the subject. Administers the Pembroke Archive Project, an activity to collect papers, memorabilia, and oral histories from University alumnae.

Publications: Meetings/Educational Activities: Offers postdoctoral fellowships and sponsors

★8175★ Business and Professional
Women's Foundation
2012 Massachusetts Ave. NW
Washington, DC 20036
Phone: (202)293-1200
Sandra Shastel, Executive Director

Founded: 1956. **Research Activities and Fields:** Women's economic issues, including wage work, family work and life, and pay equity. Awards research fellowships for doctoral and postdoctoral research on women's economic issues and for women researchers of Latin American descent or citizenship. **Publications:** *Research Summaries; Information Digests on Women and Work.* **Library:** 6,000 volumes and other materials on economic issues affecting U.S. women.

★8176★ Case Western Reserve University
Perinatal Clinical Research Center
3395 Scranton Rd.
Cleveland, OH 44109
Phone: (216)459-4246
Patrick M. Catalano, M.D., Program Director

Founded: 1964. **Research Activities and Fields:** Clinical study of pregnant women, fetuses, and newborns, especially perinatal mortality, morbidity, prenatal and postnatal pathology, including sequential study of developmental physiology, biochemistry, and immunology of subjects under varied conditions of disease. Investigates physiology of maternal exercise and alterations in maternal carbohydrate metabolism during gestation. **Meetings/Educational Activities:** Holds monthly perinatal clinical research conferences in Cleveland area. **Library:** 200 volumes on obstetrics, gynecology, pediatrics, biochemistry, and endocrinology.

★8177★ Center for Population Options
1025 Vermont Ave. NW, Ste. 210
Washington, DC 20005
Phone: (202)347-5700
Judith Senderowitz, Executive Director

Founded: 1980. **Research Activities and Fields:** Sex education, life planning for adolescents, impact of sex in television on adolescents, AIDS education, and evaluation of school-based comprehensive health care clinics that provide family planning services. **Publications:** *Make a Life for Yourself* (English, Spanish); *Options* (quarterly publication on public policy); *Passages* (quarterly publication on international issues); *Clinic News* (quarterly publication on school-based clinics and related issues); *School-based Clinics Update* (annually); Fact Sheets. **Meetings/Educational Activities:** Conducts training seminars for sexuality educators (including an AIDS workshop), sponsors the AIDS and Adolescents Conference, and operates the Life Planning Project, a pregnancy prevention strategy, through an education curriculum and workshops that promote the development of vocational goals and the planning of reproductive/family decisions. **Library:** Maintains the Public Education and Resource Center with over 2,000 books, journals, articles, curricula, and related materials on adolescent pregnancy, sex education, and family planning.

★8178★ Center for Reproductive Law and Policy
120 Wall St.
New York, NY 10005
Phone: (212)514-5534
Fax: (212)514-5538
Janet Benshoof, President

Description: Analyzes federal legislation and regulations regarding women's reproductive rights, abortion, and sexual abstinence programs. Sponsors public education programs.

★8179★ Center for the Research and Treatment of Anorexia Nervosa
10921 Wilshire Blvd., Ste. 702
Los Angeles, CA 90024
Phone: (213)824-5881
Dr. Burt Crausman, Director

Founded: 1978. **Research Activities and Fields:** Anorexia nervosa and other eating disorders, including research into their causes, detection, and treatment. **Library:** 3,000 volumes on psychology.

★8180★ Center for the Study of Anorexia and Bulimia
1 W. 91st St.
New York, NY 10024
Phone: (212)595-3449
Jane B. Supino, Executive Director

Founded: 1979. **Research Activities and Fields:** Clinical and empirical studies on the prevalence, demography, etiology, and treatment of anorexia and bulimia, and compulsive overeating. **Publications:** Pamphlets and curriculum guides. **Meetings/Educational Activities:** lectures and seminars for staff therapists, interested community groups, and schools.

★8181★ Center for Women Policy Studies
2000 P St. NW, Ste. 508
Washington, DC 20036
Phone: (202)872-1770
Leslie R. Wolfe, Executive Director

Founded: 1972. **Research Activities and Fields:** Policy issues affecting legal, social, educational, and economic status of women. Projects focus on education for women and girls of color, women and AIDS, violence against women, sexual harassment in the workplace, reproductive laws for the 1990's, work and family issues, and occupational segregation and its roots in education. Designs model legislation and develops and disseminates program models. **Meetings/Educational Activities:** Sponsors policy seminars.

★8182★ Center on Women and Public Policy
University of Minnesota
909 Social Sciences Bldg.
Minneapolis, MN 55455

★8183★ City University of New York Center for the Study of Women and Society
33 W. 42nd St.
New York, NY 10036
Phone: (212)642-2954
Dr. Sue Rosenberg Zalk, Director

Founded: 1978. **Research Activities and Fields:** Issues related to women in health and women and work. Projects include revision of college curricula to reflect scholarship on gender, race, ethnicity, and class, a study of women and substance abuse, an investigation of gender and crime, and an evaluation of women internationally. **Publications:** *Newsletter* (biannual); *Feminist Directory*; *Gender-Balancing Handbook*. **Meetings/Educational Activities:** Holds seminars and conferences on topics related to women and society. **Formerly:** Center for the Study of Women and Sex Roles.

★8184★ College of St. Catherine Abigail Quigley McCarthy Center for Women
2004 Randolph Ave.
St. Paul, MN 55105
Phone: (612)690-6783
Fax: (612)690-6024
Catherine Lupori, Contact

Specialization: Research on Women from Catholic Tradition

★8185★ Columbia University Institute for Research on Women and Gender
763 Schermerhorn Extension
New York, NY 10027
Phone: (212)854-3277
Martha Howell, Director

Research Activities and Fields: Women as related to race and class.

★8186★ Contraceptive Research and Development Program
1611 N. Kent St., Ste. 806
Arlington, VA 22209
Phone: (703)524-4744
Toll-free: 800-448-5628
Fax: (804)448-5905
Henry L. Gabelnick, Ph.D., Director

Research Activities and Fields: Improvement of contraception methods, especially for use in developing countries. Studies include new barrier methods and spermicides, long-acting injectable and implantable contraceptives for women and men, nonsurgical and/or reversible sterilization techniques for women and men, contraceptive vaccines directed against sperm, ova, or hormones, nonsteroidal gonadal proteins that regulate pituitary and/or gonadal functions, methods that are suitable for lactating women, and vaginal and transdermal delivery systems.

★8187★ Duke-UNC Center for Research on Women
Univ. of North Carolina
03 Caldwell Hall
CB 3135
Chapel Hill, NC 27599-3135
Phone: (919)684-6641
Jacquelyn Dowd Hall, Academic Director

Founded: 1982. **Research Activities and Fields:** Promotes research, curriculum development, and outreach programs in women's studies, especially in the tri-state region of North Carolina, South Carolina, and Virginia. Research projects center on the changing gender roles of women in the South with an emphasis on gender, race, and class. **Publications:** *Branches* (quarterly newsletter); *Southern Women: The Intersection of Race, Class & Gender* (a collaborative working paper series project with Center for Research on Women at Memphis State University). **Meetings/Educational Activities:** Holds monthly seminars and special programs and cosponsors conferences. **Formerly:** Duke-UNC Women's Studies Research Center.

★8188★ Eating Disorders Research & Treatment Program
Michael Reese Hospital and Medical Center
Lake Shore Dr. at 31st St.
Chicago, IL 60616
Phone: (312)791-3878
Regina Casper, M.D., Director of Biological Psychiatry

Founded: 1977. **Research Activities and Fields:** Eating disorders, particularly anorexia nervosa and bulimia nervosa, and major affective disorders, particularly depression. Conducts studies on prognostic factors, epidemiology, personality dimensions, neuroendocrine regulation, energy expenditure, family interaction patterns, and genetic factors.

★8189★ Equal Relationships Institute
PO Box 731
Pacific Palisades, CA 90272-0731
Phone: (310)276-0686
Genevieve Marcus, Ph.D., Copresident

Founded: 1982. **Research Activities and Fields:** Problems afflicting couples and families following rejection by men and women of the old relationship models, and the role and nature of equality between individuals and groups. **Publications:** *The New Relationships*; *Equal Time: Maintaining a Balance in Today's Intimate Relationships*. **Meetings/Educational Activities:** Sponsors weekend seminars for couples, mixed groups, and industry and organizations; one-day seminars for singles; and three-hour workshops. Also sponsors public lectures on such topics as equality and intimacy, power in the intimate relationship, enhancing intimacy, love between equals, and politics and equality. **Library:** Maintains a large number of books, magazines, and articles covering all aspects of relationships; Jeff Kramer, librarian.

★8190★ Equity Policy Center
2000 P St. NW
Washington, DC 20036
Phone: (202)872-1770
Dr. Irene Tinker, President

Founded: 1978. **Research Activities and Fields:** Studies and promotes more equitable distribution of income and resources worldwide, with particular attention to women. Programs concentrate on the food system, micro-enterprise, population, household energy, futures, and development policy. **Library:** 6,000 titles on women, fugitives, development policy, urban development, employment and income generation, rural development, agriculture and food, education, communications, natural resources, energy, science, population, migrations and refugees, and youth. Putting all text on CD Rom.

★8191★ Family Health International
PO Box 13950
Research Triangle Park, NC 27709
Phone: (919)544-7040
Dr. Theodore, M. King, President

Founded: 1971. **Research Activities and Fields:** New contraceptive technology, contraceptive acceptability, contraceptive effectiveness and safety, breast-feeding practices, maternal/child health, demography, interventions to reduce the transmission of sexually transmitted diseases and AIDS, technology transfer, institutional development, economics of family planning and financing of AIDS programming. **Publications:** Network (quarterly) newsletter, plus editions in French and Spanish (semiannually). **Meetings/Educational Activities:** Sponsors expert meetings and training seminars. **Library:** 5,500 volumes on contraceptive methods, family planning services, maternity care and primary health care, including clinical trials, epidemiological studies, program evaluation and AIDS prevention plus 665 periodical titles; William Barrows, information services manager. **Formerly:** International Fertility Research Program.

★8192★ The Feminist Press at the City University of New York
311 E. 94 St.
New York, NY 10128
Phone: (212)360-5790
Prof. Florence Howe, Director

Founded: 1970. **Research Activities and Fields:** Women's lives and patterns of education for women, including "lost" literature by and about women (fiction, autobiography, biography, and history). Also studies the status and treatment of women in colleges and universities and the history and status of women's studies programs and centers for research on women, both nationally and internationally. Specific projects focus on literature by and about disabled women, about disabled women and lost women writers and lost women writers of India. **Publications:** Women's Studies Quarterly. **Meetings/Educational Activities:** Sponsors programs at the annual meetings of the National Women's Studies Association and at international meetings. **Meetings/Educational Activities:** Sponsors programs at the annual meetings of the National Women's Studies Association and at international meetings. **Library:** Several thousand books, a vertical file on women's studies programs, and a major collection of international materials on women.

★8193★ Fertility Research Foundation
1430 Second Ave., Ste. 103
New York, NY 10021
Phone: (212)744-5500
Masood Khatamee, M.D., Executive Director

Founded: 1964. **Research Activities and Fields:** Fertility and human reproduction, including studies on microsurgery, fertilization, fallopian tube transplant, and artificial embryonation.

Seeks solutions to infertility. **Publications:** Infertility Journal.

★8194★ Fertility and Women's Health Care Center
130 Maple St.
Springfield, MA 01103
Phone: (413)781-8220
Ronald K. Burke, M.D., Head

Founded: 1984. **Research Activities and Fields:** Conducts basic and clinical studies of male and female infertility, with special emphasis on sperm motility and velocity, reproductive endocrinology, gender preselection, ovulation induction, vaginal ultrasonography, and gamete intrafallopian tube transfer. **Meetings/Educational Activities:** Provides resident training and conducts lectures. **Library:** Maintains a collection on gynecology and reproductive endocrinology. **Formerly:** Fertility Institute of Western Massachusetts (1991).

★8195★ George Mason University Women's Studies Research and Resource Center
4400 University Dr.
Fairfax, VA 22030
Phone: (703)323-2921
Karen Rosenblum, Contact

★8196★ George Washington University Women's Studies Program and Policy Center
Funger Hall 217
2201 G St. NW
Washington, DC 20052
Phone: (202)994-6942
Dr. Sonya A. Quitslund, Director

Founded: 1972. **Research Activities and Fields:** Women and public policy, including employment and economic status, older women and pension policies, family policy, gender roles and socialization, feminist theory, newspaper reporting on women's issues, occupational segregation in the labor market, and the Congressional Women's Caucus. **Publications:** Newsletter (monthly). **Meetings/Educational Activities:** Grants two master of arts degrees in women's studies and public policy.

★8197★ Hartford College for Women Office of Women's Research
260 Girard Ave.
Hartford, CT 06105
Phone: (203)236-1215
Sharon Toffey Shepela, Ph.D., Director

Founded: 1983. **Research Activities and Fields:** Interdisciplinary research on gender issues with emphasis on factors affecting public policy. Activities include studies on the economic effects of divorce on women and men in Connecticut; Russian women's studies; the use of justice norms in women's pay equity claims; the poetry of Soror Juana Inez de la Cruz (1651-1695), Mexican nun and poet; the writings of Dorothy Canfield Fisher (1879-1958), American novelist and essayist; women writers of the World War II era; and a revision of the myth of the House of Atreus from the point of view of the Mycenaean Queen, Clytemnestra. **Meetings/Educational Activities:** Sponsors a seminar series throughout the year as well as periodic research forums. **Formerly:** Women's Research Institute.

★8198★ Harvard University Women's Studies in Religion Program
Harvard Divinity School
45 Francis Ave.
Cambridge, MA 02138
Phone: (617)495-5705
Constance H. Buchanan, Director

Founded: 1980. **Research Activities and Fields:** Investigates the role and function of gender in the symbolization of religious traditions of the world, the institutionalization of roles in religious communities, and the interaction between religion and the personal, social, and cultural condition of women. Studies emphasize the pluralism of historical and contemporary religious traditions, racial diversity of female religious experience, and balance in representing the disciplines of theology, ethics, history of religion, Hebrew Bible, New Testament, history of Christianity, and psychology and sociology of religion. **Publications:** Essay Series; Monographs. **Meetings/Educational Activities:** Offers five seminars per year. **Library:** For information contact Charles Willard, librarian.

★8199★ Higher Education Resource Services, Mid-America (HERS)
University of Denver
Colorado Women's College Campus
7150 Montview Blvd.
Denver, CO 80220
Phone: (303)871-6866
Fax: (303)871-6897
Cynthia Secor, Director

Founded: 1975. **Research Activities and Fields:** Women in higher education administration.

★8200★ Human Lactation Center
666 Sturges Hwy.
Westport, CT 06880
Phone: (203)259-5995
Dana Raphael, Ph.D., Director

Founded: 1975. **Research Activities and Fields:** Human lactation and maternal and infant feeding behavior. **Publications:** The Lactation Review. **Meetings/Educational Activities:** Sponsors conferences on breastfeeding at hospitals. **Library:** 2,400 volumes and journal articles on lactation, research women and children.

★8201★ Institute for Reproductive Health
8721 Beverly Blvd.
Los Angeles, CA 90048
Phone: (213)854-7714
Vicki Hufnagel, M.D., Director

Founded: 1987. **Research Activities and Fields:** Repair and conservation of female reproductive organs, including multidisciplinary studies of uterine endocrinology, reconstructive surgery, sexually transmitted diseases and their effect on female infertility, and substance abuse and obstetrical problems. Analyzes the risks of hysterectomies and surveys related medical advances in women's health care. **Publications:** Women's Health Quarterly. **Meetings/Educational Activities:** Sponsors occasional educational meetings and seminars.

★8202★ **Institute for Research on Social Problems**
520 Pearl St.
Boulder, CO 80302
Phone: (303)449-7782
Dr. Phyllis Katz, Director

Founded: 1976. **Research Activities and Fields:** Conducts research on social development of children and adolescents, including sex roles and social attitudes.

★8203★ **Institute for the Study of Matrimonial Laws**
11 Park Pl., Ste. 1116
New York, NY 10007
Phone: (212)766-4030
Sidney Siller, President

Founded: 1972. **Research Activities and Fields:** Divorce, alimony, custody, and visitation laws in the U.S. Studies also focus on the emotional aspects of divorce. Compiles demographic and statistical information. **Publications:** Bulletin, published monthly except in summer. **Meetings/Educational Activities:** Sponsors an annual meeting in January in New York City. **Library:** 10,000 volumes and documents dealing with divorce, alimony, and custody.

★8204★ **Institute for Women's Policy Research**
1400 20th St. NW, Ste. 104
Washington, DC 20036
Phone: (202)785-5100
Heidi I. Hartmann, Ph.D., Director

Founded: 1987. **Research Activities and Fields:** Causes and consequences of women's poverty, particularly of minority women; costs and benefits of family and work policies; pay equity; wages and employment opportunities; and impact of tax policy on women and families; and access to and costs of health care. Specific issues include the impact of the Pregnancy Discrimination Act, the costs and benefits of family and medical leave, pay equity in 20 state civil service systems, the wage gap between women of color and white women, low-wage work, and welfare reform. **Meetings/Educational Activities:** Offers workshops, conferences, and speeches.

★8205★ **International Center for Research on Women**
1717 Massachusetts Ave. NW 302
Washington, DC 20036
Phone: (202)797-0007
Dr. Mayra Buvinic, President

Founded: 1976. **Research Activities and Fields:** The Center emphasizes applied, policy-relevant research on the social, health, and economic situation of women in developing countries at the national, local, and household levels and provides program analysis and support in the design and evaluation of strategies and projects which seek to actively incorporate women in productive activities. Studies include women, poverty, and the environment in Latin America; the role of women in fighting AIDS; maternal nutrition and health care; the aging process of women; women's access to credit; the effects of recession and stabilization policies on women; access by women farmers to agricultural extension and technology; women-headed households; and family structure and the transmission of poverty. **Publications:** *Technical Reports and Papers.* **Meet-**

ings/Educational Activities: Sponsors fellowship program for professionals and graduate students of developing countries. Holds policy roundtables and conferences irregularly. **Library:** 15,000 published and unpublished documents on women in developing countries.

★8206★ **Kent State University
Project for the Study of Gender and Education**
405 White Hall
Kent, OH 44242
Phone: (216)672-2178
Averil McClelland, Dir.

Specialization: Transformation of Teacher Education (Joint Center: The University of Akron and Kent State University).

★8207★ **Kinsey Institute for Research in Sex, Gender, and Reproduction, Inc.**
Morrison Hall, 3rd Fl.
Bloomington, IN 47405
Phone: (812)855-7686
Dr. June M. Reinisch, Director

Founded: 1947. **Research Activities and Fields:** Effects of prenatal exposure to drugs and hormones, American human sexual behavior, sexual orientation as it relates to sexually transmitted diseases, and sexual identity roles and attitudes, including studies of sexual and psychosexual development and biomedical and psychobiological approaches to sex, gender, and reproduction. **Library:** 70,000 volumes and 125 serial subscriptions on sex and erotica. **Formerly:** Institute for Sex Research (1981).

★8208★ **League of Women Voters Education Fund**
1730 M St. NW
Washington, DC 20036
Phone: (202)429-1965
Garcia Hillman, Executive Director

Founded: 1957. **Research Activities and Fields:** Government and governing, financing the federal government, national security, social policy, and natural resources and the environment including studies of the Congress, the Presidency, the budget, tax policy and deficit issues, campaign financing, federal agriculture policy, basic human needs, employment, discrimination, child care, affirmative action, education, hazardous and nuclear waste management, water, air, energy supply and demand, and health care policy. **Publications:** *The National Voter* (bimonthly); Annual Report; *Choosing the President* (quadrennially). **Meetings/Educational Activities:** Sponsors various special conferences and leadership training.

★8209★ **Masters & Johnson Institute**
24 S. Kingshighway
St. Louis, MO 63108
Phone: (314)361-2377
Virginia Johnson Masters, Director

Founded: 1964. **Research Activities and Fields:** Conceptive, contraceptive, and human sexual physiology, psychology, and endocrinology. Offers educational and clinical programs and training in human sexuality and treatment for sexual dysfunction and disorders. **Formerly:** Reproductive Biology Research Foundation (1979).

★8210★ **Maternal and Child Health Studies Project**
Information Sciences Research Institute
8375 Leesburg Pike, Ste. 439
Vienna, VA 22182
Phone: (703)255-1408
Margaret W. Pratt, Director

Founded: 1966. **Research Activities and Fields:** Maternal, infant, fetal, and child mortality rates, including analyses and trends by age, race, sex, geographic location, and relationship to socioeconomic descriptors, based upon computer-supported research operations. Seeks to identify health needs of mothers and children and evaluate maternal and child health service programs addressing those needs. **Publications:** *Health Planners Handbook for Maternal and Child Health Programs* (one to three sections added or updated annually); *50 Years of U.S. Federal Support to Promote the Health of Mothers, Children, and Handicapped Children (1935-1985).* Operates consultant network to provide training and technical assistance to Head Start projects. **Library:** 1,000 volumes on maternal and child health. **Formerly:** Maternal and Infant Health Project (1967), Operational and Demographic Analysis for Maternal and Child Health (1971), both at George Washington University.

★8211★ **Medical College of Pennsylvania Center for the Mature Woman**
3300 Henry Ave.
Philadelphia, PA 19129
Phone: (215)842-7180
Dr. Jon Schneider, Director

Founded: 1983. **Research Activities and Fields:** Health of the mature woman, including osteoporosis, mammography, urinary incontinence, and menopause.

★8212★ **Melpomene Institute for Women's Health Research**
1010 Univ. Ave.
St. Paul, MN 55104
Phone: (612)642-1951
Judy Mahle Lutter, President

Founded: 1981. **Research Activities and Fields:** Physically active women and girls, including effects of exercise on menstruation, pregnancy, menopause, body image, osteoporosis, stress, and aging, children's introduction to physical activity, and disabled women and exercise. **Publications:** *Melpomene Journal* (published three times per year); *The Bodywise Woman; Reliable Information about physical activity and health, A guide for physically active women.* **Meetings/Educational Activities:** Sponsors accredited conferences and seminars. **Library:** 200 books and over 3,000 articles; Eleanor Laursen, resource center coordinator.

★8213★ **Memphis State University Center for Research on Women**
Clement Hall-339
Memphis, TN 38152
Phone: (901)678-2770
Lynn Weber, Director

Founded: 1982. **Research Activities and Fields:** Southern women and women of color (Black, Latina, Asian American, and Native American) in the U.S., including critical examination of the intersection of gender, class, and racial oppression; perception of class among Americans; mobility strategies of minority women; working class women in the South; rural poverty; and comparative study of Black and White professional and managerial women in the Memphis area. **Publications:** Newsletter (twice per year); *Southern Women: The Intersection of Race, Class and Gender* (co-sponsored with the Duke University–University of North Carolina Women's Studies Research Center); Research Papers Curriculum Integration Publications; a printed version of the database (updated annually). **Meetings/Educational Activities:** Sponsors Workshop on Women in the Curriculum (annually) and summer research institutes (occasionally).

★8214★ Michigan State University
Women and International Development Program
202 Center for International Programs
East Lansing, MI 48824
Phone: (517)353-5040
Dr. Rita Gallin, Director

Founded: 1978. **Research Activities and Fields:** Womens' roles in production and reproduction in developing nations; effects of economic, political, and social factors on the sexual division of labor and the status of women; the impact of development programs on women; the role of women and womens' groups in change; and women and health. **Publications:** *WID Forum; Working Papers on Women in International Development; WID Bulletin* (a resource guide published three times per year). **Meetings/Educational Activities:** Sponsors seminars, study groups, and conferences. **Library:** Maintains a collection of books, articles, and reports on women in developing countries; Laura Carantza, secretary. **Formerly:** Committee on Women in International Development; Office of Women in International Development (1991).

★8215★ National Center on Women and Family Law, Inc.
799 Broadway, Rm. 402
New York, NY 10003
Phone: (212)674-8200
Mary Johnson, Office Manager

Founded: 1979. **Research Activities and Fields:** Family law, including studies on crime and violence, spouse abuse, battery, custody, child support, marital rape, divorce, and wife support. **Publications:** *The Woman's Advocate* (bimonthly newsletter). Resource packets, manuals, and handbooks available for sale. Provides technical assistance and performs advocacy activities. **Library:** Maintains a reference collection.

★8216★ National Council for Research on Women
Sara Delano Roosevelt Memorial House
47-49 E. 65th St.
New York, NY 10021
Phone: (212)570-5001
Mary Ellen S. Capek, Executive Director

Founded: 1982. **Research Activities and Fields:** Women's studies and education of women. Member centers include campus-based and independent policy centers working on a broad range of research and policy projects. Forms working groups to study specific issues such as intersections of race, class and gender, women and work, and diversity in the curriculum. Facilitates collaborative research and communication on related topics and monitors de-

velopments in public policy. Serves as a clearinghouse for research and other information resources relating to women. **Publications:** *Women's Research Network News* (newsletter); *A Women's Thesaurus; Women in Academe: Progress & Prospects;* Annual Report; also publishes periodic reports and directories. **Meetings/Educational Activities:** Sponsors annual meeting of member centers and the National Network of Women's Caucuses and Committees in the Professional Associations. Sponsors international exchange programs, including the US/USSR Women's Dialogue. Also awards international fellowships.

★8217★ National Institute for Women of Color
1301-20th St. NW, Ste. 202
Washington, DC 20036
Phone: (202)296-2661
Sharon Parker, Chair, Board of Directors

Founded: 1981. **Research Activities and Fields:** Women of color, including studies on demographic trends, education, sports, and sex equity. Assists in the formulation and implementation of public policy. **Publications:** *NIWC Network News.* **Meetings/Educational Activities:** Developed and distributes a resource packet on reproductive freedom for women of color.

★8218★ National Museum of Women in the Arts, Library and Research Center
1250 New York Ave. NW
Washington, DC 20005
Phone: (202)783-5000
Krystyna Wasserman, Director

Founded: 1981. **Research Activities and Fields:** Women in the arts. Research is mostly related to the visual arts.

★8219★ National Women's Law Center
1616 P St. NW
Washington, DC 20036
Phone: (202)328-5160
Nancy Duff Campbell, Co-President

Founded: 1972. **Research Activities and Fields:** Current and proposed policies and practices in the public and private sectors, as women are affected. Studies include women's legal rights issues, primarily in areas of employment, education, and income security, including child support, public assistance, taxes, social security, child and adult dependent care, and health and reproductive rights. Actively participates in various women's rights coalitions and in coalitions with labor, religious, and civil rights organizations. **Publications:** Annual Report; *National Women's Law Center Update* (newsletter, 3-4 times yearly). **Meetings/Educational Activities:** Provides training for second and third year law students. **Library:** Legal journals, books, and other materials; Ellen Vargyas, librarian.

★8220★ National Women's Studies Association
Univ. of Maryland
College Park, MD 20742-1325
Phone: (301)405-5573
Deborah Louis, National Director

Founded: 1977. **Research Activities and Fields:** Supports and encourages women's studies and feminist education. Conference topics have included curricular development, intersection of race and gender, and internation-

al women's studies. **Meetings/Educational Activities:** Holds an annual national conference. Offers graduate scholarships, undergraduate and graduate internships, and the Illinois-NWSA Manuscript Award. **Library:** Maintains an archive collection.

★8221★ New York Medical College Institute of Breast Diseases
Munger Pavilion, G-40
Valhalla, NY 10595
Phone: (914)285-8770
Reinhard E. Zachrau, M.D., Contact

Research Activities and Fields: Breast diseases, including skin window reactivity and second primary breast cancer.

★8222★ New York University Women's Studies Commission
10 Washington Pl.
New York, NY 10003
Phone: (212)998-7999

Specialization: Women in Human Service Professions

★8223★ Northern California Mediation Center
100 Tamel Plaza, Ste. 175
Corte Madera, CA 94925
Phone: (415)927-1422
Joan Kelly, Director

Research Activities and Fields: Mediation. Activities include a comparison of the effects of mediation and litigation on the outcomes of divorce cases involving child custody, financial support, and property division, including the psychological, legal, and economic effects on disputants and the role of gender in disputes. **Publications:** *Northern California Mediation Center Newsletter.*

★8224★ Ohio State University Center for Women's Studies
207 Dulles Hall
230 W. 17th Ave.
Columbus, OH 43210-1311
Phone: (614)292-1021
Dr. Susan M. Hartmann, Director

Founded: 1975. **Research Activities and Fields:** Develops, coordinates, and conducts interdisciplinary research projects in women's studies with focus on cultural identities, gender issues, collective history, social roles, literary and artistic productions, and individual experiences. Administers research grants program yearly for faculty, staff, and students conducting scholarly research on women and women's issues. **Publications:** *Feminisms* (quarterly review of new scholarship, fiction, poetry, films, and art by and about women); Research Directory (covering approximately 50 faculty members at the University pursuing work in women's studies). **Meetings/Educational Activities:** Sponsors a visiting lecture series and a colloquium/symposium series. **Formerly:** Office of Women's Studies (1980).

★8225★ Our Lady of the Lake University
of San Antonio
Center for Women in Development
411 SW 24th St.
San Antonio, TX 78207
Phone: (512)434-6711
Fax: (512)436-0824
Jane Shafer, Contact

★8226★ Pennsylvania State University
Center for Rural Women
201 Agricultural Administration Bldg.
University Park, PA 16802

★8227★ Pennsylvania State University,
University Park
Center for Research on Women and
Science
13 Sparks Bldg.
University Park, PA 16802
Phone: (814)865-1962
Mary Frank Fox, Contact

★8228★ Project of Equal Education Rights
99 Hudson St., 12th Fl.
New York, NY 10013
Phone: (212)925-6635
Helen Nuborne, Executive Director

Research Activities and Fields: Women's
studies, including education issues.

★8229★ Radcliffe College
Bunting Institute
34 Concord Ave.
Cambridge, MA 02138
Phone: (617)495-8212
Florence C. Ladd, Director

Founded: 1960. Research Activities and
Fields: Multidisciplinary program for women
scholars, artists, writers, musicians, and scientists, and practitioners pursuing independent
study in academic or professional fields in
creative writing, the sciences, social sciences,
humanities, or the arts. Offers six fellowships,
office or studio space, and access to Radcliffe
and Harvard resources. Publications: Working
Papers; Annual Newsletter. Meet-
ings/Educational Activities: Holds weekly public colloquia on fellows' research in progress
between October and May. Formerly: Radcliffe
Institute for Independent Study (1978); Mary
Ingraham Bunting Institute of Radcliffe College.

★8230★ Radcliffe College
Henry A. Murray Research Center
10 Garden St.
Cambridge, MA 02138
Phone: (617)495-8140
Dr. Anne Colby, Director

Founded: 1976. Research Activities and
Fields: National repository for data on American
women collected by social scientists. Houses
both computer and raw data, including interview
transcripts, questionnaires, and projective tests
for secondary analysis, followup, replication,
and other research purposes. Acts as a catalyst
for and sponsors scholarly research, including
dissertation and postdoctoral research on wom-
en. Grants awards to eligible researchers. Publications: Murray Center News (two times per
year); Guide to the Data Resources of the
Murray Center. Meetings/Educational Activities: Sponsors workshops, colloquia, and occasional conferences during the academic year.
Formerly: Radcliffe Data Resource and Research Center (1979).

★8231★ Rocky Mountain Women's
Institute
Foote Hall, Rm. 317
7150 Montview Blvd.
Denver, CO 80220
Phone: (303)871-6923
Cheryl Bezio-Gorham, Executive Director

Founded: 1976. Research Activities and
Fields: Arts and humanities. Annually offers 7-
10 one-year associateships to artists, writers,
and scholars. Meetings/Educational Activities:
Sponsors public lectures, readings, workshops,
art exhibits, and performing arts events.

★8232★ Russell Sage College
Helen Upton Center for Women's Studies
90 1st St.
Troy, NY 12180
Phone: (518)270-2306
Kristi S. Anderson, Director

Founded: 1980. Research Activities and
Fields: Women and educational equity, including identification of institutional barriers to equity, program evaluation, and studies on help
seeking behaviors of students in academic
difficulty. Publications: Green Light (bimonthly
newsletter for students); Center News (bimonthly newsletter for faculty). Meet-
ings/Educational Activities: Sponsors the following special programs: monthly faculty colloquia on a balance curriculum; Sage Women's
Issues, a discussion series on topics of concern
to women students; brown bag lunch support
group for nontraditional students; and periodic
workshops for women on assertiveness, self
confidence, demystifying academia, demystifying the machine (a computer literacy workshop),
empowerment, and decision making (a life work
planning workshop or teenage women), open to
public on a fee basis. Library: Maintains a
collection on women. Formerly: Center for
Women's Education (1990).

★8233★ Rutgers, The State University of
New Jersey, Douglass College
Center for Women's Global Leadership
27 Clifton Ave.
New Brunswick, NJ 08903
Phone: (908)932-8782
Charlotte Brunch, Contact

Formerly: Center for Global Issues and Wom-
en's Leadership.

★8234★ Rutgers University
Center for the American Woman and
Politics
Eagleton Institute of Politics
New Brunswick, NJ 08901
Phone: (908)932-9384
Dr. Ruth B. Mandel, Director

Founded: 1971. Research Activities and
Fields: The nature and extent of women's
political participation in the U.S., particularly
women in state legislatures. Surveys and profiles women candidates and women holding
elective or appointive office. Studies impact of
women in public office, routes women take into
public office, influences on their decision to
seek office, and their experiences. Research
findings used to recommend specific channels
towards office-holding and to encourage more
women to enter the electoral process. Publications: News & Notes (newsletter published
three times a year as part of a packet provided
through Subscriber Information Services). Library: Maintains books, papers, reports, and

periodicals; Kathy Kleeman, senior program
associate.

★8235★ Rutgers University
Institute for Research on Women
Douglass College
27 Clifton Ave.
New Brunswick, NJ 08903
Phone: (908)932-9072
Carol H. Smith, Director

Founded: 1976. Research Activities and
Fields: Gender integration and curricular reform, reproductive laws, women and war and
peace, black women writers, feminist theory
and methodology, women's leadership, and
development of archives on women. Publications: NETWORC (semiannual newsletter);
Women, War & Peace Bibliography and Filmog-
raphy; Women & Gender Directory; New Jersey
Project Handbook. Meetings/Educational Activities: Sponsors Consortium for Educational
Equity, Thinking About Women Seminar Series
(monthly), and a Celebration of Our Work
Conference (annually, open to the public).
Formerly: Women's Studies Institute (1982).

★8236★ Simmons College
Institute for Case Development and
Research
Graduate School of Management
409 Commonwealth Ave.
Boston, MA 02215
Phone: (617)536-8289
Cinny Little, Director

Founded: 1974. Research Activities and
Fields: Researches, publishes, and distributes
case studies on organizational behavior issues
in management. All cases feature women in
middle and senior management. Cases address
a variety of management situations as well as
the issues of career planning and development,
minority women in management, and balancing
family and career. Publications: Catalogue of
Cases on Women in Management (revised
annually). Library: Maintains a collection on
management; Jane Nash, librarian.

★8237★ Smith College
Project on Women and Social Change
138 Elm St.
Northampton, MA 01063
Phone: (413)585-3591
Dr. Susan C. Bourque, Director

Founded: 1978. Research Activities and
Fields: Women, including studies in the areas of
health and technology, cross-cultural issues,
adult development, public policy, gender, and
international development. Library: Contact organization for more information.

★8238★ Southwestern University
Center for Texas Women in the Arts
Georgetown, TX 78626
Phone: (512)863-6511
Fax: (512)863-5788
Mary Visser, Contact

Specialization: Texas Women in the Visual and
Performing Arts.

★8239★ Spelman College
Women's Research and Resource Center
Box 115
Atlanta, GA 30314
Phone: (404)681-3643
Dr. Beverly Guy-Sheftall, Director

Founded: 1981. **Research Activities and Fields:** Black women, particularly history, literature, higher education, and health care studies. Coordinates curriculum development project in black women's studies at selected southern colleges. **Publications:** *Exhibit Catalogs*; *Sage: A Scholarly Journal on Black Women* (semiannually). **Meetings/Educational Activities:** Sponsors conferences on black women; brown bag luncheon seminars; and co-sponsors workshops, symposia, lecture series.

★8240★ Stanford University
Institute for Research on Women and Gender
Serra House
Serre St.
Stanford, CA 94305-8640
Phone: (415)723-1994
Iris F. Litt, M.D., Director

Founded: 1974. **Research Activities and Fields:** Women and gender, emphasizing the historical, social, and cultural contexts of the experiences of women, including projects on gender discrimination laws, child care, womens' autobiographies, mental health, and work, family, and reproductive issues. **Publications:** Newsletter (quarterly); *Report Series*; *Working Papers*. **Meetings/Educational Activities:** Sponsors the Jing Lyman lecture series (quarterly, during the academic year), open to the public, assorted special seminars and conferences, and the annual Corporate Seminar for Corporate Associates. **Library:** 600-650 volumes on women, gender, and gender-related subjects; also maintains a tape library of all lecture series. **Formerly:** Center for Research on Women (1986).

★8241★ State University of New York at Albany
Center for Women in Government
Draper 310
135 Western Ave.
Albany, NY 12222
Phone: (518)442-3900
Florence Bonner, Director

Founded: 1978. **Research Activities and Fields:** Brings together unions, women's organizations, advocacy organizations, and government officials to address public sector employment issues of interest to women and minorities, including studies on career ladders, promotion processes, pay equity, and other barriers preventing full participation of women and minorities in public service. Other areas of study include access to public sector jobs for economically disadvantaged and inner city women, and women's public policy leadership development. **Publications:** Monographs; *Working Paper Series*; *News on Women in Government* (newsletter); Technical Reports; Guidebooks. **Meetings/Educational Activities:** Sponsors seminars and special programs, including training seminars.

★8242★ State University of New York at Albany
Institute for Research on Women
Dept. of Sociology - SS 326
1400 Washington Ave.
Albany, NY 12222
Phone: (518)442-4815
Iris Berger, Director

Research Activities and Fields: Women's issues. **Publications:** Newsletter. **Meetings/Educational Activities:** Sponsors international conferences on women's issues and special workshops to promote and facilitate grant-seeking efforts.

★8243★ State University of New York College at Binghamton
Sojourner Center for Research on Women
Library North 1105
Binghamton, NY 13901
Phone: (607)777-4273
Deborah Hertz, Contact

★8244★ State University of New York College at Brockport
Community Research Center
Brockport, NY 14420
Phone: (716)395-2682
Fax: (716)395-2246
Margaret Blackman, Dept. Head

Specialization: Gender and Cultural Diversity.

★8245★ State University of New York College at Buffalo
Graduate Group for Feminist Studies
527 O'Brien Hall
Buffalo, NY 14260
Phone: (716)636-2361
Claudia Freidefsky, Contact

★8246★ Syracuse University
Women's Studies Program
307 Hall of Languages
Syracuse, NY 13244-1170
Phone: (315)443-3707
Diane Lyden Murphy, Director

Founded: 1975. **Research Activities and Fields:** Women, including studies on women's work in the U.S. and comparative perspectives, images, and traditions of women in literature; the gendering of knowledge and the academic profession; sex role socialization; feminist theory; women's history; and women and public policy. Activities focus on feminist analysis for social change. **Publications:** *Newsletter* (semiannually). **Meetings/Educational Activities:** Coordinates conferences and sponsors a lecture series, weekly lunch seminars, and faculty seminars.

★8247★ Towson State University
Center for the Study of Women and Education
Linthicum Hall
Towson, MD 21204
Phone: (301)830-2660
Fax: (301)296-8782
Dr. Elaine Hedges, Chairperson

Specialization: Curriculum Transformation and Research Projects

★8248★ Tulane University
Newcomb College Center for Research on Women
1229 Broadway
New Orleans, LA 70118
Phone: (504)865-5238
Beth Willinger, Dir.

Specialization: Southern Women and Women's Education

★8249★ Union Institute
The Women's Project
1731 Connecticut Ave., NW, No.300
Washington, DC 20009-1146
Phone: (202)667-1313
Dr. Judith Arcana, Contact

★8250★ University of Arizona
Southwest Institute for Research on Women (SIROW)
102 Douglass Bldg.
Tucson, AZ 85721
Phone: (602)621-7338
Dr. Janice Monk, Executive Director

Founded: 1979. **Research Activities and Fields:** Women in the Southwest, with emphasis on multicultural character of the region, educational issues, and impact of regional growth on women, particularly elderly women. Also studies women's health issues and women in public policy. **Publications:** SIROW Newsletter (three per year); *SIROW Working Paper Series*; Monographs. **Meetings/Educational Activities:** Sponsors two to three conferences per year.

★8251★ University of California, Berkeley
Beatrice M. Bain Research Group
2539 Channing Way, Room 19
Berkeley, CA 94720
Phone: (415)643-7172
Aihwa Ong, Director

Founded: 1986. **Research Activities and Fields:** Women and gender. Promotes and supports research projects by faculty and graduate students. Sponsors a research affiliates program, and an annual graduate student conference, sponsors and co-sponsors lectures, symposia, colloqnia and several working groups. **Publications:** Biennial Newsletter. **Formerly:** Group in Feminist and Gender Studies.

★8252★ University of California, Davis
Women's Resources and Research Center
10 Lower Freeborn
Davis, CA 95616
Phone: (916)752-3372
Linda A. Morris, Director

Founded: 1974. **Research Activities and Fields:** Women's studies, especially women in education and academia. **Publications:** *Catalogue of Research on Gender and Women at UCD*. **Meetings/Educational Activities:** Offers educational programs throughout the academic year and holds periodic research conferences.

**★8253★ University of California, Los Angeles
Center for the Study of Women**
236A Kinsey Hall
405 Hilgard Ave.
Los Angeles, CA 90024-1504
Phone: (213)825-0590
Helen S. Astin, Acting Director

Research Activities and Fields: Women's studies in areas such as women and health, including prenatal care and birth outcomes and health and women's work; violence involving women, including rape, spouse abuse, child abuse, female offenders, and victimization; African women; women in history and literature; psychology of sex differences; close relationships; women and the media; women in the professions; and women in education, including women in higher education, sexual harassment in education, sex differences in learning, and education of the mature woman. **Publications:** Newsletter (quarterly). Sponsors higher education programs in women's studies and offers fellowships and grants. Holds conferences, symposia, public lecturer series, and faculty development and research seminars.

**★8254★ University of Cincinnati
Women's Studies Research and Resources Institute**
Center for Women's Studies
155 McMicken Hall
Cincinnati, OH 45221-0164
Phone: (513)556-6654
P. McAllister, Coordinator

Founded: 1983. **Research Activities and Fields:** Feminist studies and history of women, especially midwestern women, women in Cincinnati, women in the paid labor force, and Appalachian women. Also develops non-sexist curricula for primary and secondary schools and for non-traditional students. **Publications:** *A Century of Achievement: Women in Cincinnati* (three volumes); also produces video documentaries (seven to date, available to the public). **Meetings/Educational Activities:** Conducts quarterly faculty-student research forum and coordinates University conferences and lectures on topics in women's studies.

**★8255★ University of Connecticut
Institute for the Study of Women and Gender**
U-181
Stoors, CT 06268-1181
Phone: (203)486-2186
Fax: (503)486-4789
Patricia A. Carter, Coordinator

Description: The institute's purpose is the development of research projects that have "both a theoretical and applied nature," including gender equity in education, women and technology, women and international development, women and labor force participation, and women and disability. **Publications:** *Annual Report.* • *Working Paper Series.*

**★8256★ University of Connecticut
Women's Center**
417 Whitney Rd., Box U-118
Storrs, CT 06268
Phone: (203)486-4738

Research Activities and Fields: Conducts institutional research and other activities related to women's and gender issues, including Connecticut PEER Project for Equal Education

Rights to improve K-12 math and science education for female and minority students; the Vocational Equity Research, Evaluation and Training Center, to examine gender equity in vocational education. Other areas of interest include gender harassment, sexual harassment and violence, abortion, job discrimination, women's economic status, status of women of color, the legal meaning of marriage, sexual abuse of children, eating disorders, and black women under apartheid. **Publications:** *Annual Report*; *VERTEC Newsletter*; *Research Briefs.* Also publishes various informational pamphlets, fact sheets, and brochures. **Meetings/Educational Activities:** Conducts monthly informal lectures (open to the public), invites guest speakers to campus, and conducts various conferences, seminars, and training programs. The student-operated Rape Education and Awareness Program provides speakers and educational materials on violence against women. The Re-Entry Student Project provides support and information to older adult students. The Center also sponsors Women in the Arts Month (March); a film series by, for, and about women; and receptions for special populations. **Library:** Maintains a collection of books, magazines, and reference information.

**★8257★ University of Illinois at Chicago
Women's Studies Program**
Box 4348, M/C 360
Rm. 1022 C BSB
Chicago, IL 60680
Phone: (312)413-2300
Stephanie Riger, Dir.

Founded: 1973. **Research Activities and Fields:** Interdisciplinary studies concerning the history and role of women in society. Studies have included the development of curricula especially appropriate to women's studies in an urban area.

**★8258★ University of Michigan
Center for the Education of Women**
330 E. Liberty
Ann Arbor, MI 48104-2289
Phone: (313)998-7080
Carol Hollenshead, Director

Founded: 1964. **Research Activities and Fields:** Education and career concerns, including transitions, for women. Projects focus on precollege and undergraduate women in the fields of science and technology, and graduate and undergraduate women in higher education. **Publications:** *CEW Research Reports*; *CEW Newsletter* (one or two yearly); plus conference proceedings as they apply and bibliographies. **Meetings/Educational Activities:** Holds conferences, seminars, and Women in Science Lecture Series. **Library:** Over 20,000 articles, papers, government documents, dissertations, and monographs dealing with women's education and employment, plus women's organizational files and clipping files. **Formerly:** Center for Continuing Education of Women.

**★8259★ University of Minnesota
Center for Advanced Feminist Studies**
496 Ford Hall
224 Church St. SE
Minneapolis, MN 55455
Phone: (612)624-6310
Shirley Garner, Director

Founded: 1983. **Research Activities and Fields:** Interdisciplinary studies on gender and

the life histories of women, emphasizing women regionally, nationally, and internationally. Seeks to develop theoretical perspectives and research and analytic skills and foster a strong community of feminist scholars at the University through conferences, research projects, and colloquia. **Publications:** Annual Report; Quarterly Newsletter; Biweekly Newsletter. **Meetings/Educational Activities:** Offers internships through several agencies and a graduate minor in feminist studies on master's and doctoral levels.

**★8260★ University of Minnesota
Women, Public Policy, and Development Project**
Humphrey Institute of Public Affairs
301 19th Ave. S.
Minneapolis, MN 55455
Phone: (612)625-2505
Arvonne Fraser, Director

Founded: 1982. **Research Activities and Fields:** Teaching, research, and outreach center devoted to the following women's policy issues: research and the provision of educational materials on the changing economic roles and responsibility of women, women's organizations, and changes in public policy internationally; leadership by and among women; and followup to the U.N. Decade of Women. Monitors implementation of the Convention on the Elimination of All Forms of Discrimination Against Women, an international treaty, and examines labor force participation and economic status of women in the U.S. **Publications:** *The Women's Watch*. **Meetings/Educational Activities:** Supports student work in the Women and Public Policy master's degree program. Sponsors meetings, seminars, and conferences, including an annual international conference. **Library:** Maintains a resource center containing current and historical materials relating to women in development.

**★8261★ University of Minnesota, Duluth
Center for Research, Women's Studies Program**
10 University Dr.
Duluth, MN 55812
Phone: (218)726-7953
Fax: (218)726-6331
Charlotte MacLeod, Contact

**★8262★ University of Mississippi
Sarah Isom Center for Women's Studies**
University, MS 38677
Phone: (601)232-5916
Dr. Joanne Hawks, Director

Founded: 1979. **Research Activities and Fields:** Women, particularly from the South. Studies include women in history and women legislators. **Publications:** *Sarah Isom Center News* (semiannual newsletter). **Meetings/Educational Activities:** Offers courses on women through the Center and other academic departments at the University.

**★8263★ University of Oregon
Center for the Study of Women in Society**
Eugene, OR 97403
Phone: (503)346-5015
Dr. Sandra Morgen, Director

Founded: 1973. **Research Activities and Fields:** Disciplinary and multi-disciplinary research on gender and women in society. Activities support the development, production and dissemination of research. Provides support to local researchers, faculty and graduate students at the University of Oregon, and visiting scholars. **Publications:** Bulletin (monthly); *Review* (yearly); Working Papers. **Meetings/Educational Activities:** Cooperates in a Women's Studies Program at the University and sponsors lectures, open to the public. **Library:** Reference books and journals on gender and women. **Formerly:** Center for the Sociological Study of Women (1983).

★8264★ University of Pennsylvania
Alice Paul Research Center for the Study of Women
106 Logan Hall
249 S. 36th St.
Philadelphia, PA 19104-6304
Phone: (215)898-8740
Prof. Janice F. Madden, Director

Founded: 1984. **Research Activities and Fields:** Women's studies, especially in the disciplines of English, history, language, sociology, and economics. **Publications:** Working Paper Series. **Meetings/Educational Activities:** Sponsors the Penn Mid-Atlantic Seminar for the Study of Women and Society and the Seminar on the Role of Gender in Social, Economic and Political Life, both of which serve as research forums for faculty members and graduate students.

★8265★ University of Southern California
Institute for the Study of Women and Men
734 W. Adams Blvd., 208
Los Angeles, CA 90007
Phone: (213)743-3683
Judith Glass, Ph.D., Director

Founded: 1987. **Research Activities and Fields:** Gender issues, feminism, ethnicity and sexuality. Also studies media and its feminist movement. **Publications:** *Bi-Annual Newsletter; Faculty Research Directory.* **Meetings/Educational Activities:** Sponsors an affiliated scholars program, a distinguished visitors program, and outreach programs, including a mentoring project with minority high school girls.

★8266★ University of Texas at Arlington
Women and Minority Work Research and Resource Center
Box 19129
Arlington, TX 76019
Phone: (817)273-3131
Kathleen Underwood, Director

Research Activities and Fields: Women and work, particularly the interrelationships between work and family, women entrepreneurs and owners of small businesses, and the effect of on-site child care facilities on employee, family, company, and child. Activities encompass studies of demographic trends and projections, education, reentry of mature women to higher education, and sex equity.

★8267★ University of Tulsa
Research in Women's Literature
600 S. College
Tulsa, OK 74104
Phone: (918)631-2503
Prof. Holly A. Laird, Editor

Founded: 1982. **Research Activities and Fields:** Women's literature, with an emphasis on literary history, criticism, and bibliography. **Publications:** *Tulsa Studies in Women's Literature* (semiannual journal). **Meet-**ings/Educational Activities: Sponsors guest lecturers on women's literature each semester. **Library:** Women's literature collections are available to students in the faculty of English Language and Literature at the University. **Formerly:** Tulsa Center for the Study of Women's Literature.

★8268★ University of Washington
Northwest Center for Research on Women
AJ-50
Seattle, WA 98195
Phone: (206)543-9531
Dr. Angela B. Ginorio, Director

Founded: 1980. **Research Activities and Fields:** Curriculum integration; women, science, and technology; women in academia; and women in education. **Publications:** *Northwest Women's Report* (quarterly). **Meetings/Educational Activities:** Hosts visiting scholars.

★8269★ University of Wisconsin—Eau Claire
The Women Studies Bibliographic Center
c/o Women's Studies Program
McIntyre Library
Eau Claire, WI 54701
Phone: (715)836-5717
Fax: (715)836-2380
Sarah Harder, Contact

★8270★ University of Wisconsin—Madison
Women's Studies Research Center
209 N. Brooks St.
Madison, WI 53715
Phone: (608)263-2053
Prof. Cyrena Pondrom, Director

Founded: 1977. **Research Activities and Fields:** Feminist theory, impact of feminist policy, parental leave policy, women and development, women and aging, and women and mental health, curriculum transformation, feminist literacy analysis, women's history, gender analysis, of political transitions, and gender analysis of economics and society. **Publications:** Newsletter (semiannually); Working Paper Series; Reprint Series. **Meetings/Educational Activities:** Holds colloquia and lectures (weekly) and grant process workshops (once per semester). **Library:** Maintains a reading room of 250 volumes and 40 journals on women's studies.

★8271★ University of Wisconsin—Milwaukee
Center for Women's Studies
P.O. Box 413
Milwaukee, WI 53201
Phone: (414)229-5918
Janice D. Yoder, Director

Research Activities and Fields: Women and gender, women and politics, women and economics, spousal abuse, women and AIDS, women in history, architectural careers for women, women in music, child care, women athletes, curriculum integration, and feminist theory. **Publications:** Working Papers; *Directory of Milwaukee Area Women's Organizations; Women's Studies Newletter.* **Meetings/Educational Activities:** Administers undergraduate major and certificate programs in women's studies. Sponsors Women's History Month programming and faculty seminar series.

★8272★ Utah State University
Women and Gender Research Institute
Logan, UT 84322-3555
Phone: (801)750-2376
Dr. Caryn Beck-Dudley, Director

Founded: 1984. **Research Activities and Fields:** Women and gender studies, including women and development, migration and poverty, singleness, female and male athletes' academic achievement, and women in the inter-mountain region. Also studies women in education, including higher education for the mature woman and sex differences in learning. **Publications:** Newsletter; Working Paper Series. **Meetings/Educational Activities:** Provides assistantships to students, sponsors gender research and professional development programs, and offers internal travel awards and small grants.

★8273★ Vassar College
Women's Health Initiative
Box 115
Poughkeepsie, NY 12601
Phone: (914)437-7144
Colleen Cohen, Contact

Specialization: Women's Health.

★8274★ Virginia Polytechnic Institute and State University
Women's Research Institute
10 Sandy Hall
Blacksburg, VA 24061-0338
Phone: (703)231-7615
Dr. Carol J. Burger, Contact

★8275★ Washington State University
Women's Resource and Research Center
Pullman, WA 99164-7204
Phone: (509)335-6830
Beth Prinz, Dir.

★8276★ Wellesley College
Center for Research on Women
Wellesley, MA 02181
Phone: (617)431-1453
Dr. Susan M. Bailey, Director

Founded: 1974. **Research Activities and Fields:** Social science, applied, and policy research on women, including studies on girls in American education, child care, stress in the lives of women and men, and curriculum change, women in the sciences, employment of women, effects of public policy on women. **Publications:** Working Papers Series; Research Report (occasional newsletter); Annual Report; *Women's Review of Books.* **Meetings/Educational Activities:** Research seminars and colloquia.

★8277★ Wichita State University
Research Group on Women and Work
Psychology Dept.
1845 Fairmount, Box 34
Wichita, KS 67208
Phone: (316)689-3170
Dr. Ellie Shore, Contact

Specialization: Professional Women in the Wichita Area.

★8278★ Women Employed Institute
22 W. Monroe, Ste. 1400
Chicago, IL 60603-2505
Phone: (312)782-3902
Anne Ladky, Executive Director

Founded: 1973. **Research Activities and Fields:** Economic status of working women, working women and the law, sexual harassment in the workplace, equal employment opportunity, women's access to vocational education and job training, comparable worth, working mothers, and career development.

★8279★ Women's History Research Center
2325 Oak St.
Berkeley, CA 94708
Phone: (510)524-1582
Laura X, Executive Director

Founded: 1969. **Research Activities and Fields:** Women in world history. Distributes three microfilm collections from the Women's History Library: *Herstory* (serial), *Women and Law* (subject files), and *Women's Health/Mental Health* (subject files). **Library:** Contact organization for more information.

★8280★ Women's Research and Education Institute
1700 18th St. NW, Ste. 400
Washington, DC 20009
Phone: (202)328-7070
Betty Parsons Dooley, Executive Director

Founded: 1977. **Research Activities and Fields:** Monitors the administration and enforcement of existing laws affecting women, provides data on the impact of impending legislation, serves as a link between legislators and over thirty women's research and policy centers, and suggests new areas where congressional attention could be directed. Issues treated have included such subjects as midlife and older women, women in the military, alternative work options, employment and economic issues, the feminization of poverty, women and pension coverage, day care, and the impact of proposed budget reductions. **Publications:** *The American Woman 1990-91: A Status Report*, a biennial report on the status of women in the U.S. **Meetings/Educational Activities:** Sponsors conferences, brown bag lunches and discussion groups, symposia, and the Congressional Fellowships on Women and Public Policy (open to graduate students). **Library:** Clipping file on issues of interest to women; Anne J. Stone, research associate.

(14) Federal Government Agencies

Entries in this chapter are arranged alphabetically by agency name. See the User's Guide at the front of this directory for additional information.

★8281★ **National Science Foundation**
Women's Programs Section
1800 G. St. NW
Washington, DC 20550
Phone: (202)357-7734
Margarete S. Klein, Contact

★8282★ **U.S. Commission on Civil Rights**
1121 Vermont Ave. NW
Washington, DC 20425
Phone: (202)523-5571
Fax: (202)376-1163
Arthur A. Fletcher, Chairman

Description: The Commission on Civil Rights collects and studies information on discrimination or denials of equal protection laws because of race, color, religion, sex, age, handicap, national origin, or in the administration of justice in such areas as voting rights, enforcement of Federal civil rights laws, and equality of opportunity in education, employment, and housing.

★8283★ **U.S. Commission on Civil Rights**
Central Regional Office
Old Federal Office Bldg.
911 Walnut St.
Kansas City, MO 64106
Phone: (816)426-5253
Fax: (816)426-2233
Melvin L. Jenkins, Director

Territory Includes: Alabama, Arkansas, Iowa, Kansas, Louisiana, Mississippi, Missouri, and Nebraska.

★8284★ **U.S. Commission on Civil Rights**
Eastern Regional Office
1121 Vermont Ave. NW
Washington, DC 20425
Phone: (202)523-5264
Fax: (202)376-1163
John I. Binkley, Director

Territory Includes: Connecticut, Delaware, District of Columbia, Maine, Maryland, Massachusetts, New Hampshire, New Jersey, New York, Pennsylvania, Rhode Island, Vermont, Virginia, and West Virginia.

★8285★ **U.S. Commission on Civil Rights**
Midwestern Regional Office
175 W. Jackson St.
Chicago, IL 60604
Phone: (312)353-8311
Fax: (312)353-8324
Constance D. Davis, Director

Territory Includes: Illinois, Indiana, Michigan, Minnesota, Ohio, and Wisconsin.

★8286★ **U.S. Commission on Civil Rights**
Rocky Mountain Regional Office
Federal Office Bldg.
1961 Stout St.
PO Drawer 3585
Denver, CO 80294
Phone: (303)844-6716
Fax: (303)844-6721
William Muldrow, Director

Territory Includes: Colorado, Montana, North Dakota, South Dakota, Utah, and Wyoming.

★8287★ **U.S. Commission on Civil Rights**
Southern Regional Office
101 Marietta St.
Atlanta, GA 30303
Phone: (404)730-2476
Fax: (404)730-2480
Bobby Doctor, Director

Territory Includes: Florida, Georgia, Kentucky, North Carolina, South Carolina, and Tennessee.

★8288★ **U.S. Commission on Civil Rights**
Western Regional Office
3660 Wilshire Blvd.
Los Angeles, CA 90010
Phone: (213)894-3437
Fax: (213)894-0508
Philip Montez, Director

Territory Includes: Alaska, Arizona, California, Hawaii, Idaho, Nevada, New Mexico, Oklahoma, Oregon, Texas, and Washington.

★8289★ **U.S. Commission on Interstate**
Child Support
1120 Vermont Ave. NW, Ste. 680
Washington, DC 20005
Phone: (202)254-8093
Fax: (202)254-3047
Vernon Drew, Staff Contact

History and Authority: Commission was established under authority of P.L. 100-485, dated October 13, 1988. It is an independent advisory commission. **Description:** Commission was es-

tablished to make recommendation to the U.S. Congress on improving the interstate establishment and enforcement of child support awards and revising the Uniform Reciprocal Enforcement of Support Act.

★8290★ **U.S. Committee for the United**
Nations Fund for Women (UNIFEM)
1730 K St. NW, Ste. 304
Washington, DC 20006
Phone: (202)296-0947
Patricia Hutar, President

Description: Concerned with the development of women in Third World nations.

★8291★ **U.S. Commodity Futures Trading**
Commission
Officer of Personnel
Federal Women's Program
2033 K St. NW
Washington, DC 20581
Phone: (202)254-9531
Mary Pat O'Leary, Manager

★8292★ **U.S. Congressional Caucus for**
Women's Issues
2471 Rayburn House Office Bldg.
Washington, DC 20515
Phone: (202)225-6740
Lesley Primmer, Exec. Dir.

★8293★ **U.S. Consumer Product Safety**
Commission
Office of Equal Opportunity and Minority
Enterprise
Westwood Towers
5401 Westbard Ave.
Bethesda, MD 20816
Phone: (301)504-0570
John W. Barrett, Jr., Director

★8294★ **U.S. Department of Agriculture**
Agricultural Research Service
Equal Opportunity Office
Federal Women's Program
Administration Bldg.
14th St. & Independence Ave. SW
Washington, DC 20250
Phone: (202)720-6161
Anna Grayson, Manager

**★8295★ U.S. Department of Agriculture
Animal and Plant Health Inspection
   Service
Federal Women's Program**
South Agriculture Bldg.
Independence Ave. bet. 12th & 14th Sts.
Washington, DC 20250
Phone: (202)720-6312
Mary Ward, Mgr

**★8296★ U.S. Department of Agriculture
Cooperative State Research Service
Federal Women's Program**
Aerospace Bldg.
901 D St. SW
Washington, DC 20024
Phone: (202)401-6845
Dawn L. Britton, Manager

**★8297★ U.S. Department of Agriculture
Extension Service
Federal Women's Program**
South Agriculture Bldg.
Independence Ave. bet. 12th & 14th Sts.
Washington, DC 20250
Phone: (202)720-8070
Joyce Okpah, Mgr

**★8298★ U.S. Department of Agriculture
Food and Nutrition Service
Civil Rights Division
Federal Women's Program**
Park Office Center
3101 Park Center Dr.
Alexandria, VA 22302
Phone: (703)305-2195
Eunice Bowman, Manager

**★8299★ U.S. Department of Agriculture
Food and Nutrition Service
Supplemental Food Programs Division
National Advisory Council on Maternal,
   Infant and Fetal Nutrition**
3101 Park Center Dr.
Alexandria, VA 22302
Phone: (703)756-3746
Fax: (703)756-3420
Ronald J. Vogel, Executive Secretary

History and Authority: Council was established
September 22, 1976, under authority of Section
17 of the Child Nutrition Act of 1966, as
amended by Public Law 94-105 dated October
7, 1975. It is a public advisory council within the
Food and Nutrition Service. **Description:** Council was established to make a continuing study
of the operation of the Special Supplemental
Food Program for Women, Infants and Children
(WIC) and related programs such as the Commodity Supplemental Food Program (CSFP) to
determine how the programs may be improved.
The WIC and CSFP provide special supplemental foods and nutrition education to low-income
pregnant, breast feeding, postpartum women,
and infants and children who are at nutritional
risk. **Publications:** *Biennial Report on the Special Supplemental Food Program for Women,
Infants and Children and on the Commodity
Supplemental Food Program.*

**★8300★ U.S. Department of Agriculture
Food and Nutrition Service
Supplemental Food Programs Division
Special Supplemental Food Program for
   Women, Infants, and Children (WIC
   Program)**
Park Office Center
3101 Park Center Dr.
Alexandria, VA 22302
Phone: (703)756-2746

Description: Provides specific types of nutritious food to pregnant and nursing women and
to children up to five years of age who are
nutritionally deprived.

**★8301★ U.S. Department of Agriculture
Food Safety and Inspection Service
Federal Women's Program**
Annex Bldg.
300 12th St. SW
Washington, DC 20250
Phone: (202)205-0285
Marquerita Moody, Mgr

**★8302★ U.S. Department of Agriculture
Foreign Agriculture Service
Federal Women's Program**
South Agriculture Bldg.
Independence Ave. bet. 12th & 14th Sts.
Washington, DC 20250
Phone: (202)720-9335
Karlene Saenz, Mgr.

**★8303★ U.S. Department of Agriculture
Soil Conservation Service
Equal Opportunity Branch
Federal Women's Program**
South Agriculture Bldg.
Independence Ave. bet. 12th & 14th Sts.
Washington, DC 20250
Phone: (202)720-1710
Sandra Burgess, Manager

**★8304★ U.S. Department of the Air Force
Manpower, Reserve Affairs, Installations,
   and Environment
Equal Opportunity Agency**
Crystal Square Bldg. 4
1745 Jefferson Davis Hwy.
Arlington, VA 22202
Phone: (703)746-6992
Deputy Dora Alcala, Contact

**★8305★ U.S. Department of the Army
Manpower and Reserve Affairs
Equal Employment Opportunity Agency
Federal Women's Program**
Crystal Mall, No. 4
1941 Jefferson Davis Hwy.
Arlington, VA 20360
Phone: (703)607-1976
June Hajjar, Director

**★8306★ U.S. Department of Commerce
Office of Small and Disadvantaged
   Business Utilization
Women's Small Business Specialist**
14 and Constitution Ave. NW
Washington, DC 20230
Phone: (202)377-1472
Rosemary Mullany, Contact

**★8307★ U.S. Department of Defense
Administration and Management
   Washington Headquarters Services
Federal Women's Program**
400 Army Navy Dr.
Arlington, VA 22202
Phone: (703)693-1096
Valerie B. Mohn, Manager

**★8308★ U.S. Department of Defense
Defense Advisory Committee on Women in
   the Services and Military Women
   Matters (DACOWITS)**
The Pentagon
Washington, DC 20301
Phone: (703)697-2122
Lt. Col. M.C. Pruitt, Director

History and Authority: Committee was established in September 1951 by the Secretary of
Defense. It is a public advisory committee of the
Office of the Secretary, Department of Defense,
and operates under the provisions of DoD
Directive 5120.14. **Description:** Committee was
established to provide the Secretary of Defense
with assistance and advice on matters relating
to women in the services, to interpret to the
public the need for and the role of women in the
services, and to encourage the acceptance of
military service as a career opportunity for
qualified women.

**★8309★ U.S. Department of Defense
Defense Information Systems Agency
Federal Women's Program**
701 S. Courthouse Rd.
Arlington, VA 22204-2199
Phone: (703)692-0042
O. Homphrey, Mgr

**★8310★ U.S. Department of Defense
Defense Investigative Service
Federal Women's Program**
1900 Half St. SW
Washington, DC 20324
Phone: (202)475-0966
Stephanie Meise, Mgr

**★8311★ U.S. Department of Education
Office of the General Counsel
Educational Equity Division**
400 Maryland Ave. SW
Washington, DC 20202
Phone: (202)401-2666
Susan Craig, Contact

**★8312★ U.S. Department of Education
Women's Educational Equity Act Program**
400 Maryland Ave. SW, Rm. 2049
Washington, DC 20002
Phone: (202)401-1342
Alice Ford, Program Specialist

Description: Designed to provide educational
equity for women in the U.S. Awards funds to
individuals and non-profit organizations to develop and test model programs for local education agents in meeting requirements of Title IX;
educational programs to increase involvement
of women in math and science; improve educational opportunities for economically disadvantaged women; and programs for women discriminated against on the basis of race, sex,
ethnic origin, age, or disability.

**★8313★ U.S. Department of Health and
   Human Services
Alcohol, Drug Abuse, and Mental Health
   Administration
Federal Women's Program**
Parklawn Bldg.
5600 Fishers Ln.
Rockville, MD 20857
Phone: (301)443-4447
Anne Ambler, Manager

★8314★ **U.S. Department of Health and Human Services**
Alcohol, Drug Abuse, and Mental Health Administration
National Institute on Drug Abuse
Women and Drugs Section
5600 Fishers Ln.
Rockville, MD 20857
Phone: (301)443-6720
Gloria Weisman, Contact

★8315★ **U.S. Department of Health and Human Services**
Alcohol, Drug Abuse, and Mental Health Administration
National Institute of Mental Health
National Center for the Prevention and Control of Rape
5600 Fishers Ln., Rm. 6-C-12
Rockville, MD 20857
Phone: (301)443-3728
Eunice Raigrodski, Technical Information

★8316★ **U.S. Department of Health and Human Services**
Alcohol, Drug Abuse, and Mental Health Administration
National Institute of Mental Health
Violence and Traumatic Stress Review Committee
5600 Fishers Ln.
Rockville, MD 20857
Phone: (301)443-4266
Peggy W. Cockrill, Staff Contact

History and Authority: Committee was established February, 1992, under authority of 42 USC 290aa(j), section 501(j) of the Public Health Service Act, as amended. It is a public advisory committee of the National Institute of Mental Health. **Description:** Committee advises the Administrator, Alcohol, Drug Abuse, and Mental Health Administration, and the Director, National Institute of Mental Health, on scientific and technical merit of applications for research, research training, or research-related grants, cooperative agreements, or contracts relating to the mental health aspects of traumatic stress; criminal, delinquent, and antisocial behavior; individual violent behavior; and sexual assault. Areas included are the nature, source, prevention, and treatment of delinquent, criminal, antisocial, and individual violent behaviors, including violence within the family and sexual assault; the mental health consequences of victimization by such behaviors; and all aspects of post-traumatic stress disorder, and other disorders and adjustment problems resulting from exposure to traumatic events. Committee makes recommendations on applications to the National Advisory Mental Health Council.

★8317★ **U.S. Department of Health and Human Services**
Alcohol, Drug Abuse, and Mental Health Administration
Office of the Administrator
Women's Council
Parklawn Bldg.
5600 Fishers Ln.
Rockville, MD 20857
Phone: (301)443-4447
Dorothy H. Ragsdale, Staff Contact

History and Authority: Council was originally established in 1971 as the NIMH Women's Council; name changed in 1973. It is an internal council of the Alcohol, Drug Abuse, and Mental Health Administration (ADAMHA). **Description:** Council directs its activities toward matters concerning women that are internal to the Alcohol, Drug Abuse, and Mental Health Administration and its Institutes, and matters related to women's concerns over alcohol, drug abuse, and mental health. It addresses such issues as employment status for women within the ADAMHA; the role of women in agency policymaking; child care; sexist language; communication between women and management; and prevention of sexual harassment. **Publications:** *ADAMHA Women's Council: Report to the Administrator*, annual.

★8318★ **U.S. Department of Health and Human Services**
Alcohol, Drug Abuse, and Mental Health Administration
Office for Substance Abuse Prevention
Pregnant and Postpartum Women and Infants Review Committee
Rockwall 2 Bldg., 6th Fl.
5600 Fishers Ln.
Rockville, MD 20857
Phone: (301)443-4783
Elizabeth A. Breckinridge, Exec. Sec.

History and Authority: Committee was established April 9, 1990, by the Administrator, Alcohol, Drug Abuse, and Mental Health Administration, under authority of Section 501(j) of the Public Health Service Act, as amended. It is a public advisory committee of the office for Substance Abuse Prevention. **Description:** Committee reviews applications that focus on the prevention, treatment, and rehabilitation of drug, alcohol, and tobacco use in the target populations of pregnant and postpartum women and their infants. It advises the Alcohol, Drug Abuse, and Mental Health Administrator and the Director, Office for Substance Abuse Prevention, on the technical merit of demonstration grant applications, cooperative agreements, and contract proposals that address the areas of primary prevention and early intervention. Committee makes recommendations on applications to the Advisory Committee on Substance Abuse.

★8319★ **U.S. Department of Health and Human Services**
Centers for Disease Control
National Center for Chronic Disease Prevention and Health Promotion
Reproductive Health Division
Rhodes Bldg., Koger Center
2858 Woodcock Blvd.
Atlanta, GA 30333
Phone: (404)488-5191
Carol J. Hogue, Director

★8320★ **U.S. Department of Health and Human Services**
Food and Drug Administration
Center for Devices and Radiological Health
Obstetrics-Gynecology Devices Panel
1390 Piccard Dr.
Rockville, MD 20850-4332
Phone: (301)427-1186
Patsy Trisler, Staff Contact

History and Authority: Panel was established September 17, 1982, when the Obstetrics-Gynecology and Radiologic Devices Panel split into the Obstetrics-Gynecology Devices Panel and the Radiologic Devices Panel. It was a public advisory panel of Center for Devices and Radiological Health, and a subpanel of the Medical Devices Advisory Committee. **Description:** Panel reviews and evaluates available data on the safety and effectiveness of obstetrics-gynecology devices currently in use and makes recommendations for their classification.

★8321★ **U.S. Department of Health and Human Services**
Food and Drug Administration
Center for Drug Evaluation and Research
Fertility and Maternal Health Drugs Advisory Committee
5600 Fishers Ln.
Rockville, MD 20857
Phone: (301)443-3511
Fax: (301)443-9282
Philip A. Corfman, M.D., Designated Federal Employee

History and Authority: Committee was originally established August 31, 1965, as the Obstetrics and Gynecology Advisory Committee; name changed in 1978. It is a public advisory committee of the Center for Drug Evaluation and Research. **Description:** Committee reviews and evaluates available data concerning safety and effectiveness of marketed and investigational human drug products for use in the practice of obstetrics, gynecology, and contraception. **Publications:** *Second Report on the Oral Contraceptives* (1969) and *FDA Report on the Oral Contraceptives* (1966).

★8322★ **U.S. Department of Health and Human Services**
Food and Drug Administration
Federal Women's Program
Parklawn Bldg.
5600 Fishers Ln.
Rockville, MD 20857
Phone: (301)443-3310
Cynthia A. Barnes, Manager

★8323★ **U.S. Department of Health and Human Services**
Food and Drug Administration
Office of Consumer Affairs
Advisory Group on Women's Health Issues
Parklawn Bldg.
5600 Fishers Ln.
Rockville, MD 20857
Patricia M. Kuntze, Staff Contact

History and Authority: Group was established in 1983 as an internal advisory group of the Food and Drug Administration. **Description:** Group identifies and advises the Food and Drug Commission on areas of specific concern relative to the health of women. It also assesses research, identifies new programs that are needed, and serves as a link with members of the FDA Policy Board to assure that issues relating to women's health are considered in decisions made by the Food and Drug Administration. **Remarks:** Group was responsible for planning the Special Topic Conference on Osteoporosis held October 30, 1987.

★8324★ **U.S. Department of Health and Human Services**
Health Resources and Services Administration
Maternal and Child Health Bureau
Parklawn Bldg.
5600 Fishers Ln.
Rockville, MD 20857
Phone: (301)443-2170
Audrey Nora, Actg. Dir.

★8325★ U.S. Department of Health and
Human Services
Health Resources and Services
Administration
Maternal and Child Health Bureau
Maternal and Child Health Research
Grants Review Committee
Parklawn Bldg.
5600 Fishers Ln.
Rockville, MD 20857
Phone: (301)443-2190
Gontran Lamberty, Designated Federal
Employee

History and Authority: Committee was originally established by the Commissioner of the
Welfare Administration in 1964 under provisions
of Section 114(f) of the Social Security Act, as
the Maternal and Child Health and Crippled
Children's Services Research Grants Advisory
Group; transferred under the Secretary's Reorganization Order of April 1, 1968, to the Health
Services and Mental Health Administration;
name changed to the Maternal and Child Health
Service Research Grants Review Committee in
1972; name changed to current name in 1974. It
is a public advisory committee of the Maternal
and Child Health Bureau. **Description:** Committee provides advice to the Director of the
Bureau of Community Health Services on research grants in the field of maternal and child
health and reviews applications for grants to
improve the operation, functioning, and general
usefulness and effectiveness of maternal and
child health services of all kinds by providing
financial support for studies that contribute to
the advancement of health services for mothers
and children.

★8326★ U.S. Department of Health and
Human Services
Health Resources and Services
Administration
Maternal and Child Health Bureau
National Center for Education in Maternal
and Child Health (NCEMCH)
2000 15th St. N., Ste. 701
Arlington, VA 22201
Phone: (703)524-7802
Dr. Rochelle Mayer, Ed.D, Program Director

Founded: 1982. **Description:** NCEMCH is a
national resource which provides information
and educational services, as well as technical
assistance to organizations, agencies, and individuals with maternal and child health interests.
The Center links maternal and child health
professionals, practitioners, administrators, educators, and the lay public to sources of MCH-
related information and services and supports
their efforts to improve health care of mothers,
children, and families. Subject areas covered by
the Center include maternal health, infant
health, child health, adolescent health, children
with special health care needs, and maternal
and child health services and programs. The
Center provides information and educational
services, as well as technical assistance, to
organizations, agencies, and individuals with
maternal and child health interests. Information
responses include providing educational materials, and making referrals to voluntary and
professional organizations, service providers,
support groups, and federal or state agencies.
Publications: Numerous bibliographies, directories, proceedings, booklets, brochures, resource guides, and other informational and
educational materials are available from the
Center. Publications are listed in the *Maternal
and Child Health Publications Catalog.* Topics

include maternal, infant, child and adolescent
health, children with special health care needs,
and maternal and child health services and
programs. Directories include *Reaching Out: A
Directory of National Maternal and Child Health;*
and *Starting Early: A Guide to Federal Resources in Maternal and Child Health.* While
most are written in English, some publications
are available in Spanish, Chinese, Korean, Lao,
Tagalog, and Vietnamese. Most publications
distributed by the Center are available in limited
quantities at no cost, but others are for sale.
Remarks: The Center is funded by the Bureau
of Maternal and Child Health, U.S. Department
of Health and Human Services, and is affiliated
with the Department of Obstetrics and Gynecology at the Georgetown University School of
Medicine. NCEMCH is the sister organization to
the National Maternal and Child Health Clearinghouse.

★8327★ U.S. Department of Health and
Human Services
Health Resources and Services
Administration
Maternal and Child Health Bureau
National Maternal and Child Health
Clearinghouse (NMCHC)
8201 Greensboro Dr., Ste. 600
McLean, VA 22102
Phone: (703)821-8955
Linda Cramer, Executive Director

Description: NMCHC is the sister organization
of the National Center for Education in Maternal
and Child Health (NCEMCH)(see separate entry). It is funded by the Bureau of Maternal and
Child Health and Resources Development, U.S.
Department of Health and Human Services. The
Clearinghouse provides current information
through the collection and dissemination of
publications on maternal and child health topics.
The Clearinghouse's resources are used in
responding to requests, providing technical
assistance, and developing publications. When
a request cannot be answered by sending
publications from the Clearinghouse, it is referred to the National Center for Education in
Maternal and Child Health which responds with
appropriate information from its reference collection. This may include copies of educational
materials, bibliographies, and referral to national
and local sources for further information. **Publications:** Each month NMCHC distributes more
than 50,000 publications to over 2,000 reques-
ters. Clearinghouse maintains a large inventory
of publications on a wide range of maternal and
child health topics and makes them available to
the public through its publications catalog. Most
of the publications are produced by the Bureau
of Maternal and Child Health, the National
Center for Clinical Infant Programs, or the
Healthy Mothers, Healthy Babies Coalition.
Some publications from other sources are also
available. Most publications are in English, with
some in Spanish, Chinese, Korean, Lao, Tagalog, and Vietnamese. Most publications distributed by the Clearinghouse are available in
limited quantities at no cost. In addition,
NCEMCH has developed resource guides for
health care providers and educators on various
maternal health topics. The resource guide
provides a selected annotated bibliography and
a descriptive listing of sources of additional
information (organizations, programs, services)
related to the topic. Consumer-oriented titles
inclue: *Healthy Food, Healthy Baby; Nutrition
and Your Health-Dietary Guidelines for Americans*; and *Infant Care.* The following resource
guides are available from NMCHC: *Adolescent

Pregnancy Resource Guide; Careers in Human
Genetics Resource Guide; Children with Special
Health Needs Resource Guide; Environmental
Exposures and Pregnancy Resource Guide;
Genetic Counseling and Cytogenetic Technolo-
gy Resource Guide; Human Genetics—A Guide
to Educational Resources; Organizing Self-Help
Groups Resource Guide; Prenatal Care Re-
source Guide,* and *Preterm and Low Birth-
weight Infants Resource Guide.*

★8328★ U.S. Department of Health and
Human Services
Health Resources and Services
Administration
Office of Equal Opportunity and Civil
Rights
Federal Women's Program
Parklawn Bldg.
5600 Fishers Ln.
Rockville, MD 20857
Phone: (301)443-6824
Gladys Maquardt, Manager

★8329★ U.S. Department of Health and
Human Services
Indian Health Service
Federal Women's Program
Parklawn Bldg.
5600 Fishers Ln.
Rockville, MD 20857
Phone: (301)443-2700
Cecelia Heftel, Coordinator

★8330★ U.S. Department of Health and
Human Services
National Institutes of Health
National Institute of Child Health and
Human Development
Center for Research for Mothers and
Children
Executive Plaza N.
6130 Executive Blvd.
Rockville, MD 20852
Phone: (301)496-5097
Sumner J. Yaffe, Director

★8331★ U.S. Department of Health and
Human Services
National Institutes of Health
National Institute of Child Health and
Human Development
Maternal and Child Health Research
Committee
Scientific Review Program
Bethesda, MD 20892
Phone: (301)496-1696
Scott F. Andres, Ph.D., Executive Secretary

History and Authority: Committee was originally established June 30, 1965, as the Child
Development and Mental Retardation Training
Review Committee under authority of Section
222 of the Public Health Service Act, as amended; name changed to Growth and Development
Research and Training Committee, November
30, 1969; merged with the Perinatal Biology and
Infant Mortality Research and Training Committee, June 30, 1973, and name changed. It is a
public advisory committee of the Scientific
Review Program, National Institute of Child
Health and Human Development. **Description:**
Committee advises the Director, National Institutes of Health, and the Director, National
Institute of Child Health and Human Development, concerning research in pregnancy, infancy, developmental biology, nutrition, genetics,
human learning, and behavior. It reviews applications for program project grants, perinatal
emphasis research center grants, and national

research service awards relating to research and manpower in the fields of pregnancy, infancy, developmental biology, nutrition, and human learning, and behavior, and makes recommendations to the National Advisory Child Health and Human Development Council. Committee is also responsible for concept clearance review of contract projects in the Endocrinology, Nutrition, and Growth Branch, Pregnancy and Perinatology Branch, Genetics and Teratology Branch, and Human Learning and Behavior Branch of the Center for Research for Mothers and Children.

★8332★ U.S. Department of Health and Human Services
National Institutes of Health
National Institute of Child Health and Human Development
Office of Research Reporting
Bldg. 31, Rm. 2A-32
9000 Rockville Pike
Bethesda, MD 20205
Phone: (301)496-5133
Michaela P. Richardson, Chief

Description: The Institute conducts and supports basic and clinical research in maternal and child health, and the population sciences. The Office responds to individual inquiries concerning child health and human development, including reproductive biology and contraception, fertility and infertility, developmental biology and nutrition, mental retardation, and developmental disabilities. **Publications:** Consumer materials are available on anorexia nervosa, Cesarean childbirth, Down syndrome, oral contraception, precocious puberty, premature birth, pregnancy, smoking and pregnancy, vasectomy, childhood hyperactivity, dyslexia, learning disabilities, maternal health, and child health. A publications list is available.

★8333★ U.S. Department of Health and Human Services
National Institutes of Health
National Institute of General Medical Sciences
Coordinating Committee on Women's Health Issues
9000 Rockville Pike
Bethesda, MD 20892
Dr. Ruth L. Kirschstein, Staff Contact

History and Authority: Committee was originally established in April 1983 as the Public Health Service Task Force on Women's Health Issues; name changed after October 1985. It is an internal committee of the Public Health Service, Department of Health and Human Services. **Description:** Committee was established to assure that the health needs of women throughout the nation are effectively addressed and to make recommendations on the status of women's health in the United States. Currently, the Committee is studying issues related to AIDS in women. **Remarks:** Committee, with the Food and Drug Administration, cosponsored the National Conference on Women's Health, June 17-18, 1987.

★8334★ U.S. Department of Health and Human Services
National Institutes of Health
Office of Disease Prevention
Scientific and Technical Committee on Women's Health Initiatives
9000 Rockville Pike
Bethesda, MD 20892
Phone: (301)496-1058
Dr. William Harlan, Staff Contact

Committee is an internal committee under the National Institutes of Health.

★8335★ U.S. Department of Health and Human Services
National Institutes of Health
Office of Equal Opportunity
Federal Women's Program
9000 Rockville Pike
Bethesda, MD 20892
Phone: (301)496-6301
Lucretia Coffer, Manager

★8336★ U.S. Department of Health and Human Services
National Institutes of Health
Office of Research on Women's Health
9000 Rockville Pike
Bethesda, MD 20892
Phone: (301)402-1770
Vivian W. Pinn, Dir.

★8337★ U.S. Department of Health and Human Services
National Institutes of Health
Task Force on Opportunities for Research on Women's Health
9000 Rockville Pike
Bethesda, MD 20892

Description: Task Force is a subcommittee of the Advisory Committee to the Director, National Institutes of Health. Task Force convened a Workshop on Opportunities for Research on Women's Health, Sepetmber 4-6, 1991.

★8338★ U.S. Department of Health and Human Services
Office of the Assistant Secretary for Health
Office on Women's Health
Hubert H. Humphrey Bldg.
200 Independence Ave. SW
Washington, DC 20201
Phone: (202)690-7650
Agnes Donahue, Director

★8339★ U.S. Department of Health and Human Services
Office of Family Planning
Family Life Information Exchange
PO Box 37299
Washington, DC 20013-7299
Phone: (301)585-6636

Founded: 1976. **Description:** Originally established as the National Clearinghouse for Family Planning Information. Objective is to provide information primarily to federally-funded family planning clinics, with some information available to the general public. The facility collects and distributes materials on family planning, adoption, and adolescent pregnancy, and makes referrals to other information centers. **Publications:** Produces newsletters, directories, fact sheets, monographs, bibliographies, pamphlets, and consumer materials including *The Adoption Option: Many Teens are Saying "NO" (Muchos Jovenes Estan Diciendo "NO"); Public Health Services Guidelines/Prevent HIV and AIDS;*

Teenage Pregnancy and Fertility in the US; AIDS Education, Counseling and Testing in Title X; Family and Adolescent Pregnancy; Contraceptive Choices For Now, For Later, and a mailing list of family planning grantees and clinics supported by the Office of Family Planning. A publications list is available.

★8340★ U.S. Department of Health and Human Services
Office of the Surgeon General
Panel on Women, Adolescents and Children with HIV Infection and AIDS
Working Group on Pediatric AIDS
200 Independence Ave. SW
Washington, DC 20201
Phone: (202)472-4248
Winniford Frable, Staff Contact

History and Authority: Group was established in February 1988 by Secretary of Health and Human Services. **Description:** Group makes recommendations on pediatric AIDS to the Secretary of Health and Human Services.

★8341★ U.S. Department of Health and Human Services
Public Health Service
Agency for Health Care Policy and Research
Cesarian Section Patient Outcome Research Advisory Committee
6001 Montrose Rd., Ste. 704
Rockville, MD 20852
Steve Fox, Staff Contact

History and Authority: Committee was established in 1990 and is a public advisory committee of the Agency for Health Care Policy and Research, Department of Health and Human Services.

★8342★ U.S. Department of Health and Human Services
Public Health Service
Agency for Health Care Policy and Research
Panel on Development of Guidelines on Quality Determinants of Mammography
Off. of Forum for Quality and Effectiveness in Health Care
5600 Fishers Ln., Rm. 18-A-46
Rockville, MD 20857
Phone: (301)227-6671
Stephen H. King, M.D., Staff Contact

History and Authority: Panel was established in 1991 under authority of P.L. 101-239, the Omnibus Budget Reconciliation Act of 1989. It is a public advisory panel of the Office of the Forum for Quality and Effectiveness in Health Care. **Description:** Panel was established to develop, periodically review, and update clinical practice guidelines for the quality determinants of mammography. Panel will address the attributes of clinical practice, equipment, and personnel to ensure the highest quality of mammography. The guidelines will be used by physicians, educators, other health care practitioners, and consumers to assist in determining how diseases, disorders, and other health conditions can most effectively and appropriately be prevented, diagnosed, treated, and managed clinically.

★8343★ U.S. Department of Health and Human Services
Task Force on Women, Children, and AIDS
370 L'Enfant Promenade SW
Washington, DC 20447
Phone: (202)619-0257

★8344★ U.S. Department of Justice
Special Counsel for Sex Discrimination Litigation
10th and Pennsylvania Ave., Rm. 574
Washington, DC 20530
Phone: (202)633-4701

★8345★ U.S. Department of Labor
Women's Bureau
Frances Perkins Bldg.
200 Constitution Ave. NW
Washington, DC 20210
Phone: (202)523-6611
Elsie V. Vartanian, Director

Description: The Women's Bureau is responsible for formulating standards and policies that promote the welfare of wage earning women, improve their working conditions, increase their efficiency, and advance their opportunities for profitable employment.

★8346★ U.S. Department of Labor
Women's Bureau
Network on Female Offenders
3535 Market St.
Philadelphia, PA 19104
Phone: (215)596-1183
Hellen E. Sherwood, Regional Administrator

Description: Serves as a forum for advocates, practitioners, and researchers interested in female offender issues. Programs include panels on battered women and prison.

★8347★ U.S. Department of Labor
Women's Bureau
Region I, Boston
1 Congress St.
Boston, MA 02114
Phone: (617)565-1988
Martha Izzi, Regional Adm.

Territory Includes: Connecticut, Maine, Massachusetts, New Hampshire, Rhode Island, and Vermont.

★8348★ U.S. Department of Labor
Women's Bureau
Region II, New York
201 Varick St.
New York, NY 10014
Phone: (212)337-2389
Mary Murphree, Regional Adm.

Territory Includes: New Jersey, New York, Puerto Rico, and the Virgin Islands.

★8349★ U.S. Department of Labor
Women's Bureau
Region III, Philadelphia
Gateway Bldg.
3535 Market St.
Philadelphia, PA 13280
Phone: (215)596-1183
Helen Sherwood, Regional Adm.

Territory Includes: Delaware, District of Columbia, Maryland, Pennsylvania, Virginia, and West Virginia.

★8350★ U.S. Department of Labor
Women's Bureau
Region IV, Atlanta
1371 Peachtree St. NE
Atlanta, GA 30367
Phone: (404)347-4461
Delores Crockett, Regional Adm.

Territory Includes: Alabama, Florida, Georgia, Kentucky, Mississippi, North Carolina, South Carolina, and Tennessee.

★8351★ U.S. Department of Labor
Women's Bureau
Region V, Illinois
J.C. Kluczynski Federal Bldg.
230 S. Dearborn St.
Chicago, IL 60604
Phone: (312)353-6985
Sandra Frank, Regional Adm.

Territory Includes: Illinois, Indiana, Michigan, Minnesota, Ohio, and Wisconsin.

★8352★ U.S. Department of Labor
Women's Bureau
Region VI, Dallas
525 Griffin St.
Dallas, TX 75202
Phone: (214)767-6985
Evelyn Smith, Regional Adm.

Territory Includes: Arkansas, Louisiana, New Mexico, Oklahoma, and Texas.

★8353★ U.S. Department of Labor
Women's Bureau
Region VII, Kansas City
Federal Bldg.
911 Walnut St.
Kansas City, MO 64106
Phone: (816)426-6108
Rose Kemp, Regional Adm.

Territory Includes: Iowa, Kansas, Missouri, and Nebraska.

★8354★ U.S. Department of Labor
Women's Bureau
Region VIII, Denver
Federal Bldg.
1961 Stout St.
Denver, CO 80294
Phone: (303)844-4138
Oleta Crain, Regional Adm.

Territory Includes: Colorado, Montana, North Dakota, South Dakota, Utah, and Wyoming.

★8355★ U.S. Department of Labor
Women's Bureau
Region IX, San Francisco
71 Stevenson St.
San Francisco, CA 94105
Phone: (415)744-6678
Madeline Mixer, Regional Adm.

Territory Includes: Arizona, California, Guam, Hawaii, Nevada, and the Trust Territory of the Pacific Islands.

★8356★ U.S. Department of Labor
Women's Bureau
Region X, Seattle
1111 3rd Ave.
Seattle, WA 98101
Phone: (206)553-1534
Lazelle S. Johnson, Regional Adm.

Territory Includes: Alaska, Idaho, Oregon, and Washington.

★8357★ U.S. Department of Labor
Women's Bureau
Task Force on Women in Apprenticeships
200 Constitution Ave. NW
Washington, DC 20210
Phone: (202)523-8913
Alina Walker, Contact

★8358★ U.S. Department of Labor
Women's Bureau
Work and Family Clearinghouse
200 Constitution Ave. NW
Washington, DC 20210
Phone: (202)523-4486
Toll-free: 800-827-5335
Alina Walker, Dir.

Description: The Clearinghouse is an information center of the U.S. Department of Labor that disseminates materials on the establishment of dependent child care programs within corporations. Online searches, 800 accessibility, CIJE article delivery, and referrals are offered by the Clearinghouse. It also provides information on child welfare, child care, corporate support, and day care as related to establishing these programs within corporations. **Publications:** Directories, fact sheets, and monographs.

★8359★ U.S. Department of the Navy
Bureau of Naval Personnel
Women in the Navy
Columbia Pike & Southgate Rd.
Arlington Annex
Arlington, VA 20370
Phone: (703)695-9385
Captain Martha Whitehead, Contact

★8360★ U.S. Department of State
Bureau of International Organizational Affairs
Human Rights and Women's Affairs
2201 C St. NW
Washington, DC 20520-6319
Phone: (202)647-1534
Charlotte Ponticelli, Contact

★8361★ U.S. Department of State
Bureau of International Organizational Affairs
Human Rights and Women's Affairs
International Women's Programs
21st and C Streets NW
Washington, DC 20520
Phone: (202)647-1155
Sharon B. Kotok, Contact

★8362★ U.S. Department of Transportation
Federal Aviation Administration
Office for Civil Rights
Federal Women's Program
800 Independence Ave. SW
Washington, DC 20591
Phone: (202)267-3259

★8363★ U.S. Department of Transportation
Federal Highway Administration
Office of Civil Rights
Federal Women's Program
400 7th St. SW
Washington, DC 20590
Phone: (202)366-1596
Nancy H. Johnson, Manager

★8364★ U.S. Department of Transportation
Federal Railroad Administration
Office of Civil Rights
Federal Women's Program
400 7th St. SW
Washington, DC 20590
Phone: (202)366-0482
Elsie M. Just-Buddy, Manager

★8365★ U.S. Department of Transportation
National Highway Traffic Safety
  Administration
Office of Civil Rights
Federal Women's Program
400 7th St. SW
Washington, DC 20590
Phone: (202)366-0972
Ann Mitchell, Manager

★8366★ U.S. Department of Transportation
Office of the Deputy Secretary
Office of Civil Rights
Departmental Federal Women's Program
400 7th St. SW
Washington, DC 20590
Phone: (202)366-9367
Ella L. Graham, Manager

★8367★ U.S. Department of the Treasury
Internal Revenue Service
Affirmative Action Section
Federal Women's Program
1111 Constitution Ave. NW
Washington, DC 20224
Phone: (202)566-6416
Nicole Scheffer, Manager

★8368★ U.S. Department of the Treasury
United States Customs Service
Office of the Commissioner
Federal Women's Program
1301 Constitution Ave. NW
Washington, DC 20229
Phone: (202)927-0210
Wantalee Mayfield, Manager

★8369★ U.S. Department of Veterans
Affairs
Advisory Committee on Women Veterans
810 Vermont Ave. NW
Washington, DC 20420
Phone: (202)233-2621
Susan H. Mather, M.D., Designated Federal
Employee
History and Authority: Committee was established April 29, 1983, by the Secretary, Department of Veterans Affairs, under P.L. 98-160. It
is a public advisory committee of the Department of Veterans Affairs. **Description:** Committee reviews existing information, renders advisory opinions, and makes recommendations to
the VA Secretary's staff concerning the needs
of women veterans with respect to health care,
rehabilitation benefits, compensation, outreach
programs, and other programs administered by
the VA.

★8370★ U.S. Department of Veterans
Affairs
Assistant Secretary for Human Resources
and Administration
Affirmative Employment Service
Federal Women's Program
McPherson Sq. Bldg.
1425 K St. NW
Washington, DC 20005
Phone: (202)233-3136
Alice E. Bell, Manager

★8371★ U.S. Department of Veterans
Affairs
Veterans Health Administration
Women Veterans Program
810 Vermont Ave. NW
Washington, DC 20420
Phone: (202)535-7182
Barbara Brandau, Coordinator

★8372★ U.S. Environmental Protection
Agency
Office of Civil Rights
National Federal Women's Program
401 M St. SW
Washington, DC 20460
Phone: (202)260-4585
Barbara Gary, Mgr

★8373★ U.S. Equal Employment
Opportunity Commission
1801 L St., NW
Washington, DC 20507
Phone: (202)663-4001
Evan Kemp, Jr., Chairman
Description: The Commission's purpose is to
eliminate discrimination based on race, color,
religion, sex, national origin, or age in hiring,
promoting, firing, wages, testing, training, ap-
prenticeship, and all other conditions and terms,
to make equal employment opportunity an
actuality. The Commission is responsible for all
compliance and enforcement activities relating
to equal employment opportunity among federal
employees and applicants, including handicapped discrimination. The Commission en-
forces the Age Discrimination in Employment
Act of 1967; Title VII of the Civil Rights Act of
1964; the Equal Pay Act of 1963; and in the
federal sector only, Section 501 of the Rehabilitation Act of 1963.

★8374★ U.S. Equal Employment
Opportunity Commission
Atlanta District Office
75 Piedmont Ave., NE
Atlanta, GA 30335
Phone: (404)331-6093
Chris Roggerson, Director
Territory Includes: Georgia.

★8375★ U.S. Equal Employment
Opportunity Commission
Baltimore District Office
111 Market Pl.
Baltimore, MD 21202
Phone: (410)962-3932
Issie L. Jenkins, Director
Territory Includes: Maryland and Virginia.

★8376★ U.S. Equal Employment
Opportunity Commission
Birmingham District Office
1900 3rd Ave., N.
Birmingham, AL 35203
Phone: (205)731-0083
Warren A. Bullock, Director
Territory Includes: Alabama and Mississippi.

★8377★ U.S. Equal Employment
Opportunity Commission
Charlotte District Office
5500 Central Ave.
Charlotte, NC 28212
Phone: (704)567-7100
Marsha Drane, Director
Territory Includes: North Carolina and South
Carolina.

★8378★ U.S. Equal Employment
Opportunity Commission
Chicago District Office
536 S. Clark St.
Chicago, IL 60605
Phone: (312)353-2713
Jack Rowe, Director
Territory Includes: Northern Illinois.

★8379★ U.S. Equal Employment
Opportunity Commission
Cleveland District Office
1375 Euclid Ave.
Cleveland, OH 44115
Phone: (216)522-2001
Harold Ferguson, Director
Territory Includes: Ohio.

★8380★ U.S. Equal Employment
Opportunity Commission
Dallas District Office
8303 Elmbrook Dr.
Dallas, TX 75247
Phone: (214)767-7015
Jacqueline Bradley, Director
Territory Includes: Oklahoma and Northern
Texas.

★8381★ U.S. Equal Employment
Opportunity Commission
Denver District Office
1845 Sherman St.
Denver, CO 80203
Phone: (303)866-1300
Francisco J. Flores, Director
Territory Includes: Colorado, Montana, Ne-
braska, South Dakota, and Wyoming.

★8382★ U.S. Equal Employment
Opportunity Commission
Detroit District Office
477 Michigan Ave.
Detroit, MI 48226
Phone: (313)226-7636
A. William Schukar, Director
Territory Includes: Michigan.

**★8383★ U.S. Equal Employment
Opportunity Commission
Houston District Office**
1919 Smith St.
Houston, TX 77002
Phone: (713)653-3320
Harriet J. Ehrlich, Director

Territory Includes: Central Texas.

**★8384★ U.S. Equal Employment
Opportunity Commission
Indianapolis District Office**
46 E. Ohio St.
Indianapolis, IN 46204
Phone: (317)226-7212
Thomas P. Hadfield, Director

Territory Includes: Indiana and Louisville, Kentucky.

**★8385★ U.S. Equal Employment
Opportunity Commission
Los Angeles District Office**
3660 Wilshire Blvd.
Los Angeles, CA 90010
Phone: (213)251-7278
Dorothy Porter, Director

Territory Includes: Southern California and Nevada.

**★8386★ U.S. Equal Employment
Opportunity Commission
Memphis District Office**
1407 Union Ave.
Memphis, TN 38104
Phone: (901)722-2617
Walter Grabon, Director

Territory Includes: Kentucky (except Louisville) and Tennessee.

**★8387★ U.S. Equal Employment
Opportunity Commission
Miami District Office**
1 NE 1st St.
Miami, FL 33132
Phone: (305)536-4491
Frederico Costales, Director

Territory Includes: Florida and the Panama Canal Zone.

**★8388★ U.S. Equal Employment
Opportunity Commission
Milwaukee District Office**
310 W. Wisconsin Ave.
Milwaukee, WI 53203
Phone: (414)291-1111
Chester V. Bailey, Director

Territory Includes: Iowa, Minnesota, and Wisconsin.

**★8389★ U.S. Equal Employment
Opportunity Commission
New Orleans District Office**
701 Loyola Ave.
New Orleans, LA 70113
Phone: (504)589-2329
Patricia Fields Bivins, Director

Territory Includes: Arkansas and Louisiana.

**★8390★ U.S. Equal Employment
Opportunity Commission
New York District Office**
90 Church St.
New York, NY 10007
Phone: (212)264-7161
Spencer H. Lewis, Jr., Director

Territory Includes: Connecticut, Maine, Massachusetts, New Hampshire, Puerto Rico, Vermont, and the Virgin Islands.

**★8391★ U.S. Equal Employment
Opportunity Commission
Philadelphia District Office**
1421 Cherry St.
Philadelphia, PA 19102
Phone: (215)597-9350
Johnny J. Butler, Director

Territory Includes: Delaware, New Jersey, Pennsylvania, and West Virginia.

**★8392★ U.S. Equal Employment
Opportunity Commission
Phoenix District Office**
4520 N. Central Ave.
Phoenix, AZ 85012
Phone: (602)640-5000
Charles Burtner, Director

Territory Includes: Arizona, New Mexico, and Utah.

**★8393★ U.S. Equal Employment
Opportunity Commission
St. Louis District Office**
625 N. Euclid St.
St. Louis, MO 63108
Phone: (314)425-6523
Lynn Bruner, Director

Territory Includes: Kansas and Missouri.

**★8394★ U.S. Equal Employment
Opportunity Commission
San Antonio District Office**
5410 Fredericksburg Rd.
San Antonio, TX 78229
Phone: (512)229-4810
Pedro Esquivel, Director

Territory Includes: Southern Texas.

**★8395★ U.S. Equal Employment
Opportunity Commission
San Francisco District Office**
901 Market St.
San Francisco, CA 94103
Phone: (415)744-6500
Paula Montanez, Director

Territory Includes: American Samoa, Northern California, the Commonwealth of the Northern Mariana Islands, Guam, Hawaii, and Wake Island.

**★8396★ U.S. Equal Employment
Opportunity Commission
Seattle District Office**
2815 2nd Ave.
Seattle, WA 98121
Phone: (206)553-0968
Jeanette Leino, Director

Territory Includes: Alaska, Idaho, Oregon, and Washington.

**★8397★ U.S. Equal Employment
Opportunity Commission
Washington Field Office**
1400 L St., NW
Washington, DC 20005
Phone: (202)275-6365
Susan Reilly, Director

Territory Includes: District of Columbia.

**★8398★ U.S. Federal Deposit Insurance
Corporation
Office of Equal Opportunity
Minority and Women Outreach Program**
550 17th St. NW
Washington, DC 20429
Phone: (202)898-6742
Paul Barnes, Manager

**★8399★ U.S. House of Representatives
Judiciary Committee
Subcommittee on Civil and Constitutional
Rights**
806 O'Neill Bldg.
Washington, DC 20515
Phone: (202)226-7680

**★8400★ U.S. House of Representatives
Select Committee on Aging
Task Force on Social Security and Women**
Washington, DC 20515
Phone: (202)225-5871
Scott Frey, Contact

Description: Concerned with retirement income as it related to women.

**★8401★ U.S. Information Agency
Office of Equal Employment Opportunity
and Civil Rights
Federal Women's Program**
301 4th St. SW
Washington, DC 20547
Phone: (202)619-5151
Debbie A. Young, Director

**★8402★ U.S. International Development
Cooperation Agency
U.S. Agency for International Development
Women in Development Office**
320 21st St. NW
Washington, DC 20523
Phone: (703)875-4411

Description: Regulates economic assistance to women in Third World nations. Maintains a resource center on women's roles in economic development, which includes a library available to the public on women in development.

**★8403★ U.S. Marine Corps Headquarters
Administration and Resource Management
Division
Equal Employment Opportunity Office**
Columbia Pike and Southgate Rd.
Arlington Annex
Arlington, VA 22204
Phone: (703)614-2046
Linda Jones, Contact

**★8404★ U.S. National Aeronautics and
Space Administration
Office of Equal Opportunity Programs
Federal Women's Program**
400 Maryland Ave. SW
Washington, DC 20546
Phone: (202)453-2174
Maureen M. Yagodka, Manager

★8405★ **U.S. Nuclear Regulatory Commission**
Office of Small and Disadvantaged Business Utilization/Civil Rights
Civil Rights Program
Federal Women's Program
Maryland National Bank Bldg.
7735 Old Georgetown Rd.
Bethesda, MD 20814
Phone: (301)492-7082
Era Louis Marshall, Manager

★8406★ **U.S. Office of Personnel Management**
Government Wide Federal Women's Program
1900 E. St. NW
Washington, DC 20415
Phone: (202)606-0870
Pat Paige, Program Specialist

Description: Aimed at increasing the employment and advancement of women in the federal government.

★8407★ **U.S. Peace Corps**
Women in Development
1990 K St. NW
Washington, DC 20526
Phone: (202)606-3890
Barbara Ferris, Contact

★8408★ **U.S. Postal Service**
Employee Relations Department
Office of Equal Employment Opportunity
Women's Program
475 L'Enfant Plaza West, SW
Washington, DC 20260
Phone: (202)268-3950
Sheryl McCullough, Manager

★8409★ **U.S. Small Business Administration**
National Women's Business Council
409 3rd St. SW, Ste. 7425
Washington, DC 20416
Phone: (202)205-3850
Fax: (202)205-6825
Wilma Goldstein, Exec. Dir.

History and Authority: Council was established by P.L. 100-533, the Women's Business Ownership Act of 1988, dated October 25, 1988. It is an independent advisory council under the Small Business Administration. **Description:** Council reviews (1) the status of women-owned business nationwide, including progress made and barriers that remain, in order to assist such businesses to enter the mainstream of the American economy; (2) the role of federal, state, and local governments in assisting and promoting aid to, and the promotion of, women-owned business; (3) data collection procedures and the availability of data relating to women-owned businesses, women-owned small businesses, and small businesses owned and controlled by socially and economically disadvantaged women; and (4) government initiatives relating to women-owned business, including those related to federal procurement. Council will make recommendations on new private sector initiatives that will provide management and technical assistance to women-owned small business, ways to promote greater access to public and private sector financing and procurement opportunities for such businesses, and detailed multiyear plans of action, with specific goals and timetables for actions needed to overcome discriminatory barriers to full participation in the economic mainstream.

★8410★ **U.S. Small Business Administration**
Office of Women's Business Ownership
1441 L St. NW
Washington, DC 20416
Phone: (202)205-6673
Lindsey Johnson, Director

Description: The Women's Business Ownership Program was formed to implement a national policy to support women entrepreneurs. The Office develops and coordinates a national program to increase the strength, profitability, and visibility of women-owned businesses while making maximum use of existing government and private-sector resources.

★8411★ **U.S. Task Force on Legal Equity for Women**
Social Security Administration
West High Rise, Rm. 4413
6401 Security Blvd.
Baltimore, MD 21235
Phone: (301)965-4033
Robin E. Fournier, Coordinator

History and Authority: Task Force was established December 21, 1981, by President Reagan, by Executive Order 12336, as amended by Executive Order 12355. It is a presidential advisory task force. **Description:** The Attorney General reviewed federal laws, regulations, policies, and practices which contain language that unjustifiably discriminates on the basis of sex and reported his findings to the President through the Cabinet Council on Legal Policy. Task Force coordinates and facilitates, in their respective agencies, the implementation of changes ordered by the President in sex-discriminatory federal regulations, policies, and practices. **Publications:** *A Survey of the Reagan Administration Accomplishments on Behalf of Women* (September 1984).

(15) Federal Domestic Assistance Programs

Entries in this chapter are arranged alphabetically by agency name. See the User's Guide at the front of this directory for additional information.

**★8412★ National Science Foundation
Directorate for Computer and Information
  Science and Engineering
Engineering Grants**
1800 G St. NW, Rm. 1126e
Washington, DC 20550
Phone: (202)357-9774
Glen Larsen, Contact

Catalog Number: 47.041. **Objectives:** NSF's Directorate for Engineering seeks to promote to progress of engineering and technology, thereby contributing to national prosperity and security through its broad and long-range support of engineering research and education. Overall goals are to: strengthen the engineering science base, which provides the foundation for engineering education, research technological innovation and practice; encourage technological innovation through the support of research in emerging areas; improve the quality of engineering education; provide additional opportunities for minorities, women and the disabled. Areas of research include: chemical Reaction Processes; Interfacial Transport and Separation Processes; Fluid, Particulate and Hydraulic Systems; Thermal Systems; Dynamic Systems and control; Materials Engineering and tribology; Structures; Geomechanics and Bulding Systems; Mechanics and Material; Solid State and Microstructures; Emerging Technologies Initiation; Communication and Computational Systems; Engineering systems; Quatum Electronics, Waves, and Beams; Design and Computer-Integrated Engineering; Manufacturing Processes and Equipment; Operations Research and Product Systems; Bioengineering and Aiding the Disabled; Environmental and Ocean Systems; Earthquake Hazard Mitigation; natural and Man-made Hazard mitigation; Engineering Research Centers; Industry/university Cooperative Research Centers; Engineering Education; Human Resources Development; Physical Infrastructure; Special Studies and Analyses. Support is also provided for undergraduate student research, faculty enhancement, instrumentation, and laboratory improvement; and for research opportunities for women, minority, and disabled scientists and engineers. **Types of Assistance:** Project Grants (Cooperative Agreements). **Applicant Eligibility:** Public and private collegs and universities, nonprofit institutions, profit-making institutions including small businesses, and Federal, State, and local government agencies. The greatest percentage of support (97 percent in fiscal year 1989) goes to academic institutions. Proposals are especially welcome from (1) women, minority, and disabled individuals and (2) cooperative teams invloving universities and the private sector.

Beneficiary Eligibility: Public and private colleges and universities; nonprofit institutions; profit organizations, including small businesses; Federal, State, and local government agencies; and individuals.

**★8413★ National Science Foundation
Division of Human Resource Development
Human Resources Development**
1800 G St. NW
Washington, DC 20550
Phone: (202)357-7552
Joseph G. Danek, Director

Catalog Number: 47.069. **Objectives:** To strengthen the nation's human and institutional resource base for science and engineering; increase opportunities for women, minority, physically disabled investigators, and research faculty from predominantly undergraduate institutions to participate more fully in the nation's scientific and engineering enterprise; and to improve access to scientific and technical resources by institutions that currently underutilize such resources. Programs include: Research Improvement in Minority Institutions (RIMI); Research Careers for Minority Scholars (RCMS); Minority Research Centers of Excellence; Alliances for Minority Participation; Career Access Opportunities; Faculty Awards for Women; and Visiting Professorships for Women (VPW). **Types of Assistance:** Project Grants. **Applicant Eligibility:** Programs are open to all U.S. universities and colleges, acting on behalf of their faculty and students. Proposals may be submitted in any field supported by NSF. Those students supported must be members of an underrepresented minority group; U.S. citizens or permanent residents; and enrolled as fulltime undergraduate or graduate students. The Research Improvement in Minority Institutions (RIM) program is open to minority institutions (predominantly minority enrollment or significant enrollment of any one eligible minority) with graduate programs in science or programs in engineering. The Visiting Professorships for Women (VPW) program supports research and teaching activities by women holding doctorates in science or engineering who have independent research experience in academic, industrial, or public sectors. More details on eligibility requirements are included in individual program announcements. **Beneficiary Eligibility:** Minority women, and disabled scientists and engineers; minority institutions; predominantly undergraduate institutions; other public and private colleges and universities.

**★8414★ National Science Foundation
Division of Research Career Development
Young Scholars**
1800 G St. NW
Washington, DC 20550
Phone: (202)357-7538
Virginia J. Eaton, Contact

Catalog Number: 47.072. **Objectives:** To identify secondary school students with high potential/high ability in science, mathematics and/or engineering and to facilitate their making of informed career choices. Participation by minorities, women and the disabled and students from rural areas is strongly encouraged. **Types of Assistance:** Project Grants. **Applicant Eligibility:** Colleges and universities, their association or consortiums, scientific or professional societies with memberships of primarily university faculty or researchers, and for-profit industries and other organizations with significant advanced research activities. There are additional requirements. **Beneficiary Eligibility:** Two-year colleges, four-year colleges, and universities in the United States or its territories; scientific and professional societies; and for-profit industries with significant research activities.

**★8415★ U.S. Commission on Civil Rights
Clearinghouse Services
Civil Rights Discrimination Complaints**
1121 Vermont Ave. NW
Washington, DC 20425
Phone: (202)376-8177

Catalog Number: 29.001. **Objectives:** (1) To serve as a national clearinghouse for information to the public in respect to discrimination or denials of equal protection because of race, color, religion, sex, age, handicap or national origin; to hold public hearings and collect and study information on discrimination or denials of equal protection. (2) To receive and refer complaints alleging denial of civil rights because of the aforementioned factors; to receive, investigate, and refer complaints alleging denial of voting rights. **Types of Assistance:** Dissemination of Technical Information. **Applicant Eligibility:** Anyone can seek information; no criteria must be satisfied. **Beneficiary Eligibility:** General public.

★8416★ U.S. Department of Agriculture
Food and Nutrition Service
Supplemental Food Programs Division
Commodity Supplemental Food Program
Park Office Center
3101 Park Center Dr.
Alexandria, VA 22302
Phone: (703)305-2746
Ronald J. Vogel, Director

Catalog Number: 10.565. **Objectives:** To improve the health and nutritional status of low-income pregnant, postpartum and breastfeeding women, infants, and children up to age of 6, and elderly persons through the donation of supplemental foods. **Types of Assistance:** Sale, Exchange, or Donation of Propery and Goods; Formula Grants. **Applicant Eligibility:** Agreements are made between the Department and the State agency, or an Indian tribe, band, or group recognized by the Department of the Interior for the administration of the program, and between the Department, the State agency, and distributing agency for the distribution of commodities to eligible persons. **Beneficiary Eligibility:** To be certified as eligible to receive supplemental foods, each applicant must be: (a) Categorically eligible as an infant, child up to age 6, pregnant, postpartum or breastfeeding woman, or elderly person 60 years of age or older, residing in an area where the program operates; (b) income eligible under existing Federal, State, or local food, health, or welfare programs for low-income women, infants and children, 130 percent of Federal poverty income guidelines for newly certified elderly persons; and (c), at State agency discretion, at nutritional risk as determined by a competent health professional at the local agency. Not all States offer program benefits to low-income elderly population.

★8417★ U.S. Department of Agriculture
Food and Nutrition Service
Supplemental Food Programs Division
Special Supplemental Food Program for
**   Women, Infants, and Children (WIC**
**   Program)**
Park Office Center
3101 Park Center Dr.
Alexandria, VA 22302
Phone: (703)305-2746
Ronald Vogel, Director

Catalog Number: 10.557. **Objectives:** To supply, at no cost, supplemental nutritious foods and nutrition education, as an adjunct to good health care to low-income pregnant and post-partum women, infants and children identified to be at nutritional risk. **Types of Assistance:** Formula Grants. **Applicant Eligibility:** A local agency is eligible to apply to participate in the WIC program provided: 1. It gives health services free or at reduced cost or can arrange for such service to be provided to residents of low-income areas; 2. it serves a population of low-income women, infants, and children at nutritional risk; 3. it has the personnel, expertise, and equipment to perform measurements, tests, and data collection specified for the WIC program or can arrange for such services; 4. it maintains, or is able to maintain, adequate eligibility records; and 5. it is a public or private nonprofit health or human service agency. All local agencies must apply through the responsible State or U.S. Territory agency. **Beneficiary Eligibility:** Pregnant, postpartum or breastfeeding women, infants, and children up to 5 years of age are eligible if they are determined by a competent professional to be in need of the special supplemental foods supplied by the program, because of nutritional risk, and they have a family income that meets a level set by the State agency in compliance with standards set by USDA or are determined automatically income eligible based on their participation in certain health or welfare programs. They must also be residents of the State in which they receive benefits.

★8418★ U.S. Department of Education
Office of Assistant Secretary for
**   Elementary and Secondary Education**
Equity and Educational Excellence Division
Women's Educational Equity
400 Maryland Ave. SW
Washington, DC 20202
Phone: (202)401-1342
Janice Williams-Madison, Contact

Catalog Number: 84.083. **Objectives:** 1. To promote educational equity for women and girls at all levels of education, and 2. to provide financial assistance to educational agencies and institutions to help them meet the requirements of Title IX of the Education Amendments of 1972. **Types of Assistance:** Project Grants; Project Grants (Contracts). **Applicant Eligibility:** Through a nationwide competition, public and private nonprofit agencies, institutions, and organizations including student and community groups and individuals may apply. **Beneficiary Eligibility:** Public and nonprofit private agencies, institutions, and organizations, including student and community groups, and individuals will benefit.

★8419★ U.S. Department of Education
Office of Assistant Secretary for
**   Vocational and Adult Education**
Vocational-Technical Education Division
Vocational Education—Consumer and
**   Homemaking Education**
330 C St. SW
Washington, DC 20202
Phone: (202)732-2441
Winifred I. Warnat, Contact

Catalog Number: 84.049. **Objectives:** To assist States in conducting consumer and home-making education instructional programs, services, and activities that prepare youth and adults for the occupation of homemaking through instructional programs which include the areas of food and nutrition, individual and family health, consumer education, family living and parenthood education, child development, housing, home management (including resource management), clothing, and textiles. Emphasis is placed on projects located for residents of economically depressed areas and/or areas with high rates of unemployment. Projects are designed to assist consumers, and to help improve home environments and the quality of family life. **Types of Assistance:** Formula Grants. **Applicant Eligibility:** State Boards for Vocational Education. Eligible recipients for subgrants are local educational agencies including postsecondary institutions. **Beneficiary Eligibility:** Youth and adults preparing for the occupation of homemaking will benefit.

★8420★ U.S. Department of Energy
Office of Energy Research
Pre-College Programs Division
Pre-Freshman Enrichment (PREP)
Forrestal Bldg.
1000 Independence Ave. SW
Washington, DC 20585
Phone: (202)586-8949

Catalog Number: 81.047. **Objectives:** To alleviate manpower shortages in mathematics, science and engineering by preparing and guiding minority and women high school students in the selection of college preparatory courses in science and mathematics. **Types of Assistance:** Project Grants. **Applicant Eligibility:** Applications will be accepted only from U.S. colleges and universities granting baccalaureate degrees in at least one of the following disciplines: biological sciences; computer sciences; engineering and engineering technologies; natural resources; physical sciences; and mathematics. Nonprofit organizations, scientific and professional societies, science museums and science centers, two-year colleges, profit industries, and Federal laboratories may participate in cooperative or joint PREP projects providing the application is submitted by a four-year U.S. college or university. **Beneficiary Eligibility:** Must be a citizen of the U.S. or permanent resident alien and meet the selection requirements of the college or university administering the program.

★8421★ U.S. Department of Health and
**   Human Services**
Administration for Children and Families
Administration for Children, Youth and
**   Families**
Comprehensive Child Development Centers
330 C St. SW
Washington, DC 20201
Phone: (202)245-0566
Allen Smith, Contact

Catalog Number: 93.666. **Objectives:** To plan for and carry out projects for intensive, comprehensive, integrated and continuous supportive services for infants, toddlers, and pre-schoolers from low-income families to enhance their intellectual, social, emotional and physical development and provide support to their parents and other family members. **Types of Assistance:** Project Grants. **Applicant Eligibility:** Eligible entities include: (1) a Head Start agency; (2) an agency that is eligible to be designated as a Head Start agency under Section 641 of the Head Start Act; (3) a community based organization as defined under Section 4(5) of the Job Training Partnership Act (29 U.S.C. 1303(5)); (4) an institution of higher education as defined under Section 1201(a) of the Higher Education Act of 1965 (20 U.S.C. 11411); (5) a public hospital as defined under 42 U.S.C. 2910(c); (6) a community development corporation as defined under Section 681(a)(2)(A) of the Community Services Block Grant Act (42 U.S.C. 9910(a)(2)(A)); or (7) a public or private nonprofit agency or organization specializing in delivering social services to infants or young children (i.e., toddlers and pre-schoolers). **Beneficiary Eligibility:** Infants, toddlers and pre-schoolers from low-income families, their parents, and other family members.

★8422★ U.S. Department of Health and Human Services
Administration for Children and Families
Child Care and Development Block Grant Task Force
Payments to States for Day Care Assistance
370 L'Enfant Promenade SW
Aerospace Bldg., 5th Fl.
Washington, DC 20447
Phone: (202)401-9326

Catalog Number: 93.037. **Objectives:** To make grants available to States, Territories, and Tribal Governments to provide child care services for low-income families and to increase the availability, affordability, and quality of child care and development services. **Types of Assistance:** Formula Grants. **Applicant Eligibility:** All the States, the District of Columbia, and U.S. Territories, including the Commonwealth of Puerto Rico, Virgin Islands, Guam, American Samoa, the Northern Mariana Islands, the Trust Territory of the Pacific Islands, the federally-recognized Indian Tribal Governments Tribal organizations and Alaskan Native Organizations. **Beneficiary Eligibility:** Children under age 13 (or up to age 19, if disabled), who reside with a family whose income is at or below 75 percent of the State median income for a family of the same size, and reside with a parent who is working or attending a job-training or educational program (or are in need of or are receiving protective services, and live with a parent other than the parent described above).

★8423★ U.S. Department of Health and Human Services
Administration for Children and Families
Family Violence Prevention and Services
200 Independence Ave. SW
Washington, DC 20201
Phone: (202)245-2892

Catalog Number: 93.671. **Objectives:** To demonstrate the effectiveness of assisting States and Indian Tribes in the prevention of family violence and to provide immediate shelter and related assistance for victims of family violence and their dependents. **Types of Assistance:** Formula Grants; Projects Grants. **Applicant Eligibility:** For State and Indian Tribal grants, the 50 States, the District of Columbia, the Commonwealth of Puerto Rico, Guam, American Samoa, the Virgin Islands, the Northern Mariana Islands, Palau, and certain federally-recognized Indian Tribes. For discretionary grants, public or nonprofit private agencies and organizations. **Beneficiary Eligibility:** This program will benefit victims of family violence.

★8424★ U.S. Department of Health and Human Services
Administration for Children and Families
Office of Child Support Enforcement
Child Support Enforcement (Title IV-D)
370 L'Enfant Promenade SW, 4th Fl.
Washington, DC 20447
Phone: (202)401-9386
Elizabeth Matheson, Contact

Catalog Number: 93.023. **Objectives:** To enforce the support obligations owed by absent parents to their children, locate absent parents, establish paternity, and obtain child, spousal and medical support. **Types of Assistance:** Formula Grants. **Applicant Eligibility:** All States, the District of Columbia, Puerto Rico, Virgin Islands, and Guam. Each of these jurisdictions is required to establish or designate a single and separate State Child Support Enforcement Agency. **Beneficiary Eligibility:** The State must provide support enforcement services to: (1) all applicants for, or recipients of AFDC, Foster Care Maintenance Payments, and Medicaid, for whom an assignment to the State of support rights has been made and who are in need of such services; (2) all individuals who cease to receive AFDC; (3) individuals who provide authorization to the IV-D agency to continue support enforcement services; and (4) any other individual who is in need of such services and who has applied for them.

★8425★ U.S. Department of Health and Human Services
Administration for Children and Families
Office of Family Assistance
Child Care for Families At-Risk of Welfare Dependency
370 L'Enfant Promenade SW
Aerospace Bldg. 5th Fl.
Washington, DC 20447
Phone: (202)401-9275
Jason Turner, Director

Catalog Number: 93.036. **Objectives:** To allow States the option of providing child care to low-income families who are not receiving Aid To Families With Dependent Children (AFDC), who need child care in order to work, and who would otherwise be at-risk of becoming eligible for AFDC. **Types of Assistance:** Formula Grants. **Applicant Eligibility:** The United States, including the Commonwealth of Puerto Rico, the Virgin Islands, Guam and American Samoa. **Beneficiary Eligibility:** Approved applicants who are low-income working families with children.

★8426★ U.S. Department of Health and Human Services
Administration for Children and Families
Office of Financial Management
Child Care Improvement Grants
370 L'Enfant Promenade SW
Washington, DC 20447
Phone: (202)401-9228
Charleen M. Tompkins, Contact

Catalog Number: 93.039. **Objectives:** To allow States to improve child care licensing, registration requirements and procedures, and to enforce child care provided under the Family Support Act and Child Care for Children At-Risk of Dependency; and to provide for the training of child care providers. **Types of Assistance:** Formula Grants. **Applicant Eligibility:** All State-designated Title IV-A agencies in the United States, including the Commonwealth of Puerto Rico, the Virgin Islands, Guam and American Samoa. **Beneficiary Eligibility:** Children and their families.

★8427★ U.S. Department of Health and Human Services
Alcohol, Drug Abuse, and Mental Health Administration
Demonstration Grants on Model Projects for Pregnant and Postpartum Women and Their Infants
5600 Fishers Ln.
Rockwall II Bldg.
Rockville, MD 20857
Phone: (301)443-9110
Bernard R. McColgan, Contact

Catalog Number: 93.169. **Objectives:** (1) To promote the involvement and coordinated participation of multiple organizations in the delivery of integrated, comprehensive services for alcohol and other drugs using pregnant and postpartum women, and their families; (2) increase the availability and accessibility of prevention, early intervention, and treatment services for these populations; (3) decrease the incidence and prevalence of drug and alcohol use among pregnant and postpartum women; (4) reduce the incidence of abuse and neglect among childrn of alcohol and other drug using mothers; (5) improve the birth outcomes and reduce the infant motality of women who use alcohol and other drugs during pregnancy and decrease the incidence of infants affected by maternal substance use; (6) reduce the serverity of impairment among children born to substance using women; (7) improve the recognition of co-occurring mental and substance abuse disorders among providers; and (8) increase the availability, accessibility, and coordination of comprehensive mental health and substance abuse programs for pregnant and postpartum women who have co-occurring mental and substance abuse disorders. **Types of Assistance:** Project Grants. **Applicant Eligibility:** Public and private nonprofit or for-profit organizations such as universities, colleges, hospitals, community-based organizations, units of State or local governments and private organizations. **Beneficiary Eligibility:** For awards under Sections 509F and 509G; public or private for-profit or nonprofit organizations and the targeted population, pregnant or postpartum low-income women and their infants.

★8428★ U.S. Department of Health and Human Services
Centers for Disease Control
Cooperative Agreements for State-Based Comprehensive Breast and Cervical Cancer Control Programs
1600 Clifton Rd. NE
Mailstop K52
Atlanta, GA 30333
Phone: (404)488-5483
Alexander D. Bell, Contact

Catalog Number: 93.919. **Objectives:** To work with official State health agencies in developing comprehensive breast and cervical cancer control programs. To the extent possible, increase screening and following-up among all groups of women in the State, with special efforts to reach those women who are of low income, uninsured, underinsured, minority, and Native American. **Types of Assistance:** Project Grants. **Applicant Eligibility:** Eligible applicants are the official State health agencies of the United States, the District of Columbia, the Commonwealth of Puerto Rico, the Virgin Islands, Guam, the Northern Mariana Islands, the Federated States of Micronesia, the Republic of the Marshall Islands, the Republic of Palau, and American Samoa. **Beneficiary Eligibility:** Official State and Territorial health agencies; women, especially low-income women.

★8429★ **U.S. Department of Health and Human Services**
Centers for Disease Control
Preventive Health Services
Sexually Transmitted Diseases Control Grants
1600 Clifton Rd. NE
Atlanta, GA 30333
Phone: (404)639-3878
Willard Cates, Jr., Director

Catalog Number: 93.977. **Objectives:** To reduce morbidity and mortality by preventing cases and complications of sexually transmitted diseases (STD). Project grants under Section 318c awarded to State and local health departments emphasize the development and implementation of nationally uniform prevention and control programs which focus on disease intervention activities designed to reduce the incidence of these diseases, with applied research, demonstration, and public and professional education activities supporting these basic program activities authorized under Section 318b of the Public Health Service Act. **Types of Assistance:** Project Grants. **Applicant Eligibility:** Any State, and, in consultation with the appropriate State Health Authority, any political subdivision of a State. **Beneficiary Eligibility:** Any State or authorized subdivision.

★8430★ **U.S. Department of Health and Human Services**
Health Resources and Services Administration
Maternal and Child Health Bureau
Maternal and Child Health Federal Consolidated Programs
5600 Fishers Ln.
Rockville, MD 20857
Phone: (301)443-2170
Audrey H. Nora, Contact

Catalog Number: 93.110. **Objectives:** To carry out special projects of regional and national significance; to conduct training and research; to conduct genetic disease testing, counseling, and information development and dissemination programs; and to support comprehensive hemophilia diagnostic and treatment centers. **Types of Assistance:** Project Grants. **Applicant Eligibility:** Training grants may be made to public or private nonprofit institutions of higher learning. Research grants may be made to public or private nonprofit institutions of higher learning and public or private nonprift private agencies and organizations engaged in research or in Maternal and Child Health (MCH) or children with Special Health Care Needs (CSHCN) programs. Any public or private entity is eligible for hemophilia and genetics grants and other special projects grants. **Beneficiary Eligibility:** For training grants: (1) trainees in the MCH health professions related to MCH; and (2) mothers and children who receive services through training programs. For research grants: public or private nonprofit agencies and organizations engaged in research or in MCH or CSHCN programs. For hemophilia, genetics and special projects: (1) public or private agencies, organizations and institutions; and (2) mothers and children, and persons with hemophila (any age), who receive services through the programs.

★8431★ **U.S. Department of Health and Human Services**
Health Resources and Services Administration
Maternal and Child Health Bureau
Maternal and Child Health Services Block Grant
5600 Fishers Ln., Rm. 9-11
Rockville, MD 20857
Phone: (301)443-2170
Dr. Vince L. Hutchins, Contact

Catalog Number: 93.994. **Objectives:** To enable States to maintain and strengthen their leadership in planning, promoting, coordinating and evaluating health care for mothers and children and in providing health services for mothers and children who do not have access to adequate health care. **Types of Assistance:** Formula Grants. **Applicant Eligibility:** Maternal and Child Health Block Grants are limited to States and insular areas. **Beneficiary Eligibility:** Mothers, infants and children, particularly those of low-income families.

★8432★ **U.S. Department of Health and Human Services**
Health Resources and Services Administration
Maternal and Child Health Bureau
Maternal and Child Health Targeted Infant Mortality Initiative
5600 Fishers Ln.
Parklawn Bldg., Rm. 9-11
Rockville, MD 20857
Phone: (301)443-2170
Dr. Vince L. Hutchins, Contact

Catalog Number: 93.926. **Objectives:** To reduce infant mortality and improve infant health and well-being by targeting communities with high infant mortality rates and directing resources and interventions to improve access to, utilization of, and full participation in comprehensive maternity and infant care services. **Types of Assistance:** Project Grants. **Applicant Eligibility:** Urban and rural communities which have exceptionally high infant mortality rates. The proposal for an eligible community must be submitted by an applicant designated by the chief elected official of the eligible city or county (or, if there is more than one county, the chief elected officials acting in concert). Only a local or State health department or authority, or a not-for-profit organization may be so designated. No more than one application may be made for an eligible community, and each application must be endorsed by the Governor of the State. **Beneficiary Eligibility:** Mothers and infants in areas with exceptionally high infant mortality rates.

★8433★ **U.S. Department of Health and Human Services**
Health Resources and Services Administration
Maternal and Child Health Bureau
Pediatric AIDS Health Care Demonstration Program
5600 Fishers Ln., Rm. 9-48
Rockville, MD 20857
Phone: (301)443-9051
Beth Roy, Contact

Catalog Number: 93.153. **Objectives:** To support demonstration projects for strategies and innovative models for intervention in pediatric acquired immunodeficiency syndrome (AIDS) and coordination of services for child-bearing women and children with AIDS, or who are at-

risk of contracting AIDS. **Types of Assistance:** Project Grants. **Applicant Eligibility:** All public and private entities, nonprofit and for-profit. Proof of nonprofit status is required for nonprofit organizations. **Beneficiary Eligibility:** Women, adolescents and children with AIDS, or who are at risk of contracting AIDS.

★8434★ **U.S. Department of Health and Human Services**
National Institutes of Health
National Institute of Child Health and Human Development
Research for Mothers and Children
6130 Executive Blvd.
Rockville, MD 20852
Phone: (301)496-5097
Sumner J. Yaffe, Director

Catalog Number: 93.865. **Objectives:** To stimulate, coordinate, and support fundamental and clinical, biomedical, and behavioral research and research training associated with normal development from conception to maturity and those factors or special health problems which may delay or interfere with normal development. The Center for Research for Mothers and Children (CRMC) supports research for mothers, children, and families, and is designed to: (1) advance knowledge about fetal development, pregnancy, and birth; (2) identify the prerequisites of optimal growth and development through infancy, childhood, and adolescence; and (3) contribute to the prevention and treatment of mental retardation, developmental disabilities, and other childhood and adolescent problems. Small Business Innovation Research (SBIR); to stimulate technological innovation; to use small business to meet Federal research and development needs; to increase private sector commercialization of innovations derived from Federal research and development; and to foster and encourage participation by minority and disadvantaged persons in technological innovation. Small Instrumentation Program: To support the purchase of relatively low-cost pieces of research equipment that generally are not funded in research project grants and which also do not qualify for support under the National Institutes of Health's (NIH) larger shared instrumentation program. **Types of Assistance:** Project Grants. **Applicant Eligibility:** Grants: Universities, colleges, medical, dental and nursing schools, schools of public health, laboratories, hospitals, State and local health departments, other public or private institutions, both nonprofit and for-profit, and individuals. National Research Service Award: Support is provided for academic and research training only, in health and health-related areas which are periodically specified by the National Institutes of Health (see Preapplication Coordination). Individuals with a professional or scientific degree are eligible (M.D., Ph.D., D.D.S., D.O., D.V.M., Sc.D., D.Eng., or equivalent domestic or foreign degree). Predoctoral research training grants to institutions are also supported. Proposed study must result in biomedical or behavioral research training in a specified shortage are and which may offer opportunity to research health scientists, research clinicians, etc., to broaden their scientific background or to extend their potential for research in health-related areas. Applicants must be citizens of the United States or be admitted to the United States for permanent residency; they also must be nominated and sponsored by a public or private institution having staff and facilities suitable to the proposed research training. Domestic nonprofit organizations may apply for the institutional NRS grant. SBIR: SBIR grants can be awarded only to domestic small businesses (entities that are independently owned and operated for profit, are not dominant in the field in which research is proposed, and have no more than 500 employees). Primary employment (more than one-half time) of the principal investigator must be with the small business at the time of award and during the conduct of the proposed project. In both Phase I and Phase II, the research must be performed in the U.S. or its possessions. To be eligible for funding, a grant application must be approved for scientific merit and program relevance by a scientific review group and a national advisory council. Small Instrumentation Program: Eligible institutions or institutional components are those that (1) have received a Biomedical Research Support Grant (BRSG) in the previous fiscal year, and (2) have, at the time of application, active NIH grants that can benefit from the requested equipment. Only one application may be submitted by each eligible institution or institutional component. **Beneficiary Eligibility:** Any nonprofit or for-profit organization, company, or institution engaged in biomedical or biobehavioral research.

★8435★ **U.S. Department Health and Human Services**
Office of the Assistant Secretary for Health
Family Planning—Services
Hubert H. Humphery Bldg.
200 Independence Ave. SW, Rm. 736E
Washington, DC 20201
Phone: (202)245-0142
William R. Archer, Contact

Catalog Number: 93.217. **Objectives:** To provide educational, counseling, comprehensive medical and social sevices necessary to enable individuals to freely determine the number and spacing of their children, and by so doing helping to reduce maternal and infant mortality and promote the health of mothers and children. **Types of Assistance:** Project Grants. **Applicant Eligibility:** Any public (including city, county, local, regional, or State government) entity or nonprofit private entity located in a State (including the District of Columbia, Puerto Rico, Guam, the Commonwealth of the Northern Mariana Islands, American Samoa, the Virgin Islands, the Federated States of Micronesia, the Republic of Marshall Islands and the Republic of Palau) is eligible to apply for a grant. **Beneficiary Eligibility:** Persons who desire family planning services and who would not otherwise have access to them. Priority to be given to persons from low-income families. Individuals from other than low-income families will be charged a fee in accordance with an established fee schedual although inability to pay must not be a deterrent to services.

★8436★ **U.S. Department of Health and Human Services**
Office of Child Support Enforcement
Family Support Administration
Child Support Enforcement Research
370 L'Enfant SW, 4th Fl.
Washington, DC 20447
Phone: (202)401-5364
Gaile Maller, Contact

Catalog Number: 93.024. **Objectives:** To discover, test, demonstrate, and promote utilization of new concepts which will increase cost effectiveness, reduce welfare dependency, and increase child support collections from absent parents. **Types of Assistance:** Project Grants. **Applicant Eligibility:** Section 1110 grants may be made to State and nonprofit and for-profit organizations. Contracts may be executed with nonprofit or for-profit organizations. Section 1115 grants may be made to State Child Support Enforcement agencies. **Beneficiary Eligibility:** State agencies, local governments, nonprofit organizations, and profit organizations.

★8437★ **U.S. Department of Health and Human Services**
Office of Population Affairs
Family Planning-Service Delivery Improvement Research Grants
200 Independence Ave. SW
Hubert H. Humphrey Bldg., Rm. 736E
Washington, DC 20201
Phone: (202)245-1181
Patricia Thompson, Contact

Catalog Number: 93.974. **Objectives:** To promote service delivery improvement through research studies, and application of knowledge. **Types of Assistance:** Project Grants. **Applicant Eligibility:** Any public entity (city, county, local, regional, or State government) or private nonprofit entity located in a State (including the District of Columbia, Puerto Rico, the Commonwealth of the Northern Marianas Islands, Guam, American Samoa, the Virgin Islands, the Federated States .of Micronesia, the Republic of Marshall Islands and the Republic of Palau) is eligible to apply for a grant under this subpart. **Beneficiary Eligibility:** All levels of government and nonprofit entities responsible for the efficient and effective delivery of family planning services; providers and recipients of family planning services; and the general public.

★8438★ **U.S. Department of Justice**
Civil Rights Division
Equal Employment Opportunity
10th St. & Constitution Ave. NW
Washington, DC 20530
Phone: (202)514-2007
Amy Casner, Contact

Catalog Number: 16.101 **Objectives:** To enforce Federal laws providing equal employment opportunities for all without regard to race, religion, national origin or sex, and where authorized, handicap condition. **Types of Assistance:** Provision of Specialized Services. **Applicant Eligibility:** All persons. **Beneficiary Eligibility:** All persons.

★8439★ **U.S. Department of Labor**
Women's Bureau
Office of Administrative Management
Women's Special Employment Assistance
200 Constitution Ave. NW
Washington, DC 20210
Phone: (202)523-6606
Dora E. Carrington, Chief

Catalog Number: 17.700. **Objectives:** To provide input in the development of policies and programs affecting the employment of women; to expand training and employment opportunities for women and promote their entry into better paying jobs, especially in new technology and nontraditional occupations; to establish linkage with national and community organizations, business and industry, trade unions, research foundations, academic and Federal, State, and local government agnecies for cooperative projects that address the employment and supportive service needs of women; and to develop publications and disseminate information on women's economic status, employment rights, and job options. **Types of Assistance:** Advisory Services and Counseling; Dissemination of Technical Information. **Applicant Eligibility:** Any individual or group located in the United States or its territories. **Beneficiary Eligibility:** Individuals (particularly women) and groups.

★8440★ **U.S. Equal Employment Opportunity Commission**
Office of Communications and Legislative Affairs
Public Information Unit
Employment Discrimination—Equal Pay Act
1801 L St. NW
Washington, DC 20507
Phone: (202)663-4900
Toll-free: 800-USA-EEOC

Catalog Number: 30.010. **Objectives:** To prohibit sex discrimination in the payment of wages to men and women performing equal work in the same establishment. **Types of Assistance:** Advisory Services and Counseling; Investigation of Complaints. **Applicant Eligibility:** Individuals who believe they have been paid in violation of the Equal Pay Act or who believe that other persons are being paid in violation of the Act in any State of the United States, the District of Columbia or any territory or possession of the United States. **Beneficiary Eligibility:** Individuals covered by the Fair Labor Standards Act of 1938, as amended.

★8441★ **U.S. Equal Employment Opportunity Commission**
Office Communications and Legislative Affairs
Public Information Unit
Employment Discrimination—Title VII of the Civil Rights Act of 1964
1801 L St. NW
Washington, DC 20507
Toll-free: 800-USA-EEOC

Catalog Number: 30.001. **Objectives:** To provide for enforcement of the Federal prohibition against employment discrimination in the private and public sector based on race, color, religion, sex or national origin. **Types of Assistance:** Investigation of Complaints. **Applicant Eligibility:** Any aggrieved individual or individuals, labor union, association, legal representative, or unincorporated organization, filing on behalf of an aggrieved individual, who have reason to believe that an unlawful employment practice within the meaning of Title VII, as amended, has been committed by an employer with more than 15 employees, employment agency, labor organization or joint labor-management committee. **Beneficiary Eligibility:** Potential employees, employees and former employees of the named respondents in a charge who have been subject to unlawful employment practices.

★8442★ U.S. Equal Employment
Opportunity Commission
Office of Program Operations
Systemic Investigation and Individual
Compliance Programs
Employment Discrimination—State and
Local Anti-Discrimination Agency
Contracts
1801 L St. NW
Washington, DC 20507
Phone: (202)663-4866
Winston Robertson, Contact

Catalog Number: 30.002. **Objectives:** To assist EEOC in the enforcement of Title VII of the Civil Rights Act of 1964, as amended, and of the Age Discrimination in Employment Act of 1967 by investigating and resolving charges of employment discrimination based on race, color, religion, sex, national origin, or age. **Types of Assistance:** Direct Payments for Specified Use. **Applicant Eligibility:** Official State and local government agencies charged with the administration and enforcement of fair employment practices laws. **Beneficiary Eligibility:** Employees, potential employees and former employees covered by Title VII of the Civil Rights Act of 1964 as amended, and/or the Age Discrimination in Employment Act of 1967.

★8443★ U.S. Small Business
Administration
Office of Women's Business Ownership
Women's Business Ownership Assistance
409 3rd St. SW
Washington, DC 20416
Phone: (202)205-6673
Lindsey Johnson, Director

Catalog Number: 59.043. **Objectives:** To promote the legitimate interest of small business concerns owned and controlled by women and to remove, in so far as possible, the discriminatory barriers that are encountered by women in accessing capital and other factors of production. **Types of Assistance:** Project Grants (Cooperative Agreements or Contracts). **Applicant Eligibility:** Profit or nonprofit organizations having experience in training and counseling business women effectively. Educational institutions, State and local government, and SBA-funded Small Business Development Centers are not eligible.

(16) State Government Agencies

Entries in this chapter are arranged alphabetically by state, then alphabetically by agency name within state. See the User's Guide at the front of this directory for additional information.

Alabama

★8444★ **Alabama Department of Economic and Community Affairs**
Law Enforcement Planning Division
Family Violence and Prevention Services
3465 Norman Bridge Rd.
PO Box 2939
Montgomery, AL 36105-0939
Phone: (205)242-5891
Gilbert D. Miller, Division Chief

★8445★ **Alabama Department of Human Resources**
Child Support Enforcement Division
50 N. Ripley St.
Montgomery, AL 36130-1801
Phone: (205)242-9300
Horace Satcher, Contact

★8446★ **Alabama Department of Human Resources**
Civil Rights and Equal Employment Opportunity Office
50 N. Ripley St.
Montgomery, AL 36130-1801
Phone: (205)242-1550
Sylvester Smith, Contact

★8447★ **Alabama Department of Public Health**
Family Health Services Bureau
Public Health Service Bldg.
434 Monroe St.
Montgomery, AL 36130
Phone: (205)242-5673

★8448★ **Alabama Women's Commission**
Rte. 2, Box 204
Troy, AL 36081
Phone: (205)566-3574
Jean Boutwell, Exec. Director

Alaska

★8449★ **Alaska Council on Domestic Violence and Sexual Assault**
PO Box N
Juneau, AK 99811
Phone: (908)465-4356
Maria Lynn McKenzie, Acting Exec. Dir.

★8450★ **Alaska Department of Health and Social Services**
Division of Public Health
Family Health Section
Alaska Office Bldg., Rm. 517
PO Box H
Juneau, AK 99811-0610
Phone: (907)465-3100

★8451★ **Alaska Office of the Governor**
Administration Department
Personnel and Equal Employment Opportunity Division
PO Box 11201
Juneau, AK 99811-0201
Phone: (907)465-4430
R.H. King, Director

★8452★ **Alaska Women's Commission**
3601 C St., Ste. 742
Anchorage, AK 99503
Phone: (907)561-4227
Mary McClinton, Chairperson

Arizona

★8453★ **Arizona Attorney General**
Child Enforcement Section
1275 W. Washington
Phoenix, AZ 85003
Phone: (602)542-1655
Kirk Birch, Contact

★8454★ **Arizona Department of Economic Security**
Equal Employment Opportunity Office
PO Box 6123
Phoenix, AZ 85005
Phone: (602)255-5961

★8455★ **Arizona Department of Health Services**
Division of Family Health Services
Maternal and Child Health Bureau
1740 W. Adams
Phoenix, AZ 85007
Phone: (602)542-1870

★8456★ **Arizona Department of Health Services**
Office of Domestic Violence and Mental Health
2632 E. Thomas Rd.
Phoenix, AZ 85106
Phone: (602)255-1025
Linda Kmetz Mission, Director

★8457★ **Arizona Family Health Services Division**
Maternal and Child Health Bureau
1740 W. Adams Ave.
Phoenix, AZ 85034
Phone: (602)542-1870
Jane Pearson, Director

★8458★ **Arizona Women's Services**
State Capitol, W. Wing, Rm. 420
Phoenix, AZ 85007
Phone: (602)542-1755
Harriett Hank Barnes, Director

Arkansas

★8459★ **Arkansas Department of Health**
Bureau of Public Health Programs
Division of Maternal and Child Health
4815 W. Markham St.
Little Rock, AR 72205
Phone: (501)661-2199

★8460★ **Arkansas Office of Prosecutor Coordinator**
Family Violence Prevention and Services
323 Center, Ste. 750
Little Rock, AR 72201
Phone: (501)682-3671
Caran Curry, Prosecutor Coordinator

California

★8461★ **California Commission on the Status of Women**
1303 J. St., Ste. 400
Sacramento, CA 95814-2900
Phone: (916)445-3173
Pat Towner, Exec. Director

★8462★ **California Department of Employment Development**
Equal Employment Opportunity Office
PO Box 826880
Sacramento, CA 94280-0001
Phone: (916)654-8210
Roberto Garcia, Contact

★8463★ **California Health and Welfare Agency**
Department of Health Services
Maternal and Child Health Division
714 P St., Rm. 750
Sacramento, CA 95814
Phone: (916)327-8181

**★8464★ California Office of Criminal
Justice Planning**
Domestic Violence Branch
1130 K St., Ste. 300
Sacramento, CA 95814
Phone: (916)324-9100
Beverly Green-Simmons, Contact

Colorado

★8465★ Colorado Department of Health
Office of Health Care Services
Division of Family Health Services
4210 E. 11th Ave.
Denver, CO 80220
Phone: (303)331-8360

**★8466★ Colorado Department of Social
Services**
Family Violence Program
1575 Sherman St.
Denver, CO 80203-1714
Phone: (303)866-2855
Mary Ann Ganey, Supervisor

Connecticut

**★8467★ Connecticut Department of Health
Services**
Division of Community Health
Family Reproductive Health Division
150 Washington St.
Hartford, CT 06106
Phone: (203)566-5601

**★8468★ Connecticut Department of
Human Resources**
Bureau of Grants Management
Family Violence Prevention and Services
1049 Asylum Ave.
Hartford, CT 06105-2431
Phone: (203)566-5173
John Pikens, Director

**★8469★ Connecticut Office of the
Attorney General**
Child Support Department
55 Elm St.
Hartford, CT 06106
Phone: (203)566-4998
Donald Longley, Contact

**★8470★ Connecticut Status of Women
Commissions**
90 Washington St.
Hartford, CT 06106
Phone: (203)566-5702
Frederica Gray, Exec. Director

Delaware

★8471★ Delaware Commission for Women
820 N. French St., 6th Fl.
Wilmington, DE 19801
Phone: (302)577-2660
Ramone Fullman, Exec. Director

★8472★ Delaware Criminal Justice Council
Family Violence Prevention and Services
State Office Bldg., 4th Fl.
820 French St.
Wilmington, DE 19801
Phone: (302)577-3432
Cheryl Stallman, Sr. Planner

**★8473★ Delaware Department of Health
and Social Services**
Child Support Enforcement Division
Delaware State Hospital
New Castle, DE 19720
Phone: (302)577-4815
Barbara Paulin, Contact

**★8474★ Delaware Department of Health
and Social Services**
Division of Public Health
**Bureau of Personal and Family Health
Services**
Jesse Cooper Bldg.
802 Silver Lake Blvd.
PO Box 637
Dover, DE 19903
Phone: (302)739-4745

**★8475★ Delaware Division of Employment
Service**
University Plaza
PO Box 9499
Newark, DE 19714
Phone: (302)368-6913
Virginia Herring, Contact

District of Columbia

**★8476★ District of Columbia Commission
for Women**
2000 14th St. NW, Rm. 354
Washington, DC 20009
Phone: (202)939-8083
Carol Hill-Lowe, Exec. Director

**★8477★ District of Columbia Department
of Human Services**
Commission of Public Health
**Bureau of Maternal and Child Health
Services**
1660 L. St., NW, Ste. 904
Washington, DC 20036
Phone: (202)673-6665

**★8478★ District of Columbia Department
of Human Services**
Commission on Social Services
Family Violence Prevention and Services
609 H St. NE, 5th Fl.
Washington, DC 20024
Phone: (202)727-5951
Dr. June W. McCarron, Contact

**★8479★ District of Columbia Office of the
Mayor**
Corporation Counsel Office
Child Support Unit
1350 Pennsylvania Ave. NW
Washington, DC 20004
Phone: (202)727-3885
Sylvia Larrabee, Contact

★8480★ Government of American Samoa
Department of Human Services
Social Services Division
Family Violence Prevention and Services
1206 Longworth Bldg.
Washington, DC 20515
Phone: (202)225-8577
Suli Sataua, Contact

Florida

**★8481★ Florida Department of Health and
Rehabilitative Services**
Aging and Adult Services Office
Family Violence Prevention and Services
1317 Winewood Blvd., Bldg. 2, Rm. 323
Tallahassee, FL 32399-0700
Phone: (904)488-2881
Connie Hall, Contact

**★8482★ Florida Department of Health and
Rehabilitative Services**
**Maternal, Child and Special Health
Services Office**
1317 Winewood Blvd.
Tallahassee, FL 32399-0700
Phone: (904)487-2705

Georgia

**★8483★ Georgia Department of Human
Resources**
Division of Family and Children Services
Family Violence Prevention and Services
878 Peachtree St. NE, Rm. 502
Atlanta, GA 30309-1202
Phone: (404)894-4456
Linda Darter, Director

**★8484★ Georgia Department of Human
Resources**
Division of Public Health
Family Health Section
878 Peachtree St. NE, Ste. 217
Atlanta, GA 30309
Phone: (404)894-6622

**★8485★ Georgia Fair Employment
Practices Office**
156 Trinity Ave. SW, Ste. 208
Atlanta, GA 30303
Phone: (404)656-1736
Carla A. Ford, Administrator

Hawaii

**★8486★ Hawaii Commission on the Status
of Women**
335 Merchant St., Rm. 253
Honolulu, HI 96813
Phone: (808)586-5757
Kathleen McRae-Lunsford, Exec. Secretary

★8487★ Hawaii Department of Health
Family Health Services Division
Maternal and Child Health Branch
741 Sunset Ave.
Honolulu, HI 96816
Phone: (808)735-3056

★8488★ Hawaii Department of Human
Services
Family Violence Prevention and Services
PO Box 339
Honolulu, HI 96809-0339
Phone: (808)586-4977
Winona Rubin, Director

★8489★ Hawaii Department of Labor and
Industrial Relations
Equal Employment Opportunity Office
830 Punchbowl St.
Honolulu, HI 96813
Phone: (808)548-4533
Alice Hong, Contact

Idaho

★8490★ Idaho Council on Domestic
Violence
450 W. State, 9th Fl.
Statehouse
Boise, ID 83720
Phone: (208)334-5580
Celia Heady, Exec. Dir.

★8491★ Idaho Department of Health and
Welfare
Division of Health
Bureau of Maternal and Child Health
450 W. State, 4th Fl.
Boise, ID 83720
Phone: (208)334-5967

Illinois

★8492★ Illinois Citizen's Council on
Women
300 W. Monroe
Springfield, IL 62706
Phone: (217)782-4546
Steve Stalcup, Exec. Director

★8493★ Illinois Department of
Employment Security
**Equal Employment Opportunity and
Affirmative Action Office**
401 S. State St.
Chicago, IL 60605
Phone: (312)793-4305
Hattie Jones, Contact

★8494★ Illinois Department of Public Aid
Division of Family Support
Family Violence and Prevention Services
300 Isles Park
Springfield, IL 62718
Phone: (217)524-6034
Carol Brigman, Contact

★8495★ Illinois Department of Public
Health
Office of Health Services
Division of Family Health
535 W. Jefferson
Springfield, IL 62761
Phone: (217)782-4977

Indiana

★8496★ Indiana Family and Social
Services Administration
Family and Children Division
Family Violence Prevention and Services
402 W. Washington St.
Indianapolis, IN 46204-7083
Phone: (317)232-4241
Lena Harris, Contact

★8497★ Indiana State Board of Health
Family Health Services Bureau
Maternal and Child Health Division
1330 W. Michigan St.
PO Box 1964
Indianapolis, IN 46206
Phone: (317)633-0171

Iowa

★8498★ Iowa Commission on the Status
of Women
Lucas State Office Bldg., 1st Fl.
Des Moines, IA 50319
Phone: (515)381-4461
Charlotte Nelson, Administrator

★8499★ Iowa Department of Public Health
Division of Family and Community Health
Maternal and Child Health Bureau
Lucas State Office Bldg.
Des Moines, IA 50319
Phone: (515)281-4910

Kansas

★8500★ Kansas Administration
Department
Equal Employment Opportunity Division
State Capitol, Rm. 263-E
Topeka, KS 66612
Phone: (913)296-4278
Clyde Howard, Contact

★8501★ Kansas Department of Health and
Environment
Division of Health
Maternal and Child Health Bureau
Landon State Office Bldg.
901 SW Jackson St.
Topeka, KS 66612
Phone: (913)296-1300

★8502★ Kansas Department of Social and
Rehabilitation Services
Child Support Enforcement Division
Docking State Office Bldg.
Topeka, KS 66612
Phone: (913)296-3237
Jim Robertson, Contact

Kentucky

★8503★ Kentucky Attorney General
Child Support Enforcement Division
116 Capitol Bldg.
Frankfort, KY 40601
Phone: (502)564-7600
Robin Hite, Contact

★8504★ Kentucky Commission on Women
614A Shelby
Frankfort, KY 40601
Phone: (502)564-6643
Marsha Weinstein, Exec. Director

★8505★ Kentucky Department of Social
Services
Family Violence Prevention and Services
275 E. Main St.
Frankfort, KY 40621
Phone: (502)564-6750
Paul Doyle, Contact

★8506★ Kentucky Human Resources
Cabinet
Department for Health Services
Maternal and Child Health Division
275 E. Main St.
Frankfort, KY 40621
Phone: (502)564-4830

★8507★ Kentucky Human Resources
Cabinet
Social Insurance Department
Child Support Enforcement Division
275 E. Main St.
Frankfort, KY 40621
Phone: (502)564-2285
Maxine Stricker, Contact

Louisiana

★8508★ Louisiana Department of Health
and Hospitals
Office of Public Health Services
Health Services Programs
Maternal and Child Health Program
325 Loyola Ave., Rm. 612
New Orleans, LA 70112
Phone: (504)568-5073

★8509★ Louisiana Office of Women's
Services
150 Riverside Mall, 4th Fl.
PO Box 94095
Baton Rouge, LA 70804-9095
Phone: (504)342-2715
Glenda K. Parks, Exec. Director

**★8510★ Louisiana Office of Women's
Services**
Family Violence Prevention and Services
PO Box 94095
Baton Rouge, LA 70804-9095
Phone: (504)342-2715
Katherine Bailey, Contact

Maine

★8511★ Maine Commission for Women
State House Sta., No. 93
Augusta, ME 04333
Phone: (207)289-3418
Leslie Anderson, Exec. Director

**★8512★ Maine Department of Human
Services**
Bureau of Health
Division of Maternal and Child Health
State House, Sta. 11
Augusta, ME 04333
Phone: (207)289-3311

**★8513★ Maine Department of Human
Services**
Bureau of Social Services
Family Violence Prevention and Services
State House, Sta. 11
Augusta, ME 04333
Phone: (207)287-5060
Jeanette Talbot, Contact

Maryland

★8514★ Maryland Commission for Women
311 W. Saratoga St., Rm. 239
Baltimore, MD 21201
Phone: (301)333-0054
Lisa G. Carreno, Exec. Director

**★8515★ Maryland Department of Health
and Mental Hygiene**
Division of Public Health Services
Local and Family Health Administration
201 W. Preston St.
Baltimore, MD 21201
Phone: (301)225-5300

**★8516★ Maryland Department of Human
Resources**
Community Services Administration
Women's Services Program
311 W. Saratoga St., Rm. 239
Baltimore, MD 21201
Phone: (301)333-0059
Susan Fernandez, Director

**★8517★ Maryland Equal Employment
Opportunity Office**
217 E. Redwood St., Ste. 1123
Baltimore, MD 21202
Phone: (410)333-6626
Dale Webb, Director

Massachusetts

**★8518★ Massachusetts Administration and
Finance Executive Office**
Personnel Administration Department
Equal Employment Practices Office
1 Ashburton Pl.
Boston, MA 02108
Phone: (617)727-3777
Eugene H. Rooney, Jr., Contact

**★8519★ Massachusetts Department of
Social Services**
Family Violence Prevention and Services
150 Causeway St.
Boston, MA 02114
Phone: (617)727-0900
Pam Whitney, Director of Special Projects

**★8520★ Massachusetts Executive Office
of Human Services**
Department of Public Health
**Bureau of Parent, Child and Adolescent
Health**
150 Tremont St., 4th Fl.
Boston, MA 02111
Phone: (617)727-0941

**★8521★ Massachusetts Governor's
Advisory Committee on Women's Issues**
State House, Rm. 109
Boston, MA 02133
Phone: (617)727-7853
Vivan Li, Governor's Advisor on Women

**★8522★ Massachusetts Health and Human
Services Executive Office**
Public Welfare Department
Child Support Division
180 Tremont St.
Boston, MA 02111
Phone: (617)574-0307
Paul Alford, Contact

**★8523★ Massachusetts Minority and
Women's Business Division**
100 Cambridge St., 13th Fl.
Boston, MA 02114
Phone: (617)727-8692
Sunny Brent-Harding, Director

Michigan

★8524★ Michigan Department of Labor
Women and Work Office
201 N. Washington Sq.
PO Box 30015
Lansing, MI 48909
Phone: (517)373-9475
Hilda Curran, Contact

**★8525★ Michigan Department of Public
Health**
**Division of Program and Administrative
Services**
Maternal and Child Health Office
3423 N. Logan
PO Box 30195
Lansing, MI 48909
Phone: (517)335-8900

**★8526★ Michigan Department of Social
Services**
**Domestic Violence Prevention and
Treatment Board**
235 S. Grand Ave., Ste. 515
PO Box 30037
Lansing, MI 48909
Phone: (517)373-8144
Kathryn Young, Prog. Dir.

★8527★ Michigan Women's Commission
611 W. Ottawa St., 3rd Fl.
Lansing, MI 48933
Phone: (517)373-2884
Mary Addison, Exec. Director

Minnesota

**★8528★ Minnesota Commission on the
Economic Status of Women**
85 State Office Bldg.
St. Paul, MN 55155
Phone: (612)296-8590
Katy Olson, Chairperson

**★8529★ Minnesota Department of
Corrections**
**Program and Services for Battered
Women**
300 Bigelow Bldg.
450 N. Syndicate St.
St. Paul, MN 55104
Phone: (612)642-0253
Jean Barkey, Director

★8530★ Minnesota Department of Health
Maternal and Child Health Division
717 Delaware St. SE
Minneapolis, MN 55440
Phone: (612)623-5166

**★8531★ Minnesota Department of Human
Services**
Child Support Enforcement Division
444 Lafayette Rd.
St. Paul, MN 55155
Phone: (612)296-2499
Bonnie Becker, Contact

**★8532★ Minnesota Employee Relations
Department**
Equal Opportunity Division
Centennial Office Bldg.
658 Cedar St.
St. Paul, MN 55155
Phone: (612)296-7956
Chris Goodwill, Contact

Mississippi

★8533★ Mississippi Department of Health
Bureau of Health Services
Maternity Services Division
PO Box 1700
Jackson, MS 39215-1700
Phone: (601)960-7464

★8534★ Mississippi Department of Health
Domestic Violence Shelters Projects
PO Box 1700
2423 N. State St.
Jackson, MS 39215-1700
Phone: (601)960-7470
Ann Simms, Special Projects Coord.

★8535★ Mississippi Department of Human Services
Child Support Division
PO Box 352
Jackson, MS 39205-0352
Phone: (601)949-2090
James Graves, Contact

Missouri

★8536★ **Missouri Department of Health**
Maternal and Child Health Division
1730 E. Elm St.
PO Box 570
Jefferson City, MO 65102
Phone: (314)751-6174

★8537★ **Missouri Department of Social Services**
Child Support Enforcement Division
227 Metro Dr.
Jefferson City, MO 65102
Phone: (314)751-4301
Michael Henry, Director

★8538★ **Missouri Department of Social Services**
Division of Family Services
Family Violence Prevention and Services
PO Box 88
Jefferson City, MO 65103-1527
Phone: (314)751-6780
Pat Wojciehowski, Asst. for Special Projects

Montana

★8539★ **Montana Department of Family Services**
Program, Planning & Evaluation Bureau
Family Violence Prevention and Services
PO Box 8005
Helena, MT 59604
Phone: (406)444-5900
Judith Williams, Administrative Officer

★8540★ **Montana Department of Health and Environmental Sciences**
Division of Health Services
Family, Maternal and Child Health Bureau
Cogswell Bldg., Rm. C314
Helena, MT 59620
Phone: (406)444-4740

★8541★ **Montana Department of Social and Rehabilitation Services**
Child Support Enforcement Division
PO Box 4210
Helena, MT 59604
Phone: (406)444-4614
MaryAnn Wellbank, Contact

★8542★ **Montana Women in Employment Advisory Council**
Office of the Governor
Capitol Bldg.
Helena, MT 59624
Phone: (406)444-3111
Antoinette Rosell, Chair

Nebraska

★8543★ **Nebraska Commission on the Status of Women**
301 Centennial Mall S.
Box 94985
Lincoln, NE 68509
Phone: (402)471-2039
Rose Melle, Exec. Director

★8544★ **Nebraska Department of Health**
Division of Maternal and Child Health
301 Centennial Mall S., 3rd Fl.
PO Box 95007
Lincoln, NE 68509-5007
Phone: (402)471-2907

★8545★ **Nebraska Department of Social Services**
Domestic Violence Services
301 Centennial Mall S.
PO Box 95026
Lincoln, NE 68509
Phone: (402)471-9370
Colette Perkins, Contact

★8546★ **Nebraska Equal Opportunity Commission**
PO Box 94934
Lincoln, NE 68509
Phone: (402)471-2024
Lawrence R. Myers, Exec. Director

Nevada

★8547★ **Nevada Department of Human Resources**
Division of Health
Bureau of Maternal and Child Health
505 E. King St., Rm. 201
Carson City, NV 89710
Phone: (702)687-4885

★8548★ **Nevada Department of Human Resources**
Family Violence Prevention and Services
505 E. King St.
Carson City, NV 89710
Phone: (702)687-5943
Chris Graham, Project Mgr.

★8549★ **Nevada Equal Rights Commission**
1515 E. Tropicana Ave., Ste. 590
Las Vegas, NV 89109
Phone: (702)486-7161
Della E. Martinez, Exec. Director

New Hampshire

★8550★ **New Hampshire Commission on the Status of Women**
22 State House Annex
Concord, NH 03301-6312
Phone: (603)271-2660
Georgegett Hippauf, Chairwoman

★8551★ **New Hampshire Department of Health and Human Services**
Division of Public Health Services
Bureau of Maternal and Child Health
6 Hazen Dr.
Concord, NH 03301
Phone: (603)271-4517

New Jersey

★8552★ **New Jersey Department of Health**
Division of Family Health Services
Maternal and Child Health Services
363 W. State St., CN 364
Trenton, NJ 08625
Phone: (609)292-5656

★8553★ **New Jersey Department of Human Services**
Division of Youth and Family Services
Family Violence Prevention and Services
1 S. Montgomery St.
Trenton, NJ 08625
Phone: (609)633-2116
Ertha Drayton, Grants Mgr.

★8554★ **New Jersey Division on Women**
Department of Community Affairs
101 S. Broad St., CN 801
Trenton, NJ 08625-0801
Phone: (609)292-8840
Roberta W. Francis, Exec. Director

★8555★ **New Jersey Personnel Department**
Equal Employment Opportunity and Affirmative Action Division
44 S. Clinton Ave., CN 317
Trenton, NJ 08625-0317
Phone: (609)777-0919
S. Howard Woodson, Contact

New Mexico

★8556★ **New Mexico Commission on the Status of Women**
4001 Indian School Rd. NE, Ste. 220
Albuquerque, NM 87125
Phone: (505)841-4662
Loretta Armenta, Chairperson

★8557★ **New Mexico Department of Health and Environment**
Division of Public Health
Maternal Section
Harold Runnels Bldg.
1190 St. Francis Dr.
Santa Fe, NM 87501
Phone: (505)827-2352

★8558★ **New Mexico Department of Human Services**
Child Support Enforcement Division
PO Box 2348
Santa Fe, NM 87504-2348
Phone: (505)827-7200
Ben Silva, Contact

★8559★   New Mexico Department of Human Services
Divison of Social Services
Family Violence Prevention and Services
1100 S. Main
Rosewell, NM 88201
Phone: (505)624-6071
Al Wilson, Program Specialist

New York

★8560★   New York Department of Social Services
Child Support Enforcement Office
40 N. Pearl St.
Albany, NY 12243
Phone: (518)474-9081
Joan Keenan, Contact

★8561★   New York Department of Social Services
Family Violence Prevention and Services
11-D 40 N. Pearl St.
Albany, NY 12243-0001
Phone: (518)473-6456
Sallie D'Asaro, Contact

★8562★   New York Minority and Women's Business Development Office
Empire State Plaza
Box 2072
Albany, NY 12220
Phone: (518)474-6346
Lynn Canton, Director

★8563★   New York State Department of Health
Center for Community Health
Family Health Bureau
Tower Bldg., Empire State Plaza
Albany, NY 12237
Phone: (518)474-7922

★8564★   New York State Division for Women
Executive Chamber
Albany, NY 12224
Phone: (518)474-3612
Judith Avner, Director

North Carolina

★8565★   North Carolina Council on the Status of Women
526 N. Wilmington St.
Raleigh, NC 27604-1199
Phone: (919)733-2455
Suzanne E. Williams, Exec. Director

★8566★   North Carolina Department of Environment, Health and Natural Resources
Office of Health Director
Maternal and Child Health Division
1330 St. Mary's St.
PO Box 27687
Raleigh, NC 27611-7687
Phone: (919)733-3816

★8567★   North Carolina Division of Social Services
Family Services Section
Family Violence and Prevention Services
325 N. Salisbury St., Ste. 779
Raleigh, NC 27603
Phone: (919)733-3677
Ruth Relos, Ph.D., Mgr

★8568★   North Carolina State Personnel Office
Equal Employment Opportunity Services Division
116 W. Jones St.
Raleigh, NC 27603-8004
Phone: (919)733-0205
Nelly Reily, Contact

North Dakota

★8569★   North Dakota Department of Health and Consolidated Laboratories
Preventive Health Section
Maternal and Child Health Division
600 E. Blvd.
State Capitol
Bismarck, ND 58505
Phone: (701)224-2493

★8570★   North Dakota Department of Labor
Equal Employment Opportunity Division
605 East Blvd.
Bismarck, ND 58505
Phone: (701)224-2660
John E. Lynch, Contact

★8571★   North Dakota Governor's Commission on the Status of Women
600 E. Boulevard, 13th Fl.
Bismark, ND 58505-0250
Phone: (701)224-2970
Nerlene Yellow Bird, Exec. Director

Ohio

★8572★   Ohio Department of Health
Division of Maternal and Child Health
246 N. High St.
PO Box 118
Columbus, OH 43266-0588
Phone: (614)466-3263

★8573★   Ohio Department of Human Services
Child Support Bureau
30 E. Broad St., 32nd Fl.
Columbus, OH 43266-0423
Phone: (614)466-3233
Elizabeth Lightie, Contact

★8574★   Ohio Department of Human Services
Domestic Violence and Community Social Services Unit
65 E. State St., 5th Fl.
Columbus, OH 43215
Phone: (614)466-5392
Julia Arbini Carbonell, Contact

★8575★   Ohio Equal Employment Opportunity Division
65 E. State St., 8th Fl.
Columbus, OH 43266
Phone: (614)466-8380
Booker T. Tall, Deputy Director

Oklahoma

★8576★   Oklahoma Department of Health
Department of Personal Health Services
Maternal and Child Health Services
1000 NE 10th St.
PO Box 53551
Oklahoma City, OK 73152
Phone: (405)271-4476

★8577★   Oklahoma Department of Mental Health
Domestic Violence Services
PO Box 53277
Capitol Sta.
Oklahoma City, OK 73152
Phone: (405)271-8777
N. Ann Lowrance, Director

★8578★   Oklahoma Employment Security Commission
Equal Employment Opportunity Office
2401 N. Lincoln Blvd.
Oklahoma City, OK 73105
Phone: (405)557-7255
Barbara Williams, Contact

★8579★   Oklahoma Governor's Commission on the Status of Women
4100 Bank of Oklahoma Tower
One Williams Center
Tulsa, OK 74172
Phone: (918)588-4063
Margaret Swimmer, Chair

Oregon

★8580★   Oregon Department of Human Resources
Children's Services Division
Domestic Violence Program
198 Commercial St. SE
Salem, OR 97310
Phone: (503)378-4324
Bonnie Jean Braeutigam, Director

★8581★   Oregon Department of Human Resources
Division of Health
Office of Maternal and Child Health
State Office Bldg., Rm. 508
Portland, OR 97201
Phone: (503)229-6390

★8582★ Oregon Women's Commission
695 Summer St. NE
Salem, OR 97310
Phone: (503)378-3308
Ann Small, Chairperson

Pennsylvania

★8583★ Pennsylvania Department of Health
Bureau of Maternal and Child Preventive Health Programs
Division of Maternal and Child Health
725 Health and Welfare Bldg.
Box 90
Harrisburg, PA 17108
Phone: (717)787-7443

★8584★ Pennsylvania Department of Public Welfare
Office of Social Programs
Family Violence Prevention and Services
PO Box 2675
Harrisburg, PA 17105
Phone: (717)783-7477
Karen Habel, Contact

★8585★ Pennsylvania Women's Commission
PO Box 1326
Harrisburg, PA 17105
Phone: (717)787-8128
Janice McElroy, Exec. Director

Puerto Rico

★8586★ Puerto Rico Commission for Women's Affairs
Office of the Governor, Commonwealth of Puerto Rico
PO Box 11382 Estacion Fernandez
Santurce, PR 00910
Phone: (809)722-2977
Yolanda Cayas, Exec. Director

★8587★ Puerto Rico Department of Social Services
Office of External Affairs
Family Violence Prevention and Services
PO Box 11398
Santurce, PR 00910
Phone: (809)722-1524
Luz Berrios, Director

Rhode Island

★8588★ Rhode Island Administration Department
Equal Opportunity Office
1 Capitol Hill
Providence, RI 02908-5865
Phone: (401)277-3090
A. Vincent Igliozzi, Chief

★8589★ Rhode Island Advisory Commission on Women
67 Cedar St.
Providence, RI 02903
Phone: (401)277-6105
Sue Baker, Exec. Director

★8590★ Rhode Island Department of Health
Division of Family Health
3 Capitol Hill
Providence, RI 02908
Phone: (401)277-2312

★8591★ Rhode Island Department of Human Services
Economic and Social Services Division
Family Violence Prevention and Services
600 New London Ave.
Cranston, RI 02920
Phone: (401)464-2371
John D. Bamford, Contact

South Carolina

★8592★ South Carolina Commission on Women
2221 Devine St., Ste. 408
Columbia, SC 29205
Phone: (803)734-9143
Carolyn Matalene, Chairperson

★8593★ South Carolina Department of Health and Environmental Control
Office of Health Services
Bureau of Maternal and Child Health
J. Marion Sims Bldg. and R.J. Ayacock Bldg.
Columbia, SC 29201
Phone: (803)734-4190

★8594★ South Carolina Department of Social Services
Spouse Abuse Program
PO Box 1520
Columbia, SC 29202
Phone: (803)734-5670
Valerie Doughty, Director

South Dakota

★8595★ South Dakota Department of Health
Division of Health Services
Maternal and Child Health Program
Foss Bldg.
523 E. Capitol
Pierre, SD 57501-3182
Phone: (605)773-3737

★8596★ South Dakota Department of Social Services
Child Protection Services Office
Family Violence Prevention and Services
700 Governor's Dr.
Pierre, SD 57501
Phone: (605)773-3227
Diane Kleinsasser, Program Specialist

★8597★ South Dakota Department of Social Services
Child Support Enforcement Office
700 Governors Dr.
Pierre, SD 57501
Phone: (605)773-3641
Terry Walter, Contact

★8598★ South Dakota Personnel Bureau
Equal Employment Opportunity Office
500 E. Capitol
Pierre, SD 57501
Phone: (605)773-4919
Douglas Decker, Contact

Tennessee

★8599★ Tennessee Department of Health and Environment
Health Services Bureau
Maternal and Children's Health Section
344 Cordell Hull Bldg.
Nashville, TN 37247-0101
Phone: (615)741-7353

★8600★ Tennessee Department of Human Services
Family Violence Prevention and Services
400 Deadrick St.
Nashville, TN 37219
Phone: (615)741-5947
Dora Hemphill, Contact

Texas

★8601★ Texas Attorney General
Child Support Enforcement Division
PO Box 12548
Austin, TX 78711-2548
Phone: (512)463-2181
Ellen Abbott, Contact

★8602★ Texas Department of Health
Personal Health Services
Bureau of Maternal and Child Health
1100 W. 49th St.
Austin, TX 78756
Phone: (512)458-7700

★8603★ Texas Department of Human Services
Family Violence Prevention and Services
Mail Code W-417
PO Box 149030
Austin, TX 78714-9030
Phone: (512)450-3011
Kathlyn Redfern, CPS Provider Services

★8604★ Texas Employment Commission
Equal Employment Opportunity Division
101 E. 15th St.
Austin, TX 78778
Phone: (512)463-2320
David Laurel, Contact

★8605★ Texas Governor's Commission for Women
PO Box 12428
Auston, TX 78711
Phone: (512)463-1782
Sallie F. McKenzie, Chair

Utah

★8606★ Utah Department of Health
Division of Family Health Services
Maternal and Child Health Bureau
PO Box 16700
Salt Lake City, UT 84116-0700
Phone: (801)584-8237

★8607★ Utah Department of Human Services
Bureau of Family Services
Family Violence Prevention and Services
120 N. 200 West, 4th Fl.
Salt Lake City, UT 84145-0500
Phone: (801)538-4100
Leroy Franke, Contact

★8608★ Utah Governor's Commission on Status of Women and Families
State Capitol Bldg., Rm. B-11
Salt Lake City, UT 84114
Phone: (801)566-1000
Kathleen Mason, Chair

Vermont

★8609★ Vermont Agency of Human Services
Child Support Services Office
103 S. Main St.
Waterbury, VT 05671-1901
Phone: (802)241-2319
Jeffrey P. Cohen, Director

★8610★ Vermont Agency of Human Services
Department of Health
Bureau of Maternal and Child Health
60 Main St.
PO Box 70
Burlington, VT 05402
Phone: (802)863-7606

★8611★ Vermont Agency of Human Services
Family Violence Prevention and Services
103 S. Main St.
Waterbury, VT 05676
Phone: (802)241-2227
Dr. Ted J. Mable, Contact

★8612★ Vermont Commission on Women
126 State St.
Montpelier, VT 05633-6801
Phone: (802)828-2851
Sara Lee, Exec. Director

Virginia

★8613★ Virginia Administration Office
Personnel and Training Department
Equal Employment Opportunity Office
Monroe Bldg.
101 N. 14th St.
Richmond, VA 23219
Phone: (804)225-3462

★8614★ Virginia Council on the Status of Women
8007 Discovery Dr.
Blair Bldg.
Richmond, VA 23229-8699
Phone: (804)662-9200

★8615★ Virginia Department of Health
Division of Maternal and Child Health
James Madison Bldg.
109 Governor St.
Richmond, VA 23219
Phone: (804)786-7367

★8616★ Virginia Department of Social Services
Child Support Enforcement Division
8007 Discovery Dr.
Richmond, VA 23229-8699
Phone: (804)662-7412
Harry Wiggins, Contact

★8617★ Virginia Department of Social Services
Division of Service Programs
Spouse Abuse Prevention and Services
8007 Discovery Dr.
Richmond, VA 23288
Phone: (804)662-9008
Deb Downing, Coordinator

Washington

★8618★ Washington Department of Health
Division of Parent and Child Health Services
1300 SE Quince, EY-12
Olympia, WA 98504
Phone: (206)753-5870

★8619★ Washington Department of Social and Health Services
Division of Children and Family Services
Domestic Violence Program
Mail Stop OB-41C
Olympia, WA 98504
Phone: (206)586-2380
Barbara Gilbertson, Contact

West Virginia

★8620★ West Virginia Department of Health and Human Resources
Family Violence Prevention and Services
Charleston, WV 25305
Phone: (304)348-7980
Claire C. Leviner, Director

★8621★ West Virginia Department of Health and Human Resources
Public Health Bureau
Office of Community Health Services
Division of Maternal and Child Health
State Capitol Complex
Bldg. 3, Rm. 519
Charleston, WV 25305
Phone: (304)768-6295

★8622★ West Virginia Women's Commission
Bldg. 6, State Capitol, 8th Fl.
Charleston, WV 25305
Phone: (304)348-0070
Adrienn Worthy, Exec. Director

Wisconsin

★8623★ Wisconsin Department of Health and Social Services
Bureau for Children, Youth and Families
Family Violence Prevention and Services
PO Box 7850
Madison, WI 53707
Phone: (608)266-9305
Mary Lauby, Contact

★8624★ Wisconsin Department of Health and Social Services
Child Support Bureau
PO Box 7850
Madison, WI 53707
Phone: (608)266-9909

★8625★ Wisconsin Department of Health and Social Services
Division of Health
Bureau of Community Health and Prevention
1 W. Wilson St.
PO Box 7850
Madison, WI 53707
Phone: (608)266-1251

★8626★ Wisconsin Industry Labor and Human Relations Department
Equal Rights Division
PO Box 7946
Madison, WI 53707
Phone: (608)266-0946
Sheehan Donoghue, Administrator

★8627★ Wisconsin Women's Council
16 N. Carroll St., Ste. 720
Madison, WI 53702
Hannah Rosenthal, Exec. Director

Wyoming

★8628★ Wyoming Commission for Women
Herschler Bldg.
25th & Central
Cheyenne, WY 82002
Phone: (307)777-7349
Jan Nelson-Schroll, Exec. Director

★8629★ Wyoming Department of Employment
Fair Employment Division
Herschler Bldg., 2nd Fl. E.
Cheyenne, WY 82002
Phone: (307)777-6381
David Simonton, Contact

★8630★ Wyoming Department of Health
Division of Community Programs
Office of Family Violence and Sexual Assault
454 Hathaway Bldg.
Cheyenne, WY 82002-0710
Phone: (307)777-7115
Ruth Edwards, Contact

★8631★ Wyoming Department of Health
Division of Health and Medical Services
Family Health Services
Hathaway Bldg.
Cheyenne, WY 82002
Phone: (307)777-6186

(17) Top U.S. Women-Owned Businesses

Businesses are listed in descending order based on total sales. See the User's Guide at the front of this directory for additional information.

★8632★ Axel Johnson Group
110 E. 59th St.
New York, NY 10022
Antonia Axson Johnson, Chair

Founded: 1873. **Employees:** 2,000. **Type of Business:** Speciality metals, water-treatment and telecommunications equipment. **1991 Sales (in millions of dollars):** $829 million. **Rank in 1991:** 1.

★8633★ Minyard Food Stores
PO Box 518
Coppell, TX 75019
Phone: (214)393-8700
Gretchen Minyard Williams, Co-Chair; Liz Minyard, Co-Chair

Founded: 1932. **Employees:** 6,100. **Type of Business:** Supermarket chains. **1991 Sales (in millions of dollars):** $700 million. **Rank in 1991:** 2.

★8634★ Warnaco Group Inc.
90 Park Ave.
New York, NY 10016
Phone: (212)661-1300
Linda J. Wachner, Chair, CEO, Pres.

Founded: 1874. **Employees:** 11,800. **Type of Business:** Apparel manufacturer. **1991 Sales (in millions of dollars):** $548 million. **Rank in 1991:** 3.

★8635★ Jockey International
2300 60th St.
Kenosha, WI 53140
Phone: (414)658-8111
Donna W. Steigerwaldt, Chair, CEO

Founded: 1876. **Employees:** 5,000. **Type of Business:** Apparel manufacturer. **1991 Sales (in millions of dollars):** $450 million. **Rank in 1991:** 4.

★8636★ Esprit de Corp
900 Minnesota Ave.
San Francisco, CA 94017
Phone: (415)648-6900
Susie Tompkins, Creative Director

Founded: 1968. **Employees:** 1,400. **Type of Business:** Women's and children's apparel manufacturer and wholesaler. **1991 Sales (in millions of dollars):** $450 million. **Rank in 1991:** 5.

★8637★ Astronautics
41115 N. Teutonia
Milwaukee, WI 53209
Phone: (414)447-8200
Fax: (414)447-8231
Norma Paige, Chair and Exec.V.Pres.

Founded: 1959. **Employees:** 4,700. **Type of Business:** Aircraft and navigation equipment manufacturer. **1991 Sales (in millions of dollars):** $415 million. **Rank in 1991:** 6.

★8638★ Jenny Craig, Inc.
445 Marine View Ave., Ste. 300
Del Mar, CA 92014
Phone: (619)259-7000
Jenny Craig, Vice Chair

Founded: 1983. **Employees:** 7,000. **Type of Business:** Weight-loss centers and diet foods. **1991 Sales (in millions of dollars):** $412 million. **Rank in 1991:** 7.

★8639★ Copley Press
7776 Ivanhoe Ave.
La Jolla, CA 92307
Phone: (619)454-0411
Helen K. Copley, Chair, CEO

Founded: 1905. **Employees:** 3,500. **Type of Business:** Newspaper publishing and printing. **1991 Sales (in millions of dollars):** $405 million. **Rank in 1991:** 8.

★8640★ Charles Levy Co.
1200 N. Northbranch St.
Chicago, IL 60627
Phone: (312)440-4400
Barbara Levy Kipper, Chair

Founded: 1893. **Employees:** 1,700. **Type of Business:** Book, magazine, newspaper and video wholesaler. **1991 Sales (in millions of dollars):** $350 million. **Rank in 1991:** 9.

★8641★ Lundy Packing Co.
PO Box 49
Clinton, NC 28328
Phone: (919)592-2104
Fax: (919)592-7411
Annabelle Lundy Fetterman, Chair

Founded: 1950. **Employees:** 900. **Type of Business:** Pork processing. **1991 Sales (in millions of dollars):** $350 million. **Rank in 1991:** 10.

★8642★ Gear Holdings, Inc.
127 7th Ave.
New York, NY 10011
Phone: (212)645-8000
Bettye Martin Musham, CEO, Pres.

Employees: 30. **Type of Business:** Furniture design, home furnishings. **1991 Sales (in millions of dollars):** $280 million. **Rank in 1991:** 11.

★8643★ Johnson Publishing
820 S. Michigan Ave.
Chicago, IL 60605
Linda Johnson Rice, COO, Pres.

Founded: 1942. **Employees:** 2,753. **Type of Business:** Black media conglomerate. **1991 Sales (in millions of dollars):** $252 million. **Rank in 1991:** 12.

★8644★ Owen Healthcare, Inc.
9800 Centre Pkwy., Ste. 1100
Houston, TX 77036
Phone: (713)777-8173
Dian Graves Owen, Chair, Co-CEO

Founded: 1970. **Employees:** 2,000. **Type of Business:** Cost-control company for hospital pharmacies. **1991 Sales (in millions of dollars):** $250 million. **Rank in 1991:** 13.

★8645★ Carole Little, Inc.
102 E. Martin Luther King Blvd.
Los Angeles, CA 90011
Phone: (213)232-3100
Fax: (213)232-0377
Carole Little, Co-Chair, Co-Founder

Founded: 1975. **Employees:** 600. **Type of Business:** Women's apparel manufacturer. **1991 Sales (in millions of dollars):** $205 million. **Rank in 1991:** 14.

★8646★ Sunshine-Jr. Stores, Inc.
PO Box 2498
Panama City, FL 32402
Phone: (904)769-1661
Lana Jane Lewis-Brent, CEO, Pres., Vice Chair

Founded: 1944. **Employees:** 1,800. **Type of Business:** Convenience food stores, supermarkets, and gasoline service stations. **1991 Sales (in millions of dollars):** $203 million. **Rank in 1991:** 15.

★8647★ Tootsie Roll Industries
7401 S. Cicero Ave.
Chicago, IL 60629
Phone: (312)838-3400
Ellen R. Gordon, President
Founded: 1917. **Employees:** 1,400. **Type of Business:** Candy manufacturer. **1991 Sales (in millions of dollars):** $200 million. **Rank in 1991:** 16.

★8648★ Donna Karan Co.
550 7th Ave., 14th Fl.
New York, NY 10018
Phone: (212)398-0616
Donna Karan, CEO
Founded: 1984. **Employees:** 750. **Type of Business:** Women's apparel manufacturer. **1991 Sales (in millions of dollars):** $200 million. **Rank in 1991:** 17.

★8649★ Owen Steel Co.
PO Box 18
Columbia, SC 29202
Phone: (803)251-7680
Dorothy Owen, Chair
Founded: 1936. **Employees:** 1,500. **Type of Business:** Structural and reinforcement steel. **1991 Sales (in millions of dollars):** $192 million. **Rank in 1991:** 18.

★8650★ Resort Condominiums
International
3502 Woodview Trace
Indianapolis, IN 46268
Phone: (317)876-1692
Christel Dehaan, CEO & Pres
Employees: 2,300. **Type of Business:** Real estate, time share trading. **1991 Sales (in millions of dollars):** $180 million. **Rank in 1991:** 19.

★8651★ Adrienne Vittadini, Inc.
1441 Broadway, 1st Fl.
New York, NY 10018
Phone: (212)921-2510
Adrienne Vittadini, Chair
Founded: 1979. **Employees:** 200. **Type of Business:** Apparel. **1991 Sales (in millions of dollars):** $160 million. **Rank in 1991:** 20.

★8652★ Lillian Vernon Corp.
510 S. Fulton Ave.
Mt. Vernon, NY 15150
Phone: (914)699-4131
Lillian Vernon, CEO
Founded: 1951. **Employees:** 1,000. **Type of Business:** Mail-order gifts and novelties. **1991 Sales (in millions of dollars):** $160 million. **Rank in 1991:** 21.

★8653★ Copeland Lumber Yards Inc.
901 NE Glisan
Portland, OR 97232
Phone: (503)232-7181
Helen Jo Whitsell, Chair, CEO
Founded: 1913. **Employees:** 800. **Type of Business:** Retail lumber and building materials. **1991 Sales (in millions of dollars):** $152 million. **Rank in 1991:** 22.

★8654★ Software Spectrum
2140 Merritt Dr.
Garland, TX 75741
Phone: (214)840-6600
Judy Sims, CEO
Founded: 1983. **Employees:** 260. **Type of Business:** Software retailer. **1991 Sales (in millions of dollars):** $146 million. **Rank in 1991:** 23.

★8655★ Redken Laboratories
6625 Variel Ave.
Canoga Park, CA 91303
Phone: (818)992-2700
Paula Kent Meehan, Chair, CEO
Founded: 1960. **Employees:** 830. **Type of Business:** Hair and skin care products manufacturer. **1991 Sales (in millions of dollars):** $140 million. **Rank in 1991:** 24.

★8656★ Rose Acre Farms
6874 N. Base Rd.
Seymour, IN 47274
Phone: (812)522-8692
Lois Rust, President
Employees: 500. **Type of Business:** Egg farm. **1991 Sales (in millions of dollars):** $127 million. **Rank in 1991:** 25.

(18) Consultants and Consulting Organizations

Entries in this chapter are arranged alphabetically by organization name. See the User's Guide at the front of this directory for additional information.

★8657★ Carol Ann Valentine
2607 S. Forest Ave.
Tempe, AZ 85282
Phone: (602)967-2817

Founded: 1975. **Staff:** 2. **Principle Executive(s):** Carol Ann Valentine. **Consulting Activities:** Conducts seminars and other training programs on communication. Frequent programs focus on nonverbal communication, listening skills, interviewing and communication among women. Serves private industries as well as government agencies. Small women-owned firm. **Seminars and Workshops:** Effective Listening; Family Communication.

★8658★ Catherine Gaffigan
400 W. 43rd St., Suite 44L
New York, NY 10036
Phone: (212)594-9871

Founded: 1977. **Staff:** 7. **Principle Executive(s):** Catherine Gaffigan, CEO. **Consulting Activities:** Welfare consultant whose total focus is on ending dependency by creating wage earners. Provides training seminars. A two-session, six-hour intensive program prepares welfare recipients, including women with no work history, to free themselves from the system and take charge of their own lives. Offers individually tailored "personal action program" containing attainable and realistic training and education goals, plus job interview skills. Also identifies specific, appropriate job openings existing at the present time. Serves government agencies administering "workfare" programs, and public assistance recipients, especially single mothers. **Seminars and Workshops:** All sessions custom designed for targeted population; in house. This training is conducted in locations and for groups organized by the client organization (such as the City of New York).

★8659★ Center for Counseling and Health Resources
611 Main St.
Edmonds, WA 98020
Phone: (206)771-5166
Fax: (206)670-2807

Founded: 1980. **Staff:** 8. **Principle Executive(s):** Gregory L. Jantz. **Consulting Activities:** Consulting services of the Center include education and training, as well as counseling and treatment programs concerning family relationships, eating disorders, weight loss, and addictions and compulsions. Emphasis is on health programs, nutrition and issues concerning women. **Seminars and Workshops:** Sales Excellence; Personal Selling Power; Personal Power.

★8660★ Child Care Management Consultants, Inc.
512 Jerome St.
Davis, CA 95616
Phone: (916)753-6959

Founded: 1985 **Staff:** 2. **Principle Executive(s):** Sylvia E. Schmidt; Lisa M. Austin. **Consulting Activities:** A child care management, research and development firm offering the latest information on planning and managing a variety of child care options for client companies seeking to offer child care as part of an employee benefit plan. Consultation ranges from conducting employee child care needs surveys, and employer financing cost/benefit studies, to the development of specific dependent care assistance plans for the tax advantages and record keeping needed to manage the child care option best suited to a client firm and its employees. Firm also assists in planning on-site child care, arranges private care contacts, develops resources and referral services, gives parenting seminars, and consults about other child care and family-oriented options. **Seminars and Workshops:** Principals lecture frequently on various aspects of day care for working families.

★8661★ Consultant Services Northwest, Inc.
839 NE 96th St.
Seattle, WA 98115
Phone: (206)524-1950

Founded: 1980. **Principle Executive(s):** Charna S. Klein, President; Mardell O. Moore, Secretary-Treasurer. **Consulting Activities:** Offers human relations training and development, with emphasis on women and minorities; research, consultation, and training on social and cultural issues; training to bridge the communication gap between clients and providers of mental and medical health care; and training on issues involving select client populations, especially involving sex, age, and cultural differences. Provides foundation and library research; abstracting and writing services. Offers microcomputer software training (IBM, Apple), computer programming, word processing, spreadsheet, and data base management services. Offers services to individuals, profit, non-profit, governmental organizations and agencies, and "alternative" organizations. **Seminars and Workshops:** Ethnotheraphy and Ethnomedicine—How to Work with Diverse Clients.

★8662★ Consultants on Today's Women
361 S. Commonwealth Ave.
Elgin, IL 60123
Phone: (708)741-1739

Founded: 1976. **Staff:** 1. **Principle Executive(s):** Barbara J. Schock, Managing Director. **Consulting Activities:** Provides consulting service to businesses seeking to develop educational materials and newsletters in consumer interest areas, with emphasis on foods and textiles; to governmental agencies requiring knowledge of women's consumer interests; and to women's organizations in program development areas.

★8663★ Cosmopolitan Chamber of Commerce Contractors Division
1326 S. Michigan Ave.
Chicago, IL 60605
Phone: (312)786-0212
Fax: (312)786-9079

Founded: 1933. **Staff:** 7. **Principle Executive(s):** Consuelo M. Pope, President/CEO. **Consulting Activities:** Consults to major corporations, general contractors, government entities, municipal agencies, and participants in the construction industry on the use of minority and female contractors and subcontractors. Active in metropolitan Chicago area. Minority-owned firm. **Seminars and Workshops:** Estimating, Bonding and Financing; How to Start a Construction Company; Managing Construction Costs. **Computerized Information Services:** Maintains database of minority and female owned construction and related firms in the Chicago, Illinois, area.

★8664★ DCC, Inc./the Dependent Care Connection
PO Box 2783
Westport, CT 06880
Phone: (203)226-2680
Fax: (203)226-2852

Founded: 1984. **Staff:** 10. **Principle Executive(s):** John B. Place, President; Jeff Burki, Vice President; Peter Burki, Vice President; Norma Savarino. **Consulting Activities:** Provides consulting services that help employers to evaluate and implement child care and eldercare employee assistance programs. Works primarily with companies with 500 plus employees. Complete needs assessment and implementation assistance provide to clients. Serves the following businesses and industries: aerospace, agriculture, banking, consumer products, data processing, government, health care, insurance, manufacturing, nonprofit organizations, and pharmaceutical. Active in the United States. Small Business firm. **Publications and/or Videos:** *How to Find and Evaluate High Quality Child Care; How to Find and Evaluate High Quality Eldercare* (videos). **Seminars and Workshops:** Integrating Work and Family: Issues and Options; How to Find and Evaluate High Quality Child Care; How to Find and Evaluate High Quality Eldercare. **Computerized Information Services:** Maintains a database of over 500,000 listings of child care and eldercare resource organizations on a nationwide basis; employee resourse kiosks with database, videos and print materials. **Branch Office(s):**

■ 37 Franklin St., Westport, CT 06880

★8665★ Donald E. Maypole
123 Aspen Ln.
Duluth, MN 55803
Phone: (218)724-6029
Founded: 1979. **Staff:** 1. **Principle Executive(s):** Donald E. Maypole. **Consulting Activities:** Provides consulting services in grantwriting for social and health agencies; developing employee assistance programs in business firms, developing policies and procedures to deal with sexual harassment at work in business firms; and consultation to individuals and attorneys as expert witness. **Seminars and Workshops:** How to Write Successful Grants; Introduction to Counseling; Sexual Harassment at Work; Marketing Social and Health Agencies.

★8666★ Gender Harmony Network
Box 9173
Madison, WI 53715
Phone: (608)256-6024
Fax: (608)251-0658
Founded: 1990. **Staff:** 3. **Principle Executive(s):** Roy U. Schenk. **Consulting Activities:** Offers consulting on male perspective on gender issues. Provides expert witness testimony on sexual harassment, domestic abuse, sexual assault, and other related issues. Serves private industries as well as government agencies. Active nationally. Small business firm.

★8667★ Haskell Associates
2205 Panama St.
Philadelphia, PA 19103
Phone: (215)735-3348
Fax: (215)735-8686
Founded: 1985. **Staff:** 1. **Principle Executive(s):** Jean R. Haskell, President. **Consulting Activities:** Offers expertise in management training, career development, executive coaching, and leadership training for women. Serves manufacturing, service, financial, health care and non-profit industries, as well as government agencies. Active primarily in Delaware Valley, however no geographical restrictions. Small women-owned firm. **Seminars and Workshops:** Effective Presentations; Career Planning Leadership; Interpersonal Communication; Making Meetings Work; Coaching Skills for Managers.

★8668★ Health Associates
RD 2, Box 149
Waynesburg, PA 15370
Phone: (412)627-7557
Founded: 1980. **Staff:** 23. **Principle Executive(s):** Mona M. Counts. **Consulting Activities:** Health care consultants and trainers offering health education programs, health promo-

tion services, impaired worker seminars, seminars on issues in policy making, medical consultation for legal services, women's health strategies, communication seminars/workshops, health care issues of the older population, and community health development. **Seminars and Workshops:** Women's Health; Healthy Aspects of Aging; Health Assessment for Home Health Practitioners.

★8669★ Healy & Associates
121 Springfield Ave.
Joliet, IL 60435-6561
Phone: (815)741-0102
Founded: 1979. **Staff:** 7. **Principle Executive(s):** Carolyn B. Healy, President. **Consulting Activities:** Personal development consultant with experience in alcoholism and family treatment; employee assistance program consultation and implementation; health promotion programming on stress, smoking cessation, weight control; alcohol and drug related prevention and educational programming; and individual, group and family counseling. Serves private industries as well as government agencies. Active in Chicago metropolitan area. Small woman-owned firm. **Seminars and Workshops:** Superwoman Syndrome; Assertive Communication; Alcohol and Drug Problems in the Workplace; Chemical Dependency: Enabling vs. Intervention; Stress Management; Women and Friendship; Employee Assistance Programs; Smoking Cessation in the Workplace; Eating and Weight Issues. **Branch Office(s):**

■ 15 Spinning Wheel Rd., Suite 417, Hinsdale, IL 60521

■ 800 W. Fifth Ave., Suite 203C, Naperville, IL 60540

■ 120 W. Golf Rd., Suite 217, Schaumburg, IL 60195

■ 3411 Chicago Rd., Suite 1W, Steger, IL 60475

★8670★ Institute of Applied Philosophy & Policy Analysis (IAPPA)
1910 Wyndale St., Suite 3
Houston, TX 77030
Phone: (713)790-9862
Founded: 1989. **Staff:** 12. **Principle Executive(s):** Nader Chokr. **Consulting Activities:** Conducts policy, conceptual, philosophical, and ethical research and analysis. Focus is on major issues and problems, including social, political, cultural, artistic, and technological issues. Areas served include education, arts, health and medical, science and technology, social and political systems, and government agencies. Active in the United States, Europe, Third World (Africa, Latin America, Middle East). Small business firm. **Seminars and Workshops:** Technology and Democracy: Reasons for Hope or for Concern; The Dynamics of Health Policy: Impact on Women; Why Appropriate Progressive Technologies for the Third World; Feminism, Women's Issues, and Public Policy: Toward a General Framework for Policy Analysis.

★8671★ Institute for the Study of Sexual Assault
403 Ashbury St.
San Francisco, CA 94117
Phone: (415)861-2048
Staff: 4. **Principle Executive(s):** Judith L. Musick. **Consulting Activities:** Consultants to attorneys, victim advocacy organizations, mental health state and metropolitan systems, special-

izing in the socio-legal aspects of sexual assault. Develops technical materials for attorneys, and offers consultations and technical assistance to institutions and agencies engaged in sexual assault prevention and response. Also offers needs assessments and evaluation studies for mental health facilities as well as training and professional development for legal, administrative, advocacy and treatment staffs. **Seminars and Workshops:** Preventing Sexual Abuse.

★8672★ Interactive Arts, Inc.
800 Market Ave., N.
Canton, OH 44702
Phone: (216)454-3200
Founded: 1981. **Staff:** 6. **Principle Executive(s):** Merle D. Griff, President. **Consulting Activities:** Deals with preventing, or resolving, problems of "people-to-people" and "people-to-environment" situations. Specializes in the custom design of training at all levels, in addition to management and program development. Areas covered in this training include: creativity (creative thinking), employee assistance, image (self and corporate), communication skills (interpersonal), conflict management, corporate culture, counseling skills, dual careers, human relations, and women's issues and concerns. **Seminars and Workshops:** Examples of current programs include: Male/Female Communication Styles (a cross-cultural approach); Marketing Your Services; How to Sell the Abstract; Using Your Corporate Culture in the Planning of Office Environments.

★8673★ The Kaleel Jamison Consulting Group, Inc.
1731 Robinway Dr.
Cincinnati, OH 45230
Phone: (513)231-1007
Founded: 1970. **Staff:** 4. **Principle Executive(s):** Frederick A. Miller, President; Judith H. Katz, Vice President; Catherine S. Buntaine, Vice President; Patricia A. Volk, Vice President; Sandy Fastert, Vice President. **Consulting Activities:** Offers human resources, strategic change, and management consulting services. Provides assistance to organizations and government agencies that want to be high performing and culturally diverse; also specializing in issues such as competition for individual excellence, building traditional organizations into culturally diverse organizations, conflict resolution, team building, black/white work relationships, women/men work relationships, performance appraisal, sexual attraction, and sexual harassment. Active in North America, Europe, Asia, and Africa. Small minority, women-owned firm. **Publications and/or Videos:** Videos on racism and sexism available. **Seminars and Workshops:** Developing Diversity; Making Multiculturalism Work; Creating High Performing Culturally Diverse Organizations.

★8674★ Karen B. Werth
10604 NE 38th Pl., Ste. 114
Kirkland, WA 98033
Phone: (206)454-4510
Founded: 1983. **Staff:** 1. **Principle Executive(s):** Karen B. Werth. **Consulting Activities:** Psychotherapy and behavioral health consultant offering services in these areas: support and management group facilitation; small and large group psycho-educational programming on a variety of health and mental health related

topics; mental health program development; group psychotherapy, eating disorders treatment as examples; stress management for professionals; and interpersonal communications training. **Seminars and Workshops:** Workshops include Burn-Out; Stress Management; Communications; Women's Mental Health Care; Eating Disorders; Health-Exercise-Nutrition.

★8675★ **Kaye Phyllips**
109-10 Queens Blvd.
Forest Hills, NY 11375
Phone: (718)268-6439
Founded: 1969. **Principle Executive(s):** Kaye Phyllips. **Consulting Activities:** Management consultant on new business development for women and minority groups. Offers counsel in business administration, organization, community-based planning, management, executive search, and college level training in new enterprises development for women and disadvantaged seeking an alternative to a job.

★8676★ **Management Training Specialists**
500 Main St., Ste. 1100
Ft. Worth, TX 76102-3929
Phone: (817)332-3612
Founded: 1982. **Staff:** 15. **Principle Executive(s):** Connie Sitterly. **Consulting Activities:** Offers customized, on-site training (entry level through officer) to increase productivity and enhance effectiveness and efficiency of employees in industry, government, banks, hospitals, tailored to meet specific interests and/or needs of client organization. Also offers speeches, programs, and public workshops. Topics include attitude productivity, teamwork, quality improvement, time management, stress, conflict, supervision, communication, assertiveness, change, problem solving, negotiation, style, and decision-making. Serves the following businesses and industries: public and private sectors, business, industry, and government. Active nationally and internationally. Small women-owned firm. **Publications and/or Videos:** A series of audio cassettes, titled *A Woman's Place Management*, is available from firm. **Seminars and Workshops:** How to Start and Succeed in Your Own Business; Executive Essentials: Image, Attitude, and Performance; Moving Up! Success Strategies for Women; Women in Management; Winning at Work.

★8677★ **MG Woman's Counseling Service of New York**
61 E. 77th St.
New York, NY 10021
Phone: (212)439-0100
Founded: 1979. **Staff:** 15. **Principle Executive(s):** Mara Gleckel. **Consulting Activities:** Offers consultations and referrals to professional specialists in short term or long term therapy, individual, family, couples, and specialized woman's groups. **Seminars and Workshops:** Presents numerous workshops on topics related to The Woman in Transition; The Woman Alone; The Woman in Marriage; Women's Leadership Training; Couples Workshop; The Career Woman; Ego and Image.

★8678★ **Miranda Associates, Inc.**
2000 L St. NW, Ste. 408
Washington, DC 20036
Phone: (202)857-0430
Fax: (202)822-6399
Founded: 1975. **Staff:** 40. **Principle Executive(s):** Lourdes Miranda, President; Gerald Griffin; Jack O'Brien; John Birdsong; Richard Fera. **Consulting Activities:** Three division-Human Resources, International Services, and Environmental Information-provide diversified services to businesses and governmental organizations including: education and training; health and human services programs; social and market research; environmental programs; program evaluation; cross-cultural training; consultation; technical assistance and program support; conference planning and management; multimedia communications; customized systems development; materials development; translation; project support and implementation; and customized seminars and workshops. **Seminars and Workshops:** Offers seminars and workshops tailored to fit government, business and educational institutions' needs which focus on increasing skills and knowledge in such areas as intercultural communications, sexual harassment prevention, management and career development for women and minorities, and micro-enterprise development.

★8679★ **National Clearinghouse on Marital and Date Rape**
2325 Oak St.
Berkeley, CA 94708
Phone: (510)524-1582
Founded: 1980. **Staff:** 4. **Principle Executive(s):** Laura X, Executive Director. **Consulting Activities:** Offers publications, consulting, and training services to help victims of marital and date rape and to stop the rape of potential victims by educating the public and offering resources to battered women's shelters, crisis centers, district attorneys, legislators, campuses, etc. Active in the United States. Women-owned firm. **Publications and/or Videos:** A chart which lists state laws regarding marital rape is available from the Clearinghouse. **Seminars and Workshops:** Workshops to improve services to marital and date rape survivors and their children, and general education.

★8680★ **New Futures Enterprises**
4502 Broad Rd.
Syracuse, NY 13215
Phone: (315)469-3902
Founded: 1983. **Staff:** 3. **Principle Executive(s):** Rosemary Agonito. **Consulting Activities:** Specializes in issues relating to women, male-female dynamics, and gender equity serving education, government and business. Provides training, research, surveys, program development, evaluation, problem identification and solving, and video production. Active in New York and the northeastern United States. Women-owned firm. **Publications and/or Videos:** R. Agonito, *All About Grants: Training Video*, provides an introduction to successful grant seeking. **Seminars and Workshops:** Positive Male-Female Communications Skills; Overcoming Sexual Harassment; Women's Leadership/Management Training; Women and Minority Business Ownership Training; Sex Equity in Schools.

★8681★ **Procurement Resources, Inc.**
111 Petrol Point, Ste. 204
Peachtree City, GA 30269
Phone: (404)631-3633
Fax: (404)487-0765
Founded: 1973. **Staff:** 7. **Principle Executive(s):** Reginald Williams, President; Carla Greenlee, Vice President. **Consulting Activities:** Management consultants with specialized expertise in minority/women's purchasing programs. Services focused on: staff training, supplier sourcing, needs evaluation, and program design and development. Serves private industries as well as government agencies. Active in continental United States. Minority-owned firm. **Seminars and Workshops:** Doing Business with Minority Vendors.

★8682★ **Ruth Lang Fitzgerald**
34 Harrison St.
Newton Highlands, MA 02161
Phone: (508)244-9620
Founded: 1974. **Staff:** 2. **Principle Executive(s):** Ruth L. Fitzgerald, President. **Consulting Activities:** Health and personal development consultant working in the areas of interpersonal relations, nutrition, healthy habits, preventive medicine, human relations and child rearing, personal image, women's issues and concerns, and other health care services. Serves private industries as well as government agencies. **Seminars and Workshops:** Modes, Manners, Morals; You and Your Child; Real Women of the 80's; AIDS Conference; Legislative Issues in Health Care.

★8683★ **Womandynamics**
27 Park Ln.
Bethpage, NY 11714
Phone: (516)735-9784
Founded: 1984. **Staff:** 1. **Principle Executive(s):** Nancy Philips. **Consulting Activities:** Offers personal growth and career effectiveness counseling and workshops specialized to meet the needs of female workers at all levels of an organization, from entry level to senior management. Serves all industries. **Seminars and Workshops:** Personal Power; Career Dynamics; Balancing Multiple Roles; Dynamic Communication; Stress Management.

★8684★ **Womanhood Media**
2701 Durant Ave., Ste. 14
Berkeley, CA 94704-1733
Phone: (510)549-2970
Founded: 1975. **Principle Executive(s):** Helen R. Wheeler. **Consulting Activities:** Consultant in academic affirmative management, with specializations in areas of women studies/women's services, media, libraries, and community college, through counseling-consulting in research structure and projects, course and program innovation, staff and professional development. Professional development services include tailor made training and workshops mainly for women in academe and in management. Also offers expert witness services. Small women-owned firm. **Publications and/or Videos:** H. Wheeler, *Getting Published in Women's Studies: An International Interdisciplinary, Professional Development Guide Mainly for Women*, McFarland (1989). **Seminars and Workshops:** How to Write and Market Your First Nonfiction Book; Getting the Right Job; Women and the Media; Women and Aging; Herstory-Why Women's History; Response to Sexual Harassment;

Women's Health Issues; Working with the Mass Media to Get Publicity for your Organization, Event, and Self; Women and Politics; Women and Leadership; Censorship in U.S.A. **Computerized Information Services:** Prepares unique "Pathfinders" for individual researchers.

★8685★ **Woman's Counseling Service**
61 E. 77th St.
New York, NY 10021
Phone: (201)439-0100

Founded: 1970. **Staff:** 12. **Principle Executive(s):** Mara Gleckel; Karen Sands. **Consulting Activities:** Consultant to women's groups on such topics as image and ego, success in life, interpersonal communicating, and related issues of concern to women and men. Serves private industries and universities, as well as government agencies. Active in New York, including all boroughs and Long Island; New Jersey; and Connecticut. Women-owned firm.
Branch Office(s):

■ 28 Illingworth Ave., Tenafly, NJ 07670.

★8686★ **Women's History Research Center**
2325 Oak St.
Berkeley, CA 94708
Phone: (510)524-1582

Founded: 1968. **Staff:** 4. **Principle Executive(s):** Laura X, President. **Consulting Activities:** Consultants on establishing small special interest libraries and small scale microform publishing and information on women's libraries. Works with professors, teachers, lawyers, graduate students, doctors, nurses, etc. working on research projects dealing with women's issues. Also provides phone consultation and speaker referrals. Active in the North America. Women-owned firm.

(19) Directories

Entries in this chapter are arranged alphabetically by publication title. See the User's Guide at the front of this directory for additional information.

★8687★ Abortion Alternative Organizations Directory
American Business Information, Inc.
American Business Directories, Inc.
5711 S. 86th Circle
Omaha, NE 68127
Phone: (402)593-4600
Fax: (402)331-1505

Number of listings: 1,131. **Entries include:** Name, address, phone, size of advertisement, name of owner or manager, number of employees, year first in *Yellow Pages*. **Arrangement:** Geographical. **Frequency:** Annual. **Price:** $85.00, payment with order. Significant discounts offered for standing orders. **Other Information:** Compiled from telephone company *Yellow Pages*, nationwide.

★8688★ Albuquerque Women in Business Directory
Duval Publishing
PO Box 6133
Albuquerque, NM 87197
Phone: (505)247-9195

Description: Yellow pages for area women in business. Also contains sections on community resources and women's organizations. **Frequency:** Annual.

★8689★ Ambulatory Maternal Health Care and Family Planning Services
March of Dimes Birth Defects Foundation
Professional Education Department
1275 Mamaroneck Ave.
White Plains, NY 10605
Phone: (914)428-7100
Fax: (914)428-8203

Publication Includes: List of professional organizations concerned with family planning and newborn care. **Entries include:** Name of organization, address. **Price:** $1.00. **Other Information:** Principal content is a guide for health care professionals on providing maternal health care and family planning services.

★8690★ American National Cattle Women—Directory
American National CattleWomen (ANCW)
5420 S. Quebec
PO Box 3881
Englewood, CO 80155-8011
Phone: (303)694-0313
Fax: (303)694-0305

Covers: About 10,000 member women employed or interested in the cattle industry.

Frequency: Annual. **Price:** Available to members only. **Other Information:** Also cited as *ANCW Directory*. Former association name is American National Cowbelles (1976).

★8691★ American News Women's Club—Directory
American News Women's Club
1607 22nd St. NW
Washington, DC 20008
Phone: (202)232-6770

Covers: Approximately 450 women employed by or associated with the news media industry. **Frequency:** Annual.

★8692★ American Society of Women Accountants—Membership Directory
American Society of Women Accountants
35 E. Wacker Dr., Ste. 1068
Chicago, IL 60601
Phone: (312)726-9030
Fax: (312)726-4543

Covers: Approximately 7,300 member accountants and educators in the accounting field. **Frequency:** Annual.

★8693★ American Woman's Society of Certified Public Accountants—Roster
American Woman's Society of Certified Public Accountants
401 N. Michigan Ave.
Chicago, IL 60611
Phone: (312)644-6610
Fax: (312)321-6869

Number of listings: 4,000. **Entries include:** Name, title; company name, address, phone; home address and phone; membership classification. **Arrangement:** Classified by type of membership, then geographical. **Indexes:** Alphabetical. **Pages (approx.):** 140. **Frequency:** Annual, September. **Price:** Available to members only.

★8694★ American Women Artists: From Early Indian Times to the Present
G. K. Hall & Company
70 Lincoln St.
Boston, MA 02111
Phone: (617)423-3990
Toll-free: 800-343-2806
Fax: (617)423-3999

Covers: 285 American women artists. **Entries include:** Name personal education, and career data, awards, honors, memberships; bibliogra-

phy, works. **Arrangement:** Chronological. **Indexes:** Subject, personal name. **Pages (approx.):** 560. **Frequency:** Published 1982. **Price:** $39.95.

★8695★ American Women Managers and Administrators: A Selective Biographical Dictionary
Greenwood Publishing Group, Inc.
88 Post Rd. W.
PO Box 5007
Westport, CT 06881
Phone: (203)226-3571

Covers: 225 twentieth-century women who hold or have held administrative, managerial, or leadership positions in business, education, or government, including founders and presidents of colleges and companies, vice presidents of major corporations, and women who were first in their profession or position. **Entries include:** Name, vital statistics, education and career information, bibliography. **Arrangement:** Alphabetical. **Pages (approx.):** 320. **Frequency:** Published June 1985. **Price:** $55.00. **Also Includes:** Bibliographies on business, education, and government. **Other Information:** Former name of publisher, Greenwood Press, Inc.

★8696★ American Women Writers: A Critical Reference Guide from Colonial Times to the Present
Crossroad Publishing Company
370 Lexington Ave.
New York, NY 10017
Phone: (212)532-3650
Toll-free: 800-638-3030
Fax: (212)532-4922

Covers: In four volumes, about 1,000 American fiction writers, poets, writers in the social sciences, magazine and newspaper writers, and others, including a considerable number of contemporary figures. **Entries include:** Listings are essentially critical bibliographies, and include an evaluation of the importance of the author's work, a bibliography, and biographical information. **Arrangement:** Alphabetical. **Indexes:** Subject/author. **Pages (approx.):** 500-600 per volume. **Price:** $75.00 per volume; $300.00 per set. **Other Information:** Formerly published by Continuum Publishing Company.

★8697★ Annotated Guide to Women's Periodicals
Earlham College
Women's Center
Box E-62
Richmond, IN 47374
Phone: (317)983-1268

★8698★ Artificial Breasts Directory
American Business Information, Inc.
American Business Directories, Inc.
5711 S. 86th Circle
Omaha, NE 68127
Phone: (402)593-4600
Fax: (402)331-1505

Number of listings: 1,019. **Entries include:** Name, address, phone, size of advertisement, name of owner or manager, number of employees, year first in *Yellow Pages*. **Arrangement:** Geographical. **Frequency:** Annual. **Price:** $85.00, payment with order. Significant discounts offered for standing orders. **Other Information:** Compiled from telephone company *Yellow Pages*, nationwide.

★8699★ ASPA Women in Public Administration Directory
American Society for Public Administration (ASPA)
Women in Public Administration
1120 G St. NW, Ste. 500
Washington, DC 20005
Phone: (202)393-7878

Covers: 1,500 member women in public administration. **Entries include:** Name, title, affiliation, address, phone. **Arrangement:** Alphabetical. **Indexes:** Geographical. **Pages (approx.):** 90. **Frequency:** Biennial, February of odd years. **Price:** Available to members only. **Other Information:** Formerly published by the Society's Committee for Women (1971-81). **Former Title(s):** *ASPA Women in Public Management Directory*.

★8700★ Association for Women in Science Directory
Association for Women in Science, Inc.
1522 K St. NW, Ste. 820
Washington, DC 20005
Phone: (202)408-0742
Toll-free: 800-886-2947
Fax: (202)408-8321

Covers: Over 3,000 female scientists and engineers. **Entries include:** Name, address, phone, education, occupational background. **Arrangement:** Geographical. **Pages (approx.):** 128. **Frequency:** Biennial, even years. **Price:** Available to members only. **Former Title(s):** *National Directory of Women in the Sciences: Members of the Association for Women in Science* (1990).

★8701★ Battered Women's Directory
Terry Mehlman
2702 Fairlawn Rd.
Durham, NC 27705-2774

Covers: Over 2,000 shelters, hotlines, YWCA's, hospitals, mental health services, legal service agencies, and other organizations and agencies which offer services to abused wives in the United States and abroad; includes listings of many educational resources on the problem. **Entries include:** Name, address, phone; additional information as available. **Arrangement:** Geographical. **Pages (approx.):** 285. **Frequency:** Irregular; latest edition spring 1989. **Price:**

$12.00, postpaid, payment with order. **Former Title(s):** *Working on Wife Abuse*.

★8702★ Biannual Women's Studies Program Directory
National Women's Studies Association (NWSA)
c/o Deborah Louis
University of Maryland
College Park, MD 20742-1325
Phone: (301)405-5573

★8703★ Building Women's Studies Collections: A Resource Guide
Association of College & Research Libraries
CHOICE
CHOICE Bibliographic Essay Series
100 Riverview Center
Middletown, CT 06457
Phone: (203)347-6933
Fax: (203)346-8586

Covers: 620 feminist publishers, publishers of women's studies books, pamphlets, films, microforms, and data archives; bookstores, distributors, and book dealers; and organizations that issue publications on women's issues. **Entries include:** Company or organization name, address, phone, products. **Arrangement:** Classified by product. **Indexes:** Company or organization name. **Pages (approx.):** 50. **Frequency:** Published 1988. **Price:** $12.00. **Other Information:** Formerly published in cooperation with the American Library Association.

★8704★ Campus Gang Rape: Party Games?
Association of American Colleges
Project on the Status and Education of Women
1818 R St. NW
Washington, DC 20009
Phone: (202)387-1300

Publication Includes: List of about 10 publishers and organizations concerned with gang rape on college campuses. **Frequency:** Published November 1985. **Price:** $3.00, payment with order. **Other Information:** Principal content is a discussion of the causes, consequences, and prevention of gang rape.

★8705★ Child Abuse and Neglect and Family Violence Audiovisual Catalog
Clearinghouse on Family Violence Information
Box 1182
Washington, DC 20013
Phone: (703)821-2086
Fax: (703)506-0384

Covers: Distributors of over 550 films, videotapes, filmstrips with tapes, slides with tapes, and audiovisual packages about child abuse and neglect and family violence. **Entries include:** Title, name of producer, distributor name and address; description of materials, including length, format, and price. **Arrangement:** Alphabetical by title. **Indexes:** Product, subject, distributor name. **Pages (approx.):** 250. **Frequency:** Irregular. **Price:** $25.00.

★8706★ Child Care Service Directory
American Business Information, Inc.
American Business Directories, Inc.
5711 S. 86th Circle
Omaha, NE 68127
Phone: (402)593-4600
Fax: (402)331-1505

Number of listings: 43,368. **Entries include:** Name, address, phone (including area code), size of advertisement, year first in *Yellow Pages*, name of owner or manager, number of employees. **Arrangement:** Geographical. **Frequency:** Annual. **Price:** $1215.00, payment with order. Significant discounts offered for standing orders. **Other Information:** Compiled from telephone company *Yellow Pages*, nationwide.

★8707★ Church Funding Resource Guide
Women's Technical Assistance Project (WTAP)
733 15th St., NW, Ste. 510
Washington, DC 20005
Phone: (202)638-0449
Fax: (202)783-1839

Frequency: Annual. **Price:** $50.

★8708★ Consumer's Guide to Abortion Services
National Abortion Federation (NAF)
1436 U St. NW, Ste. 103
Washington, DC 20009
Phone: (202)667-5881

Remarks: Available in English and Spanish.

★8709★ Contemporary Concert Music by Women: A Directory of the Composers and Their Works
Greenwood Publishing Group, Inc.
88 Post Rd. W.
PO Box 5007
Westport, CT 06881
Phone: (203)226-3571

Covers: About 80 female composers, primarily living, from the United States, Europe, and Australia; publishers and archives of women's music; companies which have recorded the music included in the discographies. **Entries include:** Composer, publisher, or archive name, address; biographical information and discographies for composers are given in separate sections, along with information on availability of their works. **Arrangement:** Composers, publishers, and archives in single alphabet, record companies separate. **Indexes:** Composer name. **Pages (approx.):** 355. **Frequency:** First edition April 1981. **Price:** $39.95, postpaid, payment with order.

★8710★ Continuum Dictionary of Women's Biography
Continuum Publishing Company
370 Lexington Ave.
New York, NY 10017
Phone: (212)532-3650
Toll-free: 800-638-3030

Covers: 1,900 women selected on the basis of their achievements in such fields as government, education, entertainment, sports, and business; both living and deceased persons are listed. **Entries include:** Name, personal and career data, achievements, specialties. **Arrangement:** Alphabetical. **Indexes:** Subject. **Pages (approx.):** 675. **Frequency:** Published 1989. **Price:** $39.50. **Former Title(s):** *International Dictionary of Women's Biography*.

★8711★ *The Courage to Heal: A Guide for Women Survivors of Child Sexual Abuse*
HarperCollins
10 E. 53rd St.
New York, NY 10022
Phone: (212)207-7000
Toll-free: 800-242-7737

Publication Includes: List of organizations and support groups that provide assistance to women who were sexually abused as children; also includes publications dealing with child sexual abuse. **Entries include:** Organization name, address, phone, geographical area served, description of services. **Arrangement:** Classified by type of service provided. **Frequency:** Irregular; most recent reprint, February 1990. **Price:** $18.95. **Other Information:** Principal content of publication is recovery guide for women who were sexually abused as children.

★8712★ *Custody Handbook: A Woman's Guide to Child Custody Disputes*
Women's Legal Defense Fund
PO Box 53131
Washington, DC 20009
Phone: (202)887-0364

Publication Includes: In appendixes—List of 6 agencies in the Washington, D.C. area for mothers seeking child support and 16 legal organizations nationwide for women seeking child custody during or after divorce, including organizations for lesbian mothers. **Entries include:** Organization name, address, phone. **Arrangement:** Geographical. **Pages (approx.):** 70. **Frequency:** Irregular; latest edition October 1988. **Price:** $7.95. **Other Information:** Principal content is a discussion of legal rights and issues for women involved in child custody disputes; case law discussions of child custody issues in the District of Columbia, Maryland, and Virginia are also included.

★8713★ *Directory of Family Day Care Associations and Support Groups*
Children's Foundation
725 15th St. NW, Ste. 505
Washington, DC 20005
Phone: (202)347-3300

Description: Lists over 500 groups involved in family day care issues. **Frequency:** Annual.

★8714★ *Directory of Family Planning Grantees, Delegates, and Clinics*
Family Life Information Exchange
PO Box 37299
Washington, DC 20013-7299
Phone: (301)585-6636
Fax: (301)565-5112

Covers: About 4,500 family planning clinics and recipients of grants funded by Title X of the Public Health Service Act through the Department of Health and Human Services. **Entries include:** Name, address. **Arrangement:** Geographical by DHHS region. **Pages (approx.):** 170. **Frequency:** Irregular; latest edition 1991-1992. **Price:** Free. **Other Information:** Former name of publisher, National Clearinghouse for Family Planning Information. **Former Title(s):** *Directory of Family Planning Grantees and Clinics.*

★8715★ *Directory of Federal Women's Program Managers*
Office of Affirmative Recruiting and Employment
Office of Personnel Management
1900 E St., N.W., Rm. 6336
Washington, DC 20415
Phone: (202)606-0870

Covers: About 95 federal government departments, agencies, bureaus, etc., with equal employment opportunity programs concerned specifically with women. **Entries include:** Department or agency name, address, phone, and name of program manager. **Arrangement:** Alphabetical. **Pages (approx.):** 10. **Frequency:** Irregular; latest edition January 1990. **Price:** Available under the Freedom of Information Act.

★8716★ *Directory of Financial Aids for Women*
Reference Service Press
1100 Industrial Rd., Ste. 9
San Carlos, CA 94070
Phone: (415)594-0743
Fax: (415)594-0411

Covers: More than 1,600 scholarships, fellowships, loan sources, grants, awards, internships, and state government educational assistance programs; includes annotated list of 75 financial aid directories. Sponsors include institutions, associations, businesses, government bodies, etc. **Entries include:** Program title, sponsor name, address, phone, purpose, candidate eligibility, financial details, duration, restrictions, application details and deadline, number awarded, etc. **Arrangement:** Programs are by type (scholarship, loan, etc.). **Indexes:** Sponsoring organization name, program title, geographical, subject, deadline date. **Pages (approx.):** 490. **Frequency:** Biennial, January odd years. **Price:** $45.00 (current edition); $47.50. **ISSN:** 0732-5215. **Other Information:** Formerly published by ABC-CLIO.

★8717★ *Directory of Information Resources on Victimization of Women*
Response
4136 Leland St.
Chevy Chase, MD 20815
Phone: (301)951-0039

Covers: Special libraries, clearinghouses, and online database offering resource information on women and children as victims of abuse. **Send orders to:** Response, Box 2462, Ada, OK 74820.

★8718★ *Directory of International Networking Resources on Violence Against Women*
Response
4136 Leland St.
Chevy Chase, MD 20815
Phone: (301)951-0039

Covers: Nongovernmental organizations, United Nations offices, United States organizations with international activities, and international periodicals in the field of violence against women. **Send orders to:** Response, Box 2462, Ada, OK 74820.

★8719★ *Directory of Library and Information Profession Women's Groups*
American Library Association (ALA)
Committee on the Status of Women in Librarianship
50 E. Huron St.
Chicago, IL 60611
Phone: (312)944-6780
Toll-free: 800-545-2433
Fax: (312)280-3256

Covers: About 40 associations and other groups of women active in library sciences and information services occupations. **Entries include:** Group name, contacts' names, titles, addresses, phone numbers; membership, purpose, dates and locations of meetings. **Arrangement:** Classified by type of membership. **Pages (approx.):** 15. **Frequency:** Irregular; latest edition 1992. **Price:** Free.

★8720★ *Directory of Minority and Women-Owned Engineering and Architectural Firms*
American Consulting Engineers Council (ACEC)
1015 15th St. NW, Ste. 802
Washington, DC 20005
Phone: (202)347-7474
Fax: (202)898-0068

Covers: Approximately 525 minority and women-owned engineering and architectural firms. **Entries include:** Firm name, address, phone; owner name(s), including percentage of ownership, sex, and race of each; registered professionals, size of staff, description of activities, minority status, branches; local, state, and federal MBE/WBE certification, if applicable. **Arrangement:** Geographical. **Indexes:** Firm name, area of experience. **Pages (approx.):** 115. **Frequency:** Irregular; latest edition 1990. **Price:** $15.00. **Former Title(s):** *Directory of Minority Architectural and Engineering Firms* (1980).

★8721★ *Directory of Minority and Women-Owned Investment Bankers*
San Francisco Redevelopment Agency
770 Golden Gate Ave.
San Francisco, CA 94101
Phone: (415)749-2400

Covers: About 15 minority-owned investment banking firms. **Entries include:** Company name, address, phone, owner's name and title. **Arrangement:** Alphabetical. **Frequency:** Latest edition 1988.

★8722★ *Directory of the National Association of Women in Horticulture*
National Association of Women in Horticulture
PO Box 1483
Mt. Dora, FL 32757-1483
Phone: (904)383-8811
Fax: (904)735-2688

Covers: Women in the field of horticulture, including members and nonmembers of the National Association of Women in Horticulture. **Entries include:** Name, address, phone, fax, employer, biographical data. **Arrangement:** Geographical and alphabetical. **Pages (approx.):** 30. **Frequency:** Annual, January. **Other Information:** Formerly published by Sunbelt Marketing Services, Inc.

★8723★ Directory of National Women's Organizations (NWO)
The National Council for Research on Women (NCRW)
The Sara Delano Roosevelt Memorial House
47-49 E. 65th St.
New York, NY 10021
Phone: (212)570-5001

Description: Describes 500 U.S. national women's organizations and groups, including research centers and discipline caucuses, policy and activist organizations, foundations, government agencies, libraries and archives, political action committees and unions, sororities and religious groups, women of color organizations, and more. **Price:** $38.

★8724★ Directory of Nurse-Midwifery Practices
American College of Nurse-Midwives
1522 K St. NW, Ste. 1000
Washington, DC 20005
Phone: (202)289-0171
Fax: (202)289-4395

Covers: About 600 nurse and midwifery practices. **Entries include:** Name of practice, address, phone, name of contact, site of birth. **Arrangement:** Geographical. **Pages (approx.):** 99. **Frequency:** Annual, spring. **Price:** $10.00. **Former Title(s):** American College of Nurse-Midwives—Directory; American College of Nurse-Midwives—Registry of Birth Services; National Registry of Nurse-Midwifery Services and Practices.

★8725★ Directory of Organizations for Women
Garrett Park Press
PO Box 190 B
Garrett Park, MD 20896
Phone: (301)946-2553

Covers: Hundreds of national and regional professional, service, and other organizations of women. **Frequency:** Periodic.

★8726★ Directory of Selected Research and Policy Centers Working on Women's Issues
Women's Research and Education Institute
1700 18th St. NW, Ste. 400
Washington, DC 20009
Phone: (202)328-7070
Fax: (202)328-3514

Covers: Over 40 research and policy centers that focus on issues of concern to women. **Entries include:** Center name, address, name of director or contact person, activities, current work or research projects, areas of expertise. **Arrangement:** Alphabetical. **Indexes:** Research subject or field, activity. **Pages (approx.):** 40. **Frequency:** Biennial, latest edition fall 1992. **Price:** $12.00, postpaid; payment with order. **Also Includes:** Tables of primary activities and research activities, and appendix listing centers with particular expertise on minority issues. **Former Title(s):** Directory of Selected Women's Research and Policy Centers (1977).

★8727★ Directory of Services for the Widowed in the United States and Canada
American Association of Retired Persons (AARP)
Widowed Persons Service
601 E St. NW
Washington, DC 20049
Phone: (202)434-2260

Covers: About 500 associations, services, and agencies offering counseling and other forms of assistance to widows and widowers. **Entries include:** Organization name, address, phone. **Arrangement:** Geographical. **Pages (approx.):** 100. **Frequency:** Biennial. **Price:** Free to libraries and public service organizations.

★8728★ Directory of State and Local Child Support Advocacy Groups
Children's Foundation
725 15th St. NW, Ste. 505
Washington, DC 20005
Phone: (202)347-3300

Description: Lists peer support groups for custodial parents having difficulty with child support issues. **Frequency:** Annual.

★8729★ Directory of Women Entrepreneurs
Wind River Publications, Inc.
PO Box 450827, Northlake Branch
Atlanta, GA 30345
Phone: (404)496-5986
Fax: (404)496-5986

Covers: Approximately 3,200 women-owned businesses; companies with minority and women professional development programs, women's groups and organizations, and minority business assistance offices. **Entries include:** For women-owned businesses—Company name, address, phone, names and titles of key personnel, year founded, financial data, Standard Industrial Classification (SIC) code, description of products or services. For others—Name, address, phone. **Arrangement:** Alphabetical. **Indexes:** Geographical, Standard Industrial Classification (SIC) code. **Pages (approx.):** 600. **Frequency:** Annual, February. **Price:** $79.95. **ISSN:** 1042-2420.

★8730★ Directory of Women Historians
American Historical Association
400 A St. SE
Washington, DC 20003-3889
Phone: (202)544-2422

Covers: 1,300 women historians who hold either a master's degree or doctorate, or are employed as professional historians. **Entries include:** Name, office or home address, office phone, highest degree held, personal data, research areas and areas of specialization. **Arrangement:** Alphabetical. **Indexes:** Subject and research area. **Pages (approx.):** 125. **Frequency:** Irregular; latest edition October 1988. **Price:** $8.00, plus $1.00 shipping.

★8731★ Directory of Women-Owned Businesses in New Hampshire
University of New Hampshire
Office of Economic Initiative
Heidelberg—Harris Bldg.
Technology Dr.
Durham, NH 03824
Phone: (603)862-0710

Frequency: Annual.

★8732★ Directory of Women in Sports Business
Women's Sports Guide
3306 Maynard Rd.
Shaker Heights, OH 44122
Phone: (216)751-0910

Covers: Approximately 1,500 women involved in all aspects of sports business, including broadcasting and corporate sponsorship. **Price:** $15.00.

★8733★ Directory of Women's Health Care Centers
Oryx Press
4041 N. Central, No. 700
Phoenix, AZ 85012
Phone: (602)265-2651
Toll-free: 800-279-ORYX
Fax: 800-279-4663

Covers: More than 200 women's health care facilities and organizations. **Entries include:** Facility or organization name, address, phone, names and titles of key personnel, type of facility, year established, parent company or organization affiliation, description of facilities, services, programs, and publications. **Arrangement:** Geographical. **Pages (approx.):** 160. **Frequency:** Latest edition July 1989. **Price:** $45.00.

★8734★ Directory of Women's Media
National Council for Research on Women
Sara Delano Roosevelt Memorial House
47-49 E. 65th St.
New York, NY 10021
Phone: (212)570-5001
Fax: (212)570-5380

Covers: More than 1300 women's media resources, including print and electronic media, publishers and news services, art groups, productions, and distributors (for film, video, cable, theater, dance, music, and multimedia), writers' groups and speakers' bureaus, media organizations, bookstores, libraries, museums, and archives.

★8735★ Directory of Women's Studies Programs and Library Resources
The Oryx Press
2214 N. Central
Phoenix, AZ 85004-1483
Toll-free: 800-457-6799
Fax: (602)253-2741

Description: Contains information on over 400 women's studies programs at colleges and universities in the United States, including library holdings in women's studies, details on programs, and faculty. **Entries include:** Institution name, discipline orientation, women's studies credentials, and library collection subject strengths. Subjects include political sciences, history, literature, theater, and sociology. **Price:** $55.

★8736★ Directory of Work-in-Progress and Recently-Published Resources
National Council for Reseach on Women
Sara Delano Roosevelt Memorial House
47-49 E. 65th St.
New York, NY 10021
Phone: (212)570-5001
Fax: (212)570-5380

Description: More than 1400 citations of works-in-progress and recently-published research and resources that encompass a broad range of work by and about women, including journal articles, books, conference presentations, data collections, policy guidelines, reports, art, and media. **Remarks:** The Directory is the published version of of the Council's Work-in-Progress data base, developed in collaboration with the Schlesinger Library at Radcliffe College and the Research Libraries Group. It is available online via RLIN, the Research Libraries Information Network.

★8737★ Displaced Homemaker Program Directory
National Displaced Homemakers Network
1625 K St. NW
Washington, DC 20006
Phone: (202)628-6767
Fax: (202)628-0123

Covers: Over 1,000 counseling and career assistance centers for women who are (primarily) widowed, divorced, separated, or abandoned after full-time careers as wives and mothers. **Entries include:** Center name, address, phone, name of contact. **Arrangement:** Geographical. **Pages (approx.):** 80. **Frequency:** Annual, September. **Price:** $20.00, plus $2.00 shipping; payment must accompany order.

★8738★ Equal Rights Amendment: An Annotated Bibliography of the Issues
Greenwood Publishing Group, Inc.
88 Post Rd., W.
PO Box 5007
Westport, CT 06881
Phone: (203)226-3571

Publication Includes: List of publishers of about 700 books, articles, government publications, and ERIC documents following the efforts to ratify the Equal Rights Amendment between 1975 and 1985, as well as organizations on record as supporting or opposing the ERA. **Entries include:** Name, address, description, and title of publication. **Arrangement:** Classified by subject. **Indexes:** Subject, author. **Frequency:** Published November 1986. **Price:** $35.00 **ISSN:** 0742-6941.

★8739★ Family Planning Information Centers Directory
American Business Information, Inc.
American Business Directories, Inc.
5711 S. 86th Circle
Omaha, NE 68127
Phone: (402)593-4600
Fax: (402)331-1505

Number of listings: 3,958. **Entries include:** Name, address, phone (including area code), size of advertisement, year first in *Yellow Pages* name of owner or manager, number of employees. **Arrangement:** Geographical. **Frequency:** Annual. **Price:** $145.00, payment with order. Significant discounts offered for standing orders. **Other Information:** Compiled from telephone company *Yellow Pages*, nationwide.

★8740★ Female Artists Past and Present
Women's History Research Center
2325 Oak St.
Berkeley, CA 94708

Covers: Women in the visual arts, with international sections.

★8741★ Feminist Business and Professional Network—Directory
Feminist Business and Professional Network (FBPN)
PO Box 91214
Washington, DC 20090-1214
Phone: (703)836-5325

Covers: Approximately 85 member individuals and companies. **Frequency:** Annual. **Price:** Free.

★8742★ Feminist Periodicals: A Current Listing of Contents
University of Wisconsin System
Women's Studies
Memorial Library, Rm. 112A
728 State St.
Madison, WI 53706
Phone: (608)263-5754
Fax: (608)262-4649

Covers: Over 100 periodicals of national or midwestern readership focusing on women's issues, particularly from a feminist standpoint. **Entries include:** Periodical title, year of first publication, frequency of publication, subscription price, subscription address, name of editor, editorial address (if different), ISSN, Library of Congress catalog card number, OCLC control number, University of Wisconsin system locations, publications in which indexed, subject focus or statement of purpose. **Arrangement:** Alphabetical by periodical title. **Pages (approx.):** 116. **Frequency:** Quarterly. **Price:** $43.00 per year to libraries; $23.00 per year to others; $2.75 per issue. Subscriptions also include *Women's Studies in Wisconsin: Who's Who and Where*, *Feminist Collections: A Quarterly of Women's Studies Resources*, *New Books on Women and Feminism*, and *Wisconsin Bibliographies in Women's Studies*. **ISSN:** 0742-7433. **Also Includes:** Title and table of contents pages from listed publications.

★8743★ Fertility Awareness & Natural Family Planning Resource Directory
Fertility Awareness Services
2857 NW Tyler
PO Box 986
Corvallis, OR 97339
Phone: (503)753-8530

Pages (approx.): 200. **Frequency:** Latest edition May 1988. **Price:** $35.00. **Other Information:** Formerly published by Small World Publications. Publication also reviews books and materials on infertility, parenting, birth, infant loss, and teen sex education.

★8744★ Focus on Families: A Reference Handbook
ABC-CLIO
PO Box 1911
Santa Barbara, CA 93116-1911
Phone: (805)968-1911
Toll-free: 800-422-2546

Publication Includes: List of agencies, organizations, and hotlines that service the public for a variety of social concerns including child abuse, incest, drug abuse, poverty, step-families, communication problems, alcoholism, runaways, and single-parent families. **Frequency:** Published 1989. **Price:** $29.50, plus $1.75 shipping. **Also Includes:** Annotated bibliography of fiction, non-fiction, and audio-visual materials. **Other Information:** Part of a series entitled *Teenage Perspective Series*, the principal con-

tent of publication is discussion on the aforementioned topics.

★8745★ Gaia's Guide
Inland Book Company
PO Box 120261
East Haven, CT 06512
Phone: (203)467-4257

Covers: Resorts, entertainment facilities, and other organizations providing services for lesbians; limited international coverage. **Entries include:** Facility name, address, phone, description of services. **Pages (approx.):** 660. **Price:** $11.95.

★8746★ Gay & Lesbian Parents Coalition International—Confidential Chapter Directory
Gay & Lesbian Parents Coalition International
Box 28317
Washington, DC 20038
Phone: (703)548-3238

Covers: Approximately 2,000 member homosexual fathers and mothers and their partners. **Entries include:** Name, address, phone. **Frequency:** Annual. **Price:** Available to members only.

★8747★ Gayellow Pages: A Classified Directory of Gay Services and Businesses in USA and Canada
Gayellow Pages
Box 292
Village Station
New York, NY 10014
Phone: (212)674-0120

Covers: Gay- or lesbian-oriented business enterprises, organizations, resources, churches, bars, restaurants, and publications. Many AIDS/HIV resources. Includes a separate listing of national organizations. **Entries include:** Name, address, phone, business hours, and an annotation describing programs, products, or services. **Arrangement:** Geographical; national listings are classified by subject category. **Pages (approx.):** 255. **Frequency:** Annual, February. **Price:** $12.00; postpaid. **Other Information:** Also available in regional editions; New York/New Jersey (annual, December, $4.50); the Northeast, including Connecticut, Delaware, District of Columbia, Maine, Maryland, Massachusetts, New Hampshire, Ohio, Pennsylvania, Rhode Island, Vermont, West Virginia (annual, $4.50); and Southern and Southern Midwest, including Alabama, Arizona, Arkansas, Florida, Georgia, Kansas, Kentucky, Louisiana, Mississippi, Missouri, New Mexico, North Carolina, Oklahoma, Puerto Rico, South Carolina, Tennessee, Texas, Virginia (annual, $4.50).

★8748★ Greater Philadelphia Women's Yellow Pages
PO Box 1002
Havertown, PA 19083
Phone: (215)235-4042
Frequency: Annual.

★8749★ The Greater Phoenix Women's Yellow Pages
4425 N. Saddlebag Trl.
Scottsdale, AZ 85251
Phone: (602)945-5000
Fax: (602)941-5196

Covers: Women's businesses, services, and organizations in the greater Phoenix area. **Frequency:** Annual. **Price:** $9.00 plus $3.00 for shipping.

★8750★ Guide to Women Book Publishers in the United States
Clothespin Fever Press
5529 N. Figueroa
Los Angeles, CA 90042
Phone: (213)254-1373

Covers: Approximately 285 women publishers. **Entries include:** Publisher name, address, contact, year founded, interests. **Arrangement:** Alphabetical by publisher. **Indexes:** Personal name and interest. **Pages (approx.):** 61. **Frequency:** Biennial, odd years. **Price:** $15.95.

★8751★ Handbook of Family Day Care Associations
Children's Foundation
725 15th St. NW, Ste. 505
Washington, DC 20005
Phone: (202)347-3300

★8752★ Healthy Mothers, Healthy Babies—Directory of Educational Materials
Healthy Mothers, Healthy Babies Coalition
409 12th St., SW, Rm. 309
Washington, DC 20023
Phone: (202)863-2458
Fax: (202)963-2499

Covers: Approximately 70 member organizations providing educational services and materials (primarily literature) concerning prenatal and infant care; approximately 15 additional non-member organizations offering similar services or products. **Entries include:** Organization name and address; brief statement outlining objectives and projects; list of materials or services provided. **Arrangement:** Alphabetical. **Indexes:** Subject, title. **Pages (approx.):** 170. **Frequency:** Irregular; latest edition 1985. **Price:** Free (single copies). **Other Information:** Single copy available from National Maternal and Child Health Clearinghouse, (202-821-8955).

★8753★ Higher Education Opportunities for Minorities and Women: Annotated Selections
U.S. Office of Postsecondary Education
400 Maryland Ave., Rm. 3915
Washington, DC 20202-5151
Phone: (202)732-5656

Covers: Programs of public and private organizations and state and federal government agencies that offer loans, scholarships, and fellowship opportunities for women and minorities. **Entries include:** Organization name, address, brief description of program. **Arrangement:** Classified by subject. **Pages (approx.):** 125. **Frequency:** Irregular; latest edition 1989. **Price:** $5.00. **Send orders to:** Superintendent of Documents, U.S. Government Printing Office, Washington, DC 20402 (202-783-3238). **Former Title(s):** Selected List of Postsecondary Education Opportunities for Minorities and Women.

★8754★ How to Get Money for Research
The Feminist Press at the City University of New York
311 E. 94th St.
New York, NY 10128
Phone: (212)360-5790

Covers: About 85 organizations, associations, foundations, and institutions offering grants and fellowships for research studies conducted by or about women; about 90 libraries or publishers offering research grant information. **Entries include:** For organizations, associations, foundations, or institutions—Name, address, phone, contact person, name of fund, award, purpose of award, eligibility requirements, restrictions, application procedures and deadline, amount and number of awards granted. For publishers—Publisher name, address, phone, title, price, information offered. For libraries in the Foundation Center network—Name, address, description of service. **Arrangement:** Classified by type of service. **Indexes:** Subject, program title, sponsoring organization. **Pages (approx.):** 95. **Frequency:** Irregular; latest edition 1983; new edition expected; date not set. **Price:** $6.95. **Other Information:** Research conducted with the Business and Professional Women's Foundation.

★8755★ Ideas on Proposal Writing and Financial Technical Assistance
International Women's Tribune Centre
777 United Nations Plaza, 3rd Fl.
New York, NY 10017
Phone: (212)687-8633
Fax: (212)661-2704

Covers: Agencies that fund women's programs worldwide. **Entries include:** Organization name, address, phone, geographical area served, requirements for eligibility, description of projects/services. **Arrangement:** Classified by type of agency. **Indexes:** Agency name. **Pages (approx.):** 80. **Frequency:** Irregular; latest edition September 1989. **Price:** $8.00. **Also Includes:** A section on how to write proposals and approach donor agencies.

★8756★ Infertility: Medical and Social Choices
Office of Technology Assessment
600 Pennsylvania Ave., SE
Washington, DC 20510
Phone: (202)224-3827
Fax: (202)275-0019

Publication Includes: List of approximately 170 facilities that perform in vitro fertilization (IVF) and gamete intrafallopian transfer (GIFT) surgery; approximately 20 surrogate mothering matching services. **Entries include:** For IVF/GIFT facilities—Company or institution name, address, phone. For surrogate mothering matching services—Company name, address. **Arrangement:** Separate geographical sections for IVF/GIFT facilities and surrogate mothering matching services. **Frequency:** Published May 1988. **Price:** $16.00. (S/N 052-003-01091-7; PB 88-196464). **Send orders to:** Superintendent of Documents, U.S. Government Printing Office, Washington, DC 20402 (202-783-3238); National Technical Information Service, Springfield, VA 22161 (703-487-4780). **Other Information:** Principal content examines the scientific, economic, legal, and ethical considerations involved in conventional and novel reproductive technologies.

★8757★ Inn Places: A Guide to Gay and Lesbian Accommodations
Ferrari Publications
Box 37887
Phoenix, AZ 85069
Phone: (602)863-2408
Fax: (602)942-3839

Covers: About 1000 accommodations for the gay and lesbian traveler. **Entries include:** Accommodation name and location, description of amenities and ambiance. **Arrangement:** Geographical. **Pages (approx.):** 600. **Frequency:** Annual, winter. **Price:** $14.95.

★8758★ The International Alliance, An Association of Executive and Professional Women—Membership Directory
The International Alliance, An Association of Executive and Professional Women
8600 LaSalle Rd., Ste. 308
Baltimore, MD 21204
Phone: (410)321-6699
Fax: (410)823-2410

Covers: About 5,000 member professional and executive women. **Entries include:** Network members and Alliance Associates. **Pages (approx.):** 30. **Frequency:** Annual. **Price:** Available to members only.

★8759★ International Association for Personnel Women—Membership Roster
International Association for Personnel Women
PO Box 969
Andover, MA 01810-0017
Phone: (508)474-0750
Fax: (508)474-8091

Covers: 1,200 members-at-large and members of affiliated chapters. **Entries include:** Individual name, title, company name, mailing address, office phone. **Arrangement:** Classified by type of membership. **Pages (approx.):** 90. **Frequency:** Annual, December.

★8760★ International Centers For Research on Women
National Counil for Research on Women (NCRW)
The Sara Delano Roosevelt Memorial House
47-49 E. 65th St.
New York, NY 10021
Phone: (212)570-5001

Description: Lists over 150 research and documentation centers in 47 countries, including the U.S. member centers of the National Council. **Price:** $10.

★8761★ International Childbirth Education Association—ICEA Membership Directory
International Childbirth Education Association
Box 20048
Minneapolis, MN 55420
Phone: (612)854-8660

Covers: Cesarean educators, childbirth educators, counselors, family physicians, homebirth specialists, nurses, nurse midwives, obstetricians and gynecologists, parent educators, pediatricians, and physical therapists and other individuals and associations involved in family-centered maternity care; international coverage. **Entries include:** Personal or organization name, address, names and titles of key personnel, services. **Arrangement:** Geographical. **Pages**

(approx.): 160. **Frequency:** Annual, February. **Price:** Available to members only.

★8762★ *International Directory of Gay and Lesbian Periodicals*
Oryx Press
4041 N. Central, No. 700
Phoenix, AZ 85012
Phone: (602)265-2651
Toll-free: 800-279-ORYX
Fax: 800-279-4663

Covers: Over 2,000 publishers of gay and lesbian newspapers, newsletters, journals, magazines, and other publications. **Entries include:** Periodical name, publisher name, address, phone, former titles, frequency, first publication date, organizational affiliations, editorial staff, advertising information, subscription rates, membership fees. **Arrangement:** Alphabetical. **Indexes:** Subject, geographical. **Pages (approx.):** 240. **Frequency:** Published March 1987. **Price:** $25.00, postpaid.

★8763★ *Iota Sigma Pi—Membership Directory*
Iota Sigma Pi
Beverly J. Lee
Clear Creek High School
2035 E. Main
League City, TX 77573
Phone: (713)482-6261

Covers: 1,300 members. **Entries include:** Name, address, type of membership, employer. **Arrangement:** Geographical (by chapter and by zipcode). **Pages (approx.):** 30. **Frequency:** Triennial; latest edition 1990. **Price:** Available to members only.

★8764★ *Jewish Women's Resource Center—Rosh Chodesh Directory*
National Council of Jewish Women, New York Section
9 E. 69th St.
New York, NY 10021
Phone: (212)535-5900
Fax: (212)535-5909

Covers: Approximately 40 groups that celebrate Rosh Chodesh, a festival for Jewish women. **Entries include:** Group name, address, meeting dates, contacts, description of group purpose or philosophy. **Pages (approx.):** 5. **Frequency:** First edition June 1991. **Price:** $1.00.

★8765★ *Leadership Conference of Women Religious of the U.S.A.— Directory*
Leadership Conference of Women Religious of the U.S.A.
8088 Cameron St.
Silver Spring, MD 20910
Phone: (301)588-4955

Covers: About 800 superiors of Roman Catholic communities for women; list of organizations. **Entries include:** For members and associates—Name, address, phone. For organizations—Name, address, phone, name of administrator/officer. **Arrangement:** Geographical. **Pages (approx.):** 60. **Frequency:** Annual, fall. **Price:** Available to members only.

★8766★ *Lesbian Periodicals Index*
Naiad Press
Box 10543
Tallahassee, FL 32302
Phone: (904)539-5965
Toll-free: 800-533-1973
Fax: (904)539-9731

Publication Includes: List of nearly 40 libraries and archives with extensive holdings of lesbian periodicals. **Entries include:** Library or archive name, address. **Arrangement:** Alphabetical. **Frequency:** First edition 1986. **Price:** $29.95. **Other Information:** Principal content is subject and author indexes of articles, drawings, poems, and stories in lesbian journals.

★8767★ *Libraries and Information Centers Within Women's Studies Research Centers*
Special Libraries Association
1700 18th St., NW
Washington, DC 20009
Phone: (202)234-4700
Fax: (202)265-9317

Publication Includes: List of research centers with library and information center facilities that provide resources for women's studies. **Frequency:** Latest edition 1988. **Price:** $7.00. **Other Information:** Major content of publication is discussion of the importance of these facilities in forming an information network for women's studies research.

★8768★ *Minorities and Women: A List of Major Organizations in Librarianship*
American Library Association (ALA)
50 E. Huron St.
Chicago, IL 60611
Phone: (312)280-4277
Toll-free: 800-545-2433
Fax: (312)280-3256

Covers: About 10 minority and women librarian organizations. **Entries include:** Organization name, address, phone, names and titles of key personnel, publications. **Arrangement:** Classified by interest group. **Frequency:** Annual, summer. **Price:** Free.

★8769★ *NAPSAC Directory of Alternative Birth Services and Consumer Guide*
National Association of Parents & Professionals for Safe Alternatives in Childbirth (NAPSAC)
Rt. 1, Box 646
Marble Hill, MO 63764
Phone: (314)238-2010

Covers: 2,000 birth centers, midwifery schools, midwives, doctors attending to home births, childbirth educators, and others in the field of alternative childbirth; international coverage. **Entries include:** Name, address, phone, medically related degree, and services offered. **Arrangement:** Geographical. **Pages (approx.):** 150. **Frequency:** Annual, spring. **Price:** $5.95; payment must accompany order. **Also Includes:** List of state and regional associations and referral services belonging to NAPSAC.

★8770★ *National Association for Women Deans, Administrators, and Counselors— Member Handbook*
National Association for Women Deans, Administrators, and Counselors
1325 18th St., NW, No. 210
Washington, DC 20036
Phone: (202)659-9330

Covers: 2,000 American and foreign members. **Entries include:** Name, institution, office and home addresses, phone, education, position, committee membership. **Arrangement:** Geographical. **Indexes:** Alphabetical. **Frequency:** Annual. **Price:** Available to members only.

★8771★ *National Council of Career Women—Membership Directory*
National Council of Career Women
3203 Gemstone Ct.
Oakton, VA 22124
Phone: (703)591-4359

Covers: 450 members. **Entries include:** Name, address, title, and affiliation. **Arrangement:** Alphabetical. **Frequency:** Annual, summer. **Price:** Available to members only.

★8772★ *National Directory of College Athletics*
Ray Franks Publishing Ranch
Box 7068
Amarillo, TX 79109
Phone: (806)355-6417

Covers: Women's athletic departments at 2,000 senior and junior colleges. **Entries include:** School name, address; enrollment, colors, stadium and/or gym capacity, team nicknames; names of president, women's athletic director and physical education director, and coaches for each sport; athletic department phone number; and association affiliations. **Arrangement:** Alphabetical. **Pages (approx.):** 240. **Frequency:** Annual, August. **Price:** $12.00. **Former Title(s):** *National Directory of Women's Athletics* (1976).

★8773★ *National Directory of Facilities and Services for Lesbian and Gay Alcoholics*
National Association of Lesbian and Gay Alcoholism Professionals (NALGAP)
204 W. 20th St.
New York, NY 10011
Phone: (212)713-5074

Covers: Over 300 treatment facilities, private counselors, etc.; facilities and services are not necessarily limited to homosexuals. **Entries include:** Facility name, address, phone, name of contact, services provided, fees; eligibility requirements (if any), percentages of staff and clientele openly gay or lesbian. **Arrangement:** Geographical. **Pages (approx.):** 95. **Frequency:** Irregular; latest edition 1987. **Price:** $5.00; payment must accompany order. **Other Information:** Former name of association is National Association of Gay Alcoholism Professionals. **Former Title(s):** *NALGAP Directory of Facilities and Services....*

★8774★ National Directory of Women Elected Officials
National Women's Political Caucus
1275 K St. NW, Ste. 750
Washington, DC 20005
Phone: (202)898-1100
Covers: Women elected officeholders at the federal and state government levels, women on the Republican and Democratic National Committees, women mayors in cities with populations over 30,000, and women county officials in counties with populations over 100,000. **Entries include:** Name, address, district represented or government and population, party; profile included for members of Congress. **Arrangement:** By level of government, then geographical. **Pages (approx.):** 230. **Frequency:** Biennial, August of odd years. **Price:** Free. **Send orders to:** Corporate Public Affairs, Philip Morris Companies, Inc., 120 Park Ave., New York, NY 10017.

★8775★ National Directory of Women-Owned Business Firms
Business Research Services, Inc.
2 E. 22nd St., Ste. 202
Lombard, IL 60148
Phone: (708)495-8787
Toll-free: 800-325-8720
Fax: (708)495-8791
Covers: Over 20,000 women-owned businesses. **Entries include:** Company name, address, phone, name and title of contact, minority group, certification status, date founded, number of employees, description of products or services, sales volume government contracting experience, references. **Arrangement:** Alphabetical. **Indexes:** Standard Industrial Classification (SIC) code, geographical. **Pages (approx.):** 1,070. **Frequency:** Irregular; latest edition January 1990. **Price:** $195.00, plus $5.00 shipping. **ISSN:** 0886-389X. **Other Information:** Library edition available from Gale Research Inc., 835 Penobscot Bldg., Detroit, MI 48226 (800-877-GALE). This and *National Directory of Minority-Owned Business Firms* were formerly combined in *National Directory of Minority and Women-Owned Business Firms.*

★8776★ National Divorce and Singles Resource Directory
Divorce Support Services, Inc.
234 Main St.
Woodbridge, NJ 07095
Phone: (908)636-3802
Toll-free: 800-424-8765
Fax: (908)636-5586
Covers: Approximately 12,000 resources for single, separated, divorced persons in the United States, including clubs, support groups, associations, and periodicals. **Entries include:** Organization name, address, phone, description of purpose or activities. **Arrangement:** Geographical, then alphabetical by organization name. **Indexes:** Subject. **Pages (approx.):** 200. **Frequency:** Published June 1991. **Editor(s):** Edward Kitzis, Executive Directory. **Price:** $19.95. **Send orders to:** Divorce Support Services, Inc. PO Box 689, Woodbridge NJ 07095.

★8777★ National Guide to Funding for Women and Girls
The Foundation Center
79 5th Ave., Dept. E
New York, NY 10003
Phone: (212)620-4230
Fax: (212)807-3677
Covers: Over 700 programs sponsored by foundations and corporations which fund women's and girl's organizations and projects. **Price:** $95.

★8778★ National Intercollegiate Women's Fencing Association—Directory
National Intercollegiate Women's Fencing Association
3 Derby Ln.
Dumont, NJ 07628
Phone: (201)384-1722
Covers: About 20 colleges and universities with women's varsity fencing teams. **Entries include:** Name of institution, address, phone; name, address, and phone of the team coach and athletic director. **Arrangement:** Geographical. **Indexes:** Alphabetical. **Pages (approx.):** 5. **Frequency:** Annual, winter. **Price:** Available to members only.

★8779★ National Women's Directory of Alcohol & Drug Abuse Treatment & Prevention Programs
Human Services Institute, Inc.
4301 32nd St. W., No. C8
Bradenton, FL 34205-2743
Phone: (813)746-7088
Pages (approx.): 80. **Frequency:** Latest edition March 1988; no new edition planned. **Price:** Free; $2.00 shipping.

★8780★ National Women's Mailing List
Women's Information Exchange
Box 68
Jenner, CA 95450
Phone: (707)632-5763
Description: Mailing labels. Directories supplied as a mailing list in zip code order; can be selected on subject of women's organizations or by demographics and interests of individual women. Lists are created from a database of 10,000 women's organizations and 60,000 individual women. **Entries include:** Name, address, contact (or organization) name. **Frequency:** Supplied upon demand.

★8781★ NWSA Directory of Women's Studies Programs, Women's Centers, and Women's Research Centers
National Women's Studies Association (NWSA)
University of Maryland
College Park, MD 20742-1325
Phone: (301)405-5573
Fax: (301)314-9328
Covers: Over 600 academic programs in women's studies. **Entries include:** Name, address, phone, fax, name of administrator, degrees or credits offered. **Arrangement:** Geographical. **Pages (approx.):** 125. **Frequency:** Biennial, even years. **Price:** $7.00; payment must accompany order. **Former Title(s):** *Women's Studies Quarterly—Women's Studies Program List Issue*; *NWSA Directory of Women's Studies Programs.*

★8782★ Opportunities for Research and Study
National Council for Research on Women
Sara Delano Roosevelt Memorial House
47-49 E. 65th St.
New York, NY 10021
Phone: (212)570-5001
Covers: Approximately 60 women's research centers that offer fellowships, affiliated scholar programs, grants, and internships. **Entries include:** Organization name, address, phone, name and title of contact, description of programs. **Arrangement:** Alphabetical. **Pages (approx.):** 35. **Frequency:** Approximately annual; latest edition November 1990. **Price:** $5.00. **Also Includes:** Annotated bibliography of financial aid resources for women at all education levels.

★8783★ Over 50...AARP's Directory of Elected Women Officials
American Association of Retired Persons (AARP)
Office of Women's Activities
1909 K St. NW
Washington, DC 20049
Phone: (202)728-4332
Covers: Approximately 1,200 elected women officials at the federal, state, and local levels; 10 regional AARP offices. **Entries include:** For officials—Personal name, address, phone. For offices—Name, address, phone. **Price:** Free. **Also Includes:** Map.

★8784★ Parental Kidnapping: How to Prevent an Abduction and What to Do If Your Child Is Abducted
National Center for Missing and Exploited Children
2101 Wilson Blvd., Ste. 550
Arlington, VA 22201
Phone: (703)235-3900
Toll-free: 800-843-5678
Fax: (703)235-4067
Publication Includes: List of more than 100 support groups for parents of children who are victims of parental abduction. **Entries include:** For support groups—Name, address, phone. **Arrangement:** Geographical. **Frequency:** Irregular; latest edition August 1988. **Price:** Free. **Other Information:** Principal content is information on preventive action, legal remedies and assistance available, counseling, rights of non-custodial parents, state and federal laws and regulations, and international kidnapping. Prepared in cooperation with the Office of Juvenile Justice and Delinquency Protection of the Department of Justice.

★8785★ Planned Parenthood Affiliates, Chapter & State Public Affairs Offices Directory
Planned Parenthood Federation of America
810 7th Ave.
New York, NY 10019
Phone: (212)603-4736
Number of listings: 250. **Entries include:** Affiliate or chapter name, address, phone, code for whether medical, educational, provisional member, or public affairs office. **Arrangement:** Geographical. **Pages (approx.):** 30. **Frequency:** Annual, September. **Price:** Available only to Planned Parenthood affiliates. **Former Title(s):** *Affiliate Directory; Planned Parenthood Affiliates & Chapters.*

★8786★ Planning Consultant Roster
American Planning Association
1313 E. 60th St.
Chicago, IL 60637
Phone: (202)872-0611
Fax: (312)955-4244

Covers: Firms which specialize or are active in planning; includes women and minority owned planning firms. **Entries include:** Firm name, address, phone, names of principal executives, identification of minority group(s) in control, number of employees, years of employee experience, geographic area covered, services provided, subsidiary and branch names and locations, year founded. **Arrangement:** Alphabetical. **Indexes:** Geographical, women or minority owned firm name. **Pages (approx.):** 50. **Price:** $8.00. **Former Title(s):** *Minority and Women Planning Consultant Roster* (1987).

★8787★ Procurement Automated Source System (PASS)
U.S. Small Business Administration
Office of Procurement Assisitance
409 3rd St., SW
Washington, DC 20416
Phone: (202)205-6469

Description: Online database. Covers more than 228,000 small businesses (including some 39,000 minority-owned, 50,000 woman-owned, and 69,000 veteran-owned businesses) seeking government procurement contracts.

★8788★ Programs to Strengthen Families: A Resource Guide
Family Resource Coalition
200 S. Michigan, Ste. 1520
Chicago, IL 60604
Phone: (312)341-0900
Fax: (312)341-9361

Publication Includes: List of over 60 organizations offering programs providing a variety of service models for working with families of varied economic and ethnic backgrounds in different geographic (urban, rural, etc.) settings; includes parent education, prevention of child abuse and neglect, day care, neighborhood-based self-help and information support programs, and others. **Entries include:** Organization name, address, phone, program name, description, goals, history, community served, services, participants, staff, evaluation (by program or independent evaluator), source of funding, materials available. **Arrangement:** Classified by type of program. **Indexes:** Subject, service, geographical, demographic. **Pages (approx.):** 140. **Frequency:** Irregular; previous edition May 1988; latest edition January 1992. **Price:** $30.00.

★8789★ Reaching Out: A Directory of National Organizations Related to Maternal and Child Health
National Center for Education in Maternal and Child Health
38th & R Sts. NW
Washington, DC 20057
Phone: (202)625-8400
Fax: (202)625-8404

Covers: Over 500 national and international voluntary organizations for health professionals, educators, and the public; mutual support groups; self-help clearinghouses; and selected federal Maternal and Child Health Information Centers. **Entries include:** Name, address, phone, name of contact; code indicates whether a newsletter is published. **Arrangement:** Classified by cause or specialty. **Indexes:** Organization name, subject. **Pages (approx.):** 130. **Frequency:** Approximately biennial; previous edition December 1987; latest edition March 1989; new edition expected 1992. **Price:** Free. **Former Title(s):** *National List of Voluntary Organizations in Medical Genetics and Maternal and Child Health* (1983); *Reaching Out: A National List of Voluntary Organizations in Maternal and Child Health* (1985); *Reaching Out: A Directory of Voluntary Organizations in Maternal and Child Health* (1985).

★8790★ Recovering from Rape
Henry Holt & Co.
4375 West 1980 South
Salt Lake City, UT 84104
Phone: (801)972-2221
Toll-free: 800-247-3912
Fax: (801)977-9712

Publication Includes: List of rape crisis centers in the United States. **Frequency:** Irregular; latest edition July 1989. **Price:** $9.95. **Other Information:** Principal content is information and advice for victims of rape and their families.

★8791★ Regional Directory of Minority & Women-Owned Business Firms
Business Research Services, Inc.
2 E. 22nd St., Ste. 202
Lombard, IL 60148
Phone: (708)495-8787
Toll-free: 800-325-8720
Fax: (708)495-8791

Description: Published in 3 regional volumes: Eastern, with 22,500 listings; Central, with 23,000 listings; and Western, with 19,125 listings. Based on *National Directory of Minority-Owned Business Firms* and *National Directory of Women-Owned Business Firms* **Entries include:** Company name, address, phone, name and title of contact, minority group, certification status, date founded, number of employees, description of products or services, sales volume, government contracting experience, references. **Arrangement:** Alphabetical. **Indexes:** Standard Industrial Classification (SIC) code, geographical. **Pages (approx.):** Eastern, 520; Central, 527; Western, 440. **Frequency:** Irregular; previous editions May 1988; latest editions January 1990. **Price:** $145.00 each, plus $5.00 shipping. **Other Information:** Library editions available from Gale Research Inc., 835 Penobscot Bldg., Detroit, MI 48226.

★8792★ Roster of Women Economists
Committee on the Status of Women in the Economics Profession
c/o Joan G. Haworth
4901 Tower Ct.
Tallahassee, FL 32303
Phone: (904)562-1211
Fax: (904)562-3838

Covers: 5,000 women in economics. **Entries include:** Name, address, phone, title, affiliation, degrees, honors, specialty, number of articles and books published. **Arrangement:** Alphabetical. **Indexes:** Geographical, employer, fields of specialization. **Pages (approx.):** 287. **Frequency:** Biennial, even years. **Price:** $35.00. **Other Information:** Publisher is a standing committee of the American Economic Association.

★8793★ Safe, Strong, and Streetwise
Little, Brown & Co.
Joy Street Books
34 Beacon St.
Boston, MA 02108
Phone: (617)227-0730

Publication Includes: List of 40 organizations concerned with crisis and informative counseling and prevention of sexual assault, particularly involving teenagers. **Entries include:** Organization name, address, phone. **Arrangement:** Geographically. **Pages (approx.):** 180. **Frequency:** Published March 1987. **Price:** $14.95, cloth; $5.95, paper. **Other Information:** Principal content is discussion of types of sexual assault and methods of prevention.

★8794★ Sexual Assault and Child Abuse: A National Directory of Victim Services and Prevention Programs
Oryx Press
4041 N. Central, No. 700
Phoenix, AZ 85012
Phone: (602)265-2651
Toll-free: 800-279-ORYX
Fax: 800-279-4663

Pages (approx.): 385. **Frequency:** Published July 1989. **Price:** $55.00.

★8795★ Sigma Phi Gamma—Membership Directory
Sigma Phi Gamma
Rte. 2, Box 86
Charlotte Hall, MD 20622
Phone: (301)884-8438

Covers: About 4,500 women in business and other occupations who conduct various projects for the promotion of friendship among women. **Frequency:** Annual. **Price:** Available to members only.

★8796★ Society of Woman Geographers Bulletin—Membership Directory Issue
Society of Woman Geographers
1619 New Hampshire Ave.
Washington, DC 20009
Phone: (202)265-2669

Publication Includes: List of 500 women engaged in geographical work and allied sciences such as ethnology, archeology, botany, natural history, sociology, and folklore. **Entries include:** Name, affiliation, address, phone. **Arrangement:** Alphabetical. **Frequency:** Annual, November. **Price:** Available to members only.

★8797★ Solo Parenting: Your Essential Guide
Penguin USA
120 Woodbine St.
Bergenfield, NJ 07621
Phone: (201)387-0600

Publication Includes: List of resources intended to aid the single parent. **Frequency:** Irregular; latest edition September 1990. **Price:** $4.50. **Other Information:** Principal content is a discussion of single parent concerns, including concerns about money, child care, career, and social life.

★8798★ Sources: An Annotated Bibliography of Women's Issues
Knowledge, Ideas & Trends, Inc.
400 Prospect St.
Glen Rock, NJ 07450
Phone: (201)444-0085
Fax: (203)646-3931
Covers: 1,500 books from small and university presses in the U.S. concerned with women's issues. **Entries include:** Title, publisher, annotation; publisher's address. **Arrangement:** Classified by subject. **Indexes:** Alphabetical by title, alphabetical by author. **Pages (approx.):** 320. **Frequency:** Biennial in March of odd years. **Editor(s):** Rita I. McCullough. **Price:** $24.95 (current edition); $32.95 (tentative, 1993 edition). **Send orders to:** Knowledge, Ideas and Trends, Inc., 1131-0 Tolland Tpke., Ste. 175, Manchester, CT 06040 (203)646-1621.

★8799★ Starting Early: A Guide to Federal Resources in Maternal and Child Health
National Center for Education in Maternal and Child Health
38th & R Sts. NW
Washington, DC 20057
Phone: (202)625-8410
Fax: (202)625-8404
Covers: Federal government agencies and federally supported organizations offering over 500 print and non-print resources (posters, audiovisual materials, software) on prenatal, infant, and adolescent health; state and regional maternal and child health contacts; regional genetics services networks. **Entries include:** Agency name, address, phone; description of publication, including title, length, order number, price. **Arrangement:** Agencies are classified by subject of their focus, regional contacts are geographical. **Indexes:** Agency name, publication title, subject, foreign language material. **Pages (approx.):** 170. **Frequency:** Irregular; latest edition November 1988. **Price:** Free. **Other Information:** Published with a grant from the Department of Health and Human Services.

★8800★ T.A.P.P. Sources: A National Directory of Teenage Pregnancy Prevention
Women's Action Alliance
370 Lexington Ave.
New York, NY 10017
Phone: (212)532-8330
Covers: About 600 teenage pregnancy prevention programs. **Entries include:** Program name, address, phone, names and titles of key personnel, number of employees, geographical area served, financial data, description of services. **Arrangement:** Geographical. **Pages (approx.):** 560. **Frequency:** Published 1989. **Price:** $19.95. **Other Information:** Published jointly with Scarecrow Press. **Former Title(s):** Women Helping Women: A State by State Directory of Services.

★8801★ Tech and Tools Book: A Guide to Technologies Women Are Using Worldwide
International Women's Tribune Centre
Intermediate Technology Development Group
777 United Nations Plaza
New York, NY 10017
Phone: (212)687-8633
Fax: (212)661-2704
Covers: New and alternative technologies for agricultural, communications, health and sanitation, food, energy, and income-generation purposes. **Entries include:** Technology name, description, summary of strengths and weaknesses, names and addresses of organizations able to provide more information, user reports, related publications. **Arrangement:** Classified by function. **Pages (approx.):** 190. **Frequency:** Irregular; latest English edition 1986; new edition possible, date not set. **Price:** $10.00. **Other Information:** French version published in 1990.

★8802★ Total Nutrition for Breast-Feeding Mothers
Little, Brown & Company, Inc.
34 Beacon St.
Boston, MA 02108-1493
Phone: (617)227-0730
Publication Includes: List of about 25 resources for nursing mothers, such as organizations, books, and magazines. **Entries include:** Organization name, address, phone. **Arrangement:** Classified by subject. **Frequency:** Published July 1986. **Price:** $9.70. **Other Information:** Principal content is information on nutrition, vitamins, recipes, and breast feeding in general.

★8803★ The Tribune—"Women Organizing"
International Women's Tribune Centre
777 United Nations Plaza
New York, NY 10017
Phone: (212)687-8633
Fax: (212)661-2704
Publication Includes: List of regional organizations, nongovernmental organizations, networks, etc., concerned with women's working together in various fields; directed primarily towards the Third World. **Entries include:** Name, address, interests. **Price:** $3.00. **Also Includes:** Case histories. **Other Information:** Also available as part of a bound volume (published 1984) that includes the newsletters, Women's Networks and Women's Centres Worldwide under the title Women Organizing; $6.00.

★8804★ United States Women's Track Coaches Association—Membership Directory
United States Women's Track Coaches Association
c/o Karen Dennis, Pres.
Michigan State University
Women's Athletic Dept.
East Lansing, MI 48825
Phone: (517)353-9299
Covers: About 100 member coaches and others involved in women's track and field.

★8805★ Victim Rights and Services: A Legislative Directory
National Organization for Victim Assistance (NOVA)
1757 Park Rd. NW
Washington, DC 20010
Phone: (202)232-6682
Description: Provides state by state victim laws and legislation. **Frequency:** Periodic.

★8806★ Whole Arts Directory
Midmarch Arts Books
Box 3304
Grand Central Sta.
New York, NY 10163
Description: Lists organizations, alternative spaces, cooperative galleries, and special museums for visual artists. Focuses on women and minorities and also includes state by state resource listings, financial and legal help, arts advocacy and information services, artists' colonies, retreats and study centers, and art therapy groups. **Price:** $12.50. **Remarks:** Supercedes the Guide to Women's Art Organizations and Directory for the Arts.

★8807★ Who's Who in Professional and Executive Women
American Society of Professional and Executive Women (ASPEW)
1429 Walnut St.
Philadelphia, PA 19102
Phone: (215)563-3501
Covers: About 5,000 professional women selected by the editors for their "singular commitment to achievement." **Entries include:** Name, address, profession, birthdate and location; family, education, and career information; professional and association memberships; civic activities, awards, honors, publications. **Arrangement:** Alphabetical. **Pages (approx.):** 300. **Frequency:** Biennial, September of odd years. **Price:** $79.00. **Also Includes:** Table of abbreviations.

★8808★ A Woman's Yellow Book
Federation of Organizations for Professional Women
2001 S St., Ste. 540
Washington, DC 20009
Phone: (202)328-1415
Covers: About 575 national organizations, government agencies, research institutes, clearinghouses, and publishers concerned with women's issues. **Entries include:** Organization or agency name, address, phone, names of key personnel, year found, number of members, geographic area served, services, keyword. **Arrangement:** Alphabetical. **Indexes:** Keyword/geographical. **Pages (approx.):** 250. **Frequency:** Irregular; latest edition spring 1990. **Price:** $25.00, postpaid. **Former Title(s):** Woman's Yellow Pages (1981).

★8809★ Women in Broadcast Technology—Directory
Women in Broadcast Technology
c/o Susan Elisabeth
2435 Spaulding St.
Berkeley, CA 94703
Phone: (415)642-1311
Covers: More than 100 women technicians and operators of audio and video broadcasting equipment. **Entries include:** Name, address, phone, specialty, employment interests. **Ar-**

rangement: Classified by specialty. **Pages (approx.):** 20. **Frequency:** Annual, January. **Price:** $3.00, postpaid.

★8810★ **Women of Color and Southern Women: A Bibliography**
Memphis State University
Center for Research on Women
Clement Hall
Memphis, TN 38152
Phone: (901)678-2770
Fax: (901)678-3299
Frequency: Annual supplements.

★8811★ **Women in Communications— National Membership and Resource Directory**
Women in Communications
2101 Wilson Blvd., Ste. 417
Arlington, VA 22201
Phone: (703)528-4200
Fax: (703)528-4205
Covers: 12,500 professional and student members. **Entries include:** For professional members—Name, name of firm, business title, firm address, phone, and fax. For student members—Name. **Arrangement:** Geographical (by chapter); campus chapters are by institution name. **Indexes:** Personal name, type of business, job title. **Pages (approx.):** 200. **Frequency:** Biennial, January of odd years. **Price:** $100.00. **Former Title(s):** *National Directory of Professional Members* (1974); *Directory of Creative Communicators* (1987); *Women in Communications—National Membership Directory*.

★8812★ **Women Directors of the Top Corporate 1,000**
National Women's Economic Alliance Foundation
1440 New York Ave. NW, Ste. 300
Washington, DC 20005
Phone: (202)393-5257
Fax: (202)639-8685
Covers: About 400 women serving on the boards of Fortune 1,000 corporations, compiled from surveys of Fortune 500 Industrial and Fortune 500 Service corporations. **Entries include:** Name, title, company name, address, corporate boards on which serves. **Arrangement:** Alphabetical. **Indexes:** Corporate board affiliation. **Pages (approx.):** 65. **Frequency:** Annual, January. **Price:** $45.00. **Former Title(s):** *Women Directors of the Top 1,000 Corporations*.

★8813★ **Women and Fellowships**
Women's Equity Action League
9308 Worrell Ave.
Lanham, MD 20706-3112
Covers: About 30 organizations that offer fellowship programs to women. **Entries include:** Organization name, address, phone. **Arrangement:** Classified by field of study. **Pages (approx.):** 30. **Frequency:** Irregular. **Price:** $12.00.

★8814★ **Women and Judaism: A Selected Annotated Bibliography**
Garland Publishing, Inc.
136 Madison Ave.
New York, NY 10016
Phone: (212)686-7492
Toll-free: 800-627-6273
Fax: (212)889-9399
Publication Includes: List of publishers of nearly 180 journals concerned with Jewish women studies. **Entries include:** Periodical name, company name, address, phone. **Indexes:** Subject, author. **Pages (approx.):** 256. **Frequency:** Latest edition 1988. **Price:** $47.00.

★8815★ **Women Outdoors: The Best 1900 Books, Programs and Periodicals**
c/o Jennifer Abromowitz
RD1 345C
Williamsburg, MA 01096
Publication Includes: Listing of approximately 140 outdoor organizations offering programs and trips for women. **Frequency:** Published 1990. **Price:** $28.00. **Other Information:** Principal content of publication is an annotated bibliography of books in English related to women and outdoor interests, arranged by subject and including an author index.

★8816★ **Women Remembered: A Guide to Landmarks of Women's History**
Greenwood Publishing Group, Inc.
88 Post Rd. W.
PO Box 5007
Westport, CT 06881
Phone: (203)226-3571
Covers: Over 2,000 historic sites, monuments, statues, and other historical markers documenting women's role in American history. Basis of selection for the directory includes one of the following: the women made significant contributions to society (as determined by the editors), performed a documented heroic act, or were documented participants in a historic event. In addition, sites must be open to the public; markers for only local significance are omitted. Does not include sites for living women, spouses or daughters of commemorated men, sites closed to the public, or gravesites. **Entries include:** Name of site or marker, name of woman commemorated, location, type of landmark, hours open, description of historical event. **Arrangement:** Geographical. **Indexes:** Personal name, occupation. **Pages (approx.):** 800. **Frequency:** Published 1986. **Price:** $79.95.

★8817★ **Women Scientists from Antiquity to Present: An Index**
Locust Hill Press
Main St.
West Cornwall, CT 06796
Phone: (203)672-0060
Description: Not a directory, but an index to citations in over 130 publications of about 2,500 women in science, engineering, medicine, technology, anthropology, mathematics, psychology, sociology, and other social sciences, as well as science authors, historians, and educators. **Entries include:** Scientist name, field of study, dates of birth and death or scientific activity, nationality, publications in which cited. **Arrangement:** Alphabetical. **Indexes:** Discipline. **Pages (approx.):** 240. **Frequency:** Published 1986. **Price:** $30.00. **Also Includes:** List of sources used in compilation.

★8818★ **Women's Auxiliary of the International Chiropractors Association— Membership Roster**
Women's Auxiliary of the International Chiropractors Association (ICA)
1925 Apple Ave.
Muskegon, MI 49442
Phone: (616)777-2622
Covers: About 500 women who are chiropractic assistants, chiropractors, or related to members of the ICA. **Frequency:** Biennial.

★8819★ **Women's Foreign Policy Council Directory**
Women's Foreign Policy Council
845 3rd Ave., 15th Fl.
New York, NY 10022
Phone: (212)759-7982
Covers: Approximately 275 women foreign policy specialists available for public appearances, speaking and media engagements, and expert commentary. **Entries include:** Personal name, address, phone, and biographical data. **Arrangement:** Alphabetical. **Indexes:** Name, subject, geographical. **Pages (approx.):** 335. **Frequency:** Published 1987. **Price:** $25.00.

★8820★ **Women's History Catalog**
National Women's History Project
7738 Bell Rd.
Windsor, CA 95492
Phone: (707)838-6000
Fax: (707)838-0478
Description: Describes multicultural materials offered by the Project, including books, films, records, posters, subject index, and program planning guides on women's history. **Frequency:** Annual.

★8821★ **Women's History Network Directory**
National Women's History Project (NWHP)
7738 Bell Rd.
Windsor, CA 95492
Phone: (707)838-6000
Frequency: Semiannual.

★8822★ **Women's Information Directory**
(WID)
Gale Research Inc.
835 Penobscot Bldg.
Detroit, MI 48226
Phone: (313)961-2242
Toll-free: 800-347-GALE
Fax: (313)961-6241
Description: Nearly 10,800 entries covering national, regional, state, and local women's organizations; battered women's services; displaced homemaker programs; family planning services; university-related women's centers; library collections; museums and galleries; women's colleges and universities; women's studies programs; scholarships, fellowships, and loans; awards, honors, and prizes; research centers; federal government agencies; federal domestic assistance programs; state and local government agencies; top U.S. women-owned businesses; consultants and consulting organizations; directories; journals and magazines; newsletters; newspapers; publishers; booksellers; videos; and electronic resources. **Entries include:** Organization or publication name, address, telephone and fax numbers, name and title of contact, description of services, activi-

ties, etc. **Arrangement:** Classified by type of resource. **Frequency:** Biennial. **Price:** $75.00

★8823★ **Women's Legal Rights in the United States: A Selective Bibliography**
American Library Association (ALA)
50 E. Huron St.
Chicago, IL 60611
Phone: (312)944-6780
Toll-free: 800-545-2433
Fax: (312)440-9374

Publication Includes: List of about 30 organizations which provide information and advocacy services for women's legal rights issues. **Entries include:** Organization name, address, phone. **Arrangement:** Alphabetical. **Frequency:** Irregular; latest edition 1985. **Price:** $3.95. **Other Information:** Principal content is a bibliography on women and the law.

★8824★ **A Women's Mailing List Directory**
National Council for Research on Women
47-49 E. 65th St.
New York, NY 10021
Phone: (212)570-5001
Fax: (212)570-5380

Covers: Over 100 women's organizations offering their mailing lists for sale or exchange. **Entries include:** Organization name, address, phone, name and title of contact, mailing list formats, method of compilation and maintenance of list, geographical area served. **Arrangement:** Alphabetical. **Indexes:** Organization name. **Pages (approx.):** 160. **Frequency:** Irregular; latest edition 1990. **Price:** $20.00 plus $2.00 shipping.

★8825★ **Women's Organizations: A National Directory**
Garrett Park Press
Box 190F
Garrett Park, MD 20896
Phone: (301)946-2553

Covers: About 2,000 national and local women's organizations including professional and trade associations, government commissions, and research centers specializing in women's issues. **Entries include:** Organization name, address, description of role. **Arrangement:** Alphabetical. **Indexes:** Geographical, type of program. **Pages (approx.):** 310. **Frequency:** Irregular; latest edition 1986. **Price:** $22.50, payment with order; $25.00, billed. **Also Includes:** List of women's directories.

★8826★ **Women's Periodicals and Newspapers, from 18th Century to 1981**
State Historical Society of Wisconsin Library
816 State St.
Madison, WI 53706
Phone: (608)262-9584
Fax: (608)262-5554

Description: Index to local and national titles published by and about women.

★8827★ **Women's Programming Directory**
National Federation of Community Broadcasters
1314 14th St. NW
Washington, DC 20005

★8828★ **The Women's Traveller**
Damron Company
Box 11270
San Francisco, CA 94101
Phone: (415)255-0404
Toll-free: 800-462-6654
Fax: (415)255-9428

Covers: Approximately 3,000 lesbian bars, restaurants, women's accomodations, bookstores, newspapers, groups and services in the U.S. and Canada. **Entries include:** Company name, address, phone, description of product or service. **Arrangement:** Geographical. **Pages (approx.):** 335. **Frequency:** Annual, May. **Price:** $10.00, plus $4.50 shipping. **Also Includes:** Maps, city descriptions.

★8829★ **Women's Yellow Pages**
8835 SW Canyon Ln., Ste. 304
Portland, OR 97225
Phone: (503)297-8040

Description: Women-owned businesses and groups in the Portland, Oregon area. **Frequency:** Annual.

★8830★ **Women's Yellow Pages**
Box 66093
Los Angeles, CA 90066
Phone: (310)398-5761

Description: Women's businesses, services, and organizations in Los Angeles and Orange counties and nearby areas of southern California. **Entries include:** Company or organization name, address, phone, product or service provided, field of interest. **Frequency:** Annual.

★8831★ **Women's Yellow Pages: A Directory of Women in Business, Professions and Organizations**
Women's Yellow Pages
Women's Informational Network, Inc.
Box 421
Romeo, MI 48065
Phone: (313)752-4370

Description: Women in business and professions, women's organizations, and businesses and services geared toward women in the Flint, Saginaw, and Bay City, Michigan areas. **Entries include:** Personal or company name, address, phone, memberships, products or services provided.

★8832★ **Words to the Wise**
Firebrand Books
141 The Commons
Ithaca, NY 14850
Phone: (607)272-0000

Covers: Over 150 publishers of feminist and lesbian books and periodicals who actively solicit manuscripts from women; publishers of directories, newsletters, and other publications and resources for women writers. **Entries include:** Publisher name, address, phone, contact name; periodical or resource title, description of activities and publications. Separate charts for publishers and periodicals give year founded, frequency or number of books in print, submission requirements, type of payment for acceptance, subscription fees, and other information as appropriate. **Arrangement:** Separate sections for publishers, periodicals, and resources. **Pages (approx.):** 56. **Frequency:** Every 18-24 months; latest edition October 1990. **Price:** $4.95, plus $2.00 shipping.

★8833★ **A Working Woman's Guide to Her Job Rights**
U.S. Department of Labor
200 Constitution Ave. NW
Washington, DC 20210
Phone: (202)523-8191

Publication Includes: List of state and federal agencies in charge of enforcing the rights of working women. **Entries include:** Agency name and address. **Price:** $9.95. **Other Information:** Major content of publication is description of employment rights for women and ways to protect those rights.

★8834★ **World Federation of Methodist Women—Handbook**
World Federation of Methodist Women
c/o Edith Ming
7100 Grey Oaks Dr.
New Orleans, LA 70126
Frequency: Every five years.

(20) Journals and Magazines

Entries in this chapter are arranged alphabetically by publication title. See the User's Guide at the front of this directory for additional information.

★8835★ **AAUW Outlook**
American Association of University Women
1111 16th St. NW
Washington, DC 20036
Phone: (202)785-7728
Description: Magazine covering women's concerns including current family, education and legislative issues. **First published:** January 1989. **Frequency:** Quarterly. **ISSN:** 0161-5661. **Subscription:** $15.

★8836★ **A.B. Bookman's Weekly**
PO Box AB
Clifton, NJ 07015
Phone: (201)772-0020
Fax: (201)772-9281
Description: Book-world magazine that devotes special issues to women's studies. **Frequency:** Weekly.

★8837★ **ACHE: A Journal For Black Lesbians**
PO Box 6071
Albany, CA 94706
Description: Publication by Black lesbians. **Frequency:** 6x/year. **Subscription:** $10-$25. Single copy $2.

★8838★ **The Advocate**
Liberation Publications, Inc.
6922 Hollywood Blvd., 10th Fl.
Los Angeles, CA 90028
Phone: (213)871-1225
Subtitle: The National Gay and Lesbian Newsmagazine. **Description:** National gay news and lifestyle magazine. **First published:** September 1967. **Frequency:** Every other week. **ISSN:** 0001-8996. **Subscription:** $39.97.

★8839★ **AFFILIA: Journal of Women and Social Work**
Sage Periodicals Press
2455 Teller Rd.
Newbury Park, CA 91320
Phone: (805)499-0721
Fax: (805)499-0871
Description: Journal following women in the social work field. **First published:** 1986. **Frequency:** Quarterly. **ISSN:** 0886-1099. **Subscription:** $30; $64 institutions; $50 two years; $128 two years, institutions. $10 single issue; $19 single issue, institutions.

★8840★ **Aglow**
Women's Aglow Fellowship International
PO Box 1548
Lynnwood, WA 98046-1557
Phone: (206)775-7282
Subtitle: The Magazine for Spirit-Renewed Christian Women. **Description:** Religious magazine presenting articles and Christian testimonies. **First published:** 1969. **Frequency:** 6x/yr. **ISSN:** 0748-6677. **Subscription:** $10.97.

★8841★ **Albuquerque Woman**
Duval Publishing
PO Box 6133
Albuquerque, NM 87197
Phone: (505)247-9195
Description: Features articles on business and career issues. **Frequency:** Bimonthly. **Subscription:** $12.

★8842★ **Alternative Press Index**
PO Box 33109
Baltimore, MD 21218
Phone: (410)243-2471
Description: Alternative index including Black, Hispanic, and women's listings. **First published:** 1969. **Frequency:** 4x/yr. **ISSN:** 0002-662X. **Subscription:** $30; $125 institutions.

★8843★ **American Voice**
Kentucky Foundation for Women, Inc.
The Waldorf Astoria
301 Park Ave.
New York, NY 10022
Phone: (212)755-2539
Fax: (212)755-2539
Description: Journal contains fiction, poetry, essays, and photographs. **Frequency:** Quarterly. **Subscription:** $12; $5 single copy.

★8844★ **American Woman**
GCR Publishing Group
1700 Broadway, 34th Fl.
New York, NY 10019
Phone: (212)541-7100
Description: Lifestyle magazine for women. **First published:** 1990. **Frequency:** 6x/yr.. **Subscription:** $7.99. $1.99 single issue.

★8845★ **American Woman Motorsports Magazine**
Ladylike Enterprise, Inc.
2830 Santa Monica Blvd.
Santa Monica, CA 90404
Phone: (310)829-0012
Description: Magazine for career and family women who ride motorcycles or are involved in other adventure sports. **First published:** January 1989. **Frequency:** 6x/yr. **Subscription:** $10; $18 two years. $2 single issue.

★8846★ **Annals of Scholarship**
1841 Broadway
New York, NY 10023-7602
Description: Discusses nineteenth-century women in England and America. **Subscription:** $28/individual; $50/institution; $10 single copies.

★8847★ **Association Management**
American Society of Association Executives
1575 Eye St. NW
Washington, DC 20005
Phone: (202)626-2711
Subtitle: The Magazine for Association Executives. **Description:** National business magazine. **First published:** 1949. **Frequency:** Monthly. **Subscription:** $24.

★8848★ **Bad Attitude**
PO Box 110
Cambridge, MA 02139
Phone: (617)395-4849
Description: Journal geared toward women who have an interest in lesbian lifestyles. **Frequency:** 6x/year. **Subscription:** $24.

★8849★ **Bay Windows**
1523 Washington St.
Boston, MA 02118
Phone: (617)266-6670
Description: Magazine covering gay male and lesbian literature. **First published:** 1983. **Frequency:** Weekly. **Subscription:** $35. $1 single issue.

★8850★ BBW: Big Beautiful Woman
BBW Publishing Co.
9171 Wilshire Blvd., Ste. 300
Beverly Hills, CA 90210
Phone: (310)271-8442

Description: Fashion magazine for large-size women. **First published:** April 1979. **Frequency:** Monthly. **ISSN:** 0192-5938. **Subscription:** $14.95.

★8851★ Belles Lettres
11151 Captain's Walk Ct.
North Potomac, MD 20878
Phone: (301)294-0278

Subtitle: A Review of Books by Women. **Description:** Literary review featuring women-authored books. **First published:** 1985. **Frequency:** Quarterly. **ISSN:** 0084-2957. **Subscription:** Free to qualified subscribers; $20; $40 institutions; $15 students. $5 single issue.

★8852★ Berkeley Women's Law Journal
University of California
Periodicals Dept.
2120 Berkeley Way
Berkeley, CA 94720
Phone: (415)642-6263

Description: Journal addressing various perspectives of the legal concerns of women, especially women of color, lesbians, disabled women, and poor women. **Frequency:** Annual. **Subscription:** $35/institutions; $16/regular; $8 low income; $30-$99 friend; $100 sponsor. Add $3 for foreign postage.

★8853★ The Birth Gazette
Farm Midwifery Center
42 The Farm
Summertown, TN 38483
Phone: (615)964-2519

Description: Magazine published independently by practicing midwives.

★8854★ Birth Notes
Association for Childbirth at Home,
International
PO Box 430
Glendale, CA 91205-1025

Description: Magazine presents information for parents, childbirth educators, midwives, and physicians about childbirth at home and other alternative technologies of childbirth and perinatology. **First published:** 1977. **Frequency:** Quarterly. **Subscription:** $25.

★8855★ Bitch
San Jose Face
478 W. Hamilton Ave., Ste. 164
Campbell, CA 95008
Phone: (408)374-8073

Description: Music magazine covering rock music made by women. **First published:** 1985. **Frequency:** Monthly. **Subscription:** $15.

★8856★ Black Lace
PO Box 83912
Los Angeles, CA 90083
Phone: (213)410-0808

Description: Magazine by and for African-American lesbians. Includes erotica and politically focused articles and analysis. **Frequency:** 4x/year. **Subscription:** $16.

★8857★ Blushing Bride
114-02 Merrick Blvd.
Jamaica, NY 11434-1735
Phone: (718)739-1296

Description: Magazine catering to the black and minority bridal market. **Frequency:** Quarterly.

★8858★ Bridal Guide
Globe Communications Corp.
441 Lexington Ave.
New York, NY 10017-3910
Phone: (212)949-4040

Subtitle: The How-To For "I Do." **Description:** Magazine. **First published:** 1982. **Frequency:** 6x/yr. **ISSN:** 0882-7451. **Subscription:** $18.95.

★8859★ Bride's
The Conde Nast Publications, Inc.
350 Madison Ave.
New York, NY 10017
Phone: (212)880-8800

Description: Magazine presenting information to engaged couples on finance, travel, liquor, cars, electronics, entertaining, home furnishings, fashion, fitness, health, and beauty. **First published:** 1934. **Frequency:** 6x/yr. **Subscription:** $18. $4 single issue.

★8860★ Bridges
PO Box 18437
Seattle, WA 98118
Phone: (206)721-5008

Subtitle: A Journal for Jewish Feminists and Our Friends. **Description:** Journal of essays, fiction, and poetry combining Jewish identity and activism. **Frequency:** Biannual.

★8861★ Bridges: A Journal of Exceptional Prose and Poetry
1365 1/2 Maltman Ave.
Los Angeles, CA 90026
Phone: (213)666-8741

★8862★ Broomstick
3543 18th St., No. 3
San Francisco, CA 94110
Phone: (415)552-7460

Subtitle: By, for, and about women over forty. **Description:** Feminist magazine. **First published:** January 1978. **Frequency:** Quarterly. **Subscription:** $15; $25 institutions and other countries. $5 single issue.

★8863★ Buenhogar
America Publishing Group
Vanidades Continental Bldg.
6355 NW 36th St.
Virginia Gardens, FL 33166
Phone: (305)871-6400

Description: Magazine for the married woman featuring articles of general interest and entertainment (Spanish). **First published:** 1965. **Frequency:** Every other week. **Subscription:** $53.70. $2.95 single issue.

★8864★ Bulletin: Committee on South Asian Women
Texas A & M University
Department of Psychology
College Station, TX 77843
Phone: (409)845-2576

Description: Features original essays, reports, interviews, reviews, and creative works by and about South Asian women. **Frequency:** 2-3x/year. **Subscription:** $16/individual (per volume); $25/institution (per volume).

★8865★ California Woman
California Federation of Business and Professional Women's Clubs
1100 N St., No. 50
Sacramento, CA 95814-5627
Phone: (916)442-2633

Description: Magazine for business and professional women. **First published:** 1920. **Frequency:** Quarterly. **ISSN:** 0008-1663. **Subscription:** $6.

★8866★ Calyx: A Journal of Arts and Literature by Women
PO Box B
Corvallis, OR 97339
Phone: (503)753-9384

Description: Journal containing poetry, prose, art and book reviews, translations, and photography of women artists and writers. **Frequency:** 3x/year. **Subscription:** $18/individuals; $22.50/libraries and institutions; $15/low income; $8/single copies.

★8867★ Camera Obscura: A Journal of Feminism and Film Theory
Johns Hopkins University Press
Journals Publishing Division
701 W. 40th St., Ste. 275
Baltimore, MD 21211-2190

Description: American journal on feminism and the film industry. **Frequency:** 3x/year. **Subscription:** $18.50/individuals; $37/institutions; add $6.75 for foreign postage.

★8868★ Career Opportunities Bulletin
Women's Bar Association of DC
1819 H St. NW, Ste. 1205
Washington, DC 20006
Phone: (202)785-1540
Fax: (202)293-3388

Description: Features articles and events relating to law. Updates job listings. **Frequency:** 9/yr. **Subscription:** $90.

★8869★ Carolina Woman Today
Nason & Associates
PO Box 8204
Asheville, NC 28814
Phone: (704)258-1322

Description: Magazine for women in North and South Carolina. **First published:** 1989. **Frequency:** Monthly. **Subscription:** $30. $2.50 single issue.

★8870★ Catholic Woman
National Council of Catholic Women
1275 K St. NW, Ste. 975
Washington, DC 20005
Phone: (202)682-0334

Description: Magazine informing membership about programs and policies. **First published:** 1973. **Frequency:** 6x/yr. **Subscription:** $10.

★8871★ The Church Woman
Church Women United
475 Riverside Dr.
New York, NY 10115
Phone: (212)870-2344

Description: Magazine for churchwomen. **First published:** 1936. **Frequency:** Quarterly. **ISSN:** 0009-6598. **Subscription:** $8.

★8872★ College Woman
Alan Weston Communications, Inc.
2501 W. Burbank Blvd., No. 302
Burbank, CA 91505

Description: Lifestyle magazine for college women. **First published:** September 15, 1985. **Frequency:** 4x/yr. **Subscription:** $5.95 for 4 issues.

★8873★ Columbia Journal of Gender and Law
Columbia University School of Law
435 W. 116th St.
New York, NY 10027-7297

Description: Includes legal and interdisciplinary writings on feminism and gender issues and feminist jurisprudence. **Subscription:** $15/individuals; $25/institutions; $10/current students per volume.

★8874★ Common Lives/Lesbian Lives
PO Box 1553
Iowa City, IA 52244
Phone: (319)353-6265

Description: Magazine documenting the lives of lesbians. Contains history, biography, correspondence, journal entries, fiction, poetry, and visual art. **Frequency:** 4x/year. **Subscription:** $15/individual; $25/institution; $4.50 single copies.

★8875★ Complete Woman
1165 N. Clark, Ste. 607
Chicago, IL 60610
Phone: (312)266-8680

Subtitle: For All the Women You Are. **Description:** Women's general interest. **First published:** 1980. **Frequency:** 6x/yr. **Subscription:** $7.50.

★8876★ Conditions
PO Box 56
Van Brunt Sta.
Brooklyn, NY 11215
Phone: (718)788-8654

Description: Feminist writing magazine produced by an editorial collective. Contains and encourages submissions of poetry, fiction, essays, reviews, interviews, special event coverage, journal entries, and dialogues. **Frequency:** Annual. **Subscription:** $24.

★8877★ Connexions
Peoples Translation Service
4228 Telegraph Ave.
Oakland, CA 94609
Phone: (415)654-6725

Subtitle: An International Women's Quarterly. **Description:** Collectively-run magazine featuring news and interviews otherwise unattainable in the English-language press. **First published:** May 1981. **Frequency:** Quarterly. **ISSN:** 0886-7062. **Subscription:** $15; $24 institutions.

★8878★ Conscience
Catholics for a Free Choice
1436 U St. NW, No. 301
Washington, DC 20009
Phone: (202)638-1706

Description: Analyzes ethical discussion of reproductive issues. Monitors efforts of the organization and of others to change the attitude of the Catholic Church toward abortion and birth control. Reports legislative and court actions as well as developments in medical science and in the Church. **First published:** 1979. **Frequency:** Bimonthly. **Price:** Included in membership. **ISSN:** 0740-6835.

★8879★ Cosmopolitan
Hearst Magazines
224 W. 57th St.
New York, NY 10019
Phone: (212)262-5700

Description: Lifestyle magazine for young working women. Includes general interest features, personality profiles, movie, book, and music reviews, and service editorials on beauty, fashion, home decorating, food, nutrition, diet, health, and fitness. **First published:** 1886. **Frequency:** Monthly. **ISSN:** 0010-9541. **Subscription:** $2.50 single issue.

★8880★ Cosmopolitan en Espanol
America Publishing Group
Vanidades Continental Bldg.
6355 NW 36th St.
Virginia Gardens, FL 33166
Phone: (305)871-6400

Description: Magazine for the young modern Hispanic woman; covering fashion, relationships, travel, entertainment, and career (Spanish). **First published:** 1973. **Frequency:** Monthly. **Subscription:** $22.50. $2.50 single issue.

★8881★ Country Woman
5400 S. 60 St.
Greendale, WI 53129
Phone: (414)423-0100

Description: Magazine featuring articles on rural living and concerns of country women. **First published:** 1970. **Frequency:** 6x/yr. **ISSN:** 0892-8525. **Subscription:** $14.98.

★8882★ Crazy Quilt
PO Box 390575
Mountain View, CA 94039

Description: Journal containing letters, personal essays, including some poetry and sketches, covering a wide range of topics. **Frequency:** Quarterly. **Subscription:** $16/year; $5/single copy.

★8883★ The Creative Woman
Governors State University
University Pkwy.
University Park, IL 60466
Phone: (312)534-5000
Fax: (708)534-5459

Description: Focuses on a special topic regarding creative achievements by women in each issue. Includes fiction, poetry, book reviews, articles, photography, and original graphics. **Subscription:** $10/individual; $20/institution; $3/single copy.

★8884★ Current Literature in Family Planning
Planned Parenthood Federation of America
Katharine Dexter McCormick Library
810 7th Ave.
New York, NY 10019
Phone: (212)603-4637

Subtitle: A Monthly Classified Review of the Literature in the Field of Family Planning. **Description:** Magazine devoted to family planning. **First published:** 1972. **Frequency:** Monthly. **ISSN:** 0092-6000. **Subscription:** $40.

★8885★ Dallas Woman
Paradigm Publishing Inc.
14275 Midway Rd., Ste. 280
Dallas, TX 75244
Phone: (214)458-7383

Description: General-interest magazine for working women ages 25-54. **First published:** 1988. **Frequency:** Monthly.

★8886★ Daughters of Sarah
3801 N. Keeler
PO Box 416790
Chicago, IL 60641
Phone: (312)736-3399

Subtitle: The Magazine for Christian Feminists. **Description: First published:** November 1974. **Frequency:** 6x/yr. **ISSN:** 0739-1749. **Subscription:** $18.

★8887★ Detroit Metropolitan Woman
North Park Plaza
17117 W. 9 Mile Rd., Ste. 1115
Southfield, MI 48075-4517
Phone: (313)443-6500
Fax: (313)443-6501

Description: Magazine containing news, features, and information for women in the Metropolitan Detroit area. **Frequency:** Monthly. **Subscription:** $15.

★8888★ Differences: A Journal of Feminist Cultural Studies
Indiana University Press
10th and Morton
Bloomington, IN 47405
Phone: (812)855-9449
Fax: (812)855-7931

Description: Journal that seeks to bring together cultural studies and feminism. **Frequency:** 3x/year. **Subscription:** $28/individual; $48/institution; add $10 for foreign postage. Single copies: $10/individual; $20/institution; add $1.75 for postage.

★8889★ Dimension
Southern Baptist Convention
Women's Missionary Union
PO Box 830010
Birmingham, AL 35283-0010
Phone: (205)991-8100
Fax: (205)991-4990
Description: Administrative magazine for general officers and age-level directors. **Subscription:** $2.25/single copy.

★8890★ Dykes, Disability & Stuff
PO Box 6194
Boston, MA 02114
Description: Focuses on health, disability, and illness related to women. **Frequency:** 4x/year. **Subscription:** $8-$20.

★8891★ Earth's Daughters
Box 622
Sta. C
Buffalo, NY 14209
Phone: (716)886-2636
Description: Literary arts magazine supportive of feminist concerns; publishes poetry, fiction, and artwork. **Frequency:** 3x/year. **Subscription:** $14/individuals; $22/libraries and institutions. Sample copy $4.

★8892★ Educational Horizons
Pi Lambda Theta
4101 E. 3rd St.
Bloomington, IN 47407
Phone: (812)339-3411
Fax: (812)339-3462
Description: Journal for professionals in education. **Frequency:** Quarterly.

★8893★ Elegant Bride
Pace Communications, Inc.
1301 Carolina St.
Greensboro, NC 27401
Phone: (919)378-6065
Description: Nationally-distributed bridal publication. **First published:** 1988. **Frequency:** 6x/yr. **Subscription:** $30; $34 other countries. $4.95 single issue.

★8894★ Elle
Hachette Magazines, Inc.
1633 Broadway
New York, NY 10019
Phone: (212)767-5800
Description: Magazine covering fashion, styles, and trends for young women. **First published:** September 1985. **Frequency:** Monthly. **ISSN:** 0888-0808. **Subscription:** $19. $3 single issue.

★8895★ The Emunah Women Magazine
Emunah Women of America
370 7th Ave., No. 11N
New York, NY 10001
Phone: (212)654-9045
Description: Magazine on underprivileged children in Israel.

★8896★ Entrepreneurial Woman
Entrepreneur, Inc.
2392 Morse Ave.
Irvine, CA 92714
Phone: (714)261-2325
Description: Magazine for women business owners. **First published:** June 1989. **Frequency:** Monthly. **ISSN:** 0889-4301. **Subscription:** $19.95. $3 single issue.

★8897★ Equal Play
Women's Action Alliance
370 Lexington Ave., Rm. 630
New York, NY 10017
Phone: (212)532-8330
Fax: (212)779-2864
Description: Magazine for adults concerned with children and stereotypes. **Frequency:** Semiannually. **Subscription:** $12.50/individuals; $22/institutions.

★8898★ Essence
Essence Communications, Inc.
1500 Broadway
New York, NY 10036
Phone: (212)642-0600
Fax: (212)921-5173
Description: Magazine for contemporary black women. **First published:** 1970. **Frequency:** Monthly. **ISSN:** 0014-0880. **Subscription:** $14. $1.75 single issue.

★8899★ Ethnic Woman
Trade Union Women of African Heritage
530 W. 23rd St.
New York, NY 10003
Phone: (212)547-5656
Description: Contains information concerning discrimination against women in the labor movement. **Frequency:** 2x/year.

★8900★ Executive Female
National Association for Female Executives
127 W. 24th St., 4th Fl.
New York, NY 10011
Phone: (212)645-0770
Description: Magazine covering career and financial management for professional exexutive and entrepreneuial women. **First published:** 1978. **Frequency:** 6x/yr. **ISSN:** 0199-2880. **Subscription:** $29.

★8901★ Fairfield County Woman
FCW, Inc.
15 Bank St.
Stamford, CT 06901
Phone: (203)323-3105
Fax: (203)323-4112
Description: Tabloid written exclusively for working women; containing news on finance, health, law, education, career advancement, and topical issues. **First published:** 1982. **Frequency:** Monthly. **Subscription:** $15.

★8902★ Family Circle
The Family Circle, Inc.
110 5th Ave.
New York, NY 10011
Phone: (212)463-1000
Description: Women's magazine. **First published:** 1932. **Frequency:** Every third week. **Subscription:** $1.09 single issue.

★8903★ Feelin' Good
Ware Publishing, Inc.
400 Corporate Pointe, No. 580
Culver City, CA 90230
Phone: (213)649-3320
Subtitle: Lifestyle Guide To Healthy Living.
Description: Magazine covering healthy lifestyles for black women. **First published:** 1988. **Frequency:** 6x/yr. **Subscription:** $2.95 single issue.

★8904★ Feminist Bookstore News
PO Box 882554
San Francisco, CA 94188
Phone: (415)626-1556
Description: Trade magazine for booksellers, librarians, and publishers interested in books by and about women. **First published:** October 1, 1976. **Frequency:** 6x/yr. **ISSN:** 0741-6555. **Subscription:** $68. $5 single issue.

★8905★ Feminist Issues
2948 Hillegass
Berkeley, CA 94705
Phone: (415)843-7659
Description: Journal of feminist social and political theory, with emphasis on an international exchange of ideas. **Frequency:** 2x/year. **Subscription:** $15/individual; $34/institution. Single copies: $9/individual; $20/institution. Add $10 (surface) or $16 (air mail) for postage outside U.S.

★8906★ Feminist Periodicals: A Current Listing of Contents
University of Wisconsin
Women's Studies Librarian
430 Memorial Library
728 State St.
Madison, WI 53706
Phone: (608)263-5754
Description: Reference work containing tables of contents from feminist periodicals of interest to persons involved in women's studies. **First published:** 1981. **Frequency:** Quarterly. **ISSN:** 0742-7433. **Subscription:** $12.60 individuals and women's programs; $23 out of state individuals and women's programs; $17.95 libraries and organizations; $43 out of state libraries and organizations.

★8907★ Feminist Studies
Unversity of Maryland
Women's Studies Program
College Park, MD 20742
Phone: (301)405-7415
Description: Scholarly journal discussing issues related to women's studies. Contains original articles, essays, interviews, book reviews, and bibliographies. **Frequency:** 3x/year. **Subscription:** $25/individuals; $55/institutions.

★8908★ Feminist Teacher
Indiana University
442 Ballantine
Bloomington, IN 47405
Description: Magazine contains articles, news, and resources for feminist educators. **Frequency:** 3x/year. **Subscription:** $12/individual; $20/institution; $6 single copies. Add $5/individual and $10/institution for foreign orders.

★8909★ Fighting Woman News
Fighting Woman News
6741 Tung Ave. W.
Theodore, AL 36582
Phone: (205)653-0549

Subtitle: Quarterly Magazine of Martial Arts, Self-Defense, Combative Sports. **Description:** Provides information on martial arts for women. **First published:** 1975. **Frequency:** Quarterly. **Price:** $10/yr. for individuals, $15 for institution, U.S.; $15 elsewhere. **ISSN:** 0146-8812.

★8910★ Financial Woman Today
Financial Women International, Inc.
7910 Woodmont Ave., Ste. 1430
Bethesda, MD 20814-3015
Phone: (301)657-8288

Description: Newsmagazine for women financial executives. Covers career information, trends in the financial services industry, and workforce issues. **First published:** 1985. **Frequency:** Monthly. **ISSN:** 8778-4000. **Subscription:** $24; $28 Canada; $30 other countries.

★8911★ First for Women
Bauer Publishing Co.
270 Sylvan Ave.
Englewood Cliffs, NJ 07632
Phone: (201)569-6699

Description: Magazine for women featuring articles on fashion, food, decorating, and beauty. **First published:** 1989. **Frequency:** 16x/yr. **ISSN:** 1040-9467. **Subscription:** $27. $1.50 single issue.

★8912★ Free Focus
Women's Literary Guild
224 82nd St.
Brooklyn, NY 11209
Phone: (718)680-3899

Subtitle: Thursday's Press. **Description:** Literary magazine promoting women writers. **First published:** 1985. **Frequency:** Quarterly. **Subscription:** $4. $2 single issue.

★8913★ Friendly Woman
84889 Harry Taylor Rd.
Eugene, OR 97405
Phone: (503)344-4973

Description: Journal for the exchange of ideas, feelings, hopes, and experiences by and among Quaker women. **Frequency:** Quarterly.

★8914★ Frontiers: A Journal of Women Studies
University of New Mexico
Women's Studies Program
Mesa Vista Hall 2142
Albuquerque, NM 87131-1586
Phone: (505)277-1198
Fax: (505)277-0267

Description: Publishes scholarly and feature articles, personal essays, poetry, short fiction, book reviews, bibliographies, art, and black and white photography. Issues include those on Native American women. **Frequency:** 3x/yr. **Subscription:** $20/individual; $33/institution. Single copies $8/individual; $11/institution.

★8915★ Gender & Society
Sage Periodicals Press
2455 Teller Rd.
Newbury Park, CA 91320
Phone: (805)499-0721

Description: Journal covering theory and research in the study of gender as a primary social category and its relationship to social order; emphasizing the study of gender and feminist scholarship. **First published:** March 1987. **Frequency:** Quarterly. **ISSN:** 0891-2432. **Subscription:** $36; $96 institutions; $72 two years; $192 two years, institutions. $11 single issue; $24 single issue, institutions.

★8916★ Genders
University of Colorado
English Dept.
Campus Box 226
Boulder, CO 80309
Phone: (202)492-2853

Description: Journal seeks to aid the distribution and exchange of feminist research and ideas in the multidisciplinary, international areas of gender in education. Welcomes articles that examine the experiences of girls and women in education as well as boys and men. **Frequency:** 3x/year. **Subscription:** $12/individual; $20/institution. Add $5/individual; $10/institution for foreign postage. Single copies $6.

★8917★ Genesis
American Society for Psychoprophylaxis in Obstetrics, Inc. (ASPO/Lamaze)
1101 Connecticut Ave. NW, Ste. 700
Washington, DC 20036-4303
Phone: (703)524-7802

Description: Journal containing original research data and teaching aids for physicians, health care educators, and family members who promote and support the ASPO/Lamaze method of prepared childbirth. **Frequency:** 6x/yr. **Subscription:** Free to members; $30 libraries and institutions.

★8918★ GFWC Clubwoman Magazine
General Federation of Women's Clubs
1734 N St. NW
Washington, DC 20036
Phone: (202)347-3168
Fax: (202)835-0246

Description: Magazine covering women's clubs news and community service projects. **First published:** 1897. **Frequency:** 6x/yr. **Subscription:** $5.

★8919★ Girl Scout Leader
Girl Scouts of the U.S.A.
830 3rd Ave.
New York, NY 10022
Phone: (212)940-7500

Subtitle: For Adults in Girl Scouting. **Description:** Magazine with information and news of interest to Girl Scout adult volunteers and staff. **First published:** April 1923. **Frequency:** Quarterly. **ISSN:** 0017-0577. **Subscription:** $5.

★8920★ Glamour
Conde Nast Publications, Inc.
350 Madison Ave.
New York, NY 10017
Phone: (212)880-8800

Description: Fashion, beauty, and health magazine. **First published:** April 1939. **Frequency:** Monthly. **ISSN:** 0017-0747. **Subscription:** $15. $2.50 single issue.

★8921★ Glowing Lamp
Chi Eta Phi Sorority, Inc.
3029 13th St., NW
Washington, DC 20009
Phone: (202)232-3858

Description: Journal containing information related to nursing profession. **Frequency:** Annual.

★8922★ Golden Isis Magazine
Bldg. 105, Box 137
23233 Saticoy St.
West Hills, CA 91304

Description: Goddess-inspired journal of mystical surrealism and the occult. **Frequency:** Quarterly. **Subscription:** Subscriptions $10. Sample $2.95.

★8923★ Golden Threads
PO Box 3177
Burlington, VT 05401-0031
Phone: (802)658-5510

Description: International networking publication targeted to middle-aged lesbians. **Frequency:** Quarterly.

★8924★ Good Housekeeping
959 8th Ave.
New York, NY 10019
Phone: (212)649-2531

Description: Magazine focusing on women and the home. **First published:** 1885. **Frequency:** Monthly. **Subscription:** $16.97. $1.95 single issue.

★8925★ Hadassah Magazine
Hadassah, The Women's Zionist Organization of America
50 W. 58th St.
New York, NY 10019
Phone: (212)355-7900

Description: Information relates to health and educational programs in Israel. **Frequency:** Monthly.

★8926★ Hag Rag
PO Box 93243
Milwaukee, WI 53203
Phone: (414)372-3330

Description: Radical lesbian feminist news, analysis, reviews, political commentary, theory, letters, and calendar listing. **Frequency:** Bimonthly. **Subscription:** $10.

★8927★ Harley Women Magazine
Asphalt Angels Publications, Inc.
PO Box 374
Streamwood, IL 60107
Phone: (708)888-2645

Description: Motorcycle magazine containing personality profiles, technical tips, photos, fiction, and coverage of national motorcycle events. **First published:** 1985. **Frequency:** 6x/yr. **ISSN:** 0893-6447. **Subscription:** $12; $22 two years.

★8928★ Harper's Bazaar
1700 Broadway
New York, NY 10019
Phone: (212)903-5000

Description: Fashion and beauty magazine. **First published:** 1867. **Frequency:** Monthly. **Subscription:** $24. $2.50 single issue.

★8929★ Harper's Bazaar en Espanol
America Publishing Group
Vandidades Continental Bldg.
6355 NW 36th St.
Virginia Gardens, FL 33166
Phone: (305)871-6400

Description: Hispanic edition of Harper's Bazaar (Spanish). **First published:** 1980. **Frequency:** 8x/yr. **Subscription:** $18.90. $2.95 single issue.

★8930★ Harvard Women's Law Journal
Harvard Law School
Publications Center
Cambridge, MA 02138
Phone: (617)495-3726
Fax: (617)495-1110

Description: Journal dedicated to the development of a feminist jurisprudence and to the presentation of women's legal issues. **Frequency:** Annual. **Subscription:** $15/individual; $17/foreign, surface; $27/foreign, airmail.

★8931★ Health
Family Media, Inc.
3 Park Ave.
New York, NY 10016
Phone: (212)779-6441

Description: Health and nutrition magazine for women. **First published:** 1969. **Frequency:** 10/yr. **ISSN:** 0279-3547. **Subscription:** $22; $28 Canada; $30 other countries. $2.25 single issue.

★8932★ Health Care for Women International
Hemisphere Publishing Corp.
1101 Vermont Ave. NW, No. 200
Washington, DC 20005
Phone: (202)289-2174

Description: Interdisciplinary journal on women's health care. Covers cultural differences, psychological challenges, alternative lifestyles, aging, wife abuse, childbearing, childrearing, and ethical issues. **First published:** 1979. **Frequency:** Quarterly. **ISSN:** 0739-9332. **Subscription:** $37; $87 institutions.

★8933★ Heresies: A Feminist Publication on Art & Politics
Heresies Collective, Inc.
280 Broadway, Ste. 412
New York, NY 10013

Description: Contains essays, poetry, short fiction, satire, criticism, letters, interviews, page art, photography, and graphic and visual art. **Frequency:** 2x/year. **Subscription:** $23/individual; $33/institution; $6.75/single copies.

★8934★ Hikane: The Capable Woman
PO Box 841
Great Barrington, MA 01230

Description: Serves as a grassroots, networking tool for disabled lesbians and their allies. **Frequency:** Quarterly. **Subscription:** $14/individual; $24/institution. Subscriptions available to women only. Available in print, cassette, and braille.

★8935★ Horizons
Presbyterian Women in the Presbyterian Church
100 Witherspoon St.
Louisville, KY 40202-1396
Phone: (502)569-5366
Fax: (502)569-5018

Description: Official magazine of Presbyterian women. **Frequency:** Bimonthly. **Subscription:** $12. Overseas add U.S. $2.

★8936★ Hot Wire
Empty Closet Enterprises
5210 N. Wayne
Chicago, IL 60640
Phone: (312)769-9009

Subtitle: The Journal of Women's Music and Culture. **Description:** Covers contemporary and historical women in the arts, including writers, musicians, comediennes, and actresses. **First published:** 1985. **Frequency:** 3/yr. **Price:** $17/yr., U.S.; $19, Canada; $27, Europe; $31, Asia. **ISSN:** 0747-8887.

★8937★ Housewife-Writer's Forum
PO Box 780
Lyman, WY 82937
Phone: (307)786-4513

Description: Literary magazine for housewives. **First published:** 1988. **Frequency:** 6x/yr. **Subscription:** $15. $4 single issue.

★8938★ Human Life Issues
University of Steubenville
Human Life Center
Steubenville, OH 43952
Phone: (614)282-9953

Description: Magazine for those interested in pro-life viewpoints and natural family planning. **First published:** 1981. **Frequency:** Quarterly.

★8939★ Hurricane Alice
Hurricane Alice Foundation
207 Lind Hall
207 Church St. SE
Minneapolis, MN 55455
Phone: (612)625-1834

Subtitle: A Feminist Quarterly. **Description:** Feminist journal covering works of culture, prose, poetry, and artwork. **First published:** 1983. **Frequency:** Quarterly. **ISSN:** 0882-7907. **Subscription:** $10; $8 students, low income persons, seniors; $12 Canada; $15 other countries; $20 libraries and institutions.

★8940★ HW
Gamer Publishing Group
20 Isham Rd.
West Hartford, CT 06107-2291
Phone: (203)278-3800

Subtitle: Hartford Woman. **Description:** Magazine for business and professional women. **First**

published: 1981. **Frequency:** Monthly. **Subscription:** $12.

★8941★ Hypatia
University of South Florida
Soc-107
Tampa, FL 33620-8100
Phone: (813)974-5531
Fax: (813)974-2668

Description: Journal of feminist philosophy. **Frequency:** 4x/year. **Subscription:** $32.50/individual; $50/institutions. Add $12.50 for foreign postage.

★8942★ Ideas para su Hogar (Ideas for Your Home)
America Publishing Group
Vandidades Continental Bldg.
6355 NW 36th St.
Virginia Gardens, FL 33166
Phone: (305)871-6400

Description: Magazine for homemakers; including articles on cooking, decorating, gardening, and patterns (Spanish). **First published:** 1978. **Frequency:** Monthly. **Subscription:** $22.50. $2.50 single issue.

★8943★ Ikon
PO Box 1355
Stuyvesant Sta.
New York, NY 10009

Description: Cultural, political, and feminist magazine which shows the experiences of Third World women, lesbians, Jewish women, and working women. **First published:** 1982/83. **Frequency:** 2x/yr. **ISSN:** 0579-4315. **Subscription:** $12/individual; $15/institution; $6/single copies.

★8944★ ILWC Journal
International League of Women Composers (ILWC)
670 Southshore Rd.
Three Mile Bay, NY 13693
Phone: (315)649-5086

Description: Publication providing information for and about women concert music composers.

★8945★ Indianapolis Woman
Media Management Group
PO Box 68699
Indianapolis, IN 46268
Phone: (317)297-7465

Description: Magazine for women living in and around Indianapolis. **First published:** 1984. **Frequency:** Monthly. **ISSN:** 0897-0211. **Subscription:** $12.47.

★8946★ Initiatives: Journal of NAWE
National Association of Women in Education (NAWE)
1325 18th St., NW, Ste. 210
Washington, DC 20036-6511
Phone: (202)659-9330

Description: Journal focuses on addressing issues associated with the education of today's women and their personal and professional development. **Frequency:** 4x/yr. **ISSN:** 0094-3460. **Subscription:** $40; $50 foreign; $13 single copies.

★8947★ Inner Woman
Silver Owl Publications, Inc.
PO Box 51186
Seattle, WA 98115-1186
Phone: (206)524-9071
Description: Magazine (tabloid) devoted to women's spirituality, healing and evolution. **First published:** March 1987. **Frequency:** Quarterly. **ISSN:** 1049-9709. **Subscription:** $7.50.

★8948★ Intercambios Femeniles
National Network of Hispanic Women
12021 Wilshire Blvd., Ste. 353
Los Angeles, CA 90025
Phone: (213)225-9895
Description: Magazine profiles the career paths of successful Hispanic women and disseminates career and resource information for professional and business women. **Frequency:** Quarterly.

★8949★ International Altrusan
Altrusa International, Inc.
332 S. Michigan Ave., Ste. 1123
Chicago, IL 60604-4305
Phone: (312)427-4410
Description: Service club magazine for women executives. **First published:** September 1922. **Frequency:** Quarterly.

★8950★ International Family Planning Perspectives
The Alan Guttmacher Institute
111 5th Ave.
New York, NY 10003
Phone: (212)254-5656
Fax: (212)254-9891
Founded: 1975. **Description:** Family planning magazine. Printed in Spanish and French. **Frequency:** 6/yr.

★8951★ International League of Women Composers Journal
Abilene Christian University
Box 8274
Abilene, TX 79699
Phone: (915)674-2044
Fax: (915)674-2232
Description: Report available to members, libraries, and music organizations of the organization's activities. Also includes announcements of awards and competitions and opportunities for women composers. **Frequency:** Quarterly.

★8952★ International Review: Natural Family Planning & Human Life Issues
University of Steubenville
Human Life Center
Steubenville, OH 43952
Phone: (614)282-9953
Subtitle: Natural Family Planning & Human Life Issues. **Description:** Journal promoting natural family planning and human life issues in America and the world. **First published:** 1976. **Frequency:** Quarterly. **ISSN:** 0146-1745. **Subscription:** $20; $24 other countries; $29 Canada & Mexico (mail); $36 other countries (mail). $6 single issue.

★8953★ Interracial Books for Children Bulletin
Council on Interracial Books for Children
1841 Broadway
New York, NY 10023
Phone: (212)757-5339
Description: Journal concerning itself with elimination of racism, sexism, and other bias in children's books. **First published:** 1967. **Frequency:** 8x/yr. **ISSN:** 0146-5562. **Subscription:** $20; $28 institutions; $64 other countries, air mail.

★8954★ Iowa Image
PO Box 744
Centerville, IA 52544
Phone: (515)437-1143
Description: Lifestyle magazine for southeast and south central Iowa women. **First published:** May 1989. **Frequency:** Quarterly.

★8955★ Iowa Woman
Iowa Woman Endeavors
PO Box 680
Iowa City, IA 52244
Phone: (319)987-2879
Description: Regional journal covering literature, art, and information for women. **First published:** 1979. **Frequency:** Quarterly. **ISSN:** 0271-8227. **Subscription:** $15; $17 Canada and Pan America; $20 other countries.

★8956★ IRIS: A Journal About Women
University of Virginia
Women's Center
Box 323, HSC
Charlottesville, VA 22908
Phone: (804)924-4500
Description: Journal contains articles and news on women's political, academic, social, and artistic concerns. **Frequency:** 2x/year. **Subscription:** $8/individual; $15/institution; $5 single copies.

★8957★ Issues In Reproductive and Genetic Engineering (IRAGE)
Pergamon Press
82 Richdale Ave.
Cambridge, MA 02140
Phone: (612)491-4038
Subtitle: Journal of the International Feminist Analysis. **Description:** Designed to develop feminist analyses of the new reproductive technologies and genetic engineering and their impact on women. **Frequency:** 3x/year.

★8958★ Ivy Leaf
Alpha Kappa Alpha Sorority, Inc.
5656 S. Stony Island Ave.
Chicago, IL 60637
Phone: (312)684-1282
Description: Sorority publication for Black women. **First published:** December 1921. **Frequency:** Quarterly. **ISSN:** 0021-3276. **Subscription:** $10.

★8959★ Journal of the American Medical Women's Association
American Medical Women's Assn.
801 N. Fairfax St.
Alexandria, VA 22314
Phone: (703)838-0500
Fax: (703)549-3864
Description: Medical journal. **First published:** 1946. **Frequency:** 6x/yr. **ISSN:** 0098-8421. **Subscription:** $35; $40 other countries. $5 single issue.

★8960★ Journal of Feminist Family Therapy
The Haworth Press
3833 Woods Dr.
Des Moines, IA 50312
Phone: (515)277-2324
Description: Provides a multidisciplinary forum to explore the relationship between feminist theory and family therapy practice and theory. **Frequency:** Quarterly. **Subscription:** Subscriptions $24/individuals; $40/institutions; $75/libraries. Add 40% for foreign requests (outside Canada and Mexico).

★8961★ Journal of Feminist Studies in Religion
Harvard Divinity School
45 Francis Ave.
Cambridge, MA 02138
Phone: (617)495-5751
Description: Journal of feminist scholarship in religion. **Frequency:** 2x/year. **Subscription:** $18.

★8962★ Journal of the History of Sexuality
University of Chicago Press
5720 S. Woodlawn
Chicago, IL 60637
Phone: (312)702-7600
Fax: (312)702-0172
Description: Journal covers such topics as prostitute saints in medieval legend; sodomy and the eighteenth-century London stage; sexual politics in eighteenth-century France; novelist William Godwin and the politics of homophobia; and dominance and difference in the United States. Includes commentaries and book reviews.

★8963★ Journal of Homosexuality
The Haworth Press, Inc.
10 Alice St.
Binghamton, NY 13904
Phone: (607)722-2493
Description: Journal devoted to theoretical, empirical, and historical research on homosexuality, heterosexuality, sexual identity, social sex roles, and the sexual relationships of both men and women. **First published:** 1974. **Frequency:** Quarterly. **ISSN:** 0091-8369. **Subscription:** $40; $95 institutions; $175 libraries.

★8964★ Journal of Marriage and the Family
National Council on Family Relations
3989 Central Ave., NE, Ste. 550
Minneapolis, MN 55421
Phone: (612)781-9331
Description: Premier research publication in the family field featuring original research and theory, research interpretation, and critical discus-

sion related to marriage and the family. **First published:** 1939. **Frequency:** Quarterly. **ISSN:** 0022-2445. **Subscription:** $50; $85 institutions.

★8965★ Journal of the National Association of University Women
National Association of University Women (NAUW)
1553 Pine Forest Dr.
Tallahassee, FL 32301
Phone: (904)878-4660
Frequency: Biannual.

★8966★ Journal of Reprints of Documents Affecting Women
Today Publications & News Service, Inc.
621 National Press Building
Washington, DC 20045
Phone: (202)628-6663
Description: Journal on women's rights and opportunities. **First published:** 1975. **Frequency:** Quarterly. **Subscription:** $40.

★8967★ Journal of Women and Aging
The Haworth Press
10 Alice St.
Binghamton, NY 13904
Phone: (913)295-6616
Description: Journal designed for a wide audience covering the health and well-being of women as they age. **Frequency:** Quarterly. **Subscription:** $28/individuals; $38/institutions; $45/libraries.

★8968★ Journal of Women and Religion
Graduate Theological Union
Center for Women and Religion
2400 Ridge Rd.
Berkeley, CA 94709
Phone: (415)649-1417
Description: Journal containing information related to ending sexism and promoting justice for women in religious institutions. **Frequency:** Annual. **Price:** Available to members only.

★8969★ The Journal of Women's History
Indiana University
History Dept.
742 Ballantine Hall
Bloomington, IN 47405
Phone: (812)855-1320
Fax: (812)855-5678
Description: Feminist journal on women's history.

★8970★ The Joyful Woman
Joyful Woman Christian Ministries, Inc.
118 Shannon Lake Circle
Greenville, SC 29615-9711
Phone: (803)297-1625
Description: Magazine for Christian women. **First published:** March 1978. **Frequency:** 6x/yr. **ISSN:** 0885-8004. **Subscription:** $13.95; $17.45 other countries. $3 single issue.

★8971★ Kalliope: A Journal of Women's Art
Florida Community College at Jacksonville
3939 Roosevelt Blvd.
Jacksonville, FL 32205
Phone: (904)387-8211
Description: Supports women in the arts by publishing their poetry, fiction, interviews, reviews, and artwork. **Frequency:** 3x/yr. **Subscription:** $10.50/individual; $18/institution. Add $6 for foreign postage. Single copies $4, $7, or $8.

★8972★ Ladies' Home Journal
Meredith Publishing
100 Park Ave.
New York, NY 10017
Phone: (212)953-7070
Description: Women's magazine. **First published:** December 1883. **Frequency:** Monthly. **Subscription:** $19.95. $1.75 single issue.

★8973★ Lady's Circle
Lopez Publications, Inc.
105 E. 35th St.
New York, NY 10010
Phone: (212)689-3933
Description: Women's interest magazine. **First published:** 1964. **Frequency:** Monthly. **Subscription:** $18. $1.95 single issue.

★8974★ Lambda Book Report
Lambda Rising, Inc.
1625 Connecticut Ave. NW
Washington, DC 20009
Phone: (202)462-7924
Subtitle: A Review of Contemporary Gay and Lesbian Literature. **Description:** Magazine covering gay and lesbian literature. **First published:** 1987. **Frequency:** 6x/yr.. **ISSN:** 1048-9487. **Subscription:** $19.95. $3.95 single issue.

★8975★ Lana's World/How Do You Spell It Productions
PO Box 3633
Eugene, OR 97403
Description: Magazine dedicated to lesbian and feminist cartoons. **Frequency:** Quarterly.

★8976★ Leader In Action
American Association of University Women (AAUW)
1111 16th St. NW
Washington, DC 20036
Frequency: 3x/year. **Subscription:** $15/year.

★8977★ Lear's
Lear Publishing Co.
655 Madison Ave.
New York, NY 10021-8043
Phone: (212)888-0007
Subtitle: For the Woman Who Wasn't Born Yesterday. **Description:** Magazine. **First published:** 1988. **Frequency:** Monthly. **ISSN:** 0897-0149. **Subscription:** $18; $25 Canada. $3 single issue.

★8978★ Legacy
Pennsylvania State Press
Barbara Bldg., Ste. C
820 N. University Dr.
University Park, PA 16802
Phone: (814)865-1327
Description: Journal of seventeenth, eighteenth, nineteenth, and early twentieth-century American women writers. **Frequency:** 2x/yr. **Subscription:** $12/graduate students; $17.50/individuals; $20/institutions; $9/single copies.

★8979★ Lesbian Connection
Elsie Publishing Institute
PO Box 811
East Lansing, MI 48826
Phone: (517)371-5257
Description: National magazine by, for, and about lesbians. Collective, edited by the Ambitious Amazons. **First published:** 1974. **Frequency:** 6x/yr. **Subscription:** Free to qualified subscribers; $18 (donation).

★8980★ Lesbian Contradiction
LesCon
1007 N. 47th St.
Seattle, WA 98103
Subtitle: A Journal of Irreverent Feminism. **Description:** Newspaper (tabloid) presenting commentary, analysis, and humor. **First published:** December 1982. **Frequency:** Quarterly. **Subscription:** $6.50.

★8981★ Lesbian Ethics
LE Publications
PO Box 4723
Albuquerque, NM 87106
Description: Journal of lesbian feminist ethics and philosophy, with a focus on how lesbians behave with each other. **Frequency:** 3x/year. **Price:** $14/individual; $16/foreign individual (surface); $24/foreign individual (air); $20/foreign institution (surface); $28/foreign institution (air); $6 single copies.

★8982★ Letras Femeninas
Asociacion de Literatura Femenina Hispania
University of Nebraska
Department of Modern Languages
Lincoln, NE 68588-0315
Description: Contains contemporary Hispanic literature by women. Contributors must be members of the association. **Frequency:** Spring and Fall. **Subscription:** $20.

★8983★ Lilith
Lilith Publications
250 W. 57th, Ste. 2432
New York, NY 10107
Phone: (212)757-0818
Subtitle: The Jewish Women's Magazine. **Description:** Magazine with a feminist focus. **First published:** 1976. **Frequency:** Quarterly. **ISSN:** 0146-2334. **Subscription:** $14; $20 institutions.

★8984★ LQ (Ladies Quarterly)
Rothschild Publishing Co.
9 E. 45th St.
New York, NY 10017
Phone: (212)309-6970
Description: Women's fashion magazine. **First published:** Fall 1989. **Frequency:** Quarterly.

★8985★ Lutheran Woman Today
Augsburg Fortress, Publishers
426 S. 5th St.
Box 1209
Minneapolis, MN 55440
Phone: (612)330-3300
Description: Women of the Evangelical Lutheran Church bible study magazine. **First published:** 1908. **Frequency:** Monthly (July/Aug. issues combined). **ISSN:** 0896-209X. **Subscription:** $9.

★8986★ Mademoiselle
350 Madison Ave.
New York, NY 10017
Phone: (212)880-8800
Description: Young women's magazine. **First published:** 1935. **Frequency:** Monthly. **Subscription:** $15. $2.50 single issue.

★8987★ Madre
121 W. 27th St., Rm. 301
New York, NY 10001
Phone: (212)627-0444
Fax: (212)675-3704
Description: Offers a muti-cultural perspective on political and social issues affecting women and children in the United States and the Middle East. **Frequency:** Quarterly.

★8988★ Maize, A Lesbian Country Magazine
Word Weavers
PO Box 8742
Minneapolis, MN 55408
Description: Magazine about the rural lesbian experience and strategies for economic survival and community building. Topics include food, shelter, agriculture, environmental issues, and healing arts presented in essays, news, book reviews, interviews, and how-to articles. **Frequency:** 4x/year. **Subscription:** $10.

★8989★ Martha Stewart at Home
Time, Inc.
1271 Avenue of the Americas
New York, NY 10020
Phone: (212)522-1212
Description: Magazine featuring gardening, decorating, traveling, and home entertaining for women. **Frequency:** Quarterly.

★8990★ Matrix Women's Newsmagazine
108 Locust St., No. 14
Santa Cruz, CA 95060
Phone: (408)429-1238
Description: Feminist publication for the central coast and Bay Area regions of California. Contains news, articles, poetry, and reviews by and about women. **Frequency:** Monthly. **Subscription:** $14.

★8991★ McCall's
The New York Times Co. Magazine Group
110 5th Ave.
New York, NY 10011
Phone: (212)463-1000
Description: Women's magazine. **First published:** 1876. **Frequency:** Monthly. **Subscription:** $18; $1.75 single issue.

★8992★ Medical Digest
Planned Parenthood Federation of America
810 7th Ave.
New York, NY 10019
Phone: (212)261-4660
Description: Provides information on family planning and reproductive health care to individuals, the media, and health care professionals. **Frequency:** Semiannual.

★8993★ Melpomene: A Journal for Women's Health Research
Melpomene Institute
1010 University Ave. W.
St. Paul, MN 55104-4706
Phone: (612)642-1951
Description: Focuses on the institute's efforts to link physical activity and health through research, publication, and education.

★8994★ Metropolitan Woman
Talcott Publications
Lumber Exchange Bldg.
10 S. 5th St., Ste. 700
Minneapolis, MN 55402
Phone: (612)335-3555
Description: Women's lifestyle magazine. **First published:** August 1989. **Frequency:** 10x/yr. **Subscription:** $18. $2.50 single issue.

★8995★ Michigan Woman Magazine
TMW, Inc.
30400 Telegraph, Ste. 370
Birmingham, MI 48010
Phone: (313)646-5575
Description: Magazine for the professional Michigan woman. **First published:** 1985. **Frequency:** 6x/yr. **Subscription:** $12.

★8996★ Midwifery Today
Box 2672
Eugene, OR 97402
Phone: (503)344-7438
Description: Magazine for midwives and childbirth educators. **First published:** 1985. **Frequency:** Quarterly. **Subscription:** $25. $6.50 single issue.

★8997★ Military Lifestyle Magazine
4800 Montgomery Ln., No. 710
Bethesda, MD 20814
Phone: (301)718-7623
Fax: (301)718-7652
Description: Articles on military marriages, parenting, personal and family finances, health, beauty, and travel. Accepts outside manuscripts submission. **Frequency:** 10/yr.

★8998★ Minerva
The Minerva Center
1101 S. Arlington Ridge Rd., Rm. 210
Arlington, VA 22202
Phone: (703)892-4388
Subtitle: Quarterly Report on Women and the Military. **Description:** Journal featuring articles, reviews, fiction, and poetry. **First published:** March 1983. **Frequency:** Quarterly. **ISSN:** 0736-718X. **Subscription:** $40; $60 institutions. $10.95 single issue.

★8999★ Minerva's Bulletin Board
The Minerva Center
1101 S. Arlington Ridge Rd., Rm. 210
Arlington, VA 22202
Phone: (703)892-4388
Description: News magazine focusing exclusively on women and the military. Companion publication to the Minerva Quarterly Report. **Frequency:** 20/yr.

★9000★ Minnesota Clubwoman
General Federation of Women's Clubs of Minnesota, Inc.
5701 Normandale Rd., Ste. 315
Minneapolis, MN 55424
Phone: (612)920-2057
Description: Magazine reporting on club activities. **First published:** 1915. **Frequency:** 4x/yr. **Subscription:** Included in membership dues.

★9001★ Minorities and Women in Business
Venture X, Inc.
PO Drawer 210
Burlington, NC 27216
Phone: (919)229-1462
Description: Magazine networks with major corporations and small businesses owned and operated by minority and female entrepreneurs. **First published:** October 1984. **Frequency:** 6x/yr. **Subscription:** Free to qualified subscribers; $15; $36 three years.

★9002★ Mirabella
Murdoch Magazines
200 Madison Avenue
New York, NY 10016
Phone: (212)447-4600
Description: Lifestyle magazine for women age 30-50. **First published:** June 1989. **Frequency:** Monthly. **ISSN:** 1040-5153. **Subscription:** $17.98 or reg. $24. $2.95 single issue.

★9003★ Model
Family Media, Inc.
3 Park Ave.
New York, NY 10016
Phone: (212)340-9200
Description: Magazine edited for young women focusing on fashion, style, health, and fitness. **First published:** 1988. **Frequency:** 10x/yr.

★9004★ Modern Bride
Cahners Publishing Co.
475 Park Ave. S.
New York, NY 10016
Phone: (212)779-1999
Description: Magazine for brides. **First published:** 1949. **Frequency:** 6x/yr. **Subscription:** $18.98. $4 single issue.

★9005★ Mothers Today
24 Colonia Pkwy.
Bronx, NY 10708
Description: Baby magazine. **First published:** 1958. **Frequency:** 6x/yr. **Subscription:** $10.

★9006★ Moving Out: A Feminist Literary and Arts Journal
PO Box 21249
Detroit, MI 48221
Description: Explores feminist aesthetics in art and literature. **First published:** 1970. **Subscription:** $6/sample issue.

★9007★ Moxie
Weider Publications
21100 Erwin St.
Woodland Hills, CA 91367
Phone: (818)595-0450
Description: Magazine for women over forty. **First published:** September 1989. **Frequency:** Monthly. **Subscription:** $24.95. $3 single issue.

★9008★ Ms. Magazine
Lang Communications Inc.
230 Park Ave., 7th Fl.
New York, NY 10169
Phone: (212)551-9595
Description: Feminist magazine. **First published:** 1973. **Frequency:** 6x/yr. **ISSN:** 0047-8318. **Subscription:** $45. $4.95 single issue.

★9009★ NA'AMAT WOMAN
NA'AMAT USA
200 Madison Ave.
New York, NY 10016
Phone: (212)725-8010
Description: Magazine of NA'AMAT USA, the Women's Labor Zionist Organization of America. **First published:** 1926. **Frequency:** 5x/yr. **ISSN:** 0888-191X. **Subscription:** $5.

★9010★ National Business Woman
National Federation of Business & Professional Women's Clubs, Inc.
2012 Massachusetts Ave. NW
Washington, DC 20036
Phone: (202)293-1100
Fax: (202)861-0298
Description: Magazine for working women. **First published:** 1919. **Frequency:** 4x/yr. **ISSN:** 0027-8831. **Subscription:** $10.

★9011★ National NOW Times
National Organization for Women, Inc.
1000 16th St. NW, Ste. 700
Washington, DC 20036
Phone: (202)331-0066
Fax: (202)785-8576
Description: Feminist magazine. **Frequency:** 6x/yr. **Subscription:** $35.

★9012★ National Voter
League of Women Voters
1730 M St., NW
Washington, DC 20036
Phone: (202)429-1965
Fax: (202)429-0854
Description: Magazine covers social policy, energy, land use, the environment, government,

and international relations. **Subscription:** $2.50/single copy.

★9013★ National Women's Health Report
National Women's Health Resource Center
2440 M St. NW, Ste. 325
Washington, DC 20037
Phone: (202)293-6045
Fax: (202)293-7256
Description: Magazine concerned with women's health issues. Emphasizes preventive self-care. **First published:** 1984. **Frequency:** Quarterly. **ISSN:** 0741-9147. **Subscription:** $21; $30 institutions.

★9014★ NCJW Journal
National Council of Jewish Women (NCJW)
53 W. 23rd St.
New York, NY 10010
Phone: (212)645-4048
Fax: (212)645-7466
Description: Reports on the efforts of the NCJW to further human welfare in the Jewish and general communities, locally, nationally, and internationally.

★9015★ Network Magazine
155 E. 4905 South
Murray, UT 84107
Phone: (801)262-8091
Fax: (801)261-5623
Description: Publication for women.

★9016★ New Body Magazine
GCR Publications
1700 Broadway, 34th Fl.
New York, NY 10019
Phone: (212)541-7100
Subtitle: Health, Fitness, Lifestyles for Women on the Go. **Description: First published:** 1982. **Frequency:** 8x/yr. **Subscription:** Newsstand sales only.

★9017★ New Directions for Women
Trustees of New Directions for Women
108 W. Palisade Ave.
Englewood, NJ 07631
Phone: (201)568-0226
Fax: (201)568-6532
Description: Magazine publishing feminist analyses of political events; social commentary; and book, music, and movie reviews. **First published:** 1972. **Frequency:** 6x/yr. **ISSN:** 0160-1000. **Subscription:** $12; $20 institutions. $2 single issue.

★9018★ New England Bride
New England Publishing Group, Inc.
215 Newbury St.
Peabody, MA 01960
Phone: (508)535-4186
Subtitle: America's Only Monthly Bridal Magazine. **Description:** Magazine for brides-to-be in six New England states. **First published:** September 1972. **Frequency:** Monthly. **ISSN:** 0744-6861. **Subscription:** Free to qualified brides-to-be 18 months before their wedding; $24.

★9019★ New Jersey Woman Magazine
27 McDermott Pl.
Bergenfield, NJ 07621
Phone: (201)384-0201
Description: Emphasizes women's accomplishments and regional pride. **Subscription:** $24.

★9020★ New Woman
Murdoch Magazines
215 Lexington Ave.
New York, NY 10016
Phone: (212)685-4790
Subtitle: A New Woman is an Attitude, Not an Age. **Description:** Magazine covering women's interests including career, relationships, health, money, fashion, and beauty. Also publishes profiles of pacesetters. **First published:** 1970. **Frequency:** Monthly. **ISSN:** 0028-6974. **Subscription:** $15. $2.25 single issue.

★9021★ The Ninety-Nine News
International Women Pilots Association
The Ninety-Nines, Inc.
Will Rogers Airport
PO Box 59965
Oklahoma City, OK 73159
Phone: (405)685-7969
Description: Magazine for women pilots. **First published:** 1933. **Frequency:** Monthly. **Subscription:** $20.

★9022★ Nursing and Health Care
National League for Nursing (NLN)
350 Hudson St.
New York, NY 10014
Phone: (212)989-9393
Fax: (212)989-3710
Frequency: Monthly.

★9023★ NWSA Journal
National Women's Studies Association (NWSA)
University of Hampshire
Department of English
Durham, NH 03824
Phone: (603)862-1313
Fax: (603)862-2030
Description: Publishes feminist scholarship emerging from or supporting the feminist movement. **First published:** 1988. **Frequency:** 4/yr. **Subscription:** $35/ Individual. $95/Institution.

★9024★ Off Our Backs: A Women's Newsjournal
2423 18th St. NW
Washington, DC 20009
Phone: (202)234-8072
Description: Feminist Newsjournal featuring articles by, for, and about women. **First published:** February 1970. **Frequency:** Monthly. **ISSN:** 0030-0071. **Subscription:** $17; $30 institutions. $2 single issue.

★9025★ On the Issues
Choices Women's Medical Center, Inc.
97-77 Queens Blvd.
Forest Hills, NY 11374-3317
Phone: (718)275-6020
Subtitle: The Progressive Women's Quarterly. **Description: First published:** 1983. **Frequency:** Quarterly. **ISSN:** 0895-6014. **Subscription:**

$10.50; $20 two years; $20 institutions; $32 institutions two years.

★9026★ On Our Backs
526 Castro St.
San Francisco, CA 94114
Phone: (415)861-4723

Description: National entertainment publication for lesbians containing fiction, features, columns, and pictorials. **Frequency:** 6/yr. **Subscription:** $36. $8/issue.

★9027★ On Our Minds
Towson State University
Women's Studies Program
Baltimore, MD 21204
Phone: (301)830-2334

Description: Journal focuses on campus, community, and regional activity related to Towson's work in curriculum integration and women's education. **Frequency:** Annual. **Subscription:** Free.

★9028★ Our Life
Ukrainian National Women's League of America, Inc.
108 2nd Ave
New York, NY 10003
Phone: (212)533-4646

Frequency: Monthly.

★9029★ Our Special
National Braille Press, Inc.
88 Stephen St.
Boston, MA 02115
Phone: (617)266-6160

Description: General interest Braille magazine for blind women. **First published:** 1930. **Frequency:** Monthly. **Subscription:** Free; contributions accepted.

★9030★ OUT/LOOK, National Lesbian & Gay Quarterly
2940 16th St., Rm. 319
San Francisco, CA 94103
Phone: (415)626-7929

Description: Gay and lesbian magazine. **First published:** March 1988. **Frequency:** Quarterly. **ISSN:** 0896-7733. **Subscription:** $21; $29 institutions; $31 other countries. $5.95 single issue.

★9031★ Outweek Magazine
159 W. 25th St.
New York, NY 10010
Phone: (212)337-1200

Description: Lesbian and gay magazine covering national and international news, reviews of all media, features on health, arts and entertainment, cartoons, humor and satire, and extensive New York City listings. **Frequency:** Weekly. **Subscription:** $59.95.

★9032★ Parents Magazine's Expecting
685 3rd Ave.
New York, NY 10017
Phone: (212)878-8700

Description: Magazine for expectant mothers. **First published:** 1967. **Frequency:** Quarterly.

★9033★ The Pen Woman
National League of American Pen Women, Inc.
Pen Arts Bldg.
1300 17th St., NW
Washington, DC 20036
Phone: (202)785-1997

Description: Magazine emphasizes a how-to approach to art, music, and letters. Contains book reviews. **Frequency:** 9x/year. **Subscription:** $4; $.50/single copy.

★9034★ Perceptions
1317 Johnson
Missoula, MT 59801
Phone: (406)543-5875

Description: Devoted to the development of women writers.

★9035★ PLAINSWOMAN
Plainswoman, Inc.
PO Box 8027
Grand Forks, ND 58202
Phone: (701)777-8043

Description: Feminist journal focusing on women in the Great Plains area. Contains fiction, poetry, articles, and essays. **First published:** October 1977. **Frequency:** Monthly (except Feb. and Aug.). **ISSN:** 0148-902X. **Subscription:** $15; $10 low income; $20 supporters.

★9036★ Playgirl
Playgirl, Inc.
801 2nd Ave.
New York, NY 10017
Phone: (212)986-5100

Description: Adult entertainment magazine for women. **First published:** July 1973. **Frequency:** Monthly. **ISSN:** 0273-6918. **Subscription:** $35. $3.95 single issue.

★9037★ Polka—Polish Woman
National United Women's Societies for the Adoration of the Most Blessed Sacrament
1127 Frieda St.
Dickson City, PA 18519
Phone: (717)346-9131

Description: Magazine for women in the Polish National Catholic Church; emphasizes religion, ethnic tradition, and activity of the church membership. **First published:** July 9, 1935. **Frequency:** Quarterly. **Subscription:** $2.

★9038★ Prenatal Educator
Educational Programs, Inc.
8003 Old York Rd.
Elkins Park, PA 19117-1410
Phone: (215)635-1700

Description: Magazine for teachers of prenatal education. **First published:** 1979. **Frequency:** Quarterly.

★9039★ Press Woman Magazine
Box 99
Blue Springs, MO 64013
Phone: (816)229-1666

Description: Contains articles on journalism/communications with an emphasis on the advancement of women. **Frequency:** Monthly.

★9040★ Primavera
1448 E. 52th St., Box 274
Chicago, IL 60615

Description: Magazine contains fiction and poetry reflecting the experiences of women. **Price:** $5/single copy.

★9041★ The Professional Communicator
Women in Communications, Inc. (WICI)
2101 Wilson Blvd., Ste. 417
Arlington, VA 22201
Phone: (703)528-4200

Description: National magazine features communications management practices, how-to material, membership news, communications trends, features, opinion columns, and information about women and communications issues. **Frequency:** 5x/year. **Subscription:** $15; $3/single copy.

★9042★ ProWoman Magazine
MatriMedia, Inc.
PO Box 6957
Portland, OR 97228-6957
Phone: (503)221-1298

Subtitle: The Magazine for the Northwest Professional. **Description:** **First published:** June 1987. **Frequency:** 6x/yr. **ISSN:** 0895-7339. **Subscription:** $12. $2.50 single issue.

★9043★ Psychological Perspectives
C. G. Jung Institute of Los Angeles
10349 W. Pico Blvd.
Los Angeles, CA 90064
Phone: (213)556-1193
Fax: (213)556-2290

Description: Journal contains essays focusing on gender as a social construct and as a category of analysis, with issues divided into sections on family relations, sexual preferences, and bodies (health and aging). **Subscription:** $18/year; $12/single copy; $23/special issue copy.

★9044★ Psychology of Women Quarterly
Cambridge University Press
40 W. 20th St.
New York, NY 10011
Phone: (212)924-3900

Description: Psychology journal. **First published:** 1976. **Frequency:** Quarterly. **ISSN:** 0361-6843. **Subscription:** $34; $89 institutions.

★9045★ Quarante
Savoir, Inc.
1600 S. Eads St.
P.O. Box 2875
Arlington, VA 22202
Phone: (703)920-3333

Subtitle: Magazine for the Woman Who's Arrived. **Description:** Magazine catering to successful and affluent women over forty. **First published:** 1984. **Frequency:** Quarterly. **Subscription:** $9; $3 single issue.

★9046★ Radiance
PO Box 30246
Oakland, CA 94604
Phone: (510)482-0680

Subtitle: The Magazine for Large Women. **Description:** Magazine encouraging women to feel good about their bodies, whatever their size. Featuring articles on health, media, fashion and politics. **First published:** October 5, 1984. **Frequency:** Quarterly. **ISSN:** 0889-9495. **Subscription:** $15; $20 Canada; $23 other countries.

★9047★ *Radical America*
1 Summer St.
Somerville, MA 02143
Phone: (617)628-6585

Description: Socialist-feminist journal of politics and culture specializing in radical, labor, and women's history and theory; grassroots and community organizing; peace and disarmament issues; and Afro-American and Third World issues. **First published:** May 1967. **Frequency:** 4x/yr. **ISSN:** 0033-7617. **Subscription:** $20; $23 other countries.

★9048★ *Radical Teacher*
PO Box 102
Cambridge, MA 02142
Phone: (617)492-3468

Description: Provides "feminist and socialist considerations of education at all levels." Contains articles, photos, interviews on radical theory and practice in education, and book reviews. **Frequency:** 3x/year. **Subscription:** $8.

★9049★ *Re-Vision*
College of St. Catherine
Abigail Quigly McCarthy Center for Women
2004 Randolph Ave., Mail No. 4150
St. Paul, MN 55105
Phone: (612)690-6736
Fax: (612)690-6024

Description: Focuses on the Center's programs and feminist issues. **Frequency:** 3x/year. **Subscription:** Available with membership.

★9050★ *Redbook Magazine*
The Hearst Corporation
224 W. 57th St., 6th Fl.
New York, NY 10019
Phone: (212)262-3450

Description: Magazine containing articles and fiction features for young working mothers. **First published:** 1903. **Frequency:** Monthly. **ISSN:** 0034-2106. **Subscription:** $11.97. $1.95 single issue.

★9051★ *The Reporter*
Women's American ORT
315 Park Ave. S.
New York, NY 10010
Phone: (212)505-7700

Subtitle: The Women's American ORT Reporter. **Description:** Magazine reporting on women's issues, education, and Jewish affairs. Includes feature articles, opinion, and book reviews. **First published:** 1966. **Frequency:** Quarterly. **ISSN:** 1053-2676. **Subscription:** Free to qualified subscribers; $5 nonmembers.

★9052★ *Reproductive and Genetic Engineering*
Pergamon Press/Maxwelll House
Farfield Park
Elmsford, NY 10523
Phone: (914)345-6425
Fax: (914)592-3625

Description: Designed to facilitate the development of multi-disciplinary and feminist analysis

on reproductive technology and genetic engineering and their impact on women. **Frequency:** 3/yr.

★9053★ *Research News Reporter*
Institute for Women's Policy Research (IWPR)
1400 20th St., NW, Ste. 104
Washington, DC 20036
Phone: (202)785-5100

Description: A resource guide of reprinted newspaper articles from the New York Times, Wall Street Journal, and Washington Post on work and education; poverty and income; politics and society; family life; and health and reproductive issues. **Frequency:** Bimonthly. **Subscription:** $150/individual; $195/non-profit organization; $295/corporate.

★9054★ *Response*
The United Methodist Church
General Board of Global Ministries
Women's Division
475 Riverside Dr., 15th Fl.
New York, NY 10115
Phone: (212)870-3752

Description: Addresses the concerns and the the needs of women and children. **Frequency:** Bimonthly.

★9055★ *Response to the Victimization of Women and Children*
Guilford Publications, Inc.
72 Spring St.
New York, NY 10012
Phone: (212)431-9800

Description: Journal of research and analysis of data, programs, and legislative responses to child and wife abuse, sexual abuse, pornography, and related topics. **First published:** 1976. **Frequency:** Quarterly. **ISSN:** 0894-7597. **Subscription:** $30; $55 institutions.

★9056★ *Sacred River: A Women's Peace Journal*
PO Box 5131
Berkeley, CA 94705

Description: Local focus, but includes articles and news of interest outside California. **Subscription:** $18.

★9057★ *Sage: A Scholarly Journal on Black Women*
PO Box 42741
Atlanta, GA 30311-0741
Phone: (404)223-7528
Fax: (404)753-8383

Description: An interdisciplinary forum for black women. Includes feature articles, interviews, profiles, documents, book reviews, and bibliographies. **First published:** 1984. **Frequency:** 2/yr. **Subscription:** $15/individual. $25/institution. Overseas include $6 for postage.

★9058★ *Sagewoman Magazine*
PO Box 641
Point Arena, CA 95468

Description: Focuses on women's spirituality. **First published:** 1986. **Frequency:** 4/yr. **Subscription:** $18. Overseas add $12 for postage.

★9059★ *San Diego Woman Magazine*
4186 Sorrento Valley Blvd., Ste. M
San Diego, CA 92121
Phone: (619)452-2900

Description: Contains articles and information pertaining professional and personal growth. **Frequency:** Monthly.

★9060★ *Savvy Woman*
Family Media, Inc.
3 Park Ave.
New York, NY 10016
Phone: (212)779-6200

Subtitle: For the Successful Woman. **Description:** Magazine for career women, including money and management advice, and features on dining, travel, the arts, beauty, and fashion. **First published:** 1979. **Frequency:** Monthly. **Subscription:** $12. $2 single issue.

★9061★ *Seattle Gay News*
JT and A
704 E. Pike St.
Seattle, WA 98122
Phone: (206)324-4297

Description: Gay and lesbian magazine. **First published:** 1973. **Frequency:** Weekly. **Subscription:** $35; $.25 single issue.

★9062★ *SELF Magazine*
The Conde Nast Publications, Inc.
350 Madison Ave.
New York, NY 10017
Phone: (212)880-8800

Description: Magazine serving as sourcebook for contemporary women. **First published:** January 1979. **Frequency:** Monthly. **ISSN:** 0149-0699. **Subscription:** $15. $1.95 single issue.

★9063★ *Sex Roles: A Journal of Research*
Institute for Research on Social Problems
520 Pearl St.
Boulder, CO 80302
Phone: (303)449-7782
Fax: (303)449-6694

Description: Contains empirical research on sex roles and book reviews. **First published:** 1975. **Frequency:** 12/yr. **Subscription:** $31/individual. $37.50/foreign individual. $197.50/institution. $230/foreign institution.

★9064★ *Shape*
Weider Publications
21100 Erwin St.
Woodland Hills, CA 91367
Phone: (818)884-6800

Description: Magazine for women covering nutrition, weight control, and physical fitness. **First published:** September 1981. **Frequency:** Monthly. **Subscription:** $20. $2 single issue.

★9065★ *Short Fiction By Women*
Box 1276
Stuyvesant Sta.
New York, NY 10009
Phone: (212)316-7601

Description: Contains original fiction by women writers. **Frequency:** Triannual. **Subscription:** $18.

★9066★ Signs: Journal of Women in Culture and Society
University of Chicago Press
5720 S. Woodlawn Ave.
Chicago, IL 60637
Phone: (312)702-7600

Description: Women's studies journal. **First published:** 1975. **Frequency:** Quarterly. **ISSN:** 0097-9740. **Subscription:** $29; $65 institutions.

★9067★ Sing Heavenly Muse!
PO Box 13320
Minneapolis, MN 55414
Phone: (612)822-8713

Description: Journal containing poetry, fiction, and art primarily by women. **Frequency:** 3x/yr. **Subscription:** $17/individual; $21/institution; $7/single copy.

★9068★ The Single Parent
Parents Without Partners, Inc.
8807 Colesville Rd.
Silver Spring, MD 20910
Phone: (301)588-9356

Subtitle: Journal of Parents Without Partners. **Description: First published:** 1957. **Frequency:** 6x/yr. **ISSN:** 0037-5748. **Subscription:** $15; $18 Canada.

★9069★ Sinister Wisdom
PO Box 3252
Berkeley, CA 94703
Phone: (415)534-2335

Subtitle: Journal exploring lesbian imagination in the arts and politics. **Description: First published:** 1976. **Frequency:** Quarterly. **ISSN:** 0196-1853. **Subscription:** $17; $22 other countries; $30 institutions; $10 hardship (free to women in prison or mental institutions).

★9070★ SISTERS
National Council of Negro Women, Inc.
1211 Connecticut Ave. NW, Ste. 702
Washington, DC 20036
Phone: (202)659-0006

Description: Magazine covering diverse issues that affect the African-American woman and her community. **First published:** 1988. **Frequency:** Quarterly. **ISSN:** 0899-935X. **Subscription:** $20. $5 single issue.

★9071★ Snake Power: A Journal of Contemporary Female Shamanism
5856 College Ave.
PO Box 138
Oakland, CA 94118
Phone: (415)658-7033

Description: Journal by and about women which focuses on ''female shamanism and the Goddess.'' **Frequency:** 4x/year. **Subscription:** $23.

★9072★ Social Justice
Crime and Social Justice Associates, Inc.
PO Box 40601
San Francisco, CA 94140-0601
Phone: (415)550-1703

Description: Draws upon history, economics, and political theory to address social policy issues, including criminality, imprisonment, and women's rights in the 1990s. **Frequency:** Quarterly. **Subscription:** $15/individual;

$30/institution; $10/single copy individual; $15/single copy institution.

★9073★ Social Problems
University of California Press
Society for the Study of Social Problems
Journals Department
2120 Berkeley Way
Berkeley, CA 94720

Description: Addresses reproductive issues. **Subscription:** $66/non-members and institutions. $16.50/issue.

★9074★ Sojourner
Sojourner, Inc.
42 Seaverns Ave.
Jamaica Plain, MA 02130-2355
Phone: (617)524-0415

Subtitle: The Women's Forum. **Description:** Magazine covering various feminist viewpoints. **First published:** September 1975. **Frequency:** Monthly. **ISSN:** 0191-8699. **Subscription:** $15; $26 institutions.

★9075★ The Soroptomists of the Americas
Soroptomist International
1616 Walnut St., Ste. 700
Philadelphia, PA 19103
Phone: (215)732-0512
Fax: (212)732-7508

Description: Publication for members of Soroptomist International, a classified service organization for executive and professional women. **Frequency:** Bimonthly.

★9076★ Spokane Woman
Northwest Business Press, Inc.
S 104 Division
Spokane, WA 99202
Phone: (509)456-0203

Description: Lifestyle magazine for metropolitan Spokane, WA, women in their mid-20s to mid-50s. **First published:** July 1989. **Frequency:** Monthly. **Subscription:** $12. $1.50 single issue.

★9077★ Successful Woman in Business
American Society of Professional & Executive Women
1429 Walnut St.
Philadelphia, PA 19102
Phone: (215)563-6005

Subtitle: The Magazine of Franchise & Business Opportunity. **Description:** Magazine containing advice on resources, management strategies, personal finance, and career development for professional and executive women. **First published:** 1979. **Frequency:** Quarterly. **ISSN:** 0275-0260. **Subscription:** $48 (included in membership dues).

★9078★ Support
1935 E. Villa St., Ste. 4
Pasadena, CA 91107
Phone: (818)546-3810

Description: Magazine offering answers and solutions for single parents. **First published:** 1987. **Frequency:** Monthly. **Subscription:** $10.

★9079★ TAXI
Family Media, Inc.
3 Park Ave.
New York, NY 10016
Phone: (212)779-6200

Description: Magazine covering fashion, trends, and leisure living. **First published:** August 1986. **Frequency:** 10x/yr. **ISSN:** 0894-3249. **Subscription:** $14.97. $3 single issue.

★9080★ TenPercent
ASUCLA Communications Board
University of California, Los Angeles (UCLA)
112-B Kerckhoff Hall
Los Angeles, CA 90024
Phone: (213)825-8500

Subtitle: UCLA's Lesbian, Gay and Bisexual Magazine. **Description: First published:** 1979. **Frequency:** 2x/semester (6x/yr). **Subscription:** $16.

★9081★ Texas Woman's News
RR 5, Box 574-46
Kerrville, TX 78028

Description: Newspaper (tabloid) for working women. **First published:** October 1, 1984. **Frequency:** Monthly. **Subscription:** $13.

★9082★ 13th Moon: A Feminist Literary Magazine
SUNY-Albany
English Department
Albany, NY 12222

Description: Eclectic literary publication containing feature articles, poetry, fiction, art, and reviews. Particularly solicits feminist and working class lesbian literature. **First published:** 1973. **Frequency:** 2/yr. **Subscription:** $8.

★9083★ Today's Christian Woman
Christianity Today, Inc.
465 Gundersen Dr.
Carol Stream, IL 60188
Phone: (708)260-6200

Description: Religious magazine for contemporary Christian women. **First published:** 1978. **Frequency:** 6x/yr. **ISSN:** 0163-1799. **Subscription:** $14.95. $2.95 single issue.

★9084★ Today's Insurance Woman
National Association of Insurance Women
PO Box 4410
Tulsa, OK 74159
Phone: (918)744-5195
Fax: (918)743-1968

Description: Magazine on insurance and professional development topics for men and women in the risk and insurance field. **First published:** 1942. **Frequency:** 6x/yr. **ISSN:** 0892-4414. **Subscription:** $15.

★9085★ Together
ASUCLA Communications Board
University of California, Los Angeles (UCLA)
112 Kerckhoff Hall
Los Angeles, CA 90024
Phone: (213)206-6168

Subtitle: UCLA's Feminist Newsmagazine. **Description:** News Magazine for women and feminist students at the University and the surrounding community. **First published:** 1973. **Frequency:** 6x/yr. **Subscription:** $16.

★9086★ Tradeswomen
Tradeswomen, Inc.
PO Box 40664
San Francisco, CA 94140
Phone: (415)821-7334
Subtitle: A Quarterly Magazine for Women in Blue-Collar Work. **Description:** Magazine written by and for women in blue-collar non-traditional jobs. **First published:** January 1981. **Frequency:** Quarterly. **ISSN:** 0739-344X. **Subscription:** $25. $2.50 single issue.

★9087★ Trivia: A Journal of Ideas
PO Box 606
North Amherst, MA 01059
Phone: (413)367-2254
Description: Features radical feminist theory, experimental writing, and reviews. **First published:** 1982. **Frequency:** 2/yr. **Subscription:** $14/ 3 issues, individual. $20/3 issues, libraries and institutions;. $7/issue.

★9088★ Tu Internacional
America Publishing Group
Vandidades Continental Bldg.
6355 NW 36th St.
Virginia Gardens, FL 33166
Phone: (305)871-6400
Description: Magazine providing the young woman with information on beauty, fashion, entertainment, decorating, and cooking (Spanish). **First published:** 1981. **Frequency:** Monthly. **Subscription:** $22.50. $2.50 single issue.

★9089★ Tulsa Studies in Women's Literature
Tulsa Studies in Women's Literature (TSWL)
The University of Tulsa
600 S. College Ave.
Tulsa, OK 74104
Description: Includes articles, reviews, notes, and queries from scholars of every period, including those reading in a language other than English. **First published:** 1982. **Frequency:** 2/yr. **Subscription:** $12/individual; $14/institution; $10/student; $7/issue ($8 foreign).

★9090★ The Union Signal
National Women's Christian Temperance Union
1730 Chicago Ave.
Evanston, IL 60201
Phone: (708)864-1396
Description: Journal covers legislative and organizational news with educational features on alcohol, narcotics, and tobacco. **Frequency:** Monthly. **Subscription:** $6; $.60/single copy.

★9091★ U.S.-Japan Women's Journal: A Journal for the International Exchange of Gender Studies
US-Japan Women's Center
926 Bautista Ct.
Palo Alto, CA 94303
Phone: (415)857-9049
Fax: (415)494-8160
Description: Publication with English supplement for international exchange on women and gender.

★9092★ U.S. Woman Engineer
Society of Women Engineers
345 E. 47th St.
New York, NY 10017
Phone: (212)705-7855
Fax: (212)319-0947
Description: Magazine for engineering students and for women and men working in the engineering and technology fields. Covers career development and topical issues. **First published:** 1951. **Frequency:** 6x/yr. **ISSN:** 0272-7838. **Subscription:** $20.

★9093★ Up Against the Wall, Mother
Miriam Press
9114 Wood Spice Ln.
Lorton, VA 22079-3240
Phone: (703)690-2246
Description: Journal emphasizing poetry as therapy for women in crisis. **First published:** January 1981. **Frequency:** Quarterly. **ISSN:** 1041-9993. **Subscription:** $12. $3.50 single issue.

★9094★ Vanidades Continental
America Publishing Group
Vanidades Continental Bldg.
6355 NW 36th St.
Virginia Gardens, FL 33166
Phone: (305)871-6400
Description: Women's fashion and beauty magazine (Spanish). **First published:** 1961. **Frequency:** Every other week. **Subscription:** $53.70. $2.95 single issue.

★9095★ Victoria
The Hearst Corp.
224 W. 57th St., 4th Fl.
New York, NY 10019
Phone: (212)649-3700
Description: Lifestyle magazine for women. **First published:** 1987. **Frequency:** Monthly. **Subscription:** $2.50 single issue.

★9096★ The Villager
Bronxville Women's Club
135 Midland Ave.
Bronxville, NY 10708
Phone: (914)337-3252
Description: Magazine covering women's club news and literature. **First published:** 1928. **Frequency:** 9x/yr. **Subscription:** $7.50.

★9097★ Vintage '45
Vintage '45 Press
PO Box 266
Orinda, CA 94563
Phone: (415)254-7266
Subtitle: A Uniquely Supportive Quarterly Journal for Women. **Description:** Magazine containing articles of special interest to women, middle-aged or older. **First published:** September 1983. **Frequency:** Quarterly. **ISSN:** 0742-1494. **Subscription:** $9.45; $13.50 other countries.

★9098★ Virtue
Good Family Magazines
PO Box 850
Sisters, OR 97759
Phone: (503)549-8261
Description: Christian magazine for women. **First published:** 1978. **Frequency:** 6x/yr. **ISSN:** 0164-7288. **Subscription:** Free to qualified subscribers; $15.95.

★9099★ Visibilities
PO Box 1169
Olney, MD 20830-1169
Phone: (301)774-8591
Description: International publication by and for lesbians. Seeks to promote a strong positive image of lesbians.

★9100★ Visible
PO Box 1494
Mendocino, CA 95460
Phone: (707)964-2756
Description: Publication for older women. **Frequency:** 3/yr.

★9101★ Viva Petites!
USA Petites
537 Newport Dr.
Fashion Island
Newport Beach, CA 92660
Phone: (714)643-5008
Fax: (714)362-3013
Description: Fashion magazine for petite women. **Frequency:** Monthly. **Subscription:** $18/year.

★9102★ Vogue
Conde-Nast Publications
350 Madison Ave.
New York, NY 10017
Phone: (212)880-8800
Founded: 1982. **Description:** Women's fashion and beauty magazine. **Frequency:** 6x/yr. **Subscription:** $28. $3 single issue.

★9103★ Voices, Hawaii Women's News Journal
University of Hawaii
Kuyjebdakk 402
1733 Donaghho Rd.
Honolulu, HI 96822
Phone: (808)956-8805
Description: Feminist publication by and about women. Includes interviews, art, poetry, fiction, and non-fiction. **Frequency:** Triannual.

★9104★ W
Fairchild Publications
7 E. 12th St.
New York, NY 10003
Phone: (212)741-4277
Description: Magazine for educated, affluent women. **First published:** 1972. **Frequency:** Every other week. **Subscription:** $30. $2.50 single issue.

★9105★ Washington Sales Journal
National Association of Professional Saleswomen (NAPS)
712 W. Broad St., Ste. 5
Falls Church, VA 22046
Phone: (703)538-4390
Description: Contains chapter news, sales tips, features, and profiles.

★9106★ **Wichita WOMEN**
Watson Wordsmiths, Inc.
400 N. Woodlawn, No. 28
Wichita, KS 67208
Phone: (316)684-3620

Subtitle: To Ease, Enrich, and Celebrate the
Lives of Busy Wichita Women. **Description:**
Magazine (tabloid) for Wichita women. **First
published:** October 1986. **Frequency:** Monthly.
Subscription: $15.

★9107★ **WIF News Magazine**
Women in Film (WIF)
6464 Sunset Blvd., Ste. 900
Los Angeles, CA 90028
Phone: (213)463-6040
Fax: (213)463-0963

Description: Reports on issues of interest to
women in the film industry. **Frequency:** Monthly.

★9108★ **WIN News**
Women's International Network (WIN)
187 Grant St.
Lexington, MA 02173
Phone: (617)862-9431

Description: Women's International Network
News. Open, participatory journal written by,
for, and about women, reporting on the status
of women and women's rights around the
globe. **First published:** 1975. **Frequency:**
Quarterly. **ISSN:** 0145-7985. **Subscription:** $30;
$40 institutions.

★9109★ **Wisconsin Woman**
ECKlectic, Inc.
PO Box 10
Menomonee Falls, WI 53052-0010
Phone: (414)273-1234

Description: Magazine (tabloid) covering subjects of interest to upscale, professional wom-
en. **First published:** 1987. **Frequency:** Monthly.
Subscription: $14.95. $3.50 single issue.

★9110★ **Wisconsin Women's Law Journal**
University of Wisconsin Law School
975 Bascom Hall
Madison, WI 53706
Phone: (608)262-8294

Description: Examines legal issues facing wom-
en. Contains both traditional and nontraditional
law review articles. **First published:** 1985.
Frequency: Annual. **Subscription:**
$8/individual; $15/institution.

★9111★ **The Wise Woman**
2441 Cordova St.
Oakland, CA 94602
Phone: (415)536-3174

Description: Focuses on feminist issues,
Goddess lore, feminist spirituality, and feminist
witchcraft. Also includes original research about
witch hunts, women's heritage, and women
today. **First published:** 1980. **Frequency:**
Quarterly. **Subscription:** $15. $4/issue.

★9112★ **Wishing Well Magazine**
PO Box 713090
Santee, CA 92072-3090
Phone: (619)443-4818

First published: 1974.

★9113★ **WLW Journal**
Women Library Workers (WLW)
2027 Parker St.
Berkeley, CA 94704
Phone: (510)540-5322

Subtitle: News/Views/Reviews for Women and
Libraries. **Description:** For librarians, library
technicians, clerks, and others interested in
ending discrimination against women in libraries. Contains in-depth articles on issues affecting women and libraries, feminist management
and database building, and feminist presses.
First published: September 1975. **Frequency:**
Quarterly. **Price:** Included in membership. **Former Title(s):** Women Library Workers Newsletter, 1979.

★9114★ **Woman**
The Conde Nast Publications, Inc.
360 Madison Ave.
New York, NY 10017
Phone: (212)880-8800

Description: Women's interest magazine. **First
published:** 1980. **Frequency:** 10x/yr. **Subscription:** $1.95 single issue.

★9115★ **The Woman Activist**
The Woman Activist, Inc.
2310 Barbour Rd.
Falls Church, VA 22043
Phone: (703)573-8716

Description: Magazine covering women's rights
issues and news. **First published:** 1970. **Frequency:** 10x/yr. **Subscription:** $17.

★9116★ **Woman Bowler**
Women's International Bowling Congress
5301 S. 76th St.
Greendale, WI 53129-1191
Phone: (414)421-9000

Description: News magazine for women bowlers. **First published:** 1936. **Frequency:** 8x/yr.
ISSN: 0043-7255. **Subscription:** $6.

★9117★ **The Woman Conductor**
Women Band Directors National Association
344 Overlook Dr.
West Lafayette, IN 47906
Phone: (317)463-1738

Description: Journal reports on career improvement, conducting techniques, and association
news. **Frequency:** Quarterly.

★9118★ **The Woman CPA**
ASWA and AWSCPA
PO Box 39295
Cincinnati, OH 45239
Phone: (513)385-3998

Description: Magazine for practicing accountants and other accounting professionals. **First
published:** 1934. **Frequency:** Quarterly. **ISSN:**
0043-7271. **Subscription:** $8; $15 other countries.

★9119★ **Woman Engineer**
Equal Opportunity Publications
44 Broadway
Greenlawn, NY 11740
Phone: (516)261-8899

Subtitle: For Entry Level and Professional
Women. **Description:** Affirmative action engineer recruitment magazine. **First published:**

1980. **Frequency:** 4x/yr. **Subscription:** Controlled; $17 others.

★9120★ **Woman Entrepreneur**
American Woman's Economic Development
Corporation (AWED)
641 Lexington Ave., 9th Fl.
New York, NY 10022
Phone: (212)688-1900
Fax: (212)688-2718

Description: Magazine for women in business.
Frequency: Monthly.

★9121★ **Woman of Power**
Woman of Power, Inc.
PO Box 827
Cambridge, MA 02238
Phone: (617)625-7885

Description: Magazine includes articles, interviews, profiles, art, poetry, and photographs, on
topics that include feminism, spirituality, and
politics. **Frequency:** Quarterly. **Subscription:**
$26; $7/single copy.

★9122★ **Woman's Art Journal**
1711 Harris Rd.
Laverock, PA 19118

Description: Contains articles on art history and
other topics and reviews pertaining to women in
the visual arts. **First published:** 1980. **Frequency:** 2/yr. **Price:** $14/individual; $18/institution.

★9123★ **Woman's Day**
Hachette Magazines, Inc.
1633 Broadway
New York, NY 10019
Phone: (212)767-6000
Fax: (212)767-5610

Description: Women's magazine. **First published:** 1937. **Frequency:** 17x/yr. **ISSN:** 0043-
7336. **Subscription:** $14.77.

★9124★ **Woman's Day Crosswords**
Hachette Publications, Inc.
1633 Broadway
New York, NY 10019
Phone: (212)767-6000

Description: Publication featuring crosswords
with themes of interest to women. **First published:** August 1981. **Frequency:** Monthly.
ISSN: 0732-054X. **Subscription:** $17.95. $1.50
single issue.

★9125★ **Woman's Enterprise**
Paisano Publications Inc.
28210 Dorothy Dr.
Box 3000
Agoura Hills, CA 91301
Phone: (818)889-8740

Description: Small business magazine for wom-
en who own or would like to start their own
business. **First published:** December 1987.
Frequency: 6x/yr. **Subscription:** $9.95.

★9126★ Woman's National Farm & Garden Magazine
Women's National Farm and Garden Association
2230 Quail Lake Rd.
Findlay, OH 45840
Phone: (419)422-2466

Description: Published for members of the association. Information relates to agricultural and horticultural interests among women.

★9127★ The Woman's Pulpit
International Association of Women Ministers (IAWM)
579 Main St.
Stroudsburg, PA 18360
Phone: (717)421-7751

Description: Reports on issues of interest to women in Christian ministry. **Frequency:** Quarterly.

★9128★ Woman's Touch
General Council of the Assemblies of God/Gospel Publishing House
1445 Boonville Ave.
Springfield, MO 65802-1894
Phone: (417)862-2781

Description: Religious magazine. **First published:** July 13, 1977. **Frequency:** 6x/yr. **ISSN:** 0190-4620. **Subscription:** $6. $1.25 single issue.

★9129★ Woman's Weal
J.R.H. Cruikshank Ltd.
PO Box 264
Lynden, WA 98264-0264
Phone: (604)922-5891

Description: Women's interest magazine. **First published:** 1983. **Frequency:** Monthly. **Subscription:** $14.46.

★9130★ Woman's World
Heinrich Bauer North America Inc.
PO Box 1648
Englewood Cliffs, NJ 07632
Phone: (201)569-6699

Subtitle: The Woman's Weekly. **Description:** Woman's service and entertainment magazine. **First published:** January 27, 1981. **Frequency:** Weekly. **ISSN:** 0272-961X. **Subscription:** $65; $82 Canada. $1 single issue.

★9131★ Women in Business
The American Business Women's Association (ABWA) Co., Inc.
9100 Ward Pkwy.
PO Box 8728
Kansas City, MO 64114-0728
Phone: (816)361-6621

Description: Women's business magazine for members of the American Business Women's Association. **First published:** 1949. **Frequency:** 6x/yr. **ISSN:** 0043-7441. **Subscription:** $12. $2 single issue.

★9132★ Women & Criminal Justice
Trenton State College
Department of Law & Justice
CN 4700
Trenton, NJ 08650
Phone: (609)771-2644
Fax: (609)530-7784

Description: Devoted to interdisciplinary and international feminist scholarship dealing with all areas of criminal justice. **First published:** 1989. **Frequency:** 2/yr. **Subscription:** $24/individual; $32/institution; $48/library.

★9133★ Women & Health
117 St. John's Pl.
Brooklyn, NY 11217
Phone: (212)305-3724
Fax: (212)305-6832

Description: Includes feature articles, research, bibliographies, book reviews, news, and notes. **First published:** 1976. **Frequency:** 4/yr. **Subscription:** $36/individual; $110/institution; $200/library.

★9134★ Women Lawyers Journal
National Association of Women Lawyers
750 N. Lake Shore Dr.
Chicago, IL 60611
Phone: (312)988-6186

Description: Profesional publication for attorneys throughout the United States and abroad. **Frequency:** Quarterly. **Subscription:** $12.

★9135★ Women in Natural Resources
Unversity of Idaho
Bowers Laboratory
Moscow, ID 83843
Phone: (208)885-6754

Description: For women in forestry, wildlife, range, fisheries, recreation, and related social sciences. **Frequency:** Quarterly.

★9136★ Women Outdoors
Women Outdoors, Inc.
55 Talbot Ave.
Medford, MA 02155
Phone: (508)892-9515

Description: Magazine with outdoor and environmental focus sent to Women Outdoors members. **First published:** 1980. **Frequency:** Quarterly. **Subscription:** $20.

★9137★ Women & Performance: A Journal of Feminist Theory
New York University
721 Broadway, 6th Fl.
New York, NY 10003
Phone: (212)998-1625

Description: Feminist journal devoted to the study of theater, dance, film, music, video, and ritual and performance art. **First published:** 1983. **Frequency:** 2/yr. **Price:** $14/individual; $25/institution; $7/issue.

★9138★ Women and Politics
The Haworth Press
10 Alice St.
Binghampton, NY 13904-1580
Phone: (307)766-2983
Fax: (307)766-2697

Description: Features articles, research, bibliographies, book reviews, news, and notes. **First**

published: 1980. **Frequency:** 4/yr. **Price:** $32/individual; $75/institution; $150/library.

★9139★ Women Studies Abstracts
Rush Publishing Co.
PO Box 1
Rush, NY 14543-0001
Phone: (716)624-4418

Description: Magazine providing abstracts of journal articles. **First published:** 1972. **Frequency:** Quarterly. **ISSN:** 0049-7835. **Subscription:** $102.

★9140★ Women and Therapy
University of Vermont
Department of Psychology
John Dewey Hall
Burlington, VT 05405
Phone: (802)656-2680

Description: Covers mental health problems affecting women, women's roles in society, the special needs of minority women, lesbians, older women, and alternatives to traditional mental health treatment. **Frequency:** 4x/year. **Subscription:** $30.

★9141★ Women & Therapy
c/o Ellen Cole
Prescott College
220 Grove Ave.
Prescott, AZ 86301

Description: Journal with feminist orientation designed to facilitate dialogue about therapy experiences among therapists, consumers, and researchers. **Price:** $36/individual; $75/institution; $150/library. Add 40% for foreign postage (outside Canada and Mexico).

★9142★ Women & Work
U.S. Department of Labor
Office of Information and Public Affairs
200 Constitution Ave. NW
Washington, DC 20210
Phone: (202)523-7323

Description: Government publication covering women's legal, educational, and employment issues. **Frequency:** Monthly.

★9143★ Women's Circle
Women's Circle Publishing
306 E. Parr Rd.
Berne, IN 46711
Phone: (219)589-8741

Description: Magazine containing stories on home-based female entrepreneurs, readers' letters, patterns, handicrafts, and designs. **First published:** 1957. **Frequency:** 6x/yr. **ISSN:** 0509-089X. **Subscription:** $9.95. $1.95 single issue.

★9144★ Women's Circle Counted Cross-Stitch
Women's Circle Publishing
306 E. Parr Rd.
Berne, IN 46711
Phone: (219)589-8741

Description: Magazine containing original cross-stitch designs, book reviews, and articles on designers. **First published:** 1983. **Frequency:** 6x/yr. **Subscription:** $12.97.

★9145★ **Women's Circle Country Needlecraft**
Women's Circle Publishing
306 E. Parr Rd.
Berne, IN 46711
Phone: (219)589-8741

Description: Magazine covering sewing, patchwork, knitting, embroidery, crochet, and cross-stitch. **First published:** 1967. **Frequency:** 6x/yr. **ISSN:** 0892-8223. **Subscription:** $12.97.

★9146★ **Women's Circle Crochet**
Women's Circle Publishing
306 E. Parr Rd.
Berne, IN 46711
Phone: (219)589-8741

Description: Magazine containing patterns for fashion, children, and home. **First published:** 1981. **Frequency:** Quarterly. **ISSN:** 0279-1978. **Subscription:** $7.95.

★9147★ **Women's Circle Home Cooking**
Women's Circle Publishing
306 E. Parr Rd.
Berne, IN 46711
Phone: (219)589-8741

Description: Magazine featuring old and new recipes. **First published:** 1972. **Frequency:** Monthly. **ISSN:** 0195-2439. **Subscription:** $9.95.

★9148★ **Women's Health Issues**
Jacob's Institute of Women's Health
409 12th St., SW
Washington, DC 20024-2188
Phone: (202)863-4990
Fax: (202)863-2499

Description: Contains original articles and expert commentary on key medical, social, legal, ethical, and public policy issues. **Frequency:** Quarterly.

★9149★ **Women's Household**
Women's Circle Publishing
306 E. Parr Rd.
Berne, IN 46711
Phone: (219)589-8741

Description: Magazine containing information on homemaking. **First published:** 1960. **Frequency:** 6x/yr. **ISSN:** 0510-7385. **Subscription:** $12.97. $1.95 single issue.

★9150★ **Women's Household Crochet**
Women's Circle Publishing
306 E. Parr Rd.
Berne, IN 46711
Phone: (219)589-8741

Description: Magazine featuring crochet patterns for home decorating, toys, and fashions for children and adults. **First published:** 1981. **Frequency:** Quarterly. **ISSN:** 0147-4685. **Subscription:** $7.95.

★9151★ **Women's League Outlook**
Women's League for Conservative Judaism
48 E. 74th St.
New York, NY 10021
Phone: (212)628-1600

Description: Magazine focusing on issues of concern to contemporary Jewish women and their families. **First published:** 1929. **Frequen-**cy: 4x/yr. **ISSN:** 0043-7557. **Subscription:** $8; $10 other countries. $2 single issue.

★9152★ **The Women's Review of Books**
Wellesley College
Wellesley, MA 02181
Phone: (617)431-1453
Fax: (617)239-1150

Subtitle: Book Review **Description:** Magazine on feminist thinking and writing. **First published:** 1983. **Frequency:** Monthly (except Aug.). **ISSN:** 0738-1433. **Subscription:** $17; $30 institutions.

★9153★ **Women's Rights Law Reporter**
15 Washington St.
Newark, NJ 07102
Phone: (201)648-5320
Fax: (201)648-1249

Description: Includes full-length and feature articles, comments, review essays, and bibliographies on all areas of the law affecting women's rights and sex discrimination. **First published:** 1971. **Frequency:** 4/yr. **Subscription:** $15/students; $20/individuals; $40/institution.

★9154★ **Women's Sports & Fitness**
Sports & Fitness, Inc.
1919 14th St., Ste. 421
Boulder, CO 80302
Phone: (303)440-5111
Fax: (303)440-3313

Description: Magazine covering women's sports, fitness, nutrition, and health. **First published:** 1974. **Frequency:** 8x/yr. **Subscription:** $19.97. $2.95 single issue.

★9155★ **Women's Studies Abstracts**
Transaction Periodicals and Consortium
Rutgers University
New Brunswick, NJ 08903
Phone: (908)932-2280
Fax: (908)932-3138

Description: Abstracts and listings of articles and book reviews, covering subjects from education and socialization to prejudice, interpersonal relations, and the women's movement. **Frequency:** Quarterly. **Subscription:** $124. Also available on CD-ROM.

★9156★ **Women's Studies International Forum**
Pergamon Press, Inc.
Maxwell House
Fairview Park
Elmsford, NY 10523
Phone: (914)592-7700
Fax: (914)592-3625

Description: Journal on women's studies. **First published:** 1978. **Frequency:** 6x/yr. **ISSN:** 0277-5395. **Subscription:** $170.

★9157★ **Women's Studies Quarterly**
The Feminist Press at the City University of N.Y.
311 E. 94 St.
New York, NY 10128-5603
Phone: (212)360-5790

Description: Feminist journal focusing on education. **First published:** 1972. **Frequency:** 2x/yr. **ISSN:** 0732-1562. **Subscription:** $25; $35 institutions. $13 single issue.

★9158★ **Womyn's Words**
Women's Energy Bank
PO Box 15524
St. Petersburg, FL 33733-5524
Phone: (813)823-5353

Description: Lesbian-feminist with local focus on events. Published by a charitable, cultural organization. **Frequency:** Monthly. **Subscription:** $15.

★9159★ **Working Mother**
Lang Communications
230 Park Ave.
New York, NY 10169
Phone: (212)551-9500

Description: Magazine for working mothers. **First published:** 1978. **Frequency:** Monthly. **ISSN:** 0278-193X. **Subscription:** $7.97. $1.95 single issue.

★9160★ **Working Woman Magazine**
230 Park Ave., 7th Fl.
New York, NY 10169-0005
Phone: (212)309-9800
Fax: (212)599-4763

Description: Magazine for women in business. **First published:** November 1976. **Frequency:** Monthly. **Subscription:** $18. $2.50 single issue.

★9161★ **WREE-View**
Women for Racial and Economic Equality (WREE)
198 Broadway, No. 606
New York, NY 10036
Phone: (212)385-1103

Description: Concentrates on the problems of working and working-class women. **Frequency:** 3-4. **Subscription:** $6.

★9162★ **Yale Journal of Law and Feminism**
Box 401A Yale Sta.
New Haven, CT 06520
Phone: (203)432-4056

Description: Provides a forum for the analysis of women, society, and the law. **First published:** 1989. **Frequency:** 2/yr. **Subscription:** $16/individual; $12/student; $28/institution.

★9163★ **Zontian**
Zonta International
557 W. Randolph St.
Chicago, IL 60661
Phone: (312)930-5848

Description: Service club organization magazine of interest to women in business and professions. **First published:** 1919. **Frequency:** Quarterly. **ISSN:** 0279-3229. **Subscription:** $7.

★9164★ **Zora Neale Hurston Forum**
Morgan State University
PO Box 550
Baltimore, MD 21239
Phone: (301)444-3435

Description: Official journal of the Zora Neale Hurston Society; includes creative writing and essays writing that promote the appreciation of the life, works, and legacy of Zora Neale Hurston. **Frequency:** Biannually.

(21) Newsletters

Entries in this chapter are arranged alphabetically by publication title. See the User's Guide at the front of this directory for additional information.

★9165★ AAAA News
American Association for Affirmative Action (AAAA)
11 E. Hubbard St., Ste. 200
Chicago, IL 60611
Phone: (312)329-2512
Description: Reports on Association news and activities as well as pertinent civil rights legislation and Equal Employment Opportunity Commission (EEOC) decisions. **Price:** Included in membership. **ISSN:** 0896-8217.

★9166★ AARP WIN (Women's Initiative Network)
American Association of Retired Persons (AARP)
Women's Initiative
1909 K St. NW
Washington, DC 20049
Phone: (202)434-2642
Description: Advocates and supports policies, programs, and legislation related to improving the status of mid-life and older women.

★9167★ AAWCJC Quarterly
American Association of Women in Community and Junior Colleges (AAWCJC)
Western Wisconsin Technical College
304 N. Sixth St.
P.O. Box 908
LaCrosse, WI 54602-0908
Phone: (608)785-9100
Fax: (608)785-9205
Description: Covers topics of interest to women who are administrators, faculty members, or students at community, junior, and vocational/technical colleges. Reports Association and regional activities and programs involving women. **Frequency:** 3-4/yr. **Price:** Included in membership. **Former Title(s):** AAWCJC Newsletter, November 1981.

★9168★ Abortion Research Notes
Transnational Family Research Institute
8307 Whitman Dr.
Bethesda, MD 20817
Phone: (301)469-6313
Fax: (301)469-0461
Description: Analyzes research and provides citations for abortion-related journal articles and books. Deals with legal, social, and psychological aspects of abortion, and abortion services and techniques. Studies abortion trends and legislation on country-by-country and interna-

tional levels. **First published:** 1972. **Frequency:** Periodic. **Price:** $25/yr. **ISSN:** 0361-1116.

★9169★ ACOG Newsletter
American College of Obstetricians and Gynecologists (ACOG)
409 12th St. SW
Washington, DC 20024-2188
Phone: (202)638-5577
Fax: (202)484-5107
Description: Reviews health policy issues, clinical research, national statistics, and other information pertaining to obstetrics and gynecology. Reports on College projects, staff, and meetings. **First published:** May 1952. **Frequency:** Monthly. **Price:** Included in membership.

★9170★ ACRL Women's Studies Newsletter
Association of College & Research Libraries (ACRL)
c/o ALA/ACRL
50 E. Huron St.
Chicago, IL 60611
Description: Discusses women's issues such as feminism, sexism, lesbianism, abortion, racism, rights, and social concerns. **Price:** Included in membership. **ISSN:** 0895-691X.

★9171★ Action Alert
American Association of University Women (AAUW)
1111 16th St. NW
Washington, DC 20036
Description: Examines legislative news. **Frequency:** Monthly. **Price:** $20/yr.

★9172★ Action Voice: A Focus on Diethylstilbestrol Exposure
DES Action, U.S.A.
Long Island Jewish Medical Center
New Hyde Park, NY 11040
Phone: (516)775-3450
Frequency: Quarterly.

★9173★ Affinity
Affirmation/Gay and Lesbian Mormons
PO Box 46022
Los Angeles, CA 90046
Phone: (213)255-7251
Description: Promotes understanding, tolerance, and acceptance of gay men and lesbians as full, equal, and worthy members of the

Church of Jesus Christ of Latter-Day Saints and society. Provides a forum for dialogue between members and church leaders and examines the consistency of homosexual behavior and the Gospel. Studies ways of reconciling sexual orientation with traditional Mormon beliefs. **Frequency:** Monthly. **Price:** Included in membership; $20/yr. for nonmembers.

★9174★ African American Women's Association Newsletter
African American Women's Association
PO Box 55122
Brightwood Sta.
Washington, DC 20011
Phone: (202)966-6645
Description: Concerned with African American women developing a better understanding of their heritage. Provides charitable, cultural, educational and social activies.

★9175★ African Studies Association Women's Caucus Newsletter
Emory University
African Studies Association
Women's Caucus
Credit Union Bldg.
Atlanta, GA 30322
Phone: (404)329-6410
Description: Promotes participation of women and attention to women's issues in African studies.

★9176★ Alan Guttmacher Institute— Washington Memo
Alan Guttmacher Institute
2010 Massachusetts Ave. NW
Washington, DC 20036
Phone: (202)296-4012
Fax: (202)223-5756
Description: Covers legislative developments relating to family planning and reproductive health issues. Monitors federal appropriations for family planning and contraceptive research, congressional and court actions on abortion, international population assistance, teenage pregnancy, maternal health and pregnancy-related services, and other matters related to reproductive health and population issues in the U.S. and abroad. **First published:** 1973. **Frequency:** Ca. 20/yr. **Price:** $60/yr. **ISSN:** 0739-4179. **Former Title(s):** Planned Parenthood World Population—Washington Memo.

★9177★ ALERT
Federation of Organizations for Professional
  Women (FOPW)
2001 S St. NW, Ste. 500
Washington, DC 20009
Phone: (202)328-1415

Description: Promotes equality for all women in
all educational levels and career fields.

★9178★ The Alert
Societas Docta
2207 Glynnwood Dr.
Savannah, GA 31404
Phone: (912)354-4634

Description: Reports news of interest to minority women with doctorate degrees. Provides
news on membership activities. **First published:** 1986. **Price:** Free with membership.

★9179★ The Alliance
Association of Executive and Professional
  Women
The International Alliance
8600 LaSalle Rd., Ste. 308
Baltimore, MD 21204
Phone: (410)321-6699
Fax: (410)823-2410

Description: Networks executive and professional women and the business, not-for-profit,
and government sectors. **Frequency:** Bimonthly.

**★9180★ American Anorexia/Bulimia
Association—Newsletter**
American Anorexia/Bulimia Association, Inc.
418 E. 76th St.
New York, NY 10021
Phone: (201)734-1114

Description: Features articles on the symptoms, causes, and treatment of the eating
disorders anorexia and bulimia. Carries news of
research in the field, book reviews, and information about the services and activities of the
Association. **Frequency:** 4/yr. **Price:** Included in
membership; $40/yr. for nonmembers.

**★9181★ American Association of Women
Dentists—Chronicle**
American Association of Women Dentists
401 N. Michigan Ave.
Chicago, IL 60611-4267
Phone: (312)644-6610
Fax: (312)565-4658

Description: Discusses Association news of
interest to women dentists and women dental
students. Includes short articles on scholarships, conferences, awards, and regional career
and education opportunities. Also lists addresses and telephone numbers of officers,
district chairs, and committees of the Association. **Frequency:** Bimonthly. **Price:** Included in
membership; $30/yr. for nonmembers.

★9182★ The American Baptist Woman
American Baptist Women
PO Box 851
Valley Forge, PA 19482-0851
Phone: (215)768-2284

Description: Brings news of the organization.
Aimed towards Baptist women. **Frequency:**
3/yr.

★9183★ American Forum
Vincent F. Palazzolo
PO Box 020261
Staten Island, NY 10302-0003
Phone: (718)720-4120

Subtitle: For the Opinionated. **Description:**
Reprints news articles submitted by readers,
especially those which extol more severe penal
laws for rapists and those in which rape victims
get "revenge" on their rapists. **Frequency:**
Weekly. **Price:** $19.95/yr., U.S.; $24.95, Canada.

★9184★ The American Mother
American Mothers, Inc.
The Waldorf Astoria
301 Park Ave.
New York, NY 10022
Phone: (212)755-2539
Fax: (212)755-2539

Description: Reports information regarding the
preservation of "American family values".

**★9185★ American Society of Women
Accountants—Coordinator**
American Society of Women Accountants
1755 Lynnfield Rd., Ste. 222
Memphis, TN 38119
Phone: (901)680-0470
Fax: (901)680-0505

Description: Publishes news and information of
interest to women accountants. Carries Society
news, excerpts from chapter newsletters, and
items on professional activities of members.
Frequency: Monthly. **Price:** Included in membership. **ISSN:** 0744-8937.

**★9186★ American Women Composers,
Inc.—News Forum**
American Women Composers, Inc.
1690 36th St, NW, Ste. 409
Washington, DC 20007
Phone: (202)342-8179

Description: Recognizes active female composers in the U.S.

**★9187★ American Women in Radio and
Television—News and Views**
American Women in Radio and Television
1101 Connecticut Ave. NW, Ste. 700
Washington, DC 20036
Phone: (202)429-5102
Fax: (202)223-4579

Description: Provides news of the radio and
television industry, focusing on women who are
active in the field. Carries organization news
and program ideas. **First published:** 1951.
Frequency: 6/yr. **Price:** Included in membership.

★9188★ The AMIT Woman
AMIT Women
817 Broadway
New York, NY 10003
Phone: (212)477-4720
Fax: (212)353-2312

Description: Covers the group's efforts to
maintain a network of secondary schools,
youths, villages, and children's homes in Israel.

★9189★ APLICommunicator
Association for Population/Family Planning
  Libraries and Information Centers,
  International (APLIC)
2058 SW Olympic Club Terrace
Palm City, FL 34990

Description: Focuses on subjects related to
population and family planning. Discusses organizations, associations, and networks involved
in these issues throughout the world; and library
and information center methodology. Includes
news of members and chapters. **First published:** April 1975. **Frequency:** Quarterly. **Price:**
Included in membership; $3/yr. for nonmem-
bers. **ISSN:** 0891-0847.

**★9190★ The Arthur and Elizabeth
Schlesinger Library Newsletter**
The Arthur and Elizabeth Schlesinger Library
Radcliffe College
10 Garden St.
Cambridge, MA 02138
Phone: (617)495-8647
Patiricia M. King, Director

Description: Reports on the collection, which
contains published and unpublished materials
chronicling the history of women in the United
States from 1800 to the present. **Frequency:**
Annual.

**★9191★ Association of Black Women in
Higher Education Newsletter**
Association of Black Women in Higher
  Education
31-33 91st St.
Jackson Heights, NY 11369
Phone: (212)760-7911

Description: Concerned with the preservation
of the history and presence of Black women in
higher education. **Frequency:** Quarterly.

**★9192★ Association of Women in
Development Newsletter**
Association of Women in Development
  (AWID) Secretariat
c/o Virginia Polytechnic Institute & State
  University
International Agriculture Program
10 Sandy Hall
Blacksburg, VA 24061-0338
Phone: (703)231-3765
Fax: (703)231-6741

Description: Keeps members current on recent
issues, events, and information affecting the
field of women in development. **Frequency:**
Quarterly. **Price:** $45/yr. for individuals; $20 for
students; $10 for members from developing
countries; $100 for institutions.

**★9193★ Association for Women in
Mathematics—Newsletter**
Association for Women in Mathematics
Wellesley College
PO Box 178
Wellesley, MA 02181
Phone: (617)237-7517
Fax: (617)235-7361

Description: Concerned with the progress of
women in professional fields, particularly in
mathematics and related careers. Recounts
facets of the history of women in mathematics,
discusses issues related to education, and
highlights women being honored for studies and
achievements. **First published:** January 1971.
Frequency: 6/yr. **Price:** Included in member-

ship; $20 for nonmembers; $5 for students and retired or unemployed persons.

★9194★ *Association for Women in Social Work Newsletter*
Association for Women in Social Work (AWSW)
University of Pennsylvania
Women's Center
119 Houston Hall
3417 Spruce St.
Philadelphia, PA 19104-6306
Phone: (215)898-8611
Fax: (215)898-0843
Description: Covers concerns of women in social work.

★9195★ *Atalanta*
Atlanta Lesbian Feminist Alliance
PO Box 5502
Atlanta, GA 30307
Phone: (404)378-9769
Description: Concerned with lesbian feminism, including "herstory," discrimination and gay civil rights, lesbian spiritualism, and lesbian artists. Carries news of the Alliance's events and financial status, feminist happenings in Atlanta, and national and regional lesbian news. Discusses lesbian legal cases related to job harassment, child custody, and rape. **First published:** September 1973. **Frequency:** Monthly. **Price:** Included in membership; $15/yr. for nonmembers; $30 for institutions. **Former Title(s):** *Atlanta Lesbian Feminist Alliance—Newsletter.*

★9196★ *AUL Newsletter*
Americans United for Life (AUL)
343 S. Dearborn, Ste. 1804
Chicago, IL 60604
Phone: (312)786-9494
Description: Discusses the legal aspects of and current court cases involving abortion, euthanasia, infanticide, in vitro fertilization, genetic engineering, and medical treatment for handicapped newborn infants. Carries announcements and ordering information for new publications. **Frequency:** Quarterly. **Price:** Donation requested.

★9197★ *AVSC News*
Association for Voluntary Surgical Contraception, Inc. (AVSC)
79 Madison Ave.
New York, NY 10016
Phone: (212)561-8093
Fax: (212)779-9439
Description: Provides information on all aspects of voluntary sterilization: programs, research, legal issues, and new medical technologies. Discusses programs in the U.S. and developing countries. **First published:** 1962. **Frequency:** 4/yr. **Price:** Included in membership. **ISSN:** 0001-2904. **Former Title(s):** *AVS News.*

★9198★ *AWC News/Forum*
American Women Composers, Inc. (AWC)
1690 36th St. NW, No. 409
Washington, DC 20007
Phone: (202)342-8179
Description: Promotes the works of women composers and performers in the U.S. with the purpose of "alleviating the gross inequities that women composers have experienced in all

areas of the music world." Also carries features on personalities. **First published:** January 1977. **Frequency:** Annual. **Price:** $15/yr. **ISSN:** 0193-0850. **Remarks:** Semiannual supplement, AWC News—Update.

★9199★ *The AWC Source*
Association for Women in Computing (AWC)
41 Sutter St., Ste. 1006
San Francisco, CA 94104
Description: Focuses on issues relevant to the field of computer data processing. Carries information on conferences, regional meetings, officer reports, and career changes among members. Also provides articles on technological advances in computer use in business, industry, science, education, and government. **First published:** January 1979. **Price:** Included in membership.

★9200★ *AWIS Newsletter*
Association for Women in Science (AWIS)
1522 K St. NW, Ste. 820
Washington, DC 20005
Phone: (202)408-0742
Toll-free: 800-886-2947
Fax: (202)408-8321
Description: Covers issues, legislation, and trends related to science education for girls, women, and minorities. Includes information on grants and fellowships, job openings, educational programs, events, and notices of publications available. **First published:** 1971. **Frequency:** Bimonthly. **Price:** Included in membership.; $55 for non-members. **ISSN:** 0160-256X.

★9201★ *AWNY Matters*
Advertising Women of New York (AWNY)
153 E. 57th St.
New York, NY 10022
Phone: (212)593-1950
Subtitle: A Monthly Report from the Advertising Women of New York. **Description:** Includes personnel movements and a calendar of events of interest to women in advertising in New York.

★9202★ *AWSCPA Newsletter*
American Woman's Society of Certified Public Accountants (AWSCPA)
401 N. Michigan Ave.
Chicago, IL 60611
Phone: (312)644-6610
Description: Concerned with future developments within the accounting profession for women CPA's. Carries items on new accounting methods, job opportunities, member profiles, and other topics of interest. **First published:** 1954. **Frequency:** Quarterly. **Price:** Included in membership.

★9203★ *AWSM Newsletter*
Association for Women in Sports Media (AWSM)
PO Box 355
Alameda, CA 94501
Description: Reports information of interest to women in sports media and public relations. **Frequency:** Quarterly.

★9204★ *BACW Newsletter*
Bay Area Career Women (BACW)
55 New Montgomery, Ste. 606
San Francisco, CA 94105
Description: Offers coverage of networking, business seminars and meetings, social events, and support information. **Frequency:** Bimonthly.

★9205★ *The Beltane Papers*
Juno's Peacock Press
Northwest Graphics
PO Box 8
Clear Lake, WA 98235
Phone: (206)856-5494
Subtitle: A News-Journal of Women's Spirituality and Theology. **Description:** Explores women's life experiences, spirituality, and "the divine feminine" through articles, poetry, fiction, and artwork. Carries letters to and from the editors, news of educational opportunities, notices of publications available and book reviews, and columns titled The College of Hera and Natural Timing. **First published:** May 1984. **Frequency:** 2/yr.

★9206★ *BHP Bulletin*
Breast Health Program of New York (BHP)
28 W. 12th St.
New York, NY 10011
Phone: (212)645-0052
Description: Provides information on breast care.

★9207★ *Bi Women: Boston Bisexual Women's Network Newsletter*
Boston Bisexual Women's Network
PO Box 639
Cambridge, MA 02140
Phone: (617)247-6683
Description: Offers news and articles on regional, national and international levels of interest to bisexual women. Also contains calendar listings. **Frequency:** Bimonthly.

★9208★ *The Black Woman*
Black Women in Sisterhood for Action, Inc. (BISA)
PO Box 1592
Washington, DC 20013
Phone: (301)460-1565
Description: Provides information on alternative strategies in educational and career development, scholarship assistance, and related resources available to Black women.

★9209★ *The Bookwoman*
Women's National Book Association
160 5th Ave.
New York, NY 10010
Phone: (212)675-7805
Description: Covers major topics of interest to publishers, librarians, educators, writers, and agents in the book world. **First published:** November 1936. **Frequency:** 3/yr. **Price:** Included in membership.

★9210★ Border Crossing
International Network for Women in
 Enterprise and Trade, Inc.
PO Box 6178
McLean, VA 22106
Phone: (703)893-8541
Description: Contains articles promoting wom-
en in international transactions, short reviews of
relevant publications, directory of members, an
international events listing, and how-to articles.
Frequency: Bimonthly. **Price:** Free to members;
subscriptions $45/year.

★9211★ Boston NOW News
National Organization for Women (NOW),
 Boston Chapter
971 Commonwealth Ave.
Boston, MA 02215
Phone: (617)782-1056
Description: Provides news and information on
feminist issues on local and national levels. **First
published:** 1972. **Frequency:** 4/yr. **Price:**
$35/yr.

★9212★ Branches
Duke University
Center for Research on Women
207 E. Duke Bldg.
Durham, NC 27708
Phone: (919)684-6641
Description: Contains information on women's
studies, particularly gender, race, and class as it
relates to men's and women's experiences of
living in the South. **Frequency:** Semiannual.
Price: Free.

★9213★ Breakthrough
National Association of Commissions for
 Women
624 9th St., NW, Ste. M-10
Washington, DC 20001
Phone: (202)628-5030
Description: Reports news related to improving
the status of women.

★9214★ Breastfeeding Abstracts
La Leche League International, Inc.
9616 Minneapolis
Franklin Park, IL 60131-8209
Phone: (312)455-7730
Toll-free: 800-LA-LECHE
Description: Consists of abstracts from profes-
sional journals on the medical aspects of breast-
feeding. **First published:** Summer 1981. **Fre-
quency:** Quarterly. **Price:** $9.50/yr., U.S.;
$12.50 elsewhere.

★9215★ Breeline
PO Box 4551
Arlington, VA 22204
Description: Contains erotic humor based on
the fictional Bree Innerprizes Corporation (an all-
women corporation). **First published:** September 1991. **Frequency:** 4/yr. **Price:** $9/yr.

★9216★ Bridging the Gap
Section for Women in Public Administration
c/o Debra Martin
3214 McClure Ave.
Flint, MI 48502
Phone: (313)736-9554
Description: Disseminates information relating
to the organization's efforts to initiate action
programs appropriate to the needs and concerns of women in public administration. Discusses the equality of educational and employment opportunities for women in public service
and government. Acts as a forum for communication among professionals and students interested in women in public service administration.
First published: 1980. **Frequency:** 3/yr. **Price:**
Included in membership.

★9217★ The Campaign Report
80% Majority Campaign
PO Box 1315
Highstown, NJ 08520
Phone: (609)443-8780
Fax: (609)448-9550
Description: Discusses abortion from a pro-
choice viewpoint. **Frequency:** Semimonthly.
Price: $60/yr.

★9218★ Capital Update
American Nurses Association (ANA)
1101 14th St., NW, Ste. 200
Washington, DC 20005
Phone: (202)554-4444
Fax: (202)842-4375
Description: Provides information concerning
registered nurses in the U.S.

★9219★ CARAL Newsletter
California Abortion Rights Action League
 (CARAL)
300 Brannan St,. Ste. 501
San Francisco, CA 94118
Phone: (415)546-7211
Description: Provides updates on legislation
affecting abortion and family planning. Supports
the right to safe, legal abortion, and addresses
the concerns of those who are or who want to
be involved in working for pro-choice legislation.
First published: 1979. **Frequency:** Quarterly.
Price: Included in membership; $35/yr. for
nonmembers.

**★9220★ Caucus for Women in
 Statistics—Newsletter**
Caucus for Women in Statistics
6000 Forest Rd.
Cheverly, MD 20785
Phone: (202)272-5060
Fax: (202)233-1620
Description: Offers articles of interest to wom-
en in statistics. **First published:** 1970. **Fre-
quency:** Quarterly. **Price:** Included in member-
ship.

★9221★ CCL Family Foundations
Couple to Couple League International, Inc.
 (CCL)
PO Box 111184
Cincinnati, OH 45211
Phone: (513)661-7612
Description: Concerned with natural family
planning, its growth, social effects, health bene-
fits, and advantages to couples and families.
Carries practical helps, supportive information,

personal testimonies, and items on activities
and developments in the movement and the
League. **First published:** 1974. **Frequency:**
Bimonthly. **Price:** Included in membership. **Former Title(s):** *The CCL News.*

★9222★ CCWHP Newsletter
Coordinating Committee on Women in the
 Historical Profession (CCWHP)
c/o B. Winslow
124 Park Pl.
Brooklyn, NY 11217
Phone: (718)638-3227
Description: Focuses on the status of women
in the history profession. Concerned with wom-
en's history, discrimination against women, the
ERA (Equal Rights Amendment), educational
opportunities for women in the field of history,
and Committee affairs. **First published:** 1970.
Frequency: 3/yr. **Price:** Included in member-
ship. **Remarks:** Published alternately with
CGWH Newsletter.

★9223★ CDDR News
Coalition for the Medical Rights of Women
25 Taylor St., No. 704
San Francisco, CA 94102
Phone: (415)441-4434
Description: Focuses on women's medical
rights, particularly reproductive rights, and other
health issues. **First published:** 1977. **Frequency:** 6/yr. **Price:** $25/yr.

**★9224★ Center for Advanced Feminist
 Studies—Newsletter**
University of Minnesota
Center for Advanced Feminist Studies
496 Ford Hall
224 Church St. SE
Minneapolis, MN 55455
Phone: (612)624-6310
Fax: (612)626-1697
Description: Provides updates on the activities
of the Center, its faculty, and its graduate
students. **First published:** 1983. **Frequency:**
Quarterly. **Price:** Free.

**★9225★ Center for Research on
 Women—Center News**
Memphis State University
Center for Research on Women
Clement Hall-339
Memphis, TN 38152
Phone: (901)678-2770
Fax: (901)678-3299
Description: Features news on issues of con-
cern to women, including careers, education,
ethnic minority affairs, sexual harrassment, vio-
lence, and health care. Includes information on
Center activities and conferences. **First pub-
lished:** December 1982. **Frequency:** 2/yr. (Fall
and Spring). **Price:** Free; donations accepted.

**★9226★ Center for Research on
 Women—Research Report**
Wellesley College
Center for Research on Women
Wellesley, MA 02181
Phone: (617)431-1453
Fax: (617)239-1150
Description: Provides reports of research stud-
ies that focus on women. **Frequency:** Semian-
nually. **Price:** Free.

★9227★ *Center for the Study of Women and Society—Newsletter*
City University of New York
Center for the Study of Women and Society
33 W. 42nd St.
New York, NY 10036
Phone: (212)642-2954

Description: Reports on Center activities and provides a forum for information exchange concerning interdisciplinary research related to women and society. Carries essays discussing topics such as women in the arts, women and health, feminist social theory, and women and work. **First published:** 1972. **Frequency:** 2/yr. **Price:** Free.

★9228★ *Center for Women and Religion—Membership Newsletter*
Graduate Theological Union (GTU)
Center for Women and Religion
2400 Ridge Rd.
Berkeley, CA 94709
Phone: (510)649-2490
Fax: (510)649-1417

Description: Covers issues in religion, ministry, and theology that directly affect women's lives. Includes book reviews and poetry. **First published:** 1979. **Frequency:** 10/yr. **Price:** $20/yr. for students; $30 for others.

★9229★ *Center for Women and Religion—Student, Faculty, and Staff Newsletter*
Graduate Theological Union (GTU)
Center for Women and Religion
2400 Ridge Rd.
Berkeley, CA 94709
Phone: (510)649-2490
Fax: (510)649-1417

Description: Serves an in-house newsletter to the community of the Graduate Theological Union. **First published:** 1977. **Frequency:** 10/yr. **Price:** Free to the GTU community.

★9230★ *Centerpiece*
The Women's Center
133 Park St. NE
Vienna, VA 22180
Phone: (703)281-2657

Description: Contains news and information on the Center's services and programs. Addresses women's issues and concerns. **First published:** 1983. **Frequency:** Quarterly. **Price:** Free.

★9231★ *CGWH Newsletter*
Conference Group on Women's History (CGWH)
c/o B. Winslow
124 Park Pl.
Brooklyn, NY 11217
Phone: (718)638-3227

Description: Focuses on issues related to women's history. Publishes notes on archival sources about women's history available in the U.S. and on new books and articles by members. **First published:** 1975. **Frequency:** Semi-annually. **Price:** Included in membership. **Remarks:** Published alternately with CCWHP Newsletter.

★9232★ *Challenging Media Images of Women*
PO Box 902
Framingham, MA 01701
Phone: (617)879-8504

Description: Designed to enable readers to protest (through letterwriting or boycotting) sexist, racist, and abusive images of women in the mass media.

★9233★ *Chapter League Bulletin*
National Association of Women Business Owners (NAWBO)
600 S. Federal St., Ste. 400
Chicago, IL 60605
Phone: (312)922-0465

Description: Provides information of concern to women business owners.

★9234★ *Chicago Catholic Women Newsletter*
5249 N. Kenmore
Chicago, IL 60640
Phone: (312)561-5668

Description: Promotes structural change within the Church and society with the goal of justice for women.

★9235★ *Chicago Women in Publishing News*
43 E. Ohio St., Ste. 914
Chicago, IL 60611
Phone: (312)641-6311
Fax: (312)645-1078

Description: Announces monthly programs, courses,and job opportunities. Contains articles on trends in publishing, women, careers, book reviews, and internal organization news.

★9236★ *Child Care ActioNews*
Child Care Action Campaign
330 7th Ave., 17th Fl.
New York, NY 10001
Phone: (212)239-0138
Fax: (212)268-6516

Description: Supports the Campaign, "a coalition of leaders from a wide range of American organizations, whose long range goal is to set in place a national system of quality, affordable child care, using all existing resources, both public and private." Offers news on issues and innovations in the field of child care for children of working parents and all types of service delivery (public, private, and employer-supported, family day care, and other child care organizations). **First published:** January 1984. **Frequency:** Bimonthly. **Price:** Included in membership; $100-$250 for organizations or companies.

★9237★ *Childbirth Without Pain Education Association—Memo*
Childbirth Without Pain Education Association
20134 Snowden
Detroit, MI 48235
Phone: (313)341-3816

Description: Concerned with the Lamaze-Pavlov method of childbirth, obstetric care, parenting, and women. **First published:** 1959. **Frequency:** Bimonthly. **Price:** Included in membership; $25/yr. for physicians. **Former Title(s):** *Childbirth Without Pain Education Association—Newsletter.*

★9238★ *Choose Life*
National Right to Life Committee, Inc.
419 7th St. NW, Ste. 500
Washington, DC 20004
Phone: (202)626-8800
Fax: (202)737-9189

Description: Provides educational and religious information for religiously based pro-life groups and individuals. **First published:** June 1988. **Frequency:** Bimonthly. **Price:** $3/yr.

★9239★ *Chrome Rose's Review*
7 Lent Ave.
LeRoy, NY 14482
Phone: (716)768-6054

Description: Designed to increase networking among women motorcyclists. Contains news of upcoming events, and technical and touring tips.

★9240★ *Chronicle of Minority Business: National Newsletter*
American Association of Black Women Entrepreneurs
909 Pershing Dr., Ste. 207
Silver Spring, MD 20910
Phone: (301)565-0258

Description: Contains news for and about Black women business owners. **Frequency:** Quarterly.

★9241★ *Clearinghouse on Women's Issues Newsletter*
13905 N. Gate Dr.
Silver Spring, MD 20906
Phone: (301)871-6106

Description: Describes public and private policies affecting women. **Frequency:** Monthly.

★9242★ *CLUW News*
Coalition of Labor Union Women (CLUW)
15 Union Sq.
New York, NY 10003
Phone: (212)242-0700
Fax: (212)255-7230

Description: Contains information on the activities of the Coalition and news items relevant to union women. **First published:** April 1975. **Frequency:** Bimonthly. **Price:** Included in membership; $10/yr. for retired nonmembers.

★9243★ *CN: Career Opportunities News*
Garrett Park Press
PO Box 190 B
Garrett Park, MD 20896
Phone: (301)946-2553

Description: Focuses on new and developing careers. Includes career guidance materials and a section on items of interest to women. **Frequency:** 6/yr.

★9244★ *Collections*
The Medical College of Pennsylvania
Archives for Women in Medicine
3300 Henry Ave.
Philadelphia, PA 19129
Phone: (215)842-7124
Fax: (215)849-1380

Description: Contains news on the Archives for Special Collections on Women in Medicine.

★9245★ Committee of 200 Newsletter
Committee 200
676 N. St. Clair, No. 1900
Chicago, IL 60611
Phone: (312)280-5200
Fax: (312)751-3477
Description: Offers business ideas, solutions, and support; promotes active involvement in business and related issues, the visibility of women in business and as leaders, and the expansion of opportunities for women business leaders.

★9246★ Committee on Women in Asian Studies Newsletter
University of Pittsburgh
Asian Studies Program
Pittsburgh, PA 15260
Phone: (412)648-7510
Fax: (518)442-4936
Description: Contains reports, conference notices, and networking sources to promote the exchange of information on women and gender in Asia and Asia populations. **First published:** 1982. **Frequency:** 3/yr. **Price:** $8 for students/unemployed; $15 for employed subscribers; $25 for institutions. **ISSN:** 0738-3185.

★9247★ Common Ground/Different Planes
Women of Color Partnership Program
100 Maryland Ave., NE, Ste. 307
Washington, DC 20002
Phone: (202)543-7032
Fax: (202)543-7820
Description: Shares experiences and accomplishments of Black, Latino, Asian, and Native American Women.

★9248★ The Communicator
National Federation of Democratic Women (NFDW)
828 Lemont Dr.
Nashville, TN 37216
Phone: (615)244-4270
Fax: (615)244-4281
Description: Includes president's message and regional reports concerning the recruitment of women to run for political office on the Democratic ticket. **Frequency:** Quarterly. **Price:** $20/yr.

★9249★ Compassionate Friends—Newsletter
Compassionate Friends
PO Box 3696
Oak Brook, IL 60522-3696
Phone: (708)990-0010
Description: Offers friendship and understanding to parents whose children have died. Includes contributed letters, articles, poetry, and book reviews in support of family members. Works to achieve positive resolution of the grief experience and to foster physical and emotional health. Also provides news of research on parental bereavement. **First published:** Fall 1978. **Frequency:** Quarterly. **Price:** $10/yr.

★9250★ Concerns: Newsletter of the Women's Caucus for the Modern Languages
University of Wisconsin
English Department
Box 2000
Kenosha, WI 53141
Phone: (414)553-2644
Description: Contains information about calls for papers, new publications, research in progress, and jobs for women teaching English and other modern languages at the college level, with a focus on women's literature. **Frequency:** 3x/yr. **Subscription:** $10/yr.

★9251★ Contacts
National Network of Women in Sales
710 E. Ogden Ave., Ste. 113
Naperville, IL 60563
Phone: (708)369-2406
Description: Contains information concerning women in the sales profession.

★9252★ Cornerstone
University of Michigan
Center for Education of Women
330 E. Liberty
Ann Arbor, MI 48104-2289
Phone: (313)998-7080
Fax: (313)998-6203
Description: Examines the role of women in society, with an emphasis on education and careers. **First published:** 1965. **Frequency:** 1-2/yr. **Price:** Free.

★9253★ Counterbalance
National Association of Women Judges
300 Newport Ave.
Williamsburg, VA 23187-8798
Phone: (804)253-2000
Fax: (804)220-0449
Description: Reports information of concern to women holding judicial or quasi-judicial positions. **Frequency:** 3/yr.

★9254★ Country Council Newsletter
Country Women's Council, United States of America
3500 Henbet Dr.
West Columbia, SC 29169
Phone: (803)794-7548
Description: Covers topics concerning rural women. **Frequency:** Semiannual.

★9255★ The Courier
Cosmopolitan Associates
PO Box 1491
West Caldwell, NJ 07007
Phone: (201)992-2232
Description: Provides news and information helping foreign-born women maintain ties with their country of birth. **Frequency:** Monthly.

★9256★ The Crystal Quilt, Inc.
532 LaGuardia Pl., No.321
New York, NY 10012
Phone: (212)529-7579
Description: Includes news on workshops, support groups, courses, cultural events, personal relationships, careers, and spirituality for women. **Price:** $10 (optional).

★9257★ CSWEP Newsletter
American Economic Association
Committee on the Status of Women in Economics (CSWE)
Department of Economics
University of Arizona
Tucson, AZ 85721
Phone: (602)621-6227
Fax: (602)621-2606
Description: Information on the activities of the Committee and the advancement of women in the economics profession.

★9258★ CWAO News
National Coalition of Women's Art Organizations (CWAO)
123 E. Beutel Rd.
Port Washington, WI 53074
Phone: (414)284-4458
Description: Informs the national network about arts issues and arts legislation. **Price:** $10/yr. for members; $25 for organizations.

★9259★ CWIS Newsletter
National Association of Independent Schools
Council for Women in Independent Schools (CWIS)
75 Federal St.
Boston, MA 02110
Phone: (617)451-2444
Description: Offers news and information concerning female leadership in member schools, the quality of life for women in independent schools, and the scope of the curriculum. **Frequency:** Annual.

★9260★ CWWH Newsletter
Washington State University
Coalition for Western Women's History (CWWH)
History Dept.
Pullman, WA 99164
Phone: (509)335-1560
Description: Focuses on multicultural women's history in the American West.

★9261★ Day Care Information Service
United Communications Group
11300 Rockville Pike, Ste. 1100
Rockville, MD 20852-3030
Phone: (301)816-8950
Fax: (301)816-8950
Description: Covers policies on day care, Head Start program, early intervention, and preschool. **First published:** 1971. **Frequency:** Biweekly. **Price:** $229/yr.

★9262★ Delta DREF Chapter Network News
Delta Sigma Theta Sorority, Inc.
Delta Research and Education Foundation (DREF)
1707 New Hampshire Ave., NW
Washington, DC 20009
Phone: (202)483-5460
Description: Covers family welfare, educational development, and international awareness. **Frequency:** Quarterly.

★9263★ DES Action Voice
DES Action USA
1615 Broadway, No. 510
Oakland, CA 94612
Phone: (510)465-4011
Fax: (415)549-0320
Description: Provides medical and legal information about the drug DES (Diethylstilbestrol) and those exposed to it. Contains accounts of personal experiences, DES international outreach programs, and on lawsuits. **First published:** 1979. **Frequency:** Quarterly. **Price:** $25/yr.

★9264★ DES Litigation Reporter
Andrews Publications
PO Box 1000
Westtown, PA 19395
Phone: (215)399-6600
Toll-free: 800-345-1101
Fax: (215)399-6610
Subtitle: The National Journal of Record of Diethylstilbestrol Litigation. **Description:** "Provides unbiased coverage of the major developments in the mass tort litigation that has developed in the wake of studies linking a rare form of vaginal cancer and other abnormalities of the female genital tract to the victim's in utero exposure to diethylstilbestrol, a synthetic hormone administered to prevent miscarriage." Reprints complete texts of key decisions and pleadings along with editorial summations and "covers in-depth the litigation surrounding new, burden-shifting theories of liability." **First published:** June 1981. **Frequency:** Semimonthly. **Price:** $800/yr. **ISSN:** 0276-5675.

★9265★ Dinah
PO Box 1485
Cincinnati, OH 45201
Description: Contains ideas, articles, comments, book and music reviews, and information about upcoming events of interest to the lesbian community. Readers are encouraged to contribute. **First published:** 1975. **Frequency:** Bimonthly.

★9266★ Direct Line
Amit Women
817 Broadway
New York, NY 10003
Phone: (212)477-4720
Fax: (212)353-2312
Description: Presents information concerning the organization's recruiting of religious Zionist women in an effort to provide child care, social services, and training programs for Israeli youth and newcomers to Israel. Reports on secondary, technological and academic education, youth villages, high schools, and children's homes in Israel. **First published:** 1981. **Frequency:** 6/yr. **Price:** Included in membership. **Former Title(s):** Not for Presidents Only.

★9267★ Displaced Homemakers Center Newsletter
Cornell University
Center for Religion, Ethics and Social Policy
123 Anabel Taylor Hall
Ithaca, NY 14853
Phone: (607)255-6846
Description: Provides news of updates, upcoming events, and information on new Center projects. **First published:** 1980. **Frequency:** Semiannual. **Price:** Free.

★9268★ Division of Psychology of Women Newsletter
American Psychological Association
Division of the Psychology of Women
Women's Program Office
750 1st St., NE
Washington, DC 20002-4242
Phone: (202)336-6044
Fax: (202)336-6040
Description: Promotes the research and practice of feminist psychology. **Frequency:** Quarterly.

★9269★ Double-Time
National Clearinghouse For The Defense of Battered Women
125 S. 9th St., Ste. 302
Philadelphia, PA 19107
Phone: (215)351-0010
Description: Includes articles, legislative updates, and resources for battered women in prison. **Frequency:** 3/yr.

★9270★ Eating Disorders Review
PM, Inc.
PO Box 10172
Van Nuys, CA 91410
Phone: (818)873-4399
Toll-free: 800-365-2468
First published: July/August 1990. **Frequency:** Bimonthly. **Price:** $59/yr. **ISSN:** 1048-6984.

★9271★ The Echo
United Order True Sisters, Inc.
212 5th Ave., Rm. 1307
New York, NY 10010
Phone: (212)679-6790
Description: Highlights activities of the Order, a women's charitable organization dedicated to helping cancer patients and other sick and needy persons. Features profiles of members and local fundraising and service projects. **Frequency:** 3/yr. **Price:** Included in membership. **ISSN:** 0046-1067.

★9272★ Ecos Nacionales
National Conference of Puerto Rican Women, Inc.
5 Thomas Circle, NW
Washington, DC 20005
Phone: (202)387-4716
Description: Focuses on the rights of Puerto Rican and other Hispanic women. **First published:** 1972. **Frequency:** Quarterly.

★9273★ The 80% Majority Campaign Report
Pro-Choice Research and Information Service
PO Box 1315
Highstown, NJ 08520
Phone: (609)443-8780
Description: Focuses on analysis of events and news concerning abortion rights "that does not show up in the mainstream media." **Frequency:** 24/yr. **Price:** $60/year.

★9274★ Electrical Women's Round Table—Connections
Electrical Women's Round Table, Inc.
PO Box 292793
Nashville, TN 37229-2793
Phone: (615)890-1272
Description: Reports on the electric industry and allied fields. **Frequency:** Quarterly. **Price:** Free.

★9275★ EMILY's Newsletter
EMILY's List
1112 16th St., NW, Ste. 750
Washington, DC 20036
Phone: (202)887-1957
Fax: (202)452-7097
Description: Reports on pro-choice, democratic women candidates running in gubernatorial or Congressional races. **Frequency:** Quarterly. **Price:** Available upon request.

★9276★ Endometriosis Association Newsletter
International Endometriosis Association
8585 N. 76th Pl.
Milwaukee, WI 53223
Phone: (414)355-2200
Toll-free: 800-992-3636
Description: Publishes news and concerns of the Association, a self-help organization devoted to "offering mutual support and help to those affected by endometriosis, educating the public and medical community about the disease, and promoting research related to endometriosis." Recurring features include medical updates, letters from women with endometriosis, news of members and chapters of the Association, book reviews, and columns titled In the Mail, News/Announcements, and Research Recap. **First published:** 1980. **Frequency:** Bimonthly. **Price:** Included in membership. **ISSN:** 0897-1870. **Former Title(s):** Endometriosis Association—National Newsletter.

★9277★ Enrich!
National Chamber of Commerce for Women
10 Waterside Plaza, Ste. 6H
New York, NY 10010
Phone: (212)685-3454
Description: Analyzes opportunities, trends, and techniques for women who manage small businesses in commercial space or their homes. Includes information on how to bid, how to get consulting contracts, legal options, business plan formats, and pay comparisons. **Frequency:** Bimonthly. **Price:** $35/yr. for nonmembers.

★9278★ Entre Nous
PO Box 70933
Sunnyvale, CA 94086
Phone: (408)246-1117
Description: Geared towards lesbians. Contains comprehensive activities calendar and lists events from San Francisco to Santa Cruz. **Frequency:** Monthly. **Price:** $12/yr.

★9279★ Equal Rights
National Woman's Party
144 Constitution Ave. NE
Washington, DC 20002
Phone: (202)546-1210
Fax: (202)543-2365
Description: Publishes news of this association concerned with ratification of the Equal Rights

Amendment (ERA) and current women's issues. **First published:** Ca. 1923. **Frequency:** Quarterly. **Price:** $10/yr., U.S. and Canada.

★9280★ **Equal Rights Advocate**
Equal Rights Advocates
1663 Mission St., Ste. 550
San Francisco, CA 94103
Phone: (415)621-0672

Description: Contains information on legal issues related to women. **Frequency:** Quarterly.

★9281★ **Equal Time**
United Nations Secretariat
Rm. S-2727B
New York, NY 10017
Phone: (212)963-6209

Description: News on women employed by the United Nations. **Frequency:** Irregular.

★9282★ **Everywoman's Center Newsletter**
University of Massachusetts
Wilder Hall
Amherst, MA 01003
Phone: (415)545-0883

Description: Details the Center's activities; contains updates on staff, programs, and events.

★9283★ **The Exchange**
National Woman Abuse Prevention Project
2000 P St., NW, Ste. 508
Washington, DC 20036
Phone: (202)337-6070

Description: Concerned with the awareness and prevention of domestic violence and improvement of services offered to battered women. Includes model program highlights and resource reviews. **Frequency:** Quarterly. **Price:** $15/yr.

★9284★ **Fair Employment Practices
Summary of Latest Developments**
Bureau of National Affairs, Inc. (BNA)
1231 25th St. NW
Washington, DC 20037
Phone: (202)452-4200
Toll-free: 800-372-1033
Fax: (202)822-8092

Description: Highlights developments in employment opportunity and affirmative actions, and affirmative action programs. Reports on federal and state court decisions, Equal Employment Opportunity Commission (EEOC) rulings and Office of Federal Contract Compliance Programs (OFCCP) decisions, new laws, regulations, and agency directives. Also provides information on special programs for minorities, the handicapped, women, and older workers. **First published:** March 4, 1965. **Frequency:** Biweekly. **Price:** $96/yr. **ISSN:** 0525-2156.

★9285★ **Fair Share**
Prentice-Hall, Inc.
c/o Steve Nelson
11 Dupont Circle, Ste. 325
Washington, DC 20036
Phone: (202)328-6662
Toll-free: 800-223-0231
Fax: (202)332-7122

Description: Deals with the financial-economic issues at the heart of matrimonial law. **First published:** 1980. **Frequency:** Monthly. **Price:** $145/yr. **ISSN:** 0273-3560.

★9286★ **Fairfax County Career
Development Center for Women—
Connections**
The Fairfax County Career Development
Center for Women
5501 Backlick Rd., Ste. 110
Springfield, VA 22151
Phone: (703)750-0633
Fax: (703)658-9675

Subtitle: A Newsletter About Employment and Career Options. **Description:** Reports on career and employment issues, workshops, job and resource fairs, and other special programs sponsored by the Center. Provides a calendar of events. **Frequency:** 3/yr. **Former Title(s):** Re-Entry Women's Employment Center—Connections; Career Devlopment—Connections.

★9287★ **Family Day Care Bulletin**
Children's Foundation
815 15th St. NW, Ste. 928
Washington, DC 20005
Phone: (202)347-3300
Fax: (202)347-3382

Description: Serves as a national information resource on family day care systems and supports. Covers topics such as government program and legislative developments, day care insurance, day care licensing, and current research concerning child development and behavior. **First published:** 1977. **Frequency:** Quarterly. **Price:** $10/yr.

★9288★ **Family Health International—
Network**
PO Box 13950
Research Triangle Park, NC 27709
Phone: (919)549-7040

Description: Covers research into new methods of family planning, maternal and child health care, and the transfer of technology in these areas. Focuses on the impact of this research on the developing countries and the population problem. **First published:** October 1979. **Frequency:** Quarterly. **Price:** Free. **ISSN:** 0270-3637. **Remarks:** Also available in Spanish and French 2-3/yr.

★9289★ **Family Matters**
Center for Law and Social Policy
1616 P St., NW, Ste. 450
Washington, DC 20036
Phone: (202)328-5140
Fax: (202)328-5195

Description: Addresses the problems of low income families and the legal needs of the poor. **Frequency:** Quarterly.

★9290★ **Family Services Newsletter**
Toiyabe Indian Health Project, Inc.
Family Services Program
PO Box 1296
Bishop, CA 93515
Phone: (619)873-6394
Fax: (619)873-3935

Description: Focuses on concerns of Indian families, discussing issues such as drugs and alcohol, parenting, child abuse and neglect, and women's concerns. Provides information on the Program's counseling, educational, legal, and advocacy services. **First published:** October 1980. **Frequency:** Quarterly. **Price:** Free.

★9291★ **Feminism & Philosophy
Newsletter**
University of Delaware
American Philosophical Association (APA)
Committee on the Status of Women
Department of Philosophy
Neward, DE 19716
Phone: (302)451-1112

Description: Focuses on the status of women in the profession of philosophy.

★9292★ **Feminisms**
Ohio State University
Center for Women's Studies
207 Dulles Hall
230 W. 17th Ave.
Columbus, OH 43210-1311
Phone: (614)292-1021

Description: Contains interviews, essays, short fiction, poetry, book reviews, announcements, upcoming events, and articles. **Frequency:** Bimonthly. **Price:** $8/yr. U.S.; $9 in Canada; $10 elsewhere; $1.50 single copies. **Former Title(s):** Women's Studies Review.

★9293★ **Feminist Collections**
University of Wisconsin
430 Memorial Library
728 State St.
Madison, WI 53706
Phone: (608)263-5754
Fax: (608)262-4649

Description: Provides news and information of interest to scholars and researchers, librarians, and others in the field of women's studies. **First published:** 1980. **Frequency:** Quarterly. **Price:** $23/yr.; $43 for libraries and organizations. **ISSN:** 0742-7441.

★9294★ **Feminist Futures Network News**
Center for Women Policy Centers
2000 P St., NW, Ste. 508
Washington, DC 20036
Phone: (202)872-1770

Description: Covers educational equity, work and family issues, violence against women, reproductive rights and health, and women and AIDS.

★9295★ **Feminist Health Fund, Inc.**
PO Box 323
Yellow Springs, OH 45387
Phone: (513)767-4551

Description: Provides information related to assisting economically disadvantaged Ohio women during a serious illness.

★9296★ **Feminist Majority Report**
Fund For the Feminist Majority
1600 Wilson Blvd., No. 704
Arlington, VA 22209
Phone: (703)522-2214
Fax: (703)522-2219

Description: Reports news of the organization. **Frequency:** Quarterly.

★9297★ **Feminist News**
Columbia University
Institute for Research on Women and
    Gender
763 Schermerhorn Extension
New York, NY 10027
Phone: (212)854-1556
Fax: (212)854-7466
Description: Addresses feminist scholarship
and teaching at Columbia University.

★9298★ **FEW's News and Views**
Federally Employed Women, Inc. (FEW)
1400 Eye St. NW, Ste. 425
Washington, DC 20005-2252
Phone: (202)898-0994
Fax: (202)898-0998
Description: Concerned with women's issues,
particularly those involving women in the federal
government. Reports on administration actions
affecting the status of women and analyzes
significant legislation. **First published:** February
1969. **Frequency:** Bimonthly. **Price:** Included in
membership; $12/yr. for nonmembers. **ISSN:**
0895-3619.

★9299★ **Financial Women International—**
    Newsletter
Financial Women International (FWI)
7910 Woodmont Ave., Ste. 1430
Bethesda, MD 20814-3015
Phone: (301)657-8288
Description: Updates members on industry
issues and Financial Women International; provides group, state, and national news. **First
published:** 1985. **Frequency:** 8/yr. **Price:** Included in membership. **Former Title(s):** Financial Women International Exchange, October
1990.

★9300★ **Firework**
Women in the Fire Service
PO Box 5446
Madison, WI 53705
Phone: (608)233-4768
Description: Discusses issues related to fire-
fighting and working in non-traditional jobs.
Frequency: Monthly. **Price:** $25/yr. for individu-
als; $40 for institutions.

★9301★ **The Flame**
Coalition on Women and Religion
Church Council of Greater Seattle
4759 15th Ave. NE
Seattle, WA 98105
Phone: (206)255-7110
Description: Covers religious news and human
rights issues from a feminist viewpoint. Reports
on news of the Coalition, educational opportunities, and national conferences for women's
rights. **First published:** January 1975. **Frequency:** Quarterly. **Price:** $12/yr.

★9302★ **FLASHpoint**
Captive Audience Communications, Corp.
1564 Dixie Way
Melbourne, FL 32935
Phone: (904)736-9163
Description: Addresses medical and social is-
sues such as suicide, birth control, Acquired
Immune Deficiency Syndrome (AIDS), abortion,
and general health concerns. **Frequency:** Quar-
terly. **Price:** $10/yr.

★9303★ **Florida Caucus Communique**
Florida Women's Political Caucus
832 SW 32nd Terrace
Cape Coral, FL 33914
Description: Publicizes information of the Club,
which seeks to involve women in the Florida and
National Caucuses, politics, and women's issues. Presents news on delegations and legislation. **First published:** August 1991.

★9304★ **The Flyer**
General Commission on the Status and Role
    of Women in the United Methodist Church
1200 Davis St.
Evanston, IL 60201
Phone: (708)869-7330
Description: Provides a link between the na-
tional and the local commissions on the status
and role of women in the United Methodist
Church, in the church in general, and in society.
Speaks for a continuing commitment to full and
equal responsibility for women in the total life
and mission of the church. **First published:**
June 1978. **Frequency:** 4/yr. **Price:** $7.50/yr.

★9305★ **Footnotes**
American Sociological Association (ASA)
Committee on the Status of Women
1722 N St., NW
Washington, DC 20036
Phone: (202)833-3410
Fax: (202)785-0146
Description: Focuses on the sociology profes-
sion, the ASA, and the impact of feminist work
in sociology. **Price:** Included in membership;
$15/yr. for nonmembers.

★9306★ **The Foundation for Women's**
    Health in Alabama Newsletter
PO Box 550114
Birmingham, AL 35253
Phone: (205)933-9524
Fax: (205)933-9420
Description: Contains health information, spe-
cial events, legislation, history, conferences,
profiles, features, and news. **Price:** $10/yr. with
membership.

★9307★ **Friends of Ruth**
House of Ruth
501 H St., NE
Washington, DC 20002
Phone: (202)547-6173
Fax: (202)547-1496
Description: Focuses on homeless women,
abused women and their children, and shelter
experiences. **Frequency:** Periodic.

★9308★ **From the State Capitals: Family**
    Relations
Wakeman/Walworth, Inc.
300 N. Washington St., Ste. 204
Alexandria, VA 22314
Phone: (703)549-8606
Fax: (703)549-1372
Description: Covers state activities affecting
family relations issues, including juvenile justice,
marital rights, abortion laws, drug abuse control, child support, adoption, abuse centers,
counseling and shelter programs, and AIDS
testing. Emphasizes legislative and regulatory
measures concerning women's rights. **Frequency:** Weekly. **Price:** $215/yr. **ISSN:** 0741-

3505. Incorporates the former From the State
Capitals: Women and the Law.

★9309★ **Gaea**
Macalester College Geology Department
Association for Women Geoscientists
1600 Grand Ave.
St. Paul, MN 55105-1899
Phone: (612)696-6448
Fax: (612)696-6183
Description: Serves as an exchange of technical and professional information for the purpose
of enhancing the professional growth and advancement of women in the geosciences. Explores opportunities and careers available in the
geosciences and announces workshops and
seminars on job hunting techniques, management skills, and career and life planning. **First
published:** 1981. **Frequency:** Bimonthly. **Price:**
Included in membership.

★9310★ **Gazette of the CSWP**
American Physical Society
Committee on the Status of Women in
    Physics (CSWP)
335 E. 45th St.
New York, NY 10017
Phone: (212)682-7341
Description: Addresses the production, reten-
tion, and career development of women physi-
cists.

★9311★ **Gender and Education**
Kent State University
College of Education
405 White Hall
Kent, OH 44242
Phone: (216)672-2178
Description: Includes regular features on wom-
en's issues, creative corner, and interviews.
Frequency: Quarterly.

★9312★ **GLCA Women's Studies**
    Newsletter
Great Lakes College Association (GLCA)
2929 Plymouth Rd., Ste. 207
Ann Arbor, MI 48105
Phone: (313)761-4833
Fax: (313)761-4833
Description: Covers the women's studies activ-
ities and programs of the Great Lakes Colleges
Association, a consortium of twelve private,
liberal arts colleges.

★9313★ **Gold Star Wives of America—**
    Newsletter
Gold Star Wives of America, Inc.
5325 Beard Ave. S.
Minneapolis, MN 55410
Phone: (612)922-9120
Description: Serves as a medium of communication for widows of military servicemen or of
men who died of a service-related condition.
Publishes information on social security benefits, activities of members, and pending legislation. **First published:** 1955. **Frequency:** Quarterly. **Price:** Included in membership.

★9314★ The GP Reporter
Star Reporter Publishing Company, Inc.
Box 060377, N.D. Sta.
Staten Island, NY 10306-0004
Phone: (718)981-5703
Fax: (718)981-5713
Subtitle: A Paper for Journalists, Advertisers and Media People. **Description:** Focuses on journalism, mass communication, advertising, and marketing "to promote the growth of a professional journalistic approach to the legitimate concerns of Gay men and women." Recurring features include editorials and news briefs. **First published:** June 1982. **Frequency:** Bimonthly. **Price:** $9/yr.

★9315★ Graduate Group for Feminist Studies Newsletter
State University of New York at Buffalo
Graduate Group for Feminist Studies
c/o Law School, North Campus
305 O'Brian Hall
Buffalo, NY 14260
Phone: (716)636-2361
Fax: (716)636-2064
Description: Addresses feminist issues and research. **Frequency:** Distributed in the spring and fall.

★9316★ GS/USA News
Girl Scouts of the USA
830 3rd Ave.
New York, NY 10022
Phone: (212)940-7500
Description: Addresses Girl Scout news (including national and international highlights), profiles, programs, national meetings, membership activities, and other events in Girl Scouting/Girl Guiding. Includes obituaries. **Frequency:** Monthly. **Price:** Available free to members and former members.

★9317★ GWS News
National Association for Girls and Women in Sports (NAGWS)
1900 Association Dr.
Reston, VA 22091
Phone: (703)476-3452
Fax: (703)476-9527
Description: Focuses on women and girls in sports. **Frequency:** Quarterly.

★9318★ Headway
Women's Sports Foundation
342 Madison Ave., Ste. 728
New York, NY 10173
Phone: (212)972-9170
Fax: (212)949-8024
Description: Covers all areas of women in sports, with an emphasis on issues which affect women's participation in or leadership of sports. **Frequency:** Quarterly.

★9319★ Her Own Words: Women Writers
Her Own Words
PO Box 5264
Madison, WI 53705
Phone: (608)271-7083
Description: Provides information about "forgotten" women writers and women's history. **First published:** Fall 1987. **Frequency:** Quarterly. **Price:** $10/yr. **ISSN:** 0898-0241.

★9320★ Her Voice, Our Voices
Women's Alliance
PO Box 21454
Oakland, CA 94620-1454
Phone: (415)658-2949
Frequency: Semiannual.

★9321★ HERI Quarterly
University of California, Los Angeles
Higher Education Research Institute (HERI)
320 Moore Hall
405 Hilgard Ave.
Los Angeles, CA 90024-1521
Phone: (213)825-2709
Fax: (213)206-6293
Description: Discusses student development, equity in education, and gender differences in status attainment among faculty.

★9322★ The Hericane
Sisterspirit, Inc.
1806 Curcor Dr.
Gulfsport, MS 39507
Phone: (601)896-3196
Description: Discusses issues of interest to women in the Gulf Coast area. **Frequency:** Monthly.

★9323★ Herizon Newsletter
Herizon
PO Box 1082
Binghampton, NY 13902
Phone: (607)724-2582
Description: Promotes activities exclusively for women; contains news of interest to lesbians. **Frequency:** Monthly.

★9324★ HERS Newsletter
Hysterectomy Educational Resources and Services Foundation (HERS)
422 Bryn Mawr Ave.
Bala Cynwyd, PA 19004
Phone: (215)667-7757
Description: Features articles on information and services concerning hysterectomy and castration. Covers health issues, and chronicles of individual experiences. **First published:** Spring 1982. **Frequency:** Quarterly. **Price:** $20/yr., U.S.; $22, elsewhere. **ISSN:** 0892-628X.

★9325★ Hispa-News
Hispanic Women's Council
5803 E. Beverly Blvd.
Los Angeles, CA 90022
Phone: (213)725-1657
Description: Addresses information for and about Hispanic women, particularly career and educational development. **Frequency:** Quarterly. **Price:** Free.

★9326★ Hispanic Women's Center Network Newsletter
Hacer, Inc.
611 Broadway, Rm. 814
New York, NY 10012
Phone: (212)594-7640
Fax: (212)967-5546
Description: Reports on career and educational opportunities to Hispanic women. **Frequency:** Quarterly.

★9327★ Homeworking Mothers
Mother's Home Business Network
PO Box 423
East Meadow, NY 11554
Phone: (516)997-7394
Fax: (516)997-0839
Subtitle: The Mother's Home Business Network Newsletter. **Description:** Aims to inform and inspire mothers who choose to work at home. Explains how to get started in specific businesses and offers articles written by women who successfully combine motherhood with a money-making home business. **First published:** July 1984. **Frequency:** Quarterly. **Price:** Included in membership.

★9328★ Homosexual Information Center—Newsletter
Homosexual Information Center
115 Monroe St.
Bossier City, LA 71111
Description: Provides information on homosexuality, with articles on sexual freedom, freedom of the press, and civil rights. Serves as one of the information sources the Center offers to media, legislative bodies, libraries, and the helping professions. **First published:** 1965. **Frequency:** Periodic. **Price:** Free. **Former Title(s):** Tangents.

★9329★ Hook-up News and Views
National Hook-Up of Black Women, Inc.
5117 S. University Ave.
Chicago, IL 60615
Phone: (312)643-5866
Description: Addresses issues of concern to Black women in public service or political office.

★9330★ Hot Flash
National Action Forum for Midlife and Older Women
PO Box 816
Stony Brook, NY 11790-0609
Subtitle: A newsletter for mid-life and older women. **Description:** Addresses the health and social concerns of both mid-life and older women. **First published:** Summer 1981. **Frequency:** Quarterly. **Price:** $25/yr.

★9331★ Illinois Right to Life Committee—News
Illinois Right to Life Committee
343 S. Dearborn St., Ste. 1217
Chicago, IL 60604
Phone: (312)922-1918
Fax: (202)541-3054
Subtitle: All that is necessary for the triumph of evil is that good men do nothing. **Description:** Focuses on the issue of abortion from a right-to-life perspective. Discusses legislation, personal accounts, medical data, and living wills. Alerts those interested in the Committee's activities. **Price:** $7.50/yr.

★9332★ Illinois Women's Advocate and Legislative Watch
Midwest Women's Center
53 W. Jackson, Rm. 1015
Chicago, IL 60604
Phone: (312)922-8530
Fax: (312)922-8931
Description: Reports on state and local legislation related to employment, reproductive rights,

child welfare, and domestic violence. **Frequency:** Quarterly. **Price:** $35/yr.

★9333★ *Images*
Conference for Catholic Lesbians (CCL)
PO Box 436
Planetarium Sta.
New York, NY 10024
Phone: (718)921-0463
Description: Provides a forum on current Catholic and lesbian issues. **Frequency:** Quarterly.
Price: Free.

★9334★ *Imprints*
Birth & Life Bookstore
7001 Alonzo Ave. NW
PO Box 70625
Seattle, WA 98107
Phone: (206)789-4444
Description: Publishes reviews of books on childbirth, child care, family planning, breastfeeding, and women's health issues. Reports on forthcoming books, new editions, and paperbacks. Contains an annotated list of books available from the Bookstore. Provides an order form and information on book and shipping costs. **First published:** April 1980. **Frequency:** 3-4/yr. **Price:** $3/6 issues; free to Bookstore customers.

★9335★ *In Brief*
National Organization for Women (NOW)
Legal Defense and Education Fund (LDEF)
99 Hudson St., 12th Fl.
New York, NY 10013
Phone: (212)925-6635
Fax: (212)226-1066
Description: Focuses on the achievement of equality for women and girls. **Frequency:** Bimonthly.

★9336★ *Institute for Research on Women and Gender—Newsletter*
Institute for Research on Women and Gender
Stanford University
Serra House
Stanford, CA 94305-8640
Phone: (415)723-1994
Fax: (415)725-0374
Description: Reports on the Institute's programs, publications, research, and other activities concerning women. **First published:** 1975. **Frequency:** Quarterly. **Price:** $8/yr.

★9337★ *Institute for the Study of Women and Men in Society Newsletter*
University of Southern California
Institute for the Study of Women and Men in Society (ISWM)
Louise Kerckhoff Hall
734 W. Adams Blvd.
Los Angeles, CA 90007
Phone: (213)743-3683
Description: Reports on feminist research, professional networking, and scholarly exchange in the area of gender in culture and social structure. **Frequency:** 3/yr.

★9338★ *Intensive Caring Unlimited*
Intensive Caring Unlimited
910 Bent Ln.
Philadelphia, PA 19118
Phone: (215)233-4723
Fax: (215)233-5795
Description: Provides information and support for parents of high risk and premature babies. Deals with prematurity, hospitalization, developmental delays, high-risk pregnancy, and grieving, as well as other general parenting topics. Includes articles written by parents and professionals. **First published:** May 1983. **Frequency:** Bimonthly. **Price:** $8/yr., U.S.; $12 for professionals or in Canada.

★9339★ *The International Alliance—Newsletter*
The International Alliance
83 Phillips St.
Boston, MA 02114
Phone: (617)523-0615
Description: Offers information on network exchanges for women, summarizes meetings and conferences, and profiles members. **First published:** 1982. **Frequency:** 6/yr. **Price:** Included in membership. **Former Title(s):** The National Alliance.

★9340★ *International Women's Fishing Association Newsletter*
International Women's Fishing Association
PO Drawer 33480
Palm Beach, FL 33480
Description: Promotes fishing and competition fishing between women. **Frequency:** Bimonthly.

★9341★ *International Women's Writing Guild—Network*
International Women's Writing Guild
Box 810, Gracie Sta.
New York, NY 10028
Phone: (212)737-7536
Description: Carries a variety of items for women who write both for personal growth and professionally. Announces opportunities for retreat, study, publication, and awards. **First published:** 1978. **Frequency:** Bimonthly. **Price:** Included in membership. **ISSN:** 1044-1476.

★9342★ *IROW News*
State University of New York at Albany
Institute for Research on Women (IROW)
Social Sciences 324
Albany, NY 12222
Phone: (518)442-4670
Description: Discusses interdisciplinary research and scholarship for women faculty. **First published:** 1987. **Frequency:** Semiannual.

★9343★ *ISA Newsletter*
International Society of Women Airline Pilots (ISA)
PO Box 66268
Chicago, IL 60666
Description: Serves as an idea and information exchange for women airline pilots. Reports on Society activities and upcoming meetings. Provides industry news and information on job opportunities. **First published:** 1978. **Frequency:** Quarterly. **Price:** Included in membership.

★9344★ *ITROW News*
Towson State University
Institute for Teaching and Research on Women (ITROW)
Baltimore, MD 21204
Phone: (301)830-2334
Description: Contains articles on initiatives taken by the Institute and a bulletin board listing job vacancies, calls for papers, and more. **Frequency:** Quarterly. **Price:** $5/yr.

★9345★ *Just for the Record*
PO Box 3768
New Orleans, LA 70177
Phone: (504)943-3067
Subtitle: New Orleans Gay and Lesbian Television Show. **Description:** Covers issues and events of interest to the gay and lesbian community, such as AIDS, alcohol/drug abuse, equality legislation, arts, and fellowship. **Price:** Included in membership.

★9346★ *Justice for Women Newsletter*
United Presbyterian Church, USA Women's Unit
Justice for Women
100 Witherspoon St.
Louisville, KY 40202
Phone: (212)870-2019
Description: Promotes women to participate in the life, mission, and leadership of the church. **Frequency:** Quarterly.

★9347★ *The Kappan*
Alpha Delta Kappa
1615 W. 92nd St.
Kansas City, MO 64114
Phone: (816)363-5525
Description: Relates to women educators actively engaged in teaching, administration, or some specialized field of the teaching profession.

★9348★ *Key-Note*
Harmony, Inc.
R.F.D. 1, Box 142
East Calais, VT 05650
Description: Presents news and information on the International Organization of Women Barbershop Singers. Announces events, contests, conventions, and meetings. Discusses singing and performance techniques and training. **Frequency:** 4/yr. **Price:** Included in membership; $10/yr. for nonmembers. **ISSN:** 0899-0301.

★9349★ *Kids & Career: New Ideas and Options for Mothers*
Mother's Home Business Network
PO Box 423
East Meadow, NY 11554
Phone: (516)997-7394
Fax: (516)997-0839
Description: Provides mothers with information on home business and other flexible work options, including flex-time, part-time, and job sharing. **First published:** 1988. **Frequency:** Semiannual. **Price:** Included in membership.

★9350★ La Bella Figura
PO Box 411223
San Francisco, CA 94141-1223
Description: Offers literary items of interest to Italian-American women, particularly lesbians. **Frequency:** Quarterly.

★9351★ Lambda Update
Lambda Legal Defense & Education Fund, Inc.
666 Broadway
New York, NY 10012-2317
Phone: (212)995-8585
Description: Publishes news of Lambda, the oldest and largest legal organization in the U.S., which pursues test-case litigation to counter discrimination against gay men, lesbians, and people with HIV/AIDS. Features the Fund's educational programs and publications to raise public awareness of gay legal rights. Devoted to the nationwide effort to counter AIDS-related discrimination. Provides updates on recent state and federal legislation affecting gay civil rights and current Lambda legal cases. **First published:** 1976 **Frequency:** 3/yr. **Frequency:** 3/yr. **Price:** $40/yr. for members. **Former Title(s):** *Lambda Legal Defense & Education Fund—Newsletter.*

★9352★ Latin American Professional Women's Newsletter
Latin American Professional Women's Association
3516 N. Broadway
Los Angeles, CA 90031
Phone: (213)227-9060
Description: Focuses on cultural, educational, and vocational advancement for Latin American women.

★9353★ Lavender Letter
PO Box 1527
Harrisburg, PA 17105
Phone: (717)232-1201
Description: Provides a monthly calendar of events for lesbians in the central Pennsylvania area. **Price:** $10/yr.

★9354★ Lavender Morning
PO Box 729
Kalamazoo, MI 49005
Phone: (616)388-5656
Description: Provides information of interest to lesbians in the southwestern Michigan area. **Frequency:** Monthly. **Price:** $12.50/yr.

★9355★ Legacy
The Bethune Museum and Archives National Historic Site
1318 Vermont Ave., NW
Washington, DC 20005
Phone: (202)332-1233
Fax: (202)332-6319
Description: Contains information and events documenting Black women's history. **Frequency:** Quarterly. **Price:** Free.

★9356★ Lesbian Herstory Archives Newsletter
Lesbian Herstory Educational Foundation, Inc.
PO Box 1258
New York, NY 10116
Phone: (212)874-7232
Description: Provides news of Foundation events, activities, and source material. Lists bibliographies and reviews lesbian cultural material. **First published:** 1975. **Frequency:** Periodic. **Price:** Free; donation requested.

★9357★ A Lesbian Position—Newsletter
A Lesbian Position
PO Box 9205
New Haven, CT 06533
Description: Offers articles and news written "by, for, and about lesbians." **First published:** April 1982. **Frequency:** Monthly. **Price:** $15/yr.

★9358★ Lex Vitae
American United for Life
343 S. Dearborn, Ste. 1804
Chicago, IL 60604
Phone: (312)263-5029
Subtitle: A Reporter on Life and Death Issues in the Law. **Description:** Discusses legislation and current court cases involving abortion, euthanasia, infanticide, in vitro fertilization, and genetic engineering. **First published:** 1977. **Frequency:** Quarterly. **Price:** Donation requested.

★9359★ LFL Reports: The Newsletter of Libertarians for Life
Libertarians for Life (LFL)
13424 Hathaway Dr.
Wheaton, MD 20906
Phone: (301)460-4141
Description: Concerned with the libertarian and pro-life movements, particularly the principles and policies of the group, who contend that "dependent children, born and unborn, have the right to be provided for and protected by their parents." Recurring features include the column titled From Doris, written by the national coordinator. **First published:** August 1981. **Frequency:** Occasional. **Price:** Donation requested. **ISSN:** 0882-116X.

★9360★ Licensing Newspaper
Religious Coalition for Abortion Rights
Women of Color Partnership Program
100 Maryland Ave., NE, Ste. 307
Washington, DC 20002
Description: Informs African American, Latin American, Asian Pacific American, Native American, and other women of color in the United States about reproductive rights issues. **Frequency:** 2/yr.

★9361★ Life-Guardian
Birthright International
PO Box 98361
Atlanta, GA 30359-2061
Phone: (404)451-2273
Fax: (404)455-3913
Description: Provides information on programs operated by group members of the organization to help pregnant women find alternatives to abortion. Discusses issues involved with childbirth and parenting and offers assistance to groups wishing to form Birthright chapters. **First**

published: Autumn 1971. **Frequency:** Bimonthly. **Price:** Included in membership.

★9362★ Life Insight
National Council of Catholic Bishops (NCCB)
Secretariat for Pro-Life Activities
3211 4th St. NE
Washington, DC 20017-1194
Phone: (202)541-3070
Fax: (202)541-3054
Subtitle: The Natural Choice is Life. **Description:** Addresses the issue of abortion from a pro-life point of view; discusses the morality behind the procedure and the right to life of unborn children. Presents information on forms of abortion, such as the drug RU-486, and studies on parental involvement laws.

★9363★ LifeDate
Lutherans for Life
PO Box 819
Benton, AR 72015
Phone: (501)794-2212
Fax: (501)794-1437
Description: Devoted to "guarding and upholding the dignity and worth of all human life." Concerned about the care of children, unwed mothers, handicapped persons, the poor, and the repressed, but focuses special attention on the lives of preborn and newborn children. Covers issues such as abortion, adoption, euthanasia, infanticide, church policies and policy-making, and counseling and research related to these issues. **First published:** 1981. **Frequency:** Quarterly. **Price:** Included in membership. Replaces the former Lutherans for Life—Newsletter.

★9364★ Lifeletter
Ad Hoc Committee in Defense of Life
1187 National Press Bldg.
Washington, DC 20045
Phone: (202)347-8686
Description: Disseminates information opposing abortion and euthanasia and monitors lobbying efforts for legislation against abortion and euthanasia. Seeks to have the Roe vs. Wade decision of 1973 repealed. **Frequency:** 12/yr. **Price:** $34.95/yr.

★9365★ Listen Real Loud
American Friends Service Committee (AFSC)
1501 Cherry St.
Philadelphia, PA 19102
Phone: (215)241-7181
Description: Covers the women's liberation movement internationally, including a section on women and global corporations in every issue. Contains resources and action alerts to help build networks and a global feminist movement. **Frequency:** Quarterly. **Price:** $10/yr.

★9366★ Mainstay, Inc. Newsletter
Mainstay, Inc.
PO Box 816
Marshall, MN 56258
Phone: (507)532-1546
Description: Informs women of career development services offered by the Agency.

★9367★ **Making Success Happen Newsletter**
National Association of Black Women Entrepreneurs
PO Box 1375
Detroit, MI 48231
Phone: (313)341-7400
Fax: (313)342-3433
Description: Acts as a national support system for Black businesswomen in the U.S. and focuses on the unique problems they face. Promotes the Association's objective to enhance business, professional, and technical development of both present and future Black businesswomen. **First published:** 1978. **Frequency:** Bimonthly. **Price:** Included in membership.

★9368★ **Mama Bears News and Notes**
6536 Telegraph Ave.
Oakland, CA 94609
Description: Topics include: Reviews of lesbian fiction and non-fiction and other women's and children's books, spirituality, recovery, psychology, women's studies, and Third World women. Features non-fiction by contributing authors. **Frequency:** 6/yr. **Price:** $6/yr.

★9369★ **MANA—Newsletter**
Mexican American Women's National Association (MANA)
1030 15th St. NW, Ste. 468
Washington, DC 20005
Phone: (202)898-2036
Fax: (202)371-1405
Description: Provides news of the Association, which focuses on providing leadership and support for Hispanic women. Honors important contributions made by Hispanic women. Spotlights issues of concern, such as legislation on child care, health equity, economic equity, and civil rights. Publicizes the Association's advocacy programs. **Frequency:** Quarterly. **Price:** Included in membership.

★9370★ **Manager's Legal Bulletin**
Alexander Hamilton Institute, Inc.
197 W. Spring Valley Ave.
Maywood, NJ 07607-1700
Description: Discusses legal issues of employment layoffs, sexual preference and disability discrimination, and sexual harassment claims. **ISSN:** 0889-4493.

★9371★ **Marketing to Women**
Marketing to Women, Inc.
33 Broad St.
Boston, MA 02109
Phone: (617)723-4337
Fax: (617)723-7107
Edited by: E. Janice Leeming. **Description:** Discusses market studies aimed at women. Covers such topics as demographics, women's attitudes, family issues, consumer products, fashion, media preferences, health care, employment, recreation, food/nutrition, shopping, working women, travel, and reproduction. **Frequency:** Monthly. **Price:** $230/yr. for individuals and $200 for institutions, USC; $255 and $225 elsewhere. **Former Title(s):** Woman Scope.

★9372★ **Mary Ingraham Bunting Institute—Newsletter**
Radcliffe College
Mary Ingraham Bunting Institute
34 Concord Ave.
Cambridge, MA 02138
Phone: (617)495-8212
Description: Interviews and reports on the fellows, alumnae, and staff of the Bunting Institute, an advanced center for studies by women. Includes research by women artists, writers, scientists, and practitioners of varied arts who are or have been fellows at the Institute. Features interviews, news of research, reports of meetings, and notices of publications available. **First published:** 1983. **Frequency:** Annual. **Price:** Free.

★9373★ **The Matrimonial Strategist**
New York Law Publishing Company
Leader Publications
111 8th Ave.
New York, NY 10011
Phone: (212)741-8300
Fax: (212)463-5523
Description: Reports on legal strategy and substantive developments in the area of matrimonial law, including such topics as tax considerations, custody, visitation, division of property, and valuation. **First published:** February 1983. **Frequency:** Monthly. **Price:** $145/yr., U.S. and Canada; $165 elsewhere. **ISSN:** 0736-4881.

★9374★ **Media Report to Women**
Communication Research Associates, Inc.
10606 Mantz Rd.
Silver Spring, MD 20903-1228
Phone: (301)445-3230
Description: Discusses concerns of media women and news of current women's media events. Carries documents and reports on women's actions worldwide in areas such as devising new communications structures, the employment of women in the media, and the portrayal of women in the media. Focuses on how to increase the effectiveness od media to keep the public aware of women's news and information. **First published:** 1972. **Frequency:** Bimonthly. **Price:** $35/yr. for individuals; $50 for institutions. **ISSN:** 0145-9651.

★9375★ **Milwaukee 9to5 Newsletter**
238 W. Wisconsin, Ste. 806
Milwaukee, WI 53203
Phone: (414)272-7795
Fax: (414)272-2870
Description: Informs members of chapter efforts to increase salaries and the working conditions of office workers.

★9376★ **Missionary Magazine**
African Methodist Episcopal Church (AME) Women's Missionary Society
1134 11th St., NW
Washington, DC 20001
Phone: (202)371-8886
Fax: (202)371-8820
Description: Informs members of the Society's efforts to empower women seeking to ''break the cycle of poverty and second-class citizenship.''

★9377★ **Mom's Apple Pie**
Lesbian Mothers' National Defense Fund
PO Box 21567
Seattle, WA 98111
Phone: (206)325-2643
Description: Reports on lesbian custody cases, current legislation, alternative insemination, adoption, and other issues surrounding lesbian parenting. **First published:** 1974. **Frequency:** Quarterly. **Price:** Included in membership; $15/yr. for nonmembers.

★9378★ **MOTC'S Notebook**
National Organization of Mothers of Twins Clubs, Inc. (MOTC)
PO Box 23188
Albuquerque, NM 87192-1188
Phone: (505)275-0955
Description: Contains news of interest to the Organization, research reports, and articles of general interest to mothers of twins. **First published:** 1960. **Frequency:** Quarterly. **Price:** Included in membership; $15/yr. for nonmembers. **ISSN:** 8756-9965.

★9379★ **Ms. Foundation for Women Newsletter**
Ms. Foundation for Women
141 5th Ave., Ste. 6S
New York, NY 10010-7105
Phone: (212)353-8580
Fax: (212)475-4217
Description: Reports efforts the foundation has made in the areas of funding and assistance to women's self-help initiatives, changes in public consciousness, law, philanthropy, and social policy, and the direction of resources toward activities that discourage racial, class, age, sexual orientation, and cultural barriers.

★9380★ **Mujer Imagen de Vida**
c/o WORLD
PO Box 11535
Oakland, CA 94611
Phone: (510)658-6930
Description: Spanish-language newsletter with articles written for and by HIV-positive latina women. **First published:** 1991.

★9381★ **The Murray Research Center News**
Radcliffe College
Henry A. Murray Research Center
10 Garden St.
Cambridge, MA 02138
Phone: (617)495-8140
Fax: (617)495-8422
Description: Reports on the Center's research initiatives and archival collection of social and behavioral research data. The center houses data with an emphasis on the lives of American women. **Frequency:** 2/yr.

★9382★ **NAACOG Newsletter**
NAACOG
409 12th St. SW
Washington, DC 20024-2191
Phone: (202)638-0026
Description: Provides information on developments and activities regarding obstetrics, gynecology, and neonatal nursing. **First published:** 1967. **Frequency:** Monthly. **Price:** $30/yr.; $5 per back issue copy. **ISSN:** 0889-0579.

★9383★ **NABCO News**
National Alliance of Breast Cancer
Organizations (NABCO)
1180 Avenue of the Americas, 2nd Fl.
New York, NY 10036
Phone: (212)719-0154
Fax: (212)768-8828
Description: Furnishes information on all aspects of breast cancer and affordable detection and treatment. **Frequency:** Bimonthly. **Price:** $40 for individuals; $75 for nonprofit organizations; $150 for businesses.

★9384★ **NABWA News**
National Association of Black Women
Attorneys (NABWA)
3711 Macomb St., NW
Washington, DC 20016
Phone: (202)966-9693
Fax: (202)244-6648
Description: Focuses on Black women and all women in the legal profession. **Frequency:** Bimonthly. **Price:** Free to members.

★9385★ **NAMBAW News**
National Association of M.B.A. Women
(NAMBAW)
7701 Georgia Ave., NW
Washington, DC 20012
Phone: (202)723-1267
Description: Offers information on career opportunities, networking, and scholarship opportunities. **Frequency:** Bimonthly.

★9386★ **NAPSAC News**
International Association of Parents and
Professionals for Safe Alternatives in
Childbirth (NAPSAC)
Rt. 1, Box 646
Marble Hill, MO 63764
Phone: (314)238-2010
Description: Promotes the philosophy of natural childbirth and responsible patient self-determination and independence. Covers such topics as midwifery, home birth, breastfeeding, obstetrics, medical economics and politics, legal aspects of maternal and child health care, hospitals, and birth centers. **First published:** March 1976. **Frequency:** Quarterly. **Price:** $20/yr., U.S.; $22 elsewhere. **ISSN:** 0192-1233.

★9387★ **NARAL Newsletter**
National Abortion Rights Action League
(NARAL)
1101 14th St. NW
Washington, DC 20005
Phone: (202)408-4600
Fax: (202)408-4698
Description: Monitors legislative news regarding the issue of abortion. Contains organizational news on various NARAL affiliates and covers action taken by NARAL to help keep abortion safe and legal. **First published:** 1975. **Frequency:** Quarterly. **Price:** Included in membership. **ISSN:** 0742-7506.

★9388★ **National Association of Women Artists News**
National Association of Women Artists
41 Union Sq. W., No. 906
New York, NY 10003
Phone: (212)675-1616
Description: Presents news of women in the art field. **Price:** Included in membership.

★9389★ **National Association of Women Business Owners—Statement**
National Association of Women Business
Owners
600 S. Federal St., Ste. 400
Chicago, IL 60605
Phone: (312)922-0465
Fax: (312)922-2734
Description: Serves as a forum for women business owners to communicate and share experiences with others and to use their collective influence to broaden opportunities for women in business. Monitors trends and legislative developments affecting women in business, and provides news of the Association's services and activities on the behalf of women business owners. **Frequency:** Bimonthly. **Price:** Included in membership.

★9390★ **National Association of Women Lawyers—President's Newsletter**
National Association of Women Lawyers
American Bar Center
750 N. Lake Shore Dr.
Chicago, IL 60611
Phone: (312)988-6186
Description: Seeks to keep members up-to-date with the rulings and meetings of the Association. Announces appointments made by the president and upcoming national and regional meetings. **Frequency:** Quarterly. **Price:** Included in membership.

★9391★ **National Association of Women's Centers—Connections Newsletter**
National Association of Women's Centers
c/o Ann Hill Beuf
Cedar Crest College
100 College Dr.
Allentown, PA 18104
Phone: (215)437-4471

★9392★ **National Center for Women and Retirement Research Newsletter**
National Center for Women and Retirement
Research (NCWRR)
Long Island University
Southampton Campus
Southampton, NY 11968
Toll-free: 800-426-7386
Fax: (516)283-4678
Description: Addresses aging issues of concern to women. **Frequency:** Quarterly.

★9393★ **National Clearinghouse on Marital and Date Rape—Newsletter**
National Clearinghouse on Marital & Date
Rape
2325 Oak St.
Berkeley, CA 94708
Phone: (415)524-1582
Description: Edited by a consultant, speaker, and researcher of marital/date rape; functions as part of a campaign to protect women by changing current rape laws. Documents marital/date rape trials, court decisions, legislation, statutes, and related news. Reports on cohabitation and date rape, as well. **First published:** 1982. **Frequency:** Quarterly. **Price:** $5/yr. **Former Title(s):** *National Clearinghouse on Marital Rape—Newsletter.*

★9394★ **National Coalition Against Domestic Violence Voice**
National Coalition Against Domestic Violence
(NCADV)
PO Box 34103
Washington, DC 20043-4103
Phone: (202)638-6388
Description: Reports on the coalition's efforts to end violence against women and children. Also informs readers of urban and rural programs that support and involve women from a variety of backgrounds. **Frequency:** Quarterly.

★9395★ **National Coalition of 100 Black Women—Statement**
National Coalition of 100 Black Women
50 Rockefeller Plaza, Ste. 46
New York, NY 10020
Phone: (212)974-6140
Description: Reports on the activities and achievements of Black women involved with such issues as economic development, health, employment, education, voting, housing, criminal justice, the status of Black families, and the arts. Comments on the problems encountered by Blacks in cities and operates as a forum for the exchange of ideas on improving the conditions for Black communities. **Frequency:** Periodic. **Price:** Included in membership.

★9396★ **National Committee on Pay Equity—Newsnotes**
National Committee on Pay Equity (NCPE)
1126 16th St. NW, Rm. 422
Washington, DC 20036
Phone: (202)331-7343
Fax: (202)331-7406
Description: Covers efforts to eliminate sex- and race-based wage discrimination and achieve pay equity.

★9397★ **National Conference of Women's Bar Associations Newsletter**
National Conference of Women's Bar
Associations (NCWBA)
PO Box 77
Edenton, NC 27932-0077
Phone: (919)482-8202
Fax: (919)482-7642
Description: Provides a nationwide forum for the concerns and interests of women lawyers. Reports on the NCWBA's efforts to promote the advancement of women in law. **Frequency:** Quarterly.

★9398★ **National Council of Women of the United States—Bulletin**
National Council of Women of the United
States
777 United Nations Plaza
New York, NY 10017
Phone: (212)697-1278
Fax: (212)972-0164
Description: Promotes the participation of women in decision making at both the national and international level. Reports on Council programs and activities of member organizations. **Frequency:** Quarterly. **Price:** $15/yr.

★9399★ National Displaced Homemakers Network, Inc.—Network News
National Displaced Homemakers Network, Inc.
1411 K St. NW, Ste. 930
Washington, DC 20005
Phone: (202)628-6767
Fax: (202)628-0123

Description: Serves displaced homemakers who, through divorce, separation, widowhood, ineligibility for public assistance, or other crises, have lost their source of economic support. Also provides information for service providers and agencies working with displaced homemakers. Covers legislation, regional news, fundraising, issues of divorce and widowhood, employment, and continuing and vocational education opportunities and conferences. **First published:** 1979. **Frequency:** Quarterly. **Price:** Included in membership.

★9400★ National Foundation for Women Business Owners Newsletter
National Foundation for Women Business Owners
1825 I St., NW, Ste. 800
Washington, DC 20006
Phone: (202)833-1854
Fax: (202)833-1938

Description: Covers the Foundation's efforts to expand the horizons of women business owners. Aimed at strenghthening leadership and management skills. **Frequency:** Quarterly.

★9401★ National Grange Newsletter
National Grange
Department of Women's Activities
15 Meadowlark Rd.
West Simsbury, CT 06092
Phone: (203)658-2855

Description: Reports on the Department's efforts to provide women with opportunities to learn, lead, and grow as individuals.

★9402★ The National Museum of Women in the Art News
1250 New York Ave., NW
Washington, DC 20005
Phone: (202)783-5000

Description: Chronicles contributions of women to the history of art. **Frequency:** Quarterly.

★9403★ The National Report on Work & Family
Millin Publications, Inc.
Buraff Publications
1350 Connecticut Ave. NW
Washington, DC 20036
Phone: (202)862-0993
Fax: (202)862-0999

Description: Examines the changes in family structure and their impact on the workplace. Covers parental leave, elder care, care for sick children, flexible worktime, and other related issues. **First published:** December 15, 1987. **Frequency:** Biweekly. **Price:** $475/yr. **ISSN:** 0896-3002.

★9404★ National Right to Life News
National Right to Life Committee
419 7th St., Ste. 500
Washington, DC 20004
Phone: (202)626-8820
Fax: (202)347-3668

Description: Discusses pro-life issues, abortion, and euthanasia. **First published:** 1973. **Frequency:** Semimonthly. **Price:** $16/yr.

★9405★ National Rural Electric Women's Association—Newsline
National Rural Electric Cooperative Association (NRECA)
National Rural Electric Women's Association (NREWA)
1800 Massachusets Ave, NW
Washington, DC 20036
Phone: (202)257-9537

Description: Focuses on efforts to promote consumer and community understanding of rural electric cooperatives. Concerned with NRECA's legislative, political, and communication objectives. **Frequency:** Quarterly.

★9406★ National STOPP News
Stop Planned Parenthood, Inc. (STOPP)
PO Box 8
LaGrangeville, NY 12540
Phone: (914)452-6209

Description: Scrutinizes Planned Parenthood programs and philosophy from a pro-life perspective. Covers Supreme Court decisions and pertinent legislation and contains notices of conventions and workshops. **Price:** $10/yr. suggested donation.

★9407★ National Update
Moore College of Art
Women's Caucus for Art
20th and the Parkway
Philadelphia, PA 10103
Phone: (215)854-0922

Description: Includes articles on art history; exhibition and book reviews; employment information, exhibitions, and grants; and chapter and membership activities. **Frequency:** Quarterly. **Price:** Included in membership.

★9408★ National Women's Hall of Fame Newsletter
National Women's Hall of Fame
76 Fall St.
PO Box 335
Seneca Falls, NY 13148
Phone: (315)568-8060

Description: Covers activities of the Hall of Fame, which honors the achievements of extraordinary American women.

★9409★ National Women's Health Network—Network News
National Women's Health Network
1325 G St. NW
Washington, DC 20005
Phone: (202)347-1140
Fax: (202)347-1168

Description: Carries timely health information and medical alerts for women. Emphasizes matters affecting reproductive rights and occupational and environmental health. Reports federal health policies and local health actions affecting women, including the aged, the poor, minorities, and others termed medically neglect-

ed. **Frequency:** Bimonthly. **Price:** Included in membership. **ISSN:** 8755-867X. **Former Title(s):** National Women's Health Network—Newsletter.

★9410★ National Women's Law Center Update
National Women's Law Center
1616 P St., NW
Washington, DC 20036
Phone: (202)328-5160
Fax: (202)328-5137

Description: Contains summaries of news of interest to women in the legal profession. **Frequency:** Quarterly. **Price:** Free to members.

★9411★ The NAWIC Image
National Association of Women in Construction (NAWIC)
327 S. Adams St.
Ft. Worth, TX 76104
Phone: (817)877-5551

Description: Fosters career advancement for women in construction. Publishes Association news and information on legislation affecting the industry. **First published:** 1967. **Frequency:** Monthly. **Price:** $15/yr., U.S.; $25, Canada.

★9412★ NAWJ Counterbalance
National Association of Women Judges (NAWJ)
300 Newport Ave.
Williamsburg, VA 23187-8798
Phone: (804)253-2000
Fax: (804)220-0449

Description: Promotes the Association, which provides a "supportive network providing women judges with an opportunity to discuss common problems and gain strength, courage, and reassurance, as well as renewed energy and dedication, from our sisters on the bench." Provides information on Association activities, conventions, and various pertinent issues, including gender bias in the courts. Includes news of members and notices of appointments, elevations, and elections. **First published:** 1980. **Frequency:** 3/yr. **Price:** Included in membership. **Former Title(s):** NAWJ News and Announcements.

★9413★ NCAWE News
National Council of Administrative Women in Education (NCAWE)
2335 Chatworth Blvd.
San Diego, CA 92111
Phone: (619)233-3121

Description: Contains information of interest to women in educational administration. **Frequency:** Semiannual.

★9414★ NCDBW Newsletter
National Clearinghouse for the Defense of Battered Women (NCDBW)
125 S. 9th St., Ste. 302
Philadelphia, PA 19107
Phone: (215)351-0010
Fax: (215)351-0779

Description: Aimed towards those concerned with the legal defense of battered women.

**★9415★ NCSL Women's Network—
Network News**
National Conference of State Legislatures
(NCSL)
Women's Network
1560 Broadway, Ste. 700
Denver, CO 80202
Phone: (303)830-2200
Fax: (303)863-8003

Description: Focuses on the efforts to elevate
women's positions within the NCSL and their
state legislative bodies. Also reports on legislation that will support women and their families.
Frequency: 3/yr.

★9416★ NETWORC
Rutgers University
Institute for Research on Women
27 Clifton Ave.
Douglass College Campus
New Brunswick, NJ 08903
Phone: (908)932-9072
Fax: (908)932-1180

Description: Contains information on women's
studies and gender study activities at Rutgers
University. **First published:** 1985. **Frequency:**
2/yr. **Price:** Free.

★9417★ New Beginnings
La Leche League International, Inc.
PO Box 1209
Franklin Park, IL 60131-8209
Phone: (708)455-7730
Toll-free: 800-LA-LECHE

Description: Covers breastfeeding, childbirth
and nutrition, and child care in relation to
breastfeeding. **First published:** 1958. **Frequency:** Bimonthly. **Price:** Included in membership.
Former Title(s): *La Leche League News*, December 1984.

**★9418★ New Jersey Network on
Adolescent Pregnancy—EXCHANGES**
Rutgers University School of Social Work
Center for Community Education
New Jersey Network on Adolescent
  Programs
73 Easton Ave.
New Brunswick, NJ 08903
Phone: (908)932-8636
Fax: (908)932-7508

Description: Discusses unwanted pregnancy,
teen parenting, birth control, and related issues.
First published: 1979. **Frequency:** Quarterly.

★9419★ The New National Perspective
National Association for Family Day Care
725 15th St., Ste. 505
Washington, DC 20005
Phone: (202)347-3300

Description: Serves as a national voice for
family day care providers, who provide child
care services in a home setting. Monitors
developments pertaining to day care operations
and promotes quality standards. **First published:** Family day care and group day care
providers and support agencies. **Frequency:**
Bimonthly. **Price:** Included in membership.

★9420★ New Women/New Church
Women's Ordination Conference
PO Box 2693
Fairfax, VA 22031
Phone: (703)352-1006
Fax: (703)352-5181

Description: Provides coverage of efforts to
advance the movement to ordain women in the
Roman Catholic church. **Frequency:** Bimonthly.

**★9421★ Newcomb College Center for
Research on Women Newsletter**
Tulane University
Newcomb College Center for Research on
  Women
Caroline Richardson Bldg.
New Orleans, LA 70118-5683
Phone: (504)865-5238

Description: Focuses on the efforts to promote
scholarly research about women into the Tulane
curriculum.

★9422★ News on Women in Government
State University of New York at Albany
Center for Women in Government
Draper Hall, Rm. 302
135 Western Ave.
Albany, NY 12222
Phone: (518)442-3900
Fax: (518)442-5232

Description: News on women and minorities
employed by the government. **Frequency:** Irregular. **Price:** Free.

**★9423★ Newsletter of the Geographic
Perspectives on Women Specialty Group**
Association of American Geographers
Specialty Group on Geographic Perspectives
  on Women
Rutgers University
Department of Geography
Lucy Stone Hall
New Brunswick, NJ 08903
Phone: (201)932-4013

Description: Discusses topics relating to wom-
en and gender.

★9424★ 9to5 Newsletter
9to5, National Association of Working
  Women
614 Superior Ave. NW, Ste. 852
Cleveland, OH 44113
Phone: (216)566-9308

Description: Addresses concerns and rights of
women office workers, covering such topics as
pay equity, job stress, child care, proper use of
office technology, and respect among employees and from employers. Reports on the Association's activities, which include legislative publicity, and health and safety campaigns. **First
published:** 1973. **Frequency:** 5/yr. **Price:** Included in membership; $25/yr. for nonmembers.
Former Title(s): *Newsletter for Working Wom-
en*, March/April 1982.

★9425★ NIW Newsletter
National Institute of Womanhood (NIW)
4612 Nottingham Dr.
Washington, DC 20815
Phone: (301)654-8034

Description: Provides information pertaining to
"authentic womanhood and affecting the dignity
of women." Recurring features include a calendar of events, reports of meetings, book reviews, and notices of publications available.
First published: January 1991. **Frequency:**
4/yr. **Price:** Included in membership.

★9426★ NIWC Network News
National Istitute for Women of Color (NIWC)
1301 20th St., NW
Washington, DC 20036
Phone: (202)296-2661
Fax: (212)296-8140

Description: Discusses efforts to promote educational and economic equity for women of
color, including Hispanic Americans, African
Americans, Asian Americans, Pacific Island
Americans, and Native Americans. **First published:** 1933. **Frequency:** 10/yr. **Price:** $20/yr.

**★9427★ NLC's Constituency Group
Newsletter**
National League of Cities (NLC)
Women in Municipal Government
1301 Pennsylvania Ave., NW
Washington, DC 20004
Phone: (202)626-3181
Fax: (202)626-3043

Description: Covers membership activity. **Frequency:** Quarterly.

★9428★ The NOEL News
National Organization of Episcopalians for
  Life (NOEL)
10523 Main St.
Fairfax, VA 22030
Phone: (703)591-6635

Description: Focuses on issues concerning the
protection of human life in accordance with the
teachings of Scripture. Promotes alternatives to
abortion through discussion of religious, ethical,
and scientific perspectives. **Frequency:** Quarterly. **Price:** $10/yr. for nonmembers.

**★9429★ Non-Traditional Employment for
Women—NEWsletter**
Non-Traditional Employment for Women
  (NEW)
243 W. 20th St.
New York, NY 10011
Phone: (212)627-6252
Fax: (212)255-8021

Description: Focuses on NEW's initiatives on
behalf of women in and seeking non-traditional
blue-collar employment, such as construction.
Frequency: Quarterly.

**★9430★ North Carolina Center for Laws
Affecting Women, Inc.—Report**
North Carolina Center for Laws Affecting
  Women, Inc. (NCC-LAW)
1111 Brookstown Ave.
Winston-Salem, NC 27101
Phone: (919)722-0098

Description: Informs readers of legislative
changes in family law, reviews court cases that
affect future interpretation of laws, critiques
areas of law that affect the family and women
unfairly, and proposes reform. **First published:**
1981. **Frequency:** Quarterly. **Price:** Included in
membership.

★9431★ NOW-NYS Report
National Organization for Women-New York State (NOW-NYS)
14 Fountain Ave.
Seldon, NY 11784
Phone: (516)537-0483
Description: Contains information on women's rights legislation. **Frequency:** Quarterly.

★9432★ NWEA Outlook
National Women's Economic Alliance Foundation (NWEA)
1440 New York Ave., NW, Ste. 300
Washington, DC 20005
Phone: (202)393-5257
Description: Reports the placement of executive-level women on corporate boards. **Frequency:** Semiannual.

★9433★ NWSAction
National Women's Studies Association (NWSA)
University of Maryland
College Park, MD 20742
Phone: (301)405-5573
Description: Focuses on regional activities, conferences, association business, selected women's studies programs, and campus activities. Also contains resources and position announcements. **Frequency:** Quarterly.

★9434★ Ob/Gyn Clinical Alert
American Health Consultants, Inc.
3525 Piedmont Rd., Bldg. 6, Ste. 400
Atlanta, GA 30305
Phone: (404)262-7436
Toll-free: 800-688-2421
Fax: (404)262-7837
Subtitle: A Monthly Update of Current Developments in Female Reproductive Medicine. **Description:** Reviews medical literature and research related to obstetrics and gynecology, providing commentary on each item. Covers diseases, treatments, drugs, general health, and professional trends. **First published:** 1983. **Frequency:** Monthly. **Price:** $95/yr., U.S.; $115, Canada; $135 elsewhere. **ISSN:** 0743-8354.

★9435★ OCAW Speaks
Organization of Chinese American Women (OCAW)
1300 N St. NW, Ste. 100
Washington, DC 20005
Phone: (301)405-5573
Description: Addresses issues of interest to Chinese American women. **Frequency:** Quarterly.

★9436★ On Campus With Women
Project on the Status and Education of Women
Association of American Colleges
1818 R St., N.W.
Washington, DC 20009
Phone: (202)387-3760
Fax: (202)265-9532
Description: Focuses on issues affecting women students, faculty, and administrators in colleges and universities. **First published:** November 1971. **Frequency:** Quarterly. **Price:** $20/yr. for individuals at AAC-member institutions; $28 for others. **ISSN:** 0734-0141.

★9437★ On the Record
Women in Government Relations
1325 Massachusetts Ave., NW, Ste. 510
Washington, DC 20005-4171
Phone: (202)347-5432
Fax: (202)347-5434
Description: Reports organizational activities. **Frequency:** Bimonthly. **Price:** $24/yr.

★9438★ Online
Association for Women in Computing, Twin Cities
Box 14605, University Sta.
Minneapolis, MN 55414
Phone: (612)681-9371
Description: Promotes communication, education, and professional development and advancement of women in computing. Publishes news of the Chapter, its members, and its activities. **Frequency:** 11/yr. **Price:** Included in membership.

★9439★ Operation Big Vote Newsletter
National Coalition on Black Voter Participation
Black Women's Roundtable
1430 K St. NW, Ste. 401
Washington, DC 20005
Phone: (202)898-2220
Description: Discusses efforts to promote social justice and economic equity for African American women through increased participation in the political process.

★9440★ OSCLG News
Arizona State University
Organization for the Study of Communication, Language and Gender (OSCLG)
Communication Dept.
2607 S. Forest Ave.
Tempe, AZ 85282
Phone: (602)967-2817
Description: Information on creative projects in the areas of communication, language, and gender. **Frequency:** Quarterly. **Price:** $6/yr.

★9441★ Outdoor Adventures for Women Newsletter
235 Carmelita Dr.
Mountain View, CA 94040
Phone: (415)961-5674
Description: Covers outdoor activities for women including hiking, nature walks, biking, and camping. **Frequency:** 6/yr.

★9442★ Ovulation Method Newsletter
Ovulation Method Teachers Association
PO Box 101780
Anchorage, AK 99510
Phone: (907)344-8606
Description: Disseminates information on the ovulation method of birth control and natural family planning. **Frequency:** Quarterly.

★9443★ Pan Asian News
Organization of Pan Asian Women
PO Box 39218
Washington, DC 20016
Phone: (202)659-9370
Description: Provides a voice for the concerns of Asian Pacific-American women and encourages their participation in all aspects of American society. Also monitors legislation on national issues of concern to Asian Pacific-American women. **Frequency:** Quarterly. **Price:** Included in membership; $12/yr. for nonmembers.

★9444★ Paradoxy
3330 SE 30th Pl.
Gainesville, FL 32601
Phone: (904)376-3864
Description: Provides a forum for Florida women.

★9445★ Pa$$ IT ON
National Network of Women's Funds (NNWF)
1821 University Ave., Ste. 409N
St. Paul, MN 55104
Phone: (612)641-0742
Description: Reports on organizations and foundations with programs that benefit women and girls.

★9446★ Peace and Freedom
Women's International League for Peace and Freedom (WILPF)
1213 Race St.
Philadelphia, PA 19107
Phone: (215)563-7110
Fax: (215)864-2022
Description: Concerned with disarmament, women's empowerment, feminism, international affairs, U.S. militarism, racism, and grassroots activism. Provides articles, news items, and commentary, plus ideas for action. **First published:** 1924. **Frequency:** 6/yr. **Price:** Included in membership; $12/yr. for nonmembers. **ISSN:** 0015-9093. **Former Title(s):** Four Lights, 1970.

★9447★ Peace Links—The Connection
Peace Links
747 8th St., SE
Washington, DC 20003
Phone: (202)544-0805
Fax: (202)544-0809
Description: Provides information on the organization and its grassroot activists. Includes book and film reviews and calendar of events. **Frequency:** Bimonthly. **Price:** Free.

★9448★ People Concerned for the Unborn Child—Newsletter
People Concerned for the Unborn Child
3050 Pioneer Ave.
Pittsburgh, PA 15226
Phone: (412)531-9272
Fax: (412)531-5885
Description: Concerned with issues of importance to the right-to-life movement, including abortion, euthanasia, infanticide, fetal experimentation, and government birth control policies. Emphasizes state and federal legislation that affects these issues. Features organization news and information from allied groups. **First published:** 1970. **Frequency:** Bimonthly. **Price:** Included in membership.

★9449★ Perinatal Press, Inc.—Newsletter
Perinatal Press, Inc.
PO Box 710698
San Diego, CA 92171
Phone: (619)541-6875

Subtitle: For Persons Dedicated to Improving the Health Care of the Pregnant Woman, Fetus and Newborn. **Description:** Presents abstracts and reviews of articles concerned with research and developments in perinatal and neonatal health care. Seeks to provide practical information for perinatal clinicians. **First published:** 1977. **Frequency:** 6/yr. **Price:** $21/yr. **ISSN:** 0160-7219.

★9450★ The PH Factor
National Panhellenic Conference (NPC)
3901 W. 86th St., Ste. 380
Indianapolis, IN 46268
Phone: (317)872-3185
Fax: (317)872-3192

Description: Focuses on news concerning member Greek fraternities. **Frequency:** Semiannual.

★9451★ The Phyllis Schlafly Report
Eagle Trust Fund
PO Box 618
Alton, IL 62002
Phone: (618)462-5415

Description: Provides news and commentary on issues of concern to the "traditional family." Deals with education, national defense, economics, foreign affairs, politics, and feminism. **First published:** August 1967. **Frequency:** Monthly. **Price:** $20/yr. **ISSN:** 0556-0152.

★9452★ The Pied Piper
Organization for the Enforcement of Child Support
119 Nicodemus Rd.
Reisterstown, MD 21136
Phone: (301)833-2458

Description: Aimed toward persons seeking enforcement of laws pertaining to child support. Describes the Organization's work to improve the child support enforcement system and to inform people of their rights under current child support laws. **Frequency:** Quarterly. **Price:** $6/yr.

★9453★ Planned Parenthood of Minnesota—Network News
Planned Parenthood of Minnesota
1965 Ford Pkwy.
St. Paul, MN 55116
Phone: (612)698-2401
Frequency: Quarterly.

★9454★ PLEN Newsleter
Public Leadership Education Network (PLEN)
1001 Connecticut Ave. NW, Ste. 925
Washington, DC 20036
Phone: (202)872-1585
Fax: (202)457-0549

Description: Reports on efforts to prepare women for public leadership. **Frequency:** Semiannual.

★9455★ PMS Access—Newsletter
Madison Pharmacy Associates, Inc.
PMS Access
PO Box 9326
Madison, WI 53715
Phone: (608)833-4767
Toll-free: 800-222-4767
Fax: (608)833-7412

Description: Updates patients and health professionals on the latest developments in research into and treatment of premenstrual syndrome (PMS). Carries book reviews, information on PMS support groups, listings of workshops and symposia, and columns titled Dimensions in PMS, Ask the Expert, and PMS Cuisine. **First published:** May 1985. **Frequency:** Bimonthly. **Price:** $15/yr.

★9456★ The Positive Women
PO Box 34372
Washington, DC 20043
Phone: (202)898-0372

Description: Newsletter for HIV-positive women. **Subscription:** $15 for individuals; $55 for non-profit groups; $90 for businesses and institutions; free to HIV-positive women who cannot afford subscription.

★9457★ Priority Parenting
Tamra B. Orr
PO Box 1793
Warsaw, IN 46581-1793
Phone: (219)453-3864

Subtitle: The Newsletter for Alternative Parents. **Description:** Offers commentary "geared for those parents who raise their children according to nature, not society." Explores such topics as home birth, prolonged breastfeeding, family beds, immunizations, home schooling, and related issues. **First published:** May 1987. **Frequency:** Monthly. **Price:** $14/yr.

★9458★ Pro-Life Action League—Action News
Pro-Life Action League
6160 N. Cicero Ave.
Chicago, IL 60646
Phone: (312)777-2900

Description: Describes actions taken by the League and the results of media appearances by the League's director. **First published:** 1980. **Frequency:** Quarterly. **Price:** Free.

★9459★ Professional Women in Construction Newsletter
Professional Women in Construction (PWC)
342 Madison Ave., Ste. 453
New York, NY 10173
Phone: (212)687-0610

Description: Geared towards managerial women in construction.

★9460★ Professional Women Photographers Newsletter
Photographers Unlimited
Professional Women Photographers
17 W. 17th St.
New York, NY 10011
Phone: (212)255-9678

Description: Provides an interactive forum for photographers. Presents monographs. **Frequency:** Quarterly.

★9461★ Program and Legislative Action Bulletin
Women's International League for Peace and Freedom (WILPF)
1213 Race St.
Philadelphia, PA 19107
Phone: (215)563-7110
Fax: (215)864-2022

Description: Reflects the aims of the League, which works, through nonviolent means, for the elimination of war, want, and discrimination on any basis. Provides updates and timely action suggestions on disarmament, intervention, racial justice, and women's rights. **Frequency:** Bimonthly. **Price:** $12/yr. Incorporates the former WILPF Legislative Alert/Program Action Bulletin. **Former Title(s):** Program and Action Newsletter.

★9462★ Quickening
American College of Nurse-Midwives
1522 K St. NW, Ste. 1120
Washington, DC 20005
Phone: (202)347-5445

Description: Promotes the training and certification of nurse-midwives. **First published:** December 1970. **Frequency:** Bimonthly. **Price:** Included in membership. **ISSN:** 0196-3805.

★9463★ Radia
614 Orange St.
New Haven, CT 06511
Phone: (203)776-2658

Description: Includes events calendar and news for women in the region. **Frequency:** Monthly.

★9464★ RCC Currents
DC Rape Crisis Center
PO Box 21005
Washington, DC 20009
Phone: (202)232-0789

Description: Provides information for sexual assault survivors in the metropolitan Washington DC community. **Frequency:** Quarterly.

★9465★ Reading Women
Reading Women, Inc.
PO Box 296
Winnetka, IL 60093-9816
Phone: (708)432-8832

Subtitle: The Newsletter of Literary Ideas. **Description:** Analyzes, criticizes, and interprets contemporary fiction with a humanist/feminist perspective. Reviews novels and short stories. **Frequency:** Bimonthly. **Price:** $29/yr.

★9466★ Reel News
Women in Film
6464 Sunset, Ste. 530
Hollywood, CA 90028
Phone: (213)463-6040

Description: Contains news from within the entertainment industry about employment. Also discusses the depiction and position of women in the industry. **Frequency:** Monthly.

★9467★ Re-Entry News
City College of San Francisco
Re-Entry to Education Program
50 Phelan Ave., Box LB8
San Francisco, CA 94112
Phone: (415)239-3297

Description: Contains short articles, editorials, book reviews, and a calendar of events for adults re-entering college.

★9468★ Religious Coalition for Abortion Rights Newsletter
Religious Coalition for Abortion Rights
100 Maryland Ave. NE, No. 307
Washington, DC 20002-5625
Phone: (202)543-7032
Fax: (202)543-7820

Description: Focuses on reproductive rights and religious freedom. Carries news of national and state activities, legislative information, articles by pro-choice clergy, and conference information. **First published:** 1973. **Frequency:** 3/yr. **Price:** Included in membership; $25 for nonmembers. **Former Title(s):** Options, Fall 1990.

★9469★ Responsibility Newsletter
National Association of Negro Business and Professional Women (NANBPW)
1806 New Hampshire Ave. NW
Washington, DC 20009
Phone: (202)483-4206
Fax: (202)462-7253

Description: Provides news on activities and programs.

★9470★ Ruth Jackson Society Newsletter
American Academy of Orthopaedic Surgeons
Ruth Jackson Society
22 S. Prospect Ave.
Park Ridge, IL 60068-4058
Phone: (708)698-1632

Description: Serves as a network for women orthopaedic surgeons and a forum for the confrontation for common problems facing them. **Frequency:** Semiannual.

★9471★ Safe House
Towson State University
Campus Violence Prevention Center
Towson, MD 21204

Description: Contains news of center activities, crime statistics, conference announcements, and descriptions of available videos.

★9472★ Sarah Isom Center News
University of Mississippi
Sarah Isom Center for Women's Studies
University, MS 38677
Phone: (601)232-5916

Description: Presents news of Center activities and information on seminars regarding women's issues.

★9473★ The Sex and Gender Newsletter
Rutgers University
American Sociological Association
Sex and Gender Section
Sociology Department
PO Box 5072
New Brunswick, NJ 08904-5072
Phone: (908)932-2897

Description: Contains information on gender relations.

★9474★ Shop Talk
PO Box 64211
Lubbock, TX 79424-4211
Subtitle: Collection of Parenting Experiences.
Description: Considers one aspect of parenting per issue, such as homebirth, nursing beyond infancy, shopping with children, mothers at home, food, immunizations, family finances, circumcision, grandparents, discipline, weaning, toilet training, and education. **First published:** June 1987. **Frequency:** Bimonthly. **Price:** $12/yr., U.S.; $17, Canada, $27 elsewhere.

★9475★ SIROW Newsletter
University of Arizona
Southwest Institute for Research on Women (SIROW)
Douglass Bldg., Rm. 102
Women's Studies
Tucson, AZ 85721
Phone: (602)621-7338
Fax: (602)621-9424

Description: Contains information on projects, programs, issues, and research being done in women's studies in the southwestern U.S. **First published:** November 1979. **Frequency:** 3/academic yr. **Price:** Free.

★9476★ 630 News
Independent Federation of Flight Attendants
630 3rd Ave.
New York, NY 10017
Phone: (212)818-1130
Fax: (212)949-4058

Description: Covers topics of interest to members, including government activities, labor relations in the airline industry, and health information. **Frequency:** Quarterly.

★9477★ SOAP Newsletter
Baylor College of Medicine
Department of Anesthesiology
Society for Obstetric Anesthesia and Perinatology (SOAP)
6550 Fannin, Ste. 1003
Houston, TX 77030
Phone: (713)798-5119
Fax: (713)798-7345

Description: Offers physicians and scientists interested in perinatal health care news and information commensurate with the Society's purpose, which is to improve the health care of pregnant women and their unborn children. **Frequency:** Quarterly. **Price:** Included in membership. **Former Title(s):** Society for Obstetric and Anesthesia and Perinatology—Newsletter.

★9478★ Sobering Thoughts
PO Box 618
Quakertown, PA 18951
Phone: (215)536-8026
Toll-free: 800-333-1606

Description: Contains articles for women substance-abusers on self-esteem and overcoming depression. **Frequency:** Monthly. **Price:** $18/yr. for individuals; $8 for individuals over 65.

★9479★ Society for Menstrual Cycle Research Newsletter
The Society for Menstrual Cycle Research
10559 N. 104th Pl.
Scottsdale, AZ 85258
Phone: (602)457-9731

Description: Focuses on the health needs of women as they relate to menstruation. **Frequency:** Quarterly.

★9480★ Southern Association for Women Historians—Newsletter
Clemson University
Southern Association for Women Historians
History Department
Clemson, SC 29634
Phone: (803)656-5370
Fax: (803)656-1015

Description: Informs members of the Association's activities aimed at advancing the professional development of women historians and historians of women. Carries minutes of the annual meeting, announcements of awards and prizes available for work published in a variety of areas, and calls for papers at various conferences. **Frequency:** 3/yr. **Price:** Included in membership.

★9481★ Southern California Women for Understanding
1017 N. La Cienega Blvd., Ste. 106
West Hollywood, CA 90069
Phone: (310)657-1115
Fax: (310)657-1116

Description: Offers educational information for the lesbian community. **Frequency:** Bimonthly. **Price:** $15/year.

★9482★ Speak Out!
Single Parent Resource Center, Inc.
141 W. 28th St.
New York, NY 10001
Phone: (212)213-0047

Description: Focuses on issues of concern to the single parent population, including housing discrimination, day care, teen-parent relations and work/home conflicts. **First published:** 1975. **Frequency:** Bimonthly. **Price:** Included in membership; $5/yr. for nonmembers.

★9483★ Speak Out for Children
National Council for Children's Rights (NCCR)
220 I St. NE
Washington, DC 20002
Phone: (202)547-6227
Fax: (202)546-7689

Description: Reports on the Council's work for divorce and child custody reform, favoring joint custody (shared parenting), mediation, access (visitation) enforcement, and equitable child support. Carries legislative updates and reviews of other developments in the field. Also features court cases. **First published:** 1985. **Frequency:**

Quarterly. **Price:** Included in membership. **ISSN:** 1042-3559.

★9484★ Special Delivery
Maternity Center Association
48 E. 92nd St.
New York, NY 10128
Phone: (212)369-7300
Description: Contains information on the Association and its programs for childbearing families. Includes articles on all aspects of maternity care, maternal and infant health, and family life. **Frequency:** 2/yr. **Price:** Included in membership.

★9485★ Special Delivery
Informed Homebirth/Informed Birth & Parenting
PO Box 3675
Ann Arbor, MI 48106
Phone: (313)662-6857
Description: Provides information on alternatives in childbirth, including pregnancy, midwifery, and home birth. Discusses parenting and early childhood issues. **First published:** 1977. **Frequency:** Quarterly. **Price:** Included in membership; $15/yr. for nonmembers, U.S.; $18 elsewhere.

★9486★ Spectrum
Biophysical Society
Committee on Professional Opportunities for Women
9650 Rockville Pike
Bethesda, MD 20814
Phone: (202)727-2280
Fax: (202)638-1736
Description: Reports efforts to assure full representation for women in the scientific community.

★9487★ Status Report
New York City Commission on the Status of Women
52 Chambers St., Ste 207
New York, NY 10007
Phone: (212)788-2738
Fax: (212)406-3587
Description: Provides information on various women's groups around New York City; publicizes the Commission's events. **Frequency:** Quarterly.

★9488★ Successful Saleswomen
National Association of Professional Saleswomen
PO Box 2606
Novato, CA 94948
Phone: (415)898-2606
Fax: (415)897-5437
Description: Reports on the status of women in sales and marketing.

★9489★ The Supreme Herald
Order of the White Shrine of Jerusalem
Supreme Shrine
107 E. New Haven Ave.
Melbourne, FL 32901
Phone: (407)952-5323
Description: Reports on activities of the Shrine, a charitable organization of women relatives of Master Masons giving aid for artificial limbs, wheel chairs, hearing aids, eye glasses, and seeing eye and hearing dogs. **First published:** 1978. **Frequency:** Quarterly. **Price:** $2.50/yr.

★9490★ Synapses Messages
1821 W. Cullerton
Chicago, IL 60608
Phone: (312)421-5513
Fax: (312)421-5762
Description: Examines justice issues in a domestic and international context. Written by Filipino, South African, Salvadoran, and North American women. **Frequency:** Bimonthly.

★9491★ Tennessee Family Law Letter
M. Lee Smith, Publishers & Printers
162 4th Ave. N.
PO Box 2678
Nashville, TN 37219
Phone: (615)242-7395
Toll-free: 800-866-7729
Subtitle: A Montly Digest of Tennessee Family Law Developments. **Description:** Details Tennessee Supreme Court and Court of Appeals decisions concerning abortion, alimony, inheritance, child custody and visitation, division of marital property, and other family law matters. Contains attorney opinions, news of educational opportunities, and notices of publications available. **Frequency:** Monthly. **Price:** $80/yr. **ISSN:** 0890-5355.

★9492★ Themophoria
Women's Spirituality Forum
PO Box 11363
Oakland, CA 94611
Phone: (510)444-7724
Subtitle: Voice of the New Women's Religion. **Description:** Acts as a network for the exchange of experiences among those interested in Goddess worship. Also contains stories and poems. **First published:** June 1979. **Frequency:** 8/yr. **Price:** $10/yr., U.S. and Canada; $13 elsewhere. **Former Title(s):** Themis, Summer 1981.

★9493★ The Times
Executive Women International
965 E. 4800 S., Ste. 1
Salt Lake City, UT 84117
Phone: (801)263-3296
Description: Focuses on the networking activities of top professional women for personal and career development and community involvement.

★9494★ Today
National Association of Minority Women in Business
906 Grand Ave., Ste. 200
Kansas City, MO 64106
Phone: (816)421-3335
Description: Serves as a network for the exchange of ideas and information on business opportunities for minority women in the public and private sectors. Discusses topics of concern to minority women in business ownership and management positions. **Frequency:** Bimonthly. **Price:** Included in membership.

★9495★ Trade Trax
Tradeswomen, Inc.
PO Box 40664
San Francisco, CA 94140
Phone: (415)821-7334
Subtitle: A Newsletter for Women in Blue Collar Work. **Description:** Reports activities of the organization and other events in the California Bay Area and of national interest to women working or wishing to work in non-traditional and blue-collar jobs. **First published:** 1981. **Frequency:** Monthly. **Price:** Included in membership; $15/yr. for nonmembers.

★9496★ The Tribune
International Women's Tribune Centre
777 U.N. Plaza
New York, NY 10017
Phone: (212)687-8633
Fax: (212)661-2704
Description: Reports on women's projects and groups in the Third World, "the issues they are confronting and the actions and initiatives they are formulating." Covers specific themes such as water and sanitation, training techniques, economics, and legal issues. **First published:** 1976. **Frequency:** Quarterly. **Price:** Free to people in the Third World; $12/yr., North America; $16 Australia, Europe, Japan, and New Zealand. **ISSN:** 0738-9779. **Remarks:** Also available in French and Spanish. **Former Title(s):** Decade Update, 1987.

★9497★ Twin Services Reporter
Twin Services
PO Box 10066
Berkeley, CA 94709
Phone: (510)524-0863
Subtitle: Multiple Birth News. **Description:** Offers parenting advice and research updates on the care and development of twins, triplets, quadruplets, and quintuplets, from prenatal care through their adjustment as adults. Concerned with such issues as preventing pre-term births, multiple-pregnancy management, breastfeeding multiples, coping with toddlers, and the twin relationship. **First published:** Fall 1983. **Frequency:** Quarterly. **Price:** Included in membership. **ISSN:** 0895-0784. **Remarks:** Twinline is "the only professional service agency in the world specifically for multiple-birth families." **Former Title(s):** Twinline Reporter.

★9498★ UCLA Center for the Study of Women Newsletter
University of California, Los Angeles (UCLA)
Center for the Study of Women
236A Kinsey Hall
Los Angeles, CA 90064
Phone: (213)825-0590
Description: Covers activities of the Center, which encourages and supports research on women and gender issues. **Frequency:** Quarterly.

★9499★ Unitarian Universalist Women's Federation—The Communicator
Unitarian Universalist Women's Federation
25 Beacon St.
Boston, MA 02108
Phone: (617)742-2100
Description: Carries Federation news and reports in the fields of equality for women, responsible abortion laws, child advocacy, violence against women, and women's spirituality.

First published: October 1976. **Frequency:** 6/yr. **Price:** Included in membership. **Former Title(s):** *Speakout*; *Federation Newsletter*, March 1984; *UUWF Newsletter*.

★9500★ **United States Council for INSTRAW Newsletter**
United Nations International Research and Training Institute for the Advancement of Women (INSTRAW)
National Council for Research on Women
47-49 E. 65th St.
New York, NY 10021
Phone: (212)570-5005
Fax: (212)570-5380

Description: Reports Council and Institute news. **Frequency:** Quarterly.

★9501★ **United States Delegation for Friendship Among Women Newsletter**
United States Delegation for Friendship Among Women
2219 Caroline Ln.
South St. Paul, MN 55075
Phone: (612)455-5620

Description: Reports on the delegation's efforts to promote cultural exchange and understanding among women leaders of the world.

★9502★ **Unmarried Parents Today**
National Committee for Adoption, Inc.
1930 17th St. NW
Washington, DC 20009
Phone: (202)328-1200
Fax: (202)332-0935

Subtitle: An Information Service From National Committee for Adoption Headquarters in Washington, D.C. **Description:** Concerned with maternity services and adolescent pregnancy. Carries information "especially useful to those who operate maternity services," namely, data on various prevention, demonstration, and community education projects around the country and the grants they've received from the Federal Office of Adolescent Pregnancy Programs. **First published:** 1980. **Frequency:** Quarterly. **Price:** Included in membership.

★9503★ **Update**
Congressional Caucus for Women's Issues
2471 Rayburn House Office Bldg.
Washington, DC 20515
Phone: (202)225-6740

Description: Covers initiatives of the Caucus that improve the status of women and eliminate discrimination from federal programs and policies.

★9504★ **Violence Update**
Sage Publications
PO Box 5084
Newbury Park, CA 91359-9924

Description: Concerned with domestic violence and sexual assault. Features one or more special reports, profiles/interviews of professionals in the field, book reviews, and resource listings and discussions. **Frequency:** Monthly. **Price:** $36 for individuals; $49 for nonprofit victim service organizations; $75 for instituitions.

★9505★ **Vital Signs**
National Black Women's Health Project
1237 Gordon St. SW
Atlanta, GA 30310
Phone: (404)753-0916
Fax: (404)752-6756

Description: Encourages mutual and self-help activism among women to bring about a reduction in health care problems prevalent among black women. Reports on research conducted on the health problems of black women and discusses black women's health issues. **First published:** 1984. **Frequency:** Quarterly. **Price:** Included in membership.

★9506★ **The Voice of the Agri-Women**
American Agri-Women
Rt. 2, Box 193
Keota, IA 52248
Phone: (515)636-2293

Description: Covers agriculture from the viewpoint of the woman agriculturalist.

★9507★ **Voice of Eritrean Women**
National Union of Eritrean Women
PO Box 631
New York, NY 10025
Phone: (212)678-1977

Description: Contains articles, interviews, photographs, and information relative to women's issues and Eritrean women. **Frequency:** Quarterly.

★9508★ **WAMM Newsletter**
Women Against Military Madness (WAMM)
3255 Hennepin Ave., Ste. 125-B
Minneapolis, MN 55408
Phone: (612)827-5364
Fax: (612)827-6433

Description: Promotes the aim of the organization, which is directed toward "direct action and visible public protest against militarist resolution to conflict, proliferation of arms and the diversion of energy, money and resources from helping people." **First published:** April 1982. **Frequency:** Monthly. **Price:** Included in membership.

★9509★ **Washington WSPer/Legislative Alert**
Women Strike for Peace (WSP)
105 2nd St., NE
Washington, DC 20002
Phone: (202)543-2660

Description: Informs readers of actions taken by the U.S. and other countries on disarmament and other foreign policy issues, and offers possible action that can be taken to alter objectionable policies. Includes news of research. **Frequency:** Monthly. **Price:** $10/yr.

★9510★ **WASP News**
Women Airforce Service Pilots WWII (WASP)
PO Box 9212
Ft. Wayne, IL 46899
Phone: (219)747-7933

Description: Features news and information related to the organization. **Frequency:** 3/yr.

★9511★ **WATERwheel**
Women's Alliance for Theology, Ethics and Ritual (WATER)
8035 13th St., Stes. 1 & 3
Silver Spring, MD 20910
Phone: (301)589-2509
Fax: (301)589-3150

Description: Focuses on women's issues in religion. Topics include feminist/womanist theology and ethics, new models of church, and celebrations and rituals for women's groups. **Frequency:** Quarterly. **Price:** $35/yr. suggested donation.

★9512★ **WBA Newsletter**
Women's Bar Association (WBA) of the District of Columbia
1819 H St. NW, Ste. 1250
Washington, DC 20006
Phone: (202)785-1540
Fax: (202)293-3388

Description: Features articles, interviews, announcements, upcoming programs, a calendar of events, and items of interest to women attorneys.

★9513★ **WCC Newsletter**
American Philological Association
Women's Classical Caucus (WCC)
College of New Rochelle
Department of Classics
New Rochelle, NY 10801
Phone: (914)654-5399

Description: Reports on the Caucus' attempts to eliminate sexist, ageist, and homophobic practices and attitudes in the APA.

★9514★ **The Webb Report**
Premiere Publishing, Ltd.
145 Northwest 85th, Ste. 201
Seattle, WA 98117
Toll-free: 800-767-3062

Description: Newsletter on sexual harassment. **Frequency:** Monthly.

★9515★ **WEJC Update**
National Center for Policy Alternatives
Women's Economic Justice Center (WEJC)
1875 Connecticutt Ave. NW, Ste. 710
Washington, DC 20009
Phone: (202)387-6030
Fax: (202)986-2539

Description: Covers efforts to create sound state policy that improves the lives of economically disadvantaged women and their families.

★9516★ **What to Do about Personnel Problems—National News Update**
Business and Legal Reports, Inc.
39 Academy St.
Madison, CT 06443-1513

Description: Discusses laws and legislations on issues such as age and sex discrimination, health insurance liabilities, and bias settlements. **Frequency:** Monthly. **Price:** $216/yr.

★9517★ What She Wants
What She Wants Collective
PO Box 18465
Cleveland Heights, OH 44118
Phone: (216)321-3054

Description: Offers information on social and business events of interest to feminists. Includes a calendar of events. **First published:** 1977. **Frequency:** Monthly.

★9518★ WHISPER Newsletter
Women Hurt In Systems of Prostituiton Engaged In Revolt (WHISPER)
Lake St. Sta.
PO Box 8719
Minneapolis, MN 55408
Phone: (612)644-6301

Description: Reports resources for women in prostitution, educators, and women's advocates. **Price:** $15/yr.

★9519★ White Caps
c/o Mrs. Sue Carroll
475 E. Burke St.
Martins Key, WV 25401

Description: Provides news of women veterans. Includes address updates. **Frequency:** Bimonthly. **Price:** Included in membership.

★9520★ WIC News
Women in Cable (WIC)
500 N. Michigan Ave., Ste. 1400
Chicago, IL 60611
Phone: (312)661-1700
Fax: (312)661-0769

Description: Aimed toward women in the cable industry. Focuses on economic, professional, and personal goals, and the future of the industry. **Frequency:** Bimonthly.

★9521★ WIIS Words
University of Maryland
Center for International Studies
Women in International Security (WIIS)
School of Public Affairs
College Park, MD 20742
Phone: (301)403-8109
Fax: (301)403-8107

Description: Focuses on issues of interest to women in international security. Seeks to educate on the roles and achievements of women in the field.

★9522★ Wilderness Women
5329 Manila Ave.
Oakland, CA 94618
Phone: (510)658-2196

Description: Geared towards women interested in camping. **Frequency:** Monthly. **Price:** $5/yr.

★9523★ WILLA Newsletter
National Council of Teachers of English (NCTE)
Women in Literature and Life Assembly (WILLA)
1111 Kenyon Rd.
Urbana, IL 61801
Phone: (217)328-3870

Description: Focuses attention on the status and image of women in the English teaching profession. Also reports on WILLA's efforts to ensure equitable treatment and act a resource group for women in the NCTE's constituent group. **Frequency:** Semiannual.

★9524★ William Joiner Center for the Study of War and Social Consequences—Connection
University of Massachusetts at Boston
William Joiner Center for the Study of War and Social Consequences
Harbor Campus
Wheatley Hall, 4th Fl.
Boston, MA 02125
Phone: (617)287-5850

Description: Publicizes the work of the Women Veterans Project, which focuses on issues concerning women veterans. **First published:** August 1987. **Frequency:** Semiannual.

★9525★ WISP Newsletter
Women in Scholarly Publishing (WISP)
c/o Beacon Press
25 Beacon St.
Boston, MA 02108-2892
Phone: (617)742-2110

Description: Discusses efforts to encourage educational and professional advancement for women.

★9526★ WIT
Northern New England Tradeswomen
1 Prospect Ave.
St. Johnsbury, VT 05819
Phone: (802)748-3308

Description: Provides a network of support, information, and skill sharing for women in trade professions. **First published:** 1986. **Frequency:** Quarterly. **Price:** Included in membership; $10/yr. for nonmembers. **Also known as:** Women in Trades.

★9527★ WLDF News
Women's Legal Defense Fund (WLDF)
1875 Connecticut Ave. NW, Ste. 710
Washington, DC 20009
Phone: (202)986-2600
Fax: (202)861-0691

Description: Monitors developments in employment discrimination, family law, and other areas of sex discrimination law that affect women's status. Contains updates on the organization's services and activities, discussions of women's rights issues, and editorials. **First published:** 1971. **Frequency:** 3/yr. **Price:** Included in membership; $10/yr. for nonmembers; $15 for organizations. **ISSN:** 0736-9433. **Former Title(s):** WLDF Newsletter.

★9528★ WLUC News
Women Life Underwriters Confederation (WLUC)
6807 Old Alexandria Ferry Rd.
Clinton, MD 20735-1744
Phone: (301)868-7461
Fax: (301)868-6731

Description: Features news and information for women in the insurance industry. **Frequency:** Monthly.

★9529★ WMA 'Nouncements
Women Marines Association (WMA)
PO Box 387
Quantico, VA 22134
Phone: (703)640-6599

Description: Includes information on membership, scholarships, chapters, and current leadership positions. **Frequency:** Quarterly. **Price:** Available to members.

★9530★ WOHRC News
Women's Occupational Health Resource Center (WOHRC)
117 St. Johns Pl.
Brooklyn, NY 11217
Phone: (718)230-8822

Description: Alerts individuals to potential occupational hazards for women, recommends prevention techniques, and assists labor unions in negotiating for a more healthful work environment. Covers such topics as reproductive rights in the workplace, abatement practices in the workplace, noise pollution, radiation, workplace design, personal protective equipment, fire hazards, and genetic screening. **First published:** 1979. **Frequency:** Quarterly. **Price:** $12/yr. for individuals; $25 for institutions.

★9531★ Woman$ense
Target, Inc.
4475 Willow Rd.
Pleasanton, CA 94588-0625
Phone: (415)463-2200
Toll-free: 800-877-7833

Subtitle: A Personal Financial Guide for Women. **Description:** Provides advice on such topics as insurance, estate planning, investments, budgeting, and others. **Frequency:** Monthly. **Price:** $79/yr.

★9532★ Women Artists News
Midmarch Associates
Box 3304, Grand Central Sta.
New York, NY 10163
Phone: (212)666-6990

Description: Focuses on news for women involved in the visual arts: painting, sculpture, dance, photography, film, and crafts. **First published:** April 1975. **Frequency:** 4/yr. **Price:** $12/yr. **ISSN:** 0149-7081. **Former Title(s):** Women Artists Newsletter, December 1977.

★9533★ Women in the Arts
National Museum of Women in the Arts
1250 New York Ave. NW
Washington, DC 20005
Fax: (202)393-3235

Description: Chronicles the progress of the Museum, which is devoted to the work of women artists. Includes announcements of special events. **First published:** 1983. **Frequency:** Quarterly. **Price:** Included in membership. **ISSN:** 1058-7217. **Former Title(s):** National Museum of Women in the Arts—Newsletter.

★9534★ Women in the Arts Bulletin
Women in the Arts Foundation, Inc.
c/o Roberta Crown
1175 York Ave., Apt. 2G
New York, NY 10013
Phone: (212)751-1915

Description: Focuses on issues concerning women artists. Provides exhibit announcements and listings of opportunities. **First published:**

1972. **Frequency:** 4/yr. **Price:** Included in membership; $9/yr. for nonmembers, $15 for institutions, U.S.; $12 nonmembers, $18 institutions, Canada; $13 nonmembers, $19 institutions elsewhere.

★9535★ **Women of Color Newsletter**
National Women of Color Association (NWCA)
University of Wisconsin, LaCrosse
Department of Women's Studies
336 North Hall
LaCrosse, WI 54601
Phone: (608)785-8357

Description: Focuses on issues concerning African American, Asian American, Hispanic American, and Native American women. **Frequency:** 3/yr.

★9536★ **Women in Constant Creative Action**
Women In Constant Creative Action (WICCA)
PO Box 5080
Eugene, OR 97405
Phone: (503)345-6381

Description: Features information concerning women's spirituality, metaphysics, and feminism. **Frequency:** Monthly. **Price:** $10/yr.

★9537★ **Women Executives in Public Relations—Network**
Women Executives in Public Relations
PO Box 781
Murray Hill Sta.
New York, NY 10156
Phone: (212)683-5438

Description: Serves as a forum for ideas, experiences, contemporary issues, and the advancement of women in public relations. **Frequency:** Quarterly.

★9538★ **Women in French Newsletter**
Bell State University
Department of Foreign Languages
Women in French
Muncie, IN 47306
Phone: (317)285-1374
Fax: (317)285-1027

Description: Promotes French literature by women authors, both in metropolitan France and francophone countries.

★9539★ **Women and Gender Research Institute Newsletter**
Utah State University
Women and Gender Research Institute
College of Natural Resources
Logan, UT 84322-5200
Phone: (801)750-2580

Description: Encourages the involvement of women in research and promotes research on gender-related issues.

★9540★ **Women in Higher Education**
The Wenniger Company
2325 W. Lawn Ave.
Madison, WI 53711-1953
Phone: (608)233-0160
Fax: (608)256-3027

Description: Offers advice for college women on careers, personal success, and leadership. **Frequency:** Monthly.

★9541★ **Women & Language**
George Mason University
Communication Dept.
Fairfax, VA 22030
Phone: (703)993-1099

Description: Presents interdisciplinary research in the field of language and gender. Discusses theory, language use, acquisition, and attitudes. Coordinates information on sex-differentiated language research in linguistics, anthropology, speech communication, sociology, psychology, literature, education, medicine, women's studies, and other disciplines. **First published:** January 1976. **Frequency:** 2/yr. **Price:** $8/yr. for individuals, U.S.; $10 for individuals, Canada; $13 elsewhere. $15 for institutions, U.S. and Canada. **ISSN:** 8755-4550.

★9542★ **Women in Libraries**
American Library Association
Office for Library Outreach
The Feminist Task Force
50 E. Huron St.
Chicago, IL 60611
Phone: (312)994-6780

★9543★ **Women Make Movies**
225 Lafayette St., Rm. 207
New York, NY 10012
Phone: (212)925-0606
Fax: (212)925-2052

Description: Brings updates on fims and videos produced by and about women.

★9544★ **Women & Mathematics Education—Newsletter**
Women & Mathematics Education
Center for Science and Mathematics Education
California State Polytechnic University
3801 W. Temple Ave.
Pomona, CA 91768

Description: Promotes the study of mathematics by girls and women. Supplies information on conferences, institutes, programs, and meetings significant to members, along with reports on the activities of the organization. **First published:** October 1978. **Frequency:** 3/yr. **Price:** Included in membership. **Former Title(s):** Association for the Promotion of the Mathematics Education of Girls and Women—Newsletter.

★9545★ **Women in Medicine Update**
Association of American Medical Colleges (AAMC)
Women in Medicine Program
One Dupont Circle NW, Ste. 200
Washington, DC 20036
Phone: (202)828-0575
Fax: (202)785-5027

Description: Reports the issues affecting women in the medical professions.

★9546★ **Women and Missions**
Baptist Mid-Missions
7749 Webster Rd.
PO Box 308011
Cleveland, OH 44130-8011
Phone: (216)826-3930

Description: Lists projects and ideas for Women's Missionary Fellowships. **First published:** November 1984. **Frequency:** Quarterly. **Price:** Free.

★9547★ **Women of the Motion Picture Industry Newsletter**
Women of the Motion Picture Industry
PO Box 900
Beverly Hills, CA 90213
Phone: (213)203-4083

Description: Covers information concerning women involved in the motion picture, television, and theatrical industries. **Frequency:** Periodic.

★9548★ **Women of Nations Newsletter**
Women of Nations
PO Box 40309
St. Paul, MN 55104
Phone: (612)222-5830

Description: Contains articles, poetry, announcements, and a community calendar for Native American battered women. **Frequency:** Quarterly.

★9549★ **Women Officials of NACO Newsletter**
National Association of County Officials (NACO)
Women Officials of National Association of County Officials
440 1st St., NW
Washington, DC 20001
Phone: (202)393-6226

Frequency: Semiannual.

★9550★ **Women Police**
International Association of Women Police
1401 Landwehr Rd.
Northbrook, IL 60062
Phone: (718)721-6494

Description: Addresses law enforcement issues as they relate to women in the profession.

★9551★ **Women in Psychiatry Newsletter**
American Psychiatric Association (APA)
Association of Women Psychiatrists (AWP)
9802 Farnham Rd.
Lousville, KY 40223
Phone: (502)588-6185
Fax: (502)588-6849

Description: Discusses issues of interest to women psychiatrists.

★9552★ **Women and Revolution**
Spartacist Publishing Company
PO Box 1337 GPO
New York, NY 10118
Phone: (212)732-7862
Fax: (212)732-7861

Description: Discusses the issues surrounding women's liberation and the American culture. **Frequency:** Semiannual.

★9553★ **Women in Scholarly Publishing Newsletter**
Duke University Press
Women in Scholarly Publishing
6697 College Sta.
Durham, NC 27708

Description: Focuses on the education and professional development of women in scholarly press publishing. **Frequency:** Quarterly.

★9554★ Women Strike for Peace—Legislative Alert
Women Strike for Peace
105 2nd St. NE
Washington, DC 20002
Phone: (202)543-2660

Description: Promotes the goal of the organization, which is "the achievement of general and complete disarmament under effective international control." Informs readers of actions taken by the U.S. and other countries on disarmament and other foreign policy issues, and offers possible action that can be taken to alter objectionable policies. **First published:** 1975. **Frequency:** Monthly. **Price:** $10/yr.

★9555★ Women and Theatre Program Newsletter
Bowling Green State University
Association for Theatre in Higher Education (ATHE)
Women and Theatre Program
English Department
Bowling Green, OH 43403
Phone: (419)372-6831

Description: Focuses on services, programs, and meetings and issues of interest, including women in theatre, feminist theatre, and the theatrical representation of women.

★9556★ Women USA Fund, Inc.—News & Views
Women USA Fund, Inc.
1133 Broadway, Ste. 924
New York, NY 10010
Phone: (212)691-7316
Fax: (212)243-3609

Description: Covers women's issues related to policy making. **Frequency:** Irregular.

★9557★ Women to Watch
Women's Campaign Fund
1601 Connecticut Ave., NW, Ste. 800
Washington, DC 20009
Phone: (202)234-3700
Fax: (202)789-5600

Description: Acts as a direct-mail letter endorsing women politicians who support pro-choice and ERA.

★9558★ Women with Wheels—Newsletter
Patricia Stringer
1718 A Northfield Sq.
Northfield, IL 60093
Phone: (708)501-3519

Subtitle: Quarterly Newsletter on Automobiles for Women. **Description:** Provides information on cars and their maintenance. Features articles on anti-lock brakes, safety, leasing, purchasing, and dealing with car salespeople. **First published:** Spring 1989. **Frequency:** Quarterly. **Price:** $15/yr. for individuals; $20 for institutions. **ISSN:** 1043-979X.

★9559★ Women at Work
National Commission on Working Women (NCWW)
Wider Opportunities for Women (WOW)
1325 G St., NW
Washington, DC 20005
Phone: (202)638-3143
Fax: (202)638-4885

Description: Combines information devoted to increasing economic independence and equality of opportunities for women. **Frequency:** Quarterly.

★9560★ WOMENews
Pennsylvania Commission for the Status of Women
209 Finance Bldg.
PO Box 1326
Harrisburg, PA 17105
Phone: (717)787-8128

Description: Covers the activities of the Pennsylvania Commission for Women and similar women's organizations. **First published:** May 1977. **Frequency:** Quarterly.

★9561★ Womenpolice
International Association of Women Police
c/o Mona Moore
5800-A N. Sharon Amity Rd.
Box 252
Charlotte, NC 28215
Phone: (704)537-5997
Fax: (704)536-0635

Description: Focuses on women in police work and issues of interest to women officers around the world. Reports on relevant legislation and on recent promotions, awards, and commendations presented to female officers. Announces upcoming meetings, conferences, and training workshops. **Frequency:** 3/yr. **Price:** Included in membership; $25/yr. for nonmembers, U.S.; $35 elsewhere. **ISSN:** 0890-5894. **Former Title(s):** *Police Woman*; *IAWP Bulletin*.

★9562★ The Women's Advocate
National Center on Women and Family Law
799 Broadway, Rm. 402
New York, NY 10003
Phone: (212)674-8200
Fax: (212)533-5104

Description: "Discusses legal developments and emerging trends in such areas as domestic violence, intra-family custody, the rights of single mothers, divorce, child-snatching, child support, spousal support, rape, legal safeguards for older women." Focuses on legal avenues for dealing with economic and sex discrimination and on family law as it affects poor women. **First published:** January 1980. **Frequency:** Bimonthly. **Price:** $30/yr.

★9563★ Women's Building Newsletter/Calendar
1643 18th St.
Santa Monica, CA 90404
Phone: (213)828-6277

Description: Features announcements of interest to women artists.

★9564★ Women's Caucus Newsletter
American Public Health Association (APHA)
Women's Caucus
1015 15th St., NW
Washington, DC 20005
Phone: (202)789-5600

Description: Serves as a forum for a feminist opinion in the Association. **Frequency:** Semiannual.

★9565★ The Women's Caucus Newsletter
Speech Communications Association
Women's Caucus
5105 Backlick Rd., Ste. E
Annandale, VA 22003
Phone: (703)750-0533

Description: Disseminates information on women in communications. Supports scholarly research on women and gender. **Frequency:** Semiannual.

★9566★ Women's Caucus Quarterly
Texas A & M University
Women's Caucus for Political Science
Department of Political Science
Attn: Judith Baer
College Station, TX 77843
Phone: (409)845-2246

Description: Examines the status of women in the political science profession. **Frequency:** Quarterly. **Price:** Free.

★9567★ Women's Caucus: Religious Studies Newsletter
Women's Caucus: Religious Studies
2529 Elm St.
Youngstown, MA 44505
Phone: (216)742-1625

Description: Aimed at women working in the field of theology.

★9568★ Women's Collection Newsletter
Northwestern University Library
Evanston, IL 60208
Phone: (708)491-2895
Fax: (708)491-8306

Description: Features acquisitions, exhibits, developments, and current research. **Frequency:** Semiannual. **Price:** Free.

★9569★ The Women's College Coalition Quarterly
Women's College Coalition
1725 K St. NW, Ste. 750
Washington, DC 20006
Phone: (202)789-7556

Description: Brings news on the 85 women's colleges in the Coalition.

★9570★ Women's Cycling News
Women's Cycling Network
PO Box 73
Harvard, IL 60033
Phone: (815)943-3171

Description: Covers activities of women's cycling. **First published:** June 1984. **Frequency:** Quarterly. **Price:** $10/yr. for individuals; $40 for institutions.

★9571★ Women's Foreign Policy Council—News and Views
Women's Foreign Policy Council
845 3rd Ave., 15th Fl.
New York, NY 10022
Phone: (212)759-7982
Fax: (212)759-8647

Description: Reports Council activities. **Price:** Free.

★9572★ Women's Health Nursing Scan
Nurses Association of the American College of Obstetricians and Gynecologists (NAACOG)
409 12th St., SW
Washington, DC 20024-2188
Phone: (202)638-0026
Description: Brings updates on prenatal women's health nursing.

★9573★ Women's Heritage Museum— NEWS
Women's Heritage Museum
1509 Portola Ave.
Palo Alto, CA 94306
Phone: (415)321-5260
Description: Reports on endeavors to build a permanent structure to house its collection and increase awareness of global women's history. Contains news of exhibits, events, preservation, and research. **Frequency:** Quarterly. **Price:** $15/yr.

★9574★ Women's History Network—News
National Women's History Project
Women's History Network
7738 Bell Rd.
Windsor, CA 95492
Phone: (707)838-6000
Fax: (707)838-0478
Description: Promotes education on the history of women to reclaim the significant contributions of women and facilitate constructive social change. Carries historical articles and research reports. **First published:** 1984. **Frequency:** Quarterly. **Price:** Included in membership.

★9575★ Women's Investment Newsletter
Phoenix Communications Group, Ltd.
1837 S. Nevada Ave., Ste. 223 W.
Colorado Springs, CO 80906
Phone: (719)576-9200
Description: Presents in-depth analysis and trading strategies concerning common stocks, options, mutual funds, income/fixed securities, and tax-advantaged investments. Also considers such topics as tax planning and life insurance as they apply to investments. Written by women who are active investment/financial planners from around the U.S. and who have "a demonstrated expertise in their profession." Recurring features include letters to the editor, news of research, reports of meetings, book reviews and notices of publications available, and columns titled Uncommon Stocks and Income Investments. **First published:** 1984. **Frequency:** Monthly. **Price:** $39/yr., U.S. and Canada; $50 elsewhere.

★9576★ Women's Issues Task Force Newsletter
United Handicapped Federations
1821 University, Ste. 284
St. Paul, MN 55114
Phone: (612)645-8922
Fax: (612)649-3073
Description: Provides information on services, activities and conferences focused on the needs of disabled women. **Frequency:** Quarterly.

★9577★ Women's Legal Defense Fund Newsletter
Women's Legal Defense Fund (WLDF)
1875 Connecticut Ave., Ste. 710
Washington, DC 20009
Phone: (202)986-2600
Fax: (202)986-2539
Description: Reports activities of the WLDF. **Frequency:** Biannual. **Price:** $10/yr. for individuals. $15 for institutions and organizations.

★9578★ Women's Letter
American Federation of State, County and Municipal Employees (AFSCME)
Women's Rights Department
1625 I St., NW
Washington, DC 20036
Phone: (202)429-5090
Fax: (202)429-1293
Description: Features union news of concern to public employees. **Frequency:** 4/yr.

★9579★ Women's Liberation News and Letters
59 E. Van Buren, Ste. 707
Chicago, IL 60605
Phone: (312)663-0839
Description: Features the philosophical Marxist-Humanist works of Ray Dunayevskaya. Focuses on minorities and women. **Frequency:** Monthly. **Price:** $2.50/yr.

★9580★ The Women's National Democratic Club Calendar Notes
Women's National Democratic Club
1526 New Hampshire Ave., NW
Washington, DC 20036
Phone: (202)232-7363
Description: Serves as a vehicle for the discussion and evaluation of current issues and problems confronting the nation. **Frequency:** Monthly.

★9581★ Women's Network
American Society for Training and Development (ASTD)
Women's Network
Box 1443
1630 Duke St.
Alexandria, VA 22313
Phone: (703)683-8100
Fax: (703)683-8103
Description: Covers issues of interest to women as they relate to the human resource development field.

★9582★ Women's Network News
5804 Cary Dr.
Austin, TX 78757
Phone: (512)459-0309
Description: Examines Christian/feminist views on current controversial issues affecting women. **Frequency:** Bimonthly. **Price:** $2.50/yr.

★9583★ Women's Political Times
National Women's Political Caucus (NWPC)
1275 K St., NW
Washington, DC 20005-4051
Phone: (202)898-1100
Description: Geared towards women who are interested in politics.

★9584★ Women's Recovery Network
PO Box 141554
Columbus, OH 43214
Phone: (614)268-5847
Description: Addresses women recovering from alcoholism, codependency, drug addiction, eating disorders, domestic violence, incest, rape, and other physical and psychological disorders and injustices. **Frequency:** Bimonthly. **Price:** $27/yr. for individuals; $45 for institutions. In Canada, add $10 US; overseas, add $15 US.

★9585★ Women's Research Network News
National Council for Research on Women
Sara Delano Roosevelt Memorial House
47-49 E. 65th St.
New York, NY 10021
Phone: (212)570-5001
Fax: (212)570-5380
Description: Recurring features include interviews with prominent feminist scholars, and columns titled News from the Council, News from the Member Centers, News from Women's Caucuses in the Disciplines, News from International Women's Research Networks, Publications, Opportunities for Research and Study, and Job Opportunities. **First published:** 1988. **Frequency:** Quarterly. **Price:** Included in membership.

★9586★ Women's Rights Committee Newsletter
United Federation of Teachers (UFT)
Women's Rights Committee
260 Park Ave.
New York, NY 10010
Phone: (212)598-6879
Fax: (212)533-2704
Description: Provides curriculum information on teaching women's history. **Frequency:** Annual.

★9587★ Women's Studies Research Center—Newsletter
University of Wisconsin, Madison
Women's Studies Research Center
209 N. Brooks St.
Madison, WI 53715
Phone: (608)263-2053
Description: Presents information on research conducted at the UW - Madison, and administered by the Women's Studies Research Center. Includes topics such as motherhood, childbirth, health issues, feminism and science, technology, and women's autobiographies. **First published:** September 1979. **Frequency:** Biennially. **Price:** Free.

★9588★ The Women's Watch
Humphrey Institute of Public Affairs
International Women's Rights Action Watch
301 19th Ave., S.
Minneapolis, MN 55455
Phone: (612)625-2505
Fax: (612)625-6315
Description: Reports law and policy changes affecting the status of women worldwide. **Frequency:** Quarterly. **Price:** $20/yr.

★9589★ Womensword
Fort Wayne Women's Bureau, Inc.
303 E. Washington Blvd.
Ft. Wayne, IN 46802
Phone: (219)424-7977
Description: Features issues relevant to women, such as work, family, health, communication, and rape awareness. Lists resources, publications, activities. **Frequency:** Monthly.

★9590★ Womenwise
Concord Feminist Health Center
38 S. Main St.
Concord, NH 03301
Phone: (603)225-2739
Description: Covers women's health issues, including well-woman care, nutrition, and recent women's health news and information, with a feminist perspective. Also includes political analyses. **Frequency:** Quarterly. **Price:** $10/yr. for individuals; $20 for institutions.

★9591★ Womyn's Press
PO Box 562
Eugene, OR 97440
Description: Provides news and information on personal experience pieces, poetry, fiction, and art concerning women. **First published:** December 1970. **Frequency:** Bimonthly. **Price:** Free.

★9592★ Woodswomen News
25 W. Diamond Lake Rd.
Minneapolis, MN 55419
Phone: (612)822-3809
Description: Directed towards women interested in outdoor lifestyles. Contains philosophical and how-to articles, accounts on personal adventures, and information about guided international and domestic trips. **Frequency:** 2x/yr. **Subscription:** $15/yr.

★9593★ Working at Home
Mrs. H.C. McGarity
PO Box 200504
Cartersville, GA 30120
Phone: (404)386-1257
Description: Provides short articles about work-at-home opportunities for women who are unable to work outside of the home. **First published:** 1985. **Frequency:** Quarterly. **Price:** $12/5 issues, U.S.; $17 elsewhere.

★9594★ Working Together
National Association of Anorexia Nervosa
   and Associated Disorders (ANAD)
PO Box 7
Highland Park, IL 60035
Phone: (708)831-3438
Description: Publishes news of the Association, which is "dedicated to alleviating the problems of eating disorders." Features articles written by victims of anorexia nervosa and/or bulimia, therapists, and family members. **First published:** 1981. **Frequency:** Quarterly. **Price:** Included in membership. **Former Title(s):** ANAD.

★9595★ World CWF News
World Christian Women's Fellowship (CWF)
PO Box 1986
Indianapolis, IN 46206
Phone: (317)353-1491
Description: Reports on the international activities of the Fellowship, an organization of women in the Christian Church (Disciples of Christ). Carries photos and biographies of executive committee members and news from these women, who represent 17 countries involved in united missionary action. **First published:** 1954. **Frequency:** Semiannual. **Price:** Free. **Former Title(s):** World Christian Women's Fellowship—Newsletter, December 1987.

★9596★ World Federation of Health Agencies for the Advancement of Voluntary Surgical Contraception—Communique
World Federation of Health Agencies for the
   Advancement of Voluntary Surgical
   Contraception
122 E. 42nd St.
New York, NY 10168
Phone: (212)351-2536
Fax: (212)599-0959
Description: Covers all aspects of voluntary surgical contraception, including programs, research, legal issues, new technologies, medical guidelines, and counseling. Emphasizes voluntary sterilization issues in developing countries. **First published:** 1980. **Frequency:** 2/yr. **Price:** Free. **ISSN:** 0001-2904.

★9597★ WORLD Newsletter
PO Box 11535
Oakland, CA 94611
Phone: (510)658-6930
Description: Newsletter for women with HIV and AIDS to "share information about doctors, drugs, insurance, support groups, and life." **First published:** May 1991. **Frequency:** Monthly. **Subscription:** $50-$100 donation per year for organizations; $20-$50 for individuals who can afford a donation; free to others.

★9598★ WorldWIDE—News
WorldWIDE
1331 H St. NW, Ste. 903
Washington, DC 20005
Phone: (202)347-1514
Fax: (202)347-1524
Subtitle: World Women in Development and Environment. **Description:** Features information, successful projects, studies and reports, organizations, and policies that affect women, environment, and natural resources throughout the world. **First published:** 1982. **Frequency:** 6/yr. **Price:** $25/yr.

★9599★ WRI Newsletter
Virginia Polytechnic Institute and State
   University
Women's Research Institute (WRI)
10 Sandy Hall
Blacksburg, VA 24061-0338
Phone: (703)231-7615
Description: Publicizes the Institute's efforts to advance and promote research by, for, and about women.

★9600★ YWCA Interchange
Young Women's Christian Association of the
   U.S.A. (YWCA)
726 Broadway
New York, NY 10003
Phone: (212)614-2700
Description: Articles emphasize world responsibility, education, employment, health, recreation, and the elimination of sexism and racism. Also covers national and local YWCA news. **Frequency:** Quarterly. **Price:** Free.

(22) Newspapers

Entries in this chapter are arranged alphabetically by publication title. See the User's Guide at the front of this directory for additional information.

★9601★ Athena
Box 5028
Thousand Oaks, CA 91360
Phone: (805)379-3185
Description: International newspaper focusing on domestic violence. Contains stories, columns, and more. **Frequency:** 2x/yr. **Subscription:** $3/yr; $6/yr outside U.S.

★9602★ Binnewater Tides
Women's Studio Workshop
PO Box 489
Rosendale, NY 12472
Phone: (914)658-9133
Description: Newspaper for women artists, including writers and photographers. **Frequency:** Quarterly.

★9603★ Clarion
2956 N. Campbell, No. 310
Tucson, AZ 85719
Phone: (602)628-1518
Description: Women's newspaper.

★9604★ The Disability Rag
PO Box 145
Louisville, KY 40201
Phone: (502)459-5343
Description: Newspapers on women's disability rights. **Frequency:** 6x/year. **Subscription:** $12.

★9605★ Exclusively Connecticut
MacClaren Press, Inc.
315 Peck St.
New Haven, CT 06513-0580
Phone: (203)782-1420
Description: Targeted to women who live and work in New Haven, Fairfield, and Hartford Counties. Features local women and provides resources for networking. **Frequency:** Monthly. **Subscription:** $13.

★9606★ Exponent II
Exponent II, Inc.
PO Box 37
Arlington, MA 02174
Phone: (617)862-1928
Description: Newspaper for Mormon women. **First published:** 1974. **Frequency:** Quarterly. **Subscription:** $10.

★9607★ Freedom Socialist
Freedom Socialist Party
5018 Rainier Ave. S.
Seattle, WA 98118
Phone: (206)722-2453
Subtitle: Voice of Revolutionary Feminism. **Description:** Socialist newspaper. **First published:** 1966. **Frequency:** Quarterly. **ISSN:** 0272-4367. **Subscription:** $5.

★9608★ Glos Polek/Polish Women's Voice
Polish Women's Alliance of America
203 S. Northwest Hwy.
Parkridge, IL 60068
Phone: (312)693-6215
Description: Newspaper reporting on Polish ethnic and cultural concerns. Also includes organization news of official nature (Polish and English). **First published:** 1910. **Frequency:** 2x/mo. **ISSN:** 0199-0462. **Subscription:** Included with membership.

★9609★ Harrington Journal
PO Box 239
Harrington, DE 19952
Phone: (302)398-3206
Description: Newspaper on women's interests. **First published:** 1913. **Frequency:** Weekly (Wed.). **Subscription:** $12.

★9610★ Hera
Women's Center
PO Box 354
Binghamton, NY 13902
Phone: (607)770-9014
Subtitle: The Women's Center Newspaper. **Description:** Feminist tabloid newspaper. **First published:** May 1981. **Frequency:** Monthly (Jan./Feb. and Sept./Oct. combined issues). **Subscription:** $6.

★9611★ Houston Woman
1702 S. Post Oak Ln.
Houston, TX 77056
Phone: (713)961-0599
Fax: (713)523-8915
Description: Articles for professional women on finance, health and fitness, legal issues, career strategies, personal issues, profiles, and a calendar of events of business and professional groups in and around the Houston, Texas, area. **Frequency:** Monthly. **Subscription:** $15.

★9612★ Labyrinth
4722 Baltimore Ave.
Philadelphia, PA 19143
Phone: (215)724-6181
Description: Newspaper for Philadelphia area women. Seeks to print material that is feminist, non-racist, and non-homophobic. **Frequency:** Monthly. **Subscription:** $15.

★9613★ Minnesota Women's Press
Minnesota Women's Press, Inc.
771 Raymond Ave.
St. Paul, MN 55114-1522
Phone: (612)646-3968
Description: Feminist newspaper providing news coverage by and for women. **First published:** April 17, 1985. **Frequency:** Every other week (Wed.). **Subscription:** $25; $45 two years.

★9614★ North Shore Woman's Newspapers, Inc.
PO Box 1056
Huntington, NY 11743
Phone: (516)271-0832
Description: Feminist news, community events, financial advice, poetry, and book and film reviews. **Frequency:** Monthly. **Subscription:** $10.

★9615★ Of A Like Mind
Reformed Congregation
Box 6021
Madison, WI 53716
Phone: (608)838-8629
Description: International network and newspaper ''for spiritual womyn.'' Includes articles, reviews, graphics, and an extensive networking section. **Subscription:** $13-$33.

★9616★ The OWL Observer
Older Women's League (OWL)
730 11th St. NW, Ste. 300
Washington, DC 20001
Phone: (202)783-6686
Fax: (202)638-2356
Description: National. Includes news, views, and concerns of mid-life and older women activists. **Frequency:** 6/yr. **Subscription:** $15.

★9617★ Probe
National Assembly of Religious Women
 (NARW)
529 S. Wabash, Rm. 404
Chicago, IL 60605
Phone: (312)663-1980
Description: Tabloid includes theological reflection, social analysis, and action suggestions.
Frequency: Bimonthly. **Subscription:** $20.

★9618★ Riveting News
Hard Hatted Women
PO Box 93384
Cleveland, OH 44101
Phone: (216)961-4449
Description: Tabloid reporting on racism, affirmative action, child care, the environment, housing, and other issues relating to women. Includes book reviews. **Frequency:** Quarterly.
Subscription: $7.

★9619★ San Diego Lesbian Press
PO Box 8666
San Diego, CA 92102
Description: Newspaper providing a forum and focus for lesbian ideas and issues. **Frequency:** 6x/yr.

★9620★ Sappho's Isle
256 W. 15th St.
New York, NY 10011
Phone: (212)620-9013
Fax: (717)676-5284
Description: "The Tri-State Lesbian Newspaper." Includes articles of general interest in addition to local (New York) news. **Frequency:** Monthly. **Subscription:** $12 for postage; otherwise distributed free. $1/Issue.

★9621★ SheTotem
Panic Press
PO Box 27465
San Antonio, TX 78227-0465
Description: Tabloid covering magic and witchcraft, and regaining-remerging with the pre-Christian deities of Earth, Air, Fire, and Water. Contains book and film reviews. **Frequency:** Quarterly. **Subscription:** $10.

★9622★ Sonoma County Women's Voices
PO Box 4448
Santa Rosa, CA 95402
Phone: (707)575-5654
Description: Addresses the issues and concerns of the women of Sonoma County, CA. Includes a calendar of events, news, features, poetry, and reviews. **Frequency:** Monthly. **Subscription:** $10.

★9623★ Today's Chicago Woman
Leigh Communications, Inc.
233 E. Ontario St., Ste. 1300
Chicago, IL 60611
Phone: (312)951-7600
Description: Magazine (tabloid) providing information to working women in Chicago. **First published:** October 1982. **Frequency:** Monthly. **Subscription:** Free to qualified subscribers.

★9624★ Today's Woman
PO Box 1048
Peoria, IL 61653-1048
Phone: (309)672-2722
Description: Newspaper focusing on women's issues, news, and profiles. **First published:** 1985. **Frequency:** Monthly.

★9625★ WAND Bulletin
Women's Action for Nuclear Disarmament
 (WAND)
691 Massachusetts Ave.
Arlington, MA 02174
Phone: (617)643-6740
Fax: (617)643-6744
Description: Tabloid serves to educate women in political action so that they can work to eliminate weapons of mass destruction and redirect military spending to human and environmental needs. **Frequency:** Quarterly.

★9626★ Welfare Mothers Voice
4504 N. 47th
Milwaukee, WI 53218
Phone: (414)444-0220
Description: Written by, for, and about mothers. Supported by Aid to Families with Dependent Children (AFDC). Available in English and Spanish. **Frequency:** Quarterly.

★9627★ WIFE Line
Women Involved in Farm Economics (WIFE)
Box 191
Hingham, MT 59528
Description: Includes editorials and reports on commodities. **Frequency:** Monthly. **Subscription:** $5.

★9628★ Womanews
PO Box 220 Village Sta.
New York, NY 10014
Phone: (212)674-1698
Description: New York City feminist newspaper and calendar. Provides a forum for the NYC feminist community while focusing on issues of interest to women everywhere. **Frequency:** Monthly. **Subscription:** $1.25/sample issue.

★9629★ Women's Almanac
14301 SW 87th Ave.
Miami, FL 33176
Phone: (305)235-4356
Description: By, for, and about Florida women.
Subscription: $15.

★9630★ Women's News
PO Box 829
Harrison, NY 10528
Phone: (914)835-5400
Description: Feminist newspaper geared toward women's issues, problems, events, and causes. Features pull-out event calendar, newsbriefs, followups, classifieds, displays, letters, and special cultural issues. **First published:** December 1979. **Frequency:** Monthly. **Subscription:** $15.

★9631★ The Women's Record
JAG Publishers Ltd.
55 Northern Blvd.
Greenvale, NY 11548
Phone: (516)625-3033
Subtitle: Long Island's Premier Publication for Working Women. **Description:** Business newspaper for professional women. **First published:** August 1985. **Frequency:** Monthly. **ISSN:** 1044-3312. **Subscription:** $10; $16.95 two years.

★9632★ Women's World
B'nai B'rith Women
1828 L St. NW Ste. 250
Washington, DC 20036
Phone: (202)857-1370
Description: Jewish women's newspaper. **First published:** 1951. **Frequency:** 4x/yr. **ISSN:** 0043-759X. **Subscription:** Included in membership dues.

(23) Publishers

Entries in this chapter are arranged alphabetically by publisher's name. See the User's Guide at the front of this directory for additional information.

★9633★ **Achievement Press**
1501 Fort Mackenzie Rd.
PO Box 6
Sheridan, WY 82801

Description: Publishes consumer-oriented publications on health-related topics. Reaches market through direct mail and major small press distributors. **Subjects:** Health, Wyoming, breastfeeding, childbirth. **Number of New Titles:** 1990 - 1; Total Titles in Print - 6. **Selected Titles:** *Breastfeeding Success for Working Mothers, Breastfeeding Source Book,* both by Marilyn Grams; *Our Wyoming Heritage as Seen Through the Eyes of the Young.* **Principal Officials and Managers:** Wendell J. Robison, President; A. L. Matthews, Marketing Manager; Mary Scott, Senior Editor.

★9634★ **Advocacy Press**
PO Box 2
Santa Barbara, CA 93102
Phone: (805)962-2728

Description: Publishes works particularly relevant to today's girls and young women, ages six to twenty. Offers videos of four children's books. Also offers workshops, newsletters, and posters. Accepts manuscripts related to gender equity issues; include a self-addressed, stamped envelope. Distributes for other publishers. Reaches market through direct mail, display advertising, conventions, and major small press distributors. **Number of New Titles:** 1989 - 3, 1990 - 2, 1991 (est.) - 4; Total Titles in Print - 21. **Selected Titles:** *More Choices: A Strategic Guide for Mixing Career and Family* by Bingham and Stryker; *My Way Sally* by Melinda Bingham and Penelope Paine; *Tonia the Tree* by Sandy Stryker; *Kylie's Song* by Patty Sheehan; *Berta Benz and the Motorwagen* by Bingham; *Time for Horatio* by Penelope Paine. **Principal Officials and Managers:** Penelope Paine, Editor and Marketing Director.

★9635★ **Afro Resources, Inc.**
PO Box 192
Temple Hills, MD 20748
Phone: (301)894-3855

Subjects: Afro-American women.

★9636★ **Aglow Publications**
PO Box 15
Lynnwood, WA 98047-1557
Phone: (206)775-7282

Description: "Aglow Publications is the publishing division of Women's Aglow Fellowship International, a worldwide organization providing support, education, training, and ministry opportunities to help women discover their true identity in Jesus Christ through the power of the Holy Spirit. Readers are contemporary women of all ages who juggle many demands." Reaches market through direct mail, trade sales, and distributors. **Subjects:** Female concerns, Christianity, support groups. **Selected Titles:** *How to Pray for Your Children* by Quin Sherrer; *Friends Forever* by Janet Bly; *Love and Its Counterfeits* by Barbara Cook; *Sure Footing in a Shaky World* by Kathy Collard Miller; *How to Say Goodbye* by Joanne Smith and Judy Biggs; *Beyond Fear* by Michelle Cresse. **Principal Officials and Managers:** Susan Goodnight, Vice-President, Publications; Gloria Chisholm, Acquisitions Editor; Jennifer Hatloe, Production Manager.

★9637★ **Air-Plus Enterprises**
PO Box 1
Garrisonville, VA 22463

Description: An information agency dealing with women's health and sexuality. In addition to publishing, does some research of medical literature, provides information for students' term papers, etc. **Subjects:** Legal abortion, women's health and sexuality. **Selected Titles:** *Every Woman Has a Right to Know the Dangers of Legal Abortion; The Threat of Abortion; When Legal Means Lethal; Teachers, Counselors: Abortion Is Legal, What Could Possibly Go Wrong; Holocaust: How Could It Have Happened; Introducing the Preborn and the Newborn,* all by Ann Saltenberger. **Principal Officials and Managers:** J. Frost, Manager.

★9638★ **Alan Guttmacher Institute**
111 5th Ave.
New York, NY 10003
Phone: (212)254-5656

Description: Publishes research and policy analysis in the field of reproductive health. Offers photographic slide rentals. Accepts unsolicited manuscripts. Distributes for Yale University Press. Reaches market through direct mail. **Subjects:** Family planning, population, abortion, sex education, prenatal and maternity care, adolescent sexuality, women's rights, law, and policy. **Number of New Titles:** 1989 - 7, 1990 - 4, 1991 (est.) - 3; Total Titles in Print - 34. **Selected Titles:** *Abortion and Women's Health* by Rachel Gold; *Ru 486: The Science and the Politics* by Michael Klitsch; *Barriers to Contraceptive Services* by Jane Silverman and Aida Torres; *Readings on Teenage Pregnancy;* *Prenatal Care in the US: A State and County Inventory; Risk and Responsibility: Teaching Sex Education in America's Schools Today.* **Principal Officials and Managers:** Jeannie I. Rosoff, President; Olivia Schieffelin, Director of Publications and Editor-in-Chief; Beth Fredrick, Director of Communications and Development; Jacqueline Darroch-Forrest, Vice-President for Research; Donald L. Mullare, Director of Finance and Administration.

★9639★ **The Alaskan Viewpoint**
HCR 64, Box 453
Seward, AK 99664
Phone: (907)288-3168

Founded: 1986. **Subjects:** Reference guide to Alaskan Arts & Crafts; children's literature; Alaskan women.

★9640★ **Alicejamesbooks**
33 Richdale Ave.
Cambridge, MA 02140-2627
Phone: (617)354-1408

Founded: 1973. **Subjects:** Women and New England poets.

★9641★ **Alleluia Press**
672 Franklin Tpke.
Allendale, NJ 07401
Phone: (201)327-3513

Founded: 1969.

★9642★ **Allen and Unwin**
8 Winchester Pl.
Winchester, MA 01890
Phone: (617)729-0830

Description: Publishes women's studies books.

★9643★ **Alternative Press Center**
PO Box 33109
Baltimore, MD 21218
Phone: (410)243-2471

★9644★ **Alyson Publications, Inc.**
40 Plympton St.
Boston, MA 02118
Phone: (617)542-5679

Description: Publishes books for gay and lesbian readership. Accepts unsolicited manuscripts; must query with outline first. Include a self-addressed, stamped envelope. Distributes for GMP Publishers (England). Reaches market through direct mail, trade sales, and distributors, including Inland Book Co., BookPeople, and Carrier Pigeon Distributors. **Number of New Titles:** 1989 - 20, 1990 - 17, 1991 (est.) - 20; Total Titles in Print - 110. **Selected Titles:** *Choices* by Nancy Toder; *Cody* by J. Keith Hale; *Long Time Passing* by Marcy Adelman; *Reflections of a Rock Lobster* by Aaron Fricke; *Rocking the Cradle* by G. Hanscombe and J. Forster; *Goldenboy* by Michael Nava. **Principal Officials and Managers:** Sasha Alyson, President.

★9645★ **Am-Fem Co.**
PO Box 93, Cooper St
New York, NY 10276

Subjects: Sports. **Number of New Titles:** 1990 - 1; Total Titles in Print - 1. **Selected Titles:** *International Directory of Amateur Female Fighting, Supplement to International Directory of Amateur Female Fighting.* **Principal Officials and Managers:** A. Ripstone, Partner.

★9646★ **American Association of University Women**
1111 16th St. NW
Washington, DC 20036
Phone: (202)785-7700

Subjects: Education. **Selected Titles:** *College Admissions Tests: Opportunities or Roadblocks; Progress for Women in Financial Aid; Protecting Academic Freedom; Pay Equity Action Guide; AAUW Outlook; Action Alert.* **Principal Officials and Managers:** Sharon Schuster, President; Anne Bryant, Executive Director; Karen Johnson, Editor.

★9647★ **American Citizens Concerned for Life, Inc. (ACCL)**
Communications Center
PO Box 1
Excelsior, MN 55331
Phone: (612)474-0885

Description: A national nonprofit organization engaged in educational, research, and service activities "to promote respect for all human life in contemporary society." Also publishes a counseling manual, booklets, ideas, and a video, *Who Broke the Baby.* Reaches market through direct mail. **Selected Titles:** *New Perspectives on Human Abortion* edited by Hilgers, Horan, and Mall; *Counseling the Individual Experiencing a Troubled Pregnancy; Sex and the Illusion of Freedom* by Dr. Donald De Marco; *The First Nine Months of Life* by Geraldine Lux Flanagan; *Too Much, Too Soon* by Samuel A. Nigro; *In Good Conscience: Abortion and Moral Necessity* by David Mall. **Principal Officials and Managers:** Gloria Ford, President; William C. Hunt, Secretary-Treasurer; Carol W. Riddle, Director, Communications Center.

★9648★ **American Life League**
2721 Jefferson Davis Hwy., Ste. 101
Stafford, VA 22554
Phone: (703)659-4171

Description: Concerned with life and family issues, specifically abortion, euthanasia, anti-life organizations, and history. Offers a magazine and newsletter. Reaches market through direct mail and wholesalers. **Total Titles in Print:** 35. **Selected Titles:** *The Anti-Life Conspiracy* by Rene Bel; *Sex Is Alive and Well and Flourishing among Christians* by V. Henry Sattler; *Choices in Matter of Life and Death* by Judie Brown; *Abortion: Choice or Chance* by Ann Saltenber-

ger. **Principal Officials and Managers:** Judith A. Brown, President; Clay Mansfield, Treasurer.

★9649★ **Americans United for Life Legal Defense Fund**
343 S. Dearborn, Ste. 1804
Chicago, IL 60604
Phone: (312)786-9494

Description: The legal arm of the pro-life movement; offers legislative testimony, drafts model abortion statutes, and writes legal briefs in cases involving abortion and euthanasia. Publishes educational materials and newsletters. Offers a quarterly legal reporter, *Lex Vitae* and a monthly news summary, *Life Docket,* and others. Reaches market through direct mail. Formerly known as Americans United for Life Legal Defense Fund. **Selected Titles:** *Death, Dying, and Euthanasia* edited by Dennis J. Horan and David Mall; *Abortion and Social Justice* edited by Thomas W. Hilgers and Dennis J. Horan; *A Private Choice* by John T. Noonan; *Abortion and the Conscience of the Nation* by Ronald Reagan; *Abortion and the Constitution: Reversing Roe vs. Wade through the Courts* edited by Dennis J. Horan, Edward R. Grants, and Paige Comstock Cunningham. **Principal Officials and Managers:** Guy Condon, President; Clarke D. Forsythe, General Counsel; Laurie Anne Ramsey, Vice-President for Public Affairs.

★9650★ **Ananke's Womon Publications**
PO Box 1348, Madison Sq. St
New York, NY 10159
Phone: (212)796-1467

Description: Self-publisher of feminist literature. Offers audio and video cassettes and a quarterly publication, *The Gold Flag Bulletin.* Reaches market through direct mail and Inland Book Co. **Number of New Titles:** 1990 - 1, 1992 (est.) - 1; Total Titles in Print - 8. **Selected Titles:** *Feminism: Freedom from Wifism, How to Build a Feminist Bridge, Tricks of the Voice, The Arrest of an American Feminist, The Incompetent Gift of Violence against Masters, A Scrap of Royal Need,* all by Mia Albright. **Principal Officials and Managers:** Mia Albright, Author and Publisher.

★9651★ **Andrew Mountain Press**
PO Box 14353
Hartford, CT 06114

Founded: 1980. **Subjects:** Poetry with political or feminist slant, cookbooks, and children's books.

★9652★ **Antelope Publications**
1050 S. Monado, No. 97
Denver, CO 80224
Phone: (303)355-0504

Description: Publishes pamphlets, articles, and speeches of current feminist thought. **Total Titles in Print:** 4. **Selected Titles:** *Feminism in the 80's: Facing Down the Right, Feminism in the 80's: Going Public with Our Vision, Feminism in the 80's: Bringing the Global Home,* all by Charlotte Bunch; *Compulsory Heterosexuality and Lesbian Existence* by Adrienne Rich. **Principal Officials and Managers:** Jacqueline St. Joan, Proprietor.

★9653★ **Apprentice Academics**
PO Box 7
Claremore, OK 74018-0788
Phone: (918)342-1335

Description: Publishes on midwifery and childbirth education. Offers teaching aids, seminars, and workshops on time management, childbirth education, and midwifery. **Principal Officials and Managers:** Carla Hartley, Owner.

★9654★ **Aquarian Research Foundation**
5620 Morton St.
Philadelphia, PA 19144
Phone: (215)849-3237

Subjects: Natural birth control, alternative lifestyles, peace research. **Selected Titles:** *The Natural Birth Control Book* by Art Rosenblum. **Principal Officials and Managers:** Art Rosenblum, Director; Judy Rosenblum, Assistant Director.

★9655★ **Arachne Publishing Co.**
PO Box 41
Mountain View, CA 94040
Phone: (415)961-5709

Description: Aims to encourage feminist materials. Offers postcards. **Subjects:** Humor. **Total Titles in Print:** 3. **Selected Titles:** *I'm Not for Women's Lib. But, Dissecting Dr. Medicorpse, Sugar Daddy's a Sticky Myth,* all cartoons by Bulbul.

★9656★ **Arden Press**
PO Box 4
Denver, CO 80201
Phone: (303)239-6155

Description: Publishes in the areas of women's studies and film studies. Accepts unsolicited manuscripts. Reaches market through direct mail, wholesalers, and trade sales. **Number of New Titles:** 1989 - 2, 1990 - 5, 1991 (est.) - 2; Total Titles in Print - 10. **Selected Titles:** *Film: The Front Line 1* by Jonathan Rosenbaum; *Film: The Front Line 2* by David Ehrenstein; *Film: The Front Line 3* by Berenice Reynaud; *Behind the Spanish Lens: Spanish Cinema Under Fascism and Democracy* by Peter Besas; *Woman's Counsel: A Legal Guide for Women* by Gayle Niles and Douglas Snider; *Uncommon Eloquence: A Biography of Angna Enters* by Dorothy Mandel. **Principal Officials and Managers:** Frederick Ramey, Susan C. Holte.

★9657★ **Arkansas Women's History Institute**
PO Box 77
Little Rock, AR 72217
Phone: (501)623-7396

Description: Publishes on Arkansas women's history. Offers biannual conferences and an annual award for manuscripts on women's history. Reaches market through direct mail and publisher sales. **Total Titles in Print:** 1. **Selected Titles:** *Behold! Our Works Were Good: A Handbook of Arkansas Women's History* edited by Elizabeth Jacoway. **Principal Officials and Managers:** Janie Evins, President; Nancy Britton, Vice-President; Barbara Patty, Treasurer; Wendy Richter, Secretary.

★9658★ **Arte Publico Press**
The Americas Review
University of Houston
Houston, TX 77204
Phone: (713)749-4768

Description: Publishes literature by Hispanic authors, with an emphasis on works by Hispanic Women. Genres include poetry, plays, essays, short stories and novels. **Selected Titles:** *The House on Mango Street* by Sandra Cisneros, and *The Last of the Menu Girls* by Denise Chavez.

★9659★ **Arts & Images**
10485 Dupont Rd. S.
Bloomington, MN 55431
Phone: (612)888-7712

Description: Publishes resource manuals and how-to books on health and social service issues. Reaches market through direct mail and trade sales. **Number of New Titles:** 1990 - 2, 1991 (est.) - 3; Total Titles in Print - 1. **Selected Titles:** *Free Child Care in Your Community: How to Find It, Free Adult Day Care in Your Community: How to Find It,* both by Susan Anton-Johnson. **Principal Officials and Managers:** Susan Anton-Johnson, President.

★9660★ **Ash Tree Publishing**
PO Box
Woodstock, NY 12498
Phone: (914)246-8081

Description: Aims to "reweave the threads of the wise woman healing tradition." Publishes herbals and herbally related books and tarot decks. Offers workshops and apprenticeships in the "wise woman" tradition. Reaches market through direct mail, BookPeople, and Inland Book Co. **Number of New Titles:** 1989 - 1, 1990 - 1, 1991 (est.) - 1; Total Titles in Print - 3. **Selected Titles:** *Wise Woman Herbal for the Childbearing Year, Healing Wise,* both by Susun S. Weed. **Principal Officials and Managers:** Susun S. Weed, Owner.

★9661★ **Association of American Colleges Project on the Status and Education of Women**
1818 R St. NW
Washington, DC 20009
Phone: (202)387-3760

Description: Provides information concerning women students, faculty, and administrators. Publishes the newsletter *On Campus with Women.* Reaches market through direct mail. **Selected Titles:** *Financial Aid: A Partial List of Resources for Women* by Julie K. Ehrhart; *Campus Gang Rape: Party Games* by Julie K. Ehrhart and Bernice R. Sandler; *In Case of Sexual Harassment: A Guide for Women Students, Peer Harassment: Hassels for Women on Campus,* both by Jean Hughes and Bernice R. Sandler; *The Classroom Climate: A Chilly One for Women* by Roberta Hall and Bernice R. Sandler; *Black Women in Academe: Issues and Strategies* by Yolanda T. Moses. **Principal Officials and Managers:** Sherry Levy-Reiner, Director, Public Information and Publications.

★9662★ **Association of Part-Time Professionals**
Crescent Plaza
7700 Leesburg Pike, Ste. 216
Falls Church, VA 22043
Phone: (703)734-7975

Description: Provides information about part-time employment and trends, families and work, and older workers. Offers a newsletter and a resource kit. Reaches market through direct mail. **Number of New Titles:** 1990 - 2. **Selected Titles:** *Job Sharing Handbook* by Barney Olmsted and Suzanne Smith; *Employee Benefits for Part-Timers* 2nd ed., *Part-Time Professional,* both by Diane S. Rothberg and Barbara Ensor Cook; *A Mother's Choice: To Work or Not While Raising a Family* by Barbara Ensor Cook; *Flexible Work Options: A Selected Biography* by Maria Laqueur; *Sure-Hire Resumes* by Robbie M. Kaplan. **Principal Officials and Managers:** Maria Laqueur, Executive Director; Judith A. McVerry, President.

★9663★ **Association for Women in Science (AWIS)**
1522 K St. NW, Ste. 820
Washington, DC 20005
Phone: (202)408-0742

Description: Promotes equal opportunities for women to enter the sciences and achieve their career goals. Publishes *AWIS Newsletter.* Reaches market through membership mailings. **Selected Titles:** *Grants-at-a-Glance; Careers in Science; Gender and Science: A Panel Discussion; AWIS-CAC Compilation of Recommended Career Guidance Resources.* **Principal Officials and Managers:** Stephanie J. Bird, Ph.D., President; Catherine Diction, Executive Director.

★9664★ **Astarte Shell Press**
PO Box 104
Portland, ME 04104
Phone: (207)871-1817

Description: Publishes on feminist spirituality. Accepts unsolicited manuscripts; query first with outline and sample chapter. Reaches market through direct mail and distributors, including Inland Book Co., BookPeople, and New Leaf Distributing Co. **Number of New Titles:** 1990 - 1, 1991 - 1, 1992 (est.) - 4; Total Titles in Print - 2. **Selected Titles:** *Moon in Hand* by Eclipse; *Vision and Struggle* by Eleanor H. Haney. **Principal Officials and Managers:** Debbie Leighton, Marketing; Diane Eiker, Business Manager; Elly Haney and Sapphire, Editors; Sylvia Sims, Design.

★9665★ **Ata Books**
1928 Stuart St.
Berkeley, CA 94703
Phone: (415)841-9613

Founded: 1978.

★9666★ **Aunt Lute Book Co.**
PO Box 4106
San Francisco, CA 94141
Phone: (415)558-8116

Description: Aunt Lute Books is sponsored by the Aunt Lute Foundation, which is the non-profit entity that grew out of Spinsters/Aunt Lute Book Company. Publishes fiction and nonfiction by women, with an emphasis on work by women of color and lesbians. Accepts unsolicited manuscripts. Reaches market through direct mail, trade sales, and distribu-

tors, including BookPeople, Inland Book Co., and Pacific Pipeline. Formerly listed as Spinsters/Aunt Lute Book Co. **Number of New Titles:** 1989 - 6; Total Titles in Print - 15. **Selected Titles:** *Boarderlands/La Frontera* by Gloria Anzaldua; *The Cancer Journals* by Audre Lorde; *The Woman Who Owned The Shadows* by Paula Gunn Allen; *My Jewish Face and Other Stories* by Melanie Kaye/Kantrowitz; *Daughter of the Mountain* by Edna Escamill. **Principal Officials and Managers:** Joan C. Pinkvoss.

★9667★ **Avery Publishing Group**
120 Old Broadway
Garden City Park, NY 11040
Phone: (516)741-2155

Description: Publishes college texts, reference books, and trade titles specializing in childbirth, child care, natural cooking, health, and military books. Distributes for Prism Press, Ashgrove Press, Paper Tiger Books, and Foulshom & Co. Reaches market through direct mail and Publishers Group West. **Number of New Titles:** 1989 - 60, 1991 (est.) - 35; Total Titles in Print - 400. **Selected Titles:** *The Juicing Book* by Stephen Blaver; *The Complete Book of Homeopathy* by Michael Weiner; *The Complete Prenatal Water Workout* by Helga Hughes; *Heind Psychology* by Andrew Fitzherbert; *The Occult Experience* by Neville Drury; *The Macrobiotic Cancer Prevention Cookbook* by Avalline Kushi and Wendy Esko. **Principal Officials and Managers:** Rudy Shur, Managing Editor; Lee Solomon, Vice-President; Ken Rajman, Sales Manager.

★9668★ **B.A. Press**
1269 N. E St.
San Bernardino, CA 92405
Phone: (714)355-1100

Description: Publishes how-to information in the areas of education, prevention, and intervention for domestic violence. Reaches market through direct mail. **Total Titles in Print:** 3. **Selected Titles:** *The MAN Program: Self-Help Counseling for Child Molesters; National Directory: Domestic Violence Resources; Batterers Anonymous: Self-Help Counseling for Men Who Batter Women,* all by Jerry M. Goffman, Ph.D. **Principal Officials and Managers:** Jerry M. Goffman, Ph.D., Publisher.

★9669★ **Banned Books**
PO Box 33280, No. 292
Austin, TX 78764
Phone: (512)282-8044

Description: Books aimed at the gay/lesbian reader. Genres include erotic and short fiction, humor and mystery. **Selected Titles:** *Intricate Passions* edited by Tee Corinne and *Sugar with Spice* by Kieran.

★9670★ **Barn Owl Books**
PO Box 226
Vallecitos, NM 87581
Phone: (505)582-4226

Founded: 1982. **Description:** Planetary healing, spiritual growth, literature, feminism, transformation (cultural). **Selected Titles:** *The Lesbian Reader.*

★9671★ Battered Women's Directory
Box E-84
Earlham College
Richmond, IN 47374
Phone: (317)966-0858

Description: Promotes women's rights; opposes economic discrimination, sexual harassment, and domestic violence. Reaches market through direct mail and libraries. **Subjects:** Battered women. **Total Titles in Print:** 1. **Selected Titles:** *Battered Women's Directory* edited by Betsy Warrior. **Principal Officials and Managers:** Betsy Warrior, Author; Stacey Sewall, Terry Mehlman, Editors.

★9672★ Beacon Press
25 Beacon St.
Boston, MA 02108
Phone: (617)742-2110
Fax: (617)723-3097

Founded: 1854. **Description:** Women's studies, religion, gay and lesbian studies and environmental issues.

★9673★ Bergamot Books
PO Box 7413
Minneapolis, MN 55407
Phone: (612)722-6058

Description: Publish books written by women regarding the wilderness and environment. **Selected Titles:** *White Silk and Black Tar: A Journal of the Alaska Oil Spill* by Page Spencer; *Arctic Daughter: A Wilderness Journey* by Jean Aspen.

★9674★ Best to You! Press
PO Box 1
Cabin John, MD 20818
Phone: (301)229-6765

Description: Originally established to provide women's consumer information. Basic philosophy includes women's right to education, professional achievement, and life-plan decision-making. Formerly known as Women Matter's Press. Accepts unsolicited manuscripts; query first. Reaches market through direct mail. **Number of New Titles:** 1991 (est.) - 8; Total Titles in Print - 6. **Selected Titles:** *Cut Your Day-to-Day Household Expenses, Reduce Breakfast Costs by 50 Percent, Make Money Selling Baked Products, Wardrobe Tips Guaranteed to Save Women Money, Common Sense Guide to Diet and Exercise, Tips for Mature Women Who Plan to Re-enter the Job Market,* all by Barbara Schnipper. **Principal Officials and Managers:** Barbara Schnipper, Publisher and Owner.

★9675★ Biblio Press
1140 Broadway, R. 1507
New York, NY 10001
Phone: (212)684-1257

Description: Publishes feminist guides and Jewish women's studies books. **Number of New Titles:** 1989 - 1, 1990 - 2; Total Titles in Print - 14. **Selected Titles:** *Written Out of History: Our Jewish Foremothers* by Taitz and Henry; *Jews and the Cults* by Jack Nusan Porter; *Sex and the Modern Jewish Woman* compiled by Joan Scherer Brewer et al.; *The Jewish Woman: 1900-1985 Bibliography* compiled by A. Cantor et al.; *The Jewish Women's Studies Guide,* 2nd ed. compiled by Sue Levi Elwell; *Preparing for Sabbath* by Nessa Rapaport. **Principal Officials and Managers:** Doris B. Gold, Sole Proprietor.

★9676★ Bibliographer
270 Back River Rd.
Bedford, NH 03110
Phone: (603)623-4412

Description: Publishes material on American women and early New Hampshire legal records. Reaches market through direct mail and trade sales. **Number of New Titles:** 1992 (est.) - 1; Total Titles in Print - 3. **Selected Titles:** *Index of References to American Women in Colonial Newspapers through 1800, Vol. 1: New Hampshire 1756-1770, Vol. 2: New Hampshire 1771-1785; A Comprehensive Index of H. E. Noyes' 1889 History of Hempstead, New Hampshire,* both by Helen F. Evans. **Principal Officials and Managers:** Helen F. Evans, Owner.

★9677★ Bibulophile Press
24 Old Mt. Tom Rd.
PO Box 757
Bantam, CT 06750-0750
Phone: (203)567-5543

Founded: 1982. **Subjects:** Chemical dependency, gay/lesbian material.

★9678★ Birth Photos
7901 Park Crest Dr.
Silver Spring, MD 20910-5414
Phone: (301)428-0355

Description: Publishes explicit photos, posters, and slides of natural childbirth. Reaches market through direct mail. **Total Titles in Print:** 1. **Selected Titles:** *Miracle of Birth* (poster), *Miracle of Birth* (slides), both by Ed Downey. **Principal Officials and Managers:** Ed J. Downey, Principal.

★9679★ Bloodroot
PO Box 8
Grand Forks, ND 58206-0891
Phone: (701)775-6079

Description: Publishes works generally on women's themes. **Subjects:** Poetry, short fiction. **Selected Titles:** *Whistling Dixie* by John Little; *Poems from a Residential Hotel* by Grayce Ray; *Standing Around Outside* by Robert King. **Principal Officials and Managers:** Joan Eades, Linda L. Ohlsen, Dan Eades, Editors.

★9680★ Book Weaver Publishing Co.
PO Box 30072
Indianapolis, IN 46230
Phone: (317)253-5160

Description: Publishes books on women's issues. Reaches market through commission representatives, Inland Book Co., BookPeople, and New Leaf Distributing Co. Formerly known as Word Weaver Publishing Co. **Number of New Titles:** 1989 - 1, 1991 (est.) - 1; Total Titles in Print - 3. **Selected Titles:** *The Fourth Woman, Twice Raped, The Making of a Man,* all by Audrey Savage. **Principal Officials and Managers:** Audrey Savage, Publisher and President; Mary Jean Pies, Marketing; Charlotte Wright, Editor.

★9681★ Books & Music (U.S.A.)
PO Box 1301, Cathedral Sta.
New York, NY 10025
Phone: (212)666-7697

Description: Publishes an encyclopedia on women composers. Reaches market through direct mail. **Total Titles in Print:** 1. **Selected Titles:** *International Encyclopedia of Women Composers,* 2nd ed. by Aaron I. Cohen. **Principal Officials and Managers:** M. Hall, Business Manager.

★9682★ Boston Women's Health Book Collective, Inc.
240 A Elm St., 3rd Fl.
Somerville, MA 02144
Phone: (617)625-0271

Description: Compiles, publishes, and disseminates information on wide range of health and women's issues. **Selected Titles:** *The New Our Bodies Ourselves; Ourselves Growing Older; Changing Bodies, Changing Lives.* **Principal Officials and Managers:** Judy Norsigian, Co-Director; Susan Quass, Administrative Coordinator.

★9683★ Bowling Green State University Popular Press
838 E. Wooster St.
Bowling Green, OH 43403
Phone: (419)372-7866

Description: Publishes materials for use as classroom texts. Reaches market through direct mail. **Subjects:** Folklore, popular culture, women's studies. **Total Titles in Print:** 205. **Selected Titles:** *A Social Gospel for Millions* by John Ferre; *A Taste of the Pineapple: Essays on C. S. Lewis* by Bruce Edwards; *The Noble Savage in the New World Garden* by Gaile McGregor; *Heroines of Popular Culture* by Pat Browne. **Principal Officials and Managers:** Ray B. Browne, Director; Pat Browne, Editor.

★9684★ Bradley Boatman Productions
PO Box 41
Malibu, CA 90265

Description: Produces video cassettes on pregnancy. Distributes for Fine Media International. Reaches market through direct mail and Baker & Taylor. **Subjects:** Pregnancy, divining. **Selected Titles:** *A Gift for the Unborn Children* (video cassette) by Bradley Boatman; *Discover Dowsing* (video cassette) by Bill and Davina Cox. **Principal Officials and Managers:** Bradley Boatman, Owner.

★9685★ Branden Publishing Co., Inc.
17 Station St.
PO Box 8
Brookline Village
Boston, MA 02147
Phone: (617)734-2045

Description: Publishes general trade fiction, nonfiction, biographies and autobiographies with an emphasis on books by or about women. Reaches market through commission representatives, direct mail, telephone sales, trade sales, Ingram, Baker & Taylor, and Publishers Marketing Service. **Number of New Titles:** 1989 - 15; Total Titles in Print - 250. **Selected Titles:** *Barbra–An Actress Who Sings* by James Kimbrell; *Pay Dirt–Divorces of the Rich and Famous* by James Albert; *The Saving Rain* by Elsie Webber; *Miss Emily Martine and Other Stories* by Lynn Thorsen; *Ten Soviet Sports Stars* by Yuri Khromov and Russel Ramsey; *Jack Johnson* by Sal Fradella. **Principal Officials and Managers:** Adolph Caso, President and Editor; Bernice Danburg, Vice-President; Liana C. Caso, C.E.O.

★9686★ Bridal Sense Publications
111 E. Main St.
Hopkinton, MA 01748
Phone: (617)435-3504
Description: Publishes a wedding and bridal guide. Reaches market through direct mail and Baker & Taylor (wholesaler). **Total Titles in Print:** 1. **Selected Titles:** *Bridal Sense: How to Get Married without Going Crazy or Broke* by Melanie Sonsini-Goodrich. **Principal Officials and Managers:** Melanie Sonsini-Goodrich.

★9687★ Brighton Publications
PO Box 127
New Brighton, MN 55112
Phone: (612)636-2220
Description: Publishes how-to books providing information on weddings, showers, and decorating. Reaches market through direct mail, trade sales, and wholesalers. **Subjects:** Home management, decorating, culinary arts, weddings. **Number of New Titles:** 1991 (est.) - 2; Total Titles in Print - 8. **Selected Titles:** *Baby Shower Fun, Folding Table Napkins: A New Look at a Traditional Craft, Wedding Plans: 50 Unique Themes for the Wedding of Your Dreams,* all by Sharon Dlugosch; *Food Processor Receipes for Conventional and Microwave Cooking* by Sharon Dlugosch and Joyce Battcher; *Wedding Shower Fun, Games for Wedding Shower Fun,* both by Sharon Dlugosch and Florence Nelson. **Principal Officials and Managers:** Sharon Dlugosch, President; Jessica Fallon, Marketing Manager.

★9688★ Business and Professional Women's Foundation
2012 Massachusetts Ave. NW
Washington, DC 20036
Phone: (202)293-1200
Description: A nonprofit organization whose aim is to promote full participation, equity, and economic self-sufficiency for working women through programs of financial assistance, research, and information collection and dissemination. Reaches market through direct mail. **Total Titles in Print:** 2. **Principal Officials and Managers:** Linda Colvard Dorian, Executive Director.

★9689★ Calyx Books
PO Box
Corvallis, OR 97339
Phone: (503)753-9384
Description: Publishes books by women. Offers posters, art cards, and calendars. Accepts unsolicited manuscripts; query for guidelines. Distributed by BookPeople, Inland Book Co., The Distributors, Pacific Pipeline, Airlift, and Bookslinger. **Subjects:** Aging, women, literature, art. **Number of New Titles:** 1990 - 3, 1991 - 4, 1992 (est.) - 3; Total Titles in Print - 12. **Selected Titles:** *The White Junk of Love, Again; In China with Harpo and Karl,* both by Sibyl James; *Killing Color* by Charlotte Watson Sherman; *Women and Aging: An Anthology by Women; The Forbidden Stitch: An Asian American Women's Anthology* edited by Shirley Geok-lin Lim et al.; *Indian Singing in Twentieth Century America* by Gail Tremblay. **Principal Officials and Managers:** Margarita Donnelly, Managing Editor; Catherine Holdorf, Bev McFarland, Vice-President; Cheryl McLean, President.

★9690★ Cardinal Press
76 N. Yorktown
Tulsa, OK 74110
Phone: (918)583-3651
Founded: 1978. **Subjects:** Southwest poets; socialist; feminist humanist/non-racist, non-sexist, non-classist, non-agist. **Selected Titles:** *The Experience of Common People; The Experience of Southern Ladies.*

★9691★ Carolina Wren Press
PO Box 277
Carrboro, NC 27510
Phone: (919)560-2738
Description: Publishes the fiction, poetry and drama of women and black writers working on the cultural edge.

★9692★ Carousel Press
PO Box 6061
Albany, CA 94706-0061
Phone: (415)527-5849
Founded: 1976. **Description:** Publishes family-oriented travel guides.

★9693★ Cassiopeia Press
PO Box 2
Morrison, CO 80465-0208
Phone: (303)986-4370
Description: Publishes women's history material. Reaches market through direct mail, Baker & Taylor, Yankee Book Peddler, Inc., Blackwell North America, Midwest Library Service, and John Coutts Library Services. **Number of New Titles:** 1990 - 1; Total Titles in Print - 1. **Selected Titles:** *In Red Hats, Beads, and Bags: 1908 Graduates Sharing Their Lives through Letters (Wellesly College)* compiled by Dolores Avelleyra Murphy. **Principal Officials and Managers:** Dolores Avelleyra Murphy, Publisher.

★9694★ Catalyst
PO Box 205
Sarasota, FL 34276-3572
Phone: (813)349-1613
Description: Self-publishes a book dealing with cancer. Accepts unsolicited manuscripts. Reaches market through direct mail and commission representatives. **Total Titles in Print:** 1. **Selected Titles:** *Journey to Justice: A Woman's True Story of Breast Cancer and Medical Malpractice* by Diane Craig Chechik. **Principal Officials and Managers:** Diane Craig Chechik, President.

★9695★ Catalyst
250 Park Ave. S.
New York, NY 10003
Phone: (212)777-8900
Description: Works with corporations to effect change for women in business. Offers a monthly newsletter and an information center to members. Reaches market through direct mail and telephone sales. **Number of New Titles:** 1989 - 3, 1990 - 6, 1991 (est.) - 4; Total Titles in Print - 21. **Selected Titles:** *The Corporate Guide to Parental Leaves; Report on a Nationwide Survey of Parental Leaves; Flexible Benefits: How to Set Up a Plan When Your Employees Are Complaining, Your Costs Are Rising, and You're Too Busy to Think about It; Women in Corporate Management; Flexible Work Arrangements: Establishing Options for Managers and Professionals; Female Management Style*

Bibliography. **Principal Officials and Managers:** Felice Schwartz, President and Founder; Leslie Levin, Vice-President, Marketing; Gloria Markfield, Executive Vice-President; Mary C. Mattis, Ph.D., Vice-President, Research; Janet Andre, Vice-President, Advisory Services.

★9696★ Cayuse Press
PO Box 9086
Berkeley, CA 94709
Phone: (510)525-8515
Founded: 1985. **Subjects:** Literary/feminist.

★9697★ Celestial Arts
PO Box 7327
Berkeley, CA 94707
Phone: (510)845-8414
Toll-free: 800-841-2665
Fax: (510)524-1052
Founded: 1968. **Selected Titles:** *Sexual Evolution.*

★9698★ Center for the Study of Multiple Birth
333 E. Superior St., Ste. 464
Chicago, IL 60611
Phone: (312)266-9093
Description: Stimulates and fosters medical and social research in the area of mulitple birth and provides help to mothers with the special problems they and their offspring will encounter. Reaches market through advertising, direct mail, and featured articles. **Total Titles in Print:** 3. **Selected Titles:** *The Care of Twin Children,* 2nd ed. by Theroux and Tingley; *Gemini: The Psychology and Phenomena of Twins* by Hagedorn and Kizziar; *A Full House* by Ziner. **Principal Officials and Managers:** Donald Keith, Board Chairor; Louis Keith, M.D., President; Linda Neglia, Manager.

★9699★ Center for Women Policy Studies
2000 P St. NW, Ste. 508
Washington, DC 20036
Phone: (202)872-1770
Description: A feminist research organization disseminating results of research on employment, economic, educational, and domestic violence issues affecting women and girls. **Number of New Titles:** 1989 - 5; Total Titles in Print - 12. **Selected Titles:** *The SAT Gender Gap* by Phyllis Rosser; *Earnings Sharing in Social Security* by Fierst and Campbell; *The Guide to Resources on Women and AIDS; The Law and Pregnancy: Protection or Punishment; Sexual Abuse of Children; Women of Color in Mathematics, Science, and Engineering: A Review of the Literature.* **Principal Officials and Managers:** Leslie R. Wolfe, Executive Director.

★9700★ Center for Women's Studies and Services (CWSS)
2467 E St.
San Diego, CA 92102
Phone: (714)233-8984
Description: Publishes on feminism. Offers a bimonthly newsletter. Reaches market through direct mail. **Selected Titles:** *Double Jeopardy: Young and Female in America* by Allenby, Cicalo, and Lemke; *Bylines by Women: A Young Women's Guide to Journalism and Independent Publishing* by Lynette Thwaites; *Year of the Fires* by Joyce Nower. **Principal Officials and Managers:** Lisa Cobbs, Board President.

★9701★ Chas. Franklin Press
7821 175th St. SW
Edmonds, WA 98026
Phone: (206)774-6979

Subjects: Childbirth, women's issues, child safety. **Total Titles in Print:** 14. **Selected Titles:** *I Take Good Care of Me* by Linda Meyer; *Strangers Don't Look Like the Big Bad Wolf* by Janis Buschman and Debbie Hunley; *Welcome Home: A Child's View of Alcoholism* by Judith Jance; *Into the Light: A Guide for Battered Women* by Leslie Cantrell; *Conquering Pre-Menstrual Syndrome* by Barbara Clarke; *Trapped in Kuwait: Countdown to Armageddon* by John and Roberta Hogan. **Principal Officials and Managers:** Linda Doreen Meyer, President and General Manager; D. Lee Meyer, Vice-President; Barbara Davidson, Marketing Manager.

★9702★ Chicory Blue Press
East St. N.
Goshen, CT 06756
Phone: (203)491-2271

Description: Publishes materials written by women. Reaches market through direct mail, trade sales, Bookslinger, and Inland Book Co. **Number of New Titles:** 1991 (est.) - 2; Total Titles in Print - 3. **Selected Titles:** *A Wider Giving: Women Writing after a Long Silence* edited by Sondra Zeidenstein; *Memoir* by Honor Moore; *Heart of the Flower: Poems for the Sensuous Gardener* edited by Sondra Zeidenstein. **Principal Officials and Managers:** Sondra Zeidenstein, Publisher.

★9703★ Child Welfare League of America, Inc. (CWLA)
440 1st St. NW, Ste. 310
Washington, DC 20001
Phone: (202)638-2952

Description: Accepts unsolicited manuscripts. Reaches market through direct mail. **Subjects:** Child welfare and development. **Number of New Titles:** 1989 - 15, 1990 - 20, 1991 (est.) - 20; Total Titles in Print - 200. **Selected Titles:** *Prediction in Child Development* by Janet L. Hoopes; *Establishing Parent Involvement in Foster Care Agencies* edited by Karen Blumenthal and Anita Weinberg; *Group Care of Children: Toward the Year 2000* edited by Edwin A. Balcerzak; *Child Neglect: Understanding and Reaching the Parent* by Norman A. Polansky et al.; *The One Girl in Ten: Self Portrait of the Teenage Mother* by Sallie Foster; *The Family and Children's Services Curriculum* by June Brown. **Principal Officials and Managers:** David S. Liederman, Executive Director; Joyce Strom, Deputy Director; Susan Brite, Director of Publications.

★9704★ Children's Defense Fund
122 C St. NW
Washington, DC 20001
Phone: (202)628-8787

Description: A national public charity formed as a voice for children, who do not vote, lobby, or speak for themselves when critical policy decisions are made that affect their lives. Offers the monthly newsletter *CDF Reports*, the journal *CDF's Child, Youth and Family Futures Clearinghouse*, calendars, and posters. Reaches market through direct mail and conference sales. **Subjects:** Child health, education, child care, youth employment, adolescent pregnancy prevention. **Number of New Titles:** 1991 (est.) - 8; Total Titles in Print - 54. **Selected Titles:** *The State of America's Children; Your Child's School Records; Preventing Children Having Children: What You Can Do; Welcome the Child: A Child Advocacy Guide for Churches; Who Knows How Safe: The Status of State Efforts to Ensure Quality Child Care; Outside the Dream: Child Poverty in America.* **Principal Officials and Managers:** Marian Wright Edelman, President; Kati Haycock, Executive Vice-President; Donna M. Jablonski, Publications Director.

★9705★ Children's Foundation
725 15th St. NW, Ste. 505
Washington, DC 20005
Phone: (202)347-3300

Description: Produces easy-to-understand materials on child care, especially family day care and child support enforcement. Offers the quarterly newsletters *Family Day Care Bulletin* and *Child Support Bulletin*. Reaches market through direct mail. **Number of New Titles:** 1989 - 2, 1990 - 2; Total Titles in Print - 15. **Selected Titles:** *Child Support: An Overview, Child Support Action: How to Start a Grassroots Group*, both by Worth Cooley-Prost; *Family Day Care: An Overview of Issues and Trends* by Loribeth Weinstein; *Family Day Care: Implications for the Black Community* by Costella Tate; *Better Baby Care: A Book for Family Day Care Providers* by C. Tate and M. Nash; *1990 Family Day Care Licensing Study.* **Principal Officials and Managers:** Kay Hollestelle, Director.

★9706★ CHOICE (Concern for Health Options: Information Care & Education)
1233 Locust St., 3rd. Fl.
Philadelphia, PA 19107
Phone: (215)985-3355

Description: A consumer education and advocacy organization concerned with reproductive health care, AIDS, sexuality education, maternity care, and child care. It is a nonprofit agency which produces educational books, pamphlets, brochures, and flyers for teens, working parents, women, and anyone interested in AIDS and reproductive health. Most materials are free. Reaches market through direct mail. **Selected Titles:** *Changes: You and Your Body.* **Principal Officials and Managers:** Mary Hale Meyer, Executive Director; Germaine Ingram, President, Board of Directors; Ernesta Ballard, Advisor.

★9707★ Civetta Press
PO Box 1043
Portland, OR 97207-1043
Phone: (503)228-6649
Founded: 1989.

★9708★ Cleis Press
PO Box 89
Pittsburgh, PA 15221
Phone: (412)937-1555

Description: Publishes "progressive books by women" on many different issues. Reaches market through distributors and wholesalers. **Subjects:** Feminism, literature, politics, lesbianism. **Number of New Titles:** 1989 - 6, 1991 (est.) - 6; Total Titles in Print - 19. **Selected Titles:** *Fight Back: Feminist Resistance to Male Violence* edited by Newman and Delacoste; *Voices in the Night: Women Speaking about Incest* edited by Morgan and McNaron; *Woman-Centered Pregnancy and Birth* by Ginny Cassidy Brinn; *Long Way Home: The Odyssey of a Lesbian Mother and Her Children* by Jeanne Jullion; *With the Power of Each Breath: A Disabled Women's Anthology* edited by Browne, Conners, and Stern; *The Little School: Tales of Disappearance and Survival in Argentina* by Partnoy. **Principal Officials and Managers:** Felice Newman, Frederique Delacoste, Editors.

★9709★ Clothespin Fever Press
5529 N. Figueroa
Los Angeles, CA 90042
Phone: (213)254-1373

Founded: 1986. **Subjects:** Lesbian/feminist. **Selected Titles:** *A Dyke's Bike Repair Handbook; In a Different Light: An Anthology of Lesbian Writers.* **Publications:** *Lesbian Line* (newsletter).

★9710★ Coalition on Women and Religion
4759 15th Ave. NE
Seattle, WA 98105
Phone: (206)525-1213

Description: Publishes "to encourage women in their spiritual journeys, to reveal new and evolving forms of feminist spirituality, to support women working for change and equality, and to examine religious concepts and expressions from a feminist perspective." Offers a quarterly newsletter, *The Flame.* **Subjects:** Feminism, religion. **Selected Titles:** *The Woman's Bible* by Elizabeth Cady Stanton; *The Word for Us: Non-Sexist Scripture Translation, Flame Cartoons, The Spirited Woman's Cartoon Book* all by Joann Haugerud; *Study Guide to the Woman's Bible.* **Principal Officials and Managers:** Carol Van Buren, Chairor; Nancy Goodno, Jessie Kinnear Kenton, Eleanor Bilimoria, Board.

★9711★ Committee for Single Adoptive Parents, Inc.
PO Box 150
Chevy Chase, MD 20825

Description: An information service for single women and men interested in adoption. Supports right of all children to a loving family, regardless of age, race, ethnic or national origin or handicap. Promotes worth of single people as parents. Offers a list of sources that will accept single applicants. **Total Titles in Print:** 1. **Selected Titles:** *Handbook for Single Adoptive Parents* edited by Hope Marindin. **Principal Officials and Managers:** Hope Marindin, Executive Director.

★9712★ Committee on the Status of Women in the Economics Profession
4901 Tower Ct.
Tallahassee, FL 32303
Phone: (904)562-1211

Description: Publishes an updated roster of all women economists. Offers newsletters, mailing lists, mailing labels, and data on women economists. **Number of New Titles:** 1990 - 1; Total Titles in Print - 1.

★9713★ **Communication Dynamics**
10601-A Tierrasanta Blvd., Ste. 201
San Diego, CA 92124
Phone: (619)292-6949

Description: Publishes books on parenting. Reaches market through direct mail, Inland Book Co., and Quality Books, Inc. **Number of New Titles:** 1990 - 1, 1991 (est.) - 3; Total Titles in Print - 1. **Selected Titles:** *Mom to Mom: A Valuable Collection of Tips and Hints for the Mother-to-Be and the New Mother* by Lynett Root Cabler. **Principal Officials and Managers:** Lynett Cabler, President.

★9714★ **Consultant Services Northwest, Inc.**
839 NE 96th St.
Seattle, WA 98115
Phone: (206)524-1950

Description: Publishes on lesbian/gay counseling services and the mental health movement in the United States. Reaches market through direct mail, and telephone sales, Baker & Taylor, and Inland Book Co. **Number of New Titles:** 1991 (est.) - 1; Total Titles in Print - 3. **Selected Titles:** *Counseling Our Own: Lesbian/Gay Subculture Meets the Mental Health System* 1st and 2nd eds. by Charna Klein; *The Washington Foundation Directory: How to Get Your Slice of the Pie 1991* by Mardell Moore and Charna Klein. **Principal Officials and Managers:** Charna Klein, President; Mardell Moore, Treasurer.

★9715★ **Consumer Awareness Learning Laboratory**
PO Box 3
Penns Grove, NJ 08069-0386
Phone: (609)935-6264

Description: Publishes on child support enforcement, research, and volunteer help. **Subjects:** Social sciences, family studies, women, divorce. **Total Titles in Print:** 1. **Selected Titles:** *The Child Support Survivors Guide* by Barry T. Schnell. **Principal Officials and Managers:** Barry T. Schnell.

★9716★ **Cornell University Press**
124 Roberts Pl.
Ithaca, NY 14853
Phone: (607)257-7000

Description: Academic press. Publishes women's studies books.

★9717★ **Cottonwood Press**
PO Box 1947
Boulder, CO 80306
Phone: (303)433-4166

Founded: 1976. **Description:** Emphasis is on women and ethnic groups in Western America. **Selected Titles:** *Western Women in History and Literature: Annotated Bibliography.*

★9718★ **Council on Interracial Books for Children, Inc.**
1841 Broadway
New York, NY 10023
Phone: (212)757-5339

Description: Publishes "to identify–and more recently to counteract–racism, sexism, and other anti-human values in children's learning materials and in society." Offers books, maps, filmstrips, catalogs, and booklists. Reaches market through direct mail. **Total Titles in Print:** 30. **Selected Titles:** *Embers: Stories for a Changing World; Guidelines for Selecting Bias-Free Textbooks and Storybooks; Stereotypes, Distortions and Omissions in U.S. History Textbooks; Violence, the Ku Klux Klan and the Struggle for Equality; Chronicles of American Indian Protest; Unlearning "Indian" Stereotypes,* all by the CIBC. **Principal Officials and Managers:** Melba Kgositsile, Executive Director.

★9719★ **Cranehill Press**
708 Comfort Rd.
Spencer, NY 14883

Description: Publishes a children's book that emphasizes positive images of women. Reaches market through wholesalers and distributors. **Subjects:** Children, feminist, New age. **Total Titles in Print:** 2. **Selected Titles:** *The Wisewoman, The Wisewoman's Sacred Wheel of the Year,* both by Naomi Strichartz, illustrated by Ella Moore.

★9720★ **Crones' Own Press**
PO Box 4
Durham, NC 27702
Phone: (919)688-3521

Description: Publishes feminist works by older women. Accepts unsolicited manuscripts; query for guidelines. Reaches market through direct mail, Inland Book Co., BookPeople, and Baker & Taylor. **Subjects:** Women, poetry, feminism, fiction. **Number of New Titles:** 1989 - 1, 1991 - 1; Total Titles in Print - 6. **Selected Titles:** *Seven Windows: Stories of Women* by F. Zarod Rominski; *Splinters* by Margaret Budicki; *Pacific Soul: Poems and Sketches* by Bonnie Davidson; *Button, Button, Who Has the Button* by Ruth Harriet Jacobs; *Clais and Clock* by Jean Kadmon; *Widdershins* by Judith W. Monroe. **Principal Officials and Managers:** Elizabeth Freeman, Publisher.

★9721★ **Crossing Press**
PO Box 10
Freedom, CA 95019
Phone: (408)722-0711

Description: Publishes general fiction and nonfiction for adults. Also offers postcards and calendars. Reaches market through commission representatives, direct mail, trade sales, and wholesalers and distributors, including Baker & Taylor, Ingram Book Co., BookPeople, and Inland Book Co. **Subjects:** Feminism, literature, cookbooks, homosexuality. **Number of New Titles:** 1989 - 34, 1990 - 38, 1991 (est.) - 38; Total Titles in Print - 120. **Selected Titles:** *All Good Women* by Valerie Miner; *Red Flower: Rethinking Menstruation* by Dena Taylor; *Street Food* by Rose Grant; *Island Cooking: Recipes from the Caribbean* by Dunstan A. Harris; *Quiet Fire: Memoirs of Older Gay Men* by Keith Vacha; *Walk When the Moon Is Full* by Frances Hamerstrom. **Principal Officials and Managers:** John Gill, Elaine G. Gill, Publishers.

★9722★ **Crossroads**
370 Lexington Ave.
New York, NY 10017
Phone: (212)532-3650

Founded: 1980.

★9723★ **Cybele Society**
1603 W. 9th Ave.
Spokane, WA 99204-3406
Phone: (509)838-2332

Subjects: Family-centered maternity care. **Total Titles in Print:** 4. **Selected Titles:** *Family-Centered Maternity Care: How to Achieve It* by Jan Bishop; *The Cybele Cluster: A Single Room Maternity Care System for High- and Low-Risk Families* by Loel Fenwick, M.D. and Ruthie Dearing. **Principal Officials and Managers:** Loel Fenwick, M.D., Executive Director; John Moyer, M.D., and Helen Berglund, Vice-Presidents; Jeanne Tomlin, Administrator; Larry Brewer, M.D., Secretary-Treasurer.

★9724★ **Damron Co., Inc.**
PO Box 4224
San Francisco, CA 94142-2458
Phone: (415)255-0404

Description: "Publishes the largest selling, most widely circulated gay travel guide on the market. It lists bars, baths, hotels, restaurants, etc. in the U.S., Canada, Puerto Rico, Virgin Islands, and Mexico which cater to and are frequented by gays and lesbians." Reaches market through commission representatives and direct mail. Formerly listed as Bob Damron Enterprises, Inc. **Total Titles in Print:** 3. **Selected Titles:** *Bob Damron's Address Book* edited by Gatta and Robert Ian Philips; *The Women's Traveller, The Damron Road Atlas,* both edited by Gina Gatta. **Principal Officials and Managers:** Edward Gatta, President.

★9725★ **Daughter Culture Publications**
1840 41st Ave., Ste. 102-301
Capitola, CA 95010

Description: Publishes inspirational literature and art which honor and illustrate the value, the power, and the pride of young girls. Reaches market through direct mail, and the Daughter Culture Programs and Projects. **Total Titles in Print:** 2. **Selected Titles:** *Celebrations of Daughterhood* by Suellen M. Fast. **Principal Officials and Managers:** Suellen M. Fast, Founder and Director; Alba I. Daniel, Assistant Director.

★9726★ **Delphi Press**
PO Box 15
Oak Park, IL 60304
Phone: (708)524-7900

Description: Accepts unsolicited manuscripts with return postage. Reaches market through wholesalers. **Subjects:** Women's spirituality, occult. **Number of New Titles:** 1990 - 1, 1991 (est.) - 6, 1992 (est.) - 8; Total Titles in Print - 7. **Selected Titles:** *To Know: A Guide to Women's Magic and Spirituality* by Jade; *Loving the Goddess Within: Sex Magic for Women* by Nan Hawthorne; *The Eye Goddess* by O.G.S. Crawford; *She Changes* by Teressa Mark. **Principal Officials and Managers:** Karen Jackson, President.

★9727★ **Designs III Publishers**
515 W. Commonwealth Ave.
Ste. 105
Fullerton, CA 92632
Phone: (714)871-9100

Description: Publishes books by women writers and on computers. Reaches market through direct mail. **Total Titles in Print:** 2. **Selected Titles:** *Young Woman Citizen* by Mary Austin;

The Whole Computer Catalog by Narda L. Schwartz. **Principal Officials and Managers:** Marie Schwartz, Leonard Schwartz, Publishers.

★9728★ Diemer, Smith Publishing Co.
3377 Solano Ave., Ste. 322
Napa, CA 94558
Phone: (707)224-4251

Description: Publishes on women's history, aging, and the history of culture. Reaches market through direct mail, seminars, and Baker & Taylor. **Total Titles in Print:** 5. **Selected Titles:** *Women's Roots, It's All Right to Get Old, A Lie Is a Debt, Humanity's Search for the Meaning of Life, Womankind,* all by June Stephenson. **Principal Officials and Managers:** June Stephenson, Owner; Evelyn Smith, Business Manager; Christine Diemer, Senior Editor.

★9729★ Diotima Books
PO Box
Glen Carbon, IL 62034
Phone: (618)345-1374

Subjects: Feminism. **Total Titles in Print:** 4. **Selected Titles:** *Lockout, Override, Breakout, Pilgrimage,* all by Kathryn Anger; *We Live and Remember* by Doreen Anwar. **Principal Officials and Managers:** D. Anwar, Secretary; Beatrice Ann, Publisher.

★9730★ Divorce Support Services, Inc.
234 Main St.
Woodbridge, NJ 07095
Phone: (908)636-3802

Description: Publishes on separation and divorce. Offers databases, newsletters, support groups, workshops, and seminars. Reaches market through direct mail, telephone and trade sales, speaking engagements, and support groups. **Number of New Titles:** 1991 - 2; Total Titles in Print - 2. **Selected Titles:** *Answers: A Divorce/Separation Survival Handbook, National Divorce & Singles Resource Directory.* **Principal Officials and Managers:** Edward Kitzis, Executive Director; Robert Dato, President.

★9731★ Down There Press
PO Box 20
Burlingame, CA 94011-2086
Phone: (415)342-2536

Description: Publishes exclusively sexual self-help books for adults and children. Alternate telephone number: (415) 550-0912. Accepts unsolicited manuscripts; send query letter with table of contents and sample chapters first. Reaches market through direct mail, BookPeople, Inland Book Co., Pacific Pipeline, and The Distributors. **Number of New Titles:** 1989 - 1, 1990 - 1, 1991 (est.) - 1; Total Titles in Print - 10. **Selected Titles:** *Men Loving Themselves, Anal Pleasure and Health,* both by Jack Morin; *Good Vibrations: Complete Guide to Vibrators, A Kid's First Book about Sex,* all by Joani Blank; *Herotica: A Collection of Women's Erotic Fiction* edited by Susie Bright; *Erotic by Nature* edited by David Steinberg. **Principal Officials and Managers:** Joani Blank, Publisher; Leigh Davidson, Managing Editor.

★9732★ Druid Press
2724 Shades Crest Rd.
Birmingham, AL 35216
Phone: (205)967-6580

Founded: 1982. **Subjects:** Literary, primarily women's literature.

★9733★ Dustbooks
PO Box 100
Paradise, CA 95969
Phone: (916)877-6110
Toll-free: 800-477-6110
Fax: (916)877-0222

Founded: 1963.

★9734★ E-Heart Press, Inc.
3700 Mockingbird Ln.
Dallas, TX 75205
Phone: (214)741-6915

Description: Distributor. Publisher undertook distributing to help several small press publishers unite and sell more books than they could singly. Reaches market through commission representatives and direct mail. **Subjects:** Women, folklore, children's books, Texana. **Principal Officials and Managers:** Frances B. Vick, President.

★9735★ Earth Books
PO Box 7
Redwood Valley, CA 95470
Phone: (707)485-5684

Description: Publishes fiction, nonfiction and poetry by women. Also offers audio cassettes and cards. Reaches market through trade sales, BookPeople, Inland Book Co., Baker & Taylor, and New Leaf Distributing Co. **Number of New Titles:** 1991 (est.) - 2; Total Titles in Print - 3. **Selected Titles:** *Being: Guide to a New Way, Womonseed, Meditations for Being* (cassette), all by Sunlight. **Principal Officials and Managers:** Dorothy Lane.

★9736★ Edgepress
PO Box
Point Reyes, CA 94956
Phone: (415)663-1511

Description: Publishes academic works in the fields of philosophy evaluation, feminist studies, and technology. Offers *University Micro News,* a newsletter. Reaches market through direct mail and trade sales. **Number of New Titles:** 1989 - 2, 1990 - 1; Total Titles in Print - 5. **Selected Titles:** *Evaluation Thesaurus,* 3rd ed., *Logic of Evaluation,* both by Michael Scriven; *The Nature of Woman* by Mary Anne Warren; *Informal Logic* edited by Johnson and Blair. **Principal Officials and Managers:** Michael Scriven, Director.

★9737★ Edwin Mellen Press
415 Ridge St.
PO Box 450
Lewiston, NY 14092
Phone: (716)754-2266
Fax: (716)754-4335

Founded: 1975. **Selected Titles:** *Woman's Transformation: A Psychological Theology; Flannery O'Connor: Her Life, Library and Book Reviews.*

★9738★ Eighth Mountain Press
624 SE 29th Ave.
Portland, OR 97214
Phone: (503)233-3936

Description: Publishes feminist literature. Accepts unsolicited manuscripts. Sponsors an annual poetry contest for women. Reaches market through commission representatives, trade sales, BookPeople, Inland Book Co., Bookslinger, and other major distributors. **Number of New Titles:** 1990 - 3, 1991 (est.) - 3; Total Titles in Print - 12. **Selected Titles:** *Cows and Horses* by Barbara Wilson; *History and Geography,* both by Judith Barrington; *The Eating Hill* by Karen Mitchell; *A Few Words in the Mother Tongue, Dreams of an Insomniac,* both by Irene Klepfisz; *Incidents Involving Mirth* by Anna Livia. **Principal Officials and Managers:** Ruth Gundle, Publisher.

★9739★ Ellen C. Temple, Publishing, Inc.
5030 Champions Dr., Ste. 100
Uffkin, TX 75901
Phone: (409)639-4707

Subjects: Women in Texas history, children's books (for 8-14 year olds). **Number of New Titles:** 1989 - 2, 1990 - 2, 1991 (est.) - 2; Total Titles in Print - 14. **Selected Titles:** *The Train to Estelline* by Jane Roberts Wood; *A Texas Suffragist: Diaries and Writings of Jane Y. McCallum* by Janet Humphrey; *Maggie and a Horse Named Devildust, Maggie and the Search for Devildust, Maggie and Devildust Ridin' High,* all by Judy Alter; *A Vampire Named Fred* by Bill Crider. **Principal Officials and Managers:** Ellen C. Temple, Owner.

★9740★ Emma Goldman Clinic
227 N. Dubuque St.
Iowa City, IA 52245
Phone: (319)337-2112

Founded: 1973. **Subjects:** Feminist approach to women's health; alternative healthcare; cervical cap.

★9741★ Empty Closet Enterprises
5210 N. Wayne
Chicago, IL 60640
Phone: (312)769-9009

Description: Publishes a directory and a periodical pertaining to feminist music and culture. Offers *HotWire: The Journal of Women's Music and Culture* and *Paid My Dues: Journal of Women and Music.* Offers t-shirts and notecards with *Hotwire* logo. Accepts unsolicited manuscripts. Reaches market through commission representatives and direct mail. Formerly listed as Not Just a Stage, Inc. **Total Titles in Print:** 1. **Selected Titles:** *Women's Music Plus Directory* edited by Toni Armstrong. **Principal Officials and Managers:** Toni Armstrong, Publisher and Managing Editor; Lynn Siniscalchi and Toni Armstrong, Jr., Editors; Annie Lee, Chris Crosby, Production Managers; Deb Dettman and Ginny Newsom, Office Managers.

★9742★ ERA Impact Project
99 Hudson St.
New York, NY 10013
Phone: (212)925-6635

Description: Nonprofit agency working to eliminate sex discrimination in education, family law, employment, in the media, and in the judiciary. Publishes individual summaries of state ERA experience for fifteen states. **Selected Titles:**

The ERA and Family Law: Making Equality Work for Men and Women by Marsha Levick; *Legal Reference Guide to State ERAs; ERA Impact Project Information Kit; Litigation Packet: The State Action Requirement; State ERAs Litigation Packet: Valuing Homemakers Services under the State ERAs; Implementing Your State Equal Rights Amendment: An Action Manual.* **Principal Officials and Managers:** Marsha Levick, Susan Cary Nicholas, Directors.

★9743★ Essential Medical Information Systems, Inc.
PO Box 16
Durant, OK 74702-1607

Description: Publishes medical texts and handbooks for physicians and clinicians. Reaches market through direct mail. Formerly Creative Infomatics, Inc. **Number of New Titles:** 1990 - 6, 1991 (est.) - 6; Total Titles in Print - 21. **Selected Titles:** *Estrogen Replacement Therapy* by Gambrell; *Hypertension* by Kaplan; *Breastfeeding* by Saunders; *Oral Contraceptives* by Dickey; *PMS* by Chihal. **Principal Officials and Managers:** J. P. Wells, President; Phyllis Jones, General Manager.

★9744★ Family Health International
RTP Branch
PO Box 139
Durham, NC 27709
Phone: (919)544-7261

Description: Conducts, analyzes, and disseminates research on contraceptive methods, family planning services, maternity care, and primary health care. Research reported in journals and in an occasional monograph series. Offers a newsletter, *Network*, in English, French, and Spanish. Reaches market through direct mail. **Total Titles in Print:** 3. **Selected Titles:** *Long-Term IUD Use in Ljubljana, Yugoslavia* by Andolsek et al.; *Reproductive Health in Africa: Issues and Options* by B. Janowitz et al.; *Sante Reproductive en Afrique Subsahariene: Les Questions et Les Choix.* **Principal Officials and Managers:** Malcolm Potts, President Emeritus; William Schellstede, Senior Vice-President; JoAnn Lewis, Vice-President, Programs; Robert Hughes, Vice-President, Administration; Alfredo Perez, Vice-President, Health.

★9745★ Family Publications
PO Box 4903
Maitland, FL 32794-0398
Phone: (407)539-1411

Description: Publishes on childbirth education and consumer health education. Offers audio cassettes. Reaches market through direct mail and trade sales. **Selected Titles:** *All about Childbirth, Women and Hormones,* both by Alice T. MacMahon. *Everything Makes a Difference* by Betram and Moon. **Principal Officials and Managers:** James R. MacMahon, Alice T. MacMahon, Partners.

★9746★ Federally Employed Women Legal and Education Fund, Inc.
PO Box 48
Washington, DC 20008
Phone: (202)462-5235

Description: "Purpose is to eliminate unlawful discrimination in federal employment by educating federal workers and policy makers about their rights and responsibilities." Offers training, lawyer referral, and employee counseling.

Reaches market through direct mail. **Number of New Titles:** 1991 (est.) - 2; 1992 (est.) - 2; Total Titles in Print - 7. **Selected Titles:** *Sexual Harassment in the Workplace* by Janet Cooper; *Making Waves without Drowning, How to Find an EEO Attorney,* both by June Chewning et al. *Federal EEO: A Complete Guide to Court Cases* edited by Helen Cohn Needham; *Federal Managers and EEO* by Valerie Voorhees; *The Privacy Act: What You Should Know About It* by Florence Perman. **Principal Officials and Managers:** Janet Cooper, President, Board of Directors; Bill Jefferson, Treasurer; Karen Scott, Vice-President; Marie Argana, Secretary; Elsa Dik-Glass , General Counsel.

★9747★ Federation of Organizations for Professional Women
2001 S. St. NW, Ste. 540
Washington, DC 20009
Phone: (202)328-1415

Description: A national nonprofit federation publishing information on professional women. Reaches market through direct mail. **Selected Titles:** *A Woman's Yellow Pages; Woman and Psychotherapy; What's Left of Federal Funding for Sex Equity in Education and Social Science Research; Washington's Women's Directory; Career Guides for Professionals* (3 booklets) by Geraldine V. Cox. **Principal Officials and Managers:** Viola M. Young Horvath, Executive Director; Jo Ann Jackson, Treasurer; Janis Campbell, Secretary.

★9748★ Feminist Institute Clearinghouse (FIC)
PO Box 30563
Bethesda, MD 20814
Phone: (301)951-9040

★9749★ Feminist Press at the City University of New York
311 E. 94th St.
New York, NY 10128
Phone: (212)360-5790

Description: Publishes women's studies, feminist biographies, reprints, non-sexist children's books, and educational materials. Also publishes a journal, *Women's Studies Quarterly.* Accepts unsolicited manuscripts, send proposal, resume, sample pages and outline. Reaches market through commission representatives and Talman Co., Inc. **Subjects:** Women's studies, feminism, women's literature. **Number of New Titles:** 1989 - 12, 1990 - 10, 1991 (est.) - 10; Total Titles in Print - 110. **Selected Titles:** *Women Activists* by Anne Witte Garland; *Writing Red: An Anthology of Women Writers, 1930-1940* by Charlotte L. Nekola and Paula Rabinowitz; *Sultana's Dream and Selections from the Secluded Ones* by Rokeya Sakhawat Hossain; *Get Smart: A Woman's Guide to Equality on Campus* by S. Montana Katz and Veronica Vieland; *The Yellow Wallpaper* by Charlotte Perkins Gilman; *Reena and Other Stories* by Paule Marshall. **Principal Officials and Managers:** Florence Howe, Publisher; Susannah Driver, Senior Editor; Paula Martinac, Art and Production Director.

★9750★ Feminist Women's Health Center
330 Flume St.
Chico, CA 95928
Phone: (916)891-1917
Fax: (916)893-9347

Description: Women's health center. **Selected Titles:** *A New View of a Woman's Body; Woman-Centered Pregnancy and Birth.*

★9751★ Ferrari Publications
PO Box 355
Phoenix, AZ 85069
Phone: (602)863-2408

Description: Publishes gay travel guidebooks to the United States, Canada, Caribbean, Europe, Mexico, Australia, New Zealand, and Tahiti. Specializes in covering gay and lesbian events and tours. Offers an illustrated calendar and mailing labels to gay and lesbian businesses and organizations. Reaches market through direct mail, wholesalers, and retailers. **Number of New Titles:** 1989 - 4, 1991 (est.) - 4; Total Titles in Print - 4. **Selected Titles:** *Places of Interest: Gay Travel Guide with Maps, Places of Interest to Women, Places for Men, INN Places: A Definitive Source on Gay Accommodations,* all by Marianne Ferrari. **Principal Officials and Managers:** Marianne Ferrari, Editor and Publisher.

★9752★ Fertility Awareness Services
2857 NW Tyler
PO Box 9
Corvallis, OR 97339
Phone: (503)753-8530

Description: Publishes on fertility and birth control. Offers consulting. Reaches market through direct mail. **Number of New Titles:** 1990 - 1, 1992 (est.) - 1; Total Titles in Print - 6. **Selected Titles:** *A Fertility Awareness Self Instruction Course, The Ovulation Method Charting Booklet,* both by Cooper-Doyle; *A Fertility Awareness and NFP Resource Directory* edited by Cooper-Doyle, *Fertility Factsheets Series G 1-20* by Doyle et al.; *Infertility Self-Help: What You Can Do to Regain Fertility* by Doyle. **Principal Officials and Managers:** Suzannah Cooper Doyle, Lyris Kyla, Directors.

★9753★ Fintapes, Inc.
PO Box 97
Washington, DC 20016
Phone: (202)337-3636

Description: Produces audio cassettes on financial matters for women. **Number of New Titles:** 1990 - 1, 1991 (est.) - 1; Total Titles in Print - 6. **Selected Titles:** *Put Your Money to Work; What Every Wife Should Know; Suddenly Single; Single, Together and Savvy; Eldercare: When You Can't Do It All Yourself,* (all audio cassettes). **Principal Officials and Managers:** Liane W. Atlas, President; Maryann Friedman, Secretary-Treasurer.

★9754★ Firebrand Books
141 The Commons
Ithaca, NY 14850
Phone: (607)272-0000

Description: Publishes on feminist and lesbian topics. Reaches market through direct mail, trade sales, and distributors, including Bookpeople and Inland Book Co. **Number of New Titles:** 1990 - 10, 1991 (est.) - 10; Total Titles in Print - 58. **Selected Titles:** *A Burst of Light, Essays* by Audre Lorde; *The Fires of Bride* by

Ellen Galford; *Getting Home Alive* by Aurora Levins Morales and Rosario Morales; *A Letter to Harvey Milk* by Leslea Newman; *A Restricted Country* by Joan Nestle; *Shoulders* by Georgia Cotrell. **Principal Officials and Managers:** Nancy K. Bereano, Editor and Publisher.

★9755★ First Amendment Press
PO Box 9
Mill Valley, CA 94942-0963
Description: Publishes on First Amendment rights, justice for women. **Selected Titles:** *Curious What You Might Find When You Go Out to Look for Elephants; How to Bring Up Your Brother; The Three Wives of Robert X; Up the Escarpment,* all by M. Macur. **Principal Officials and Managers:** Mary Macur.

★9756★ Flower Press
Flowerfield Enterprises
10332 Shaver Rd.
Kalamazoo, MI 49002
Phone: (616)327-0108
Founded: 1976.

★9757★ Food Research and Action Center, Inc. (FRAC)
1875 Connecticut Ave. NW, Ste. 540
Washington, DC 20009
Phone: (202)986-2200
Description: In addition to books, publishes a bimonthly newsletter, *Foodlines.* **Subjects:** Federal food assistance programs. **Selected Titles:** *Feeding the other Half: Mothers and Children Left Out of WIC; The Nutritional Status of Low Income Preschool Children in the United States; WIC Facts; The Relationship between Nutrition and Learning; FRAC's Guide to the Food Stamp Program; Fuel for Excellence: FRAC's Guide to School Breakfast Expansion.* **Principal Officials and Managers:** Robert J. Fersh, Executive Director; Edward Cooney, Deputy Director.

★9758★ ForLIFE, Inc.
Depot St. P.O. Drawer 1279
Tryon, NC 28782
Phone: (704)859-5392
Description: Publishes pro-life literature and films. Reaches market through direct mail. **Total Titles in Print:** 10. **Selected Titles:** *This'll Kill You, The Key Question,* both by Senander; *The Bible Does Speak on Abortion* by Overduin; *Abortion, Poverty, and Black Genocide* by Craven; *Abortion in Theological Context* by Eichhorst; *Bible and the Abortion Problem* by Lonning. **Principal Officials and Managers:** Ralph D. Kuether, Executive Director.

★9759★ Foundation for Women's Resources
PO Box 502
Austin, TX 78763
Phone: (512)476-6112
Description: Formerly listed as Texas Foundation for Women's Resources. **Subjects:** Women's history, Texas women. **Total Titles in Print:** 4. **Selected Titles:** *A Multicultural Instructional Guide to Texas Women: A Celebration of History* by Candace O'Keefe; *Texas Women: A Celebration of History* by Mary Beth Rogers; *Texas Women's History Project Bibliography* by Ruthe Winegarten; *Texas Women in Politics* by Weddington, Hickle, and Fitzgerald. **Principal**

Officials and Managers: Cathy Bonner, President of the Board of Directors.

★9760★ Foxmoor Press
Rte. 6, Box 28
Tahlequah, OK 74464
Description: A cooperative that publishes poetry by new poets, particularly women poets. Reaches market through direct mail and poetry readings. **Selected Titles:** *Foxgrapes: Poems of the Plains and the People, The Moon in Five Disguises,* both by Joan S. Isom; *Sun-Catcher: Children of Earth* edited by Joan S. Isom. **Principal Officials and Managers:** Joan Isom, Co-op Coordinator.

★9761★ Freedom Enterprise
6915 Wilcox
Fremont, MI 49412
Phone: (616)924-4660
Description: Publishes self-help books for women. Accepts unsolicited manuscripts. Reaches market through commission representatives, direct mail, and Baker & Taylor. **Total Titles in Print:** 1. **Selected Titles:** *Divorce: Play the Game to Win* by Jan Elizabeth. **Principal Officials and Managers:** Jan Ross, President.

★9762★ Freestone Publishing Co.
PO Box 398
Monroe, UT 84754
Phone: (801)527-3738
Founded: 1978. **Subjects:** Women's health, sexuality and fertility. **Selected Titles:** *Conscious Conception.*

★9763★ Frog in the Well
PO Box 1700
San Francisco, CA 94117
Phone: (415)431-2113
Description: Publishes feminist literature. Accepts unsolicited manuscripts with a self-addressed stamped envelope. Reaches market through direct mail and a number of wholesalers, including BookPeople, Inland, Bookslinger, and Pacific Publishers Cooperative. **Subjects:** Feminism, social change, women in literature. Total Titles in Print - 9. **Selected Titles:** *Marx and Gandhi Were Liberals, The New Woman's Broken Heart,* both by Andrea Dworkin; *Against Sadomasochism* edited by Linden, Pagano, Russell, and Star; *Ariadne* by Batya Podos; *For Nights Like This One* by Becky Birtha; *Crimes Against Women: Proceedings of the International Tribunal* compiled and edited by Diana E. H. Russel and Nicole Van de Ver; *The Honesty Tree* by Carole Spearn McCauley. **Principal Officials and Managers:** Susan Hester, Owner.

★9764★ G. K. Hall and Company
70 Lincoln St.
Boston, MA 02111
Phone: (617)423-3990
Description: Trade press. Publishes women's studies books.

★9765★ Garrett Park Press
PO Box 190
Garrett Park, MD 20896
Phone: (301)946-2553
Founded: 1968. **Description:** Publishes in the areas of women's issues, affirmative action, international affairs, career education, and gen-

eral reference. **Selected Titles:** *Directory of Special Opportunities for Women; Minority Organizations: A National Directory.*

★9766★ Germainbooks
91 St. Germain Ave.
San Francisco, CA 94114
Phone: (415)731-8155
Subjects: Feminism. **Selected Titles:** *Married Women v. Husbands' Names, Mrs. Man,* both by Una Stannard. **Principal Officials and Managers:** John W. Backus, Publisher; B. Miller, Managing Editor.

★9767★ Girls Inc.
30 E. 33rd St.
New York, NY 10016
Phone: (212)689-3700
Description: A nonprofit organization dedicated to the research and development of informal educational programs for girls. Formerly listed as Girls Clubs of America. **Total Titles in Print:** 6. **Selected Titles:** *Choices: A Teen Woman's Journal for Self Awareness and Personal Planning* by Mindy Bingham et al.; *Facts and Reflections on Female Adolescent Sexuality; What Do We Know about Girls; Facts and Reflections on Girls and Substance Use; Operation SMART Research Tool Kit; An Action Agenda for Equalizing Girl's Options.* **Principal Officials and Managers:** Margaret Gates, National Executive Director.

★9768★ Glad Hag Books
PO Box 29
Washington, DC 20013
Phone: (202)526-0049
Total Titles in Print: 2. **Selected Titles:** *Making a Way: Lesbians out Front* by JEB. **Principal Officials and Managers:** Joan E. Biren.

★9769★ Glenhurst Publications, Inc.
6300 Walker St.
St. Louis Park, MN 55416
Phone: (612)925-3632
Description: Publishes secondary-school-level curriculum, women's history and culture, and materials on women in development. Also produces filmstrips, videos, teachers' guides, manuals, and slides. Distributes for Gem Publications, Inc. Reaches market through direct mail and telephone sales. **Total Titles in Print:** 20. **Selected Titles:** *Women in Ancient Greece and Rome, Women in Medieval/Renaissance Europe, Toward Achieving Historical Symetry: A Manual for Teaching Women's History and Culture in a Global Setting, Women in Latin America the 20th Century, Women in Africa, Vols. I-II; Third World Women: Family, Work, and Empowerment,* all by Susan Hill Gross and Marjorie Wall Bingham. **Principal Officials and Managers:** Janet Donaldson, President; Susan Hill Gross, Vice-President; Bert M. Gross; Eileen F. Soderberg, Treasurer.

★9770★ Glover Press
500 Country Ave.
Secaucus, NJ 07096
Phone: (201)867-5840
Description: Publishes books on maternal childcare in English, Spanish, and Chinese. Offers advertising and marketing services. Accepts unsolicited manuscripts. Reaches market through direct mail and trade sales. **Number of**

New Titles: 1989 - 1, 1990 - 2; Total Titles in Print - 4. **Selected Titles:** *Breastfeeding Your Baby* by Joyce Fischer; *Mother and Baby Care* (English, Spanish, and Chinese editions) by Roseann Neuberg and Lisa Kugler; *A New Baby for Us* by Lisa Kugler; *A Passage Through the Land of Sleepy Hollow* by Lynn Butler; *Hey What About Me, Diapers and Delirium* (video cassette). **Principal Officials and Managers:** Alice Glover, Director; Sara Tucker, Associate Director.

★9771★ **Good Gay Poets**
PO Box 277, Astor St
Boston, MA 02123
Phone: (617)492-7713

Description: Publishes books of poetry by lesbians and gay males. The press is collectively run and operated; income is supplemented by grants and benefits. **Selected Titles:** *Behind the State Capitol* by John Weiners; *Only as Far as Brooklyn* by Maurice Kenny; *Desert Journal* by Ruth Weiss; *Amusement Business* by Freddie Greenfield; *Black and Queer* by Adrian Stanford; *25 Years of Malcontent* by Stephanie Byrd. **Principal Officials and Managers:** Charles Shively, Walta Borawski, Collective Members.

★9772★ **Grace and Goddess Unlimited**
PO Box 4367
Boulder, CO 80306

Description: Holistic health careers and feminist hypnosis books and tapes. Distributors include Ladyslipper (see separate entries) and New Leaf.

★9773★ **Greenfield Review Press**
2 Middle Cove Rd.
PO Box 308
Greenfield Center, NY 12833
Phone: (518)584-1728
Fax: (518)583-9741

Founded: 1970. **Description:** Includes poetry by ethnic minorities, women, and people in prison.

★9774★ **Greenwood Press/Praeger Publishers**
88 Post Rd. W.
Westport, CT 06881
Phone: (203)226-3571

Description: Trade press. Publishes women's studies books.

★9775★ **Greyfalcon House**
496-A Hudson St.
New York, NY 10014
Founded: 1968.

★9776★ **Grinnen-Barrett Publishing Co.**
36 Winchester St., No. 8
PO Box 7
Brookline, MA 02146
Phone: (617)232-1993

Description: Publishes on pregnancy and nutrition. Offers posters and dieting materials. Reaches market through direct mail. **Number of New Titles:** 1990 - 1; Total Titles in Print - 1. **Selected Titles:** *D.I.E.T. During Pregnancy: The Complete Guide and Calendar* by Miriam Erick. **Principal Officials and Managers:** Miriam Er-

ick, President and C.E.O.; Dianne Friend, Office Manager.

★9777★ **Guilford Publications, Inc.**
72 Spring St.
New York, NY 10012
Phone: (212)431-9800

Description: Publishes books, cassettes, educational programs, and journals in psychology, psychiatry, sociology, communication, family studies, criminology, geography, and molecular biology for clinical and academic readers. Offers journals, a newsletter, and audio and video cassettes. Accepts unsolicited manuscripts. Reaches market through direct mail, space advertising, convention exhibits, and trade sales. **Number of New Titles:** 1989 - 50, 1990 - 50, 1991 (est.) - 60; Total Titles in Print - 385. **Selected Titles:** *Black Families in Therapy* by Nancy Boyd-Franklin; *Therapeutic Paradox* by Michael Ascher; *Healing Brain* by Robert E. Ornstein and Charles Swencionis; *Eating Disorders* by L. K. George Hsu; *Intimate Environments* by David Kantor and Barbara F. Okun; *Pain in Children* by Patricia McGrath. **Principal Officials and Managers:** Robert Matloff, President; Seymour Weingarten, Editor-in-Chief; Marian Robinson, Marketing Manager; David Mitchell, Business Manager.

★9778★ **Harrington Park Press**
10 Alice St.
Binghamton, NY 13904-1580
Toll-free: 800-342-9678
Fax: (607)722-1424

Description: Topics include gay/lesbians, abortion and theocracy. **Selected Titles:** *God's Country: A Case Against Theocracy* by Sandy Rapp, *Embryos, Ethics, and Women's Rights* edited by Elaine Hoffman Baruch, Amadeo F. D'Adamo, Jr. and Jone Seager, and *The Criminalization of A Woman's Body* edited by Clarice Feinman, Ph.D. **Remarks:** An imprint of The Harworth Press, Inc.

★9779★ **Hart to Heart Publishing**
PO Box 2293
Sausalito, CA 94966
Phone: (415)389-1016
Sylvia K. Hart, Contact

Founded: 1988. **Subjects:** Love addiction and recovery.

★9780★ **Harvard University Press**
79 Garden St.
Cambridge, MA 02138
Phone: (617)495-2600

Description: Academic press. Publishes women's studies books.

★9781★ **Hayes Publishing Co., Inc.**
6304 Hamilton Ave.
Cincinnati, OH 45224
Phone: (513)681-7559

Subjects: Sex education, pro-life publication on abortion. **Selected Titles:** *Sex Education in the Classroom, Abortion and Slavery: History Repeats, Human Life and Abortion: The Hard Questions, How Babies Grow, Abortion: Questions and Answers,* all by Dr. and Mrs. J. C. Willke; *Abortion, Bible, and the Christian* by Donald Shoemaker; *German Euthanasia* by Dr. Frederic Wertham. **Principal Officials and**

Managers: H. B. Hayes, President; Margery Lammers, Office Manager.

★9782★ **Helaine Victoria Press, Inc.**
PO Box 17
Martinsville, IN 46151
Phone: (812)331-0444

Description: Nonprofit, educational organization; publishes women's history materials, mainly postcards. Accepts unsolicited manuscripts. Reaches market through direct mail and wholesalers. Also distributes related materials for Fotofolio and Crossing Press. Total Titles in Print - 105. **Selected Titles:** *Susan B. Anthony and Elizabeth Cady Stanton; Emma Goldman; Sojourner Truth; Rosie the Riveter; Amelia Earhart and Eleanor Roosevelt; Women in Social: The U.S. since 1915.* **Principal Officials and Managers:** Jocelyn H. Cohen, Director; Lydia Bagwell, Interim Director.

★9783★ **Helicon Nine**
PO Box 22412
Kansas City, MO 64113
Phone: (913)722-2999

Description: Small press publishing company emphasizing literature, music, and the visual and performing arts. **Selected Titles:** *The Helicone Nine Reader.*

★9784★ **Her Own Words**
PO Box 52
Madison, WI 53705
Phone: (608)271-7083

Description: Publishes on women's literature and history for general and academic audiences. Offers *Her Own Words* newsletter four times yearly. Also offer audio and video cassettes and t-shirts. Reaches market through direct mail, Baker & Taylor, Ingram Book Co., and Victory. **Subjects:** Women's studies, American literature, social studies, quilts. **Number of New Titles:** 1990 - 6, 1991 - 6, 1992 (est.) - 6; Total Titles in Print - 24. **Selected Titles:** *The Literature of Quilts, Belle Case La Follette, Votes for Women!, Zona Gale, Pioneer Women's Diaries, Norwegian Pioneer Women,* all by Jocelyn Riley. **Principal Officials and Managers:** Jocelyn Riley, President and Owner.

★9785★ **Her Publishing**
32 Gretna Blvd.
Gretna, LA 70053
Phone: (504)368-1934

Founded: 1976. **Description:** Publishes unknown women authors.

★9786★ **HerBooks**
PO Box 74
Santa Cruz, CA 95061
Phone: (408)425-7493

Description: Publishes books on lesbianism and feminism with a Jewish emphasis. Reaches market through commission representatives, dierct mail, trade sales, and Inland Book Co. **Number of New Titles:** 1990 - 1, 1992 (est.) - 2; Total Titles in Print - 11. **Selected Titles:** *Cats (and their Dykes)* edited by Irene Reti and Shoney Sien; *Bubbe Meiseh by Shayneh Maidelehs* edited by Leslea Newman; *Love Me Like You Mean It* by Leslea Newman; *Love, Politics and "Rescue" in Lesbian Relationships* by Diana Rabenold. **Principal Officials and Managers:** Irene Reti, Owner.

★9787★ Heron Press
51 Melcher St., 4th Fl.
Boston, MA 02210
Phone: (617)482-3615
Founded: 1968.

★9788★ Holistic Exchange
PO Box 16
Muncie, IN 47308
Phone: (317)741-7850
Description: Publishes books and catalogs on holistic health, women, and black studies. Offers a quarterly newsletter *Nature's Aid First Aid Kits.* Also offers herbs, vitamins, and health products. Distributes for Nature's Sunshine, Carlton Press, Earth Pride, and Nutrition Express. Reaches market through direct mail, wholesalers, and trade sales. **Total Titles in Print:** 20. **Number of New Titles:** 1992 (est.) - 2; **Selected Titles:** *Black History Comic Books* by Baylor; *An Apple A Day; Road to Riches; New and Different Friends,* all by Miller; *System Guide to Natural Health; The Seven Basic Lesson of Black History.* **Principal Officials and Managers:** Melvia F. Miller, President.

★9789★ Home Team Press
2206 20th St.
Cuyahoga Falls, OH 44223
Phone: (216)928-8083
Description: Publishes on parenting. Reaches market through direct mail and trade sales. **Number of New Titles:** 1990 - 1; Total Titles in Print - 1. **Selected Titles:** *The Child Influencers: Restoring the Lost Art of Parenting* by Dan Adams. **Principal Officials and Managers:** Daniel J. Adams, Owner.

★9790★ Homosexual Information Center, Inc.
PO Box 82
Universal City, CA 91608-0252
Phone: (318)742-4709
Description: Accepts unsolicited manuscripts. Alternate address: 115 Monroe, Bossier City, LA 7111-4539. **Subjects:** Homosexuality, pornography, abortion, prostitution. **Selected Titles:** *Seeds of the American Sexual Revolution; Selected Bibliography of Homosexuality; Directory of Homosexual Organizations and Publications.* **Principal Officials and Managers:** Don Slater, Chairor; William Edward Glover, Vice-Chairor; Ursula Copely, Secretary.

★9791★ Hot Flash Press
PO Box 215
San Jose, CA 95151
Phone: (408)292-1172
Description: Publishes on religion and feminism. Reaches market through direct mail and BookPeople. **Selected Titles:** *Readings for Women's Programs, Memorial Services for Women, Dramatic Readings on Feminist Issues, Vol. 1,* all by Meg Bowman; *Readings for Older Women* edited by Meg Bowman and Diane Haywood; *Sexist Language* edited by Meg Bowman and Rosemary Matson; *Famous Unitarian Universalist Women.* **Principal Officials and Managers:** Meg Bowman, Owner.

★9792★ How(ever) Press
1936 Leavenworth
San Francisco, CA 94133
Phone: (415)474-8911
Founded: 1983. **Subjects:** Innovative poetry by women. Spin-off from magazine of same name.

★9793★ Hughes Press
500 23rd St. NW, B203
Washington, DC 20037
Phone: (202)293-2686
Description: Publishes books dealing with the legal, medical, economic, and social aspects of sex discrimination. Reaches market through commission representatives, direct mail, bibliographic listings, trade sales, and wholesalers. **Subjects:** Law, medicine, social science, physics. **Total Titles in Print:** 1. **Selected Titles:** *The Sexual Barrier: Legal, Medical, Economic and Social Aspects of Sex Discrimination; Computer Health Hazards.* **Principal Officials and Managers:** Marija Matich Hughes, Proprietor.

★9794★ Ide House
4631 Harvey Dr.
Mesquite, TX 75150
Phone: (214)686-5332
Description: Feminist press that publishes liberal social/economic scholarly books. Accepts unsolicited manuscripts; query first. Reaches market through direct mail, trade sales, and major wholesalers and distributors. **Subjects:** Women, lesbian/gay, liberal politics, health. **Number of New Titles:** 1990 - 1, 1991 - 2, 1992 (est.) - 5; Total Titles in Print - 106. **Selected Titles:** *Woman in Yorkist England* by Darlene Tempelton; *Education of Italian Renaissance Women* by Belinda Blade; *Chinese Women: Past and Present* by Esther S. Yao; *Peppertree III* by Shyree Latham; *Magic Washing Machine: Diary of Single Parenthood* by Beverly Slapin; *Woman as Priest, Bishop and Laity* by Arthur Frederick Ide. **Principal Officials and Managers:** Ruby Borchardt, President; Mary Helen Potter, Executive Vice-President; Mary Dahmusi, Vice-President, Sales; Anna Pahl, Senior Editor; Lacy Ruth Lovi, Vice-President, Contracts.

★9795★ ILR Press
Cornell University
School of Industrial and Labor Relations
Ithaca, NY 14851
Phone: (607)255-3061
Description: Academic press. Publishes women's studies books.

★9796★ Ilut Publications
c/o Lane & Associates
5268 La Jolla Blvd.
La Jolla, CA 92037-8109
Description: Provides contacts beyond networking for upcoming professional people. **Selected Titles:** *Who's Who among San Diego Women: The Power Source* edited by Lorraine Andren and Gloria Lane. **Principal Officials and Managers:** Lorraine Andren, Gloria Lane, Co-Publishers and Editors.

★9797★ Imp Press
270 Potomac Ave.
Buffalo, NY 14213-1257
Phone: (716)881-5391
Founded: 1979. **Selected Titles:** *Seed of a Woman; Pictures from the Past.*

★9798★ In Her Image: A Gallery of Women's Art
3208 SE Hawthorne
Portland, OR 97214
Phone: (503)231-3726
Description: Gallery maintains a small art publishing operation.

★9799★ Incunabula Collection Press, Ltd. (ICP)
277 Hillside Ave.
Nutley, NJ 07110
Phone: (201)667-8502
Subjects: Feminist studies. **Selected Titles:** *Cinderella's Housework Dialectics* by Lela and Paul Meinhardt. **Principal Officials and Managers:** Lela and Paul Meinhardt, Owners.

★9800★ Indiana University
Kinsey Institute for Research in Sex, Gender & Reproduction, Inc.
Morrison Hall 313
Bloomington, IN 47405
Phone: (812)855-7686
Description: Conducts research on human sexuality and has established library, art, film, and photo collections to support such research. **Subjects:** Sex behavior, attitudes, education, erotic art and literature. **Selected Titles:** *Sexuality and Disease* edited by Bowell, Hexter, and Reinisch; *Homosexuality/Heterosexuality: Concepts of Sexual Orientation,* edited by McWhirter, Sanders and Reinisch; *AIDS and Sex: An Integrated Biomedical and Biobehavioral Approach* edited by Voeller, Reinisch, and Gottlieb; *Adolescence and Puberty* by Bancroft and Reinisch; *Sex and Morality in the United States: An Empirical Enquiry under the Auspices of the Kinsey Institute* by Klassen, Williams and Levitt; *Sexuality and Disease: Metaphors, Perceptions, and Behavior in the AIDS Era.* **Principal Officials and Managers:** June Machover Reinisch, Director; Stephanie A. Sanders, Assistant Director.

★9801★ Indiana University Press
10th and Morton Sts.
Bloomington, IN 47405
Phone: (812)855-4203
Description: Academic press. Publishes women's studies books.

★9802★ Information Systems Development
44 East Ave., Ste. 201
Austin, TX 78701
Phone: (512)477-1604
Description: Offers books and databases on minority issues, specifically pertaining to Hispanics, Blacks, and women, in the Austin area. Reaches market through commission representatives and direct mail. **Subjects:** Bilingual and ethnic studies materials, women's studies, bibliographies. **Selected Titles:** *Chicana Feminist, Diosa y Hembra, Multicultural Women Sourcebook: Materials Guide for Bilingual Education Women Studies Programs,* all by Martha P. Cotera; *La Mujer Chicana* by Evey Chapa and

Sally Andrade; *Women of Hispanic Origin in U.S.; Austin Hispanic Directory.* **Principal Officials and Managers:** Martha P. Cotera, Director.

★9803★ **Institute for Childhood Resources**
210 Columbus Ave., Rm. 611
San Francisco, CA 94133
Phone: (415)864-1169
Subjects: Parent education, child care, toys. **Selected Titles:** *The Whole Child: A Sourcebook, Choosing Child Care: A Guide for Parents, The Toy Chest: A Sourcebook, Confronting the Child Care Crisis, Child Care: A Comprehensive Guide,* all by S. Auerbach; *Tips on Toys* (audio cassette). **Principal Officials and Managers:** Stevanne Auerbach, Director.

★9804★ **Institute of Lesbian Studies**
PO Box 602
Palo Alto, CA 94306
Description: Publishes on lesbian theory for classroom use in women's studies, lesbian studies, feminist theory, and philosophy. Reaches market through direct mail, trade sales, and distributors, including Inland Book Co. and BookPeople. **Selected Titles:** *Lesbian Philosophy: Explorations* by Jeffner Allen; *Lesbian Ethics* by Sarah Lucia Hoagland; *Are We There Yet A Continuing History of Lavender Woman, A Chicago Lesbian Newspaper 1971-1976* by Michal Brody. **Principal Officials and Managers:** Ann Seawall, Coordinator.

★9805★ **International Childbirth Education Association, Inc. (ICEA)**
PO Box 200
Minneapolis, MN 55420
Phone: (612)854-8660
Description: Publishes for health care professionals and consumers who work with the childbearing family. Also offers four periodicals per year, a review book catalog, and teaching aids for childbirth educators. **Total Titles in Print:** 20. **Selected Titles:** *Parents Guide* by Peg Beals; *Labor and Birth* by Linda Todd; *Unnecessary Cesareans* by Diony Young; *Humanizing Maternity Services through Family Centered Care* by Susan McKay; *Maternal-Child Health Care for the Young and the Poor* edited by Joanne Nicholson; *Outreach Teaching* edited by Barbara McCormick. **Principal Officials and Managers:** Jeanne Rose, President; Mickey Gillmor, Treasurer; Doris Olson, Office Manager; Trudy Keller, President-Elect; Pam Staurt, Secretary.

★9806★ **International Women's Tribune Centre**
777 United Nations Plaza
New York, NY 10017
Phone: (212)687-8633
Description: Makes information by, for, and about Third World women more widely available. Offers books, a quarterly newsletter, posters, postcards, and slide tapes. **Number of New Titles:** 1990 - 6; Total Titles in Print - 40. **Selected Titles:** *Ideas on Funding and Proposal Writing; It's Our Move Now: A Community Action Guide to the U.N. Nairobi Forward-Looking Strategies for the Advancement of Women; Clip Art: Women, the Password Is Action; The Tech and Tools Book: A Guide to Technologies Women Are Using Worldwide; Women and Small Business; Women Using Media for Social Change.* **Principal Officials and Managers:** Anne S. Walker, Executive Director, Vicki J. Semler, Associate Director.

★9807★ **International Women's Writing Guild (IWWG)**
PO Box 810, Gracie St
New York, NY 10028
Phone: (212)737-7536
Description: "A network for the personal and professional empowerment of women through writing." Publishes a bimonthly newsletter and occasional anthologies of the work of its members. Offers conferences, workshops, and retreats throughout the United States. Reaches market through direct mail and telephone and trade sales. **Number of New Titles:** 1990 - 6, 1991 (est.) - 6. **Selected Titles:** *The Ethics of Fiction Writing; Hope, Courage, Inspiration and Creativity; Aspects of Transformation; Writing as an Act of Faith* by Hannelore Hahn; *In the Valley of the Moon* by Carol Logue; *Mosaic: Poems from an IWWG Workshop.* **Principal Officials and Managers:** Hannelore Hahn, Founder and Executive Director; Tatiana Stoumen, "Network" Editor; Lyle Benjamin, Typesetter.

★9808★ **Ism Press**
PO Box 12447
San Francisco, CA 94112
Phone: (415)333-7641
Founded: 1982. **Description:** Publishes "radical books in history, politics, and people's cultures, with a focus on third world and women's movements." **Selected Titles:** *Lesbian Origins.*

★9809★ **Ivy Hill Press**
2024 Waterbury
Chula Vista, CA 92013
Description: Specializes in women's publications, stressing literary quality and experimentation in fiction, nonfiction, and poetry. **Selected Titles:** *The Other Me, Finding Voice, Homeland, Sidereality,* all by Ella Blanche. **Principal Officials and Managers:** Roxanne Flom, Business Manager.

★9810★ **Janes Publishing**
25671 Fleck Rd.
Veneta, OR 97487
Phone: (503)935-7654
Description: Publishes on alternative communities and midwifery. Offers a quarterly magazine *Midwifery Today.* Reaches market through direct mail, New Leaf Distributing Co., Armadillo, and Ubiquity Distributors. **Total Titles in Print:** 2. **Selected Titles:** *New Age Community Guidebook* by Corcoran. **Principal Officials and Managers:** Bobbi Corcoran, President and Managing Editor; Michael Richards, Marketing Director.

★9811★ **Jeffers/Carr Associates**
307 E. 44th St.
New York, NY 10017
Phone: (212)599-2327
Subjects: Women's issues. **Total Titles in Print:** 1. **Selected Titles:** *How to Find a Job: A Woman's Handbook* by Susan J. Jeffers and Ellen F. Carr. **Principal Officials and Managers:** Susan J. Jeffers, Ellen F. Carr, Partners.

★9812★ **Jewels Graphics and Publishing**
304 15th St.
Oakland, CA 94612
Phone: (415)763-9671
Fax: (415)763-1245
Description: Publishes magazines, books, and newsletters for organizations and businesses. Also produces camera-ready feminist, non-sexist, all-ages, all-races clip art.

★9813★ **Jewish Women's Resource Center (JWRC)**
9 E. 69th St.
New York, NY 10021
Phone: (212)535-5900
Description: Publishes texts intended to advance the movement for Jewish renewal, with a special focus on feminist approaches and perspectives. Also publishes various guides for ritual performance and a newsletter. Offers audio cassettes. Accepts unsolicited manuscripts. Reaches market through direct mail. **Subjects:** Women and Judaism, Jewish life. **Total Titles in Print:** 15. **Selected Titles:** *Feminist Passover Haggadah, Tu B'Shevat Feminist Haggadah,* both by Rabbi Julie Gordon; *Ladies of Genesis: Poems of Women in the Bible* by Barbara Holender; *International Rosh Chodesh Group Directory* edited by Beth Edberg; *Experimental Guide to Celebrating the Birth of a Daughter; Rosh Chodesh Ceremonies.* **Principal Officials and Managers:** Alice Zacharius, Chairor; Bernice Friedes, Vice-President; Helen Caplin Heller, Executive Director.

★9814★ **Joanna Taylor Books**
2461 El Pavo Way
Cordova, CA 95670
Phone: (916)362-6963
Description: Private publisher of books by and about women. Reaches market through direct mail. **Total Titles in Print:** 2. **Selected Titles:** *Literary Ladies: A Selection of First Books of Women Writers* by Joanna Taylor; *December 24th, A Poem* by Hildegarde Flanner. **Principal Officials and Managers:** Joanna Taylor, Owner.

★9815★ **Joanne Friedman**
66 N. Mitchell Ave.
Livingston, NJ 07039
Phone: (201)994-6644
Description: Publishes on nutrition during pregnancy and infancy. Reaches market through direct mail. **Total Titles in Print:** 1. **Selected Titles:** *Nourishing Your Child: Pregnancy and Infancy* by Joanne Faust-Friedman. **Principal Officials and Managers:** Joanne Friedman.

★9816★ **Johari M. Rashad**
1245 4th St. SW, Ste. 406
Washington, DC 20024
Founded: 1982. **Subjects:** Women's concerns, black women's issues; Afro American issues. **Formerly:** Writely So, (1982); Rashad Association, (1988).

★9817★ **Joyful Woman**
PO Box 900
Chattanooga, TN 37412
Phone: (615)698-7318
Description: Publishes on women. Reaches market through direct mail and trade sales. **Total Titles in Print:** 15. **Selected Titles:** *The*

Organized Joyful Woman, The Joyful Woman Leadership Manual, Making Your Marriage Magnificent, all by Joy Rice Martin; *Pain, the Gift Nobody Wants* by Grace Rice MacMullen; *Forgiving the Unforgivable* by Elizabeth Rice Handford. **Principal Officials and Managers:** Walter Handford, President; Roger Martin, Vice-President; Joy Martin, Treasurer; Elizabeth Handford, Secretary.

★9818★ Judith's Room: Books for Women and their Friends
681 Washington St.
New York, NY 10014
Phone: (212)727-7330

★9819★ Keegan Press
PO Box 25
Palm Springs, CA 92263
Phone: (619)320-5089
Description: A feminist press currently working on in-house publications. May branch out in the future to solicited feminist manuscripts. Reaches market through Island Book Co., Inc., East Haven, CT. **Subjects:** Feminism, mystery novels, short fiction. **Total Titles in Print:** 1. **Selected Titles:** *Alimony or Death of the Clock* by Lynn Watson. **Principal Officials and Managers:** Lynn Watson, Owner and Manager.

★9820★ Kelsey Street Press
PO Box 92
Berkeley, CA 94709
Phone: (415)845-2260
Description: Established to encourage women writers and to publish new experimental writing. Accepts unsolicited manuscripts. Reaches market through direct mail and distributors. **Subjects:** Poetry, short stories, art. **Number of New Titles:** 1989 - 2, 1990 - 2, 1991 (est.) - 2; Total Titles in Print - 20. **Selected Titles:** *Musicality* by Barbara Guest; *Dreams in Harrison Railroad Park* by Nellie Wong; *Biting Sun* by Thalia Kitrilakis; *Something: Even Human Voices* by Kathleen Fraser; *Bake-Face and Other Guava Stories* by Opal Palmer Adisa; *Like Roads* by Laura Moriarty. **Principal Officials and Managers:** Rena Rosenwasser, Director; Thalia Kitrilakis, Editorial; Marian Chapman, Manager, Business and Grants; Lori Paulson, Publicity.

★9821★ KIDS Project/Squeaky Wheels Press Anthology
PO Box 448
Berkley, CA 94701-0448
Phone: (415)587-2885
Description: Disabled writers and artists annual anthology edited and published by disabled women.

★9822★ Kitchen Table: Women of Color Press
PO Box 9
Latham, NY 12110
Description: "The first publisher in North America with a commitment to publishing and distributing the work of Third World women of all racial/cultural heritages, sexualities, and classes." **Principal Officials and Managers:** Myrna Bain, Audre Lorde, Cherrie Moraga, Mariana Romo-Carmona, Barbara Smith, Collective Members.

★9823★ KM Associates
4711 Overbrook Rd.
Bethesda, MD 20816
Phone: (301)652-4536
Description: Produces, publishes, and markets educational materials on natural family planning and related topics. Reaches market through New Leaf Distributing Co. **Total Titles in Print:** 2. **Selected Titles:** *Challenge to Love* by Mary Shivanandan; *Breastfeeding and Natural Family Planning* edited by Mary Shivanandan. **Principal Officials and Managers:** Mary Shivanandan, Director.

★9824★ Knowledge, Ideas & Trends, Inc.
1131-0 Tolland Tpke., Ste. 175
Manchester, CT 06040
Phone: (203)646-0745
Description: Nonfiction trade publisher. Accepts unsolicited manuscripts; should pertain to the environment, multiculturalism, women's issues, or business. Reaches market through direct mail, telephone sales, and wholesalers and distributors, including Inland Book Co., The Distributors, and Baker & Taylor. **Selected Titles:** *Be an Outrageous Older Woman* by Ruth Harriet Jacobs; *Telling It Like It Is* by Elayne Clift; *Sources: Annotated Bibliography of Women's Issues* edited by Rita I. McCullough; *The Yellow Slicker: A Woman's Fable* by Pegi Clark Pearson; *Delights, Dilemmas, and Decisions: Balance Stress and Success* by Margaret Bedrosian; *Making Peace with My Mother* by Edith Grossman. **Principal Officials and Managers:** Sandra L. Brown, President; Rita I. McCullough, Vice-President.

★9825★ La Leche League International, Inc.
9616 Minneapolis Ave.
PO Box 12
Franklin Park, IL 60131-8209
Phone: (708)455-7730
Description: Publishes and distributes information about breastfeeding, including books, periodicals, and calendars. Reaches market through direct mail. Distributes books on the subject by other publishers. **Subjects:** Breastfeeding, child care, nutrition, family life. **Number of New Titles:** 1989 - 1; Total Titles in Print - 15. **Selected Titles:** *Nightime Parenting, Safe and Healthy: A Parent's Guide to Children's Accidents and Illnesses, Becoming a Father, Growing Together: A Parent's Guide to Baby's First Year,* all by William Sears; *The Womanly Art of Breastfeeding* by La Leche League International; *Learning a Loving Way of Life* by Virginia Sutton Hatonen and Nancy Mohrbacher. **Principal Officials and Managers:** Betty Wagner, Executive Director; Sandra Tauber, Business Manager; Mary Lofton, Director of Special Projects; Sally Murphy, Publications Director.

★9826★ Lactation Associates Publishing Co.
1818 Stonecrest Ct.
PO Box 70
Lakeland, FL 33813
Phone: (813)644-7714
Description: Self-publishes on breast-feeding. Reaches market through direct mail and trade sales. **Selected Titles:** *Why Should I Nurse My Baby* by Pamela K. Wiggins. **Principal Officials and Managers:** Pamela K. Wiggins, Owner, Publisher, and Author.

★9827★ Ladyslipper
PO Box 31
Durham, NC 27705
Phone: (919)683-1570
Description: Publishes catalog of recorded titles by women. Also offers compact discs, LP records, audio tapes, and videos. Reaches market through direct mail and telephone sales. **Total Titles in Print:** 1. **Selected Titles:** *Ladyslipper Catalog and Resource Guide of Records, Tapes, Compact Discs, and Videos by Women.* **Principal Officials and Managers:** Laurie Fuchs, Director; Reggae P. J. Dodson, Buyer.

★9828★ Lake Press
PO Box 7934, Avondale St
Paducah, KY 42002
Phone: (502)575-2200
Description: Publishes women's health books. Reaches market through direct mail. **Number of New Titles:** 1990 - 1; Total Titles in Print - 2. **Selected Titles:** *The Women's Health Handbook, The Year of Birth: A Guide for Expectant Parents,* both by Laverne Kindred Brown. **Principal Officials and Managers:** Laverne Brown, Owner.

★9829★ Lambda Rising, Inc.
1625 Connecticut Ave. NW
Washington, DC 20009
Phone: (202)462-6969
Description: Publishes books and periodicals on homosexuality and offers thousands of current and out-of-print titles on homosexuality, lesbianism, and gay rights. Reaches market through direct mail and telephone sales. **Selected Titles:** *Parents of Gays* by Betty Fairchild; *Lambda Rising Book Report* edited by Jane Troxell; *The Whole Gay Catalog, Lambda Rising News,* both edited by Michael Brickey. **Principal Officials and Managers:** L. Page Maccubbin, President; James M. Bennett, Vice-President, Retail Operations; R. Kent Fordyce, Book Buyer.

★9830★ Lane & Associates, Inc.
6202 Friars Rd., Ste. 311
San Diego, CA 92108
Phone: (714)275-3030
Description: Primarily a technical and educational publishing house, currently concentrating on training books for women in business and management. **Subjects:** Data systems, communication, management. **Selected Titles:** *The Creative Touch* by B. Evans; *Who's Who among San Diego Women: The Power Source* edited by Lane and Andren; *The Woman's Basic Training Manual, Take Back the Power,* both by G. Lane; *Management Training for the Female Executive* by L. Romine; *It's All in How You Look at Things* by R. Kuehne. **Principal Officials and Managers:** Gloria J. Lane, President; Julie K. Lane, Comptroller; Lorraine Andren, Editor-in-Chief.

★9831★ Leonarda Productions
PO Box 1736, Cathedral Sta.
New York, NY 10025
Phone: (212)666-7697
Description: A nonprofit recording company that publishes classical and contemporary concert music. Offers compact discs, LPs, and cassettes, including cassette tapes corresponding to a book about women composers condu-

cive to classroom use. Accept written inquiries regarding making recordings. Reaches market through direct mail, Albany Music Distributors (U.S.A.) and Albany Records (U.K.). **Subjects:** Music, women. **Number of New Titles:** 1990 - 2, 1991 (est.) - 1; Total Titles in Print - 35. **Selected Titles:** *Women Composers: The Lost Tradition Found* (2 cassettes); *The London Philharmonic Celebrates American Composers; Masques: The Huntingdon Trio; The American Chamber Ensemble; Five: Johnathan Kramer: Five Compositions* (all compact discs); *Journey: Orchestral Works by American Women Composers.* **Principal Officials and Managers:** Marnie Hall, Executive Director.

★9832★ **Lexington Books**
125 Spring St.
Lexington, MA 02173
Phone: (617)862-6650

★9833★ **Liberal Arts Press**
PO Box 1603
Las Colinas, TX 75016
Phone: (214)686-5332

Description: Publishes on women's history, religion, and gay studies. Reaches market through commission representatives, direct mail, and reviews. **Total Titles in Print:** 7. **Selected Titles:** *From Pink Triangles to Growing Up Gay* by J. Michael Clark; *Unfolding Misconceptions: The Arkansas State Penetentiary* by Clyde Crosley; *Loving Women: A Study of Lesbianism to 500 CE* by Arthur Frederick Ide; *Women* by Marie Mapes; *Rhetoric and Change, Echoing Voices,* both edited by William R. Tanner. **Principal Officials and Managers:** Arhatha Jmsoi, President; Belinda Bapez, Vice-President; Brenda Jones, Senior Editor.

★9834★ **Liberation Publications Inc.**
6922 Hollywood Blvd., 10th Fl.
Los Angeles, CA 90028
Phone: (213)871-1225

Description: Publishes *The Advocate*, a national gay newsmagazine. Books published are on topics of interest to lesbians and gay men. **Selected Titles:** *Drawing on the Gay Experience* by Gerard Donelan; *The Advocate Gay Visitors Guide to San Francisco; The Advocate Gay Visitors Guide to Los Angeles; An Index to the Advocate, 1967-1982.* **Principal Officials and Managers:** Niles Merton, C.E.O.; John Knoebel, Chief Operations Officer.

★9835★ **Lida Rose Press**
PO Box 141017, University Sta.
Minneapolis, MN 55414
Phone: (612)331-6567

Description: Publishes popular history of current topics. Accepts unsolicited manuscripts; write for information and guidelines. Reaches market through Ingram Book Co., BookPeople, and Quality Books, Inc. **Number of New Titles:** 1990 - 1, 1991 (est.) - 1; Total Titles in Print - 1. **Selected Titles:** *Mothers of Thyme: Customs and Rituals of Infertility and Miscarriage* by J. L. Sha. **Principal Officials and Managers:** Janet L. Hatfield, Publisher.

★9836★ **Life Force Press**
303 W. Brooks St.
Howell, MI 48843
Phone: (517)548-9369

Description: Publishes on alternative subjects, especially feminism. Accepts unsolicited manuscripts; include a self-addressed, stamped envelope. Reaches market through direct mail. **Number of New Titles:** 1989 - 1, 1990 - 2; Total Titles in Print - 1. **Selected Titles:** *The Book of Woman* by Lea Souran. **Principal Officials and Managers:** Elizabeth E. De Courcy-Wernette, Owner and President; Christopher H. Romney, Owner and Vice-President.

★9837★ **Light Cleaning Press**
PO Box
Guttenberg, NJ 07093
Phone: (201)868-8106

Description: Publishes poetry with a feminist, spiritual, or astrological interest. Formerly Karmic Revenge Laundry Shop Press. **Selected Titles:** *Extra Footage, This Moment Is Your Momma,* both by R. Karman; *Cinderella* by Leah Kavablum; *Dyke Tracy* by Anna Mae Xerox; *On the Eve of God's 40th Yes* by Ziporah de los Angeles; *Between a Rock* by Rita Karman and Leah Kavablum. **Principal Officials and Managers:** Rita Karman, Editor.

★9838★ **Lioness Books**
52 Gramercy Park
New York, NY 10010
Phone: (212)505-6946

★9839★ **LivingQuest**
Box 3306
Boulder, CO 80307
Phone: (303)444-1319

Description: Publishes on addiction, eating disorders, and personal and planetary transformation. **Number of New Titles:** 1990 - 4; Total Titles in Print - 3. **Selected Titles:** *The Healing Power of Inner Light-Fire, Living Binge Free: A Personal Guide to Victory over Compulsive Eating,* both by Jane Evans Latimer; *The Gaia Mission* by Gene Latimer. **Principal Officials and Managers:** Gene Latimer, President; Jane Evans Latimer, Board Chairor.

★9840★ **Lollipop Power**
PO Box 2
Carrboro, NC 27510
Phone: (919)560-2738

Description: Publishes non-sexist, multi-cutural and bilingual children's books. Offers a newsletter and writing consultation service via mail. Accepts unsolicited manuscripts with a self-addressed, stamped envelope. Reaches market through trade sales, New Leaf Distributing Co., Baker & Taylor, and Inland Book Co. **Number of New Titles:** 1990 - 1, 1992 (est.) - 2; Total Titles in Print - 14. **Selected Titles:** *The Boy Toy* by Phyllis Johnson; *Jo, Flo, Yolanda* by Carol de Poix; *Grown Ups Cry Too* by Nancy Hazen; *In Christina's Toolbox* by Diane Homan; *Maria Theresa* by Mary Atkinson; *Joshua's Day* by Sandra Lucas Surowiecki. **Principal Officials and Managers:** Shelley Day, Executive Director; David C. Donelson, President; Elaine Goolsby, Editor-in-Chief.

★9841★ **Lowell House**
1875 Century Park E., No. 220
Los Angeles, CA 90067
Phone: (213)203-8407

Subjects: Women's issues, health, parenting. **Number of New Titles:** 1989 - 10, 1990 - 16, 1991 (est.) - 20; Total Titles in Print - 26. **Selected Titles:** *Adult Children of Abusive Parents* by Steven Farmer; *Teach Your Child to Draw* by Mia Johnson; *What Mona Lisa Knew* by Barbara Mackoff; *Overcoming the Legacy of Overeating* by Nan Kathryn Fuchs; *The Emotionally Abused Woman* by Beverly Engel, *Meeting the Challenge of Arthritis* by George Yates and Michael Shermer. **Principal Officials and Managers:** Jack Artenstein, President and C.E.O.; Janice Gallagher, Vice-President and Editor-in-Chief; Elizabeth Wood, Marketing Manager; Derek Gallagher, Production Manager.

★9842★ **The Luna Press**
Box 511, Kenmore Sta.
Boston, MA 02215
Phone: (617)427-9846

Selected Titles: *The Lunar Calendar: Dedicated to the Goddess in Her Many Guises*

★9843★ **LuraMedia**
7060 Miramar Rd., Ste. 104
San Diego, CA 92121
Phone: (619)578-1948

Description: Publications deal with psychology, religion, and women. Offers cassette tapes. Accepts unsolicited manuscripts; send for brochure. Reaches market through direct mail, telephone and trade sales, Spring Arbor Distributors, Inland Book Co., and New Leaf Distributing Co. **Number of New Titles:** 1990 - 6, 1991 (est.) - 5; 1992 (est.) - 6. Total Titles in Print - 28. **Selected Titles:** *Guerrillas of Grace: Prayers for the Battle, Tracks in the Straw: Tales Spun from the Manger,* both by Ted Loder; *Braided Streams: Esther and a Woman's Way of Growing, Seasons of Friendship: Naomi and Ruth as a Pattern,* both by Marjory Zoet Bankson; *Just a Sister Away: A Womanist Vision of Women's Relationships in the Bible* by Renita J. Weems; *The Star in My Heart* by Joyce Rupp. **Principal Officials and Managers:** Lura Jane Geiger, Publisher; Nan E. Coulter, Business Manager; Marcia Broucek, Managing Editor; Philip Dawdy, Marketing Manager.

★9844★ **Lynne Rienner Publishers**
1800 30th St., No. 314
Boulder, CO 80301
Phone: (303)444-6684
Fax: (303)444-0824

Founded: 1984. **Subjects:** Women's studies course materials.

★9845★ **MacMurray & Beck Communications**
PO Box 42
Aspen, CO 81612
Phone: (303)925-5284

Description: Publishes nonfiction on personal relationships. Accepts unsolicited manuscripts. Intends to produce audio cassettes. Reaches market through direct mail and SCB Distributors. **Subjects:** Women's studies, psychology, mythology. **Selected Titles:** *The Passion of Being Woman: A Love Story from the Past for the Twenty-First Century, Some Midnight*

Thoughts: A Little Collection of Unlicensed Poems and Uncertified Essays, First Edition of the Better-Balanced Dictionary for Smart People Who Want to Be Happy: New Meanings for New Realities, all by Mary Hugh Scott; *For Men Only: A Manual to Coach Men Who Love Women but Don't Know How to Live with Them, Lifequakes: What to Do in the Worst of Times,* both by Richard Corriere. **Principal Officials and Managers:** Russell Scott, Jr., President; Heidi Benson, Research Manager.

★9846★ Magic Circle Press
10 Hyde Ridge Rd.
Weston, CT 06883
Phone: (203)226-1903

Description: Publishes books for women and children. **Total Titles in Print:** 15. **Selected Titles:** *Cubal Analysis* by Karin Blair; *Brisburial* by Edward Pomerantz; *Maria Montessori, Francis Steloff, Anais Nin/Stars in My Sky* by Valerie Harms; *Little Boat Lighter Than a Cork, Somebody Else's Nut Tree and Other Tales from Children,* both by Ruth Krauss; *Feeling Mad, Sad, Bad, Glad* by Ann McGovern. **Principal Officials and Managers:** Valerie Harms, Director.

★9847★ Malafemmina Press
PO Box 411223
San Francisco, CA 94141-1223

★9848★ Manpower Demonstration Research Corp.
3 Park Ave.
New York, NY 10016
Phone: (212)532-3200

Description: Purpose is to test alternative approaches to the solution of social problems in the U.S. Reaches market through direct mail. **Subjects:** Work welfare, teen pregnancy, supported work for mentally retarded. **Number of New Titles:** 1989 - 2; Total Titles in Print - 63. **Selected Titles:** *Work Initiatives for Welfare Recipients* by J. Gueron; *The Challenge of Serving Pregnant and Parenting Teens: Lessons from Project Redirection* by J. Quint and J. Riccio; *Lessons on Transitional Employment: The STETS Demonstration for Mentally Retarded Workers* by M. Bangser; *The Community Service Projects: A New York State Adolescent Pregnancy Prevention and Services Program* by C. Guy et al.; *Tenant Management: Findings from a Three-Year Experiment in Public Housing; Findings on Youth Employment: Lessons from MDRC Research.* **Principal Officials and Managers:** Judith Gueron, President; Robert Ivry, Michael Bangser, Senior Vice-Presidents; Karen Paget, Barbara Goldman, Vice-Presidents.

★9849★ Margaret Media
421 Manases Pl.
New Orleans, LA 70119
Phone: (504)822-9305

Founded: 1981. **Subjects:** New Orleans women; women's history.

★9850★ Martha Rosler
143 McGuinness Blvd.
Brooklyn, NY 11222
Phone: (212)834-1466

Description: Publishes on women and their relation to household work, food, class, and economics. Distributed by Printed Matter, Inc.,

Art in Form, and Visual Studies Workshop. Alternate telephone number: (212) 383-2277. Reaches market through direct mail, trade sales, and wholesalers. **Total Titles in Print:** 5. **Selected Titles:** *A Budding Gourmet; McTowersMaid; Tijuana Maid; A New-Found Career; Letters on Abusing Women and Trying to Blame Them for It.* **Principal Officials and Managers:** Martha Rosler, Publisher and Editor.

★9851★ Maternity Center Association
48 E. 92nd St.
New York, NY 10128
Phone: (212)369-7300

Description: A national nonprofit health agency dedicated to the improvement of maternal and child health. Publishes booklets, a newsletter, pamphlets, teaching charts, books, and slide sets. Reaches market through direct mail. **Number of New Titles:** 1991 (est.) - 1, 1992 (est.) - 2; Total Titles in Print - 37. **Selected Titles:** *Birth Atlas; Preparing Children for Birth: A Professional's Guide; Preparation for Childbearing; For the Expectant Father; Growing Uterus Charts; Environmental Hazards During Pregnancy.* **Principal Officials and Managers:** Ruth Watson Lubic, General Director; Elizabeth Haak, Director, Public Information.

★9852★ Matrix Press
PO Box 327
Palo Alto, CA 94302
Phone: (415)325-7166

Founded: 1979. **Selected Titles:** *Women Writing Poetry in America.*

★9853★ Mayapple Press
PO Box 54
Saginaw, MI 48603-0473

Description: Publishes Great Lakes regional literature, especially poetry, fine literature by women, and craft books. Distributes for Tout Press, Earth's Daughters, and Allegany Mountain Press. Reaches market through sales at author readings. **Number of New Titles:** 1991 (est.) - 1; Total Titles in Print - 4. **Selected Titles:** *Letters to My Daughters* by Judith Minty; *As If Anything Could Grow Back Perfect* by Toni Ortner-Zimmerman; *Soft Sculpture: The Fantasy Real World of Kelli Rumfola* by Kelli Rumfola; *To Catch a Comet: Souvenir Book* by Judith Kerman. **Principal Officials and Managers:** Judith B. Kerman, Proprietor.

★9854★ McQueen & Son Publishing Co.
6302 Van Maren Ln.
Citrus Heights, CA 95621
Phone: (916)725-3285

Description: Publishes books on effective management. Also provides films, games, and interactive exercises. Reaches market through direct mail. **Total Titles in Print:** 1. **Selected Titles:** *The Management View: Sexual Harassment in the Workplace* by Iris McQueen. **Principal Officials and Managers:** Iris McQueen.

★9855★ Meadowbrook Press, Inc.
18318 Minnetonka Blvd.
Deephaven, MN 55391
Phone: (612)473-5400

Description: Publishes books on pregnancy, newborn and child care, the environment, travel, and cooking. Also offers mugs, cards, baby calendars, travel guides, games, and humor

books. Distributed to the trade by Simon & Schuster. Accepts unsolicited manuscripts; include a proposal, sample letter, and a self-addressed, stamped envelope. **Number of New Titles:** 1989 - 15, 1990 - 9, 1991 (est.) - 9. **Selected Titles:** *Grandma Knows Best, but no One ever Listens* by Mary McBride; *Baby and Child Medical Care* by Terril H. Hart; *Haitian without Words* by John Bertsch and Joseph Della Carpini; *Best Baby Name Book in the Whole Wide World, Baby Name Personality Survey,* both by Bruce Lansky; *Shopping for a Better Environment* by Laurence Tasaday; *Free Stuff for Kids.* **Principal Officials and Managers:** Bruce Lansky, President and Marketing Director; Stan Sergot, National Sales Manager; Kerstin Gorham, Editor; Joann Krueger, Production Manager; Dan Verdick, Subrights Manager.

★9856★ Merging Media
516 Gallows Hill Rd.
Cranford, NJ 07016
Phone: (201)276-9479

Description: Publishes works by women and sensitive men. Combines writing with the visual arts, including photos and graphics. Also offers editing and workshops. Reaches market through direct mail. **Number of New Titles:** 1990 - 2, 1991 - 1, 1992 (est.) - 3; Total Titles in Print - 48. **Selected Titles:** *Rand House* by Etienne Noir; *Upstream* edited by Virginia Love Long; *Underground-Aboveground: Her Poetic Voices* edited by Rochelle L. Holt; *A Warning* by Karl Miller; *Author's Choice, Stream of Consciousness,* both by Rochelle L. Holt. **Principal Officials and Managers:** Diane C. Erdmann, Publisher and Owner.

★9857★ Michigan State University Office of Women in International Development
202 International Center
East Lansing, MI 48824-1035
Phone: (517)353-5040

Description: Publishes articles about women's historical and changing participation in political, economic, and religious spheres, inter- and intra-family relationships, and health and health care. Also offers the newsletter *WID Bulletin.* Accepts unsolicited manuscripts; send two double-spaced copies. Reaches market through direct mail and Yankee Book Peddler. **Total Titles in Print:** 214. **Selected Titles:** *Women's Movements in Contemporary Pakistan: Results and Prospects* by Shahnaz J. Rouse; *Women, Work, and Ideology in Post-Revolutionary Iran* by V. Moghadam; *Women's Participation in the "People's Church": A Critical Appraisal* by S. Alvarez; *Zimbabwe: State, Class, and Gendered Models of Land Resettlement* by S. Jacobs; *From the Ground Up: An Anthropological Version of a Women's Development Movement in Polynesia* by C. Small; *Extending Credit to Rural Women: NGO Models from South Asia* by V. Viswanath. **Principal Officials and Managers:** Rita S. Gallin, Director.

★9858★ MidCoast Publications
65 Aberdeen Pl.
St. Louis, MO 63131
Phone: (314)721-3568

Description: Publishes on women and modeling. Offers video cassettes. Reaches market through Baker & Taylor and Quality Books, Inc. **Total Titles in Print:** 3. **Selected Titles:** *The Inside Secrets to a Modeling Career!, Model-*

ing.*How to Make it in Modeling Without Having to go to Modeling School,* both by Marilyn Stafford; *Swimming; The Art of the Stroke* by Mark Gerard. **Principal Officials and Managers:** Masrilyn Hanish, President and Director of Research and Development; Ann Terschluse, Editor and Marketing Director; Val Terschluse, Legal Counsel/Attorney at Law.

★9859★ Midmarch Associates
300 Riverside Dr.
New York, NY 10025
Phone: (212)666-6990
Description: Provides publications focusing on women in the arts. Accepts unsolicited manuscripts. Reaches market through direct mail. **Total Titles in Print:** 9. **Selected Titles:** *Women Artists of the World* by Cindy Lyle and Sylvia Moore; *Whole Arts Directory, American Women in Art, Guide to Women's Art Organizations/Directory for the Arts,* all by Cynthia Navaretta; *International Directory of Women in the Arts* by C. Lyle; *Voices of Women* edited by Lucy Lippard. **Principal Officials and Managers:** Rena Hansen, Managing Editor; Lynda Hulkower, Circulation Manager.

★9860★ Midwest Health Center for Women
825 S. 8th St., No. 902
Minneapolis, MN 55404
Phone: (612)332-2311
Description: Publishes books for and about women. Also produces newsletters, brochures, and family planning information. Reaches market through direct mail and telephone sales. **Total Titles in Print:** 2. **Selected Titles:** *Loving* by Linda Crawford and Lee Lanning; *The Pregnant Male.* **Principal Officials and Managers:** Jeri Rasmussen, Executive Director.

★9861★ Milwaukee Feminist Writer's Guild
2119 W. Juneau
Milwaukee, WI 53233
Phone: (414)342-9538
Description: Publishes an anthology of writing by Milwaukee feminists. **Selected Titles:** *Five-Petalled Blossom.* **Principal Officials and Managers:** Michaelle Deakin-Schall, Coordinator; Jean Ross, Editor.

★9862★ MND Publishing, Inc.
7163 Old Harding Rd.
Nashville, TN 37221
Phone: (615)646-9879
Description: Publishes on natural family planning for family planning agencies, book trade, health food markets, and libraries. Offers a printed temperature chart for use with this method of birth control. Reaches market through reviews and trade sales. **Selected Titles:** *Signs of Fertility: The Personal Science of Natural Birth Control.* **Principal Officials and Managers:** Margaret Dotzler, President.

★9863★ Monthly Review Press
122 W. 27th St.
New York, NY 10001
Phone: (212)691-2555
Fax: (212)727-3676
Founded: 1949.

★9864★ Monument Press
PO Box 1603
Las Colinas, TX 75016-0361
Phone: (214)686-5332
Description: Publishes liberal, feminist, and scholarly/academic books. Reaches market through direct mail, trade sales, and wholesalers. **Number of New Titles:** 1989 - 3, 1990 - 7; Total Titles in Print - 22. **Selected Titles:** *And Justice for Some: Judge Jack Hampton and the Richard Lee Bednarski Gang, Tomorrow's Tyrants: The Radical Right and the Politics of Hate, AIDS Hysteria, Origins of the Female Species,* all by Arthur Frederick Ide; *The Blood Tattoo* by Ebi Gabor; *Memories Are Forever* by Ruth Johnson. **Principal Officials and Managers:** Nicholas Lashmet, C.O.O.; Joanne Gonjales, Senior Editor; Valerie Gonz, Editor.

★9865★ Moon of New Ferns
12150 W. Calle Seneca
Tucson, AZ 85743
Description: Publishes a poetry and art book. Reaches market through direct mail and trade sales. **Subjects:** Lesbian feminism, self-sufficient living. **Total Titles in Print:** 1. **Selected Titles:** *herb womon* by zana. **Principal Officials and Managers:** Zana Siegel.

★9866★ Morning Glory Press, Inc.
6595 San Haroldo Way
Buena Park, CA 90620
Phone: (714)828-1998
Description: Specializes in books dealing with pregnant adolescents and school age parents. Reaches market through direct mail, trade sales, and wholesalers. **Subjects:** Adolescent pregnancy, parenthood, single parenthood, early marriage, adoption. **Number of New Titles:** 1990 - 1, 1991 (est.) - 7; Total Titles in Print - 16. **Selected Titles:** *Pregnant Too Soon: Adoption Is an Option; Do I Have a Daddy? A Story about a Single-Parent Child; Teenage Marriage: Coping with Reality; Open Adoption: A Caring Option,* all by Jeanne Warren Lindsay; *Teens Parenting: Your Pregnancy and Newborn Journey* by Jeanne Lindsay and Jean Brunelli; *Surviving Teen Pregnancy: Your Choices, Dreams, and Decisions* by Shirley Arthur. **Principal Officials and Managers:** Jeanne Lindsay, President; Robert E. Lindsay, Vice-President; Carole Blum, Director, Marketing; Eric W. Lindsay, Secretary.

★9867★ Mother Courage Press
1533 Illinois St.
Racine, WI 53405
Phone: (414)634-1047
Description: Publishes lesbian/feminist fiction and nonfiction. Reaches market through direct mail, trade sales, Baker & Taylor, BookPeople, Inland Book Co., and other wholesalers and distributors. **Number of New Titles:** 1989 - 2, 1990 - 2, 1991 (est.) - 4; Total Titles in Print - 18. **Selected Titles:** *Something Happened to Me* by Phyllis Sweet; *Why Me? Help for Victims of Child Sexual Abuse (Even If They Are Adults Now)* by Lynn B. Daugherty; *Fear or Freedom: A Woman's Option is Social Survival and Physical Defense* by Susan B. Smith; *Warning! Dating may be Hazardous to your Health!* by Claudette McShane; *I Couldn't Cry When Daddy Died* by Iris Galey; *The Woman Inside, from Incest Victim to Survivor* by Patty Barnes. **Principal Officials and Managers:** Barbara

Lindquist, Chief Executive Officer; Jeanne Arould, Editor-in-Chief.

★9868★ Mother Tongue Ink
37010 SE Snuffin Rd.
Estacada, OR 97023
Phone: (503)630-7848
Founded: 1979. **Description:** Publishes an Astrological Moon Calender reflecting natural cycles and sources through international women's culture.

★9869★ Mothering Magazine
PO Box 16
Santa Fe, NM 87504
Phone: (505)984-8116
Description: Publishes *Mothering Magazine,* an alternative parenting magazine. Also publishes books and booklets pertaining to pregnancy, birth, and parenting. Formerly known as Mothering Publications, Inc. Reaches market through direct mail. **Total Titles in Print:** 8. **Selected Titles:** *Circumcision; Immunizations; Midwifery and the Law.* **Principal Officials and Managers:** Peggy O'Mara, Publisher.

★9870★ Motheroot Publications
PO Box 83
Pittsburgh, PA 15218
Phone: (412)731-4453
Description: Publishes serious work by women reflecting women's culture and combining the art and politics inherent to the female experience. Also publishes *Motheroot Journal,* a quarterly review of books published by the small press dealing in women's interests. Reaches market through direct mail. **Total Titles in Print:** 8. **Selected Titles:** *Women and Honor: Some Notes on Lying* by Adrienne Rich; *Notes from a Daughter from the Old Country* by Melanie Perish; *Mother, May I* by Alma Villanueva; *The Uprising of the 20,000* by Donna Ippolito; *The Odyssey of Katinou Kalokovich* by Natalie L. M. Petesch; *We Speak in Code* by Melanie Kaye. **Principal Officials and Managers:** Anne Pride, President; Paulette Balogh, Treasurer.

★9871★ Mountain Moving Press
315 S. 4th East
Missoula, MT 59801
Phone: (406)543-4523

★9872★ Moving Parts Press
220 Baldwin St.
Santa Cruz, CA 95060
Phone: (408)427-2271
Founded: 1977.

★9873★ Multi-Medea Enterprises/Water Press
PO Box 194
Minneapolis, MN 55419-0437
Phone: (612)489-0704
Description: Multi-Medea is a sponsoring and publishing organization for the production of feminist performances, newspapers, broadsides, brochures, and books. Offers exchange of extensive (1000) mailing list of alternative/feminist/pacifist organizations and affiliates. Also offers, *Nine All Mine: A Woman's Self-Healing Video.* Reaches market through direct mail and conferences. **Subjects:** Feminism, pacifism, religious studies, oral history, erotica, children's rights, health. **Total Titles in Print:** 5.

Selected Titles: *It's Quite a Thing to Live All These Years, What We Will.Nos. 1-3,* both edited by Wendy Knox; *People, Places, and Words; Roaring Mouth: A Necklace for the Reckless; Warring and Whoring: Memoir Poems,* all by Wendy Joan Knox; *Levi Strauss, You've Left Your Mark on the Ass of America and Other Poems of the Seventies* by Roy McBride. **Principal Officials and Managers:** Wendy Knox, Publisher; Becky Knight, Roy McBride, Editors; Craig Cox, Sarah Maas, Advisors.

★9874★ Naiad Press, Inc.
PO Box 105
Tallahassee, FL 32302
Phone: (904)539-5965

Description: Publishes lesbian literature. Offers video cassettes. Accepts unsolicited manuscripts; query first. Alternative phone number: (904) 539-5965. Reaches market through direct mail, trade sales, wholesalers, and distributors, including Blackwell North America, John Coutts Library Services, Baker & Taylor, Inland Book Co., BookPeople, Ingram Book Co., and Pacific Pipeline. **Number of New Titles:** 1989 - 24, 1990 - 24, 1991 (est.) - 24; Total Titles in Print - 160. **Selected Titles:** *Double Daughter* by Vicki P. McConnell; *The Beverly Malibu* by Katherine V. Forrest; *After the Fire* by Jane Rule; *Lifting Belly* by Gertrude Stein; *There's Something I've Been Meaning to Tell You* edited by Loralee Macpike; *Lesbian Queries: The Book of Lesbian Questions* edited by Jennifer Hertz and Martha Ertman. **Principal Officials and Managers:** Barbara Grier, Vice-President and General Manager; Donna J. McBride, Vice-President.

★9875★ Nanny Goat Publications
PO Box 8
Laguna Beach, CA 92652
Phone: (714)494-7930

Description: Founded to bring feminist humor, outlook, etc. to "underground" style comic books. Much of subject matter is sexual satire from a woman's point of view. Reaches market through direct mail and Last Gasp (San Francisco, CA). **Total Titles in Print:** 9. **Selected Titles:** *Abortion Eve, Pandoras Box,* both by Farmer and Lyveley; *Tits and Clits.* **Principal Officials and Managers:** Joyce Farmer, Owner.

★9876★ NAPSAC International
PO Box 6
Marble Hill, MO 63764
Phone: (314)238-2010

Subjects: Childbirth, maternity care, obstetrics, pediatrics, early infant rearing, home birth. **Number of New Titles:** 1989 - 1; Total Titles in Print - 6. **Selected Titles:** *NAPSAC Directory of Alternative Birth Services* by Jamy Braun et al.; *The Five Standards for Safe Childbearing* by David Stewart; *Safe Alternatives in Childbirth; Compulsory Hospitalization or Freedom of Choice,* both edited by David and Lee Stewart; *Home Schooling* by Lee Stewart; *Childrearing and the Roots of Violence* by David and Lee Stewart; *Transitions in Midwifery* by Reichman. **Principal Officials and Managers:** Lee Stewart, President; David Stewart, Editor-in-Chief.

★9877★ Nathan Star Press
3602 Chestnut St.
Grand Forks, ND 58201
Phone: (701)772-1342

Subjects: Women. **Total Titles in Print:** 1. **Selected Titles:** *Women's Journeys through Crisis* by Myrna Olson. **Principal Officials and Managers:** Myrna R. Olson, Owner and Manager.

★9878★ National Association of Women Business Owners
600 S. Federal St., Ste. 400
Chicago, IL 60605
Phone: (312)346-2330

Description: Publishes material to encourage and support women who own and operate businesses. **Principal Officials and Managers:** Natalie P. Holmes, CAE, Executive Director.

★9879★ National Association for Women Deans, Administrators, and Counselors
1325 18th St. NW, Ste. 210
Washington, DC 20036
Phone: (202)659-9330

Description: Committed to strengthening educational and career opportunities of women in education, counseling, and academic administration. Publishes quarterly journal and reports. **Subjects:** Women in education. **Selected Titles:** *Women in Educational Administration: A Book of Readings* edited by Margaret Berry; *Women in Higher Education: A Contemporary Bibliography* by Kathryn Moore and Peter Wollitzer; *Returning Women Students: A Review of Research and Descriptive Studies* by Nancy A. Scott; *Organizational Barriers and Their Impact on Women in Higher Education* by Myra Jean Stokes; *Strategies and Attitudes: Women in Educational Administration* edited by Patricia A. Farrant. **Principal Officials and Managers:** Patricia Rueckel, Executive Director.

★9880★ National Center on Women and Family Law, Inc.
799 Broadway, Rm. 402
New York, NY 10003
Phone: (212)674-8200

Description: Publishes texts and a newsletter on developments in family law issues. Reaches market through direct mail. **Subjects:** Family law, support, custody, battery, incest, rape. **Number of New Titles:** 1990 - 8, 1991 (est.) - 6, 1992 (est.) - 6; Total Titles in Print - 200. **Selected Titles:** *Interstate Child Custody Disputes: Policy, Practice, and Law; Child Support: A National Disgrace; Annotated Battered Women Bibliography; Battered Women: The Facts; Marital Rape.* **Principal Officials and Managers:** Laurie Woods, Director.

★9881★ National Council of Jewish Women
53 W. 23rd St.
New York, NY 10010
Phone: (212)645-4048

Description: Publishes on women's issues, children and youth, and Israel. Also publishes a magazine. Reaches market through direct mail. **Total Titles in Print:** 20. **Selected Titles:** *Pro-Choice Guidelines; Choosing Family Child Care; Soviet Jewry Resettlement.* **Principal Officials and Managers:** Joan Bronk, President; Iris Gross, Executive Director.

★9882★ National Gay and Lesbian Task Force Policy Institute (NGLTF)
1734 14th St. NW
Washington, DC 20009-4309
Phone: (202)332-6483

Description: Publishes resource materials aimed at informing the public about the homosexual community and the reasons why civil rights protections are needed. Also publishes a quarterly newsletter, *Task Force Report.* Offers a map in connection with the Privacy Project. Reaches market through direct mail and the gay press. **Subjects:** Lesbianism, homosexuality, gay civil rights, AIDS lobbying. **Number of New Titles:** 1990 - 3, 1991 (est.) - 4; Total Titles in Print - 30. **Selected Titles:** *Anti-Gay Violence and Victimization in 1985-90; Anti-Gay Violence: Causes, Consequences, Responses* by Kevin Berrill; *Military Disservice; Anti-Gay/Lesbian Victimization; Hate Crimes Legislation Packet; Gay Rights Protection in the U.S.* **Principal Officials and Managers:** Urvashi Vaid, Executive Director; Robert Bray, Public Information Director; Kevin Berrill, Anti-Violence Project Director; Tim Drake, Director of Privacy Project and Military Freedom Initiative; Ivy Young, Director of Families Project.

★9883★ National Radical Women Publications
608 22nd Ave.
Seattle, WA 98122
Phone: (202)722-6057

Description: Publishes radical women's theoretical documents relevant to countering racism, sexisim, anti-gay bigotry, and labor exploitation.

★9884★ National Women's History Project
7738 Bell Rd.
Windsor, CA 95492
Phone: (707)838-6000

Description: Publishes on women's history. Accepts unsolicited manuscripts for women's history curriculum units only. Offers videotapes, newsletters, posters, research, teacher-training, and writing services. **Number of New Titles:** 1989 - 3, 1990 - 1, 1991 (est.) - 2; Total Titles in Print - 25. **Principal Officials and Managers:** Mary Ruthsdotter, Project Director.

★9885★ Network Publications
PO Box 18
Santa Cruz, CA 95061-1830
Phone: (408)438-4060

Description: Nonprofit publisher of family life, health, and sex education books, videos curricula, research reports, and pamphlets. Also publishes a quarterly magazine, *Family Life Educator.* Reaches market through direct mail and telephone sales. **Number of New Titles:** 1989 - 26, 1990 - 27, 1991 (est.) - 24; Total Titles in Print - 190. **Selected Titles:** *Am I in Trouble* by Curwin and Mendler; *Here We Go. Watch Me Grow!* by Hendricks and Smith; *Tobacco Talk* by D'Onofrio; *The Multicultural Caterpillar* by Matiella; *Ending the HIV Epidemic* edited by Petrow et al; *Reducing Adolescent Pregnancy* edited by Brindis. **Principal Officials and Managers:** Sandra Ludlow, Executive Director; Steven Bignell, Marketing Director; Mary Nelson, Editorial Director; Susan Bagby, Sales Manager; Judith Carey, Marketing Manager.

★9886★ **New Nativity Press**
PO Box 62
Leawood, KS 66206
Phone: (913)341-8369

Description: Publishes on childbirth. **Selected Titles:** *Birth and the Dialogue of Love* by Marilyn A. Moran; *Happy Birth Days* edited by Marilyn A. Moran. **Principal Officials and Managers:** Marilyn A. Moran, Manager.

★9887★ **New Pages Press**
4426 S. Belsay Rd.
Grand Blanc, MI 48439
Phone: (313)743-8055
Founded: 1980.

★9888★ **New Seed Press**
PO Box 9488
Berkeley, CA 94709
Phone: (510)540-7576

Founded: 1971. **Subjects:** Non-sexist, non-racist children's books. Feminist collective. **Selected Titles:** *My Mother and I Are Growing Strong.*

★9889★ **New Society Publishers**
4527 Springfield Ave.
Philadelphia, PA 19143
Phone: (215)382-6543
Fax: (215)222-1993
Founded: 1980.

★9890★ **New Victoria Publishers**
PO Box
Norwich, VT 05055-0027
Phone: (802)649-5297

Description: A feminist literary and cultural organization which publishes fiction with lesbian/feminist content. Offers an audio tape. Accepts unsolicited manuscripts send sample chapter and outline along with self-addressed, stamped envelope. Reaches market through direct mail and distributors. **Subjects:** Mystery, humor, romance, adventure, short stories, history. **Number of New Titles:** 1989 - 4, 1990 - 5, 1991 (est.) - 6; Total Titles in Print - 20. **Selected Titles:** *As the Road Curves* by Elizabeth Dean; *Found Goddesses: Asphalta to Viscera* by Morgan Grey and Julia Penelope; *Heterodoxy: A Club for Radical Feminists*, 2nd ed. by Judith Schwarz; *Stoner McTavish, Lesbian Stages*, both by Sarah Dreher; *All Out* by Judith Alguire. **Principal Officials and Managers:** Claudia Lamperti, Editor; Beth Dingman, Vice-President.

★9891★ **New York City Commission on the Status of Women**
52 Chambers St., Ste. 207
New York, NY 10007
Phone: (212)566-3830

Description: Issues occasional publications on women's issues and interests. Produces an annual women's history calendar. Also publishes a quarterly newsletter, *Status Report,* and a monthly, *Women's Bulletin.* Reaches market through direct mail and wholesalers, including Inland Book Co. **Total Titles in Print:** 4. **Selected Titles:** *Cruises for and about Women: A New City Guide, Women's Organizations: A New York City Directory,* 3rd ed., both edited by Maxine Gold; *Exploring Attitudes toward Women with Disabilities* edited by Mary Bliss; *New York City Boards and Task Forces: What They Are and How to Get Appointed; Guide to*

Women's Studies; Women Making History: Conversations with Fifteen New Yorkers. **Principal Officials and Managers:** Marcella Maxwell, Chairor; Marilyn J. Flood, Executive Director; Ginny Vida, Program Director; Maxine Gold, Communications Director; Dr. Anne Briscoe, Vice-Chair.

★9892★ **NewSage Press**
PO Box 410
Pasadena, CA 91114-8029
Phone: (213)641-8912

Description: Publishes primarily photo-essay books on social issues, family issues, and women's studies. Reaches market through Consortium Book Sales & Distribution for trade sales. **Number of New Titles:** 1991 (est.) - 2, 1992 (est.) - 3; Total Titles in Print - 6. **Selected Titles:** *Pasadena 100 Years* by Maureen Michelson; *Common Heroes: Facing a Life Threatening Illness* by Eric Blau; *The New Americans* by Ulli Steltzer; *Gentle Birthing Choices for the '90s* by Barbara Harper, R.N.; *Women and Work: Photographs and Personal Writings; A Portrait of American Mothers and Daughters.* **Principal Officials and Managers:** Maureen R. Michelson, Publisher; Gary Spoerle, Director, Sales and Marketing.

★9893★ **Northeastern University Press**
360 Huntington Ave.
Boston, MA 02115
Phone: (617)437-5480

Description: Academic press. Publishes women's studies books.

★9894★ **Northland Press of Winona**
1522 E Southern Ave., No. 2161
Tempe, AZ 85282-5678
Phone: (507)452-3686

Description: Publishes poetry, progressive issues in both fiction and nonfiction, and women's issues. Distributes for Earth Review Press. Reaches market through direct mail, trade sales, Baker & Taylor, and Bookslinger. **Selected Titles:** *Saving the Planet: The Politics of Hope* by Walbek; *A Thousand Rainy Days* by Wallace; *Coyote Dream Cantos* by Lagier; *The Silence of Light* by Platz; *Legends of the Lost* by Robinson; *Natural Law* by Hyett. **Principal Officials and Managers:** Jody Namio-Wallace, Publisher and Owner; James Namio, Art Director.

★9895★ **Northwest Matrix**
3383 Bayview Rd.
Waldport, OR 97394
Phone: (503)563-4988

Description: Founded as a feminist press. Since 1980, emphasis has been on book production and marketing for academic and professional self-publishers. Alternate phone number: (503) 563-5234. **Selected Titles:** *Fair by Eleven: Railroading in Oregon* by Hagan Moore; *One Woman's West: Recollections of the Oregon Trail and Settling the Northwest Country* by Lois Barton; *A Guide to Shipwrecks along the Oregon Coast* by Victor West and R. E. Wells; *On Therapy: Essays on Wellness* by Mary Ediert; *Of Life and Joy* by Ethel E. Ownley. **Principal Officials and Managers:** Charlotte Mills, Publisher.

★9896★ **Old Harbor Press**
PO Box 97
Sitka, AK 99835
Phone: (907)747-3584

Founded: 1982. **Subjects:** Alaskan subjects written and illustrated by women.

★9897★ **Omega Cottonwood Press**
PO Box 5
Alma, NE 68920
Phone: (308)799-2010

Description: Self-publisher of poetry and non-fiction. Offers fine art collages, broadsides, and postcards. Accepts unsolicited manuscripts that pertain to the author or the author's works. Reaches market through direct mail, readings, and workshops. **Subjects:** The Great Plains, feminism. **Number of New Titles:** 1990 - 4, 1991 - 5, 1992 (est.) - 4; Total Titles in Print - 66. **Selected Titles:** *Potpourri, Eostre: Celebrations of Spring, Ridin' the Rails: A Pastiche, Mas-tur-ba-tion,* all by Marilyn Coffey; *The Battle of Orleans: An Illustrated Documentary of the Marcella Marathon* edited by Marilyn Coffey; *Figures of Speech* by Marilyn Coffey and Renae Taylor. **Principal Officials and Managers:** Marilyn Coffey, Founder.

★9898★ **OmniComm Publications**
7233 Alliance Ct.
San Diego, CA 92119
Phone: (619)465-7960

Description: Publishes health information booklets. Offers social-medical research, editing, and typesetting services. Reaches market through commission representatives and direct mail. **Subjects:** Sexuality, nutrition, fitness, family life. **Total Titles in Print:** 7. **Selected Titles:** *Understanding Sexual Desire; Talking with Your Sex Partner; Multiple Orgasms for Men; Recovering from Rape and Sexual Assault; G-Spot and Female Ejaculation; Woman's Guide to the Man over Forty.* **Principal Officials and Managers:** Joann S. Sandlin, Editor and Publisher.

★9899★ **Omnicorn Productions, Inc.**
PO Box 15
Sedona, AZ 86336
Phone: (602)282-3666

Description: Publishes self-help books on abused women. **Number of New Titles:** 1991 (est.) - 3; Total Titles in Print - 1. **Selected Titles:** *Battered without Bruises* by Marlene and Monty Wilson. **Principal Officials and Managers:** Marlene Wilson, President; Monty Wilson, Secretary.

★9900★ **Open Hand Publishing**
PO Box 22048
Seattle, WA 98122
Phone: (206)447-0597

Founded: 1981. **Subjects:** Books to promote positive social change. Some bilingual children's books.

★9901★ **Orbis Books**
Maryknoll, NY 10545
Phone: (914)941-7590

Description: Trade press. Publishes women's studies books.

★9902★ Organizing Against Pornography
310 E. 38th St., No. 109
Minneapolis, MN 55409
Phone: (612)822-1476
Description: Distributes feminist anti-pornography material. Offers newsletters, information packets, and occasional audio cassettes. Reaches market through direct mail and trade sales. **Selected Titles:** *Pornography and Civil Rights: A New Day for Women's Equality* by Andrea Dworkin and Catharine A. MacKinnon. **Principal Officials and Managers:** Jeanne M. Barkey, Executive Director.

★9903★ Ovulation Method Teachers Association
PO Box 10-17
Anchorage, AK 99510
Phone: (907)344-8606
Subjects: Ovulation. **Selected Titles:** *The Ovulation Method: Cycles of Fertility* by Denise Guren and Nealy Gillette. **Principal Officials and Managers:** Suzzannaha Cooper, President; Denise Guren, Vice-President; Fran Butzke, Secretary; Diane Moxness, Treasurer.

★9904★ OWL (Ohio Women Librarians)
PO Box 5
Northfield, OH 44067
Description: Publications consist of research addressing feminist issues and professional concerns. Also offers a newsletter. Reaches market through direct mail. **Subjects:** Employment, organizational values, salaries, leadership preferences. **Number of New Titles:** 1990 - 1; Total Titles in Print - 6. **Selected Titles:** *Sex of Director, Salary, and Size of Library* by Jeanne M. Patterson and Linda R. Silver; *Deference to Authority in Feminized Professions, Partial Answers to Economic Perspectives on Occupational Sex Segregation and the Wage Gap, The Outsider's Eye: A Critique of Male Management Model and Its Impact on Women in Organizations,* all by Linda R. Silver; *Selecting a Director: Professional and Managerial Characteristics Preferred by Ohio Public Library Boards* by Anne S. McFarland et al; *Appointing Library Board Members.* **Principal Officials and Managers:** Margaret Cooper, President; Patricia Holsworth, Vice-President; Sheryl Jacober, Secretary; Linda Silver, Treasurer.

★9905★ Oxford University Press
200 Madison Ave.
New York, NY 10016
Phone: (212)679-7300
Description: Academic press. Publishes women's studies books.

★9906★ P.P.R.J. Enterprises
7439 La Palma Ave.
Ste. 250
Buena Park, CA 90620
Subjects: Women, automotive maintenance. **Selected Titles:** *A Ladies Automotive Recovery Manual* by Polly P. Long. **Principal Officials and Managers:** Polly Long, Peggy Prien, Jack Macy, Ronnie Ouellette, Partners.

★9907★ Pacific Coast Publisher
710 Silver Spur Rd., Ste. 126-B
Rolling Hills Estates, CA 90274
Phone: (213)547-9560
Description: Publishes on the family, communication, and female-owned business operations. **Number of New Titles:** 1989 - 3, 1990 - 3; Total Titles in Print - 4. **Principal Officials and Managers:** Vivianne Israel, President; Ann Christie, Production Supervisor; Robert Reynolds, Marketing Director.

★9908★ Pandit Press
24843 Del Prado, No. 405
Dana Point, CA 92629
Phone: (714)240-7151
Description: Publishes on politics and abortion. Reaches market through direct mail, trade sales, Baker & Taylor, Quality Books, Inc., BookPeople, and Brodart Co. **Number of New Titles:** 1989 - 1, 1990 - 2; Total Titles in Print - 3. **Selected Titles:** *The One-Term Solution, Abortion Is Not a Sin,* both by Kent Welton. **Principal Officials and Managers:** Kent Welton, Owner.

★9909★ Papier-Mache Press
795 Via Manzana
Watsonville, CA 95076
Phone: (408)726-2933
Description: Publishes poetry and fiction by, for, and about women. Offers t-shirts, posters, and audio cassettes. Accepts unsolicited manuscripts; send self-addressed, stamped envelope for guidelines. Reaches market through direct mail, trade sales, and wholesalers, including BookPeople, Inland Book Co., and Baker & Taylor, Ingram Book Co., Moving Books, Select Books, and New Leaf Distributing Co. **Number of New Titles:** 1990 - 3, 1991 (est.) - 4, 1992 (est.) - 4; Total Titles in Print - 16. **Selected Titles:** *When I Am an Old Woman I Shall Wear Purple; If I Had a Hammer: Women's Work in Poetry and Fiction,* both edited by Sandra Martz; *Fragments I Saved from the Fire* by Mary Anne Ashley; *Flight of the Wild Goose* by Janet Carncross Chandler; *Ric Masten Speaking* by Ric Masten; *Another Language* by Sue Saniel Elkind. **Principal Officials and Managers:** Sandra Martz, Publisher and Editor.

★9910★ Paradise Press
PO Box 53
Santa Monica, CA 90409
Phone: (213)473-4972
Description: Established to print artists' books and literary work that combine innovative form with content. Reaches market through direct mail and wholesalers. **Subjects:** Art, printing, women. **Total Titles in Print:** 7. **Number of New Titles:** 1990 - 1, 1991 (est.) - 1; 1992 (est.) - 2; **Selected Titles:** *Say, See, Bone, Lessons from French; Lessons from the South, Support Living Artists!,* all by Susan King; *She* by Martha Ronk Lifson; *Ordinary Wisdom* by Eloise Klein Healy; *Life in Los Angeles* by Grand, Healy, et al. **Principal Officials and Managers:** Susan E. King, Founder.

★9911★ Parent Education Programs Press
3007 22nd St.
Lubbock, TX 79410
Phone: (806)799-6021
Description: Publishes teaching materials for Lamaze childbirth preparation class use. Se-

lected **Titles:** *Joyful Beginnings with Lamaze Preparation for Childbirth* by Rosemary Cogan, Suzanne Logan, and Linda Tipton. **Principal Officials and Managers:** Rosemary Cogan, Suzanne Logan, Linda Tipton.

★9912★ Parkhurst Press
PO Box 1
Laguna Beach, CA 92652
Phone: (714)499-1032
Subjects: Women's rights, peace, solar power, humor. **Selected Titles:** *Alida: An Erotic Novel* by Edna MacBrayne. **Principal Officials and Managers:** Lynne Thorpe, Editor.

★9913★ Pemberton Publishers
PO Box 4415
Somerville, MA 02144
Phone: (617)868-6065
Description: Publishes works in the area of women's studies, emphasizing those written by Boston University faculty members. Accepts unsolicited manuscripts; query for guidelines and fees. Reaches market through direct mail, trade sales, and Midwest Library Service. **Number of New Titles:** 1990 - 1, 1991 - 1; Total Titles in Print - 2. **Selected Titles:** *Women's Inferior Education: An Economic Analysis, Woman Traveler: How to Get Over the Economic Hurdles along the Way,* both by Blanche Fitzpatrick. **Principal Officials and Managers:** Blanche Fitzpatrick, President.

★9914★ Pennypress, Inc.
1100 23rd Ave. E.
Seattle, WA 98112
Phone: (206)325-1419
Description: Publishes pamphlets and books exploring controversial issues and new areas of concern in maternity care. Offers an audiotape, *Relax for Childbirth* and a newsletter, *P.S. for Pennypress.* Accepts unsolicited manuscripts. Distributes for Meadowbrook and Harvard Common Press. Reaches market through direct mail and trade sales. **Subjects:** Childbirth, parenting. **Number of New Titles:** 1990 - 3; 1992 (est.) - 3; Total Titles in Print - 30. **Selected Titles:** *Birth: Through Children's Eyes* by Sandra VanDam Anderson and Penny Simkin; *Mom and Dad and I Are Having a Baby, Our Brand New Baby,* both by Maryann Malecki, R.N.; *Episiotomy and the Second Stage of Labor* by Sheila Kitzinger and Penny Simkin; *The New Parent: The Spectrum of Postpartum Adjustment* by Dawn Gruen. **Principal Officials and Managers:** Penny Simkin, President and Editor-in-Chief.

★9915★ People's Translation Service
4228 Telegraph Ave.
Oakland, CA 94609
Phone: (415)654-6725
Description: Publishes an international women's quarterly based on translations and information from the international women's press, for a U.S. audience. **Subjects:** Women, international affairs. **Number of New Titles:** 1989 - 4; Total Titles in Print - 31. **Selected Titles:** *Connexions, 1-30; Women on Work; Lesbian Activism; Feminism and Religion; Girls Speak Out; Reproductive Rights.*

★9916★ Pergamon Press
Maxwell House, Fairview Park
Elmsford, NY 10523
Phone: (914)592-7700
Fax: (914)592-3625
Founded: 1952.

★9917★ Perinatal Loss
2116 NE 18th Ave.
Portland, OR 97212
Phone: (503)284-7426
Description: Publishes on how to deal with the death of a baby. Offers two videos and birth/death announcement cards. Reaches market through direct mail, ICEA Centering Corp., and Birth & Life. **Total Titles in Print:** 2. **Selected Titles:** *When Hello Means Goodbye, Still to Be Born,* both by Pat Schwiebert and Paul Kirk. **Principal Officials and Managers:** Pat Schwiebert, Director; Ann Huntwork, Research Assistant.

★9918★ Personal Press
1515 Riebli Rd.
Santa Rosa, CA 95404
Phone: (707)525-1338
Description: Reaches market through direct mail, BookPeople, Inland Book Co., and DeVorss and Co. **Subjects:** Feminism. **Selected Titles:** *Emerging Woman: A Decade of Midlife Transitions* by Natalie Rogers. **Principal Officials and Managers:** Natalie Rogers, Owner and Author.

★9919★ Pin Prick Press
2664 S. Green Rd.
Shaker Heights, OH 44122
Phone: (216)932-2173
Founded: 1978. **Selected Titles:** *Survival Manual for the Independent Woman Traveler.*

★9920★ Pink Inc.! Publishing
PO Box 8
Atlantic Beach, FL 32233-0866
Phone: (904)731-7120
Description: Publishes on pregnancy, birth, and parenting. Reaches market through direct mail, telephone and trade sales, Childbirth Graphics, ICEA, and Birth and Life Books. **Number of New Titles:** 1989 - 1; Total Titles in Print - 1. **Selected Titles:** *Young and Pregnant* by Ginny Brinkley and Sherry Sampson. **Principal Officials and Managers:** Sherry Sampson, Marketing; Ginny Brinkley, Accounting; Gail Cooper, Design.

★9921★ Pizzazz Press, Inc.
5114 Chicago
Omaha, NE 68132
Phone: (402)466-5311
Subjects: Fitness for women. **Selected Titles:** *Be a Natural Woman: Fitness for Teens, Everything You Need to Know about Cellulite,* both by Judy Lessmann. **Principal Officials and Managers:** Stan Lessmann, President; Judy Lessmann, Editor.

★9922★ Placenta Music, Inc.
314 Woodward Way NW
Atlanta, GA 30305
Phone: (404)355-4242
Description: Offers cassette tapes and compact discs combining womb sounds with music to sooth crying babies and relax mothers during labor. Reaches market through commission representatives and wholesalers and distributors, including American Baby Concepts, New Leaf Distributing Co., Music Design, and BookPeople. **Number of New Titles:** 1990 - 1, 1992 (est.) - 1; Total Titles in Print - 2. **Selected Titles:** *Transitions; Transitions 2: Music to Help Baby Sleep.* **Principal Officials and Managers:** Fred J. Schwartz, M.D., President.

★9923★ Plain View Press, Inc.
2009 Arthur Ln.
Austin, TX 78704-3235
Phone: (512)441-2452
Founded: 1976. **Subjects:** Feminist, women's literature, family history, video art, fine printing and handmade books; distributes In Between Books.

★9924★ Planned Parenthood of Central California
633 N. Van Ness
Fresno, CA 93728
Phone: (209)486-2647
Description: Publishes on family life and reproduction health. Reaches market through direct mail and reviews and also through ETR Associates, Inland Book Co., and other distributors. **Total Titles in Print:** 2. **Selected Titles:** *Let's Talk about S-e-x, Hablemos acerca del S-e-x-o,* both by Gitchel and Foster. **Principal Officials and Managers:** Lorraine Foster, Director, Community Services.

★9925★ Planned Parenthood Federation of America, Inc.
Marketing Dept.
810 7th Ave.
New York, NY 10019
Phone: (212)541-7800
Description: Publishes information on reproductive health, sexuality, and family planning. Also offers videos and teaching aids. Reaches market through direct mail and telephone sales. **Number of New Titles:** 1992 (est.) - 6; Total Titles in Print - 55. **Selected Titles:** *How to Talk with Your Child about AIDS; Teensex: It's OK to Say No Way; Sexually Transmitted Disease: The Facts; Facts about Birth Control; The Condom: What It Is, What It Is For, How to Use It; Planned Parenthood Resource Catalog for Educators and Health Professionals.* **Principal Officials and Managers:** Faye Wattleton, President; Kenneth Edelin, Board Chairor.

★9926★ Pocahontas Press, Inc.
2805 Wellesley Ct.
PO Drawer F
Blacksburg, VA 24063-1020
Phone: (703)951-0467
Founded: 1984. **Subjects:** Feminist fiction. Publishes poetry, memoirs and other historical subjects.

★9927★ Population Council
One Dag Hammarskjold Plaza
New York, NY 10017
Phone: (212)644-1300
Description: An international, nonprofit organization; undertakes social science and biomedical research, advises and assists governments and international agencies, and is a leading source of information on population issues. Also publishes two journals, *Population and Development Review* quarterly and *Studies in Family Planning* bimonthly. Also offers software. Accepts unsolicited manuscripts; please write for information. Reaches market through direct mail. **Subjects:** Population, development, economics, women's and children's health, and family planning programs. **Number of New Titles:** 1989 - 1, 1990 - 1. **Selected Titles:** *Population and Resources in Western Intelletual Traditions* edited by M. S. Teitelbaum and J. M. Winters; *Below-Replacement Fertility in Industrial Societies* edited by Kingsley Davis et al.; *Resources, Environment, Population: Present Knowledge, Future Options* edited by Kingsley Davis and Mikhail S. Bernstam; *Rural Development and Population: Institutions and Policy* edited by Geoffrey McNicoll and Mead Cain; *Child Survival: Strategies for Research* edited by W. Henry Mosley and Lincoln C. Chen. **Principal Officials and Managers:** George Zeidenstein, President.

★9928★ Positive Press
PO Box 31
Joliet, IL 60436
Phone: (815)372-3163
Description: Publishes motivational works as an "inspiration to women to be the best they can be." Also publishes women's success stories. Offers a *Women and Self-Confidence* seminar. Alternate phone number: (708)482-3669. Reaches market through direct mail. **Total Titles in Print:** 1. **Selected Titles:** *Women and Self-Confidence: How to Take Charge of Your Life.* **Principal Officials and Managers:** Carol V. Havey, Owner; M. Ann Canaday, Director of Marketing.

★9929★ The Post-Apollo Press
35 Marie St.
Sausalito, CA 94965
Phone: (415)332-1458
Founded: 1982. **Subjects:** Poetry and fiction by women.

★9930★ Pre-Birth Parenting, Inc.
2554 Lincoln Ave., Ste. 509
Marina del Rey, CA 90291
Phone: (213)417-3663
Description: Offers a video tape about the prenatal bonding process. Reaches market through direct mail and telephone and trade sales. **Selected Titles:** *Knowing the Unborn* (video cassette). **Principal Officials and Managers:** Royda Ballard, President.

★9931★ Premiere Publishing, Ltd.
145 NW 85th St., Ste. 201
Seattle, WA 98117
Phone: (206)782-8310
Toll-free: 800-767-3062
Description: Publisher and producer of sexual harassment products and resources, including videos. **Subjects:** Sexual harassment. **Selected Titles:** *Sexual Harassment: Shades of Gray.*

★9932★ Prestwick Poetry Publishing Co.
2235 Calle Guaymas
La Jolla, CA 92037
Subjects: Feminist poetry. **Total Titles in Print:**
1. **Selected Titles:** *In a Nutshell* by Natasha Josefowitz. **Principal Officials and Managers:** Natasha Josefowitz, President.

★9933★ Psytec, Inc.
PO Box 5
De Kalb, IL 60115
Phone: (815)758-1415
Description: Provides books and testing materials that benefit psychologists, social workers, and family court mediators in dealing with family violence and divorce. Accepts unsolicited manuscripts. Distributes for Guilford, Josey Bass, and Research Press. Reaches market through direct mail and wholesalers. **Selected Titles:** *The Child Abuse Potential Inventory: Manual,* 2nd ed. by Joel S. Milner; *Children of Divorce: A Developmental Approach to Residence and Visitation* by Mitch Baris and Carla Garrity; *A Social Learning Approach to Marital Therapy* by Richard B. Stuart; *Applications of Social Learning to Family Life* by Gerald R. Patterson; *The Power of Imagery for Personal Enrichment* by Arnold A. Lazarus; *Growing Up on Purpose* by Robert W. Parkinson. **Principal Officials and Managers:** Joel S. Milner, President; Renanne Brock, Vice-President.

★9934★ R & R Publishers
408-D Leafmore Rd.
Rome, GA 30161
Phone: (404)234-2683
Description: Publishes self-help books for women. Reaches market through direct mail and telephone sales. **Total Titles in Print:** 2. **Selected Titles:** *Become the Woman You Want to Be, Florida Employment Guide,* both by Ray Fricks. **Principal Officials and Managers:** Rose M. Fricks, Ray E. Fricks.

★9935★ Radical America
Alternative Education Project, Inc.
1 Summer St.
Somerville, MA 02143
Phone: (617)628-6585
Description: Publishes on history, labor, community organizing, feminism, and black history. Reaches market through direct mail. **Total Titles in Print:** 22. **Selected Titles:** *Women's Place Is at the Typewriter* by Davies; *Women on the Integrated Circuit* by Rachel Grossman; *Fleetwood Wildcat* by Jon Lippert; *Common Ground, Separate Fate* by John Demeter; *The Mel King Campaign in Boston; Youth and Popular Culture* by Shirley Holmes. **Principal Officials and Managers:** Marla Erlien, Publisher; John Demeter, Editor; James Stark, Review Editor.

★9936★ Radical Women
523-A Valencia St.
San Francisco, CA 94110
Phone: (415)864-1278
Description: A socialist, feminist organization involved in ''the concerns of all women–women of color, lesbians, working women.'' Publishes documents associated with its cause. **Selected Titles:** *Radical Women Manifesto: Theory, Program, and Structure; Women's Psychology: Mental Illness as a Social Disease* by Susan

Williams; *Women Who Work* by Melba Windoffer; *The Emancipation of Women, Which Road toward Women's Liberation: The Movement as a Radical Vanguard or a Single-Issue Coalition,* both by Clara Fraser. **Principal Officials and Managers:** Constance Scott, National Organizer.

★9937★ Rainbow Books
PO Box 1069
Moore Haven, FL 33471
Phone: (813)946-0293
Description: Rainbow specializes in self-help, reference and resource books with an emphasis on women and women's issues. **Selected Titles:** *Beyond Victim: You Can Overcome Childhood Abuse...Even Sexual Abuse* and *Self Sabotage* both by Martha Baldwin.

★9938★ Rashad Associates/Raw Ink Press
1245 4th St. SW, Ste. 406
Washington, DC 20024
Phone: (202)484-2171
Description: Publishes poetry dealing with black affairs, women's issues, and single parenting. Reaches market through direct mail. **Number of New Titles:** 1991 (est.) - 1; Total Titles in Print - 2. **Selected Titles:** *(R)evolutions; Woman, Too,* both by Johari M. Rashad. **Principal Officials and Managers:** Johari M. Rashad, President.

★9939★ Red Alder Books
PO Box 29
Santa Cruz, CA 95063
Phone: (408)426-7082
Description: Publishes books of ''conscious, imaginative erotica–prose, poetry, photographs, and drawings that touch the heart of sexual experience with aliveness, joy, and humor.'' Also publishes on feminism and men's liberation from traditional sex roles. Reaches market through direct mail and wholesalers. **Total Titles in Print:** 6. **Selected Titles:** *Erotic by Nature: A Celebration of Love and of Our Wonderful Bodies* edited by David Steinberg; *Welcome, Brothers: Poems of a Changing Man's Consciousness; Beneath This Calm Exterior,* both by David Steinberg; *Yellow Brick Road: Steps toward a New Way of Life* edited by Ann Dilworth and David Steinberg. **Principal Officials and Managers:** David Steinberg, Publisher.

★9940★ Red Flag Green Flag Resources
PO Box 29
Fargo, ND 58108
Description: A nonprofit agency serving victims of sexual abuse, sexual assault, and domestic violence through educational materials for children and young adults. Also holds training seminars. Provides materials in coloring book form, storybook form, workbooks, manuals, videotapes, and filmstrips. Reaches market through direct mail and telephone sales. **Number of New Titles:** 1990 - 2, 1991 (est.) - 1, 1992 (est.) - 2; Total Titles in Print - 8. **Selected Titles:** *Red Flag Green Flag People: A Personal Safety Program for Children; T Is for Touching, Annie; New Beginnings: A Facilitater's Manual for Implementing a Support Group for Female Adolescent Sexual Assault Victims; I Wish the Hitting Would Stop.* **Principal Officials and Managers:** Beth Haseltine, Executive Director;

Dawn Ganje, Director, Marketing; Greg Diehl, Customer Service.

★9941★ Red Lyon Publications
c/o Midwifery Today
PO Box 26
Eugene, OR 97402
Phone: (503)753-5019
Subjects: Midwifery, birthing, women's health, biography, self development. **Selected Titles:** *Mabel: The Story of One Midwife* by Elizabeth Redditt-Lyon. **Principal Officials and Managers:** Elizabeth Redditt-Lyon, Publisher.

★9942★ Redstockings of the Women's Liberation Movement
255 Fort Washington Ave., No. 33
New York, NY 10032
Phone: (212)777-9241
Description: Publishes materials on the women's liberation movement. Offers audio cassettes. Accepts unsolicited manuscripts; include a self-addressed, stamped envelope. Reaches market through direct mail. **Subjects:** Feminism, women's liberation history, the 1960's, censorship, national health care. **Selected Titles:** *Feminist Revolution: An Abridged Edition with Additional Writings, The Censored Section of Feminist Revolution,* both by Redstockings; *Notes from the First Year: 1968* by New York Radical Women; *Toward a Female Liberation Movement* by Judith Brown and Beverly Jones. **Principal Officials and Managers:** Marisa Figuereido, Secretary; Kathie Sarachild, President.

★9943★ Remi Books, Inc.
205 E. 78th St.
New York, NY 10021
Phone: (212)570-6265
Description: Publishes on social issues. Accepts query letters for manuscripts. Reaches market through direct mail, trade sales, and wholesalers. **Selected Titles:** *An Adopted Woman, Pregnant by Mistake: The Stories of Seventeen Women,* both by Katrina Maxtone-Graham. **Principal Officials and Managers:** Katrina Maxtone-Graham, President and Publisher; Alicia Adams, Office Manager.

★9944★ Remington Press
4141 E. 6th Ave.
Denver, CO 80220
Phone: (303)377-1047
Description: Publishes a book on womens' issues. Offers seminars, workshops, keynote addresses, and an audio and video presentation of seminars. **Number of New Titles:** 1990 - 1; Total Titles in Print - 1. **Selected Titles:** *Women in the Workplace: A Man's Perspective* by Lloyd Lewan. **Principal Officials and Managers:** Lloyd Lewan, President and C.E.O.

★9945★ Rhiannon Press
1105 Bradley Ave.
Eau Claire, WI 54701
Phone: (715)835-0598
Founded: 1977. **Subjects:** Midwest women's poetry. **Selected Titles:** *A Change of Weather: Midwest Women Poets.*

★9946★ Ribe
13A Ware St., No. 8
Cambridge, MA 02138
Description: Publishes on women's history tours and women's art. Offers a video tape and slides. Reaches market through direct mail. **Number of New Titles:** 1989 - 3, 1990 - 2; Total Titles in Print - 2. **Selected Titles:** *The Grandes Dames of Boston; Women's Walkabouts Down Under.* **Principal Officials and Managers:** Ann Rollins, Publisher.

★9947★ Rising Tide Press
5 Kivy St.
Huntington Station, NY 11746
Phone: (516)427-1289
Description: Publishes fiction and nonfiction lesbian books. Accepts unsolicited manuscripts. **Principal Officials and Managers:** Lee Boojamra and Alice Frier.

★9948★ River Bend Publishing
B2 Heather Lynn
Muscatine, IA 52761
Phone: (319)264-2963
Description: Publishes on Iowa women; also offers a cookbook. Reaches market through direct mail and trade sales. **Number of New Titles:** 1992 (est.) - 1; Total Titles in Print - 2. **Selected Titles:** *Remarkable Iowa Women, My Lady's Fare,* both by Ethel W. Hanft. **Principal Officials and Managers:** Ethel W. Hanft, Owner.

★9949★ Rowman and Littlefield, Publishers
81 Adams Dr.
Totowa, NJ 07512
Phone: (201)256-8600
Description: Trade press. Publishes women's studies books.

★9950★ Rush Publishing Company
PO Box 1
Rush, NY 14543
Phone: (716)533-1376
Selected Titles: *Women's Studies Abstracts.*

★9951★ Rutgers University Press
109 Church St.
New Brunswick, NJ 08903
Phone: (201)932-7762
Description: Academic press. Publishes women's studies books.

★9952★ Safer Society Press
RR 1, Box 24-B
Orwell, VT 05760
Phone: (802)897-7541
Description: A nonprofit religious organization publishing books and other materials on nonrepressive alternatives for sex-crime victims and offenders, including strategies for prevention. Consults with state and county agencies on plans for treatment of sexual offenses. Offers educational seminars and conferences and a video and audio series. Reaches market through direct mail and seminars. **Number of New Titles:** 1990 - 5, 1991 (est.) - 4, 1992 (est.) - 6; Total Titles in Print - 24. **Selected Titles:** *Remedial Intervention in Adolescent Sex Offenses, Retraining Adult Sex Offenders: Meth-*

ods and Models, The Youthful Sex Offender: The Rationale and Goals of Early Intervention and Treatment, all by Fay Honey Knopp; *Treating the Young Male Victim of Sexual Assault* by Eugene Porter; *Who Am I and Why Am in Treatment, Why Did I Do It Again,* both by R. Freeman-Longo and L. Bayes. **Principal Officials and Managers:** Arleon Kelly, Executive Director; Fay Honey Knopp, Director, Safer Society Programs and Press.

★9953★ Sage Publications
275 S. Beverly Dr.
Beverly Hills, CA 90212
Phone: (213)274-8003
Description: Trade press. Publishes women's studies books.

★9954★ Sage Women's Educational Press
PO Box 42741
Atlanta, GA 30311-0741
Phone: (404)223-7528
Fax: (404)753-8383
Description: Publishes teaching materials in black women's studies and related work. **Selected Titles:** *Sage: A Scholarly Journal*

★9955★ St. Martin's Press
175 5th Ave.
New York, NY 10010
Phone: (212)674-5151
Description: Trade press. Publishes women's studies books.

★9956★ San Joaquin Eagle Publishing
5640 W. Sweet Dr.
PO Box 42
Visalia, CA 93291
Description: Publishes books on law and on family life. Reaches market through telephone sales, trade sales, and Baker & Taylor. **Number of New Titles:** 1989 - 2; Total Titles in Print - 2. **Selected Titles:** *Settlement Conference* by Kenneth E. Conal; *Real Grandmas Don't Bake Cookies Anymore* by Therese McGee. **Principal Officials and Managers:** Carmelita Jarvis Conn, Publisher.

★9957★ Sanguinaria Publishing
85 Ferris St.
Bridgeport, CT 06605
Phone: (203)576-9168
Description: Formed to publish the Bloodroot restaurant's recipes and feminist political philosophy. Expects to publish other books of special interest to feminists. Reaches market through direct mail and wholesalers. **Total Titles in Print:** 3. **Selected Titles:** *The Political Palate: A Feminist Vegetarian Cookbook, The Second Seasonal Political Palate,* both by the Bloodroot Collective; *Carried Away* by Abbe Smith. **Principal Officials and Managers:** Selma Miriam, Noel Furie, Betsey Beaven, Partners.

★9958★ Sarah Lawrence College Women's Studies Program
Bronxville, NY 10708
Phone: (914)395-2405
Description: Publishes bibliographies and books on women. Reaches market through direct mail. **Total Titles in Print:** 6. **Selected Titles:** *Bibliography in the History of European Women* by Joan Kelly et al.; *Selected Bibliogra-*

phy of Chinese-American Women by Ginger Chih; *Conceptual Frameworks for the Study of Women's History* by Marilyn Arthur et al.; *Feminist Perspectives on Housework and Childcare* by Amy Swerdlow et al.; *Bibliography in the History of Women in the Progressive Era* by Judith Papachristou. **Principal Officials and Managers:** Kay Griffin Jeuchter, Coordinator.

★9959★ Saturday Press, Inc.
PO Box 884
Upper Montclair, NJ 07043
Phone: (201)256-5053
Founded: 1975. **Subjects:** Women poets over forty. Sponsors the Eileen W. Barnes Award for a first book of poems by a woman over forty. **Selected Titles:** *Saturday's Women, The Life of Mary.*

★9960★ Scarecrow Press
52 Liberty St.
Metuchen, NJ 08840
Phone: (201)548-8600
Description: Trade press. Publishes women's studies books.

★9961★ Sea Horse Press Ltd.
PO Box 294, Village Sta.
New York, NY 10014
Phone: (212)691-9066
Description: "Founded in order to publish and distribute fine and accessible fiction, poetry, drama, and selected nonfiction written by and for lesbians and gay men by new as well as established authors." Distributes for Gay Presses of New York. **Total Titles in Print:** 24. **Selected Titles:** *Safe* by Dennis Cooper; *Male Fantasies/Gay Realities* by George Stambolion; *Lasting Relations* by Rudy Kikel; *Jailbait and Other Stories* by Brad Gooch; *Forty-Deuce: A Play* by Alan Bowne; *About Time: Exploring the Gay Past* by Marty Duberman. **Principal Officials and Managers:** Felice Picano, Publisher.

★9962★ Seal Press
3131 Western Ave., Ste. 410
Seattle, WA 98121
Phone: (206)283-7844
Description: Provides a forum for women writers and feminist issues in fiction and nonfiction, including mysteries, contemporary stories, books on domestic violence and recovery, and other women's studies issues. Offers an audio tape series. Accepts unsolicited manuscripts; send query letter first. Reaches market through direct mail, commission representatives, and several major distributors. **Subjects:** Feminist fiction, nonfiction. **Number of New Titles:** 1990 - 10, 1991 (est.) - 12; Total Titles in Print - 56. **Selected Titles:** *Murder in the Collective* by Barbara Wilson; *Getting Free: You Can End Abuse and Take Back Your Life* by Ginny N. Carthy; *To Live and to Write: Selections by Japanese Women Writers, 1913-1938* edited by Yukiko Taraka; *Bird Eyes* by Madelyn Arnold; *Ladies' Night* by Elisabeth Bowers; *Hard-Hatted Women: Stories of Stuggle and Success in the Trades* edited by Molly Martin. **Principal Officials and Managers:** Faith Conlon, Barbara Wilson, Publishers and Editors; Judy Schick, Operations Manager; Pam Horino, Marketing Director; Leah Kosik, Business Manager.

★9963★ Seismograph Publications
PO Box 1701
San Francisco, CA 94117
Phone: (415)567-5530
Description: Publishes avant garde poetry and literature, especially works by gay and lesbian authors. Reaches market through direct mail, trade sales, Blackwell North America, John Coutts Library Service, and Small Press Distribution, Inc. **Number of New Titles:** Total Titles in Print - 2. **Selected Titles:** *Practising Angels: A Contemporary Anthology of San Francisco Bay Area Poetry* edited by Michael Mayo; *All Fall Down* by Michael Mayo. **Principal Officials and Managers:** Michael J. Mayo, Publisher.

★9964★ Seven Cycles
c/o Mary Beth Edelson
110 Mercer St.
New York, NY 10012
Phone: (212)226-0832
Description: Self-publisher of works with experimental forms and content. Reaches market through direct mail, the feminist network, and personal contact with museums and galleries. **Subjects:** Feminism, occult, religion, photography, visual arts, women's spirituality, new age. **Total Titles in Print:** 3. **Selected Titles:** *Seven Cycles: Public Rituals, Seven Sites: Painting on the Wall, Shape Shifter: Seven Mediums,* all by Mary Beth Edelson. **Principal Officials and Managers:** Mary Beth Edelson, Publisher.

★9965★ Sheba Review Foundation
PO Box 16
Jefferson City, MO 65102
Description: Publishes on Missouri women writers. Conducts book signings, readings, performances, and workshops. Offers seminars. Also offers posters and a calendar of events. Reaches market through commission representatives and direct mail. Formerly listed as Sheba Review, Inc. **Total Titles in Print:** 3. **Selected Titles:** *Tyrants Tears: A Collection of Poems* by Betty Cook Rottmann, *The First Anthology of Missouri Women Writers, Art Museums and Galleries in Missouri: A Directory, Women's Issues/Minority Concerns,* all edited by Sharon Kinney-Hanson; *Writings: Poetry, Song, Verse; Writing Memories.* **Principal Officials and Managers:** Sharon Kinney-Hanson, President and Managing Editor.

★9966★ Sidewalk Revolution Press
PO Box 9062
Pittsburgh, PA 15224
Phone: (412)361-8927
Description: Publishes lesbian feminist poetry.

★9967★ Silverleaf Press, Inc.
PO Box 701
Seattle, WA 98107
Description: Publishes fiction by feminist writers. Reaches market through direct mail, trade sales, Baker & Taylor, Pacific Pipeline, BookPeople, and Inland Book Co. **Number of New Titles:** 1990 - 1, 1991 (est.) - 1; Total Titles in Print - 4. **Selected Titles:** *Three Glasses of Wine Have Been Removed from this Story* by Marian Michener; *Crossing the Mainstream: New Fiction by Women Writers* edited by Larson and Carr. **Principal Officials and Managers:** Ann E. Larson, Editor and Publisher.

★9968★ Sis Enterprises
2174 Louis Rd.
Palo Alto, CA 94303
Phone: (415)322-8927
Description: Seeks to improve the status of women by publishing pertinent books, measurement instruments, and programs. **Selected Titles:** *The Woman's Machiavelli* by Prudence Freeman; *Dedication and Courage Works, A Program for Economic Justice for Homemakers, Not for Cowards,* all by Dorothy Woodworth. **Principal Officials and Managers:** D. C. Woodworth, President.

★9969★ Sisters' Choice Press
1450 6th St.
Berkeley, CA 94710
Phone: (415)524-5804
Description: Publishes materials on non-sexist storytelling and songs. **Selected Titles:** *Just Enough to Make a Story, Plum Pudding: Stories and Songs,* both by Nancy Schimmel; *All in This Together* (cassette) by Nancy Schimmel and C. Forest. **Principal Officials and Managers:** Nancy Schimmel, Owner; Ruth Burnstein, Manager.

★9970★ The Smith Publishers
69 Joralemon St.
Brooklyn, NY 11201
Phone: (718)522-0623
Description: Publishes poetry and books on women's issues. Offers a newsletter, *The Generalist Papers.* Accepts unsolicited manuscripts; query first with sample chapter. Distributes for Birch Brook Press. Reaches market through direct mail, trade sales, Baker & Taylor, Blackwell North America, and John Coutts Library Services. **Number of New Titles:** 1990 - 4; Total Titles in Print - 81. **Selected Titles:** *A Sense of Direction* by Karen Swenson; *Old Soldiers* by Richard Nason; *Night Feet* by Celia Watson; *Crocodile Man* by Bradley Strahan. **Principal Officials and Managers:** Harry Smith, Editor and Publisher.

★9971★ Smooth Stone Press, Inc.
PO Box 198
St. Louis, MO 63144
Phone: (314)968-2596
Description: Publishes on women's health. Accepts unsolicited manuscripts with a self-addressed, stamped envelope. Reaches market through commission representatives, trade sales, Baker & Taylor, BookPeople, Ingram, Inland Book Co., Nutri-Books Corp., New Leaf Distributing Co., Pacific Pipeline, and Quality Books, Inc. **Selected Titles:** *Your Fertility Signals: Using Them to Achieve or Avoid Pregnancy Naturally* by Merryl Winstein. **Principal Officials and Managers:** M. Winstein, Vice-President.

★9972★ South End Press
Attn: Publicity Dept.
116 St. Botolph St.
Boston, MA 02115
Phone: (617)266-0629
Description: Publishes books related to politics, social movements, women, Third World, sexuality, disarment, economics, Central America, and U.S. foreign policy. Reaches market through commission representatives, direct mail, and distributors, including BookPeople, Inland Book Co., and Baker & Taylor. **Number of New Titles:** 1990 - 15, 1991 (est.) - 15; Total Titles in Print - 160. **Selected Titles:** *Necessary Illusions* by Noam Chomsky; *Under the Big Stick: Nicaragua and the US Since 1848* by Karl Bermann; *Sex and Germs: The Politics of AIDS* by Cindy Patton; *Agents of Repression: The FBI's Secret Wars against the American Indian Movement and the Black Panther Party* by Ward Churchill and Jim Vander Wall; *Keep Hope Alive: Jesse Jackson's 1988 Presidential Campaign* edited by Frank Clemente; *Talking Back: Thinking Feminist, Thinking Black* by Bell Hooks. **Principal Officials and Managers:** Karin A. San Juan, Steve Chase, Promotion and Editorial; Tanya McKinnon, Finance and Editorial; Loie Hayes, Cynthia Peters, Production and Editorial.

★9973★ Spinster's Book Co.
PO Box 4106
San Francisco, CA 94141
Phone: (415)558-9586
Description: Publishes fiction and nonfiction by women, with an emphasis on work by women of color and lesbians. Accepts unsolicited manuscripts. Distributes for Glad Hag Books and Bergamont Books. Reaches market through direct mail, trade sales, BookPeople, Inland Book Co., and Pacific Pipeline. Formerly known as Spinsters/Aunt Lute Book Co. **Selected Titles:** *Elise* by Claire Kensington; *Modern Daughters and the Outlaw West* by Melissa Kwasny; *The Lesbian Erotic Dance* by JoAnn Loulan; *Lesbians at Midlife* edited by Barbara Sang, Joyce Warshaw, and Adrienne Smith; *Final Session* by Mary Morrell. **Principal Officials and Managers:** Joan C. Pinkvoss and Sherilyn Thomas, Partners.

★9974★ Stanford University Press
Stanford, CA 94305
Phone: (415)497-9434
Description: Academic press. Publishes women's studies books.

★9975★ Star Publishing
1000 Jousting
Austin, TX 78746
Phone: (512)327-8310
Description: Publishes information on birth, parenting, the family, metaphysics, and spiritual life. Reaches market through direct mail, BookPeople, and New Leaf Distributing Co. **Total Titles in Print:** 3. **Selected Titles:** *Celebration, Healing Power of Birth,* both by Rima Star. **Principal Officials and Managers:** Rima Beth Star, President.

★9976★ Starogubski Press
Westbeth
55 Bethune St., Ste. H658
New York, NY 10025
Phone: (212)222-5070
Subjects: Women, feminism. **Total Titles in Print:** 1. **Selected Titles:** *Woman to Woman: European Feminists* by Bonnie Bluh. **Principal Officials and Managers:** Bonnie Bluh, President; Lana Crow, Sales Manager; Helen Charles, Public Relations Manager.

★9977★ Steppingstone Press
3113 Falling Brook Ln.
Boise, ID 83706
Phone: (208)384-1577
Description: Publishes self-help books for women. Also offers seminars for women. **Se-**

lected Titles: *Feed My Sheep* by Dorris Murdock; *You Are Worth a Million* by Dorris Murdock et al. **Principal Officials and Managers:** Martha Miller, Publisher; Dorris Murdock, Editor.

★9978★ Still Waters Press
112 W. Duerer
Galloway, NJ 08201-9402
Phone: (609)652-1790

Description: Publishes works by, for, or about women. Accepts unsolicited manuscripts. Reaches market through direct mail. **Number of New Titles:** 1990 - 4, 1991 - 5, 1992 (est.) - 4; Total Titles in Print - 20. **Selected Titles:** *Going off on Her Own* by Pamela Aiken Rock; *The Good Child* by Lynne H. deCourcy; *Labors* by Kevin Griffith; *Mary of Migdal* by Madeline Tiger; *Somewhere Between, Zeroes for Zorba: A Feminist Critique of "Zorba the Greek"*, both by Shirley Warren. **Principal Officials and Managers:** Shirley A. Warren, Managing Editor.

★9979★ Success Publications
PO Box 46
McAllen, TX 78502
Phone: (512)687-8747

Description: Publishes materials for women. Reaches market through direct mail, trade sales, The Distributors, Quality Books, Inc., Gordon's Books, Inc., and Baker & Taylor. **Total Titles in Print:** 1. **Selected Titles:** *Pregnancy in the Executive Suite* by Valerie Lee. **Principal Officials and Managers:** Charlie Woerner, Owner.

★9980★ Sun Life Books
Greystone
Thaxton, VA 24174
Phone: (703)586-4898

Description: Independent publishing arm of the pro-life movement. Reaches market through direct mail and advertisements in right-to-life publications. **Selected Titles:** *Abortion and Social Justice* edited by Thomas Hilgers, M.D., and Dennis Horan; *And Now Infanticide* by Effie A. Quay; *The Position of Modern Science on the Beginning of Human Life* edited by Edward Freiling, Ph.D. **Principal Officials and Managers:** Gerald J. Brunning, Manager.

★9981★ Syndicated Capital Publishing Co., Inc.
1410 E. Silver Springs Blvd.
Ocala, FL 32670-6820
Phone: (904)237-6414

Subjects: Child care education. **Selected Titles:** *All You Wanted to Know about Daycares and Didn't Know Who to Ask.* **Principal Officials and Managers:** Lawrence P. O'Reilly, President.

★9982★ Syracuse Cultural Workers
PO Box 6367
Syracuse, NY 13217
Phone: (315)474-1132

Founded: 1982. **Description:** Native Americans, feminism, gay liberation and civil rights.

★9983★ Syracuse University Press
1600 Jamesville Ave.
Syracuse, NY 13210
Phone: (315)423-2596

Description: Academic press. Publishes women's studies books.

★9984★ Tabor Sarah Books
2419 Jefferson Ave.
Berkeley, CA 94703
Phone: (510)843-2779

Founded: 1985. **Subjects:** Children's nonsexist, nonracist books.

★9985★ Talman Company
150 5th Ave.
New York, NY 10011-4311
Phone: (212)620-3182
Toll-free: 800-537-8894
Fax: (212)627-4682

Description: Specializes in health, travel, women's issues and children's books.

★9986★ Tangelwuld Press
PO Box 1603
Las Colinas, TX 75016-0361
Phone: (214)686-5332

Description: Publishes books on liberal theology and women's studies. Accepts unsolicited manuscripts. Reaches market through direct mail, trade sales, wholesalers, and distributors. **Number of New Titles:** 1990 - 2; Total Titles in Print - 10. **Selected Titles:** *God's Girls: Ordination of Women* by Arthur Frederick Ide; *A Place to Start: Toward an Unapologetic Gay Theology* by J. Michael Clark; *Richard I in England* by Harry Steven Howser. **Principal Officials and Managers:** Ruby Borlaug, President; Ruthra Edi, Publisher.

★9987★ Tara Educational Services
65 Cretin Ave. N.
St. Paul, MN 55104
Phone: (612)645-4427

Description: Publishes books and presentations on women's life experiences. Offers video tapes. Distributes for North Star Press. Reaches market through Inland Book Co. and New Leaf Distributing Co. **Number of New Titles:** 1991 (est.) - 2; Total Titles in Print - 3. **Selected Titles:** *Many Faces of the Great Mother: A Coloring Book for all Ages, Winter Solstice Celebrations Through Time, Gala Celebrations for Children*, all by Terri Berthiaume Hawthorne and Diane Berthiaume Brown. **Principal Officials and Managers:** Terri Hawthorne, John C. Hawthorne, Directors.

★9988★ Texas Foundation for Women's Resources
PO Box 50224
Austin, TX 78763
Phone: (512)476-6112

Founded: 1974. **Subjects:** Texas women; women's history.

★9989★ Thelphini Press
1218 Forest Rd.
New Haven, CT 06515
Phone: (203)389-6830

Founded: 1978. **Selected Titles:** *Greek Women Poets*; *Greek Women in Resistance*.

★9990★ Third Side Press
2250 W. Farragut
Chicago, IL 60625
Phone: (312)271-3029

★9991★ Third Woman Press
Chicano Studies
University of California
Dwinelle Hall 3412
Berkeley, CA 94720
Phone: (415)642-0240

Description: Publishes works by and about U.S. Latinas, Hispanic women, and Third World women in general. **Number of New Titles:** 1990 - 4, 1992 (est.) - 5; Total Titles in Print - 15. **Selected Titles:** *Variaciones Sobre una Tempestad* by Lucha Corpi; *My Wicked Wicked Ways* by Sandra Cisneros; *The Margarita Poems* by Luz Maria Umpierre-Herrera; *Speak to Me from Dreams* by Barbara Brinson Curiel; *Chicana Lesbians: The Girls Our Mothers Warned Us About*, edited by Carla Trujillo; *The Sexuality of Latinas*, edited by Norma Alarcon, Ana Castillo, and Cherrie Moraga. **Principal Officials and Managers:** Norma Alarcon, Editor and Publisher; James Opiat, Business Manager.

★9992★ Tide Book Publishing Co.
PO Box 101
York Harbor, ME 03911-0101
Phone: (207)363-4534

Founded: 1979. **Description:** Publishes on social science, health, aging, women and the arts.

★9993★ Timely Books
4040 Mountain Creek Rd., No. 1304
Chattanooga, TN 37415
Phone: (615)875-9447

Description: Publishes on alternative lifestyles and feminism. Accepts unsolicited manuscripts, query first. **Total Titles in Print:** 9. **Selected Titles:** *By Sanction of the Victim* by Patte Wheat; *The Cruise, Amanda, Love Is Where You Find It, The Others Side of Desire*, all by Paula Christian. **Principal Officials and Managers:** R. Jo Anne Prather, Yvonne MacManus, Publishers.

★9994★ Times Change Press
PO Box 13
Ojai, CA 93023
Phone: (805)646-8595

Description: Publishes books and posters to further social and political change and personal growth. Accepts unsolicited manuscripts; include a self-addressed, stamped envelope. Reaches market through trade sales and several wholesalers. **Subjects:** Feminism, gay and youth liberation, men's consciousness-raising, social change. **Number of New Titles:** 1990 - 2, 1991 - 2, 1992 (est.) - 2; Total Titles in Print - 27. **Selected Titles:** *Fatherjournal* by David Steinberg; *The Traffic in Women and Other Essays on Feminism* by Emma Goldman; *The Early Homosexual Rights Movement, 1864-1935* by John Lauristen and David Thorstad; *Momma: A Start on All the Untold Stories* by Alta; *Generations of Denial: 75 Short Biographies of Women in History* by Kathry Taylor; *The Great Harmony: Teachings and Observations of the Way of the Universe* edited by Su Negrin. **Principal Officials and Managers:** Lamar Hoover, Publisher; Sally Hoover, Senior Editor.

★9995★ Tough Dove Books
PO Box 1999
Redway, CA 95560
Selected Titles: *Lesbian Bedtime Stories II.*

★9996★ Triad Publishing Co.
1110 NW 8th Ave.
Gainesville, FL 32601
Phone: (904)373-5800
Fax: (904)373-1488
Founded: 1978. **Selected Titles:** *Women Take Care: The Consequences of Caregiving in Today's Society.*

★9997★ University of California Press
2120 Berkeley Way
Berkeley, CA 94720
Phone: (510)642-4247
Description: Academic press. Publishes women's studies books.

★9998★ University of Chicago Press
5801 Ellis Ave.
Chicago, IL 60637
Phone: (312)962-7700
Description: Academic press. Publishes women's studies books.

★9999★ University of Georgia Press
Athens, GA 30602
Phone: (404)542-2830
Description: Academic press. Publishes women's studies books.

★10000★ University of Illinois Press
54 E. Gregory Dr.
Champaign, IL 61820
Phone: (217)333-0950
Description: Academic press. Publishes women's studies books.

★10001★ University of Massachusetts Press
PO Box 429
Amherst, MA 01004
Phone: (413)545-2217
Description: Academic press. Publishes women's studies books.

★10002★ University of Michigan Press
839 Greene St.
PO Box 1104
Ann Arbor, MI 48106
Phone: (313)764-4394
Description: Academic press. Publishes women's studies books.

★10003★ University of Minnesota Press
2037 University Ave., SE
Minneapolis, MN 55414
Phone: (612)624-2516
Description: Academic press. Publishes women's studies books.

★10004★ University of Nebraska Press
901 N. 17th St.
Lincoln, NE 68588
Phone: (402)472-3581
Description: Academic press. Publishes women's studies books.

★10005★ University of North Carolina, Chapel Hill
Carolina Population Center
CB No. 8120, University Sq.
Chapel Hill, NC 27516-3997
Phone: (919)966-2152
Description: Publishes and distributes scholarly works in various disciplines relating to population studies. **Selected Titles:** *Family Planning for Health in Africa* edited by Abdel R. Omran and Alan G. Johnston; *The Media and Family Planning* by J. Richard Udry; *Abortion to Zoophilia: A Source Book of Sexual Facts* by Anne Mandetta and Patricia Gustaveson; *Introduction to Sexual Counseling* by R. Reid Wilson; *Adolescent Sexuality and Teenage Pregnancy: A Selected, Annotated Bibliography with Summary Forewords* by Karen Robb Stewart; *Counseling Skills in Family Planning: Trainer's Handbook* by Deborah E. Bender and Cydne Bean. **Principal Officials and Managers:** Lynn Igoe, Editor, Publications; Frank Twiford, Director, Educational Materials.

★10006★ University of Wisconsin
Women's Studies Librarian
430 Memorial Library
728 State St.
Madison, WI 53706
Phone: (608)263-5754
Description: Publishes bibliographies for women's studies. Offers three periodicals. Reaches market through direct mail. **Number of New Titles:** 1991 - 1, 1992 (est.) - 2; Total Titles in Print - 2. **Selected Titles:** *Women, Race, and Ethnicity: A Bibliography* Susan Searing, Linda Shult, and Elli Lester-Massman; *The History of Women and Science, Health, and Technology: A Biliographic Guide to the Professions and the Disciplines* by Susan Searing and Rita Apple. **Principal Officials and Managers:** Phyllis Weisbard, Acting Women's Studies Librarian.

★10007★ Vanessapress
PO Box 827
Fairbanks, AK 99708
Phone: (907)479-0172
Description: Publishes Alaskan women authors writing about Alaska. Accepts unsolicited manuscripts; include $10.00 for costs of editorial review. Reaches market through direct mail and distributors, including Inland Book Co. **Subjects:** Autobiography, poetry, anthology. **Number of New Titles:** 1991 - 1, 1992 (est.) - 1; Total Titles in Print - 5. **Selected Titles:** *Growing Up Stubborn at Gold Creek* by Melody Erickson; *O'Rugged Land of Gold* by Martha Martin; *Tides of Morning* by Mei Mei Evans et al.; *On Why the Quiltmaker Became a Dragon: A Visionary Poem* by Sheila Nickerson; *Bits of Ourselves: Women's Experiences with Cancer.* **Principal Officials and Managers:** Liz Biesiot, President; Janet Baird, Vice-President; Melody Erickson, Treasurer.

★10008★ Veritie Press
PO Box 222
Novelty, OH 44072
Phone: (216)338-3374
Founded: 1975. **Subjects:** Women in history; early Norse women explorers. **Selected Titles:** *Marguerite de la Rogue: A Story of Survival.*

★10009★ Vintage '45 Press
PO Box 2
Orinda, CA 94563
Phone: (415)254-7266
Description: Publishes the work of women writers for "active, introspective women who have outgrown traditional women's publications." Also offers audio cassettes. Distributes for Papier Mache, Volcano, and others. Reaches market through direct mail, trade sales, and Inland Book Co. **Total Titles in Print:** 25. **Selected Titles:** *Maternal Legacy: A Mother-Daughter Anthology* edited by Susan L. Aglietti; *If I Had A Hammer* edited by Sandra Martz; *Feminist Convert: A Portrait of Mary Ellen Chase* by Evelyn Hyman Chase; *A Primer for Buford* by Wilma McDaniel; *Late Bloomer: Stories of Successful Aging* (audio cassette) edited by Connie Goldman; *Reaching* by Connie Hunt. **Principal Officials and Managers:** Susan L. Aglietti, Editor and Publisher.

★10010★ Volcano Press, Inc.
PO Box 2
Volcano, CA 95689
Phone: (209)296-3445
Description: Publishes titles with a "feminist consciousness." Also offers audio cassettes. Accepts unsolicited manuscripts with self-addressed stamped envelope; query first. Reaches market through direct mail, trade sales, and distributors, including BookPeople and Inland Book Co. **Subjects:** Women's health, domestic violence, art, children's books. **Total Titles in Print:** 19. **Selected Titles:** *Berchick* by Esther Silverstein Blanc; *The Infertility Book: A Comprehensive Medical and Emotional Guide* by Carla Harkness; *Menopause Naturally: Preparing for the Second Half of Life* by Sadja Greenwood; *Learning to Live without Violence* by Daniel Sonkin and Michael Durphy; *Conspiracy of Silence: The Trauma of Incest* by Sandra Butler; *Mighty Mountain and the Three Strong Women* by Hedlund. **Principal Officials and Managers:** Ruth Gottstein, President; Ann Sharkey, Business Manager.

★10011★ VSE Publisher
212 S. Dexter
Denver, CO 80222
Phone: (303)322-7450
Description: Publishes children's books on issues of women history. Reaches market through direct mail, trade sales, telephone sales, and major small press distributors. **Subjects:** Children's books on issues of women history. **Total Titles in Print:** 3. **Selected Titles:** *History of Women Artists for Children, History of Women for Children, The ABC's of What a Girl Can Be,* all by Vivian Sheldon Epstein. **Principal Officials and Managers:** Vivian Sheldon Epstein.

★10012★ Waterwomen Books
3022 Ashbrook Ct.
Oakland, CA 94601
Phone: (415)532-3545

Description: Publishes a lesbian photo album and provides consultation on self-publishing, production, and marketing.

★10013★ Wellesley College
Center for Research on Women
Wellesley, MA 02181
Phone: (617)431-1453

Description: Develops and disseminates knowledge about women; sponsors policy-oriented projects. Publishes working papers series and a semi-annual newsletter. Selected Titles: The Role of Day Care in Serving the Needs of School-Age Parents and Their Children: A Review of the Literature by Marx; Employment and Health among Older Black Women: Implications for Their Economic Status by Brown; A Quiet Fight All the Way: A Report on the Need for Child Care among Parents of School-Age Children with Handicapping Conditions by Fink; Developmental Changes in Menstrual Attitudes by Stubbs, Rierdan, and Keff; White Privilege and Male Privilege: A Personal Account of Coming to See Correspondences through Work on Women's Studies by McIntosh. Principal Officials and Managers: Susan Bailey, Director; Jan Putnam, Assistant Director.

★10014★ West End Press
PO Box 27334
Albuquerque, NM 87125
Phone: (505)345-5729

Description: Publishes feminist, progressive and working-class titles. Selected Titles: Coming Home: Peace Without Complacency by Margaret Randall and The Girl by Meridel LeSueur.

★10015★ West Pine Publishing Co.
912 W. Pine St.
Hattiesburg, MS 39401
Phone: (601)582-1978

Description: Publishes a self-help book on women's health. Reaches market through direct mail and Baker & Taylor. Number of New Titles: 1989 - 1; Total Titles in Print - 1. Selected Titles: Sexocize: A Female Genitourinary Program by Janan Clark.

★10016★ Westview Press
5500 Central Ave.
Boulder, CO 80301
Phone: (303)444-3541
Fax: (303)449-3356
Founded: 1975.

★10017★ Wider Opportunities for Women
1325 G St. NW
Washington, DC 20005
Phone: (202)638-3143

Description: An independent, national nonprofit resource organization that works to promote equal employment opportunity for women. Selected Titles: Suit Yourself. Shopping for a Job by Roberta Kaplan; Nontraditional Work Programs: A Guide, Working for You: A Guide to Employing Women in Nontraditional Jobs, all by Wider Opportunities for Women. Principal Officials and Managers: Cynthia E. Marano, Executive Director.

★10018★ Wild Violet Publishing
PO Box1311
Hamilton, MT 59840
Phone: (406)363-2696

Description: Publishes books on women's spirituality. Selected Titles: Beyond the Eagle: An Intervibrational Perspective on Women's Spirituality by Chambers and Grace.

★10019★ Wildfire Books
PO Box 105
Albuquerque, NM 87184
Phone: (505)344-4790

Description: Publishes books on feminist theory. Offers audio and video cassettes. Accepts unsolicited manuscripts. Reaches market through direct mail, BookPeople, Inland Book Co., New Leaf Distributing Co., Ingram Book Co., The Distributors, and Baker & Taylor. Number of New Titles: 1990 - 3, 1992 (est.) - 1; Total Titles in Print - 2. Selected Titles: Wildfire: Igniting the She/Volution, Housewife to Heretic, both By Sonia Johnson. Principal Officials and Managers: Christine Champion, Sonia Johnson, Co-Publishers.

★10020★ Wildwood Resources, Inc.
9085 E. Mineral Circle, Ste. 300
Englewood, CO 80112
Phone: (303)790-7580

Description: Publishes and distributes educational books and materials for parents, family day care homes, day care centers, and preschools. Reaches market through direct mail. Subjects: Nutrition, child care. Selected Titles: Off to a Good Start by C. Romaniello and N. Van Domelen.

★10021★ Willowood Press
PO Box 1846
Minot, ND 58702
Phone: (701)838-0579

Description: Offers mailing lists of American libraries and educational institutions.

★10022★ W.I.M. Publications
10203 Parkwood Dr., No. 7
Cupertino, CA 95014-1466
Phone: (408)253-3329
Fax: (408)253-3329

Description: Publishes feminist and lesbian poetry. Offers mail order directories, mailing lists, book reviews, and self-publishing consulting. Reaches market through direct mail and telephone and trade sales. Subjects: Feminism, lesbian literature, writing, religion. Number of New Titles: 1989 - 4, 1990 - 2, 1991 (est.) - 3; Total Titles in Print - 18. Selected Titles: Dyke Hands, Poet's Poetry Workbook, both by Bogus; Intro to Fine by Sebastian; Who's Who in Mail Order by Sherilynn Posey; The Book of Lives by Sherilynn Posey; Buddhism for My Friends. Principal Officials and Managers: Dr. S. Diane Bogus, Publisher; T. Nelson Gilbert, Business Manager. Also known as: Woman in the Moon Publications

★10023★ Wind River Publications Inc.
2359 Henderson Mill Ct.
Atlanta, GA 30345
Phone: (404)496-4986

Description: Publishes a directory of women-owned businesses nationwide. Reaches market

through direct mail. Selected Titles: Directory of Women Enterprenuers. Principal Officials and Managers: Patricia A. Morrall, Publisher.

★10024★ Wingbow Press
2929 5th St.
Berkeley, CA 94710
Phone: (415)549-3030

Description: Publishes original works, reprints, and audio cassettes. Accepts unsolicited manuscripts; query first. Subjects: Women's studies, occult, New Age, self-help, psychology, astrology, spirituality. Number of New Titles: 1989 - 3; Total Titles in Print - 28. Selected Titles: The Motherpeace Tarot Playbook: Astrology and Motherpeace Cards by Vicki Noble and Jonathan Tenney; Astrology for Yourself by Douglas Bloch and Demetra George; The Holy Book of Women's Mysteries by Zsuzsanna Budapest; Constructive Criticism by Gracie Lyons; The God of the Labyrinth by Colin Wilson; The Heart of the Goddess: Art, Myth and Meditations of the World's Sacred Feminine by Hallie Inglehart Austen. Principal Officials and Managers: Randy Fingland, Managing Editor; Stanton Nelson, Acquisitions Editor.

★10025★ Woman Activist Fund, Inc.
2310 Barbour Rd.
Falls Church, VA 22043
Phone: (703)573-8716

Subjects: Politics, feminists, government. Total Titles in Print: 11. Selected Titles: The Almanac of Virginia Politics, 1987; 1986 Supplement; Virginia General Assembly Voting Record, 1979. Principal Officials and Managers: Flora Crater, President; Jayne Conrad, Vice-President; Joanna Rubin, Treasurer.

★10026★ Woman-to-Woman Press
Lowell House
1875 Century Park E., No. 220
Los Angeles, CA 90067
Phone: (213)552-7555

★10027★ Woman's Institute for Continuing Jewish Education
4126 Executive Dr.
La Jolla, CA 92034
Phone: (619)442-2666

Description: Publishes educational books for women. Reaches market through direct mail. Total Titles in Print: 6. Selected Titles: Taking the Fruit: Modern Women's Tales of the Bible edited by Jane Zones; Educating the New Jewish Woman by Irene Fine; On a Spiritual Journey: A Woman's Siddur edited by Jackie Tolley; Women Speak to God: The Prayers and Poems of Jewish Women edited by Marcia Spiegel. Principal Officials and Managers: Irene Fine, Director.

★10028★ Womanshare Books
PO Box 6
Grants Pass, OR 97526
Phone: (503)862-2807

Description: Publishes work by women. Selected Titles: Country Lesbians by the Woman Share Collective. Principal Officials and Managers: Billie Mericle, Secretary-Treasurer.

★10029★ **Women in the Arts Foundation**
c/o Roberta Crown
1175 York Ave., Apt. 2G
New York, NY 10021
Phone: (212)691-0988

Description: Publishes catalogs of exhibits of women's artwork and newsletter. Reaches market through direct mail. **Subjects:** Art. **Total Titles in Print:** 2. **Selected Titles:** *Women Choose Women, Artists/Choice,* both by Women in the Arts. **Principal Officials and Managers:** Roberta Crown, Executive Coordinator; Joyce Weinstein, Recording Coordinator; Freda Pond, Financial Coordinator; Jacquelin Skiles, Editor.

★10030★ **Women-in-Literature, Inc.**
PO Box 605
Reno, NV 89506
Phone: (702)972-1671

Description: Publishes regional anthologies of poetry by women, providing supplemental criticism, interviews, photos, and biographies of featured poets. Reaches market through direct mail, wholesalers, and Inland Book Co. **Total Titles in Print:** 3. **Selected Titles:** *Woman Poet: The West; Woman Poet: The East; Woman Poet: The Midwest; Woman Poet: The South.* **Principal Officials and Managers:** Dr. Elaine Dallman, President; Laurel Ross, Secretary; Pamela Pavlovsky, Treasurer.

★10031★ **Women for Sobriety, Inc.**
PO Box 6
109 W. Broad St.
Quakertown, PA 18951
Phone: (215)536-8026

Description: Publishes material for women alcoholics in recovery. Offers books, booklets, cassettes, video tapes, and posters. Accepts unsolicited manuscripts from alcoholic women. Also publishes a monthly newsletter, *Sobering Thoughts.* Distributes for Bantam and Ballantine. Reaches market through direct mail. **Total Titles in Print:** 60. **Selected Titles:** *Turnabout: Help for a New Life, A Fresh Start, Nutrition and the Woman Alcoholic, Goodbye Hangovers–Hello Life, Depression, The Difference Gender Makes,* all by Kirkpatrick. **Principal Officials and Managers:** Dr. Jean Kirkpatrick, Executive Director.

★10032★ **Women & Their Work, Inc.**
1137 W. 6th St.
Austin, TX 78703
Phone: (512)477-1064

Description: Publishes catalogs for major group exhibitions. Also produces a quarterly newsletter. Reaches market through direct mail. **Subjects:** Visual, literary and performing arts. **Number of New Titles:** 1990 - 1, 1991 (est.) - 1; Total Titles in Print - 4. **Selected Titles:** *Metis; College: 31 Artists Mix It Up,* both by Meridel LeSeur et al.; *Woman-in-Sight: New Art in Texas* introduction by Marcia Tucker; *Review: 10 Years of Women and Their Work; Women of the Big State: Current Art.* **Principal Officials and Managers:** Chris Cowden, Executive Director; Cindy Noe, Assistant Director; Pat Land, Operations Manager; Genny Duncan, Project Coordinator.

★10033★ **Women in Transition**
125 S. 9th St., Ste. 502
Philadelphia, PA 19107-5125
Phone: (215)922-7177

Description: Publishes on counseling for women. Also provides training and consultation services. **Total Titles in Print:** 3. **Selected Titles:** *A Facilitator's Guide to Working with Separated and Divorced Women; Stepping Out to Work: A Facilitator's Guide; Child Support: How You Can Obtain and Enforce Support Orders.* **Principal Officials and Managers:** Roberta L. Hacker, Executive Director.

★10034★ **Women in Translation**
3131 Western Ave., Ste. 410
Seattle, WA 98121-1028

Description: Publishes translations of books by Asian women. **Selected Titles:** *How Many Miles to Babylon?; Two Women in One; Unmapped Territories: New Women's Fiction from Japan.* **Remarks:** Previously an imprint of Seal Press (see separate entry).

★10035★ **Women on Words and Images**
30 Valley Rd.
Princeton, NJ 08540
Phone: (609)921-8653

Description: Publishes research on sex role stereotyping in education and television. **Selected Titles:** *Dick and Jane as Victims; Help Wanted: Sex Stereotyping in Career Education Materials; Channeling Children: Sex Stereotyping in Prime Time TV.* **Principal Officials and Managers:** Carol Jacobs, President.

★10036★ **Women's Action Alliance, Inc.**
370 Lexington Ave.
New York, NY 10017
Phone: (212)532-8330

Description: A national center on women's issues and programs. Develops, coordinates, assists and administers programs committed to full equality for all persons. Annual Sales: $25,000. **Number of New Titles:** 1989 - 1, 1990 - 2; Total Titles in Print - 11. **Selected Titles:** *Struggling through Tight Times* by Sara Gould; *T.A.P.P. Sources: A National Directory of Teenage Pregnancy Prevention Programs* by Dominique Treboux; *Nuts and Bolts of NTO: Nontraditional Occupations* by Jo Sanders; *The Forgotten Five Million: Women in Public Employment; Non-Sexist Education for Young Children: A Practical Guide; Women's Centers and Aids: A Guidebook for Community Groups.* **Principal Officials and Managers:** Gail Chasin, Acting Executive Director.

★10037★ **Women's Caucus for Art**
Moore College of Art
20th and The Parkway
Philadelphia, PA 19103
Phone: (215)854-0922

Subjects: Art, feminist studies, women's issues. **Total Titles in Print:** 2. **Selected Titles:** *Honors Catalog; WCA Directory.* **Principal Officials and Managers:** Iona Deering, President; Essie Karp, National Administrator.

★10038★ **Women's College Coalition**
1090 Vermont Ave. NW, 3rd Fl.
Washington, DC 20005
Phone: (202)842-3600

Description: Publishes information about women's colleges and sex education. **Number of New Titles:** 1992 (est.) - 1; Total Titles in Print - 12. **Selected Titles:** *Expanding Options: A Profile of Older Graduates of Women's Colleges; A Study of the Learning Environment at Women's Colleges: Highlights of the Study; 67/77: A Profile of Recent Women's College Graduates; List of Women's Colleges; Alumnae Giving at Women's Colleges: A Ten-Year Study, 1988; Women's College Directory.* **Principal Officials and Managers:** Marcia Sharp, Executive Director; Mary Huchette, Associate Director; Peter Mirijanian, Associate Director.

★10039★ **Women's Educational Equity Act Publishing Center**
55 Chapel St.
Newton, MA 02160
Phone: (617)969-7100
Toll-free: 800-225-3088
Katherine Henson, Director

Founded: 1976. **Description:** The Center publishes, reviews and disseminates a broad range of print materials to promote educational equity for girls and women.

★10040★ **Women's Foreign Policy Council**
835 3rd Ave., 15th Fl.
New York, NY 10022-6601
Phone: (212)759-7982

Description: Publishes a directory of women foreign policy specialists. Offers a newsletter, *News & Views.* **Total Titles in Print:** 1. **Selected Titles:** *Women's Foreign Policy Council Directory: A Guide to Women Foreign Policy Specialists and Listings of Women and Organizations Working on International Affairs.* **Principal Officials and Managers:** Bella Abzug, Mim Kelber, Chairors.

★10041★ **Women's History Research Center**
2325 Oak St.
Berkeley, CA 94708
Phone: (415)524-1582

Description: Collects, preserves, and distributes materials by and about women, through microfilms of the collections of the Women's History Library and through the National Clearinghouse on Marital and Date Rape. **Subjects:** Women, the health-care system, sex discrimination, the women's movement. **Selected Titles:** *Women and Health/Mental Health; Women and Law; Herstory.* **Principal Officials and Managers:** Laura Murra, Executive Director.

★10042★ **Women's Institute for Freedom of the Press**
3306 Ross Pl.
Washington, DC 20008
Phone: (202)966-7783

Description: Publishes works on women and the media. **Total Titles in Print:** 2. **Selected Titles:** *Women in Media: A Documentary Source Book* by Beasley and Gibbons; *Syllabus Sourcebook on Media and Women* edited by Dana Densmore. **Principal Officials and Managers:** Martha Leslie Allen, Director.

★10043★ **Women's League for Conservative Judaism**
48 E. 74th St.
New York, NY 10021
Phone: (212)628-1600

Description: Publishes "books of Jewish interest for women and children especially, with accent on various aspects of Jewish education and Jewish family living." Also publishes *Women's League Outlook*, a quarterly magazine and *Ba Olam*, a bimonthly newsletter. Offers an annual calendar-diary with English and Hebrew entries. Also offers teaching audio cassettes of Hebrew prayers and blessings. Accepts unsolicited manuscripts. Reaches market through direct mail and wholesalers. **Number of New Titles:** 1990 - 2, 1991 (est.) - 4, 1992 (est.) - 4; Total Titles in Print - 12. **Selected Titles:** *Adventures of K'tonton* by Sadie Rose Weilerstein; *Count Your Blessings* by Connie Reisner; *Welcome to the World - A Jewish Baby's Record Book; Quantity Kosher Cooking; A Doorway to Understanding; Celebration Series - Holiday Manuals.* **Principal Officials and Managers:** Audrey Citak, National President; Rhonda Kahn, Public Relations Director; Bernice Balter, Executive Director.

★10044★ **Women's Legal Defense Fund**
1875 Connecticut Ave. NW, Ste. 710
Washington, DC 20009
Phone: (202)986-2600

Description: Publishes legal materials for lawyers, policymaker advocates, and laypersons about employment, family law and work, and family policy. Reaches market through direct mail. Total Titles in Print - 15. **Selected Titles:** *Representing Primary Caretakers Parents in Custody Disputes; The Custody Handbook: A Woman's Guide to Child Custody Disputes; Sex Discrimination in the Workplace: A Legal Handbook; Expanding Employment Opportunities for Women: A Blueprint for the Future; Legal Remedies for Sexual Harassment: A Handbook; Critical Issues, Critical Choices: Special Topics in Child Support Guidelines Development.* **Principal Officials and Managers:** Judith Lichtman, President; Donna Lenhoff, Legal Policy Director.

★10045★ **The Women's Project**
2224 Main St.
Little Rock, AR 72206
Phone: (501)372-5113

Founded: 1981. **Subjects:** Violence against women and children; women's economic issues; social justice such as sexism, racism, homophobia, ageism, ableism, classism, and anti-Semitism.

★10046★ **Women's Research Action Project**
72 Cornell St.
Roslindale, MA 02131
Phone: (617)442-1707

Selected Titles: *Corporations and Child Care* by C. Avrin and G. Sassen. **Principal Officials and Managers:** Frances Avrin, President; Georgia Sassen, Secretary and Treasurer.

★10047★ **Women's Research & Education Institute (WREI)**
1700 18th St. NW, No. 400
Washington, DC 20009
Phone: (202)328-7070

Description: Helps translate policy into action by identifying and coordinating research, by analyzing the effects on women of proposed legislation and by putting practical and timely analyses in the hands of decisionmakers. Reaches market through direct mail. **Subjects:** Women's economic issues. **Number of New Titles:** 1990 - 2, 1991 (est.) - 2, 1992 (est.) - 3; Total Titles in Print - 13. **Selected Titles:** *The American Woman 1990-91* edited by Sara E. Rix; *Family and Medical Leave* by Heidi Hartmann and Roberta Spalter-Roth; *Parental Leave and Woman's Place* by Susanne Stoiber; *Home-Based Employment* by Cynthia Costello; *Women at State* by Olmsted et al.; *Directory of Selected Research and Policy Centers: Working on Women's Issues 1989.* **Principal Officials and Managers:** Betty Parsons Dooley, Executive Director; Jean Stapleton, President of the Board; Paula Ries, Research Director.

★10048★ **Women's Studio Workshop Print Center**
PO Box 489
Rosendale, NY 12472
Phone: (914)658-9133

Founded: 1974. **Subjects:** Letterpress, fine printing.

★10049★ **Women's Times Publishing**
PO Box 2
Grand Marais, MN 55604
Phone: (707)829-0558

Description: Publishes northeastern Minnesota literature, literature by or for women, and native literature. Reaches market through direct mail, reviews, and wholesalers. **Number of New Titles:** 1990 - 1; Total Titles in Print - 6. **Selected Titles:** *Woman of the Boundary Waters* by Justine Kerfoot; *Ingeborg's Isle Royale* by Ingeborg Holte; *In These Hills* by Hart and Gagnon; *I Walk on the River at Dawn* by Joanne Hart; *Kid's Northwoods Activity Book* by Lind; *At Home in the Heart of Alaska* by Pat Shuffner. **Principal Officials and Managers:** Jane Lind, Owner and Publisher.

★10050★ **Women's Yellow Pages**
3942 Sawtelle
Los Angeles, CA 90066
Phone: (213)398-5761

Description: Publishes an annual directory of women-owned businesses, professional women, and their organizations and services. Reaches market through commission representatives, direct mail, and telephone sales. **Number of New Titles:** 1991 (est.) - 1, 1992 (est.) - 1; Total Titles in Print - 1. **Selected Titles:** *The 1991 Women's Yellow Pages* (Los Angeles edition); *1990/1991 Women's Yellow Pages* (Orange County edition).

★10051★ **Womenspace**
1101 Euclid Ave.
Cleveland, OH 44114
Phone: (216)696-3100

Description: Nonprofit organization focused on reducing negative impact of divorce. Publishes divorce manuals designed for men, for women, and for parents. Currently manuals are tailored

for Ohio law. Offers a quarterly newsletter, workshops, seminars, and conferences. Reaches market through direct mail and telephone sales. **Subjects:** Divorce law and procedures, child custody, child support guidelines. **Number of New Titles:** 1989 - 2; Total Titles in Print - 4. **Selected Titles:** *Getting Out: A Divorce Manual for Women in Ohio; Getting Out: A Divorce Manual for Men in Ohio; Child Custody: What Are the Options.*

★10052★ **Womyn's Braille Press**
PO Box 8475
Minneapolis, MN 55408
Phone: (612)872-4352

Description: Provides feminist and lesbian literature on tape and in braille.

★10053★ **Word Weavers**
Box 8742
Minneapolis, MN 55408

Description: Lesbian publishing company.

★10054★ **WREE (Women for Racial and Economic Equality)**
198 Broadway, Rm. 606
New York, NY 10038
Phone: (212)385-1103

Subjects: Women's issues, racism. **Selected Titles:** *It Begins Softly, Seeds of Ourselves,* both by Bernadine; *Fannie Lou Hamer: A Biography* by Susan Kling; *Facts about U.S. Women 1991.* **Principal Officials and Managers:** Sally Chaffee Maron, Camille Looper, National Chairors.

★10055★ **Yale University Press**
302 Temple St.
New Haven, CT 06520
Phone: (203)436-7584

Description: Academic press. Publishes women's studies books.

★10056★ **ZiZi Press**
610 W. 110th St.
New York, NY 10025
Phone: (212)866-1356

Description: Publishes feminist work to further the cause of women's liberation through humor. **Selected Titles:** *Majority Report* by the Women's Collective; *The Little Prick* by ZiZi; *Collected Works of Chelsea Gilbert.* **Principal Officials and Managers:** Chelsea Dreher, Editor and Publisher; Laura Collins, Business and Office Manager; Willow West, Accounting and Sales.

(24) Booksellers

Entries in this chapter are arranged alphabetically by state and city, then by organization name within city. See the User's Guide at the front of this directory for additional information.

Alabama

Birmingham

★10057★ Lodestar Books
2020 11th Ave. S
Birmingham, AL 35205
Phone: (205)939-3356

Description: Alternative bookstore with gay/lesbian and feminist titles, cards and music.

Huntsville

★10058★ Ibis Books
3301 Governors Dr.
Huntsville, AL 35805
Phone: (205)536-9604

★10059★ Opening Books
403 Pratt Ave.
Huntsville, AL 35801
Phone: (205)536-5880

Montgomery

★10060★ Trade N' Books
5145 Atlanta Hwy.
Montgomery, AL 36109

Alaska

Anchorage

★10061★ Alaska Women's Bookstore
2440 E. Tudor Rd., No. 304
Anchorage, AK 99507
Phone: (907)562-4716

Description: Feminist, lesbian and spiritual titles.

Arizona

Flagstaff

★10062★ Aradia Bookstore
116 W. Cottage
Flagstaff, AZ 86002
Phone: (602)779-3617

Description: Feminist bookstore.

Phoenix

★10063★ Humanspace Books, Inc.
1617 N. 32nd St., #5
Phoenix, AZ 85008
Phone: (602)220-4419

Description: Bookstore/information center, lesbian, feminist, new age, children's books.

Tucson

★10064★ Antigone Books
600 N. 4th Ave.
Tucson, AZ 85705
Phone: (602)792-3715

Description: Feminist books, music and jewelry.

★10065★ Enchanted Room
808 E. University Blvd., Ste. 100
Tucson, AZ 85710
Phone: (602)622-8070

Description: General bookstore with a women's/feminist/lesbian section.

California

Auburn

★10066★ Lotus Bookstore
100 Brewery Ln.
Auburn, CA 95603
Phone: (916)885-6685

Description: Feminist bookstore.

Bakersfield

★10067★ Eucalyptus Lesbian & Feminist Bookstore
1926 Maple St.
Bakersfield, CA 93304
Phone: (805)834-3769

Berkeley

★10068★ GAIA Bookstore and Catalogue Co.
1400 Shattuck Ave., No. 15
Berkeley, CA 94709
Phone: (510)548-4172

Description: Eco-Spiritual, feminist, goddess and lesbian books and materials, jewelry.

★10069★ Shambhala Booksellers
2482 Telegraph Ave.
Berkeley, CA 94704
Phone: (510)848-8443

Description: Feminist section, goddess-related items, music.

Claremont

★10070★ Huntley Bookstore
175 E. 8th
Claremont, CA 91711
Phone: (714)621-8168

★10071★ Wild Iris Bookstore
143 Harvard Ave., Ste. A
Claremont, CA 91711
Phone: (714)626-8283

Description: Feminist bookstore with jewelry, music, gifts, and art.

Coulterville

★10072★ Blue Heron Connections
3717-L Stoney Oak Rd.
Coulterville, CA 95311

Description: Mail order store.

Eureka

★10073★ Bookleggger
402 E. 2nd St.
Eureka, CA 95501
Phone: (707)445-1344

Fresno

★10074★ Valley Women Books
1118 N. Fulton St.
Fresno, CA 93728
Phone: (209)233-3600

Description: Women's books, feminist and lesbian titles.

Gualala

★10075★ Gualala Books
39225 Hwy. One S.
Gualala, CA 95445
Phone: (707)884-4255

Guerneville

★10076★ **Storyteller Bookstore**
16350 Third St.
Guerneville, CA 95446
Phone: (707)869-2852

Hollywood

★10077★ **A Different Light**
4014 Santa Monica Blvd.
Hollywood, CA 90029
Phone: (213)668-0629
Description: Gay/lesbian bookstore.

La Jolla

★10078★ **Groundworks Books**
D-023C UCSD Student Center
La Jolla, CA 92093
Phone: (619)452-9625
Description: "Radically left-of-center" bookstore; gay/lesbian section.

Laguna Beach

★10079★ **A Different Drummer Bookshop**
1027 N. Coast Hwy., Ste. A
Laguna Beach, CA 92657
Phone: (714)497-6699
Description: Women's gay and feminist titles, metaphysics, self-help and recovery titles.

★10080★ **Fahrenheit 451 Books**
540 S. Coast Hwy, Ste. 100
Laguna Beach, CA 92651
Phone: (714)494-5151
Description: Bookstore with gay/lesbian section.

Long Beach

★10081★ **Chelsea Books**
2501 E. Broadway
Long Beach, CA 90803
Phone: (310)434-2220
Description: Bookstore with a large lesbian/gay section, women's music and magazines.

★10082★ **Lavender Books**
Gay/Lesbian Community Center
1213 N. Highland Ave.
Long Beach, CA 90038
Phone: (213)464-7400
Description: New and used women's titles, shirts, music, art.

★10083★ **Pearls**
358 Rosewell Ave.
Long Beach, CA 90814
Phone: (213)439-5484
Description: Feminist bookstore.

★10084★ **Womontyme Distribution Company**
PO Box 50145
Long Beach, CA 90815-6145
Toll-free: 800-247-8903
Fax: (213)425-4258
Description: Feminist, lesbian-owned company specializing in books and tapes. Topics include incest, sexual assault, domestic violence, codependency, recovery, parenting, prevention, and self-esteem. Includes the work of women artists.

Los Angeles

★10085★ **Circus of Books**
4001 Sunset Blvd.
Los Angeles, CA 90029
Phone: (213)656-7199

★10086★ **MCC Bookstore**
5300 Santa Monica Blvd. #304
Los Angeles, CA 90029
Phone: (213)646-5100

★10087★ **Sisterhood Bookstore**
1351 Westwood Blvd.
Los Angeles, CA 90024
Phone: (213)477-7300
Description: Feminist bookstore also has music, periodicals, etc.

Menlo Park

★10088★ **Two Sisters Bookshop**
605 Cambridge Ave.
Menlo Park, CA 94025
Phone: (415)323-4778
Description: Feminist bookstore. Also offers Goddess art, jewelry, music tapes and CD's, tinkerbells, Native American crafts, drums and rattles, crystals, incense, oils, smudge, posters, T-shirts and weekly events and workshops.

Oakland

★10089★ **Bay Bridge Books**
901 Broadway
Oakland, CA
Phone: (415)835-5845
Description: General bookstore with a strong women's section.

★10090★ **Mama Bears Bookstore and Coffeehouse**
6536 Telegraph Ave.
Oakland, CA 94609
Phone: (510)428-9684
Description: Feminist bookstore. Also offers performance theater, socials, readings, book parties.

Orinda

★10091★ **Vintage '45 Press**
PO Box 266
Orinda, CA 94563
Phone: (510)254-7266
Description: Mail order store.

Palo Alto

★10092★ **Stepping Stones**
226 Hamilton Ave.
Palo Alto, CA 94301
Phone: (408)296-7136
Description: Feminist bookstore.

Pasadena

★10093★ **Page One - Books By and For Women**
966 N Lake Ave.
Pasadena, CA 91104
Phone: (818)798-8694
Description: Feminist bookstore.

Sacramento

★10094★ **Lioness Book Store**
2224 J St.
Sacramento, CA 95016
Phone: (916)442-4657
Description: Feminist books, crafts, music.

San Diego

★10095★ **Paradigm Women's Bookstore**
3343 Adams Ave.
San Diego, CA 92116
Phone: (619)563-1981
Description: Feminist bookstore

San Francisco

★10096★ **Books Etc.**
538 Castro St.
San Francisco, CA 94114
Phone: (415)621-8631
Description: Used books with large gay/lesbian section.

★10097★ **Books 'n Birds**
456 14th St #6G
San Francisco, CA 94103
Description: Feminist bookstore.

★10098★ **Castro Kiosk**
554 Castro St.
San Francisco, CA
Phone: (415)431-1003
Description: Gay/lesbian periodicals and international newspapers.

★10099★ **A Different Light**
489 Castro St.
San Francisco, CA 94114
Phone: (415)431-0891
Description: Gay/lesbian and feminist bookstore; music videos.

★10100★ **Good Vibrations and the Sexuality Library**
1210 Valencia St.
San Francisco, CA 94110
Phone: (415)550-0827

★10101★ **Modern Times Bookstore**
968 Valencia St.
San Francisco, CA 94110
Phone: (415)282-9246
Description: General bookstore with large feminist and gay/lesbian section.

★10102★ Old Wives' Tales Bookstore
1009 Valencia St.
San Francisco, CA 94110
Phone: (415)821-4675
Description: Women's books, jewelry, music.

★10103★ Womancrafts West
1007 1/2 Valencia St.
San Francisco, CA 94110
Phone: (415)648-2020

San Jose

★10104★ Sisterspirit
175 Stockton Ave.
San Jose, CA 95126
Phone: (408)293-9372
Description: Women's bookstore/coffeehouse.

Santa Barbara

★10105★ Choices Books and Music
913 De La Vina St.
Santa Barbara, CA 93101
Phone: (805)965-5477
Description: Bookstore for women.

Santa Cruz

★10106★ Bookshop Santa Cruz
1547 Pacific Ave.
Santa Cruz, CA 95060
Phone: (408)423-0900
Description: General bookstore with large selection of feminist and lesbian/gay titles.

Santa Rosa

★10107★ ClaireLight Books
1110 Petaluma Hill Rd., Ste. 5
Santa Rosa, CA 95404
Phone: (707)575-8879
Description: Feminist books and music.

Sherman Oaks

★10108★ Bread and Roses Books
13812 Ventura Blvd.
Sherman Oaks, CA 91423
Phone: (818)986-5376
Description: Feminist books, music, cards, jewelry.

Visalie

★10109★ Kindred Spirit Bookshop
1110 N. Ben Maddox Way
Visalie, CA 93291
Phone: (209)625-0978

West Hollywood

★10110★ A Different Light
8853 Santa Monica Blvd.
West Hollywood, CA 90069
Phone: (213)854-6601
Description: Gay/lesbian bookstore.

★10111★ Unicorn Book Store
8940 Santa Monica Blvd.
West Hollywood, CA 90069
Phone: (213)652-6253
Description: Gay/lesbian bookstore.

Colorado

Aurora

★10112★ Isis Metaphysical Supplies and Books
9511 E. Colfax
Aurora, CO 80220
Phone: (303)341-7562

Boulder

★10113★ Ambrosia Books and Treasures for Women
4396 Snowberry Ct.
Boulder, CO 80304
Phone: (303)440-4146
Description: Feminist bookstore.

Colorado Springs

★10114★ Abaton Books
2525 Pikas Peak, Ste. C
Colorado Springs, CO 80904
Phone: (719)475-2508
Description: Feminist bookstore.

Denver

★10115★ Book Garden
2625 E. 12th Ave.
Denver, CO 80206
Phone: (303)399-2004
Description: Feminist bookstore, jewelry, posters and specialty items.

★10116★ Category Six Books
1029 E. 11th Ave.
Denver, CO 80218
Phone: (303)832-6263
Description: Gay/lesbian and feminist books, records, jewelry.

★10117★ Isis Bookstore
5701 E. Colfax Ave.
Denver, CO 80220
Phone: (303)321-0867
Description: Metaphysical, new age, and women's books.

Durango

★10118★ Ponder Pocket
125 E. 10th St.
Durango, CO 81301
Phone: (303)259-9335

Lafayette

★10119★ Leadership Dynamics
10951 Isabelle Rd.
Lafayette, CO 80026
Phone: (303)499-2719

Louisville

★10120★ Beebo's Books
925 Spruce St.
Louisville, CO 80027
Phone: (303)666-4914

Connecticut

Bridgeport

★10121★ Bloodroot
85 Ferris St.
Bridgeport, CT 06605
Phone: (203)576-9168
Description: Feminist bookstore.

Hartford

★10122★ Reader's Feast Bookstore Cafe
529 Farmington Ave.
Hartford, CT 06105
Phone: (203)232-3710
Description: A "feminist progressive" bookstore/cafe.

New Haven

★10123★ Golden Thread Booksellers
915 State St.
New Haven, CT 06511
Phone: (203)777-7807
Description: Feminist bookstore; gifts, book readings, special events.

South Norwalk

★10124★ Liberation Book Club
PO Box 453
South Norwalk, CT 06856
Phone: (203)322-7829
Description: Mail order store.

Delaware

Rehoboth

★10125★ Lambda Rising
39 Baltimore Ave.
Rehoboth, DE 19971
Phone: (302)227-6969

District of Columbia

Washington

★10126★ Lambda Rising 2
1625 Connecticut Ave. NW
Washington, DC 20009
Phone: (202)462-6969

★10127★ Lammas Women's Books and More
1426 21st St. NW
Washington, DC 20036
Phone: (202)775-8218
Description: Reading series, lesbian and women's titles, music and cards.

Florida

Coconut Grove

★10128★ **Lambda Passages Bookstore**
3025 Fuller St.
Coconut Grove, FL 33133
Phone: (305)443-6411
Description: Gay/lesbian and feminist bookstore.

Coral Gables

★10129★ **Gables Booksellers**
222 Andalusia Ave.
Coral Gables, FL 33134
Phone: (305)446-7215

Ft. Lauderdale

★10130★ **Dangerous Ideas, Inc.**
2416 Wilton Dr.
Ft. Lauderdale, FL 33305
Phone: (305)753-2969

Key West

★10131★ **Key West Island Books**
513 Fleming St.
Key West, FL 33040
Phone: (305)294-2904
Description: New and used books of gay and lesbian interest.

Miami

★10132★ **Lambda Passages**
7545 Biscayne Blvd.
Miami, FL 33138
Phone: (305)754-6900

Pensacola

★10133★ **Silver Chord**
615 Stafford Ln.
Pensacola, FL 32507
Phone: (904)453-6652
Description: Feminist bookstore.

St. Petersburg

★10134★ **Brigit Books**
3434 4th St. N, No. 5
St. Petersburg, FL 33704
Phone: (813)522-5775
Description: Feminist bookstore, gifts, cards.

★10135★ **MCC Bookstore (4)**
4825 9th Ave. N.
St. Petersburg, FL 33713

Tallahassee

★10136★ **Rubyfruit Books**
666-4 W. Tennessee St.
Tallahassee, FL 32304
Phone: (904)222-2627
Description: Alternative bookstore with feminist titles.

Tampa

★10137★ **Three Birds Bookstore and Coffee Room**
1518 7th Ave.
Tampa, FL 33605
Phone: (813)247-7041

★10138★ **Tomes and Treasures**
202 S. Howard Ave.
Tampa, FL 33606
Phone: (813)251-9368
Description: Gay/lesbian bookstore.

West Palm Beach

★10139★ **Back Door Bookstore**
6507 S. Dixie Hwy.
West Palm Beach, FL 33405
Phone: (407)582-6553
Toll-free: 800-354-3822
Description: Lesbian/gay literature and videos, gifts, recovery and new age items.

Georgia

Atlanta

★10140★ **Charis Books and More**
419 Moreland Ave. NE
Atlanta, GA 30307
Phone: (404)524-0304
Description: Feminist bookstore.

Hawaii

Honolulu

★10141★ **Laughing Goddess Wymyn's Bookstore**
1020 Keeaumoko, #303-A
Honolulu, HI 96822
Phone: (808)523-0906
Description: Women's books, cards, calendars, music, etc. Mail order address: 2002 Hunnewell St., Honolulu, HI 96822.

Illinois

Champaign

★10142★ **Jane Addams Books**
208 N. Neil
Champaign, IL 61820
Phone: (217)356-2555
Description: Antiquarian bookstore with women's/gay/lesbian/children's titles.

Chicago

★10143★ **Barbara's Bookshop**
330 N. Broadway
Chicago, IL 60657
Phone: (312)477-0411

★10144★ **People Like Us Books**
3321 N. Clark St.
Chicago, IL 60657
Phone: (312)248-6363
Description: Feminist bookstore.

★10145★ **Something Else Books**
2805 N Sheffield Ave.
Chicago, IL 60657
Phone: (312)549-0495

★10146★ **Women and Children First**
5233 N. Clark St.
Chicago, IL 60640
Phone: (312)769-9299
Women's bookstore. Also features videos and music.

Evanston

★10147★ **Platypus Book Shop**
606 Dempster St.
Evanston, IL 60202
Phone: (708)866-8040
Description: Feminist bookstore.

Oak Park

★10148★ **Barbara's Bookstore**
1110 W. Lake St.
Oak Park, IL 60301
Phone: (708)848-9140

Indiana

Bloomington

★10149★ **Aquarius Books Inc.**
116 N Grant St.
Bloomington, IN 47408
Phone: (812)336-0988
Description: Feminist bookstore.

Indianapolis

★10150★ **Dreams and Swords**
828 E. 64th St.
Indianapolis, IN 46220
Phone: (317)253-9966
Description: Feminist bookstore.

★10151★ **Works**
4120 N Keystone Ave.
Indianapolis, IN 46205

Kentucky

Louisville

★10152★ **Open Door Bookstore**
3434 Allison Way
Louisville, KY 40220
Phone: (502)452-1435
Description: Feminist bookstore.

Louisiana

Baton Rouge

★10153★ **Hibiscus Bookstore**
PO Box 44370
Baton Rouge, LA 70801
Phone: (504)387-4264

Metairie

★10154★ **Mystic Moon**
412 Jefferson Ave.
Metairie, LA 70005
Phone: (504)891-4266
Description: Women's bookstore.

New Orleans

★10155★ **Faubourg Marigny Bookstore**
600 Frenchmen St.
New Orleans, LA 70116
Phone: (504)943-9875
Description: Gay/lesbian and feminist books.

Maine

Portland

★10156★ **Cunningham and Co. Books**
188 State St.
Portland, ME 04102
Phone: (207)775-2246

West Rockport

★10157★ **New Leaf Books**
PO Box 159
West Rockport, ME 04865
Phone: (207)596-0040
Description: Feminist bookstore.

Maryland

Baltimore

★10158★ **Lambda Rising**
241 W. Chase St.
Baltimore, MD 21201
Phone: (410)234-0069
Description: Gay/lesbian and feminist titles; periodicals, gifts, jewelry, and videos.

★10159★ **Thirty-First St. Book Store**
425 E. 31st St.
Baltimore, MD 21218
Phone: (301)243-3131
Description: Women's and children's books.

Massachusetts

Amherst

★10160★ **Food for Thought Books**
106 N Pleasant St.
Amherst, MA 01002
Phone: (413)253-5432

Boston

★10161★ **Glad Day Books**
673 Boylston St., 2nd Fl.
Boston, MA 02116
Phone: (617)267-3010
Description: Gay/lesbian bookstore with videos, cards and novelties.

★10162★ **New Words Bookstore**
186 Hampshire St.
Boston, MA 02139
Phone: (617)876-5310
Description: Women's bookstore with lesbian titles.

★10163★ **Unicorn Books**
1210 Massachusetts Ave., Arlington
Boston, MA 02174
Phone: (617)646-3680
Description: Spiritual bookstore with gay/lesbian titles.

Cambridge

★10164★ **House of Sarah Books**
225 Hampshire St.
Cambridge, MA 02139
Phone: (617)547-3447
Description: Used bookstore specializing in rare and out-of-print women's books.

Haverhill

★10165★ **Radzukina's**
714 N. Broadway
Haverhill, MA 01832
Phone: (502)521-1333
Description: Womyn-made fine arts and crafts, books, jewelry, and music.

Jamaica Plain

★10166★ **Crone's Harvest**
761 Centre St.
Jamaica Plain, MA 02130
Phone: (617)983-9530
Description: Feminist bookstore.

Northampton

★10167★ **Lunaria**
90 King St.
Northampton, MA 01060
Phone: (413)586-7853
Description: Feminist books and music, new and used titles.

Pittsfield

★10168★ **Crystal Works**
301 N St.
Pittsfield, MA 01201
Phone: (413)442-5532
Description: Feminist bookstore.

Provincetown

★10169★ **Now Voyager**
357 Commercial St.
Provincetown, MA 02657
Phone: (508)487-3146
Description: Mystery and gay/lesbian bookstore.

★10170★ **Recovering Hearts Book and Gift Store**
4 Standish St.
Provincetown, MA 02657
Phone: (508)487-4875
Description: Feminist bookstore.

★10171★ **Womencrafts**
376 Commercial St.
Provincetown, MA 02657
Phone: (508)487-2501
Description: Offers feminist and lesbian/gay books; women's crafts, jewelry, cards, and T-shirts.

Michigan

Ann Arbor

★10172★ **Common Language**
214 S. 4th Ave.
Ann Arbor, MI 48104
Phone: (313)663-0036
Description: Feminist bookstore.

Ferndale

★10173★ **A Woman's Prerogative**
175 W. Nine Mile
Ferndale, MI 48220
Phone: (313)543-4769
Description: Feminist bookstore.

Grand Rapids

★10174★ **Haven Book Club**
PO Box 1668
Grand Rapids, MI 49501
Description: Mail order store.

★10175★ **Sons & Daughters**
962 Cherry St. SE
Grand Rapids, MI 49506
Phone: (616)459-8877

Haslett

★10176★ **Room of Our Own**
PO Box 129
1486 Haslett Rd.
Haslett, MI 45840
Phone: (517)339-0270
Description: Feminist bookstore.

Kalamazoo

★10177★ **Hidden Room Book Shoppe**
7018 W. H Ave.
Kalamazoo, MI 49009
Phone: (616)375-9398

★10178★ **Pandora Books for Open Minds**
226 Lovell St.
Kalamazoo, MI 49007
Phone: (616)388-5656
Description: Feminist, lesbian, and gay men's books and music and children's books.

Royal Oak

★10179★ **Chosen Books**
120 W. 4th St.
Royal Oak, MI 48067
Phone: (313)864-0485
Description: Gay/lesbian bookstore.

Southfield

★10180★ **Sons and Daughters Bookstore**
30715 Southfield Rd.
Southfield, MI 48076
Phone: (313)645-2210

Minnesota

Mankato

★10181★ **Half the Sky Bookstore**
417 Byron St.
Mankato, MN 56001
Phone: (507)345-5790
Description: Feminist bookstore.

★10182★ **Our Mother's Gardens Books**
417 Byron St.
Mankato, MN 56001
Phone: (507)345-5790

Minneapolis

★10183★ **Amazon Book Store**
1612 Harmon Pl.
Minneapolis, MN 55403
Phone: (612)338-6560
Description: Women's bookstore, jewelry, music and videos.

★10184★ **A Brothers Touch**
2327 Hennepin
Minneapolis, MN 55405
Phone: (612)377-6279
Description: Lesbian periodicals.

St Paul

★10185★ **Minnesota Women's Press Bookstore**
771 Raymond
St Paul, MN 55114
Phone: (612)646-3968
Description: Feminist bookstore.

Winona

★10186★ **Women's Resource Center**
77 E. 5th St.
Winona, MN 55987
Phone: (507)452-4440

Missouri

Harrisburg

★10187★ **Sunday Women's Bookstore**
12450 N Rte. E.
Harrisburg, MO 65256
Phone: (314)874-5969
Description: Feminist bookstore.

Kansas City

★10188★ **Phoenix Books**
6 W. 39th St.
Kansas City, MO 64111
Phone: (816)931-5794
Description: Gay/lesbian bookstore, music, jewelry and crystals.

St. Louis

★10189★ **Left Bank Books**
399 N. Euclid Ave.
St. Louis, MO 63108
Phone: (314)367-6731
Description: Women's/gay titles, records, tapes.

★10190★ **Our World Too**
11 S. Vandeventer
St. Louis, MO 63108
Phone: (314)533-5322
Description: Gay/lesbian titles, gifts, jewelry and art.

Springfield

★10191★ **Renaissance Books and Gifts**
1337 E. Montclair
Springfield, MO 65804
Phone: (417)883-5161
Description: Women's music, jewelry, books and new age materials.

Montana

Billings

★10192★ **Barjon's**
2718 Third Ave.
Billings, MT 59101
Phone: (406)252-4398

Nebraska

Lincoln

★10193★ **Arbor Moon**
440 S. 44th St.
Lincoln, NE 68510
Phone: (402)489-4634
Description: Feminist bookstore.

Nevada

Las Vegas

★10194★ **Bright Pink Literature**
4637 Paradise Rd.
Las Vegas, NV 89109
Phone: (702)737-7780
Description: Gay/lesbian bookstore.

Reno

★10195★ **Grapevine Books**
290 California Ave.
Reno, NV 89509
Phone: (702)786-4869
Description: Feminist bookstore.

New Hampshire

Hopkinton

★10196★ **Women's Words Books**
RR 4, Box 322 Straw Rd.
Hopkinton, NH 03229
Phone: (603)228-8000
Description: Feminist bookstore.

New Jersey

Englewood

★10197★ **Pandora Book Peddlers**
68 W. Palisade Ave
Englewood, NJ 07631
Phone: (201)894-5404
Description: Feminist bookstore and book club.

Merchantville

★10198★ **WelWoman's Books**
135 Park Ave.
Merchantville, NJ 08109
Phone: (609)663-3782
Description: Feminist bookstore.

New Mexico

Albuquerque

★10199★ **Full Circle Books**
2205 Silver SE
Albuquerque, NM 87106
Phone: (505)266-0022
Description: Women's bookstore.

★10200★ **Sisters and Brothers Bookstore**
PO Box 8768
Albuquerque, NM 87198
Phone: (505)266-7317

Santa Fe

★10201★ **Downtown Subscription**
376 Garcia St.
Santa Fe, NM 87501
Phone: (505)983-3085
Description: Gay/lesbian periodicals.

★10202★ **Galisteo News**
201 Galisteo St.
Santa Fe, NM 87501
Phone: (505)984-1316
Description: Gay/lesbian periodicals.

New York

Albany

★10203★ Boulevard Bookstore
15 Central Ave.
Albany, NY 12210
Phone: (518)436-8848

Glens Falls

★10204★ Lavender Jade's
Box 3308
Glens Falls, NY 12801
Phone: (518)798-3304

Ithaca

★10205★ Borealis Bookstore
113 N. Aurora St.
Ithaca, NY 14850
Phone: (607)272-7752
Description: Large selection of lesbian titles.

★10206★ Smedley's Bookshop
307 W. State St.
Ithaca, NY 14850
Phone: (607)273-2325
Description: Women's books, music and jewelry, community board.

Kingston

★10207★ Author, Author for the Serious
Reader
89 Broadway Roundout
Kingston, NY 12401
Phone: (914)339-1883

New York

★10208★ Alternatives Corner Bookstore
Women's Alternative Community Center
669 Woodfield Rd.
Long Island
New York, NY 11746
Phone: (516)483-2050
Description: Gay/lesbian and feminist books.

★10209★ Black Books Plus
702 Amsterdam Ave.
New York, NY 10025
Phone: (212)749-9632

★10210★ A Different Light
548 Hudson St.
New York, NY 10014
Phone: (212)989-4850
Description: Gay/lesbian bookstore.

★10211★ Judith's Room
681 Washington St.
New York, NY 10014
Phone: (212)727-7330
Description: Women's bookstore.

★10212★ MosaicBooks
167 Ave. B
New York, NY 10009
Phone: (212)475-8623

★10213★ Oscar Wilde Memorial Bookshop
15 Christopher St.
New York, NY 10014
Phone: (212)255-8097
Description: Lesbian and gay titles.

★10214★ Womankind Books
5 Kivy St., Huntington Sta.
Long Island
New York, NY 11746
Phone: (516)427-1289
Description: Large selection of lesbian titles, music and jewelry. Free mail order catalog.

Rochester

★10215★ Silkwood Books
633 Monroe Ave.
Rochester, NY 14607
Phone: (716)473-8110
Description: Women's bookstore.

★10216★ Wild Seeds Bookstore and Cafe
704 University Ave.
Rochester, NY 14607
Phone: (716)244-9310
Description: Gay/lesbian bookstore.

Schenectady

★10217★ Open Door Bookstore
136 Jay St.
Schenectady, NY 12305
Phone: (518)346-2719

South Fallsburg

★10218★ The Gallery
PO Box 94
South Fallsburg, NY 12779
Phone: (914)446-4674

Syracuse

★10219★ My Sister's Words
304 N. McBride St.
Syracuse, NY 13203
Phone: (315)428-0227
Description: Women's bookstore and bulletin board.

North Carolina

Asheville

★10220★ Malaprop's Bookstore/Cafe
61 Haywood St.
Asheville, NC 28801
Phone: (704)254-6734

Chapel Hill

★10221★ Orange County Women's Center
Women's Book Exchange
Henderson St.
Chapel Hill, NC 27514
Phone: (919)968-4610
Description: Membership, lending library.

Charlotte

★10222★ Baker and Taylor Books
5 LakePoint Plaza, Ste. 500
2709 Water Ridge Pkwy.
Charlotte, NC 28217
Phone: (201)218-0400
Fax: (201)722-7420
Description: Distributes to schools, academic libraries, booksellers and the general public. Features a strong women's studies collection.

★10223★ Rising Moon Books and Beyond
316 E. Blvd.
Charlotte, NC 28203
Phone: (704)332-7473
Description: Feminist bookstore.

Durham

★10224★ Ladyslipper
602 W. Chapel Hill St.
Durham, NC
Phone: (919)683-1570
Description: Women's music and videos.

★10225★ Regulator Bookstore
720 9th St.
Durham, NC 27705
Phone: (919)286-2700

★10226★ South of the Garden Books
PO Box 7725
Durham, NC 27708
Phone: (919)687-0408
Description: Mail order store.

★10227★ Southern Sisters
411 Morris St.
Durham, NC 27701
Phone: (919)682-0739
Description: Feminist bookstore, crafts and jewelry.

Greensboro

★10228★ White Rabbit Books
1833 Spring Garden St.
Greensboro, NC 27403
Phone: (919)272-7604
Description: Gay/lesbian bookstore, women's music.

Raleigh

★10229★ White Rabbit Books (Raleigh)
309 W Martin St.
Raleigh, NC 27601
Phone: (919)956-1429

Wilmington

★10230★ Doorways for Wimmin
105 Kenwood Ave.
Wilmington, NC 28405
Description: Feminist bookstore.

North Dakota

Fargo

★10231★ Food for Thought
314 10th St. N.
Fargo, ND 58102
Phone: (218)236-5434
Description: Feminist bookstore.

Ohio

Cincinnati

★10232★ Crazy Ladies Bookstore
4039 Hamilton Ave.
Cincinnati, OH 45223
Phone: (513)541-4198
Description: Women's bookstore.

Cleveland

★10233★ Six Steps Down
1921 W. 25th St.
Cleveland, OH 44113
Phone: (216)566-8897
Description: Women's records, tapes, and books.

Cleveland Heights

★10234★ Gifts of Athena
2199 Lee Rd.
Cleveland Heights, OH 44118
Phone: (216)371-1937
Description: Women's bookstore.

Columbiana

★10235★ For Women Only
4471 Signal Rd.
Columbiana, OH 44408
Description: Mail order store.

Columbus

★10236★ Fan the Flame
65 S. 4th St.
Columbus, OH 43215
Phone: (614)291-7756
Description: Books, music and cards for lesbians, feminists, and women of color.

★10237★ Our Voices
21 E Lincoln St.
Columbus, OH 43215
Phone: (614)221-9424
Description: Feminist bookstore.

Loveland

★10238★ Grailville Art and Book Shop
932 O'Bannonville Rd.
Loveland, OH 45140
Phone: (513)541-4198
Description: Specializes in books about women, spirituality, empowerment, and global perspectives.

Oklahoma

Oklahoma City

★10239★ Herland Sister Resources, Inc.
2312 NW 39th St.
Oklahoma City, OK 73112
Phone: (405)521-9696
Description: Women's bookstore.

Oregon

Corvallis

★10240★ Grass Roots Bookstore
227 S.W. 2nd St.
Corvallis, OR
Phone: (503)754-7668
Description: Alternative lifestyle/women's books.

Eugene

★10241★ Mother Kali's Bookstore
2001 Franklin Blvd.
Eugene, OR 97403
Phone: (503)343-4864
Description: Lesbian, feminist and women of color books, music, and jewelry.

★10242★ Peralandra Books and Music
1016 Willamette St.
Eugene, OR 97401
Phone: (503)485-4848
Description: Lesbian and feminist books.

La Grande

★10243★ Sunflower Books Etc.
1114 Washington St.
La Grande, OR 97850

Newport

★10244★ Woman's View Bookstore
PO Box 28
1001 SW Hurbert St.
Newport, OR 97365
Phone: (503)265-7721
Description: Feminist bookstore.

Portland

★10245★ Blue Earth
8215 SE 13th Ave.
Portland, OR 97202
Phone: (503)234-2224

★10246★ Ladd's Editions
1864 SE Hawthorne Blvd.
Portland, OR 97214
Phone: (503)236-4628

★10247★ A Woman's Place Bookstore
1431 N.E. Broadway
Portland, OR
Phone: (503)284-1110
Description: Feminist books, music, jewelry, crafts and women's information center.

Pennsylvania

Lancaster

★10248★ The Closet
25 N. Prince St.
Lancaster, PA 17603
Phone: (717)399-8818
Description: Gay/lesbian bookstore featuring buttons, books, t-shirts, jewelry.

Lewisburg

★10249★ Dwelling Place
200 Market St.
Lewisburg, PA 17837
Phone: (717)523-7878
Description: Feminist bookstore.

Narberth

★10250★ Earthworks Quality Handmade Gifts
227 Haverford Ave.
Narberth, PA 19072
Phone: (215)667-1143

New Hope

★10251★ Book Gallery
19 W Mechanic St.
New Hope, PA 18938
Phone: (215)862-5110
Description: Feminist bookstore.

Philadelphia

★10252★ Giovanni's Room
345 S. 12th St.
Philadelphia, PA 19107
Phone: (215)923-2960
Toll-free: 800-222-6996
Description: Gay/lesbian bookstore.

★10253★ Girlfriends Bookstore
1540 South St.
Philadelphia, PA 19072
Phone: (215)424-6422

Pittsburgh

★10254★ Gertrude Stein Memorial Bookshop
1003 E. Carson St.
Pittsburgh, PA 15203
Phone: (412)481-9666
Description: Women's bookstore.

★10255★ Saint Elmo's
2214 E Carson
Pittsburgh, PA 15203
Phone: (412)431-9100

Springfield

★10256★ Step-by-Step Books
PO Box 387
Springfield, PA 19064
Phone: (215)622-2492
Description: Mail order women's books. Specialists in 12-step recovery literature.

★10257★ Womanvision Books, Inc.
PO Box 387
Springfield, PA 19064
Phone: (215)622-2492
Description: Mail order store.

Rhode Island

Providence

★10258★ Barbara Walzer Books
PO Box 2536
Providence, RI 02906
Phone: (401)785-2277
Description: Old and rare books relating to women's history.

★10259★ Dorrwar Bookstore
312 Wickenden
Providence, RI 02906
Phone: (401)521-3230

★10260★ Visions and Voices
255 Harris Ave.
Providence, RI 02909
Phone: (401)273-9757
Description: Gay/lesbian/feminist bookstore.

South Carolina

Columbia

★10261★ Bluestocking Books
829 Gervals St.
Columbia, SC 29201
Phone: (803)929-0114
Description: Feminist bookstore.

Tennessee

Memphis

★10262★ Meristom
930 S Cooper St.
Memphis, TN 38104
Phone: (901)276-0282
Description: Feminist bookstore.

★10263★ Solutions A Recovery Bookstore
3145 Poplar
Memphis, TN 38111
Phone: (901)452-1999

Nashville

★10264★ The Book Oasis: Books and More for Women
2824 Dogwood Pl.
Nashville, TN 37209
Phone: (615)292-7100
Description: Women's bookstore.

Thompsons Ste

★10265★ It's A Scream
4616 Old Harpeth Paytonsville
Thompsons Ste, TN 37179
Phone: (615)244-7346

Texas

Austin

★10266★ Book Connections
PO Box 9700
Austin, TX 78766
Description: Mail order store.

★10267★ Book Woman
324 E. 6th
Austin, TX 78701
Phone: (512)472-2785
Description: Women's bookstore, cards, jewelry, music.

★10268★ Celebration
108 W. 43rd
Austin, TX 78751
Phone: (512)453-6207
Description: Women's earth magic store; jewelry, cards, music, books, oils.

★10269★ Congress Avenue Booksellers
718 Congress Ave.
Austin, TX 78701
Phone: (512)478-1157
Description: Gay/lesbian titles.

★10270★ Liberty Books
1014-B N. Lamar Blvd.
Austin, TX 78703
Phone: (512)495-9737
Description: Gay/lesbian titles, cards, periodicals.

Dallas

★10271★ Crossroads Market
3930 Cedar Springs Rd.
Dallas, TX 75219
Phone: (214)521-8919

★10272★ Curious Times
4008-D Cedar Springs Rd.
Dallas, TX 75219
Phone: (214)528-4087
Description: Gay/lesbian bookstore, cards and gifts, jewelry and music.

Danton

★10273★ Athena's Attic
108 Austin St.
Danton, TX 76201
Phone: (817)565-9755
Description: Feminist bookstore.

El Paso

★10274★ E & J Books and More
827 Pueblo
El Paso, TX 79903
Phone: (915)564-0524

Houston

★10275★ Inklings
1846 Richmond
Houston, TX 77090
Phone: (713)521-3369
Description: Women's bookstore.

Lubbock

★10276★ Ellie's Garden: Women's Books and More
2812 34th St.
Lubbock, TX 79410
Phone: (806)796-0880
Description: Feminist bookstore.

San Angelo

★10277★ Books Etc.
2410 W. Ave. N.
San Angelo, TX 76904
Phone: (915)942-1544

Utah

Salt Lake City

★10278★ Rhino Nest
235 W. 400 S.
Salt Lake City, UT 84101
Phone: (801)532-1555
Description: Feminist bookstore.

★10279★ A Woman's Place Bookstore
Foothill Village, Ste. 240
Salt Lake City, UT 84108
Phone: (801)583-6431
Description: Women, lesbian, feminist titles; art, jewelry.

Vermont

Brattleboro

★10280★ Everyone's Books
71 Elliott St
Brattleboro, VT 05301
Phone: (802)254-8160

Virginia

Annandale

★10281★ Womanstuff
7306 Maple Pl.
Annandale, VA 22003
Phone: (703)256-8383
Description: Feminist bookstore.

Newport News

★10282★ Out of the Dark
530 Randolph Rd.
Newport News, VA 23601
Phone: (804)596-6220

Description: Women's bookstore; goddess worship.

Norfolk

★10283★ Max Images
537 W 21st St
Norfolk, VA 23517

Richmond

★10284★ Richmond Womensbooks
2132 W. Main St.
Richmond, VA 23220
Phone: (804)788-1607

Description: Women's books.

Virginia Beach

★10285★ OutRight Books
485 S Independence Blvd #110
Virginia Beach, VA 23452
Phone: (804)490-6658

Washington

Seattle

★10286★ Beyond The Closet Bookstore
1501 Belmont Ave.
Seattle, WA 98122
Phone: (206)322-4609

★10287★ Red & Black Books
432-15th Ave. E.
Seattle, WA 98117
Phone: (206)322-7323

Tacoma

★10288★ Imprints Bookstore and Gallery
917 N. 2nd
Tacoma, WA 98403
Phone: (206)383-6322

Description: Lesbian, women's, feminist books; cards and jewelry. Mail order catalog available.

Wisconsin

Beloit

★10289★ A Different World Bookstore
414 E. Grand Ave.
Beloit, WI 53511
Phone: (608)365-1000

Description: Women's and children's books.

Madison

★10290★ A Room of One's Own
317 W. Johnson St.
Madison, WI 53703
Phone: (608)257-7888

Description: Women's books and music.

Milwaukee

★10291★ Peoples Books
1808 N. Farwell Ave.
Milwaukee, WI 53202
Phone: (414)272-1232

**★10292★ Planned Parenthood of
  Wisconsin**
**Maurice Ritz Resource Library and
  Bookstore**
302 N. Jackson St.
Milwaukee, WI 53202
Phone: (414)271-7930
Fax: (414)271-1935

Description: Family planning, reproductive health, sexuality education, contraception, obstetrics/gynecology nursing education, and population materials.

Waterloo

★10293★ The Untamed Shrew Books
N7609 Airport Rd.
Waterloo, WI 53594
Phone: (414)478-3644

Description: Specializes in rare and out-of-print books by and about women.

(25) Videos

Entries in this chapter are arranged alphabetically by video title. See the User's Guide at the front of this directory for additional information.

★10294★ The ABC's of Breastfeeding
Lifecircle
2378 Cornell Dr.
Costa Mesa, CA 92626
Phone: (714)546-1427

1987. **Description:** Shows techniques that will help the new nursing mother. Covers latch-on, positioning, storing milk, breast care and nighttime nursing. **Length:** 30 mins. **Acquisition:** Rent/Purchase.

★10295★ Abdominal Hysterectomy
Milner-Fenwick, Inc.
2125 Greenspring Dr.
Timonium, MD 21093
Phone: (301)252-1700

1988. **Description:** The steps involved in an abdominal hysterectomy are shown here as an aid to women who are unsure about the nature of the operation. **Length:** 12 mins. **Format:** Beta, VHS, 3/4″ U-matic. **Acquisition:** Purchase.

★10296★ Abortion in Adolescence
Emory Medical Television Network
Emory University
1440 Clifton Rd. NE, Dept. C
Atlanta, GA 30322
Phone: (404)727-5817

1983. **Description:** A discussion of the Center for Disease Control's statistics on teenage pregnancies and abortions in the United States. **Length:** 58 mins. **Format:** Beta, VHS, 3/4″ U-matic. **Acquisition:** Rent/Lease, Purchase, Subscription.

★10297★ Abortion Clinic
Fanlight Productions
47 Halifax St.
Boston, MA 02130
Phone: (617)524-0980

1989. **Description:** This program, from the PBS series Frontline, explores the painful and complex decisions faced by four young women with unwanted pregnancies. The video presents both the pro-life and pro-choice viewpoints. **Length:** 52 mins. **Format:** Beta, VHS, 3/4″ U-matic. **Acquisition:** Rent/Lease, Purchase.

★10298★ Abortion: The Divisive Issue
Video Free America
442 Shotwell
San Francisco, CA 94110
Phone: (415)648-9040

Description: The pros and cons of abortion are discussed in interviews with leaders from both sides including the President of National Right to Life and the President of National Abortion Rights Action League. **Length:** 28 mins. **Format:** 3/4″ U-matic, Other than listed. **Acquisition:** Rent/Lease, Purchase.

★10299★ Abortion: Stories from North and South
National Film Board of Canada
1251 Avenue of the Americas, 16th Fl.
New York, NY 10020-1173
Phone: (212)586-5131

1989. **Description:** An examination into the world wide practice of abortion and the degree it has crossed religious, social, racial, and cultural boundaries. **Length:** 55 mins. **Format:** Beta, VHS, 3/4″ U-matic. **Acquisition:** Rent/Lease, Purchase.

★10300★ Abuse
American Journal of Nursing Company
Educational Services Division
555 West 57th Street
New York, NY 10019
Phone: (212)582-8820

1983. **Description:** This tape is part of a series on home care and discusses a nurse's reaction to a wife who claims to have been beaten by her husband. **Length:** 36 mins. **Format:** 3/4″ U-matic, Other than listed. **Acquisition:** Rent/Lease, Purchase.

★10301★ Acquaintance Rape Prevention
Great Plains National Instructional Television Library (GPN)
University of Nebraska at Lincoln
PO Box 80669
Lincoln, NE 68501-0669
Phone: (402)472-2007

1981. **Description:** A series which shows what can be done to help prevent this violence committed against classmates, dates, and even casual friends. **Length:** 30 mins. **Format:** Beta, VHS, 3/4″ U-matic, Other than listed. **Acquisition:** Rent/Lease, Purchase.

★10302★ Acting Our Age
Direct Cinema Limited, Inc.
Box 69799
Los Angeles, CA 90069
Phone: (213)652-8000

1987. **Description:** Elderly women talk candidly about such subjects as sexuality, loneliness, financial difficulties, dealing with death and growing old in America. **Length:** 58 mins. **Format:** Beta, VHS, 3/4″ U-matic. **Acquisition:** Purchase, Rent/Lease.

★10303★ After Childbirth: The Post-Partum Experience—Revised
Professional Research, Inc.
930 Pitner Ave.
Evanston, IL 60202
Phone: (708)328-6700

1987. **Description:** A look at the physical and emotional adjustments mothers must make immediately after birth. **Length:** 14 mins. **Format:** Beta, VHS, 3/4″ U-matic. **Acquisition:** Rent/Lease, Purchase.

★10304★ After Your Mastectomy
Professional Research, Inc.
930 Pitner Ave.
Evanston, IL 60202
Phone: (708)328-6700

1989. **Description:** A look at the emotional traumas women who have had a mastectomy are apt to go through. **Length:** 9 mins. **Format:** Beta, VHS, 3/4″ U-matic. **Acquisition:** Purchase, Rent/Lease.

★10305★ Ain't Nobody's Business
New Orleans Video Access Center
2010 Magazine St.
New Orleans, LA 70130
Phone: (504)524-8626

Description: Battered women express the agony of sharing life with men who constantly beat them. **Length:** 21 mins. **Format:** Beta, VHS, 1/2″ reel, 3/4″ U-matic, Other than listed. **Acquisition:** Rent/Lease, Purchase.

★10306★ All of Our Lives
Film Library
3450 Wilshire Blvd., No. 700
Los Angeles, CA 90010-2215
Phone: (213)384-8114

1984. **Description:** A celebration of elderly women who have achieved much despite their situation, banding together to fight for senior citizen's rights. **Length:** 29 mins. **Format:** Beta, VHS, 3/4″ U-matic. **Acquisition:** Rent/Lease, Purchase.

★10307★ Alternative Conceptions
Women Make Movies
225 Lafayette St., Ste. 212
New York, NY 10012
Phone: (212)925-0606

1985. **Description:** The controversy surrounding artificial insemination for lesbians is examined. **Length:** 35 mins. **Format:** Beta, VHS, 3/4″ U-matic. **Acquisition:** Purchase, Rent/Lease.

★10308★ The American Parade: We the Women
Phoenix/BFA Films
468 Park Ave., S.
New York, NY 10016
Phone: (212)684-5910

1974. **Description:** Narrated by Mary Tyler Moore, the program traces the history of the women's movement. **Length:** 30 mins. **Format:** Beta, VHS, 3/4″ U-matic. **Acquisition:** Purchase.

★10309★ And Baby Makes Two
PBS Video
1320 Braddock Pl.
Alexandria, VA 22314-1698
Phone: (703)739-5380

1982. **Description:** This program follows the lives of five single women who are raising their children alone. **Length:** 30 mins. **Format:** Beta, VHS, 3/4″ U-matic. **Acquisition:** Rent/Lease, Purchase, Duplication, Off-Air Record.

★10310★ ...And Everything Nice
Phoenix/BFA Films
468 Park Ave., S.
New York, NY 10016
Phone: (212)684-5910

1974. **Description:** The program shows the process of consciousness-raising (CR) during which women develop new expectations. In an actual CR group, Gloria Steinem and Shirley Chisholm provide insights. **Length:** 20 mins. **Format:** Beta, VHS, 3/4″ U-matic. **Acquisition:** Purchase.

★10311★ And What Does Your Mother Do?
Women Make Movies
225 Lafayette St., Ste. 212
New York, NY 10012
Phone: (212)925-0606

1983. **Description:** Lively salsa music accompanies this look at women's work in the home. **Length:** 20 mins. **Format:** Beta, VHS, 3/4″ U-matic. **Acquisition:** Purchase, Rent/Lease.

★10312★ Anorexia Nervosa
Professional Research, Inc.
930 Pitner Ave.
Evanston, IL 60202
Phone: (708)328-6700

1988. **Description:** Different aspects of this particular eating disorder are examined. **Length:** 10 mins. **Format:** Beta, VHS, 3/4″ U-matic. **Acquisition:** Purchase, Rent/Lease.

★10313★ Another Look at Cesarean
Lifecircle
2378 Cornell Dr.
Costa Mesa, CA 92626
Phone: (714)546-1427

1989. **Description:** Covers the indications for a Cesarean as well as ultrasound, amniocentesis, and fetal monitoring. **Length:** 28 mins. **Acquisition:** Rent/Purchase.

★10314★ Are You Listening?
Martha Stuart Communications, Inc.
PO Box 246
Hillsdale, NY 12529
Phone: (518)325-3900

197?. **Description:** This program series is an in-depth look at women in all phases, positions and stages in life. Each program concerns itself with women's role and function in the structures of society. Programs are available individually. **Length:** 28 mins. **Format:** 3/4″ U-matic, 2″ Quad. **Acquisition:** Rent/Lease, Purchase.

★10315★ The Art of Self Defense for Women
Kartes Video Communications (KVC)
7225 Woodland Dr.
PO Box 68881
Indianapolis, IN 46268-0881
Phone: (317)297-1888

1990. **Description:** Third-degree black belt Robin Cooper shows women a number of strategies and defenses to use in confrontational situations. This course conncentrates on improving your attitude and inner strength as well as practicing simple moves alone, or with a partner. **Length:** 90 mins. **Format:** VHS. **Acquisition:** Purchase.

★10316★ The Artist was a Woman
MTI Teleprograms, Inc.
108 Wilmot Rd.
Deerfield, IL 60015-9990
Phone: (708)940-1260

1981. **Description:** The achievements of women artists in Europe and America from the late Renaissance to the early 20th century are chronicled. Interviews with Ann Sutherland Harris and Linda Nochlin of the Los Angeles County Museum are included. **Length:** 58 mins. **Format:** Beta, VHS, 3/4″ U-matic. **Acquisition:** Purchase.

★10317★ Asians Now: International Women's Day
Chinese for Affirmative Action
17 Walter U. Lum Pl.
San Fransisco, CA 94108
Phone: (415)274-6750

1975. **Description:** Discusses the significance of International Women's Day for Chinese women. Two Asian women express the difficulties they encounter being a worker and a wife. **Length:** 30 mins. **Format:** EJ. **Acquisition:** Loan.

★10318★ Assertiveness for Women in Health Care
Marshfield Regional Video Network
1000 N. Oak Ave.
Marshfield, WI 54449-5777
Phone: (715)387-5127

1979. **Description:** This program is a candid look at the women working in the health field.

Length: 46 mins. **Format:** Beta, VHS, 3/4″ U-matic. **Acquisition:** Rent/Lease, Purchase.

★10319★ Assignment: Life
Jeremiah Films
PO Box 1710
Hemet, CA 92343
Phone: (714)652-1006

198?. **Description:** Noted journalist Ann Sommers presents a report on the abortion controversy in America through interviews, live births, and live abortions. **Length:** 52 mins. **Format:** VHS. **Acquisition:** Purchase.

★10320★ At the Houston Women's Conference
Martha Stuart Communications, Inc.
PO Box 246
Hillsdale, NY 12529
Phone: (518)325-3900

1977. **Description:** Participants active in women's issues discuss the media's impact on the women's movement. **Length:** 29 mins. **Format:** 3/4″ U-matic, 2″ Quad. **Acquisition:** Rent/Lease, Purchase.

★10321★ Attention: Women at Work!
National Film Board of Canada
1251 Avenue of the Americas, 16th Fl.
New York, NY 10020-1173
Phone: (212)586-5131

1989. **Description:** A documentary which focuses on women in non-traditional jobs, such as hovercraft pilot and construction worker. **Length:** 29 mins. **Format:** Beta, VHS, 3/4″ U-matic. **Acquisition:** Purchase, Rent/Lease.

★10322★ Babies and Special Consideration
Lifecircle
2378 Cornell Dr.
Costa Mesa, CA 92626
Phone: (714)546-1427

1986. **Description:** Shows the care of the newborn in the delivery room and nursery along with the characteristics of the newborn and the physical exam. The program also discusses jaundice, circumcision, PKU, and basic infant care. **Length:** 33 mins. **Acquisition:** Rent/Purchase.

★10323★ Baby Basics
Great Plains National Instructional Television Library (GPN)
University of Nebraska at Lincoln
Post Office Box 80669
Lincoln, NE 68501-0669
Phone: (402)472-2007

1989. **Description:** This video has eight chapters and provides parents-to-be with instructions on how to care for an infant. **Length:** 110 mins. **Format:** Beta, VHS, 3/4″ U-matic. **Acquisition:** Rent/Lease, Duplication License.

★10324★ Baby Booming
Pyramid Film & Video
Box 1048
2801 Colorado Ave.
Santa Monica, CA 90406
Phone: (310)828-7577

1989. **Description:** The transformations that take place in a pregnant woman's body are displayed. **Length:** 2 mins. **Format:** Beta, VHS,

3/4″ U-matic. **Acquisition:** Purchase, Rent/Lease.

★10325★ **Baby Care**
Lifecircle
2378 Cornell Dr.
Costa Mesa, CA 92626
Phone: (714)546-1427

1986. **Description:** Demonstrates the basic skills needed by new parents during the first month. Topics include infant holds, cord and circumcision care, diapering, sponge and tub baths, dressing, needed supplies and safety. **Length:** 28 mins. **Acquisition:** Rent/Purchase.

★10326★ **Baby Clock**
Centre Productions, Inc.
1800 30th St., Ste. 207
Boulder, CO 80301
Phone: (303)444-1166

1988. **Description:** This film takes a sensitive look at the lives of five career women who must face the issues as their biological clocks continue to tick. **Length:** 30 mins. **Format:** Beta, VHS, 3/4″ U-matic. **Acquisition:** Purchase.

★10327★ **Back Inside Herself**
Women Make Movies
225 Lafayette St., Ste. 212
New York, NY 10012
Phone: (212)925-0606

1984. **Description:** This poetic film urges black women to reject imposed notions and create their own identities. **Length:** 5 mins. **Format:** Beta, VHS, 3/4″ U-matic. **Acquisition:** Purchase, Rent/Lease.

★10328★ **Battered**
Ambrose Video Publishing
1290 Avenue of the Americas, Ste.2245
New York, NY 10104
Phone: (212)696-4545

198?. **Description:** A documentary on the problem of domestic violence, focusing on women who have been abused by husbands or boyfriends. Includes interviews with offenders now in treatment. **Length:** 56 mins. **Format:** VHS, 3/4″ U-matic. **Acquisition:** Purchase, Duplication.

★10329★ **Battered Wives, Shattered Lives**
New Jersey Network
1573 Parkside Ave.
Trenton, NJ 08625
Phone: (609)292-5252

1984. **Description:** An analysis of this common form of domestic violence and the motivation behind it. **Length:** 90 mins. **Format:** VHS, 3/4″ U-matic. **Acquisition:** Purchase.

★10330★ **The Battered Woman**
Maryland Center for Public Broadcasting
11767 Bonita Ave.
Owings Mills, MD 21117
Phone: (301)356-5600

197?. **Description:** Insight to the crime of wife-beating with interviews with battered women. A psychiatrist, lawyer, judge, and hospital administrator discuss the problem at different levels in our society. **Length:** 60 mins. **Format:** Beta, VHS, 3/4″ U-matic. **Acquisition:** Rent/Lease, Purchase.

★10331★ **The Battered Woman Syndrome**
Marshfield Regional Video Network
1000 N. Oak Ave.
Marshfield, WI 54449-5777
Phone: (715)387-5127

1982. **Description:** This tape looks at incidence, police involvement, traditional social role, relationships, abusers, abused and the impact on the children in cases of domestic violence. **Length:** 40 mins. **Format:** Beta, VHS, 3/4″ U-matic. **Acquisition:** Rent/Lease, Purchase.

★10332★ **Battered Women**
Maryland Center for Public Broadcasting
11767 Bonita Ave.
Owings Mills, MD 21117
Phone: (301)356-5600

1979. **Description:** Documentary focusing on the problem of domestic violece in America. Included is testimony from battered women, psychologists and law enforcement officials. **Length:** 30 mins. **Format:** Beta, VHS, 3/4″ U-matic. **Acquisition:** Rent/Lease, Purchase.

★10333★ **Battered Women: Violence Behind Closed Doors**
MTI Teleprograms, Inc.
108 Wilmot Rd.
Deerfield, IL 60015-9990
Phone: (708)940-1260

1977. **Description:** A look at the causes for wife battering, and how many women come to accept it. **Length:** 24 mins. **Format:** Beta, VHS, 3/4″ U-matic. **Acquisition:** Rent/Lease, Purchase.

★10334★ **The Beauty Queens**
Public Media Video
5547 N. Ravenswood Ave.
Chicago, IL 60640
Phone: (312)878-2600

1989. **Description:** A documentary series examining three women who helped shape the beauty industry. The first tape tells the history of Helena Rubinstein's rise from poverty. The second tape discusses Elizabeth Arden and her introduction of the health-farm concept. The final tape shares the life of marketing genius Estee Lauder. **Length:** 60 mins. **Format:** VHS. **Acquisition:** Purchase.

★10335★ **Beginning Breastfeeding**
Polymorph Films
118 South St.
Boston, MA 02111
Phone: (617)542-2004

1986. **Description:** Mothers learn how to make the first nursing stages safe, effective and comfortable. **Length:** 23 mins. **Format:** Beta, VHS, 3/4″ U-matic. **Acquisition:** Rent/Lease, Purchase.

★10336★ **Behind the Veil: Nuns**
National Film Board of Canada
1251 Avenue of the Americas, 16th Fl.
New York, NY 10020-1173
Phone: (212)586-5131

1984. **Description:** An analogy is made between the invisibility of nuns in history, and the invisibility of women, whose achievements are minimally documented. **Length:** 130 mins. **Format:** Beta, VHS, 3/4″ U-matic. **Acquisition:** Purchase, Rent/Lease.

★10337★ **Belinda**
Appalshop Film & Video
306 Madison St.
Whitesburg, KY 41858
Phone: (606)633-0108
Fax: (606)633-1009

1992. **Description:** After becoming infected with the HIV virus, Belinda Mason became a powerful advocate for AIDS prevention, education, treatment, and human rights. **Length:** 40 minutes. **Acquisition:** Rent/Lease, Purchase.

★10338★ **Bella Abzug**
KPBS-TV15
San Diego State University
San Diego, CA 92182
Phone: (714)265-6415

1978. **Description:** Feminist leader Bella Abzug discusses her background and her view of the American women's movement. **Length:** 30 mins. **Format:** 3/4″ U-matic. **Acquisition:** Purchase.

★10339★ **The Best Time of My Life: Portraits of Women in Mid-Life**
National Film Board of Canada
1251 Avenue of the Americas, 16th Fl.
New York, NY 10020-1173
Phone: (212)586-5131

1987. **Description:** This film attempts to deal with the so called mid-life crisis by examining the lives of a group of women, ages 40-60, who feel they are experiencing the best period of their lives. **Length:** 59 mins. **Format:** Beta, VHS, 3/4″ U-matic. **Acquisition:** Rent/Lease, Purchase, Duplication.

★10340★ **A Better Way**
Daughters of Saint Paul
50 Saint Paul's Ave.
Jamaica Plain
Boston, MA 02130
Phone: (617)522-8911

1988. **Description:** Ways to deal with unwanted pregnancies are discussed. **Length:** 30 mins. **Format:** Beta, VHS, 3/4″ U-matic. **Acquisition:** Purchase.

★10341★ **Beware the Rapist**
Film Library
3450 Wilshire Blvd., No. 700
Los Angeles, CA 90010-2215
Phone: (213)384-8114

1977. **Description:** A dramatization of several incidents in which women ignored the fundamentals of rape protection. The film points out how each woman could have avoided the situation. **Length:** 20 mins. **Format:** VHS, 3/4″ U-matic. **Acquisition:** Rent/Lease.

★10342★ **Beyond Rape: Seeking an End to Sexual Assault**
Learning Corporation of America
108 Wilmot Rd.
Deerfield, IL 60015-9990
Phone: (708)940-1260

1984. **Description:** A look at preventing rape through precaution and an understanding of the motivations behind sexual violence. **Length:** 28 mins. **Format:** Beta, VHS, 3/4″ U-matic. **Acquisition:** Rent/Lease, Purchase.

★10343★ **The Biblical Role of Women**
Bob Jones University Press
Greenville, SC 29614
Phone: (803)242-5100

1985. **Description:** A program comparing the current roles of women and their ancient Biblical counterparts. **Length:** 29 mins. **Format:** Beta, VHS, 3/4″ U-matic. **Acquisition:** Purchase.

★10344★ **Biography of the Unborn**
Britannica Films
310 South Michigan Avenue
Chicago, IL 60604
Phone: (312)347-7958

1987. **Description:** Find out what's going on during the development of a fertilized egg. **Length:** 17 mins. **Format:** Beta, VHS, 3/4″ U-matic. **Acquisition:** Purchase, Trade-in.

★10345★ **Birth**
Milner-Fenwick, Inc.
2125 Greenspring Drive
Timonium, MD 21093
Phone: (301)252-1700

197?. **Description:** Animated program depicting the woman's generative organs. Includes detailed descriptions and illustrations of the three stages of labor. **Length:** 15 mins. **Format:** Beta, VHS, 3/4″ U-matic. **Acquisition:** Purchase.

★10346★ **Birth Control: Your Responsibility, Your Choice**
Professional Research, Inc.
930 Pitner Ave.
Evanston, IL 60202
Phone: (708)328-6700

1990. **Description:** This tape stresses the importance of a woman's individuality in her choice of contraception. Among the forms described are the pill, diaphragm, sponge, condoms, spermicides and fertility awareness. **Length:** 14 mins. **Format:** Beta, VHS, 3/4″ U-matic. **Acquisition:** Rent/Lease, Purchase.

★10347★ **Birth Day—Through the Eyes of the Mother**
Lawren Productions, Inc.
PO Box 666
Mendocino, CA 95460
Phone: (707)937-0536

1970. **Description:** A sensitive treatment of labor and delivery from the mother's point of view. The use of a subjective camera provides a gentle treatment of human birth, and a feeling of a warm, positive relationship between the patient and her doctors. **Length:** 29 mins. **Format:** 3/4″ U-matic, Other than listed. **Acquisition:** Purchase.

★10348★ **Birth: How Life Begins**
Britannica Films
310 S. Michigan Ave.
Chicago, IL 60604
Phone: (312)347-7958

1981. **Description:** This film investigates the new attitudes about childbirth. A look at natural childbirth as an alternative birth technique is also included. **Length:** 23 mins. **Format:** Beta, VHS, 3/4″ U-matic. **Acquisition:** Rent/Lease, Purchase, Trade-in.

★10349★ **Birth in the Lateral Position**
University of Arizona
Biomedical Communications
Arizona Health Sciences Center
The University of Arizona
Tucson, AZ 85724
Phone: (602)626-7343

1989. **Description:** Natural childbirth is a huge trend recently, and this video helps those who would like to try it by proposing an alternative positioning of the birthing mother for greater ease in childbirth. **Length:** 14 mins. **Format:** Beta, VHS, 3/4″ U-matic. **Acquisition:** Purchase, Rent/Lease.

★10350★ **Birth Series**
Videograph
2833 25th Street
San Francisco, CA 94110
Phone: (415)282-6001

1979. **Description:** These videotapes offer prenatal and childbirth education culturally and linguistically tailored to Spanish and Afro-American patients and their partners. The psychological and physical state of the pregnant woman, her partner, and family is approached within a cultural context. Programs available individually. **Length:** 11 mins. **Format:** Beta, VHS, 3/4″ U-matic. **Acquisition:** Purchase.

★10351★ **The Birth of Your Baby: Revised**
Professional Research, Inc.
930 Pitner Ave.
Evanston, IL 60202
Phone: (708)328-6700

1987. **Description:** An overview for mothers-to-be of the process of childbirth in a hospital environment. **Length:** 14 mins. **Format:** Beta, VHS, 3/4″ U-matic. **Acquisition:** Rent/Lease, Purchase.

★10352★ **Blue Collar Women**
New Orleans Video Access Center
2010 Magazine St.
New Orleans, LA 70130
Phone: (504)524-8626

1986. **Description:** A mini-documentary about a New Orleans program placing women in high-paying blue collar jobs traditionally reserved for men, predominantly construction work. **Length:** 6 mins. **Format:** Beta, VHS, 1/2″ reel, 3/4″ U-matic, Other than listed. **Acquisition:** Rent/Lease, Purchase.

★10353★ **Body & Mind Fitness for the Last Trimester of Pregnancy**
Wishing Well Distributing
PO Box 2
Wilmot, WI 53192
Phone: 800-888-9355

198?. **Description:** A guide to proper fetal care during the final stages of pregnancy, using an exclusive non-aerobic method. **Length:** 40 mins. **Format:** VHS. **Acquisition:** Purchase.

★10354★ **The Bond of Breastfeeding**
Perennial Education, Inc.
930 Pitner Ave.
Evanston, IL 60202
Phone: (708)328-6700

1978. **Description:** A clear, concise look at the pros and cons of breastfeeding, intending to provide the new mother with enough information to make the decision on whether or not to breastfeed. **Length:** 20 mins. **Format:** 3/4″ U-matic, Other than listed. **Acquisition:** Rent/Lease, Purchase, Trade-in, Duplication License.

★10355★ **Breaking Through**
Phoenix/BFA Films
468 Park Ave., S.
New York, NY 10016
Phone: (212)684-5910

1982. **Description:** This program looks at the many women who are pursuing jobs that are traditionally considered "men's work." **Length:** 28 mins. **Format:** Beta, VHS, 3/4″ U-matic. **Acquisition:** Purchase.

★10356★ **Breast Cancer**
National AudioVisual Center
National Archives & Records Administration
Customer Services Section PZ
8700 Edgeworth Dr.
Capitol Heights, MD 20743-3701
Phone: (301)763-1896

1980. **Description:** Dr. Marc Lippman increases our awareness about breast cancer through an engrossing review of the nature, diagnosis, and treatment of the disease. Part of the "Medicine for the Layman" series. **Length:** 60 mins. **Format:** Beta, VHS, 3/4″ U-matic, Other than listed. **Acquisition:** Purchase.

★10357★ **Breast Cancer 1**
WNET/Thirteen Non-Broadcast
356 W. 58th St.
New York, NY 10019
Phone: (212)560-3045

1979. **Description:** Gives a step-by-step demonstration of breast self-examination, then explains detection and treatment of breast cancer. **Length:** 26 mins. **Format:** Beta, VHS, 3/4″ U-matic. **Acquisition:** Rent/Lease, Purchase.

★10358★ **Breast Cancer 2**
WNET/Thirteen Non-Broadcast
356 W. 58th St.
New York, NY 10019
Phone: (212)560-3045

1979. **Description:** The emotional and physical impact of losing a breast to cancer is described by three women who have been through the experience. **Length:** 26 mins. **Format:** Beta, VHS, 3/4″ U-matic. **Acquisition:** Rent/Lease, Purchase.

★10359★ **Breast Cancer: Adjusting to It**
Focus International, Inc.
14 Oregon Dr.
Huntington Station, NY 11746
Phone: (516)549-5320

1983. **Description:** Nine women talk about how their lives have been since cancerous lumps were removed from their breasts. **Length:** 20 mins. **Format:** Beta, VHS, 3/4″ U-matic. **Acquisition:** Purchase, Rent/Lease.

★10360★ **Breast Cancer: A Curable Disease**
Creative Vision
935 E. South Union Ave., Ste. D-202
Midvale, UT 84047
Phone: (801)562-5136

1991. **Description:** The American Cancer Society has endorsed this video, which discusses prevention by self-examination, alternative treatments and profiles of women who have beaten breast cancer. **Length:** 72 mins. **Format:** VHS. **Acquisition:** Purchase.

★10361★ **Breast Cancer: Finding the Lump**
Focus International, Inc.
14 Oregon Dr.
Huntington Station, NY 11746
Phone: (516)549-5320

1983. **Description:** Women talk about finding a lump on their breast and what happened from there. **Length:** 20 mins. **Format:** Beta, VHS, 3/4″ U-matic. **Acquisition:** Purchase, Rent/Lease.

★10362★ **Breast Cancer, A Personal Challenge**
Professional Research, Inc.
930 Pitner Ave.
Evanston, IL 60202
Phone: (708)328-6700

1987. **Description:** Several women talk about their reactions to the diagnosis of breast cancer, progressing from self-violation to hopeful acceptance. **Length:** 23 mins. **Format:** Beta, VHS, 3/4″ U-matic. **Acquisition:** Rent/Lease, Purchase.

★10363★ **Breast Cancer and Reconstruction**
San Francisco Regional Cancer Foundation
2107 Van Ness Ave., Ste. 408
San Francisco, CA 94109
Phone: (415)775-9956

1979. **Description:** This program documents different types of breast cancer and where a woman can seek help for breast reconstruction. **Length:** 15 mins. **Format:** 3/4″ U-matic. **Acquisition:** Purchase, Duplication License.

★10364★ **The Breast Cancer Video**
Increase Video
6914 Conby Ave., Ste. 110
Reseda, CA 91335
Phone: (818)342-2880

1989. **Description:** How to perform a self-exam, treatment methods, and reconstruction possibilities are discussed. **Length:** 30 mins. **Format:** VHS. **Acquisition:** Purchase.

★10365★ **Breast Cancer as Viewed by Three Patients**
San Francisco Regional Cancer Foundation
2107 Van Ness Ave., Ste. 408
San Francisco, CA 94109
Phone: (415)775-9956

1979. **Description:** Three women tell about their respective experiences and the support of their families and friends. **Length:** 60 mins. **Format:** 3/4″ U-matic. **Acquisition:** Purchase, Duplication License.

★10366★ **The Breast Center Video**
Tapeworm Video Distributors
12420 Montague St., Ste. B
Arleta, CA 91331
Phone: (818)896-8899

1990. **Description:** Information on detecting breast cancer and the latest methods for treatment. **Length:** 37 mins. **Format:** VHS. **Acquisition:** Purchase.

★10367★ **Breast Feeding**
Medfact, Inc.
PO Box 418
Massillon, OH 44648
Phone: (216)837-9251

1981. **Description:** A complete discussion of all aspects of breast feeding, with emphasis of the do's and dont's. **Length:** 22 mins. **Format:** Beta, VHS, 3/4″ U-matic. **Acquisition:** Purchase.

★10368★ **Breast Feeding**
Milner-Fenwick, Inc.
2125 Greenspring Dr.
Timonium, MD 21093
Phone: (301)252-1700

1979. **Description:** This detailed explanation of how to be a nursing mother discusses preparing ahead, the first weeks of nursing, and how to involve the children and the family. **Length:** 15 mins. **Format:** Beta, VHS, 3/4″ U-matic. **Acquisition:** Purchase.

★10369★ **Breast Pumping: A Worthwhile Experience**
Care Video Productions
PO Box 45132
Cleveland, OH 44145
Phone: (216)835-5872

1982. **Description:** How new mothers and nurses can use the three types of breast pumping equipment that is available. **Length:** 14 mins. **Format:** Beta, VHS, 3/4″ U-matic. **Acquisition:** Rent/Lease, Purchase.

★10370★ **Breast Self-Examination**
Professional Research, Inc.
930 Pitner Ave.
Evanston, IL 60202
Phone: (708)328-6700

1986. **Description:** This revised program encourages monthly self-examination of the breasts, and gives viewers detailed instruction in how to do so. Also covered: mammography and its benefits. **Length:** 13 mins. **Format:** Beta, VHS, 3/4″ U-matic. **Acquisition:** Rent/Lease, Purchase.

★10371★ **Breastfeeding: A Practical Guide**
Motion, Inc.
3138 Highland Pl. NW
Washington, DC 20008
Phone: (202)363-9450

1982. **Description:** Two 15-minute segments, each available separately, comprise this program, which covers all facets of preparation for and management of breastfeeding. **Length:** 15 mins. **Format:** 3/4″ U-matic, Other than listed. **Acquisition:** Rent/Lease, Purchase.

★10372★ **Breastfeeding: A Special Closeness**
Motion, Inc.
3138 Highland Pl. NW
Washington, DC 20008
Phone: (202)363-9450

1977. **Description:** Designed to spark discussion and provide a well-structured educational tool covering such issues as parental roles, nutrition, modesty, sexuality, siblings, and working mothers. Features noted neonatologist David Abramson, who addresses the typical questions and concerns of expectant parents. A highly motivational program to breastfeed. **Length:** 23 mins. **Format:** 3/4″ U-matic, Other than listed. **Acquisition:** Rent/Lease, Purchase.

★10373★ **Breastfeeding Your Baby: A Mother's Guide**
Twin Tower Enterprises
18720 Oxnard Str., Ste. 101
Tarzana, CA 91356
Phone: (818)344-8424

1987. **Description:** A complete guide to breastfeeding techniques, with an analysis of its benefits as opposed to formula feeding. **Length:** 64 mins. **Format:** Beta, VHS. **Acquisition:** Purchase.

★10374★ **Bulimia**
Health Sciences Consortium
201 Silver Cedar Ct.
Chapel Hill, NC 27514
Phone: (919)942-8731

1986. **Description:** A thorough examination of the illness through interviews, medical expertise and dramatization. Upon the purchaser's request the phone number of that person's local help resource will be recorded at the end of the tape before shipping. **Length:** 24 mins. **Format:** Beta, VHS, 3/4″ U-matic. **Acquisition:** Purchase, Rent/Lease.

★10375★ **Bulimia and the Road to Recovery**
Women Make Movies
225 Lafayette St., Ste. 212
New York, NY 10012
Phone: (212)925-0606

1988. **Description:** The symptoms and possible causes of this eating disorder are explored through interviews with recovered bulimics. **Length:** 27 mins. **Format:** Beta, VHS, 3/4″ U-matic. **Acquisition:** Purchase, Rent/Lease.

★10376★ **Burning Bridges**
Women Make Movies
225 Lafayette St., Ste. 212
New York, NY 10012
Phone: (212)925-0606

1988. **Description:** The difficulties immigrant women face when they move to a new country with different values are examined. Many of the women in the film have been battered by their husbands. **Length:** 10 mins. **Format:** Beta, VHS, 3/4″ U-matic. **Acquisition:** Purchase, Rent/Lease.

★10377★   Caesarean Childbirth
Academy Communications
Box 5224
Sherman Oaks, CA 91423-5224
Phone: (818)788-6662

1986. **Description:** For laymen, a look at the surgical technique and the conditions that necessitate it. **Length:** 24 mins. **Format:** Beta, VHS, 3/4″ U-matic. **Acquisition:** Purchase.

★10378★   Cancer: Just a Word...Not a Sentence
Willow Mixed Media, Inc.
PO Box 194
Glenford, NY 12433
Phone: (914)657-2914

1989. **Description:** The idea that breast cancer does not mean an end to a woman's life is reinforced. **Length:** 45 mins. **Format:** VHS. **Acquisition:** Purchase.

★10379★   Caution: Women Working
Michigan Media
University of Michigan
400 4th St.
Ann Arbor, MI 48109
Phone: (313)764-8228

1980. **Description:** A musical portrayal of the role of American women in society and as members of the work force. Folksinger-composer Sheila Ritter weaves a story about women through rich comic and serious songs. **Length:** 29 mins. **Format:** 3/4″ U-matic, Other than listed. **Acquisition:** Rent/Lease, Purchase.

★10380★   Cervical Cancer
Pyramid Film & Video
Box 1048
2801 Colorado Avenue
Santa Monica, CA 90406
Phone: (310)828-7577

1989. **Description:** This program features information which every woman needs to know—what causes cervical cancer, who is at risk, how to prevent it, plus information on how the human papilloma virus causes cancer cells to develop in the cervix. **Length:** 10 mins. **Format:** Beta, VHS, 3/4″ U-matic. **Acquisition:** Purchase, Rent/Lease, Duplication License.

★10381★   Child Care Choices
Perennial Education, Inc.
930 Pitner Ave.
Evanston, IL 60202
Phone: (708)328-6700

1983. **Description:** An examination of the options available for working mothers regarding the acquisition of proper care for their children. **Length:** 14 mins. **Format:** Beta, VHS, 3/4″ U-matic. **Acquisition:** Rent/Lease, Purchase, Trade-in.

★10382★   Childbirth Preparation
Center for Humanities, Inc.
Communications Park
Box 1000
Mt. Kisco, NY 10549
Phone: (914)666-4100

1988. **Description:** This film offers information on pregnancy, labor, and delivery for the pregnant woman. **Length:** 60 mins. **Format:** VHS, 3/4″ U-matic. **Acquisition:** Purchase.

★10383★   Childbirth Preparation Program
Feeling Fine Programs
3575 Cahuenga Blvd. W., Ste. 440
Los Angeles, CA 90068
Phone: (213)851-1027

1985. **Description:** Dr. Ulene demonstrates techniques that pregnant women in labor can use to promote relaxation and relieve discomfort. **Length:** 56 mins. **Format:** Beta, VHS. **Acquisition:** Purchase.

★10384★   The Childhood of Susan B. Anthony
Film Fair Communications
10900 Ventura Blvd.
PO Box 1728
Studio City, CA 91604
Phone: (818)985-0244

1987. **Description:** The formative years of the women's rights activist, the only woman ever to be on U.S. currency. **Length:** 17 mins. **Format:** Beta, VHS, 3/4″ U-matic. **Acquisition:** Purchase, Duplication License.

★10385★   Children of Children
Coronet/MTI Film & Video
108 Wilmot Rd.
Deerfield, IL 60015-9990
Phone: (708)940-1260

1988. **Description:** During this conservative time when abortion, birth control and sex education in schools are being fought over, this video takes an intelligent and insightful look at the problem of teenage pregnancy. Many of these very young mothers, some even pre-teens, were raised by children as well, and the program raises questions as to why history seems to repeat itself. **Length:** 30 mins. **Format:** Beta, VHS, 3/4″ U-matic. **Acquisition:** Purchase.

★10386★   Chlamydia
Milner-Fenwick, Inc.
2125 Greenspring Dr.
Timonium, MD 21093
Phone: (301)252-1700

1989. **Description:** Prevention and treatment of the "silent STD" are covered. **Length:** 9 mins. **Format:** Beta, VHS, 3/4″ U-matic. **Acquisition:** Purchase.

★10387★   Chlamydia: Never Heard of It!
Focus International, Inc.
14 Oregon Dr.
Huntington Station, NY 11746
Phone: (516)549-5320

1986. **Description:** Chlamydia is one thousand times more common than AIDS, and potentially more serious than herpes, but it can be cured or prevented if people have the facts. **Length:** 25 mins. **Format:** Beta, VHS, 3/4″ U-matic. **Acquisition:** Purchase, Rent/Lease.

★10388★   A Circle of Women
Island Visual Arts
5959 Triumph St.
Commerce, CA 90040
Phone: (213)723-0997

1991. **Description:** Modern women meet women elders of Native American Tribes in an effort to link their cultures, and create an awareness of wisdom long discarded by the modern world. **Length:** 60 mins. **Format:** VHS. **Acquisition:** Purchase.

★10389★   The Climacteric Years
Design Media
2235 Harrison St.
San Francisco, CA 94110
Phone: (415)641-4848

1988. **Description:** Women are interviewed about what it feels like to be middle-aged. **Length:** 14 mins. **Format:** Beta, VHS, 3/4″ U-matic. **Acquisition:** Purchase.

★10390★   Clorae and Albie
Education Development Center
39 Chapel St.
Newton, MA 02160
Phone: (617)969-7100

197?. **Description:** "Clorae and Albie" deals with the need for women to prepare for the responsibilities of life in or out of marriage, with or without children. The program underscores the need for young women to grow up assuming that they will be self-supporting; that they have options with regard to education and careers and should consider them carefully. Students can compare their own lives to those documented in the program and learn a great deal from the experiences of others who have been or are in similar situations. Part of the "Role of Women·in American Society" series. **Length:** 36 mins. **Format:** 3/4″ U-matic, Other than listed. **Acquisition:** Rent/Lease, Purchase.

★10391★   Coalmining Women
Appalshop Films
306 Madison St.
Box 743A
Whitesburg, KY 41858
Phone: (606)633-0108

1982. **Description:** Through interviews with women coal miners at home and on the job, this program traces women's significant contributions to coalfield struggles and the importance of their new position as working miners. **Length:** 40 mins. **Format:** Beta, VHS, 3/4″ U-matic. **Acquisition:** Purchase.

★10392★   Community Services for Battered Women
Marshfield Regional Video Network
1000 N. Oak Ave.
Marshfield, WI 54449-5777
Phone: (715)387-5127

1982. **Description:** This tape looks at the outlets available to aid victims of wife beating. **Length:** 45 mins. **Format:** Beta, VHS, 3/4″ U-matic. **Acquisition:** Rent/Lease, Purchase.

★10393★   The Confrontation: Latinas Fight Back Against Rape
Women Make Movies
225 Lafayette St., Ste. 212
New York, NY 10012
Phone: (212)925-0606

1983. **Description:** A docudrama which pits the friends and rape counselors of a rape victim against the violent attacker. **Length:** 37 mins. **Format:** Beta, VHS, 3/4″ U-matic. **Acquisition:** Purchase, Rent/Lease.

★10394★ **Considrando Una Opcion**
University of California at Berkeley Extension
  Media Center
2176 Shattuck Ave.
Berkeley, CA 94704
Phone: (510)642-0460

1986. **Description:** A brief discussion concerning women who are considering sterilization. **Length:** 26 mins. **Format:** VHS, 3/4″ U-matic. **Acquisition:** Purchase, Rent/Lease.

★10395★ **Contraceptive Choices**
Milner-Fenwick, Inc.
2125 Greenspring Dr.
Timonium, MD 21093
Phone: (301)252-1700

1988. **Description:** Different birth control methods available are compared against one another. **Length:** 16 mins. **Format:** Beta, VHS, 3/4″ U-matic. **Acquisition:** Purchase.

★10396★ **Coping with the Discomforts of Pregnancy**
Milner-Fenwick, Inc.
2125 Greenspring Dr.
Timonium, MD 21093
Phone: (301)252-1700

1989. **Description:** Dizziness, fatigue, and nausea are only some of the problems that pregnant women may have. **Length:** 10 mins. **Format:** Beta, VHS, 3/4″ U-matic. **Acquisition:** Purchase.

★10397★ **Cramps!**
Churchill Films
12210 Nebraska Ave.
Los Angeles, CA 90025
Phone: (213)207-6600

1985. **Description:** A layman's look at menstrual cramps and how to allay them. **Length:** 26 mins. **Format:** Beta, VHS, 3/4″ U-matic, Other than listed. **Acquisition:** Purchase, Duplication License.

★10398★ **Crimes against Women**
International Training Company
3301 Allen Pky.
PO Box 3881
Houston, TX 77001
Phone: (713)529-5928

1984. **Description:** This program discusses purse snatching, sexual assault and other crimes women face most often. **Length:** 38 mins. **Format:** Beta, VHS, 3/4″ U-matic. **Acquisition:** Purchase.

★10399★ **Crisis Pregnancy**
Jeremiah Films
PO Box 1710
Hemet, CA 92343
Phone: (714)652-1006

198?. **Description:** A compassionate and sensitive look at the choices a woman can make when confronted with an unwanted pregnancy. **Length:** 26 mins. **Format:** VHS. **Acquisition:** Purchase.

★10400★ **Crisis Shelter Alternative**
Washington University in St. Louis
Learning Resources Video Center
George W. Brown School of Social Work
Campus Box 1196
St. Louis, MO 63130
Phone: (314)889-6612

1981. **Description:** Three women currently at a crisis shelter share their experiences with sexual abuse, emotional abuse, and violence. **Length:** 25 mins. **Format:** 1/2″ reel, 3/4″ U-matic. **Acquisition:** Purchase.

★10401★ **Cuidado Prenatal Serie (Prenatal Care Series)**
Professional Research, Inc.
930 Pitner Ave.
Evanston, IL 60202
Phone: (708)328-6700

1987. **Description:** A series on prenatal care in Spanish with English subtitles. Covers every aspect of prenatal care, including exercise, rest, nutrition, activities to avoid and seeing a doctor. **Length:** 13 mins. **Format:** Beta, VHS, 3/4″ U-matic. **Acquisition:** Purchase, Rent/Lease.

★10402★ **Cycles**
Women Make Movies
225 Lafayette St., Ste. 212
New York, NY 10012
Phone: (212)925-0606

1988. **Description:** A lively experimental film that reflects on black womanhood. **Length:** 15 mins. **Format:** Beta, VHS, 3/4″ U-matic. **Acquisition:** Purchase, Rent/Lease.

★10403★ **Dark Secrets, Bright Victory: One Woman's Recovery from Bulimia**
Carle Medical Communications
110 West Main St.
Urbana, IL 61801-2700
Phone: (217)384-4838

1987. **Description:** The life-threatening disorder of bulimia and the correlation between the onset of binging and purging and family problems is discussed in this presentation. The story follows Heidi's bulimic reaction to her mother's extramarital affairs and the breakup of the family. **Length:** 13 mins. **Format:** Beta, VHS, 3/4″ U-matic. **Acquisition:** Rent/Lease, Purchase.

★10404★ **Date Rape: No Means No!**
Phoenix/BFA Films
468 Park Ave., S.
New York, NY 10016
Phone: (212)684-5910

1985. **Description:** The focus is on a high school couple in which the girl is raped after a school dance. **Length:** 25 mins. **Format:** Beta, VHS, 3/4″ U-matic. **Acquisition:** Purchase.

★10405★ **Daughter Rite**
Women Make Movies
225 Lafayette St., Ste. 212
New York, NY 10012
Phone: (212)925-0606

1979. **Description:** Mother/daughter and sibling/sister relationships are provocatively explored in this film. **Length:** 53 mins. **Format:** Beta, VHS, 3/4″ U-matic. **Acquisition:** Purchase, Rent/Lease.

★10406★ **Dealing with the Cesarean Epidemic**
Academy Communications
Box 5224
Sherman Oaks, CA 91423-5224
Phone: (818)788-6662

1988. **Description:** A discussion of childbirth is presented with experts on the subject. **Length:** 109 mins. **Format:** Beta, VHS, 3/4″ U-matic. **Acquisition:** Purchase.

★10407★ **Decisions: Teens, Sex and Pregnancy**
Kidsrights
3700 Progress Blvd.
Mt. Dora, FL 32757
Phone: 800-892-KIDS

1991. **Description:** The lives of three girls are examined to determine the problems in facing teenage pregnancy. The decisions of the girls are looked at and the consequences of their actions are discussed. **Length:** 26 mins. **Format:** Beta, VHS, 3/4″ U-matic, Other than listed. **Acquisition:** Purchase.

★10408★ **Delayed Parenthood: Pros and Cons**
Carousel Film & Video
260 5th Ave., Rm. 705
New York, NY 10001
Phone: (212)683-1660

1983. **Description:** This program looks at the social and medical questions that arise with women who wait until they are established in a career before having children. **Length:** 22 mins. **Format:** 3/4″ U-matic. **Acquisition:** Purchase.

★10409★ **DES: The Timebomb Drug**
Filmakers Library, Inc.
124 E. 40th St.
New York, NY 10016
Phone: (212)808-4980

1983. **Description:** This tape exposes the medical problems encountered by children whose mothers had been prescribed DES during pregnancy. **Length:** 27 mins. **Format:** Beta, VHS, 3/4″ U-matic. **Acquisition:** Purchase.

★10410★ **D.E.S.: An Uncertain Legacy**
University of California at Berkeley Extension
  Media Center
2176 Shattuck Ave.
Berkeley, CA 94704
Phone: (510)642-0460

1986. **Description:** A report is given on an ineffective, unhealthy synthetic estrogen that was prescribed to over a million women. **Length:** 58 mins. **Format:** VHS, 3/4″ U-matic. **Acquisition:** Purchase, Rent/Lease.

★10411★ **The Diaphragm, Vaginal Sponge, and Cervical Cap**
Milner-Fenwick, Inc.
2125 Greenspring Dr.
Timonium, MD 21093
Phone: (301)252-1700

1989. **Description:** Demonstrates the proper use of these birth control devices. **Length:** 10 mins. **Format:** Beta, VHS, 3/4″ U-matic. **Acquisition:** Purchase.

★10412★ The Disabled Women's Theatre Project
Women Make Movies
225 Lafayette St., Ste. 206
New York, NY 10012
Phone: (212)925-0606
Fax: (212)925-2052
1982. **Description:** This tape is a dynamic series of skits and performances by the Disabled Women's Theatre Project. In exploring and communicating the experience of disability through theater, the Company conveys the outrageous, absurd, funny, painful and dramatic moments of their lives. **Length:** 60 mins. **Format:** VHS, Beta, 3/4 " U-matic. **Acquisition:** Rent/Lease, Purchase.

★10413★ Divorce
WTL Productions
600 N. Jackson St.
Media, PA 19063
Phone: (215)626-7470
1979. **Description:** A look at the impact of no-fault divorce, grounds for divorce, custody, and alimony. Produced for Seton Hall U Law Center. From the ''Women and the Law'' series. **Length:** 30 mins. **Format:** Beta, VHS, 1/2" reel, 3/4" U-matic, Other than listed. **Acquisition:** Rent/Lease, Purchase.

★10414★ Doctors, Liars, and Women: AIDS Activists Say No To Cosmo
American Federation of Arts
41 E. 65th St.
New York, NY 10021
Phone: (212)988-7700
1988. **Description:** A vitriolic response by AIDS activists to a controversial article on AIDS and heterosexual women in the January 1988 issue of ''Cosmopolitan'' magazine. Includes new footage as well as segments from many popular TV talk shows on the subject. **Length:** 30 mins. **Format:** Beta, VHS, 3/4" U-matic. **Acquisition:** Purchase, Rent/Lease.

★10415★ Domestic Bliss
Women Make Movies
225 Lafayette St., Ste. 212
New York, NY 10012
Phone: (212)925-0606
1984. **Description:** A comic lesbian soap opera, which touches on the issues of mothering, relationships, alternative lifestyles and wacky neighbors. **Length:** 52 mins. **Format:** Beta, VHS, 3/4" U-matic. **Acquisition:** Purchase, Rent/Lease.

★10416★ Donna: Women in Revolt
Women Make Movies
225 Lafayette St., Ste. 212
New York, NY 10012
Phone: (212)925-0606
1980. **Description:** The history and development of Italian feminism is documented in this film. **Length:** 65 mins. **Format:** Beta, VHS, 3/4" U-matic. **Acquisition:** Purchase, Rent/Lease.

★10417★ Drugs, Smoking and Alcohol During Pregnancy
Polymorph Films
118 South St.
Boston, MA 02111
Phone: (617)542-2004
1984. **Description:** Clear and compelling information about how three substances in a mother's blood can affect the growth of the baby. **Length:** 12 mins. **Format:** Beta, VHS, 3/4" U-matic. **Acquisition:** Rent/Lease, Purchase.

★10418★ Early Abortion
Milner-Fenwick, Inc.
2125 Greenspring Dr.
Timonium, MD 21093
Phone: (301)252-1700
197?. **Description:** This program uses the story of a young woman faced with an unwanted pregnancy to explain the operation used to terminate the pregnancy. **Length:** 15 mins. **Format:** Beta, VHS, 3/4" U-matic. **Acquisition:** Purchase.

★10419★ Early Discharge
Lifecircle
2378 Cornell Dr.
Costa Mesa, CA 92626
Phone: (714)546-1427
1986. **Description:** Prepares parents for their first days at home. Care and characteristics of the newborn, sleeping, stool changes, cord and circumcision care, the sponge bath and jaundice are covered. **Length:** 30 mins. **Acquisition:** Rent/Purchase.

★10420★ Eating Disorders
Research Press
2612 N. Mattis Ave.
Box 3177
Champaign, IL 61821
Phone: (217)352-3273
1989. **Description:** Teenagers seem especially prone to eating disorders such as bulimia, anorexia, and compulsive overeating. **Length:** 21 mins. **Format:** Beta, VHS, 3/4" U-matic. **Acquisition:** Purchase.

★10421★ Eating Disorders: You Are Not Alone
RMI Media Productions, Inc.
2807 W. 47th St.
Shawnee Mission, KS 66205
Phone: (913)262-3974
1987. **Description:** Various aspects of eating disorders such as anorexia and bulimia are described, including symptoms, physical and mental consequences, treatment, and recovery. **Length:** 20 mins. **Format:** Beta, VHS, 3/4" U-matic. **Acquisition:** Purchase.

★10422★ The Eleanor Roosevelt Story
Video Communications, Inc.
Drawer 111
PO Box 21338
Tulsa, OK 74121-1338
Phone: 800-331-4077
1965. **Description:** Oscar winning documentary about one of the most important women in the history of the U.S. **Length:** 90 mins. **Format:** VHS. **Acquisition:** Purchase.

★10423★ The Emerging Woman
Cinema Guild
1697 Broadway, Rm. 802
New York, NY 10019
Phone: (212)246-5522
1980. **Description:** Using old engravings, photographs, newsreels and other film clips, the film traces the history of woman in America. **Length:** 40 mins. **Format:** 3/4" U-matic, Other than listed. **Acquisition:** Purchase.

★10424★ Endometriosis
Milner-Fenwick, Inc.
2125 Greenspring Dr.
Timonium, MD 21093
Phone: (301)252-1700
197?. **Description:** The nature of endometriosis is explained, as are theories on its causes and possible treatments. **Length:** 15 mins. **Format:** Beta, VHS, 3/4" U-matic. **Acquisition:** Purchase.

★10425★ Enterprising Women
AIMS Media, Inc.
6901 Woodley Ave.
Van Nuys, CA 91406-4878
Phone: (818)785-4111
1989. **Description:** Profiles of five different businesses and the women who run them. **Length:** 27 mins. **Format:** Beta, VHS, 3/4" U-matic. **Acquisition:** Purchase, Duplication License.

★10426★ Equality
New Jersey Network
1573 Parkside Ave.
Trenton, NJ 08625
Phone: (609)292-5252
1977. **Description:** This study of age, sex, race and economic equality features interviews with Gloria Steinem, the Rev. Jesse Jackson and Marabel Morgan. **Length:** 60 mins. **Format:** VHS, 3/4" U-matic. **Acquisition:** Rent/Lease, Purchase.

★10427★ Every Woman's Guide to Breast Self-Examination
Wishing Well Distributing
PO Box 2
Wilmot, WI 53192
Phone: 800-888-9355
1990. **Description:** A presentation of the proper techniques of breast self-examination, complete with a step-by-step demonstration. **Length:** 18 mins. **Format:** VHS. **Acquisition:** Purchase.

★10428★ Every Woman's Guide to Osteoporosis
Wishing Well Distributing
PO Box 2
Wilmot, WI 53192
Phone: 800-888-9355
1990. **Description:** Advice on preventing the bone disease through diet, exercise, and medical screening. **Length:** 28 mins. **Format:** VHS. **Acquisition:** Purchase.

★10429★ **Exercise and Pregnancy**
Milner-Fenwick, Inc.
2125 Greenspring Dr.
Timonium, MD 21093
Phone: (301)252-1700

1989. **Description:** Helpful exercises for pregnant women are demonstrated, and movements that are too stressful are pointed out so they can be avoided. **Length:** 12 mins. **Format:** Beta, VHS, 3/4″ U-matic. **Acquisition:** Purchase.

★10430★ **Experiment in Equality**
WTL Productions
600 N. Jackson St.
Media, PA 19063
Phone: (215)626-7470

1984. **Description:** A unique, legal and historical perspective on the loss of woman's rights and the significance of the right for women to vote. **Length:** 60 mins. **Format:** Beta, VHS, 1/2″ reel, 3/4″ U-matic, Other than listed. **Acquisition:** Rent/Lease, Purchase.

★10431★ **Facing Tomorrow**
Lucerne Media
37 Ground Pine Rd.
Morris Plains, NJ 07950
Phone: (201)538-1401

1988. **Description:** The United Nations conference in Nairobi, Kenya was the site of the largest women's gathering in history. **Length:** 56 mins. **Format:** Beta, VHS, 3/4″ U-matic. **Acquisition:** Purchase.

★10432★ **Fast Food Women**
Appalshop Film & Video
306 Madison St.
Whitesburg, KY 41858
Phone: (606)633-0108
Fax: (606)633-1009

1991. **Description:** Looks at the lives of women who work at four fast food restaurants in eastern Kentucky. **Length:** 28 minutes. **Acquisition:** Rent/Lease, Purchase.

★10433★ **The Fear that Binds Us**
Intermedia Arts of Minnesota, Inc.
425 Ontario St. SE
Minneapolis, MN 55414
Phone: (612)627-4444

1982. **Description:** An acclaimed video about the effects of violence against women. Personal interviews with abused women, social workers and medical professionals are featured. **Length:** 52 mins. **Format:** 3/4″ U-matic. **Acquisition:** Purchase, Rent/Lease.

★10434★ **Fear of Fat: Dieting and Eating Disorders**
Churchill Films
12210 Nebraska Ave.
Los Angeles, CA 90025
Phone: (213)207-6600

1988. **Description:** Many young people, mostly women, feel that eating will make them ugly and bloated and subsequently unpopular. **Length:** 26 mins. **Format:** Beta, VHS, 3/4″ U-matic. **Acquisition:** Purchase, Rent/Lease, Duplication License.

★10435★ **Feeling Good Again: Coping with Breast Cancer**
Carle Medical Communications
110 W. Main St.
Urbana, IL 61801-2700
Phone: (217)384-4838

1987. **Description:** This program provides women with a realistic yet optimistic look at life after a mastectomy. Some of the hurdles that must be overcome are the woman's changed physical appearance, illness caused by chemotherapy, and the fear of the cancer returning. **Length:** 20 mins. **Format:** Beta, VHS, 3/4″ U-matic. **Acquisition:** Rent/Lease, Purchase.

★10436★ **Female Cycle**
Texture Films, Inc.
5547 N. Ravenswood Ave.
Chicago, IL 60640
Phone: (312)878-7300

197?. **Description:** The story of menstruation is simply told from the development of the immature egg, its passage through the fallopian tube, the preparation of the uterus in the event of fertilization and the final disintegration of the vascular walls of the uterus. **Length:** 8 mins. **Format:** Beta, VHS, 3/4″ U-matic, Other than listed. **Acquisition:** Purchase.

★10437★ **Female Head of Household**
New Jersey Network
1573 Parkside Ave.
Trenton, NJ 08625
Phone: (609)292-5252

1983. **Description:** An examination and explanation of why so many Puerto Rican women are heads of their households. **Length:** 30 mins. **Format:** VHS, 3/4″ U-matic. **Acquisition:** Rent/Lease, Purchase.

★10438★ **Female Sexual Dysfunctions**
Milner-Fenwick, Inc.
2125 Greenspring Dr.
Timonium, MD 21093
Phone: (301)252-1700

1988. **Description:** A few of the sexual problems that women have are described. **Length:** 17 mins. **Format:** Beta, VHS, 3/4″ U-matic. **Acquisition:** Purchase.

★10439★ **Female Sterilization**
National AudioVisual Center
National Archives & Records Administration
Customer Services Section PZ
8700 Edgeworth Dr.
Capitol Heights, MD 20743-3701
Phone: (301)763-1896

1979. **Description:** Combining dramatization, discussion, and drawings, this program delivers the facts about female sterilization. **Length:** 34 mins. **Format:** Beta, VHS, 3/4″ U-matic, Other than listed. **Acquisition:** Purchase.

★10440★ **Feminism and the Church**
UMCom Video
810 12th Ave. S.
Nashville, TN 37203
Phone: (615)256-0530

1982. **Description:** This tape looks at the ever-changing role of women in the Christian Churches. **Length:** 30 mins. **Format:** 3/4″ U-matic. **Acquisition:** Rent/Lease, Purchase.

★10441★ **Feminist Visions of the Future**
California State University at Chico
Instructional Media Center
Chico, CA 95929
Phone: (916)895-6112

1979. **Description:** Content of this program includes goals for women in future society. Women's architectural ideas, relationships in the future, artistic abilities, and spirituality are discussed. **Length:** 50 mins. **Format:** Beta, VHS, 3/4″ U-matic. **Acquisition:** Purchase.

★10442★ **Feminization of Poverty**
National Film Board of Canada
1251 Ave. of the Americas, 16th Fl.
New York, NY 10020-1173
Phone: (212)586-5131

1987. **Description:** Series concerning the world-wide increasing tendency for women to be poor. **Length:** 30 mins. **Format:** Beta, VHS, 3/4″ U-matic. **Acquisition:** Purchase, Rent/Lease.

★10443★ **Fight Back! Emergency Self-Defense for Women**
Cambridge Career Products
1 Players Club Dr.
Charleston, WV 25311
Phone: (304)344-8550

1986. **Description:** Women don't have to be helpless victims to any assault; now they can learn how to take care of themselves. **Length:** 55 mins. **Format:** VHS. **Acquisition:** Purchase.

★10444★ **Financial Planning for Women**
Cambridge Career Products
1 Players Club Dr.
Charleston, WV 25311
Phone: (304)344-8550

1986. **Description:** This tape was designed to help women handle their finances. **Length:** 40 mins. **Format:** VHS. **Acquisition:** Purchase.

★10445★ **Firewords: Louky Bersianik, Jovette Marchessault, Nicole Brossard**
National Film Board of Canada
1251 Ave. of the Americas, 16th Fl.
New York, NY 10020-1173
Phone: (212)586-5131

1986. **Description:** The three feminist writers of the title are profiled, with excerpts from the works of each woman. **Length:** 85 mins. **Format:** Beta, VHS, 3/4″ U-matic. **Acquisition:** Purchase, Rent/Lease.

★10446★ **First Lady of the World: Eleanor Roosevelt**
AIMS Media, Inc.
6901 Woodley Ave.
Van Nuys, CA 91406-4878
Phone: (818)785-4111

1974. **Description:** Depicts Eleanor's early life through old pictures and shows her involvement in political, national, and world affairs after the death of her husband. **Length:** 25 mins. **Format:** Beta, VHS, 3/4″ U-matic. **Acquisition:** Purchase, Duplication License.

★10447★ Fitness for the Last Trimester of Pregnancy
Wishing Well Distributing
PO Box 2
Wilmot, WI 53192
Phone: 800-888-9355

1990. **Description:** Light exercise for the last three months of pregnancy, with emphasis on relaxation. **Length:** 45 mins. **Format:** VHS. **Acquisition:** Purchase.

★10448★ The Flapper Story
Cinema Guild
1697 Broadway, Rm. 802
New York, NY 10019
Phone: (212)246-5522

1985. **Description:** An engaging historical look at the new woman of the Roaring 20's, better known as the flapper. Through interviews and rare footage, this video explores the values these women were rebelling against, as well as the limits of their new found independence. **Length:** 29 mins. **Format:** Beta, VHS, 3/4" U-matic. **Acquisition:** Rent/Lease, Purchase.

★10449★ Four Corners of Earth
Native American Public Broadcasting Consortium
1800 N. 33rd St.
PO Box 86111
Lincoln, NE 68501
Phone: (402)472-3522

1984. **Description:** A film documenting the cultural evolution of Seminole women. Changing traditional values in the modern world are viewed from the perspective of women living on South Floridas' Seminole reservations. **Length:** 30 mins. **Format:** VHS, 3/4" U-matic, 1" Broadcast type C, 2" Quad. **Acquisition:** Rent/Lease, Purchase.

★10450★ Four Pregnant Teenagers: Four Different Decisions
Focus International, Inc.
14 Oregon Dr.
Huntington Station, NY 11746
Phone: (516)549-5320

1988. **Description:** Adoption, marriage, and abortion are some of the suggestions made to deal with the problem of teenage pregnancy. **Length:** 60 mins. **Format:** Beta, VHS, 3/4" U-matic. **Acquisition:** Purchase, Rent/Lease.

★10451★ Four Women Artists
Center for Southern Folklore
1216 Peabody Avenue
PO Box 40105
Memphis, TN 38104
Phone: (901)726-4205

1977. **Description:** Interviews with four women artists (novelist Eudora Welty, quilter Pecolia Warner, embroiderer Ethel Mohamed, painter Theora Hamblett) reveal the creative spirit that drives all artists, as they discuss their creative lives and personal motivations. **Length:** 25 mins. **Format:** Beta, VHS, 3/4" U-matic. **Acquisition:** Purchase.

★10452★ Four Women over Eighty
MTI Teleprograms, Inc.
108 Wilmot Rd.
Deerfield, IL 60015-9990
Phone: (708)940-1260

1979. **Description:** Four women octogenarians discuss aging, physical activity, gainful employment, and related topics. **Length:** 10 mins. **Format:** Beta, VHS, 3/4" U-matic. **Acquisition:** Rent/Lease, Purchase.

★10453★ From Conception to Birth
Lifecircle
2378 Cornell Dr.
Costa Mesa, CA 92626
Phone: (714)546-1427

1992. **Description:** Emphasizes the responsibility and lifetime commitment of pregnancy and covers preconception along with the needs and rights of the newborn. **Length:** 42 mins. **Acquisition:** Rent/Purchase.

★10454★ From the Heart
American Federation of Arts
41 E. 65th St.
New York, NY 10021
Phone: (212)988-7700

1982. **Description:** Examines the art created by twentieth-century women, focusing particularly on nine of the thirteen artists in the Gihon art collection, "Works by Women." **Length:** 58 mins. **Format:** Beta, VHS, 3/4" U-matic. **Acquisition:** Rent/Lease, Purchase.

★10455★ From Pregnant Worker to Working Mother
Perennial Education, Inc.
930 Pitner Ave.
Evanston, IL 60202
Phone: (708)328-6700

1984. **Description:** The attitudes and emotional reactions of the future mother and her business associates during all stages of pregnancy are discussed. **Length:** 22 mins. **Format:** 3/4" U-matic, Other than listed. **Acquisition:** Rent/Lease, Purchase, Trade-in, Duplication License.

★10456★ Gender Politics
United Learning, Inc.
6633 W. Howard St.
Niles, IL 60648
Phone: (708)647-0600

1990. **Description:** Jinx Melia, author of "Breaking Into the Boardroom," explains the differences in the ways men and women relate to the world and the business environment, and how women can get ahead in their careers. **Length:** 25 mins. **Format:** Beta, VHS, 3/4" U-matic. **Acquisition:** Purchase, Rent/Lease.

★10457★ Girls at 12
Education Development Center
39 Chapel St.
Newton, MA 02160
Phone: (617)969-7100

1975. **Description:** The video program looks at three capable youngsters for whom many avenues are open as they make the transition from the end of childhood into adolescence and womanhood. This tape is also concerned with specific socialization processes they are experiencing. Part of the "Role of Women in American Society" series. **Length:** 30 mins. **Format:** 3/4"

U-matic, Other than listed. **Acquisition:** Rent/Lease, Purchase.

★10458★ Gloria Steinem
KPBS-TV15
San Diego State University
San Diego, CA 92182
Phone: (714)265-6415

1981. **Description:** The founder and editor of Ms. Magazine talks about priorities for the American women's movement in the eighties. **Length:** 30 mins. **Format:** 3/4" U-matic. **Acquisition:** Purchase.

★10459★ Goddess Remembered
National Film Board of Canada
1251 Avenue of the Americas, 16th Fl.
New York, NY 10020-1173
Phone: (212)586-5131

1984. **Description:** This is a film documenting the recent feminist attempt to revive a primal matriarchal religion centered on "the Goddess." **Length:** 54 mins. **Format:** Beta, VHS, 3/4" U-matic. **Acquisition:** Purchase, Rent/Lease.

★10460★ Good Monday Morning
Fanlight Productions
47 Halifax St.
Boston, MA 02130
Phone: (617)524-0980

1985. **Description:** A documentary about woman office workers and how they adjust to the pressures of chauvinism, skill deprivation and trivial labor. **Length:** 30 mins. **Format:** Beta, VHS, 3/4" U-matic. **Acquisition:** Purchase.

★10461★ Guilty Madonnas
University of California at Berkeley Extension Media Center
2176 Shattuck Avenue
Berkeley, CA 94704
Phone: (510)642-0460

1981. **Description:** A look at contemporary studies which show that day care centers can have a positive influence on a child's socialization, besides allowing mother to get out and work. **Length:** 51 mins. **Format:** 3/4" U-matic. **Acquisition:** Rent/Lease, Purchase.

★10462★ Hairpiece: A Film for Nappy-Headed People
Women Make Movies
225 Lafayette St., Ste. 212
New York, NY 10012
Phone: (212)925-0606

1985. **Description:** An irreverent, animated satire on the standards of beauty imposed on Black women in our society. **Length:** 10 mins. **Format:** Beta, VHS, 3/4" U-matic. **Acquisition:** Purchase, Rent/Lease.

★10463★ Hands Off!
WNET/Thirteen Non-Broadcast
356 West 58th Street
New York, NY 10019
Phone: (212)560-3045

1978. **Description:** This program in the "Turnabout" series focuses on unnerving sexual harassment received by women on college campuses and at work. **Length:** 30 mins. **Format:** Beta, VHS, 3/4" U-matic. **Acquisition:** Rent/Lease, Purchase.

★10464★ Hard-hatted Women
WNET/Thirteen Non-Broadcast
356 W. 58th St.
New York, NY 10019
Phone: (212)560-3045
1978. Description: Women who assume blue-collar jobs are facing prejudice and harassment. This segment of the "Turnabout" series looks at some of the women entering trades. Length: 30 mins. Format: Beta, VHS, 3/4″ U-matic. Acquisition: Rent/Lease, Purchase.

★10465★ Hard Work
MTI Teleprograms, Inc.
108 Wilmot Rd.
Deerfield, IL 60015-9990
Phone: (708)940-1260
1978. Description: Documentary about Margo St. James and her fight to legalize prostitution. Length: 29 mins. Format: Beta, VHS, 3/4″ U-matic. Acquisition: Rent/Lease, Purchase.

★10466★ Health Update: What's New for Women
Health Communications Network
Division of Continuing Education
Medical University of South Carolina
171 Ashley Ave.
Charleston, SC 29425
Phone: (803)792-4435
1980. Description: This program discusses home pregnancy tests and new discoveries relating to amenorrhea and prostaglandin antagonists. Length: 29 mins. Format: Beta, VHS, 3/4″ U-matic. Acquisition: Rent/Lease, Purchase, Subscription.

★10467★ Her Own Words: Wisconsin Pioneer Women's Diaries
Jocelyn Riley
PO Box 5264
Hilldale
Madison, WI 53705
Phone: (608)271-7083
1986. Description: Learn about pioneer life by reading through the diaries of various Wisconsin women. Length: 15 mins. Format: Beta, VHS, 3/4″ U-matic. Acquisition: Purchase, Rent/Lease.

★10468★ Hidden Alcoholics: Why is Mommy Sick?
CRM/McGraw-Hill Films
674 Via de la Valle
PO Box 641
Del Mar, CA 92014
Phone: (619)453-5000
1977. Description: An examination of female alcoholism, presenting two actual case histories of women with drinking problems. Length: 22 mins. Format: Beta, VHS, 3/4″ U-matic. Acquisition: Rent/Lease, Purchase.

★10469★ The Hidden Army
International Historic Films, Inc.
Box 29035
Chicago, IL 60629
Phone: (312)436-8051
1944. Description: A salute to the "hidden army" of women who worked in American industry during World War II, replacing the men who were fighting overseas. Made as a morale booster to bolster sagging production in the last year of the war. Length: 17 mins. Format: Beta, VHS, 3/4″ U-matic. Acquisition: Purchase.

★10470★ An Historical View of Abortion Around the World
Keep the Faith Inc.
PO Box 8261
810 Belmont Ave.
North Haledon, NJ 07508
Phone: (201)423-5395
1990. Description: A survey of abortion through the years, from a Catholic pro-life position. Length: 30 mins. Format: Beta, VHS. Acquisition: Purchase.

★10471★ Hope Is Not a Method—III
Perennial Education, Inc.
930 Pitner Ave.
Evanston, IL 60202
Phone: (708)328-6700
1984. Description: A demonstration of the current birth control methods available. Length: 22 mins. Format: 3/4″ U-matic, Other than listed. Acquisition: Rent/Lease, Purchase, Trade-in, Duplication License.

★10472★ How Far Is Too Far?
Coronet/MTI Film & Video
108 Wilmot Rd.
Deerfield, IL 60015-9990
Phone: (708)940-1260
1988. Description: Hugh Downs and Barbara Walters host this 20/20 look at recent court decisions that have enlarged the legal definition of sexual discrimination and harassment. Length: 18 mins. Format: VHS, 8mm, 3/4″ U-matic. Acquisition: Purchase, Rent/Lease, Duplication License.

★10473★ How to be a Financially Secure Woman
Maryland Center for Public Broadcasting
11767 Bonita Ave.
Owings Mills, MD 21117
Phone: (301)356-5600
1983. Description: This series offers information about investment tips, saving money and financial management for women. Length: 60 mins. Format: Beta, VHS, 3/4″ U-matic. Acquisition: Rent/Lease, Purchase.

★10474★ How Many Eves?
Walter J. Klein Company, Ltd.
6311 Carmel Rd.
PO Box 2087
Charlotte, NC 28211
Phone: (704)542-1403
1976. Description: The story of Eve Parada and her confrontation with an employer who has accepted women only in traditional roles. An important program on employment barriers for women. Length: 15 mins. Format: Beta, VHS, 1/2″ reel, 3/4″ U-matic, Other than listed. Acquisition: Purchase.

★10475★ How to Say No to a Rapist— And Survive
Learning Corporation of America
108 Wilmot Rd.
Deerfield, IL 60015-9990
Phone: (708)940-1260
1975. Description: Demonstrates rape prevention methods. Length: 52 mins. Format: Beta, VHS, 3/4″ U-matic. Acquisition: Rent/Lease, Purchase.

★10476★ Humanism and Feminism: New Directions
American Humanist Association
7 Harwood Dr.
PO Box 146
Amherst, NY 14226-0146
Phone: (716)839-5080
1972. Description: Betty Friedan (founder of the National Organization for Women) and Jacqueline Ceballos (eastern regional director of NOW) tell how feminists and humanists can work together to develop full personhood for all—men, women, and children. Part of the "Humanists Alternative" series. Length: 30 mins. Format: 3/4″ U-matic, Other than listed. Acquisition: Rent/Lease, Purchase.

★10477★ I Can See and I Can Breathe
UMCom Video
810 12th Ave., S.
Nashville, TN 37203
Phone: (615)256-0530
1981. Description: This tape explores incarcerated women and the overall criminal justice system. Length: 20 mins. Format: VHS, 3/4″ U-matic. Acquisition: Rent/Lease, Purchase.

★10478★ I Know All Three
Women Make Movies
225 Lafayette St., Ste. 212
New York, NY 10012
Phone: (212)925-0606
1985. Description: A trio of women provide support and solidarity for each other during their personal struggles with romance, self-fulfillment, and ultimately male violence. Length: 55 mins. Format: Beta, VHS, 3/4″ U-matic. Acquisition: Purchase, Rent/Lease.

★10479★ I Need Your Full Cooperation
Women Make Movies
225 Lafayette St., Ste. 206
New York, NY 10012
Phone: (212)925-0606
Fax: (212)925-2052
1989. Description: Chronicles the relationship between women and the medical institution using experimental techniques. Archival footage from educational and Hollywood films reveals the persistent image of male doctors' control of female patients. Critical commentary is provided by feminist scholars Barbara Ehrenreich and Carroll Smith-Rosenberg. Length: 28 min.

★10480★ I Want to be an Engineer
Arthur Mokin Productions, Inc.
PO Box 1866
Santa Rosa, CA 95402-1866
Phone: (707)542-4868
1984. Description: A documentary that examines the professional and personal lives of three female engineers. Length: 28 mins. Format: Beta, VHS, 3/4″ U-matic, Other than listed. Acquisition: Purchase.

★10481★ Ideas, Impressions, Images: American Women in the Visual Arts
Michigan Media
University of Michigan
400 4th St.
Ann Arbor, MI 48109
Phone: (313)764-8228

1980. **Description:** This program examines the contribution women have made to the visual arts in America. **Length:** 30 mins. **Format:** 3/4" U-matic, Other than listed. **Acquisition:** Rent/Lease, Purchase.

★10482★ Illuminated Lives: A Brief History of Women's Work in the Middle Ages
National Film Board of Canada
16th Floor
1251 Avenue of the Americas
New York, NY 10020-1173
Phone: (212)586-5131

1982. **Description:** Using manuscript illuminations, this film quickly examines the contributions women made to the working world during the Middle Ages. **Length:** 6 mins. **Format:** Beta, VHS, 3/4" U-matic. **Acquisition:** Purchase, Rent/Lease.

★10483★ I'm Not a Feminist, But...
Perennial Education, Inc.
930 Pitner Ave.
Evanston, IL 60202
Phone: (708)328-6700

1986. **Description:** A tongue-in-cheek view of traditional and contemporary roles for women in marriage. Animated. **Length:** 9 mins. **Format:** Beta, VHS, 3/4" U-matic, Other than listed. **Acquisition:** Purchase.

★10484★ Image of Women
Michigan Media
University of Michigan
400 4th St.
Ann Arbor, MI 48109
Phone: (313)764-8228

1977. **Description:** A look at the stereotypes and traditions which influence both self and sex concepts and the relationships of men and women to each other. Part of the "Worlds of Women" series. **Length:** 29 mins. **Format:** 3/4" U-matic, Other than listed. **Acquisition:** Rent/Lease, Purchase.

★10485★ Images of Women: Shaping a Spirituality
William C. Brown Company Publishers/ROA Media
Religious Education Division
2460 Kerper Blvd.
PO Box 539
Dubuque, IA 52001
Phone: 800-922-7696

1987. **Description:** Four women discuss how females can experience spirituality. **Length:** 30 mins. **Format:** VHS. **Acquisition:** Purchase.

★10486★ Infertility in Women
Design Media
2235 Harrison St.
San Francisco, CA 94110
Phone: (415)641-4848

1989. **Description:** Patients are reassured that most instances of infertility can be treated. Also, different infertility tests are demonstrated.

Length: 14 mins. **Format:** Beta, VHS, 3/4" U-matic. **Acquisition:** Purchase.

★10487★ Inserts for: Bradley Classes Videotape No. 1
Academy Communications
Box 5224
Sherman Oaks, CA 91423-5224
Phone: (818)788-6662

1988. **Description:** A collection of videotapes on the Bradley Method of childbirth. **Length:** 28 mins. **Format:** Beta, VHS, 3/4" U-matic. **Acquisition:** Purchase.

★10488★ Inserts for: Bradley Classes Videotape No. 2
Academy Communications
Box 5224
Sherman Oaks, CA 91423-5224
Phone: (818)788-6662

1988. **Description:** Another selection of Bradley childbirth method tapes. **Length:** 58 mins. **Format:** Beta, VHS, 3/4" U-matic. **Acquisition:** Purchase.

★10489★ Is it Hot in Here? A Film about Menopause
AIMS Media, Inc.
6901 Woodley Ave.
Van Nuys, CA 91406-4878
Phone: (818)785-4111

1989. **Description:** Important questions about menopause are answered through interviews with health and medical professionals. **Length:** 38 mins. **Format:** Beta, VHS, 3/4" U-matic. **Acquisition:** Purchase, Duplication License.

★10490★ It's Not Always Happy at My House
Coronet/MTI Film & Video
108 Wilmot Rd.
Deerfield, IL 60015-9990
Phone: (708)940-1260

1987. **Description:** This dramatized video deals with domestic violence and seeks to help battered women and children find the strength to speak out against their batterers and stop the violence. **Length:** 34 mins. **Format:** VHS, 8mm, 3/4" U-matic. **Acquisition:** Purchase, Rent/Lease, Duplication License.

★10491★ Jeannette Rankin: The Woman Who Voted No
PBS Video
1320 Braddock Pl.
Alexandria, VA 22314-1698
Phone: (703)739-5380

1984. **Description:** The story of America's first Congresswoman and her efforts to promote world peace. First elected to Congress by Montana voters in 1916, Ms. Rankin made history by being the only member of Congress to vote against America's entry into both World Wars. **Length:** 30 mins. **Format:** Beta, VHS, 3/4" U-matic. **Acquisition:** Rent/Lease, Purchase, Off-Air Record.

★10492★ A Joyous Labor
Filmakers Library, Inc.
124 East 40th
New York, NY 10016
Phone: (212)808-4980

1986. **Description:** This film provides women with an unbiased look at the many childbirth options available to them. **Length:** 30 mins. **Format:** VHS, 3/4" U-matic. **Acquisition:** Rent/Lease, Purchase, Duplication.

★10493★ Just Because of Who We Are
Women Make Movies
225 Lafayette St., Ste. 212
New York, NY 10012
Phone: (212)925-0606

1986. **Description:** Violence against lesbians is explored in this film, which includes personal accounts of family rejection, unprovoked violence and the clash between activists and anti-gay forces. **Length:** 28 mins. **Format:** Beta, VHS, 3/4" U-matic. **Acquisition:** Purchase, Rent/Lease.

★10494★ Labor and Birth
Lifecircle
2378 Cornell Dr.
Costa Mesa, CA 92626
Phone: (714)546-1427

1987. **Description:** Follows couples through prenatal care, classes, practicing at home, early labor and births in a positive, family-centered hospital environment. Part II "Options and Interventions" includes pros and cons of the prep, enema, I.V., fetal monitoring and episiotomy. **Length:** 42 mins. **Acquisition:** Rent/Purchase. Also available in Spanish.

★10495★ Labor Coaching
Lifecircle
2378 Cornell Dr.
Costa Mesa, CA 92626
Phone: (714)546-1427

1987. **Description:** Supports and prepares the coach for the realities of labor. Gives information on how to recognize, cope, and provide relief during each stage of labor. **Length:** 30 mins. **Acquisition:** Rent/Purchase.

★10496★ Labor of Love: Childbirth without Violence
Perennial Education, Inc.
930 Pitner Avenue
Evanston, IL 60202
Phone: (312)328-6700

1977. **Description:** The subject of this program is the controversial and radically new technique of birth advocated by Dr. Frederick Leboyer. The Leboyer method attempts to soften the traditionally violent process of childbirth. **Length:** 27 mins. **Format:** 3/4" U-matic, Other than listed. **Acquisition:** Rent/Lease, Purchase, Trade-in, Duplication License.

★10497★ Labor More than Once
Women Make Movies
225 Lafayette St., Ste. 212
New York, NY 10012
Phone: (212)925-0606

1983. **Description:** This documentary follows a lesbian mother's struggle to regain parental rights to her son and the judicial system's denial of those rights based solely on the grounds of her sexual preference. **Length:** 52 mins. **For-**

mat: Beta, VHS, 3/4″ U-matic. **Acquisition:** Rent/Lease, Purchase.

★10498★ **Landing a Job: Strategies for Women**
RMI Media Productions, Inc.
2807 W. 47th St.
Shawnee Mission, KS 66205
Phone: (913)262-3974
1988. **Description:** It shouldn't be difficult or intimidating for a woman to go out and interview for a job, as this program shows. **Length:** 25 mins. **Format:** Beta, VHS, 3/4″ U-matic. **Acquisition:** Purchase.

★10499★ **The Last to Know**
New Day Films
121 West 27th Street
Suite 902
New York, NY 10001
Phone: (212)645-8210
1981. **Description:** Through personal interviews and social and historical perspectives, this program considers the widespread problems of alcoholism and prescription drug abuse among women. **Length:** 55 mins. **Format:** Beta, VHS, 3/4″ U-matic. **Acquisition:** Rent/Lease, Purchase.

★10500★ **A League of Their Own**
Filmakers Library, Inc.
124 E. 40th St.
New York, NY 10016
Phone: (212)808-4980
1987. **Description:** During World War II, a women's baseball league was formed. Playing under professional rules, the women's league drew over a million fans a year. This film explores the league, its ten teams, and the athletes who helped change America's attitude towards women in sports. (Not to be confused with the 1992 film of the same name.) **Length:** 27 mins. **Format:** VHS, 3/4″ U-matic. **Acquisition:** Rent/Lease, Purchase, Duplication.

★10501★ **Learning about Pregnancy Series**
Professional Research, Inc.
930 Pitner Ave.
Evanston, IL 60202
Phone: (708)328-6700
1989. **Description:** A series designed to educate women on the workings of their bodies during pregnancy. Also examines health care and child birth preparation. **Length:** 13 mins. **Format:** Beta, VHS, 3/4″ U-matic. **Acquisition:** Purchase, Rent/Lease.

★10502★ **Let's Talk About: Breastfeeding**
Academy Communications
Box 5224
Sherman Oaks, CA 91423-5224
Phone: (818)788-6662
1988. **Description:** The former president of La Leche League discusses all aspects of breastfeeding. **Length:** 44 mins. **Format:** Beta, VHS, 3/4″ U-matic. **Acquisition:** Purchase.

★10503★ **Lies**
Women Make Movies
225 Lafayette Street
Suite 212
New York, NY 10012
Phone: (212)925-0606
1983. **Description:** This is a comic, yet dramatic video study of the lies women tell in order to negotiate the hurdles of everyday living in a sexist world. **Length:** 30 mins. **Format:** Beta, VHS, 3/4″ U-matic. **Acquisition:** Rent/Lease, Purchase.

★10504★ **Life after Breast Cancer**
San Francisco Regional Cancer Foundation
2107 Van Ness Avenue
Suite 408
San Francisco, CA 94109
Phone: (415)775-9956
1980. **Description:** Three women talk about choices they made prior to breast cancer treatment. **Length:** 30 mins. **Format:** 3/4″ U-matic. **Acquisition:** Purchase, Duplication License.

★10505★ **Living with Breast Cancer**
Trainex Corporation
PO Box 116
Garden Grove, CA 92642
Phone: 800-854-2485
19??. **Description:** The alternatives that women with breast cancer have are discussed. Double mastectomies, radiation implants, and reconstructive surgery are covered. **Length:** 25 mins. **Format:** Beta, VHS, 3/4″ U-matic. **Acquisition:** Rent/Lease, Purchase.

★10506★ **Living with Menopause Series**
Professional Research, Inc.
930 Pitner Ave.
Evanston, IL 60202
Phone: (708)328-6700
1988. **Description:** A complete series on the problems experienced during menopause, including emotional, pyschological, and social issues, symptoms, treatments, and the expectations women can have for their future life. **Length:** 14 mins. **Format:** Beta, VHS, 3/4″ U-matic. **Acquisition:** Purchase, Rent/Lease.

★10507★ **A Lost History**
CC Films
National Council of Churches
475 Riverside Dr., Rm. 860
New York, NY 10115-0050
Phone: (212)870-2575
1984. **Description:** Lynn Redgrave narrates this documentary looking at three great American women: Harriet Tubman, Francis Willard and Mary M. Bethune. **Length:** 60 mins. **Format:** 3/4″ U-matic. **Acquisition:** Purchase.

★10508★ **Louder Than Our Words: Women and Civil Disobedience**
Women Make Movies
225 Lafayette St., Ste. 212
New York, NY 10012
Phone: (212)925-0606
1983. **Description:** This historical and current overview of women and civil disobedience addresses such critical issues as political and personal conflicts surrounding civil disobedience; the relationship between feminism and non-violent resistance; and the significance of

women organizing for social change. **Length:** 36 mins. **Format:** Beta, VHS, 3/4″ U-matic. **Acquisition:** Rent/Lease, Purchase.

★10509★ **Management Principles for New Women Managers**
1st Financial Video Network
1701 E. Woodfield Rd., Ste. 412
Schaumburg, IL 60173-5133
Phone: (708)605-0222
1987. **Description:** Women who have just been given a managerial job see what their new job entails. **Length:** 25 mins. **Format:** Beta, VHS, 3/4″ U-matic. **Acquisition:** Purchase, Rent/Lease.

★10510★ **Margaret Sanger**
University of Connecticut
Media & the Arts for Social Services
U-Box 127
Storrs, CT 06268
Phone: (203)486-4888
1979. **Description:** In 1916 Margaret Sanger opened the first birth control clinic in Brooklyn. This program highlights one episode of Margaret's struggle to establish her clinic. This lesson is a tribute to her pioneering efforts in family planning. Note: The EJ format is only available in black and white. **Length:** 23 mins. **Format:** Beta, VHS, 1/2″ reel, 3/4″ U-matic. **Acquisition:** Purchase.

★10511★ **The Martial Art of Self-defense**
Crocus Entertainment, Inc.
762 Twelve Oaks Center
15500 Wayzata Boulevard
Wayzata, MN 55391
Phone: (612)473-9002
1988. **Description:** An easy to follow, step-by-step demonstration of effective self-defense techniques. Includes techniques especially designed for women. **Length:** 30 mins. **Format:** VHS. **Acquisition:** Purchase.

★10512★ **Medications and Anesthesia**
Lifecircle
2378 Cornell Dr.
Costa Mesa, CA 92626
Phone: (714)546-1427
1984. **Description:** Discusses medication used during labor and childbirth and stresses techniques that might be substituted. Covers relaxant and analgesic drugs, paracervicals, pudendals, local, regional and general anestesia. **Length:** 15 mins. **Acquisition:** Rent/Purchase.

★10513★ **Menopause**
Medfact, Inc.
PO Box 418
Massillon, OH 44648
Phone: (216)837-9251
1981. **Description:** A discussion of the nature of menopause, with emphasis on both the physiological and the psychological aspects of this condition. **Length:** 7 mins. **Format:** Beta, VHS, 3/4″ U-matic. **Acquisition:** Purchase.

★10514★ **Menopause: Myths and Realities**
Perennial Education, Inc.
930 Pitner Ave.
Evanston, IL 60202
Phone: (708)328-6700

1980. **Description:** A positive program dealing with menopause, which reassures the woman reaching her middle years that the symptoms are neither painful nor permanent. **Length:** 22 mins. **Format:** 3/4″ U-matic, Other than listed. **Acquisition:** Rent/Lease, Purchase, Trade-in, Duplication License.

★10515★ **The Menopause Story**
Churchill Films
12210 Nebraska Ave.
Los Angeles, CA 90025
Phone: (213)207-6600

1983. **Description:** A look at the causes and treatments of female menopause. **Length:** 30 mins. **Format:** Beta, VHS, 3/4″ U-matic, Other than listed. **Acquisition:** Purchase, Duplication License.

★10516★ **Miss, Mrs. or Ms.—What's it all about?**
Carousel Film & Video
260 Fifth Avenue
Room 705
New York, NY 10001
Phone: (212)683-1660

198?. **Description:** Shows how the term ''Ms.'' has become and established part of our vocabulary and how women are becoming newsmakers rather than onlookers in our society. **Length:** 25 mins. **Format:** Beta, VHS, 3/4″ U-matic. **Acquisition:** Purchase.

★10517★ **Miss...or Myth?**
Cinema Guild
1697 Broadway, Rm. 802
New York, NY 10019
Phone: (212)246-5522

1986. **Description:** An examination into the increasingly controversial world of beauty pageants with a special emphasis on the Miss California contest. Promoters see pageants as legitimate avenues for success for girls and young women. Anit-pageant forces see these events as sexist and demeaning to all women. Contains footage of the Miss America and Miss California Pageants as well as interviews with beauty contest winners, protesters, and feminist authors. **Length:** 60 mins. **Format:** Beta, VHS, 3/4″ U-matic. **Acquisition:** Rent/Lease, Purchase.

★10518★ **Modern Moves for Pregnancy Fitness**
Rudra Press
PO Box 1973
Harvard Sq.
Cambridge, MA 02238
Phone: (617)576-3394

1991. **Description:** Exercise program for pregnant women emphasizes yoga stretches and non-impact exercise. Includes 20-minute routines and a relaxation session. **Length:** 60 mins. **Format:** VHS. **Acquisition:** Purchase.

★10519★ **A Moveable Feast: A Film about Breastfeeding**
Professional Research, Inc.
930 Pitner Ave.
Evanston, IL 60202
Phone: (708)328-6700

1982. **Description:** A look at the most common myths, fallacies, prejudices and fantasies about breastfeeding, as well as the benefits. **Length:** 22 mins. **Format:** Beta, VHS, 3/4″ U-matic. **Acquisition:** Rent/Lease, Purchase.

★10520★ **Mrs. Breadwinner**
MTI Teleprograms, Inc.
108 Wilmot Rd.
Deerfield, IL 60015-9990
Phone: (708)940-1260

1982. **Description:** A look at the increasing number of women who work and out- earn their husbands and how it affects their families. **Length:** 12 mins. **Format:** Beta, VHS, 3/4″ U-matic. **Acquisition:** Rent/Lease, Purchase.

★10521★ **My Husband Is Going to Kill Me**
PBS Video
1320 Braddock Pl.
Alexandria, VA 22314-1698
Phone: (703)739-5380

1988. **Description:** The true story of Pamela Guenther whose abusive husband threatened repeatedly to kill her. She tried to get protection from friends, social workers, the police and the court to no avail, and was eventually shot to death by David Guenther in a parking lot. **Length:** 60 mins. **Format:** Beta, VHS, 3/4″ U-matic. **Acquisition:** Purchase, Rent/Lease.

★10522★ **Natural Family Planning**
Liguori Publications
1 Liguori Dr.
Liguori, MO 63057-9999
Phone: 800-527-1153

1989. **Description:** An introduction to family planning done the natural way. **Length:** 10 mins. **Format:** Beta, VHS. **Acquisition:** Purchase.

★10523★ **New Method**
Videotakes
187 Parker Ave.
Rte. 71
Manasquan, NJ 08736
Phone: (908)528-5000

1991. **Description:** Breathing techniques and the LaMaze method are taught via color and music association. **Length:** 72 mins. **Format:** VHS. **Acquisition:** Purchase.

★10524★ **New Mothers and Infant Care**
AIMS Media, Inc.
6901 Woodley Ave.
Van Nuys, CA 91406-4878
Phone: (818)785-4111

1989. **Description:** New mothers are told how to properly care for their new child. **Length:** 15 mins. **Format:** Beta, VHS, 3/4″ U-matic. **Acquisition:** Purchase, Rent/Lease.

★10525★ **No Alibis**
Bridgestone Production Group
1991 Village Park Way, Ste. 180
Encinitas, CA 92024
Phone: (619)943-9200

1988. **Description:** This drama focuses on the rights of the unborn. **Length:** 30 mins. **Format:** Beta, VHS. **Acquisition:** Purchase.

★10526★ **No Means No: Avoiding Date Abuse**
MTI Film & Video
108 Wilmot Rd.
Deerfield, IL 60015
Phone: (708)940-1260

1988. **Description:** Through dramatized examples of typical behavior leading to rape and other forms of date abuse, the program stresses the importance of communicating expectations and sexual limits and helps alleviate the fear of being rejected for standing up for personal rights. **Length:** 18 mins. **Format:** Beta, VHS, 3/4″ U-matic. **Acquisition:** Purchase, Rent/Lease.

★10527★ **No More Nice Girls**
Women Make Movies
225 Lafayette St., Ste. 212
Suite 212
New York, NY 10012
Phone: (212)925-0606

1989. **Description:** Veteran feminists converse about their politics against the backdrop of the 1980s. **Length:** 44 mins. **Format:** Beta, VHS, 3/4″ U-matic. **Acquisition:** Purchase, Rent/Lease.

★10528★ **No Place to Hide**
Landmark Films, Inc.
3450 Slade Run Dr.
Falls Church, VA 22042
Phone: (703)241-2030

1989. **Description:** A look at domestic violence and what can be done about it from all sides: battered wives, abusive husbands and children caught in the crossfire. **Length:** 57 mins. **Format:** Beta, VHS, 3/4″ U-matic. **Acquisition:** Purchase, Rent/Lease.

★10529★ **Not All Parents are Straight**
Cinema Guild
1697 Broadway, Rm. 802
New York, NY 10019
Phone: (212)246-5522

1986. **Description:** This film takes the viewer inside households where children are being raised by gay and lesbian people. Examines the social and legal problems these families face. **Length:** 58 mins. **Format:** Beta, VHS, 3/4″ U-matic. **Acquisition:** Rent/Lease, Purchase, Duplication.

★10530★ **Not Mine to Deny**
Broadman
127 9th Ave., N.
Nashville, TN 37234
Phone: (615)251-3697

1989. **Description:** A Christian view of why abortion is wrong. **Length:** 35 mins. **Format:** VHS. **Acquisition:** Purchase.

★10531★ Nutrition: Teen Pregnancy
Lifecircle
2378 Cornell Dr.
Costa Mesa, CA 92626
Phone: (714)546-1427

1990. **Description:** Stresses the importance of good nutrition throughout pregnancy for both the growing teenager and her baby. Looks at common teenage food habits and how they can be altered to meet the needs of both mother and baby. **Length:** 14 mins. **Acquisition:** Rent/Purchase.

★10532★ Nutrition: The Third Trimester
Lifecircle
2378 Cornell Dr.
Costa Mesa, CA 92626
Phone: (714)546-1427

1989. **Description:** Motivates expectant couples regarding their nutrition. It covers nutritional needs of the last trimester and the benefits for mother, baby, birth and lactation. Covers weight gain, special needs of Cesarean mothers, high risk pregnancies and common pregnancy discomforts. **Length:** 18 mins. **Acquisition:** Rent/Purchase.

★10533★ Of Snakes, Moons, and Frogs
Video Data Bank
School of the Art Institute of Chicago
37 S. Wabash Ave.
Chicago, IL 60603
Phone: (312)443-3793

1991. **Description:** This unique, mind-expanding video focuses on woman's role in society throughout history. It becomes apparent that woman's status is reaching an all-time low. What happened to the days of goddesses and high priestesses? More than just a Woman's Studies film, the process of history, religion and the modifications of time are captured. **Length:** 27 mins. **Format:** VHS, 3/4″ U-matic. **Acquisition:** Purchase.

★10534★ Older and Bolder
Education Development Center
39 Chapel St.
Newton, MA 02160
Phone: (617)969-7100

19??. **Description:** An upbeat film about the experience of aging. Showing a small group of older women in Massachusetts who meet weekly to talk, laugh, and share their joys and problems. All of these women have had to face the problem of loneliness but have taken control of their own lives and continue to enjoy active outside interests. **Length:** 14 mins. **Format:** 3/4″ U-matic, Other than listed. **Acquisition:** Rent/Lease, Purchase.

★10535★ On Equal Terms: Sex Equity in the Workforce
Centre Productions, Inc.
1800 30th St., Ste. 207
Boulder, CO 80301
Phone: (303)444-1166

1987. **Description:** This video explores how young women can be brought to understand and accept the fact that they will need self-supporting careers. **Length:** 29 mins. **Format:** Beta, VHS, 3/4″ U-matic. **Acquisition:** Purchase.

★10536★ On Guard
Women Make Movies
225 Lafayette St., Ste. 212
New York, NY 10012
Phone: (212)925-0606

1983. **Description:** A political satire about four lesbians who conspire to sabotage UTERO, a reproductive engineering factory. **Length:** 51 mins. **Format:** Beta, VHS, 3/4″ U-matic. **Acquisition:** Purchase, Rent/Lease.

★10537★ One Fine Day
National Women's History Project
7738 Bell Rd.
Windsor, CA 95492
Phone: (707)838-6000

19??. **Description:** Black and white stills of women who broke down the barriers of history set to the music of Kay Weaver. **Length:** 6 mins. **Format:** VHS, Other than listed. **Acquisition:** Purchase.

★10538★ One for My Baby
Film Library
3450 Wilshire Blvd., No. 700
Los Angeles, CA 90010-2215
Phone: (213)384-8114

198?. **Description:** This is an in-depth examination of Fetal Alcohol Syndrome and the means of preventing this disease. **Length:** 28 mins. **Format:** VHS, 3/4″ U-matic. **Acquisition:** Rent/Lease.

★10539★ Osteoporosis
Milner-Fenwick, Inc.
2125 Greenspring Dr.
Timonium, MD 21093
Phone: (301)252-1700

1988. **Description:** Women have to be more careful than men when it comes to preventing this particular bone disease, and this video provides a great deal of information about it. **Length:** 12 mins. **Format:** Beta, VHS, 3/4″ U-matic. **Acquisition:** Purchase.

★10540★ Out of Our Time
Women Make Movies
225 Lafayette St., Ste. 212
New York, NY 10012
Phone: (212)925-0606

1988. **Description:** A feminist discovers her grandmother's similar dreams in this contemporary/historical narrative. **Length:** 70 mins. **Format:** Beta, VHS, 3/4″ U-matic. **Acquisition:** Purchase, Rent/Lease.

★10541★ The Pap Test and Self Breast Examination
Medfact, Inc.
Post Office Box 418
Massillon, OH 44648
Phone: (216)837-9251

1971. **Description:** A comprehensive discussion of the nature of the pap test including a discussion of what is done during a pelvic examination. An illustrated description of the proper method of examining the breast is given. **Length:** 9 mins. **Format:** Beta, VHS, 3/4″ U-matic. **Acquisition:** Purchase.

★10542★ Pay Equity for Women
New York State Education Department
Center for Learning Technologies
Media Distribution Network
Rm. C-7, Concourse Level
Albany, NY 12230
Phone: (518)474-1265

1984. **Description:** A group of female clerical workers sue their company for comparative pay to their male counterparts. **Length:** 30 mins. **Format:** Beta, VHS, 1/2″ reel, 3/4″ U-matic, 2″ Quad. **Acquisition:** Duplication, Free Duplication.

★10543★ Personal Decisions
Cinema Guild
1697 Broadway, Rm. 802
New York, NY 10019
Phone: (212)246-5522

1986. **Description:** This video examines the complex social and emotional issues of abortion. By presenting the stories of real life men and women, the filmmakers attempt to show why and how the decision to have an abortion was reached and the importance of maintaining this right. **Length:** 30 mins. **Format:** Beta, VHS, 3/4″ U-matic. **Acquisition:** Rent/Lease, Purchase.

★10544★ Perspectives on Breast Cancer Treatment: It's Come a Long Way
University of Michigan Medical Campus
Media Library
R4440 Kresge 1 Box 56
Ann Arbor, MI 48109
Phone: (313)763-2074

1986. **Description:** The history of treatment for breast cancer is told by a group of women who have battled the disease themselves. **Length:** 33 mins. **Format:** Beta, VHS, 3/4″ U-matic. **Acquisition:** Purchase, Rent/Lease.

★10545★ The Pill: A Young Woman's Guide
Polymorph Films
118 South St.
Boston, MA 02111
Phone: (617)542-2004

1989. **Description:** The advantages and disadvantages of taking birth control pills are discussed in this film. How to use this form of contraception is also explained. **Length:** 11 mins. **Format:** Beta, VHS, 3/4″ U-matic. **Acquisition:** Rent/Lease, Purchase.

★10546★ A Place to Go
MTI Teleprograms, Inc.
108 Wilmot Rd.
Deerfield, IL 60015-9990
Phone: (708)940-1260

1981. **Description:** This is an examination of the battered woman's plight in finding refuge, and how one community rose to the challenge. Produced by the CBS News series "Sixty Minutes." **Length:** 15 mins. **Format:** Beta, VHS, 3/4″ U-matic. **Acquisition:** Rent/Lease, Purchase.

★10547★ Pornography: The Double Message
Filmakers Library, Inc.
124 E. 40th St.
New York, NY 10016
Phone: (212)808-4980
1985. Description: Is there a correlation between hardcore pornography and society's desensitized response to sexual violence? This film examines research studies that suggest images of rape, domination, and bondage lead to insensitivity and unsympathetic attitudes towards victims of rape. Contains explicit material. Length: 28 mins. Format: VHS, 3/4" U-matic. Acquisition: Rent/Lease, Purchase, Duplication.

★10548★ Portrait of an Artist
Women Make Movies
225 Lafayette St., Ste. 212
New York, NY 10012
Phone: (212)925-0606
1984. Description: A vibrant documentary of painter, sculptor and pioneer video artist Dorothy Chase. Length: 28 mins. Format: Beta, VHS, 3/4" U-matic. Acquisition: Purchase, Rent/Lease.

★10549★ Portraits of Anorexia
Churchill Films
12210 Nebraska Ave.
Los Angeles, CA 90025
Phone: (213)207-6600
1988. Description: Anorexia affects over two million people in America. Seven of them are interviewed in this program. Also available in a 28 minute version. Length: 51 mins. Format: Beta, VHS, 3/4" U-matic. Acquisition: Purchase, Rent/Lease, Duplication License.

★10550★ Positive Images: Portraits of Women with Disabilities
Women Make Movies
225 Lafayette St., Ste. 212
New York, NY 10012
Phone: (212)925-0606
1989. Description: This tape features profiles of three women with disabilities who are overcoming discrimination while dealing constructively with their physical limitations. Length: 58 mins. Format: Beta, VHS, 3/4" U-matic. Acquisition: Purchase, Rent/Lease.

★10551★ Post Partum Exercises
Care Video Productions
PO Box 45132
Cleveland, OH 44145
Phone: (216)835-5872
1980. Description: A Physical Therapist demonstrates hospital and home exercises that can help women who have just had babies to regain a well-conditioned body. Length: 16 mins. Format: Beta, VHS, 3/4" U-matic. Acquisition: Rent/Lease, Purchase.

★10552★ Postpartum
Lifecircle
2378 Cornell Dr.
Costa Mesa, CA 92626
Phone: (714)546-1427
1986. Description: Looks at the emotional ups and downs and the physical changes following birth along with the comfort techniques to cope with these changes. Postpartum checkup, birth control and sexuality are also discussed. Length: 30 mins. Acquisition: Rent/Purchase.

★10553★ Postpartum: A Bittersweet Experience
Lifecycle Productions
PO Box 183
Newton, MA 02165
Phone: (617)890-2303
1986. Description: a tape for recent mothers about the emotional setbacks that sometimes appear after giving birth. Length: 30 mins. Format: Beta, VHS, 3/4" U-matic. Acquisition: Purchase.

★10554★ The Postpartum Period
Churchill Films
12210 Nebraska Ave.
Los Angeles, CA 90025
Phone: (213)207-6600
1988. Description: Women who have just given birth sometimes need a little help getting back into a normal life. Length: 12 mins. Format: Beta, VHS, 3/4" U-matic. Acquisition: Purchase, Rent/Lease, Duplication License.

★10555★ Poverty Shock: Any Woman's Story
Centre Productions, Inc.
1800 30th St., Ste. 207
Boulder, CO 80301
Phone: (303)444-1166
1986. Description: This documentary on the new "feminization of poverty" focuses on real-life situations in which women's lifestyles have been severely disrupted, whether by divorce, loss of husband's income or teen pregnancy. Length: 29 mins. Format: Beta, VHS, 3/4" U-matic. Acquisition: Purchase.

★10556★ Pre- & Post-Natal Yoga
Rudra Press
PO Box 1973
Harvard Sq.
Cambridge, MA 02238
Phone: (617)576-3394
1990. Description: Several women in different stages of pregnancy demonstrate yoga stretching exercises to help expectant mothers prepare for a natural and relaxed birth. Length: 35 mins. Format: VHS. Acquisition: Purchase.

★10557★ Pregnancy After 35
Polymorph Films
118 South St.
Boston, MA 02111
Phone: (617)542-2004
1980. Description: This program deals with both the physical and emotional problems of late pregnancy. Statistics relating to Down's Syndrome are given and a woman is shown undergoing amniocentesis. Length: 22 mins. Format: Beta, VHS, 3/4" U-matic. Acquisition: Rent/Lease, Purchase.

★10558★ Pregnancy: Caring for Your Unborn Baby
AIMS Media, Inc.
6901 Woodley Avenue
Van Nuys, CA 91406-4878
Phone: (818)785-4111
1984. Description: The strict how-tos of unborn infant care are examined, emphasizing the kind and quality of food ingested by the mother. Explains why drugs, alcohol and smoking are detrimental to the fetus. Length: 20 mins. Format: Beta, VHS, 3/4" U-matic. Acquisition: Rent/Lease, Purchase, Duplication License.

★10559★ Pregnancy and the Newborn Child
Vision Productions, Ltd.
PO Box 8778
Moscow, ID 83843
Phone: (208)883-0105
1980. Description: A complete pregnancy instruction program is provided, along with demonstrations of holding, washing, and diapering a newborn baby. Length: 72 mins. Format: Beta, VHS, 3/4" U-matic. Acquisition: Purchase.

★10560★ Pregnancy and Nutrition
Milner-Fenwick, Inc.
2125 Greenspring Dr.
Timonium, MD 21093
Phone: (301)252-1700
1988. Description: Proper nutrition before and during pregnancy is explained in this film. Also available in Spanish. Length: 12 mins. Format: Beta, VHS, 3/4" U-matic. Acquisition: Rent/Lease, Purchase.

★10561★ Pregnancy Prevention: Options
AIMS Media, Inc.
6901 Woodley Ave.
Van Nuys, CA 91406-4878
Phone: (818)785-4111
1980. Description: In this program, teenagers discuss what they think they know about birth control, as well as their attitudes, feelings, questions, and fears. Length: 17 mins. Format: Beta, VHS, 3/4" U-matic. Acquisition: Purchase, Duplication License.

★10562★ Pregnancy on the Rocks
Kinetic Film Enterprises, Ltd.
255 Delaware Ave., Ste. 340
Suite 340
Buffalo, NY 14202
Phone: (716)856-7631
1984. Description: This program examines the effects on the child of limited as well as excessive use of alcohol during pregnancy. Length: 28 mins. Format: 3/4" U-matic. Acquisition: Rent/Lease, Purchase.

★10563★ Pregnancy and Work
Milner-Fenwick, Inc.
2125 Greenspring Dr.
Timonium, MD 21093
Phone: (301)252-1700
1988. Description: Women talk about how they are able to deal with the discomforts of pregnancy while on the job. Length: 14 mins. Format: Beta, VHS, 3/4" U-matic. Acquisition: Purchase.

★10564★ Pregnancy in the Workplace
Spectrum Films, Inc.
Box 801
2755 Jefferson St., Ste. 103
Carlsbad, CA 92008
Phone: (619)434-6191
1990. Description: Outlines things that a pregnant woman can do to remain more active and keep a positive attitude, making the pregnancy

easier and the baby healthier. **Length:** 26 mins. **Format:** Beta, VHS, 3/4″ U-matic. **Acquisition:** Purchase, Rent/Lease.

★10565★ **Pregnant but Equal**
Icarus Films
200 Park Ave., S., Ste. 1319
New York, NY 10003
Phone: (212)674-3375

1982. **Description:** This program documents the fight for equal rights on the job by highlighting the story of one group of factory workers and their fight for maternity benefits. **Length:** 24 mins. **Format:** 3/4″ U-matic. **Acquisition:** Purchase.

★10566★ **Premenstrual Syndrome**
Milner-Fenwick, Inc.
2125 Greenspring Dr.
Timonium, MD 21093
Phone: (301)252-1700

1988. **Description:** A young career woman's life is interrupted by PMS. **Length:** 18 mins. **Format:** Beta, VHS, 3/4″ U-matic. **Acquisition:** Purchase.

★10567★ **Premenstrual Syndrome Series**
Professional Research, Inc.
930 Pitner Ave.
Evanston, IL 60202
Phone: (708)328-6700

1989. **Description:** A series that covers the problems and treatment of premenstrual syndrome. **Length:** 11 mins. **Format:** Beta, VHS, 3/4″ U-matic. **Acquisition:** Purchase, Rent/Lease.

★10568★ **Prenatal Care**
Polymorph Films
118 South St.
Boston, MA 02111
Phone: (617)542-2004

1989. **Description:** This film prepares women for the changes they will experience during pregnancy. The harmful effects of smoking, alcohol and drugs are addressed as well. Also available in Spanish. **Length:** 12 mins. **Format:** Beta, VHS, 3/4″ U-matic. **Acquisition:** Rent/Lease, Purchase.

★10569★ **Preventing the Reality of Rape**
Program Source
1415 Lenox Rd.
Bloomfield Hills, MI 48013
Phone: (313)647-2220

1982. **Description:** Nancy Hightshoe, a former detective with the St. Louis County sexual assault investigative unit, presents a program designed to decrease the incidence of rape in this country. She describes the psychological make-up of the rapist, behavioral patterns of potential victims, and how to deal with an assault if it occurs. A 29-minute program is also available. **Length:** 53 mins. **Format:** Beta, VHS, 3/4″ U-matic. **Acquisition:** Rent/Lease, Purchase.

★10570★ **Pro-Life Under Attack**
Keep the Faith Inc.
PO Box 8261
810 Belmont Ave.
North Haledon, NJ 07508
Phone: (201)423-5395

1990. **Description:** A video designed for Catholics that talks about the Pro-life position and the recent debates on abortion. **Length:** 30 mins. **Format:** Beta, VHS. **Acquisition:** Purchase.

★10571★ **The Promise of Equality in the U.S. Constitution**
WTL Productions
600 N. Jackson St.
Media, PA 19063
Phone: (215)626-7470

1979. **Description:** The Fourteenth Amendment is examined, along with the history of stereotypes about women and the Equal Rights Amendment. Produced for Seton Hall U Law Center. From the ''Women and the Law'' series. **Length:** 30 mins. **Format:** Beta, VHS, 1/2″ reel, 3/4″ U-matic, Other than listed. **Acquisition:** Rent/Lease, Purchase.

★10572★ **The Prostitutes of Forsyth Street**
Downtown Community TV Center
87 Lafayette St.
New York, NY 10013
Phone: (212)966-4510

1983. **Description:** This is a documentary about the prostitutes who work New York's Lower East Side. **Length:** 4 mins. **Format:** 1/2″ reel, 3/4″ U-matic, Other than listed. **Acquisition:** Rent/Lease, Purchase.

★10573★ **Rape: An Act of Hate**
Kidsrights
3700 Progress Blvd.
Mt. Dora, FL 32757
Phone: 800-892-KIDS

1990. **Description:** This Emmy award winner features Victoria Hamel dealing with the ugly aftermath of rape and characterizes the likely inflictors of rape. **Length:** 58 mins. **Format:** Beta, VHS, 3/4″ U-matic, Other than listed. **Acquisition:** Purchase.

★10574★ **Rape: The Boundaries of Fear**
Centre Productions, Inc.
1800 30th St., Ste. 207
Boulder, CO 80301
Phone: (303)444-1166

1986. **Description:** This program is about the fear of rape and how that fear affects women's lives. Women from all walks of life, some who have been raped and some who have not, describe the boundaries they put around their lives because of their fear. **Length:** 30 mins. **Format:** Beta, VHS, 3/4″ U-matic. **Acquisition:** Purchase.

★10575★ **Rape! A Crime of Violence**
Master Arts Video
11549 Amigo Ave.
Northridge, CA 91326
Phone: (818)368-9220

1982. **Description:** Awareness, precaution and defense of rape are exposed in this docudrama. **Length:** 48 mins. **Format:** Beta, VHS. **Acquisition:** Purchase.

★10576★ **Rape/Crisis**
Cinema Guild
1697 Broadway, Rm. 802
New York, NY 10019
Phone: (212)246-5522

1983. **Description:** An investigation of the aftermath of rape and how volunteers at the Rape Crisis Center in Austin, Texas care for rape victims. **Length:** 87 mins. **Format:** Beta, VHS, 3/4″ U-matic. **Acquisition:** Rent/Lease, Purchase, Duplication.

★10577★ **Rape: Face to Face**
Filmakers Library, Inc.
124 E. 40th St.
New York, NY 10016
Phone: (212)808-4980

1984. **Description:** The causes and consequences of rape are examined in this documentary. **Length:** 55 mins. **Format:** Beta, VHS, 3/4″ U-matic. **Acquisition:** Purchase.

★10578★ **Rape: It Can Happen to You**
Film Library
3450 Wilshire Blvd., No. 700
Los Angeles, CA 90010-2215
Phone: (213)384-8114

1983. **Description:** Five rape victims discuss the situations that led up to their individual violations. **Length:** 17 mins. **Format:** VHS, 3/4″ U-matic. **Acquisition:** Rent/Lease.

★10579★ **Rape: A Matter of Survival**
Bullfrog Films, Inc.
PO Box 149
Oley, PA 19547
Phone: (215)779-8226

198?. **Description:** In this program myths are exploded, types of rapists are described, and every woman is challenged to develop her own prevention and survival plan. **Length:** 28 mins. **Format:** Beta, VHS, 3/4″ U-matic. **Acquisition:** Purchase, Duplication License.

★10580★ **Rape Prevention**
Coronet/MTI Film & Video
108 Wilmot Rd.
Deerfield, IL 60015-9990
Phone: (708)940-1260

1988. **Description:** Most rape victims report a feeling of uneasiness or of being in danger, which they suppressed, before the attack occurred. This video helps women get in touch with their natural awareness of situations, and to better understand and heed subliminal danger signs. **Length:** 20 mins. **Format:** VHS, 8mm, 3/4″ U-matic. **Acquisition:** Purchase, Rent/Lease, Duplication License.

★10581★ **Rape Stories**
Women Make Movies
225 Lafayette St., Ste. 212
New York, NY 10012
Phone: (212)925-0606

1989. **Description:** In October 1979, Margie Strosser was raped in the elevator of her apartment building. Two weeks later, she asked a friend to interview her about the incident. Ten years later, she remembers and recounts the same incident. An emotionally moving film, in which the experience of rape is reshaped through memory. **Length:** 25 mins. **Format:** Beta, VHS, 3/4″ U-matic. **Acquisition:** Purchase, Rent/Lease.

★10582★ **Rape: Taking Back the Night**
Washington University in Street Louis
Learning Resources Video Center
George W. Brown School of Social Work
Campus Box 1196
St. Louis, MO 63130
Phone: (314)889-6612

1981. **Description:** This program provides a comprehensive look at the problem of violence against women. **Length:** 20 mins. **Format:** 1/2″ reel, 3/4″ U-matic. **Acquisition:** Purchase.

★10583★ **Ready, Willing and Able...**
University of Wisconsin at Madison
 Vocational Studies Center
964 Educational Sciences Building
1025 W. Johnson St.
Madison, WI 53706
Phone: (608)263-2929

1987. **Description:** A set of programs about the difficulties and struggles that women today experience when trying to have both a family and a job. **Length:** 30 mins. **Format:** VHS. **Acquisition:** Purchase.

★10584★ **Real People: Meet a Teenage Mother**
Human Relations Media (HRM)
175 Tompkins Ave., No. V212
Pleasantville, NY 10570-9973
Phone: (914)769-7496

1989. **Description:** Lauri, who became a mother at 15, talks about what has happened in her life. **Length:** 18 mins. **Format:** Beta, VHS, 3/4″ U-matic. **Acquisition:** Purchase.

★10585★ **Science—Woman's Work**
Media Design Associates, Inc.
PO Box 3189
Boulder, CO 80307-3189
Phone: (303)443-2800

1988. **Description:** This program looks into the theory that girls are not as interested in math and science as boys are, and what, if anything, can be done about it. **Length:** 27 mins. **Format:** Beta, VHS. **Acquisition:** Purchase.

★10586★ **A Second Chance**
Icarus Films
200 Park Ave., S., Ste. 1319
New York, NY 10003
Phone: (212)674-3375

1984. **Description:** A documentary about women who seek a new career after major changes in their lives. **Length:** 28 mins. **Format:** 3/4″ U-matic. **Acquisition:** Purchase.

★10587★ **Seeking Justice: One Victim's Experience**
Alexandria Office on Women
2525 Mt. Vernon Ave., Unit No. 6
Alexandria, VA 22301
Phone: (703)838-0970

1984. **Description:** A mock trial based on an actual acquaintance rape case prosecuted in Alexandria, with the actual judge and DA acting in the roles they held in reality; designed to inform in regards to the courtroom experience of rape victims and cases. **Length:** 30 mins. **Format:** VHS. **Acquisition:** Purchase.

★10588★ **Self Breast Examination**
San Francisco Regional Cancer Foundation
2107 Van Ness Ave., Ste. 408
San Francisco, CA 94109
Phone: (415)775-9956

1979. **Description:** This program shows how to examine the breast for possible signs of cancer. **Length:** 5 mins. **Format:** 3/4″ U-matic. **Acquisition:** Purchase, Duplication License.

★10589★ **Sexual Abuse and Harassment: Causes...Prevention...Coping**
Center for Humanities, Inc.
Communications Park
Box 1000
Mt. Kisco, NY 10549
Phone: (914)666-4100

1987. **Description:** This video alerts students to the wide range of inappropriate behavior that can be considered sexual harassment, whether it be from peers, professors or employers. **Length:** 30 mins. **Format:** Beta, VHS, 3/4″ U-matic. **Acquisition:** Purchase.

★10590★ **Sexual Assault Crimes**
Human Relations Media (HRM)
175 Tompkins Ave., No. V212
Pleasantville, NY 10570-9973
Phone: (914)769-7496

1988. **Description:** Students are given ways to avoid sexual attacks. **Length:** 30 mins. **Format:** VHS. **Acquisition:** Purchase.

★10591★ **Sexual Harassment: No Laughing Matter**
SouthWestern Publishing Company
5101 Madison Rd.
Cincinnati, OH 45227
Phone: (513)271-8811

1984. **Description:** A program outlining the legal parameters of sexual harassment, with the concentrated purpose of alerting employees if they are a victim of it. **Length:** 15 mins. **Format:** Beta, VHS, 3/4″ U-matic, 2″ Quad. **Acquisition:** Rent/Lease, Purchase.

★10592★ **Sexual Harassment: No Place in the Workplace**
Michigan Media
University of Michigan
400 4th St.
Ann Arbor, MI 48109
Phone: (313)764-8228

1979. **Description:** Gloria Steinem and Lynn Farley discuss the problem of sexual harassment in the workplace. **Length:** 29 mins. **Format:** 3/4″ U-matic, Other than listed. **Acquisition:** Rent/Lease, Purchase.

★10593★ **Sexual Harassment: The Other Point of View**
United Learning, Inc.
6633 W. Howard St.
Niles, IL 60648
Phone: (708)647-0600

1987. **Description:** This video demonstrates types of sexual abuse and details ways they can be avoided or stopped in the workplace. **Length:** 33 mins. **Format:** Beta, VHS, 3/4″ U-matic. **Acquisition:** Purchase, Rent/Lease.

★10594★ **Sexual Harassment: Shades of Gray**
Premiere Publishing, Ltd.
145 Northwest 85th St., Ste. 201
Seattle, WA 98117
Phone: (206)782-8310
Toll-free: 800-767-3062

1991-1992. **Description:** A series of five tapes addressing sexual harassment on the job. Titles include: "What Are We Doing Here?", "What is Sexual Harassment?", "Why Should I Worry About It?", "What Does the Law Say?", and "What Am I Supposed to Do?". **Format:** VHS, 3/4″ U-matic cassette. **Acquisition:** Purchase, rental.

★10595★ **Sexual Harassment in the Workplace: The Power Pinch**
Bureau of Business Practice
24 Rope Ferry Rd.
Waterford, CT 06386
Phone: (203)442-4365

1981. **Description:** Interviews are conducted to explore the legal and sociological definitions of sexual harrassment. **Length:** 20 mins. **Format:** Beta, VHS, 3/4″ U-matic, Other than listed. **Acquisition:** Rent/Lease, Purchase.

★10596★ **Sexually-Transmitted Diseases**
Films for the Humanities
743 Alexander Rd.
Princeton, NJ 08540
Phone: (609)452-1128

1989. **Description:** An overview for laymen of various venereal diseases, including syphilis, vaginitis, gonorrhea, herpes, chlymydia and AIDS. **Length:** 19 mins. **Format:** Beta, VHS, 3/4″ U-matic. **Acquisition:** Rent/Lease, Purchase.

★10597★ **Shattered!**
MTI Teleprograms, Inc.
108 Wilmot Road
Deerfield, IL 60015-9990
Phone: (312)940-1260

198?. **Description:** The social, emotional, and legal aftermath of a rape attack and how victims can be helped to cope with the trauma. **Length:** 21 mins. **Format:** Beta, VHS, 3/4″ U-matic. **Acquisition:** Rent/Lease, Purchase.

★10598★ **She's a Railroader**
Phoenix/BFA Films
468 Park Ave., S.
New York, NY 10016
Phone: (212)684-5910

1980. **Description:** This program tells the story of a woman who works on the railroad and how she manages in a traditionally male field. **Length:** 10 mins. **Format:** Beta, VHS, 3/4″ U-matic. **Acquisition:** Purchase.

★10599★ **The Silent Scream**
Keep the Faith Inc.
PO Box 8261
810 Belmont Ave.
North Haledon, NJ 07508
Phone: (201)423-5395

1977. **Description:** This graphic anti-abortion film presents actual footage of an abortion with a spoken narration by the aborted infant. **Length:** 30 mins. **Format:** Beta, VHS. **Acquisition:** Purchase.

★10600★ **The Single Parent Family**
Educational Consortium for Cable
24 Beechwood Rd.
Summit, NJ 07901
Phone: (201)277-2870

1987. **Description:** An educational film about the unique stresses and tribulations of single parenthood. **Length:** 26 mins. **Format:** Beta, VHS, 3/4″ U-matic. **Acquisition:** Rent/Lease, Purchase.

★10601★ **Single Parenting: A New Page in America's Family Album**
Centre Productions, Inc.
1800 30th St., Ste. 207
Boulder, CO 80301
Phone: (303)444-1166

1987. **Description:** This program not only looks at the traditional divorced single parent mother who often ends up in poverty, but also presents case histories of the single parent father, women who choose to have children without marriage, and co-operating, the joint responsibility of rearing children outside the nuclear family. **Length:** 25 mins. **Format:** Beta, VHS, 3/4″ U-matic. **Acquisition:** Purchase.

★10602★ **Smoking, Drinking and Drugs During Pregnancy**
March of Dimes
1275 Mamaroneck Ave.
White Plains, NY 10605
Phone: (914)428-7100

1988. **Description:** The risks of substance abuse while a woman is pregnant are defined. **Length:** 13 mins. **Format:** VHS, 3/4″ U-matic. **Acquisition:** Purchase.

★10603★ **So Many Voices: A Look at Abortion in America**
Phoenix/BFA Films
468 Park Ave., S.
New York, NY 10016
Phone: (212)684-5910

1982. **Description:** This program explores the issue of abortion in the United States today and, through interviews with people personally affected by this issue, examines the human implications of both sides of this important question. **Length:** 30 mins. **Format:** Beta, VHS, 3/4″ U-matic. **Acquisition:** Purchase.

★10604★ **Some American Feminists**
Arthur Mokin Productions, Inc.
PO Box 1866
Santa Rosa, CA 95402-1866
Phone: (707)542-4868

1980. **Description:** A series of interviews, interspersed with newsreel footage, place the American Feminist movement into historical perspective. **Length:** 56 mins. **Format:** Beta, VHS, 3/4″ U-matic, Other than listed. **Acquisition:** Purchase.

★10605★ **Some Girls**
Fanlight Productions
47 Halifax St.
Boston, MA 02130
Phone: (617)524-0980

1989. **Description:** This documentary follows the lives of four teenage girls as they receive pregnancy prevention counseling and parenting education. The video attempts to explain the reasons for teenage pregnancy and its impact on society. **Length:** 30 mins. **Format:** Beta, VHS, 3/4″ U-matic. **Acquisition:** Rent/Lease, Purchase.

★10606★ **Some of These Days**
Media Project, Inc.
PO Box 4093
Portland, OR 97208
Phone: (503)223-5335

1980. **Description:** The film profiles women grappling with the process of aging in America. **Length:** 60 mins. **Format:** Beta, VHS, 1/2″ reel, 3/4″ U-matic. **Acquisition:** Rent/Lease, Purchase.

★10607★ **Someone You Know: Acquaintance Rape**
Coronet/MTI Film & Video
108 Wilmot Rd.
Deerfield, IL 60015-9990
Phone: (708)940-1260

1986. **Description:** One in every seven women will be raped in her lifetime, and more than half of those rapes will be committed by someone the victim knows, even trusts. This video will help women see the magnitude of the problem and to understand that reporting an assault may be emotionally painful, but it is necessary for healing and for justice. **Length:** 30 mins. **Format:** VHS, 8mm, 3/4″ U-matic. **Acquisition:** Purchase, Rent/Lease, Duplication License.

★10608★ **Special Delivery: Creating the Birth You Want for You and Your Baby**
Videotakes
187 Parker Ave.
Rte. 71
Manasquan, NJ 08736
Phone: (908)528-5000

1991. **Description:** What prospective parents need to know about birthing options, where to have the baby, whether to use a doctor or a midwife, and the latest natural birth information. Video shows three babies being born. **Length:** 42 mins. **Format:** VHS. **Acquisition:** Purchase.

★10609★ **Starving for Perfection**
Wishing Well Distributing
PO Box 2
Wilmot, WI 53192
Phone: 800-888-9355

1990. **Description:** A look at the problem of eating disorders, and how they are exacerbated by the media's constant attention on thinness. **Length:** 30 mins. **Format:** VHS. **Acquisition:** Purchase.

★10610★ **Stepping Out/Stepping In**
University of Wisconsin at Madison Vocational Studies Center
964 Educational Sciences Building
1025 W. Johnson St.
Madison, WI 53706
Phone: (608)263-2929

1987. **Description:** A guide for women who want to know what to expect when they enter the working world. **Length:** 30 mins. **Format:** VHS. **Acquisition:** Purchase.

★10611★ **Sterilization by Minilaparotomy**
Milner-Fenwick, Inc.
2125 Greenspring Dr.
Timonium, MD 21093
Phone: (301)252-1700

1989. **Description:** Minilaparotomy is a safe and permanent method for a women to be sterilized. **Length:** 11 mins. **Format:** Beta, VHS, 3/4″ U-matic. **Acquisition:** Purchase.

★10612★ **Stop Date Rape!**
Cornell University
Media Services Distribution Center
7-8 Research Park
Ithaca, NY 14850
Phone: (607)255-2091

1987. **Description:** A discussion of things that can be done to prevent acquaintance rape. **Length:** 23 mins. **Format:** VHS. **Acquisition:** Purchase, Rent/Lease.

★10613★ **Successful Breast Feeding Right From the Start**
Teaching Films, Inc.
930 Pitner Ave.
Evanston, IL 60202
Phone: (708)328-6700

1984. **Description:** This program shows mothers the proper techniques and routines for breast feeding their babies. **Length:** 24 mins. **Format:** Beta, VHS, 3/4″ U-matic. **Acquisition:** Rent/Lease, Purchase.

★10614★ **Suffering in Silence: Sexual Assault Survivors**
Kidsrights
3700 Progress Blvd.
Mt. Dora, FL 32757
Phone: 800-892-KIDS

1990. **Description:** The trauma of rape and sexual abuse is discussed by several victims, including an adult survivor of incest, a young boy who was sexually abused by his babysitter, a college student raped by her roommate's friend, a man attacked at knifepoint by a male attacker, and a woman raped by her estranged husband as their small child looked on. **Length:** 22 mins. **Format:** Beta, VHS, 3/4″ U-matic, Other than listed. **Acquisition:** Purchase.

★10615★ **Sugar and Spice and All Is Not Nice**
Learning Corporation of America
108 Wilmot Rd.
Deerfield, IL 60015-9990
Phone: (708)940-1260

1984. **Description:** The myths and realities of rape are examined by June Callwood using victims' interviews. **Length:** 19 mins. **Format:** Beta, VHS, 3/4″ U-matic. **Acquisition:** Rent/Lease, Purchase.

★10616★ **Take Charge of Your Pregnancy**
CBS/Fox Video
1330 Avenue of the Americas, 5th Fl.
New York, NY 10019
Phone: (212)819-3200

1989. **Description:** A guide to pre-natal care with advice from twenty-two experts. **Length:** 90 mins. **Format:** Beta, VHS. **Acquisition:** Purchase.

★10617★ **Technology and Women's Future**
KPBS-TV15
San Diego State University
San Diego, CA 92182
Phone: (714)265-6415
1981. **Description:** Why technology is a women's issue is the focus of this discussion of women's involvement with technological change. **Length:** 30 mins. **Format:** 3/4″ U-matic. **Acquisition:** Purchase.

★10618★ **Teenage Mothers: Beyond the Baby Shower**
Perennial Education, Inc.
930 Pitner Avenue
Evanston, IL 60202
Phone: (312)328-6700
1989. **Description:** Three women serve as examples of what happens to teenage mothers. **Length:** 27 mins. **Format:** VHS, 3/4″ U-matic, Other than listed. **Acquisition:** Purchase.

★10619★ **Tender Places**
Coronet/MTI Film & Video
108 Wilmot Road
Deerfield, IL 60015-9990
Phone: (312)940-1260
1987. **Description:** This film, adapted from the play by Jason Brown, shows how one boy deals with a custody fight during his parents divorce. It is designed to help children understand why divorces occur, that it is not their fault, and to come to grips with their conflicting feelings. **Length:** 25 mins. **Format:** VHS, 8mm, 3/4″ U-matic. **Acquisition:** Purchase, Rent/Lease, Duplication License.

★10620★ **There's No Such Thing as Woman's Work**
National Women's History Project
7738 Bell Rd.
Windsor, CA 95492
Phone: (707)838-6000
1987. **Description:** Photographs, cartoons and newsreels depicting womens' changing influence in the U.S. workforce. **Length:** 30 mins. **Format:** VHS. **Acquisition:** Purchase.

★10621★ **They're Doing My Time**
Cinema Guild
1697 Broadway, Rm. 802
New York, NY 10019
Phone: (212)246-5522
1988. **Description:** The plight of children of women incarcerated in America's prisons is the focus of this film. **Length:** 56 mins. **Format:** Beta, VHS, 3/4″ U-matic. **Acquisition:** Purchase.

★10622★ **Things My Mother Never Told Me**
Perennial Education, Inc.
930 Pitner Ave.
Evanston, IL 60202
Phone: (708)328-6700
1989. **Description:** Myths about the female body, contraception, and reproduction are cleared up. **Length:** 15 mins. **Format:** VHS, 3/4″ U-matic, Other than listed. **Acquisition:** Purchase, Rent/Lease, Trade-in.

★10623★ **Things Your Mother Never Told You**
Filmakers Library, Inc.
124 E. 40th St.
New York, NY 10016
Phone: (212)808-4980
1987. **Description:** A revealing look at the demands and rewards of modern motherhood. **Length:** 58 mins. **Format:** VHS, 3/4″ U-matic. **Acquisition:** Rent/Lease, Purchase, Duplication.

★10624★ **39, Single and Pregnant**
Filmakers Library, Inc.
124 E. 40th St.
New York, NY 10016
Phone: (212)808-4980
1982. **Description:** This program is a portrait of Jane Davis, a secretary who had never married, yet decided at the age of 39 to have a child on her own, following her life from late pregnancy to the toddler age of her child. **Length:** 18 mins. **Format:** Beta, VHS, 3/4″ U-matic. **Acquisition:** Purchase.

★10625★ **This Film is about Rape**
MTI Teleprograms, Inc.
108 Wilmot Rd.
Deerfield, IL 60015-9990
Phone: (708)940-1260
1980. **Description:** This tape gives information on how women can reduce their exposure to rape and how to respond both physically and psychologically should an attack occur. **Length:** 30 mins. **Format:** Beta, VHS, 3/4″ U-matic. **Acquisition:** Rent/Lease, Purchase.

★10626★ **Time Out Series**
MTI Teleprograms, Inc.
108 Wilmot Road
Deerfield, IL 60015-9990
Phone: (312)940-1260
1982. **Description:** A series about the effects of domestic violence on the family and the abusive behavior of the spouses in three separate households. **Length:** 15 mins. **Format:** Beta, VHS, 3/4″ U-matic. **Acquisition:** Rent/Lease, Purchase.

★10627★ **A Time to Tell: Teen Sexual Abuse**
Coronet/MTI Film & Video
108 Wilmot Road
Deerfield, IL 60015-9990
Phone: (312)940-1260
1990. **Description:** A peer group of teenagers talks about date rape, incest and molestation. They learn the importance of sharing their feelings and protecting themselves. **Length:** 20 mins. **Format:** Beta, VHS, 1/2″ reel, 3/4″ U-matic, Other than listed. **Acquisition:** Purchase, Rent/Lease.

★10628★ **To Have and Not to Have a Pregnancy**
Emory Medical Television Network
Emory University
Emory Medical Television Network-Department C
1440 Clifton Road, NE
Atlanta, GA 30322
Phone: (404)727-5817
1986. **Description:** A speech by Dr. Luella Klein about the extraordinary amount of unwed, unwanted teen pregnancy in the country, and what must be done to stop it. **Length:** 20 mins. **Format:** Beta, VHS, 3/4″ U-matic. **Acquisition:** Rent/Lease, Purchase, Subscription.

★10629★ **Too Young to Parent**
Maryland Center for Public Broadcasting
11767 Bonita Avenue
Owings Mills, MD 21117
Phone: (301)356-5600
1988. **Description:** Nine teenagers from Maryland talk about pregnancy. **Length:** 30 mins. **Format:** Beta, VHS, 3/4″ U-matic. **Acquisition:** Purchase.

★10630★ **Trade Secrets: Blue Collar Women Speak Out**
Women Make Movies
225 Lafayette St., Ste. 212
New York, NY 10012
Phone: (212)925-0606
1985. **Description:** Four women talk about what it's like to do work traditionally done by men. **Length:** 23 mins. **Format:** Beta, VHS, 3/4″ U-matic. **Acquisition:** Purchase, Rent/Lease.

★10631★ **The Trial of Susan B. Anthony**
Phoenix/BFA Films
468 Park Avenue South
New York, NY 10016
Phone: (212)684-5910
1972. **Description:** Part of the "You Are There" series. CBS newsman Walter Cronkite acts as anchorman as correspondents cover "The Trial of Susan B. Anthony." One of 15 programs. **Length:** 23 mins. **Format:** Beta, VHS, 3/4″ U-matic. **Acquisition:** Purchase.

★10632★ **A Truck Driver Named Gret**
Carousel Film & Video
260 5th Ave., Rm. 705
New York, NY 10001
Phone: (212)683-1660
1983. **Description:** A look at a 38-year-old woman who is a wife, a mother and a truck driver, yet manages to juggle all three careers at once. **Length:** 11 mins. **Format:** Beta, VHS, 3/4″ U-matic. **Acquisition:** Purchase.

★10633★ **Turnaround: A Story of Recovery**
National Film Board of Canada
1251 Avenue of the Americas, 16th Fl.
New York, NY 10020-1173
Phone: (212)586-5131
1987. **Description:** The Aurora House, a three-month recovery center for drug addicted women, is described. **Length:** 47 mins. **Format:** Beta, VHS, 3/4″ U-matic. **Acquisition:** Purchase, Rent/Lease.

★10634★ **The 21st Century**
Sensor
708 Venice Blvd., Ste. 2
Venice, CA 90291
Phone: (310)823-3428
1979. **Description:** A program exploring women's future in space exploration. **Length:** 30 mins. **Format:** Beta, VHS, 3/4″ U-matic, 1″ Broadcast type C. **Acquisition:** Rent/Lease, Purchase.

★10635★ Two Lies
Women Make Movies
225 Lafayette Street
Suite 212
New York, NY 10012
Phone: (212)925-0606

1989. **Description:** A Chinese-American woman's search for identity is told from the perspective of her daughter. **Length:** 25 mins. **Format:** Beta, VHS, 3/4" U-matic. **Acquisition:** Purchase, Rent/Lease.

★10636★ Two Million Women: Domestic Violence
Coronet/MTI Film & Video
108 Wilmot Rd.
Deerfield, IL 60015-9990
Phone: (708)940-1260

1987. **Description:** Collin Siedor hosts this look at battered women, focusing especially on the question of why these victims stay with the men who continually beat and abuse them and why men beat their wives. **Length:** 29 mins. **Format:** VHS, 8mm, 3/4" U-matic. **Acquisition:** Purchase, Rent/Lease, Duplication License.

★10637★ The Ultimate Test Animal
Cinema Guild
1697 Broadway
Room 802
New York, NY 10019
Phone: (212)246-5522

1985. **Description:** This video explores the issues raised by the controversial birth control method of injecting the drug Depo Provera into women. **Length:** 40 mins. **Format:** Beta, VHS, 3/4" U-matic. **Acquisition:** Rent/Lease, Purchase.

★10638★ Understanding Breast Cancer
AIMS Media, Inc.
6901 Woodley Ave.
Van Nuys, CA 91406-4878
Phone: (818)785-4111

1989. **Description:** The nature of breast cancer as well as some of its causes are covered. **Length:** 12 mins. **Format:** Beta, VHS, 3/4" U-matic. **Acquisition:** Purchase, Rent/Lease.

★10639★ Understanding Common Breast Problems
Design Media
2235 Harrison Street
San Francisco, CA 94110
Phone: (415)641-4848

1988. **Description:** Two women are confused about breast abnormalities. This tape describes and explains such problems. **Length:** 11 mins. **Format:** Beta, VHS, 3/4" U-matic. **Acquisition:** Purchase.

★10640★ Understanding Labor
Professional Research, Inc.
930 Pitner Ave.
Evanston, IL 60202
Phone: (708)328-6700

1988. **Description:** This program describes and explains what goes on during the course of labor and delivery. Guidelines are given for recognizing the onset and course of true labor. **Length:** 11 mins. **Format:** Beta, VHS, 3/4" U-matic. **Acquisition:** Rent/Lease, Purchase.

★10641★ Understanding the Pill
Professional Research, Inc.
930 Pitner Ave.
Evanston, IL 60202
Phone: (708)328-6700

1982. **Description:** This program examines oral contraceptives and how they work. **Length:** 9 mins. **Format:** 1/4" compact videocassette, Beta, VHS, 3/4" U-matic. **Acquisition:** Rent/Lease, Purchase.

★10642★ Vaginal Birth after Cesarean (VBAC)
Lifecircle
2378 Cornell Dr.
Costa Mesa, CA 92626
Phone: (714)546-1427

1986. **Description:** Shows "positive birth sequences" and stresses Cesarean birth prevention techniques. **Length:** 40 mins. **Acquisition:** Rent/Purchase.

★10643★ Veronica 4 Rose
Women Make Movies
225 Lafayette St., Ste. 212
New York, NY 10012
Phone: (212)925-0606

1985. **Description:** Stereotypes about lesbians are addressed in this film which includes candid discussions with several British teenage girls who are coming out. **Length:** 45 mins. **Format:** Beta, VHS, 3/4" U-matic. **Acquisition:** Purchase, Rent/Lease.

★10644★ Visions of the Spirit: A Portrait of Alice Walker
Women Make Movies
225 Lafayette St., Ste. 212
New York, NY 10012
Phone: (212)925-0606

1989. **Description:** Pulitzer Prize-winning author Alice Walker is profiled in this documentary which shows the writer as mother, daughter, philosopher and activist. **Length:** 58 mins. **Format:** Beta, VHS, 3/4" U-matic. **Acquisition:** Purchase, Rent/Lease.

★10645★ Voices of Power
Indiana University Audio-Visual Center
Franklin 004
Bloomington, IN 47405-5901
Phone: (812)855-4848

1987. **Description:** A look at the arduous process of recovering from rape, featuring interencounter group dramatizations and support group therapy. **Length:** 47 mins. **Format:** VHS, 3/4" U-matic. **Acquisition:** Rent/Lease, Purchase, Duplication License.

★10646★ Voices from the Well
University of California at Santa Barbara
Instructional Development
Santa Barbara, CA 93106
Phone: (805)961-3518

1984. **Description:** A dramatized conglomeration of portraits of history's greatest women, from Georgia O'Keefe to Mother Jones to George Sand. **Length:** 45 mins. **Format:** Beta, VHS, 3/4" U-matic. **Acquisition:** Rent/Lease, Purchase.

★10647★ The Waist Land: Eating Disorders
Coronet/MTI Film & Video
108 Wilmot Rd.
Deerfield, IL 60015-9990
Phone: (708)940-1260

1985. **Description:** The social and psychological forces behind anorexia nervosa and bulimia, especially in teen-age girls, are examined in this video. **Length:** 23 mins. **Format:** VHS, 8mm, 3/4" U-matic. **Acquisition:** Purchase, Rent/Lease, Duplication License.

★10648★ The Waiting Room
Carousel Film & Video
260 5th Ave., Rm. 705
New York, NY 10001
Phone: (212)683-1660

1981. **Description:** A provocative discussion of the pros and cons in the abortion issue. Pressures from the family, church, political groups, and medical profession are examined. **Length:** 29 mins. **Format:** Beta, VHS, 3/4" U-matic. **Acquisition:** Purchase.

★10649★ Water Baby: Experiences of Water Birth
Point of View Productions
2477 Folsom Street
San Francisco, CA 94110
Phone: (415)821-0435

1987. **Description:** Leading experts in the field provide comprehensive information on the use of water for labor, birth and early childhood. Includes scenes of actual water births and water training exercises for babies. **Length:** 57 mins. **Format:** Beta, VHS, 3/4" U-matic. **Acquisition:** Rent/Lease, Purchase.

★10650★ We Dig Coal
Cinema Guild
1697 Broadway, Rm. 802
New York, NY 10019
Phone: (212)246-5522

1982. **Description:** This film examines the rigors faced by women coal miners in the U.S. **Length:** 58 mins. **Format:** Beta, VHS, 3/4" U-matic. **Acquisition:** Rent/Lease, Purchase.

★10651★ Weight, Nutrition and Exercise During Pregnancy
Professional Research, Inc.
930 Pitner Ave.
Evanston, IL 60202
Phone: (708)328-6700

1986. **Description:** This revised program explains why the physiological changes a woman experiences during pregnancy increase her need for both nutrition and exercise. The value of a balanced diet is made clear, and exercises for the pregnant woman are demonstrated. **Length:** 14 mins. **Format:** 1/4" compact videocassette, Beta, VHS, 3/4" U-matic. **Acquisition:** Rent/Lease, Purchase.

★10652★ We're Here Now
Filmakers Library, Inc.
124 East 40th
New York, NY 10016
Phone: (212)808-4980

1983. **Description:** Seven former call girls debunk the myths surrounding prostitution. **Length:** 35 mins. **Format:** Beta, VHS, 3/4" U-matic. **Acquisition:** Purchase.

★10653★ WFS Program in Levels of
Recovery
Women For Sobriety, Inc. (WFS)
109 W. Broad St.
PO Box 618
Quakertown, PA 18951
Phone: (215)536-8026
1987. **Description:** The thirteen-step program
specifically designed for female alcoholics is
outlined. **Length:** 95 mins. **Format:** Beta, VHS,
3/4″ U-matic. **Acquisition:** Purchase,
Rent/Lease.

★10654★ What Does She Want?
Video Data Bank
School of the Art Institute of Chicago
37 S. Wabash Ave.
Chicago, IL 60603
Phone: (312)443-3793
1986. **Description:** A series of experimental,
free-form video pieces by and about women.
Each title in the series includes approximately
seven shorts dealing with feminist issues. Experimental short titles include "Suburban
Queen," "A Chevrolet Impala," "Kleenex Napkins Cling Like Cloth," "A Crack in the Tube,"
"In My Merry Oldsmobile," "Christine Choy,"
and numerous others by artists such as Mindy
Faber, Julie Dash, Cecelia Condit, Laurel Chi-
ten, and many other contemporary artists.
Length: 60 mins. **Format:** Beta, VHS, 3/4″ U-
matic. **Acquisition:** Rent/Lease, Purchase.

★10655★ What People Are Calling PMS
Carle Medical Communications
110 W. Main St.
Urbana, IL 61801-2700
Phone: (217)384-4838
1989. **Description:** Some of the many myths
about PMS are examined. **Length:** 28 mins.
Format: Beta, VHS, 3/4″ U-matic. **Acquisition:**
Purchase, Rent/Lease.

★10656★ What You Don't Know CAN Kill
You: Sexually Transmitted Diseases and
AIDS
Guidance Associates, Inc.
Box 3000
90 South Bedford Road
Communications Park
Mt. Kisco, NY 10549
Phone: (914)666-4100
1991. **Description:** A frank look at STD's, AIDS
and real life situations that put a person in
danger of contracting a virus through sexual
contact. **Length:** ? mins. **Format:** VHS. **Acqui-
sition:** Purchase.

★10657★ What You Take for Granted
Women Make Movies
225 Lafayette St., Ste. 212
New York, NY 10012
Phone: (212)925-0606
1983. **Description:** A creative look at women's
experiences in jobs traditionally held by men.
Length: 75 mins. **Format:** Beta, VHS, 3/4″ U-
matic. **Acquisition:** Purchase, Rent/Lease.

★10658★ When the Honeymoon is Over
Lucerne Media
37 Ground Pine Rd.
Morris Plains, NJ 07950
Phone: (201)538-1401
1979. **Description:** This program presents the
personal experiences of four women who suffered mental and physical cruelty at the hands
of their husbands. Part of the "Women" series.
Length: 30 mins. **Format:** Beta, VHS, 3/4″ U-
matic. **Acquisition:** Purchase.

★10659★ When Mom has to Work
Professional Research, Inc.
930 Pitner Ave.
Evanston, IL 60202
Phone: (708)328-6700
1988. **Description:** Women should be able to
have a family and a job without feeling exhaust-
ed or guilty about it. **Length:** 23 mins. **Format:**
Beta, VHS, 3/4″ U-matic. **Acquisition:** Purchase, Rent/Lease.

★10660★ When Sex Means Trouble
Kidsrights
3700 Progress Boulevard
Mt. Dora, FL 32757
Phone: 800-892-KIDS
1990. **Description:** This video discusses the
definitions of sex exploitation, sexual abuse and
acquaintance rape by relating experiences of
teenagers who have encountered these situations and have learned how to cope with them.
Length: 20 mins. **Format:** Beta, VHS, 3/4″ U-
matic, Other than listed. **Acquisition:** Purchase.

★10661★ When Teens Get Pregnant
Polymorph Films
118 South St.
Boston, MA 02111
Phone: (617)542-2004
1982. **Description:** Young girls speak openly
about their lives before becoming pregnant and
the changes in their lives since. **Length:** 19
mins. **Format:** Beta, VHS, 3/4″ U-matic. **Acquisition:** Rent/Lease, Purchase.

★10662★ When a Woman Fights Back
PBS Video
1320 Braddock Pl.
Alexandria, VA 22314-1698
Phone: (703)739-5380
1980. **Description:** Legal and social questions
are raised about four recent court cases in the
state of Washington involving women who killed
men in self-defense. One of the trials set a legal
precedent when the Washington State Supreme
Court reversed a conviction. **Length:** 59 mins.
Format: Beta, VHS, 3/4″ U-matic. **Acquisition:**
Rent/Lease, Purchase, Off-Air Record.

★10663★ Who Remembers Mama?
Media Project, Inc.
PO Box 4093
Portland, OR 97208
Phone: (503)223-5335
1988. **Description:** A documentary exploring
the plight of divorced, middle aged women
showing the emotional, economic, and legal
problems of the divorcee. **Length:** 60 mins.
Format: Beta, VHS. **Acquisition:** Rent/Lease,
Purchase.

★10664★ Who's There for the Victim?
MTI Teleprograms, Inc.
108 Wilmot Rd.
Deerfield, IL 60015-9990
Phone: (708)940-1260
1981. **Description:** An in-depth look at a group
of dedicated volunteers serving the special
needs of rape victims. **Length:** 22 mins. **Format:** Beta, VHS, 3/4″ U-matic. **Acquisition:**
Rent/Lease, Purchase.

★10665★ Why Women Stay
Women Make Movies
225 Lafayette St., Ste. 212
New York, NY 10012
Phone: (212)925-0606
1979. **Description:** A study of the position of
the battered woman in today's society: why
many women stay in violent homes and possible
alternatives. **Length:** 30 mins. **Format:** 3/4″ U-
matic. **Acquisition:** Rent/Lease, Purchase.

★10666★ Windows on Women
CC-M Productions
7755 16th St. NW
Washington, DC 20012
Phone: (301)588-4095
1986. **Description:** A look through interviews
and statistics at the changing role of women in
today's world. **Length:** 60 mins. **Format:** Beta,
VHS, 3/4″ U-matic. **Acquisition:** Purchase.

★10667★ With Babies and Banners
New Day Films
121 W. 27th St., Ste. 902
New York, NY 10001
Phone: (212)645-8210
1978. **Description:** A look at the Women's
Emergency Brigade of 1937, the backbone of
the General Motors sitdown strike which was
the key to the success of the C.I.O's national
drive for industrial unionism. **Length:** 45 mins.
Format: Beta, VHS, 3/4″ U-matic. **Acquisition:**
Rent/Lease, Purchase.

★10668★ With a Vengeance: The Fight
for Reproductive Freedom
Women Make Movies
225 Lafayette St., Ste. 212
New York, NY 10012
Phone: (212)925-0606
1990. **Description:** Produced by and for young
women, this powerful video draws parellels
between the fights for abortion rights in the '60s
and again in the '80s. Focusing on the strength
of the women's movement, "With a Vengeance" provides inspiration for women of all
colors and economic backgrounds to unite
together to protect their reproductive rights.
Length: 40 mins. **Format:** Beta, VHS, 3/4″ U-
matic. **Acquisition:** Purchase, Rent/Lease.

★10669★ Without Consent
Pyramid Film & Video
Box 1048
2801 Colorado Ave.
Santa Monica, CA 90406
Phone: (310)828-7577
1987. **Description:** This thought-provoking drama will stimulate discussions about acquaintance rape as it challenges viewers to consider
what rape is, why it occurs, how it might be
prevented, and who is ultimately responsible.
Length: 25 mins. **Format:** Beta, VHS, 3/4″ U-

matic. **Acquisition:** Purchase, Rent/Lease, Duplication License.

★10670★ **Woman Entrepreneur: Do You Have What it Takes?**
United Home Video
4111 S. Darlington St., Ste. 600
Tulsa, OK 74135
Phone: (918)622-6460

1987. **Description:** A motivational look at starting a business for women, featuring interviews with a half dozen women who have made it. **Length:** 55 mins. **Format:** Beta, VHS. **Acquisition:** Purchase.

★10671★ **The Woman Rebel**
King Features Entertainment
235 E. 45th St.
New York, NY 10017
Phone: (212)682-5600

1977. **Description:** A docu-drama about the life and work of Margaret Sanger who was largely responsible for acceptance of the birth control pill. **Length:** 58 mins. **Format:** Beta, VHS, 3/4″ U-matic. **Acquisition:** Rent/Lease, Purchase.

★10672★ **The Woman's "How To" of Self-Defense**
Cambridge Career Products
1 Players Club Dr.
Charleston, WV 25311
Phone: (304)344-8550

1985. **Description:** Ward off rapists and muggers with the tips given here. **Length:** 50 mins. **Format:** VHS. **Acquisition:** Purchase.

★10673★ **A Woman's Place**
V.I.E.W. Video
34 E. 23rd St.
New York, NY 10010
Phone: (212)674-5550

1989. **Description:** Rare film footage and still photography highlight this documentary which examines the contributions of women who dared to be "first" in the arts, sciences, business and athletics. Narrated by Julie Harris. **Length:** 25 mins. **Format:** Beta, VHS. **Acquisition:** Purchase.

★10674★ **Women and AIDS: A Survival Kit**
University of California at Berkeley Extension
  Media Center
2176 Shattuck Ave.
Berkeley, CA 94704
Phone: (510)642-0460

1989. **Description:** Heterosexual women are not free from the dangers of AIDS. This program tells them how to avoid it. **Length:** 22 mins. **Format:** VHS, 3/4″ U-matic. **Acquisition:** Purchase, Rent/Lease.

★10675★ **Women in America**
Dallas County Community College District
Center for Telecommunications
4343 N. Hwy. 67
Mesquite, TX 75150-2095
Phone: (214)324-7988

1980. **Description:** This program provides a historical prospective on the women's movement in America. **Length:** 28 mins. **Format:** 3/4″ U-matic. **Acquisition:** Purchase.

★10676★ **Women and the American Family**
Video Knowledge, Inc.
29 Bramble Ln.
Melville, NY 11747
Phone: (516)367-4250

1987. **Description:** The role of women - past, present, and future - is examined from a historical perspective. **Length:** 28 mins. **Format:** VHS. **Acquisition:** Purchase.

★10677★ **Women in American Life—Video Series**
National Women's History Project
7738 Bell Rd.
Windsor, CA 95492
Phone: (707)838-6000

1989. **Description:** This five-part series features over 700 historical photographs selected from dozens of photo archives throughout the United States. Each video focuses on a particular time in the country's history and emphasizes women's daily life experiences, work and involvements with social issues. Also available individually. **Length:** 88 mins. **Format:** VHS. **Acquisition:** Purchase.

★10678★ **Women in Business**
Direct Cinema Limited, Inc.
Box 69799
Los Angeles, CA 90069
Phone: (213)652-8000

1984. **Description:** Six different women discuss their business problems and successes. **Length:** 24 mins. **Format:** Beta, VHS, 3/4″ U-matic, Other than listed. **Acquisition:** Rent/Lease, Purchase.

★10679★ **Women in Business: The Risks, Rewards & Secrets of Running Your Own Company**
Wishing Well Distributing
PO Box 2
Wilmot, WI 53192
Phone: 800-888-9355

1990. **Description:** Five successful businesswomen give insights and advice on the business world. **Length:** 75 mins. **Format:** VHS. **Acquisition:** Purchase.

★10680★ **Women, Drugs and Alcohol**
MTI Teleprograms, Inc.
108 Wilmot Rd.
Deerfield, IL 60015-9990
Phone: (708)940-1260

1980. **Description:** A look at the monumental problem of drug and alcohol abuse among women in our society, with special emphasis on prescription drugs. **Length:** ? mins. **Format:** Beta, VHS, 3/4″ U-matic. **Acquisition:** Rent/Lease, Purchase.

★10681★ **Women, Drugs and the Unborn Child**
Pyramid Film & Video
Box 1048
2801 Colorado Ave.
Santa Monica, CA 90406
Phone: (310)828-7577

1987. **Description:** A package of two films on the dangers of prenatal drug and alcohol abuse. **Length:** 54 mins. **Format:** Beta, VHS, 3/4″ U-matic. **Acquisition:** Purchase, Rent/Lease, Duplication License.

★10682★ **Women and Family**
California State University at Chico
Instructional Media Center
Chico, CA 95929
Phone: (916)895-6112

1979. **Description:** This program includes role models of egalitarian marriage, a call for change from traditional male-female roles, child care, and communication skills. **Length:** 50 mins. **Format:** Beta, VHS, 3/4″ U-matic. **Acquisition:** Purchase.

★10683★ **Women: The Hand That Cradles the Rock**
Cinema Guild
1697 Broadway, Rm. 802
New York, NY 10019
Phone: (212)246-5522

198?. **Description:** This film presents both the concepts of individuals in the Women's Liberation movement, as well as the opinions of those satisfied with their traditional roles. **Length:** 20 mins. **Format:** 3/4″ U-matic, Other than listed. **Acquisition:** Purchase.

★10684★ **Women: Hope of the World**
Keep the Faith Inc.
PO Box 8261
810 Belmont Ave.
North Haledon, NJ 07508
Phone: (201)423-5395

1990. **Description:** This Catholic video talks about the role women can play in the future. **Length:** 30 mins. **Format:** Beta, VHS. **Acquisition:** Purchase.

★10685★ **Women and the Law**
WTL Productions
600 N. Jackson St.
Media, PA 19063
Phone: (215)626-7470

1980. **Description:** This series explores selected aspects of the law as it has affected women. **Length:** 30 mins. **Format:** Beta, VHS, 1/2″ reel, 3/4″ U-matic, Other than listed. **Acquisition:** Rent/Lease, Purchase.

★10686★ **Women Make the Difference**
New York State Education Department
Center for Learning Technologies
Media Distribution Network
Rm. C-7, Concourse Level
Albany, NY 12230
Phone: (518)474-1265

197?. **Description:** Women can enrich their lives by volunteering their services to the community, as this program shows. **Length:** 28 mins. **Format:** Beta, VHS, 1/2″ reel, 3/4″ U-matic, 2″ Quad. **Acquisition:** Duplication.

★10687★ **Women in Ministry**
William C. Brown Company Publishers/ROA
  Media
Religious Education Division
2460 Kerper Blvd.
PO Box 539
Dubuque, IA 52001
Phone: 800-922-7696

1987. **Description:** Women are becoming more and more involved in church ministries. **Length:** 30 mins. **Format:** VHS. **Acquisition:** Purchase.

★10688★ Women in Politics
King Features Entertainment
235 E. 45th St.
New York, NY 10017
Phone: (212)682-5600
1983. **Description:** This program follows the origins of the women's rights movement right up to the contemporary issues of women's political power. **Length:** 14 mins. **Format:** Beta, VHS, 3/4″ U-matic. **Acquisition:** Rent/Lease, Purchase.

★10689★ Women, Power, and Politics
New Jersey Network
1573 Parkside Ave.
Trenton, NJ 08625
Phone: (609)292-5252
1988. **Description:** This documentary examines the history of women's rights from the early 20th century to Geraldine Ferraro's nomination for the Vice Presidency of the country. **Length:** 30 mins. **Format:** VHS, 3/4″ U-matic. **Acquisition:** Rent/Lease, Purchase.

★10690★ Women in Science
Agency for Instructional Technology
Box A
Bloomington, IN 47402
Phone: (812)339-2203
1988. **Description:** A videotape which explains to females what scientific careers are open to them. **Length:** 30 mins. **Format:** Beta, VHS, 3/4″ U-matic. **Acquisition:** Purchase, Rent/Lease, Duplication License.

★10691★ Women and Society
Journal Films, Inc.
930 Pitner Ave.
Evanston, IL 60202
Phone: (708)328-6700
1988. **Description:** The history of women in a male-dominated society is chronicled. **Length:** 26 mins. **Format:** Beta, VHS, 3/4″ U-matic. **Acquisition:** Purchase, Rent/Lease.

★10692★ The Women of the Summer
Filmakers Library, Inc.
124 E. 40th St.
New York, NY 10016
Phone: (212)808-4980
1986. **Description:** This documentary examines the Bryn Mawr Summer School for Women Workers. In operation from 1921 to 1938, the school brought together seventeen hundred blue collar women of different economic backgrounds and races, to study the humanities and political science. In the end, its funders, including the Rockefellers, DuPonts, and Carnegies, found the school too radical. **Length:** 55 mins. **Format:** VHS, 3/4″ U-matic. **Acquisition:** Rent/Lease, Purchase, Duplication.

★10693★ Women Who Changed the Century, Vol. 1
Minnesota Studio
430 Oak Grove St., Ste. 222
Minneapolis, MN 55403
Phone: (612)879-0493
1986. **Description:** A retrospective look at the century's important women, from Helen Keller to Mata Hari to Eleanor Roosevelt. **Length:** 60 mins. **Format:** VHS. **Acquisition:** Purchase.

★10694★ Women, Wine & Wellness: Alcohol & Your Body
Gerald T. Rogers Productions, Inc.
5215 Old Orchard Rd., Ste. 410
Skokie, IL 60077
Phone: (708)967-8080
1991. **Description:** This two-part series speaks candidly to women between the ages of 16 and 30. Part one details the physiological impact of alcohol, including diseases and nutritional impairment. Part two deals with the risk of drinking alcohol during pregnancy and the detrimental effects of advertising on women. **Length:** 9 mins. **Format:** VHS, 3/4″ U-matic. **Acquisition:** Rent/Lease, Purchase.

★10695★ Women's Guide to B.S.E.
Pyramid Film & Video
Box 1048
2801 Colorado Ave.
Santa Monica, CA 90406
Phone: (310)828-7577
1986. **Description:** This program presents a detailed, logical presentation of the three steps of breast self-examination as promoted by the American Society and the National Cancer Institute. **Length:** 18 mins. **Format:** Beta, VHS, 3/4″ U-matic. **Acquisition:** Purchase, Rent/Lease, Duplication License.

★10696★ Women's Voices: The Gender Gap Movie
New Day Films
121 W. 27th St., Ste. 902
New York, NY 10001
Phone: (212)645-8210
1985. **Description:** A look at modern feminist outrage, using interviews, statistics and satiric animated skits. **Length:** 16 mins. **Format:** Beta, VHS, 3/4″ U-matic. **Acquisition:** Rent/Lease, Purchase.

★10697★ A Word in Edgewise
Women Make Movies
225 Lafayette St., Ste. 212
New York, NY 10012
Phone: (212)925-0606
1986. **Description:** An inventive, necessary video which insightfully exposes the numerous biases against women in the English language. **Length:** 26 mins. **Format:** Beta, VHS, 3/4″ U-matic. **Acquisition:** Purchase, Rent/Lease.

★10698★ Working and Breast Feeding
University of Minnesota Media Distribution
Box 734 Mayo Bldg.
420 Delaware St. SE
Minneapolis, MN 55455
Phone: (612)624-7906
1988. **Description:** The pros and cons of a working woman trying to nurse an infant are weighed. **Length:** 10 mins. **Format:** Beta, VHS, 3/4″ U-matic. **Acquisition:** Purchase, Rent/Lease.

★10699★ The Working Mom's Survival Guide
Xenejenex
300 Brickstone Sq.
Andover, MA 01810
Phone: 800-228-2495
1990. **Description:** Successful career women with families give tips for survival to working moms. Expectant mothers who plan a return to

the office will find this useful. A 15-minute workout is included. **Length:** 30 mins. **Format:** VHS. **Acquisition:** Purchase.

★10700★ Workshop Materials for In-Service Training Developed by National Women's History Project
National Women's History Project
7738 Bell Rd.
Windsor, CA 95492
Phone: (707)838-6000
1989. **Description:** An educational video for educators who want to integrate women's role in history into their curriculum. **Length:** 12 mins. **Format:** Beta, VHS, 3/4″ U-matic. **Acquisition:** Purchase.

★10701★ World Feminists
Martha Stuart Communications, Inc.
Post Office Box 246
Hillsdale, NY 12529
Phone: (518)325-3900
1980. **Description:** This program is an international women's effort in realizing the primary issues affecting women today. Material discussed includes sex descrimination, role of male feminists, and the media's perception and view of women in societies throughout the world. **Length:** 28 mins. **Format:** 3/4″ U-matic, 2″ Quad. **Acquisition:** Rent/Lease, Purchase.

★10702★ You CAN Be Too Thin: Understanding Anorexia and Bulimia
Guidance Associates, Inc.
Box 3000
90 S. Bedford Rd.
Communications Park
Mt. Kisco, NY 10549
Phone: (914)666-4100
1991. **Description:** This video explains eating disorders and offers approaches to solving them. **Length:** ? mins. **Format:** VHS. **Acquisition:** Purchase.

★10703★ You are the Game: Sexual Harassment on Campus
Indiana University Audio-Visual Center
Franklin 004
Bloomington, IN 47405-5901
Phone: (812)855-4848
1985. **Description:** A dramatization and following discussion about students harassed on campus by professors. **Length:** 59 mins. **Format:** Beta, VHS, 3/4″ U-matic. **Acquisition:** Rent/Lease, Purchase.

★10704★ Young, Single and Pregnant: A New Perspective
Center for Humanities, Inc.
Communications Park
Box 1000
Mt. Kisco, NY 10549
Phone: (914)666-4100
1981. **Description:** This program offers several case histories which point out the problems that attend any teenage pregnancy and sexual activity, and reliable birth control is discussed. **Length:** 50 mins. **Format:** Beta, VHS, 3/4″ U-matic. **Acquisition:** Purchase.

★10705★ You've Come a Long Way,
    Maybe?
Indiana University Audio-Visual Center
Franklin 004
Bloomington, IN 47405-5901
Phone: (812)855-4848

1981. **Description:** A documentary based upon
the question "Are women paid less than men
because of marketplace factors, or because of
subtle, historical patterns of discrimination?"
Length: 55 mins. **Format:** 3/4" U-matic. **Acquisition:** Rent/Lease, Purchase, Duplication License.

(26) Electronic Resources

Entries in this chapter are arranged alphabetically by resource name. See the User's Guide at the front of this directory for additional information.

★10706★ Data Archive on Adolescent Pregnancy and Pregnancy Prevention
Sociometrics Corporation
170 State St., No. 260
Los Altos, CA 94022
Phone: (415)949-3282

Description: Covers studies dealing with adolescent family life, sexuality, contraception, pregnancy, childbearing, parenting, and family planning. **Language Used in Database:** English. **Subject Coverage:** Adolescent sexuality, health, marriage, employment, and education; general information on family planning, infant health, and attitudes toward sexual issues; information on social demographics. **Format:** CD-ROM (known as NATASHA: National Archive on Sexuality, Health, & Adolescence); diskette; magnetic tape.

★10707★ Data Resources of the Henry A. Murray Research Center of Radcliffe College
Henry A. Murray Research Center
Radcliffe College
Garden St.
Cambridge, MA 02138
Phone: (617)495-8140

Description: Contains social science data on the lives and experiences of American Women. **Language Used in Database:** English. **Subject Coverage:** American women in sociology. **Format:** Diskette; magnetic tape.

★10708★ Database of Third World Women's Literary Works
Folke Bernadotte Memorial Library
Gustavus Adolphus College
St. Peter, MN 56082
Phone: (507)933-7553
Barbara Fister, Contact

Description: Contain a list of more than 600 novels, short story collections, plays, collections of poetry, and personal narratives derived from third world women writers. Typical data elements include title, author, region, and country. **Language Used in Database:** English. **Subject Coverage:** Third world women writers. **Format:** Producer provides search services.

★10709★ EDUCOM-W

Description: Provides a forum for the exchange of information dealing with issues in technology and education that are of interest to women. **Language Used in Database:** English. **Subject Coverage:** Technological and educational is-

sues of interest to women. **Format:** Electronic bulletin board. **Electronic mail address:** LISTSERV@BITNIC (BITNET); LISTSERV@BITNIC.EDUCOM.ORG (Internet).

★10710★ Endometriosis Association Research Registry
Endometriosis Association
8585 N. 76th Place
Milwaukee, WI 53223
Phone: (414)355-2200

Description: Contains detailed case histories of individuals diagnosed with endometriosis, a female disorder in which endometrial tissue, which lines the uterus, is found in other locations in the body, usually the abdomen. Provides coded and analyzed questionnaire responses that cover each respondent's experiences with the disease, including symptoms, diagnosis, treatment, and outcome of treatment. **Language Used in Database:** English. **Subject Coverage:** Endometriosis, including etiology, symptoms, treatment, psychosocial aspects, and coping methods. **Format:** Producer provides search services.

★10711★ Family Resources Database
National Council on Family Relations (NCFR)
3989 Central Ave. NE, Ste. 550
Minneapolis, MN 55421
Phone: (612)781-9331

Description: Provides references and abstracts of journal and nonjournal literature covering marriage and the family as well as descriptions of the programs and services offered by research centers and other organizations in the field. Includes the Human Resource Bank, which lists family specialists willing to be contacted by the general public; and the Idea Bank, which covers research work in progress. **Language Used in Database:** English. **Subject Coverage:** Marriage and family, including trends and changes; organizations and services for families; family relationships and dynamics; mate selection; marriage and divorce; issues related to reproduction; sexual attitudes and behavior; families with special problems; psychology and sociology; counseling, therapy, and education; minority groups; and aids for theory and research. **Format:** Online; magnetic tape.

★10712★ FEMAIL

Description: Provides a forum for the discussion issues of interest to women. **Language Used in Database:** English. **Subject Coverage:**

Women's issues. **Format:** Electronic bulletin board. **Electronic mail address:** FEMAIL-REQUEST%HPDLH@HPLABS.HP.COM.

★10713★ FEMECON-L
Jean Shackelford, Contact

Description: Provides a forum for the exchange of information involving economics, including research, syllabi, pedagogy discussions, resources, job listings, and general concerns. **Language Used in Database:** English. **Subject Coverage:** Feminist economics. **Format:** Electronic bulletin board. **Electronic mail address:** MAILSERVE@BUCKNELL.EDU; MAILSERV@BKNLVMS.BITNET.

★10714★ FEMINIST
Feminist Task Force of the American Library Association

Description: Provides a forum for the exchange of information dealing sexism in the libraries and librarianship field. Includes issues such as pornography and censorship in the libraries and racism and ethnic diversity in librarianship field. **Language Used in Database:** English. **Subject Coverage:** Sexism. **Format:** Electronic bulletin board. **Electronic mail address:** LISTSERV@MITVMA (BITNET); LISTSERV@MITVMA.MIT.EDU (Internet).

★10715★ FEMREL-L
Cathy Quick, Contact

Description: Provides a forum for the discussion of topics dealing with women and religion and feminist theology. **Language Used in Database:** English. **Subject Coverage:** Women and religion. **Format:** Electronic bulletin board. **Electronic mail address:** LISTSERV@UMCVMB (BITNET).

★10716★ GENDER

Description: Provides a forum for the discussion of questions and issues pertaining to the study of communication and gender from an academic perspective. **Language Used in Database:** English. **Subject Coverage:** Communications and gender. **Format:** Electronic bulletin board. **Electronic mail address:** COMSERVE@RPIECS (BITNET); COMSERVE@VM.ECS.RPI.EDU. (Internet).

★10717★ Human Sexuality
Clinical Communications, Inc.
132 Hutchin Hill
Shady, NY 12409
Phone: (914)679-2217

Description: Provides information and advice on sexuality and sex-related topics as well as emotional support groups for participants. Organized into three basic sections:

The Hotline receives approximately 500 user messages each week; many are referred to the service's consulting medical editors.

The Information Service contains more than 1500 replies to user questions and lists special features on major issues, online transcripts of conversations with experts, and a reader exchange on relationship experiences.

Support Groups enable users to share feelings through live conferencing and message boards; each group has a leader who serves as discussion facilitator. One group is geared toward specific relationship groups such as couples, parents, singles, women, and homosexuals; the other focuses on specific topics such as passages, breaking up, encounter groups, and bisexuality.

Language Used in Database: English. **Subject Coverage:** Sexuality and sex-related topics, including relationships, contraception, homosexuality, sexual dysfunctions, and sexually transmitted diseases, as well as other areas of urology, gynecology, psychiatry, and pharmacology. **Format:** Online.

★10718★ Kinsey Institute for Research in Sex, Gender, and Reproduction Bibliographic Database
Kinsey Institute for Research in Sex, Gender, and Reproduction
Information Services
Morrison Hall, 4th Fl.
Indiana University
Bloomington, IN 47405
Phone: (812)855-7686

Description: Provides full bibliographic descriptions of books received by the Kinsey Institute's library. **Language Used in Database:** English. **Subject Coverage:** Sex, gender, reproduction, and sexual behavior. **Format:** Producer provides search services.

★10719★ Legislative Responses to Women's Suffrage and ERA
Political Science Department
Marquette University
Milwaukee, WI 53233
Janet Boles, Contact

Description: Comprises two data sets dealing with the socioeconomic and political status of women. The ERA set contains 74 variables for 50 states; the suffrage set contains 39 variables for 49 states. Most measures are from a common time period close to the policy itself. Legislative responses are measured in terms of direction, speed, and consensus of ratifications. **Language Used in Database:** English. **Subject Coverage:** ERA and suffrage legislative responses. **Format:** Producer provides search services.

★10720★ LEXIS Family Law Library
Mead Data Central, Inc. (MDC)
LEXIS
9393 Springboro Pike
PO Box 933
Dayton, OH 45401
Phone: (513)865-6800

Description: Provides statutes and case law from 50 states and the District of Columbia covering 20 areas of family-related law. **Language Used in Database:** English. **Subject Coverage:** Family-related law, including abortion, child support, and divorce. **Format:** Online.

★10721★ Library and Information Network
Planned Parenthood Federation of America, Inc.
Education Department
810 7th Ave.
New York, NY 10019
Phone: (212)603-4637

Description: Cites books, journal articles, and papers held in Planned Parenthood Federation's Katharine Dexter McCormick (KDM) Library covering 1973 to the present, as well as programs, program materials, curricula, audiovisual resources, and pamphlets held in the Federation's Clearinghouse of Educational Resources (CLH) covering 1980 to the present. **Language Used in Database:** English. **Subject Coverage:** Sexuality education, birth control, human sexuality, family planning, reproductive health, population, and related topics. **Format:** Producer provides search services.

★10722★ Marguerite Rawalt Resource Center Database
Business and Professional Women's Foundation
2021 Massachusetts Ave. NW
Washington, DC 20036
Phone: (202)293-1200

Description: Contains information dealing with the status of women in the United States, workplace trends, economic issues affecting women workers, and balancing work and family life. **Language Used in Database:** English. **Subject Coverage:** Women in the United States. **Format:** Producer provides search services.

★10723★ Marketing to Women
Marketing to Women, Inc.
33 Broad St.
Boston, MA 02109
Phone: (617)723-4337
Fax: (617)723-7107

Description: Contains the complete text of *Marketing to Women*, a monthly newsletter discussing market studies aimed at women. Covers such topics as demographics, women's attitudes, family issues, consumer products, fashion, media preferences, health care, employment, recreation, food and nutrition, shopping, working women, travel, and reproduction. Includes interviews, research news, and book reviews. **Language Used in Database:** English. **Subject Coverage:** Advertising and marketing directed towards women. **Format:** Online.

★10724★ The National Report on Work and Family
The Bureau of National Affairs, Inc. (BNA)
BNA ONLINE
1231 25th St. NW
Washington, DC 20037
Phone: (202)452-4132

Description: Provides information on social issues concerning work and family, including related court cases and legal requirements. **Language Used in Database:** English. **Subject Coverage:** Work and family issues, including day care, alternative work schedules, paternity and maternity leave, relocation, sick child care, pay equity and nondiscrimination insurance, and elder care. **Format:** Online; producer provide search services.

★10725★ National Women's Mailing List
Women's Information Exchange
PO Box 68
Jenner, CA 95450
Phone: (707)632-5763

Description: Contains names and addresses of individuals and groups interested in women's and feminist issues. **Language Used in Database:** English. **Subject Coverage:** Women's and feminist issues. **Format:** Producer provides search services.

★10726★ Obstetrics and Gynecology on Disc
Elsevier Science Publishing Co., Inc.
655 Avenue of the Americas
New York, NY 10010
Phone: (212)989-5800

Description: Contains the complete text of each issue of Obstetrics and Gynecology, the journal of the American College of Obstetricians and Gynecologists (ACOG). Includes all articles, tables, color and black and white images, and references cited. **Language Used in Database:** English. **Subject Coverage:** Obstetrics and gynecology, especially the medical and surgical treatment of female conditions, obstetrics management, and clinical evaluation of drugs and instruments. **Format:** Online.

★10727★ Political Culture and Female Political Representation
Department of Political Science
Texas A&M University
College Station, TX 77843
David Hill, Contact

Description: Contains information on the political culture and political representation of women. Provides indicators of political culture, status of women, historical treatment of women, legislative and institutional arrangements, and female membership in each state legislature. **Language Used in Database:** English. **Subject Coverage:** Female political represention. **Format:** Magnetic tape.

★10728★ Pregnant Professionals: Balancing Career & Family
The Bureau of National Affairs, Inc. (BNA)
1231 25th St. NW
Washington, DC 20037
Phone: (202)452-4132
Toll-free: 800-452-7773
Fax: (202)882-8092

Description: Contains the complete text of Pregnant Professionals: Balancing Career and Family, a special report providing information on problems associated with balancing a professional career, pregnancy, and family. Includes possible solutions to a given problems. **Language Used in Database:** English. **Subject Coverage:** Family and family life. **Format:** Online.

★10729★ **Promoting Minorities & Women**
The Bureau of National Affairs, Inc. (BNA)
1231 25th St. NW
Washington, DC 20037
Phone: (202)452-4132
Toll-free: 800-452-7773
Fax: (202)822-8092
Description: Contains the complete text of *Promoting Minorities & Women*, a special report on affirmative action policies in the 1990s. Includes information on changing demographics of the U.S. labor pool, with projections of labor force growth by sex and race. Provides examples of major corporate affirmative action programs and reviews of several case studies. **Language Used in Database:** English. **Subject Coverage:** Employment of women and minorities and family life. **Format:** Online.

★10730★ **Research Clearinghouse on Women of Color and Southern Women**
Center for Research on Women
Memphis State University
Clement Hall, Rm. 339
Memphis, TN 38152
Phone: (901)678-2770
Description: Provides bibliographic citations to the social science and historical works on women of color (African American, Asian American, Latinas, and Native Americans) in the United States and women of the Southern United States since 1975. Covers anthropology, criminal justice, economics, education, health, history, psychology, political science, and sociology of women of color and southern women. **Language Used in Database:** English. **Subject Coverage:** Literature on women of color and southern women. **Format:** Diskette; producer provides search services.

★10731★ **Research-in-Progress**
National Council for Research on Women (NCROW)
Sara Delano Roosevelt Memorial House
47-49 E. 65th St.
New York, NY 10021
Phone: (212)570-5001
Description: Contains citations to books, articles, dissertations, working papers, curricula, art, software, and reports pertaining to research in the field of women's studies. **Language Used in Database:** English. **Subject Coverage:** Women's studies. **Format:** Online.

★10732★ **Retirement Income versus Family Responsibilities: 10 Ways to Protect Working Women's Pension Benefits**
Executive Telecom System International (ETSI), Human Resource Information Network (HRIN)
College Park North
9585 Valparaiso Court
Indianapolis, IN 46268
Phone: (317)421-8884
Description: Contains the complete text of *Retirement Income Versus Family Responsibilities: 10 Ways to Protect Working Women's*

Pension Benefits, a special report covering continuing retirement benefits for women who may temporarily drop out of the workforce. **Language Used in Database:** English. **Subject Coverage:** Employee benefits and pension plans for women. **Format:** Online.

★10733★ **Roper Center for Public Opinion Research**
The Roper Center for Public Opinion Research, Inc.
University of Connecticut
U-164 R
Storrs, CT 06268
Phone: (203)486-4440
Description: Contains a collection of more than 9000 survey data sets covering information from some 75 countries dealing with domestic political attitudes and behavior, public policy, market research, and mass media. **Language Used in Database:** English. **Subject Coverage:** Global sociology and demographics. **Format:** Diskette; magnetic tape.

★10734★ **Sexual Harassment in the Federal Workplace, 1978-1980**
United States Merit Systems Protection Board
1120 Vermont Ave. NW
Washington, DC 20419
Description: Contains the responses to a mail survey on sexual harassment. Provides demographic information on the respondent, attitudinal and demographic information on the respondent's workplace, attitudes regarding sexual behavior that may occur at work, respondent definition of sexual harassment, general data on the incidence level of sexual harassment, and information about whether the respondent has been accused of sexual harassment. **Language Used in Database:** English. **Subject Coverage:** Sexual harassment. **Format:** Producer provides search services.

★10735★ **Survey of Women-Owned Businesses**
U.S. Bureau of the Census
Economic Surveys Division
Washington, DC 20233
Phone: (301)763-5470
Description: Covers basic economic data on businesses owned by women in the United States. **Language Used in Database:** English. **Subject Coverage:** U.S. women-owned businesses. **Format:** CD-ROM.

★10736★ **SWIP-L**
Society for Women in Philosophy (SWIP)
University of South Florida
Women's Studies
Tampa, FL 33620
Phone: (813)974-5531
Linda Lopez McAlister, Contact
Description: Provides a forum for the discussion of issues in feminist philosophy. Intended primarily for academic and professional people involved with women's studies such as teachers, researchers, and program administrators. **Language Used in Database:** English. **Subject Coverage:** Women's Studies. **Format:** Electronic bulletin board. **Electronic mail address:** LISTSERV@CFRVM; LISTERV@CFRVM.CFR.USF.EDU.

★10737★ **Systers**
Digital Equipment Corporation
Western Research Laboratory
250 University Ave.
Palo Alto, CA 94301
Phone: (415)688-1500
Anita Borg, Contact
Description: Provides a forum for female computer scientists for the exchange of research and career information. **Language(s) used in text:** English. **Subjects:** Women in computer science. **Format:** Electronic bulletin board. **Electronic mail address:** SYSTERS-REQUEST@WRL.DEC.COM.

★10738★ **WISENET**
University of Illinois at Chicago
Computer Center
Chicago, IL 60612
Phone: (312)996-2479
Harriet Coleman, Contact
Description: Provides a forum for the discussion of women in science, mathematics, and engineering. **Language Used in Database:** English. **Subject Coverage:** Women in the sciences. **Format:** Electronic bulletin board. **Electronic mail address:** U35049@UICVM.

★10739★ **WMST-L**
Description: Provides a forum for the discussion of questions and issues pertaining to women's studies. Intended primarily for academic and professional people involved with women's studies such as teachers, researchers, and program administrators. **Language Used in Database:** English. **Subject Coverage:** Women's Studies. **Format:** Electronic bulletin board. **Electronic mail address:** LISTSERV@UMDD (BITNET); LISTSERVL@UMDD.UMD.EDU (Internet).

★10740★ **Woman, Water and Sanitation**
National Information Services Corporation (NISC)
Wyman Towers, Ste. 6
3100 St. Paul St.
Baltimore, MD 21218
Phone: (301)243-0797
Fax: (301)454-8061
Description: Contains the complete text of major documents dealing with environmental issues, sanitation concerns, health practices, and the education and training of health care workers released by international development associations. Includes small- and large-scale studies of community-based development projects. Covers documents released by such agencies as the U.S. Agency for International Development (USAID), Cooperative for American Relief Everywhere (CARE), United Nations Development Programm/PROWNESS, United Nations Children's Fund (UNICEF), World Health Organization (WHO), Pan American Health Organization (PAHO), International Reference Centre for Community Water Supply and Sanitation, United Nations International Research and Training Institute for the Advancement of Women (INSTRAW), International Drinking Water Supply and Sanitation Decade (IDWSSD), World Bank, United Nations Interagency Task Force on Women, and NGO Committee on UNICEF/Kenya. **Language Used in Database:** English. **Subject Coverage:** Health and sanitation concerns, practices, and education. **Format:** CD-ROM.

★10741★ Women: Partners in Development
CD Resources, Inc.
118 W. 74th St., Ste. 2A
New York, NY 10023
Phone: (212)580-2263

Description: Contains the complete text of overviews, mandates, case studies, training materials, resource and bibliographic directories, and other materials covering all aspects of women's development. **Language Used in Database:** English. **Subject Coverage:** Women's development in such areas as agriculture, business and employment, communications, education, health, law, and science and technology. **Format:** CD-ROM.

★10742★ Women Writers Project List
Women Writers Project (WWP)
Brown University
Box 1941
Providence, RI 02912
Elaine Brennan, Assistant Director

Description: Provides the text of some 200 literary works produced by women from pre-1830 for British, Scottish, Irish, and Welsh women writers and from pre-1850 for North American, Australian, Indian, South African women writers; includes works from other colonies. Also offers a forum for the discussion of the works. **Language Used in Database:** English. **Subject Coverage:** Women writers. **Format:** Electronic bulletin board. **Electronic mail address:** FEMINIST@MITVMA.BITNET.

★10743★ Women's Health Care Centers
Oryx Press
4041 N. Central Ave.
Phoenix, AZ 85012-3399
Phone: (602)265-2651
Toll-free: 800-279-6799
Fax: (602)265-6250

Description: Contains mailing information for more than 300 facilities offering health services for women. For each facility, provides name, contact persons, and address information. Covers medical, psychological, preventive medicine, and obstetric and gynecological programs and services. Also covers facilities offering onsite childcare, patient/client libraries, educational workshops, publications and periodicals, crisis hotlines, and information and referral services for women. Enables the user to obtain mailing lists or labels based on personnel, facility type, and ownership. **Language Used in Database:** English. **Subject Coverage:** Health care and social services for women. **Format:** Diskette and magnetic tape.

Master Name and Subject Index

This index provides an alphabetical arrangement of all the organizations, publications, and other entities in the Directory. Subject terms are bolded with the appropriate citations listed immediately below. Publication names appear in italics. Index references are to book entry numbers rather than page numbers. Entry numbers appear in **boldface** type if the reference is to the unit for which information is provided in WID and in lightface if the reference is to a program, former, or alternate name included within the text of the cited entry.

U.S. Department of Health and Human Services
Health Resources and Services Administration • Maternal and Child Health Bureau • Pediatric AIDS Health Care Demonstration Program **8433**
Office of the Surgeon General • Panel on Women, Adolescents and Children with HIV Infection and AIDS • Working Group on Pediatric AIDS **8340**
University of Wisconsin—Milwaukee • Center for Women's Studies **8271**
What You Don't Know CAN Kill You: Sexually Transmitted Diseases and AIDS **10656**
Women and AIDS: A Survival Kit **10674**
Women and AIDS Resource Network **2573**
Women Organized to Respond to Life-threatening Diseases; WORLD— **1188**
Women's Action Alliance • Library **6980**
WORLD Newsletter **9597**
Aiken County Women's Advocates **3972**
Aiken Technical College • Single Parents/Displaced Homemakers Program **5906**
Aims Community College—South Campus • Displaced Homemakers Program **5139**
Ain't Nobody's Business **10305**
Air-Plus Enterprises **9637**
Air Products and Chemicals, Inc. Scholarship **7790**
Aitkin County Women's Advocates **3937**
Akron Business and Professional Women **2670**
Akron City Schools • Displaced Homemakers Program **5761**
ALA Equality Award **7914**
ALA Gay & Lesbian Task Force • Clearinghouse **6723**
Alabama Abortion Rights Action League **1197**
Alabama Association of Women's and Youth Clubs **1209**
Alabama Aviation and Technical College • Displaced Homemaker/Single Parent Program **4992**
Alabama Coalition Against Domestic Violence **1212**
Alabama Department of Economic and Community Affairs • Law Enforcement Planning Division • Family Violence and Prevention Services **8444**
Alabama Department of Human Resources
Child Support Enforcement Division **8445**
Civil Rights and Equal Employment Opportunity Office **8446**
Alabama Department of Public Health • Family Health Services Bureau **8447**
Alabama Federation of Women's Clubs **1198**
Alabama Women's Commission **8448**
Alamo Community College District • Displaced Homemaker/Single Parent Program **6026**
Alan Guttmacher Institute **12, 8169, 9638**
Alan Guttmacher Institute—Washington Memo **9176**
Alaska Council on Domestic Violence and Sexual Assault **8449**
Alaska Department of Health and Social Services • Division of Public Health • Family Health Section **8450**

Alaska Network On Domestic Violence and Sexual Assault **1216**
Alaska Office of the Governor • Administration Department • Personnel and Equal Employment Opportunity Division **8451**
Alaska Pacific University • Women's Resource Center **6367**
Alaska Women's Bookstore **10061**
Alaska Women's Commission **8452**
Alaska Women's Resource Center **3273**
The Alaskan Viewpoint **9639**
Albany Arbor House **4186**
Albany Catholic Family and Community Services • Domestic Violence Services **4187**
Albany Displaced Homemakers Center **5670**
Albany Law School • Women's Studies Program **7489**
Albany-Schoharie-Schenectady Board of Cooperative Education Service • Jobs for Success **5671**
Albany Technical Institute • New Connections **5245**
Alberta E. Crowe Star of Tomorrow **7915**
Albertus Magnus College • Continuing Education **6430**
Albia Woman's Club **1876**
Albion College
Women's Center **6518**
Women's Studies Program **7384**
Albion Fellows Bacon Center **3710**
Albright College • Women's Center **6644**
Albuquerque Woman **8841**
Albuquerque Women in Business Directory **8688**
Alcoholism see Substance Abuse
Alcoholism Center for Women **13**
Alcoholism Program for Women **13**
Alcorn County Vocational Center • Single Parent Displaced Homemaker Program **5526**
ALERT **9177, 9178**
Battered Women's Task Force **4073**
Alexandra Apostolides Sonenfeld Award **7791**
Alexandra House **3950**
Alfred University • Women's Studies Program **7491**
Alice E. Smith Fellowship **7792**
Alice Paul Award **7916**
Alice Paul House **4532**
Alicejamesbooks **9640**
Alimony see Child Custody; Child Support; Divorce; Matrimonial Law
Alimony Limited **654**
ALIVE **4056, 4128, 4440**
South Bay Coalition **3408**
All About Issues American **14**
All-Craft Foundation **15**
All Nations Women's League **16**
All of Our Lives **10306**
Allan Hancock College • Single Parent/Displaced Homemaker Project **5103**
Alle-Kiski Area Hope Center **4565**
Allegan Business and Professional Women's Club **2139**
Allegany Community College • Displaced Homemaker Program **5424**
Alleghany Highlands Community Services Board **4778**
Allegheny College • Women's Studies Program **7648**
Alleluia Press **9641**
Allen County Community College • Single Parent/Homemaker Program **5377**
Allen Scholarship; Dr. J. Frances **7962**
Allen and Unwin **9642**
Allen Women's Resource Center **4247**
The Alliance **9179**

Alliance Against Domestic Violence **3496**
Alliance Against Family Violence **3347, 3775**
Alliance Area Domestic Violence Shelter **4398**
Alliance of Black Women Attorneys **2044**
Alliance City Schools • Displaced Homemaker Program **5762**
Alliance of Minority Women for Business and Political Development **17**
Alliance Task Force on Domestic Violence **4090**
Alliance of Women Bikers **18**
Alliance of Women Entrepreneurs **2178**
Alliant Health System • Library/Media Services **6724**
Alma College • Women's Studies Program **7386**
Alpena Community College • Displaced Homemakers Program **5465**
Alpha Chapter Chi Eta Phi Sorority **1542**
Alpha Delta Kappa **19**
Alpha Epsilon Iota Scholarship Fund **7793**
Alpha Iota Sorority, Jacksonville Alumnae Chapter **1751**
Alpha Kappa Alpha **20**
Alpha Kappa Alpha National Achievement Awards **7917**
Alpha Kappa Alpha Sorority, Delta Rho Omega Chapter **2491**
Alpha Phi International Fraternity **21**
Alpha Phi Sorority **1967**
Alpha Sigma Alpha Sorority **22**
Alpharetta Women's Club **1622**
Alternative Conceptions **10307**
The Alternative Counseling Center • Domestic Violence Services **4196**
Alternative Education Project, Inc. • *Radical America* **9935**
Alternative Health
Ash Tree Publishing **9660**
Birth Notes **8854**
ERA Impact Project **9742**
Grace and Goddess Unlimited **9772**
Holistic Exchange **9788**
NAPSAC Directory of Alternative Birth Services and Consumer Guide **8769**
Alternative Horizons **3475**
Alternative House **3866**
Alternative Press Center **9643**
Alternative Press Index **8842**
Alternatives to Abortion **23**
Alternatives to Abortion International/Women's Health and Education Foundation **23**
Alternatives for Abused Adults **4814**
Alternatives for Battered Women **4293**
Alternatives Corner Bookstore **10208**
Alternatives to Domestic Violence **3696, 4151**
Horizon House **3410**
YWCA **4864**
Alternatives to Family Violence **3465**
Alternatives for Girls **2154**
Alternatives to Violence **3491, 3610, 3613, 3631, 4830**
Altoona Area Vocational Technical School • New Choices **5848**
Alverno College **7019**
Research Center on Women **6712, 6725, 8170**
Alvin Community College • Displaced Homemaker/Single Parent Program **5982**
Always Causing Legal Unrest **24**
Alyson Publications, Inc. **9644**
Alza Corporation • Research Library **6726**
Am-Fem Co. **9645**
Amador County Crisis Line • Operation Care **3378**
Amaranth Fund Awards **7794**

Amarillo College
Displaced Homemakers Program • Adult Students and Women's Service **5983**
Women's Programs **7690**
Amazon Book Store **10183**
Ambrosia Books and Treasures for Women **10113**
Ambulatory Maternal Health Care and Family Planning Services **8689**
Amelia Earhart Fellowship Awards **7795**
Amelia Greenbaum Scholarship Fund **7796**
Amend **3468**
America/Israel Friendship Award **7918**
American Academy of Husband-Coached Childbirth **25**
American Academy of Natural Family Planning **26**
American Academy of Obstetrics and Gynecology **62**
American Academy of Religion • Women's Caucus **27**
American Agri-Women **28**
American Agri-Women Awards **7919**
American Agri-Women Resource Center **29**
American Anorexia/Bulimia Association **30**
American Anorexia/Bulimia Association— Newsletter **9180**
American Anorexia Nervosa Association **30**
American Anthropological Association • Association for Feminist Anthropology **31**
American Association for Adult and Continuing Education • Women's Issues, Status and Education Unit **32**
American Association for the Advancement of Science • National Network of Women in Science **33**
American Association of Black Women Entrepreneurs **158**
American Association for Counseling and Development • Committee on Women **34**
American Association for Higher Education • Women's Caucus **35**
American Association of Immunologists • Committee on the Status of Women **36**
American Association of Law Schools • Committee on Women **37**
American Association for Maternal and Child Health **38**
American Association for Maternal and Infant Health **38**
American Association of ProLife Obstetricians and Gynecologists **39**
American Association of Pro-Life Pediatricians **40**
American Association for Protecting Children • National Resource Center on Child Abuse and Neglect • American Humane Association **6732**
American Association of Retired Persons • Women's Initiative Network **41**
American Association of University Professors • Committee on the Status of Women in the Academic Profession **42**
American Association of University Women **43, 9646**
Educational Foundation Library and Archives **6727**
American Association of University Women, Alabama Division **1213**
American Association of University Women, Alliance Branch **2343**
American Association of University Women, Arlington Branch **2990**
American Association of University Women, Austin Branch **2247**
American Association of University Women, Bartlesville Branch **2749**
American Association of University Women, Baton Rouge **2000**

American Association of University Women, Bedford Chapter **3096**
American Association of University Women, Bennington Chapter **3078**
American Association of University Women, Benton Harbor/St. Joseph Branch **2146**
American Association of University Women, Bluefield Branch **3182**
American Association of University Women, Bowling Green Branch **2674**
American Association of University Women, Brownsburg Chapter **1817**
American Association of University Women, Brunswick Chapter **1633**
American Association of University Women, Burlington Branch **3081**
American Association of University Women, California State Division **1367**
American Association of University Women, Carthage Branch **1695**
American Association of University Women, Charleston-Mattoon Area Branch **1702**
American Association of University Women, Clarinda Chapter **1889**
American Association of University Women, Clearwater Branch **1568**
American Association of University Women, Cortland Chapter **2520**
American Association of University Women, Crystal River Branch **1588**
American Association of University Women, De Kalb County Branch **1807**
American Association of University Women, Dearborn Branch **2151**
American Association of University Women, Delaware Branch **2717**
American Association of University Women, Delaware Chapter **1532**
American Association of University Women, Des Moines Branch **1895**
American Association of University Women, Dunkirk-Fredonia Branch **2513**
American Association of University Women Educational Foundation **44**
American Association of University Women, Fairborn Branch **2719**
American Association of University Women, Falls Church Branch **3091**
American Association of University Women, Federal Way Branch **3134**
American Association of University Women, Fenton Branch **2189**
American Association of University Women, Flint Branch **2240**
American Association of University Women, Florida Division **1604**
American Association of University Women, Georgia Chapter **1650**
American Association of University Women, Grand Rapids Chapter **2179**
American Association of University Women, Hillsboro Branch **2720**
American Association of University Women, Idaho Chapter **1676**
American Association of University Women, Illinois Division **1794**
American Association of University Women, Iowa Division **1877**
American Association of University Women, Kalamazoo Branch **2193**
American Association of University Women, Kingsport Branch **2972**
American Association of University Women, Kokomo Branch **1849**
American Association of University Women, Louisiana Division **2015**
American Association of University Women, Lower Connecticut Valley **1501**
American Association of University Women, Maine Division **2032**

American Association of University Women, Manistee Branch **2211**
American Association of University Women, Marshall Branch **2212**
American Association of University Women, Maryland Division **2045**
American Association of University Women, Michigan Division **2197**
American Association of University Women, Minnesota Division **2251**
American Association of University Women, Mississippi Division **2295**
American Association of University Women, Mobridge Chapter **2958**
American Association of University Women, Montana Chapter **2337**
American Association of University Women, Montclair Chapter **2424**
American Association of University Women, Mooresville Branch **1856**
American Association of University Women, Morristown Branch **2981**
American Association of University Women, Moscow Branch **1679**
American Association of University Women, Muleshoe Branch **3046**
American Association of University Women, Nebraska Division **2362**
American Association of University Women, Nevada Chapter **2370**
American Association of University Women, New Jersey Division **2446**
American Association of University Women, New Mexico Division **2462**
American Association of University Women, North Carolina Chapter **2637**
American Association of University Women, North Dakota **2664**
American Association of University Women, Odessa Branch **3043**
American Association of University Women, Ontario County Branch **2501**
American Association of University Women, Orange Branch **3049**
American Association of University Women, Oregon Chapter **2779**
American Association of University Women, Port Murray Branch **2440**
American Association of University Women, Presque Isle Branch **2039**
American Association of University Women, Reston Chapter **3106**
American Association of University Women, Rhinelander Branch **3214**
American Association of University Women, Rhode Island Division **2922**
American Association of University Women, Ripon Branch **3237**
American Association of University Women, Roseburg Branch **2801**
American Association of University Women, Salina Branch **1960**
American Association of University Women, San Bruno Chapter **1381**
American Association of University Women, Scottsbluff Branch **2348**
American Association of University Women, Shenandoah Branch **1938**
American Association of University Women, South Carolina Chapter **2938**
American Association of University Women, South Haven **2233**
American Association of University Women, Springfield Branch **2736**
American Association of University Women, Taunton Area Branch **2129**
American Association of University Women, Tucumcari Chapter **2474**
American Association of University Women, Utica Branch **2216**

American Association of University Women, Varney Branch **1997**

American Association of University Women, Vermont Branch **3088**

American Association of University Women, Virginia Division **3105**

American Association of University Women, Washington Division **3133**

American Association of University Women, West Virginia Division **3184**

American Association of University Women, Western Springs Branch **1811**

American Association of University Women, Wilmington Branch **1536**

American Association of University Women, Wilson County Branch **2652**

American Association of University Women, Wyoming Chapter **3246**

American Association of University Women, Yakima Branch **3178**

American Association of Women **45**

American Association of Women in Community and Junior Colleges **46**

American Association of Women Dentists **47**

American Association of Women Dentists— Chronicle **9181**

American Association for Women Podiatrists **48**

American Association of Women Radiologists **49**

American Association of Women Voters **45**

American Astronomical Society • Committee on the Status of Women in Astronomy **50**

American Atheist Women **51**

The American Baptist Woman **9182**

American Baptist Women, Livingston Chapter **2340**

American Bar Association
    Center on Children and the Law **6728**
    Commission on Women in the Profession **52**
    Section on Individual Rights and Responsibilities • Committee on the Rights of Women **53**

American Birth Control League **836**

American Business Women - Crossroads of America Chapter **2743**

American Business Women's Association **54**

American Business Women's Association, Boca Raton Chapter **1563**

American Business Women's Association, Campbell Chapter **1272**

American Business Women's Association, Carolina Morning Chapter **2644**

American Business Women's Association, Centennial Chapter **1670**

American Business Women's Association, Challenge Chapter **1896**

American Business Women's Association, Charleston Branch **1684**

American Business Women's Association, Chippewa Falls Chapter **3203**

American Business Women's Association, De Ridder Chapter **2009**

American Business Women's Association, Eden Charter Chapter **2630**

American Business Women's Association, El Paso New Horizons Chapter **3017**

American Business Women's Association, Franklin Chapter **1828**

American Business Women's Association, Gainesville Chapter **1580**

American Business Women's Association, Georgian Chapter **1634**

American Business Women's Association, Grand Forks Chapter **2661**

American Business Women's Association, Greer Charter Chapter **2941**

American Business Women's Association, Heritage Hills Chapter **2363**

American Business Women's Association, Hopewell Chapter **2180**

American Business Women's Association, Howdy Pardner Chapter **3047**

American Business Women's Association, Indian Capital Chapter **2754**

American Business Women's Association, Kerrville Chapter **3038**

American Business Women's Association, Key Wakota Chapter **2282**

American Business Women's Association, Metrolina Chapter **2648**

American Business Women's Association, Ozark Paradise Chapter **2305**

American Business Women's Association, Pine Cone Chapter **1244**

American Business Women's Association, Roseburg Chapter **2802**

American Business Women's Association, Sand Dollar Chapter **3028**

American Business Women's Association, Scenic Cactus Chapter **3007**

American Business Women's Association, Seminole Chapter **1613**

American Business Women's Association, Three Bridges Chapter **1894**

American Business Women's Association, Triple Crown Chapter **2358**

American Business Women's Association, Tuit Chapter **2755**

American Business Women's Association, Tulsey Town High Noon Chapter **2762**

American Business Women's Association, Vivon Chapter **2138**

American Business Women's Association, West Point Chapter **1660**

American Business Women's Association, Wolf Creek Carter Chapter **2832**

American Chemical Society • Women Chemists Committee **55**

American Child Custody Alliance **56**

American Citizens Concerned for Life, Inc. • Communications Center **9647**

American Citizens Concerned for Life Education Fund • ACCL Communications Center **57**

American Citizens for Life **57**

American Civil Liberties Union **58**

American Civil Liberties Union Foundation **59**

American Civil Liberties Union, Gay Rights Chapter **1399**

American Coalition for Life **60**

American College of Nurse-Midwifery **61**

American College of Nurse-Midwives **61**

American College of Obstetricians and Gynecologists **62**
    Nurses Association **63**
    Resource Center **6729**

American Collegians for Life **64**

American Committee on Maternal Welfare **38**

American Council for Career Women **65**

American Council on Education • Office of Women in Higher Education **66**

American Council of Railroad Women **67**

American Council of Women Chiropractors **312**

American Economics Association • Committee on the Status of Women in the Economics Profession **68**

American Educational Research Association • Research on Women and Education Group **69**

American Educational Research Association Women's Caucus **1025**

American Farm Bureau Federation • Women's Committee **70**

American Federation of State, County and Municipal Employees • Women's Rights Department **71**

American Federation of Teachers
    Library **6730**
    Women's Rights Committee **72**

American Federation of Television and Radio Artists • National Women's Division **73**

American Film Institute • Directing Workshop for Women **74**

American Folklore Society • Women's Section **75**

American Forum **9183**

American Foundation for the Blind • Helen Keller Archives **6731**

American Foundation for Maternal and Child Health **76**

American Friends Service Committee • Nationwide Women's Program **77**

American German Library for Women in Enterprise and Trade at Humboldt University **475**

American GI Forum Auxiliary **78**

American GI Forum Women **78**

American Gold Star Mothers **79**

American Gynecological and Obstetrical Society **80**

American History Association **81**

American Home Economics Association **82**

American Humane Association • American Association for Protecting Children • National Resource Center on Child Abuse and Neglect **6732**

American Humanist Association • Feminist Caucus **83**

American Indian Women's Circle Against Domestic Abuse **3991**

American Institute of Architects • Women in Architecture Committee **84**

American Institute of Certified Planners • Women's Rights Committee **85**

American Jewish Congress • Commission for Women's Equality **86**

American Legion Auxiliary **87**

American Library Association
    ACRL Women's Studies Section **88**
    Committee on Pay Equity **89**
    Committee on the Status of Women in Librarianship **90**
    LAMA Women Administrators Discussion Group **91**
    RASD Discussion Group on Women's Materials and Women Library Users **92**
    Social Responsibilities Round Table Feminist Task Force **93**
    Gay and Lesbian Task Force **94**

American Life Education and Research Trust **95**

American Life League **95, 9648**

American Life Lobby **96**
    Library **6733**

American Lithuanian Roman Catholic Women's Alliance **530**

American Lutheran Church Women **97**

American Mathematical Society • Joint Committee on Women in the Mathematics Sciences **98**

American Medical Women's Association **99**
    American Women's Hospitals Service Committee **100**

American Meteorological Society • Board on Women and Minorities **101**

American Mizrachi Women **149**

The American Mother **9184**

American Mothers, Inc. **102**

American Mothers Committee **102**

American Musicological Society • Committee on the Status of Women **103**

American National Cattle Women **104**

Supreme Lodge of the Danish Sisterhood of America **928**

Ukrainian National Women's League of America **942**

United Daughters of the Confederacy **950**

Wampetuc Colony of New England Women **1926**

And Baby Makes Two **10309**

...And Everything Nice **10310**

And What Does Your Mother Do? **10311**

Anderson County Republican Women **2927**

Anderson County Woman's Club **2928**

Anderson-Oconee Council on Teen Pregnancy Prevention **2929**

Anderson Scholarship; Gladys C. **7836**

Andrew Mountain Press **9651**

Angel of the Year **7924**

Angeles Girl Scout Council **1312**

Angelina College • Women's Support Services **6018**

Angola Business and Professional Women's Club **1814**

Ann May School of Nursing Library & Media Center • Jersey Shore Medical Center **6818**

Anna Bixby Women's Center **3678**

Anna Lord Strauss Library • Foundation for Citizen Education **6795**

Anna Louise Hoffman Award for Outstanding Achievement in Graduate Research **7925**

Annals of Scholarship **8846**

Anne O'Hare McCormick Scholarship **7800**

Annie Jump Cannon Award in Astronomy **7926**

Annotated Guide to Women's Periodicals **8697**

Annual Roundtable for Women in Prison **719**

Anoka-Ramsey Community College • Women's Studies Program **7410**

Anorexia Nervosa see Eating Disorders

Anorexia Nervosa **10312**

Anorexia Nervosa Aid Society **30**

Anorexia Nervosa and Associated Disorders **150**

Anorexia Nervosa and Related Eating Disorders **151**

Anorexic Aid Society **577**

Another Look at Cesarean **10313**

Anson Community College • Women's Center **6602**

Anson County Crisis Council **4366**

Antelope Publications **9652**

Anthony; The Childhood of Susan B. **10384**

Anthony House; Susan B. **7008**

Anthony Post-doctoral Fellowship; Susan B. **7898**

Anthony Project; Susan B. **3518**

Antigone Books **10064**

Antioch College
   Women's Center **6618**
   Women's Studies Program **7608**

Antoinette Brown Award **7927**

APLICommunicator **9189**

Apollo Career Center • Displaced Homemaker Program **5778**

Appalachian State University • Women's Studies Program **7564**

Apparel (see also Fashion)
   American Women Buyers Club **143**
   Ladies Apparel Contractors Association **502**
   National Women's Neckwear and Scarf Association **780**
   U.S.A. Petites **968**
   Women's Apparel Chains Associations **1096**
   Women's Fashion Fabrics Association **1122**

Apprentice Academics **9653**

Aquarian Research Foundation **9654**

Aquarius Books Inc. **10149**

Aqudath Israel of America • Fresh Start **5680**

Aquinas College • Women's Center **6525**, **7398**

Aquinas Junior College—Milton **7020**

Aquinas Junior College—Newton **7021**

Arab Americans
   Arab-Jewish Women's Dialogue for Peace **152**
   Institute for Women's Studies in the Arab World **439**
   Lebanese American Women's Club of El Paso **3019**
   Middle East Studies Association • Association of Middle East Women's Studies **547**
   Najda: Women Concerned About the Middle East **568**
   SSRC-MacArthur Foundation Fellowships on Peace and Security in a Changing World Dissertation Fellowships **7897**
   Union of Palestinian Women's Association in North America **944**

Arab-Jewish Women's Dialogue for Peace **152**

Arachne Publishing Co. **9655**

Aradia Bookstore **10062**

Arbor Moon **10193**

Arbuckle Women's Club **1258**

Arcadia Woman's Club **1561**

Arcadia Women's Club **2143**

Archaeology
   ASOR National Endowment for the Humanities Post-Doctoral Research Fellowships, Jerusalem **7801**
   ASOR National Endowment for the Humanities Post-Doctoral Research Fellowships, Nicosia **7802**
   Sibley Fellowship; Mary Isabel **7865**

Archconfraternity of Christian Mothers **153**

Architecture
   AAUW Science/Technology Fellowships **7780**
   American Institute of Architects • Women in Architecture Committee **84**
   Association of Women in Architecture **189**
   Directory of Minority and Women-Owned Engineering and Architectural Firms **8720**
   Henderson Scholarship; Edith H. **7824**
   Organization of Women Architects and Design Professionals **1408**
   University of Wisconsin—Milwaukee • Center for Women's Studies **8271**
   Virginia Polytechnic Institute and State University • International Archive of Women in Architecture **6972**
   Wimmer Scholarship; Harriett Barnhardt **7837**

Archives see Libraries and Archives

Archuleta County Educational Center, Inc. • Displaced Homemaker Program **5147**

Arctic Women in Crisis **3275**

Arden Press **9656**

Are You Listening? **10314**

Area and Ethnic Studies
   Association of Asian Studies • Committee of Women in Asian Studies (CWAS) **164**
   Central Piedmont Community College • Women's Studies Program **7566**
   Committee on Women in Asian Studies **291**
   Cottonwood Press **9717**

Delegation for Friendship Among Women • Library **6783**

Emory University • Special Collections Department **6788**

Glos Polek/Polish Women's Voice **9608**

Latin American Studies Association • Task Force on Women in Latin American Studies **515**

Middle East Studies Association • Association of Middle East Women's Studies **547**

Modern Language Association • Coalition of Women in German **555**

Native Daughters of the Golden West **784**

Panel of American Women **824**

Polka—Polish Woman **9037**

Swedish Women's Educational Association International **933**

Thelphini Press **9989**

Tulane University • Newcomb College Center for Research on Women **8248**

University of Southern California • Institute for the Study of Women and Men **8265**

Wichita State University • Research Group on Women and Work **8277**

Women of Color and Southern Women: A Bibliography **8810**

Women in French **1040**

Area Women's Center **4462**

Arizona Association of Midwives **1220**

Arizona Attorney General • Child Enforcement Section **8453**

Arizona Business and Professional Women's Foundation **1230**

Arizona Coalition Against Domestic Violence **1223**

Arizona Department of Economic Security • Equal Employment Opportunity Office **8454**

Arizona Department of Health Services Division of Family Health Services • Maternal and Child Health Bureau **8455**
   Office of Domestic Violence and Mental Health **8456**

Arizona Family Health Services Division • Maternal and Child Health Bureau **8457**

Arizona Family Planning Council **1224**

Arizona Right to Choose **1236**

Arizona State University • Women's Studies Program **7108**

Arizona Woman Image Now **1235**

Arizona Women's Education and Employment **1229**

Arizona Women's Education & Employment (AWEE) **5013**

Arizona Women's Employment and Education (AWEE) • Northern Arizona Council of Governments **5016**

Arizona Women's Services **8458**

Arkansas Coalition Against Violence to Women and Children **1247**

Arkansas Department of Health • Bureau of Public Health Programs • Division of Maternal and Child Health **8459**

Arkansas Office of Prosecutor Coordinator • Family Violence Prevention and Services **8460**

Arkansas Valley Women's Resource Center **3487**

Arkansas Women's History Institute **9657**

Arlington Community Temporary Shelter **4773**

Arlington County Victims of Violence Program **4774**

Armed Forces see Military

Armenian Women's Welfare Association **154**

Pan Pacific and Southeast Asia Women's Association of the U.S.A., Chicago Chapter **1741**
Research Clearinghouse on Women of Color and Southern Women **10730**
Sarah Lawrence College • Women's Studies Program **9958**
Two Lies **10635**
Women of Color Newsletter **9535**
Women in SelfHelp **2619**
Women in Translation **10034**
Asian-Indian Women in America **157**
Asian-Pacific Sisters **1400**
Asian Resources Center • Displaced Homemaker Program **5090**
Asian Women's Shelter **3420**
Asians Now: International Women's Day **10317**
Asnuntuck Community College • Student Services **6423**
Asociacion Nacional de Mujeres Cubanoamericanas, de los Estados Unidos de America **592**
Asociatia Reuniunilor Femeilor Ortodoxe Romane-Americane **184**
ASOR National Endowment for the Humanities Post-Doctoral Research Fellowships, Jerusalem **7801**
ASOR National Endowment for the Humanities Post-Doctoral Research Fellowships, Nicosia **7802**
ASPA Women in Public Administration Directory **8699**
Assault Care Center Extending Shelter and Support **3732**
Assault Victim Services **3052**
Assertiveness for Women in Health Care **10318**
Assignment House of Chicago • Single Parent/Displaced Homemaker Building Opportunity Project **5299**
Assignment: Life **10319**
Associated Lesbians of Puget Sound **3151**
Associated Mennonite Seminary • Women's Advisory Council **6458**
Association of African-American Women Business Owners **158**
Association of American Colleges • Project on the Status and Education of Women **159, 9661**
Association of American Geographers
Committee on the Status of Women in Geography **160**
Specialty Group on Geographic Perspectives on Women **161**
Association of American Law Schools • Section on Women in Legal Education **162**
Association of American Medical Colleges • Women in Medicine Program **163**
Association of American Women Dentists **47**
Association of Asian Studies • Committee of Women in Asian Studies (CWAS) **164**
Association for the Behavioral Treatment of Sexual Abusers **165**
Association for the Behavioral Treatment of Sexual Aggression **165**
Association of Black Women Attorneys **2540**
Association of Black Women in Higher Education **166**
Association of Black Women in Higher Education Newsletter **9191**
Association of Black Women Historians **167**
Association of Business and Professional Women in Construction **856**
Association for Childbirth at Home **168**
Association for Childbirth at Home, International **168**

Association for Children for Enforcement of Support **169**
Association of College and Research Libraries • Women's Studies Section **170**
Association of Collegiate Alumnae **43**
Association of Contemplative Sisters **171**
Association for Education in Journalism and Mass Communication • Committee on Status of Women **172**
Association of Executive and Professional Women • The International Alliance **173**
Association of Federal Woman's Award Recipients **174**
Association for Gay, Lesbian, and Bisexual Issues in Counseling **175**
Association for Gay and Lesbian Issues in Counseling **175**
Association of Girl Scout Executive Staff **176**
Association of Girl Scout Professional Workers **176**
The Association of Junior Leagues International **177**
Association of Libertarian Feminists **178**
Association Management **8847**
Association of Maternal and Child Health Programs **179**
Association of Part-Time Professionals **180, 9662**
Association for Population/Family Planning Libraries and Information Centers, International **181**
The Association for the Prevention of Domestic Violence **3594**
Association for the Prevention of Family Violence **4899**
Association for Professional Insurance Women **182**
Association on Programs for Female Offenders **183**
Association for the Promotion of the Mathematics Education of Girls and Women **1060**
Association for the Promotion of the Mathematics Education of Girls and Women—Newsletter **9544**
Association of Romanian-American Orthodox Ladies Auxiliaries **184**
Association for the Sexually Harassed **185**
Association of State and Territorial Maternal and Child Health and Crippled Children's Directors **179**
Association of Teachers of Maternal and Child Health **186**
Association for Theatre in Higher Education • Women and Theatre Program **187**
Association for Union Democracy • Women's Project for Union Democracy **188**
Association for Voluntary Surgical Contraception • Library **6735**
Association of Women in Architecture **189**
Association of Women Business Owners **614**
Association for Women in Computing **190**
Association of Women Contractors, Iowa Chapter **1941**
Association for Women in Development **191**
Association of Women in Development Newsletter **9192**
Association of Women Gemologists **192**
Association of Women Geoscientists **193, 193**
Association of Women Lawyers of Greater Kansas City **2310**
Association of Women Mathematicians **194**
Association for Women in Mathematics **194**
Association for Women in Mathematics— Newsletter **9193**
Association of Women in the Metal Industries, Pittsburgh Chapter **2817**

Association of Women in Natural Foods **195**
Association of Women in the Natural Foods Industry **195**
Association of Women Painters and Sculptors **613**
Association for Women Psychiatrists **196**
Association for Women Psychologists **197**
Association for Women in Psychology **197**
Association for Women in Science **198, 9663**
Association for Women in Science, Alaska Chapter **1215**
Association for Women in Science, Albany Area Chapter **2617**
Association for Women in Science, Baltimore Chapter **2046**
Association for Women in Science, Boston Chapter **2073**
Association for Women in Science, Brooklyn Chapter **2492**
Association for Women in Science, Buffalo Chapter **2497**
Association for Women in Science, Central Illinois Chapter **1809**
Association for Women in Science, Central Ohio Chapter **2695**
Association for Women in Science, Chicago Area Chapter **1760**
Association for Women in Science, Claremont Colleges Chapter **1275**
Association for Women in Science, Corvallis Chapter **2775**
Association for Women in Science, Dartmouth Chapter **2383**
Association for Women in Science, Detroit Area Chapter **2173**
Association for Women in Science, Devry Atlanta Chapter **1637**
Association for Women in Science Directory **8700**
Association for Women in Science, East Tennessee Chapter **2987**
Association for Women in Science, Fort Collins Chapter **1485**
Association for Women in Science, Fullerton Chapter **1294**
Association for Women in Science, Gulf Court/Houston Chapter **3031**
Association for Women in Science, Hawaii Chapter **1663**
Association for Women in Science, Illinois Chapter **1738**
Association for Women in Science, Indiana Chapter **1837, 1839**
Association for Women in Science, Kansas Flint Hills Chapter **1957**
Association for Women in Science, La Jolla Chapter **1304**
Association for Women in Science, Lake Superior Chapter **2257**
Association for Women in Science, Lansing Area Chapter **2167**
Association for Women in Science, Little Rock Chapter **1250**
Association for Women in Science, Long Island Chapter **2502**
Association for Women in Science, Metropolitan New York Chapter **2541**
Association for Women in Science, New England Chapter **2126**
Association for Women in Science, New York State Chapter **2508**
Association for Women in Science, NJS Chapter **2406**
Association for Women in Science, Northern Utah Chapter **3067**
Association for Women in Science, Palo Alto Chapter **1347**

Association for Women in Science, Philadelphia Chapter **2858**
Association for Women in Science, San Diego Chapter **1383**
Association for Women in Science, San Francisco Chapter **1401**
Association for Women in Science, Seattle Chapter **3152**
Association for Women in Science, Southern Nevada Chapter **2367**
Association for Women in Science, Syracuse Chapter **2607**
Association for Women in Science, Tallahassee Chapter **1610**
Association for Women in Science, Triangle Area Chapter **2645**
Association for Women in Science, University of New Hampshire Chapter **2380**
Association for Women in Science, Washington, DC Chapter **1543**
Association for Women in Science, West Virginia Chapter **3190**
Association for Women in Science, Wilmington Chapter **1537**
Association for Women in Social Work **199**
Association for Women in Social Work Newsletter **9194**
Association of Women Soil Scientists **200**
Association for Women in Sports Media **201**
Association for Women Students **202**
Association for Women Veterinarians **203**
Association for Women Veterinarians Distinguished Service Award **7930**
Association of Women's Music and Culture **204**
Associations and Organizations
 Coalition of Leading Women's Organizations **268**
 Coalition on Women and the Budget **271**
 The Council of Presidents of United States Women's Organizations **311**
 Directory of Organizations for Women **8725**
 GFWC Clubwoman Magazine **8918**
 Greater Philadelphia Women's Yellow Pages **8748**
 The Greater Phoenix Women's Yellow Pages **8749**
 Minnesota Clubwoman **9000**
 National Association of Commissions for Women **590**
 National Association of Women's Centers **625**
 National Association of Women's Centers—Connections Newsletter **9391**
 National Council of Negro Women **671**
 National Council for Research on Women **672**
 National Women's Mailing List **778, 8780**
 PanAmerican Liaison Committee of Women's Organizations **822**
 PanPacific and Southeast Asia Women's Association of the U.S.A. **825**
 State University of New York at Buffalo • University Archives **6933**
 Status Report **9487**
 The Tribune—"Women Organizing" **8803**
 A Woman's Yellow Book **8808**
 A Women's Mailing List Directory **8824**
 Women's Organizations: A National Directory **8825**
 Women's Roundtable **1171**
 Women's Yellow Pages **8829, 8830**

Women's Yellow Pages: A Directory of Women in Business, Professions and Organizations **8831**
Ast Resource Collection; Birdie Goldsmith • Barnard College • Barnard Center for Research on Women **6738**
Astarte Shell Press **9664**
Astraea National Lesbian Action Foundation **205**
Astronautics **8637**
Astronomy (see also Space Sciences)
 American Astronomical Society • Committee on the Status of Women in Astronomy **50**
 Bunting Institute Science Scholars Fellowships **7815**
 Cannon Award in Astronomy; Annie Jump **7926**
At the Houston Women's Conference **10320**
Ata Books **9665**
Atalanta **9195**
AT&T Bell Laboratories Dual Degree Scholarships **7803**
AT&T Bell Laboratories Engineering Scholarships **7804**
AT&T Bell Laboratories Graduate Research Fellowships for Women **7805**
AT&T Bell Laboratories Graduate Research Grants for Women **7806**
AT&T Bell Laboratories Summer Research Program for Minorities & Women **7807**
Athena **9601**
Athena's Attic **10273**
Athens Area Technical Institute • New Connections **5246**
Athletics see Sports and Recreation
Athol Woman's Club **2071**
Atlanta Area Vocational Technical School • New Connections **5247**
Atlanta Lesbian Feminist Alliance **1623**
 Southeastern Lesbian Archives **6736**
Atlanta Lesbian Feminist Alliance— Newsletter **9195**
Atlantic City Women's Chamber of Commerce **2397**
Atlantic County Women's Center **4161**
Attala County Lady Landowner League **2300**
Attention: Women at Work! **10321**
Auburn Business and Professional Women's Club **1816**
Auburn University • Women's Studies Program **7102**
Augsburg College
 Women's Awareness House **6530**
 Women's Studies Program **7414**
Augusta Ada Lovelace Award **7931**
Augusta Technical Institute
 Library **6737**
 New Connections **5248**
Augustana College • Women's Studies Program **7272**
AUL Newsletter **9196**
Aunt Lute Book Co. **9666**
Aurora University • Women's Studies Program **7245**
Austin AAU Women's Basketball Club **2993**
Austin Area Vocational Technical Institute • Expanded Career Choices **5506**
Austin Business and Professional Women's Club **2248**
Austin Community College
 Displaced Homemaker/Single Parent Program **5985**
 Women's Center—Northridge Campus **6658**
 Women's Studies Program **7692**
Austin Peay State University • Women's Studies Program **7682**

Author, Author for the Serious Reader **10207**
Auxiliaries of Our Lady of the Cenacle **206**
AVA Crisis Shelter **3327**
AVAIL **4890**
Avalon: A Center for Women and Children **4821**
Avenues, Inc. **4038**
Averett College • Women's Resource Center **6678**
Averill Career Center **5498**
Avery Publishing Group **9667**
Aviation
 Earhart Fellowship Awards; Amelia **7795**
 Ferdinand Award; Marguerite **8026**
 Independent Federation of Flight Attendants **428**
 International Society of Women Airline Pilots **480**
 ISA Newsletter **9343**
 Mullen Memorial Flight Scholarship; Doris **7822**
 National Agriculture Aviation Association Most Active Woman Award **8050**
 The Ninety-Nine News **9021**
 Ninety-Nines, International Organization of Women Pilots, Blue Ridge Chapter **2949**
 Ninety-Nines, International Organization of Women Pilots, New York-New Jersey Section **2516**
 Ninety-Nines, International Women Pilots **797**
  Library **6883**
 Ninety-Nines NIFA Achievement Award **8067**
 Richardson Memorial Flight Scholarship; Gini **7834**
 Scott Memorial Scholarship; Sheila **8098**
 630 News **9476**
 U.S. Department of Transportation • Federal Aviation Administration • Office for Civil Rights • Federal Women's Program **8362**
 WASP News **9476**
 Whirly-Girls (International Women Helicopter Pilots) **984**
 Women Airforce Service Pilots WWII **1010**
 Women Military Aviators **1062**
 Women of the National Agricultural Aviation Association **1068**
Avila College • Women's Studies Program **7437**
AVS News **9197**
AVSC News **9197**
Awards (see also Financial Aid, Educational; Funding; Chapter 11: Scholarships, Fellowships, and Loans; Chapter 12: Awards, Honors and Prizes)
 American Association of University Women Educational Foundation **44**
 Association of Federal Woman's Award Recipients **174**
 Directory of Financial Aids for Women **8716**
 National Women's Hall of Fame **773**
 National Women's Hall of Fame Newsletter **9408**
 Opportunities for Research and Study **8782**
 PEO Sisterhood **829**
 Radcliffe College • Bunting Institute **8229**
 Rocky Mountain Women's Institute **8231**
 Womanhood Media **8684**
 Women and Fellowships **8813**

Aware [Lakeport, CA] **3381**
AWARE **3909, 4562, 4759**
AWC News/Forum **9198**
The AWC Source **9199**
AWIS Newsletter **9200**
AWIS Predoctoral Awards **7808**
AWNY Advertising Woman of the Year **7932**
AWNY Matters **9201**
AWSCPA Newsletter **9202**
AWSM Newsletter **9203**
Axel Johnson Group **8632**
B.A. Press **9668**
B. Robert Lewis House **3956**
Babies and Special Consideration **10322**
Baby Basics **10323**
Baby Booming **10324**
Baby Care **10325**
Baby Clock **10326**
Back Door Bookstore **10139**
Back Inside Herself **10327**
BACW Newsletter **9204**
Bad Attitude **8848**
Bainbridge College • Vocational-Technical Education • STEP/New Connections **5249**
Baker Memorial Library; Blanche M. • ONE, Inc. **6887**
Baker Mission Shelter/Porterville Women's Shelter; Mary • Porterville Mission Project **3404**
Baker and Taylor Books **10222**
Bakersfield Community College • Women's Studies Program **7113**
Bald Knob School District • CHOICES: Career Development Center **5025**
Ball State University • Women's Studies and Gender Studies **7284**
Baltic Women's Council **207**
Bangor Hall, University College • Transitions: A Displaced Homemaker Program **5406**
Banking see Business and Management
Banned Books **9669**
Baptists for Life **208**
Baraga County Shelter Home **3911**
Barat College • Committee on Women **7264**
Barbara Deming Memorial Fund • Money for Women **209**
Barbara Kettle Gundlach Shelter **3890**
Barbara V. Ferraro Award **7933**
Barbara Walzer Books **10258**
Barbara's Bookshop **10143**
Barbara's Bookstore **10148**
Bard College
    Women's Center **6567**
    Women's Studies Program **7492**
Barjon's **10192**
Barn Owl Books **9670**
Barnard Center for Research on Women • Birdie Goldsmith Ast Resource Collection • Barnard College **6738**
Barnard College **7022**
    Barnard Center for Research on Women **8171**
        Birdie Goldsmith Ast Resource Collection **6738**
    Women's Studies Program **7530**
Barnard New Women Poets Prize **7934**
Barnes Library • Lambda, Inc. **6825**
Barre Regional Vocational Technical Center • Single Parent Displaced Homemaker Program **6060**
Barrer Journalism Award; Myra E. **8045**
Barry University • Women's Studies Program **7221**
Bartlesville Women and Children in Crisis **2750**
Bates College • Women's Studies Program **7323**

Baton Rouge Association of Women Attorneys **2002**
Battered **10328**
Battered Families Services **4176**
Battered Person's Advocacy Project **4506**
Battered Service Action Center **3386**
Battered Wives, Shattered Lives **10329**
The Battered Woman **10330**
The Battered Woman Syndrome **10331**
Battered Women (see also Domestic Violence; Rape; Violence Against Women; Chapter 3: Battered Women's Services)
    Abuse **10300**
    Ain't Nobody's Business **10305**
    American Women's Clergy Association **146**
    Asian-Indian Women in America **157**
    B.A. Press **9668**
    Battered **10328**
    Battered Wives, Shattered Lives **10329**
    The Battered Woman **10330**
    The Battered Woman Syndrome **10331**
    Battered Women **10332**
    Battered Women: Violence Behind Closed Doors **10333**
    Battered Women's Directory **8701, 9671**
    Burning Bridges **10376**
    Center for Women's Studies and Services **250**
    Community Services for Battered Women **10392**
    Directory of Information Resources on Victimization of Women **8717**
    Domestic Violence Institute **337**
    Double-Time **9269**
    The Exchange **9283**
    Fayette County Council on Battered Women **1639**
    Feminist Karate Union **368**
    Franklin Press; Chas. **9701**
    Friends of Ruth **9307**
    House of Ruth **418**
    It's Not Always Happy at My House **10490**
    Legal Advocates for Women **519**
    Massachusetts Coalition of Battered Women's Service Groups **2078**
    Minnesota Coalition for Battered Women **2285**
    Minnesota Department of Corrections • Program and Services for Battered Women **8529**
    My Husband Is Going to Kill Me **10521**
    Napa Emergency Women's Service **1332**
    National Association of Women's Centers **625**
    National Center on Women and Family Law, Inc. **636, 8215, 9880**
        Information Center **6863**
    National Clearinghouse for the Defense of Battered Women **640**
    National Clearinghouse on Marital and Date Rape **641, 8679**
    National Coalition Against Domestic Violence **643**
    National Woman Abuse Prevention Project **759**
    NCDBW Newsletter **9414**
    Omnicorn Productions, Inc. **9899**
    A Place to Go **10546**
    Placer Women's Center **1261**
    Soroptimist International **914**
    Two Million Women: Domestic Violence **10636**

U.S. Department of Labor • Women's Bureau • Network on Female Offenders **8346**
University of California, Los Angeles • Center for the Study of Women **8253**
University of Wisconsin—Milwaukee • Center for Women's Studies **8271**
When the Honeymoon is Over **10658**
Why Women Stay **10665**
Women in Crisis **1022**
Women of Nations Newsletter **9548**
Women's Crisis Center **3080**
Women's Crisis Center of Northern Kentucky **1995**
Women's Health Resources **6982**
Battered Women **10332**
Battered Women, Inc. **4631**
Battered Women: Violence Behind Closed Doors **10333**
Battered Women's Alternatives **3359**
Battered Women's Directory **8701, 9671**
Battered Women's Network **4070**
Battered Women's Project [Houlton, ME] **3822**
Battered Women's Project [Taos, NM] **4185**
Battered Women's Services of Hubbard County, Inc. **3992**
Battered Women's Services of Montpelier **4760**
Battered Women's Services of San Mateo County **3349**
Battered Women's Shelter of Akron **4397**
Battered Women's Shelter of Bexar County **4724**
    Outreach: Women's and Children's Resource Center **4725**
The Battered Women's Shelter of Visalia **3450**
Battle Creek Area Organization Against Domestic Violence • Safe Place **3885**
Bauer Prize; Evelyn **7973**
Bay Area Black Women's Health Project **1334**
Bay Area Evangelical and Ecumenical Women's Caucus **1335**
Bay Area Women's Center **4660**
Bay Bridge Books **10089**
Bay County League of Democratic Women **2144**
Bay County Women's Center **3886**
Bay De Noc Community College • Single Parent/Homemaker Program **5477**
Bay Path College **7023**
    Women's Studies Program **7362**
Bay State Centers for Displaced Homemakers [Hyannis, MA] **5450**
Bay State Centers for Displaced Homemakers [Northampton, MA] **5455**
Bay State Centers for Displaced Homemakers **5459**
    Greater Lowell, YWCA **5451**
    Higher Education Information Center **5444**
    New Bedford YWCA **5454**
    Quincy Junior College **5458**
    Women's Services Center, **5457**
    Worcester Community Action County **5464**
Bay Windows **8849**
Bayfront Medical Center, Inc. • Health Sciences Library **6739**
Bayonne Public Schools • Project RITE (Reaching Independence Through Employment) **5619**
Bayou Area Young Women's Christian Association **2011**
BBW: Big Beautiful Woman **8850**
Beacon College • Women's Studies Program **7164**

Brooklyn College • Womens Center **4208**
Brooklyn College of the City University of New York
    Women's Center **6571**
    Women's Studies Program **7501**
Brooklyn Public Library • Social Science/Philosophy Division **6748**
Broome Community College • Displaced Homemaker Program **5676**
Broome County Coalition for Free Choice **2485**
Broome County Republican Women's Club **2486**
Broome-Tioga Board of Cooperative Educational Services • Displaced Homemaker Program **5677**
Broomstick **8862**
Brother Charlie Rescue Center **3598**
A Brothers Touch **10184**
Broward Community College
    Project You **5197**
    WINGS (Women Investigating New Goals and Services) **5192**
Brown Award; Antoinette **7927**
Brown School of Social Work; George Warren • Library & Learning Resources Center • Washington University **6973**
Brown University
    Christine Dunlap Farnham Archives **6749**
    Pembroke Center for Teaching and Research on Women **8174**
        Library **6750**
    Sarah Doyle Center **6650**
    Women's Studies Program **7671**
Bryn Mawr College **7027**
    Feminist and Gender Studies **7633**
    Women's Center **6634**
Buck Woman's Award; Pearl S. **8079**
Buckeye Joint Vocational School • Displaced Homemaker Program **5787**
Bucknell University
    Women's Resource Center **6640**
    Women's Studies Program **7646**
Bucks County Emergency Pregnancy Service **2847**
Bucyrus Business and Professional Women's Club **2675**
Buddhist Churches of America • Federation of Buddhist Women's Associations **226**
BUDDY Award (Bring Up Daughters Differently) **7938**
Buenhogar **8863**
Buffalo State College
    Women's Resource Center **6574**
    Women's Studies Program **7505**
Buffalo Women's Bowling Association **2498**
Building Opportunity Project [Perkin, IL] **5328**
Building Opportunity Project [Urbana, IL] • Single Parent/Displaced Homemakers Program **5335**
Building Women's Studies Collections: A Resource Guide **8703**
Bulimia see Eating Disorders
Bulimia **10374**
Bulimia and the Road to Recovery **10375**
Bulletin: Committee on South Asian Women **8864**
Bunker Hill Community College • Single Parent/Homemakers Program **5447**
Bunting Fellowship **7812**
Bunting Institute Affiliation Program **7813**
Bunting Institute—Newsletter; Mary Ingraham **9372**
Bunting Institute Peace Fellowships **7814**
Bunting Institute of Radcliffe College; Mary Ingraham **8229**
Bunting Institute Science Scholars Fellowships **7815**

Burlington Area Vocational Technical Center • Displaced Homemaker Program/National Skill Building: Working in Vermont **6058**
Burlington College • Feminist Studies **7712**
Burning Bridges **10376**
Business and Management
    AAUW Focus Professions Fellowships **7779**
    Advertising Women of New York **2539**
    Advertising Women of New York President's Award **7911**
    AFL-CIO • Committee on Salaried and Professional Women **6**
    Akron Business and Professional Women **2670**
    Albuquerque Woman **8841**
    Albuquerque Women in Business Directory **8688**
    Allegan Business and Professional Women's Club **2139**
    The Alliance **9179**
    Alliance of Minority Women for Business and Political Development **17**
    Alliance of Women Entrepreneurs **2178**
    Alpha Iota Sorority, Jacksonville Alumnae Chapter **1751**
    American Association of University Women, Fairborn Branch **2719**
    American Business Women - Crossroads of America Chapter **2743**
    American Business Women's Association **54**
    American Business Women's Association, Boca Raton Chapter **1563**
    American Business Women's Association, Campbell Chapter **1272**
    American Business Women's Association, Carolina Morning Chapter **2644**
    American Business Women's Association, Centennial Chapter **1670**
    American Business Women's Association, Challenge Chapter **1896**
    American Business Women's Association, Chippewa Falls Chapter **3203**
    American Business Women's Association, De Ridder Chapter **2009**
    American Business Women's Association, Eden Charter Chapter **2630**
    American Business Women's Association, El Paso New Horizons Chapter **3017**
    American Business Women's Association, Franklin Chapter **1828**
    American Business Women's Association, Gainesville Chapter **1580**
    American Business Women's Association, Georgian Chapter **1634**
    American Business Women's Association, Grand Forks Chapter **2661**
    American Business Women's Association, Greer Charter Chapter **2941**
    American Business Women's Association, Heritage Hills Chapter **2363**
    American Business Women's Association, Hopewell Chapter **2180**
    American Business Women's Association, Howdy Pardner Chapter **3047**
    American Business Women's Association, Indian Capital Chapter **2754**

American Business Women's Association, Kerrville Chapter **3038**
American Business Women's Association, Key Wakota Chapter **2282**
American Business Women's Association, Metrolina Chapter **2648**
American Business Women's Association, Ozark Paradise Chapter **2305**
American Business Women's Association, Pine Cone Chapter **1244**
American Business Women's Association, Roseburg Chapter **2802**
American Business Women's Association, Sand Dollar Chapter **3028**
American Business Women's Association, Scenic Cactus Chapter **3007**
American Business Women's Association, Seminole Chapter **1613**
American Business Women's Association, Three Bridges Chapter **1894**
American Business Women's Association, Triple Crown Chapter **2358**
American Business Women's Association, Tuit Chapter **2755**
American Business Women's Association, Tulsey Town High Noon Chapter **2762**
American Business Women's Association, Vivon Chapter **2138**
American Business Women's Association, West Point Chapter **1660**
American Business Women's Association, Wolf Creek Carter Chapter **2832**
American Council for Career Women **65**
American Institute of Certified Planners • Women's Rights Committee **85**
American Planning Association • Planning and Women Division **113**
American Society of Professional and Executive Women **129**
American Society for Public Administration • Section for Women in Public Administration **131**
American Society of Women Accountants **133**
American Society of Women Accountants, Baton Rouge Chapter **2001**
American Society of Women Accountants, Columbus Chapter **2694**
American Society of Women Accountants—Coordinator **9185**
American Society of Women Accountants, Ft. Worth Chapter **3022**
American Society of Women Accountants, Grand Rapids Chapter **2196**
American Society of Women Accountants—Membership Directory **8692**
American Society of Women Accountants, Tulsa Chapter **2763**
American Woman's Economic Development Corporation **141**
American Woman's Society of Certified Public Accountants **142**
American Woman's Society of Certified Public Accountants of Alabama **1199**
American Woman's Society of Certified Public Accountants of Baltimore **2056**

Institute for Managerial and Professional Women **2788**
Interactive Arts, Inc. **8672**
Intercambios Femeniles **8948**
The International Alliance, An Association of Executive and Professional Women **443**
The International Alliance, An Association of Executive and Professional Women—Membership Directory **8758**
The International Alliance— Newsletter **9339**
International Altrusan **8949**
International Black Women's Congress **451**
International Network for Women in Enterprise and Trade **475**
International Women's Tribune Centre • Library **6816**
Junction City Business and Professional Women's Club **2780**
Kansas Business and Professional Women **1945**
Katharine Gibbs School, Boston • Library **6822**
Kievman Leadership Award; NNWS Beverly **8069**
Kingman Business and Professional Women's Club **1949**
Kirkland Business and Professional Women's Club **3138**
Ladies Apparel Contractors Association **502**
Ladies at Work **1245**
Lane & Associates, Inc. **9830**
Latin American Professional Women's Newsletter **9352**
Latrobe Business and Professional Women's Club **2849**
Lewin Award; Elizabeth **7968**
Lewiston-Auburn Business and Professional Women **2041**
Making Success Happen Newsletter **9367**
Management Principles for New Women Managers **10509**
Management Training Specialists **8676**
Manitowoc-Two Rivers Business and Professional Women's Club **3219**
Marketing to Women **9371, 10723**
Massachusetts Minority and Women's Business Division **8523**
Merrillville Business and Professional Women's Club **1857**
MG Woman's Counseling Service of New York **8677**
Michigan Federation of Business and Professional Women's Clubs **2200**
Michigan Woman Magazine **8995**
Middletown Business and Professional Women's Club **2741**
Milwaukee Business and Professional Women's Club **3221**
Minorities and Women in Business **9001**
Minority Women Business Enterprise **1598**
Miranda Associates, Inc. **8678**
Monticello Business and Professional Women's Club **1930**
Morgan City-Berwick Business and Professional Women's Club **2019**
Moscow Business and Professional Women's Club **1680**
Mothers' Home Business Network **560**
Moundsville Business and Professional Women's Club **3188**
Mountain Grove Business and Professional Women's Club **2316**

MS. Magazine Making a Difference Advertising Award **8043**
Municipal Bond Women's Club of New York **2555**
Municipal Bond Women's Club of New York **2437**
Murphysboro Business and Professional Women's Club **1766**
Nash Club of National Association of Negro Business and Professional Women's Clubs **2977**
National Alliance of Homebased Businesswomen **576**
National Alliance of Homebased Businesswomen, Northern Illinois Chapter **1765**
National Association of Bank Women **580**
National Association of Black Women Entrepreneurs **582**
National Association of Business and Industrial Saleswomen **583**
National Association for Female Executives **595**
National Association of Minority Women in Business **605**
National Association of Negro Business and Professional Women's Clubs **607**
National Association for Professional Saleswomen **609**
National Association for Professional Saleswomen Achievers' Circle **8057**
National Association of Women Business Owners **614, 9878**
    Austin Chapter **2997**
    Baltimore Chapter **2051**
    Boca/Delray Chapter **1577**
    Capital Area Chapter **1549**
    Cedar Rapids/Iowa City Chapter **1919**
    Central Arkansas Chapter **1253**
    Central Illinois Chapter **1777**
    Central Iowa Chapter **1903**
    Chattanooga Chapter **2970**
    Chicago Area Chapter **1748**
    Colorado Chapter **1464**
    Dallas/Ft. Worth Chapter **3012**
    Ft. Lauderdale Chapter **1572**
    Greater Detroit Chapter **2161**
    Houston Chapter **3035**
    Kansas City Chapter **1959**
    Lexington Chapter **1984**
    Long Island Chapter **2515**
    Los Angeles Chapter **1299**
    Louisville Chapter **1990**
    Miami Chapter **1593**
    Minnesota Chapter **2259**
    Mobile Chapter **1211**
    Nashville Chapter **1308**
    New Jersey Chapter **2401**
    New York Chapter **2556**
    North Carolina Chapter **2641**
    Northern Nevada Chapter **2369**
    Oklahoma City Chapter **2759**
    Omaha Chapter **1893**
    Orange County Chapter **1358**
    Palm Beach Chapter **1596**
    Philadelphia Chapter **2890**
    Phoenix Chapter **1232**
    Pittsburgh Chapter **2876**
    Quad Cities/Davenport Chapter **1744**
    Rhode Island Chapter **2921**
    Richmond Chapter **3109**
    Rochester Chapter **2588**
    Sacramento Chapter **1373**
    San Diego Chapter **1388**
    San Francisco Chapter **1405**
    Sarasota Chapter **1607**
    Silicon Valley Chapter **1451**

    Springfield Chapter **1803**
    Tidewater Chapter **2971**
    Tulsa Chapter **2768**
    Waterloo/Cedar Falls Chapter **1914**
    Wichita Chapter **1969**
National Association of Women Business Owners—Statement **9389**
National Association for Women in Careers **615**
National Association for Women in Careers, West Suburban Chapter **1767**
National Association of Women in Chambers of Commerce **616**
National Association of Women Government Contractors **620**
National Business Woman **9010**
National Chamber of Commerce for Women **638**
    Elizabeth Lewin Business Library & Information Center **6864**
National Coalition for Women's Enterprise **650**
National Council of Administrative Women in Education Leadership Award **8061**
National Council of Career Women **663**
National Council of Career Women— Membership Directory **8771**
National Directory of Women-Owned Business Firms **8775**
National Federation of Business and Professional Women's Clubs • Women's Clubs Political Action Committee **687**
National Federation of Business and Professional Women's Clubs, Inc. of the U.S.A. **686**
National Forum for Executive Women **696**
National Foundation for Women Business Owners **697**
National Foundation for Women Business Owners Newsletter **9400**
National Negro and Professional Women's Clubs, New Metropolitan Detroit Chapter **2162**
National Network of Hispanic Women **717**
National Network of Women in Sales **720**
National Network of Women in Sales, Northwest Suburban Chicago Chapter **1683**
National Women's Automotive Association **767**
National Women's Economic Alliance Foundation **771**
National Women's Hall of Fame **8065**
The NAWIC Image **9411**
Network of Entrepreneurial Women **3112**
Network for Professional Women **788**
New England Women Business Owners **2091**
New Futures Enterprises **8680**
New Jersey Woman Magazine **9019**
New Mexico Graduate Fellowships **7876**
New Women Council of Boise **1671**
New York Minority and Women's Business Development Office **8562**
Newburyport Business and Professional Women's Organization **2124**
Norfolk Business and Professional Women's Club **2357**
NWEA Outlook **9432**

Center for Family Crisis [Grand Marais, MN] **3961**
Center for Family Planning Program Development **12, 8169**
Center For Displaced Homemakers [Shreveport, LA] **5404**
Center for Global Issues and Women's Leadership **8233**
Center for Humane Options in Childbirth Experiences **238**
    Library **6762**
Center for International Studies • Women in International Security **239**
Center for Law and Social Policy **240**
Center for Loss in Multiple Birth **241**
Center for New Directions [Columbus, OH] **5774**
Center for New Directions [Glendale, AZ] **5009**
Center for New Directions [Mesa, AZ] **5011**
Center for New Directions [Phoenix, AZ] **5014**
Center for the Pacific Asian Family **3387**
Center for Population Options **242, 8177**
    Resource Center **6763**
Center for Prevention of Domestic Violence **3464, 4402**
Center for Prevention of Sexual Abuse and Domestic Violence **4856**
Center for Psychologically and Physically Abused Persons **4239**
Center for Reproductive Law and Policy **8178**
Center for Reproductive and Sexual Health **243**
Center for the Research and Treatment of Anorexia Nervosa **8179**
Center for Research on Women **8240**
Center for Research on Women—Center News **9225**
Center for Research on Women—Research Report **9226**
Center for Sexual Assault and Domestic Violence Survivors **4094**
Center for the Sociological Study of Women **8263**
Center for the Study of Anorexia and Bulimia **8180**
Center for the Study, Education and Advancement of Women **244**
Center for the Study of Multiple Birth **9698**
Center for the Study of Population • Florida State University **6793**
Center for the Study of Social Policy **245**
Center for the Study of Women and Sex Roles **8183**
Center for the Study of Women and Society—Newsletter **9227**
Center for Surrogate Parenting **246**
Center for Training and Careers [San Jose, CA] • Displaced Homemakers Program **5096**
Center for a Woman's Own Name **247**
Center for Women [Tampa, FL] **5239**
Center for Women and Families
    Creative Employment Project **5393**
    Spouse Abuse Center **3724**
Center for Women in Government **248**
Center for Women Policy Studies **249, 8181, 9699**
Center on Women and Public Policy **8182**
Center on Women and Religion **1265**
Center for Women and Religion— Membership Newsletter **9228**
Center for Women and Religion—Student, Faculty, and Staff Newsletter **9229**
Center for Women in Transition [Holland, MI] • Displaced Homemakers Program **5483**
Center for Women in Transition **3904**

Center for Women's Economic Alternatives **2623**
Center for Women's Education **8232**
Center for Women's Global Leadership • Rutgers, The State University of New Jersey, Douglass College **8233**
Center for Women's Studies **250**
Center for Women's Studies and Services **250, 3418, 6406, 9700**
Centerpiece **9230**
Central Alabama Community College, Childersburg Campus • Displaced Homemakers Program **4974**
Central Arizona College • Displaced Homemaker Program **5007**
Central California Coalition On Domestic Violence **1327**
Central Coast Women's Soccer Association **1260**
Central College • Committee on the Role of Women **7303**
Central Community College • Explore Your World • Displaced Homemaker Program **5591**
Central Connecticut State University
    Women's Center **6429**
    Women's Studies Program **7200**
Central Florida Community College
    Single Parent/Homemakers Program **5221**
    Women and Family Center **6444**
Central High School • Single Parent/Displaced Homemaker Program • COPE **5963**
Central Maine Technical College • Women Unlimited **6482**
Central Michigan University • Women's Studies Program **7402**
Central Missouri State University • Women's Studies Program **7444**
Central Nebraska Task Force on Domestic Abuse and Sexual Assault **4093**
Central Oklahoma Vocational Technical School • Displaced Homemaker/Single Parent Program **5823**
Central Oregon Battering and Rape Alliance **4479**
Central Oregon Community College • Changing Directions **5833**
Central Piedmont Community College
    Wider Opportunities for Women **5733**
    Women's Studies Program **7566**
    Womenshare **6598**
Central Savannah River Girl Scout Council **1630**
Central Texas College • American Education Complex System • Single Parent Homemaker Program **6014**
Central Vermont Shelter Project **4761**
Central Washington University
    Women's Resource Center **6690**
    Women's Studies Program **7731**
Central Wisconsin Women's Caucus for Art **3215**
Central Wyoming College • Single Parent/Homemaker Project **6182**
Centralia Woman's Club **1698**
Centre County Area Vocational-Technical School • New Choices **5850**
Centre County Women's Resource Center **4563**
Cervical Cancer **10380**
Cesarean Birth see Childbirth
Cesarean Prevention Movement **251**
Cesarean Prevention Movement of Boulder **1466**
Cesarean Prevention Movement of Fairfield County **1502**
Cesarean Prevention Movement of Greater Philadelphia **2859**

Cesarean Prevention Movement of Greater Phoenix **1218**
Cesarean Prevention Movement of Houston **3032**
Cesarean Prevention Movement of Ithaca **2524**
Cesarean Prevention Movement of Long Beach **1309**
Cesarean Prevention Movement of Marietta **1645**
Cesarean Prevention Movement of Marin County **1325**
Cesarean Prevention Movement of New Mexico **2463**
Cesarean Prevention Movement of Northern Arizona **1221**
Cesarean Prevention Movement of Northern New York **2613**
Cesarean Prevention Movement of Northwest Ohio **2730**
Cesarean Prevention Movement of Ogden/Northern Utah **3069**
Cesarean Prevention Movement of San Diego **1385**
Cesarean Prevention Movement of San Francisco Bay Area **1290**
Cesarean Prevention Movement of San Gabriel/San Bernardino **1459**
Cesarean Prevention Movement of Santa Clara Valley **1436**
Cesarean Prevention Movement of Sonoma **1448**
Cesarean Prevention Movement of South Orange County **1420**
Cesarean Prevention Movement of Southeast Florida **1571**
Cesarean Prevention Movement of Southern Oregon **2784**
Cesarean Prevention Movement of Suffolk **2506**
Cesarean Prevention Movement of Tampa **1614**
Cesarean Prevention Movement of Westchester/Putnam **2489**
Cesarian Section Patient Outcome Research Advisory Committee • U.S. Department of Health and Human Services • Public Health Service • Agency for Health Care Policy and Research **8341**
CGWH Newsletter **9231**
Chabot College • Women in Transition • Displaced Homemakers Program **5059**
Chace House; Elizabeth Buffum **4588**
Chaffey College • Single Parent/Displaced Homemaker Project **5083**
The Chagrin Valley Woman's Exchange **2680**
Challenging Media Images of Women **9232**
Chambersburg Woman's Club **1699**
Chaminade University of Honolulu • Women's Studies **7241**
Champaign/Ford Vocational System • Building Opportunity Project **5330**
Champion Player of the Year Award **7946**
Champlain College • Displaced Homemaker Program **6059**
Champlin Valley Birthright **3082**
Chances and Changes **4233**
Chapter League Bulletin **9233**
Charis Books and More **10140**
Charities see Philanthropy; Volunteers
Charles Andrew Rush Learning Center/Library • Special Collections • Birmingham Southern College **6743**
Charles County Community College • Project Transition **5430**
Charles Levy Co. **8640**
Charleston Business and Professional Women's Club **1703**

Charleston Career Center • Displaced Homemakers Program **5780**
Charleston Woman's Club **1704**
Charlotte Danstrom Award **7947**
Charlotte Vocational Technical School Center • ENCORE! **5230**
Chas. Franklin Press **9701**
Chasman Scholarship; Renate W. **7888**
Chatham College **7030**
Chattahoochee Technical College • New Connections **5262**
Chattahoochee Valley State Community College • Displaced Homemakers Program **4993**
Chattanooga Urban League • Single Parent/Displaced Homemaker Program **5946**
Chelsea Books **10081**
Chelsea Help for Battered Women **4757**
Chemeketa Community College
Services for the New Workforce • Skills for Independence **5845**
Women's Studies Program **7629**
Chemistry
Air Products and Chemicals, Inc. Scholarship **7790**
American Business Women's Association, Charleston Branch **1684**
American Chemical Society • Women Chemists Committee **55**
American Society of Bio-Chemistry and Molecular Biology • Committee on Equal Opportunities for Women **125**
Association for Women Geoscientists **193**
AT&T Bell Laboratories Graduate Research Fellowships for Women **7805**
AT&T Bell Laboratories Graduate Research Grants for Women **7806**
Bunting Institute Science Scholars Fellowships **7815**
Emerson Scholarship; Gladys Anderson **7835**
Garvan Medal **7982**
Gerry Fellowships; Eloise **7829**
Hoffman Award for Outstanding Achievement in Graduate Research; Anna Louise **7925**
IBM Fellowships for Women **7841**
Iota Sigma Pi **488**
Iota Sigma Pi Award for Professional Excellence **8003**
Iota Sigma Pi National Honorary Member **8004**
Iota Sigma Pi Undergraduate Award for Excellence in Chemistry **7842**
Morgan Research Award; Agnes Faye **7912**
NCAR Graduate Research Assistantships **7875**
New Jersey Department of Human Services • Division of Youth and Family Services • Family Violence Prevention and Services **8553**
Post Doctoral Support in the Atmospheric Sciences **7886**
Undergraduate Award for Excellence in Chemistry **8119**
Chenango County Mental Health Clinic • Domestic Violence Services **4280**
Cherokee County Crisis Center **4699**
Cherokee Family Violence Center **3591**
Chesapeake Area Group of Women Historians **3093**
Chesapeake College • New Horizons **5440**
Chester County Citizens Concerned About Life **2900**
Chester Women's Club **1761**

Chesterfield County Victim/Witness Assistance Office **4777**
Chesterfield-Marlboro Technical College • Single Parent/Displaced Homemaker Program **5910**
Chestnut Hill College **7031**
Women's Studies Program **7650**
Chez Hope, Inc. **3804**
Chi Eta Phi Sorority, Inc. **252**
Chi Upsilon Sorority **2224**
Chicago Abused Women Coalition **3653**
Chicago Area Women's History Conference **1706**
Chicago Catholic Women Newsletter **9234**
Chicago City-Wide College
Displaced Homemaker Program **5300**
Single Parent/Displaced Homemaker Building Opportunity Project **5301**
Chicago Department of Human Services • Domestic Violence Services **3654**
Chicago Foundation for Women **1707**
Chicago Historical Society • Library and Archives **6764**
Chicago Public Library **6765**
Chicago Society of Women Certified Public Accountants **1708**
Chicago Women in Government Relations **1709**
Chicago Women in Publishing **1710**
Chicago Women in Publishing News **9235**
Chicago Women's Conference **1773**
Chicana Research & Learning Center, Inc. • Library **6766**
Chicana Rights Project **253**
Chicana Service Action Center • East Los Angeles/Free Spirit Shelter **3388**
Chicanas see Hispanic Americans
Chicano Por LaCausa • Displaced Homemaker/Single Parent Program **5019**
Chicanos por la Causa • De Colores **3313**
Chicory Blue Press **9702**
Child Abuse
American Bar Association • Center on Children and the Law **6728**
American Humane Association • American Association for Protecting Children • National Resource Center on Child Abuse and Neglect **6732**
B.A. Press **9668**
C. Henry Kempe National Center for the Prevention and Treatment of Child Abuse and Neglect • Library **6752**
Child Abuse and Neglect and Family Violence Audiovisual Catalog **8705**
Child Welfare League of America, Inc. **9703**
Clearinghouse on Child Abuse and Neglect Information **6770**
The Courage to Heal: A Guide for Women Survivors of Child Sexual Abuse **8711**
Defense for Children International— United States of America • Library **6782**
Domestic Violence Institute **337**
Focus on Families: A Reference Handbook **8744**
Giarretto Institute **397**
Human Lactation Center, Ltd. • Library **6805**
International Child Resource Institute • Information Clearinghouse **6812**
Mexican-American Opportunity Foundation • Resource and Referral Service • Lending Library **6849**
Mother Courage Press **9867**
Programs to Strengthen Families: A Resource Guide **8788**

Sexual Assault and Child Abuse: A National Directory of Victim Services and Prevention Programs **8794**
U.S. Department of Justice • National Institute of Justice • Library **6941**
University of California, Los Angeles • Center for the Study of Women **8253**
University of Connecticut • Women's Center **8256**
Women Organized Against Rape **2869**
Women's Crisis Center **3080**
Child Abuse and Neglect and Family Violence Audiovisual Catalog **8705**
Child Bereavement see Infant Death
Child Care (see also Day Care; Parenting)
American Federation of Teachers Library **6730**
Women's Rights Committee **72**
Arts & Images **9659**
Baby Care **10325**
Child Care Action Campaign **254**
Child Care Management Consultants, Inc. **8660**
Child Care Service Directory **8706**
Child Welfare League of America, Inc. **9703**
Children's Defense Fund **9704**
Children's Foundation **256, 9705**
CHOICE **258**
CHOICE (Concern for Health Options: Information Care & Education) **9706**
Day Nursery Association **2487**
DCC, Inc./the Dependent Care Connection **8664**
Early Discharge **10419**
ERIC Clearinghouse on Elementary and Early Childhood Education **6789**
Fairfax County Mothers of Multiples **3121**
Fitzgerald; Ruth Lang **8682**
Glover Press **9770**
Imprints **9334**
Indiana Association for Child Care Resource and Referral **1844**
Institute for Childhood Resources **9803**
International Child Resource Institute • Information Clearinghouse **6812**
International Nanny Association **474**
Kins (Mothers) of Twins Southtowns **2586**
League of Women Voters Education Fund **8208**
Maryland Committee for Children, Inc. • MCC Resource Center **6844**
Mature Women Scholarship Grant **8031**
Meadowbrook Press, Inc. **9855**
Missouri Women's Network **2322**
Mothers Matter **562**
Nanny Pop-Ins Association **569**
National Association of Negro Business and Professional Women's Club National Youth Award **8056**
National Center for Policy Alternatives • Women's Economic Justice Center **635**
National Coalition for Campus Child Care **647**
National Commission for Women's Equality **652**
National Commission on Working Women **653**
National Council of Jewish Women **9881**
National Organization of Mothers of Twins Clubs **728**
The National Report on Work and Family **10724**
National Women's Law Center **8219**

Child Health (continued)

Michigan Department of Public Health • Division of Program and Administrative Services • Maternal and Child Health Office **8525**

Michigan Midwives Association **2187**

Minnesota Department of Health • Maternal and Child Health Division **8530**

Mississippi Department of Health • Bureau of Health Services • Maternity Services Division **8533**

Missouri Department of Health • Maternal and Child Health Division **8536**

Montana Department of Health and Environmental Sciences • Division of Health Services • Family, Maternal and Child Health Bureau **8540**

Mother and Unborn Baby Care of York **2909**

NAPSAC News **9386**

National Center for Education in Maternal and Child Health **633**

National Maternal and Child Health Clearinghouse **715**

National Sudden Infant Death Syndrome Clearinghouse **6872**

Nebraska Department of Health • Division of Maternal and Child Health **8544**

Nevada Department of Human Resources • Division of Health • Bureau of Maternal and Child Health **8547**

New Hampshire Department of Health and Human Services • Division of Public Health Services • Bureau of Maternal and Child Health **8551**

New Jersey Department of Health • Division of Family Health Services • Maternal and Child Health Services **8552**

New Jersey Healthy Mothers, Healthy Babies **2455**

New Mexico Department of Health and Environment • Division of Public Health • Maternal Section **8557**

New Mothers and Infant Care **10524**

New York State Department of Health • Center for Community Health • Family Health Bureau **8563**

North Carolina Department of Environment, Health and Natural Resources • Office of Health Director • Maternal and Child Health Division **8566**

North Dakota Coalition for Healthy Mothers, Healthy Babies **2663**

North Dakota Department of Health and Consolidated Laboratories • Preventive Health Section • Maternal and Child Health Division **8569**

Ohio Department of Health • Division of Maternal and Child Health **8572**

Oklahoma Department of Health • Department of Personal Health Services • Maternal and Child Health Services **8576**

Oregon Department of Human Resources • Division of Health • Office of Maternal and Child Health **8581**

Pennsylvania Department of Health • Bureau of Maternal and Child Preventive Health Programs • Division of Maternal and Child Health **8583**

Planned Parenthood of Northern New England • PPNNE Resource Center **6898**

Reaching Out: A Directory of National Organizations Related to Maternal and Child Health **8789**

Rhode Island Department of Health • Division of Family Health **8590**

South Carolina Department of Health and Environmental Control • Office of Health Services • Bureau of Maternal and Child Health **8593**

South Dakota Department of Health • Division of Health Services • Maternal and Child Health Program **8595**

Starting Early: A Guide to Federal Resources in Maternal and Child Health **8799**

Tennessee Department of Health and Environment • Health Services Bureau • Maternal and Children's Health Section **8599**

Texas Department of Health • Personal Health Services • Bureau of Maternal and Child Health **8602**

U.S. Department of Agriculture Food and Nutrition Service • Supplemental Food Programs Division • Commodity Supplemental Food Program **8416**

Food and Nutrition Service • Supplemental Food Programs Division • Special Supplemental Food Program for Women, Infants, and Children (WIC Program) **8300, 8417**

U.S. Department of Health and Human Services

Alcohol, Drug Abuse, and Mental Health Administration • Demonstration Grants on Model Projects for Pregnant and Postpartum Women and Their Infants **8427**

Health Resources and Services Administration • Maternal and Child Health Bureau **8324**

Health Resources and Services Administration • Maternal and Child Health Bureau • Maternal and Child Health Federal Consolidated Programs **8430**

Health Resources and Services Administration • Maternal and Child Health Bureau • Maternal and Child Health Services Block Grant **8431**

Health Resources and Services Administration • Maternal and Child Health Bureau • Maternal and Child Health Targeted Infant Mortality Initiative **8432**

Health Resources and Services Administration • Maternal and Child Health Bureau • National Center for Education in Maternal and Child Health **8326**

Health Resources and Services Administration • Maternal and Child Health Bureau • National Maternal and Child Health Clearinghouse **8327**

National Institutes of Health • National Institute of Child Health and Human Development • Office of Research Reporting **8332**

National Institutes of Health • National Institute of Child Health and Human Development • Research for Mothers and Children **8434**

Office of the Surgeon General • Panel on Women, Adolescents and Children with HIV Infection and AIDS • Working Group on Pediatric AIDS **8340**

Utah Department of Health • Division of Family Health Services • Maternal and Child Health Bureau **8606**

Vermont Agency of Human Services • Department of Health • Bureau of Maternal and Child Health **8610**

Virginia Department of Health • Division of Maternal and Child Health **8615**

Washington Department of Health • Division of Parent and Child Health Services **8618**

West Virginia Department of Health and Human Resources • Public Health Bureau • Office of Community Health Services • Division of Maternal and Child Health **8621**

Wisconsin Department of Health and Social Services • Division of Health • Bureau of Community Health and Prevention **8625**

Wyoming Department of Health • Division of Health and Medical Services • Family Health Services **8631**

CHILD, Inc. • Family Violence Program **3522**

Child Support

Alabama Department of Human Resources • Child Support Enforcement Division **8445**

American Bar Association • Center on Children and the Law **6728**

Arizona Attorney General • Child Enforcement Section **8453**

Association for Children for Enforcement of Support **169**

Center for Law and Social Policy **240**

Children's Foundation **256, 9705**

Congressional Caucus for Women's Issues **299**

Connecticut Office of the Attorney General • Child Support Department **8469**

Consumer Awareness Learning Laboratory **9715**

Delaware Department of Health and Social Services • Child Support Enforcement Division **8473**

Directory of State and Local Child Support Advocacy Groups **8728**

District of Columbia Office of the Mayor • Corporation Counsel Office • Child Support Unit **8479**

For Our Children's Unpaid Support **379**

From the State Capitals: Family Relations **9308**

Illinois Women's Advocate and Legislative Watch **9332**

Institute for the Study of Matrimonial Laws **8203**

Kansas Department of Social and Rehabilitation Services • Child Support Enforcement Division **8502**

Kentucky Attorney General • Child Support Enforcement Division **8503**

Kentucky Human Resources Cabinet • Social Insurance Department • Child Support Enforcement Division **8507**

LEXIS Family Law Library **10720**

Massachusetts Health and Human Services Executive Office • Public Welfare Department • Child Support Division **8522**

Minnesota Department of Human
Services • Child Support Enforcement
Division **8531**
Mississippi Department of Human
Services • Child Support
Division **8535**
Missouri Department of Social Services
• Child Support Enforcement
Division **8537**
Montana Department of Social and
Rehabilitation Services • Child Support
Enforcement Division **8541**
National Association of Childbirth
Assistants **586**
National Center on Women and Family
Law, Inc. **636, 8215, 9880**
Information Center **6863**
National Child Support Enforcement
Association **639**
National Organization to Insure Survival
Economics **726**
National Women's Law Center **8219**
New Jersey Child Support
Council **2459**
New Mexico Department of Human
Services • Child Support Enforcement
Division **8558**
New York Department of Social
Services • Child Support Enforcement
Office **8560**
North Carolina Child Support
Council **2642**
Northern California Mediation
Center **8223**
Ohio Department of Human Services •
Child Support Bureau **8573**
Organization for the Enforcement of
Child Support, Wisconsin
Chapter **3236**
The Pied Piper **9452**
South Dakota Department of Social
Services • Child Support Enforcement
Office **8597**
Speak Out for Children **9483**
Texas Attorney General • Child Support
Enforcement Division **8601**
U.S. Commission on Interstate Child
Support **8289**
U.S. Department of Health and Human
Services
Administration for Children and
Families • Office of Child Support
Enforcement • Child Support
Enforcement (Title IV-D) **8424**
Office of Child Support
Enforcement • Family Support
Administration • Child Support
Enforcement Research **8436**
Vermont Agency of Human Services •
Child Support Services Office **8609**
Virginia Department of Social Services •
Child Support Enforcement
Division **8616**
Wisconsin Department of Health and
Social Services • Child Support
Bureau **8624**
Women in Transition **1081, 10033**
The Women's Advocate **9562**
Women's Legal Defense Fund **10044**
Womenspace **10051**
Child Trends, Inc. • Library **6768**
Child Welfare League of America, Inc. **9703**
**Childbirth (see also Maternal Health;
Pregnancy)**
Achievement Press **9633**
*After Childbirth: The Post-Partum
Experience—Revised* **10303**
American Academy of Husband-
Coached Childbirth **25**

American College of Nurse-
Midwives **61**
American College of Obstetricians and
Gynecologists • Nurses
Association **63**
American Society for Psychoprophylaxis
in Obstetrics **130**
Another Look at Cesarean **10313**
Apprentice Academics **9653**
Arizona Association of Midwives **1220**
Association for Childbirth at Home,
International **168**
Avery Publishing Group **9667**
Birth Community **2270**
*Birth Day—Through the Eyes of the
Mother* **10347**
The Birth Gazette **8853**
Birth: How Life Begins **10348**
Birth in the Lateral Position **10349**
Birth Notes **8854**
Birth Options in Pregnancy **1606**
Birth Photos **9678**
Birth Series **10350**
*The Birth of Your Baby:
Revised* **10351**
Birthright of Greater Glens Falls **2517**
Boston Association for Childbirth
Education **2113**
C/SEC **229**
Caesarean Childbirth **10377**
Carolina Home Birth Alliance **2943**
Center for Humane Options in Childbirth
Experiences **238**
Library **6762**
Center for the Study of Multiple
Birth **9698**
Cesarean Prevention Movement **251**
Cesarean Prevention Movement of
Boulder **1466**
Cesarean Prevention Movement of
Fairfield County **1502**
Cesarean Prevention Movement of
Greater Philadelphia **2859**
Cesarean Prevention Movement of
Greater Phoenix **1218**
Cesarean Prevention Movement of
Houston **3032**
Cesarean Prevention Movement of
Ithaca **2524**
Cesarean Prevention Movement of Long
Beach **1309**
Cesarean Prevention Movement of
Marietta **1645**
Cesarean Prevention Movement of
Marin County **1325**
Cesarean Prevention Movement of New
Mexico **2463**
Cesarean Prevention Movement of
Northern Arizona **1221**
Cesarean Prevention Movement of
Northern New York **2613**
Cesarean Prevention Movement of
Northwest Ohio **2730**
Cesarean Prevention Movement of
Ogden/Northern Utah **3069**
Cesarean Prevention Movement of San
Diego **1385**
Cesarean Prevention Movement of San
Francisco Bay Area **1290**
Cesarean Prevention Movement of San
Gabriel/San Bernardino **1459**
Cesarean Prevention Movement of
Santa Clara Valley **1436**
Cesarean Prevention Movement of
Sonoma **1448**
Cesarean Prevention Movement of
South Orange County **1420**
Cesarean Prevention Movement of
Southeast Florida **1571**

Cesarean Prevention Movement of
Southern Oregon **2784**
Cesarean Prevention Movement of
Suffolk **2506**
Cesarean Prevention Movement of
Tampa **1614**
Cesarean Prevention Movement of
Westchester/Putnam **2489**
Childbirth Education Association **1386**
Childbirth Education Association of
Cleveland **2691**
Childbirth Education Association of
Greater Philadelphia **2844**
Childbirth Education Foundation **255**
Childbirth Education Services **2128**
Childbirth Preparation **10382**
Childbirth Preparation Program **10383**
Childbirth Without Pain Education
Association **2155**
*Childbirth Without Pain Education
Association—Memo* **9237**
Cleis Press **9708**
Dayton Childbirth Education
Association **2710**
*Dealing with the Cesarean
Epidemic* **10406**
Depression After Delivery **333**
*Directory of Nurse-Midwifery
Practices* **8724**
Family Life and Maternity Education of
Dunn Loring **3101**
Family Publications **9745**
Feminist Women's Health Center **9750**
*Fertility Awareness & Natural Family
Planning Resource Directory* **8743**
Flagstaff Association of Parents and
Professionals for Safe Alternatives in
Child Birth **1222**
Franklin Press; Chas. **9701**
Genesis **8917**
Georgia Midwifery Association **1627**
Home Birth Support Group **2318**
Homebirth Information Group **1497**
Human Lactation Center, Ltd. •
Library **6805**
Imprints **9334**
Informed Homebirth/Informed Birth and
Parenting **431**
*Inserts for: Bradley Classes Videotape
No. 1* **10487**
*Inserts for: Bradley Classes Videotape
No. 2* **10488**
International Association of Parents and
Professionals for Safe Alternatives in
Childbirth **446**
International Childbirth Education
Association **453, 9805**
*International Childbirth Education
Association—ICEA Membership
Directory* **8761**
Janes Publishing **9810**
A Joyous Labor **10492**
Kentucky Alliance for the Advancement
of Midwifery **1987**
Labor and Birth **10494**
Labor Coaching **10495**
Madisonville Mothers of Twins **1994**
Massachusetts Association for Parents
and Professionals for Safe Alternatives
in Childbirth **2085**
Maternity Center Association **539**
Reference Library **6846**
Medications and Anesthesia **10512**
Michigan Midwives Association **2187**
Midwest Parentcraft Center **1720**
Midwifery Today **8996**
Midwives Alliance of North
America **549**
*NAPSAC Directory of Alternative Birth
Services and Consumer Guide* **8769**

Coordinating Committee on Women's Health Issues • U.S. Department of Health and Human Services • National Institutes of Health • National Institute of General Medical Sciences **8333**

Coordinating Council on Women in the Historical Profession, Upstate New York Chapter **2583**

Coos County Family Health Services • RESPONSE to Sexual and Domestic Violence **4129**

Coos County Women's Crisis Service **4481**

Coosa Valley Technical Institute • CHIPS/New Connections **5267**

Cope **4786**

COPE [Alamogordo, NM] **4171**

Cope House [Elmira, NY] **5689**

Copeland Lumber Yards Inc. **8653**

Copeland Scholarship; Helen **7993**

Copiah-Lincoln Community College • Single Parent/Homemaker Program **5550**

Copiah-Lincoln Community College—Natchez Campus • Single Parent/Homemaker Program **5541**

Coping with the Discomforts of Pregnancy **10396**

Copley Press **8639**

Corbett Scholarship; Lucy **7860**

Cornell College • Women's Studies Program **7302**

Cornell Scholarship; Holly A. **7840**

Cornell University
    Institute for Women and Work **305**
    New York State School of Industrial and Labor Relations • Sanford V. Lenz Library **6779**
    Women's Center **6580**
    Women's Studies Program **7522**

Cornell University Press **9716**

Cornerstone **9252**

Cornerstone Advocacy Service **3942**

Correctional Facility • Displaced Homemaker Program **5939**

Cosby Coalition Against Domestic Violence • Safe Space **4647**

Cosmetic Career Women **306**

Cosmetic Executive Women **306**

Cosmopolitan **8879**

Cosmopolitan Associates **307**

Cosmopolitan Chamber of Commerce Contractors Division **8663**

Cosmopolitan en Espanol **8880**

Cosumnes River College • Women's Studies Program **7160**

Cotee River Women's Republican Club **1587**

Cottey College **7040**

Cottonwood County Crisis Center **4020**

Cottonwood Press **9717**

Council for Advancement and Support of Education • Commission for Opportunity and Equity **308**

Council Against Domestic Abuse **3738, 3758**

Council Against Domestic Assault **3912**

Council of Asian American Women **309**

Council on Battered Women **3568**

Council of Collegiate Women's Athletic Administrators **588**

Council of Communication Organizations • A Woman's Network **310**

Council on Domestic Abuse **3729**

Council on Domestic Violence for Page County • Choices, Inc. **4813**

Council on Domestic Violence and Sexual Assault **3917**

Council on Families in Crisis **4050**

Council on Interracial Books for Children, Inc. **9718**

The Council of Presidents of United States Women's Organizations **311**

Council for the Prevention of Domestic Violence [Estherville, IA] **3748**

Council on Sexual Assault and Domestic Violence **3759**

Council of Women Chiropractors **312**

Council for Women in Independent Schools **313**

Council of Women's Clubs **1350**

Counseling (see also Mental Health; Psychiatry; Psychology)
    American Association for Counseling and Development • Committee on Women **34**
    Association for Gay, Lesbian, and Bisexual Issues in Counseling **175**
    California Family Study Center • Library **6753**
    Compassionate Friends— Newsletter **9249**
    Consultant Services Northwest, Inc. **9714**
    The Courage to Heal: A Guide for Women Survivors of Child Sexual Abuse **8711**
    The Family Institute • Crowley Library **6791**
    MG Woman's Counseling Service of New York **8677**
    Minnesota Women's Center **2276**
    National Association for Women Deans, Administrators, and Counselors **9879**
    National Association for Women Deans, Administrators, and Counselors— Member Handbook **8770**
    Options **2864**
    Pinellas County Juvenile Welfare Board • Mailande W. Holland Library **6891**
    Safe, Strong, and Streetwise **8793**
    Schoolcraft College • Women's Resource Center **6923**
    University of Michigan • Center for the Education of Women • Library **6954**
    Womandynamics **8683**
    Woman's Counseling Service **8685**
    Women & Therapy **9141**
    Women in Transition **10033**

The Counseling Institute • Domestic Violence Program **4742**

Counterbalance **9253**

Countering Domestic Violence • Mid-Central Community Action, Inc. **3647**

Country Acres Women's Association **2384**

Country Council Newsletter **9254**

Country Woman **8881**

Country Women's Council United States of America **314**

County College of Morris • Women's Studies Program **7477**

Couple to Couple League **315**

The Courage to Heal: A Guide for Women Survivors of Child Sexual Abuse **8711**

The Courier **9255**

Covina Woman's Club **1278**

Cowley County Community College • Single Parent/Homemaker Program **5368**

Cowley County Safe Homes **3783**

COYOTE **755**

Coyote Howls **755**

Cramps! **10397**

Crandall Center for Women; Prudence **3512**

Crandall Museum; Prudence **7005**

Cranehill Press **9719**

Cranston Adult Education • Single Parent Program **5901**

Craven County Council on Women • Rape/Sexual Assault Program **4354**

Crawford County Area Vocational Technical School • New Choices **5878**

Crawford County Democratic Women's Club **1790**

Crawford County Federated Republican Women **1772**

Crawford County Republican Woman's Club **1791**

Crazy Ladies Bookstore **10232**

Crazy Quilt **8882**

Creative Services • Rape Crisis/Spouse Abuse Center **3551**

The Creative Woman **8883**

Crescent House **3812**

Crime Victims Assistance Center **4197**

Crime Victim's Center of Chester County **2901**

Crime Victims Program **4281**

Crime Victims Services and Crisis Assistance in Putnam County **4432**

Crimes against Women **10398**

Crimes Against Women Task Force • Albemarle Hopeline **4331**

Criminal Justice
    Aid to Incarcerated Mothers **2072**
    Association on Programs for Female Offenders **183**
    Double-Time **9269**
    Friends of Guest House, Inc. **3092**
    I Can See and I Can Breathe **10477**
    National Coalition of 100 Black Women **648**
    Operation Sisters United **811**
    Program for Female Offenders of South Central Pennsylvania **2837**
    Research Clearinghouse on Women of Color and Southern Women **10730**
    Social Justice **9072**
    They're Doing My Time **10621**
    U.S. Department of Labor • Women's Bureau • Network on Female Offenders **8346**
    When a Woman Fights Back **10662**
    Women & Criminal Justice **9132**
    Women in Crisis **1022**
    Women's Prison Association **1162**

Crisis Assistance Response Emergency Shelter **4798**

Crisis Care Line **4445**

Crisis Center [Marble Falls, TX] **4706**

Crisis Center **3764, 3776, 4100, 4663**
    Cooke County Friends of the Family **4680**

Crisis Center North **4510, 4554**

Crisis Center for South Suburbia **3698**

Crisis Center for South Suburbia **3702**

Crisis Control Center **4458**

Crisis Council, Inc. **4365**

Crisis Hotline **3627**

Crisis Intervention Center **3637, 4493**

Crisis Intervention Service **3754**

Crisis Intervention Services **4949**

Crisis Pregnancy **10399**

Crisis and Referral Emergency Services **4946, 4957**

Crisis Services **3761**

Crisis Shelter Alternative **10400**

Crone's Harvest **10166**

Crones' Own Press **9720**

Crossing Press **9721**

Crossroads **3477, 4425, 4558, 9722**

Crossroads Market **10271**

Crowder College • New Horizons • Displaced Homemakers Program **5565**

Crowe Star of Tomorrow; Alberta E. **7915**

Crowley's Ridge Vocational-Technical School • Single Program/Homemaker Program **5030**

Crystal Award **7954**

The Crystal Quilt, Inc. **9256**

Crystal Works **10168**

CSWEP Newsletter **9257**

Cubana Women's Club **1592**
Cuesta Community College • Women's Studies Program **7172**
Cuidado Prenatal Serie (Prenatal Care Series) **10401**
Cultural Exchange see International Relations
Cultural Studies (see also Social Science; Sociology)
 American Folklore Society • Women's Section **75**
 American Studies Association • Women's Committee **138**
 Brown University • Pembroke Center for Teaching and Research on Women **8174**
 City University of New York • Center for the Study of Women and Society **8183**
 Columbia University • Institute for Research on Women and Gender **8185**
 Data Resources of the Henry A. Murray Research Center of Radcliffe College **10707**
 Diemer, Smith Publishing Co. **9728**
 Differences: A Journal of Feminist Cultural Studies **8888**
 Duke-UNC Center for Research on Women **8187**
 Hartford College for Women • Office of Women's Research **8197**
 Harvard University • Women's Studies in Religion Program **8198**
 Institute for Research on Social Problems **8202**
 International Center for Research on Women **8205**
 Memphis State University • Center for Research on Women **8213**
 National Council for Research on Women **8216**
 National Women's History Project **6876**
 Ohio State University • Center for Women's Studies **8224**
 Smith College • Project on Women and Social Change **8237**
 The Spring Foundation for Research on Women in Contemporary Society **920**
 University of Arizona • Southwest Institute for Research on Women (SIROW) **8250**
 University of Cincinnati • Women's Studies Research and Resources Institute **8254**
Cumberland Career Equity Center **5949**
Cumberland Council on Adolescent Pregnancy **2632**
Cumberland County Department of Social Services • Domestic Violence Services **4332**
Cumberland County Women's Center **4169**
Cunningham and Co. Books **10156**
Curious Times **10272**
Current Literature in Family Planning **8884**
Curry College • Women's Studies Program **7365**
Custody see Child Custody; Divorce
Custody Action for Lesbian Mothers **316**
Custody Handbook: A Woman's Guide to Child Custody Disputes **8712**
Cuyahoga Community College
 Displaced Homemaker Program **5777**
 Institute on Human Relations **7587**
Cuyahoga Community College, Metropolitan Campus • Displaced Homemaker Program **5773**
CVAN Battered Women's Shelter **4329**
CWAO News **9258**

CWCMH • Kittitas Services **4832**, **4866**, **4874**
CWIS Newsletter **9259**
CWWH Newsletter **9260**
Cybele Society **9723**
Cycles **10402**
D.C. Commission for Women **1545**
D.C. Public Schools • Office of Sex Equity [Washington, DC] • A Step Towards Employment Program **5180**
Dabney S. Lancaster Community College • Single Parent/Displaced Homemaker Program **6083**
Dahlonega Woman's Club **1636**
Dakota Women of All Red Nations **317**
Dallas Woman **8885**
Dallas Women's Coalition **3010**
Dallas Women's Foundation **3011**
Dalton College • New Connections **5254**
Dalton Vocational School of Health Occupations • CHIPS/New Connections **5255**
Damron Co., Inc. **9724**
Dana Point Woman's Club **1282**
Dance see Performing Arts
Dane County Advocates for Battered Women **4910**
Dangerous Ideas, Inc. **10130**
Danstrom Award; Charlotte **7947**
Danville Area Community College • Project Hope **6084**
Danville Business Women's Club **3099**
Danville Women's Club **1283**
Danzig Award; Sarah Palfrey **8093**
Dark Secrets, Bright Victory: One Woman's Recovery from Bulimia **10403**
Dartmouth College
 Women's Resource Center **6554**
 Women's Studies Program **7454**
Data Archive on Adolescent Pregnancy and Pregnancy Prevention **10706**
Data Resources of the Henry A. Murray Research Center of Radcliffe College **10707**
Database of Third World Women's Literary Works **10708**
Databases (see also Online Networks; Chapter 26: Electronic Resources)
 Center for International Studies • Women in International Security **239**
Date Rape: No Means No! **10404**
Daughter Culture Publications **9725**
Daughter Rite **10405**
Daughters of the American Colonists **318**
Daughters of the Cincinnati **319**
Daughters of the Elderly Bridging the Unknown Together **320**
Daughters of Isabella Caribou Chapter **2029**
Daughters of Isabella Faribault Council **2262**
Daughters of Isabella Hastings Chapter **2265**
Daughters of Isabella, International Circle **321**
Daughters of Isabella, National Circle **321**
Daughters of Isabella, Supreme Circle **321**
Daughters of the King **813**
Daughters of the Nile, Supreme Temple **322**
Daughters of Penelope **323**
Daughters of Penelope, Mason City Chapter **1923**
Daughters of Penelope Past Grand Presidents Award **7818**
Daughters of the Republic of Texas **324**, **2994**
Daughters of Sarah **8886**
Daughters of Scotia **325**
Daughters of Union Veterans of the Civil War, 1861-1865 **326**

Daughters of Zion **409**
David Sarnoff Research Center Scholarship **7819**
Davidson County Domestic Violence Services **4345**
Davis Area Vocational-Technical School • Turning Point **6046**
DAWN **4839**
 Family Rescue Shelter **4098**
Dawson Community College • New Directions **5580**
Dawson County Parent/Child Center **4103**
Dawson County Spouse Abuse Program **4076**
Day Care (see also Child Care)
 Child Care ActioNews **9236**
 Child Care Choices **10381**
 Child Care Management Consultants, Inc. **8660**
 Child Care Service Directory **8706**
 Children's Foundation **9705**
 Day Care Information Service **9261**
 DCC, Inc./the Dependent Care Connection **8664**
 Directory of Family Day Care Associations and Support Groups **8713**
 Family Day Care Bulletin **9287**
 Guilty Madonnas **10461**
 Handbook of Family Day Care Associations **8751**
 Maryland Committee for Children, Inc. • MCC Resource Center **6844**
 National Association for Family Day Care **594**
 National Association of Negro Business and Professional Women's Club National Youth Award **8056**
 National Child Day Care Association **1550**
 The National Report on Work and Family **10724**
 New Bedford Young Women's Christian Association **2110**
 The New National Perspective **9419**
 Parent's Alternative to Latch Key **2042**
 Programs to Strengthen Families: A Resource Guide **8788**
 Speak Out! **9482**
 Syndicated Capital Publishing Co., Inc. **9981**
 U.S. Department of Labor • Women's Bureau • Work and Family Clearinghouse **8358**
 Wellesley College • Center for Research on Women **10013**
 Wildwood Resources, Inc. **10020**
 Women's Research Action Project **10046**
 Women's Research and Education Institute **8280**
Day Care Information Service **9261**
Day House; Dorothy **4303**
Day Nursery Association **2487**
Daybreak, Inc. **3880**
Daybreak Family Resource Center of Northwest Alabama **3265**
Dayton Childbirth Education Association **2710**
Dayton and Montgomery County Public Library • Adult Services Department **6780**
Daytona Beach Community College
 Fresh Start for Displaced Homemakers—Women's Center **5194**
 Women's Center • Single Parent/Homemaker Program **5195**
DC Feminists Against Pornography **1546**
DCC, Inc./the Dependent Care Connection **8664**

Displaced Homemakers Program [Dubuque, IA] **5361**

Displaced Homemakers Program [Fargo, ND] **5755**

Displaced Homemakers Program [Houlton, ME] **5409**

Displaced Homemakers Program [Skowhegan, ME] **5413**

Displaced Homemakers Program, Inc. [Thief River Falls, MN] • Crossroads **5518**

Displaced Homemakers Resource Center [Portland, ME] **5411**

Distinguished American Woman Award **7959**

Distinguished Engineering Educator Award **7960**

Distinguished Women of Northwood Institute **7961**

District of Columbia Coalition Against Domestic Violence **1547**

District of Columbia Commission for Women **8476**

District of Columbia Department of Human Services

    Commission of Public Health • Bureau of Maternal and Child Health Services **8477**

    Commission on Social Services • Family Violence Prevention and Services **8478**

District of Columbia Office of the Mayor • Corporation Counsel Office • Child Support Unit **8479**

District VI HRDC—Human Resources Development Council • Displaced Homemakers Center **5585**

Division of Girl's and Women's Sports of the American Association of Health, Physical Education, and Recreation **598**

Division of Psychology of Women Newsletter **9268**

Divorce (see also Child Custody; Child Support; Displaced Homemakers; Family Issues; Matrimonial Law)

    Chicago Public Library **6765**

    Child Custody Services of Philadelphia, Inc. • Resource Center **6767**

    Consumer Awareness Learning Laboratory **9715**

    Divorce **10413**

    Divorced and Separated Women's Group, New London Chapter **1517**

    The Family Institute • Crowley Library **6791**

    Forty Upward Network **381**

    Freedom Enterprise **9761**

    Institute for the Study of Matrimonial Laws **435, 8203**

    Irene Josselyn Clinic • Mental Health Library **6817**

    Joint Custody Association **493**

    Judean Society **494**

    LADIES - Life After Divorce Is Eventually Sane **508**

    LEXIS Family Law Library **10720**

    National Center on Women and Family Law, Inc. **636, 8215**

        Information Center **6863**

    National Committee for Fair Divorce and Alimony Laws **654**

    National Displaced Homemakers Network—Network News **9399**

    National Divorce and Singles Resource Directory **8776**

    National Organization to Insure Survival Economics **726**

    National Organization for Women, Alice Paul Chapter **2403**

    Northern California Mediation Center **8223**

Psytec, Inc. **9933**

Who Remembers Mama? **10663**

Women on Their Own **1080**

Women in Transition **1081, 10033**

Women's Action Alliance • Library **6980**

The Women's Advocate **9562**

Womenspace **10051**

Working Opportunities for Women • W.O.W. Resource Center **6988**

Divorce **10413**

Divorce Support Services, Inc. **9730**

Divorced and Separated Women's Group, New London Chapter **1517**

Dixie College • Turning Point **6051**

Dixie District Schools • Single Parents or Homemakers **5193**

Dr. B. Olive Cole Graduate Educational Grant **7821**

Dr. J. Frances Allen Scholarship **7962**

Doctoral Dissertation Grants in Women's Studies **7963**

Doctors, Liars, and Women: AIDS Activists Say No To Cosmo **10414**

Dodge City Community College • Single Parent/Displaced Homemaker Program **5372**

Domestic Abuse Advocates of Wabasha County **3967, 3993**

Domestic Abuse Council **3535**

Domestic Abuse Family Shelter **4027**

Domestic Abuse Intervention Project **3954**

Domestic Abuse Prevention Center **3735**

Domestic Abuse Project [Minneapolis, MN] **3975**

Domestic Abuse Project **4511, 4544**

Domestic Abuse and Rape Crisis Center **4142**

Domestic Abuse Services, Inc. **4160**

Domestic Abuse/Sexual Assault Crisis Center **4097**

Domestic Abuse/Sexual Assault Services **4106**

Domestic Abuse Shelter **3546**

Domestic Assault Program **3563**

Domestic Assault and Rape Elimination Services **3929**

Domestic Assistance for You **4782**

Domestic Bliss **10415**

Domestic Harmony **3903**

Domestic Intervention Program • Family and Victim Services **3548**

Domestic Violence (see also Battered Women; Child Abuse; Rape; Chapter 3: Battered Women's Services)

    Action Ohio Coalition for Battered Women **2693**

    Aegis Association; Womancare/ **2030**

    Alabama Coalition Against Domestic Violence **1212**

    Alabama Department of Economic and Community Affairs • Law Enforcement Planning Division • Family Violence and Prevention Services **8444**

    Alaska Council on Domestic Violence and Sexual Assault **8449**

    Alaska Network On Domestic Violence and Sexual Assault **1216**

    American Rape Prevention Association **123**

    Arizona Coalition Against Domestic Violence **1223**

    Arizona Department of Health Services • Office of Domestic Violence and Mental Health **8456**

    Arkansas Coalition Against Violence to Women and Children **1247**

    Arkansas Office of Prosecutor Coordinator • Family Violence Prevention and Services **8460**

Athena **9601**

B.A. Press **9668**

Bartlesville Women and Children in Crisis **2750**

Battered **10328**

Battered Wives, Shattered Lives **10329**

The Battered Woman Syndrome **10331**

Battered Women **10332**

Battered Women's Directory **9671**

California Office of Criminal Justice Planning • Domestic Violence Branch **8464**

Carteret County Domestic Violence Program **2626**

Cass County Coalition Against Domestic Violence **2149**

Center Against Rape and Domestic Violence **2776**

Center for Women Policy Studies **249, 9699**

Central California Coalition On Domestic Violence **1327**

Chicago Public Library **6765**

Child Abuse and Neglect and Family Violence Audiovisual Catalog **8705**

Cincinnati Coalition of Domestic Violence **2681**

Clearinghouse on Family Violence Information **264, 6771**

Colorado Coalition Against Domestic Violence **1475**

Colorado Department of Social Services • Family Violence Program **8466**

Connecticut Coalition Against Domestic Violence **1508**

Connecticut Department of Human Resources • Bureau of Grants Management • Family Violence Prevention and Services **8468**

Delaware Commission for Women • Department of Community Affairs **1539**

Delaware Criminal Justice Council • Family Violence Prevention and Services **8472**

Directory of Information Resources on Victimization of Women **8717**

District of Columbia Coalition Against Domestic Violence **1547**

Divorced and Separated Women's Group, New London Chapter **1517**

Domestic Violence Institute **337**

Domestic Violence Intervention of Lebanon County **2846**

The Exchange **9283**

Florida Coalition Against Domestic Violence **1597**

Florida Department of Health and Rehabilitative Services • Aging and Adult Services Office • Family Violence Prevention and Services **8481**

Friends of Ruth **9307**

Gender Harmony Network **8666**

Georgia Advocates for Battered Women and Children **1626**

Georgia Department of Human Resources • Division of Family and Children Services • Family Violence Prevention and Services **8483**

Government of American Samoa • Department of Human Services • Social Services Division • Family Violence Prevention and Services **8480**

Greater Cleveland Community Shares **2692**

Hawaii Department of Human Services • Family Violence Prevention and Services **8488**

Hawaii State Committee on Family Violence **1666**
Idaho Council on Domestic Violence **8490**
Idaho Network to Stop Violence Against Women **1677**
Illinois Coalition Against Domestic Violence **1801**
Illinois Department of Public Aid • Division of Family Support • Family Violence and Prevention Services **8494**
Illinois Women's Advocate and Legislative Watch **9332**
Indiana Coalition Against Domestic Violence **1853**
Indiana Family and Social Services Administration • Family and Children Division • Family Violence Prevention and Services **8496**
Iowa Coalition Against Domestic Violence **1897**
It's Not Always Happy at My House **10490**
Kentucky Department of Social Services • Family Violence Prevention and Services **8505**
Louisiana Office of Women's Services • Family Violence Prevention and Services **8510**
Maine Department of Human Services • Bureau of Social Services • Family Violence Prevention and Services **8513**
Massachusetts Department of Social Services • Family Violence Prevention and Services **8519**
Mexican-American Opportunity Foundation • Resource and Referral Service • Lending Library **6849**
Michigan Coalition Against Domestic Violence **2217**
Michigan Department of Social Services • Domestic Violence Prevention and Treatment Board **8526**
Mineral County Advocates to End Domestic Violence **2366**
Mississippi Department of Health • Domestic Violence Shelters Projects **8534**
Missouri Coalition Against Domestic Violence **2309**
Missouri Department of Social Services • Division of Family Services • Family Violence Prevention and Services **8538**
Missouri Women's Network **2322**
Montana Coalition Against Domestic Violence **2331**
Montana Department of Family Services • Program, Planning & Evaluation Bureau • Family Violence Prevention and Services **8539**
Mothers Support Group of New London **1518**
My Husband Is Going to Kill Me **10521**
National Center on Women and Family Law, Inc. **9880**
National Clearinghouse on Marital and Date Rape **641, 6865**
National Coalition Against Domestic Violence **643**
National Coalition Against Domestic Violence Voice **9394**
National Council on Child Abuse and Family Violence **665**
National Organization for Victim Assistance **729**

National Woman Abuse Prevention Project **759**
Nebraska Department of Social Services • Domestic Violence Services **8545**
Nebraska Domestic Violence and Sexual Assault Coalition **2352**
Nevada Department of Human Resources • Family Violence Prevention and Services **8548**
Nevada Network Against Domestic Violence **2374**
New Hampshire Coalition Against Domestic and Sexual Violence **2378**
New Jersey Coalition for Battered Women **2454**
New Mexico Department of Human Services • Divison of Social Services • Family Violence Prevention and Services **8559**
New Mexico State Coalition Against Domestic Violence **2473**
New York Department of Social Services • Family Violence Prevention and Services **8561**
New York State Coalition Against Domestic Violence **2479**
No Place to Hide **10528**
North Carolina Coalition Against Domestic Violence **2628**
North Carolina Division of Social Services • Family Services Section • Family Violence and Prevention Services **8567**
North Dakota Council on Abused Women's Services **2654**
Northern California Coalition Against Domestic Violence **1430**
Ohio Department of Human Services • Domestic Violence and Community Social Services Unit **8574**
Ohio Domestic Violence Network **2726**
Oklahoma Coalition on Domestic Violence and Sexual Assault **2757**
Oklahoma Department of Mental Health • Domestic Violence Services **8577**
Oregon Coalition Against Domestic and Sexual Violence **2791**
Oregon Department of Human Resources • Children's Services Division • Domestic Violence Program **8580**
Pennsylvania Coalition Against Domestic Violence **2836**
Pennsylvania Department of Public Welfare • Office of Social Programs • Family Violence Prevention and Services **8584**
Psytec, Inc. **9933**
Puerto Rico Coalition Against Domestic Violence **2911**
Puerto Rico Department of Social Services • Office of External Affairs • Family Violence Prevention and Services **8587**
Red Flag Green Flag Resources **9940**
Response to the Victimization of Women and Children **9055**
Rhode Island Council on Domestic Violence **2918**
Rhode Island Department of Human Services • Economic and Social Services Division • Family Violence Prevention and Services **8591**
Seal Press **9962**
South Carolina Coalition Against Domestic Violence and Sexual Assault **2936**
South Carolina Department of Social Services • Spouse Abuse Program **8594**

South Dakota Coalition Against Domestic Violence and Sexual Assault **2951**
South Dakota Department of Social Services • Child Protection Services Office • Family Violence Prevention and Services **8596**
Southern California Coalition on Battered Women **1441**
Suffering in Silence: Sexual Assault Survivors **10614**
Tennessee Department of Human Services • Family Violence Prevention and Services **8600**
Tennessee Task Force on Family Violence **2983**
Texas Council on Family Violence **2999**
Texas Department of Human Services • Family Violence Prevention and Services **8603**
Time Out Series **10626**
Two Million Women: Domestic Violence **10636**
U.S. Department of Health and Human Services • Administration for Children and Families • Family Violence Prevention and Services **8423**
U.S. Department of Justice • National Institute of Justice • Library **6941**
Utah Department of Human Services • Bureau of Family Services • Family Violence Prevention and Services **8607**
Vermont Agency of Human Services • Family Violence Prevention and Services **8611**
Vermont Network Against Domestic Violence and Sexual Assault **3086**
Virginia Department of Social Services • Division of Service Programs • Spouse Abuse Prevention and Services **8617**
Virginians Against Domestic Violence **3119**
Washington Department of Social and Health Services • Division of Children and Family Services • Domestic Violence Program **8619**
Washington State Domestic Violence Hotline **3141**
West Virginia Coalition Against Domestic Violence **3196**
West Virginia Department of Health and Human Resources • Family Violence Prevention and Services **8620**
Widows Support Group of New London **1519**
Wisconsin Coalition Against Domestic Violence **3217**
Wisconsin Department of Health and Social Services • Bureau for Children, Youth and Families • Family Violence Prevention and Services **8623**
Women in Crisis Coalition **2968**
The Women's Advocate **9562**
Women's Crisis Center **3080**
Women's Crisis Center of Northern Kentucky **1995**
Women's History Research Center **10041**
Women's Political Action Committee of New Jersey **2407**
Women's Recovery Network **9584**
Wyoming Coalition Against Domestic Violence and Sexual Assault **3245**
Wyoming Department of Health Division of Community Programs • Office of Family Violence and Sexual Assault **8630**

Education (continued)

National Education Association • Women's Caucus **682**

National Federation of Business and Professional Women's Clubs, Inc. of the U.S.A. **686**

National Institute for Women of Color **8217**

National Judicial Education Program to Promote Equality for Women and Men in the Courts **707**

National Organization for Women • Legal Defense and Education Fund • Project on Equal Education Rights **731**

National Women Student's Coalition **765**

National Women's Education Fund **772**

National Women's Hall of Fame **8065**

National Women's History Project **776**

National Women's Law Center **8219**

National Women's Studies Association **782, 8220**

NCAWE News **9413**

NOW Legal Defense and Education Fund **802**

Organization for Equal Education of the Sexes **816**

PEO Sisterhood, DW Chapter **1785**

Pi Lambda Theta **834**

Project on Equal Education Rights **859, 8228**

Radcliffe College
Arthur and Elizabeth Schlesinger Library on the History of Women in America **6911**
Henry A. Murray Research Center **6912**

Research Clearinghouse on Women of Color and Southern Women **10730**

Russell Sage College • Helen Upton Center for Women's Studies **8232**

Schoolcraft College • Women's Resource Center **6923**

Sex Equity in Education Program **892**

Shute Award; Gladys G. **7986**

Smith Award; Georgina **7984**

Soroptimist International **914**

Towson State University • Center for the Study of Women and Education **8247**

Tri-County Council of Women in Education Administration **2166**

Tulane University • Newcomb College Center for Research on Women • Vorhoff Library **6939**

U.S. Department of Education • Office of Assistant Secretary for Elementary and Secondary Education • Equity and Educational Excellence Division • Women's Educational Equity **8418**

University of California, Davis • Women's Resources and Research Center **8252**

University of California, Los Angeles • Center for the Study of Women **8253**

University of Cincinnati • Women's Studies Research and Resources Institute **8254**

University of Connecticut • Women's Center **8256**

University of Michigan
Center for the Education of Women **8258**
Center for the Education of Women • Library **6954**

University of Minnesota • Women, Public Policy, and Development Project **8260**

University of North Carolina at Greensboro • Woman's Collection **6960**

University of Washington • Northwest Center for Research on Women **8268**

Utah State University • Women and Gender Research Institute **8272**

WAND Education Fund **982**

Wellesley College
Archives **6974**
Center for Research on Women **8276**

Western Michigan University • Women's Center • Library **6977**

Willowood Press **10021**

WMST-L **10739**

Woman's Education and Leadership Forum **994**

Woman's Institute for Continuing Jewish Education **10027**

Women and Mathematics Education **1060**

Women: Partners in Development **10741**

Women on Words and Images **10035**

Women's Action Alliance, Inc. **1087**

Women's Economic Rights Project **1118**

Women's Institute **1131**

Women's Research and Education Institute **1168, 8280**

Women's Studies Quarterly **9157**

Workshop Materials for In-Service Training Developed by National Women's History Project **10700**

YWCA of Houston Outstanding Women's Award **8168**

Education, Adult

American Association for Adult and Continuing Education • Women's Issues, Status and Education Unit **32**

Gaffigan; Catherine **8658**

National University Continuing Education Association • Division of Programs for Women **758**

Re-Entry News **9467**

Utah State University • Women and Gender Research Institute **8272**

Education for Cooperative Living **3977**

Education, Higher

AAUW American Fellowships **7774**

AAUW Community Action Grants **7777**

AAUW Outlook **8835**

AAWCJC Quarterly **9167**

The Alert **9178**

American Association for Higher Education • Women's Caucus **35**

American Association of University Women **43, 9646**

American Association of University Women, Alabama Division **1213**

American Association of University Women, Alliance Branch **2343**

American Association of University Women, Arlington Branch **2990**

American Association of University Women, Austin Branch **2247**

American Association of University Women, Bartlesville Branch **2749**

American Association of University Women, Baton Rouge **2000**

American Association of University Women, Bedford Chapter **3096**

American Association of University Women, Bennington Chapter **3078**

American Association of University Women, Benton Harbor/St. Joseph Branch **2146**

American Association of University Women, Bluefield Branch **3182**

American Association of University Women, Bowling Green Branch **2674**

American Association of University Women, Brownsburg Chapter **1817**

American Association of University Women, Brunswick Chapter **1633**

American Association of University Women, Burlington Branch **3081**

American Association of University Women, California State Division **1367**

American Association of University Women, Carthage Branch **1695**

American Association of University Women, Charleston-Mattoon Area Branch **1702**

American Association of University Women, Clarinda Chapter **1889**

American Association of University Women, Clearwater Branch **1568**

American Association of University Women, Cortland Chapter **2520**

American Association of University Women, Crystal River Branch **1588**

American Association of University Women, De Kalb County Branch **1807**

American Association of University Women, Dearborn Branch **2151**

American Association of University Women, Delaware Branch **2717**

American Association of University Women, Delaware Chapter **1532**

American Association of University Women, Des Moines Branch **1895**

American Association of University Women, Dunkirk-Fredonia Branch **2513**

American Association of University Women Educational Foundation **44**

American Association of University Women, Falls Church Branch **3091**

American Association of University Women, Federal Way Branch **3134**

American Association of University Women, Fenton Branch **2189**

American Association of University Women, Flint Branch **2240**

American Association of University Women, Florida Division **1604**

American Association of University Women, Georgia Chapter **1650**

American Association of University Women, Grand Rapids Chapter **2179**

American Association of University Women, Hillsboro Branch **2720**

American Association of University Women, Idaho Chapter **1676**

American Association of University Women, Illinois Division **1794**

American Association of University Women, Iowa Division **1877**

American Association of University Women, Kalamazoo Branch **2193**

American Association of University Women, Kingsport Branch **2972**

American Association of University Women, Kokomo Branch **1849**

American Association of University Women, Louisiana Division **2015**

American Association of University Women, Lower Connecticut Valley **1501**

American Association of University Women, Maine Division **2032**

American Association of University Women, Manistee Branch **2211**

National Ecumenical Coalition, Inc. • Library **6867**

National Education Association • Women's Caucus **682**

National Organization for Women **730**

National Woman's Party **761**

National Women's Conference Committee **770**

National Women's Political Caucus **781**

Northwestern University • Special Collections • Women's Collection **6884**

Off Our Backs: A Women's Newsjournal **9024**

Paul Award; Alice **7916**

The Promise of Equality in the U.S. Constitution **10571**

Redstockings of the Women's Liberation Movement **868, 9942**

St. Joan's International Alliance • U.S. Section **883**

Sewall-Belmont House **7006**

Smithsonian Institution • Museum of American History • Division of Political History • National Women's History Collection **7007**

Stop Equal Rights Amendment **922**

Women in America **10675**

Women: The Hand That Cradles the Rock **10683**

Women in Politics **10688**

Women, Power, and Politics **10689**

Women and Society **10691**

Women to Watch **9557**

Women's History Research Center **10041**

Equal Rights Amendment: An Annotated Bibliography of the Issues **8738**

Equal Rights Congress **350**

Equal Time **9281**

Equality **10426**

Equinox • Domestic Violence Services **4188**

The Equity Institute, Inc. **351**

Equity Policy Center **352, 8190**

ERA see Equal Rights Amendment

ERA Impact Project **9742**

ERIC Clearinghouse on Elementary and Early Childhood Education **6789**

Erie Community College, North Campus • Women's Center/Caucus **6597**

Erie Community College, South Campus • Women's Center **6590**

Erie County Technical School • New Choices **5867**

Erie No. 2 BOCES—Board of Cooperative Educational Services • Project New Ventures **5673**

Erv Lind Award **7971**

Esperanza **4182**

Esprit de Corp **8636**

Essence **8898**

Essential Medical Information Systems, Inc. **9743**

Essex Community College • Turning Point **5417**

Essex County College • WISE Women's Center **5642**

Essex County Family Violence Program **4159**

Essex County National Organization for Women **2421**

Essex County Women's Bowling Association **2399**

Essex District Republican Women's Club **2069**

Essex Junction Area Vocational Center • Single Parent/Homemakers Program **6062**

Esther Haar Award **7972**

Eta Phi Beta Sorority, Inc. **353**

Ethnic Studies see Area and Ethnic Studies

Ethnic Woman **8899**

Etowah City School District • Displaced Homemaker/Single Parent Programs **5954**

ETS Postdoctoral Fellowship **7830**

Eucalyptus Lesbian & Feminist Bookstore **10067**

Eugene Lang College • New School for Social Research • Women's Studies Program **7536**

European Americans

Daughters of Penelope **323**

Daughters of Scotia **325**

Federation of French American Women **361**

First Catholic Slovak Ladies Association **378**

Glos Polek/Polish Women's Voice **9608**

Legion of Young Polish Women **520**

Lithuanian Catholic Women **530**

National Council of Women of Free Czechoslovakia **676**

National Organization of Italian-American Women **727**

National Society, Daughters of the British Empire in the United States of America **749**

Our Life **9028**

Polish Women's Alliance of America **838**

Polka—Polish Woman **9037**

Sarah Lawrence College • Women's Studies Program **9958**

Slovenian Women's Union **899**

Society of Daughters of Holland Dames **902**

Supreme Lodge of the Danish Sisterhood of America **928**

Turkish Women's League of America **941**

Ukrainian National Women's League of America **942**

Women's Welsh Clubs of America **2734**

Evangelical and Ecumenical Women's Caucus **354**

Evansville Career Women of Business and Professional Women's Club **1822**

Evansville-Vanderburgh School Corporation • Single Parent/Homemaker Program **5339**

Evansville Young Women's Christian Association **1823**

Eveleth United Methodist Women **2261**

Evelyn Bauer Prize **7973**

Everett Community College • Women's Programs **6115, 6691, 7732**

Evergreen Human Services **4868**

The Evergreen State College
Women's Center **6692**
Women's Studies Program **7735**

Evergreen Woman's Club **2428**

Every Woman Opportunity Center, Inc. **2500**

Every Woman's Guide to Breast Self-Examination **10427**

Every Woman's Guide to Osteoporosis **10428**

Every Woman's House **4448**

Every Woman's Place **5493**
Crisis Center **3924**

Everyone's Books **10280**

Everywoman Opportunity Center [Buffalo, NY] **5684**

Everywoman Opportunity Center [Dunkirk, NY] **5688**

Everywoman Opportunity Center [Olean, NY] **5710**

Everywoman Opportunity Center [Tonawanda, NY] **5724**

Everywoman's Center Newsletter **9282**

Ex-Victims Empowered, Inc. **4427, 4789**

EXCEL! The Initiative for Entrepreneurial Excellence **2157**

Exceptional Merit Media Award (EMMA) **7974**

The Exchange **9283**

Exclusively Connecticut **9605**

Executive Female **8900**

Executive Women International **355**

Executive Women International, Omaha Chapter **2359**

Executive Women International, Orange County Chapter **1357**

Executive Women International, Reno Chapter **2371**

Executive Women International, Tulsa Chapter **2765**

Executive Women of the Palm Beaches **1600**

Executive Women's Division **696**

Executives see Business and Management

Executives' Secretaries **355**

Exercise and Pregnancy **10429**

Experiment in Equality **10430**

Exponent II **9606**

Extended Services Center • Single Parent/Homemakers Program **5345**

F.W. Olin Library • Special Collections • Mills College **6853**

Facing Tomorrow **10431**

Fahrenheit 451 Books **10080**

Fair Employment Practices Summary of Latest Developments **9284**

Fair Share **9285**

Fairbanks Native Association • Careers in Nontraditional Occupations for Single Parent Homemakers **5002**

Fairfax County Career Development Center for Women **6100**

Fairfax County Career Development Center for Women—Connections **9286**

Fairfax County Mothers of Multiples **3121**

Fairfax County Victim Assistance Network **4770**

Fairfax County Women's Shelter **4817**

Fairfax County YWCA Women's Network **3100**

Fairfield Career Center • Discover **5764**

Fairfield County Woman **8901**

Fairfield University • Women's Resource Center **6424**

Fairleigh Dickinson University • Women's Studies Program **7478**

Faith House **3301, 3319, 3808**

Faith Mission and Help Center **4664**

Fall River Crisis Intervention Team **4607**

Falls City General Women's Club **2347**

Families in Crisis **4701**

Families First, Inc. • Domestic Crisis Intervention Unit **3569**

Family Abuse Center **4735**

Family Abuse Services of Alamance County **4325**

Family Abuse Shelter **4424, 4444**

Family Advocacy Network **4818**

Family Advocate Program, Inc. • Parent Aids and CASA Programs **3618**

Family Advocates **4924**

Family of the Americas Foundation **356**

The Family Center **4945**
Domestic Violence/Sexual Assault Prevention Program **4766**

Family and Children's Services **3978, 4002, 4198**
Domestic Violence Program **4629**
Passage Program **4278**
Turning Point **4336**

Family and Children's Services of Central
Maryland • Battered Spouse
Program 3830, 3848
Family Circle 8902
Family Counseling Agency • Battered
Women's Program 3802
Family Counseling Center 4803
Family Violence Project 4236
Family Counseling and Children's
Services 3882
Family Counseling Service of the Finger
Lakers • Domestic Violence Services 4273
Family Counseling Service of the Finger
Lakes • Domestic Violence Services 4234
Family Counseling Service of Orange
County 4274
Family Counseling Services of Jefferson
County 4313
Family Counseling Services of Newark •
New Beginnings Shelter 4431
Family Counseling and Shelter
Services 3918
Family Crisis Center [Baltimore, MD] 3831
Family Crisis Center [Bastrop, TX] 4658
Family Crisis Center [Brentwood, MD] 3835
Family Crisis Center [Cleburne, TX] 4669
Family Crisis Center [Farmington, NM] 4175
Family Crisis Center [Great Bend, KS] 3767
Family Crisis Center [Harlingen, TX] 4685
Family Crisis Center [Keyser, WV] 4881
Family Crisis Center [Polson, MT] 4087
Family Crisis Center [Redfield, SD] 4618
Family Crisis Center [Ruidoso, NM] 4181
Family Crisis Center [Stevens Point,
WI] 4935
Family Crisis Intervention Center of Region
V 4885
Family Crisis Network 4405, 4846
Family Crisis Resource Center 3838
Family Crisis Service 3462
Domestic Violence Program 3766
Family Crisis Shelter 3601, 3707, 3824,
4396
Family Crisis Support Services • Hope
House 4796
Family Day Care Bulletin 9287
Family Focus of Richmond County •
Haven 4820
Family Guidance Center • First Step Spouse
Abuse Program 4340
Family Haven 3580, 4715
Family Health International 8191, 9744
Library 6790
Family Health International—Network 9288
The Family Institute • Crowley Library 6791
Family Issues (see also Child Abuse;
Child Care; Child Custody; Divorce;
Domestic Violence; Homemakers;
Parenting; Reproductive Issues)
American Bar Association • Center on
Children and the Law 6728
The American Mother 9184
Burning Bridges 10376
C. Henry Kempe National Center for
the Prevention and Treatment of Child
Abuse and Neglect • Library 6752
California Family Study Center •
Library 6753
Catalyst 9695
Center for Women Policy Studies 8181
Child Custody Services of Philadelphia,
Inc. • Resource Center 6767
Child Trends, Inc. • Library 6768
Cleis Press 9708
Columbia University • Whitney M.
Young, Jr. Memorial Library of Social
Work 6777
Committee for Single Adoptive Parents,
Inc. 9711
Concerned Women for America 295

Consumer Awareness Learning
Laboratory 9715
Daughter Rite 10405
*Delta DREF Chapter Network
News* 9262
Delta Sigma Theta Sorority, Inc. • Delta
Research and Education
Foundation 331
ERIC Clearinghouse on Elementary and
Early Childhood Education 6789
Family Health International 8191
The Family Institute • Crowley
Library 6791
Family Matters 9289
Family Resources Database 10711
Family Services Newsletter 9290
Female Head of Household 10437
Feminist Futures Network News 9294
*Focus on Families: A Reference
Handbook* 8744
*From the State Capitals: Family
Relations* 9308
Institute for the Study of Matrimonial
Laws 8203
Institute for Women's Policy
Research 8204
International Center for Research on
Women • Resource Center 6811
Irene Josselyn Clinic • Mental Health
Library 6817
*Journal of Feminist Family
Therapy* 8960
Joyful Woman 9817
LEXIS Family Law Library 10720
Los Angeles Public Library • Social
Sciences, Philosophy and Religion
Department 6832
Margaret Sanger Center-Planned
Parenthood New York City • Abraham
Stone Library 6842
Mexican-American Opportunity
Foundation • Resource and Referral
Service • Lending Library 6849
Michigan Association of American
Mothers 2241
Montclair State College • Women's
Center Library 6856
National Association of Negro Business
and Professional Women's Club
National Youth Award 8056
National Center for Lesbian Rights 634
National Center for Policy Alternatives •
Women's Economic Justice
Center 635
National Center on Women and Family
Law, Inc. 636, 8215, 9880
National Committee for Adoption •
Library 6866
National Council on Family Relations •
Feminism and Family Studies 667
*The National Report on Work &
Family* 9403, 10724
New York Public Library • Early
Childhood Resource and Information
Center 6880
NewSage Press 9892
9 to 5, National Association of Working
Women 795
9 to 5 Working Women Education
Fund 796
*North Carolina Center for Laws
Affecting Women, Inc.—Report* 9430
Northern California Mediation
Center 8223
Not All Parents are Straight 10529
OmniComm Publications 9898
Pennsylvania State University •
Gerontology Center • Human
Development Collection 6890
The Phyllis Schlafly Report 9451

Pinellas County Juvenile Welfare Board
• Mailande W. Holland Library 6891
Planned Parenthood Association • Leslie
Resource Center 6892
Planned Parenthood of Central
California 9924
Planned Parenthood of Cleveland, Inc. •
Library 6894
Planned Parenthood of Northern New
England • PPNNE Resource
Center 6898
Planned Parenthood of Southwestern
Indiana, Inc. • Resource Center 6902
Pregnant Professionals: Balancing
Career & Family 10728
*Programs to Strengthen Families: A
Resource Guide* 8788
Promoting Minorities & Women 10729
Rawalt Resource Center Database;
Marguerite 10722
Ready, Willing and Able... 10583
San Joaquin Eagle Publishing 9956
Stanford University • Institute for
Research on Women and
Gender 8240
University of North Carolina at
Greensboro • Woman's
Collection 6960
Urban Institute • Program of Policy
Research on Women and
Families 973
Utah Association of Women 3075
Washington University • George Warren
Brown School of Social Work •
Library & Learning Resources
Center 6973
*Women and the American
Family* 10676
Women Employed 1026
Women and Family 10682
Women's Action Alliance •
Library 6980
The Women's Advocate 9562
Women's Research & Education
Institute 10047
Womensword 9589
*The Working Mom's Survival
Guide* 10699
Family Law see Matrimonial Law
Family Leave see Employment; Family
Issues
Family Life Abuse Center 3794
Family Life Bureau 887
Family Life Center 3531
Family Life Division 887
Family Life Information Exchange 6792
Family Life and Maternity Education of Dunn
Loring 3101
Family Life Ministry United States Catholic
Conference 887
Family Life and Population Program/Church
World Service 357
Family Matters 9289
Family Peace Center 3603
The Family Place 4671
Family Planning see Reproductive Issues
Family Planning Association of New
Jersey 2452
Family Planning Council of Western
Massachusetts 2118
*Family Planning Information Centers
Directory* 8739
Family Planning-Service Delivery Improvement
Research Grants • U.S. Department of
Health and Human Services • Office of
Population Affairs 8437
Family Planning—Services • U.S. Department
Health and Human Services • Office of the
Assistant Secretary for Health 8435
Family Publications 9745

Family Refuge Center **4882**
Family Renewal Shelter **4869**
Family Rescue **3655**
Family Rescue Services **4099**
Family Resource Center [Davenport, WA] **4831**
Family Resource Center [Rocky Mount, VA] **4811**
Family Resource Center [Wytheville, VA] **4824**
Family Resources Database **10711**
Family Resources Domestic Violence Advocacy Program **3742**
Family Service Center **4691**
Family Service Domestic Abuse Program • Multi-Service Center at Bellevue **4091**
Family Service of Greenville • Women in Crisis **4593**
Family Service of Northwest Ohio **4442**
Family Services [Marion, NC] **4348**
Family Services [Seattle, WA] **4857**
Family Services [Winston-Salem, NC] **4374, 4375**
Family Services • Domestic Violence Program **4808**
Family Services Newsletter **9290**
Family Shelter [San Angelo, TX] **4723**
The Family Shelter **4031**
Family Shelter House **4484**
Family Shelter Service **3677**
Family Stress Services of the District of Columbia • Fact Hotline **3524**
Family Support Center **3825, 4897**
Battered Women's Project **3819**
Family Support Council of Douglas County **4124**
Family Violence see Domestic Violence
Family Violence Center [Houston, TX] **4692**
Family Violence Center **3259, 3744, 3749, 4063, 4901**
Family Violence Counseling **3433**
Family Violence Diversion Network **4656**
Family Violence Intervention Program **3482, 4339**
Family Violence Law Center **3350**
Family Violence Network **3968**
Family Violence Prevention Fund **3422**
Family Violence Prevention Program **4816**
Family Violence Prevention and Services
Connecticut Department of Human Resources • Bureau of Grants Management **8468**
U.S. Department of Health and Human Services • Administration for Children and Families **8423**
Family Violence Program • Division of Indian Work **3979**
Family Violence Project [Van Nuys, CA] **3447**
Family Violence Project **3817, 3828**
Family Violence Protection, Inc. **3333**
Family Violence and Rape Crisis Services in Chatham County **4355**
Family Violence and Sexual Assault Services **4965**
Family Violence Shelter **4713**
Family Violence Support Network **3733**
Family Violence Task Force of Allegany County **4315**
Family of Woodstock • Family Shelter **4251**
Fan the Flame **10236**
Fannin County Church Women United **3008**
Fargo Women of Today **2656**
Farm Bureau Women **1917**
Farming see Agriculture
Farnham Archives; Christine Dunlap • Brown University **6749**
Fashion (see also Apparel)
BBW: Big Beautiful Woman **8850**
Blushing Bride **8857**

Bridal Guide **8858**
Bridal Sense Publications **9686**
Bride's **8859**
Brighton Publications **9687**
Cosmopolitan en Espanol **8880**
Elegant Bride **8893**
Elle **8894**
Essence **8898**
First for Women **8911**
Glamour **8920**
Harper's Bazaar **8928**
Harper's Bazaar en Espanol **8929**
LQ (Ladies Quarterly) **8984**
Mademoiselle **8986**
MidCoast Publications **9858**
Model **9003**
Modern Bride **9004**
New England Bride **9018**
Savvy Woman **9060**
TAXI **9079**
U.S.A. Petites **968**
Vanidades Continental **9094**
Viva Petites! **9101**
Vogue **9102**
Women's Circle Country Needlecraft **9145**
Fast Food Women **10432**
Faubourg Marigny Bookstore **10155**
Favorhouse of Northwest Florida, Inc. **3554**
Fayette County Council on Battered Women **1639, 3584**
Fayette County Family Abuse Council **4517, 4570**
Fayetteville Junior Woman's Club **3187**
Fayetteville Technical Institute • Single Parent/Homemaker Program **5736**
The Fear that Binds Us **10433**
Fear of Fat: Dieting and Eating Disorders **10434**
Federally Employed Women **358**
Federally Employed Women Legal and Education Fund, Inc. **9746**
Federated Estonian Women's Clubs **1182**
Federated Women in Timber **359**
Federation of Colored Women's Clubs - Tulsa Chapter **2766**
Federation Employment and Guidance Service • Displaced Homemakers Programs **5694**
Federation Feminine Franco-Americaine **361**
Federation of Feminist Women's Health Centers **360**
Federation of French American Women **361**
Federation of Jewish Women, Terre Haute Chapter **1868**
Federation of Jewish Women's Organizations **2547**
Federation Newsletter **9499**
Federation of Organizations for Professional Women **362, 9747**
Federation of Sisterhoods **2547**
Federation of Woman's Exchanges **363**
Federation of Woman's Exchanges, Baton Rouge Chapter **2003**
Federation of Women Lawyers • Judicial Screening Panel **364**
Feelin' Good **8903**
Feeling Good Again: Coping with Breast Cancer **10435**
Fellowships see Awards; Financial Aid, Educational
FEMAIL **10712**
Female Artists Past and Present **8740**
Female Benevolent Society at South Danvers **2121**
Female Composers of America **144**
Female Cycle **10436**
Female Head of Household **10437**
Female Sexual Dysfunctions **10438**
Female Sterilization **10439**

FEMECON-L **10713**
Feminism (see also Equal Rights; Women's Studies)
AAUW Outlook **8835**
Abzug Memorial Award; Martin **8028**
ACRL Women's Studies Newsletter **9170**
ALA Gay & Lesbian Task Force • Clearinghouse **6723**
All Nations Women's League **16**
Alverno College • Research Center on Women **6725**
Always Causing Legal Unrest **24**
American Anthropological Association • Association for Feminist Anthropology **31**
American Humanist Association • Feminist Caucus **83**
American Library Association • Social Responsibilities Round Table • Feminist Task Force **93**
American Philological Association • Women's Classical Caucus **109**
American Philosophical Association • Committee on the Status of Women **110**
American Public Health Association • Women's Caucus **122**
American Sociological Association • Committee on the Status of Women **134**
Ananke's Womon Publications **9650**
Andrew Mountain Press **9651**
Antelope Publications **9652**
Arachne Publishing Co. **9655**
Association of American Law Schools • Section on Women in Legal Education **162**
Association of Libertarian Feminists **178**
Association for Women in Social Work **199**
Association of Women's Music and Culture **204**
Astarte Shell Press **9664**
Atalanta **9195**
Atlanta Lesbian Feminist Alliance **1623**
Southeastern Lesbian Archives **6736**
Barn Owl Books **9670**
Barnard College • Barnard Center for Research on Women • Birdie Goldsmith Ast Resource Collection **6738**
Bay Area Evangelical and Ecumenical Women's Caucus **1335**
Bella Abzug **10338**
Biblio Press **9675**
Black Women in Church and Society **215**
Research/Resource Center **6744**
Boston NOW News **9211**
Boyer Award; Elizabeth **7966**
Camera Obscura: A Journal of Feminism and Film Theory **8867**
Cardinal Press **9690**
Cayuse Press **9696**
Center for Advanced Feminist Studies— Newsletter **9224**
Center for Women's Studies and Services **250, 9700**
Chicago Historical Society • Library and Archives **6764**
Cleis Press **9708**
Clothespin Fever Press **9709**
Coalition on Women and Religion **273, 9710**
Committee to Expose, Oppose, and Depose Patriarchy **280**

Garden City Community College • Single
Parent Homemaker Program **5375**
Gardner Woman's Club **2093**
Garland County Community College •
CHOICES: Career Development
Center **5033**
Garrett Community College • New
Horizons **5432**
Garrett Park Press **9765**
Garvan Medal **7982**
Gary Business and Professional Women's
Club **1833**
Gary Commission for Women
The Ark Shelter **3713**
The Rainbow **3714**
Gastineau Human Services • Single
Parent/Displaced Homemaker Corrections
Program **5004**
Gaston County Department of Social
Services • Battered Spouse
Program **4334**
Gateway Battered Women's Shelter **3460**
Gateway Community Services **3896**
Gateway House [Gainesville, GA] **3586**
Gateway Technical College • Wisconsin
Displaced Homemakers Networth **6170**
Gateway Vocational Technical School •
CHOICES: Career Development
Center **5026**
Gatorade Rookie of the Year **7983**
Gay see Homosexuality; Lesbians
Gay AA **393**
Gay Alliance of the Genesee Valley Inc. •
Library **6797**
Gay Archives; Lesbian and • Naiad Press,
Inc. **6860**
Gay and Lesbian Media Coalition **394**
*Gay & Lesbian Parents Coalition
International—Confidential Chapter
Directory* **8746**
Gay and Lesbian Press Association **541**
Gay Task Force of ALA **94**
Gay Task Force of ALA—Information
Center **6723**
Gay Women's Alliance **524**
*Gayellow Pages: A Classified Directory of
Gay Services and Businesses in USA and
Canada* **8747**
Gays Against Abortion **851**
Gazette of the CSWP **9310**
Gear Holdings, Inc. **8642**
Geary County Business and Professional
Women's Clubs **1947**
GENDER **10716**
Gender and Education **9311**
Gender Equity Program [Los Angeles,
CA] **5063**
Gender Harmony Network **8666**
Gender Politics **10456**
**Gender Research (see also Women's
Studies)**
Alverno College • Research Center on
Women **8170**
American Philosophical Association •
Committee on the Status of
Women **110**
American Psychological Association •
Women's Caucus, Council of
Representatives **121**
American Sociological Association
Committee on the Status of
Women **134**
Sex and Gender Section **135**
American Studies Association •
Women's Committee **138**
Association of American Law Schools •
Section on Women in Legal
Education **162**

Association of Asian Studies •
Committee of Women in Asian
Studies (CWAS) **164**
Association for Women in
Psychology **197**
Barnard College
Barnard Center for Research on
Women **8171**
Barnard Center for Research on
Women • Birdie Goldsmith Ast
Resource Collection **6738**
Branches **9212**
Brown University
Pembroke Center for Teaching and
Research on Women **8174**
Pembroke Center for Teaching and
Research on Women •
Library **6750**
Center for Women Policy Studies **249**
City University of New York • Center
for the Study of Women and
Society **8183**
Clairol Take Charge Awards
Program **7951**
*Columbia Journal of Gender and
Law* **8873**
Columbia University • Institute for
Research on Women and
Gender **8185**
Committee on Women in Asian
Studies **291**
Duke-UNC Center for Research on
Women **8187**
Equal Relationships Institute **8189**
Feminist News **9297**
GENDER **10716**
Gender and Education **9311**
Gender Harmony Network **8666**
Gender Politics **10456**
Gender & Society **8915**
Genders **8916**
George Washington University •
Women's Studies Program and Policy
Center **8196**
Girls Incorporated • National Resource
Center **6799**
Hartford College for Women • Office of
Women's Research **8197**
Harvard University • Women's Studies
in Religion Program **8198**
How to Get Money for Research **8754**
Institute for Research on Social
Problems **8202**
*Institute for Research on Women and
Gender—Newsletter* **9336**
*Institute for the Study of Women and
Men in Society Newsletter* **9337**
IROW News **9342**
ITROW News **9344**
Journal of Homosexuality **8963**
Kent State University • Project for the
Study of Gender and Education **8206**
Kinsey Institute for Research in Sex,
Gender, and Reproduction
Bibliographic Database **10718**
Kinsey Institute for Research in Sex,
Gender, and Reproduction, Inc. **8207**
Library and Information
Service **6823**
Masters & Johnson Institute **8209**
Memphis State University • Center for
Research on Women **8213**
National Council for Research on
Women **672, 8216**
National Network of Women's
Caucuses **673**
New Futures Enterprises **8680**
*Newcomb College Center for Research
on Women Newsletter* **9421**

Northern California Mediation
Center **8223**
Ohio State University • Center for
Women's Studies **8224**
*Opportunities for Research and
Study* **8782**
Organization for the Study of
Communication, Language and
Gender **818**
OSCLG News **9440**
Psychological Perspectives **9043**
Rutgers University • Institute for
Research on Women **8235**
The Sex and Gender Newsletter **9473**
*Sex Roles: A Journal of
Research* **9063**
Smith College • Project on Women and
Social Change **8237**
Speech Communications Association •
Women's Caucus **919**
Stanford University • Institute for
Research on Women and
Gender **8240**
State University of New York College
at Brockport • Community Research
Center **8244**
Syracuse University • Women's Studies
Program **8246**
*UCLA Center for the Study of Women
Newsletter* **9498**
The Union Institute • The Center for
Women **943**
*U.S.-Japan Women's Journal: A Journal
for the International Exchange of
Gender Studies* **9091**
University of California, Berkeley •
Beatrice M. Bain Research
Group **8251**
University of California, Davis •
Women's Resources and Research
Center **8252**
University of California, Los Angeles
Center for the Study of
Women **8253**
Higher Education Research
Institute **969**
University of Connecticut
Institute for the Study of Women
and Gender **8255**
Women's Center **8256**
University of Minnesota • Center for
Advanced Feminist Studies **8259**
University of Missouri—St. Louis •
Women's Center **6958**
University of Oregon • Center for the
Study of Women in Society **8263**
University of Pennsylvania • Alice Paul
Research Center for the Study of
Women **8264**
University of Southern California •
Institute for the Study of Women and
Men **8265**
University of Wisconsin—Madison •
Women's Studies Research
Center **8270**
University of Wisconsin—Milwaukee •
Center for Women's Studies **8271**
Utah State University • Women and
Gender Research Institute **8272**
*Women and Gender Research Institute
Newsletter* **9539**
Women & Language **9541**
The Women's Caucus Newsletter **9565**
Women's Information Exchange **1130**
*Women's Research Network
News* **9585**
WRI Newsletter **9599**
Gender & Society **8915**
**Gender Studies see Gender Research;
Women's Studies**

Gynecology (continued)
    Maternity Center Association •
      Reference Library **6846**
    Mature Women Scholarship
      Grant **8031**
    NAACOG Newsletter **9382**
    NAACOG: The Organization for
      Obstetric, Gynecologic, and Neonatal
      Nurses **566**
    Ob/Gyn Clinical Alert **9434**
    Obstetrics and Gynecology on
      Disc **10726**
    *The Pap Test and Self Breast
      Examination* **10541**
    Planned Parenthood of Wisconsin •
      Maurice Ritz Resource Library and
      Bookstore **6903**
    Searle Research Library **6924**
    SOAP Newsletter **9477**
    U.S. Department of Health and Human
      Services • Food and Drug
      Administration • Center for Devices
      and Radiological Health • Obstetrics-
      Gynecology Devices Panel **8320**
    University of Minnesota • Department of
      Obstetrics and Gynecology •
      Litzenberg-Lund Library **6956**
    Women's Health Care Centers **10743**
    Women's Health Nursing Scan **9572**
Haar Award; Esther **7972**
HACER - National Hispanic Women's
    Center **2551**
Hadassah Magazine **8925**
Hadassah, The Women's Zionist
    Organization of America **409**
Hadassah, The Women's Zionist
    Organization of America, Chicago
    Chapter **1713**
Hag Rag **8926**
Hagerstown Business College • Women's
    Center **6488**
Hagerstown Junior College • Chapter II
    Homemakers in Transition **5429**
*Hairpiece: A Film for Nappy-Headed
    People* **10462**
Hale County Crisis Center **4719**
Hale Laiku **3609**
Half the Sky Bookstore **10181**
Halifax County Community Action • Domestic
    Violence Program **4812**
Halifax County Mental Health Center •
    Services for Battered Women **4358**
Hamblen County Board of Education •
    Single Parent/Displaced Homemaker
    Program **5970**
Hamburg Business and Professional
    Women's Club **2521**
Hamilton College
    Women's Center **6576**
    Women's Studies Program **7509**
Hamilton County Republican Women's
    Club **1815**
Hamilton County Schools • Displaced
    Homemaker Program **5947**
Hamilton Women's Club **2336**
Hamline University • Women's Studies
    Program **7424**
Hammond Client Service Center • Single
    Parent/Displaced Homemaker
    Program **5342**
Hampshire College
    Feminist Studies **7339**
    Women's Center **6492**
Hancock County Schools • Displaced
    Homemaker Program **5977**
*Handbook of Family Day Care
    Associations* **8751**
Handicapped see Disabled
Hands Off! **10463**

Haney Vocational Technical Center • Single
    Parent/Displaced Homemaker
    Program **5224**
Hannah's Place **4359**
Hapoel Hamizrachi Women's
    Organization **345**
Happiness of Womanhood **410**
Harbor, Inc. **4363**
Harbor House **3730, 4430**
Harbor House/Women's Center **3916**
Harbor Me **3854**
Harcum Junior College **7047**
    New Choices **5858**
Hard-hatted Women **10464**
Hard Work **10465**
Harkness Scholarship; Georgia **7833**
Harley Women Magazine **8927**
Harmony House • YWCA **3564**
Harmony Women's Fund **2274**
Harney Helping Organization for Personal
    Emergencies **4480**
Harold Washington University • Women's
    Studies Program **7251**
Harper College • Project Turning
    Point **5325**
Harper House **3453**
Harper's Bazaar **8928**
Harper's Bazaar en Espanol **8929**
Harriet Tubman Shelter **3656, 3980**
Harriett Barnhardt Wimmer
    Scholarship **7837**
Harrington Journal **9609**
Harrington Park Press **9778**
Harris Public Service Fellowship; Patricia
    Robert **7885**
Harrison Center for Career Education **5181**
Harrisonville Business and Professional
    Women's Club **2307**
Harry S. Truman College • Single
    Parent/Displaced Homemaker Building
    Opportunity Program **5302**
Hart to Heart Publishing **9779**
Hartford Area Vocational Center • Single
    Parents/Homemaker Project **6078**
Hartford College for Women **7048**
    The Counseling Center • Look
      Forward **5159**
    Office of Women's Research **8197**
Hartford Interval House **3509**
Hartnell College
    Re-Entry Center **5092**
    Women's Programs **7162**
Hartwick College • Women's Studies
    Program **7541**
Harvard Divinity School • Women's Studies
    in Religion **7351**
Harvard Extension School • Women's
    Studies Program **7352**
Harvard University
    Women's Studies Program **7353**
    Women's Studies in Religion
      Program **8198**
Harvard University Press **9780**
Harvard Women's Law Journal **8930**
Harvey Mudd College • Women's Studies
    Program **7121**
Haskell Associates **8667**
Haskell Indian Junior College • Academic
    Support Center **6473**
The Hastings Center • Library **6800**
Hasty Pudding Theatricals Woman of the
    Year **7989**
Havana Business and Professional Women's
    Club **1747**
HAVEN **3928, 4080, 4916**
Haven Book Club **10174**
Haven from Domestic Violence **4483**
Haven Hills **3354**
Haven of Hope **4403, 4649**

Haven House **3402, 3715, 4051, 4216,
    4627**
    Family Services Center **4115**
Haven of Lake and Sumter Counties,
    Inc. **3545**
Haven of Peace • Women's Shelter **3369**
Haven Women's Center of Stanislaus **3393**
Haverford College
    Feminism and Gender Studies **7643**
    Women's Center **6639**
HAVIN **4535**
Hawaii Abortion Rights Action League **1665**
Hawaii Commission on the Status of
    Women **8486**
Hawaii Department of Health • Family Health
    Services Division • Maternal and Child
    Health Branch **8487**
Hawaii Department of Human Services •
    Family Violence Prevention and
    Services **8488**
Hawaii Department of Labor and Industrial
    Relations • Equal Employment Opportunity
    Office **8489**
Hawaii Planned Parenthood **6226**
Hawaii State Committee on Family
    Violence **1666**
Hawaii Women Lawyers • Domestic Violence
    Legal Hotline **3604**
The Hawthorn Press, Inc. **9778**
Hayes Publishing Co., Inc. **9781**
Hays County Women's Center **4726**
Hazard Community College • Career
    Awareness for the Single Parents and
    Homemakers **5388**
Hazleton Woman's Club **2840**
Headliner Award **7990**
Headway **9318**
Health **8931**
Health Associates **8668**
**Health Care (see also Medicine; Mental
    Health; Specific Health Issues, e.g.
    Breastfeeding)**
    Air-Plus Enterprises **9637**
    Alliant Health System • Library/Media
      Services **6724**
    American College of Obstetricians and
      Gynecologists
        Nurses Association **63**
        Resource Center **6729**
    American Library Association •
      Committee on Pay Equity **89**
    American Medical Women's Association
      • American Women's Hospitals Service
      Committee **100**
    American Society of Allied Health
      Professions • Women's Issues
      Section **124**
    *Assertiveness for Women in Health
      Care* **10318**
    Bay Area Black Women's Health
      Project **1334**
    BHP Bulletin **9206**
    Boston University • Women's Center •
      Library **6746**
    Boston Women's Health Book
      Collective, Inc. **9682**
    Case Western Reserve University •
      Perinatal Clinical Research
      Center **8176**
    CDDR News **9223**
    CHOICE **258**
    CHOICE (Concern for Health Options:
      Information Care & Education) **9706**
    Colorado Department of Health • Office
      of Health Care Services • Division of
      Family Health Services **8465**
    *Directory of Women's Health Care
      Centers* **8733**
    Eastern Women's Center **339**
    Emma Goldman Clinic **9740**

Index

Indian Capital Area Vocational Technical School • Displaced Homemaker Program **5816**

Indian Health Board of Minneapolis • Counseling and Support Clinics **3983**

Indian Hills Community College • Women's Center **6470**

Indian Meridian Area Vocational Technical School • Displaced Homemaker Program **5825**

Indian River Community College
    Single Parent/Displaced Homemakers Program **5200**
    Women's Program **7217**

Indiana Abortion Rights Action League **1843**

Indiana Association for Child Care Resource and Referral **1844**

Indiana Coalition Against Domestic Violence **1853**

Indiana Family and Social Services Administration • Family and Children Division • Family Violence Prevention and Services **8496**

Indiana State Board of Health • Family Health Services Bureau • Maternal and Child Health Division **8497**

Indiana State University
    Women's Resource Center **6465**
    Women's Studies Program **7290**

Indiana University • Kinsey Institute for Research in Sex, Gender & Reproduction, Inc. **9800**

Indiana University Bloomington • Women's Studies Program **7276**

Indiana University Northwest • Women's Studies Program **7279**

Indiana University of Pennsylvania
    Center for Vocational Personnel Preparation • New Choices **5871**
    Women's Studies Program **7644**

Indiana University Press **9801**

Indiana University—Purdue University at Fort Wayne
    Center for Women and Returning Adults **6459**
    Women's Studies Program **7277**

Indiana University—Purdue University at Indianapolis
    Office of Women's Research **6461**
    Women's Studies Program **7283**

Indiana University, School of Medicine • Institute of Women's Health **429**

Indiana University at South Bend
    Women's Resource Center **6464**
    Women's Studies Program **7289**

Indiana University Southeast
    Adult Student Center **6462**
    Women's Studies Certificate **7285**

Indiana Women in Agriculture **1864**

Indiana Women's Political Caucus **1845**

Indianapolis Woman **8945**

Indigenous Women's Network **430, 2266**

Individual and Family Counseling [Grand Junction, CO] **3483**

Industry and Trade
    All-Craft Foundation **15**
    American Council of Railroad Women **67**
    American Women Buyers Club **143**
    Association of Women Contractors, Iowa Chapter **1941**
    Association of Women Gemologists **192**
    Association of Women in the Metal Industries, Pittsburgh Chapter **2817**

Association of Women in Natural Foods **195**

Club of Printing Women of New York **2544**

Coal Employment Project **266**

Cosmetic Executive Women **306**

Electrical Women's RoundTable **342**

Electrical Women's RoundTable, Bluegrass Chapter **1975**

Electrical Women's RoundTable— Connections **9274**

Electrical Women's RoundTable, Indiana Chapter **1842**

Electrical Women's RoundTable, New York Chapter **2546**

Electrical Women's RoundTable, North Central Chapter **2273**

Electrical Women's RoundTable, North Texas Chapter **3023**

Electrical Women's RoundTable, South Texas Chapter **2995**

Federated Women in Timber **359**

Financial Women International **377**

Goodyear Women's Club **1640**

Ladies Apparel Contractors Association **502**

Midwest Women's Center **6852**

National Association of Railway Business Women **610**

National Association of Women in Construction **617**

National Association of Women in Construction, Albany Chapter **1621**

National Association of Women in Construction, Dubuque Chapter **1911**

National Association of Women in Construction, Fargo/Moorhead Chapter **246 2658**

National Association of Women in Construction, Grand Rapids Chapter **2183**

National Association of Women in Construction, Greater Birmingham Chapter **1202**

National Association of Women in Construction, Kankakee Chapter **1757**

National Association of Women in Construction, San Diego Chapter 21 **1389**

National Forum for Executive Women **696**

National Rural Electric Cooperative Association • National Rural Electric Women's Association **744**

National Rural Electric Women's Association—Newsline **9405**

National Women's Automotive Association **767**

National Women's Neckwear and Scarf Association **780**

The NAWIC Image **9411**

Network of Women in Trade and Technical Jobs **789**

New England Lumber Women's Association **1522**

New York Metro Roundtable for Women in Foodservice **2563**

Non-Traditional Employment for Women **798**

Petroleum Women's Club of Liberal **1956**

Professional Women in Construction **856**

Roundtable for Women Food-Beverage-Hospitality **878**

Society for Women in Plastics **911**

Trade Trax **9495**

Trade Union Women of African Heritage **939**

Tradeswomen, Inc. **940**

Tradeswomen of Philadelphia/Women in Non-Traditional Work **2867**

United Food and Commercial Workers International Union • Civil Rights and Women's Affairs **952**

University of Massachusetts at Lowell • Center for Lowell History **6953**

WIT **9526**

Women Grocers of America **1044**

Women in Mining National **1064**

Women on Wine **1085**

Women's Apparel Chains Associations **1096**

Women's Jewelry Association **1144**

Infant Death
    Center for Loss in Multiple Birth **241**
    Compassionate Friends, Nebraska Panhandle Chapter **2364**
    Compassionate Friends— Newsletter **9249**
    Empty Arms **1781**
    Fertility Awareness & Natural Family Planning Resource Directory **8743**
    Intensive Caring Unlimited **9338**
    Perinatal Loss **9917**
    Pregnancy and Infant Loss Center **843**
    Project Comfort **1826**
    Resolve Through Sharing **875**
    Unite **946**

Infertility see Reproductive Issues

Infertility: Medical and Social Choices **8756**

Infertility in Women **10486**

Info-Line **4227**

INFORM **6815**

Information Science see Library and Information Science

Information Systems Development **9802**

Informed Homebirth **431**

Informed Homebirth/Informed Birth and Parenting **431**

Ingram State Technical Institute • Displaced Homemakers Program **4975**

Initiatives: Journal of NAWE **8946**

Inklings **10275**

Inn Places: A Guide to Gay and Lesbian Accommodations **8757**

Inner Woman **8947**

Inserts for: Bradley Classes Videotape No. 1 **10487**

Inserts for: Bradley Classes Videotape No. 2 **10488**

Institute of Applied Philosophy & Policy Analysis **8670**

Institute for Childhood Resources **9803**

Institute for the Development of Human Resources • Displaced Homemakers Program **5175**

Institute of Electrical and Electronic Engineers • Task Force on Women and Minorities **432**

Institute for Feminist Studies **433**

Institute for Human Research and Development • Displaced Homemaker Center **5215**

Institute of Lesbian Studies **9804**

Institute for Managerial and Professional Women **2788**

Institute for Modern Psychoanalysis • Domestic Violence Services **4264**

Institute for Reproductive Health **434, 8201**

Institute for Research on Social Problems **8202**

Institute for Research on Women and Gender—Newsletter **9336**

Institute for Sex Research **8207**

Institute for the Study of Matrimonial Laws **435, 8203**

Institute for the Study of Sexual Assault **436, 8671**

Knoxville Women's Center • Single Parent/Displaced Homemaker Program **5961**
Korean American Women Artists and Writers Association **1404**
Korean American Women in Need **1716**
Korean Family Counseling and Research Center **4231**
La Bella Figura **9350**
La Casa **4179**
La Casa de las Madres **3423**
La Cosa de Don Pedro • Vocational Outreach for Single Parents and Homemakers **5643**
La Grange Junior Woman's Club **1642**
La Isla Pacifica • South County Alternatives **3371**
La Leche League of Clearwater **1570**
La Leche League of the Golden Strip **2946**
La Leche League of Greenville County **2947**
La Leche League International **499, 9825** Library **6824**
La Leche League International, Arizona Chapter **1237**
La Leche League International, Corning Chapter **2504**
La Leche League International, Dillon Chapter **2334**
La Leche League International, East New York Chapter **2530**
La Leche League International of Evansville **1825**
La Leche League International, Florida Chapter **1602**
La Leche League International, Front Royal Chapter **3123**
La Leche League International, Gainesville Florida Association **1584**
La Leche League International, Georgia Chapter **1648**
La Leche League International, Illinois Chapter **1754**
La Leche League International, Indiana Chapter **1875**
La Leche League International, Kingsport Chapter **2973**
La Leche League International, Mason City/Clear Lake Chapter **1890**
La Leche League International, Michigan **2186**
La Leche League International, Minnesota/Dakotas **2258**
La Leche League International, New Jersey Chapter **2414**
La Leche League International, Newfane Chapter **2483**
La Leche League International, North California/Hawaii Chapter **1263**
La Leche League International, Rhode Island Chapter **2920**
La Leche League International, Salina Chapter **1944**
La Leche League International, South California/Nevada **1454**
La Leche League International, Spearfish Chapter **2967**
La Leche League International, Temple Terrace Chapter **1617**
La Leche League International, West Pennsylvania Chapter **2875**
La Leche League International, Western Nebraska Chapter **2365**
La Leche League International, Worland Chapter **3255**
La Leche League of Massachusetts/Rhode Island/Vermont **2105**
La Leche League News **9417**
La Leche League North Carolina **2624**

La Mesa Community Welfare Association **1307**
Labette Community College • Single Parent/Displaced Homemaker Program **5382**
Labor see Employment
Labor and Birth **10494**
Labor Coaching **10495**
Labor of Love: Childbirth without Violence **10496**
Labor More than Once **10497**
Labor Relations; New York State School of Industrial and • Sanford V. Lenz Library • Cornell University **6779**
Labor Unions see Unions
Labyrinth **9612**
Lac du Flambeau Domestic Abuse Program **4908**
Laconia Woman's Club **2386**
Lact-Aid International **500**
Lactation see Breastfeeding
Lactation Associates Publishing Co. **9826**
Ladd's Editions **10246**
Ladies Against Women **501**
Ladies Apparel Contractors Association **502**
Ladies Association of Walden **3045**
Ladies' Auxiliary of the American Beekeeping Federation **503**
Ladies Auxiliary, Military Order of the Purple Heart, United States of America **504**
Ladies Auxiliary to the Veterans of Foreign Wars of the United States **505**
Ladies Auxiliary to the VFW Junior Girls Scholarship **7858**
Ladies of the Grand Army of the Republic **506**
Ladies' Home Journal **8972**
Ladies Kennel Association of America **507**
Ladies' Kennel Association of New York **2533**
LADIES - Life After Divorce Is Eventually Sane **508**
Ladies Oriental Shrine of North America **509**
Ladies Pennsylvania Slovak Catholic Union **2905**
Ladies Professional Bowlers Tour **510**
Ladies Professional Golf Association **511**
Ladies Professional Golf Association Hall of Fame **8014**
Ladies Professional Golf Association Leading Money Winners **8015**
Ladies Professional Golf Association Professional of the Year **8016**
Ladies Village Improvement Society **2507**
Ladies at Work **1245**
Lady Reelers **2534**
Lady's Circle **8973**
Ladyslipper **512, 9772, 9827, 10224**
Lafayette College • Women's Studies Program **7639**
Lafayette House **4041**
LaGuardia Community College Project Enable **5701** Women's Studies Program **7525**
Laguna Family Shelter Program **4178**
Lake Area Vocational Technical Institute • Single Parent/Homemaker Project **5941**
Lake Area Vocational Technical School • Single Parent/Homemakers Program **5752**
Lake Cable Women's Club **2677**
Lake City Community College • Continuing Education Department • Displaced Homemakers Program **5206**
Lake County Area Vocational System • Building Opportunity Project **5314**
Lake County Area Vocational-Technical Center • DAWN (Dealing Affirmatively With Needs Program) **5196**

Lake Erie College • Women's Studies Program **7601**
Lake Forest College • Women's Studies **7265**
Lake Geneva Woman's Club **3213**
Lake Land College • Building Opportunity Project **5323**
Lake Michigan College Single Parent/Homemaker Program **5471** Women's Studies Program **7390**
Lake Press **9828**
Lake Sumter Community College • Women's Program **5211, 6443**
Lake Tapawingo Women's Club **2302**
Lake Washington Vocational Technical Institute • Displaced Homemakers Program **6116**
Lakeland College • Women's Studies Program **7767**
Lakeland Community College Displaced Homemaker Program **5784** Women's Studies Program **7596**
Lakes Area Service for Rape and Domestic Violence **3953**
Lakes Region Stop Family Violence Program **4134**
Lakeshore Technical College Life Work Planning **6158, 6705** Women's Studies Program **7751**
Lamar Coalition of Women **1632**
Lamar Community College • Displaced Homemaker Program **5144**
Lamaze Birth Without Pain Education Association **2155**
Lambda, Inc. • Barnes Library **6825**
Lambda Book Report **8974**
Lambda Legal Defense & Education Fund— Newsletter **9351**
Lambda Passages **10132**
Lambda Passages Bookstore **10128**
Lambda Rising **10125, 10158**
Lambda Rising 2 **10126**
Lambda Rising, Inc. **9829**
Lambda Update **9351**
Lammas Women's Books and More **10127**
Lamme Scholarship; Westinghouse Bertha **7902**
Lamoille Area Vocational Center • Displaced Homemaker Program **6063**
LaMoine Valley Vocational System • Building Opportunity Project **5321**
Lana's World/How Do You Spell It Productions **8975**
Lancaster County, Area Vocational-Technical School at the YWCA • New Directions-Employment and Counseling Center. **5873**
Lancaster Shelter for Abused Women **4536**
Lander County Committee Against Domestic Violence **4116**
Lander Women's Bowling Association **3249**
Landing a Job: Strategies for Women **10498**
Lane & Associates, Inc. **9830**
Lane Community College Transition to Success • Displaced Homemaker/Single Parent Project **5836** Women's Awareness Center **6623** Women's Studies Program **7615**
Lane County Women for Agriculture **2781**
Laney College • Women's Studies Program **7150**
Language and Linguistics
American Speech-Language-Hearing Association • Committee on the Equality of the Sexes **136**
Committee on the Status of Women in Linguistics **286**

Waterwomen Books **10012**
W.I.M. Publications **10022**
Wishing Well **989**
Womanshare Books **10028**
Women in Touch **2390**
Women's Resource Center
Library **6987**
The Women's Traveller **8828**
Womyn's Braille Press **10052**
Womyn's Words **9158**
Word Weavers **10053**
Words to the Wise **8832**
Lesbians United Non-Nuclear Action **525**
Lesley College **7054**
Leti Study Club **3037**
Letras Femininas **8982**
Let's Talk About: Breastfeeding **10502**
Lewin Award; Elizabeth **7968**
Lewin Business Library & Information
Center; Elizabeth • National Chamber of
Commerce for Women **6864**
Lewis and Clark College • Gender
Studies **7623**
Lewis & Clark Community College • Building
Opportunity Project **5319**
Lewis and Clark Republican Women's
Club **2338**
Lewis-Clark State College • Center for New
Directions **5287**
Lewis House **3966**
Lewis House; B. Robert **3956**
Lewis University
Women's Programs **7273**
Women's Studies Center **6457**
Lewiston-Auburn Business and Professional
Women **2041**
Lewiston/Auburn College University of
Southern Maine/University of Maine—
Augusta • Displaced Homemakers
Program **5410**
Lewisville Area Republican Women's
Club **3021**
Lex Vitae **9358**
Lexington Books **9832**
Lexington Planned Parenthood Center **6248**
Lexington Vocational Center • Single
Parent/Displaced Homemaker
Program **5923**
LEXIS Family Law Library **10720**
*LFL Reports: The Newsletter of Libertarians
for Life* **9359**
Liberal Arts (see also Humanities)
National League of American Pen
Women **711**
Radcliffe College • Bunting
Institute **8229**
Rocky Mountain Women's
Institute **8231**
University of Tulsa • Research in
Women's Literature **8267**
Liberal Arts Press **9833**
Liberation Book Club **10124**
Liberation Publications Inc. **9834**
Libertarians for Life **526**
Liberty Books **10270**
Liberty Godparent Ministry **527**
Liberty House **3565**
Liberty Shelter **4048**
**Libraries and Archives (see also Chapter
7: Library Collections; Chapter 8:
Museums and Galleries)**
American Library Association
Committee on the Status of
Women in Librarianship **90**
Social Responsibilities Round Table
• Feminist Task Force **93**
Social Responsibilities Round Table
• Gay and Lesbian Task
Force **94**

Art Libraries Society/North America •
Women and Art Round Table **155**
Association of College and Research
Libraries • Women's Studies
Section **170**
Association for Population/Family
Planning Libraries and Information
Centers, International **181**
Directory of Women's Media **8734**
*Directory of Women's Studies Programs
and Library Resources* **8735**
FEMINIST **10714**
Freedom Information Service **386,
6796**
*International Centers For Research on
Women* **8760**
Lesbian Periodicals Index **8766**
*LFL Reports: The Newsletter of
Libertarians for Life* **9359**
*Libraries and Information Centers Within
Women's Studies Research
Centers* **8767**
OWL (Ohio Women Librarians) **9904**
Society of American Archivists •
Women's Caucus **901**
Willowood Press **10021**
Womanhood Media **8684**
Women in Libraries **9542**
Women Library Workers **1054**
Women in the Mainstream **1056**
Women's History Research
Center **8686**
Women's National Book Association,
Detroit Chapter **2239**
Women's National Book Association,
Nashville Chapter **2986**
*Libraries and Information Centers Within
Women's Studies Research Centers* **8767**
Library of Congress
Public Service and Collections
Management I
Manuscript Division **6827**
Music Division **6828**
Prints and Photographs
Division **6829**
Public Service and Collections
Management II • Microform Reading
Room **6830**
Rare Book & Special Collections
Division **6831**
Library and Information Network **10721**
Library and Information Science
ALA Equality Award **7914**
AT&T Bell Laboratories Graduate
Research Fellowships for
Women **7805**
AT&T Bell Laboratories Graduate
Research Grants for Women **7806**
AT&T Bell Laboratories Summer
Research Program for Minorities &
Women **7807**
*Directory of Library and Information
Profession Women's Groups* **8719**
*Minorities and Women: A List of Major
Organizations in Librarianship* **8768**
WLW Journal **9113**
Women in Data Processing **1023**
Women in Information Processing **1049**
Licensing Newspaper **9360**
Licking County Employment Training Office •
Displaced Homemaker Program **5788**
Lida Rose Press **9835**
Lies **10503**
Life after Breast Cancer **10504**
Life Crisis Center **3845**
Life Force Press **9836**
Life-Guardian **9361**
Life Insight **9362**
Life Span **3672**

Life-Work Planning Center • Nichols Office
Center **5510**
LifeDate **9363**
Lifeletter **9364**
Lifeline for the Battered **3725**
Light Cleaning Press **9837**
Lighthouse **4423**
Lilac Tree Women in Transition **1719**
Lilith **8983**
Lillian Gish Award **8018**
Lillian Moller Gilbreth Scholarship **7859**
Lillian Vernon Corp. **8652**
Lincoln Land Community College • Project
Fresh Start Displaced Homemakers
Program **5334**
Lincoln Shelter and Services **4494**
Lincoln Trail Domestic Violence
Program **3788**
Lincoln University • Women's Technical
Program **6641**
Lind Award; Erv **7971**
Linfield College • Abigail Scott Duniway
Women's Center **6626**
Linguistic Society of America • Committee
on the Status of Women in
Linguistics **528**
Linguistics see Language and Linguistics
The Links, Inc. **529**
Linn-Benton Community College
Turning Point Transition Program **5831**
Women's Center **6620**
Linn-Henley Library for Southern Historical
Research • Department of Archives and
Manuscripts • Birmingham Public and
Jefferson County Free Library **6742**
Linn Technical College • Careers
Unlimited **5562**
Linnfield College • Women's Programs **7620**
Linton Award; Margaret M. **8025**
Lioness Book Store **10094**
Lioness Books **9838**
Lisle Woman's Club **1762**
Listen Real Loud **9365**
Literacy
Church Women United Literacy
Council **1493**
Soroptimist International **914**
Tri-County Business and Professional
Women's Luv Council **1978**
Literature (see also Fiction)
Barn Owl Books **9670**
Belles Lettres **8851**
Boston University • Women's Center •
Library **6746**
*Bridges: A Journal of Exceptional Prose
and Poetry* **8861**
Brown University • Christine Dunlap
Farnham Archives **6749**
Calyx Books **9689**
*Calyx: A Journal of Arts and Literature
by Women* **8866**
Carthage Woman's Club **1697**
Cayuse Press **9696**
*Concerns: Newsletter of the Women's
Caucus for the Modern
Languages* **9250**
The Creative Woman **8883**
Database of Third World Women's
Literary Works **10708**
Druid Press **9732**
Earth's Daughters **8891**
Fogelson Cultural and Creative Arts
Program; Gertrude **7985**
Free Focus **8912**
Gillette Scholarship; R.L. **7887**
Helicon Nine **9783**
Housewife-Writer's Forum **8937**
*Kalliope: A Journal of Women's
Art* **8971**
Kelsey Street Press **9820**

Manchester Community College
Look Forward/Beginning Again **5161**
Women's Center **6427**
Manhattan Area Vocational Technical School
• Single Parent/Homemaker Program **5380**
Manhattanville College • Women's Studies
Program **7548**
Maniilaq Regional Women's Crisis
Program **3288**
Manitou Springs Women's Club **1472**
Manitowoc County Domestic Violence
Center **4911**
Manitowoc-Two Rivers Business and
Professional Women's Club **3219**
Mankato State University
Women's Centre **6529**
Women's Studies Program **7413**
Manpower Demonstration Research
Corp. **9848**
Maple Woods Community College •
Displaced Homemakers Program **5558**
Maquoketa Community Center • Project
Stepping Stone **5365**
March of Dimes Birth Defects Foundation •
Reference Room **6841**
March for Life **536**
Margaret H. Zimmerman Award **8024**
Margaret M. Linton Award **8025**
Margaret Media **9849**
Margaret Sanger **10510**
Margaret Sanger Center-Planned Parenthood
New York City • Abraham Stone
Library **6842**
Margaret Stroock Clinic **1498**
Marguerite Ferdinand Award **8026**
Marguerite Rawalt Resource Center •
Business and Professional Women's
Foundation **6751**
Marguerite Rawalt Resource Center
Database **10722**
Maria Goeppert-Mayer Award **8027**
Marian Court Junior College **7055**
Marian House **4520**
Maricopa County Task Force Against
Domestic Violence **3325**
Marietta College • Women's Studies
Program **7595**
Marin Abused Women's Services **3430**
Marin County Office of Education • SOLO
Single Parent/Displaced Homemaker
Project **5100**
Marin County Women's PAC **1445**
Marion County Democratic Woman's
Club **3186**
Marion Junior Woman's Club **3108**
Marist College • Women's Studies
Program **7546**
Marital Law see Matrimonial Law
Marjaree Mason Center • YWCA **3370**
Marketing see Business and Management
Marketing to Women **9371, 10723**
Marlboro College • Women's Studies
Program **7715**
Marquette/Alger Planned Parenthood **6259**
Marquette University
Department of Special Collections and
University Archives • Manuscript
Collections Memorial Library **6843**
Women's Center **6713**
Women's Studies Program **7761**
Marriage (see also Matrimonial Law)
Blushing Bride **8857**
Bouey Memorial Award; E.C. **7964**
Bridal Guide **8858**
Bridal Sense Publications **9686**
Bride's **8859**
Brighton Publications **9687**
Buenhogar **8863**
California Family Study Center •
Library **6753**

Chicago Public Library **6765**
Elegant Bride **8893**
The Family Institute • Crowley
Library **6791**
I'm Not a Feminist, But... **10483**
Institute for the Study of Matrimonial
Laws **8203**
*Journal of Marriage and the
Family* **8964**
Joyful Woman **9817**
Modern Bride **9004**
New England Bride **9018**
Orr Award; Joan **8013**
Pennsylvania State University •
Gerontology Center • Human
Development Collection **6890**
Pinellas County Juvenile Welfare Board
• Mailande W. Holland Library **6891**
Wives-SelfHelp Foundation **990**
Women's Action Alliance •
Library **6980**
Marriott President's Award; Phyllis B. **8081**
Marshall County Vocational Center •
Displaced Homemaker/Single Parent
Program **5534**
Marshall University • Women's Studies
Program **7747**
Martha Rosler **9850**
Martha Stewart at Home **8989**
The Martial Art of Self-defense **10511**
Martin Abzug Memorial Award **8028**
Martin County Women's Council **2651**
Martin Luther King Center • Building
Opportunity Project **5312**
Mary Baker Mission Shelter/Porterville
Women's Shelter • Porterville Mission
Project **3404**
Mary Baldwin College **7056**
Women's Studies Program **7728**
Mary Butler Scholarship **7863**
Mary Connolly Livingston Grant **7864**
Mary Egging Memorial Award **8029**
Mary Elizabeth Hudson Library • Planned
Parenthood of Houston and Southeast
Texas **6896**
*Mary Ingraham Bunting Institute—
Newsletter* **9372**
Mary Ingraham Bunting Institute of Radcliffe
College **8229**
Mary Isabel Sibley Fellowship **7865**
Mary Lawson Foreman House of
CMV **3855**
Mary and Martha House **3557**
Mary Washington College • Race and
Gender Project **7723**
Maryknoll Sisters of St. Dominic **537**
Maryland Abortion Rights Action
League **2064**
Maryland Association for Anorexia Nervosa
and Bulimia **2050**
Maryland Association of Women Highway
Safety Leaders **2065**
Maryland Commission for Women **8514**
Maryland Committee for Children, Inc. •
MCC Resource Center **6844**
Maryland Department of Health and Mental
Hygiene • Division of Public Health
Services • Local and Family Health
Administration **8515**
Maryland Department of Human Resources •
Community Services Administration •
Women's Services Program **8516**
Maryland Equal Employment Opportunity
Office **8517**
Maryland Mothers of Twins **2062**
Maryland New Directions, Inc. **5418**
Marylhurst College • Women's Studies
Programs **7619**
Marymount College **7057**
Women's Studies Program **7561**

Marymount Manhattan College **7058**
Mary's Pence **538**
Marysville Women's Club **2213**
Mason Center; Marjaree • YWCA **3370**
**Mass Media (see also Electronic Mail;
Online Networks; Public Relations;
Publishing; Radio; Television; Visual Arts)**
American Federation of Television and
Radio Artists • National Women's
Division **73**
American News Women's Club **105**
*American News Women's Club—
Directory* **8691**
American Women in Radio and
Television Achievement Award **7921**
American Women in Radio and
Television Commendation
Awards **7922**
AWSM Newsletter **9203**
*Challenging Media Images of
Women* **9232**
Clarion Awards **7952**
Communications Consortium **294**
*Directory of Women in Sports
Business* **8732**
Directory of Women's Media **8734**
Distinguished Women of Northwood
Institute **7961**
Exceptional Merit Media Award
(EMMA) **7974**
Frontrunner Award **7978**
Fund for the Feminist Majority **390**
Gay and Lesbian Media Coalition **394**
The GP Reporter **9314**
Heart of America **7991**
International Women's Media
Project **484**
Marketing to Women **9371**
Matrix Award **8030**
Media Fund for Human Rights **541**
Media Report to Women **9374**
Media Watch **542**
Media Women **2449**
Multi-Medea Enterprises/Water
Press **9873**
National Association of Media
Women **602**
National Federation of Press
Women **692**
National News Service for Women and
Minorities **722**
Newswomen's Club of New York **2569**
Shute Award; Gladys G. **7986**
Silver Satellite Award **8102**
*Women in Communications, Inc.—
National Membership and Resource
Directory* **8811**
Women at Work Broadcast
Awards **8156**
Women's Institute for Freedom of the
Press **1132, 10042**
Women's Media Project **1151**
YWCA of Houston Outstanding
Women's Award **8168**
Massachusetts Administration and Finance
Executive Office • Personnel Administration
Department • Equal Employment Practices
Office **8518**
Massachusetts Association for Parents and
Professionals for Safe Alternatives in
Childbirth **2085**
Massachusetts Bay Community College •
Single Parent/Homemakers Program **5462**
Massachusetts Choice **2077**
Massachusetts Citizens for Life, Arlington
Chapter **2070**
Massachusetts Citizens for Life, Needham
Chapter **2108**
Massachusetts Coalition of Battered
Women's Service Groups **2078**

Massachusetts Department of Social
Services • Family Violence Prevention and
Services **8519**
Massachusetts Executive Office of Human
Services • Department of Public Health •
Bureau of Parent, Child and Adolescent
Health **8520**
Massachusetts Governor's Advisory
Committee on Women's Issues **8521**
Massachusetts Health and Human Services
Executive Office • Public Welfare
Department • Child Support Division **8522**
Massachusetts Institute of Technology
Humanities Library **6845**
Women's Studies Program **7354**
Massachusetts Minority and Women's
Business Division **8523**
Massachusetts Mothers of Twins
Association **2086**
Massachusetts Women's Political
Caucus **2079**
Massasoit Community College
Center for Women **6502**
Single Parent/Displaced Homemakers
Program **5445**
Masters & Johnson Institute **8209**
MASWE Memorial Scholarship **7866**
Matagorda County Women's Crisis
Center **4659**
Maternal and Child Health Bureau
Health Resources and Services
Administration • U.S. Department of
Health and Human Services **8324**
Maternal and Child Health Federal
Consolidated Programs • U.S.
Department of Health and Human
Services • Health Resources and
Services Administration **8430**
Maternal and Child Health Research
Grants Review Committee • U.S.
Department of Health and Human
Services • Health Resources and
Services Administration **8325**
Maternal and Child Health Services
Block Grant • U.S. Department of
Health and Human Services • Health
Resources and Services
Administration **8431**
Maternal and Child Health Targeted
Infant Mortality Initiative • U.S.
Department of Health and Human
Services • Health Resources and
Services Administration **8432**
National Center for Education in
Maternal and Child Health • U.S.
Department of Health and Human
Services • Health Resources and
Services Administration **8326**
National Maternal and Child Health
Clearinghouse • U.S. Department of
Health and Human Services • Health
Resources and Services
Administration **8327**
Pediatric AIDS Health Care
Demonstration Program • U.S.
Department of Health and Human
Services • Health Resources and
Services Administration **8433**
Maternal and Child Health and Crippled
Children's Services Research Grants
Advisory Group **8325**
Maternal and Child Health Federal
Consolidated Programs • U.S. Department
of Health and Human Services • Health
Resources and Services Administration •
Maternal and Child Health Bureau **8430**

Maternal and Child Health Research
Committee • National Institute of Child
Health and Human Development • National
Institutes of Health • U.S. Department of
Health and Human Services **8331**
Maternal and Child Health Research Grants
Review Committee • U.S. Department of
Health and Human Services • Health
Resources and Services Administration •
Maternal and Child Health Bureau **8325**
Maternal and Child Health Service Research
Grants Review Committee **8325**
Maternal and Child Health Services Block
Grant • U.S. Department of Health and
Human Services • Health Resources and
Services Administration • Maternal and
Child Health Bureau **8431**
Maternal and Child Health Studies
Project **8210**
Maternal and Child Health Targeted Infant
Mortality Initiative • U.S. Department of
Health and Human Services • Health
Resources and Services Administration •
Maternal and Child Health Bureau **8432**
Maternal Health (see also Pregnancy)
Advocates for Infants and
Mothers **1541**
Alabama Department of Public Health •
Family Health Services Bureau **8447**
Alaska Department of Health and Social
Services • Division of Public Health •
Family Health Section **8450**
*Ambulatory Maternal Health Care and
Family Planning Services* **8689**
American Association for Maternal and
Child Health **38**
American College of Nurse-
Midwives **61**
American College of Obstetricians and
Gynecologists • Nurses
Association **63**
American Foundation for Maternal and
Child Health **76**
Arizona Department of Health Services
• Division of Family Health Services •
Maternal and Child Health
Bureau **8455**
Arizona Family Health Services Division
• Maternal and Child Health
Bureau **8457**
Arkansas Department of Health •
Bureau of Public Health Programs •
Division of Maternal and Child
Health **8459**
Association of Maternal and Child
Health Programs **179**
Association of Teachers of Maternal
and Child Health **186**
California Health and Welfare Agency •
Department of Health Services •
Maternal and Child Health
Division **8463**
Case Western Reserve University •
Perinatal Clinical Research
Center **8176**
CHOICE (Concern for Health Options:
Information Care & Education) **9706**
Colorado Department of Health • Office
of Health Care Services • Division of
Family Health Services **8465**
Connecticut Department of Health
Services • Division of Community
Health • Family Reproductive Health
Division **8467**
Cybele Society **9723**
Delaware Department of Health and
Social Services • Division of Public
Health • Bureau of Personal and
Family Health Services **8474**
Depression After Delivery **333**

District of Columbia Department of
Human Services • Commission of
Public Health • Bureau of Maternal
and Child Health Services **8477**
Family Health International **8191**
*Family Health International—
Network* **9288**
Family Life and Population
Program/Church World Service **357**
Federation of Feminist Women's Health
Centers **360**
Florida Department of Health and
Rehabilitative Services • Maternal,
Child and Special Health Services
Office **8482**
Friedman; Joanne **9815**
Georgia Department of Human
Resources • Division of Public Health
• Family Health Section **8484**
Glover Press **9770**
Grinnen-Barrett Publishing Co. **9776**
Guttmacher Institute; Alan **8169, 9638**
*Guttmacher Institute—Washington
Memo; Alan* **9176**
Hawaii Department of Health • Family
Health Services Division • Maternal
and Child Health Branch **8487**
Healthy Mothers, Healthy Babies **412**
Healthy Mothers, Healthy Babies
Coalition of Broward County **1576**
*Healthy Mothers, Healthy Babies—
Directory of Educational
Materials* **8752**
Healthy Mothers, Healthy Babies,
Maryland State Coalition **2049**
Healthy Mothers, Healthy Babies
Virginia State Coalition **3094**
Human Lactation Center **419, 8200**
Idaho Department of Health and
Welfare • Division of Health • Bureau
of Maternal and Child Health **8491**
Illinois Department of Public Health •
Office of Health Services • Division of
Family Health **8495**
Indiana State Board of Health • Family
Health Services Bureau • Maternal
and Child Health Division **8497**
International Center for Research on
Women **8205**
Resource Center **6811**
*International Childbirth Education
Association—ICEA Membership
Directory* **8761**
International Planned Parenthood
Federation • Western Hemisphere
Region • Library **6814**
Iowa Department of Public Health •
Division of Family and Community
Health • Maternal and Child Health
Bureau **8499**
Kansas Department of Health and
Environment • Division of Health •
Maternal and Child Health
Bureau **8501**
Kentucky Human Resources Cabinet •
Department for Health Services •
Maternal and Child Health
Division **8506**
La Leche League International **499**
Louisiana Department of Health and
Hospitals • Office of Public Health
Services • Health Services Programs •
Maternal and Child Health
Program **8508**
Maine Department of Human Services •
Bureau of Health • Division of
Maternal and Child Health **8512**
March of Dimes Birth Defects
Foundation • Reference Room **6841**

Woman's Organization of the National Association of Retail Druggists **1000**
Women in Endocrinology **1029**
Women in Medicine Update **9545**
Women Scientists from Antiquity to Present: An Index **8817**
Women's Auxiliary of the International Chiropractors Association— Membership Roster **8818**
Women's Caucus of the Endocrine Society **1106**
YWCA of Houston Outstanding Women's Award **8168**
Medina County Vocational Center • Women's Connection **5783**
Medina County Women's Crisis Center **4688, 4732**
Meiklejohn Civil Liberties Institute • Library **6848**
Melpomene Institute for Women's Health Research **544, 8212**
Melpomene: A Journal for Women's Health Research **8993**
Memphis City Schools • Single Parent/Displaced Homemakers Program **5965**
Memphis Planned Parenthood **6336**
Memphis State University
Center for Research on Women **8213**
Women's Studies Program **7684**
Memphis YWCA • PEP **5966**
MEND - Mothers Embracing Nuclear Disarmament **545**
Mendocino County Office of Education • Regional Occupational Programs • SOLO Single Parent/Displaced Homemaker Project **5112**
Menominee County Domestic Violence Program **4906**
Menopause
Essential Medical Information Systems, Inc. **9743**
Hot Flash **9330**
Is it Hot in Here? A Film about Menopause **10489**
Living with Menopause Series **10506**
Medical College of Pennsylvania • Center for the Mature Woman **8211**
Melpomene Institute for Women's Health Research **8212**
Menopause **10513**
Menopause: Myths and Realities **10514**
The Menopause Story **10515**
National Women's Health Network • Women's Health Information Service • Library **6875**
North American Menopause Society **800**
Society of General Internal Medicine • Women's Caucus **903**
Menopause **10513**
Menopause: Myths and Realities **10514**
The Menopause Story **10515**
Menstruation (see also Premenstrual Syndrome)
Cramps! **10397**
Female Cycle **10436**
Melpomene Institute for Women's Health Research **8212**
Society for Menstrual Cycle Research **904**
Society for Menstrual Cycle Research Newsletter **9479**
Wellesley College • Center for Research on Women **10013**
Mental Health (see also Psychiatry)
Depression After Delivery **333**
The Family Institute • Crowley Library **6791**

Irene Josselyn Clinic • Mental Health Library **6817**
Love-N-Addiction **532**
National Coalition for Women's Mental Health **651**
Postpartum Support, International **842**
Radcliffe College • Henry A. Murray Research Center **6912**
U.S. Department of Health and Human Services • Alcohol, Drug Abuse, and Mental Health Administration • Federal Women's Program **8313**
University of Wisconsin—Madison • Women's Studies Research Center **8270**
Washington University • George Warren Brown School of Social Work • Library & Learning Resources Center **6973**
Werth; Karen B. **8674**
Women and Therapy **9140**
Women's Growth and Therapy Center **1558**
Women's Health Resources **6982**
Women's History Research Center **8279**
Women's History Library **6983**
Women's Psychotherapy Institute **1167**
Meramec Community College • Careers for Homemakers **5572**
Merced College • Single Parent/Displaced Homemaker Project **5067**
Merced County Regional Occupational Program • SOLO Single Parent/Displaced Homemaker Project **5068**
Mercer County Area Vocational-Technical School • New Choices **5880**
Mercer County Community College • Women's Studies Concentration **7480**
Mercer County Vocational-Technical School • Single Parent Homemaker Program **5647**
Mercer University • Women's Studies Program **7236**
Merchantville Woman's Club **2422**
Mercy College • Women's Studies Program **7511**
Mercy Home **4078**
Mercy House **3634, 4189**
Meredith College **7059**
Merging Media **9856**
Meriden/Wallingford Chrysalis **3510**
Meridian Community College • Single Parent/Displaced Homemaker Program **5539**
Meristom **10262**
Mermod Award; Camille **7940**
Merrillville Business and Professional Women's Club **1857**
Merrimack College • Women's Studies Program **7367**
Merritt College • Women's Center/Career Center **5075**
Mesa Community College
Displaced Homemaker Program **5012**
Mesa Community College Re-Entry Center **6369**
Mesa County Women's Network **1486**
Metro/Dade Advocates for Victims **3549**
Metro Nashville Public Schools • Career Directions Program **5972**
Metro Tech [Oklahoma City, OK] • Displaced Homemaker Program **5819**
Metropolitan Battered Women's Program **3807**
Metropolitan Community College • Expanded Services for Homemakers and Single Parents **5598**
Metropolitan Development Council [Tacoma, WA] • Displaced Homemaker Program **6135**

Metropolitan New York Right to Life Foundation **2554**
Metropolitan State College of Denver
Women's Services **6417**
Women's Studies Program **7190**
Metropolitan State University • Women's Program **6538, 7426**
Metropolitan Woman **8994**
Mexican-American Opportunity Foundation • Resource and Referral Service • Lending Library **6849**
Mexican American Women's National Association **546**
Mexican American Women's National Association - Kansas City Office **2311**
Meyer-Schutzmeister Award; Luise **7861**
MG Woman's Counseling Service of New York **8677**
Mi Casa Resource Center For Women **5131**
Miami-Dade Community College
Vocational Educational Opportunity Grant • Single Parent/Homemaker Program **5216**
Vocational Training for Single Parents and Homemakers **5217**
Miami University • Women's Studies Program **7600**
Miami Valley Aborted Women **2712**
Michael Scholarship; Edwin G. and Lauretta M. **7826**
Michigan Abortion Rights Action League **2234**
Michigan Association of American Mothers **2241**
Michigan Coalition Against Domestic Violence **2217**
Michigan Council for Maternal and Child Health **2199**
Michigan Democratic Women's Caucus **2168**
Michigan Department of Civil Rights • Civil Rights Library **6850**
Michigan Department of Labor • Women and Work Office **8524**
Michigan Department of Public Health • Division of Program and Administrative Services • Maternal and Child Health Office **8525**
Michigan Department of Social Services • Domestic Violence Prevention and Treatment Board **8526**
Michigan ERAmerica **2219**
Michigan Federation of Business and Professional Women's Clubs **2200**
Michigan Federation of Democratic Women **2159**
Michigan Metro Girl Scout Council **2160**
Michigan Midwives Association **2187**
Michigan Press Women **2243**
Michigan Religious Coalition for Abortion Rights **2225**
Michigan State Association of Colored Women's Clubs **2190**
Michigan State University
Division of Women's Programs **6523**
Office of Women in International Development **9857**
Women and International Development Program **8214**
Women's Studies Program **7396**
Michigan Woman Magazine **8995**
Michigan Women's Bowling Association **2214**
Michigan Women's Commission **8527**
Michigan Women's Foundation **2201**
Michigan Women's Historical Center and Hall of Fame **2202**
Michigan Women's Political Caucus **2235**

Minnesota Citizens Council on Crime and Justice • Crime Victim Center **3984**
Minnesota Clubwoman **9000**
Minnesota Coalition for Battered Women **2285**
Minnesota Commission on the Economic Status of Women **8528**
Minnesota Correctional Facility **4014**
Minnesota Department of Corrections • Program and Services for Battered Women **8529**
Minnesota Department of Health • Maternal and Child Health Division **8530**
Minnesota Department of Human Services • Child Support Enforcement Division **8531**
Minnesota Employee Relations Department • Equal Opportunity Division **8532**
Minnesota Historical Society • Minnesota Women's History Project **7000**
Minnesota Korean Women's Association **2264**
Minnesota Migrant Council • Hispanic Battered Women Program **3997**
Minnesota NARAL **2275**
Minnesota Pork Council Women **2246**
Minnesota Women for Agriculture **2254**
Minnesota Women's Campaign Fund **2286**
Minnesota Women's Center **2276**
Minnesota Women's Consortium **2287**
Minnesota Women's Fund **2277**
Minnesota Women's History Project • Minnesota Historical Society **7000**
Minnesota Women's Press **9613**
Minnesota Women's Press Bookstore **10185**
Minorities
    AAUW Focus Professions Fellowships **7779**
    The Alert **9178**
    Alliance of Minority Women for Business and Political Development **17**
    Alternative Press Index **8842**
    Aunt Lute Book Co. **9666**
    Berkeley Women's Law Journal **8852**
    Center for Research on Women— Center News **9225**
    Center for Women Policy Studies **8181, 9699**
    Common Ground/Different Planes **9247**
    Consortium of Doctors **303**
    Council for Advancement and Support of Education • Commission for Opportunity and Equity **308**
    Directory of Minority and Women- Owned Engineering and Architectural Firms **8720**
    Directory of Minority and Women- Owned Investment Bankers **8721**
    Directory of Women Entrepreneurs **8729**
    ETS Postdoctoral Fellowship **7830**
    Garrett Park Press **9765**
    Higher Education Opportunities for Minorities and Women: Annotated Selections **8753**
    Information Systems Development **9802**
    Institute for Women's Policy Research **8204**
    Kitchen Table: Women of Color Press **9822**
    LeNoire Award; Rosetta **8089**
    Licensing Newspaper **9360**
    Memphis State University • Center for Research on Women **8213**
    Minority Women Business Enterprise **1598**
    Minority Women's Network **550**
    Miranda Associates, Inc. **8678**

National Association of Minority Political Women **604**
National Association of Minority Women in Business **605**
National Bar Association • Association of Black Women Attorneys **626**
National Institute for Women of Color **704, 8217**
National Network of Minority Women in Science **718**
National News Service for Women and Minorities **722**
National Recreation and Parks Association • Women and Minority Programs **739**
National Women of Color Association **764**
New Futures Enterprises **8680**
NIWC Network News **9426**
NSF Minority Graduate Fellowships for Women **7883**
Panel of American Women **824**
Phyllips; Kaye **8675**
Procurement Resources, Inc. **8681**
Promoting Minorities & Women **10729**
Radical Women **9936**
Research Clearinghouse on Women of Color and Southern Women **10730**
Society of General Internal Medicine • Women's Caucus **903**
Spinster's Book Co. **9973**
State University of New York at Albany • Center for Women in Government **921, 8241**
Today **9494**
United States Student Association • Women's Coalition/Women of Color Caucus **963**
University of Connecticut • Women's Center **8256**
University of Texas at Arlington • Women and Minority Work Research and Resource Center **8266**
The Woman Activist Fund **992**
Women of Color Newsletter **9535**
Women of Color Partnership Program **1019**
Women of Color and Southern Women: A Bibliography **8810**
Women's History Research Center • Women's History Library **6983**
Women's Resource Center Library **6987**
Working Opportunities for Women • W.O.W. Resource Center **6988**
Minorities and Women in Business **9001**
Minorities and Women: A List of Major Organizations in Librarianship **8768**
Minority Women Business Enterprise **1598**
Minority Women's Network **550**
Minot Regional Area Learning Center • Displaced Homemakers Program **5759**
Minyard Food Stores **8633**
Mirabella **9002**
Miranda Associates, Inc. **8678**
Miscarriage see Infant Death; Pregnancy
Miss America Pageant Scholarships **7868**
Miss America Women's Achievement Award **8038**
Miss Mom **551**
Miss Mom/Mister Mom **551**
Miss, Mrs. or Ms.—What's it all about? **10516**
Missing Children (see also Kidnapping)
    Missing Children Minnesota • Resource Center **6854**
Missing Children Minnesota • Resource Center **6854**
Mission College • Single Parent/Displaced Homemaker Project **5102**

Missionaries (see also Religion and Theology)
    African Methodist Episcopal Church • Women's Missionary Society **11**
    Aglow Publications **9636**
    Bethlehem Lutheran Women's Missionary League **1922**
    Dimension **8889**
    International Lutheran Women's Missionary League **472**
    Maryknoll Sisters of St. Dominic **537**
    Medical Mission Sisters **543**
    Missionary Sisters of the Society of Mary - Marist Missionary Sisters **553**
    Missionary Women International **554**
    Southern Baptist Convention • Women's Missionary Union **915**
    Woman's Home and Foreign Mission Society **995**
    Woman's Missionary Union **996**
    Women of the Church of God **1018**
    Women and Missions **9546**
    Women's Home and Overseas Missionary Society **1126**
    Women's Missionary Society, AME Church **1154**
Miss...or Myth? **10517**
Missionary Association of Catholic Women **552**
Missionary Magazine **9376**
Missionary Sisters of the Society of Mary - Marist Missionary Sisters **553**
Missionary Women International **554**
Mississippi Delta Community College • Displaced Homemakers Program **5540**
Mississippi Department of Health
    Bureau of Health Services • Maternity Services Division **8533**
    Domestic Violence Shelters Projects **8534**
Mississippi Department of Human Services • Child Support Division **8535**
Mississippi Federation of Women's Club **2297**
Mississippi Gulf Coast Community College, Jackson County Campus • Displaced Homemaker/Single Parent **5529**
Mississippi Gulf Coast Community College, Jefferson Davis Campus • Displaced Homemaker/Single Parent Program **5531**
Mississippi Gulf Coast Community College, Parkinston Campus • Single Parent Displaced Homemaker Program **5543**
Mississippi State University • Women's Studies Concentration **7432**
Mississippi University for Women **7062**
    Women's Studies Program **7429**
Missouri Abortion Rights Action League **2320**
Missouri Branch of National Abortion Rights Action League **2312**
Missouri Coalition Against Domestic Violence **2309**
Missouri Department of Health • Maternal and Child Health Division **8536**
Missouri Department of Social Services
    Child Support Enforcement Division **8537**
    Division of Family Services • Family Violence Prevention and Services **8538**
Missouri Pork Council Women **2303**
Missouri Shores Women Resource Center • Single Parent/Homemaker Project **5935**
Missouri Shores Women's Resource Center **4615**
Missouri Western State College • Women's Educational Resource Center **6544**
Missouri Women's Action Fund **2321**
Missouri Women's Network **2322**

NAACOG: The Organization for Obstetric, Gynecologic, and Neonatal Nurses **566**

NAACP Legal Defense and Educational Fund • Law Library • National Association for the Advancement of Colored People **6862**

Na'amat U.S.A. **567**

NA'AMAT WOMAN **9009**

NABCO News **9383**

NABWA News **9384**

NABWA Scholarship Award **7870**

Naiad Press, Inc. **9874**
Lesbian and Gay Archives **6860**

Naismith All-American Teams **8046**

Naismith College Coach of the Year **8047**

Naismith Hall of Fame Award; Frances Pomeroy **7976**

Naismith High School Awards **8048**

Najda: Women Concerned About the Middle East **568**

NAMBAW News **9385**

Nanny Goat Publications **9875**

Nanny Pop-Ins Association **569**

Naomi Berber Memorial Award **8049**

Napa Emergency Women's Service **1332, 3396**

Napa Valley College
Single Parent/Displaced Homemaker Project **5072**
Women's Re-Entry Center **6393**

NAPSAC Directory of Alternative Birth Services and Consumer Guide **8769**

NAPSAC International **9876**

NAPSAC News **9386**

NARAL New Jersey **2425**

NARAL Newsletter **9387**

Nash Club of National Association of Negro Business and Professional Women's Clubs **2977**

Nashua Adult Learning Center • Project PLACE (People Learning About Careers and Entry) **5616**

Nashville State Technical Institute • Displaced Homemaker/Single Parent Program **5973**

Nassau Community College
Adult Students Multi-Service Center **5725**
AIMS Program **5692**

Nassau County Coalition Against Domestic Violence **4225**

Nassau County Office of Women's Services **5696**

Nassau County Pro-Life **1620**

Nassau County Women's Services **2589**

Nathan Star Press **9877**

National Abortion Federation **570**
Resource Center **6861**

National Abortion Rights Action League **571**

National Abortion Rights Action League, Colorado Chapter **1480**

National Abortion Rights Action League of Illinois **1722**

National Abortion Rights Action League of Iowa **1943**

National Abortion Rights Action League of New Hampshire **2377**

National Abortion Rights Action League of North Carolina **2627**

National Abortion Rights Action League of Ohio **2700**

National Abortion Rights Action League of Pennsylvania **2862**

National Academy of Sciences • Committee on Women in Science and Engineering **572**

National Action for Former Military Wives **573**

National Action Forum for Midlife and Older Women **574**

National Action Forum for Older Women **574**

National Advisory Council on Maternal, Infant and Fetal Nutrition • U.S. Department of Agriculture • Food and Nutrition Service • Supplemental Food Programs Division **8299**

National Agriculture Aviation Association Most Active Woman Award **8050**

The National Alliance **9339**

National Alliance of Breast Cancer Organizations **575**

National Alliance Daughters of Veterans **326**

National Alliance of Homebased Businesswomen **576**

National Alliance of Homebased Businesswomen, Northern Illinois Chapter **1765**

National Alliance of Professional and Executive Women's Networks **443**

National American Woman Suffrage Association **518**

National Anorexic Aid Program, Ohio Chapter **2701**

National Anorexic Aid Society **577**

National Assembly of Religious Women **578**

National Assembly of Women Religious **578**

National Association for the Advancement of Colored People • NAACP Legal Defense and Educational Fund • Law Library **6862**

National Association of Anorexia Nervosa and Associated Disorders **579**

National Association of Bank Women **377, 580**

National Association of Black Women Attorneys **581**

National Association of Black Women Attorneys Scholarship Award **8051**

National Association of Black Women Entrepreneurs **582**

National Association of Business and Industrial Saleswomen **583**

National Association of Chicano Studies • Mujeres Activas en Letras y Cambio Social **584**

National Association of Childbearing Centers **585**

National Association of Childbearing Centers [Milwaukie, OR] **2785**

National Association of Childbearing Centers [Southfield, MI] **2236**

National Association of Childbearing Centers, Monroe Maternity Center **2978**

National Association of Childbirth Assistants **586**

National Association of Childbirth Education **587**

National Association of College Women **612**

National Association of Collegiate Women Athletic Administrators **588**

National Association of Colored Girls Clubs **597**

National Association of Colored Women's Clubs **589**

National Association of Commissions for Women **590**

National Association of County Officials • Women Officials of the National Association of County Officials **591**

National Association of Cuban-American Women of the U.S.A. **592**

National Association of Deans of Women **619**

National Association of Extension Home Economists **593**

National Association for Family Day Care **594**

National Association for Female Executives **595**

National Association of Full Figured Women **596**

National Association of Future Women **615**

National Association of Gay Alcoholism Professionals **8773**

National Association of Girl Scout Executives **176**

National Association of Girls Clubs **597**

National Association for Girls and Women in Sport **598**

National Association to Improve Support Enforcement **726**

National Association of Independent Schools • Council for Women in Independent Schools **599**

National Association of Insurance Women **600**

National Association of Insurance Women - International **600**

National Association of Insurance Women of Virginia/West Virginia **3193**

National Association of MBA Women **601**

National Association of Media Women **602**

National Association of Military Widows **603**

National Association of Ministers' Wives **445**

National Association of Ministers' Wives and Ministers' Widows **445**

National Association of Minority Political Women **604**

National Association of Minority Women in Business **605**

National Association of Mothers' Centers **606**

National Association of Negro Business and Professional Women's Club National Achievement Award **8052**

National Association of Negro Business and Professional Women's Club National Appreciation Award **8053**

National Association of Negro Business and Professional Women's Club National Community Service Award **8054**

National Association of Negro Business and Professional Women's Club National Scholarship Award **8055**

National Association of Negro Business and Professional Women's Club National Youth Award **8056**

National Association of Negro Business and Professional Women's Clubs **607**

National Association of Parents and Professionals for Safe Alternatives in Childbirth **446**

National Association of Professional Asian-American Women **608**

National Association for Professional Saleswomen **609**

National Association for Professional Saleswomen Achievers' Circle **8057**

National Association of Railroad Women **67**

National Association of Railway Business Women **610**

National Association for Repeal of Abortion Laws **571**

National Association of Surrogate Mothers **611**

National Association of University Women **612**

National Association of Women Artists **613**

National Association of Women Artists News **9388**

National Association of Women Business Owners **614, 9878**
Austin Chapter **2997**
Baltimore Chapter **2051**
Boca/Delray Chapter **1577**
Capital Area Chapter **1549**
Cedar Rapids/Iowa City Chapter **1919**
Central Arkansas Chapter **1253**

Planned Parenthood Association of Southwestern Michigan **6254**

Planned Parenthood Association of Utah **6352**

Planned Parenthood of Broome and Chenango Counties **6284**

Planned Parenthood of Buffalo and Erie County **6285**

Planned Parenthood of Cameron and Willacy Counties **6341**

Planned Parenthood of the Capitol Region **6326**

Planned Parenthood Center of Austin **6340**

Planned Parenthood Center of El Paso **6344**

Planned Parenthood Center of San Antonio **6350**

Planned Parenthood Center of Syracuse **6299**

Planned Parenthood Center of Walla Walla **6362**

Planned Parenthood Centers of West Michigan **6257**

Planned Parenthood of Central California **6195, 9924**

Planned Parenthood of Central Florida **6218**

Planned Parenthood of Central Indiana **6237**
Resource Center **6893**

Planned Parenthood of Central Missouri **6263**

Planned Parenthood of Central and Northern Arizona **6191**

Planned Parenthood of Central Ohio **6312**

Planned Parenthood of Central Oklahoma **6320**

Planned Parenthood of the Central Ozarks **6266**

Planned Parenthood of Central Pennsylvania **6332**

Planned Parenthood of Central South Carolina **6334**

Planned Parenthood of Central Texas **6351**

Planned Parenthood of Central Washington **6363**

Planned Parenthood of Chester County **6331**

Planned Parenthood of Cleveland, Inc. • Library **6894**

Planned Parenthood of Columbia/Willamette **6324**

Planned Parenthood Committee of Sioux City **6245**

Planned Parenthood of Connecticut **6212**

Planned Parenthood of Dallas and Northeast Texas **6343**

Planned Parenthood of Decatur **6231**

Planned Parenthood of Delaware **6213**

Planned Parenthood of Dutchess/Ulster **6296**

Planned Parenthood of East Central Georgia **6225**

Planned Parenthood of East Central Indiana **6240**

Planned Parenthood of East Tennessee **6338**

Planned Parenthood of Eastern Oklahoma and Western Arkansas **6321**

Planned Parenthood of Essex County **6277**

Planned Parenthood Federation of America **836, 8169**
Northern Region Office **6232**
Southern Region Office **6224**
Western Region Office **6202**

Planned Parenthood Federation of America, Inc. **9925**
Katharine Dexter McCormick Library **6895**

Planned Parenthood Federation of America (PPFA) Margaret Sanger Award **8084**

Planned Parenthood of the Finger Lakes **6288**

Planned Parenthood of Greater Arkansas **6193**

Planned Parenthood of the Greater Camden Area **6274**

Planned Parenthood of Greater Charlotte **6304**

Planned Parenthood of Greater Cleveland **6311**

Planned Parenthood of Greater Kansas City **6264**

Planned Parenthood of Greater Northern New Jersey **6275**

Planned Parenthood of Greater Raleigh **6305**

Planned Parenthood Health Services of Northeastern New York **6298**

Planned Parenthood of Houston and Southeast Texas **6346**
Mary Elizabeth Hudson Library **6896**

Planned Parenthood of Kansas **6246**

Planned Parenthood of Lancaster County **6327**

Planned Parenthood League of Detroit **6255**

Planned Parenthood League of Massachusetts **6252**

Planned Parenthood League of Middlesex County **6276**

Planned Parenthood of Lincoln **6270**

Planned Parenthood of Linn County **6243**

Planned Parenthood of Louisiana **6250**

Planned Parenthood of Louisville **6249**

Planned Parenthood of the Low Country **6335**

Planned Parenthood of Mahoning Valley **6319**

Planned Parenthood of Marin, Sonoma, and Mendocino **6205**

Planned Parenthood of Metropolitan Washington, DC **6214**

Planned Parenthood of Mid-Central Illinois **6228**

Planned Parenthood of Mid-Iowa **6244**

Planned Parenthood of Mid-Michigan **6253**

Planned Parenthood of Minnesota **6261**
Phyllis Cooksey Resource Center **6897**

Planned Parenthood of Minnesota—Network News **9453**

Planned Parenthood of Mississippi **6262**

Planned Parenthood of Missoula **6269**

Planned Parenthood of Monmouth County **6279**

Planned Parenthood of Monterey County **6197**

Planned Parenthood of Nassau County **6290**

Planned Parenthood of New York City **6291**

Planned Parenthood of Niagara County **6293**

Planned Parenthood of North Central Florida **6216**

Planned Parenthood of North Central Indiana **6241**

Planned Parenthood of North Central Ohio **6315**

Planned Parenthood of North East Pennsylvania **6330**

Planned Parenthood of North Texas **6345**

Planned Parenthood of Northeast Florida **6217**

Planned Parenthood of Northeast Missouri **6265**

Planned Parenthood of Northern Nevada **6273**

Planned Parenthood of Northern New England **6353**
PPNNE Resource Center **6898**

Planned Parenthood of Northern New York **6301**

Planned Parenthood of Northwest/Northeast Indiana **6239**

Planned Parenthood of Northwest Ohio **6318**

Planned Parenthood of Omaha/Council Bluffs **6271**

Planned Parenthood of Orange County **6303**

Planned Parenthood of Orange and San Bernardino Counties **6206**

Planned Parenthood of Orange/Sullivan **6292**

Planned Parenthood of the Palm Beach Area **6222**

Planned Parenthood of Pierce County **6361**

Planned Parenthood Program **357**

Planned Parenthood of Rhode Island **6333**

Planned Parenthood of Rochester and Genesee Valley **6297**

Planned Parenthood of the Rocky Mountains **6211, 6364**

Planned Parenthood of Sacramento Valley **6199**

Planned Parenthood of the St. Louis Region **6267**
Education Department • Library **6899**

Planned Parenthood of San Antonio and South Central Texas • Library **6900**

Planned Parenthood of San Diego and Riverside Counties **6200**

Planned Parenthood of San Joaquin Valley **6209**

Planned Parenthood of San Mateo County **6204**

Planned Parenthood of Santa Barbara, Ventura, and San Luis Obispo Counties **6207**

Planned Parenthood of Santa Cruz County **6208**

Planned Parenthood of Seattle/King County **6359**

Planned Parenthood of Shasta/Diablo **6210**

Planned Parenthood of Snohomish County **6358**

Planned Parenthood of South Palm Beach and Broward Counties **6215**

Planned Parenthood of South Texas **6342**

Planned Parenthood of Southeast Iowa **6242**

Planned Parenthood of Southeast Ohio **6308**

Planned Parenthood Southeastern Pennsylvania • Resource Center **6901**

Planned Parenthood of Southeastern Virginia **6354**

Planned Parenthood of Southern Arizona **6192**

Planned Parenthood of Southern Indiana **6235**

Planned Parenthood of Southern Nevada **6272**

Planned Parenthood of Southern New Mexico **6282**

Planned Parenthood of Southern Oregon **6323**

Planned Parenthood of the Southern Tier **6287**

Planned Parenthood of Southwest Florida **6220**

Planned Parenthood of Southwest Virginia **6356**

Planned Parenthood of Southwestern Indiana **6236**

Planned Parenthood of Southwestern Indiana, Inc. • Resource Center **6902**

Planned Parenthood of Spokane and Whitman Counties **6360**

Presbyterian Women **845**
Priests for Equality **847**
Probe **9617**
Project Priesthood **860**
Putnam Alliance Church of the
Unity **2135**
Reformed Church Women **869**
Religious Coalition for Abortion
Rights **871**
Religious Coalition for Abortion Rights,
Illinois Affiliate **1729**
Religious Coalition for Abortion Rights,
New York State **2608**
*Religious Coalition for Abortion Rights
Newsletter* **9468**
Religious Coalition for Abortion Rights,
Ohio Affiliate **2673**
Religious Coalition for Abortion Rights,
Wisconsin Affiliate **3198**
Religious Network for Equality for
Women **872**
Response **9054**
Robinson Church Women United **1792**
Safer Society Press **9952**
Sagewoman Magazine **9058**
St. Joan's International Alliance • U.S.
Section **883**
Schutze Memorial Scholarship; Katherine
J. **7856**
Seamless Garment Network **886**
Secretariat for Family, Laity, Women,
and Youth **887**
Seven Cycles **9964**
Seventh Day Baptist Historical Society
Robe of Achievement **8097**
SheTotem **9621**
Sisters of St. Joseph of Carondelet •
St. Paul Province • Archives **6928**
SisterSpirit **2798**
Society of Our Lady of the Way **906**
Southern Baptist Convention • Women's
Missionary Union **915**
Southern Baptist Women in
Ministry/Folio **916**
Spartanburg Christian Women's Club
II **2945**
Supreme Ladies Auxiliary Knights of St.
John **927**
Tangelwuld Press **9986**
Task Force on Equality of Women in
Judaism **935**
Themophoria **9492**
Today's Christian Woman **9083**
Unitarian Universalist Women's
Federation **945**
*Unitarian Universalist Women's
Federation—The Communicator* **9499**
United Church of Christ Coordinating
Center for Women in Church and
Society **949**
The United Methodist Church
General Board of Global Ministries
• Women's Division **953**
General Commission on the Status
and Role of Women **954**
United Presbyterian Church • USA
Women's Unit • Justice for
Women **958**
U.S. Catholic Award **8120**
Valley City Christian Women's
Club **2665**
Virtue **9098**
WATERwheel **9511**
Wild Violet Publishing **10018**
W.I.M. Publications **10022**
Winning Women **2210**
Woman's Home and Foreign Mission
Society **995**
Woman's National Auxiliary Convention
of Free Will Baptists **997**

The Woman's Pulpit **9127**
Woman's Touch **9128**
Women Church Convergence **1017**
Women of the Church of God **1018**
Women in Community Service **1021**
Women of the ELC Scholarship **7903**
Women of the Evangelical Lutheran
Church in America **1851**
Women: Hope of the World **10684**
Women in Ministry **10687**
Women in Ministry Project **1065**
Women and Missions **9546**
Women in Theology and Church
History **2585**
Women in United Methodist History
Research Grant **7905**
Women's Aglow Fellowship
International **1091**
Women's Aglow Fellowship of
Loveland **1489**
Women's Alliance for Theology, Ethics
and Ritual **1093**
Women's Caucus: Religious
Studies **1109**
*Women's Caucus: Religious Studies
Newsletter* **9567**
Women's Christian Temperance
Union **1887**
Women's Christian Temperance Union,
Rapid City Chapter **2963**
Women's Division of the Board of
Global Ministries of the United
Methodist Church **1116**
Women's Fellowship of the First
Congregational Church of
Greenfield **2095**
Women's Fellowship of the First
Congregational Church of Turners
Falls **2131**
Women's Home and Overseas
Missionary Society **1126**
Women's League for Conservative
Judaism **1148**
Women's Missionary Council of the
Christian Methodist Episcopal
Church **1152**
Women's Missionary and Service
Commission of the Mennonite
Church **1153**
Women's Missionary Society, AME
Church **1154**
Women's Network News **9582**
Women's Ordination Conference **1159**
Women's Spirituality Center **3163**
Women's Spirituality Forum **1172**
Women's Theological Center **1176**
World CWF News **9595**
*World Federation of Methodist
Women—Handbook* **8834**
World Federation of Methodist Women,
North America Area **1184**
Yankton Christian Women's
Council **2969**
Young Ladies Institute **1190, 1415**
Young Women of the Church of Jesus
Christ of Latter-Day Saints **1191**
Religious Coalition for Abortion Rights **871**
Religious Coalition for Abortion Rights,
Illinois Affiliate **1729**
Religious Coalition for Abortion Rights,
Missouri Chapter **2326**
Religious Coalition for Abortion Rights, New
Jersey Chapter **2430**
Religious Coalition for Abortion Rights, New
Mexico Chapter **2468**
Religious Coalition for Abortion Rights, New
York State **2608**
*Religious Coalition for Abortion Rights
Newsletter* **9468**

Religious Coalition for Abortion Rights, Ohio
Affiliate **2673**
Religious Coalition for Abortion Rights,
Oklahoma Chapter **2771**
Religious Coalition for Abortion Rights,
Oregon Chapter **2797**
Religious Coalition for Abortion Rights,
Washington Chapter **3157**
Religious Coalition for Abortion Rights,
Wisconsin Affiliate **3198**
Religious Committee for the ERA **872**
Religious Network for Equality for
Women **872**
Remi Books, Inc. **9943**
Remington Press **9944**
Renaissance Books and Gifts **10191**
Renate W. Chasman Scholarship **7888**
Rend Lake College • Building Opportunity
Project **5318**
Renew, Inc. **3466**
Renewal House **3873, 4220**
Reno County Victims of Abuse
Network **3770**
The Reporter **9051**
Reproductive Biology Research
Foundation **8209**
Reproductive and Genetic Engineering **9052**
Reproductive Health Care Center of South
Central Michigan **6258**
**Reproductive Issues (see also Abortion;
Population; Pregnancy; Pro-Choice;
Chapter 5: Family Planning Services)**
Abdominal Hysterectomy **10295**
Air-Plus Enterprises **9637**
Alternative Conceptions **10307**
*Ambulatory Maternal Health Care and
Family Planning Services* **8689**
American Academy of Natural Family
Planning **26**
American Association of ProLife
Obstetricians and Gynecologists **39**
American College of Obstetricians and
Gynecologists • Resource
Center **6729**
American Foundation for the Blind •
Helen Keller Archives **6731**
American Life Lobby **96**
Library **6733**
APLICommunicator **9189**
Aquarian Research Foundation **9654**
Arizona Family Planning Council **1224**
Assignment: Life **10319**
Association for Population/Family
Planning Libraries and Information
Centers, International **181**
Association for Voluntary Surgical
Contraception • Library **6735**
AVSC News **9197**
Baby Clock **10326**
Barnard College • Barnard Center for
Research on Women • Birdie
Goldsmith Ast Resource
Collection **6738**
*Birth Control: Your Responsibility, Your
Choice* **10346**
Carolina Population Center •
Library **6756**
Catholics for a Free Choice **235**
Catholics United for Life **6758**
CCL Family Foundations **9221**
CDDR News **9223**
Center for Population Options **242,
8177**
Resource Center **6763**
Center for Reproductive Law and
Policy **8178**
Center for Reproductive and Sexual
Health **243**
Center for Surrogate Parenting **246**
Center for Women Policy Studies **8181**

Richardson Memorial Flight Scholarship;
Gini **7834**
Richland College • Adult Resource
Center **5997**
Richland Community College
Options for Displaced
Homemakers **5309**
Options for Displaced Homemakers and
Single Parents **6453**
Richland County Coalition Against Domestic
Violence **4088**
Richmond County Council on the Status of
Women **2647**
Richmond Mental Health Center • Domestic
Violence Intervention Project **4804**
Richmond Womensbooks **10284**
Ride College • Women's Studies
Program **7466**
Rider College • Women's Center **6558**
Ridgeland Federated Women's Club **1836**
Ridgewood Unit of Republican
Women **2441**
Right to Life of Illinois **1730**
Right to Life of Indianapolis **1847**
Right to Life League of Southern California •
Library **6913**
Right to Life of Louisville **1993**
Right to Life of Michigan [Lansing, MI] •
Resource Center **6916**
Right to Life of Michigan [Lincoln Park, MI]
• Resource Center **6917**
Right to Life of Michigan [Novi, MI] •
Resource Center **6915**
Right to Life of Michigan **2184**
Macomb County Education/Resource
Center **6914**
State Central Resource Center **6918**
Right-to-Life (see also Abortion;
Pregnancy; Pro-Choice; Reproductive
Issues)
Abortion Clinic **10297**
Abortion: The Divisive Issue **10298**
Ad Hoc Committee in Defense of
Life **2**
All About Issues American **14**
Alternatives to Abortion
International/Women's Health and
Education Foundation **23**
American Association of ProLife
Obstetricians and Gynecologists **39**
American Association of Pro-Life
Pediatricians **40**
American Citizens Concerned for Life
Education Fund • ACCL
Communications Center **57**
American Citizens Concerned for Life,
Inc. • Communications Center **9647**
American Coalition for Life **60**
American Collegians for Life **64**
American Life League **95, 9648**
American Life Lobby **96**
Library **6733**
American ProLife Council **116**
Americans United for Life **147**
Legal Defense Fund **148**
Library **6734**
Americans United for Life Legal
Defense Fund **9649**
AUL Newsletter **9196**
Baptists for Life **208**
Birthright of Antigo **3197**
Birthright of Assabet Valley **2092**
Birthright of Berks County **2886**
Birthright of Central
Westmoreland **2830**
Birthright Counseling **2387**
Birthright of Delaware **1538**
Birthright of Dubuque **1907**
Birthright, Essex County Chapter **2400**
Birthright-Freehold **2410**

Birthright of Greater New
Bedford **2109**
Birthright of Holland **2188**
Birthright of Huntsville **1210**
Birthright of Kirksville **2315**
Birthright of Lexington **1983**
Birthright of Lindenwold **2418**
Birthright of Maquoketa **1920**
Birthright of Marin **1429**
Birthright of Mt. Pleasant **1931**
Birthright of Rensselaer **1861**
Birthright of St. Marys **1649**
Birthright of Seattle **3153**
Birthright, United States of
America **212**
Birthright of Washington **3174**
Birthright of Wheaton **2067**
Birthright of Worland **3254**
Birthrights **1687**
Black Americans for Life **213**
Catholics United for Life **236, 6758**
Champlin Valley Birthright **3082**
Chester County Citizens Concerned
About Life **2900**
Choose Life **9238**
Christian Americans for Life **259**
Columbia County Right to Life **3231**
Committee to Resist Abortion **282**
Crisis Pregnancy **10399**
Diocese of Allentown • Pro-Life
Library **6784**
Educational Center for Life **6787**
Feminists for Life of America **376**
Feminists for Life of Chicago **1712**
Feminists for Life of Illinois **1780**
Feminists for Life of Minnesota **2279**
Feminists for Life of New Jersey **2429**
ForLIFE **380, 9758**
Grand Rapids Right-to-Life **2182**
Guernsey County Right to Life
Society **2676**
Hayes Publishing Co., Inc. **9781**
An Historical View of Abortion Around
the World **10470**
Howard County Right to Life **1850**
Human Life Alliance of
Minnesota **2283**
Human Life Center **420**
Library **6806**
Human Life Foundation **421**
Human Life International **422**
Library **6807**
Human Life Issues **8938**
Illinois Right to Life Committee—
News **9331**
Justice for Women **496**
Lex Vitae **9358**
LFL Reports: The Newsletter of
Libertarians for Life **9359**
Libertarians for Life **526**
Liberty Godparent Ministry **527**
Life-Guardian **9361**
Life Insight **9362**
LifeDate **9363**
Lifeletter **9364**
Lutherans for Life **534**
Library **6837**
March for Life **536**
Massachusetts Citizens for Life,
Arlington Chapter **2070**
Massachusetts Citizens for Life,
Needham Chapter **2108**
Metropolitan New York Right to Life
Foundation **2554**
Mills County Iowans for Life **1916**
Nassau County Pro-Life **1620**
National Committee for a Human Life
Amendment **655**
National Federation of Officers for
Life **691**

National Organization of Episcopalians
for Life **725**
National Pro-Life Democrats **737**
National Right to Life Committee **742**
Library **6870**
National Right to Life Educational Trust
Fund **743**
National Right to Life News **9404**
National Youth Pro-Life Coalition **783**
No Alibis **10525**
The NOEL News **9428**
Not Mine to Deny **10530**
Nurses Concerned for Life, Wabash
Chapter **1872**
Operation Rescue **810**
Pennsylvanians for Human Life **2888**
People Concerned for the Unborn
Child—Newsletter **9448**
People for Life **831**
Pharmacists for Life **832**
Pro-Family Press Association **849**
Pro-Life Action League **850**
Library **6910**
Pro-Life Action League—Action
News **9458**
Pro-Life Alliance of Gays and
Lesbians **851**
Pro-Life Direct Action League **852**
Pro-Life Education Association **2037**
Pro-Life Nonviolent Action Project **853**
Pro-Life of San Mateo County **1426**
Pro-Life Under Attack **10570**
Protect Life in All Nations **862**
Right to Life of Illinois **1730**
Right to Life of Indianapolis **1847**
Right to Life League of Southern
California • Library **6913**
Right to Life of Louisville **1993**
Right to Life of Michigan • Resource
Center **6915**
Right to Life of Michigan • Resource
Center **6916**
Right to Life of Michigan • Resource
Center **6917**
Right to Life of Michigan **2184**
Macomb County
Education/Resource Center **6914**
State Central Resource
Center **6918**
Rosary Novena for Life
Organization **877**
Save a Baby **884**
Schenectady County Right to
Life **2601**
Seamless Garment Network **886**
Sharon Long - Private Collection **6926**
The Silent Scream **10599**
Sun Life Books **9980**
Texas Feminists for Life of
America **3002**
U.S. Coalition for Life **961**
Value of Life Committee **975**
Library **6968**
Vermont Right to Life Committee **3087**
Williston Chapter Right to Life **2669**
Wisconsin Right to Life **3225**
Women Exploited **1035**
Women Exploited by Abortion **1036**
Library **6979**
World Federation of Doctors Who
Respect Human Life
Library **6989**
U.S. Section **1181**
Rio Grande Planned Parenthood **6281**
Rio Hondo College • Career and Equity
Services **6415**
Rio-Pecos Family Crisis Center **4651, 4677,**
4707
Ripon College • Women's Studies
Program **7765**

Shelley and His Circle Collection; Carl H. Pforzheimer • New York Public Library **6879**
The Shelter [Alpena, MI] **3883**
The Shelter [Charlotte, NC] **4326**
The Shelter [Columbia, MO] **4035**
The Shelter [Gadsden, AL] **3263**
The Shelter [Lawrenceburg, TN] **4638**
The Shelter [Mansfield, OH] **4426**
The Shelter [Omaha, NE] **4111**
Shelter for Abused Spouses and Children **3607**
The Shelter for Abused Women **4822**
Shelter for Abused Women and Children **3600**
Shelter for Abused Women of Collier County **3550**
Shelter Against Violent Environments **3368**
Shelter/Domestic Violence Resource Center **4488**
Shelter From Violence **4420**
Shelter for Help in Emergency **4776**
Shelter Home of Caldwell County **4344**
Shelter House **4019**
Shelter, Inc. • Displaced Homemaker Program **5466**
Shelter Our Sisters **4152**
Shelter Plus **3413**
Shelter Services for Women **3384, 3431, 3434**
Shelter from the Storm **4492**
Shelter for Victims of Domestic Violence **4172, 4174**
Shelter of Wayne County **4335**
Shelton State Community College • New Options Program **4998**
Shenandoah Women's Center **4883**
Shenandoah Women's Service Club **1915**
Sheridan College • Transitional Support Services for Single Parent/Displaced Homemakers **6185**
She's a Railroader **10598**
SheTotem **9621**
Shippenburg University of Pennsylvania • Women's Center **6645**
Shippensburg University of Pennsylvania • Women's Studies Program **7662**
Shoals Community College • Choices for Success **4989**
Shop Talk **9474**
Shore Up, Inc. • Project Renaissance **5437**
Shoreline Community College
    Women's Center **6696**
    Women's Program **7737**
    Women's Programs **6129**
Shores Women's Club **2227**
Short Fiction By Women **9065**
Shute Award; Gladys G. **7986**
Sibley Fellowship; Mary Isabel **7865**
SIDS see Infant Death
Siena College • Women and Minority Studies **7526**
Sierra College
    Single Parent/Displaced Homemaker Project **5088**
    Women's Studies Program **7157**
Sierra Madre Woman's Club **1449**
Sigma Alpha Iota Inter-American Music Awards **7894**
Sigma Delta Epsilon **894**
Sigma Delta Epsilon Fellowships **8099**
Sigma Delta Epsilon, Graduate Women in Science **894**
Sigma Delta Epsilon Honorary Member **8100**
Sigma Gamma Rho Sorority, Inc. **895**
Sigma Phi Gamma—Membership Directory **8795**

Signs: Journal of Women in Culture and Society **9066**
The Silent Scream **10599**
Silicone Breast Implants see Breast Implants
Silkwood Books **10215**
Silver Baton Award **8101**
Silver Chord **10133**
Silver Satellite Award **8102**
Silver Snail Award **8103**
Silverleaf Press, Inc. **9967**
Simmons College **7084**
    Archives **6927**
    Institute for Case Development and Research **8236**
    Women's Center **6497**
    Women's Studies Program **7345**
Simmons High School • Single Parent Displaced Homemaker Program **5532**
Simon's Rock of Bard College
    Women's Center **6506**
    Women's Studies Program **7360**
Simpson College • Women's Studies Program **7300**
Sing Heavenly Muse! **9067**
Single Mothers (see also Displaced Homemakers; Family Issues; Mothers; Parenting)
    And Baby Makes Two **10309**
    Arizona Women's Education and Employment **1229**
    Center for the Study of Social Policy **245**
    Committee for Single Adoptive Parents, Inc. **9711**
    Focus on Families: A Reference Handbook **8744**
    Miss Mom/Mister Mom **551**
    National Center on Women and Family Law, Inc. • Information Center **6863**
    Rashad Associates/Raw Ink Press **9938**
    The Single Parent **9068**
    The Single Parent Family **10600**
    Single Parenting: A New Page in America's Family Album **10601**
    Solo Parenting: Your Essential Guide **8797**
    Speak Out! **9482**
    Support **9078**
    39, Single and Pregnant **10624**
    Unmarried Parents Today **9502**
    Unwed Parents Anonymous **971**
    Welfare Mothers Voice **9626**
    Women on Their Own **1080**
Single Mothers By Choice **896**
The Single Parent **9068**
Single Parent/Displaced Homemakers Program [Tampa, FL] **5241**
The Single Parent Family **10600**
Single Parent/Homemakers Program [Bismarck, ND] **5749**
Single Parent/Homemakers Program of Southeastern Indiana **5338**
Single Parent Resource Center **897**
Single Parenting: A New Page in America's Family Album **10601**
Sinister Wisdom **9069**
Siphers Scholarship; Kathryn G. **7857**
SIROW Newsletter **9475**
Sis Enterprises **9968**
Siskiyou County Domestic Violence Program **3455**
SISTER-HELP **4597**
Sister United **4596**
SISTERCARE, Inc. **4591**
Sisterhood Bookstore **10087**
Sisterhood Is Global Institute **898**
SISTERS **9070**
Sisters and Brothers Bookstore **10200**

Sisters' Choice Press **9969**
Sisters of the Congregation of St. Agnes **298**
Sisters of St. Joseph of Carondelet • St. Paul Province • Archives **6928**
SisterSpirit **2798, 10104**
Sitkans Against Family Violence **3292**
Six College Conference Admissions Programs **297**
Six Rivers Planned Parenthood **6194**
Six Steps Down **10233**
630 News **9476**
Skagit Rape Relief and Battered Women's Services **4844**
Skagit Valley College • Women's Program **7734**
Skamania County Council on Domestic Violence and Sexual Assault **4865**
Skidmore College • Women's Studies Program **7553**
Skyline College • Women in Transition Program **6405**
Slippery Rock University of Pennsylvania • Women's Studies Program **7663**
Slovenian Women's Union **899**
Small Business Advocates of the Year **8104**
Small Businesses see Business and Management
Smedley's Bookshop **10206**
Smith Award; Georgina **7984**
Smith Collection; Sophia • Women's History Archive • Smith College **6929**
Smith College **7085**
    Project on Women and Social Change **8237**
    Sophia Smith Collection • Women's History Archive **6929**
    Women's Resource Center **6510**
    Women's Studies Program **7369**
Smith Fellowship; Alice E. **7792**
Smith House; Grace **4290**
The Smith Publishers **9970**
Smithsonian Institution • Museum of American History • Division of Political History • National Women's History Collection **7007**
Smoking, Drinking and Drugs During Pregnancy **10602**
Smooth Stone Press, Inc. **9971**
Snake Power: A Journal of Contemporary Female Shamanism **9071**
Snohomish County Center for Battered Women **4833**
Snow College • Turning Point **6045**
So Many Voices: A Look at Abortion in America **10603**
SOAP Newsletter **9477**
Sobering Thoughts **9478**
Social Justice **9072**
Social Problems **9073**
Social Science
    ACLS Grants for East European Studies—Dissertation Fellowships **7783**
    ACLS Grants for East European Studies—Fellowships for Advanced Graduate Training **7785**
    ACLS Grants for East European Studies—Fellowships for Postdoctoral Research **7786**
    ACLS Grants for Latin American Studies—
        Advanced Grants Competition **7789**
        Doctoral Research Fellowships **7788**
    American Anthropological Association • Association for Feminist Anthropology **31**
    AWIS Predoctoral Awards **7808**

Social Services (continued)

Young Women's Christian Association of the Harbor Area **1428**

Young Women's Christian Association of Haverhill **2097**

Young Women's Christian Association of Hawaii Island **1662**

Young Women's Christian Association of Hazleton **2841**

Young Women's Christian Association of Houston **3036**

Young Women's Christian Association of Huron **2955**

Young Women's Christian Association of Indianapolis **1848**

Young Women's Christian Association of Jamestown **2527**

Young Women's Christian Association of Janesville **3209**

Young Women's Christian Association of Jersey City **2416**

Young Women's Christian Association of Johnstown **2843**

Young Women's Christian Association of Kalamazoo **2195**

Young Women's Christian Association of Kankakee **1759**

Young Women's Christian Association of Kansas City **1948, 2314**

Young Women's Christian Association of Kauai County **1669**

Young Women's Christian Association of Kitsap County **3132**

Young Women's Christian Association of Kokomo **1852**

Young Women's Christian Association of La Crosse **3212**

Young Women's Christian Association of Lafayette **1854**

Young Women's Christian Association of Lake County **1810**

Young Women's Christian Association of Lakewood and Ocean County **2417**

Young Women's Christian Association of Lancaster **2845**

Young Women's Christian Association of Lea County **2481**

Young Women's Christian Association of Leavenworth **1953**

Young Women's Christian Association of Lewiston-Auburn **2033**

Young Women's Christian Association of Lewiston-Clarkston **1678**

Young Women's Christian Association of Licking County **2731**

Young Women's Christian Association of Lima **2723**

Young Women's Christian Association of Lincoln **2355**

Young Women's Christian Association of Lockport **2532**

Young Women's Christian Association of Long Beach **1311**

Young Women's Christian Association of Lorain **2724**

Young Women's Christian Association of Los Angeles **1323**

Young Women's Christian Association Los Angeles, South Valley Center **1324**

Young Women's Christian Association of Lowell **2104**

Young Women's Christian Association of Lubbock **3041**

Young Women's Christian Association of Madison **3218**

Young Women's Christian Association of Malden **2106**

Young Women's Christian Association of Manchester **2389**

Young Women's Christian Association of Mansfield **2725**

Young Women's Christian Association of Maricopa County **1228**

Young Women's Christian Association of Marion **1855**

Young Women's Christian Association of Marshalltown **1921**

Young Women's Christian Association of Massillon **2727**

Young Women's Christian Association of McKeesport **2850**

Young Women's Christian Association of McLean County **1692**

Young Women's Christian Association of Meadville **2851**

Young Women's Christian Association of Medina County **2728**

Young Women's Christian Association of Metropolitan Chicago **1732**

Young Women's Christian Association of Metropolitan Dallas **3016**

Young Women's Christian Association of Metropolitan Denver **1483**

Young Women's Christian Association of Metropolitan St. Louis **2327**

Young Women's Christian Association of Minot **2667**

Young Women's Christian Association of Missoula **2342**

Young Women's Christian Association of Mitchell **2957**

Young Women's Christian Association of Monroe **2018**

Young Women's Christian Association of Montclair-North Essex **2426**

Young Women's Christian Association of the Monterey Peninsula **1329**

Young Women's Christian Association of Mt. Desert Island **2026**

Young Women's Christian Association of Muncie **1859**

Young Women's Christian Association of Muscatine **1932**

Young Women's Christian Association of Nashua **2391**

Young Women's Christian Association of New Britain **1513**

Young Women's Christian Association of New Haven **1516**

Young Women's Christian Association of New London **1504**

Young Women's Christian Association of New Orleans **2020**

Young Women's Christian Association of Newburgh **2538**

Young Women's Christian Association of Newburyport **2112**

Young Women's Christian Association of North Orange County **1295**

Young Women's Christian Association of Northern Rhode Island **2925**

Young Women's Christian Association of Northwest Louisiana **2022**

Young Women's Christian Association of Oahu **1668**

Young Women's Christian Association of Oakland **1343**

Young Women's Christian Association of Ogden/Northern Utah **3070**

Young Women's Christian Association of Oil City **2857**

Young Women's Christian Association of Oklahoma City **2761**

Young Women's Christian Association of Olympia **3143**

Young Women's Christian Association of Omaha **2361**

Young Women's Christian Association of Oskaloosa **1933**

Young Women's Christian Association of Ottumwa **1935**

Young Women's Christian Association of Paris and Lamar County **3050**

Young Women's Christian Association of Passaic-Clifton **2435**

Young Women's Christian Association of Paterson **2436**

Young Women's Christian Association of Pekin **1776**

Young Women's Christian Association of Peoria **1779**

Young Women's Christian Association of Philadelphia **2872**

Young Women's Christian Association of Piqua **2733**

Young Women's Christian Association of Plainfield/North Plainfield **2439**

Young Women's Christian Association of Pocatello **1681**

Young Women's Christian Association of Pontiac-North Oakland **2223**

Young Women's Christian Association of Portland **2038, 2800**

Young Women's Christian Association of Pottstown **2884**

Young Women's Christian Association of Pottsville **2885**

Young Women's Christian Association of Pueblo **1492**

Young Women's Christian Association of Quincy **1789**

Young Women's Christian Association of Racine **3233**

Young Women's Christian Association of Redlands **1361**

Young Women's Christian Association of Reno-Sparks **2373**

Young Women's Christian Association of Richmond **1863**

Young Women's Christian Association of Ridgewood **2443**

Young Women's Christian Association of Riverside **1363**

Young Women's Christian Association of Rochester and Monroe County **2597**

Young Women's Christian Association of Rock Island **1796**

Young Women's Christian Association of Rockford **1799**

Young Women's Christian Association of Sacramento **1379**

Young Women's Christian Association of St. Clair County **1690**

Young Women's Christian Association of St. Joseph **2317**

Young Women's Christian Association of St. Joseph-Benton Harbor **2230**

Young Women's Christian Association of St. Joseph County **1866**

Young Women's Christian Association of Salem **2735, 2805**

Young Women's Christian Association of Salina **1962**

Young Women's Christian Association of Salt Lake City **3077**

Young Women's Christian Association of San Antonio **3055**

Young Women's Christian Association of San Bernardino **1380**

Young Women's Christian Association of San Diego County **1397**

Young Women's Christian Association of San Gabriel Valley **1463**

Young Women's Christian Association of Santa Clara Valley **1419**

Young Women's Christian Association of Bellingham **3131**

Young Women's Christian Association of Berkeley **1269**

Young Women's Christian Association of Bethlehem **2811**

Young Women's Christian Association of Billings **2329**

Young Women's Christian Association of Binghamton and Broome County **2488**

Young Women's Christian Association of Bisbee **1217**

Young Women's Christian Association of Black Hawk County **1940**

Young Women's Christian Association of Boise **1672**

Young Women's Christian Association of Boston **2083**

Young Women's Christian Association of Boulder County **1469**

Young Women's Christian Association of Bradford **2812**

Young Women's Christian Association of Brooklyn **2496**

Young Women's Christian Association of Bucks County **2856**

Young Women's Christian Association of Burlington **1882**

Young Women's Christian Association of Butler **2814**

Young Women's Christian Association of Cambridge **2089**

Young Women's Christian Association of Canton **1693, 2679**

Young Women's Christian Association of Carlisle **2816**

Young Women's Christian Association of Cedar Rapids and Linn County **1888**

Young Women's Christian Association, Central Branch **3020**

Young Women's Christian Association of Central Jersey **2433**

Young Women's Christian Association of Central Orange County **1345**

Young Women's Christian Association of Chemung County **2509**

Young Women's Christian Association of Chester **2820**

Young Women's Christian Association of Cincinnati **2684**

Young Women's Christian Association of the City of New York **2582**

Young Women's Christian Association of Cleveland **2690**

Young Women's Christian Association of Coatesville **2821**

Young Women's Christian Association of Cobb County, Marietta Center **1646**

Young Women's Christian Association of Columbus **2708**

Young Women's Christian Association of Contra Costa County **1362**

Young Women's Christian Association of Corpus Christi **3009**

Young Women's Christian Association of Cortland **2505**

Young Women's Christian Association of Coshocton **2709**

Young Women's Christian Association of Danville **1736**

Young Women's Christian Association of Darien-Norwalk **1499**

Young Women's Christian Association of Dayton **2716**

Young Women's Christian Association of Decatur **1737**

Young Women's Christian Association of Douglas **1219**

Young Women's Christian Association of Downtown Youngstown **2746**

Young Women's Christian Association of Dubuque **1913**

Young Women's Christian Association of Dutchess County **2592**

Young Women's Christian Association of Easton **2824**

Young Women's Christian Association of El Dorado **1246**

Young Women's Christian Association of Elgin **1740**

Young Women's Christian Association of Elkhart County **1820**

Young Women's Christian Association of Elyria **2718**

Young Women's Christian Association of Enid **2753**

Young Women's Christian Association of Erie **2827**

Young Women's Christian Association of Essex and West Hudson **2434**

Young Women's Christian Association of Evanston/North Shore **1742**

Young Women's Christian Association of Fargo-Moorhead **2660**

Young Women's Christian Association of Flint **2177**

Young Women's Christian Association of Fontana **1289**

Young Women's Christian Association of Ft. Smith **1249**

Young Women's Christian Association of Ft. Wayne **1827**

Young Women's Christian Association of Ft. Worth and Tarrant County **3027**

Young Women's Christian Association of Fresno **1293**

Young Women's Christian Association of Gardena Valley **1298**

Young Women's Christian Association of Gary **1834**

Young Women's Christian Association of Gateway Branch **1892**

Young Women's Christian Association of Genesee County **2484**

Young Women's Christian Association of Gettysburg **2829**

Young Women's Christian Association of Glendale **1300**

Young Women's Christian Association of Gloversville **2518**

Young Women's Christian Association of Grand Island **2349**

Young Women's Christian Association of Grand Rapids **2185**

Young Women's Christian Association of Great Falls **2335**

Young Women's Christian Association of Greater Bridgeport **1495**

Young Women's Christian Association of Greater Des Moines **1906**

Young Women's Christian Association of the Greater Harrisburg Area **2838**

Young Women's Christian Association of Greater Lansing **2208**

Young Women's Christian Association of Greater Lawrence **2099**

Young Women's Christian Association of Greater Little Rock **1255**

Young Women's Christian Association of Greater Pittsburgh **2883**

Young Women's Christian Association of Greater Pittsburgh, Carnagie Center **2818**

Young Women's Christian Association of Greater Pittsburgh, Wilkinsburg Center **2906**

Young Women's Christian Association of Greater Pomona Valley **1328**

Young Women's Christian Association of Greater Rhode Island **2919**

Young Women's Christian Association of Greater West Chester **2902**

Young Women's Christian Association of Green Bay-De Pere **3205**

Young Women's Christian Association of Greensburg **2831**

Young Women's Christian Association of Greenwich **1503**

Young Women's Christian Association of Hackensack **2412**

Young Women's Christian Association of Hanover **2834**

Young Women's Christian Association of the Harbor Area **1428**

Young Women's Christian Association of Haverhill **2097**

Young Women's Christian Association of Hawaii Island **1662**

Young Women's Christian Association of Hazleton **2841**

Young Women's Christian Association of Houston **3036**

Young Women's Christian Association of Huron **2955**

Young Women's Christian Association of Indianapolis **1848**

Young Women's Christian Association of Jamestown **2527**

Young Women's Christian Association of Janesville **3209**

Young Women's Christian Association of Jersey City **2416**

Young Women's Christian Association of Johnstown **2843**

Young Women's Christian Association of Kalamazoo **2195**

Young Women's Christian Association of Kankakee **1759**

Young Women's Christian Association of Kansas City **1948, 2314**

Young Women's Christian Association of Kauai County **1669**

Young Women's Christian Association of Kitsap County **3132**

Young Women's Christian Association of Kokomo **1852**

Young Women's Christian Association of La Crosse **3212**

Young Women's Christian Association of Lafayette **1854**

Young Women's Christian Association of Lake County **1810**

Young Women's Christian Association of Lakewood and Ocean County **2417**

Young Women's Christian Association of Lancaster **2845**

Young Women's Christian Association of Lea County **2481**

Young Women's Christian Association of Leavenworth **1953**

Young Women's Christian Association of Lewiston-Auburn **2033**

Young Women's Christian Association of Lewiston-Clarkston **1678**

Young Women's Christian Association of Licking County **2731**

Young Women's Christian Association of Lima **2723**

Young Women's Christian Association of Lincoln **2355**

Young Women's Christian Association of Lockport **2532**

Sports and Recreation (continued)

Young Women's Christian Association of Long Beach **1311**

Young Women's Christian Association of Lorain **2724**

Young Women's Christian Association of Los Angeles **1323**

Young Women's Christian Association Los Angeles, South Valley Center **1324**

Young Women's Christian Association of Lowell **2104**

Young Women's Christian Association of Lubbock **3041**

Young Women's Christian Association of Madison **3218**

Young Women's Christian Association of Malden **2106**

Young Women's Christian Association of Manchester **2389**

Young Women's Christian Association of Mansfield **2725**

Young Women's Christian Association of Maricopa County **1228**

Young Women's Christian Association of Marion **1855**

Young Women's Christian Association of Marshalltown **1921**

Young Women's Christian Association of Massillon **2727**

Young Women's Christian Association of McKeesport **2850**

Young Women's Christian Association of McLean County **1692**

Young Women's Christian Association of Meadville **2851**

Young Women's Christian Association of Medina County **2728**

Young Women's Christian Association of Metropolitan Chicago **1732**

Young Women's Christian Association of Metropolitan Dallas **3016**

Young Women's Christian Association of Metropolitan Denver **1483**

Young Women's Christian Association of Metropolitan St. Louis **2327**

Young Women's Christian Association of Minot **2667**

Young Women's Christian Association of Missoula **2342**

Young Women's Christian Association of Mitchell **2957**

Young Women's Christian Association of Monroe **2018**

Young Women's Christian Association of Montclair-North Essex **2426**

Young Women's Christian Association of the Monterey Peninsula **1329**

Young Women's Christian Association of Mt. Desert Island **2026**

Young Women's Christian Association of Muncie **1859**

Young Women's Christian Association of Muscatine **1932**

Young Women's Christian Association of Nashua **2391**

Young Women's Christian Association of New Britain **1513**

Young Women's Christian Association of New Haven **1516**

Young Women's Christian Association of New London **1504**

Young Women's Christian Association of New Orleans **2020**

Young Women's Christian Association of Newburgh **2538**

Young Women's Christian Association of Newburyport **2112**

Young Women's Christian Association of North Orange County **1295**

Young Women's Christian Association of Northern Rhode Island **2925**

Young Women's Christian Association of Northwest Louisiana **2022**

Young Women's Christian Association of Oahu **1668**

Young Women's Christian Association of Oakland **1343**

Young Women's Christian Association of Ogden/Northern Utah **3070**

Young Women's Christian Association of Oil City **2857**

Young Women's Christian Association of Oklahoma City **2761**

Young Women's Christian Association of Olympia **3143**

Young Women's Christian Association of Omaha **2361**

Young Women's Christian Association of Oskaloosa **1933**

Young Women's Christian Association of Ottumwa **1935**

Young Women's Christian Association of Paris and Lamar County **3050**

Young Women's Christian Association of Passaic-Clifton **2435**

Young Women's Christian Association of Paterson **2436**

Young Women's Christian Association of Pekin **1776**

Young Women's Christian Association of Peoria **1779**

Young Women's Christian Association of Philadelphia **2872**

Young Women's Christian Association of Piqua **2733**

Young Women's Christian Association of Plainfield/North Plainfield **2439**

Young Women's Christian Association of Pocatello **1681**

Young Women's Christian Association of Pontiac-North Oakland **2223**

Young Women's Christian Association of Portland **2038, 2800**

Young Women's Christian Association of Pottstown **2884**

Young Women's Christian Association of Pottsville **2885**

Young Women's Christian Association of Pueblo **1492**

Young Women's Christian Association of Quincy **1789**

Young Women's Christian Association of Racine **3233**

Young Women's Christian Association of Redlands **1361**

Young Women's Christian Association of Reno-Sparks **2373**

Young Women's Christian Association of Richmond **1863**

Young Women's Christian Association of Ridgewood **2443**

Young Women's Christian Association of Riverside **1363**

Young Women's Christian Association of Rochester and Monroe County **2597**

Young Women's Christian Association of Rock Island **1796**

Young Women's Christian Association of Rockford **1799**

Young Women's Christian Association of Sacramento **1379**

Young Women's Christian Association of St. Clair County **1690**

Young Women's Christian Association of St. Joseph **2317**

Young Women's Christian Association of St. Joseph-Benton Harbor **2230**

Young Women's Christian Association of St. Joseph County **1866**

Young Women's Christian Association of Salem **2735, 2805**

Young Women's Christian Association of Salina **1962**

Young Women's Christian Association of Salt Lake City **3077**

Young Women's Christian Association of San Antonio **3055**

Young Women's Christian Association of San Bernardino **1380**

Young Women's Christian Association of San Diego County **1397**

Young Women's Christian Association of San Gabriel Valley **1463**

Young Women's Christian Association of Santa Clara Valley **1419**

Young Women's Christian Association of Santa Cruz **1438**

Young Women's Christian Association of Santa Monica **1442**

Young Women's Christian Association of Schenectady **2602**

Young Women's Christian Association of Seattle-King County **3164**

Young Women's Christian Association of Shiawassee County **2220**

Young Women's Christian Association of Sioux Falls **2966**

Young Women's Christian Association of Sonoma County **1444**

Young Women's Christian Association of South Orange County **1432**

Young Women's Christian Association of Southern Alameda County **1302**

Young Women's Christian Association of Spokane **3168**

Young Women's Christian Association of Springfield **1805**

Young Women's Christian Association of Stateline Area **3201**

Young Women's Christian Association of Steubenville **2737**

Young Women's Christian Association of Summit **2448**

Young Women's Christian Association of Sussex County **2447**

Young Women's Christian Association of Sweetwater County **3253**

Young Women's Christian Association of Syracuse and Onondaga County **2609**

Young Women's Christian Association of Tacoma and Pierce County **3171**

Young Women's Christian Association of Terre Haute **1870**

Young Women's Christian Association of Texarkana **3058**

Young Women's Christian Association of Titusville **2893**

Young Women's Christian Association of Toledo **2740**

Young Women's Christian Association of the Tonawandas **2584**

Young Women's Christian Association of Topeka **1966**

Young Women's Christian Association of Torrance **1457**

Young Women's Christian Association of Trenton **2456**

Young Women's Christian Association of Troy-Cohoes **2610**

Young Women's Christian Association of Tucson **1243**

Young Women's Christian Association of Tulsa **2773**

Young Women's Christian Association of Ulster County **2529**

United Tribes Technical College • Displaced Homemakers Program **5750**
United Women's Societies of the Adoration of the Most Blessed Sacraments **757**
The Unity Group **3840**
Unity Home **3379**
Unity House • Families in Crisis **4309**
The University of Akron • Women's Studies Program **7579**
University of Alabama • Women's Studies Program **7104**
University of Alabama at Birmingham • Women's Studies Program **7103**
University of Alaska • Center for Women and Men **6368, 7105**
University of Alaska, Anchorage • Center for Women and Men **5001**
University of Arizona
    Associated Studies of the University of Arizona **6370**
    College of Agriculture • Project for Homemakers Seeking Employment **5023**
    Southwest Institute for Research on Women (SIROW) **8250**
    Women's Studies Program **7109**
University of Arkansas at Little Rock • Women's Studies Program **7110**
University of Baltimore • Women's Studies Program **7329**
University of California, Berkeley
    Beatrice M. Bain Research Group **8251**
    Women's Resource Center **6375**
    Women's Studies Department **7116**
University of California, Davis
    Women's Resources and Research Center **8252**
        Library **6947**
    Women's Studies Program **7126**
University of California, Irvine
    Women's Center **6384**
    Women's Studies Program **7134**
University of California, Los Angeles
    Center for the Study of Women **8253**
    Higher Education Research Institute **969**
    Women's Resource Center **6389**
    Women's Studies Program **7143**
University of California Press **9997**
University of California, Riverside
    Special Collections **6948**
    Women's Resource Center **6401**
    Women's Studies Program **7156**
University of California, San Diego
    Women's Resource Center **6385**
    Women's Studies Program **7136**
University of California, Santa Barbara
    Women's Center **6410**
    Women's Studies Program **7176**
University of California, Santa Cruz
    Dean E. McHenry Library **6949**
    Feminist Studies Focused Research Activity **970**
    Women's Center **6412**
    Women's Studies Program **7178**
University of Chicago Press **9998**
University of Cincinnati
    Center for Women's Studies Program **7583**
    Women's Programs and Services **6606**
    Women's Studies Research and Resources Institute **8254**
University City Police Department • Victim Services Unit **4065**
University of Colorado, Boulder
    Multicultural Center for Counseling and Community Development **6416**
    Western Historical Collections/University Archives **6950**

Women's Studies Program **7187**
University of Colorado, Colorado Springs • Women's Studies Program **7189**
University of Connecticut
    Institute for the Study of Women and Gender **8255**
    Women's Center **6433, 8256**
    Women's Studies Program **7204**
University of Dayton • Women's Studies Program **7589**
University of Delaware • Women's Studies Program **7209**
University of Denver • Women's Studies Program **7191**
University of Detroit • Women's Studies Program **7393**
University of Florida • Women's Studies Program **7218**
University of Georgia, Athens • Women's Studies Program **7229**
University of Georgia Press **9999**
University of Hartford • Women's Studies Program **7206**
University of Hawaii at Hilo
    Single Parent/Homemaker Program **5276**
    Women's Center **6448**
    Women's Studies Program **7240**
University of Hawaii at Manoa
    Women's Center **6449**
    Women's Studies Program **7243**
University of Houston, Clear Lake • Women's Studies Program **7701**
University of Idaho • Women's Center **3632**
University of Illinois at Chicago
    University Library • Midwest Women's Historical Collection **6951**
    Women's Studies Program **7256, 8257**
University of Illinois Press **10000**
University of Illinois at Urbana-Champaign
    Women in International Development **7248**
    Women in International Development Library **6952**
    Women's Studies Program **7275**
University of Illinois Young Women's Christian Association **1701**
University of Iowa
    Women's Research and Action Center **6469**
    Women's Studies Program **7301**
University of Kansas
    Women's Resource Center **6474**
    Women's Studies Program **7306**
University of Kentucky • Women's Studies Program **7313**
University of Louisville • Women's Studies Program **7314**
University of Lowell **6953**
    Women's Center **6507**
    Women's Studies Program **7363**
University of Maine
    Thomaston Center • Displaced Homemakers Program **5414**
    Women's Studies Program **7324**
University of Maine—Augusta, Stoddard House • Displaced Homemaker Program **5405**
University of Maine—Farmington • Look House Basement • Displaced Homemakers Program **5408**
University of Maryland, Baltimore County • Women's Studies Program **7330**
University of Maryland at College Park
    Women's Center **6486**
    Women's Studies Program **7331**
University of Massachusetts at Amherst
    Everywoman's Center **6493**
    Women's Studies Program **7340**

University of Massachusetts at Boston Harbor Campus
    Women's Center **6499**
    Women's Studies Program **7347**
University of Massachusetts at Dartmouth • Women's Studies Program **7368**
University of Massachusetts at Lowell • Center for Lowell History **6953**
University of Massachusetts Press **10001**
University of Michigan
    Center for Education of Women **6519, 8258**
        Library **6954**
    School of Public Health • Department of Population Planning and International Health • Reference Collection **6955**
    Women's Studies Program **7388**
University of Michigan, Dearborn • Women's Studies Program **7392**
University of Michigan, Flint
    Re-Entry Program **6524**
    Women's Studies Program **7397**
University of Michigan Press **10002**
University of Minnesota
    Center for Advanced Feminist Studies **8259**
    Department of Obstetrics and Gynecology • Litzenberg-Lund Library **6956**
    Social Welfare History Archives **6957**
    Women, Public Policy, and Development Project **8260**
University of Minnesota, Duluth
    Center for Research, Women's Studies Program **8261**
    Women's Resource and Action Center **6528**
    Women's Studies Program **7412**
University of Minnesota, Morris • Women's Studies Program **7418**
University of Minnesota Press **10003**
University of Minnesota, Twin Cities
    Women's Center **6531**
    Women's Studies Program **7416**
University of Mississippi
    Sarah Isom Center for Women's Studies **8262**
    Women's Studies Program **7431**
University of Missouri, Columbia
    Women's Center **6542**
    Women's Studies Program **7435**
University of Missouri, Kansas City
    Women's Center **6543**
    Women's Studies Program **7438**
University of Missouri, St. Louis
    Women's Center **6545, 6958**
    Women's Studies Program **7441**
University of Montana
    Women's Center **6550**
    Women's Studies Program **7447**
University of Nebraska, Lincoln
    Women's Resource Center **6552**
    Women's Studies Program **7450**
University of Nebraska Press **10004**
University of Nevada, Las Vegas • Women's Studies Program **7451**
University of Nevada—Reno
    Special Collections Department/University Archives **6959**
    Women's Center **6553**
    Women's Studies Program **7452**
University of New England • Women's Studies Program **7321**
University of New Hampshire • Women's Studies Program **7453**
University of New Mexico
    Women's Center **6565**
    Women's Studies Program **7486**

University of New Mexico—Gallup • Sex Equity Program **5664**
University of New Mexico—Los Alamos • Single Parent/Low Income Homemakers Internship Program **5665**
University of New Orleans
Women's Center **6481**
Women's Studies Program **7319**
University of North Carolina • Southeastern Women's Studies **7563**
University of North Carolina, Chapel Hill
Carolina Population Center **10005**
Women's Studies Program **7565**
University of North Carolina at Charlotte • Women's Studies Program **7567**
University of North Carolina at Greensboro
Woman's Collection **6960**
Woman's Detective Fiction Collection **6961**
Women's Studies Program **7572**
University of North Carolina at Wilmington • Women's Studies Program **7574**
University of North Dakota
Devils Lake Regional Area Learning Center • Displaced Homemakers Program **5753**
Elwyn B. Robinson Department of Special Collections **6962**
Women's Center **6604**
Women's Studies Program **7578**
University of North Florida
Women's Center **6442**
Women's Studies Program **7219**
University of Northern Colorado • Women's Studies Program **7194**
University of Northern Iowa • Women's Studies Program **7295**
University of Notre Dame • Gender Studies **7287**
University of Oklahoma • Women's Studies Program **7610**
University of Oregon
Center for the Study of Women in Society **8263**
Knight Library • Special Collections Department **6963**
Women's Center **6624**
Women's Studies Program **7616**
University of Pennsylvania
Alice Paul Research Center for the Study of Women **8264**
Women's Center **6642**
Women's Studies Program **7655**
University of Pittsburgh • Women's Studies Program **7659**
University of Portland • Women's Studies Program **7626**
University of Puget Sound • Women's Studies Program **7742**
University of Redlands
Women's Center **6400**
Women's Studies Program **7154**
University of Rhode Island
Women's Center **6649**
Women's Studies Program **7670**
University of Richmond
Women's Resource Center **6685**
Women's Studies Program **7726**
University of Rochester
Government Documents and Microtext Center **6964**
Susan B. Anthony Center for Women's Studies Program **7551**
University of San Diego • Women's Studies Program **7166**
University of Scranton • Women's Studies Program **7661**
University of South Carolina
Women's Student Services **6653**

Women's Studies Program **7678**
University of South Dakota • Women's Studies Program **7681**
University of South Florida
Everywoman's Center **6447**
Women's Studies Program **7226**
University of Southern California
Institute for the Study of Women and Men **8265**
Study of Women/Men in Society **7144**
Women's Issues Advocate Office **6390**
University of Southern Colorado
Women's Center **6420**
Women's Studies Program **7195**
University of Southern Maine
Women's Forum **6484**
Women's Studies Program **7325**
University of Tampa • Women's Studies Program **7227**
University of Tennessee at Chattanooga • Life Planning Services for Displaced Homemakers **5948**
University of Tennessee, Knoxville
Women's Center **6654**
Women's Studies Program **7683**
University of Tennessee, Memphis • Women's Studies Program **7686**
University of Texas at Arlington
Center for Women's Studies Program **7691**
Women and Minorities Research and Resource Center **6657**
Women and Minority Work Research and Resource Center **8266**
University of Texas at Austin • Women's Studies Program **7693**
University of Texas at Dallas • Women's Studies Program **7704**
University of Texas at El Paso
Women's Center **6662**
Women's Studies Program **7698**
University of Toledo
Catharine S. Eberly Center for Women • Project Succeed **5796**
Center for Women **6616**
Ward M. Canaday Center **6965**
Women's Studies Program **7605**
University of Tulsa
Center for Study of Women's Literature **7612**
Research in Women's Literature **8267**
University of Utah
Women's Resource Center **6671**
Women's Studies Program **7710**
University of Vermont • Women's Studies Program **7714**
University of Virginia
Women's Center **6677**
Women's Studies Program **7721**
University of Washington
Northwest Center for Research on Women **8268**
Women's Information Center **6697**
Women's Studies Program **7738**
University of West Florida • Women's Studies Program **7222**
University of Wisconsin • Women's Studies Librarian **10006**
University of Wisconsin—Eau Claire
The Women Studies Bibliographic Center **8269**
Women's Center **6706**
Women's Studies Program **7752**
University of Wisconsin—Green Bay
Women's Center **6707**
Library **6966**
Women's Studies Program **7753**
University of Wisconsin—La Crosse
Women's Center **6709**
Women's Studies Program **7755**

University of Wisconsin—Madison
Memorial Library • Department of Special Collections **6967**
Women's Center **6711**
Women's Studies Program **7759**
Women's Studies Research Center **8270**
University of Wisconsin—Milwaukee • Center for Women's Studies **7762, 8271**
University of Wisconsin—Oshkosh
M.F. Berry Women's Resource Center Board **6715**
Women's Studies Program **7763**
University of Wisconsin—Parkside
Women's Center **6708**
Women's Studies Program **7754**
University of Wisconsin—Platteville
Women's Center **6717**
Women's Studies Program **7764**
University of Wisconsin—River Falls
Women's Center **6718**
Women's Studies Program **7766**
University of Wisconsin—Stevens Point
Women's Resource Center **6719**
Women's Studies Program **7768**
University of Wisconsin—Stout • Women's Studies Program **7760**
University of Wisconsin—Superior
Women's Resource Center **6720**
Women's Studies Program **7769**
University of Wisconsin—Whitewater • Women's Studies Program **7771**
University of Wyoming
Women's Center **6721**
Women's Studies Program **7773**
Unmarried Parents Today **9502**
Unsung Heroine Award **8121**
The Untamed Shrew Books **10293**
Unwed Parents Anonymous **971**
Up Against the Wall, Mother **9093**
Update **9503**
Upper Cumberland Alliance Against Domestic Violence **4630**
Upper Hudson Planned Parenthood **6283**
Upper Midwest Women's History Center **972**
Upper Midwest Women's History Center for Teachers **2281**
Upper Valley Joint Vocational School • Discovering Hope **5789**
Upson Technical Institute • New Connections **5271**
Upstate New York Women's History Organization **2525**
Uptown Center Hull House • Woman Abuse Action Project **3666**
Upward Mobility Award **8122**
Urban Institute • Program of Policy Research on Women and Families **973**
Urban League [Seattle, WA] • Displaced Homemaker Program **6131**
Urban Resource Institute • Urban Women's Retreat **4268**
Urban Women's Center **5624**
Urban Women's Retreat **4237**
Ursinus College • Women's Studies Program **7637**
Ursuline College **7093**
USO Woman of the Year **8123**
USRowing Athlete of the Year (Female) **8124**
USRowing Woman of the Year **8125**
USTA/ITHOF Tennis Educational Merit Award for Women **8126**
USWCA Senior Ladies Trophy **8127**
Utah Abortion Rights Action League **3074**
Utah Association of Women **3075**
Utah Basin Applied Technology Center • Turning Point **6050**

Washtenaw Community College
Adult Resource Center **6520**
Single Parent/Homemaker
Program **5468**
Women's Studies Program **7389**
Washtenaw County Community Mental
Health Center • Assault Crisis
Center **3936**
Washtenaw County Women's Action for
Nuclear Disarmament **2142**
WASP News **9510**
*Water Baby: Experiences of Water
Birth* **10649**
Waterbury Job Training Agency • Displaced
Homemakers Program **5168**
WATERwheel **9511**
Waterwomen Books **10012**
Watkins Glen Business and Professional
Women's Club **2536**
Watkins Memorial Library; Jessie Beach •
Seneca Falls Historical Society **6925**
Waubonsee Community College • Building
Opportunity Project **5291**
Waubonsie Mental Health Center **3739**
Waukesha County Technical College
Cooperative Employment Services for
Displaced Homemakers **6169**
Women's Development Center **6716**
Wauwatosa Event **8132**
Wava Turner Award **8133**
WAVES National **983**
Waves National Corporation **983**
Wayne Community College • Second
Wind **6600**
Wayne County Community College
Displaced Homemaker Program **5475**
Women's Studies Program **7394**
Wayne State University
Women's Resource Center **6522**
Women's Studies Program **7395**
WBA Newsletter **9512**
WCA Honors **8134**
WCC Newsletter **9513**
We Dig Coal **10650**
Weakley County Board of Education • Single
Parents Success Program **5952**
Weatherford College • Single
Parent/Displaced Homemaker
Program **6041**
Webb House Museum **7009**
The Webb Report **9514**
Weber State College • Women in Higher
Education **7708**
Webster University
Women's Resource Center **6547**
Women's Studies Advisory
Committee **7443**
Wedge Women's Economic Development
Group Enterprises **1905**
*Weight, Nutrition and Exercise During
Pregnancy* **10651**
WEJC Update **9515**
Welfare (see also Social Services)
Gaffigan; Catherine **8658**
Welfare Mothers Voice **9626**
Welfare Mothers Voice **9626**
Wellesley College **7094**
Archives **6974**
Center for Research on Women **8276,
10013**
Women's Studies Program **7376**
Wells College **7095**
Women's Resource Center **6568**
Women's Studies Program **7493**
WelWoman's Books **10198**
Wenatchee Rape Crisis and Domestic
Violence Center **4872**
Wenatchee Valley College • Community
Services **6142**

Wentworth Institute of Technology •
Women's Task Force **6500**
We're Here Now **10652**
Werth; Karen B. **8674**
Wesley Shelter **4373**
Wesleyan College **7096**
Wesleyan University
Women's Resource Center **6428**
Women's Studies Program **7199**
West Central Community Action [Elbow
Lake, MN] • Pathfinders **5509**
West Central Domestic Abuse Project **4915**
West Chester University of Pennsylvania
Women's Center **6647**
Women's Studies Program **7667**
West End Press **10014**
West Georgia Technical Institute • New
Connections **5259**
West Haven Junior Women's Club **1527**
West Haven Laurel Woman's Club **1528**
West Los Angeles College
Center for New Options **6382**
Single Parent/Displaced Homemaker
Project **5048**
West Pine Publishing Co. **10015**
West Shore Community College • Single
Parent/Homemaker Program **5500**
West Valley College
Single Parent/Displaced Homemaker
Project **5106**
Women's Studies Program **7179**
West Virginia Abortion Rights Action
League **3185**
West Virginia Branch of National Abortion
Rights Action League **3194**
West Virginia Coalition Against Domestic
Violence **3196**
West Virginia Department of Health and
Human Resources
Family Violence Prevention and
Services **8620**
Public Health Bureau • Office of
Community Health Services • Division
of Maternal and Child Health **8621**
West Virginia Institute of Technology
Community and Technical College •
Options for Adult Women **6155**
West Virginia Library Commission • Film
Services Department **6975**
West Virginia Northern Community College •
Wider Opportunities for Women **6157**
West Virginia University • Women's Studies
Program **7748**
West Virginia Women's Commission **8622**
Westark Community College • CHOICES:
Career Development Center **5031**
Westchester Association of Women
Business-Owners **2537**
Westchester Community College • Project
Transition-AAB 302 **5728**
Westchester Office for Women • Displaced
Homemaker Program **5729**
Western Association of Women
Historians **1268**
Western Colorado Employment and Training
• Single Parent/Displaced Homemaker
Program **5127**
Western Colorado Employment and Training
Service • Displaced Homemaker
Program **5134**
Western Connecticut State University •
Women's Studies Program **7196**
Western Dakota Vocational Technical
Institute • Displaced Homemakers
Programs **5937**
Western Evangelical Seminary • Women's
Studies Program **7628**
Western Historical Collections/University
Archives • University of Colorado—
Boulder **6950**

Western Historical Manuscript
Collection **6976**
National Women and Media
Collection **6874**
Western Illinois University
Women's Center **6456**
Women's Studies Program **7266**
Western Maryland College • Women's
Studies Program **7336**
Western Michigan University
Women's Center • Library **6977**
Women's Studies Program **7401**
Western Nebraska Community College
Displaced Homemakers and Single
Parent Program **5600**
Vocational Education for
Homemakers **5601**
Western Nevada Community College • Single
Parent/Displaced Homemaker
Program **5602**
Western New Mexico University • Pathways
to Success **5668**
Western Political Science Association
Awards **8135**
Western Reserve Girl Scout Council **2671**
Western Tidewater Mental Health Center •
Domestic Violence Services **4815**
Western University • Fairhaven College •
Chrysalis Art Gallery **7010**
Western Vocational Technical School •
Displaced Homemaker Program **5806**
Western Washington University
Women's Center **6688**
Women's Studies **7729**
Western Wisconsin Technical College
Displaced Homemaker Program **6164**
The Opportunity Center **6710**
Western Wyoming College • Women's
Center **6183**
Western Wyoming Community College •
Women's Center **6722**
Western York Business and Professional
Women's Club **2950**
Westfield State College • Women's Studies
Program **7377**
Westhampton College **7097**
Westinghouse Bertha Lamme
Scholarship **7902**
Weston Woman's Club **1661**
Westside Women's Club **2526**
Westview Press **10016**
Westwood Woman's Club **2460**
WFS Program in Levels of Recovery **10653**
Wharton County Junior College • Single
Parent/Displaced Homemaker
Program **6042**
*What to Do about Personnel Problems—
National News Update* **9516**
What Does She Want? **10654**
What People Are Calling PMS **10655**
What She Wants **9517**
*What You Don't Know CAN Kill You:
Sexually Transmitted Diseases and
AIDS* **10656**
What You Take for Granted **10657**
Whatcom Community College • Women's
Programs **6110**
Whatcom County Crisis Services • Domestic
Violence Program **4826**
Wheatland Career Center • Displaced
Homemakers Program **6188**
Wheaton College • Women's Studies
Program **7370**
When the Honeymoon is Over **10658**
When Mom has to Work **10659**
When Sex Means Trouble **10660**
When Teens Get Pregnant **10661**
When a Woman Fights Back **10662**
Whirly-Girls (International Women Helicopter
Pilots) **984**

Whisper **985**
W.H.I.S.P.E.R. **4007**
WHISPER Newsletter **9518**
White Bear Lake Business & Professional Women's Club **2293**
White Buffalo Calf Woman Society Shelter **4613**
White Caps **9519**
White Mountain Apache Committee for Family Peace • White Mountain Indian Hospital **3330**
White Mountain Indian Hospital • White Mountain Apache Committee for Family Peace **3330**
White Mountain SAFE House **3323**
White Rabbit Books **10228**
White Rabbit Books (Raleigh) **10229**
Whiteville State Area Vocational-Technical School • Displaced Homemaker/Single Parent Program **5981**
Whitman College
    Women's Resource Center **6701**
    Women's Studies Program **7744**
Whitney M. Young, Jr. Memorial Library of Social Work • Columbia University **6777**
Who Remembers Mama? **10663**
Whole Arts Directory **8806**
Wholeness Center **4604**
Who's There for the Victim? **10664**
Who's Who in Professional and Executive Women **8807**
Why Women Stay **10665**
WIC News **9520**
WIC Program; Special Supplemental Food Program for Women, Infants, an d Children • U.S. Department of Agriculture • Food and Nutrition Service • Supplemental Food Programs Division **8300**, **8417**
Wichita National Organization for Women **1970**
Wichita State University
    Center for Women's Studies Program **6476**, **7310**
    Research Group on Women and Work **8277**
Wichita WOMEN **9106**
Wichita YWCA • Employment and Resource Network **5385**
Wider Community Assistance Program **4008**
Wider Opportunities for Women **986**, **5182**, **10017**
Widowed Information and Consultation Services **6132**
Widows (see also Displaced Homemakers)
    Directory of Services for the Widowed in the United States and Canada **8727**
    Forty Upward Network **381**
    Gold Star Wives of America **405**
    Gold Star Wives of America—Newsletter **9313**
    International Association of Ministers Wives and Ministers Widows **445**
    National Association of Military Widows **603**
    National Displaced Homemakers Network—Network News **9399**
    New Encounters **1884**
    Radcliffe College • Henry A. Murray Research Center **6912**
    Society of Military Widows **905**
    Widows Support Group of New London **1519**
    Widows of World War I **987**
    Women on Their Own **1080**
Widows Support Group of New London **1519**
Widows of World War I **987**
WIF News Magazine **9107**
WIFE Line **9627**

WIIS Words **9521**
Wild Iris Bookstore **10071**
Wild Iris Women's Services **3353**, **3391**
Wild Seeds Bookstore and Cafe **10216**
Wild Violet Publishing **10018**
Wilderness Women **9522**
Wildfire Books **10019**
Wildwood Resources, Inc. **10020**
Wilkes University • Women's Studies Program **7668**
Wilkinson County Vocational Center • Single Parent/Displaced Homemaker Program **5551**
WILLA Newsletter **9523**
Willamette University • Women's Center **6631**
Willard Memorial Library; Frances E. • National Woman's Christian Temperance Union **6873**
William Joiner Center for the Study of War and Social Consequences—Connection **9524**
William and Mousie Powell Award **8136**
William Paterson College of New Jersey • Women's Studies Program **7484**
William Rainey Harper College • Women's Programs **7269**
William Smith College **7098**
    Women's Studies Program **7518**
William Woods College **7099**
Williams College
    Feminist Alliance **6515**
    Women's Studies Program **7379**
Williams, Sr. Health Sciences Library; John R. • Highland Hospital **6802**
Williamsburg Technical College • Single Parents/Displaced Homemakers Program **5922**
Williamson County Crisis Center **4722**
Williston Chapter Right to Life **2669**
Willmar Community College
    Non-Traditional Student Center **6540**
    Women's Studies Program **7428**
Willowood Press **10021**
Wilshire Club **988**
Wilson College **7100**
    Directions Unlimited **5860**
    Women's Studies Program **7636**
Wilson Women's Studies Research Grant; Woodrow **7908**
W.I.M. Publications **10022**
Wimmer Scholarship; Harriett Barnhardt **7837**
WIN News **9108**
Wind River Publications Inc. **10023**
W.I.N.D.O.W. **4013**
Windows on Women **10666**
Windsor Republican Women's Club **1530**
Windward Community College
    Single Parent/Homemaker Program **5281**
    Women's Studies Program **7244**
Wingbow Press **10024**
Wings [St. Cloud, MN] • Tri-County Action Program Inc. **5515**
Winner Area Crisis-Line **4625**
Winning Women **2210**
Winthrop College • Women's Studies Program **7679**
Wippman Scientific Research Award; Arthur and Edith **7928**
Wisconsin Abortion Rights Action League **3224**
Wisconsin Association of Women Highway Safety Leaders **3207**
Wisconsin Business Women's Coalition **3200**
Wisconsin Coalition Against Domestic Violence **3217**

Wisconsin Department of Health and Social Services
    Bureau for Children, Youth and Families • Family Violence Prevention and Services **8623**
    Child Support Bureau **8624**
    Division of Health • Bureau of Community Health and Prevention **8625**
Wisconsin Indianhead Technical College • New Perspectives **6173**
Wisconsin Industry Labor and Human Relations Department • Equal Rights Division **8626**
Wisconsin Right to Life **3225**
Wisconsin Sportwomen's Club **3241**
Wisconsin Woman **9109**
Wisconsin Women's Council **8627**
Wisconsin Women's Law Journal **9110**
Wisconsin Women's Political Caucus **3208**
WISE Award for Engineering Achievement **8137**
WISE Award for Scientific Achievement **8138**
WISE Lifetime Achievement Award **8139**
Wise Loan; E.K. **7823**
Wise Options for Women **4537**, **4579**
The Wise Woman **9111**
WISENET **10738**
WISER, Inc. **4034**
WISH List **1771**
WISH (Women in Self Help) [Brooklyn, NY] **5683**
Wishing Well **989**
Wishing Well Magazine **9112**
WISP Newsletter **9525**
WIT **9526**
With Babies and Banners **10667**
With a Vengeance: The Fight for Reproductive Freedom **10668**
Without Consent **10669**
Witness/Victim Service Center • Family Violence Program of Cuyahoga County **4410**
Wittenberg University
    Women's Studies Progam **7603**
    Womyn's Center **6615**
Wives-SelfHelp Foundation **990**
WLDF News **9527**
WLDF Newsletter 9527
WLUC News **9528**
WLW Journal **9113**
WMA National Service Award **8140**
WMA 'Nouncements **9529**
WMST-L **10739**
WOHRC News **9530**
Wolfe Art Club Annual Open Exhibition; Catherine Lorillard **7945**
Woman **9114**
Woman of Achievement Award **8141**
The Woman Activist **991**, **9115**
The Woman Activist Fund **992**, **10025**
Woman Bowler **9116**
Woman Care of Washington **2058**
Woman Centered [Montpelier, VT] **6067**
The Woman Conductor **9117**
The Woman CPA **9118**
Woman Engineer **9119**
Woman Entrepreneur **9120**
Woman Entrepreneur: Do You Have What it Takes? **10670**
Woman House **3999**
Woman Lawyer of the Year **8142**
Woman in the Moon Publications **10022**
Woman Officer of the Year **8143**
Woman of Power **9121**
The Woman Rebel **10671**
Woman Scope 9371
Woman Shelter **4435**
Woman-to-Woman Press **10026**

Woman, Water and Sanitation **10740**
Womancare/Aegis Association **2030, 3820**
Womancrafts West **10103**
Womandynamics **8683**
Woman$ense **9531**
Womanews **9628**
Womanhaven [El Centro, CA] **3363**
Womanhood Media **8684**
Womankind **3823**
    Support Services for Battered
       Women **3987**
    Support Systems for Battered
       Women **3946**
Womankind Books **10214**
WomanKraft **993**
WomanReach, Inc. **5734**
Woman's Art Journal **9122**
A Woman's Choices of Columbus
    County **2650**
Woman's Civic Club of Garden Grove **1297**
Woman's Civic League of Pasadena **1356**
Woman's Club of Arcadia **1259**
Woman's Club of Cheyenne **3248**
Woman's Club of Falls Church **3104**
Woman's Club of Hilton Village **3110**
Woman's Club of Kenosha **3211**
Woman's Club of New Britain **1511**
Woman's Club of Penns Grove and Carneys
    Point **2438**
Woman's Club of Plymouth **2222**
Woman's Club of Reading **2887**
Woman's Club of Ridgewood **2442**
Woman's Club of Upper Montclair **2458**
Woman's Club of Warren **2895**
Woman's Counseling Service **8685**
Woman's Day **9123**
Woman's Day Crosswords **9124**
Woman's Education and Leadership
    Forum **994**
Woman's Enterprise **9125**
Woman's Exchange of Memphis **2980**
A Woman's Fund • A Woman's Place **3699**
Woman's Home and Foreign Mission
    Society **995**
*The Woman's "How To" of Self-
    Defense* **10672**
Woman's Institute for Continuing Jewish
    Education **10027**
Woman's Missionary Union **996**
Woman's National Auxiliary Convention of
    Free Will Baptists **997**
Woman's National Democratic Club **998**
Woman's National Farm and Garden
    Association **999**
*Woman's National Farm & Garden
    Magazine* **9126**
Woman's Organization of the National
    Association of Retail Druggists **1000**
A Woman's Place **3392, 3485, 4521,
    10673**
    Montgomery County Government
       Commission for Women **2063**
A Woman's Place Bookstore **10247, 10279**
A Woman's Prerogative **10173**
The Woman's Pulpit **9127**
Woman's Touch **9128**
Woman's View Bookstore **10244**
Woman's Weal **9129**
Woman's Workshop **1001**
Woman's World **9130**
A Woman's Yellow Book **8808**
Woman's Yellow Pages **8808**
Womanshare Books **10028**
Womanshelter/Companeras **3861**
Womanspace, Inc. **4168**
    Outreach Office **4155**
Womansplace **3852, 4542**
Womanstuff **10281**
Womanvision Books, Inc. **10257**
Women, Inc. **1048**

Women Accepted for Volunteer Emergency
    Service **983**
Women Achieving Greater Economic
    Status **1003**
Women in Advertising and Marketing **1004**
Women in Aerospace **1005**
Women Against Abuse **4552**
Women Against Domestic Violence **3626**
Women Against Military Madness **1006**
Women Against Pornography **1007**
Women Against Rape **1008**
Women Against Violence [Rapid City,
    SD] **4617**
Women in Agribusiness **1009**
Women and AIDS Resource Network **2573**
Women and AIDS: A Survival Kit **10674**
Women Airforce Service Pilots WWII **1010**
Women of All Red Nations **317**
Women in America **10675**
Women and the American Family **10676**
*Women in American Life—Video
    Series* **10677**
Women Artists News **9532**
Women Artists News/Midmarch Arts •
    Archives **6978**
Women Artists Newsletter **9532**
Women in the Arts **1011, 9533**
Women in the Arts Bulletin **9534**
Women in the Arts Crown Award **8144**
Women in the Arts Foundation **1012,
    10029**
Women Aware **4157**
    Outreach Office **4158**
Women Band Directors National
    Association **1013**
Women Band Directors National Association
    Achievement Award **8145**
Women Band Directors National Association
    Citation of Merit Award **8146**
Women Band Directors National Association,
    Mississippi Chapter **2294**
Women Band Directors National Association
    Performing Artists Award **8147**
Women Band Directors National Association
    Scroll of Excellence **8148**
Women in Broadcast Technology **1014**
*Women in Broadcast Technology—
    Directory* **8809**
Women in Business **3066, 9131, 10678**
Women in Business of the New London
    Area **2392**
Women Business Owners of New York
    Corporate Awards **8149**
Women Business Owners of New York Up
    and Coming Award **8150**
Women in Business, Pocono Mountains
    Chamber of Commerce **2892**
*Women in Business: The Risks, Rewards &
    Secrets of Running Your Own
    Company* **10679**
Women in Cable **1015**
Women in Cable, Michigan Chapter **2739**
Women in Cable, Wisconsin Chapter **3206**
Women in Cell Biology **1016**
Women Certified Public Accountants of
    Seattle **3160**
Women and Children in Crisis **4454, 4745**
Women and Children First **10146**
Women in the Church Coalition **1017**
Women Church Convergence **1017**
Women of the Church of God **1018**
Women of Color Newsletter **9535**
Women of Color Partnership Program **1019**
*Women of Color and Southern Women: A
    Bibliography* **8810**
Women in Communications, Inc. **1020**
*Women in Communications, Inc.—National
    Membership and Resource Directory* **8811**
Women in Community Service **1021, 1410**

Women in Community Service, Region
    III **2868**
Women of Conscience Award **8151**
Women in Constant Creative Action **9536**
Women Counseling and Career Center
    [Rockville, MD] **5436**
Women & Criminal Justice **9132**
Women in Crisis **1022, 3458**
Women in Crisis Coalition **2968**
Women in Crisis Counseling and
    Assistance **3280**
Women in Data Processing **1023**
Women on Death Row Project • National
    Coalition to Abolish the Death
    Penalty **1024**
Women in Development Award **8152**
*Women Directors of the Top Corporate
    1,000* **8812**
Women and Disability Awareness
    Project **341**
Women in Distress of Broward
    County **3537**
Women, Drugs and Alcohol **10680**
*Women, Drugs and the Unborn
    Child* **10681**
Women Educators **1025**
Women of the ELC Scholarship **7903**
Women Employed **1026**
Women Employed Institute **1027, 5306,
    8278**
Women and Employment **1028, 6148**
Women in Endocrinology **1029**
Women in Energy **1030**
Women of Enterprise Awards **8153**
Women Entrepreneurs **1031**
Women Escaping a Violent
    Environment **3412**
Women of the Evangelical Lutheran Church
    in America **1851**
Women Executives International Tourism
    Association **1032**
Women Executives in Public Relations **1033**
*Women Executives in Public Relations—
    Network* **9537**
Women Executives in State
    Government **1034**
Women Exploited **1035**
Women Exploited by Abortion **1036**
    Library **6979**
Women Exploited by Abortion, Wisconsin
    Chapter **3199**
Women and Family **10682**
Women and Fellowships **8813**
Women in Film **1037**
Women in Film International Award **8154**
Women in Fire Service **1038**
Women in Fire Suppression **1038**
Women For: **1271**
Women and Foundations/Corporate
    Philanthropy **1039**
Women in French **1040**
Women in French Newsletter **9538**
*Women and Gender Research Institute
    Newsletter* **9539**
Women in Government **1041**
Women in Government Relations **1042**
Women in Government Relations
    Distinguished Member Award **8155**
Women in Government Relations LEADER
    Foundation **1043**
Women in Government Relations Leader
    Fund **1043**
Women Grocers of America **1044**
Women for Guatemala **1045**
*Women: The Hand That Cradles the
    Rock* **10683**
Women & Health **9133**
Women and Health Roundtable **1046**
Women Helping Battered Women **4755**
Women Helping Women **3612, 4249**

Young Women's Christian Association of
Boise **1672**

Young Women's Christian Association of
Boston **2083**

Young Women's Christian Association of
Boulder County **1469**

Young Women's Christian Association of
Bradford **2812**

Young Women's Christian Association of
Brooklyn **2496**

Young Women's Christian Association of
Bucks County **2856**

Young Women's Christian Association of
Burlington **1882**

Young Women's Christian Association of
Butler **2814**

Young Women's Christian Association of
Cambridge **2089**

Young Women's Christian Association of
Canton **1693, 2679**

Young Women's Christian Association of
Carlisle **2816**

Young Women's Christian Association of
Cedar Rapids and Linn County **1888**

Young Women's Christian Association,
Central Branch **3020**

Young Women's Christian Association of
Central Jersey **2433**

Young Women's Christian Association of
Central Orange County **1345**

Young Women's Christian Association of
Chemung County **2509**

Young Women's Christian Association of
Chester **2820**

Young Women's Christian Association of
Cincinnati **2684**

Young Women's Christian Association of the
City of New York **2582**

Young Women's Christian Association of
Cleveland **2690**

Young Women's Christian Association of
Coatesville **2821**

Young Women's Christian Association of
Cobb County, Marietta Center **1646**

Young Women's Christian Association of
Columbus **2708**

Young Women's Christian Association of
Contra Costa County **1362**

Young Women's Christian Association of
Corpus Christi **3009**

Young Women's Christian Association of
Cortland **2505**

Young Women's Christian Association of
Coshocton **2709**

Young Women's Christian Association of
Danville **1736**

Young Women's Christian Association of
Darien-Norwalk **1499**

Young Women's Christian Association of
Dayton **2716**

Young Women's Christian Association of
Decatur **1737**

Young Women's Christian Association of
Douglas **1219**

Young Women's Christian Association of
Downtown Youngstown **2746**

Young Women's Christian Association of
Dubuque **1913**

Young Women's Christian Association of
Dutchess County **2592**

Young Women's Christian Association of
Easton **2824**

Young Women's Christian Association of El
Dorado **1246**

Young Women's Christian Association of
Elgin **1740**

Young Women's Christian Association of
Elkhart County **1820**

Young Women's Christian Association of
Elyria **2718**

Young Women's Christian Association of
Enid **2753**

Young Women's Christian Association of
Erie **2827**

Young Women's Christian Association of
Essex and West Hudson **2434**

Young Women's Christian Association of
Evanston/North Shore **1742**

Young Women's Christian Association of
Fargo-Moorhead **2660**

Young Women's Christian Association of
Flint **2177**

Young Women's Christian Association of
Fontana **1289**

Young Women's Christian Association of Ft.
Smith **1249**

Young Women's Christian Association of Ft.
Wayne **1827**

Young Women's Christian Association of Ft.
Worth and Tarrant County **3027**

Young Women's Christian Association of
Fresno **1293**

Young Women's Christian Association of
Gardena Valley **1298**

Young Women's Christian Association of
Gary **1834**

Young Women's Christian Association of
Gateway Branch **1892**

Young Women's Christian Association of
Genesee County **2484**

Young Women's Christian Association of
Gettysburg **2829**

Young Women's Christian Association of
Glendale **1300**

Young Women's Christian Association of
Gloversville **2518**

Young Women's Christian Association of
Grand Island **2349**

Young Women's Christian Association of
Grand Rapids **2185**

Young Women's Christian Association of
Great Falls **2335**

Young Women's Christian Association of
Greater Bridgeport **1495**

Young Women's Christian Association of
Greater Des Moines **1906**

Young Women's Christian Association of the
Greater Harrisburg Area **2838**

Young Women's Christian Association of
Greater Lansing **2208**

Young Women's Christian Association of
Greater Lawrence **2099**

Young Women's Christian Association of
Greater Little Rock **1255**

Young Women's Christian Association of
Greater Pittsburgh **2883**

Young Women's Christian Association of
Greater Pittsburgh, Carnagie Center **2818**

Young Women's Christian Association of
Greater Pittsburgh, Wilkinsburg
Center **2906**

Young Women's Christian Association of
Greater Pomona Valley **1328**

Young Women's Christian Association of
Greater Rhode Island **2919**

Young Women's Christian Association of
Greater West Chester **2902**

Young Women's Christian Association of
Green Bay-De Pere **3205**

Young Women's Christian Association of
Greensburg **2831**

Young Women's Christian Association of
Greenwich **1503**

Young Women's Christian Association of
Hackensack **2412**

Young Women's Christian Association of
Hanover **2834**

Young Women's Christian Association of the
Harbor Area **1428**

Young Women's Christian Association of
Haverhill **2097**

Young Women's Christian Association of
Hawaii Island **1662**

Young Women's Christian Association of
Hazleton **2841**

Young Women's Christian Association of
Houston **3036**

Young Women's Christian Association of
Huron **2955**

Young Women's Christian Association of
Indianapolis **1848**

Young Women's Christian Association of
Jamestown **2527**

Young Women's Christian Association of
Janesville **3209**

Young Women's Christian Association of
Jersey City **2416**

Young Women's Christian Association of
Johnstown **2843**

Young Women's Christian Association of
Kalamazoo **2195**

Young Women's Christian Association of
Kankakee **1759**

Young Women's Christian Association of
Kansas City **1948, 2314**

Young Women's Christian Association of
Kauai County **1669**

Young Women's Christian Association of
Kitsap County **3132**

Young Women's Christian Association of
Kokomo **1852**

Young Women's Christian Association of La
Crosse **3212**

Young Women's Christian Association of
Lafayette **1854**

Young Women's Christian Association of
Lake County **1810**

Young Women's Christian Association of
Lakewood and Ocean County **2417**

Young Women's Christian Association of
Lancaster **2845**

Young Women's Christian Association of
Lea County **2481**

Young Women's Christian Association of
Leavenworth **1953**

Young Women's Christian Association of
Lewiston-Auburn **2033**

Young Women's Christian Association of
Lewiston-Clarkston **1678**

Young Women's Christian Association of
Licking County **2731**

Young Women's Christian Association of
Lima **2723**

Young Women's Christian Association of
Lincoln **2355**

Young Women's Christian Association of
Lockport **2532**

Young Women's Christian Association of
Long Beach **1311**

Young Women's Christian Association of
Lorain **2724**

Young Women's Christian Association of
Los Angeles **1323**

Young Women's Christian Association Los
Angeles, South Valley Center **1324**

Young Women's Christian Association of
Lowell **2104**

Young Women's Christian Association of
Lubbock **3041**

Young Women's Christian Association of
Madison **3218**

Young Women's Christian Association of
Malden **2106**

Young Women's Christian Association of
Manchester **2389**

Young Women's Christian Association of
Mansfield **2725**

Young Women's Christian Association of
Maricopa County **1228**

Young Women's Christian Association of Marion **1855**

Young Women's Christian Association of Marshalltown **1921**

Young Women's Christian Association of Massillon **2727**

Young Women's Christian Association of McKeesport **2850**

Young Women's Christian Association of McLean County **1692**

Young Women's Christian Association of Meadville **2851**

Young Women's Christian Association of Medina County **2728**

Young Women's Christian Association of Metropolitan Chicago **1732**

Young Women's Christian Association of Metropolitan Dallas **3016**

Young Women's Christian Association of Metropolitan Denver **1483**

Young Women's Christian Association of Metropolitan St. Louis **2327**

Young Women's Christian Association of Minot **2667**

Young Women's Christian Association of Missoula **2342**

Young Women's Christian Association of Mitchell **2957**

Young Women's Christian Association of Monroe **2018**

Young Women's Christian Association of Montclair-North Essex **2426**

Young Women's Christian Association of the Monterey Peninsula **1329**

Young Women's Christian Association of Mt. Desert Island **2026**

Young Women's Christian Association of Muncie **1859**

Young Women's Christian Association of Muscatine **1932**

Young Women's Christian Association of Nashua **2391**

Young Women's Christian Association of New Britain **1513**

Young Women's Christian Association of New Haven **1516**

Young Women's Christian Association of New London **1504**

Young Women's Christian Association of New Orleans **2020**

Young Women's Christian Association of Newburgh **2538**

Young Women's Christian Association of Newburyport **2112**

Young Women's Christian Association of North Orange County **1295**

Young Women's Christian Association of Northern Rhode Island **2925**

Young Women's Christian Association of Northwest Louisiana **2022**

Young Women's Christian Association of Oahu **1668**

Young Women's Christian Association of Oakland **1343**

Young Women's Christian Association of Ogden/Northern Utah **3070**

Young Women's Christian Association of Oil City **2857**

Young Women's Christian Association of Oklahoma City **2761**

Young Women's Christian Association of Olympia **3143**

Young Women's Christian Association of Omaha **2361**

Young Women's Christian Association of Oskaloosa **1933**

Young Women's Christian Association of Ottumwa **1935**

Young Women's Christian Association of Paris and Lamar County **3050**

Young Women's Christian Association of Passaic-Clifton **2435**

Young Women's Christian Association of Paterson **2436**

Young Women's Christian Association of Pekin **1776**

Young Women's Christian Association of Peoria **1779**

Young Women's Christian Association of Philadelphia **2872**

Young Women's Christian Association of Piqua **2733**

Young Women's Christian Association of Plainfield/North Plainfield **2439**

Young Women's Christian Association of Pocatello **1681**

Young Women's Christian Association of Pontiac-North Oakland **2223**

Young Women's Christian Association of Portland **2038, 2800**

Young Women's Christian Association of Pottstown **2884**

Young Women's Christian Association of Pottsville **2885**

Young Women's Christian Association of Pueblo **1492**

Young Women's Christian Association of Quincy **1789**

Young Women's Christian Association of Racine **3233**

Young Women's Christian Association of Redlands **1361**

Young Women's Christian Association of Reno-Sparks **2373**

Young Women's Christian Association of Richmond **1863**

Young Women's Christian Association of Ridgewood **2443**

Young Women's Christian Association of Riverside **1363**

Young Women's Christian Association of Rochester and Monroe County **2597**

Young Women's Christian Association of Rock Island **1796**

Young Women's Christian Association of Rockford **1799**

Young Women's Christian Association of Sacramento **1379**

Young Women's Christian Association of St. Clair County **1690**

Young Women's Christian Association of St. Joseph **2317**

Young Women's Christian Association of St. Joseph-Benton Harbor **2230**

Young Women's Christian Association of St. Joseph County **1866**

Young Women's Christian Association of Salem **2735, 2805**

Young Women's Christian Association of Salina **1962**

Young Women's Christian Association of Salt Lake City **3077**

Young Women's Christian Association of San Antonio **3055**

Young Women's Christian Association of San Bernardino **1380**

Young Women's Christian Association of San Diego County **1397**

Young Women's Christian Association of San Gabriel Valley **1463**

Young Women's Christian Association of Santa Clara Valley **1419**

Young Women's Christian Association of Santa Cruz **1438**

Young Women's Christian Association of Santa Monica **1442**

Young Women's Christian Association of Schenectady **2602**

Young Women's Christian Association of Seattle-King County **3164**

Young Women's Christian Association of Shiawassee County **2220**

Young Women's Christian Association of Sioux Falls **2966**

Young Women's Christian Association of Sonoma County **1444**

Young Women's Christian Association of South Orange County **1432**

Young Women's Christian Association of Southern Alameda County **1302**

Young Women's Christian Association of Spokane **3168**

Young Women's Christian Association of Springfield **1805**

Young Women's Christian Association of Stateline Area **3201**

Young Women's Christian Association of Steubenville **2737**

Young Women's Christian Association of Summit **2448**

Young Women's Christian Association of Sussex County **2447**

Young Women's Christian Association of Sweetwater County **3253**

Young Women's Christian Association of Syracuse and Onondaga County **2609**

Young Women's Christian Association of Tacoma and Pierce County **3171**

Young Women's Christian Association of Terre Haute **1870**

Young Women's Christian Association of Texarkana **3058**

Young Women's Christian Association of Titusville **2893**

Young Women's Christian Association of Toledo **2740**

Young Women's Christian Association of the Tonawandas **2584**

Young Women's Christian Association of Topeka **1966**

Young Women's Christian Association of Torrance **1457**

Young Women's Christian Association of Trenton **2456**

Young Women's Christian Association of Troy-Cohoes **2610**

Young Women's Christian Association of Tucson **1243**

Young Women's Christian Association of Tulsa **2773**

Young Women's Christian Association of Ulster County **2529**

Young Women's Christian Association of the United States of America **1192**

Young Women's Christian Association of Utica **2611**

Young Women's Christian Association of Van Wert County **2742**

Young Women's Christian Association of Vancouver-Clark County **3173**

Young Women's Christian Association of Waco **3062**

Young Women's Christian Association of Wake County **2643**

Young Women's Christian Association of Walla Walla **3175**

Young Women's Christian Association of Warren **2896**

Young Women's Christian Association of Washington **1939, 2898**

Young Women's Christian Association of Waterbury **1526**

Young Women's Christian Association of Watertown **2615**

Young Women's Christian Association of Watsonville **1462**

Young Women's Christian Association of Wausau **3244**

Young Women's Christian Association of Wenatchee Valley **3177**

Index